1. "Bride & Groom" by Artaffects, Ltd.
2. "Time For Bed" from Enesco Memories of Yesterday Society
3. "1990 Betsy Ross" by Annalee Mobilitee Dolls, Inc.
4. "Father Christmas" by Lenox Collections
5. "Glorya" by The Constance Collection
6. The Night Before Christmas Collection by Goebel Miniatures
7. "Santa Entry/Fireplace" by Whitley Bay
8. "Springtime Gathering" by Hamilton Gifts, Ltd.
9. "We Are God's Workmanship" from Enesco Precious Moments Club
10. "Autumn Magic" by ANRI
11. "Feeding Time" by Royal Doulton
12. "Fifty Years of Oz" by The Hamilton Collection
13. "On the Threshold" by Woodmere China-copyright The Balliol Corporation
14. "A Child Is Born" by Reco International Corp.
15. "The Finishing Touch" by Flambro Imports
16. "Sitting Pretty" by The Norman Rockwell Gallery
17. "Crossroads" (Hum 331) Commemorative Edition by Goebel
18. British Traditions Books and Bookends-"The Printers" and "The Bookbinders" by John Hine Studios, Inc.
19. "Gurneyfoot and Shadra" by Precious Art/Panton
20. "Victoria Station" by Department 56, Inc.
21. "St. Peter's Cove" by Lilliput Lane Limited
22. "Tee Time at St. Andrew's" by Roman, Inc.
23. "Unexpected Rescuer" by LEGENDS
24. "Nicole" by Goebel, Inc.
25. "Aubrey" by Nahrgang Collection
26. "Cherie" by Gorham, Inc.
27. "Attack" by The Lance Corporation
28. "Delicate Motion" by Maruri U.S.A.
29. Carolers by Byers' Choice
30. "Argos" by Kaiser Porcelain USA, Inc.
31. "Medieval Santa" by Duncan Royale

Contents

Reference Section

About the Editors

Executive Editor
Diane Carnevale Jones

Diane Carnevale Jones is the principal of Professional Marketing Services, a Grand Rapids, Michigan based firm which specializes in media relations, market research and promotions for companies in the collectibles, gourmet cookware and manufacturing fields.

As an experienced collector herself, Ms. Carnevale Jones takes a special interest in the limited edition collectibles field and is very knowledgeable about the secondary market. Since September 1986, she has been Executive Director of the COLLECTORS' INFORMATION BUREAU. Prior to this, Ms. Carnevale Jones provided enthusiastic and innovative service to the BUREAU almost since its inception and was the Managing Editor for prior editions of this book.

Ms. Carnevale Jones researches and prepares secondary market columns for *Collector Editions* and *Collections* magazines and is a guest writer for other collectible publications. She also lectures and conducts seminars on a number of collectible topics.

Ms. Carnevale Jones holds a B.A. degree in English and journalism from the University of Michigan and resides in Grand Rapids with her husband and two children.

Managing Editor
Cindy Zagumny

Cindy Zagumny is the Executive Administrator and Managing Editor of the *Collectibles Market Guide & Price Index*. She graduated from Michigan State University with a Bachelor of Science Degree in retailing and business from the College of Human Ecology.

Ms. Zagumny previously worked in the retail, medical and insurance fields for several Midwest firms before joining the COLLECTORS' INFORMATION BUREAU in 1987. She currently resides in Grand Rapids, Michigan with her husband and two teenage children.

About the Writers

Susan K. Jones

Susan K. Jones has spent more than eighteen years in the limited edition collectibles field. She is the owner of Susan K. Jones and Associates, a consulting firm for direct marketers and limited edition marketers. She has been a Marketing Manager for The Hamilton Collection, and she worked with The Bradford Exchange in the mid-1970s.

Today Ms. Jones serves a number of collectibles clients and contributes to several collectibles publications. She authored *Creative Strategy in Direct Marketing* (NTC Business Books, 1991), and co-authored two business books published by Charles Scribner's Sons. Since 1990, Ms. Jones has served as an Associate Professor of Marketing at Ferris State University in Big Rapids, Michigan and has taught direct marketing at Northwestern University.

Ms. Jones was the first Executive Director of COLLECTORS' INFORMATION BUREAU and now serves as its Special Consultant. Ms. Jones' expertise in the collectibles field led her to write many of the company feature and background articles for this book.

Educated at Northwestern University, she holds a master's degree in advertising. She lives in East Grand Rapids, Michigan with her husband and two sons.

Catherine Bloom is a newspaper columnist and a writer for the COLLECTORS' INFORMATION BUREAU since 1983. She attended Loretto Heights College in Denver, Colorado and earned a bachelors degree from Creighton University in Omaha, Nebraska and her graduate studies were through The University of Michigan.

Ms. Bloom worked in the promotion departments of a number of radio and television stations in the Midwest. She currently lives in Grand Rapids, Michigan where her regular column "With Us Today" appears in the *Grand Rapids Press*.

In 1990, she did the text for *Capidomonte Collectibles*, published by Publications International, Inc. Since 1987, Ms. Bloom has also written the "C.I.B. Hotline" for *Collectors News*.

Ann Saigeon is a free-lance writer residing in Alto, Michigan. She was an adjunct professor of English at Calvin College in Grand Rapids, Michigan where she also has done research in publications for the art department. Ms. Saigeon's hobbies include gardening, travelling and Celtic studies.

A professional copy writer in the direct mail business for six years, Katherine Holden Trotti has also published magazine articles in such diverse publications as *New Woman*, *Collector Editions*, *Los Angeles Times Magazine* and *Palm Springs Life*. Her photographs have appeared in *Islands Magazine*. She lives in Santa Barbara, California.

Gail Cohen was introduced to the giftware/collectibles industry as trade show and sales and communications manager for The Bradford Exchange in 1980. In 1987, she became director of marketing for Roman, Inc., and in 1990 established The Gail Cohen Company, Inc., a full-service creative agency.

Ms. Cohen holds a masters degree in anthropology from the University of Georgia at Athens. Formerly a book reviewer for *The Library Journal*, her writings include articles for *Family Circle*, *Military Lifestyle*, *GSB*, *Northshore* (Chicago) and other magazines, as well as features in *The Chicago Tribune* and *The* (Chicagoland) *Daily Herald*.

Acknowledgments

The Collectors' Information Bureau would like to thank the following persons who have contributed to the creation of this book: Gail Cohen, Barbara Dike of Enesco Corporation, Ronald Frey of Interiors by Town & Country, Robert Groters of Klingman Furniture Company, Linda Joswick of Trade Typographers, Inc., Ray and Lorrie Kiefer of the National Association of Limited Edition Dealers, Todd Mellema of Philip B. Schaafsma Photography, Dan Nichols of Wm. C. Brown Publishers, Ann Saigeon, Philip Schaafsma of Philip B. Schaafsma Photography, Laurie Schaut and Carla Siegle of Trade Typographers, Inc., Pat Shaw of Enesco Corporation, John Spoelma of Klingman Furniture Company, Dave Stafford and Joy Versluys of Trade Typographers, Inc. and Katherine Holden Trotti.

In addition, the Collectors' Information Bureau would like to thank its panel of over one hundred limited edition dealers, whose dedication has helped make our ever-expanding 125 page-plus Price Index possible. We wish we could thank them by name, but they have agreed that to be singled out in this manner might hinder their continued ability to obtain an unbiased view of the marketplace.

The executive editor also wishes to express heartfelt appreciation to the following persons whose dedication, hard work and encouragement have made this book possible: Catherine P. Bloom, John Conley, Nancy Hart, Ron Jedlinski, Paul F. Jones, Susan K. Jones, Sue Knappen, Bruce Kollath, Heio W. Reich, Michelle Satterthwaite, James P. Smith, Jr., Carol Van Elderen and Cindy Zagumny.

By Heio W. Reich

President of COLLECTORS' INFORMATION BUREAU
and
President of RECO INTERNATIONAL CORP.

Foreword

Dear Collector:

It has been a decade since a group of dedicated collectibles marketers and producers met at the International Collectible Exposition in South Bend, Indiana. Their mission was to explore ideas for an important new means of communication with collectors. These visionary leaders foresaw an "information explosion" in the collectibles field. And they banded together to develop an organization that would be the "voice of the industry" serving collectors by sharing this growing body of information on limited editions.

That exploratory meeting led to more conferences, brainstorming and planning sessions. By November 1982—just four months after their initial meeting — the founders of COLLECTORS' INFORMATION BUREAU were ready to unveil their concept. Sponsored by a total of fourteen charter members, the COLLECTORS' INFORMATION BUREAU has now more than quadrupled its original membership with a Regular Members' roster that now includes 70 of the world's most honored marketers and manufacturers of fine art collectibles. Through the years, the BUREAU has expanded its services to collectors with the introduction of the "Collectibles Hotline" and the publishing of the "C.I.B. Report" Newsletter, the *Collectibles Price Guide* and its latest book, *Directory to Secondary Market Retailers*. This would not have been possible without the continued dedication and support of the CIB Board members, charter and regular member companies, secondary market retailers and countless others who have helped shape this dynamic organization. The CIB welcomes the numerous letters and phone calls it receives from enthusiastic collectors who enjoy their hobby, and thanks them for utilizing the CIB's resources.

The CIB was founded to be a direct link to collectors offering information on the most fascinating companies, artists, craftsmanship processes and product introductions in the world of limited editions. Even more important, the CIB pledged to create and publish an authoritative Price Index listing thousands of the most actively traded works of art in contemporary limited edition collecting. The initial medium for this information was to be a totally unique book: the first edition of what now is known as the COLLECTIBLES MARKET GUIDE & PRICE INDEX.

Our first GUIDE, published in 1984, contained 192 pages including a thirty-page Price Index. Today the COLLECTORS' INFORMATION BUREAU proudly presents the Tenth Edition of the COLLECTIBLES MARKET GUIDE & PRICE INDEX.

The GUIDE we introduce to you today comprises more than 575 pages, including an expanded 150-plus page Price Index that covers nearly 27,000 of today's most widely traded plates, figurines, bells, graphics, ornaments, dolls and steins.

Page through this comprehensive book and I feel sure you will agree it has become a "work of art" in and of itself. Our readers have praised the GUIDE as "The Collector's Bible" and "A Treasure Trove of Information." Novice collectors and seasoned veterans alike enjoy the GUIDE, which is based on recent developments, discoveries and events in the world of collectibles.

In these pages you will find historical perspectives on collecting plates, figurines, dolls and other limited edition categories...an up-to-date guide to the secondary market...ideas from a top interior designer on how to decorate your home with collectibles. You will also learn the best ways to protect your valuable holdings—both within your home and with insurance policies that guard against loss.

You will learn where to travel to see your favorite collectibles made, enjoy collectibles conventions and view noteworthy collections in museums and other exhibitions. And of course, there is the Price Index with its recent quote prices drawn from the combined experience of over 250 respected dealers all over North America.

So indulge yourself. Pour a cup of your favorite beverage and sit down prepared for a reading adventure! The members of COLLECTORS' INFORMATION BUREAU commend this volume to you as the latest edition of our authoritative book—devoted to enjoyment by you, the collector.

Cordially,

Heio W. Reich

Heio W. Reich
Port Washington, NY
November, 1992

Members

During its first year of existence, the CIB Membership Roster included fourteen member firms and six associate members. Today, the roster of member firms numbers seventy — an all-time record membership! Here is our current membership roster.

Kurt S. Adler, Inc./Santa's World
1107 Broadway
New York, NY 10010

Anheuser-Busch, Inc.
Retail Sales Department
2700 South Broadway
St. Louis, MO 63118

Annalee Mobilitee Dolls, Inc.
Box 708 Reservoir Road
Meredith, NH 03253

ANRI
c/o Goebel United States
Goebel Plaza
P.O. Box 10
Pennington, NJ 08534

Armani
c/o Miller Import
300 Mac Lane
Keasbey, Woodbridge
Township, NJ 08832

Artaffects, Ltd.
P.O. Box 98
Staten Island, NY 10307

The Ashton-Drake Galleries
9200 N. Maryland Avenue
Niles, IL 60648

The Bradford Exchange
9333 Milwaukee Avenue
Niles, IL 60648

Byers' Choice Ltd.
P.O. Box 158
Chalfont, PA 18914

The Cat's Meow
2163 Great Trails Drive
Wooster, OH 44691

Classic Carolina Collections/ C.U.I., Inc./DRAM TREE
1502 North 23rd Street
Wilmington, NC 28405

The Collectables
Rt. 4, Box 503
Rolla, MO 65401

The Constance Collection
Rte 1, Box 538
Midland, VA 22728

M. Cornell Importers, Inc.
1462- 18th Street N.W.
St. Paul, MN 55112

Corolle/Timeless Creations
333 Continental Blvd.
El Segundo, CA 90245-5012

Creart
4517 Manzanillo Drive
Austin, TX 78749

Cross Gallery
P.O. Box 4181
Jackson Hole, WY 83001

Department 56, Inc.
PO Box 44456
Eden Prairie, MN 55344-1456

The Walt Disney Company
500 South Buena Vista Street
Burbank, CA 91521

Duncan Royale
1141 So. Acacia Avenue
Fullerton, CA 92631

Dynasty Doll
P.O. Box 99
400 Markley Street
Port Reading, NJ 07064

Enesco Corporation
1 Enesco Plaza
Elk Grove Village, IL 60007

Flambro Imports
1260 Collier Road N.W.
Atlanta, GA 30318

The Franklin Mint
U.S. Route One
Franklin Center, PA 19091

Gartlan USA, Inc.
15502 Graham Street
Huntington Beach, CA 92649

Georgetown Collection
One Foden Rd.
Portland, ME 04104-5030

Goebel United States
Goebel Plaza
P.O. Box 10
Pennington, NJ 08534-0010

Goebel Miniatures
c/o Goebel United States
P.O. Box 10, Rt. 31
Pennington, NJ 08534

Gorham Inc.*
P.O. Box 2011
Penndel, PA 19047

The Hamilton Collection*
4810 Executive Park Court
Jacksonville, FL 32216-6069

Hand & Hammer Silversmiths
Hand & Hammer Collectors' Club
2610 Morse Lane
Woodbridge, VA 22192

John Hine Studios, Inc.
4456 Campbell Road
P.O. Box 800667
Houston, TX 77280-0667

M.I. Hummel Club*
Division of Goebel Art GmbH
Goebel Plaza
P.O. Box 11
Pennington, NJ 08534-0011

Kaiser Porcelain USA Inc.
2045 Niagara Falls Blvd.
Niagara Falls, NY 14304

Ladie & Friends, Inc.
220 North Main Street
Sellersville, PA 18960

Lance Corporation
321 Central Street
Hudson, MA 01749

Lawtons
548 North First
Turlock, CA 95380

Ron Lee's World of Clowns
2180 Agate Court
Simi Valley, CA 93065

LEGENDS
2665D Park Center Drive
Simi Valley, CA 93065

Lenox Collections
1170 Wheeler Way
Langhorne, PA 19047

Lightpost Publishing
Ten Almaden Blvd. 9th Floor
San Jose, CA 95113

Lilliput Lane Limited
c/o Gift Link, Inc.
9052 Old Annapolis Road
Columbia, MD 21045

Lladro Collectors Society
43 W. 57th Street
New York, NY 10019

Seymour Mann, Inc.
225 Fifth Avenue,
Showroom #102
New York, NY 10010

Maruri U.S.A.
7541 Woodman Place
Van Nuys, CA 91405

June McKenna Collectibles Inc.
P.O. Box 846
Ashland, VA 23005

Midwest Importers of Cannon Falls, Inc.
P.O. Box 20, Consumer Inquiries
Cannon Falls, MN 55009-0020

Nahrgang Collection
1005 First Avenue
Silvis, IL 61282

Novelino, Inc.
12-A Mason
Irvine, CA 92718

PenDelfin Sales Inc.
750 Ensminger Road,
Suite 108
Tonawanda, NY 14150

Polland Studios
P.O. Box 1146
Prescott, AZ 86302

Possible Dreams
6 Perry Dr.
Foxboro, MA 02035

Precious Art/Panton
110 E. Ellsworth Road
Ann Arbor, MI 48108

Reco International Corp.*
150 Haven Avenue
Port Washington, NY 11050

The Norman Rockwell Gallery
9200 Center for the Arts
Niles, IL 60648

Roman, Inc.*
555 Lawrence Avenue
Roselle, IL 60172-1599

Royal Copenhagen/Bing & Grondahl
27 Holland Ave.
White Plains, NY 10603

Royal Doulton
700 Cottontail Lane
Somerset, NJ 08873

Sarah's Attic
126-1/2 West Broad
Chesaning, MI 48616

Schmid
55 Pacella Park Drive
Randolph, MA 02368

Silver Deer, Ltd.
4824 Sterling Drive
Boulder, CO 80301

Summerhill Crystal & Glass
P.O. Box 1479
Fairfield, IA 52556

Swarovski America Ltd.
2 Slater Road
Cranston, RI 02920

Takara
230 Fifth Avenue,
New York, NY 10001

Timeless Creations
333 Continental Blvd.
El Segundo, CA 90245-5012

Turner Dolls Inc.
P.O. Box 36
Heltonville, IN 47436

United Design
P.O. Box 1200
Noble, OK 73068

VickiLane, Inc.
515 Colonial Dr.
Springfield, OR 97477

WACO Products Corporation
One North Corporate Drive
Riverdale, NJ 07457

**Charter Member*

—— *Associate Members* ——

Custom China Creations
13726 Seminole Drive
Chino, CA 91710

Mattheyprint Corporation
1397 King Road
West Chester, PA 16105

The Joy of Collecting

American Collectors Share Their Enthusiasm for Limited Edition Plates, Figurines, Bells, Graphics, Ornaments and Dolls

Unique home decor...the lure of the chase...a retirement pastime...an investment for the future. These are but a few of the reasons why today's collectors enjoy their beautiful limited editions. Their motives are as varied as their collections, but these enthusiasts have at least one thing in common: they love their beautiful works of art.

To gain insight into the strong and steady growth of the limited edition field, Collectors' Information Bureau interviewed male and female collectors from every U.S. region, age group and walk of life. Here we share the highlights of this fascinating survey.

It wouldn't be Christmas without Sandi Hight's doll collection, which is attractively displayed throughout the Hight home during the holidays. A large Annalee Mobilitee Santa makes himself comfortable on the family piano bench, while other Annalee dolls sing holiday favorites.

The Inspiration to Collect

Some collectors insist that the hobby is "in their blood" — a passion that was passed down to them by parents or grandparents who filled their childhood homes with cherished objects. Others knew nothing of collecting until a special friend or relative gave them a gift: a plate, bell or figurine that turned out to be a limited edition.

Michael G. Brennan of Cherry Hill, New Jersey claims he "married into a family of collectors." While visiting shops that sold the Bing and Grondahl and Royal Copenhagen plates enjoyed by his wife and mother-in-law, David Winter's charming cottages caught Brennan's eye. Now he says of the David Winter line, "They have become a passion with me. I greatly admire the uniqueness and artistry that goes into each and every cottage."

Dara Bise of Crossville, Tennessee received a Precious Moments "Time Heals" figurine instead of flowers after major surgery, from a sister-in-law who loves Sam Butcher's heartwarming designs. Karin Warner of Christianburg, Virginia, was already a raccoon collector when her mother purchased several collectible raccoons for her as gifts. Now Ms. Warner collects every raccoon she can find in the form of plates, figurines, graphics, and even ornaments.

Like Ms. Warner, many collectors become intrigued when they discover a collector's item that ties in with a favorite subject. As a Shrine clown, Frank Yetner of Warwick, Rhode Island became an admirer and collector of Duncan Royale figurines and other clown-subject works.

A love of "The Nutcracker" ballet spurred Donna Arthur's collecting hobby in Rowland Heights, California, while Diane K. McCarrick first discovered plate collecting when she learned her favorite comedian, Red Skelton, would attend the International Plate and Collectible Exposition in South Bend, Indiana. Ms. McCarrick traveled to the South Bend show from her home in Lansing, Michigan in 1977, and has attended each annual convention since. "We went to see Red Skelton, but once I stepped on that floor, I was hooked," she explains. Now Ms. McCarrick owns works by Lowell Davis, Swarovski, Lladro, and many other collectibles firms.

Fran Oldrigde uses two stunning Lalique crystal cats to accessorize her end table.

This is just a small sampling of Karin Warner's ever-growing raccoon collection! Attractively displayed are Roger Brown's "Reggie," Maruri USA raccoon, Schmid's "Coon Capers Moonraiders" by Lowell Davis, "Bobby Coon" by Goebel, Schmid's "Anybody's Home," by Lowell Davis, "Ruffles" by Cybis, Boehm Studios' raccoon and Lowell Davis' "Creek Bank Bandit."

Joyce Lambert displays her cottages in aquariums. "My cottages are dust-free and away from children's little hands as long as they are in the aquarium." There is a David Winter emblem at the top of the aquarium, etched by Joyce's son.

The Fun of Sharing a Collection

The collectors we surveyed agreed that home display is one of the most rewarding aspects of their pastime. Their decor ideas abound all year long, but their Christmas displays are especially elaborate. Beverly A. Thyssen of Little Chute, Wisconsin uses her dolls and teddy bears for a Christmas display in her front bay window. She combines "Mr. and Mrs. Claus, elves, dolls and bears. Cars actually stop to look," she reports proudly.

Even her normally skeptical sons insist that Sandi Hight decorate their Skowhegan, Maine home with all the holiday collectibles she has gathered. "My two boys are always having a fit about dolls being all over the house," she smiles. "So one year I decided not to decorate so extensively. About the second week into December my boys said, 'Aren't we having Christmas?'" It goes without saying that Ms. Hight then "decked the halls" with all her seasonal Annalee Dolls and Hallmark Merry Miniatures.

Although Billie Lou Frandsen of Rock Springs, Wyoming started out wanting only a simple village scene to place under her Christmas tree, she and her whole family have become Department 56 enthusiasts. "I enjoy putting a large village scene on the entertainment center," she says. "We have two cobblestone 'roads' with street lights and our favorite pieces, lots of snow and people. Trees and coaches also decorate the scene." As of this writing, Ms. Frandsen owned 56 buildings, seven coaches and sleighs, and scores of people, trees, animals and street lights for her grand holiday display.

Christmas isn't the only time for decoration, however, and Joyce Lambert of Coal Grove, Ohio has devised a clever way to show off her cottage collection all year long. "I have three 20-gallon aquariums that I display my cottages in," she explains. "The aquariums are stacked and have a light on top to shine down through the tanks." A unique display indeed!

Fran Oldridge of Anaheim Hills, California treasures her two Lalique crystal cat sculptures above all other possessions. "My Lalique cats are on a lamp table between my sofa and loveseat," she says. "People — myself included — who sit on the end of the sofa or loveseat usually end up stroking or 'petting' the cats as they talk, unaware of what they are doing!"

People with extensive collections often plan their furniture arrangements with display in mind. The owner of 250 collector plates, Inez B. Tillison of Atlanta, Georgia has a twelve-foot-long shelf in her living room especially for her Bjorn Wiinblad plates. "We also have a china cabinet full," she adds.

Georgiana Bodemer of Green Brook, New Jersey houses her collectibles on shelves and glassed-in cabinets. "It keeps them so clean and new looking," she exclaims. Ms. Bodemer has two large collector's cabinets and one attorney's book case in which to store her favorite works of art. And a roll-top desk plays host to Quinn Dahlstrom's Krystonia dragons and English miniature cottages in Bonney Lake, Washington.

A Never-Ending Passion for Collecting

Our collector "panel" tells us that their enjoyment of limited editions has no bounds. Some people who collect the works of a certain artist or firm are spurred on to acquire the newest items in that line. Others enjoy seeking out back issues or rare pieces — some even call or travel all over the country looking for special treasures.

Still others find collecting is a wonderful way to fill spare hours — either during their retirement years or as a happy diversion from the world of work. Florence Zulick of Hazel Park, Michigan goes so far as to call her collecting hobby "great therapy in times when life held many disappointments."

The comments and encouragement of friends and relatives spur on some collectors, as Rose Patterson knows. Ms. Patterson, of San Pedro, California, says that "When family and friends come to my home, the first thing they say is how warm and cozy it feels to be there. I know that a lot of that has to do with my different collections."

Barbara Ann Hart, a doll collector in La Porte, Texas, says that friends "tease me about my 'babies,' but they always ask about what I'm watching for (to acquire) and have surprised me many times with new additions."

The Importance of a Good Dealer

Many collectors prefer selecting a special dealer whose shop they can visit, and who alerts them

Georgiana Bodemer's collectibles are stored safely in glassed-in cabinets. She uses the back wall in the case to hang some of her pieces, as well as the ornaments that hang from the shelves themselves. This technique adds interest to her arrangement and gives Georgiana more space to work with.

Quinn Bahlstrom arranges his fantasy figurines and cottages in a cozy setting. From left to right are "Owhey" from Precious Art/Panton, "Secret Garden" from Lilliput Lane, "Stoope" from Precious Art/Panton and "Hometown Depot" from Lilliput Lane.

Two husband and wife teams take great joy at arranging their Department 56 villages for the holidays. Above, Billie Lou Frandsen and her husband put their favorite and/or newest pieces in front to construct a main road and continue creating the village from there. Shown left, is just a partial collection of a Department 56 village as displayed by Florence Zulick and her husband, whose entire collection spans three walls. The village is displayed from late October until February.

when new collectibles come on the market. Dealers who feature favorite artists at get-togethers and signing parties win high marks from their customers, as do firms that buy and sell on the secondary market. Indeed, while few of our survey respondents buy mainly for investment purposes, they do like to know that there is an outlet available if they ever should wish to participate in secondary market trading.

Other collectors enjoy purchasing collectibles by mail for a number of reasons: selection, convenience, and payment terms, to name a few.

Toni Meyer of Wausau, Wisconsin says she buys "a lot of collectibles by mail, because I cannot always find what I'm looking for in town. I buy from advertisements, and I get retired pieces from collectible exchanges."

As a senior citizen, Doris M. Foster of Telford, Pennsylvania likes the convenience of buying from home. And Judy Anderson of Mukwonago, Wisconsin appreciates the mail-order policy of installment buying, which allows her to spread her payments.

Collectors Share Their Joy of Collecting

When asked what special comments they would like to share with fellow collectors, our respondents were most eloquent. Philip L. Field of Norwalk, Connecticut finds collecting to be "educational, profitable, and a wonderful pastime for rainy or winter days."

Edith Smith poses with a few of her David Winter cottages. She enjoys looking for retired pieces and plans to continue collecting them until she runs out of space to show them!

Edith Smith of Richmond, Virginia compares collecting to an addiction or habit — "except it is a wonderful one that can be enjoyed for years to come. It is one of the great joys of my life."

Rita K. Clark of Salinas, California appreciates the monetary value of her favorite pieces as well as their appeal. "Through collecting things I love for their beauty and artistry, I always have my money's worth. But knowing their values — some of which are growing — gives me a wonderful sense of security."

Collectibles and Your Home Design

A Top Interior Designer's Advice Sparks New Ideas for Showing Off Your Favorite Works of Limited Edition Art

Imagine a living room furnished in neutral tones with wall-to-wall carpet, white painted walls, a sofa, two pull-up chairs, coffee table and floor lamps. Sounds functional...even comfortable. But charming? Inviting? Not really. A room may be fitted with all the basics of seating and lighting, but without accessories and a few special touches of personality and style, it remains as cold and impersonal as a public waiting area!

We all sense the difference between a "ho-hum room" and one that sings with joy and warmth. But few of us possess a natural flair for home design: we need the advice of an expert to turn our favorite rooms into cozy retreats that are sought out happily by family and friends. Nothing adds personal style to a room more effectively that one's carefully chosen plates, bells, figurines, graphics, ornaments and dolls. But some collectors are unsure as to how to display their treasures for maximum enjoyment and beauty. That's why Collectors' Information Bureau has enlisted the guidance of Interior Designer Ronald Frey.

Ronald Frey

A member of the American Society of Interior Designers (A.S.I.D.), Frey is certified by the National Council for Interior Design Qualification (NCIDQ) — and he is listed in the current International Edition of Barons *Who's Who In Interior Design*. Based in Allendale, Michigan at Interiors by Town & Country, Frey holds a B.F.A. in Interior Design from the renowned Kendall College of Art and Design in Grand Rapids, Michigan, and is a member of Kendall's adjunct faculty. In an exclusive interview with C.I.B. Special Consultant Susan K. Jones, Frey shared his authoritative tips on adorning the home with collectibles.

Even Novices Can Design With Style

At one time home design was constrained by certain musts, but according to Ronald Frey, "There are no longer any rules for displaying objets d'art — only that the display be executed with taste."

Frey cautions, however, that working without rules does not mean that "anything goes."

"The trained eye will be able to discern problem areas immediately. But for the person with little or no training in design, a few suggestions on displaying collectibles may be of help."

This oriental plate rail from Van Hygan & Smythe demonstrates an excellent way to attractively display many plates in a limited space.

Be Aware of Scale. "Relating the size of an object to the space around it is very important," Frey cautions. "The obvious mistake to avoid here is displaying too small an item in too large a space, or vice-versa. Think of proportion: relating one part to another, each part to the whole, and each object to the other objects."

Frey says that some especially interesting, unique and imposing items may be strong enough

Swarovski crystal ornaments and train create an elegance at Chrismas time, that collectors will certainly admire. The ornaments hang attractively on a tree trimmed with bows, while a Swarovski train sits on a track that encircles the tree.

to stand alone and become focal elements in the room. A large sculpture of a bird or animal, for instance, might command its surrounding space while a smaller wildlife sculpture would need to be grouped with other items.

How To Unify Collectibles in Groups. When grouping items together, Frey suggests that you find some way to relate each piece to the overall display. "For example, one approach I take is to place different objects with similar colors together for harmony. Or, I may place objects of varying heights side by side for contrast and variation."

Frey suggests that when showing a group of objects that differ in size, an asymmetrical composition is best. On the other hand, pieces of the same size look well when combined in a straight row, or stacked above and below each other.

Using the Design Principle of Rhythm. According to Frey, "When you repeat elements either by size, texture or color to form a regular pattern, you employ the concept of rhythm. A properly composed and balanced display, whether symmetrical or asymmetrical, will naturally seem correct because the objects will achieve a 'state of being' in which they equal each other."

The key is to avoid haphazard placement of objects, yet take a risk from time to time. "Crystal objects can take on a very avant garde look when displayed in a straight line at a further than normal distance from each other," Frey suggests. Of course, some collectors may still prefer to show off their crystal pieces in a more traditional cluster on a tabletop or curio cabinet shelf.

Experiment With Eclectic Displays. Ronald Frey encourages collectors to mix and match items whose periods and "statements" are totally unrelated — antique pieces with contemporary works of art, for example, or child-subject works mixed with wildlife pieces. "This is one of my most fun and favorite things to do," Frey explains.

"On a tabletop, for instance, mix and layer items of different heights from back to front. Remember to unify all the items in some way — perhaps harmonizing colors. Though this is challenging, when it's executed correctly, this type of mix can lead to a visually surprising room that awakens every one of the human senses."

A Wide Range of Areas for Display. "There are many different places to display collections," according to Ronald Frey. "Two or three pieces combined with a few art books, some magazines and a plant or cut flowers in a vase make for a stunning cocktail table," he believes. "Other tables and

Doll artist Phyllis Parkins decorates her home, using many of her own lovely dolls as accents. Pictured is "Kallie," the second collector club exclusive from Phyllis' Collectors Club. The wall grouping of three child-subject graphics adds to this lovely setting.

desktops can combine photos, pottery, ornaments, plates, paintings and candlesticks — all of which do *not* have to match.

"Bookshelves are excellent pedestals for smaller objects and look very charming when their contents are mixtures of books, periodicals and items of display. And try this: by painting the back of the bookcase black or another dark color, the elements on display seem to pop out at you for notice."

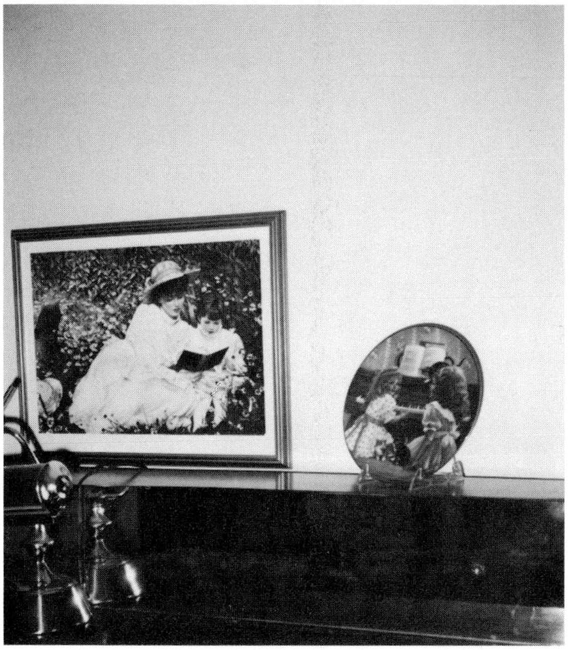

Try displaying the same artist's works, but in different forms, as shown here. Sandra Kuck's artwork is attractively displayed, with "Afternoon Recital" appropriately set upon this collector's piano, while Ms. Kuck's "The Reading Lesson" graphic by V.F. Fine Arts completes this charming scene.

More "Homes" for Collectibles. "Armoires with glass doors and shelves, lit from above, become dramatic settings for collections of all kinds," Ronald Frey suggests. "Use the tops of armoires and bookcases for additional display for special objects. Use walls for mounting photos, graphics and other artworks. These are particularly interesting when placed in a low position to create a more intimate feeling. Deep window sills and even the floor are other perfect areas to stack and prop things."

The Importance of Lighting. Frey emphasizes good lighting above all else in creating a handsome home. "I could utilize everything mentioned above, yet without the proper lighting, displays die quickly," he cautions. "There are a hundred different solutions to lighting, all correct, yet the one I come back to again and again for collections is the

Many collectors display their favorite holiday ornaments all year long. Above: Hallmark wooden ornament trees house miniature ornaments. Below: This angel collection is shown on a folding white metal display rack,with ribbon woven throughout to soften the setting.

Several M.I. Hummel figurines were used to create this lovely vignette.

pinspot or narrow spot. Used in a recessed incandescent fixture or with a small, unobtrusive track fixture, these low-voltage, tungsten-halogen lamps will thrust narrow beams of light with great precision. The result is an exciting and dramatic look, with dark shadows surrounding the objects that are highlighted."

Frey borrowed this lighting concept from his retail designs, where he focuses intense beams of light on featured objects. "It works in residential design as well, and why shouldn't we have as much fun in our homes as when we go shopping?" Another tip from Frey: use reostats to vary the intensity of light depending on the time of day and the effect you seek.

Have Fun and Be Daring. Ronald Frey's final word of advice concerns "taking the plunge" with your home display and showing off those offbeat objects that say "you." "Many times the items I select as accessories for my clients are objects they currently own and just never considered. I find them stored away somewhere because they were thought of as 'old' or 'inappropriate.' The main thing to remember is to have fun, be daring, and take the risk to display some objects you like in a creative way. When you do this, you can only enhance the collectibles you are displaying!"

Here are some specific ideas for each of the collectible categories featured in this book:

Plates

* Try hanging four or more plates of the same size in a straight vertical line — one on top of the other.
* Mix plates on a theme with other objects that amplify that theme: Victorian lace, a children's tea cup and saucer and a fairy tale book with a nostalgic, child-subject plate for example.
* Show off your plates in every room of the home: including the bathroom and kitchen. Porcelain is the ideal art medium for these rooms because it is durable and easy to clean.
* Today's plate frames add elegance and style to porcelain art. Try rustic oak frames for plates in the family room...polished dark wood frames for the living room.

Figurines and Bells

* Add interest to a display by placing some pieces on pedestals to vary their heights.
* Keep your finest and most delicate figurines and bells safe and clean by investing in a lighted glass cabinet or shelving unit.
* Christmas pieces may be displayed all year: don't limit your enjoyment to just a few weeks annually.
* Add a favorite piece or two to your bedroom, or rotate figurines and bells from your living room to your private quarters: you'll enjoy waking up to beauty each day!

Dolls

* There's nothing more charming than a child-size chair or rocker adorned by one or more pretty dolls
* Let your porcelain "babies" slumber in a real baby's cradle or wicker basket
* If you own a number of elegant lady dolls, set up a child-size table, chairs and tea set for a tea party vignette
* A standing doll shows off her costume to best advantage: many contemporary dolls come with their own unobtrusive stands at no additional charge

Graphics

* White walls serve as a complementary backdrop for a large collection of graphics in different sizes and varied frames
* Group graphics and collector plates for an eclectic look; unify them by theme or style
* If you enjoy traditional decor, try hanging your graphics Victorian style with ribbons, or with wires suspended from the crown molding
* Consider frames as carefully as you do the graphics you choose: a handsome frame can double the impact of a work of art

Ornaments

* Don't be afraid to decorate more than one Christmas tree: many ornament collectors now boast a tree for every room of the home at holiday time!
* Show off some of your favorite ornaments all year 'round: suspend them from hooks and hangers to brighten rooms no matter what the season
* When you "deck the halls" with pine boughs, add some of your favorite ornaments to the display
* Carefully chosen ornaments make a pretty centerpiece when piled in a crystal bowl

The Secondary Market

Leading Dealers Share Their Hard-Won Knowledge About Buying and Selling Collectibles on the Secondary Market

I recently overheard a well-known collectibles producer bemoaning the fact that one of his loveliest plates would never see significant secondary market action. "We introduced it in a limited edition of just 1,000," the gentleman explained, "and so few people have ever heard of it or seen it that it has never penetrated the market"!

Imagine that: a limited-edition collectible whose edition is *too small* to ensure its opportunity for secondary market price rises! Novices in the field would be sure to surmise just the opposite: aren't we all taught from childhood that the rarer an item is, the more likely it is to appreciate in value?

The fact is that in today's international collectibles market, with millions of enthusiastic art lovers vying to own the most popular works, a piece with a relatively large edition may well "outperform" an extremely limited plate, figurine or other collectible. Why? Because the key to the market is supply and demand.

If available supply is less than pent-up demand for a given work of art, that piece's price most often will begin to climb on the auction market. Demand cannot be stimulated without collectors' knowledge of the item's existence. And those items which are seen throughout the marketplace are most likely to attract and sustain the interest of a broad range of collectors.

This short "object lesson" is meant to illustrate a point. Today's market for limited edition collectibles is complex, exciting and fast-paced. And its patterns of success do not necessarily "square" with a collector's experience in financial markets or other aspects of life.

Going Once, Going Twice — This doll auction in Plymouth, Michigan, conducted by International Doll Exhibitions and Auctions Ltd. and sponsored by Georgia's Gift Gallery, was part of an all-day event attended by over 2,500 doll enthusiasts.

There is a great deal to learn and understand in order to make the best buying and selling decisions. And to gather this valuable knowledge for our readers, Collectors' Information Bureau has interviewed more than 20 top limited edition dealers who are actively involved in today's secondary market for plates, figurines, bells, graphics, ornaments and dolls.

What Is the Secondary Market?

To begin, let us establish the step-by-step process by which a limited edition collectible enters the secondary market.

1. A collectible is introduced to the market and made available to collectors. Collectors may purchase the item through a dealer (in person or by mail or phone), or direct from the manufacturer/marketer (usually by mail or phone only). Items are sold at "original issue price," which is their retail price level. This method of selling is known as the "primary market."
2. After a period which may vary from days to years, the collectible becomes "sold out." This means that neither the dealers nor the manufacturer/marketers have any additional pieces to sell to collectors on the primary market.
3. When a collector wishes to buy a piece which is "sold out," he or she must enter the "secondary market" to purchase it. Because the piece is no longer available at retail, the new buyer must locate someone who already owns it and pay whatever price the market will bear. Most buyers enlist the help of a dealer, exchange, or matching service to help them in this process, while some place want ads in collectibles publications, or "network" with fellow collectors.
4. If new buyers continue to seek to acquire the piece long after its edition is sold out, the secondary market for that item may become stronger

and stronger and the price it can command may multiply over and over. Such market action is reported in the Collectors' Information Bureau Price Index at the back of this book.

Of course, some collectibles never sell out completely, while others sell out but never attract sufficient demand to command a higher price than the issue-price level. Some collectibles peak soon after their editions close, while others remain dormant for years and then begin rising in value because of changing market dynamics.

Manufacturers, dealers, and collectibles experts alike caution all collectors to *buy items that they like and want to display*, without regard for possible price rises. No one knows for certain whether a given item will end up rising in value on the secondary market.

How Collectible Editions are Limited

The term "limited edition" is one that many collectors find confusing, since studios limit production of their collectibles in many different ways. Here is an explanation of the most common methods of edition limitation.

Limited by Number: The producer sets a worldwide edition limit which may be a round number, or a number with special significance. Gartlan U.S.A., for example, often limits its sports collectibles to numbers that have importance in the careers of the sports celebrities they depict. Such items may carry their own sequential numbers within the edition.

Limited by Time: The producer pledges to craft an item only during a specific time period: the year 1992, for instance. A Christmas plate might close its edition on Christmas Eve of the year of issue, as another example. Or a commemorative figurine might be offered for the two years prior to a historic event, then close its edition on the date of the event. Such items may carry their own sequential numbers within the edition.

Limited by Firing Period: This designation has to do with the number of items that can be kiln-fired by a marketer or producer in a given number of days. It is stated in terms such as "limited to a total of 14 firing days." Items limited by firing period most often are sequentially numbered on the backstamp or bottomstamp.

Limited to Members: In recent years, many collectibles clubs have offered "members-only" items that are available only during a set time period, and only to individuals who have joined the club. A secondary market for these items develop when individuals join the club in later years and wish to acquire earlier editions of "members-only" collectibles that are no longer available at retail.

Open Editions that are Closed or Retired: While open editions are not strictly considered limited editions, they may stimulate secondary market action when they are closed or retired, and are no longer available at original-issue price.

Advice to Collectors Entering the Secondary Market

Deciding how to go about buying and selling on the secondary market, and what "philosophy of collecting" to adopt can be challenging to collectors. Here, some words of wisdom from experienced dealers provide guidelines to new and seasoned collectors.

When considering the sale of an item, the first step is to "determine the present secondary market value of the collectible," according to Lynda Blankenship of Dickens' Exchange in Metairie, Louisiana. Ms. Blankenship advises collectors to check this book or monthly update reports in collectibles magazines for prices. "Or contact a secondary broker for an opinion," she suggests.

Being realistic in setting a price is important, says Bob Phillips of The Wishing Well in Solvang, California. "Don't think that your piece is worth more than the other person's or you'll be hanging onto it longer than you want," Phillips cautions. Sandie Ellis of Ellis in Wonderland, Sacramento, California, echoes his advice and adds a comment of her own. "If you are looking for a quick sale, set the price below market; otherwise be prepared to wait," she says.

Sometimes a buyer is waiting in the wings in your own "back yard," according to Reda Walsh of The Kent Collection in Englewood, Colorado. That's why Ms. Walsh advises collectors to "check with your local retail dealer first to see if they are looking" for the item or items you have to sell. Another possibility, according to Marge Rosenberg of Carol's Gift Shop, Artesia, California, is selling through a local collectors club. "Most of them have Swap and Sell events at their meetings," she explains.

In setting prices, collectors should understand that the amount they clear from the sale of an item will depend upon how they arrange to sell it. The prices quoted in most price guides — including the one at the back of this book — are retail prices. Any brokerage fees, commissions, consignment fees or cost of ads will be deducted from this price. What's more, price quotes represent averages: an item may command more at certain times and in certain areas of the country and less in others depending upon supply and demand.

In addition, price quotes assume that the item is perfect — in mint condition. Chips, repairs, discolorations, production flaws, damage, or other imperfections will negatively impact the selling price in most cases. As the seller, you should be straightforward about your collectible's condition, says Patricia M. Cantrell of Village Realty Miniature Properties, Fort Worth, Texas. "If any problems are found, they should be noted and the prospective buyer made aware of them," she cautions.

Sandy Forgach of Collectibles etc., Inc. Match Service and Gift Shop says that cleaning one's collectibles before selling them will help maximize the price they can command. "People often make no effort to clean them," Ms. Forgach says, but a dusty and dingy piece is much less likely to bring a top price than one which is mint-condition clean.

Making Smooth Buying Transactions on the Secondary Market

In addition to the often-heard advice to "buy only what you like," experienced dealers have much to share in the way of guidelines for secondary market buyers. Their most frequent comment is to be sure that you know whom you are dealing with: the choice of a broker, buy-sell service or other "go-between" is often even more important for the buyer than it is for the seller.

Sandy Forgach suggests paying with a charge card when you buy from an ad. This offers you protection in case the item is not in mint condition or does not arrive as promised. "When you pay by check, you assume all the risks," she explains.

Connie Eckman of Collectible Exchange Inc. in New Middletown, Ohio, advises collectors to buy only the items they need to fill in collections they're working on. She has found that people who purchase an item only in the hopes that it will rise in value — so they can sell at a profit — are often disappointed. "Speculating at secondary prices rarely pays off," she says.

"Don't just shop in your own back yard," says Linda Blankenship. Take advantage of possible regional differences in price by checking around. "If a piece is constantly available at the same price, it is obviously not a fabulous deal," Ms. Blankenship continues. Education, patience and staying abreast of the market will yield the best possible bargain, she believes.

Those who plan on buying via the secondary market should "go on mailing lists of as many reputable secondary market dealers as possible," says Becky Flynn of Dollsville Dolls and Bearsville Bears in Palm Springs, California. This will enable the collector to research items just by reading over the mail they receive.

While there is some controversy over the necessity of obtaining boxes, certificates and other materials that originally accompanied the collectible, it is in the buyer's best interest to receive this material if at all possible. In this case, an experienced and reputable dealer or broker can be of help in determining what came with the collectible upon its arrival from the producer. "Be certain all necessary papers, Certificates of Authenticity, etc. are available at the time of purchase," says Karen Wilson of Callahan's of Calabash Nautical Gifts, Calabash, North Carolina.

Finally, a collector should rationally assess what a piece is worth to him or her, and make buying decisions accordingly. In the heat of an auction situation, collectors may bid a piece up to 20 or 30 times its original price, and still be happy to get it. Other collectors are more conservative, perhaps to their later regret. As Renee Tyler of Collector's Marketplace in Montrose, Pennsylvania says, "I've seen people miss a great chance to get something special because of a $25.00 difference in price."

The C.I.B. Price Index Offers a Starting Point for Secondary Prices

As our experts have said, one good first step to take before buying or selling a collectible is to

The first step before buying or selling a collectible is to check its recent price quote from a reliable source such as the Collectors' Information Bureau's Collectibles Price Guide.

check on its recent quote price from one or more reliable sources. To get started, check the Collectors' Information Bureau Price Index in the back of this book. It's the most comprehensive Price Index for limited edition plates, figurines, bells, graphics, ornaments and dolls available in the marketplace today!

As with any Price Index, a collector must look upon secondary information as a guide and not the value of an item right down to the penny. Some collectibles retain the same value for years, while others rise or fall faster than the information is printed.

The Collectors' Information Bureau Price Index is prepared very carefully. Manufacturers supply all pertinent product information to the C.I.B. This data is then entered into a computer. Copies of the Price Index are then mailed to our panel of dealers located all across the country. These knowledgeable store owners report actual selling prices back to the C.I.B. headquarters.

As mentioned above, collectibles may sell for different prices throughout the country. Therefore, a price or a price range is determined for each entry based upon careful analysis of the dealer reports. The Price Index is printed for this book and also updated one more time during the year.

Should collectors ever question a secondary market quote, they are advised to seek a second source or to write to the Collectors' Information Bureau for an updated value.

Collectors can place buy and sell orders for limited edition plates by calling The Bradford Exchange's Trading Floor.

Specific Ways to Buy and Sell Collectibles

Experts recommend several avenues for the collector who wishes to buy or sell a collectible once it is sold out at the retail level. Here are details on each procedure.

Contact the Manufacturer. While most manufacturers consider it unethical to directly determine their products' secondary market values, they may offer services to interested collectors who would otherwise find it difficult to purchase or sell a collectible on the secondary market.

Such services may include listings or ads in a company or club newsletter or publication, a matching service which helps prospective buyers and sellers make contact, or referrals to dealers who are actively involved in trading the firm's collectibles. In addition, some manufacturers help arrange for auctions at which collectors or club members may offer their pieces for sale to the highest bidder. Results of these auctions then may be reported in company or club newsletters.

Place a Classified Ad. Collectors may elect to place a classified ad in a collector publication to avoid paying a commission to a third party. The cost of the ad will be deducted from the profit, but if a collector sells directly to another collector, the seller can normally expect to receive a value closer to an item's secondary market quote price. Refer to the listing of "Magazines and Newsletters" elsewhere in this book for publications to contact.

According to Cherie Henn of *Collectors News*, the more details that appear in the ad, the more likely it is that a transaction will result. She suggests including a specific price you are willing to pay or to accept, along with a phone number instead of or in addition to an address. If you are responding to an ad, promptness is essential, as both buyers and sellers are anxious to proceed once the ad is in print.

The Bradford Exchange. Bradford is a long-established exchange for buyers and sellers of limited edition plates only. The Exchange acts as an agent for its clients, and guarantees that the trader-seller will be paid. Bradford also guarantees that the buyer will receive a plate in mint condition with proper certification. The Exchange acts as a broker to ensure trustworthy and fair transactions.

There is no fee for listing a plate on the Exchange, but a thirty percent fee will be subtracted from the sale price when a plate is sold. These sales are recorded and maintained on a computer to provide information about secondary market sales. Collectors can place buy and sell orders simply by calling the Exchange's toll-free number for the Trading Floor at 1-800-323-8078.

Retail Dealers. There are many dealers and store owners across the country who will work with collectors interested in selling their collectibles. Some dealers will work with regular customers to make trades if the dealer needs what the collector has, permitting them to trade up to a more valuable or newer item. Others may offer to take items on consignment. Since each dealer operates differently, collectors should expect policies to vary.

Another avenue for buying or selling collectibles is through retail dealers who specialize in the secondary market.

Our survey of dealers revealed that they charge commissions and brokerage fees ranging from 5% to 35%. While in most cases the seller absorbs this cost, it is sometimes split between the buyer and the seller. Shipping and insurance costs are another matter: they may be paid by the seller, split by buyer and seller, or in rare cases, absorbed by the dealer out of his/her commission. Sometimes the dealer takes the item into possession and displays it in the shop until it is sold. In other cases, the seller retains the item until a bargain is made.

Some dealers prefer to purchase items outright from collectors, in which case the collector should expect to receive as little as 50% of the current quote price; perhaps even less. In this case, the dealer considers the secondary market transaction the same as a regular retail sale: he or she buys the item at about 50% of retail and then takes it into inventory. When it is sold, the proceeds cover overhead, inventory costs, and costs of doing business as well as profit.

A continuing trend among dealers is to specialize in the secondary market for just one or two lines. There are still a handful of dealers who are knowledgeable on a wide range of collectibles and are willing to buy and sell them. However, collectors may have to contact the manufacturer's customer service department or an organization such as Collectors' Information Bureau to locate a "specialist" who can sell their particular piece of artwork.

Secondary Market Action is Sought by Only a Few

Our dealer experts agree that the vast majority of collectors purchase their items with very little thought of secondary market potential. At the most, they look forward to showing off their "smart buys" to friends as they watch prices rise for their favorite collectibles.

Most secondary market buys, our experts say, are executed by collectors who are hoping to fill out a series or acquire an item of special significance that they were unable to purchase on the primary market.

Some sellers enjoy "trading up" to more expensive collectibles, and finance their new purchases by selling items that once were quite affordable — but now command high prices on the auction market. There are also a number of collectors who wish to sell certain items because of a lifestyle change, move to smaller quarters, or financial hardship. And sometimes those who inherit collections are not in a position to keep and display them.

Whatever a collector's reason for buying or selling on the secondary market, the keys to success are education, patience, rational thinking, and advice from the experts. That includes ready access to the resources of Collectors' Information Bureau. For answers to your secondary market questions, send a self-addressed, stamped envelope to the Collectors' Information Bureau at 2420 Burton S.E., Grand Rapids, Michigan 49546.

Insuring Your Collectibles

How to Establish Your Collection's Worth...and Protect Your Treasures Against Loss or Theft

Imagine returning from an evening on the town to discover that your home has been ransacked...your favorite artwork and collectibles stolen. The feelings of violation and fear would be difficult enough to deal with. But imagine your shock if you should find that your insurance policy did not cover the full value of your favorite works of art!

In a very short time, plates, figurines and other collectibles may double, triple or even soar in value to ten times their original prices or more. And collectors who started out to buy "just a few things to display here and there" may soon find themselves the proud owners of scores of pieces — worth many thousands of dollars.

So how does the intelligent collector protect those precious assets? Experts suggest a plan that combines prevention and risk management. Begin by doing all you can to make sure your home does not become a target for crime. Then find out how much each of your art pieces is worth, and work with an insurance specialist to develop a protection plan that fits your needs and budget.

Prevent Theft Through Home Preparedness

In today's society, electronic protection devices have become the "locks" of ultimate security. The first choice for any burglar is a home or site that has no electronic security system. There are many excellent companies now offering home systems that can be especially designed for your particular home and collection. These firms can be easily located by checking your local yellow pages under the "security" heading.

There are several points to consider when purchasing a security system. Some systems operate with batteries at the point of contact, and these batteries either need to be replaced on occasion or checked regularly by the security firm's employees. A system that relies primarily on batteries and constant maintenance by company employees may not be the most effective form of protection. The most effective systems ring into a central station where the local police are dispatched on a 24-hour basis.

While having a burglar alarm installed, it is usually wise to also connect a smoke/fire alarm to the system, thereby offering yourself further protection against another type of loss that could occur. In any case, shop around and compare systems before making your selection. Speak with other collectors that you respect and get their comments regarding systems they have purchased.

Your precautionary measures may well reap benefits on your insurance policy: such items as deadbolt locks, central alarms, smoke detectors and available fire extinguishers may result in valuable credits against the cost of your coverage.

How to Plan for Out-of-Town Travel

Russell J. Lindemann, Assistant Vice-President of Hilb, Rogal, and Hamilton Company of Grand Rapids, Michigan, offers his insurance clients a few simple tips that may help avoid break-ins during vacations or business trips. "If you're going away, take your most valuable items to someone else's house for safe keeping, or put them in a bank vault," Lindemann suggests. "You might place smaller and less fragile items in your safety deposit box.

"It's worth reminding people to leave some lights on timers when they go out of town," Lindemann continues. "I suggest one or two upstairs, one or two downstairs, and one in the kitchen. I vary their times a bit each day. I leave a radio on a timer, too. Mine goes on from about 11 p.m. to 3 a.m. If someone approaches the house and hears that sound from outside, they'll be less likely to try to enter.

"The less people who know you are away from home, the better," Lindemann counsels. "While some advisors will tell you to stop your mail and newspaper delivery, you never know who might overhear that order. I prefer to have a family member, trusted neighbor or close friend pick up the mail and newspaper each day while I'm gone." Lindemann has some suggestions for winter travelers, too. "Have someone shovel your driveway and a path up to the front walk. Or arrange to have someone pull up to your garage to make tracks. It's a dead giveaway that no one's home if your driveway is left unshoveled for days after a major snowstorm." The same goes for summertime lawn mowing if you'll be gone for more than a week.

Lindemann's associate, Kay Scoville, says it's a good idea to have someone go in and check on your home periodically while you are away. "Don't leave the storm door unlocked for them," Ms. Scoville says. "It's best to have as many locks and deterrents as possible. One idea is to leave your garage door down and give the garage door opener or key to the person who's checking your house. When they leave and put down the door, the house is locked up tight again."

Establishing the Value of Your Collectibles

While some collectors assume that their favorite works of art are automatically covered under the "contents" provisions of their homeowners or renters policies, Lindemann and Ms. Scoville warn that it's never safe to assume.

"The 'contents' amount is usually determined as a percentage of your home's value, but it can be increased. The percentage differs from company to company, but the majority are in the area of 50 to 70% of your home's replacement cost," Lindemann explains. In the case of a total loss, problems may arise if an individual owns a relatively modest home but has a large collection of valuable pieces — or pieces that have risen substantially in value.

"In addition, there's the question of irreplaceable, one-of-a-kind items," Lindemann continues. "How do you set a value on them? They need to be appraised, and scheduled individually on your insurance policy."

Insurance agent Thomas A. Mier from Universal Insurance Services, Inc., Grand Rapids, Michigan, explains the types of coverage available to collectors and the importance of adequately insuring valuable possessions.

While the prices listed in books such as this *Collectibles Market Guide and Price Index* may be considered adequate documentation by many insurance firms, Lindemann emphasizes that especially rare, valuable or controversial pieces often may require individual appraisal.

What is an Appraiser, and How Do I Choose One?

Some collectors are unsure as to whether they need the services of an appraiser, and if so, how they should choose the best appraiser for their needs. To provide guidance in this important area, Collectors' Information Bureau solicited the advice of Emyl Jenkins, author of *Emyl Jenkins' Appraisal Book: Identifying, Understanding, and Valuing Your Treasures* (Crown Publishers). Ms. Jenkins' book is available for $24.95 in major bookstores or by writing her for an autographed copy at Emyl Jenkins Appraisals, P.O. Box 12465, Raleigh, NC 27605.

An appraiser is a person who determines the value of an item or items for insurance purposes, and can supply the necessary information for the settlement of damage claims. The professional appraiser is also the person who can determine the value of a collection at the time it is donated to a tax-exempt institution or charity.

While the *New York Times* estimates that there are an estimated 125,000 appraisers in the United States, it is up to the individual collector to evaluate an appraiser's qualifications. Ms. Jenkins offers this advice:

"The American Society of Appraisers is recognized as this country's only multidisciplinary appraisal testing designation society. Membership in the ASA is not necessarily proof of ability. It does mean, however, that the ASA member has submitted his appraisals for examination by his peers, has taken and passed a multisection examination on ethics, appraisal principals, and his specialized area, and is experienced.

"Because of the rigid requirements imposed on its members, the American Society of Appraisers is often referred to as the most prestigious of the appraisal organizations. The ASA and the International Society of Appraisers both have excellent educational programs conducted under college and university auspices. These two professional associations also grant their members different levels of professional proficiency as a result of successful course completion and/or testing. The Appraisers

Association of America is also widely recognized, and applicants must submit appraisals and meet AAA requirements before they are accepted as members.

"Locally, you may find personal property appraisers listed in the yellow pages, but if not, call your insurance agent, bank, attorney, or museum. A call to a college or university art department may be worthwhile. You can also check with antique shops, interior decorators, or auction houses. They may offer appraisal services or refer you to an independent appraiser."

According to Ms. Jenkins, the cost of appraisal services should be comparable to that of other professional services in your locale — attorney or accounting fees, for example. Hourly rates range from $35 to $150 per hour or $350 to $1,500 per day. Do not expect to be charged only for the time your appraiser spends with you. Appraisers must also charge for their research and appraisal preparation time. You will be wise to negotiate a contract spelling out prices and services before beginning to work with your appraiser.

Keep a Detailed Inventory of Your Holdings

Even items which do not call for individual appraisal should be carefully documented in your collectibles records. With some insurance policies, it may not be possible to receive reimbursement for the full value of your collection without a comprehensive list. Record the following basic information for each item:

- Manufacturer Name
- Edition Limit/Your Item's Number if Numbered
- Artist Name
- Your Cost
- Series Name
- Added Expenses (Shipping, Framing, Restoration, etc.)
- Item Name
- Special Markings (Artist's Signature, etc.)
- Year of Issue
- Secondary Market History (If Purchased on Secondary Market)
- Size/Dimensions
- Place of Purchase
- Location in Your Home (For Burglary or Loss)
- Date of Purchase
- Insurance Company/Policy or Rider Number

Of course, you will also keep any appraisal documents with your inventory list. Record each new item you buy at the time of purchase. Large index cards will handle the pertinent information, or you may prefer to invest in one of the published record books that may be available in your local bookstore.

The Importance of Video Documentation

Collectors should take advantage of today's video technology to provide a full-color, close-up record of all valuable possessions on tape. If you do not own a video camera, rent one for an afternoon and equip yourself with this essential "video documentation."

Begin with a general overview of the entire collection to provide a "feel" for how extensive it is, and how you normally display your pieces. Then tape a detailed close-up of each individual piece. Hold up each item so that the markings on base or backstamp can be read. Close-ups should offer special views of details and any printed wording on the items.

After you have finished with your video record, replay the film to check the quality and then rewind for storage with your written inventory in a site off-premises: perhaps in your safe deposit box. Make a copy of your video and written inventory so that another set can be kept at home.

Options and Choices for Collectibles Insurance

Once you have "burglar proofed" your home, established values for your collectibles, and documented your holdings, you are ready to make an informed decision about your fine arts insurance coverage. It is a good idea to get two or three different companies to quote you a price, since different insurance companies specialize in certain kinds of policies. Or talk with a multi-line firm like Hilb, Rogal, and Hamilton, where Russell J. Lindemann and other staff members do the legwork for you and present you with recommendations of the best company and policy for your needs.

There are several types of coverage available today: valuable articles coverage (VAC), homeowner's or renter's, a separate endorsement to an existing policy, an endorsement on a business policy, or a completely separate policy.

Once you have established your insurance coverage, you can breathe easy for a time. But don't

It is important to keep an accurate record of your collectible purchases. Both record books above provide space for photographs and pertinent information.

forget to consider the impact of new acquisitions: should they be appraised? Should they be listed individually on your fine arts rider? As Lindemann says, "You have to keep up. If you don't modify your policy and a loss occurs, you can't collect more than what's shown on the policy. And if something you own is going up in value, make sure you adjust the value shown for it in your policy at least every year or two."

Protecting one's collection may seem like an arduous task, but the time invested is well worth the rewards of peace of mind and proper coverage. And like many collectors, you may even find that you enjoy the process of documentation and valuation — as it reinforces the growing scope and value of your wonderful collection!

The Collectors' Information Bureau thanks Dean A. Genth of Miller's Gift Gallery, Eaton, Ohio, for his substantial contributions to this article.

C.I.B. Associate Members

Mattheyprint and Custom China Work Behind the Scenes to Produce Some of the World's Most Honored Collector Plates

The gleaming porcelain plates that you see in your favorite collectibles shop — or admire in ads and direct mailings — require months of skilled and devoted work to design and produce. And two firms whose outstanding efforts have contributed to many an award-winning plate are Mattheyprint Corporation, a decal maker, and Custom China Creations, a collector plate decorator.

Mattheyprint's work comes first: using the original artwork selected for a plate as the basis for the creation of perfectly faithful ceramic art transfers. Custom China uses such transfers in the decoration, firing and finishing of plates to beautifully reflect the artist's original. As this story unfolds, you will come to understand the intricacy and care which are necessary for the successful completion of this step-by-step process of art reproduction on porcelain.

A Decal Maker of International Stature

Mattheyprint Corporation is the United States sales office for ceramic decals printed at Matthey Transfers, England and Matthey Beyrand et Cie of Limoges, France. These two factories have long and respected histories for supplying ceramic decals to the world's finest names in tableware, glassware and collectible plates. Familiar brand names such as Royal Doulton, Wedgwood, Spode and Ainsley all are decorated with Matthey ceramic decals.

For the past fifteen years, the French firm of Matthey Beyrand et Cie has concentrated on the production of high-quality collectible plate decals and is now considered one of the premiere suppliers for the limited edition market. The Johnson Matthey Group, of which Matthey Transfers, Matthey Beyrand and Mattheyprint are parts, have made a commitment to quality and customer service on behalf of their over 7,000 worldwide employees.

One of the most knowledgeable of these employees, Norm D. Cote, serves as U.S. Sales Manager for Johnson Matthey. His expertise in the crafting of ceramic decals has led to his authorship of an authoritative description of the process, which is quoted liberally with his permission in the paragraphs to follow.

The Art of Decal Making Stage I: Planning

Norm Cote stresses the importance of pre-planning before any collector plate decal is produced. Indeed, as he says, "a ceramic decal is a complex art within itself; an amalgamation of artistry, printing and ceramics.

"Long before reproduction of the artwork is begun, even before a ceramic decal manufacturer is involved, the producer should have clearly outlined his goals: number of plates to be produced, size of the plate, and retail price." According to Cote, all of these factors help determine how the decal manufacturer will proceed.

Choosing the ceramic colors to match the artwork from previously printed color palette.

The Color Separation Process

Collector plate decals "are printed one color at a time," Cote explains, "using ceramic pigments to 'build' the final design. The printed image is held together by a covercoat or 'carrier'." This "carrier" becomes volatile when high-temperature firing takes place, leaving behind the ceramic colors, which fuse into the glaze of the plate.

Some ceramic decals are printed in a four-color process, like that used in commercial printing. In this case, the four basic "process" colors of black, magenta (red), yellow and cyan (blue) are used in combination to create all other necessary colors. This process does not allow for the exact reproduction of every color in an artist's palette or in nature, however. Thus many producers elect to use "picked" colors — sometimes twenty or more for an individual transfer.

As Cote tells us, "We have never been able to influence the DeGrazias, Rockwells and Hibels of the world to create their fine art in just the four primary colors. Their subtle nuances of color are at the same time an integral part of their attraction and the basis for much time consumption in their reproduction.

"The color separation expert must predetermine, for instance, what percentage of red and yellow will faithfully capture the facial tones of a Rockwell painting. Too much red will give a sunburned appearance; too much yellow, and 'jaundice' will be the diagnosis!"

Reproduction artist "separating" colors prior to printing.

How Collector Plate Decals are Printed

A familiar tale from Norm Cote helps explain the challenges that beset the printer of collector plate decals. "The house needs a fresh coat of paint. A quick trip to the hardware store and we're ready. Little by little, stroke by stroke, a new gleaming finish is applied. But — a breeze springs up and our still tacky finish is covered with airborne particles of dust and grit, not to mention a few members of the insect world. A disappointing result at best.

"However, it is precisely this basic phenomenon which is an integral part of the printing of a ceramic decal for a collectible plate. Basically, the decal manufacturer substitutes clear varnish for the house paint and ceramic color (in powder form) for the airborne dust and grit. In the controlled atmosphere of a pressroom, the two are combined. The dry ceramic dust adheres itself to the clear, wet varnish in specific areas designated by the color separation. This two-step process, the laying on of a clear varnish on each sheet and the 'dusting' of ceramic color is collectively referred to as the printing stage of lithographic ceramic decal manufacture."

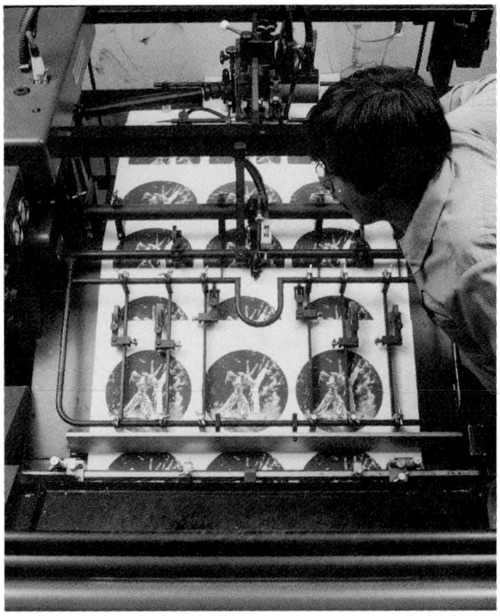

Nearly completed collectible plate decals in production.

The paper used for the making of a ceramic decal is like ordinary paper in that it originates from wood fiber. But unlike the paper in this book, decal paper has a smooth, glossy coating on one side only. The coating disintegrates when dipped in water, so that the decal can slide off the paper and onto a plate.

Norm Cote cautions that the actual printing process for decals is much more complex than a trip to the neighborhood speedy printer. "Because of the special varnish used and its drying characteristics, only one color can be printed per day." That means that a twenty-five color decal would require five full working weeks to complete.

The Decals Arrive at Custom China

Once Matthey's richly colored, top-quality decals are completed, finally inspected, packaged and ready for shipment to the decorator, a firm like Custom China Creations takes center stage in the plate production process. In business for a dozen years, Custom China is capably run by its president, Bob Perkins — an expert with twenty-five years' experience in the field of ceramics.

Perkins holds a master's degree in ceramic engineering, and he worked in ceramics research before joining the famed Franciscan dinnerware firm some years ago. He ran the fine china production department at Gorham, Inc. for five years before opening the California-based Custom China Creations in 1979.

Perkins attributes his firm's success to the level of expertise his staff members bring to their work. "Each of our employees is hand-picked, and many of them have ten years' experience or more," Perkins explains.

When Custom China begins work on an edition of plates, the first step — in addition to the selection of appropriate ceramic ware and added decorations like gold banding — is the "proofing" of the plate. This process requires the concentration not only of decal maker and decorator, but of artist and producer. All four parties are equally concerned that the resulting "proof plate" offers the best possible image of the artist's original.

In "proofing," the decal maker provides a decorator like Custom China with a sample of the decals it has produced, before the full edition of decals is printed. Then Custom China uses the decals to decorate and fire some border or rim adornments. It is Custom China's job to determine the correct firing temperature and timing, in collaboration with the decal maker. According to Bob Perkins, sometimes experimentation is necessary to "fine tune" the firing process. And in some cases, the fired plates may show that the colors of the decals need adjustment before the full edition is printed.

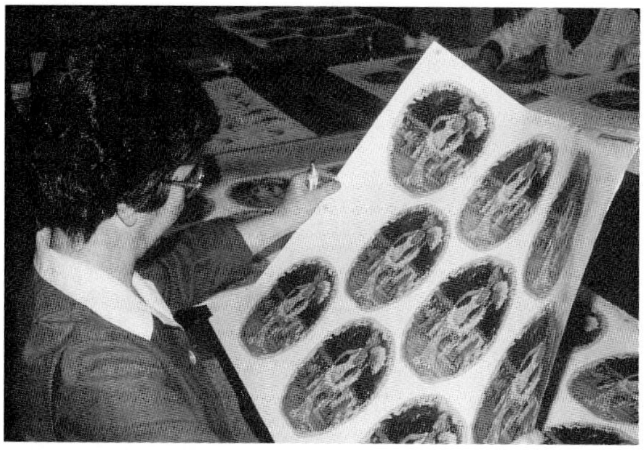

Final, decal by decal, inspection prior to shipment to the decorator.

How Plates are Decorated and Fired at Custom China

With 40,000 square feet of production space available, Custom China is already considered a "state of the art" facility for collector plate decorating and firing. Yet Bob Perkins is committed to staying "ahead of the times." He has a 60,000 square foot facility on the drawing board, for completion within the next few years. "The equipment will be all-new," Perkins says. "We will be able to implement automated gold banding equipment, and we'll use newest continuous belt kiln design, called a 'lehr'."

Yet even with his firm's up-to-date equipment in place, Perkins understands full well that it is the human touch that sets Custom China apart. Each plate that is decorated and fired in this facility is monitored from beginning to end by highly trained, quality-conscious artisans.

The creation of a single collector plate requires a multi-step process that begins with inspection of each decal and plate blank. For many firms, Custom China is entrusted with the selection and purchase of blank plates in sizes ranging from a "micro mini" of 1" in diameter to a dramatic, 16" round piece.

"When the plate blanks arrive here," Bob Perkins tells us, "we thoroughly inspect them for warpage, pinholes, black spots and edge quality. We also 'dry spot' the decals, an inspection process that ensures that each has outstanding quality of registration and uniformity of color, with no stray color deposits.

"After eliminating blanks and decals that are not completely perfect, we decorate a small number of plates for a test firing. We use only deionized water in the decoration process, to avoid any sodium or calcium deposits that might mar the finished plates. When the test firing is approved, we implement the production run.

"As each plate is decorated and hand-numbered, it is re-inspected to ensure that it has no visible flaws of any kind. After each plate is numbered, it is allowed to dry for a full twenty-four hours before firing," Perkins explains.

The kilns used for collector plate firing allow each plate to be slowly and uniformly heated to the temperature level necessary to allow the ceramic colors to fuse forever to the porcelain. They come out of the kiln already cooled, and then are taken to a final inspection center.

"At the time of this final inspection," Bob Perkins relates, "each plate is supplied with its own Certificate of Authenticity, numbered to match the number on its backstamp. Then the plates are packaged along with any literature the producer or marketer has supplied. Of course, all of our packaging is tested for its protective qualities and safety for transportation via United Parcel Service and the U.S. Postal Service."

Once a plate leaves the care of Custom China, it may be on its way initially to a retail store or dealer, or to the warehouse of a direct mail marketer. In any event, each plate is created in the hope that it will ultimately reside in the care of an individual collector who appreciates its handsome art...and its intricate production process.

The Production Process
How Figurines Are Made

Leaf through the pages of this book and you will view an endless variety of handsome collectibles that fall into the broad categories of "figurines." The elegant, hand-painted porcelains of Lenox and Kaiser...the shimmering crystal birds and animals of Swarovski...the appealing wood carvings of ANRI...the charming cottages of John Hine, Lilliput Lane, and Department 56.

Some figurines are crafted using age-old processes like the Goebel Miniatures' lost wax method, while others utilize state-of-the-art techniques like porcelain cold casting. Some pieces are left unadorned so that the innate beauty of polished bronze or pristine white bisque porcelain may be admired in all its glory. Others are painted in myriad individual colors...underglazed...overglazed...or burnished.

When collectors come to understand the complexity and care invested in even the simplest limited edition figurines, their enjoyment and appreciation may be greatly heightened. What's more, such knowledge enables collectors to evaluate possible purchases based upon the value of their materials and the intricacy of their design and production, as well as the appeal of their subject matter. This article provides a brief introduction to several of the step-by-step processes that bring today's figurines alive in three dimensions.

The Classic Limited Edition Porcelain Figurine

The limited edition figurine is a Twentieth Century invention: in the 1930s, Royal Worcester and its master artist, Dorothy Doughty, first perfected a method for casting exact replicas from an original, master sculpture. A very similar process still is used today by fine porcelain studios, as exemplified by this step-by-step technique employed at the American studios of Lenox Collections.

First, an artist creates an original sculpture, from which intricate molds are made. A phenomenal number of mold-parts are required for each porcelain: a single, three and one-half inch bird sculpture might require thirty-eight parts! While using so many individual mold parts is costly, Lenox considers it well worthwhile to produce lifelike poses and deeper detailing.

Next, liquid porcelain "slip" is poured into each mold. The formula of the porcelain slip will be varied to meet specific artist requirements for color and detail. Lenox, like most fine porcelain studios, limits the "lifetime use" of each mold. Thus, the sculptured detail stays especially crisp and sharp.

The resulting fragile castings, called "greenware," must be hand-assembled and propped for firing. If this is not done correctly, the sculpture

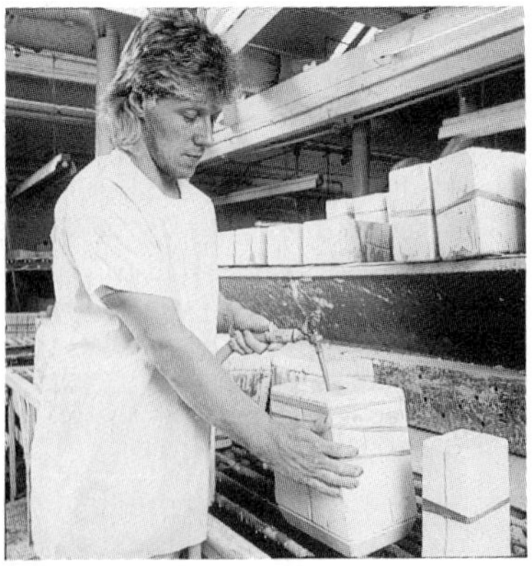

#1 — The making of a classic Royal Doulton Character Jug begins as liquid slip is poured into a mold. The porous mold absorbs the moisture from the china "slip" and leaves a coating of china in the form of the character jug inside.

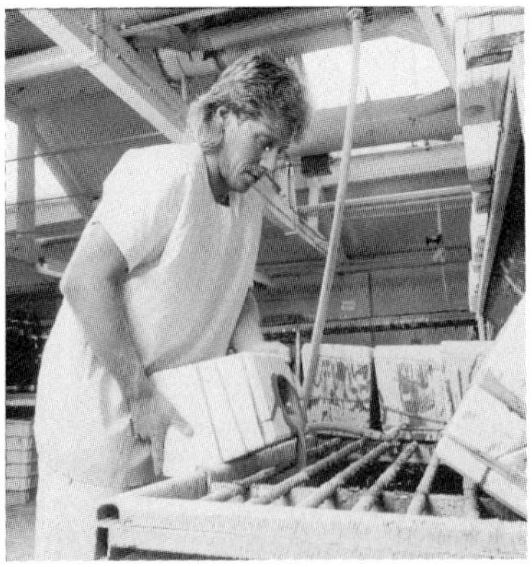

#2 — Excess slip is poured away after approximately twenty minutes.

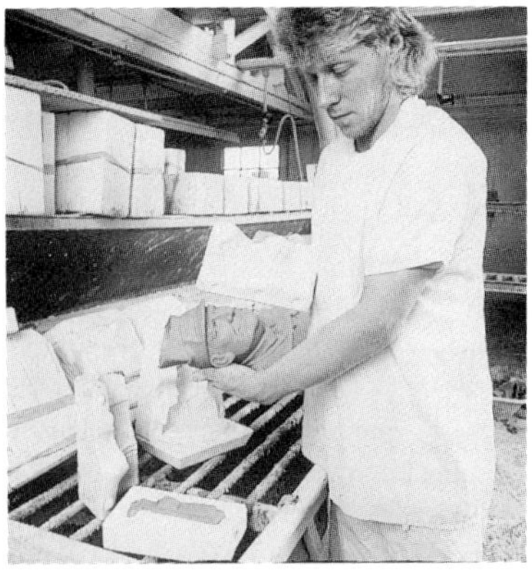

#3 — The mold is carefully opened to reveal a character jug inside.

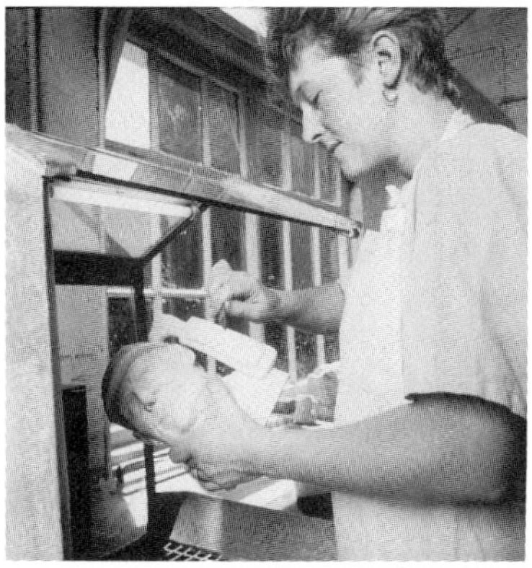

#4 — The handle of "The Golfer," modeled to portray a bag of golf clubs, is attached to the main body of the piece.

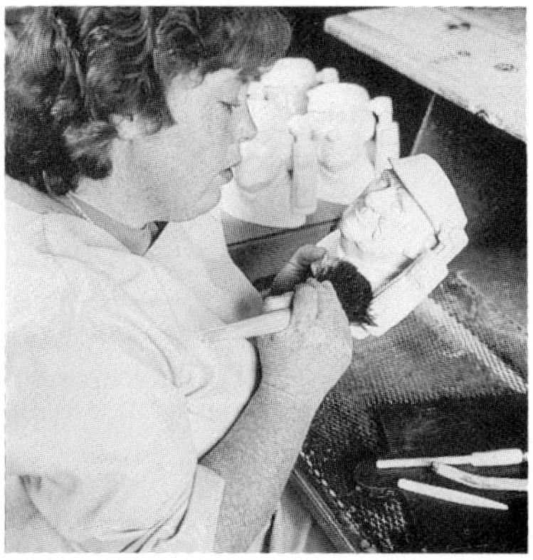

#5 and #6 — After drying, the jug is brushed and smoothed to remove any mold marks or rough edges of china.

will "slump" in the kiln and compromise the desired effect. Craftsmen at Lenox reject even minor "slumps" to ensure the artistic integrity of each sculpture.

A typical Lenox sculpture is fired in the kiln four separate times. The first firing takes place at temperatures as high as 1330 degrees Centigrade, and can last as long as thirteen to twenty-four hours.

From the fiery tips of an autumn leaf to the blush of a shy young maiden, details come to life only if painted to perfection. Lenox-trained artisans take extra care in hand-painting every sculpture, often using an unusually rich palette of colors. Each hand-painted work then is kiln-fired to fuse the ceramic colors to the porcelain.

A Time-Consuming Creative Process

While the Lenox process described above offers an overview of porcelain craftsmanship, some large and complex porcelain works may require many more steps — and much more time — for completion. As an example, WACO's "The Grand Carousel" consumed more than two years of research and development time and an investment of over $1,000,000 before its completion. In addition to the carousel itself, this sculptural work also includes a music box.

Other sculptures — notably those of Boehm and Royal Worcester — may combine porcelain with another sculptural medium such as burnished bronze. In these cases, delicate floral petals are cast in porcelain and fashioned into flowers by hand; then joined to stems and leaves of bronze which allow for durability as well as incredible detail work.

LEGENDS has gained fame and praise for its dynamic works of art — often on Western themes — which combine two or more precious metals for a rich and dramatic sculptural effect. Portions in bronze, silver, or other metals are cast individually, then joined together, adding dimension and beauty to the finished figurine.

An Up-and-Coming Art Form: Cold-Cast Porcelain

Renowned figurine makers including Border Fine Arts and Duncan Royale employ a fine art process called cold-casting. The formula for cold-casting may call for chips or dust of bronze, wood, or — most often — porcelain, combined with resin. The advantages of cold-casting include the cost savings of avoiding kiln firing, and the remarkable detail work that is possible when a figurine is cast in resin-based materials. This narrative describes the step-by-step process that takes place at the Border Fine Arts Studios to make popular figurines, such as those of Lowell Davis for Schmid.

Like the classic porcelain crafting process, each cold-cast porcelain figurine begins with an original sculpture, most often created in modeling wax. Next, a special mold-making silicone compound is carefully applied over the wax original to produce the master mold. There must be no mistakes during this operation, as the original may be lost and with it scores or even hundreds of hours of work.

Next, a metal composition casting is poured, and the resulting piece is used as a production master. The master is reworked with engraving tools to ensure that every detail is sharp and crisp. Then production molds and cases are made from this master, and injected with a liquid "slip" combining the resin and porcelain dust. A chemical reaction takes place under pressure, resulting in a white, porcelain-like casting that offers a faithful rendering of the sculptor's original.

These "whiteware" castings then are removed from their molds and set aside to cure. The castings are inspected for quality, and any which are not absolutely perfect are destroyed.

In a process called "fettling," a team of skilled artisans prepares the raw, white castings for painting. Seams on the whiteware are removed with delicate dentistry drills, and sculptures with multiple parts are assembled in the fettling department. Another quality control inspection precedes the careful process of hand-painting.

In many cases, handsome wooden bases are added to the finished pieces, which are then enhanced by felt bottoms that protect the furniture in collectors' homes.

Mold-Making is the Key to a Successful Cottage

As collectible cottages gain more and more admirers each year, there is growing interest in the production process for these charming miniature homes, shops and public buildings. Here is an overview of the making of one of the much-loved David Winter cottages for John Hine Limited.

The most difficult and fundamental part of the production work is the making of the molds for each original cottage. Indeed, the sole purpose of every craftsperson who works on the cottages is to produce exact replicas of David Winter's own intricately modeled pieces. This stage requires scrupulous care, since each cottage emerges from one single mold, which must capture every nuance of detail.

The successful mold is passed to the casters who use it to produce a perfect cast in a special material called Crystacal. Crystacal is a form of natural gypsum which is filtered, dried and ground to a powder. When added to water, it becomes an excellent, perfectly pure casting material.

Each minute feature inside the mold must be fingered carefully to ensure that none of the finer

#7 — Jug being placed onto a kiln car which will transport it through a tunnel kiln for its first firing. This firing process takes 18 hours at 1260 degrees C.

#8 — Character jugs on cart at entrance of the kiln.

#9 — The Royal Doulton backstamp is applied to the bottom of the jug.

#10 — Each jug is carefully hand-painted. Jugs are painted on the biscuit body before glazing to achieve a stronger, more character-like look or style of decoration.

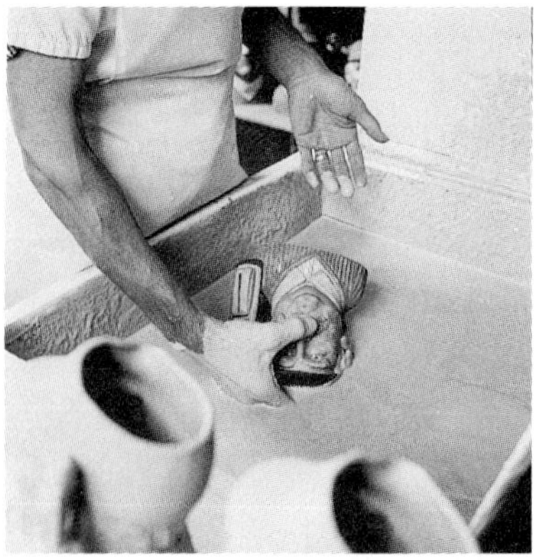

#11 — After decoration, the jug is hand dipped in a vat of glaze and then will be fired in the kiln a final time.

details is missed. The exact position of everything inside the mold is essential, and thus the craftspeople who carry out this process must employ the greatest possible degree of concentration.

Next the mold is removed from the cast slowly and deliberately, to ensure that the model itself is not damaged. If the emerging cast piece is anything less than perfect, it is destroyed.

After the cast has been removed from the mold, "flashes" of Crystacal are still attached to it. These small pieces of excess material are delicately "fettled" away and the base is made smooth and even.

At this stage, the cast is set, but not yet completely dry. To allow the cottage to reach the correct consistency for the next process, it is "rested" in a temperature controlled room in conditions of suitable humidity. A sealing solution of shellac and white polish is used to coat the models next; this acts as an undercoat for the painting. Then when the sealing solution has dried fully, the unpainted models are delivered to the homes of John Hine Limited's skilled team of painters.

Those selected as painters are taught the delicate skill of staining the cottages in a manner which highlights the artistry and detailing of David Winter's work. The subtle colors, and the special techniques used by the painters, emphasize the realism of Winter's miniature cottages. A final inspection, the addition of felt on each cottage base, and careful packaging complete the creation of a handsome new collectible cottage.

ANRI Wood Carvings Carry on the European Tradition

Also included in the category of figurines are the wonderful wood carvings of Italy's ANRI Workshops, which are presented in the United States by Schmid. Each wood carving begins with the unblemished wood of an Austrian Alpine maple tree, which is prepared with care and hand-carved by a skilled craftsperson.

Once a rough cut for carving is prepared on a lathe, the sculptor uses progressively smaller and finer tools to gradually work toward an extremely fine detailed carving. After many hours of painstaking carving, ANRI figures arrive in the hands of the painters. Special, transparent oil colors are produced for ANRI in Italy, while stains for the sculptures are produced in Germany.

The Sparkling Story of Crystal Sculpture

Often today, the term "crystal" is used loosely to describe any fine glass. But the regulations of the European Economic Community (EEC) make the legal definition of this substance very specific — indeed, "crystal clear." In order to be sold as Full Lead Crystal, a glass product must be made with at least 30% lead. Crystal that contains 30% lead or more has the potential for incredible brilliance and maximum refraction when the crystal stones are cut and polished.

While some of us think of handsome dinner goblets when we hear the word "crystal," today this coveted substance is used to make a menagerie of animals, birds and other handsome, sculptural collectibles by Swarovski America.

Whether you prefer your three-dimensional collectibles in fine porcelain, cold-cast porcelain, precious metal, wood or crystal, today's art studios offer you a wide variety of elegant figurines. In all price ranges...all sizes...and every degree of complexity, figurines make a superb addition to any home. And when you understand the careful process by which they are created, your enjoyment of these works of sculptural art increases all the more!

#12 — Golfer character jugs being removed from the kiln.

#13 — Each jug is carefully inspected to ensure that it meets quality control before it is allowed to leave the factory.

The Finished Product

"When Coffee Never Tasted So Good" by Lowell Davis from Schmid

Club ANRI's "Twenty Years of Love" by Juan Ferrandiz

"The Grand Carousel" from WACO Products Corporation

"Squires Hall" from John Hine Studios

Lenox Collections' "Polar Bear"

Flambro Imports' "65th Birthday Commemorative"

"Hippopotamus," "Elephant" and "Rhinoceros" from Swarovski America

Duncan Royale's "May" from the Calendar Secrets *collection*

LEGENDS' "Pursued" by C.A. Pardell

Travel for Collectors

Broaden Your Knowledge of Collecting by Visiting Museums and Touring Collectible Production Facilities

Collectors who vacation in the United States, Canada and abroad are invited to browse through this chapter to discover the locations of exciting collectible tours and museums offered by manufacturers and other firms.

Attend a barbecue. Participate in an auction. Tour your favorite collectible factory and enjoy their step-by-step production process. The opportunities are endless. Collectors who take the opportunity to experience their hobby first-hand, are certain to gain a deeper appreciation of their artwork and how it was crafted.

United States Museums and Tours

AMERICAN MUSEUM OF WILDLIFE ART
P.O. Box 26
3303 North Service Drive
Red Wing, MN 55066
612/388-0755

Open Monday-Saturday, 10 A.M.-5 P.M. Sunday, Noon-4 P.M. Closed all major holidays.

Located in Red Wing, Minnesota, fifty-five miles southeast of St. Paul and Minneapolis on U.S. 61.

Admission free, donations welcome, nature shoppe.

It is a non-profit organization established to further interest in wildlife art — collecting, presenting, honoring and preserving art in this field. The museum has five rotating exhibits yearly.

ANNALEE DOLL·MUSEUM
P.O. Box 708
Meredith, NH 03253
800/433-6557

The factory is open only during the Barbecue & Auction weekend to the public. Tour hours are 8 A.M.-4 P.M. both days.

Located at the end of Reservoir Road and Hemlock Drive in Meredith, New Hampshire.

The Barbecue & Auction event includes two auctions, tours of the factory, special offers to attendees, live music, food and a 'meet-the-artist' party.

Tickets are $15.00 for each Doll Society member, $15.00 for first guest and $20.00 for each additional guest thereafter.

Call for date of this wonderful event.

BABYLAND GENERAL® HOSPITAL
19 Underwood St.
Cleveland, GA 30528
404/865-2171

Hospital hours are Monday thru Saturday, 9 A.M.-5 P.M. and Sunday, 1-5 P.M.

Admission is free.

Visitors will see where the Magic Crystal Tree grows within early 1900s medical clinic and Licensed Patch Nurses performing deliveries of original Cabbage Patch Kids®. The gift shop is open during tour hours and guided tours are available. Cabbage Patch Kids are available for adoption at the hospital as well as everything needed to care for them at the gift shop.

Ready to be "adopted" just minutes after birth, original Cabbage Patch Kids® are "delivered" daily from the Mother Cabbages near the Magic Crystal Tree at Babyland General® Hospital in Cleveland, Ga. A Licensed Patch Nurse proudly presents a brand new baby to enchanted visitors who have witnessed the entire birth!

MARTY BELL GALLERY

9424 Eton Avenue
Chatsworth, CA 91311
800/637-4537

The Gallery is open on Mondays only from 9 A.M. to 5 P.M.

Reservations are required by calling. The tour is limited to members of the *Marty Bell Collector's Society*.

The guided tour is approximately one hour. Visitors will see Marty Bell's publishing facility including Marty's originals' gallery. The originals' gallery features many original oil paintings never seen by the general public.

BELL HAVEN

c/o Iva Mae Long
R.D. #4 Box 54
Tarentum, PA 15084
412/265-2872

Tours are by appointment only.

Located on one acre of wooded grounds with bells located inside and out of the workshop.

Admission is $4.00.

Collectors will marvel at the 30,000 bells on display that have been gathered through the years beginning in the late 1950s.

BELLINGRATH GARDENS AND HOME/ BOEHM GALLERY

12401 Bellingrath Garden Rd.
Theodore, AL 36582
205/973-2217

Open daily 7 A.M.-dusk.

Located twenty miles southwest of Mobile off Interstate 10, Exit 15A to Theodore.

Reservations recommended for group tours and for groups of twenty or more.

Admission for the Garden is $5.00 adults, children 6-11 $2.50. Under 6 free. Home tour is $6.25 (except babes in arms). Boehm Gallery included in gardens.

Boehm Gallery has the largest public display of Boehm porcelains in the world. Over 225 porcelains are exhibited in lighted cases behind glass. The Bellingrath Home has a large collection of porcelains, crystal, silver, paintings and furniture from around the world. Hostesses conduct tours of the homes. The Bellingrath Gardens consist of sixty-five acres which include a bird sanctuary and chapel. The gardens are planned so as to be in bloom year-round.

Gift shop opens at 7 A.M. Cafeteria serves breakfast and lunch from 7 A.M.-3 P.M.

THE BRADFORD MUSEUM OF COLLECTOR'S PLATES

9333 Milwaukee Avenue
Niles, IL 60648
708/966-2770

Located in the Chicago suburb of Niles, Illinois.

The Bradford Museum of Collector's Plates is the world's largest permanent exhibit of limited edition collector's plates.

The museum's collection contains porcelain, china, silver and wood plates which were produced by over seventy makers from more than sixteen countries.

In the center of the museum is The Bradford Exchange Trading Floor where brokers help clients buy and sell plates over the telephone. The trading floor is the heart of the dynamic international collector's plate market in North America, Europe and Australia.

Since its opening in 1978, the museum has attracted more than 100,000 visitors from all fifty states and nine foreign countries.

The museum is currently under renovation and is slated to open in the fall of 1991. For more information on tour hours and admission prices, contact the museum.

THE BYERS' CHOICE MUSEUM

Wayside Country Store
1015 Boston Post Road Rt. 20
Marlborough, MA 01752
508/481-3458

Open seven days a week from 10 A.M.-5 P.M.

Located at the famous Wayside Country Store on the Marlborough/Sudbury Massachusetts line.

The museum houses many old and rare collectible Byers Choice Carolers. Many of them are pieces that collectors have never seen.

The historical Wayside Country Store was restored and operated by Henry Ford in 1929. The Wayside Country Store has fourteen specialty shops. Nearby is the very famous Longfellow's "Wayside Inn," The Little Red School House that the poem "Mary Had a Little Lamb" was written about. The Martha/Mary Chapel, a very picturesque non-denominational chapel where hundreds of weddings are performed each year is also close by. Both the chapel and the beautiful Stone Grist Mill were built by Heny Ford. It is a very picturesque New England setting.

There is no admission fee.

CIRCUS WORLD MUSEUM

426 Water St.
Baraboo, WI 53913
608/356-8341
608/356-0800 — seasonal information line

Museum exhibit buildings and grounds are open 9 A.M.-6 P.M. early May thru mid-September except late July through late August when the grounds are open until 10 P.M. The grounds include live shows.

Irvin Field Exhibit Hall and Visitor Center open year round. Located in south central Wisconsin, 12 miles from the Wisconsin Dells in Baraboo.

Admission charge is $8.95 for adults, seniors $7.95, children 3-12 $5.50 and under 3 free. Includes all shows, exhibits and demonstrations.

The world's largest facility devoted to the circus, it is located on the site of the Ringling Brothers Circus original winterquarters (1884-1918). The world's largest repository of circus antiques, artifacts and information is recognized by the American Association of Museums and is a National Historic Site. (Collectors of Flambro's Emmett Kelly, Jr. collectibles would find this museum especially interesting.)

LOWELL DAVIS' RED OAK II

Rt. 1
Carthage, MO 64836
417/358-1943

Tour hours are 10 A.M.-6 P.M., Monday-Saturday.

Admission is free for the self-guided tour.

The tour includes buildings from the 1930s era on forty acres of land. Buildings that will be open to visitors are a school house, general store, gas station, church, blacksmith shop, saw mill and the reception center which includes original art works by Lowell Davis. The Belle Starr Museum is also in the area and admission is $1.00.

FAVELL MUSEUM OF WESTERN ART AND INDIAN ARTIFACTS

125 West Main Street
Klamath Falls, OR 97601
503/882-9996

Monday-Saturday, 9:30-5:30, closed on Sundays.

Admission: $4 adults, $3 seniors, $1 children 6-16.

The museum overlooks the outlet of the largest natural lake in Oregon and its 17,000 square feet of display space is laid out like the spokes of a wagon wheel. Includes works by renowned western artists such as Donald Polland, John Clymer, Joe Beeler, Frank McCarthy, and Mort Kunstler, as well as more than eighty collections of artifacts, including miniature firearms. Gift shop and art gallery.

FENTON ART GLASS COMPANY

420 Caroline Avenue
Willaimstown, WV 26187
304/375-7772

Fenton Art Glass Company offers a free forty minute factory tour.

The factory tour runs Monday-Friday, beginning at 8:30 A.M. and the last leaving at 2:30 P.M. The factory is closed on national holidays and during an annual two week vacation always around the first two weeks of July.

Located in Williamstown, West Virginia, just across the Ohio River from Marietta, Ohio. The factory is easily reached by Interstate I-77, Exit 185, from West Virginia State Routes 2, 14, and US Route 50.

No reservations necessary for groups under 20; highly recommended for more than 20.

Admission free.

Tour of plant allows you to watch highly skilled craftsmen create handmade glass from molten state to finished product. Majority of factory tour handicap accessible.

The museum craftshop hours are: September-May, Monday-Saturday, 8 A.M.-5 P.M., except Tuesday and Thursday, open till 8 P.M.; Sunday 12 P.M.-5 P.M. June-August, Monday-Friday, 8 A.M.-8 P.M.; Saturday, 8 A.M.-5 P.M.; Sunday 12 P.M.-5 P.M.

The museum gift shop is closed only on Easter, Christmas, Thanksgiving and New Years Day.

Admission charges are $1 adults, 50 cents children 10-16, under 10 free and a 20% discount for groups of 20 or more.

The museum offers examples of Ohio Valley glass with major emphasis on Fenton glass made 1905-1955. Representative glass of other Ohio Valley companies is displayed along with items of historical interest. A thirty-minute movie on the making of Fenton Glass is shown at regular times throughout the day.

FJ DESIGNS CATS MEOW FACTORY

2163 Great Trails Drive
Wooster, OH 44691
216/264-1377

Tours at 10 A.M. and 1 P.M., Monday-Friday.

Admission is free. Reservations required with groups of more than six persons. No bus tours are available.

The tour is 45 minutes long and begins in the lobby area. In the lobby are displays of all retired and new products from FJ Designs, beginning in 1982. During the tour through the factory, the production processes of five different departments will be observed. These processes include sanding, spray painting, screen printing, and the finishing of the Cats Meow *Village* pieces.

FRANKLIN MINT MUSEUM

Franklin Center, PA 19091
215/459-6168

Closed Monday. Open Tuesday-Saturday 9:30 A.M.-4:30 P.M., Sunday 1:00 P.M.-4:30 P.M.

No reservations required.

Free admission.

The Franklin Mint Museum houses original masterpieces by such world-famous American artists as Andrew Wyeth and Norman Rockwell, as well as re-creations of works commissioned by the National Wildlife Federation, the Royal Shakespeare Theatre, the Louvre and The White House. You'll also see the finest works created by the world-famous artists of The Franklin Mint Studio. Extraordinary sculptures in porcelain, crystal, pewter and bronze. Award-winning collector dolls. Die-cast automotive classics. Uniquely designed and minted coins. Philatelics of historic significance. Handicap facilities provided. Special events, gallery store, free parking.

FRANKOMA POTTERY TOUR

P.O. Box 789
2400 Frankoma Road
Sapulpa, OK 74067
800/331-3650 or 918/224-5511

The gift shop is open 8 A.M.-6 P.M., Monday-Saturday, and 12:30-5 P.M. on Sunday. Tours begin at 9 A.M. until 3:15 P.M., Monday-Friday.

Admission is free. Reservations are highly recommended for large groups to ensure that not too many groups arrive at one time. Tours are every thirty minutes.

Located four miles southwest of Tulsa on Frankoma Road in Sapulpa, Oklahoma.

A very interesting tour for young and old of the pottery factory. On exhibit are 275 pieces of pottery made in thirteen colors, plus gift items. Frankoma has been producing fine pottery for fifty-eight years.

GALLERY IN THE SUN

6300 N. Swan Road
Tucson, AZ 85718
602/299-9191

Open seven days a week, 10 A.M.-4 P.M.

No admission charge.

Reservations needed for free guided tours.

Exhibits in this all-adobe museum include thirteen rooms of the works of Ted DeGrazia. Two of the rooms are rotated during the year, one being seasonal. Exhibits cover all types of DeGrazia sculptures and paintings, including his first painting, which he painted at the age of 16.

At Easter you can see The Way of The Cross which is DeGrazia's interpretations of the Fifteen Stations of The Cross. A series of Madonnas and angels are on display at Christmas time along with celebrating the Fiesta of Guadalupe. The museum closes promptly at 4 P.M. in keeping with DeGrazia's policy when he was alive. A gift shop is also open during tour hours.

GOEBEL MINIATURES STUDIOS/FACTORY

4820 Adohr Lane
Camarillo, CA 93012
805/484-4351

All tours must be booked in advance. Call the studio to make arrangements. The most common time for tours is Thursdays at 10 A.M.

No admission is charged.

Visitors will see a brief film about the production of the miniature figurines and then walk through the studios/factory to see close-up the developmental and decorative processes. The tour takes approximately one hour.

Goebel Miniature figures receive a priming coat of paint and are inspected for bubbles and mold marks in the grinding room before they go into the decorating studios.

SONJA HARTMANN ORIGINALS DOLL STUDIO

1230 Pottstown Pike
Glenmoore, PA 19343
215/458-1120

The studio is open 9 A.M.-5 P.M., Monday-Friday.

Tours are by appointment only. Bus groups are welcome.

Visitors will see the production of porcelain and vinyl dolls from the pouring of porcelain into the molds to the dressing and hair styling of the charming dolls.

Admission is free.

HIBEL MUSEUM OF ART

150 Royal Poinciana Plaza
Palm Beach, FL 33480
407/833-6870

Tours are Tuesday-Saturday, 10 A.M.-5 P.M.; Sunday, 1-5 P.M.

Admission is free. Reservations are requested for groups of ten or more. Bus tours are invited.

The museum opened in January 1977, as a tribute to artist Edna Hibel by the late Ethelbelle and Clayton B. Craig.

The Hibel Museum of Art has an extensive collection of Edna Hibel oil paintings, drawings, lithographs, porcelain collectables and dolls. Visitors will see antique snuff bottles, dolls and paperweight collection. The museum has a collection of rare art books and antique Oriental, English and Italian furniture.

The museum shop is open during tour hours.

JERRI DOLL'S COLLECTION ROOM

Dolls by Jerri Factory
651 Anderson St.
Charlotte, NC 28205
704/333-3211

The factory is open 9 A.M.-4 P.M., Monday-Friday.

No admission is charged. Tours are by appointment only and group size is limited to twenty visitors.

Visitors will see the showroom with a complete collection of every Jerri doll, plate, ornament, figurine created by Jerri since 1976. The steps in creating a Jerri doll can be seen on the tour, which includes the creative beginnings to shipping of the product from the factory.

LAWTONS' WORKSHOP

548 North First St.
Turlock, CA 95380
209/632-3655

Tours are by special arrangement to groups only.

No admission charge.

Guests are treated to a step-by-step demonstration of Lawtons' actual doll production. Guests will see the process from the first pour of porcelain slip to the final inspection and packaging.

Lawtons provides a fascinating tour of its doll company to interested groups, including school tours.

LLADRO MUSEUM AND GALLERIES

43 West 57th Street
New York, NY 10019
212/838-9341

Open Tuesday-Saturday 10 A.M.-5:30 P.M.

Reservations required for large groups.

Free Admission.

The museum houses the largest collection of retired Lladro porcelains. Display features appoximately 2,500 pieces, and museum occupies three floors of the building.

The Lladro Art Gallery on the sixth floor is dedicated to inroducing the works of contemporary Spanish art to people in the United States.

LEE MIDDLETON ORIGINAL DOLLS

1301 Washington Boulevard
Belpre, Ohio 45714
800/233-7479

There is no charge for tours of the factory.

Lee Middleton Original Doll Company opens its doors to countless visitors from around the world. A larger-than-life doll house in every way, Lee's new manufacturing facility is discreetly hidden behind a beautiful pastel "gingerbread" facade which fronts her 37,000 square foot state-of-the-art production plant. Each tour provides a clear understanding of the creative process behind Lee's porcelain and vinyl collectible dolls. Visitors will see the mixing and pouring of liquid porcelain, the vinyl molding and curing process and the hand-painting of each doll's face.

The company schedules tours seven times daily, Monday-Friday, 9 A.M.-3 P.M., and is always pleased to host large group tours at requested times with adequate advance notice.

The Middleton Doll Company tour includes an opportunity to see how liquid porcelain is carefully poured into a plastic mold. To preserve the detail required in Lee's fine porcelain dolls, the plaster mold is destroyed after only a few pourings and replaced with a fresh mold.

PRECIOUS MOMENTS CHAPEL & VISITORS CENTER

P.O. Box 802
Carthage, MO 64836
800/543-7975

No admission fee. Free Guided Tours.

Reservations requested for large groups of fifteen or more. Please call for more information.

The chapel is open daily at 9 A.M., Monday-Sunday.

In a quiet setting, just outside the Victorian town of Carthage, Missouri stands the realization of a dream that was born in the heart of one of America's most famous artists, Sam Butcher.

Sam Butcher began the preliminary sketches of his dream four years ago on a flight to Asia. One finds the Precious Moments Chapel, a gallery of reverence nestled among the dogwood in the beautiful meadows of the Ozarks.

The fifteen stained glass windows are among the most exquisite treasures in the Chapel. The windows, with some containing over 1,200 individually cut pieces of glass, were painstakingly leaded by the artist's family.

The fifty-four murals, covering a total of almost five thousand square feet, are perhaps the most important works of Sam's life. Thirty-five feet above the marble floor, angels wing their way across a twenty-six hundred square foot ceiling as they celebrate the victory of our saviour's resurrection.

REED & BARTON FACTORY

144 W. Britannia St.
Taunton, MA 02780
800/822-1824, X308

Tours are by appointment only. The factory is open Monday-Friday, 8 A.M.-2 P.M. Located in scenic New England, the Reed & Barton factory is over 160 years old and is listed on the National Register of historic places.

See how Reed & Barton flatware is handcrafted during a forty-five minute guided tour. Visitors will see the artists create from start to finish — transferring raw materials into elegant flatware.

Admission for the tour is free.

The Reed & Barton factory tour includes a look at the die-cutting operation.

NORMAN ROCKWELL CENTER/ FRANCES HOOK MUSEUM

315 Elizabeth Street
P.O. Box 91
Mishicot, WI 54228
414/755-4014

Monday through Saturday, 10 A.M.-4 P.M., Sunday 1-4 P.M., evenings by appointment.

Located in the Old School in the Village of Mishicot, Wisconsin.

Reservations requested for groups. (Contact Carol Anderson)

One of the largest Norman Rockwell collections in the world, free slide shows, shop displays of art, limited edition prints and collectibles. The Frances Hook Museum/Art Gallery features her limited edition issues and sponsors an annual Frances Hook Celebration in June, complete with Frances Hook Look-Alike Contest.

NORMAN ROCKWELL MUSEUM

601 Walnut Street
Philadelphia, PA 19106
215/922-4345

Open Monday-Saturday, 10 A.M.-4 P.M. and 11 A.M.-4 P.M. on Sunday.

Open everyday of the year except Christmas, New Year's, Thanksgiving and Easter.

Located 601 Walnut Street, lower level.

Reservations necessary for groups of 10 or more. Admission charge: adults, $2.00, seniors over 62 and AAA members, $1.50, children 12 and under free. Group rates available.

Exhibits include one of three complete sets of Saturday Evening Post covers (324 pieces), over 700 pieces of additional art including the original art for Rockwell's famous War Bond Poster, a replica of his studio, the Four Freedoms Theater which has an eight minute video. Extensive gift shop. Tour should take thirty to forty-five minutes.

THE NORMAN ROCKWELL MUSEUM

Main Street
Stockbridge, MA 01262
413/298-4239

From May through October the museum is open 10 A.M.-5 P.M., Monday-Sunday and November through April, 11 A.M.-4 P.M. Monday-Friday and 10 A.M.-5 P.M. Saturday and Sunday. Guided tours stop at 4:40 P.M. Closed Thanksgiving, Christmas, New Year's Day and last two weeks of January.

Located on Main Street, Stockbridge, Massachusetts.

Reservations requested for groups of ten or more.

Admission fee is charged.

This museum contains two floors and shows only original paintings, drawings and sketches by Norman Rockwell which include about fifty paintings on view at any one time. Temporary exhibitions focus on different aspects of Rockwell's Art and the field of illustrations. It offers the public the opportunity to see original art that is so familiar in prints.

THE OFFICIAL SEBASTIAN MINIATURES MUSEUM

Stacy's Gifts and Collectibles
Route One
Walpole Mall
East Walpole, MA 02032
508/668-4212

Monday-Saturday 9:30 A.M.-9:30 P.M. Sunday 1 P.M.-5 P.M.

Admission in free.

Located in the center of the renovated Stacy's Gifts and Collectibles in the Walpole Mall in East Walpole, Massachusetts. The original museum was dedicated on October 29, 1983 by Sebastian creator Prescott W. Baston.

After a complete store renovation, in 1989, the museum was rededicated by Woody Baston, son of Prescott and now sole sculptor of Sebastian Miniatures.

The museum is comprised of over 1,000 Sebastian Miniatures from the personal collection of the store owners, Sherman and Doris Edwards. It also contains scrapbooks of some early drawings and advertisements that were used as models for many of the original figurines. In the museum are videos that feature the annual Sebastian Festivals and interviews with both Prescott and Woody Baston.

The Official Sebastian Miniatures Museum is located in East Walpole, Massachusetts at Stacy's Gifts & Collectibles. Pictured are owners of Stacy's, Sherman and Doris Edwards, front, along with Woody Baston, son of Prescott and now sole sculptor of Sebastian Miniatures.

UNITED DESIGN PLANT

1600 North Main
Noble, OK 73068
800/727-4883

Plant tours are at 9:30 A.M.and 10:30 A.M., Monday-Friday.

A tour group listens to their tour guide before beginning a tour of United Design's 230,000 square foot manufacturing facility. The tour participants are standing outside the company Gift Shop, where one of every design manufactured is on display and where many are available for purchase by tourists.

Admission is free. Reservations for large groups are requested.

Visitors will see the manufacturing process of United Design figurines. All are produced in Noble, Oklahoma by American artists and craftsmen. The plant is 230,000 square feet and includes the manufacturing, distribution and administration facilities.

The gift shop open during tour hours has one of every design manufactured on display and available for purchase by tourists.

VAILLANCOURT FOLK ART
145 Armsby Rd.
Sutton, MA 01590
508/865-9183

The studio is open Monday-Friday from 9 A.M.-5 P.M., Saturday 11 A.M.-5 P.M. and Sunday 12-5 P.M. Tours are 11 A.M., Monday-Friday.

Admission is free. Reservations are required for groups larger than ten people.

Vaillancourt Folk Art is located in an 1820 New England farmhouse surrounded by stone walls.

The complete tour of the painting studios begins in the moulding room and viewing the antique chocolate moulds. Then the visitors proceed through the painting rooms and then see the finishing process. This shows the creation of the chalkware originals from beginning to end.

Foreign Museums and Tours

THE HOUSE OF ANRI
1-39047 St. Christina
Val Gardena, Italy
617/961-3000 ANRI Headquarters

Tours require advance reservations with Club ANRI to ensure an English-speaking guide. There is no admission charged. To participate in the tour of the workshop Club membership is required.

Mastercarver Ulrich Bernardi takes a moment to pose with a young man who is touring The House of ANRI in Italy.

Located in Northern Italy near the Austrian border.

Visitors to the workshop will see the artists at work: the step-by-step process of how an ANRI woodcarving is created.

Call for train schedule or car route to the factory.

BELLEEK POTTERY
Belleek Co. Fermanagh
Northern Ireland
Phone 011-44-365-65501 ask for Patricia McCauley

Located in County Fermanagh, Northern Ireland. Free guided tours.

Demonstrations of Belleek's distinctive porcelain weaving and hand assembly. Call before visit to verify when the pottery will be open.

Tours are every half-hour Monday-Friday and the Visitor Center is open Monday-Saturday. The Visitor Center includes a showroom, museum, audio visual room, and restaurant.

The tours provide a chance to see the tradition behind the 133 years of Belleek pottery. On display are all collectible pieces ever made by Belleek and antique pieces dating from 1857. A film of how Belleek pottery is made step-by-step is shown in the audio visual room.

Admission is one British pound, call for American equivalency.

THE ENESCO PRECIOUS MOMENTS COLLECTORS' CLUB TRIP TO THE ORIENT
P.O. Box 1466
Elk Grove Village, IL 60007
Julia Kirkwood
708/640-3195

Tour offered annually every spring. Open to all club members, family and friends.

Precious Moments Collectors' Club members can enjoy a memorable 13-day tour to the Orient. The trip includes stops in Japan, Taiwan, Hong Kong and China. Members tour the Design Studio in Nagoya, Japan, where they will meet the Master Sculptor Yasuhei Fujioka, who personally oversees the original sculpting of each and every Precious Moments figurine. They will also visit the Precious Moments production facilities in Miaoli, Taiwan.

W. GOEBEL PORZELLANFABRIK FACTORY
Postfach 1146/47
W8633 Roedental
From U.S.: 01149-9563920
From Germany: 9536/92303

The factory is located in the county of Coburg, just a few kilometers from the city of the same name.

Factory hours are Monday-Friday, 9 A.M.-12 noon, and Monday-Friday, 1-5:00 P.M.

Visitors will see a film, a special demonstration and be able to shop in the factory store. Members of the M.I. Hummel Club may also be the factory's guest for lunch (but must be there by noon, and advise the receptionist as soon as they arrive); non-members traveling with them pay a nominal amount.

Goebel Factory artist at work.

THE STUDIOS AND WORKSHOPS OF
JOHN HINE LIMITED
2 Hillside Road
Aldershot, Hampshire
England GU113NQ
Phone (0252) 334672

The studios and workshops tours are at 10 A.M. and 2 P.M., Monday-Friday.

Admission is free. Reservations are required and can be made by phone or by writing in advance.

Visitors will see the artists' workplaces and demonstrations. On display are new and retired pieces. And visitors are able to browse through the gardens of the restored 16th century barn which houses the studios and workshops.

KAISER PORZELLAN FACTORY TOUR
Alboth & Kaiser GmbH & Co. KG — Postfach 1160
8623 Staffelstein — Germany
Phone (09573) 336-0

Tours can be arranged through Kaiser Porcelain in Niagara Falls (716) 297-2331. No admission charge. Contact Betsy Braun.

Collectors tour the Kaiser factory in Staffelstein, Germany — the heart of Bavarian porcelain making.

KRYSTONIA FACTORY
1 Winpenny Rd.
Chestertow, Staffs., England
Phone (0782) 566636

Tours are by appointment only, Monday-Friday. No admission is charged.

The factory which opened in late 1990 has a guided one-hour tour. Visitors will see the step-by-step process of how a Krystonia figure is produced and decorated. The painters, moldmakers and fettlers will be seen creating the mystical creatures of the Krystonia collection.

Prior to the painting and spraying process, each Krystonia figure is fettled, whereby mold lines are either smoothed or removed.

LLADRO: A COLLECTOR'S ODYSSEY
Lladro Collectors Society
43 West 57th Street
New York, NY 10019-3498

Several tours available for Collector Society members.

Ten day to two week tours of sights in Spain, as well as a tour of the Lladro factory in Valencia. If traveling on own call for appointment to tour factory.

ROMAN HOLIDAY
555 Lawrence Avenue
Roselle, IL 60172
708/529-3000

There will be ten trips in 1992 and the dates will be available in the Spring and Fall of the year. The trips are only available to dealers. For details of trips please call Roman, Inc.

Reservations are required. The cost is tentatively set at $1,992.00 per person (double occupancy).

The trip to Italy will include a full tour of the fascinating process of crafting figurines at the

Fontanini facility in Bagni di Lucca. Travelers will also tour Milan, Ortisei, Florence and many other exciting places.

ROYAL COPENHAGEN
PORCELAIN FACTORY
Smallegade 45
2000 Frederikberg, Copenhagen
Denmark
Phone 31 86 48 48

The factory is open from May 15th to September 14th: tours from Monday-Friday, at 9 A.M., 10 A.M., 11 A.M., 1 P.M. and 2 P.M. From September 15th to May 14th: tours from Monday-Friday, at 9 A.M., 10 A.M. and 11 A.M.

Reservations are recommended. For groups of more than five persons, other times for tours can be arranged by prior agreement.

During the tour of the factory, visitors will be told what porcelain is and shown an impressive assortment of porcelain. Visitors will also have the opportunity of seeing porcelain painters at work.

The talk during the one-hour tour is given in Danish, English, German and French.

ROYAL DOULTON FACTORY
Nile Street
Burslem, Stoke-on-Trent
England ST6 2AJ
800/582-2102
Phone (0782) 575454

Admission is free to club members and the non-member admission price is two British pounds per person. Visits for parties of students and senior citizens can be pre-booked at specially reduced rates.

Visitors will see the entire production process starting with raw materials to the finished product. The Sir Henry Doulton Gallery is open to visitors which features archives, early wares and the Figures Collection. Tours can be pre-arranged through the Collectors Club or the factory. The tour is completed with a visit to the gift shop and tea room.

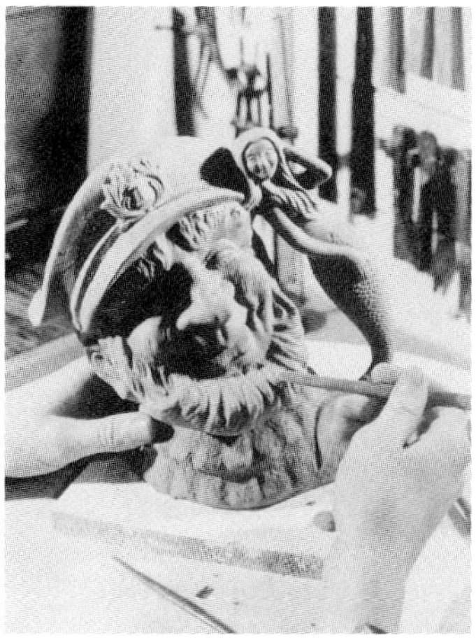

The artisan is modeling the "Old Salt" character jug at The Royal Doulton factory located in Stoke-on-Trent, England.

ROYAL WORCESTER —
DYSON PERRINS MUSEUM
Severn Street
Worcester WR1 2NE
England
Phone (0905) 23221

Open Monday-Friday 9:30 A.M.-5:00 P.M. Saturday 10:00 A.M.-5:00 P.M. Free admission.

Collectors are invited to view the largest collection of Worcester porcelain in the world.

ROYAL WORCESTER FACTORY TOURS
Severn Street
Worcester WR1 2NE
England
Phone (0905) 23221

Factory tours are arranged through the Dyson Perrins Museum. They can be booked in advance by phoning Pam Savage at (0905) 23221.

Two tours are offered:

A standard guided tour of the factory that takes in all stages of the making and decorating processes. Tours last approximately one hour and leave from the Museum at ten minute intervals between 10:25 A.M. and 11:25 A.M. and 1:15 P.M. and 3:15 P.M. Maximum group size twelve. Cost $2.50 (children 8-16 years old $1.50).

The Connoisseurs tour is a more detailed tour for those with more specialized interest. Includes visits to departments not usually open to the general public. Tours last two hours. Two tours a day only — leaving the Museum at 10:15 A.M. and 1:30 P.M. Maximum group size ten (but normally 2 or 4 — very personal!) Cost $7.50 per person includes full color guide book plus morning coffee or afternoon tea.

Note — Safety regulations preclude children less than 8 years old. These tours are also unsuitable for very elderly or disabled persons, due to the number of flights of stairs.

SWAROVSKI CRYSTAL SHOP
A-6112 Wattens
Innstrasse 1
Austria
Phone 05224/5886

May-September, Monday-Saturday, 8 A.M.-6 P.M., Sunday 8 A.M.-12 noon. October-April, Monday-Friday, 8 A.M.-6 P.M., Saturday 8 A.M.-12 noon.

From the Autobahn, take the Wattens exit between Innsbruck and Salzburg/Munich onto Swarovski Strasse.

Visitors can see Swarovski crystal products. Tours highlight artisans cutting, engraving, painting and blowing glass. Gift shop and cafe.

SWAROVSKI COLLECTORS SOCIETY
EUROPEAN TOUR
2 Slater Road
Cranston, RI 02920
1-800-426-3088

Tours offered twice a year in the Fall and Spring and limited to members of the Swarovski Collectors Society.

The first part of the tour is spent in Austrian Tyrol, then moves on to the Lake Geneva region of Switzerland. In the Austrian Tyrol, a special visit will be made to Wattens, the home of the Swarovski Company. In Wattens, special exhibits are constructed and members are able to meet Swarovski craftsmen, designers, and technical experts. A private members only shopping experience at the Swarovski Crystal Shop is arranged.

Arrangements are made via an outside travel service.

Information on Other Tours

Factories and museums not listed here may also welcome collectors, even if they do not post specific visiting hours. See addresses in "Company Summaries" to contact any firms that you especially want to visit.

A parent's most cherished memories are those of a child...the first steps...the walks to church Sunday morning...and lullabies to a babe in mother's arms. From left to right and top to bottom are: "One Step at a Time" figurine from Enesco Precious Moments Collectors' Club, Hamilton's "Sacajawea" plate, The Constance Collection's figurines "Sunday Morning" and "Santa's Walk," Artaffects' "My Sunshine" plate, "Lullaby" mother and child doll produced by Reco International Corp. under the hallmark of the W.S. George China Company, Roman, Inc.'s "Legacy of Love" plate and "A Gift of Love" figurine from Lladro Collectors Society.

The animals that brighten our daily lives are captured by renowned artists who create them singing in trees, hunting and playing. From left to right and top to bottom are: "Ruby-throated Hummingbird" figurine by Maruri U.S.A., "Sam Squirrel's Visit" plate by Kaiser Porcelain USA, Inc., "Cardinal with Cherry Blossom" figurine by Maruri U.S.A., Schmid's "Warm Milk" figurine, The Hamilton Collection's "Double Take" figurine, "Screech Owl" figurine by Kaiser Porcelain USA, Inc., Hamilton's "Wide Retriever" plate, Reco International Corp.'s "The Retrieval" plate, "Robin with Baby — Azalea" figurine by Maruri U.S.A., Seymour Mann, Inc.'s "Puss in Boot" figurine and Schmid's "Outing with Grandpa" figurine.

'Man's best friend' comes in all shapes and sizes. They are there to listen and help and most of all to cuddle. From left to right and top to bottom are: Enesco Corporation's "Where Shall We Go?" figurine, The Norman Rockwell Gallery's "Splish, Splash" figurine, "Welcome To Your New Home" figurine from Enesco Memories of Yesterday Collectors' Society, Reco International Corp.'s "Puppy" plate, M.I. Hummel Figurine by Goebel "Sensitive Hunter" (HUM 6/0), "We Belong Together" figurine from Enesco Memories of Yesterday Collectors' Society, Flambro Imports' "Artist at Work" figurine, The Constance Collection's "New Pups" figurine, "Kitty's Lunch" figurine by Hamilton Gifts Ltd., "Sharing A Gift of Love" figurine from Enesco Precious Moments Collectors' Club, Armani's "Girl with Chicks" figurine, Lawtons' "To Market, To Market" doll and Reco International Corp.'s "Kitten" plate.

Authentic buildings mark the treasures of the past and present that every tourist should include on their itinerary. From left to right and top to bottom are: Lilliput Lane Limited's "Falls Mill" figurine, The Norman Rockwell Gallery's "Rockwell's Residence" figurine, Lilliput Lane Limited's "The King's Arms" figurine, The Hamilton Collection's "The Periwinkle Tea Rooms" plate, Schmid's "Nel's Diner" figurine, John Hine Studios, Inc.'s "Moonlight Haven" figurine, Flambro Imports' "Pleasantville Department Store Lamp" figurine, John Hine Studios, Inc.'s "New England Lighthouse" figurine, Lilliput Lane Limited's "Double Cottage" figurine, Legends' "Cape Hatteras" figurine, Lilliput Lane Limited's "Covered Memories" figurine and Flambro Imports' "Bakery/Sweet Shoppe Lamp" figurine.

Welcoming faces await the arrival of visitors from other places and reach out to collectors with warmth and friendship. From left to right and top to bottom are: "The Carriage" figurine by Kaiser Porcelain USA, Inc., "Tutankhamun and His Princess" plate from The Bradford Exchange, "Friendship Has No Boundaries" figurine from Enesco Memories of Yesterday Collectors' Society, Royal Doulton's "Christopher Columbus" jug, M.I. Hummel figurine by Goebel "Merry Wanderer" (HUM 7/0), "St. Basil's Moscow" plate from The Bradford Exchange, M.I. Hummel figurine by Goebel "Going to Grandma's" (HUM 52/0), Lawtons' "Midsommar" doll, Duncan Royale's "October" figurine, Lawtons' "Ndeko/Zaire" doll and Roman, Inc.'s "Christopher Columbus" figurine.

The Indians are the symbol of bravery and a simpler way of life, where a horse is a trophy and a friend comes to the rescue on horseback. From top to bottom and left to right are: Polland Studios' "The Signal" and "War Drummer" figurines, Artaffects, Ltd.'s "Christmas Journey" plate, Legends' "The Tables Turned" figurine, Polland Studios' "War Trophy" and "Running Wolf" figurines, Artaffects, Ltd.'s "The Cheyenne Carousel" figurine, Polland Studios' "Hot Pursuit" figurine, Legends' "Unexpected Rescuer" and "Defiant Comanche" figurines and Hamilton's "The Lone Ranger and Tonto" plate.

Patriotism and the theme of freedom remind Americans of those that fought and those that will not be forgotten. From left to right and top to bottom are: "Freedom" plate from The Bradford Exchange, "Double American Bald Eagle" figurine by Maruri U.S.A., Lance Corporation's "Quantrill's Raiders" figurine, "Bless Those Who Serve Their Country" figurines representing the Army, Navy, Air Force, and Marines from Enesco Precious Moments Collectors' Club, Lance Corporation's "Marines in the Solomons" figurine, "You'll Always Be My Hero" figurine from Enesco Memories of Yesterday Collectors' Society, Lenox Collections' "Lord of the Skies" figurine, Sarah's Attic's tribute to Operation Desert Storm "Forever In Our Hearts" figurine, Nahrgang Collection's "Sailor" doll and Legends' "American Allegiance" figurine.

Sports…the favored pastime of millions. From baseball, basketball and football evolve heroes that fulfill the fans' dreams. From left to right and top to bottom are: Sports Impressions' "Boomer Esiason Gold Edition" plate, Lou Gehrig porcelain stein and Nolan Ryan figurine, Gartlan USA, Inc.'s "Comeback Kid" plate, "Cool Papa" Bell signed figurine and Kareem Abdul-Jabbar mini figurine, Hamilton's "Casey Stengel" and "Mickey Mantle" porcelain baseball cards, Gartlan USA, Inc.'s "Hitting for the Hall — Rod Carew" plate, Polland Studios' "Double Play" figurine, "Bubba Batboy" by Lee Middleton Original Dolls, Sports Impressions' "Nolan Ryan 5000K" porcelain baseball card, Gartlan USA, Inc.'s Ted Williams and "Stride For Victory" figurines and Sports Impressions' "Lawrence Taylor Gold Edition."

Varied occupations of the working world are exemplified by an accountant rejoicing, a doctor comforting a worried patient, and fishermen bringing in their catch. From left to right and top to bottom are: Flambro Imports' "The Finishing Touch" figurine, WACO Product Corporation's "Peanut Vendor" figurine, Lance Corporation's "Hudson Depot" with "Billy Mitchell," "Mr. LeClair," "Mr. & Mrs. Howard" and "Mrs. Berry" figurines, The Norman Rockwell Gallery's "Love Cures All" figurine, John Hine Studios, Inc.'s "The Sherlock Holmes" figurine, Lance Corporation's "Dory Fisherman" figurine, Duncan Royale's "The Accountant" figurine, Flambro Imports' "Follow the Leader" figurine, Armani's "Lady Pierrot with Doll" figurine and Duncan Royale's "Banjo Man" figurine.

Mystical creatures, fairies and legendary heroes and heroines represent some of the fanciful creations by renowned artists in the collectibles field. On the left page, from left to right and top to bottom are: Lance Corporation's "The Dream" figurine, The Collectables "Natasha" doll and unicorn, Precious Art/Panton's "Maj-Dron Migration" and "N'Borg on Throne" figurines, United Design's "Fire It Up" figurine, John Hine Studios, Inc.'s "The Shoemaker's Dream Boot Tavern" figurine, Schmid's "Cinderella Kitty" figurine, Gorham, Inc.'s "Alexandra" doll, Precious Art/Panton's "Twilyght" figurine and Gorham, Inc.'s "Juliet" doll.

On the right page, from left to right and top to bottom are: John Hine's "Knight's Castle" figurine, WACO's "Robin Hood" figurine, ANRI's "The Mad Dog" figurine, Goebel Miniatures' *Cinderella Collection* with "Cinderella's Dream Castle," "Drizella," "Anastasia," "Cinderella," "Gus," "Jaq" and "Lucifer" figurines, Precious Art/Panton's "Flayla and Jumbly" figurine, Goebel Miniatures' *Fantasia Collection* with the "Dancing Brooms Display" and "Sorcerer's Apprentice" figurine, Polland Studios' "The Mermaid" figurine, Duncan Royale's "Almond Blossom" figurine, Precious Art/Panton's "Graffyn on Grunch" figurine, Goebel Miniatures' *Pinocchio Collection* with "Geppetto's Toy Shop," "J.W. Foulfellow," "Gideon," "Geppetto /Figaro," "Jiminy Cricket" and "Pinocchio" figurines, WACO's "Little John" figurine, Precious Art/Panton's "Tokkel" figurine and Lenox Collection's "Guinevere" figurine.

The wilderness allures and mystifies with the majesty and grace of its animals. From left to right and top to bottom are: Lenox Collection's "African Elephant Calf" figurine, The Hamilton Collection's "Autumn in the Mountains" plate, "Dolphin and Baby" figurine by Kaiser Porcelain USA, Inc., Reco International Corp.'s "Whale Song" plate, Maruri U.S.A.'s "Baby Harp Seals" figurine, Artaffects, Ltd.'s "Hortense Hippo" figurine, Legends' "Old Tusker" figurine, Swarovski America Ltd.'s "Penguin" and "Walrus" figurines and "Fleeting Encounter" plate from The Bradford Exchange.

The memories of childhood, loved ones and favorite things are captured by renowned artists with the joy and love they bring to collectors. From left to right and top to bottom are: Reco International Corp.'s "Flower Swing" graphic, United Design's "Betty Button's Surprise" figurine, M.I. Hummel figurine by Goebel "Art Critic" (HUM 318), Sarah's Attic's "Sassafras" doll, M.I. Hummel figurine by Goebel "Apple Tree Boy" (HUM 142/I), The Norman Rockwell Gallery's "Sitting Pretty" figurine, WACO Product Corporation's "Accordion Boy" figurine, The Constance Collection's "Sweet Dreams" figurine, WACO Product Corporation's "Grandfather's Clock" figurine, Hamilton Gifts Ltd.'s "Susanna" figurine, Hamilton Heritage Dolls' "Sara" doll, Sarah's Attic's "Classroom Memories" plate and "Sitting Pretty" figurine from Lladro Collectors Society.

The secrets of a garden are unlocked, and the flowers and animals that have been hidden are enjoyed by those who seek them out. From left to right and top to bottom are: Lilliput Lane Limited's "Periwinkle Cottage" figurine, "We Are God's Workmanship" figurine from Enesco Precious Moments Collectors' Club, Swarovski America Ltd.'s "Pineapple" figurine, "Delicate Motion" figurine by Maruri U.S.A., Hamilton Gifts Ltd.'s "A Flower for You" figurine, Schmid's "Peter Rabbit in the Garden" figurine, Goebel Miniature's *Historical Series* with "Country Garden Display" and figures, Lenox Collections' "Calla Lily" figurine, Hamilton Gifts Ltd.'s "Spring Frolic" figurine, Swarovski America Ltd.'s "Grapes" figurine, "Iris Quartet" plate from The Bradford Exchange, Lawtons' "Spring Blossom" doll, "Collecting Makes Good Scents" figurine from Enesco Precious Moments Collectors' Club, Hamilton's "Virginia" doll and "I'm Nuts Over My Collection" figurine from Enesco Precious Moments Collectors' Club.

The first moments of love fill the sentimental hearts of collectors in these beautiful creations of brides and sweethearts. From left to right and top to bottom are: "He Loves Me…" figurine from Enesco Memories of Yesterday Collectors' Society, "Over the Threshold" figurine from Lladro Collectors Society, Armani's "Oriental Girl with Column" figurine, Reco International Corp.'s "The Magic of Love" plate, "Let's Make Up" figurine from Lladro Collectors Society, Royal Doulton's "Thinking of You," "Thank You," "Forget Me Not" and "Loving You" figurines, Sarah's Attic's "Groom Whimpy" and "Bride Katie" on the "Heart Tree" figurines, Lenox Collections' "Love's Promise" figurine, Hand & Hammer Silversmiths' "Wedding Keepsake" cake topper, "Flora" doll produced by Roman, Inc. under the hallmark of the W.S. George China Company, Goebel Inc.'s "Claudia" doll and Armani's "Lady on Horse" figurine.

Dolls...dolls...dolls. Each with expressions of wonderment and joy, dressed in authentic dresses and many with a cherished companion — a rocking horse or rag doll. On the left page, from left to right and top to bottom are: "Rebeccah" available through the Ashton-Drake Galleries, The Collectables' "Yvette," Goebel Inc.'s "Brandy," Lee Middleton Original Dolls' "Baby Grace," "Sincerity Apricots and Cream" and "Serenity Apples and Spice," Goebel Inc.'s "Samantha," "Emily" available through The Ashton-Drake Galleries and Gorham, Inc.'s "Jessica."

On the right page, from left to right and top to bottom are: Hamilton's "Jessica," The Collectables' "Lauren," Nahrgang Collection's "Karmin," Seymour Mann, Inc.'s "Lady Caroline," Reco International Corp.'s "Katie The Tightrope Walker," Lee Middleton Original Dolls' "Missy Buttercup" on her rocking horse, Goebel Inc.'s "Helga" and "Gigi," The Collectables' "Toddler Boy" and Nahrgang Collection's "McKinsey."

Religious themes are delicately portrayed to please collectors who appreciate their inspirational messages and true beauty. From left to right and top to bottom are: "Angel with Flute" figurine by Kaiser Porcelain USA, Inc., Roman, Inc.'s *Fontanini Signature Collection* figures and stable, and "Madonna and Child" graphic, Artaffects, Ltd.'s "The Last Supper" plate, "Angel with Lute" figurine by Kaiser Porcelain USA, Inc., Roman, Inc.'s "Noah" figurine, Goebel Miniatures *DeGrazia Collection* with "DeGrazia Chapel Display" and figurines, Duncan Royale's "The Pageant" figurine, Roman, Inc.'s "Bless This Child" plate, Lenox Collections' "The Good Shepherd" figurine and Lilliput Lane Limited's "Convent in the Woods" figurine.

It's Christmas time...sledders are gliding down hillsides and carolers are filling the streets and air with tunes of joy. From left to right and top to bottom are: Department 56's "C.H.Watt Physician," and "Tutbury Printer" with Carolers figurines, Duncan Royale's "Julinesse" figurine, M.I. Hummel Figurine by Goebel "Ride Into Christmas" (HUM 396/1), Enesco Corporation's "Have a Coke and a Smile" ornament, United Design's "A Wild Ride" figurine, Flambro Imports' "1991 Emmett Kelly, Jr." dated ornament, Seymour Mann's "The Christmas Village" figurine, Byers' Choice Ltd.'s "Carolers®" figurines and Department 56's "Wong's In Chinatown" figurine.

Christmas time means Santa's busy making lists, test driving his sleigh and keeping his elves busy at work creating toys. On the left page, from left to right and top to bottom are: Annalee Mobilitee Dolls, Inc.'s "Santa In Tub With Rubber Duckie" doll, WACO Product Corporation's "Santa Claus-1990" figurine, Whitley Bay's "Santa" figurine, United Design's "For Santa" figurine, The Norman Rockwell Gallery's "Santa's Workshop" figurine, Whitley Bay's "Felix" figurine, Department 56's "Santa and Mrs. Claus" and "Santa's Workshop" figurines, Whitley Bay's "Sleigh" figurine, Enesco Corporation's "All We Want For Christmas" figurine, Annalee Mobilitee Dolls, Inc.'s "Day-After-Christmas Santa" and "Santa With Pot Belly Stove" dolls.

On the right page, from left to right and top to bottom are: Whitley Bay's "Hug" and "Lists" figurines, Goebel Miniatures' *Night Before Christmas Collection* with display and figurines, Whitley Bay's "Gus" figurine, Hand & Hammer Silversmiths' "I Love Santa" ornament, The Norman Rockwell Gallery's "Christmas Dream" figurine, Hand & Hammer Silversmiths' "Prancer" ornament, Sarah's Attic's "Masquerade" figurine, Hand & Hammer Silversmiths' "The Night Before Christmas" ornaments, Annalee Mobilitee Dolls, Inc.'s "Collector Santa with Reindeer Golfing" doll and The Constance Collection's "Santa's Dance" figurine.

As the city becomes a winter wonderland, thoughts of angels and heavenly moments warm collectors' hearts. From left to right and top to bottom are: United Design's "The Gift" figurine, The Collectables' "Snowfairy Tree Topper" doll, The Constance Collection's "Heavenly Blessings" figurine, Department 56's "Twinkle Little Stars," set of two figurines, 1991 Christmas Bell from Lladro Collectors Society, Artaffects, Ltd.'s "Forever Friends" figurine, Department 56's "Wishing on a Star" figurine, Nahrgang Collection's "Laura" doll, Lawtons' "Crystal Winter" doll, The Collectables' Doll Head Ornament and Gorham, Inc.'s "Emily" doll.

Sophisticated ladies don their hats and parasols as they attend the races at Ascot, a tea or their first party. From left to right and top to bottom are: "Eliza At Ascot" doll from The Ashton-Drake Galleries, Hamilton Heritage Dolls' "First Party" doll, Royal Doulton's "Lady Worsley" figurine, Goebel, Inc.'s "Priscilla" doll, "Tea Time" figurine from Lladro Collectors Society, Armani's "Lady with Sunshade" figurine, Seymour Mann, Inc's "Sheila" doll, Nahrgang Collection's "Aubrey" doll, Armani's "Lady with Powder Puff" figurine and Seymour Mann, Inc.'s "Felicia" doll.

The artwork above exhibits the variety of subject matter and detail-rich artistry which characterizes the field of limited edition collectibles. From left to right and top to bottom are: Annalee Mobilitee Dolls' "Easter Parade Boy and Girl" dolls, John Hine Studios' "Pudding Cottage" figurine, The Hamilton Collection's "Star Trek®, 25th Anniversary Commemorative Plate," Sports Impressions' "Andre Dawson Gold Edition" plate, Lance Corporation's "Barber" figurine, "68 Comeback Special" plate from The Bradford Exchange, Hand & Hammer Silversmiths' "Mrs. Rabbit" ornament, Swarovski America Ltd.'s "Airplane" and "Oldtimer Automobile" figurines, "Johanna" by Lee Middleton Original Dolls, Hand & Hammer Silversmiths' "Peter Rabbit" ornament, Hamilton Gifts Ltd.'s "Little Boy Blue" figurine and Lawtons' "The Blessing" doll.

Young women can be beautiful in a multitude of activities and moods—romantic, patriotic, energetic, quiet, simple, elegant.... From left to right and top to bottom are: "Francesca" from Seymour Mann, Inc., "Sara's Teatime" from Gorham Inc., Dynasty Doll's "Carley," "English Lady" figurine by Lladro, the "1992 Cherub Stein" and the "1893 Columbian Exposition" plate produced by Anheuser-Busch, Inc., "Kiyoshi — The Japanese Bride" figurine from Lenox Collections, "Grace Valentine" from Ladie & Friends, Inc., "Rosapina" graphic by Cross Gallery, "Twilight — Lady With Violin" by Armani and Dynasty Doll's "Adele."

Little boys and girls are captured in motion by renowned artists who portray them dancing a ballet, reading a book, playing baseball and making music. From left to right and top to bottom are: "La Danseuse" (The Dancer) and "Marie Lavande" dolls from Corolle/Timeless Creations, "Katie's Bedtime Story" doll by Georgetown Collection, "10-inch Baseball Player" doll from Annalee Mobilitee Dolls, Inc., "Children Skaters" figurines by Byers' Choice Ltd., Artaffects' "Rainbow Patrol" figurine, "Claire Valentine" from Ladie & Friends, Inc. and "Bavarian Moving Van" figurine from Midwest Importers of Cannon Falls, Inc.

Precious memories of childhood are these: walking to school, cuddling a stuffed toy and fishing with a friend on a lazy summer afternoon. From left to right and top to bottom are: The Hamilton Collection's "Jennifer," "Gift of Love" figurine by ANRI, "Catch Me If You Can!" doll from The Ashton-Drake Galleries, "Nancy Bowman" by Ladie & Friends, Inc., Novelino's "Castle Building" figurine, "Skier" figurine from M.I. Hummel Club, "Patience" plate by Reco International Corp., Cross Gallery's "Thick Lodge Clan Boy: Crow Indian" graphic, "Amy with Doll Carriage" from Kurt S. Adler/Santa's World and Lawtons' "The Little Emperor's Nightingale" doll.

Favorite story book, cartoon and fantasy characters are skillfully represented in stunning figurines and sculptures. On the left page from left to right and top to bottom are: "Graffyn On Grunch" from Precious Art/Panton, "The Scarecrow" from Ron Lee's World of Clowns, "Tweety Bird" by Summerhill Crystal & Glass, "The Little Mermaid" by Ron Lee's World of Clowns, "Princess Coach" from Summerhill Crystal & Glass, Silver Deer's "Joe Cool 'Vette" and "Strong to the Finish" by Ron Lee's World of Clowns.

On the right page from left to right and top to bottom are: "Castle In The Air" from John Hine Studios, Inc., "Merlin the Magician" smoking figure from Kurt S. Adler/Santa's World, "For Better For Worse" by Ron Lee's World of Clowns, "Large Mickey Mouse" and "Minnie Mouse" by Summerhill Crystal & Glass, "The Swami" and "Woody 1940" figurines from Ron Lee's World of Clowns and "Farm Gnome" by Flambro Imports.

Santa Claus never goes out of style. He is internationally known and loved in every type of ethnic costume and performing every type of activity. On the left page from left to right and top to bottom are: Rockwell's "Balancing the Budget" figurine by Possible Dreams, "Christmas Is In The Air" by Kurt S. Adler/Santa's World, "Fisherman Santa" from Midwest Importers of Cannon Falls, Inc., United Design's "Santa & Mrs. Claus, Victorian" figurine, "Santa Claus 1992" from WACO Products Corporation, "The Department Store — Santa & Santa's Helper" dolls from Ladie & Friends, Inc., "Reach for the Star" from The Constance Collection, "Santa's Arrival" by June McKenna Collectibles, Inc., The Norman Rockwell Gallery's "Making His List," and Novelino's "Father Christmas."

On the right page, from left to right and top to bottom are: "Santa Nykolai" figurine by Midwest Importers of Cannon Falls, Inc., "Santa's Hot Air Balloon" figurine from June McKenna Collectibles, Inc., "Father Christmas" nutcracker from Midwest Importers of Cannon Falls, Inc., "1940's Traditional Santa" figurine by Possible Dreams, Duncan Royale's "Nast and Sleigh," "Christmas Gathering" by June McKenna Collectibles, Inc., "Heralding the Way" from Possible Dreams and "Santa on the Roof" plate by Royal Copenhagen/Bing & Grondahl.

Winter and Christmas are magical times of the year. The mention of the Christmas holiday brings to mind visions of carolers, snow-covered landscapes, nativity scenes and gifts of toys. On the left page from left to right and top to bottom are: "Little Guardian Angel" figurine by June McKenna Collectibles, Inc., Charles Dickens' "A Christmas Carol" ornaments by Hand & Hammer Silversmiths, "Crown & Cricket Inn" from Department 56 Inc., Silver Deer's "Dalmatian Christmas Animal" figurine, "Christmas In San Francisco" plate by Royal Copenhagen/Bing & Grondahl, Takara's "Train Engine With Elf" figurine, *Hometown Christmas* from The Cat's Meow and "Christmas Shopping" plate by Royal Copenhagen/Bing & Grondahl.

On the right page from left to right and top to bottom are: "Toy Shop" from PenDelfin Sales Inc., The Franklin Mint's "Winter's Eve" plate, "Snowman" by Takara, "Lion Standing Holding Lamb" and "Cookie Peddler" figurines from VickiLane, Inc., Takara's "Elves With Sleigh" figurine, *Sugar Town* by Enesco Corporation and "The Crows" plate from Royal Copenhagen/Bing & Grondahl.

A variety of dolls created by renowned artists are styled with authentic outfits and memorable expressions. On the left page from left to right and top to bottom are: Georgetown Collection's "Baby Bunting," "Annie at Play" from Dynasty Doll, "Kitty Kay" by Turner Dolls Inc., "Marty" and "Matia" dolls from The Collectables and "Liliane," "Shireem" and "Neblina" dolls by Annette Himstedt for Timeless Creations, Div. of Mattel.

On the right page from left to right and top to bottom are: "Victoria, The Littlest Gibson" doll from The Franklin Mint, Turner Doll's "Terrance" and "Nikkeya," "Hannah" by Turner Dolls, Inc., Goebel United States' "Cindy" doll, "Marie Claudine" from Corolle/Timeless Creations and Dynasty Doll's "Corinne."

Small woodland animals can be whimsical, enchanting and captivating. Artists have represented some of these little creatures performing many human tasks, such as camping or holding tea parties. From left to right and top to bottom are: Takara's "Deer with Rabbits," Schmid's "Don't Play With Fire," "Scout" from PenDelfin Sales Inc., "Tea Time" by VickiLane, Inc., Thumper's Sisters: "Hello, Hello There!," Thumper: "Hee! Hee! Hee!," Bambi & Flower: "He Can Call Me A Flower If He Wants To" and Friend Owl: "What's Going On Around Here?" by The Walt Disney Company, "Mother & Kids Baking" and "Mama Pig, Piglets & Apple" from VickiLane, Inc., Silver Deer's "Make a Wish" and "Schoolhouse Mouse," Novelino Inc.'s "Eastern Fox Squirrel," "Jacky" from PenDelfin Sales Inc. and "The Beaver Family" by Swarovski America Ltd.

Hear the call of the wild... Large animals of the wilderness intrigue and fascinate with their majesty and grace. From left to right and top to bottom are: "Sound of Warning" and "Breaking Away" sculptures by Creart U.S., "Timber Wolf Stein" from M. Cornell Importers, Inc., "Reticulated Giraffe with Baby" figurine by Novelino, Inc., "Giant Panda Stein" from Anheuser-Busch, Inc., Silver Deer's "Gorillas" figurine, Creart's "Puma Head" sculpture, "Rainforest Magic" stein by Classic Carolina Collections, "The Imperial Panda" figurine from Maruri U.S.A. and Creart's "Standing Whitetail Deer."

History is an interesting category on which to reflect and study. Ancient events are fascinating as well as history in the making. From left to right and top to bottom are: "Olde Porterfield Tea Room" plate from The Bradford Exchange, "Berlin Wall II Stein" by M. Cornell Importers, Inc., Steinbach "Abraham Lincoln" Nutcracker by Kurt S. Adler/Santa's World, "General Grant Stein" by Anheuser-Busch, Inc., "Birth of a Nation" stein from Classic Carolina Collections, "Oakwood Smithy" cottage by Lilliput Lane Limited, The Franklin Mint's "1912 Packard Victoria," "Hank Aaron Signed Figurine" by Gartlan USA, Inc., "Boys Night Out" figurine from Sarah's Attic, Inc., Classic Carolina Collections' "Attack On Fort Sumter" and "Jackhammer" steins, "Albert" Londonshire figurine by Possible Dreams, "Promontory Point Stein" from M. Cornell Importers, Inc. and Royal Doulton's "King Charles I Character Jug."

Mystery and allure enshroud Indian heritage and traditions. From left to right and top to bottom are: "The Fur Trapper" and "Prince of the Plains" figurines from Roman, Inc., Nahrgang Collection's "Pocahantas" doll, "Esteemed Warrior" sculpture by LEGENDS, The Hamilton Collection's "Deliverance" plate, "Warrior's Farewell" figurine and "Polland Cabinet Sign" by Polland Studios, "Buffalo Hunt Stein" by M. Cornell Importers, Inc., Lance Corporation's "Chief Joseph" figurine and The Franklin Mint's "Spirit of the Sioux" figurine.

Lovely lithographs adorn a room with vibrant or subtle hues. These graphics depict exquisite Indian, building and landscape scenes. From left to right and top to bottom are: "Agnjnauq Amaguut; Inupiaq (Woman With Her Wolves)" from Cross Gallery, Inc., "The Broadwater Bridge" and "Home Is Where The Heart Is" from Lightpost Publishing, "Wooltalkers" from Cross Gallery, Inc., "Evening At Swanbrook Cottage, Thomashire" and "New York: Snow on Seventh Avenue, 1932" from Lightpost Publishing.

Annalee Mobilitee Dolls

Annalee Doll Society Offers Whimsical Dolls to Benefit Worthy Charities and Causes

It has been more than half a century since Annalee Davis married Charles ("Chip") Thorndike and moved to his family chicken farm in Meredith, New Hampshire. The Harvard-educated Chip wanted nothing more than to enjoy the simple life of a farmer, but after World War II the chicken industry began its inevitable migration south.

Faced with the challenge of changing careers — and with two young sons to provide for — the Thorndikes turned their energies to the dollmaking craft that Annalee had initiated as a girlhood hobby.

Soon Annalee's happy little skiers, Santa Clauses and other delightful figures won an enthusiastic audience throughout New England. And over the years, Annalee Mobilitee dolls have become favorites of collectors throughout the United States and beyond.

As Annalee and Chip's son Townsend says, "The company has grown significantly since the early days when Mom and Dad labored at the kitchen table to perfect each doll, and the local bankers maintained that 'It will never work!'."

Those New England bankers were wrong, for what was once a classic "cottage industry" based in the Thorndikes' 200-year-old brick house has now grown into a thriving business which employs more than 400 people — including the family's two sons.

But most important to Annalee Thorndike and her family is that their venture retain its "down-home" atmosphere and friendly, low-key manner. The company's concern for community and for people shines through as well, considering its many joint ventures creating dolls to benefit charitable organizations and causes.

The New Hampshire Music Festival Conductor Doll

Tom Nee has been the New Hampshire Music Festival conductor for 25 years — and his orchestra has been a favorite of the Thorndike family for nearly all that time. Now Annalee has created a doll in his honor, with ten percent of the proceeds donated to the Festival's Permanent Endowment Fund.

A master of the stage, Nee brings his skilled musicians into perfect harmony and soothes his audiences with the beauty of music. Now his likeness has been captured in a conductor doll with white hair and moustache, formal attire, and baton at the ready. Each doll includes a numbered brass plaque signed by its artist and creator, Annalee Thorndike, as well as a wooden base and glass dome.

The Annalee Victory Ski Doll

Annalee Mobilitee has high aspirations for its U.S. Olympic-hopeful Chris Pedersen, a young man from the Thorndikes' hometown of Meredith, New Hampshire. Annalee has created a special doll to help provide funds for its sponsorship of young Pedersen — and to help sponsor the Christa McAuliffe Ski Invitational.

The "Annalee Victory Ski Doll" portrays a happy young skier who is holding a huge loving cup and is wearing a gold medal around his neck. The skier looks as if he just claimed the ultimate Olympic prize.

At the affordable price of $49.95 each, the "Annalee Victory Ski Doll" includes a membership in the Annalee Doll Society and all attendant Society benefits.

Five percent of the proceeds will be donated to Chris Pedersen and the U.S. Ski Team, while ten percent of the proceeds will go to the Christa McAuliffe Sabbatical Trust Fund through the Christa McAuliffe Ski Invitational. Ms. McAuliffe, a New Hampshire school teacher, was tragically killed in the Challenger space shuttle disaster of 1986. In one recent year, Annalee Mobilitee provided $14,000 to the Trust Fund through doll proceeds.

The Annalee Earth Day and Sheriff Mice

For decades, Annalee has delighted collectors with her charming little mouse dolls on a wide range of themes. Now two of her mice have "gone to work" for good causes: one to further the cause of Earth Day, and another to fight for drug rehabilitation.

10" New Hampshire Music Festival doll

The Annalee "Earth Day Mouse" looks for all the world like a modern-day Johnny Appleseed with his backpack and bright felt costume. He's digging a hole with his shiny shovel, doing his best to preserve Mother Earth for the future. A portion of the proceeds from his sale is going to the New Hampshire Trust for Land Conservation.

The Spirit of '76 Tableau

In just the first few months of its existence, Annalee's "The Spirit of '76" tableau generated over $10,000 for the Veterans of Foreign Wars (V.F.W.), with much more funding to come.

Suggested by the famous painting that hangs in the Selectmen's Office in Abbot Hall, Marblehead, Massachusetts, "The Spirit of '76" portrays a bandaged fife player and two drummers. Indomitable in spirit, these three revolutionary warriors step forth proudly against the background of a 13-star American flag. Each tableau is signed and numbered and has its own glass dome.

Annalee herself spent many long hours with her design team to ensure that this tableau would realize its full potential and historic significance. "I wanted to do something special to commemorate those who have served this nation, and help the organization that cares for them," she says.

Annual Barbecue Highlights Annalee Doll Society Membership

Year by year, membership in the Annalee Doll Society grows as collectors discover its many benefits. Perhaps the most famous and unique of these is the annual barbecue at the Thorndikes' home in Meredith, New Hampshire. Visitors enjoy food, friendship, a factory tour, and the opportunity to acquire rare Annalee dolls at a lively auction.

At the auction, the most knowledgeable Annalee collectors in the world settle down to bid on pieces that have risen from just a few dollars in value to hundreds or even thousands of dollars apiece. Also auctioned are many artist proofs and prototypes. New Society dolls are unveiled for the first time, creating an atmosphere of excitement and anticipation.

Since The Society began in 1983, membership has soared to over 23,000 collectors. Today, The Society keeps in touch with its members through a colorful, quarterly magazine called *The Collector,* which is supplemented by other publications throughout the year.

Additional Society membership privileges include: a free 7" "Logo Kid" whose design changes each year; a free Annalee Doll Society Membership pin; free admission to the Annalee Doll Museum; and the opportunity to purchase limited

Annalee Victory Ski Doll

edition, signed and numbered dolls designed exclusively for members of the Annalee Doll Society. For more information on Society membership, contact the Annalee Doll Society at P.O. Box 1137, Meredith, New Hampshire 03253-1137.

7" Earth Day Mouse

"Spirit of '76"

ANRI Nativities

Woodcarved Creche Scenes Capture the Birth of Jesus in ANRI's Traditional Heirloom Style

For more than 750 years, the glory of Christmas has been celebrated with the recreation of Jesus' humble birth in Bethlehem. And for more than 300 years, woodcarvers in Europe's Groden Valley — the home of The House of ANRI — have lent their talents to the creation of exquisite nativity figures.

It was on December 24, 1233 when St. Francis of Assisi stood in a candlelit forest to sing the Christmas gospel. In the background, for the first time since that holy night so many centuries before, was a stable complete with ox and ass, and an infant in swaddling clothes.

On that eventful night, the tradition of the nativity was born. And before the end of that century, freestanding figures of the Holy Family were sculpted for the Basilica of St. Mary Major — a practice that spread quickly throughout the churches of Europe. Soon, people brought nativities into their homes, adding to the beauty and the number of elements included as time went by.

On Christmas Eve, 1741, the first nativity reached the New World. Brought from the Old World and set up by missionaries in Bethlehem, Pennsylvania, it consisted of the Holy Family surrounded by waterfalls, bridges, fountains and hundreds of figurines — a grand nativity in the European tradition.

The History of ANRI's Woodcarved Nativities

While nativities were capturing the hearts of Europe in the 15th century, a unique transformation was taking place in the Groden Valley, where ANRI makes its home. Grodeners, already well-known for their fine lace and cloth, were turning their skills to the art of woodcarving. In time, their nativity figures and other woodcarvings virtually replaced their lace and cloth in the markets of Europe.

Grodeners left a permanent mark on the history of nativities. They were the first to add snow to the Bethlehem scene. This unique feature, coupled with the intricate detail of their carvings, quickly endeared Groden nativities to churches and collectors throughout Europe. By the 18th century, the Groden Valley had become one of the primary sources of handcarved nativities in the world.

During the 1800s, Luis Riffeser and later his son, Anton, set as their goal the creation of woodcarvings that would meet the highest standards of artistry and quality. Anton Riffeser founded The House of ANRI (from ANton RIffeser), where he brought together the Valley's finest woodcarvers under one roof. Today, four generations of Riffesers later, The House of ANRI is still home to world-famous artists, Groden master woodcarvers, and painters. And faithful to the philosophy of its founder, ANRI proudly continues the tradition of nativity woodcarvings begun by their ancestors more than 300 years ago.

ANRI Presents Precious Gift Nativities as Heirlooms for Future Generations

When today's collector makes the decision to invest in an ANRI nativity, he or she is presented with a wide range of options in terms of artistry and pieces to select. ANRI offers collectors a

Juan Ferrandiz captures the birth of Christ in this nativity starter set from The Message Collection. *Like all the handcarved figurines in this collection from The House of ANRI, the nativity is enhanced by the brilliance of a perfectly cut Swarovski crystal. The set consists of Mary, Joseph, Jesus and a lamb, and measures four and one-half inches in height.*

choice of "Starter Sets," which include a preliminary purchase of six pieces — usually the three-piece Holy Family plus one King, one Shepherd and one Sheep. In this case, a stable is included as a special gift from ANRI at no additional charge. Other starter sets may include just the Holy Family, or as many as ten pieces. In any case, a free stable is part of every ANRI starter set.

Choosing the style and size of nativity should be a very careful decision-making process. Some collectors enjoy the cherubic style of Juan Ferrandiz, where his message of peace, harmony and love among man and beast shine through. Others prefer the traditional touch in the designs of German artist Karl Kuolt or Groden-born Ulrich Bernardi. The renowned Bernardi began his traditional set over 30 years ago, but he also offers the "Florentine" set, which is more ornate.

Another consideration is size. Collectors need to consider exactly where they will display the creche, so that the correct scale may be selected. With the starter set in a place of honor, many collectors buy more figurines year by year: the wise men, angel, ox, donkey, more shepherds, sheep, and perhaps a camel and camel driver.

The work of acclaimed sculptor Karl Kuolt is faithfully reproduced by master woodcarvers at The House of ANRI, where this six-piece starter set nativity scene, complete with free stable, was created. Carved and painted by hand, using time-honored techniques, the Kuolt nativity set includes the Holy Family, one king, one shepherd, and a lamb, as well as the stable. The wood sculptures measure from three inches to six inches in height.

The Innocent Charm of the Ferrandiz Nativities

For more than twenty years, the gifted Juan Ferrandiz has shared his genius with ANRI collectors. Two of the most renowned Ferrandiz creations are his nativities: a traditional creche and the new *Message Collection* nativity adorned with genuine Swarovski crystals.

Ferrandiz' gentle vision is that "The innocence of children incites us to create a world where communication and love lead to that sublime desire which is Peace." He plays out his world view with a nativity that celebrates the innocence of children. Each beloved character appears in the guise of a happy child, while the animals are invested with an appealing, fantasy-like quality.

Along with the Holy family and traditional nativity characters, Ferrandiz has recently added geese, ducks and dogs to his array of offerings. This artist's unique vision — portraying the blessed event through the innocence of youth — continues to enthrall collectors all over the world.

The Beautifully Realistic Creche Of Professor Karl Kuolt

Through the centuries there have been countless artistic interpretations of the birth of Jesus presented through a nativity. Among these a few stand out as exceptional, and one is the nativity of Professor Karl Kuolt. Kuolt's design, made at the House of ANRI's woodcarving workshop, has over the years proven itself to be one of the most admired and collected woodcarved nativities of its kind.

During his life, which began in Germany in 1878 and lasted until 1937, Kuolt established himself as an artist extraordinaire. He began his art training at the Munich School of Art and continued his education at the Munich Academy. His works, which include monuments and memorial chapels as well as figurines, are well-known, respected and admired worldwide. A collection of his works can be seen in The Glass Palace in Munich.

ANRI has crafted its Kuolt nativity in both a three-inch and a six-inch size, with each set including over forty figurines. All are painted in lovely muted shades of blues, yellow, reds, browns and golds. These colors capture the essence and spirit of the blessed event while also enhancing the intricate detail of each figurine.

In recent years, there have been wonderful additions to the Kuolt creches, notably a new sheep and a cow. There are also several newer shepherds and a shepherdess to enrich the scene surrounding the Holy Family. New or traditional, each Kuolt piece is designed differently, but they all send the same message: "Peace on Earth."

The Wonder of Ulrich Bernardi's Masterworks

Since he was a child, Ulrich Bernardi dreamed of becoming a woodcarver. His famous Madonna earned him the rank of master carver at age 30. A Master of Art, he has been producing religious carvings for ANRI for more than 30 years — including the famous traditional and Florentine nativities of his own design.

Characterized by exquisite detail, Bernardi's creches are renowned by collectors for their wide range of sizes: from a miniature two-inch series to four-inch, six-inch, and eight-inch collections. The Florentine creche, at five inches in size, recaptures the glory of Italy's most fabled city of Renaissance art.

In recent years, Bernardi has added a brown sheep and other animals to his traditional nativity, as well as an older shepherd and two young shepherd boys. Bernardi also expanded his Florentine nativity to include a camel driver from a faraway land, and camel. These two woodcarvings complement the set by adding two very detailed and interesting characters.

Whether a collector prefers the magical charm of Ferrandiz, the life-like realism of Kuolt, or the elegance of Bernardi, The House of ANRI can provide a stunning creche to fulfill his or her desires and complement any display space. As the nativity scene is enhanced by the addition of more lovely pieces, its value as a collector's item — and as a treasured family heirloom — is destined to grow year by year.

Italian wood sculptor Ulrich Bernardi presents a traditional interpretation of the nativity scene with this ten-piece miniature figurine set from The House of ANRI. The Bernardi nativity is carved and painted by hand using age-old techniques that have been handed down from generation to generation. Each hand-carved sculpture measures two inches in height. Bernardi's de signs are also available to collectors in the 4", 6" and 8" sizes.

Armani Collection from Miller Import Corporation

His Fair Ladies: The Splendid, Romantic Sculptures of Giuseppe Armani

Travelers to the region of Tuscany in Italy know they have reached a magical place the moment they arrive.

Tall, graceful poplar trees point toward heaven along roadsides as though telling the world that this region is central to God's masterplan for the universe. Towns rise up like medieval dreams... compact wedding cake-dwellings, with tier upon tier of earthen-colored residences, separated by cobblestone streets and steep alleys, tiny courtyards and slamming doors.

The air smells sweet and rich, and everyone, from the oldest man sipping espresso at an outdoor table to the tiniest baby in baptismal gown, seems to be incredibly enchanting. Indeed, they really are.

This is Tuscany...and home to sculptor Giuseppe Armani. If the talented artist has his way, it is here that he will spend the rest of his days on earth. After all, how much closer can one be to heaven than Tuscany, the cradle of artistic civilization and home to several centuries worth of artistic masters?

Giuseppe Armani was born in this, the richest artistic region on earth. His background gave no clue that he would join the ranks of 20th Century Italian master sculptors. The only son of an agricultural products broker and his wife, Giuseppe Armani came into the world in 1935 in Calci, a small village near Pisa. It was here that he spent his childhood years. And, it was here that he first began to show an emerging talent for art that took advantage of Calci's resources. Armani constantly and voraciously drew the faces of friends and the faces of strangers...and when he ran out of real models, Armani turned to his vivid imagination and conjured visions of people in his head.

Not one to limit himself to just paper or canvas surfaces, the boy also took to decorating the walls of his boyhood village. The resulting art work made bold statements about his future as a gifted artist.

We do not know if the young Armani ran out of wall space to sketch his fanciful murals...or if his father simply found a new job in Pisa. We do know, however, that the Armani family moved to Pisa, famous for its leaning tower, when the artist was just fourteen. The move was to be the last one Armani would make. Pisa came to be his artistic and spiritual home. He resides there to this day.

In Pisa, Armani undertook a rigorous, ten-year-long curriculum in art and anatomy. He patiently developed his very own style, all the while immersing himself in the textures and nuances of the masters he worshipped: Michaelangelo, daVinci, Donatello and Pisano. He explored Renaissance works and the splendor of Rococo. Eventually, Armani came to apprentice with a master sculptor at a world-renown studio. Working with this sculptor changed Armani's life. He soon came to a personal understanding that three dimensional art would be his future course. Though the gifted artist truly loved the splendid oils and watercolors of famous Italian painters, it was only through the medium of sculpture that Giuseppe Armani felt his art really come alive.

Exacting Standards that Bring a Lifetime of Enjoyment to Collectors

If Pisa is on the road to heaven, surely Florence is its gate! Ornate cathedrals sparkle in the sun and their spires reach for the clouds. Inside, breathtaking frescos shimmer across vaulted ceilings, illuminated by what appear to be thousands of candles. Streets teem with cosmopolitan life and everywhere you look, there is beauty and art.

In a small village just outside this mecca, Giuseppe Armani found a haven for his creative muse at the Florence Sculture d'Arte Studios. For it is at this modern facility that the artist's sculptures are reproduced for the world marketplace and where Armani performs his many functions as a premier sculptor for the Studios.

To insure that his artistic perspective remains unclouded by the many commercial aspects of the Florence studios, Armani creates each original sculpture in his private studio in Pisa. Each morning, the sculptor sets out just after dawn to walk the tranquil Pisa countryside. His eyes take in the lush greens of the landscape and his lively imagination pulsates with new ideas for sculptures. Armani believes that this essential walk sets the pace for his day.

By 8:30 AM, charged by nature and his brisk walk, Armani takes a seat at his studio work table and begins his day; he starts to massage lifeless clay into extraordinary forms.

While working, he often thinks back to his first days as a sculptor when he did not have the pliable medium of clay as a base for his creations. Like many well-trained artists around the world, Armani's first sculpting medium was marble, an unforgiving, hard substance that forces the artist to decide, before making the first chisel, exactly what the final piece will look like. A dedicated artist, Armani worked with the unyieldingly hard material...until he discovered the magic of clay. Once he found the clay, he would never return to the marble. Clay allowed Armani's creations to unfold like flower petals growing toward the light. We see the miracle in each of his works.

It takes Armani about twenty days to sculpt a new figure of medium size and difficulty. Once a sculpture is complete, Armani transfers it to the Florence Sculture d'Arte Studios where the detailed process of reproduction begins. Each of the artisans in the Florence Studios is an expert in his or her own right. However, Armani remains an integral part of each phase of the manufacturing process. At one moment he might oversee the modeling of the prototype that prepares his work for the mold. At another, he can be found checking the quality of carefully mixed kaolin and resin, two of the materials used to fabricate his figurines for the world market.

Only 1991 G. Armani Society members may purchase this lively clown who is precariously balanced atop a swirling chair and whose arms are full of just-picked daisies. The figure is limited to 1991 distribution, and will be retired at year's-end.

You might find him inspecting figures as they come out of the molds and are prepared for painting. And, his supervision follows the figures all the way to a unique painting system selected by the master. For while most collectibles are decorated with only one color pallet, Armani selects many! Each color is painstakingly mixed and applied at the Florence Studios.

While the full-color painting is very labor-intensive, requiring an enormous amount of time investment on the part of the highly skilled painter, all three styles are painted with identical, meticulous attention to detail. It's an Armani hallmark and a source of great pride to the entire Florence Studio.

Once the painting is complete, each detail is checked and re-checked by the master himself. Stringent rules and regulations prevent any facet of this complex manufacturing and decoration process to be taken outside of the Florence Studios. And, it is the orderly inspection system that insures that Armani sculptures maintain their integrity of design and production.

As you can see, figurines in the "Armani Collection" are carefully monitored by their designer. And, while it takes the artist twenty days or more to create each figure in the clay, it may take six months, a year or more before that figurine is ready for the world marketplace!

The Long, Lean Ladies of Armani

Let your eyes travel the length of an Armani sculpture and the journey will take longer than you had imagined. His figures bring to mind the lithe, willowy bodies of graceful Erte paintings, and indeed the entire Art Deco movement. But what prevents just a cursory glance at Armani's figures are the stops the eyes must make along the way. The detailing on every sculpture is quite extraordinary.

Flowing silks and satins and gauzy, draped jerseys fall from Armani's figures like fragile gossamer butterfly wings moving against the breeze. You know it's a sculpture, because affixed to the rich wood base that comes with each Armani work of art is a tiny, bronze signature plaque delivering that message. But, tell your eyes that! Armani's sculptures beg to be touched. Particularly his striking figures of women and couples. They manage to move while standing still and are typical of the fluid body poses captured by the sculptor.

The Armani women are many...too many to describe them all here...but certain sculptures in his enormous collection require that we stop a moment to spotlight just a few of his lovely ladies.

They are the pieces for which Armani may be best remembered.

"Lady With Peacock" is certainly such a figure. It's showcased within the very popular My *Fair Ladies*™ series, and the fully painted figure has been retired after market demand for the $400-plus figurine took the Lady on a whirlwind journey from introduction to sell-out. Nearly 20" high, "Lady With Peacock" features a pencil-thin woman reminiscent of the glamorous 1920s with a regal peacock atop her shoulder. The bird's highly detailed feathers cascade down her back, nearly reaching her knees.

Other sculptures in the My *Fair Ladies*™ series introduced in 1988, are equally dramatic and gorgeous. In place of the peacock, we find Armani's women reading books, dancing, tucking hands into a fur muff or preparing to unfurl a fan with feathers so real, you're tempted to wait for the breeze. Armani must have decided that ladies as lovely as these were not meant to be alone, for his My *Fair Ladies*™ series was expanded to include a romantic selection of couples. In addition, select figures from the collection were ultimately fashioned into lamps with hand-made silk shades atop polished wood or marble bases.

Giuseppe Armani's global love affair with women is evident in all of his works. From Neopolitan maidens to exotic, Oriental opera heroines to chaste Madonnas, and from sultry gypsy dancers to post-Victorian fashion figures, Armani's inspired touch is everywhere, transcending his sculptures of people.

Morning walks in the country must have inspired the magnificent animals Armani's hands have molded from clay, and their variety is mind-boggling. Majestic eagles. Romantic doves. Ducks in pairs awaiting the Spring. Exotic flamingos perched amid flowers and reeds. Exquisite peacocks and birds of paradise. Every imaginable harbinger of the seasons is found in the Armani kingdom: wrens, robins, swallow and goldfinch, each superbly finished down to the tiniest detail of wing tint and beak.

In case you think Armani stopped with birds, think again. His domestic cats are shown at play and *Fun Time*, a whimsical nursery of tiny puppies, kittens and other animal babies, reveals still another side of Armani's artistic style. The Armani collection also boasts powerful, bronze-finished wildlife (one 25" falcon anchors this small grouping, dwarfing a 12½" elephant with trunk and tusks raised).

If we have not already taken your breath away, please note that the Armani universe of sculptures also includes sweet and playful sculptures of children, remarkable clowns and even fabulous clocks wrapped with the master's sculptures.

In the past few years, an awe-inspiring series of ballet dancers has taken the marketplace by storm. And, when word got out that Herschel Walker, Minnesota Vikings tailback (an unlikely collector of dancing figurines) was a serious collector of Armani ballet sculptures, it became evident that the Armani charisma and talent was capable of turning the world into his personal fan club.

The G. Armani Society: Icing on the Cake

When the G. Armani Society was launched in January of 1990, it didn't waltz onto the collectibles scene with the slow grace of an Armani ballerina. Rather, the club burst into the world, championed by member number one, none other than the aforementioned Herschel Walker! The Society was proud to confer a first Members-Only offering "The Awakening" upon Walker. It's not often that a new organization finds a celebrity endorsement without even trying.

This is the kind of good fortune that's bound to carry the G. Armani Society well beyond the 6,000 members it predicted upon its debut. Statistics published by the collector club six months into its first year substantiate organizer's optimistic predictions: by summer of 1990, there were already 3,000 members on the books. Each enjoys a bountiful selection of benefits.

The G. Armani Review, a slick quarterly magazine, updates members with timely news of product introductions, rich lore about wondrous Italian cities and sites and practical, secondary market news. It's all wrapped around profiles of collectors, open house locations and editorial messages from both sides of the ocean. In addition to this impressive magazine, members receive a handsome binder to store Society materials, a porcelain member's plaque signed by Armani, special gifts and the opportunity to purchase Members-Only art at special prices.

Could we add Giuseppe Armani's name to the list of "things Italian" that make us think of heaven? Probably. His passion for his art is encased in every aspect of his work and we think that a good deal of the inspiration the artist receives to pursue his life's passion comes directly from his roots in Tuscany. For while many of us may move from city to city...chase rainbows and dreams to exciting ports-of-call...Giuseppe Armani has found fulfillment in Pisa. His journeys to enchantment take place every day in his head and travel down to the gifted hands that create the treasures we know simply as "Armani."

Artaffects

Teaching the Fine Art of Collectibles

Morning settles over New York City as a gentle sun spills across five boroughs of diversity. On Manhattan Island, building-fingers reluctantly stretch, while Brooklyn's ethnic neighborhoods push back covers and proffer greetings in all of the languages you'll find in the neighboring United Nations building. The Bronx, with its tough neighborhoods, greets the day with a mixture of hope and anticipation, while Queens yawns and allows the sun to flow over its boundaries, pushing toward the bedroom community of Long Island.

For Americans from Bangor to La Jolla, this is New York. Brash. Teeming. Loud. Honking cars and shouting voices. Racks of clothing crossing streets pushed by frantic clothiers. Delicatessens with boulder-sized salamis hanging like so many military weapons in glass windows. The flavor of New York.

But is it? Look a little closer and you'll find a fifth jewel in New York City's crown. Another borough also awakens to the morning. It's called Staten Island. Staten Island is a huge community situated directly across the river from New Jersey. Crammed with shopping centers, homes and offices, there's also a fascinating 18th century historical district that's been lovingly preserved by Staten Islanders. Amid this combination of old and new, you will also find a renovated, turn-of-the-century home that occupies space on a transitional block. This is the headquarters of Artaffects®, a fifteen-year-old collectibles company with product, goals and ambitions to match this eclectic city.

"Forever Friends" is part of the Simple Wonders *collection, created by Carol Roeda.*

Artaffects has all of the bustle of Manhattan, the artistic mix of Brooklyn, the tenacity of The Bronx and the diversity of Queens. Artaffects balances old with new in ways that have allowed it to grow from fledgling mail order distributor of limited edition collectors plates to well-respected manufacturer of distinctive figurines, dolls, lithographs and plates. It's a careful growth that has been engineered by Richard J. Habeeb, sole owner of Artaffects since its organization.

Habeeb's introduction to the limited edition collectibles industry is a story that's very similar to other tales of entrepreneurial zeal, though not all corporate start-ups were as unexpected as Habeeb's. But, perhaps it's the city. In a place like New York, it would be almost impossible *not* to reach for a compelling idea once it presents itself, no matter how far it is from what you'd planned... and that's exactly what Richard Habeeb did.

From Teacher to Investor to Art Dealer

Richard Habeeb earned a degree in education and expected to spend his life teaching children and raising his own. Newly married in 1971, the Habeebs set up housekeeping in a small apartment and held down teaching jobs to save for the future. As part of his regular reading, Habeeb routinely consulted *The Wall Street Journal* for information that would enable him to invest his money wisely. During one fateful reading of the *Journal*, Habeeb happened upon an article about newly issued, silver collectors plates featuring the work of Norman Rockwell. The article talked not only about the distinctive beauty of Rockwell's work, but it implied that plates in the series might hold investment potential.

For the newlyweds, the idea to purchase collectors plates seemed ideal. They could decorate their apartment with hand-picked art, and the plates offered a fabulous bonus: the potential to see their investment dollars grow. Thus began the Habeeb

"*The Last Supper" is part of* The Life of Jesus *series created by Lou Marchetti.*

"Christmas Journey" is the 1991 annual plate in the Perrillo Christmas *series.*

Rob Sauber, acknowledged as the American 'Master of Romantic Art,' designed "My Sunshine" to commemorate mothers in this lovely plate featuring the American Blues hallmark.

family's passion for limited edition, collectible art.

Fast forward three years. It's 1975, and Geraldine and Richard Habeeb are at the same address. They've settled into a comfortable lifestyle and picked out new furniture. There are also lots of limited edition plates on the walls. Everywhere.

"Our entire house was literally filled with them," Habeeb remembers. "We loved them all. Just about every manufacturer was represented, as well as art styles and mediums from around the world." The Habeebs had no wish to move to find the wall space their huge collection would need, so they placed an ad in their local paper and sold a few plates to make room for new discoveries. This ad was to hold another puzzle piece to the future. It literally opened a new world that would take Habeeb away from public school teaching for good.

From One Classified Ad to 20,000 Collectors

In what seemed like an instant, Habeeb found himself juggling two careers. Each day, he instructed the children of the New York school system, and when the bell rang at 3:00 p.m., he joined them in rushing down the steps of the school. For the kids, milk, cookies and play clothes awaited their pleasure. For Habeeb, it was the mail. A post office box brimming with surprises and treasures each day.

"Richard's Limited Editions" quickly became more than a mail order business devoted to buying and selling collectible plates. Striving to refine his expertise, Habeeb began to publish information on the plate market. Not one to make guarantees, he provided sound advice on the state-of-the-market gleaned from an ever-increasing research effort. The experience provided a rich base for what was to become a full-time career as collectibles dealer and later, producer.

By 1977, Richard Habeeb decided to risk all for what he knew to be his future and formed a company called Vague Shadows. Initially, Vague Shadows would serve as a showcase for the work of Gregory Perillo, a fellow New Yorker whose bold, exciting Native American portraits and wildlife art had attracted followers across the nation for decades. Perillo was a studio-trained master with a rich heritage of experience and a powerful painting and drawing style.

Perillo's work spoke volumes about the history and culture of our land and Habeeb was quick to recognize its universal appeal. He invited the artist into the world of limited edition art, and Perillo soon became one of the most collected artists in the land. His work enjoyed explosive growth on the secondary market.

To guide Vague Shadows' growth, Habeeb sought out other artists whose work supplemented the distinctive painting and sculpting of Perillo. Romantic portrait painter Rob Sauber, with his visually enticing, gown-clad 19th century women and sensuous landscapes, proved a perfect balance to Perillo's rugged portraits. Perillo and Sauber were joined by Jim Deneen, a master painter of sleek trains and American cars; MaGo, whose innocent children are delicately rendered, and versatile Lou Marchetti, creator of the *Life of Jesus* series of collectors plates.

Due to this diversity of style and medium, Habeeb chose names for his series that would mirror each. He picked Curator Collection and Signature Collection as two, but quickly realized that as his company gained recognition, a single hallmark would help collectors identify Habeeb's offerings from the rest. After careful consideration, research and discussion, the name Artaffects was selected in 1988. The new name combined all of the elements that propel people toward collecting art. Emotion. Influence. Desire for beauty. The name of Artaffects would move the former teacher's company into the new decade with a high profile and bright, recognizable talent.

All This, and Heaven Too!

Skilled at examining the "big picture," Richard Habeeb knew that the 1990s would call for a careful balance of yesterday and tomorrow. He began to search for new talent to drive Artaffects forward and found just what he was looking for in the sculpting magic of Michigan artist Carol Roeda. Roeda had used pottery and sculpture as her creative outlet while raising her children and doing community work. Her artistic style, rendered in terra cotta clay, reflected her deepest values. Fashioning children and angels from this earthy material, Roeda shaped her little figures, and when she was done, each bore her distinctive trademark of hope: a rounded mouth singing God's praises as only a child can do.

In addition to the angels and children, the artist had also designed a whimsical nativity set, using it as the focus of her craft show displays. The public must have recognized Carol Roeda's gift, for she gained great local attention and soon afterwards, that of Artaffects. The *Simple Wonders*™ Collection officially joined the family in 1991, and was first shown at the Long Beach Plate and Collectibles Convention to delighted retailers and collectors in attendance.

Spurred on by new artists such as Carol Roeda and continued strength in the Perillo collection, Artaffects determined that the Perillo Collectors Society, supported by the artist's legion of fans, had to be reactivated. Demand for the club was met in 1991 with the revitalization of The Artaffects Perillo Collectors Club™. The newly revamped Club, with its exciting package of benefits, was given a bold new Southwest look. A binder, membership card, newsletter called "Drumbeats," gift of a delicate little Navajo girl figurine named "Sunbeam," and other benefits were produced for new members. To celebrate the Club's new look, Perillo designed two Members-Only offerings: a bold, colorful sculpture of "Crazy Horse" with hand-tooled wood base and brass nameplate, and four mini-plates rendered in dramatic black and white porcelain. Members have the option to buy one of each using their special redemption form.

In addition to the two Artaffects Perillo Collectors Club offerings, Perillo was commissioned to sculpt some of the most complex figures he had ever attempted for the collectible market: his new *The Great Chieftains* series. The figures salute five of this nation's most outstanding Native American leaders: "Sitting Bull," "Chief Joseph," "Geronimo," "Cochise" and "Red Cloud." Limited to only 5,000 of each figure, Artaffects elected to fashion these figures of cast artist resin so that Perillo's fine undercuts would not be lost in the molding process. These figures, long awaited by Perillo collectors, debuted in 1991.

A fanciful grouping of baby animals, dubbed *Blue Ribbon Babies*™ for their award-winning appeal, also joined the Artaffects family in 1991. *Blue Ribbon Babies* offer a world of charm and collectibility. "Elmont the Elephant," "Penelope the Pig," "Petunia the Penguin," "Siegfried the Seal," "Chauncey the Camel," and "Hortense the Hippo" wear blue ribbons and come with humorous gift cards.

While it may seem to Richard Habeeb that the past fifteen years have flashed by like a meteor, in actuality they have been cram-packed with careful planning, forward-thinking and the same methodical analysis that went into the purchase of the Rockwell plate featured in *The Wall Street Journal* in 1971. Taking his company through many stages of growth that began with offerings from such classic painters as Remington, Cassatt, Jessie Wilcox-Smith, Charlotte Becker and Bessie Pease Gutmann, Habeeb's success has evolved splendidly through today's artisans: Perillo, Sauber, Roeda, Deneen, Marchetti and MaGo. Pride, diversity and quality have been Artaffects' strengths in the past. These strengths will carry the company forward in the years ahead.

This hand-painted porcelain figurine by Greg Perillo, entitled "The Cheyene Carousel," is limited to 5,000.

Ashton-Drake Galleries

Ashton-Drake Artists Breathe Life into Little Porcelain People

For every collector who harbors cherished memories of her children's early years, Ashton-Drake Galleries has dolls that can bring back specific memories at a glance. Whether it's a sleepy baby just waking up from a nap, an independent little girl pouting or a child hugging her own doll, the little people created by Ashton-Drake's artists are moments of long ago back again.

These same artists also recreate the children of nursery rhymes, fairy tales and history, in series like *Born to Be Famous*, which includes "Florence Nightingale." Other little porcelain people represent different cultures, such as "Chen, a Little Boy of China," by Kathy Barry-Hippensteel, or "Rebeccah," an Amish child by Julie Good-Krüger.

Together, the extensive collection of dolls from Ashton-Drake creates a family of fascinating children for collectors to hold and love. And each Ashton-Drake doll is designated "premiere grade," indicating that it meets all ten of the Uniform Grading Standards for Dolls.

The Uniform Grading Standards are a checklist for evaluating the merits of an individual doll. Key criteria include the artist's credentials, sculptural artistry, costume artistry, thematic detail and authenticity. Other standards have been established to rate craftsmanship, distinction of pose, quality of handpainting, reputation of the maker and the statement of edition.

The artists who create Ashton-Drake dolls adhere to the strictest standards of doll making. Each of these creative women has her own unique approach to the challenge of designing high quality porcelain people.

Yolanda Bello

Originally from Caracas, Venezuela, Yolanda Bello cares about capturing memorable times with her dolls. The recipient of more than sixty doll awards, Bello works to purify an emotion, to isolate a moment that is immediately identifiable. It may be the instant captured with "Lisa" from *Yolanda's Picture-Perfect Babies*, when a baby first opens her eyes from a nap and — still half-asleep — recognizes her mother. Or, as with "Michael," another doll in this series, it may be the first time a baby reaches for a ball.

Bello begins work on a new doll by first imagining what the baby is trying to say. She works from the inside out, envisioning the child's soul before she begins to shape the face, eyes and mouth. Love and tenderness are essential ingredients in each doll she creates.

Perhaps this is why virtually every letter of the hundreds she receives from collectors is prompted by the same experience: a Bello-designed doll that reminds the writer of one of her own children or grandchildren.

This bond is particularly important to the artist who feels the oneness of all human beings. No wonder she loves her art so intensely. Her creations reunite families, bringing a child's early years back home again.

Kathy Barry-Hippensteel

Her love for children is so great that, if she could, Kathy Barry-Hippensteel would adopt every child in need of a home. When her own daughter was born prematurely and the medical bills soared, Barry-Hippensteel wondered how she would be able to afford to buy dolls for her little girl.

She solved the problem by learning how to make dolls herself, taking her first class from Yolanda Bello. In the process, doll making has become a "family affair" for the artist. Not only did

With her eyes half-open, this little sleepyhead has just awakened from her afternoon nap. "Lisa" is one of the latest issues in Yolanda's Picture-Perfect Babies, *an award-winning collection designed by popular doll artist Yolanda Bello.*

it furnish her with a way to provide her daughter with dolls, it also offered her the opportunity to involve her mother in her artistic endeavors. Barry-Hippensteel's mother designs the clothing for many of her daughter's dolls, including "Chen" and "Molly" from *International Festival of Toys and Tots* and "Elizabeth" and "Christopher" from *Baby Book Treasures*.

The artist gets all her ideas from real children and subscribes to every baby magazine published just to review the photographs they contain. She looks for character and delights in children who border on what she describes as "the slightly odd side," perhaps because they are laughing very hard or squinting their eyes. Barry-Hippensteel feels that dolls that are *only* good looking are too simple.

She works on several dolls at a time and finds herself talking to them, saying such things as "Oh, you're looking better and better; wait until your nose is done." She even feels that her little people have notions of their own.

How does she know when a doll is finished? When she sits back, looks at her sculpture and smiles. It's easy to imagine her dolls smiling back in agreement.

Dianna Effner

Flour-and-salt dough proved to be a crucial ingredient in Dianna Effner's recipe for success as a doll artist. Twelve years ago, Effner was making figurines out of the mixture when some dollmakers saw her work and asked her to make porcelain parts for them. However, after attending her first doll show with a friend, Effner knew that she would never be satisfied by making porcelain parts for someone else to use. She wanted to create her own dolls.

Today, she is doing just that. Her Ashton-Drake portfolio includes two series featuring characters from classics of children's literature: *Heroines from the Fairytale Forests* and *Dianna Effner's Mother Goose*.

For "Snow White," the artist worked hard to capture the "gentle grace and inner glow of a person who is truly beautiful inside as well as out." And her "Mary Mary, Quite Contrary" wears an enchanting little pout to show just how headstrong and independent she can be.

Effner works from candid photographs she takes of children who live around her in rural Missouri. She usually focuses on one doll at a time, drawing on her photographs for ideas for facial expressions. When she is sculpting a doll, she keeps at it until she achieves the mood and personality she's after.

Recognizable by her sweetly pouting face, "Mary, Mary, Quite Contrary," is hard at work taking care of her little "garden": a pail of flowers. This green-eyed, rosy-cheeked blonde is the first issue in Dianna Effner's Mother Goose *collection.*

Dolls "come alive" for Effner at different stages. It may happen once the face is painted or it may occur when the hair or clothes are added.

A member of the National Institute of American Doll Artists (NIADA), Effner also continues to be inspired by her colleagues and the techniques they use for dollmaking.

Julie Good-Krüger

Although she is a newcomer to Ashton-Drake Galleries, Julie Good-Krüger has been involved with dolls for most of her life. Her grandmother gave her an antique doll when she was eight years old, and at about the same time, her father bought her a doll that was in pieces at an auction.

Good-Krüger learned about dolls quickly and by the age of ten, she was giving presentations about the history of dolls to groups such as Future Farmers of America, 4-H, Brownies and the Girl Scouts. Then, she grew up and put her dolls away in boxes. Eventually, she earned a college degree in the classics, and philosophy replaced dolls until she had a dream that she was making dolls. The dream seemed so real and the message so true, that she immediately began to experiment with dollmaking.

"Rebeccah" is the first issue in Amish Blessings, *a series that reflects the gentle nature of Amish children and their appreciation of life's simple pleasures. "Rebeccah's" hairstyle, clothing and hand-crafted faceless doll are all reflections of Amish traditions.*

Unhappy with the vacant look of many antique dolls, Good-Krüger tries to give her creations thoughtful, realistic expressions. She wants each doll's face and body language to convey real feelings. Typically, each doll is a composite of many influences, including children pictured in magazines and her own six-year-old daughter.

The artist usually works on several dolls at a time and she admits to being a little irritable in the early stages. She begins to feel cheerful when she notices an expression in the clay she's sculpting. When one of her dolls starts to "speak to her," Good-Krüger's mood immediately shifts.

Good-Krüger, her husband and their daughter live in Pennsylvania's Amish country, an experience that is reflected in her first series for Ashton-Drake: *Amish Blessings*. "Rebeccah," the initial doll in this collection, is the result of Good-Krüger's effort to portray how a child feels when she is cradling her own doll. "Rebeccah" sits with her legs crossed and her arms around a traditional faceless Amish doll.

Good-Krüger has been making dolls for fourteen years and her new series for Ashton-Drake promises to be a blessing for doll collectors everywhere.

This brief look at four of the artists who create Ashton-Drake dolls indicates why the company has become a leader in the growing field of contemporary collectible dolls. The commitment of their artists, combined with the strict requirements of the Uniform Grading Standards, ensures high quality porcelain creations full of personality and soul.

Ashton-Drake dolls are available at dealers throughout the country. Collectors may also contact the company directly to find a wide array of dolls depicting babies, older children, costumed characters and historical fashions.

Kurt S. Adler, Inc./Santa's World

A Delightful Array of Christmas Collectibles From Artists All Over the World

Christmas may come but once a year, but at the offices of Kurt S. Adler, Inc./Santa's World, it always looks like December 25. As an importer of more than 20,000 holiday items from over 200 factories in more than twenty nations, this famous firm reigns as one of the leading Christmas marketers on the international scene.

Kurt Adler enjoys reminiscing about his more than forty years in business, bringing yuletide joy in many art forms. "It was a one-man operation when I started," he recalls. Adler had finished his hitch in the army at the end of World War II and was ready to work for himself. "I didn't want to take orders anymore," he jokes. "I started exporting consumer goods, everything from candy to detergent to fluorescent lights to cups and saucers. But I saw the handwriting on the wall."

Adler's new firm was sending American goods to European countries: a lucrative business until the factories overseas could be rebuilt after World War II. But once European manufacturing was up to speed once again, American imports that were the firm's stock-in-trade were banned.

Using the profits from his export business, Adler began to reverse the direction of his trade. He traveled the world in search of unique art forms that would capture the imagination of well-heeled, post-war American consumers.

Adler's own good taste and business sense — along with the help of his two sons — have enabled Kurt S. Adler/Santa's World to grow from a "one-man band" to a 250-person operation including administration, marketing, sales and warehouse capabilities. And that is just the tip of the iceberg. "I would imagine it takes 10,000 people working all year long to make the merchandise we sell," Adler estimates. Adler currently serves as president of Kurt S. Adler/Santa's World. Assisting him with management of the firm are his sons, Clifford and Howard, who serve as vice-presidents.

Presidents Abraham Lincoln and George Washington are portrayed in these hand-crafted and hand-painted wooden nutcrackers from the famed German factory of Steinbach. Exclusive to the KSA Collectibles line, the nutcrackers are offered in limited editions of 12,000 each. Issue price for each 17" piece is $195.

Included in the Smithsonian Museum collection, Kurt S. Adler/Santa's World introduced this "Holiday Drive" figure crafted of Fabriché™ — a special fabric maché material. The 10 1/2"x10 1/2" piece features Santa contemplating his list as he prepares to deliver toys from his antique automobile. It sells for $155.

Looking as if he has just stepped out of the woods, "Black Forest Santa" greets admirers in his "fur" trimmed outfit. His forest friends surround him as this Fabriché™ Santa makes his historic debut. Designed by Jocelyn Mostrom, "Black Forest Santa" measures 12 1/2" tall and carries an issue price of $100.

"Merlin the Magician" carries his trusty owl in one hand and his crystal ball in the other. This limited edition smoking figure was produced at the famed Steinbach Nutcracker Factory in Hohenhameln, Germany for Kurt S. Adler/Santa's World.

American Collectors Discover the Charms of German Steinbach Nutcrackers

The complete Kurt S. Adler/Santa's World line includes everything from figurines and musicals to waterglobes, ornaments, trees, and lights — and of course, St. Nick himself in many guises. In addition to these Christmas classics, the executives and artists of Kurt S. Adler/Santa's World have been very gratified by the excitement surrounding their first limited edition offerings.

A "Merlin the Magician" nutcracker led the limited edition parade, being introduced at $185 in an edition of 7,500 pieces which sold out promptly. A recent sale of "Merlin the Magician" showed the piece commanding $1000 on the secondary market. And "Merlin the Magician" was followed in 1992 by a limited edition "Merlin" smoking figure limited to 7,500 pieces with a retail price of $150. Another new issue in this *Camelot* series is "King Arthur," a wooden monarch in a robe and crown, holding the Holy Grail and carrying an Excalibur sword. "King Arthur" sells for $195 in an edition of 10,000.

Both "Merlin the Magician" and "King Arthur" were produced at the famed Steinbach Nutcracker Factory in Hohenhameln, Germany. While Kurt S. Adler/Santa's World has been importing nutcrackers into the United States for some years, "There has been tremendous interest for our new designs," Adler explains. "I'm glad," he is quick to add.

Among the most recent Kurt S. Adler/Santa's World nutcracker introductions is a series entitled *Great Americans*. "George Washington," and "Abraham Lincoln" both have been captured in nutcracker form: Washington in full-dress General's regalia complete with white gloves, and Lincoln waving the American flag and holding the Emancipation Proclamation. Each of these 18" nutcrackers has been hand-crafted and hand-painted in an edition of 12,000 for worldwide distribution. The original issue price for each is $195.

Just as coveted is the new "Happy Santa" nutcracker, featuring a wooden Santa holding a miniature Christmas tree and sled. At 16½" in height, the hand-crafted "Happy Santa" carries an original price of $190. Kurt S. Adler/Santa's World also has limited edition Zuber nutcrackers in its line featuring such beloved folk characters as "Gepetto the Toymaker," "Paul Bunyan," "Bronco Billy the Cowboy," and more.

Collectors Find Enchantment In Fabriché™ Works of Art

Drawing upon the innovations of *The Fabriché™ Collection* of fabric maché figurines, Kurt S. Adler/Santa's World has also introduced several series of elegant works crafted by hand. This unique Fabriché™ allows for wonderfully realistic representations of Santa and other beloved holiday characters.

Mrs. Claus herself is the star of "Apron Full of Love," a 10" Fabriché™ figure who holds her apron while carrying a basket. Marjorie Grace Rothenberg, Chief Designer for Kurt S. Adler/Santa's World for many years, created this heartwarming image.

It may not be well known that Santa enjoys hot air ballooning as a hobby, but now the "Christmas Is In The Air" Fabriché™ figure of Santa tells the tale. Santa looks down to the earth below through his telescope, while he enjoys a ride in a Christmas-decorated balloon that bears the legend, "Peace on Earth." A "Homeward Bound" Santa features Santa with his suitcase, while Marjorie Grace Rothenberg's "Santa's Ice Capades" showcases a musical Santa on ice skates.

"Bundles of Joy" features Santa with a little child on his back, a miniature tree in his left hand, and a bag of gifts suspended over his shoulders. Meanwhile, Santa joins his wife in Ms. Rothenberg's "Santa Steals a Cookie and a Kiss": unbeknownst to Mrs. Claus, her husband is taking one cookie from her tray. Just as heartwarming is "Bringing in the Yule Log," a limited edition figurine designed by Ms. Rothenberg and showing Santa on his sleigh, pulled by a stalwart St. Bernard dog.

Other inspirations by Marjorie Grace Rothenberg include: "Santa's Cat Nap," with Old St. Nick snoozing in his chair; "Santa Fiddler," a musical design in which Santa plays the fiddle; "Merry Kissmas," where Santa and Mrs. Claus exchange gifts while they share a kiss under the mistletoe; and "A Stitch in Time," a limited edition figure of an elf sewing Santa's hat. Many other Santas, angels, teddy bears, carolers, and even Scrooge himself round out this stunning Fabriché™ group.

The Smithsonian Museum Collection

Another Fabriché™ favorite is the "Holiday Drive" figure from the *Smithsonian Museum Christmas Collection*, showing Santa driving an antique automobile. The 10½" by 10½" figurine carries a $155 price tag. Also from the *Smithsonian Museum* group, favorites include "Santa on a Bicycle," the angel figurines called "Peace on Earth," and the angelic "Heavenly Messenger" ornament.

Every year, Kurt S. Adler/Santa's World introduces two new *Smithsonian* Carousel Figures, and retires two figures from this renowned and popular

Jocelyn Mostrom's porcelain Christmas In Chelsea *dolls are cleverly designed so that they may also be used as ornaments. Dolls in this collection capture the charms of turn-of-the-century storybook characters and depict garden fairies, party children and heavenly angels.*

collection. In 1991, the firm retired "The Rabbit" and "The Goat." In 1992, it introduced "The Camel" and "The Elephant." Also available in this group are two "Carousel Horses," "The Giraffe," "The Seahorse," "The Zebra," "The Rooster," "The Lion," and "The Cat." These figurines, which are available in authentic Smithsonian gift boxes, have antique finishes and range in height from four to five inches. They carry retail prices of $14.50 each.

Jocelyn Mostrom's Christmas In Chelsea *Collection*

Featured in the *Christmas In Chelsea* Collection are porcelain dolls that — very cleverly — double as ornaments. The group has been designed by award-winning artist Jocelyn Mostrom exclusively for Kurt S. Adler/Santa's World.

Inspired by the famous English Gardens, these dolls have an ethereal quality of turn-of-the-century storybook pictures that depict garden fairies, party children, and heavenly angels. Newly introduced are several *Garden Party* doll ornaments, including "Amy" in a white party dress and "Allison" in pink. Each blonde-haired, blue-eyed ornament doll stands 5" high. Ms. Mostrom also designed a collection of limited edition Santas for Kurt S. Adler/Santa's World.

Licensed Collectibles, Musicals and More Round Out The Kurt S. Adler/Santa's World Line

Kurt S. Adler/Santa's World also offers many licensed collections which feature collectibles inspired by beloved characters from Disney, Jim Henson's Muppets, and Sesame Street. The *Disney* licensed c ollection features "Mickey Mouse Sorcerer" and "Mickey Mouse Toy Solder" nutcrackers, as well as a nutcracker depicting "Goofy Toy Soldier." The *Vintage Disney* series features Disney characters with an antiqued look of the 1930s. *Disney* Collections offer ornaments, snow globes, figurines, stockings and accessories which are much sought-after by collectors. And the *Disney Little Mermaid* series features ornaments and stockings, as well.

The *Jim Henson's Muppets* group showcases a "Kermit the Frog" nutcracker, as well as stockings, snowglobes, and ornaments. The *Sesame Street* Collection combines a "Big Bird" nutcracker, stockings and snowglobes with a Fabriché™ "Big Bird" figurine and ornaments.

A Growth Area for Collectors: Snowglobes and Ornaments

Kurt S. Adler/Santa's World takes note of significant collecting trends, and one stands out for the 1990s. It seems that collectors have been seeking out handsome snowglobes, ornaments and musicals that date back to the 1960s. These collectibles feature a variety of traditional holiday tunes, and they foreshadow collectors' continued fascination with these Christmas collectible classics.

More Holiday Treasures for 1993 And Beyond

What's in store for Kurt S. Adler/Santa's World? More and more Christmas collectibles, according to the firm's founder. Nutcrackers from Steinbach and Zuber, more Fabriché™ figurines from Marjorie Grace Rothenberg, new Santas from Jocelyn Mostrom, and pieces inspired by more lovable fantasy characters are all in the works.

To assist collectors in finding a convenient dealer from whom to acquire the many offerings of Kurt S. Adler/Santa's World, the firm has established a Collectible Dealer Network of retail stores that sell complete lines of the nutcrackers and/or Fabriché™ figurines. Collectors are invited to contact the firm for more information and referrals.

After so many years of "Christmas every day," Kurt Adler and his family might understandably become jaded about their "close relationship with Santa." Yet Adler insists that he loves every piece in his line, and he never tires of his holiday focus. He does take one yearly reprieve from his nutcrackers and figures and ornaments, however. "Christmas Eve I put them away and we go to Florida," he admits with a wink and a smile worthy of Old St. Nick himself!

The Bradford Exchange

World's Largest Trading Center Expands The International Plate Market With Innovative Subjects and Diverse Art Styles

As the world's largest trading center for limited-edition collector's plates, The Bradford Exchange provides an organized, orderly market where collectors can buy and sell plates. The company is also one of the world's most successful marketers of collector's plates. Since the early 1970s, The Bradford Exchange has demonstrated its unique vision of plate collecting — and its ability to attract new art lovers to the field. Today Bradford's headquarters in Niles, Illinois, serves as an international hub for plate collecting activities around the globe: the coordinating link for all eleven worldwide offices of The Bradford Exchange.

This international focus has enabled Bradford to play a special role for plate collectors. With representatives all over the globe, Bradford has been able to offer American collectors many "firsts" based on geography and art media. These landmark issues include the world's first collector's plates from the People's Republic of China, the U.S.S.R., Greece and Egypt, the first plate series clad in Florentine bronze, and the first plate series executed in aggregate Carrara marble.

In addition, the Exchange has acted in response to the worldwide environmental movement to present a wide range of nature and wildlife plates. And to round out its impressive repertoire, Bradford offers a colorful range of celebrity and movie plates including recent introductions paying tribute to Elvis Presley and Marilyn Monroe.

Bradford Paves the Way for International Art Appreciation With Plates from Distant Lands

When Bradford first introduced its *Beauties of the Red Mansion* plate series in 1986, collectors in many countries flocked to own the premiere series of plates from the People's Republic of China. Inspired by a classic Chinese novel, this series of handsome plates continues the age-old tradition of Ching-te Chen, a renowned porcelain center that produced the world's very first porcelain between 600 and 900 A.D.

"Pao-chai," the first issue in the series, was honored as 1988 "Market Performer" — an award based on a combination of trading activity and appreciation during a plate's initial year on the secondary market. Readers of *Plate World* magazine named "Pao-chai" their all-time favorite plate in 1989. That same year, the second issue in the *Red Mansion* series, "Yuan-chun" earned "Market Performer" honors of its own.

The success of this initial Chinese series created demand for additional issues featuring artwork from the Far East. Subsequent series in this category introduced by Bradford include *Scenes From The Summer Palace*, *Blessings From a Chinese Garden*, *China's Imperial Palace: The Forbidden City*, *Legends Of West Lake*, and most recently, *Flower Goddesses Of China*.

Fresh from its success with the Chinese plate premiere, The Bradford Exchange broke new ground in 1988 with the first plate series from the U.S.S.R: *Russian Legends*. These dramatic plates translated the Russian art form of miniature paint-

"St. Basil's, Moscow" is the premiere issue in Jewels Of The Golden Ring *plate collection by Byliny Porcelain. This 1990 introduction continues Bradford's concentration on well-loved Russian art which began when the Exchange introduced the world's first collector's plate crafted in the U.S.S.R.*

ing on lacquer to the porcelain collector's plate medium. The Master Artists of Palekh, Russia created the delicate artwork of the original lacquer paintings in the tradition of their ancestors, who were medieval icon painters.

In 1989, "Ruslan and Ludmilla," first issue in the series, won the Silver Chalice Award for Best Plate Under $50 at the California Plate & Collectibles Show — and it was selected "Plate of the Year" by the National Association of Limited Edition Dealers (NALED). This tremendous reception by American collectors encouraged Bradford to introduce other series featuring Russian artwork, including *The Firebird, The Legend Of The Snowmaiden, Village Life Of Russia,* and *Jewels Of The Golden Ring.*

More "Firsts" Keep Bradford in the News

When the Exchange introduced the first collector's plates from Greece, the subject was Greek mythology, interpreted specifically as the *Great Love Stories From Greek Mythology.* Greek painter and sculptor Yiannis Koutsis was commissioned to create the art as his first venture in bas-relief plates. The series was produced by Delos Apollo Studios.

The material selected for the 1988 series is also a significant first. Never before had aggregate marble been used in the creation of a bas-relief plate series. This represents a brilliant, modern treatment of the favorite stone used by all classic Greek sculptors. The plates in the series are hand-cast in white aggregate marble, deeply shadowed by a warm, antique patina, and hand-polished to bring out the finest details.

The Exchange's "collector's plate travelogue" continued to Florence, Italy, in 1989. Here the glories of the 15th-century East Doors of the San Giovannie Baptistery served as inspiration for the *Gates Of Paradise,* the first collector's plate series ever to be clad in Florentine bronze. Crafted at the famed Studio Dante di Volteradici, and sculpted by award-winning portraitist Ennio Furiesi, the plates exhibit a rich patina and depth of color that belie their modern lineage.

While the Exchange introduced collectors to the use of aggregate marble with its first Greek collector plate series, never before had any plate been presented in aggregate *Carrara* marble until the 1990 debut of *Masterpiece Madonnas.* This series depicts famous interpretations of the Madonna and child theme, including pieces by Raphael and Della Robbia. Each plate is realized using "the living stone of the Renaissance masters," which is mined only from the soaring peaks of solid marble that surround the Tuscan town of Carrara, Italy.

The first collector's plate from Egypt is "Tutankhamun & His Princess," the 1991 first issue in The Legend Of Tutankhamun *plate collection from Osiris Porcelain.*

Moving on to Egypt, Bradford presented *The Legend Of Tutankhamun* as its 1991 "first ever" plate series. Crafted in the tradition of the Land of the Pharaohs, each plate combines sixteen distinct ceramic pigments as well as rich applications of 22K gold. Artist Nageh Nassif Bichay studied the Eighteenth Dynasty Egyptian art style (1550-1307 B.C.) under the tutelage of Dr. Hassan Ragbah, founder of the Papyrus Institute and Museum of Giza.

Bradford Reflects the Art World's Love of Nature

Natural and wildlife-theme collector's plates have become an increasingly important part of today's market, due, at least in part to the public's concern over endangered species, conservation and ecology. A growing number of plates from Bradford feature artwork on every conceivable aspect of this subject: majestic mountains and other natural wonders, graceful waterfowl, exotic animals, and more.

A number of these series benefit wildlife and conservation organizations. In fact, as a direct result of plates purchased through The Bradford Exchange, almost $1,000,000 has been contributed to various animal welfare and conservation causes since 1985.

Charles Fracé, a respected and popular wildlife artist whose limited edition prints have sold out for the past two decades, burst onto the plate scene with three series available from the Exchange: *Nature's Lovables*, *The World's Most Magnificent Cats*, and *Soaring Majesty*. Other recent nature/wildlife series from Bradford include *Nature's Legacy*, *The Beauty Of Polar Wildlife*, and *Treasures Of The Arctic*.

"Comeback Special" features Elvis Presley dressed in sleek black leather. It's the first issue in the Delphi series Elvis Presley: In Performance, *presented by The Bradford Exchange.*

Plates Pay Tribute to Celebrities and Stars

Movie plates have always been a popular category with Bradford collectors, but recent years have seen an expansion of this category to include plates featuring individual celebrities. Two of the most popular personalities depicted on plates are Elvis Presley and Marilyn Monroe.

The first Elvis series marketed by Bradford was *Elvis Presley: Looking At a Legend*, introduced in 1988. The enthusiastic reception of this collection of portraits led to the debut of a second series featuring "The King" in 1990, *Elvis Presley: In Performance*. Both series are endorsed by the late entertainer's estate. "Elvis at the Gates of Graceland," the first issue in the *Looking at a Legend* series, was named 1990 "Market Performer," as the plate appreciated by 163% to $65 during its initial year on the secondary market.

The Marilyn Monroe Collection premiered in 1989. Authorized by The Estate of Marilyn Monroe and Twentieth Century Fox Film Corp., this series features scenes from Marilyn's best-known Fox film roles. The first issue depicts the single motion picture moment most closely identified with Marilyn, the "billowing skirt" scene from "The Seven Year Itch."

The Bradford Exchange Expands to Meet Collectors' Needs

A recent survey by the Exchange showed that collectors consider plates their second most favorite collecting medium behind figurines. This popularity is attested to in the steady growth of Bradford's client list and its facilities. The award-winning, atrium-style U.S. headquarters of Bradford completed a $4,500,000 addition in 1991, the German Exchange has a new office, and Bradford has recently established a presence in France.

With offices all over the world — and a strong international and historical focus — The Bradford Exchange plans to continue its impressive list of "firsts" and achievements, fulfilling the needs and wishes of collectors in America, and all around the globe.

Byers' Choice®, Ltd.

A Dickens of an Idea

During a trip to London many years ago, Joyce and Bob Byers found a unique series of porcelain figures in an antique shop. These pieces, which appeared to step right from the pages of a Charles Dickens novel, captured the spirit of 19th century England for Joyce, and she immediately fell in love with them.

Upon returning home, Joyce saw a set of papier-mache choir figures that seemed to capture the true spirit of Christmas. While debating whether or not to purchase these as gifts, she was struck by an idea...she could try to create caroling figures with the feeling of the 19th century.

As an amateur artist with a degree in fashion design, Joyce began working on the project using materials she had at home: plaster, papier-mache, wire, paints, and almost every kind of fabric imaginable. She was already adept at handcrafts and enjoyed seeing her creations come to life; figurines that resulted from this effort were no exception. Joyce fashioned each character with a singing posture and called them "Carolers®" to convey a connection both to Christmas and to Dickens' *A Christmas Carol*. These early figurines were quite different than "The Carolers" as we know them today.

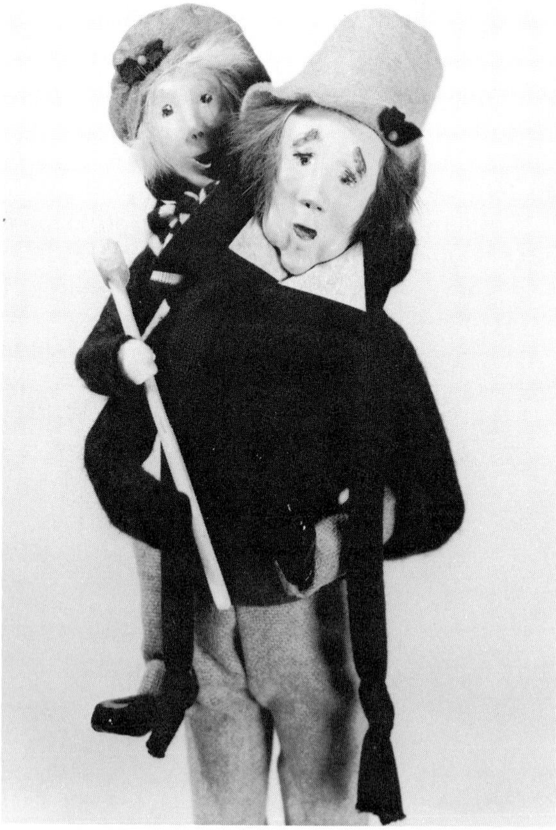

In 1990, Byers' Choice added the eagerly anticipated figurine "Bob Cratchit & Tiny Tim" to The Dickens — A Christmas Carol *series.*

When family members saw the Carolers at Christmastime, they adored them. All of a sudden, Christmas shopping became that much easier, as over the next few years all of the Byers' friends and relatives received the figurines as gifts. A neighbor suggested taking the figurines to craft and antique shows. The first Carolers sold out quickly, but Bob was fortunate enough to be approached by someone from a New York display company who said that his company would be interested in buying the figurines if they could be enlarged and altered according to their customers' needs. Joyce rose to the challenge, thus determining the fate of Byers' Choice.

Over the next years, Joyce, Bob and their two sons spent much of each fall making figurines for friends, craft fairs, a few stores and the display company. As the demand for handicrafts grew, the family found itself even busier. After the Carolers began overwhelming the dining room, the garage was converted to a workshop. In 1981, with the addition of full-time helpers, the family hobby was incorporated, and Bob and Joyce cast their lot with The Carolers. By then the facial features, dress, materials of construction and finish details of the figurines had also evolved into the common features by which the Carolers are now recognized.

Today Byers' Choice Ltd. is still a cottage industry that hires skilled handcrafters and professionally trained artists. In order to meet a growing demand, it was necessary to make significant changes in both the method of manufacture and, to a limited extent, the appearance of the figurines. While today's Carolers are very different from those produced in the early years, almost everyone agrees that they are far better and more attractive. Joyce still sculpts all of the faces and

This family grouping of Carolers® figurines joyously sings under the flickering light of a street lamp. The accessory lamp is a working electrical light.

designs most of the clothes for the Carolers. Meanwhile, Bob takes care of the financial and administrative side of the business, trying to serve the customer in any way possible. In 1987, the job of overseeing each figurine through production fell to son Robert, while son Jeffrey joined the family business in 1990 as marketing manager. Virtually everyone agrees that the family of Carolers figurines gets better each year, and many of the older ones have become valuable collectors' items.

The history of the Carolers is a good old "made in the USA" story. With a lot of hard work and imagination, Bob and Joyce Byers have seen their hobby grow into a family business dedicated to serving the customer. With the boundless energy of the Byers' Choice family, the Carolers should only get better.

Byers' Choice Expands Its Line

In 1978 Byers' Choice crafted only traditional adult caroling figures, an Old World Santa and a New World Santa. Only 100 of each style of the traditional adults were made. In the ensuing years more than 100 special characters have been created. These include many different Santas and musicians and figures representing various occupations and the four seasons. In 1983 Scrooge was unveiled as the first in a series featuring characters from Charles Dickens' A *Christmas Carol*. Both the first and second editions of these figures have been very well received. Through the years the most popular figures continue to be those caroling. Of these no more than 100 of any one style is made.

"Mr. & Mrs. Claus," dressed in luxurious red velvet, are two of the most popular Byers' Choice figurines.

The Collectors Speak

From the beginning Byers' Choice received many wonderful letters from fans telling how much the Caroler figurines mean to them. An overwhelming number of questions prompted the firm to publish the *Caroler Chronicle*. In this newsletter which is published three times a year, the company attempts to respond to the more than 15,000 collectors who have indicated an interest in learning more about Byers' Choice Caroler figurines. The *Chronicle* highlights various figures, both new and retired, and tells how and why they came to be. Information about signings and other special Caroler happenings are included. A chronological index of Byers' Choice characters and their years of production is also published.

One fan compared collecting Byers' Choice figurines to eating peanuts: once she had one, she couldn't resist going back for another, and another, and another...

Byers' Choice creates a wide range of Carolers® depicting characters in various occupations. No more than 100 of any one style is made.

The Collectables

Phyllis Parkins Creates Fine Porcelain Dolls Which are Made With Pride in the U.S.A.

If Phyllis and John Parkins had been blessed with four sons instead of their four lovely daughters, their life might have been very different indeed. For it was the four Parkins daughters — Leigh Ann, Jennifer, Heather, and Brenda, who inspired their mother to create her very first baby doll.

Years ago when her daughters were young, Phyllis crafted and dressed a little reproduction German doll to entertain them. It was all porcelain with movable arms and legs, and the 5½" "Tiny Bye-Lo" was an immediate hit with the Parkins clan.

Around this time, the mid-1970s, Phyllis Parkins had retired from her real estate career to spend more time at home with her children. She delighted in the freedom to pursue various crafts, especially china painting. Mrs. Parkins began showing her jewelry, plates, and bells — and then a few of the little reproduction dolls — at nearby craft shows. Lo and behold, the "Tiny Bye-Los" practically leaped off the table into customers' hands!

In 1977, contemporary dolls made from molds were a rarity at craft shows, and Mrs. Parkins found herself a pioneer in the field. Craft show customers — and collectibles shops as word spread — urged Mrs. Parkins to create more and different dolls.

Phyllis and John Parkins made the decision to pursue the doll market as husband-and-wife team. Mrs. Parkins would run the little business, while her husband retained his career as a salesman in the petroleum field. John Parkins would assist on evenings and weekends, but his full-time earnings would allow the couple to "plow back" any profits into their fledgling doll studio.

At first, making the dolls was difficult. There was a lot of breakage and much frustration. But week by week, Phyllis improved her skills with the molds as John patiently assisted every step of the way. Within months the couple acquired the necessary proficiency to produce the astonishing number of "Tiny Bye-Los" necessary to meet demand. Then they could turn their attention to additional, more complicated dolls.

A Family Hobby Grows into a Booming Business

Meanwhile at the Parkins' home, the dolls threatened a "friendly take-over" as ever-growing demand required the Parkins to attend — and create inventory for — as many as twenty to twenty-five craft shows per year. In 1980, an addition to the family home provided a temporary solution. But by 1982 it was clear that the Parkins were at a turning point. Either they "toned down" their business or went full speed ahead. They chose the latter course, and soon broke ground on a 3,200-square-foot factory near their home in Rolla, Missouri.

John Parkins himself designed the building to fit the needs of the company that he and his wife had christened The Collectables. "Looking back, when we first built the building and the amount of sales

With soft blonde hair and striking blue eyes, "Bethany" is irresistible in her white batiste, with a pinafore of pale pink organdy. She comes complete with porcelain kitten, baby blocks and blanket.

we made compared to what the building cost — we were crazy to do it," John Parkins marvels. "But it worked out." Indeed, since then The Collectables has made two additions, bringing the total to 8,400 feet of work space. What's more, John Parkins joined the company full-time in 1984, enabling his wife to concentrate on artistic endeavors while he manages business operations.

The Collectables Expands to Create Original Dolls

When the Parkins began their business, the demand for reproductions of classic dolls was steady and strong. But as the doll market became more sophisticated during the 1980s, The Collectables was ready to make the transition to original dolls, sculpted exclusively for the firm. At the same time, The Collectables completed a gradual change from selling via retail craft shows to distributing their creations through wholesale gift marts. This allowed for nationwide availability of The Collectables dolls in gift shops, Christmas shops, small department stores, and florist shops.

At first, all of The Collectables' original dolls were sculpted by the renowned doll artist Diana Effner, who began an association with the firm in 1980. The most popular doll produced by The Collectables from a sculpture by Ms. Effner was for the "Mother's Little Treasures, Series I." It shows a little sister looking adoringly at her older sister, and it was nominated for a "Doll of the Year" award by *Doll Reader* magazine in 1985.

"Natasha" rides through her world of dreams and make-believe with her unicorn. Limited to an edition of 750, she is 14" in height with blue eyes and blonde hair.

Meanwhile, Phyllis Parkins was hard at work perfecting her own sculptural skills so that she could design original dolls. Mrs. Parkins' natural gift for dollmaking shone through from the very beginning: her first doll, "Ashley," won the hearts of collectors. This dark-haired little girl was beautifully dressed as well, with a ruffled white dress and a hat trimmed with lovely lace and pink ribbon.

The Collectables Dolls Tell Stories With Their Elaborate Settings

The next Parkins original was "Tatiana," the first in the very successful fairy series. Later fairy dolls were presented in more and more intricate settings. For instance, little "Tasha" was seated on a plush duck — and won a "Doll of the Year" award in 1987, as well as the *Dolls* magazine Award of Excellence.

Mrs. Parkins earned a second "Doll of the Year" award in 1987 for the charming "Sarah Jane — Storytime." This work of art — which sold out very promptly — shows a little girl seated on the floor, reading to her doll who sits in a rocker. The 1988 "Tabatha" has her own tree swing and woodland setting. The tree was cast from a real tree branch, and the pond base was crafted of cold-cast porcelain.

More Honors and Prompt Sell-Outs Continue The Story of Success for The Collectables

Each year, The Collectables has earned a prominent place in the nominations and awards of both *Doll Reader's* "Doll of the Year" honors and the "Awards of Excellence" from *Dolls* magazine. In addition, in 1989 The Collectables was honored to participate in "The World Showcase of Dolls" at Disney World in Orlando, Florida. Phyllis Parkins sculpted and produced her first-ever, one-of-a-kind doll for the event, which was auctioned off at Disney World for $2,000. The doll, named "Tiffany," wore a silk chiffon dress featuring one hundred hand-made silk rose buds, sequins, beads and pearls. "Tiffany's" dangling "diamond" earrings provided the final touch of elegance.

A highlight of 1990 came when The Collectables was commissioned by The White House in Washington, D.C. to produce fifty large dolls

"Lauren" is an 18" porcelain doll with a poseable body. Hand-made rosebuds accent her exquisite blue charmeuse satin dress with embroidered net overskirt.

Sculpted and designed by Phyllis Parkins, "Toddler Boy" and "Toddler Girl" are part of a series of 10" all-porcelain dolls, limited to an edition of 1,000 each.

which would be used to decorate the official White House Christmas Tree.

Then in 1991, The Collectables announced plans for "Designs by Phyllis," a new company that will bring Mrs. Parkins' skills for designing and sculpting to a new vinyl line at a most affordable price. These vinyl dolls will be made overseas, but will be supervised at every stage of production to ensure that they meet the high standards of The Collectables.

Dolls Made in America With Exquisite Care

In creating new dolls for The Collectables line, Phyllis and John Parkins pay close attention to the desires of collectors. They personally read every registration card that arrives at their firm to get new ideas from their loyal collector friends. Time spent with collectors at shows like the International Plate and Collectibles Convention in South Bend, Indiana can also spark ideas and concepts.

Phyllis Parkins combines a remarkable gift for sculpture with a great love of costuming. As a child, she designed countless paper doll dresses on her Big Chief Tablet, and then made doll houses for her paper dolls to live in using shirt cardboards. Today she can create most anything she can envision, for it is the policy of The Collectables for each doll to meet its artist's concept. No doll is ever simplified in any way to facilitate the production process.

While she and her husband are intimately involved at each stage of crafting, painting and costuming, Mrs. Parkins is quick to give credit to her staff of artists and seamstresses. John Parkins agrees, saying that "We have a team organization and a team spirit. Everybody pulls together to get a job done."

Collectors Join "The Inner Circle" as Members of Phyllis' Collectors Club

"Caravans" of collectors descend each May on Rolla, Missouri to enjoy a special weekend sponsored by The Collectables popular "members-only" group, Phyllis' Collectors Club. An invitation to spend time with Mrs. Parkins, her family and employees is just one of the many benefits of membership, which also includes a subscription to "The Inner Circle" newsletter, advance notification of new doll issues, "members only" Club doll acquisition opportunities, and much more.

Joining Phyllis' Collectors Club is the best way to join The Collectables "family" and stay abreast of the Parkins' innovations, activities and new products. For more information, contact Phyllis' Collectors Club, Rt. 4, Box 503, Rolla, MO 65401.

The Constance Collection

All Things Bright and Beautiful: The Constance Collection

When Constance Guerra was an idealistic, young art student not too many years ago, she proudly turned in a portfolio of what she considered "my best work" and awaited the professor's verdict. Like most students, she had a passion for her art and was neither too critical nor too sure of her efforts...but one thing she didn't expect was the reaction her art teacher handed back without so much as a blink of the eye.

"You'll never succeed in the art field," he told her emphatically. "Your work is 'too round.' "

It was a day Guerra never forgot, for it changed her life's direction. She took his word for her "lack of talent" and immediately dropped her entire creative curriculum for a program in business administration. Does she regret the move? Not Connie.

"The business courses were heaven-sent," she says emphatically. "I needed those classes from the moment I first started my own business, and they help me survive in it today. Besides, getting out of the art program in such a discouraging way made me strong. Like other things that happen to us in life, moving into the business school was for the best. I never walked into another art class again. Everything I did from that day forward was self-taught."

How does a woman manage to carve out a successful one-woman art business with no "formal" art education and a professor who thinks that getting one wouldn't matter? Simple, reflects Connie. She continued to sketch everything she saw... mountains, trees, people and everything in between. Then one day, Constance picked up a woman's magazine and ripped out an article that gave her professional life the second biggest push she'd received since the day she was "fired" by her art professor.

Santa holds tight to the hand of little boys everywhere in Constance Guerra's "Little Boys Santa." An impressive 9½" tall, "Little Boys Santa" (SC91) is limited to 2,500 pieces at just $95.00 each.

Sacred vows and loving commitment...sculpted into every detail of "Endless Love" (GA26) by artist Constance Guerra. The "Endless Love" wedding couple measures 6¼" X 4¼" and makes a sweet memento at $70.00.

Connie's Bread Dough Experiment

Maybe it's her fiery Portuguese heritage. Maybe it's fighting for attention in a household filled with women. Or maybe it's just that "X" quality that comes with God's package when He sorts out "who gets what" in the talent department. Whatever it is, Constance Guerra had 'The X-Factor:' an eye for a great idea combined with the guts to carry it out.

"The idea" came to her after she'd finished up her business education and found a good job with the United States Government in Washington, D.C., just a jog away from her home in Maryland. Working for the National Institutes of Health by day, she spent her evenings and weekends sketching and reading for new ideas. Just about every sort of magazine was fodder for her creative mill.

During one casual perusal of a woman's magazine, Connie became intrigued by an article about bread dough art. Using a few ingredients, all of which could be found in the kitchen, one could craft an amazing array of little sculptures which could then be baked, painted and formed into everything from table to wall art. She tried the recipe over and over, each time getting a bit more daring with her subjects and colors. A friend saw, and quickly fell in love with, Connie's little creations. Encouragement from other friends, an offer of support from Connie's three sisters and the announcement of an upcoming craft show sealed the commitment. Connie and her sisters would launch "the line" with a huge, two day supply of bread dough sculptures and a collective enthusiasm that stays with Constance today.

Connie's bread dough figures drew instant attention...wallets began to come out of purses... and the entire collection was sold out in three hours! Connie's head was buzzing like the Santa Ana Freeway. She had a success on her hands, and she would go after it.

The Adventure (and Fun) of an Entrepreneur Begins

Those first bread dough sculptures hit the craft show tables just short of ten years ago, and Connie will tell you that it was only the beginning of her good fortune. While her sisters drifted off to a smorgasbord of lifestyles (one to dental school, one to teaching and one to "having lots of babies"), Connie carried on the tradition. And like the student whose love of creating pushed her toward sketching every tree and mountain in sight, so Connie's figures and style unfolded.

Enchanting women in turn-of-the-Century dress. Farm boys in overalls and bandannas. Winsome little animals rendered in detail that stopped lookers in their tracks. All of this and more greeted craft show shoppers for the first few years of Connie's new found career. Over and over again, her product sold out, regardless of the city in which the show was held.

By this time, Connie had adopted the corporate name "Doughlightfully Yours" and was showing at some of the most prestigious craft shows in the nation. It was at such a show, in 1985, that Connie began talking to an interested customer at her booth in New York about a more sophisticated crafting method that might give her line year-round distribution possibilities. By the end of his visit, the gentleman had convinced Connie that having molds made and using a popular cold cast medium would surely improve the quality of her product. Not one to ignore good advice, Connie looked into the process just as soon as the show closed.

Using the new molding methodology would mean that Constance could create even more figures. Once the process of doing the actual manufacturing of the sculptures was in the hands of professional mold pourers, she could spend more time creating new items and supervising finishing and painting details. And because her passion for research is nearly as strong as her love for her art, she could devote more time into the background data necessary to enhance the costuming and experiences of her figurines.

Most of us aren't lucky enough to have the Library of Congress to turn to when we need data, but then Constance has had something of a charmed life. Her trips into Washington became lengthy ones ("If I could, I would move into the Library of Congress," Constance confides), for they involved the exploration of book after book of clothing and face styles, customs and designs. Ideas came faster than she could get them down on paper or clay. By 1990, over 500 separate figures had come from the mind and heart of Constance Guerra. And if you ask Connie, she'll tell you that she's just begun to tap the well.

A Few of Her Favorite Things

As we write this article about Constance Guerra, she has produced 700 limited edition collectibles for The Constance Collection and retired 125 of them. The variety of her subject matter is enough to take your breath away!

Take, for instance, Constance's *Kitty Kat Club* and *Dog Pound* series. If you're expecting to find your everyday pups and kittens, think again. For every kitten with a ball of twine, there's one dressed in a long prairie dress with straw hat! There's floppy-eared dogs with perky bows and a black kitten clutching a big, red heart. *The Cattle Club* and *Pig Pack* are just as sweet. Connie portrays some of her pigs and cows in just their "birthday suits," while others wear ruffled pinafores or overalls.

The *Briar Patch* series of bunnies, chicks and kids shows such an amazing array of Easter characters, you wonder how one person could possibly come up with so many ideas, and the *Bear Den* grouping featured in Constance's brochure is...well...we can't resist saying it...unbearably cute! Most of the groupings have an angel or two sitting amid the the animals to keep a spiritual eye on the rest.

If animals aren't your collectible, you'll find the most amazing array of "humans" imaginable in The Constance Collection. Homespun Amish family members in a wide array of sizes, tell a story of simplicity and devotion. Because Connie's research indicated that the Amish do not feel comfortable with faces painted on dolls, she respected that tradition and left the faces off of each of her *Traditional Amish Collection*. But, there's no mistaking the sect. Each figure is rendered in the classic blue and black clothing styles best known as Amish, and the activities many are involved with are typical of the Amish lifestyle.

If one series of minority figures were showcased for their sheer dignity and strength, *The American Heritage* and Connie's other Black American collections would be the ones selected. They accurately depict the life of black people in the south before emancipation. While adult males and females are beautifully represented in the collection, it's the children that catch your eye when you gaze across the array of figures. Playful and inquisitive, loving and just a bit rambunctious, each is caught in a magical moment of childhood from infancy to the brink of first love.

The challenge of so accurately replicating an entire society of people gave Connie the idea for her next project, one so ambitious, she still remembers the hours, days and nights of research that went into the *Exclusive State Santas* series. Imagine: fifty different Santa Clauses, each rendered holding a state flag, the state bird perched upon one gloved hand, the state's flower and tree tucked in at the hem of Santa's red robe, and in addition, each state Santa has embellishments unique to that state! Multiply fifty Santa Clauses times at least five separate decorative touches and you have some idea of the lengths to which Connie will go to create a unique collection! As you could guess, each Santa (as well as the other figures big and small in The Constance Collection) are made right here in America.

The Personal Touch That Makes the Difference

Like America, Connie Guerra is fiercely independent, changing, growing and ready for the next bend in the road. One of the reasons she's so receptive to change and all that it brings comes from being solidly grounded in real values, a sense of loyalty and tradition and a strength that allows her to trust her instincts.

How many business women do you know who won't do a trade show without Mom and Dad along to help anchor the booth? How many artists do you know who sew their own table ruffles to make sure the product looks exactly right when it's on display? And how many sculptors do you know who crafted an entire line of figures based upon the life of the nanny who cared for them throughout childhood?

Constance Guerra is such a woman. Her favorite sculpting tools are her mom's knitting needle and a selection of other household tools contributed by family members. They go with Connie wherever she goes, but strangely enough, these sculpting tools never go into her studio!

"I never go in there to work," Connie confides with the twinkle in her eye that you learn to recognize whenever she's about to make a statement that might sound strange if it came from anyone's mouth other than hers. "I sculpt everywhere else! At home. In the car. In hotel rooms."

If ever you see a woman sitting on a park bench working away on a little figure, there's a good chance it's Connie. The world is her studio.

But we were curious. Exactly why does she maintain her Virginia studio when her work goes on everywhere but within the confines of its walls ...and what does goes on in there?

The answer seemed perfectly logical once it was out, and we can almost imagine what the room looks like, based upon Connie's description.

"It's filled with letters from collectors," Constance confides, her eyes lighting up as she describes the studio. "They hang from the ceiling to the floor and they're from my loyal fans. I keep them hanging there to remind me of the pleasure my art brings people, just in case I get a little discouraged," she concludes.

Hard to imagine? Definitely. The Constance Collection is most assuredly a bold reflection of one woman's determination to create her dream and the word discouraged doesn't seem to fit anyplace in that scenario.

What do you suppose that art professor would say if he could see Constance Guerra today?

Department 56, Inc.

Just Imagine...Snowladen Trees, Wreaths At The Windows and Welcome Mats Out... The Tradition Begins

"Department 56" may seem a curious name for a firm that designs and manufactures nostalgic, collectible villages. How the name "Department 56" originated is a rather unusual story.

Before Department 56, Inc. became an independent corporation, it was part of a large parent company that used a numbering system to identify each of its departments. While Department 21 was administration and Department 54 was the gift warehouse, the name assigned to wholesale gift imports was "Department 56."

Department 56, Inc. originally began by importing fine Italian basketry, however, a new product line introduced in 1977 set the groundwork for the collectible products we know today. Little did the company realize that their appealing group of four lighted houses and two churches would pave the way for one of today's most popular collectibles.

These miniature buildings were the beginning of *The Original Snow Village*©. Each design was handcrafted of ceramic, and hand-painted to create all the charming details of an "olden day" village. To create the glow from the windows, a switched cord and bulb assembly was included with each individually boxed piece.

Collectors could see the little lighted buildings as holiday decorations under a Christmas tree or on the mantel. Glowing lights gave the impression of cozy homes and neighborhood buildings with happy, bustling townsfolk in a wintry setting. Sales were encouraging, so Department 56, Inc. decided to develop more *Snow Village* pieces to add to their 1978 line.

Word of mouth and consumer interest helped Department 56 realize that *The Original Snow Village* collection would continue. Already there were reports of collectors striving to own each new piece as it was introduced.

By 1979, Department 56, Inc. made an important operational decision; in order to keep *The Original Snow Village* at a reasonable size, buildings would have to be retired from production each year to make room for new designs. Being new to the world of collectibles, they did not realize the full impact of this decision. Collectors who had

The North Pole Collection *depicts the wonderful Santa Claus legend with great charm and detail.*

not yet obtained a retired model would attempt to seek out that piece on the secondary market. This phenomenon had led to reports that early *Snow Village* pieces may be valued at considerably more than their original issue price.

Since its beginning in 1977, over 136 lighted designs have been produced. In 1991, *The Original Snow Village* consisted of thirty lighted models, over thirty-nine accessory pieces, frosted trees, street lamps, and even flashing stop and go lights.

The Heritage Village™ Collection *From Department 56, Inc.*

Love of holiday traditions sparked the original concept of *The Heritage Village Collection*. When decorating our homes, we are often drawn to objects reminiscent of an earlier time. Holiday memories wait, hidden in a bit of wrinkled tissue or a dusty box, until that time each year, when rediscovered, we unpack our treasures and are magically transported to a beloved time and place.

The first Heritage Village grouping was *The Dickens' Village© Collection* introduced in 1984. Extensive research, charming details and the fine hand-painting of the seven original porcelain shops and "Village Church" established them as a favorite among collectors.

Other series followed with the introduction of *The New England Village© Collection, The Alpine Village© Collection, The Christmas in the City© Collection,* the presentation of *The Little Town of Bethlehem© Collection* in 1987, and in 1991, the introduction of *The North Pole© Collection.* Each of these ongoing collectible series has been researched for authenticity and has the same attention to detail as the original *Dickens' Village.*

As each of the villages began to grow, limited edition pieces were added, along with trees, street lamps, and accessory groupings to complete the nostalgic charm of each collection. Each lighted piece is stamped in the bottom with its designated series name, title, year of introduction, and Department 56, Inc. logo to assure authenticity.

Each model is packed in its own individual styrofoam storage carton and illustrated sleeve. A special compartment in the boxing of all lighted pieces holds a UL approved switched cord and bulb. This method not only protects the pieces during shipping, but provides a convenient way of repacking and storing your collection for many years.

Each grouping within *The Heritage Village Collection* captures the holiday spirit of a bygone era. *The Dickens' Village Collection,* for instance, portrays the bustling, hearty and joyous atmosphere of the holidays in Victorian England. *The New England Village Collection* brings back memories of "over the river and through the woods," with a journey through the countryside.

The Alpine Village Collection recreates the charm of a quaint mountain town, where glistening snow and clear lakes fed by icy streams dot the landscape. *The Christmas in the City Collection* evokes memories of busy sidewalks, street corner Santas, friendly traffic cops and bustling crowds amid cheery shops, townhouses and theaters.

In 1987, Department 56, Inc. introduced *The Little Town of Bethlehem Collection.* The unique twelve-piece set authentically reproduces the essence of the birthplace of Jesus. This complete village scene will continue to inspire and hearten those who celebrate Christmas for many years to come.

Two delightful Snowbaby angels decorate a tree with stars in "We Will Make It Shine." This figurine issued in 1990 for $45.00 and is part of the Snowbabies *collection.*

Life in 'the big city' is brimming with activity in The Christmas in the City Collection. *Tall buildings, city buses and a hint of subway adds to the authenticity of this collection.*

In 1991, Department 56, Inc. presented *The North Pole Collection,* a new ongoing *Heritage Village* series. The brightly lit North Pole buildings and accompanying accessories depict the wonderful Santa Claus legend with charm and details that bring childhood dreams to life for the young and the young-at-heart.

Celebrate Snowbabies©

Another series from Department 56, Inc. is *Snowbabies*. These adorable, whimsical figurines have bright blue eyes and white snowsuits covered by flakes of new-fallen snow. They sled, make snowballs, ride polar bears and frolic with their friends.

Since their introduction five years ago, *Snowbabies* have enchanted collectors around the country and have brightened the imagination of all of us who celebrate the gentle play of youthful innocence.

Each of the finely detailed bisque porcelain collectibles, with handpainted faces and hand-applied frosty bisque snow crystals, are complete in their own gold foil stamped storybook boxes.

Every year, new Snowbaby friends are introduced in this very special collection.

"Christmas Classic," the Beginning of a Holiday Tradition

Department 56, Inc. has joined with award-winning artist Roberto Innocenti in creating an elegant new dinnerware pattern entitled "Christmas Classic."

Through exquisite illustrations and warm holiday colors, Mr. Innocenti's interpretation of Charles Dickens' *A Christmas Carol* has brought fresh insight into these timeless characters. From the chilling meagerness of Scrooge's apartment to the plum-pudding richness of his nephew's celebration, Innocenti's watercolors are unforgettable, and eight of his most beautiful illustrations have been incorporated into this splendid new holiday dinnerware.

The Wide Range of Department 56, Inc. Products

In addition to the popular collectibles already mentioned, Department 56, Inc. continues to develop colorful and innovative giftware and collectibles of many types.

Collectors Discover Department 56, Inc.

Seldom does a firm win the attention and loyalty of collectors as quickly as Department 56, Inc. has done since its first *Original Snow Village* buildings debuted in 1977. As one consumer stated, "A company can't make an item collectible. People have to make it collectible, and the people have discovered Department 56."

The hustle and bustle of the Christmas season is cheerily portrayed in this grouping of figures and buildings, all part of The Dickens' Village Collection.

Duncan Royale

A Studio Creating Unique and Historic Art Collections... Where the Stories Never End

Nearly a decade ago, Duncan Royale captured the imagination of collectors with its landmark *The History of Santa Claus* Collection. Based upon the ground-breaking research of company president Max Duncan, the first twelve cold cast porcelain Santa Claus figures celebrated the customs and personages of Santa over his 4000-year history.

In 1985, twelve additional Santas have made their debuts in *The History of Santa Claus II* — a dozen more heartwarming and historically significant figures exhibiting the holiday customs and traditions of nations all over the world.

Almost since the day of their introduction, the Santa Claus figures have been among the most talked-about issues in today's world of collectibles. Some of the Santa Clauses have soared in value to five...ten...or even fifty times their original prices: notably the beloved "Nast" Santa issued in 1983 for $90.00, which often sells for more than $5000 on the secondary market.

And now for the 1990s, Duncan Royale has responded to popular demand for more wonderfully detailed, historical Santas with the introduction of *The History of Santa Claus III*. The announcement of plans for twelve upcoming Santas is well in keeping with the Duncan Royale slogan: "The stories never end..."

"Star Man" of Poland and "St. Basil" of Greece are the first two Santas introduced in Duncan Royale's The History of Santa Claus III *collection.*

Polish and Greek Santas Headline the New Series

The Christmas customs of Poland and Greece will be the highlights of the first two issues in this third Santa collection, featuring exceptionally intricate, three-dimensional renderings of "Star Man," and "St. Basil."

In Poland the first star in the evening sky on Christmas Eve sets the theme for the Celebration of the Polish Christmas, the Festival of the Star, which commemorates the Star of Bethlehem. Before the evening meal is served, families gather around the dinner table to honor the Holy Child. The head of the household distributes wafers to each member of the family, symbolizing friendship and peace on Earth.

After the meal, the "Star Man" arrives. He is usually the village priest or a friend in disguise. He quizzes the children on their religious knowledge and rewards them with gifts. Star Boys accompany him, carrying illuminated stars and singing carols as they go along.

In Greece, St. Basil's Day or New Year's Day is the time of exchanging gifts. "St. Basil" is considered the gift giver and is highly honored by the Greeks.

As a young man, St. Basil was sent to Athens to complete his education. He was a good student, and often after a hard day of study, he liked to relax by walking and singing hymns. One day, he encountered some boys who made fun of him. They tried to start a fight. But they were taken aback when suddenly the staff young Basil was holding burst into bloom as the Christmas Rose! Frightened and bewildered, the boys retreated.

The people of Greece remember this event each year on St. Basil's Feast Day. Model ships, commemorating St. Basil's coming to Athens, are carried around by carolers who collect money in them for the poor. And now American collectors can experience these colorful traditions as well, as the owners of "St. Basil" from Duncan Royale.

The Calendar Secrets *figurine collection features this charming tribute to "May," in which a lovely mother helps her little daughter enjoy a traditional May Pole Dance.*

Greet Each New Month With Calendar Secrets

One of Duncan Royale's newest collections — created to greet the 1990s — is called *Calendar Secrets.* This twelve-piece, limited edition series depicts the celebrations, traditions, and legends of our calendar.

Each of the twelve calendar months is commemorated with its own figurine. January, for instance, begins with "Janus," the Roman god who rings the bell of the New Year and carries the key to the future. The month of February derives from the Latin Februare, which means to purify. It shows a lovely feminine creature with cupid ready to take his aim.

March used to be the first month in the Roman calendar: it started the year as nature seemed ready to begin the new cycle of life. Thus the figure for March is a Roman gladiator, complete with shield and golden helmet. Most agree that April evolved from the goddess Venus, known to the Greeks as Aphrodite. The figural subject for April is a pretty shepherdess with a basket of Easter treats.

The month of May is marked by pole dances and Mother's Day, and owes its name to the goddess Maia. For this month, the figure is of a lovely mother, sharing the fun of a pole dance with her daughter. June received its name from Juno, the wife of Jupiter, who is portrayed in classic splendor for this month's elegant figurine.

July was named after the Roman emperor Julius Caesar, and two great revolutions — the American and the French — were fought starting in July. Thus the month has come to symbolize Liberty, and a lovely "Lady Liberty" is portrayed in Duncan Royale's stunning work of art. Named after a Roman emperor, Caesar Octavius Augustus, the month of August is often portrayed by the image of the sun. This month's figurine captures a summer rite of dance by a Native American brave.

A gracious harvester is the subject for September's figurine. Known as the barley month, September is the time of year when all good things come to fruition. October was called "brumaire," the foggy month, during the aftermath of the French Revolution. Duncan Royale pays tribute to the concept of Oktoberfest with a German gent ready to enjoy beer from his fancy stein.

The year draws to a close with bare trees and fading colors in fall, showing that winter is settling in. An American Indian chief in full cold-weather attire shows off a cornucopia of fruits and vegetables in remembrance of the first Thanksgiving for American settlers and their Native friends. Finally, the year ends in December, a month that has been called "fumusus," "canus," and "nivose" in reference to the smoke in the air, the frost, and the snow. The character for December is "Father Time," portrayed with his hourglass nearly spent and his clock ticking rapidly toward midnight.

Each of the *Calendar Secrets* figurines has been

Duncan Royale's Ebony *collection depicts black heritage, as these appealing characters illustrate.*

lovingly hand-crafted with exceptional attention to detail, and each has been hand-painted to emphasize the charm and character of its subject. To enhance collectors' enjoyment of the *Calendar Secrets* all the more, Duncan Royale has prepared a hard-cover book that shares these historic "secrets" from history, legend and lore.

The Ebony Collection Depicts Black Heritage

Another new Duncan Royale collection is entitled *Ebony*, and it focuses on the history of black Americans. The first piece, "Banjo Man," has been received with such an overwhelming response that many dealers placed orders for the entire, upcoming collection, sight-unseen.

This photograph illustrates the exceptional ranges of sizes and art media in which collectors may enjoy Duncan Royale Santas.

In addition to "Banjo Man," figures are now available depicting a harmonica player and an older man playing his fiddle while a youngster — perhaps his grandson — looks on.

Duncan Royale Pieces Come in Many Sizes

Some Duncan Royale collectors are intrigued by miniatures, while others enjoy owning more sizable pieces that make a dramatic statement in home decor. To accommodate the wishes — and the pocketbooks — of its many admirers, Duncan Royale has developed a wide range of sizes and media in which to present its handsome collectibles.

For example, the famous Duncan Royale Santas may be acquired in an eighteen-inch cold cast version in limited editions of 1,000, or in a twelve-inch cold cast version in limited editions of 10,000. Collectors who are partial to wood carvings may be intrigued by Duncan Royale's 10" wooden Santas, hand-carved in Italy by Dolfi.

There are also six-inch, cold-cast Santas on wooden bases, and three-inch pewter miniature Santas — all capturing the incredible detail work for which Duncan Royale is justly famous. Finally, plate collectors may enjoy owning Duncan Royale's three-inch mini-plates on the Santa Claus theme.

This versatility is typical of the Duncan Royale philosophy. The firm prides itself on developing exceptional products with a firm historical research base, outstanding sculptural craftsmanship, and intricate hand-painting. Then Duncan Royale looks to collectors for direction on sizes, art media, and subject matter. With an enthusiastic audience of admirers providing constant feedback and ideas, Max Duncan and his staff assure collectors once again that at Duncan Royale, "the stories never end..."

Enesco

The *Precious Moments* Collection . . . *Memories of Yesterday* Collection . . . and Collectibles for Every Collector

When the Enesco *Precious Moments* Collection was introduced to the marketplace in 1978, few would have predicted that these teardrop-eyed little children with their inspirational messages would be powerful enough to change the entire collectibles industry, but that's exactly what happened. Often called a "phenomenon," the *Precious Moments* Collection not only catapulted Enesco into the leader among producers, but the Collection awakened an entirely new market: men and women of modest means, who had never before been "collectors."

It was almost by chance that artist Sam Butcher's inspirational drawings found a new dimension when they did. Enesco President Eugene Freedman saw Butcher's cards and posters during a stopover in Los Angeles and immediately set into motion the contact that would shortly bring the *Precious Moments* Collection to the world.

Enesco was formed in 1959 with the concept of developing and importing giftware products from the Orient. As the company grew to become a designer as well as importer, so did the role of Freedman as a pioneer in the giftware industry. His leadership in setting trends became legend, and his ability to foresee collectors' needs set Enesco apart from its competition. The *Precious Moments* Collection bears witness to his vision.

Precious Moments Collectors Continue to Increase

One of the remarkable aspects of the Enesco *Precious Moments* Collection is the fierce loyalty of its legion of collectors and the continued growth of the Collection's collector base. After more than a decade, new collectors continue to swell the demand for the figurines in stores and shops, as well as through an active secondary market. Even Freedman, with his remarkable vision for the Collection, could not have foreseen the deep attachment of collectors for these little teardrop-eyed children.

In 1981, responding to requests and urging from collectors, Freedman formed the Enesco Precious Moments Collectors' Club, which continues to be the largest collectors' club of its kind. Providing a forum for collectors and initiating programs to further collector interest, the Club has enjoyed steady growth over the years, just as the Collection has grown.

Enesco Introduces Lucy & Me Collection

In 1979, Freedman made another monumental move in collectibles. He discovered the handmade "Rigglets" — teddy bears made of baker's clay — being produced in the kitchen of Seattle artist Lucy Rigg. Demand for her teddy bears had grown to the point that she was producing hundreds every day in her make-shift "factory."

Relying on the reputation of Enesco and Eugene Freedman, Lucy Rigg licensed her delightful bears for a collection to be called "Lucy & Me." Its popularity as porcelain bisque figurines and musicals

A little boy looks at his thumb, while a teardrop-eyed girl holding a hammer has a sorry expression on her face in the inspirationally titled "Thumb-Body Loves You" Precious Moments *figurine.*

continues after more than a decade.

Ms. Rigg continues to operate Lucy & Company in Seattle, producing cards, calendars and paper accessories to complement the *Lucy & Me* Collection. She has also authored children's books, one of which — "Lucylocks" — became the first in the *Storybook Classics* series for the *Lucy & Me* Collection.

Creating unique dress-up characters for the *Lucy & Me* teddy bears keeps collector interest high, and these delightful little figurines in demand. A Lucy & Me Collectors Club continues to grow and is headquartered in Seattle.

Memories of Yesterday *Collection Develops Strong Following*

Based on the work of famed English artist Mabel Lucie Attwell, regarded as the foremost illustrator of children in England in this century, the *Memories of Yesterday* Collection was introduced by Enesco in 1988. In its premiere year, the nostalgic porcelain bisque collection was named the most promising new collectible of the year, and within another year, it was ranked among the top ten collectibles in the United States.

The Collection portrays chubby-legged children of the 1920s and 1930s, regarded by most as the apex of Miss Attwell's lengthy career. Each figurine poses a nostalgic situation, complete with a title that is as germane today as when the artist first created it more than a half-century ago.

"The Majestic" from the Enesco Small World of Music™ Collection features an intricate turn-of-the-century ferris wheel. The deluxe action musical won Collector Editions magazine's 1990 Award of Excellence.

This delightful ornament "Have a Coke and a Smile" features an old-time soda fountain. It is the second issue in the Coca-Cola series for the Enesco Treasury of Christmas *Ornaments*.

As the popularity of the Collection grew, so did demand for a collectors' club. Enesco responded to collector and retailer requests by forming the Enesco Memories of Yesterday Collectors' Society in 1991. Before the Charter Year even began on January 1, 1991, there were more than 10,000 members registered for the Society.

Using artwork by Miss Attwell from the 1920s, Enesco introduced a 1991 limited edition figurine "Dedicated to World Peace" and titled "Friendship Has No Boundaries." Twelve 9-inch porcelain bisque figurines were produced for presentation to world leaders, and the regular size figurine was limited to 1991 production.

Enesco Treasury of Christmas Ornaments *Draws Collectors*

With Christmas ornaments continuing as the fastest growing form of popular collecting, the Enesco *Treasury of Christmas Ornaments* has shown increased favor among collectors. Since 1989, Enesco has published an annual collector's guide to the Collection, illustrating every ornament available, its title, series and length of production.

An increased collector following has also led to the publishing of the first Greenbook "Guide to Christmas Ornaments" in 1990. At the same time, a secondary market for *Treasury of Christmas Ornaments* has gained strength.

Subjects for the Enesco *Treasury of Christmas Ornaments* includes classic characters — "Coca Cola;" "Twelve Days of Christmas;" "McDonald's;" Marilyn Monroe; Paddington Bear; Baskin Robbins; Cheerios and Wheaties cereals; and World Wildlife Fund, GARFIELD; Ziggy; and Grimmy, among others.

Intricate detail and unique situations characterize the Collection, along with use of familiar objects — such as eyeglasses, teacups, baskets, utensils — to convey the titles. To celebrate the 10th anniversary of the Collection, a commemorative toy chest ornament filled with miniature replicas was issued in 1991, limited to year of production.

Introducing the Enesco Small World of Music *Collection*

More than a decade ago, Enesco introduced the first of its action musicals, a clown rotating with a ball that balanced precariously on his upturned foot. As subjects and action became more complex, collector interest in Enesco action musicals grew. Several years ago, the company developed its Enesco *Small World of Music* concept, and each year, Enesco introduces additions to its extraordinary line of action musicals.

Subjects for the action musicals have been limitless and range from a scene in a barber shop to mice repairing an electric fan and toy chests with moving toys to a miniature sewing machine — and much, much more. One of the most ambitious is the 1990 "Majestic," an old fashioned ferris wheel with calliope, that was more than three years in developing. This unique action musical was the recipient of a 1990 *Collector Editions* magazine Award of Excellence. As new technology has evolved, Enesco has utilized new musical workings, new materials and more ambitious engineering techniques to achieve its unusual results.

As collectibility of these deluxe action musicals has increased, retailers and collectors called for a collectors organization. In 1990, Enesco announced that the Enesco Musical Society would begin in 1991, offering numerous benefits to members, including a miniature musical as the Charter Year symbol of membership.

Kinka *and Other Emerging Collectibles Complete the Enesco Roster*

Since its introduction in 1989, the *Kinka* Collection — based on illustrations of Ohio artist Kinka, whose greeting cards have captivated consumers for many years — has gained a faithful collector following. Kinka's subjects are characterized by muted pastels and a long, flowing, clean line to create her poignant figures. The Collection has been nominated for national awards, and Kinka has made numerous appearances at national and regional collectors exhibitions.

Following the successful introduction of National Audubon Society porcelain bisque figurines and musicals in 1989, Enesco has also added a second statement to the preservation and conservation of wildlife with the 1991 introduction of animal figurines licensed by World Wildlife Fund. Certificates of Authenticity accompany each figurine, to verify the painstaking accuracy of each interpretation. A portion of sales from both collections is donated to further the programs of these organizations.

Two popular collectibles from England have joined Enesco for the 1990s. *Brambly Hedge*, based on artist/author Jill Barklem's enchanting stories of the community of mice who live in English hedgerows, premiered in 1990 with a variety of resin and pewter miniature figurines and musicals. Michael Bond's storybook classic *Paddington Bear* has come to Enesco in a 1991 collection of porcelain figurines and musicals. With built-in followings, both can be expected to rise in popularity among Enesco collectors.

As collectors discriminately seek out new collections for lasting appeal and interest, Enesco continually looks for both classics and new art to fill demand. From its leadership position in the industry, Enesco and its visionary President Eugene Freedman see a bright future for collectibles in the 1990s and beyond. From its success with the *Precious Moments* Collection, Enesco has used its experience and expertise in collectibles to nurture and develop its newest collections with collectors.

These teddy bears, attired as a honey bee and a lady bug, are part of the enchanting Enesco Lucy & Me *Collection.*

Anheuser-Busch, Inc.

Budweiser® Collector Series Steins Celebrate the Time-Honored Brewer's Art

For 500 years, the beer stein has symbolized the care, the craftsmanship and the cherished tradition of the brewer's trade. And over the last century, steins have become works of art in their own right. While hundred-year-old antique steins from Villeroy & Boch and Gerz may bring tens of thousands of dollars at auction, today's collector has scores of affordable new choices as well. Notable among these is the popular *Collector Series* from Anheuser-Busch.

Since 1975, this renowned American brewer has created steins of character and celebration, with classic and contemporary themes and styles to please a wide range of collectors. All are crafted with the same dedication to perfection that beer drinkers have come to expect from Anheuser-Busch.

The Tradition of Anheuser-Busch

Founded in St. Louis, Missouri in 1852, Anheuser-Busch has reigned as the world's largest brewer for over thirty-five years with record –annual sales of 86,000,000 barrels of beer in 1991 alone. Since 1975, Anheuser-Busch has produced fine steins to commemorate special occasions and as a promotional tool for its beer wholesalers.

Working in close collaboration with the Ceramarte stein manufactory in Brazil as well as classic German stein makers like Gerz, Thewalt and Rastal, Anheuser-Busch was able to add more steins and greater variety to its offerings each year. The response from collectors was tremendous: so much so that Anheuser-Busch tested the actual retail sale of steins for the first time in 1980. In that year, 50,000 Holiday Steins were sold to avid stein lovers. Less than ten years later, the annual sales of the Holiday Stein had reached more than 1,000,000 units!

Loyal Collectors Seek Anheuser-Busch Steins

After more than fifteen years of stein introductions, some aficionados boast near-complete collections of all Anheuser-Busch steins. While some of these enthusiasts collect steins only, others are intrigued by what is called "breweriana" — an assortment of bottles, cans, labels and signs as well as steins.

The selection of Anheuser-Busch steins includes a wide range of subjects. Some owe their visual matter to brewery heritage, others to holidays and celebrations, and still others to non-profit organizations which Anheuser-Busch supports. Local and national artists are commissioned based on the style that best reflects the theme used for a particular stein. Anheuser-Busch constantly reviews new talent, and once an artist is chosen, the firm provides direction and guidance on design and production.

Brazilian Studios Expand as Demand Grows

The majority of Anheuser-Busch steins are crafted in Brazil at Ceramarte, because this firm has proven its unique ability to produce large quantities while retaining high quality and superior detailing. Year by year, Ceramarte expands to keep up with the ever-growing interest in Anheuser-Busch stein issues.

The Brazilian steins are completely handcrafted, and the decal process and painting are all done by hand so no two steins are exactly alike. The machine that mixes the clay is the only mechanized process.

These five colorful steins in the Anheuser-Busch Sports Series *depict (from left) baseball, (retired) football, golf, auto racing and basketball. Each stein features a handle with a motif typical of the sport it inspired. Retail price for each stein is $22.00.*

"Columbian Exposition" debuts as the first commemorative stein in the Anheuser-Busch Archives *Series. With a pewter lid and ceramic inlay, the stein features art from the 1893 Columbian Exposition in which the United States symbolically raises a toast to Christopher Columbus.*

Some Anheuser-Busch collectors prefer the old-world craftsmanship of Gerz, Thewalt and Rastal, although their traditional methods yield higher prices in most cases. All three firms strive to keep up the century-old tradition of German art steins, while Gerz and Rastal have added some advanced technology. While certain procedures are mechanized, hand-painting is still a feature of all the German steins.

Thewalt manufactures its steins completely by hand as it did generations ago. This limits the number of steins that can be produced in a short time frame: for instance, only 500 of Anheuser-Busch's "Bevo Fox" steins can be made each month. Since 7,000 of the 10,000 steins in the "Bevo Fox" limited edition were spoken for in its first six months of production, many collectors have found themselves waiting to welcome this striking work of art into their homes.

Developed in 1916, the Bevo Fox is a symbol of the non-alcoholic beverage, Bevo, manufactured during the Prohibition era. This sly fox adorns all corners of Anheuser-Busch's thirty-one acre packaging plant in St. Louis. And now his image graces a handcrafted stein in the rich German tradition of Thewalt.

Steins in Series Intrigue Anheuser-Busch Collectors

Anheuser-Busch has found that collectors enjoy acquiring steins in related series, and the firm has obliged with a number of handsome collections. The *Discover America* grouping, for example, includes three steins: one each for Columbus' three exploring ships. The 8" tall "Nina," "Pinta" and "Santa Maria" steins feature pewter lids with ceramic inlays, and the main image of each stein depicts a different moment from Christopher Columbus' historic voyage 500 years ago.

A handsome *Sports Series* offers a retrospective on five popular American sports in handcrafted, 7½" steins. Each stein's handle features the motif of a particular sport: a baseball bat, golf club handle, football down-marker, racing car stick shift, and basketball hoop. Retail price for each stein is $22.00. The most recent stein, golfing's "Par for the Course," is still widely available while the earlier editions will be offered on the primary market until supplies are exhausted.

Steins Feature the Heritage of Anheuser-Busch

Ask beer drinkers what they think of when they hear the name "Budweiser," and the famous Clydesdale horses are always top-of-mind. Thus it comes as no surprise that Anheuser-Busch offers an ongoing series of *Clydesdales* steins, now presented in gift boxes. The newest of these issues is "Clydesdales on Parade," featuring the majestic horses in full regalia as they have appeared for Budweiser over the past half-century.

Another Budweiser series salutes the world-renowned beer's classic labels and offers a retrospective of how the famous packaging has evolved over the years. First in the collection was the current Bud Label design, followed by an 1891 antique label with stylized eagles and German script. The "Bottled Beer Stein" offers a colorful reproduction of an 1890s advertisement. Each 5½" stein in this series is handcrafted in detailed relief so they are especially attractive in display.

Historical landmarks are featured on the *National Historical Landmark Series* in which all four editions are retired. Brewery scenes are depicted on the *Limited Edition Series* in which four of the five editions are now retired.

Many new stein series are available. The *Birds Of Prey Series* features the "American Bald Eagle" as the first edition and the "Peregrine Falcon" as the second edition. Both ceramic steins with pewter lids are 10 ½" tall and retail for $125.00 each.

This handsome, cherry-stained shelf makes the perfect display piece for a set of Archives *steins from Anheuser-Busch. The unit is also available in a natural stain finish.*

Now available is the first edition in the *Civil War Series*, "General Grant," which was introduced in May. This stein is 12$^{3}/_{4}$" tall and has a pewter lid and base. It retails for $150.00. Look for the "General Lee" stein in January of 1993 and the third and final edition in this series, "Abraham Lincoln" in August next year.

Collector Plates From Anheuser-Busch Continue Popular Themes

In addition to its famous steins, Anheuser-Busch now has unveiled several series of collector plates, all limited to a total of twenty-five firing days and measuring 8$^{1}/_{2}$" in diameter. The plates all feature 24K gold rims, but their topics are quite varied: from *1992 Olympic Team* to *Man's Best Friend* and *Holiday* subjects.

The "1992 Olympic Team Summer Plate" depicts the summer sports of diving, basketball, baseball, gymnastics, equestrian and track. The "1992 Olympic Team Winter Plate" pays tribute to the winter sports of figure skating, skiing, ice hockey, luge, speed skating and bobsled.

Dedicated to our canine companions, the *Man's Best Friend* series currently features plates inspired by the antics of puppies. "Something's Brewing," the third edition, shows three playful labrador puppies — each with a different color coat — tugging on a Budweiser hunting hat.

Susan Renae Sampson is the artist for the heart-warming *Holiday* Plate Series from Anheuser-Busch. Her "An American Tradition" plate sold out recently as the second issue in the series, while "The Season's Best" still is available in limited quantities. Both plates show wintry scenes including the beloved Budweiser Clydesdales and their bright red cart. The 1992 Holiday Plate is titled "A Perfect Christmas".

The Joy of Displaying Anheuser-Busch Steins

Because much of the enjoyment of stein collecting derives from home or office display, Anheuser-Busch has created two striking shelving units which are perfect for showing off favorite stein specimens. Especially popular for the *Archives* and *Endangered Species* series, the Archives Series Shelves may be acquired in a rich cherry stain or a natural stain finish. Each shelf measures 14$^{1}/_{2}$"x27$^{1}/_{2}$"x8$^{3}/_{4}$", with room for two steins per shelf as well as a customized Anheuser-Busch plaque for each. The shelves are affordably priced at $44.00 each.

One of the steins that "shows off" best on the Archives Shelves is "Columbian Exposition," an *Archives* series stein commemorating the 400th anniversary of the 1893 Columbian Exposition. It also includes a symbolic image of the U.S. toasting Christopher Columbus. Hand-crafted in detailed relief with pewter lid and ceramic inlay, this $35.00, 6$^{1}/_{2}$" stein is the first in a new series offered in a 150,000-piece edition.

With prices for a number of Anheuser-Busch steins rising week by week on the secondary market — and the current growth of the stein market in general — prospects for Anheuser-Busch stein collectors look strong. With expansion continuing into collector plates, ornaments and figurines, the firm continues to research new designs and styles to continue the steinmaking quality and tradition established by Anheuser-Busch nearly twenty years ago.

Corolle®

From the Heart of France Comes a Delightful Collection of Traditional Dolls Inspired by Real Children

"To me, a doll represents the first child of a little girl and she is able to become the mother, the friend, the confidant," says the renowned French doll artist Catherine Refabert. "As a result, the doll is an object that receives all the child's emotions. This quality of a doll, that which encourages the affections of a child, is extremely important. I have always insisted on this symbolic aspect of the doll."

Madame Refabert's great sensitivity to the doll as a cultural object — and her remarkable talents for concept and painting — have made her one of the world's most honored doll designers. For more than twenty-five years she has created "play dolls" for children to cherish, cuddle and love. And now — to the delight of doll connoisseurs in more than twenty countries — Madame Refabert has expanded her horizons to collector dolls as well. Yet her goal is still to fulfill the universal needs of children.

"I know that there are many adult collectors in the United States who are very taken with Corolle®, and although I appreciate the interest of collectors, it is not for them specifically that I create dolls. I create them for children," the artist explains. "And if my dolls also capture the interest of collectors, then I am all the more delighted as this creates an additional bond between the child and the adult, between the mother and the daughter. For me, a doll is an indispensable toy for a child."

Corolle Dolls Charm American Collectors

While Madame Refabert's dolls are still crafted in the picturesque Loire Valley of France with its fertile vineyards and graceful castles, today Corolle is part of the Mattel, Inc. family. As American collectors discover Corolle dolls, they become entranced by their true-to-life looks, their soft, cuddly bodies and their fashionable attire. Collectors also comment on the delicately scented, soft-to-the-touch vinyl that gives Corolle dolls the translucent look of real skin.

In her native France, Catherine Refabert has been the recipient of many honors — and she has been the featured designer in a special doll exhibit in the Louvre's Museum of Decorative Arts. Now she has won praise from the American doll world as well, as evidenced by her several award nominations including the U.S. "Doll of the Year" award for "Marie Lavande" in 1991 and the *Dolls* magazine "Awards of Excellence" for "Angelique La Marieé" in 1992. What's more, her first porcelain collector doll, "Esperance," sold out almost immediately.

All of Madame Refabert's signed and numbered, and limited edition collector dolls reflect her delicate artistry and capture the romantic magic of their Loire Valley birthplace. The *Catherine Refabert* collection includes series such as "Friends Around Our World," "They Changed Our World" and a stunning "Connoisseur Collection" of baby, toddler and little girl dolls.

All three of the "Friends Around the World" dolls are named for their creator, Catherine, as her name would appear in Holland ("Kaatje"), France ("Katie"), and Russia ("Katioucha"). All are dressed in authentic costumes from their native countries and have soft bodies, blonde wigs, and blue eyes that open and close. "They Changed Our World" includes tributes to "Christopher Columbus" and "Queen Isabella," as well as a stunning doll inspired by "Marie Antoinette."

"Kaatje," "Katie" and "Katioucha" all are named for their gifted creator, Catherine Refabert, who has costumed these pretty doll children in traditional attire from Holland, France's Alsace region, and Russia.

All three of these historic dolls wear authentic-looking costumes fashioned of rich fabrics with elegant trimmings and accessories.

The "Connoisseur Collection" includes romantic English children like "Jenny" and "Juliette," a Southern Belle named "Carolina," a French beauty named "Danielle," a graceful bride doll called "Angelique, La Marieé," "Christina" the christening baby and a classic in porcelain, "Baby Desiré," only the second porcelain doll ever created by Madame Refabert.

As she turns more of her attention toward the creation of dolls for collectors, Madame Refabert retains her ultimate concern for children as her audience and inspiration. As she concludes, "Through all my design processes, it is my final wish that children enjoy my dolls, play with them, and above all, love them. My dolls are created for the collector's eye and the child's heart."

Dolls Form an Image for the Child

Madame Refabert never considers her work as a mere consumer product. To her, a doll is "an object of affection, and a symbolic object which provides emotional communication for a child. In fondling, cajoling, or scolding his or her doll, the child is looking for an image of himself or herself."

According to Madame Refabert, "A doll helps form a child's personality by allowing him or her to discover his or her place in relation to his or her surroundings. It represents, on a child's scale, the people with whom he or she is in contact; it acts as a link between the child and the world of adults, natural events and daily routine.

Here Comes the Bride. . . "Angelique, La Marieé," designed by Catherine Refabert, is a lovely little girl, dressed in pure white finery, dreaming of the beautiful wedding dress she will wear some day.

"I believe that the best doll of all is one which helps a child to create a world suited to his or her own dimensions," says Madame Refabert. "A doll which does nothing more than come to life under his or her admiring gaze; a doll which will make him or her 'a creator and not just a spectator.' For this reason, it is essential that I make dolls, before anything else, for children."

The Artist Continues a Family Tradition

Now chairman and renowned designer of Corolle of France, Catherine Refabert was born in Paris in 1938 into a family well known in the fine arts. Her grandfather was a world-famous miniature painter and her mother specialized in plastic and graphic arts. From her earliest years, Catherine was surrounded by an appreciation of art and beauty.

She studied mathematics and history in Paris but her first loves were painting and design. In 1960, after meeting her husband Jacques Refabert at the Sorbonne in Paris, the pair joined Clodrey, the Refabert family's doll firm which was founded in 1952. After studying the many aspects of fabrication, Madame Refabert decided to specialize in designing new doll models.

"I started creating dolls for my own children in 1965," she recalls, "and now design them for children around the world. The doll business is very ironic because it is always adults who create, make, buy, and sell articles designed for children. Between the doll and the child come designers, manufacturers, marketers, retailers and parents — in a word, adults! Fortunately these adults are nothing more than grown-up children, with hidden fantasies and a desire to interpret, understand and somehow grasp the needs and wants of children.

"Right from the start I was obsessed by the fact that it was necessary to break through this barrier between adults and children, and try to do something corresponding to the deep-down desires of the latter. I devoted myself to listening to children, trying to understand them, encouraging them to speak out, and watching them play. Then I attempted to build something concrete from all the information gathered through my observations."

Many Influences Lead to a Corolle Doll's "Birth"

Before she creates each new doll, Madame Refabert draws upon a multi-faceted program of research and exposure that she has perfected over the years. As she explains, "As far as I am con-

While most of Madame Refabert's dolls to date have been crafted of delicately scented vinyl, "Desiré" has head, arms and legs of finest French bisque porcelain and a soft body. This limited edition doll is dressed in exquisite French ivory lace trimmed in peach-colored ribbons.

cerned, a doll cannot be created exclusively in a design studio. A doll is not the result of a sudden vision or a flash of inspiration. On the contrary, it is the result of long reflection — a project which slowly appears and progressively takes shape. I absorb all the information I can, including the remarks of children; and the influences of the media, advertising, fashion, and new research techniques at my disposal.

"When designing a doll, I often start with a remark made by a child. One of the collections that I created, started with a request from my daughter who wanted a doll that looked like one of her drawings. These drawings represented a very stylized little girl with a round and cheerful face and two little black dots instead of eyes. I used them as inspiration to create a very simple rag doll with a very sketchy molded vinyl face. This doll was very successful as it was a symbolic representation of something which was familiar to children.

"More recently, the idea of making newborn babies for Corolle came from a remark by a little girl, who asked me for a baby doll that looked like a real live newborn because she had a new baby brother whom her mother prevented her from handling. I remember her telling me that my dolls were very beautiful but that they did not look like newborn babies. Now she wanted a baby doll that looked like her little brother, so that she could play with him and copy the way her mother cared for her brother."

Each New Personality Begins With a Sketch

The step-by-step process of doll creation and production requires considerable time and effort from Madame Refabert. As she describes, "When I finally sit down to design, I start with a sketch. As that sketch progresses and becomes more detailed, the features become more distinctive and the toddler or baby doll takes shape. I give this sketch to a sculptor, who gives it three-dimensional form. Implementing infinite care, we use the time-consuming 'lost-wax' method of sculpture. To achieve a mold we are truly satisfied with takes anywhere from three months to one year. The most agonizing moment comes when the mold is stripped and the plastic is checked for shrinkage and deformation in relation to the wax.

"If the first cast is not absolutely identical to our initial sculpture, then we make a wax mold to correct the defects that appear on the casting. This casting process is similar to the actual birth of a child in that it takes shape very slowly, as the result of many different functions."

Doll Fashions Take a Cue from Children's Clothing

Once the face of each doll is painted and the hair is styled, it is time for the clothing to be designed. Madame Refabert considers the clothing to be one of a Corolle doll's most unique attributes.

"In France, the country known for haute couture fashion, Corolle is considered the grand couturier of dolls. One talks of the 'look' for dolls just as one talks of the 'look' for the fashions of adults or children," Madame Refabert explains. "Because there is a strong fashion current for children in France created by ready-to-wear fashion houses as well as the grand couturiers of international reputation, nothing gives a little girl more pleasure than to dress her doll in a dress similar to the one that she wears."

Details such as the size of prints, however, must be carefully scrutinized. "A print which appears small on a seven or eight-year-old child appears large on a doll 14-inches high," Madame Refabert says. "Small prints have to be found. If I fail to find anything suitable, I have the required size of pattern printed especially for Corolle."

Flambro Imports Inc.

Flambro's Twenty-Five Years of Success Includes Ten Years for America's Favorite Clown and a New Year for Small Town, America

Chalking up twenty-five years of success seems to be only the beginning for Flambro, importers of fine quality giftware. The idea of resting on their laurels probably hasn't occurred to them. Instead, Flambro is celebrating the past ten years of "Weary Willie," America's favorite clown, planning for his future and bringing Small Town, America of 100 years ago into the collectibles Main Street.

Ten Years of Clowning Around

The lovable clown Weary Willie comes to life thanks to Emmett Kelly, Jr., and comes to collectors from Flambro's figurines. 1991 is the tenth anniversary of the Emmett Kelly, Jr. Collectors Society and to celebrate, Flambro has created a "Members Only" figurine available for purchase by members via the redemption coupon mailed to them.

The figurine is titled "10 Years of Collecting" and it will be limited to only the quantity ordered by the members in the EKJ Collectors Society. It is seven-and-a-half inches high, just about as high as clowns may be in your memory when, as a child, you may have perched high up in the bleachers at the circus and watched the clowns pouring out of a tiny car.

"10 Years of Collecting" finds Emmett standing tall, engrossed in reading the *EKJournal*, the Society's publication. A stack of journals sits on the floor next to him. Holding the paper firm, his eyes are focused on the page. He's probably intrigued to catch up on all the events covered in the journal. For him, it may be as if he were reading his own diary. He may well be reading memories of the very first two limited edition Emmetts, "Looking Out To See" and "Sweeping Up."

It's certain this important ten year commemorative figurine will become one-of-a-kind to collectors just as "Merry-Go-Round," the very first "Members Only" Emmett figurine. With the success of the EKJ figurines, Flambro looks forward to ten year commemorative pieces for decades to come.

New Clown Faces for 1991

Three new Emmett pieces were released in 1991, each limited to an edition of 7,500 pieces. They include "Follow the Leader," "The Finishing Touch," and "Artist at Work." Like the "Members Only" commemorative piece, these new releases all include wooden bases and brass name plaques.

Here is Emmett, catching up on all the news in the EKJournal *which carries stories covering his ten years in the collectibles field. This is the commemorative "Members Only" piece, something all Emmett lovers will treasure.*

Emmett Kelly, Jr. gets "Weary Willie" involved in all kinds of activities sure to entice collectors, from making music and brightening up a wagon wheel, to showing what a fine artist he is.

"Follow the Leader" is the tallest, at eleven-and-a-half inches high. Here is Emmett poised behind a podium which holds an open music book. He is holding a baton in his hand, ready to begin "Oh Promise Me." His audience, or perhaps his assistant, stands on a crate alongside, waiting for the show to begin. His side kick is a monkey in a tall hat and tails, so monkey business may be close at hand.

"Artist at Work" is nine inches tall and depicts Emmett engrossed in a self-portrait he's creating on canvas. He is looking into a hand-mirror to see clearly each detail of his clownface. This figurine takes collectors into the heart of Emmett, for he is re-creating himself right before our eyes. This time his assistant is his patient dog, helping as best he can by holding the palette close to Emmett's brush.

The third figurine, "The Finishing Touch," is seven and three-quarters inches high and shows Emmett painting the circus wagon wheel. He's nearly done. Again, his faithful dog is close by, this time duty-free, basking in the warm sun.

Careful detailing of Emmett is the hallmark of the Flambro figurines and it takes the collector directly into the moment depicted, from Emmett conducting and painting to self-scrutiny and reading the *EKJournal*. Whether it's celebrating the past or creating new Emmett figurines, Flambro can be counted on to bring the clown everybody loves home to collectors.

Yesterday's Small Town Wins Collectors' Hearts Today

Flambro is delighting 20th Century collectors by reaching into America's past and bringing back the charm, warmth and simplicity of Small Town, America a hundred years ago. Introduced in 1990, *Pleasantville 1893*® is a series of hand-crafted bisque porcelain houses and buildings depicting how Americans lived at the turn-of-the-century. Accessories include people, horses, carriages, even street lamps. Each building comes with its own story, its own history.

This mythical town is the creation of artist Joan

Berg Victor. Flambro took her vision and created an initial series of nine pieces in the collection and in 1991 added four more buildings.

What is it like strolling down the main street of Pleasantville? There's the house of Reverend Edwin Littlefield and his wife, Emily, and their two boys. They live in the great brick house to the right of the Pleasantville Church. Directly across the town square from the bakery is the Pleasantville Department Store, founded in 1877 by John Tubbs. His son and grandson run it now. The Gerber House is home to Sam Gerber and his wife Rose (his childhood sweetheart), his two sons, Toddy and Carl, and an old Coon cat named Harry, and his hunting hound called Skip. The Sweet Shoppe and Bakery is the place to go to find out what's going on in town. Charlie Hubbard, the owner, was skinny as a rail when he first opened his doors for business but as the years go by, he's more and more his own best advertisement. The Sanford Toy Store faces the town square and it holds more than toys — it's a fountain of fantasy for all the children of Pleasantville. The Band Stand sits right in the town square and here is where everyone gathers on Christmas Eve to begin a caroling tour of Pleasantville. The Neo-Gothic design of the Pleasantville library lends a classical touch to the town and the First Church of Pleasantville, directly across the town square from the library, is where the minister Edwin Littlefield can be found not only on Sundays, but whenever someone needs him.

This is Pleasantville as first created by Joan Berg Victor and Flambro. Four structures have been added — a schoolhouse, a firehouse, a courthouse and a Methodist church. It's as though the town has a heartbeat of its own, and is growing as small towns everywhere tend to. A hard cover storybook about Pleasantville 1893 and its residents became available in the Fall of 1991.

Here is late 19th Century America, porch-deep in fresh snow, just before Christmas. The warmth of the homes and the sense of belonging make an open invitation to come to this small town for a visit.

The Best of the Past Returns

Artist Victor says *Pleasantville 1893* represents the best of every small town in the 1890s — not that people didn't get thrown from a horse now and then, or escaped winter colds or kids didn't bicker — but life unfolded with friends and neighbors there to help. There was a sense of community, of belonging, and no matter what, laughter and love prevailed.

Pleasantville 1893 almost guarantees collectors will smile every time they hold one of the buildings, rearrange them on a table, or just see them all together and imagine life on Main Street a long, long time ago.

Pleasantville 1893 comes in two sizes, which is an intriguing idea in itself. The regular size offers actual lighted houses, and the buildings range from four and three-quarters inches in height to eight inches. The people who accompany this size are from one to two inches high. There is also a miniature *Pleasantville 1893* with buildings from two-and-a-half to four inches high.

All the buildings have natural colors — browns, yellows, greens and reds, as if recently painted. The firehouse is more muted, perhaps because it's one of the older buildings in town. The people sport colorful clothing and animate the town in a charming matter.

A Love of Storytelling

For artist Victor, the road to Pleasantville began with summers spent with her parents, sister and grandmother on the shore of Lake Michigan in a big, old Victorian house. It was filled with enticing old items her grandmother brought from Europe. Later, Victor began writing and illustrating children's books. Then came the idea to create her own village, complete with stories and anecdotes. Thus, *Pleasantville 1893* is far more than static buildings — Victor adds the people and stories that make the town come alive.

Flambro and Victor will be busy developing *Pleasantville 1893* together. They will add more buildings and see that as the population grows, each building comes with a history, and each new person has a scrapbook of memories to share with all the collectors who come to visit.

Gartlan USA

Signed Collectibles Featuring World-Class Athletes Celebrate "The Art of Winning"

While misguided fans stole the hubcaps from the Rolls Royce of Earvin "Magic" Johnson, those bootleg collectibles don't promise the same lasting value as the more than 900 collector plates he autographed on the driveway next to his Corniche!

More than 1,900 plates altogether, featuring original artwork of Magic "at work" on the basketball court, were individually autographed by the NBA superstar. Produced by Gartlan USA, the plates are just one example of the burgeoning demand for sports memorabilia and collectibles — especially those personally signed by their subjects.

"Since starting the company in 1985, we've had do to a lot of dancing and weaving," says Bob Gartlan, president of the fine-art sports collectibles firm that bears his name. "Working with a multitude of personalities — athletes, attorneys, agents, and artists — keeps us jumping."

Many of Gartlan USA's limited edition plates, figurines and lithographs are personally signed, enhancing the products' value. Additionally, licensing, autographs, and reputation of the company work together to reinforce the collectibility of the company's products.

Joe Montana expresses his pleasure upon viewing the hand-painted figurine inspired by his stellar career with the San Francisco 49ers. That's Gartlan USA president Bob Gartlan at right.

Attention to the Needs and Desires of Each Athlete and His Fans

"The personalities and styles of doing business vary drastically with each athlete we sign," Gartlan says. "Players from baseball's golden age — for example, Joe DiMaggio, Yogi Berra, Whitey Ford and Luis Aparicio all negotiate their respective contracts individually. They also exercise an incredible work ethic. Luis Aparicio flew up from Venezuela and signed 2,300 plates in one sitting. Same thing with Ford," Gartlan marvels.

"Conversely, today's players — inundated by media and merchandising demands — are a tougher sell. The hours spent working with agents and assistants are innumerable: tracking them down and getting them to sign for even two to three hours can be extremely difficult. Usually, we'll transport the plates directly to their houses," Gartlan explains.

Controversy Sometimes Spurs Sales

While a Super Bowl win or an MVP award for a current player can stimulate sales of products inspired by his image, controversy doesn't necessarily hurt sales, Gartlan reveals.

"Pete Rose was our first project. Back in 1985, we tracked Rose while he pursued Ty Cobb's all-time career base-hit record of 4,192 hits. In 1989, we introduced a plate and a ceramic baseball card that celebrated Rose's retirement from baseball. As the gambling scandal and IRS investigation festered, the demand for Pete Rose collectibles gained momentum.

"Sports fanatics only look at the record books, plus — with his banishment from baseball — we were about the last licensed company to produce an authentic Pete Rose product. His autograph isn't as accessible and future products can't be in an official Cincinnati Reds uniform. I've been told, in fact, that while he was in prison, his meal pass was stolen because he was required to sign it!"

A Booming Market is Buoyed by Gartlan Collectibles

The Gartlan baseball collection is extensive, reflecting universal interest in our national pastime and the fact that more than 57 million tickets were sold for Major League baseball games in one year. Hall of Famers and contemporary All-Stars, including Luis Aparicio, Reggie Jackson, Mike Schmidt, Yogi Berra, Darryl Strawberry, Johnny Bench, George Brett, Monte Irvin, and Whitey Ford thrill their fans with personally signed figurines, ceramic baseball cards, collector plates, and more. There is even a collection inspired by one of the greatest baseball umpires of all time, Al Barlick.

Like all Gartlan collectibles, these pieces are offered in strict limited editions, whose numbers often are tied to a statistic relevant to the athlete's life or career. When Gartlan limited editions sell out, they often rise sharply in value due to their quality craftsmanship, the appeal of their subjects, and the extra value of their personally signed autographs.

Singing the Praises of the "Unsung Baseball Heroes"

Until Jackie Robinson broke the color line in 1947, black players — no matter how talented — were destined to toil their entire careers in the segregated Negro Leagues. One of Gartlan's newest product lines offers a well-deserved tribute to three of the greatest stars of baseball's old Negro Leagues — "Cool Papa" Bell, Buck Leonard, and Ray Dandridge. A portion of the proceeds from sales of these artworks is donated to the Negro League Baseball Players Association (NLBPA).

A handsome, hand-painted figurine has been crafted to honor each of these unsung heroes — all of whom have now been awarded their rightful place at the Baseball Hall of Fame in Cooperstown, New York. Each $8^1/_2$" figurine exactly captures the image of the player in his prime. The figurines are available in matched, numbered sets — and each comes autographed by its favorite sports hero. Issue price is $195.00 per figurine; $500 for the set of three.

These three hand-painted figurines pay tribute to some of the greatest athletes ever to play baseball in the old Negro Leagues. From left, the figurines honor Ray Dandridge, "Cool Papa" Bell, and Buck Leonard.

All-time greats Wayne Gretzky and Gordie Howe are commemorated on this Gartlan USA collector plate.

Gartlan Pays Tribute to the Legends of Basketball, Football and Hockey

Although Gartlan USA gained its initial fame by producing collectibles for baseball enthusiasts, the company soon fueled the interest and avid following among fans and collectors of basketball, football and hockey memorabilia as well.

The Kareem Abdul-Jabbar *Sky-Hook* Collection celebrates this basketball legend's retirement after a lifetime of sports achievement with a hand-painted figurine, a striking, gold-rimmed collector plate, and a handsome mini-plate. Earvin "Magic" Johnson stars on his own *Gold Rim* Collection, including two figurines, a full-size collector plate and a mini-plate.

Gartlan USA proudly presents works of art inspired by two of the world's most renowned and beloved football quarterbacks: Joe Montana and

Roger Staubach. And in the realm of hockey, Gartlan has created something especially unique: its first plate ever to capture two Hall-of-Fame performers at once. The plate features signatures in gold from both of its revered subjects, Wayne Gretzky and Gordie Howe. A similar plate honoring the father-son combo of Brett and Bobby Hull followed the Gretzky-Howe plate.

The company embodied America's four major sports in 1991 — football, baseball, basketball and hockey — in its first series of pewter figurines. The personally signed figurines commemorated *Joe Montana, Ted Williams, Kareem Abdul-Jabbar and Wayne Gretzky* respectively.

The Gartlan USA Collectors' League

As more and more collectors have discovered Gartlan USA collectibles, the firm felt a need to recognize and reward its loyal collector-friends. Thus in 1989, Gartlan USA inaugurated the Gartlan USA Collectors' League. This subscription-based club provides members with a free gift each year in which they enroll. In addition, members may purchase as many as two different yearly "members-only" collectibles that are distributed through authorized Gartlan USA dealers.

Just as important, club members are placed on the Gartlan USA mailing list, which provides them advance information about new collectibles. Thus they have the opportunity to reserve upcoming issues at their favorite dealers, as much as two months before the general public is aware of production. Club members also receive a quarterly newsletter, chock-full of news, background and "inside looks" at the sports celebrities featured on Gartlan USA collectibles.

Rod Carew was inducted into the Hall of Fame July, 1991. Artist Michael Taylor created this plate in honor of Carew, whose lifetime batting average was .328.

Although Gartlan USA does not benefit directly from the strong secondary market trading that now takes place on many of its issues, President Bob Gartlan is justly proud of his products' "track record." With each passing year, his firm's well-made products — and the personal signatures that accompany them — become more treasured by sports aficionados and collectors. As Gartlan says, "MVP doesn't just stand for Most Valuable Player — in my book, it means Most Valuable Plate (or figurine, plaque, or lithograph)!"

Goebel, Inc.

Bette Ball and Karen Kennedy Keep Yesterday's Memories Alive With Victoria Ashlea Originals®

Remember when you played house...and offered your guests a cup of tea? Remember when you wished you were grown-up...and admired the girls who went to school? Remember when you giggled at parties...and your favorite doll was your best friend who shared your dreams, and listened to whispered secrets? Dreams of parties and weddings ...when fantasy seemed so real...family gatherings around beautiful Christmas trees? When holidays were magic...a winter wonderland?

Bette Ball and Karen Kennedy have never forgotten these cherished childhood memories of innocence and delight. And now these gifted doll designers share their visions of gentle days gone by in a marvelous array of limited edition musical porcelain dolls: the *Victoria Ashlea Originals®*.

Each creation for *Victoria Ashlea Originals* is a masterpiece of fine detailing, craftsmanship and tasteful design. The goal of Ms. Ball and Ms. Kennedy is to capture the imagination and love of discerning collectors today...and for many generations to come.

Like the excitement of finding a treasured collectible in Grandmother's attic, or a trip down memory lane in a fine antique shop, each exquisite designer doll is destined to evoke memories of the carefree child in each of us.

The Success of Dolly Dingle Sets the Stage For Victoria Ashlea

Goebel, Inc. International Designer Bette Ball graduated from Philadelphia's Moore College of Art, but marriage and motherhood placed her ambitions as a fashion designer on the "back burner" for some years. Then in 1977, Ms. Ball's husband started a new importing company for Wilhelm Goebel. "That's when my life came full circle," Ms. Ball recalls. "I was back in the 'fashion' business designing limited edition porcelain dolls."

In 1983, Ms. Ball and her daughter Ashlea were browsing through an antique shop and happened upon a box of old cut-outs. Ms. Ball recalls that, "As a child, I made an 'army' of paper dolls and supplied them with enormous wardrobes." Thus the cut-out character of "Dolly Dingle" — found in that dusty antique store box — was destined to win her heart. Soon Ms. Ball convinced Goebel to buy the rights to this early 20th-century cut-out doll originally created by Grace Drayton.

By 1985, "Dolly Dingle" had become "America's Sweetheart" in the form of three-dimensional dolls created by Bette Ball. That year, Ms. Ball earned the prestigious Doll of the Year (DOTY) Award for "Dolly Dingle."

Today the "Dolly Dingle" line continues to win admirers all over the globe: indeed, Dolly's baby brother "Dickie Dingle" resides in the Yokohama Doll Museum, Yokohama, Japan. Dolly and the other residents of Dingle Dell will welcome a new character for 1992: an orange cat named "PussyKins."

But while Bette Ball will always reserve a special place in her heart for "Dolly Dingle," she and Karen Kennedy are now the "mothers" to a whole new family of musical, limited edition dolls: the *Victoria Ashlea Originals.*

Exquisitely Dressed Dolls with Musical Flair

The Victoria Ashlea line, named after Ms. Ball's daughter, was created in 1982 by Bette Ball. Karen Kennedy became Ms. Ball's protegee and assistant directly after her graduation from the Philadelphia College of Textiles and Science with a major in fashion design. As an award-winning doll designer herself, she shares Bette Ball's great love of fabrics, her eye for detail, and her demand for the utmost in quality. Their creativity flourished in an atmosphere of friendship and artistic collaboration. As Ms. Kennedy explains, "We work really well together. Each of us does her own individual designs and then we critique each other to make sure each doll is as special as she can be."

The two designers also agree that adding a fine, 18-note musical movement to each doll provides an additional dimension to their creations. Bette Ball's inspiration for this concept came from an antique German doll she was given as a child. "It

To commemorate the seventy-fifth anniversary of "Dolly Dingle," Bette Ball lovingly designed this festive costume for her famous doll creation. Complete with a simulated diamond pendant, this musical porcelain doll plays "Diamonds Are a Girl's Best Friend." Introduced in 1987, this "Dolly Dingle Diamond Jubilee" doll is now sold out. The doll is in the private collection of actress Carol Channing, and is on display at the McCurdy Historical Doll Museum in Provo, Utah, and the Doll Castle Doll Museum in Washington, New Jersey.

had a music box concealed in its cloth body. I will always remember the joy it gave me when I found it. It seemed so personal."

The selection of each doll's name and her musical accompaniment is a source of great pleasure for Ms. Ball, Ms. Kennedy, and the entire doll design studio staff. In addition, the artists will often design dolls to represent specific relatives or friends. As Ms. Ball says, "I feel these have been some of my best creations because of the personal feeling I have for the special person."

The Crafting of a Victoria Ashlea Original

Each Victoria Ashlea doll begins with a drawing that serves as the basis for costuming and porcelain production. The doll may be a Victorian-style lady, at 18" to 36" in height, or a toddler at 14" to 24" in height. The designers are particularly concerned about proportion. As Ms. Ball explains, "If the proportion is correct, the doll looks more life-like. It's the same as with a person, if you are proportioned correctly you look better in your clothes."

The costumes are made from Ms. Ball's and Ms. Kennedy's drawings and fabric choices. Patterns are drafted for each outfit, the material cut out and sewn. Each limited edition doll has its own individual pattern. Upon completion, the doll is photographed and sent to the factory along with a description sheet, enough fabric to make a sample, the pattern and photograph.

At the factory they copy the doll and return it to the designer along with her sample. After the factory's work is approved, the limited edition is authorized. At that time, a description tag for the doll's wrist, a Certificate of Authenticity, and a designer gift box are printed.

Excellent Fabrics Make Victoria Ashlea Designs Outstanding

Because of their interest and educational background in fashion design, Bette Ball and Karen Kennedy share a love of fine fabrics. This they joyfully express in the varied costumes of their Victoria Ashlea dolls.

As Bette Ball explains, "Quality fabric has always been a passion of mine. I've been called a 'fabric freak,' and I consider this a great compliment. It was never difficult for me to understand why Scarlett O'Hara used the rich, opulent dining room draperies when she wanted to impress and

Bright-eyed "Samantha" was created by Bette Ball for the Victoria Ashlea Originals® *Collection. The 20" porcelain beauty plays "You Are My Sunshine." She wears a dress of luxurious black velvet trimmed in white bridal lace, and her suggested retail price is $185.00.*

capture a suitor. I've always maintained that it is a waste of time to make anything out of inferior fabric." Fabrics for Victoria Ashlea dolls are selected four times a year at eight top fabric houses.

Most Victoria Ashlea Dolls are Limited Editions

While there are several ways in which the editions for collectible items may be limited, Victoria Ashlea dolls are limited strictly by number. Only the quantity of the edition that is hand-numbered on the back of the doll's neck will be sold worldwide.

For example, "L/E 1000" means that only 1,000 dolls like the original drawing, plus the designer's artist proof, will be produced. Most Victoria Ashlea dolls are limited to 500 or 1,000 worldwide, although a few small dolls and a few animal dolls carry edition limits of 2,500.

Doll Designers Keep New Ideas Flowing

Both Bette Ball and Karen Kennedy seem to have a never-ending "idea bank" for their Victoria Ashlea dolls. Karen Kennedy gets many of her ideas from real children, and she is also inspired by magazines and Victorian books for themes, fashion ideas, and costuming concepts.

Ms. Kennedy says that the 20" "Amie" doll is a personal favorite; dressed in a colorful, feminine clown suit, this blonde charmer with the Dutch boy haircut features a musical movement that plays "Put on a Happy Face."

Bette Ball relies on frequent museum visits, window shopping in world capitals, and gallery openings for her inspiration. She loves to see what's new — colors in decorating, fashions, and other trends that keep her designs fresh and unique.

A Large and Growing Family of Lovely Dolls

The *Victoria Ashlea Originals*® now number more than 700 "personalities" in all. In fact, "Alicia," "Jody," "Christie," and several more have already seen their editions completed. Scores more are still available on the primary market at prices ranging from \$12.00 for a tiny 4¼" doll to \$575 for the stunning, 36" "Nicole" playing "I Could Have Danced All Night."

To see all of the Victoria Ashlea dolls in a full-color, 24-page catalog costing \$3.00, collectors may call the Goebel, Inc. Doll Design Studio at 1-800-366-4632, press 4 — or visit one of the many doll shops, gift shops and fine department stores that carry this popular line.

Karen Kennedy created "Joanne" as a part of the Victoria Ashlea Originals® *Collection for Goebel, Inc. The 18" doll wears a warm-weather cotton dress and a faux pearl necklace, and plays "Last Rose of Summer." Suggested retail price for "Joanne" is \$165.00.*

A personal favorite doll of Karen Kennedy's, pretty "Amie" wears a charmingly feminine clown outfit and boasts bright heart designs on her pretty cheeks. "Amie" is a recent addition to the Victoria Ashlea Originals® *line.*

The M. I. Hummel Club

Collectors Enjoy "The Magic of Membership" in a Club Celebrating the Delightful Children of Sister Maria Innocentia Hummel

Today — nearly sixty years after the renowned German firm of Goebel began offering M. I. Hummel art in the form of charming figurines — collectors all over the world treasure their beautiful "M. I. Hummels." Many thousands experience the "Magic of Membership," by joining the M. I. Hummel Club. And all M. I. Hummel collectors and admirers share in the delight of the story that brought Sister M. I. Hummel and the artists of Goebel together.

A Child's Love of Art Fuels a Worldwide Phenomenon

Berta Hummel was born in the town of Massing in Lower Bavaria, Germany, on May 21, 1909. She was one of six children of Adolph and Viktoria Hummel.

Four years of instruction at the Institute of English Sisters prepared young Berta for a unique adventure. In a time and place when few girls were able to pursue an individual dream of success, Berta was supported by her father in her enrollment at Munich's Academy of Fine Arts. Her residence there was in a dormitory run by a religious order.

While Berta's mentor at the Academy hoped that she would remain after graduation as his assistant, her friendship with two Franciscan nuns who were also studying at the Academy became even more compelling. With the military and politic threat of the Nazis on the horizon, young Berta Hummel sensed a need for the quiet, withdrawn life of a nun.

In March, 1931, Berta Hummel graduated from the Academy. On April 22 of that same year, she entered the Convent of Siessen at Saulgau, and two years later was ordained Sister Maria Innocentia of the Sisters of the Third Order of St. Francis.

Franz Goebel Discovers the Genius of Sister M. I. Hummel

Several decades before the birth of Berta Hummel, Franz Detleff Goebel and his son William founded The Goebel Company to create marble, slates and slate pencils. When the Duke of Saxe-Coburg-Gotha gave the Goebels permission to introduce a kiln, the stage was set for the creation of figurines.

In 1890, the first Goebel porcelain figurines were produced, and by 1933, there was an extensive line of three-dimensional Goebel pieces. Even so, Franz Goebel, the fourth generation of the family to head the company, was always on the lookout for promising new artists. It was this quest that took him to Munich to visit various gift shops, looking for inspiration.

In one shop that specialized in religious art, a display of art cards caught his eye. They were simple and touching in their innocence, and it struck him that these sketches would be the perfect basis for a new line of figurines. The artist was Sister Maria Innocentia Hummel!

The renewal figurine for returning M. I. Hummel Club members during 1991-92 is the sweet, four-inch-high "Two Hands, One Treat."

The Long-Standing Relationship of Goebel and Sister M. I. Hummel

In 1934, Franz Goebel wrote a letter to Sister M. I. Hummel, proposing that Goebel artists translate her two-dimensional drawings into three-dimensional figurines. At first she hesitated, but Franz Goebel persisted. He arranged a meeting at the Convent with Sister Maria Innocentia and the Mother Superior. He assured them that the figurines would be true to her artwork and that they would be handcrafted to meet the highest quality standards.

Franz Goebel also granted Sister M. I. Hummel and the convent final artistic control. In fact, he stated that once she approved, the M. I. Hummel signature would be incised on the base of each piece. Under these conditions, Sister M. I. Hummel and her Mother Superior agreed to the manufacture of M. *I. Hummel* figurines by Goebel — a licensing agreement that continues to this day.

The introduction of the first M. I. Hummel figurines at the 1935 Liepzig Fair was a tremendous success. Only World War II interrupted forward progress. Severe hardships were inflicted upon the Convent by the Nazi regime, and Sister Maria Innocentia became ill. Although she continued to draw as much as she could, her condition worsened and in 1946 she died at the age of 37.

The popularity of M. I. Hummel collectibles led to the establishment in 1977 of the Goebel Collectors' Club, whose name was changed in 1989 to the M. I. Hummel Club to better reflect the strong interest of its members in the works of this unassuming, yet brilliant, master artist.

How to Enjoy "The Magic of Membership"

Each year, more and more collectors experience "a new sense of wonder" when they join the M. I. Hummel Club. Membership costs just $35.00 U.S. currency or $47.50 in Canadian funds, yet it brings each member a whole world of benefits worth several times its cost: what the Club calls "the joys of belonging."

The magic begins with a present: the "I Brought You a Gift" figurine, worth $65.00 in U.S. currency or $85.00 Canadian. Members also are entitled to own exclusive items available only to Club members. Because they are never sold to the general public, these treasures automatically become some of the rarest and most sought after M. I. Hummels in the contemporary world of collecting.

Through *Insights*, the Club's beautiful, full-color quarterly magazine, collectors become insiders to news about the figurines' inspirational history...

Goebel Miniatures created this adorable "Gift From a Friend" figurine exclusively for members of the M. I. Hummel Club in Club Year 15 (1991-92).

the artists who create them by hand...and the newest releases. Members even have opportunities to embark on luxurious tours to Europe and other destinations with fellow Club members.

Additional benefits abound. All Club members receive a membership card, and a handsome binder filled with a collector's log, price list and facts about M. I. Hummel history and production. There are Club services such as the Research Department and Collectors' Market to match buyers and sellers of M. I. Hummel collectibles. And Local Chapters of the M. I. Hummel Club help collectors expand their friendships and learn even more about M. I. Hummel.

Exciting Opportunities Mark the Club's Fifteenth Anniversary

It has been fifteen years since the charter members banded together to form what is now the M. I. Hummel Club. To celebrate this landmark anniversary in 1991-92, the Club has announced a number of attractive "Club Exclusives." These include a free renewal figurine, a special figurine for charter members, and both regular and miniature size "Club Exclusives" to purchase.

As a special thank-you to renewing members during 1991-92, the M. I. Hummel Club unveiled "Two Hands, One Treat." Standing four inches high, the figurine is a charming portrayal of a favorite childhood game (guess which hand?) and comes complete with the special backstamp assuring Club members that this unique piece was created exclusively for them.

For members who have been involved since the Club's inception, a very special opportunity exists to acquire the M. I. Hummel figurine "Honey Lover." In this first year of availability, only members who have belonged to the Club continuously since its first year will qualify to receive a redemption card for this memorable piece. In subsequent years, each member who renews for his or her fifteenth consecutive year will become eligible. And for those whose 1991-92 renewal is for either the fifth or tenth consecutive year of membership, their renewal kits will also include a redemption form for the figurines — "Flower Girl" and "The Little Pair" respectively — created to mark those membership milestones.

These renewal kits will also include redemption forms for all members to acquire two "Club Exclusives": the charming "Gift from a Friend," and the miniature "Morning Concert." This new miniature comes with its very own Bavarian Bandstand and glass display dome. It measures just 7/8" in height and is a hand-painted, bronze replica of a longtime favorite M. I. Hummel Club figurine.

M. I. Hummel Enthusiasts Enjoy Luxury Travel

"Collecting Memories at Home and Abroad" is the theme of the M. I. Hummel Club's famous travel adventures, which are open exclusively to Club members, their family and friends. European itineraries of eleven to sixteen days include opportunities to visit: the Convent of Siessen, where much of Sister M. I. Hummel's artwork is beautifully displayed; the Goebel factory, including a behind-the-scenes tour; and an interlude in Coburg.

To celebrate the fifteenth anniversary of the M. I. Hummel Club, "Honey Lover" has been introduced. It will be available to charter members of the Club during the fifteenth anniversary year, 1991-92. After that, Club members will be invited to acquire the figurine as soon as they have completed fifteen consecutive years of membership.

Each itinerary enables travelers to indulge their favorite travel fantasies. The "France and Germany" tour spotlights magical Monte Carlo in a sixteen-day adventure that includes Monaco, Avignon, Strasbourg, Coburg, and the Rhine. The twelve-day "Heritage Tour" combines stops at Hamburg, Hamilin and Coburg with an opportunity for those of German descent to trace their ancestry from Germany to the U.S.A. "Christmas Markets" features eleven days of European holiday shopping.

In 1992 we've added a whole new facet to the Club's travel program with the introduction of two luxurious sea cruises. New tours include "A Voyage Through the Lands of the Midnight Sun," a cruise that includes stops in Copenhagen, Estonia, Leningrad, Helsinki and much more. "Seven Islands, Seven Days & Seventh Heaven" is a cruise that begins in San Juan, Puerto Rico and includes a number of exotic ports of call. Details on any of the tours are available by calling 1-800-666-CLUB.

Local Chapters Bring the Magic Close to Home

For many M. I. Hummel collectors, the joy of collecting has been greatly enhanced by their experiences as part of an M. I. Hummel Club Local Chapter. In August, 1978, the first Local Chapter was founded in Atlanta, Georgia, and by the early 1990s, there were over 100 active chapters formed and operated by M. I. Hummel Club members.

Local Chapter members cite sharing, education and social aspects as their greatest club benefits, along with opportunities for community service, and lots of fun. In addition, there is "Local Chapter Chatter," a quarterly M. I. Hummel Club publication written exclusively for Local Chapter members, as well as early release of "M. I. Hummel news," and a Local Chapter Patch for each member.

For generations now, the gentle innocence of Sister Maria Innocentia Hummel's children has delighted collectors all over the world. And for more than fifteen years, M. I. Hummel Club membership has enabled the Sister's many admirers to maximize their enjoyment of her fine art legacy. For more information about Club membership, contact the M. I. Hummel Club 1-800-666-CLUB, or write the Club at Goebel Plaza, P. O. Box 11, Pennington, NJ 08534-0011.

Goebel Miniatures

Goebel Art Masters Capture the Intricate Charms of People, Animals and Flowers on a Lilliputian Scale

To fully appreciate the magic of Goebel Miniatures, collectors are wise to keep a magnifying glass at the ready. For as remarkable as Goebel's tiny miniature figurines appear to the naked eye, a closer look yields even more enjoyment. The quizzical expression of "Alice in Wonderland" ...the delicate plumage of a blue jay...the flower-print dress of a lovely, miniature Capodimonte lady.

Miniature figures have been prized by royalty and patrons of the arts for centuries: the Egyptians cherished finely detailed pieces more than 5,000 years ago, and relics of similar works may be found in the museum collections of Europe and Asia. Their popularity stems first from the novelty of their tiny size and wonderful details. But just as important, miniatures allow collectors to create a complete, tiny, scale-model world of their own.

At Goebel Miniatures, the master of this magical world is artist Robert Olszewski. Ever since Olszewski was discovered by Goebel Miniatures in the late 1970s, his brilliant vision has guided the company's creative output, with world renowned results. Here, we take a step-by-step look at the sculpting, crafting and finishing of a delightful Goebel Miniature — from the original wax sculpture to the finished work of art.

Olszewski Employs the Age-Old "Lost Wax" Process

While technology advances at a breathless pace, there is still no artistic substitute for the classic method of creating metal figurines developed in the Middle East circa 2000 B.C. Called the "lost wax" process, this method allows for castings of the utmost precision and detail, even in miniature sizes. Robert Olszewski and the artists of Goebel Miniatures still utilize this painstaking process to achieve the unique qualities of their works. Here, this fine art technique is explained from beginning to end.

Step One: Wax Carving. Robert Olszewski begins each of his miniatures with a small block of carving wax, which he sculpts using incredibly fine carving tools. Each miniature sculpture may require anywhere from 100 to 400 hours of concentrated work to complete.

Step Two: Lost Wax. Next the wax sculpture is placed inside a crucible and covered with plaster. Once the plaster becomes solid, it is heated, which causes the wax to melt and drain out of tiny holes which are placed in the plaster for this purpose. Thus the original wax figure is "lost," replaced by a hard plaster cavity or cast in its exact image.

Master Artist, Robert Olszewski, carves an original wax sculpture.

A finished wax, in this case, "The Hunt with Hounds."

Here, the wax carving is cast to produce a sterling silver master.

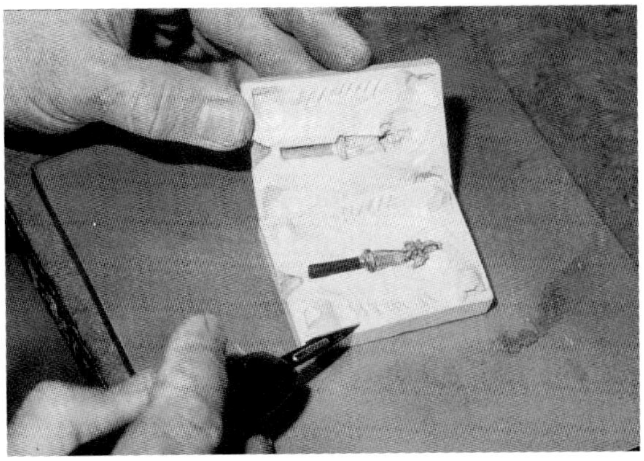

A rubber latex mold is made from the sterling master. Wax is then injected into this mold.

Step Three: The Sterling Master. Now the hard plaster mold is filled with molten sterling silver. When the precious metal hardens, the plaster mold is broken open to reveal what is called a "sterling master." When a one-of-a-kind piece, such as an item of jewelry, is being made, this may end the creative process. But for limited edition Goebel Miniatures, the sterling master now becomes the subject of a latex mold.

Step Four: The Latex Mold. The sterling master now is placed between multiple, thin sheets of a special latex rubber. When the latex is pressed together and heated, it becomes a solid piece of rubber. Once the rubber cures, a sharp knife is used to remove the sterling master. The result is a perfect rubber mold — and now the sterling master can be locked away for safekeeping.

Step Five: Wax Production Master. Next the latex rubber mold is reclosed and clamped shut. Hot wax is injected under pressure so that it fills in every tiny detail of the rubber mold. After the wax has been allowed to cool and harden, the mold is opened with special care. Now there is another wax which represents a faithful reproduction of the original wax carving. At this point, Master Modeler Robert Olszewski looks over this initial production wax to recarve any rough areas and eliminate possible problems in producing the limited edition. Then this revised wax is used for a repetition of the entire process from plaster to sterling production master.

Step Six: The Wax Tree. The final sterling production master serves as the original from which a number of waxes are made. These waxes are attached to a cylinder of wax to form what is called the "wax tree." The "wax tree" then is invested with plaster, and next the plaster molds are filled with molten bronze. The result of this process is a bronze "tree of figurines."

Step Seven: Finishing and Painting. Each individual bronze figurine is separated from its tree and turned over to a skilled artisan who finishes and "fine tunes" it with care. Finally, intricate hand-painting emphasizes the features, costumes, colora-

After the wax figurines are removed from the mold, they are attached to a stem, forming a "tree."

Molten bronze is poured into a plaster cast of the wax tree.

tions and accessories that make each Goebel Miniature such a fascinating work of art.

Each finished Goebel Miniature may require as many as 25 separate steps and over six weeks to complete. No two are ever alike, but each represents an inspiring modern-day masterwork, crafted with the same care as miniature bronzes made centuries ago in the Middle East and Europe.

The Variety of the Goebel Miniature Line

The Goebel Miniatures line offers an incredible array of subjects to intrigue most any collector:

Storybook Lane is a new collection name; a collection of groups whose inspiration has come from great children's classics.

Marquee Classics is another new collection name. It reflects the inspiration for the lavish retelling of Walt Disney's Pinocchio, the Sorcerer's Apprentice from Fantasia, Snow White, and Cinderella.

Ted DeGrazia's World is the collection that couples the talent of Olszewski with the talent of Ted DeGrazia, the noted painter of southwestern Indian children.

Portrait of America is a remarkable collection. Inspired by the art of Norman Rockwell, Goebel Miniatures' artists have captured the essence of Rockwell's uniquely American vision.

And finally...

The Art of Miniatures, the broadest of the collections, provides an umbrella for all the miniatures sculpted by Olszewski. And so, it's the most unique collection in the world.

Whatever the subject matter, Robert Olszewski invests each miniature with his own brand of genius and lively art style. As Olszewski says, "I want you to find each of my miniature sculptures to be a new statement in an old art form...a surprise; a discovery. That surprise and your personal satisfaction is what makes my work so exciting to me."

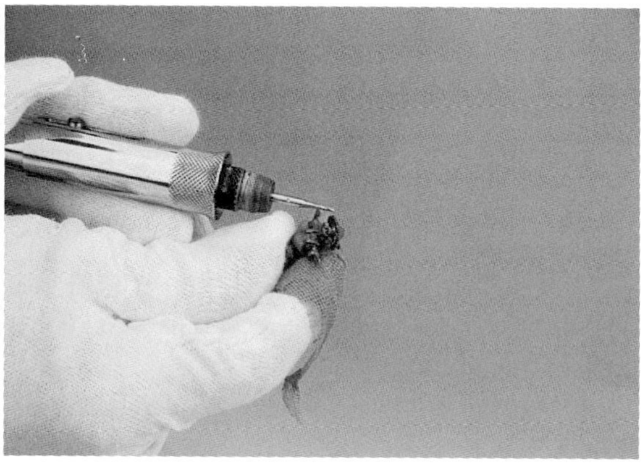

The bronze figurines are cut off the tree; bases and mold lines are ground off.

Figurines are airbrushed white and decorated by hand.

The finished product: a striking Goebel Miniature. This is the "Moor with Spanish Horse."

The Gorham Doll Collection
What Little Girls' Dreams and Precious Heirlooms Are Made Of

The most treasured dolls are inspired by the joy and innocence of little girls' dreams. They appeal to the child in all of us. And, if they are truly exceptional, they grow to become prized heirlooms.

For years, Gorham has gone to great lengths to create such remarkable dolls. Gorham begins with the most talented artists — women who combine rich imagination and warm childhood memories with the talent to make dreams of youth come true.

Indeed, in the world of collectible dolls, Gorham is celebrated for exceptional artistry, workmanship, and exquisite detailing. Many Gorham dolls have appreciated in value far beyond their original issue prices, attracting collectors with their wondrous combination of sculptural quality, costuming and craftsmanship. Many Gorham dolls are limited editions, whose rarity makes them all the more desirable. And the extra attention Gorham pays to each doll makes her so captivating, she will be cherished as a treasured family heirloom for generations to come. Then Gorham brings the artists' visions to life with superb craftsmanship: meticulous detailing, luxurious materials and those special little flourishes that set Gorham heirloom dolls apart.

"Cherie" represents Susan Stone Aiken's elegant Les Belles Bebes *collection of dolls created exclusively for Gorham. With her lavish costume and large, expressive eyes, "Cherie" hearkens back to the priceless French bebes of Leon-Casmir Bru and Emil Jumeau.*

Today Gorham reigns among the world's most elite doll manufacturers. Yet this respected American firm refuses to rest upon its laurels. Year after year, Gorham continues to invest considerable resources and attention to cultivating new doll artists and designs. And if history repeats itself, many of these new dolls will grow more valuable in the years to come.

Susan Stone Aiken: The First Lady of Gorham Dolls

For more than a decade, the gifted doll artist, Susan Stone Aiken, has been creating elegant dolls for Gorham. Not only have Ms. Aiken's dolls been honored with many awards, but they are also so coveted that many have increased significantly in market value over time. Acclaimed for her rare ability to capture the style of priceless French antique dolls, Ms. Aiken personally selects the fabrics, laces, trims, ribbons, flowers and feathers for each original creation.

A native of Massachusetts, Ms. Aiken trained as an artist at the University of Maine and the Rhode Island School of Design. She began creating her elegant doll outfits as a labor of love. "I sewed, loved dolls, loved antiques and was a free-lance artist," she recalls. "And I was able to apply all these elements when Gorham approached me to design their first doll collection in 1981."

Ms. Aiken gets her inspiration from books and photos of turn-of-the-century fashions. Her research is enhanced by her instinctive feel for the bygone era, and for the combinations of materials that are authentic and correct. "I am from an old, New England family," she explains, "and I grew up surrounded by antiques. When I create a costume for a doll, it is like discovering an old friend. It is important to me that each doll has its own personality."

With her blonde hair coiled about each tiny ear, "Samantha" listens to her precious Gingerbread dollhouse play "Brahms' Lullaby." She is the result of a collaboration between doll connoisseur and collector, John T. Young, and doll artist, Brenda Elizabeth Gerardi.

The Romantic Dolls of Brenda Elizabeth Gerardi

"Expressing a gentle touch" with her dolls is the goal of Brenda Elizabeth Gerardi, creator of Gorham's *Victorian Cameo Collection.* Ms. Gerardi says that each doll takes on its own personality as she is designing it — so much so that "each doll's character helped to inspire its name."

Ms. Gerardi attended the Vesper School of Art and the Boston Museum School of Art to enhance her background in wood carving and sculpture. Her first collection for Gorham, entitled *Bonnets and Bows*, was extremely well received in 1988 — in fact, each of the ten dolls has shown an impressive price increase on the secondary market.

"Alexandra" and "Victoria," the premiere dolls in the *Victorian Cameo Collection,* — were inspired by the elegance of the Victorian era. Dressed in luxurious finery, each nineteen-inch doll wears the hallmark of this collection: an intricate cameo.

Her newest collection for Gorham, the *Victorian Cameo Collection*, was designed with a sensitivity to the nostalgic Victorian period. Each reflects a different vignette of Victorian life. "Victoria" is engaged in the classic pastime of gardening, while "Alexandra" is dressed for the event of the season — an elegant ball.

Modern Classics Reflect the Elegance of the Past

A century ago, the doll bebes of Leon-Casmir Bru and Emil Jumeau took Paris by storm with their elegant images of children in grown-up finery. Today the original Bru and Jumeau works are priceless. But through Ms. Aiken's artistry, *Les Belles Bebes* collection brings the enchantment of French doll mastery to contemporary American collectors.

"Cherie" and "Desiree" — the number one and two dolls respectively in the collection are lavishly outfitted in voile, taffeta, delicate laces and elegant hats which frame their original French-style faces. Each carries a miniature hat box which cleverly conceals an 18-note musical movement.

Ms. Aiken is also adept at translating the Kate Greenaway look into modern collectibles. *Gifts of the Garden*, features floral bouquets from the English countryside, and each is outfitted in floral prints and pastel fabrics.

Another collection by Ms. Aiken is *Legendary Heroines*. Inspired by romance, they step right out of timeless literary classics and all reflect their historic period. "Lara," "Guinevere," "Juliet," and "Jane Eyre" are accompanied by their own musical storybooks.

Gift of Dreams *Doll Collection Enhanced by Distinctive Dollhouses*

Collectors will marvel at the unique collection of four dolls entitled *Gift of Dreams* — a series that celebrates little girls, their dreams and their very special dollhouses.

Gift of Dreams is an original creation by doll connoisseur and collector John T. Young, who collaborated with renowned doll artist Brenda Elizabeth Gerardi.

Ms. Gerardi's use of lavish detail is evident in her selection of luxurious doll fabrics, trims, ribbons and imported laces which outfit each doll to perfection. Sculptured teeth, dimpled cheeks and lifelike hands that "hold" dollhouses, are just a few of the features that make this extraordinary collection a true heirloom.

Each *Gift of Dreams* doll is accompanied by her own dollhouse that opens to reveal interior rooms. An 18-note musical movement, cleverly concealed within each house, plays a favorite lullaby.

"Samantha's" Gingerbread dollhouse plays "Brahms' Lullaby." "Melissa's" Southern Colonial mansion plays "Rousseau's Lullaby." Strains of "Mozart's Lullaby" can be heard from "Katherine's" Georgian Colonial. "Shubert's Lullaby" can be heard from "Elizabeth's" Victorian dollhouse.

"Christina," the first and only Christmas issue in the *Gift of Dreams* collection, is accompanied by her own holiday-decorated musical dollhouse which plays "Silent Night."

Dolores Valenza Shares Her Childhood Memories

For years, Dolores Valenza has been a favorite artist among America's connoisseurs of porcelain collectibles. So the news that Ms. Valenza would create her very first doll for Gorham represents an exciting event for collectors. The results of her efforts are captivating: *Childhood Memories* is a collection of irresistible "little girls" sharing very special moments with their enchanting playtime "friends."

Each doll is crafted of hand-painted porcelain with lifelike eyelashes. And they're as cute as can be in cotton prints and silky stripes, laces and satin ribbon trim. The cherished playtime companions are every bit as captivating and carefully crafted as the dolls: a fuzzy bunny, a smiling rag doll, a stuffed elephant, and a teddy bear. Each delightful doll has a sitting height of nine and one-half inches, and all are hallmarked with the artist's signature and presented in gift packaging.

Wide-eyed and full of wonder at the sight of her first Christmas tree, "Baby's First Christmas" gets ready to decorate the tree with her own silverplated angel ornament. She is the creation of Estelle Ansley Worrell, celebrated doll and costume expert.

International Dolls Featured in The Friendship Dolls *Series*

The Friendship Dolls is a collection of international dolls created by celebrated artists from around the world. Each doll, handcrafted in fine bisque porcelain and hand-painted with special care, captures the unique character and distinctive fashion of her native country.

The first four dolls in the collection include "Peggy — The American Traveler," designed by Patricia Seamen; "Meagan — The Irish Traveler," created by Laura O'Connor; "Angela — The Italian Traveler," designed by Silvano M. Nappo; and "Kinuko — The Japanese Traveler," created by Susumu Ueki.

Each doll carries her very own travel bag and also bears the signature of the artist on the hallmark.

Childhood "Firsts" Captured in Special Moments *Collection*

Gorham and Estelle Ansley Worrell have created and introduced a beautiful doll collection — *Special Moments* — which captures and preserves those memorable 'first' milestones in a baby's life.

Each doll in the collection has a silverplated accessory to remember each special occasion: "The Christening" holds a traditional rattle; "Baby's First Christmas" clutches an angel ornament; "Baby's First Birthday" clasps an alphabet block; and, "Baby's First Steps" wears a heart necklace.

Ms. Worrell is renowned for her rare ability to design lifelike detail. A popular authority on dolls and costume, she has been revered on national television for her accomplishments. The enchanting *Special Moments* collection is the result of Ms. Worrell's remarkable talents.

Gorham prides itself on creating "dolls as precious as little girls' dreams." Gorham pledges that collectors are not just buying dolls when they deal with this long-established manufacturer. Instead they are acquiring valuable possessions of unmistakable heirloom quality.

Hamilton Heritage Dolls

An Exquisite Line of Collectible Dolls in the Hamilton Tradition of Quality

There is something about a doll created in the image of a lovely child that captures all of our hearts. And when that doll is hand-crafted in fine porcelain...and dressed from head to toe in an adorable hand-tailored outfit...she's destined to become a member of the family and an heirloom to cherish for generations.

In recent years, one U.S.-based doll studio has earned a special place of honor with collectors for its exquisite porcelain collector dolls. Inspired by works from beloved artists of the past and present, these wonderful dolls are the creations of Hamilton Heritage Dolls, a division of The Hamilton Collection of Jacksonville, Florida.

Hamilton first made its mark on the world of collecting by producing some of the world's most honored collector plates, figurines, bells and other works of limited edition art. Now Hamilton Heritage Dolls gains more renown each year for its elegant dolls inspired by childhood memories. Many of these popular works have been inspired by the art of classic illustrators like Bessie Pease Gutmann and Maud Humphrey Bogart. In addition, Hamilton has made news with contemporary doll creations, based upon the brilliant, original sculptures of Connie Walser Derek.

The Adorable "Jessica" and "Sara"

Connie Walser Derek is renowned as one of America's most respected creators of original doll designs. She has developed a line of exquisite and unique dolls — each of which boasts its own special personality. Two of these little charmers have been created exclusively for The Hamilton Collection, and their names are "Jessica" and "Sara."

"Jessica" is as precious as she can be...and has received accolades from collectors across the country! Pretty as a picture and sweet as sugar, she delights everyone she meets. "Daddy, will you pick me up?" this wide-eyed little one seems to say, as she waits patiently in her picture-perfect outfit. Ms. Derek was inspired by a photograph of her own pretty daughter to create the original sculpture for "Jessica," a work of doll art that is as appealing as it is unique.

"Jessica" is known for her poseable qualities, her tiny porcelain hands that rest together or apart. She is dressed in ruffles and bows, for Ms. Derek finds that this is the perfect formula for melting hearts. Rows of embroidered ruffles frame "Jessica's" face, and her crisp white pinafore is accented at the shoulders with big pink bows. "Jessica's" pink shoes are trimmed in lace and have "pearl" buttons; a fine match for her flower-print dress.

The perfect little friend for "Jessica" is "Sara," a barefoot sweetheart who hugs her very own cuddly bunny and blanket. While "Jessica" is a blue-eyed blonde, pretty "Sara" has huge brown eyes and soft auburn hair. Her flower-print romper is adorned with piping, lace, and a crisp ribbon bow at the neckline. A hair bow of the same ribbon and lace add a feminine touch to "Sara's" attire.

Both "Jessica" and "Sara" debuted at an original-issue price of $155.00, exclusively through The Hamilton Collection.

As precious as she can be, Connie Walser Derek's "Jessica" is one of the most popular collector dolls today. This blue-eyed charmer is an exclusive presentation of Hamilton Heritage Dolls.

Inspired by a classic painting from Bessie Pease Gutmann, lovely little "Virginia" has just returned from an afternoon of picking flowers. This porcelain work of art displays the charm and attention to detail that have won praise for Hamilton Heritage Dolls.

A Bessie Pease Gutmann Beauty: "Virginia"

While Connie Walser Derek reigns as a top contemporary doll artist, collectors also flock to own Hamilton Heritage Dolls inspired by child-subject "classics" from the turn-of-the-century. The art of Bessie Pease Gutmann has delighted collectors in many forms: most recently in wonderful dolls created exclusively by Hamilton. And one of the most beloved Gutmann dolls is pretty "Virginia," inspired by Mrs. Gutmann's portrait of a little girl wearing a crown of summer flowers. As a mother of three and a gifted painter, Mrs. Gutmann had ample opportunity to observe such happy, healthy little ones — and to capture their innocent glow on canvas.

Now all the beauty...appeal...and timeless charm of "Virginia" are portrayed in this breathtaking new porcelain collector doll. Her floral print dress is extra-feminine with its ruffles and lace, and she carries a woven basket just brimming with colorful blossoms. Perhaps even the delicate rosettes that adorn her shining curls were also picked that day. Peeking out from below the ruffled hem of her dress are pristine white pantalettes and a slip, trimmed in a delicate white lace. And her real leather shoes are tied with blue satin bows to complete her outfit.

"Virginia's" lovely, ivory skin boasts a gentle blush at the cheeks, brought on by a sunny afternoon in the garden. Her delicate eyelashes have been carefully painted by hand to gently frame her luminous blue eyes. Her face, arms and legs are crafted of fine bisque porcelain and hand-painted with the utmost care. Truly, "Virginia" is just as enchanting as the Bessie Pease Gutmann portrait that inspired her. And at $135.00, she represents a most affordable acquisition from Hamilton Heritage Dolls.

The Gentle Art of Maud Humphrey Bogart Inspires "First Party" and "The First Lesson"

Maud Humphrey Bogart was famous as an artist in her own right long before her actor-son, Humphrey, was born. As a young protégé of James McNeill Whistler, she studied in Paris and won commissions to paint the portraits of well-to-do French

She looks into her little flowered mirror one last time before inviting guests in for her "First Party." This Hamilton Heritage Doll is inspired by the art of Maud Humphrey Bogart.

children before returning to the United States. Before her marriage to Dr. Belmont DeForest Bogart, Maud Humphrey established her reputation as one of the nation's finest painters of children.

Like Bessie Pease Gutmann, Mrs. Bogart used her children as a constant source of inspiration. Her paintings always contain an ideal quality...her children dressed in "Sunday Best" attire with every hair in place, ever happy, ever serene. Now two of these timeless paintings, "First Party" and "First Lesson," have inspired popular new creations from Hamilton Heritage Dolls.

"First Party" captures a little girl's moment of joy as she puts the finishing touches on her curly coiffeur before her guests arrive. Her eyes sparkle with delight as she catches her reflection in the mirror. "Everything is just perfect," she thinks to herself, and takes one last twirl around the room.

Crafted of fine porcelain, the face, arms and legs of "First Party" are painstakingly hand-painted to capture the delicate complexion of a young girl. This exquisite doll is made using fifteen separate molds. Four distinct firings are necessary to ensure that her youthful beauty will be maintained over the years.

The doll's bow-trimmed pink "shoes" peek out from her flowing, pink chiffon dress which is lavishly trimmed with ribbons, rosettes and fine lace. Underneath, she wears a pristine white slip and lace-trimmed pantalettes. And as the perfect complement to her dress, she proudly wears a gold-toned necklace displaying five lustrous faux pearls. Even the mirror in her hand is rich in detail: adorned with delicately painted rosebuds.

A wonderful friend for "First Party" is the lovely "The First Lesson," another heirloom-quality doll inspired by the art of Maud Humphrey Bogart. "The First Lesson" portrays a sweet little girl, all ready for her first day of school. She's been up since dawn, dressed in her finest. Now she's just moments away from that long-awaited event. Carrying her own little slate...with a strapful of books to swing as she walks...this wistful child can hardly wait for "The First Lesson."

Pretty little "Sara" cuddles her bunny and her blanket. This charming porcelain doll was created by Connie Walser Derek exclusively for The Hamilton Collection.

Crafted of porcelain with the same care invested in "First Party," "The First Lesson" wears a costume that is the picture of turn-of-the-century Victorian fashion. Her starched, off-white frock boasts crisp ruffles and eyelet trim, while underneath is a lacy petticoat. The doll's blonde curls peek out from beneath a blue plaid Scottish tam that matches the plaid piping on her dress. Like "First Party," the beautiful "The First Lesson" doll has been introduced at an issue price of $135.00, exclusively by Hamilton Heritage Dolls.

Year by year, Hamilton Heritage Dolls brings contemporary collectors a carefully chosen mix of elegant dolls — inspired by classic art from the past or crafted from the original sculptures of some of today's most gifted art masters. Each doll exhibits the care in craftsmanship and costuming that has earned it the Hamilton Heritage Dolls "Seal of Excellence"...and each is destined to become a cherished family heirloom.

The Hamilton Collection

"Plate of the Year" Honor Confirms Hamilton's Leading Role Producing Entertainment-Theme Plates for the 1990s

The South Bend, Indiana audience fell silent in anticipation of the long-awaited announcement of the National Association of Limited Edition Dealers (NALED) "Plate of the Year." A NALED representative tore open a crisp white envelope and looked out over the packed banquet hall. "And the winner is...'Fifty Years of Oz' from The Hamilton Collection!"

Amid thunderous applause, Hamilton's Chairman, J. P. Smith, walked to the stage to accept the award on behalf of his company and the plate's gifted artist, Thomas Blackshear. And now it was official, The Hamilton Collection's Golden Anniversary Tribute to "The Wizard of Oz" had earned a place in history as the first "Plate of the Year" for the 1990s.

This singular honor confirms what plate collectors have known for some time: that The Hamilton Collection has a unique ability to produce market-leading works of art inspired by movies, television shows and celebrities. From Dorothy, Toto and their "Oz" friends to the Kramdens and the Nortons of "Honeymooners" fame...from "Star Wars" and "Star Trek" to "I Love Lucy," Hamilton's plate subjects have kept pace with collectors' desires for artwork capturing their favorite stars on porcelain.

The Golden Anniversary of "The Wizard of Oz"

To commemorate the 50th anniversary of "The Wizard of Oz," The Hamilton Collection immediately chose Thomas Blackshear for this coveted commission. Renowned for his movie posters, illustrations and "popular culture" collector plates, Blackshear has the unique ability to capture favorite movie and television stars with the utmost realism and emotional appeal.

Thomas Blackshear's award-winning "Fifty Years of Oz" plate offers a magical view of this beloved land, complete with "appearances" by Dorothy and Toto, Glinda the good witch, the Wicked Witch of the West, Scarecrow, Cowardly Lion and Tin Man, and of course, the mysterious Wizard of Oz himself.

Another Blackshear original, "There's No Place Like Home," is one of the most coveted issues in The Hamilton Collection's *The Wizard Of Oz Commemorative* plate series. The plate shows Glinda encouraging Dorothy and her friends to close their eyes and chant "There's no place like home...there's no place like home..." in an effort to return the young girl and her pet to their Kansas "roots." So popular is this plate — complete with its "Yellow Brick Road" border of 23K gold — that it was reported trading at more than twice its issue price in a matter of months after the edition closed.

T.V. Retrospectives Bring Back Favorite Stars on Porcelain

Another popular "performer" for The Hamilton Collection is "The Honeymoon Express," one of the plates in *The Official Honeymooners* Plate Collection authorized by Jackie Gleason before his death. This plate shows Gleason and his television "family" aboard his New York bus. The enduring popularity of Ralph and Alice Kramden and Ed and Trixie Norton inspired such active trading for "The Honeymoon Express" that it multiplied more than six times in value during the first two years after its edition closed.

With television classics like "I Love Lucy" and "The Lone Ranger" still going strong in re-runs, it comes as no surprise that Hamilton collectors are showing great interest in collector plates featuring the Ricardos and Mertzes, and the Lone Ranger with his faithful companion, Tonto.

"California, Here We Come" has won favor as part of *The Official I Love Lucy* Plate Collection from Hamilton. It shows Lucy, Ricky, Ethel and Fred singing their way out of New York on their way to Hollywood, driving across the Brooklyn Bridge in their convertible. "The Lone Ranger and Tonto," introduced to commemorate the 40th anniversary of the Ranger's famous television show, portrays the masked rider of the plains and his American Indian friend astride their horses. It is the first in the *Classic TV Westerns* plate series, another Hamilton Collection exclusive.

"Fifty Years of Oz" won "Plate of the Year" honors for The Hamilton Collection and Thomas Blackshear at the 1990 International Plate and Collectibles Exposition in South Bend, Indiana. The National Association of Limited Edition Dealers honored this commemorative of the Golden Anniversary of one of the most beloved films of all time, "The Wizard of Oz."

The Science Fiction Dramas of "STAR TREK®" and "Star Wars®"

Ever since The Hamilton Collection introduced its very first "STAR TREK®" plate, "Mr. Spock®," in 1984, this studio has been renowned among fans and plate collectors alike as THE source for collectibles inspired by the STARSHIP ENTERPRISE® and its crew. Now that the Silver Anniversary of the original "Star Trek" television program is upon us, Hamilton has called upon Thomas Blackshear — creator of the outstanding "Plate of the Year," "Fifty Years of Oz," to create two special anniversary tributes to Spock, Kirk, and their loyal 23rd-century crew.

Both fully authorized by Paramount Pictures and endorsed by The Official STAR TREK Fan Club, the "STAR TREK 25th Anniversary Commemorative Plate" and the *STAR TREK 25th Anniversary Commemorative Collection* feature the characters from the show that first captured the imagination of America back in 1966.

The Commemorative Plate shows Captain James Kirk with Mr. Spock and Dr. McCoy at his side. In the background we see Sulu, Chekov, Uhuru and Scotty — all just as they appeared a quarter-century ago as the stars of the most original, innovative and daring television program of all time. The stunning plate features an 8mm decorative border of 23K gold, bearing its title and the anniversary dates, 1966-1991.

"SPOCK," a portrait of Mr. Spock displaying his familiar Vulcan salute, premieres the *STAR TREK 25th Anniversary Commemorative Collection.* Set against a dramatic backdrop of deep space — a natural "canvas" of planets, nebulae and stars — the half-Vulcan, half-human First Officer extends his hand in the traditional greeting of his people. Blackshear's riveting portrayal of Spock is highlighted by a lavish, commemorative border of 23K gold inscribed with the words "Star Trek."

In addition to The Hamilton Collection's many successful STAR TREK collectible artworks, the firm has won fame as the creator of Star Wars commemoratives and collector plates. Notable among these is "Luke Skywalker and Darth Vader" from the *Star Wars* Plate Collection, a dramatic work of art that has doubled in market price since its introduction in the late 1980s.

The enduring popularity of the "Star Wars" films is proved once again in the secondary market strength of this Hamilton Collection plate favorite, "Luke Skywalker™ and Darth Vader™."

Hamilton Also Makes News with Limited-Edition Child-Subject Plates

In addition to its demonstrated fame as the creator of some of the world's most coveted show business collector plates, The Hamilton Collection continues to please its patrons with plate series by some of the greatest child-subject art

The Hamilton Collection has issued the "STAR TREK®" Commemorative Plate by award-winning artist Thomas Blackshear.

"The Lone Ranger" represents The Hamilton Collection's popular series of plates entitled Classic TV Westerns. *This work of art shows the masked man himself with his faithful Indian friend, Tonto.*

masters in our history. Since Bessie Pease Gutmann's "In Disgrace" premiered *A Child's Best Friend* Plate Collection in 1985, Hamilton has introduced many popular works of art on porcelain from her classic paintings to those of Maud Humphrey Bogart.

The incredibly popular "In Disgrace" depicts a charming little girl and her faithful dog after having made a mess in mother's prized flower bed! Another beloved plate is the one inspired by Mrs. Gutmann's "Awakening," a portrait of a newborn reaching up to Mother, just as her eyes open for a new day of discovery. Both of these plates have seen considerable secondary market action, with "In Disgrace" having risen nearly five times in value, and "Awakening" recently bringing three times its issue price.

Maud Humphrey Bogart, also created wonderful child-subject art that has inspired a number of very popular Hamilton plates. One of the most beloved of these is "Playing Bridesmaid," a dress-up "make believe" portrait that premiered the *Little Ladies* Plate Collection.

Hamilton Commissions Top Artists for Plates

As evidenced in the show business plates by Thomas Blackshear and the child-subject works inspired by Bessie Pease Gutmann and Maud Humphrey Bogart, The Hamilton Collection strives to bring the finest artists of the past and present to the porcelain plate medium. This goal has led Hamilton to offer works of art on a variety of subjects: the dog and puppy-subject plates of Jim Lamb, for example, and the Native American Indian works of David Wright.

Lamb's *Puppy Playtime*, *Good Sports* and *A Sporting Generation* have won him tens of thousands of loyal collectors, while Wright's *Noble American Indian Women* are considered a triumph of Indian-subject art.

As the 1990s progress, The Hamilton Collection will strive to continue its impressive record as the presenter of some of the world's most honored show business plates. At the same time, this award-winning firm will remain constantly alert to find art opportunities in its quest to provide collectors with the most distinguished porcelain plates featuring exceptional art from the past... and the present.

Cross Gallery, Inc.

Penni Anne Cross Portrays the Dignity and Drama of Native Americans in Her Paintings and Graphic Prints

"All Crow Indians are given an 'Indian' name, in addition to their birth name," says Native American artist Penni Anne Cross of Jackson Hole, Wyoming. "The Crow Indian name 'Alawa-sta-wa-ches' was given to me by my great-grandfather on my Indian mother's side of the family. The literal translation of 'Alawa-sta-wa-ches' is 'Travels the Good Road,' and of course that has paved my way and time in life."

"No matter where I have gone I have always come home healthy and happy and far richer because of the people and experiences I have been involved with. I am a born-again Christian and do feel that my whole life has been lovingly planned for me by God," Ms. Cross explains.

Today this gifted artist lends her name to the Cross Gallery, Inc. of Jackson Hole, the publisher and distributor of her limited edition prints and hand-pulled originals. Working in both oils and pastels, Ms. Cross has developed a place in the art world by portraying the subjects that are close to home for her — her Native American family and the people among whom she has lived.

Although prominent investors and museums continue to acquire her work, Ms. Cross is most grateful that collectors purchase her art for the appeal of image and subject matter. "I won't do something I don't know; and if I don't, I'll find out," she insists, referring to her passion for accuracy. This quest may involve years of research in the field for a single image, culminating in a piece of art which is beautiful, true to history and culture, and deeply meaningful.

A Self-Taught Artist Becomes a Caring Teacher

"I did not necessarily choose this occupation," Ms. Cross says of her art career, "as I feel God chose it for me. My original direction was to become a concert pianist, and an auto accident cut that short with some irreversible damage to my hand. I was always able to draw and consequently began to paint."

Ms. Cross soon discovered that she had a talent for painting, and took steps to nurture it by befriending the owners of her local art store. These two elderly people counted on sales of supplies and art lessons for their livelihood. When Ms. Cross inquired about signing up for lessons, the owners confided sadly that the art teacher had recently passed away.

"Would I please take the classes for a few weeks, until they found a replacement? That's what they asked me," Ms. Cross recalls with a smile. "They had surmised from my drawings that I would be accomplished enough to hold the classes together for awhile at least until they could locate a qualified replacement teacher. I protested, and did tell them that while I could not lead the students to believe I was formally trained, I could at least help and assist each student with the little knowledge I had, until they found a replacement. And teach I did!"

Ms. Cross continued that "temporary assignment" for six years, literally conducting her own art studies as she mentored the students. Each night she would go home and pick a lesson from a current Walter Foster book, teach herself, and then go in the next day and teach the students. This seemed to thrill the students, as they never thought of Penni as their teacher — more that she was their friend.

"There never seemed to be a problem painting-wise that we could not solve together," Ms. Cross recalls. "These times were not only precious and warm for me and the students that I grew to know, teach and love, but I ultimately taught myself the hard way, through trial and error." Ms. Cross found that she and the students were able to become quite innovative in approaching new ideas and solutions for all types of paintings.

Penni Anne Cross Studies the "Window of the Soul"

During this time of extensive study, Ms. Cross became fascinated by the importance of eyes in creating a painting. She made an appointment with a police forensics expert, who gave her quite a lesson in how victims are traumatized. She learned that long after a person's death, the expression of the eyes still reflects their previous situation — be it peace, violence or pain.

To pursue her theory that the eyes are the

"window and record of the soul," Ms. Cross paid an ophthalmologist for several hours of his time. She had him teach her about "the eye" and all its functioning powers. "I made him explain to me why eyes do what they do," she says. "Where does the light come from? What happens to eyes when a person is getting ready to cry, or when he's happy? I'm fascinated with eyes. I can look at people's faces and almost tell you what they're experiencing."

In addition to sharing what she learned about eyes with her students, Ms. Cross took them through rigorous anatomical discovery. First, they studied bones and muscle structure of their own hands, arms, legs and feet. Then they would draw the actual bone placement directly on themselves. After memorizing, they translated this work to paper: a marvelous exercise in rendering realistic human art.

Created from an original oil painting in an edition of 475 with forty-seven artist proofs, "The Blue Shawl" lithograph has been hand-signed, titled and numbered by its artist, Penni Anne Cross. The issue price is $185. The following poem sets the tone for this evocative painting of a lovely Native American woman.

He never really saw the stars at night.
Never seen were the stars and the sparkle at night
Nor the red-gold sunset that blisters horizons of finished days
Nor the laggard blue of day-weary skies at twilight
And not even the pewtered neutral of some hovering clouds.
But then...he never sought these things out.
And then, one night at the dance in the Roundhouse, for it was Winter, someone sat quietly as he passed by.
A sunset? no, just the sheen of splendid orange-gold pattern
A midnight-laced sky? no, just a lapis-laced shawl covering someone
And stars? no, just the quick glance as she dropped her gaze ever so demurely
And then he saw the stars that night.
And the Blue Shawl as well.

A Professional Art Career Beckoned Ms. Cross

It was a hard decision for Penni Anne Cross to give up her classes and become a professional. She had proven her belief that you could find out how to do anything if you really wanted to know. And she had made wonderful friends among her students. But Ms. Cross felt a pull toward her artistic endeavors, and she was driven to maximize her talent.

As a full-time artist, Ms. Cross enjoys her career, "Firstly because it is my ministry and what God has called me to do. He has given me not only the talent, but also the ability, expertise and knowledge in how to paint as well as the opportunity to present my work to the world." Before beginning each painting, Ms. Cross prays to have people see the Creator first, and then the "Creation." "My inspiration is Jesus Christ," she says. "I asked God a long time ago to live inside of me, and if my paintings touch the inner part of a person, then God IS working and living through my art."

Penni Anne Cross' original oil painting of "Woman With Her Wolves" has been introduced in an edition of 1,050 prints at an issue price of $325. The following sets the scene in Ms. Cross' own words: "There is a Race. One that is run each year in Alaska...the Iditarod. A race that calls from each participating man and woman every fragmented vestige of strength, courage and endurance that can be scraped from the lining of one's soul. A race of time where dog and man become one, where safety has no face...and the wolf and Eskimo past return to see a story acted out for eleven-plus days and nights. A story that is told only by long nights, cold winds and blinding snow — the true Lords of Winter."

Each Penni Anne Cross creation is a spiritual ticket into the subject's life. "An artist's downfall comes when they let their gift possess them instead of possessing their gift," she says. If an artist is an expression of a painter's soul, then it is easy to see why Penni Anne's art is characterized by confidence, serenity and love. Her life has not been without its upheavals, but through them all, a strong Christian faith bolstered by the Native American's philosophy has enriched both her understanding and portrayal of life.

Working With Young People Invigorates Penni Anne Cross

One of Ms. Cross' favorite things to do is to lecture at junior and senior high schools, which would come as no surprise to those who know her and her love for children. "Part of my obligation of ownership of my own talent rests in the ability to inspire children to use their talents, whether it be for a future career or education, or for a sense of self-esteem, self-worth, and self-satisfaction," Ms. Cross explains. "If meeting me inspires just one student to reach his or her potential of achievement, it is worth everything. I have always felt it is a privilege to share my views and feelings on the 'road' I travel."

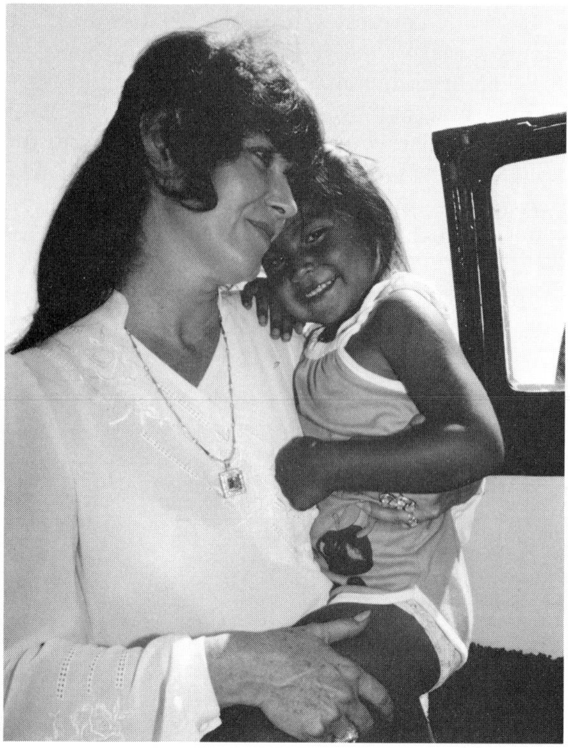

Artist Penni Anne Cross is shown with one of her many young friends in the Native American community of Montana.

For all the critical acclaim received for her stunning and sensitive Indian portraiture, it is a remark made several years ago by a second grade student which remains Penni's most treasured compliment. After seeing a particularly dramatic piece of work portraying a beautiful Indian woman whose shiny black hair is blowing freely in the wind, the little girl timidly approached Penni. "Are you the artist?" she asked. When Penni Anne Cross responded that she was indeed, the little girl asked in genuine amazement, "How did you glue each piece of hair on that picture?" To this day Ms. Cross insists, "Children are the best critics in the world!"

Penni Anne Cross has a truly beautiful view of herself, saying "I would describe myself as just another grateful servant of my Lord Jesus Christ and my Father, God. They truly are the artists, life around me becomes the colors, and I am merely the paintbrush that wields and executes the components for a successful recreation of what already exists."

For "Ach-Hua Dlubh: (Body Two), Half-Breed," Penni Anne Cross takes inspiration from a beautiful young woman who represents two cultures. "I dream of wonderful rides between the two villages," Ms. Cross writes in the accompanying poem, as she describes the way in which the woman does her best to remain part of all her heritage. The original oil painting now is presented in an edition of 475 lithographic prints with forty-seven artist's proofs. The issue price is $190.

Hand & Hammer Silversmiths

Silversmiths to Presidents and Royalty Create Elegant Ornaments for American Collectors

By the time he was ten years old, Chip deMatteo had begun "paying his dues" as a third-generation silversmith for his family's thriving business. Today Chip follows in the footsteps of his famous father and grandfather, the premier silversmiths William deMatteo Sr. and Jr.

At the helm of Hand & Hammer Silversmiths along with his partner, Philip Thorp, deMatteo oversees a team of world-class silver craftsmen. The Hand & Hammer artists design and produce the finest in silver collectible ornaments and jewelry — both under their own hallmark, and for some of the world's most honored institutions, museums and private firms.

The Heritage of Hand & Hammer Silversmiths

Chip's father, William deMatteo Jr., was for many years the Master Silversmith of Colonial Williamsburg. His grandfather, William deMatteo Sr., was a premier silversmith in New York. The deMatteo name is so justly renowned in the world of silver craftsmanship that William deMatteo Jr. has been commissioned to design and fashion unique silver gifts for several presidents.

John F. Kennedy selected a pair of solid silver lanterns for the Oval Office. Richard Nixon commissioned a silver globe on a graceful stand, and Gerald R. Ford was presented with a miniature Liberty Bell of shimmering silver. Especially for President Jimmy Carter, Hand & Hammer fashioned a beautiful Rose Bowl in sterling and gold. And each year a group of Hand & Hammer ornaments is selected to decorate a tree in the President's quarters at the White House in Washington, D.C.

In addition, various American Presidents have commissioned important State Gifts from Hand & Hammer Silversmiths, including selections for Queen Elizabeth II, Anwar Sadat and Menacham Begin, President Lyndon Johnson, and Winston Churchill.

Also especially notable is the fact that Hand & Hammer is the sole supplier of Phi Beta Kappa keys to the eminent academic society.

Hand & Hammer Artists Work in Shimmering Silver

The deMatteos have always been strong advocates for the preservation of traditional craftsmanship. As William deMatteo once said, "If we ever lose this feeling for the esthetic, this feeling of doing things with our hands for other people, we'll have lost something from our way of life." Indeed, Hand & Hammer Silversmiths is dedicated to the idea that the care and the attention artisans of the past lavished on their creations should continue today.

That is why Hand & Hammer artists prefer to work in silver above any other material. Indeed, they consider silver the most wonderful element known to man. Bright white and lustrous, it is the most reflective material on earth and is the best conductor of heat and electricity. It is also remarkably malleable and ductile — an ounce of silver can be drawn into a fine wire many miles long!

Silversmithing is an art which predates written history. In an ancient treatise on metals Birincuccio wrote, "He who wishes to be acclaimed a master silversmith must be a good universal master in many arts, for the kind of work which comes to his hand are infinite. Those who work in silver must outdistance all other craftsmen in learning and achievement to the same degree that their materials outdistance other metals in nobility."

Many families have heirlooms of silver passed down through the generations. These antiques were handmade and many are now priceless museum pieces. Today most silver is machine-made, and while some machine-made pieces are beautiful and many are valuable, none will be regarded in the future as highly as the handmade work of the skilled silversmith.

The Hand & Hammer Tradition of Excellence Continues in Contemporary Designs

Because of its unique dedication to hand-craftsmanship in silver and other fine materials, Hand & Hammer has won commissions from virtually every major museum in the United States. Many smaller museums, as well as the United States Historical Society, are also Hand & Hammer clients. For these institutions, the silversmiths create specially designed and exclusively made ornaments, jewelry and collectibles.

Since 1963, Shreve Crump & Low of Boston has commissioned annual ornaments from Hand & Hammer, while the studio has designed sterling annual commemoratives of famous Boston and national American landmarks for this famed Boston store since 1985.

Lord and Taylor department stores have featured exclusive Hand & Hammer ornament designs each year since 1984, centered upon beloved Hans Christian Andersen fairy tale subjects. These include "The Wild Swan," "The Little Mermaid," "The Nightingale," "The Snow Queen," "Thumbelina," "The Ugly Duckling," and "The Steadfast Tin Soldier."

The Sterling Qualities of Beatrix Potter

One of the most satisfying recent associations for Hand & Hammer Silversmiths has been the studio's licensing agreement with Frederick Warne Co. in London, publisher of the original Beatrix Potter books. Hand & Hammer's collection of hand-made ornaments and jewelry depicts characters from the famous *Peter Rabbit* books written and illustrated by Miss Potter — charming volumes that have enchanted children throughout the world for four generations. Each prospective design was submitted to London for approval, first as drawings and then as actual samples.

Beatrix Potter was born in London in 1866, and during her lonely childhood she studied art and natural history. The inspiration for Peter Rabbit was a schoolroom pet of hers. She learned to love the countryside and its animal inhabitants during childhood holidays in Scotland and later in the English Lake District, where she made her home for the last thirty years of her life.

The story of the naughty Peter Rabbit in Mr. McGregor's garden first appeared in a letter Beatrix Potter wrote to a young friend in 1893. Published by Frederick Warne in 1902, the initial tale and the many that followed have since been translated into many foreign languages — and have captured the imagination of children and adults alike.

Initial offerings in the Beatrix Potter ornament suite include two pieces featuring that rascal, Peter Rabbit; two tributes to Mrs. Rabbit and Peter's three siblings — Flopsy, Mopsy and Cottontail; The Tailor of Gloucester taking a break from his work for a "good read"; and a silver portrait of Jeremy Fisher doing what comes naturally: fishing. There are also wonderful keepsake ornament/lockets, charms, pendants and a brooch, all capturing

From Beatrix Potter's beloved Tale of Peter Rabbit *comes "Mrs. Rabbit," a limited edition sterling silver ornament from Hand & Hammer. The piece was created under license from Frederick Warne Co., London, and was produced only during 1991. Retail price is $39.50.*

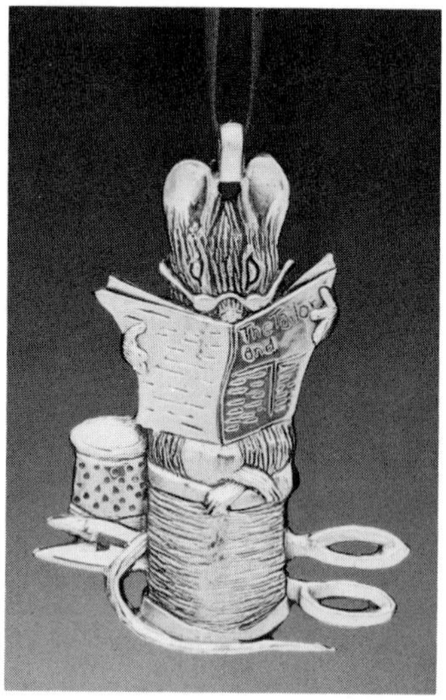

The whimsical "Tailor of Gloucester" stars on his own sterling silver ornament from Hand & Hammer. Reading as he sits atop his thimble of thread, the tailor carries a retail price of $39.50.

The form of antique carousel horses inspired this "Carousel Horse" designed by Chip deMatteo and crafted by the Hand & Hammer Silversmiths. The edition is limited to 5,000, and this is the third in a limited edition series. Retail price: $36.00.

the enduring appeal of Beatrix Potter's wonderful animal characters.

Historical and Whimsical Ornaments Abound

One of Hand & Hammer's most challenging recent commissions has been that of Jeff Stewart Antiques, a North Carolina firm that asked Chip deMatteo to make a series of sterling silver ornaments representing the fifty State Capitol buildings. The first four pieces completed were North Carolina, South Carolina, Georgia, and Florida, with more to follow.

The United States Historical Society of Richmond, Virginia, has been working with Hand & Hammer to develop a beautiful set of silver ornaments boasting faithful reproductions of the homes of the great presidents. Chip deMatteo drew the designs from blueprints of the Historic American Buildings Survey at the National Archives in Washington, D.C.

Hand & Hammer's own wonderful line of silver Christmas ornaments began with a set of silver icicles just like those which hang on the deMatteo family's Christmas tree. Since then, scores of striking ornaments — all in shimmering sterling silver — have been introduced to the delight of American collectors. In addition to the open edition ornaments, each year Hand & Hammer introduces dated annuals as well as limited edition sets to please the growing numbers of serious Christmas ornament collectors.

"Silver Tidings" Keeps Collectors Informed

The Hand & Hammer Collector's Club began in 1989 with the printing of the first edition of the club's official newsletter, "Silver Tidings." There is no charge to join the Collector's Club, and members receive four issues of "Silver Tidings" each year. The Club also sponsors store and show appearances by Chip deMatteo and Philip Thorp. Collectors may sign up for the Club through participating Collector Club retailers or by calling Hand & Hammer at 1-800-SILVERY.

America's "ultimate ornament collector" and noted author, Clara Scroggins, has long been an admirer of Hand & Hammer ornaments. At holiday time, she could not do without her large Hand & Hammer collection, as she explains: "I decorate several trees in my home from my collection of special Christmas ornaments. Out of my collection, I always choose a selection of sterling silver ornaments hand-made with expert skills and loving care by the artisans at Hand & Hammer."

All grown up now, and carrying on the tradition of fine silver craftsmanship begun by his father and grandfather, Chip deMatteo poses with his partner, Phil Thorp, at Hand & Hammer.

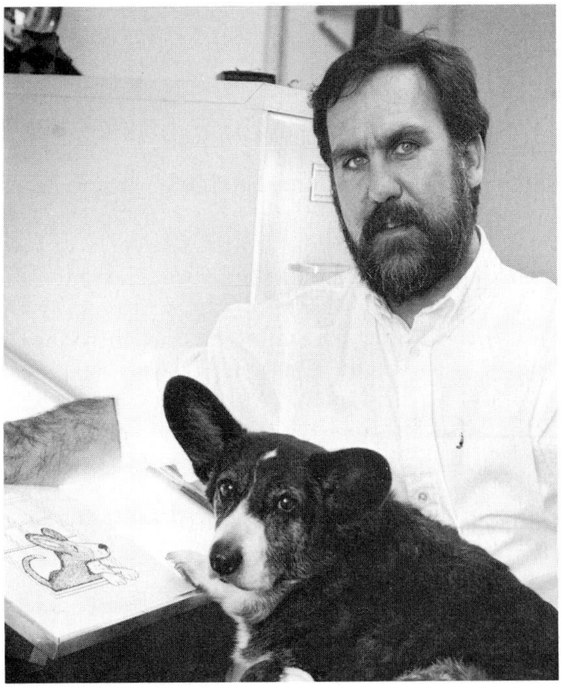

Chip deMatteo poses with Club mascot "Ember," who supervised the drawing of the 1990 Club ornament.

John Hine Studios

John Hine and David Winter Foster the Genius of Artists and Craftspeople in Their Award-Winning Studios and Workshops

It was a meeting of the minds and hearts from the very beginning. When John Hine and David Winter first discovered their mutual fascination with the lifestyles of their British ancestors, they sensed that this special bond could set the stage for a once-in-a-lifetime collaborative effort. With Hine as the visionary and business manager and Winter as the researcher and sculptor, this pair of gifted entrepreneurs embarked on the adventure that has today earned worldwide renown for The Studios and Workshops of John Hine.

While David Winter's beloved cottages feature few figures of people, their shapes and functions imply a busy group of inhabitants from many walks of life. It is this human connection — based on historical research of lifestyles and architectural details — that makes his enduring partnership with John Hine so fruitful. And from the early days of their work together (when their operations fit snugly in an old coal shed on Winter's parents' property) the twosome have showered each new artist, craftsperson and collector with their personal attention and caring.

A Tale of Serendipity

The story of John Hine Studios begins in 1978, when Hine paid a visit to his old friend, the renowned British sculptor Faith Winter. Hine had an idea for a heraldic art project, and wanted to commission Mrs. Winter for the sculptures. She was booked ahead for months, but introduced Hine to her nineteen-year-old son and sculptural assistant, David Winter.

As Hine recalls, "There has never been the slightest doubt in my mind about the talent of David Winter. (At that time) only a handful of people knew him and nobody thought of him as a highly significant sculptor who would one day become a household name. Yet there was, even then, the first glimmering signs of something truly outstanding.

"Instinct has always been my lodestar and the bristling of the hairs on the back of my neck when I watched David at work reinforced that fundamental intuition. It led me to believe that here, in

Following in his traditional Dickens theme, David Winter sculpts the 1991 David Winter Cottage Christmas piece, "Fred's House: A Merry Christmas, Uncle Ebeneezer," said Scrooge's nephew Fred, "and a Happy New Year."

front of my eyes, was the chrysalis of an immense emerging talent."

When the heraldic shields concept proved less than successful, Hine settled upon a much more challenging subject for his new partner and protege. In 1979, John Hine and David Winter set out to create miniature houses inspired by the rich history of their native Great Britain.

The Craftspeople Make The Studios and Workshops Hum

Much has been written about David Winter — his genius for sculpture, his love of British history, his many awards from collectors and dealers on both sides of the Atlantic. But Hine and Winter both agree that their staff of devoted craftsmen and craftswomen are the "unsung heroes" of the Studios and Workshops.

As Hine says, "They not only work night and day to guarantee that every piece ordered will be satisfactorily delivered, they also drive their craftsmanship to exceptional heights of quality to show that although many people seek David's sculptures, it could never be said that they have dropped their self-imposed standards to clear the order quickly."

Hine speaks for all the craftspeople when he

says, "We take the most immense pride in our work and are driven by the realization that we carry the responsibility for David Winter's reputation in what we do each hour of every day. Get it right — and we have done what we are there to do; but get it ever so slightly wrong, and we have sullied the name of the sculptor who entrusted us with his creations."

New Art Masters Expand Upon the Repertoire of John Hine Studios

Since 1979, David Winter has created a remarkable array of cottages and buildings, which are crafted in The Studios and Workshops of John Hine. There are the original *David Winter Cottages*, the *Scottish Collection*, *British Traditions*, and a number of pieces which have already been retired — and are available only on the secondary market.

In recent years, John Hine Studios have welcomed several exceptional artists to their gifted band — each a proven talent with a remarkable specialty of his or her own. Prominent among these art masters are Sandra Kuck, Maurice Wideman, Malcolm Cooper, Christopher Lawrence, and Jon Herbert.

Victorian Mother-and-Child Figurines from Sandra Kuck

In announcing Sandra Kuck's affiliation with his studios, John Hine said, "We are proud to have Sandra join us and are especially excited to have an artist of her caliber to create an entire new line for us." Ms. Kuck, winner of the National Association of Limited Edition Dealers (NALED) Artist of the Year Award for six consecutive years during the 1980s, says she chose John Hine Studios because of the creative freedom Hine gives his artists, as well as the reputation of his craftspeople.

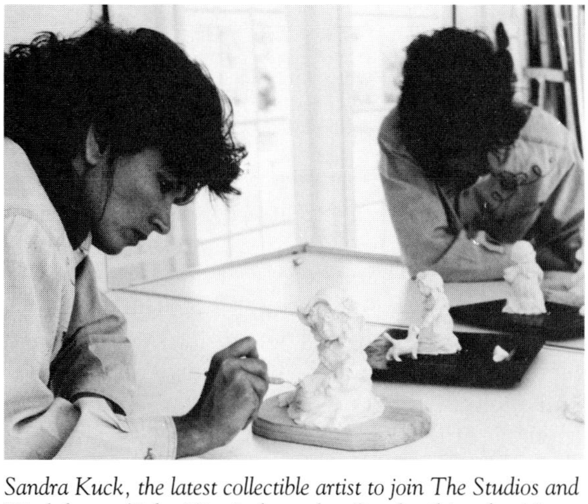

Sandra Kuck, the latest collectible artist to join The Studios and Workshops of John Hine Ltd., sculpts fine detail into her Victorian mother-and-child theme figurines at her Florida studio.

Sandra Kuck's figurines for John Hine Studios, entitled *Heartstrings*, will be consistent with the artist's popular Victorian mother-and-child theme. Already Ms. Kuck has won collector admiration and awards for her dolls, plates and lithographs in this genre. In addition to many North American honors since the mid-1980s, Ms. Kuck has been named International Collectibles Artist of the Year for 1991.

Although Ms. Kuck is beloved for her skills as a painter, she is also an accomplished sculptor. The figurines inspired by her sketches will possess the same beauty, delicacy, luminosity and palette as those previous works familiar to her collectors. The sculptures will be produced in cold-cast porcelain and will utilize special production techniques developed by The Studios and Workshops. The first four figurines were introduced in 1991.

Maurice Wideman Creates The American Collection

Although he was born in Aldershot, Hampshire, England, Maurice "Mo" Wideman claims a variety of heritage in his bloodstream, including American Indian and European lineage. Now a Canadian citizen, this renowned artist spent his boyhood traveling with his family around England and North America, and experienced many climates and many regional lifestyles. He found each new way of life more fascinating than the last. And thus his youthful experiences served as a backdrop for the rich legacy of *The American Collection* for John Hine Studios.

Upon his commission from John Hine to create a series of miniature homes and buildings in the American tradition, Wideman and his family spent a delightful year in England at The Studios and Workshops of John Hine Ltd. There he developed the initial pieces in *The American Collection*, including small-town buildings like the "Barber Shop," "Cherry Hill School," and "Town Hall," and regional pieces like the "Cajun Cottage," "California Winery," and "New England Lighthouse."

Indulging his love of travel, Wideman spent six months during 1991 on a "Hats Off to America" tour, visiting 21 cities from coast to coast. He designed a special collector's piece commemorating the journey, which was available only through dealers hosting Wideman in the cities slated for the tour. Designed to complement *The American Collection*, the 6"x4" plaque depicts Maurice Wideman at work in his studio.

Jon Herbert Portrays "The Shoemaker's Dream"

An imaginative young artist named Jon Herbert has created a fanciful collection of miniature cottages, clock towers and taverns for The Studios and Workshops of John Hine, capturing the vivid images of a shoemaker's dream. As the story goes, Crispin the shoemaker is descended from a long line of cobblers. No longer a young man, Crispin sometimes nods off while working at his bench, particularly on hot summer afternoons after lunch.

When this occurs, Crispin has brilliant dreams when he vividly sees ordinary shoes and boots take on magical forms and become exotic homes with elaborate designs and incredible decorations. When Crispin wakes, he can still remember every detail. He goes to work to make the houses he saw in his idyllic dream.

"The Gate Lodge" looks for all the world like a typical lodge, except that two laced boots stand guard on either side of its "oaken" door. "The Clocktower Boot" shows its origins as footwear at the base, but climbs to an English Tudor-style top with a "clock" at its peak. There is even a "Baby Booty," available in the collector's choice of pink or blue, with a charming cottage growing from inside a classic example of infant footwear!

The David Winter Cottages Collectors Guild

While the John Hine "family" of artists continues to grow, interest in the studios' first creations — the cottages of David Winter — soars in popularity year by year. Stories of collectors lining up at dawn to meet David Winter at conventions and personal appearances are legendary in the collectibles field. And today, more than 40,000 American collectors have joined the David Winter Cottages Collectors Guild.

Members are entitled to purchase pieces which Winter sculpts exclusively for the Guild. What's more, David Winter prepares a special gift yearly for members of the Guild. In 1991, this gift piece was "Pershore Mill," a hand-painted, bas-relief plaque inspired by John Hine's descriptions of the mill in his sleepy home town of Pershore, England.

The quarterly Guild magazine, *Cottage Country*, is sent free of additional charge to all dues-paying Guild members. Upon joining the Guild, members also are sent a handsome leather binder to hold copies of the magazine. Other membership benefits include a Certificate of Membership and a Membership Card.

Guild members who attend the annual International Plate and Collectible Exposition in South Bend, Indiana may be treated to a special event — such as a lavish tea. And for those who travel to England, John Hine offers prearranged tours of the Studios and Workshops of John Hine Limited, Aldershot, Hampshire. There visitors enjoy a complete tour of the facility where they share smiles and pleasant chats with the craftspeople about their favorite David Winter creations. Thus the "human connection" comes full circle — from visionary to artist to craftspeople to collectors — all focused on the wonderful cottages of David Winter.

Maurice Wideman's American Collection *includes many historical structures such as this "Cherry Hill School." His miniature homes and public buildings reflect America's varied heritage and colonial spirit.*

"Moonlight Haven" captures the cozy beauty of a typical English cottage in a design by David Winter for The Studios and Workshops of John Hine Limited.

Kaiser Porcelain

One of the World's Great Porcelain Studios Creates Collector Figurines and Plates on Wildlife and Fairy Tale Themes

The wondrous evolution of Germany's famed Kaiser Porcelain Studio is closely connected with the mysterious and ancient saga of porcelain. Located in the quaint old town of Staffelstein, Kaiser is close to the famous center of Bavarian porcelain making — an artistic tradition that extends back to the sixteenth century

Kaiser's own history of creating fine porcelains represents a family legacy with origins 120 years ago. Today Kaiser Porcelain is as devoted to high quality and meticulous workmanship as was its founder, August Alboth, in 1872. Kaiser is renowned worldwide as a leader in the limited edition sculpture and porcelain plate markets. Current choice selections from the Kaiser line focus on dramatic wildlife works as well as whimsical visions of fairy tale worlds inhabited by people and animals alike.

Kaiser Unveils the Fanciful Characters of English Artist Robert Hersey

One of Kaiser's newest artists, Robert Hersey, spent his early childhood in the West Country of England where he grew to appreciate the countryside and its diverse wildlife. While young Bob's father was a baker by trade, the elder Hersey prepared sketches and paintings as a hobby — and he encouraged his talented son to join him in this enjoyable pursuit. The family kept household pets and animals — many of whose quirks and charms show up in the characters that inspire Hersey's figurines and paintings today.

"The Carriage" from Dear of Italy is proudly presented to North American audiences by Kaiser Porcelain. This richly detailed work of hand-painted porcelain art is the masterwork of Italian sculptor Auro Belcari.

While the Hersey clan moved back to suburban London when Bob was ten, the artist founded his own home in the countryside of Kent as soon as his career afforded him the necessary money and freedom. There he continues to explore the wonderful world of nature — and to capture it in his artwork.

Bob Hersey has created a delightful collection of six porcelain plates for Kaiser, entitled *Through a Woodland Window*. The collector plate medium allows Hersey to develop visual stories for his viewers, just as if they were able to peep through the cherry blossom-framed windows of their woodland friends. There they may enjoy a glimpse at the homes and private moments of these happy little creatures.

"Sam Squirrel's Visit," for instance, shows Granny's kitchen on a day when young Sammy Squirrel is paying her a visit. She pours him a cup of tea as he kneels on a three-legged stool at her table. The squirrel pair are surrounded by Granny's treasures; the dresser with its blue-and-white china, the shelves with her well-used pots, and of course her nuts and jam.

"The Woodmice Larder" lets us enter a snug little room where a mouse couple store the good things of summer. They've collected nuts, berries, fruits and flowers — and now it is time to save them for the cold days ahead. They fill the shelves and cupboards so that there will be plenty to eat until next year's warm weather arrives.

Kaiser's Master Artist Pays Tribute to Grimm Fairy Tales

While Bob Hersey has envisioned his own fairy tale world of woodland creatures, Kaiser's famed master artist, Wolfgang Gawantka, has chosen to capture the enduring magic of Classic Fairy Tales from the Brothers Grimm. In six porcelain figurines, realized in fine bisque Kaiser porcelain, Gawantka honors "Hansel and Gretel," "Frog King," "Puss'n Boots," "Cinderella," "Sleeping Beauty," and "Little Red Riding Hood."

Gawantka, who has been with Kaiser for his entire art career, studied for six years at the Meissen School of Art and one year at the School of Ceramics at Hermsdorf, Thuringia, to prepare for his career as a sculptor. He currently holds the position of Master Sculptor at the Kaiser Porcelain Factory in Staffelstein, Germany. His three-dimensional portraits of *The Grimm Brothers Fairy Tales* offer a heartfelt retrospective of some of the world's most beloved "once upon a time" stories.

Gawantka Creates a Dolphin Masterpiece

For years, Wolfgang Gawantka and the artists of Kaiser have been renowned for their sculptures inspired by dolphins. Gawantka's newest dolphin work, "Dolphin Mother and Baby," was one of the most popular pieces unveiled at a recent, international art buyers' show at Frankfurt, Germany.

The grace and motion of these beautiful mammals have been artistically captured in white bisque porcelain in a figurine measuring approximately 7¼"x11". Worldwide environmental awareness coupled with the basic maternal instinct are two important factors in the strong initial showing of Gawantka's "Dolphin Mother and Baby." The general appeal and quality of this lovely, open edition figurine will ensure its popularity for years to come.

A Lipizzaner Horse in Flawless Bisque

Another recent Gawantka masterpiece is "Argos," a work of art first unveiled in 1989 and offered in a worldwide limited edition of 3,000 pieces. The sculpture is inspired by the proud bearing of the Lipizzaner stallion, the renowned horse first bred at the Imperial Austrian stud farm near Trieste.

Gawantka has presented "Argos" in two versions. The first is crafted in pristine white bisque, while the second is hand-painted to reflect the natural color and markings of the famed Lipizzaners.

Robert May Honors Man's "Faithful Companions"

Like Robert Hersey of *Woodland Window* fame, the creator of Kaiser's *Faithful Companions* collector plate series is a native of Great Britain. A keen dog lover himself, Robert J. May has joined forces with Kaiser to present porcelain portraits of fourteen dog breeds representing some of the most popular pets and companions in the world.

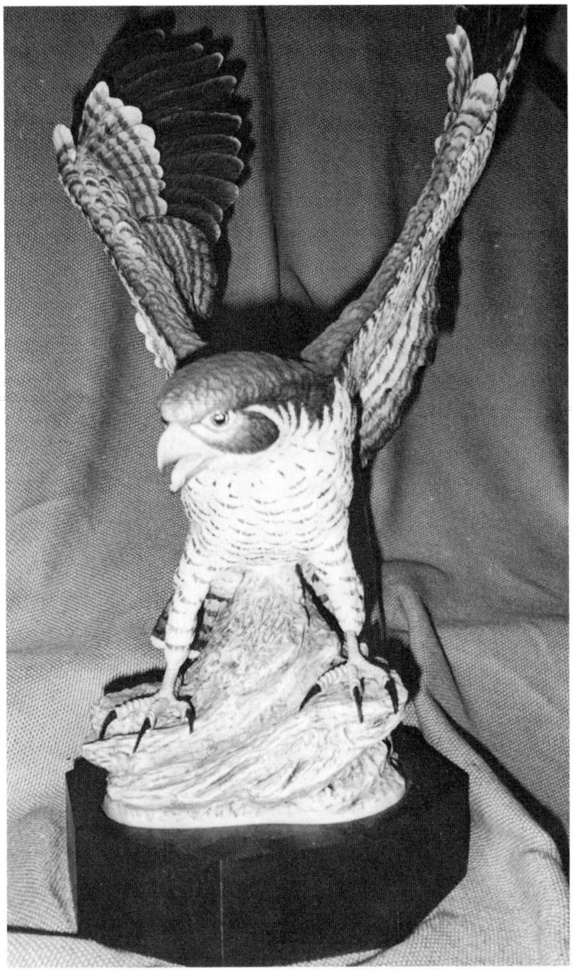

This Tandy "Peregrine Falcon" illustrates Kaiser's long-established mastery of bird and animal sculpture. Now considered a "classic," it was introduced in 1984 in a limited edition of 1500.

From the bold "German Shepherd" to the pampered "Poodle"...the adorable "Yorkshire Terrier" to the hard-working "Rough Collie," May's portraits capture the endearing qualities of each breed. Some collectors may choose to acquire only the plate or plates that represent their own favorite dog breeds, while others will make a display of any number of these *Faithful Companions*, paying tribute to "Man's Best Friend."

Feline Enthusiasts Will Enjoy "American Cats"

Kaiser called on an American art master, Gerald Williams, to create its new series of porcelain plates featuring *American Cats*. The collection of four plates honors Siamese, Persian, and two American short hair breeds. An upcoming group-

One of the most dramatic new additions to the Kaiser line is Wolfgang Gawantka's "Dolphin and Baby," an open edition in pristine white bisque porcelain.

Kaiser now proudly represents the "Dear" sculptures of Italy as this firm's exclusive North American agents. "Lady and Wolfhound" shows off the new black and white finish from "Dear."

ing by Williams, called *International Cats*, will offer portraits of the British, Birmans, Turkish Van and Maine Coon breeds.

Gerald Williams became intrigued with the idea of painting cats when he created an oil painting of his daughter's two Russian Blue cats for her birthday. He researched the origins of various cat breeds and discovered the enchanting allure of each cat — that special something to portray with new insight in each of his portraits for the porcelain medium.

Kaiser Now Offers Italian "Dear" Sculptures in North America

In addition to its own extensive offerings in sculptures, figurines and collector plates, Kaiser is proud to announce its status as the exclusive North American representatives for the "Dear" sculptured articles of Italy.

The Dear studio, located in Siena, Italy, has long been the home of famous artists like Auro Belcari, Marcello Salvestrini and Ermanno Farina. Through Dear, these masters produce works of art reflecting realism, richness of detail, and naturalness of movement and color.

The first "Dear" sculpture introduced through Kaiser is entitled "The Carriage" — a creation of the Italian master artist Auro Belcari. In fine porcelain, this highly complex work portrays an elegant, 19th-century lady embarking on a leisurely ride in her small and finely decorated carriage. Every detail of her costume has been beautifully rendered, from the lace on her parasol to the porcelain feathers adorning her fashionable hat.

The carriage master wears a handsome top hat and carries a buggy whip. The horse has been masterfully crafted as well, and painted with care to enhance his white markings on a coat of rich brown. With "The Carriage" as a stunning debut, Kaiser looks forward to presenting new additions to the Dear line as they are introduced.

The Kaiser Tradition of Exclusivity and Quality

Today, Kaiser enjoys a worldwide reputation for exquisite lines of fine collector pieces, magnificent figurines in limited editions, enchanting gift items and elegant dinnerware.

Kaiser porcelains have been sought after by connoisseurs since the days of August Alboth before the turn of the twentieth century. Experienced collectors know that items bearing the Kaiser name are not only objects of great beauty, but also a worthwhile art investment for the future.

The Lance Corporation

New England Studios of Chilmark, Hudson and Sebastian Create Fine Art Sculptures on Popular American Themes

From its base in picturesque Hudson, Massachusetts, The Lance Corporation offers three renowned lines of fine art sculpture — each with its own personality and collectors' following. Some pieces are crafted in polished metal...others are hand-painted over a metal base...while still others are hand-painted over cast porcelain. Yet all the works produced by Chilmark, Hudson and Sebastian are unified by their adherence to the highest quality standards in all stages of production...and by their exceptional detail.

Until the American Bicentennial celebration began in the mid-1970s, Lance was known mainly as a caster of specialty items for high-tech industries. But within a matter of a few years, the firm offered a memorable range of Bicentennial commemoratives and forged associations with some of the finest sculptors of our time — including Don Polland and the late Prescott W. Baston.

Chilmark Captures America's Legacy in Three Dimensions

When the renowned Western sculptor Don Polland brought his "Cheyenne" model to Lance for pewter casting in 1974, the artist and studio began a fruitful association that continues to this day. The most recent collaboration between Polland and Chilmark has resulted in the introduction of two striking Western masterpieces.

Lance's Sebastian Miniatures span many different subjects, as well as avenues of distribution. Shown here are an adaptation of the Yankee Clipper, a private label miniature done for the Grand Lodge F & AM of Michigan; "The Leprechaun," second in the Holiday Memories *series available only to members of the Sebastian Miniatures Collectors Society, and two pieces for the open retail line — "The Checkers Players" from the* Sunday Afternoon in the Park *grouping and "Justice" from the* Professionals *series.*

Cast in metal and beautifully hand-painted, the Shoshone warrior and Northern Plains chief sculptures must be seen in color to be fully appreciated. Polland worked with Chilmark's patina colorist, Isaura Dalinda Parrish, to ensure that the "Eagle Dancer" and the "Running Wolf" would capture these historic subjects with drama and accuracy.

Ms. Parrish also works with a young and gifted sculptress named Anne McGrory to create three-dimensional images from the famed paintings of Frederic Remington. Called *OffCanvas*™, these sculptures offer Remington's admirers the chance to enjoy some of his 2,400 two-dimensional paintings and illustrations of the American West in a three-dimensional form.

Each figure and horse is modeled carefully in three dimensions, then colored with Chilmark's exclusive deNatura® coloring process deNatura®, with its authentic accents, allows the metal to "come through" the color, preserving Remington's scene in both form and appearance.

When the finished sculpture is placed in front of a reproduction of the painting, there is a feeling of the painting coming to life, and the figure, now fully formed, springs out of the flat background. A warrior attacks, Indians send smoke signals, and cowboys ride hell-for-leather with breathtaking vitality.

Chilmark Captures Turning Points from The Civil War and World War II

Recent issues from Chilmark will be of special interest to military history buffs as well as collectors of sculpture. "Quantrill's Raiders" by sculptor Francis Barnum shows the team of William Clarke Quantrill, Frank James (brother of Jesse James) and Cole Younger joining forces as the loosely attached guerilla band of the Confederate Army in the disastrous raid at Lawrence, Kansas in 1863. The James and Younger brothers achieved legendary fame years later as the western saga's most famous bank robbers.

The sixth sculpture in Hudson Pewter's Generations of Mickey *series, "The Band Concert" pays tribute to Mickey's First Color Cartoon (1935). The pewter version is a limited edition of 2,000 and with a low edition limit of 500, the elegantly hand-painted version will quickly become a prized Disney collectible.*

The colorful, powerful and fearsome "Yellow Boy" is part of Don Polland's Warrior *series for Chilmark.*

Barnum's sculpture reflects his painstaking research. With guns blazing and horses rearing back, "Quantrill's Raiders" make their appearance as one of the latest in Barnum's collection of Civil War sculptures. This remarkable Chilmark grouping portrays the trials and triumphs of the War Between the States through its creator's remarkable gift for detailed sculpture.

A series of striking sculptures entitled *Days of Anger* premieres Chilmark's World War II commemorative collection marking the Fiftieth Anniversary of America's participation in the war: December 7, 1941 to August 14, 1945. This landmark collection combines the work of three top artists. William T. Wilson created the weapons models, David LaRocca sculpted the four scenes, and Richard Hazen, Chilmark's master tooling engineer, broke down these complex originals into castable parts.

Hudson Wins Top Honors from Disney

While Lance's Chilmark line concentrates on historical and Western sculptural art, the Hudson brand enjoys widespread renown for its whimsical and warmhearted works in fine metal. Hudson has enjoyed an association with Disney that dates back to 1974 — a long and happy association that culminated in a very special award for Hudson in 1990.

A limited-edition Hudson set entitled *Sorcerer's Apprentice Collectors Series* won Disney Licensing's "Best New Product of the Year" award — the top prize from Disney and an honor that no company in this category had ever earned before.

Hudson's Disney line continues to earn praise and collector enthusiasm with appealing pieces like the gold and pewter editions of "Hollywood Mickey," the wonderful *Generations of Mickey* sculptures, and works inspired by the famous mouse's many Disney pals. Pewter pieces in a range of sizes portray the world's most beloved mouse in roles from his 133 movies and cartoons.

A Mickey Mouse *Christmas Village*, *Barnyard Symphony* and *Stairway to the Stars* round out a Hudson/Disney collection that is sure to please all of Mickey's multi-generational fans.

Hudson's The Villagers *and* Fantasy *Figures*

While there are many village scenes available in today's collectibles market, Hudson's works are special because of the crisp detail that hand-painted fine pewter allows. *The Villagers*™ offer up a wide variety of buildings, townspeople and accessories that let collectors create an ideal "small town U.S.A." from days gone by. Each of the pewter pieces is enhanced by bright, hand-painted touches that make the shimmering metal seem all the more beautiful.

Villagers pieces celebrate the joys of hometown

Christmas, complete with Santa's arrival...last-minute shopping at the bakery and toy shop...a visit to church...bringing home the Christmas tree...and much more. *The Villagers* offers Hudson collectors the opportunity to build a fine art collection in pewter that tells a happy story and provides year-round enjoyment in home display.

While *The Villagers* line stays firmly rooted in the reality of small-town America, Hudson's *Fantasy* series offers up a wild and wonderful world of make-believe. Wizards, dragons, castles, and a host of unique creatures inhabit this world in the form of highly detailed pewter sculptures. Hudson *Fantasy* designs showcase the talents of Dennis Liberty, one of the most gifted sculptors of fantasy pieces in today's art world.

Liberty's *The Book of Zorn*™ collection traces the legend of Zorn, through sculpture. Genuine rubies, emeralds and sapphires adorn the limited sculptures, as well as quartz and Austrian cut crystals. A series of Liberty *Wizards*, as well as whimsical dragons, handsome castles, sorcerers and warriors round out this fantastic collection.

Christmas and Main Street Themes Charm Sebastian Collectors

Prescott W. Baston began creating his delightful Sebastian Miniatures in 1938, and he first joined forces with Lance in 1969. Since then the names of Lance and Sebastian have become synonymous with quality in hand-painted, miniature figurines. Today, the late Prescott Baston's son Woody continues his father's legacy as the featured artist for the Lance Sebastian line.

"Tickling a Dragon's Fancy" is typical of Dennis Liberty's work for Hudson Pewter's Fantasy *line. The highly detailed composition displays Liberty's attention to detail and his subtle humor.*

Among the most beloved Sebastian pieces today are those on Christmas themes such as Woody Baston's "Santa at His Workbench." Here, Santa shows off his handiwork as he presents a newly finished nutcracker that will soon be on its way to some lucky boy or girl. Another popular piece is "December 26," which shows Santa resting his feet and enjoying a refreshing beverage as he dozes in his favorite easy chair.

Main Street U.S.A. is a series of pieces inspired by small-town America. Drawing on inspiration from his father's most cherished works, Woody has created recent introductions including "Soda Fountain," "Baker's Dozen," "Butcher," "Barber," and "Florist."

On a similar theme, Baston's *Sunday Afternoon at the Park* figures capture the gentle joys of leisure in a simpler time and place: bicycling, baseball, and much more.

Sebastian Collectors Seek "Members Only" Pieces

Since 1980, admirers of the works of Prescott and Woody Baston have banded together as members of the Sebastian Miniature Collectors Society. One of the finest membership benefits of this group is the opportunity to acquire "members only" pieces, which are announced through the group's "Collectors Society News." Since these pieces are available only to an exclusive group of collectors — for a limited period of time — they are among the most likely candidates for price appreciation when their editions close.

With the historic significance of Chilmark Gallery works...the whimsical charm of pieces from Hudson...and the all-American tradition of Sebastian...Lance continues to reign as one of America's most versatile producers in the world of three-dimensional art. While the media and decoration processes may vary, all Lance pieces have two important concepts in common: devotion to the utmost quality, and exceptional detail in fine art sculpture.

Lawtons
Exquisite Limited Edition Dolls That Tell a Story as Time Goes By...

For Wendy Lawton, every beloved childhood memory seems highlighted by dolls. Looking back on her youth in San Francisco, this gifted doll sculptor and costumer can't ever recall a time when dolls were not an important part of her life.

"My very first dolls were a pair of two and one-half inch, hard plastic, Renwal joined babies (purchased at Woolworths for five cents each), carefully sewn into a twin bunting made of soft cotton flannel," Ms. Lawton recalls fondly. "My mother understood the importance of having a doll scaled to fit in a tiny pocket or a child-sized hand. I can still remember the comforting feel of the soft flannel bunting as I'd suck my thumb while holding the babies in the other four fingers. Those battered little babies are still a treasured part of my doll collection to this day."

Not long ago, Ms. Lawton went through her family photo album to see if she could find photographs of some of her first dolls. Not surprisingly, she found it difficult to locate a photo of herself *without* a doll in her arms, or close at hand.

"My younger sister, Linda, and I played dolls hour after hour for years, from Tiny Tears through Barbie," Ms. Lawton smiles. "We sewed for them, cooked for them and curled and styled their hair. We even took our dolls along in strollers when we went shopping downtown. We were blessed with a magical childhood, rich with make-believe and "let's pretend." My parents believed in the importance of creative play.

"We were provided with the tools of childhood — which for me were dolls — and plenty of time in which to learn to exercise our imaginations. Who would have guessed that all those years of play were actually job training for me!"

Dolls and Beloved Books and Stories Inspire Wendy Lawton's Art

While Wendy Lawton enjoyed work as a graphic artist, kindergarten teacher and daycare administrator after completing her education at San Jose State University, she found her true vocation after the birth of her first child, Rebecca. In the early years of her marriage to her husband, Keith, Ms. Lawton spent lots of time experimenting with doll making. She made many cloth dolls and even experimented with bread dough and plaster as dollmaking media.

Soon after the arrival of Rebecca, the artist began to search out someone who could teach her porcelain dollmaking. "I had a profound desire to somehow capture Rebecca at that moment in time," Ms. Lawton recalls. She found a wonderful teacher who had been making and repairing dolls for nearly fifty years. "She taught me doll making from the first clay sculpture all the way through moldmaking to the final china paint. I even learned how to make a hand wefted wig!" Ms. Lawton recalls.

Wendy Lawton began to work in porcelain by doing commissioned portrait dolls. Then a few copies of these portraits were sold in local California shops. From that point on, it seems there were never quite enough Lawtons Dolls to go around!

Today Rebecca Lawton is a lovely teenager, and the Lawtons have a handsome young son, Patrick, as well. Keith and Wendy Lawton, along with partners Jim and Linda Smith, are kept busy by the ever-growing demands of Lawtons — now a booming doll making business in Turlock, California. And while Lawtons has won fame and numerous awards for beautiful dolls on many subjects, the studio is best known for Wendy Lawton's porcelain characters inspired by the beloved heroes and heroines of favorite children's storybooks.

The Loving Creation of a Lawtons Doll

Collectors and dealers praise Lawtons for the uniqueness of its dolls and their costumes — especially the fact that Ms. Lawton sculpts a new head for each and every new edition. Many companies use the same doll sculpture over and over, simply re-dressing the doll. All Lawtons dolls are entirely made in the U.S.A., in the firm's own California workshops. Wendy Lawton guides each step of the production process personally.

Each edition of Lawtons dolls is strictly limited, with most offered in editions of 250, 350, or 500 dolls. The one exception is the firm's licensed doll, "Marcella." This unique work of art features a mini-

As eagerly anticipated as the first spring crocus, "Spring Blossom," is the final issue of Lawton's first collection of dolls celebrating the four seasons.

Carrying her tray of threads and notions and dressed in the traditional plain garb of her people, little Hannah is on her way to a "Frolic"—an Amish working party.

ature Raggedy Ann in the arms of a doll who looks just like the real "Marcella" whose father, Johnny Gruelle, created Raggedy Ann at the turn-of-the-century.

Much thought and research goes into the "theming" of each doll. As Louise Fecher of *Dolls* magazine said, "With guides like Heidi, Hans Brinker and Laura Ingalls, (Ms. Lawton) travels through the pages of children's classic literature." Lawtons dolls have been inspired by literary characters, holidays, seasons, poetry, and memorable childhood events.

Lawtons Step-by-Step Creative Process

Once Wendy Lawton has completed her research for a particular doll, she creates a prototype — a process that can consume an incredible amount of time. That first sculpt is subjected to three different molding stages, with refinements in between each stage. At the same time, initial sketches for costuming give way to fabric selection, pattern drafting and sample garment creation. Meanwhile, wigs are selected and props are designed or sourced. These initial stages require anywhere between three weeks and three months — sometimes longer.

Then the edition of dolls is created, one by one, following the same process for each doll in the edition. The costume is cut and sewed, props or hats are made, greenware is poured, and body parts are soft-fired and then detailed. Next, the body parts are high-fired and the head is detailed, with the eye openings cut and beveled before the head is high-fired.

Once all six porcelain parts are complete, they are sanded before the cheeks are painted and fired. Painting and shading, and highlighting the lips come next, before firing once again. Then the eyelashes and eyebrows are painted on before a final firing.

To put the doll's parts together, Lawtons craftspeople set hooks in the body parts, then string the doll together. The doll's eyes are set and cleaned, and she is dressed in all her finery. Finally, each doll is numbered and registered, her pate is affixed, her wig is added and styled, and she is carefully boxed for shipment.

Not counting the processes involved in making the costume, props, wigs and accessories, there are fifty-six different hand operations required to make a single Lawtons doll. Because of Lawtons strict quality control requirements, more than half of all dolls are rejected at one step or another before they win the right to represent the studio in the marketplace. Each doll requires no less than twenty to twenty-five hours of individual attention, including firing time and up to ten hours of hand labor on creation and costuming.

Highlights of the Lawtons Doll Line

Lawtons collectors eagerly await new introductions in several of the studio's popular doll lines including *Childhood Classics*, *Christmas Collection*, *Special Occasions Collection*, *Cherished Customs*, and *Seasons Collection*. Among the *Childhood Classics* are beautiful, well-appointed dolls inspired by "Rebecca of Sunnybrook Farm," the "Poor Little Match Girl," and the "Little Princess." *Christmas Collection* dolls are issued annually on holiday themes, including "Christmas Joy," "Noel," and "Christmas Angel."

Special Occasions highlighted to date by Lawtons include losing one's first tooth and getting a shiny new Indian head penny, and "First Day of School," in which a sweet little redhead prepares for kindergarten. *Cherished Customs* offers an international panorama of festivals and special days, including "Girl's Day" in Japan, "The Blessing" in Mexico, "High Tea" in England, and "Midsommar" in Sweden. Each of the four seasons will have its own lovely Lawtons doll, including "Summer Rose" and "Crystal Winter." New dolls are added regularly to the Lawtons line, and open editions close, often leading to market appreciation within just a few months' time.

Lawtons Collector's Guild Members May Acquire "Members-Only" Dolls

Each year, members of the Lawtons Collector's Guild are afforded a special, no-obligation opportunity to purchase an exclusive doll that Wendy Lawton will design for Guild members only. This is just one of the several benefits of Guild membership, which requires a $15.00 initial fee and a yearly renewal at just $5.00 annually.

Members of the Guild receive a membership card, Lawtons logo pin in delicate cloisonne enamel, a subscription to Lawtons Collector's Guild Quarterly newsletter, a vinyl-covered three-ring binder to protect copies of the Quarterly, and a set of postcards featuring the current collections of Lawtons dolls. For more information about Guild membership, contact Lawtons Collector's Guild at P.O. Box 969, Turlock, California 95381.

Freddie and Flossie, the younger set of twins from the classic, "The Bobbsey Twins," are charming in their crisp blue and while pique outfits. The dolls, sold as a set only, are limited to an edition of 350 sets.

As joyful and festive as the season itself, "Yuletide Carole" is the fourth doll in the Annual Christmas Collection *from Lawtons.*

Legends

A Tradition of Fine Art Sculpture in Mixed Media™...

"Zev Beckerman is a guy who knows how to take a good idea and run with it. If you start with that and add an exceptional group of artists and a demand for quality work, you've got the beginning of a legend."

Mario Pancino, owner of Collector's World in Montrose, California, spoke these prophetic words about the fast-rising California art studio of Legends. In a *Collector Editions* article entitled "Creating a Legend," Pancino continued, "As far as I'm concerned, this company really has no competition in the marketplace."

Since its founding in 1986, Legends has enjoyed what may seem an "overnight success" with its exquisite sculptures in bronze, pewter and other fine metals. Yet the Beckermans' firm rests on a solid foundation of experience: its parent company, Starlite Originals, Inc., founded by Bob Beckerman has been producing sculptures for Disney, American Express, Franklin Mint and other discerning clients since 1972.

"Angakchina" and "Ahote" represent two of the stunning American Indian art sculptures in Christopher Pardell's The Kachina Dancers Collection *for Legends. Each piece is limited to an edition of 2,500, and each is crafted in Legends' striking Mixed Media™ which combines bronze, fine pewter, and 24K gold vermeil (and cultured turquoise).*

Four Brothers Express Their Artistic Vision

Before they founded Legends, Zev Beckerman and his three brothers presided over a thriving business producing sculptures for others. But their talents extended far beyond mere reproduction: the Beckermans longed to express their own ideas in three dimensions. That is how Legends evolved. The next step was to forge relationships with some of today's most outstanding sculptors — and to convince them to work exclusively for Legends.

Today the Legends "family" of artists includes: Christopher Pardell, who captures the pride and dignity of the American Indian; Kitty Cantrell, who specializes in three dimensional wildlife portraits; Larry Steorts, whose miniature Victorian homes capture the nostalgic charm of an era; and Dan Medina, a fine nautical sculptor who also serves as Legends' in-house art director.

The Legends line ranges from small collectibles to large gallery bronzes — but each piece is priced with care to remain accessible to "middle America." Indeed, even a major work of art like Christopher Pardell's 11" "Songs of Glory," from the *Legendary West Premier Edition* Collection, originally sold for less than $1000. And Kitty Cantrell's 8" "Forest Spirit," from the *Endangered Wildlife* Collection, allows collectors to own a distinctive Mixed Media™ masterwork for less than $300.

The Uniqueness and Richness of Mixed Media Sculpture

All of Legends' works in bronze and pewter have attracted collector attention for their bold artistry, attention to detail, and quality in every aspect of production and packaging. Yet collectors and dealers reserve their highest praise for the Legends Mixed Media sculptures: works of art that combine bronze and pewter and brass vermeil with the striking addition of 24-karat gold vermeil.

Zev Beckerman says that while some other firms may decorate pewter pieces with bronze or gold-colored paints, Legends is the only firm making this combination "for real." Indeed, Mixed Media™ is the inventive creation of Legends — a new art medium developed to transcend the traditional limitations of the pewter art form by including the beauty of natural color.

Each component part of the Mixed Media sculptures is exceptional in its own right — and indeed, many Legends pieces are crafted using just one of these fine substances. Legends Bronze is fine metal finished in genuine bronze, and highlighted to enhance the original bronze patina. Legends Fine Pewter contains semi-precious tin and is considered to be one of the handsomest and most malleable pewters available. Legends 24-Karat Gold Vermeil is a fine metal finished with the bright beauty of pure 24-karat gold.

The American Indian Art of Chris Pardell

The sculptures of Chris Pardell first brought Legends to national prominence. Mario Pancino calls Pardell "The best Western artist now working. His great plus is that he can take an actual character and capture the essence of the person. His work just doesn't look like anyone else's. Pardell does his homework. And he pays great attention to detail."

Chris Pardell honed his considerable skills in a five-year apprenticeship with Italian masters Gino Bonvi, Aldo Gregory and Vertitio Bonofazi. A free-lance sculptor before he joined Legends, Pardell has enjoyed remarkable success with his historic Native American works of art. His "Red Cloud's Coup" sculpture was the first Legends piece to sell out — and it more than doubled in value quite promptly.

Other sell-outs and secondary market price rises have followed in quick succession, leading collectors to anticipate each new Pardell introduction with even more enthusiasm. In addition to his Indian works, the prolific Pardell has paid tribute to a wide range of outdoors and wildlife subjects for Legends.

Kitty Cantrell's Personal Commitment to Wildlife

Through award-winning artist, Kitty Cantrell's, faithful attitude, hard work and escalating talent, she continues to grace the world with her commitment to wildlife and the environment. The first four Mixed Media™ releases of Cantrell's *Endangered Wildlife Collection* — "Unbounded," "Sentinel," "Outpost," and "Aguila Libre" — gloriously embodied the majesty of the American Bald Eagle. Shortly thereafter, collectors were mesmerized by her captivating busts of the Timber Wolf, "Forest Spirit" and the African Cheetah, "Savannah Prince." Admiring collectors anxiously anticipate each new release of this unique collection.

Her exquisite sense of detail and brilliant perception of balance, tension and form enable her to embody the true beauty of the endangered wildlife. Cantrell strives to draw attention to people's perception of what wildlife is for. "Animals should not have to justify their existence. They should be allowed to be, simply because they are."

Larry Steorts Captures America's Victorian Era

As an avid admirer of Victorian architecture and a master of miniature sculpture, Larry Steorts was the obvious choice to create Legends' *The Victorian Homes* Collection. Beautifully crafted in Legends' stunning Mixed Media, the six homes offer a remarkable array of Victorian buildings.

Steorts' Queen Anne, and Stick houses feature the peaked towers, lacy gables, pointed finials, hooded windows, and columned doorways that set Victorian architecture apart.

Larry Steorts loves paying tribute to this era in American design, for he says, "To me, modern architecture is cold, sterile and unfriendly... nothing more than variations on a rectangle. I love the Victorian details which, as scale is reduced, increasingly challenges my vision as an artist and my skills as a craftsman."

Larry also exhibits his appreciation for some of the coastline's most historic forms of architecture in his enchanting *Lighthouse Collection*. With his first four Mixed Media™ releases, "Old Point

In addition to his charming Victorian houses, Larry Steorts also has introduced The Lighthouse Collection *for Legends. The first two releases, shown here, are "North Head" and "Old Point Loma." Limited to editions of 950 each, these exquisitely detailed lighthouse sculptures are crafted in Mixed Media™.*

Loma," "North Head," "Cape Hatteras," and "Boston Light," he has managed to capture the legendary beauty of these famous landmarks. (These sculptures are also handsomely accented with full lead crystal in each tower.)

The Process of Creation for Legends Art Masterworks

The step-by-step creative process for each Legends sculpture helps explain why collectors and dealers hold these works of art in such high regard. In present-day Southern California, the Beckermans' artisans take the kind of care one might expect to see invested in a Renaissance masterwork.

First, the sculptor's original serves as the basis for an epoxy figure. Then the sculptor spends considerable time "fine-tuning" the epoxy — a medium that allows for what Beckerman calls "terrific detail." Next, the finished epoxy piece is separated into an average of 26 component parts for moldmaking. Multiple molds also enhance the exquisite detail that characterizes Legends' sculptures.

When the molds are complete, molten metal is poured into each individual mold under great pressure. After the cast metal comes out of the mold, craftspeople use tiny steel picks — similar to dental instruments — to enhance any details that may have been lost in the molding process.

Next, the individual pieces are welded together and finished so that no weld marks are ever noticeable. The result is a piece that combines "old world" craftsmanship with the artistry of some of today's most gifted contemporary sculptors.

The Legends Collectors Society

In response to the requests of its many loyal collectors, Legends has introduced an exclusive membership program called the Legends Collectors Society. Society members enjoy the opportunity to acquire new sculptures before their open-market release, help with secondary market activities, a subscription to the quarterly publication "The Legends Collector," and other benefits.

Each individual who purchases a Legends sculpture is invited to join the Society through his or her dealer. Legends dealers also facilitate the acquisition of a special Legends Certificate of Ownership for each collector purchase. This Cer-

The wildlife artistry of Kitty Cantrell gains superb expression in "Forest Spirit," an edition limited to 950 pieces and cast in Legends' Mixed Media™.

tificate highlights the collector's name, the sculpture's title, edition number and size, the Chief Registrar's signature, the date, and the Legends gold craftsmanship seal.

The Legends Buy and Sell Program

Because Legends realizes that there is a significant need to bring together collectors who wish to buy or sell Legends sculptures on the secondary market, the firm has devised a simple, step-by-step program that is facilitated through the collector's local Legends dealer.

To ensure proper certification, an official "Transfer of Ownership" policy allows a sculpture's new owner to acquire a new, personalized Certificate of Ownership to document the secondary market transaction.

In the few short years since Legends began its tradition of fine art sculpture, this California-based firm has earned a strong reputation for integrity, sculptural excellence, and innovation. Considering these factors — and the studio's commitment to old-world craftsmanship in fine metal, the "Legends tradition" stands to grow in stature and renown for many years to come.

Lenox Collections

"The Lenox Difference" Makes Lenox Collections Dolls Special

Lenox Collections introduces an important new line of collector dolls, each set apart by certain very special characteristics. The "Lenox Difference" makes Lenox Collections dolls especially appealing to contemporary collectors.

The "difference" begins with a focus on the future and an appreciation of the past. Each Lenox doll is created with heirloom quality, emotional impact, and nostalgic appeal in mind. The goal of Lenox is to strive for incredible realism in each doll sculpture: not only in pose and expression, but also in the doll's situation and her wonderfully detailed costuming.

The porcelain parts for every Lenox doll are individually sculpted and tailored for that doll alone — no common parts ever are used. The highest quality fabrics are selected for each doll's costume, and clothing is designed with intricate details before being finished by a skilled dressmaker.

To document each doll for the future, the Lenox logo/backstamp is incised into the back of the neck on each doll. A hardwood doll display is shipped with every "standing" doll, and other display devices are included with non-standing dolls. Examples include an elegant pillow with the "Christening" doll, and a colorful quilt with "Tea for Teddy."

Many Lenox dolls are complemented by a piece of Lenox china jewelry in the form of a pin/brooch, a bracelet, or a locket. The "Bride" and "Christening" dolls each have a Lenox brooch as part of their costumes.

Most Lenox Collections dolls are part of themed groupings which include *The Victorian Doll Collection*, *Children of the World*, *Ellis Island Dolls*, and new series inspired by children and toys, brothers and sisters, and "The Nutcracker" ballet.

Lovely Dolls in Authentic Victorian Costumes

"The Lenox Victorian Bride" made a delightful debut as the first introduction for *The Victorian Doll Collection*. She's the picture of pure romance in hand-tailored taffeta, velvet, tulle, satin and lace — and her costume is rich with hand beading and accents of 24K gold. Radiantly beautiful, this lovely bride's features have been painted by hand to capture her blush of joy. Her upswept hair is arranged by hand, and she carries a hand-made bouquet of silken roses.

The next doll in this series continues the Victorian family theme with "The Lenox Victorian Christening Doll." This sweet, sleeping baby doll wears a flowing satin christening gown of satin, accented with lace, satin bows and seed pearls. A hand-tucked satin pillow and a delicate, heart-shaped pendant of fine Lenox china are the perfect accessories for this adorable baby. Her sculpted porcelain face is delicately hand-painted to reveal softly rounded, rosy cheeks, a rosebud mouth, and a truly angelic expression.

This stunning turn-of-the-century bride doll premieres Lenox Collections' Victorian Doll Collection.

Children Of The World *Celebrate Native Folk Costumes and Events*

To pay tribute to the world's many cultures, pageants and holidays, Lenox presents these colorful events through the eyes of children. Each *Children of the World* doll carries a special accessory to illustrate the event he or she represents, beginning with "Hannah, The Little Dutch Maiden," and "Heather, The Little Highlander."

"Hannah" is bright and fresh as springtime...as delicate and lovely as the tulips she carries. From her crisp white cap to her shoes of hand-carved wood, "Hannah" is a collector doll as superbly detailed as she is beautiful. Her festive costume and her braided hair represent the same classic styles worn by little Dutch maidens for many centuries past. Her pale blue cotton frock boasts a pretty provincial design created for "Hannah" alone. And her dainty apron is gathered with a band of delicate embroidery in the favorite Dutch tulip motif.

"Heather" is authentically costumed in a Scottish ensemble of velvet, lace, and custom-loomed tartan. One look and her admirers can almost hear the bagpipes ring! "Heather" holds her hand-painted porcelain Scottie dog and awaits her turn to dance in her real leather Highland pumps. The tartan she wears has been specially woven in perfect scale to her size, and the ten buttons of her black vest are traditional. A crisp white blouse and feather-trimmed tam complete her pretty costume.

Also available from the *Children of the World* collection are an adorable African child in an authentic and boldly patterned ceremonial dance costume, and a striking Japanese girl in a lavish silken Kimono. Lenox plans many more additions to this wonderful series — providing collectors with a "trip around the world" through exquisite doll craftsmanship.

Elizabeth Presents Her Gift for a Victorian Christmas

As a magnificent single issue, Lenox has captured all the charm and delight of a Victorian Christmas in a magnificent collector doll entitled "Elizabeth — Her Christmas Gift." Her green eyes shining with anticipation, young Elizabeth is all dressed up for a Christmas Eve visit to someone special. She holds a gift that she has wrapped with loving care — and she wears a costume that is completely hand-tailored just for her.

From her holly-bedecked bonnet of rich Christmas green to the hem of her sumptuous, satin-lined velvet cape, "Elizabeth's" costume is extraordinary! Her taffeta dress shows the Victorian love of rich fabric and detail, for it is trimmed in lace, velvet, and golden-threaded plaid. And her beautifully wrapped gift has a real velvet bow. What's more, the delicately sculptured features of "Elizabeth" are painted by hand with tiny brushstrokes to capture the graceful arch of her brows,

Continuing the popular Victorian theme, Lenox presents this lovely "Christening" doll dressed in an elegant satin gown accented with lace, satin bows and seed pearls.

the blush of excitement on her cheeks, and the happy smile on her lips.

"Megan" and "Tea for Teddy" Highlight New Collections

To celebrate the centennial of Ellis Island, Lenox Collections plans a commemorative series in tribute to this monument that reminds us all of America's immigrant heritage. Children of five major nationalities which passed through Ellis Island, New York will be represented in original porcelain sculptors from the acclaimed doll artist, Patricia Thompson. The collection has been developed in association with the Statue of Liberty/Ellis Island Commission and a portion of the proceeds will be donated to the Ellis Island Foundation.

First in the collection is "Megan — An Irish Lass," whose features and costume are typical of the early 1890s. With her curly red hair and smiling green eyes, "Megan" is the picture of an Irish colleen. Her costume befits a child who has just completed a very long journey: a faded corduroy coat and hat with missing button, worn boots, and a bundle of clothes to start her new life.

Another new Lenox Collections doll grouping focuses on children and toys, with each doll to feature a child at play, accompanied by a favorite toy accouterment. The first issue is entitled "Tea for Teddy," and it captures a little girl and her teddy bear, sitting on a quilt to enjoy an afternoon cup of tea. The blonde-haired child wears a pastel blue romper and white cotton blouse with an eyelet collar, while her plush friend "Teddy" sports a striped sailor tee shirt and straw hat. A porcelain tea pot, cup, and saucer, all decorated with a delicate floral motif, make appropriate additions to this wonderful doll presentation.

Doll Pairs and "Nutcracker" Ballet Issues Complete the Lenox Collections

The special bond between siblings will provide several enchanting portraits of childhood in a new collection of Lenox doll pairs that begins with "The Skating Lesson." Designed by famed doll artist Alice Lester, the doll set includes a little sister and big sister on a roller skating outing. Little sister's face is aglow with excitement as she takes her first shaky roller-skate step, while big sister proudly helps and guides her along. Their costumes are hand-tailored, contemporary children's outfits, with big sister in a red corduroy skirt and yellow turtleneck, and little sister in a plaid cotton jumper.

"Clara" premieres a collection of Lenox dolls portraying favorite characters from "The Nutcracker" Ballet to commemorate this most popular of all the world's ballets on its 100th anniversary. In a flowing white nightgown of satin, tulle, and silken flowers, "Clara" poses ever so gracefully. She carries her precious Nutcracker, sculpted of fine bisque porcelain and meticulously hand-painted in bright colors.

The wonderful dolls already introduced by Lenox Collections represent an auspicious beginning. This year, doll collectors can look forward to ten new collections, plus subsequent issues to all collections already introduced. And all of these lovely dolls will exemplify "The Lenox Difference" of heirloom quality, nostalgic appeal, craftsmanship and uniquely appealing accessories.

With her tulips at hand, "Hannah — The Dutch Maiden" portrays the colorful cultural tradition of her native Holland.

Lilliput Lane

The Little Cottages that Dreams are Made of: David Tate and the Story of Lilliput Lane

If you have ever travelled to England, you know that the country has a mystic quality not found elsewhere in the world. The air is crisp and fresh. And then there are the people: imaginative, frank and proper, bursting with the pride of a culture that developed with wisdom and humor that's enviable in the world community.

All of England and Europe are represented in what has been called this decade's most welcome family of collectibles: *The Lilliput Lane Collection.* And unless you have just recently discovered figurine collecting, you are aware of the fact that Lilliput's original series of award-winning English cottages has expanded to include unique examples of period architecture from all parts of the globe: Scotland, Germany...even the United States.

An unlikely gathering of treasures to be prized by limited edition collectors? Not if you've seen the detail in Lilliput Lane's cottages. And certainly not if you've had a chance to discover the heart and soul of Lilliput Lane's founder, David J. Tate. His cottages are charming. His life story is the sort that gives us all a good set of goose bumps, for it tells of a man who would not stop chasing his life's dream...even when it meant risking all of his money, the security of a salaried position, and a major family move. All for the chance to preserve some of England's finest architectural heritage.

Meet David Tate: The Founder of Lilliput Lane

Success stories such as the Lilliput Lane tale rarely evolve without revealing a charismatic mastermind...someone whose dream to succeed knows no limits. You find such a beginning in the story of David J. Tate. His vision of Lilliput Lane actually took root during his childhood in post-war England. David was born in 1945 in the legendary Yorkshire district, the only son of a small, close-knit family. He was bright and curious, showing exceptional talent for drawing that earned an art scholarship at the tender age of ten.

David Tate's art career took a slight detour when he turned fifteen and left school to support his mother with a series of jobs, but his love of creating and his perseverance sustained him. Every job gave David knowledge and skills necessary for future dream-building. He was a salesman, gaining insight into people. He became an accomplished photographer, learning to record on film the beauty that is uniquely England. David moved from public relations through the ceramics industry and ultimately proved his determination and self-belief by becoming a senior executive in the fiberglass industry of England.

David Tate's eyes saw the colors and textures of the world. His heart waited for just the right moment, and in 1982, the thirty-seven year old (who claims he does not know the meaning of the word "impossible") gathered up his talents and experience and set out to start his own business. Adopting the name Lilliput Lane from the much beloved *Gulliver's Travels* he'd read and re-read as a child, David Tate and his wife embarked upon "the dream."

Moving to Penrith in the north of England, not far from David's birthplace and the Scottish border, the Tate family set up shop in an old farm

A babbling brook and dappled sunlight streaming into cut-glass chapel windows are two striking features of "Convent in the Woods." The magnificent sculpture from Lilliput Lane™ took "Best Collectible of Show" honors at the 16th annual South Bend International Plate and Collectibles Exposition in 1990.

house where the very first Lilliput Lane cottage was sculpted. It was here, in England's Lake District, that the dream took shape. And with that dream came rewards that even David could not have imagined.

From Seven Employees to One Thousand: David Tate's Enthusiastic Team Grows

Look behind the talent of a Renaissance man or woman, and one usually finds a complex individual with revolutionary ideas that surpass the work they have chosen. Look behind David Tate, and you will find not just a sculptor, but a student of human motivation...a man who understands that commitment to excellence sometimes includes an aptitude for innovation.

As a Lilliput Lane employee, for instance, you might be expected to laugh a lot on the job. It's one of the unwritten requirements for employment at Lilliput Lane, where hard work combined with having fun are key reasons for the firm's growth from about seven to nearly one thousand employees since 1982 (that's just about 100 new employees a year!).

When a project begins, David personally supervises the search for a unique cottage style that's representative of a region. His method for spotting unusual shapes and materials takes time. Months of study and hundreds of photographs may go into the production of a single cottage of particular vernacular styling (this refers to a distinctive style of building that's found only in one, small area of the country). Then it's time to breathe life into the study by rendering the building in three dimensions.

The sculpting process is a painstaking step. Any "reminders" of twentieth century living must be eliminated in order to make the cottage an authentic representation of its day. Gardens and foliage found in the region are added for warmth and detail, then the wax is meticulously carved and inspected until the Lilliput Lane team confers a collective "thumbs up." Only then is a silicone mold undertaken at great expense...sealing the design forever.

Casting a Lilliput Lane cottage begins a whole new phase of production. A material named "amorphite" is carefully mixed and poured into the delicate molds. Amorphite is a strong, hard substance, specially suited to the fine undercuts and minute details collectors prize. Once set, a sculpture is removed from its mold and "fettled." This process cleans the cottage and prepares it for dipping in a special sealant before the unpainted cottage is finally dried.

Then comes the painting! Over 500 painters bring their talents through the doors of Lilliput Lane studios each morning; no home workers are permitted by the company as this ensures extremely high finishing standards and supervision. Each cottage is painted with pride by a single "Lilliputian," and each takes their responsibility very seriously, for a painting position at the Lilliput studios is prized throughout the region.

During this process, over eight separate inspections take place during the crafting. It's a hallmark of David Tate's work ethic that will never change.

The Love Affair with Lilliput Cottages Leads to a Collectors Club

"Ash Nook." "Beacon Heights." "The Briary." "Buttercup Cottage." Gently sloping roofs with thatch so detailed, one must touch the cottage to see if it's real! That's the secret of Lilliput. Cottages. Stores. Churches. Pubs. Inns. Whole neighborhoods. Most are wrapped in Spring and Summer greenery, but a few are all dressed up for Winter in their icy cloaks of snow.

As of this writing, there are almost one hundred and fifty pieces in the current line. An equal number of pieces are retired and highly sought after on the secondary market! Nearly every style of building created during the medieval period is represented, and while the collector initially finds a detailed representation of a piece of yesterday, he also discovers the lore behind the architecture. A stickler for detail, David creates a feeling of authentic English history through his sculptures.

Booklets filled with everything from typical landscaping materials to roofing styles accompany the Lilliput Lane cottages. Poetry and facts are intertwined with fascinating details of how the people lived while occupying these quaint homes. We even learn what a meal might have cost in 1863 and how many pounds were collected in tolls at the opening of a new bridge that same year!

David Tate's thirst for data on Britain's unique housing periods was barely quenched, when he turned his camera to the north and west and began to depict the romantic stories behind Scottish and Irish architecture. Once more, a huge panorama of diverse styling confronted his inquiring mind.

In his first ventures beyond the British Isles, David discovered the world of German architecture and brought ten styles of houses to market. He followed with an American collection in 1989, inviting well-known plate artist and watercolorist Ray Day to create the *American Landmarks Collection* for a growing American market. What was once a company known only to the United Kingdom, Lilliput Lane now finds itself at home in the United States, Canada, Italy, Japan, New Zealand and twenty other countries around the world. Enthusiastic collectors from across the globe patiently hope that David will, some day, include the distinctive architectural styling of their homeland in his diverse mix of masterpieces. Until that time, Lilliput Lane collectors continue to speak a common language, but nowhere is it better understood than in the United States.

Several factors have gone into the widespread popularity of Lilliput Lane in America. Roger Fitness was hand-picked to head up the United States operation under the name Gift Link, Inc. in 1988. From its Columbia, Maryland headquarters, Gift Link, Inc. has made available to the American collecting public a wide range of Lilliput Lane product, excellent service and attention to detail, and a collectors' club that will probably go down in history as one of the fastest-growing organizations in the collecting world. Multinational in scope, the Lilliput Lane Collectors Club now boasts tens of thousands of members...and it's only a few years old.

Excellent benefits tell the Club story. In addition to a Members-Only cottage that's eagerly awaited by devoted collectors each year, Lilliput publishes a colorful, quarterly magazine packed full of information. Bold, cheery photographs flow across the pages, and readers are given glimpses of the history, tradition, and people in Lilliput's world. The publication is called *Gulliver's World*, and while the cottages are the "stars" of the articles, each story is steeped in gloriously rich folklore that gives members a wealth of enjoyment each time they pick up an issue.

But, a gift cottage and a subscription to *Gulliver's World* are just the beginning of a Lilliput Lane membership adventure. Exclusive cottages, not available to the general public, await a member's reservation. Conventions and retail open houses across the country are plentiful, and Lilliput collectors eagerly await personal invitations to these events. In sum, Lilliput Lane takes great pride in the club's growth and never misses an opportunity to thank members for their loyalty.

All Things Come to Those Who Believe

When David Tate left school at fifteen to help support his family, he might have envisioned employing 1000 people or seeing his art sold across the world; but he could hardly have imagined being among those on the 1988 Honors List compiled annually to salute British citizens making revolutionary contributions to England's prestige and economy. With great pride and humility, David found his name on that list. Soon after, he visited Buckingham Palace where he was invested as a M.B.E. (Member of the Order of the British Empire) by Queen Elizabeth II.

"We try to speak to our customers' desire for peace and tranquility in a difficult world," David Tate once said during an interview. "From the beginning, I cared about these tiny cottages, about the heritage they represented."

There followed a series of other awards, each of which is specially treasured by David. Twice named one of the United Kingdom's Five Top Companies (given by the Confederation of British Industry), David also accepted The Queen's Award for Export given to Lilliput Lane at a personal audience with former Prime Minister Margaret Thatcher.

Then came the American industry awards: South Bend's "Best Collectible of Show" for "Convent in the Woods" in 1990 and *Collector Editions* "Award of Excellence" presented to Lilliput Lane for "Periwinkle Cottage" that same year. This impressive combination of honors has been awarded in less than three years and attests to the stamina and fortitude of David Tate, M.B.E. and the talented staff working for Lilliput Lane.

The future? It's as limitless as the imagination. Lilliput Lane, headed up by the master sculptor, David Tate, is sure to lead us toward the new century with surprises and delights when we least expect them. That's what collectors love most about Lilliput's past, and what we most look forward to in the future.

Lladro Collectors Society

Lladro Marks its Collectors Society's Fifth Anniversary With Exclusive Works of Spanish Porcelain Art

When the famed Spanish porcelain firm of Lladro first announced plans for an international Collectors Society in 1985, few could have predicted its worldwide impact. Today, the Lladro Collectors Society looks back upon more than five successful years as a source of inspiration, information and enjoyment for Lladro aficionados in nations spanning the globe.

One of the most cherished membership benefits of the Lladro Collectors Society is the opportunity to acquire exclusive figurines which are introduced annually, and made available to Society members only. In 1985, the first of these charming works of art, "Little Pals," made its debut at an original price of $95.00.

At a recent Lladro Auction, "Little Pals" commanded $4000 in intense bidding. The next Members-Only figurine, "Little Traveler," brought as much as $1250 at the same fast-paced event. Indeed, each retiring Members-Only figurine has attracted strong secondary market trading as new Society members seek to complete their collections with previous years' issues.

Hugh Robinson, Director of the Lladro Collectors Society since its inception, looks back proudly on the Members-Only collection. "Each year we have seen a figurine introduced that combines artistry and individuality," he explains. "From the boyish rogues like 'Little Pals,' 'Little Traveler,' 'My Buddy,' and most recently, 'Can I Play?' to the girlishly sweet 'School Days,' 'Spring Bouquets,' and now 'Summer Stroll,' each has enchanted us with a personality all its own."

Yet for most Lladro collectors, the demonstrated investment potential of their beloved figurines plays only a minor part in their enjoyment. For upon the celebration of its Fifth Anniversary, the Lladro Collectors Society offers its members a remarkable array of opportunities and services.

A Superb Commemorative Marks a Lladro Anniversary

In a special message to Collectors Society members, Hugh Robinson stated that "Anniversaries are traditionally a time to reminisce contentedly and to proudly plan ahead. On the occasion of the Lladro Collectors Society's Fifth Anniversary, those ambitious plans included a special commemorative figurine created and offered to thank Society members for their active involvement.

"Picture Perfect" defines the classic Lladro style in every precious detail. This graceful figurine portrays a lovely young lady, resting under a parasol as she plays with her perky puppy — a special companion and confidante. The little canine's upturned nose and devoted expression remind us of the origin of the term "puppy love."

The young girl's sweet face is beautifully rendered, and the details of her costume are superb: from the remarkably delicate floral pattern "woven" into her blouse, to the gossamer "embroidery" in the hem of her skirt.

Lladro performs a near-miracle in transforming real lace into a dainty porcelain parasol trimmed with tiny, lifelike flowers. And just as artistic details flourish in "Picture Perfect," so do graceful lines frame her form. Movement is suggested in the flowing shape of her skirt. Lady-like dignity is captured in the turn of her ankle and the bend of her wrist.

The sum of these nuances adds up to a perfect portrait of love...a tribute to the love of beauty ...and an appreciation of loyalty. That loyalty is expressed both in the mutual devotion of youngster and pet, and — more significantly — a salute to the mutual loyalty between Lladro and its collectors.

At $8^1/_2$" in height, "Picture Perfect" made its debut at $350, with an edition closing forever on December 31, 1991. It seems a foregone conclusion that "Picture Perfect" will attract considerable secondary market interest as the Members-Only edition marking the Collectors Society's first major anniversary.

The Charms of a "Summer Stroll"

While "Picture Perfect" commanded a great deal of attention among Lladro collectors during 1990 and 1991, the Lladro Collectors Society 1991 Members-Only offering, "Summer Stroll,"

"Picture Perfect" marks the Fifth Anniversary of the Lladro Collectors Society. This elegant porcelain work of art debuted at $350 as an offering for Society members only.

The most recent annual Members-Only Lladro Collectors Society figurine is "Summer Stroll," a charming porcelain portrait of a young girl mediating between a bird and a kitten. Its original price was set at $195.

also caught the eyes and captured the hearts of many admirers.

"Summer Stroll" portrays the dainty, elongated figure of a child with a sensitive expression and a grace far beyond her tender years. Her perfect parasol boasts a faux pearl handle, and her gracefully flowing skirt features a tiny, decorative pattern: both examples of Lladro craftsmanship at its best. This young lady appears to be a peacemaker as she gently extends her hand to a dove with her kitten at her feet.

Like all of the finest Lladro figurines, "Summer Stroll" combines consummate artistry and sublime sensitivity. She was designed and produced by the Lladro family of artisans exclusively for the Lladro Collectors Society family. This finely glazed, 9" porcelain figurine was introduced in 1991 at an original price of $195. The redemption period was set to conclude on June 30, 1992.

A Four-Year Series of Gifts for New and Renewing Members of the Lladro Collectors Society

Each year since its inception, the Lladro Collectors Society has bestowed a special gift upon its members as a token of thanks and appreciation. For 1991 — and for each year through 1994 — that gift will be a beautiful bell.

Lladro Collectors Society members expressed their preference for a thank-you gift that was an actual Lladro porcelain. Thus the artists of Lladro created a limited-edition series of four bells depicting the four seasons. Members will receive the first bell upon joining or renewing their memberships and each additional bell upon subsequent renewals. These renewal gifts are particularly exciting because the value of each of the Four Seasons Bells is more than the $35.00 annual cost of renewing the Society membership.

The first bell in the series features a spring scene conceived by Lladro's sculptors and created by master craftsmen. Set off by a lush lilac trim, the Spring Bell was available for those memberships due for renewal beginning January, 1991.

The remaining bells in the series continue the four seasons theme, with the Summer Bell trimmed in a fresh garden green, the Fall Bell shaded in a distinctive amber, and the Winter Bell featuring a brisk blue. Each bell comes with a matching satin-finish ribbon.

Lladro Collectors Society Members Enjoy a Host of Outstanding Benefits

Originally formed to enhance the appreciation of exceptional porcelain figurines, the Lladro Collectors Society is an association of individuals who admire fine craftsmanship, enjoy exclusive opportunities to acquire limited edition figurines, and wish to become more knowledgeable about the fascinating world of Lladro porcelains.

In addition to an annual opportunity to acquire a Members-Only figurine like "Summer Stroll," members receive a free subscription to Lladro's *Expressions* magazine. This well-written, full-color publication has achieved world-wide recognition and several awards. It is filled with articles and features of special interest to collectors.

One of the newer columns in *Expressions* notes the current standing of Lladro limited editions' availability. This service alerts collectors when certain pieces are nearing their edition limits, so that they may be sure to acquire the pieces at the original price.

Expressions readers will also be among the first to learn of special U.S. appearances by Juan, Jose and Vicente Lladro as well as other members of the Lladro family and Society Director Hugh Robinson.

Members of the Society receive a leather-like binder designed especially to keep their *Expressions* magazines stored and organized.

All new members receive a handsome porcelain membership plaque depicting Don Quixote and bearing the signatures of the Lladro brothers: Juan, Jose and Vicente. Members also are honored with a handsomely embossed membership card. In addition, each Society member becomes an Associate Member of the Lladro Museum in New York City, with full rights to utilize its research facilities.

A highlight for many Lladro Collectors Society members is the opportunity to join their fellow collectors on a Society tour of Lladro headquarters in Valencia, Spain — the capstone of one of several luxurious journeys throughout Spain available only to Society members. Full details of these memorable tours are made available in *Expressions*.

For more information on the many benefits and opportunities of Lladro Collectors Society membership, contact the organization's United States office at 43 West 57th Street, New York, New York 10019-3498.

The first of four bells created expressly for Society members, Lladro's Spring Bell features a delicate, bas-relief design and pretty trimmings in lilac. Upcoming annual bells will celebrate Summer, Fall, and Winter, and each will be a gift to new and renewing members of the Lladro Collectors Society.

Seymour Mann

Seymour Mann Transcends Collectibles to an Art Form

In March of 1991, Seymour Mann was nominated for three Awards of Excellence by *Dolls* Magazine. This is the first time a supplier has been nominated for three of those awards in one year. In addition, the firm was nominated for the DOTY Award by *Doll Reader* Magazine in April, 1991. These accomplishments have reaffirmed that Seymour Mann dolls are more important to collectors than ever before. And here's how it all began...

Thirty Years Filled With New Beginnings

Take an energetic, artistic woman, add her creative and business-wise husband, blend in four decades of success, and it's possible to begin to add up all that the collectibles market has in Seymour Mann, Inc. Seymour Mann is the company of Seymour and Eda Mann, a husband and wife team that creates collectibles, decorative accessories, tableware, and connoisseur dolls for the giftware and collectibles market.

Ten years ago Eda Mann turned her artistry to designing dolls for their company and already has nearly 1,200 designs, enough to fill an entire floor of Seymour Mann's New York showroom. Considering her background and her talent, this isn't surprising.

From a Family of Artists

Originally from England, Eda Mann represents the third generation of artists in her family. Her father and two uncles, all professional artists, guided her natural creativity until she was sixteen. Then she moved to America and began studying at the National Academy of Design in New York City.

Like the artists in her family, Eda wanted to be a professional artist. Her father, Samuel Mirsky, was a well-known society painter of the 1930s and 1940s, and then went on to create many of the great movie posters for such companies as Columbia Pictures, United Artists and MGM.

Eda studied at the National Academy of Design for four years, then began a career as a fashion and fabric designer. She was successful in her field before meeting Seymour Mann, an accomplished musician. One of her most noted accomplishments included having two of her paintings recently accepted by the Metropolitan Museum of Art in New York City.

Their partnership has brought forth a family of three daughters (one of whom is the noted author Erica Jong) and a remarkably successful business.

The Artistry of Dolls

Eda Mann has designed much of the giftware and tableware items for the family company. Ten years ago she began designing dolls and Seymour Mann's *Connoisseur Doll Collection* line came into being. The phenomenal number of designs to date, well over a thousand, speak of the artistry that flows from Eda Mann.

Turning to dolls in a business sense was a natural extension of the doll collecting and doll making Eda Mann had done for her children. Eda sculpts dolls from the originals in her collection. Already there are more than 350 dolls in the *Connoisseur Doll Collection.* Edition sizes vary — they can be 2,500, 3,500 or 7,500, and each doll has a hang tag stating the edition size of the series. Furthermore, each doll has a hallmark imprinted with the Seymour Mann name and patent number on the back of its neck. Prices vary, with the mid-price porcelain dolls selling for between $50 and $150.

This Chalet lights up and beckons everyone who sees it. It almost seems possible to come in for a cozy evening in front of a crackling fire with a cup of hot cocoa and a favorite Christmas story to share.

Seymour Mann, President, and Master Designer Eda Mann, continue to create and produce quality giftware and collectibles that delight people everywhere. This dynamic husband and wife team give added meaning to the word "success."

Delightful Dolls

Three new dolls recently released in the *Connoisseur Doll Collection* include "Betty Ann," "Andrea" and "Pauline." "Betty Ann" has vibrant red hair, blue eyes, and a red dress. She is sixteen inches tall. "Andrea" has blonde hair with blue eyes, a blue dress and is eighteen inches tall. She also comes in a pink dress. "Pauline" is another beautiful blonde doll with blue eyes. She comes in either a pink or blue dress, and is also eighteen inches tall. Each looks like a little princess with her rich and detailed clothing, beautiful coiffure and wide-eyed, adorable face.

Another Connoisseur Doll is the appealing "Ashley" who looks as if she stepped out of a turn-of-the-century storybook with her white cotton middy blouse and skirt with black satin ribbon accents. She has a matching hairbow, black open-weave tights and Mary Jane shoes. It's easy to imagine her blowing her black plastic whistle tied around her neck and waiting for a friend to look out the window and see Ashley ready to play. "Ashley" is porcelain and fifteen inches high.

Along with dolls created by master designer Eda Mann, the company produces designs by other designers, and has recently expanded into a new category — collectible vinyl dolls. This expansion demonstrates the company's innovative movement — and it's movement that works.

Being surrounded by hundreds of dolls she and others design for their company might be enough for many artists, but not Eda Mann. She is now also painting portraits of the dolls she creates. Her husband says it is the final step in Eda's creations — a complete cycle of art, from the drawing, to the sculpture of the doll to the painting. The Manns are finding that people who purchase their dolls want to buy the paintings, and Eda is working on a series of paintings of her dolls for public exhibition. Thus the lace on the dress she has designed, the blush on the cheek, the curl in the hair, and the stocking on the leg, move from the three dimensional doll one can hold and cuddle, to the original oil framed on the wall. It's almost as though a child one loves sits for a portrait and that work of art then adorns the home.

Although dolls with a Victorian theme account for many of the Seymour Mann dolls, other themes and designs are constantly being created. For example, the company has the popular series called *Dolls of the Month*, where each doll is dressed to represent a particular month. Not only is the costume appropriate for the month, such as a child in yellow boots and slicker for April, each doll also comes with the birthstone and the flower of the month. Priced at $37.50, this series makes the dolls affordable for nearly everyone who wishes to collect dolls. The company has created a

Three new faces in the Connoisseur Doll Collection *belong to "Betty Ann," "Andrea" and "Pauline." Their bright eyes, beautiful faces and richly detailed dresses are nearly irresistible.*

group called the *Signature Series*, designed by Pat Kolesar, which includes an Eskimo doll called "Enoc." The *Signature Series* features collectible dolls designed by new artists.

It seems as though Seymour Mann may develop nearly as many different dolls as there are children in the world. In only ten years, this company has made a major entrance into the collectibles doll market. The diverse and growing family of dolls from Seymour Mann will continue to delight doll collectors everywhere.

Christmas Collectibles to Light Up the Season

Christmas collectibles are another interest of Seymour Mann, and the company recently unveiled its "Christmas Village of Lights." Five ceramic light-up houses are featured, including a light-up Chalet noted for its "Dickensian Look." The Chalet is hand-sculpted in cold cast porcelain and is naturally colored. It is ten inches long, six inches deep and seven and a half inches high. It is extremely translucent, and beckons with a warm glow to the miniature town people who come with the collection.

The Christmas collectibles and collectible dolls represent a reaching out by Seymour Mann into the collectibles market as a whole. Seymour Mann says his company has embarked on a collectible campaign because the collectible business is growing and the consumer wants something that may increase in value. Offering more collectibles is also a way Seymour Mann can work even closer with speciality stores which, Mann believes, are getting stronger, and more and more of them are getting into collectibles.

This movement to boost speciality store presence while still working closely with department store groups is another example of how Seymour Mann studies and anticipates the giftware and collectibles market, then shifts and expands in appropriate ways to provide customers with what they want and love.

Also playing a major role in the firm's success is Gideon Oberweger, Senior Executive Vice President and Managing Director. Mr. Oberweger is responsible for overseeing much of the company's administrative and marketing responsibilities. Yet it all begins with two very creative people — Seymour and Eda Mann — and from their creativity, commitment and business acumen, come the innovative and beautiful items collectors love to take home.

"Enoc The Eskimo Boy" is a vinyl doll designed by Pat Kolesar for Seymour Mann, Inc. and a nominee for Dolls Magazine's *Award of Excellence.*

"Ashley" is a collectible porcelain doll recently added to the Connoisseur Doll Collection *of Seymour Mann. Her turn-of-the-century charm is heart-warming.*

Maruri USA

Maruri Studio Creates Stunning Sculptures of Beloved Birds, Flowers and Animals

The art of fine porcelain sculpture requires two things above all else: art masters of exceptional talent, and total devotion to quality. In the entire world, there are no more than a score of studios which have achieved true excellence in porcelain.

Some — like Royal Worcester or Meissen in Europe — earned their reputations centuries ago and retain them today by continued greatness. Others — like Cybis and Boehm in the U.S. — represent 20th-century porcelain masters who learned the secrets discovered in Asia thousands of years ago.

Until a decade ago, American collectors were largely unaware of another contemporary porcelain studio with the potential for a "world class" reputation. Then Maruri — a Japanese firm with roots in the age-old Ceramic Capital of Seto — introduced some magnificent wildlife sculptures. Within months, Maruri became a respected name in the U.S. collectibles market. And since then, Maruri's honor and fame have grown with each passing year.

Only a few years after its introduction, the Maruri "American Bald Eagle I" by renowned artist W.D. Gaither, commanded $600 on the secondary market — up from its modest issue price of $165. By 1991 — a decade after its introduction — the piece was selling regularly in the $1150 range. Since then, Maruri has introduced scores of stunning works by Gaither and other superb artists — capturing the glories of nature in hand-painted porcelain.

The Ceramic Capital of the World is Home to Maruri

Maruri was originally founded hundreds of years ago in Seto, the fabled ceramic capital of Japan. At that time, porcelain craftsmanship flourished among family-oriented workshops, one of which was the family business of Mizuno. The Mizuno brothers named their business Maruri, and soon this studio earned a wide reputation for excellent bone china, figurines, and true-to-nature bird and animal sculptures.

Maruri prides itself on its studied approach in the creation of limited-edition sculptures. Each piece takes many days to complete, using a multi-step process that has been followed faithfully over the years.

The Maruri Process of Distinctive Hand-Crafting

As their ancestors did centuries ago, Maruri's contemporary craftsmen follow an exacting process to create each of their porcelain masterworks. They begin by creating as many molds as are needed to capture all of the individual nuances or details of a figure. Then they use the ancient Grand Feu formula for porcelain to create a creamy, feldspar-containing mixture in the form of liquid slip.

Each mold is filled with just the right thickness of porcelain, then allowed to dry slowly until the exact degree of dryness is achieved and the molds are removed. Then the pieces are assembled, after which all seam lines and points of juncture are smoothed and refined by hand to eliminate creases or other signs of joining.

Support molds are then strategically positioned to assure proper drying and the pieces are placed in a temperature-controlled room for several days to continue the drying process. Each piece is then kiln-fired for at least sixteen hours. The temperature is carefully controlled as it gradually builds to a maximum heat and then is slowly reduced.

After firing, Maruri artisans carefully inspect each piece for flaws, and as many as 35 to 40% may be discarded. Each surviving piece is then sandblasted to achieve a flawless, smooth surface, and again is checked for defects. At this point, the porcelain is brilliant and strong. Once the sandblasting is finished, artists painstakingly hand-paint each piece in many subtly differentiated colors.

Songbirds of Beauty Combine North American Birds and Exquisite Flowers

One of Maruri's most recent collections marries fine porcelain and bronze and pays tribute to some

Three of Maruri's elegant new Songbirds Of Beauty *are, clockwise from top, "Double Bluebird with Peach Blossom," "Goldfinch with Hawthorn," and "Robin with Lily."*

From Maruri's Wings of Love Collection *comes "Double Dove with Cherry Blossom," one of many charming tributes to the bird of love and peace.*

of North America's loveliest songbirds and their floral habitats. "Robin and Baby with Azalea" portrays what is perhaps the best-known songbird on the continent. "Cardinal with Cherry Blossom" is complemented by "Double Cardinal with Dogwood," a duet of sculptures inspired by the bright red creatures that delight birdwatchers from the Southeastern United States up to the Canadian border.

"Chickadee with Rose" offers a true-to-life portrait of the trusting songbird recognized by the distinctive call that named it: "chick-a-dee-dee." "Bluebird with Apple Blossom" makes a wonderful contrast, what with the bright blue plumage of the bird and the delicate pink of the blossoms on the apple tree's graceful branches. The "Double Bluebird with Peach Blossom" captures a male and female pair enjoying a moment of rest.

To round out the *Songbirds Of Beauty* Collection, Maruri's art masters have selected a handsome "Robin with Lily" and a brightly colored "Goldfinch with Hawthorn." Both sculptures depict the birds with their wings outstretched, the better to show off their exquisitely rendered plumage. Sizes for the collection range from 5½" to 7½" in height, and prices are from $85.00 to $145.00, depending upon complexity and size.

A Maruri Studio Limited Edition: "Delicate Motion"

From time to time, Maruri introduces a very special work of art that combines numerous figures in a composition of rare delicacy and intricacy. Just such an event has occurred with the unveiling of "Delicate Motion," which displays three Violet-Crowned Hummingbirds frolicking amid a spray of Morning Glories.

Individually numbered and limited to only 3,500 pieces for worldwide distribution, the 11¼" "Delicate Motion" is crafted of porcelain and bronze and comes complete with its own polished wooden base and Certificate of Authenticity. Its issue price has been set at $325.00.

Maruri Invites Collectors on a Polar Expedition

Few of us will ever be privileged to view polar bears, harp seals, arctic foxes and penguins in the wild. But now Maruri has created a group of amazingly life-like replicas that can be enjoyed in the comfort of home. The *Polar Expedition* Collection offers beautifully crafted reproductions of some of nature's most fascinating creatures in hand-painted porcelain.

From the legendary strength of the mighty Polar Bear...to the delightfully playful Baby Seal...the waddling Emperor Penguin...the gracefully sleek Arctic Fox...these works of art are beautiful to see and wonderful to touch. Each figure in the *Polar Expedition* Collection comes with a Certificate of Authenticity: your assurance that it has been made with all quality and care for which Maruri is renowned.

A Line of Remarkable Depth and Breadth

In addition to these most recent introductions, Maruri offers a wide range of figurines and sculptures inspired by eagles, owls, hummingbirds, doves, and even the animals seen on African safaris.

Ever since Maruri created their first eagle figurine, the studio has been renowned throughout the world for its three-dimensional tributes to this majestic bird. Indeed, Maruri's newest eagle masterwork is entitled "Majestic Eagles," and is sculpted in porcelain and bronze to show off two handsome birds with wings outspread.

Maruri's *Eyes Of The Night* help discover the truths behind the fascinating myths surrounding the owl. The collection of nine owls is crafted in hand-painted porcelain, and they offer breathtakingly real depictions of this wide-eyed bird in its natural habitat.

The delicate and elusive hummingbird appears in a Maruri collection that portrays these tiny creatures close to full size, in tandem with the flower that attracts it most readily. *The Maruri Hummingbirds* range in size from $4^1/_2$" to $8^1/_2$" in height, and each comes with its own polished wooden base and Certificate of Authenticity.

As the birds of love and peace, doves have fascinated man for centuries. Maruri honors these snow-white beauties with a splendid collection entitled *Wings of Love*. Whether presented in pairs or all alone, the doves in this group of figurines offer perfect portraits of heavenly innocence — the perfect gifts for weddings.

W.D. Gaither's *African Safari* series resulted from the sculptor's personal experience on "photo safari" in Zululand, South Africa. There he sketched and photographed the elephants, rhinos, buffalo, lions, leopards, kudus, impalas and other great beasts that served as inspiration for his masterful sculptures.

Ever since its origins more than a decade ago, Maruri has been renowned as the creator of some of the world's most compelling eagle sculptures. Here is one example — in which some eagle nestlings prepare to receive their dinner from a proud parent.

As Maruri broadens and extends its line of brilliant naturalist sculptures, one thing is certain: the firm will continue to craft each work of art individually, with no shortcuts. Maruri's age-old process has yielded lasting works of fine art for generations. Today, Maruri continues this tradition, providing an enduring tribute to some of the world's most enchanting creatures.

Dynasty Doll Collection

A Family Business Provides Designer Dolls in Exquisite Costumes...at Uniquely Affordable Prices

The award-winning studios of Dynasty Dolls have earned a special place in the hearts of American collectors. With their distinct personalities, faces and expressions, these lavishly costumed Dynasty "ladies" enjoy an especially loyal following. But few Dynasty collectors know the "inside story" of their favorite studio's origins. For Dynasty began as the dream of three young American men ...and the path of their dream took several turns before they discovered their "niche" in today's thriving world of collectible dolls.

World War II had just ended when three brothers-in-law, Sidney Darwin, Samuel Kronman and Charles Dengrove, joined forces to launch a ceramic factory in Carteret, New Jersey. Samuel was a ceramic engineer in college, and Sidney and Charles were just out of the service. Both Sidney and Charles had business experience before going into the armed forces. The intention of this ambitious trio was to produce a line of ceramics at popular prices, and distribute these items under the name of Cardinal China.

"They tried for quite awhile to develop some items," explains Gary Darwin, son of founder Sidney and today the Vice President-Sales for Cardinal, Inc. and Dynasty Dolls. "They had many technical problems getting started, due to some innovative ceramic techniques that Samuel pioneered."

Before long the entrepreneurs saw their patience rewarded when they launched their first big item: a measuring spoon holder. Even in this common household item there was a hint of the artistry to come, because the spoon holder was fashioned to look like a flower pot with leaves. "Then you put brightly colored plastic measuring spoons in it and it formed what looked like a flower pot," Gary Darwin recalls. "They sold well over three million pieces. That's what got the company off the ground."

A Force in the Fledgling Gift Industry

In the late 1940s, the American gift industry was relatively small and close-knit, according to Gary Darwin. "That's where they got distribution heavily entrenched," Darwin says of his father and two uncles. "Their line included piggy banks, butter melters, sprinklers for ironing, napkin holders, decorative switch plates, and many other practical and attractive items."

A fire in the early 1950s became the impetus for a move to larger quarters in Carteret, when they bought a multi-story brick building that had been owned by General Cigar. "They set up another pottery with state-of-the-art equipment," Gary Darwin recounts. "This included a high speed and more efficient tunnel kiln. My uncle Samuel was responsible for developing some unique methods in ceramic manufacturing. In those days they employed on the average of 150 people, and operated the pottery twenty-four hours a day, seven days a week until 1960."

Japanese Ceramics Prompt a Change of Focus

"During the 1950s, the Japanese were coming on very strong in their ceramic production, offering the world great prices. It became more and more difficult to compete as a domestic resource," Darwin explains. The pottery was shut down, and the company was transformed into an import concern, with Sidney Darwin making his first buying trip to the Far East in 1960.

"Importing as opposed to manufacturing let us become a multi-media resource, not just ceramics," Darwin says. Sidney traveled extensively during the 1960s and 1970s, selecting an impressive array of giftware merchandise that was sold both to shops and to the leading mail order companies. Darwin recalls, "With the change to importing, my Uncle Samuel became Operations Manager, and my Uncle Charles was Office Manager. To make room for the warehouse, "The kiln was literally pulled out brick by brick, and I did partake in that operation," Gary Darwin smiles.

Pride Creations Becomes Part of Cardinal, Inc.

In the early 1970s, Cardinal, Inc. purchased another giftware firm called Pride Creations, thereby gaining valuable personnel like Sales

Dynasty's 1992 Annual Christmas Doll, "Angelique," plays "White Christmas" and wears a rich red costume. Crafted of bisque porcelain with hand-painted facial features, "Angelique" is limited to an edition of 5,000 pieces. The doll measures 19" in height and carries an issue price of $155.

"Princess Aurora" represents Dynasty's Classic Ballet Collection *with a lovely ballerina atop a hardwood base with embossed medallion. At 16" in height, "Princess Aurora's" issue price is $230, and the edition is 7,500 hand-numbered pieces.*

For the first time, Dynasty presents an annual bride doll with an extra-fine quality porcelain bisque head, arms and hands. Sculpted by Hazel Tertsakian, the doll boasts an exclusive wedding gown, hand-painted face, and real eyelashes. Limited to one year of production, the 22" "Victorian Bride" sells for $175.

Manager Stanley Wahlberg. Stanley remained with the company until early 1992, and he and his wife Irene were instrumental in shaping the concept and product line of Dynasty Dolls. But the doll business became part of Cardinal, Inc. in a very round-about way.

"In the mid-1970s, Stanley Wahlberg purchased six pieces of doll house furniture and put them in the line," Gary Darwin says. "The six miniatures absolutely took off, even though collectors and dealers told us they were all wrong: wrong size, wrong color, wrong dimensions. We learned very quickly and a new division, Concord Miniature Collection, was born. Today, the Concord line is part of Cardinal, Inc. and it is the largest creator and importer of one-inch to one-foot miniature furniture in the world.

"As the Concord division grew, we were looking for other categories of merchandise to sell to miniature retailers or doll house retailers. That's how we got into the doll business," Gary Darwin recalls. "Stan Wahlberg purchased a couple of dolls in frontier-type costumes, in velvet as well as some calicos. They took off, but in the giftware trade — not the miniature trade. Talk about backing into a business!" Darwin chuckles.

"At the same time, we were a major supplier in the catalog showroom industry. Dolls did very well through those channels of distribution. We were encouraged by our catalog reps to build a special identity for our dolls and to package them distinctively," Darwin explains. The resulting Dynasty Dolls concept built rapidly into a recognizable favorite among many doll collectors.

Famed Artists and Designers Create Dynasty Dolls

After the death of founder Samuel Kronman and the retirement of founder Charles Dengrove, Cardinal, Inc. and Dynasty Dolls were entrusted completely to the care of Sidney Darwin and his sons, Gary and Allen. The Darwins encouraged Stanley Wahlberg to continue the development of Dynasty Dolls into a distinctive doll line that fits the desires of today's collectors.

"Our theory with Dynasty Dolls is to give the collector a popular priced collector doll with all the personality, style, costuming and accessories of the higher-priced models. We currently offer between 400 and 500 styles with a variety of heads. Some are antique reproductions, but mainly we work with a variety of artists who design their own products," Darwin says.

These artists include Hazel T. Tertsakian, Gail Hoyt, Teena Halbig, Sonya Hartman, Karen Henderson, and Li Po Nan. With the Wahlbergs no longer part of the Dynasty team, the well-known giftware and doll expert Anne Dolan now merchandises the Dynasty line.

"Ideas for new dolls come from designers, from our suppliers, and from historical books, among other places," Darwin says. "We source our fabrics in the markets of Hong Kong and Taiwan, and our chief costume designer, Genevieve Casalco has much to do with our dolls' elegant outfits. In addition, we read all of the mail we receive from collectors, and some terrific ideas both for doll designs and for names have come from their correspondence."

The Unique Niche of Dynasty Dolls

"For a long time we sensed a real void in the under-$200 price range for collectible dolls," Gary Darwin asserts, "and that is where Dynasty has made its mark with well-designed, well-made, collector-quality dolls. Most of the selections doll shops were carrying were artist-type pieces, which were very expensive, hard to come by, and out of the reach of the average collector.

"A lot of what collectors could obtain was put together in series by color theme: a group of dolls with the same expression and outfit that basically all looked the same," Darwin recalls. "The key to any good collectibles program is selection, and that is what Dynasty provides. Today we offer limited editions, annual dolls, artist-designed pieces, and exclusives, along with a few antique reproductions."

Dynasty Doll's own Swiss Miss is "Carley," designed by Gail Hoyt with sparking blue eyes, long eyelashes, and rosy red lips. With flower basket in hand, "Carley" shows off her red taffeta dress with its white apron overlay, flowers, and lace trim. The 17" doll can be part of your collection for $115.

"Dynasty Dolls has been honored to receive a number of nominations for Awards of Excellence as well as a Doll of the Year (DOTY) nomination. We have won our categories a couple of times," Darwin recalls with pride. "These honors strengthen our name and place in the minds of our doll collectors, and we are very gratified to receive them."

A Wide Array of Lovely Dynasty Ladies

Leafing through the Dynasty Dolls catalog...or encountering a range of these elegant dolls in a retail shop...Gary Darwin's explanation of the line's uniqueness becomes all the more real. Here we have a quartet of *Victorian Ladies* designed and sculpted by Hazel Tertsakian, dressed in fine satins, silks, jacquards and laces. Next we see the coveted *Dynasty Annual Dolls*: an exquisite bride, a holiday doll who plays "White Christmas," a Victorian mother and daughter, and "Corinne," a Southern belle with her very own teddy bear.

Ballerinas from Dynasty Dolls include sweet little girls like "Amy," young ladies in toe shoes like "Lana," and the *Great Ballet* series featuring "Princess Aurora," "Giselle," and "Crystal." "Masha" from "The Nutcracker Suite," part of this coveted collection, was nominated for the *Dolls* magazine "Awards of Excellence."

Many doll lines include creations inspired by the months of the year, but Dynasty's *Flower Of The Month* dolls are especially outstanding. Each little girl boasts a different sculptured head and distinct expression, eye color, and style and color of hair. And each is dressed in a designer outfit chosen to complement the flower she represents. *Four Seasons* dolls are equally special, with their musical accompaniments and costumes to fit the time of year they represent. "Merrie, Miss Winter," for instance, wears a "fur" jacket, carries ice skates, and plays "Winter Wonderland."

International dolls from Dynasty include "Pocahontas" and "Rory," Native American and cowgirl dolls from the U.S.A.; a little Asian girl named "Su-Wen"; and pretty "Basha from Poland." "Basha" carries a porcelain plate of traditional welcome buns.

From the post-war dream of three young entrepreneurs to an internationally renowned creator of elegant-yet-affordable collectible dolls, the history of Cardinal, Inc. and Dynasty Dolls is fascinating and rich. Now under the leadership of the Darwin clan, Dynasty's goal is to continue developing and producing dolls with uniquely designed faces, superb crafting, and costumes worthy of proud display in homes across the land.

Nahrgang Collection
Dolls of Perfection a Family Affair

Perfect, handmade dolls dressed to the nines are the hallmark of dolls created by artist Jan Nahrgang and her family. Along the banks of the Mississippi River in Moline, Illinois, come their precious dolls which are handmade in every detail, from the highest curl of the hair, to the tip of the well-shoed toe. All are beguiling with their individual touches and come in very limited editions, ranging from 250 in porcelain up to 2,000 in vinyl.

It all began several years ago when Jan Nahrgang's daughter, then a senior in high school, wanted a very beautiful and very expensive doll. Her daughter was Jan's eldest child and, as she has several children, buying such a doll was financially impossible. Jan solved the problem by making her daughter a doll.

One doll led to another. Family members, then friends wanted the dolls, and by 1980, the Nahrgang family was officially in the collectibles doll business. Jan learned doll making first from local teachers, then from experts in New York, and she continues to practice new techniques and develop new ideas. What hasn't changed, and never will, is her commitment to designing every aspect of each doll, from hand-painting the face to designing the hand-sewn clothing. Jan is a perfectionist, and each doll must pass her own incredibly high standards.

From Classroom to Doll Studio

Along with Jan's total absorption with each doll is the fact that Jan still teaches elementary school. She works with children in special education.

Her schoolchildren are often her inspiration for a particular doll. There are lots of different traits, emotions and moods she sees in her children that she admires, and those are often carried into her dolls. It could be a little rebellion, a touch of shyness, even a little smug look. Some of her dolls are

"Aubry" is ready to take your hand and go for a stroll in the park. She's nineteen inches of satin and lace. She comes in porcelain or vinyl. All eyes on the boulevard will turn toward her the moment she steps outside.

"Laura" is a vision in white. She comes in porcelain or vinyl and is nineteen inches tall. The softness of her coat, muff and hat, the sheen of her dress and the directness of her sky-blue eyes, all add the elegance and perfection she can bring to any doll lovers collection.

named after particular children. Her close proximity to children gives her a firsthand "artist's studio" full of models to work with and draw from. Private collectors around the world enjoy Jan's dolls, many of whom were modeled after Jan's schoolchildren.

The Nahrgang Collection

Perfection with each doll is the foundation, the one truth, Jan requires. To ensure this, she is in charge of the total concept of each doll. With each outfit, Jan uses an extravagance of lace and fabric, ending up with what she calls "simple abundance." The result is individual dolls of amazing beauty that ask to be touched and held. Who can resist velvet, lace, and satin? Who could resist any of the dolls described below?

"Aubry," at nineteen inches, comes in both porcelain and vinyl. She's a Victorian lady dressed in mint-colored batiste, adorned with white lace. She has a hat with pink roses tucked into the brim, and a matching parasol, which she may open if the day gets even a little warmer. Certainly she's ready for a stroll. Lace caresses her neck, shelters her wrists and gently touches the ground. Seven tiers of snow-white lace ring the full skirt of her dress, from her pink-ribboned waist to the hem of her skirt. "Aubry" is limited to an edition of 250 in porcelain. It's clear at a glance that all the heirloom sewing in her outfit, with its lace inserts and tucks, turns her instantly into a lady of high fashion.

"Laura" is limited to an edition of 250. She is also nineteen inches high and comes in both porcelain and vinyl. Inspired by Laura in Dr. Zhivago, she looks like a winter goddess wrapped in white fur, white satin, white lace, white stockings and white leather boots with double stitching at the top. Again, pink is the accent, as with "Aubry." Pink silk flowers and pink ribbons brighten up her white fur hat and fur muff. White pearls glisten, and double pink and white bows complete her elegant look.

"Laura" is ready to put her other hand into the cozy muff, climb into her winter sleigh, and let a pair of prancing horses carry her through the countryside where her long blond curls will dance in the wind, and her pink cheeks and lips will tingle with the fresh air.

"McKinsey" comes directly from one of Jan's students whom Jan says is both a little smug and a little shy. "McKinsey" measures nineteen inches in height, and her big blue eyes would melt any heart. Jan gives her a simple dark dress with a full skirt and mutton sleeves. The dress is accented with white lace at the neck and bodice, creating a stunning contrast against the dark fabric.

The doll's full, slightly pursed lips, speak of the pride she feels for her basket of pink and white roses. She seems to be offering them, albeit a little shyly, to someone nearby. She has a full pink bow at her waist, tied with loving care, and charming ringlets on either side of her face. Ribbons and roses adorn her hair. No wonder "McKinsey" seems pleased. She's picture-perfect.

"Karmin" is Nahrgang's gypsy doll. Her nineteen inches include wild black hair, a skirt with ruffled black and purple material, gold braiding, gold bangles and even gold lacing on her dark stockings. She has a crystal ball in her hand, ready to tell someone's fortune. There's a vibrancy about "Karmin" one sees at a glance. It's in the tilt of her head, the purse in her lips and the light in her huge brown eyes. It's almost as if, in another moment, she'll twirl in a dance whose movements have been handed down — gypsy mother to gypsy daughter — for generations.

Looking for Challenge

As committed as Jan is to the perfection of each doll, there is also the need in her for change and new challenges in the kinds of dolls she creates.

"McKinsey" is a porcelain doll with a basket of roses to share and a tilt to her head that just asks collectors to look her way. Who could resist those blue eyes? Hand- made lace adorns the bodice of her dress, giving her a slightly old-fashioned look.

She says that when she achieves one level of accomplishment, she's ready for the next challenge. She's never content to stay with what she's already done.

One new challenge for the future is to create historical characters — women from the past who can help serve as role models for young women today, including Jan's students. Thus there would be the sense of bringing back to the students who inspire her, dolls which can inspire the children.

Jan would love to create a Dolly Madison doll, because of Dolly Madison's courage. She is also enamored with Beatrix Potter because she spent so much time and effort protecting the little wild animals in England. Creating such dolls, dolls filled with meaning as well as beauty, is something Jan looks forward to.

These dolls are to be in porcelain-like vinyl so children can hold them close and so more people can afford to own them. Jan's vinyl dolls are about half the price of her porcelain dolls, which retail for around $400.

Each doll will continue to have what Jan considers a must — something that makes each doll special, whether it's the English hand-smocking or heirloom sewing in the outfit.

Nahrgang just released a new line of eight vinyl dolls in May of 1991. Each is eighteen and a half inches tall, all are girls, and each is limited to an edition of either 250 or 500 dolls. This is Nahrgang's first line of strictly vinyl dolls. A quick glance at these dolls shows that "Molly" is a peasant girl, happy with her bare feet in the grass. She even has flowers around her left foot. She's a child of the earth and loves it. "Ann Marie" is beautiful in her peaches and cream outfit which echoes "Aubry's" outfit, described above. "Alexis" is a Victorian bride dressed in ecru, satin and lace. "Brooke" is a contemporary bride in a gorgeous white satin gown. "Beatrix" is an English country lady elegant in her imported peach batiste and happy with the bunny in her basket. "Vanessa" is wearing an exquisite Victorian evening gown with satin, lace and pearls. "Angela" is an innocent Mexican-American girl in an authentic dance dress. Like "Molly," she is barefoot. These eight dolls are beautiful both individually and in the variety they offer.

Non-stop Growth

Women all over the world collect Nahrgang dolls. A few individuals own one hundred dolls, and many own fifty or more. Jan now has a list of collectors who insist on buying one of every doll she makes, sight unseen.

Until 1990, Jan's collectors were primarily repeat collectors. Now, with national advertising and exposure, many first-time Nahrgang doll collectors are everywhere, across America.

What pleases Jan is that she knows the collectors who purchase her dolls want them because they truly love them, not because they're banking on any possible future rise in value, nor because they have "money to burn." There seems to be a link of love between the doll collector and each Nahrgang doll.

Fortunately Jan loves to meet her public, because with the national network of distribution her company is developing, along with toy fairs and gift shows, she's in ever-growing demand. She intends to retire from teaching in two years, and this will allow her more time to focus not only on the creation of her dolls, but on the business side of her dolls.

Certainly the business is mushrooming. Jan is proud her husband and children are part of the business, and she depends heavily on their assistance and expertise. Jan's husband, Larry, handles the company bookkeeping, her daughter, Jennifer, is the production manager, one son, Ray, is the business manager, and her other son, Leonard, supervises the production pouring of all the molds. The entire production team for the company involves less than ten people. Each person has a specialty, yet there is never a sense of mass production. Each doll receives total individual attention to reach the state of perfection Jan demands.

One concession to growth is the establishment of a new factory in a town close to Moline, where the porcelain-like vinyl dolls are now created. The Nahrgang Collection intends to remain a small business with the unique feature of creating handmade collectibles which doll lovers all over America can treasure. Considering how each doll is handmade from start to finish, it isn't surprising collectors consider them family heirlooms as soon as the dolls come into their homes.

Polland Studios

Grounded in Western Art of the Past, Polland Studios is Busy Outfitting Itself for the Future

Don Polland is a feast of a man — artist, designer, historian, storyteller, manufacturer, businessman, family man and alchemist, ever-ready to experiment with new materials to bring his sculpture alive in new ways.

Beginning with large bronze sculptures depicting life in the Old West, Polland has, since the 1960s, received recognition from the leading western art galleries and museums in the country. His sculptures are in private collections around the world, including the homes of his peers. However, in many respects, all this is just a beginning for Don Polland and Polland Studios because this is an outfit dedicated to the future. And this is good news for everyone interested in collecting Polland's art.

A Nostalgia for the Old West

It's hard to imagine Don Polland knowing just how powerful his summers in Utah between the years 1940 and 1950 would be. He spent those summers on his uncles' ranches, surrounded by cowboys, Indians and even miners. That environmental exposure, starting when he was eight years old, immersed his artistic spirit in a feeling and love for the West which, with passing years, Polland translated into his life's work.

Don Polland at work enticing the life of the Old West out of the clay he deftly works with. Already the horse and rider seem to be galloping directly toward Polland.

The cornerstone of Polland's artistic talent is the amazing realism and detail captured in each work, whether it is one of the magnificent large bronzes he created years ago, or the miniature pieces in pewter or porcelain he creates today. It's as if looking at, touching, or holding one of Polland's pieces puts the collector immediately into the moment depicted. Whether it's an Indian, with the string of his bow and the muscles in his arms taut the instant before the release of the arrow, or the last touch between the cowboy and the bucking bronc, as the bronc succeeds in discharging its rider directly toward heaven, the life force pulses in Polland's works.

Polland has become quite an historian about America's West and now has an extensive western reference library. He doesn't get involved with current cowboy life — he's sentimental and nostalgic about the older period. He feels there's a wealth of subjects still to be touched upon, and brought to life through his sculpture. Over the years, Polland has shifted how he translates his western subjects from the large and mighty bronzes, to the miniatures he creates in pewter and hand-painted cold cast porcelain. His miniatures vary from just a few inches (sometimes as small as an inch) up to nearly nine inches. Polland has designed eighty pewter miniatures for The Lance Corporation's Chilmark© line and currently creates four or more pewter miniatures each year for Chilmark©.

This reflects one aspect of Polland Studios — creating designs to license to other companies. Polland's art is now licensed to such companies as The Lance Corporation, The Franklin Mint, Danbury Mint and Border Fine Arts.

A Family Business

The other part of Polland Studios is creating designs and manufacturing and marketing them through their own family company, called Chardon (a combination of Don's and his wife Charolette's first names). The Pollands have four grown children, and while the children grew up in the

Each of the three pewter pieces from the Polland Studios line, is limited to an edition of 1,500. Within each piece from "Hunting Cougar" to "Running Free" to "Federal Stallion," the realism is breathtaking.

family business, they left for several years. The two youngest sons and a daughter-in-law are now back, bringing with them a bevy of talents which add to the font of talents Polland possesses. (The oldest two children, a daughter and son, may join the family business later). This makes it an especially exciting time for Chardon, because it is now poised to gauge the pulse of the collectibles market and create exquisitely detailed art in additional mediums and at price points attractive to the collectibles field.

The first Polland Studios was established in Laguna Beach, California in 1972. It is now located in Prescott, Arizona. The second Polland Studios is a brand new addition to the Boston area of Massachusetts. Expansion for the company goes far beyond establishing a second studio and adding personnel. The Polland Studios are a reflection of the many-faceted talents of Don Polland and his family. Polland's art, which began with a focus on our western heritage, is coming into expression in different mediums and themes as never before.

A Man for All Seasons

Polland is proud to be a 1990s man, happy to take the buyer's pulse and create what the market demands. This fits in perfectly with his thrust for innovation and his desire to find new ways to express his art. Polland finds challenge in new kinds of materials, new themes and new market trends. He loves the collectibles field because he feels collectors have a high level of taste and they know what they want. Furthermore, they are extremely friendly, and he views their appreciation for his art as a form of payment.

No wonder Polland Studios is busy exploring new themes and new mediums. Polland's art of the Old West will continue to be the main topic of his artwork, but new themes are emerging. Collectors can look forward to sculpture pieces depicting endangered animals, as well as other themes, and these may be executed in materials other than pewter or porcelain.

Coupled with Polland's family commitment is his own seven-day-a-week commitment to his art and his business. He's a self-proclaimed workaholic, beginning at four in the morning and often working until ten at night. He keeps to this schedule because he loves what he's doing — it energizes him.

No wonder Polland Studios is in such a good position to create designs for other companies as well as create artwork it can market directly to the collectibles field. It's a non-stop outpouring of new art and new materials, new methods of marketing and new ways of reaching people who love the realism Polland brings to each piece he creates.

The Polland Collectors Society

For a special group of people who love Polland's work, there is The Polland Collectors Society. Founded in 1986, it is now in its fifth year. Each year Society members have the opportunity to acquire "members only" pewter sculptures, and each year the sculpture depicts a single western subject in stunning reality. The 1991 "members only" piece is called "War Drummer" and it shows the Indian with his hand raised, ready to strike the drum he holds under his other arm, next to his side. It is nearly possible to hear the beat of the drum while watching the dance he is performing. Every part of the brave's body is involved in movement and this membership figurine brings the collector into the circle of the dance.

The Collectors Society is based in Prescott, Arizona, and people interested in joining can contact Polland Studios for full information.

The circle of involvement from Polland's art is impressive. Beginning with Polland himself, it moves outward to include all the people involved with manufacturing his designs. Polland is very pleased that every time he finishes a new piece, he puts from thirty to fifty people to work — in factories, dealers and their representatives, and salespeople. This of course involves his own family members, which is especially pleasing to Polland. Then there is the collector — from the person who buys a single piece from one of the nearly 400 stores Chardon now ships to across the country, to the collector who belongs to the Collectors Society, a real connoisseur of Polland's art and committed buyer.

Leadership Through Quality

For all the innovation and expansion that now marks the Polland Studios, uppermost in importance is the commitment to quality. Although the materials used have changed, and new themes evolve, quality is never sacrificed. The Polland Studios looks forward to being a leader in the collectibles field and that leadership will continue to be grounded in quality.

The Old West still beckons to Polland, and his art will still reflect the nostalgia of days-gone-by with cowboys and Indians. The West is in Polland's blood and experience, and collectors can look forward to new pieces each year that reflect Polland's interpretation of our western heritage.

Added to that is the Don Polland of today who is taking the challenge of the collectibles field and delighting in turning his talents into creating works of art in new ways, in new materials, for new markets. This whirlwind of a man is a true gift for art lovers everywhere.

Five years of "members only" pewter figurines for The Polland Collectors Society include "I Come In Peace," "The Hunter," "Crazy Horse," "Chief Pontiac" and "War Drummer." The wooden display base adds a museum-quality feeling to the display.

The five Collectors Specials for The Polland Collectors Society from 1987-1991 include "Silent Trail," "Disputed Trail," "Apache Birdman," "Buffalo Pony" and "The Signal."

Precious Art/Panton

The World of Krystonia Brings Fantasy Characters With Shimmering Krystals to Eager Collectors

All collectors are hereby invited to enter the whimsical World of Krystonia, a land full of adventures both mysterious and magical. These stories are told in the books *Chronicles of Krystonia* and *Krystonian Adventures*, and now exist in three dimensions, with the characters coming to life in the hand-painted figurines created by Panton International.

Krystonia is a land of extremes, from towering mountains to barren plains, from lush green valleys to shifting dunes of expansive deserts which sweep over the cities of long ago. Here, the magical krystal can be found by those who search to find it. The wizards and their allies must keep their supplies high or bow to the winter of no end the evil N'Borg wishes to cast upon them.

The council of wizards wields great power when working together, but unfortunately this is not always the case. Try as they may, things do not always go as planned. Working in the Krystalette Obelisk, they consult the ancient books and translate their incantations. Whispering their charm-words, they weave their magic through the magical krystals to provide for the good of Krystonia. Every wizard has his own specialty or area which is his forte. Rueggan is a tinkerer who loves to experiment with the machines of the ancient civilizations — sometimes with unexpected results. Sheph casts his spells to create proper weather, that is, when he's not too busy letting the wind dry and fluff his beard. Turfen works to make wonderful dreams and peaceful slumbers. There are many more wizards on the council, such as the incorrigible Haapf who is forever playing practical jokes on others, and he is always full of mirth.

The dragon society of Krystonia is led by the ever-complaining Grumblypeg Grunch. Residing in Cairn Tor, he negotiates all transport agreements with the wizards. Cairn Tor has quite an assortment of characters all its own. Spyke the singer, Stoope the self-titled 'magician,' and Flayla the nanny, for example. Younger dragons and babies are everywhere in Krystonia. There are sleeping dragons like Grazzi, dragons just hatching from the egg, like Tokkel, and even the dragon Koozl, who carries his best friend with him at all times (a stuffed bear he found in the ruins). And who can forget Owhey, who would love nothing more than to learn to fly? Pultzr may speak with a lisp but none can compare with his desire to learn.

As you travel throughout Krystonia, you may encounter the Om-ba-Don, led by Moplos. You might meet Shigger, leading the Maj-Dron through the searing deserts. If you hear a noise under a bridge, don't be alarmed — it may just be a troll fast asleep.

Kephren, the recorder, tells the tales about Krystonia. These tales are translated by Mark Scott, Pat Chandok and David Lee Woodard. The transcripts are brought to him by dragon transport, and he carefully stores them in his chest so they cannot be damaged. These stories are printed in the books *Chronicles of Krystonia* and *Krystonian Adventures*. In these stories, you find many of the mysteries and confrontations of Krystonia. How did Koozl find his bear? Why is Grunch even more unhappy than usual? What happens when N'Borg unleashes his legions in an evil conquest?

Speaking of evil conquest brings one to N'Borg

Wise in his years but his health failing, "Gurneyfoot" thought it time to step down as leader of Dragon Transport, Inc. Here "Shadra" joins him for a walk to hear him tell his stories of the "grand old days" of Krystonia.

and his desire to rule Krystonia. He is not alone in his desires. N'Chakk, master of the dark arts, and the hench-dragon N'Grall, are waiting in the wings to share in any ill-gotten gains. From Krak N'Borg in the barren wastelands, N'Borg plots his next move.

Creating the Krystonia Story Lines

Pat Chandok and Dave Woodard work with Mark Scott to make up plots and devise the Krystonia story lines. English author Scott then writes the stories in true Krystonia form. Krystonia stories are not just fantasy stories. They are a combination of fantasy, make-believe, and just the right amount of whimsy blended together. As in real life, sometimes the best made plans go awry, and in Krystonia, it seems this happens on a regular basis.

New characters are created every year. In some cases, the character is written into the story line first, but often, the character is created and his own special story is created to explain his being.

Created in Merry Old England

Krystonia figurines are produced in Stoke-on-Trent, England. Why England? Because of its tradition of excellence and wealth of expert painters. The intent was to create a high-quality collectible. Every piece of Krystonia is hand painted with great care and attention to detail. Pat and Dave head a creative team which includes talented English sculptors and painters. When creating a new figurine, it is extremely important to capture the exact personality and whimsical touch that makes the figurine unique and perfect. Because Pat and Dave had fifteen years of giftware experience, they knew that Krystonia would be successful if they could get a real, heartwarming feeling into every character. England seemed the perfect place to get exactly what they wanted, and judging from the reaction people have when first seeing a new figurine — everything from a smile to outright laughter — England was the right choice.

Each piece comes with a sparkling Swarovski crystal, and a name tag explaining how the character fits into the story line. Most of the figurines are limited editions, but some are open stock. Just because it is open, doesn't mean the character won't be retired at some point, as in the case of the 1990 retirement of Owhey.

The Growing World of Krystonia

Krystonia is ever growing. In 1987, there were only nineteen characters. In 1991, there are forty-three, and in 1992, there will be fifty-one. Krystonia figurines come in several different forms. Eight musical waterballs were introduced in 1989, adding even more to this whimsical world. 1990 saw the first Krystonia miniatures, and even a miniature 'Lands of Krystonia' to set them on. Krystonia plaques offer a perfect way for collectors to complete their displays.

"Twilyght" gazes at the stars and thinks about all the good things that will happen tomorrow.

"Graffyn" practices harnessing the magical powers of the krystal. Unfortunately, the vibrating krystal has given poor "Grunch" a severe headache.

The Krystonia Collector's Club

The Krystonia Collector's Club continues to grow. People of all ages and occupations are members, drawn to the pleasure the World of Krystonia offers. The 1991 collector's figurine is "Dragon's Play," which shows two young dragons playing with a magical krystal. Members receive a free gift when they pay their yearly dues. The free gift for 1991 is "Kephren's Chest." This is the chest where Kephren keeps his scrolls before they are translated. The whimsical fantasy of Krystonia continues to attract new collectors, young and old alike, and certainly all are young-at-heart.

Panton's New Porcelain Animals

Panton has created a new collection of cold-cast porcelain animals — animals so real they capture the feeling of being on an African safari, or peeking out a window at the world of animals right in the backyard. Introduced in 1990, the *Safari Animal Kingdom* includes animals such as zebras, giraffes, foxes and bears. All are limited editions, each is hand painted, and comes on a base that reflects its natural habitat, such as the panther in the branch, or the lion in the tawny-colored grass.

Giraffe and Zebra mother and babes. A part of the new Chesterton cold-cast porcelain collection, and so realistic it's almost possible to feel the mother giraffe washing her baby and the contentment of the baby zebra resting alongside its grazing mother.

Panton also unveiled a new collection in 1990 of adorable mice busily munching on apples, cheese, pears and bananas, and other mice out in the garden, in broken flower pots, next to a trowel, or nestled in a big autumn leaf. All are made out of cold-cast porcelain and are hand painted in England. *Baby Animals in Play* was introduced in 1991, including otters, bears, foxes, elephants and others, and all show the animals' playful antics in their natural habitats.

Exquisite Little Mice

The make-believe world of Malcolm Merriweather arrived on America's shores in 1991. These finely detailed mice tell the story of Malcolm Merriweather and the other mice he encounters. They may be doing something as simple as drinking a cup of coffee, or picking flowers, but these small, beautifully executed figurines are charming, and surely will be treasured for years to come. Each is a limited-edition creation.

Precious Art/Panton creates many different collectible lines in its English facilities. From dragons and wizards to nature's animals, both large and small, they bring a combination of whimsy and stunning reality to collectors world-wide.

Reco International Corp.

America's Most Honored Artists Make Reco International Their Home Studio

When Heio Reich founded Reco International Corp. in 1967, he pledged to provide American collectors with the world's finest collectible art. As a native of Berlin, Germany, Reich enjoyed a great many excellent contacts with European art studios. Thus Reco gained fame by introducing plates from some of Europe's most celebrated makers, including Fuerstenberg, Royale, Dresden, Royal Germania Crystal, King's, and Moser.

Many of the plates Reco imported to the United States have risen substantially in value since their introduction in the late 1960s and early 1970s. But Heio Reich sensed a golden opportunity in 1977, and he steered his business in a whole new direction. Since then, Reco International has reigned as one of the nation's top producers of limited edition plates by gifted American painters like Sandra Kuck, John McClelland, Jody Bergsma, and Dot and Sy Barlowe.

Home Studio to the "First Lady of Plates" — Sandra Kuck

Since "Sunday Best" was introduced by Reco International and Sandra Kuck in 1983, the Reco-Kuck connection has been renowned as one of the strongest bonds in the limited edition world. When Ms. Kuck met Heio Reich, she was known primarily as a children's portraitist and gallery artist. Reich knew instinctively that Sandra Kuck's combination of Old Master colorations and detail with child subjects would capture the imagination of plate collectors.

Sandra Kuck and Reco began to work together in a process of experimentation, looking for just the right concept to establish Ms. Kuck in the world of plates. Their work paid off with "Sunday Best" — a nostalgic vision of two sweet little girls in their dress-up bonnets.

"Sunday Best" won multiple honors including the coveted "Plate of the Year" and "Silver Chalice" awards. And it earned Ms. Kuck her very first "Artist of the Year" award from the National Association of Limited Edition Dealers (NALED). When she accepted this singular honor at the 1984 NALED Banquet in South Bend, Indiana, Ms. Kuck had no idea that another FIVE consecutive "Artist of the Year" honors would follow. This sustained leadership of the plate art field has made Ms. Kuck the "First Lady of Plates" — the most honored artist in collector plate history.

Sandra Kuck Keeps Getting "Better and Better"

Never one to rest on her laurels, Sandra Kuck continues to expand her horizons in association with Reco. Ms. Kuck has always enjoyed painting mothers and children in turn-of-the-century finery, for she loves to explore intricate patterns and textures. Thus her current Mother's Day series features a Victorian theme, with both mothers and children dressed in frills, lace and pretty picture hats. The most recent addition to the *Victorian Mother's Day* series is "A Precious Time," which depicts a lovely blonde mother and her tow-headed daughter amid the splendor of an old-fashioned greenhouse conservatory and its many blooming plants.

For years, Ms. Kuck has enjoyed portraying beloved pets along with her child subjects for plates. Now she has embarked on a new edition of two plates that focus more attention on these pampered pets and their proud young owners. Introduced during 1991, "Puppy" and "Kitten" feature dramatic jewel tones and a burnished-gold filigreed border design. The generous 10¼" china plates are limited to 7,500 each for worldwide distribution.

Also in the works is a new Kuck series entitled *Hearts and Flowers*, which is sure to capture the hearts of collectors everywhere. In addition, Ms. Kuck shows her versatility with dolls and ornaments created in association with Reco International. Her newest doll is called "Lullaby," and it portrays a mother and child with sensitivity and tenderness. Her most recent additions to the *Reco Ornament Collection* are "Amy" and "Johnny," both limited to the year of issue; and "Peace on Earth," limited to 17,500 pieces worldwide.

"Kitten" and "Puppy" represent two of the most recent plate introductions by Sandra Kuck and Reco International. Presented on a generous porcelain "canvas" of 10¼" each, these plates boast a burnished-gold filigreed border design. Each is limited to an edition of 7,500.

John McClelland: A "Breakthrough Artist" for Reco

The art of John McClelland inspired Heio Reich to change the direction of Reco International. So impressed was Reich with the charming, child-subject paintings of McClelland that he became a plate producer in order to introduce John McClelland originals on porcelain.

A great admirer of classic illustrators like J. C. Leyendecker, Norman Rockwell, Al Parker and Dean Cornwall, McClelland began his New York art career in the later years of the "Golden Age of Illustration." When illustrated magazines gave way to television in the early 1950s, McClelland turned his attention to portraiture, working from his Connecticut home. He is also renowned to millions as the painter of covers for the Miles Kimball catalog.

When John McClelland and Heio Reich introduced their first plate together, "Rainy Day Fun" became an overnight success. Collectors were hungry for paintings of children on porcelain, and they flocked to own this vision of a smiling child in her bright yellow slicker. McClelland's *Mother Goose* plate series, which began with "Mary, Mary" the contrary little girl, amplified his fame and won the artist a "Plate of the Year" award in 1980. Since then, Reco and McClelland have collaborated on works of art in various media including plates, figurines, dolls, and ornaments.

John McClelland is currently working on a new series of Reco collector plates to be announced in the near future. In the meanwhile, his latest doll from the *Children's Circus Dolls* collection is "Katie the Tightrope Walker." Inspired by the successful plate by the same name, "Katie" is an adorable little girl all dressed up in her tutu and carrying her parasol.

Jody Bergsma Shares Her Fanciful Art Vision

When Jody Bergsma was a child, her mother encouraged her to "draw her dreams" to overcome her youthful fears. It was an imaginative solution to a small problem — but it led to great things. Jody soon fell in love with sketching and painting, and she began to develop her unique artistic style. In addition, she found that she had been blessed with a very special gift: the ability to capture the fleeting, magical world which most of us see only in our dreams.

John McClelland's painting of "Katie the Tightrope Walker" inspired this lovely doll from Reco International.

While she began selling paintings at the age of fifteen, Ms. Bergsma did not commit herself wholeheartedly to an art career until she traveled to Europe in 1978. There, drinking in the wonders of the Old Masters and Impressionists in Amsterdam's many galleries and museums, she vowed that she would create paintings to inspire other people.

Today, Ms. Bergsma works from her own sunny gallery in Bellingham, Washington, creating prints and plates that feature her trademark "little people." Over the past few years, she has forged a successful association with Reco International to create the *Guardians of the Kingdom* series as well as a Christmas plate series featuring the 1991 second issue, "A Child is Born." A favorite with collectors, Ms. Bergsma often attends plate shows where her charm and unique perspective win her new admirers.

"A Child is Born" is the 1991 issue in Jody Bergsma's Christmas plate series for Reco International.

The Husband-and-Wife Team of Dot and Sy Barlowe

Since the 1940s, Dot and Sy Barlowe have collaborated in their art and in their lives. Equally gifted as artists, the pair have spent their married lives working on individual and dual projects that express their love for and deep understanding of the natural world.

The Barlowes' most recent projects for Reco International include: *Town and Country Dogs*, a series of portraits of favorite breeds in beautiful, natural settings; and *Our Cherished Seas*, depicting the life and natural beauty of our oceans.

The Hallmark of Reco: Versatility

Reco International also enjoys fruitful associations with a number of renowned and talented plate artists including: Clemente Micarelli, creator of *The Nutcracker Ballet* series; Garri Katz, painter for *Great Stories of the Bible;* and Inge Dreschler, artist for a series of tranquil landscapes called *God's Own Country*.

In addition, Reco is producing the beloved works of the late Cicely Mary Barker in a *Flower Fairies Year* Plate Collection. Special occasion plates, music boxes, and figurines by Sandra Kuck and John McClelland, and the *Sophisticated Ladies* Collection of cat plates, figurines and musicals by Aldo Fazio, round out this prolific studio's current line.

As one of the first American firms to sense the true potential for limited edition plates, Reco International strives to remain on the "cutting edge" of today's art collectibles world. Under the strong guidance of Heio Reich, Reco pledges to remain a versatile and innovative leader among limited edition studios.

The Norman Rockwell Gallery

Offering Collectibles Inspired by America's Best-Loved Artist

To protect Norman Rockwell's historic legacy of artwork — and to allow today's Americans to share in that treasury of art — The Norman Rockwell Family Trust is working closely with The Norman Rockwell Gallery to faithfully translate the work of America's best-loved artist into distinctive and unique collectible products.

The Family Trust ensures that Rockwell's artwork, name and likeness are used with taste and integrity. To signify that collectibles available through the Gallery meet these high standards, each one bears a seal attesting to their authorization by the Family Trust. This seal serves as the collector's assurance of a faithful, high-quality collectible.

Current offerings of The Norman Rockwell Gallery include two remarkable series of sculptures capturing the charming buildings of the artist's hometown of Stockbridge, Massachusetts, and several collections of figurines inspired by Rockwell's classic paintings. Christmas ornaments and snow globes are among the other artforms offered by the Gallery.

"Rockwell's Residence" offers a perfect miniature image of Norman Rockwell's famous home in Stockbridge, Mass. Handcrafted and hand-painted, this sculpture has been authorized by The Norman Rockwell Family Trust for presentation by The Norman Rockwell Gallery.

Rockwell's Hometown *and* Rockwell's Main Street *Portray the Artist's Beloved Stockbridge*

Norman Rockwell first settled in Stockbridge, Massachusetts, in 1953, with his second wife, Mary. After her death, the artist remained in the house that was to be his home for 25 years until his death in 1978. Stockbridge is a wonderfully quaint New England town that enjoyed a quiet love affair with its famous resident.

Rockwell's fondness for this Massachusetts town is evident in his famous painting entitled "Main Street, Stockbridge." Considered by many to be his greatest landscape, this wide-angle view of the town is the inspiration behind the seven landmark sculptures that comprise *Rockwell's Main Street:* "Rockwell's Studio," "The Antique Shop," "The Town Offices," "The Country Store," "The Library," "The Bank" and "The Red Lion Inn."

Other distinctive buildings in Stockbridge are showcased in detail in a second collection — *Rockwell's Hometown* — which begins with "Rockwell's Residence." Built in 1783 when Stockbridge was a small mission settlement, Rockwell's white clapboard home was one of the town's first grand homes.

As Thomas Rockwell, the artist's son, biographer and administrator of the Family Trust, remembers, "Pop gave a lot to Stockbridge. But Stockbridge gave a lot to him, too. Its physical beauty never failed to soothe him. The townsfolk provided him with a steady supply of models and picture ideas. I'm sure he would have approved of these wonderful sculptures that, in a way, are a show of thanks to the town that inspired him."

Figurines Feature Favorite Rockwell Children and Adults

Wherever he lived, it was Norman Rockwell's habit to seek out "real people" as his models. Some of these delightful children and adults have been selected as subjects for The Norman Rockwell Gallery's array of hand-painted figurines.

For example, *Age of Wonder* figurines feature children experiencing the simple joys of youth.

Typical of this heartwarming collection is "Splish Splash," a three-dimensional portrait of a young brother and sister washing their not-too-cooperative pup in an old metal wash tub.

As Tom Rockwell recalls, his father always had a unique knack for capturing the traumas and triumphs of youth. "There was always something special about my father's relationship with kids," he says. "Even when his own sons were grown up, he never lost that uncanny ability to penetrate right to the heart of what a child was feeling."

"Splish, Splash" is a wonderful beginning for a collection which has its roots in the post-war era when the gentle humor of a Rockwell painting meshed beautifully with the positive spirit of the people.

Just as appealing as the *Age of Wonder* works are *Rockwell's Beautiful Dreamers*, a suite of figurines inspired by young women; and *Gems of Wisdom*, a figurine series showing young children interacting with older adults.

"Sitting Pretty," the premier sculpture in the *Beautiful Dreamers* collection, is the first figurine to be endorsed by both the Norman Rockwell Family Trust and the *Saturday Evening Post*. Inspired by Rockwell's June 27, 1925, *Saturday Evening Post* cover, "Sitting Pretty" portrays a young woman lost in a reverie while reading a magazine. Next to her wing chair, a little Scotty begs for his mistress' attention.

Throughout his long career, Rockwell demonstrated time and time again his unmatched ability to capture the emotional connection between children eager to learn and older adults happy to teach them. The *Gems of Wisdom* figurines successfully translate into three-dimensional works some of Rockwell's most sensitive paintings on this subject. "Love Cures All," the initial issue, shows a kindly family doctor pausing to reassure a little girl by giving her favorite doll "a check-up."

Another important subject of Rockwell's work was Santa Claus, so it is especially appropriate that *Rockwell's Heirloom Santa Collection* be presented by the Norman Rockwell Gallery. This annual series of hand-painted figurines will re-create the many faces, sizes, shapes and moods of Rockwell's vision of the legendary elf.

Collectors Enjoy Many Benefits Through The Norman Rockwell Gallery

Collectors automatically become a Gallery Member the first time they purchase an item from the Gallery or receive one as a gift. In addition to

Every whimsical detail of Norman Rockwell's classic Christmas painting comes to life in "Santa's Workshop," one of an annual series of figurines from The Norman Rockwell Gallery.

Inspired by a cover illustration that Rockwell created for the June 27, 1925, Saturday Evening Post, "Sitting Pretty" is the first figurine to earn the endorsement of both the Rockwell Family Trust and the Post.

the assurance of authenticity indicated by the Family Trust seal, Gallery Members enjoy a variety of services and advantages.

For example, Members receive the "Norman Rockwell Gallery Collector Newsletter" which contains timely news and features about the world of Norman Rockwell. It includes information on special exhibits, previews of new Rockwell collectibles, insightful stories from those who knew the artist and much more.

An Unconditional 365-Day Guarantee protects each collectible acquired through the Gallery. If a collector is not completely satisfied with any Gallery offering, he or she may return it within one year for a full refund with no questions asked.

In addition, every Gallery piece is accompanied by a Certificate of Authenticity and literature on the artwork. Members also enjoy priority notification of new issues from The Norman Rockwell Gallery.

"People still relate to my father's work because he painted ordinary people in their everyday lives," says Tom Rockwell. "The situations he depicted are one that we all have shared or observed, no matter when or where we live: a brother and sister washing their dog, a couple making wedding plans, a kindly doctor reassuring a young girl, a young woman starting out on her own.

"These are universal experiences," he explains. "They embody American ideals of family and patriotism, humor and compassion; ideals which people still strive for and appreciate. Even though the physical settings may have changed, the human emotions remain the same. That is what people responded to when my father originally created them and that is what people still respond to today."

Norman Rockwell, who captured the emotions and experiences of the American scene for more than 60 years, left a unique artistic legacy which collectors still treasure today. Copyright Louie Lamone

The continuing demand for Rockwell collectibles is proof of the timeless appeal of the artist's work. Novice and veteran collectors alike will appreciate the high-quality Rockwell-inspired limited-edition pieces and the unique member benefits available through The Norman Rockwell Gallery. And with each acquisition, they are assured of the opportunity to celebrate American life through the eyes of America's best loved artist.

Roman, Inc.

Collectibles are a Kaleidoscope of Rich Family Life Experience — Children, Marriage, Relationships, History and Religion

It is only natural that Roman, Inc., a company with strong family ethics and respect for traditional values, consistently seeks talented artists whose subject matter for inspirational and religious collectibles reflects these qualities. Over the past two decades, this Midwestern firm has steadily developed into an inspirational collectibles leader with superb limited editions eloquently portraying the full and varied spectrum of the family life experience. Birth, childhood, marriage, religion, relationships with friends and family, holidays and history, all vital threads of the rich fabric of our lives, are prevailing themes in impressive Roman collections of sculptures, hanging ornaments, plates, dolls and bells. They are meticulously crafted in a variety of mediums — delicate porcelain bisque, durable poly resin, rich wood, brilliant crystal — each faithfully capturing the essence of the artists' original artwork.

The fresh beauty and ingenuous joy of childhood...a bride's nuptial grace and elegance... the power of faith...the preservation of traditions that bond families together...history instilling a strong sense of belonging and continuity...these are the vital universal themes predominant in Roman collectibles.

This choice of subjects has struck a strong responsive chord in collectors. They react to these themes because they represent all that is good in life...all to which they aspire. Lovers of fine art pieces also appreciate the magnificent artistry of Roman offerings.

Innocence, Vitality, Exuberance of Modern-Day American Children In Collectibles by Hook, Williams

The close and abiding friendship of two of Roman's foremost children's artists, Frances Hook and Abbie Williams, is indicative of the strong personal influence inherent in all Roman-artist relationships.

The gifted Hook was a successfully established children's illustrator when Roman President Ron Jedlinski approached her about translating her work into figurines in 1979. Her Northern Tissue children had already captured America's hearts; therefore, her work debuting in 1980 was quickly recognized once rendered in three-dimensional porcelain. Her understanding of child anatomy and youthful postures brought an innate realism to her art. The final element that caused Hook to rise above the proverbial crowd...the quality that shows through in her beloved works...was her love of children and boundless joy in capturing their emotions and expressions.

Long after Hook's death, the steady growth in value of closed issues of her wonderful works supports the theory she is "the Berta Hummel of America." Working with Hook's daughter, Barbara Hook Ham, Roman maintains production of translations of Hook's timeless art.

Hook's three short, but prolific, years with Roman proved long enough to establish a rich heritage. This legacy has been passed on to the able

Focal point of and inspiration for the Fontanini Heirloom Nativity, *the Holy Family, set in a humble stable is a reminder of the humility and humanity of the birth of Jesus. As the source for the exquisite "Fontanini Collectible Creche," Roman provides a vast array of nativity figurines in nine sizes, ranging from the miniature 6.5 cm to the stunning life-sized 125 cm version.*

The Bible passage, Mark 10:14-16 inspired Frances Hook's beloved subject, "Little Children, Come To Me." The aura of universal love and caring emanates from the luminous faces of children encirling Christ as He protectively holds a child in His arms.

Meet devotees of the game from days past — "A Gentleman's Game," "The Caddie" and "Tee Time at St. Andrew's" by Angela Tripi.

This "Legacy of Love" keepsake plate was designed by Abbie Williams for infant celebrations. The backstamp provides space for that all-important personal information about the newest family addition.

and talented hands of Abbie Williams — Hook's close friend and protegee. Destiny must have played a role in bringing these artists together at critical stages in their lives. The older Hook was in the last phase of her ongoing battle with cancer yet enjoying the fruits of unprecedented collectibles success with Roman. Young Williams, spurred by financial necessity and love of art, sought entry into the world of fulltime artistry.

Their special focus on children and shared specialty of the highly demanding medium of pastels were natural magnets that drew them together. Their personal affinity sealed the relationship. Hook encouraged and assisted Williams in resuming her child portraiture career and introduced her to Roman.

Williams delights in depicting her young subjects as they revel in such universal experiences as childhood relationships with animals and caring friendships among children. Her renderings exhibit great strength and vibrancy which Williams attributes to her special interest in working with light to create a sense of health, joy and vitality synonymous with childhood. Williams' vision of youthful spontaneity is celebrated on limited and open edition plate collections and music boxes enjoying enthusiastic collector reception. Her newest efforts for Roman include *Legacy of Love* newborn commemorative and *Bless the Child* especially conceived for the growing segment of Black American collectors. Next on the horizon for Williams is delving into the delights of "firsts" in babies' lives with her *God Bless You, Little One* keepsake collection.

Turn-of-Century, Winsome European Youngsters by Lisi Martin

Collectors are drawn to Lisi Martin's pensive children as they go about their business in their magical world of make-believe. As a child in post-World War II Spain, Martin dreamed of creating unique drawings of youngsters at play.

Martin captures the pensive nature of European juveniles — a little wise for their years —in her greeting card illustrations. Even the rich hues of her intricate figures are carefully formulated to impart an old world charm to her small fry. Eloquent translations of Martin's art into valuable wood carvings and affordable StoneArt sculptures are performed at the Dolfi Studios in Ortisei, Italy.

All Brides Are Beautiful... Especially Those by Ellen Williams

Superb artistry, exquisite craftsmanship and accuracy of historical detail combined for Ellen Williams' award-winning *Classic Brides of the Century*™ Collection. Williams' embarked on many months of research to authenticate her designs for nine brides from 1900 to 1990 — each the epitome of her decade. Her painstaking efforts earned the *1989 Collectible of Show* honors at the California International Collectibles Exposition for the limited edition series.

"I felt that an evolution of fashion, as shown through the wedding tradition, would give an interesting perspective of life in this twentieth century," Williams asserts. And the bride representing each 10-year span is, indeed, a portrait of grace and elegance. Each also marks an important milepost in the transformation of woman's role in society.

Williams has expanded her concept of brides as a reflection of social and political trends into a limited edition series of bridal dolls based on the popular *Classic Brides of the Century* figurines. "Flora" — The 1900s Bride walked down the col-

"Flora" — The 1900s Bride is the first issue in the Classic Brides of the Century *collection of porcelain bisque dolls based on original designs by award-winning artist Ellen Williams.*

lectors' aisle in 1991. She is the embodiment of the lingering Victorianism and Edwardian extravagances of her times.

"Jennifer" — The 1980s Bride, second in the doll series, will celebrate her nuptials late in 1991. This young bride closer to modern times exemplifies the Hollywood glamour so popular in this decade. With slender silhouette in a heavily beaded satin gown...every feature chosen for dramatic effect ...she reflects '80s women coming into their own with an independence carrying over into fashion.

Angela Tripi — Chronicler of Times Past, Present For Sense of Belonging, Continuity

Gallery-quality masterpieces exploring Christian, Judaic and historic themes are Italian sculptor Tripi's specialty and contribution to the Roman kaleidoscope of life collectibles. Her creative hands, skilled from years of working with clay, infuse Tripi's unique perception of life into her vibrant and expressive subjects. She commemorates the 500th anniversary in 1992 of the discovery of America with salutes to "Christopher Columbus" and "The Nina, The Pinta and The Santa Maria." Her masterful depictions of golf's early days, "The Caddie," "Tee Time at St. Andrew's" and "A Gentleman's Game," are reminders of this sport's interesting beginnings in Scotland.

Tripi also focuses on "St. Francis of Assisi," whose desire to share his wonder at the miracle of Christ's birth with all people led to the first live enactment of the Nativity in Greccio, Italy, in 1223. As a result, he transformed perception and celebration of Christmas and the devotion to the Nativity forevermore into the beloved observances maintained to the present.

The Fontanini® Heirloom Nativity — An Abiding Core of Religious Tradition That Bonds Families Together

The time-honored custom of celebrating the Nativity continues as a major tradition in the lives of millions of Christians around the world. Moravian settlers brought their "putz," or Christmas tree yard, practice to America's shores in the 1740s. Brave and hardy immigrants from all corners of the world wove their forefathers' rituals into their new lives. And the American Nativity came into being.

Roman assumes a pivotal role in this widespread Nativity ethic as the exclusive source for the exquisite "Fontanini® Collectible Creche" from Italy's famed house of Fontanini. Since 1908, three generations of the Fontanini family have crafted figures and decorations of heirloom quality echoing the heritage of the Renaissance ever present in Tuscany. In accord with Roman philosophy, the creation of Fontanini figures is truly a family affair from concept to completion. The exquisite sculptures begin in the skilled hands of master sculptor Elio Simonetti. A meticulous molding process follows under vigilant Fontanini supervision. Finally, each figure is painstakingly painted by hand by artisans utilizing skills passed from generation to generation in their families.

American families increasingly choose Fontanini Nativities for their beauty and year 'round availability. To keep up with growing North American demand in 1991, Roman expanded offerings with the versatile *The Fontanini Signature Collection*™. This 11 cm. collection of 18 figurines blends perfectly with existing 10 and 12 cm. pieces. Beautifully conceived Story Cards bring added dimension to gift-boxed sculptures in this stunning series. While gathering together to set up their Nativities, families enjoy readings that unfold fascinating stories about life in the Holy Land at the time of Christ's birth.

Royal Doulton

Modern Works of Ceramic Art From a Fine Art Studio With a Two-Century Heritage of Excellence

When John Doulton invested his life savings in a small Thameside pottery at Lambeth, England, he surely had no idea that the Doulton name would become a dominating force in the ceramic industry over the next two centuries. Doulton began his business creating everyday goods like stoneware vessels and drainpipes. But he and his descendants soon began to perfect methods of creation for some of the world's finest dinnerware and decorative collectibles.

John Doulton's son, Henry, became an apprentice to his father at the age of 15, in 1835. Young Henry enjoyed a strong interest in the arts, and he convinced his father to devote some of their studio's energies to decorative wares. Even though Doulton was primarily concerned with and noted for its production of utility wares like pipes and garden vases, Henry began to devote some production of more artistically inspired designs. These designs were merely considered a side interest until the Paris Exhibition of 1867. There, some seventy pieces of Royal Doulton decorative wares were shown.

These elegant works of ceramic art impressed critics and the viewing public, and also won the appreciation of Queen Victoria. She ordered some pieces to be sent to London, and throughout the rest of her long reign she showed a great personal interest in Doulton works. A Doulton artist named George Tinworth created a figure of Queen Victoria. And in 1877, Henry Doulton was knighted by the Queen for his contributions to the ceramic industry.

"The Fortune Teller" is Royal Doulton's annual Character Jug of the Year, issued in 1991.

Doulton Earns the Title "Royal"

In addition to his knighthood, Henry Doulton reached another milestone in 1877 with the purchase of an old, established pottery at Burslem, in Staffordshire. This new pottery enabled Doulton to craft works in fine earthenware and bone china, and spurred the recruitment of a distinguished staff of designers, sculptors, and artists. Many of these artists achieved long service records for thirty, forty, fifty years and more — paving the way for years of great accomplishment for Doulton...and then for Royal Doulton potteries.

Queen Victoria bestowed the Royal Warrant upon Doulton, in 1901, which enabled the firm to call itself Royal Doulton forever after. By this time, Royal Doulton's fame was such that the studio was called upon to design wares for royalty in far-off countries as well as Britain.

A Mysterious Royal Commission

Indeed, in 1907, Royal Doulton received a mysterious, exclusive special order for a cobalt-blue dinner service of 3,000 pieces, including vases, all to be heavily gold-encrusted. The design chosen, Royal Doulton craftsmen began the careful production of the china, a two-year task. When the magnificent set was complete, the identity of the buyer was revealed as Abdul-Hamid II, Sultan of Turkey. The valuable china was carefully crated, insured, and shipped to the Sultan's royal Turkish palace.

Its Constantinople arrival coincided with a revolution. Abdul-Hamid had been taken prisoner and exiled to Salonica. The cargo ship's officers warehoused the Sultan's china and notified

London. The exiled Sultan would have no use for the china, nor could he pay the bill, so it was decided to return the china to England. The underwriters insisted it must be packed by a skilled Royal Doulton employee.

A packer named Tom Clarke made the necessary journey to Turkey to perform the job. On the last lap of the return voyage, the ship carrying the china caught fire in the Bay of Biscay and went to the bottom with its priceless treasure! When the set was originally produced, several original pieces were made as a safeguard against damage in transit. Today, these pieces are part of Doulton's archival collection which has been on exhibition in the United States and abroad and is admired by thousands for its fabulous detail.

The Making of a Royal Doulton Figurine

The famous collection of Royal Doulton figurines — now totaling more than 2,000 separate figures — have emanated from the Royal Doulton factory at Burslem only since 1912. Loved by all are a series of bone china figurines representing characters from the stories of Charles Dickens. During the first part of this century, the series won the approval of Alfred Tennyson Dickens, the author's son, who wrote a letter of praise to the company when the figurines first appeared.

The creation of one of these figures has always demanded the close collaboration of the sculptor, the potter, and the painter. Success has always depended on the expertise of each man in the team, and Doulton's constant insistence upon high artistic and technical standards has ensured that the necessary talent is readily available.

Even today, when Doulton figurine production is counted in thousands, each figure is a unique creation. Every piece is sculpted by hand, and the various sections are cast in molds. The statuette base is usually molded whole, but the other pieces, such as the body torso, head, arms and any other detailed parts are cast separately.

More elaborate figures need to be built up from an even greater number of component parts. After a model has received its initial firing, it is glazed; after the second firing, it is assigned to an artist who is responsible for the delicate painting of the figure. To obtain the subtle color effects which — in addition to the careful sculpting — distinguish these figures from all imitations, five or more separate firings are sometimes necessary, one color being fired before the next is applied. The facial expressions are particularly important, and are normally entrusted to the most talented painters. Considerable care is taken to ensure that the finished product is perfect in every detail.

Royal Doulton's English Toby Mugs and Character Jugs

Among the most famous of all Royal Doulton creations are the firm's Character Jugs and Toby Mugs, known by collectors around the world. Such

Crafted in pristine white bone china, "The Bridesmaid" shows Royal Doulton's ability to create elegant figurines to enhance contemporary decor.

These Royal Doulton Age of Innocence *figures are, from left, "Puppy Love," "Feeding Time," and "Making Friends." Retail prices range from $225 to $250.*

Royal Doulton's 1991 "Figure of the Year" is a hand-painted bone china masterwork entitled "Amy." From her flouncy skirts to her flowered fan, "Amy" is dressed in the height of period fashion. Her delicate features, graceful arms and tiny waist make "Amy" a beauty to be cherished forever.

is the fascination of the English Toby Mug and its near relation, the Character Jug, that anyone fortunate enough to become the owner of even one or two examples, is almost irresistibly fired with the desire to become a collector.

The number of genuine eighteenth-century specimens still in existence is small, and the scope for forming a collection of these items is quite difficult. On the other hand, thousands of enthusiasts find interest and pleasure in collecting Royal Doulton pieces created currently.

These are the twentieth-century descendants of a long historical line of tankards and jugs, fashioned in human likenesses by potters through the ages. The early Toby Mugs were made so each corner of the tricorn hat formed a convenient spout for drinking. Today vivid likenesses of William Shakespeare, Rip Van Winkle, Sir Winston Churchill and George Washington have been colorfully produced by Doulton craftsmen.

In 1991, Royal Doulton initiated the concept of "Character Jug of the Year," introducing a "Fortune Teller" jug in a large size, sculpted by Stanley James Taylor. At the end of 1991, it was retired from the collection, never to be reintroduced, with a new annual piece unveiled for 1992. Other Character Jugs currently in the Royal Doulton line include sports and military tributes, and a circus "Ring Master."

Royal Doulton Figurines: Heirlooms of Tomorrow

The contemporary Royal Doulton figurine collection offers pieces with clean, modern lines as well as works that reflect the Victorian grace of the firm's first patroness. The *Images* line — a perfect choice for contemporary homes — features "Bridesmaid" in pure white bone china. *Character Studies* premieres "Winning Putt," a portrait of a lady golfer that would be ideal as a trophy or commemorative.

The *Age of Innocence* Collection comprises three delightful childhood studies, each issued in a limited edition of 9,500. They are, "Puppy Love," "Feeding Time," and "Making Friends," and each portrays a lovely little girl with her animal friend or friends.

For 1991, Royal Doulton offered a superb "Figure of the Year" entitled "Amy," a special-edition, fine bone china figure whose edition closed at the end of the calendar year. Each year, Royal Doulton will offer another lovely work of art that may be acquired during that year only.

Collectors Club and Special Appearances Make For Enjoyment by Royal Doulton Admirers

The Royal Doulton International Collectors Club represents a pioneer in the collectors club field, having been founded in 1980. With thousands of members in the United States, England, Australia, Canada, Europe and New Zealand, the Club provides a vital information service to further awareness and understanding of Royal Doulton. Members receive frequent, beautifully presented newsletters as well as regular opportunities to acquire exclusive Royal Doulton pieces.

Club members and other Royal Doulton admirers often are treated to local appearances by Royal Doulton craftspeople — and exclusive appearances by a descendant of John Doulton himself: Michael Doulton. For more information about an American membership in the Royal Doulton International Collectors Club, write the club at 700 Cottontail Lane, Somerset, New Jersey 08873.

Sarah's Attic

Sarah Schultz's Charming Figurines Capture the Heritage of African Americans, Native Americans, and Country Life in the U.S.A.

Sarah Johnston Schultz was born on February 23, 1943 to William (Bill) and Louise Johnston. As a young girl, Sarah was quite a tomboy. She walked around the small town of Chesaning, Michigan as the town's first papergirl. Older residents of Chesaning can still remember this dirty, ragged looking, but somehow adorable, little girl personally delivering papers to their doorsteps.

At a young age, Sarah developed a serious case of rheumatic fever. She was sick for quite some time and her father seriously worried about the fate of his little girl. In a move to cheer her up and somehow appeal to God to take care of her, Sarah's father bought a collection of angels for her while she was sick. With many prayers, Sarah recovered with no permanent side effects. Sarah honestly believes that her father and the angels he had so lovingly purchased for her had everything to do with her recovery. When Sarah moved out of her house, she stored the angels in her attic so her young children would not break them. As a dedication to her father who passed away and to everyone who has lost a loved one, Sarah created her collection, *Angels in the Attic*.

An Afro-American family lived in an apartment near Sarah when she was young. Sarah had very close ties to this family. She would visit them daily and they would all sit around a table and tell stories. The elder members of the family had very interesting stories to tell Sarah. She was so intrigued by these stories, that she never forgot them. Many of the pieces in Sarah's Attic's *Black Heritage Collection* are inspired by these stories from this special family.

On August 17, 1963 Sarah Johnston married her high school sweetheart, John (Jack) Schultz. Because Jack was still in pharmacy school, Sarah began working for Michigan Bell Telephone Company to help put her husband through school. After Jack graduated, he began working in his father's pharmacy in Chesaning and eventually purchased it. Shortly after their marriage, Jack and Sarah began their family. They had five children — Mark, Tim, Tom, Julie, and Michael. As all mothers, Sarah felt as if her children grew overnight, so she brought back the memory of her children growing up. These children are in the *Daisy Collection*, and it is no surprise that daisies are Sarah's favorite flower.

Harpster and his family, "Whoopie," "Wooster," and "Baby Tansy" are enjoying an outing together in this grouping of figurines from the Sarah's Attic Black Heritage Collection.

Just as daisies have brightened Sarah's days, her children have brought a brightness to her days that could never be replaced. Sarah hopes that all her pieces come alive for collectors and bring back one of their own loving memories.

As her children grew older and began leaving home for college, Jack and Sarah knew they were going to need added income to put their five children through college. With this in mind, Sarah knew that she would never get her shabby, torn-up, old couch replaced. So in 1983, she decided to turn her hobby of making crafts into a wholesale business. That tiny business that was started by one woman has now grown and become one of the most popular collectible lines in the country.

Because of the upbringing that Sarah had, she feels very strongly that everyone should love one another. This strong feeling of love, which is instilled in every piece that Sarah designs, comes straight from Sarah's heart. Hence, Sarah's Attic logo — The very best always comes from the heart! This strong feeling of loving one another is also shown on every piece by the signature heart, a registered trademark of Sarah's Attic. Sarah started the signature heart because she feels that everyone has the same color heart no matter what color they may be. And the heart is the true quality of a person. So, no matter what race a Sarah's Attic figurine portrays, it will always have the signature heart on it to represent peace and equality in the world.

A Scene in the Park from the Black Heritage Collection

Sarah Schultz has the heart of a storyteller, and collectors may share in her visions as they arrange *Black Heritage* figurines in special groupings. For instance, when "Harpster with Harmonica," "Whoopie & Wooster in Sweaters," and "Baby Tansy" are shown together, we can imagine a cool autumn evening when father Harpster takes his family to the park.

Harpster plays a song on his harmonica...a special tune written just for his family. Clinging to Mama's knees, little Wooster is not quite used to all the people in the park. He's not ready to run over to the swings and slides just yet! Baby Tansy enjoys the deep sound of her father's music, and we can imagine her joining in with a soft "coo" of contentment.

Little Angels Make a Heavenly Combination

As the mother of five children, Sarah is known for capturing youngsters' mischief in many of her figurines. But her "Adora Angel with Bunny" and "Enos Angel with Frog" show two black children in heavenly harmony. But as a mother, Sarah

Angel "Adora" and her friend, Angel "Enos," have taken time out from their heavenly schedule to act like children. "Enos" has a frog and baseball equipment, while "Adora" is busy coloring a picture.

Sarah's Attic pays tribute to Native Americans with this set of family figurines dressed in traditional clothing. From left to right their names are, "Little Dove," "Bright Sky," "Iron Hawk," and "Spotted Eagle."

knows that all little boy and girl angels need a break from being heavenly once in awhile — they deserve time for play, too!

Not unlike many little girls on earth, Adora enjoys coloring pictures and giving them to people. She has just finished drawing and coloring a picture with her crayons, and she plans to give it to the Heavenly Guardian Angel. Someday Adora would like to become a Guardian Angel, too! Besides her picture and crayons, she also holds her pet bunny in her lap.

Between his heavenly duties, Enos, too, has fun doing boyish things. He likes to play catch with the other small boy angels, or sometimes takes an interest in catching frogs. If it were not for his wings, Enos would appear to be a normal young boy, in his baseball cap, T-shirt, and jeans!

Proud Native American Family

In addition to her well-received *Black Heritage* Collection, Sarah has created a collection of figurines capturing the pride and tradition of America's Native People. An attractive grouping features, "Iron Hawk," "Bright Sky," "Little Dove," and "Spotted Eagle."

"Iron Hawk," a fearless warrior and trusted protector, wears the soft deerskin clothing and beaded jewelry native to his people. His beautiful wife, "Bright Sky," a skilled weaver and craftsperson, is busy finishing a gathering basket made from twigs. Dressed in sun-bleached white leather, "Bright Sky" also wove the wool blanket her daughter, "Little Dove," wears to ward off the autumn chill. "Little Dove" and her brother, "Spotted Eagle," have just returned from the meadow where they picked some of the last wild daisies of the season. "Spotted Eagle," a little brave with chubby cheeks,

This hand-painted figurine, "Forever In Our Hearts," offers a tribute to those who have served the American Armed Forces in the past or present. Proceeds will go to the USO.

is upset because he could not find a feather for his headband. "Iron Hawk" assures him it will only be a matter of time before he earns his own feathers, explaining that it is much more honorable to earn a feather than to find one.

A Special Honor for the American Armed Forces

A tribute to both current and past members of the Armed Forces who have helped build this great Nation, "Forever in Our Hearts" is a hand-painted limited edition (10,000 pieces).

Waiting patiently for word from far away loved ones, two children have tied a yellow ribbon around the mailbox to show their support for American servicemen and women.

Sarah's Attic will show its support by donating the proceeds from this collectible to USO which aids those who, by serving America, remain "Forever In Our Hearts."

Forever Friends Collectors' Club

Collectors are invited to become a Charter Year Member of the Sarah's Attic Forever Friends Collectors' Club! Sarah's Attic has created the *Forever Friends* Collection, an exclusive collection for members only. For years to come, members of the Forever Friends Collectors' Club will be the only collectors eligible to purchase figurines from this collection.

Remember sitting on the back porch, both you and your friend, dreaming of new games to play or places to explore? Before you knew it, the day had already passed. Still sitting on the back porch, you found that you and your friend did not have to dream of things to do, because you had each other to laugh with, talk with, and share everything with. Sarah's Attic would like to keep these childhood memories alive by offering the first two pieces from the *Forever Friends* Collection, "Diamond" and "Ruby." Collectors who join between June 1, 1991 and May 31, 1992 will receive two Redemption Certificates for these Members Only figurines which collectors will be able to purchase at any Sarah's Attic Dealer. Collectors will also receive other special benefits for being a club member as well as beginning a special friendship that will last forever.

SCHMID

Three Generations of Schmids Share the Best of Contemporary Collectible Art With American Collectors

"From the time my grandfather first started selling giftware to New England shopkeepers in the 1930s, he insisted that Schmid must be known for its quality and service," says Paul Schmid III, the firm's current President. "He'd be very proud to know those same values are still the guiding force at Schmid nearly sixty years later."

Today Paul Schmid III continues the Schmid legacy with a thriving firm that was born when his grandfather sensed opportunity in the aftermath of the Stock Market Crash of 1929. While many New Englanders were stymied by the Great Depression, the sixty-nine-year-old Schmid had a vision for a brand-new business. His successful career in commodities at an end, Schmid enlisted the help of his sons, Paul II and John, to make his new dream a reality.

Schmid Shares the Art Mastery of His Native Germany

Paul Schmid had long believed that Americans would enjoy owning many of the beautiful art objects created in the land of his birth, Germany.

The critters in Lowell Davis' sketchbook jump to life on "When Coffee Never Tasted So Good," created at the Border Fine Arts Studio in Langholm, Scotland. The figurine is limited to 1,250 and is available at $800 issue price.

These giftware items and collectibles were not yet available in the United States in the early 1930s. Even though few could afford such "extras" during the Depression, by 1935 Paul Schmid could see his plan falling into place. The key was the discovery of the charming Goebel figurines of Sister M. I. Hummel by Paul's son John.

John Schmid was attending the Frankfurt Fair in Germany when he first saw the hand-painted porcelain M. I. Hummels, and placed an immediate order for seventy-two pieces. At that time, Hummel Figurines retailed for about $2.00 apiece: a tidy sum for Depression-weary Americans to pay for a decorative item. Yet the Hummel pieces sold well that year and thus began the long and fruitful association of Schmid and the works of Sister M. I. Hummel.

The next year also saw a triumph for Schmid, when the company began importing ANRI woodcarvings from Italy. The Hummel and ANRI lines comprised the bulk of Schmid's business for the next few years, until World War II forced Schmid into a four-year hiatus. Paul II and John Schmid donned the uniforms of the U.S. Armed Forces, and President Franklin D. Roosevelt suspended American trading relationships with Germany for the duration of the war.

Post-War Prosperity for Schmid Brothers

After World War II, Schmid & Co. reopened its doors as Schmid Brothers. During the next twenty-five years, demand for ANRI woodcarvings and M. I. Hummel figurines grew slowly and steadily, and Schmid Brothers prospered. The company grew to include fifty employees and distribution expanded across the United States.

In the 1960s and 1970s, Schmid expanded its business by acquiring some of the most sought-after licenses in the collectibles and giftware fields, including Disney, Beatrix Potter and Gordon Fraser. Schmid also began developing its own brands of music boxes, dolls, ornaments, and other gift and collectible items. And in 1979, Schmid formed what is now a long and highly successful association with the Missouri farmer-turned-artist, Lowell Davis.

Tick, tock — Peter Rabbit's a clock! This hand-painted clock features a fine quartz movement, and large, easy-to-read numbers.

Market-Driven Strategy Helps Schmid Serve Collectors

Today Schmid has grown to become one of the world's leading suppliers of fine gifts and collectibles. Schmid's enduring strength lies in its commitment to listen to its customers, and to provide them with the artists, artwork and media that they want most.

"While we always knew that the 1990s would be demanding and difficult for manufacturers and retailers alike," says Schmid's C.O.O. Jim Godsill, "we recognized that no one can forecast precisely the directions collectors will take as the events in their lives evolve. The real benefit of a market-driven strategy is that it is not cast in bronze. It contains mechanisms for listening, measuring, taking the beginning pulse of change, then has the built-in flexibility to respond to change quickly."

An example of Schmid's ability to react quickly and provide collectors with timely works of art is the "Crossroads" figurine from the M. I. Hummel line. Introduced to celebrate the new freedom in Eastern Europe, it depicts two boys at a juncture in which one sign points East, and another West. Inspired by a similar 1955 design, in which a "Halt" sign stands at the midpoint, this limited edition carries the "Halt" sign, cast on the ground.

" 'Crossroads' immediately captured Americans' joy at the events abroad," says Schmid's Paul Johnson, Vice-President, M.I. Hummel Division. "It sold out in ten days." Schmid plans many more timely issues that will allow collectors to celebrate special events and historic occurrences, and to indulge their evolving interests.

Lowell Davis Shares Rural America With "City Slickers"

As a farmer, husband, father and artist, Missouri's Lowell Davis is dedicated to preserving the memory of American rural life. Schmid — under the "third generation" leadership of Paul Schmid III — forged an association with this gifted farmer-turned-artist in 1979. And now Davis draws upon his vivid childhood memories of American farm life to create his popular collector plates, figurines, and ornaments.

Not content with mere memories of the days "way back when", Davis has recreated it with a farm complete with vintage buildings and implements, and a barnyard full of animals for inspiration. These "critters" take on human qualities in charming works like "When Coffee Never Tasted So Good," a limited edition, wood-based porcelain figurine from Schmid. This work of art is part of the *Little Critters* series, all of which portray animals with human characteristics.

Lowell Davis collectors enjoy the opportunity to become members of the Lowell Davis Farm Club — a service of Schmid which keeps them informed about the artist's newest works and activities. For their annual membership fee, club members receive a free "members only" figurine, a free club cap with the Lowell Davis Farm Club insignia, a Lowell Davis Farm Club Membership Card, and a free annual renewal gift. In addition, mem-

Kitty Cucumber acts out the fantasy of "Cinderella" as she is whisked away to the ball in a horse-drawn coach! The musical plays "Cinderella's Dream of the Ball," measures 9¹/₄" in height and carries an issue price of $75.00.

Mickey and Minnie Mouse celebrate Mother's Day and Father's Day on this pair of hand-painted figurines from the Disney Characters Collection *by Schmid. Each figurine is gift-boxed and sells for $17.50.*

bers receive periodic invitations to visit Lowell Davis on his farm, announcements of his local appearances, the "Lowell Davis Farm Gazette," and the opportunity to buy exclusive "members only" Lowell Davis figurines.

Beatrix Potter® — More Beloved Than Ever Before

For years, Schmid collectors have enjoyed acquiring Schmid's delightful recreations of Beatrix Potter's famous animal characters. Ever since 1902, when Peter Rabbit first squeezed his way into Mr. McGregor's garden in one of her storybooks, Miss Potter's mischievous bunny and all his friends have been favorites of children and adults alike.

From the pages of those tales, Beatrix Potter's unforgettable characters come to life — in a beautifully hand-crafted, hand-painted earthenware and porcelain collection of animated music boxes, ornaments, waterballs, and nightlights. In addition, there is now a charming Peter Rabbit Clock, capturing this beloved bunny with two carrots in his paws and a look of delight on his furry face. Perfect for a child's room — or a whimsical gift for an adult, the 11½" clock sells for $60.00.

Kitty Cucumber® Plays "Cinderella"

Ever since Kitty Cucumber made her Schmid debut in 1985, this adorable feline and her friends have delighted collectors as the stars of a wonderful line of figurines, music boxes, ornaments, tins, and other gifts and collectibles. Licensed by B. Shackman & Company, Kitty and her friends — J. P. Buster, Ellie, Albert, Priscilla, Miss Fish, Muffin, and Baby Pickles — are in a "Cat"-egory all their own!

Most recently, Kitty Cucumber has taken on a fairy tale quality as she acts out the fantasy of Cinderella in a new, limited edition porcelain bisque musical from Schmid. As she is whisked away to the ball in a horse-drawn coach, Kitty plays "Cinderella's Dream of the Ball." The creation of New York artist Mary Lillemoe, Kitty Cucumber is based on Ms. Lillemoe's own favorite cat remembered from her Minnesota childhood.

Mickey and Minnie Mouse Join Forces With Schmid

Schmid welcomes you to Disney's Magic Kingdom, where Mickey Mouse and Minnie are forever young...Donald Duck is forever rascally...and Daisy is a fiery Southern Belle. Pluto, of course, is forever "friendly" and Goofy will always be..."Goofy"!

Under license with The Walt Disney Company, Schmid has been creating a world of fantasy and charm for collectors for more than 20 years. In addition to Mickey Mouse and friends, the collection is augmented by all the well-known Disney Characters that have become as familiar as the folks next door.

Hand-crafted and hand-painted by the world's finest craftsmen, there are animated music boxes, porcelain and hand-carved wooden dolls, figurines, ornaments, limited edition vignettes, nightlights, musical picture frames, and more.

From the whimsical farm animal art of Lowell Davis to the beloved figurines of Sister M. I. Hummel, Schmid's product lines shine with quality and uniqueness. Whether one collects Disney Characters, Beatrix Potter or Kitty Cucumber designs, all Schmid patrons are assured of the utmost in fine craftsmanship and charm — just as they were two generations ago under the watchful eye of the company's founder, Paul Schmid.

Swarovski America Limited

Swarovski America Celebrates Our Environmental Riches With Swarovski Collectors Society Pieces

The Swarovski Collectors Society may seem like an "overnight success" to collectors who have recently discovered the dazzling Silver Crystal figurines of this celebrated Austrian firm. Yet the remarkable popularity of Swarovski crystal animals and decorative items is firmly rooted in their rich 100-year history: a saga that began when Daniel Swarovski applied for a patent on his first invention: a machine capable of cutting glass jewelry stones with perfect precision.

Through two world wars and the Great Depression of the 1930s, the Swarovski company endured as one of Europe's most trusted sources for crystal jewelry stones and other decorative products. But it was not until 1977 that Daniel Swarovski's heirs introduced the first piece in the Swarovski Silver Crystal collection.

The Swarovski Silver Crystal legend began with a menagerie of animals, an elegant selection of candleholders, and decorative accessories. Then, ten years after the first animal was unveiled, the firm launched what is today one of the most renowned collectible associations in the world: the Swarovski Collectors Society.

In addition to its many Silver Crystal pieces inspired by animals, Swarovski creates other works of naturalist art like this exquisite, shimmering "Apple," introduced during 1991.

The Sharing and Caring *Series*

The Swarovski Collectors Society introduced its first piece in 1987, and since then the shimmering "Togetherness" — the Lovebirds has become one of the most renowned works of art in today's world of collectibles. This elegant crystal figurine of two lovebirds has reached new secondary market heights with each passing year.

Two more pieces completed the *Sharing and Caring* series: the wonderful "Sharing" — the Woodpeckers in 1988, and the heartwarming "Amour" — the Turtledoves in 1989. Now each of these editions has closed, paving the way for a new suite of annual Collectors Society editions that premiered in 1990: the *Maternal Love* series.

A Dolphin Pair Celebrates Mother's Love

Swarovski America Limited introduced the three-piece *Maternal Love* series in 1990 with a three-day extravaganza in Orlando, Florida — an event orchestrated especially for Collectors Society members. Called "Design Celebration '90," the gathering attracted more than 500 collectors from throughout the United States and Canada.

A highlight of the celebration was the unveiling of "Lead Me" — the Dolphins, the 1990 Collectors Society piece and first of three offerings in the *Maternal Love* series. Crystal art master Michael Stamey presented "a breathtaking look at a dolphin and her calf, exquisitely rendered in Swarovski crystal," according to a Swarovski Collectors Society spokesperson.

"...Stamey has captured the grace, beauty, and special closeness of the dolphins as they leap in harmony over a cresting wave." The artist himself has been overwhelmed by the reception he is given whenever he appears at Collectors Society events such as the one in Orlando. "They all seem to think I'm a great artist — but I'm just a craftsman doing something I enjoy and am good at," he comments modestly.

The readers of Collector Editions *magazine chose "Lead Me" — the Dolphins as the winner of one of its coveted Readers' Choice awards during the piece's year of introduction, 1990.*

Award-Winning "Lead Me" — the Dolphins Highlights Environmental Concerns

Dolphins have captured the imaginations — and hearts — of artists like Stamey for centuries. In 1500 B.C., the Minoans looked upon them as symbols of joy and music. Years later, the ancient Greeks dedicated their temple at Delphi to a dolphin god. Indeed, the word "dolphin" comes from the Greek word "delphi."

Considered among the wisest of mammals, dolphins today continue to enchant humans with their intelligence, physical grace, and special rapport — with each other as well as with people. Their charm and beauty have inspired a protective instinct among their human admirers — and thus dolphins have become a special concern to environmentalists.

To call attention to the efforts of three major U.S. tuna companies which decided to stop buying tuna caught in gill or drift nets — nets that also kill dolphins — Swarovski America Limited made a very special presentation in May of 1990. They bestowed "Lead Me" — the Dolphins upon the Chief Executive Officers of H. J. Heinz Company (owner of Starkist), Pet, Inc. (owner of Chicken of the Sea), and Bumblebee Tuna Company.

"Lead Me" — the Dolphins also earned a special honor during 1990: the piece won the *Collector Editions* magazine "Awards of Excellence" contest for 1990 in the category of Glass Objects: $100 and over. Sold originally for $225.00, the edition "Lead Me" — the Dolphins closed on December 31, 1990 and the piece is now available only on the secondary market.

"Save Me" — the Seals Continues Maternal Love Series

"The trouble with seals is that they don't do spectacular things like leaping out of the ocean, and they look pretty helpless on land," says Michael Stamey, creator of the 1991 Annual Edition for the Swarovski Collectors Society's "Save Me" — the Seals. Stamey says the reason he chose to depict the mother seal and her pup huddled together on an ice floe was because they do not spend any time together in the ocean. As soon as the pup has been weaned, which takes place out of the water, it leaves its mother to make its own way. So the poignancy of the moment depicted in the Swarovski piece is as short-lived as it is emotive.

Although seals are now protected by the laws of most countries and the damage of commercial exploitation of the past has largely been repaired, other dangers threaten these creatures' survival. Epidemics caused by pollution, death caused by eating plastic packaging discarded by humans, or — like the dolphins — becoming caught in fishing nets all are threats to the seal.

"Save Me" — the Seals seeks to draw attention to these noble animals by depicting the mother-and-child relationship with exquisite poignancy. Available only to Swarovski Collectors Society members, "Save Me" — the Seals is available until December 31, 1991 at an original price of $225. The 1992 *Maternal Love* issue will complete this exquisite, three-piece series.

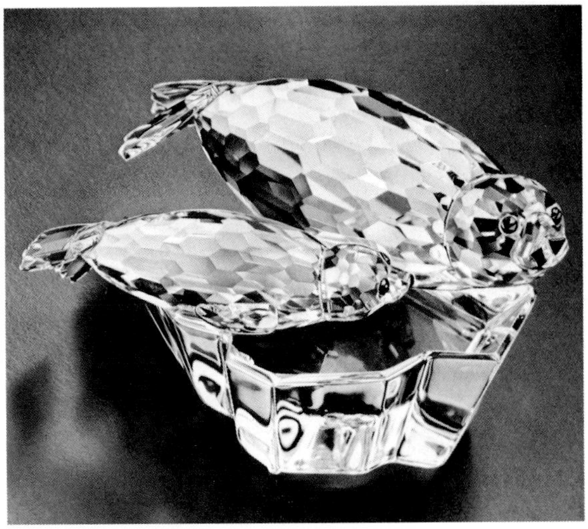

"Save Me" — the Seals debuted in 1991 as the second in Swarovski Collectors Society series entitled Maternal Love.

Endangered Species Series Features Animals Who Need Our Compassion

Elegant works of art from Swarovski focus much-needed attention on several of the world's endangered species: the whale, the koala bear, the falcon, and the tortoise. Modern hunting techniques have outwitted the clever whale, while the burning of the woodlands and merciless hunting have proved fatal to the friendly koala of eastern Australia. The falcon is known as the fastest inhabitant of the air, but recent events have shown that he must be protected as carefully and specifically as the deliberate tortoise.

To draw attention to these endangered creatures, Swarovski Silver Crystal has created a series of figurines with the utmost care, grace, and the essential extra ingredient: depth of feeling. The pieces are available in a range of sizes and prices from highly affordable to imposing, investment-quality pieces.

Swarovski Boasts the Four C's of Crystal

To be considered an excellent crystal specimen, a piece must score well on four important guidelines of quality: clarity, cut, caliber, and collectibility. Swarovski crystal scores high on all four C's established by crystal connoisseurs and has achieved incredible brilliance and maximum refraction when the crystal stones are cut and polished.

But while the purity of raw materials, and technical expertise in finishing make Swarovski crystal flawless in transparency, brilliance and weight, it is another quality that sets them apart. Originality of design creates the Swarovski magic that attracts thousands of new collectors — and Collectors Society members — with each passing year.

The Many Benefits of Membership in the Swarovski Collectors Society

Today there are more than 100,000 Swarovski Collectors Society members worldwide. For just $30.00 per year, U.S. members are offered a wide range of privileges and advantages. Perhaps most important of all, they have the exclusive opportunity to purchase the Swarovski Collectors Society Annual Editions, spectacular pieces of dazzling crystal designed exclusively for members.

They also receive tips on cleaning and caring for their precious collection and are informed in advance of all new and soon-to-be retired Swarovski Silver Crystal products in a twice-yearly, full-color magazine, the *Swarovski Collector*. Special opportunities to attend gala events such as the Orlando extravaganza held in 1990 are also announced. Authorized Swarovski Collectors Society retailers organize special activities and events and invite members to attend.

Invaluable as the tangible benefits of membership are, it is perhaps the human element that is most important and attractive to Collectors Society members. Membership brings crystal lovers together, enabling them to share with others the joy their collections give them.

United Design

Charming Collectible Figurines... Sculpted and Crafted With Pride in the U.S.A.

They've come a long way from their backyard chicken coop studio to a stunning 200,000-square-foot physical plant in Noble, Oklahoma — but the husband-and-wife team of Gary and Jean Clinton still share the same values that inspired their business from the very beginning. Devotion to creativity, quality, and "hands-on" craftsmanship, has set United Design and its appealing products apart.

Both Clintons studied ceramic art at Oklahoma University, and they both made pottery and craft items for classes and just for pleasure. But when they sold $300 worth of their creations at their very first craft show in 1973, Gary and Jean knew they were on to something.

"We took half the $300 and made a down payment on two pottery kilns, which we moved and rebuilt in an orchard next to our house. Then we ran electricity to a deserted chicken coop in our backyard and turned it into a studio." Since then the Clintons' business — soon christened United Design — has grown at an astounding rate.

Today during peak periods, the United Design team can produce an average of 20,000 pieces daily. Both Gary and Jean remain actively involved in the creative life of United Design — overseeing product development and working with sculptors and artists to guide the overall vision of the firm. The company owes its rapid growth and unparalleled success to its corporate philosophy, which includes an all-encompassing concern for animals and the environment.

Limited Edition Craftsmanship Draws Collectors to United Design

While many United Design "fans" have long been familiar with the firm's giftware items such as Stone Critters® and Itty Bitty Critters®, the company has made large strides in the limited edition collectible field in recent years. Collectors have been intrigued both with the charm of unique lines such as *The Legend of Santa Claus*™, *PenniBears*™, and *Lil' Doll*™, and with the exceptional detail work that United Design's cold-casting techniques allow. Each figurine takes up to fifteen steps before it is ready to ship, and each step requires the talents of several dedicated American artisans or craftsmen.

United Design's lush, green atrium, complete with lagoon. Schools of Koi fish populate the lagoon. Guests at United Design's manufacturing, administration and distribution facilities are greeted by a large Galapagous tortoise as they enter the atrium.

The first step in the process is an original sculpture created by one of the master artists on the United Design team. These include the gifted Ken Memoli, Larry Miller, Dianna Newburn, Donna Kennicutt, Suzan Bradford — and Penni Jo Jonas, creator of the beloved *PenniBears*™. Using a variety of tools and a lot of imagination, the sculptor will create an original from clay, sculpting in all the intricate detail to be molded into the finished piece.

Once the original clay sculpture is complete, the piece is carefully delivered to the mold room. A thin layer of silicon or latex is poured over the sculpture and the mold maker uses an air brush to blow the silicon or latex into all the fine cracks and crevices that make up the detail of the piece. Additional layers are applied until this first mold is strong enough to make the first master. When the mold is ready, the clay sculpture is removed, a process which almost always destroys the clay original.

The first master is then cast, using a thick polyurethane resin compound. This first master is sent back to the sculptor for any necessary rework or final finishing. Extra detail can be carved or cut into the master at this stage, ensuring the production pieces will be exactly as the sculptor designed the piece.

Hundreds of American artisans and craftsmen are employed at United Design's manufacturing facility in Noble, Oklahoma.

From this resin master, a series of production molds are made, again using silicon or latex. Each production mold is prepared with a thick surrounding "back-up" mold, which ensures the casting process does not stretch the initial mold out of shape.

Following the mold making process, actual casting begins. At this stage, the production molds are filled with a white liquid gypsum product called hydrastone, a rocklike substance that sets up extremely hard. Other United Design pieces are crafted of cold-cast porcelain, a combination of the dry elements of porcelain with resin substances. In either case, the resulting castings are removed from the molds, then dried and cured by passing through a heat chamber.

Once the pieces are completely dry, a step called "fettling" begins. In this process, craftsmen use knives, dental tools and dental drills to cut away mold flashings and etch any needed detail back into the molded piece. After fettling, the molded pieces are ready for staining and painting.

Staining gives an overall undercoat to the piece, which is then overpainted in oils, acrylics, or a combination of each. The artists who hand-paint each piece use both regular brush and air-brush techniques, depending on the effect desired. Once the final touches are added, each piece is adorned by an American flag tag that says 'Made in U.S.A.,' and packed for shipment in a handsome, protective gift box.

"The artistry and craftsmanship in the figurines we produce is fascinating to watch," says Gary Clinton. "We've had many people ask to visit our facilities and now, with our modern new production lines, we can accommodate several large groups each day." United Design also welcomes tours and visitors to its on-site gift shop, which displays and sells all of the company's items at retail prices.

Penni Jo Jonas' PenniBears™ *Make Their Home at United Design*

Like Gary and Jean Clinton, Penni Jo Jonas began her career as sculpting and figurine making as a "cottage industry." Indeed, Ms. Jonas used homey tools such as a food processor and toaster oven to create the very first of her highly popular *PenniBears*™.

Back in 1982, Penni Jo Jonas decided to make a special gift for her daughter's birthday. The result was a set of doll house dishes that were adorable — and Ms. Jonas found she could sell the little hand-painted dishes, cups, saucers and plates to an admiring audience of collectors. Working in a German clay called *Fimo*, Ms. Jonas perfected her technique for intricate miniature sculpting. While making items to furnish a doll house one day, she experimented with her first tiny teddy bear, and the rest is history!

The *PenniBears* became a part of the United Design family when Ms. Jonas found herself unable to keep up with the growing demand of her "kitchen table" business. "I actually went to United Design to see if they could make some molds so I could cast pieces myself. Gary Clinton, the owner, showed my work to several people on his product development staff. They were all so delighted with the *PenniBears* they asked me to come to work for them. I was so delighted with what I saw at the company that I said okay."

Today's *PenniBears* command the attention and the love of collectors nationwide who thrill to each new vignette. The button-eyed bears can be acquired in a wide range of poses and activities, from "Baking Goodies" and "Summer Sailing" to "Country Lullaby," and "Goodnight Sweet Prince" /"Goodnight Sweet Princess."

Legends of Santa and Little People Enthrall United Design Collectors

To honor the legendary figure of Santa Claus and provide cherished Christmas memories for collectors, the artists of United Design have created a series of richly detailed, limited edition figurines called *The Legend of Santa Claus*™. Some of these bright, hand-painted pieces depict Santa as he appears in various cultures, while others pay tribute to an All-American Santa engaged in his yearly ritual.

While the earlier Santas, beginning in 1986, were sculpted primarily by Larry Miller and Suzan Bradford, the team of Ken Memoli and Penni Jo Jonas got into the act during 1990 with the introduction of "Safe Arrival." Memoli sculpted a grandfatherly Santa with a big empty sack, while Ms. Jonas created six tiny Victorian toys which can be placed in the sack or removed.

Two of the newest additions to *The Legend of Santa Claus*™ series are "Victorian Santa" and "Victorian Santa with Teddy." Created by Suzan Bradford, these designs appeal to the growing interest in all things Victorian.

Sculptor Larry Miller is the force behind *The Legend of The Little People*™, introduced in 1989 in a limited edition. These appealing little characters live deep in the woods with their animal friends. In his mind's eye, Miller has conjured up a world of Leprechauns, Brownies, Menehunes and others, who frolic through the forest with friends such as the turtle, frog, mole and owl, virtually forgotten by the Large Folk. Each figurine, cast in hydrastone, is accompanied by a Certificate of Authenticity and a collector's book.

This charming figurine from The Legend of the Little People™ *by sculptor Larry Miller is entitled "Fire It Up."*

Easter Bunnies Hop into Collectors' Hearts

Although United Design's *The Easter Bunny Family*™ was not introduced as a limited-edition line, collectors have made these 'critters' collectible and much sought-after. Created by United Design sculptor Donna Kennicutt, the bunnies boast colorful eggs, ducklings and chicks to help in the celebration of a joyous Easter. United Design has announced plans to retire some of the *Easter Bunny* designs periodically, and to continue to introduce new ones.

United Design Communicates With Collectors

One of the pleasures of collecting United Design's limited edition lines is the opportunity to receive newsletters about *PenniBears*™, *The Legend of Santa Claus*™, and other products, simply by registering one's purchases with the company. This communication link is enhanced by frequent appearances by United Design artists at annual collectibles shows in California, New York, and South Bend, Indiana. So while United Design retains its strong roots in Noble, Oklahoma, its owners and artists will continue to expand their horizons by reaching out to collectors all over the nation.

Making wise use of her harvested fruit by "Baking Goodies," this miniature figurine is from the PenniBears™ *collection.*

WACO Products Corporation

An Innovative Manufacturer Combines Music and Movement in Figurines of Fantasy, Humor and Nostalgia

Since their introduction in 1985, WACO's unique "Melody In Motion®" figurines have captivated collectors worldwide, both for the beauty of their characters and for the quality of the studio-recorded music to which the figures move. Today, WACO stands alone in the world of porcelain figurines for its combination of artistry and technology.

The Art and Science Behind "Melody In Motion®"

The U.S.-based firm of WACO has forged an association with the renowned porcelain sculptors of Seto, Japan to bring its "Melody In Motion®" figurines to life. Each of these coveted works of art combines three classic arts: fine porcelain making, beautiful music, and graceful motion. The images themselves are sensitive and heartwarming: but through the addition of music and animation, they come to life with the touch of a finger, offering visual and musical delights to those who own them.

The sculptures of the award-winning Japanese master sculptor Seiji Nakane are used to make the molds from which the figurines are produced. Specially trained craftsmen reproduce Nakane's visions using the pure clays which are found only in Seto, Japan. No two pieces are exactly alike, for all are essentially and uniquely hand-made.

After each figurine is formed into Seto clay, it is fired to a bisque finish before hand-painting by skilled artisans. Careful inspections at each stage of production ensure that every piece meets the specifications of the artist. When final assembly is completed, each figurine is inspected and tested.

State-of-the-Art Sound Reproduction

The wizardry of sound and movement that sets "Melody In Motion®" figurines apart begins with a unique electro-mechanical device that activates the music and gracefully animates the characters.

A high-quality precision motor drives a gear train that activates a multitude of cams and levers to create the synchronized movements of each figurine. Each part of the mechanical device is custom made for that style of figurine, with each mechanism designed and engineered to achieve a specific movement. This state-of-the-art technology is truly unique in the world of porcelain mastery.

"Willie The Fisherman" whistles the cheerful tune "Summertime." His upper body and fishing pole move back and forth while the cat eagerly tries to snatch the fish.

Music and Art That Tell a Story

Combining music with the characterization and the movement of each figurine is achieved by selecting the appropriate tune and musical instrument, and then recording the selected tune in a sound studio with professional instrumentalists. The high quality of the music is evident in pieces that play a Tchaikovsky theme as rendered by a professional concert cellist, or the carousel music actually recorded from working carousel band organs from around the world.

Explaining the appeal of these musical figurines, WACO Vice President Jack Miller says, "Each 'Melody In Motion®' figurine sparks the imagination and captures personal visions and nostalgia. The music and the figurine bring back warm memories to our collectors."

Combining the art of porcelain with precision technology, each figurine is presented as a tableau. Accompanied by a pet or an appropriate setting, it tells a story, sparking the imagination of the collector. "Melody In Motion®" figurines can only be produced in limited quantities due to their complex design and painstaking craftsmanship. The crafting of one prototype requires two weeks and the work of hundreds of skilled artisans.

"Lull'aby Willie's" head moves from side to side as the soothing tune of "Rock-A-Bye Baby" lulls him to sleep. May be switched on manually or set to play every hour on the hour.

The "Woodchopper" plays the graceful rendition of "The Happy Farmer" as he swings his ax from side to side.

The Sherwood Forest *Collection*

One of the newest additions to the "Melody In Motion®" line is the *Sherwood Forest* Collection, a group of limited edition figurines that bring the legend of Robin Hood to life. These beautiful figurines capture the romance and adventure of the famous outlaws of Sherwood Forest. There, Robin Hood and his band of merry men plotted their course of kindness to the poor, while avoiding capture by the Sheriff of Nottingham. Robin Hood was joined by the lovely Maid Marian and a band of colorful characters, including the seven-foot Little John, Friar Tuck, Alan a'Dale, and Will Scarlet.

WACO's "Robin Hood" moves from side to side while drawing his bow, and "Little John" moves his upper body and points his staff, each to the tune of "Riding Through the Glen." One figurine features a song played on a flute recorder, while the other features a bugle. Additional characters from the legendary tale will also become a part of this historic collection.

Jim Unger's "Herman" Delights WACO Collectors

Ask his creator Jim Unger who "Herman" is, and Jim might tell you that "Herman" is everyman. And everywoman. And everykid, and everydog. In short, Unger's "Herman" is a state of mind, hilariously illustrated by Unger in a series of cartoons that charm the readers of more than 350 newspapers in over twenty countries around the world.

Now "Herman" comes to life in a new series of figurines created exclusively by WACO in fine bisque-finish porcelain. Each hand-crafted figurine is based on an original Jim Unger cartoon, and is individually painted by hand to capture every detail of Unger's unique characters.

One "Herman" figurine shows our hero with a tennis racquet unceremoniously squashed over his head and down around his neck as his wife looks on. "Okay, that does it! No more doubles," the hapless "Herman" exclaims. In another, "Herman" plays a doctor who confronts his blimp-like patient with the unfortunate news, "Your skeletal structure can't support your weight anymore." When his friend is victimized by a fallen set of file drawers, "Herman" has his priorities in order. "Quick...call a lawyer," he orders. So far there are a dozen knee-slapping "Herman" figurines in WACO'S *The Herman Collection* — enough to keep most any Jim Unger fan in stitches!

"Don't let them see the frying pan!" from The Herman Collection *is based on an original Jim Unger cartoon. This hand-crafted figurine is individually painted by hand to capture every detail of Unger's unique characters.*

Georgetown Collection

Design Skills of Some of the World's Most Distinguished Doll Artists Make Georgetown Dolls Extraordinary

In just a few short years since its founding in 1987, Georgetown Collection has become established as one of America's premier collectible doll studios. With the help of the renowned "godfather of fine art dolls," Thomas Boland, this New England firm has forged bonds with several of the world's most honored doll artists.

With Brigitte Deval, Terri DeHetre and Linda Mason as part of its inspirational design team, Georgetown already has premiered two dozen exceptional dolls. And while each artist brings his or her own special brilliance to every assignment, all Georgetown dolls boast the same distinctions of quality control and edition limitation.

The highest designation for a Georgetown doll is an Artist's Edition. From the designer's original sketches to the final accessories and touches, Georgetown Artist's Editions must meet standards usually seen only in old-fashioned heirloom dolls.

Hand-crafted of the finest bisque porcelain, each doll is costumed in rich fabrics and accompanied by the charming accessories and props that help establish beloved doll personalities in collectors' hearts. Most important of all, the artist exercises total control over product quality. If an individual doll fails to meet the artist's own high standards, it is destroyed.

Oops! Little "Sarah" needs to tie that canvas sneaker before she embarks on her game of baseball. But Brigitte Deval has decked this little girl out for success with bat and ball, rough-and-tumble overalls, and even a bright red baseball cap over her shining brunette pigtails!

This attention to detail — and the unique vision of Georgetown artists — has charmed collectors from the very first Artist's Edition. Indeed, when Avigail Brahms' "Hansel & Gretel" debuted in late 1987, collectors were immediately intrigued by this storybook pair.

The Remarkable Art of Brigitte Deval

Called "...among the superlative few, the very best" by doll expert John Darcy Noble, Brigitte Deval was the first of the "realistic" school of doll artists. She began making her stunning dolls over twenty years ago, and still she reigns as the world's most eminent creator of realistic dolls. So rare is her gift that her dolls have been proudly displayed in museums, and shown in the windows of Tiffany's.

Ms. Deval's relationship with Georgetown Collection began in 1988 when her adorable "Emma" was introduced as the first in the *Little Loves* collection. Nominated for a coveted "Doll of the Year" award along with her 1989 companion, "Katie," both of these *Little Loves* plus their 1990 friend "Laura" have now seen their editions close. Also tapped for a "Doll of the Year" award nomination was Ms. Deval's 1989 "Faerie Princess," which has sold out along with the 1989 *Little Loves* "Megan."

A close-up look at sweet little "Megan" shows just how captivating Brigitte Deval's children can be. "Megan" and her kitten "Marmalade" represent pure mischief in hand-painted porcelain. "Megan" is the kind of child we all love like crazy, even when she makes us crazy. She's brought home a cuddly orange-and-white kitten and now she's looking soulfully into our eyes and begging, "Can I keep her...please?"

It comes as no surprise that "Megan" has already named the kitten "Marmalade." We can almost hear her promising to feed and play with her new

"Peek-a-Boo Beckie" has posable arms so that she can hide her eyes or pull her hands away and play her very favorite game with you! Her crisp print jumpsuit and lace-trimmed cap make her a fashionable baby, and her bright blue eyes are sure to win every heart for this Terri DeHetre doll original.

friend...and take good care of her, too. So how can we say no? And we know that Megan will bring us joy every day...what with her hand-painted freckles and her hand-tailored plaid dress with organza pinafore trimmed in cotton lace. Matching pantaloons peek out from below. And Marmalade the kitten is crafted with the same care: every stripe is painted by hand and her eyes gleam with the same bright spirit as those of her little mistress.

Still open for collectors to acquire and love are three *Small Wonders* dolls from Brigitte Deval and Georgetown: "Corey" from 1990, "Abbey" from 1991, and "Sarah" from 1992. Typical of this appealing collection is "Sarah," the little slugger: dressed for the big leagues and ready to steal our hearts.

While Sarah is dressed for a rough-and-tumble outdoor game, her gentle and expressive face shows that she would be just as at home at a dance recital. Big blue eyes shining, her brunette tresses plaited into pigtails, she adds blue ribbons to her hair for a touch of femininity. The rest of her costume is pure "sports utility": hand-tailored overalls, real canvas sneakers, and bright red baseball cap. And she carries her baseball bat and ball with such authority that we just know she's about to make a hit!

The Delightful Children of Terri DeHetre

A two-time winner of the renowned "Doll of the Year" award, Terri DeHetre has earned international acclaim for her porcelain portraits of children. From the age of two she was destined for greatness: her family dentist found her toddler finger paintings so intriguing that he wanted to purchase them to decorate his office! (Terri's mother refused.) By the age of fifteen, Terri saw her paintings displayed at the Ford Art Exhibit in Dearborn, Michigan, making her the youngest exhibitor at that time.

"Children have always been my inspiration," Ms. DeHetre explains. "I'm continually amazed at their range of depth and emotion. Working with the children of my friends and neighbors as models, I'm fortunate to have had the luxury of sculpting from real life. My greatest reward is knowing that my collectors find some similarities between my babies and their own."

Ms. DeHetre's first doll for Georgetown Collection, the 1990 "Baby Bunting," already has seen its edition close. "Baby Bunting" and the next *Nursery Babies*™ issue, "Patty Cake" from 1990, both earned "Doll of the Year" nominations, while "Baby Bunting" also was nominated for the "Dolls Award of Excellence." Still open in the *Nursery Babies* series are "Patty Cake" along with the 1991 "Diddle Diddle Dumpling," 1991 "Little Girl With a Curl," 1991 "This Little Piggy," and 1992 "Rock-a-bye Baby."

It comes as no surprise that these sweet baby dolls have earned the love of collectors and award nominators alike — as a glimpse at "Baby Bunting" clearly reveals. While the famous nursery rhyme actually says "bye baby bunting..." this wide-eyed infant is such a little cutie that we could never say good-bye. She's all dressed up for a hug in her fleecy bunny bonnet and flannel flap-seat jammies. A little pink cottontail and pink bunny buttons continue the theme, and she holds her own baby bunny close in one chubby hand.

In 1992, Terri DeHetre caught the fancy of collectors with the first edition in a new series: "Peek-a-boo Beckie" from the *Kid's Play*™ collection. When little Beckie plays peek-a-boo, we can almost hear her giggle as she pulls her hands away to see us. And every detail of the doll is so real that each observer is tempted to pick her up and hug her. She is sculptured of fine bisque porcelain so her chubby baby cheeks and dimpled hands and arms are remarkably true-to-life. Her arms are posable, so she can play peek-a-boo in many positions, too.

Every bit as pretty as she is playful, Beckie has big blue eyes and she's dressed in a floral calico romper. Her bib collar is edged in lace, and her matching sun bonnet has a ruffle of embroidered eyelet lace that complements her bright red hair. Just as adorable as Beckie is another 1992 DeHetre creation, little "Michelle" from Georgetown's brand-new *Baby Kisses*™ collection.

Linda Mason Wins Dolls of Excellence Awards

Imagine a doll artist so sought-after that her limited edition studio dolls are sold out years in advance of their introduction! There is just such an artist: Linda Mason. And Georgetown Collection is proud that this remarkable sculptor's works now make up a major portion of the firm's doll line.

As a three-time winner of the renowned "Dolls of Excellence" award, Linda Mason has cultivated a wide and admiring following for her historically significant works of art. Her *American Diary Dolls*™ for Georgetown Collection premiered in 1990 with "Jennie Cooper," and continued with "Bridget Quinn," "Christina Merovina," and "Many Stars," all introduced during 1991.

It's a moment of faith...a moment of pride for lovely "Bridget Quinn," a little girl from turn-of-the-century Boston who is making her First Communion. Created by multiple award winner Linda Mason, Bridget's serene expression and beautiful white costume make her a very special doll indeed.

Each of these exquisite dolls tells the story of a child with a mind of her own, dressed in period costume and placed in historical perspective by her accessories and her personal biography. "Jennie Cooper," for instance, lives in the seaport town of Sag Harbor circa 1905. Her dream is to learn to sail and someday to become a sea captain!

Linda Mason has created Jennie as a sweet-faced child with a determined expression. She wears an authentic boater hat trimmed with navy satin ribbon, and her chestnut curls are gathered by a white satin ribbon. Her nautical "middy" top is trimmed with white piping and two embroidered stars on the back collar. A lace-trimmed slip and pantaloons complete Jennie's custom-tailored outfit.

"Bridget Quinn" is a little Roman Catholic girl from Boston, Massachusetts, circa 1899. Today is the long-awaited day of her First Communion, and we see her just as she is ready to join the procession down the aisle. It's clear that Bridget is proud of her beautiful Communion dress — hand-tailored especially for her and trimmed with delicate embroidered lace. She is also wearing a veil of illusion net, gathered into a crown of flowers and satin ribbons. Her golden cross necklace gleams, and her emerald green eyes flash with excitement as she clutches her prayer book tight. One look at Bridget and it comes as no surprise that she won Linda Mason the 1991 "Dolls of Excellence" award.

Another collection by Linda Mason for Georgetown Collection, *Sugar & Spice*™, already has two dolls available: the 1991 issues "Little Sweetheart" and "Red Hot Pepper." "Little Sweetheart" was recently nominated for the prestigious "Doll of the Year" award from *Dolls* magazine.

In just over five years' time, Georgetown Collection has delighted the doll world with works of art combining first-rate sculptural mastery, unique themes and imaginative costuming. In the years to come, Georgetown's pledge is to continue its mission of "making the finest collectibles available" — especially in coveted Artist's Editions of beautiful dolls.

Lightpost Publishing

"Painter of Light"™ Thomas Kinkade Captures the Warm Glow of Art in the Style of the 19th-Century Luminists

"I've been fascinated by the effects of light ever since my days as a painter for the movie business," recalls Thomas Kinkade, the artistic force behind Lightpost Publishing of San Jose, California. "Back then I became known as a 'painter of light' — and I've devoted myself to creating a sense of light as the dominant theme in all of my paintings."

Since 1983, Kinkade has disciplined himself to a rigorous six-day-a-week schedule of research, field work and painting. The artist's favorite subjects are quaint towns, tranquil landscapes and charming cottages — and his concern for accuracy leads him to spend long hours researching historical documents and vintage photographs. He also visits each location as often as necessary to capture its intimate details and its unique patterns of light.

Kinkade's "quest for the light" has led him to study techniques from the Renaissance and the Impressionist periods. "In the Renaissance, the concept was that shadows are transparent. Artists threw everything into a relief of light and shadow," the voluble Kinkade explains. "The Impressionists' goal was to create radiant light effects."

Kinkade's most direct inspiration comes from a group of 19th-century American artists known as The Luminists. In California's Oakland Museum hang the canvases Kinkade admires most: landscapes by Thomas Hill, William Keith, Albert Bierstadt, John F. Kensett and Frederick Edwin Church. As for the effect of The Luminists on his work, Kinkade has several observations. He strives for "depth and mood," while combining a "warm palette, enhancement and softening of the edges, and an overall sense of light" in his unabashedly romantic paintings.

Kinkade sees his art as a way to express his deep faith in daily life. As a devout Christian, he sets time aside for regular church activities — and he considers his artistic abilities to be a special gift from God. "Everyone who is a believer has a ministry," Kinkade asserts. "I try to remember that I am a minister with a paint brush. I simply want to use pigment and canvas and paint brushes to create images that are uplifting to others."

Sometimes the healing power of art becomes especially clear, as in a recent encounter Kinkade enjoyed with one of his collectors. "At a show a lady approached me and told me that her house was one of those destroyed in the big Oakland fire. 'The art collection I inherited from my mother all was burned,' she told me. 'Collecting your work has given me a new start.' She actually felt that these paintings were giving her new hope and meaning," Kinkade recounts with joy.

"The Broadwater Bridge, Thomashire" portrays a Victorian bridge spanning "one of the most delightful, most tranquil stretches of watercourse I've yet seen," according to Thomas Kinkade. This hand-signed collector print is available in several limited editions.

A Natural-Born Artist Finds His Niche

Thomas Kinkade was born in 1958 and grew up in the foothills of the Sierra Mountains. From the age of four his calling as an artist was evident, and by sixteen he was an accomplished painter in oil. An apprenticeship under the well-known California representational painter Glenn Wessels won Kinkade a world of knowledge as well as a special legacy: Wessels gifted Kinkade with photographer Ansel Adams' paint brushes.

Kinkade next embarked on studies at the University of California, Berkeley, and Art Center College of Design in Pasadena. His fierce devotion to his craft is evident in that to remain in school, the impoverished young artist often lived only on potatoes for weeks on end. What's more, he had to cook his spuds at a friend's place because Kinkade's modest flat did not include an oven!

The artist's next adventure took place in the summer of 1982, when he and his Berkeley roommate, Jim Gurney, decided to ride the rails and sketch the countryside. In Yuma, Arizona the twosome discovered that they could make plenty of money to pay for their trip by sketching portraits at a cowboy bar for two dollars apiece. Continuing their journey as far as New York City, the pair had another inspiration. They convinced Watson-Guptill publishing to give them a contract on a book: *The Artist's Guide to Sketching* The resulting volume became a best-selling art instructional book.

Kinkade's association with the movie industry began at the tender age of twenty-two, when he was commissioned to create over 600 background paintings for the animated feature film, *Fire and Ice*. Constant attention to the effects of light was essential to movie background painting, and this experience fueled Kinkade's fascination with The Luminists. By 1983, Kinkade was ready to leave the film industry to pursue his vision as a painter of light-filled landscapes.

Since then his career has been documented in a host of magazines, he has become a regular guest on talk shows, and he has won an impressive list of honors. These include two Certificates of Merit from the New York Society of Illustrators, two Founder's Awards from the National Parks Academy for the Arts, a two-man show at the C.M. Russell Museum in Great Falls, Montana, and more than ten one-man shows. Other awards are Kinkade's selection as official artist for the 1989 National Parks Collector's Print, and the 1990 Commemorative Press Collector's Print honoring Rotary International.

Thomas Kinkade and his family discovered this charming cottage during a stroll through the English countryside. The inviting cottage and its babbling brook inspired the artist to paint "Evening at Swanbrooke Cottage, Thomashire," and to capture the gentle play of light as night descends.

Kinkade Blends Studio Time with Field Work

Today, Thomas Kinkade has returned to his roots in northern California's Sierra foothills. Amidst rolling orchards, his studio is located in a huge, 19th-century barn set among pines and oaks. The Kinkade family home is just 100 yards away — a distance advocated by Norman Rockwell because "It's far enough away that you don't hear your kids playing, but near enough so you can come home for lunch."

As for his work day, Kinkade considers his two young children as "built-in alarm clocks." He and his wife, Nanette, get the little girls ready for the day and Kinkade attends to his daily three-mile run, breakfast and prayer before arriving at his studio by 9 a.m. He breaks briefly for lunch and continues working until about 6 p.m., six days a week. Sunday is reserved for church and family activities.

To enhance his solitary time in the studio retreat, Kinkade listens to an extensive collection of musical recordings. His taste ranges from symphonic to 40s swing, "with many stops in between." The artist also loves listening to books on tape — especially when the subject matter keys in to what he is painting. "As I work on a painting, of, for example, an English scene, I have Charles Dickens in the background describing the countryside!" Kinkade explains.

While the artist spends most of his year in the California studio, he finds location work to be very stimulating. A favorite "studio base" is in the Cotswold district of England. When Kinkade sets out across the Atlantic, he prepares a complete "studio in a suitcase" including canvases, painting materials, a folding easel and a portable drying rack for storing wet paintings.

A Summer in England Yields Favorite Paintings

Thomas Kinkade is bursting with stories about his most recent trip to England, where he leased a studio for the summer and set up in various locations to paint in the open air. One of his subjects was "The Broadwater Bridge, Thomashire," an Elizabethan bridge over a stream that is part of an exclusive gentlemen's fishing syndicate.

"Non-members were not really allowed in, but I

was told, 'If you want to paint, have at it!'" Kinkade recalls. "I worked on the basic painting up to six hours a day — as long as the light would last. I met some incredible people. British gentlemen with their flyrods would drive up in Bentleys and say 'Oh, I say, what are you working on?' And when they saw my painting, they would tip their tweed caps at me and say, 'Oh, I say, jolly good show!' or something equally as charming.

"'Broadwater Bridge' spans one of the most delightful, most tranquil stretches of watercourse I've yet seen. Just beyond the bridge is a spillway that acts as a tiny dam to back up the normally small stream to a width of perhaps twenty or thirty yards. Flowering shrubs and lush trees line this wide part of the stream, casting dappled shade along the well mown green banks. In all directions nothing interrupts the unbelievably pastoral beauty of the setting."

As for "Evening at Swanbrooke Cottage, Thomashire," Kinkade found this delightful spot upstream from the Broadwater Bridge. "In England, walking trails accompany even the smallest stream, and on a summer's evening, a peaceful stroll beside a gently whispering brook is guaranteed to restore even the most burdened soul. On one such evening walk in England, my family and I came upon the cottage on which I based this painting.

"The cottage hung over the water, and I was fascinated by the way it was integrated with the stream. I think we all have fantasies of living in a cottage right on the water, and this was mine," Kinkade recalls. As Kinkade worked for several days to capture the cottage on canvas, "I began to imagine myself living in this idyllic cottage, with the entrancing sound of the tiny brook as a constant backdrop to a peaceful life."

Like many of his previous works, both "The Broadwater Bridge, Thomashire" and "Evening at Swanbrooke Cottage, Thomashire" are available through Lightpost Publishing as hand-signed collector's prints in two editions, each with 980 signed and numbered prints. One edition for each image has been produced on 100% rag paper, and the other on cotton fiber artist's canvas. Additional offerings include 200 artist's proofs 200 gallery proofs, and 100 publisher's proofs of each image.

Thomas Kinkade is quick to point out that these two works from "The Thomashire Collection" are not inspired by a real area of England, but by an "imaginary realm, filled with quaint vil-

From his studio at the base of the Sierra Mountains, Thomas Kinkade continues to perfect his craft as America's "Painter of Light"™. Painstaking research and field work are supplemented by long hours in the studio to create works of art that serve as "a window for the imagination."

lages and tranquil streams, with enchanting castles and quiet country lanes. Thomashire is a countryside that is completely full of beauty and peace, where morning mist and sunshine and luminous sunsets combine each day to reveal a lush and resplendent landscape that is without time or place. In short, Thomashire is my attempt as an artist to capture in an ongoing series of paintings all that I hold dear about England. I invite collectors to join me, through these paintings, on a visit to the enchanting realm of Thomashire!"

With subjects ranging from small-town America to landscapes and the English countryside, Thomas Kinkade's oil paintings and reproductions communicate deeply with viewers. Kinkade paints a simpler, idyllic world which seems to radiate an inner light. This is consistent with his goals as an artist. As he puts it, "I try to create paintings that are a window for the imagination. If people look at my work and are reminded of the way things were or perhaps the way they could be, then I've done my job."

Cat's Meow Village/FJ Designs

Faline Jones' Village Collectibles Truly Are The Cat's Meow

Each miniature building in the Cat's Meow *Village* collection features a tiny black feline resting on a window ledge or waiting patiently at the door, a sign as sure as paw prints on a freshly washed auto that the piece has been touched by the artistry of Faline Jones.

Faline Jones (yes, some people call her "Feline"), the originator of Cat's Meow *Village* collectibles, says she gets some of her most creative ideas for new designs in her sleep. But the fantastic success of her line of two-dimensional miniature historical buildings must surpass even her most optimistic dreams.

Jones began the business she now runs with her husband, Terry, in the fall of 1982 in the basement of their Wooster, Ohio home. Beginning with a $39 piece of pine and her grandfather's old band saw, she designed, cut, painted and stenciled sets of miniature wooden buildings and sold them as quickly as they could be supplied to local gift shops. Terry helped with buying and cutting the wood, and he devised a way to spraypaint the background colors in their garage. From this modest beginning, their business would soon grow to employ 150 people.

Sudden Popularity of Their Miniatures Forces the Joneses to Expand

The phenomenal growth of Faline and Terry Jones' business over the next several years reads like a textbook chapter on the triumph of the free enterprise system. Beginning with a display of their *Village* wares at the 1983 Columbus Gift Mart, they were swamped with orders and forced to find a more efficient way to meet the demand for their product.

The Gift Mart success allowed Faline to move operations out of her basement and into the backroom of another business in 1984, only to take over that entire building's space within the year. That year she also hired nineteen employees, and she decided that her business needed a new name. "How was I to hire any male employees and expect to keep them if they had to tell people they worked at 'The Cat's Meow'?" she says. "That's when I came up with the generic FJ Designs name."

Two years later, in 1986, her husband, formerly an auto parts salesman, officially joined the company, taking over personnel and maintenance operations. By the spring of 1989 the business had once more outgrown its facilities; the reputation of Cat's Meow had spread across the country, and a new building was constructed to house its now 120-member team of employees.

By this time not only the location of the business but the product itself had undergone a change. Previously, in the first two years of her business, Jones' miniature buildings were personal interpretations; each of them might feature elements of architectural detail from buildings that she admired, but none of them really existed. However, starting the third year, she began to pattern her designs after actual buildings and historic landmarks. From this impulse, the concept of the *Village* developed. Today, each *Village* series of ten buildings faithfully reproduces examples of typical American architecture, chosen with respect for the craftsmanship, commerce, culture and activities that are part of every community.

The Selection and Design Process

Although today designs are created by staff designers who use computers to aid in the process, Jones has final approval over all patterns. She also chooses the buildings that will be reproduced, and this can be a lengthy process. It begins with Jones sorting through her library of possible subjects. She loves to study and collect literature on historic places and architecture, and she garners fresh inspiration from the historic buildings in towns that she visits. "I don't travel specifically to search out buildings, but I always have my camera with me when I do travel," she says. According to the artist, her library is packed with postcards, newspaper clippings, photographs and books. Jones adds that whenever she begins to pick out a series, she pays careful attention to what customers have been asking for.

To develop a new series, Jones selects about 100 suitable buildings from her collection and then narrows this group down to just ten. Once her staff develops designs from these ten buildings that meet with Jones' approval, the designers construct a paper pattern with specifications for the work to be done and a black and white design for screen printing. Next, an adjoining business uses the paper patterns to cut the pieces.

Finally, these pieces are returned to FJ Designs where employees complete the process. Each building is sanded smooth and spraypainted in one of the soft colonial colors used for the entire line of *Village* series. Crisp touches of black and white are screen printed to highlight structural details such as archways, Palladian windows and clapboard siding. Roofs are finished off either by handbrushing or by dipping. Although the process is exacting, with improvements in production over the years, the company currently turns out over 4,500 pieces a day in two shifts.

Every building is designed within a 6"x6" scale and is cut from a $^{3}/_{4}$" thick piece of pine. Each piece is finished both front and back, resulting in a two-dimensional effect, and allowing collectors to display their pieces where they are visible from all angles. A flat finish is used, and since no overcoat varnishes are applied, the buildings must be handled and stored with care. To help collectors identify authentic Cat's Meow *Village* buildings, each is stamped on the bottom with a copyright stamp indicating the year of introduction, and includes the Cat's Meow name, the building name and the name of the series to which it belongs.

Jones and her team of designers have also created a line of *Village* accessories, which are manufactured by the same process as the collections of buildings. Dozens of these accessories capture impressions of several historical eras. They include trees, old-time street signs and picket fences, some gaily festooned for the winter holidays. Collectors can people their miniature towns, too, with children building a snowman, a load of kids on the "School of Hard Knox" bus, or a proper Victorian nanny airing the baby. All accessories are reproduced in the same muted golds, blues, greens and brick reds of the *Village* buildings.

Jones' Imaginative Personal Touch Makes Her Collections Unique

Besides being intimately involved with the design of each series, Jones also often adds her own imaginative, sometimes playful personal touches to her line of miniatures. For example, the *Village VI History* collection features the "Stiffenbody Funeral Home." And an "FJ Realty Company" was included in the *1990 Series VIII* collection. "We joke with local realtors about how many houses we sell in a year," Jones says, "so I thought we'd better set up a realty company just to make things legitimate."

Jones frequently adds details to her designs

A Cat's Meow Village *assortment captures the architectural variety of the American past.*

which allude to her love of cats. At times her household has been home to eight of them at once. "O'Malley's Livery Stable" in the *Village IV History* collection is named after her fourth cat, O'Malley the Alley Cat.

The inspiration for the black cat logo which graces each *Village* collectible was "Casper," Jones' brown and white tabby. The original trademark cats used by Jones during her first eight months of manufacturing were of all colors. These "colored cat" pieces are all being hoarded by collectors. Jones never kept a copy of any of these early pieces, and those she has been able to locate are not for sale. "No one will sell them back to me, no matter how much I offer them," she says.

Along with her whimsical cats, Jones often adds other design details that are related to her own family background. Jenny Lillich, the proprietor of the "Fashionable Dressmaker" shop in *Series VI*, for example, is Jones' great-grandmother. And the "Murray Hotel" from the *Village V History* group is a hotel where Jones and her husband stayed on a trip to Mackinac Island, Michigan.

System of Retiring Village Pieces Adds Value For Collectors

The collectibility of the *Village* pieces began to increase as Faline devised a system of retiring old patterns as new ones were developed. Currently, new pieces are presented twice a year. In January a ten-piece Series is released, which is identified by a Roman numeral which corresponds with the number of years that FJ Designs has been in business. This series will be retired after five years of production. Eight to ten new accessory pieces that coordinate with the *Village* themes for a particular year are released in June.

January is the release month for each new four-piece Theme Series, consisting of four buildings all related to and named after a specific theme. Past themes have included a *Main Street Series* (1987), a *Wild West Series* (1989) and a *Washington D.C. Series* (1991). The Theme Series are also retired after five years.

An annual four-piece *Christmas Series* is also released on June first each year. All four buildings are decorated for the holiday. The *Christmas Series* is produced and sold from June through December of that year only and then retired.

Collector's Club Formed

To accommodate the increasing number of *Village* collectors, FJ Designs formed The National Cat's Meow Collector's Club in June of 1989. By the end of that year, over 4,000 collectors had joined. The club continues to grow today with over 13,000 members nationally. Dealers who belong to the club display a redemption center decal provided by FJ Designs.

"That tells us we are definitely in the collector's market at this point, and we are working on our secondary resale market next," says Jones.

A Village *street featuring the 1991 "Limberlost Cabin" (far right) and the* American Songwriters Series *collection, both members-only issues, is brought to life with accessories from the regular line.*

A sampler of buildings and accessories from the 1992 Series X *and* Barn Series, *ready to take its place in a* Village *recreation of the American past.*

An official membership card is included in the club's $22 membership fee, along with a notebook filled with current collection history sheets (background information on individual buildings), a personal checklist to keep track of collections, a year's subscription to the club newsletter, a buying list of all custom designs, a redemption card for that year's four-piece series produced exclusively for members and a T-shirt.

Jones Emphasizes the Importance of Meeting Customer Needs

Another way in which Jones strives to keep a personal touch despite her expanding business is reflected in the size of the shops in which Jones markets her collectibles. Her miniatures are available primarily in small to mid-size gift shops since, Jones notes, "in order for the product to sell in a store, you need to know the histories behind the houses and have an interest to pass along to the customers." That doesn't happen in large stores, she adds. Currently, *Village* collectibles are sold in forty-eight states and retail between $7.50 and $10.

Custom Service A Growing Part of FJ Design's Business

FJ Designs also responds to customer needs by offering custom service. Cat's Meow dealers may request a special individual piece or a small special theme series. For a fee, the company will design and produce a minimum of 150 copies for which that store will have exclusive sales rights. Custom work is becoming an increasingly large part of FJ Design's business. In 1990, replicas of 437 buildings from across the country were reproduced. Some of the more unusual items in this eclectic collection include the "Big Chicken" Kentucky Fried Chicken building near Atlanta, Georgia; the Lancaster County Prison in Pennsylvania and the Ohio State football stadium complete with the OSU band.

The popularity of the Cat's Meow *Village* Collection continues to grow as FJ Designs expands its line of products and works hard to please customers. And for Faline Jones, there is no city limit boundary to inhibit the number of her miniature historical treasures. "Every piece in the Cat's Meow *Village* has a little bit of history," she says. "There is always something new to add about the American way of life. Just as history is never ending, neither is the *Village*."

Midwest Importers of Cannon Falls, Inc.
Celebrating Holidays Year-Round With Seasonal Collectibles From the Old World

When Ken Althoff was diagnosed with multiple sclerosis some forty years ago, he realized that his work as a Lutheran pastor might soon present problems of stamina and mobility. He and his wife decided to look "for another way to get through the world" — and discovered a whole new life in the process.

Amazingly, Ken is healthy and active even now. And just as miraculous as Ken's good health is the growth of the little business he and his wife began in Minnesota during the 1950s. From its beginnings as a small-scale importer of traditional European collectibles, today Midwest Importers of Cannon Falls, Inc. has grown to be an industry leader in the business of designing and importing fine-crafted gifts and decorations.

From the quaint little town of Cannon Falls, Minnesota (Population: 2,653) Ken's daughter, Kathleen Brekken, now presides over a line that includes thousands of seasonal gifts and decorations. With charming offerings for Christmas, Easter, Valentine's Day, Halloween, Thanksgiving and more, Ms. Brekken keeps her in-house staff of designers busy all year long.

In addition to its midwestern U.S. headquarters, the firm has a base of operations in the United Kingdom and offices in Manila, Hong Kong and Taipei. Yet even though Midwest Importers of Cannon Falls now enjoys a worldwide reach, its roots in European craftsmanship remain an essential focus for the business.

The Rich History of Erzgebirge Nutcrackers

The romance of the Nutcracker Prince from Tchaikovsky's *Nutcracker Fantasy* has inspired many an American collector to seek out handsome wooden nutcrackers from the Erzgebirge region of Germany. Rich with heritage and tradition, this area is dense with lavish forests — a natural resource that encouraged villagers to develop many unique wood-crafted items. Over the centuries, the woodworkers of the Erzgebirge have stayed true to their handcrafted roots, creating items of superb craftsmanship and quality.

The development of the nutcracker began in the 18th century, when Erzgebirge villagers began to craft simple figures equipped with a lever device for cracking nuts. It is often said in Germany that one who faces a difficult problem has to "crack a tough nut," so the Erzgebirge craftsmen often shaped their nutcrackers as authority figures such as kings, policemen and military officers — putting these figures to work for *them* to crack nuts! Later, figures from folklore and fantasy were designed as well. Today as then, Erzgebirge nutcrackers are characterized by limited availability, for they are crafted completely by hand — and there are very few woodworkers who have developed this painstaking skill.

Midwest Importers proudly offers a wonderful variety of Erzgebirge nutcrackers in all sizes, including life-size nutcrackers standing six feet tall. In addition to the traditional Christmas-themed pieces, the Midwest Importers' line includes Easter and year-round designs as well.

The Christian Ulbricht Nutcrackers of Bavaria

When Christian Ulbricht was born in the toymaking village of Seiffen in the Erzgebirge, he found himself immersed in the woodworking craft of his ancestors. As an adult, Ulbricht found a new home in Bavaria, where he carries on the same Erzgebirge tradition with a twist: his nutcrackers mix traditional designs with whimsical interpretations of hobbies and professions.

Vibrantly colored and beautifully crafted, Christian Ulbricht's nutcrackers are renowned for their wonderful details. Favorite Christian Ulbricht nutcrackers include toy-makers, coin collectors, musicians, even *Hofbrau Haus* beer drinkers!

The highlight of Midwest Importers' line of Christian Ulbricht nutcrackers is an exclusive, limited edition "Father Christmas" nutcracker, introduced in an edition of 2,500. Designed by Ulbricht exclusively for Midwest, each "Father Christmas" is not only beautifully crafted, but also is hand-signed by Christian Ulbricht himself. Another exciting Midwest exclusive is Christian

Based on Tchaikovsky's Nutcracker Suite, *these distinctive wooden nutcrackers are a wonderful example of the craftsmanship and character development of skilled artisans in the German Erzgebirge. "Herr Drosselmeyer" stands 14 1/2" tall, and "The Prince" is 12 3/4" tall.*

Members of the Heritage Santa Collection™ *include: (back row) "MacNicholas," the Highlands Santa; "Father Christmas" of England; "Santa Nykolai," the Slavic Santa; "Herr Kristmas" of Germany's Black Forest; (front) "Santa Niccolo," the Italian Santa; and "Père Noël" of France. (Not pictured are "Scanda Klaus" and "Papa Frost," soon to be retired.)*

Ulbricht's collection of *Nutcracker Fantasy* characters — including "Clara," "The Prince," "The Mouse King," and "Herr Drosselmeyer," the magical toymaker.

For those interested in nutcrackers as collectibles, there are many exciting opportunities in store for the thriving secondary market. With the reunification of Germany, older nutcrackers with "East" or "West" Germany stickers or trademarks are expected to become more valuable. The first nutcrackers with the new "Germany" stickers are also much in demand.

Midwest Importers Presents Wendt und Kühn

More than seventy-five years have passed since Grete Wendt and her friend Grete Kühn first created their little hand-turned wood figurines in the German village of Grunhainichen. The tradition they founded — of uncompromising quality and commitment to craftsmanship in every detail — continues today under the direction of Grete Wendt's nephew Hans.

Among the best-loved Wendt und Kühn figures are their delightful little angels. One group of angels with green-and-white polka dot wings carry musical instruments to create a precious angel orchestra. Another group, the "Margarita Angels," are distinguished by their blue-and-white wings and white halo wreaths. Uniquely crafted Santas, charming village children, and vividly colored angels add to this heartwarming collection. Each piece is made by hand from the finest quality woods, then beautifully hand-painted and hand-finished by craftsmen who give full attention to each intricate detail.

Imaginatively designed and meticulously crafted, *The Wendt und Kühn Collection* has become a favorite of collectors around the world. In the United States, Midwest Importers is proud to be the exclusive distributor of these wooden treasures.

The Nativity Figures of Spain's Belenes Puig

While Midwest Importers brings American collectors many superb items from Germany, the firm also enjoys a strong relationship with fine art studios in other lands. Notable among these is the Old World firm of Belenes Puig (formerly known as J. Puig Llobera), creators of hand-crafted nativity figures in Barcelona, Spain.

Each nativity figure is meticulously hand-crafted and lovingly detailed, beginning with an original sculpture in chalk. This chalk figure is used to create limited-use molds for reproduction. Refined terra-cotta from the south of Spain is hand-pressed into the molds and left until slightly hardened. At this point, the terra-cotta pieces are removed from the molds and joined together to form each full figure. While the clay is still soft, additional details are hand-sculpted into the figure.

The fully dimensional figures are dried for two

to three days on studio roof tops, soaking up the warm Barcelona sun. Next, kiln firing changes the fragile, unfired terra-cotta into its final, hardened state. Clothing is draped upon each figure, using fabric which has been dipped in a liquid that rapidly hardens to create dramatic, flowing costumes. In the final stage, the figures are hand-painted with multi-hued finishes, imparting the beautifully rich patina characteristic of the works of Belenes Puig.

Heritage Santas™ *Feature St. Nick Around the World*

To honor the international tradition of Santa Claus, Midwest Importers has created an exclusive family of Santas inspired by the legends and lore of Christmas around the world, *The Heritage Santa Collection*™.

There is kilted "MacNicholas" of the Highlands, and proud "Papa Frost," the Santa of the Great North. Cheery "Scanda Klaus" visits from Scandinavia, and regal "Herr Kristmas" resides in Germany's Black Forest. "Santa Niccolo" hails from Italy, and "Father Christmas" travels throughout the English countryside. The newest members of the collection are "Santa Nykolai," who delivers presents throughout the Slavic lands, and "Père Noël," the generous gift-giving spirit of France.

Wonderfully detailed and beautifully crafted, Each *Heritage Santa* character comes with his own unique Christmas legend and is available in sizes and product categories to please a variety of collectors: Fabric Maché figure, sculpted figurine, whimsical Roly-Poly, sculpted dimensional ornament, figural porcelain music box and musical snow scene.

The Folk Art of Woodcarver Leo R. Smith III

Woodcarver Leo R. Smith III believes that "the artist is a reflection of the environment." His choice of inspirational surroundings is the picturesque little town of Fountain City on the Mississippi, in Wisconsin. This area of river and woodlands holds not only beauty, but also a rich trove of the legend and folklore captured in Smith's compelling folk art pieces.

Largely self-taught, Smith creates each of his original carvings in a studio attached to his gallery. Working from life, legends and dreams, he strives to bring his personal vision of a character to life. To begin, he sculpts a rough clay model of the design to establish the basic shape and character. Then comes the meticulous hand carving of the wood sculpture, a process that often takes months to complete. Once the carving is done, Smith and his wife Marilyn develop a color scheme and hand-paint the figure.

Since 1991, Midwest Importers has offered an exclusive, limited edition collection of Smith's designs. Each sculpture in Midwest's *Leo R. Smith III Collection* is hand-cast in resin to precisely reproduce the beauty of the original woodcarving, then is hand-painted with incredible richness and detail. Each sculpture in this handsome collection of folk pieces is limited to an edition of 5,000, and is accompanied by a Certificate of Authenticity and a description of the inspiration behind the sculpture. Beautifully crafted and strikingly unique, each member of *The Leo R. Smith III Collection* is a treasured gift and the delight of serious collectors.

The Worldwide Vision of Midwest Importers

From their home in Cannon Falls to art studios around the world, the Midwest Importers' family share their vision of excellence with friends across America. For Christmas, Easter, Valentine's Day, Halloween, Thanksgiving and all year round, Midwest Importers offers a marvelous and ever-growing range of items to intrigue art lovers and collectors alike.

"Dreams of Night Buffalo" and "Santa of Peace" are two of the new members of the Leo R. Smith III Collection *of folk art introduced in 1992. "Fisherman Santa" is one of the charter members of the collection. Each piece is limited to an edition of 5,000.*

The Royal Copenhagen Group

Jack Woodson Shares the Charms of Christmas in America With Collectors of Classic Danish Plates

It's been nearly a century since the Danish porcelain maker Harald Bing had his holiday "inspiration" — yet even today, every collector cherishes the history of "Behind the Frozen Window." In 1895, Bing's family firm introduced this blue-and-white beauty as the world's first limited edition Christmas plate. Intrigued by the success of "Behind the Frozen Window," Royal Copenhagen of Denmark followed the lead of Bing & Grondahl with its own cobalt blue Christmas plate series.

Generations later, both Bing & Grondahl and Royal Copenhagen still reign supreme as creators of the world's most cherished Danish porcelains. And today the works of both renowned studios are available to North American collectors through The Royal Copenhagen Group. What's more, since the mid-1980s, this remarkable merger has also included two other prominent Danish art firms: Georg Jensen Silversmiths and Holmegaard Glassworks.

Creators of Fine Arts for Danish Royalty And Collectors All Over the World

The oldest of these studios is Royal Copenhagen itself, founded in 1775. As a purveyor to Her Majesty the Queen of Denmark, the firm earned its royal appellation as well as international renown for rare porcelains and exceptional hand-painted dinnerware. Like Royal Copenhagen, Bing & Grondahl gained recognition with its famous cobalt "Copenhagen Blue" underglaze decoration. It was founded in 1853 and already was well established when Harald Bing unveiled "Behind the Frozen Window" some forty-two years later.

Holmegaard Glassworks has been renowned for the best in hand blown glassware and art pieces since 1825. In modern times, Holmegaard has united the centuries-old craft of the glassblower with striking contemporary designs. Meanwhile Georg Jensen Silversmiths, founded in 1904, is widely recognized for breathtaking creations in precious silver and other metals including jewelry, cutlery, and holloware.

For his 1992 tribute to Christmas In America, *Jack Woodson takes us to the West Coast for "Christmas in San Francisco." A father and son head home with fir tree and presents in hand as the famous cable car pauses for a moment at the top of a hill. A 3" bell and a 2" ornament, both trimmed in gold, have been crafted at Bing & Grondahl to complement the 5" plate of Copenhagen blue and white.*

An American Artist Forges Ties With The Royal Copenhagen Group

While Danish plate collecting was largely a European phenomenon until after World War II, Americans have since become some of the world's great patrons of this delightful pastime. Recognizing the Americans' appreciation of Copenhagen blue-and-white designs — and their abiding love for U.S. landmarks — Bing & Grondahl developed a remarkable connection with American artist Jack Woodson in the late 1980s.

When Woodson's first *Christmas In America* plate was unveiled in 1986, collectors purchased the entire year's production of "Christmas Eve in Williamsburg" in a matter of months. Then when the 1987 issue, "Christmas Eve at the White

House," was unveiled, many people who had not acquired the first plate decided that they wanted both. Because the 1986 issue was sold out, secondary market trading began. This phenomenon has continued each year since, as more and more collectors discover the appeal of Jack Woodson's art as portrayed in classic blue and white.

Jack Woodson Chronicles The American Scene

"The day I said, 'I am a professional artist,' was the happiest day of my life," recalls Jack Woodson of the days in the late 1920s when he cast his fate as what he calls a "paint thrower." In a soft drawl that reveals his Richmond, Virginia roots, Woodson recalls his few private art lessons as a schoolboy. This was to remain his only formal art training. "At least it got me started, gave me exposure, and some technical background," he explains.

Woodson soon learned that his talent could lead to what he calls "saleable art" and a professional career. As he remembers, "I liked to go down to Williamsburg, long before the Rockefeller restoration, and sketch the original 18th-century buildings. Well, one of my teachers had a sister who was a Williamsburg librarian. She displayed my sketches around the library, and somebody bought them for three dollars apiece. I couldn't get over it. Three dollars was a lot of money in those days; I'd cut all the grass in the neighborhood for thirty cents. I learned right then that people were willing to pay for it if it was something they wanted."

This practical attitude served Woodson well as he crafted advertising art, theater posters, and stage sets throughout the 1930s. By 1938, Woodson was anxious to make it on his own, and he set up a studio in Richmond. Then he was ready to branch out with a wider range of commissions — including many that required him to recreate historical settings with absolute accuracy.

To this end Woodson spent long hours in the field studying everything from historic buildings to his personal favorites: boats and ships. And like the great Norman Rockwell, he keeps period costumes and accessories at the ready in his studio so that he can dress up models and pose them in scenes for inspiration. Woodson's wife, Iris, has played many a part, while Richmond friends have enjoyed dressing up as pirates, soldiers and other characters. The artist is so particular that when he was commissioned to paint a clown on a unicycle playing a banjo, he would not begin until he could stage the scene completely: unicyclist and all.

Woodson's legendary attention to detail attracted Robert Kline of the Richmond-based United States Historical Society, who eventually commissioned the artist to create more than forty-five plates including the series *America's Christmas Carols*, *200 Years Of Flight*, and *Buffalo Bill's Wild West*. It was through the creation of the Buffalo Bill plates in Denmark that Jack Woodson met Paul Steffensen of Bing & Grondahl.

The Christmas In America Collection

As Woodson recalls, "The *Christmas In America* series was an idea from Bing & Grondahl and Paul Steffensen. It was highly flattering to me to be asked to produce work for Bing & Grondahl." With his characteristic attention to research and detail, Woodson made it his business to learn everything he could about the age-old Copenhagen blue underglaze technique. "I wanted to make sure that my Christmas subjects would be adaptable to the unique process used to achieve the typical Bing & Grondahl look," Woodson explains.

"Location, recognition value, and most importantly popularity of subject" are the main criteria for selection of *Christmas In America* topics, Woodson says. While topics to date have centered mostly on the Eastern United States, the selection of San Francisco for 1992 may signal a move toward more diverse geography — "From Alaska to Western," as Woodson hints.

Since 1908, plate collectors have looked forward to the annual introduction of the classic Royal Copenhagen Christmas plate. The 1992 creation, "The Queen's Carriage," pictures Her Majesty the Queen of Denmark leaving Christiansborg Castle in her 1840-vintage carriage.

The 1992 "Christmas Shopping" plate is the second of an upbeat, unconventional collection created in color by Hans Henrik Hansen of Royal Copenhagen. An associated motif is reproduced in miniature on the Christmas ornament.

Born in 1913, Woodson admits that he tried retiring once but that it didn't work out. He did shut down his Richmond studio several years back, and now works at a slightly more leisurely pace from a studio cottage behind his 18th-century house. Richly decorated with Woodson art and creations, the studio also features a long shelf of books illustrated by Woodson himself. With hundreds of potential sites for the *Christmas In America* collection, Jack Woodson and Bing & Grondahl consider that they're just getting started. After all, the original Bing & Grondahl Christmas series has featured a new issue every single year since 1895!

Traditional Holiday Plates Lead the Collectible Art Line-up From The Royal Copenhagen Group

In addition to the popular *Christmas In America* series, Royal Copenhagen and Bing & Grondahl offer a stunning array of collector's items each year. Perhaps best known of these are the annual Christmas plates offering beloved scenes of snowy Denmark. For 1992, Bing & Grondahl introduced "Christmas at the Rectory," capturing the spirit of the holidays at the rectory of Noddebo on North Zealand. Royal Copenhagen portrayed "The Queen's Carriage," with Her Majesty the Queen leaving Christiansborg Castle in the splendid Christian VIII carriage built by wainwright Henry Fife in 1840.

In addition to the classic plates, there are other collectibles crafted to portray the same holiday scene: a bell and an ornament from both Bing & Grondahl and Royal Copenhagen; and a Christmas cup and saucer from Royal Copenhagen only.

A Preview: The Bing & Grondahl Centennial Collection

In 1995 it will be 100 years since the first Christmas plate was issued by Bing & Grondahl. But the celebrations have already started with the issue of the *Centennial* Collection, a limited series of five issues reproducing some of the best-loved motifs since 1895. The first edition of the series bears the motif "Crows Enjoying Christmas" from the 1899 Christmas plate, recreated from artist Dahl Jensen's original drawings.

The second edition, "The Christmas Tree in City Hall Square," is recreated from H. Flugenring's drawings for the plate that first appeared in 1930. Both plates have a hand-painted border of 24K gold. They are individually numbered, come with Certificates of Authenticity, and are strictly limited editions.

Now Danish Plates Come in Full Color

While both Royal Copenhagen and Bing & Grondahl first won fame among collectors for their blue underglaze plates, both firms now have introduced handsome works of art in an array of elegant colors. Notable for 1992 are the "Santa's Arrival" plate from Bing & Grondahl, and the "Christmas Shopping" plate from Royal Copenhagen. Each plate also is complemented by a Christmas ornament that picks up its motif in miniature.

Another collection from Royal Copenhagen, entitled *Flower Of The Year*, utilizes earthenware and Art Nouveau styling to portray lovely flowers in warm colors. *The Carl Larsson Home* reproduces six of this Swedish artist's most beloved images on fine porcelain, released successively during 1992 and framed in gold-trimmed wood. A handsome range of porcelain figurines created by both Royal Copenhagen and Bing & Grondahl add depth and intrigue to each line of collectibles.

From "Behind the Frozen Window" to Jack Woodson's *Christmas In America* and beyond, the art masters of Bing & Grondahl, Royal Copenhagen, Georg Jensen and Holmegaard Glass pledge to maintain a high standard of Danish decorative art — and to remain perennial favorites of international collectors.

Editor's note: Jack Woodson passed away on August 3, 1992. This was his last major interview.

Summerhill Crystal
The Multifaceted, Magical, Magnificent World of Summerhill Crystal

At first glance, it looks like a child's room. Chock full of cartoon characters in every shape and size. There's every possible rendition of Walt Disney's classic alter-ego, "Mickey Mouse." There's the innocent yet exasperating foe to pussycats everywhere, "Tweety Bird." There's the Oscar-winning rabbit, "Bugs Bunny." And in all his glory, it's the famous "Tasmanian Devil."

But wait. This room is populated by adults — not children. And they're not adults at play — although they look like they're having a great deal of fun. We've entered a world of gifted adults at work. At work at Summerhill Crystal.

These are the artists who have created the world's first three-dimensional crystal cartoon characters. The toys that pack the room are samples that Summerhill consulted so that they could perfectly reproduce Disney and Warner Brothers characters as crystal figurines. And one look at the finished product proves these artists' success.

It's a success that's built on a strong foundation. The firm has been in the crystal market for more than a decade now. It was Marcus Wagner, founder of Summerhill, who led the way in the marketing of simple crystal figurines through Sears, under the name Crystal Forest. A few years later Marcus began Summerhill to create more exclusive, refined crystal designs.

Marcus and Imal Wagner Unlock the Secrets of Crystal

The success of Summerhill has made Marcus Wagner, and his wife and "teammate" Imal, justifiably proud. According to Imal Wagner, chief designer, "When I joined Summerhill, our original concept was that rather than imitate or repeat what has already been done, I'd focus more on discovering new and unique designs and techniques in crystal. Instead of going into pewter or porcelain figurines, I was going to take the medium that we're using — crystal and glass — and go as far as I could, as quickly as I could, as perfectly as I could. Summerhill is trying and succeeding in creating more dimension within the structure. We're unlocking the secrets of crystal."

Those secrets have resulted in the January, 1992 creation of "Mickey Mouse" and "Minnie Mouse" in crystal and the line Summerhill recently introduced — a complete collection of sixteen Warner Brothers characters. The Warner Brothers collection includes "Tweety Bird," "Bugs Bunny," the "Tasmanian Devil" and "Speedy Gonzales." Twelve more pieces were unveiled at the 1992 summer gift shows, as well.

All of this artistry grew out of a challenge by Marcus Wagner to Imal Wagner. "He asked me to design a face," Ms. Wagner recalls. "He would be really, really thrilled if I could do something that's never been done before. For me, it couldn't just be a face. It had to be a face with personality. And it had to artistically challenge me. Cartoon characters are challenging."

While the challenge was far from an easy one, it was accomplished within one year. Trained as a fabric and textile designer, she found that one experience in design helped the other. According to her, "Traditional crystal designing was enjoyable, but going beyond the existing boundaries was the challenge that the classically trained artist in me was looking for."

Ms. Wagner adds, "I have learned the way to succeed in designing anything that has not been done before is to just go ahead and do it. Believe you can and you will. Surround yourself with a team that has great enthusiasm and create the challenge. The fun is in succeeding."

How the Summerhill Crystal Characters Come to Life

This philosophy of teamwork is how "Mickey Mouse" and "Bugs Bunny" — and the entire world of three-dimensional faces in Summerhill Crystal — took hold. Summerhill starts with crystal components and looks at restructuring them. According to Ms. Wagner, "We're working in the realm of infinite potential and the creativity is endless."

"It was the greatest moment when Mickey's face really started to take shape," she recalls. "He's such a wonderful personality and we captured that personality. We got the smile. We got the twinkle in his eye. We got Mickey!" adds a delighted Imal Wagner.

Technologically the design of these characters will go down in crystal sculpting history. Crystal collectors who have seen them have already started to talk about crystal in a new way. They gaze at a character and they see how he's crafted. Then they start talking about the number of facets in the design. They ask about the number of grinds. It's a way of looking at crystal as more than just building blocks. Summerhill has opened up a whole new crystal dimension.

Imal Wagner is especially excited about the unique personalities in the design challenge of "Bugs Bunny" and the "Tasmanian Devil." She says, "When you see 'Bugs Bunny,' you immediately notice his posture is exactly like his posture in the closing credits of each cartoon, where he lies on his side nonchalantly, focusing on the audience. He is totally cool and collected. There is no doubt he is an international cartoon superstar!"

"The 'Tasmanian Devil' is the same," Ms. Wagner says. "He's an awesome character. You can see at a glance that the figurine's physiology is very, very powerful. The amount of detail and intricacy will delight crystal collectors."

Summerhill expects the crystal cartoon designs to open up an entirely new world of collectors — not only those who collect crystal, but also those who collect cartoon characters. The Warner Brothers pieces are available to collectors through gift retailers nationwide. They include a line of crystal figurines as well as a line of glass and crystal etchings in paperweights and pendants. The price for the etchings ranges from $18.00 to $100 suggested retail, while the figurines range from $120 to $360.

Research Fires Imal Wagner's Sculptural Creativity

According to Imal Wagner, the initial challenge of creating a personality's face was very intense. "It took hundreds of hours to get a breakthrough with the first three-dimensional design," she recalls. "Once we knew the principles, it took much less time to move on to other characters.

"First I purchased books about the company such as Warner Brothers or Disney, their characters, and the artists who drew them. Then I read and read. Next came the videos and movies to watch the personalities in action. Only after that was I ready to begin the actual designs."

According to Ms. Wagner, each character is first rendered in clay. The clay model is fashioned using

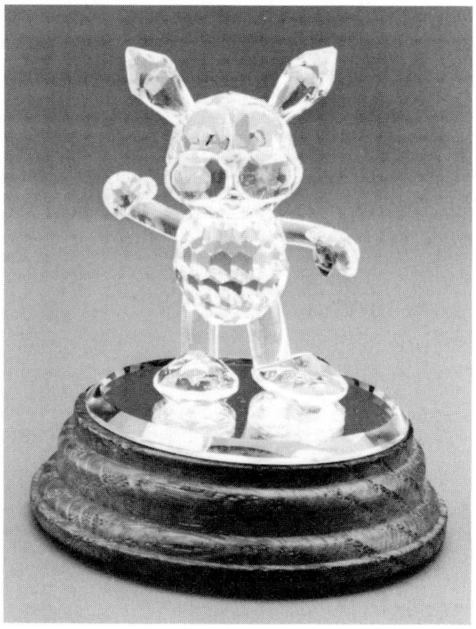

Through April 1, 1993, charter member of the Summerhill Crystal Collectors Society are invited to own "Robbie Rabbit," the exclusive "members-only" club piece.

Winning an "Award of Excellence" in 1992 from Collector Editions magazine is "The Princess Coach." This magnificent Summerhill Crystal piece, which was introduced in January 1992, has an edition limit of 1,500 and an issue price of $700.

artwork provided by the character's original artists. From the clay model, Summerhill's artists then do regular drawings and specialized crystal drawings. Next, they sit with the drawings and various crystal components and figure out how they have to restructure the crystal. Then starts the grinding. "Sometimes I get so enthusiastic that I begin grinding right away," Ms. Wagner admits. "Then, of course, I have to go back and reestablish exactness through the drawings."

In between each phase, the artist refers to the original drawings again. The finishing process consists of hours of regrinding and restructuring until the character is perfect. Much of this is possible through the use of proprietary manufacturing tools designed and built especially for Summerhill.

All of the designs are done by hand by a small group of artists who work as a team. "I've worked with this group for two years now," says Imal Wagner. "We've created our own world. We're a world that works in the magic of crystal and the beauty of crystal design. The licensed figures are a perfect fit. Crystal is magical. It's light and color. Cartoon characters are magical, too. The companies that create them create a world of inner feelings of happiness and joy. They stand for quality projects that make you feel the wonder of happiness."

Summerhill Thrives in the Heart of the Midwest

The atmosphere at Summerhill's Fairfield, Iowa headquarters is one of commitment. The location is idyllic. Nestled in-between rolling corn fields, Summerhill is a close-knit company. The town is small. It has a population of only 10,000 people. Summerhill employs about 80 of them. Everyone is on a first-name basis and the entire emphasis of Summerhill is on creativity and growth. No idea is too unusual. No design is out of reach.

Summerhill was the first to introduce a human figure in crystal — a nude. This figure, "Venus DeMilo," recently was nominated for *Collector Editions* magazine's achievement award. "Venus DeMilo" was one of three Summerhill designs nominated. The firm also received recognition for "The Princess Coach" and for a design called "Glass Iris."

Summerhill's ability to gain a three-dimensional look with its crystal is what has really put the company on the map. Dealers now report that their collectors are specifically asking for Summerhill pieces by name. According to Imal Wagner, "Even other crystal designers have come to us to see what we do and ask how we've created these pieces."

The Summerhill Collectors Society

All this led to the recent introduction of the Summerhill Collectors Society. Summerhill started signing up dealers and collectors at collectibles shows during 1992 and will continue making opportunities available through more channels, including applications at dealer outlets and inserts in Summerhill product boxes.

Collectors who enroll in the Society will enjoy a wide range of benefits beginning with a shimmering, octagonal crystal desk paperweight bearing the Summerhill hallmark. In addition, charter Society members will be invited to own the first exclusive "members-only" piece, "Robbie Rabbit." A membership card and a regular newsletter for Society members round out the initial package of benefits — all available at a first-year dues level of $25.00. Renewal dues will be just $20.00 per year.

With a licensing agreement from Turner Home Entertainment for Hanna Barbera's beloved "Tom & Jerry" on Summerhill's horizon, it's clear that this Iowa-based firm has only just begun. Indeed, there's a "many-faceted" future ahead for Summerhill Crystal collectors!

Summerhill Crystal has won the coveted licensing rights of Warner Brothers as well as Disney for the creation of remarkable and appealing pieces like this tribute to the "Tasmanian Devil."

Takara U.S.A. Corp.

Tom Rubel Invites Collectors to Explore the Delightful Fantasy World of *Nature's Woods*

Imagine a land where fantasy and reality combine in dream-like adventures. A place where there are no regulations to make life predictable. A woodland paradise where anything can happen. This is the world of *Nature's Woods*: the ultimate creation of renowned collectibles artist Tom Rubel. In Rubel's first *Nature's Woods* tale, we enter the winter woods to join precocious little Sally, her fantasy friend Buster the Elf, and the holiday world of Santa Claus!

Only a firm with the creative flair of Takara U.S.A. could envision *Nature's Woods* and encourage Tom Rubel to bring his dream land to life. As creator of some of the most popular toys and gift items of the 1980s and 1990s, Takara U.S.A. now has set the stage for an equally successful entry into the world of collectible art.

This firm first captured the imagination of American children in the 1980s when it introduced the famous "Transformers." Its gift division took the nation by storm with the "Rock'N Flower" in 1989 and the "Dancin' Coke Can" a year later. A mixture of toy and gift items, these attention-getters rocked 'n rolled to the sound of any music they "heard."

Now Takara has made a 100% commitment to the U.S. collectibles industry. And to ensure the firm's success in appealing to American collectors, Takara U.S.A. has forged an association with one of the most prolific, talented and imaginative artists in today's world of collectibles: Tom Rubel.

The Premiere of Nature's Woods

The *Nature's Woods* line includes character figurines, cottages and accessories — all created to help tell the "once upon a time" tale of Sally, Buster, Santa Claus and friends. Beginning with winter figures including Santa and his elves, the *Nature's Woods* ensemble will soon encompass all four seasons of the year with real and fantasy characters, and charming stories to unite them all.

There's so much to do in Santa's Workshop, that some of the elves have moved their finished toys outside to do the wrapping! Santa Claus supervises their activities in this Nature's Woods *preview rendering by Tom Rubel.*

Careful Craftsmanship Supervised by Tom Rubel

Each *Nature's Woods* piece begins with a painstaking drawing by Tom Rubel himself. These original drawings then form the basis for sculpting by a team of artists in the Far East. Frequent trips to these Asian studios enable Rubel to give each original sculpture his own finishing touches. Then he supervises mold-making and casting, and hand-paints a prototype of each piece to serve as the master for production.

Every detail of presentation for the *Nature's Woods* pieces bespeaks the special concern for quality and uniqueness that is shared by Takara U.S.A. and Tom Rubel. Each piece arrives nestled in its own handsome gift box, and each is accompanied by a special, four-color brochure with a note from the artist, and photographs of all the *Nature's Woods* characters, cottages and accessories.

Works of Art to Bring Joy to the Hearts and Homes of Collectors

One look at the kindly face of Buster or the inquisitive, lively Sally is enough to make most every viewer fall under the spell of *Nature's Woods*. The wonderful detail made possible by the resin medium brings out every nuance of charm and personality instilled by Tom Rubel in his characters. And Rubel himself has created cottages and a complete environment for Santa Claus, his elves, animals and friends: works of art that allow each collector to arrange his or her own *Nature's Woods* at home.

Each of the initial sixty pieces may be purchased individually. But when displayed together, they form a picturesque scene of the snowy outdoors at Christmas. It is all part of Tom Rubel's vision of the joy that nature can bring to people, especially during the holidays.

There's Santa looking over the children's toys...elves with pointed ears, rosy cheeks and round noses getting ready for the big day...snow-covered houses and trees...Christmas carolers...a singing snowman and woodsmen...deer and bunnies in the snow...and even mushrooms! It's a fascinating scene, and each character and accessory plays a part in the story that constantly unfolds in Tom Rubel's mind. In the months and years to come, collectors will find out what happens in *Nature's Woods* during the spring, summer and fall — all progressing in a unified story that combines fairytale fantasy with joyful reality.

A Distinguished Career in Collectibles Leads Tom Rubel to Takara U.S.A.

Tom Rubel knew he would be an artist from earliest childhood. And it was clear that he would work in three dimensions when he directed the rest of the youngsters in his school in creating outdoor displays for holidays and special events. After graduating with honors from the American Academy of Art in Chicago, Rubel held positions as an art director until he became intrigued by a new concept: the private mint. He spent many years as an innovative designer in precious metals for both The Lincoln Mint and The Hamilton Mint, and then later worked as the creative director for the diversified collectibles firm, Roman, Inc.

Now in association with Takara U.S.A., Rubel lives and works in picturesque Falmouth, Massachusetts, on Cape Cod. As a nature lover, he photographs many of his subjects before painting them or preparing for the creation of sculpture. He is fascinated by the opportunity to observe, study and draw the small and large creatures of our earth.

Inquisitive and precocious, little "Sally" serves as protagonist for the first Nature's Woods *story. Her adventures with "Buster" the elf will be chronicled in a forthcoming book from Takara with illustrations by the collection's creator, Tom Rubel.*

Like the beloved American artist Norman Rockwell, Tom Rubel paints subjects as he would like them to be. As he puts it, "Some are happy, some are sad, and some are humorous, but all have the joy of life." When portraying nature's creatures, Rubel uses his own special approach. "I try to capture a moment when the animal is caught out of the corner of your eye, and always with an unsurprised natural feeling."

According to Rubel, "The one thing that is always foremost in my mind is to learn to see beauty. The subjects that I draw never really change, but the way I think about them does. My imagination and inner feeling develop the ideas and principles of the art and shape the form. One thing that I am always aware of is the finished product. I ask myself: 'Does it express my original excitement? Have I organized the design and sustained the emotion or thrill I initially felt?'"

Portraying Santa Claus is a special pleasure for Rubel. "Santa is a fascinating creature," Rubel believes. "He is what the imagination makes him. To depict him in various ways is truly an experience of excitement and emotion. One doesn't know what Santa really looks like, except by the depiction of him through the ages. Santa to me is how my imagination pictures him at the time I imagine him."

Rubel's own youth and experiences with his four children color his Santa Claus creations. As he explains, "Santa is alive in all of us with memories going back to our childhood. I try to convey these memories in my figurines. My depictions of Santa are always different — whether he is conferring with his elves, checking his list, or even sewing on a button. Each portrays a holiday spirit which only Santa can truly express and the excitement he brings not only to the young, but to all ages. Santa is peace, kindness and friendships throughout the world. These are the qualities I try to convey in every piece I do."

The Story of Nature's Woods *Unfolds in a Charming New Book*

Collectors will learn more about *Nature's Woods* in a richly illustrated book entitled *Nature's Woods* (A Winter Story). This volume will combine Tom Rubel's illustrations and concept with a heart-warming tale from mother-and-son authors, Susan K. Jones and Scott C. Jones.

The story begins as Tom Rubel himself falls asleep over his drawing pad, and some of the characters on the pad come alive in Rubel's dreams. They lead him into the world of *Nature's Woods*, where we watch a wonderful tale unfold through Rubel's sleepy eyes.

The story revolves around a precocious little girl named Sally, and her *Nature's Woods* "mentor" — Santa's most trusted and oldest elf, Buster. Sally dreams of visiting Santa's Workshop (a magical place that readers of the story get to see in all its glory!) but Buster knows that her visit there would break the spell of Christmas Eve for children all over the world. To help divert Sally's attention from the workshop, Buster guides her on a whirlwind trip through *Nature's Woods*. On their way, the pair meet many remarkable characters including a singing snowman, the lovely Snow Queen, mischievous Jack Frost, and many more.

As the book concludes, we see a glimpse of Sally's upcoming springtime adventure with a whole new cast of *Nature's Woods* characters. Tom Rubel already is at work creating figurines, cottages and accessories to bring these next scenes from *Nature's Woods* alive. And under the care of Takara U.S.A., a whole world of seasonal figurines, dolls and collectibles will continue to unfold in the months and years to come — all from the vivid imagination of Tom Rubel.

A whole range of Nature's Woods *characters appear in a heartwarming winter scene in which a smiling snowman comes alive to lead a holiday carol! These hand-painted figures capture the magic of Christmas just outside Santa's Workshop.*

Timeless Creations™

Annette Himstedt's™ Barefoot Dolls Capture the Gentle and Free-Spirited Qualities of Children Around the World

"I always wanted to do 'children in porcelain,' never dolls," says German doll designer and sculptor Annette Himstedt™. Yet to make her porcelain children truly lifelike, Ms. Himstedt knew that she would need to "break the mold" on traditional dollmaking and come up with her own unique method for capturing a child's lively qualities in three dimensions.

"Usually dolls are premodeled and then these molds are used for a porcelain founding," the artist explains. "But so much of the facial expression is lost in this process." Ms. Himstedt was convinced that in order to get the likeness that she wanted, she would have to teach herself to form porcelain with her hands: an idea that was considered impossible by many experts.

Perhaps because she is a self-taught artist free of the constraints of academic learning — yet a stickler for accuracy in all that she does — Ms. Himstedt did not allow herself to be dissuaded by the traditional dollmakers. Trained originally to work in the insurance business, she waited to indulge her dream of sculpting dolls until her own children were past nursery age. Then in 1977, she modeled her first exquisitely detailed doll, with her daughter as the subject.

It took a good deal of perseverance to bring that first doll to life. "I was naive when I first started out. I only knew what I wanted. I didn't know that porcelain was liquid. I didn't know anything," Ms. Himstedt recalls with a smile.

Friends and neighbors knew that this doll was special, however, and they prevailed upon Annette to create portrait dolls of themselves, their children and grandchildren. Flattered by these requests, Ms. Himstedt obliged, even though each individual commission required more than 250 hours of her undivided attention.

She was not satisfied until she captured every nuance of expression, posture, pose, movement and temperament for each subject. These early "Himstedts" are not only treasured as family heirlooms, but also are destined to become a priceless record of a fine doll artist's evolution.

Himstedt Dolls are Now Available to Collectors

Before long, the demands upon her time were such that Annette Himstedt had to consider ways in which to create more dolls within the bounds of her personal energy. As she remembers, "At first I didn't want to make industrially manufactured dolls, as I had only produced unique ones so far. But these are so expensive that they are unobtainable for many and, above all, are not toys for children."

In her quest for a way in which to retain her standards of absolute quality, Ms. Himstedt "considered, worked and fought like fury" until she found a factory in Spain which she could acquire, right down to the tools on the workbenches. And even though she now relies on a team of handpicked doll artisans for support, Ms. Himstedt insists on complete control of the creative process. She never forgets that she was once told her dolls could not be made by individuals considered "experts" in the field of porcelain sculpture.

Now that her dolls can be had by collectors, Ms. Himstedt's fame has spread around the world. Not surprisingly, she attracted the attention of Mattel, which has become the sole distributor in the United States of several popular Himstedt doll series in vinyl.

Several tours throughout the U.S. have earned Annette Himstedt the affection and regard of thousands of doll collectors, and today her works can even be found in museums. Yet when she returns to Germany and Spain, she still creates each new doll according to the same simple, solitary process she pioneered over a decade ago.

The Birth of an Annette Himstedt Original

Wooden sticks and knives were all that Ms. Himstedt had to work with when she first started making dolls, and she sharpened them into shapes that enabled her to capture all the necessary details. These tools have been refined over the years to exactly suit the artist's needs.

When four of Annette Himstedt's dolls get together, they look for all the world like a quartet of real children! These charmers are from the Summer Dream Collection.

Before she begins a new doll, Ms. Himstedt chooses a subject: be it a neighbor child from Germany or a new friend from a land far away. As she explains, "I especially love to model children from other parts of the world. Because, despite their different appearance, they are similar in their characters, wishes and feelings."

Once the child is selected, Ms. Himstedt needs a wealth of photographic references. Unlike many dolls on the market, hers are faithful to their subjects right down to the fingers and toes! And since each child is barefoot, the realistic rendering of those cute little toes is a Himstedt hallmark. Coloring of skin, hair and eyes is a passion of Ms. Himstedt's as well, and her many photographs enable her to perfectly capture each subject's individual attributes.

A stickler for accuracy, Ms. Himstedt hand-inserts real hair eyelashes on many of her porcelain and vinyl portrait dolls. The dolls' cotton clothes are fashioned from materials woven and dyed to resemble old material Ms. Himstedt collects and saves for just the right doll. These multi-layered costumes of all-natural fabrics feature their designer's personal label.

As worldwide demand for her dolls increased, Ms. Himstedt began to work in vinyl in addition to porcelain. She still retains complete control over every stage of the production process — and all of her vinyl dolls are marked on the back of the head and dated the year they were produced.

Each vinyl doll's face features delicate, hand-sketched eyebrows and round, glistening eyes that are full of emotion. In addition, the dolls' eyelashes are hand-applied and each wig is individually styled. For realistic coloring, the doll's complexion is air-brushed and the lips are hand-painted by a team of artists trained by Ms. Himstedt herself. And under her direction, the toes, fingers and nails of each doll are carefully sculpted for a realistic look.

Collectors Inspire Ms. Himstedt's Creativity

When Annette Himstedt's dolls were unveiled at the Nuremberg Toy Fair in 1986, she learned something very touching about her work: it had as much impact on men as it did upon women and children. Indeed, the dolls stirred the emotions of many men so greatly that they became teary-eyed. Seeing children become attached to her dolls moves the artist deeply as well, for as a poor refugee child after World War II, Annette never

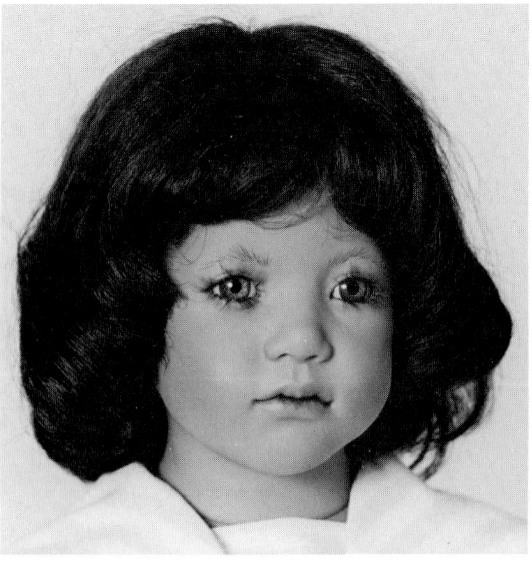

had the means nor the opportunity to play with dolls herself.

Today, dolls in her newest collection for Mattel's Timeless Creations™ division, entitled *The Summer Dream Collection* (part of Ms. Himstedt's *Barefoot Series*), enable the doll artist to share the joy of "childhood deferred" with all of her collector friends. This collection includes four dolls: "Jule," "Enzo," "Pemba," and "Sanga." "Jule" is a blonde beauty with long braids from Sweden; "Enzo" is an adorable Italian brunette; and "Pemba" and "Sanga" are two sweet Black dolls from the Southern United States.

These four dolls join Ms. Himstedt's family of international dolls in her *Faces Of Friendship Collection*, which includes "Liliane," "Shireem," and "Neblina." "Liliane" is a red-haired beauty from the Netherlands; "Shireem" with beautiful black hair wears an authentic costume from Bali; and "Neblina" is a lovely young girl from Switzerland. Each of these dolls is approximately 28" tall, and each comes with a registration card and a Certificate of Authenticity.

Achievement Awards Are Bestowed Upon Annette Himstedt

Universally recognized by collectors and her peers, Ms. Himstedt's many awards include the "Doll of the Year" awards from *Doll Reader* magazine in 1987 and 1989. In 1990, the same magazine recognized "Fiene" as "Doll Face of the Year," their highest honor. "Liliane" recently earned a "Doll of the Year" nomination from *Doll Reader* and an "Awards of Excellence" nomination from *Dolls* magazine. From the latter publication, Ms. Himstedt already has logged two "Awards of Excellence" in addition to "Sanga's" nomination for the "Awards of Excellence" in 1992.

The ultimate thrill for an Annette Himstedt collector is to see a grouping of these wonderful dolls posed as if they were children at play or at a party. Their expressions and gestures are so true-to-life that most every observer is compelled to "do a double take," just to be sure. Their designer finds this "confusion with reality" the ultimate compliment, for her goal is to capture the free-spirited gentle qualities of childhood in each of her precious, barefoot creations.

"Sanga," "Jule," and "Enzo" all are part of Annette Himstedt's Summer Dream Doll Collection. *"Sanga" (top) has black, braided human hair and a salmon-pink white checkered cotton dress. She captures the spirit of Cakecrumb City, Tennessee. "Jule" (center) is a Scandinavian beauty with blue eyes and braided blonde hair, while "Enzo" (bottom) hails from Italy.*

CREART™

Living Sculptures From a Team of Gifted Artists Whose Passion Is to CREate ART

When Carlos and Minerva Estevez took a trip to Mexico in 1986, they had no idea that they would discover an untapped source of remarkable wildlife art. While strolling through a store, Carlos happened upon some hand painted sculptures that intrigued him because of his love of nature. He and Minerva both were deeply moved by these stunning sculptures of African wildlife, equestrian subjects, and all manner of American animals, both wild and domestic. And the Estevezs were astounded to learn that the works of Creart had not yet been introduced into the United States market.

A few months later, Carlos and Minerva Estevez met Norma Galvan and Leon Del Rio. Soon a strong working relationship was forged between the Estevezs of Austin, Texas and the brilliant Mexican sculptors and craftspeople of Creart. And thus American collectors are privileged to experience the glories of Creart.

Among the most recent Creart masterpieces is *The Wild American Edition* — a collection of eight animal busts with facial features as focal points. The idea is not to represent a hunting trophy, but to portray nature itself as a companion in our daily habitat. Vicente Perez is the creator of two stunning examples: "Puma Head," and "Deer Head." The 15¼"-tall "Puma Head" has a retail price of $320. The 24¾"-tall "Deer Head" is a majestic 12-pointer with a retail price of $472.

After finishing the first two *Wild American* pieces, Maestro Vicente said, "My feelings as a naturalist have been touched, and I wish that every collector who has the opportunity to own one of these busts will feel an obligation to nature and conservation of our environment. It is our desire that when one of these pieces is physically touched, it won't be considered as a trophy, but a companion representative of wildlife."

Also new within the past year is Vicente Perez's "Pegasus." This fantasy horse appears to be lifting out of a magical cloud. The edition limit is 1,500 and the price is $420. Emilio Martinez Skossowksa created "The Standing Whitetail Deer," shown in a natural setting and offered in an edition of 1,500 at $364. Vicente Perez also created "The Soaring Royale Eagle," which looks as if it is balanced by a cloud. This intricately detailed work has an edition limit of 1,500 and a price of $560.

Considering the excellence of the sculpture and the intricacy of the hand painting, American collectors already consider the works of Creart remarkably affordable. Yet the firm's sculptors and marketers are concerned that even more collectors should find Creart pieces to be within their price range.

Thus they have introduced a new line called *The Stylus*, in which they present decorative art in a dramatic, bronze-like finish. The same pieces also may be acquired in a gray, light brown, or dark brown finish as the collector prefers. *The Stylus* pieces will be designed simply, while maintaining the quality, anatomy, proportion and balance of each design. Early additions to *The Stylus* line include a $100 "Imperial Eagle," a $100 "Mare," a $150 "Horse Head," a $60.00 "Puma" bust, a $100 "Mustang," and "Recoil" at $100.

The Masterful Sculptors of Creart

Creart began in Mexico in 1979, when five professional sculptors — also experts in manufacturing science — realized their dream of forming a company. Their goal was to produce high-quality sculpture of extraordinary realism. These art masters were searching for a "living dimension" of amazingly lifelike animal sculpture. In their early years, the founding sculptors experimented with different materials — even metals — to find combinations that achieved the desired excellence and accuracy in reproduction.

Creart's limited edition figures now are made using a bonded marble, for this substance produces a piece that is stable, impermeable, hard, and provides an excellent surface for intricate painting.

Among the artistic minds and spirits contributing to the Creart legacy today are Emilio Martinez, Vicente Perez, Gaston Gonzalez, Francisco Quesada, and Francisco "Paco" Contreras.

Master Sculptor Emilio Martinez attended the National School of Plastic Arts in his native Mexico City. He was tutored in painting by

Maestro Rafael Rodriguez and studied composition and enamel on copper under the tutelage of Maestro Ayaco Tsuru. As a founder of Creart, Martinez's love for nature and wildlife shines through in sculptures of great realism and superb detail. In the peaceful surroundings of his Creart studio in Mexico, where life moves at a slow pace, he faces each day by saying, "Today I am working on my masterpiece."

Master Sculptor Vicente Perez started as an artist in the studios of two maestros: Humberto Pedraza, and well-known sculptor and painter Francisco Zuñiga. He went on to teach modeling with clay and plastics for fifteen years at The Technical School of Mexico. Working for several years at the National Institute of Anthropology and History, Vicente Perez made replicas of prehispanic sculptures. This position helped him to gain experience in molding and casting, as well as in sculpture. As a founder of Creart, his concept is to "give life" to his pieces. In his opinion, "Realism is the beauty of our work."

Master Sculptor Gaston Gonzalez graduated from Mexico's National School of Plastic Arts San Carlos and received his first prize as a sculptor in 1962. In 1965, he produced a monumental stone sculpture for "Expo 65" in New York. Then in 1967, he was commissioned to create a sculpture in iron and wood for the Mexican pavilion of "Expo 67" in Montreal, Canada. Gaston has studied in Paris under a scholarship from the French government, and he has produced sculptures for buildings and gardens all over the world. "I believe in Creart, where perfection and quality are our goals and realism our incomparable mark," he says.

Newly arrived at Creart as a Master Sculptor is Francisco "Paco" Contreras, whose first works will be unveiled soon as part of the ever-growing Creart line. He was initiated in the Institute of Bellas Artes until 1975, when he began studies under the direction of the monumental sculptor Modesto Barrios. In 1983, he became a professor of the National School of Plastic Arts.

How Creart Sculptures Are Made

From the drawing board to the finished product, every Creart sculpture is created in a climate of excellence, with the collector's wishes paramount in the minds of sculptors and producers. The conception of every sculpture begins with Creart's dealers and collectors. Twice a year they survey their clientele and the public to learn what subjects they are interested in seeing, how large pieces should be, how much they should cost, and how each subject should be portrayed. They base their final choices on the motifs that are most in demand.

After a subject is chosen, the sculptor documents its potential positions and angles. The most appropriate or characteristic form for that subject is selected: be it a standing or sitting position, or

The "Soaring Royale Eagle" looks as if it is balanced by a cloud! This intricately detailed sculpture is the creation of Maestro Vicente Perez. It measures 10¼"x13½"x16¾". The edition of 1,500 carries a suggested retail price of $560.

From Creart's new line called The Stylus *comes this "Horse Head," a masterful bust of a proud and majestic horse. Each* Stylus *figure is available in a bronze-like finish, or in gray, light brown, or dark brown. Suggested retail price is $150.*

"Breaking Away" Gazelles, as portrayed by the artist Francisco Quezada Garcia, displays a very elegant pair in flight, surrounded by a background of brush. It measures 15"x8"x20" and is presented in an edition of 1,500 at a suggested retail price of $650.

perhaps rearing up in the case of a horse, or spreading wings in flight in the case of an eagle.

When a consensus is reached on the portrayal, a scale model sketch is developed. The sketch details each animal's anatomy, proportion and muscle tone. Creart sculptors work "from the inside out." Next, an original modeling clay statue of the subject is created, and up to three matrix models are obtained from this original.

The best of the matrix models is trimmed, and small hand drills are used to complete detail work. Some details are accentuated, while others are minimized: this is part of the sculptor's artistry. The finished model is then photographed from different angles to preserve it as a work of art.

Now skilled artisans are called upon to construct molds to faithfully reproduce copies of the subject's original form. Parts of the sculpture which may be delicate or weak are subtly reinforced with steel or fiberglass rods, which will be invisible in the completed piece.

The mold is then filled with the material selected for this particular piece. Creart can use different materials, when desired. They have found, however, that the best results are achieved using their own formula for marble compound. This compound has exceptional reproduction qualities — stability, hardness, weight, resistance, impermeability, high density, balance, and less rigidity than marble. What's more, because of the nature of this material, Creart pieces can be repaired when damaged so that they look just like new.

After the piece is unmolded, all the mold junctions are trimmed and each is carefully checked for flaws. When the piece passes quality control, it is numbered as part of the limited edition. Creart never reopens an expired edition for any reason.

Next comes the painting stage. First a base coat is applied to ensure that the oil pigments will adhere to the figure. Highly skilled artisans hand-decorate each figure. Some figures are painted with up to twenty-four different colors to achieve a natural texture not found in glass and porcelain figurines. A fine, transparent, lusterless lacquer is applied to ensure that the colors stay fresh and that Creart pieces may be cleaned with a damp cloth. A lifelike luster is applied to the eyes of each figure.

Finally, each figure is set in an appropriate mount featuring a felt underlay. Each piece is individually boxed, and a certificate request card is enclosed so that collectors may receive a letter-sized, personalized, limited-edition certificate by mail.

With the desires of collectors as their utmost concern, and excellence in wildlife sculpture as their ultimate goal, the Maestros of Creart pledge to continue their artistic journey. And under the guidance of Carlos and Minerva Estevez, these wonderful artworks will be available throughout the United States to collectors with a true love of nature and all of her elegant creatures.

The Franklin Mint

American Purveyors of International Art, Collectibles and Home Decor

For a generation, the name "Franklin Mint" has been renowned for fine medallic art and commemoratives in precious metals. But today, The Franklin Mint's "umbrella" shelters a marvelous range of collectible product offerings: porcelain plates, sculpture, Franklin Heirloom Dolls, originals from the House of Fabergé, as well as jewelry, The Franklin Library, Franklin Mint Precision Models, home decor items, historic and artistic arms reproductions, and elegant collector games.

The mission of The Franklin Mint is to offer works of enduring beauty in a diverse range of artistic media and genres; to create collectibles that can be displayed and enjoyed today, and passed on with pride to future generations. In short, the heirlooms of tomorrow.

The emphasis is on originally designed, upscale works distributed directly and exclusively by The Franklin Mint. Renowned as one of the world's largest direct response marketers, the company also is preeminent in its design leadership. In-house design studios at The Franklin Mint's Pennsylvania headquarters and in London are supplemented through collaborations with internationally acclaimed designers such as Bill Blass, Mary McFadden, Bob Mackie, Stuart Devlin, Adolfo and Givenchy.

The Franklin Mint maintains close affiliations with world-renowned museums, associations, companies and individuals who sponsor and authenticate the company's products. The complete roster spans hundreds of names regarded as the definitive experts in their fields — from the American Lung Association to the National Wildlife Federation, from the Louvre Museum to Metro-Goldwyn-Mayer and The Walt Disney Company.

The Franklin Mint staffs eighteen offices in countries on four continents. More than half of the firm's employees are based at its world headquarters at Franklin Center, Pennsylvania, in suburban Philadelphia.

Artists Provide the Creative Prowess of The Franklin Mint

To create its diverse artistic offerings, The Franklin Mint boasts a concentration of creative talent unique in our times. In Pennsylvania and London, the company employs hundreds of full-time artists representing every discipline — design, sculpture, medallic art, bookbinding, doll making and model making. In addition, The Franklin Mint works with the world's most influential designers and fine artists as well as important museums, associations, companies and individuals.

A partial list of artists with whom The Franklin Mint has collaborated includes: Chagall, Dali, Norman Rockwell, Felix de Weldon, Peter Max, Jeanne Holgate, Margaret Keane, Jamie Carpenter, Ben Nighthorse, and Guy Coheleach, among many others. The Franklin Mint Studio has also been privileged to introduce new types of work from artists known for their achievements in other media. Thus, The Franklin Mint issued Andrew Wyeth's first art in porcelain, James Wyeth's first work in silver, and Hanae Mori's first limited edition jewelry.

The Franklin Mint works with artists throughout the world: England's animal artist Peter Barrett; Russian theatre and costume designer Natasha Beshenkovsky; Chinese painters Zhe Zhou Jiang and Yao Youxin; and Indian master

Your favorite Looney Tunes characters — Bugs Bunny, Sylvester, Daffy Duck and the rest — are captured in "The Looney Tunes Christmas Plate." Available exclusively from The Franklin Mint, the plate sells for $29.50 and is hand-decorated with 24K gold.

Fully authorized and authenticated by the Milton Bradley Company, "The Classic Collector's Edition of Scrabble" is the first and only classic collector's edition of America's favorite word game. All 100 letter tiles are spectacularly minted into ingots and embellished with 24K gold. The game sells for $495, and comes complete with a player's dictionary and official score sheets.

jeweler Shaill Jhaveri. Perhaps most importantly, The Franklin Mint takes pride in discovering and nurturing new talent — carefully drawn from the nation's premier art schools and local art and craft exhibitions — and sets out to bring tomorrow's masters to international prominence.

The Franklin Mint and Its Collectors

The most valuable treasure to The Franklin Mint is its collectors — people with avid interests in acquiring the best heirloom quality items. To support the varied interests of its collectors, the Mint has formed several clubs.

The Franklin Mint Collectors Society was founded in 1970, and since then it has grown to be one of the largest organized groups of collectors in the world. Members receive biannual issues of The Franklin Mint's own publication, *Almanac*, and many other benefits at no cost. Members also are invited to purchase an annual minted membership card. And each year, collectors are offered the opportunity to join fellow Society members on an exciting vacation trip designed especially for them.

The Franklin Heirloom Doll Collectors Society is dedicated to the tradition of doll collecting. Society members receive a quarterly newsletter that keeps them up-to-date with the latest doll information and includes columns on collectors, how to recognize quality collectible dolls, doll artists and designers. Members also have use of an exclusive toll-free "doll" number and are eligible for valuable gift premiums with their purchases of Franklin Heirloom Dolls.

The Franklin Mint Precision Models Car Club is an extension of The Franklin Mint Precision Models division, dedicated to "Keeping Automotive History Alive." Car Club members receive "WHEELS," a quarterly newsletter with the latest information including columns on collectors, how to recognize quality precision models, and automobiles of historic significance. Members receive complimentary passes to automotive museums and use of an exclusive toll-free events "hotline."

The Franklin Mint Museum and Gallery Stores

The Franklin Mint Museum is located at The Franklin Mint's world headquarters outside Philadelphia. In addition to its current array of magnificent collectibles encompassing jewelry, sculpture, and medallic works of art, the Museum recently added three new permanent exhibitions. These new exhibits showcase the creation of porcelain heirloom dolls, precision die-cast models, and authentic *Star Trek* collectibles.

On a regular basis, the Museum features changing exhibits that highlight the extraordinary personal artwork — sculpture, photography and paintings — of The Franklin Mint's in-house and affiliated artists. Many of the collectible items created and crafted at the Mint are available at The Gallery Store, which is located within the museum. In addition, there are gallery stores in Florida, Michigan, Maryland and Virginia.

The Franklin Mint's Sculpture Studio

Dedicated to "breaking the mold" with original works that push the bounds of technical capability, The Franklin Mint's Sculpture Studio brings new, fascinating art to a broad audience of collectors. With a strong background in the field of medallic sculpture, the studio also is a pioneer in the use of mixed media — creating exciting combinations of crystal and porcelain as well as metals and porcelain.

Sculpture from The Franklin Mint covers a wide range of subjects. The Mint was among the first companies to realize the untapped potential of dramatic porcelain sculpture for men. The company also is rediscovering classic genres such as Art Deco and Art Nouveau.

Known for its work in areas such as wildlife and nature, The Franklin Mint regularly works with prominent organizations such as the National Wildlife Federation, the Humane Society of the United States and the World Wildlife Fund. In the area of western art, the Mint works with the Western Heritage Museum and the Frederick Remington Museum, to name a few.

Collector Plates from The Franklin Mint

The newest line of collectibles from The Franklin Mint is collector plates. The Mint's porcelain plates are high-quality works of art. Each is crafted in fine porcelain and hand-decorated with

24K gold. Each plate is hand-numbered to the edition and is signed by the artist of record.

Some of the most noteworthy artists working with the Mint to create new plates are Max Ginsburg, Jane Wooster Scott, Margaret Keane, Maureen Drdak-Jensen, and Bill Bell. Various sponsors such as the American Lung Association, the Ellis Island Foundation, the USO and Matt Groening, creator of the cartoon series, "The Simpsons," lend their expertise to the new plate line.

Franklin Heirloom Dolls

For centuries, dolls have been collected for their beauty, charm, and importance as works of fine art. Today, doll collecting is more popular than ever before — and Franklin Heirloom Dolls is a leading creator of fine porcelain collectible dolls. The firm prides itself on authenticity, imaginative artistry, attention to detail, and extraordinary high quality.

Each doll issued by Franklin Heirloom Dolls is lovingly sculptured and hand painted to make it remarkably lifelike. Sculpted fingers help achieve a delicate, refined, even eloquent pose. Eyes are hand painted, using dozens of strokes to create a sparkle of life. Colors for lips and cheeks are usually custom blended, and some dolls even have individually polished nails.

Exacting detail and high quality are evident in the costumes and accessories as well. Research authenticates the dolls' custom-designed wigs, accessories and gowns. Embroidery and other touches of splendor combine with genuine precious gems — cultured pearls, rubies, diamonds, 14K gold, and sterling silver — to enhance the appeal of many dolls.

The company is a five-time winner of the coveted *Doll Reader* magazine "Doll of the Year" award. Winning dolls include "Vivien Leigh as Scarlett O'Hara," "Olivia De Havilland as Melanie," "The Gibson Bride Doll," "The Anniversary Edition of Scarlett O'Hara," and most recently, "The Gibson Boudoir Doll."

Other Franklin Collectible Creations Abound

With The House of Fabergé, The Franklin Mint creates fine jewelry, enamelled eggs, and other art objects in the tradition of master jeweler Igor Carl Fabergé. Fabergé is best known for its dazzling, bejeweled eggs — the first of which was made in 1884 for Empress Maria Fedorovna.

Franklin Mint Jewelry designs are inspired by the creative vision of Artistic Director Alfred Durante. For two decades, Durante was Vice President of Design at Cartier, and is best known for the private-commission pieces he created for Hollywood celebrities and business luminaries. With a complete line of fashion and traditional jewelry ranging in price from $195 to $9,500, the Mint offers the lasting beauty of precious gems and precious metals in designs to last a lifetime.

Home Decor pieces from The Franklin Mint range from tapestries and Christmas ornaments to crystal candlesticks, wall hangings, and reproductions of ancient art forms. Franklin Mint Precision Models offer reasonably priced, die-cast cars in 1:24 to 1:43 scale, in association with world-class automotive experts, historians, museums and collectors.

Collector Games including the famous "Civil War Chess Set" and other fine chess sets, backgammon games, and a spectacular version of "Monopoly" add a historical or whimsical note to any home. And The Franklin Library combines the lost art of fine bookbinding with the opportunity for collectors to acquire the classics and to display them with special pride.

True to its origins as a renowned private mint, The Franklin Mint creates originally designed coinage for foreign nations such as the British Virgin Islands and the Arab Republic of Egypt. The Franklin Mint also creates exceptional artistic commemorative medals that honor monumental and historic subjects. *Historic and Artistic Weaponry* round out the wide-ranging collections of The Franklin Mint with authentic replicas of some of the world's most famous firearms and other weapons.

Although The Franklin Mint began a generation ago as a creator of fine minted items in precious metal, the 1990s find the Mint as a thriving, diverse purveyor of art with worldwide recognition. Drawing upon the gifts of internationally renowned artists and designers, The Franklin Mint — under the caring direction of Stewart and Lynda Resnick — pledges to remain in the forefront of decorative heirloom-quality art.

In 1925, the glorious era of the Silver Ghost came to an end when the last Silver Ghost to be made at Rolls-Royce's Derby facility was delivered to its fortunate owner. Now, this legendary car is available in 1:24 scale, exclusively from Franklin Mint Precision Models. "The 1925 Rolls-Royce Silver Ghost Tourer" precision model sells for $120.

Turner Dolls

Virginia Ehrlich Turner Creates Adorable Babies and Toddlers From Her Studio in the Rolling Countryside Near Heltonville, Indiana

Imagine a successful lady doll designer who never played with dolls as a child! Sound far-fetched? Well, not in the case of Virginia Ehrlich Turner — for this successful Indiana artist spent her childhood caring for real-life babies and toddlers.

"I was the oldest of six, and my four younger brothers always tore up my dolls. In my family there was a new (real) baby every three years," Mrs. Turner reminisces. So who needed dolls when the latest bundle of joy wanted a big sister's help with feeding, diapering and playtime?

Art was also an important part of Virginia Turner's life, because both of her parents were artists and they "lived for art," as she recalls. "Dad taught art on the high school level. I loved taking art from him. I especially loved oil painting. I always liked anything that was realistic," Mrs. Turner asserts.

Doll sculpture and design began as an adult career for Virginia Turner, spurred on by her sister-in-law, Judy Turner. Virginia and her husband, Boyce, opened their Indiana factory in 1981 to produce Judy Turner's dolls. Then one day Virginia was inspired to strike out on her own, with Judy's enthusiastic blessing. She sought the help of sculptor Lewis Goldstein.

"It was very, very intense," Mrs. Turner recalls. "I sculpted this little head. He looked at it and told me, 'you really do have a talent for sculpting.'" The aim was to create a smiling baby doll — and the result was an immediate hit. With her sparkling blue eyes, upswept blonde hairdo and dimpled grin, "Jeannie" debuted to unanimous raves in 1990. Since then, Virginia Turner has expanded her horizons to create a complete line of life-like (and often life-size) children and portrait dolls. The doll world has reacted with immediate praise: already two Turner originals have been nominated for the coveted *Doll* magazine "Awards of Excellence."

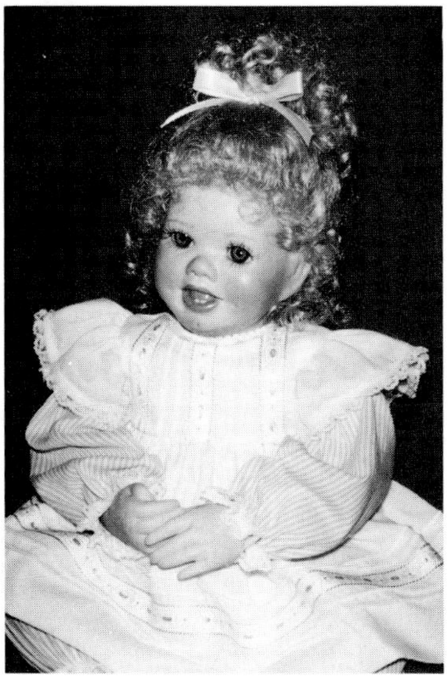

Virginia Turner's first doll, "Jeannie," fulfilled collectors' desires for a baby doll with a happy, smiling face. The edition of 500 was sold out within five months after "Jeannie" debuted in 1990.

"Terrance" and "Nikkeya" are two of Virginia Turner's most recent creations: a pair of adorable African-American children dressed for a day of happy playtime. Cuddled together, they could be brother and sister.

"Kitty Kay" is dressed for a big day in her pink checkered outfit with matching, eyelet-trimmed bonnet. Her huge and expressive eyes are sure to win your heart!

A Tour Through the Family-Run Studios of Turner Dolls

While collectors are very welcome at the Turners' Indiana outpost, an "armchair tour" can help all of Virginia Turner's admirers to visualize the down-home atmosphere of Turner Dolls, Inc. Our "tour" begins in Virginia's own studio, where she's likely to be working on a sculpture of a new little boy or girl.

Mrs. Turner works from a turntable that supports the clay bust she is working on. Surrounding her are various devices such as calipers to measure with, sculpting knives, palette knives, water spray bottles, and rags to keep the clay moist. All of this — plus Mrs. Turner's great talent — is necessary to work a piece of clay from a formless lump into a beautiful doll.

Just a short walk across the yard from the studio is the main factory building for Turner Dolls. The first person a visitor sees is Boyce Turner, Virginia's husband. He is the designer and maker of the molds for all of Virginia Turner's dolls. Good mold making is an art form in itself, with a great deal of planning and hand work involved.

Turner designs the molds with the necessary number of pieces that will let the porcelain part release without incident. This is where experience pays off because too many pieces to the mold would make it more like working a jigsaw puzzle than making doll parts. Also, the more pieces a mold has, the more seams there are to sand down in making a smooth porcelain piece.

Once a new mold is made, it has to be tested to see if it works properly. One of the key factors is to determine whether the porcelain piece can be removed from the mold without breaking. After the mold is made and tested, several identical working molds are made. Molds can wear out, so several are made so that a few porcelain doll parts are made, then that mold is thrown away. Then, another mold is used to make sure that each piece is of the same fine quality throughout the limited edition.

In this same area of the factory, we find another Turner: Tim. Tim Turner is the slip-caster and handyman. He is the one who pours the porcelain into the molds and casts the various parts. He works with "slip," a term for liquid porcelain. This slip is poured into the molds which will sit for a certain length of time before the slip is poured back out. What remains becomes a porcelain part that is ready to be taken out.

At this stage, the porcelain is called greenware. It can be cut with a knife, to open the eyeholes. Holes also are made at this stage in the shoulder plates, so that the body can be securely attached later on. Now the pieces go back to Boyce, who trims out the eye openings, sizes them, and does any necessary trim work needed to prepare each part for the porcelain cleaners.

Each Doll Comes to Life as Production and Painting Continue

Up to this point, the porcelain has not yet been fired, so it is still rather soft and can be worked somewhat when necessary. As the porcelain piece comes out of the mold, there will be small ridges where the pieces of the mold fit together. These and other bits of so-called "flashing" have to be cleaned off to make a nice, smooth piece. If they are not, the ridges of the seam lines are left behind: a tell-tale sign of lesser quality porcelain works of art.

At Turner Dolls, Gyla Kinser, Myra Apple, Gina Smith, Vickie Stidam and Sharon Ingle all work diligently to make sure that each piece of porcelain is painstakingly cleaned. Sharon is a detail cleaner, who works mostly on the porcelain hands and feet. She details the tiny fingernails and lines in fingers and toes that the porcelain in the mold can't quite produce perfectly.

The painting process for each new doll is overseen by Virginia Turner herself. After Boyce casts prototypes in porcelain and the initial cleaning and firing are complete, Virginia will paint one or more complete dolls to serve as a master for the painters. Then in the painting room, Ann Hillenburg and Virginia and Boyce's daughter, Teri, paint most of the doll heads. Virginia likes to paint and does so as time permits. During or after painting, the porcelain is fired again to ensure the permanence of the colors.

Another of Virginia and Boyce's daughters, Julie, makes all of the bodies for the dolls being crafted at the factory. She does all of this work at her own home, a sort of "extension factory" she has set up with all the necessary machinery and equipment.

Just as Virginia Turner paints the first one or two of each doll design, she also serves as the "mastermind" for the creation of each doll's costume and accessories. Carol Ziegler, one of the Turner Doll seamstresses, then brings the outfits to reality and makes patterns for them in partnership with Lois Flynn. Carol, Lois, and two other seamstresses named Pauline Stafford and Doris Picou have the responsibility of providing the outfits worn by the Turner creations. These ladies all work out of their homes.

Painted Porcelain, Bodies and Costumes Are Assembled To Complete Each Turner Doll

In the doll assembly area of Turner Dolls, the painted porcelain parts, doll bodies, and clothing and accessories all await the orchestration of Nellie Fortune, plant manager. Everything is neatly organized, with clothes racks of brand-new, hand-made outfits, shelves of porcelain doll heads, several shelves of wigs, and more shelves full of other doll necessities.

Sitting on either side of a large table covered with doll parts are Fran Cobb and Genia Fitzgerald, the doll assemblers. They take the various pieces and put them together to make beautiful dolls. Then under Nellie Fortune's supervision, dolls are placed lovingly into their boxes for shipment to a doll shop — and ultimately to the lucky person who will welcome this work of art into their home.

Turner Dolls, Inc. Proudly Presents the Current Line

Just a few short years since she began designing original dolls, Virginia Turner, her family and employees are producing a complete line of dolls in limited editions. They have even forged an association with The Hamilton Collection for the creation and direct marketing of a doll called "Michelle."

Some of the newest members of the Turner Doll family include "Nikkeya" and "Terrance," two delightful African-American children. Each is offered in an edition of 350, with "Nikkeya" standing 27" tall and "Terrance" at 25". "Nikkeya" smiles shyly and her luminous brown eyes shine as she prepares for play in her brightly printed jumpsuit. She has been crafted with an armatured body, which means that this pretty toddler can be posed in many ways. "Terrance" wears suspenders with his plaid pants, and with his armatured body, he can raise his arms to "put on" his matching plaid cap. These two dolls look like brother and sister when posed together. Their issue prices are $800 for "Nikkeya" and $750 for "Terrance."

Another newer favorite is "Bucky" the paper boy, who can visit your home complete with his paper bag and a newspaper he'll deliver to you personally. At 25" tall, "Bucky" comes in an edition of 200. There's another "Bucky" just for Christmastime, in an edition of only fifty dolls. This young charmer has red curls and a velvety holiday outfit. The newsboy "Bucky" retails at $650, while the Christmas "Bucky" sells for $900. Lovely "Raven" comes in 25" and 28" sizes, each classically beautiful in her own way. "Raven" also is available in three seasonal versions: a 28" Autumn in an edition of 150 at $900, a 25" Spring in an edition of 250 at $900, and a 25" Christmas Raven in an edition of fifty at $1,100. Each "Raven" has long, wavy curls and a sweet expression.

"Sarah Chang" is one of Virginia Turner's portrait dolls, and she is presented in a 25" version in a bright spring costume. In an edition of 150 with armatured body for "poseability," this "Sarah" sells for $600 retail. In a 30" ballerina version, "Sarah Chang" wears an elaborate tutu. The limited edition of fifty dolls carries a retail price of $1,200 each.

The babies of the collection are "Baby Joe Michael" and "Makenzie," a pair of heart-stealers with their wide-eyed good looks and adorable costumes. "Baby Joe Michael" comes with red, brown or blonde hair and brown or blue eyes. He is a lifelike 21", offered in a limited edition of 450 at $470. Pretty "Makenzie" wiggles her bare toes and smiles to show off her new teeth. She wears a costume in a choice of pink, blue, or polka-dot black, white and golden yellow. At 26", the edition of 250 carries an original issue price of $600.

Rounding out the collection is wonderful "Kitty Kay," a vinyl doll who comes with a choice of red, brown or blonde hair, all with blue eyes. Her outfit comes in blue or pink, is trimmed with lace and zig-zag applique, and her dimpled hands are beautifully expressive. Collectors may choose any combination of hair and outfit color. "Kitty Kay" is remarkably affordable at $189.

A Cottage Industry in a Farming Community

What with all the activity in the Turner doll factory, the surrounding countryside is surprisingly pastoral and tranquil. In fact, Boyce Turner makes it a point to stay on top of his "other" profession: farming and taking care of the family's forty acre homestead. A wide variety of livestock thrives on the Turner spread: cattle, chickens, sheep, ducks, and even a guinea hen or two.

Inside the Turner home, dolls reign supreme. They rest on the sofa, peer out from behind chairs, and command the best places at the table, just as real children do. And with Virginia Turner's love for doll sculpture and her remarkable empathy for children, surely there will be more and more porcelain and vinyl "youngsters" to join the Turner family...and to delight collectors who celebrate the lifelike qualities of Turner Dolls.

CUI, Inc.

Premiere Designers of Collectible Steins Support Wildlife Conservation and Offer Fine Commemoratives of Companies, Sports Teams and Historic Events

Just after the turn-of-the-century, an American entrepreneur named Percy Hexter launched a small manufacturing business in Bay Ridge, New York. His goal was to create and manufacture the finest ceramic and porcelain works available in the United States. The enterprise has changed its name and its focus since those early days, but there is still a Hexter at the helm — and the firm now known as CUI, Inc. is still committed absolutely to the utmost service and quality.

In 1979, the college football and wrestling coach, Peter K. Hexter, Jr., joined his family business. And Hexter has found that many of the same principles that made him a successful coach have been essential in building CUI as a major force in the world of collectible steins. Hexter's original "game plan" was to create and market decorated mugs and glassware to colleges and businesses.

Soon an alliance with Miller Brewing Company introduced CUI to the world of collectible steins. Stein programs with Stroh's and Coors followed — and at the same time collector interest in steins began to soar to the point where today over 2,000,000 of these collectibles are sold during the Christmas season alone!

While the beer stein concept was highly successful, it became just one aspect of CUI's remarkable growth. In 1987, CUI diversified its market and produced its first collectible stein for the waterfowl conservation group, Ducks Unlimited. Used as a fund raiser, the organization receives a percentage of the purchase price for each stein sold. This first successful stein has been followed by more — and to date, CUI has donated over $400,000 back to Ducks Unlimited from stein royalty proceeds.

The Ducks Unlimited program generated many other notable conservation-related collaborations for CUI including National Wild Turkey Federation, Quail Unlimited, Ruffed Grouse Society, Whitetails Unlimited, Trout Unlimited, Pheasants Forever, and Bass Research Foundation, to name a few. This inspired combination — producing unique and distinctive products while assisting in the funding of important habitat restoration and conservation projects — is one of CUI's most meaningful achievements.

1. CUI employs a multi-step method of painstaking craftsmanship to create each handsome stein. The process begins with decals, which are individually hand-applied for perfect positioning. Decals may display only one color, or may be done using four-color process or as many as seven individual colors.

2. Only the steady hands of skilled decorators may apply finishing details to the steins.

3. *With a capacity of 20,000 pieces per day, the 100-foot-long CUI Lear Kiln can handle the largest jobs.*

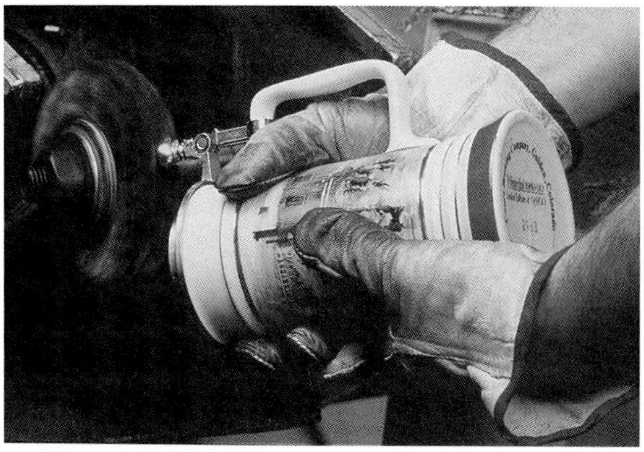

4. *Every solid pewter lid is attached by an exclusive, automated process. Thumbpieces are buffed to a smooth consistency for good looks and ease of handling.*

Classic Carolina Collections Continues the 450-Year Stein Legacy

We probably have the dreaded bubonic plague to thank for the creation of steins as we know them today. In Europe, the covered container law was instituted in the 1500s to keep infested flies out of drinking vessels. This was thought to be one cure for the transmission of Black Death.

As sanitation standards improved, so did the quality of beer. People became accustomed to having their very own drinking vessels, no matter how primitive they may have been. Experimentation with earthenware firing resulted in a vitrified substance that we now call stoneware, a much improved but costly material. These new and expensive steins then became worthy of decorative art. Colored glazes to go with art provided by Renaissance artists became the forerunner for decoration as we see it now.

The development of the stein crafting art continued for centuries into what we now call the modern period. Breweries throughout Europe developed the tradition of promoting their brands through a new stein each year. Europe is afloat with new editions each and every holiday season.

Through CUI's collectible stein business, the company has evolved as a "major player" in the marketing of steins direct to American collectors. Today this division, Classic Carolina Collections, boasts a preferred collector's list of over 100,000 names. Collectors across the country have enjoyed the wide spectrum of subjects available through Classic Carolina Collections.

The firm forges relationships with wildlife conservation groups, professional sports figures and teams, and many other organizations: now boasting a total of more than 30 licenses in all. Both Miller Brewing Company and Coors have been so impressed by the steins' artistic quality and the strong collector response that they have named CUI their "Licensee of the Year."

The Wide-Ranging Line of Classic Carolina Collections

Collectors who receive the mailings of Classic Carolina Collections have an outstanding array of products to choose from. Ducks Unlimited steins include *The Waterfowl* Series, with tributes to the "Wood Duck," "Mallard," "Canvasback," "Pintails" and "Canada Geese." A *Civil War* series features a first edition called "Attack on Fort Sumter," while Paul Kethley's "Hunt for the Buffalo" art is portrayed both on a handsome stein and on an $8^1/_2$" collector plate.

Miller Beer licensed products include a "Girl in the Moon" plate as well as a range of steins inspired by history, architecture, holidays and sports. A grouping of Federal Duck Stamp steins feature the same award-winning art that appears on stamps by Neal Anderson, Jim Hautman, and other top wildlife painters. Coors steins highlight nostalgic Rocky Mountain activities like cross-country skiing and white water rafting. A collection called the *Coors Rodeo Series* features original art by Colorado painter Marci Haynes Scott, and benefits the Cowboy Crisis Fund.

Stroh's steins take on a Bavarian theme, while a stein licensed by Germany's Beck's Beer is crafted of bas-relief pewter, porcelain and bronze. A handsome range of *Sportsteins*™ helps round out the Classic Carolina Collections offerings, including pieces honoring championship teams from football, basketball, baseball and hockey.

Dram Tree offers CUI Collectibles Through Dealers

In addition to its direct-to-collector distribution through Classic Carolina Collections, CUI now offers fine collectibles through retail dealer channels under the trademark of Dram Tree. The name comes from a gnarled, moss-draped oak known as "The Dram Tree."

For over 200 years, seafaring vessels passed the Dram Tree as this stately old oak stood sentinel on the banks of the Cape Fear River, several miles south of the bustling port of Wilmington, North Carolina. For sailors, the sight of the famous tree raised a blend of hope and anticipation. Upon the sighting of the Dram Tree, the ship's captain signaled for the traditional round of rum for the thirsty crew, in celebration of a safe entry into port. This Dram Tree celebration was a custom of many ports, and remains part of America's nautical heritage.

From the Rathskellers of Germany to the Pubs of Merry Old England, to the Country Taverns of Colonial America, steins have proclaimed a centuries-old tradition of festivity and celebration. And Dram Tree celebrates this classic heritage with a unique offering of commemorative steins and other special collectibles, establishing a Dram Tree hallmark of quality, collectibility and value.

Each special collector's edition is designed by the artisans of Dram Tree to recreate the exacting detail found in steins and other pieces with old-world craftsmanship. The 1990s are the "Green" decade, and thus Dram Tree has aligned itself with a group of dedicated organizations to help fund habitat restoration and conservation projects. To design pieces for these projects, Dram Tree commissions images from some of the most highly regarded wildlife artists in America today. Sports licensing — including licenses with the NFL, MLB, NBA and NHL — and breweries round out the Dram Tree "line-up" of collectible products.

Many of the same exceptional products offered direct-to-collectors through Classic Carolina Collections may be acquired through authorized Dram Tree dealers, but Dram Tree boasts some of its own exclusive designs as well.

In less than ten years, CUI has found a market niche, secured its position with technology and strong licensed relationships, and built a reputation as one of the leaders in the world of collectible steins. During this decade of growth, the stein category has exploded from a relatively unknown American collectible to one that generates over 5,000,000 unit sales annually. And most who follow the collectibles field consider this only the tip of the iceberg. With its leadership role in place, CUI is poised for continued strong growth and remarkable success.

This first-edition stein features Donald Boncela's realistic rendering of two 1930s Bert Graves mallard decoys. Each stein is $9\frac{1}{2}$" in height and individually numbered. An intricately detailed, hand painted remarque figurine of the drake is affixed to the custom, solid pewter lid. A portion of every sale is earmarked for the crucial wetland habitat conservation programs of Ducks Unlimited.

The first edition in the Coors Rodeo *series, which benefits the Cowboy Crisis Fund, features original art, "Jackhammer," by Colorado artist Marci Haynes Scott. Each stein is fitted with a solid pewter lid which is adorned with a hand-crafted figurine of a bucking bronco and rider. Each stein is $10\frac{1}{2}$" in height and numbered in an edition of 20,000.*

Featuring Ernie Nevers and his Duluth Eskimos uniform from 1926, and the crest of every NFL team, each first-edition "Historically Speaking" NFL Collector Series *stein is $8\frac{1}{2}$" in height, and individually numbered. The gold edition series is limited to 950 and adorned with a hand painted remarque figurine.*

June McKenna® Collectibles, Inc.

Santa's Twinkling Eyes and Time-Honored Image Inspire June McKenna's Beloved Figurines

"With your talent, we can do big things!" Dan McKenna insisted to his wife the day June McKenna won first prize at the Fredericksburg, Virginia doll show. Naturally cautious, June was amazed at her husband's determination — especially when, as she recalls, "He quit his job as an electrician the next day!"

Energized by Dan McKenna's faith in her natural gift for art, June set up shop on the kitchen table with her husband by her side. And ever since that day in 1982, the McKennas have been partners in one of the most remarkable collectibles success stories of the decade. Today, June McKenna is the sole creator and designer of her own remarkable line of figurines: and she is one of only a handful of artists who still takes such a completely "hands-on" approach.

While June McKenna is renowned for her appealing Santa Claus figures, Old St. Nick was not the first sculpture she attempted. The idea for her three-dimensional craft came about almost by accident when her son — then twelve years old — asked for help on a school science project. The youngster was studying dinosaurs and asked his mother for help in modeling a brontosaurus.

"I said, 'If we're going to do this, let's do it good,'" June McKenna recalls. "We looked it up in the encyclopedia and it said that people used to make models of cornstarch and salt. So that's what we did. If I may say so myself, it looked good." The youngster earned a high mark on his dinosaur project, and his mother got an inspiration: soon she was modeling her first Santa Claus as a gift for her own mother!

After that, Mrs. McKenna was unstoppable. She began making hand-painted clay Kate Greenaway figurines and Santas in her kitchen, then selling them at Virginia craft shows. Then came the fateful day in Fredericksburg, where June McKenna not only took top prize, but also sold $1,000 worth of figurines.

Special Santas Intrigue Collectors Year-Round

Today, many of the early June McKenna Santas are long since sold out, with one particularly popular piece, the 1983 "Father Christmas," commanding over $5,000 on the secondary market. Celebrities including Happy Rockefeller and Sugar Ray Leonard are counted among Mrs. McKenna's collectors, and foreign diplomats even took her Santas home after an international summit in Williamsburg, Virginia.

June McKenna's "Father Christmas, 1983"™ has proven so popular among collectors that it has been reported at a fair market value of $5,000. This limited edition piece — and other McKenna closed editions — are traded actively on the secondary market.

"What makes my Santas special are their faces," June McKenna explains. Dealers agree, commenting on the "character and detail" that set June McKenna Santa figures apart from the rest. Those who know the McKennas say that June's Santas look a lot like her husband, Dan: with high cheekbones, twinkling brown eyes, and a full beard.

For ideas, June McKenna has studied the long and rich history of Santa Claus in many lands, but she finds her greatest joy in Santa's history during the 18th and 19th centuries. "I try to center everything in that period," she explains. "Each piece is stained so it looks like something your grandmother had on the shelf for years and years." To ensure complete authenticity, Mrs. McKenna constantly researches clothes, toys and legends from eras past.

Although her sculptural methods have become a bit more sophisticated since those early days of cornstarch and flour, Mrs. McKenna finds simple dental tools, toothbrushes, toothpicks and sticks to be the perfect instruments for her original work. Each clay "carving" then becomes the subject of molds for production in epoxy resin. The prototype for each Santa is painted by June McKenna herself, and then the editions are turned over to a "family" of ladies who have been trained as painters — a group so caring that they add a dash of love fit for Santa himself to each piece they produce.

A Country Girl Copes With Sudden Fame

Unassuming and humble, June McKenna has been surprised to learn that her collectors consider her a celebrity. "I'm just a country girl," she explains modestly. "I used to be embarrassed. I would go to Richmond, and write a check, and somebody would say, 'Are you the Santa Claus lady?' Now, over the years, I have become used to the recognition and enjoy their enthusiasm."

Even so, the artist retains her wonder at the esteem her collectors hold for her. She recounts a visit to Lathan, New York — one of the many personal in-store appearances she makes each year to meet collectors. A man came in with four special books and asked June McKenna to sign each one of them. "He had one book for each grandchild. All of the famous people that had come through that town, he had had sign there. In front of me was Tony Randall! He had Babe Ruth in there, too."

Collector Communications are a June McKenna Specialty

To keep in touch with her many collector friends, June McKenna offers a twice-yearly newsletter with a friendly, family tone. She updates collectors about new works of art and delivery of pieces that have been previously announced. She introduces the people "behind the scenes" who help with the creation of her beloved artworks. And she reports on secondary market values and where collectors may be able to purchase sold-out or retired pieces. June McKenna also publishes her travel schedule and tells about her visits with collectors at shops and shows across the country.

A highlight for many collectors at these events is the opportunity to acquire pieces from the *Personal Appearance Santa* collection. Each piece is a replica of a sold-out limited edition from the past, beginning with "Father Christmas, 1983." Much smaller than the coveted originals, these Santas feature the same appealing image right down to

"Fishing John" and "Sweet Sister Sue" are the first signed and numbered limited edition figurines of June McKenna's Black Folk Art Collection. This collection consists of many figurines depicting Black Folk Art of the early 18th century.

June McKenna recaptures memories of "my visits to Santa, sitting on his knee, sharing secrets with him" in "Bedtime Stories," a heartwarming figurine picturing Old St. Nick surrounded by admiring little ones from around the world.

the twinkle in St. Nick's eye. And because they are available only at Mrs. McKenna's personal appearances, only a very small number will ever be made and circulated.

Santa Appears in Many Happy Guises

A small number of new Santa Claus images are introduced each year by June McKenna Collectibles, usually in limited editions ranging from a 4,000 to 10,000 circulation. The company reserves the right to retire a figurine before its maximum circulation is reached, but pledges that circulation will never exceed the number announced originally.

Among the most limited Registered Editions, now sold out or retired, are "Colonial, 1986," "Jolly Ole St. Nick, 1988," and "Traditional Santa, 1989." Each of these signed and numbered Santas has a circulation no higher than 4,000. The colonial Santa gives us a glimpse of Early American times, when Christmas was celebrated with fruit, festive meals and handmade toys. St. Nick's overstuffed sack of toys begins to fall to the ground in the 1988 issue, as the Jolly Old Elf breaks a twig of holly for decorating. The traditional Santa has his sack of toys over one shoulder and a fresh-cut Christmas tree over the other — ready for an Eve of celebration.

The 1988 "Remembrance of Christmas Past" work of art is 17" in height, and shows Santa walking through the snow-covered forest with his burro. They are preparing to bring many toys for all the children of the world. The 18" "Kris Kringle" from the previous year shows Santa coming to town with his fir tree, toys, and a sturdy sack of candy.

Santa doesn't always wear red, as evidenced in "Seasons Greetings," a 1989 limited edition where St. Nick dresses elegantly in a flowing white robe. His clothing is blue and gold in "Bringing Home Christmas," a 1988 limited edition that finds Santa strolling through the woods with decorations for the family Christmas tree and presents for the children.

Santa and Friends Bring Holiday Cheer

While many of June McKenna's works depict Santa all by himself, others show our favorite Christmas visitor in tandem with other people or special props. In "Last Gentle Nudge," a 1989 limited edition, we see Mrs. Claus trying to rouse her sleepy spouse in time to complete his Christmas rounds. It measures 9" in height and is offered in a signed and numbered circulation of 4,000.

"Santa's Magic Sleigh" from 1989 shows Santa waving goodbye as he sets off on his Christmas Eve journey. This signed and numbered piece depicts Santa, sleigh and full regalia — and another figurine called "Santa's Reindeer" complements and completes the scene.

A very limited work of art, "Santa's Wardrobe," was introduced in 1989 showing our Christmas friend getting ready for his long journey. Still barefoot, Santa opens his free-standing wardrobe to select his jacket, boots and other attire. At his feet, his bag of toys and goodies awaits. This 16" piece is limited to a circulation of just 1,500.

"Bedtime Stories," a limited edition from 1991, shows youngsters from many cultures along with Santa Claus. Every child around the world dreams of sitting on Santa's knee, each with his or her own secret wishes for Christmas. This collectible brings forth the love and enjoyment shared by all as a young boy reads stories of Christmas.

"Santa's Hot Air Balloon Ride" captures the Jolly Old Elf on an amazing adventure. His basket is loaded up with many toys for children around the world, while "Rocky" the dog awaits the excitement of Christmas morning. The blue balloon is adorned with sprays of holly and red ribbons, and a netting of gold holds the balloon in place.

June McKenna "Spreads Her Wings" With Angels and Other New Collectibles

While she has made her reputation with Santa Claus sculptures, recently Mrs. McKenna's horizons also include a series of pieces inspired by Amish families, and her continuous collection of Black Folk Art figurines, *Memories of Yesteryear*, based on the 18th-century era. Her Nativity Set features several additions each year, and for the 10th anniversary of June McKenna Collectibles, the artist created a charming "Little Guardian Angel."

With her natural art talent, vivid imagination and "can-do" attitude, June McKenna is only just beginning to make her mark on the world of collectibles. Husband Dan's faith in her potential has long since paid off, and with each new collector who discovers Mrs. McKenna's art, the couple savor new friendships and associations. As June McKenna wrote in her newsletter recently, "My sincere wishes are that these figurines brighten your home and help preserve memories year after year, that your blessings are as limitless as the toys in Santa's bag, and that the joy of the holiday season stays with you throughout the year."

Silver Deer

An Endearing Menagerie of Sparkling Crystal and Hand Painted Sculptures

Every successful business begins with a burst of discovery. And for Lester Ronick and Mike Saunders, that inspirational moment came in the mid-1970s at a Colorado Christmas Fair. The two friends found themselves dazzled by the beauty of a sparkling crystal prism. Within months, this fascination led them to import fine prisms from Austria. From there it was just a matter of time before Silver Deer was launched in Boulder, Colorado — creating unique crystal figurines of animals, people, places and things.

Those early days saw Silver Deer introducing a number of significant "firsts" to the crystal market. They created a limited edition "Pinocchio," adorable "Winnie the Pooh" and "Babar the Elephant" pieces, and even a series inspired by the animals of Beatrix Potter. Silver Deer intrigued collectors with the very first crystal people as well: notably an elegant bride and groom.

Today the Ronick and Saunders team has been joined by current Silver Deer President Michael McKeown, and the firm is celebrated worldwide for its breakthroughs in crystal artistry and craftsmanship. And while crystal is still the major focus of Silver Deer, the firm's artists have not been constrained in their choice of media. Today Silver Deer offers works of art in painted porcelain and polyresin as well. And two successful collector clubs support Silver Deer's most prominent lines: The Crystal Zoo and Silver Deer's Ark.

The Award Winning Designs of The Crystal Zoo

Silver Deer's Crystal Zoo Collection offers a showcase for that lovable "Peanuts" beagle, Snoopy, as well as a host of collectible crystal figurines inspired by animals, fantasy, and romance. Two gifted crystal artists — Gina Truex and Susan Dailey — are the heart and soul of The Crystal Zoo.

Gina Truex earned her B.F.A. from the Tyler School of Fine Arts in Philadelphia and later completed her M.F.A. at the University of Colorado. Her countless Silver Deer designs include both limited edition and licensed pieces: notably "Bride and Groom," "Snoopy," "Country Birdhouse" and "Bloomer." Designing pieces for The Crystal Zoo is a way for Ms. Truex to reflect her love for animals and the happiness they bring her.

Susan Dailey joined The Crystal Zoo design team in 1990, bringing a new and individual style. Her education includes a B.F.A. from Indiana University at Bloomington and an M.A. in Education from Colorado State University. She has spent over twenty years sharing her love for art and design by teaching in private and public schools throughout the country. Ms. Dailey has a typically western, carefree style that she incorporates into her work. Favorites created by her include "Joe Cool Jammin'," "Into the Wind" and "Ice Palace."

Snoopy and Joe Cool Win Collectors' Hearts

Whether he is playing the role of one of his alter-egos, (Joe Cool, World War I Flying Ace or Literary Ace) or just being Snoopy, Charlie Brown's favorite canine is sure to bring a smile. Silver Deer's *Snoopy* collection includes a "Literary Ace" piece inspired by that famous saying, "It was a dark and stormy night." We see Snoopy hunched over his typewriter, looking for the second line of his Great American Novel.

In a more playful mode, we celebrate carefree Snoopy in "Joe Cool 'Vette," a limited edition of 1,500 that has the Snoopster showing off his bright red sports car. Thanks to Silver Deer's crystal artistry and the liberal use of wonderful props, collectors can enjoy "Joe Cool Hockey," "Joe Cool Jammin'," and several more. Snoopy even takes off in his own crystal prop plane in "Flying Ace."

"Tea for Two" Wins "Best Crystal Design" Award

Another work of art from The Crystal Zoo is the delightful "Tea for Two," chosen by attendees at the 17th Annual Collectible Exposition in South Bend, Indiana as the year's best design in crystal. Capturing the whimsy of two teddy bears at tea time, this 3" piece was issued in a limited edition of 1,500.

Other limited and special editions in The Crystal Zoo cover a wonderful array of topics, from animals and clowns to bride and groom, and even

Silver Deer was honored to receive a blue ribbon for the best design in crystal at the 17th Annual Collectible Exposition in South Bend, Indiana. The winning entry was "Tea for Two," a 3" crystal sculpture offered in a limited edition of 1,500 at a $150 retail price.

the beloved storybook character "Pinocchio." *Crystal Fantasy* pieces from The Crystal Zoo are inspired by monumental castles and fortresses including the romantic "Camelot," and the stunning "Castle of Dreams."

The range of subject matter is amazing, with appealing little creatures like "Schoolhouse Mouse" and "Forest Owl" as well as dramatic works like "The Archer" and "Gabriel" the angel. And for those with a sense of humor, there's "Teetering Twosome," which captures the predictable result when an elephant sits on one end of a seesaw and a tiny mouse "holds down" the other.

The Crystal Zoo Collectors' Club

Collectors who enjoy the delights of The Crystal Zoo are invited to join The Crystal Zoo Collectors' Club. Membership benefits include: an exclusive Members Only limited edition figurine, free with enrollment; an official Club Membership Card and Certificate; a subscription to the informative and fun-to-read quarterly newsletter, "Facets"; and a registry of the current Crystal Zoo Collection.

Club members will also receive special, Members Only limited edition Redemption Certificates for upcoming figurines. These entitle members to order these special figurines through their local authorized Silver Deer dealer. All of these benefits are available for a yearly membership fee of $25.00.

Silver Deer's Ark Explores the Natural Beauty of Animals

Silver Deer also invites collectors to "come aboard" Silver Deer's Ark, a playful parade of coldcast creatures designed by famed collectibles artist Tom Rubel. Each sculpture is carefully hand crafted and hand painted with life-like detail and coloring. The line includes several popular series including *Peaceful Creatures*, *Animal Friendship*, *Parent and Child* and *Christmas Animals*. Each has its own endearing qualities to warm the heart.

The *Peaceful Creatures* are portrayed in candid instants from nature, each capturing a glimpse of the animal's genuine spirit at the hand of the gifted Rubel.

Domesticated pets like the "Poodle" and "American Shorthair Cat," are joined by wildlife such as "Brown Bear," "American Elk," and even exotic creatures like the "Lion" and "African Elephant."

The *Animal Friendship* sculptures allow collectors to delight in the gentle kindness and mutual harmony exuded by pairs of animals and birds. Parent-and-child scenes such as "Big Horn Sheep" and "Raccoons" as well as pairs of similar animals such as "Lambs" and "Polar Bears" make this collection a special favorite. The *Parent and Child* collection focuses specifically on the profound warmth of the animal parent-and-child relationship, with images such as "American Quarter Horses," "Kangaroos," "Giraffes," and many more.

Among the delightful creatures in The Crystal Zoo's Playful Parade *is "Schoolhouse Mouse," a 2-1/16" portrayal of a very studious little fellow. Designed by Susan Dailey, the piece sells for $45.00.*

Tom Rubel is especially renowned for his *Christmas Animals*, a very special collection that portrays favorite animals adorned with holiday wreaths, ornaments and other finery. For holiday decorating and gift-giving, these works of art have proven extraordinarily popular. A gentle "Cow" wears a red ribbon with bells around her neck, and boasts a bright green wreath with matching red ribbon bows. A sweet-faced "Bear" wears his wreath around his neck, as does the "Giraffe" and the "Clydesdale." The "Poodle" is all wrapped up in bows like a gift, and the "Squirrel" has discovered a bright red-and-white candy cane.

In addition to the regular *Christmas Animals* sculptures, Tom Rubel has created five limited editions in a larger, 12" size. They are the "Christmas Dog," "Christmas Cat," "Christmas Bear," "Christmas Horse" and "Christmas Dalmatian." To round out Silver Deer's Ark, there are snowglobes in Christmas animal motifs, and *Christmas Animal* ornaments to grace the boughs of a holiday evergreen.

Tom Rubel Offers a Fresh Aspect on Animal Sculpture

Tom Rubel brings years of successful experience as a collectibles artist and designer to his creation of Silver Deer's Ark. As a nature lover, he is fascinated with the opportunity to observe, study and draw the large and small creatures of our earth. In his meticulous presentation of detail in color and form, Rubel has developed a unique artistic style.

"I try to capture a moment when the animal is caught out of the corner of your eye," he explains. "Always with an unsurprised, natural feeling. The one thought that is always foremost in my mind is to learn to see beauty."

The Silver Deer's Ark Collectors' Club

Animal lovers everywhere can enjoy Silver Deer's Ark all the more as members of the Collectors' Club founded in response to demand of collectors across the nation. The primary purpose of the Club is to provide collectors with information about the animals, the artist, advance notice of retirements and other vital news. In addition, the Club serves as the source for exclusive, Members Only Limited Editions.

Club membership benefits include: a free limited edition figurine with enrollment; future opportunities to acquire other limited edition figurines through Dealer Club Members; a complimentary subscription to the Club's official newsletter; a Charter Membership Certificate; a Membership Card; and special Club promotions.

Although Silver Deer began as a maker of sparkling crystal figurines, the studio now has broadened its horizons to include porcelains, polyresins, and many other products. But always the memory of that multi-faceted crystal prism will inspire Silver Deer to "catch the sparkle" — and share its brilliant fire with collectors everywhere.

One of Tom Rubel's Peaceful Creatures *for Silver Deer's Ark is "Tiger" — a handcrafted and hand-painted sculpture that comes with its own gift box and carries a retail price of $25.00.*

Possible Dreams®

Celebrating Christmas and the Seasons of the Year With Clothtique® Originals

On one of his frequent international buying trips, Possible Dreams President Warren Stanley once made a very remarkable discovery. He came upon a centuries-old process for stiffening cloth — and as he learned more about it, he was greatly intrigued. Originally developed in Europe, this process was used by a handful of artists in various countries — but only in a limited way. Stanley predicted amazing potential for this technique, because he saw that it allowed designers and artisans to make extremely realistic costumes for porcelain figures. Every fold, crease, texture and trim could be brought to life in the process Possible Dreams christened "Clothtique®!"

Today — nearly a decade after Stanley's successful journey — the Clothtique Originals of Possible Dreams thrive as one of America's most popular collectible lines. What started out as a conservative offering of seven Clothtique designs now has grown to embrace scores of elegant works from artists like Tom Browning, Mark Alvin, Judith Ann Griffith, Lynn Bywaters, Jan Brett, Judi Vaillancourt and Thomas Blackshear. What's more, a number of the great Norman Rockwell and J. C. Leyendecker's most memorable covers from *The Saturday Evening Post* now reign in three dimensions, thanks to Clothtique.

The initial Clothtique Originals were angels and nativities. Then for the next Christmas season, Possible Dreams introduced the first Clothtique *Santa Claus* collection. Confined to just three pieces, the line represented a broad look at Santa Claus around the world. It was an immediate hit with collectors — so much so that the Santas sold out to dealers within five months of issue. As soon as these Santas hit the stores, collectors began writing Possible Dreams asking for more information and to be kept informed of new additions to the line. Today, Possible Dreams fields thousands of pieces of mail to keep collectors informed about the growing world of Clothtique Originals.

Tom Browning's "A Friendly Visit" showcases the American Artist *collection of Clothtique Santas by famed U.S. designers. At 11½" high, this work of art has an issue price of $99.50.*

The Art of Clothtique

There is no mystery to the charm, the beauty, and the special, lifelike "feel" that Clothtique brings to a character. But collectors often express curiosity as to how this unique process evolved. The earliest records of a technique similar to Clothtique can be traced to southern Europe. For Possible Dreams, a well-known sculptor named Paul Chang perfected the process based upon his success with papier maché.

Chang's search for just the right compounds and materials to complement his talent brought him to the process now known as Clothtique. The blend of old-world magic and new technology — and Chang's own expertise with porcelain, resin and cloth — gave birth to a product that looks as close to real life as humanly possible. We can feel the rich texture of Santa's "fur" trimmed coat, hat and pants...experience the richness of tapestry next to the smoothness of "woolen" cloth.

Today the Clothtique® line of figures includes four special collections: the *Clothtique Santa* Collection,™ *The American Artist* Collection,™ *The Citizens of Londonshire,*™ and the Clothtique *Saturday Evening Post Covers*. Each features its own gifted designers, seasonal themes, and unique appeal to collectors.

The Clothtique Santa *Collection*

Alive with details, color and artistry, the Clothtique Santas range from the American traditional St. Nick in many guises and poses to portrayals of

One of the lovable citizens of the mythical land of Londonshire is "Tiffany Sorbet," a sweet lady hippo who runs the local ice cream parlor. This Clothtique® figure is 8½" in height and sells for $65.00.

the "Jolly Old Elf" in costumes from around the world. In "Santa on Reindeer," we see St. Nick taking off for a ride over rooftops on the back of one of his trusty friends. We also see "Santa on Motorbike," "Santa Skiing," "Santa on Sled" and "Santa on Sleigh," ensuring that St. Nicholas has many different ways to make it to our homes on Christmas Eve. In the world of Possible Dreams, there's also an "Engineer Santa" who steams into town with a Christmas Express full of toys for good little girls and boys.

Santa's multicultural nature shines through in designs like "Siberian Santa," "Santa with White Coat," ornaments inspired by "Father Christmas" and "Kris Kringle," and the "Black Santa" and "African-American Santa" pieces. There are also 10" "Kris Kringle" and "Nicholas" figures to add an international flair to home display.

Limited edition collectors are intrigued by the Clothtique "Patriotic Santa," "Father Christmas," and "Traditional USA Santa and Elf" designs, each offered in a sequentially numbered edition of 10,000 pieces. Each of these Santas stands 17" high, bears a commemorative brass tag, and comes nestled inside a handsome gift box. Considering the number of Clothtique Santas that have already been retired, interest surrounding these special limited editions has been particularly strong.

The American Artist *Collection*

In cooperation with some of today's most honored contemporary American artists, Possible Dreams has introduced the *American Artist* collection. The detail and accuracy that are captured in these Clothtique Santas are a testament to the talent of their designers.

Tom Browning, a member of the prestigious Northwest Rendezvous Group in Helena, Montana, offered images from his famous "Santa's Time Off"™ greeting cards for his Clothtique® Originals. We visit with Santa "up close and personal" as he pets a kitten, cooks a meal, feeds wildlife and makes music with his elves.

Mark Alvin's Santa is entitled "Peace on Earth," and it shows Santa with the traditional gift of peace, the Lion and the Lamb, added to his traditional sack of toys. Alvin, whose works include posters, Christmas ornaments and greeting cards, says, "Into each of my paintings I put my love of finely crafted objects. I always think of the viewer and try to fill my work with a light that we may share for a fleeting moment."

Judith Ann Griffith loves the great outdoors, and she has spent much of her life in the woods of Pennsylvania and Arkansas. She says that her artwork "celebrates a deep reverence for life and for the beauty and peace which truly exist on earth." Her Santas are taken from greeting card images which she prepared for Sunrise Publications. "An Angel's Kiss" shows Santa smiling as a sweet little angel kisses him on the cheek. "Heralding the Way" offers a Santa richly dressed in forest green, waving a banner as he approaches with his bag of toys.

Whether Lynn Bywaters portrays an engaging furry animal, a mythological creature, or a mother and child, there is an ever-present vision of realism in each illustration. Her Santa Claus images were taken from Sunrise Publications greeting cards. They include: "The Magic of Christmas," with Santa riding a handsome horse; "A Peaceful Eve," with Santa posing alongside one of his reindeer; and "Lighting the Way," in which Santa's Clothtique costume is enhanced by "fur" and gold brocade trimmings.

In describing her work, Jan Brett says, "I remember the special quiet of rainy days when I felt that I could enter the pages of my beautiful picture books. Now I try to recreate that feeling believing that the imaginary place I'm drawing really exists. The detail in my work helps to convince me, and I hope others, that such places might be real." Ms. Brett's gift for detail is confirmed in her "Alpine Santa," a figure with costume trimmings in intricate motifs. Even Santa's reindeer boasts a fancy cloth "costume" draped over his back.

Judi Vaillancourt began experimenting in 1984 with Santa Claus in three dimensions. She filled antique chocolate molds with chalkware and then hand painted each piece. Soon Vaillancourt Folk Art was born — and now two of Ms. Vaillancourt's wonderful designs come to life in Clothtique. "Father Christmas" shows Santa arriving with a bag full of apples, while "Out of the Forest" features a stunning cape for Santa. Both pieces are trimmed in "fur."

Thomas Blackshear is renowned for his dramatic lighting and sensitivity to mood. With commissions from the U.S. Postal Service, Jim Henson Studios, National Geographic, Disney, and Universal Studios, he has become one of America's preeminent illustrators. For Possible Dreams, Blackshear presents "Traditions" — an old-fashioned American Santa smoking a pipe and bearing a crystal "light" in his hand.

The Citizens of Londonshire

Already as famous as the *Clothtique Santa* collections are the characters in the appealing *Londonshire* collection, based on a land "Beyond the Third Rainbow." Londonshire has become almost real to the 3,000 subscribers to this land's special newspaper, "The Londonshire Daily Mail," and the thousands of others who receive one of these characters as a gift.

As the story of Londonshire goes...in the land that we now call Great Britain, there once lived a famed nobleman: Lord Roland Holloway. Lord Holloway was one of the animal kingdom's best friends. He devoted his life to his animal family, as he had no human one. It is fabled that as Lord Holloway lay dying, he clutched a magic jewel which had once belonged to Merlin of King Arthur's Court. The jewel was famed to contain three rainbows.

As Lord Holloway drew his last breath, the crystal started to emit a brilliant light and Lord Holloway uttered his dying wish: "That all animals should enjoy the human happiness he had enjoyed, in a faraway land they could call their own." The animals fulfilled that dying wish by sailing away on the ship they called the "Rainbow," to a new life in "Londonshire."

Norman Rockwell's classic "Triple Self Portrait" now has inspired a Clothtique® work of art in three dimensions. The detail work is exceptionally fine, and the piece is completely faithful to the Saturday Evening Post *cover of February 13, 1960. The figure measures 14" high and sells for $230 retail.*

The *Londonshire* collection features the original captain of the "Rainbow," "Admiral Waldo," as well as such lovable characters as the "Earl of Hamlett," a pig who serves as the local magistrate and chef, and his children, "Walter" and "Wendy." The most recent addition to the line is "Tiffany Sorbet," a lady hippo and proprietor of the local ice cream parlor. From the ruddy masculinity of "Officer Kevin" to the delicate grace of "Lady Ashley" and "Lady Margaret," the Citizens of Londonshire are a whimsical link between past and present.

The Saturday Evening Post *Collection*

Possible Dreams is especially proud to bring the art of Norman Rockwell and J. C. Leyendecker to life through a licensing agreement with The Curtis Publishing Company. Inspired by classic *Saturday Evening Post* covers, these Clothtique treasures now may be enjoyed in three dimensions and vivid color.

The Rockwell collection includes Christmas favorites such as "Santa's Helpers," "Gramps at the Reins," "Santa Plotting His Course," and "Balancing the Budget." There are also several pieces marking other seasons, such as "Springtime," and "The Marriage License." And Norman Rockwell's beloved "Triple Self Portrait" now is available in Clothtique, with incredibly lifelike detailing. Leyendecker's "Hugging Santa," and "Santa on the Ladder" round out this marvelous, historic set of offerings.

The Clothtique Line Continues to Grow

Today, Clothtique Originals have expanded to cover every season. There are Clothtique nativities, angels, and treetops, as well as spring ducks, bunnies and Easter pieces. In addition, Possible Dreams' skill with Clothique has won them the coveted Pepsi licenses. They now produce two Pepsi Santas, including the very famous one by Norman Rockwell.

Leni Miller, C.E.O. of Possible Dreams, sees many more Clothtique Originals in the company's future. The firm's designers are always experimenting with new characters and ways in which to use the process. From Santa to Londonshire to *Saturday Evening Post* and beyond, most all Clothtique dreams seem possible for the company called Possible Dreams!

VickiLane

Vicki Anderson Shares Her Gift for Art in a Heartwarming Array of Collectibles

The world of VickiLane is a realm of imagination, innocent delight, and subtle expressions. There, make-believe and reality thrive side-by-side in creations with a message for living. Each precious work of art stirs something unique inside the beholders. These originals transmit the feelings, thoughts and blessings of Vicki Elaine Anderson to every collector with love.

For Vicki, art has always been as much a part of life as breathing. She grew up in a household brimming with creativity. Her parents, Jack and Viletta West, met while attending Denver Art School. And the Wests maintained an active interest in art all their lives, leading Vicki's mother to found the renowned Viletta China Company.

As a high school student, Vicki West met and fell in love with Ron Anderson, and after attending community college the two embarked on a marriage and partnership that has thrived both personally and professionally. The Andersons' artistic collaboration began with a plan to fulfill their dreams of higher education.

From Craft Markets to the World through VickiLane

It was the early 1970s, and mushroom sculptures were all the rage. Vicki and Ron needed a way to pay their tuition at the University of Oregon. Vicki was an art major, and Ron was majoring in computer science and math. They pooled their talents to design and market a line of sculptured mushrooms, whimsical turtles, children, and calligraphy prints — works of art that were soon among the most coveted Saturday Market "finds."

Back then, the Andersons believed that their little business would only be a temporary part of their lives. They sold it in 1977 after Ron completed his ministerial studies at Portland Bible College, and they were called to pastor a church in a small community. In 1985, in the midst of that ministry, Ron and Vicki began to realize that their study, experience and faith had prepared them for a new arena of service. Even though VickiLane Inc. became their full-time occupation at that time, they still have continued to devote many hours as lay ministers in their local church, and much support to its missions.

Vicki Anderson is truly the heart of VickiLane. This creative lady has a remarkable ability to bring ideas to life through her skills and imagination. With a twinkle in her eyes, she designs one masterpiece of make-believe after another.

With a sense of destiny in their hearts, Ron and Vicki set out to make a mark in the gift and collectible business. "Create an experience of beauty and delight that will uplift every heart." "Make a positive impact through the products we design, the ideas we stimulate, and the jobs we create." These and other similar phrases have been part of a chosen philosophy underlying every step of their journey.

A Natural Talent for Pleasing Collectors

In continuation of the experience that began with the 1970s, Vicki's work continues to be in demand and in touch with the times. Currently, most of her design time is being devoted to the creation of figurines and prints for her various series of bunnies, mice, cats, pigs, teddy bears, lambs, dogs and sea life. Each animal is a charming character with a story to tell. And Ron Anderson says his wife has a "sixth sense" for knowing what collectors want in a figurine or painting.

To keep up-to-date, Vicki is constantly developing her skills. It's a way of life. She carefully observes current design trends, the desires and needs of people, and analyzes the best of contemporary artists. Then she lets her creativity wander freely. "It's not an analytical or scientific thing," she says of her mental process. "But rather a felt thing — stemming from a desire to express my true self." Vicki has a deep appreciation for the best art from every era of history and is aware that it subtly influences her own work, helping her to meld current trends with long-standing traditions.

There is a sense of anticipation among those closely acquainted with Vicki Anderson's work. Items she created years ago are still popular, yet each new piece seems to elevate the artist's "personal best." As Ron Anderson says, "Collectors are always curious to know what Vicki will come up with next. I, too, am full of a sense of anticipation as to how her creative talents will unfold. I believe we have only seen a thumb sketch of the high quality work she will create in the years to come." For the near future, Vicki is working on concepts for new lines of children, fancy little girls and ladies, people of character and a series of floral prints.

While Vicki's original pieces were crafted in three dimensions, she has turned her energies recently to the realm of watercolors to be offered as collectible prints. The success she has found there came as no surprise to her husband. "I have known in my heart for years that as the areas of sculpting, drawing, lettering, design, pastels, watercolor and oils were developed more fully by Vicki, the results would be amazing. You can count on a few hands the artists that can do all these things well."

She Designs With a Twinkle in Her Eye

Vicki Anderson's *Mice Memories* and *Sweet Thumpins* are but two examples of the animal worlds this warmhearted artist creates from her imagination. In and of itself, each figurine is a delight. But with knowledge of the characters and their personalities, collectors find themselves falling in love with these make-believe worlds.

Mice Memories features Earnest and Sunshine as its central personalities. This loving couple appears in a limited edition figurine called "Happiness Together," where they rest on a log and express their caring and mutual interest. Earnest and Sunshine have two adorable children named Willie and Rosebud.

To celebrate the warmth of motherhood and the beauty and security of home, Mrs. Anderson has portrayed the mother mouse, Sunshine, preparing cookies for her little youngsters. We can almost smell the sweet scent of baking when we view the figurine and watercolor on this subject. Another motherly moment takes center stage as Sunshine serves a birthday cake for one of her beloved family. In "Bathtime," Sunshine helps her little son Willie get his ears clean while Rosebud chuckles and plays with her floating rubber ducky. Willie knows he's loved, but he can't help wincing as Mama loosens every last speck of dirt!

"Mice in a Shoe" shows Willie out on his own with friends Bramble and Toby. They're all sound asleep in a tennis shoe that Earnest found on one of his hikes. Willie prefers a sardine can for a bed, however — he says it's much better than those paper matchbox beds most of his friends have. Another image features Willie enjoying a perfectly ripened strawberry at the Country Fair. For this little mouse, one berry is enough for a meal!

Even in the mouse community, some ladies thrive on status, and Sunshine's friend Virginia plays this up in "Sunday Stroll." She's all dressed up and her baby and stroller are adorned "just so." She's hoping to "run into" a few close friends and interested neighbors who can "ooh" and "aah" over her little one and her finery. Another mouse friend named Susie thrives on life at the beach. We see her collecting sea shells as she enjoys the fresh breeze on a warm, sunny day.

Earnest and Sunshine Share a Great Adventure

In addition to their appearances in figurines, now Earnest and Sunshine are the stars of one of Vicki Anderson's new watercolors. Entitled "Life's a Great Adventure," it shows the mouse couple discovering a place they have never seen before. They are walking along a path, and somehow they know in their hearts that this is the road they should follow. It's a beautiful path, yet as the flowers become more dense, towering above, they create dark shadows and unclear steps.

Earnest and Sunshine share both delight in the new discoveries and uncertainty as to what risk or danger they might encounter. Sunshine clings to Earnest's arm. Earnest speaks a word of courage and comfort, moving forward while at the same time taming his own doubts by faith and prayer. As one of eight watercolors in a series from Mrs. Anderson, "Life's a Great Adventure" is available in a choice of frames at retail prices between $25.00 and $40.00.

The Sweet Thumpins *of Blackberry Hill*

Vicki Anderson tells another "once upon a time" story through her creation of the *Sweet Thumpins*. This charming community of bunnies lives snugly at the bottom of Blackberry Hill, just past Smiling Stream. Their bright and cheerful land is filled with truth, hope and love.

The first limited edition piece in this figurine collection captures Rachael Rabbit as she passes through the gate to see her friend Jessica. "Venture into Sweet Thumpins" symbolizes each person's entrance through the gate of imagination and down the path that is VickiLane. Rachael has a fascinating story to tell her friend Jessica as they share tea and tender gourmet carrots. This scene is portrayed in another limited edition piece: "Tea Time."

Meanwhile a father bunny named Albert works with his little son Briar to build a toy airplane. Briar is just amazed that such a detailed toy can be made from blank pieces of wood. The moment is caught in the limited edition figurine known as "Building Memories."

There are many more personalities in *Sweet Thumpins* land, all delightful to know and enjoy as they embark upon new antics. We meet Violet and her son Benjamin after their Christmas shopping is complete. They rest in the park before heading home with their treasures.

Several scenes feature the energetic Huckleberry. He proposes to Heather as the pair are seated on a wooden bench. She looks so shy and sweet and he — with flowers in hand — just knows that she will say yes. Next we greet Huckleberry and Heather on their marriage day in the charming "Wedding Bunnies" piece. Soon their new baby son and daughter, Gregory and Sweet Pea, appear with Heather in "Mother Rocking Babies." And then Huckleberry delights his son with something special — but first he teases little Gregory by holding the surprise behind his back.

It's also a pleasure to meet Jeffrey the farmer bunny, and Allison, who holds her special bunny doll. And in "Bunny First Steps," Ivy can't hide her excitement as her son Willard takes those first few strides on his own. Poor Benjie has had a rough day of school in "Hurt Bunny." He got into a bit of a scuffle, tore his clothes, and got a little bruised. He knows he may be scolded, but he's also in need of motherly sympathy and care! And finally little "Blossom" enjoys a special interlude of reading and reflection in "Quiet Time."

Stroll Down VickiLane For More Adventures

These few tales of *Mice Memories* and *Sweet Thumpins* offer just a taste of the delights that await collectors as they begin their "walk down VickiLane." A prolific and enthusiastic artist, Vicki Anderson has many more stories to spin and many more figurines, prints and other collectibles to design and produce for her friends. From their studios in Springfield, Oregon, the Andersons vow to continue sharing the beauty of their magical world for many years to come.

Two lady bunnies are dressed in their Sunday best for an afternoon of conversation in a beautiful outdoor setting! It's "Tea Time," and artist Vicki Anderson has captured the charm of this bright-eyed twosome as well as their elegant accessories. At 6" wide by 4" tall, this hand painted piece has a retail issue price of $82.00.

The same charming lady bunnies that star in the "Tea Time" figurine are also on display in Vicki Anderson's graphic print by the same name. This 8" x 10" "Tea Time" print comes alive in pretty pastel colors, and it arrives framed and ready for home display.

In her "Cookie Peddler" figurine, Vicki Anderson has captured the feeling of sharing and the special bond that exists between children and older people. Limited to 1,500 pieces, this 6" x $4^1/_2$" figurine features Grandpa Winky selling some of his "secret recipe" cookies at a special low price "for children only." Retail price is $90.00.

The Walt Disney Classics Collection

Capturing Magical, Memorable Moments from Classic Disney Animated Films and Short Cartoons

One late night in 1934, Walt Disney gathered a group of his animators on a studio soundstage. With them as his audience, he proceeded to tell a story, acting out all the roles himself. Years later, one animator said, "That performance lasted us three years. Whenever we'd get stuck, we'd remember how Walt did it that night."

The story was *Snow White and the Seven Dwarfs*, and what Walt "did that night" — what he continually inspired his talented staff to do in every film — was to make the characters as fascinating and real as living, breathing people. As his nephew, Roy E. Disney, explains, "That lifelikeness and believability is at the heart of every Disney film. It's why we still chuckle at Thumper's ingenuous remarks and smile at Bambi's first attempts to talk; why we never stop cheering for Cinderella, or laughing at Mickey's desperate attempts to halt those multiplying brooms!"

And now, that same striving for the "illusion of life" has inspired today's gifted group of Disney artists to create the *Walt Disney Classics Collection*. The collection represents the first Disney character figurines created by Disney artists and the first time Disney animation principles have been applied directly to a three-dimensional art program. With each piece, the Disney artists have applied the exacting principles developed over years of animated filmmaking to capture the living spirit of the original characters and scenes.

Recreating Disney Film Moments of Storytelling Magic

To ensure that the *Walt Disney Classics Collection* would please Disney's millions of loyal admirers, The Walt Disney Studios conducted formal, extensive research among collectors. Their efforts were aimed at learning exactly what collectors want in a fine sculpture program from Disney.

"We found that collectors were looking for figurines that would bring to life special, memorable moments from Disney films, a collection that would reflect the Disney heritage of quality and entertainment and would recreate the magic they remember from the first time they saw these films," explains Susanne Lee, Director of the *Walt Disney Classics Collection*. "We spent two years developing the *Walt Disney Classics Collection*. The culminating proof of our success is that the figurines have earned the endorsement of Roy E. Disney, Walt's nephew and President of Disney Animation."

Scenes were carefully selected to "tell a story," and each figurine and grouping reflects special moments from films such as *Bambi*, *Cinderella*, and *Fantasia*, as well as short cartoons starring Mickey Mouse, Donald Duck, and other beloved Disney characters. One of the highlights in the initial collection is a tribute to *Bambi*, which celebrated its fiftieth anniversary in 1992. The first thirty-two works in the collection, introduced in 1992, will be supplemented regularly with pieces from many more classic films and with more favorite cartoon characters.

Even though there have been Disney figurines in many media over the years, this collection marks quite a few firsts for Disney including the first time some characters have ever been represented in three dimensions. Examples are the adorable "Field Mouse" from *Bambi*, and Mickey and Minnie as they appeared in the early cartoon, *The Delivery Boy*.

"We see this collection as having limitless potential," Ms. Lee says. "We did not set out to do the single quintessential Cinderella, but rather Cinderella as seen in particular magical and memorable story scenes. Because there are as many potential Cinderella figurines as there are special moments in the film, we have a rich repertoire of untapped story moments from which to choose future pieces to surprise and delight our audience."

How Disney Creates in a New Dimension

The *Walt Disney Classics Collection* starts with a challenge: "Translate beloved Disney film characters from two-dimensional drawings to three-dimensional sculptures, capturing their personalities and ephemeral quality of life." Every step taken in the creation of a sculpture — from the initial choice of characters to the final title — is made with the ultimate goal of meeting that challenge.

Before the first sculpting tool is picked up, hundreds of hours of videotapes are viewed. Then the

To celebrate the fiftieth anniversary of Bambi, *the* Walt Disney Classics Collection *presents a three-dimensional hand-painted portrait of Bambi and Flower, "He Can Call Me A Flower If He Wants To." At 6" in height, this hand-numbered limited edition of 10,000 sells for $295 (suggested retail) and is complemented by other figurines portraying Thumper and his sisters as well as wise old Friend Owl.*

original animation drawings made for each character and scene are researched as reference. These rough study sketches, production drawings and beautiful, painted cels provide valuable information about how the characters' physical attributes and personalities were originally brought to life. What gesture or expression communicates Cinderella's sense of humor or Mickey's flirty sauciness? What tilt of the head tells us immediately that shy little Flower is tickled pink with his new name?

Concept sketches are drawn to analyze various poses from the films and find the perfect combination of emotion and story. The artists study live-action models and original animators' models (maquettes) to help the translation into three dimensions. As they work, they often answer different questions than those posed in animation: "What does the space between Thumper's ears look like from a top view? How does Lucifer look from behind?"

As final drawings progress to initial sculptures, Disney animators continue to make suggestions to improve composition, structure, and emotional impact. Many of the animators bring their experience from work on the original films to bear on the sculpture creation. With their input, Thumper's cheeks were puffed up more when he smiles, making his eyes crinkle a bit — and suddenly — you could almost hear him giggle! Mickey's nemesis — that determined broom — grew thinner, while Cinderella took on a fuller, more womanly shape.

Once the original model is approved, the individual pieces for each sculpture are cast, then hand-assembled, hand-detailed and fired. World-class manufacturing resources brought their expertise to this exacting process. Finally, the gleaming whiteware is ready for painting.

The Disney Ink and Paint labs are called upon to prepare original paints from the special Disney color palettes used in the film. Using the same color principles developed to create mood, character and emotion in the original animation, Disney painters paint the whiteware prototypes. As the factory adapts the rich, original animation colors for ceramic painting, the Disney artists find that ceramic painting provides opportunities for special effects and textures that animation only hints at. The painters use a rough brushstroke to give Bambi and his friends a natural look, while the cartoon characters called for a smoother, flatter cartoon effect.

Many figurines are "plussed" — a Disney term for adding special extras — from films to theme parks — to enhance the magic. The *Walt Disney Classics Collection* figurines are enhanced by blown glass, platinum, or other materials to further the Disney "illusion of life." For example, blown glass was used for a soap bubble in Cinderella's hand, while platinum stars emphasized the magical look of Mickey's sorcerer's hat.

To increase collectibility, each figurine bears a backstamp or bottomstamp that includes the Walt Disney signature logo, the name of the film represented, and a special symbol to denote the year in which the figurine was produced. Roy E. Disney, President of Disney Animation and Walt's nephew, endorses them on a Certificate of Authenticity included with each piece.

While this development process is lengthy, in some ways, the entire process has brought each character even closer to Walt Disney's original

In "They Can't Stop Me From Dreaming," Cinderella ponders a bubble made of blown glass as she dreams of happier days. Lucifer, the Stepmother's sly, nasty-tempered cat, and faithful Bruno are natural enemies as "Meany, Sneaky, Roos-A-Fee" and "Just Learn to Like Cats."

A cast of truly delightful characters from Cinderella *are portrayed in these figurines from the* Walt Disney Classics Collection. *Jaq and Gus have just liberated a string of beads from beneath Lucifer's nose to make a necklace for Cinderella while Suzy, the needle mouse, the bluebirds and the chalk mouse sew Cinderella a ballgown using implements larger than themselves!*

vision of complete believability. For here they are — Cinderella, Bambi, Thumper, Mickey, and Donald...looking as if they had paused in mid-movement on screen.

A Sampling from the First Pieces in the Walt Disney Classics Collection

To celebrate the fiftieth anniversary of *Bambi*, the *Walt Disney Classics Collection* presents a group of delightful pieces that look marvelous together — just as they appeared in the classic film. Bambi and Flower, the skunk, star in "He Can Call Me A Flower If He Wants To," while Thumper and his sisters look on in "Hee! Hee! Hee!" and "Hello, Hello There!" From his perch in a gnarled old tree, Friend Owl adds his two cents worth with "What's Going On Around Here?" In celebration of the 50th anniversary, each of these pieces produced in 1992 will carry a special gold 50th Anniversary marking.

As the first full-length animated story from Disney since 1942, *Cinderella* was welcomed with open arms by critics and audiences on February 15, 1950. Collectors will do the same when they see the appealing "They Can't Stop Me from Dreaming," a vision of the pretty young girl pausing to dream with her soap bubbles as she scrubs the floor. For comic relief, we have Lucifer, portrayed in three dimensions as "Meany, Sneaky, Roos-A-Fee," and Bruno, a cat-wary canine who's trying to heed Cinderella's advice in "Just Learn to Like Cats."

Who can forget Mickey Mouse in one of his most dramatic starring roles: that of the Sorcerer's Apprentice in *Fantasia*. To commemorate this art treasure on film, the *Walt Disney Classics Collection* introduced Sorcerer Mickey as the "Mischievous Apprentice." He is accompanied by his "Bucket Brigade" of brooms.

From the world of Disney cartoons come classics vignettes. We see Donald and his best girl Daisy cutting a rug in "Oh Boy, What a Jitterbug," while Donald's nephew vies for Daisy's attention with a box of candy and says "I Got Somethin' for Ya" in a humorous moment from the cartoon, *Mr. Duck Steps Out*. "Maestro Michel Mouse" conducts in scenes from *Symphony Hour* entitled "Clarabelle's Crescendo," "Horace's High Notes," and "Goofy's Grace Notes." And a dancing Mickey, Minnie and Pluto from the 1931 cartoon, *The Delivery Boy*, round out this captivating part of the collection.

With open stock pieces ranging in price from $55 to $300 and limited edition figurines selling from $200 to $800, the *Walt Disney Classics Collection* offers a wide range of opportunities for collectors to participate in this exciting new program. On the drawing board already is a Walt Disney collectors society, as well as many more characters in scenes from the fabled Disney archives. With collectors' desires firmly in mind and the treasuries of Disney at their disposal, the creators of the *Walt Disney Classics Collection* have only just begun!

M. Cornell Importers

Importers and Creators of Handsome Steins Combining Old-World Elegance With Contemporary Art Mastery

M. Cornell Importers, Inc. of St. Paul, Minnesota began as a family business in 1959 when Morris and Maria Cornell started importing cuckoo clocks, nutcrackers and steins. Today, their son Henry and his wife Gail oversee a multi-faceted business encompassing the development, importation, and nationwide distribution of collectible steins.

After the devastation of two World Wars, the German beer stein industry was forced to regroup in the late 1940s and 1950s. There was little demand for steins except on the home market, and thus those pieces produced were very functional and inexpensive for the most part.

Outside of the domestic market, however, steins remained popular souvenir items with veterans who served in Europe, and with the 20,000,000 people of German ancestry in the United States. At that time, the United States had little impact on stein development.

The "Santa Maria" stein commemorates the 500-year anniversary of Christopher Columbus' arrival on American shores. This limited edition of 4,000 pieces features an unusual, deep relief figural motif. Each German-made stein is individually numbered and registered.

Cornell Helps Shape a Growing, Changing Stein Market

In the early 1970s, M. Cornell Importers noticed that the stein market was beginning to change as collectors recognized and appreciated steins for their artistic qualities. Steins are true works of art. Designing the subject area, making the master molds, and hand-decorating the body and lid have been done by master craftsmen since the 1500s. Finely detailed master molds were used to produce hand-decorated steins of great beauty.

The German stein industry responded to requests from companies like Cornell for higher-quality steins in the tradition of earlier generations. Many surviving original German factories started creating limited editions and experimenting with materials, color techniques and lids. They retrieved the old master molds made by artists seventy-five to 100 years ago. These rejuvenated molds had more detailing added, as well. The first few stein editions sold out quickly and limited edition steins soon became the most exciting part of the industry.

In the past decade, Cornell has worked in very close cooperation with numerous German manufacturers, developing hundreds of new steins over the years. Always focusing on the American market, Cornell has consistently introduced new artists, molds, color combinations, handles and lids to the stein industry.

The Heritage of the Stein Lid

A variety of lids — pewter, stoneware and figurine inlay — grace the steins imported by Cornell. Though these lids today are very decorative, the original purpose of the beer stein lid is far from glamorous. The first beer steins were simple drinking vessels, and the primary reason for the lid was functional — a common sense precaution to keep insects and other contaminants away from an aromatic liquid. In addition to this, early functions of lids were to keep the liquid at a constant temperature as well as to prevent spillage. Lids, even in early days, provided an attractive finishing touch.

Today, the "finishing touch" aspect is by far the

Multiple subjects for horse lovers are portrayed on the "Equestrian" stein from Cornell. The main subject area depicts this beautiful animal's head with bridal. On the left side is a horse with jockey leaping over a fence in a steeplechase. The right side captures a young quarter horse romping freely on a ranch. Made in Germany, the stein features an ornamental pewter lid, and is offered in a registered, individually numbered limited edition of 10,000 pieces.

The "Promontory Point" stein is a hand-painted, raised-relief work of art commemorating the completion of the first transcontinental railway line in the United States. The stein features the Jupiter engine of the Central-Pacific railway and Engine No. 119 of the Union-Pacific Railway, as well as a gold spike signifying the line's completion at Promontory Point, Utah, on May 10, 1869. The limited edition of 4,000 German-made pieces are registered and individually numbered. The lid is made of pewter, complete with a pewter engine figurine resting upon tracks.

most important reason for the lid. In many cases, the lid is the most outstanding feature of the stein. Lids have a tremendous impact on price as well, sometimes more than doubling the cost of a stein. Hundreds of different lids are currently available on Cornell steins — including conical, flat, ornamental, inlay/figurine and stoneware. The figurine inlay lids come in designs including: wildlife, medieval, occupations and sports, to name just a few.

Cornell Steins Make Marvelous Gifts for Men

Today's Cornell steins appeal to so many collectors because they satisfy the persistent demand for men's gifts — and because the great variety of themes and subjects appeal to many different types of buyers. As Henry Cornell explains, "Cornell steins priced in the $20.00 to $60.00 retail range are among the most popular. However, very ornate limited edition steins retailing from $100 to $200 are also in great demand."

According to Cornell, "Steins, mugs and tankards are popular throughout the year as gifts for birthdays, Father's Day, Christmas and groomsmen." The Cornell line today includes over 800 different steins, including over 200 limited editions. This abundant collection includes the works of forty-five different German stein factories.

Steins Come in Many Materials and Sizes

The classical stoneware which can only be produced in "Westerwald" of Germany provides collectors with a combination of old-world tradition and modern technology which allows for handsome and reasonably priced, limited edition steins. Actual stoneware is hard, fired in high-temperature kilns until they vitrify (turn glass-like). Because the result is a stein that is less than two percent porous, glazing is optional for stoneware. The vast majority of Cornell steins are made of stoneware and are glazed.

In addition to stoneware, steins may be crafted of ceramic substances known as earthenware, creamware, porcelain or the generic term ceramic. Virtually non-existent in the Cornell collection are earthenware and creamware steins.

True porcelain, known as hard paste, is made of kaolin (white clay) and petuntse (pulverized granite). When fired at a temperature of 1300 to 1400 degrees Centigrade, these ingredients produce a white, more or less translucent, glass-like material. The generic term "ceramics" refers to slightly porous, light colored ware that must be glazed to make it impermeable. Cornell offers a significant selection of porcelain steins. Hand-painted relief porcelain pieces are in the collection, as are regimental porcelain steins with lithophanes (translucent, see-through pictures on the bottom).

In addition to the ceramic steins of various types, Cornell offers steins made of European pewter with a minimum tin content of 92%. The higher the tin content, the more silvery the final color of a pewter stein. Crystal steins from Cornell are cased, hand-cut, mouth-blown, and entirely lead-free. Glass steins are quite affordable, and are crafted by molding and the addition of transfer decorations.

Conventional-sized steins are joined in the Cornell line by over fifty miniature steins with between one and three-ounce capacity. These steins intrigue traditional stein collectors as well as those who seek miniatures and shot glasses. Henry Cornell adds, "These miniatures often serve practical decorative purposes such as salt and pepper shakers, match holders and tooth pick holders." There are also impressive oversized steins ranging in height from 12" to 30" and in volume from 33.8 oz. to two gallons. Cornell's "largest stein in the world" stands four feet tall and holds eight gallons!

Cornell now offers an exclusive series of stoneware steins designed by internationally renowned artists James A. Meger and Jon Q Wright. The four new wildlife steins by Meger are (left to right, back row): "Timber Wolf," "North American Buffalo," "Grizzly Bear" and "Moose." Each is framed by an original elk horn design. Three steins featuring North American fish by Wright are (front row): "Large Mouth Bass," "Crappie," and "Muskie and Northern Pike." Each is framed by an aquatic life border decoration.

Steins Feature Special Themes and Characters

The Cornell collection includes forty different "character" or "figural" steins deriving their names from their unconventional shapes. Rather than having bodies in standard cylindrical or conical forms, character steins are more like hollow figurines, in which the body and lid are clearly modeled after a real subject, such as a person, animal or building.

Within the Cornell collection are numerous special-theme pieces, representing nautical, wildlife, fantasy, firefighter, musical, railroad, golf, fishing, sports, Harley-Davidson®, American and Germania steins.

A recent and exciting addition to the Cornell line is an exclusive series of stoneware steins designed by internationally renowned artists James A. Meger and Jon Q Wright. The four new wildlife steins by James A. Meger are "Grizzly Bear," "Moose," "Timber Wolf" and "North American Buffalo." Six steins featuring North American fish by Jon Q Wright are "Large Mouth Bass," "Muskie and Northern Pike," "Crappie," "Salmon," "Trout" and "Walleye." The transfer decoration on each stein is beautifully framed with an original elk horn design or aquatic life border decoration. Each stein is seven inches high, one-half liter in capacity, and retails for less than $36.00.

In July of 1992, Cornell introduced 100 new steins, including many limited editions. Expansions of existing themes as well as the introduction of new themes are included in generous numbers. A full-color catalog and reference book shows off all of the new and returning Cornell steins and provides background information on the fascinating hobby of stein collecting.

The Cornell Collectible Teapots

Recently, Cornell also introduced a complete selection of collectible teapots made in England from a variety of manufacturers. Styles vary from the very traditional English floral teapot, the *English Life* series from Wade, to the whimsical themes featuring animals, Noah's Ark, and many more. With one hundred different styles, variety is the key to this line's immediate success.

With handsome wooden boxes from Poland and candleholders, oil lamps and picture frames crafted in Italy, M. Cornell Importers has become a versatile importer — building upon its long-time base in the field of collectible German steins.

Ron Lee

Clowns Are Only the Beginning of Ron Lee's Contributions to the World of Collectible Art

They stand on long tables in neat rows of ten as if they were soldiers poised for battle. But what's this? Each "soldier" in the regiment has a round, red nose! Upon closer inspection, we realize we are looking at a diverse array of hundreds of white-face clowns. As we move down the table, we see red tags being placed on each clown as they are inspected one last time before being shipped from their "birthplace" in Simi Valley, California.

The clowns' gifted creator is Ron Lee — considered a pioneer of clown and circus-theme collectibles. This prolific artist has created well over 1,000 designs in the past fifteen years, many of them on clown themes. But today Ron Lee's versatility has resulted in a multi-dimensional collectibles firm creating wonderful images of beloved cartoon characters and carousels as well as the ever-popular clowns. And all of Lee's designs come to life at home in America, in his spacious Simi Valley factory.

The Inspiration for The Ron Lee Collection

The company was born in 1976 when Lee began creating sculptures of his original and now-famous "Hobo Joe." After a successful run which included collector plates, Lee began focusing more attention on "Hobo Joe" while developing other designs in classic clown styles. It was also as early as 1976 that Ron Lee began establishing his strong following and enticing clown enthusiasts to his product line.

"I have always been fascinated with the circus and clowns," Lee explains. "It started when I was a child, now you could call it an obsession. When I finish a new sculpture, it's like the birth of a child — it's just very exciting. It's a new little character that's come into the world," Lee enthuses.

Soon after his company was formed, Ron Lee began creating one of his most ambitious and mesmerizing designs — a replication of an amusement park carousel. With miniaturized, finely detailed giraffes, camels, lions and horses, the carousel slowly rotates while also moving up and down. All the while, 128 flashing lights glitter to the beat of the music. The carousel project — considered one of Lee's absolute masterpieces — took over three years to create using the latest in computer technology and Ron Lee's masterful skill.

A signed Ron Lee limited edition is easily identified when displayed on a shelf. All Ron Lee sculptures are finely detailed and mounted on polished onyx with tiny gold beading at the base of each piece. But what makes Ron Lee sculptures all the more desirable and unique are several additional facts. First, each edition is made of fine metal that is 24K gold plated. Second, each is manufactured completely in the United States. And third, each is individually hand-painted by a group of artisans selected by Ron Lee himself.

Once Lee designs a sculpture — from the concept and sculpting to painting the original — he shows his team of artists how to follow his painting methods meticulously. Since each design is hand-painted, each sculpture sold is truly a one-of-a-kind collectible.

One of Ron Lee's most popular characters is "Hobo Joe," a self-portrait in clown make-up. This sculpture of Joe, entitled "Business is Business," finds the clown in competition with a canine balloon seller with decidedly low prices. The edition limit is 1,500 and the suggested retail price is $115.

Ron Lee Attracts Prestigious Art Commissions

While creating and manufacturing sculptures for his own national network of over 3,000 dealers and retail stores, Ron Lee continues to receive major commissions for his work. Due to his ability to capture the essence and a certain "irrestible" quality in his sculptures, Ron Lee continues to create exclusive designs for The Walt Disney Company and Warner Bros. Studio Stores.

The San Francisco Music Box Company secured Ron Lee to create three original designs that will become fanciful music boxes and will be available exclusively through their stores.

"Ron Lee" Becomes a Household Name to Collectors

In recent years, Ron Lee has become a celebrity in his own right, with requests for guest appearances made by his dealers and retailers. The guest appearances have included numerous local television and radio shows, as well as his existing busy schedule of national exhibitions and trade shows, along with mall and gallery openings. In addition, Lee appears at a number of gift and collectibles shows where his company exhibits its diverse and colorful line.

On a recent broadcast of the local Nashville, Tennessee, TV show, "The Talk of the Town," Ron Lee appeared with country singing star Crystal Gayle to promote her store called Crystal's for Fine Gifts & Jewelry. The store carries a wide variety from the Ron Lee Collection of limited editions. The next day when Lee was scheduled to appear at the store, collectors turned out in overflow numbers to meet Ron Lee and secure his signature on their purchases. This phenomenon has occurred over and over when Lee makes guest appearances.

The Ron Lee Collectors Club continues to grow by over 300 new members per month. With regular updates, member-collectors learn about new sculpture introductions, along with numerous incentives, special designs and items created specifically for the Collectors Club. Each day, Lee receives numerous letters describing the enjoyment his sculptures have brought to his ever-growing number of collectors.

Why Collectors Love Ron Lee Clowns

What is the "love affair" with clowns that makes a supposed one-time purchase of a Ron Lee clown into an avid collector? With a twinkle in his eye, Ron Lee replies, "Hasn't humor and fun

After receiving numerous accolades for creating his award-winning, first offering of Looney Tunes sculptures, Ron Lee presents "Leopold and Giovanni" as part of a new collection featuring Bugs Bunny and his looney friends. Here, Bugs reprises one of his most memorable roles as an orchestra conductor.

been the guideline for my whole life? When have I not gone for the punchline, to make someone laugh, to see a happy smile, to entertain, and who do you know more dedicated to that concept than the high-spirited, energetic clown?"

Lee adds, "As we sit in the audience, captivated, haven't we all wondered about what (behind the garish makeup and the bright colorful costumes) clowns are feeling as they commit their own being to making us laugh? I guess there is no better reflection of myself; the entertainer, the clown, the sculptor."

Ron Lee Expands His Horizons to Become a Premiere Sculptor of Beloved Cartoon Characters

In the year 1992 alone, Ron Lee sculpted and produced over 100 new pieces. Many of these have brought Lee center stage in the world of cartoons, what with coveted licenses to create sculptures based on animated cartoon "classics" such as Looney Tunes™ characters, Rocky and Bullwinkle, Betty Boop, and Woody Woodpecker. In addition, Ron Lee is creating a marvelous series of "Wizard of Oz" scenes, and he has earned the commission of The Walt Disney Company to create pieces that sell exclusively in Disney theme park company stores.

The Disney commission was Lee's first grouping of animated characters, but he soon arranged to license and market products inspired by characters from Warner Brothers, MCA, Hanna-Barbera, and other entertainment firms. Although he remains committed to clowns, Lee finds the cartoon theme an exciting new challenge. As he explains, "I wanted to recreate the characters that had an impact on my life so I could share them with my own children, fans of the characters and my collectors."

Ron Lee Presents Looney Tunes™

Mounted on his trademark onyx bases, Ron Lee's Looney Tunes™ character sculptures capture the unique antics of cartoon favorites like "Bugs Bunny," "Tweety," "Daffy Duck," "Porky Pig," "Wile E. Coyote and "Roadrunner," and many more.

The brilliant colors that made these cartoons such a treat to watch are captured with painstaking hand-painting. Each piece is reproduced in the finest metal and pewter, and enhanced by 24K gold plating. The sculptures are offered in limited editions of 2,750 each.

"Wizard of Oz" Collection Captures Memorable Moments from the Movie

Twelve of the most dramatic scenes from the beloved film classic *The Wizard of Oz* now may be enjoyed in the form of Ron Lee originals — part of the *Ron Lee "Wizard Of Oz" Collection*. Interacting with other characters such as "Auntie Em," "Uncle Henry," "Scarecrow," "Cowardly Lion," "Tin Woodsman" and "Toto," as well as the "Munchkins," "Glinda," "The Wicked Witch of the West," and "The Wizard," "Dorothy" follows the yellow brick road in this limited edition series.

Each piece is hand-poured, hand-finished, plated in 24K gold, and then hand-painted before Ron Lee adds his personal signature. The first six "Oz" pieces became available during 1992, while the remaining six are to be introduced during 1993.

Ron Lee Helps Hanna-Barbera Fans Remember Their Favorite TV Characters

"The Flintstones" made television history for Hanna-Barbera Productions by starring in the first animated situation comedy on nighttime television. And now, Ron Lee helps "The Flintstones" to make history again with the introduction of a series of original sculptures presenting Bedrock's most famous residents. As Lee explains, "Fred Flintstone and Barney Rubble are like old friends. I suppose that is why I wanted to recreate Fred and Barney in my medium."

Another Hanna-Barbera hit was "The Jetsons," earth's foremost space age family. Airing for fourteen years on all three major television networks, this twenty-first century ensemble cast established themselves as enduring favorites. Now Ron Lee takes favorite moments from "The Jetsons" episodes and captures them in sculpture form, from "I Rove Roo" featuring George Jetson and his dog, Astro, to "The Jetsons," which shows these cosmic characters in their futuristic space ship.

"Quick Draw McGraw," "Huckleberry Hound," "Yogi Bear & Boo Boo," and "Scooby-Doo & Shaggy" round out Ron Lee's Hanna-Barbera offerings. The artist found special joy in these creations because, as he says, "Hanna-Barbera set a standard when they courageously introduced evening comedy starring animated characters. I feel I recaptured a happy part of my youth as I sculpted these wonderful, old friends. In many ways, they are part of the symbols which represent a simpler and very charming period of innocence in America's history."

Circus carousels...lovable clowns...cartoon characters. Ron Lee already has proven his incredible versatility. But what's next for Ron Lee? There are endless possibilities for an artist of his energy and spirit. As Lee himself attests, "The world is filled with ideas. A day doesn't go by that new ideas do not emerge. If I live to be 500, I couldn't produce all the fantasies in my head!"

Sold exclusively at The Disney Store nationwide, "Lady & The Tramp" is one of many designs Ron Lee has created under the commission of The Walt Disney Company. Here we see lovely Lady and her suitor, the Tramp, enjoying a romantic meal with musical accompaniment. Limited to an edition of 1,500, the sculpture carries a retail price of $295.

Ladie And Friends™

Barbara and Peter Wisber Present The Family and Friends of Lizzie High® Dolls

It was Christmas, 1984, and Barbara Wisber was enjoying a happy family holiday with her husband Peter, her children Marisa and Little Pete, and Peter's parents. The Wisber family had been immersed in the giftware business for several years, ever since Barbara's successful innovations with decorated grapevine wreaths.

Just weeks before, Barbara had made another discovery. "She's always been a step ahead of everyone else," her husband, Peter, says admiringly. While working on new samples for the coming season, Barbara realized that a wooden ball could be used for the head of a doll. She took paper and pencil in hand, and drew a simple body to go with the wooden ball "head." As her sketch developed, she drew a dress, added hair, and in that moment a new American folk art concept was born.

Barbara shared her sketches with Peter, a professional carpenter, and he went to work turning a block of pine and a two-inch wooden ball into a childlike figure that would be the keeping place for all the whimsy Barbara would create.

Now it was late December, and a whole family of dolls were in mid-production to be unveiled at the January trade show. Barbara and her husband had created a little "tale" to explain each doll's reason for being, but the cute little creatures did not yet have names

Suddenly the Wisber family's old heirloom Bible caught Barbara's eye. "LIZZIE HIGH" was the name embossed in large gold letters on its time-worn leather cover. Lizzie was Peter Wisber's maternal great-great-grandmother, and in her Bible was a record of scores of marriages, births and deaths that had occurred in the family over a century ago. The Good Book was rich with good old-fashioned names — names perfect for the folk dolls Barbara was creating.

Since then, Peter's and Barbara's family trees and the names of beloved friends have served to supplement Lizzie's Bible as the source of names for most of the dolls in *The Family And Friends Of Lizzie High®* collection. There are now twenty-seven dolls with the last name of High, thirty-seven dolls are Valentines (Peter's mother's maiden name), and over fifty dolls have the last name of Bowman.

The Distinctive Charms of Lizzie High® Dolls

Today the Lizzie High® family of dolls extends all across the United States and into several foreign lands as collectors succumb to the simple charms of Barbara and Peter Wisber's folk art designs. Each Lizzie High® doll features that same distinctive "blank round face with two dots for eyes," which is a trademark of Ladie and Friends, Inc.

Their unique personalities emerge in their poses and costumes, as well as the tags that explain a charming reason for each doll's existence. One of the "Lizzie" dolls, for instance, is leading a goose on a leash. Its accompanying tag reads, "Lizzie walks her goose, Lily, to the pond every day before school...she's always late."

The Family Behind Lizzie High®

The "ladie" behind the company Ladie and Friends™ is Barbara Kafka Wisber, a creative woman who has been an innovator in crafts and fine arts since childhood. She and her husband, Peter Wisber, have been married since 1971 and have two children: Marisa, 15, and Little Pete, 9. Marisa has inherited much of her mother's artistic ability, and, on several occasions, has amazed her parents with wonderful creative input. Little Pete

The first hand-painted wooden folk doll in The Family And Friends Of Lizzie High® *collection was "Lizzie High®" herself, introduced in January of 1985.*

"Kathryn Bowman," *the first limited edition from Ladie and Friends*™, *was inspired by the oldest surviving Bowman cousin. Born in 1899, she is portrayed as a child, playing the piano with her little sister at her side.*

Generations ago, "The Thanksgiving Play" was presented by Mrs. Poole's fifth-grade class each year in an effort to bring true meaning to the holiday. These wonderful dolls with names from the High, Valentine and Yocum families play pilgrims, an Indian, and a papoose.

prefers to channel his talent toward futuristic creations; he leaves the nostalgia to the other members of the family.

The Wisbers share their old stone farmhouse in rural Bucks County, Pennsylvania, with several cats, one hamster, and a collection of tropical fish. This happy country life, along with recollections of her own childhood, have provided much inspiration for Barbara's creations. Another rich source of creativity has been her husband's ancestral history, especially the Bowman branch of the family tree.

The Bowman Family Legend

The Bowman side of Peter Wisber's family has had extensive genealogical research done. While the ancestry has been traced back to Uly Buman, born 1369 in Zurich, Switzerland, Barbara and Peter find the more recent relatives, Wendel and Johannes Bowman, particularly interesting. The names of their heirs have been especially useful in christening dolls.

Wendel Bowman (1681-1735) was the patriarch of the American Bowmans. He arrived in America with his wife, Annie, in 1707, and they became one of the first nine families to settle in the frontier that we now know as Lancaster, Pennsylvania. Within a year Wendel's younger brother, Johannes (1685-1738), his wife and two children, joined the "Swiss Pequea Settlement." The Pequea Creek is southeast of the city of Lancaster.

The Bowmans were Mennonites and America was the final stop on their flight from religious persecution. They had migrated from Switzerland to Holland with their parents in 1698 but the attraction of the New World was too strong for the young men to resist. With the courage many Americans take for granted in their forebearers, they and their wives braved the Atlantic Ocean for three months, and the Pennsylvania wilderness for weeks, until they established their sanctuary along the Pequea Creek.

Wendel and Johannes could have had no idea what the future had in store for their descendants. Theirs was a simpler time; the world was a great deal smaller. *The Family And Friends Of Lizzie High® Dolls* conjure up memories of the times — real or imagined — in our own past when our worlds were smaller and our lives a lot less complicated.

The Passing of a Grand Lady Brings the Lizzie High® Clan into Focus

During the early years of Lizzie High, Barbara and Peter enjoyed the direct inspiration of Peter's grandmother. Mary Bowman Valentine was the original Lizzie High's granddaughter, and a descendant of the Bowmans who settled Pennsylvania's picturesque Lancaster and Bucks County areas. This lovely lady led a full and wonderful life, even into her 85th year. She was actively involved in the Philadelphia community and a patron of the arts.

When Mary Bowman Valentine was laid to rest in the family plot in Newville, Pennsylvania, it was an emotional experience for the Wisber family. There they viewed the resting places of so many ancestors with now-familiar names: Luther Bowman, Flossie High, Lizzie High, and now Mary Valentine.

Frequent visits to Peter's relatives help Barbara Wisber to keep the Bowman and High legacy alive in her work. The very first limited edition from Ladie and Friends™, for example, has been inspired by "Kathryn Bowman," the oldest surviving Bowman cousin. Kathryn Bowman Gidley, born in 1899, is portrayed playing the piano along with her sister as she remembers doing so many years ago. As "Kathryn's" tag reads, "...refrains of 'Heart and Soul' can still bring a smile to this day."

This lovely little girl is sitting at an upright piano with her little sister by her side. Their cat is lounging on top of music books alongside a miniature portrait of great-great-great grandmother Lizzie High. From their brown curly hair tied in pink ribbons, to their coordinated pinafores in warm shades of taupe and rose; from the classic book of lullabies to the dusty rose braided rug, the detailing on these special little girls is extraordinary.

Kathryn's younger sister also comes alive in a doll created by Barbara: "Rebecca Bowman" is a little girl character taking her baby brother for a walk. Rebecca and Kathryn's brother Luther was seven years younger than Rebecca.

A Family Photo Portrays Four Lizzie High® Favorites

Another rich source of ideas for Barbara Wisber is the family photo album. One marvelous 1930 snapshot depicts four generations of a family posed on a front porch in Newville, Pennsylvania.

Seated in her rocker we see Lizzie High, still active in her eighty-first year. On the steps before her sits her second-born, Flossie, a sixty-one-year-old grandmother. Seated next to Flossie is her daughter Mary and her granddaughter, two-and-one-half-year-old Joanna. Now all of these wonderful individuals have been captured in folk art dolls that celebrate their personalities and interests.

This classic snapshot from 1930 depicts four generations of the Lizzie High family, posed on a front porch in Newville, Pennsylvania. The oldest lady, seated in the rocker, is Lizzie High herself. On the steps are her second-born child, Flossie, her grand-daughter, Mary, and her great-granddaughter, Joanna. Now these family members have been remembered as subjects for delightful folk art dolls at the hand of the gifted Barbara Wisber.

The Lizzie High® Notebook Teaches Reading, History, Arithmetic and Art

In keeping with the whimsical charms of their delightful folk art dolls, the people of Ladie and Friends have created a warm and personal way of sharing news through a unique newsletter. Called the "Lizzie High® Notebook," it is designed to look much like a child's school notebook. Inside the newsletter covers four important "school subjects" that offer insights into Lizzie's world.

The Reading section provides information about Ladie and Friends™ and answers questions raised by curious collectors. The History section sheds light on the family history that has inspired the naming of many of the dolls. Arithmetic tells about additions to the Family And Friends Of Lizzie High®, and about dolls that will be retiring. In addition, the Arithmetic section features messages from collectors who would like to add to or subtract from their own Lizzie High collections. Finally, in the Art section, items other than dolls that may be of interest to Lizzie High collectors are featured.

A New Home for Ladie and Friends™

As a fast-growing concern, Ladie and Friends™ found itself outgrowing its original space in Dublin, Pennsylvania. So in early 1992, the company moved its offices, production and shipping departments, as well as its wood shop, all together into a new home on Main Street in Sellersville, Pennsylvania. The Country Gift Shoppe, where Ladie and Friends™ dolls are sold, can still be found in Dublin.

Everyone in the Ladie and Friends™ organization delights in the family atmosphere of their place of work — and in the charming dolls they create. As they agree in one of their favorite poems:

There is not vocabulary
For love within a family,
love that's lived in
But not looked at,
love within the light of which
All else is seen,
the love within which
All other love finds speech.
This love is silent.
— T.S. Eliot

Novelino, Inc.

Concern for Animal Preservation Sparks Novelino's Celebrity-Sponsored Figurine Collections

Black-maned lions sunning themselves on a cool patch of ground...a mother elephant nurturing her baby...a graceful spotted leopard ready to pounce on its prey. When the late American actor William Holden first visited Kenya in 1956, he found himself enthralled by the natural beauty of wildlife scenes like these. Yet Holden was saddened by threats to the animals' very survival — and from then on he devoted much of his time to ensuring that Africa's endangered species would be valued and protected.

Today, years after Holden's death, his dear friend and fellow actor Stefanie Powers continues the work of The William Holden Wildlife Foundation, which is dedicated to breeding and protecting endangered species. The Foundation achieves this by exposing Africans of all ages to the principles of conservation. And one of the most vibrant sources of support for this vital effort comes from the sale of finely crafted Novelino wildlife figurines.

William Holden Figurines Feature Mothers and Babies of Endangered Kenyan Species

Located in Irvine, California, the artists and marketers of Novelino work in close communication with the directors of The William Holden Wildlife Foundation to create collectible African wildlife figurines. The initial offering was twelve figurines in a collection featuring an adult and a baby of a dozen beloved endangered species.

Hand-crafted by Novelino master artisans, the cold-cast resin figurines have an edition limit of 9,500 each and a price range of $50.00 to $90.00. The most minute detail is conveyed in each figure, just as the animal appears in nature. And as Ms. Powers, President of the Foundation, explains: "A portion of your investment in each magnificent animal in this limited edition series represents a donation to further the work of The William Holden Wildlife Foundation. We are deeply grateful for your support."

For years, Ms. Powers has donated her time to ensure that animal lovers around the world would know of — and have the opportunity to contribute to — the work of the Holden Foundation. Since the Novelino figurines have been introduced, she has spent part of this time promoting these works of art to collectors.

"Stefanie's been wonderful," asserted a company representative for Novelino, in a recent interview. "Whenever possible, she makes in-store appearances at department stores and collectibles shops. She tries to coordinate these with her theater work." Ms. Powers' charm and her knowledge of African wildlife figurines combine with the Novelino pieces' beauty to make for impressive sales. At one of her appearances in Dillard's, a Dallas department store, more than 150 figurines were sold in two hours.

The figurines themselves deserve credit as well, for they offer uniquely realistic images of African animals enjoying loving, parent-and-child relationships. Each figurine represents a charming vignette that combines the animal's natural behavior with a special moment of intimacy between mother and baby.

The "Colobus Monkey," for example, shows a tiny baby snuggling close to its mother's chest as the mother wraps protective arms around a branch, shielding her little one from harm. The "Spotted Leopard" combines a regal mother leopard with a playful baby, showing off his spotted stomach as he rolls over on his back, teasing his mother to join in his games. Mother and child "Hippopotamus" are equally lazy as they nap the afternoon away on a muddy riverbank.

Novelino's Single Animals Portray The Majesty of African Wildlife

In addition to the mother-and-child figurines created with The William Holden Wildlife Foundation, Novelino has also joined forces with the Foundation to create six sculptured and hand-painted single animals: the "Grevy's Zebra," "Spotted Leopard," "African Elephant," "Black-Maned Lion," "Rhinoceros" and "Reticulated Giraffe." While the animal pairs capture gentle moments at rest, these individual sculptures portray the animals in a more active mode. The "Spotted Leopard" and "Black-Maned Lion," for instance, appear ready to pounce upon their prey or to attack an intruder at the next instant.

For collectors who enjoy smaller pieces, Novelino has developed a collection of 3" pewter figurines which are hand-painted to mirror the colorations of African wildlife. The ten pieces in this series include a stately "Crested Crane," a sweet-faced "Chimpanzee," a striking "Grevy's Zebra" and seven more. There are also six wonderful revolving 6" musical waterglobes in *The William Holden Wildlife Foundation Collection*, each of which plays "Born Free."

Novelino Helps Foster the Crucial Mission of the National Wildlife Federation

In addition to its partnership with The William Holden Wildlife Foundation, Novelino has forged an important bond with the National Wildlife Federation. This organization's vital mission is "to create and encourage an awareness among the people of the world of the need for wise use and proper management of those resources of the Earth upon which our lives and welfare depend; the soil, the air, the water, the forests, the minerals, the plant life and the wildlife."

To further this work, Novelino has crafted thirteen sculptured and hand-painted, cold-cast figurines inspired by some of America's most distinctive animals. A portion of the investment in each animal in this collection represents a donation to the National Wildlife Federation.

The creatures portrayed in this handsome series range from the gentle little "Eastern Fox Squirrel" to the endangered "Bison" and the fascinating "Orca (Killer Whale)." Some are familiar, domestic animals like the "White-Tailed Deer and Fawn," while others live far away, like the "Polar Bear and Cub" found only in the frigid Arctic Circle.

Each animal has been selected for something unique to be portrayed in sculpture. The "Moose and Calf," for example, represents the largest member of the deer family in which some males weigh over 1,000 pounds and sport 80-pound antlers. The "Red Fox" was selected for his stunning, russet-colored coat, while the "Bighorn Sheep" shows off his horns that coil, spiral and twist to form a full arc.

Ranging in size from 3½" to 10" and in price from $35.00 to $160, these figurines provide a marvelous perspective of the world's intriguing animals. Each piece is created to exact scale, with some at a one-to-six size ratio, and others measuring one-to-eight.

An "African Elephant" mother and child enjoy a playful game of "tickle the trunk" in this heartwarming figurine from Novelino. The hand-painted piece represents an edition of 9,500, and a portion of the proceeds of each sale are earmarked for The William Holden Wildlife Foundation.

The "Mountain Lion and Cub" represents Novelino's collection created in collaboration with the National Wildlife Federation. Also known as cougars, catamounts and pumas, these large cats have the greatest natural distribution of any mammal in the western hemisphere.

My Friends And Me Collection *Helps Fund Actors and Others for Animals*

In addition to its relationships with wildlife organizations, Novelino has forged an important bond with Actors and Others for Animals, a nonprofit group founded in 1971 to promote the humane treatment of animals.

A little girl in nostalgic, 19th-century attire stages "Bathtime" for her apprehensive dog in this work of art from the My Friend And Me *figurine collection. Some of the proceeds from each sale of "Bathtime" go to benefit the organization Actors and Others for Animals.*

This "Clement Moore Santa," circa 1829, is one of twelve unique, historical American Santas in a collection of hand-painted figurines from Novelino. A portion of each purchase supports The National Alliance to End Homelessness.

Members of "A&O," as it is called, use their prominence as actors to bring the public's attention to the unfortunate plight of many animals in the United States. Earl Holliman is President of the organization, and Connie Sellecca is among its active members. A portion of each investment in Novelino's *My Friends And Me* collection goes to help Actors and Others for Animals alleviate needless suffering and cruelty to animals.

There are twelve sculptured and hand-painted pieces in the collection, each measuring 3½" to 6" in height. Each figurine depicts an adorable child with an animal friend, and each captures a heart-warming moment of interaction between the two.

"Fishing Buddies," for example, shows a young man and his frisky pup on their way to the pond in search of a worthy catch. "Bathtime" has a little girl giving her dog a not-much-wanted sudsing, while "Grooming Time" has a young lad putting the finishing touches on his sheepdog's coiffeur.

Classic Santas *and* Wild Things *Round Out the Novelino Line*

Twelve unique, historical American Santas representing periods from 1624 to the present intrigue Novelino collectors with their colorful costumes and active poses. These appealing works of art range from the 17th-century "St. Nicholas" to the "Modern Santa" of the 1990s, with appropriate figures and costumes in-between. A portion of each purchase from the *Classic American Santa* collection goes to support The National Alliance to End Homelessness.

Just as remarkable are the *Wild Things Of The West*, a crew of colorful pets dressed up in western attire. Each of the fourteen hand-painted, cold-cast figurines captures some of the magic of the Wild West from a canine or feline point of view. There's the "Orange Tabby Cook" and the "Golden Retriever Marshall," not to mention the "Poodle Showgirl" and the "St. Bernard Bartender!"

With dual concerns for today's issues of endangered species and homelessness, plus a remarkable track record for excellent sculptural art, Novelino, Inc. has earned a fine reputation. In the future, Novelino plans to continue its tradition of adding value to its collectible lines, with investment in additional timely causes and worthy charitable foundations.

PenDelfin

A Whimsical World of Hand-Painted Stonecraft from the Imagination of Two Delightful Englishwomen

London, England, 1953. Elizabeth the Second is crowned Queen. And on the same day, in the County of Lancashire, and in the shadow of majestic Pendle Hill, PenDelfin is born.

On that day thunder rolled across the valley, and rain fell in torrents onto the roof of the tiny garden-hut where two good friends, Jeannie Todd and Jean Walmsley Heap, began the hobby that would become their claim to international fame. Jean Walmsley Heap, being the artist of the pair, designed and modeled their very first piece — a witch, flying against the moon, with her "familiar," a wide-eyed cat on her shoulder.

The witch sculpture was crafted in honor of Pendle Hill, which is known far and wide as the Hill of Witches. Various other models followed, but it was not until Miss Heap modeled a sturdy, bossy-looking rabbit and christened him "Father Rabbit," that orders for him began to roll in. The "hobby" then threatened to overtake the two friends, and they needed help.

This charming bunny figurine is titled "Herald," and he is offered free to each Charter Member in the "PenDelfin Family Circle" Collectors' Club.

The Original "Cast of Characters" at PenDelfin

Enter Doreen Noel Roberts, who began to share in the "joys" of clearing the drains of paint, stone mix and lost diamond rings. She learned rapidly that oil paint spilled on clothing never washes out! And after absorbing each step of production over the years, Doreen herself ultimately became a designer and sculptor of the famous PenDelfin rabbits.

Doreen Noel Roberts was born in Burnley and comes from a long line of artists. Her natural talents were developed by Jean Walmsley Heap so that Doreen now designs and models full-time for PenDelfin and is a member of its board of directors as well as a partner in the PenDelfin Design Unit.

Jean Walmsley Heap trained as an artist at Burnley School of Art under the guidance of distinguished artist Noel H. Leaver A.R.C.A. He had great faith in Jean's talents: teaching her clay-modeling as well as painting and composition. All the things taught to her by Noel Leaver, and many Jean herself has originated, have been put to good use in the development of PenDelfin. As Chairman of PenDelfin Studios Ltd., Jean Walmsley Heap F.R.S.A. gracefully occupies her rightful place.

Jeannie Todd, meanwhile, charmed creditors about the rent, and bullied her engineer brothers about kilns and driers. The late Jeannie Todd's greatest gift to PenDelfin was enthusiasm. She was often to be discovered late at night, shading models for the artists to color the next day. Shading is a "dirty" and hard job, during which one becomes covered to the elbows in dark brown paint, but this never worried Jeannie. She was proud of her talent as the "best" shader on the job. Her main work always was dealing with the Office and all the things that go on there. Although she died in 1974, she would be proud and amazed to be "boss" of the present staff.

Indeed, for artists and collectors alike, it seems, the PenDelfin obsession quickly strikes. In those early days, the staff grew; orders for the rabbits also grew; and grew and grew and grew. Now PenDelfin employs over one hundred dedicated, full-time craft-workers, most of whom love their work and return smiling from each weekend break.

The Process of Crafting a PenDelfin Piece

There are many steps in the complex process needed to produce a piece of PenDelfin. First, the Studio receives a master model from either Jean or Doreen. These painstaking sculptors may spend from several weeks to several months designing and modeling each new piece. Usually these pieces are rabbits, but sometimes a Village Shop or a Jetty or a new Cottage have appeared. The architectural pieces have formed the nucleus of a Village for the Rabbit Family to live in.

No one ever knows what type of piece will come next; the designers say they have to wait until they receive a certain type of inspiration. They call this a "request" from Mother and Father Rabbit about just what is needed in PenDelfin Village to make their lives more comfortable. The "Old Schoolhouse" by Jean Walmsley Heap and "The Toyshop" by Doreen Noel Roberts are results of the latest requests for "new buildings."

After receiving the master model from the designers, the Studio molding department goes into action, producing working molds for the casters. Casting is the men's side of the business (as is molding), as both these jobs are heavy and more suited to muscles.

After casting and drying (firing in a kiln is not necessary for the special PenDelfin stonecast medium) the models are sealed and underpainted before shading. All of this produces a suitable base for the PenDelfin artists to begin the serious, but enjoyable process of painting. The finest paints obtainable are used, making certain all are lead-free.

When all these processes are complete, the models are finished with a special "waxy" finish, and their eyes and teeth are hard-glossed, so that you see the twinkle in their eyes (or, in young "Barney's" case, a tear sparkling). Fine quality green felt bases are put on all the rabbits before they are lovingly packed into their attractive boxes.

Thousands are "Stricken" with "PenDelfinitis"

The word "obsession" comes up time and again when people endeavor to describe their relationship with PenDelfin. This happy "malady" has earned the joking name of "Pendelfinitis," but few have ever sought after a cure. Many of the employees, the designers, the tea-lady and retired staff return regularly to "snoop" through the PenDelfin Studio in search of new discoveries. People who were given a PenDelfin rabbit as a child have added yearly to their collections until they own (or are owned by!) complete sets of these appealing creations.

"Bosun," with Scrimshaw parrot, was sculpted exclusively for "Pendelfin Family Circle" Collectors' Club Founder Year members by Doreen Noel Roberts. This adorable sailor is on a quest for buried treasure!

For long-time PenDelfin lovers and new collectors alike, the formation of the "PenDelfin Family Circle" Collectors' Club is exciting news indeed. For $30.00 U.S. or $40.00 Canadian, members receive: a free gift of a special PenDelfin piece; a chance to win a coveted retired model; an official member's certificate, a regular club newsletter called "The PenDelfin Times"; a membership card; and the opportunity to enjoy a Studio tour for members whose travels bring them to Burnley, England. In addition, members of the "PenDelfin Family Circle" will be invited to purchase a yearly "members-only" figurine through their favorite retail store.

Another treat for those with "PenDelfinitis" is *The Pendelfin Story*, a book by Jean Walmsley Heap. This collector's guide tells the full and fascinating story of the rabbits, their Village, their designers and the many other interesting people who have contributed so much to the company. There is also a series of "PenDelfin Village Tales" in book form, telling the stories of several favorite characters. Each volume is rich in full-color illustrations and fascinating information, and each provides a delightful introduction to the riverbank world of PenDelfin Village.

The Family, for instance, tells the early history of the celebrated Rabbit Family, from the Great Cabbage Rush and the building of the Large House, to the very first Rabbit Band Contest on PenDelfin Village Green.

The PenDelfin Line Offers a Wide Variety of Whimsical Works of Art

Of course, PenDelfin is best known for the classic, three-dimensional stoneware figures of adorable rabbits. But there are also a number of fine, limited edition collector's plates especially created by the PenDelfin designers for lovers of the Rabbit Family. The series includes vignettes of "Mother and Baby" (sold out), "Father," and a number of events in the lives of these charming rabbits. There's "Gingerbread Day," "The Old Schoolhouse," "Whopper at Cobble Cottage" and "The Caravan."

Mother with her baby, "Charles Thomas," is dressed in her Sunday best for a family outing.

Because of the popularity of the "PenDelfin Village Tales," the Studio now offers block-mounted pictures from these beautiful books in 18" x 14" size, perfect for home display. Recent issues include "The Old Hole Homestead," "The Dance" and "The Auction."

A recent collection of classic PenDelfin artwork centers around the younger members of the Rabbit Family, and their adventures at "The Old Schoolhouse," "The Toy Shop" and "The Grandstand." There are gentle characters like "New Boy," the latest pupil to be enrolled at PenDelfin Village School. There are excellent students like the brainy "Euclid" and the determined "Digit," and lazybones like "Snuggles Awake," who's not quite ready for school.

"Angelo" is a fully-qualified Associate of the R.R.A. (Rabbit's Royal Academy), with some rather extravagant ideas. He plans to paint the dusty ceiling of "The Old Schoolhouse" with the Story of Creation! Less ambitious, perhaps, is little "Duffy," who is late to school again and not too happy about the hasty job he has done on his homework! Trying to keep the whole crew together is the long-suffering "Boswell," a helpful and patient teacher.

With offices in Canada and the United States as well as England, PenDelfin now enchants collectors on both sides of the Atlantic. The Studio's firm commitment to quality and excellence has not changed since the early days in that quaint garden hut. PenDelfin has never been successfully copied, although many have tried. These individual rabbit personalities and their delightful world have charmed collectors for four decades. And PenDelfin will continue to bring a smile to many discerning collectors for many years to come!

National Collector Conventions

A whole new world opens to collectors who take the opportunity to travel to the two manufacturer-sponsored collector conventions! Collectors are invited to visit several hundred booths, where new products are on display and where artists are often on hand to meet the public. Collectors may further enhance their visit by attending seminars on a whole host of topics or by visiting the 'swap and sell,' where collectors sell retired collectibles to interested parties. For more information on the conventions, contact the exposition management at McRand International, Ltd., One Westminster Place, Lake Forest, Illinois, 60045.

Featured artists from past collectible expositions join Edna Hibel, the recipient of the 1992 International Collectible Artist Award during the award presentation at Memories in South Bend (left to right: Michal McClure, President of the Collectible Expositions, with Edna Hibel, Gregory Perillo, P. Buckley Moss, Lowell Davis, Sandra Kuck, and John McClelland.

M.I. Hummel® Look-Alikes COME TO SOUTH BEND... *All decked out looking like M.I. Hummel figurines, a group of children ranging in ages from six to twelve vied for top honors in the Look-Alike contest held at the International Collectibles Exposition, Century Center, South Bend, Indiana, on July 18, 1992. Winners were presented valuable gift certificates by Goebel Master painter Ulrich Tendera. To add to the fun, St. Nikolaus gave all contestants a special Christmas stocking filled with "goodies."*

During the Collector's Club 10th Anniversary Gala, Lilliput Lane unveiled an extraordinary birthday cake, which was donated by Mrs. Joy Jones (right), owner of the Tudor Rose Tearoom in Salem Oregon. The cake was an exact replica of their special dinner piece, "Ashberry Cottage." Tonya Bredehoft (left), President of Retail Resources, bid $675 for the cake, which was auctioned. All profits from the auction were donated to The Frances Hook Scholarship Fund, at Ms. Bredehoft's request. The monies will help to provide scholarships for up and coming young artists.

Three exhibit halls featuring 321 exhibits from 121 manufacturers of Limited Edition Collectibles were packed full during public days at the International Collectible Exposition. The show played host to over 15,000 retailers and collectors, and set a new attendance record for the exposition.

1993 Show Schedule:

Long Beach, California: March 11-14
Long Beach Convention Center
March 11-12: Dealer days
March 13-14: Open to the public
(swap and sell on the 14th)

South Bend, Indiana: July 14-18
South Bend Century Center
July 14-15: Dealer days
July 16-17: Open to the public
July 18: Swap and sell

The History of Limited Edition Collectibles

The Bells and Dolls of Bygone Eras Foreshadow Today's Lively Market for Plates, Figurines, Graphics, and Ornaments

In 1995, the world of collectibles will celebrate an important milestone: the 100th anniversary of plate collecting. Bing & Grondahl's charming "Behind the Frozen Window" — introduced in 1895 — marked the beginning of the "modern era" for collectors. This work of art in blue-and-white porcelain launched the very first series of limited edition plates.

Yet many centuries before Harald Bing unveiled his annual Christmas collectible, people of diverse nations and cultures cherished their pretty bells, dolls and other decorative pieces. Today, the Collectors' Information Bureau concentrates its reporting efforts on six of the world's most popular limited edition art forms: plates, figurines, bells, graphics, ornaments and dolls. This brief history will provide a perspective on the origins of each of these celebrated collectors' art media.

Designer Bette Ball has created a colonial costume in apropos 100% American cotton fabric, worn by "Priscilla." This doll is part of the Victoria Ashlea Originals *collection and is available through Goebel, Inc.*

Bells Sound the Call of Joy and Warning

Centuries before collectors thought to display their bells as home decor, bells played important roles in religion, war and commerce. In ancient Greece, Rome, Egypt and Asia, bells heralded religious ceremonies — just as church bells still ring out each Sunday in Europe and North America.

Battle diaries tell us that long ago, large bells sounded out warnings of the enemy's approach. Once the skirmish was complete, the bells were rung again to signal "all clear." During Great Britain's terrifying World War II air raids, booming brass bells were used to warn the citizenry. The bells' bright surfaces were temporarily blackened with soot so that no enemy aircraft could spot them from above.

Visitors to Philadelphia consider the trip incomplete without a glimpse of the Liberty Bell, one of the world's most renowned symbols of freedom. Yet while tales of famous bells light the pages of our history books, we all cherish memories of everyday bell sounds, too — the old school bell, sleigh bells in winter, or even the sound of the Salvation Army bell ringer at holiday time.

"Angelic Guide" is the 1991 M.I. Hummel Ornament, the fourth in the annual series. "Hear Ye, Hear Ye," the 1991 M.I. Hummel Christmas Bell, is the third in a four-bell Christmas series.

Collector club memberships entitle collectors to purchase exclusive pieces and to learn more about the artists who create them, and the Polland Collectors Society is no exception. "Chief Pontiac," the 1990 Society gift, measures $3^1/_2$ inches high and is made of pewter.

A Bell Collector's Chronicle

While the sound of a mechanized alarm or siren can never compete with the rich tone of a hand-rung bell, technology has found "modern" replacements for most of the bells we once used every day. Yet bells remain as much a part of our lives as ever — for they have evolved into one of today's most popular collector's items.

When bells were considered mostly as work-a-day items, they were crafted of iron, bronze and other durable metals. But in recent centuries, bells began their wondrous transition from utilitarian to decorative forms. As European monarchs encouraged their court artisans to explore various forms of artistic expression, superb ceramic materials, glassware and crystal were developed.

Soon, pretty bells emerged in porcelain and bone china...Venetian glass...and full lead crystal. Ladies and gentlemen of leisure used these delicate bells to call their servants or ring for tea — and in the competition for social status, bell designs became ever more intricate and elegant.

Generations ago, art lovers began to collect and display pretty bells in their homes — and later to give their fine collections to museums. Over the years, bell collecting became more formalized, leading to the organization of the American Bell Association (ABA) in 1940. Since then, thousands of bell hobbyists have met in local groups and at annual conventions — all planned to allow these enthusiasts to share in the joy of their collections.

One of the highlights of ABA membership is the opportunity to travel the world with fellow bell aficionados, celebrating the "roots" of bell collecting in such far-flung locales as India, Asia, and Europe.

Contemporary Bell Collections Gain Popularity

Until recently, most bell collectors concentrated their energies on obtaining rare bells from the Far East, or charming specimens from European art studios like Lalique, Meissen, Dresden, Wedgwood or Delft. Yet even at the turn-of-the-century, today's strong market for contemporary bells was foreshadowed in Royal Bayreuth's "Sunbonnet Babies." This grouping is renowned as one of the first related series of bells. At the same time, Royal Bayreuth introduced some whimsical nursery rhyme bells, while another firm launched a collection of flint glass bells, each boasting a different figure on its handle.

Today a host of firms offer handsome bells in series, or individually. The annual M. I. Hummel bells feature the artwork of the famous German nun in bas-relief, while Gorham has revived the traditional "figural" and "school bell" forms. For a round-up of some of today's most widely traded contemporary bells, check the Price Index at the end of this volume.

When Precious Moments artist Sam Butcher speaks through his little messengers, it is often with wisdom, and that is perhaps why this collection has captured the hearts of tens of thousands of collectors around the world. "Don't Let The Holidays Get You Down" was first introduced in 1989 and is a powerful reminder that Christmas means more than the decorations!

Henry Wadsworth Longfellow's Song of Hiawatha *was the inspiration for this "Hiawatha" doll created by Wendy Lawton for Lawton Dolls. This doll is part of the* Childhood Classics *collection.*

Robert Bateman, both conservationist and artist, captures the spirit of this eagle in his graphic, "Majesty on the Wing - Bald Eagle," distributed by Mill Pond Press, Inc.

Dolls: The Oldest Collectibles of All

When the ruins of Pompeii and Herculaneum were uncovered centuries after the eruption of Mt. Vesuvius in A.D. 79, the perfectly preserved body of a little girl was found still clutching her doll. Yet this treasured old friend was already part of a 2000-year-old tradition: Egyptian dolls have been found in tombs dating from 2000 B.C.!

Even in ancient times, dolls were seen as more than playthings. The Greeks, for example, were known to offer their favorite dolls to show their respect for the gods. The poet Sappho wrote to the goddess Aphrodite, "Despise not my doll's little purple neckerchief. I, Sappho, dedicate this precious gift to you."

Children's Playthings and Adults' Diversions

In the Middle Ages, boys played with dolls in the image of knights on horseback, while girls enjoyed dolls crafted of wood, wax, or a paper-like material. During the 15th century, the Germans began carving dolls of wood: in fact, history's first recorded, professional doll artisans were the Germans Ott and Mess, who began their "Docken Macher" (doll maker) firm circa 1465.

Around the same period as Ott and Mess, French dollmakers began to ply their trade in Paris. Most early French dolls were made for adults as miniature "fashion mannequins" to display the latest designs. Made of wood or wax and known as "pandores," their popularity foreshadowed the "Golden Age of Dollmaking." which took place in Germany and France during the 19th century.

Like the French "pandores," traditional Japanese dolls are created as works of art to be admired and displayed, rather than as rough-and-tumble playthings. Part of the Japanese festival tradition are events known as "Boy's Doll Day" and "Girl's Doll Day," when young people showed off their richly clothed "children" of porcelain or papier mache. Japanese Hakata dolls (named for their town of origin) are made completely of hand-painted bisque porcelain: even their clothing is created as part of the sculpture.

Dolls of the Modern Era

French and German lady dolls and bisque "bebes" were beloved on both sides of the Atlantic at the turn-of-the-century, when most dolls sold in the United States still came from Europe. Then World War I called a halt to imports, and American ingenuity took hold. Madame Alexander and Effanbee dolls burst upon the scene, along with a wide range of advertising character dolls: Campbell Kids, Aunt Jemima, and Buster Brown to name a few.

The Great Depression and World War II slowed down the doll market for a time, but the invention of hard plastic in 1949 heralded a "boom" that brought us Barbie and G.I. Joe. While these children's dolls may seem remote from the world of art collectibles, mint-condition Barbies and Joes are often "star performers" on the auction market!

Today's Collectible Doll Scene

The few remaining doll specimens of ancient times and the Middle Ages are closely guarded in museums: priceless beyond measure. Yet some collectors are fortunate enough to acquire elegant dolls of the 19th and 20th centuries on the secondary market.

Even more collectors have discovered the joys of purchasing contemporary dolls — many of which are crafted in the image of some of the finest doll "classics" of previous generations. To survey the wealth of doll acquisition opportunities available today, turn to the Price Index at the end of this volume.

A Year-Round Celebration of Ornaments

Visit the home of one of today's enthusiastic ornament collectors, and you're likely to think it's "Christmas in July"! Ornaments are no longer relegated to a one-month show at holiday time: today there are ornaments on a wide range of themes from childhood adventure to crystal fantasy. Yet the history of ornament collecting is firmly rooted in Christmas tradition: a legacy that stretches back to Germany in circa 1820.

In those early days of the 19th century, most German families decorated their Christmas "tannenbaums" with homemade ornaments and candles. But in the little town of Lauscha, a center for glass making since the 16th century, the glass craftsmen happened upon a new use for their talents.

Once their daily work was done, the Lauscha glass makers would compete to see how large they could blow a glass ball. Then they embellished their prizes with lead or zinc "silvering," and took them home to decorate their living quarters. Soon it occurred to some of the glass makers that their silvery balls would look beautiful on dark green pine, and by 1848 the "Weihnachtsbaum Kugeln," or Christmas Tree Balls, had become standard items in the glass factory's order book.

During the 1850s, a glass master named Louis Greiner-Schlotfeger perfected the formula for silvering, and ever since then our classic ball ornaments have been graced with a bright and mirror-like shine. This same clever inventor also developed a paper-thin glass ideal for creating lightweight ornaments, as well as the first ornament ever crafted of molded glass.

Americans first learned of the Lauscha discoveries when the young dime store magnate, Frank Woolworth, imported his first $25 worth of German glass ornaments in 1880. The ornaments sold out in two days, and Woolworth sensed a revolution in the making. By 1890, he was ordering

Hudson's hand painted, fine pewter sculpture entitled "The Dream" is from the limited edition Sorcerer's Apprentice Collector Series. *This piece, distributed by The Lance Corporation, stands 6¼ inches high and issued at $225.00.*

200,000 ornaments annually for his 14 stores. Since then, glass ornaments have been joined by charming Christmas artworks crafted of wax, paper, tinsel, crystal, porcelain, and — an American favorite — shimmering silver.

Silver Ornaments Enthrall American Collectors

Drawing upon an old English custom, two American companies began annual series of sterling silver bell ornaments in 1963. Both Halls of Kansas City, Missouri and Shreve, Crump and Lowe of Boston have continued their collections every year since, marking three decades of family memories and holidays.

While sterling silver has become prohibitively expensive for many collectors, the 1960s and 1970s saw a wide range of sterling ornaments hallmarked by some of America's most celebrated silver companies: Franklin Mint, Reed and Barton, Towle, Lunt, Steiff, Kirk, Oneida, Wallace, Hand & Hammer Silversmiths and International Silversmiths. While some ornaments still are created in sterling today, many more are just as lovely in silverplate or highly polished pewter.

An Ornament Explosion in the 1980s and Beyond

While Hallmark began introducing dated ornaments in the 1970s, this famous firm became a "major player" in the ornament field during the 1980s, as did Enesco, American Greetings and many other companies. And while some of us still decorate our holiday trees with cranberries, popcorn and paper chains, this volume's Price Index shows the growing importance of ornaments in today's collectibles market.

Graphics Bring Fine Art Home to Everyone

At one time — not so many generations ago — only royalty and the wealthy could afford to display artwork on the walls of their homes. Original paintings were far too costly for working people to afford. But with the proliferation of reproduction techniques such as lithography, woodcuts, engraving, and serigraphy, the works of top artists could be made available to many, at reasonable prices.

Most of today's art reproduction methods have roots in the ancient past. The Sumerians invented engraving circa 3000 B.C., using stone cylinder seals which were engraved and then rolled over soft clay tablets. The Chinese reproduced wood blocks on cloth around 150 A.D., and they transferred their wood block art to paper by the ninth century. In fourteenth century Japan, the woodcut relief process was perfected, while at the same time European craftsmen were using woodcuts to decorate playing cards and books.

In the late 1700s, a German named Aloys Senefelder changed the direction of printmaking. While searching for a way to reproduce sheet music, he stumbled upon a new form of printing now known as lithography. Mass produced lithography was not perfected until the 1890s, however, when the French developed the first printing press to use large litho-stones. These stones could handle more than one image at a time, which greatly decreased the time and cost of production. It was quite a fad at the turn-of-the-century to collect posters and color lithographs created in this manner.

Early Print Artists Set the Stage for Today's Market

Some of history's finest American painters are far more renowned for reproductions of their work than for the originals themselves. Just a few of the classic artists whose prints have made them "household names" include John James Audubon, Currier and Ives, and Bessie Pease Gutmann.

Audubon's "Birds of America" were the result of sixteen years' research in which this inspired artist traveled the United States and Canada to study birds in the wild. The resulting folio of 435 plates — in which each bird is shown life-size — originally sold for $1000 a set in the 1840s. Today a complete "double elephant folio" of Audubon's original aquatint engravings would sell for several hundred thousand dollars — and individual prints might bring thousands of dollars apiece.

Nathaniel Currier and James Ives developed a wildly successful business creating and selling lithographs in the middle and late 1800s. The genius of this studio was in its understanding of the American public's taste for idyllic seasonal scenes, clipper ships, and current events.

Because Currier and Ives prints originally sold for just a dollar or two apiece, most every American family could afford to display at least one of these attractive works of art. If you were to locate a "mint condition" Currier and Ives print tucked away in an attic today, however, it might bring hundreds or even thousands of dollars on the secondary market.

Just as Currier and Ives dominated the print world of the 19th century, Bessie Pease Gutmann became the star of the American art scene during the 1920s and 1930s. In fact, it is said that most every home in the United States featured at least one of her adorable babies and toddlers.

The art form of painted bronze miniatures, pioneered by Goebel Miniatures with Robert Olszewski as Master Artist, is an established and sought after medium in the field of collecting. Shown above is the Three Little Pigs Display, with "Little Sticks Pig," "Little Straw Pig," "Little Bricks Pig" and "The Hungry Wolf."

After art studies in Philadelphia, Bessie Pease married Hellmuth Gutmann, owner of a graphic arts studio. The two forged a strong relationship both personally and professionally, raising three children while they created and promoted Bessie's prints. In recent years, Mrs. Gutmann's art has seen a strong resurgence of popularity. Indeed, her paintings have inspired many successful collector plates, figurines, and other handsome items.

Today, collectible prints are more popular than ever before in history. With growing affluence and greater art appreciation, most Americans now consider fine art a "must" to decorate their homes. They enjoy owning graphics that bring both Old Masters and contemporary talents into their living rooms for daily enjoyment. For an overview of today's print market, check the Price Index at the end of this book.

Harald Bing's Christmas Inspiration: The Limited Edition Plate Collection

Elegant displays in the world's great porcelain museums illustrate that plates have long been considered much more than utilitarian vessels. Yet until Harald Bing hit upon the idea of an annual Christmas plate, there was no formal concept of "plate collecting."

In 1895, Bing had the craftsmen at his Bing & Grondahl studio fire about 400 of one special plate called "Behind the Frozen Window." Decorated in Copenhagen blue and white underglaze, the plate bore the words "Jule Aften 1895," which means "Christmas Eve 1895" in Danish. Bing anticipated that his customers would pile the pretty plates with Christmas treats and offer them as gifts. This was the custom in Denmark, especially between employer and employee.

"Behind the Frozen Window" sold out, and Bing made plans to continue the tradition year after year. And soon Bing & Grondahl and the plate world at large will celebrate an unbroken century of annual Bing & Grondahl Christmas plates!

A Charming Gift Becomes a Collectible

If fate had not intervened, "Behind the Frozen Window" might have remained in the china cabinet and used only to serve cookies and cakes. But before long, the Danes who owned these blue-and-white beauties began to use them as wall decorations, adding another annual plate each year. Some Danish immigrants to the United States brought their "plate display" custom with them, but until World War II plate collecting was largely unknown in America.

In the late 1940s, returning G.I.s brought European collector plates home with them as souvenirs. Several U.S.-based antique dealers — notably William Freudenberg, Jr. of Chicago and Pat Owen of Ft. Lauderdale, Florida — sensed the potential for plate collecting in America, and began importing blue-and-white plates crafted by Bing & Grondahl, Royal Copenhagen, Rosenthal, Royal Delft and other European firms.

Plate Collecting Enters the Modern Era

Until the mid-1960s, the "European blue" plates enjoyed a small audience of enthusiasts who traded them quietly among themselves. Then a major breakthrough occurred: the first limited edition collector plate made in a material other than blue-and-white porcelain, with a theme other than Christmas.

"Deux Oiseaux" was the creation of France's famed Lalique crystal studio. This incised design of two handsome birds on full lead crystal opened the horizons for plate producers and collectors all over the world. If Lalique could develop and sell a crystal plate on a general theme, the sky was the limit!

In the next decade, the floodgates opened and

Seymour Mann's designing process begins with an original sculpture, which is produced into a doll, and then re-created into a painting — a complete evolution in art. Pictured above is "Ashley," just one of the dolls from the Connoisseur Doll Collection.

creativity flourished as never before in the previous 70 years of plate collecting. Goebel of Germany introduced hand-painted, bas-relief plates featuring the endearing art of Sister M. I. Hummel. Wedgwood of England crafted limited-edition plates of jasperware, featuring British historical scenes. Veneto Flair of Italy fashioned plates of majolica and adorned them with rich gold. And in the United States, the first of many plate collections emerged in tribute to America's favorite illustrator, Norman Rockwell.

In the early 1970s, the late Rod MacArthur launched The Bradford Exchange as a medium for buying and selling limited edition plates on the secondary market. Bradford helped stabilize and organize the plate market, as did the establishment of the National Association of Limited Edition Dealers and the Collector Platemakers Guild.

Today there are several million plate collectors in the United States, Canada, and throughout the world. From its simple beginnings in Denmark, plate collecting has become a fascinating pastime. Today, plates of porcelain, wood, crystal, and many other materials feature the art of some of the world's most celebrated painters and sculptors of the past and present. Themes range from wildlife, holidays and history to children and popular culture. The Price Index at the end of this volume lists thousands of the most actively traded issues in today's diverse and fast-paced plate market.

Each Hand & Hammer Silversmiths design begins at artist Chip deMatteo's drawing table, where he turns his quick idea sketches into finished scaled drawings. These exacting drawings are used to produce the master pattern models, which may be sculpted in either wax or metal. Shown above is one of the nearly 300 ornaments designed by deMatteo over the years.

In recent years, The Hamilton Collection has attracted fans all over America with its colorful range of collectibles, capturing memorable moments in entertainment. Hamilton commemorates the science fiction field with its Star Trek Plate Collection *and USS Enterprise Plate (center).*

The Historical Roots of Figurine Collecting

In today's world of collectibles, figurines may be crafted of porcelain, precious metal, cold-cast bronze, crystal, or high-quality resins combined with porcelain or metal materials. No other area of collecting has seen such incredible expansion of material, subject and form. Yet whether we collect cottages or crystal..."cute little children" or elegant sculptures from world-class art studios...the "roots" of our passion are the same. Today's limited edition figurine market continues the tradition of porcelain craftsmanship and quality that began in Asia and Europe many centuries ago.

When Marco Polo returned to Europe with his precious cargo of Chinese porcelain circa 1300 A.D., monarchs began a fierce competition to see which nation could develop its own formula for this delicate, creamy-white material. The quest for what the kings called "white gold" took several hundred years, but by the 1700s porcelain craftsmanship flourished in Germany and France.

Until the 20th century, however, only the wealthy could afford to own porcelain art objects. Each was one of a kind, and the time and care invested in sculpture and hand-painting made the price prohibitive for most. Then in the 1930s, Royal Worcester of England joined forces with the sculptress Dorothy Doughty to create the first limited edition collection of sculptures.

Miss Doughty had an exceptional ability to sculpt birds and flowers with outstanding fidelity to nature. Thus her *Birds of America* sculptures often were enhanced by delicate flowers and branches. To complete each of her sculptures, Miss Doughty supervised the creation of between twenty and forty molds to capture every detail of the original.

Because of their intricacy, the *Birds of America*

Norman Rockwell created a pictorial history of his times and illuminated the lives of his fellow Americans with gifted warmth and insight. "Quiet Reflections" is the first issue in Rockwell's Treasured Memories *series by Edwin M. Knowles China for the Rockwell Society of America. This series features beautiful women in moments of quiet reflection.*

sold for several hundred dollars apiece, even in the 1930s. Yet at that price, an upper middle class audience could afford to own and display figurines in their homes for the first time ever. And soon other European and American art studios introduced limited edition figurines at even more affordable prices, opening up the world of collecting to middle class people as well.

During the 1930s, Royal Doulton of England and Kaiser and Goebel of Germany began to create fine art pieces in limited editions. Royal Doulton's "Toby Jugs," Kaiser's animal sculptures and Goebel's M. I. Hummel figurines became favorites of collectors on both sides of the Atlantic.

In the United States, Edward Marshall Boehm and Boleslaw Cybis established separate studios bearing their names and devoted to crafting the finest three-dimensional porcelain art. Not long after that, the Lladro brothers — Juan, Jose and Vicente — opened their famous Lladro porcelain studio in Valencia, Spain.

Today's Figurine World Includes Cottages and Crystal

Over the past decade or two, figurine makers have experimented with various media and subject matter. Today the Collectors' Information Bureau Price Index for figurines includes the cottages of Lilliput Lane and David Winter, lighted houses by Department 56, and shimmering crystal collectibles from Swarovski. These works of art are listed side by side with classic porcelain pieces from Boehm and Cybis, Goebel's timeless M.I. Hummel figurines, and scores of other series from around the world. To learn more about this panorama of three-dimensional art, turn to the Price Index at the end of this volume.

Company Summaries
About the Marketers and Manufacturers of Limited Edition Collectibles

There are several hundred firms actively involved in today's world of limited edition collectibles, with bases of operation in the United States, Canada, and in many other countries. Here you'll find some basic background information about some of the more prominent firms in the field. With each there is an address, and in many cases a contact person, which you may use to inquire about a firm's products and services. There is also a listing of the types of limited edition products each firm makes or markets.

ALEXANDER DOLL COMPANY, INCORPORATED

615 West 131 Street
New York, New York 10027
(212) 283-5900

Dolls

As a child, Beatrice Alexander Behrman was touched by the tears of the little girls who brought their broken dolls to her father to be mended. Later when World War I halted the shipment of European dolls, young Beatrice began making and selling "Made in America" dolls.

One of the first and most successful doll companies in the United States, the Alexander Doll Company was founded in 1923 by Beatrice who later became known throughout the world as "Madame Alexander." In the 1920s and 1930s, the demand for Madame Alexander Dolls exceeded the supply. Some of the most popular dolls were the Dionne Quintuplets, Scarlett O'Hara and the Princess Elizabeth and the Princess Margaret Rose.

To date, more than 5,000 different styles of dolls have been produced by the company. Madame Alexander received the first Doll of the Year (DOTY) Lifetime Achievement Award. In addition, Madame Alexander Dolls was nominated for *Doll Reader* magazine's Doll of the Year Award and was awarded the "Dolls of Excellence" award from *Dolls* magazine. The Madame Alexander Doll Club currently has more than 10,000 members.

AMERICAN ARTIST PORTFOLIO INC.

Pauline Ward
Rt. 1, Box 316-G
Somerset, Virginia 22972
(703) 672-0400

Graphics

American Artist Portfolio Inc. was founded in 1988 to publish and market the works of realist artist Adolf Sehring. Located in Somerset, Virginia, American Artist Portfolio's first offerings were eight still lifes and landscapes. A year later, two more graphics were added to the edition. Sehring created three more lithographs depicting African wildlife in 1990.

Renowned for his portraits of children and dignitaries, Sehring is the only American artist to be commissioned by the Vatican to paint the official portrait of Pope John Paul II.

Sehring's offset lithographs and mixed-media serigraphs are reproduced from the artist's original oils and are sold through select galleries throughout the continental United States, Alaska, Hawaii and Japan.

AMERICAN ARTISTS/ GRAPHICS BUYING SERVICE

Peter Canzone
43 Sherwood Terrace Suite 7
Lake Bluff, Illinois 60044
(708) 295-5355
Fax: (708) 295-5491

Plates, Figurines, Graphics

Graphics Buying Service (GBS) originated ten years ago as a firm devoted to the commissioning and marketing of limited edition graphic art. The company was the first of its kind — offering quality, limited edition prints by top plate artists, at affordable prices.

GBS artists have included James Auckland, Irene Spencer, Frank Russell and Gertrude Barrer, Donald Zolan, Richard Zolan, Fred Stone, Dave Chapple and Mary Vickers. Currently American Artists handles only Fred Stone lithographs. Each original edition is signed and sequentially numbered by the artist. These editions are very limited — especially compared to the plate market — and thus they have made for some impressive secondary market gains in a short period of time.

In 1981, GBS began a new division called American Artists, dedicated to the creation of the finest in limited edition collector plates. Today, American Artists/GBS continues in both the graphics field and the realm of limited edition plates. The firm is currently producing plates by the award winning equine artist Fred Stone, cat plates by Zoe Stokes and Susan Leigh, and works by Donald Zolan.

AMERICAN GREETINGS

10500 American Road
Cleveland, Ohio 44144
(216) 252-7300

Christmas Ornaments, Plates

American Greetings is the world's largest publicly owned manufacturer and distributor of greeting cards and personal communications merchandise, including stationery, calendars, gift wrap, party goods, candles, toys and gift items, dedicated to meeting the personal communications needs of an ever-changing society.

The firm is one of the industry's innovative leaders in the creation and licensing of characters, such as their exclusive Holly Hobbie, Ziggy, Strawberry Shortcake, Care Bears, Care Bear Cousins and Popples, which are featured on thousands of retail products and seen nationally on television and in motion pictures.

The staff of talented artists and writers creates and produces more than 20,000 new designs each year for their diverse lines of merchandise. Products of American Greetings, their subsidiaries, licensees and affiliates are distributed through a global network of 90,000 retail outlets located throughout the Free World.

American Greetings is headquartered in Cleveland, Ohio, where it was founded in 1906. They employ approximately 20,000 people and operate 49 plants and facilities in the United States, Canada, Continental Europe, Mexico, Monaco and the United Kingdom.

ANNA-PERENNA PORCELAIN, INC.

Klaus D. Vogt
71-73 Weyman Avenue
New Rochelle, New York 10805
(914) 633-3777
(800) 627-2550
Fax: (914) 633-8727

Plates, Figurines

ANNA-PERENNA Porcelain is an international firm specializing in limited edition art plates made of hard-paste Bavarian porcelain, miniature figurines, limited edition sculptures and hand made carrousel music boxes.

Founded in 1977 by Klaus D. Vogt, the former president of Rosenthal, U.S.A., ANNA-PERENNA has translated the art of Thaddeus Krumeich, Count Bernadotte, Al Hirschfeld and Pat Buckley Moss into limited edition art plates.

The ten year collaboration of ANNA-PERENNA Porcelain and Pat Buckley Moss provides collectors with a number of notable series including: *American Silhouettes*, *Christmas*, *Celebration Series*, the *Carrousel Triptych*, the *Four Seasons Quartet*, the *Grandparent Diptych* and the *Heartland Series*. The "Wedding" plate and the first Mother's Day plate was issued in the anniversary year 1991.

ANNA-PERENNA Porcelain will introduce a unique collection of limited edition porcelain figurines designed by P. Buckley Moss and produced to its uncompromising standards of porcelain manufacturing.

Other ANNA-PERENNA collectible lines include the *ADORABLES*, hand-made and hand painted miniatures by Scottish artist Peter Fagan. These whimsical pieces, which frequently incorporate cats and teddy bears, have generated thousands of loyal members of the ADORABLES COLLECTORS SOCIETY in Europe and the United States.

ANNA-PERENNA also represents Art Foundation Studios of Spain, and the famous sculptors Joseph Bofill, Jose Luis de Casasola and NICO.

ANNALEE MOBILITEE DOLLS INC.

Reservoir Road, Box 708
Meredith, New Hampshire 03253-0708
(603) 279-3333
Fax: (603) 279-6659

Dolls, Christmas Ornaments

In 1934, a young girl carefully adapted a pattern and created her own doll. Barbara Annalee Davis was pleased with it, but eventually dollmaking was put aside in favor of all the adventures of growing up.

As a youngster, Annalee spent her summers in Meredith, New Hampshire. In 1941, she married Charles "Chip" Thorndike, a Harvard man and native of Boston. They decided that Meredith was where they would make their home.

Chip started the Thorndike Chicken Farm. But in 1955, the price of eggs plummeted and they abandoned chicken farming. By then they had two sons, Charles and Townsend, and didn't want to forsake the lifestyle they had established in Meredith.

Annalee had rediscovered the art of dollmaking. Handmade of felt, her dolls had soft felt shapes and arms and legs that could be bent. The whimsical, hand-painted expressions of all her dolls reveal her sense of humor. Her early dolls were skiers, fishermen, angels and dancers, to name a few.

Annalee's big break came when the New Hampshire Department of Parks and Recreations ordered her ski and other sports-related dolls for displays. The publicity brought in unprecedented orders.

With the help of her sons, Annalee began making more dolls while Chip handled the business side, using the family's Volkswagen "Bug" to deliver the dolls.

When demand for the "Annalee Dolls" exceeded their production capabilities, the Thorndikes turned to their neighbors who began making dolls in their own homes. As the fame of Annalee's dolls spread, the Thorndikes erected a workshop and gift shop near their home.

Ultimately the company constructed the Factory in the Woods on their farmland where today more than 400 craftspeople are engaged in making the dolls in an extended complex of buildings.

In 1983, the Annalee Doll Society was formed. Among the benefits available to its 23,000 worldwide members include "The Collector" newsletter, an opportunity to purchase a limited edition doll designed exclusively for members and an invitation to the annual Society Barbecue and Auction held each year in Meredith, New Hampshire.

In 1985, a new Annalee Doll Museum was also opened with more than 450 of Annalee's dolls displayed.

Although Annalee remains the company's creative director, son Townsend is president, chief executive officer and

Annalee Mobilitee introduced this 7" "Desert Mouse" as a tribute to the service personnel in the Persian Gulf.

Chairman of the Board of this American success story.

ANRI WOODCARVINGS

April Bargout
55 Pacella Park Drive
Randolph, Massachusetts 02368
(617) 961-3000
Fax: (617) 986-8168

Plates, Figurines, Christmas Ornaments

The House of ANRI, located in the South Tyrol, Italy, was founded in 1912 by Anton Riffeser. Since that time, an ANRI Woodcarving has come to be one of the most sought-after collectible art forms. The woodcarved and handpainted limited editions include relief plates and figurines by such renowned artists as Juan Ferrandiz, Walt Disney and Sarah Kay and beautiful wood sculpted nativity sets by Ulrich Bernardi. CLUB ANRI, a society for all ANRI Woodcarvings, was formed in 1983.

Among the specific benefits offered to members are: An official member plaque, a club newsletter, an ANRI collector's guidebook, special annual figurine offerings by Sarah Kay, Juan Ferrandiz and Walt Disney, an authorized dealer listing, and an annual value survey which includes issue prices and current values of selected retired woodcarvings.

Members who renew always receive a free gift. For example, the 1991 renewal gift was the Fence Display on which members can display the Club figurines,

"Fore!" is a limited edition wood sculpture by Sarah Kay, available in 4" and 6" sizes and limited to 2,000 each.

"Kiss Me" and "A Little Bashful," by Sarah Kay.

Events are held throughout the year so that Club Members can get together during woodcarving promotions and collector shows.

CLUB ANRI is a service of Schmid.

ARMANI COLLECTION

c/o Miller Import Corporation
300 Mac Lane
Keasbey, Woodbridge Township,
New Jersey 08832
(908) 417-0330
Fax: (908) 417-0031

Figurines

The dream of providing American collectors with some of the world's finest collectibles and giftware prompted Herb Miller to found Miller Import Corporation in 1953. Using his savings as capital, Miller began searching the world for quality products.

One of Miller's first real discoveries was high quality, full-lead crystal from Germany. The *Byrdes Crystal Collection*, which contains over 175 pieces of crystal, soon became one of his most popular lines. Later, Miller added Capodimonte flowers and other products from Italy, Germany and Poland.

But it was Miller's discovery of a small porcelain works in Italy that was to make collectibles history. Giuseppe Armani, a sculptor in the Renaissance tradition, produced figurines with an unusual style and color. Working closely together, Miller and Armani created subjects — both wildlife and human — which would appeal to American collectors. These figurines were destined to become known as the Armani Collection.

According to Miller, the latest Armani collectible series is the master sculptor's *Moonlight Masquerade* series. This group of figurines consists of five women in various "masquerade" poses, all standing in front of a crescent moon. Presented in the age-old Renaissance style of Tuscany, Armani's ladies retain the contemporary charm of today's energetic, independent and beautiful women. Miller also advises of Armani's new wildlife introductions, which include a large, limited edition eagle, a limited edition group of doves and a limited edition bird of paradise.

Armani first executes his sculptural masterworks in clay, and then draws upon the expertise of the Florence Sculture d' Arte studios to recreate his works for collectors. Produced in the finest cold-cast porcelain, Armani's limited edition *My Fair Ladies*, *Pearls Of The Orient*, *Premiere Ballerinas*, and selections from his *Wildlife* collection have become immediate successes for Miller Import's U.S. market and for the artist's worldwide market.

Miller Import Corporation is the exclusive U.S. importer and distributor of the Armani Collection and is founder of the G. Armani Society, the collector club for fans of Armani's works.

"Ballerina with Drape" is part of the Premiere Ballet Series.

ART WORLD OF BOURGEAULT

Monica or Robert Bourgeault
20538 Therese Drive
Mount Clemens, Michigan 48043
(313) 791-8569

CANADIAN DISTRIBUTION:
KAISER PORCELAIN CO. LTD.
Brian Cleary
RR 3, Shelburne
Ontario, Canada L0N 1S0
(705) 466-2246

Plates, Graphics

Artist Robert Bourgeault has created a work of art that is new and exciting with the development of the "Lisa-

Caroline" Plate, commencing the *Royal Gainsborough Series*.

Robert's talents do not stop with landscapes. He is a versatile artist, sketching life around him, as a pastime, and incorporating models in many of these sketches. It was no surprise to anyone who knows Bourgeault's artistic abilities when he had his daughter, Lisa-Caroline pose in front of an English country cottage resulting in the beautiful "Lisa-Caroline" plate. This $9^{1}/_{4}$ inch, $^{1}/_{4}$ inch gold bordered, porcelain plate is a collector's delight.

Bourgeault developed a loyal following after the release of his first series, *The English Countryside*, and his hand-painted exclusive issues, such as "Lilac Cottage." His series, *The Royal Literary Series*, began with the "John Bunyan Cottage" and continued with the "Thomas Hardy Cottage," "John Milton Cottage," and "Anne Hathaway Cottage." Bourgeault has also released four beautiful prints to match the plates. The meeting of the artist's expression with the viewer's response puts the collection in the elite class — both exclusive as well as educational. Bourgeault has brought to each collector his own "original painting" to be enjoyed forever.

Followers of Bourgeault's work are familiar with the obscure birds that he cleverly projects into his canvases and collector's plates; in each and every creative garden there is a finch, a tiny wren, robin or a nightingale — you can almost hear its song as you view the creative, artistic work of a Bourgeault.

ARTAFFECTS, LTD.

Richard Habeeb
P.O. Box 98
Staten Island, New York 10307
(718) 948-6767
Fax: (718) 967-4521

Plates, Figurines, Graphics, Dolls, Bells, Christmas Ornaments

Artaffects is a company with a new name, yet a long history in the field of fine limited edition collectibles and gift issues.

In 1971 Richard J. Habeeb read an article in the *Wall Street Journal* describing how newly issued silver collector plates featuring artwork by Norman Rockwell were quickly oversubscribed and were climbing in price. The article implied that collector plates held investment potential. Newly married, Richard felt that plate collecting would enable he and his wife Geraldine to decorate their new apartment nicely with works of art that appealed to them, and at the same time offered some appreciation potential.

By 1974, the small apartment was filled. There was no more wall space to be found. The Habeebs wished to continue collecting so there seemed no alternative but to place a classified ad offering some pieces for sale. Unexpectedly, a business was born. Richard would hurry home from his teaching position to check the post office box appropriately labeled 'Richard's Limited Editions'. A family of 20,000 collectors was developed, collectors who listened to Richard's recommendations.

This background as a collector and dealer made Habeeb uniquely sensitive to the needs of fellow collectors and it spurred him on to develop collectibles under his own hallmark.

Vague Shadows was formed in 1977 to produce and market the works of Gregory Perillo. Both the Curator Collection and Signature Collection were formed to feature the works of outstanding artists whose paintings set standards of excellence in their fields. In 1988 all three collections were consolidated under one hallmark, Artaffects. It is a most appropriate name, in that it reflects Richard Habeeb's goal to present art that moves us deeply on an emotional level.

The art of Gregory Perillo moves people deeply. He has produced many award winning collectibles for Artaffects, which range from plates to figurines, lithographs, porcelain collector dolls, pewter belt buckles and the exquisitely detailed sculptures of *The Great Chieftains*. The emergence of the Artaffects Perillo Collectors Club has proven very popular with Perillo collectors both old and new.

Artaffects also represents the work of Carol Roeda who, with her little children singing praises to the Lord, her "Simple Wonders" became an immediate success for Artaffects. The romantic artwork of Rob Sauber's *Winter Mindscapes* plate series has been a proven winner as well as his beautiful doll "Caroline," the same Southern Belle that graced the first issue of his enormously successful plate series *Portraits of American Brides*.

Jim Deneen's very popular series of classic trains and classic cars illustrate why he has been called America's foremost painter of classic modes of transportation. The artwork of MaGo (Maurizio Goracci) has also found wide acceptance with his *Reflections of Youth* and *Studies of Early Childhood* being highly sought after. Lou Marchetti has captured the *Life of Jesus* with realism that only the old masters could have rendered.

Besides the outstanding roster of contemporary artists, Artaffects, under the Curator Collection designation, presented works by Norman Rockwell, Frederick Remington, Mary Cassatt, Jessie Wilcox Smith, Charlotte Becker, and Bessie Pease Gutmann. In fact, Curator Collection's presentation of Gutmann pieces helped to spark the revival of interest in her work.

What began as a passion and hobby for Richard Habeeb has evolved into Artaffects, a company that reproduces fine quality artwork in various formats, artwork that speaks to people and moves them on an emotional, human level.

Gregory Perillo's Indian artwork is highly coveted by collectors worldwide.

ARTISTS OF THE WORLD

Thomas R. Jackson
2915 North 67th Place
Scottsdale, Arizona 85251
(602) 946-6361
Fax: (602) 941-8918

Plates, Figurines, Christmas Ornaments

Artists of the World was founded in 1976 to represent Arizona artist, Ettore (Ted) De Grazia. However, over the years they have represented many artists, including Don Ruffin, Larry Toschik, and Kee Fun Ng.

To this day, Artists of the World is still primarily focused in reproducing the works of Ted De Grazia. A variety of products with De Grazia's unique style are currently available, such as collector plates, figurines, blankets, miniature figurines, and miniature plates.

Artists of the World is also the exclusive U.S. Distributor of Elisa figurines. These classic pieces, which are created by Monserrat Ribes, possess a fresh contemporary look.

Artists of the World's main showroom is located in Scottsdale, and collectors are welcome to call and make arrangements to visit when they are in Arizona.

THE ASHTON-DRAKE GALLERIES

9200 North Maryland Avenue
Niles, Illinois 60648

Dolls

The Ashton-Drake Galleries is a leading collectibles company specializing in limited-edition dolls. Ashton-Drake uses the Uniform Grading Standards for Dolls to evaluate the dolls it reviews. Only dolls which meet all ten standards and are judged to be of the highest quality, or "premiere" grade, are recommended to collectors.

Its first collection — *Yolanda's Picture-Perfect Babies* — was designed by popular doll artist Yolanda Bello. Since then, Ashton-Drake has introduced a variety of doll collections by other accomplished artists, including Cindy McClure, Dianna Effner, Kathy Barry-Hippensteel, Ellen Williams, Pat Ryan Brooks, Merri Roderick, Sandra Kuck, John McClelland, Maryanne Oldenburg, Julie Good-Krüger and Susan Krey. Baby, children, fashion and character dolls are all represented in the company's product line.

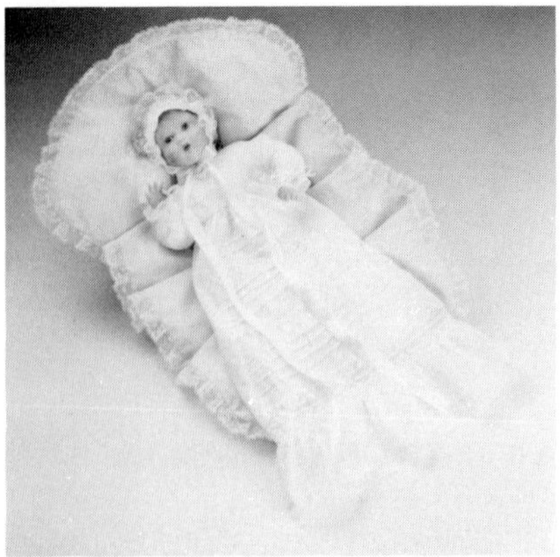

Kathy Barry-Hippensteel created "Catherine's Christening" for the Baby Book Treasures *series.*

Ashton-Drake dolls are available at dealers throughout the country or by contacting the company directly.

THE B & J COMPANY

P.O. Box 67
Georgetown, Texas 78626
(512) 863-8318
Fax: (512) 863-0833

Plates, Dolls, Graphics

The B & J Company was started in 1975 in Tempe, Arizona by Bill and Jan Hagara to produce and market prints of Jan Hagara's work. In 1977, they moved the business to Georgetown, Texas for a more central location.

Their first offerings were cards and fine art prints, featuring children with an old-fashioned look — a look that has become Jan's trademark.

Jan's first plate series, *Yesterday's Children*, introduced in 1978, followed by three other series, were very successful and had tremendous secondary market activity. Jan's prints are extremely popular, selling out in a few months, with editions of 1,000 or 2,000.

The popularity of Jan's work also led to the formation of the Jan Hagara Collectors' Club in 1987. In a recent move designed to enhance their marketing effort, the Hagaras bought the Royal Orleans company.

THE BALLIOL CORPORATION

Marvin Mitchell
Karen Choppa
1353 Elm Avenue
Lancaster, Pennsylvania 17603
(717) 293-2779
Fax: (717) 293-2781

Plates, Figurines, Dolls, Christmas Ornaments, Graphics

The Balliol Corporation is a major licensor to the collectibles industry of such prominent artists as Bessie Pease

"On the Threshold" is the first issue in the Bessie Pease Gutmann Special Moments Collection.

Gutmann and Maud Humphrey, the famous illustrators of children, and contemporary artists Gré Gerardi, Tim Hildebrandt, Sally Evans and Lynne Yancha.

Balliol has issued licenses to Lenox Collectibles for porcelain collector plates; Hallmark and Willitts Designs for figurines; The Hamilton Collection and Danbury Mint for porcelain collector plates and dolls; Hamilton Gifts and Enesco for figurines, Christmas ornaments, mugs, tins, music boxes, and other collectible items; Bradley Collectibles and the Georgetown Collection for dolls and other collectibles; Portal Publications, Limited and Thomas Nelson Inc. for posters, greeting cards, calendars, and journals; The Stephen Lawrence Company for gift wrap and gift bags; Antioch for bookplates and bookmarks; and Keller-Charles Company for tinware. Balliol also licenses major publishers, such as Putnam, Crown Publishing, and Wallace-Homestead Book Company, a division of Chilton.

One of the Balliol Corporation's top licenses is Bessie Pease Gutmann, and one of the most popular Gutmann collectibles has been The Hamilton Collection's plate series, *A Child's Best Friend*. The first plate in that series, "In Disgrace," began appearing on the secondary market only months after introduction. These plates were recently issued in miniature to honor the fiftieth anniversary of the original publication of "In Disgrace" and its companion piece, "The Reward." Another plate series, *Special Moments Collection*, features some of Gutmann's adult subjects.

Gré Gerardi is another exclusive

license of The Balliol Corporation. Since her discovery by Balliol in 1988, Gerardi has produced two collector plate series for The Hamilton Collection. An entire giftware line also has been developed around her charming portrayal of cats and other animals.

Of major impact on the collectibles market have been the products from Balliol's doll licenses which collectors have bought up eagerly. Among the most popular have been the Maud Humphrey and Bessie Pease Gutmann dolls produced by The Hamilton Collection. Bradley Collectibles offers dolls based on Balliol's collection of Kate Greenaway art.

BAND CREATIONS

28427 North Ballard
Lake Forest, Illinois 60045
708-816-0900

Dolls, Figurines

Although Band Creations is only two years old, the direct importers of collectibles and giftware lines has achieved an enviable place in today's market.

The firm's most successful lines are the *Christmas* figurines and their limited edition *Gallery Doll Collection*. The *Christmas* line features a wide variety of attractive Santas and Christmas angel figurines and extremely popular treetoppers.

The *Gallery Doll Collection* currently contains nineteen imported dolls which are limited to 1,000 dolls per edition. Each doll is packaged in an attractive gift box with a certificate of authenticity. According to Dennis Sowka, president of Band Creations, their ballerina dolls are among the most popular dolls in the line.

Band Creation's newest item introduced in 1991 was *Deer Ones*, a collection of reindeer who help Santa prepare for his annual Christmas journey around the world.

BAREUTHER

c/o Wara Intercontinental Co.
Walter A. Rautenberg
20101 West Eight Mile Road
Detroit, Michigan 48219
(313) 535-9110
Fax: (313) 535-9112

Plates, Bells

The Bareuther & Company porcelain factory of Germany began producing giftware, vases and dinnerware in 1867. Established by Johann Matthaeus Reis, the shop contained a porcelain kiln and an annular brick kiln.

The business later was sold to Oskar Bareuther, who continued to produce quality tableware.

To celebrate the 100th anniversary of Bareuther, the company began to issue limited edition Christmas plates in 1967, which are Cobalt blue. Their *Father's Day* series, which features many of the great German castles, was initiated in 1969. The *Mother's Day* series was also initiated in 1969, and the first issue of the *Christmas Bell* series was produced in 1973.

BEADAZZLED CRYSTAL

1451 Fifth Street
Berkeley, California 94710
(415) 527-5796

Figurines

Beadazzled Crystal specializes in smaller crystal figurines. The firm takes pride in offering a wide selection of quality, detailed figurines, including such figures as Raggedy Ann, and a junior train set.

Beadazzled Crystal had the good fortune of making arrangements with Black and Paterno Crystal to reproduce some of their fine designs. The company also markets larger crystal figurines, prisms, crystal prism hangers, and crystal jewelry.

MARTY BELL FINE ART, INC.

Eric Abel
9424 Eton Avenue
Chatsworth, California 91311
(800) 637-4537

Plates, Graphics

Marty Bell paints the charm of country England. Quaint cottages, elegant manor houses and lovely landscapes are captured in the softly detailed work of her brushes.

Marty Bell is an American born artist whose love for the beauty of the English countryside has created her international popularity. Collectors enjoy her peaceful, serene images both for their romantic charm as well as the investment value of her work.

A successful secondary market has sprouted, and prices for sold-out editions are soaring.

Founded in 1987, Marty Bell Fine Art, Inc. has published over 100 of Marty's paintings under the leadership of her husband — President Steve Bell. This family run, multi-million dollar company markets lovely gift and collectible products featuring her images — including note cards, needlepoint kits, and music tapes commissioned by the artist.

The Hamilton Collection has released many of Marty's paintings as collector plates. Currently in production is an eight plate series titled *The English Country Cottage Collection*. Marty's original oil paintings can be viewed in her gallery in Chatsworth, California.

BING & GRONDAHL

27 Holland Avenue
White Plains, New York 10603
(914) 428-8222
Fax: (914) 428-8251

Plates, Figurines, Bells, Christmas Ornaments

In 1853 when brothers Meyer and Jacob Bing joined Frederik Grondahl in starting a new porcelain factory named Bing & Grondahl, their dreams were modest. The company produced figurines in bisque, and dinnerware and porcelain objects that were all replicas of the work of Danish sculptor, Thorvaldsen. In 1895, Bing & Grondahl produced, "Behind the Frozen Window." It became the world's first Christmas plate and is also considered to be the plate that began the tradition of plate collecting.

The quality of the firm's collections became well known, and Bing & Grondahl pieces began appearing in museums around the world. The firm also serves by appointment to the courts of Denmark, Sweden and Great Britain.

In addition to collector plates and tableware, Bing & Grondahl also introduced a variety of figurines and other porcelain pieces. In 1969, Bing & Grondahl introduced the first *Mother's Day* plate and in 1985, the first annual *Children's Day* plate. The *Mother's Day* series also has a hand-painted companion figurine. Selected Bing & Grondahl *Annual Figurines* were later used as models when Bing & Grondahl entered the doll market with "Mary," their first porcelain doll.

The *Christmas Collectibles* collection currently contains the annual Christmas plate, bell, and matching porcelain ornament. The popular *Christmas in America* series contains a plate, matching ornament and bell. Another series from Bing & Grondahl is the *Santa Claus Collection* introduced in 1989. Bing & Grondahl also features the limited edition *Annual Egg* and *Annual Year Figurine* series.

THOMAS BOLAND & COMPANY

230 West Superior Street
Chicago, Illinois 60610
(312) 266-0494
Fax (312) 266-0123

Dolls

For Thomas Boland, one of the greatest joys in the doll business is finding and developing truly fine doll artists. Ironically, Boland entered the doll market quite by accident nearly fifteen years ago when Aletha Kendall brought her dolls to Boland's gift showroom in the Chicago Merchandise Mart. Once they were displayed, people flocked to see her dolls. When the House of Global Art, Gorham, Ebeling & Reuss and Schmid entered the doll market a short time later, Boland knew a doll trend had begun.

Over the next few years, Boland brought to the forefront doll artists like Avigail Brahms, Marla Florio, Karen Henderson, Peter Wolf, Beth Cameron and Pat Thompson. Boland recently has been instrumental in bringing the work of many contemporary artists to the attention of collectors in more moderately priced dolls. Boland also has been called upon to arrange exhibits by his doll artists at Tiffany & Company, New York's Lincoln Center and the Museum of the City of New York.

BOEHM STUDIOS

Virginia Perry
25 Fairfacts
Trenton, New Jersey 08638
(609) 392-2242

Plates, Figurines

In 1950, Edward Marshall Boehm, a sculptor, naturalist-farmer opened a basement studio in Trenton, New Jersey. Blessed with an innate talent and an intense desire to excel, Boehm specialized in artworks portraying birds, flowers and animals.

His wife and partner, Helen Boehm, was an energetic, brilliant tactician who was determined to see her husband's work receive its just recognition and respect. Boehm's art was just beginning to be recognized when Edward died unexpectedly in 1969.

Most people assumed that Boehm Studios would close, but they hadn't counted on Helen Boehm's determination and business sense. She had always taken an active role in bringing his ideas from the studio to the marketplace, and in the discussions on new projects.

She continues to assume responsibility for the studio's designs. Fortunately, her husband left behind a talented, well-trained staff of artists.

Today, Boehm porcelains can be found in hundreds of museums and institutes throughout the world, including the Metropolitan Museum of Art, the White House, the Smithsonian Institution, Buckingham Palace and the Vatican.

Traditionally, Boehm's artworks were only marketed through art galleries and fine jewelers. However, in 1970 Boehm entered the direct mail market in association with Lenox China Company. Later, Boehm plates and bisque sculptures were introduced to collectors through direct-mail marketing programs with American Express, The Hamilton Collection and the Audubon Society.

With so many retail outlets at the mercy of takeovers and staff changes, Boehm Studios began opening galleries where the staff can be trained to assist collectors properly. The first gallery was opened in Trump Towers in New York, and it was soon followed by galleries in Costa Mesa, California; Chicago, Illinois; and Houston and Dallas, Texas. In all, ten galleries are planned.

MICHAEL BOYETT STUDIO & FOUNDRY

Michael Boyett
P.O. Box 632012
Nacogdoches, Texas 75963-2012
(409) 560-4477

Figurines

Michael Boyett Studio and Foundry was founded in 1987. After years of having his work produced by other companies, Michael began production of all his new work. The line currently has twenty sculptures and one print. Subjects for his sculptures are Christian, wildlife, military, and western themes. Small limited editions are a special attraction for collectors and are available in both fine pewter and real bronze. His realistic and moving style have captivated collectors for over seventeen years.

THE BRADFORD EXCHANGE

9333 N. Milwaukee Avenue
Niles, Illinois 60648
(708) 966-2770

Plates

As the world's largest trading center for limited edition collector's plates, The Bradford Exchange provides an organized, orderly market where collectors can buy and sell plates.

The company is also one of the world's most successful marketers of collector's plates and the leading publisher of information on the international collector's plate market.

Over the years, the exchange has introduced collectors to many innovative plate series featuring art from around the world, including *Beauties of the Red Mansion*, the first series of collector's plates from the People's Republic of China; *Russian Legends*, the first series of collector's plates from the U.S.S.R.; *The Legend of Tutankhamun*, the first series from Egypt; and *Great Love Stories of Greek Mythology*, the first series from Greece.

Plates marketed by the exchange include those produced under the hallmarks of Dominion China, Imperial Ching-te Chen, D'Arceau-Limoges, Furstenberg, Konigszelt Bayern, Crown Davenport, Royal Grafton, Studio Dante di Volteradici, Byliny Porcelain, Kholui Art Studios, Leningrad Porcelain Factory, v-Palekh Art Studios, Delphi, W.S. George, Edwin M. Knowles, Morgantown Crystal, Rhodes Studios and the Rockwell Society of America.

To help inform collectors about the thousands of different collector's plates on the market, the exchange publishes *The Bradford Book of Collector's Plates*, an annual reference guide to the international hobby of plate collecting. The quarterly "Bradford Exchange Current Quotations" contains the issue, high bid, low ask, close and estimated market prices for the more than 2,000 plates listed on the exchange.

In addition to its headquarters located in the Chicago suburb of Niles, Illinois, Bradford has offices in ten other locations around the world. Plates are available directly from the exchange or from authorized gift and collectible dealers.

The eagle is featured in "Freedom," the first issue in the Soaring Majesty *series.*

BRADLEY COLLECTIBLES

Danny Dimont
1424 North Spring Street
Los Angeles, California 90012
(213) 221-4162
Fax: (213) 221-8272

Figurines, Bells, Dolls, Christmas Ornaments

Over thirty-five years ago, Bradley Collectibles was founded with a total of six dolls. Now, in 1991, Bradley offers collectors more than four hundred unique selections.

This company built its early reputation on its now classic silk face doll. Subsequently, Bradley Collectibles brought forth a series of top-quality, exquisitely-costumed porcelain dolls and clowns, all at affordable price points. In fact, Bradley was the first company to bring out a quality, limited edition porcelain doll for under $50.00.

Decades have passed. During that time, the company has brought collectors innovation after innovation. But, some things never change. In fact, Bradley still employs many of the same factories with which it originally contracted more than thirty-five years ago. All the costumes are still researched, designed and authenticated by Bradley's in-house staff. Bradley still issues only small limited editions of usually 1,500 pieces, and certainly no more than 3,500 pieces in order to protect the collector and the value of the collectible.

Fashions do change, even in collectibles, but one thing that will never change at Bradley is the proud family tradition of excellence, quality and service.

Joanna Hartstein, president, has transformed Bradley into one of the premier collectible companies in the country. Her own personal taste and style are evident in every collectible. She works tirelessly to maintain a high level of quality and service, to carry on the family traditions.

Artist Beth Ilyssa is the head designer of Bradley collectible designs. She carefully researches and designs the costumes for many dolls to ensure their authenticity.

Bradley also sponsors the Bradley Collectible Doll Club which keeps collectors informed about the Bradley Dolls. Also available to members only is a limited edition porcelain doll designed especially for collectors.

A recent addition to the Bradley "family," Danny Dimont, executive vice president and general manager, brings with him years of experience in marketing, sales and licensing of fine collectibles. He has added unique products to the Bradley line, including the new *Kate Greenaway* series. With boundless energy and enthusiasm, he will continue to extend the marketing capabilities of this company, to bring collectors what is new, and what is very special.

BROWN & BIGELOW, INC.

Ida M. Johnson
345 Plato Blvd. E.
St. Paul, Minnesota 55107
(612) 293-7046
Fax: (612) 293-7277

Plates, Figurines

Brown & Bigelow, the world's largest calendar manufacturer and distributor of Advertising Specialties, was founded in 1896 and soon became a respected leader in calendar advertising promotion. Brown & Bigelow calendars are distributed worldwide. Every year new, original and exclusive artwork and photography are purchased or commissioned for Brown & Bigelow calendars. Their archives include calendar art from the early 1900s until today.

Heading the list of human interest artists is Norman Rockwell. The center of the entire Brown & Bigelow calendar line is always his incomparable "Four Seasons" art. Rockwell's continuing popularity is based on his ability to arouse sympathy for his characters. His subjects are average people who display common emotions, set in familiar situations.

America's wildfowl are painted by Brown & Bigelow's franchise artist, David Maass, an expert naturalist/artist and twice the winner of the Federal Duck Stamp competition. Other well-known Brown & Bigelow wildlife artists include Manfred Schatz and Fred Sweney.

The popularity of Cassius Coolidge's poker-playing dogs is ageless. The first series was issued in 1906 and the canines with human characteristics have remained in print and popular to the present time. One of the most famous illustrators to have a long association with Brown & Bigelow was Maxfield Parrish. He was commissioned by the company in 1936 at the age of sixty-six and went on to produce three decades of calendar art. The beautiful Parrish landscapes are among the best calendar art ever created.

Also included in Brown & Bigelow's outstanding collection of artists are the Western artists Charles M. Russell, Frank Hoffman and Tom Ryan and famous etchers like Al Mettel, R.H. Palenske and Lionel Barrymore.

The names mentioned represent just a handful of the widely recognized artists who are enrolled in the Brown & Bigelow roster.

Brown & Bigelow's exclusive artwork also appears on limited edition collectibles such as fine china plates, Christmas ornaments and figurines.

BUCCELLATI, INC.

Mariangela N. Risso
46 East 57th Street
New York, New York 10022
(212) 308-2900
Fax: (212) 750-1323

Christmas Ornaments

When Mario Buccellati founded the House of Buccellati at the turn-of-the-century in Milan, he was backed by the Buccellati tradition of creating superb gold and silver art which began in the 18th century. It was a family enterprise in which craftsmen were trained in the ancient techniques of engraving.

Initially available only in Italy, the demand for Buccellati designs became so strong that Luca Buccellati, the son of the founder, opened the family's first store in the United States in 1952.

Heavily involved in the design of

their silver and fine jewelry, Luca also took over the presidency of the American operation after Mario's death in 1965. Today, the American operation is headed by the founder's namesake and grandson, Mario Buccellati II.

Buccellati remains one of the few companies in the world that produces hundreds of entirely handmade pieces each year using the classical and baroque influences.

Gold, silver, precious and semi-precious stones — as well as other rare and semi-precious materials — are combined with the Buccellati attention to detailing, to create jewelry and collectibles sought by discriminating collectors everywhere.

BYERS' CHOICE, LTD.

P.O. Box 158
Chalfont, Pennsylvania 18914
(215) 822-6700
Fax: (215) 822-3847

Figurines

In 1981 Bob and Joyce Byers incorporated Byers' Choice, Ltd., a company which sprang from a hobby begun many years before. An interest in the history of Christmas prompted Joyce to blend her artistic skills into the creation of caroling figurines reminiscent of the 19th century. With wire, paper and assorted fabrics, she fashioned a Christmas decoration which became the first step in the development of this multimillion dollar handcraft enterprise.

Byers' Choice is a family business. Joyce sculpts the original faces and designs the large variety of costumes. Bob Sr. takes care of the financial and administrative aspects of the business. Bob Jr. oversees production and son Jeff is involved in the marketing of the product.

Approximately fifty craftsmen and professionally-trained artists account for the company's ability to produce this quality handcrafted figurine.

Byers' Choice Caroler figurines have increased in collectibility since 1983 when "Scrooge" initiated the introduction of their Charles Dickens *A Christmas Carol* series. Other seasonal figures have been produced; however, the overwhelming emphasis has been on Christmas.

The Byers have enjoyed watching their company grow. They receive great satisfaction in listening to and serving their ever-expanding loyal collector base.

This group of Victorian Carolers is produced by Byers' Choice, Ltd.

CFC DAUM, INC.

Beverley Gould
41 Madison Avenue 9th Floor
New York, New York 10010
(212) 481-0288
Fax: (212) 685-7327

Figurines, Christmas Ornaments

Since the acquisition of a glassworks in Nancy, France in 1875, five generations of the Daum family have left their unique mark on every artistic period with their sparkling crystal transcending into works of art.

Daum's work with crystal in the Art Nouveau, Art Deco, Free Form and Contemporary styles set the stage in 1968 for the re-introduction of Pate de verre, a technique which is now synonymous with Daum and allows for three dimensional and sculptured pieces to be created-attracting renowned artists and designers like Cesar, Dali, Picasso, McConnico and Phillipe Starck to work with Daum craftsmen.

Each year limited edition sculptures in Pate de verre and new additions to the Daum line of crystal and Pate de verre become available to collectors. The Daum line includes vide-poches, animals, perfume bottles, bowls and vases in clear crystal and Pate de verre and Christmas ornaments.

CARRIAGE HOUSE STUDIO INC.

Jerry Alexander
210 State Street
Salem, Oregon 97301
(503) 363-6004
Fax: (503) 371-0676

Christmas Ornaments

An abstract landscape artist with a master's degree in fine arts from the University of Nebraska, the last thing that Margaret Furlong ever thought she'd be doing was handcrafting porcelain angels.

But, eleven years ago when a friend suggested she make a bisque angel, Ms. Furlong accepted the challenge and the result was so lovely that she continued the enterprise.

Ms. Furlong's angels are handmade bisque, fired without a glaze to retain the detailing. In 1981, Ms. Furlong's angels adorned the White House Christmas tree.

Ms. Furlong and her husband, Jerry Alexander, now own Carriage House Studio Inc. which has twenty-five full-time employees.

Although the angels remain the most popular offering in the line, Carriage House has added hearts, stars, shell stars, wreaths and a line of porcelain pins and earrings.

Involved with every aspect of the line, Ms. Furlong also designs the boxes for her pieces. The boxes are adorned with quotations, hearts and stars.

CAZENOVIA ABROAD, LTD.

Glen Trush
67 Albany Street
Cazenovia, New York 13035
(315) 655-3433
Fax: (315) 655-4249

Christmas Ornaments

Cazenovia Abroad, Ltd. was established as a retail store for fine gifts in 1967. Its founder, Pat Trush, in the second year of operation, found sterling silver teething rings in Portugal, and adapted them to Christmas ornaments. The initial six pieces were completely sold out in the small retail operation during the first year. From the reaction, the decision was made to market the ornaments at wholesale, to other fine gift and jewelry stores. Each year, additional ornaments were added to the collection. The collection now numbers forty, and this year, miniatures have been introduced.

At the request of its customers, Cazenovia Abroad expanded to other sterling and silverplated collectibles. Cazenovia Abroad is now a major force in the silver industry, that offers its customers over 950 items, ranging from the inexpensive silverplated tussy mussy flower holders, (for brides as a keepsake),to a $52,000 sterling silver chess set with amethyst and pearls.

Products are imported from Portugal, Italy, Spain, France, England, Holland, Brazil, and Argentina.

CHARDON

114 West Street
Wilmington, Massachusetts 01887
(508) 658-5114
Fax: (508) 658-0730

Figurines

Chardon, located in Wilmington, Massachusetts, was formed in 1990. This newly formed company is rapidly establishing a name for itself in the collectible market. The company specializes in the marketing of fine, limited edition figurines by renowned artists such as Donald Polland, America's leading western miniature sculptor; Robert Simpich, known for his intriguing character dolls; and Leo Osborne, the winner of several national awards for his superb wood carvings.

These hand finished, quality figurines are made in a large variety of media, including cast porcelain, cold-cast bronze, pewter and cast ivory. Themes include such captivating subjects as Don Polland's *American West* porcelain Indians, *The Simpich Caroler Collection* of endearing porcelain Christmas characters, reproduction of Leo Osborne's award winning, bird carvings and *The Wildlife Series* by Daniel Parker. All of Chardon's studio lines are made of only the highest quality materials and craftsmanship. The figurines can be purchased at affordable prices and promise to enrich the lives of many for generations.

CHRISTIAN BELL PORCELAIN LTD.

P.O. Box 940
Mount Forest, Ontario
Canada N0G 2L0
(519) 323-1742
(800) 265-2688
Fax: (519) 323-1762
P.O. Box 930
Tustin, California 92680
(714) 731-7044
(800) 448-7246

Plates

Christian Bell Porcelain was founded in 1979 by Horst Muller, who had apprenticed as a china painter in Germany and sold china for a number of companies before forming his own firm. Christian Bell's first artist, Canada's renowned Peter Etril Snyder, has completed three plate series based on Mennonite lifestyles - *Preserving A Way Of Life, Chapter I, Chapter II, Chapter III.* Their next artist was American Ted Xaras and his phenomenally popular series of railroad plates, beginning with *The Age of Steam* series and its award-winning leadoff plate "Symphony In Steam," CALED 1981 Plate Of The Year award. Other series which followed were: *American Steam, The Men Of The Rails, Steam On The CPR*, and commemorative issues for the CPR's Last Spike centennial in 1985.

More recent issues include Doug Manning's eight-plate series *Big Cats Of The World*, portraying mysterious and powerful cats in their natural habitats. Also new is Eric Copeland's two-plate set called *Pigs*, based on recollections of his apprenticeship on a pig farm. He has also painted an eight-plate bird series titled *Feathered Friends*. Two other releases are available from Eric Copeland, both based on the classic children's story *The Wind In The Willows;* a series of four collector plates, and a set of twelve signed and numbered limited edition prints.

Christian Bell Porcelain is continually expanding their product line with innovative ideas to reach new collectors.

CHRISTIAN FANTASY COLLECTIBLES

Pris Dailey
125 Woodland Avenue
Rutherford, New Jersey 07070
(201) 933-4836

Plates

Christian Fantasy Collectibles was founded in 1984, and the company's formation actually reads like a fantasy.

Enter Priscilla Dailey, a spiritually moved woman, who suddenly heard the phrase "prayer bear" in her mind while riding in her car and regarded this as a message from God.

Three weeks later, Ms. Dailey awoke at 3 A.M. with a poem in her mind. With the help of her husband Bob, the poem was polished, and the search began in earnest for just the right illustrator.

Where else would you locate the perfect illustrator for the poem but from a recommendation from a direct sales person selling encyclopedias! Tim Hildebrandt was that referral — a man who has illustrated fantasy for over twenty years, including a commission from Twentieth Century Fox to do the original *Star Wars* movie poster, illustrating JRR Tolkien calendars, as well as "Dungeons and Dragons" calendars and three calendars for Landmark.

With Hildebrandt's superb illustrations, Priscilla and Bob Dailey created *The Legend of the Prayer Bear* plate series including the original heartwarming lyrical poem as part of the backstamp. It is the story of Christ's first night on Earth and the tender love of a poor orphaned bear cub. Hence, a Christian Fantasy; a three plate series.

Christian Fantasy Collectibles has also introduced the Rita and Tim Hildebrandt *Fantasy Cookbook* plate series, featuring four recipes selected by Rita from her natural food cookbook and backstamped on each plate. Also available is *The Realms of Wonder I* and *The Realms of Wonder II* series by artist Hildebrandt with poetry on the backstamp written by Rita. Each is a four-plate series and embodies the new Matrix Collectible System.

THE COLLECTABLES, INC.

John Parkins
Rt.4 Box 503
Rolla, Missouri 65401
(314) 364-7849
(800) 874-7120
Fax: (314) 364-2448

Dolls, Christmas Ornaments

The Collectables, Inc. was established in 1975 when Phyllis Parkins began making a small porcelain baby doll which she sold at Silver Dollar City craft shows. Each year, more dolls were added, and in 1981 the first original limited edition dolls were made. Now the original dolls are the dominant part of The Collectables line. Each year Phyllis Parkins sculpts and designs eight to ten new dolls; about thirty dolls are included in this year's collection along with tree top angels and doll head ornaments. The Collectables are sold in all fifty states as well as several foreign countries. Last year Phyllis' Collector's Club was formed and the first exclusive Collector's Club doll was introduced. The Collectables dolls have received several major awards including the *Doll Reader* DOTY two times and *Dolls* magazine Award of Excellence three times.

Phyllis Parkins created "Yvette" for The Collectables.

THE CONSTANCE COLLECTION

P.O. Box 250
Route 1 Box 538
Midland, Virginia 22728
(703) 788-4500

Figurines

Blessed with a flair for art, Constance Angela Guerra was encouraged by friends to sell her bread dough figurines at craft shows. When her figurines sold out during the first three hours of a two-day show, Guerra — with help from her three sisters — became a regular at local and county fairs and craft shows.

While attending college and working, Guerra continued producing her bread dough figurines and ornaments. Her passion for authenticity and creativity gradually became her hallmark. In addition to her animal figures, Guerra also sculpted an array of *Santas* and began her *Golden American Collection*.

Guerra eventually abandoned her mixture of flour, salt and water for a newer medium containing crushed pecan shells and resins. She creates all her original models in clay, which are then sent to one of three casting factories where the finely detailed figures are produced.

Guerra formed The Constance Collection five years ago. The company's only designer-sculptor, Constance is also president of the company. But, it also is a family business. Her father, Serf, handles the marketing and her mother, Amber, manages the office.

Guerra designs and produces about seventy-five new figurines each year. Some of her most popular collections are the *Golden Americans, State Santas* (fifty Santas representing all fifty states in limited editions), *Bear Den, Briar Patch, Cattle* and *Pig Pack Collections*.

One of the newest and most successful series is the *Golden American Collection* which features historical black heroines and heroes such as Harriet Tubman and Frederick Douglas. Another new series heralds *Black Professionals*. To make these pieces as authentic as possible, Guerra consults with a member of the Howard University faculty in addition to doing a great deal of research at the Library of Congress.

"Teddy Claus" is the first issue in the annual Santa Series *from The Constance Collection.*

COROLLE

A Division of Mattel
333 Continental Boulevard
El Segundo, California 90245
213-524-2496
Fax (213) 524-4214

Dolls

Born in Paris, France, Catherine Refabert came from a family well known for their fine arts. Her grandfather was a famous miniature painter, while her mother specialized in plastic and graphic arts and her father was an industrial designer.

Refabert grew up in a home where beauty was appreciated and carefully nurtured. As a student, Catherine studied mathematics and design. In 1960, she married Jacques Refabert and became a doll designer for Clodrey, the family's doll firm.

In 1979, Catherine and Jacques established their own company, Corolle, to design and produce their own line of dolls which ranges from dolls designed to withstand the rigors of being loved by children to a line of limited edition collector dolls. Some of Refabert's most popular limited edition dolls are "La Danseuse," "Melisande," "Marie Lavande," "Ludivine," "Marie Claudine," "Colombe" and "Princesse Maya."

CROSS GALLERY, INC.

Mary Schmidt
P.O. Box 4181
Jackson, Wyoming 83001
(307) 733-2200
Fax: (307) 733-1414

Plates, Figurines, Dolls, Christmas Ornaments, Graphics

Cross Gallery, Inc., located in Jackson Hole, Wyoming, publishes and distributes limited editions, offset reproductions and handpulled originals. Cross Gallery is the exclusive limited publisher of Penni Anne Cross. They offer her limited edition lithographs, serigraphs, stone lithographs, etchings, plates and ornaments. They also handle Ms. Cross' original sketches, drawings and paintings.

Penni Anne Cross is an honorary adopted member of the Crow nation in Montana, with the Indian name, Alawa-sta-we-ches, "Travels the Good Road." She began painting years ago after signing up for a local art class and ended up teaching it for six years! She learned anatomy by reading medical books and then drawing the bones in her own hand. A two hour visit to an ophthalmologist taught her about the structure of the eyes and how they reveal emotion. "I made him explain to me why eyes do what they do. Where does the light come from? What happens to eyes when a person is getting ready to cry, or when he's happy? I'm fascinated with eyes," she said. "I can look at people's faces and almost tell you what they've experienced, if they've gone through traumas," Penni says. "But I don't know why I can do it."

For her first exhibition, Cross copied old Indian portraits done by other artists. Now she concentrates on her own people, capturing them first in photographs used as models for her work on canvas.

A versatile artist, Cross has enjoyed a collectible career encompassing plates, figurines, original graphics, and most extensively, limited edition prints. She has a waiting list of up to three years for originals. Working in both oil and pastel mediums, Cross found her niche in the art world in 1973 while working with subjects close to home - Native American people. Although prominent investors and museums are among her acquisitors, Cross is most grateful that collectors purchase her works of art for the appeal of the image and subject matter. "I won't do something I don't know. And if I don't know, I'll find out," says Cross, referring to her passion for accuracy. This quest may involve years of research in the field for a single image, culminating in art which is both beautiful and meaningful.

Before beginning each picture, Cross prays to have people see the Creator first in her work, and then the creation. "My inspiration is Jesus Christ," she says. "I asked God a long time ago to live inside of me, and if my painting is a way of making people happy, then God is working through my art." Each Penni Cross creation is a spiritual ticket into someone's life. "An artist's downfall comes when they let their gift control them instead of controlling their gift," she says.

If art is an expression of an artist's soul, then it is easy to see why Cross's art is characterized by confidence, serenity and love. Her life has not been without it's own upheavals, but through them all, a strong Christian faith bolstered by the Indian philosophy taught by her friends has enriched both her understanding and portrayal of life.

Ms. Cross received the NALED "Special Recognition" award in July 1991 at the South Bend Collectibles Exposition for her contribution to the collectibles field.

CROWN PARIAN, LTD.

James L. Carter
7215 Crider Avenue
Pico Rivera, California 90660
(213) 942-7655
Fax: (213) 942-0553

Plates, Christmas Ornaments

Crown Parian, Ltd. was founded in 1979 as a manufacturer and distributor of specialty collector plates and ornaments in ceramic glass (otherwise known as "Ceragraph"). They also design and produce products on a contract basis.

THE CRYSTAL WORLD

3 Caesar Place
Moonachie, New Jersey 07074
(201) 896-0336
(800) 445-4251
Fax: (201) 896-0795

Figurines

Founded in 1984, The Crystal World has become one of the most respected names in the world for production of 32% lead crystal collectibles. With their unique designs, they have become the center of innovation - from their trend setting *Original Rainbow Castle* Collection to the award winning "Curious Cat." Drawing from the talents of an international staff of accomplished designers, their collectibles have inspired millions. In 1986, The Crystal World took the entire collectible industry by surprise with the introduction of *The Rainbow Castle. The Rainbow Castle* launched an entire new generation of rainbow crystal collectibles.

Master Designer Ryuji Nakai, Nicolo Mulargia, Tom Suzuki and Gary Veith are The Crystal World's principal crystal artists. Each designer invests his sincere heart into each creation, by breathing life into each of their designs. Their underlying motivation is to bring true joy to the collector.

One of the areas in which The Crystal World excells is in the creation of architectural masterpieces. The Empire State Building, The Eiffel Tower, The Taj Majal, and The US Capitol Building are just a few of these limited edition wonders. To commemorate the 100th anniversary of the founding of Ellis Island, The Crystal World has recently introduced "Ellis Island," in a limited edition of 1,000. Each piece comes with a signed certificate of authenticity by the artist.

Headquartered in New Jersey, The Crystal World offers one of the largest varieties of crystal figurines available anywhere. From the whimsical teddy bear and animal series to the sophisticated limited edition pieces, The Crystal World will be appreciated for years to come.

CYBIS

65 Norman Avenue
Trenton, New Jersey 08618
(609) 392-6074

Figurines, Christmas Ornaments

Cybis, America's oldest existing porcelain Art Studio, has been dubbed "An American Treasure" by collectors throughout the world. The Cybis response, with a sense of pride of accomplishment, has created a renewed excitement in the collector world with the introduction of the Cybis *Hall of Fame* Collection.

This collection of figures is being released to honor the 100th birth date of Boleslaw Cybis, internationally acclaimed artist and founder of the renowned Cybis Studio. The collection, which will continue through the 1990s, features reproductions of selected Cybis sculptures which were produced over the last half century. Selection is based on aesthetic value, collector demand and artistic achievement.

Although subjects will be changed in size and decoration, they will be produced in the fine museum quality that is synonymous with Cybis.

Initial introductions to the *Cybis Hall of Fame* include "Holy Child of Prague," "The Pope," "American Bald Eagle," "Madonna with Bird," "Liberty II," "Little Miss Liberty II" and "Persephone."

One of the most outstanding Cybis works of art, which is part of the *Commemorative* Collection, is "Knight In Shining Armor" which depicts a handsome knight rescuing a beautiful damsel from a dragon. This magnificent sculpture, which is 21" high and 18½" wide, is priced at $25,000 retail.

The "Children to Cherish" Collection has been further enhanced by *The Games Children Play* series. This grouping includes a "Baseball," a "Football" and a "Soccer" player, a "Young Cowboy," "Gymnast" and "Girl with Lamb." A new "Bride," a new "Cinderella" and a lovely "Girl Gathering Flowers with Chipmunk" are also new to this collection.

Carrousel collectors will look in awe at the piece de resistance of the Cybis *Carrousel* Collection, "Golden Thunder," which is a horse with the previous thirteen carrousel sculptures' heads in bas relief on the 24 karat gold armor saddle blanket.

Joseph W. Chorlton is Chairman and Chief Executive Officer of Cybis.

DANFORTH PEWTERERS

Peggy Zilinsky
P.O. Box 828
52 Seymour Street
Middlebury, Vermont 05753
(802) 388-8666
Fax: (802) 388-0099

Christmas Ornaments

Fred and Judi Danforth founded Danforth Pewterers in Vermont in 1975. Judi's training as a silversmith at R.I.T.'s School for American Craftsmen inspired her interest in pewtersmithing. Fred is a direct descendant of Thomas Danforth and his family, who were 18th century Connecticut pewtersmiths.

Fred and Judi's career began with an apprenticeship in New Brunswick, Canada. Living in Vermont with their two daughters, they maintain a growing business creating handcrafted pewter hollowware and cast pewter ornaments, buttons, and jewelry.

Judi specializes in Christmas ornaments, and each year she designs a new ornament to commemorate that year. Some of her recent designs include the 1990 "Peace Dove," the 1989 "Reindeer," and the 1988 "Father Christmas." These future heirlooms are exquisitely crafted of fine lead-free pewter, and each comes with its own flannel pouch and gift box.

In 1989, the Walt Disney Company, recognizing the lovely "old world quality" of Judi's designs, chose Danforth Pewterers to offer a charming collection of classic Winnie-the-Pooh pins, buttons, earrings, and ornaments. Danforth will also be making a line of handcrafted pewter pieces to celebrate the nationwide Christopher Columbus quincentenary events.

For antique pewter collectors, a piece of today's Danforth Pewter hollowware will surely add interest to any collection. Each piece is original in design, is signed and dated, and bears the lion touchmark based upon one that was used by Fred's ancestors in Colonial America.

ANDREW D. DARVAS, INC.

2165 Dwight Way
Berkeley, California 94704
(415) 843-7838
Fax: (415) 843-1815

Figurines

The firm of Andrew D. Darvas Incorporated has been a major importer of Bossons Character Wall Masks since 1963 and plays an integral part in their distribution and promotional efforts in the U.S. Darvas Company is proud of their efforts to bring quality, affordable collectibles to the American market, and in January 1991 created a limited edition poster celebrating their long association with the Bossons Factory.

The W.H. Bossons Company grew out of a retiree's hobby. After a managerial career in the English ceramic-tile industry, W.H. Bossons retired to Congleton, an endearing English town eight miles north of Stoke-on-Trent. There he began making lead soldiers and plaster Christmas figures. Possessing a wide range of technical skills he improved the production of plaster and the complementary mold making.

Working at home with only makeshift equipment, Bossons' small business flourished. In 1946, his son Ray, after serving six years in World War II as an Officer of the 79th Field Regiment, joined him in the business.

Ray, like his father, had been trained in pottery-making at the Burslem School of Art in Stoke-on-Trent. He also completed the Federation of Master Printers course at Manchester University and separately qualified as a Diploma Member of the Advertising Association of London.

Together with his father, Ray Bossons moved the existing operations to Brook Mills, a collection of brick buildings in Congleton made vacant by the war. W.H. Bossons died in 1951, but his son continued to operate the business.

In 1958, Ray Bossons, an extremely talented artist in his own right, designed the first of the internationally recognized "Character Wall Masks," which went into production in 1959. This first design is the now much sought after "Snake Charmer."

Each "character" is designed and created with extraordinary regard to anatomical detail, artistic excellence and historical accuracy.

The entire production process, from the initial sketching and sculpting, through the plaster mixing and pouring, to the skilled painting and even the final packing is all done by hand! There are no machines at W.H. Bossons Ltd.

A perfectionist, Ray Bossons has purposefully limited the size of his company to better allow close supervision of every step in the production process. In this way he can ensure the superior quality of Bossons Artware.

DEPARTMENT 56 INCORPORATED

P.O. Box 5562
Hopkins, Minnesota 55343
(800) 548-8696
Fax: (612) 943-4500

Figurines

"Department 56, Inc." may seem a curious name for a firm that designs and manufactures nostalgic, collectible villages. How the name "Department 56" originated is a rather unusual story.

Before Department 56, Inc. became an independent corporation, it was part of a large parent company that used a numbering system to identify each of its departments. While Department 21 was administation and Department 54 was the gift warehouse, the name assigned to wholesale gift imports was "Department 56."

Department 56, Inc. originally began by importing fine Italian basketry. However a new product line introduced in 1977, called *The Original Snow Village*©, set the groundwork for the collectible products we know today.

1977 sales of these six original building pieces were encouraging, so Department 56, Inc. decided to develop more *Snow Village* pieces to add to their 1978 line. By 1979, Department 56, Inc. made an important operational decision: in order to keep *The Original Snow Village* at a reasonable size, buildings would have to be retired from production each year to make room for new designs.

The Department 56, Inc. Master Sculptors form the clay models for each building with an emphasis on fine detail. From the original concept to drawings, sculpting, casting, firing, handpainting and packaging, craftsmanship and quality is evident. Each piece is stamped in the bottom with its designated series name, title, year of introduction, and Department 56, Inc. logo, all assurances of authenticity.

Since its beginning in 1977, over 136 lighted designs have been produced. In 1991 *The Original Snow Village Collection* consisted of thirty lighted models, over thirty-nine accessory pieces, frosted trees, street lamps, and even flashing stop and go lights.

In 1990 a totally new book for collectors, The *Original Snow Village Collectors' Album* was published. The album includes a full history of the series, including detailed information on design, manufacturing and packaging. In addition, there are full-color photographs of every lit piece and accessory, as well as fold-out spreads of entire village scenes grouped according to yearly collections. It has become an important history for collectors of *The Original Snow Village*.

The first introduction of *The Heritage Village Collection*™ was *The Dickens' Village Collection*©, introduced in 1984. Extensive research, charming details and the fine hand-painting of the seven original porcelain shops and "Village Church" established them as a favorite among collectors.

The Heritage Village Collection sign by Department 56.

Other series followed with the introduction of *The New England Village Collection*, *The Alpine Village Collection*, *The Christmas in the City Collection*, *The Little Town of Bethlehem Collection* in 1987, and in 1991, the introduction of *The North Pole Collection*. Also available in 1989 was a collectors book entitled *The Heritage Village Collection*, which provided collectors with an interesting narrative and photographs of this complete collectible series.

As with *The Original Snow Village*, each piece of *The Heritage Village Collection* is bottom stamped and packed in an individual styrofoam storage carton with illustrated sleeve. Each year, Department 56, Inc. continues to unveil intriguing new lighted pieces and accessories for their collectors.

DOLLS BY JERRI

651 Anderson Street
Charlotte, North Carolina 28205
(704) 333-3211
Fax: (704) 333-7706

Dolls

One of the oldest commercial porcelain doll companies in the United States today, Dolls by Jerri is a name widely recognized as a guarantee of excellence in collectible dolls, plates and figurines.

Beginning in 1976 as a cottage industry producing limited editions of Jerri's imaginative all-porcelain dolls, the company has continued to expand and increase in stature through a combination of Jerri's prolific creative talents and husband Jim McCloud's experienced marketing and management skills.

Jerri's sculpting artistry is clearly defined in the exquisitely detailed features of her elegant high fashion dolls and her real-to-life toddlers and babies. Her dolls are painted by hand with the "softest" of colorations that have become distinctive hallmarks of a Jerri doll. Costuming is authentic and meticulously detailed, using the finest of fabrics and trims.

Jointed full bodied bisque porcelain limited edition dolls are a speciality of Dolls by Jerri. However, in 1990, the company successfully introduced several groups of her delightfully "huggable" vinyl dolls. Recognizing the unique merits of both porcelain and vinyl, the company adheres to the strict policy of never making vinyl dolls from their porcelains, nor porcelain dolls from their vinyls. Dolls by Jerri does not sell its molds and there are no seconds or irregulars. Dolls blemished during production are destroyed.

Over the years, dolls from this fine company have received many awards including the coveted DOTY from Doll Reader Magazine and the Award of Excellence from *Dolls* Magazine. It is little wonder that among discriminating collectors, a Dolls by Jerri is a highly prized possession.

DRAM TREE

(A Division of CUI, Inc.)
1502 North 23rd Street
Wilmington, North Carolina 28405
(919) 251-1110
Fax: (919) 251-3587

Plates, Figurines, Bells, Steins

Over six decades ago, Percy K. Hexter purchased a small manufacturing business in New Jersey. The concept was to create and manufacture America's finest quality porcelain products.

Although the enterprise has changed its name since the early days, the same tradition of excellence in quality, service, and guaranteed customer satisfaction remains the driving force of the company.

Today, Peter K Hexter, Jr. grandson of the founder, is CUI's President. He is quick to point out that CUI's success has been built on a total commitment from management and employees. Collectively they share a common desire to be the best in the world.

Licensing during the '80s blossomed to become a multi-billion dollar business. Breweries, as well as professional sports leagues, capitalized on the popularity of their brands and teams to lead the way in licensed merchandise marketing.

CUI's eye for design and unique approach to maximizing full market potential with its pretigious licenses have earned several "Licensee of the Year" awards. Moreover, serious collectors have recognized the beauty and value of CUI products, elevating its position in the collectibles marketplace to that of a leader and trendsetter.

The 1990s have been predicted to be the "Green" decade, the dawning of an awareness to global conservation heretofore never fully realized. Aligning themselves with such dedicated organizations as "Ducks Unlimited," "The Ruffed Grouse Society," "Whitetails Unlimited," "Bass Research Foundation," to name a few, reflects a corporate objective to directly contribute back to the important effort at hand.

Commissioned fish and wildlife art from the most highly regarded artists embrace their products. Wildlife art, one of the fastest growing art categories in America, rises to new levels in CUI's exciting collectibles medium. The combination of producing truly unique and distinctive products, while assisting in the funding of important habitat restoration and conservation projects, is one of their most meaningful achievements.

In years to come, CUI's focus will not change. They will continue to set trends in the market through excellence in products and unconditionally guaranteed customer satisfaction.

DUNCAN ROYALE

1141 South Acacia Avenue
Fullerton, California 92631
(714) 879-1360
Fax: (714) 879-4611

Figurines, Plates

Duncan Royale was founded more than thirty years ago by its president Max E. Duncan. The company's early years were devoted to importing a variety of figurines and porcelain items. During the last decade, the company has turned to designing and creating limited edition, copyrighted collectibles.

In 1983 Duncan Royale introduced the first twelve cold-cast porcelain figurines in the *History of Santa Claus*. The second group of Christmas personalities, including some women, was added in 1986, and the final twelve figurines completed the series in 1990. The completed *History of Santa Claus* contains thirty-six figurines in limited editions of 10,000 and portrays Santas from 2000 B.C. through the 20th century. Companion pieces are available in miniature pewter painted sculptures, limited edition plates, mini-plates and intricate Dolfi woodcarvings. Once a piece is retired, it is brought out in the eighteen-inch size.

Following the success of the *History of Santa Claus* collection, Duncan Royale introduced in June 1987, a *History of Classic Entertainers*, tracing the evolution of entertainers from the Greek-Roman times through the 20th century. This twenty-four piece collection of limited edition cold-cast porcelain figurines has proven to be a tremendous success.

In 1988 Duncan Royale introduced *The Greatest Gift...Love*, a series of three beautifully sculpted figurines depicting "The Annunciation," "Nativity" and "Passion" of Christ. In contrast to previous Duncan Royale figurines, this collection emphasizes body form rather than clothing, and is produced in cold cast marble.

Duncan Royale also entered into the world of fantasy in 1988. A magical limited edition collection of fourteen *Woodland Fairies* was created to the delight of collectors. Each figurine has its own mini-book that tells the story behind each character.

In keeping with the motto, "the stories never end...," Duncan Royale introduced two new series in 1990. The *Calendar Secrets* are sophisticated sculptures representing the legend, curiosities, and facts behind our calendar months. Each figurine depicts a different month and tells the story. This collection is accompanied by its own hardcover book.

The 1990s also brought in *Ebony*. This limited edition collection of Black figurines has been warmly received by collectors nation wide. The primary focus of this ongoing series is a musical theme, with the first introductions being "Banjo Man," "Harmonica Man" and "Fiddler Man."

Duncan Royale presents "March," featuring this Roman gladiator, from the Calendar Secrets *collection.*

The Early Americans are another new introduction for the 1990s. These charming characters depict life when times were simpler. Among your favorites you will find "The Lawyer," "The Homemaker," "The Nurse" and "The Doctor.

Christmas Images focus on that special time of year as seen through the eyes of children. These limited editions convey the warmth that we feel during this special time.

Duncan Royale will continue to introduce collections that relate a story. They allow the collector the chance to enjoy beautiful art as well as experience history and legend that can be shared with others.

DYNASTY DOLL COLLECTION

Gary R. Darwin V.P. Sales
P.O. Box 99
Port Reading, New Jersey 07064
(908) 636-6160
Fax: (908) 636-6215

Dolls

The Dynasty Doll Division of Cardinal Inc. was started in 1980, in response to the demand for high-quality porcelain collector dolls at affordable prices. The line, which began with a small selection, has grown to over 250 styles, including limited editions, annual dolls, reproductions and original pieces in a broad variety of costumes.

In 1987, Dynasty received its first "Dolls Award of Excellence" from *Dolls* Magazine for "Gayle." In 1989, two dolls were nominated for awards — "Amber," the 1989 Dynasty annual doll, and "Cayala." A third award was given to the firm for the 1990 annual doll "Marcella," in the category of porcelain, under $150.

Cardinal Inc., the parent company, was founded in 1946 by its current president, Sidney Darwin. Originally a ceramics manufacturer, Cardinal ceased domestic production in 1960. Its entire line is imported, primarily from the far East.

EBELING & REUSS

477 N. Lewis Road
Royersford, Pennsylvania 19468

Plates, Figurines, Bells, Christmas Ornaments

Ebeling & Reuss Co., founded in 1886, is a major importer of fine giftware and collectibles.

Ronald D. Rapelje was named President and Chief Executive Officer of Ebeling & Reuss in 1990.

Among the many collectible lines that Ebeling & Reuss offers are an assortment of nutcrackers, steins, and figurines from Europe.

EFFANBEE DOLL COMPANY

200 Fifth Avenue
New York, New York 10010

Dolls

Effanbee is one of the oldest and most respected American doll makers. The company was organized in 1910 and was known as Kleischaker and Baum, jobbers and retailers of toys. In 1913, Effanbee was formed and began producing rag dolls and dolls of a crude, hard composition. When the First World War cut off the doll supply from Europe, Effanbee accelerated production to fill the need.

Their first major success was "Patsy," introduced in 1928 and long regarded as a classic. It was followed in 1934 by the "DyDee" doll — the first doll to drink and wet. When "DyDee" celebrated her 50th birthday in 1984, Effanbee produced a Commemorative Edition "DyDee" doll for one year only.

In 1976, Effanbee began to develop its first collectible series. Those include the *International* series, *Grande Dames Collection* and the *Storybook Collection*. The current limited edition doll series from Effanbee include *The President's Collection*, *The Eugenia Dukas Collection*, *Thank Heaven for Little Girls Collection*, and the *Namesake Collection*.

THE EHLERS COMPANY, INCORPORATED

2675 Skypark Drive #303
Torrance, California 90505

Dolls

The Ehlers Company was founded in 1962 to import gift items from West Germany for sale at such locations as Disneyland and the German Pavillion in Epcot Center, Florida.

In the early 1980s, Ehlers began handling limited edition and one-of-a-kind dolls. Some of their current artists are: Gaby Rademann, Ute Kase Lepp, Christine Heath, Hilary Pugh, Pauline Middleton, Sue Hammerschmidt, Cynthia Dutra, Beverly Stoehr, Shirley Baran, Sabrina Haas and Linda Mason. Known for their high quality, these dolls range in price from $500 to $6,000.

ELLENBROOKE DOLLS, INCORPORATED

1450 Marcy Loop
Grants Pass, Oregon 97527

Dolls

In 1976, Connie Walser-Derek started Connie's Dolls and Company, a retail and mail-order business that caters to aspiring doll makers and doll collectors. But Derek's real fame within the doll industry rests on her original dolls produced in mediums as diverse as porcelain, wax and even vinyl.

Derek got started reproducing and repairing antique dolls, but by 1985 her dolls had earned her a reputation as a maker of museum-quality dolls. Inspired by Maud Humphrey's paintings of turn-of-the-century children, Derek created the *Seasons of Playtime* doll series and recently signed a contract to do a series of porcelain dolls for The Hamilton Collection.

To meet the demand for a more affordable line, Derek formed Ellenbrooke Dolls, Inc., which produces dolls in a number of different editions, including a limited production edition, the exclusive signature edition in porcelain or wax and limited artist's proofs. Derek's "Sweet Cherub" doll was nominated for the 1990 *Doll Reader* "Collectible Porcelain Doll of the Year."

ENESCO CORPORATION

One Enesco Plaza
Elk Grove Village, Illinois 60007
(800) 323-0636
Fax: (708) 640-6151

Figurines, Plates, Bells, Dolls, Christmas Ornaments

Founded in 1959, Enesco Corporation has built its reputation as a leader in the gift and collectibles industry. Today, Enesco is the anchor company of Enesco Worldwide Giftware Group, an umbrella that includes Hamilton Gifts Ltd., Sports Impressions, Tomorrow-Today Corporation, Via Vermont, Ltd. — all U.S. companies — as well as subsidiary companies in Canada, the United Kingdom, Germany, Australia and Hong Kong. Enesco Worldwide Giftware Group is a wholly-owned division of Stanhome Inc., Westfield, Massachusetts, a New York Stock Exchange-listed business.

Industry leadership for Enesco was firmly established in 1978 with the introduction of the *Enesco Precious Moments*© Collection. Based on the work of inspirational artist Sam Butcher, the initial twenty-one teardrop-eyed porcelain bisque figurines with their messages of love, caring and sharing captured the imagination, affection and loyalty of collectors.

The overwhelming popularity of the *Precious Moments* Collection led to formation of the Enesco Precious Moments Collectors' Club℠ in 1981. Today, the club has more than a half-million members, making it the largest collectors club of its kind. In 1985, the Enesco Precious Moments Birthday Club was established to encourage collecting for and by children.

Today, there are several hundred figurines, plates, bells, thimbles and ornaments in the collection, and collector interest keeps the collection the number one collectible in the United States. The *Precious Moments* Collection has earned many awards over the years, including being named Collectible of the Year in 1985 by the National Association of Limited Edition Dealers.

The number two collectible at Enesco is the *Memories of Yesterday* Collection©, based on the illustrations of English artist Mabel Lucie Attwell. Since its introduction in 1988, the *Memories of Yesterday* Collection of nostalgic little children reminiscent of the 1920s and 1930s has developed a strong collector following, making it one of the top ten collections in the United States.

In 1990, Enesco announced that the Enesco Memories of Yesterday Collectors' Society℠ would begin its Charter Year in 1991. The Charter Year Symbol of Membership figurine is "We Belong Together." Enesco also announced the first two retirements in the collection in 1990 and three more figurines were retired in 1991.

A fourth collectors' club sponsored

"Wishful Thinking" is a charming addition to the Memories of Yesterday *collection.*

by Enesco premiered in 1991: the Enesco Musical Society, in support of the Enesco *Small World of Music*™ action musicals. For more than a decade, Enesco has pioneered intricate action musicals, utilizing new technology and familiar subjects to create unique musical masterpieces.

The Enesco *Treasury of Christmas Ornaments*® has grown as rapidly as ornament collecting itself. This unusual collection of highly detailed classic and whimsical Christmas ornaments has a very strong collector base around the world.

Other noted collectibles from Enesco include *Lucy & Me*® porcelain bisque teddy bears by Lucy Rigg; *Kinka*® Collection of satin-finish porcelain figurines by Ohio artist Kinka; *National Audubon Society*™ and *World Wildlife Fund* collections of authentic wildlife subjects; *Brambly Hedge*™ by artist Jill Barklem; *Paddington*™ *Bear* based on Michael Bond's literary classics for children; *GARFIELD* by Jim Davis; *Treasured Memories*® limited edition figurines; limited edition musicals and figurines by Enesco artists Karen Hahn and G.G. Santiago; and miniature collections by Merri Roderick.

Enesco has a strong sense of social responsibility, and in 1987, the company became a National Corporate Sponsor of the National Easter Seal Society. In its first five campaigns, the company raised over $6.5 million for programs and services to disabled children and adults.

International headquarters for Enesco and a 33,000-square foot Plaza Showroom are located in Elk Grove Village, northwest of Chicago. The company also operates eleven permanent showrooms in major U.S. cities.

FENTON ART GLASS COMPANY

Shelly Fenton-Ash
700 Elizabeth Street
Williamstown, West Virginia 26187
(304) 375-6122
Fax: (304) 375-6459

Plates, Figurines, Bells

The Fenton Art Glass Company was founded in 1905 by Frank L. Fenton and his two brothers, John and Charles. The company started first as a decorating company in Martins Ferry, Ohio; but by January of 1907, it began to manufacture its own glass at a new factory in Williamstown, West Virginia. For over eighty-five years, Fenton has made a varied line of colored glass, tableware and giftware. In the early years of the company, it was best known for having originated iridescent glass which is now called Carnival glass. In its second twenty-five years, opalescent glass and milk glass were the best known products. In more recent years, Fenton has recreated Burmese glass, Cranberry and overlay glass and a fine line of hand-decorated, opaque glasses.

The second and third generations of the Fenton family now lead the company, with Wilmer C. Fenton as Chairman of the Board, George W. Fenton as President, Thomas K. Fenton as Vice President of Manufacturing and Don A. Fenton as Vice President of Sales.

In 1990, Fenton introduced the first edition of the *Christmas At Home* series of four entitled, "Sleigh Ride." Designed by Frances Burton, this series includes an 8" plate, 6½" bell, fairy light, clock and lamp. The bell, plate and fairy light are limited to 3,500 pieces, the clock to 1,500 and the lamp to 1,000. The 1991 second edition is entitled "Christmas Eve."

Each year (beginning in 1988) Fenton introduces one or two antique offerings. The basis of these offerings is twofold. First, Fenton brings to collectors antique reproductions from moulds made by their own firm, as well as other well known glass companies. Most of these pieces have a history that will be recognized by knowledgeable glass collectors. Secondly, Fenton brings these collectibles to collectors in exotic colors and treatments to enhance their collectibility. The items in each collection are limited to a one-year production. The 1991 offering is Stiegel Blue Opalescent which was first made in 1908. The items are made from a combination of moulds from the late Westmoreland and McKee glass companies as well as Fenton. Past offerings have been Pink Opalescent and Topaz Opalescent in 1988, Persian Blue Opalescent in 1989 and Sapphire Blue Opalescent in 1990.

Another annual offering from Fenton is the *Connoisseur Collection* which involves very rare glass treatments in limits between 500 and 5,000 pieces. The 1989 offering was Rosalene Glass, and the 1990 85th Anniversary Offering was exotic Burmese. The 1991 offering is Favrile glass made with silver.

There are two Fenton collectors' clubs that are not sponsored by the manufacturer. For more information, contact The Fenton Art Glass Collectors of America, P.O. Box 384, Williamstown, WV 26187 or National Fenton Glass Society, P.O. Box 4008, Marietta, OH 45750.

FLAMBRO IMPORTS INCORPORATED

1260 Collier Road N.W.
Atlanta, Georgia 30318
(404) 352-1381
Fax (404) 352-2150

Bells, Christmas Ornaments, Figurines, Plates

When Louis and Stanley Flamm started Flambro Imports Incorporated in 1965, they had no idea how successful the company would become. Located in Atlanta, Georgia, Flambro is recognized for its lines of collectible clowns and circus-related giftware. Flambro also handles a number of porcelain collectibles which appeal to lovers of Americana and nostalgia.

In 1972, Allan Flamm joined his father, Louis, in the business. Stanley passed away in 1975, and in 1982 Allan succeeded his father as president of the company. An experienced importer, Flamm continued to provide retailers with quality collectible lines and seasonal decorations for Easter, Halloween and Christmas.

In 1980, the Flamms signed their first licensing agreement for figurines depicting Emmett Kelly, Jr., America's best known clown. The first Emmett Kelly, Jr. figurines were introduced the following year. The line was greeted with enthusiasm by collectors who appreciated the high quality of the porcelain craftmanship and the careful attention to details.

Over the past decade, the values of the Emmett Kelly, Jr. figurines and plates have increased dramatically on the secondary market. Although they are open editions, the miniature Emmett Kelly, Jr. figurines have also become extremely popular with collectors.

An exciting edition to the Flambro line is the *Pleasantville 1893* series, featuring Small Town America, created by Joan Berg Victor. Introduced in 1990, *Pleasantville 1893* is a series of handcrafted bisque porcelain houses and buildings depicting life at the turn-of-the-century. Accessories, including prominent town people, round out this lovely collection. Each building comes with its own heartwarming story, relating a history about the structures and its residents or owners and employees. Collectors can also enjoy a richly illustrated and detailed account of this town in a recently released hard-cover storybook entitled *Pleasantville 1893; A Charming Piece of Americana That Never Existed.*

Pleasantville 1893 *"Swirl Snow Globes" are available in four styles: "Teddy Bear," "The Boy and Girl on Rocking Horse," "Santa" and "The Christmas Tree."*

THE FRANKLIN MINT

Jack Wilkie
Franklin Center, Pennsylvania 19091
(215) 459-7494
Fax: (215) 459-6880

Plates, Figurines, Bells, Graphics, Dolls, Christmas Ornaments

The Franklin Mint is a leading creator of fine, heirloom-quality collectibles and objets d'art. The company offers originally designed, luxury products, including high-fashion jewelry; upscale home decor and table accessories (from fine porcelain sculpture to exquisite crystal); collector plates; precision-crafted die-cast automobile replicas and porcelain collector dolls; medallics and philatelics; historic weapons replicas; recreations of famous works housed in the world's most prestigious museums, and classic collector books in fine bindings. The company also publishes *ALMANAC* the world's largest collectors' magazine, with an active circulation of more than one million readers.

FRANKOMA POTTERY, INC.

A Division of Frankoma Industries Inc.
Ms. Joniece Frank
Box 789 2400 Frankoma Road
Sapulpa, Oklahoma 74067
(918) 224-5511

Plates

Frankoma Pottery first opened in Norman, Oklahoma in 1933. John Frank moved his business to Sapulpa in 1938, where he continued to create ceramics from the Oklahoma clay found there on "Sugar Loaf Hill."

Frankoma's *American Bicentennial Commemorative* plates are a series of five, with the first produced in 1972 and the last plate made in 1976. These were created to celebrate 200 years of American independence. The series was significant because it was made of American clay. Each plate portrays a significant event in the American Revolution. On the back of the plates are signatures of the signers of the Declaration of Independence. John Frank created the plate art for 1972 and 1973, and his daughter, Joniece, created the remaining three plates.

The firm also created a *Teen-Agers of the Bible* annual plate collection which debuted in 1973 and ran for ten years, ending in 1982.

Perhaps most significant among Frankoma limited editions is the firm's 1965 Christmas plate — the first annual Christmas plate made in America, and a series that continues today. The plates are inspired by the Christmas story and the life of Christ. They are done in a semi-translucent "Della Robbia" white glaze.

John Frank designed a five ounce "Elephant Mug" in 1968 as a fund raiser for the National Republican Womans Club. This was the start of the *Political Mug* Series. The next year, the mug was modified and offered as a collector's item. "Nixon-Agnew" was printed on the side along with the date, as was on the original mug. This was the first of the *Presidential* Mug Series. Later, Joniece designed the "Donkey Mug" to represent the Democratic Party.

Both the "Elephant" and "Donkey" Mugs have continued to be made annually since their inceptions. Each year a new color is chosen, and the date is changed. In an inaugural year, the presidential names are added on the appropriate mug.

In September, 1983, Frankoma Pottery was destroyed by fire. The firm was rebuilt and reopened on July 1, 1984.

In 1985, a "Phoenix Plate" was introduced in remembrance of the 1983 fire. This flame-colored plate depicts the mythological bird coming out of the ashes, just as Frankoma Pottery came out of the ashes to rebuild and reopen in 1984.

GARTLAN USA, INC.

15502 Graham Street
Huntington Beach, California 92649
(714) 897-0090
Fax: (714) 892-1034

Plates, Figurines, Graphics

The tradition of collecting sports memorabilia has taken on an entirely new dimension since Gartlan USA introduced its extraordinary line of fine-art sports collectibles, ranging from limited edition lithographs, plates and figurines, to open editions of mini-plates and ceramic players cards.

Headquartered in Huntington Beach, California, Gartlan USA was established in 1985. Robert H. Gartlan envisioned this totally new concept in commemorating the achievements of some of America's leading athletes, including the Hall-of-Fame performances of Joe DiMaggio, Kareem Abdul-Jabbar, Wayne Gretzky and Joe Montana.

The career of each superstar selected for this honor is telescoped into a montage of images by skilled sports artists. This artwork is recreated as a limited edition lithograph or limited edition plate. In some cases, an open edition collector plate is also issued.

The companion figurine of each athlete, coach or official captures the vitality and skill that brought each individual to prominence in his or her field. In some cases, figurines are available in two different sizes. As an added incentive, all limited edition lithographs, plates and figurines are signed by the athlete.

Among the other sports greats honored are: Earvin "Magic" Johnson, Pete Rose, Mike Schmidt, George Brett, Roger Staubach, Reggie Jackson, Ted Williams, Johnny Bench, Carl Yastrzemski, Hank Aaron, Ray Dandridge and Buck Leonard.

New additions to the Gartlan USA line include Hall-of-Famer Yogi Berra, umpire Al Barlick and baseball greats Whitey Ford, Darryl Strawberry, Ken Griffey Jr. and Rod Carew. Gartlan USA's foray into hockey also includes Brett and Bobby Hull.

In commemorating these players, and then executing such a wide line of high-quality sports collectibles, Gartlan USA has earned the respect of today's sports fans. The true measure of these commemorative collectibles, however, will come from tomorrow's collectors who will appreciate Gartlan's vision.

Part of the Joe Montana Collection, *this 10¼" 24-karat personally signed plate was offered in a worldwide edition of 2,250.*

W.S. GEORGE POTTERY COMPANY

9333 N. Milwaukee Ave.
Niles, Illinois 60648

Plates, Dolls

The W.S. George Pottery Co. is proud of its rich tradition and history. In 1865, William S. George's grandfather was born in the Ohio River Valley, an area famous for its chinamaking.

Grandfather George learned the craft of chinamaking as a boy from "the bottom up" and in 1902 formed his own company.

The company soon became known for its fine workmanship and advanced ceramics technology. The family tradition for quality china is now carried on by grandson William, who recently founded a new company affiliated with The Bradford Exchange: W.S. George Pottery Company.

Among the most popular offerings from W.S. George is *Critic's Choice: Gone With the Wind* by Paul Jennis. Other movie series premiered under the W.S. George hallmark are *The Sound of Music: 25th Anniversary Series* by Victor Gadino and *Dr. Zhivago* by George Bush.

Collectors of bird and animal plates will enjoy *Nature's Lovables, Soaring Majesty* and *The World's Most Magnificent Cats* by Charles Fracé; as well as *Vanishing Gentle Giants* by Anthony Casay, *Last of Their Kind: The Endangered Species* by Will Nelson and *The Secret World of the Panda* by Joyce Bridgett.

Recent nature series include *Symphony of Shimmering Beauty* and *Nature's Poetry* by Lena Liu, *Nature's Legacy* by Jean Sias and *Flowers from Grandma's Garden* by Glenna Kurz. The company has also introduced three holiday series: *Spirit of Christmas* by Jean Sias, *Scenes of Christmas Past* by Lloyd Garrison and *Bonds of Love*, a Mother's Day collection by Brenda Burke.

Several doll series have also been produced under the W.S. George hallmark. They are *The King and I* and *My Fair Lady* by Pat Ryan Brooks; and *Romantic Flower Maidens* by Merri Roderick. In addition, W.S. George has produced two doll series in conjunction with other collectibles firms: *Precious Memories of Motherhood* by Sandra Kuck with Reco and *Brides of the Century* by Ellen Williams with Roman.

NUMA LTD.-THE GHENT COLLECTION

Ruth Krise
1653 Merriman Road
Suite 103
Akron, Ohio 44313
(216) 867-5880
Fax: (216) 867-0269

Plates, Figurines, Graphics

The Ghent Collection, the limited edition collectibles division of NUMA, Ltd., has offered a variety of fine artwork to collectors over the past fifteen years. The direct mail firm began with a line of heraldic products displaying family crests, and has gone on to offer custom greeting cards, sculptures, medallics, limited edition lithographs and serigraphs, as well as an exclusive line of collector plates.

Master artists including Harry Moeller, Guy Tudor, Edward Bierly, Jay Matternes, Charles Frace, Dean Fausett and Alton Tobey have worked for Ghent Collection. This firm has produced pieces of historical interest such as the *Treasures of Tutankhamun* plate series, and the *American Bicentennial Wildlife Collection*.

A pioneer in new techniques in porcelain, Ghent works with manufacturers including Kaiser, Fairmont, Viletta, Lenox, Gorham, Woodmere, Caverswall, and Porcelaine Etienne.

Other notable issues include the Ghent *Christmas* and *Mother's Day* series, a collection called *From Sea to Shining Sea*, the official 1980 Olympic Summer Games plate, and Norman Rockwell's *April Fools Day* plates. Ghent's most recent contributions have been the *American Classics* series, *Lands of Fable*, *Hans Brinker Delft* plate collection and Official XXIII Olympiad Plate, *Lands of Enchantment*, *Man's Dream of Flight*, and the annual *Memory* plates.

The president of Ghent Collection is Dennis B. Haslinger.

GOEBEL, INC.

Goebel Plaza
P.O. Box 10 Route 31
Pennington, New Jersey 08534
(609) 737-8700
Fax: (609) 737-8685

Figurines, Dolls, Christmas Ornaments

Founded in 1871, Goebel Germany has maintained a special relationship with the United States since before the turn-of-the-century. Today, as Goebel products enjoy increasing popularity in nearly ninety countries, its major audience on a worldwide basis is still the American consumer.

While the company's three dimensional figurines reflect popular collecting and gift-giving trends, Goebel figurines evoke traditional values. They represent a certain timeless quality which spans the years. Dedicated to top-of-the-line craftsmanship, coupled with

"Ashlea," designed by Bette Ball, is limited to an edition of 1,000 and plays "As Time Goes By."

an upscale family image, Goebel, Inc.'s many successful lines include *Victoria Ashlea Originals*® limited edition dolls, DeGrazia figurines, Goebel miniatures, Goebel crystal and Christmas collectibles and Norman Rockwell figurines and plates.

This unique product mix reflects original creations designed by Goebel artists as well as licensed two-dimensional art developed outside the Goebel studios.

GOEBEL MINIATURES

4820 Adohr Lane
Camarillo, California 93012
(805) 484-4351
Fax: (805) 482-2143

Figurines

Formed in 1978, Goebel Miniatures produces fine collectible miniature figurines and jewelry by using the centuries old "lost wax" process developed by Egyptian and Chinese artists more than 5,000 years ago.

After first embarking on a line of miniature furniture known as the *Butterfly Collection* for the dollhouse market, the company soon discovered that the tiny handcrafted figurines produced by Master Artist Robert Olszewski would be the company's future. The furniture line was discontinued in early years.

In 1980 the company moved to larger offices in order to accommodate its growing staff, and by 1984 was doubling its size every year.

One of the goals of Goebel Miniatures is to reproduce in miniature some of the finest examples of antique and contemporary masterpieces. Goebel Miniatures takes great pride in honoring the companies and artists who produced the fullscale originals.

Although some designs are released as limited editions (usually due to the amount of difficulty involved in reproduction), it is rare for the company to do so. Goebel Miniatures believes that limiting an edition is no guarantee of artistic worth. The real value of a work of art comes from its artistic quality. Goebel Miniatures' first limited edition "Alice in the Garden," based on the Lewis Carroll works and commissioned in 1981 by *Miniature Collector Magazine*, was released at $60.00 per figurine and now commands as much as $1,000 per figurine on the secondary market.

Goebel Miniatures figurines range in themes from children, women, wildlife, and history, to the art of Ted DeGrazia, Walt Disney, Norman Rockwell and M.I. Hummel. Each piece is cast in bronze, is no more than one-and-a-half inches tall and has a display environment to accompany the series.

Owned by W. Goebel Porzellanfabrik, the German firm that produces M.I. Hummel figurines, Goebel Miniatures has grown from two people, President Charles Harley and Master Artist Robert Olszewski, to a staff of over 100 and is today the largest studio producing miniature figurines, objects of art and collectible jewelry in the United States.

From the Pinocchio Series *comes "Geppetto's Toy Shop" with (from left to right) "J.W. Foulfellow," "Gideon," "Geppetto/Figaro," "Pinocchio" and "Jiminy Cricket."*

GORHAM, INC.

Ann Holbrook
P.O. Box 906
Mt. Kisco, New York 10549
(914) 242-9300
Fax:(914) 242-9379

Plates, Figurines, Dolls, Christmas Ornaments

When Jabez Gorham, the company founder, began making silver spoons in 1831, Gorham prided itself on providing quality merchandise with popular appeal. By the dawn of the 20th century, Gorham was being hailed as "Silversmiths to the World," winning first prize awards and acclaim at international exhibitions by offering intricate, meticulously crafted hollowware pieces. Silver pieces in the martelé — meaning hammered — tradition, produced only by Gorham, are now found in the permanent collections of museums like the Smithsonian and Metropolitan and are treasured by private collectors.

Now 160 years later, Gorham continues their commitment to design excellence and superior American craftsmanship. While sterling silver flatware and hollowware, stainless and silverplated flatware, china and crystal have historically been Gorham's primary products, it is now equally committed to the production of collectibles inspired by works from their archives and original designs by leading doll artists.

Since 1981, Gorham's major collectible has been the Gorham doll collection, recognized for its exceptional artistry and appreciating value. These original, limited edition dolls feature fine porcelain heads, hands and feet, as well as, elaborate outfits reflecting the historic period which they represent. Artists like Susan Stone Aiken, combine rich imagination and warm childhood memories to capture the style and personality that make her Gorham dolls possessions of unmistakable heirloom quality.

Another favorite with collectors is renowned New England doll artist and sculptress, Brenda Elizabeth Gerardi, who modeled the memorable faces and designed the elegant, turn-of-the-century fashions for three exclusive Gorham doll collections. And new to Gorham is a premiere collection by Dolores Valenza, one of the world's elite porcelain artists, portraying irresistible little girls sharing special moments with enchanting playtime "friends."

Gorham has also been very successful in creating china and porcelain collectibles featuring the art of Norman

"Cherie," the first doll in the new Les Belles Bebes Collection, *was created by award-winning artist Susan Stone Aiken.*

Rockwell, Betty Felder and John Clymer. Other original collectibles have included the animal and bird figurines of the Country Artists of Stratford-on-Avon in England and the unique chalkware of July Vaillancourt, inspired by turn-of-the-century ice cream and candy molds.

Gorham has also produced Christmas ornaments in sterling silver, silverplate and crystal for the past two decades. In fact, the 1990 Sterling Snowflake, the 20th anniversary design in Gorham's classic Christmas series, won an Award of Excellence in the first annual competition sponsored by *Collector Editions* magazine.

THE GREENWICH WORKSHOP, INC.

30 Lindeman Drive
Trumbull, Connecticut 06611
(800) 243-4246
(203) 371-6568

THE GREENWICH WORKSHOP, LTD.

3781 Victoria Park Avenue
Unit 6
Scarborough, Ontario M1W 3K5
(800) 263-4001 (Inside Canada)
(416) 490-8342

Graphics

In the early 1970s, printing techniques and the public interest in quality art matured together. Into this environment was founded The Greenwich Workshop with a clearly expressed dedication and commitment to provide a quality product to the collector.

Quality and innovation are the words that bind together the world of The Greenwich Workshop and set it apart from many other publishers. Quality of artists, of subject matter, of production processes and service. Innovation of new products and subjects. The firm pioneered Western, Aviation and Fantasy art in limited edition print form. Examples are the introduction of the *Personal Commission*™, the *Cameo Collection* and *Master Work*™ prints. One of the latest innovations is the introduction of *The Living Canvas*™, which brings the art experience to life with award-winning videos produced by The Greenwich Workshop to accompany select prints and to profile individual artists. Their offerings also include Americana, Marine, Wildlife, the art of Bev Doolittle and Contemporary Realism from the Peoples' Republic of China. The Greenwich Workshop also publishes books, most recently *The Art of Bev Doolittle* in association with Bantam Books.

The Greenwich Workshop looks at the world through the eyes of some of the finest artists at work today, including Charles Wysocki, Howard Terpning, Frank C. McCarthy, Stephen Lyman, Rod Frederick, William S. Phillips and Simon Combes among others. Each is a distinguished painter or sculptor. They are diverse. Their techniques vary. They span all ages. They live throughout the United States, Canada and Europe. Each sees the world a little differently, yet each holds a reverence for life and nature, and an artist's passion that enables them to express it visually.

DAVE GROSSMAN CREATIONS

J. Kevin Horth
1608 North Warson Road
St. Louis, Missouri 63132
(314) 423-5600
Fax: (314) 423-7620

Plates, Figurines, Christmas Ornaments

Dave Grossman Designs began producing collectibles, most notably Norman Rockwell figurines in 1975. The company began and has remained in St. Louis, Missouri since 1968 and is owned and run solely by Dave Grossman. Mr. Grossman originally began his business by creating and marketing metal sculptures and has since expanded into many areas of collectible art.

Mr. Grossman is a native of St. Louis. After graduating from the University of Missouri, he was commissioned to do architectural sculptures for banks, hospitals, hotels and other public and private buildings. One of his works is in Lincoln Center in New York. He also was commissioned to create sculptures for Presidents Johnson and Nixon.

In 1975 Grossman became the first company to produce a collectible line inspired by the work of Norman Rockwell doing so under a license from Curtis Publishing Company. The firm has continued to produce Rockwell items for sixteen years, and this year introduces a Christmas plate, waterglobe and figurine in addition to the annual ornaments.

Grossman also has other licensed lines including Emmett Kelly, Gone With The Wind, and The Wizard of OZ. Emmett Kelly was the most famous circus clown of all time, and this line is licensed through his estate. Gone With The Wind and The Wizard of OZ are licensed through Turner Entertainment Co.

Grossman also produces other figurine lines and plans to expand on existing lines while also marketing new collectibles. Mr. Grossman takes pride in the quality of his work and his devotion to the collector.

H&G STUDIOS, INC.

Dick Gabbe
8259 North Military Trail
Palm Beach Gardens, Florida 33410
(407) 626-4770
Fax: (407) 775-1290

Plates, Figurines, Dolls, Graphics

H&G Studios, Inc. was founded in 1987, at which time it referred to itself as "a new company with years and years of experience." The two founders, Bill Hibel and Dick Gabbe, had collectively committed over fifty years in the gift and collectibles industry, creating products that the discriminating consumer/collector demanded at the best possible quality for affordable prices.

H&G's product line includes music boxes, collector plates, collector dolls, prints and lithographs and figurines. Talented and well-known artists such as Brenda Burke, Ado Santini, John Akers and Francois Cloutier create the paintings, sculptures and designs that form the backbone of the company's products. Then the finest quality producers in Italy, England, the USA and the Far East are employed to perform the manufacturing functions. The result is a continuing line of artistic, collectible and gift-oriented products that perform in the stores due to their acceptablility by the consuming public.

At the company headquarters in Palm Beach Gardens, Florida, all merchandise is received from the global producers, examined, repacked and shipped to the customers. The executive offices, design studios and accounting are at this location as well. All the facilities are well equipped to handle the multi-million dollar volume that H&G has attained. Several plans are in the works for product expansion, and the company foresees a continuation of its growth pattern in the years to come.

THE HADLEY HOUSE

Joan Lee
11001 Hampshire Avenue South
Bloomington, Minnesota 55438
(612) 943-8474
Fax: (612) 943-8098

Plates, Graphics

The Hadley Companies grew from a hobby into an enterprise that includes the country's largest manufacturer of hand-carved decoys; a major publisher of limited edition art; a chain of retail galleries and one of the country's leading galleries of original art.

Ray E. Johnson founded the company in 1975 with the help of two friends. Their original intent was to create wooden decoys on a lathe which replicated a Wisconsin antique. A showroom, opened next to the factory, was so popular, the trio opened the first retail gallery in Rosedale Center the following year. Currently, The Wooden Bird galleries have twenty locations in Minnesota, Michigan, Illinois and California and is still expanding at a controlled pace.

Today, The Hadley Companies market lithographs, limited edition plates and porcelains by some of America's most renowned Americana, wildlife, western and figure artists such as Terry Redlin, Ozz Franca, Martin Grelle, Les Didier, Ted Blaylok, Jerry Raedeke, Bryan Moon, Peter Skirka, Olaf Wieghorst, Kenneth Riley, John Clymer and Clark Hulings through Hadley House publishing and the Special Markets divisions of the company as well as The Wooden Bird.

Hadley House has an international dealer network spanning the United States and Canada, and the Special Markets division is purveyor to major conservation groups and many Fortune 500 companies.

THE HAMILTON COLLECTION

Gwen Hunter
4810 Executive Park Court
P.O. Box 2567
Jacksonville, Florida 32232

Plates, Dolls, Figurines, Christmas Ornaments, Bells

The Hamilton Collection is an international purveyor of fine limited editions, including plates, dolls, figurines, bells, boxes and ornaments.

In the early 1970s, the firm's Hamilton Mint division created a wide range of precious metal ingots, medallions, plates and jewelry. In 1978, the company moved into the collector plate realm with a series of plates honoring *The Nutcracker Ballet*, premiering with "Clara and Nutcracker." A series by Thornton Utz soon followed, beginning with the first-issue "A Friend in the Sky."

For more than a decade, Hamilton has offered a number of extremely successful collections of plates and fiurines. Many of these have been produced in conjunction with some of the world's most renowned names in collectibles — including Wedgwood, Royal Worcester, Boehm Studios, Pickard, Maruri Studios, Hutschenreuther, Spode, Kaiser, Roman, Villeroy & Boch, and Reco International.

Many other products were researched and developed, entirely by Hamilton's staff artists, including several types of collectibles from the Orient never previously seen in limited edition plates. These include the first cloisonne plate, the first Japanese cloisonne and porcelain plates, and the first translucent cloisonne plate.

Hamilton is also well known for its entertainment themes, including the theater, ballet, opera, television and the movies. Successes include plates featuring *The Wizard of Oz*, *I Love Lucy*, *The Honeymooners* as well as *Star Wars* and *Star Trek* plate collections. In 1990, Hamilton introduced "Fifty Years of Oz" by Thomas Blackshear. This popular issue won the coveted 1990 "Plate of the Year" award.

Bird and animal subjects have been major areas of interest. This includes bird figurines from Royal Worcester and Maruri Studios, as well as Venetian glass birds, Royal Worcester plates featuring cats from artist Pam Cooper, other cat-subject plates from artist Gré Gerardi and Bob Harrison, dog-subject plates by artist Jim Lamb and Bob Christie, and owl and other bird-subject plates from several well-known artists including John Seerey-Lester, Ron Parker and Rod Lawrence.

Perhaps, the best-known category of collectibles offered by The Hamilton Collection has been the child-subject plates. In this area, Hamilton has played a large role in making available to collectors several important series from award-winning artists. These include several plates, some featuring works by two great American artists Bessie Pease Gutmann and Maud Humphrey Bogart produced by Balliol; the *Pride of America's Indians* and *America's Indian Heritage* plates by Gregory Perillo from Artaffects; and a number of plates issued by Reco International which featured the famed artist Sandra Kuck.

The newest category for The Hamilton Collection is collectible dolls, beginning with three very popular issues — Bessie Pease Gutmann's "Love Is Blind," Maud Humphrey Bogart's "Playing Bride," and a doll crafted in the image of a priceless antique Bru Bebé, "Nicole." One of the biggest doll hits ever occurred in 1990 when The Hamilton Collection introduced the adorable baby doll, "Jessica," by Connie Walser Derek. The response from collectors was truly astounding.

Today, The Hamilton Collection continues to introduce fine collector dolls *always with an eye for quality and value*. Clearly, this is a company that collectors will want to watch in the future.

The 1990 "Plate of the Year" — Thomas Blackshear's "Fifty Years of Oz" issued by The Hamilton Collection.

HAMILTON GIFTS LTD.

Maud Humphrey Bogart Collectors' Club
P.O. Box 4009
Compton, California 90224-4009

Figurines, Plates, Bells, Dolls

Hamilton Gifts Ltd. was actually begun when its founder was able to acquire a company that held the license to produce collectibles based on artwork of Bessie Pease Gutmann and Louis Icart — two of the most formidable collections in the Hamilton Gifts line. This is only the beginning of a history that only dates back to 1986 but is filled with excitement and innovation.

Hamilton Gifts Ltd. was formed with the acquisition of Tomy Giftware in 1986 by The Hamilton Group. Subsequently, Hamilton Group became a wholly owned subsidiary of Stanhome Inc., in 1989, which is also the parent company of Enesco and Enesco Worldwide Giftware Group.

In 1991, Hamilton Gifts Ltd. became a separate company owned by Enesco Worldwide Giftware Group, and it operates as an independent business. Hamilton Gifts has come to be synonymous with creative licensing and fine collectibles.

Its Presents Division has such unique collectibles as Star Trek®, I Love Lucy, Super Heroes, Betty Boop™, Captain America™ and Spiderman™, among others. The Heirloom Tradition produces the collections of Bessie Pease Gutmann, Louis Icart, Pricilla of Boston and the most popular of them all — the Maud Humphrey Bogart Collection, which was introduced by Hamilton Gifts in 1988.

Based on the art of famed American artist Maud Humphrey Bogart, this collection capitalizes on the extraordinarily beautiful victorian illustrations for which Miss Humphrey is famous. Born in 1863, she studied both in New York and Paris, and built a formidable reputation for the period. At one time, she was reputed to have been the highest paid woman artist of her day.

"Magic Kitten" and "Susanna" are two miniature figurines in the new Petite Collection of Maud Humphrey.

Aside from her art, Miss Humphrey is also renowned as the mother of Humphrey Bogart, the famous actor. He was the first child of her marriage to a prominent New York physician, and ultimately became the model for some of her most famous advertising campaigns.

Hamilton Gifts Ltd. extended its commitment to the Maud Humphrey Bogart Collection with the 1990 formation of the Maud Humphrey Bogart Collectors' Club, marking its Charter Year during 1991. The company is based in Compton, California, but many of its support services are now combined with Enesco Worldwide Giftware Group through its Elk Grove Village, Illinois headquarters.

HAND & HAMMER SILVERSMITHS

2610 Morse Lane
Woodbridge, Virginia 22192
(703) 491-4866
Fax: (703) 491-2031

Christmas Ornaments

The tradition of master silver craftmanship is rapidly disappearing from the scene. Fortunately, William deMatteo apprenticed with his father, a silversmith who willingly passed on the skill and love needed to work in gold and silver.

Once his apprenticeship was completed, deMatteo became the master silversmith at Colonial Williamsburg in Virginia. In 1979, deMatteo, his assistant Philip Thorp and deMatteo's son, Chip, founded Hand & Hammer Silversmiths.

William deMatteo has been recognized by the American Institute of Architects which awarded him its Gold Medal. In 1975, he became the first American silversmith to be honored with a membership in the Goldsmiths' Company of London. DeMatteo has designed and fashioned silver gifts for every president since John F. Kennedy, as well as many gifts of state for world leaders.

Hand & Hammer Silversmiths has a number of commercial, corporate and academic society customers. It also has developed ornaments and jewelry for some of the country's most prestigious museums, historical societies, stores and organizations.

Since 1981, Chip deMatteo has created more than 300 ornament designs for organizations like the U.S. Historical Society, the Boston Museum, Frederick Warne Co. of London, Lord & Taylor, Gump's, Tiffany's, Cartier and Neiman-Marcus. In 1987, Hand & Hammer introduced its first limited edition dated series, *Bells*. It was soon followed by the equally limited *Santa* and *Carousal* series.

Also of interest to serious collectors is the five-piece *The Night Before Christmas* limited edition ornament collection and the four-piece limited edition *Victorian Village* collection based on Currier & Ives lithographs. Since 1990, Hand & Hammer has had the exclusive license to produce silver ornaments and jewelry based on the popular Beatrix Potter stories and characters.

"Peter Rabbit" is a handcrafted sterling silver ornament adapted from Beatrix Potter's Tale of Peter Rabbit *and crafted by Chip deMatteo and Hand & Hammer Silversmiths.*

HEIRLOOM EDITIONS

Barbara Ringer
25100-B South Normandie Avenue
Harbor City, California 90710
(213) 539-5587
(800) 433-4785
Fax: (213) 539-8891

Bells

Heirloom Editions Ltd. was founded by Barbara Ringer in 1977. The original idea was to provide thimbles to collectors of the fourth leading worldwide collectible from one large source. Heirloom manufactures the largest line of thimbles in the world. They produce porcelain, pewter and bronze thimbles in their California factory. Exclusive designs are produced for Heirloom in Europe. The creative ideas are done by Barbara. This company has over 3,500 different style thimbles making them the largest thimble company in the world.

Two new additions have been introduced by Heirloom editions: porcelain bells and English Staffordshire teapots for collectors.

EDNA HIBEL STUDIO

Andy Plotkin
P.O. Box 9967
Riviera Beach, Florida 33419
(407) 848-9633
Fax: (407) 848-9640

Plates, Figurines, Graphics, Christmas Ornaments, Dolls

Edna Hibel is among America's foremost artists of international renown. Edna Hibel Studio offers her limited edition graphics, sculptures, plates and other collectible art.

Since 1940, museums, galleries and private collectors worldwide have recognized Ms. Hibel's talents. Many of her collectibles are displayed alongside her original oil paintings and drawings in the Hibel Museum of Art in Palm Beach, Florida. This is the world's only non-profit, public museum dedicated to the art of a living American woman. Included in the museum's collection is Hibel's original "Mother Earth" painting which was recently reproduced as a United Nations commemorative stamp.

Her two exhibitions in the People's Republic of China and in the Soviet Union represent the first time any foreign artist has been invited to display artwork in these countries more than once. Hibel's collectibles have received numerous awards from the National Association of Limited Edition Dealers and The Bradford Exchange.

Her latest "Vertu" collections of table arts, jewelry and dolls is an innovation in the collectibles industry. Hibel's art products are sold by many distributors world-wide, including Canada through Kaiser Porcelain, 5572 Ambler Dr., Mississauga, Ontario L4W 2K9.

JOHN HINE STUDIOS, INC.

4456 Campbell Road
P.O. Box 801207
Houston, Texas 77280-1207
(713) 690-4477

Figurines

John Hine and David Winter met in 1979 and quickly discovered that they shared an interest in the past. A sculptor, Winter had fashioned a number of sculptured cottages which Hine found so charming that he suggested that they go into business together. Later that year, they formed John Hine Ltd. Winter designed the cottages, and Hine handled the manufacturing and marketing.

David Winter's "Staffordshire Vicarage" is part of the British Traditions *series.*

The first cottage was introduced in the spring of 1980. Although the partners had envisioned a small English craft company, the popularity of the cottages soon made the David Winter cottages one of the leading collectibles of the decade. In 1987, the David Winter Cottage Collectors Guild was formed. Currently, there are more than eighty cottages in the line, in addition to approximately fifty-five cottages and buildings now retired.

Hine later put another facet of British life under the microscope with the introduction of Malcolm Cooper's *Great British Pubs* series which features finely detailed miniatures of some of Britian's most beloved pubs.

Hine turned to silversmith Christopher Lawrence for a whimsical look at *Mushrooms*, a mythical village bearing a striking resemblance to exotic mushrooms.

In 1990, Hine introduced the *American Collection* by Canadian sculptor Maurice Wideman. This more traditional series contains about forty miniature homes and buildings that range from a California winery to a New England town hall.

Fantasy reigns supreme in Jon Herbert's *Shoemaker's Dream*, a series of miniature English buildings that seem to spring from equally astonishing footwear.

The latest artist to join John Hine is Sandra Kuck, one of America's most popular plate artists who recently added figurines to her accomplishments. Kuck has designed a series of Victorian mother and child figurines which were released in late 1991.

HOPKINS SHOP

John Hopkins Sr.; John Hopkins, Jr.
347 West Sierra Madre Blvd.
Sierra Madre, California 91024
(818) 355-1813
Fax: (818) 355-1982

Figurines

Hopkins Shop was founded in 1973 by John Hopkins Sr., a builder and furniture designer, and his son, John Jr., an art major in college. Originally, they manufactured wood products for the craft and hobby market. In 1985 they created the *Village Lights*, a series of lighted English and turn-of-the-century American style cottages.

Hopkins Shop then produced the *Enchanted Kingdom*, a collection of fantasy castles accented with Swarovski crystals. This grouping includes the original "Enchanted Kingdom" pieces, "Ravenstone Ruins," "Birthstone Castles" and the "Dream Castles."

Rounding out the fantasy theme is *Peanut Patch Village*, a new series of whimsical cottages, the originals constructed from materials such as gourds, pumpkins and peanut shells.

M.I. HUMMEL CLUB

Division of GmbH Inc.
Goebel Plaza
P.O. Box 11
Pennington, New Jersey 08534-0011
1-800-666-CLUB

Figurines, Plates, Bells

The M.I. Hummel Club (formerly the Goebel Collector's Club) was formed in 1977. This organization is designed to serve and inform those who enjoy figurines, plates, bells, miniatures and other works based upon the art of Sister M.I. Hummel.

The M.I. Hummel Club offers many benefits to its members, including a free figurine valued at $65. Club members receive the four-color quarterly magazine, *Insights*, filled with informative articles to keep the reader knowledgeable on all things pertaining to the art of M.I. Hummel.

The M.I. Hummel Club membership kit contains an official membership card which is the member's passport to excitement. Enclosed within a specially designed binder are inserts detailing the history of the Goebel company, the intricacies in the handcrafting of *M.I. Hummel* figurines, as well as the always important current *M.I. Hummel* figurines and a current M.I. Hummel price list. Club members have the opportunity to buy *M.I. Hummel* exclusive collectibles, created only for members, with redemption cards they redeem through participating retailers.

One of the most exciting benefits of Club membership is the opportunity to travel on custom designed trips with others who share their hobby. On all trips, members are treated to deluxe accomodations and care with a Club ambassador, a tour guide and a travel agency principal, all as part of the experienced team. Each year the itinerary changes. European trips always include the behind-the-scenes tour of the factory in Roedental, Bavaria and the visit to the Convent of Siessen where Sister M.I. Hummel lived and worked for the last fifteen years of her life.

Beginning with the Club year June 1, 1991, all charter members were rewarded with the right to own the M.I. Hummel figurine "Honey Lover."

Members benefit from the exclusive Collector's Market, through which, they can buy and sell on a confidential basis. Because of the Club's link to the factory archives, members also can have their research questions answered in depth.

Local Chapters are a vital ingredient for Club membership. They give individuals the opportunity to meet one another in small regional groups to learn, to study and to expand their friendships. Through newsletters and other publications developed by the Chapters themselves, a nationwide network of friendship has developed. There's so much to gain by joining the M.I. Hummel Club, so don't miss out!

HUTSCHENREUTHER CORP.

85 Price Parkway
Farmingdale, New York 11735

HUTSCHENREUTHER (Canada) Ltd.
55 H East Beaver Creek Road
Richmond Hill, Ontario, Canada L4B 1E8

Plates, Figurines

Hutschenreuther is a famed German maker of porcelain items, located in the Selb region of Bavaria. A long-time leader in superb quality figurines and other collector's items, as well as fine dinnerware. Hutschenreuther entered the limited edition market in 1922.

Since then, the firm has introduced several series of plates by the husband-and-wife team of Charlotte and William Hallett. In 1982, the Hamilton Collection offered Hutschenreuther's *The Roses of Redoute* collection of eight plates. Other artists whose works have been produced by Hutschenreuther include Ole Winther, Gunther Granget, Hans Achtziger and Dolores Valenza.

VICTORIA IMPEX CORPORATION

2150 John Glenn Drive, Ste. 400
Concord, California 94520
(415) 685-6787
Fax: (415) 685-8839

Dolls, Figurines

Since its founding in 1979, Victoria Impex has made a name for itself in the collectible doll market. They are currently listed as the number three doll company in a survey conducted by *Giftware News*, January 1989 issue. The firm maintains that quality, creativity and customer service are of utmost importance. "Our customers come first... without them we would never have come so far, so fast."

Victoria Impex was founded in 1979 by Victoria and Paul Chang. Mr. and Mrs. Chang have been involved in the gift industry for over twenty years with the ownership and operation of their trading company Victradco LTD in Taiwan. Victradco acts as an agent for Victoria as well as for some of the biggest names in the gift industry — Enesco, Schmid and Gorham.

Victoria experimented with a number of different gift products in the early years, but it was their porcelain dolls, clowns and pierrots, many designed by Mrs. Chang herself, which really took off. In 1983 Victoria chose to concentrate all of its efforts in the collectible market.

Moving up the ladder in the collectible doll market was not due to chance or luck, but rather a result of Victoria and Paul Chang's knowledge of the industry, and their ability to spot and recreate original, new designs.

It was this insight that led the Changs to discover the works of artist Cindy M. McClure. Mrs. McClure's *Legend of the Fairies* Collection brought Victoria international recognition in 1986 with the prestigious Doll of the Year Award from *Doll Reader* Magazine.

With the popularity of Mrs. McClure, came the introduction of two new artists in 1988 — Linda Blood and Rick St. Dennis. The original designs of Ms. Blood and Mr. St. Dennis were a delightful addition to the Victoria family. Full of fun and frolic, they have won the hearts of doll and clown collectors throughout the country.

Recently, the company added the dolls of Donna Bloom. The *Bloom Babies* are true-to-life expressions of the "inner child" — both the joyful loving child and the hurting tearful child. For each *Bloom Baby* sold, Victoria Impex makes a contribution to the National Committee for the Prevention of Child Abuse.

In 1988, Victoria expanded its distribution to include the United Kingdom. Heredities Limited, itself a manufacturer and wholesaler of figurines, began distributing their product line throughout the U.K. With distribution already in the United States, Canada and Puerto

Rico, the U.K. provided Victoria with a European base.

Today, Victoria has a total of fifteen sales organizations, with 130 sales representatives on the road to serve the needs of its customers. Victoria plans to continue growing and expanding its operations as well as its product categories.

With growth will come greater product variety, innovation and creativity. Yet, their fundamental principle will always remain, "quality and customer service."

INCOLAY STUDIOS INC.

445 North Fox Street
P.O. Box 711
San Fernando, California 91340
(818) 365-2521
Fax: (818) 365-9599

Plates

One of the most ancient forms of art was the detailed carving of cameos from multi-layered gemstones. The figures and scenes were carved on the white layer, while the multi-colored layers formed the background.

The artisans of Incolay Studios Inc. have revived this lost art, using a totally different medium, handcrafted Incolay Stone. The process for creating Incolay Stone is a closely guarded secret in which various colored minerals and coupling agents are combined in the stratified background to reproduce the same variegated formations and beauty of natural stone.

In 1977, Incolay Studios entered the limited edition collector plate market with the *Romantic Poets* series. It was followed by *The Great Romances of History* and *Life's Interludes*. Other series are the *Four Elements*, *Voyages of Ulysses*, *Fall of Troy* and *Enchanted Moments*, *The Sonnets of Shakespeare* and the *Shakespearean Lovers*.

Recent Incolay introductions include *Love Themes from the Grand Opera* and *The Christmas Cameo Collection*. Incolay also produces limited edition music boxes using Reuge movements from Switzerland. "Le Magnifique" and "Amore" are limited to 2,500 pieces. "Minuet" is numbered but not limited.

IRIS ARC CRYSTAL

Edwin Rosenblatt
114 East Haley Street
Santa Barbara, California 93101
(805) 963-3661
Fax: (805) 965-2458

Figurines, Christmas Ornaments

Jonathan Wygant and Francesca Patruno founded Iris Arc Crystal in 1976. Initially, Iris Arc marketed faceted crystal in the form of prisms and jewelry. The name for their firm came from the Greek myth of Iris, the goddess of the rainbow who was sent by Zeus to Earth on a rainbow to give a message to mortals. Eventually, they added the tag line "The Gift of Light."

"Light is the essence of what crystal is all about. Consequently, every single piece we have in our collection is a prism — cut and faceted so the light plays through it, breaking up into rainbows of color," said Wygant.

From their early experience selling prisms, Wygant and Patruno graduated in 1979 to become the first American manufacturer of faceted crystal figurines. Using imported full-lead crystal, each figurine is handcrafted at their company in Santa Barbara, California. One of the first companies to promote the halogen lighting of crystal figurines, Iris Arc offers a number of fine limited edition pieces.

Cottages are one of Iris Arc's most popular items. Iris Arc has also designed a limited edition "Country Cottage" and "Vase of Flowers." *The Enchanted Castle* series, the "Honeymoon Cottage" and "Baseball Bear" are a few of Iris Arc's latest and most popular items.

Iris Arc has trademarked the name of Rainbow Crystal as part of its commitment to collectors' desire for colorful crystal collectibles.

JESCO IMPORTS INCORPORATED

923 South Myrtle Avenue
Monrovia, California 91016
(818) 303-3787

Dolls

JESCO Imports Incorporated was founded in 1976 by James E. Skahill. The firm currently produces and markets both limited edition porcelain and vinyl dolls. According to the company's vice-president Tom Skahill, JESCO currently holds licenses for 107 original dolls molds from the Cameo Doll Company which includes classic dolls like Scootles©, Baby Mine©, Baby Peanut©, Miss Peep© and the all-time favorite, the Kewpie© doll.

The Cameo Kewpies© are considered by many to be the original, authentic Kewpie© dolls. Based on illustrations by Rose O'Neill, the Cameo Kewpie© was sculpted and produced by Joseph Kallus, the owner of Cameo. The Kewpie© dolls currently being produced use these original molds. In 1991, JESCO issued a limited edition 27-inch Kolonial Kewpie© before permanently retiring the original molds.

KAISER PORCELAIN (US) INC.

2045 Niagara Falls Blvd. Unit 11 & 12
Niagara Falls, New York 14304
(716) 297-2331
Fax: (716) 297-2749

KAISER PORCELAIN CO. LTD.
5572 Ambler Drive
Mississauga, Ontario L4W 2K9

KAISER PORCELAIN LTD.
Bangors Road North
Iver Heath, Bucks SLO OBL
England

VIKING IMPORT HOUSE
412 S.E. 6th Street
Fort Lauderdale, Florida 33301

Plates, Figurines, Bells, Dolls, Christmas Ornaments

In 1872, August Alboth, a talented artist and craftsman established his porcelain workshop in Coburg, Germany. The product "porcelain," derived from this area's kaolin clay, was called "White Gold" due to its beauty and purity.

Eventually, Alboth was joined by his son, Ernst, who helped him design and execute exquisite porcelains. They moved the porcelain works to Kronach, Bavaria and later Ernst's daughter married Georg Kaiser, who became a partner in the business. The company's trademark "Alka-Kunst" was created in 1925. It combined the first two letters of "Alboth" and "Kaiser." The other word "Kunst" means art in German.

In 1953, a new state-of-the-art factory was constructed in Staffelstein, Germany. To commemorate the enormous process initiated by the Kaiser family, and because of the international recognition of the name, the firm's name was changed to Kaiser Porcelain in 1970. The chief executive of the family-owned company is Hubert Kaiser.

A leader in the limited edition sculpture and plate markets, Kaiser has produced notable series like the *Birds of America* figurine series. In addition to its annual *Christmas* and *Mother's Day* plate series, Kaiser has recently introduced *American Cats, Through a Woodland Window*, and *Arabian Nights*.

"Scheherazade" is the first plate in the Arabian Nights *series by artist Robert Hersey.*

KALEIDOSCOPE, INC.

Leonard E. Padgett
P.O. Box 415
Clinton, Maryland 20735
(301) 856-1250

Plates, Bells, Christmas Ornaments

Kaleidoscope, Inc., who celebrated its 10th anniversary during 1991, offers affordable, limited edition gift items with a wide range of wares including miniature glass plates, cups and saucers, mugs, steins, thimbles, bells, Christmas ornaments and presentation pieces.

The firm offers choice items in small quantity and can produce personalized pieces decorated with company logos, historical sites, and other themes which the customer wishes to provide.

The company offers a unique line of miniature glass cup plates featuring a wide variety of designs pressed into high quality glass plates. Decaled designs are also available. Kaleidoscope, Inc. will be publishing catalogue sheets featuring their recent miniature plates.

All pieces are done on high quality glass, china, porcelain and ceramics. The firm won a special award from the Society of Glass and Ceramic Decorators and from the State of Maryland for a special line commemorating the 350th Anniversary celebration of the founding of Maryland.

KEIRSTEAD GALLERY LIMITED

40 Grant Timmins Drive
Kingston, Ontario
Canada K7L 4V4
(613) 549-4066
Fax: (613) 549-5783

Plates

Keirstead Gallery was established in 1977 to distribute the work of James Lorimer Keirstead and Janice Dawn Keirstead. The firm's objective is to create reproductions that look and feel like originals, by capturing mood, texture, and vibrant exciting color. Even the framing is the artist's choice.

Lithographic reproductions of Keirstead paintings are produced to the highest standards. Skilled craftspeople are trained to apply clear acrylic varnish on images to create a texture similar to the artist's original oil paintings. Each print is presented in a wooden frame with linen matting.

Classic yet contemporary, the products are popular in residential, hotel, and office settings. The complete Keirstead collectible line is impressive, encompassing handtextured reproductions, collector plates, plate frames, limited edition reproductions, art cards, gift enclosure cards, placemats, and coasters.

Swift delivery, exacting reproduction, and consistent fine quality have established Keirstead Gallery's name as a guarantee of integrity.

KEVIN FRANCIS

Stoke-on-Trent
England
011-44-81-081-693-9184
Fax: 011-44-81-299-1513

U.S.A. Office
13540 North Florida Avenue
Suite 103
Tampa, Florida 33613
(813) 961-9487
Fax: (813) 961-9332

Figurines, Steins

Kevin Francis Ceramics Studio launched their Toby Jug of David Winter at the 1991 California Collectibles show. The jug is number four in their series *Great English Artists and Potters*. Limited to an edition of 950 and priced at $450 with half the edition reserved for John Hine retailers, the retail allocation sold out the first day of the 1991 Long Beach Collectibles Exposition.

The jug, sculpted by Douglas V. Tootle, has been produced with the full approval of David Winter and John Hine. It features David Winter in blue jeans and a maroon sweater sitting on Blossom Cottage and holding the "Dower House" in his arms. Each cottage is an exact reproduction of the original. The toby is assembled by hand from nine separate moulds before being hand painted and fired twice to produce a high gloss finish. Each jug is individually numbered and comes with a certificate.

Three different trial colourways were shown at the 1991 Long Beach convention and the final colourway was selected on the basis of collectors' comments. One of the two discarded colourways was then auctioned for charity where it made $2,000. The other remaining colourway was auctioned for charity at the South Bend Collectibles Show in July, 1991.

Kevin Francis is a studio pottery based in Stoke-on-Trent England with a U.S.A. office in Tampa, Florida. The company is a partnership between Kevin Pearson and Francis Salmon, who between them, have written and published several books on Toby Jugs. They formed the company in 1987, with the simple criteria of producing the finest toby jugs possible using studio pottery techniques.

Part of the company's philosophy is to only produce low size editions ranging from 350 to 1,500. They never reproduce a character once sold out, and the partners take great delight in holding ceremonial mould smashing exercises to highlight this point.

Each Kevin Francis jug is an exacting likeness of the character, featuring aspects of that character in the handle and detail on the side of the jug. For example, "President Gorbachev," who is seated on a broken Berlin Wall, also contains an actual piece of the wall in the side as well as a cracked bust of Stalin and the Russian Bear and Flag on the handle. Their latest release of "General Schwarzkopf" features a shield with a U.S. Flag, the Kuwaiti Towers and a storm cloud.

To date, the company has released

over forty characters, twenty-five percent of which have sold out. A discontinued market for these already exists in England, and there are signs of one beginning in the States as new collectors start to seek old releases. Future plans include several more "American" subjects, including a series of *Great American Potters and Artists*.

KIRK STIEFF, DIVISION OF LENOX, INC.

Linda H. Rindone
800 Wyman Park Drive
Baltimore, Maryland 21211
(301) 338-6091
Fax: (301) 338-6097

Bells, Christmas Ornaments

In 1979, two of America's oldest and most prestigious names in silversmithing were united. At the time of the union, Samuel Kirk & Son, Inc. was already 164 years old and the Stieff Company, eighty-seven. Think of the American history through which they have flourished, the precipitous times and the glorious — their products graced the tables of the visionary and the influential — Kirk Stieff became the hallmark of a great young society.

During the post-Revolutionary period when our young country was setting its course as an independent nation, Samuel Kirk came to Baltimore, Maryland, and in 1815 opened his first shop. As Kirk developed his personal silversmithing style and as American tastes progressed, he introduced the world famous Repousse' style in 1820, a fabulous flower and foliage design, created in raised relief by hammering.

Prized for its superb quality and beauty, Kirk sterling silver has graced many of the finest homes in America, the owners a virtual "who's who" of American social and political history. One of the first was Major General Marquis de Lafayette, hero of the American Revolution. Other distinguished patrons followed; Robert E. Lee, Jefferson Davis, the Carrolls, the Warfields, the Astors, the Biddles, and the Roosevelts. Many of their highly treasured pieces are now part of the Kirk Collection — a collection that has travelled to museums throughout the United States.

Women were still wearing bustles and favoring elaborate Victorian styles when Charles C. Stieff opened his first sterling manufacturing facility for flatware and hollowware in 1892. One of Stieff's greatest contributions to the silver industry was his single-handed drive to have the quality and authenticity of sterling silver assured by law. He succeeded and greatly served both the industry and the consumer by influencing passage of the Silver Laws Registration, which insures that only true sterling may be marked "sterling" and advertised as such, the legal content defined as no less than 92.5 percent fine silver.

Springboarding on its selection in 1939 as the manufacturer of authentic Colonial Williamsburg Foundation Reproductions, Stieff expanded its pewter line to become the world leader in authentic antique reproductions. The firm's reputation for high quality and exacting standards continues today for historic organizations like Colonial Williamsburg, Historic Newport, The Smithsonian Institution, The Boston Museum of Fine Arts, The Thomas Jefferson Memorial Foundation, Historic Charleston, and others.

EDWIN M. KNOWLES CHINA COMPANY

9333 N. Milwaukee Avenue
Niles, Illinois 60648

Plates, Dolls, Figurines

The history of the Edwin M. Knowles China Co. is also the story of a family. Early in the 19th century, Isaac Knowles established Knowles, Taylor and Knowles as a family business in East Liverpool, Ohio. His son, Edwin, apprenticed with his father and then established his own company in Newell, West Virginia.

After Edwin Knowles' death, the firm ceased operations until entering into an affiliation with The Bradford Exchange.

The first proprietary collector's plate series issued by Knowles was *The Wizard of Oz* by James Auckland. It was followed by the *American Holidays* by Don Spaulding and the *Gone With The Wind* series by Ray Kursar.

Since 1975, the Knowles name had appeared on plates issued by The Rockwell Society of America. Series sponsored by the society included *Christmas, Mother's Day, Heritage, Rockwell's Rediscovered Women, Rockwell on Tour* and *Rockwell's Light Campaign*.

In 1985, Knowles was granted an official endorsement from the children of Norman Rockwell to produce collector's plates featuring their father's artwork. The first plate series to be endorsed by the Norman Rockwell Family Trust was *Rockwell's American Dream*. It was followed by *Rockwell's Colonials; The Rarest Rockwells, A Mind of Her Own: Rockwell's Studies of Girlhood* and *Rockwell's Golden Moments*. The newest series based on Rockwell's artwork is *Rockwell's Treasured Memories*.

Another popular plate theme is famous movies. Recently issued offers are *Singin' in the Rain* by Mark Skolsky and *Casablanca* by James Griffin. Scenes from several of Disney's animated film classics — such as *Cinderella, Pinocchio, Fantasia, Sleeping Beauty* and *Snow White* — have also been captured on plates.

Plates featuring children include *Nature's Child* by Mimi Jobe and *The March of Dimes: Our Children, Our Future* by various artists. Knowles produced the March of Dimes series in conjunction with five other leading collectibles firms.

The continuing popularity of plates featuring birds and animals has prompted the introduction of a variety of series, such as *Baby Owls of North America* by Joe Thornburgh, *Pussyfooting Around* by Christine Wilson, *Birds of the Season* by Sam Timm and *Field Trips* by Lynn Kaatz. Other series featuring nature scenes are *Jewels of the Flowers* by T.C. Chiu and *Old Mill Stream* by Craig Tennant. And the beauty of simple, household items, such as handmade quilts and Shaker-style chairs, is highlighted in *Cozy Country Corners* by Hannah Hollister Ingmire.

The Knowles hallmark has also become associated with high quality, limited-edition baby, children and character dolls, beginning with *Yolanda's Picture-Perfect Babies* by Yolanda Bello. Additional baby doll collections are *Baby Book Treasures* by Kathy Barry-Hippensteel, *The Littlest Clowns* by Mary Tretter and Maude Fangel's *Cover Babies*.

Series portraying older children include *My Closest Friend* by Jan Goodyear, *Polly's Tea Party* by Susan Krey, *Amish Blessings* by Julie Good-Krüger, *Yesterday's Dreams* by Maryanne Oldenburg, *Cindy's Playhouse Pals* by Cindy McClure and *Born to Be Famous* and *International Festival of Toys and Tots* by Kathy Barry-Hippensteel.

Three collections featuring characters from children's literature are available from Knowles: *The Children of Mother Goose* by Yolanda Bello, *Heroines from the Fairytale Forests* and *Dianna Effner's Mother Goose* by Dianna Effner.

KURT S. ADLER, INC.

1107 Broadway
New York, New York 10010-2872
(212) 942-0900
Fax: (212) 807-0575

Christmas Ornaments, Figurines

For more than forty years, Kurt S. Adler, Inc. has become the nation's leading importer, designer and supplier of Christmas ornaments, decorations and accessories. During the past few years, the company has introduced several groups of collectibles.

The first major group of collectibles is the *"Fabriché" Collection of Old World Santas*, which are crafted of fabric-mache. The first issue was inspired by Thomas Nast, and another issue depicts a Fabriché Old World "Santa on A Bicycle" which is licensed by The Smithsonian Museum.

Collectible Santas also include the *Visions of Santa* group, which features Old World Santas crafted of cold cast resin and a group of limited edition, painted fabric Santas.

Hand-crafted nutcrackers are an important group of collectibles. Kurt S. Adler, Inc. has introduced a collectibe Steinbach nutcracker portraying "Merlin The Magician." Other limited edition German nutcrackers stand fifteen inches high and depict characters such as Paul Bunyan, Gepetto The Toymaker, a Tyrolean, etc.

Other collectibles offered by the firm are Christmas ornaments and accessories featuring popular characters from Walt Disney, Sesame Street and Norman Rockwell covers from the *Saturday Evening Post*. If the strong demand for Kurt S. Adler collectibles continues, then you can expect the firm to expand the line greatly in the very near future.

LALIQUE

11, Rue Royale
8e Paris, France

Plates

Lalique is a family-owned maker of exceptionally fine crystal products, including one of the most famous plates in the limited edition market: the first-issue, 1965 "Deux Oiseaux." This plate opened the way for a new variety in collectible issues: it was the first non-blue-and-white, non-Christmas, non-porcelain collector plate ever introduced.

The founder of the firm was Rene Lalique, a goldsmith and jeweler. He began his business late in the nineteenth century, and then purchased a small glassworks in 1902. Lalique built a reputation for fine, Art Deco-style items including perfume bottles, vases and figurines. After the death of Rene Lalique, his son Marc took over the presidency until his death in 1977. Then Marie-Claude Lalique, Marc's daughter, stepped in to head the firm. She is also its chief designer, and she was the creator of the famous "Deux Oiseaux" and the other plates in the twelve-year annual.

LANCE CORPORATION

321 Central Street
Hudson, Massachusetts 01749
(508) 568-1401
Fax: (508) 568-8741

Plates, Figurines, Christmas Ornaments

In the 1960s, a group of Boston-based foundry experts began shifting their skills from industrial to artistic metal casting. Working under the name, Lance Laboratories, these men had experimented with mold materials and casting techniques to produce precision metal products for the aerospace and research and development industries around Boston. The material and techniques they developed allowed them to cast a variety of metals with amazing accuracy and detail.

By the late 1960s, New England silver companies began using Lance's technical expertise to cast detail metal parts. It wasn't long before Lance was casting metal sculptures for silver and porcelain producers.

In 1974, Don Polland, an established bronze sculptor, brought his "Cheyenne" model to Lance for casting in pewter. This began a long and successful collaboration that continues today. Now known as Chilmark, this limited edition line of pewter sculpture features, in addition to Polland, the works of well known artists such as Francis Barnum, Anne McGrory, David LaRocca, Michael Boyett, Star York and Amy Kann.

Lance also produces a less expensive pewter line of whimsical and contemporary pieces under the name of Hudson Pewter. The line has expanded through the years and now includes a wide representation of products and themes including the very successful *Disney*, *Noah's Ark*, *Christmas Villagers* and *Fantasy* categories.

Hudson Pewter's *The Sorcerer's Apprentice Collector Series*, a collection of five sculptures portraying the major scenes in Mickey Mouse's most popular role, won the coveted *Disney Best New Product of 1990* award. The series was chosen in competition with all new Disney licensed merchandise introduced in 1990, from figurines to games to books to clothing, etc.

In contrast to the pewter lines Lance offers, they have manufactured and distributed Sebastian Miniatures on a national basis since 1975. The highly decorated and colorful cast porcelain Sebastian Miniatures are America's oldest continually produced collectible line. First introduced in 1938 by artist Prescott W. Baston, they are currently designed and sculpted by Baston's son, Woody Baston and sought after by avid collectors.

Cast porcelain is also an integral part of Lance's pewter lines. Hudson Pewter incorporates porcelain backdrops with pewter figurines in such groupings as the *Villagers*, *Mickey's Barnyard Symphony* and the *Santa's Elves* series. Chilmark has combined white porcelain and pewter for some of their fine art sculpture: Francis Barnum's *Summit*, Anne McGrory's *High and Mighty* and Don Polland's *WinterSet* series.

"A Dash for Timber" is from Anne McGrory's OffCanvas series for Lance's Chilmark Pewter.

LAWTONS

548 North First Street
Turlock, California 95380
(209) 632-3655
Fax: (209) 632-6788

Dolls

More than a dozen years ago, Wendy and Keith Lawton formed Lawtons, a company dedicated to the manufacturing and marketing of Wendy's original porcelain dolls. Even from the beginning, it seems they could never make quite enough Lawtons dolls to meet the demand. In 1987, they were joined by Jim and Linda Smith of Tide-Rider, a firm which has been importing European toys for over twenty-five years. The partners have built a strong business based on the high standards that collectors have come to expect from Lawtons dolls.

"Ndeko," a doll from the Cherished Customs™ *series, proudly carries her little Zairian sister, Kimia.*

Wendy still sculpts an original face for each new issue. And the skilled artists who work at Lawtons, take pride in every detail, still crafting each doll the same way Wendy did, back in 1978. Each doll is made entirely by hand in Lawtons' workshops in the San Joaquin Valley of California. Not counting the processes involved in making the costume, shoes, wigs and accessories, there are fifty-six different hand operations in making a single doll.

Lawtons' goal remains the same as it was in the beginning; to make the finest doll it is possible to produce; to maintain the Lawtons "look" — crisp and realistic portraits, with a straightforward American appeal; to work hard to maintain a price that offers real value for each dollar spent on a Lawtons doll; and to continue to do the research necessary to create dolls that illustrate the human experience — from beloved literature to the customs and celebrations of people the world over.

Lawtons dolls have been the recipients of many industry awards. Eleven Lawtons dolls have been nominated for *Doll Reader's* "Doll of the Year (DOTY) Award," and in 1988 Lawtons won two DOTY awards. Lawtons has also been nominated five times for *Dolls* magazine's "Dolls of Excellence" Award and twice received the "Dolls of Excellence" gold medal.

LEGACY DOLLS INC.

5400 Dixie Highway
Holiday, Florida 34690

Dolls

Terri DeHetre began creating reproduction dolls in 1984. Working out of her home, she and her husband traveled to local shows in Florida selling her dolls. Her success led Terri to begin doing original dolls and in 1986, her first original doll was introduced.

She opened a retail shop in Tarpon Springs, Florida and started teaching students. By 1987, the shop had almost doubled in size and her husband, Al, quit the building contracting business to help with the growing new doll business.

In 1988, the company moved into a larger manufacturing facility in Holiday, Florida. Today, thirty-six people are employed and all the limited edition porcelain dolls and vinyl rotational molding is done in that facility.

Terri's most popular original is her lifelike baby "Punkin" which won the prestigious "Doll of the Year" award in 1988.

LEGENDS

Zev Beckerman
2665-D Park Center Drive
Simi Valley, California 93065
(805) 520-9660
Fax: (805) 520-9670

Figurines

LEGENDS' parent, Starlite Originals Inc., was founded in 1972 for the purpose of creating fine art metal sculptures for prestigious companies such as American Express and Walt Disney Productions.

Since its 1986 inception, Starlite's prodigy, LEGENDS, has dramatically impacted the market with its creation of affordable fine art sculpture. The foundry's conception and mastery of Mixed Media™ — the combination of multiple precious metals; LEGENDS Bronze, fine Pewter and Brass Vermeil, and 24 karat Gold Vermeil — has established LEGENDS as one of the industry leaders while redefining the limitations of the artform. LEGENDS sculptures combine the traditional sculptural composite of balance, tension and form with the beauty of awe-inspiring natural color.

Intricately detailed, LEGENDS handcrafted certified limited edition sculptures are registered for the secondary market. The work of prominent LEGENDS artist, Christopher A. Pardell, is appreciating at an unprecedented 500% annual increase. The first four releases of *The Legendary West Premier Edition* — "Red Cloud's Coup," "Pursued," "Songs of Glory," and "Crow Warrior" — sold out within weeks of their scheduled release date and have set a precedent for many of Pardell's other premier collections.

"Defiant Comanche" is the third release from the Legacies of the West Premier Edition *by C.A. Pardell.*

The first and second release of Pardell's *Legacies of the West Premier Edition* — "Mystic Vision" and "Victorious" — have both sold out within weeks of their release, and "Mystic Vision" was honored with a 1990 Award of Excellence from *Collector Editions* Magazine.

LEGENDS' many collections encompass subjects ranging from Native American to western to oceanic to equestrian. They also incorporate the beauty of wildlife through Kitty D. Cantrell's *Endangered Wildlife Collection* and the symmetry of historic architecture through Larry Steorts' two enchanting collections — *The Victorian Homes Collection* and *The Lighthouse Collection*.

LENOX

Rhea E. Goldman
1170 Wheeler Way
Langhorne, Pennsylvania 19047
(215) 750-6900

Figurines, Plates, Bells, Christmas Ornaments, Dolls

At sixteen, Walter Scott Lenox became an apprentice porcelain maker. He dreamed of raising American ceramic art to world prominence. In 1889, Lenox and his partner, Jonathan Coxon Sr., founded the Ceramic Art Company in Trenton, New Jersey. Six years later, Lenox became the sole proprietor and renamed the firm Lenox, Incorporated.

Lenox's determination to improve the quality of American porcelain led him to develop fine china tableware with an ivory lustre and delicate patterns which replaced American's preference for European china. Considered America's premier tableware, Lenox china has graced the tables of four presidents — Woodrow Wilson, Franklin D. Roosevelt, Harry S. Truman and Ronald Reagan.

Lenox Collections, a division of Lenox, Inc., maintains the company's reputation for heirloom-quality porcelain and full-lead crystal. Some of the division's most successful lines have been the *Garden Birds*, *Carousel Animals*, *Legendary Princesses* and the *Nativity* series.

Lenox recently began work on a number of commemorative products. In all cases, a portion of the proceeds help support the efforts of the sponsoring institution. Lenox and The Smithsonian Institution are cooperating on two projects: *Kings of the Sky*, a porcelain sculpture collection of bald eagles, and *Endangered Baby Animals*, porcelain figurines featuring the newborn of endangered species. In cooperation with the PBS Program NATURE, Lenox recently introduced *Gentle Majesty*, a collection of porcelain sculptures demonstrating the maternal bonds between wild animals and their young.

The "Peony Vase" and the "Imperial Bowl from the Ch'ing Emperor" are the first two issues in a collection of porcelain reproductions based on items displayed in The Palace Museum in Peking, China.

Lenox also is working with organizations interested in issuing commemorative pieces celebrating the Bicentennial of the Constitution (1987), the Bicentennial of the Bill of Rights (1991), and the Quincentenary of the Discovery of America by Christopher Columbus (1992).

Dolls programs have also been developed to commemorate important occasions. *Ellis Island Dolls* celebrate the Centennial of Ellis Island (1992), while *Nutcracker Dolls* celebrate the 100th anniversary of the beloved Nutcracker Ballet (1992).

Other new Lenox doll collections include *Children of the World*, the *Victorian Doll Collection* and *Children with Toys*. Lenox also produces a line of decorative kitchen accessories. The *Lenox Village* includes "Lenox Spice Village," "Lenox Village Canisters" and a "Lenox Village Teapot."

"Hannah, The Dutch Maiden" is the first issue in the Children of the World Collection.

LIGHTPOST PUBLISHING

10 Almaden Blvd., 9th Floor
San Jose, California 95113
(408) 279-4777
Fax: (408) 287-1169

Graphics

Lightpost Publishing is most widely known in the limited edition field for its publishing of fine art prints by artist Thomas Kinkade. Kinkade is widely regarded as one of the foremost living painters of light.

Thomas Kinkade grew up in the foothills of the Sierra mountains and began painting seriously at the age of fourteen. After studies at the University of California, Berkeley, and Art Center College of Design in Pasadena, California, Kinkade began work for the motion picture industry at age twenty-two. He personally created over 600 background paintings for the animated feature film, *Fire and Ice*. Also during this period, he and fellow artist James Gurney authored a best selling book entitled *The Artist's Guide to Sketching*.

In 1983, Kinkade left the film industry to pursue his vision as a painter of romantic landscapes and city scenes. Since then, his career has been documented in feature articles in such magazines as *Southwest Art*, *Sierra Heritage*, *U.S. Art*, *Worldwide Challenge* and *Lively Arts and Leisure*. In addition, Kinkade's painting, "Artist's Point," was chosen from nearly 2,700 entrants nationwide, as the official 1989 National Parks Collector Print and stamp.

To research his paintings, Kinkade regularly transports elaborate painting gear to locations ranging from the glaciers of Alaska to the busy streets of Paris. Kinkade spares no effort in creating his works, feeling that painting on location lends energy and mood to his compositions.

Thomas Kinkade works in an enormous studio within a 100-year-old barn on his rural northern California property. In addition to a rigorous six day a week painting schedule, he and his family are highly involved with a nearby Christian church where Kinkade serves faithfully on the board of counsel.

LILLIPUT LANE LIMITED

Gift Link Incorporated
9052 Old Annapolis Road
Columbia, Maryland 21045

(301) 964-2202
Fax: (301) 964-5673

Figurines

Lilliput Lane Limited was founded in September 1982 by David J. Tate with six other family members and friends. From the company's modest beginnings in an old run-down barn, Lilliput Lane has evolved into a leader in the cottage collectibles market. Lilliput Lane is based in Penrith, which is in the Northwest of England in an area known as the Lake District, not far from the Scottish Border.

As the founder and master sculptor, David Tate established high standards and new manufacturing techniques essential for the vernacular reproductions of extremely detailed sculptures. David has spent years researching the architecture of England and has a collection of reference books and thousands of photographs that he utilizes for his designs. He and his team of skilled artists and technicians work on new pieces for months at a time to ensure that all the historical features are accurately portrayed in the finest detail. In recognition for his accomplishments, David J. Tate was invested as a M.B.E. (Member of the Order of the British Empire) in the 1988 New Years Honors List, an award for which he gives credit to everyone in the company.

Lilliput Lane's collection of architecture includes English, Scottish, Irish, German and French Cottages, *The Blaise Hamlet Village Collection*, and *The American Landmarks* series. New sculptures are introduced each and every year to broaden and expand the collectibility of the various ranges.

Lilliput Lane has enjoyed outstanding success and was named one of the top five companies by the Confederation of British Industry in 1987 and 1988. Lilliput Lane was also awarded the Queen's Award for Export in 1988 and a National Training Award in 1989. In the USA, Lilliput Lane was voted 'Best Collectible of Show' in South Bend 1990 for the piece "Convent in the Woods." In the same year, *Collector Editions* magazine presented an "Award of Excellence" from their collectors to Lilliput Lane for "Periwinkle Cottage."

Lilliput Lane is distributed exclusively in the United States by Gift Link, Inc.

David Tate's "Convent in the Woods" is part of the English Cottage Collection.

LLADRO

225 Fifth Avenue
New York, New York 10010
(201) 807-1177
Fax: (201) 807-1168

Figurines, Bells, Ornaments

In 1951, three brothers named Juan, Jose and Vicente Lladro pooled their talents and finances to start a ceramic-making operation in Valencia, Spain. After building a kiln on the family patio, the brothers began to produce ceramics that made the name Lladro synonymous with superb quality and craftmanship.

From the very beginning, they concentrated almost exclusively on the production of figurines at the expense of the utilitarian wares that commonly provided the backbone of such a company's prosperity. This emphasis, however, reflected the sculptural sympathies of the brothers, and continues even today in the wide range of Lladro figurines.

Many of their first offerings were decorated with delicate, miniature, sculpted porcelain flowers. Their vases were modeled after Dresden and Sevres porcelains. But it wasn't long before the Lladro brothers developed their own highly stylized "signature" figures with their own sense of grace and movement.

In order to create these highly specialized works of art, teams of talented workers of unparalled experience in porcelain manufacture were assembled. They were to become the cornerstone of the present-day company.

Today, the company sells a wide range of both limited and open-ended edition figurines. The subjects range from flowers and animals to nativity sets and sports activities. In addition, Lladro manufactures vases, lamp bases and miniatures. In a recent effort to expand its scope, the firm founded the Lladro Collectors Society, which is open to those who decorate with or collect Lladro.

Members of the Collectors Society receive a host of benefits, including a free porcelain plaque with the signatures of the three Lladro brothers, a complimentary leatherette binder to store copies of the Society magazine, and a subscription to the award winning publication, *Expressions*, full of everything a collector might want to know about Lladro and its products. The personalized Society card shows associate membership in the Lladro Museum, which opened to the public in October 1988, and enables members to purchase the specially designed annual members-only figurine. Collectors catalogs are available to active members for a fifty percent savings on the normal suggested retail price. Society memberships are $35 for one year and $60 for two years.

"Flowers of the Season," L1454G is an excellent example of Lladro's attention to delicate floral detailing.

LYNN'S PRINTS

Diane or Ted Graebner
P.O. Box 133
Lodi, Ohio 44254
(216) 948-4607

Graphics

Lynn's Prints was established in 1986 due to an overwhelming response to

Diane Graebner's artistic portrayal of the Amish living near her home.

Phenomenal growth has taken place in a very short time. Her simple statement of the Amish, and the respect she has for their way of life, shows in their wonderful family interactions. She respects the Amish and their beliefs and therefore does not take photographs or paint facial features. Simple elegance with much family love and respect for their religion is the strength Diane Graebner sees, and wants to share with everyone.

Mrs. Graebner's limited edition prints can be found in galleries in thirty-eight states and Canada. Among her releases are yearly special Mothers Day and Christmas editions. Many of Diane Graebner's sold out editions are commanding many times their release price.

SEYMOUR MANN, INCORPORATED

225 Fifth Avenue
New York, New York 10010
(212) 683-7262

Dolls, Figurines

Eda and Seymour Mann have combined their diverse talents in business enterprises since marrying in the 1940s. Seymour has always handled the business and marketing details. And, Eda designed the figurines and other decorative accessories for lines including their highly successful "Americana" collection.

They founded Seymour Mann Inc. in the 1960s. In addition to raising a family and designing giftware, Eda also was an artist and a doll collector who made dolls for her children and grandchildren as a hobby. So it was not surprising that in 1981, Eda's first limited edition dolls in her *Connoisseur Doll Collection* were introduced by Seymour Mann, Inc.

Over the past decade, Eda has designed more than 1,500 limited edition dolls. Some of her most popular series have been the *Dolls of All Nations* and the *Dolls of the Month*.

In 1991, the Manns introduced the *Signature* series which features new doll artists and a number of new doll lines.

The Manns have been nominated for and have won numerous awards for their collectibles. In 1990 their doll/treetopper was nominated for a *Collector Editions* award. Two of Eda's dolls were nominated for *Doll* magazine's "Awards of Excellence" and *Doll Reader* magazine's DOTY Award in 1991. The firm also received two other nominations for the "Awards of Excellence" for other dolls by its designers.

"Lady Caroline" was nominated for the 1991 Awards of Excellence by Dolls Magazine.

MARURI USA CORPORATION

Ed Purcell
7541 Woodman Place
Van Nuys, California 91405
(818) 780-0704

CANADIAN DISTRIBUTOR
Lisser & James Rothschild
53 Courtland Avenue
Concord, Ontario, Canada L4K 3T2
(416) 738-8877

Figurines, Plates

Until 1982, American collectors were largely unaware of a superb porcelain studio in Japan — a firm with roots in the age-old ceramic capital of Seto. In that year, Maruri introduced its wildlife sculptures by renowned artist W.D. Gaither. Within months, Maruri became a respected name in the United States collectibles market.

Less than two years after its introduction, the Maruri-Gaither "American Bald Eagle I" brought $600 on the secondary market — up from its modest issue price of $165. The exceptional quality of Maruri which attracted such attention, is the result of high standards set generations ago, and observed just as strictly today.

Maruri was founded generations ago in Seto, the fabled Ceramic Capital of Japan. At that time, porcelain craftsman flourished among family-oriented workshops, one of which was the family business of Mizuno. The Mizuno brothers named their business Maruri, and soon this studio earned a wide reputation for excellent bone china and porcelain figurines, and true-to-nature bird and animals sculptures.

Maruri prides itself on its studied approach to the creation of limited edition figurines. Each piece takes thirty days or more to complete, using a multi-step process that has been followed faithfully over the years. The studio's premier master sculptor is Ito, who oversees the Seto operation. Ito's understanding of classic porcelain artistry is evident in every Maruri piece. In addition to Ito's many works, Maruri carries on its association with many great artists, creating a wide variety of superb sculptures.

Maruri introduced a series of six Hummingbirds in porcelain and bronze. Single and double Hummingbirds are featured with bronze branches and hand-painted flowers.

The firm recently introduced the *Maruri Studio* collection, which is intended to bring to collectors the very finest quality editions using various subjects and edition sizes. In this collection, "Majestic Eagles" features two American Bald Eagles in fine porcelain and bronze. One of the latest pieces in the collection is "Delicate Motion," which features three violet crowned hummingbirds amid a spray of morning-glories.

From the Maruri Studio *collection, comes "Delicate Motion."*

McGUFFEY DOLLS

1300 East Bay Drive, Unit 1
Largo, Florida 34641

Dolls

In 1989, Karen McGuffey Miller and Melva McGuffey formed McGuffey Dolls and Jomel Studios. Proud descendants of William Holmes McGuffey, the educator who influenced millions through the old McGuffey Eclectic Readers, the McGuffeys are determined to bring the same integrity and basic values to the art of dollmaking.

While Melva has been making reproduction dolls since 1982, Karen made her debut in 1989 with her original porcelain doll, "Samantha Jo," sculpted from a picture of her niece. "Samantha Jo" was the first in a series of babies. Dolls like "Snookums," "Joey," "Joy," "Stephanie Nichole" and "Todd" soon followed. All are based on children within the family. The McGuffey dolls are usually limited to an issue of only 300 dolls. Each doll is numbered, signed and accompanied by a certificate of authenticity.

School teacher dolls named "Miss Melzie" and "Professor McGuffey" have become the company's logo dolls, and both were produced in limited editions of only 150 dolls each.

All McGuffey dolls are hand finished in the United States and dressed in authentic costumes created by meticulous seamstresses.

JUNE MCKENNA COLLECTIBLES, INC.

Donna M. Gomer
205 Haley Road P.O. Box 846
Ashland, Virginia 23005
(804) 798-2024

Figurines, Christmas Ornaments

Exquisite attention to detail marked by authentic period clothing and toys, a whimsical face highlighted by an upturned nose and twinkling brown eyes — these are the trademarks of June McKenna's famous Santa Claus figurines. Focusing on Santa Claus as he was known in the 16th through the 19th centuries, June McKenna works to include just the right touches to make each figurine the highly sought after collectible that it is.

The artist, using minute dental tools sculpts the figurine in clay, achieving such realism that people are often seen touching the lace collar on one piece or the gold braid on another to see whether they are made of fabric or wood resin. Next, a mold is formed and wood resin poured into it and allowed to harden. Finally, artists meticulously hand-paint each individual figure and then cover the finished piece with the antique finish which gives the distinctive old world appearance which is such a striking part of June McKenna's work.

There are, perhaps, two ways in which the success of a collectible line can easily be measured, and June McKenna Collectibles achieves high marks on both counts. Although June McKenna only began carving her Santa Claus figures in 1982, her major limited edition pieces for 1983 through 1988 have already sold out — quite a feat for a collectible line. And the second criterion for success, one set by June McKenna herself, is that her pieces are designed to be both attractive and affordable to everyone from the young child who loves Santa to the most serious collector.

June McKenna figurines, which range in size from five to seventeen inches, are available in a wide variety of prices, starting at $20.00 each, marked by old world charm and intricate attention to detail. The artist creates approximately fifteen new pieces each year.

LEE MIDDLETON ORIGINAL DOLLS

1301 Washington Boulevard
Belpre, Ohio 45714
(614) 423-1717
Fax: (614) 423-5983

Dolls

While most successful corporate executives would not consider "seeing the world through a mother's eyes" an asset, Lee Middleton, the co-founder and artistic force behind Lee Middleton Original Dolls, knows that her sensitive motherly insights are essential in sculpting the dolls which have made her company a success.

A deeply religious person, Lee attributes her ability to capture the innocence and wonder of infants and children to God. This trust was born out in 1978 when Lee entered her first doll show. Her "Little Angel" doll was named best of show for design excellence. As a token of "giving credit where credit is due," each of Lee's original dolls leaves the factory accompanied by a tiny Bible.

When she started out, Lee used her children as models. She taught herself to sculpt, mold and cast her dolls. Lacking capital to buy new materials, Lee adorned her dolls with scraps from thrift store clothiers and wigs. Used purses were cut up to make shoes.

With the encouragement of family and friends, Lee started Lee Middleton Original Dolls in 1980. During her fledgling years, her dolls were sold on the regional doll show circuit, but by late 1980 enough wholesale orders had been placed for Lee to move her business from her kitchen table to a series of rented locations.

Although all of her early dolls were handcrafted porcelains, Lee was searching for another medium in which to produce more affordable dolls. In 1984, Lee introduced porcelain-looking vinyl versions of her dolls. Undetectable from porcelain except by touch, and more affordable, the sale of these dolls soon skyrocketed.

Lee's "extended family" of 140-plus full and part-time employees are among the doll industry's most talented artisans. Working to the most exacting standards of pride and excellence, they collectively give life to each of Lee's extraordinary designs. A new, 37,000 square-foot state-of-the-art production plant on the Ohio River in Belpre, Ohio now houses this dynamic and ever-growing company.

A Middleton Collectors' Club has recently been started to keep collectors informed about Lee's newest offerings, and tours of Lee Middleton Original

Limited to 5,000, "Baby Grace" features soft flaxen hair and striking lavender-blue eyes.

Dolls are conducted on a regular basis for interested collectors.

MIDWEST IMPORTERS INC. OF CANNON FALLS

Attn: Consumer Inquiries
P.O. Box 20
Cannon Falls, MN 55009
(800) 377-3335

Figurines

Midwest Importers of Cannon Falls, Inc. was founded as a retail gift shop in 1955. This store specialized in imported handcrafted articles from Europe, and offered an extensive line of religious products. In 1964, the retail store was closed in favor of establishing a wholesale distribution business serving retail stores across the U.S. Over the past quarter century, the company has grown to a prominent position among the industry leaders in seasonal giftware, offering over 4,500 items.

The company entered the collectible market in 1990 with the introduction of *The Heritage Santa Collection*. Inspired by the legends, lore, and folk traditions surrounding this gift-bearing spirit, the collection features Santas from different countries, including "Herr Kristmas" from the Black Forest of Germany; "MacNicholas" from the Scottish Highlands; "Papa Frost" from the Russian Steppes; "Scanda Klaus" from the Scandinavian countries; "Santa Niccolo" from Italy; and "Father Christmas" from England. Each character is originally designed, meticulously sculpted and handpainted, and highly detailed with accessory pieces which reflect their unique heritage. Two new characters are added to the collection each year.

Collectors of folk art will appreciate *The Leo Smith Collection*, a numbered limited edition collection designed by Leo R. Smith III. Working from his home in the picturesque Mississippi River town of Fountain City, Wisconsin, Leo Smith creates wood sculptures that combine the spirit of the wood with the legends of the land to create truly magical and compelling figures. To begin, he sculpts a rough clay model of the design to establish the basic shape and character. Then come the meticulous handcarving of the wood sculpture, a process that can take months to complete. Once complete, Leo and his wife Marilyn develop a color scheme and handpaint the figure. These original figures are then reproduced in handcast resin to precisely capture the beauty of the original woodcarving, then handpainted based on the color schemes developed by the Smiths. Richly detailed and imaginatively sculpted, this collection brings to life the legends of the Mississippi Valley.

MILL POND PRESS, INC.

310 Center Court
Venice, Florida 34292

Graphics, Sculptures

Mill Pond Press, Venice, Florida, a family-owned art print publishing company, is proud of its reputation for creating some of the finest limited edition prints in the country. Quality is the foundation upon which the firm has built its reputation over the last eighteen years.

As publisher, Mill Pond Press closely supervises the reproduction process of each limited edition print. The artists are consulted at each stage, and their input is vital. As many colors as necessary are used to match the original artwork. Advances in offset lithography printing have made it possible to do this with incredible accuracy. The printing is done by fine craftsmen who find it a particular challenge to meet Mill Pond's high standards. The prints are published on luxurious all-rag, neutral pH paper made to Mill Pond's specifications. With proper care, the paper will last generations.

Mill Pond publishes a monthly publication *Art For Collectors*, which announces the release of ten to twelve new prints each month. The prints are distributed through a network of dealers in the U.S., Canada and England.

Mill Pond Press has an extensive line of limited edition prints by more than fifty artists of national and international acclaim.

Subjects range from nature and sporting prints to landscapes, florals and primitives to nudes.

In 1986, the company further expanded its offerings to collectors by adding original hand-colored etchings.

NAHRGANG COLLECTION

1005 1st Avenue
Silvis, Illinois 61282
(309) 792-9180

Dolls

The Nahrgang Collection evolved from a small family business in Moline, Illinois on the banks of the Mississippi River. Jan Nahrgang with the help of her husband, Larry and daughter Jennifer, started the business in 1980. What began as a hobby led to a thriving and booming business involving more family members and numerous employees. The business has doubled every year for the past ten years.

Nahrgang dolls are sold in fine doll and gift shops across the country and as far away as Australia. Nahrgang dolls are recognized for their fine detailed sculpture, delicate hand painting exclusively by Jan, and exquisitely hand sewn costumes. All the dolls and costumes are hand made in Illinois and are usually designed from children Jan has had contact with in her teaching position at Franklin Elementary School. In addition to children dolls, exquisite fashion dolls are also produced. All editions are very small — usually 250.

Nahrgang dolls have received numerous awards and recognition. The most prestigious to date has been the 1990 Doll of The Year award from *Doll Reader* magazine for "Karissa."

Due to the demand and extreme amount of time to produce hand-crafted Nahrgang porcelain dolls, exquisite porcelain-like vinyl dolls are being produced by the Nahrgang Collection in the new factory in Silvis, Illinois (a neighboring town). At the new facility,

Exquisitely outfitted, "Carmen," the gypsy, authentically looks into her crystal ball.

the famous Nahrgang porcelain dolls will continue to be produced in small quantities along with the new limited edition vinyl designs.

The company intends to remain a small business in America's Heartland with the unique feature of producing hand-made collectible treasures for doll lovers around the world.

NEW MASTERS PUBLISHING CO., INC.

Connie Hardin
2301 14th Street Suite 105
Gulfport, Mississippi 39501
(601) 863-5145
800 647-9578
Fax: (601) 863-5145

Graphics

Very few artists in the world, past or present, have portrayed the delicacy, sensitivity, and mystery of women with the skill and insight of Pati Bannister. She is a master of feminine portraiture and exquisite detail, as evidenced by the limited edition prints that are issued by New Masters Publishing Co., Inc.

Pati Bannister was born in north London, England, into a family of accomplished artists. After an early career as an illustrator for children's books and the famous English equestrian publication, *Riding*, she worked as a special effects artist for the J. Arthur Rankin film studios where she further developed a keen and sensitive eye for detail and color mixing, and their impact on all aspects of design and composition in a work of art.

In 1952, Pati Bannister moved to the U.S. and later settled on the Mississippi Gulf Coast overlooking a wildlife sanctuary. There she explores the female psyche, posing the young ladies of her imagination with exotic flowers, gossamer fabrics, and filigreed lace in fine Victorian parlors, beside rain-swept windows, along lone country roads. Her juxtaposition of delicate natural beauty with steadfast matter is a key element of Pati Bannister's unique style and extraordinary popularity.

But it's the intangible quality of her women toward which people of all ages and backgrounds are irresistibly drawn. From innocent child to sensual maiden, there exists in Bannister's females an ethereal vulnerability one wants to protect along with an inherent strength one wants to know. Here is an artist who is master of the feminine mystique.

Pati Bannister's continuous endeavor to capture and preserve the tranquility, beauty, and aura of her astute vision through painting and sculpture is the essence of her life.

OLDENBURG ORIGINALS

Hidden Meadow Farm
W5061 Pheasant Valley Road
Waldo, Wisconsin 53093
414-528-7127

Dolls

Maryanne Oldenburg's love for children is evident in her work. Trained as a commercial artist, Oldenburg began making dollhouses and miniatures in 1970 before learning to make dolls with polyform clay. By the late 1970s, she had mastered the porcelain and mold making processes needed to make high quality porcelain dolls.

Oldenburg's dolls are all based on "real" children and events. Many of her models are her grandchildren and local school children. Working from photos and facial measurements, the artist molds a clay model from which all the working molds will be taken.

Oldenburg's limited edition dolls are signed and numbered with most editions limited from 30 to 50 dolls. The artist also designs dolls for Ashton-Drake Galleries and teaches sculpturing in traveling seminars and doll conventions. Oldenburg is also a member of ODACA (Original Doll Artist Council of America).

OLDHAM PORCELAINS, LTD.

Victoria L. Oldham
18 Hemlock Road
Lansdowne, Pennsylvania 19050
(215) 259-4444
Fax: (215) 622-3037

Figurines, Dolls

Oldham Porcelains, Ltd. was established in 1989 for the design and production of a new line of collectible sculptures and dolls in fine porcelain.

The founders, Charles and Victoria Oldham, are not newcomers to the collectibles field; they have already created more than 150 original designs, produced in porcelain or crystal, and marketed under the names of other famous porcelain makers, including Cybis, The Franklin Mint, and Lenox. Sculptures designed by Oldham were also selected by two U.S. Presidents as gifts to leaders of foreign nations, and by The Cousteau Society and The National Wildlife Federation. In addition, they developed limited edition and one-of-a-kind porcelains for retail jewelers and specialty shops across the U.S.

Works designed by Oldham Porcelains, Ltd. are the result of extensive market research and comprise a wide variety of subjects. Charles and Victoria are known for their accurate and dramatic portrayals of wildlife (some almost two feet tall), fanciful carousel animals, realistic flowers, and elegant figurines of women and children.

ORIGINAL APPALACHIAN ARTWORKS, INC.

Diane Cobb
P.O. Box 714
Cleveland, Georgia 30528
(404) 865-2171
Fax: (404) 865-5862

Dolls

In 1977, a young art student, Xavier Roberts, combined an interest in sculpture with age-old quilting skills of the Appalachian Mountains. The results were life-size cloth "babies" who were so homely they were adorable. He called them "Little People®" and began making them available for adoption at craft shows in the Southeast.

A year later, Roberts and five college friends established "Babyland General® Hospital" in Cleveland, Georgia. A short time later more than 500,000 of these hand-stitched babies had been adopted for fees that ranged from $150 to $650.

In August 1982, Roberts granted Coleco Industries, Inc. the license to produce a small, mass-market version of the babies and the name was changed to "Cabbage Patch Kids.®" In July 1989, Hasbro Inc., one of the world's largest toy companies, assumed the licensing agreement previously held by Coleco.

Collectors will find Cabbage Patch Kids, both the hand-stitched, limited edition originals as well as the mass market version, capturing the trends and fashions of the times while maintaining an eternal child-like innocence.

ORREFORS OF SWEDEN

Robin Spink
140 Bradford Drive
Berlin, New Jersey 08009

(609) 768-5400
Fax: (609) 768-9726

Christmas Ornaments

Orrefors, one of the world's leading producers of fine crystal art glass, tableware and accessories, was established in 1726 as a foundry in the forest area of southern Sweden. In 1898, it began manufacturing glass bottles, eau de cologne holders, and simple tableware.

Orrefors' direction began changing again in 1916 and 1917 when it became the first glass producer to retain fine artists and designers like Simon Gate, a portrait and landscape painter, and Edward Hald, a former student of Matisse.

In 1925, Orrefors won grand prizes at the Paris Exposition. This was only the first of countless prizes and prestigious exhibits of Orrefors art glass in the leading museums around the world.

In 1991, Orrefors released the eighth in its series of collectible crystal Christmas ornaments. The entire *Christmas Ornament* collection has been created by renowned Orrefors artist Olle Alberius.

OSTROM COMPANY

P.O. Box 4729
Portland, Oregon 97208-4729
(503) 281-6469
FAX: (503) 281-6469

Christmas Ornaments

A Revolutionary War heroine, Abigail Lefferts Lloyd, enjoyed the art of ornamental paper-cutting. Her artistically shaped birds and flowers were passed from generation-to-generation as family mementos. It was Roger Ostrom, her great-great-great-great grandson, who recognized the creative potential of her paper-cuttings, and after a series of experiments, transformed them into satin brass Christmas ornaments.

In 1973, Ostrom founded the Ostrom Company, which is recognized nationally for its glass and metal etchings and engravings. At the request of his customers, Ostrom began experimenting with small pieces for awards and corporate gifts. These experiments led Ostrom to see these antique paper-cuttings from a different perspective. He produced his first filigreed, through-etched brass ornaments based on one of Abigail's paper-cuttings in 1983 and presented them to members of the family as gifts.

Other family members and friends who saw these original ornaments, begged to be included in the tradition. In 1988, the first annual limited editon Ostrom-Lloyd ornament was introduced to collectors. Both the beauty and the historical significance of these ornaments made them an immediate success with collectors. This series is expected to be limited to thirteen ornaments. The 1991 Abigail Lefferts Lloyd ornament was nominated for the Awards of Excellence by *Collectors Editions* magazine. Ostrom recently announced plans to release a second series in 1992 which will celebrate the art of paper-cutting around the world.

PAST IMPRESSIONS

Caroline Doss
P.O. Box 188
Belvedere, California 94920
(415) 435-1625 or
(415) 358-9075
Fax: (415) 435-1625

FREDERICK DICKSON & CO.
28, Carnforth Road
Toronto, Ontario Canada M4A 2K7
(416) 751-4685

Graphics

Alan Maley, internationally acclaimed artist, is highly regarded for his sensitive interpretation of life at the turn-of-the-century. Stimulating activities as well as everyday events are beautifully interwoven with historic locales to create intriguing vignettes of people and places. The absorbing and romantic scenes of the late 19th century invite the viewer to wander in and participate in the meaningful moments of another lifetime.

Born in England, Maley's artistic talents were recognized at an early age and encouraged by his family. He attended the Reigate College of Art and then had the opportunity to attend the Royal Academy of Art in London or enter the British movie industry. His first love, the movies, won, and he served a five year apprenticeship learning his art from some of the finest European masters. He distinguished himself as one of the foremost artists in the motion picure industry with his work appearing in many of the best known and well loved movies of our time.

Maley's dream to work in Hollywood was achieved in 1964, when he was invited to work at the Walt Disney Studios where he spent many happy years. His skillful recreations of reality earned him widespread recognition and respect from his colleagues, culminating in a prestigious OSCAR from the Academy of Motion Picture Arts & Sciences. For the past twenty years, his superb impressionistic easel paintings have captured the attention of serious collectors both in the USA and abroad who have eagerly acquired his works as soon as they have become available.

In 1984, Alan Maley formed his own publishing company, Past Impressions, to produce limited editions of his own paintings. All prints produced under his close supervision are of the finest quality. They are a tribute to his unique talent and keen perception in interpreting the style, grace and elegance of a bygone era, captured with remarkable inventiveness and presented through an appealing intimate perspective.

PEMBERTON & OAKES

Mary Hugunin
133 E. Carrillo
Santa Barbara, California 93101
(805) 963-1371

Plates, Figurines, Graphics

Pemberton & Oakes is most widely known in the limited edition field for its Donald Zolan collector plates on child subjects.

Beginning with Zolan's 1978 "Erik and Dandelion," the firm issued eight Zolan series: *Zolan's Children*, the *Children at Christmas* collection, the *Wonder of Childhood Collection*, the *Children and Pets Collection*, the *Childhood Friendship Collection*, the *Best of Zolan in Miniature* collection, the *Special Moments of Childhood* series, and the *Adventures of Childhood* series. It also has produced figurines and limited edition lithographs by Zolan.

The Pemberton & Oakes Gallery in Santa Barbara, California offers original works, and displays original paintings for the plates in the series named above.

The president of Pemberton & Oakes is John Hugunin, former president of The Bradford Exchange.

PENDELFIN SALES INCORPORATED

P.O. Box 884
750 Ensinger Road Suite 108
Tonawanda, New York 14150
800-263-4491

Figurines

On the day that Elizabeth the Second was crowned Queen of England, two young English women founded their business. It began as a quiet hobby for Jeannie Todd and Jean Walmsley Heap who enjoyed molding small clay figures as gifts for their friends. Soon their enterprise grew too large for the garden hut where it started and spilled over into Todd's kitchen. Later, they moved their business to a small shop where customers soon began arriving.

Since they lived in the shadow of Pendle Hill (the old Witch Hill of "Mist over Pendle") and were creating elfin characters, the partners selected Pendle and Elfin hence "PenDelfin" for the name of their company. A broomstick was added to their trademark for luck.

Made of a durable stone-based compound, the PenDelfin line includes a collection of cottages, shops and landmarks like the bandstand and jetty. These charming display pieces provide the perfect backdrop for the diverse members of the Rabbit Family who inhabit this magical land.

In addition to their figurines, PenDelfin also produces limited edition collector plates, books and pictures.

PICKARD CHINA

Patti Kral
782 Corona Avenue
Antioch, Illinois 60002
(708) 395-3800
Fax: (708) 395-3827

Plates

Pickard China was founded in 1893 by Wilder Austin Pickard and has the distinction of being the only American china company still owned and operated by its founding family. The earliest Pickard pieces were hand-painted pottery made by Pauline Jacobus of Edgerton, Wisconsin, supplemented with porcelain blanks imported from France and Germany to keep the studio of thirteen artists busy.

In 1937, the studio was moved to Antioch, Illinois where a factory was built and a formula for fine china was developed. The emphasis then switched from hand-painted, one-of-a-kind entertaining pieces and decorative accessories to fine china dinnerware under the direction of Wilder's son, Henry Austin Pickard.

In the 1960s, current president Henry Austin (Pete) Pickard, Jr. became involved and began to diversify Pickard's product line. In addition to dinnerware and gifts, Pickard entered the field of limited editions, first offering the landmark plate series, *Lockhart Wildlife*, and expanding to the elaborate *Christmas* series, then a limited edition Christmas bell collection. Plate series like *Children of Renoir*, *A Mother's Love*, *Children of Mexico* and *Symphony of Roses* led to "Best Manufacturer" awards from the National Association of Limited Edition Dealers for eight years running.

Recent plate offerings include the *Wings of Freedom* series produced in conjunction with the Fountainhead Corporation, *Gems of Nature: The Beautiful Hummingbirds* currently being offered by the Bradford Exchange, and *The Romantic Castles of Europe* series being co-marketed with the Hamilton Collection.

In addition to plates, Pickard has been a catalyst in bringing the bowl into acceptance as a limited edition collectible, first teaming up with The Greenwich Workshop in producing "The Americana Bowl" by artist Charles Wysocki, and then with the U.S. Historical Society in the production of "The Presidential Bowl" and the "Waterfowl of Maynard Reece." Currently in production is "The Triple Crown Bowl" by equine artist Fred Stone for American Artists.

POLLAND STUDIOS

c/o Donald J. Polland
P.O. Box 1146
Prescott, Arizona 86302
(602) 778-1900
FAX: (602) 778-4034

Figurines

Donald Polland's early works were ambitious, cast-bronze sculptures, but in the late 1960s he began rethinking his entire concept of art. Gradually, he realized he wanted to create different, miniature "jewels" with the same detailing as his larger works.

In 1972, he established the Polland Studios in Laguna Beach, California and a short time later Polland entered the gift and collectibles market. Finding that the cost of casting bronze was too prohibitive, he searched for a suitable, less costly material. The search ended in January 1974 when Polland's first pewter sculptures were introduced by The Lance Corporation. This remains one of Polland's most successful associations.

In 1979, Polland became affiliated with Border Fine Arts which produced a line of Polland cold-cast porcelains which were distributed by Schmid. A decade later, Polland Studios took over the entire design, manufacturing and marketing of this line in the United States.

A second Polland Studio has been established in Boston so he and his staff can be closer to The Lance Corporation and other clients of Polland's design services. Polland has earned a unique place in the collectible's world, yet his credo remains the same, "Quality at a fair price."

"Running Wolf" is part of the American West *cast porcelain series, created by Don Polland and limited to 2,500 pieces, available through Chardon.*

PORSGRUNDS PORSELAENSFABRIK A/S

Porselensvn.12, P.O. Box 100
N-3901 Porsgrunn/NORWAY
+47 3 550040
Fax: +47 3 559110

PORSGRUND USA INC.
2920-3000 Wolff Street
Racine, Wisconsin 53404
(414) 632 3433
Fax: (414) 632 2529

Plates, Figurines, Bells, Christmas Ornaments

A happy accident led to the establishment of Porsgrund, Norway's first and leading porcelain factory. Johan Jeremiassen of Telemark in southern Norway was convalescing in Germany after an illness. He noticed that German porcelain manufacturers imported large quantities of quartz and feldspar from Norway, and wondered why porcelain was not produced in his native land. Upon returning home, he looked into the situation and discovered that not only raw materials but also manpower and even a building site with shipping facilities were right at hand.

He soon convinced his wife's family that a porcelain factory would be an excellent investment for them. This family, the Knudsens, were prominent in the shipping business, and to this day their contribution to the company is acknowledged by the anchor in the Porsgrund trademark.

Porsgrund makes fine porcelain of outstanding design, and has received numerous national and international awards and prizes for the past forty years. In 1985 Porsgrund celebrated its 100th anniversary. The firm created its first Christmas plate in 1909, and resumed a series in 1968 which continues today. Porsgrund also has offered Castle, Traditional Christmas, Deluxe Christmas, Easter, Father's Day, Jubilee and Mother's Day plates over the past two decades.

PRECIOUS ART / PANTON INTERNATIONAL

110 E. Ellsworth
Ann Arbor, Michigan 48108-2203
(313) 677-3510
Fax: (313) 677-3412

Figurines

Precious Art/Panton International is a leading distributor and producer of fine limited edition collectibles. Since its conception in 1981, Precious Art has been a source for many innovative lines. Sam and Pat Chandok own Precious Art, and the company headquarters are in Ann Arbor, Michigan. From carousel ponies to fantasy figures, Precious Art has an ongoing dedication to bringing new and exciting products to the market.

With a new state-of-the-art factory in Chestertown, England, Panton stands ready to follow the success of last year's *Safari Kingdom* and *Mischievous Mice* series. These realistic quality figures were introduced by the company in 1991, one of the most exciting being a new series of babies from the animal kingdom.

Malcolm Merriweather collectibles hit American shores in 1991. These small mice figures, whimsical in nature, are made of cold cast porcelain, and are hand painted in the Panton factory.

Leading the pack in Precious Art's stable of collectibles is the ever popular *World of Krystonia*. A whimsical fantasy line of wizards and dragons, it continues to be one of the most sought-after collectibles. Collectors can now read two books, *Chronicles of Krystonia* and *Krystonian Adventures* which follow the exploits of the haphazard Krystonian inhabitants. Not only do these books tell of the struggle for control of Krystonia, but tell of the adventures of its lovable characters. Pat Chandok and David Woodard designed many new characters which were released in 1991, as well as the second year Collector's Club figurine, "Dragons Play."

Gurneyfoot shares the history of the "World of Krystonia" with young Shadra while walking hand in hand in this figurine entitled "Gurneyfoot and Shadra."

PRESTIGE DOLLS

Caroline Kandt-Lloyd
2208-10 NW Birdsdale
Gresham, Oregon 97030
(503) 667-1008

Dolls

Prestige Dolls began in 1989 with a line of original porcelain dolls by Caroline Kandt-Lloyd. These dolls were limited in production and ranged from editions of 5 to 250. Although during 1990, one-of-a-kind dolls were also added to the line.

Caroline began her doll career after spending time outside the U.S. studying tropical medicine and then teaching in a nursing program in Africa. On return, a hobby soon turned into a part-time job and then a career change. Caroline taught classes and seminars before beginning to sculpt her own creations.

Happy children's faces are Caroline's trademark. She knows personally each of the children she has taken from human form to doll form. Caroline and her husband Stewart share the responsibilities of production. Caroline sculpts and designs, while Stewart takes her clay model into the mold stage. Stewart also handles the production and business details. Family members and friends complete the staff who all take special delight in creating these works of love.

Prestige Dolls introduces new faces each year to its selection, taking great pains in putting the best materials into each doll.

RECO INTERNATIONAL CORP.

Marlene Marcus
150 Haven Avenue, P.O. Box 951
Port Washington, New York 11050
(516) 767-2400
Fax: (516) 767-2409

Bells, Christmas Ornaments, Dolls, Figurines, Graphics, Plates

Reco International Corp. was founded in 1967 by Heio Reich, a native of Berlin, Germany. From its inception, Reco has been dedicated to the world of limited editions. Reco's first offerings were collector plates created in association with renowned porcelain manufacturers like Fuerstenberg, Royale, Dresden, Royal Germania Crystal, King's and Moser. All of these series are complete and now available only on the secondary market.

In 1977, Reco discovered John McClelland, a well-known illustrator and artist who specialized in child-subject art. McClelland's first series, *The World of Children*, was introduced in 1977 and was immediately followed by *The Mother Goose* and the *McClelland Children's Circus* series. Reco later introduced a number of McClelland figurine series — *Porcelains in Miniature*, *Clowns* and *Angels*. In 1987, McClelland returned to collector plates with the release of *Becky's Day* which was followed by *The*

Treasured Songs of Childhood. McClelland also was among the artists selected to participate in the *Our Children, Our Future* plate series honoring the 50th anniversary of the March of Dimes.

McClelland designed a series of music boxes for Reco and in 1990, McClelland entered the collectible doll market with "Tommy the Clown," the first doll in his *Children's Circus* doll series. Second doll in the series is "Katie the Tightrope Walker."

Another noted Reco artist is Sandra Kuck. Ms. Kuck has created a number of popular series; *Games Children Play, The Grandparents Collector's Plates, Little Professionals, A Childhood Almanac, A Children's Christmas Pageant* and the award-winning *Days Gone By* series. Ms. Kuck's most recent series include the *Mother's Day, Barefoot Children* and the *Victorian Mother's Day* series. Sandra Kuck was also selected to create plate art for the March of Dimes series, *Our Children, Our Future.* She has won several awards, including the coveted N.A.L.E.D. award for Artist of the Year for six years in a row.

In addition to lines of music boxes and Christmas ornaments, Kuck also has successfully entered the doll market with "Loving Steps," the first doll in *Precious Memories of Motherhood* series. The second mother and infant dolls are titled "Lullaby."

In 1985, Reco introduced Aldo Fazio's *The Sophisticated Ladies* plate collection depicting cats in elegant poses. It was later followed by *Sophisticated Ladies* figurines and musicals.

Reco added the plate series by nature artists, Dot and Sy Barlowe in 1986. The Barlowe's plate series include *The Vanishing Animal Kingdoms, Gardens of Beauty, Town and Country Dogs,* and *Our Cherished Seas.* In 1987, Reco introduced *Great Stories from the Bible* by Garri Katz.

The first plate in the annual *Nutcracker Ballet* series by Clemente Micarelli was introduced in 1989. The following year, Reco introduced series by three fine artists. Artist Jody Bergsma created three new series; *Guardians of the Kingdom, Mother's Day* and *Christmas.* Inge Drechsler's new series is entitled *God's Own Country.* Another popular series is *The Flower Fairies Year Collection* based on the art of Cicely Mary Barker.

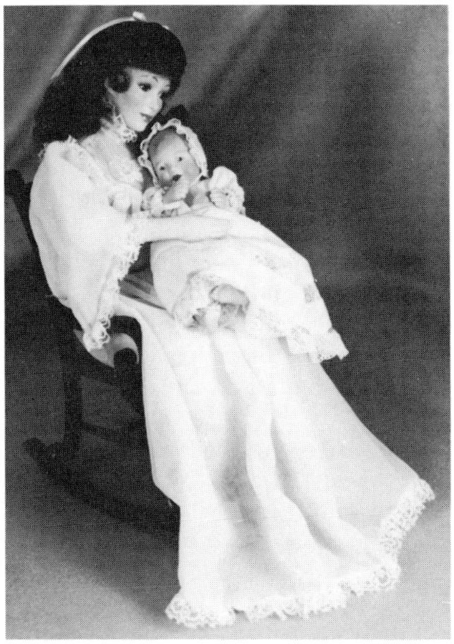

"Lullaby" is the second doll in the Precious Memories of Motherhood *series, created by Sandra Kuck.*

RED MILL MFG., INC.

Karen S. McClung
1023 Arbuckle Road
Summerville, West Virginia 26651
(304) 872-5231
Fax: (304) 872-5234

Figurines

Red Mill Mfg. was established in 1980 as a manufacturer of handcrafted collectibles made from crushed pecan shells. The line consisted of twelve different collectibles for that first year.

Since then, a number of pieces have retired from the line annually, and new designs added. The 1992 line of collectibles consists of over 105 different designs.

An annual limited edition angel is a favorite of many collectors along with the limited edition eagles in the *Red Mill Heritage Collection.*

Red Mill Mfg. offers a great variety for all collectors — turtles, owls, frogs, horses — appealing to collectors' interests.

REED & BARTON

144 West Britannia Street
Taunton, Massachusetts 02780
(508) 824-6611

Bells, Christmas Ornaments, Plates

Reed & Barton has been one of America's leading silversmiths since its founding in 1824. The company has been manufacturing fine sterling silver, silverplate, and stainless flatware and giftware for more than 160 years.

The Reed & Barton *Christmas Ornament Collection* represents one of the finest, most extensive assortment of silver and gold ornaments in the world. Since the introduction of the sterling silver and 24 K gold-over-sterling *Christmas Crosses* in 1971, Reed & Barton has added a number of highly successful annual series like the *Holly Bell, The Twelve Days of Christmas* (sterling and lead crystal), *Marching Band, Flora of Christmas, Carousel Horse, Colors of Christmas, and Cathedrals.* Ornaments like the golden "Lace Basket," "Yuletide Bell" and *Mini-Tree* ornaments in silver-plate also have been popular with collectors.

For bell collectors, Reed & Barton introduced the *Twelve Days of Christmas,* a twelve-bell series of silver and porcelain in 1990.

HAROLD RIGSBY GRAPHICS

P.O. Box 769
Glasgow, Kentucky 42142

Graphics

In 1978, Harold Rigsby formed his own graphics company, Harold Rigsby Graphics, Inc. to produce and distribute both his open issues and his limited edition wildlife prints.

Harold Rigsby earned a degree with honors from Herron School of Art at Indiana University and studied at Western Kentucky University, the Louisville School of Art and the Instituto-Allende in Mexico.

After art school, Rigsby worked as a portrait artist at a tourist attraction. He later became the advertising director for a pharmaceutical company. In 1978, Rigsby released his first print which sold out within three weeks. The income from this piece allowed Rigsby to paint daily.

Rigsby seeks out and studies his subjects in zoos across the country. Working from a series of sketches and photos, the artist then completes his artwork in the comfort of his studio.

RIVER SHORE

Gwen Hunter
4810 Executive Park Court
P.O. Box 2567
Jacksonville, Florida 32232

Plates, Figurines, Bells

River Shore was founded in 1975, and in 1976 introduced its *Famous Americans* series — the first-ever copper collector plates. The plates were based on artwork by Norman Rockwell and sculpted by Roger Brown to create a bas-relief effect.

Other popular issues from River Shore and Brown have included several series of baby animal figurines. His most recent collections were the *Babies of Endangered Species*, premiering with an adorable, blue-eyed, Eastern cougar named "Sydney;" and the *Wilderness Babies*, beginning with "Penelope" the fawn. Other collections include *Puppy Playtime* and *Delights of Childhood* by Jim Lamb, and *America at Work* by Norman Rockwell.

River Shore has focused its attention on Americana themes in the area of collector plates. A favorite has been the *America at Work* series, featuring Americans in interesting occupations, as portrayed by the legendary Norman Rockwell on the covers of *The Saturday Evening Post*.

Renowned western artist Don Crook was featured in two of River Shore's plate series — one portraying mischievous *Children of the American Frontier*; and the other honoring the U.S. Constitution's 200th Anniversary, called *We the Children*, and featuring playful scenes of the Bill of Rights in action.

THE NORMAN ROCKWELL GALLERY

9200 Center for the Arts
Niles, Illinois 60648

Figurines, Ornaments

The Norman Rockwell Gallery is dedicated to faithfully translating the work of America's best-loved artist into distinctive and unique collectible products. Only collectibles which have been authorized by The Norman Rockwell Family Trust are offered by the Gallery, and each work bears a bronze seal attesting to this important endorsement.

The Gallery publishes a quarterly newsletter for its members which provides updates on special exhibits, previews of new Rockwell collectibles and comments and interviews from friends and associates who knew the artist.

Rockwell's Main Street, a series of landmark sculptures re-creating Rockwell's famous painting, "Main Street, Stockbridge," was one of the Gallery's early successes. It was soon followed by a second sculpture series entitled *Rockwell's Hometown*.

Figurines translating Rockwell's original artwork into three-dimensional interpretations are also an important part of the Gallery's product line. Rockwell's affection for children was demonstrated in dozens of paintings throughout his career, and two of the Gallery's figurine collections are based on some of these paintings. *Rockwell's Age of Wonder* features children enjoying the simple pleasures of youth; and *Gems of Wisdom* focuses on children interacting with older adults. Young women are the subject of *Rockwell's Beautiful Dreamers* figurine collection, while the artist's numerous illustrations of Old Saint Nick provided the inspiration for *Rockwell's Heirloom Santa Collection*.

In addition to cottages and figurines, other collectible product forms authorized by The Norman Rockwell Family Trust — including snow globes and Christmas ornaments — are also offered by the Gallery.

"Love Cures All" was authorized by The Norman Rockwell Family Trust released by The Norman Rockwell Gallery. Copyright 1990 Rhodes.

ROMAN, INC.

555 Lawrence Avenue
Roselle, Illinios 60172-1599
(708) 529-3000
Fax: (708) 529-1121

Plates, Figurines, Dolls, Christmas Ornaments, Bells, Graphics

Roman, Inc. is proof that the American dream lives. With a family background in giftware retailing, it was inevitable that Ronald Jedlinski would enter some facet of the collectibles and giftware fields. Jedlinski formed Roman, Inc. independently as a wholesaler of religious products in 1963.

By 1973, his eye for product development, business acumen and supplier relationships resulted in regular imports of Italy's finest offerings. At this point, Jedlinski's successful association with the famous House of Fontanini in Tuscany developed into Roman becoming the exclusive North American source for their creations. Roman's best-known Fontanini line, *The Collectible Creche*, has been expanded with the addition of *The Fontanini Signature Collection*.

Roman expanded its presence in the collectible and giftware markets with the mid-1970s introduction of the entirely handcrafted *Ceramica Excelsis* limited edition porcelain bisque figurines devoted to biblical and inspirational subjects. This collection led to Roman's association with Japan's House of Maruri and other porcelain makers and has enabled the firm to produce major works by noted artists.

The company roster of leading American and European artists features talented award-winners with strong and devoted followings.

Frances Hook, noted creator of the original Northern Tissue children was the first artist to design an entire collection for Roman. Her sensitive collector plates, prints and figurines for Roman have endeared her to countless collectors. Continuing releases since Hook's death in 1983 are supervised by her daughter, Barbara, and include busts inspired by her acclaimed portraits of Jesus — "The Carpenter" and "Little Children, Come to Me."

Abbie Williams, to whom Hook was friend and mentor, is one of America's foremost child portraitists. Williams' limited edition plates include *The Magic of Childhood, The Lord's Prayer, Love's Prayer*, and a special March of Dimes fund-raising edition, "A Time to Laugh" in association with the Bradford Exchange. Williams' lithograph, "Mary, Mother of The Carpenter," is a moving tribute to her friend, Hook's "The Carpenter." Williams' newest effort for Roman is the "Legacy of Love" keepsake plate.

Award-winning collectibles artist, Irene Spencer, also creates for Roman.

Spencer's latest creative renderings include the limited edition commemorating the 500th anniversary in 1992 of *The Discovery of America* — delightful miniature art print and porcelain hanging ornaments of feline "Kistopher Kolumbus" and "Queen Kitsabella."

"Christopher Columbus" by gifted Italian sculptor, Angela Tripi, demonstrates her special talent for infusing life into her subjects.

Ellen Williams, winner of the 1989 Pasadena "Collectible of Show" award for her *Classic Brides of the Century* figurines, now turns her attention to exquisite, limited edition dolls based on this series. "Flora" — the 1900s Bride is the first of her meticulously researched porcelain dolls. Other new Williams creations include her nostalgic our *First Christmas Together* collection and *Heaven's Little Angels* birthday commemoratives bearing her signature faux pearls.

Newest creations from Dolfi woodcarving studios of Ortisei, Italy, are a family of sixteen limited edition boy and girl dolls. Their expressive faces are carved by hand entirely from aged alpine maple...even their hair. Others are soft-bodied with real hair. Dolfi has pioneered a unique, ball-jointed design, allowing these dolls to assume lifelike poses. *Dolls Magazine* judges have nominated "Susie" for the "Doll of the Year" in the All-Wood Category of the 1991 Awards of Excellence.

Newcomer to Roman is gifted Italian sculptor Angela Tripi. Roman has captured every intricate detail of her powerful works in durable poly resin and presents them in *The Museum Collection of Angela Tripi* — a distinctive gallery of Old Testament subjects and seven new limited editions with Christian, Judaic and secular themes.

RON LEE'S WORLD OF CLOWNS

2180 Agate Court
Simi Valley, California 93065
(805) 520-8460
Fax: (805) 520-8472

Figurines

Recognized as a pioneer of clown and circus theme collectibles, the prolific and mega-talented Ron Lee has created over 1,000 designs in the past fifteen years. Headed by Ron Lee, designer and sculptor, and his wife Jill, who is Vice President and General Manager of the complete operation, this California-based company is dedicated to creating heirloom quality collectibles, while providing personalized service to their dealers and collectors.

The company was born in 1976 when Ron Lee began creating sculptures of his original and now famous "Hobo Joe." Occupying a 20,000 square foot building, Ron Lee employs over 100 artisans, casters, mold makers, finishing, shipping and office personnel. The collector's club is also located in the facility.

A signed Ron Lee limited edition is easily identified when displayed on a shelf. All sculptures are finely detailed and mounted on polished onyx with tiny gold beading at the base of each statue. Each edition is made of fine metal, that is 24K gold plated, manufactured in the United States, and they are individually hand painted by a group of artisans handpicked by Ron Lee himself. Being that each design is hand painted, each sculpture is truly a one-of-a-kind collectible.

While creating and manufacturing sculptures for a national and international network of dealers and retail stores, Ron Lee continues to receive major commissions for his art. Presently he has created thirteen designs and is manufacturing sculptures for Service Merchandise Company, Inc. based in Nashville, Tennessee. These special statues will only be sold through their national network of 350 retail outlets.

The San Francisco Music Box Company secured Ron Lee to create three original designs that will become fanciful music boxes and available exclusively through their stores.

Although Ron Lee designs have focused on clowns and circus themes, and have an established consumer base collectors club of over 13,000-plus, (which continues to grow by 300 new members per month), designs will break ground in a new arena of collectibles.

The *Ron Lee Collection* will now include many of America's best loved and most memorable animated characters, from numerous classic animation entertainment companies, which began in the summer of 1991.

"To have grown-up with these wonderful characters — and now to have an opportunity to bring them to my collectors — this is absolutely the highlight of my career," stated Ron Lee.

THE ROSEBUD DOLL STUDIO

Patricia Rose
200 Alymer Court
Westminster, Maryland 21157
(301) 848-6735

Dolls

The Rosebud Doll Studio is in its second year of operation. It is owned and operated by Patricia Rose, contemporary doll artist. Patricia has been a photo realist portrait artist since 1969. Her love for detail and realistic human proportions has been carried over into her sculpting of her popular lady dolls.

Her "Delta Dawn" doll, first in the *Painted Lady* series, was nominated at the 1991 New York Toy Fair by *Dolls* Magazine for the "Award of Excellence" in the $300 to $500 price category.

Rosebud Dolls introduced a new series in August 1991 called the *Dancer* series. The first in this series was an elegant ballerina from the Swan Lake ballet. The doll's name is "Brianna." "Brianna" is eighteen inches tall, with an all porcelain body, rotating arms, and movable legs. She is anatomically correct and sells for $895 retail.

At the 1992 Toy Fair, Patricia promises many innovative ideas and new dolls that will surprise and delight all who are interested in realistic, lifelike lady dolls at reasonable prices.

ROSENTHAL U.S.A.

Melissa Wiener
66-26 Metroplitan Avenue
Middle Village, New York 11379
(718) 417-3400
Fax: (718) 417-3407

Plates

Rosenthal was founded by Philipp Rosenthal in 1879, in Selb, Bavaria. At first, Rosenthal bought white ware from other porcelain manufacturers and painted it with his own designs. Then in 1895, he established his own factory at Kronach, where he produced fine porcelain with his signature on the back.

The Rosenthal Christmas plate series began in 1910, and ended in 1974. Some cobalt blue plates were reissued in small quantities. The plates all bear a post-1957 backstamp. However, this practice was discontinued after 1971.

A second traditional Christmas series was introduced in the 1970s. This blue-and-white plate series depicts churches and public buildings, and bears the Classic Rose backstamp.

In 1971, Rosenthal issued the first of its Studio-Linie collections with the *Wiinblad Christmas* series. These plates feature intricate modern designs, partially hand-painted in as many as eighteen colors, and embellished with platinum and 18K gold. The series was completed in 1980. A second series by Bjorn Wiinblad entitled *Fantasies and Fables* began in 1976 and contains two plates. From 1976 to 1981, Wiinblad designed a series of crystal Christmas plates for Rosenthal. Based on scenes from the traditional Christmas story, Wiinblad used the traditional Danish colors of blue and white in a unique manner, with 24k gold.

Two series featuring the work of Edna Hibel, *The Nobility of Children*, and *Oriental Gold*, were introduced by Rosenthal in 1976.

In 1981, Rosenthal introduced a new series entitled *Christmas Carols on Porcelain*. The plates feature famous carols, which are created with the same coloration as the other series and shaped somewhat like a Japanese square.

Philip Rosenthal, son of the founder, recently retired as president and chief executive officer of Rosenthal A.G. He holds citizenship in both England and Germany and is a former member of the Bundestag, the German Congress.

ROYAL COPENHAGEN

27 Holland Avenue
White Plains, New York 10603
(914) 428-8222
Fax: (914) 428-8251

Plates, Figurines, Christmas Ornaments

The original Royal Copenhagen Porcelain Manufactory Ltd. is Denmark's oldest porcelain maker. It was established in 1755 by Franz Heinrich Muller, a pharmacist and chemist who was the first to duplicate porcelain in Denmark. He was supported by Denmark's dowager queen, Juliane Marie.

In 1779, "The Danish Porcelain Factory" came under royal control where it remained until 1868, when it passed into private ownership. However, the firm still is a purveyor to the royal court. The royal control is symbolized by a crown in the firm's trademark. Three wavy lines under the crown part of the trademark represent Denmark's three ancient waterways: the Sound, the Great Belt, and the Little Belt.

The first Royal Copenhagen commemorative plate was produced in 1888, but it was not until 1908 that Royal Copenhagen introduced its *Christmas* series. The first three plates were six inches in diameter, but after 1911 the size was changed to seven inches.

The *Christmas* plates were issued with the text in English, German, French and Czechoslovakian until 1931, when Dutch was added. Two years later, the Dutch edition was dropped. The other foreign texts were dropped in 1945. The Royal Copenhagen *Christmas* series remains one of the most popular series in the world.

The first Royal Copenhagen *Mother's Day* series was added in 1971 and ended in 1982. A second *Motherhood* series by Svend Vestergaard premiered the same year. In 1988, Royal Copenhagen introduced the *American Mother's Day* series.

In 1991 Royal Copenhagen proudly introduced the first edition of its second *Christmas Plate* series since 1908. "Christmas in Denmark" is a brilliantly colorful and romantic collectible *Christmas Plate* series designed by renowned Danish artist Hans Henrik Hansen, the very same artist who designs the *Santa Claus Christmas* plates for Bing & Grondahl.

ROYAL COPENHAGEN INC./ BING & GRONDAHL

27 Holland Avenue
White Plains, New York 10603

Plates, Figurines, Bells, Christmas Ornaments

In 1987, two of the world's most respected porcelain companies, Bing & Grondahl and Royal Copenhagen merged under the umbrella of Royal Copenhagen A/S. (Royal Copenhagen Inc. is now owned by Carlsberg A/S, a conglomerate made up of sixty other companies including Holmegaard Glass and Georg Jensen Silver.)

The Royal Copenhagen group of companies is made up of Royal Copenhagen Porcelain and Bing & Grondahl, Georg Jensen Silver and Holmegaard Glass. These companies each retain separate identities and product lines.

ROYAL DOULTON USA, INC.

Hattie Purnell-Burson
700 Cottontail Lane
Somerset, New Jersey 08873
(201) 356-7880
Fax: (201) 356-9467

ROYAL DOULTON CANADA, INC.
Shona McCleod
850 Progress Avenue
Scarborough, Ontario M1H 3C4

Plates, Figurines

Royal Doulton, founded in 1815 as Doulton and Company, has developed a fine reputation worldwide for quality and excellence in dinnerware, crystal, figurines and other fine collectibles.

In 1901, the company was awarded a Royal Warrant, and the right to incorporate the word Royal into the company name. Founded by John Doulton, the company truly began to flourish under the direction of John Doulton's son, Henry Doulton, who employed some of the finest artists of that time.

His commitment and desire for excellence was contagious and was quickly adopted by the fine artists who worked for Royal Doulton.

Charles J. Noke, Art Director, 1914-1936, also had that same commitment. Noke was responsible for the growth of the range of Royal Doulton figurines and character jugs. By 1920, Noke had succeeded in producing figurines acclaimed by the critics and public alike.

"Bedtime Bunnykins" is part of the Bunnykins *figurine series by Royal Doulton.*

In 1991, Royal Doulton introduced several new product concepts in the figurine product category. The *Figurine of the Year* will bring a special edition fine bone china figurine to enthusiasts annually, and will be retired at the end of the year. The first in this new annual series is "Amy."

The *Age of Innocence Collection*, currently comprised of three delightful childhood studies, are all issued in a limited edition of 9,500. Each subject is exquisitely modeled and hand-decorated, capturing the beauty and innocence of children enjoying the pleasures of the countryside from days gone by.

As with all Royal Doulton limited editions, *Age of Innocence* is certain to arouse great interest from collectors, particularly as childhood studies are rarely introduced in limited numbers.

ROYAL ORLEANS

40114 Industrial Park Circle
Georgetown, Texas 78626

Figurines

Royal Orleans of Georgetown, Texas, is owned and operated by Bill and Jan Hagara who design, market and distribute products by Jan Hagara. These figurines, miniatures, tins, mugs, sachet and cards all have the familiar Hagara trademark of her "romantic Victoriana" look.

Figurines are priced from about $40.00 to $600.00, while the tins, mugs, cards and sachet are well within the reach of most collectors.

Jan's tremendously loyal following of collectors makes her products some of the most popular in today's collectible market.

ROYAL WORCESTER LIMITED

Mrs. Elizabeth Collins
Severn Street
Worcester, England WR1 2NE
0905 23221
Fax: 0905 23601

Plates, Figurines

Founded in 1751, Royal Worcester is the oldest continuously operating manufacturer of porcelain in the United Kingdom. Following the visit of George III and Queen Charlotte, the company was granted a Royal Warrant in 1789 and warrants have since been granted by every successive Monarch.

Throughout its history, Royal Worcester has produced prestigious tableware and giftware in porcelain and bone china which are still sought by collectors the world over. The company claims the honor of making the first limited edition, in 1935, and this was followed over the years by superb bone china figurines and sculptures by Dorothy Doughty, Doris Lindner, Ruth and Ronald Van Ruyckevelt, and others. Birds, horses, cattle, kings and queens and historical figures are just a few of the subjects modelled by these talented artists.

In 1789 Royal Worcester achieved its first Royal patronage from King George III and has retained a Royal Warrant continuously ever since. In 1989 the Company introduced a *200th Anniversary Collection* to commemorate the event. This collection of ten beautiful ornamental bone china pieces, each issued in a limited edition of 200, provides the opportunity to collect faithful reproductions of some extremely valuable originals.

SARAH'S ATTIC

126 1/2 West Broad Street
Chesaning, Michigan 48616
(517) 845-3990
Fax: (517) 845-3477

Dolls, Figurines

When Sarah Schultz needed a new couch, she decided to turn her favorite hobby into a wholesale company. Sarah was inspired by a love of antiques and a desire to create complimentary accents for them. Sarah started her own business on the family dining room table in 1983. Because the unique handcrafted items were like treasures from the past, Sarah called her business Sarah's Attic, Granny's Favorites. She also signed each piece with a little red heart as a personal guarantee of quality and originality.

With the help of her husband, five children, and many friends, Sarah originally began to supply the family pharmacy with unique gifts to complement the country decor. It was not long before Sarah's Attic began to grow, and Sarah had to hire employees. She hired a salesperson and two artists who worked on the products in their own homes. When orders poured in and space ran out, the business moved to the "attic" above the pharmacy in late 1984. By mid-1989, Sarah's Attic had expanded to four times the original size, still using the original attic above the pharmacy.

As business expanded, so did the line to include collectibles and wood items that complement any decor. Through all this growth and the many changes, one thing remained the same — Sarah's devotion to fine quality. From woodcutters to painters to salespeople, everyone at Sarah's is devoted to the objective of producing unique collectibles of the highest quality — quality that will satisfy even Sarah. That is why each piece will always bear the signature heart, which is the firm's trademark of quality. Sarah's Attic has turned into an

"Percy and Pearl" were released January 1, 1991, offered by Sarah's Attic.

extremely successful company, which is no surprise to Sarah's customers. They know that once they have purchased a Sarah's Attic original, they have purchased a quality treasure of timeless value. By the way, Sarah eventually earned enough to buy that new couch she needed so badly. Worn from years of use by her family, it still rests before the fireplace in her family room...but Sarah has never had a chance to sit on it.

SCHMID

April Bargout
55 Pacella Park
Randolph, Massachusetts 02368
(617) 961-3000
Fax: (617) 986-8168

Plates, Figurines, Bells, Dolls, Christmas Ornaments, Graphics

Since 1931, the name Schmid has been synonymous with the finest gifts and collectibles. Founded by Paul A. Schmid, the company is still family-owned and remains dedicated to the same uncompromising standards of design and workmanship that have made it a leader in the industry for over fifty years.

Schmid has expanded considerably over the years in offering the very best. Today, the company boasts a number of sought-after licenses. The collection of licensed Walt Disney characters which first made its debut at Schmid in 1969 encompasses innovative designs transformed into figurines, music boxes and ornaments.

The *Kitty Cucumber Collection* has become one of the most sought-after collectible lines on the market in just five years. Kitty has proven the premise that old-fashioned whimsy, coupled with contemporary themes will never be out of style.

For over a decade, Schmid has recreated the delightful characters of Beatrix Potter into a collection of musicals and ornaments enchanting collectors of Flopsy, Mopsy, Cotton-Tail and Peter.

Schmid also represents some of the most talented artists in the world including Missouri-born Lowell Davis. In his studio in Carthage, Missouri, Lowell immortalizes farmlife of the 1930s in a style that is unique among American folk artists. To his continual surprise, his art has captured the hearts and imaginations of people around the world.

Lowell Davis recalls the days before self service with "Just Check the Air," a recent limited edition porcelain figurine from the Route 66 *collection at Schmid.*

"I've often tried to figure out what's made my things so popular," Lowell once mused. "And I think it boils down to this: people can see in them a life we once had, a simpler life."

Being the exclusive United States distributor of world-famous M.I. Hummel figurines, Schmid first marketed Hummel figurines in this country back in 1935. Schmid is also the exclusive distributor of ANRI Woodcarvings.

SCULPTURE WORKSHOP DESIGNS

William Graham
P.O. Box 420
Blue Bell, Pennsylvania 19422
(215) 643-7447

Christmas Ornaments

Sculpture Workshop Designs issued its first sterling silver Christmas ornament in 1985 entitled "The Return of the Christmas Comet," and has continued issuing one or two ornaments each year. Commemorative editions, such as the 1987 "The Bicenntenial of the U.S. Constitution," and "The Presidential Signatures," issued in 1989, were offered in very small editions of just 200 works. Traditional Christmas designs, such as the 1990 "Joyful Angels," are offered in editions of 2,500 works. Ornaments are designed and sculpted by artist F. Kreitchet. In 1991, the company issued a 200th year commemorative for the Bill of Rights and also offered a traditional design to collectors. Ornaments are $3^1/_4$ inches in diameter, and include approximately one troy ounce. Registration numbers are hand-engraved.

SILVER DEER, LTD.

Karen Brown
4824 Sterling Drive
Boulder, Colorado 80301
(800) 729-3337
(303) 449-6771
Fax: (303) 449-0653

Figurines, Bells, Christmas Ornaments

Founded over twelve years ago, Silver Deer, Ltd. was one of the first North American companies to design and manufacture crystal figurines using 32% full-lead Austrian crystal. Comprising over 200 designs, the *Crystal Zoo Collection* has become recognized as a standard of excellence for design innovation, quality and craftsmanship.

Silver Deer also holds the distinction of capturing licensed characters in crystal. From Walt Disney's Winnie-the-Pooh to Beatrix Potter's Peter Rabbit and Charles Schulz's Snoopy, Silver Deer has won the hearts of crystal collectors everywhere.

The *Crystal Zoo Collection* is created by master designers Gina Truex, Olga Plam and Susan Dailey. Each of these accomplished artists have earned an MFA degree and are individually recognized for their works in other media including papier-mache, jewelry and sculpting.

Silver Deer is also proud of the *Christmas Animals Collection* designed by renowned artist Tom Rubel. Inspired by the tide of popular demand for his animals, Mr. Rubel has expanded his menagerie of the large and small creatures of our earth in the creation of a new line — Silver Deer's *Ark Collection*. Also new from Silver Deer and Tom Rubel is *Santa's Celebration*, a collectible series of Santa figurines, music boxes, bells and ornaments.

SPORTS IMPRESSIONS

1501 Arthur Avenue
Elk Grove, Illinois 60007
(800) 368-5553
Fax: (708) 290-8322

Plates, Figurines

Sports Impressions is a leading producer of high quality porcelain collector plates, figurines and other sports-related memorabilia featuring more than 100 prominent personalities and legends in baseball, football, basketball and boxing.

Sports Impressions was founded in 1985 by Joseph Timmerman, a sports enthusiast and owner of three major gift and collectibles retail stores on Long Island. Timmerman began his business with licensing agreements from two well-known baseball figures: Mickey Mantle and Don Mattingly.

Since then, the roster of players in the company's line has significantly increased. Baseball players now under license to Sports Impressions include Nolan Ryan, Willie Mays, Ted Williams, Ernie Banks, Jackie Robinson, Bo Jackson, Darryl Strawberry, Orel Hershiser and Andre Dawson. Baseball Hall of Fame member Mickey Mantle is spokesman for Sports Impressions.

A new NFL series features Joe Montana, Lawrence Taylor, John Elway and others. Sports Impressions will be introducing an NBA series with Michael Jordan, Patrick Ewing, Larry Bird, Charles Barkley and others in porcelain figurines and collector plates.

Baseball star Nolan Ryan appears on a porcelain figurine, and San Francisco '49ers quarterback Joe Montana is featured on a ceramic mug by Sports Impressions.

The growth and popularity of sports-related collectibles continues to increase, according to Sports Impressions. In response to collector demand, Timmerman launched the Sports Impressions Collectors' Club in 1989. Many of the club's 5,000 members are men, unique among collectors' clubs.

Sports Impressions is an independent business of Enesco Worldwide Giftware Group.

SWAROVSKI AMERICA LIMITED

2 Slater Road
Cranston, Rhode Island 02920
(401) 463-3000
Fax: (401) 463-8459

Figurines

For over a decade, collectors all over the world have been charmed and excited by Silver Crystal collectibles from Swarovski. The originality of design and quality of workmanship in each exclusive piece is no accident. Swarovski is one of the leading crystal manufacturers in the world, that designs and manufactures faceted crystal specifically for the collector. D. Swarovski & Co. was founded in 1895 in Georgenthal/Bohemia by Daniel Swarovski, who learned the art of crystal production as an apprentice in his father's company. When he established his own firm, he extended the state of the art by developing automatic crystal cutting methods and harnessing the natural energy of the water available in the mountainous Tyrol region. He established the exacting standards that Swarovski is known for today: 100% Austrian crystal, original designs, and exquisite workmanship.

Headquartered in Zurich, Switzerland, Daniel Swarovski Corporation employs over 8,000 people worldwide. Production/Design headquarters remain in Wattens, Austria. Manufacturing facilities are located in eleven countries worldwide, including the United States (Cranston, RI). Swarovski America distributes Silver Crystal (decorative accessories: figurines) and limited edition pieces created exclusively for collectors by the Swarovski Collectors Society.

In 1987 the International Swarovski Collectors Society was formed, offering exclusive, limited edition pieces available only to Swarovski Collectors Society members. Members also receive the *Swarovski Collector*, a full color magazine full of information on new products, articles on crystal production, profiles of Swarovski designers and travel tips when visiting the Tyrol.

The SCS 1990 Annual Edition, "Lead Me" - the Dolphins was created exclusively for members of the Swarovski Collectors Society. This piece was Swarovski America's best-selling item in 1990.

T.S.M. & COMPANY

Teresa Schiavi
98 Rose Hill Avenue
New Rochelle, New York 10804
(914) 235-5675
Fax: (914) 576-0533

Graphics

T.S.M. & Company is a partnership established to produce and sell the artwork of sporting and wildlife artist Adriano Manocchia. The artist's line includes original oil paintings, limited edition offset lithographs and hand-pulled etchings. In the past, Adriano has also created bronzes and porcelain sculptures.

Board member of the Society of Animal Artists and member of the Outdoor Writers Association of America, his renderings have attracted the attention of a growing number of collectors, and his images have been published in a number of magazines not only in the United States, but also in Europe and Japan.

Adriano began as a photojournalist and ran a successful photo and film agency before switching from photography to painting. In 1979, he dedicated most of his time to painting wildlife and later, outdoor sporting art. His painting of a Bald Eagle was chosen by the U.S. Bicentennial Committee to commemorate the 200th anniversary of the Constitution. It has been reproduced as a limited edition plate and poster. He was also selected by the New York State Audubon as the official Earth Day artist for 1990, and has created artwork for Ducks Unlimited, the Sportsman's Alliance of Maine and the Atlantic Salmon Federation for their conservation programs. He was also commissioned to create paintings for The Bradford Exchange for one of their plate series.

CAT'S MEOW/F.J. DESIGNS, INC.

2163 Great Trails Dr., Dept. C
Wooster, OH 44691
(216) 264-1377
Fax: (216) 263-0219

Figurines

In the fall of 1982, The *Cat's Meow Village* company began in the basement of Terry and Faline Jones' home. Mrs. Jones opened the firm with a $39 piece of pine, a creative concept and a lot of ingenuity. She created the *Cat's Meow Village*, a product line of two-dimensional miniature historical buildings and accessories. Husband Terry joined the company on a full time basis in 1986.

At first Mrs. Jones designed, cut, painted and stenciled all of the small wooden buildings using whatever supplies and tools she could find close at hand. Terry soon started helping with the buying and cutting of the wood. He also devised a way to spraypaint the background colors in their garage.

During 1983, Mrs. Jones shipped the *Village* to store owners throughout Ohio and western Pennsylvania. In the spring of 1984, the Cat's Meow moved from the Jones' basement into the backroom of a woodworking shop, only to take over the entire building by the spring of the following year! At this point, Mrs. Jones decided to change the name of the company to the generic FJ Designs name. "How was I to hire any male employees and expect to keep them if they had to tell people they worked at The Cat's Meow," she humorously related.

Beginning her third year of business, Faline Jones began to pattern her designs after actual buildings and historic landmarks no longer in existence. That's when the concept for the *Village* was developed. The *Village* would include faithful reproductions of typical American architecture, chosen with respect for the craftsmanship, commerce, culture and activities that are part of every community. Mrs. Jones draws upon her vast collection of books and literature, as well as her camera, to develop her ideas.

The collectibility of the *Village* began to increase as Mrs. Jones devised a system of retiring old patterns as new ones were developed. A *Village* series retires after five years of production, with the special annual Christmas series retiring each year.

The company formed The National Cat's Meow Collector's Club in June 1989. By the end of that year, over 4,000 collectors had joined. The club is still growing today, with over 14,000 members nationally.

The Village *from Cat's Meow/F.J. Designs, Inc. includes numerous patterns and accessories.*

TOWLE SILVERSMITHS

Karen Daly
144 Addison St.
Boston, Massachusetts 02128
(617) 561-2200
Fax: (617) 569-8484

Christmas Ornaments

Towle represents 301 years of craftsmanship 1690-1991. One of the most important crafts in Colonial America was silversmithing. The Moultons of Newburyport, Massachusetts followed this craft for over 200 years. More members of this family followed the silversmith's profession than any other early American family.

The Towle tradition of craftsmanship is still being carried on today. Many of Towle's present employees are second and third generations of the family to work at Towle. From this unique heritage, comes the understanding and respect that distinguishes their work today.

Towle Silversmiths creates and produces beautiful sterling Christmas ornaments. Some of these ongoing limited edition series include the *Floral Medallion, Story of Christmas* and the *Towle Old Master Snowflake* collections. New for 1991 are the *Twelve Days of Christmas* and *Christmas Angel* series.

TURNER DOLLS INC.

P.O. Box 36
Heltonville, Indiana 47436
(812) 834-6692
Fax: (812) 834-1501

Dolls

Although artistic in her own right, Virginia Turner didn't expect to hold any other position at Turner Dolls than assistant to her doll artist sister-in-law, Judith Turner. However, with encouragement from husband Boyce and her own determination, Virginia was inspired to experiment with making her own dolls. That was the beginning of a beautiful career.

Virginia's first doll was "Jeannie," a happy, perky-faced porcelain baby. All 500 dolls in the edition sold out in just five months. Virginia was on her way and firmly established as a doll artist.

Virginia studies the faces of children constantly, collecting ideas for more dolls. She explains, "I'm always looking for the next doll. To be able to see a face in your mind and then to see it in a real-life doll is wonderful!"

Since "Jeannie," Virginia has introduced several dolls including "Hannah," a nominee for *Doll* Magazine's "Award of Excellence." Boyce and Virginia are at home at Heltonville, Indiana, where Virginia continues her work as a doll artist, keeping collectors of all ages looking forward to her new designs.

UNITED DESIGN CORPORATION

Gary and Jean Clinton
P.O. Box 1200
Noble, Oklahoma 73068
(405) 872-3468
Fax: (405) 360-4442

Figurines, Dolls, Christmas Ornaments

In 1973, Gary and Jean Clinton, both graduates of the University of Oklahoma School of Art, founded a company which was to become United Design Corporation in Noble, Oklahoma. Their goal was to produce figurines with a uniquely American look, a look that would reflect both the vitality and the good humor of the American perspective.

Once their sculptor's clay is molded into a design, the Clintons and their skilled artisans make production molds. Two raw materials are then used for casting their pieces. One is Hydrostone, a finely ground gypsum mined in northern Oklahoma and southern Kansas. In its finely crushed, powder-like form, it mixes easily with water to form a pourable slurry which fills product molds completely and sets up in a matter of minutes.

Once the Hydrostone is dried to remove the moisture, items can be handpainted and finished.

Experts at United Design have also developed their techniques for the use of "bonded porcelain." In this process, the dry ingredients that would normally go into fired porcelain clay mix, are instead blended with a polyester resin compound which bonds or fuses to create bonded porcelain. The finished pieces have characteristics which match fired porcelain in hardness, strength, whiteness, translucency, and absorption of water. While this material will not accept a fired glaze, making it unsuitable for tableware or kitchen use, the process allows the creation of surface details that would not be possible with fired porcelain.

United Design's animal figurines, especially the *Stone Critters®* collection, is one of the fastest growing lines of animal figurines in the world. Every two years, beginning in 1984, United Design introduced special edition *Party Animals*™ — a Republican elephant and a Democrat donkey.

A limited edition line of Santa Claus figurines, *The Legend of Santa Claus*™, was introduced in 1986. Each edition is limited to 15,000, 10,000 or 7,500. In the fall of 1988, the firm also introduced *The Legend of The Little People*™ collection of limited edition figurines. The collection includes two designs, each limited to 7,500 pieces.

In 1990 United Design introduced *PenniBears*™, a limited edition collection of miniature teddy bears. Each *PenniBear*™ design is limited by a production run of three years or less. United Design also sponsors a PenniBears Collectors Club. Membership benefits include the opportunity to purchase annual members-only designs, as well as advance information about introductions and retirements.

Part of the Legend of Santa Claus *collection, "Victorian Santa with Teddy" was introduced for the 1991 Christmas season.*

The *Easter Bunny Family*™ is a collection of bunnies introduced in 1988. Though not produced in limited edition, this line has become very popular among collectors. The original seven designs were retired by United Design after the 1991 Easter season.

The *Lil' Doll*™ collection of limited edition doll figurines was introduced at Christmas in 1991. This collection is limited to 10,000 pieces.

All of the products produced by United Design are created by artists and craftsmen who adhere to the philosophy expressed by the company's mission statement: "...to provide giftware creations inspired by the joy and wonder of the world around us, thereby prospering through serving and satisfying customers the world over."

U.S. HISTORICAL SOCIETY

Jackie Dickinson
First and Main Streets
Richmond, Virginia 23219
(804) 648-4736
Fax: (804) 648-0002

Plates, Figurines, Dolls, Christmas Ornaments

The United States Historical Society is a private, non-governmental organization dedicated to historical research and the sponsorship of projects and issuance of objects which are artistically and historically significant. The Society works with museums, educational institutions, foundations and other organizations to create objects for collection that have historic significance, artistic value and a high level of craftsmanship.

Organizations with whom the Society has worked include Monticello; the Folger Shakespeare Library; the Metropolitan Museum of Art and the Museum of Fine Arts, Boston; the Field Museum of Natural History; Ringling Museum; Unicef; and the Tower of London.

Among the projects of the Society are the reproductions of George Washington's Flintlock Pistols and his Inaugural Sword, reproductions of Thomas Jefferson's Queen Anne Pistols and his Telescope. The Society also issued the Young America of Winslow Homer plates, Battle of Yorktown prints from the painting commissioned for President Ronald Reagan, and doll series including *Living Image Portrait Dolls*, *Great American Women*, the *American Women of Arts and Letters* and the *School's Out* collection. Also issued are the *Seven Ages of Man Stained Glass Tableau* from the Folger Shakespeare Library, Centennial of Golf statues and the *Greatest Story Ever Told* collection of stained glass medallions of the Life of Christ. Other projects included White House China by Haviland for the USS Abraham Lincoln Commissioning Committee; stained glass tableau for the 50th anniversary of the Airline Owners and Pilots Association; statues and other objects for the U.S. Navy Memorial Foundation in Washington, DC; the book *Paperweights of the Bergstrom-Mahler Museum* in Wisconsin; the Robert E. Lee Saber with the Lee family; the book *Reminiscences of General Robert E. Lee* with Washington and Lee University; the Chuck Yeager Shotgun to benefit the Yeager Fund at Marshal University; the Presidential Bowl in observance of the 200th anniversary of the U.S. Presidency; stained glass plates for the National Wildlife Federation and the Vietnam Veterans Association.

Among the current projects of the Society are: Monitor and Virginia (Merrimac) Navy Revolver in cooperation with the Portsmouth Naval Shipyard Museum; the Wyatt Earp Revolver, *The American Lawman* statue and *The Lawman* book in cooperation with the U.S. Marshals Foundation; stained glass rounds of songbirds for the National Audubon Society; the Arnold Palmer Shotgun; the Ducks Unlimited Waterfowl Bowl by Maynard Reece; the Wood Duck Stained Glass and Pewter Plate by David Maass; *Homes of the Great American Presidents* sterling silver ornaments; and the Columbus statue, the *Log of Christopher Columbus* and Columbus Bowl in honor of the 500th anniversary of Columbus' first voyage to the New World.

D.H. USSHER LTD.

Des Ussher
1132 West 15th Street
North Vancouver, British Columbia
Canada V7P 1M9
(604) 986-0365
Fax: (604) 986-9984

Plates

D.H. Ussher Ltd. was incorporated in 1979 as a distributor of limited edition collectibles. Its main office, showroom, and warehouse are located in Vancouver. The firm has representatives covering every province in Canada.

D.H. Ussher represents a wide range of U.S.-based collectible firms in Canada. These include Armstrong's, Hollywood, American Legacy, Artists of the World, American Artists, Porter & Price Inc., Sports Impressions, and Artaffects. The firm also distributes brass hangers and plate stands for Briant & Sons and frames for Lynette Decor Products. In 1985, D.H. Ussher Ltd. began producing for the limited edition market and is currently active with products under the labels Reefton Meadows and Western Authentics.

In 1989 and 1990, N.H.L. personalities were signed to be featured on plates. These athletes include Lanny McDonald, Darryl Sittler, Gordie Howe, Vladislav Tretiak and Tiger Williams. In 1991, a personally signed 10¼ inch plate featuring three shots of two-time world figure skating champion Kurt Browning was released.

V.F. FINE ARTS

P.O. Box 246
Lisbon, Ohio 44432
(216) 424-5231
Fax: (216) 424-5203

Figurines, Graphics

V.F. Fine Arts was founded to promote Sandra Kuck's limited edition prints and original artworks. The company is named in honor of Sandra's father, Vermont Franklin, or V.F.

Sandra Kuck has been chosen for virtually every major award including the Silver Chalice, Print of the Year, and NALED's Artist of the Year for six consecutive years. She was honored as the International Artist of the Year by the International Collectible Exposition held in July 1991 in South Bend, Indiana.

Sandra's distinctive Victorian style has made her a creative force in the collectible market for over fourteen years.

V.F. Fine Arts is under the direction of Sandra's husband, John, in Boca Raton, Florida and is operated by Sandra's brother and his wife in Ohio.

V.F. Fine Arts offers through its dealership, some of Sandra's most memorable original oil paintings and also receives inquiries for her personal commissioned portraits. In 1990, V.F. Fine Arts established the long awaited Sandra Kuck Collectors' Club, offering the figurine "Kitten" as a gift for joining along with two newsletters per year to keep her collectors well informed. The club also offers unique "Members only" redemption pieces, created for these special collectors.

As always, Sandra Kuck's signature means her collectors are receiving only the best in quality and a real investment for tomorrow.

VAILLANCOURT FOLK ART

Gary Vaillancourt
145 Armsby Road
Sutton, Massachusetts 01590
(508) 865-9183
Fax: (508) 865-4140

Figurines, Christmas Ornaments

Vaillancourt Folk Art was founded in 1984 by Judi and Gary Vaillancourt. It is located in Sutton, Massachusetts, a small New England town located outside of Worcester. The company employs twenty-seven people.

Vaillancourt Folk Art's main product line is chalkware cast from antique moulds that were originally used to make chocolate or ice cream forms. The moulds date from the mid-1800s to the early 1900s. A plaster-like substance, chalkware first appeared in the mid-1800s and was referred to as "poor man's Staffordshire." It since has developed into a popular collectible.

Each piece of Vaillancourt chalkware is an original; individually hand-painted, signed and numbered.

Additional Vaillancourt products include hand-painted clocks and special production pieces such as the Vaillancourt Chess Set and Noah's Ark.

Beginning in 1991, Vaillancourt offered two limited edition series: *The Vaillancourt Collection*, consisting of thirty finely-detailed, high quality chalkware pieces with a limited production of 500 copies; and *The Vaillancourt Mould Collection*, consisting of approximately ten moulds per year. From each of these ten moulds, Judi casts and paints a one-of-a-kind chalkware piece which is then sold with the mould. Of special interest to collectors is the fact that the first copy of each piece in *The Vaillancourt Mould Collection* is being sold in special packaging with its antique mould.

Vaillancourt Folk Art is distributed through folk art dealers, specialty gift stores, art galleries, museum gift shops, leading department stores and fine furniture stores throughout the U.S.

In 1986, Queen Elizabeth II of England was presented with a collection of Vaillancourt Folk Art during her visit to the United States.

VILETTA CHINA COMPANY

R. S. Toms
8000 Harwin Drive, #150
Houston, Texas 77036-1891
(713) 785-0761
800 231-5762
Fax: (713) 977-4333

Plates, Bells, Christmas Ornaments

Viletta China Company was started in 1959 in Roseberg, Oregon, by Viletta West, who hand painted china and sold it through stores in the Pacific Northwest. In 1978, Viletta China relocated to Houston, Texas and expanded its distribution throughout the U.S. and Canada.

The firm is involved in many areas of fine china including commemorative pieces, fine giftware, dinnerware and limited edition collector plates. Recently the firm has enhanced its offerings with crystal and 24% lead crystal products.

VILLEROY & BOCH

41 Madison Avenue
New York, New York 10010
(212) 683-1747

VILLEROY & BOCH
45 Railside Road
Don Mills, Ontario M3A 1B2

Plates

Villeroy & Boch is a German firm with a long heritage of quality in tableware and art items. The firm was founded in 1748, when Francois Boch opened his first pottery studio at Auden-le-Tiche. The Villeroy family joined with the Bochs in 1836. Together the families became renowned for their innovations and artistic flair — and today an eighth-generation descendant of the Boch family sits as Managing Director of the firm.

Today, Villeroy & Boch is an internationally-known maker of dinnerware and accessories in addition to collector plates, plaques, and steins. The firm has as many as 16,000 employees in its eighteen locations across France, Luxembourg, Italy and Germany. Headquarters are at Mettlach, West Germany.

Villeroy & Boch has a well-deserved reputation as the world's finest maker of steins. The firm developed both the Chromolith (etched or incised) process and the Phanolith (cameo) process. Although stein production stopped at Mettlach in 1927, the firm has offered several contemporary limited editions in recent years.

The Heinrich Studios in the Bavarian town of Selb create most of Villeroy & Boch's collector plates, including three "Flower Fairies" series, the elegant *Russian Fairy Tales*, a current collection sponsored by the World Wildlife Fund and a six-plate series entitled *The Magical Fairy Tales from Old Russia* by Gero Trauth.

WACO PRODUCTS CORPORATION

One North Corporation Drive
Riverdale, New Jersey 07457
(201) 616-1660

Figurines

Founded in New York City in 1978, WACO Products Corporation is a leading creator, manufacturer and distributor of collectible figurines, executive games and novelties. In 1984, WACO introduced its first *Melody in Motion* porcelain figurines.

Each of the *Melody in Motion* figurines is based on an original created by master sculptor Seiji Nakane. Nakane's art is then faithfully translated into high-quality porcelain by skilled artisans in Seto, Japan. Concealed within each figurine are two special mechanisms — one plays an appropriate tune, while the other allows portions of the figurine to move gracefully. The musical selections in all of the *Melody in Motion* figurines were recorded in studios and are superior to most musicals on the market.

In 1985, WACO introduced the first three figurines in the *Melody in Motion Willie* series and the first offerings in the *Melody in Motion Variety* series. In 1986, the popular annual *Santa* series was added. In 1987, six more clown musicians were added to the collection and the charming *Vendor* series which includes an "Organ Grinder," "Peanut Vendor" and "Ice Cream Vendor."

The seven-piece *Melody in Motion*

"Willie The Trumpeter," issued by Waco, plays 'When The Saints Go Marching In.'

Madames series was added in 1988. In 1989, "Clockpost Willie," the first porcelain timepiece, was added to the collection. In 1990, WACO added the comic career series and *The Herman Collection*. Four limited edition *Melody in Motion* figurines — "Woodchopper," "Blacksmith," "Accordian Boy" and "Shoemaker" — and the Grand Carousel, the largest moving, hand-painted porcelain carousel in the world, also were introduced. In 1991, the first figurines in *Melody in Motion Sherwood Forest Collection* appeared.

SUSAN WAKEEN DOLL COMPANY

106 Powder Mill Road Box 1007
Canton, Connecticut 06019

Dolls

Dollmaker Susan Wakeen is unassuming and delicate in appearance, but she is both a determined and talented artist. After graduating from college, Wakeen moved to Boston where she taught, took classes in art (her first love), and met and married Thomas Wallace.

Fascinated by dolls, Wakeen began making and selling reproduction dolls at craft shows, but a gift of a box of doll clothes changed the focus of her work. The box contained a tutu. When Wakeen dressed one of her dolls in the costume, she found a new inspiration. In 1982, Wakeen began sculpting and produced her own original porcelain dolls and incorporated her business as the Littlest Ballet Company in 1985. The company's named was changed to the Susan Wakeen Doll Company in 1989 .

Wakeen's porcelain and vinyl dolls have won numerous honors. She has become a regular in the nominations for *Doll Reader's* DOTY and *Dolls* magazine's "Awards of Excellence" and has won four awards. Her most popular dolls have been "Love Me Tender" and "Amberley." Wakeen plans to add baby, fairy tale and play dolls to her line in the near future.

THE WALKER TOY COMPANY, INCORPORATED

363 North Main Street
Clinton, Tennessee 37716
(615) 457-4949

Dolls

Vickie Walker began learning the art of dollmaking in 1983 with purchased molds and a desire to make the most authentic reproductions of the old French and German dolls possible. Through study and hard work, she began to hone her artistic skills and design talents, creating beautiful dolls that soon became popular in her local market.

By 1985, her reproductions were selling for $300 to $500 each. Out of this beginning, the Walker Doll Company started and quickly caught the attention of a number of dealers in the Southeast. In 1986, Vickie was commissioned to create a doll for the Tennessee Homecoming '86 celebration. In 1987, WDC was the licensed manufacturer of the official doll commemorating the Bicentennial Celebration for the U.S. Constitution for We The People 200.

In 1986, Vickie began sculpting her own original doll heads. Today, all of her dolls are designed exclusively on her own original sculptures and are sold throughout the United States, Canada and in Japan. In addition to her own line of quality American made porcelain dolls, Vickie has also created original dolls for Reed & Barton Silver Company, Walt Disney, Opryland USA, plus a number of other special commissioned pieces.

WALLACE SILVERSMITHS

Janice Crowley
P.O. Box 9114
East Boston, Massachusetts 02128

Christmas Ornaments

In 1833, young Robert Wallace, a farmer's son learned the art of making Britannia spoons and set up his own spoon factory in an old grist mill in Cheshire, Connecticut. A year later, Wallace was introduced to "German" or "Nickel" silver, a durable alloy of copper, zinc and nickel. Recognizing the superiority of this metal, Wallace and his partner, Deacon Hall, moved to Wallingford to begin manufacturing "German Spoons."

In 1854, he migrated West to take up farming, but a short time later Wallace returned and took a new partner, Samuel Simpson. They eventually formed, Wallace, Simpson & Company Inc., but in 1871 it was changed to R. Wallace & Sons Manufacturing Company. In 1875, the firm began manufacturing sterling silver flatware and several years later, Wallace Brothers was formed to manufacture silverplated cast steel flatware. The two companies eventually merged as R. Wallace & Sons Mfg. Co., producing flatware, hollowware and a complete line of articles in which silver was a component.

During World War I, the factory was converted to defense production. In 1924, a Canadian plant was opened in Quebec to produce tinned spoons and forks and in 1944 sterling flatware was added.

In the 1920s, Wallace was introducing new sterling patterns annually and by 1934, William S. Warren, the company's most influential designer, was taking advantage of the inherent beauty and sculptural qualities of silver to create "Third Dimension Beauty" in sterling flatware.

Wallace purchased the Watson Company, Tuttle Silversmiths, and the Smith and Smith Company in 1955. In 1956, the company name was changed to Wallace Silversmiths.

Wallace entered the limited edition bell market in 1971 with the introduction of the first *Annual Sleigh Bell.* This series remains popular with collectors. In 1980, the first ornament in the *Christmas Cookie Series* was introduced, and in 1988 Wallace added a series of 24 karat Goldplate sculptured ornaments.

WATERFORD CRYSTAL

41 Madison Avenue
New York, New York 10010
(212) 532-5950

Bells, Christmas Ornaments

More than 200 years ago, the craftsmen in Waterford on the southeastern coast of Ireland began creating a crystal of such preeminence of design, clarity and luminescence that the very name Waterford meant quality.

Waterford crystal seems to glow with a bottomless light. The secret lies in the purity of ulta-white silica sand and the addition of minerals which distinguish true crystal from ordinary glass. Soft to the touch, Waterford crystal has a sweet singing ring when it is tapped. But, it is the weight and substance of the crystal which accommodates Waterford's prismatic cuts, ranging from flat shallow cuts and wedges to a myriad of fluted and diamond patterns. None of these opulent, timeless Waterford patterns is ever discontinued.

After a hundred-year reign, the Waterford factory closed and an entire century passed before the priceless Waterford heritage was resumed. The founders of the new Waterford chose not to simply bask in past glory, but rather to rekindle the ancient Irish art. Ancient methods of hand manufacturing were revived, and once again, Irish craftsmen fashioned the elegant and timeless patterns from the white-hot molten crystal.

WEDGWOOD

41 Madison Avenue
New York, New York 10010
(212) 532-5950

Bells, Christmas Ornaments, Plates

In 1759, Josiah Wedgwood founded his own potteryworks. It was the first step in fulfilling his dreams of creating classic pottery and dinnerware of such magnificent quality that it would set new standards and endure beyond his time. He would succeed far beyond his dreams. Born in 1730, Wedgwood was a fourth-generation potter who, at the age of nine, became his brother's apprentice. His talent was quickly recognized, and while still a young man, he became the partner of Thomas Whieldon, England's finest potter of that period.

His eagerness to explore new techniques of English pottery making prompted Josiah to strike out on his own in 1759. Less than five years later, he perfected a cream-colored earthenware with a rich and brilliant glaze which withstood both heat and cold. Queen Charlotte so loved it, that she promptly decreed that all creamware thenceforth be known as "Queen's Ware."

Thomas Bentley later joined the firm as a partner, bringing with him a knowledge of the arts and valuable social contacts. Wedgwood's most prestigious commission during this period was a 952-piece set of "Queen's Ware" dinnerware for Catherine the Great of Tsarist Russia.

In addition to his "useful wares," Wedgwood experimented with a new Black Basalt which became one of the company's most popular products. His most famous invention was Jasper; unglazed, vitreous, fine stoneware which could be stained various colors such as blue, green, lilac, yellow or black. It provided a suitable background for white relief work on classic subjects or portraits.

Wedgwood became one of the earliest and most active members of the current collectibles field, producing Christmas plates, thimbles, bells and mugs in its famous Jasper. The firm also produces several plate series in fine bone china and earthenware.

WHITLEY BAY

1009 Central
Kansas City, Missouri
816-221-8200

Figurines

Although Whitley Bay is a relatively new company, the quality and imaginative charm of their figurines has already won the company a loyal following among collectors.

In 1989, Whitley Bay introduced its first entry into the collectible field, with an eight-piece limited edition *Santa Series* and a ten-piece collectors edition *Elf Series.* Both series are extremely detailed and equisitely painted.

The *Santa Series* figurines are based on myths and legends that we have grown up with — Santa checking his list or riding in a sleigh. The Santa figurines seen to awaken long-forgotten memories of childhood. The first eight in the series are now gradually being retired, and three new Santas are being introduced in 1992. Each Santa in the current series is limited to 10,000 pieces.

The *Elf* collection features eight elves, Santa and Santa's Workshop. Booklets included with each elf will give collectors insights as to the European troop each is from, his duties at the North Pole and his characteristics. Using your imagination, you will probably find someone you know in these elves.

A great deal of historical research takes place before renowned artist, Lawrence Heyda, begins the process of sculpting each model. Once all the details of this prototype are approved, the molds are prepared and the colors selected for the artists who hand paint the figurines.

Modern technology and materials are employed to produce finely detailed cold-cast porcelain figurines with an old world look.

"Entry" depicts Santa, loaded down with his traditional goodies. The Christmas stocking, the mantle and the hearth have played an important role in the Santa Claus legends.

WILDLIFE INTERNATIONALE, INC.

John A. Ruthven
6290 Old U.S. 68
Georgetown, Ohio 45121

Graphics, Plates

Founded in 1971, Wildlife Internationale, Inc. publishes the artwork of John A. Ruthven.

Born in Cincinnati, Ohio, John A. Ruthven served in the Navy during World War II and later attended the Cincinnati Art Academy. The opportunity to build a career in wildlife art arose in 1960, when Ruthven won the U.S. Department of Interior's federal duck stamp art competition with "Redhead Ducks."

Ruthven is a prolific artist, turning out several important works per year. In undertaking any project, Ruthven generally likes to go to the source and finish up in the studio. Each painting is planned very carefully in advance. Essentially all of Ruthven's work is commissioned these days. Ruthven's work has been accepted in major judged shows and he has received numerous major commissions. In 1976, the artist was honored with a White House unveiling of his Bald Eagle. As a member of the Explorers Club in New York, Ruthven carried their flag to the Phillipines on an expedition which discovered a bird new to science.

John Ruthven manages to sum it all up by saying, "I'm never at work, I'm away from work. To be able to paint what I see and record it — it's just an exciting thing for me. I'll never retire."

WILLITTS DESIGNS

Mary Beggs
1129 Industrial Blvd.
P.O. Box 750009
Petaluma, California 94975
(707) 778-7211
Fax: (707) 769-0304

Figurines, Plates, Bells, Christmas Ornaments, Graphics

Since William G. Willitts, Sr. and Elda Willitts founded Willitts Imports in 1961, the company has followed the doctrine of hard work, long hours and "the customer is always right" motto. The strong foundation they created, helped foster the company's successful growth.

Bill Willitts, Jr. joined the company on a full-time basis beginning in 1973, eventually taking over the company presidency. The company now has its own design team as well as licenses with Walt Disney, United Media (PEANUTS), Tobin Fraley, Coca-Cola and others.

Bill Willitts has based his management philosophy on treating everyone, from his best clients to co-workers, with respect, courtesy and encouragement. Employees are encouraged to "Be Healthy" and are paid each time they work out, up to three times a week. The company also has a unique monthly "Speak Freely" meeting — a kind of town meeting for all employees to discuss their ideas and make suggestions.

In 1987, NBC's *Today* show featured a lengthy segment on the company. Willitts has also been featured in magazines including *American Way*, the magazine of American Airlines. Willitts Designs is one of the fastest growing companies in the gift industry with customers and representatives across the United States, in Puerto Rico, Canada, Australia and Japan.

JOHANNES ZOOK ORIGINALS

1519 South Badour
Midland, Michigan 48640
(517) 835-9388

Dolls

In 1983, Joanna Secrist was thinking of opening a doll and toy store. Searching for original marketing ideas, her husband Pat thought it would be a nice touch to offer a unique doll to customers, one that couldn't be found anywhere else. Pat, who had learned sculpting as a child, would create the faces while Joanna would design and make the costumes. They bought a kiln and books on doll making and for the next few months, focused their attention on a workshop in the middle of the kitchen of their basement apartment. Unfortunately, their first doll looked "as if it had hit a wall at full speed."

They didn't give up, and by late 1984 had produced thirty porcelain dolls. The following year they added two baby dolls to their line, explored the technical aspect of vinyl doll production and formed Johannes Zook Originals. By 1986, they were producing their own vinyl dolls.

The year 1987 was a watershed year for their company. Zook's "Sara" doll won the coveted DOTY (Doll of the Year) Award by *Doll Reader* as the best doll in its category. Zook's "Patrick" also was nominated by the International Academy for a DOTY award and won the "Award of Excellence" from *Dolls* magazine.

The Zook line has now increased to thirty different dolls and includes both black and Asian Zook Kids. The Secrists now manufacture their dolls in a factory in Midland, Michigan. Johannes Zook Originals is a division of Secrist Toys, Inc.

Meet the Artists

Biographies of Some of Today's Most Popular and Talented Limited Edition Artists

Limited edition artists are the objects of a great deal of interest and admiration on the part of collectors. Some collectors will travel hundreds of miles to attend an open house or convention featuring that special artist or craftsman. Here is some brief biographical information about some of the best-known artists in today's world of limited editions. This listing is not comprehensive, but it will provide an introduction to a good number of the talented men and women whose works bring pleasure to collectors all over the world.

SUSAN STONE AIKEN

This year marks Susan Stone Aiken's tenth anniversary as Gorham's first lady of dolls. Having initially agreed to sketch some outfits for the newly developing doll program at Gorham, her illustrations were so exciting that she was chosen as the designer for Gorham's original collection of ten dolls introduced in 1981. Since then, she's designed well over 100 dolls for the company.

From "Rosamond" and "Christopher" in 1981 to "Amey," Gorham's tenth anniversary issue, every doll dressed by Ms. Aiken is renowned for its original, heirloom quality. In fact, she has had the distinct honor of seeing many of her dolls appreciate in value far beyond their original issue price. And her newest, limited edition collector doll series, *Les Belles Bebes* and *Legendary Heroines*, are also destined to be passed on through generations.

A native of Massachusetts, Ms. Aiken trained as an artist at the University of Maine and the Rhode Island School of Design. She has taken courses in fashion illustration and pattern making, and her talent as a seamstress is a natural gift. Ms. Aiken gets much of her inspiration from books and photos of turn-of-the-century fashions. But she does have an instinctive feeling for the combinations of materials that are authentic and correct.

"I'm from an old New England family," she says, "and I grew up surrounded by antiques. When I create a costume for a doll, it is like discovering an old friend."

After researching her ideas, she begins with a sketch, then personally selects fabrics, laces and trims to create an original sample. She works with the sculptor so that the face, coloring and hairstyle coordinate with the costume she has designed.

Aiken finds her work especially rewarding because she gets to make artist appearances for Gorham and is able to meet collectors who appreciate the love and effort she puts into each design. The culmination of her talents and efforts can be seen in the *Gorham Doll Collection*.

PAULETTE APRILE

A native of California, Paulette Aprile loved art, making clothes for her dolls, and later designing and sewing her own clothes. Years later, she resumed making doll clothes, this time for her daughters' dolls. Ms. Aprile then decided to learn all that she could about ceramics. She bought every book she could find on ceramics and doll making. For the next few years, she experimented with slip (liquid porcelain), molds and a few tools. She proved to be a stern taskmaster, but she acquired a good working knowledge of sculpting and doll making.

A member of three doll clubs, she made numerous reproduction dolls which won ribbons in area competitions.

In 1987, Ms. Aprile's "Cynthia" doll won the "Best Sculpture Award" and the *Doll* magazine's "Awards of Excellence." Ms. Aprile enjoys doing the research for her authentic period dolls, especially her bride dolls.

In 1991, she had three limited edition dolls in her line. Her "Stephanie" doll was nominated for *Doll* magazine's "Awards of Excellence."

Ms. Aprile recently was selected by Seymour Mann to design dolls for the company's new *Signature Collection*. This milestone marks Ms. Aprile's first venture with a commercial doll supplier. She trusted the firm to manufacture outstanding reproductions without devaluing her doll originals. Seymour Mann, Inc.'s international reputation as a high-quality collectible supplier with strong marketing expertise persuaded her to design collectible porcelain dolls for the firm.

GIUSEPPE ARMANI

For many years, collectors have been delighted by the elegance and grace of Giuseppe Armani's many fine figurines.

The Italian master sculptor has a unique talent for translating both human and animal form, and for capturing the emotion and ambience of the occasion into each of his works.

Born in Calci, Italy in 1935, Armani began his artistic career as a child in his village. Working with chalk, he sketched his many childhood friends, real and imaginary, on whatever surface he could find. "The walls of my village were full of my drawings," Armani recalled.

Armani was about fourteen years old when his family moved to Pisa. There he studied art and anatomy for the next ten years. Although Armani started as a painter, the artist confesses that he always envisioned his art in three-dimensional form. And so, he eventually turned to sculpture for expression. Although he has sculpted in alabaster, wood and marble, Armani prefers working in clay.

As with any artist, Armani's style has evolved over the years. He now describes his works as "light, slender and bright."

The artist still lives in Pisa where he has a sculpture studio in his home. In addition, he works with the artists and artisans at the Florence Sculture d'Arte Studios where his works are reproduced, painted and prepared for the worldwide market. At the Florence Studios, Armani is the premiere designer and sculptor, and it is there that he supervises all aspects of his sculptures which are known as the *Armani Collection*.

Armani has made several trips to the United States, meeting collectors of his works and promoting his newly-formed collector club, the G. Armani Society. His most recent visit was in November, 1990, and he is again scheduled to tour the United States in late 1991.

The Armani Collection is imported to the United States exclusively by Miller Import Corporation of Keasbey, Woodbridge Township, New Jersey. And, the G. Armani Society is managed by this company.

MABEL LUCIE ATTWELL

British artist Mabel Lucie Attwell was born in London, the ninth of ten children. Her father, a successful butcher, encouraged his large musical family to pursue artistic interests. Mabel Lucie was not musical, and she secretly turned to her drawings at a very early age.

A shy child, she was educated at home and relied on her imagination to pass the time. With an older sister, she would make up stories about families and children, illustrating the stories herself.

She sold her first drawing before she was sixteen years old to a London publisher, receiving two pounds (about $4 U.S.) for it. From that humble beginning, Miss Attwell was a working artist. She paid her own way through art school by selling her work, unusual for a young woman before the turn-of-the-century.

She no doubt benefitted from the Victorian Era interest in women's art, which created great demand for illustrations by talented women. Among her Victorian contemporaries were artists Cicely Mary Barker, Kate Greenawald, Bessie Pease Gutmann and Maud Humphrey, some of whom were art school classmates.

It was during her studies in art school that Mabel Lucie Attwell met and married a fellow art student, illustrator Harold Earnshaw. They had two sons and a daughter. Her daughter Peggy, who was born in 1909, became the "Attwell child," the adorable toddler with large eyes, a winsome expression and often with a large bow in her hair.

Miss Attwell's earliest published illustrations appeared in "That Little Limb", issued in 1905. For many years, she illustrated gift books for Raphael Tuck, as well as many children's books and fairy tales.

She continued her work, surviving two world wars and reflecting changes in public taste. Throughout her career, her art was always in demand — even by the Royal Family. As a toddler, Prince Charles was presented with a set of nursery china bearing Miss Attwell's illustrations, and Princess Margaret chose Miss Attwell's artwork for personal Christmas cards when she was a child in the 1930s.

Mabel Lucie Attwell died peacefully on November 5, 1964. Enesco continued the legacy of Mabel Lucie Attwell in 1987, by licensing the rights to translate her artwork into porcelain bisque figurines through the *Enesco Memories of Yesterday Collection®*. Her artwork is held by her estate, which is managed in England by her grandson, John, and his wife, Hilary.

The Collection premiered in 1988 and was soon ranked among the Top Ten Collectibles in the United States. The Collection is now available throughout the world, and in 1991, Enesco formed the Memories of Yesterday Collectors' Society℠, in support of the Collection.

BETTE BALL

Betty Ball is the award-winning designer of the highly acclaimed *Betty Jane Carter®*, *Carol Anne®*, *Dolly Dingle®* and *Victoria Ashlea Originals®* porcelain dolls. She is known and appreciated by doll collectors for her uncompromising quality of design.

Ms. Ball double majored in Fine Arts and Costume Design in art school. Her paintings hang in many private collections around the world. She also enjoys an international reputation for her design in fine china and giftware.

She is a member of the International Foundation of Doll Makers, The Society of Professional Doll Makers, as well as a recipient of the prestigious DOTY award and NALED, Doll of the Year awards.

Bette's dolls have been honored by acceptance in many museums such as The Yokohama Doll Museum in Japan; The McCurdy Historical Doll Museum, Utah; The White Castle Doll Museum, California; Arizona Toy and Doll Museum, Arizona; Doll Castle Museum, New Jersey; San Francisco Doll Museum, California; and Mary Stoltz Doll & Toy Museum, Pennsylvania.

Bette Ball has endeared herself to countless admirers through personal and television appearances, where she lends her vibrant personality to discussions on designing and collecting dolls.

Bette is director of doll design for Goebel United States.

CICELY MARY BARKER

English artist Cicely Mary Barker, whose Flower Fairies have thrilled generations of children, has won the hearts of yet another generation of collectors of fantasy and romance. Born in Surrey, England in 1895, Ms. Barker demonstrated her artistic talent at a very early age. A frail child, she was educated at home and spent a considerable amount of time sketching seascapes and children. Although she had no formal training, her talents were developed during her association with artists she met through the local Croydon Art Society.

In 1923, the first volume of her Flower Fairies was published. Whimsical and sensitive in every detail, her Flower Fairies reflected an art nouveau style with the color richness and subtlety of

that period. Her *Children's Book of Hymns* was published in 1929 and was re-issued fifty years later. Cicely Mary Barker died in 1973, shortly after the 50th anniversary of her first Flower Fairies book.

A Festival of Flower Fairies was recently introduced by Enesco Corporation. Based on Ms. Barker's artwork, the collection contains fantasy figurines, musicals, miniatures and accessories.

W.S. George has also introduced a limited edition plate series based on Ms. Barker's sketches entitled *Beloved Hymns of Childhood.*

Reco International Corp. has released the *Flower Fairies Year Plate Collection.* Each plate has a portion of the artist's poems printed on the backstamp.

JILL BARKLEM

Jill Barklem began drawing the mice who reside in the mythical community of Brambly Hedge while traveling by train from her home in Epping, England, to art classes in London. During the long rides, Jill created her own private world: a community of self-sufficient mice who live in a hedgerow. She carefully researched every aspect of Brambly Hedge, keeping notebooks and diaries.

In 1980, four picture books were published chronicling the astonishing lives and adventures of the mice of Brambly Hedge. *Spring Story, Summer Story, Autumn Story* and *Winter Story* were a phenomenal success and have since been published in thirteen languages. Two more books soon followed: *The Secret Staircase* and *The High Hills.* Her seventh book, *Sea Story,* was released in 1991.

Readers of all ages are captivated by her beautiful illustrations and stories that portray a "loving environment where everyone is valued and where the earth itself is appreciated and respected."

In 1990, Enesco Corporation recreated her book's heartwarming adventures and characters into charming figurines, musicals, waterballs, gift bags, plush toys and other accessories. From Mrs. Apple's kitchen with its open hearths and wooden hutch to Primrose's nursery, every small detail captures Jill's original artwork.

Growing up in Epping, Jill always loved nature. One of her favorite pastimes was hiding in a patch of wild grass under a chestnut tree in the family garden. It was in this special hiding place that Jill would draw and paint.

At thirteen, she suffered a detached retina and had to give up many childhood activities. She became more involved in art and later attended the famous St. Martin's School of Art in London.

Today Jill is married and has two young children. But she still retreats to her fantasy world of Brambly Hedge to continue creating the adventures of the mice whose lives she now shares with the world.

DOT AND SY BARLOWE

When Dot and Sy Barlowe first collaborated as fellow artists at New York's Museum of Natural History in the 1940s, they began a harmonious personal and working relationship that has been preserved to this day. Four years after their marriage in 1946, they began working as free-lance illustrators. Since then — together and separately — they have earned national recognition for their historic and naturalist art.

Together, the Barlowes have illustrated nature books for some of the largest publishing houses in America, including Knopf, Random House, Morrow, Follett, American Heritage Press, Putnam, Harper & Row, McGraw-Hill, and Grosset and Dunlap. For the Golden Press alone they illustrated fifteen books, including such well-known nature identification volumes as *Seashores, Trees of America,* and *Amphibians of North America.*

In addition, the Barlowes have contributed illustrations to several Audubon Society guides and to *The Audubon Society Encyclopedia of North American*

Birds. They also share their knowledge of nature illustration and botany by teaching at the Parsons School of Design in New York. The artists have done features for publications including *The New York Times* and *Newsday*, and their works have been honored with numerous awards and exhibitions at the Society of Illustrators in New York and Expo '67 in Montreal.

For the past thirty years, the Barlowes have lived on Long Island. Their two children are Amy, a concert violinist and music professor; and Wayne, an award-winning illustrator in his own right.

Reco International Corp. has presented an eight-plate *Vanishing Animal Kingdoms* collection by Sy Barlowe, and a *Gardens of Beauty* Plate Collection by Dorothea Barlowe. The artists also introduced a series of animal figurines through Reco. Two recent introductions include *Town & Country Dogs* and *Our Cherished Seas* plate series.

FRANCIS J. BARNUM

Francis J. Barnum of Loveland, Ohio joined the Chilmark Gallery of artists in the midst of a twenty-six year career as a designer, modelmaker and sculptor. His career — from commercial illustrator to serious artist of American subjects — parallels the careers of Frederic Remington, Charles M. Russell and many of today's best cowboy artists.

Born and raised in Ohio's Cuyahoga River Valley, the family farm had been the site of countless Shawnee Indian encampments. As a boy he began saving and cataloging Indian artifacts, a hobby that paved the way for Barnum's lifelong interest in archeological history and Indian culture.

He has created dioramas for museums, corporate displays for trade and consumer fairs and toys like the Star Wars figures (working with Lucasfilm Inc.) and the Six Million Dollar Man. One of his sculptures for the College Football Hall of Fame is used as the logo for all televised football games.

Painstaking research and attention to even the smallest detail is obvious in all of Barnum's work. In addition to bringing a sense of high drama to his scenes, Barnum has the ability to capture the very emotions of his characters. Barnum's sculptures for the Lance's Chilmark line are as diverse as his previous experiences spanning the *Old West*, *Wildlife* and most recently the *American Civil War*.

Barnum has designed a series of *Civil War* sculptures for Chilmark Pewter. Numbering over twenty pieces in 1991, with more in the planning stages, Barnum takes us from Gettysburg to Shiloh to Antietam and runs the gamut of emotions from victory to defeat. His "Burnside's Bridge," the *Civil War* flagship sculpture, stands as a memorial to America's most remembered war.

KATHY BARRY HIPPENSTEEL

Kathy Hippensteel sculpts only baby dolls and she has dedicated her career to creating the most lifelike dolls possible. This dedication has earned her awards in virtually every show she has entered, including a top award from the Illinois Doll Makers' Association.

"Chen," the first doll in her *International Festival of Toys & Tots* collection, was nominated for a prestigious 1989 Award of Excellence by *Dolls* magazine and received a 1990 Achievement Award from the National Association of Limited Edition Dealers. Her other collections available from Ashton-Drake are *Born to Be Famous* and *Baby Book Treasures*.

Today, Ms. Hippensteel's dolls are displayed with the most celebrated dolls of this century in doll museums in Paris, France, and in the United States. Private collectors consider her works to be some of their most valued acquisitions.

PRESCOTT "WOODY" BASTON, JR.

In 1981, Sebastian Miniatures reached a landmark when the first *Sebastian Miniature* sculpted by Prescott "Woody" Baston, Jr., the son of Prescott Baston, was introduced.

A trained artist, Woody had wanted to try his hand at making Sebastian miniatures from the time he was a boy. He began working part-time in the studio during his junior year in high school and spent summers learning all phases of production. Following four years of study at Boston University, he graduated with a bachelor's degree in fine arts,

majoring in Sculpture.

After a stint in the Army, Woody joined the Lance Corporation in Hudson as Production Manager. In 1968, his father had begun designing miniature figurines to be cast by Lance into Hudson pewter.

In 1975, operations at the Marblehead plant were halted and production continued in the Hudson facility. At the present time, Woody is Vice-President of Marketing Services and the sole sculptor of *Sebastian Miniatures* since the death of his father in 1984. Woody has sculpted more than 150 miniatures for the Lance Sebastian retail line and private commissions.

PRESCOTT WOODBURY BASTON

Prescott Woodbury Baston was born in Arlington, Massachusetts in 1909 and received his formal art training at the Vesper George School of Art in Boston in the late 1920s.

Baston began sculpting under his own name in 1938, and in 1940, formed the Sebastian Miniature Company. The success of his tiny figurines prompted him to move his company from the basement of his home to a studio in Marblehead, Massachusetts. He produced over 900 different "Sebastian Miniatures" for his retail line and private commissions. His tiny, hand-painted miniatures were distributed initially through gift shops in New England and later, throughout the nation. He also designed and produced advertising giveaway pieces for over 100 corporations.

In 1969, Baston, then over sixty years old, turned his design attention to plates and figurines that were cast in pewter by other gift manufacturers. They included *The Birth of a Nation* and the *Currier & Ives* plate series for Royal Worcester.

In 1976, the Lance Corporation began producing 100 of Baston's most popular designs for national distribution. Paralleled with an explosion of American interest in nostalgic collectibles, Sebastian Miniatures started to attract an attention they had never enjoyed over the forty previous years.

Prescott Woodbury Baston died in May 1984, after seeing his son, Woody, begin sculpting his own *Sebastian Miniatures*, and the love of the man and his art still continue today.

YOLANDA BELLO

Award-winning doll artist Yolanda Bello began "restyling" her dolls when she was a young child in Caracas, Venezuela. With each change, Bello's imagination helped transform her ordinary dolls into new and exciting characters.

Bello moved to Chicago, Illinios when she was fourteen, bringing her love of dolls with her. She eventually began working as a figurine sculptor while pursuing her interest in doll design and sculpture in her spare time. In 1981, Ms. Bello created her first porcelain dolls — a pair of Spanish girls — and the reaction was so favorable that within a year, dollmaking had become her full-time profession.

Since then, Yolanda Bello has designed and produced dolls which have earned her critical acclaim and more than fifty prizes in major juried exhibitions, including five Best of Show awards, a prestigious Doll of the Year award in 1985 and First Place in Doll Achievement from the National Association of Limited Edition Dealers in 1987, 1988 and 1989.

Ms. Bello's designs range from one-of-a-kind dolls portraying the characters in the opera *Carmen* for the New York Metropolitan Galleries, to her most sought-after limited edition dolls. Both *Yolanda's Picture-Perfect Babies*, her first collection produced by the Edwin M. Knowles China Co. exclusively for the Ashton-Drake Galleries, and *Children of Mother Goose* have been enthusiastically received by collectors.

JODY BERGSMA

The whimsical world of Jody Bergsma's "Little People" may be pure fantasy, but its simplicity and beauty has touched the hearts of collectors. Born in 1953 in Bellingham, Washington, Bergsma came from a family of five children where her early artistic efforts were encouraged and prominently displayed. When Bergsma was fifteen, her aunt Eileen Knight invited her to Port Angeles to enter her first art show. She made sixty dollars, which motivated both her artistic and entrepreneurial efforts.

In 1973, Bergsma attended a small college in Vancouver, Canada where she came under the influence of the Canadian impressionists called "the group of seven." In 1978, she began a year-long journey through Europe where she visited the museums in Amsterdam, London and Paris. She painted in southern France, Venice and Florence and ended her studies in Athens and the Greek Islands. Returning home, Bergsma withdrew from her engineering studies and became a serious, full-time artist.

Bergsma has had numerous one-woman shows of her abstract watercolors and has released over 300 different "Little People" prints through the Jody

Bergsma Gallery. Jody's first collector plate series for Reco International was *Guardians of the Kingdom*, which is also available through The Hamilton Collection. In 1990, Reco International introduced the Jody Bergsma *Christmas Series*, premiering with "Down the Glistening Lane" and continuing in 1991 with "A Child Is Born." In addition, a new *Mother's Day* series premiered with "The Beauty of Life." A new figurine line was also recently introduced. Each Jody Bergsma plate offers a poetic message from the artist on the backstamp.

ULRICH BERNARDI

While many artists often fear they will suffer from "creative block," mastercarver Ulrich Bernardi has just the opposite problem: he bemoans the fact that there simply isn't enough time for him to carry out all the ideas swirling around in his head.

Bernardi dreamed of creating exquisite figurines from blocks of wood even when he was a little boy. Inspired by the work of his grandfather, an altar builder, and grandmother, an ornamental wood sculptress, Bernardi vowed to learn the art himself one day. Today, as a mastercarver for ANRI, Bernardi creates masterpieces which reflect his lifelong dream and his dedication.

"I became a carver in a very natural way, and it's perfectly fitting with my personality," says Bernardi. "I like to communicate with other people, but I love to work quietly by myself."

Since becoming a mastercarver for ANRI, Bernardi has earned acclaim for his nativity figures, creche sets and other religious pieces, and for his evocative interpretations of Sarah Kay's children.

Born in 1925 in St. Ulrich in the Groden Valley, Bernardi developed his talent in drawing, modelling and woodcarving at the Academy of Art in St. Ulrich, and later in studies which earned him the master of arts degree. While working in his first apprenticeship with a master woodcarver, Bernardi encountered the area of art which continues to be his deepest passion and greatest joy — the carving of nativity scenes. Through his nativity sets, Bernardi says, he is able to give his deepest expression and sentiment.

From the window of his studio in the Groden Valley, Bernardi can view the quiet village of St. Ulrich below and the magnificent mountains above. "The feeling of freedom and detachment combined with a sense of belonging and community is an inspiration for my work," he explains. "Living in the Groden Valley is so beautiful. I feel so comfortable and protected, so close to nature."

An active member of the men's and church choir, as well as an avid hiker and skier, Bernardi enjoys the simple life of family and nature. He also practices figure drawing in his leisure time. To Bernardi, the three greatest artists of all time are Michelangelo, Raphael and Botticelli.

Of his several trips to the United States, Bernardi says: "I have a very good impression of Americans and their culture, especially their heartiness and candor. I have enjoyed my visits there very much and would like to see it again."

THOMAS BLACKSHEAR

As an admirer of turn-of-the-century art masters like N.C. Wyeth and J.C. Leyendecker, Thomas Blackshear strives to capture the mood and the inherent drama in each of his subjects. Yet, Blackshear is very much a man of the present day, and thus he draws upon contemporary techniques and art media to create his true-to-life cinematic masterworks.

Through the use of gouache, acrylics, pastels and oils, Blackshear captures the personality and drama of some of the world's best-loved cinematic characters. His unique talent has been represented on movie posters for *Indiana Jones and Temple of Doom*, *The Black Cauldron*, *Legend* and *Star Wars* and has earned him the admiration of moviegoers.

Blackshear has worked hard for success. He credits his teachers at Chicago's American Academy of Art, and the famous contemporary illustrator, Mark English, as his formative influences. Working for Disney Studios, 20th Century Fox, Lucasfilm and Universal Studios has allowed him to paint his favorite subjects.

Blackshear's talent earned him gold and silver awards from the Kansas City Directors Club in 1982, and many of his works were on display in Society of Illustrators shows during this time.

In 1986, Blackshear created the original art for a series of collector plates entitled the *Star Wars* plate collection. This very popular plate series issued by The Hamilton Collection, paved the way for Blackshear's growing notoriety in the collector plate field. On the heels of that success, Blackshear was commissioned to create the first officially authorized plate collection celebrating the 50th anniversary of *The Wizard of Oz* for The Hamilton Collection.

Then, in 1990, Blackshear created a major new commemorative work that won him the prestigious "Plate of the Year" Award. This stunning plate-painting, entitled "Fifty Years of Oz," firmly established Blackshear as one of the most gifted cinematic artists of our time.

Most recently, Thomas Blackshear has been working with The Hamilton Collection on a new series of officially authorized commemorative plates in conjunction with the 25th Anniversary of one of the most acclaimed television shows of all time, *STAR TREK*.

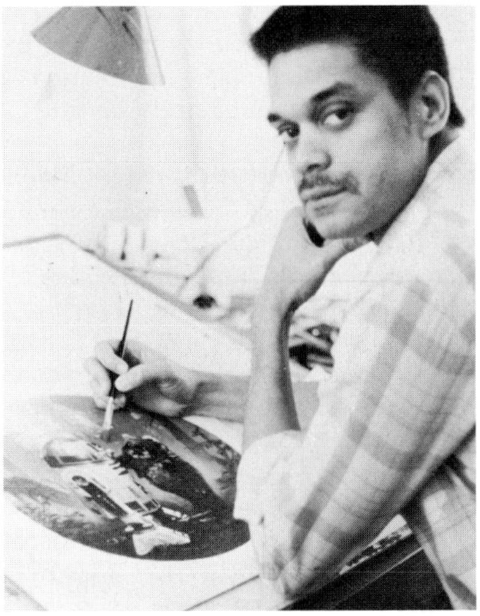

MAUD HUMPHREY BOGART

Long before her only son Humphrey Bogart won worldwide fame as an actor, Maud Humphrey established herself as one of the country's most gifted artists. Her turn-of-the-century paintings of adorable children brilliantly combined the elegance of the Victorian age with the joys of childhood.

As one of the most talented artists from America's "Golden Age of Illustration," Maud Humphrey always loved to draw and paint. She left her home in Rochester, New York, to study at the famous Art League in New York City. Her training continued in Paris at the Julian Studios where she worked under several master painters. Impressed by her outstanding gift for children's portraiture, several prominent Parisian families commissioned Ms. Humphrey to capture their sons and daughters on canvas.

Upon returning to New York, Ms. Humphrey was hired to produce illustrations for Christmas cards as well as for books, calendars and advertisements. She became one of the country's most sought-after artists as more requests poured in from magazines, book publishers and advertising companies. In several months, Maud Humphrey's illustrations became the talk of the nation.

"This artist apparently has the pleasing faculty of seeing only the beauty and innocence of youth in her subjects — bright, happy, pretty children, with pleasant surroundings," wrote an admiring art critic nearly a century ago. "One feels the wholesome and sweet atmosphere in all her work: her little ones are always good, and when she came to draw a little lamb under her transforming pencil, it immediately became a good little lamb."

When she was thirty-three, Maud Humphrey married Belmont DeForest Bogart, a prominent doctor in Manhattan. Their first son, Humphrey Bogart, would eventually become the famed Hollywood star. But Humphrey Bogart actually entered the public eye much earlier when his mother painted his portrait as a baby and sent it to a New York advertising agency. His picture showed up on all the labels and advertisements of a popular baby food company. Soon he became famous as the "Original Maud Humphrey Baby."

The Bogarts also had two daughters, Frances and Catherine. Maud Humphrey gracefully combined marriage, motherhood and career during an era when such a combination was very uncommon. Remarkably, she continued painting until she was well into her seventies.

Though she died in 1940, her artwork lives on and has become more popular today than ever before. Offered by The Balliol Corporation and The Hamilton Collection, original creations inspired by her illustrations are now reaching a wide new audience of collectors — the *Little Ladies* plate collection, the "Playing Bride" and "First Lesson" porcelain collector dolls and an array of fanciful figurines. In mid-1988, Hamilton Gifts Limited unveiled the first works of art in the *Maud Humphrey Bogart* Collection with nine limited edition figurines. Since then, this fanciful line of collector's items — all inspired by the adorable children in Miss Humphrey's paintings — have won nationwide acclaim. "My First Dance," a hand-painted figurine of a little girl admiring her reflection in a mirror, became the first figurine to retire in 1989.

While resin and porcelain bisque figurines dominate the *Maud Humphrey Bogart Collection*, some of the artist's works have been used as the basis for accessories such as music boxes, picture frames, vanity trays and jewelry boxes.

HIGGINS BOND

Higgins Bond's artwork is the result of a lifetime spent drawing, painting, studying and practicing her craft. Born Barbara Higgins, the artist began signing her paintings with her last name only while studying at Memphis College of Arts, where she earned a Bachelor of Fine Arts degree. Upon her marriage, she modified her professional signature to "Higgins Bond," although friends still know her as Barbara.

Ms. Bond has earned the commissions of major corporations and book publishers for her original paintings. She has created illustrations for books, magazines and calendars as well as personal portraits for firms including Houghton-Mifflin, Anheuser-Busch, RCA, NBC, McGraw-Hill, Crown Publishers, The Bell System, and Random House. Her works have been exhibited at the Metropolitan Museum of Art in New York, and numerous other museums in New York, Chicago, Indiana and New Jersey.

The artist is an award winner from the Society of Illustrators, and was presented the "Key to the City" of Indianapolis for her artworks. She has been a guest lecturer at numerous colleges, universities and schools, and now resides and works in Teaneck, New Jersey.

The first limited edition collector plate by Higgins Bond, "Ashley," portrayed a little girl discovering a butterfly in a field of flowers. It premiered an eight-plate collection offered exclusively by The Hamilton Collection: *Treasured Days*. As one would expect from so diversely talented an artist, Higgins Bond changed subject matter for her second plate collection to that of the fascinating coral seas in "The Living Oasis." This colorful 'underwater' plate-painting was the first issue in her eight plate collection offered by The Hamilton Collection, entitled *Coral Paradise*.

MICHAEL BOYETT

Texan Michael Boyett is recognized as one of the most important sculptors of the American West. His works are exhibited in Western art galleries and museums throughout the United States. Special invitational exhibitions of his works have included the inauguration of President Jimmy Carter (Washington D.C.), The George Phippen Memorial Art Show (Prescott, Arizona), Texas Rangers Hall of Fame (Waco, Texas), and the Texas Art Classic (Fort Worth, Texas).

Born in Boise, Idaho in 1943, Boyett began painting and sculpturing as a child. He received recognition at the age of twelve when one of his paintings was chosen to hang in the governor's office in Topeka, Kansas. Boyett attended the University of Texas Art School and holds bachelor and master's degrees in fine arts from the Stephen F. Austin State University.

Boyett worked exclusively in bronze until 1979 when the Chilmark foundry of Hudson, Massachusetts, began casting his miniature scale sculptures in pewter.

SUZAN BRADFORD

Suzan's love of art stemmed from age two, as she watched oil paintings develop at her artist-mother's knee. Her Air Force pilot father supplied the rough carpentry/three-dimensional side of her life's vantage point and also a catalytic viewing of the Louvre's "Winged Victory of Samothrace" at the age of six. At age ten, she vowed to "be a sculptor like Michelangelo." Though short of that mark, her empathy and striving for life-like forms has remained kindled over the years, as many friends, family, and animal critters have graced her life in Florida, Kansas, Colorado and Oklahoma. The latter included almost a dozen horses, a herd of Holsteins, range ewes at lambing time, barnyard fowl of

many types, dogs (some of whom travel well to Santa Fe and beyond), cats, parakeets, turtles, and a saucy cockateil.

Suzan's freelance and commissioned artworks are in private collections across the country and venture into the mediums of drawing, oil painting, watercolor, mixed media, stoneware pottery, terra-cotta sculptures, bronzes and lithographs.

Ms. Bradford has been with United Design for seven years and is the creator of several lines: *Backyard Birds*™, the original *Fancy Frames*™, and *Candlelights*™; she has also sculpted many of *The Legend of Santa Claus*™ limited edition figurines, and pieces in the *Pet Pin*™ line, as well as the *Animal Magnetism*™ line.

CLARK BRONSON

Clark Bronson's career began at age twenty-one when he became a staff artist for the Utah Fish and Game Department. Nine years later, Bronson was recognized as one of the leading wildlife painters in America. His artwork graced the covers of wildlife publications and he was commissioned to illustrate Rand McNally's books, *The Album of North American Birds* and *The Album of North American Animals*.

He then turned his attention to another medium and began sculpting in bronze. Bronson set up his own bronze foundry, the Big Sky Casting Corporation, so he could oversee every phase of the casting process. Since 1971, the year he began issuing his sculptures, Bronson has averaged four to five works each year. In the last few years, he has cut back on his sculpting to host wildlife tours in Canada and Alaska.

Bronson's "Eagle Rock," a striking eagle with a wingspan of nineteen inches, was introduced in 1988 and is his premier work for the Lance Corporation. This magnificent sculpture was done for Lance's Chilmark line.

PATRICIA BROOKS

As a youngster in her native Australia, Patricia Brooks could draw and paint beautifully — so well that she was nominated for a scholarship to art school. But young Patricia was impatient with art theory: she couldn't wait to try her skills in the real world. So at a tender age, she set out on her own and won a job as junior artist for one of Rupert Murdoch's newspapers.

Patricia's sense of adventure and promise compelled her to seek a greater challenge, and before long she was on her way to England. Her "can-do" manner served her well, and within a short time she established herself as a graphics designer in advertising.

Her years in advertising provided Ms. Brooks with a special ability that serves her to this day: she steps into the shoes of her viewer whenever she creates a painting. "I meld what I know to what my viewers like," she explains. "For each new subject, I analyze what will be most appealing to a viewer...what will be the most emotionally effective way of touching him or her."

In her search for flexible work as a young wife, Patricia Brooks took the pseudonym "Patrick" and designed greeting cards for the Gordon Fraser greeting card company in the mid-1960s. She experimented with all manner of art media and means of expression during her prolific greeting card

career. Ms. Brooks' work style is quite active and lively and she prefers to work with art media that allow for speed: watercolors, poster colors, gouache, and even air brush.

Although Ms. Brooks is renowned throughout the world for her illustrations done under the name of "Patrick," she had never before accepted a commission for the creation of limited edition porcelain plates. In cooperation with The Hamilton Collection, she presented a series of eight original works of art portraying children and animals together: the *Growing Up Together* Plate Collection.

PATRICIA RYAN BROOKS

Patricia Ryan Brooks has achieved a stature among collectors and her fellow artists that would be the envy of many. She has been a member of the National Institute of American Doll Artists (NIADA) — one of the most prestigious professional organizations of artists in the United States — since 1981 and has held several offices.

Although Brooks comes from a family of artists and dollmakers, she is largely self-taught, creating her first dolls (which became prize winners) without previous dollmaking training. Brooks is renowned for her commitment to authenticity in her dolls, and designs every detail — from wigs to jewelry to shoe styles — entirely herself. No doubt it's this commitment to excellence that has earned Brooks a top prize in every doll competition she has ever entered, including several Best of Show awards.

Known for her wooden dolls, she recently unveiled her first design in porcelain. Entitled "Shall We Dance?," it is a set of two dolls portraying Deborah Kerr and Yul Brynner in perhaps their most

famous roles: Anna and the King of Siam from the movie *The King and I*. Her second porcelain doll is also a celebrity portrait called "Eliza Doolittle at Ascot." It recaptures the wonderful costume which Audrey Hepburn wore as Eliza at the Ascot races in the 1964 Academy Award-winning film *My Fair Lady*.

Produced by W.S. George, Brooks' porcelain dolls are available from the Ashton-Drake Galleries.

SAM BUTCHER

Inspirational artist Sam Butcher was struggling to feed his young family as a "chalk minister" using illustrations to teach young children about God. Because the pay was small, Sam supplemented his income by working as a janitor.

It was the mid-1970s when Sam's friend Bill Biel encouraged Sam to share his artistic ministry with the world: the little teardrop-eyed, innocent children with the soulful expressions that Bill named "Precious Moments." The little messengers would appear on a small line of greeting cards.

Sam worked non-stop for thirty days to create the first line that was to be shown in a tiny booth at the International Christian Booksellers Association Annual Convention in Anaheim, California. The new line was an instant hit at the CBA show, as competing exhibitors left their booths to come over and help write orders for the overwhelmed newcomers. It was the beginning of artistic and financial success for Sam.

He was born in Jackson, Michigan, on New Year's Day 1939, the third child of an English-Irish mechanic and his young Lebanese-Syrian wife. Like many artists, Sam was lonely as a young child and would spend long hours alone, making up stories and drawing pictures to illustrate them.

Encouraged by his teachers who recognized his unique talent, Sam recalls that he began to reach out to people with his art, as he discovered that drawing for them made people happy. When he was a high school senior in 1957, he was awarded a scholarship to the College of Arts and Crafts in Berkeley, California. That same year, he met young Katie Cushman, who shared his interest in art. Two years later, they were married.

When their first son, Jon, was born in 1962, Sam left school and set aside art to work full time to support his family. Philip was born in 1963, and Sam and his family began attending a small church near their home.

He says that his study of the Bible and his love of God brought about many changes in his life. He accepted a job as an artist at the international Child Evangelism Fellowship in Grand Rapids, Michigan. Over the next ten years, Sam's reputation as a fine artist grew, as did his family.

By 1974, there were seven children, and he says they have been a constant inspiration for his Precious Moments art. In the beginning, his drawings were for family and friends, and he called them "messengers of love, caring and sharing" as they reached out to touch people with the simple inspirational messages Sam wrote.

It was in 1978 that Sam's cards and posters found their way into the hands of Enesco President Eugene Freedman, who recognized the potential for fine porcelain figurines. Although Sam feared commercializing the inspirational aspect of his art, he ultimately agreed to allow Enesco to translate the drawings into figurines.

Within a short time, the new *Precious Moments Collection* was hailed as a "phenomenon in the giftware industry." Sam became one of the most sought after artists for personal appearances, as the collection became the number one collectible in the United States.

He has earned many awards through the years, and in 1988, he was presented with a Special Recognition Award by the National Association of Limited Edition Dealers (NALED) during the International Plate and Collectibles Exposition in South Bend, Indiana. His appearances draw thousands of collectors, some traveling hundreds of miles to meet him and have him sign a figurine.

His devotion to his faith and to his art has led to construction of a Precious Moments Chapel near his home in Carthage, Missouri. The chapel was under construction for several years and opened in the summer of 1989.

Inspired by the Sistine Chapel, Sam has painted the ceiling in a special Precious Moments scene, and giant Precious Moments murals and stained glass windows adorn the chapel. Sam calls the chapel his life's work and says he never expects it to be "completely finished."

He divides his time between Carthage and the Philippines, which he regards as his second home. Butcher's affection for children has led him to set up scholarship funds for deserving students both in the United States and the Philippines.

JOYCE F. BYERS

Born and raised in a small, quiet community in southern Lancaster County, Pennsylvania, Joyce Fritz Byers developed an early sense of creative design. She has fond early memories of creating wonderful costumes for her dolls with her grandmother's treadle sewing machine. By the age of twelve, her artistic curiosity had expanded to include sculpture and oil painting.

Joyce's practical Pennsylvania Dutch heritage steered her to Drexel University for a degree in Home Economics. Her creative nature drew her towards fashion design, and upon graduation she took a position designing children's clothing.

While attending Drexel, Joyce met Bob Byers. They married, and by the late 1960s, found themselves and their two small sons settled into a home in Bucks County, Pennsylvania.

Joyce was never without an artistic project. While the children were very young, she began making caroling Christmas figures; first for herself and then as gifts for her family and friends. As the children grew, so did the hobby. For about ten years, Joyce perfected the methods of construction and refined her sculpture skills.

In the late 1970s, the demand for the *Carolers®* figurines became so great that with Bob's assistance, they turned a Christmas hobby into a business.

Joyce has remained responsible for the creation of each character. She sculpts each original face in clay and designs the costumes for each of the hundreds of different figures they produce each year. She has taught the skills necessary for quantity production to artisans, so that each Byers' Choice figurine is completely hand made. It is this intensive hand work which imparts into each figurine the delightful personality sought by more than 15,000 collectors.

The incredible success of the Byers' Choice figurines has enabled Bob and Joyce to share the joy of giving in the true spirit of Christmas. Each year, they give more than twenty-five percent of their company's profits to charities.

KITTY D. CANTRELL

Award winning artist Kitty D. Cantrell conceives on canvas the visions she sculpturally incarnates for LEGENDS. In a style reminiscent of Remington and James, her work is a narrative of an artistic philosophy linked to the physical composite of the medium in which she creates.

Kitty Cantrell is a realist. Her sculpture is intricately detailed yet impressionistic, the dichotomy of which is realized in the intensity of her work.

Alienated from academia by professors who counselled, "Animals are not art," Ms. Cantrell reinvested her tuition in supplies. The year was 1972. Since, the California native has pursued her passion for wildlife through the accomplishment of her art.

Ms. Cantrell's freelance career has culminated in a technical proficiency in chasing, mold making, casting and patinas. She has achieved an artistic maturity, as a painter, mastering perception, line, depth and color; as a sculptor, volume, balance, tension and form.

Eloquently addressing the endangerment of our wildlife, Kitty Cantrell's discovery and definition of individual personality through the width of a brow and the slant of an eye has distinguished her with such prestigious awards as the Juror's Choice, 1986 San Diego Wildlife Show; 1987 World Wilderness Congress Art Exhibit, Denver; First Place Award, 1987 San Diego Wildlife Show; 1988 Audubon Exhibiton of Alaska Wildlife, Anchorage, and the 1988 Endangered Species Exhibition, Los Angeles.

A conservationist, she is active in World Wildlife Fund, National Wildlife Federation, National Audubon Society, American Endangered Species Foundation, Grounded Eagle Foundation, Nature Conservancy and San Diego Zoologist Society. She strives to "draw attention to people's perception of what wildlife is for . Animals should not have to justify their existence. They should be allowed to be simply because they are."

The artist resides in Southern California with her husband, sculptor Eric Fredsti.

JOSEPH CATALANO

From the age of two, Joseph Catalano was destined to paint. His earliest training came from his grandfather Ralph Miele, a realist painter who displayed his work in Greenwich Village in the '40s and '50s. Catalano's talents blossomed under the guidance of his grandfather. Today he is regarded as one of the premiere sports artists.

Catalano's professional career started at age sixteen, when a portrait of John Wayne he had displayed at a school art fair, led to a commission to paint a First Day Cover Stamp for a New York company. That successful project led to other covers for the governments of China, Germany, Ireland, Italy, Japan and the United States. Catalano ended up designing more than 500 portraits for the company, producing about 120 works a year.

Although Catalano had been painting sports art for various companies since 1980, a portrait of pitcher Dwight Gooden brought the artist to the attention of Sports Impressions, a leading producer of figurines, plates and other memorabilia.

Catalano's first assignment for Sports Impressions was an illustration for a collector plate titled "Yankee Tradition" featuring New York Yankees' greats Mickey Mantle and Don Mattingly. The Gold Plate Edition became the fastest sellout in Sports Impressions' history. He followed this success with more captivating plate designs of Jose Canseco, Ted Williams, Nolan Ryan and Will Clark.

Since 1987, Catalano has designed more than 110 items for Sports Impressions including plates, mini-plates, ceramic cards, steins and lithographs. He recently created a series of plates for an NFL collection, with football stars such as Joe Montana, Lawrence Taylor, Randall Cunningham and Dan Marino. Other projects feature basketball superstars and boxing legends Joe Louis and Rocky Marciano.

"I can never pick a favorite painting because they have all been like children to me," Catalano says. "From conception you're with them, so they all become part of you."

Catalano is a perfectionist. Each work of art requires a meticulous eight-stage process. He starts with ten to fifteen thumbnail sketches to decide the painting's basic composition. He researches his subject through photographs and film to help define the features, lighting and color. Once both artist and Sports Impressions are satisfied with the color sketch, Catalano spends days creating a detailed drawing and painting his composition on canvas.

Catalano has won numerous awards, including the 1990 Awards of Excellence from *Collector Editions* magazine for his plate of Mickey Mantle titled "The Greatest Switch Hitter."

Catalano, who lives in Rocky Point, New York, studied at The Art Students League of New York and the Parsons School of Art and Design.

PAT CHANDOK AND DAVE WOODWARD

Every Krystonian character starts in the imagination of Pat Chandok and David Lee Woodard, of Precious Art/Panton. When a character is being designed, great caution must be taken to assure that it fits in the Krystonian kingdom. For fifteen years, Pat and Dave have used their sales and marketing experience in the gift industry. Their one goal is to continue the huge success of their whimsical characters. Developing stories is one of their most challenging tasks, but already the outline for the third Krystonia book is underway.

Pat and Dave lead a team of very talented individuals. English writer Mark Scott adds background and develops the story lines into written book form. After conception, the characters must be drawn and sculpted. Illustrator Bob Sparks draws the pictures for Krystonia. To bring the figurines to life, accomplished sculptor Robert Worthington spends a long period of time to make sure every detail is portrayed. Whether it is a classic Moment or a miniature Krystonian, each figurine exemplifies his fine craftsmanship. Master painter Phil Bryan uses combination after combination to give the piece its final personality. After all the initial stages, the piece again returns to Pat and Dave's hands to make sure their newest creation correctly reflects the Krystonian character they had in mind.

"We created a whole new category by doing whimsical fantasy and we're very protective of our special characters. Even our *Phargol Horn* newletter from the collector's club is written in a whimsical way that our collectors enjoy. I think we're like our collectors — it gives us escape from the everyday routine."

MALCOLM COOPER

For centuries, the British Pub has been far more than a mere watering hole. It is the center of British social and cultural activity, where great battles are re-fought, politics are endlessly debated, and football (soccer) matches are replayed.

The historical riches to be found in British Pubs are infinite. Everything from the headquarters of notorious highwaymen to the not-so-secret meeting place of Kings and their mistresses can all be found within these walls.

The rich lore inherent in British Pubs fascinated Malcolm Cooper, a young British sculptor who received national acclaim as a leading gold and silversmith in London's Hatton Gardens where he worked on gifts ordered by Queen Elizabeth for members of royal families.

Born in 1958, Malcolm Cooper spent his boyhood in Devon and Dorset and, from the outset, showed unmistakable talent in arts and crafts. On leaving school, he studied silversmithing in Medway College of Design in Kent. During his four years there, he won three major awards from the Worshipful Company of Goldsmiths all for outstanding design and for accomplished craftsmanship. An exquisite silver tea set, exhibited countrywide, won him a First Prize, as did his engraving of the Tower of London, undertaken to commemorate its 900th anniversary.

It was while he was still working in Hatton Garden that Malcolm met John Hine and rapidly concluded that they shared an artistic appreciation of Britain's past. After several joint projects, work began on a series of models of famous London buildings, including "The George in the Strand."

Each day on his way to work at Hatton Gardens, Malcolm had passed by the George in the Strand. This London pub (now called "Mr. Toby's Carving Room"), is said to be haunted by a 17th century Cavalier who stands in the corner staring into space. Malcolm was fascinated with the lore and decided to sculpt the pub. He was so satisfied with the results that he opted to do two more. The interest generated by these pieces compelled him to pursue the series and complete the collection now known as *The Great British Pubs.*

PAM COOPER

From early childhood, animals played an important part in Pam Cooper's life. Born in rural Lancashire, England, she spent most of her early life in Cheshire. Almost as soon as she could hold a brush, young Pam painted likenesses of the animals around her, and also modeled them in clay.

Her natural art skill led her to the Royal College of Art in Manchester. After graduation, Pam Cooper set out for London, where she earned a position as illustrator of children's magazines and also studied under noted cartoonist, Hugh McNeill. Later she began to specialize in her first love, animals and wildlife, illustrating and painting for a wide variety of publications. She also created cards and lithographic prints.

Miss Cooper's work has been exhibited at the Assembly Room, Norwich, and also at the Fermoy Gallery, Kings Lynn, Norfolk. She now lives in a cottage in the beautiful Conway Valley, North Wales, with her family and various animals. There she continues to paint her favorite subjects — animals, flowers and the countryside.

In recent years, she has created several plate collections for Royal Worcester in association with The Hamilton Collection: *Kitten Classics*, *Kitten Encounters*, *A Child's Blessing*, and *Mixed Company*.

EUGENE DAUB

After an early career in advertising and graphic design, Eugene Daub — husband and father of four — made a daring mid-life switch to full-time sculptor. He resigned his position in an advertising agency and attended the Pennsylvania Academy of Fine Art and Princeton's Johnson Atelier Technical Institute of Sculpture. Then, little by little, he began to develop a clientele of his own.

Over the past decade, Daub earned a number of major awards and coveted commissions for his sculptures in porcelain, pewter and crystal. The famed Artists' Guild has honored him with three separate awards, and he is also the recipient of recognition from the National Academy of Design, FAO International Sculpture Competition, American Numismatic Society, and others.

Daub sculpted "Something Like a Star," a magnificent bronze sculpture, created under the commission of the Philadelphia Center for Older People, developed for the Klein Foundation; and more than 200 figurative sculptures and bas-relief portraits for Franklin Mint, Lance and The Hamilton Collection.

A ballet aficionado of long standing, Daub turned his attention to ballet sculpture for the first time. Living just six blocks from the Pennsylvania Ballet in Philadelphia, he was able to attend numerous performances — and to have top ballerinas pose for the various subjects in his *The Splendor of the Ballet* Figurine Collection. Created under the commission of The Hamilton Collection, this series includes eight masterworks inspired by some of the most beloved ballet heroines of all time.

LOWELL DAVIS

Painter and sculptor Lowell Davis appreciates the nostalgic search by Americans for the "good ol' days." Born on a farm near Red Oak, Missouri, he was only a boy when his father lost the family farm during the drought of the 1930s. The Davis family moved into quarters behind his uncle's general store and Lowell began drawing animals under the guidance of his grandfather, an amateur artist. Later, the old-timers, who sat around the family store, taught him the art of whittling.

When Davis began his career as an artist, he left this peaceful setting in Southwest Missouri and headed for the Dallas area, where he became the art director for a major ad agency. Pursuing his career in Dallas, Davis longed for the simpler life of his childhood. He returned to the Ozark Mountains of Missouri. where he found a farmhouse that retained the style of the 1930s and began to paint and sculpt what he knew best, capturing on canvas — in porcelain and bronze — the America of the 1930s, the fast fading days of the family farm, the values of the simple life and the good humor of a gentler time. Schmid recognized Davis' talent and began to produce his complete line of figurines, limited edition plates and other collectibles.

Over the years, Davis has scoured the countryside for buildings and farm implements to make his Fox Fire Farm a truly authentic 1930s working farm and to recreate the town of his youth.

When Davis came home from Texas, he found his beloved Red Oak to be a ghost town. He began buying up the homes and businesses of Red Oak, moving them twenty-three miles to his farm near Carthage, Missouri, and restoring them to their original grandeur, which he now calls Red Oak II. The general store, schoolhouse, feedstore, church and even a gas station from days gone by, join the blacksmith shop, the bed and breakfast and the Belle Starr home and Museum in their new locale next to the farm.

Collectors from all over the world have come to visit Davis' farm. They see the animals, implements and buildings and return home with the knowledge that their collectibles, so carefully crafted by Lowell Davis, are truly an authentic slice of Americana.

RAY DAY

Ray Day is an artist involved in a broad spectrum of creative interest — sculptor, watercolorist, educator, businessman, and preservationist, to name a few.

Ray began his professional career in 1962 as an Art teacher at his high school Alma Mater, and whose credits include a B.A. in Art and Business as well as a Masters of Fine Arts in Painting, Sculpture, and Theater. As founder and chairman of the school's Fine Arts Department, he has developed a renowned theater program. He still continues these efforts today, teaching studio art and theater at the school.

Ray began his painting career in earnest in 1973 with the introduction of his *Old Road* series, the first of thirty-five limited edition prints that have been enthusiastically received by collectors across the country. In 1986, he entered the porcelain plate market with the *Once Upon A Barn* series of collector plates featuring barnside advertisements. Day's national success soared during 1988 when he captured "Best of Show" honors at both the Pasadena and South Bend Plate and Collectible Shows. Early in 1989, he was invited by Lilliput Lane Limited to create the *American Landmarks Collection* of American churches, barns and various buildings.

Ray Day is actively involved in preserving the subjects he paints and sculpts. He is a frequent guest speaker at many civic functions, seminars, and exhibits around the country encouraging support of preservation societies.

Featuring rural landmarks and barnside advertising, Day's art continues to visually preserve the memorable sites of our rural past. Through his paintings and sculptures, the artist captures the charm, uniqueness, and nostalgia of our most treasured memories.

NORMAN N. AND HERMAN DEATON

Norman N. (Neal) Deaton and his brother Herman are two of the most talented sculptors of animals living in the world today. Even as youngsters, they were fascinated by the opportunity to observe, study — and model in clay — the small wild creatures of their native Iowa.

The Deatons are especially noted for their famous hand-painted animal sculptures for The National Wildlife Federation. Their works are exhibited at such prominent museums as The Smithsonian Institution in Washington, D.C., and The National Museum of Canada in Ottawa, and Deaton works are also held in many important private collections — including those of such notables as United States Senators Morris Udall and Frank Church.

In all of their works, the Deatons combine an eye for natural beauty with a passion for authenticity — qualities that distinguish the two groups of hand-painted, cold-cast bronze figurines they have created for The Hamilton Collection — *The Audubon Bronzes* and *An American Wildlife Bronze Collection.*

In 1983, Herman Deaton introduced an eight-piece sculpture collection through Hamilton, entitled *Great Animals of the American Wilderness.* A few years later, he premiered a second eight-issue collection, the *Majestic Wildlife of North America* figurines.

TED DEGRAZIA

Ettore "Ted" DeGrazia. Born June 14, 1909. Died September 17, 1982. In the span of those seventy-three years, he became not only a beloved artist of the southwest, but a legend among the people with whom he lived.

He was a man of the southwest who captured the essence of his beloved region in thirty-three successful books which he both authored and illustrated. His art was showcased in the magazine *Arizona Highways*, where it was seen in 1958 by the Hallmark greeting card company which signed him to a contract. Two short years later, his painting "Los Ninos" was selected by UNICEF to grace the cover of its annual fundraising Christmas card, over 100 million of which have been sold.

It was in DeGrazia's later years that collectors of plates were afforded the opportunity to bring some of his vision into their homes. In 1976 he approved the first limited edition plate bearing the motif of his now familiar "Los Ninos." The plate sold out immediately and DeGrazia, at sixty-seven, was "an overnight success."

Early in 1983, Goebel was approached to develop a figurine series based on his works. Now they are before the public — an exciting, innovative line which Goebel is proud to bring to collectors. It represents a harmonious liaison between the more than a century-old tradition of fine German craftsmanship and the distinctly American cut of one of our outstanding individualists.

In 1985 Goebel Miniatures introduced a new dimension to his artwork with the *DeGrazia* miniature figurines. Each stands less than an inch-and-a-half tall, yet every piece accurately captures the very essence of DeGrazia's artwork.

Ted DeGrazia. With each new interpretation of his artwork, his genius is further revealed. He has become a symbol for the land he loved so well and to which he paid such high tribute.

CHIP DEMATTEO

Chip deMatteo began his apprenticeship when he was still a boy. He grew up in a restored home in Colonial Williamsburg and each morning watched his father, William deMatteo, set off for his silversmith's shop on the grounds of Williamsburg.

As a child, Chip enjoyed spending time in his father's shop and by the time he was ten, he was actually doing small

jobs for his father. Eventually, Chip went to college where he studied art. After completing his education, Chip spent a few years as a "starving artist" in Washington D.C., all the while supplementing his income with silver work for his father.

In the late 1970s, Chip, his father and a partner Philip Thorp formed Hand & Hammer Silversmiths in Alexandria, Virginia. Since 1981, Chip has been the sole designer for Hand & Hammer where he has created more than 300 ornament designs.

Using the "lost-wax" technique, Chip has designed a number of highly sought-after series. Especially popular are the *Bell, Santa,* and *Carousel* series, in addition to the *Beatrix Potter, Night Before Christmas* and *Victorian Village* collections.

JIM DENEEN

Jim Deneen is widely recognized as the foremost North American painter of various modes of transportation. His paintings are characterized by careful detailing and complete authenticity. In addition to his technical expertise, Deneen displays a special talent for capturing the romantic and nostalgic aspects of his subjects.

Deneen's technique is unique because of the dramatic sweep of his paintings and his unerring perspective. He has a special gift for capturing spatial relationships which give his work a remarkable three-dimensional quality. Vast numbers of Americans enjoy Deneen's collectible prints. It is estimated that there currently are ten million of his graphics in circulation.

The Great Trains, the artist's first limited edition collector plate series created under the commission of Artaffects, was a huge success. Since then the collaboration of Deneen and Artaffects has resulted in the equally successful series of *Classic American Trains* and *Classic American Cars*. Jim Deneen currently is at work on a new series for Artaffects.

CONNIE WALSER DEREK

From her early childhood, Connie Walser Derek found her personal expression in the world of art, school art classes, home sewing projects and summer technical drawing jobs. She developed a natural gift for design, painting and creating in three dimensions. It wasn't until many years later that Ms. Derek discovered how to put her love of sculpture and costumes together as the creator of delightful and collectible porcelain dolls. Today, she is the owner of a thriving business that employs her children, mother and sister.

The inspiration for many of her current dolls comes from contemporary baby pictures, including those of her own children. But Ms. Derek also is a fan of Maud Humphrey Bogart and other turn-of-the-century artists.

In 1990, The Hamilton Collection introduced Derek's charming "Jessica" doll. "Jessica" was based on a photo of the artist's daughter, and the doll's pinafore was inspired by a lovely turn-of-the-century dress she found in an old Victorian book. Not surprisingly, collector response for "Jessica" was extraordinary. In 1991, Ms. Derek introduced another new creation with The Hamilton Collection — "Sara." Once again, the response was overwhelming. The artist's dolls are all exceptional because they each "do something." For example, instead of simply looking pretty, "Jessica" can clasp and unclasp her hands, move her head and even sit up or lie down.

MAX DUNCAN

In recent years, collectors throughout the United States met the driving force behind the "stories that never end..." — Max Duncan, founder and president of Duncan Royale. Before Christmas 1990, Max traveled in twenty-three states and made appearances at sixty-seven Duncan Royale dealer galleries. His itinerary included television interviews, radio spots, signature sessions, seminars and visits with many collectors. Max enjoys these personal meetings with collectors and has planned several promotional tours.

Born in Indiana, Max moved to California as a toddler and only lightly claims the "Hoosier" status. A Navy veteran from World War II, Max graduated from Woodbury College in Los Angeles in 1952, with a Bachelor of Arts degree in advertising and public relations. After five years with the Sunbeam Corporation, he began his successful career in the visual arts, advertising and giftware industry.

Known for his innovation and creativity, as well as for enthusiasm and a warm personality, Max masterminded and developed the concept of Duncan Royale collections with an eye toward serious collectors everywhere. His subjects are familiar to most of us and often reveal how little we know about something we know well — but do we? The character and charisma embodied in each Duncan Royale personality — whether Santa Claus, clowns, entertainers, fairies, people of the Scriptures, early Americans or others — challenge us to discover deeper meanings to things we often take for granted.

What is next? Rest assured that Max Duncan has some lofty new ideas. You will be hearing from your favorite storyteller, because the stories "never end!"

DIANNA EFFNER

Dianna Effner brings an unusual sensitivity and depth of emotion to the doll-making world. By selecting children's characters as the subject of dolls, Ms. Effner has found the freedom to explore the world of fanstasy and inner feelings.

As a child, Ms. Effner made dolls from old socks and papier-mache. Later, she studied sculpture at Bradley University where she earned her degree in fine art. Ms. Effner then began making her dolls in porcelain because it allowed her more control over the process of creating lifelike features.

Today, Dianna Effner's dolls are part of private collections across the U.S. Her first doll for Knowles China, "Little Red Riding Hood" from the *Heroines of the Fairy Tale Forests*, was nominated for an Award of Excellence by *Dolls* magazine in 1989 and a Doll Achievement Award from The National Association of Limited Edition Dealers in 1990. Her latest series is *Dianna Effner's Mother Goose*. Both of these collections of limited edition dolls are available from Ashton-Drake.

BRUCE EMMETT

Artist Bruce Emmett, who first gained plate-world fame with his *Elvis Presley: Looking at a Legend* series, created the *Elvis Presley: In Performance* collection marketed by The Bradford Exchange. He spent hours studying Elvis movies and documentary tapes, thousands of photographs — many of them extremely rare — and listened over and over again to the classic recordings of the music that made Elvis Presley a legend.

Emmett has always been interested in both art and Elvis Presley, buying his first Elvis recording in 1956 when he was seven, and drawing pictures and sketches from his earliest childhood. He received his fine-art training from Syracuse University, and graduated in 1973 with a Bachelor of Fine Arts degree.

As a professional illustrator and portraitist, Emmett has created art for many distinguished clients, including *Reader's Digest*, ABC, NBC, CBS, Ralph Lauren, publishers Harper and Row, Macmillan,

Dell, Avon, Berkley, Warner, Zebra, and Scholastic Books. He has also created posters for such Broadway hits as "Sugar Babies," and "The Gin Game." His work has been exhibited in several prestigious Society of Illustrators Annual Shows. Emmett lives and works in New York.

ALDO FAZIO

The work of Aldo Fazio has earned this Larchmont, New York artist international fame. As the winner of the coveted Hall of Fame Award for Equestrian Sculpture, Fazio established his status as a sculptor of animals. His designs have won him prestigious commissions from Abercrombie & Fitch, FAO Schwarz and the Audubon Society, among others.

Fazio began his career with private study under noted sculptors James Earl Fraser and Bethold Nevel, and muralist Barry Faulkner. Under their tutelage, he became fascinated with the animal world and began to create his award-winning masterworks. Four of his horse paintings appear today in the Museum of Sports, New Haven, Connecticut.

Now Aldo Fazio has added a new dimension to his artistry with the creation of two limited edition collector plate series: *The Sophisticated Ladies Plate Collection*, introduced by Reco International in 1985. In addition, Fazio and Reco have created a grouping of figurines and musicals to match his *Sophisticated Ladies* plates.

JUAN FERRANDIZ

Juan Ferrandiz believes deeply in the creative energies of children, their ability to accept new ideas, to speak freely and to be continually thrilled by life.

Ferrandiz' art reflects these qualities

with gleeful images of cherub-faced children harmoniously joined by small creatures of the earth. Yet, his paintings go beyond capturing the fleeting moments of childhood. They transcend the physical constraints of youth, revealing the innocence and honesty that lives in each child's soul.

A native of Barcelona, Spain, Ferrandiz studied fine arts at the School of Arts in Barcelona, working on Sundays to earn extra money. In his spare time, he drew comic strips, exchanging them for pencils, pencil boxes, and other drawing supplies.

In addition to his artistic background, Ferrandiz is also a prolific writer and poet. He has delighted young audiences with a series of cleverly illustrated children's books, and his poetry can be found in several books published in his native language, as well as in a popular collection of Christmas greeting cards.

Regardless of the medium, Ferrandiz' message is ever-present. The artist wishes to share his dream for a sensitive and tender world — one filled with fondness, peace and harmony.

HELMUT FISCHER

A mind soaring with imagination and a careful attention to detail are two qualities that Helmut Fischer blends together in every piece of sculpture. Since entering the W. Goebel Porzellanfabrik apprentice program over twenty years ago, Fischer has demonstrated that skilled creativity in the more than 700 varied models he has created for Goebel.

As a schoolboy, he showed a marked creative aptitude. His father, who was a craftsman in Bavaria, recognized his son's talent while Helmut was still quite young and encouraged his development.

In 1964, at the age of fourteen, Fischer followed his father's suggestion and enrolled in the Goebel apprentice program. Since that time he has created models for a fascinating variety of Goebel series, including the DeGrazia figurines, which are a striking example of his artistic expertise and creative versatility. Fischer captures the essence of the American Southwest with an amazing feeling. Using Ted DeGrazia's colorful and vibrant paintings, Fischer creates in each figurine with the same love DeGrazia put on canvas. For the past few years, Fischer's career has focused on the sculpting of M.I. Hummel figurines. As Master Sculptor, he has created many new figurines including the 1991 *Century Collection* piece "We Wish You The Best" (Hum 600). All this makes Helmut Fischer a leading artist at Goebel.

In honor of Mickey Mouse's 60th birthday, Fischer recently created a very special commemorative piece for Goebel Collector's Club members (since June 1989, the M.I. Hummel Club).

Through Goebel figurines, Fischer shares with the world his special talent for capturing a moment in time and immortalizing it for all eternity.

TERRENCE FOGARTY

When Mickey Mantle received a painting by Terrence Fogarty, the Baseball Hall of Famer was said to have shed a tear. Mantle liked the painting so much that he placed it over his favorite table at his New York restaurant.

With love for art and sports, Fogarty naturally combined his interests to capture athletes and sports events with a lifelike attention to detail and remarkable color perception.

Fogarty, who describes himself as a realist painter strongly influenced by the human condition of athletics, has become one of the country's leading sports artists.

For the past five years, Fogarty's artwork has appeared on plates for Sports Impressions, a leading producer of sports figurines and other collectibles. His plate designs include such baseball greats as Nolan Ryan, Rickey Henderson, Ryne Sandberg, Roger Clemens, Mark McGuire and Paul Molitor.

A partial list of Fogarty's clients include Kent Hrbek of the Minnesota Twins, Dave Winfield of the California Angels, several Seattle Seahawks players, CBS/Columbia Records and numerous universities. Chrysler Motors Corp. commissioned Fogarty for a painting portraying the 1988 America's Cup Yacht Race.

A skilled portraitist, Fogarty also paints more than sports-related subjects. "The Wrangler," a painting depicting a ranch hand, won the National Sweepstakes Award at the prestigious Wind River National Juried Show in Wyoming.

His paintings have been exhibited in galleries from Toronto to San Francisco and are in the collections at the Canadian Baseball Hall of Fame, United States Baseball Hall of Fame and the United States Hockey Hall of Fame.

CHARLES FRACÉ

Surprisingly, the illustrious career of Charles Fracé began by chance. In 1962, photographer Shelley Grossman invited Fracé to work as an assistant on a Florida wildlife assignment. Working alongside Grossman and respected naturalist John Hamlet, Fracé developed a reverence for the wonders of nature. In

fact, Fracé recollects that it was the beauty of the outdoor world which had first inspired him to draw, as a child on eastern Pennsylvania's Bear Mountain.

Upon his return from Florida, Fracé worked ten-hour days in his studio, and he traveled into the wild to live alongside his subjects. Soon, he was earning recognition as a respected illustrator of wildlife.

Fracé's work has been featured in over 300 one-man shows throughout the United States and Canada. He has been honored by a number of prestigious museums, including the Denver Museum of Natural History and the Leigh Yawkey Woodson Art Museum. Additionally, the artist has spent several weeks each year appearing at exhibits and visiting with collectors.

While art collectors and critics have praised Fracé for his mastery of design and technique, it is his attention to detail which has earned him the respect of naturalists. Jack Hanna, director of Ohio's Columbus Zoo, has said of Fracé's work, "He knows his subjects so well. Every feather, every curvature, every habitat is so correct." Indeed, Fracé labors to help people better understand their world and the complicated interrelationships among all of its inhabitants.

To commemorate twenty-five years as a wildlife artist, Fracé established the Fracé Fund for Wildlife Preservation in 1987. This organization has made funds available to the Atlanta Zoo, the Carnivore Preservation Trust and other organizations dedicated to preserving the balance of nature. The non-profit fund is subsidized through the sale of Fracé's highly valued Artist's Proofs.

Fracé's artwork can also be seen in the limited edition plate market. Fracé's first limited edition plate series, *Small Wonders of the Wild* was issued in 1989 and 1990 by The Hamilton Collection. Fracé recently introduced four series for W.S. George — *Nature's Lovables, Soaring Majesty, The World's Most Magnificent Cats* and *Nature's Playmates.*

Throughout most of the year, Fracé is found hard at work in his studio. There, he is close to his wife and sons — and close to nature. Fracé remains committed to his belief in the power of art, stating, "My goal is to strive to be even better, to push each painting a step further."

TOM FREEMAN

When he was a teenager in Pontiac, Michigan, Tom Freeman gained national attention for a painting he contributed to an exhibition held for the International Red Cross.

But several years would pass before Tom Freeman began to "chart his course" as a marine artist. During a sailing trip aboard a schooner in the North Atlantic, the young man first answered the "call of the sea" — in its beauty and mystery he discovered the theme that would shape his career as an artist.

Tom Freeman now enjoys the respect of his peers, as well as great popularity. His limited edition prints are widely sought by collectors, as are his original paintings, which command prices as high as $15,000.

A member of the exclusive American Society of Marine Artists, Freeman has been honored with exhibitions at prominent galleries throughout the country, including the Smithsonian Institution, the Mystic Seaport Gallery, and Grand Central Galleries. His works may be found in numerous private collections, and four of his original paintings have

been on display at the Executive Mansion of the White House.

Freeman turned his talents to the collector plate medium for the first time, with his dramatic portrayals of this nation's most historic sailing vessels — The Hamilton Collection's eight-plate series, *America's Greatest Sailing Ships*.

W.D. GAITHER

W.D. "Bill" Gaither is a multi-faceted artist with hundreds of thousands of paintings and prints on display in galleries and private collections all over America. In addition to his work in the limited edition art realm, Gaither is actively involved in dozens of environmental and wildlife conservation organizations, reflecting his consuming interest in animals and birds.

As a sculptor and painter, Gaither's special gift stems from his immersion in the world of wildlife. His workshops hold books on a myriad of subjects, mounted specimens, dozens of sketches, and partially completed sculptures.

The artist prides himself on creating works which are always active, fluid and alive — never static or frozen. His wildlife studies reflect a living moment in time in the animal's life in the wild — feeding, running, attacking, playing, leaping, soaring or charging.

Gaither's first sculpture in association with the Maruri Studio premiered in 1982. In just two years' time, his "American Bald Eagle II" rose in value from $165 to $600. Since then, wildlife art connoisseurs eagerly await each Maruri-Gaither introduction — many of which sell out immediately and begin rising in value.

WOLFGANG GAWANTKA

Artist and sculptor Wolfgang Gawantka was born in Dresden in 1930. At the age of sixteen, he began six years of intensive study at the Meissen School of Art, where his teachers included A. Struck, Heinrich Thein, Munch-Khe, and E. Oehme.

An additional year of study at the School of Ceramics at Hermsdoft, Thuringia, netted him a diploma, and readied him for an immediate position as professional sculptor at the world-renowned Meissen Porzellan Manufaktur.

Gawantka later immigrated to West Germany where he joined the Kaiser Porcelain design staff as a full-time sculptor.

He currently holds the position of master sculptor at the Kaiser Porcelain Factory in Staffelstein, West Germany.

BRENDA ELIZABETH GERARDI

Brenda Elizabeth Gerardi captures a wonderful, child-like innocence in each of her dolls. The Newport, Rhode Island artist has been designing dolls for Gorham since 1985. The original, lifelike faces she sculpts in clay at her home workshop "express a gentle touch," she says, "with each facial expression inspired by children within my family."

Having attended the Vesper George School of Art and the Boston Museum School of Art in Massachusetts, Gerardi has a background in painting, woodcarving and sculpture. Creating dolls evolved from her early childhood love for dolls and her talents as a sculptor.

In partnership with Gorham, Gerardi has introduced exclusive collections of all porcelain, delicately hand painted, fully jointed dolls. Her most recent limited edition series, the *Victorian Cameo Collection*, is inspired by the elegance and romance of the Victorian period, which has powerful appeal among collectors today.

Sculpted and designed with a sensitivity to this nostalgic period, the lavish and authentic detailing of Gerardi's creations gives each doll a personality all its own. Her choice of fabrics, laces, ribbons and accessories are selected to match the image that begins emerging with the plaster mold she casts to make each porcelain head.

In addition to the *Victorian Cameo Collection*, Gerardi has introduced three exclusive collections for Gorham: *Small Wonders*, *Joyful Years*, and *Bonnets and Bows*.

GRÉ GERARDI

Although not formally trained as an artist, Gré Gerardi, says she has been painting since she was five years old. She paints animals and country and farm scenes in what she calls the old-fashioned style.

Ms. Gerardi claims to have led "an uneventful life," although many would argue that raising five children while developing an original style of art doesn't quite fit their definition of "uneventful."

Still, life has changed dramatically during the past several years for this northern New Jersey artist. For like other gifted artists who have managed to reach a broad audience, she has been "discovered."

After years of having her work admired by a loyal regional following, Ms. Gerardi is today represented by The Balliol Corporation. And, art lovers across the country are discovering the artist's charming cat-subject paintings and sweetly nostalgic images from days gone by.

Her debut in the collector plate medium brought her work to the attention of a new, ever wider audience. Her first-ever plate series, the *Country Kitties* collection was presented by The Hamilton Collection. Her second series, entitled *Little Shopkeepers*, couples her delightful cats with mischievous puppies.

JULIE GOOD-KRÜGER

For Julie Good-Krüger, creating an Amish doll seems perfectly natural. After all, Julie and husband Tim live in a renovated stone grist mill in Strasburg, Pennsylvania, which is in the very heart of Lancaster County's Amish community.

Julie's interest in dolls goes back to childhood when her grandmother gave her some antique dolls. In high school, she enjoyed reading doll magazines and creating small sculptures on plaques. Her interest in dolls waned during her college years, but in the late 1970s, she began experimenting with doll making, hoping to earn extra money for graduate school.

She spent three years learning to make dolls before she allowed anyone to see her work. In 1980, her lifelike child dolls were introduced to the public. Over the past decade, Julie has earned

the admiration of her peers and collectors. Her dolls have won numerous awards, and in 1988 and 1989 Ms. Good-Krüger's dolls were nominated for "Doll of the Year" (DOTY) Awards.

Amish Blessings is Julie Good-Krüger's first doll series for Ashton-Drake Galleries. "In *Amish Blessings*, I've attempted to capture as authentically as possible the love these special people have for their children and the traditions they hold close to their hearts," the artist said.

JAN GOODYEAR

When Jan Goodyear's young daughter was crowned Little Miss Brevard (Florida), Jan's mother made an appropriate dress for the occasion. Wanting to capture the joyous event, Jan attempted to make a porcelain doll to mark the event. Disappointed with the results, Ms. Goodyear began to seriously study dollmaking. Soon she was teaching and lecturing on the subject.

In 1987, she created "Kahlie," her first original porcelain doll, and immediately became well known among doll crafters for the realism and appeal of her sculpture. Today her doll designs are

sought after by both doll professionals and collectors alike.

Ashton-Drake Galleries recently introduced Ms. Goodyear's *My Closest Friend* collection. The artist explained the concept for the series by saying "So many children form an attachment to something that makes them feel safe and secure in the world. As adults, we may never understand quite where the attraction lies...but we do understand how adorable these children seem to us when they seek this security. It's this special kind of appeal that I hope to recreate in this doll collection."

KATE GREENAWAY

Kate Greenaway is one of the best-loved illustrators of children's books. Her images have endured for over a century. K.G., as she was called by family and friends, was born in England in 1846. By the time of her death in 1901, her illustrations were cherished not only in England, but throughout the European continent and America.

Beginning with Christmas card and Valentine illustrations, by 1877 Ms. Greenaway was illustrating books of her own verse. Her first such book, *Under the Window*, made Kate Greenaway a household name. *Kate Greenaway's Birthday Book for Children* in 1880 inspired Robert Louis Stevenson to write about his own recollections of childhood, *A Child's Garden of Verses*.

Greenaway was a quiet, modest woman who devoted most of her time to her work. When not painting or writing verse, her life was rounded out with her family, a few intimate friends, letter-writing, her dog, and her beloved garden.

Greenaway's art is peopled with graceful children in garden, flower-filled meadow, and blossoming orchard settings, for early in life, Greenaway had "struck up a friendship" with flowers. Her style is marked with a lyrical look built on delicate line and color.

But it is the frolicking children in "frocks and frills" that Greenaway collectors love best. As a child, Greenaway and her two sisters were devoted to a large family of dolls. Greenaway delighted in making clothes for her dolls, the beginning of her interest in costuming which played such an important role in her art. Later she fashioned dresses for the models she used. It was not the fashion of her own day that filled her art; instead, Greenaway turned to the fashion look of the late 1700s for its quaint and charming appeal. As her popularity as an illustrator grew, this style she had adopted for her artwork became the latest rage in children's fashions.

Today Bradley Collectibles offers a line of Kate Greenaway dolls, licensed by the Balliol Corporation, complete with all the "frocks and frills." Each doll is true to the spirit of Greenaway with the charm, authentic costuming, and artistry that makes her a favorite of generations past, present, and future.

CONSTANCE GUERRA

Maryland-born Constance Angela Guerra has always had a flair for art. In high school she designed posters and backdrops for student plays. Later, she studied art at the University of Maryland. Ms. Guerra was working as a secretary at the National Health Institute in the early 1980s when her supervisor suggested that she enter some of her craft items in a local show.

Working from her original designs, Ms. Guerra and her three sisters created dough ornaments and figurines for a two-day show, only to sell everything during the first three hours. Additional orders for her "Doughlightfully Yours" line of figurines kept Constance and her family busy for several weeks. A short time later, she began devoting all of her time to creating her figurines.

In the mid-1980s, Ms. Guerra formed her own company, The Constance Collection. By then she had abandoned bread dough art and after experimenting with a number of materials, she selected a material made of powdered pecan shells and resins. Considered a wood product, this medium could achieve the fine detailing essential to her figures.

A prolific artist, Constance Guerra has produced more than 800 figurines and usually introduces about seventy-five new offerings each year. Some of her most popular series are her *State Santas* and her *Golden American Collection*.

BESSIE PEASE GUTMANN

Born in the late 1800s, young Bessie Pease was influenced by the "Brandywine School" of illustration that was prevalent in her native Philadelphia, practiced by such artists as Howard Pyle, Maxfield Parrish, and Jessie Willcox Smith. Early in life she developed her natural art talent at the Philadelphia School of Design for Women.

The young artist continued her studies at the Chase School of Art and the Art Student's League in New York. She was privileged to learn from prominent artists including Robert Henri, William Merritt Chase, Kenyon Cox, Frederick Dielman, Arthur W. Dow and Mobray DeCamp.

Her dual career of art and family began in 1906, when Bessie Pease fell in love with and married Hellmuth Gutmann. Mrs. Gutmann's three children often were subjects for her paintings. She also drew inspiration from her many nieces and nephews, and later grandchildren. Her illustrations in children's books and her prints were quite popular in the early 1900s — not only in the United States, but in Canada, England, Europe, Australia, Japan and South Africa.

This famous artist did not do simple portraits; rather she used her subjects to create expressions, positions and attitudes in her completed works. She would often take a photograph of children for reference, or do a quick sketch in pencil, charcoal or pastel. These sketches show great detail and expression and clearly demonstrate her ability to capture the spirit and life of children.

Mrs. Gutmann's successful career spanned nearly five decades. It was not until the 1950s, when she began to suffer from poor vision, that she ceased painting. She died in Centerport, New York, on September 29, 1960, at the age of 84.

Today, the works of Bessie Pease Gutmann have seen a remarkable resurgence of popularity. The growing number of Gutmann collectors can learn more about their favorite artist from a recently published biography, *Bessie Pease Gutmann: Her Life and Works*. Recent collector plate series from Balliol and the Hamilton Collection include *A Child's Best Friend* in miniature and *Childhood Reflections*. Another Gutmann series, the *Special Moments Collection*, commemorates special events and holidays. The most recent release from this collection is "Blossom Time."

ALLEN HACKNEY

Allen Hackney always keeps in mind Leonardo Da Vinci's advice whenever he paints or teaches art students.

"I'm chiefly known for my egg tempera landscapes and still lifes, but I've tried to follow Da Vinci's admonition that a good artist can paint anything he pleases rather than having only one capability," Hackney says.

For that reason, Hackney paints everything from wildlife and sports to Americana and western subjects.

One of Hackney's most popular works titled "After the Game" features a still life of NBA superstar Larry Bird's uniform, shoes, basketball and net. His other paintings of the Boston Celtics' player also represent the dimensions of Bird's talents and achievements. Bird has called Hackney his favorite artist.

Hackney recently entered a new venture with Sports Impressions, a leading producer of high quality figurines, plates and other memorabilia featuring prominent sports personalities. Hackney designed several paintings of prominent professional basketball players for a series of limited and open edition collector plates.

A realist painter, Hackney mainly works in egg tempera, one of the most difficult mediums. Tempera painting first appeared in Europe in about the 12th or 13th century and was practiced before the invention of oils. The ancient process produces beautiful luminosity and depth.

Hackney often spends three months on one work, giving his brilliant color paintings psychological and spiritual qualities.

"My goal is to paint with truth to nature, pride in craftsmanship, precision of execution, fidelity to detail and perfection of drawing and beauty of color," says Hackney, who lives in Terre Haute, Indiana.

Born in Madison, Indiana, Hackney

is a graduate of Indiana State University where he received bachelor and master's degrees in art.

He taught art at a junior high school in Indiana for twenty-six years and has won thirty-two awards for painting. His works appear in both private and public collections in the United States, Canada, Puerto Rico and England.

Hackney is listed in *Who's Who In American Art* and *Who's Who in the World*. He has twice been awarded prizes by the National Gallery of Art in Washington, D.C. and is a member of the National Society of Casein and Acrylic Painters.

JAN HAGARA

"I can't remember when I didn't draw," recalls Jan Hagara. Although her family was considered poor, they loved beautiful things and learned to create them at home. Jan's father carved wood figures, and her mother did needlepoint and made rugs. Young Jan soon had a sketchbook which she carried everywhere.

Realizing that Jan had talent, her mother traded one of her rugs for a few basic art classes for her. This was Jan's only formal art training. Over the next few decades, she taught herself painting, sculpture, dollmaking and porcelain production. From her mother, Jan acquired a lasting interest in vintage fashions, dolls and other treasures. In addition to a collection of vintage clothes, she also has a vast collection of books on dolls and antique clothing.

It wasn't until her marriage to Bill Hagara in 1974 that Jan emerged as a prominent artist of Victorian-inspired paintings. At first, Hagara's work was only available in the form of limited editon prints. Later, Hagara's first collector

plate, "My Heart's Desire," was created to benefit the American Heart Association. Her works included figurines, porcelain and vinyl dolls, musical jewelry boxes and even calendars and cards.

Recently, Ms. Hagara introduced a collection of plate-paintings in association with The Hamilton Collection, entitled *Dear To My Heart*. Each plate features a Victorian child holding or surrounded by his or her most treasured toys and belongings.

KAREN HAHN

Artist Karen Hahn has greatly contributed to the giftware industry and Enesco product line over the past several years. As Enesco Art Director, Karen continues developing and designing new products which show her fine attention to detail and gentle creative touch.

Inspired by her daughter, Karen created a new collection of detailed coldcast figurines called *Laura's Attic*. The emotional and appealing collection reflects Karen's memorable childhood activities and those of her little daughter, Laura.

White Lace and Promises, her collection which captures traditional wedding customs, was honored as a winner in the Frances Hook Scholarship Fund's licensing program. Her "Rapunzel" jack-in-the-box musical won the Fund's 1987 Licensed Art award, while her "Wee Wedding Wishes" action musical won in the 1991 licensing contest.

Karen's other designs include deluxe action musicals, Christmas ornaments, *Tulip Town*™, *Long Ago and Far Away*™, *A Christmas Carol*, *The Nutcracker* and *The Greatest Gift Is Love*.

Prior to joining Enesco in 1985, Karen worked as a free-lance illustrator. She holds a degree in illustration from Northern Illinois University.

WILLIAM K. HARPER

A respected figurine designer for Royal Doulton, William K. Harper spent more than a decade learning his profession. In a recent interview, Harper noted that while a figurine designer employs the same aesthetic elements as a fine artist, the designer must also create a piece which will please collectors and still be profitable. The inspirations for Harper's figures range from his childhood memories of visiting the circus, to historical personalities who are developed only after careful research.

According to Harper, each image selected must be in keeping with the other Doulton characters in style, coloring, size and price. It is the designer's role to create a figure which will evoke an immediate response from collectors while at the same time telling a story and/or revealing the character of the subject through body movements, clothing and a few appropriate props. The figurine designer also must take special care in considering all of the stages of production and as much as possible, avoid designs which would be too difficult to execute.

Harper's figures range from comic figures like the "Clown" and "Punch and Judy Man," to imaginative figures like "St. George and the Dragon," "The Centurion" and "Votes for Women." He is also the designer of the popular eleven-piece *Gilbert and Sullivan* series. Harper also modelled the Henry VIII Jug which received rave reviews from collectors.

ROBERT HERSEY

Robert (Bob) Hersey was born in London in 1936. A short time later, the family moved to Britain's West Country where Hersey learned to appreciate the beauty of the countryside and its wildlife. Also accustomed to the usual household pets and animals, Hersey soon learned to endow his animal paintings with charming, almost human characteristics.

A "Sunday painter" himself, Hersey's father encouraged his son's interest in art. Hersey was about ten when the family returned to London. The boy felt restricted by city life and sought solace and subjects for his drawings in the city's parks.

At fifteen, Hersey left school to learn his craft, working in an advertising agency. Over the next few years, Hersey studied and perfected his painting technique. It wasn't long before the individuality of Hersey's paintings was sought by galleries and collectors. The artist now lives in Kent where he continues to chronicle the wonders of nature. In addition to being the local naturalist, Hersey also provides a home for injured or homeless wildlife. In return, many of these creatures become subjects in his paintings.

Hersey recently entered the collectibles market with a series of limited edition wallplates entitled *Through a Woodland Window*. This series is being produced by Kaiser-Porcelain of Germany.

LAWRENCE HEYDA

Lawrence Heyda was born in Chicago on February 8, 1944. He grew up in the peaceful suburb of Elmhurst and became an Eagle Scout. His college days were spent at the University of Illinois with a dual major in engineering and English, working during the summer for McDonnell Aircraft on the Gemini Space Capsule. After graduating with Honors in 1966, he returned to the University to receive another Bachelors with Honors in Painting in 1969.

After college he worked with a company producing animated figures and multi-media displays. During that time, Heyda perfected a technique for creating very realistic human figures run by computer. In 1973, he signed with Movieland Wax Museum and produced full figures of Johnny Cash, George C.

Scott, Lorne Greene, Ali McGraw and Ryan O'Neal. Following this, he was commissioned by Sports World in Dallas, Texas to sculpt the busts of twenty-four famous athletes. Since that time, Heyda has been doing numerous commissions for corporate and private clients. In 1983, he sculpted a figure of Humphrey Bogart for a restaurant in Venice, California, and in 1984 he sculpted a full figure of Governor Edwin W. Edwards for a historical museum in New Orleans.

Recently he completed a series of sports figures, including Joe DiMaggio, Ted Williams, Steve Carlton, Kareem Abdul-Jabbar, Darryl Strawberry, Wayne Gretzky and Bobby and Brett Hull for Gartlan USA. In 1989 he completed a full figure of the jazz clarinetist, Pete Fountain, for a museum in Louisiana. Since then, he has immersed himself in creating the characters of Whitley Bay's *Christmas Line*, as well as designing an entirely new line for Whitley Bay. In addition to this work, he has received a commission from the Ronald Reagan Foundation to sculpt a bust of the former President for the Presidential Library in California.

TIM HILDEBRANDT

Although the term, "realistic fantasy" is frequently used to describe Tim Hildebrandt's work, it doesn't adequately depict the artist's ability to transport viewers into other worlds. Early in his career, Hildebrandt was inspired by the work of realistic illustrator Howard Pyle and the animated classics from the Walt Disney Studios.

But Hildebrandt's style was clearly apparent in the publicity posters he created for George Lucas' movie *Star Wars*. From 1976 to 1978, Hildebrandt and his brother Greg illustrated the J.R. Tolkien calendars. The pair also conceived and illustrated the best selling book *Urshurak*.

Hildebrandt won the Gold Medal Award given by the Society of Illustrators and is represented in the Society's Bicentennial Collection. The first plate in Hildebrandt's *Christian Fantasy* plate series was introduced in 1985. It was followed by the *Santa's Night Out* and the *Realms of Wonder* plate series.

Hildebandt's latest artwork for The Balliol Corporation features Casey at the Bat, which will be utilized in the collectibles field.

FRANCES HOOK

The collectibles, art and publishing business communities have saluted the inimitable artistry and spirit of the late Frances Hook with their highest tribute by establishing a foundation in her name to foster young artists' studies. The Frances Hook Scholarship Fund has grown since its inception following Hook's death in 1983. During 1984, the fund gave $9,000 in awards and scholarships to deserving students enabling them to further their studies. In 1991, the foundation awarded over $50,000 following a two-stage annual National Art Competition for art students from first grade through college undergraduates.

Frances Hook serves as a wonderful role model for aspiring artists of all ages. From the moment she could put pen to paper, Mrs. Hook knew she liked drawing more than anything else. Born in Ambler, Pennsylvania, she studied art while in high school. This resulted in a scholarship at the Pennsylvania Museum of Art. Here, she studied under illustrator Harry Pitz, developing her style in the exacting pastel discipline and her unique manner of capturing children.

Following graduation, Frances Hook married her husband whom she had met in school. They both pursued careers in commercial art. Mrs. Hook's first ad was a two-page spread for the Saturday Evening Post.

With time, Frances Hook's sensitive portrayals of children drew increasing public attention to her artistic endeavors. She had a unique talent for capturing the spirit and vitality of youngsters' activities in their natural settings. Outstanding among her renderings are the famous 1960s Northern Tissue children.

With the expanded role of television reducing the demand for commercial art, the artist turned to illustrating children's books. She joined her husband, Richard, in several collaborations. One of the most successful was their illustration of *The Living Bible* by Tyndale House Publishers.

Frances Hook and her husband worked closely and well. They also bravely battled cancer together. Following the death of her husband, Mrs. Hook entered a new and rewarding stage of her career. Roman, Inc. approached her about designing a collection of porcelain figurines. The resultant sculptures proved to be a resounding collector success. Mrs. Hook's limited editions were enthusiastically received by thousands of collectors nationwide. Her collector following grew as she toured across the country engaging in warm dialogue with her devoted fans. This wonderful beginning developed into a strong relationship with Roman and the introduction of a series of collector editions by Frances Hook — plates, prints and more figurines.

The late artist's most famous print, "The Carpenter," has commanded as much as twenty times issue price on the secondary market since its 1981 closing. Pickard produced a memorial plate based on "The Carpenter" following Mrs. Hook's death in 1983. This piece has also enjoyed a high degree of collectible success after closing. A limited edition porcelain bust of the same subject produced by Roman in 1986 has experienced similar popularity.

All releases since Frances Hook's death are issued under the direction and supervision of her daughter, Barbara. Mrs. Hook's daughter is sharing her mother's work with the public by converting Mrs. Hook's home in Maine into the Frances Hook Gallery. She also continues to work closely with Roman on faithful translations of her mother's art including a bust based on the "Little Children, Come to Me" print and plate; giftware featuring her renowned Northern Tissue children; six *Portraits of Love* limited edition prints of children; a continuing series of collector bells; and large-scale reproductions of her most popular figurines.

SISTER MARIA INNOCENTIA HUMMEL

Sister Maria Innocentia Hummel was the creator of hundreds of colorful and charming sketches, drawings and paintings of children. Her work is the basis for scores of appealing, hand-painted fine earthenware figurines, as well as limited edition plates and bells, created and offered exclusively by W. Goebel Porzellanfabrik of Germany.

She was born Berta Hummel in Bavaria in 1909. Her father had inclinations toward art, and so did Berta, from earliest youth. She was graduated from the Munich Academy of Applied Art, meanwhile devoting much of her energies toward her religion as well.

Much to the dismay of her art teachers, Berta Hummel entered a convent upon her graduation, taking the name Sister Maria Innocentia. Because the convent of Siessen, a teaching order, was quite poor, she gained permission to raise money by selling some of her artwork for postcards. In 1934 Franz Goebel, the fourth-generation head of the porcelain-producing firm bearing the family name, discovered her art at a time when he was searching for ideas for a new line of figurines.

The first M.I. Hummel figurines debuted at the Leipzig Fair in 1935, and since then have been popular with collectors around the world. Sadly, Sister M.I. Hummel died much too soon, not yet aware of her full triumph as an artist. She succumbed to tuberculosis in 1946 at the age of thirty-seven.

HANNAH HOLLISTER INGMIRE

Hannah Hollister Ingmire began her award-winning career in kindergarten, when her painting of a "choo-choo" which was selected for a traveling exhibit of children's art. At ten, she began taking private watercolor lessons. Hannah's education also was influenced by the experience of living in England for three years with her family. There Hannah's mother exposed her daughters to the joys of antique collecting.

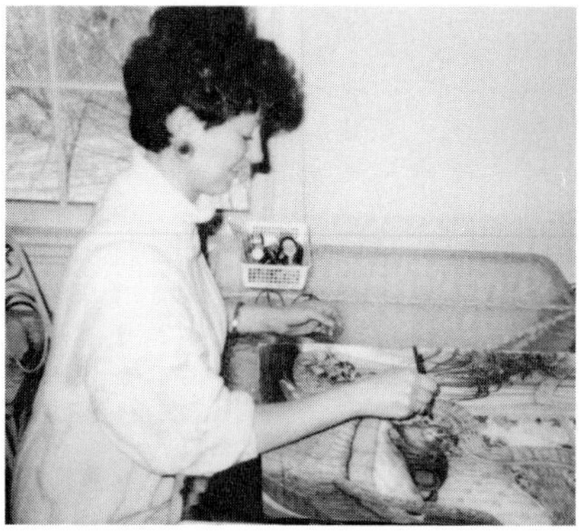

Ms. Ingmire was not comfortable with the 1960s emphasis on abstract art. Fortunately, her instructors at Grinnell College in Iowa allowed her to develop her own finely detailed and textured style. She later continued her education at Stetson University, the University of Iowa and Carnegie Institute of Pittsburgh.

She married a Lutheran minister, and the next few years were spent raising a family. By the late 1970s, Ms. Ingmire again had time for painting. Her early works during this period were sold through juried art shows and festivals, which led to gallery contracts and numerous commissions. In 1988, she opened the Hannah Ingmire Gallery in Hannibal, Missouri.

In 1990, Ms. Ingmire's first collector's plate, "Lazy Morning," the first issue in the *Cozy Country Corners* series, was introduced by Edwin M. Knowles. This skillful combination of a "Carolina Lily" quilt, a blue mixing bowl and a pair of snoozing kittens has touched the hearts of many collectors.

BRIAN JOHNSON

What began as a childhood fascination with archaeology and drawing dinosaurs led Brian Johnson to pursue art professionally. Although he doesn't draw prehistoric animals anymore, Johnson still remembers the encouragement he received from his elementary school principal to continue studying art.

He took the advice to heart. Johnson received an associates degree in art advertising and design/ illustrating from the Stevenson Academy of Art. He also attended the State University of New York at Farmingdale.

Since he always participated in sports, Johnson decided to combine his interest in athletics and art.

Several years ago, Johnson was browsing through a retail store that sold sports figurines, plates and other limited edition collectibles produced by Sports Impressions. He innocently inquired about the display and artwork featured in the products. Then he arranged an appointment to show his work to Sports Impressions.

Four years later, Johnson's illustrations of major league baseball stars appear on collector plates, mini-plates, porcelain baseball cards and posters for the company. His designs include Wade Boggs, Don Mattingly, Babe Ruth, Lou Gehrig, Mickey Mantle, Willie Mays, Duke Snider and Whitey Ford.

To design one of the products, Johnson draws several thumbnail pencil sketches and spends several days accumulating reference material. Then he makes several small color sketches before drawing the original.

Johnson's own participation in sports gives him an understanding of illustrating mood, action, emotion and authenticity. "I also receive my inspiration spiritually which gives me an inner strength, tenacious work ethic and commitment to excellence," Johnson says.

Besides painting sports figures, Johnson had artwork exhibited at the "Paris Air Show 1991" in France and was recently commissioned by Grumman Corp. to render a portrait of the company's president.

Johnson lives in Lindenhurst, New York, with his wife, Sue Ann, and his two children, Megan and Christopher.

PENNI JO JONAS

Just a few short years ago, Penni Jo was a homemaker with no idea she would have such a successful artistic career. But the phenomenon of her teddy bear creations has propelled her into the national spotlight among collectible figurine artists.

Penni Jo's first creations were made in her kitchen, using colored clays she mixed in her food processor and baked in her toaster oven. A miniature teddy bear she made for her daughter's dollhouse became the inspiration for a series of similar bears. The little bears were soon sculpted with clothes and accessories and eventually became known as PenniBears. Her local following of collectors blossomed into a national following and in 1989 Penni Jo joined the staff of United Design, where all the intricate detail of *PenniBears* are now reproduced by talented production artists and craftsmen.

In addition to *PenniBears*™, Penni Jo designs and sculpts several other collectible figurine editions, including *Tiny Tree*™ Christmas ornaments, Angel ornaments, *Itty Bitty Critters*™ and *Lil' Doll*™.

Delightfully open and candid about her transition from homemaker to nationally renowned artist, Penni Jo loves to meet collectors and fans as much as they love her and the exquisitely detailed miniatures she sculpts.

FALINE FRY JONES

Born in Wooster, Ohio, Faline Fry Jones took an active interest in art — a talent she traces back to her mother's side of the family. She actively pursued several arts and crafts, including candlemaking, leatherworking, tie dying and macrame. These craft items were taken to a consignment shop, where they were sold on a regular basis.

Always interested in cats, Faline began crafting cat doorstops out of fabric. One day, when she dropped her doorstops at the consignment shop, she noticed a small wooden house for sale. Thinking that she could make a nicer one, Faline sat down and made her very first building.

Thus began Faline Fry Jones' business, which she initially named Cat's Meow. Started in her basement in 1982, Faline patterned her designs after actual buildings and historic landmarks no longer in existence and named these pieces the *Cat's Meow Village*. By 1989, a new facility was built to house the 130-member team of employees, and the name of the firm was changed to FJ Designs. Today, Faline and her husband, Terry, run a highly successful multi-million dollar international collectible company.

The collectiblity of the *Village* began to increase as Faline devised a system of retiring a *Village* series after five years of production. She also retires a special annual *Christmas* series each year. The demand for a collector's club resulted in the formation of the Cat's Meow Collectors Club in 1989, which now boasts over 14,000 members nationally.

Faline Jones has won several awards for her business and artistic efforts, including the Small Business Person of the Year Award by the Wooster Chamber of Commerce and the Recognition Award from Ohio Small Business Revitalization, both in 1989. She is active in sev-

eral local and national organizations, including the International Screen Print Association. Faline's interest also lies with the good education of our nation's youth. Serving this purpose, she is on the board of directors of her local Junior Achievement chapter.

GARRI KATZ

Garri Katz was born in the Soviet Union when the dark cloud of war spread over all the nations of Europe. As a child he found comfort in drawing and painting on scraps of paper — an activity which helped calm his fears during the difficult days of World War II. After the war, young Katz completed his schooling at the Odessa Institute of Fine Arts, where he studied for four years before launching his career as a painter and illustrator.

In 1973, Katz and his family immigrated to Israel. His paintings of religious and historic subjects and his celebrations of everyday life in Israel soon earned Katz many invitations to display his works in one-man shows in that land. Then in 1984, Katz began a series of shows in the United States sponsored by patrons who had discovered his genius during trips to Israel. Today, art connoisseurs from many different nations purchase Katz paintings and watercolors at prices of up to $12,000 each. His works are on display in Israel, Belgium, Germany, Canada and the United States. Katz resides in Florida.

Garri Katz's first limited edition collector plate series for Reco represents a commission from Reco International. Entitled *Great Stories from the Bible*, each of eight plates portrays a memorable moment in one of the world's most beloved Bible stories.

LYNN KAATZ

Lynn Kaatz grew up on a farm in Elyria, Ohio where he was a child of the great outdoors. His early curiosity about nature and its creatures was quickly replaced by the desire to capture its beauty with sketches and paintings.

Kaatz studied art at Ohio State University for two years before transferring to the Cooper School of Art in Cleveland. After graduating, he accepted a job in Southern California as a graphic designer for Buzza Cardoza, a subsidiary of the Gibson Greeting Card Co. Kaatz stayed there for three years before joining with Mort Solberg in forming their own greeting card firm, California Graphics.

Gradually, Kaatz began producing more wildlife and outdoor art. These works evoked in him a strong desire to return to Ohio. So after nine years with California Graphics, Kaatz returned home.

In his studio on the shores of Lake Erie, Kaatz found the inspiration he needed to produce thirty to thirty-five original paintings a year. Discovered by Knowles China, Kaatz was originally slated to do a landscape plate series. But after viewing his portfolio, Knowles decided to produce a series called *Field Puppies*, featuring different breeds of hunting dogs. A second dog series, called *Field Trips*, followed.

In addition, Kaatz has created artwork for *Classic Waterfowl: The Ducks Unlimited Collection*. Produced by W.S. George, it is the first plate series to earn the sponsorship of the Ducks Unlimited conservation organization.

SARAH KAY

During the past ten years, Australian artist Sarah Kay has achieved worldwide recognition for her flawless interpretation of everyday childhood activities. Yet, she remains a shy, private woman, and enjoys nothing more than watching her children and their pets at play in her suburban Sydney home.

Sarah Kay is acutely aware of the complexities of rural youth, and that brief moment in a child's life when total innocence is coupled with the first blush of adulthood. With an unusual artistic sensitivity, these are the images which Sarah Kay transfers into colorful drawings reflecting the everyday experiences of childhood.

Although Sarah Kay's neighbors and friends have always recognized her special talent for evoking emotion and mood, it took considerable effort to convince her to share that talent with a larger public. Only after an Australian greeting card manufacturer approached her about producing a series of greeting cards bearing her illustrations, did she agree to market her designs. In 1982, ANRI approached Sarah Kay about translating her childhood themes into handcarved figurines. Working together, Schmid and ANRI have introduced several collections interpreting the works of Sarah Kay — and each has been phenomenally successful.

As one might expect, Sarah Kay continues to maintain a simple lifestyle in Australia, and anyone who happens to visit her home, would most likely find her sitting at her kitchen table surrounded by paints, brushes and sketchpads, creating inspiration for future ANRI woodcarvings.

KAREN KENNEDY

A love affair with fashion design and dolls began at an early age for Goebel's talented doll designer Karen Kennedy. In the artistic atmosphere of their atelier, she is free to combine both loves by creating exclusive costumes for *Victoria Ashlea Originals®* and their other doll lines.

Ms. Kennedy has had two of her designs accepted into museums: The

Doll Castle Museum in Washington, New Jersey and the Mary Stolz Doll and Toy Museum in East Stroudsburg, Pennsylvania.

She loves to meet with collectors personally to share her knowledge and thoughts on collecting and has appeared on television many times prior to promotional appearances.

Karen is a fast rising young star for Goebel United States.

DONNA KENNICUTT

Known best for her bronze sculptures of animal wildlife, Donna Kennicutt's philosophy is simple: "Doing is also learning." A native of Oklahoma, Kennicutt took art classes during her school years. She studied with Robert Burns Wilson and Irene Bradford. Her artworks are now in private collections

across the United States, France and other countries.

During her nine years at United Design Corporation, Ms. Kennicutt has created and sculpted the popular *Easter Bunny Family*™, as well as *Snowshoe Mountain*™ and *Bouquet*™.

JIM KILLEN

Jim Killen's career as an artist has spanned more than a quarter century. After he completed his art education at Mankato State University in Mankato, Minnesota, Killen accepted a job as an artist and designer.

In 1964, Killen moved to Philadelphia where he entered his first show and received his earliest recognition. Initially, his paintings were primarily landscapes chronicling the abandoned farms and machinery of the American heartland, in a style that incorporated both

realism and Impressionism. But eventually, Killen returned to Minnesota to work to be closer to his favorite subject, wildlife. Today, Jim exhibits in numerous galleries throughout the United States and Canada, specializing in upland game, waterfowl and sporting dogs.

A committed conservationist, Killen recently won a string of national competitions. His art won the stamp and print competitions for the 1988 Quail Unlimited, the 1987 National Wild Turkey Federation and the 1985 Minnesota Pheasant stamp and print. Killen also was named the National Ducks Unlimited "Artist of the Year" for 1984.

In 1990, The Hamilton Collection introduced the "Ring-necked Pheasant" plate, the first in Killen's *North American Gamebirds* plate collection. Some of the other popular birds featured in the series are the Bobwhite Quail, Puffed Grouse, Gambel Quail and the Mourning Dove.

KINKA

Kinka was predestined to become an artist. Born in Cleveland, Ohio to an exceptionally artistic family, Kinka studied art and music from a very early age. She turned down a career in ballet to pursue her first love: painting.

She went on to earn degrees in painting and instruction from the Cleveland Institute of Art and Bachelor of Science and Master of Arts degrees from the Flora Stone-Mather College of Western Reserve University.

From her earliest days as an artist, Kinka received awards for her work, including a *Mademoiselle Magazine* national competition award for painting. By the time she was twenty-two, she had been commissioned to illustrate stories in two national magazines and had been the subject of numerous newspaper and magazine articles.

She designed her own line of "Katy Cards" as an illustrator for American Greetings. She also created the popular Designer's Collection and contributed to the Hi Brow line. Both are still successful lines for American Greetings.

Furthering her career, Kinka designed illustrations for advertising agencies in Cleveland and later in New York. Her credits include national advertising campaigns for such major accounts as Clairol and Tishman Buildings.

Kinka's work is identified by a loose, unstructured flow of line, combined with subtle, muted color. It is categorized as feminine, delicate and whimsical. Her characters reflect the fantasy world of a little girl — innocent and filled with gentleness and love.

Kinka now owns her own greeting card company, designing both the cards and writing the messages inside. She says by doing both aspects she is "able to lock in the sentiment of the image with an always appropriate copy line." Her cards are currently available in thousands of card and gift shops throughout the United States.

In January 1989, Enesco Corporation introduced the *Kinka® Collection* of porcelain figurines and accessories. The collection meticulously translates Kinka's characters into three dimensions, maintaining the innocent images with the soft delicate colors so synonymous with the artist.

PAT KOLESAR

Back in 1979, Pat Kolesar was an avid doll collector who began to notice that all dolls looked the same. At that time, she unleashed her creative talents to design dolls that reflected the various and unpredictable moods of children. Her doll faces were atypically realistic with very distinct looks.

Since her debut, Ms. Kolesar has earned more than forty Blue Ribbons at regional doll shows and national conventions of the United Federation of Doll Clubs held throughout the U.S. Most recently, she received two Awards of Excellence nominations from *Dolls* Magazine, one for "Enoc the Eskimo Boy," which was designed for Seymour Mann, one of the most prestigious brand names in dolls. Several of her dolls currently are on display at museums across the country.

Ms. Kolesar signed with Seymour Mann, Inc. because she trusted the firm to manufacture excellent interpretations of her doll originals in collectible vinyl. Seymour Mann, Inc.'s international reputation as a high-quality collectible doll supplier with strong marketing capabilities convinced her to develop new faces for the firm.

The vivacious artist is an accomplished painter and sculptress who studied with Nat Ramer and other well-known artists. She recently was commissioned to design a portrait doll of William Simon, former Secretary of the Treasury. When she is not designing dolls, Ms. Kolesar is busy making public appearances at doll exhibitions across the U.S.

SUSAN KREY

Susan Krey was raised in the countryside of Middlesex, England. Her mother, an artist, acquainted Ms. Krey with the basics of color, light, and form. Ms. Krey attended a London art school, then emigrated to Melbourne, Australia, where she taught art and worked as a fabric designer.

Ms. Krey later moved to America, and in 1981 decided to combine her artistic talent with her love for children (she has five of her own). She began to create dolls which are noted for their simple, thoughtful design, gentle personalities, and astonishingly realistic sculpt.

Ms. Krey has earned several blue ribbons, and her dolls are displayed in museums and private collections across Australia, Canada, and the United States.

"One of my goals as a doll artist is to use interaction between dolls to tell a story," says Ms. Krey. "With the little girls in *Polly's Tea Party*, I've not only attempted to create natural, childlike expressions and soft, subtle costumes, but also to bring a favorite playtime tradition to life. *Polly's Tea Party* is available from Ashton-Drake Galleries.

SANDRA KUCK

Sandra Kuck's paintings of children display a rare gift for capturing the true spirit of childhood. The creator of several series of plates and an ongoing collection of lithographs, Ms. Kuck lives in Florida.

She was educated at U.C.L.A., where she discovered that she loved to paint and draw. She moved to New York and entered the Art Students League where she learned to do portraiture and figure drawing. She disliked drawing and painting inanimate objects and soon discovered that people, and in particular children, interested her most. Within a year, she began to win commissions from galleries for portraits and paintings.

Before long Ms. Kuck's children's paintings were on display in many New York-area galleries: she has sold more than 1,200 original paintings. In a Long Island gallery, Reco International president Heio Reich spotted her work and approached her to create a series of plates, *Games Children Play*. Soon she added *The Grandparent Collector's Plates* series and one entitled *Little Professionals*.

Ms. Kuck's other collections include *Days Gone By*, *A Childhood Almanac*, annual Christmas and Mother's Day series, and *Barefoot Children*, which are being offered by Reco, through The Hamilton Collection. One of the most celebrated plates of the 1980s, the *Days Gone By* first issue, "Sunday Best," won Plate of the Show, Silver Chalice, and Plate of the Year awards among others. In addition, Ms. Kuck has earned the NALED Artist of the Year award six years running — an unprecedented honor. She is also the recipient of numerous Print and Plate of the Year, Plate of the Show, Silver Chalice and Award of Excellence for her limited edition fan "Summer Outing."

The last issue in Ms. Kuck's four plate annual Christmas series, "We Three Kings," was released in 1989. That same year also marked the release of the first issue in the *Victorian Mother's Day* series, "Mother's Sunshine," which won Plate of the Show at Pasadena.

Sandra entered a new medium in 1989 with the introduction of "Loving Steps," for which she won Doll of the Year. "Loving Steps" is the first in a

series of mother and child porcelain dolls, entitled *The Precious Memories of Motherhood Doll Collection*. "Lullaby" was the second issue.

She has also been honored by being asked to contribute to the March of Dimes plate series, with "A Time to Love."

1991 was a very exciting year for Ms. Kuck. First, her beautiful portraits of children from an era gone by, "Puppy" and "Kitten," were introduced as part of *The Premier Collection* from Reco International.

Her new plate series *Hearts and Flowers* also made its debut. And to recognize all of her achievements, Ms. Kuck was honored with a retrospective of her work at the 1991 South Bend Collectible Exposition.

Sandra Kuck also joined together with The John Hine Studios in 1991 to present a series of figurines entitled *Heartstrings*.

GLENNA KURZ

Glenna Kurz was born in Fullerton, California. Her artistic talent emerged early, and her efforts were appreciated and encouraged by her family. Her first commission was for a series of deer paintings. She was only thirteen at the time and has been painting seriously ever since. One of her most recent commissions was a series of California missions, done for a financial institution.

She has participated in numerous exhibitions and competitions and has received many awards for her paintings. She was one of two California artists accepted (out of 18,000 entries) in the National American Artists Show in New York City.

Ms. Kurz' respect for the traditional values that prevailed in the art of the nineteenth and twentieth centuries is evident in her approach to landscapes and still-life subjects.

Her appreciation for beauty and meticulous portrayal of atmosphere, color and texture achieve realization through many hours of patient concentration.

The W.S. George series *Flowers From Grandma's Garden* marked Ms. Kurz' debut in the collector's plate medium.

JIM LAMB

When Jim Lamb was a boy, his artist-father developed a unique way to keep his active son quiet during Sunday church services. The elder Lamb would give young Jim a pencil and pad to doodle with during sermons. Then after church, the father would go over the drawings with his son, helping him to improve his art technique. His father's influence shaped Lamb in another important way as well, for they made frequent trips into the country to observe the nature of the Great Northwest. And regular trips to art galleries allowed Jim Lamb to develop his great appreciation for the Old Masters.

After a time spent in college, young Lamb joined the Navy, and spent those four years devoting all his spare time to art. During that period he put together a portfolio that he used to make his mark in Los Angeles, soon developing a clientele for book illustrations, sports paintings, advertising, and movie posters.

Yet for all his success as an illustrator, Lamb longed for the freedom to create art on his own terms. What's more, Lamb's family wanted to return to the artist's northwestern "roots." Today the Lambs live in Issaquah, Washington, where the artist works on a variety of projects, including fine art collector prints and limited edition plates.

Many of Lamb's animal and bird prints have sold out within days of their issuance. In addition, his works have been selected for a U.S. postage stamp, the Smithsonian Institution, U.S. Air Force, and the U.S. Forestry Service. Jim Lamb's first venture in the field of limited edition plates came about as the result of a commission from River Shore and The Hamilton Collection. The series, entitled *Puppy Playtime*, included eight lively puppy portraits honoring America's favorite purebred dogs. "Double Take," the premiere issue in the collection, has already been quoted at twice its original issue price on the secondary market.

Recently, The Hamilton Collection introduced another popular collection of Lamb originals, entitled *Good Sports* — a whimsical look at adorable puppies doing sports-type activities.

Lamb's newest series is *A Sporting Generation*, a collection featuring an adult sporting dog and his offspring in each image. "Like Father, Like Son" from this collection has been very well received by collectors.

A frequent award-winner, Jim Lamb was named the 1991 "Artist of the Year" by the Southeast Wildlife Exposition.

DAVID LAROCCA

Born in May 1954, in Cambridge, Massachusetts, David LaRocca received his formal art education at the Massachusetts College of Art. His early artistic efforts were the result of his attempts to copy in miniature his father's collection of statuary, armor and weapons. Later, he began researching these pieces to improve his accuracy and detailing.

While his teachers stressed abstract

forms and texture, LaRocca tended toward perfecting his exacting representational work in miniature. After getting into body building, LaRocca became equally fascinated with the human anatomy and its movements. To ensure accurate body movements, LaRocca does his figures nude and then clothes them in authentic costumes.

Through his painstaking research, LaRocca verifies the authentic details of every shield, gun, and canteen. LaRocca's rendering of his Chilmark Pewter *World War II* series, reveals a unique rendering of military art.

In addition to his military and western sculptures for the Chilmark line, LaRocca had sculpted pieces for Lance's highly successful *Villagers* series, marketed through the Hudson Line, and a miniature version of Frederic Hart's Vietnam War Memorial for the Franklin Mint.

CHRISTOPHER LAWRENCE

Christopher Lawrence is a silversmith and industrial designer who lives in Essex, England. After high school, he went to the Central School of Arts and Crafts and obtained his National Diploma in Design and the Full Technical Certificate of the City and Guilds of London. He was apprenticed to a silversmith and then started his own workshops in 1968. He has held five one-man exhibitions and has completed many commissions from the British Government, City Livery Companies, banks and leading manufacturing companies. He is a judge and external accessor for leading art colleges and is a specialist in symbolic presentation pieces and limited editions of decorative pieces including pewter mushrooms. All mushrooms are limited edition pieces — the "Princess' Palace" has a limited edition of 750 pieces and the "Gift Shop's" edition is limited to 1,250. All other pewter mushroom pieces have limited editions of 2,500 pieces. Lawrence was awarded the Jacques Cartier Memorial award for Craftsman of the Year in 1960, 1963 and 1967 — a unique achievement. When not working, he enjoys cruising in his canal narrowboat and walking in the English countryside.

Christopher Lawrence's splendid Mushroom sculptures feature a group of dwellings resembling actual mushrooms. Inside is an entire community of "Mushpeople" whose activities are described in John Hine's book *Capricious Mushrooms*. Through the gifted artistry of Lawrence, we have the privilege of looking at, and into, the homes and lives of those impulsive, gentle characters of Mushland — the Mushpeople.

Collectors won't believe their eyes when they peek into the wonderful world of Christopher Lawrence Mushrooms — the delightful lifestyle and Mushland philosophy may just rub off on the world!

WENDY LAWTON

Born in San Francisco in 1950, Wendy Lawton grew up in a large, happy family. When she was ten, her family moved to the East Bay suburb of Union City where she attended grammar and high school. Wendy then enrolled in San Jose State University where she majored in home economics and art. She worked her way through college, scooping ice cream and teaching summer art classes and later worked as a graphic artist, kindergarten teacher and daycare administrator.

In 1971, Wendy married Keith Lawton. Although she had always loved dolls, Wendy began to experiment with cloth, bread dough and even plaster for making dolls. The birth of the Lawtons' daughter Rebecca prompted her to seek out a dollmaker who would teach her the intricate processes needed to make porcelain dolls and hand-wefted wigs.

Wendy's first dolls were commissioned portrait dolls, but once retailers saw her work they immediately began placing orders. Wendy's dolls are recognized for their fresh, all-American look.

In the late 1970s, Wendy and Keith formed Lawtons to produce and market Wendy's dolls. Lawtons dolls have been nominated nineteen times for *Doll Reader's* "Doll of the Year Award" (DOTY) and *Dolls* magazines "Doll of Excellence," winning two Dolls of Excellence gold medals and two DOTYs. In 1987, the Lawtons were joined in the doll business by Jim and Linda Smith of Tide-Rider, the toy importing firm.

RON LEWIS

When Ron Lewis moved to New York City from his small hometown in Idaho, he knew getting art assignments would be a challenge. But he never imagined the difficult task of finding housing.

Ironically, his exhaustive search for a place to live led to his first break into the highly competitive New York art world. When Lewis went into a typesetting and graphics business to inquire about housing, the owner asked to see his portfolio. After looking at his work, the owner commissioned Lewis to do a magazine cover. Other assignments and opportunities soon followed.

Lewis eventually began illustrating baseball cards and now concentrates on posters, prints and magazine covers of baseball athletes, events and teams.

In 1987, Lewis started designing artwork for limited edition collector plates, steins and ceramic baseball cards for Sports Impressions. His work has appeared on items featuring Nolan Ryan, Rickey Henderson, Andre Dawson, Ty Cobb and other baseball greats.

He draws rough sketches, researches the subject and studies photographs before he paints the final design on canvas with oil paints.

Besides his work with Sports Impressions, Lewis also designs ten to fifteen card sets, promotional paintings for sports memorabilia conventions and commissioned paintings. In 1989 Lewis was featured on ESPN's "Baseball Magazine" show.

As a senior in high school, Lewis lettered in four sports and played college football and baseball. He naturally combined his love for sports with his artistic talent, which started with a fascination with designs on paperback book and record covers.

Lewis graduated with an art degree from Idaho State University and then attended the New School of Visual Concept in Seattle. Lewis, who lives in Brooklyn, New York, is married and has two children.

DENNIS LIBERTY

Dennis Liberty has been an artist since he was ten years old. He says he was "always making figures" out of clay and wax. Liberty attended Florida State University, the Husian Art School in Philadelphia, Norfolk Museum School and earned his bachelor's degree in fine arts from the University of New Mexico in Albuquerque. During this period, he also sandwiched in a four year hitch in the Navy, serving as a photographer on the USS Independence.

His sculptures are on permanent display in several museums and galleries and are part of many private galleries.

Liberty has been making metal

objects for many years. They range from bronze sculptures to small pewter figurines. He also designs bronze small pewter specialty belt buckles. His *Crystals of Zorn* figurine series for The Lance Corporation represents his first effort in the fine art pewter sculpture market. In addition to Zorn, Liberty's fantasy and whimsical fantasy are an important part of Lance's Hudson Pewter Line.

Since 1990, Liberty's work for the Hudson line has expanded to include *Santa's Elves, Inc.* and miniatures for *Lighthouse Point* and the *Circle H Ranch* groupings. In 1991, he sculpted his first pieces for Lance's Chilmark line, "The Patriot" and "Proud Hunter" for *The Eagle Gallery*.

MARY LILLEMOE

When Mary Lillemoe was a little girl growing up in Minneapolis, her favorite pet was a cat. Somehow, a cat seemed to fit right into a family with eight children and a mother who "painted."

Mary eventually studied art at the University of Minnesota, moved to New York and married. She abandoned art and instead became a nurse. For a time after the birth of her children, painting was relegated to a hobby. But, when the children were older, she once again began to pursue a professional art career. Her illustrations began appearing in children's books, on greeting cards and on gift items.

When she began sketching whimsical drawings of her childhood pet, it was her five-year-old daughter who said, "That's Kitty Cucumber." The name seemed to fit and as Kitty's family grew, Mary's family continued to help name her playful creatures.

Kitty Cucumber made her debut in a book published by B. Shackman & Co. in 1984. Kitty and friends became so popular that they soon began appearing on greeting cards and other paper products. In 1985, Schmid began transforming Mary's characters into the *The Kitty Cucumber Collection*, handcrafted and handpainted collectibles for the entire family. Today, the *Kitty Cucumber Collection* is one of the top five collectibles in America.

As for Mary Lillemoe, she continues to pursue her artistic career in her Riverdale, New York studio, where she lovingly creates Kitty Cucumber and friends.

LENA LIU

Lena Liu was born in Tokyo during her father's tour of duty as a liaison officer for the Chinese Nationalist government. Her mother came from a well-to-do family and her father was trained as a military officer, attending schools in England and the United States. The family later moved to Taipei, Taiwan.

Lena's talent was recognized early, and she began taking Oriental art lessons under Professor Sun Chia-Chin and later under Professor Huang Chun-Pi before coming to the United States with her family.

She graduated from the School of Architecture and Design at the State University of New York/Buffalo in 1974 and later went to graduate school at U.C.L.A. She worked for an architectural firm until 1977 when she began painting fulltime.

Lena's art combines traditional Chinese art with today's Western culture. Working on silk canvas, she uses natural dyes and a "wet on wet" technique to obtain her delicate, transparent colors.

To guarantee their authenticity, she carefully researches all her subjects. Ms. Liu's first plate series, *On Gossamer Wings*, was produced by W.S. George under the sponsorship of the Xerces Society.

Since then, two other W.S. George series have debuted featuring her artwork; *Nature's Poetry* and *Symphony of Shimmering Beauty*. Lena Liu's limited-edition plates are available through The Bradford Exchange.

DAVID THOMAS LYTTLETON

As a child in England's Stoke-on-Trent region, David Thomas Lyttleton knew that when he grew up, he would do something artistic. Lyttleton was quite young when he began winning prizes for his drawings and illustrations. Eventually, his attention shifted to the sculptured ceramics, one of the chief products in the area.

As a young man, Lyttleton was hired by Royal Doulton and was placed in a day-released program which allowed him to attend the local polytechnic art college where he earned his design technician certificate.

Assigned to the Beswick factory of Royal Doulton, Lyttleton created a number of animal figures that currently are in private collections. He spent fourteen years at Royal Doulton before opening his studio. During this start-up period, he worked briefly for Aynsley China. Since that time, he has received commissions from porcelain companies in England, Ireland and Italy, as well as The Hamilton Collection in the United States.

In 1990, The Hamilton Collection introduced two Lyttleton sculptures: "Tawny Owl" and "Barn Owl" from his *Little Night Owl* collection. Before beginning work on his owl sculptures, the artist observed and photographed his subjects in zoos and wildlife parks. He then skillfully posed each owl as they are found in nature. For example, Lyttleton's "Tawney Owl" is perched in the hollow of a tree, the "Snow Owl" is on the ground, and the "Barn Owl" is posed in the window frame of a barn. Clearly, Lyttleton's great strength is his ability to capture the owl and its 'habitat' so artistically in his works, with remarkable detail and amazingly realistic colorings.

EDA MANN

Born in London, England, Eda studied art under two uncles and her father, Samuel Mirsky, all professional artists. Eda was sixteen when she immigrated to the United States to study at the National Academy of Design in New York. After graduation, Eda began her professional career as a fabric and fashion designer. While vacationing she met Seymour Mann, an accomplished musician. Shortly after their marriage, the Manns formed a professional partnership in which Seymour handled the business affairs and Eda designed figurines and other decorative accessories for their popular giftware lines such as the *Americana Collection*.

In the 1960s, they founded Seymour Mann, Inc. In addition to raising a family and designing their giftware line, Eda continued to paint. Her work was praised by critics, and two of her paintings, including "Portraits of Lee Krasner," have been acquired by the Metropolitan Museum of Art in New York.

A doll collector for many years, Eda made dolls for her children and grandchildren. In 1981, Eda's first limited edition dolls were introduced in the *Connoisseur Doll Collection*. In the past decade, Eda has designed more than 1,500 dolls for this collection. In 1991, two of her dolls received major award nominations: an Award of Excellence from *Dolls* Magazine and the DOTY award from *Doll Reader*.

JOHN BOYD MARTIN

John Boyd Martin is fast becoming one of the country's most respected and popular portrait artists, especially in the sports field. Commissioned by major universities, professional sports franchises and associations, Mr. Martin brings an emotional realism to his art that communicates in dramatic fashion.

Mr. Martin began his career as an advertising art director/illustrator winning more than 150 awards for his work across the country. He then turned his full attention to his first love: portraiture.

Some of his best-known portrait commissions are: baseball greats Joe DiMaggio, Ted Williams and Stan Musial; former Baseball Commissioners Happy Chandler, Ford Frick and Bowie Kuhn; Dallas businessman Lamar Hunt; and golfer Lee Trevino.

Mr. Martin also has done portrait commissions for such institutions as The University of Michigan, The University of South Carolina, Louisiana State University, The Kansas City Chiefs, The Kansas City Royals, The Atlanta Braves, The Detroit Tigers, major League Baseball Promotions Corporation and NFL Properties.

Mr. Martin was also commissioned by Gartlan USA, Inc. to create *The Gold Crown Collection* commemorating George Brett's 2000th hit. The collection includes a custom oak-framed ceramic plaque which portrays Brett superimposed against three action shots which illustrate the sports hero in action, at the bat and in the field. "Royalty in Motion" is personally autographed by Brett and Martin.

Artist Martin still keeps his hand in as an illustrator, having done program covers for the World Series, the All-Star Game, the NBA All-Star Game and Game Day.

Although Mr. Martin's work has

been oriented to sports, he has received noted recognition for his work for business institutions and private collections, as well.

JOHN McCLELLAND

The life-sized portrait of his daughter, Susan, which John McClelland created some years back may well have been the major turning point of his career. An art director used the portrait for an ad in a trade magazine, and Miles Kimball, the mail order company, spotted it and asked John McClelland to do a Christmas cover for their catalog. That was the beginning of an association which continues today.

Brigitte Moore of Reco International saw McClelland's Miles Kimball art in the mid-1970s, and Reco arranged for the artist to create limited edition plates. McClelland today is one of the field's most celebrated artists, with numerous "Plate of the Year" and "Artist of the Year" awards to his credit.

He also has designed several figurine series, including subjects such as children, clown heads and angels, and is the creator of a number of limited edition lithographs pulled from eight to fourteen individual plates.

A native of Georgia, McClelland pursued his art career in New York after a hitch in the service. He met and married Alice Stephenson, a fashion artist, and they moved to Connecticut, where they resided for thirty years. In early 1986, the McClellands returned to their native Georgia where they have built a lovely home.

In addition to his many limited edition offerings and his Miles Kimball work, McClelland is a portraitist with a large following. He also has created scores of illustrations for publications including *The Saturday Evening Post, Redbook, American*, and *Readers Digest*.

McClelland has written two "how-to" books for artists: one on painting flowers and the other on portrait painting. He also has taught both intermediate and advanced classes in portrait painting.

The *Treasured Songs of Childhood* is McClelland's latest series, which was completed in 1990 with the release of the final issue, "Hush Little Baby."

John is one of the renowned artists who was asked to paint a childhood image for *The March of Dimes* series. McClelland's plate is entitled "A Time to Plant."

McClelland added to his long list of achievements by creating *The Children's Circus Doll Collection*, based upon the popular Reco plate series. 1989 marked a tribute to John McClelland with a retrospective of the artist's work at the South Bend Collectibles Exposition, where John's greatest work was on display.

In 1991, John's first Christmas series debuted: the title of the series is *The Wonder of Christmas*.

CINDY M. McCLURE

Cindy M. McClure has the distinction of being one of the few artists in the world to win the prestigious Doll of the Year Award from the International Doll Academy for two consecutive years. In addition to winning the Doll of the Year Award in 1986 and 1987, Ms. McClure has captured more than twenty major awards in her dollmaking career.

Today, Ms. McClure's dolls are eagerly sought by collectors because many of her original artist dolls, even those made only a few years ago, have appreciated significantly in value on the secondary market.

Ms. McClure's dolls are also in demand because of her sensitive portrayal of children. This is not surprising, because her dolls are inspired by real children she has met. Even the names that she selects for her dolls are names that belong to real children. The artist's new series for Edwin M. Knowles China Co. is *Cindy's Playhouse Pals* and is available through Ashton-Drake Galleries.

ANNE TRANSUE McGRORY

Anne Transue McGrory began drawing at the age of three. Although she was interested in wildlife and nature, her fascination was thwarted because of childhood allergies which prevented her from exploring the outdoors.

Between school sessions at the Rhode Island School of Design, Ms. McGrory worked for a newspaper, doing photography, layout and paste-up. She also spent two years designing and producing jewelry for a firm in Lexington, Massachusetts.

With a college major in illustration which emphasized wildlife art, Ms. McGrory received her bachelor's degree from the Rhode Island School of Design in 1981. She did wildlife illustrations for the Massachusetts Audubon Society, and for the next three years, designed jewelry for a manufacturer in Belmont, Massachusetts. From this experience, Anne developed an interest in three-dimensional art.

Ms. McGrory began her sculpting career for The Lance Corporation in 1985 and has created several series for the Hudson line including the twelve-piece *Classical Nativity* and the *Songs of Christmas* plate grouping.

Her work for the Chilmark line includes wildlife, reproductions of Frederic Remington works in miniature and a series of new sculptures based on the paintings of Remington. The *OffCanvas* sculptures, totalling eight pieces in 1991, interpret in three dimension Remington paintings such as "Smoke Signals," "The Emigrants," "Downing the Nigh Leader," "A Dash for the Timber" and "Blanket Signal." The first three pieces in her *Off-Canvas* series, introduced in January 1990, sold out within six months of issue.

KEN MEMOLI

"I never knew my grandfather, but he was a big influence in my life. His name was Karl Lang and he was one of the sculptors who worked under Gutzon Borglum on the carving of Stone Mountain, Georgia, and the Mount Rushmore Memorial in South Dakota. I guess it must be in the genes, because I'm very attracted to sculpture. It's just sort of a feeling."

Now a sculptor for United Design, Ken was born in Stamford, Connecticut and studied art at both the University of Hartford and the University of Oklahoma. Eager to learn, he's done landscape designing and limited edition cookie jars for a woman who specialized in Black collectibles. One of his biggest commissions was to carve a Statue of Liberty for Oklahoma City's celebration of the United States' Bicentennial.

In 1970, Memoli began as a freelancer for United Design, and is now a full time sculptor for the company. One of the first series he was involved in was the *Little Prince and Princess*™ done in bonded porcelain. His more recent works include several larger *Animal*

Classics™ and a *Legend of Santa Claus*™ figurine which was released as a limited edition.

CLEMENTE MICARELLI

The spirited festivities of Christmas Eve and the fairytale-like story of Clara and her nutcracker provide artist Clemente Micarelli with the perfect vehicle for his entry into the collector plate market. Micarelli studied art at both the Pratt Institute and The Art Students Leagues in New York and the Rhode Island School of Design.

His paintings have been exhibited in numerous shows where he has won many awards. Represented nationally by Portraits, Inc. and C.C. Price Gallery in New York, Micarelli has painted the portraits of prominent personalities throughout the United States and Europe.

Micarelli also has done fashion illustrations for Gimbels, Jordan Marsh, Filene's and Anderson Little in Boston. He has taught at the Rhode Island School of Design, the Art Institute of Boston and the Scituate Arts Association and South Shore Art Center.

In 1991, Reco International introduced the fourth issue in Micarelli's *Nutcracker Ballet Series*, "Dance of the Snow Fairies." Each plate in the series is based on an actual performance from the renowned Boston Ballet.

The talented portraitist has recently painted a *Wedding Series*, commissioned by Reco International, for plates and bells.

LEE TAYLOR MIDDLETON

Born in Springfield, Ohio, Lee was the oldest of three children. Growing up in this supportive family environment, Lee was constantly encouraged by her parents to explore her natural talents. Although she was fascinated with art as a means of self-expression, there were no art courses at Springfield's Northeastern High School. She opted for mechanical drawing, her first formal art training. Over the next few years, Lee refined her unique style of painting.

From her first doll designs sculpted at her kitchen table, through the early stages of her company's founding and the growth of her current position as America's pre-eminent doll art/manufacturer, Lee Taylor Middleton has remained ever mindful of her family's support in the development of her talents and the realization of her present success.

Middleton's first dolls were sculpted in the likeness of her children, daughter Brynn and son Michael. It was the artist's ability to capture the likenesses of children that led to her early commissions from family, friends and collectors.

It seems to be no mere coincidence that Lee's "Little Angel" won the "Best of Show" at the first doll show she entered in the late 1970s. Lee's intense faith in God and commitment to Christian values prompted her to "give credit where credit is due." Each of her original dolls leaves her factory with a tiny Bible tucked inside the box.

In 1980, Lee founded the Middleton Doll Company, which produced sculpted portrait dolls for private commissions and for sale at regional doll shows. To meet the demand for her dolls in 1984, Lee introduced a porcelain-looking vinyl version of her designs. Less labor intensive, the vinyl dolls had lower retail prices. Sales of these dolls skyrocketed.

The growth of the Middleton Doll Company continued during throughout the 1980s. After a series of rented quarters, her business moved into a new facility in Belpre, Ohio in August 1989. That same year, Lee was selected Small Business Person of the Year for the State of Ohio and was honored by President Bush during a Washington, D.C. ceremony for state winners.

LARRY MILLER

Raised in a small mining town in Arizona, Larry Miller graduated from the University of Arts and Sciences of Oklahoma, and the University of Oklahoma. He spent five years in the U.S. Army Corps of Engineers where he worked as an illustrator.

Miller's experience as a sculptor has undergone a series of transitions. In college, he concentrated on welding sculptures, but his interest later shifted to bronze. Three of his bronzes are in the permanent collection of the Gil Crease Museum in Tulsa, Oklahoma.

A member of United Design's staff for ten years, Miller has sculpted pieces for the *Stone Critters*®, *Animal Classics*™, *The Legend of Santa Claus*™ and *The Legend of the Little People*™ product lines.

"I love fantasy. That's one of the reasons I like doing the *Legends* series. I've done leprechauns and little people, and I'm at my best when my sculptures highlight fantasy."

SUSIE MORTON

Susie Morton has been creating original art for Porter and Price (formerly Ernst Enterprises) in the form of limited edition plates since 1978. In addition,

she has collaborated with other well-known collectibles firms, including The Hamilton Collection, The Danbury Mint and Duncan Royale.

A resident of Orange County, California, Morton had early schooling at the Ringling School of Art in Sarasota, Florida. She worked in pen and ink and in watercolor, and later studied painting and sculpture in California.

For the past nineteen years, Morton has been recognized as one of America's leading portraitists, earning acclaim for her realistic style and her ability to capture the "personalities" of her subjects.

The artist's most popular works combined her love of art with a love of the great stars of music and film. "Marilyn Monroe," "John Wayne" and "Elvis Presley" are among the stars honored on her plates in the 1980s. Each of these issues — as well as a number of other celebrity-subject plates — has since entered into secondary market trading and appreciated significantly in value.

In addition to her portraiture, Morton is a proficient sculptress and an expert painter of animals and wildlife.

JAN NAHRGANG

As the mother of six and a full-time special education teacher of grade school children, Jan Nahrgang experiences firsthand, all the bliss and the disappointments that fill young children's lives. Over the past ten years, Nahrgang also has developed a rare gift for translating her love of children into dolls that capture their innocence and charm.

Nahrgang made her first porcelain doll more than ten years ago to fulfill a Christmas request. One doll led to another and after a number of sculpting classes and study, she moved from copying reproduction dolls to designing originals.

For a number of years, Jan has helped each of her students make an all-porcelain doll that looks something like themselves. She sculpts the individual heads, and students clean the greenware, paint the features and assemble the dolls. Ms. Nahrgang then completes each doll with an appropriate costume.

Although she continues to teach full time, her doll business, The Nahrgang Collection, is very much a family-run business in Moline, Illinois. Almost all of her family have become involved in the enterprise. Husband Larry pours the doll heads and keeps the books. Daughter Jennifer Caldwell is the company manager. Jennifer's husband Michael is the production manager, and Jan's son, Ray Monterestelli, handles the marketing.

Still very much committed to creating original dolls, Ms. Nahrgang spends a great deal of time sculpting her dolls. She designs and makes the first dress and paints all the faces herself. She attempts to paint about twenty dolls a night which is about equal to the factory's daily production.

The originality and subtle humor of Jan Nahrgang's dolls is best expressed in dolls like "Grant," which features a little uniformed baseball player forced to delay his departure for the game because he has been ordered to practice with his violin. Although she is a newcomer to the industry, the quality of Ms. Nahrgang's dolls was recognized in 1990 when her "Karissa" doll was nominated for *Doll Reader* magazine's 1990 "Doll of the Year" (DOTY) award in the collectible porcelain doll category.

SEIJI NAKANE

Seiji Nakane, award winning master sculptor, was born in Tajimi, Gifu Prefecture of Japan in 1938 and is a graduate of Tajimi Art and Industrial School. Fascinated by the porcelain-making industry in Seto, he began working in clay at eighteen, fashioning sculptures for the European export market. In 1984, WACO Products Corporation became fascinated with his works and decided to craft their unique *Melody In Motion*® bisque porcelain figurines by using molds which were made from his original sculptures. These figurines offer both visual and musical delights to those who own them, and range from Willie's clowns, cowboys, madames and craftsmen, to Santas, carousels and porcelains with quality quartz clocks.

Nakane's sculpture expertise represents an important contribution to the *Melody In Motion*® series. His sculptures provide the ability to develop production molds of such size that only a few of them are required for the final porcelain. This and the high quality of the Seto clay allow the very small manufacturing tolerances needed when combining porcelain with the other necessary materials which make up the final WACO product. Among the awards bestowed upon Nakane, and the one of which he is most justifiably proud, was the sculpture competition for the porcelain handrails of the bridge over the river Seto, Japan. Competing against some of the finest Japanese porcelain artists, it was Seiji Nakane who was chosen to sculpt the model for the porcelain handrails which create the special effect on the bridge.

A modest man, Nakane still lives in Seto with his wife, and continues to create beautiful porcelain models for WACO Products Corporation.

WILL NELSON

Will Nelson's childhood was spent on a cattle ranch in southern Idaho where the animals and outdoor life of a working ranch provided Nelson with insights into the relationship of natural settings for animal studies.

After attending the Art Center College in Los Angeles, Nelson began his professional career in the Midwest. His illustrations were well received and he earned a number of professional awards

over the years. Nelson and his wife Elaine returned to Idaho in 1960 where they raised their three daughters and Will began working from a studio in Boise. Nelson began doing wildlife and landscape paintings, but in 1985 a series of animal illustrations prompted him to seriously study wildlife and become concerned for endangered species throughout the world.

In 1987, Nelson was a member of a scientific expedition to China — hosted by the China Science and Technology Exchange Center — where he met scientists involved in captive propagation programs and the preservation of the panda in the wild. After sketching and photographing the panda in major zoos throughout central China and hiking into the panda habitat in Eastern China, Nelson compiled extensive material on the panda in its rugged mountain home. This study has become the basis of much of his *Last of Their Kind: The Endangered Species* and *Gentle Beginnings* plate series for W.S. George.

Nelson is a member of the San Francisco Society of Illustrators and the Academic Artists Association.

GERDA NEUBACHER

Gerda Neubacher is a Canadian realist artist who was born in Austria. Artistically inclined since childhood, she studied art at the Grace Kelly School of Art in Zurich, Switzerland. In Zurich she met and married Fred Neubacher, another Canadian realist painter. In 1968 they took up residence in Toronto.

Ms. Neubacher's love for rural scenery and studies of people are reflected in her highly realistic and detailed works of art, such as the popular *Classic Fairy Tales* Plate Collection she created for Kaiser Porcelain. In her delightful *Christmas Plate* series for Kaiser Porcelain, the children seem to come alive as Ms. Neubacher focuses on the various aspects of the holiday season.

The artist has had major exhibitions in Toronto with Juliane Galleries and Christel Galleries as well as the National Art Center in Ottawa, The Galleria in Houston, the OMNI in Miami, the O'Keefe Centre in Toronto, and many more. Gerda's more recent offerings, *America The Beautiful* and *Forest Surprises*, express the artist's love of nature and wildlife, which is very welcome in the plate collector's market.

GUNTHER NEUBAUER

A better indication of the quality of talent attracted to the Goebel company, both past and present, would be hard to find than Gunther Neubauer. With Goebel for the last thirty years, Herr Neubauer has attained the highest distinctions.

In 1948, one month following his sixteenth birthday, he entered W. Goebel Porzellanfabrik as an apprentice in the painting department. He was taken under the wing of one of the masters, Arthur Moller, who trained him in all phases from designing to painting, even some sculpting. It soon became clear, however, that his strengths lay in designing and painting, and it was in those areas where his burgeoning career concentrated.

Just three years later, he distinguished himself by passing with highest honors a demanding professional test given in Coburg. In appreciation of this, and in an unusual move, Goebel promoted him quickly. He was now respon-

sible for the decoration of particularly difficult models. It is rare, even today, to find an artist equally at home in both onglaze and underglaze decoration, but Gunther Neubauer is a specialist in both areas.

By 1953, he had become head of a large section of the painting department. And he was only twenty-one! From this time on, his progression through the artistic ranks of the company was secure. By 1955, he was entrusted with the development of totally new designs. Needless to say, this is a most important and responsible position in a porcelain factory.

From the early 1960s through the present, Herr Neubauer has been directly concerned with the education of the apprentices in the decorating department. He is a recognized teacher, and has as his pupils all apprentices in all production departments of W. Goebel Porzellanfabrik. At the vocational school in Coburg, he has the rank of master.

Gunther Neubauer was born in the Sudetenland, the northern part of Bohemia (now Czechoslovakia), an area famed not only for the Bohemian glass so treasured, but also for porcelain. Swimming and skiing are important to him, but for a busman's holiday he prefers to paint! He is also an experienced photographer.

DIANNA NEWBURN

"I love making the children, especially the little girl dolls, because I love dressing them up in all the frilly clothes," says Dianna Newburn.

Being an avid doll collector, Dianna experimented with making miniature clay dolls of her own. "Then, of course, the dolls had to have tiny toys to play with and miniature furniture to sit on," she says. Soon she had a whole doll's room full of clay miniatures.

She went to miniature shows with a friend and soon had a national following of her work, *Collectibles by Dianna*, among miniature collectors. Eventually she began making her dolls out of porcelain rather than clay. She called her dolls *My Precious*.

By 1990, her work had become so popular that it sold out at a miniature show in Kansas City just seven minutes after the show opened. She was exhausted from making all the reproductions, and the demand was exceeding her ability to produce in her home studio.

She joined the staff of artists at United Design where she continues to create original dolls and other figurines. The American craftsmen at United Design reproduce the originals with exact detail.

Currently, she is sculpting figurines for the *Lil' Doll*™ collection, the *Itty Bitty Critters*™ collection, a line of miniature toys and children, and a line of miniature clocks, frames and figurines with a storybook theme.

CHRIS NOTARILE

A native of Brooklyn, New York, Chris Notarile is a graduate of the Parsons School of Design in New York City. He originally dreamt of becoming a comic illustrator and, in fact, was publishing his own comic strip while still a teenager. However, while in school, his interest in realistic art soon took precedence. His work has been seen in numerous magazines, and his portraits have appeared on everything from book covers to movie posters. His celebrity subjects have included Bill Cosby, Clint Eastwood, Kevin Costner, and Michael J. Fox. Notarile's plates are available from The Bradford Exchange.

Notarile lives in New Jersey with his wife and two young children.

MARYANNE OLDENBURG

Maryanne Oldenburg has been creating her own original dolls from images of real children since 1973. She has won hundreds of awards, including more than sixty blue ribbons, and one "Silver Cup" Best of Show from the International Doll Maker's Association.

Ms. Oldenburg maintains a high profile in her profession as Second Vice President of the Original Doll Artist Council of America (O.D.A.C.A.), a teacher of sculpting and dollmaking, and a competition judge.

Ms. Oldenburg recently designed a doll collection available through Ashton-Drake Galleries. "Andy," the first issue in *Yesterday's Dreams*, is authentically garbed in a railroad engineer's outfit.

"Andy's modest dream of becoming a railroad engineer echoes back to a simpler time in history," says Ms. Oldenburg. "Now, collectors can step back from our fast-paced society and experience another era through the innocent, imaginative eyes of a child."

ROBERT OLSZEWSKI

Growing up on the edge of a small town near Pittsburgh, Pennsylvania, Robert Olszewski was free to roam the countryside and make drawings of the things that pleased him. His efforts were encouraged, and as he grew older, he began buying poster boards for his sketches and paintings.

Olszewski continued to draw and paint throughout high school and college, but he was enough of a realist to also earn a Bachelor's Degree in Art Education. After graduation, Olszewski and his wife set out for California where he taught during the day and painted at night.

A series of unrelated incidents then propelled Olszewski into miniatures. Classroom space was at a premium so he began assigning students scaled down projects. Next, one of his paintings was stolen from a gallery. He had no photo of the stolen work so he painted a copy for the police. Ironically, he liked the miniature copy better. The final nudge came when Olszewski began building a dollhouse for his daughter.

Intrigued by miniatures, he began to study and experiment with increasingly smaller works of art. Olszewski eventually began working in the ancient "lost wax" technique, and in 1977 produced his first one-twelfth scale figurine. Two years later he signed an exclusive contract to produce for and oversee the creative directions for Goebel Miniatures studios in Camarillo, California.

A short decade later, the art form of painted bronze miniatures (Cire Perdue Bronze Poly Chromes) pioneered by Goebel Miniatures with Robert Olszewski as Master Artist, is an established and sought after medium in the field of collecting. Today, Robert Olszewski conducts the artistic course of the world's largest studio producing fine miniatures and objects of art.

Olszewski's dedication to his talent and his art form has earned him international acclaim. It's a long way from the classroom to directing a major international creative studio. Bob handles it in stride. "The hardest thing for someone who likes to teach is to give up his favorite class at the end of the term. I've had a chance to work for ten years with virtually the same nucleus of talented people. It's a dream come true...and every day we get better than the day before," says Olszewski. At middle age, Olszewski feels his best creative years are still ahead of him.

CHRISTOPHER A. PARDELL

Christopher A. Pardell, gifted young American sculptor, attributes his international acclaim to a natural passion for art and a five year apprenticeship studying under Italian masters, Gino Bonvi, Aldo Gregory and Vertitio Bonofazi.

Influenced early on in his thirty-four year career by the work of renowned sculptors Russell, Remington and Rodin, Pardell wanted to pursue his passion for realism, a passion unchallenged by the abstraction-obsessed classrooms of ivory tower academia.

Through pantomimed conversations with accomplished artists and craftsmen whose European dialects he could not understand, Pardell became proficient at the many schools of sculptural design. He achieved a classic style. He closed his apprenticeship.

Over the next four years, Pardell explored the potential of his gift as a freelance sculptor, playing with volume, balance, tension and form in a subject range encompassing wildlife to western, oceanic to equestrian and outdoorsman to nudes. A master of technique and design, he joined LEGENDS.

Since that time, his natural talent, dedication and unique artistic vision have culminated in the creation of compositions commended by fellow artists, craftsmen and collectors of fine art.

A conservationist, he works closely with the Sierra Club, The Rocky Mountain Elk Foundation, Trout Unlimited, Conservation for Big Horn Sheep Society, Ducks Unlimited and Wildlife Way Station. A humanist, he supports Green Peace and the United Sioux of America in an effort to protect a quality of life threatened by the age of technological revolution — a present and a past which he further preserves through the everlastingness of his art.

In founding "Aesthetic Associates" — an organization committed to young artists struggling to realize their artistic identities — Pardell has afforded the opportunity of apprenticeship to other gifted, young Americans.

Born in Oakland, Pardell has travelled extensively. He now resides in Southern California with his wife, Nancy, and their two sons, P.J. and Sean.

PHYLLIS PARKINS

Phyllis Parkins loved china painting and a variety of craft projects. So it really wasn't very surprising when she began making her first porcelain dolls for her young daughters.

In 1977, Phyllis' husband was transferred to Rolla, Missouri. Shortly after they arrived, a neighbor, Mable Scoville, came to welcome them to the area. Mrs. Scoville also was a crafter and skilled seamstress. After seeing some of Phyllis' dolls, Mable offered to sew dresses for them. That fall, Phyllis' dolls sold out at a large craft show in St. Louis, and dealers approached her about making dolls for their shops. Phyllis' fledging doll company, The Collectables, was on its way.

The company continued to grow slowly. In 1982, a new factory was built and in 1984, John Parkins came into the business full time, freeing Phyllis to devote more time to design work.

Recognizing that original dolls were the next trend, Phyllis taught herself to sculpt. In 1987, she won two "Doll of the Year" (DOTY) Awards for her original dolls, "Tasha" and "Sarah Jane." "Tasha" also was the winner of *Dolls* Magazine's "Award of Excellence." In 1989, Phyllis' Collectors Club was founded. Her dolls were nominated for *Dolls* Magazine's "Award of Excellence" in 1988-1990. "Welcome Home" won the Award and was also nominated for a DOTY award in 1989. In 1990, "Kristen" was the winner. A new company, Designs by Phyllis, was formed in 1991 to handle the artist's new vinyl doll line.

GREGORY PERILLO

When Gregory Perillo was a child in Staten Island, New York, his Italian immigrant father would tell the youngster colorful stories about the Old West. Young Greg would sketch what he envisioned from those grand tales, always choosing to portray the Indians rather than the cowboys. And he dreamed of the day that he would visit the American Indians for himself.

While in the Navy, Perillo shared some of his western sketches with a friend from Montana. Before long, the pair was on their way West, and Perillo had the opportunity to come face-to-face with American Indians he had read and dreamed so much about. Except for his curly hair, they mistook the Italian Perillo for a full-blooded Indian. When they asked what tribe he was from, he quickly replied "The Neapolitan tribe." Being mistaken for a Native American solidified his identification with the people he was to paint for the rest of his life.

Perillo dedicated himself to portraying the American Indian culture with fidelity and respect. He studied under the late western art master, William R. Leigh, whose individual works now command fees into the millions. In fact, it is a matter of great pride with Perillo that he was Leigh's one and only student. In 1959, Perillo was inducted into the Hudson Valley Art Association. With the association's magazine and exposure as a starting point, Perillo soon earned national exposure, and then international attention.

The artist began a series of one-man shows and gallery exhibitions that continues even today. In addition, his works were chosen for the permanent collections of museums and institutions including: the Pettigrew Museum in Sioux Falls, South Dakota; the Denver Museum of Natural History; and the University of Mexico.

In the late 1970s, Perillo began creating limited edition plates, figurines and graphics under the commission of Vague Shadows (Artaffects). Since then he has won numerous awards — both personally, and for his two and three-dimensional portrayals of American Indian life. In 1991, the Artaffects Perillo Collectors Club began and met with great response and enthusiasm.

Among the latest of Perillo's Collectible offerings is the magnificent series of highly detailed sculptures titled *The Great Chieftains* and Perillo's award-winning lithograph "The Pack." His wonderful portrayal of Navajo Village life is found in *The Village of the Sun* series. Perillo's most recent plate series include *The Council of Nations* featuring the plate "The Strength of the Sioux," the *Indian Bridal* series and the *Four Seasons*, which is done in the distinctive American Blue.

Gregory Perillo is now in the process of building The Perillo Museum of Western Art located on Hutchinson Island, Florida. The museum will include the masterworks of American Western Artists and a variety of Native American Artifacts.

MICHAEL PETRONELLA

From caricatures to lifelike portraits, Michael Petronella has made a career of capturing personalities in sports, entertainment and politics. His serious and often humorous work has appeared throughout the country in newspapers, television and collector plates.

Petronella attended the Ridgewood Art Institute in New Jersey where he studied portrait painting and technique. Upon graduation, he worked for a New Jersey newspaper where he polished his skills.

His interest in playing and following sports led to his desire to portray athletes in his artwork. So two years ago, Petronella teamed up with Sports Impressions, a producer of sports figurines, plates and memorabilia.

Petronella has designed porcelain collector plates and mini-plates of Nolan Ryan as well as football and basketball stars. He recently created *The Golden Years* collection featuring Willie Mays, Mickey Mantle and Duke Snider. The limited edition plates take a nostalgic look back at the 1950s and America's favorite pastime.

Working in watercolors, Petronella takes several weeks to research his subject and design each illustration.

For the past few years, Petronella has been free-lancing for clients such as The Associated Press, *Video Magazine*, *Personal Computing*, Harper and Roe and Showtime, a cable television station. Michael's caricatures and cartoons appear regularly in the *National Sports Daily* and *Giants Extra News*. He also draws sports cartoons for *The New York Times* and celebrity caricatures for the *New York Daily News*.

Petronella, who lives in Oradell, New Jersey, is a member of the Graphic Artist Guild in New York.

DON POLLAND

In early childhood, Don Polland carved his own toy cowboys and Indians. Living in Utah, Arizona, Colorado and Nevada, he developed an intense interest in the golden days of the American West, which he has continued to express in three-dimensional art throughout each phase of his life.

Polland's first career was that of an illustrator for space age industries. He became a professional artist in 1959. His goal as an artist is to express his personal thoughts and beliefs as a storyteller. He strives to communicate his ideas visually, without the need for words of explanation.

A self-taught and highly motivated artist, Don Polland considers creativity his way of life. His subject matter ranges from working cowboys to wild animals to Indians of the past and present. Because of their great challenge and long history in the world of art, Polland especially enjoys creating miniature sculptures. For commissions by such firms as The Franklin Mint and American Express, Polland has traveled widely, including a voyage to Africa on a research trip.

Polland's extensive list of museum showings includes the Whitney Gallery of Western Art, Buffalo Bill Historical Center, C.M. Russell Gallery and Museum, The Favell Museum of Western arts and Artifacts, and the Montana Historical Society. His awards and honors include numerous Best of Show and First Place awards at art shows nationwide. He was awarded the 1980 Favell Museum Western Heritage Award for excellence in portraying America's west and wildlife in sculpture. In addition, Polland is listed in *Who's Who in American Art, Who's Who in the West,* and *American Artists of Renown* and *Artists of Arizona.*

Today, Polland continues to work on his beloved miniature figurines. From the studio which bears his name, he also has introduced more than fifty gallery and museum bronzes as well as works for Franklin Mint, Chilmark, and other fine art firms.

CONNIE PRACHT

Born in Council Bluffs, Iowa, Connie Pracht grew up in Southern California where she began drawing at a very early age. Her first subjects were horses, but gradually she became intrigued by the challenge of recreating the emotions and the character traits of human beings.

Ms. Pracht attended Long Beach City College and California State University in Long Beach, California. While in college, she was introduced to photography and went on to study with Al Belson of the Newport School of Photography at UCLA. Her photographic training has been an immense help in obtaining the photo "studies" from which she draws or paints.

Until recently a resident of the Los Angeles area, Ms. Pracht has moved to a big old house in New Castle, Virginia. While she once had to visit nature centers for inspiration, Connie can now look out her windows for a panoramic view of the Blue Ridge Mountains.

Connie Pracht's limited edition *Daddy Loves You* series for Flambro

Imports represents the artist's first offerings in the collectibles market.

LUCY RIGG

Lucy Rigg began making baker's clay teddy bear figurines in 1969 while awaiting the birth of her daughter, Noelle. She decorated the nursery with her first teddy bears. But friends and family were so enchanted with the original creations, that Lucy began making them for others.

Teddy bear collectors bought her hand-painted clay dough bears, known as "Rigglets," at street fairs. To keep up with the growing demand, she imposed a quota on herself to make 100 teddy bears per day and often stayed up until the wee hours of the morning to meet her goal.

As her teddy bears became more popular, Lucy branched into other areas. In 1977, Lucy and her friend Judi Jacobsen, began a greeting card business known as Lucy & Me™. The partnership ended in 1984, and each artist formed her own company.

In the late 1970s, Enesco Corporation President Eugene Freedman approached Lucy and proposed turning her handmade teddy bears into a line of porcelain bisque figurines and accessories. She was operating her growing business from a small studio, already bulging at the seams with orders for her bears. Since Enesco introduced the collection in 1978, it has enjoyed steady support from collectors and teddy bear lovers.

Lucy continues to operate Lucy & Company, designing diaries, baby announcements, calendars and her "teddy bear" version of popular children's books. *Lucylocks*, a beautifully illustrated variation of *Goldilocks and the Three Bears*, formed the basis for the Enesco *Storybook Classics* series of porcelain bisque figurines.

Lucy was born in Seattle, Washington. The former Lucy Weygan was the second of four girls, and has lived most of her life in Seattle, attending Seattle public schools and the University of Washington.

Lucy has been a teddy bear collector herself since 1968. Her Seattle home is filled with toys and collector items, which project the warmth and joy of her artwork. She has created a special room to display the Enesco *Lucy & Me®* Collection, which now includes several hundred porcelain bisque figurines, plus many accessory items, including tins, plates, mugs, covered dishes, laminated bags and more — each adorned with her lovable teddy bears.

A lover of hats, Lucy often wears one and collects them, too. She is known for her religious convictions and her delightful personality, and is recognized as one of the most prolific teddy bear artists in the world.

In the last few years, she has divided her time between her business and home in Seattle and extensive overseas travel.

NORMAN ROCKWELL

"I paint life as I would like it to be," Norman Rockwell once said. "If there was a sadness in this creative world of mine, it was a pleasant sadness. If there were problems, they were humorous problems."

In his thousands of works, Norman Rockwell created a pictorial history of his times and illuminated the lives of his fellow Americans with gifted warmth and insight. Rockwell gained national prominence as an illustrator for *The Saturday Evening Post, Life, Look, Boy's Life*, Boy Scout calendars and major advertisers, all of which brought him close to the hearts of people the world over.

The man, who was to become the twentieth century's most popular American artist and illustrator, was born in a brownstone in New York on February 3, 1894. He began drawing at five, and attended the Chase School of Fine and Applied Arts and the National Academy of Design. He sold his first *Post* cover in 1916, and by 1920 he was the *Post's* top cover illustrator.

One of his most distinguished pro-

jects was a series of more than seventy sketches depicting the American Family for the Massachusetts Mutual Life Insurance Company, a collection which is now on display at The Norman Rockwell Museum. During World War II, Rockwell's "Four Freedoms" art helped raise more than $130 million in war bond money. Beginning in the early 1970s, Rockwell's works became some of the most frequently sought-out subjects for limited edition collectibles. Today Rockwell limited editions are marketed by firms including The Gorham Company, The Hamilton Collection, The Bradford Exchange and The Norman Rockwell Gallery.

Norman Rockwell continued his productive life as an artist and illustrator in his Stockbridge, Massachusetts studio until his death in November 1978.

MERRI RODERICK

For Merri Roderick, sculpting was either a "happy accident" or "meant to be." From the moment she began working in clay, she says she knew her calling was to be a sculptress. And in the years since, Merri has honed her skills to become one of the most highly regarded artisans in the collectibles industry.

After earning her fine arts degree from the University of Illinois, Merri worked as an apprentice to a well-known artist/designer in an environment known as the "fantasy factory" because of the mechanized Christmas decorations employees created for department stores.

She worked mainly as a seamstress, designing and making coverings and clothes for the animals. But one day, when all the sculptors were busy, Merri asked to sculpt a new figure. Although this was her first time using clay, she says she immediately "knew how to sculpt."

Over the years, this award-winning artist has perfected her talent and sculpting skills to create exquisite one-of-a-kind sculptures, bas relief and crystal collector plates, dolls and miniature environments.

Merri created her first collection for Enesco Corporation in 1989. *Looking Glass Legends*™ captivated collectors with its richly detailed miniature environments. Merri says she was inspired by the secret fantasy world of childhood when she reached into her imagination to sculpt the heroes, villains and dragons that live, love and cavort among the lush settings in "The Queen's Garden," "Grandyoak Wizard's Castle" and "Indigo Bay." The collection was nominated as the "Most Original Collectible" in the 1990 *Collector Editions* Magazine Awards of Excellence.

In 1990, she introduced her second Enesco collection, *Lieblings*™, a fanciful, whimsical community of woodland elves. The collection features an assortment of figurines, waterballs and other accessories.

Merri is married to a former Chicago television news anchorman, whom she credits with having encouraged her to develop her career.

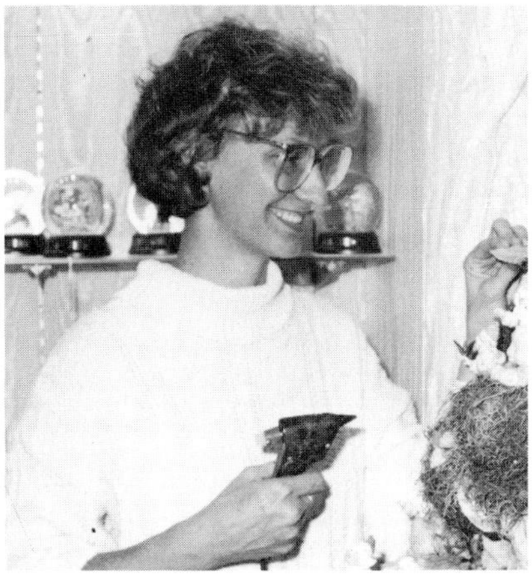

CAROL ROEDA

Carol Roeda may be the only artist in America who can boast about reading "at least two novels" a week while she works. The secret? "I have a passion for books on tape," explains Carol, whose hands playfully craft delightful collectible figures while a soothing voice reads a best-seller aloud in her bright, airy stu-

dio. While most artists may complain of a solitary life, Roeda's is anything but lonely! Each day, Carol comes into her cheerful studio to sculpt a merry band of inspirational figures. Her colorful angels and sweet children each bear the Carol Roeda hallmark: mouths shaped into big O's as though we were catching each figure in mid-song.

Her sculptures sing to deliver a message, Carol explains and that message is ageless: "Let all that breathes sing praise to the Lord." It is a theme that is laced throughout her work and her life...a life that is crowded with meaningful work, a loving family and the delightful surprise of seeing her art so well received by the public. Did she ever expect that her life would wind up as it has? Not really. Carol was born and raised in Grand Rapids, Michigan, finishing a four-year program at Calvin College with a degree in Special Education. She taught high school for one year before marrying and turning her attention to caring for her family. A four year move to Exeter (Ontario, Canada) with her minister husband and growing family brought many happy experiences, but Carol was glad to return to her lifelong home in Grand Rapids.

Needing a creative outlet, Carol turned to pottery as a young wife and mother. By 1985, she had developed a unique style for portraying children and angels with the trademark singing mouth. Fashioning a delightfully innocent nativity set as a centerpiece for her work at a big craft show, Carol was astonished to find that the nativity set sold immediately...as did every creche scene she placed on her table. Carol Roeda knew that she "was onto something."

That feeling was as accurate as her designs were compelling: soon Artaffects, Ltd., a well-known distributor of limited edition art, saw in Carol, the magical appeal shoppers had already noted at craft shows. A contract was signed, and Carol Roeda was welcomed into the Artaffects family. Her initial pieces for this firm included six ethnic angels, six angel ornaments (with their toes peeking from beneath their hems), four charming children, a bride and groom and a captivating nativity.

Look beyond Carol Roeda's inspirational figures, and you will find that her motivation to create comes from her deep religious beliefs. She once said that a goal of hers was to spread the message that Christmas should extend beyond December in our hearts. Toward that end, her angels are reminders that we are protected twelve months a year and must be responsible for keeping the Christmas spirit in our lives from January to December.

"The real work of Christmas begins after the pageant is over, the costumes are hung in the closet, and the star is put back on the shelf," Carol has often quoted. "That is the time when Christians must give hope to the broken, food to the hungry and freedom to the oppressed." It's a message Carol lives 365 days a year.

Right now, Carol juggles a demanding day at The Carol Roeda Studios and goes home to a husband, three children and a revolving door of guests from across the globe arriving on their doorstep in Grand Rapids on a regular basis. When asked if all this bustling activity stops her from getting any work done, she simply shrugs and tells you that her figures are inspired by the big and little people she meets every day. They are truly life's simple pleasures...or perhaps we should say simple wonders!

G.G. SANTIAGO

G.G. Santiago has devoted the past thirty years to capturing the innocence of children and animals through her distinctive art style. As Enesco Senior Creative Director for Product Design, G.G. has contributed her artistic talents to developing and expanding the company's line of fine giftware and collectibles.

Her designs for Enesco include such successes as *Elusive Legend*™, *Baby Tenderfeet*™, *Graceful Glory*™, *Style, Jenny, Classical Ballerina, White Whisper* and *Madonna and Child.* She also provides the creative direction for *Treasured Memories*®, a popular collection of figurines featuring families in Victorian-era settings. Most recently, G.G. designed a delightful collection of baby giftware based on "A Child's Gift of Lullabyes®," an uplifting collection of children's songs.

G.G. has earned numerous awards and recognition, including winning the Frances Hook Scholarship Fund's licensed art competition three times. "Swimming Mermaid" from the *Elusive Legend* series won the 1990 *Collector Editions* Awards of Excellence, an honor voted by the magazine's 70,000 readers.

Prior to joining Enesco, G.G.'s artwork appeared on highly successful products of two leading greeting card companies. While working six years for Hallmark Cards, G.G. created the "Rainbow Brite" character, a charming little girl with brightly colored hair. She also spent nineteen years with American Greetings.

ROB SAUBER

His lovely ladies are often portrayed in period attire so it comes as no surprise that Rob Sauber maintains a romantic view of life. His own story reads like a tale from a novel, filled with turns of fortune and lucky coincidences.

Out on his own at age eighteen, Sauber caught on as a fashion designer for a department store in Raleigh, North Carolina. Then he embarked upon a whirlwind of other occupations, including food service, free-lance photography and illustration. Saving money along the way, Sauber eventually accumulated enough to attend the prestigious Art Center in Los Angeles.

Stints as a studio artist and free-lancer followed his schooling. Then Sauber left California for New York at age thirty. Soon a famous artists' agent

signed Sauber, and since then he has advanced steadily as an illustrator, watercolor painter and limited edition plate artist.

Sauber has been working with Artaffects since 1982. He is widely known for his *Portraits of American Brides* series and his *Winter Mindscapes* series done in the distinctive American Blue.

Rob is currently working on more new and exciting collectibles for Artaffects.

SARAH SCHULTZ

When Sarah Schultz needed a new couch, she decided to turn her favorite hobby into a wholesale company. Sarah was inspired by a love of antiques and a desire to create complimentary accents for them. Sarah started her own business on the family dining room table in 1983. Because the unique handcrafted items were like treasures from the past, Sarah called her business Sarah's Attic, Granny's Favorites. She also signs each piece with a little heart as a personal guarantee of quality and originality.

Many of Sarah's creations come from memories of her past. For example, when Sarah was a little girl, she delivered newspapers in her hometown. She loved to deliver the newspaper to a black family who was on her paper route. The mother would invite Sarah into their home and she would fill her tummy with cookies and milk. While eating the cookies, they would tell her story after story. In 1984, she wanted to bring this memory and their stories alive so she introduced "Willie" and "Tillie," a little black girl and boy. These two children were introduced to *Sarah's Gang*, and the *Black Heritage Collection* started. Another memory that Sarah has brought to life is her children's youth. As all mothers, Sarah felt as if her children grew overnight so she has brought back the characteristics of her children when they were growing up. These children are in the *Daisy Collection*, and it is no surprise that daisies are Sarah's favorite flower. Just as daisies have brightened Sarah's days, her children have brought a brightness to her days that could never be replaced. Sarah hopes that all her pieces come alive for collectors and bring back one of their own loving memories.

There are many different races in the world, but we all have one heart which is the same color: RED. Sarah created the signature heart from this idea because she feels that everyone was created equal. Sarah has created all her pieces with dignity to display this equality. No matter what race a Sarah's Attic figurine portrays, it will always have the signature heart on it to represent peace and equality in the world. Sarah introduced the *United Hearts* in June 1991. The *United Hearts* shows Sarah's collections coming together to unite their love. They commemorate the months of the year portraying eternal love and unity. These collections join together for a common good. Sarah brings her collections together to form a message that no matter how many races there are in the world, everyone should join together for a common good of love and peace.

Sarah's Attic has a motto: "Remember, the very best always comes from the heart." All of Sarah's Attic employees instill love from their hearts into the pieces because they have pride in their work. Sarah treats her employees as family members because she is very family oriented. She is always telling her employees, "This is OUR company, not my company." When a collector buys a Sarah's Attic piece, they can be assured that much love and pride in creating, painting, shipping, etc. was put into each piece. That is why each piece will always bear the signature heart, which is the firm's trademark of quality and love.

JEAN SIAS

"I try to make my paintings real enough that the viewer believes that they could actually be in them, and beautiful and dramatic enough so that they want to be," said Jean Sias, one of W.S. George's newest artists.

Born and raised in Winter Park, Florida, Jean Sias began painting at the age of seven. By the time she was nine, Ms. Sias was painting portraits and is still surprised at how good they were. Later, she attended the University of Southern Florida on an art scholarship and spent a number of years studying watercolor and oil-painting techniques and theory.

Ms. Sias' paintings have won many prizes at shows and festivals including the Festival of the Masters at Disneyworld, the Aspen Artists' Gallery, the San Diego Art Institute and the Artist's Society International Gallery in San Francisco. Her work also is represented in private collections across the country, and Ms. Sias is sought after as a portrait artist.

She has always strived to reveal the "magic" of nature through a mixture of realism, design and mood. The *Spirit of Christmas* and *Nature's Legacy* plate series for W.S. George represent Jean

Sias' entry into collectible art and is an exciting new offering for discriminating collectors.

GERHARD SKROBEK

Gerhard Skrobek, a master sculptor of the Goebel company, was born in Silesia, the northernmost part of Germany, subsequently moving with his family to Berlin. There, surrounded by museum art treasures and encouraged by his artist mother, young Skrobek became immersed in the heady climate of artistic tradition. From early childhood, he was fascinated with sculpture and its many artistic forms. He studied at the Reimannschule in Berlin, a renowned private academy of the arts. Later, he continued his studies in Coburg. Through one of his professors, he was introduced to porcelain sculpture at the Goebel studios.

Skrobek joined Goebel in 1951, and soon became one of its leading sculptors and eventually the predominant interpreter of Sister Maria Innocentia Hummel's drawings. Only Skrobek could have created the six-foot replica of the "Merry Wanderer," the famous landmark that stands in front of W. Goebel Porzellanfabrik in Roedental, Germany.

"I am accustomed to creating normal-sized figurines from a lump of modeling clay," says Skrobek, "but here I had to work with a very brittle material, and had to bring many forces into play — I became an architect, mason and sculptor all in one!"

In addition to his world-renowned ability of capturing the quality of the two-dimensional artwork of Sister Maria Innocentia Hummel into three-dimensional joyous presentations, Skrobek has contributed his talents to the delightful

"The Surprise" and "Hello World" for members of the Goebel Collectors' Club (now the M.I. Hummel Club). Always delighted to meet with collectors, Gerhard looks forward to his visits to North America, and opportunities to meet friends, both old and new.

JOE SLOCKBOWER

Although Joe Slockbower's tan and build — what his Huntington Beach peers might appropriately call "cut" — lend more to a surfer moniker than sculptor, his sculpting legacy is strong, one crafted in sports, legends and sports legends.

A naturalist at heart, Joe is at home in the sun and the studio.

His work includes busts of John Wayne and Will Rogers; his art recreates the rich history of Native Americans; and he has captured such sports stars in action as O.J. Simpson and for Gartlan USA, Luis Aparicio, Ken Griffey Jr. and Rod Carew.

Joe holds a Bachelor of fine Arts degree from the California State University at Long Beach and has been sculpting professionally for more than a decade.

Displayed in galleries throughout the Southwestern United States, his art also has been purchased by such luminaries as the late Danny Thomas and John Wayne, and by Evel Knievel and Barbra Streisand.

Recently, Joe sculpted the artwork for the James R. Smith Award — in recognizing outstanding contributions to the sport of water polo.

Joe places a special emphasis on artistic endeavors that reinforce man's balance with nature. "Hopefully my art will convey a message: one that says man must fight to protect our wildlife and to begin living our lives joyously and in harmony."

JACQUELINE BARDNER SMITH

Born in Pennsylvania, artist Jacqueline Bardner Smith studied at the Philadelphia College of Art and Pennsylvania Academy of Fine Art, before pursuing her career in sculpting, painting, and illustration.

Today, she lives and works in Southern Florida's west coast, and her studio faces the Intercoastal Waterway. "I have always loved the water," she explains. But it is the artist's other loves — animals, children, and of course, painting and sculpting — which combined to give us some of the most popular and charming porcelain sculptures ever issued in collectible form. In addition, the artist has earned acclaim as an illustrator of popular children's books published by Harper & Row Atheneum.

Jacqueline Bardner Smith created a delightful collection of porcelain figurines exclusively for The Hamilton Collection. Entitled *Snuggle Babies*, each porcelain creation is actually composed of two separate "snuggling" pieces. This body of work demonstrates the beauty, wit and originality which have defined the art of Jacqueline Bardner Smith.

CHARLES R. SOILEAU

Charles Soileau was born in 1949 in Eunice, Louisiana where he lived and later graduated from Eunice High School. Charles' artistic talent was self-taught; and although he was offered a partial scholarship in fine arts at Tulane University, Charles married and moved to Houston, Texas to pursue a career in commercial art.

Charles was employed by Boone Advertising as its Senior Art Director in 1972. In 1980, Charles formed Soileau Studio, an illustration and graphic design firm. He has since grown from a one-man operation to a six-person advertising agency now called Soileau & Associates.

During his career, Charles has received thirty-two different awards for his illustrations and design achievements.

In 1987, Soileau created *The Roger Staubach Sterling Collection* for Gartlan USA, Inc. to honor Staubach's lifetime of achievement. The line includes ce-

ramic plates, miniature plates, plaques, football cards and lithographs. Soileau painstakingly researched and studied photographs and films of Staubach's playing years from the Cowboy's archives, which enabled him to portray the winning intensity in Staubach's face and penetrating blue eyes.

IRENE SPENCER

Since her first visit to Chicago's Art Institute at age nine, Irene Spencer knew she wanted to become an artist. Her dream was to create art that moved beholders as she had been stirred by the masterpieces she had viewed. There followed nine years of intensive formal training at the Institute where Mrs. Spencer shaped what was to become her guiding philosophy: the purpose of art is to improve the quality of life.

Seeking adventure at age twenty, Mrs. Spencer acted out an impulse many people only dream of...she joined a circus. During two years as an assistant elephant trainer, she discovered vivid and colorful inspiration in the world of clowns, animals and other performers she later captured on her earliest canvases.

Looking for steadier employment, Mrs. Spencer returned home to Chicago and entered the American Academy of Art. Following graduation, she worked as a commercial artist for several agencies tackling projects from comic strips to children's books. This variety laid the foundation for her proficiency at a wide spectrum of subjects from Western characters and cats to Christmas scenes. By 1964, Mrs. Spencer had relocated in California and developed her own clientele. Commissioned works from a Beverly Hills gallery eased her transition over a period to full-time painting.

Becoming the first female to design a limited edition plate stands high on the list of Irene Spencer's notable achievements in 1972. Today, Mrs. Spencer ranks as one of the industry's most popular artists. Honors she has earned include: Litho of the Year (1980, 1981), Plate of the Year (1981) and the Silver Chalice Awards at the California Plate Collectors Convention (1982, 1983). In 1986, she was voted Artist of the Year. One of her first creations for Roman, Inc., the oriental figurine, "Flower Princess," was named Figurine of the Year at the same awards ceremony. Mrs. Spencer's most recent honor is a special diamond award for excellence bestowed at the 1989 Silver Chalice Awards.

True to her philosophy that art improves the quality of life, Irene Spencer spends many hours approving every detail of her collector editions to ensure they evoke lasting enjoyment for viewers. "My intention in creating is to express with my best technical ability, a depth of feeling that defies verbal description," Mrs. Spencer explains.

Such strength of emotions is aroused by her many collectibles for such noted producers as Pickard, Franklin Mint and Gorham. Roman produced plates and sculptures celebrating Irene Spencers's renowned themes of mother and child as well as *Catnippers* ornaments and Glitterdomes™. Her newest renderings for Roman are charming commemoratives for the 500th anniversary in 1992 of the discovery of America. Delightful felines "Kistopher Kolumbus" and "Queen Kitsabella" are featured in lighthearted limited edition ornaments and an art print titled, "The Discovery of America."

MICHAEL STAMEY

Crystal designer Michael Stamey was born in Munich, West Germany to an Austrian mother and an American father. His first years were spent in the U.S.A. in Georgia and North Carolina. Then his parents moved to Austria where Stamey was brought up and educated in the provinces of Styria and Tyrol.

One of his studies was a four year specialist course at the Glass School in Kramsach, Tyrol, and after graduation, he practiced his skills in the local glass industry. He furthered his education in the U.S.A. by studying art and biology in Florence, South Carolina for two years. During this time he also worked as a freelance textile designer, and upon returning to Austria, he became a designer for D. Swarovski & Co.

Michael's wife, Gabriele, is also a crystal designer, having met her husband while studying at the Glass School in Dramsach. The Stameys have two children, Immanuel and Michael. They live in the Inn Valley, in a tiny village called Angath near the market town of Worgl.

Stamey is a keen botanist and a cacti enthusiast. He has a collection of up to thirty different species of cacti and other succulents in his house and garden. His interest in cacti began when he first saw them in the wild in the Sonora desert near Mexico.

He is a very versatile crystal designer, contributing his talents to various projects, including the hand-cut chandelier components for the renovation of the Versailles chandelier. Among his designs in the *Swarovski Silver Crystal* collection are the South Sea shell, sitting cat and apple — all new for 1991. One of his micro designs of exotic cacti was chosen as the 1988 Swarovski Collectors Society membership renewal gift. Stamey is also the designer of the 1990 and 1991 *Swarovski Collectors Society Annual Editions* — "Lead Me" - the Dolphins and "Save Me" - the Seals, respectively.

LARRY E. STEORTS

Larry Steorts is a master of miniature. His genuine fascination and appreciation for Victorian architecture — which, in the mid and late 1800s, forever altered the expression of American streetscapes — is magnificently expressed in each detailed model. His "studio" is a three-foot pine plank and his tools — an x-acto knife, fine sandpaper and a set of jewelry files — can fit into the palm of his hand.

An ex-San Diego policeman and degreed criminal attorney, Steorts contends he should have been an architect a century ago. He feels no rapport with contemporary design. "To me, modern architecture is cold, sterile and

unfriendly...nothing more than variations on a rectangle. I love the Victorian details which, as scale is reduced, increasingly challenge my vision as an artist and my skills as a craftsman."

Using photographs as "models," Steorts reconstructs missing details from his knowledge of period architecture. Each model is meticulously scaled and built from rough, penciled sketches used as blueprints and the thin sheets of basswood are individually fashioned and formed to create perfect replicas of this artist's imagination. He has created several sculptures for Legends.

Born in Spokane, Washington, Steorts has traveled extensively. Perhaps his many travels have contributed to his keen eye and genuine sense of quality and realism. He now resides in Southern California with his wife, Andrea, and two children, Taylor and Aleksandra.

ADI STOCKER

Adi Stocker, Austrian designer for Swarovski, successfully balances his two main interests — crystal and mountains — pursuing both with the same intensity.

Born in Kizbuhel, a small walled town set in the mountains, Stocker was interested in arts and crafts from an early age. He studied at the Glass School in Kramsach, Tyrol, a specialist school where all the skills of glassmaking are taught, including glassblowing, cutting, engraving, painting, and the art of crystal making. He remained there for four years, perfecting his craft.

He first began to practice his skills in the mountains of New Hampshire with Pepi Herrmann Crystal Inc. He stayed with the company for four years, acquiring extensive knowledge as an all-round glass maker.

In 1981, Stocker undertook a world trip, visiting such exotic places as Japan, China, Thailand, Nepal and India, before returning to live and work in his native Austria a year later.

In Austria, Stocker pursued both his passions: crystal designing and mountaineering. His favorite "Alpine game" is rock-climbing, which demands constant training to build up the stamina — both mental and physical — required to tackle a rock face. To Stocker, however, it represents the ultimate form of relaxation.

His love of nature is transmitted in his animal studies for the *Swarovski Silver Crystal* collection. He is fascinated by the qualities of crystal. Stocker has brought his sensitivities and talents to bear on his designs "Sharing" - the Woodpeckers (1988) and "Amour" - the Turtledoves (1989), the second and last Annual Editions in the series *Caring and Sharing* designed exclusively for members of the Swarovski Collectors Society.

PAUL J. SWEANY

For more than forty years, Paul J. Sweany has combined his interests in science and art in the creation of excep-

tionally beautiful naturalist masterworks. Today he reigns as one of America's most honored painters of butterflies, birds and flowers, earning accolades like "a man for all media"..."a vibrant and distinguished artist-teacher"...and "his masterful paintings make the best use of watercolor and composition."

A native of Indiana, Sweany served in the United States Naval Reserve during World War II before completing a Bachelor of Fine Arts degree at the Herron School of Art in Indianapolis. He taught at the Herron School from 1946 to 1976 in many capacities, beginning while still a student. Over the years, Sweany has combined teaching duties with his own naturalistic artwork.

Sweany believes that his style of painting has developed through his love of nature. For him, light and atmosphere are tools as important as brush and pigment. He draws heavily upon the traditions of the Old Masters while composing in dramatic and contemporary ways. Sweany believes that a true artist paints what is as natural to him as eating and breathing.

Paul Sweany has exhibited in more than 125 one-man shows throughout the United States and Europe. He is the recipient of more than 250 awards and has been a keynote speaker for several national and state teachers' conventions. Sweany's works may be found in many private and public collections all over the world.

Sweany's first limited edition collector plate series centered upon beautiful butterflies and flowers. Entitled the *Butterfly Garden* Plate Collection, it was a presentation of The Hamilton Collection. The famed naturalist also created *The American Rose Garden* Plate Collection, which honors an outstanding variety of America's national flowers.

ROBERT TABBENOR

Although Robert Tabbenor admits that he was born and bred in the Potteries, he did not set foot in a porcelain factory until 1973 when he began working at Royal Doulton.

Tabbenor was keenly interested in art at school, but learning to use clay was an entirely new experience for him when he began his apprenticeship under Eric Griffiths, director of sculpture at Royal Doulton. It would take him many years to learn human anatomy and to recreate the body and the garments which clothe it. This knowledge was then carefully translated into a workable clay model.

In 1979, Tabbenor's first model, "All Aboard," was accepted for production and it was soon followed by popular pieces like "Prized Possessions," "Pride and Joy," and the "Auctioneer." All of these sculptures were offered through the Royal Doulton International Collectors Club. Another popular figure, "China Repairer," commemorates the long career of Doulton repairmen in Toronto, Canada.

Through the years, Tabbenor has designed a wide variety of collectibles, ranging from character jugs of an "American Fireman," "Henry V" and "Buffalo Bill," to a miniature collection of jugs based on Dickens' characters like "Oliver Twist," "Fagan" and "Mr. Bumble." Tabbenor also created a series of ladies for the *Vanity Fair* Collection and a number of small animals for the *Little Likeables* which were made in Beswick pottery.

DAVID TATE

At the age of ten, David Tate won a scholarship to Art School that he was destined never to take. Instead, he had to leave school to help support his mother.

Although he had many jobs in the intervening years, he always maintained his keen interest in art, often painting and drawing in his spare time. David's art has been shown in many art exhibitions, notably in the United Kingdom and Singapore.

During the mid 1970s, David's career took him into the world of the fiberglass industry, where with his thirst for knowledge and inquiring mind, he became a leading authority on molds and moldmaking. It is these skills that have proven most useful and contributed most to the success of Lilliput Lane Ltd.

The need for attention to detail and thorough research was a valuable lesson that Tate learned while assisting Robert Glen, a famous Kenyan artist, complete a sculpture of nine 25-foot horses at Las Colinas, between Dallas and Fort Worth.

It was during the 1960s that David first started drawing and painting the thatched cottages of the Oxfordshire and Buckinghamshire countryside where many of the people owning such homes possess David's originals.

David started Lilliput Lane in October, 1982, with just six other people and has been an integral part of its growth and success ever since. His fine sculptures and management style have won the company many accolades, culminating in 1988 with the inclusion of David Tate in the Queen of England's New Year's Honours List. David was made a Member of the Order of the British Em-

pire for his contribution to the success of Lilliput Lane and to the social obligation the company gave to the 500 plus employees, in areas where previously there was extremely high unemployment.

Today, David is at the pinnacle of his career, researching and developing new systems and designs to increase the company's competitive edge in the chosen field of collectibles.

David now spends many weeks traveling both the United Kingdom and the United States, researching and meeting his public. One of David's greatest satisfactions in life is seeing the joy his work brings to so many of the Lilliput Lane Collectors.

MICHAEL J. TAYLOR

Influenced by an artistic correspondence course and more formal training during his collegiate days, Gartlan USA artist Michael J. Taylor, has spent more than a dozen years doing commercial and advertising illustrations.

In addition, during summer months in his native Michigan, Taylor began creating drawings and paintings for local art shows in his spare time. With a passion for sports, his moonlighting efforts featured many local heroes. "Occasionally I was asked to draw, by parents, their son or daughter student athlete," he recalls.

In 1984 Taylor began creating original portraits of renowned athletes and

worked to get their autographs on such artworks. Taylor repeated such efforts, getting autographs on paintings of many professional athletes, including Magic Johnson, Kareem Abdul-Jabbar, members of the Detroit Tigers and the Chicago Cubs.

A shameless Cubs fan, Taylor's enthusiasm for sports and his talent as an artist attracted the critical eye of Gartlan USA. Subsequently, Taylor has created original art for limited edition plates of Kareem Abdul-Jabbar, Johnny Bench, Wayne Gretzky, John Wooden, Yogi Berra, Whitey Ford, Darryl Strawberry, Rod Carew and Brett and Bobby Hull, as well as the unique limited edition lithographs of Kareem Abdul-Jabbar, Darryl Strawberry and Isiah Thomas.

ANNALEE THORNDIKE

As the oldest of three daughters, Annalee Davis Thorndike was infatuated with dolls from early childhood. Raised in a large white house in a residential section of Concord, New Hampshire, she grew up in a world of enchantment, her mother an artist and her father a candy maker.

Annalee fondly remembers her childhood activities, particularly her winters spent sledding, skiing and skating. Her dolls are reminiscent of these pastimes, complete with whimsical faces, which display the utter delight experienced by each and every creation.

As a youngster, Annalee loved to make paper dolls and costume them. Her first doll was created at the age of nineteen and can be seen today at the Annalee Doll Museum.

Annalee married Chip Thorndike in 1941, and it was after World War II when their chicken farm failed that Annalee turned her doll hobby into a business — with Chip's assistance and eventually that of her family.

The first dolls created were used in displays at department stores like Jordan Marsh, Macy's and Bambergers. Ski dolls were also sold to the New Hampshire State Park and Recreation Department. As the demand for Annalee dolls grew, so did the variety and the facilities. Today, those early dolls, made in 1951-54 during the founding years of Annalee Mobilitee Dolls and originally selling for less than $10 in most instances, have soared over 3000% in resale value. In the last seven years, 600 early and more recent dolls have been sold at the annual Annalee Doll auction. The actual range of resale value is from $50 to $3,600 depending upon the doll. These auctions, now in their eighth year, and the nationwide interest and membership in the Annalee Doll Society, now over 23,000 strong, have established the Annalee doll as a viable collectible medium.

Today, Annalee creates her dolls at the "Factory in the Woods," nestled among mountains and lakes at the site of the original chicken farm. There are more than 200 dolls in the line, including Santas, ducks, mice, bears, frogs, historical figures and many more, and they are all involved in delightful activities — skiing, playing instruments, sledding, carolling.

What makes Annalee dolls so unique are their faces. As mentioned in an *Annalee* magazine, "She perfected the art of drawing faces by drawing her own face in the mirror in every possible expression...possibly the reason she is said to resemble her dolls. The smile, the grin, the impishness of childhood, the spontaneous response of boys and girls are all reflected in the faces and poses of Annalee Dolls."

SAMUEL J. TIMM

To his congregation in a small Wisconsin town, he's the Reverend Samuel Timm, but most people know him as simply "Sam." An avid trout fisherman, wingshooter, bowhunter and self-taught artist, Timm has spent the past fifteen years learning to paint the wildlife he loves.

His extraordinary success is evident by the number of wildlife awards his work has won. In 1990, Timm was the winner of the National Wildlife Federation Conservation Stamp Print and the 1989-90 Wisconsin Turkey Stamp competition. In 1988, he won the Wisconsin Duck Stamp competition and displayed his original painting at the prestigious Leigh Yawkey Woodson Art Museum. In 1985, he won both the Wisconsin Inland Trout Stamp and the Great Lakes Trout and Salmon Stamp competitions, the only artist to win all four of the state stamp design contests. Timm was named the 1985-86 Wisconsin Wildlife Artist of the Year when his painting "Old Farm Mascots — Black-capped Chickadees" was unanimously selected from a field of eighty-nine entries.

Timm's first venture into the limited edition collector's plate market was *Birds of the Seasons* for Edwin M. Knowles.

ANGELA TRIPI

Determination and a lifelong dream have brought Italy's Angela Tripi to her current status as a world-class artist with a growing U.S. collector following. Today, Tripi fulfills her aspirations by creating masterpiece sculptures in her workshop in Corso Vittorio Emanuele 450, in her birthplace — Palermo, Sicily. Tripi is gratified her *Museum Collection by Angela Tripi* for Roman, Inc. was named "Collectible of Show" sculpture at the 1991 Long Beach Collectibles Exposition. She still remembers the days when, out of filial duty, she abandoned her hopes of studying in art school. Instead, she applied her energies to learning accounting in order to help out with family finances.

Born in 1941, the gifted sculptor showed early signs of talent inherited from her father, a well known painter in his own right. Tripi painted her first childhood creative efforts; very soon, she crossed over to the medium that was to become second nature to her — sculpting in terra cotta. The young Sicilian's initial primitive figures were fired in a makeshift oven.

For fifteen years, Tripi toiled in an office by day, all the while contemplating working after hours at what she loved best — infusing life into sculptures in her garden haven. She devoted all her spare time to working clay... shaping...smoothing until she created a figurine satisfying to her demanding eye. As she created her masterpieces, Tripi drew on the source she knows so well — everyday Sicilian peasants.

Tripi comments on the expressive faces and stances of her wonderful characters, "I sculpt the characters I see in the wonderful faces around me."

Before coming to the perceptive eye of Ron Jedlinski, president of Roman, Tripi's renderings achieved recognition with major exhibitions in Italy, France and Japan in 1986. Tripi's first efforts for Roman in *The Museum Collection by Angela Tripi* were a series of biblical sculptures — Old Testament subjects — in 1988. Tripi contributed her first Judaic piece, "The Mentor," in 1990.

Following the success of this first collection, Tripi ventured into secular themes and a second figure in the Judaic series for seven new limited editions in 1991: "Christopher Columbus" — Tripi's salute to the explorer commemorating the 500th anniversary in 1992 of the discovery of America. "The Caddie," "Tee Time at St. Andrew's" and "A Gentleman's Game" are masterful representations of golf's early days. "St. Francis of Assisi" is her tribute to the patron saint of ecology. Following the warm reception given her first Jewish subject, Tripi presents the expressive second in this series — "The Fiddler."

With skill culled from her many years of working in her specialty of clay, Tripi sculpts her figures. After firing and painting by hand, she proceeds to clothe her creations in richly patterned garments inspired by 16th-century paintings. She carefully drapes and folds the fabric achieving the desired effect; then fixes the costumes to a hard finish utilizing a secret family formula dating back hundreds of years.

Tripi's delicate originals are then translated into durable poly resin by Roman, Inc. Every meticulous detail... even the look and texture of cloth...is faithfully captured. The artist personally approves each museum-quality reproduction Roman offers at affordable prices to admirers of fine art.

As Tripi continues to perfect her craft, she now has the added gratification of watching two of her four children following in her artistic footsteps with a capacity and passion reminiscent of the creative force that has driven Tripi all her life.

THORNTON UTZ

The limited edition field has added an exciting new dimension to the many-faceted career of portraitist, fine art painter, illustrator and sculptor Thornton Utz.

Along with Norman Rockwell, Utz provided scores of cover paintings for *The Saturday Evening Post*. His career as an illustrator spanned several decades and included work for nearly every major magazine in the United States.

And during the past ten years or so, Thornton Utz has become known for his portraits and fine art paintings. Utz's appealing style that combines an impressionistic, free-flowing background and a very realistic facial expression has won him international praise.

His list of famous portrait subjects includes the late Princess Grace of Monaco, Astronaut Alan Shepherd, Rosalyn and Amy Carter and other members of the Carter Family.

In 1979, Utz and The Hamilton Collection introduced the first issue in his first series of limited edition plates — a piece called "A Friend in the Sky." The plate won the title of "Top First Issue of 1979" in a poll of dealers and collectors.

Later Utz and Hamilton plate offerings include an annual child-subject series which began in 1981, the *Carefree*

Days series of boy subjects which premiered in 1982, the *Summer Days of Childhood* series of boy-girl subjects which debuted in 1983, a commemorative plate titled "Princess Grace," and Mother's Day issues for 1983, 1984 and 1985.

Another popular Utz plate collection was entitled *Springtime of Life*. It was the creation of Reco International, in cooperation with The Hamilton Collection. Signed and numbered limited edition prints by Utz are published by Mill Pond Press Inc.

DOLORES VALENZA

Gorham has the distinction of working with one of America's most elite porcelain artists, Dolores Valenza. Her works have been exhibited in galleries throughout the United States and have been presented to celebrities such as Pope John Paul, Queen Elizabeth and former first lady, Betty Ford.

In partnership with Gorham, Ms.

Valenza has created her very first doll collection, *Childhood Memories*. Her exceptional talent captures the innocence and charm of childhood and portrays four toddlers enjoying special moments with their favorite playtime companions. Each doll includes unusually lifelike details, including lifelike eyelashes, finely sculptured hands and fine fabrics of silky stripes, satins and laces. And, each has a special armature that allows the collector to bend and pose the dolls' arms to 'hold' her playtime companion. Beautifully gift boxed, they are hallmarked with the artist's signature and come with a certificate of authenticity from Gorham.

JOAN BERG VICTOR

Joan Berg Victor was born and raised in Chicago. As a child, she spent summers in a big old Victorian home on the shores of Lake Michigan, looking at the wonderful array of old things that had belonged to her grandmother.

After graduating from high school, Ms. Victor attended Newcomb College in New Orleans — the women's college of Tulane University. Later, she earned her master's degree with honors in fine arts from Yale University.

Ms. Victor then moved to New York where she married and began doing magazine and book illustrations. Eventually, she began writing and illustrating children's books. As her children grew, the level of Victor's writing became more mature.

The artist's interest in collecting antiques also is evident in her stories of life at the turn-of-the-century in her mythical village of Pleasantville.

Ms. Victor's *Pleasantville 1893* figurine series captures the warmth and simplicity of small town American life before the turn-of-the-century. Here, both the joy and sorrows of everyday life have been carefully chronicled. Made of bisque porcelain for Flambro Imports, each of the lighted buildings has its own personality and accompanying story written by Joan Berg Victor.

MAURICE WIDEMAN

Maurice Wideman, the creator of the delightful *American Collection* from the John Hine Studios, Inc., was born in Aldershot, Hampshire, England to Canadian parents serving in the military during World War II. Raised in Canada, Wideman frequently traveled throughout the United States as a child with his parents, visiting relatives from Maine to California.

Wideman earned a university degree in sculpting and worked in a number of art-related jobs in the Canadian Northwest. Later, Wideman traveled throughout America before returning to Ontario, where he was the art director for the Ministry of Agriculture and Food. It was a handful of miniature frontier buildings that Wideman created after his stateside travels which brought him to the attention of John Hine.

Wideman spent a year working in the John Hine Studios in England, developing the first in a series of miniature replicas of America's homes and public buildings. Introduced on July 4, 1990, Wideman's *American Collection* reveals the rich diversity expressed in American architecture and culture. His first annual piece, introduced on July 4, 1991, is a replica of "Paul Revere's home," the first Wideman piece to be based on an actual structure.

ABBIE WILLIAMS

The pattern of Abbie Williams' life and career makes a perfect case for believers in the role of fate in shaping our destiny.

If her great grandparents had not honeymooned in East Boothbay, Maine in the early 1900s, and if Williams' family had not established an annual tradition of spending summers in the small coastal town, the artist might never have come to love this area enough to make it her permanent residence in the early 1970s.

East Boothbay became the setting where the paths of two talented child portrait artists, Frances Hook and Williams, met for the first time and became good friends. Visits were spent sharing their lifelong love of art and working together. The result? With Hook's encouragement, Williams successfully resumed her career in child portraiture.

Williams had studied art and design at Moore College, Philadelphia, but marriage and raising a family had taken priority over her aspirations for several years. The need to become self-supporting for the sake of her family, provided added impetus to Williams' re-entry into the world of full-time artists. Williams notes, "...for me to meet someone like Frances who was making a living at her work was really inspiring."

Through Hook, Williams obtained valuable illustration and portrait commissions. Hook arranged for Williams' introduction to Ron Jedlinski of Roman, Inc. The resultant relationship with Roman has brought a series of collectible and commemorative plates featuring heart-warming portraits of her favorite subject — children.

Williams' initial collector plate series, *The Magic of Childhood*, portrays the special friendships only children and animals have. She followed with two Christian-themed series using youngsters in moving depictions. The first collection is composed of eight illustrations of phrases of *The Lord's Prayer*. The second series, *Love's Prayer*, is based on 1 Corinthians 13. Each aspect of love is illustrated with a sweet child's vignette. These collections are also available through The Hamilton Collection.

Her ability to capture the spontaneity of children in her art extends to a series of sculptured music boxes, *Children of the Month*; a special March of Dimes fund-raising edition, *A Time to Laugh*, in association with The Bradford Exchange; and "Mary, Mother of the Carpenter" lithograph presented to John Paul II at the Vatican. This prolific artist's newest efforts for Roman include *Legacy of Love* child's commemorative and the wonderfully conceived *Bless This Child* for Black American collectors and gift-givers. New plate series available early in 1992 devoted to babies' first birthdays and "firsts" in babie's lives will be titled *God Bless You, Little One*.

Williams comments on her art: "I've always been interested in working with light. I try to use lighting in my work to create a sense of color and life."

Because "Most artists operate in an isolated world," according to Williams, she has organized "The Artist's Network" on a national level. Since 1989, this supportive organization has helped alleviate the "isolation" artists experience because "they don't benefit from the emotional support most on-the-job workers get."

The strength of her work, while sensitive to the subtleties of her subjects, draws collectors to Williams' art in increasing numbers. It has also earned her an appointment to the prestigious Pastel Society of America bringing about realization of her late mentor Frances Hook's prediction, "You have the potential of becoming one of America's great artists."

ELLEN WILLIAMS

As one of the foremost giftware artists, Ellen Williams combines her interest in historic fashion and talent for design to create superlative collectibles.

Born in Indiana, Williams was the only one of five children in her family to pursue art as her life's work. After studying fine arts and design at Indiana University, Williams moved to Chicago to

embark on her successful career. After twenty years in giftware design, several of them as vice-president of product development for a major gift and collectibles firm, Williams formed her own design company, EHW Enterprises, Inc.

Her bridal collections have reached out to the hearts of America, making her creations the choice of countless brides and wedding gift-givers nationwide. Television's Delta Burke of *Designing Women* and Gerald McRainey of *Major Dad* chose the musical wedding couple figurine from Williams' *Congratulations* Collection to top their wedding cake.

Williams' *Classic Brides of the Century*™ collection depicts bridal fashion as a reflection of historical and social trends from 1900 to 1990. The artist devoted much time to meticulous research of historic clothing design and concerned herself with each detail to ensure her exacting standards would be met. "I might make fifty sketches for each bride just to get each gesture to my satisfaction," she comments. Williams' desire to authenticate the designs of each bride's decade and insistence on high standards were rewarded when the series bowed to collector accolades. These exquisite, porcelain bisque sculptures further distinguished themselves by earning 1989 "Collectible of Show" honors at the California International Collectible Exposition.

Williams expanded this concept into limited edition bridal dolls based on the popular *Classic Brides of the Century*™ figurines. "Flora" — the 1900s Bride collectors' doll walked down the proverbial aisle in 1991. She is the reflection of all a woman wishes to be on her wedding day. The second in this charming doll collection "Jennifer" — the 1980s Bride debuted late in 1991. Both limited edition dolls are produced by Roman, Inc. under the hallmark of W.S. George Company.

Earlier limited edition dolls created by Williams for Roman include "Noelle," "Chelsea" and "Carole" — *Christmas Annual Edition* dolls — and "Rebecca," a charming traditional bridal doll. Another Ellen Williams collectible series of four *Victorian Mother and Daughter* musical figurines debuted in 1990 with The San Francisco Music Box Company.

GERALD WILLIAMS

Gerald Williams has set a goal to portray cats in the environment and historical context they so richly deserve. Williams was raised in Davenport, Iowa, "Where the American West begins." After service in the Navy, he received his BFA degree from the School of the Art Institute of Chicago, where he studied under renowned painter Paul Wieghardt.

A career in advertising coexisted with one in painting. His subjects were the cities of this country and Europe, and were added to the collections of companies such as Western Electric, Teletype Corporation, LaSalle Casualty Company and private collections throughout the Midwest.

It was when he painted an oil of his daughter-in-law's two Russian Blue cats for her birthday, that he became intrigued with the cat. He felt the felines were due a new perspective and he pursued that idea. He researched their origins and discovered the enchanting allure of the cat that could be bold with new insight.

Leaving advertising and concentrating on this interest, the many breeds of the world have appeared on his canvases. Williams has created for Kaiser Porcelain the *American Cat* and the *International Cat Plate* Collections.

DAVID WINTER

The son of an army captain and internationally famous sculptress Faith Winter, David Winter was born in Catterrick, Yorkshire, England. Winter's mother is renowned for her Falklands War Memorial, a critically acclaimed bust of Princess Anne, and the recently unveiled Statue of Lord Dowding, Commander-In-Chief of The Royal Air Force's fighter Command during World War II. Originally from Ireland, Mrs. Winter's family includes numerous architects which may help explain the life work of her son; combining three-dimensional art with miniature architecture in the creation of his David Winter Cottages.

Winter studied sculpture in school where he developed a keen appreciation of the lives of his ancestors. When he met John Hine in 1978, he found a friend and partner who shared his enthusiasm for the buildings and way of life of the past. In 1979, Winter and Hine developed and crafted the first David Winter cottage — "The Millhouse."

Before long, many English shops were requesting the miniature cottages from the fledgling firm. Operating from an old coal shed, Winter did the artwork while Hine concentrated on selling the cottages inspired by beloved old buildings of the English countryside.

In the studio, Winter becomes completely absorbed in his work. He seems to imagine the movements of the people who might be inside a cottage he is preparing, whether they be royalty, lords of the manor, or simply peasants. He insists that every window frame, brick and roof tile be completely authentic to the period. Since many of the buildings are old, Winter includes crooked, old beams, warped roofs and twisted chimneys just as they might be found in a tour of historical Great Britain.

Winter often makes his own tools for sculpting to ensure that he can achieve the effects that he seeks. Some tools are crafted from bits of wire, while others involve matchsticks or bits of wood. Once his wax models are complete, the Studios of John Hine cast, trim and paint each cottage by hand according to Winter's own careful instructions. Since the first cottage was introduced over a decade ago, David Winter has created an impressive range including castles, manor houses, shops, mills, cottages and hamlets of many sizes and styles.

David Winter and John Hine Studios, Inc. have received numerous awards for their contribution to the limited edition collectibles field. In 1988, the firm proudly received The Queen's Award for Export Achievement. Winter has also been honored many times by NALED. Most recently, he won Figurine of the Year award for "A Christmas Carol" at the 1990 South Bend Collectibles Exposition. He also received First Runner-Up for the Collectible of the Year that same evening. The awards continued in 1991, with the "Cottage of the Show" award at the Long Beach, California International Collectible Exposition for Winter's 1991 Christmas cottage, "Fred's Home: 'A Merry Christmas, Uncle Ebeneezer,' said Scrooge's nephew Fred, 'and a Happy New Year'."

DAVID WRIGHT

While many artists are willing to research the subjects in the relative safety of the library, David Wright prefers to step back in time and travel throughout the West just as the early pioneers and fur traders must have done more than two centuries ago.

Instead of choosing a well-appointed motor home, Wright and his companions travel by horseback with buckskin clothing and camping gear, just like those used by the trailblazers on their treks across the western frontier. In this

way, Wright gains a special understanding for life on the American Frontier.

Born in Kentucky and raised in Tennessee, Wright grew up in the country where he learned to hunt and fish. His outdoor experiences have provided him with a special feel for nature. After studying art in Europe, Wright spent a number of years as a designer and illustrator. However, Wright turned his full attention to fine art in 1978. Since then his range of subjects has grown to include characters from the Old West — explorers, hunters, trappers, mountain men and Native Americans.

Wright's limited edition prints for Grey Stone Press have done extremely well on the secondary market. One of his print subjects was Sacajawea, the young and beautiful Indian guide for the Lewis and Clark expedition. Wright was so fascinated with the Shoshoni woman that when he began to consider subjects for his *Noble American Indian Women* plate series for The Hamilton Collection, he chose Sacajawea as the subject of the first plate. Other issues in the collection include "Pocahontas," "Minnehaha," "Pine Leaf," "Lily of the Mohawk" and "White Rose."

LYNNE YANCHA

Lynne Yancha enters the collectibles field through collector plates. The porcelain allows the pure, translucent hues of her watercolors to shine through.

Ms. Yancha is an accomplished watercolor artist, achieving national status in 1986 through her induction into The American Watercolor Society. Twice she has won their coveted Mary S. Litt Medal of Honor.

Beginning with an idea with which she feels "emotionally involved," Ms. Yancha romanticizes that idea. As a mother, she finds herself "emotionally involved" with the mother-and-child subjects that introduced her to the collectibles field.

In the creation process, the artist begins pre-studies of her subject with a camera session. "I love the art of photography and consider the process as important and challenging as the painting itself." In the photography session, Ms. Yancha shoots from all conceivable angles. Then, after assembling and piecing photos together, she does quick thumbnail sketches to work out the basic problems of composition and design.

The paintings themselves are done in stages of washes and layers of color. "The real magic begins in the final stages of my work," Ms. Yancha says. "Now I keep working on an area with detail and washes until I am satisfied with the depth and richness. It all seems to pull together and read like poetry."

It is this "poetry," the fluid movement of an artist's spirit into a painting, that characterizes the work of Lynne Yancha. In the over two decades she has been painting, her work has continually evolved. Yancha admits, "I am filled with wonder at how far I've come and am delighted with the prospects for the future."

Ms. Yancha's artwork is licensed through the Balliol Corporation.

Collector Clubs

Artists and Companies Invite Collectors to Add An Extra Dimension of Pleasure to Their Hobby

Many collectors want to learn more about their favorite artists and companies. And there is no better way to enhance their collecting experience than by joining collector clubs! Nearly every club welcomes its members with a beautiful membership kit and the opportunity to purchase exclusive "members-only" collectibles. Listed below are several nationally sponsored collector clubs. If you know of a club which has not been mentioned here, please contact Collectors' Information Bureau so that we may list it in our next update.

Adorables Collectors Society
71-73 Weyman Avenue
New Rochelle, NY 10805
(914) 633-3777
Annual membership fee: $7.50

Collectors can enjoy the whimsically sculpted cats and teddy bear collection by creator Peter Fagan. Club members receive newsletters, a club pin and the opportunity to purchase collector club exclusive pieces.

All God's Children Collector's Club
P.O. Box 8367
Gadsden, AL 35902
(205) 549-0340
Annual membership fee: $15.00

This collector club offers its members a subscription to its quarterly magazine, *All God's Children*, a membership card, a personal checklist and an opportunity to purchase collector club exclusive figurines.

American Bell Association
P.O. Box 172
Shoreham, VT 05770
(802) 897-7371
Annual membership fee: $20.00;
Couple-$22.00

Bell collectors will enjoy membership in the American Bell Association. Members receive a year's subscription to *Bell Tower Magazine* which includes six issues and one special issue. Association members also have the opportunity to attend an annual bell collectors convention. Information on local chapters and their events is also provided.

Angel Collectors' Club of America
c/o Mrs. Mary Winemiller
2706 Greenacre Drive
Sebring, FL 33872
(813) 385-8426
Annual membership fee: $10.00

This national organization is geared toward those who collect angels and enjoy sharing their hobby with fellow angel collectors. Upon joining, collectors receive a membership card, a quarterly newsletter "Halo Everybody!," an invitation to the biannual convention and the opportunity to participate in several additional activities.

Annalee Doll Society
P.O. Box 1137
Meredith, NH 03253-1137
1-800-433-6557 In NH (603) 279-6542
Annual membership fee: $19.50

Members receive a 7" Logo Kid, subscription to *THE COLLECTOR*, a full-color quarterly magazine, membership card, and pin. Members also have the exclusive opportunity to purchase signed and numbered limited editions. Other benefits include free admission to the Annalee Doll Museum and an invitation to the annual Barbecue/Auction weekend.

Annalee Society members are invited to an annual Barbecue every summer which includes a tour of the facility, an auction and much more. Pictured is Annalee, who starts the bidding for the artist proof of "The Thorndike Chicken."

G. Armani Society
300 Mac Lane
Keasbey, Woodbridge Township, NJ 08832
(908) 417-0330
Annual membership fee: 1st year: $37.50;
Renewal $25.00

Members receive a membership card, subscription to *Armani Review*, binder, membership plaque and gift. Members also have the opportunity to purchase members-only collectibles.

Artaffects® Perillo Collectors Club™
Box 98
Staten Island, NY 10307
(718) 948-6767
Annual membership fee: $35.00

Collectors who enjoy award-winning artist, Gregory Perillo's portrayal of Indians will appreciate the quality of his collectors club as well. Member benefits include a full color catalog, three-ring binder, membership card, invitations to personal appearances, a subscription to "Drumbeats," the official Perillo newsletter, secondary market fact sheet *Arta-Quote* and a free membership gift. Members also have the exclusive opportunity to purchase members-only offerings and receive advance notice of new introductions.

The Marty Bell Collector's Society

9424 Eton Avenue
Chatsworth, CA 91311
(818) 700-0754
Annual membership fee: $30.00

Members receive a free signed and numbered lithograph, the quarterly newsletter, "The Sound of Bells," a membership card, a map of England indicating Marty's cottage locations and a Cloisonne Collector's Society pin. Members also receive a voucher to purchase the special members-only issue. Other benefits for members are gallery tours and priority announcements and invitations about upcoming events occurring around the country.

The Belleek Collectors' Society

144 W. Britannia Street
Taunton, MA 02780
1-800-822-1824
Annual membership fee: $20.00

Members receive a membership certificate, full color catalog, information on all local Belleek Collectors' Society chapter meetings and local dealers and a subscription to *The Belleek Collector*, the illustrated quarterly society journal. Members also have the exclusive opportunity to purchase Limited Edition Collectors' Society pieces available only to members. Members also receive an invitation to visit the Pottery and take the yearly Belleek Collectors' Tour — a twelve-day tour of Ireland.

The Boehm Porcelain Society

P.O. Box 5051
Trenton, NJ 08638
1-800-257-9410
Annual membership fee: $15.00

Club members receive the "Advisory" newsletter, membership card, literature about products and upcoming activities, and an opportunity to purchase a collector society exclusive porcelain piece.

Maud Humphrey Bogart Collectors' Club

P.O. Box 4009
Compton, CA 90224-4009
(708) 956-5401
Annual membership fee: $37.50

Together, collectors will retrace their steps through this nostalgic era as seen through the eyes of this gifted artist. The membership kit includes an exclusive club figurine, a year's subscription to the "Victorian Times" newsletter, a Club notebook, a full-color catalog featuring Hamilton Gifts' complete Maud Humphrey Bogart collection, a Maud Humphrey Bogart Collectors' Club Membership Card and an invitation to purchase a Members Only figurine.

Maud Humphrey Bogart Collectors' Club

The Bradley Collectible Club

1424 North Spring Street
Los Angeles, CA 90012
(213) 221-4162
Annual membership fee: $7.00

Members receive a quarterly news bulletin, Membership Card, catalog, list of club headquarter stores and the opportunity to purchase a collector club, exclusive doll.

The Byers' Choice Club

Wayside Country Store
1015 Boston Post Rd Rt. 20
Marlborough, MA 01752
(508) 481-3458
Annual membership fee: $5.00

Members receive a year's subscription to the Club's quarterly newsletter which includes the history of the Carolers. Members also receive redemption cards for special discounts. In September, members are invited to participate in the special event Dickens-of-a-Day combined with an auction.

Cabbage Patch Kids® Collectors Club

P.O. Box 714
Cleveland, GA 30528
(404) 865-2171
Annual membership fee: $25.00

Doll collectors who join this club will receive a year's subscription to "Limited Edition," the bi-monthly newsletter, membership card, pin and customized binder. Members also have the opportunity to purchase special club offerings.

Cat's Meow Collectors Club

2163 Great Trails Dr. Dept. C
Wooster, OH 44691
(216) 264-1377
Annual membership fee: 1st year: $22.00; Renewal: $20.00

New members receive an official Club notebook with color brochure, Club T-shirt, an ID card with membership number, the Collector's Buying List and subscription to the club newsletter, "The Village Mews." Members who renew receive a gift. Members also receive exclusive members-only, Cats Meow pieces and a redemption form for the annual series.

Cat's Meow Collectors Club

The Chilmark Gallery

The Lance Corporation
321 Central Street
Hudson, MA 01749
(508) 568-1401
Annual membership fee: Free upon registering a piece of Chilmark sculpture

The Gallery offers information about limited edition fine pewter sculpture. Registered owners receive quarterly issues of *Chilmark Report* and the annually updated *Aftermarket Reports*. Owners also receive Redemption Certificates for registered collectors only sculptures.

Club ANRI

55 Pacella Park Dr.
Randolph, MA 02368-1795
(617) 961-3575
Annual membership fee: $25.00

Members benefits include a binder, wooden plaque, the color newsletter published tri-annually, announcements of upcoming events, collectors guide and an annual value survey of selected retired woodcarvings. Members-only figures are also offered.

Club ANRI

Malcolm Cooper Pub Club

The Studios and Workshops of
John Hine Limited
2 Hillside Road
Aldershot, Hampshire
GU11 3NB England
(0252) 334672
Annual membership fee: U.S.- $10.00

Collectors of Malcolm Coopers' Great British Pubs will be kept up-to-date with all the latest news about Malcolm Cooper Pubs upon joining the Club. Pub Club Members receive four issues of the *Pub Club Magazine* plus the option to purchase items available exclusively to members.

Crystal Zoo Collectors' Club

4824 Sterling Drive
Boulder, CO 80301
(303) 449-6771
Annual membership fee: $25.00

Each membership kit includes a beautiful crystal "thank-you" creation, a Membership Card, a beautiful Charter Member Certificate, copies of the club newsletter, "Facets," a registry of the complete *Crystal Zoo* Collection, Redemption Coupons for exclusive figurine offerings and an invitation to special club activities and promotions.

Lowell Davis Farm Club

55 Pacella Park Dr.
Randolph, MA 02368-1795
(417) 358-1943
Annual membership fee: $25.00

Members receive a members-only figurine, official Club cap, membership card, Lowell Davis Collector's Guide and Dealer's Listing, a subscription to the *Lowell Davis Farm Club Gazette*, and coloring book written and illustrated by Lowell himself. Members also have the opportunity to acquire exclusive members-only figurines. Benefits also include a special invitation to visit Lowell Davis at his farm and announcements of in-store appearances by Lowell Davis.

Lowell Davis Farm Club

Down's Collectors Club

2200 S. 114 Street
Milwaukee, WI 53227
(414) 327-3300

Duncan Royale Collectors Club

1141 S. Acacia Ave.
Fullerton, CA 92631
(714) 879-1360
Annual membership fee: $30.00

Members receive a porcelain bell ornament, an attractive cloisonne lapel pin, a subscription to the quarterly newsletter "Royale Courier," an elegant binder, a membership card, a Charter Member Certificate and a catalog of Duncan Royale Limited Editions. Members also have the opportunity to purchase exclusive members-only figurines. Members are also extended an invitation to travel with the Club to the "lands behind the stories...".

Duncan Royale Collectors Club

EKJ Collectors Society

P.O. Box 93507
Atlanta, GA 30377-0507
(404) 352-1381
Annual membership fee: Initial: $25.00; Renewal: $15.00.

Members receive the Society publication, *EKJOURNAL*, a ring binder for the Journals, a lapel pin, membership card, special gift and a "Members Only" plaque. Members also receive the opportunity to purchase exclusive merchandise to Society Members and a "Members Only" figurine. Free registration and Certificates of Authenticity for EKJ Collectibles and invitations to special club-sponsored events are also benefits the members receive.

Enchantica Collectors Club

Munro Collectibles
P.O. Box 200
Waterville, OH 43566
(419) 878-0034
Annual membership fee: $25.00

Adventurers who decide to embark on this latest voyage into The Enchantica experience will receive a membership pack which includes: a free Enchantica piece, a pen bearing the Enchantica Logo and Collectors Club inscription, and a Membership Card. Members of the Enchantica Collectors Club will receive periodic newsletters packed with news, views, illustrations and information including details of two specially commissioned figurines available only to members each year. Other benefits include sneak previews of new characters, new ideas, new story lines and first chance to buy special figurines.

The Enesco Memories of Yesterday Collectors' Society
One Enesco Plaza
P.O. Box 245
Elk Grove Village, IL 60009-0245
(708) 640-5200
Annual membership fee: $17.50

Collectors are invited to learn more about the exquisite porcelain bisque Collection inspired by the drawings of famous British artist, Mabel Lucie Attwell.

The Welcome Kit includes a Society porcelain bisque figurine, a complete Gift Registry featuring every subject in the *Memories of Yesterday* Collection, the *Sharing Memories*...quarterly publication, a Membership Card and the opportunity to purchase a members only offering.

The Enesco Memories of Yesterday Collectors' Society

The Enesco Musical Society
One Enesco Plaza
P.O. Box 245
Elk Grove Village, IL 60009-0245
(708) 640-5200
Annual membership fee: $10.00

Collectors can expand their knowledge of the history and development of music through the ages and become better acquainted with the Enesco *Small World of Music*™ Collection. Upon joining, members will receive an official Enesco Musical Society Membership Card, a subscription to the quarterly newsletter, periodic news bulletins sent only to members and the opportunity to purchase a members only musical offering.

The Enesco Precious Moments Birthday Club
One Enesco Plaza
P.O. Box 1529
Elk Grove Village, IL 60009-1529
(708) 640-5200
Annual membership fee: $13.50

Collectors are invited to celebrate a special birthday in an extra special way.

Birthday Club Members receive a personalized ready-to-frame Certificate of Membership, a year's subscription to the *Good News Parade*, a Happy Birthday card mailed directly from the Club Headquarters, and the invitation to acquire limited edition Birthday Club Members Only porcelain bisque subjects.

The Enesco Precious Moments Collectors' Club
One Enesco Plaza
P.O. Box 1466
Elk Grove Village, IL 60009-1466
(708) 640-5200
Annual membership fee: $22.50

Upon joining, collectors will learn more about the *Precious Moments* Collection and its talented creator, Sam Butcher. Club members receive a "Symbol of Friendship" figurine, the Club's full-color quarterly publication, *GOODNEWSLETTER*, a Club binder, a personal copy of the full color *Pocket Guide to the Enesco Precious Moments Collection*, the official *Gift Registry*, a Club Membership Card and the privilege of acquiring two members only figurines.

The Enesco Precious Moments Collectors' Club

Fenton Art Glass Collectors of America, Inc. (FAGCA)
P.O. Box 384
Williamstown, WV 26187
(304) 375-6196
Annual membership fee: $15.00
($2 Associate — for each additional membership in the same household)

For collectors of Fenton Art Glass this club offers the chance to learn more about one of America's great heritages, the glass-making industry, and Fenton Art Glass in particular. Members enjoy an annual convention usually in the first week of August which is held in Williamstown, West Virginia and historic Marietta, Ohio. The week-long gala includes a private guided tour of the Fenton factory, seminars, special sales and a banquet and auction of unusual glass created especially for FAGCA members.

The Fontanini Collectors' Club
c/o Roman, Inc., Dept. 596
555 Lawrence Avenue
Roselle, IL 60172-1599
(708) 529-3000
Annual membership fee: $19.50

Members receive an exclusive gift figurine, a subscription to "The Fontanini Collector," the quarterly newsletter, a care guide, a Fontanini Story Card, membership card, and portfolio. Members also have the exclusive opportunity to purchase members-only figurines and receive special invitations to meet members of the Fontanini family when they visit America.

The exclusive gift figurine for members, "I Found Him," was just one of many benefits available to collectors joining The Fontanini Collectors' Club in 1991.

Franklin Heirloom Doll Club
The Franklin Mint
Franklin Center, PA 19091
(215) 459-6553
Annual membership fee: Complimentary

The Franklin Heirloom Doll Collectors Society is dedicated to the tradition of doll collecting. Society members receive a quarterly newsletter, "The Doll Collector," that keeps doll collectors up-to-date with the latest doll information and includes columns on collectors, how to recognize quality collectible dolls, doll artists and designers. Members also have use of an exclusive toll-free "doll" number and are eligible for valuable gift premiums with their purchases of Franklin Heirloom Dolls.

Franklin Mint Collectors Society
The Franklin Mint
Franklin Center, PA 19091
(215) 459-6553
Annual membership fee: Complimentary; fee for minted card

Founded in 1970, The Franklin Mint Collectors Society has grown to be one of the largest organized groups of collectors in the world. Members receive a number of exciting benefits at no cost. Every Collectors Society member receives biannual issues of The Franklin Mint's own publication, *ALMANAC*. The Society offers an annual minted membership card for members to purchase. Each year, members are offered the opportunity to join fellow Society members on an exciting vacation trip designed especially for the Collectors Society.

Gartlan USA's Collectors' League
15502 Graham St.
Huntington Beach, CA 92649
(714) 897-0090
Annual membership fee: $30.00

Sports enthusiasts will learn more about their favorite sports heroes from Gartlan USA. Members receive a one-year subscription to the "Collectors' Illustrated" newsletter, a members-only collectible gift, notification of Gartlan USA new issues before the open market and certificate of membership. Collectors may also purchase a members-only figurine.

Graebner Collectors Society
c/o Studio On The Square
P.O. Box 125
Lodi, OH 44254
(216) 948-4607
Annual membership fee: $20.00

Society members who enjoy Diane's simple but elegant portrayal of family love will receive a small print remarked by the artist, a Certificate of Membership, the latest information on new releases and notification of personal appearances by artist Diane Graebner.

Gutmann Collectors Club
1353 Elm Avenue
Lancaster, PA 17603
(717) 293-2780
Annual membership fee: Initial-$25.00; Renewal-$17.50

Members receive a gift figurine for joining and an option to purchase a members-only figurine, the quarterly newsletter, members only offers, and an Artist Information Service.

Jan Hagara Collectors Club
40114 Industrial Park Circle
Georgetown, TX 78626
(512) 863-9499
Annual membership fee: Initial-$22.50; Renewal-$17.50

Collectors who enjoy Jan Hagara's warm and tender child-subject art will also enjoy her collectors club, which offers a free miniature figurine to each member, in addition to a tiffany cloisonne membership pin, custom three-ring binder, membership card, subscription to the club's quarterly newsletter and the opportunity to purchase special members-only offerings. Club members are also invited to attend the annual national meeting each Spring.

Hallmark Keepsake Ornament Collector's Club
P.O. Box 412734
Kansas City, MO 64141-2734
Annual membership fee: $20.00

Ornament collectors will enjoy an array of club benefits within this club's membership kit. Benefits include a cloisonne membership pin, Keepsake of Membership ornament, "Collector's Courier" newsletter, Keepsake Ornament Treasury binder, club folder, *Dream Book* highlighting the year's ornaments, and the opportunity to purchase members-only and limited edition ornaments exclusively available through the club.

Hand & Hammer Collectors Club
2610 Morse Lane
Woodbridge, VA 22192
1-800-SILVERY or (703) 491-4866
Annual membership fee: Free

Members receive the quarterly newsletter "Silver Tidings" and an ornament collectors guide. Members also have the opportunity to purchase special releases.

Edna Hibel Society
P.O. Box 9721
Coral Springs, FL 33075
(407) 848-9663
Annual membership fee: $20.00

Admirers of Edna Hibel honor her humanitarian achievements, and enjoy her art in many media, including paintings, drawings, lithographs, serigraphs and sculptures. Society members will receive a free Hibel commemorative poster, personalized membership card, "Hibeletter" newsletter, invitations to cultural events, society tours, private tour of the Hibel Museum of Art, advance previews of Hibel artworks and the exclusive opportunity to acquire members-only limited edition Society collectibles.

M.I. Hummel Club
Goebel Plaza, P.O. Box 11
Pennington, NJ 08534-0011
1-800-666-CLUB
Annual membership fee: U.S.-$35.00, Canada-$47.50

Members receive a gift figurine, a year's subscription to *INSIGHTS*, the Club's colorful quarterly magazine, membership card, information on Local Chapters of the M.I. Hummel Club and Club services such as the Research Department and Collectors' Market. Members also have the opportunity to purchase the Special Club Exclusive fig-

M.I. Hummel Club new member kit

urines. Members are able to participate in Club trips to Europe with a members-only tour of the Goebel factory.

Jerri Collector's Society
651 Anderson St.
Charlotte, NC 28205
(704) 333-3211
Annual membership fee: $10.00

Members receive a Collector's Society pin, membership card and the quarterly newsletter. Members also have the opportunity to purchase an annual members-only doll. Other members benefits include early mail-ins on new dolls and an invitation to the annual convention of the Collector's Society which is a weekend event including factory tours, a banquet and an auction.

Krystonia Collector's Club
110 E. Ellsworth
Ann Arbor, MI 48108
(313) 677-3510
Annual membership fee: $20.00

Collectors of fantasy figurines will learn more about this popular subject as a Krystonia member. Members receive a complimentary gift and newsletter. Members also have the opportunity to purchase collectors only pieces.

"Dragon's Play" was the 1991 collector club exclusive figurine offered to members of the Krystonia Collectors Club.

Sandra Kuck Collectors Club
P.O. Box 28
Lisbon, OH 44432
(216) 726-5750
Annual membership fee: $30.00

Upon joining, members receive a limited edition figurine, a subscription to the biannual newsletter "The Artists Diary," and the opportunity to purchase Sandra Kuck collectibles for members-only through selected redemption centers.

Lalique Society of America
400 Veteran's Blvd.
Carlstadt, NJ 07072
1-800-CRISTAL
Annual membership fee: $30.00

Connoisseurs of fine crystal will appreciate the special benefits afforded Lalique Society members. They include a subscription to the quarterly *LALIQUE* Magazine, an enrollment gift: an embossed print of a Rene Lalique jewelry design signed by Madame Lalique, invitations to exclusive society events and chartered trips, as well as access to annual limited edition, members-only crystal designs.

Lawtons Collector's Guild
P.O. Box 969
Turlock, CA 95381
(209) 632-3655
Annual membership fee: Initial: $15.00; Renewal: $5.00

Members receive a membership card, cloisonne Lawtons logo pin, a year subscription to *Lawtons Collector's Guild Quarterly*, three-ring binder logo and a set of postcards featuring the current collection of Lawtons Dolls. Members also have the opportunity to purchase the special doll designed for Guild members only.

Ron Lee Collector's Club
2180 Agate Court
Simi Valley, CA 93065
(805) 520-8474 or (805) 520-8482
Annual membership fee: $25.00

Known for his outstanding renderings of clowns, Ron Lee makes available to clown enthusiasts, the opportunity to join his club. Each enrollee receives a special clown sculpture gift, a beautiful certificate printed and signed by the artist, a Club ID Card, the "Collectible News" newsletter, the opportunity to purchase Special Club Novelty Items, full-color pictures of Lee's latest work, an autographed greeting card and the opportunity to purchase a Ron Lee sculpture designed exclusively for club members.

LEGENDS Collectors Society
2665-D Park Center Dr.
Simi Valley, CA 93065
(805) 520-9660
Annual membership fee: Free upon purchase of sculpture

Collectors who enjoy exceptional fine art sculptures will want to learn more about LEGENDS and their distinctive Mixed Media™ masterworks. Members receive monthly mailers that contain new release information and newsletter. Members benefits also include previews of new sculptures before open release, secondary market registration, acquisition and sale. Members may purchase a collector club exclusive figurine annually.

Lilliput Lane Collectors' Club
c/o Gift Link, Inc.
The Oakland Building
9052 Old Annapolis Road
Columbia, MD 21045
(301) 964-2202
Annual membership fee: $25.00

Collectors joining the Lilliput Lane Collectors' Club will receive a free cottage, membership card and complimentary gift as well as a subscription to the colorful, quarterly club magazine, *Gullivers World*. Members have the chance to participate in competitions and receive invitations to exclusive events. Club members also have the opportunity to purchase Special Edition Club pieces.

Lilliput Lane Land of Legend
c/o Gift Link, Inc.
The Oakland Building
9052 Old Annapolis Rd.
Columbia, MD 21045
(301) 964-2202
Annual membership fee: $25.00

Members receive a membership card, a bookmark, a free annual sculpture and *Land of Legend Chronicle* magazine, a full color quarterly publication. Members also receive a Redemption Certificate for a members-only piece.

Lladro Collectors Society
43 West 57th Street
New York, NY 10019-3498
1-800-937-3667
Annual membership fee: $35.00

Upon joining, members receive an exclusive Lladro fine porcelain bell, a subscription to *Expressions* magazine, a binder to store the magazines, a bas-relief porcelain plaque bearing the signatures of the three Lladro brothers and a personalized membership card, an opportunity to acquire a members-only figurine and an associate membership to the Lladro Museum in New York City.

The Seymour Mann Collectible Doll Club

P.O. Box 2046
Madison Square Station
New York, NY 10159
(212) 683-7262
Annual membership fee: $17.50

Members receive a membership card, 20" x 24" full color doll poster and newsletter. Members also have the opportunity to purchase limited edition dolls available only to club members, participate in contests and take advantage of special offers.

Melody In Motion Collectors Society

c/o WACO Products Corporation
One N. Corporate Drive
Riverdale, NJ 07457
(201) 616-1660
Annual membership fee: To Be Established

Collectors are invited to become charter members of this Society in 1992. Members will receive an exclusive porcelain figurine, an opportunity to purchase a members' only edition figurine, a complimentary subscription to the "Melody In Motion Collectors Society" Newsletter, discount coupons to purchase *Melody In Motion* figurines, a personalized membership card entitling members to all the club benefits and upcoming events and a Melody In Motion folder containing four-color catalog, "Retirement" and "Purchase" logs, and a membership certificate.

Lee Middleton Collectors' Club

1301 Washington Boulevard
Belpre, OH 45714
1-800-843-9572
Annual membership fee: Charter members (limited to 500) Initial fee: $150.00

Members receive a Certificate of Membership, a photograph personally signed by Lee Middleton, the Club newsletter, "Lee's Dolls Today," an updated catalog and an exclusive Lee Middleton doll.

P. Buckley Moss Society

8015 E. Market St.
Warren, OH 44484
(216) 856-5775
Annual membership fee: $25.00

Society members receive a pewter geese membership pin, membership certificate and card, the "Sentinel" newsletter, binder, porcelain renewal pin and are entitled to purchase a members only print.

Original Print Collectors Group, Ltd.

19 East 70th Street
New York, NY 10021

PenniBears Collectors Club

P.O. Box 1200
Noble, OK 73068
1-800-727-4883
Annual membership fee: $5.00

Penni Jo Jonas creates delightful figurines in miniature. Miniature enthusiasts who join this club will receive a subscription to the quarterly newsletter, "PenniBears Post." Members also have the opportunity to purchase annual members-only PenniBears pieces.

PenniBears Collectors Club

Phyllis' Collectors Club

RR 4 Box 503
Rolla, MO 65401
(314) 364-7849
Annual membership fee: Initial-$20; Renewal-$15

Collectors are invited to become part of a network of discerning collectors who recognize the beauty and value of Phyllis Parkins' dolls. Annual Club benefits include a membership card, cloisonne lapel pin, color catalog, three newsletters, padded Collectors Club album to organize and protect newsletters and the right to purchase an Exclusive Membership doll. Members are also invited to the annual Spring convention, "An Evening with Phyllis," including a factory tour and a weekend of activities with the artist.

Phyllis' Collectors Club members are entitled to spend "An Evening with Phyllis," a Club extravaganza that takes place the first weekend in May. Photographed is Phyllis conducting a sculpting seminar during the tour of The Collectables production facilities.

PJ's Carousel Collection

P.O. Box 532
Newbern, VA 24126
(703) 674-4300
Annual membership fee: $40.00

This club is dedicated to preserving the American Carousel and making general information of carousel history available to collectors. Upon joining, members will receive a distinctive PJ Club plaque, PJ's color catalog, club newsletter, membership card and the right to purchase an exclusive members-only carousel animal.

Polland Collectors Society

P.O. Box 2468
Prescott, AZ 86302
(602) 778-1900
Annual membership fee: $35.00

The American West comes alive in Don Polland's three-dimensional figurines. Members receive newsletters, an annual gift figurine and information on the secondary market on all Polland sculptures. Members also have the opportunity to purchase members-only figurines and receive the dates of special appearances by Don.

Red Mill Collectors Society
One Hunters Ridge
Summersville, WV 26651
(304) 872-5237
Annual membership fee: $15.00

Upon joining, collectors will receive a membership card, the Society's newsletter published three times annually, advance information on new products and soon-to-be-retired pieces and secondary market information.

Royal Doulton International Collectors Club
700 Cottontail Lane
Somerset, NJ 08873
1-800-582-2102
Annual membership fee: $25.00

Members receive a year's subscription to the Club's quarterly magazine, announcements of special events featuring Michael Doulton and company artisans, access to the historical research information service on Royal Doulton products and information on local chapters of the Club. Members also have the opportunity to purchase specially commissioned pieces and are able to participate in the "Sell and Swap" column of the U.S. newsletter. Another benefit is the exclusive guided tours for club members to the Royal Doulton Potteries in Stoke-on-Trent, England.

Sarah's Attic Forever Friends Collectors' Club
126 1/2 West Broad
P.O. Box 448
Chesaning, MI 48616
(517) 845-3990
Annual membership fee: $25.00

Forever Friends members receive a Membership card, a subscription to the biannual magazine *From the Heart*, a quarterly newsletter, flyers, a folder to keep printed matter stored for easy reference, a checklist of Sarah's Attic collectibles dating back to 1983 and two redemption certificates to purchase "members-only" figurines.

Sebastian Miniatures Collectors' Society
The Lance Corporation
321 Central Street
Hudson, MA 01749
(508) 568-1401
Annual membership fee: $20.00

Upon joining, members receive a free miniature, quarterly issues of *Sebastian Collectors News* and *The Sebastian Exchange Quarterly*, an annual value register. Members also receive a Redemption Certificate for a members-only miniature.

Silver Deer's Ark Collectors' Club
4824 Sterling Drive
Boulder, CO 80301
(303) 449-6771
Annual membership fee: $25.00

Artist Tom Rubel has expanded his menagerie of creatures, large and small, as collectors joining this club will see firsthand. Membership kits include a members only figurine, a Membership Card, a beautiful Charter Membership Certificate, a copy of "The Peaceable Kingdom" club newsletter, a registry of the complete *Ark* Collection, Redemption Coupons for exclusive limited edition offerings and an invitation to special club activities and promotions.

Sports Impressions Collectors' Club
P.O. Box 633
Elk Grove Village, IL 60007-0633
(708) 640-5200
Annual membership fee: $20.00

Collectors can bring today's hottest NBA, NFL and Major League Baseball stars, as well as legends of the past, into their homes through exclusive collectors' plates and figurines. Upon joining, Club Members receive a thank-you gift, a folder for Club literature, a button bearing the official Club logo, brochures featuring the newest Sports Impressions collectibles, a Membership Card, "The Lineup" newsletter and the opportunity to purchase collector club exclusive pieces.

The "Mick/7" was part of the 1991 Sports Impressions Collectors' Club membership kit.

Fred Stone Collectors Club
42 Sherwood Terrace, Suite 7
Lake Bluff, IL 60044
(708) 295-5355
Annual membership fee: Initial-$35.00; Renewal-$30.00

Equestrian enthusiasts will appreciate this club, featuring the artwork of award-winning artist Fred Stone. Club members receive a Fred Stone poster, membership card and monthly newsletters announcing advance information on new products.

Swarovski Collectors Society
2 Slater Road
Cranston, RI 02920
1-800-426-3088
Annual membership fee: Initial-$30; Renewal-$20

Upon joining, members receive a special member gift of Swarovski crystal, and a subscription to the *Swarovski Collector* magazine. Members also are able to visit the Swarovski Collectors Society's newly remodeled Visitors' Liaison Office in Austria. Collectors may elect to purchase a collector club exclusive crystal figurine annually.

United Federation of Doll Clubs
P.O. Box 14146
Parkville, MO 64152

United States Historical Society
First and Main Streets
Richmond, VA 23219
(804) 648-4736

The United States Historical Society is a private, non-governmental organization dedicated to historical research and the sponsorship of projects and issuance of works of art which are historically and artistically significant.

David Winter Cottages Collectors Guild
4456 Campbell Road
P.O. Box 800667
Houston, TX 77280-0667
(713) 690-4490 or (713) 690-4489
Annual membership fee: Initial-$55.00; Renewal-$40.00

Members receive a year subscription to the quarterly magazine, *Cottage Country*, a complimentary members-only piece, leather magazine binder and two redemption certificates for special Guild pieces.

Robin Woods Doll Club
P.O. Box 1504
Florence, AL 35631
Annual membership fee: $20.00

This club was formed for collectors of the beautiful Robin Woods dolls. Members receive a membership card, logo club pin, quarterly newsletter and invitations to national meetings and shows.

The Donald Zolan Collector's Society
c/o Pemberton & Oakes
133 E. Carrillo Street
Santa Barbara, CA 93101
(805) 963-1371
Annual membership fee: $15.00

Known for his award-winning portrayal of child art, Donald Zolan invites collectors to join his Society. Benefits include a choice of a free miniature plate or framed miniature lithograph, quarterly newsletter, the opportunity to own Zolan originals at prices only available to Society members, a chance to have your Zolan collection hand-signed and hand-dated by the artist, and many additional benefits announced annually.

Reading Suggestions/Special Events Pictorial

Enrich Your Collecting Experience Through Additional Reading Sources and Photo Stories

Books

Whether your special area of interest is plates, figurines, bells, graphics, ornaments or dolls — or some combination of these collecting media — you'll find a great deal of material available to you in collectibles books and periodicals. The books listed here are some of the most prominent in the limited edition collectibles field — there are many more available. To find more books in your area of interest, check "Books in Print" by subject at your local library, or contact a book seller that specializes in limited editions.

The Blue Book of Dolls and Values by Jan Foulke. Hobby House Press, Inc., Cumberland, Maryland.

The Bradford Book of Collector's Plates, edited by the staff of The Bradford Exchange, Ltd., Niles, Illinois 60648.

The Chilmark Collection by Glenn S. Johnson and James E. Secky. Published by Commonwealth Press, Worcester, MA.

Chronicle of Krystonia by Scott. Published by Precious Art/Panton.

Collectibles: A Compendium by Marian Klamkin. Published by Dolphin Books, Doubleday & Company Inc., Garden City, New York.

Collecting David Winter Cottages by John Hine. Published by the John Hine Co.

The Collectors Encyclopedia of Dolls by Dorothy S. Coleman. Published by Crown Publishers, One Park Avenue, New York, New York 10016.

The Collector's History of Dolls by Constance Aileen King. Published by Bonanza Books, New York.

Contemporary Western Artists. Published by Southwest Art Publishing.

Developing Your Doll Collection by Loretta Holz. Published by Crown Publishers, One Park Avenue, New York, New York 10016.

The Encyclopedia of Collectibles. Published by Time-Life Books, Time & Life Building, Chicago, Illinois 60611.

The Goebel Miniatures of Robert Olszewski by Dick Hunt. Published by Collectibles Reference Press.

The Golden Anniversary Album: M.I. Hummel. Published by Portfolio Press, R.D.1, Huntington, New York 11743.

Gorham Silver 1831-1981 by Charles H. Carpenter, Jr. Published by Dodd, Mead & Co., New York.

Greenbook Guide to the Enesco Precious Moments® Collection. Published by Greenbook, Old Coach at Main, Box 515, East Setauket, New York 11733.

Greenbook Guide to the Memories of Yesterday™ Collection by Enesco. Published by Greenbook, Old Coach at Main, Box 515, East Setauket, New York 11733.

Greenbook Guide to Ornaments. Published by Greenbook, Old Coach at Main, Box 515, East Setauket, New York 11733.

The History of Santa. Published by Duncan Royale.

Keepsake Ornaments: A Collector's Guide by Clara Johnson Scroggins. Published by Hallmark Cards, Inc., Kansas City, MO 64108.

Kovel's Antiques and Collectibles Price List by Ralph and Terry Kovel. Published by Crown Publishers, 201 East 50th Street, New York, New York 10022.

Kovel's Guide to Selling Your Antiques and Collectibles by Ralph and Terry Kovel. Published by Crown Publishers, Inc., 201 East 50th Street, New York, New York, 10022.

Limited Edition Collectibles, Everything You May Ever Need to Know by Paul Stark. Published by The New Gallery Press, Wilkes-Barre, PA.

The Miniature Art of Robert Olszewski — An Authoritative Reference and Price Guide by Dick Hunt. Published by Dick Hunt, Satellite Beach, FL 32937.

Norman Rockwell Art and Collectibles by Carl F. Lucky. Published by Books Americana Inc., Florence, Alabama 35630.

Norman Rockwell Collectibles Value Guide by Mary Moline. Published by Rumbleseat Press, Inc., San Francisco, California 94123.

The No. 1 Price Guide to M.I. Hummel by Robert L. Miller. Published by Portfolio Press, Huntington, New York 11743.

The Official Price Guide to Collector Plates. Published by The House of Collectibles, Inc. New York, New York 10022.

The Official Guide to Collector Prints. Published by The House of Collectibles, Inc. New York, New York 10022.

Plate Collecting by Eleanor Clark. Published by Citadel Press, Secaucus, New York 07094.

Price Guide to Twentieth Century Dolls by Carol Gast Glassmire. Published by Wallace-Homestead Book Company, 1912 Grand Avenue, Des Moines, Iowa 50305.

The Sebastian Miniature Collection by Glenn Johnson. Published by Commonwealth Press, Worcester, MA.

Wildlife and Wilderness: An Artist's World by Keith Chackleton. Published by Watson-Guptill Publications, New York, New York 10036.

Wildlife Painting: Techniques of Modern Masters. Published by Watson-Guptill, New York, New York 10036.

With a Little Luck...by Helen Boehm. Published by Rawson Associates, New York, New York.

Magazines and Newsletters

The following are independent periodicals about the limited editions field. Many firms also publish newsletters and magazines which they provide free or at nominal cost to their collectors or preferred customers. For subscription information on the publications listed here, write them directly.

AMERICAN ARTIST
1 Color Court
Marion, Ohio 43302
1-800-347-6969

ANTIQUE & COLLECTING HOBBIES
1006 S. Michigan
Chicago, Illinois 60605
(312) 939-4767

THE ANTIQUE TRADER
P.O. Box 1050
Dubuque, Iowa 52001
(319) 588-2073

COLLECTIONS
P.O. Box 333
Tazewell, Tennessee 37879
(615) 626-8250

COLLECTOR EDITIONS
170 Fifth Avenue
New York, New York 10010
(212) 989-8700

COLLECTOR'S MART
650 Westdale Drive
Wichita, Kansas 67209
(316) 946-0600

COLLECTORS NEWS
P.O. Box 156
Grundy Center, Iowa 50638
(319) 824-6981

CONTEMPORARY DOLL MAGAZINE
30595 8 Mile
Livonia, Michigan 48152-1798
(313) 477-6650

DOLL CRAFTER
30595 8 Mile
Livonia, Michigan 48152-1798
(313) 477-6650

DOLLS MAGAZINE
170 Fifth Avenue
New York, New York 10010
(212) 989-8700

THE DOLL READER
c/o Hobby House Press
900 Frederick Street
Cumberland, Maryland 21502
(301) 759-3770

DOLL NEWS
P.O. Box 14146
Parkville, Missouri 64152
(816) 741-1002

FINE ART & AUCTION REVIEW
1683 Chestnut Street
Vancouver, B.C.
V6J 4M6
(604) 734-4944

INSIGHT ON COLLECTIBLES
103 Lakeshore Road, Suite 202
St. Catherines, Ontario
L2N 2T6
(416) 646-7744

KOVELS ON ANTIQUES AND COLLECTIBLES
P.O. Box 22200
Beachwood, Ohio 44122

PLATE WORLD
9200 N. Maryland Avenue
Niles, Illinois 60648
(708) 581-8310

ROCKWELL SOCIETY NEWS
597 Saw Mill River Road
Ardsley, New York 10502
(914) 693-8800

SOUTHWEST ART
P.O. Box 460535
Houston, Texas 77256-0535
(713) 850-0990

WILDLIFE ART NEWS
3455 Dakota Avenue S.
St. Louis, Minnesota 55416
(612) 927-9056

Special Events

Special Events within the collectibles industry come in many different forms — an award, a special gathering, friends. All events help to shape the industry, perhaps tell the "story behind the story," and share with the collectors that special feeling that comes with owning a treasured piece of limited edition artwork.

Michael McClure, president of McRand, the producer of the International Collectible Exposition, awards Gregory Perillo with the "Featured Artist of the Show" award during the opening ceremonies at the Westchester Collectible Exposition.

Wendy Lawton, designer, holds little Jennie Hodgens, a look-alike of Lawtons' award winning doll "Marcella" and "Raggedy Ann" at the Dolly Dears annual doll show in Birmingham, Alabama. The look-alike fashion show is greeted with much anticipation by both young and old doll enthusiasts.

Ronald McDonald Children's Charities received a special contribution of $225,000 from John Hine Studios. Pictured are John Hine(left) and David Winter(right) presenting the commemorative piece, the "Cartwright's Cottage" to Ronald McDonald. The donation was made possible through the sales of the "Cartwright's Cottage" as a 'thank you' for the enthusiasm and support which thousands of North American collectors have given David Winter over the past ten years.

The Lowell Davis Farm Event which occurs annually in Carthage, Missouri includes a Barbecue at the Davis farm and tours of the farm and Red Oak II, hayrides, fireworks, dinner, music, a bonfire and shopping at the General Store.

Hall of Famer and former New York Yankee, Whitey Ford, is pictured with Gartlan USA's President Robert Gartlan at the International Collectible Exposition in Westchester, New York, where he met collectors and signed their collectibles at the Gartlan USA booth.

Shrine clowns "Applejack" and "Strawberry" flank Ron Lee of Ron Lee's World of Clowns with the awards they presented during the International Shrine Clown Association's Imperial Session of North America held in San Francisco, California. A special Ron Lee sculpture was designed, with a percentage of the profits donated directly to the I.S.C.A. "sneaker fund" which in turn contributes to the Shrine burn centers across America.

Stephen Bogart, son of the late actor Humphrey Bogart, made a special appearance at the Bradford booth at the International Collectible Exposition in White Plains, New York, to introduce "Here's Looking at You, Kid," the first plate in the Casablanca series of limited edition plates. Bogart discussed his father's life and career with collectors who attended the show.

The Collectors' Information Bureau's booth at the International Collectible Exposition was staffed by (L to R) Diane Carnevale Jones, Sue Knappen and Cindy Zagumny. This show, held each July in South Bend, Indiana and one other collector show held in the Spring on either the East or West Coast, is managed by McRand International, Ltd. of Lake Forest, Illinois.

NALED

National Association of Limited Edition Dealers

Here is the 1991 roster of the limited edition dealers who are members of NALED, a national group of retail and wholesale merchants who are in the specialized market of selling limited edition plates, dolls, figurines and other collectible items. The group was formed in 1976. This list will help collectors to locate limited edition dealers in various areas of the United States. The National Headquarters for NALED is located at 508 Harlan Road, Mansfield, Ohio 44903.

ALABAMA
CHRISTMAS TOWN, *Mobile*, 205-661-3608
COLLECTIBLE COTTAGE, *Birmingham*, 205-988-8551
COLLECTIBLE COTTAGE, *Gardendale*, 205-631-2413
OLD COUNTRY STORE, *Gadsen*, 205-492-7659
OLDE POST OFFICE, *Gadsen*, 205-655-7292

ARIZONA
CAROUSEL GIFTS, *Phoenix*, 602-997-6488
FOX'S GIFTS & COLLECTABLES, *Scottsdale*, 602-947-0560
MARYLYN'S COLLECTIBLES, *Tucson*, 602-742-1501
MUSIC BOX & CLOCK SHOP, *Mesa*, 602-833-6943
RUTH'S HALLMARK SHOP, *Cottonwood*, 602-634-8050

CALIFORNIA
BLEVINS PLATES 'N THINGS, *Vallejo*, 707-642-7505
CAMEO GIFTS & COLLECTIBLES, *Rancho Temecula*, 714-676-1635
CARDTOWNE HALLMARK, *Garden Grove*, 714-537-5240
CAROL'S GIFT SHOP, *Artesia*, 213-924-6335
COLLECTIBLE CORNER, *Brea*, 714-529-3079
COLLECTIONS UNLIMITED, *Woodland Hills*, 818-713-9390
COLLECTOR'S CORNER, *Merced*, 209-383-5967
COLLECTOR'S WORLD, *Montrose*, 818-248-9451
CRYSTAL AERIE, *Larkspur*, 415-925-9280
CRYSTAL AERIE, *Danville*, 415-820-9133
DODIE'S FINE GIFTS, *Woodland*, 916-668-1909
EASTERN ART, *Victorville*, 619-241-0166
ENCORE CARDS & GIFTS, *Cypress*, 714-761-1266
EVA MARIE DRY GROCER, *Redondo Beach*, 213-375-8422
FORTE OLIVIA GIFTS, *West Covina*, 818-962-2588
GALLERIA GIFTS, *Reedley*, 209-638-4060
HOLIDAY GIFT SHOP, *Visalia*, 209-733-5654
LENA'S GIFT GALLERY, *San Mateo*, 415-342-1304
LOUISE MARIE'S FINE GIFTS, *Livermore*, 415-449-5757
MARGIE'S GIFTS & COLLECTIBLES, *Torrance*, 213-378-2526
MARY ANN'S CARDS, GIFTS & COL, *Yorba Linda*, 714-777-0999
MUSICAL MOMENTS & COLLECTIBLES, *Cameron Park*, 916-677-2221
NORTHERN LIGHTS, *San Rafael*, 415-457-2884
NYBORG CASTLE GIFTS & COLLECTIBLES, *Martinez*, 415-930-0200
OUR HOUSE COLLECTIBLE GIFT GALLERY, *San Diego*, 619-692-4454
P M COLLECTABLES, *Cupertino*, 408-725-8858
RUMMEL'S VILLAGE GUILD, *Montebello*, 213-722-2691
RYSTAD'S LIMITED EDITONS, *San Jose*, 408-279-1960
SUTTER STREET EMPORIUM, *Folsom*, 916-985-4647
TOMORROW'S TREASURES, *Riverside*, 714-354-5731
TOWN & COUNTRY DRUG, *Porterville*, 209-781-1925
TREASURE CHEST-CHRISTMAS & COLLECTABLES, *Calimesa*, 714-795-1220
VILLAGE PEDDLER, *La Habra*, 213-694-6111
WEE HOUSE FINE COLLECTIBLES, *Irvine*, 714-552-3228
WILSON GALLERIES, *Fresno*, 209-224-2223

COLORADO
KENT COLLECTION, *Englewood*, 303-761-0059
KING'S GALLERY OF COLLECTABLES, *Colorado Springs*, 719-636-2828
NOEL-THE CHRISTMAS SHOP, *Vail*, 303-476-6544
PLATES ETC, *Arvada*, 303-420-0752
QUALITY GIFTS & COLLECTOBLES, *Colorado Springs*, 719-599-0051
SWISS MISS SHOP, *Cascade*, 719-684-9679

CONNECTICUT
CARDS & GIFTS ETC, *Danbury*, 203-743-6515
J B'S COLLECTIBLES, *Danbury*, 203-790-1011
MAURICE NASSER, *New London*, 203-443-6523

DELAWARE
BOAMAN'S GIFTS, *Dover*, 302-734-3002
WASHINGTON SQUARE LIMITED, *Newark*, 302-453-1776

FLORIDA
CHRISTMAS COLLECTION, *Altamonte Springs*, 407-862-5383
CHRISTMAS SHOPPE, *Goulds*, 305-258-1418
CLASSIC CARGO, *Destin*, 904-837-8171
CORNER GIFTS, *Pembroke Pines*, 305-432-3739
COUNTRY PINE NEWTIQUES, *Mount Dora*, 904-735-2394
ELLIE'S HALLMARK, *Davie*, 305-434-2807
HEIRLOOMS OF TOMORROW, *North Miami*, 305-899-0920
HUNT'S COLLECTIBLES, *Satellite Beach*, 407-777-1313
MC NAMARA'S GALLERY OF GIFTS, *Ft Lauderdale*, 305-565-3368
MOLE HOLE OF FT LAUDERDALE, *Ft Lauderdale*, 305-564-6555
SIR RICHARD, *Ft Myers*, 813-936-6660
SUN ROSE GIFTS, *Indian Harbor Beach*, 407-773-0550
VILLAGE PLATE COLLECTOR, *Cocoa*, 407-636-6914

GEORGIA
BECKY'S SMALL WONDERS, *Helen*, 404-878-3108
CHAMBERHOUSE, *Canton*, 404-479-9115
DIAMOND JEWLERY, *Kennesaw*, 404-428-6170
GALLERY II, *Atlanta*, 404-872-7272
GIFTS & SUCH, *Martinez*, 404-738-4574
GLASS ETC, *Tucker*, 404-493-7936
MARTHA JANE'S, *Cave Springs*, 404-777-3608
MTN CHRISTMAS-MTN MEMORIES, *Dahlonega*, 404-864-9115
PAM'S HALLMARK SHOP, *Fayetteville*, 404-461-3041
PID-LIN PAD, *Macon*, 912-743-9897
PIKE'S PICKS FINE GIFTS, *Roswell*, 404-998-7828
PLUM TREE, *Tucker*, 404-491-9433
SWAN GALLERIES, *Stone Mountain*, 404-498-1324
TINDER BOX AT LENOX, *Atlanta*, 404-231-9853
TUDOR COTTAGE INC, *Snellville*, 404-978-3026
WESSON'S, *Helen*, 404-878-3544
WHIMSEY MANOR, *Warner Robins*, 912-328-2500

ILLINOIS
CARD & GIFT GALLERY, *Schaumburg*, 708-843-7744
CHRYSLER BOUTIQUE, *Effingham*, 217-342-4864
COVE GIFTS, *Bloomingdale*, 708-980-9020
CROWN CARD & GIFT SHOP, *Chicago*, 312-282-6771
DORIS COLLECTIBLES, *St Peter*, 618-349-8780
EUROPEAN IMPORTS, *Niles*, 708-967-5253
GUZZARDO'S HALLMARK, *Kewanee*, 309-852-5621
HALL JEWELERS & GIFTS, *Moweaqua*, 217-768-4990
HAWK HOLLOW, *Galena*, 815-777-3616
JBJ THE COLLECTOR SHOP, *Champaign*, 217-352-9610
C A JENSEN, LA SALLE, 815-223-0377
KATHLEEN'S HALLMARK, *Lincoln*, 217-732-7504
KIEFER'S GALLERIES LTD, *LaGrange*, 708-354-1888
KIEFER'S GALLERY OF CREST HILL, *Plainfield*, 815-436-5444
KRIS KRINGLE HAUS, *Geneva*, 708-208-0400
LYNN'S & COMPANY, *Arlington Heights*, 708-870-1188
M PANCER'S GIFTS, *Cicero*, 708-652-3512
MAY HALLMARK SHOP, *Woodridge*, 708-985-1008
MC HUGH'S GIFTS & COLLECTIBLES, *Rock Island*, 309-788-9525
PAINTED PLATE GIFTS, *Ofallin*, 618-624-6987
ROYALE IMPORTS, *Lisle*, 708-357-7002
RUTH'S HALLMARK, *Bloomingdale*, 708-980-9717
SANDY'S DOLLS & COLLECTABLES INC, *Palos Hills*, 708-423-0070
SIR RICHARD OF RANDHURST, *Mt Prospect*, 708-394-1699
SIR TIMOTHY OF STRATFORD, *Bloomingdale*, 708-980-9797
SOMETHING SO SPECIAL, *Rockford*, 815-226-1331
STONE'S HALLMARK SHOPS, *Rockford*, 815-399-4481
STONE'S ON THE SQUARE, *Woodstock*, 815-338-0072
STRAWBERRY HOUSE, *Libetyville*, 708-816-6129
STROHL'S LIMITED EDITIONS, *Shelbyville*, 217-774-5222
TOWER SHOP, *Riverside*, 708-447-5258
WHYDE'S HAUS, *Canton*, 309-668-2363
WONDERFUL WORLD OF DOLLS, *Centralia*, 618-532-2527

INDIANA
COUNTRY GOOSE, *Monticello*, 219-583-6340
CURIO SHOPPE, *Greensberg*, 812-663-6914
NANA'S STICHIN STATION, *Butler*, 219-868-5634
OUR PLACE, *Greensburg*, 812-663-8242
ROSE MARIE'S, *Evansville*, 812-423-7557
ROSIE'S CARD & GIFT SHOP, *Newburgh*, 812-853-3059
TEMPTATIONS GIFTS, *Valparaiso*, 219-462-1000
TOMORROW'S TREASURES, *Muncie*, 317-284-6355
WALTER'S COLLECTIBLES, *Plainfield*, 317-839-2954
WATSON'S, *New Carlisle*, 219-654-8600

IOWA
COLLECTION CONNECTION, *Des Moines*, 515-276-7766
DAVE & JANELLE'S, *Mason City*, 515-423-6377
DAVIS SALES, *Waterloo*, 319-232-0050
HAWK HOLLOW, *Bellevue*, 319-872-5467
HEIRLOOM JEWELERS, *Centerville*, 515-856-5715

KANSAS
HOURGLASS, *Wichita*, 316-942-0562
HOURGLASS, *Mission*, 913-384-9510

KENTUCKY
ANN'S HALLMARK, *Lexington*, 606-266-7302
ANN'S HALLMARK, *Lexington*, 606-266-9101
KAREN'S GIFTS, *Louisville*, 502-425-3310
STORY BOOK KIDS, *Florence*, 606-525-7743

LOUISIANA
ALLY'S HALLMARK, *Chalmeete*, 504-271-3480
LA TIENDA, *Lafayette*, 318-984-5920
PLATES & THINGS, *Baton Rouge*, 504-753-2885
PONTALBA COLLECTIBLES, *New Orleans*, 504-524-8068

MAINE
COUNTRY STORE XMAS & COL SHOPPE, *Trenton*, 207-667-5922
GIMBEL & SONS COUNTRY STORE, *Boothbay Harbor*, 207-633-5088
HERITAGE GIFTS, *Oakland*, 207-465-3910

MARYLAND
BODZER'S COLLECTIBLES, *Baltimore*, 301-931-9222
CALICO MOUSE, *Annapolis*, 301-261-2441
CHERRY TREE CARDS & GIFTS, *Laurel*, 301-498-8528
FIGURINE WORLD, *Gaithersburg*, 301-977-3997
GREETINGS & READINGS, *Towson*, 301-825-4225
MARG'S MANIA, *Lanham/Seabrook*, 301-552-2425
PLATE NICHE, *Annapolis*, 301-268-5106
TIARA GIFTS, *Wheaton*, 301-949-0210
TOMORROW'S TREASURES, *Bel Air*, 301-836-9075
WANG'S GIFTS & COLLECTIBLES, *Bel Air*, 301-838-2626

MASSACHUSETTES
CRYSTAL PINEAPPLE, *West Barnstable*, 508-362-3128
FIFTH AVENUE GALLERY, *Danvers*, 508-922-0490
GIFT BARN, *North Eastham*, 508-255-7000
GIFT GALLERY, *Webster*, 508-943-4402
GOLDEN PHOENIX, *South Hadley*, 413-533-5211
HONEYCOMB GIFT SHOPPE, *Wakefield*, 617-245-2448
LEONARD GALLERY, *Springfield*, 413-733-9492
MERRY CHRISTMAS SHOPPE, *Whitman*, 617-447-6677
SHROPSHIRE CURIOSITY SHOP I, *Shrewsbury*, 508-842-4202
SHROPSHIRE CURIOSITY SHOP II, *Shrewsbury*, 508-799-7200
STACY'S GIFTS & COLLECTIBLES, *East Walpole*, 508-668-4212
WARD'S, *Medford*, 617-395-2420
WAYSIDE COUNTRY STORE, *Marlboro*, 508-481-3458

MICHIGAN
ALLIE'S GIFT GALLERY, *Livonia*, 313-473-5750
BETTY'S HALLMARK, *Farmington Hills*, 313-476-5077
CARAVAN GIFTS, *Fenton*, 313-629-4212
COLLECTOR'S CONNECTION, *Muskegon*, 616-739-4401
COPPER CRICKET, *Westland*, 313-425-6977
CURIO CABINET COL & XMAS COTTAGE, *Lexington*, 313-359-5040
DEE'S HALLMARK, *Mt Clemens*, 313-792-5510
DOLL CARRIAGE, *Milford*, 313-684-1833
ELSIE'S HALLMARK SHOP, *Petoskey*, 616-347-5270
FLO'S HALLMARK, *Grayling*, 517-348-3161
FRITZ CHINA & GIFTS, *Monroe*, 313-241-6760
GEORGIA'S GIFT GALLERY, *Plymouth*, 313-453-5619
HARPOLD'S, *South Haven*, 616-637-3522
HOUSE OF CARDS, *Mt Clemens*, 313-247-2000
JACQUELYNS GIFTS, *Warren*, 313-296-9211
KEEPSAKE GIFTS, *Port Huron*, 313-985-5855
KNIBLOE GIFT CORNER, *Jackson*, 517-782-6846
LAKEVIEW CARD & GIFT SHOP, *Battle Creek*, 616-962-0650
MARION'S COLLECTIBLES, *Livonia*, 313-522-8620
PLATE LADY, *Livonia*, 313-261-5220
SALLY ANN'S COLLECTIBLES, *Waterford*, 313-623-6441
SANTINI GIFT & COLLECTIBLES, *Ironwood*, 906-432-4121
SCHULTZ GIFT GALLERY, *Pinconning*, 517-879-3110
SPECIAL THINGS, *Sterling Heights*, 313-739-4030
THEN & NOW GIFT SHOP, *Union Lake*, 313-363-1360
TROY STAMP & COIN EXCHANGE, *Troy*, 313-528-1181
YOUNG'S GARDEN MART & CHRISTMAS FANTASY, *Warren*, 313-573-0230

MINNESOTA
ANDERSON HALLMARK #3, *Albert Lea*, 507-373-0996
GUSTAF'S, *Lindstrom*, 612-257-6688
HUNT HALLMARK CARD & GIFT, *Rochester*, 507-289-5152
HUNT SILVER LAKE DRUG & GIFT, *Rochester*, 507-289-0749
HUTCH & MANTLE, *Minneapolis*, 612-869-2461
MARY D'S DOLLS & BEARS & SUCH, *Minneapolis*, 612-424-4375
ODYSSEY, *Mankato*, 507-388-2004
ODYSSEY, *Rochester*, 507-282-6629
SEEFELDT'S GALLERY, *Roseville*, 612-631-1397

MISSISSIPPI
CHRISTMAS WORLD, *Gulfport*, 601-896-9080

MISSOURI
CARDIALLY YOURS, *Maryland Heights*, 314-434-6637
CITY ZOO, *Kansas City*, 816-753-1886
CITY ZOO, *Kansas City*, 816-765-0063
DICKENS GIFT SHOP, *Branson*, 417-334-2992
ELLY'S, *Kimmswick*, 314-467-5019
GAMBLE'S, *Springfield*, 417-881-7555
HOURGLASS, *Kansas City*, 816-761-5777
OAK LEAF GIFTS, *Osage Beach*, 314-348-0190
SHIRLOCK I, *Joplin*, 417-781-6345
TOBACCO LANE, *Cape Girardeau*, 314-651-3414
UNIQUE GIFT SHOPPE, *Springfield*, 417-887-5476
YE COBBLESTONE SHOPPE, *Sikeston*, 314-471-8683

MONTANA
TRADITIONS, *Missoula*, 406-543-3177

NEBRASKA
COLLECTOR'S GALLERIA, *Lincoln*, 402-483-5620
GERBER'S FINE COLLECTIBLES, *Kearney*, 308-237-5139
L & L GIFTS, *Fremont*, 402-727-7275
MARIANNE K FESTERSEN, *Omaha*, 402-393-4454
SHARRON SHOP, *Omaha*, 402-393-8311

NEVADA
SERENDIPITY GALLERY OF COLLECTABLES, *Las Vegas*, 702-733-0036

NEW HAMPSHIRE
STRAW CELLAR, *Wolfeboro*, 603-569-1516

NEW JERSEY
CHINA ROYALE INC, *Englewood*, 201-568-1005
CHRISTMAS CAROL, *Flemington*, 908-782-0700
COLLECTORS CELLAR, *Pine Beach*, 201-341-4107
COLLECTORS EMPORIUM, *Secaucus*, 201-863-2977
EMJAY SHOP, *Stone Harbor*, 609-368-1227
GIFT CARAVAN, *North Arlington*, 201-997-1055
GIFT GALLERY, *Paramus*, 201-845-0940
GIFT WORLD, *Pennsauken*, 609-663-2126
GIFTS DU JOUR, *Burlington*, 609-387-8188
H K GIFT WORLD, *Livingston*, 201-992-8605
J C HALLMARK, *Perth Amboy*, 908-826-8208
JIANA, *Bloomingdale*, 201-492-1728
MATAWAN CARD & GIFT, *Aberdeen*, 908-583-9449
MEYER HOUSE GIFT SHOP, *Newfoundland*, 201-697-7122
NOTES-A-PLENTY GIFT SHOPPE, *Flemington*, 908-782-0700
OAKWOOD CARD & GIFT SHOP, *Edison*, 201-549-9494
OLD WAGON GIFTS, *Colts Neck*, 201-780-6656
SOMEONE SPECIAL, *W Berlin*, 609-768-7171
SOMEONE SPECIAL, *Cherry Hill*, 609-424-1914
STATION GIFT EMPORIUM, *Whitehouse Station*, 908-534-1212
TENDER THOUGHTS, *Freehold*, 201-462-6411
TENDER THOUGHTS, *Paramus*, 201-845-8585
TENDER THOUGHTS, *Rockaway*, 201-989-5444
TOM'S GARDEN WORLD, *McKee City*, 609-641-4522
WESTON'S LIMITED EDITIONS, *Eatontown*, 201-542-3550
WESTON'S PRESENTS, *Sea Girt*, 201-449-8333
ZASLOW'S FINE COLLECTIBLES, *Matawan*, 908-583-1499
ZASLOW'S FINE COLLECTIBLES, *Middleton*, 908-957-9560

NEW MEXICO
LORRIE'S COLLECTIBLES, *Albuquerque*, 505-292-0020
MOUNTAIN ANNIE'S, *Ruidoso*, 505-257-4445

NEW YORK
A LITTLE BIT OF CAMELOT, *Warwick*, 914-986-4438
ALBERT'S ATTIC, *Clarence*, 716-759-2231
ANN'S HALLMARK CARDS & GIFTS, *Newburgh*, 914-564-5585
ANN'S HALLMARK SHOPPE, *Newburgh*, 914-562-3149
ARISTICRAFTS PLUS, *Farmingdale*, 516-420-9669
CANAL TOWN COUNTRY STORE, *Rochester*, 716-225-5070
CANAL TOWN COUNTRY STORE, *Irondequoit*, 716-338-3670
CANAL TOWN COUNTRY STORE, *Rochester*, 716-424-4120
CERAMICA GIFT GALLERY, *New York*, 212-354-9216
CHINA CONNECTION, *West Hempstead*, 516-481-8050
CLIFTON PARK COUNTRY STORE, *Clifton Park*, 518-371-0585
CLOCK MAN GALLERY, *Poughkeepsie*, 914-473-9055
COLLECTIBLY YOURS, *Spring Valley*, 914-425-9244
CORNER COLLECTIONS, *Hunter*, 518-263-4141
COUNTRY GALLERY, *Fishkill*, 914-897-2008
CROMPOND COUNTRY STORE, *Crompond*, 914-737-4937
ELLIE'S LTD ED & COLLECTIBLES, *Selden*, 516-698-3467
GIFT GALLERY, *Manhasset*, 516-627-6500
ISLAND TREASURES, *Staten Island*, 718-698-1234
JOY'S LAMPLIGHT SHOPPE, *Avon*, 716-226-3341
LAWTON'S GIFTS & COLLECTIBLES, *Binghamton*, 607-770-8628
LIMITED COLLECTOR, *Corning*, 607-936-6195
LIMITED EDITION, THE, *Merrick*, 516-623-4400
LOCK STOCK & BARREL GIFTS, *Pittsford*, 716-586-8992
PANDORAS BOX, *White Plains*, 914-997-9160
PAUL'S ECONOMY PHARMACY, *Staten Island*, 718-442-2924
PLATE COTTAGE, *St James*, 516-862-717
PRECIOUS GIFT GALLERY, *Franklin Square*, 516-352-8900
PRECIOUS GIFT GALLERY, *Levitlawn*, 516-579-3562
PREMIO, *Massapequa*, 516-795-3050
SIX SIXTEEN GIFT SHOPS, *Port Jefferson*, 516-928-1040
SIX SIXTEEN GIFT SHOPS, *Bellmore*, 516-221-5829
TENDER THOUGHTS, *Lake Grove*, 516-360-0578
TODAY'S PLEASURE TOMORROW'S TREASURE, *Jeffrsonville*, 914-482-3690
VILLAGE GIFT SHOP, *Amherst*, 716-691-4425

NORTH CAROLINA
BRASS PONY, *Hendersonville*, 704-693-1037
COLLECTIBLY YOURS, *Asheville*, 704-665-9565
COUNTRY PINE NEWTIQUES, *Blowing Rock*, 704-295-3719
GIFT ATTIC, *Raleigh*, 919-781-1822
MC NAMARA'S GALLERY OF GIFTS, *Highlands*, 704-526-2961
OLDE WORLD CHRISTMAS SHOPPE, *Asheville*, 704-274-4819
STRICKLAND LIMITED EDITIONS, *Winston-Salem*, 919-721-4766

NORTH DAKOTA
BJORNSON IMPORTS, *Grand Forks*, 701-775-2618
HATCH'S COLLECTORS GALLERY, *Minot*, 701-852-4666
HATCH'S COLLECTORS GALLERY, *Bismarck*, 701-255-4821
HATCH'S COLLECTORS GALLERY, *Fargo*, 701-282-4457
JOY'S HALLMARK SHOP II, *Bismarck*, 701-258-4336

OHIO
ADDED TOUCH GIFTS N THINGS, *Hilliard*, 614-777-0557
ALADDIN LAMP, *Lima*, 419-224-5612
ANN'S HALLMARK, *Cincinnati*, 513-662-2021
BEEHIVE GIFT SHOP, *North Olmsted*, 216-777-2600
CABBAGES & KINGS, *Grand Rapids*, 419-832-2709
CELLAR CACHE, *Put-In-Bay*, 419-285-2738
COLLECTOR'S GALLERY, *Marion*, 614-387-0602
COMSTOCK'S COLLECTIBLES, *Medina*, 216-725-4656
CURIO CABINET, *Worthington*, 614-885-1986
DAVIDSON'S FINE GIFTS, *Columbus*, 614-846-1925
GIFT GARDEN, *Euclid*, 216-289-0116
HERFORE GIFTS, *Solon*, 216-248-8166
HOUSE OF TRADITION, *Perrysburg*, 419-874-1151
IVA'S GALLERY & GIFTS, *Cincinnati*, 513-793-1700
LEFT BANK SHOP, *Sandusky*, 419-627-1602
LITTLE RED GIFT HOUSE, *Birmingham*, 216-965-5420
LITTLE SHOP ON THE PORTAGE, *Woodville*, 419-849-3742
MUSIK BOX HAUS, *Vermilion*, 216-967-4744
NORTH HILL GIFT SHOP, *Akron*, 216-535-4811
OAK & BARN, *Alger*, 419-634-6213
ROCHELLE'S FINE GIFTS, *Toledo*, 419-472-7673
SAXONY IMPORTS, *Cincinnati*, 513-621-7800
SCHUMM PHARMACY HALLMARK & GIFTS, *Rockford*, 419-363-3630
STRAWBERRY PATCH, *Brunswick*, 216-225-7796
TOWNE CENTER SHOPPE, *Bedford*, 216-232-7655

OKLAHOMA
COLONIAL FLORISTS, *Stillwater*, 405-372-9166
DODY'S HALLMARK, *Lawton*, 405-353-8379

NORTH POLE CITY, *Oklahoma City*, 405-685-6635
RATHBONES FLAIR FLOWERS, *Tulsa*, 918-747-8491
SUZANNE'S COLLECTORS GALLERY, *Miami*, 918-542-3808
THOMPSON'S OFFICE SUPPLY & GIFTS, *El Reno*, 405-262-3552
W D GIFTS, *Okmulgee*, 918-756-2229

OREGON
ACCENT ON COLLECTIBLES, *Portland*, 503-253-0841
CROWN SHOWCASE, *Portland*, 503-243-6502
DAS HAUS-AM-BERG, *Salem*, 503-363-0669
PRESENT PEDDLER, *Portland*, 503-639-2325
TREASURE CHEST GIFT SHOP, *Gresham*, 503-667-2999

PENNSYLVANIA
BANKUS GIFTS, *Pocono Lake*, 717-646-9528
COLLECTOR'S CHOICE, *Pittsburgh*, 412-366-4477
CRAYON SOUP, *King of Prussia*, 215-265-0458
DEBBIE-JEANS, *Norristown*, 215-539-4563
THE DEN, *Lahaska*, 215-794-8493
DESIGN GALLERIES, *Wilkes-Barre*, 717-822-6704
EMPORIUM COLLECTIBLES GALLERY, *Erie*, 814-833-2895
EUROPEAN TREASURES, *Pittsburgh*, 412-421-8660
GIFT DESIGN GALLERIES, *Whitehall*, 215-266-1266
GIFT WORLD, *Strouesburg*, 717-424-7530
GILLESPIE JEWELER COLLECTORS GALLERY, *Northampton*, 215-261-0882
LAUCHNOR'S GIFTS & COLLECTABLES, *Treslertown*, 215-398-3008
LE COLLECTION, *Belle Vernon*, 412-483-5330
LIMITED PLATES, *Collegeville*, 215-489-7799
LINDENBAUM'S COLLECTORS SHOWCASE, *Pittsburgh*, 412-367-1980
RED CARDINAL, *Ambler*, 215-628-2524
ROBERTS GALLERY, *Pittsburgh*, 412-279-4223
SAVILLE'S LIMITED EDITIONS, *Pittsburgh*, 412-366-5458
SIDE DOOR, *McMurray*, 412-941-3750
SOMEONE SPECIAL, *Bensalem*, 215-245-0919
TODAY'S COLLECTABLES, *Philadelphia*, 215-331-3993
WISHING WELL, *Reading*, 215-921-2566

RHODE ISLAND
GOLDEN GOOSE, *Smithfield*, 401-232-2310

SOUTH CAROLINA
CURIOSITY SHOP, *Florence*, 803-665-8686
DUANE'S HALLMARK CARD & GIFT SHOP, *Columbia*, 803-772-2624
LUCILLE WAITS GIFTS, *Charleston*, 803-723-5906

SOUTH DAKOTA
AKERS GIFTS & COLLECTIBLES, *Sioux Falls*, 605-339-1325

TENNESSEE
BARBARA'S ELEGANTS, *Gatlinburg*, 615-436-3454
CALICO BUTTERFLY, *Memphis*, 901-362-8121
GIFT GALLERIA, *Maryville*, 615-983-4438
GLASS MENAGERIE, *Memphis*, 901-362-3215
LEMON TREE, *Gatlinburg*, 615-436-4602
OLD COUNTRY STORE, *Jackson*, 901-668-1223
PAT'S PLATES, *Goodlettsville*, 615-859-1598
PIANO'S FLOWERS & GIFTS, *Memphis*, 901-345-7670
STAGE CROSSING GIFTS & COLLECTIBLES, *Bartlett*, 901-372-4438

TEXAS
AUSTIN-BROWN GALLERY, *Irving*, 214-438-1045
BETTY'S COLLECTABLES LTD, *Harlingen*, 512-423-8234
COLLECTIBLES & GIFTS BY JEAN, *Austin*, 512-447-7002
COLLECTIBLE HERILOOMS, *Friendswood*, 713-486-5023
COLLECTOR'S COVE, *Greenville*, 214-454-2572
ELOISE'S COLLECTIBLES, *Katy*, 713-578-6655
ELOISE'S COLLECTIBLES, *Houston*, 713-783-3611
ELOISE'S GIFTS & ANTIQUES, *Rockwall*, 214-771-6371
HEARTSTRINGS, *Galveston*, 409-744-6860
KEEPSAKES & KOLLECTIBLES, *Spring*, 713-353-9233
LIMITED ADDITIONS, *Ft Worth*, 817-732-1992
LOUJON'S GIFTS, *Sugar Land*, 713-980-1245
MR C COLLECTIBLE CORNER, *Carrollton*, 214-242-5100
OPA'S HOUSE, *New Brauwfels*, 512-629-1191
SUNSHINE HOUSE GALLERY, *Plano*, 214-424-5015
TIS THE SEASON, *Ft Worth*, 817-332-1377

VERMONT
CHRISTMAS LOFT, *Jay*, 802-988-4358

VIRGINIA
BIGGS LIMITED EDITIONS, *Richmond*, 804-266-7744
CHRISTMAS GOOSE COLLECTIBLES, *Waynesboro*, 703-943-5225
GAZEBO GIFTS, *Newport News*, 804-838-3270

WASHINGTON
CHALET COLLECTORS GALLERY, *Tacoma*, 206-564-0326
GOLD SHOPPE, *Tacoma*, 206-473-4653
JANSEN FLOWERS INC, *Longview*, 206-423-0450
KAREN'S COLLECTORS COTTAGE, *Spokane*, 509-924-5687
NATALIA'S COLLECTIBLES, *Woodinville*, 206-481-4575
NUSSKNACKER HAUS, *Bellevue*, 206-455-8097
ODYSSEY IN GLASS, *Seattle*, 206-935-3875
SLUYS GIFTS, *Poulsbo*, 206-779-7171
STEFAN'S EUROPEAN GIFTS, *Yakima*, 509-457-5503
TANNENBAUM SHOPPE, *Leavenworth*, 509-548-7014

WEST VIRGINIA
ARACOMA DRUG GIFT GALLERY, *Logan*, 304-752-3812

WISCONSIN
A COUNTRY MOUSE, *Milwaukee*, 414-281-4210
BOOK & GIFT COLLECTIBLES, *Manitowoc*, 414-684-4300
CENTURY COIN SERVICE, *Green Bay*, 414-494-2719
CINNAMON WINDMILL, *Brookfield*, 414-781-7680
DOWN'S COLLECTORS SHOWCASE, *Milwaukee*, 414-327-3300
KIE'S PHARMACY, *Racine*, 414-886-8160
KRISTMAS KRINGLE SHOPPE, *Fond Du Lac*, 414-923-8210
MAXINE'S CARD'S & GIFTS, *Beaver Dam*, 414-887-8289
NUTCRACKER GIFT HOUSE, *Delavan*, 414-728-8447
P J COLLECTIBLES, *Green Bay*, 414-437-3443
P J'S HALLMARK, *Marinette*, 715-735-3940
RED CROSS PHARMACY, *Spooner*, 715-635-2117
SANSONE DRUGS & GIFTS, *Slinger*, 414-644-5246
SANSONE DRUGS & GIFTS, *Hubertus*, 414-628-3550
SANSONE GIFT & CARD, *Mequon*, 414-241-3633
TIVOLI IMPORTS, *Milwaukee*, 414-774-7590

CANADA
BARGOON PALACE COLLECTIBLES & GALLERY, *Richmond Hill*, Ont 416-883-4655
CHARLES' HOUSE OF PLATES, *Bloomfield*, Ont 613-393-2249
CHORNYS'-HADKE, *Sault Ste Marie*, Ont 705-253-0315
HAPPINESS IS, *Durham*, Ont 519-369-2115
PERTH GALLERY, *Stratford*, Ont 519-271-1185
PLATE RAIL, *Ottawa*, Ont 613-731-9965
TOMORROW'S TREASURES, *Bobcaygeon*, Ont 705-738-2147

Glossary

You can better appreciate your hobby by acquainting yourself with commonly used terms referred to by collectors and dealers to describe limited edition collectibles. This list is not all-inclusive, but it will provide a good starting point for approaching the collectibles field. When a term that you don't understand is used, chances are you can find it here. If not, write the COLLECTORS' INFORMATION BUREAU *and we'll do our best to define the term for you — and add it to next year's list.*

ALABASTER. A compact, fine-textured gypsum which is usually white and translucent. Some collector plates are made of a material called ivory alabaster, which is not translucent, but has the look and patina of old ivory.

ALLOTMENT. The number within a limited edition which a manufacturer allows to a given dealer, direct marketer or collector.

ANNUAL. The term commonly used to describe a plate or other limited edition which is issued yearly, i.e. the Goebel Hummel *annual* plate. Many *annual* plates commemorate holidays or anniversaries, but they are commonly named by that special date, i.e. the Bing & Grondahl *Christmas* plate, issued annually to commemorate Christmas.

ARTIST PROOF. Originally, the first few in an edition of lithographs or prints created for the artist's approval. Now, many editions contain a small number of prints which are marked A/P instead of numbering — basically as a means of increasing the number in the edition.

BABY DOLL. A doll with the proportions of a baby, with lips parted to take a nipple, and chubby, short-limbed body.

BACKSTAMP. The information on the back of a plate or other limited edition, which serves to document it as part of its limited edition. This information may be hand-painted onto the plate, or it may be incised, or applied by means of a transfer (decal). Typical information which may appear on the backstamp includes the name of the series, name of the item, year of issue, some information about the subject, the artist's name and/or signature, the edition limit, the item's number within that edition, initials of firing master or other production supervisor, etc.

BAND. Also known as a rim, as in "24K gold banded, or rimmed." A typical method of finishing or decorating a plate or bell is to band it in gold, platinum or silver. The firing process allows the precious material to adhere to the piece.

BAS-RELIEF. A technique in which the collectible has a raised design. This design may be achieved by pouring liquid material into a mold before firing, or by applying material to the flat surface of a plate, figurine, or other "blank" piece.

Studio Dante di Volteradici introduced "Silent Night, Holy Night" from the Christmas Creche Series. *The bas-relief plate is made of ivory alabaster.*

BAVARIA. A section of Germany known as one of the world's richest sources of kaolin clay — an essential component for fine porcelain production. Bavaria is home to a number of renowned porcelain factories.

BEDROOM DEALER. Slang term for an individual who functions as a small scale seller of limited edition collectibles, usually from his or her home. Often unable to purchase at wholesale direct from manufacturers, these dealers may buy items at a discount from a larger dealer and then resell at a small profit.

BISQUE OR BISCUIT. A fired ware which has neither a glaze nor enamel applied to it. Bisque may be white or colored. It gets its name from its biscuit-like, matte texture.

BLUE CHIP. Slang for a well-established series that some believe represents a safe and sound collectibles investment. An interesting play on words in that many of the plate series that fall into this category are Copenhagen or Cobalt blue.

BODY. The basic form of a plate, figurine, bell or other item, or its component materials.

BONE ASH. By means of heat, animal bones are reduced to powder as an ingredient for bone china or porcelain. The name of the resulting powder is calcium phosphate, or bone ash.

BONE CHINA/BONE PORCELAIN. Bone porcelain is similar to hard porcelain in its ingredients, except that calcined bone ash comprises a large percentage of the mix and is the primary contributor to the vitrification and translucency. Bone clay allows for extreme thinness and translucency without the sacrifice of strength and durability.

BOTTOMSTAMP. Same idea as the backstamp, but usually refers to documentation material which appears on the bottom of a figurine. On a bell, such information may appear on the inside.

BYE-LO BABY. Grace Storey Putnam copyrighted this life-sized baby (three days old) in 1922. This style of baby doll is much in fashion today among limited edition collectors.

CAMEO. Relief decoration with a flat surface around it, similar to the look of a jeweler's cameo. A technique used by Wedgwood, Incolay and Avondale among others.

CAST. When liquid clay, or slip, is poured into a mold and hardened. Most often used for figurines, bells, and many other forms.

CERAMIC. The generic term for a piece which is made of some form of clay and finished by firing at high temperatures.

CERTIFICATE/CERTIFICATE OF AUTHENTICITY. A document which accompanies a limited edition item to establish its place within the limited edition. Such a Certificate may include information such as the series name, item title, artist's name and/or signature, brief description of the item and its subject, signatures of sponsoring and marketing organization representatives, and other documentation material along with the item's individual number or a statement of the edition limit.

The Christmas Cameos *collection from Incolay Studios began in 1990 with "Home with the Tree."*

CHARACTER DOLLS. Usually made of bisque or composition, these dolls are created to resemble a real person, usually an actor or other celebrity.

CHASING. A sculpting process in which tiny hammers and punches are used to create decorative details on ornaments.

CHINA. Originally "china" referred to all wares which came from China. Now this term means products which are fired at a high temperature. China usually is comprised of varying percentages of kaolin clay, feldspar and quartz. Also known as "porcelain."

CHRISTMAS SERIES. Plates, figurines, bells, and other collectible items which are issued to commemorate this yearly holiday, but which normally are sold and displayed all year.

CINNABAR. A red mineral found in volcanic regions, and a principal ingredient in mercury. This material is frequently used to create collectors' items.

CIRE PERDUE. See lost wax.

CLAY. A general term for the materials used to make ceramic items. Malleable when moist, clay becomes hard and strong when fired. It may be composed of any number of earthen materials.

CLOISONNE. An enameling process in which thin metal strips are soldered in place on a base to create a pattern, and then enamel is poured in to provide the color.

CLOSED-END SERIES. A group of limited edition plates, figurines or other collectibles which comprise a specific number — be it 2, 4, 6, 8, 12 or more. This number normally is disclosed when the series begins.

COBALT BLUE. Also known as Copenhagen blue, this rich color is a favorite of ceramicists because it can withstand high firing temperatures. Cobalt oxide is a black powder when applied, but fires to a deep blue.

COLD CAST. A metal powder and a binder are forced into a mold or die under high pressure, and thus a forging process occurs. Allows for exceptional detail and creates pieces which take well to handpainting.

COLLECTOR PLATE. A limited edition plate which is created with the expressed intent that it be collected.

COMMEMORATIVE. An item created to mark a special date, holiday or event.

DEALER. The individual or store from whom a collector purchases plates, bells, and other items at retail.

DECAL. Also known as a transfer, this is a lithographic or silkscreen rendering or a piece of artwork, which is applied to a ceramic, metal, glass or other material and then fired on to fuse it to the surface.

DELFTWARE. Heavy earthenware with a tin glaze. First developed in Delft, Holland in the 16th century.

DIE CUTTING. Process by which a design or pattern is cut out of a piece of steel to form a die.

DISTRIBUTOR. A person in the collectibles market who buys from a manufacturer and sells to dealers, who in turn sell to individual collectors.

DRAFTING. Process of drawing metal into a shape with a plunger and die for making holloware.

EARTHENWARE. A non-vitrified ceramic, composed of ball clay, kaolin, and pegmatite. Most often glazed and fired.

EDITION. The term which refers to the number of items created with the same name and decoration.

EMBOSSED DESIGN. Raised ornamentation produced by the mold or by stamping a design into the body of the item.

ETCHED DESIGN. Decoration produced by cutting into the surface with acid. The object is first covered with an acid resistant paint or wax, and the design is carved through this coating. When immersed in acid, the acid "bites" into the surface in the shape of the design.

FAIENCE. Named after an Italian town called Faenza, faience is similar to Delftware in that it is a tin-glazed earthenware. Also similar to Majolica.

FELDSPAR. When decomposed, this mineral becomes kaolin, which is the essential ingredient in china and porcelain. When left in its undercomposed form, feldspar adds hardness to a ware.

FIRE. To heat, and thus harden, a ceramic ware in a kiln.

FIRING PERIOD. A time period — usually 10 to 100 days — which serves to limit an edition, usually of plates. The number of items made is limited to the capacity of the manufacturer over that 10-to-100 day period.

FIRST ISSUE. The premiere item in a series, whether closed-ended or open-ended.

FRENCH BRONZE. Also known as "spelter," this is zinc refined to 99.97% purity. This material has been used as an alternate to bronze for casting for more than a century.

GLAZE. The liquid material which is applied to a ware to serve various purposes: cosmetically, it provides shine and decorative value. It also makes the item more durable. Decorations may be applied before or after glaze is applied.

GRAPHIC. A print produced by one of the "original" print processes such as etchings, engravings, woodblocks, lithographs and serigraphs.

HALLMARK. The mark or logo of the manufacturer of an item.

HARD PASTE PORCELAIN. The hardest porcelain made, this material uses feldspar to enhance vitrification and translucency, and is fired at about 2642 degrees Fahrenheit.

INCISED. Writing or design which is cut into the piece — may provide a backstamp or a decorative purpose.

INCOLAY STONE. A man-made material combining minerals including carnelian and crystal quartz. Used to make cameo-style plates by Incolay Studios.

INLAY. To fill an etched or incised design with another material such as enamel, metal or jewels.

IN STOCK. Refers to prints in a given edition which are still available from the publisher's inventory.

ISSUE. As a verb, to introduce. As a noun, this term means an item within a series or edition.

ISSUE PRICE. The original price upon introduction of a limited edition, established by its manufacturer or principle marketer.

JASPER WARE. Josiah Wedgwood's unglazed stoneware material, first introduced in the 1770s. Although Jasper is white in its original form, it can be stained throughout in various colors. Wedgwood typically offers Jasper in the medium blue called "Wedgwood Blue," as well as darker blue, black, green, lilac, yellow, brown and grey. Some other colors have resulted through continued experimentation. Colored Wedgwood "bodies" often are decorated with white bas-relief, or vice-versa.

KAOLIN. The essential ingredient in china and porcelain, this special clay is found in quantity at several spots throughout the world — and it is there that many famous porcelain houses have developed. These areas include Bavaria in Germany, and the Limoges region of France.

LEAD CRYSTAL. Lead oxide gives this glass its weight and brilliance, as well as its clear ring. Lead crystal has a lead oxide content of 24%, while "full" lead crystal contains more than 30%.

LIMITED EDITION. An item produced only in a certain quantity or only during a certain time period. The typical ways in which collectibles editions are limited include: limited by number; limited by year; limited by specific time period; limited by firing period.

LIMOGES. A town in France which boasts a large deposit of kaolin clay, the essential ingredient in china and porcelain. Home of a number of top porcelain manufacturers.

LOST WAX. A wax "positive" is created by a sculptor, and used to create a ceramic "negative" shell. Then the ceramic shell becomes the original mold — basis for working molds used in the creation of an edition. A classic method of creating three-dimensional pieces.

LOW INVENTORY. Is the classification given an edition which has been 85% or more sold out by the publisher.

MAJOLICA. Similar to Delftware and Faience, this is a glazed earthenware first made on the Spanish island, Majorca.

MARKET. The buy-sell medium for collectibles.

MARKS OR MARKINGS. The logo or insignia which certifies that an item is made by a particular firm.

MINT CONDITION. A term originally related to the coin collecting hobby, this means that a limited edition item is still in its original, like-new condition, with all accompanying documents.

M.I. Hummel Exclusive New Backstamp

W. Goebel Porzellanfabrik, the producer of M.I. Hummel, introduced this backstamp in 1991. This prestigious crown mark with the intertwined WG monogram, (initials of Goebel company founder William Goebel), appeared on the first figurines introduced at the Leipzig Fair in 1925.

MOLD. The form which supplies the shape of a plate, figurine, bell, doll, or other item.

OPEN-ENDED SERIES. A collection of plates or other limited editions which appear at intervals, usually annually, with no limit as to the number of years in which they will be produced. As an example, the Bing & Grondahl Christmas series has been produced annually since 1895, with no end in sight.

OVERGLAZE. A decoration which is applied to an item after its original glazing and firing.

PASTE. The raw material of porcelain before shaping and firing.

PEWTER. An alloy consisting of at least 85% tin.

PORCELAIN. Made of kaolin, quartz and feldspar, porcelain is fired at up to 1450 degrees Centigrade. Porcelain is noted for its translucency and its true ring. Also called "china."

POTTERY. Ceramic ware, more specifically that which is earthen ware or non-vitrified. Also a term for the manufacturing plant where such objects are made and fired.

PRIMARY MARKET. The buy-sell arrangement whereby individuals purchase collectibles direct from their manufacturer, or through a dealer, at issue price.

PRINTED REMARQUE. A hand drawn image by the artist that is photomechanically reproduced in the margin of a print.

PRINT. A photomechanical reproduction process such as offset lithography, collotypes and letterpress.

QUEEN'S WARE. Cream-colored earthenware developed by Josiah Wedgwood, now used as a generic term for similar materials.

QUOTE. The average selling price of a collectible at any given time — may be at issue, or above or below.

RELEASE PRICE. Is that price for which each print in the edition is sold until the edition is Sold Out and a secondary market (collector price) is established.

RELIEF. A raised design in various levels above a background.

REMARQUE. A hand drawn original image by the artist, either pencil, pen and ink, watercolor or oil that is drawn in the margin of a limited edition print.

SECOND. An item which is not first quality, and should not be included in the limited edition. Normally such items should be destroyed or at least marked on the backstamp or bottomstamp to indicate that they are not first quality.

SECONDARY MARKET PRICE. The retail price that a customer is willing to sell/buy a collectible that is no longer available on the primary market. These prices will vary from one territory to another depending upon the popularity and demand for the subject in each particular area.

SERIGRAPHY. A direct printing process whereby the artist designs, makes and prints his own stencils. A serigraph differs from other prints in that its images are created with paint films instead of printing inks.

SIGNED & NUMBERED. Each individual print is signed and consecutively numbered by the artist, in pencil, either in the image area or in the margin. Edition size is limited.

SIGNED IN THE PLATE. The only signature on the print is printed from the artist's original signature. Not necessarily limited in edition size.

SIGNED ONLY. Usually refers to a print that is signed without consecutive numbers. Not limited in edition size.

SILVERPLATE. A process of manufacturing ornaments in which pure silver is electroplated onto a base metal, usually brass or pewter.

SOLD OUT. Is the classification given an edition which has been 100% sold out by the publisher.

SPIN CASTING. A process of casting multiple ornaments from rubber molds; most commonly used for low temperature metals such as pewter.

STERLING SILVER. An alloy of 92½% pure silver and 7½% copper.

STONEWARE. A vitrified ceramic material, usually a silicate clay that is very hard, rather heavy and impervious to liquids and most stains.

TERRA COTTA. A reddish earthenware, or a general term for any fired clay.

TIN GLAZE. The glaze used on Delftware, Faience or Majolica, this material allows for a heavy, white and opaque surface after firing.

TRANSFER. See Decal.

TRANSLUCENCY. Allowing light to shine through a non-transparent object. A positive quality of fine porcelain or china.

TRIPTYCH. A three-panel art piece, often of religious significance.

UNDERGLAZE. A decoration which is applied before the final glazing and firing of a plate or other item. Most often, such a decoration is painted by hand.

VITRIFICATION. The process by which a ceramic body becomes vitrified, or totally non-porous, at high temperatures.

1. "Springtime in Japan" by Lladro
2. "Queen of Hearts" by Armani
3. "The Grand Carousel" by WACO Products Corporation
4. "Jessica" by Hamilton Heritage Dolls
5. "Victorian Santa with Teddy" by United Design
6. "A Victorian Village" by Hand & Hammer Silversmiths
7. "Forever in Our Hearts" by Sarah's Attic
8. "Angel Locks" by Lee Middleton Original Dolls
9. "Passing Perfection" by Gartlan USA, Inc.
10. "The Koala" from The Bradford Exchange
11. "Michael" from The Ashton-Drake Galleries
12. "The Signal" and "War Drummer" by Polland Studios
13. "Great American Chicken Race" by Schmid
14. "Marcella and Raggedy Ann" by Lawtons
15. "The Merry Widow" by Seymour Mann, Inc.
16. "Yvette" by The Collectables
17. "Save Me" — The Seals by Swarovski America Ltd.
18. "The Majestic Ferris Wheel" by Enesco Corporation

Collectors' Information Bureau's

PRICE INDEX

Limited Edition: Plates, Figurines, Bells, Graphics, Christmas Ornaments, Dolls and Steins

1993

Collectors' Information Bureau's

PRICE INDEX•1993

Limited Edition: Plates • Figurines • Bells • Graphics • Christmas Ornaments • Dolls • Steins

This index includes several thousand of the most widely-traded limited editions in today's collectibles market. It is based upon interviews with more than a score of the most experienced and well-informed limited edition dealers in the United States, as well as several independent market advisors.

HOW TO USE THIS INDEX

Listings are set up using the following format:

Company		Series			
Number	**Name**	**Artist**	**Edition Limit**	**Issue Price**	**Quote**
❶ **Enesco Corporation**		❷ **Retired Precious Moments Figurines**			
79-13-002	Praise the Lord Anyhow-E1374B	S. Butcher	Retrd.	8.00	75-125.00
❸❹❺	❻	❼	❽	❾	❿

❶ Company = Company Name

❷ Retired Precious Moments Figurines = Series Name

❸ 79 = 1979 (year of issue)

❹ 13 = Series number for Enesco Corporation. This number indicates that this series is the 13th listed for this particular company. Each series is assigned a series number.

❺ 002 = Item number within series. For example, this is the second listing within the series. Each item has a sequential number within its series.

❻ Praise the Lord Anyhow-E-1374B = Proper title of the collectible. Many titles also include the model number as well, for further identification purposes.

❼ S. Butcher = Artist's name. The first initial and last name is indicated most often, however a studio name may also be designated in this slot. (Example: Walt Disney).

❽ Retrd. = Retired. In this case, the collectible is no longer available. The edition limit category generally refers to the number of items created with the same name and decoration. Edition limits may indicate a specific number (i.e. 10,000) or the number of firing days for plates (i.e. 100-day, the capacity of the manufacturer to produce collectibles during a given firing period). Refer to "Open," "Suspd.," "Annual," and "Yr. Iss." under "Terms and Abbreviations" below.

❾ 8.00 = Issue Price in U.S. Dollars.

❿ 75-125.00 = Current Quote Price reflected may show a price or price range. Quotes are based on interviews with retailers across the country, who provide their actual sales transactions.

A Special Note to All Precious Moments Collectors: *Each ENESCO Precious Moments subject is engraved with a special annual mark. This emblem changes with each production year. The Collector value for each piece varies because of these distinctive yearly markings. Our pricing reflects an average for all years.*
A Special Note to All Hallmark Keepsake Ornament Collectors: *All quotes in this section are for ornaments in mint condition in their original box.*
A Special Note to All Department 56 Collectors: *Year of Introduction indicates the year in which the piece was designed, sculpted and copyrighted. It is possible these pieces may not be available to the collectors until the following calendar year.*

TERMS AND ABBREVIATIONS

Annual-Issued once a year

Closed-An item or series no longer in production

N/A -Not Available

Open-Not limited by number or time-available until manufacturer stops production, "retires" or "closes" the item or series

Retrd.-Retired

S/O-Sold Out

Set-Refers to two or more items issued together for a single price

Suspd.-Suspended (not currently being produced: may be produced in the future)

Undis.-Undisclosed

Unkn.-Unknown

Yr. Iss.-Year of issue (limited to a calendar year) 28-day, 10-day, etc.-limited to this number of production (or firing) days-usually not consecutive

Company / Number	Name	Series / Artist	Edition Limit	Issue Price	Quote
ANRI		**ANRI Wooden Christmas Bells**			
76-01-001	Christmas	J. Ferrandiz	Yr.Iss.	6.00	50.00
77-01-002	Christmas	J. Ferrandiz	Yr.Iss.	7.00	42.00
78-01-003	Christmas	J. Ferrandiz	Yr.Iss.	10.00	40.00
79-01-004	Christmas	J. Ferrandiz	Yr.Iss.	13.00	30.00
80-01-005	The Christmas King	J. Ferrandiz	Yr.Iss.	17.50	18.50
81-01-006	Lighting The Way	J. Ferrandiz	Yr.Iss.	18.50	18.50
82-01-007	Caring	J. Ferrandiz	Yr.Iss.	18.50	18.50
83-01-008	Behold	J. Ferrandiz	Yr.Iss.	18.50	18.50
85-01-009	Nature's Dream	J. Ferrandiz	Yr.Iss.	18.50	18.50
ANRI		**Juan Ferrandiz Musical Christmas Bells**			
76-02-001	Christmas	J. Ferrandiz	Yr.Iss.	25.00	80.00
77-02-002	Christmas	J. Ferrandiz	Yr.Iss.	25.00	80.00
78-02-003	Christmas	J. Ferrandiz	Yr.Iss.	35.00	75.00
79-02-004	Christmas	J. Ferrandiz	Yr.Iss.	47.50	60.00
80-02-005	Little Drummer Boy	J. Ferrandiz	Yr.Iss.	60.00	63.00
81-02-006	The Good Shepherd Boy	J. Ferrandiz	Yr.Iss.	63.00	63.00
82-02-007	Spreading the Word	J. Ferrandiz	Yr.Iss.	63.00	63.00
83-02-008	Companions	J. Ferrandiz	Yr.Iss.	63.00	63.00
84-02-009	With Love	J. Ferrandiz	Yr.Iss.	55.00	55.00
Artaffects		**Bells**			
87-01-001	Newborn Bell	R. Sauber	Unkn.	25.00	25.00
87-01-002	Motherhood Bell	R. Sauber	Unkn.	25.00	25.00
87-01-003	Sweet Sixteen Bell	R. Sauber	Unkn.	25.00	25.00
87-01-004	The Wedding Bell (White)	R. Sauber	Unkn.	25.00	25.00
87-01-005	The Wedding Bell (Silver)	R. Sauber	Unkn.	25.00	25.00
87-01-006	The Wedding Bell (Gold)	R. Sauber	Unkn.	25.00	25.00
Artaffects		**Bride Belles Figurine Bells**			
88-02-001	Caroline	R. Sauber	Unkn.	27.50	27.50
88-02-002	Jacqueline	R. Sauber	Unkn.	27.50	27.50
88-02-003	Elizabeth	R. Sauber	Unkn.	27.50	27.50
88-02-004	Emily	R. Sauber	Unkn.	27.50	27.50
88-02-005	Meredith	R. Sauber	Unkn.	27.50	27.50
88-02-006	Laura	R. Sauber	Unkn.	27.50	27.50
88-02-007	Sarah	R. Sauber	Unkn.	27.50	27.50
88-02-008	Rebecca	R. Sauber	Unkn.	27.50	27.50
88-02-009	Groom	R. Sauber	Unkn.	22.50	22.50
Artaffects		**Indian Brave Annual Bell**			
89-03-001	Christmas Pow-Pow	G. Perillo	Yr.Iss.	24.50	30.00
90-03-002	Indian Brave	G. Perillo	Yr.Iss.	24.50	24.50
91-03-003	Indian Brave	G. Perillo	Yr.Iss.	24.50	24.50
Artaffects		**Indian Princess Annual Bell**			
89-04-001	The Little Princess	G. Perillo	Yr.Iss.	24.50	30.00
90-04-002	Indian Princess	G. Perillo	Yr.Iss.	24.50	24.50
Artists of the World		**DeGrazia Bells**			
80-01-001	Los Ninos	T. DeGrazia	7,500	40.00	95.00
80-01-002	Festival of Lights	T. DeGrazia	5,000	40.00	85.00
Bing & Grondahl		**Annual Christmas Bell**			
80-01-001	Christmas in the Woods	H. Thelander	Yr.Iss.	39.50	39.50
81-01-002	Christmas Peace	H. Thelander	Yr.Iss.	42.50	42.50
82-01-003	The Christmas Tree	H. Thelander	Yr.Iss.	45.00	45.00
83-01-004	Christmas in the Old Town	E. Jensen	Yr.Iss.	45.00	45.00
84-01-005	The Christmas Letter	E. Jensen	Yr.Iss.	45.00	45.00
85-01-006	Christmas Eve at the Farmhouse	E. Jensen	Yr.Iss.	45.00	45.00
86-01-007	Silent Night, Holy Night	E. Jensen	Yr.Iss.	45.00	45.00
87-01-008	The Snowman's Christmas Eve	E. Jensen	Yr.Iss.	47.50	47.50
88-01-009	The Old Poet's Christmas	E. Jensen	Yr.Iss.	49.50	49.50
89-01-010	Christmas Anchorage	E. Jensen	Yr.Iss.	52.00	52.00
90-01-011	Changing of the Guards	E. Jensen	Yr.Iss.	55.00	55.00
91-01-012	The Copenhagen Stock Exchange at Christmas	E. Jensen	Yr.Iss.	59.50	59.50
92-01-013	Christmas At the Rectory	J. Steensen	Yr.Iss.	62.50	62.50
93-01-014	Father Christmas in Copenhagen	J. Steensen	Yr.Iss.	62.50	62.50
Bing & Grondahl		**Christmas in America Bell**			
88-02-001	Christmas Eve in Williamsburg	J. Woodson	Yr.Iss.	27.50	100.00
89-02-002	Christmas Eve at the White House	J. Woodson	Yr.Iss.	29.00	75.00
90-02-003	Christmas Eve at the Capitol	J. Woodson	Yr.Iss.	30.00	30.00
91-02-004	Independence Hall	J. Woodson	Yr.Iss.	35.00	35.00
92-02-005	Christmas in San Francisco	J. Woodson	Yr.Iss.	37.50	37.50
93-02-006	Coming Home For Christmas	J. Woodson	Yr.Iss.	37.50	37.50
Brown & Bigelow Inc.		**A Boy and His Dog Silver Bells**			
80-02-001	Mysterious Malady	N. Rockwell	9,800	60.00	60.00
80-02-002	Pride of Parenthood	N. Rockwell	9,800	60.00	60.00
C.U.I./Carolina Collection/Dram Tree		**Sterling Classic**			
91-01-001	Small Tortoiseshell	J. Harris	10,000	100.00	100.00
91-01-002	Swallowtail	J. Harris	10,000	100.00	100.00
91-01-003	Camberwell Beauty	J. Harris	10,000	100.00	100.00
91-01-004	Large Blue	J. Harris	10,000	100.00	100.00
91-01-005	Peacock	J. Harris	10,000	100.00	100.00
91-01-006	Clouded Yellow	J. Harris	10,000	100.00	100.00
91-01-007	Mouse	J. Harris	10,000	100.00	100.00
91-01-008	Kingfisher	J. Harris	10,000	100.00	100.00
91-01-009	Barn Owl	J. Harris	10,000	100.00	100.00
Danbury Mint		**Various**			
75-01-001	Doctor and Doll	N. Rockwell	None	27.50	54.00
76-01-002	Grandpa Snowman	N. Rockwell	None	27.50	44.00
76-01-003	Freedom From Want	N. Rockwell	None	27.50	44.00
76-01-004	No Swimming	N. Rockwell	None	27.50	44.00
76-01-005	Saying Grace	N. Rockwell	None	27.50	44.00
76-01-006	The Discovery	N. Rockwell	None	27.50	44.00
77-01-007	The Runaway	N. Rockwell	None	27.50	40.00
77-01-008	Knuckles Down	N. Rockwell	None	27.50	40.00
77-01-009	Tom Sawyer	N. Rockwell	None	27.50	40.00
77-01-010	Puppy Love	N. Rockwell	None	27.50	40.00
77-01-011	Santa's Mail	N. Rockwell	None	27.50	40.00
77-01-012	The Remedy	N. Rockwell	None	27.50	40.00
Danbury Mint		**The Wonderful World of Norman Rockwell**			
79-02-001	Grandpa's Girl	N. Rockwell	None	27.50	29.50
79-02-002	Leapfrog	N. Rockwell	None	27.50	29.50
79-02-003	Baby-Sitter	N. Rockwell	None	27.50	29.50
79-02-004	Batter Up	N. Rockwell	None	27.50	29.50
79-02-005	Back to School	N. Rockwell	None	27.50	29.50
79-02-006	Gramps at the Reins	N. Rockwell	None	27.50	29.50
79-02-007	Friend in Need	N. Rockwell	None	27.50	29.50
79-02-008	Puppy in the Pocket	N. Rockwell	None	27.50	29.50
Danbury Mint		**The Norman Rockwell Commemorative Bell**			
79-03-001	Triple Self-Portrait	N. Rockwell	None	29.50	35.00
Enesco Corporation		**Precious Moments Annual Bells**			
83-01-001	Surrounded With Joy-E-0522	S. Butcher	Closed	18.00	60-75.00
82-01-002	I'll Play My Drum for Him-E-2358	S. Butcher	Closed	17.00	65-85.00
84-01-003	Wishing You a Merry Christmas-E-5393	S. Butcher	Closed	19.00	40-55.00
81-01-004	Let the Heavens Rejoice-E-5622	S. Butcher	Closed	15.00	165-180.
85-01-005	God Sent His Love-15873	S. Butcher	Closed	19.00	38-43.00
86-01-006	Wishing You a Cozy Christmas-102318	S. Butcher	Closed	20.00	38.00
87-01-007	Love is the Best Gift of All-109835	S. Butcher	Closed	22.50	30-44.00
88-01-008	Time To Wish You a Merry Christmas-115304	S. Butcher	Closed	25.00	40-45.00
89-01-009	Oh Holy Night-522821	S. Butcher	Closed	25.00	35-45.00
90-01-010	Once Upon A Holy Night-523828	S. Butcher	Closed	25.00	30-35.00
91-01-011	May Your Christmas Be Merry-524182	S. Butcher	Closed	25.00	32.00
92-01-012	But The Greatest Of These Is Love-527726	S. Butcher	Yr.Iss.	25.00	25-35.00
Enesco Corporation		**Precious Moments Various Bells**			
81-02-001	Jesus Loves Me-E-5208	S. Butcher	Suspd.	15.00	40-50.00
81-02-002	Jesus Loves Me-E-5209	S. Butcher	Suspd.	15.00	40-60.00
81-02-003	Prayer Changes Things-E-5210	S. Butcher	Suspd.	15.00	40-55.00
81-02-004	God Understands-E-5211	S. Butcher	Retrd.	15.00	40-75.00
81-02-005	We Have Seen His Star-E-5620	S. Butcher	Suspd.	15.00	40-50.00
81-02-006	Jesus Is Born-E-5623	S. Butcher	Suspd.	15.00	40-55.00
82-02-007	The Lord Bless You and Keep You-E-7175	S. Butcher	Suspd.	17.00	35-38.00
82-02-008	The Lord Bless You and Keep You-E-7176	S. Butcher	Suspd.	17.00	40-55.00
82-02-009	The Lord Bless You and Keep You- E-7179	S. Butcher	Open	22.50	35-55.00
82-02-010	Mother Sew Dear-E-7181	S. Butcher	Suspd.	17.00	35-50.00
82-02-011	The Purr-fect Grandma-E-7183	S. Butcher	Suspd.	17.00	35-50.00
Goebel/Schmid		**M. I. Hummel Collectibles Annual Bells**			
78-01-001	Let's Sing 700	M. I. Hummel	Closed	50.00	150-275.
79-01-002	Farewell 701	M. I. Hummel	Closed	70.00	75-165.00
80-01-003	Thoughtful 702	M. I. Hummel	Closed	85.00	85-160.00
81-01-004	In Tune 703	M. I. Hummel	Closed	85.00	100-155.
82-01-005	She Loves Me, She Loves Me Not 704	M. I. Hummel	Closed	90.00	120-150.
83-01-006	Knit One 705	M. I. Hummel	Closed	90.00	90-120.00
84-01-007	Mountaineer 706	M. I. Hummel	Closed	90.00	90-125.00
85-01-008	Sweet Song 707	M. I. Hummel	Closed	90.00	125.00
86-01-009	Sing Along 708	M. I. Hummel	Closed	100.00	125-200.
87-01-010	With Loving Greetings 709	M. I. Hummel	Closed	110.00	150-225.
88-01-011	Busy Student 710	M. I. Hummel	Closed	120.00	120.00
89-01-012	Latest News 711	M. I. Hummel	Closed	135.00	135.00
90-01-013	What's New? 712	M. I. Hummel	Closed	140.00	140-200.
91-01-014	Favorite Pet 713	M. I. Hummel	Closed	150.00	150-200.
92-01-015	Whistler's Duet 714	M. I. Hummel	Yr.Iss.	165.00	165.00
93-01-016	Celestial Musician 779	M. I. Hummel	Yr.Iss.	Unkn.	Unkn.
Gorham		**Various**			
75-01-001	Sweet Song So Young	N. Rockwell	Annual	19.50	50.00
75-01-002	Santa's Helpers	N. Rockwell	Annual	19.50	30.00
75-01-003	Tavern Sign Painter	N. Rockwell	Annual	19.50	30.00
76-01-004	Flowers in Tender Bloom	N. Rockwell	Annual	19.50	40.00
76-01-005	Snow Sculpture	N. Rockwell	Annual	19.50	45.00
77-01-006	Fondly Do We Remember	N. Rockwell	Annual	19.50	55.00
77-01-007	Chilling Chore (Christmas)	N. Rockwell	Annual	19.50	35.00
78-01-008	Gaily Sharing Vintage Times	N. Rockwell	Annual	22.50	22.50
78-01-009	Gay Blades (Christmas)	N. Rockwell	Annual	22.50	22.50
79-01-010	Beguiling Buttercup	N. Rockwell	Annual	24.50	26.50
79-01-011	A Boy Meets His Dog (Christmas)	N. Rockwell	Annual	24.50	30.00
80-01-012	Flying High	N. Rockwell	Annual	27.50	27.50
80-01-013	Chilly Reception (Christmas)	N. Rockwell	Annual	27.50	27.50
81-01-014	Sweet Serenade	N. Rockwell	Annual	27.50	27.50
81-01-015	Ski Skills (Christmas)	N. Rockwell	Annual	27.50	27.50
82-01-016	Young Mans Fancy	N. Rockwell	Annual	29.50	29.50
82-01-017	Coal Season's Coming	N. Rockwell	Annual	29.50	29.50
83-01-018	Christmas Medley	N. Rockwell	Annual	29.50	29.50
83-01-019	The Milkmaid	N. Rockwell	Annual	29.50	29.50
84-01-020	Tiny Tim	N. Rockwell	Annual	29.50	29.50
84-01-021	Young Love	N. Rockwell	Annual	29.50	29.50
84-01-022	Marriage License	N. Rockwell	Annual	32.50	32.50
84-01-023	Yarn Spinner	N. Rockwell	5,000	32.50	32.50
85-01-024	Yuletide Reflections	N. Rockwell	5,000	32.50	32.50
86-01-025	Home For The Holidays	N. Rockwell	5,000	32.50	32.50
86-01-026	On Top of the World	N. Rockwell	5,000	32.50	32.50
87-01-027	Merry Christmas Grandma	N. Rockwell	5,000	32.50	32.50
87-01-028	The Artist	N. Rockwell	5,000	32.50	32.50
88-01-029	The Homecoming	N. Rockwell	15,000	37.50	37.50
Gorham		**Currier & Ives - Mini Bells**			
76-02-001	Christmas Sleigh Ride	Currier & Ives	Annual	9.95	35.00
77-02-002	American Homestead	Currier & Ives	Annual	9.95	25.00
78-02-003	Yule Logs	Currier & Ives	Annual	12.95	20.00
79-02-004	Sleigh Ride	Currier & Ives	Annual	14.95	20.00
80-02-005	Christmas in the Country	Currier & Ives	Annual	14.95	20.00
81-02-006	Christmas Tree	Currier & Ives	Annual	14.95	17.50
82-02-007	Christmas Visitation	Currier & Ives	Annual	16.50	17.50
83-02-008	Winter Wonderland	Currier & Ives	Annual	16.50	17.50
84-02-009	Hitching Up	Currier & Ives	Annual	16.50	17.50
85-02-010	Skaters Holiday	Currier & Ives	Annual	17.50	17.50
86-02-011	Central Park in Winter	Currier & Ives	Annual	17.50	17.50
87-02-012	Early Winter	Currier & Ives	Annual	19.00	19.00
Gorham		**Mini Bells**			
81-03-001	Tiny Tim	N. Rockwell	Annual	19.75	19.75
82-03-002	Planning Christmas Visit	N. Rockwell	Annual	20.00	20.00
Dave Grossman Designs		**Norman Rockwell Collection**			
75-01-001	Faces of Christmas NRB-75	Rockwell-Inspired	Retrd.	12.50	35.00
76-01-002	Drum for Tommy NRB-76	Rockwell-Inspired	Retrd.	12.00	30.00
76-01-003	Ben Franklin (Bicentennial)	Rockwell-Inspired	Retrd.	12.50	25.00
80-01-004	Leapfrog NRB-80	Rockwell-Inspired	Retrd.	50.00	60.00
Hamilton Gifts		**Bells**			
92-01-001	Susanna 999377	M. Humphrey	Open	22.50	22.50
92-01-002	Sarah 999385	M. Humphrey	Open	22.50	22.50
92-01-002	Hollies 996095	M. Humphrey	Open	22.50	22.50
Kaiser		**Kaiser Christmas Bells**			
78-01-001	The Nativity	T. Schoener	15,000	60.00	60.00

BELLS

Company / Number	Name	Series / Artist	Edition Limit	Issue Price	Quote
79-01-002	Eskimo Christmas	N. Peter	15,000	60.00	60.00
80-01-003	Sleigh Ride at Christmas	K. Bauer	15,000	60.00	60.00
81-01-004	Snowman	K. Bauer	15,000	60.00	65.00
Kaiser		**Kaiser Tree Ornament Bells**			
79-02-001	The Carolers	K. Bauer	Yr.Iss.	27.50	44.00
80-02-002	Holiday Snowman	K. Bauer	Yr.Iss.	30.00	44.00
81-02-003	Christmas at Home	K. Bauer	Yr.Iss.	30.00	44.00
82-02-004	Christmas in the City	K. Bauer	Yr.Iss.	30.00	44.00
Kirk Stieff		**Musical Bells**			
77-01-001	Annual Bell 1977	Kirk Stieff	Closed	17.95	40-120.00
78-01-002	Annual Bell 1978	Kirk Stieff	Closed	17.95	70.00
79-01-003	Annual Bell 1979	Kirk Stieff	Closed	17.95	50.00
80-01-004	Annual Bell 1980	Kirk Stieff	Closed	19.95	50.00
81-01-005	Annual Bell 1981	Kirk Stieff	Closed	19.95	60.00
82-01-006	Annual Bell 1982	Kirk Stieff	Closed	19.95	60-120.00
83-01-007	Annual Bell 1983	Kirk Stieff	Closed	19.95	50.00
84-01-008	Annual Bell 1984	Kirk Stieff	Closed	19.95	35.00
85-01-009	Annual Bell 1985	Kirk Stieff	Closed	19.95	40.00
86-01-010	Annual Bell 1986	Kirk Stieff	Closed	19.95	40.00
87-01-011	Annual Bell 1987	Kirk Stieff	Closed	19.95	30.00
88-01-012	Annual Bell 1988	Kirk Stieff	Closed	22.50	35.00
89-01-013	Annual Bell 1989	Kirk Stieff	Closed	25.00	25.00
90-01-014	Annual Bell 1990	Kirk Stieff	Closed	27.00	27.00
91-01-015	Annual Bell 1991	Kirk Stieff	Closed	28.00	28.00
92-01-016	Annual Bell 1992	Kirk Stieff	12/92	30.00	30.00
Kirk Stieff		**Bell**			
92-02-001	Santa's Workshop Christmas Bell	Kirk Stieff	3,000	40.00	40.00
Lance Corporation		**Hudson Pewter Bicentennial Bells**			
74-01-001	Benjamin Franklin	P.W. Baston	Closed	Unkn.	75-100.00
74-01-002	Thomas Jefferson	P.W. Baston	Closed	Unkn.	75-100.00
74-01-003	George Washington	P.W. Baston	Closed	Unkn.	75-100.00
74-01-004	John Adams	P.W. Baston	Closed	Unkn.	75-100.00
74-01-005	James Madison	P.W. Baston	Closed	Unkn.	75-100.00
Lenox China		**Songs of Christmas**			
91-01-001	We Wish You a Merry Christmas	Unknown	Yr.Iss.	49.00	49.00
92-01-002	Deck the Halls	Unknown	Yr.Iss.	49.00	49.00
Lenox Collections		**Crystal Christmas Bell**			
81-01-001	Partridge in a Pear Tree	Lenox	15,000	55.00	55.00
82-01-002	Holy Family Bell	Lenox	15,000	55.00	55.00
83-01-003	Three Wise Men	Lenox	15,000	55.00	55.00
84-01-004	Dove Bell	Lenox	15,000	57.00	57.00
85-01-005	Santa Claus Bell	Lenox	15,000	57.00	57.00
86-01-006	Dashing Through the Snow Bell	Lenox	15,000	64.00	64.00
87-01-007	Heralding Angel Bell	Lenox	15,000	76.00	76.00
91-01-008	Celestial Harpist	Lenox	15,000	75.00	75.00
Lenox Collections		**Bird Bells**			
91-02-001	Bluebird	Unknown	Open	57.00	57.00
91-02-002	Hummingbird	Unknown	Open	57.00	57.00
91-02-003	Chickadee	Unknown	Open	57.00	57.00
92-02-004	Robin Bell	Unknown	Open	57.00	57.00
Lenox Collections		**Carousel Bell**			
92-03-001	Carousel Horse	Unknown	Open	45.00	45.00
Lladro		**Lladro Christmas Bell**			
87-01-001	Christmas Bell - L5458M	Lladro	Annual	29.50	100-200.
88-01-002	Christmas Bell - L5525M	Lladro	Annual	32.50	75-100.00
89-01-003	Christmas Bell - L5616M	Lladro	Annual	32.50	100-200.
90-01-004	Christmas Bell - L5641M	Lladro	Annual	35.00	40-100.00
91-01-005	Christmas Bell - L5803M	Lladro	Annual	37.50	37.50-56.00
92-01-006	Christmas Bell - L5913M	Lladro	Annual	37.50	37.50
Lincoln Mint		**Lincoln Bells**			
75-01-001	Downhill Daring	N. Rockwell	None	25.00	70.00
Museum Collections, Inc.		**Collectors Bells**			
82-01-001	Wedding/Anniversary	N. Rockwell	Open	45.00	45.00
82-01-002	25th Anniversary	N. Rockwell	Open	45.00	45.00
82-01-003	50th Anniversary	N. Rockwell	Open	45.00	45.00
82-01-004	For A Good Boy	N. Rockwell	Open	45.00	45.00
Reco International		**Special Occasions**			
89-01-001	The Wedding	S. Kuck	Open	15.00	15.00
Reco International		**Special Occasions-Wedding**			
91-02-001	From This Day Forward	C. Micarelli	Open	15.00	15.00
91-02-002	To Have And To Hold	C. Micarelli	Open	15.00	15.00
Reed & Barton		**Noel Musical Bells**			
80-01-001	1980 Bell	Reed & Barton	Closed	20.00	50.00
81-01-002	1981 Bell	Reed & Barton	Closed	22.50	45.00
82-01-003	1982 Bell	Reed & Barton	Closed	22.50	35.00
83-01-004	1983 Bell	Reed & Barton	Closed	22.50	45.00
84-01-005	1984 Bell	Reed & Barton	Closed	22.50	50.00
85-01-006	1985 Bell	Reed & Barton	Closed	25.00	40.00
86-01-007	1986 Bell	Reed & Barton	Closed	25.00	35.00
87-01-008	1987 Bell	Reed & Barton	Closed	25.00	30.00
88-01-009	1988 Bell	Reed & Barton	Closed	25.00	27.50
89-01-010	1989 Bell	Reed & Barton	Closed	25.00	27.50
90-01-011	1990 Bell	Reed & Barton	Closed	27.50	27.50
91-01-012	1991 Bell	Reed & Barton	Closed	30.00	30.00
92-01-013	1992 Bell	Reed & Barton	Yr.Iss.	30.00	30.00
Reed & Barton		**Yuletide Bell**			
81-02-001	Yuletide Holiday	Reed & Barton	Closed	14.00	14.00
82-02-002	Little Shepherd	Reed & Barton	Closed	14.00	14.00
83-02-003	Perfect Angel	Reed & Barton	Closed	15.00	15.00
84-02-004	Drummer Boy	Reed & Barton	Closed	15.00	15.00
85-02-005	Caroler	Reed & Barton	Closed	16.50	16.50
86-02-006	Night Before Christmas	Reed & Barton	Closed	16.50	16.50
87-02-007	Jolly St. Nick	Reed & Barton	Closed	16.50	16.50
88-02-008	Christmas Morning	Reed & Barton	Closed	16.50	16.50
89-02-009	The Bell Ringer	Reed & Barton	Closed	16.50	16.50
90-02-010	The Wreath Bearer	Reed & Barton	Closed	18.50	18.50
91-02-011	A Special Gift	Reed & Barton	Closed	22.50	22.50
92-02-012	My Special Friend	Reed & Barton	Yr.Iss.	22.50	22.50

Company / Number	Name	Series / Artist	Edition Limit	Issue Price	Quote
River Shore		**Rockwell Children Series I**			
77-01-001	School Play	N. Rockwell	7,500	30.00	75.00
77-01-002	First Day of School	N. Rockwell	7,500	30.00	75.00
77-01-003	Football Hero	N. Rockwell	7,500	30.00	75.00
77-01-004	Flowers for Mother	N. Rockwell	7,500	30.00	60.00
River Shore		**Rockwell Children Series II**			
78-02-001	Dressing Up	N. Rockwell	15,000	35.00	50.00
78-02-002	Future All American	N. Rockwell	15,000	35.00	52.00
78-02-003	Garden Girl	N. Rockwell	15,000	35.00	40.00
78-02-004	Five Cents A Glass	N. Rockwell	15,000	35.00	40.00
River Shore		**Norman Rockwell Single Issues**			
81-03-001	Looking Out to Sea	N. Rockwell	7,000	45.00	95.00
81-03-002	Spring Flowers	N. Rockwell	347	175.00	175.00
81-03-003	Grandpa's Guardian	N. Rockwell	7,000	45.00	45.00
Roman, Inc.		**The Masterpiece Collection**			
79-01-001	Adoration	F. Lippe	Open	20.00	20.00
80-01-002	Madonna with Grapes	P. Mignard	Open	25.00	25.00
81-01-003	The Holy Family	G. Notti	Open	25.00	25.00
82-01-004	Madonna of the Streets	R. Ferruzzi	Open	25.00	25.00
Roman, Inc.		**F. Hook Bells**			
85-02-001	Beach Buddies	F. Hook	15,000	25.00	27.50
86-02-002	Sounds of the Sea	F. Hook	15,000	25.00	27.50
87-02-003	Bear Hug	F. Hook	15,000	25.00	27.50
Roman, Inc.		**Annual Fontanini Christmas Crystal Bell**			
91-03-001	1991 Bell	E. Simonetti	Closed	30.00	30.00
92-03-002	1992 Bell	E. Simonetti	Yr.Iss.	30.00	30.00
Roman, Inc.		**Annual Nativity Bell**			
90-04-001	Nativity	I. Spencer	Closed	15.00	15.00
91-04-002	Flight Into Egypt	I. Spencer	Closed	15.00	15.00
92-04-003	Gloria in Excelsis Deo	I. Spencer	Yr.Iss.	15.00	15.00
93-04-004	Three Kings of Orient	I. Spencer	Yr.Iss.	15.00	15.00
Royal Copenhagen		**Christmas**			
92-01-001	The Queen's Carriage	S. Vestergaard	Yr.Iss.	69.50	69.50
93-01-002	Christmas Guests	S. Vestergaard	Yr.Iss.	69.50	69.50
Sandstone Creations		**A Fantasy Edition**			
80-01-001	Little Prayer	T. DeGrazia	7,500	40.00	40.00
81-01-002	Flower Vendor	T. DeGrazia	7,500	40.00	40.00
XX-01-003	Wee Three	T. DeGrazia	7,500	40.00	40.00
XX-01-004	Party Time	T. DeGrazia	7,500	40.00	40.00
Schmid		**Berta Hummel Christmas Bells**			
72-02-001	Angel with Flute	B. Hummel	Yr.Iss.	20.00	75.00
73-02-002	Nativity	B. Hummel	Yr.Iss.	15.00	80.00
74-02-003	The Guardian Angel	B. Hummel	Yr.Iss.	17.50	45.00
75-02-004	The Christmas Child	B. Hummel	Yr.Iss.	22.50	45.00
76-02-005	Sacred Journey	B. Hummel	Yr.Iss.	22.50	25.00
77-02-006	Herald Angel	B. Hummel	Yr.Iss.	22.50	50.00
78-02-007	Heavenly Trio	B. Hummel	Yr.Iss.	27.50	40.00
79-02-008	Starlight Angel	B. Hummel	Yr.Iss.	38.00	45.00
80-02-009	Parade into Toyland	B. Hummel	Yr.Iss.	45.00	55.00
81-02-010	A Time to Remember	B. Hummel	Yr.Iss.	45.00	55.00
82-02-011	Angelic Procession	B. Hummel	Yr.Iss.	45.00	50.00
83-02-012	Angelic Messenger	B. Hummel	Yr.Iss.	45.00	55.00
84-02-013	A Gift from Heaven	B. Hummel	Yr.Iss.	45.00	75.00
85-02-014	Heavenly Light	B. Hummel	Yr.Iss.	45.00	75.00
86-02-015	Tell the Heavens	B. Hummel	Yr.Iss.	45.00	45.00
87-02-016	Angelic Gifts	B. Hummel	Yr.Iss.	47.50	47.50
88-02-017	Cheerful Cherubs	B. Hummel	Yr.Iss.	52.50	52.50
89-02-018	Angelic Musician	B. Hummel	Yr.Iss.	53.00	53.00
90-02-019	Angel's Light	B. Hummel	Yr.Iss.	53.00	53.00
91-02-020	Message From Above	B. Hummel	5,000	58.00	58.00
92-02-021	Sweet Blessings	B. Hummel	5,000	65.00	65.00
Schmid		**Berta Hummel Mother's Day Bells**			
76-03-001	Devotion for Mothers	B. Hummel	Yr.Iss.	22.50	55.00
77-03-002	Moonlight Return	B. Hummel	Yr.Iss.	22.50	45.00
78-03-003	Afternoon Stroll	B. Hummel	Yr.Iss.	27.50	45.00
79-03-004	Cherub's Gift	B. Hummel	Yr.Iss.	38.00	45.00
80-03-005	Mother's Little Helper	B. Hummel	Yr.Iss.	45.00	45.00
81-03-006	Playtime	B. Hummel	Yr.Iss.	45.00	45.00
82-03-007	The Flower Basket	B. Hummel	Yr.Iss.	45.00	45.00
83-03-008	Spring Bouquet	B. Hummel	Yr.Iss.	45.00	45.00
84-03-009	A Joy to Share	B. Hummel	Yr.Iss.	45.00	45.00
Schmid		**Peanuts Annual Bells**			
79-06-001	A Special Letter	C. Schulz	10,000	15.00	25.00
80-06-002	Waiting For Santa	C. Schulz	10,000	15.00	25.00
81-06-003	Mission For Mom	C. Schulz	10,000	17.50	20.00
82-06-004	Perfect Performance	C. Schulz	10,000	18.50	18.50
83-06-005	Peanuts in Concert	C. Schulz	10,000	12.50	12.50
84-06-006	Snoopy and the Beagle Scouts	C. Schulz	10,000	12.50	12.50
Schmid		**Peanuts Christmas Bells**			
75-07-001	Woodstock, Santa Claus	C. Schulz	Yr.Iss.	10.00	25.00
76-07-002	Woodstock's Christmas	C. Schulz	Yr.Iss.	10.00	25.00
77-07-003	Deck the Doghouse	C. Schulz	Yr.Iss.	10.00	20.00
78-07-004	Filling the Stocking	C. Schulz	Yr.Iss.	13.00	15.00
Schmid		**Peanuts Mother's Day Bells**			
73-08-001	Mom?	C. Schulz	Yr.Iss.	5.00	15.00
74-08-002	Snoopy/Woodstock/Parade	C. Schulz	Yr.Iss.	5.00	15.00
76-08-003	Linus and Snoopy	C. Schulz	Yr.Iss.	10.00	15.00
77-08-004	Dear Mom	C. Schulz	Yr.Iss.	10.00	15.00
78-08-005	Thoughts That Count	C. Schulz	Yr.Iss.	13.00	15.00
Schmid		**Peanuts Special Edition Bell**			
76-09-001	Bi-Centennial	C. Schulz	Yr.Iss.	10.00	20.00
Schmid		**Disney Annuals**			
85-10-001	Snow Biz	Disney Studios	10,000	16.50	16.50
86-10-002	Tree for Two	Disney Studios	10,000	16.50	16.50
87-10-003	Merry Mouse Medley	Disney Studios	10,000	17.50	17.50
88-10-004	Warm Winter Ride	Disney Studios	10,000	19.50	19.50
89-10-005	Merry Mickey Claus	Disney Studios	10,000	23.00	23.00
90-10-006	Holly Jolly Christmas	Disney Studios	10,000	26.50	26.50
91-10-007	Mickey & Minnie's Rockin' Christmas	Disney Studios	10,000	26.50	26.50

Company Number	Name	Series Artist	Edition Limit	Issue Price	Quote
Schmid		**Lowell Davis Mini Bell**			
92-11-001	New Day	L. Davis	Yr.Iss.	10.00	10.00
Schmid/B.F.A.		**RFD Bell**			
79-01-001	Blossom	L. Davis	Closed	65.00	300-400.
79-01-002	Kate	L. Davis	Closed	65.00	300-400.
79-01-003	Willy	L. Davis	Closed	65.00	400.00
79-01-004	Caruso	L. Davis	Closed	65.00	300.00
79-01-005	Wilbur	L. Davis	Closed	65.00	300-350.
79-01-006	Old Blue Lead	L. Davis	Closed	65.00	275-300.
80-01-007	Cow Bell "Blossom"	L. Davis	Open	65.00	65.00
80-01-008	Mule Bell "Kate"	L. Davis	Open	65.00	65.00
80-01-009	Goat Bell "Willy"	L. Davis	Open	65.00	65.00
80-01-010	Rooster Bell "Caruso"	L. Davis	Open	65.00	65.00
80-01-011	Pig Bell "Wilbur"	L. Davis	Open	65.00	65.00
80-01-014	Dog Bell "Old Blue and Lead"	L. Davis	Open	65.00	65.00
Waterford Wedgwood USA		**New Year Bells**			
79-01-001	Penguins	Unknown	Annual	40.00	40.00
80-01-002	Polar Bears	Unknown	Annual	50.00	50.00
81-01-003	Moose	Unknown	Annual	55.00	55.00
82-01-004	Fur Seals	Unknown	Annual	60.00	60.00
83-01-005	Ibex	Unknown	Annual	64.00	64.00
84-01-006	Puffin	Unknown	Annual	64.00	64.00
85-01-007	Ermine	Unknown	Annual	64.00	64.00

CHRISTMAS ORNAMENTS

Company Number	Name	Series Artist	Edition Limit	Issue Price	Quote
Kurt S. Adler/Santa's World		**Fabriché™ Collection**			
92-01-001	Hello Little One! W1561	K.S. Adler	Open	22.00	22.00
92-01-002	Not a Creature Was Stirring W1563	K.S. Adler	Open	22.00	22.00
92-01-003	Hugs And Kisses W1560	K.S. Adler	Open	22.00	22.00
92-01-004	Merry Chrismouse W1565	K.S. Adler	Open	10.00	10.00
Kurt S. Adler/Santa's World		**Smithsonian Fabriché™ Collection**			
92-02-001	Holiday Drive W1580	K.S. Adler	Open	38.00	38.00
92-02-002	Santa On a Bicycle W1547	K.S. Adler	Open	31.00	31.00
92-02-003	Fabriche Santa Bear W1563	K.S. Adler	Open	22.00	22.00
Kurt S. Adler/Santa's World		**Steinbach Ornament Collection**			
92-03-001	The King's Guards ES300	K.S. Adler	Open	27.00	27.00
All God's Children		**Christmas Ornaments**			
87-01-001	Cameo Ornaments (set of 12)	M. Holcombe	Retrd.	24.00/ea	100.00/ea.
87-01-002	Doll Ornaments (set of 24)	M. Holcombe	Retrd.	28.00/ea	100.00/ea.
Anheuser-Busch, Inc.		**A & Eagle Collector Ornament Series**			
91-01-001	Budweiser Girl-Circa 1890's N3178	A.-Busch, Inc.	Open	15.00	15.00
92-01-002	1893 Columbian Exposition N3649	A.-Busch, Inc.	Open	15.00	15.00
92-01-003	Clydesdales Mini Plate Ornaments N3650 (3 pc. set)	S. Sampson	Open	23.00	23.00
Annalee Mobilitee		**Christmas Ornaments**			
86-01-001	Clown Head	A. Thorndike	5,701	7.95	25.00
86-01-002	Angel Head	A. Thorndike	Unkn.	7.95	30.00
84-01-003	Snowman Head	A. Thorndike	13,677	7.95	25.00
82-01-004	Elf Head	A. Thorndike	1,908	2.95	25.00
85-01-005	Sun Ornament	A. Thorndike	1,692	6.50	25.00
84-01-006	Star Ornament	A. Thorndike	3,275	5.95	25.00
83-01-007	Gingerbread Boy	A. Thorndike	11,835	10.95	35.00
86-01-008	Baby Angel	A. Thorndike	N/A	11.95	35.00
85-01-009	3" Angel On Cloud	A. Thorndike	Unkn.	6.50	30.00
Anna-Perenna Porcelain		**Annual Christmas Ornaments**			
91-01-001	Noel	P. Buckley Moss	Numbrd.	25.00	25.00
92-01-002	Sleighride	P. Buckley Moss	Numbrd.	27.50	27.50
ANRI		**Ferandiz Message Collection**			
89-01-001	Let the Heavens Ring	J. Ferrandiz	1,000	215.00	215.00
90-01-002	Hear The Angels Sing	J. Ferrandiz	1,000	225.00	225.00
ANRI		**Ferrandiz Woodcarvings**			
88-02-001	Heavenly Drummer	J. Ferrandiz	1,000	175.00	225.00
89-02-002	Heavenly Strings	J. Ferrandiz	1,000	190.00	190.00
ANRI		**Disney Four Star Collection**			
89-03-001	Maestro Mickey	Disney Studios	Yr.Iss.	25.00	25.00
90-03-002	Minnie Mouse	Disney Studios	Yr.Iss.	25.00	25.00
Armani		**Christmas**			
91-02-001	1991 Christmas Ornament 799A	G. Armani	Retrd.	11.50	11.50
92-02-002	1992 Christmas Ornament 788F	G. Armani	Yr. Iss.	23.50	23.50
Artaffects		**Annual Christmas Ornaments**			
85-01-001	Papoose Ornament	G. Perillo	Unkn.	14.00	65.00
86-01-002	Christmas Cactus	G. Perillo	Unkn.	15.00	50.00
87-01-003	Annual Ornament	G. Perillo	Unkn.	15.00	35.00
88-01-004	Annual Ornament	G. Perillo	Yr.Iss.	17.50	25.00
89-01-005	Annual Ornament	G. Perillo	Yr.Iss.	17.50	25.00
90-01-006	Annual Ornament	G. Perillo	Yr.Iss.	17.50	17.50
91-01-007	Annual Ornament	G. Perillo	Yr.Iss.	19.50	19.50
Artaffects		**Annual Bell Ornaments**			
85-02-001	Home Sweet Wigwam	G. Perillo	Yr.Iss.	14.00	14.00
86-02-002	Peek-A-Boo	G. Perillo	Yr.Iss.	15.00	15.00
87-02-003	Annual Bell Ornament	G. Perillo	Yr.Iss.	15.00	15.00
88-02-004	Annual Bell Ornament	G. Perillo	Yr.Iss.	17.50	17.50
89-02-005	Annual Bell Ornament	G. Perillo	Yr.Iss.	17.50	17.50
90-02-006	Annual Bell Ornament	G. Perillo	Yr.Iss.	17.50	17.50
91-02-007	Annual Bell Ornament	G. Perillo	Yr.Iss.	19.50	19.50
Artaffects		**Sagebrush Kids Bell Ornaments**			
87-03-001	The Fiddler	G. Perillo	Open	9.00	9.00
87-03-002	The Harpist	G. Perillo	Open	9.00	9.00
87-03-003	Christmas Horn	G. Perillo	Open	9.00	9.00
87-03-004	The Gift	G. Perillo	Open	9.00	9.00
87-03-005	Christmas Candle	G. Perillo	Open	9.00	9.00
87-03-006	The Carolers	G. Perillo	Open	9.00	9.00
Artaffects		**Kachina Ornaments**			
91-04-001	Sun Kachina	G. Perillo	Open	17.50	17.50
91-04-002	Old Kachina	G. Perillo	Open	17.50	17.50
91-04-003	Snow Kachina	G. Perillo	Open	17.50	17.50
91-04-004	Dawn Kachina	G. Perillo	Open	17.50	17.50
91-04-005	Kachina Mother	G. Perillo	Open	17.50	17.50
91-04-006	Totem Kachina	G. Perillo	Open	17.50	17.50
Artaffects		**Sagebrush Kids Collection**			
91-05-001	Tee-Pee Ornament	G. Perillo	Open	15.00	15.00
91-05-002	Tee-Pee Ornament	G. Perillo	Open	15.00	15.00
91-05-003	Shield Ornament	G. Perillo	Open	15.00	15.00
91-05-004	Moccasin Ornament	G. Perillo	Open	15.00	15.00
Artaffects		**Simple Wonders**			
91-06-001	Kim	C. Roeda	Open	22.50	22.50
91-06-002	Brittany	C. Roeda	Open	22.50	22.50
91-06-003	Nicole	C. Roeda	Open	22.50	22.50
91-06-004	Megan	C. Roeda	Open	22.50	22.50
91-06-005	Little Feather	C. Roeda	Open	22.50	22.50
91-06-006	Ashley	C. Roeda	Open	22.50	22.50
92-06-007	Sweet Surprise	C. Roeda	Yr.Iss.	15.00	15.00
Artists of the World		**De Grazia Annual Ornaments**			
86-01-001	Pima. Indian Drummer Boy	T. De Grazia	Yr.Iss.	27.50	300-450.
87-01-002	White Dove	T. De Grazia	Yr.Iss.	29.50	75.00
88-01-003	Flower Girl	T. De Grazia	Yr.Iss.	32.50	45-50.00
89-01-004	Flower Boy	T. De Grazia	Yr.Iss.	35.00	45-50.00
90-01-005	Pink Papoose	T. De Grazia	Yr.Iss.	35.00	45-50.00
90-01-006	Merry Little Indian	T. De Grazia	10,000	87.50	95-100.00
91-01-007	Christmas Prayer	T. De Grazia	Yr.Iss.	49.50	49.50
92-01-008	Bearing Gift	T. De Grazia	Yr.Iss.	55.00	55.00
93-01-009	Lighting the Way	T. De Grazia	Yr.Iss.	57.50	57.50
Bing & Grondahl		**Christmas In America**			
86-01-001	Christmas Eve in Williamsburg	J. Woodson	Closed	12.50	90-150.00
87-01-002	Christmas Eve at the White House	J. Woodson	Closed	15.00	15-60.00
88-01-003	Christmas Eve at Rockefeller Center	J. Woodson	Closed	18.50	18.50
89-01-004	Christmas in New England	J. Woodson	Closed	20.00	20-35.00
90-01-005	Christmas Eve at the Capitol	J. Woodson	Closed	20.00	25-45.00
91-01-006	Independence Hall	J. Woodson	Closed	23.50	23.50
92-01-007	Christmas in San Francisco	J. Woodson	Yr.Iss.	25.00	25.00
93-01-008	Coming Home For Christmas	J. Woodson	Yr.Iss.	25.00	25.00
Bing & Grondahl		**Santa Claus**			
89-02-001	Santa's Workshop	H. Hansen	Yr.Iss.	20.00	20.00
90-02-002	Santa's Sleigh	H. Hansen	Yr.Iss.	20.00	20.00
91-02-003	The Journey	H. Hansen	Yr.Iss.	23.50	23.50-45.
92-02-004	Santa's Arrival	H. Hansen	Yr.Iss.	25.00	25.00
93-02-005	Santa's Gifts	H. Hansen	Yr.Iss.	25.00	25.00
Buccellati		**Christmas Ornaments**			
86-01-001	Snowy Village Scene -2464	Buccellati	500	195.00	400.00
87-01-002	Shooting Star-2469	Buccellati	500	240.00	350.00
88-01-003	Santa Claus-2470	Buccellati	Closed	300.00	300.00
89-01-004	Christmas Tree-2471	Buccellati	750	230.00	230.00
90-01-005	Zenith-2472	Buccellati	750	250.00	250.00
91-01-006	Wreath-3561	Buccellati	750	300.00	300.00
92-01-007	Cherubs-3562	Buccellati	500	300.00	300.00
Carriage House Studio, Inc.		**Musical Series**			
80-01-001	The Caroler	M. Furlong	3,000	50.00	100.00
81-01-002	The Lyrist	M. Furlong	3,000	45.00	75.00
82-01-003	The Lutist	M. Furlong	3,000	45.00	75.00
83-01-004	The Concertinist	M. Furlong	3,000	45.00	75.00
84-01-005	The Herald Angel	M. Furlong	3,000	45.00	55-100.00
Carriage House Studio, Inc.		**Gifts from God**			
85-02-001	The Charis Angel	M. Furlong	3,000	45.00	100.00
86-02-002	The Hallelujah Angel	M. Furlong	3,000	45.00	125.00
87-02-003	The Angel of Light	M. Furlong	3,000	45.00	100.00
88-02-004	The Celestial Angel	M. Furlong	3,000	45.00	100.00
89-02-005	Coronation Angel	M. Furlong	3,000	45.00	45-75.00
Carriage House Studio, Inc.		**Joyeux Noel**			
90-03-001	Celebration Angel	M. Furlong	10,000	45.00	45-55.00
91-03-002	Thanksgiving Angel	M. Furlong	10,000	45.00	45.00
92-03-003	Joyeux Noel Angel	M. Furlong	10,000	45.00	45.00
Cazenovia Abroad		**Christmas Ornaments**			
68-01-001	Teddy Bear-P101TB	Unknown	Unkn.	9.00	34-45.00
68-01-002	Elephant-P102E	Unknown	Unkn.	9.00	34-45.00
68-01-003	Duck-P103D	Unknown	Unkn.	9.00	34-45.00
68-01-004	Bunny-P104B	Unknown	Unkn.	9.00	34-45.00
68-01-005	Cat-P105C	Unknown	Unkn.	9.00	34-45.00
68-01-006	Rooster-P106R	Unknown	Unkn.	10.00	34-45.00
68-01-007	Standing Angel-P107SA	Unknown	Unkn.	9.00	39-52.50
68-01-008	Tiptoe Angel-P108TTA	Unknown	Unkn.	10.00	34-45.00
69-01-009	Fawn-P109F	Unknown	Unkn.	12.00	45.00
70-01-010	Snow Man-P110SM	Unknown	Unkn.	12.00	45.00
70-01-011	Peace-P111P	Unknown	Unkn.	12.00	45.00
70-01-012	Porky-P112PK	Unknown	Unkn.	15.00	45.00
71-01-013	Kneeling Angel-P113KA	Unknown	Unkn.	15.00	48-65.00
72-01-014	Rocking Horse-P114RH	Unknown	Unkn.	15.00	48-65.00
73-01-015	Treetop Angel-P115TOP	Unknown	Unkn.	10.00	37-50.00
74-01-016	Owl-P116O	Unknown	Unkn.	15.00	45.00
75-01-017	Star-P117ST	Unknown	Unkn.	15.00	45.00
76-01-018	Hatching Chick-P118CH	Unknown	Unkn.	15.00	45.00
77-01-019	Raggedy Ann-P119RA	Unknown	Unkn.	17.50	39-52.50
78-01-020	Shell-P120SH	Unknown	Unkn.	20.00	34-45.00
79-01-021	Toy Soldier-P121TS	Unknown	Unkn.	20.00	34-45.00
80-01-022	Burro-P122BU	Unknown	Unkn.	20.00	34-45.00
81-01-023	Clown-P123CL	Unknown	Unkn.	25.00	34-45.00
82-01-024	Rebecca-P124RE	Unknown	Unkn.	25.00	34-45.00
83-01-025	Raggedy Andy-P125AND	Unknown	Unkn.	27.50	39-52.50
83-01-026	Mouse-P126MO	Unknown	Unkn.	27.50	39-52.50
84-01-027	Cherub-P127CB	Unknown	Unkn.	30.00	39-52.50
85-01-028	Shaggy Dog-P132SD	Unknown	Unkn.	45.00	50.00
86-01-029	Peter Rabbit-P133PR	Unknown	Unkn.	50.00	50.00
86-01-030	Big Sister-P134BS	Unknown	Unkn.	60.00	60.00
86-01-031	Little Brother-P135LB	Unknown	Unkn.	55.00	55.00
87-01-032	Lamb-P136LA	Unknown	Unkn.	60.00	60.00
87-01-033	Sea Horse-P137SE	Unknown	Unkn.	35.00	26-35.00
88-01-034	Partridge-P138PA	Unknown	Unkn.	70.00	70.00
88-01-035	Squirrel-P139SQ	Unknown	Unkn.	70.00	70.00
84-01-036	Reindeer & Sleigh-H100	Unknown	Unkn.	1250.00	1500.00
89-01-037	Swan-P140SW	Unknown	Open	45.00	45.00

CHRISTMAS ORNAMENTS

Number	Name	Artist	Edition Limit	Issue Price	Quote
90-01-038	Moravian Star-P141PS	Unknown	Open	65.00	65.00
91-01-039	Hedgehog-P142HH	Unknown	Open	65.00	65.00
91-01-040	Bunny Rabbit-P143BR	Unknown	Open	65.00	65.00
91-01-041	Angel-P144A	Unknown	Open	63.00	63.00
92-01-042	Humpty Dumpty-P145HD*	Unknown	Open	70.00	70.00
Cybis	**Christmas Collection**				
83-01-001	1983 Holiday Bell	Cybis	Yr.Iss.	145.00	1000.00
84-01-002	1984 Holiday Ball	Cybis	Yr.Iss.	145.00	700.00
85-01-003	1985 Holiday Angel	Cybis	Yr.Iss.	75.00	500.00
86-01-004	1986 Holiday Cherub Ornament	Cybis	Yr.Iss.	75.00	500.00
87-01-005	1987 Heavenly Angels	Cybis	Yr.Iss.	95.00	400.00
88-01-006	1988 Holiday Ornament	Cybis	Yr.Iss.	95.00	375.00
Department 56	**Snowbabies Ornaments**				
86-01-001	Sitting, Lite-Up, Clip-On, 7952-9	Department 56	Closed	7.00	25-39.00
86-01-002	Crawling, Lite-Up, Clip-On, 7953-7	Department 56	Open	7.00	7.00
86-01-003	Winged, Lite-Up, Clip-On, 7954-5	Department 56	Closed	7.00	28-33.00
86-01-004	Snowbaby on Brass Ribbon, 7961-8	Department 56	Closed	8.00	55-75.00
87-01-005	Moon Beams, 7951-0	Department 56	Open	7.50	7.50
87-01-006	Snowbaby Adrift Lite-Up, Clip-On, 7969-3	Department 56	Closed	8.50	30-40.00
87-01-007	Mini, Lite-Up, Clip-On, 7976-6	Department 56	Open	9.00	9.00
88-01-008	Twinkle Little Star 7980-4	Department 56	Closed	7.00	20-30.00
89-01-009	Noel, 7988-0	Department 56	Open	7.50	7.50
89-01-010	Surprise, 7989-8	Department 56	Open	12.00	12.00
89-01-011	Star Bright, 7990-1	Department 56	Open	7.50	7.50
90-01-012	Rock-A-Bye Baby 7939-1	Depatrment 56	Open	7.00	7.00
90-01-013	Penguin, Lite-Up, Clip-On 7940-5	Department 56	Open	5.00	5.00
90-01-014	Polar Bear, Lite-Up, Clip-On 7941-3	Department 56	Open	5.00	5.00
91-01-015	Swinging On a Star 6810-1	Department 56	Open	9.50	9.50
91-01-016	My First Star 6811-0	Department 56	Open	7.00	7.00
Department 56	**CCP Ornaments**				
86-02-001	Christmas Carol Village, set of 3	Department 56	Closed	13.00	32-45.00
86-02-002	Fezziwig's Warehouse	Department 56	Closed	4.35	N/A
86-02-003	Scrooge and Marley Countinghouse	Department 56	Closed	4.35	N/A
86-02-004	The Cottage of Bob Cratchit & Tiny Tim	Department 56	Closed	4.35	N/A
86-02-005	New England Village, set of 7	Department 56	Closed	25.00	N/A
86-02-006	Apothecary Shop	Department 56	Closed	3.50	10-20.00
86-02-007	General Store	Department 56	Closed	3.50	10-20.00
86-02-008	Nathaniel Bingham Fabrics	Department 56	Closed	3.50	10-20.00
86-02-009	Livery Stable & Boot Shop	Department 56	Closed	3.50	10-20.00
86-02-010	Steeple Church	Department 56	Closed	3.50	10-20.00
86-02-011	Brick Town Hall	Department 56	Closed	3.50	10-20.00
86-02-012	Red Schoolhouse	Department 56	Closed	3.50	10-20.00
Department 56	**Christmas Carol Character Ornaments**				
86-03-001	Christmas Carol Characters, set of 3	Department 56	Closed	13.00	30-45.00
86-03-002	Bob Cratchit & Tiny Tim	Department 56	Closed	4.35	16.00
86-03-003	Scrooge	Department 56	Closed	4.35	16.00
86-03-004	Poulterer	Department 56	Closed	4.35	16.00
Department 56	**Village Light-Up Ornaments**				
85-04-001	Dickens' Village, set of 8	Department 56	Closed	48.00	135-165.
85-04-002	Crowntree Inn	Department 56	Closed	6.00	15-16.00
85-04-003	Candle Shop	Department 56	Closed	6.00	15-16.00
85-04-004	Green Grocer	Department 56	Closed	6.00	15-20.00
85-04-005	Golden Swan Baker	Department 56	Closed	6.00	15-20.00
85-04-006	Bean and Son Smithy Shop	Department 56	Closed	6.00	15-20.00
85-04-007	Abel Beasley Butcher	Department 56	Closed	6.00	15-20.00
85-04-008	Jones & Co. Brush & Basket Shop	Department 56	Closed	6.00	15-20.00
85-04-009	Dickens' Village Church	Department 56	Closed	6.00	16-35.00
87-04-010	Christmas Carol Cottages, set of 3	Department 56	Closed	16.95	35-55.00
87-04-011	Fezziwig's Warehouse	Department 56	Closed	6.00	15.00
87-04-012	Scrooge & Marley Countinghouse	Department 56	Closed	6.00	15.00
87-04-013	The Cottage of Bob Cratchit & Tiny Tim	Department 56	Closed	6.00	15.00
87-04-014	Dickens' Village, set of 6	Department 56	Closed	36.00	120-130.
87-04-015	Blythe Pond Mill House	Department 56	Closed	6.00	16-20.00
87-04-016	Barley Bree Farmhouse	Department 56	Closed	6.00	15-20.00
87-04-017	The Old Curiosity Shop	Department 56	Closed	6.00	15-18.00
87-04-018	Kenilworth Castle	Department 56	Closed	6.00	18-25.00
87-04-019	Brick Abbey	Department 56	Closed	6.00	35-75.00
87-04-020	Chesterton Manor House	Department 56	Closed	6.00	15-25.00
86-04-021	New England Village, set of 7	Department 56	Closed	42.00	200.00
86-04-022	Apothecary Shop	Department 56	Closed	6.00	12-20.00
86-04-023	General Store	Department 56	Closed	6.00	18-25.00
86-04-024	Nathaniel Bingham Fabrics	Department 56	Closed	6.00	16-21.00
86-04-025	Livery Stable & Boot Shop	Department 56	Closed	6.00	16-20.00
86-04-026	Steeple Church	Department 56	Closed	6.00	75-132.00
86-04-027	Brick Town Hall	Department 56	Closed	6.00	16-22.00
86-04-028	Red Schoolhouse	Department 56	Closed	6.00	60-75.00
87-04-029	New England Village, set of 6	Department 56	Closed	36.00	200.00
87-04-030	Timber Knoll Log Cabin	Department 56	Closed	6.00	24-30.00
87-04-031	Smythe Woolen Mill	Department 56	Closed	6.00	25.00
87-04-032	Jacob Adams Farmhouse	Department 56	Closed	6.00	25.00
87-04-033	Jacob Adams Barn	Department 56	Closed	6.00	20-25.00
87-04-034	Craggy Cove Lighthouse	Department 56	Closed	6.00	100.00
87-04-035	Weston Train Station	Department 56	Closed	6.00	20-25.00
Department 56	**Miscellaneous Ornaments**				
84-05-001	Dickens 2-sided Tin Ornaments, set of 6	Department 56	Closed	12.00	165.00
84-05-002	Crowntree Inn	Department 56	Closed	2.00	N/A
84-05-003	Green Grocer	Department 56	Closed	2.00	N/A
84-05-004	Golden Swan Baker	Department 56	Closed	2.00	N/A
84-05-005	Bean and Son Smithy Shop	Department 56	Closed	2.00	N/A
84-05-006	Abel Beasley Butcher	Department 56	Closed	2.00	N/A
84-05-007	Jones & Co. Brush & Basket Shop	Department 56	Closed	2.00	N/A
88-05-008	Christmas Carol- Scrooge's Head	Department 56	Closed	12.95	20-28.00
88-05-009	Christmas Carol- Tiny Tim's Head	Department 56	Closed	10.00	20-28.00
88-05-010	Christmas Carol- Bob & Mrs. Cratchit	Department 56	Closed	18.00	33-38.00
88-05-011	Balsam Bell Brass Dickens' Candlestick	Department 56	Closed	3.00	5-10.00
83-05-012	Snow Village Wood Ornaments, set of 6	Department 56	Closed	30.00	N/A
83-05-013	Gabled House	Department 56	Closed	5.00	N/A
83-05-014	Swiss Chalet	Department 56	Closed	5.00	N/A
83-05-015	Countryside Church	Department 56	Closed	5.00	N/A
83-05-016	Carriage House	Department 56	Closed	5.00	N/A
83-05-017	Centennial House	Department 56	Closed	5.00	N/A
83-05-018	Pioneer Church	Department 56	Closed	5.00	N/A
Duncan Royale	**History Of Santa Claus**				
92-01-001	Santa I (set of 12)	Duncan Royale	Open	144.00	144.00
92-01-002	Santa II (set of 12)	Duncan Royale	Open	144.00	144.00

Number	Name	Artist	Edition Limit	Issue Price	Quote
Enesco Corporation	**Precious Moments Ornaments**				
83-01-001	Surround Us With Joy-E-0513	S. Butcher	Yr.Iss.	9.00	60-65.00
83-01-002	Mother Sew Dear-E-0514	S. Butcher	Open	9.00	15-30.00
83-01-003	To A Special Dad-E-0515	S. Butcher	Suspd.	9.00	35-45.00
83-01-004	The Purr-fect Grandma-E-0516	S. Butcher	Open	9.00	15-30.00
83-01-005	The Perfect Grandpa-E-0517	S. Butcher	Suspd.	9.00	25-40.00
83-01-006	Blessed Are The Pure In Heart -E-0518	S. Butcher	Yr.Iss.	9.00	40-55.00
83-01-007	O Come All Ye Faithful-E-0531	S. Butcher	Suspd.	10.00	45-55.00
83-01-008	Let Heaven And Nature Sing-E-0532	S. Butcher	Retrd.	9.00	35-50.00
83-01-009	Tell Me The Story Of Jesus-E-0533	S. Butcher	Suspd.	9.00	35-55.00
83-01-010	To Thee With Love-E-0534	S. Butcher	Retrd.	9.00	30-60.00
83-01-011	Love Is Patient-E-0535	S. Butcher	Suspd.	9.00	40-55.00
83-01-012	Love Is Patient-E-0536	S. Butcher	Suspd.	9.00	35-70.00
83-01-013	Jesus Is The Light That Shines- E-0537	S. Butcher	Suspd.	9.00	45-60.00
82-01-014	Joy To The World-E-2343	S. Butcher	Suspd.	9.00	33-55.00
82-01-015	I'll Play My Drum For Him-E-2359	S. Butcher	Yr.Iss.	9.00	100-150.
82-01-016	Baby's First Christmas-E-2362	S. Butcher	Suspd.	9.00	25-70.00
82-01-017	The First Noel-E-2367	S. Butcher	Suspd.	9.00	40-65.00
82-01-018	The First Noel-E-2368	S. Butcher	Retrd.	9.00	45-65.00
82-01-019	Dropping In For Christmas-E-2369	S. Butcher	Retrd.	9.00	45-60.00
82-01-020	Unicorn-E-2371	S. Butcher	Retrd.	10.00	45-75.00
82-01-021	Baby's First Christmas-E-2372	S. Butcher	Suspd.	9.00	35-45.00
82-01-022	Dropping Over For Christmas-E-2376	S. Butcher	Retrd.	9.00	45-59.00
82-01-023	Mouse With Cheese-E-2381	S. Butcher	Suspd.	9.00	90-125.00
82-01-024	Our First Christmas Together-E-2385	S. Butcher	Suspd.	10.00	15-55.00
82-01-025	Camel, Donkey & Cow (3 pc. set)-E2386	S. Butcher	Suspd.	25.00	55-75.00
84-01-026	Wishing You A Merry Christmas-E-5387	S. Butcher	Yr.Iss.	10.00	35-45.00
84-01-027	Joy To The World-E-5388	S. Butcher	Retrd.	10.00	40-55.00
84-01-028	Peace On Earth-E-5389	S. Butcher	Suspd.	10.00	30-50.00
84-01-029	May God Bless You With A Perfect Season -E-5390	S. Butcher	Suspd.	10.00	25-50.00
84-01-030	Love Is Kind-E-5391	S. Butcher	Suspd.	10.00	30-50.00
84-01-031	Blessed Are The Pure In Heart-E-5392	S. Butcher	Yr.Iss.	10.00	40.00
81-01-032	But Love Goes On Forever-E-5627	S. Butcher	Suspd.	6.00	70-100.00
81-01-033	But Love Goes On Forever-E-5628	S. Butcher	Suspd.	6.00	90-110.00
81-01-034	Let The Heavens Rejoice-E-5629	S. Butcher	Yr.Iss.	6.00	200-250.
81-01-035	Unto Us A Child Is Born-E-5630	S. Butcher	Suspd.	6.00	40-65.00
81-01-036	Baby's First Christmas-E-5631	S. Butcher	Suspd.	6.00	45-60.00
81-01-037	Baby's First Christmas-E-5632	S. Butcher	Suspd.	6.00	45-65.00
81-01-038	Come Let Us Adore Him (4pc. set)-E-5633	S. Butcher	Suspd.	22.00	65-115.00
81-01-039	Wee Three Kings (3pc. set)-E-5634	S. Butcher	Suspd.	19.00	100-129.
81-01-040	We Have Seen His Star-E-6120	S. Butcher	Retrd.	6.00	60-80.00
85-01-041	Have A Heavenly Christmas-12416	S. Butcher	Open	12.00	20-30.00
85-01-042	God Sent His Love-15768	S. Butcher	Yr.Iss.	10.00	35-75.00
85-01-043	May Your Christmas Be Happy-15822	S. Butcher	Suspd.	10.00	22-45.00
85-01-044	Happiness Is The Lord-15830	S. Butcher	Suspd.	10.00	20-37.00
85-01-045	May Your Christmas Be Delightful-15849	S. Butcher	Open	10.00	15-35.00
85-01-046	Honk If You Love Jesus-15857	S. Butcher	Open	10.00	15-27.00
85-01-047	Baby's First Christmas-15903	S. Butcher	Yr.Iss.	10.00	38.00
85-01-048	Baby's First Christmas-15911	S. Butcher	Yr.Iss.	10.00	30-40.00
86-01-049	Shepherd of Love-102288	S. Butcher	Open	10.00	15-25.00
86-01-050	Wishing You A Cozy Christmas-102326	S. Butcher	Yr.Iss.	10.00	30-40.00
86-01-051	Our First Christmas Together-102350	S. Butcher	Yr.Iss.	10.00	15-39.00
86-01-052	Trust And Obey-102377	S. Butcher	Open	10.00	15-35.00
86-01-053	Love Rescue Me-102385	S. Butcher	Open	10.00	15-35.00
86-01-054	Angel Of Mercy-102407	S. Butcher	Open	10.00	15-35.00
86-01-055	It's A Perect Boy-102415	S. Butcher	Suspd.	10.00	25-40.00
86-01-056	Lord Keep Me On My Toes-102423	S. Butcher	Retrd.	10.00	30-45.00
86-01-057	Serve With A Smile-102431	S. Butcher	Suspd.	10.00	20-35.00
86-01-058	Serve With A Smile-102458	S. Butcher	Suspd.	10.00	20-45.00
86-01-059	Reindeer-102466	S. Butcher	Yr.Iss.	11.00	150-250.
86-01-060	Rocking Horse-102474	S. Butcher	Suspd.	10.00	19-29.00
86-01-061	Baby's First Christmas-102504	S. Butcher	Yr.Iss.	10.00	22-40.00
86-01-062	Baby's First Christmas-102512	S. Butcher	Yr.Iss.	10.00	20-35.00
87-01-063	Bear The Good News Of Christmas-104515	S. Butcher	Yr.Iss.	12.50	25-35.00
87-01-064	Baby's First Christmas-109401	S. Butcher	Yr.Iss.	12.00	35-45.00
87-01-065	Baby's First Christmas-109428	S. Butcher	Yr.Iss.	12.00	35-45.00
87-01-066	Love Is The Best Gift Of All-109770	S. Butcher	Yr.Iss.	11.00	35-50.00
87-01-067	I'm A Possibility-111120	S. Butcher	Suspd.	11.00	29-49.00
87-01-068	You Have Touched So Many Hearts-112356	S. Butcher	Open	11.00	15-30.00
87-01-069	Waddle I Do Without You-112364	S. Butcher	Open	11.00	15-39.00
87-01-070	I'm Sending You A White Christmas-112372	S. Butcher	Suspd.	11.00	20.00
87-01-071	He Cleansed My Soul-112380	S. Butcher	Open	12.00	19-25.00
87-01-072	Our First Christmas Together-112399	S. Butcher	Yr.Iss.	11.00	25-35.00
88-01-073	To My Forever Friend-113956	S. Butcher	Open	16.00	20-35.00
88-01-074	Smile Along The Way-113964	S. Butcher	Open	15.00	20.00
88-01-075	God Sent You Just In Time-113972	S. Butcher	Suspd.	13.50	25-35.00
88-01-076	Rejoice O Earth-113980	S. Butcher	Retrd.	13.50	35-45.00
88-01-077	Cheers To The Leader-113999	S. Butcher	Suspd.	13.50	25-35.00
88-01-078	My Love Will Never Let You Go-114006	S. Butcher	Suspd.	13.50	25-35.00
88-01-079	Baby's First Christmas-115282	S. Butcher	Yr.Iss.	15.00	25-35.00
88-01-080	Time To Wish You A Merry Christmas -115320	S. Butcher	Yr.Iss.	13.00	50-60.00
88-01-081	Our First Christmas Together-520233	S. Butcher	Yr.Iss.	13.00	20-28.00
88-01-082	Baby's First Christmas-520241	S. Butcher	Yr.Iss.	15.00	22-35.00
88-01-083	You Are My Gift Come True-520276	S. Butcher	Yr.Iss.	12.50	30-50.00
88-01-084	Hang On For The Holly Days-520292	S. Butcher	Yr.Iss.	13.00	45.00
89-01-085	Christmas is Ruff Without You-520462	S. Butcher	Yr.Iss.	13.00	25-45.00
89-01-086	May All Your Christmases Be White-521302 (dated)	S. Butcher	Yr.Iss.	17.50	25-35.00
89-01-087	Our First Christmas Together-521588	S. Butcher	Yr.Iss.	17.50	30.00
89-01-088	Oh Holy Night-522848	S. Butcher	Yr.Iss.	13.50	30-50.00
89-01-089	Make A Joyful Noise-522910	S. Butcher	Open	15.00	17.00
89-01-090	Love One Another-522929	S. Butcher	Open	17.50	20-25.00
89-01-091	I Believe In The Old Rugged Cross-522953	S. Butcher	Open	15.00	17.00
89-01-092	Peace On Earth-523062	S. Butcher	Yr.Iss.	25.00	75-105.00
89-01-093	Baby's First Christmas-523194	S. Butcher	Yr.Iss.	15.00	23.00
89-01-094	Baby's First Christmas-523208	S. Butcher	Yr.Iss.	15.00	25.00
90-01-095	Dashing Through The Snow-521574	S. Butcher	Open	15.00	15-18.00
90-01-096	Baby's First Christmas-523798	S. Butcher	Yr.Iss.	15.00	25.00
90-01-097	Baby's First Christmas-523771	S. Butcher	Yr.Iss.	15.00	25.00
90-01-098	Once Upon A Holy Night-523852	S. Butcher	Yr.Iss.	15.00	25-30.00
90-01-099	Don't Let the Holidays Get You Down-521590	S. Butcher	Open	15.00	15.00
90-01-100	Wishing You A Purr-fect Holiday-520497	S. Butcher	Yr.Iss.	15.00	20-35.00
90-01-101	Friends Never Drift Apart-522937	S. Butcher	Open	17.50	17.50
90-01-102	Our First Christmas Together-525324	S. Butcher	Yr.Iss.	17.50	20-28.00
90-01-103	Glide Through The Holidays-521566	S. Butcher	Retrd.	13.50	125-150.
90-01-104	May Your Christmas Be A Happy Home-523704	S. Butcher	Yr.Iss.	27.50	35-45.00
91-01-105	Our First Christmas Together-522945	S. Butcher	Yr.Iss.	17.50	25.00
91-01-106	Happy Trails Is Trusting Jesus-523224	S. Butcher	Open	15.00	15.00
91-01-107	The Good Lord Always Delivers-527165	S. Butcher	Open	15.00	15.00
91-01-108	Sno-Bunny Falls For You Like I Do-520438	S. Butcher	Yr.Iss.	15.00	30.00
91-01-109	Baby's First Christmas (Girl)-527092	S. Butcher	Yr.Iss.	15.00	15.00

Company / Number	Name	Series / Artist	Edition Limit	Issue Price	Quote
91-01-110	Baby's First Christmas (Boy)-527084	S. Butcher	Yr.Iss.	15.00	15.00
91-01-111	May Your Christmas Be Merry (Ornament On Base)-526940	S. Butcher	Yr.Iss.	30.00	30.00
91-01-112	May Your Christmas Be Merry-524174	S. Butcher	Yr.Iss.	15.00	15.00
92-01-113	Baby's First Christmas-527475	S. Butcher	Yr.Iss.	15.00	15.00
92-01-114	Baby's First Christmas-527483	S. Butcher	Yr.Iss.	15.00	15.00
92-01-115	But The Greatest of These Is Love-527696	S. Butcher	Yr.Iss.	15.00	15.00
92-01-116	Our First Christmas-528870	S. Butcher	Yr.Iss.	17.50	17.50
92-01-117	But The Greatest of These Is Love-527734 (Ornament on Base)	S. Butcher	Yr.Iss.	30.00	30.00
92-01-118	Good Friends Are For Always-524131	S. Butcher	Yr.Iss.	15.00	15.00
92-01-119	Lord, Keep Me On My Toes-525332	S. Butcher	Yr.Iss.	15.00	15.00
92-01-120	I'm Nuts About You-520411	S. Butcher	Yr.Iss.	15.00	15.00
Enesco Corporation		**Memories of Yesterday Ornaments**			
88-02-001	Baby's First Christmas 1988-520373	M. Attwell	Yr.Iss.	13.50	25-30.00
88-02-002	Special Delivery! 1988-520381	M. Attwell	Yr.Iss.	13.50	25-45.00
89-02-003	Baby's First Christmas-522465	M. Attwell	Open	15.00	15-20.00
89-02-004	Christmas Together-522562	M. Attwell	Open	15.00	15-25.00
89-02-005	A Surprise for Santa-522473 (1989)	M. Attwell	Yr.Iss.	13.50	20-25.00
90-02-006	Time For Bed-524638	M. Attwell	Yr.Iss.	15.00	15-25.00
90-02-007	New Moon-524646	M. Attwell	Open	15.00	15-25.00
90-02-008	Moonstruck-524794	M. Attwell	Retrd.	15.00	15-20.00
91-02-009	Just Watchin' Over You-525421	M. Attwell	Open	17.50	17.50
91-02-010	Lucky Me-525448	M. Attwell	Open	16.00	16.00
91-02-011	Lucky You-525847	M. Attwell	Open	16.00	16.00
91-02-012	Star Fishin'-525820	M. Attwell	Open	16.00	16.00
91-02-013	S'no Use Lookin' Back Now!-527181(dated)	M. Attwell	Yr.Iss.	17.50	17.50
92-02-014	Merry Christmas, Little Boo-Boo-528803	M. Attwell	Open	37.50	37.50
92-02-015	I'll Fly Along To See You Soon-525804 (1992 Dated Bisque)	M. Attwell	Yr.Iss.	16.00	16.00
92-02-016	Mommy, I Teared It-527041 (Five Year Anniversary Limited Edition)	M. Attwell	Yr.Iss.	15.00	15.00
92-02-017	Star Light, Star Bright-528838	M. Attwell	Open	16.00	16.00
92-02-018	Swinging Together-580481 (1992 Dated Artplas)	M. Attwell	Yr.Iss.	17.50	17.50
92-02-019	Sailin' With My Friends-587575 (Artplas)	M. Attwell	Open	25.00	25.00
Enesco Corporation		**Memories of Yesterday Society Member's Only Ornament**			
92-03-001	With Luck And A Friend, I's In Heaven-MY922	M. Attwell	Yr.Iss.	16.00	16.00
Enesco Corporation		**Enesco Treasury of Christmas Ornaments**			
83-04-001	Wide Open Throttle-E-0242	Enesco	3-Yr.	12.00	35.00
83-04-002	Baby's First Christmas-E-0271	Enesco	Yr.Iss.	6.00	N/A
83-04-003	Grandchild's First Christmas-E-0272	Enesco	Yr.Iss.	5.00	N/A
83-04-004	Baby's First Christmas-E-0273	Enesco	3-Yr.	9.00	N/A
83-04-005	Toy Drum Teddy-E-0274	Enesco	4-Yr.	9.00	N/A
83-04-006	Watching At The Window-E-0275	Enesco	3-Yr.	13.00	N/A
83-04-007	To A Special Teacher-E-0276	Enesco	7-Yr.	5.00	15.00
83-04-008	Toy Shop-E-0277	Enesco	7-Yr.	8.00	N/A
83-04-009	Carousel Horse-E-0278	Enesco	7-Yr.	9.00	20.00
81-04-010	Look Out Below-E-6135	Enesco	2-Yr.	6.00	N/A
82-04-011	Flyin' Santa Christmas Special 1982-E-6136	Enesco	Yr.Iss.	9.00	75.00
81-04-012	Flyin' Santa Christmas Special 1981-E-6136	Enesco	Yr.Iss.	9.00	N/A
81-04-013	Sawin' Elf Helper-E-6138	Enesco	2-Yr.	6.00	N/A
81-04-014	Snow Shoe-In Santa-E-6139	Enesco	2-Yr.	6.00	N/A
81-04-015	Baby's First Christmas 1981-E-6145	Enesco	Yr.Iss.	6.00	N/A
81-04-016	Our Hero-E-6146	Enesco	2-Yr.	4.00	N/A
81-04-017	Whoops-E-6147	Enesco	2-Yr.	3.50	N/A
81-04-018	Whoops, It's 1981-E-6148	Enesco	Yr.Iss.	7.50	N/A
81-04-019	Not A Creature Was Stirring-E-6149	Enesco	2-Yr.	4.00	N/A
84-04-020	Joy To The World-E-6209	Enesco	2-Yr.	9.00	35.00
84-04-021	Letter To Santa-E-6210	Enesco	2-Yr.	5.00	30.00
84-04-022	Lucy & Me Photo Frames-E-6211	Enesco	3-Yr.	5.00	N/A
84-04-023	Lucy & Me Photo Frames-E-6211	Enesco	3-Yr.	5.00	N/A
84-04-024	Lucy & Me Photo Frames-E-6211	Enesco	3-Yr.	5.00	N/A
84-04-025	Lucy & Me Photo Frames-E-6211	Enesco	3-Yr.	5.00	N/A
84-04-026	Lucy & Me Photo Frames-E-6211	Enesco	3-Yr.	5.00	N/A
84-04-027	Lucy & Me Photo Frames-E-6211	Enesco	3-Yr.	5.00	N/A
84-04-028	Baby's First Christmas 1984-E-6212	Gilmore	Yr.Iss.	10.00	N/A
84-04-029	Merry Christmas Mother-E-6213	Enesco	3-Yr.	10.00	30.00
84-04-030	Baby's First Christmas 1984-E-6215	Enesco	Yr.Iss.	6.00	N/A
84-04-031	Ferris Wheel Mice-E-6216	Enesco	2-Yr.	9.00	N/A
84-04-032	Cuckoo Clock-E-6217	Enesco	2-Yr.	8.00	40.00
84-04-033	Muppet Babies Baby's First Christmas-E6222	J. Henson	Yr.Iss.	10.00	N/A
84-04-034	Muppet Babies Baby's First Christmas-E6223	J. Henson	Yr.Iss.	10.00	45.00
84-04-035	Garfield Hark! The Herald Angel-E-6224	J. Davis	2-Yr.	7.50	N/A
84-04-036	Fun in Santa's Sleigh-E-6225	J. Davis	2-Yr.	12.00	N/A
84-04-037	"Deer!" Odie-E-6226	J. Davis	2-Yr.	6.00	N/A
84-04-038	Garfield The Snow Cat-E-6227	J. Davis	2-Yr.	12.00	N/A
84-04-039	Peek-A-Bear Baby's First Christmas-E-6228	Enesco	3-Yr.	10.00	N/A
84-04-040	Peek-A-Bear Baby's First Christmas-E-6229	Enesco	3-Yr.	9.00	N/A
84-04-041	Owl Be Home For Christmas-E-6230	Enesco	2-Yr.	10.00	N/A
84-04-042	Santa's Trolley-E-6231	Enesco	3-Yr.	11.00	40.00
84-04-043	Holiday Penguin-E-6240	Enesco	3-Yr.	1.50	15.00
84-04-044	Little Drummer-E-6241	Enesco	5-Yr.	2.00	N/A
84-04-045	Happy Holidays-E-6248	Enesco	2-Yr.	2.00	N/A
84-04-046	Christmas Nest-E-6249	Enesco	2-Yr.	3.00	N/A
84-04-047	Bunny's Christmas Stocking-E-6251	Enesco	Yr.Iss.	2.00	N/A
84-04-048	Santa On Ice-E-6252	Enesco	3-Yr.	2.50	25.00
84-04-049	Treasured Memories The New Sled-E-6256	Enesco	2-Yr.	7.00	N/A
84-04-050	Up On The House Top-E-6280	Enesco	6-Yr.	9.00	N/A
84-04-051	Penguins On Ice-E-6280	Enesco	2-Yr.	7.50	N/A
84-04-052	Grandchild's First Christmas 1984-E-6286	Enesco	Yr.Iss.	5.00	N/A
84-04-053	Grandchild's First Christmas1984-E-6286	Enesco	Yr.Iss.	5.00	N/A
84-04-054	Godchild's First Christmas-E-6287	Enesco	3-Yr.	7.00	N/A
84-04-055	Santa In The Box-E-6292	Enesco	2-Yr.	6.00	N/A
84-04-056	Carousel Horse-E-6913	Enesco	2-Yr.	1.50	N/A
83-04-057	Arctic Charmer-E-6945	Enesco	2-Yr.	7.00	N/A
82-04-058	Victorian Sleigh-E-6946	Enesco	4-Yr.	9.00	N/A
83-04-059	Wing-A-Ding Angel-E-6948	Enesco	3-Yr.	7.00	N/A
82-04-060	A Saviour Is Born This Day-E-6949	Enesco	8-Yr.	4.00	12-20.00
82-04-061	Crescent Santa-E-6950	Gilmore	4-Yr.	10.00	45.00
82-04-062	Baby's First Christmas 1982-E-6952	Enesco	Yr.Iss.	10.00	N/A
82-04-063	Polar Bear Fun Whoops,It's 1982-E-6953	Enesco	Yr.Iss.	10.00	N/A
82-04-064	Holiday Skier-E-6954	J. Davis	5-Yr.	7.00	N/A
82-04-065	Toy Soldier 1982-E-6957	Enesco	Yr.Iss.	6.50	N/A
82-04-066	Merry Christmas Grandma-E-6975	Enesco	3-Yr.	5.00	N/A
82-04-067	Carousel Horses-E-6958	Enesco	3-Yr.	8.00	20.00
82-04-068	Dear Santa-E-6959	Gilmore	8-Yr.	10.00	17.00
82-04-069	Penguin Power-E-6977	Enesco	2-Yr.	6.00	15.00
82-04-070	Bunny Winter Playground 1982-E-6978	Enesco	Yr.Iss.	10.00	N/A
82-04-071	Baby's First Christmas 1982-E-6979	Enesco	Yr.Iss.	10.00	N/A
83-04-072	Carousel Horses-E-6980	Enesco	4-Yr.	8.00	N/A
82-04-073	Grandchild's First Christmas 1982-E-6983	Enesco	Yr.Iss.	5.00	73.00
82-04-074	Merry Christmas Teacher-E-6984	Enesco	4-Yr.	7.00	N/A
83-04-075	Garfield Cuts The Ice-E-8771	J. Davis	3-Yr.	6.00	N/A
84-04-076	A Stocking Full For 1984-E-8773	J. Davis	Yr.Iss.	6.00	N/A
83-04-077	Stocking Full For 1983-E-8773	J. Davis	Yr.Iss.	6.00	N/A
85-04-078	Santa Claus Balloon-55794	Enesco	Yr.Iss.	8.50	N/A
85-04-079	Carousel Reindeer-55808	Enesco	4-Yr.	12.00	40.00
85-04-080	Angel In Flight-55816	Enesco	4-Yr.	8.00	20.00
85-04-081	Christmas Penguin-55824	Enesco	4-Yr.	7.50	35.00
85-04-082	Merry Christmas Godchild-55832	Gilmore	5-Yr.	8.00	N/A
85-04-083	Baby's First Christmas-55840	Enesco	2-Yr.	15.00	N/A
85-04-084	Old Fashioned Rocking Horse-55859	Enesco	2-Yr.	10.00	N/A
85-04-085	Child's Second Christmas-55867	Enesco	5-Yr.	11.00	N/A
85-04-086	Fishing For Stars-55875	Enesco	5-Yr.	9.00	N/A
85-04-087	Baby Blocks-55883	Enesco	2-Yr.	12.00	N/A
85-04-088	Christmas Toy Chest-55891	Enesco	5-Yr.	10.00	N/A
85-04-089	Grandchild's First Ornament-55921	Enesco	5-Yr.	7.00	8.00
85-04-090	Joy Photo Frame-55956	Enesco	Yr.Iss.	6.00	N/A
85-04-091	We Three Kings-55964	Enesco	Yr.Iss.	4.50	N/A
85-04-092	The Night Before Christmas-55972	Enesco	2-Yr.	5.00	N/A
85-04-093	Baby's First Christmas 1985-55980	Enesco	Yr.Iss.	6.00	N/A
85-04-094	Baby Rattle Photo Frame-56006	Enesco	2-Yr.	5.00	N/A
85-04-095	Baby's First Christmas 1985-56014	Gilmore	Yr.Iss.	10.00	N/A
85-04-096	Christmas Plane Ride-56049	L. Rigg	6-Yr.	10.00	N/A
85-04-097	Scottie Celebrating Christmas-56065	Enesco	5-Yr.	7.50	8.00
85-04-098	North Pole Native-56073	Enesco	2-Yr.	9.00	N/A
85-04-099	Skating Walrus-56081	Enesco	2-Yr.	9.00	N/A
85-04-100	Ski Time-56111	J. Davis	Yr.Iss.	13.00	N/A
85-04-101	North Pole Express-56138	J. Davis	Yr.Iss.	12.00	N/A
85-04-102	Merry Christmas Mother-56146	J. Davis	Yr.Iss.	8.50	N/A
85-04-103	Hoppy Christmas-56154	J. Davis	Yr.Iss.	8.50	N/A
85-04-104	Merry Christmas Teacher-56170	J. Davis	Yr.Iss.	6.00	N/A
85-04-105	Garfield-In-The-Box-56189	J. Davis	Yr.Iss.	6.50	N/A
85-04-106	Merry Christmas Grandma-56197	Enesco	Yr.Iss.	7.00	N/A
85-04-107	Christmas Lights-56200	Enesco	2-Yr.	8.00	N/A
85-04-108	Victorian Doll House-56251	Enesco	Yr.Iss.	13.00	N/A
85-04-109	Tobaoggan Ride-56286	Enesco	4-Yr.	6.00	N/A
85-04-110	Look Out Below-56375	Enesco	Yr.Iss.	8.50	N/A
85-04-111	Flying Santa Christmas Special-56383	Enesco	2-Yr.	10.00	N/A
85-04-112	Sawin Elf Helper-56391	Enesco	Yr.Iss.	8.00	N/A
85-04-113	Snow Shoe-In Santa-56405	Enesco	Yr.Iss.	8.00	N/A
85-04-114	Our Hero-56413	Enesco	Yr.Iss.	5.50	N/A
85-04-115	Not A Creaturxe Was Stirring-56421	Enesco	2-Yr.	4.00	N/A
85-04-116	Merry Christmas Teacher-56448	Enesco	Yr.Iss.	9.00	N/A
85-04-117	A Stocking Full For 1985-56464	J. Davis	Yr.Iss.	6.00	N/A
85-04-118	St. Nicholas Circa 1910-56659	Enesco	5-Yr.	6.00	N/A
85-04-119	Christmas Tree Photo Frame-56871	Enesco	4-Yr.	10.00	N/A
90-04-120	Deck The Halls-566063	Enesco	3-Yr.	12.50	N/A
88-04-121	Making A Point-489212	G.G. Santiago	3-Yr.	10.00	N/A
88-04-122	Mouse Upon A Pipe-489220	G.G. Santiago	2-Yr.	10.00	12.00
88-04-123	North Pole Deadline-489387	Enesco	3-Yr.	13.50	N/A
88-04-124	Christmas Pin-Up-489409	Enesco	2-Yr.	11.00	N/A
88-04-125	Airmail For Teacher-489425	Gilmore	3-Yr.	13.50	N/A
86-04-126	1st Christmas Together 1986-551171	Enesco	Yr.Iss.	9.00	15.00
86-04-127	Elf Stringing Popcorn-551198	Enesco	4-Yr.	10.00	20.00
86-04-128	Christmas Scottie-551201	Enesco	4-Yr.	7.00	15.00
86-04-129	Santa and Child-551236	Enesco	4-Yr.	13.50	25.00
86-04-130	The Christmas Angel-551244	Enesco	4-Yr.	22.50	40.00
86-04-131	Carousel Unicorn-551252	Gilmore	4-Yr.	12.00	30.00
86-04-132	Have a Heavenly Holiday-551260	Enesco	4-Yr.	9.00	N/A
86-04-133	Siamese Kitten-551279	Enesco	4-Yr.	9.00	N/A
86-04-134	Old Fashioned Doll House-551287	Enesco	4-Yr.	15.00	N/A
86-04-135	Holiday Fisherman-551309	Enesco	3-Yr.	8.00	N/A
86-04-136	Antique Toy-551317	Enesco	3-Yr.	9.00	N/A
86-04-137	Time For Christmas-551325	Gilmore	4-Yr.	13.00	N/A
86-04-138	Christmas Calendar-551333	Enesco	2-Yr.	7.00	N/A
86-04-139	Merry Christmas-551341	Gilmore	3-Yr.	8.00	45.00
86-04-140	The Santa Claus Shoppe Circa1905-551562	J. Grossman	4-Yr.	8.00	15.00
86-04-141	Baby Bear Sleigh-551651	Gilmore	3-Yr.	9.00	30.00
86-04-142	Baby's First Christmas 1986-551678	Gilmore	Yr.Iss.	10.00	N/A
86-04-143	First Christmas Together-551708	Enesco	3-Yr.	6.00	10.00
86-04-144	Baby's First Christmas-551716	Enesco	3-Yr.	5.50	10.00
86-04-145	Baby's First Christmas 1986-551724	Enesco	Yr.Iss.	6.50	N/A
86-04-146	Peek-A-Bear Grandchild's First Christmas-552004	Enesco	Yr.Iss.	6.00	N/A
86-04-147	Peek-A-Bear Present-552089	Enesco	4-Yr.	2.50	N/A
86-04-148	Peek-A-Bear Present-552089	Enesco	4-Yr.	2.50	N/A
86-04-149	Peek-A-Bear Present-552089	Enesco	4-Yr.	2.50	N/A
86-04-150	Peek-A-Bear Present-552089	Enesco	4-Yr.	2.50	N/A
86-04-151	Merry Christmas 1986-552186	L. Rigg	Yr.Iss.	8.00	N/A
86-04-152	Merry Christmas 1986-552534	L. Rigg	Yr.Iss.	8.00	N/A
86-04-153	Lucy & Me Christmas Tree-552542	L. Rigg	3-Yr.	7.00	N/A
86-04-154	Santa's Helpers-552607	Enesco	3-Yr.	2.50	N/A
86-04-155	My Special Friend-552615	Enesco	3-Yr.	6.00	N/A
86-04-156	Christmas Wishes From Panda-552623	Enesco	3-Yr.	6.00	N/A
86-04-157	Lucy & Me Ski Time-552658	L. Rigg	2-Yr.	6.50	N/A
86-04-158	Merry Christmas Teacher-552666	Enesco	3-Yr.	6.50	N/A
86-04-159	Country Cousins Merry Christmas, Mom-552704	Enesco	3-Yr.	7.00	N/A
86-C4-160	Country Cousins Merry Christmas, Dad-552704	Enesco	3-Yr.	7.00	N/A
86-04-161	Country Cousins Merry Christmas, Mom-552712	Enesco	4-Yr.	7.00	N/A
86-04-162	Country Cousins Merry Christmas, Dad-552712	Enesco	4-Yr.	7.00	N/A
86-04-163	Grandmother's Little Angel-552747	Enesco	4-Yr.	8.00	N/A
87-04-164	Puppy's 1st Christmas-552909	Enesco	2-Yr.	4.00	N/A
87-04-165	Kitty's 1st Christmas-552917	Enesco	2-Yr.	4.00	N/A
87-04-166	Merry Christmas Puppy-552925	Enesco	2-Yr.	3.50	N/A
87-04-167	Merry Christmas Kitty-552933	Enesco	2-Yr.	3.50	N/A
86-04-168	I Love My Grandparents-553263	Enesco	Yr.Iss.	6.00	N/A
86-04-169	Merry Christmas Mom & Dad-553271	Enesco	Yr.Iss.	6.00	N/A
86-04-170	S. Claus Hollycopter-553344	Enesco	4-Yr.	13.50	N/A
86-04-171	From Our House To Your House-553360	Enesco	3-Yr.	15.00	N/A
86-04-172	Christmas Rattle-553379	Enesco	3-Yr.	8.00	N/A
86-04-173	Bah, Humbug!-553387	Enesco	4-Yr.	9.00	N/A
86-04-174	God Bless Us Everyone-553395	Enesco	4-Yr.	10.00	N/A
87-04-175	Carousel Mobile-553409	Enesco	3-Yr.	15.00	50.00
86-04-176	Holiday Train-553417	Enesco	4-Yr.	10.00	N/A
86-04-177	Lighten Up!-553603	J. Davis	5-Yr.	10.00	N/A
86-04-178	Gift Wrap Odie-553611	J. Davis	Yr.Iss.	7.00	N/A
86-04-179	Merry Christmas-553646	Enesco	4-Yr.	8.00	N/A
87-04-180	M.V.B. (Most Valuable Bear)-554219	Enesco	2-Yr.	3.00	N/A

CHRISTMAS ORNAMENTS

Company Number	Name	Series Artist	Edition Limit	Issue Price	Quote
87-04-181	M.V.B. (Most Valuable Bear)-554219	Enesco	2-Yr.	3.00	N/A
87-04-182	M.V.B. (Most Valuable Bear)-554219	Enesco	2-Yr.	3.00	N/A
87-04-183	M.V.B. (Most Valuable Bear)-554219	Enesco	2-Yr.	3.00	N/A
88-04-184	1st Christmas Together-554537	Gilmore	3-Yr.	15.00	N/A
88-04-185	An Eye On Christmas-554545	Gilmore	3-Yr.	22.50	30.00
88-04-186	A Mouse Check-554553	Gilmore	3-Yr.	13.50	N/A
88-04-187	Merry Christmas Engine-554561	Enesco	2-Yr.	22.50	25.00
89-04-188	Sardine Express-554588	Gilmore	2-Yr.	17.50	22.50
88-04-189	1st Christmas Together 1988-554596	Enesco	Yr.Iss.	10.00	N/A
88-04-190	Forever Friends-554626	Gilmore	2-Yr.	12.00	N/A
88-04-191	Santa's Survey-554642	Enesco	2-Yr.	35.00	45.00
89-04-192	Old Town's Church-554871	Gilmore	2-Yr.	17.50	20.00
88-04-193	A Chipmunk Holiday-554898	Gilmore	3-Yr.	11.00	N/A
88-04-194	Christmas Is Coming-554901	Enesco	3-Yr.	12.00	12.00
88-04-195	Baby's First Christmas 1988-554928	Enesco	Yr.Iss.	7.50	N/A
88-04-196	Baby's First Christmas 1988-554936	Gilmore	Yr.Iss.	10.00	N/A
88-04-197	The Christmas Train-554944	Enesco	3-Yr.	15.00	N/A
88-04-198	Li'l Drummer Bear-554952	Gilmore	3-Yr.	12.00	12.00
87-04-199	Baby's First Christmas-555061	Enesco	3-Yr.	12.00	N/A
87-04-200	Baby's First Christmas-555088	Enesco	3-Yr.	7.50	15.00
87-04-201	Baby's First Christmas-555118	Enesco	3-Yr.	6.00	N/A
87-04-202	Sugar Plum Bearies-555193	Enesco	2-Yr.	4.50	N/A
87-04-203	Garfield Merry Kissmas-555215	J. Davis	3-Yr.	8.50	N/A
87-04-204	Sleigh Away-555401	Enesco	3-Yr.	12.00	N/A
87-04-205	Merry Christmas 1987-555428	L. Rigg	Yr.Iss.	8.00	N/A
87-04-206	Merry Christmas 1987-555436	L. Rigg	Yr.Iss.	8.00	N/A
87-04-207	Lucy & Me Storybook Bear-555444	L. Rigg	3-Yr.	6.50	N/A
87-04-208	Time For Christmas-555452	L. Rigg	3-Yr.	12.00	N/A
87-04-209	Lucy & Me Angel On A Cloud-555487	L. Rigg	3-Yr.	8.00	N/A
87-04-210	Teddy's Stocking-555940	Gilmore	3-Yr.	10.00	N/A
87-04-211	Kitty's Jack-In-The-Box-555959	Enesco	3-Yr.	11.00	N/A
87-04-212	Merry Christmas Teacher-555967	Enesco	3-Yr.	7.50	N/A
87-04-213	Mouse In A Mitten-555975	Enesco	3-Yr.	7.50	N/A
87-04-214	Boy On A Rocking Horse-555983	Enesco	3-Yr.	12.00	N/A
87-04-215	Peek-A-Bear Letter To Santa-555991	Enesco	2-Yr.	8.00	N/A
87-04-216	Garfield Sugar Plum Fairy-556009	J. Davis	3-Yr.	8.50	12.50
87-04-217	Garfield The Nutcracker-556017	J. Davis	4-Yr.	8.50	N/A
87-04-218	Home Sweet Home-556033	M. Gilmore	3-Yr.	15.00	35-50.00
87-04-219	Baby's First Christmas-556041	Enesco	4-Yr.	10.00	N/A
87-04-220	Little Sailor Elf-556068	Enesco	3-Yr.	10.00	N/A
87-04-221	Carousel Goose-556076	Enesco	3-Yr.	17.00	35-40.00
87-04-222	Night Caps-556084	Enesco	2-Yr.	5.50	N/A
87-04-223	Night Caps-556084	Enesco	2-Yr.	5.50	N/A
87-04-224	Night Caps-556084	Enesco	2-Yr.	5.50	N/A
87-04-225	Night Caps-556084	Enesco	2-Yr.	5.50	N/A
87-04-226	Rocking Horse Past Joys-556157	Enesco	3-Yr.	10.00	15.00
87-04-227	Partridge In A Pear Tree-556173	Gilmore	3-Yr.	9.00	20.00
87-04-228	Carousel Lion-556025	M. Gilmore	3-Yr.	12.00	25.00
87-04-229	Skating Santa 1987-556211	Enesco	Yr.Iss.	13.50	N/A
87-04-230	Baby's First Christmas 1987-556238	Gilmore	Yr.Iss.	10.00	N/A
87-04-231	Baby's First Christmas 1987-556254	Enesco	Yr.Iss.	7.00	N/A
87-04-232	Teddy's Suspenders-556262	Enesco	4-Yr.	8.50	N/A
87-04-233	Baby's First Christmas 1987-556297	Enesco	Yr.Iss.	2.00	N/A
87-04-234	Baby's First Christmas 1987-556297	Enesco	Yr.Iss.	2.00	N/A
87-04-235	Beary Christmas Family-556300	Enesco	2-Yr.	2.00	N/A
87-04-236	Beary Christmas Family-556300	Enesco	2-Yr.	2.00	N/A
87-04-237	Beary Christmas Family-556300	Enesco	2-Yr.	2.00	N/A
87-04-238	Beary Christmas Family-556300	Enesco	2-Yr.	2.00	N/A
87-04-239	Beary Christmas Family-556300	Enesco	2-Yr.	2.00	N/A
87-04-240	Beary Christmas Family-556300	Enesco	2-Yr.	2.00	N/A
87-04-241	Merry ChristmasTeacher-556319	Enesco	2-Yr.	2.00	N/A
87-04-242	Merry ChristmasTeacher-556319	Enesco	2-Yr.	2.00	N/A
87-04-243	Merry ChristmasTeacher-556319	Enesco	2-Yr.	2.00	N/A
87-04-244	Merry ChristmasTeacher-556319	Enesco	2-Yr.	2.00	N/A
87-04-245	1st ChristmasTogether 1987-556335	Enesco	Yr.Iss.	9.00	N/A
87-04-246	Country Cousins Katie Goes Ice Skating-556304	Enesco	3-Yr.	8.00	N/A
87-04-247	Country Cousins Scooter Snowman-556386	Enesco	3-Yr.	8.00	N/A
87-04-248	Santa's List-556394	Enesco	3-Yr.	7.00	N/A
87-04-249	Kitty's Bed-556408	Enesco	3-Yr.	12.00	N/A
87-04-250	Grandchild's First Christmas-556416	Enesco	3-Yr.	10.00	N/A
87-04-251	Two Turtledoves-556432	Gilmore	3-Yr.	9.00	N/A
87-04-252	Three French Hens-556440	Gilmore	3-Yr.	9.00	N/A
88-04-253	Four Calling Birds-556459	Gilmore	3-Yr.	11.00	N/A
87-04-254	Teddy Takes A Spin-556467	Enesco	4-Yr.	13.00	N/A
87-04-255	Tiny Toy Thimble Mobile-556475	Enesco	2-Yr.	12.00	N/A
87-04-256	Bucket O'Love-556491	Enesco	2-Yr.	2.50	N/A
87-04-257	Bucket O'Love-556491	Enesco	2-Yr.	2.50	N/A
87-04-258	Puppy Love-556505	Enesco	3-Yr.	6.00	N/A
87-04-259	Peek-A-Bear My Special Friend-556513	Enesco	4-Yr.	6.00	N/A
87-04-260	Our First Christmas Together-556548	Enesco	3-Yr.	13.00	N/A
87-04-261	Three Little Bears-556556	Enesco	3-Yr.	7.50	N/A
87-04-262	Lucy & Me Mailbox Bear-556564	L. Rigg	4-Yr.	3.00	N/A
87-04-263	Twinkle Bear-556572	Gilmore	3-Yr.	8.00	N/A
87-04-264	I'm Dreaming Of A Bright Christmas-556602	Enesco	2-Yr.	2.50	N/A
87-04-265	I'm Dreaming Of A Bright Christmas-556602	Enesco	2-Yr.	2.50	N/A
87-04-266	Christmas Train-557196	Enesco	3-Yr.	10.00	N/A
88-04-267	Dairy Christmas-557501	M. Cook	2-Yr.	10.00	15.00
88-04-268	Merry Christmas 1988-557595	L. Rigg	Yr.Iss.	10.00	N/A
88-04-269	Merry Christmas 1988-557609	L. Rigg	Yr.Iss.	10.00	N/A
88-04-270	Toy Chest Keepsake-558206	L. Rigg	3-Yr.	12.50	N/A
88-04-271	Teddy Bear Greetings-558214	L. Rigg	3-Yr.	8.00	8.00
88-04-272	Jester Bear-558222	L. Rigg	2-Yr.	8.00	N/A
88-04-273	Night-Watch Cat-558362	J. Davis	3-Yr.	13.00	N/A
88-04-274	Christmas Thim-bell-558389	Enesco	Yr.Iss.	4.00	N/A
88-04-275	Christmas Thim-bell-558389	Enesco	Yr.Iss.	4.00	N/A
88-04-276	Christmas Thim-bell-558389	Enesco	Yr.Iss.	4.00	N/A
88-04-277	Christmas Thim-bell-558389	Enesco	Yr.Iss.	4.00	N/A
88-04-278	Baby's First Christmas-558397	D. Parker	3-Yr.	16.00	N/A
88-04-279	Christmas Tradition-558400	Gilmore	2-Yr.	10.00	N/A
88-04-280	Stocking Story-558419	G.G. Santiago	3-Yr.	10.00	N/A
88-04-281	Winter Tale-558427	G.G. Santiago	2-Yr.	6.00	N/A
88-04-282	Party Mouse-558435	G.G. Santiago	3-Yr.	12.00	N/A
88-04-283	Christmas Watch-558443	G.G. Santiago	2-Yr.	11.00	14.00
88-04-284	Christmas Vacation-558451	G.G. Santiago	3-Yr.	8.00	N/A
88-04-285	Sweet Cherub-558478	G.G. Santiago	3-Yr.	7.00	8.00
88-04-286	Time Out-558486	G.G. Santiago	2-Yr.	11.00	N/A
88-04-287	The Ice Fairy-558516	G.G. Santiago	3-Yr.	23.00	N/A
88-04-288	Santa Turtle-558559	Enesco	2-Yr.	10.00	N/A
88-04-289	The Teddy Bear Ball-558567	Enesco	3-Yr.	10.00	N/A
88-04-290	Turtle Greetings-558583	Enesco	2-Yr.	8.50	N/A
88-04-291	Happy Howladays-558605	Enesco	Yr.Iss.	7.00	N/A
88-04-292	Special Delivery-558699	J. Davis	3-Yr.	9.00	N/A
88-04-293	Deer Garfield-558702	J. Davis	3-Yr.	12.00	N/A
88-04-294	Garfield Bags O' Fun-558761	J. Davis	Yr.Iss.	3.30	N/A
88-04-295	Garfield Bags O' Fun-558761	J. Davis	Yr.Iss.	3.30	N/A
88-04-296	Garfield Bags O' Fun-558761	J. Davis	Yr.Iss.	3.30	N/A
88-04-297	Garfield Bags O' Fun-558761	J. Davis	Yr.Iss.	3.30	N/A
88-04-298	Gramophone Keepsake-558818	Enesco	2-Yr.	13.00	N/A
88-04-299	North Pole Lineman-558834	Gilmore	2-Yr.	10.00	N/A
88-04-300	Five Golden Rings-559121	Gilmore	3-Yr.	11.00	N/A
88-04-301	Six Geese A-Laying-559148	Gilmore	3-Yr.	11.00	N/A
88-04-302	Pretty Baby-559156	R. Morehead	3-Yr.	12.50	N/A
88-04-303	Old Fashioned Angel-559164	R. Morehead	3-Yr.	12.50	20.00
88-04-304	Two For Tea-559776	Gilmore	3-Yr.	20.00	N/A
88-04-305	Merry Christmas Grandpa-560065	Enesco	3-Yr.	8.00	N/A
90-04-306	Reeling In The Holidays-560405	M. Cook	2-Yr.	8.00	10.00
91-04-307	Walkin' With My Baby-561029	M. Cook	2-Yr.	10.00	N/A
89-04-308	Scrub-A-Dub Chipmunk-561037	M. Cook	2-Yr.	8.00	10.00
89-04-309	Christmas Cook-Out-561045	M. Cook	2-Yr.	9.00	10.00
89-04-310	Sparkles-561843	S. Zimnicki	3-Yr.	17.50	17.50
89-04-311	Bunkie-561835	S. Zimnicki	3-Yr.	22.50	22.50
89-04-312	Popper-561878	S. Zimnicki	3-Yr.	12.00	12.50
89-04-313	Seven Swans A-Swimming-562742	Gilmore	3-Yr.	12.00	12.00
89-04-314	Eight Maids A-Milking-562750	Gilmore	3-Yr.	12.00	12.00
89-04-315	Nine Dancers Dancing-562769	Gilmore	3-Yr.	15.00	12.00
89-04-316	Baby's First Christmas 1989-562807	Enesco	Yr.Iss.	8.00	N/A
89-04-317	Baby's First Christmas 1989-562815	Gilmore	Yr.Iss.	10.00	N/A
89-04-318	First Christmas Together 1989-562823	Enesco	Yr.Iss.	11.00	N/A
89-04-319	Travelin' Trike-562882	Gilmore	3-Yr.	15.00	15.00
89-04-320	Victorian Sleigh Ride-562890	Enesco	3-Yr.	22.50	22.50
91-04-321	Santa Delivers Love-562904	Gilmore	2-Yr.	17.50	17.50
89-04-322	Chestnut Roastin'-562912	Gilmore	2-Yr.	13.00	13.00
90-04-323	Th-Ink-In' Of You-562920	Gilmore	2-Yr.	20.00	20.00
89-04-324	Ye Olde Puppet Show-562939	Enesco	2-Yr.	17.50	17.50
89-04-325	Static In The Attic-562947	Enesco	2-Yr.	13.00	13.00
89-04-326	Mistle-Toast 1989-562963	Gilmore	Yr.Iss.	15.00	22.50
89-04-327	Merry Christmas Pops-562971	Gilmore	3-Yr.	12.00	12.00
90-04-328	North Pole Or Bust-562998	Gilmore	2-Yr.	25.00	25.00
89-04-329	By The Light Of The Moon-563005	Gilmore	3-Yr.	12.00	12.00
89-04-330	Stickin' To It-563013	Gilmore	2-Yr.	10.00	12.00
89-04-331	Christmas Cookin'-563048	Gilmore	3-Yr.	22.50	22.50
89-04-332	All Set For Santa-563080	Gilmore	3-Yr.	17.50	17.50
90-04-333	Santa's Sweets-563196	Gilmore	2-Yr.	20.00	20.00
90-04-334	Purr-Fect Pals-563218	Enesco	2-Yr.	8.00	8.00
89-04-335	The Pause That Refreshes-563226	Enesco	3-Yr.	15.00	25.00
89-04-336	Ho-Ho Holiday Scrooge-563234	J. Davis	3-Yr.	13.50	13.50
89-04-337	God Bless Us Everyone-563242	J. Davis	3-Yr.	13.50	13.50
89-04-338	Scrooge With The Spirit-563250	J. Davis	3-Yr.	13.50	13.50
89-04-339	A Chains Of Pace For Odie-563269	J. Davis	3-Yr.	12.00	12.00
90-04-340	Jingle Bell Rock 1990-563390	G. Armgardt	Yr.Iss.	13.50	20.00
89-04-341	Joy Ridin'-563463	J. Davis	2-Yr.	15.00	N/A
89-04-342	Just What I Wanted-563668	M. Peters	3-Yr.	13.50	13.50
90-04-343	Pucker Up!-563676	M. Peters	3-Yr.	11.00	11.00
89-04-344	What's The Bright Idea-563684	M. Peters	3-Yr.	13.50	13.50
90-04-345	Fleas Navidad-563978	M. Peters	3-Yr.	13.50	13.50
90-04-346	Tweet Greetings-564044	J. Davis	2-Yr.	15.00	15.00
90-04-347	Trouble On 3 Wheels-564052	J. Davis	3-Yr.	20.00	20.00
89-04-348	Mine, All Mine!-564079	J. Davis	Yr.Iss.	15.00	15.00
89-04-349	Star of Stars-564389	J. Jonik	3-Yr.	9.00	9.00
90-04-350	Hang Onto Your Hat-564397	J. Jonik	3-Yr.	8.00	8.00
90-04-351	Fireplace Frolic-564435	N. Teiber	2-Yr.	25.00	25.00
89-04-352	Hoe! Hoe! Hoe!-564761	Enesco	Yr.Iss.	20.00	25.00
91-04-353	Double Scoop Snowmouse-564796	M. Cook	3-Yr.	13.50	13.50
90-04-354	Christmas Is Magic-564826	M. Cook	2-Yr.	10.00	10.00
90-04-355	Lighting Up Christmas-564834	M. Cook	2-Yr.	10.00	10.00
89-04-356	Feliz Navidad! 1989-564842	M. Cook	Yr.Iss.	11.00	25.00
89-04-357	Spreading Christmas Joy-564850	M. Cook	3-Yr.	10.00	10.00
89-04-358	Yuletide Tree House-564915	J. Jonik	3-Yr.	20.00	20.00
90-04-359	Brewnig Warm Wishes-564974	Enesco	2-Yr.	10.00	10.00
90-04-360	Yippie-I-Yuletide-564982	K. Hahn	3-Yr.	15.00	15.00
90-04-361	Coffee Break-564990	K. Hahn	3-Yr.	15.00	15.00
90-04-362	You're Sew Special-565008	K. Hahn	Yr.Iss.	20.00	22.50
90-04-363	Full House Mouse-565016	K. Hahn	2-Yr.	13.50	15.00
89-04-364	I Feel Pretty-565024	K. Hahn	3-Yr.	20.00	20.00
90-04-365	Warmest Wishes-565032	K. Hahn	3-Yr.	15.00	15.00
90-04-366	Baby's Christmas Feast-565040	K. Hahn	3-Yr.	13.50	13.50
90-04-367	Bumper Car Santa-565083	G.G. Santiago	Yr.Iss.	20.00	20.00
89-04-368	Special Delivery(Proof Ed.)-565091	G.G. Santiago	Yr.Iss.	12.00	12.00
90-04-369	Ho! Ho! Yo-Yo!(Proof Ed.)-565105	G.G. Santiago	Yr.Iss.	12.00	12.00
89-04-370	Weightin' For Santa-565148	G.G. Santiago	3-Yr.	7.50	7.50
89-04-371	Holly Fairy-565199	C.M. Baker	Yr.Iss.	15.00	25.00
90-04-372	The Christmas Tree Fairy-565202	C.M. Baker	Yr.Iss.	15.00	22.50
89-04-373	Christmas 1989-565210	L. Rigg	Yr.Iss.	12.00	N/A
89-04-374	Top Of The Class-565237	L. Rigg	3-Yr.	11.00	11.00
89-04-375	Deck The Hogs-565490	M. Cook	2-Yr.	12.00	14.00
89-04-376	Pinata Ridin'-565504	M. Cook	2-Yr.	11.00	N/A
89-04-377	Hangin' In There 1989-565598	K. Wise	Yr.Iss.	10.00	19.50
90-04-378	Meow-y Christmas 1990-565601	K. Wise	Yr.Iss.	10.00	15.00
90-04-379	Seaman's Greetings-566047	Enesco	2-Yr.	11.00	11.00
90-04-380	Hang In There-566055	Enesco	3-Yr.	13.50	13.50
91-04-381	Pedal Pushin' Santa-566071	Enesco	Yr.Iss.	20.00	N/A
90-04-382	Merry Christmas Teacher-566098	Enesco	2-Yr.	11.00	11.00
90-04-383	Festive Flight-566101	Enesco	2-Yr.	11.00	11.00
90-04-384	Santa's Suitcase-566160	Enesco	3-Yr.	25.00	25.00
89-04-385	The Purr-Fect Fit!-566462	Enesco	3-Yr.	15.00	15.00
90-04-386	Tumbles 1990-566519	S. Zimnicki	Yr.Iss.	16.00	20.00
90-04-387	Twiddles-566551	S. Zimnicki	3-Yr.	15.00	15.00
91-04-388	Snuffy-566578	S. Zimnicki	3-Yr.	17.50	17.50
90-04-389	All Aboard-567671	Gilmore	2-Yr.	17.50	17.50
89-04-390	Gone With The Wind-567698	Enesco	Yr.Iss.	13.50	N/A
89-04-391	Dorothy-567760	Enesco	Yr.Iss.	12.00	25.00
89-04-392	The Tin Man-567779	Enesco	Yr.Iss.	12.00	18.00
89-04-393	The Cowardly Lion-567787	Enesco	Yr.Iss.	12.00	18.00
89-04-394	The Scarecrow-567795	Enesco	Yr.Iss.	12.00	18.00
90-04-395	Happy Holiday Readings-568104	Enesco	2-Yr.	8.00	8.00
89-04-396	Christmas 1989-568325	L. Rigg	Yr.Iss.	12.00	N/A
91-04-397	Holiday Ahoy-568368	Enesco	2-Yr.	12.50	12.50
91-04-398	Christmas Countdown-568376	Enesco	3-Yr.	20.00	20.00
89-04-399	Clara-568406	Enesco	Yr.Iss.	12.50	15.00
90-04-400	The Nutcracker-568414	Enesco	Yr.Iss.	12.50	12.50
91-04-401	Clara's Prince-568422	Enesco	Yr.Iss.	12.50	12.50
89-04-402	Santa's Little Reindear-568430	Enesco	2-Yr.	15.00	N/A
91-04-403	Tuba Totin' Teddy-568449	Enesco	3-Yr.	15.00	15.00
90-04-404	A Calling Home At Christmas-568457	Enesco	2-Yr.	15.00	15.00
91-04-405	Love Is The Secret Ingredient-568562	L. Rigg	2-Yr.	15.00	15.00

Company		Series			
Number	Name	Artist	Edition Limit	Issue Price	Quote
90-04-406	A Spoonful of Love-568570	L. Rigg	2-Yr.	10.00	10.00
90-04-407	Christmas Swingtime 1990-568597	L. Rigg	Yr.Iss.	13.00	N/A
90-04-408	Christmas Swingtime 1990-568600	L. Rigg	Yr.Iss.	13.00	N/A
90-04-409	Bearing Holiday Wishes-568619	L. Rigg	3-Yr.	22.50	22.50
90-04-410	Smitch-570184	S. Zimnicki	3-Yr.	22.50	22.50
91-04-411	Twinkle & Sprinkle-570206	S. Zimnicki	3-Yr.	22.50	22.50
90-04-412	Blinkie-570214	S. Zimnicki	3-Yr.	15.00	15.00
90-04-413	Have A Coke And A Smile™-571512	Enesco	3-Yr.	15.00	15.00
90-04-414	Fleece Navidad-571903	M. Cook	2-Yr.	13.50	13.50
90-04-415	Have a Navaho-Ho-Ho 1990-571970	M. Cook	Yr.Iss.	15.00	17.50
90-04-416	Cheers 1990-572411	T. Wilson	Yr.Iss.	13.50	N/A
90-04-417	A Night Before Christmas-572438	T. Wilson	2-Yr.	17.50	17.50
90-04-418	Merry Kissmas-572446	T. Wilson	2-Yr.	10.00	10.00
91-04-419	Here Comes Santa Paws-572535	J. Davis	3-Yr.	20.00	20.00
90-04-420	Frosty Garfield 1990-572551	J. Davis	Yr.Iss.	13.50	13.50
90-04-421	Pop Goes The Odie-572578	J. Davis	2-Yr.	15.00	15.00
91-04-422	Sweet Beams-572586	J. Davis	2-Yr.	13.50	13.50
90-04-423	An Apple A Day-572594	J. Davis	2-Yr.	12.00	12.00
90-04-424	Dear Santa-572608	J. Davis	3-Yr.	17.00	17.00
91-04-425	Have A Ball This Christmas-572616	J. Davis	Yr.Iss.	15.00	15.00
90-04-426	Oh Shoosh!-572624	J. Davis	3-Yr.	17.00	17.00
90-04-427	Little Red Riding Cat-572632	J. Davis	Yr.Iss.	13.50	13.50
91-04-428	All Decked Out-572659	J. Davis	2-Yr.	13.50	13.50
90-04-429	Over The Rooftops-572721	J. Davis	2-Yr.	17.50	17.50
90-04-430	Garfield NFL Los Angeles Rams-572764	J. Davis	2-Yr.	12.50	12.50
90-04-431	Garfield NFLCincinnati Bengals-573000	J. Davis	2-Yr.	12.50	12.50
90-04-432	Garfield NFLCleveland Browns-573019	J. Davis	2-Yr.	12.50	12.50
90-04-433	Garfield NFL Houston Oiliers-573027	J. Davis	2-Yr.	12.50	12.50
90-04-434	Garfield NFL Pittsburg Steelers-573035	J. Davis	2-Yr.	12.50	12.50
90-04-435	Garfield NFL Denver Broncos-573043	J. Davis	2-Yr.	12.50	12.50
90-04-436	Garfield NFLKansas City Chiefs-573051	J. Davis	2-Yr.	12.50	12.50
90-04-437	Garfield NFL Los Angeles Raiders-573078	J. Davis	2-Yr.	12.50	12.50
90-04-438	Garfield NFL San Diego Chargers-573086	J. Davis	2-Yr.	12.50	12.50
90-04-439	Garfield NFL Seattle Seahawks-573094	J. Davis	2-Yr.	12.50	12.50
90-04-440	Garfield NFL Buffalo Bills-573108	J. Davis	2-Yr.	12.50	12.50
90-04-441	Garfield NFL Indianapolis Colts-573116	J. Davis	2-Yr.	12.50	12.50
90-04-442	Garfield NFL Miami Dolphins-573124	J. Davis	2-Yr.	12.50	12.50
90-04-443	Garfield NFL New England Patriots-573132	J. Davis	2-Yr.	12.50	12.50
90-04-444	Garfield NFL New York Jets-573140	J. Davis	2-Yr.	12.50	12.50
90-04-445	Garfield NFL Atlanta Falcons-573159	J. Davis	2-Yr.	12.50	12.50
90-04-446	Garfield NFL New Orleans Saints-573167	J. Davis	2-Yr.	12.50	12.50
90-04-447	Garfield NFL San Francisco 49ers-573175	J. Davis	2-Yr.	12.50	12.50
90-04-448	Garfield NFL Dallas Cowboys-573183	J. Davis	2-Yr.	12.50	12.50
90-04-449	Garfield NFL New York Giants-573191	J. Davis	2-Yr.	12.50	12.50
90-04-450	Garfield NFL Philadelphia Eagles-573205	J. Davis	2-Yr.	12.50	12.50
90-04-451	Garfield NFL Phoenix Cardinals-573213	J. Davis	2-Yr.	12.50	12.50
90-04-452	Garfield NFL Washington Redskins-573221	J. Davis	2-Yr.	12.50	12.50
90-04-453	Garfield NFL Chicago Bears-573248	J. Davis	2-Yr.	12.50	12.50
90-04-454	Garfield NFL Detroit Lions-573256	J. Davis	2-Yr.	12.50	12.50
90-04-455	Garfield NFL Green Bay Packers-573264	J. Davis	2-Yr.	12.50	12.50
90-04-456	Garfield NFLMinnesota Vikings-573272	J. Davis	2-Yr.	12.50	12.50
90-04-457	Garfield NFL Tampa Bay Buccaneers-573280	J. Davis	2-Yr.	12.50	12.50
91-04-458	Tea For Two-573299	K. Hahn	3-Yr.	30.00	30.00
91-04-459	Hot Stuff Santa-573523	Enesco	Yr.Iss.	25.00	25.00
90-04-460	Merry Moustronauts-573558	M. Cook	3-Yr.	20.00	20.00
91-04-461	Santa Wings It-573612	J. Jonik	3-Yr.	13.00	13.00
90-04-462	All Eye Want For Christmas-573647	Gilmore	3-Yr.	27.50	27.50
90-04-463	Stuck On You-573655	Gilmore	2-Yr.	12.50	12.50
90-04-464	Professor Michael Bear, The One Bear Band-573663	Gilmore	3-Yr.	22.50	22.50
90-04-465	A Caroling Wee Go-573671	Gilmore	3-Yr.	12.00	12.00
90-04-466	Merry Mailman-573698	Gilmore	2-Yr.	15.00	15.00
90-04-467	Deck The Halls-573701	Gilmore	3-Yr.	22.50	22.50
90-04-468	You're Wheel Special-573728	Gilmore	3-Yr.	15.00	15.00
91-04-469	Come Let Us Adore Him-573736	Gilmore	2-Yr.	9.00	9.00
91-04-470	Moon Beam Dreams-573760	Gilmore	3-Yr.	12.00	12.00
91-04-471	A Song For Santa-573779	Gilmore	3-Yr.	25.00	25.00
90-04-472	Warmest Wishes-573825	Gilmore	Yr.Iss.	17.50	24.50
91-04-473	Kurious Kitty-573868	Gilmore	3-Yr.	17.50	17.50
90-0¢-474	Old Mother Mouse-573922	Gilmore	2-Yr.	17.50	17.50
90-04-475	Railroad Repairs-573930	Gilmore	2-Yr.	12.50	12.50
90-04-476	Ten Lords A-Leaping-573949	Gilmore	3-Yr.	15.00	15.00
90-0¢-477	Eleven Drummers Drumming-573957	Gilmore	3-Yr.	15.00	15.00
90-04-478	Twelve Pipers Piping-573965	Gilmore	3-Yr.	15.00	15.00
90-04-479	Baby's First Christmas 1990-573973	Gilmore	Yr Iss.	10.00	N/A
90-04-480	Baby's First Christmas 1990-573981	Gilmore	Yr.Iss.	12.00	N/A
91-04-481	Peter, Peter Pumpkin Eater-574015	Gilmore	2-Yr.	20.00	20.00
90-04-482	Little Jack Horner-574058	Gilmore	2-Yr.	17.50	17.50
91-04-483	Mary, Mary Quite Contrary-574066	Gilmore	2-Yr.	22.50	22.50
91-04-484	Through The Years-574252	Gilmore	Yr.Iss.	17.50	17.50
91-04-485	Holiday Wing Ding-574333	Enesco	3-Yr.	22.50	22.50
91-04-486	North Pole Here I Come-574597	Enesco	3-Yr.	10.00	10.00
91-04-487	Christmas Caboose-574856	Gilmore	2-Yr.	25.00	25.00
90-04-488	Bubble Trouble-575038	K. Hahn	3-Yr.	20.00	20.00
91-04-489	Merry Mother-To-Be-575046	K. Hahn	3-Yr.	13.50	13.50
90-04-490	A Holiday 'Scent' Sation-575054	K. Hahn	3-Yr.	15.00	15.00
90-04-491	Catch Of The Day-575070	K. Hahn	3-Yr.	25.00	25.00
90-04-492	Don't Open 'Til Christmas-575089	K. Hahn	3-Yr.	17.50	17.50
90-04-493	I Can't Weight 'Til Christmas-575119	K. Hahn	3-Yr.	16.50	16.50
91-04-494	Deck The Halls-575127	K. Hahn	2-Yr.	15.00	15.00
90-04-495	Mouse House-575186	Enesco	3-Yr.	16.00	16.00
91-04-496	Dream A Little Dream-575593	Enesco	2-Yr.	17.50	17.50
91-04-497	Christmas Two-gether-575615	L. Rigg	3-Yr.	22.50	22.50
91-04-498	Christmas Trimmings-575631	Gilmore	2-Yr.	17.00	17.00
91-04-499	Gumball Wizard-575658	Gilmore	2-Yr.	13.00	13.00
91-04-500	Crystal Ball Christmas-575666	Gilmore	2-Yr.	22.50	22.50
90-04-501	Old King Cole-575682	Gilmore	2-Yr.	20.00	20.00
91-04-502	Tom, Tom The Piper's Son-575690	Gilmore	2-Yr.	15.00	15.00
91-04-503	Tire-d Little Bear-575852	L. Rigg	Yr.Iss.	12.50	12.50
90-04-504	Baby Bear Christmas 1990-575860	L. Rigg	Yr.Iss.	12.00	N/A
91-04-505	Crank Up The Carols-575887	L. Rigg	2-Yr.	17.50	17.50
90-04-506	Beary Christmas 1990-576158	L. Rigg	Yr.Iss.	12.00	12.00
91-04-507	Christmas Swingtime 1991-576166	L. Rigg	Yr.Iss.	13.00	13.00
91-04-508	Christmas Swingtime 1991-576174	L. Rigg	Yr.Iss.	13.00	13.00
91-04-509	Christmas Cutie-576182	Enesco	3-Yr.	13.50	13.50
91-04-510	Meow Mates-576220	Enesco	3-Yr.	12.00	12.00
91-04-511	Frosty The Snowman™-576425	Enesco	3-Yr.	15.00	15.00
91-04-512	Ris-ski Business-576719	T. Wilson	2-Yr.	10.00	10.00
91-04-513	Pinocchio-577391	J. Davis	3-Yr.	15.00	15.00
90-04-514	Yuletide Ride 1990-577502	Gilmore	Yr.Iss.	13.50	13.50
90-04-515	Tons of Toys-577510	Enesco	Yr.Iss.	13.00	13.00
90-04-516	McHappy Holidays-577529	Enesco	2-Yr.	17.50	17.50
90-04-517	Heading For Happy Holidays-577537	Enesco	3-Yr.	17.50	17.50
90-04-518	'Twas The Night Before Christmas-577545	Enesco	3-Yr.	17.50	17.50
90-04-519	Over One Million Holiday Wishes!-577553	Enesco	Yr.Iss.	17.50	17.50
90-04-520	You Malt My Heart-577596	Enesco	2-Yr.	25.00	25.00
91-04-521	All I Want For Christmas-577618	Enesco	2-Yr.	20.00	20.00
91-04-522	Things Go Better With Coke™-580597	Enesco	3-Yr.	17.00	17.00
91-04-523	Christmas To Go-580600	M. Cook	Yr.Iss.	22.50	22.50
91-04-524	Have A Mariachi Christmas-580619	M. Cook	2-Yr.	13.50	13.50
91-04-525	Christmas Is In The Air-581453	Enesco	Yr.Iss.	15.00	15.00
91-04-526	Holiday Treats-581542	Enesco	Yr.Iss.	17.50	17.50
91-04-527	Christmas Is My Goal-581550	Enesco	2-Yr.	17.50	17.50
91-04-528	A Quarter Pounder With Cheer®-581569	Enesco	3-Yr.	20.00	20.00
91-04-529	From The Same Mold-581798	Gilmore	3-Yr.	17.00	17.00
91-04-530	The Glow Of Christmas-581801	Enesco	2-Yr.	20.00	20.00
91-04-531	All Caught Up In Christmas-583537	Enesco	2-Yr.	10.00	10.00
91-04-532	Lights..Camera..Kissmas!-583626	Gilmore	Yr.Iss.	15.00	15.00
91-04-533	Sweet Steed-583634	Gilmore	3-Yr.	15.00	15.00
91-04-534	Dreamin' Of A White Christmas-583669	Gilmore	2-Yr.	15.00	15.00
91-04-535	Merry Millimeters-583677	Gilmore	3-Yr.	17.00	17.00
91-04-536	Here's The Scoop-583693	Enesco	2-Yr.	13.50	13.50
91-04-537	Happy Meal® On Wheels-583715	Enesco	3-Yr.	22.50	22.50
91-04-538	Christmas Kayak-583723	Enesco	2-Yr.	13.50	13.50
91-04-539	Marilyn Monroe-583774	Enesco	Yr.Iss.	20.00	20.00
91-04-540	A Christmas Carol-583928	Gilmore	3-Yr.	22.50	22.50
91-04-541	Checking It Twice-583936	Enesco	2-Yr.	25.00	25.00
91-04-542	Merry Christmas Go-Round-585203	J. Davis	3-Yr.	20.00	20.00
91-04-543	Holiday Hideout-585270	J. Davis	2-Yr.	15.00	15.00
91-04-544	Our Most Precious Gift-585726	Enesco	Yr.Iss.	17.50	17.50
91-04-545	Christmas Cheer-585769	Enesco	2-Yr.	13.50	13.50
91-04-546	Fired Up For Christmas-586587	Gilmore	2-Yr.	32.50	32.50
91-04-547	One Foggy Christmas Eve-586625	Gilmore	3-Yr.	30.00	30.00
91-04-548	For A Purr-fect Mom-586641	Gilmore	Yr.Iss.	12.00	12.00
91-04-549	For A Special Dad-586668	Gilmore	Yr Iss.	17.50	17.50
91-04-550	With Love-586676	Gilmore	Yr.Iss.	13.00	13.00
91-04-551	For A Purr-fect Aunt-586692	Gilmore	Yr.Iss.	12.00	12.00
91-04-552	For A Dog-Gone Great Uncle-586706	Gilmore	Yr.Iss.	12.00	12.00
91-04-553	Peddling Fun-586714	Gilmore	Yr.Iss.	16.00	16.00
91-04-554	Special Keepsakes-586722	Gilmore	Yr.Iss.	13.50	13.50
91-04-555	Hats Off To Christmas-586757	K. Hahn	Yr.Iss.	22.50	22.50
91-04-556	Baby's First Christmas 1991-586935	Enesco	Yr.Iss.	12.50	12.50
91-04-557	Jugglin' The Holidays-587028	Enesco	2-Yr.	13.00	13.00
91-04-558	Santa's Steed-587044	Enesco	Yr.Iss.	15.00	15.00
91-04-559	A Decade of Treasures-587052	Gilmore	Yr.Iss.	37.50	37.50
91-04-560	Mr. Mailmouse-587109	Gilmore	2-Yr.	17.00	17.00
91-04-561	Starry Eyed Santa-587176	Enesco	2-Yr.	15.00	15.00
91-04-562	Lighting The Way-588776	Enesco	2-Yr.	20.00	20.00
91-04-563	Rudolph-588784	Enesco	2-Yr.	17.50	17.50
89-04-564	Tea For Two-693758	N. Teiber	2-Yr.	12.50	14.00
90-04-565	Holiday Tea Toast-694770	N. Teiber	2-Yr.	13.50	13.50
91-04-566	It's Tea-lightful-694789	Enesco	2-Yr.	13.50	13.50
89-04-567	Tea Time-694797	N. Teiber	2-Yr.	12.50	N/A
89-04-568	Bottom's Up 1989-830003	Enesco	Yr Iss.	11.00	11.00
90-04-569	Sweetest Greetings 1990-830011	Gilmore	Yr.Iss.	10.00	10.00
90-04-570	First Class Christmas-830038	Gilmore	3-Yr.	10.00	10.00
89-04-571	Caught In The Act-830046	Gilmore	3-Yr.	12.50	12.50
89-04-572	Readin' & Ridin'-830054	Gilmore	3-Yr.	13.50	13.50
91-04-573	Beary Merry Mailman-830151	L. Rigg	3-Yr.	13.50	13.50
90-04-574	Here's Looking at You!-830259	Gilmore	2-Yr.	17.50	17.50
91-04-575	Stamper-830267	S. Zimnicki	Yr.Iss.	13.50	13.50
91-04-576	Santa's Key Man-830461	Gilmore	2-Yr.	11.00	11.00
91-04-577	Tie-dings Of Joy-830488	Gilmore	Yr.Iss.	12.00	12.00
90-04-578	Have a Cool Yule-830496	Gilmore	3-Yr.	12.00	12.00
90-04-579	Slots of Luck-830518	K. Hahn	2-Yr.	13.50	13.50
91-04-580	Straight To Santa-830534	J. Davis	2-Yr.	13.50	13.50
91-04-581	Letters To Santa-830925	Gilmore	2-Yr.	15.00	15.00
91-04-582	Sneaking Santa's Snack-830933	Gilmore	3-Yr.	13.00	13.00
91-04-583	Aiming For The Holidays-830941	Gilmore	2-Yr.	12.00	12.00
91-04-584	Ode To Joy-830968	Gilmore	3-Yr.	10.00	10.00
91-04-585	Fittin' Mittens-830976	Gilmore	3-Yr.	12.00	12.00
91-04-586	The Finishing Touch-831530	Gilmore	Yr.Iss.	10.00	10.00
91-04-587	A Real Classic-831603	Gilmore	Yr.Iss.	10.00	10.00
91-04-588	Christmas Fills The Air-831921	Gilmore	3-Yr.	12.00	12.00
91-04-589	Deck The Halls-860573	M. Peters	3-Yr.	12.00	12.00
91-04-590	Bathing Beauty-860581	K. Hahn	3-Yr.	13.50	13.50
92-04-591	Sparky & Buffer-561851	S. Zimnicki	3-Yr.	25.00	25.00
92-04-592	Moonlight Swing-568627	L. Rigg	3-Yr.	15.00	15.00
92-04-593	Carver-570192	S. Zimnicki	Yr. Iss.	17.50	17.50
92-04-594	A Rockin' GARFIELD Christmas-572527	J. Davis	2-Yr.	17.50	17.50
92-04-595	The Nutcracker-574023	Gilmore	3-Yr.	25.00	25.00
92-04-596	Humpty Dumpty-574244	Gilmore	2-Yr.	25.00	25.00
92-04-597	Music Mice-Tro!-575143	Enesco	2-Yr.	12.00	12.00
92-04-598	On Target Two-Gether-575623	Enesco	Yr. Iss.	17.00	17.00
92-04-599	Rock-A-Bye Baby-575704	Gilmore	2-Yr.	13.50	13.50
92-04-600	Queen of Hearts-575712	Gilmore	2-Yr.	17.50	17.50
92-04-601	Tasty Tidings-575836	L. Rigg	Yr. Iss.	13.50	13.50
92-04-602	Bearly Sleepy-578029	Gilmore	Yr. Iss.	17.50	17.50
92-04-603	Spreading Sweet Joy-580465	Enesco	Yr .Iss.	13.50	13.50
92-04-604	Ring My Bell-580740	J. Davis	Yr. Iss.	13.50	13.50
92-04-605	4 x 4 Holiday Fun-580783	J. Davis	2-Yr.	20.00	20.00
92-04-606	The Holidays Are A Hit-581577	Enesco	2-Yr.	17.50	17.50
92-04-607	Tip Top Tidings-581828	Enesco	2-Yr.	13.00	13.00
92-04-608	Christmas Lifts The Spirits-582018	Enesco	2-Yr.	25.00	25.00
92-04-609	A Pound Of Good Cheers-582034	Enesco	2-Yr.	17.50	17.50
92-04-610	Sweet as Cane Be-583642	Gilmore	3-Yr.	15.00	15.00
92-04-611	Sundae Ride-583707	Enesco	2-Yr.	20.00	20.00
92-04-612	The Cold, Crisp Taste Of Coke™-583766	Enesco	3-Yr.	17.00	17.00
92-04-613	Sew Christmasy-583820	Enesco	3-Yr.	25.00	25.00
92-04-614	Catch A Falling Star-583944	Gilmore	2-Yr.	15.00	15.00
92-04-615	Swingin' Christmas-584096	Enesco	2-Yr.	15.00	15.00
92-04-616	Mc Ho, Ho, Ho-585181	Enesco	3-Yr.	22.50	22.50
92-04-617	Holiday On Ice-585254	J, Davis	3-Yr.	17.50	17.50
92-04-618	Fast Track Cat-585289	J. Davis	3-Yr.	17.50	17.50
92-04-619	Holiday Cat Napping-585319	J. Davis	2-Yr.	20.00	20.00
92-04-620	The Finishing Touches-585610	T. Wilson	2-Yr.	17.50	17.50
92-04-621	Jolly Ol' Gent-585645	J. Jonik	3-Yr.	13.50	13.50
92-04-622	A Child's Christmas-586358	Enesco	3-Yr.	25.00	25.00
92-04-623	Festive Fiddlers-586501	Enesco	Yr. Iss.	20.00	20.00
92-04-624	La Luminaria-586579	M. Cook	2-Yr.	13.50	13.50
92-04-625	Cozy Chrismas Carriage-586730	Gilmore	2-Yr.	22.50	22.50
92-04-626	Small Fry's First Christmas-586749	Enesco	2-Yr.	17.00	17.00
92-04-627	Friendships Preserved-586765	K. Hahn	Yr. Iss.	22.50	22.50
92-04-628	Window Wish List-586854	Gilmore	2-Yr.	30.00	30.00
92-04-629	Through The Years-586862	Gilmore	Yr. Iss.	17.50	17.50
92-04-630	Baby's First Christmas 1992-586943	Enesco	Yr. Iss.	12.50	12.50
92-04-631	Firehouse Friends-586951	Gilmore	Yr. Iss.	22.50	22.50
92-04-632	Bubble Buddy-586978	Gilmore	2-Yr.	13.50	13.50

Company / Number	Name	Series / Artist	Edition Limit	Issue Price	Quote
92-04-633	The Warmth Of The Season-586994	Enesco	2-Yr.	20.00	20.00
92-04-634	It's A Go For Christmas-587095	Gilmore	2-Yr.	15.00	15.00
92-04-635	Post-Mouster General-587117	Gilmore	2-Yr.	20.00	20.00
92-04-636	To A Deer Baby-587168	Enesco	Yr.Iss.	18.50	18.50
92-04-637	Moon Watch-587184	Enesco	2-Yr.	20.00	20.00
92-04-638	Guten Cheers-587192	Enesco	Yr.Iss.	22.50	22.50
92-04-639	Put On A Happy Face-588237	Enesco	2-Yr.	15.00	15.00
92-04-640	Beginning To Look A Lot Like Christmas-588253	Enesco	2-Yr.	15.00	15.00
92-04-641	A Christmas Toast-588261	Enesco	2-Yr.	20.00	20.00
92-04-642	Merry Mistle-Toad-588288	Enesco	2-Yr.	15.00	15.00
92-04-643	Tic-Tac-Mistle-Toe-588296	Enesco	3-Yr.	23.00	23.00
92-04-644	Heaven Sent-588423	J. Penchoff	2-Yr.	12.50	12.50
92-04-645	Holiday Happenings-588555	Gilmore	3-Yr.	30.00	30.00
92-04-646	Seed-son's Greetings-588571	Gilmore	3-Yr.	27.00	27.00
92-04-647	Santa's Midnight Snack-588598	Gilmore	2-Yr.	20.00	20.00
92-04-648	Trunk Of Treasures-588636	Enesco	Yr.Iss.	20.00	20.00
92-04-649	Festive Newsflash-588792	Enesco	2-Yr.	17.50	17.50
92-04-650	A-B-C-Son's Greetings-588806	Enesco	2-Yr.	16.50	16.50
92-04-651	Hoppy Holidays-588814	Enesco	Yr.Iss.	13.50	13.50
92-04-652	Fireside Friends-588830	Enesco	2-Yr.	20.00	20.00
92-04-653	Christmas Eve-mergency-588849	Enesco	2-Yr.	27.00	27.00
92-04-654	A Sure Sign Of Christmas-588857	Enesco	2-Yr.	22.50	22.50
92-04-655	Holidays Give Me A Lift-588865	Enesco	2-Yr.	30.00	30.00
92-04-656	Yule Tide Together-588903	Enesco	2-Yr.	20.00	20.00
92-04-657	Have A Soup-er Christmas-588911	Enesco	2-Yr.	17.50	17.50
92-04-658	Christmas Cure-Alls-588938	Enesco	2-Yr.	20.00	20.00
92-04-659	Dial 'S' For Santa-589373	Enesco	2-Yr.	25.00	25.00
92-04-660	Joy To The Whirled-589551	K. Hahn	2-Yr.	20.00	20.00
92-04-661	Merry Make-Over-589586	K. Hahn	3-Yr.	20.00	20.00
92-04-662	Campin' Companions-590282	K. Hahn	3-Yr.	20.00	20.00
92-04-663	Fur-Ever Friends-590797	Gilmore	2-Yr.	13.50	13.50
92-04-664	Tee-rific holidays-590827	Enesco	3-Yr.	25.00	25.00
92-04-665	Spinning Christmas Dreams-590908	K. Hahn	3-Yr.	22.50	22.50
92-04-666	Christmas Trimmin'-590932	Enesco	3-Yr.	17.00	17.00
92-04-667	Wrappin' Up Warm Wishes-593141	Enesco	Yr.Iss.	17.50	17.50
92-04-668	Christmas Biz-593168	Enesco	2-Yr.	22.50	22.50
92-04-669	Holiday Take-Out-593508	Enesco	Yr Iss.	17.50	17.50
92-04-670	A Christmas Yarn-593516	Gilmore	Yr.Iss.	20.00	20.00
92-04-671	Treasure The Earth-593826	K. Hahn	2-Yr.	25.00	25.00
92-04-672	Toyful' Rudolph-593982	Enesco	2-Yr.	22.50	22.50
92-04-673	Take A Chance On The Holidays-594075	Enesco	3-Yr.	20.00	20.00
92-04-674	Lights..Camera..Christmas!-594369	Enesco	3-Yr.	20.00	20.00
92-04-675	Spirited Stallion-594407	Enesco	Yr.Iss.	15.00	15.00
92-04-676	A Watchful Eye-595713	Enesco	Yr.Iss.	15.00	15.00
92-04-677	Good Catch-595721	Enesco	Yr.Iss.	12.50	12.50
92-04-678	Squirrelin' It Away-595748	K. Hahn	Yr.Iss.	12.00	12.00
92-04-679	Checkin' His List-595756	Enesco	Yr.Iss.	12.50	12.50
92-04-680	Christmas Cat Nappin'	Enesco	Yr.Iss.	12.00	12.00
92-04-681	Bless Our Home-595772	Enesco	Yr.Iss.	12.00	12.00
92-04-682	Salute the Season-595780	K. Hahn	Yr.Iss.	12.00	12.00
92-04-683	Fired Up For Christmas-595799	Enesco	Yr.Iss.	12.00	12.00
92-04-684	Speedin' Mr. Snowman-595802	M. Rhyner	Yr.Iss.	12.00	12.00
92-04-685	Merry Christmas Mother Earth-595810	K. Hahn	Yr.Iss.	11.00	11.00
92-04-686	Wear The Season With A Smile-595829	Enesco	Yr.Iss.	10.00	10.00
92-04-687	Jesus Loves Me-595837	K. Hahn	Yr.Iss.	10.00	10.00
92-04-688	Merry Kisses-831166	Enesco	2-Yr.	17.50	17.50
92-04-689	Christmas Is In The Air-831174	Enesco	2-Yr.	25.00	25.00
92-04-690	To The Point-831182	Gilmore	2-Yr.	13.50	13.50
92-04-691	Poppin' Hoppin' Holidays-831263	Gilmore	Yr.Iss.	25.00	25.00
92-04-692	Tankful Tidings-831271	Gilmore	2-Yr.	30.00	30.00
92-04-693	Ginger-Bred Greetings-831581	Gilmore	Yr.Iss.	12.00	12.00
92-04-694	A Gold Star For Teacher-831948	Gilmore	3-Yr.	15.00	15.00
92-04-695	A Tall Order-832758	Gilmore	3-Yr.	12.00	12.00
92-04-696	Candlelight Serenade-832766	Gilmore	2-Yr.	12.00	12.00
92-04-697	Holiday Glow Puppet Show-832774	Gilmore	3-Yr.	15.00	15.00
92-04-698	Christopher Columouse-832782	Gilmore	Yr.Iss.	12.00	12.00
92-04-699	Cartin' Home Holiday Treats-832790	Enesco	2-Yr.	13.50	13.50
92-04-700	Making Tracks To Santa-832804	Gilmore	2-Yr.	15.00	15.00
92-04-701	Special Delivery-832812	Enesco	2-Yr.	12.00	12.00
92-04-702	A Mug Full Of Love-832928	Gilmore	Yr.Iss.	13.50	13.50
92-04-703	Have A Cool Christmas-832944	Gilmore	Yr.Iss.	13.50	13.50
92-04-704	Knitten' Kittens-832952	Gilmore	Yr.Iss.	17.50	17.50
92-04-705	Holiday Honors-833029	Gilmore	Yr.Iss.	15.00	15.00
92-04-706	Christmas Nite Cap-834424	Gilmore	3-Yr.	13.50	13.50
92-04-707	North Pole Peppermint Patrol-840157	Gilmore	2-Yr.	25.00	25.00
92-04-708	A Boot-iful Christmas-840165	Gilmore	Yr.Iss.	20.00	20.00
92-04-709	Watching For Santa-840432	Enesco	2-Yr.	25.00	25.00
92-04-710	Special Delivery-840440	Enesco	Yr.Iss.	22.50	22.50
Flambro Imports		**Emmett Kelly Jr. Christmas Ornaments**			
89-01-001	65th Birthday	Undis.	Closed	24.00	40-95.00
90-01-002	30 Years Of Clowning	Undis.	Closed	30.00	40-125.00
91-01-003	EKJ With Stocking And Toys	Undis.	Yr.Iss.	30.00	30.00
92-01-004	Home For Christmas	Undis.	Yr.Iss.	24.00	24.00
Flambro Imports		**Raggedy Ann and Andy Ornaments**			
89-02-002	Raggedy Andy w/Gift Stocking	Undis.	Yr.Iss.	13.50	18.00
89-02-002	Raggedy Andy w/Candy Cane	Undis.	Yr.Iss.	13.50	18.00
Goebel Inc.		**Co-Boy Annual Ornaments**			
86-01-001	Coboy with Wreath	G. Skrobek	Closed	18.00	25.00
87-01-002	Coboy with Candy Cane	G. Skrobek	Closed	25.00	25.00
88-01-003	Coboy with Tree	G. Skrobek	Closed	30.00	30.00
Goebel Inc.		**Charlot Byj Annual Ornaments**			
86-02-001	Santa Lucia Angel	Charlot Byj	Closed	18.00	25.00
87-02-002	Christmas Pageant	Charlot Byj	Closed	20.00	20.00
88-02-003	Angel with Sheet Music	Charlot Byj	Closed	22.00	22.00
Goebel Inc.		**Charlot Byj Baby Ornaments**			
86-03-001	Baby Ornament	Charlot Byj	Closed	18.00	18.00
87-03-002	Baby Snow	Charlot Byj	Closed	20.00	20.00
88-03-003	Baby's 1st Stocking	Charlot Byj	Closed	27.50	27.50
Goebel Inc.		**Annual Christmas Bell Ornaments**			
84-04-001	Christmas Tree	Goebel	Yr.Iss.	14.00	25.00
85-04-002	Santa	Goebel	Yr.Iss.	14.00	15.00
86-04-003	Wreath	Goebel	Yr.Iss.	15.00	15.00
87-04-004	Teddy Bear	Goebel	Yr.Iss.	17.25	17.25
88-04-005	Crystal Bell	Goebel	Yr.Iss.	7.50	15.00
Goebel Inc.		**Angel Bells Annual Ornaments**			
76-05-001	Angel with Flute-white	Goebel	Yr.Iss.	7.00	28-70.00
76-05-002	Angel with Flute-blue	Goebel	Yr.Iss.	9.00	100.00
76-05-003	Angel with Flute-pink	Goebel	Yr.Iss.	9.00	100.00
76-05-004	Angel with Flute-red	Goebel	Yr.Iss.	9.00	100.00
77-05-005	Angel with Banjo-white	Goebel	Yr.Iss.	7.00	30.00
77-05-006	Angel with Banjo-green	Goebel	Yr.Iss.	9.00	35.00
77-05-007	Angel with Banjo-purple	Goebel	Yr.Iss.	9.00	35.00
77-05-008	Angel with Banjo-yellow	Goebel	Yr.Iss.	9.00	35.00
78-05-009	Angel with Harp-white	Goebel	Yr.Iss.	9.00	30.00
78-05-010	Angel with Harp-rust	Goebel	Yr.Iss.	11.00	35.00
78-05-011	Angel with Harp-blue	Goebel	Yr.Iss.	11.00	25-35.00
78-05-012	Angel with Harp-pink	Goebel	Yr.Iss.	11.00	35.00
79-05-013	Angel with Accordion-white	Goebel	Yr.Iss.	9.00	30.00
79-05-014	Angel with Accordion-green	Goebel	Yr.Iss.	11.00	35.00
79-05-015	Angel with Accordion-purple	Goebel	Yr.Iss.	11.00	35.00
79-05-016	Angel with Accordion-yellow	Goebel	Yr.Iss.	11.00	35.00
80-05-017	Angel with Saxaphone-white	Goebel	Yr.Iss.	11.50	30.00
80-05-018	Angel with Saxaphone-rust	Goebel	Yr.Iss.	13.50	35.00
80-05-019	Angel with Saxaphone-pink	Goebel	Yr.Iss.	13.50	25-35.00
80-05-020	Angel with Saxaphone-blue	Goebel	Yr.Iss.	13.50	35.00
81-05-021	Angel with Song Sheet-white	Goebel	Yr.Iss.	12.00	25-30.00
81-05-022	Angel with Song Sheet-green	Goebel	Yr.Iss.	14.00	35.00
81-05-023	Angel with Song Sheet-yellow	Goebel	Yr.Iss.	14.00	35.00
81-05-024	Angel with Song Sheet-purple	Goebel	Yr.Iss.	14.00	35.00
82-05-025	Angel with French Horn-white	Goebel	Yr.Iss.	12.00	30.00
82-05-026	Angel with French Horn-rust	Goebel	Yr.Iss.	14.00	35.00
82-05-027	Angel with French Horn-green	Goebel	Yr.Iss.	14.00	35.00
82-05-028	Angel with French Horn-red	Goebel	Yr.Iss.	14.00	35.00
83-05-029	Angel with Reed Pipe-white	Goebel	Yr.Iss.	12.00	30.00
83-05-030	Angel with Reed Pipe-orange	Goebel	Yr.Iss.	14.00	35.00
83-05-031	Angel with Reed Pipe-purple	Goebel	Yr.Iss.	14.00	35.00
83-05-032	Angel with Reed Pipe-brown	Goebel	Yr.Iss.	14.00	35.00
84-05-033	Angel with Drum-white	Goebel	Yr.Iss.	12.00	30.00
84-05-034	Angel with Drum-red	Goebel	Yr.Iss.	14.00	35.00
84-05-035	Angel with Drum-green	Goebel	Yr.Iss.	14.00	35.00
85-05-036	Angel with Trumpet-white	Goebel	Yr.Iss.	12.00	30.00
85-05-037	Angel with Trumpet-red	Goebel	Yr.Iss.	14.00	25-35.00
85-05-038	Angel with Trumpet-green	Goebel	Yr.Iss.	14.00	35.00
85-05-039	Angel with Trumpet-blue	Goebel	Yr.Iss.	14.00	35.00
86-05-040	Angel with Bells-white	Goebel	Yr.Iss.	12.50	30.00
86-05-041	Angel with Bells-red	Goebel	Yr.Iss.	15.00	35.00
86-05-042	Angel with Bells-green	Goebel	Yr.Iss.	15.00	35.00
86-05-043	Angel with Bells-yellow	Goebel	Yr.Iss.	15.00	35.00
87-05-044	Angel Conductor-white	Goebel	Yr.Iss.	15.00	25-30.00
87-05-045	Angel Conductor-blue	Goebel	Yr.Iss.	17.25	35.00
87-05-046	Angel Conductor-red	Goebel	Yr.Iss.	17.25	35.00
87-05-047	Angel Conductor-green	Goebel	Yr.Iss.	17.25	35.00
88-05-048	Angel with Star-white	Goebel	Yr.Iss.	17.00	23.00
88-05-049	Angel with Star-yellow	Goebel	Yr.Iss.	20.00	20.00
88-05-050	Angel with Star-green	Goebel	Yr.Iss.	20.00	20.00
88-05-051	Angel with Star-red	Goebel	Yr.Iss.	20.00	20.00
Goebel Inc.		**Annual Ornaments**			
78-06-001	Santa (white)	Goebel	Yr.Iss.	7.50	12.00
78-06-002	Santa (color)	Goebel	Yr.Iss.	15.00	17.00
79-06-003	Angel/Tree (white)	Goebel	Yr.Iss.	8.00	13.00
79-06-004	Angel/Tree (color)	Goebel	Yr.Iss.	16.00	18.00
80-06-005	Mrs. Santa (white)	Goebel	Yr.Iss.	9.00	14.00
80-06-006	Mrs. Santa (color)	Goebel	Yr.Iss.	17.00	17.00
81-06-007	The Nutcracker (white)	Goebel	Yr.Iss.	10.00	10.00
81-06-008	The Nutcracker (color)	Goebel	Yr.Iss.	18.00	18.00
82-06-009	Santa in Chimney (white)	Goebel	Yr.Iss.	10.00	10.00
82-06-010	Santa in Chimney (color)	Goebel	Yr.Iss.	18.00	18.00
83-06-011	Clown (white)	Goebel	Yr.Iss.	10.00	10.00
83-06-012	Clown (color)	Goebel	Yr.Iss.	18.00	18.00
84-06-013	Snowman (white)	Goebel	Yr.Iss.	10.00	10.00
84-06-014	Snowman (color)	Goebel	Yr.Iss.	18.00	18.00
85-06-015	Angel (white)	Goebel	Yr.Iss.	9.00	9.00
85-06-016	Angel (color)	Goebel	Yr.Iss.	18.00	18.00
86-06-017	Drummer Boy (white)	Goebel	Yr.Iss.	9.00	9.00
86-06-018	Drummer Boy (color)	Goebel	Yr.Iss.	18.00	18.00
87-06-019	Rocking Horse (white)	Goebel	Yr.Iss.	10.00	10.00
87-06-020	Rocking Horse (color)	Goebel	Yr.Iss.	20.00	20.00
88-06-021	Doll (white)	Goebel	Yr.Iss.	12.50	12.50
88-06-022	Doll (color)	Goebel	Yr.Iss.	22.50	22.50
89-06-023	Dove (white)	Goebel	Yr.Iss.	12.50	12.50
89-06-024	Dove (color)	Goebel	Yr.Iss.	20.00	20.00
90-06-025	Girl In Sleigh	Goebel	Yr.Iss.	30.00	30.00
91-06-026	Baby On Moon	Goebel	Yr.Iss.	35.00	35.00
Goebel Inc.		**Annual Ornaments - Glass**			
79-07-001	Santa	Goebel	15,000	12.00	12.00
80-07-002	Angel with Tree	Goebel	15,000	12.00	12.00
81-07-003	Mrs. Santa	Goebel	15,000	12.00	12.00
82-07-004	The Nutcracker	Goebel	15,000	4.00	4.00
Goebel Inc.		**Christmas Ornaments**			
87-08-001	Three Angels with Toys-(Set)	Goebel	Open	30.00	30.00
87-08-002	Three Angels with Instruments-(Set)	Goebel	Open	30.00	30.00
88-08-003	Snowman	Goebel	Open	10.00	10.00
88-08-004	Santa's Boot	Goebel	Open	7.50	7.50
88-08-005	Saint Nick	Goebel	Open	15.00	15.00
88-08-006	Nutcracker	Goebel	Open	15.00	15.00
86-08-007	Teddy Bear - Red Hat	Goebel	Open	5.00	5.00
86-08-008	Teddy Bear - Red Scarf	Goebel	Open	5.00	5.00
86-08-009	Teddy Bear - Red Boots	Goebel	Open	5.00	5.00
86-08-010	Angel - Red with Song	Goebel	Open	6.00	6.00
86-08-011	Angel - Red with Book	Goebel	Open	6.00	6.00
86-08-012	Angel - Red with Bell	Goebel	Open	6.00	6.00
86-08-013	Angel with Lantern (color)	Goebel	Open	8.00	8.00
86-08-014	Angel with Lantern (white)	Goebel	Open	6.00	6.00
86-08-015	Angel with Horn (color)	Goebel	Open	8.00	8.00
86-08-016	Angel with Horn (white)	Goebel	Open	6.00	6.00
86-08-017	Angel with Lute (color)	Goebel	Open	8.00	8.00
86-08-018	Angel with Lute (white)	Goebel	Open	6.00	6.00
88-08-019	Angel with Toy Teddy Bear	Goebel	Open	10.00	10.00
88-08-020	Angel with Toy Rocking Horse	Goebel	Open	10.00	10.00
88-08-021	Angel with Toy Train	Goebel	Open	10.00	10.00
88-08-022	Angel with Toys-(Set of three)	Goebel	Open	30.00	30.00
88-08-023	Angel with Banjo	Goebel	Open	10.00	10.00
88-08-024	Angel with Accordian	Goebel	Open	10.00	10.00
88-08-025	Angel with Violin	Goebel	Open	10.00	10.00

Number	Name	Artist	Edition Limit	Issue Price	Quote
88-08-026	Angel with Music Set	Goebel	Open	30.00	30.00
Goebel/Schmid	**M.I. Hummel Annual Figurine Ornaments**				
88-01-001	Flying High 452	M.I. Hummel	Closed	75.00	125-135.
89-01-002	Love From Above 481	M.I. Hummel	Closed	75.00	80-135.00
90-01-003	Peace on Earth 484	M.I. Hummel	Closed	80.00	85-105.00
91-01-004	Angelic Guide 571	M.I. Hummel	Closed	95.00	95.00
92-01-005	Light Up The Night 622	M.I. Hummel	Yr.Iss.	100.00	100.00
93-01-006	Herald on High 623	M.I. Hummel	Yr.Iss.	Unkn.	Unkn.
Goebel/Schmid	**M.I. Hummel Collectibles Annual Bell Ornaments**				
89-02-001	Ride Into Christmas 775	M.I. Hummel	Closed	35.00	35-85.00
90-02-002	Letter to Santa Claus 776	M.I. Hummel	Closed	37.50	37.50-50.00
91-02-003	Hear Ye, Hear Ye 777	M.I. Hummel	Closed	39.50	39.50
92-02-004	Harmony in Four Parts 778	M.I. Hummel	Yr.Iss.	50.00	50.00
93-02-005	Celestial Musician 779	M.I. Hummel	Yr.Iss.	Unkn.	Unkn.
Gorham	**Archive Collectible**				
88-01-001	Victorian Heart	Gorham	Open	50.00	50.00
89-01-002	Victorian Wreath	Gorham	Open	50.00	50.00
90-01-003	Elizabethan Cupid	Gorham	Open	60.00	60.00
91-01-004	Baroque Angels	Gorham	Open	55.00	55.00
92-01-005	Madonna and Child	Gorham	Yr.Iss.	50.00	50.00
Gorham	**Annual Snowflake Ornaments**				
70-02-001	Sterling Snowflake	Gorham	Closed	10.00	250-325.
71-02-002	Sterling Snowflake	Gorham	Closed	10.00	90-125.00
72-02-003	Sterling Snowflake	Gorham	Closed	10.00	75-125.00
73-02-004	Sterling Snowflake	Gorham	Closed	10.95	65-110.00
74-02-005	Sterling Snowflake	Gorham	Closed	17.50	45-75.00
75-02-006	Sterling Snowflake	Gorham	Closed	17.50	45-75.00
76-02-007	Sterling Snowflake	Gorham	Closed	20.00	45-75.00
77-02-008	Sterling Snowflake	Gorham	Closed	22.50	45-70.00
78-02-009	Sterling Snowflake	Gorham	Closed	22.50	45-70.00
79-02-010	Sterling Snowflake	Gorham	Closed	32.80	70.00
80-02-011	Silverplated Snowflake	Gorham	Closed	15.00	75.00
81-02-012	Sterling Snowflake	Gorham	Closed	50.00	85.00
82-02-013	Sterling Snowflake	Gorham	Closed	37.50	75.00
83-02-014	Sterling Snowflake	Gorham	Closed	45.00	45-80.00
84-02-015	Sterling Snowflake	Gorham	Closed	45.00	45-75.00
85-02-016	Sterling Snowflake	Gorham	Closed	45.00	45-75.00
86-02-017	Sterling Snowflake	Gorham	Closed	45.00	45-60.00
87-02-018	Sterling Snowflake	Gorham	Closed	50.00	60.00
88-02-019	Sterling Snowflake	Gorham	Closed	50.00	50.00
89-02-020	Sterling Snowflake	Gorham	Closed	50.00	50.00
90-02-021	Sterling Snowflake	Gorham	Closed	50.00	50.00
91-02-022	Sterling Snowflake	Gorham	Closed	55.00	55.00
92-02-023	Sterling Snowflake	Gorham	Yr.Iss.	50.00	50.00
Gorham	**Annual Crystal Ornaments**				
85-03-001	Crystal Ornament	Gorham	Closed	22.00	22.00
86-03-002	Crystal Ornament	Gorham	Closed	25.00	25.00
87-03-003	Crystal Ornament	Gorham	Closed	25.00	25.00
88-03-004	Crystal Ornament	Gorham	Closed	28.00	28.00
89-03-005	Crystal Ornament	Gorham	Closed	28.00	28.00
90-03-006	Crystal Ornament	Gorham	Closed	30.00	30.00
91-03-007	Crystal Ornament	Gorham	Closed	35.00	35.00
92-03-008	Crystal Ornament	Gorham	Yr. Iss.	32.50	32.50
Gorham	**Baby's First Christmas Crystal**				
91-04-001	Baby's First Rocking Horse	Gorham	Open	35.00	35.00
Dave Grossman Creations	**Emmett Kelly Annual Figurine Ornaments**				
86-01-001	A Christmas Carol	B. Leighton Jones	Closed	12.00	12.00
87-01-002	Christmas Wreath	B. Leighton Jones	Closed	14.00	14.00
88-01-003	Christmas Dinner	B. Leighton Jones	Closed	15.00	15.00
89-01-004	Christmas Feast	B. Leighton Jones	Closed	15.00	15.00
90-01-005	Just What I Needed	B. Leighton Jones	Closed	15.00	15.00
91-01-006	Emmett the Snowman	B. Leighton Jones	Closed	15.00	25-30.00
92-01-007	Christmas Tunes	B. Leighton Jones	Yr.Iss.	15.00	15.00
Dave Grossman Creations	**Gone With the Wind Ornaments**				
87-02-001	Tara	D. Geenty	Closed	15.00	45.00
87-02-002	Rhett	D. Geenty	Closed	15.00	45.00
87-02-003	Scarlett	D. Geenty	Closed	15.00	45.00
87-02-004	Ashley	D. Geenty	Closed	15.00	45.00
88-02-005	Rhett and Scarlett	D. Geenty	Closed	20.00	40.00
89-02-006	Mammy	D. Geenty	Closed	20.00	20.00
90-02-007	Scarlett (Red Dress)	D. Geenty	Closed	20.00	20.00
91-02-008	Prissy	R. Brown	Closed	20.00	20.00
92-02-009	Scarlett (Green Dress)	Rockwell-Inspired	Yr.Iss.	20.00	20.00
Dave Grossman Designs	**Norman Rockwell Collection-Annual Rockwell Figurine Ornaments**				
78-01-001	Caroler NRX-03	Rockwell-Inspired	Retrd.	15.00	45.00
79-01-002	Drum for Tommy NRX-24	Rockwell-Inspired	Retrd.	20.00	30.00
80-01-003	Santa's Good Boys NRX-37	Rockwell-Inspired	Retrd.	20.00	30.00
81-01-004	Letters to Santa NRX-39	Rockwell-Inspired	Retrd.	20.00	30.00
82-01-005	Cornettist NRX-32	Rockwell-Inspired	Retrd.	20.00	30.00
83-01-006	Fiddler NRX-83	Rockwell-Inspired	Retrd.	20.00	30.00
84-01-007	Christmas Bounty NRX-84	Rockwell-Inspired	Retrd.	20.00	30.00
85-01-008	Jolly Coachman NRX-85	Rockwell-Inspired	Retrd.	20.00	30.00
86-01-007	Grandpa on Rocking Horse NRX-86	Rockwell-Inspired	Retrd.	20.00	30.00
87-01-008	Skating Lesson NRX-87	Rockwell-Inspired	Retrd.	20.00	30.00
88-01-009	Big Moment NRX-88	Rockwell-Inspired	Retrd.	20.00	25.00
89-01-010	Discovery NRX-89	Rockwell-Inspired	Retrd.	20.00	20.00
90-01-011	Bringing Home The Tree NRX-90	Rockwell-Inspired	Retrd.	20.00	20.00
91-01-012	Downhill Daring B NRX-91	Rockwell-Inspired	Retrd.	20.00	20.00
92-01-013	On The Ice	Rockwell-Inspired	Yr.Iss.	20.00	20.00
Dave Grossman Designs	**Norman Rockwell Collection-Annual Rockwell Ball Ornaments**				
75-02-001	Santa with Feather Quill NRO-01	Rockwell-Inspired	Retrd.	3.50	25.00
76-02-002	Santa at Globe NRO-02	Rockwell-Inspired	Retrd.	4.00	25.00
77-02-003	Grandpa on Rocking Horse NRO-03	Rockwell-Inspired	Retrd.	4.00	12.00
78-02-004	Santa with Map NRO-04	Rockwell-Inspired	Retrd.	4.50	12.00
79-02-005	Santa at Desk with Mail Bag NRO-05	Rockwell-Inspired	Retrd.	5.00	12.00
80-02-006	Santa Asleep with Toys NRO-06	Rockwell-Inspired	Retrd.	5.00	10.00
81-02-007	Santa with Boy on Finger NRO-07	Rockwell-Inspired	Retrd.	5.00	10.00
82-02-008	Santa Face on Winter Scene NRO-08	Rockwell-Inspired	Retrd.	5.00	10.00
83-02-009	Coachman with Whip NRO-9	Rockwell-Inspired	Retrd.	5.00	10.00
84-02-010	Christmas Bounty Man NRO-10	Rockwell-Inspired	Retrd.	5.00	10.00
85-02-011	Old English Trio NRO-11	Rockwell-Inspired	Retrd.	5.00	10.00
86-02-012	Tiny Tim on Shoulder NRO-12	Rockwell-Inspired	Retrd.	5.00	10.00
87-02-013	Skating Lesson NRO-13	Rockwell-Inspired	Retrd.	5.00	10.00
88-02-014	Big Moment NRO-14	Rockwell-Inspired	Retrd.	5.50	6.00
89-02-015	Discovery NRO-15	Rockwell-Inspired	Retrd.	6.00	6.00
90-02-016	Bringing Home The Tree NRO-16	Rockwell-Inspired	Retrd.	6.00	6.00
91-02-017	Downhill Daring NRO-17	Rockwell-Inspired	Retrd.	6.00	6.00
92-02-018	On The Ice NRO-18	Rockwell-Inspired	Yr.Iss.	6.00	6.00
Dave Grossman Designs	**Norman Rockwell Collection-Character Doll Ornaments**				
83-03-001	Doctor and Doll NRD-01	Rockwell-Inspired	Retrd.	20.00	30.00
83-03-002	Lovers NRD-02	Rockwell-Inspired	Retrd.	20.00	30.00
83-03-003	Samplers NRD-03	Rockwell-Inspired	Retrd.	20.00	30.00
Hallmark Keepsake Ornaments	**1973 Hallmark Keepsake Collection**				
73-01-001	Betsey Clark 250XHD100-2	Keepsake	Yr.Iss.	2.50	85.00
73-01-002	Betsey Clark-First Edition 250XHD 110-2	Keepsake	Yr.Iss.	2.50	125.00
73-01-003	Manger Scene 250XHD102-2	Keepsake	Yr.Iss.	2.50	75.00
73-01-004	Christmas Is Love 250XHD106-2	Keepsake	Yr.Iss.	2.50	80.00
73-01-005	Santa with Elves 250XHD101-5	Keepsake	Yr.Iss.	2.50	75.00
73-01-006	Elves 250XHD103-5	Keepsake	Yr.Iss.	2.50	75.00
Hallmark Keepsake Ornaments	**1973 Keepsake Yarn Ornaments**				
73-02-001	Mr. Santa 125XHD74-5	Keepsake	Yr.Iss.	1.25	27.50
73-02-002	Mrs. Santa 125XHD75-2	Keepsake	Yr.Iss.	1.25	22.50
73-02-003	Mr. Snowman 125XHD76-5	Keepsake	Yr.Iss.	1.25	24.50
73-02-004	Mrs. Snowman 125XHD77-2	Keepsake	Yr.Iss.	1.25	22.50
73-02-005	Angel 125XHD78-5	Keepsake	Yr.Iss.	1.25	27.50
73-02-006	Elf 125XHD79-2	Keepsake	Yr.Iss.	1.25	24.50
73-02-007	Choir Boy 125XHD80-5	Keepsake	Yr.Iss.	1.25	27.50
73-02-008	Soldier 100XHD81-2	Keepsake	Yr.Iss.	1.00	22.00
73-02-009	Little Girl 125XHD82-5	Keepsake	Yr.Iss.	1.25	22.50
73-02-010	Boy Caroler 125XHD83-2	Keepsake	Yr.Iss.	1.25	29.50
73-02-011	Green Girl 125XHD84-5	Keepsake	Yr.Iss.	1.25	22.50
73-02-012	Blue Girl 125XHD85-2	Keepsake	Yr.Iss.	1.25	22.50
Hallmark Keepsake Ornaments	**1974 Hallmark Keepsake Collection**				
74-03-001	Norman Rockwell 250QX111-1	Keepsake	Yr.Iss.	2.50	80.00
74-03-002	Norman Rockwell 250QX106-1	Keepsake	Yr.Iss.	2.50	75.00
74-03-003	Betsey Clark-Second Edition 250QX 108-1	Keepsake	Yr.Iss.	2.50	70-78.00
74-03-004	Charmers 250QX109-1	Keepsake	Yr.Iss.	2.50	52.00
74-03-005	Snowgoose 250QX107-1	Keepsake	Yr.Iss.	2.50	75.00
74-03-006	Angel 250QX110-1	Keepsake	Yr.Iss.	2.50	65.00
74-03-007	Raggedy Ann and Andy(4/set) 450QX114-1	Keepsake	Yr.Iss.	4.50	75.00
74-03-008	Little Miracles (Set of 4) 450QX115-1	Keepsake	Yr.Iss.	4.50	55.00
74-03-009	Buttons & Bo (Set of 2) 350QX113-1	Keepsake	Yr.Iss.	3.50	50.00
74-03-010	Currier & Ives (Set of 2) 350QX112-1	Keepsake	Yr.Iss.	3.50	50.00
Hallmark Keepsake Ornaments	**1974 Keepsake Yarn Ornaments**				
74-04-001	Mrs. Santa 150QX100-1	Keepsake	Yr.Iss.	1.50	22.50
74-04-002	Elf 150QX101-1	Keepsake	Yr.Iss.	1.50	22.50
74-04-003	Soldier 150QX102-1	Keepsake	Yr.Iss.	1.50	21.50
74-04-004	Angel 150QX103-1	Keepsake	Yr.Iss.	1.50	27.50
74-04-005	Snowman 150QX104-1	Keepsake	Yr.Iss.	1.50	22.50
74-04-006	Santa 150QX105-1	Keepsake	Yr.Iss.	1.50	23.50
Hallmark Keepsake Ornaments	**1975 Keepsake Property Ornaments**				
75-05-001	Betsey Clark (Set of 4) 450QX168-1	Keepsake	Yr.Iss.	4.50	25-50.00
75-05-002	Betsey Clark (Set of 2) 350QX167-1	Keepsake	Yr.Iss.	3.50	40.00
75-05-003	Betsey Clark 250QX163-1	Keepsake	Yr.Iss.	2.50	40.00
75-05-004	Betsey Clark-Third Ed. 300QX133-1	Keepsake	Yr.Iss.	3.00	55-70.00
75-05-005	Currier & Ives (Set of 2) 250QX164-1	Keepsake	Yr.Iss.	2.50	16-40.00
75-05-006	Currier & Ives (Set of 2) 400QX137-1	Keepsake	Yr.Iss.	4.00	35-40.00
75-05-007	Raggedy Ann and Andy(2/set) 400QX 138-1	Keepsake	Yr.Iss.	4.00	65.00
75-05-008	Raggedy Ann 250QX165-1	Keepsake	Yr.Iss.	2.50	50.00
75-05-009	Norman Rockwell 250QX166-1	Keepsake	Yr.Iss.	2.50	60.00
75-05-010	Norman Rockwell 300QX134-1	Keepsake	Yr.Iss.	3.00	60.00
75-05-011	Charmers 300QX135-1	Keepsake	Yr.Iss.	3.00	20-40.00
75-05-012	Marty Links 300QX136-1	Keepsake	Yr.Iss.	3.00	35.00
75-05-013	Buttons & Bo (Set of 4) 500QX139-1	Keepsake	Yr.Iss.	5.00	30-47.50
75-05-014	Little Miracles (Set of 4) 500QX140-1	Keepsake	Yr.Iss.	5.00	30-50.00
Hallmark Keepsake Ornaments	**1975 Keepsake Yarn Ornaments**				
75-06-001	Raggedy Ann 175QX121-1	Keepsake	Yr.Iss.	1.75	35.00
75-06-002	Raggedy Andy 175QX122-1	Keepsake	Yr.Iss.	1.75	39.50
75-06-003	Drummer Boy 175QX123-1	Keepsake	Yr.Iss.	1.75	24.50
75-06-004	Santa 175QX124-1	Keepsake	Yr.Iss.	1.75	15-22.50
75-06-005	Mrs. Santa 175QX125-1	Keepsake	Yr.Iss.	1.75	21.50
75-06-006	Little Girl 175QX126-1	Keepsake	Yr.Iss.	1.75	19.50
Hallmark Keepsake Ornaments	**1975 Handcrafted Ornaments: Nostalgia**				
75-07-001	Locomotive (dated) 350QX127-1	Keepsake	Yr.Iss.	3.50	175.00
75-07-002	Rocking Horse 350QX128-1	Keepsake	Yr.Iss.	3.50	175.00
75-07-003	Santa & Sleigh 350QX129-1	Keepsake	Yr.Iss.	3.50	200-275.
75-07-004	Drummer Boy 350QX130-1	Keepsake	Yr.Iss.	3.50	150.00
75-07-005	Peace on Earth (dated) 350QX131-1	Keepsake	Yr.Iss.	3.50	125-175.
75-07-006	Joy 350QX132-1	Keepsake	Yr.Iss.	3.50	275.00
Hallmark Keepsake Ornaments	**1975 Handcrafted Ornaments: Adorable**				
75-08-001	Santa 250QX155-1	Keepsake	Yr.Iss.	2.50	55.00
75-08-002	Mrs. Santa 250QX156-1	Keepsake	Yr.Iss.	2.50	55.00
75-08-003	Betsey Clark 250QX157-1	Keepsake	Yr.Iss.	2.50	350.00
75-08-004	Raggedy Ann 250QX159-1	Keepsake	Yr.Iss.	2.50	300.00
75-08-005	Raggedy Andy 250QX160-1	Keepsake	Yr.Iss.	2.50	400.00
75-08-006	Drummer Boy 250QX161-1	Keepsake	Yr.Iss.	2.50	325.00
Hallmark Keepsake Ornaments	**1976 First Commemorative Ornament**				
76-09-001	Baby's First Christmas 250QX211-1	Keepsake	Yr.Iss.	2.50	75-80.00
Hallmark Keepsake Ornaments	**1976 Bicentennial Commemoratives**				
76-10-001	Bicentennial '76 Commemorative 250QX211-1	Keepsake	Yr.Iss.	2.50	65.00
76-10-002	Bicentennial Charmers 300QX198-1	Keepsake	Yr.Iss.	3.00	50.00
76-10-003	Colonial Children (Set of 2) 4 400QX 208-1	Keepsake	Yr.Iss.	4.00	40-65.00
Hallmark Keepsake Ornaments	**1976 Property Ornaments**				
76-11-001	Betsey Clark-Fourth Ed.300QX 195-1	Keepsake	Yr.Iss.	3.00	150.00
76-11-002	Betsey Clark 250QX210-1	Keepsake	Yr.Iss.	2.50	42.50
76-11-003	Betsey Clark (Set of 3) 450QX218-1	Keepsake	Yr.Iss.	4.50	50.00
76-11-004	Currier & Ives 250QX209-1	Keepsake	Yr.Iss.	2.50	40.00
76-11-005	Currier & Ives 300QX197-1	Keepsake	Yr.Iss.	3.00	42.00
76-11-006	Norman Rockwell 300QX196-1	Keepsake	Yr.Iss.	3.00	65.00
76-11-007	Rudolph and Santa 250QX213-1	Keepsake	Yr.Iss.	2.50	65-95.00
76-11-008	Raggedy Ann 250QX212-1	Keepsake	Yr.Iss.	2.50	55.00
76-11-009	Marty Links (Set of 2) 400QX207-1	Keepsake	Yr.Iss.	4.00	45.00

Company / Number	Name	Series / Artist	Edition Limit	Issue Price	Quote
76-11-010	Happy the Snowman (Set of 2) 350QX216-1	Keepsake	Yr.Iss.	3.50	50.00
76-11-011	Charmers (Set of 2) 350QX215-1	Keepsake	Yr.Iss.	3.50	75.00
Hallmark Keepsake Ornaments		**1976 Decorative Ball Ornaments**			
76-12-001	Chickadees 225QX204-1	Keepsake	Yr.Iss.	2.25	50.00
76-12-002	Cardinals 225QX205-1	Keepsake	Yr.Iss.	2.25	55.00
Hallmark Keepsake Ornaments		**1976 Handcrafted Ornaments: Yesteryears**			
76-13-001	Train 500QX181-1	Keepsake	Yr.Iss.	5.00	155.00
76-13-002	Santa 500QX182-1	Keepsake	Yr.Iss.	5.00	175.00
76-13-003	Partridge 500QX183-1	Keepsake	Yr.Iss.	5.00	125.00
76-13-004	Drummer Boy 500QX184-1	Keepsake	Yr.Iss.	5.00	128-135.00
Hallmark Keepsake Ornaments		**1976 Handcrafted Ornaments: Twirl-Abouts**			
76-14-001	Angel 450QX171-1	Keepsake	Yr.Iss.	4.50	150-175.00
76-14-002	Santa 450QX172-1	Keepsake	Yr.Iss.	4.50	125.00
76-14-003	Soldier 450QX173-1	Keepsake	Yr.Iss.	4.50	80-120.00
76-14-004	Partridge 450QX174-1	Keepsake	Yr.Iss.	4.50	195.00
Hallmark Keepsake Ornaments		**1976 Handcrafted Ornaments: Tree Treats**			
76-15-001	Shepherd 300QX175-1	Keepsake	Yr.Iss.	3.00	90-150.00
76-15-002	Angel 300QX176-1	Keepsake	Yr.Iss.	3.00	195.00
76-15-003	Santa 300QX177-1	Keepsake	Yr.Iss.	3.00	225.00
76-15-004	Reindeer 300QX 178-1	Keepsake	Yr.Iss.	3.00	150.00
Hallmark Keepsake Ornaments		**1976 Handcrafted Ornaments: Nostalgia**			
76-16-001	Rocking Horse 400QX128-1	Keepsake	Yr.Iss.	3.50	160.00
76-16-002	Drummer Boy 400QX130-1	Keepsake	Yr.Iss.	3.50	155.00
76-16-003	Locomotive 400QX222-1	Keepsake	Yr.Iss.	3.50	185.00
76-16-004	Peace on Earth 400QX223-1	Keepsake	Yr.Iss.	3.50	195.00
Hallmark Keepsake Ornaments		**1976 Yarn Ornaments**			
76-17-001	Raggedy Ann 175QX121-1	Keepsake	Yr.Iss.	1.75	35.00
76-17-002	Raggedy Andy 175QX122-1	Keepsake	Yr.Iss.	1.75	39.50
76-17-003	Drummer Boy 175QX123-1	Keepsake	Yr.Iss.	1.75	22.50
76-17-004	Santa 175QX124-1	Keepsake	Yr.Iss.	1.75	23.50
76-17-005	Mrs. Santa 175QX125-1	Keepsake	Yr.Iss.	1.75	21.50
76-17-006	Caroler 175QX126-1	Keepsake	Yr.Iss.	1.75	27.50
Hallmark Keepsake Ornaments		**1977 Commemoratives**			
77-18-001	Baby's First Christmas 350QX131-5	Keepsake	Yr.Iss.	3.50	35-59.50
77-18-002	Granddaughter 350QX208-2	Keepsake	Yr.Iss.	3.50	150.00
77-18-003	Grandson 350QX209-5	Keepsake	Yr.Iss.	3.50	150.00
77-18-004	Mother 350QX261-5	Keepsake	Yr.Iss.	3.50	75.00
77-18-005	Grandmother 350QX260-2	Keepsake	Yr.Iss.	3.50	150.00
77-18-006	First Christmas Together 350QX132-2	Keepsake	Yr.Iss.	3.50	75.00
77-18-007	Love 350QX262-2	Keepsake	Yr.Iss.	3.50	85.00
77-18-008	For Your New Home 350QX263-5	Keepsake	Yr.Iss.	3.50	85.00
Hallmark Keepsake Ornaments		**1977 Property Ornaments**			
77-19-001	Charmers 350QX153-5	Keepsake	Yr.Iss.	3.50	50.00
77-19-002	Currier & Ives 350QX130-2	Keepsake	Yr.Iss.	3.50	55.00
77-19-003	Norman Rockwell 350QX151-5	Keepsake	Yr.Iss.	3.50	70.00
77-19-004	Disney 350QX133-5	Keepsake	Yr.Iss.	3.50	35-55.00
77-19-005	Disney (Set of 2) 400QX137-5	Keepsake	Yr.Iss.	4.00	75.00
77-19-006	Betsey Clark -Fifth Ed. 350QX264-2	Keepsake	Yr.Iss.	3.50	550.00
77-19-007	Grandma Moses 350QX150-2	Keepsake	Yr.Iss.	3.50	175.00
Hallmark Keepsake Ornaments		**1977 Peanuts Collection**			
77-20-001	Peanuts 250QX162-2	Keepsake	Yr.Iss.	2.50	65.00
77-20-002	Peanuts 350QX135-5	Keepsake	Yr.Iss.	3.50	35-50.00
77-20-003	Peanuts (Set of 2) 400QX163-5	Keepsake	Yr.Iss.	4.00	65.00
Hallmark Keepsake Ornaments		**1977 Christmas Expressions Collection**			
77-21-001	Bell 350QX154-2	Keepsake	Yr.Iss.	3.50	65.00
77-21-002	Ornaments 350QX155-5	Keepsake	Yr.Iss.	3.50	65.00
77-21-003	Mandolin 350QX157-5	Keepsake	Yr.Iss.	3.50	65.00
77-21-004	Wreath 350QX156-2	Keepsake	Yr.Iss.	3.50	65.00
Hallmark Keepsake Ornaments		**1977 The Beauty of America Collection**			
77-22-001	Mountains 250QX158-2	Keepsake	Yr.Iss.	2.50	30-55.00
77-22-002	Desert 250QX159-5	Keepsake	Yr.Iss.	2.50	30-55.00
77-22-003	Seashore 250QX160-2	Keepsake	Yr.Iss.	2.50	30-50.00
77-22-004	Wharf 250QX161-5	Keepsake	Yr.Iss.	2.50	30-50.00
Hallmark Keepsake Ornaments		**1977 Decorative Ball Ornaments**			
77-23-001	Rabbit 250QX139-5	Keepsake	Yr.Iss.	2.50	95.00
77-23-002	Squirrel 250QX138-2	Keepsake	Yr.Iss.	2.50	115.00
77-23-003	Christmas Mouse 250QX134-2	Keepsake	Yr.Iss.	3.50	85.00
77-23-004	Stained Glass 250QX152-2	Keepsake	Yr.Iss.	3.50	65.00
Hallmark Keepsake Ornaments		**1977 Colors of Christmas**			
77-24-001	Bell 350QX200-2	Keepsake	Yr.Iss.	3.50	35-55.00
77-24-002	Joy 350QX201-5	Keepsake	Yr.Iss.	3.50	35-60.00
77-24-003	Wreath 350QX202-2	Keepsake	Yr.Iss.	3.50	25-55.00
77-24-004	Candle 350QX203-5	Keepsake	Yr.Iss.	3.50	75.00
Hallmark Keepsake Ornaments		**1977 Holiday Highlights**			
77-25-001	Joy 350QX310-2	Keepsake	Yr.Iss.	3.50	40.00
77-25-002	Peace on Earth 350QX311-5	Keepsake	Yr.Iss.	3.50	45-75.00
77-25-003	Drummer Boy 350QX312-2	Keepsake	Yr.Iss.	3.50	70.00
77-25-004	Star 350QX313-5	Keepsake	Yr.Iss.	3.50	50.00
Hallmark Keepsake Ornaments		**1977 Twirl-About Collection**			
77-26-001	Snowman 450QX190-2	Keepsake	Yr.Iss.	4.50	50-65.00
77-26-002	Weather House 600QX191-5	Keepsake	Yr.Iss.	6.00	125.00
77-26-003	Bellringer 600QX192-2	Keepsake	Yr.Iss.	6.00	50-65.00
77-26-004	Della Robia Wreath 450QX193-5	Keepsake	Yr.Iss.	4.50	85-135.00
Hallmark Keepsake Ornaments		**1977 Metal Ornaments**			
77-27-001	Snowflake Collection (Set of 4)500QX 210-2	Keepsake	Yr.Iss.	5.00	95.00
Hallmark Keepsake Ornaments		**1977 Nostalgia Collection**			
77-28-001	Angel 500QX182-2	Keepsake	Yr.Iss.	5.00	125.00
77-28-002	Toys 500QX183-5	Keepsake	Yr.Iss.	5.00	110-145.
77-28-003	Antique Car 500QX180-2	Keepsake	Yr.Iss.	5.00	45-75.00
77-28-004	Nativity 500QX181-5	Keepsake	Yr.Iss.	5.00	175.00
Hallmark Keepsake Ornaments		**1977 Yesteryears Collection**			
77-29-001	Angel 600QX172-2	Keepsake	Yr.Iss.	6.00	100-125.00
77-29-002	Reindeer 600QX173-5	Keepsake	Yr.Iss.	6.00	95-135.00
77-29-003	Jack-in-the-Box 600QX171-5	Keepsake	Yr.Iss.	6.00	100-125.00
77-29-004	House 600QX170-2	Keepsake	Yr.Iss.	6.00	75-115.00
Hallmark Keepsake Ornaments		**1977 Cloth Doll Ornaments**			
77-30-001	Angel 175QX220-2	Keepsake	Yr.Iss.	1.75	55.00
77-30-002	Santa 175QX221-5	Keepsake	Yr.Iss.	1.75	95.00
Hallmark Keepsake Ornaments		**1978 Commemoratives**			
78-31-001	Baby's First Christmas 350QX200-3	Keepsake	Yr.Iss.	3.50	55-75.00
78-31-002	Granddaughter 350QX216-3	Keepsake	Yr.Iss.	3.50	50.00
78-31-003	Grandson 350QX215-6	Keepsake	Yr.Iss.	3.50	50.00
78-31-004	First Christmas Together 350QX218-3	Keepsake	Yr.Iss.	3.50	45-55.00
78-31-005	25th Christmas Together 350QX269-3	Keepsake	Yr.Iss.	3.50	30.00
78-31-006	Love 350QX268-3	Keepsake	Yr.Iss.	3.50	50.00
78-31-007	Grandmother 350QX267-6	Keepsake	Yr.Iss.	3.50	50.00
78-31-008	Mother 350QX266-3	Keepsake	Yr.Iss.	3.50	27.00
78-31-009	For Your New Home 350QX217-6	Keepsake	Yr.Iss.	3.50	75.00
Hallmark Keepsake Ornaments		**1978 Peanuts Collection**			
78-32-001	Peanuts 250QX204-3	Keepsake	Yr.Iss.	2.50	50.00
78-32-002	Peanuts 350QX205-6	Keepsake	Yr.Iss.	3.50	75.00
78-32-003	Peanuts 350QX206-3	Keepsake	Yr.Iss.	3.50	50.00
78-32-004	Peanuts 250QX203-6	Keepsake	Yr.Iss.	2.50	50.00
Hallmark Keepsake Ornaments		**1978 Property Ornaments**			
78-33-001	Betsey Clark-Sixth Edition 350QX 201-6	Keepsake	Yr.Iss.	3.50	55.00
78-33-002	Joan Walsh Anglund 350QX221-6	Keepsake	Yr.Iss.	3.50	85.00
78-33-003	Spencer Sparrow 350QX219-6	Keepsake	Yr.Iss.	3.50	50.00
78-33-004	Disney 350QX207-6	Keepsake	Yr.Iss.	3.50	75.00
Hallmark Keepsake Ornaments		**1978 Decorative Ball Ornaments**			
78-34-001	Merry Christmas (Santa) 350QX202-3	Keepsake	Yr.Iss.	3.50	50.00
78-34-002	Hallmark's Antique Card Collection Design 350QX 220-3	Keepsake	Yr.Iss.	3.50	55.00
78-34-003	Yesterday's Toys 350QX250-3	Keepsake	Yr.Iss.	3.50	55.00
78-34-004	Nativity 350QX253-6	Keepsake	Yr.Iss.	3.50	150.00
78-34-005	The Quail 350QX251-6	Keepsake	Yr.Iss.	3.50	10-40.00
78-34-006	Drummer Boy 350QX252-3	Keepsake	Yr.Iss.	3.50	55.00
78-34-007	Joy 350QX254-3	Keepsake	Yr.Iss.	3.50	50.00
Hallmark Keepsake Ornaments		**1978 Holiday Highlights**			
78-35-001	Santa 350QX307-6	Keepsake	Yr.Iss.	3.50	95.00
78-35-002	Snowflake 350QX308-3	Keepsake	Yr.Iss.	3.50	50.00
78-35-003	Nativity 350QX309-6	Keepsake	Yr.Iss.	3.50	95.00
78-35-004	Dove 350QX310-3	Keepsake	Yr.Iss.	3.50	125.00
Hallmark Keepsake Ornaments		**1978 Holiday Chimes**			
78-36-001	Reindeer Chimes 450QX320-3	Keepsake	Yr.Iss.	4.50	60.00
Hallmark Keepsake Ornaments		**1978 Little Trimmers**			
78-37-001	Thimble Series (Mouse)-First Ed.250QX133-6	Keepsake	Yr.Iss.	2.50	250-300.00
78-37-002	Santa 250QX135-6	Keepsake	Yr.Iss.	2.50	45-65.00
78-37-003	Praying Angel 250QX134-3	Keepsake	Yr.Iss.	2.50	95.00
78-37-004	Drummer Boy 250QX136-3	Keepsake	Yr.Iss.	2.50	85.00
78-37-005	Set of 4 - 250QX355-6	Keepsake	Yr.Iss.	10.00	400.00
Hallmark Keepsake Ornaments		**1978 Colors of Christmas**			
78-38-001	Merry Christmas 350QX355-6	Keepsake	Yr.Iss.	3.50	80.00
78-38-002	Locomotive 350QX356-3	Keepsake	Yr.Iss.	3.50	75.00
78-38-003	Angel 350QX354-3	Keepsake	Yr.Iss.	3.50	35-55.00
78-38-004	Candle 350QX357-6	Keepsake	Yr.Iss.	3.50	125.00
Hallmark Keepsake Ornaments		**1978 Handcrafted Ornaments**			
78-39-001	Dove 450QX190-3	Keepsake	Yr.Iss.	4.50	85.00
78-39-002	Holly and Poinsettia Ball 600QX147-6	Keepsake	Yr.Iss.	6.00	85.00
78-39-003	Schneeberg Bell 800QX152-3	Keepsake	Yr.Iss.	8.00	199.00
78-39-004	Angels 800QX150-3	Keepsake	Yr.Iss.	8.00	325-400.00
78-39-005	Carrousel Series-First Edition600QX 146-3	Keepsake	Yr.Iss.	6.00	325-400.00
78-39-006	Joy 450QX138-3	Keepsake	Yr.Iss.	4.50	80.00
78-39-007	Angel 400QX139-6	Keepsake	Yr.Iss.	4.50	85.00
78-39-008	Calico Mouse 450QX137-6	Keepsake	Yr.Iss.	4.50	160-200.00
78-39-009	Red Cardinal 450QX144-3	Keepsake	Yr.Iss.	4.50	150-175.00
78-39-010	Panorama Ball 600QX145-6	Keepsake	Yr.Iss.	6.00	90-135.00
78-39-011	Skating Raccoon 600QX142-3	Keepsake	Yr.Iss.	6.00	60-95.00
78-39-012	Rocking Horse 600QX148-3	Keepsake	Yr.Iss.	6.00	65-95.00
78-39-013	Animal Home 600QX149-6	Keepsake	Yr.Iss.	6.00	150-175.00
Hallmark Keepsake Ornaments		**1978 Yarn Collection**			
78-40-001	Green Boy 200QX123-1	Keepsake	Yr.Iss.	2.00	20.00
78-40-002	Mrs. Claus 200QX125-1	Keepsake	Yr.Iss.	2.00	19.50
78-40-003	Green Girl 200QX126-1	Keepsake	Yr.Iss.	2.00	17.50
78-40-004	Mr. Claus 200QX340-3	Keepsake	Yr.Iss.	2.00	20.00
Hallmark Keepsake Ornaments		**1979 Commemoratives**			
79-41-001	Baby's First Christmas 350QX208-7	Keepsake	Yr.Iss.	3.50	25-30.00
79-41-002	Baby's First Christmas 800QX154-7	Keepsake	Yr.Iss.	8.00	175.00
79-41-003	Grandson 350QX210-7	Keepsake	Yr.Iss.	3.50	28.00
79-41-004	Granddaughter 350QX211-9	Keepsake	Yr.Iss.	3.50	28.00
79-41-005	Mother 350QX251-9	Keepsake	Yr.Iss.	3.50	15.00
79-41-006	Grandmother 350QX252-7	Keepsake	Yr.Iss.	3.50	14.50
79-41-007	Our First Christmas Together350-QX 209-9	Keepsake	Yr.Iss.	3.50	39-45.00
79-41-008	Our Twenty-Fifth Anniversary350QX 250-7	Keepsake	Yr.Iss.	3.50	15-19.00
79-41-009	Love 350QX258-7	Keepsake	Yr.Iss.	3.50	30.00
79-41-010	Friendship 350QX203-9	Keepsake	Yr.Iss.	3.50	17.50
79-41-011	Teacher 350QX213-9	Keepsake	Yr.Iss.	3.50	12-18.00
79-41-012	New Home 350QX212-7	Keepsake	Yr.Iss.	3.50	29.00
Hallmark Keepsake Ornaments		**1979 Property Ornaments**			
79-42-001	Betsey Clark-Seventh Edition350QX 201-9	Keepsake	Yr.Iss.	3.50	29.50
79-42-002	Peanuts (Time to Trim) 350QX202-7	Keepsake	Yr.Iss.	3.50	25.00
79-42-003	Spencer Sparrow 350QX200-7	Keepsake	Yr.Iss.	3.50	30.00
79-42-004	Joan Walsh Anglund 350QX205-9	Keepsake	Yr.Iss.	3.50	25-35.00
79-42-005	Winnie-the-Pooh 350QX206-7	Keepsake	Yr.Iss.	3.50	35.00
79-42-006	Mary Hamilton 350QX254-7	Keepsake	Yr.Iss.	3.50	30.00
Hallmark Keepsake Ornaments		**1979 Decorative Ball Ornaments**			
79-43-001	Night Before Christmas 350QX214-7	Keepsake	Yr.Iss.	3.50	29.50
79-43-002	Christmas Chickadees 350QX204-7	Keepsake	Yr.Iss.	3.50	19.00
79-43-003	Behold the Star 350QX255-9	Keepsake	Yr.Iss.	3.50	35-45.00
79-43-004	Christmas Traditions 350QX253-9	Keepsake	Yr.Iss.	3.50	32.50
79-43-005	Christmas Collage 350QX257-9	Keepsake	Yr.Iss.	3.50	17.50
79-43-006	Black Angel 350QX207-9	Keepsake	Yr.Iss.	3.50	10-20.00
79-43-007	The Light of Christmas 350QX256-7	Keepsake	Yr.Iss.	3.50	20.00

Number	Name	Artist	Edition Limit	Issue Price	Quote
Hallmark Keepsake Ornaments		**1979 Holiday Highlights**			
79-44-001	Christmas Angel 350QX300-7	Keepsake	Yr.Iss.	3.50	85.00
79-44-002	Snowflake 350QX301-9	Keepsake	Yr.Iss.	3.50	40.00
79-44-003	Christmas Tree 350QX302-7	Keepsake	Yr.Iss.	3.50	75.00
79-44-004	Christmas Cheer 350QX303-9	Keepsake	Yr.Iss.	3.50	55.00
79-44-005	Love 350QX304-7	Keepsake	Yr.Iss.	3.50	87.50
Hallmark Keepsake Ornaments		**1979 Colors of Christmas**			
79-45-001	Words of Christmas 350QX350-7	Keepsake	Yr.Iss.	3.50	85.00
79-45-002	Holiday Wreath 350QX353-9	Keepsake	Yr.Iss.	3.50	39.50
79-45-003	Partridge in a Pear Tree 350QX351-9	Keepsake	Yr.Iss.	3.50	45.00
79-45-004	Star Over Bethlehem 350QX352-7	Keepsake	Yr.Iss.	3.50	65.00
Hallmark Keepsake Ornaments		**1979 Little Trimmer Collection**			
79-46-001	Thimble Series-Mouse 300QX133-6	Keepsake	Yr.Iss.	3.00	225.00
79-46-002	Santa 300QX135-6	Keepsake	Yr.Iss.	3.00	55.00
79-46-003	A Matchless Christmas 400QX132-7	Keepsake	Yr.Iss.	4.00	75.00
79-46-004	Angel Delight 300QX130-7	Keepsake	Yr.Iss.	3.00	100.00
Hallmark Keepsake Ornaments		**1979 Handcrafted Ornaments**			
79-47-001	Holiday Scrimshaw 400QX152-7	Keepsake	Yr.Iss.	4.00	225-250.
79-47-002	Christmas Heart 650QX140-7	Keepsake	Yr.Iss.	6.50	95.00
79-47-003	Christmas Eve Surprise 650QX157-9	Keepsake	Yr.Iss.	6.50	55.00
79-47-004	Santa's Here 500QX138-7	Keepsake	Yr.Iss.	5.00	65.00
79-47-005	Raccoon 650QX142-3	Keepsake	Yr.Iss.	6.50	85.00
79-47-006	The Downhill Run 650QX145-9	Keepsake	Yr.Iss.	6.50	150.00
79-47-007	The Drummer Boy 800QX143-9	Keepsake	Yr.Iss.	8.00	125.00
79-47-008	Outdoor Fun 800QX150-7	Keepsake	Yr.Iss.	8.00	100-150.
79-47-009	A Christmas Treat 500QX134-7	Keepsake	Yr.Iss.	5.00	85.00
79-47-010	The Skating Snowman 500QX139-9	Keepsake	Yr.Iss.	5.00	85.00
79-47-011	Christmas is for Children 500QX135-9	Keepsake	Yr.Iss.	5.00	95.00
79-47-012	Ready for Christmas 650QX133-9	Keepsake	Yr.Iss.	6.50	150.00
Hallmark Keepsake Ornaments		**1979 Collectible Series**			
79-48-001	Carrousel-Second Edition 650QX146-7	Keepsake	Yr.Iss.	6.50	150-200.
79-48-002	Thimble-Second Edition 300QX131-9	Keepsake	Yr.Iss.	3.00	195.00
79-48-003	Snoopy and Friends 800QX141-9	Keepsake	Yr.Iss.	8.00	125.00
79-48-004	Here Comes Santa-First Edition 900QX 155-9	Keepsake	Yr.Iss.	9.00	400-550.
79-48-005	Bellringer-First Edition 10QX147-9	Keepsake	Yr.Iss.	10.00	300-400.
Hallmark Keepsake Ornaments		**1979 Holiday Chimes**			
79-49-001	Reindeer Chimes 450QX320-3	Keepsake	Yr.Iss.	4.50	75.00
79-49-002	Star Chimes 450QX137-9	Keepsake	Yr.Iss.	4.50	75.00
Hallmark Keepsake Ornaments		**1979 Sewn Trimmers**			
79-50-001	The Rocking Horse 200QX340-7	Keepsake	Yr.Iss.	2.00	15.00
79-50-002	Merry Santa 200QX342-7	Keepsake	Yr.Iss.	2.00	15.00
79-50-003	Stuffed Full Stocking 200QX341-9	Keepsake	Yr.Iss.	2.00	19.00
79-50-004	Angel Music 200QX343-9	Keepsake	Yr.Iss.	2.00	17.50
Hallmark Keepsake Ornaments		**1980 Commemoratives**			
80-51-001	Baby's First Christmas 400QX200-1	Keepsake	Yr.Iss.	4.00	20-40.00
80-51-002	Black Baby's First Christmas 400QX 229-4	Keepsake	Yr.Iss.	4.00	20-25.00
80-51-003	Baby's First Christmas 12QX156-1	Keepsake	Yr.Iss.	12.00	40-45.00
80-51-004	Grandson 400QX201-4	Keepsake	Yr.Iss.	4.00	25.00
80-51-005	Granddaughter 400QX202-1	Keepsake	Yr.Iss.	4.00	25.00
80-51-006	Son 400QX211-4	Keepsake	Yr.Iss.	4.00	17.00
80-51-007	Daughter 400QX212-1	Keepsake	Yr.Iss.	4.00	29.50
80-51-008	Dad 400QX214-1	Keepsake	Yr.Iss.	4.00	14.50
80-51-009	Mother 400QX203-4	Keepsake	Yr.Iss.	4.00	13.50
80-51-010	Mother and Dad 400QX230-1	Keepsake	Yr.Iss.	4.00	12.00
80-51-011	Grandmother 400QX204-1	Keepsake	Yr.Iss.	4.00	13.50
80-51-012	Grandfather 400QX231-4	Keepsake	Yr.Iss.	4.00	13.50
80-51-013	Grandparents 400QX213-4	Keepsake	Yr.Iss.	4.00	29.50
80-51-014	25th Christmas Together 400QX206-1	Keepsake	Yr.Iss.	4.00	12.50
80-51-015	First Christmas Together 400QX205-4	Keepsake	Yr.Iss.	4.00	21.50
80-51-016	Christmas Love 400QX207-4	Keepsake	Yr.Iss.	4.00	32.50
80-51-017	Friendship 400QX208-1	Keepsake	Yr.Iss.	4.00	16.00
80-51-018	Christmas at Home 400QX210-1	Keepsake	Yr.Iss.	4.00	20.00
80-51-019	Teacher 400QX209-4	Keepsake	Yr.Iss.	4.00	13.00
80-51-020	Love 400QX302-1	Keepsake	Yr.Iss.	4.00	50.00
80-51-021	Beauty of Friendship 400QX303-4	Keepsake	Yr.Iss.	4.00	55.00
80-51-022	First Christmas Together 400QX305-4	Keepsake	Yr.Iss.	4.00	25-55.00
80-51-023	Mother 400QX304-1	Keepsake	Yr.Iss.	4.00	35.00
Hallmark Keepsake Ornaments		**1980 Property Ornaments**			
80-52-001	Betsey Clark-Eighth Edition 400QX 215-4	Keepsake	Yr.Iss.	4.00	29.50
80-52-002	Betsey Clark 650QX307-4	Keepsake	Yr.Iss.	6.50	65.00
80-52-003	Betsey Clark's Christmas 750QX194-4	Keepsake	Yr.Iss.	7.50	25.00
80-52-004	Peanuts 400QX216-1	Keepsake	Yr.Iss.	4.00	20-25.00
80-52-005	Joan Walsh Anglund 400QX217-4	Keepsake	Yr.Iss.	4.00	21.00
80-52-006	Disney 400QX218-1	Keepsake	Yr.Iss.	4.00	25.00
80-52-007	Mary Hamilton 400QX219-4	Keepsake	Yr.Iss.	4.00	17.50-80.00
80-52-008	Muppets 400QX220-1	Keepsake	Yr.Iss.	4.00	25-37.50
80-52-009	Marty Links 400QX221-4	Keepsake	Yr.Iss.	4.00	15.00
Hallmark Keepsake Ornaments		**1980 Decorative Ball Ornaments**			
80-53-001	Christmas Choir 400QX228-1	Keepsake	Yr.Iss.	4.00	150.00
80-53-002	Nativity 400QX225-4	Keepsake	Yr.Iss.	4.00	125.00
80-53-003	Christmas Time 400QX226-1	Keepsake	Yr.Iss.	4.00	20.00
80-53-004	Santa's Workshop 400QX223-4	Keepsake	Yr.Iss.	4.00	12-19.50
80-53-005	Happy Christmas 400QX222-1	Keepsake	Yr.Iss.	4.00	28.00
80-53-006	Jolly Santa 400QX227-4	Keepsake	Yr.Iss.	4.00	22.50
80-53-007	Christmas Cardinals 400QX224-1	Keepsake	Yr.Iss.	4.00	35.00
Hallmark Keepsake Ornaments		**1980 Holiday Highlights**			
80-54-001	Three Wise Men 400QX300-1	Keepsake	Yr.Iss.	4.00	22.50
80-54-002	Wreath 400QX301-4	Keepsake	Yr.Iss.	4.00	85.00
Hallmark Keepsake Ornaments		**1980 Colors of Christmas**			
80-55-001	Joy 400QX350-1	Keepsake	Yr.Iss.	4.00	25.00
Hallmark Keepsake Ornaments		**1980 Frosted Images**			
80-56-001	Drummer Boy 400QX309-4	Keepsake	Yr.Iss.	4.00	20.00
80-56-002	Santa 400QX310-1	Keepsake	Yr.Iss.	4.00	20.00
80-56-003	Dove 400QX308-1	Keepsake	Yr.Iss.	4.00	35.00
Hallmark Keepsake Ornaments		**1980 Little Trimmers**			
80-57-001	Clothespin Soldier 350QX134-1	Keepsake	Yr.Iss.	3.50	45.00
80-57-002	Christmas Teddy 250QX135-4	Keepsake	Yr.Iss.	2.50	125.00
80-57-003	Merry Redbird 350QX160-1	Keepsake	Yr.Iss.	3.50	55.00
80-57-004	Swingin' on a Star 400QX130-1	Keepsake	Yr.Iss.	4.00	75.00
80-57-005	Christmas Owl 400QX131-4	Keepsake	Yr.Iss.	4.00	45.00

Number	Name	Artist	Edition Limit	Issue Price	Quote
80-57-006	Thimble Series-A Christmas Salute 400QX 131-9	Keepsake	Yr.Iss.	4.00	150.00
Hallmark Keepsake Ornaments		**1980 Handcrafted Ornaments**			
80-58-001	The Snowflake Swing 400QX133-4	Keepsake	Yr.Iss.	4.00	45.00
80-58-002	Santa 1980 550QX146-1	Keepsake	Yr.Iss.	5.50	95.00
80-58-003	Drummer Boy 550QX147-4	Keepsake	Yr.Iss.	5.50	95.00
80-58-004	Christmas is for Children 550QX135-9	Keepsake	Yr.Iss.	5.50	95.00
80-58-005	A Christmas Treat 550QX134-7	Keepsake	Yr.Iss.	5.50	75.00
80-58-006	Skating Snowman 550QX139-9	Keepsake	Yr.Iss.	5.50	75.00
80-58-007	A Heavenly Nap 650QX139-4	Keepsake	Yr.Iss.	6.50	50.00
80-58-008	Heavenly Sounds 750QX152-1	Keepsake	Yr.Iss.	7.50	90.00
80-58-009	Caroling Bear 750QX140-1	Keepsake	Yr.Iss.	7.50	150.00
80-58-010	Santa's Flight 550QX138-1	Keepsake	Yr.Iss.	5.50	95.00
80-58-011	The Animals' Christmas 800QX150-1	Keepsake	Yr.Iss.	8.00	65.00
80-58-012	A Spot of Christmas Cheer 800QX 153-4	Keepsake	Yr.Iss.	8.00	160.00
80-58-013	Elfin Antics 900QX142-1	Keepsake	Yr.Iss.	9.00	225.00
80-58-014	A Christmas Vigil 900QX144-1	Keepsake	Yr.Iss.	9.00	110.00
Hallmark Keepsake Ornaments		**1980 Special Editions**			
80-59-001	Heavenly Minstrel 15QX156-7	Keepsake	Yr.Iss.	15.00	350-375.
80-59-002	Checking it Twice 20QX158-4	Keepsake	Yr.Iss.	20.00	125-175.
Hallmark Keepsake Ornaments		**1980 Holiday Chimes**			
80-60-001	Snowflake Chimes 550QX165-4	Keepsake	Yr.Iss.	5.50	30.00
80-60-002	Reindeer Chimes 550QX320-3	Keepsake	Yr.Iss.	5.50	55.00
80-60-003	Santa Mobile 550QX136-1	Keepsake	Yr.Iss.	5.50	60.00
Hallmark Keepsake Ornaments		**1980 Collectible Series**			
80-61-001	Norman Rockwell-First Edition650QX 306-1	Keepsake	Yr.Iss.	6.50	225.00
80-61-002	Frosty Friends-First Edition650QX 137-4	Keepsake	Yr.Iss.	6.50	535-650.00
80-61-003	Snoopy & Friends-Second Ed. 900QX 154-1	Keepsake	Yr.Iss.	9.00	95.00
80-61-004	Carrousel-Third Edition 750QX141-4	Keepsake	Yr.Iss.	7.50	135-155.00
80-61-005	Thimble-Third Edition 400QX132-1	Keepsake	Yr.Iss.	4.00	175.00
80-61-006	Here Comes Santa-Second Ed.12QX 143-4	Keepsake	Yr.Iss.	12.00	115-175.00
80-61-007	The Bellringers-Second Edition15QX 157-4	Keepsake	Yr.Iss.	15.00	55-75.00
Hallmark Keepsake Ornaments		**1980 Yarn Ornaments**			
80-62-001	Santa 300QX161-4	Keepsake	Yr.Iss.	3.00	20.00
80-62-002	Angel 300QX162-1	Keepsake	Yr.Iss.	3.00	20.00
80-62-003	Snowman 300QX163-4	Keepsake	Yr.Iss.	3.00	20.00
80-62-004	Soldier 300QX164-1	Keepsake	Yr.Iss.	3.00	20.00
Hallmark Keepsake Ornaments		**1981 Commemoratives**			
81-63-001	Baby's First Christmas-Girl450QX 600-2	Keepsake	Yr.Iss.	4.50	20.00
81-63-002	Baby's First Christmas-Boy450QX 601-5	Keepsake	Yr.Iss.	4.50	20.00
81-63-003	Baby's First Christmas-Black450QX 602-2	Keepsake	Yr.Iss.	4.50	18-25.00
81-63-004	Baby's First Christmas 550QX516-2	Keepsake	Yr.Iss.	5.50	29.50
81-63-005	Baby's First Christmas 850QX513-5	Keepsake	Yr.Iss.	8.50	15.50
81-63-006	Baby's First Christmas 1300QX440-2	Keepsake	Yr.Iss.	13.00	30-49.00
81-63-007	Godchild 450QX603-5	Keepsake	Yr.Iss.	4.50	12.50
81-63-008	Grandson 450QX604-2	Keepsake	Yr.Iss.	4.50	23.00
81-63-009	Granddaughter 450QX605-5	Keepsake	Yr.Iss.	4.50	25.00
81-63-010	Daughter 450QX607-5	Keepsake	Yr.Iss.	4.50	25.00
81-63-011	Son 450QX606-2	Keepsake	Yr.Iss.	4.50	25.00
81-63-012	Mother 450QX608-2	Keepsake	Yr.Iss.	4.50	19.00
81-63-013	Father 450QX609-5	Keepsake	Yr.Iss.	4.50	12.00
81-63-014	Mother and Dad 450QX700-2	Keepsake	Yr.Iss.	4.50	12.50
81-63-015	Friendship 450QX704-2	Keepsake	Yr.Iss.	4.50	12.50
81-63-016	The Gift of Love 450QX705-5	Keepsake	Yr.Iss.	4.50	17.50
81-63-017	Home 450QX709-5	Keepsake	Yr.Iss.	4.50	14.50
81-63-018	Teacher 450QX800-2	Keepsake	Yr.Iss.	4.50	12.00
81-63-019	Grandfather 450QX701-5	Keepsake	Yr.Iss.	4.50	12.00
81-63-020	Grandmother 450QX702-2	Keepsake	Yr.Iss.	4.50	12.50
81-63-021	Grandparents 450QX703-5	Keepsake	Yr.Iss.	4.50	12.00
81-63-022	First Christmas Together 450QX706-2	Keepsake	Yr.Iss.	4.50	25.00
81-63-023	25th Christmas Together 450QX707-5	Keepsake	Yr.Iss.	4.50	15.00
81-63-024	50th Christmas 450QX708-2	Keepsake	Yr.Iss.	4.50	12.00
81-63-025	Love 550QX502-2	Keepsake	Yr.Iss.	5.50	19.50
81-63-026	Friendship 550QX503-5	Keepsake	Yr.Iss.	5.50	29.50
81-63-027	First Christmas Together 550QX505-5	Keepsake	Yr.Iss.	5.50	22.50
81-63-028	25th Christmas Together 550QX504-2	Keepsake	Yr.Iss.	5.50	19.50
Hallmark Keepsake Ornaments		**1981 Property Ornaments**			
81-65-001	Betsey Clark Cameo 850QX512-2	Keepsake	Yr.Iss.	8.50	30.00
81-65-002	Betsey Clark 900QX423-5	Keepsake	Yr.Iss.	9.00	65.00
81-65-003	Betsey Clark-Ninth Edition450QX 802-2	Keepsake	Yr.Iss.	4.50	25.00
81-65-004	Muppets 450QX807-5	Keepsake	Yr.Iss.	4.50	25-35.00
81-65-005	Kermit the Frog 900QX424-2	Keepsake	Yr.Iss.	9.00	75-95.00
81-65-006	The Divine Miss Piggy 1200QX425-5	Keepsake	Yr.Iss.	12.00	95.00
81-65-007	Mary Hamilton 450QX806-2	Keepsake	Yr.Iss.	4.50	19.50
81-65-008	Marty Links 450QX808-2	Keepsake	Yr.Iss.	4.50	15.00
81-65-009	Peanuts 450QX803-5	Keepsake	Yr.Iss.	4.50	24.50
81-65-010	Joan Walsh Anglund 450QX804-2	Keepsake	Yr.Iss.	4.50	15.00
81-65-011	Disney 450QX805-5	Keepsake	Yr.Iss.	4.50	22.00
Hallmark Keepsake Ornaments		**1981 Decorative Ball Ornaments**			
81-66-001	Christmas 1981 450QX809-5	Keepsake	Yr.Iss.	4.50	22.50
81-66-002	Christmas Magic 450QX810-2	Keepsake	Yr.Iss.	4.50	19.50
81-66-003	Traditional (Black Santa) 450QX801-5	Keepsake	Yr.Iss.	4.50	95.00
81-66-004	Let Us Adore Him 450QX811-5	Keepsake	Yr.Iss.	4.50	50.00
81-66-005	Santa's Coming 450QX812-2	Keepsake	Yr.Iss.	4.50	19.50
81-66-006	Christmas in the Forest 450QX813-5	Keepsake	Yr.Iss.	4.50	175.00
81-66-007	Merry Christmas 450QX814-2	Keepsake	Yr.Iss.	4.50	17.50
81-66-008	Santa's Surprise 450QX815-5	Keepsake	Yr.Iss.	4.50	19.50
Hallmark Keepsake Ornaments		**1981 Crown Classics**			
81-67-001	Angel 450QX507-5	Keepsake	Yr.Iss.	4.50	25.00
81-67-002	Tree Photoholder 550QX515-5	Keepsake	Yr.Iss.	5.50	25.00
81-67-003	Unicorn 850QX516-5	Keepsake	Yr.Iss.	8.50	22.50
Hallmark Keepsake Ornaments		**1981 Frosted Images**			
81-68-001	Mouse 400QX508-2	Keepsake	Yr.Iss.	4.00	20.00
81-68-002	Angel 400QX509-5	Keepsake	Yr.Iss.	4.00	65.00
81-68-003	Snowman 400QX510-2	Keepsake	Yr.Iss.	4.00	25.00
Hallmark Keepsake Ornaments		**1981 Holiday Highlights**			
81-69-001	Shepherd Scene 550QX500-2	Keepsake	Yr.Iss.	5.50	5.50-25.00
81-69-002	Christmas Star 550QX501-5	Keepsake	Yr.Iss.	5.50	9-24.50
Hallmark Keepsake Ornaments		**1981 Little Trimmers**			
81-70-001	Puppy Love 350QX406-2	Keepsake	Yr.Iss.	3.50	40.00
81-70-002	Jolly Snowman 350QX407-5	Keepsake	Yr.Iss.	3.50	50.00
81-70-003	Perky Penguin 350QX409-5	Keepsake	Yr.Iss.	3.50	60.00

Number	Name	Artist	Edition Limit	Issue Price	Quote
81-70-004	Clothespin Drummer Boy 450QX408-2	Keepsake	Yr.Iss.	4.50	45.00
81-70-005	The Stocking Mouse 450QX412-2	Keepsake	Yr.Iss.	4.50	95.00
Hallmark Keepsake Ornaments	**1981 Hand Crafted Ornaments**				
81-71-001	Space Santa 650QX430-2	Keepsake	Yr.Iss.	6.50	125.00
81-71-002	Candyville Express 750QX418-2	Keepsake	Yr.Iss.	7.50	125.00
81-71-003	Ice Fairy 650QX431-5	Keepsake	Yr.Iss.	6.50	65-85.00
81-71-004	Star Swing 550QX421-5	Keepsake	Yr.Iss.	5.50	50.00
81-71-005	A Heavenly Nap 650QX139-4	Keepsake	Yr.Iss.	6.50	49.50
81-71-006	Dough Angel 550QX139-6	Keepsake	Yr.Iss.	5.50	80.00
81-71-007	Topsy-Turvy Tunes 750QX429-5	Keepsake	Yr.Iss.	7.50	40-75.00
81-71-008	A Well-Stocked Stocking 900QX154-7	Keepsake	Yr.Iss.	9.00	75.00
81-71-009	The Friendly Fiddler 800QX434-2	Keepsake	Yr.Iss.	8.00	45-75.00
81-71-010	The Ice Sculptor 800QX432-2	Keepsake	Yr.Iss.	8.00	95.00
81-71-011	Christmas Dreams 1200QX437-5	Keepsake	Yr.Iss.	12.00	225.00
81-71-112	Christmas Fantasy 1300QX155-4	Keepsake	Yr.Iss.	13.00	75.00
81-71-113	Sailing Santa 1300QX439-5	Keepsake	Yr.Iss.	13.00	250.00
81-71-114	Love and Joy 900QX425-2	Keepsake	Yr.Iss.	9.00	95.00
81-71-115	Drummer Boy 250QX148-1	Keepsake	Yr.Iss.	2.50	50.00
81-71-116	St. Nicholas 550QX446-2	Keepsake	Yr.Iss.	5.50	35-45.00
81-71-117	Mr. & Mrs. Claus 1200QX448-5	Keepsake	Yr.Iss.	12.00	125-150.00
81-71-018	Checking It Twice 2250QX158-4	Keepsake	Yr.Iss.	22.50	195.00
Hallmark Keepsake Ornaments	**1981 Holiday Chimes**				
81-72-001	Snowman Chimes 550QX445-5	Keepsake	Yr.Iss.	5.50	25.00
81-72-002	Santa Mobile 550QX136-1	Keepsake	Yr.Iss.	5.50	40.00
81-72-003	Snowflake Chimes 550QX165-4	Keepsake	Yr.Iss.	5.50	25.00
Hallmark Keepsake Ornaments	**1981 Collectible Series**				
81-73-001	Rocking Horse - 1st Edition900QX 422-2	Keepsake	Yr.Iss.	9.00	425-595.
81-73-002	Bellringer - 3rd Edition 1500QX441-5	Keepsake	Yr.Iss.	15.00	95.00
81-73-003	Norman Rockwell - 2nd Edition850QX 511-5	Keepsake	Yr.Iss.	8.50	30-45.00
81-73-004	Here Comes Santa - 3rd Ed.1300QX 438-2	Keepsake	Yr.Iss.	13.00	225-245.
81-73-005	Carrousel - 4th Edition 900QX427-5	Keepsake	Yr.Iss.	9.00	95.00
81-73-006	Snoopy and Friends - 3rd Ed.1200QX 436-2	Keepsake	Yr.Iss.	12.00	75.00
81-73-007	Thimble - 4th Edition 450QX413-5	Keepsake	Yr.Iss.	4.50	105.00
81-73-008	Frosty Friends - 2nd Edition800QX433-5	Keepsake	Yr.Iss.	8.00	325.00
Hallmark Keepsake Ornaments	**1981 Fabric Ornaments**				
81-74-001	Cardinal Cutie 300QX400-2	Keepsake	Yr.Iss.	3.00	19.00
81-74-002	Peppermint Mouse 300QX401-5	Keepsake	Yr.Iss.	3.00	32.50
81-74-003	Gingham Dog 300QX402-2	Keepsake	Yr.Iss.	3.00	15.00
81-74-004	Calico Kitty 300QX403-5	Keepsake	Yr.Iss.	3.00	5-15.00
Hallmark Keepsake Ornaments	**1981 Plush Animals**				
81-75-001	Christmas Teddy 500QX404-2	Keepsake	Yr.Iss.	5.50	22-25.00
81-75-002	Raccoon Tunes 550QX405-5	Keepsake	Yr.Iss.	5.50	22.00
Hallmark Keepsake Ornaments	**1982 Commemoratives**				
82-76-001	Baby's First Christmas-Photoholder 650QX 312-6	Keepsake	Yr.Iss.	6.50	24.50
82-76-002	Baby's First Christmas 1300QX455-3	Keepsake	Yr.Iss.	13.00	42.50
82-76-003	Baby's First Christmas (Boy)450QX 216-3	Keepsake	Yr.Iss.	4.50	20.00
82-76-004	Baby's First Christmas (Girl)450QX 207-3	Keepsake	Yr.Iss.	4.50	22.00
82-76-005	Godchild 450QX222-6	Keepsake	Yr.Iss.	4.50	17.50
82-76-006	Grandson 450QX224-6	Keepsake	Yr.Iss.	4.50	17.50
82-76-007	Granddaughter 450QX224-3	Keepsake	Yr.Iss.	4.50	24.50
82-76-008	Son 450QX204-3	Keepsake	Yr.Iss.	4.50	25.00
82-76-009	Daughter 450QX204-6	Keepsake	Yr.Iss.	4.50	25.50
82-76-010	Father 450QX205-6	Keepsake	Yr.Iss.	4.50	12.00
82-76-011	Mother 450QX205-3	Keepsake	Yr.Iss.	4.50	15.00
82-76-012	Mother and Dad 450QX222-3	Keepsake	Yr.Iss.	4.50	12.00
82-76-013	Sister 450QX208-3	Keepsake	Yr.Iss.	4.50	22.50
82-76-014	Grandmother 450QX200-3	Keepsake	Yr.Iss.	4.50	12.00
82-76-015	Grandfather 450QX207-6	Keepsake	Yr.Iss.	4.50	12.00
82-76-016	Grandparents 450QX214-6	Keepsake	Yr.Iss.	4.50	12.00
82-76-017	First Christmas Together 850QX306-6	Keepsake	Yr.Iss.	8.50	35.00
82-76-018	First Christmas Together 450QX211-3	Keepsake	Yr.Iss.	4.50	20.00
82-76-019	First Christmas Together-Locket 1500QX 456-3	Keepsake	Yr.Iss.	15.00	45.00
82-76-020	Christmas Memories 650QX311-6	Keepsake	Yr.Iss.	6.50	19.50
82-76-021	Teacher 450QX214-3	Keepsake	Yr.Iss.	4.50	10.00
82-76-022	New Home 450QX212-6	Keepsake	Yr.Iss.	4.50	19.00
82-76-023	Teacher 650QX312-3	Keepsake	Yr.Iss.	6.50	15.00
82-76-024	25th Christmas Together 450QX211-6	Keepsake	Yr.Iss.	4.50	14.00
82-76-025	50th Christmas Together 450QX212-3	Keepsake	Yr.Iss.	4.50	14.00
82-76-026	Moments of Love 450QX209-3	Keepsake	Yr.Iss.	4.50	14.00
82-76-027	Love 450QX209-6	Keepsake	Yr.Iss.	4.50	15.00
82-76-028	Friendship 450QX208-6	Keepsake	Yr.Iss.	4.50	15.00
82-76-029	Teacher-Apple 550QX301-6	Keepsake	Yr.Iss.	5.50	15.00
82-76-030	Baby's First Christmas 550QX302-3	Keepsake	Yr.Iss.	5.50	19.50
82-76-031	First Christmas Together 550QX302-6	Keepsake	Yr.Iss.	5.50	27.50
82-76-032	Love 550QX304-3	Keepsake	Yr.Iss.	5.50	27.00
82-76-033	Friendship 550QX304-6	Keepsake	Yr.Iss.	5.50	24.50
Hallmark Keepsake Ornaments	**1982 Property Ornaments**				
82-77-001	Miss Piggy and Kermit 450QX218-3	Keepsake	Yr.Iss.	4.50	40.00
82-77-002	Muppets Party 450QX218-6	Keepsake	Yr.Iss.	4.50	40.00
82-77-003	Kermit the Frog 1100QX495-6	Keepsake	Yr.Iss.	11.00	95.00
82-77-004	The Divine Miss Piggy 1200QX425-5	Keepsake	Yr.Iss.	12.00	105.00
82-77-005	Betsey Clark 850QX305-6	Keepsake	Yr.Iss.	8.50	24.50
82-77-006	Norman Rockwell-3rd ed.850QX305-3	Keepsake	Yr.Iss.	8.50	20-29.50
82-77-007	Betsey Clark-10th edition450QX215-6	Keepsake	Yr.Iss.	4.50	29.50
82-77-008	Norman Rockwell 450QX202-3	Keepsake	Yr.Iss.	4.50	16-29.50
82-77-009	Peanuts 450QX200-6	Keepsake	Yr.Iss.	4.50	25.00
82-77-010	Disney 450QX217-3	Keepsake	Yr.Iss.	4.50	25-33.00
82-77-011	Mary Hamilton 450QX217-6	Keepsake	Yr.Iss.	4.50	17.00
82-77-012	Joan Walsh Anglund 450QX219-3	Keepsake	Yr.Iss.	4.50	18.00
Hallmark Keepsake Ornaments	**1982 Designer Keepsakes**				
82-78-001	Old World Angels 450QX226-3	Keepsake	Yr.Iss.	4.50	19.50
82-78-002	Patterns of Christmas 450QX226-6	Keepsake	Yr.Iss.	4.50	22.50
82-78-003	Old Fashioned Christmas 450QX227-6	Keepsake	Yr.Iss.	4.50	39.50
82-78-004	Stained Glass 450QX228-3	Keepsake	Yr.Iss.	4.50	19.50
82-78-005	Merry Christmas 450QX225-6	Keepsake	Yr.Iss.	4.50	15.00
82-78-006	Twelve Days of Christmas 450QX203-6	Keepsake	Yr.Iss.	4.50	29.50
Hallmark Keepsake Ornaments	**1982 Decorative Ball Ornaments**				
82-79-001	Christmas Angel 450QX220-6	Keepsake	Yr.Iss.	4.50	18.00
82-79-002	Santa 450QX221-6	Keepsake	Yr.Iss.	4.50	19.00
82-79-003	Currier & Ives 450QX201-3	Keepsake	Yr.Iss.	4.50	16.00
82-79-004	Season for Caring 450QX221-3	Keepsake	Yr.Iss.	4.50	20.00
Hallmark Keepsake Ornaments	**1982 Colors of Christmas**				
82-80-001	Nativity 450QX308-3	Keepsake	Yr.Iss.	4.50	40.00
82-80-002	Santa's Flight 450QX308-6	Keepsake	Yr.Iss.	4.50	30-39.50
Hallmark Keepsake Ornaments	**1982 Ice Sculptures**				
82-81-001	Snowy Seal 400QX300-6	Keepsake	Yr.Iss.	4.00	12-19.50
82-81-002	Arctic Penguin 400QX300-3	Keepsake	Yr.Iss.	4.00	12-19.50
Hallmark Keepsake Ornaments	**1982 Holiday Highlights**				
82-82-001	Christmas Sleigh 550QX309-3	Keepsake	Yr.Iss.	5.50	75.00
82-82-002	Angel 550QX309-6	Keepsake	Yr.Iss.	5.50	25.00
82-82-003	Christmas Magic 550QX311-3	Keepsake	Yr.Iss.	5.50	27.50
Hallmark Keepsake Ornaments	**1982 Handcrafted Ornaments**				
82-83-001	Three Kings 850QX307-3	Keepsake	Yr.Iss.	8.50	22.50
82-83-002	Baroque Angel 1500QX456-6	Keepsake	Yr.Iss.	15.00	150.00
82-83-003	Cloisonne Angel 1200QX145-4	Keepsake	Yr.Iss.	12.00	95.00
Hallmark Keepsake Ornaments	**1982 Brass Ornaments**				
82-84-001	Santa and Reindeer 900QX467-6	Keepsake	Yr.Iss.	9.00	32-45.00
82-84-002	Brass Bell 1200QX460-6	Keepsake	Yr.Iss.	12.00	15-22.50
82-84-003	Santa's Sleigh 900QX478-6	Keepsake	Yr.Iss.	9.00	20-29.50
Hallmark Keepsake Ornaments	**1982 Handcrafted Ornaments**				
82-85-001	The Spirit of Christmas 1000QX452-6	Keepsake	Yr.Iss.	10.00	125.00
82-85-002	Jogging Santa 800QX457-6	Keepsake	Yr.Iss.	8.00	45.00
82-85-003	Santa Bell 1500QX148-7	Keepsake	Yr.Iss.	15.00	60.00
82-85-004	Santa's Workshop 1000QX450-3	Keepsake	Yr.Iss.	10.00	85.00
82-85-005	Cycling Santa 2000QX435-5	Keepsake	Yr.Iss.	20.00	150.00
82-85-006	Christmas Fantasy 1300QX155-4	Keepsake	Yr.Iss.	13.00	59.00
82-85-007	Cowboy Snowman 800QX480-6	Keepsake	Yr.Iss.	8.00	40-50.00
82-85-008	Pinecone Home 800QX461-3	Keepsake	Yr.Iss.	8.00	100-175.
82-85-009	Raccoon Surprises 900QX479-3	Keepsake	Yr.Iss.	9.00	150-175.
82-85-010	Elfin Artist 900QX457-3	Keepsake	Yr.Iss.	9.00	37.50-45.
82-85-011	Ice Sculptor 800QX432-2	Keepsake	Yr.Iss.	8.00	75.00
82-85-012	Tin Soldier 650QX483-6	Keepsake	Yr.Iss.	6.50	39.50
82-85-013	Peeking Elf 650QX419-5	Keepsake	Yr.Iss.	6.50	32.50
82-85-014	Jolly Christmas Tree 650QX465-3	Keepsake	Yr.Iss.	6.50	75.00
82-85-015	Embroidered Tree - 650QX494-6	Keepsake	Yr.Iss.	6.50	25.00
Hallmark Keepsake Ornaments	**1982 Little Trimmers**				
82-86-001	Cookie Mouse 450QX454-6	Keepsake	Yr.Iss.	4.50	55-60.00
82-86-002	Musical Angel 550QX459-6	Keepsake	Yr.Iss.	5.50	100-125.
82-86-003	Merry Moose 550QX415-5	Keepsake	Yr.Iss.	5.50	49.50
82-86-004	Christmas Owl 450QX131-4	Keepsake	Yr.Iss.	4.50	35.00
82-86-005	Dove Love 450QX462-3	Keepsake	Yr.Iss.	4.50	55.00
82-86-006	Perky Penguin 400QX409-5	Keepsake	Yr.Iss.	4.00	35.00
82-86-007	Christmas Kitten 400QX454-3	Keepsake	Yr.Iss.	4.00	32.00
82-86-008	Jingling Teddy 400QX477-6	Keepsake	Yr.Iss.	4.00	39.50
Hallmark Keepsake Ornaments	**1982 Collectible Series**				
82-87-001	Holiday Wildlife-1st Ed. 700QX 313-3	Keepsake	Yr.Iss.	7.00	350-475.
82-87-002	Tin Locomotive-1st Ed. 1300QX 460-3	Keepsake	Yr.Iss.	13.00	575-650.
82-87-003	Clothespin Soldier-1st Ed. 500QX 458-3	Keepsake	Yr.Iss.	5.00	90-125.00
82-87-004	The Bellringer-4th Ed. 1500QX 455-6	Keepsake	Yr.Iss.	15.00	97.50
82-87-005	Carrousel Series-5th Ed. 1000QX 478-3	Keepsake	Yr.Iss.	10.00	99.00
82-87-006	Snoopy and Friends-4th Ed.1000QX 478-3	Keepsake	Yr.Iss.	13.00	85.00
82-87-007	Here Comes Santa-4th Edition 1500QX 464-3	Keepsake	Yr.Iss.	15.00	95-125.00
82-87-008	Rocking Horse-2nd Ed. 1000QX 502-3	Keepsake	Yr.Iss.	10.00	375.00
82-87-009	Thimble-5th Edition 500QX451-3	Keepsake	Yr.Iss.	5.00	75.00
82-87-010	Frosty Friends-3rd Ed. 500QX 451-3	Keepsake	Yr.Iss.	8.00	225.00
Hallmark Keepsake Ornaments	**1982 Holiday Chimes**				
82-88-001	Tree Chimes 550QX484-6	Keepsake	Yr.Iss.	5.50	49.00
82-88-002	Bell Chimes 550QX494-3	Keepsake	Yr.Iss.	5.50	30.00
Hallmark Keepsake Ornaments	**1983 Commemoratives**				
83-89-001	Baby's First Christmas 750QX301-9	Keepsake	Yr.Iss.	7.50	14.50
83-89-002	Baby's First Christmas 1400QX402-7	Keepsake	Yr.Iss.	14.00	34.50-37.50
83-89-003	Baby's First Christmas 450QX200-7	Keepsake	Yr.Iss.	4.50	20.00
83-89-004	Baby's First Christmas 450QX200-9	Keepsake	Yr.Iss.	4.50	20.00
83-89-005	Baby's First Christmas 700QX302-9	Keepsake	Yr.Iss.	7.00	25.00
83-89-006	Grandchild's First Christmas400Q 430-9	Keepsake	Yr.Iss.	14.00	34.50
83-89-007	Child's Third Christmas 450QX226-9	Keepsake	Yr.Iss.	4.50	19.00
83-89-008	Grandchild's First Christmas600QX 312-9	Keepsake	Yr.Iss.	6.00	20.00
83-89-009	Baby's Second Christmas 450QX226-7	Keepsake	Yr.Iss.	4.50	25.00
83-89-010	Granddaughter 450QX202-7	Keepsake	Yr.Iss.	4.50	22.50
83-89-011	Grandson 450QX201-9	Keepsake	Yr.Iss.	4.50	22.50
83-89-012	Son 450QX202-9	Keepsake	Yr.Iss.	4.50	24.50
83-89-013	Daughter 450QX203-7	Keepsake	Yr.Iss.	4.50	32.50
83-89-014	Godchild 450QX201-7	Keepsake	Yr.Iss.	4.50	14.00
83-89-015	Grandmother 450QX205-7	Keepsake	Yr.Iss.	4.50	12.00
83-89-016	Mom and Dad 650QX429-7	Keepsake	Yr.Iss.	6.50	17.50
83-89-017	Sister 450QX206-9	Keepsake	Yr.Iss.	4.50	17.00
83-89-018	Grandparents 650QX429-9	Keepsake	Yr.Iss.	6.50	14.50
83-89-019	First Christmas Together 450QX208-9	Keepsake	Yr.Iss.	4.50	20.00
83-89-020	First Christmas Together 600QX310-7	Keepsake	Yr.Iss.	6.00	30-39.50
83-89-021	First Christmas Together 750QX301-7	Keepsake	Yr.Iss.	7.50	20.00
83-89-022	First Christmas Together-Brass Locket 1500QX 432-9	Keepsake	Yr.Iss.	15.00	40-45.00
83-89-023	Love Is a Song 450QX223-9	Keepsake	Yr.Iss.	4.50	20-25.00
83-89-024	Love 1300QX422-7	Keepsake	Yr.Iss.	13.00	29.50
83-89-025	Love 600QX310-9	Keepsake	Yr.Iss.	6.00	35.00
83-89-026	Love 450QX207-9	Keepsake	Yr.Iss.	4.50	25.00
83-89-027	Teacher 600QX304-9	Keepsake	Yr.Iss.	6.00	10.00
83-89-028	First Christmas Together 600QX306-9	Keepsake	Yr.Iss.	6.00	19.50
83-89-029	Friendship 600QX305-9	Keepsake	Yr.Iss.	6.00	14.50
83-89-030	Love 600QX305-7	Keepsake	Yr.Iss.	6.00	17.50
83-89-031	Mother 600Qx306-7	Keepsake	Yr.Iss.	6.00	14.50
83-89-032	25th Christmas Together 450QX224-7	Keepsake	Yr.Iss.	4.50	17.00
83-89-033	Teacher 450QX224-9	Keepsake	Yr.Iss.	4.50	14.00
83-89-034	Friendship 450QX207-7	Keepsake	Yr.Iss.	4.50	15.00
83-89-035	New Home 450QX210-7	Keepsake	Yr.Iss.	4.50	15.00
83-89-036	Tenth Christmas Together 650QX430-7	Keepsake	Yr.Iss.	6.50	20.00
Hallmark Keepsake Ornaments	**1983 Property Ornaments**				
83-90-001	Betsey Clark 650QX404-7	Keepsake	Yr.Iss.	6.50	29.50
83-90-002	Betsey Clark 900QX440-1	Keepsake	Yr.Iss.	9.00	27.50
83-90-003	Betsey Clark-11th Edition 450QX211-9	Keepsake	Yr.Iss.	4.50	30-50.00
83-90-004	Peanuts 450QX212-7	Keepsake	Yr.Iss.	4.50	22.00
83-90-005	Disney 450QX212-9	Keepsake	Yr.Iss.	4.50	30-50.00
83-90-006	Shirt Tales 450QX214-9	Keepsake	Yr.Iss.	4.50	22.50
83-90-007	Mary Hamilton 450QX213-7	Keepsake	Yr.Iss.	4.50	39.50

Number	Name	Artist	Edition Limit	Issue Price	Quote
83-90-008	Miss Piggy 1300QX405-7	Keepsake	Yr.Iss.	13.00	195.00
83-90-009	The Muppets 450QX214-7	Keepsake	Yr.Iss.	4.50	30-50.00
83-90-010	Kermit the Frog 1100QX495-6	Keepsake	Yr.Iss.	11.00	32.50
83-90-011	Norman Rockwell-4th Edition750QX 300-7	Keepsake	Yr.Iss.	7.50	30-40.00
83-90-012	Norman Rockwell 450QX215-7	Keepsake	Yr.Iss.	4.50	42.50
Hallmark Keepsake Ornaments	**1983 Decorative Ball Ornaments**				
83-91-001	Currier & Ives 450QX215-9	Keepsake	Yr.Iss.	4.50	15-17.00
83-91-002	Christmas Joy 450QX216-9	Keepsake	Yr.Iss.	4.50	22.50
83-91-003	Here Comes Santa 450QX217-7	Keepsake	Yr.Iss.	4.50	34.50
83-91-004	Oriental Butterflies 450QX218-7	Keepsake	Yr.Iss.	4.50	15-20.00
83-91-005	Angels 500QX219-7	Keepsake	Yr.Iss.	5.00	22.00
83-91-006	Season's Greeting 450QX219-9	Keepsake	Yr.Iss.	4.50	15.00
83-91-007	1983 450QX220-9	Keepsake	Yr.Iss.	4.50	19.00
83-91-008	The Wise Men 450QX220-7	Keepsake	Yr.Iss.	4.50	30-39.50
83-91-009	Christmas Wonderland 450QX221-9	Keepsake	Yr.Iss.	4.50	95.00
83-91-010	An Old Fashioned Christmas450QX 2217-9	Keepsake	Yr.Iss.	4.50	15.00
83-91-011	The Annunciation 450QX216-7	Keepsake	Yr.Iss.	4.50	22.50
Hallmark Keepsake Ornaments	**1983 Holiday Highlights**				
83-92-001	Christmas Stocking 600Qx303-9	Keepsake	Yr.Iss.	6.00	39.50
83-92-002	Star of Peace 600QX304-7	Keepsake	Yr.Iss.	6.00	15.00
83-92-003	Time for Sharing 600QX307-7	Keepsake	Yr.Iss.	6.00	34.50
Hallmark Keepsake Ornaments	**1983 Crown Classics**				
83-93-001	Enameled Christmas Wreath900QX 311-9	Keepsake	Yr.Iss.	9.00	12.50
83-93-002	Memories to Treasure 700QX303-7	Keepsake	Yr.Iss.	7.00	22.00
83-93-003	Mother and Child 750QX302-7	Keepsake	Yr.Iss.	7.50	34.50
Hallmark Keepsake Ornaments	**1983 Holiday Sculptures**				
83-94-001	Santa 400Qx308-7	Keepsake	Yr.Iss.	4.00	32.50
83-94-002	Heart 400QX307-9	Keepsake	Yr.Iss.	4.00	49.50
Hallmark Keepsake Ornaments	**1983 Handcrafted Ornaments**				
83-95-001	Embroidered Stocking 650QX479-6	Keepsake	Yr.Iss.	6.50	19.50
83-95-002	Embroidered Heart 650QX421-7	Keepsake	Yr.Iss.	6.50	19.50
83-95-003	Scrimshaw Reindeer 800QX424-9	Keepsake	Yr.Iss.	8.00	32.50
83-95-004	Jack Frost 900QX407-9	Keepsake	Yr.Iss.	9.00	54.50
83-95-005	Unicorn 1000QX426-7	Keepsake	Yr.Iss.	10.00	58-63.00
83-95-006	Porcelain Doll, Diana 900QX423-7	Keepsake	Yr.Iss.	9.00	25.50
83-95-007	Brass Santa 900QX423-9	Keepsake	Yr.Iss.	9.00	19.00
83-95-008	Santa's on His Way 1000QX426-9	Keepsake	Yr.Iss.	10.00	20-29.50
83-95-009	Old-Fashioned Santa 1100QX409-9	Keepsake	Yr.Iss.	11.00	65.00
83-95-010	Cycling Santa 2000QX435-5	Keepsake	Yr.Iss.	20.00	150.00
83-95-011	Santa's Workshop 1000QX450-3	Keepsake	Yr.Iss.	10.00	60.00
83-95-012	Ski Lift Santa 800QX418-7	Keepsake	Yr.Iss.	8.00	65.00
83-95-013	Hitchhiking Santa 800QX424-7	Keepsake	Yr.Iss.	8.00	39.50
83-95-014	Mountain Climbing Santa 650QX407-7	Keepsake	Yr.Iss.	6.50	34.50
83-95-015	Jolly Santa 350QX425-9	Keepsake	Yr.Iss.	3.50	35.00
83-95-016	Santa's Many Faces 600QX311-6	Keepsake	Yr.Iss.	6.00	30.00
83-95-017	Baroque Angels 1300QX422-9	Keepsake	Yr.Iss.	13.00	57.50
83-95-018	Madonna and Child 1200QX428-7	Keepsake	Yr.Iss.	12.00	18-39.50
83-95-019	Mouse on Cheese 650QX413-7	Keepsake	Yr.Iss.	6.50	44.50
83-95-020	Peppermint Penguin 650QX408-9	Keepsake	Yr.Iss.	6.50	35-48.00
83-95-021	Skating Rabbit 800QX409-7	Keepsake	Yr.Iss.	8.00	35-49.50
83-95-022	Skiing Fox 800QX420-7	Keepsake	Yr.Iss.	8.00	35-40.00
83-95-023	Mouse in Bell 1000QX419-7	Keepsake	Yr.Iss.	10.00	50-65.00
83-95-024	Mailbox Kitten 650QX415-7	Keepsake	Yr.Iss.	6.50	60.00
83-95-025	Tin Rocking Horse 650QX414-9	Keepsake	Yr.Iss.	6.50	38-42.50
83-95-026	Bell Wreath 650QX420-9	Keepsake	Yr.Iss.	6.50	27.50
83-95-027	Angel Messenger 650QX408-7	Keepsake	Yr.Iss.	6.50	95.00
83-95-028	Holiday Puppy 350QX412-7	Keepsake	Yr.Iss.	3.50	29.50
83-95-029	Rainbow Angel 550QX416-7	Keepsake	Yr.Iss.	5.50	100-125.00
83-95-030	Sneaker Mouse 450QX400-9	Keepsake	Yr.Iss.	4.50	38-45.00
83-95-031	Christmas Koala 400QX419-9	Keepsake	Yr.Iss.	4.00	29.50
83-95-032	Caroling Owl 450QX411-7	Keepsake	Yr.Iss.	4.50	39.50
83-95-033	Christmas Kitten 400QX454-3	Keepsake	Yr.Iss.	4.00	35.00
Hallmark Keepsake Ornaments	**1983 Collectible Series**				
83-96-001	The Bellringer-5th Edition1500QX 403-9	Keepsake	Yr.Iss.	15.00	135.00
83-96-002	Holiday Wildlife-2nd Edition 700QX 309-9	Keepsake	Yr.Iss.	7.00	25-75.00
83-96-003	Here Comes Santa-5th Edition1300QX 403-7	Keepsake	Yr.Iss.	13.00	200-225.
83-96-004	Snoopy and Friends-5th Ed.1300QX 416-9	Keepsake	Yr.Iss.	13.00	75.00
83-96-005	Carrousel-6th Edition 1100QX401-9	Keepsake	Yr.Iss.	11.00	47.50
83-96-006	Porcelain Bear-1st Edition700QX 428-9	Keepsake	Yr.Iss.	7.00	75-95.00
83-96-007	Clothespin Soldier-2nd Edition500QX 402-9	Keepsake	Yr.Iss.	5.00	40-45.00
83-96-008	Rocking Horse-3rd Edition1000QX 417-7	Keepsake	Yr.Iss.	10.00	150-225.
83-96-009	Frosty Friends-4th Edition800QX 400-7	Keepsake	Yr.Iss.	8.00	225.00
83-96-010	Thimble - 6th Edition 500QX401-7	Keepsake	Yr.Iss.	5.00	39.50
83-96-011	Tin Locomotive - 2nd Edition1300QX 404-9	Keepsake	Yr.Iss.	13.00	225-250.
Hallmark Keepsake Ornaments	**1984 Commemoratives**				
84-97-001	Baby's First Christmas 1600QX904-1	Keepsake	Yr.Iss.	16.00	40-55.00
84-97-002	Baby's First Christmas 1400QX438-1	Keepsake	Yr.Iss.	14.00	25-45.00
84-97-003	Baby's First Christmas 700QX300-1	Keepsake	Yr.Iss.	7.00	17.00
84-97-004	Baby's First Christmas 600QX340-1	Keepsake	Yr.Iss.	6.00	25-37.50
84-97-005	Baby's First Christmas-Boy450QX 240-4	Keepsake	Yr.Iss.	4.50	20-23.00
84-97-006	Baby's First Christmas-Girl450QX 340-1	Keepsake	Yr.Iss.	4.50	20-23.00
84-97-007	Baby's Second Christmas 450QX241-1	Keepsake	Yr.Iss.	4.50	27.50
84-97-008	Child's Third Christmas 450QX261-1	Keepsake	Yr.Iss.	4.50	20.00
84-97-009	Grandchild's First Christmas110QX 460-1	Keepsake	Yr.Iss.	11.00	25-33.00
84-97-010	Grandchild's First Christmas450QX 257-4	Keepsake	Yr.Iss.	4.50	14.00
84-97-011	Godchild 450QX242-1	Keepsake	Yr.Iss.	4.50	15.00
84-97-012	Grandson 450QX242-4	Keepsake	Yr.Iss.	4.50	20.00
84-97-013	Granddaughter 450QX243-1	Keepsake	Yr.Iss.	4.50	20.00
84-97-014	Grandparents 450QX256-1	Keepsake	Yr.Iss.	4.50	15.00
84-97-015	Grandmother 450QX244-1	Keepsake	Yr.Iss.	4.50	15.00
84-97-016	Father 600QX257-1	Keepsake	Yr.Iss.	6.00	12.00
84-97-017	Mother 600QX343-4	Keepsake	Yr.Iss.	6.00	12.50
84-97-018	Mother and Dad 650QX258-1	Keepsake	Yr.Iss.	6.50	17.00
84-97-019	Sister 650QX259-4	Keepsake	Yr.Iss.	6.50	14.50
84-97-020	Daughter 450QX244-4	Keepsake	Yr.Iss.	4.50	24.50
84-97-021	Son 450QX243-4	Keepsake	Yr.Iss.	4.50	25.00
84-97-022	The Miracle of Love 600QX342-4	Keepsake	Yr.Iss.	6.00	29.50
84-97-023	First Christmas Together 600QX342-1	Keepsake	Yr.Iss.	6.00	19.50
84-97-024	First Christmas Together 1600QX904-4	Keepsake	Yr.Iss.	16.00	65.00
84-97-025	First Christmas Together 1500QX436-4	Keepsake	Yr.Iss.	15.00	29.50
84-97-026	First Christmas Together 750QX340-4	Keepsake	Yr.Iss.	7.50	17.00
84-97-027	First Christmas Together 450QX245-1	Keepsake	Yr.Iss.	4.50	15-19.00
84-97-028	Heartful of Love 1000QX443-4	Keepsake	Yr.Iss.	10.00	45.00
84-97-029	Love...the Spirit of Christmas450QX 247-4	Keepsake	Yr.Iss.	4.50	24.50
84-97-030	Love 450QX255-4	Keepsake	Yr.Iss.	4.50	14.50
84-97-031	Ten Years Together 650QX258-4	Keepsake	Yr.Iss.	6.50	19.50
84-97-032	Twenty-Five Years Together650QX 259-1	Keepsake	Yr.Iss.	6.50	19.50
84-97-033	Gratitude 600QX344-4	Keepsake	Yr.Iss.	6.00	10.00
84-97-034	The Fun of Friendship 600QX343-1	Keepsake	Yr.Iss.	6.00	32.50
84-97-035	Friendship 450QX248-1	Keepsake	Yr.Iss.	4.50	15.00
84-97-036	A Gift of Friendship 450QX260-4	Keepsake	Yr.Iss.	4.50	15.00
84-97-037	New Home 450QX245-4	Keepsake	Yr.Iss.	4.50	60-107.50
84-97-038	From Our Home to Yours 450QX248-4	Keepsake	Yr.Iss.	4.50	12.00
84-97-039	Teacher 450QX249-1	Keepsake	Yr.Iss.	4.50	12.50
84-97-040	Baby-sitter 450QX253-1	Keepsake	Yr.Iss.	4.50	12.50
Hallmark Keepsake Ornaments	**1984 Property Ornaments**				
84-98-001	Betsey Clark Angel 900QX462-4	Keepsake	Yr.Iss.	9.00	29.50
84-98-002	Katybeth 900QX463-1	Keepsake	Yr.Iss.	9.00	24.50
84-98-003	Peanuts 450QX252-1	Keepsake	Yr.Iss.	4.50	17.50-24.50
84-98-004	Disney 450QX250-4	Keepsake	Yr.Iss.	4.50	29.50
84-98-005	The Muppets 450QX251-4	Keepsake	Yr.Iss.	4.50	29.50
84-98-006	Norman Rockwell 450QX251-4	Keepsake	Yr.Iss.	4.50	20.00
84-98-007	Currier & Ives 450QX250-1	Keepsake	Yr.Iss.	4.50	15-20.00
84-98-008	Shirt Tales 450QX252-4	Keepsake	Yr.Iss.	4.50	12-15.00
84-98-009	Snoopy and Woodstock 750QX439-1	Keepsake	Yr.Iss.	7.50	42.50-75.00
84-98-010	Muffin 550QX442-1	Keepsake	Yr.Iss.	5.50	25-30.00
84-98-011	Kit 550QX453-4	Keepsake	Yr.Iss.	5.50	25-30.00
Hallmark Keepsake Ornaments	**1984 Traditional Ornaments**				
84-99-001	White Christmas 1600QX905-1	Keepsake	Yr.Iss.	16.00	65-95.00
84-99-002	Twelve Days of Christmas1500QX 415-9	Keepsake	Yr.Iss.	15.00	95.00
84-99-003	Gift of Music 1500QX451-1	Keepsake	Yr.Iss.	15.00	95.00
84-99-004	Amanda 900QX432-1	Keepsake	Yr.Iss.	9.00	20-29.50
84-99-005	Holiday Jester 1100QX437-4	Keepsake	Yr.Iss.	11.00	32.50
84-99-006	Uncle Sam 600QX449-1	Keepsake	Yr.Iss.	6.00	38-42.50
84-99-007	Chickadee 600QX451-4	Keepsake	Yr.Iss.	6.00	37.50
84-99-008	Cuckoo Clock 1000QX455-1	Keepsake	Yr.Iss.	10.00	40-49.50
84-99-009	Alpine Elf 600QX452-1	Keepsake	Yr.Iss.	6.00	37.50
84-99-010	Nostalgic Sled 600QX442-4	Keepsake	Yr.Iss.	6.00	24.50
84-99-011	Santa Sulky Driver 900QX436-1	Keepsake	Yr.Iss.	9.00	32.50
84-99-012	Old Fashioned Rocking Horse750QX 346-4	Keepsake	Yr.Iss.	7.50	17.50
84-99-013	Madonna and Child 600QX344-1	Keepsake	Yr.Iss.	6.00	40.00
84-99-014	Holiday Friendship 1300QX445-1	Keepsake	Yr.Iss.	13.00	24.50
84-99-015	Peace on Earth 750QX341-4	Keepsake	Yr.Iss.	7.50	15-22.50
84-99-016	A Savior is Born 450X254-1	Keepsake	Yr.Iss.	4.50	19.50
84-99-017	Holiday Starburst 500QX253-4	Keepsake	Yr.Iss.	5.00	20.00
84-99-018	Santa 750QX458-4	Keepsake	Yr.Iss.	7.50	14.50
84-99-019	Needlepoint Wreath 650QX459-4	Keepsake	Yr.Iss.	6.50	15.00
84-99-020	Christmas Memories Photoholder 650QX 300-4	Keepsake	Yr.Iss.	6.50	24.50
Hallmark Keepsake Ornaments	**1984 Holiday Humor**				
84-100-001	Bell Ringer Squirrel 1000QX443-1	Keepsake	Yr.Iss.	10.00	32-39.50
84-100-002	Raccoon's Christmas 900QX447-7	Keepsake	Yr.Iss.	9.00	50-57.50
84-100-003	Three Kittens in a Mitten 800QX431-1	Keepsake	Yr.Iss.	8.00	45.00
84-100-004	Marathon Santa 800QX456-4	Keepsake	Yr.Iss.	8.00	40.50
84-100-005	Santa Star 550QX450-4	Keepsake	Yr.Iss.	5.50	25-40.00
84-100-006	Snowmobile Santa 650QX431-4	Keepsake	Yr.Iss.	6.50	34.50
84-100-007	Snowshoe Penguin 650QX453-1	Keepsake	Yr.Iss.	6.50	49.00
84-100-008	Christmas Owl 600QX444-1	Keepsake	Yr.Iss.	6.00	25-30.00
84-100-009	Musical Angel 550QX434-4	Keepsake	Yr.Iss.	5.50	43-60.00
84-100-010	Napping Mouse 550QX435-1	Keepsake	Yr.Iss.	5.50	49.50
84-100-011	Roller Skating Rabbit 500QX457-1	Keepsake	Yr.Iss.	5.00	29.00
84-100-012	Frisbee Puppy 500QX444-4	Keepsake	Yr.Iss.	5.00	44.50
84-100-013	Reindeer Racetrack 450QX254-4	Keepsake	Yr.Iss.	4.50	16.00
84-100-014	A Christmas Prayer 450QX246-1	Keepsake	Yr.Iss.	4.50	16.00
84-100-015	Flights of Fantasy 450QX256-4	Keepsake	Yr.Iss.	4.50	20.00
84-100-016	Polar Bear Drummer 450QX430-1	Keepsake	Yr.Iss.	4.50	29.00
84-100-017	Santa Mouse 450QX433-4	Keepsake	Yr.Iss.	4.50	39.50
84-100-018	Snowy Seal 400QX450-1	Keepsake	Yr.Iss.	4.00	19.00
84-100-019	Fortune Cookie Elf 450Q452-4	Keepsake	Yr.Iss.	4.50	39.50
84-100-020	Peppermint 1984 450Q452-1	Keepsake	Yr.Iss.	4.50	50.00
84-100-021	Mountain Climbing Santa 650QX407-7	Keepsake	Yr.Iss.	6.50	34.50
Hallmark Keepsake Ornaments	**1984 Limited Edition**				
84-101-001	Classical Angel 2750QX459-1	Keepsake	Yr.Iss.	27.50	105.00
Hallmark Keepsake Ornaments	**1984 Collectible Series**				
84-102-001	Nostalgic Houses and Shops-1st Edition 1300QX 448-1	Keepsake	Yr.Iss.	13.00	120-175.
84-102-002	Wood Childhood Ornaments- 1st Edition 650QX 439-4	Keepsake	Yr.Iss.	6.50	30-45.00
84-102-003	The Twelve Days of Christmas- 1st Edition 600QX	Keepsake	Yr.Iss.	6.00	250.00
84-102-004	Art Masterpiece - 1st Edition650QX 349-4	Keepsake	Yr.Iss.	6.50	12-15.00
84-102-005	Porcelain Bear - 2nd Edition700QX 454-1	Keepsake	Yr.Iss.	7.00	30-45.00
84-102-006	Tin Locomotive - 3rd Edition1400QX 440-4	Keepsake	Yr.Iss.	14.00	60-85.00
84-102-007	Clothespin Soldier -3rd Edition 500QX 447-1	Keepsake	Yr.Iss.	5.00	20-29.50
84-102-008	Holiday Wildlife - 3rd Edition 725QX 347-4	Keepsake	Yr.Iss.	7.25	20-29.50
84-102-009	Rocking Horse - 4th Edition 1000QX 435-4	Keepsake	Yr.Iss.	10.00	40-75.00
84-102-010	Frosty Friends -5th Edition 800QX 437-1	Keepsake	Yr.Iss.	8.00	45-60.00
84-102-011	Norman Rockwell - 5th Edition750QX 341-1	Keepsake	Yr.Iss.	7.50	34.50
84-102-012	Here Comes Santa -6th Edition1300QX 438-4	Keepsake	Yr.Iss.	13.00	72.50
84-102-013	The Bellringer - 6th & Final Ed.1500QX 438-4	Keepsake	Yr.Iss.	15.00	45.00
84-102-014	Thimble - 7th Edition 500QX430-4	Keepsake	Yr.Iss.	5.00	39.50
84-102-015	Betsey Clark - 12th Edition500QX 249-4	Keepsake	Yr.Iss.	5.00	35.00
Hallmark Keepsake Ornaments	**1984 Keepsake Magic Ornaments**				
84-103-001	Village Church 1500QLX702-1	Keepsake	Yr.Iss.	15.00	50.00
84-103-002	Sugarplum Cottage 1100QLX701-1	Keepsake	Yr.Iss.	11.00	45.00
84-103-003	City Lights 1000QLX701-4	Keepsake	Yr.Iss.	10.00	45-50.00
84-103-004	Santa's Workshop 1300QLX700-4	Keepsake	Yr.Iss.	13.00	62.50
84-103-005	Santa's Arrival 1300QLX702-4	Keepsake	Yr.Iss.	13.00	65.00
84-103-006	Nativity 1200 QLX700-1	Keepsake	Yr.Iss.	12.00	20-27.50
84-103-007	Stained Glass 800QLX703-1	Keepsake	Yr.Iss.	8.00	19.50
84-103-008	Christmas in the Forest 800QLX703-4	Keepsake	Yr.Iss.	8.00	15-19.50
84-103-009	Brass Carrousel 900QLX707-1	Keepsake	Yr.Iss.	9.00	55-85.00
84-103-010	All are Precious 800QLX704-1	Keepsake	Yr.Iss.	8.00	18-25.00
Hallmark Keepsake Ornaments	**1985 Commemoratives**				
85-104-001	Baby's First Christmas 1600QX499-5	Keepsake	Yr.Iss.	16.00	40-45.00
85-104-002	Baby's First Christmas 1500QX499-2	Keepsake	Yr.Iss.	15.00	40-44.50
85-104-003	Baby Locket 1600QX401-2	Keepsake	Yr.Iss.	16.00	35.00
85-104-004	Baby's First Christmas 575QX370-2	Keepsake	Yr.Iss.	5.75	17.50
85-104-005	Baby's First Christmas 700QX478-2	Keepsake	Yr.Iss.	7.00	14.50
85-104-006	Baby's First Christmas 500QX260-2	Keepsake	Yr.Iss.	5.00	15.00
85-104-007	Baby's Second Christmas 600QX478-5	Keepsake	Yr.Iss.	6.00	29.50
85-104-008	Child's Third Christmas 600QX475-5	Keepsake	Yr.Iss.	6.00	27.50

Company / Number	Name	Series / Artist	Edition Limit	Issue Price	Quote
85-104-009	Grandchild's First Christmas500QX 260-5	Keepsake	Yr.Iss.	5.00	12.00
85-104-010	Grandchild's First Christmas1100QX 495-5	Keepsake	Yr.Iss.	11.00	24.00
85-104-011	Grandparents 700QX380-5	Keepsake	Yr.Iss.	7.00	10.00
85-104-012	Niece 575QX520-5	Keepsake	Yr.Iss.	5.75	10.50
85-104-013	Mother 675QX372-2	Keepsake	Yr.Iss.	6.75	10.00
85-104-014	Mother and Dad 775QX509-2	Keepsake	Yr.Iss.	7.75	18.50
85-104-015	Father 650QX376-2	Keepsake	Yr.Iss.	6.50	10.50
85-104-016	Sister 725QX506-5	Keepsake	Yr.Iss.	7.25	14.50
85-104-017	Daughter 550QX503-2	Keepsake	Yr.Iss.	5.50	12-15.00
85-104-018	Godchild 675QX380-2	Keepsake	Yr.Iss.	6.75	9.50
85-104-019	Son 550QX502-5	Keepsake	Yr.Iss.	5.50	42.50
85-104-020	Grandmother 475QX262-5	Keepsake	Yr.Iss.	4.75	15.00
85-104-021	Grandson 475QX262-2	Keepsake	Yr.Iss.	4.75	24.50
85-104-022	Granddaughter 475QX263-5	Keepsake	Yr.Iss.	4.75	11-25.00
85-104-023	First Christmas Together 1675QX400-5	Keepsake	Yr.Iss.	16.75	25.00
85-104-024	Love at Christmas 575QX371-5	Keepsake	Yr.Iss.	5.75	37.50
85-104-025	First Christmas Together 675QX370-5	Keepsake	Yr.Iss.	6.75	16-20.00
85-104-026	First Christmas Together 1300QX493-5	Keepsake	Yr.Iss.	13.00	25.00
85-104-027	Holiday Heart 800QX498-2	Keepsake	Yr.Iss.	8.00	25.00
85-104-028	First Christmas Together 800QX507-2	Keepsake	Yr.Iss.	8.00	13.00
85-104-029	Heart Full of Love 675QX378-2	Keepsake	Yr.Iss.	6.75	9.50
85-104-030	First Christmas Together 475QX261-2	Keepsake	Yr.Iss.	4.75	17.50
85-104-031	Twenty-Five Years Together800QX 500-5	Keepsake	Yr.Iss.	8.00	19.50
85-104-032	Friendship 775QX506-2	Keepsake	Yr.Iss.	7.75	10.00
85-104-033	Friendship 675QX378-5	Keepsake	Yr.Iss.	6.75	9.50
85-104-034	From Our House to Yours 775QX520-2	Keepsake	Yr.Iss.	7.75	11.00
85-104-035	Teacher 600QX505-2	Keepsake	Yr.Iss.	6.00	19.50
85-104-036	With Appreciation 675QX375-2	Keepsake	Yr.Iss.	6.75	9.50
85-104-037	Special Friends 575QX372-5	Keepsake	Yr.Iss.	5.75	10.00
85-104-038	New Home 475QX269-5	Keepsake	Yr.Iss.	4.75	25.00
85-104-039	Baby-sitter 475QX264-2	Keepsake	Yr.Iss.	4.75	10.00
85-104-040	Good Friends 475QX265-2	Keepsake	Yr.Iss.	4.75	22.50
Hallmark Keepsake Ornaments		**1985 Property Ornaments**			
85-105-001	Snoopy and Woodstock 750QX491-5	Keepsake	Yr.Iss.	7.50	39.50
85-105-002	Muffin the Angel 575QX483-5	Keepsake	Yr.Iss.	5.75	24.00
85-105-003	Kit the Shepherd 575QX484-5	Keepsake	Yr.Iss.	5.75	24.00
85-105-004	Betsey Clark 850QX508-5	Keepsake	Yr.Iss.	8.50	22.50
85-105-005	Hugga Bunch 500QX271-5	Keepsake	Yr.Iss.	5.00	19.50
85-105-006	Fraggle Rock Holiday 475QX265-5	Keepsake	Yr.Iss.	4.75	19.50
85-105-007	Peanuts 475QX266-5	Keepsake	Yr.Iss.	4.75	24.50
85-105-008	Norman Rockwell 475QX266-2	Keepsake	Yr.Iss.	4.75	22.50
85-105-009	Rainbow Brite and Friends 475QX 268-2	Keepsake	Yr.Iss.	4.75	20.00
85-105-010	A Disney Christmas 475QX271-2	Keepsake	Yr.Iss.	4.75	22.50
85-105-011	Merry Shirt Tales 475QX267-2	Keepsake	Yr.Iss.	4.75	19.00
Hallmark Keepsake Ornaments		**1985 Traditional Ornaments**			
85-106-001	Porcelain Bird 650QX479-5	Keepsake	Yr.Iss.	6.50	20-29.50
85-106-002	Sewn Photoholder 700QX379-5	Keepsake	Yr.Iss.	7.00	22.50
85-106-003	Candle Cameo 675QX374-2	Keepsake	Yr.Iss.	6.75	14.50
85-106-004	Santa Pipe 950QX494-2	Keepsake	Yr.Iss.	9.50	22.50
85-106-005	Old-Fashioned Wreath 750QX373-5	Keepsake	Yr.Iss.	7.50	19.50
85-106-006	Peaceful Kingdom 575QX373-2	Keepsake	Yr.Iss.	5.75	15-18.00
85-106-007	Christmas Treats 550QX507-5	Keepsake	Yr.Iss.	5.50	15.00
85-106-008	The Spirit of Santa Claus -Special Ed. 2250QX 498-5	Keepsake	Yr.Iss.	22.50	75-95.00
85-106-009	Nostalgic Sled 600QX442-4	Keepsake	Yr.Iss.	6.00	19.50
Hallmark Keepsake Ornaments		**1985 Holiday Humor**			
85-107-001	Night Before Christmas 1300QX449-4	Keepsake	Yr.Iss.	13.00	44.50
85-107-002	Nativity Scene 475QX264-5	Keepsake	Yr.Iss.	4.75	25.00
85-107-003	Santa's Ski Trip 1200QX496-2	Keepsake	Yr.Iss.	12.00	60.00
85-107-004	Mouse Wagon 575QX476-2	Keepsake	Yr.Iss.	5.75	55.00
85-107-005	Children in the Shoe 950QX490-5	Keepsake	Yr.Iss.	9.50	44.50
85-107-006	Do Not Disturb Bear 775QX481-2	Keepsake	Yr.Iss.	7.75	24.50
85-107-007	Sun and Fun Santa 775QX492-2	Keepsake	Yr.Iss.	7.75	35.00
85-107-008	Bottlecap Fun Bunnies 775QX481-5	Keepsake	Yr.Iss.	7.75	22-33.00
85-107-009	Lamb in Legwarmers 700QX480-2	Keepsake	Yr.Iss.	7.00	20.00
85-107-010	Candy Apple Mouse 750QX470-5	Keepsake	Yr.Iss.	6.50	43-45.00
85-107-011	Skateboard Raccoon 650QX473-2	Keepsake	Yr.Iss.	6.50	36.50
85-107-012	Stardust Angel 575QX475-2	Keepsake	Yr.Iss.	5.75	35.00
85-107-013	Soccer Beaver 650QX477-5	Keepsake	Yr.Iss.	6.50	24.50
85-107-014	Beary Smooth Ride 650QX480-5	Keepsake	Yr.Iss.	6.50	22.50
85-107-015	Swinging Angel Bell 1100QX492-5	Keepsake	Yr.Iss.	11.00	25-37.00
85-107-016	Doggy in a Stocking 550QX474-2	Keepsake	Yr.Iss.	5.50	36.50
85-107-017	Engineering Mouse 550QX473-5	Keepsake	Yr.Iss.	5.50	25.00
85-107-018	Kitty Mischief 500QX474-5	Keepsake	Yr.Iss.	5.00	24.50
85-107-019	Baker Elf 575QX491-2	Keepsake	Yr.Iss.	5.75	29.50
85-107-020	Ice-Skating Owl 500QX476-5	Keepsake	Yr.Iss.	5.00	25.00
85-107-021	Dapper Penguin 500QX477-2	Keepsake	Yr.Iss.	5.00	27.50
85-107-022	Trumpet Panda 450QX471-2	Keepsake	Yr.Iss.	4.50	22.00
85-107-023	Merry Mouse 450QX403-2	Keepsake	Yr.Iss.	4.50	20-22.00
85-107-024	Snow-Pitching Snowman 450QX470-2	Keepsake	Yr.Iss.	4.50	22.50
85-107-025	Three Kittens in a Mitten 800QX431-1	Keepsake	Yr.Iss.	8.00	34.50
85-107-026	Roller Skating Rabbit 500QX457-1	Keepsake	Yr.Iss.	5.00	19.00
85-107-027	Snowy Seal 400QX450-1	Keepsake	Yr.Iss.	4.00	16.00
Hallmark Keepsake Ornaments		**1985 Country Christmas Collection**			
85-108-001	Old-Fashioned Doll 1450QX519-5	Keepsake	Yr.Iss.	14.50	30-34.50
85-108-002	Country Goose 775QX518-5	Keepsake	Yr.Iss.	7.75	10-15.00
85-108-003	Rocking Horse Memories1000QX518-2	Keepsake	Yr.Iss.	10.00	12.00
85-108-004	Whirligig Santa 1250QX519-2	Keepsake	Yr.Iss.	12.50	15-24.50
85-108-005	Sheep at Christmas 825QX517-5	Keepsake	Yr.Iss.	8.25	29.50
Hallmark Keepsake Ornaments		**1985 Heirloom Christmas Collection**			
85-109-001	Keepsake Basket 1500QX514-5	Keepsake	Yr.Iss.	15.00	18.50
85-109-002	Victorian Lady 950QX513-2	Keepsake	Yr.Iss.	9.50	20-25.00
85-109-003	Charming Angel 975QX512-5	Keepsake	Yr.Iss.	9.75	24.50
85-109-004	Lacy Heart 875QX511-2	Keepsake	Yr.Iss.	8.75	20-29.50
85-109-005	Snowflake 650QX510-5	Keepsake	Yr.Iss.	6.50	20.00
Hallmark Keepsake Ornaments		**1985 Limited Edition**			
85-110-001	Heavenly Trumpeter 2750QX405-2	Keepsake	Yr.Iss.	27.50	99.00
Hallmark Keepsake Ornaments		**1985 Collectible Series**			
85-111-001	Windows of the World-1st Ed.975QX490-2	Keepsake	Yr.Iss.	9.75	95.00
85-111-002	Miniature Creche-1st Ed.875QX482-5	Keepsake	Yr.Iss.	8.75	30-60.00
85-111-003	Nostalgic Houses and Shops-Second Ed.-1375QX497-5	Keepsake	Yr.Iss.	13.75	65-95.00
85-111-004	Art Masterpiece-2nd Ed.675QX377-2	Keepsake	Yr.Iss.	6.75	15.00
85-111-005	Wood Childhood Ornaments-2nd Ed. 700QX472-2	Keepsake	Yr.Iss.	7.00	39.50

Company / Number	Name	Series / Artist	Edition Limit	Issue Price	Quote
85-111-006	Twelve Days of Christmas-2nd Ed. 650QX371-2	Keepsake	Yr.Iss.	6.50	40-50.00
85-111-007	Porcelain Bear-3rd Ed.750QX479-2	Keepsake	Yr.Iss.	7.50	42.50
85-111-008	Tin Locomotive-4th Ed.1475QX497-2	Keepsake	Yr.Iss.	14.75	64.50
85-111-009	Holiday Wildlife-4th Ed.750QX376-5	Keepsake	Yr.Iss.	7.50	29.50
85-111-010	Clothespin Soldier-4th Ed.550QX471-5	Keepsake	Yr.Iss.	5.50	22-24.50
85-111-011	Rocking Horse-5th Ed.1075QX493-2	Keepsake	Yr.Iss.	10.75	40-60.00
85-111-012	Norman Rockwell-6th Ed.750QX374-5	Keepsake	Yr.Iss.	7.50	27.50
85-111-013	Here Comes Santa-6th Ed.1400QX496-5	Keepsake	Yr.Iss.	14.00	52.50
85-111-014	Frosty Friends-6th Ed.850QX482-2	Keepsake	Yr.Iss.	8.50	45-53.00
85-111-015	Betsey Clark-13th & final Ed.500QX263-2	Keepsake	Yr.Iss.	5.00	29.50
85-111-016	Thimble-8th Ed.550QX472-5	Keepsake	Yr.Iss.	5.50	22-29.50
Hallmark Keepsake Ornaments		**1985 Keepsake Magic Ornaments**			
85-112-001	Baby's First Christmas 1650QLX700-5	Keepsake	Yr.Iss.	16.50	39.50
85-112-002	Katybeth 1075QLX710-2	Keepsake	Yr.Iss.	10.75	42.50-47.50
85-112-003	Chris Mouse-1st edition1250QLX703-2	Keepsake	Yr.Iss.	12.50	50-85.00
85-112-004	Swiss Cheese Lane 1300QLX706-5	Keepsake	Yr.Iss.	13.00	42-78.00
85-112-005	Mr. and Mrs. Santa 1450QLX705-2	Keepsake	Yr.Iss.	14.50	75-85.00
85-112-006	Little Red Schoolhouse 1575QLX711-2	Keepsake	Yr.Iss.	15.75	85-95.00
85-112-007	Love Wreath 850QLX702-5	Keepsake	Yr.Iss.	8.50	29.50
85-112-008	Christmas Eve Visit 1200QLX710-5	Keepsake	Yr.Iss.	12.00	22-27.50
85-112-009	Season of Beauty 800QLX712-2	Keepsake	Yr.Iss.	8.00	22-29.50
Hallmark Keepsake Ornaments		**1986 Commemoratives**			
86-113-001	Baby's First Christmas 900QX412-6	Keepsake	Yr.Iss.	9.00	35-38.00
86-113-002	Baby's First Christmas Photoholder 800QX379-2	Keepsake	Yr.Iss.	8.00	22.50
86-113-003	Baby's First Christmas 600QX380-3	Keepsake	Yr.Iss.	6.00	20-25.00
86-113-004	Baby's First Christmas 550QX271-3	Keepsake	Yr.Iss.	5.50	15-18.00
86-113-005	Grandchild's First Christmas1000QX411-6	Keepsake	Yr.Iss.	10.00	16.00
86-113-006	Baby's Second Christmas 650QX413-3	Keepsake	Yr.Iss.	6.50	27.50
86-113-007	Child's Third Christmas 650QX413-6	Keepsake	Yr.Iss.	6.50	9-20.00
86-113-008	Baby Locket 1600QX412-3	Keepsake	Yr.Iss.	16.00	24.50
86-113-009	Husband 800QX383-6	Keepsake	Yr.Iss.	8.00	15.00
86-113-010	Sister 675QX380-6	Keepsake	Yr.Iss.	6.75	15.00
86-113-011	Mother and Dad 750QX431-6	Keepsake	Yr.Iss.	7.50	17.50
86-113-012	Mother 700QX382-6	Keepsake	Yr.Iss.	7.00	15.00
86-113-013	Father 650QX431-3	Keepsake	Yr.Iss.	6.50	13.00
86-113-014	Daughter 575QX430-6	Keepsake	Yr.Iss.	5.75	20-27.00
86-113-015	Son 575QX430-3	Keepsake	Yr.Iss.	5.75	20-28.00
86-113-016	Niece 600QX426-6	Keepsake	Yr.Iss.	6.00	10.00
86-113-017	Nephew 675QX381-3	Keepsake	Yr.Iss.	6.25	12.50
86-113-018	Grandmother 475QX274-3	Keepsake	Yr.Iss.	4.75	16.50
86-113-019	Grandparents 750QX432-3	Keepsake	Yr.Iss.	7.50	17.00
86-113-020	Granddaughter 475QX273-6	Keepsake	Yr.Iss.	4.75	22.50
86-113-021	Grandson 475QX273-3	Keepsake	Yr.Iss.	4.75	20.00
86-113-022	Godchild 475QX271-6	Keepsake	Yr.Iss.	4.75	10-14.50
86-113-023	First Christmas Together 1600QX400-3	Keepsake	Yr.Iss.	16.00	27.50
86-113-024	First Christmas Together 1200QX409-6	Keepsake	Yr.Iss.	12.00	24.00
86-113-025	First Christmas Together 7000QX379-3	Keepsake	Yr.Iss.	7.00	15-20.00
86-113-026	First Christmas Together 475QX270-3	Keepsake	Yr.Iss.	4.75	20.00
86-113-027	Ten Years Together 750QX401-3	Keepsake	Yr.Iss.	7.50	24.50
86-113-028	Twenty-Five Years Together800QX410-3	Keepsake	Yr.Iss.	8.00	24.50
86-113-029	Fifty Years Together 1000QX400-6	Keepsake	Yr.Iss.	10.00	18.00
86-113-030	Loving Memories 900QX409-3	Keepsake	Yr.Iss.	9.00	13-34.50
86-113-031	Timeless Love 600QX379-6	Keepsake	Yr.Iss.	6.00	24.50
86-113-032	Sweetheart 1100QX408-6	Keepsake	Yr.Iss.	11.00	39.50
86-113-033	Season of the Heart 4750QX270-6	Keepsake	Yr.Iss.	4.75	12.50
86-113-034	Friendship Greeting 800QX427-3	Keepsake	Yr.Iss.	8.00	15.00
86-113-035	Joy of Friends 675QX382-3	Keepsake	Yr.Iss.	6.75	12.50
86-113-036	Friendship's Gift 600QX381-6	Keepsake	Yr.Iss.	6.00	12.00
86-113-037	From Our Home to Yours 600QX383-3	Keepsake	Yr.Iss.	6.00	12.00
86-113-038	Gratitude 600QX432-6	Keepsake	Yr.Iss.	6.00	9.50
86-113-039	Friends Are Fun 475QX272-3	Keepsake	Yr.Iss.	4.75	30.00
86-113-040	New Home 475QX274-6	Keepsake	Yr.Iss.	4.75	22.50
86-113-041	Teacher 475QX275-3	Keepsake	Yr.Iss.	4.75	12.00
86-113-042	Baby-Sitter 475QX275-6	Keepsake	Yr.Iss.	4.75	10.00
Hallmark Keepsake Ornaments		**1986 Property Ornaments**			
86-114-001	The Statue of Liberty 600QX384-3	Keepsake	Yr.Iss.	6.00	15-33.00
86-114-002	Snoopy and Woodstock 800QX434-6	Keepsake	Yr.Iss.	8.00	22-33.00
86-114-003	Heathcliff 750QX436-3	Keepsake	Yr.Iss.	7.50	22.50
86-114-004	Katybeth 700QX435-3	Keepsake	Yr.Iss.	7.00	22.50
86-114-005	Paddington Bear 600QX435-6	Keepsake	Yr.Iss.	6.00	39.50
86-114-006	Norman Rockwell 475QX276-3	Keepsake	Yr.Iss.	4.75	24.50
86-114-007	Peanuts 475QX276-6	Keepsake	Yr.Iss.	4.75	24.50
86-114-008	Shirt Tales Parade 475QX277-3	Keepsake	Yr.Iss.	4.75	14.50
Hallmark Keepsake Ornaments		**1986 Holiday Humor**			
86-115-001	Santa's Hot Tub 1200QX426-3	Keepsake	Yr.Iss.	12.00	39.75
86-115-002	Playful Possum 1100QX425-3	Keepsake	Yr.Iss.	11.00	35.00
86-115-003	Treetop Trio 975QX424-6	Keepsake	Yr.Iss.	11.00	29.50
86-115-004	Wynken, Blynken and Nod 975QX424-6	Keepsake	Yr.Iss.	9.75	35-42.50
86-115-005	Acorn Inn 850QX424-3	Keepsake	Yr.Iss.	8.50	23-30.00
86-115-006	Touchdown Santa 800QX423-3	Keepsake	Yr.Iss.	8.00	42.50
86-115-007	Snow Buddies 800QX423-6	Keepsake	Yr.Iss.	8.00	32.50
86-115-008	Open Me First 725QX422-6	Keepsake	Yr.Iss.	7.25	29.50
86-115-009	Rah Rah Rabbit 700QX421-6	Keepsake	Yr.Iss.	7.00	39.50
86-115-010	Tipping the Scales 675QX418-6	Keepsake	Yr.Iss.	6.75	20-27.50
86-115-011	Li'l Jingler 675QX419-3	Keepsake	Yr.Iss.	6.75	25-34.50
86-115-012	Ski Tripper 675QX420-6	Keepsake	Yr.Iss.	6.75	22.50
86-115-013	Popcorn Mouse 675QX421-3	Keepsake	Yr.Iss.	6.75	35-43.00
86-115-014	Puppy's Best Friend 650QX420-3	Keepsake	Yr.Iss.	6.50	27.50
86-115-015	Happy Christmas to Owl 600QX418-3	Keepsake	Yr.Iss.	6.00	24.50
86-115-016	Walnut Shell Rider 600QX419-6	Keepsake	Yr.Iss.	6.00	24.00
86-115-017	Heavenly Dreamer 575QX417-3	Keepsake	Yr.Iss.	5.75	35.00
86-115-018	Mouse in the Moon 550QX416-6	Keepsake	Yr.Iss.	5.50	20-28.00
86-115-019	Merry Koala 500QX415-3	Keepsake	Yr.Iss.	5.00	22.50
86-115-020	Chatty Penguin 575QX417-6	Keepsake	Yr.Iss.	5.75	19.00
86-115-021	Special Delivery 500QX415-6	Keepsake	Yr.Iss.	5.00	24.50
86-115-022	Jolly Hiker 500QX483-2	Keepsake	Yr.Iss.	5.00	20-30.00
86-115-023	Cookies for Santa 450QX414-6	Keepsake	Yr.Iss.	4.50	15-25.00
86-115-024	Merry Mouse 450QX403-2	Keepsake	Yr.Iss.	4.50	22.00
86-115-025	Skateboard Raccoon 650QX473-2	Keepsake	Yr.Iss.	6.50	39.50
86-115-026	Beary Smooth Ride 650QX480-5	Keepsake	Yr.Iss.	6.50	19.50
86-115-027	Snow-Pitching Snowman 450QX470-2	Keepsake	Yr.Iss.	4.50	22.50
86-115-028	Kitty Mischief 500QX474-5	Keepsake	Yr.Iss.	5.00	24.50
86-115-029	Soccer Beaver 650QX477-5	Keepsake	Yr.Iss.	6.50	24.50
86-115-030	Do Not Disturb Bear 775QX481-2	Keepsake	Yr.Iss.	7.75	24.50
Hallmark Keepsake Ornaments		**1986 Special Edition**			
86-116-001	Jolly St. Nick 2250QX429-6	Keepsake	Yr.Iss.	22.50	50-73.00

Company / Number	Name	Series / Artist	Edition Limit	Issue Price	Quote
Hallmark Keepsake Ornaments		**1986 Limited Edition**			
86-117-001	Magical Unicorn 2750QX429-3	Keepsake	Yr.Iss.	27.50	100-125.
Hallmark Keepsake Ornaments		**1986 Christmas Medley Collection**			
86-118-001	Joyful Carolers 975QX513-6	Keepsake	Yr.Iss.	9.75	30-40.00
86-118-002	Festive Treble Clef 875QX513-3	Keepsake	Yr.Iss.	8.75	27.50
86-118-003	Favorite Tin Drum 850QX514-3	Keepsake	Yr.Iss.	8.50	29.50
86-118-004	Christmas Guitar 700QX512-6	Keepsake	Yr.Iss.	7.00	24.50
86-118-005	Holiday Horn 800QX514-6	Keepsake	Yr.Iss.	8.00	29.50
Hallmark Keepsake Ornaments		**1986 Country Treasures Collection**			
86-119-001	Country Sleigh 1000QX511-3	Keepsake	Yr.Iss.	10.00	23-30.00
86-119-002	Remembering Christmas 865QX510-6	Keepsake	Yr.Iss.	8.75	25-30.00
86-119-003	Little Drummers 1250QX511-6	Keepsake	Yr.Iss.	12.50	34.50
86-119-004	Nutcracker Santa 1000QX512-3	Keepsake	Yr.Iss.	10.00	38-45.00
86-119-005	Welcome, Christmas 825QX510-3	Keepsake	Yr.Iss.	8.25	30-35.00
Hallmark Keepsake Ornaments		**1986 Traditional Ornaments**			
86-120-001	Holiday Jingle Bell 1600QX404-6	Keepsake	Yr.Iss.	16.00	45.00
86-120-002	Memories to Cherish 750QX427-6	Keepsake	Yr.Iss.	7.50	24.50
86-120-003	Bluebird 725QX428-3	Keepsake	Yr.Iss.	7.25	49.50
86-120-004	Glowing Christmas Tree 700QX428-6	Keepsake	Yr.Iss.	7.00	12.75
86-120-005	Heirloom Snowflake 675QX515-3	Keepsake	Yr.Iss.	6.75	21.50
86-120-006	Christmas Beauty 600QX322-3	Keepsake	Yr.Iss.	6.00	10.00
86-120-007	Star Brighteners 600QX322-6	Keepsake	Yr.Iss.	6.00	16.50
86-120-008	The Magi 475QX272-6	Keepsake	Yr.Iss.	4.75	12.75
86-120-009	Mary Emmerling: American Country Collection 795QX275-2	Keepsake	Yr.Iss.	7.95	24.50
Hallmark Keepsake Ornaments		**1986 Collectible Series**			
86-121-001	Mr. and Mrs. Claus-1st Edition1300QX402-6	Keepsake	Yr.Iss.	13.00	75-85.00
86-121-002	Reindeer Champs-1st Edition750QX422-3	Keepsake	Yr.Iss.	7.50	125.00
86-121-003	Betsey Clark: Home for Christmas-1st Edition 500QX277-6	Keepsake	Yr.Iss.	5.00	35.00
86-121-004	Windows of the World-2nd Ed.1000QX408-3	Keepsake	Yr.Iss.	10.00	49.50
86-121-005	Miniature Creche-2nd Edition900QX407-6	Keepsake	Yr.Iss.	9.00	59.50
86-121-006	Nostalgic Houses and Shops-3rd Edition 1375QX403-3	Keepsake	Yr.Iss.	13.75	125-175.
86-121-007	Wood Childhood Ornaments-3rd Edition 750QX407-3	Keepsake	Yr.Iss.	7.50	29.50
86-121-008	Twelve Days of Christmas-3rd Edition 650QX378-6	Keepsake	Yr.Iss.	6.50	43-50.00
86-121-009	Art Masterpiece-3rd & Final Ed. 675QX350-6	Keepsake	Yr.Iss.	6.75	13-24.50
86-121-010	Porcelain Bear-4th Edition 775QX405-6	Keepsake	Yr.Iss.	7.75	35.00
86-121-011	Tin Locomotive-5th Edition 1475QX403-6	Keepsake	Yr.Iss.	14.75	60-75.00
86-121-012	Holiday Wildlife-5th Edition 750QX321-6	Keepsake	Yr.Iss.	7.50	25-29.50
86-121-013	Clothespin Soldier-5th Edition 550QX406-3	Keepsake	Yr.Iss.	5.50	23-29.50
86-121-014	Rocking Horse-6th Edition 1075QX401-6	Keepsake	Yr.Iss.	10.75	35-53.00
86-121-015	Norman Rockwell-7th Edition 775QX321-3	Keepsake	Yr.Iss.	7.75	25.50
86-121-016	Frosty Friends-7th Edition 850QX405-3	Keepsake	Yr.Iss.	8.50	52.50
86-121-017	Here Comes Santa-8th Edition 1400QX404-3	Keepsake	Yr.Iss.	14.00	54.50
86-121-018	Thimble-9th Edition 575QX406-6	Keepsake	Yr.Iss.	5.75	24.50
Hallmark Keepsake Ornaments		**1986 Lighted Ornament Collection**			
86-122-001	Baby's First Christmas1950QLX710-3	Keepsake	Yr.Iss.	19.50	35-50.00
86-122-002	First Christmas Together2200QLX707-3	Keepsake	Yr.Iss.	14.00	39.50
86-122-003	Santa and Sparky-1st Edition2200QLX703-3	Keepsake	Yr.Iss.	22.00	75-125.
86-122-004	Christmas Classics-1st Edition1750QLX704-3	Keepsake	Yr.Iss.	17.50	60-85.00
86-122-005	Chris Mouse-2nd Edition1300QLX705-6	Keepsake	Yr.Iss.	13.00	60-70.00
86-122-006	Village Express 2450QLX707-2	Keepsake	Yr.Iss.	24.50	60-110.
86-122-007	Christmas Sleigh Ride 2450QLX701-2	Keepsake	Yr.Iss.	24.50	115.00
86-122-008	Santa's On His Way 1500QLX711-5	Keepsake	Yr.Iss.	15.00	69.50
86-122-009	General Store 1575QLX705-3	Keepsake	Yr.Iss.	15.75	53-60.00
86-122-010	Gentle Blessings 1500QLX708-3	Keepsake	Yr.Iss.	15.00	150-175.
86-122-011	Keep on Glowin' 1000QLX707-6	Keepsake	Yr.Iss.	10.00	49.50
86-122-012	Santa's Snack 1000QLX706-6	Keepsake	Yr.Iss.	10.00	57.50
86-122-013	Merry Christmas Bell 850QLX709-3	Keepsake	Yr.Iss.	8.50	25.00
86-122-014	Sharing Friendship 850QLX706-3	Keepsake	Yr.Iss.	8.50	22.00
86-122-015	Mr. and Mrs. Santa 1450QLX705-2	Keepsake	Yr.Iss.	14.50	95.00
86-122-016	Sugarplum Cottage 1100QLX701-1	Keepsake	Yr.Iss.	11.00	45.00
Hallmark Keepsake Ornaments		**1987 Commermoratives**			
87-123-001	Baby's First Christmas 975QX411-3	Keepsake	Yr.Iss.	9.75	25.00
87-123-002	Baby's First Christmas Photoholder 750QX4661-9	Keepsake	Yr.Iss.	7.50	29.50
87-123-003	Baby's First Christmas 600QX372-9	Keepsake	Yr.Iss.	6.00	15-17.00
87-123-004	Baby's First Christmas-Baby Girl 475QX274-7	Keepsake	Yr.Iss.	4.75	20.00
87-123-005	Baby's First Christmas-Baby Boy475QX274-9	Keepsake	Yr.Iss.	4.75	20-25.00
87-123-006	Grandchild's First Christmas900QX460-9	Keepsake	Yr.Iss.	9.00	24.50
87-123-007	Baby's Second Christmas 575QX460-7	Keepsake	Yr.Iss.	5.75	20-30.00
87-123-008	Child's Third Christmas 575QX459-9	Keepsake	Yr.Iss.	5.75	25.00
87-123-009	Baby Locket 1500QX461-7	Keepsake	Yr.Iss.	15.00	29.50
87-123-010	Mother and Dad 700QX462-7	Keepsake	Yr.Iss.	7.00	18.00
87-123-011	Mother 650QX373-7	Keepsake	Yr.Iss.	6.50	15.00
87-123-012	Dad 600QX462-9	Keepsake	Yr.Iss.	6.00	39.50
87-123-013	Husband 700QX373-9	Keepsake	Yr.Iss.	7.00	12.00
87-123-014	Sister 600QX474-7	Keepsake	Yr.Iss.	6.00	15.00
87-123-015	Daughter 575QX463-7	Keepsake	Yr.Iss.	5.75	19.50
87-123-016	Son 575QX463-9	Keepsake	Yr.Iss.	5.75	19.50
87-123-017	Niece 475QX275-9	Keepsake	Yr.Iss.	4.75	12.50
87-123-018	Grandmother 475QX277-9	Keepsake	Yr.Iss.	4.75	12.50
87-123-019	Grandparents 475QX277-7	Keepsake	Yr.Iss.	4.75	15-17.50
87-123-020	Grandson 475QX276-9	Keepsake	Yr.Iss.	4.75	15.00
87-123-021	Granddaughter 600QX374-7	Keepsake	Yr.Iss.	6.00	7-15.00
87-123-022	Godchild 475QX276-7	Keepsake	Yr.Iss.	4.75	15.00
87-123-023	First Christmas Together 1500QX446-9	Keepsake	Yr.Iss.	15.00	29.50
87-123-024	First Christmas Together 950QX446-7	Keepsake	Yr.Iss.	9.50	25-30.00
87-123-025	First Christmas Together 800QX445-9	Keepsake	Yr.Iss.	8.00	21-27.50
87-123-026	First Christmas Together 650QX371-9	Keepsake	Yr.Iss.	6.50	15.50
87-123-027	First Christmas Together 475QX272-9	Keepsake	Yr.Iss.	4.75	15-25.00
87-123-028	Ten Years Together 700QX444-7	Keepsake	Yr.Iss.	7.00	24.50
87-123-029	Twenty-Five Years Together750QX443-9	Keepsake	Yr.Iss.	7.50	24.50
87-123-030	Fifty Years Together 800QX443-7	Keepsake	Yr.Iss.	8.00	22.50
87-123-031	Word of Love 800QX447-7	Keepsake	Yr.Iss.	8.00	30.00
87-123-032	Heart in Blossom 600QX372-7	Keepsake	Yr.Iss.	6.00	24.50
87-123-033	Sweetheart 1100QX447-9	Keepsake	Yr.Iss.	11.00	25-29.50
87-123-034	Love is Everywhere 475QX278-7	Keepsake	Yr.Iss.	4.75	19.50
87-123-035	Holiday Greetings 600QX375-7	Keepsake	Yr.Iss.	6.00	12.75
87-123-036	Warmth of Friendship 600QX375-9	Keepsake	Yr.Iss.	6.00	12.00
87-123-037	Time for Friends 475QX280-7	Keepsake	Yr.Iss.	4.75	17.00
87-123-038	From Our Home to Yours 475QX279-9	Keepsake	Yr.Iss.	4.75	12.00
87-123-039	New Home 600QX376-7	Keepsake	Yr.Iss.	6.00	29.50
87-123-040	Babysitter 475QX279-7	Keepsake	Yr.Iss.	4.75	12.00
87-123-041	Teacher 575QX466-7	Keepsake	Yr.Iss.	5.75	19.50
Hallmark Keepsake Ornaments		**1987 Holiday Humor**			
87-124-001	Snoopy and Woodstock 725QX472-9	Keepsake	Yr.Iss.	7.25	30-45.00
87-124-002	Bright Christmas Dreams 725QX440-7	Keepsake	Yr.Iss.	7.25	40.00
87-124-003	Joy Ride 1150QX440-7	Keepsake	Yr.Iss.	11.50	35-50.00
87-124-004	Pretty Kitten 1100QX448-9	Keepsake	Yr.Iss.	11.00	34.50
87-124-005	Santa at the Bat 775QX457-9	Keepsake	Yr.Iss.	7.75	15-29.50
87-124-006	Jogging Through the Snow725QX457-7	Keepsake	Yr.Iss.	7.25	29.50
87-124-007	Jack Frosting 700QX449-9	Keepsake	Yr.Iss.	7.00	36.50
87-124-008	Raccoon Biker 700QX458-7	Keepsake	Yr.Iss.	7.00	25.00
87-124-009	Treetop Dreams 675QX459-7	Keepsake	Yr.Iss.	6.75	24.50
87-124-010	Night Before Christmas 650QX451-7	Keepsake	Yr.Iss.	6.50	20-32.50
87-124-011	"Owliday" Wish 650QX455-9	Keepsake	Yr.Iss.	6.50	25.00
87-124-012	Let It Snow 650QX458-9	Keepsake	Yr.Iss.	6.50	22.00
87-124-013	Hot Dogger 650QX471-9	Keepsake	Yr.Iss.	6.50	24.00
87-124-014	Spots 'n Stripes 550QX452-9	Keepsake	Yr.Iss.	5.50	20.00
87-124-015	Seasoned Greetings 625QX454-9	Keepsake	Yr.Iss.	6.25	10-25.00
87-124-016	Chocolate Chipmunk 600QX456-7	Keepsake	Yr.Iss.	6.00	35-40.00
87-124-017	Fudge Forever 500QX449-7	Keepsake	Yr.Iss.	5.00	30-35.00
87-124-018	Sleepy Santa 625QX450-7	Keepsake	Yr.Iss.	6.25	30-33.00
87-124-019	Reindoggy 575QX452-7	Keepsake	Yr.Iss.	5.75	25-30.00
87-124-020	Christmas Cuddle 575QX453-7	Keepsake	Yr.Iss.	5.75	30-35.00
87-124-021	Paddington Bear 550QX472-7	Keepsake	Yr.Iss.	5.50	30.00
87-124-022	Nature's Decorations 475QX273-9	Keepsake	Yr.Iss.	4.75	20-33.00
87-124-023	Dr. Seuss: The Grinch's Christmas 475QX278-3	Keepsake	Yr.Iss.	4.75	30.00
87-124-024	Jammie Pies 475QX283-9	Keepsake	Yr.Iss.	4.75	14.50
87-124-025	Peanuts 475QX281-9	Keepsake	Yr.Iss.	4.75	29.50
87-124-026	Happy Santa 475QX456-9	Keepsake	Yr.Iss.	4.75	29.50
87-124-027	Icy Treat 450QX450-9	Keepsake	Yr.Iss.	4.50	20-25.00
87-124-028	Mouse in the Moon 550QX416-6	Keepsake	Yr.Iss.	5.50	21.00
87-124-029	L'il Jingler 675QX419-3	Keepsake	Yr.Iss.	6.75	27.50
87-124-030	Walnut Shell Rider 600QX419-6	Keepsake	Yr.Iss.	6.00	18.00
87-124-031	Treetop Trio 1100QX425-6	Keepsake	Yr.Iss.	11.00	29.50
87-124-032	Jolly Hiker 500QX483-2	Keepsake	Yr.Iss.	5.00	17.50
87-124-033	Merry Koala 500QX415-3	Keepsake	Yr.Iss.	5.00	17.00
Hallmark Keepsake Ornaments		**1987 Old-Fashioned Christmas Collection**			
87-125-001	Nostalgic Rocker 650QX468-9	Keepsake	Yr.Iss.	6.50	29.50
87-125-002	Little Whittler 600QX469-9	Keepsake	Yr.Iss.	6.00	25-29.50
87-125-003	Country Wreath 575QX470-9	Keepsake	Yr.Iss.	5.75	29.50
87-125-004	In a Nutshell 550QX469-7	Keepsake	Yr.Iss.	5.50	32.50
87-125-005	Folk Art Santa 525QX474-9	Keepsake	Yr.Iss.	5.25	25-33.00
Hallmark Keepsake Ornaments		**1987 Christmas Pizzazz Collection**			
87-126-001	Doc Holiday 800QX467-7	Keepsake	Yr.Iss.	8.00	28-35.00
87-126-002	Christmas Fun Puzzle 800QX467-9	Keepsake	Yr.Iss.	8.00	24.50
87-126-003	Jolly Follies 850QX466-9	Keepsake	Yr.Iss.	8.50	29.50
87-126-004	St. Louie Nick 775QX453-9	Keepsake	Yr.Iss.	7.75	24.50
87-126-005	Holiday Hourglass 800QX470-7	Keepsake	Yr.Iss.	8.00	22.50
87-126-006	Mistletoad 700QX468-7	Keepsake	Yr.Iss.	7.00	29.50
87-126-007	Happy Holidata 650QX471-7	Keepsake	Yr.Iss.	6.50	29.50
Hallmark Keepsake Ornaments		**1987 Traditional Ornaments**			
87-127-001	Goldfinch 700QX464-9	Keepsake	Yr.Iss.	7.00	80.00
87-127-002	Heavenly Harmony 1500QX465-9	Keepsake	Yr.Iss.	15.00	34.50
87-127-003	Special Memories Photoholder675QX 464-7	Keepsake	Yr.Iss.	6.75	22.50
87-127-004	Joyous Angels 775QX465-7	Keepsake	Yr.Iss.	7.75	25-30.00
87-127-005	Promise of Peace 650QX374-9	Keepsake	Yr.Iss.	6.50	24.50
87-127-006	Christmas Keys 575QX473-9	Keepsake	Yr.Iss.	5.75	29.50
87-127-007	I Remember Santa 475QX278-9	Keepsake	Yr.Iss.	4.75	20-25.00
87-127-008	Norman Rockwell: Christmas Scenes 475QX282-7	Keepsake	Yr.Iss.	4.75	20-22.50
87-127-009	Currier & Ives: American Farm Scene 475QX282-9	Keepsake	Yr.Iss.	4.75	15-22.50
Hallmark Keepsake Ornaments		**1987 Limited Edition**			
87-128-001	Christmas Time Mime 2750QX442-9	Keepsake	Yr.Iss.	27.50	38-59.50
87-128-002	Christmas is Gentle 1750QX444-9	Keepsake	Yr.Iss.	17.50	35-84.50
Hallmark Keepsake Ornaments		**1987 Special Edition**			
87-129-001	Favorite Santa 2250QX445-7	Keepsake	Yr.Iss.	22.50	45.00
Hallmark Keepsake Ornaments		**1987 Artists' Favorites**			
87-130-001	Three Men in a Tub 800QX454-7	Keepsake	Yr.Iss.	8.00	20-29.50
87-130-002	Wee Chimney Sweep 625QX451-9	Keepsake	Yr.Iss.	6.25	25-28.00
87-130-003	December Showers 550QX448-7	Keepsake	Yr.Iss.	5.50	30-35.00
87-130-004	Beary Special 475QX455-7	Keepsake	Yr.Iss.	4.75	27.50
Hallmark Keepsake Ornaments		**1987 Collectible Series**			
87-131-001	Holiday Heirloom-1st Ed./limited ed. 2500QX485-7	Keepsake	Yr.Iss.	25.00	35-50.00
87-131-002	Collector's Plate-1st Edition 800QX481-7	Keepsake	Yr.Iss.	8.00	50-75.00
87-131-003	Mr. and Mrs. Claus-2nd Edition 2nd Edition 132QX483-7	Keepsake	Yr.Iss.	13.25	30-53.00
87-131-004	Reindeer Champs-2nd Edition 750QX480-9	Keepsake	Yr.Iss.	7.50	35-45.00
87-131-005	Betsey Clark: Home for Christmas-2nd edition 500QX272-7	Keepsake	Yr.Iss.	5.00	25.00
87-131-006	Windows of the World-3rd Edition 1000QX482-7	Keepsake	Yr.Iss.	10.00	18-24.50
87-131-007	Miniature Creche -3rd Edition 900QX481-9	Keepsake	Yr.Iss.	9.00	34.50
87-131-008	Nostalgic Houses and Shops-4th Edition 483QX483-9	Keepsake	Yr.Iss.	14.00	50-65.00
87-131-009	Twelve Days of Christmas-4th Edition 650QX370-9	Keepsake	Yr.Iss.	6.50	37.50
87-131-010	Wood Childhood Ornaments-4th Edition 750QX441-7	Keepsake	Yr.Iss.	7.50	24.50
87-131-011	Porcelain Bear-5th Edition 775QX442-7	Keepsake	Yr.Iss.	7.75	34.50
87-131-012	Tin Locomotive-6th Edition 1475QX484-9	Keepsake	Yr.Iss.	14.75	55-63.00
87-131-013	Holiday Wildlife -6th Edition 750QX371-7	Keepsake	Yr.Iss.	7.50	22.50
87-131-014	Clothespin Soldier-6th & Final Ed. 550QX480-7	Keepsake	Yr.Iss.	5.50	25-30.00
87-131-015	Frosty Friends -8th Edition 850QX440-9	Keepsake	Yr.Iss.	8.50	40-55.00
87-131-016	Rocking Horse-7th Edition1075QX482-9	Keepsake	Yr.Iss.	10.75	40-53.00
87-131-017	Norman Rockwell-8th Edition775QX370-7	Keepsake	Yr.Iss.	7.75	24.50
87-131-018	Here Comes Santa-9th Edition 1400QX484-7	Keepsake	Yr.Iss.	14.00	45-53.00
87-131-019	Thimble-10th Edition 575QX441-9	Keepsake	Yr.Iss.	5.75	29.50

Hallmark Keepsake Ornaments — 1987 Keepsake Magic Ornaments

Number	Name	Artist	Edition Limit	Issue Price	Quote
87-132-001	Baby's First Christmas 1350QLX704-9	Keepsake	Yr.Iss.	13.50	30-40.00
87-132-002	First Christmas Together 1150QLX708-7	Keepsake	Yr.Iss.	11.50	42.50
87-132-003	Santa and Sparky-2nd Edition1950QLX701-9	Keepsake	Yr.Iss.	19.50	75.00
87-132-004	Christmas Classics-2nd Ed.1600ZLX702-9	Keepsake	Yr.Iss.	16.00	75.00
87-132-005	Chris Mouse-3rd Edition1100QLX705-7	Keepsake	Yr.Iss.	11.00	45-53.00
87-132-006	Christmas Morning 2450QLX701-3	Keepsake	Yr.Iss.	24.50	49.50
87-132-007	Loving Holiday 2200QLX701-6	Keepsake	Yr.Iss.	22.00	52.50
87-132-008	Angelic Messengers 1875QLX711-3	Keepsake	Yr.Iss.	18.75	40-59.00
87-132-009	Good Cheer Blimp 1600QLX704-6	Keepsake	Yr.Iss.	16.00	49.00
87-132-010	Train Station 1275QLX703-9	Keepsake	Yr.Iss.	12.75	45-50.00
87-132-011	Keeping Cozy 1175QLX704-7	Keepsake	Yr.Iss.	11.75	34.50
87-132-012	Lacy Brass Snowflake 1150QLX709-7	Keepsake	Yr.Iss.	11.50	25.00
87-132-013	Meowy Christmas I 1000QLX708-9	Keepsake	Yr.Iss.	10.00	62.50
87-132-014	Memories are Forever Photoholder 850QLX706-7	Keepsake	Yr.Iss.	8.50	27.50
87-132-015	Season for Friendship 850QLX706-9	Keepsake	Yr.Iss.	8.50	19.50
87-132-016	Bright Noel 700QLX705-9	Keepsake	Yr.Iss.	7.00	29.50

Hallmark Keepsake Ornaments — 1987 Keepsake Collector's Club

Number	Name	Artist	Edition Limit	Issue Price	Quote
87-133-001	Wreath of Memories QXC580-9	Keepsake	Yr.Iss.	Unkn.	75.00
87-133-002	Carrousel Reindeer QXC580-7	Keepsake	Yr.Iss.	Unkn.	85.00

Hallmark Keepsake Ornaments — 1988 Commemoratives

Number	Name	Artist	Edition Limit	Issue Price	Quote
88-134-001	Baby's First Christmas 975QX470-1	Keepsake	Yr.Iss.	9.75	24.50
88-134-002	Baby's First Christmas 750QX470-4	Keepsake	Yr.Iss.	7.50	20.00
88-134-003	Baby's First Christmas 600QX372-1	Keepsake	Yr.Iss.	6.00	20.00
88-134-004	Baby's Second Christmas 600QX471-1	Keepsake	Yr.Iss.	6.00	12-29.50
88-134-005	Child's Third Christmas 600QX471-4	Keepsake	Yr.Iss.	6.00	27.50
88-134-006	Baby's First Christmas (Boy)475QX272-1	Keepsake	Yr.Iss.	4.75	20.00
88-134-007	Baby's First Christmas (Girl)475QX272-4	Keepsake	Yr.Iss.	4.75	20.50
88-134-008	Mother and Dad 800QX414-4	Keepsake	Yr.Iss.	8.00	20.00
88-134-009	Sister 800QX499-4	Keepsake	Yr.Iss.	8.00	17.50
88-134-010	Dad 700QX414-1	Keepsake	Yr.Iss.	7.00	24.50
88-134-011	Mother 650QX375-1	Keepsake	Yr.Iss.	6.50	12.50
88-134-012	Daughter 575QX415-1	Keepsake	Yr.Iss.	5.75	40-45.50
88-134-013	Son 575QX415-4	Keepsake	Yr.Iss.	5.75	36.50
88-134-014	Grandmother 475QX276-4	Keepsake	Yr.Iss.	4.75	12.50
88-134-015	Grandparents 475QX277-1	Keepsake	Yr.Iss.	4.75	15-17.50
88-134-016	Granddaughter 475QX277-4	Keepsake	Yr.Iss.	4.75	19.50
88-134-017	Grandson 475QX278-1	Keepsake	Yr.Iss.	4.75	19.50
88-134-018	Godchild 475QX278-4	Keepsake	Yr.Iss.	4.75	6-22.50
88-134-019	Sweetheart 975QX490-1	Keepsake	Yr.Iss.	9.75	20-27.00
88-134-020	First Christmas Together 900QX489-4	Keepsake	Yr.Iss.	9.00	20-23.00
88-134-021	First Christmas Together 675QX373-1	Keepsake	Yr.Iss.	6.75	20-24.50
88-134-022	Twenty-Five Years Together 675QX373-4	Keepsake	Yr.Iss.	6.75	13.50
88-134-023	Fifty Years Together 675QX374-1	Keepsake	Yr.Iss.	6.75	19.00
88-134-024	Love Fills the Heart 600QX374-4	Keepsake	Yr.Iss.	6.00	19.50
88-134-025	First Christmas Together 475QX274-1	Keepsake	Yr.Iss.	4.75	25.00
88-134-026	Five Years Together 475QX274-4	Keepsake	Yr.Iss.	4.75	19.50
88-134-027	Ten Years Together 475QX275-1	Keepsake	Yr.Iss.	4.75	18-25.00
88-134-028	Love Grows 475QX275-4	Keepsake	Yr.Iss.	4.75	19.00
88-134-029	Spirit of Christmas 475QX276-1	Keepsake	Yr.Iss.	4.75	15.50
88-134-030	Year to Remember 700QX416-4	Keepsake	Yr.Iss.	7.00	14.50
88-134-031	Teacher 625QX417-1	Keepsake	Yr.Iss.	6.25	16.50
88-134-032	Gratitude 600QX375-4	Keepsake	Yr.Iss.	6.00	12.00
88-134-033	New Home 600QX376-1	Keepsake	Yr.Iss.	6.00	19.50
88-134-034	Babysitter 475QX279-1	Keepsake	Yr.Iss.	4.75	10.50
88-134-035	From Our Home to Yours 475QX279-4	Keepsake	Yr.Iss.	4.75	12.00

Hallmark Keepsake Ornaments — 1988 Hallmark Handcrafted Ornaments

Number	Name	Artist	Edition Limit	Issue Price	Quote
88-135-001	Peanuts 475QX280-1	Keepsake	Yr.Iss.	4.75	24.50
88-135-002	Jingle Bell Clown 1500QX477-4	Keepsake	Yr.Iss.	15.00	34.50
88-135-003	Travels with Santa 1000QX477-1	Keepsake	Yr.Iss.	10.00	30-32.50
88-135-004	Goin' Cross-Country 850QX476-4	Keepsake	Yr.Iss.	8.50	24.00
88-135-005	Winter Fun 850QX478-1	Keepsake	Yr.Iss.	8.50	24.50
88-135-006	Go For The Gold 800QX417-4	Keepsake	Yr.Iss.	8.00	20-26.50
88-135-007	Party Line 875QX476-1	Keepsake	Yr.Iss.	8.75	26.50
88-135-008	Soft Landing 700QX475-1	Keepsake	Yr.Iss.	7.00	18.00
88-135-009	Feliz Navidad 675QX416-1	Keepsake	Yr.Iss.	6.75	25.00
88-135-010	Squeaky Clean 675QX475-4	Keepsake	Yr.Iss.	6.75	25.00
88-135-011	Christmas Memories 650QX372-4	Keepsake	Yr.Iss.	6.50	19.50
88-135-012	Purrfect Snuggle 625QX474-4	Keepsake	Yr.Iss.	6.25	24.50
88-135-013	Snoopy and Woodstock 600QX474-1	Keepsake	Yr.Iss.	6.00	25.00
88-135-014	The Town Crier 550QX473-4	Keepsake	Yr.Iss.	5.50	23-25.00
88-135-015	Christmas Scenes 475QX273-1	Keepsake	Yr.Iss.	4.75	17.50
88-135-016	Jolly Walrus 450QX473-1	Keepsake	Yr.Iss.	4.50	22.50
88-135-017	Slipper Spaniel 450QX472-4	Keepsake	Yr.Iss.	4.50	19.50
88-135-018	Arctic Tenor 400QX472-1	Keepsake	Yr.Iss.	4.00	17.00
88-135-019	Christmas Cuckoo 800QX480-1	Keepsake	Yr.Iss.	8.00	22.50
88-135-020	Peek-a-boo Kittens 750QX487-1	Keepsake	Yr.Iss.	7.50	17.00
88-135-021	Cool Juggler 650QX487-4	Keepsake	Yr.Iss.	6.50	17.00
88-135-022	Sweet Star 500QX418-4	Keepsake	Yr.Iss.	5.00	20-26.50
88-135-023	Hoe-Hoe-Hoe! 500QX422-1	Keepsake	Yr.Iss.	5.00	15.00
88-135-024	Nick the Kick 500QX422-4	Keepsake	Yr.Iss.	5.00	18.00
88-135-025	Holiday Hero 500QX423-1	Keepsake	Yr.Iss.	5.00	15.50
88-135-026	Polar Bowler 500QX478-1	Keepsake	Yr.Iss.	5.00	17.00
88-135-027	Par for Santa 500QX479-1	Keepsake	Yr.Iss.	5.00	17.00
88-135-028	Gone Fishing 500QX479-4	Keepsake	Yr.Iss.	5.00	14.00
88-135-029	Kiss the Claus 500QX486-1	Keepsake	Yr.Iss.	5.00	17.00
88-135-030	Love Santa 500QX486-4	Keepsake	Yr.Iss.	5.00	17.00
88-135-031	Teeny Taster 475QX418-1	Keepsake	Yr.Iss.	4.75	25.00
88-135-032	Filled with Fudge 475QX419-1	Keepsake	Yr.Iss.	4.75	24.50
88-135-033	Santa Flamingo 475QX483-4	Keepsake	Yr.Iss.	4.75	20-29.50
88-135-034	Kiss from Santa 450QX482-1	Keepsake	Yr.Iss.	4.50	19.50
88-135-035	Oreo 400QX481-4	Keepsake	Yr.Iss.	4.00	20-25.00
88-135-036	Noah's Ark 850QX490-4	Keepsake	Yr.Iss.	8.50	24.50-30.00
88-135-037	Sailing! Sailing! 850QX491-1	Keepsake	Yr.Iss.	8.50	20-25.00
88-135-038	Americana Drum 775Qx488-1	Keepsake	Yr.Iss.	7.75	25.00
88-135-039	Kringle Portrait 750QX496-1	Keepsake	Yr.Iss.	7.50	19-29.50
88-135-040	Uncle Sam Nutcracker 700QX488-4	Keepsake	Yr.Iss.	7.00	15-27.50
88-135-041	Kringle Tree 650QX495-4	Keepsake	Yr.Iss.	6.50	36.50
88-135-042	Glowing Wreath 600QX492-1	Keepsake	Yr.Iss.	6.00	14.50
88-135-043	Sparkling Tree 600QX483-1	Keepsake	Yr.Iss.	6.00	8-15.00
88-135-044	Shiny Sleigh 575QX492-4	Keepsake	Yr.Iss.	5.75	15.00
88-135-045	Kringle Moon 550QX495-1	Keepsake	Yr.Iss.	5.00	17-27.50
88-135-046	Loving Bear 475QX493-4	Keepsake	Yr.Iss.	4.75	19.50
88-135-047	Christmas Cardinal 475QX494-1	Keepsake	Yr.Iss.	4.75	15-19.50
88-135-048	Starry Angel 475494-4	Keepsake	Yr.Iss.	4.75	14.50
88-135-049	Old-Fashioned School House 400QX497-1	Keepsake	Yr.Iss.	4.00	16.50
88-135-050	Old-Fashioned Church 400QX498-1	Keepsake	Yr.Iss.	4.00	16.50

Hallmark Keepsake Ornaments — 1988 Special Edition

Number	Name	Artist	Edition Limit	Issue Price	Quote
88-136-001	The Wonderful Santacycle 2250QX411-4	Keepsake	Yr.Iss.	22.50	40-45.00

Hallmark Keepsake Ornaments — 1988 Artist Favorites

Number	Name	Artist	Edition Limit	Issue Price	Quote
88-137-001	Little Jack Horner 800QX408-1	Keepsake	Yr.Iss.	8.00	12-24.50
88-137-002	Merry-Mint Unicorn 850QX423-4	Keepsake	Yr.Iss.	8.50	19.50
88-137-003	Midnight Snack 600QX410-4	Keepsake	Yr.Iss.	6.00	20.00
88-137-004	Cymbals of Christmas 550QX411-1	Keepsake	Yr.Iss.	5.50	25.00
88-137-005	Baby Redbird 500QX410-1	Keepsake	Yr.Iss.	5.00	20.00
88-137-006	Very Strawbeary 475QX409-1	Keepsake	Yr.Iss.	4.75	17.00

Hallmark Keepsake Ornaments — 1988 Collectible Series

Number	Name	Artist	Edition Limit	Issue Price	Quote
88-138-001	Holiday Heirloom-Second Ed.2500QX406-4	Keepsake	Yr.Iss.	25.00	50.00
88-138-002	Tin Locomotive-Seventh Ed.1475QX400-4	Keepsake	Yr.Iss.	14.75	35-50.00
88-138-003	Nostalgic Houses and Shops-Fifth Edition -1450QX401-4	Keepsake	Yr.Iss.	14.50	35-50.00
88-138-004	Here Comes Santa-Tenth Ed.1400QX400-1	Keepsake	Yr.Iss.	14.00	33-43.00
88-138-005	Mr. and Mrs. Claus-Third Ed.1300QX401-1	Keepsake	Yr.Iss.	13.00	20-40.00
88-138-006	Rocking Horse-Eighth Ed.1075QX402-4	Keepsake	Yr.Iss.	10.75	30-40.00
88-138-007	Windows of the World-Fourth Edition 1000QX402-1	Keepsake	Yr.Iss.	10.00	15-35.00
88-138-008	Frosty Friends-Ninth Ed.875QX403-1	Keepsake	Yr.Iss.	8.75	40-52.50
88-138-009	Miniature Creche-Fourth Ed.850QX403-4	Keepsake	Yr.Iss.	8.50	12-24.50
88-138-010	Porcelain Bear-Sixth Ed.800QX404-4	Keepsake	Yr.Iss.	8.00	28-37.00
88-138-011	Collector's Plate-Second Ed.800QX406-1	Keepsake	Yr.Iss.	8.00	25-35.00
88-138-012	Norman Rockwell-Ninth Ed.775QX370-4	Keepsake	Yr.Iss.	7.75	22.50
88-138-013	Holiday Wildlife-Seventh Ed.775QX371-1	Keepsake	Yr.Iss.	7.75	22.50
88-138-014	Wood Childhood-Fifth Ed.750QX404-1	Keepsake	Yr.Iss.	7.50	24.50
88-138-015	Reindeer Champs-Third Ed.750QX405-1	Keepsake	Yr.Iss.	7.50	25-35.00
88-138-016	Five Golden Rings-Fifth Ed.650QX371-4	Keepsake	Yr.Iss.	6.50	22.50
88-138-017	Thimble-Eleventh Ed.575QX405-4	Keepsake	Yr.Iss.	5.75	12-25.00
88-138-018	Mary's Angels-First Ed.500QX407-4	Keepsake	Yr.Iss.	5.00	20-35.00
88-138-019	Betsey Clark: Home for Christmas-Third Edition 500QX271-4	Keepsake	Yr.Iss.	5.00	22.50

Hallmark Keepsake Ornaments — 1988 Keepsake Magic Ornaments

Number	Name	Artist	Edition Limit	Issue Price	Quote
88-139-001	Baby's First Christmas 2400QLX718-4	Keepsake	Yr.Iss.	24.00	50-55.00
88-139-002	First Christmas Together 1200QLX702-7	Keepsake	Yr.Iss.	12.00	32.50
88-139-003	Santa and Sparky-Third Ed.1950QLX719-1	Keepsake	Yr.Iss.	19.50	25-50.00
88-139-004	Christmas Classics-Third Ed.1500QLX716-1	Keepsake	Yr.Iss.	15.00	30-50.00
88-139-005	Chris Mouse-Fourth Ed.875QLX715-4	Keepsake	Yr.Iss.	8.75	35-42.50
88-139-006	Country Express 2450QLX721-1	Keepsake	Yr.Iss.	24.50	35-59.50
88-139-007	Kringle's Toy Shop 2450QLX701-7	Keepsake	Yr.Iss.	24.50	50-55.00
88-139-008	Parade of the Toys 2200QLX719-4	Keepsake	Yr.Iss.	22.00	30-49.50
88-139-009	Last-Minute Hug 1950QLX718-1	Keepsake	Yr.Iss.	19.50	35-58.00
88-139-010	Skater's Waltz 1950QLX720-1	Keepsake	Yr.Iss.	19.50	49.50
88-139-012	Kitty Capers 1300QLX716-4	Keepsake	Yr.Iss.	13.00	37.50
88-139-013	Christmas is Magic 1200QLX717-1	Keepsake	Yr.Iss.	12.00	49.50
88-139-014	Heavenly Glow 1175QLX711-4	Keepsake	Yr.Iss.	11.75	16-27.50
88-139-015	Radiant Tree 1175QLX712-1	Keepsake	Yr.Iss.	11.75	21.50
88-139-016	Festive Feeder 1150QLX720-4	Keepsake	Yr.Iss.	11.50	44.50
88-139-017	Circling the Globe 1050QLX712-4	Keepsake	Yr.Iss.	10.50	27.50
88-139-018	Bearly Reaching 950QLX715-1	Keepsake	Yr.Iss.	9.50	29.50
88-139-019	Moonlit Nap 875QLX713-4	Keepsake	Yr.Iss.	8.75	24.50
88-139-020	Tree of Friendship 850QLX710-4	Keepsake	Yr.Iss.	8.50	22.50
88-139-021	Song of Christmas 850QLX711-1	Keepsake	Yr.Iss.	8.50	17.50

Hallmark Keepsake Ornaments — 1988 Keepsake Miniature Ornaments

Number	Name	Artist	Edition Limit	Issue Price	Quote
88-140-001	Baby's First Christmas	Keepsake	Yr.Iss.	6.00	15.00
88-140-002	First Christmas Together	Keepsake	Yr.Iss.	4.00	20.00
88-140-003	Mother	Keepsake	Yr.Iss.	3.00	12.50
88-140-004	Friends Share Joy	Keepsake	Yr.Iss.	2.00	15.00
88-140-005	Love is Forever	Keepsake	Yr.Iss.	2.00	15.00
88-140-006	Holy Family	Keepsake	Yr.Iss.	8.50	14.50
88-140-007	Sweet Dreams	Keepsake	Yr.Iss.	7.00	22.50
88-140-008	Skater's Waltz	Keepsake	Yr.Iss.	7.00	10-22.00
88-140-009	Little Drummer Boy	Keepsake	Yr.Iss.	4.50	20-26.50
88-140-010	Three Little Kitties	Keepsake	Yr.Iss.	6.00	18.50
88-140-011	Snuggly Skater	Keepsake	Yr.Iss.	4.50	20-27.50
88-140-012	Happy Santa	Keepsake	Yr.Iss.	4.50	19.00
88-140-013	Sneaker Mouse	Keepsake	Yr.Iss.	4.00	19.50
88-140-014	Country Wreath	Keepsake	Yr.Iss.	4.00	12.00
88-140-015	Joyous Heart	Keepsake	Yr.Iss.	3.50	25-30.00
88-140-016	Candy Cane Elf	Keepsake	Yr.Iss.	3.00	19.50
88-140-017	Folk Art Lamb	Keepsake	Yr.Iss.	2.50	19.50
88-140-018	Folk Art Reindeer	Keepsake	Yr.Iss.	2.50	19.50
88-140-019	Gentle Angel	Keepsake	Yr.Iss.	2.00	19.50
88-140-020	Brass Star	Keepsake	Yr.Iss.	1.50	19.50
88-140-021	Brass Angel	Keepsake	Yr.Iss.	1.50	19.50
88-140-022	Brass Tree	Keepsake	Yr.Iss.	1.50	19.50
88-140-023	Jolly St. Nick	Keepsake	Yr.Iss.	8.00	25-36.50
88-140-024	Family Home-First Edition	Keepsake	Yr.Iss.	8.50	35-45.00
88-140-025	Kittens in Toyland-First Edition	Keepsake	Yr.Iss.	5.00	10-29.50
88-140-026	Rocking Horse-First Edition	Keepsake	Yr.Iss.	4.50	30-45.00
88-140-027	Penguin Pal-First Edition	Keepsake	Yr.Iss.	3.75	25-30.00

Hallmark Keepsake Ornaments — 1988 Hallmark Keepsake Ornament Collector's Club

Number	Name	Artist	Edition Limit	Issue Price	Quote
88-141-001	Our Clubhouse QXC580-4	Keepsake	Yr.Iss.	Unkn.	50.00
88-141-002	Sleighful of Dreams 800QC580-1	Keepsake	Yr.Iss.	8.00	35-75.00
88-141-003	Holiday Heirloom-Second Edition 2500QXC406-4	Keepsake	Yr.Iss.	25.00	37.50-65.00
88-141-004	Christmas is Sharing 1750QXC407-1	Keepsake	Yr.Iss.	17.50	25-40.00
88-141-005	Angelic Minstrel 2750QXC408-4	Keepsake	Yr.Iss.	27.50	37.50-40.00
88-141-006	Hold on Tight QXC570-4	Keepsake	Yr.Iss.	Unkn.	80.00

Hallmark Keepsake Ornaments — 1989 Commemoratives

Number	Name	Artist	Edition Limit	Issue Price	Quote
89-142-001	Baby's First Christmas Photoholder 625QX468-2	Keepsake	Yr.Iss.	6.25	25.00
89-142-002	Baby's First Christmas-Baby Girl475QX272-2	Keepsake	Yr.Iss.	4.75	17.50
89-142-003	Baby's First Christmas-Baby Boy475QX272-5	Keepsake	Yr.Iss.	4.75	15-18.00
89-142-004	Baby's First Christmas 675QX381-5	Keepsake	Yr.Iss.	6.75	10-20.00
89-142-005	Granddaughter's First Christmas 675QX382-2	Keepsake	Yr.Iss.	6.75	15.00
89-142-006	Grandson's First Christmas675QX382-5	Keepsake	Yr.Iss.	6.75	15.00
89-142-007	Baby's First Christmas 725QX449-2	Keepsake	Yr.Iss.	7.25	40.00
89-142-008	Baby's Second Christmas 675QX449-5	Keepsake	Yr.Iss.	6.75	25.00
89-142-009	Baby's Third Christmas 675QX469-5	Keepsake	Yr.Iss.	6.75	17.50
89-142-010	Baby's Fourth Christmas 675QX543-2	Keepsake	Yr.Iss.	6.75	16.50
89-142-011	Baby's Fifth Christmas 675QX543-5	Keepsake	Yr.Iss.	6.75	16.50
89-142-012	Mother 975QX440-5	Keepsake	Yr.Iss.	9.75	22.50
89-142-013	Mom and Dad 975QX442-5	Keepsake	Yr.Iss.	9.75	20.00
89-142-014	Dad 725QX442-5	Keepsake	Yr.Iss.	7.25	14.50
89-142-015	Sister 475QX279-2	Keepsake	Yr.Iss.	4.75	15.00

Number	Name	Artist	Edition Limit	Issue Price	Quote
89-142-016	Grandparents 475QX277-2	Keepsake	Yr.Iss.	4.75	15.00
89-142-017	Grandmother 475QX277-5	Keepsake	Yr.Iss.	4.75	19.50
89-142-018	Granddaughter 475QX278	Keepsake	Yr.Iss.	4.75	19.50
89-142-019	Grandson 475QX278-5	Keepsake	Yr.Iss.	4.75	13.50
89-142-020	Godchild 625QX311-2	Keepsake	Yr.Iss.	6.25	12.50
89-142-021	Sweetheart 975QX486-5	Keepsake	Yr.Iss.	9.75	22.00
89-142-022	First Christmas Together 675QX485-2	Keepsake	Yr.Iss.	9.75	19.50
89-142-023	First Christmas Together 675QX383-2	Keepsake	Yr.Iss.	6.75	20.00
89-142-024	First Christmas Together 475QX273-2	Keepsake	Yr.Iss.	4.75	19.50
89-142-025	Five Years Together 475QX273-5	Keepsake	Yr.Iss.	4.75	19.50
89-142-026	Ten Years Together 475QX274-2	Keepsake	Yr.Iss.	4.75	19.50
89-142-027	Twenty-five Years Together Photoholder 875QX485-5	Keepsake	Yr.Iss.	8.75	12-17.50
89-142-028	Forty Years Together Photoholder 875QX545-2	Keepsake	Yr.Iss.	8.75	9-17.50
89-142-029	Fifty Years Together Photoholder 875QX486-2	Keepsake	Yr.Iss.	8.75	17.50
89-142-030	Language of Love 625QX383-5	Keepsake	Yr.Iss.	6.25	16.50
89-142-031	World of Love 475QX274-5	Keepsake	Yr.Iss.	4.75	16.50
89-142-032	Friendship Time 975QX413-2	Keepsake	Yr.Iss.	9.75	32.50
89-142-033	Teacher 575QX412-5	Keepsake	Yr.Iss.	5.75	24.50
89-142-034	New Home 475QX275-5	Keepsake	Yr.Iss.	4.75	19.50
89-142-035	Festive Year 775QX384-2	Keepsake	Yr.Iss.	7.75	15.00
89-142-036	Gratitude 675QX385-2	Keepsake	Yr.Iss.	6.75	13.50
89-142-037	From Our Home to Yours 625QX384-5	Keepsake	Yr.Iss.	6.25	12.50
89-142-038	Daughter 625QX443-2	Keepsake	Yr.Iss.	6.25	15.00
89-142-039	Son 625QX444-5	Keepsake	Yr.Iss.	6.25	15.00

Hallmark Keepsake Ornaments — 1989 Holiday Traditions

Number	Name	Artist	Edition Limit	Issue Price	Quote
89-143-001	Joyful Trio 975QX437-2	Keepsake	Yr.Iss.	9.75	15.00
89-143-002	Old-World Gnome 775QX434-5	Keepsake	Yr.Iss.	7.75	19.50
89-143-003	Hoppy Holidays 775QX469-2	Keepsake	Yr.Iss.	7.75	17.50
89-143-004	The First Christmas 775QX547-5	Keepsake	Yr.Iss.	7.75	15.50
89-143-005	Gentle Fawn 775QX548-5	Keepsake	Yr.Iss.	7.75	19.50
89-143-006	Spencer Sparrow, Esq. 675QX431-2	Keepsake	Yr.Iss.	6.75	20.00
89-143-007	Snoopy and Woodstock 675QX433-2	Keepsake	Yr.Iss.	6.75	12-15.50
89-143-008	Sweet Memories Photoholder 675QX438-5	Keepsake	Yr.Iss.	6.75	19.00
89-143-009	Stocking Kitten 675QX456-5	Keepsake	Yr.Iss.	6.75	14.50
89-143-010	George Washington Bicentennial 625QX386-2	Keepsake	Yr.Iss.	6.25	14.50
89-143-011	Feliz Navidad 675QX439-2	Keepsake	Yr.Iss.	6.75	19.50
89-143-012	Cranberry Bunny 575QX426-2	Keepsake	Yr.Iss.	5.75	14.50
89-143-013	Deer Disguise 575QX426-5	Keepsake	Yr.Iss.	5.75	24.50
89-143-014	Paddington Bear 575QX429-2	Keepsake	Yr.Iss.	5.75	20.00
89-143-015	Snowplow Santa 575QX420-5	Keepsake	Yr.Iss.	5.75	15.50
89-143-016	Kristy Claus 575QX424-5	Keepsake	Yr.Iss.	5.75	11.50
89-143-017	Here's the Pitch 575QX545-5	Keepsake	Yr.Iss.	5.75	13.50
89-143-018	North Pole Jogger 575QX546-2	Keepsake	Yr.Iss.	5.75	13.50
89-143-019	Camera Claus 575QX546-5	Keepsake	Yr.Iss.	5.75	15.50
89-143-020	Sea Santa 575QX415-2	Keepsake	Yr.Iss.	5.75	13.50
89-143-021	Gym Dandy 575QX418-5	Keepsake	Yr.Iss.	5.75	15.50
89-143-022	On the Links 575QX419-2	Keepsake	Yr.Iss.	5.75	14.50
89-143-023	Special Delivery 525QX432-5	Keepsake	Yr.Iss.	5.25	14.50
89-143-024	Hang in There 525QX430-5	Keepsake	Yr.Iss.	5.25	25-34.50
89-143-025	Owliday Greetings 400QX436-5	Keepsake	Yr.Iss.	4.00	15.00
89-143-026	Norman Rockwell 475QX276-2	Keepsake	Yr.Iss.	4.75	19.50
89-143-027	A Charlie Brown Christmas 475QX276-5	Keepsake	Yr.Iss.	4.75	25-30.00
89-143-028	Party Line 875QX476-1	Keepsake	Yr.Iss.	8.75	26.50
89-143-029	Peek-a-Boo Kitties 750QX487-1	Keepsake	Yr.Iss.	7.50	17.00
89-143-030	Polar Bowler 575QX478-4	Keepsake	Yr.Iss.	5.75	17.00
89-143-031	Gone Fishing 575QX479-4	Keepsake	Yr.Iss.	5.75	17.00
89-143-032	Teeny Taster 475QX418-1	Keepsake	Yr.Iss.	4.75	17.00
89-143-033	A Kiss™ From Santa 450QX482-1	Keepsake	Yr.Iss.	4.50	19.50
89-143-034	Oreo® Chocolate Sandwich Cookies 400QX481-4	Keepsake	Yr.Iss.	4.00	15.00

Hallmark Keepsake Ornaments — 1989 New Attractions

Number	Name	Artist	Edition Limit	Issue Price	Quote
89-144-001	Sparkling Snowflake 775QX547-2	Keepsake	Yr.Iss.	7.75	24.50
89-144-002	Festive Angel 675QX463-5	Keepsake	Yr.Iss.	6.75	18.00
89-144-003	Graceful Swan 675QX464-2	Keepsake	Yr.Iss.	6.75	17.50
89-144-004	Nostalgic Lamb 675QX466-5	Keepsake	Yr.Iss.	6.75	13.50
89-144-005	Horse Weathervane 575QX463-2	Keepsake	Yr.Iss.	5.75	14.50
89-144-006	Rooster Weathervane 575QX467-5	Keepsake	Yr.Iss.	5.75	13.50
89-144-007	Country Cat 625QX467-2	Keepsake	Yr.Iss.	6.25	16.50
89-144-008	Nutshell Holiday 575QX465-2	Keepsake	Yr.Iss.	5.75	20-27.50
89-144-009	Nutshell Dreams 575QX465-5	Keepsake	Yr.Iss.	5.75	20-27.50
89-144-010	Nutshell Workshop 575QX487-2	Keepsake	Yr.Iss.	5.75	20-27.50
89-144-011	Claus Construction 775QX488-5	Keepsake	Yr.Iss.	7.75	15-19.50
89-144-012	Cactus Cowboy 675QX411-2	Keepsake	Yr.Iss.	6.75	30-40.00
89-144-013	Rodney Reindeer 675QX407-2	Keepsake	Yr.Iss.	6.75	13.50
89-144-014	Let's Play 725QX488-2	Keepsake	Yr.Iss.	7.25	40.00
89-144-015	TV Break 625QX409-2	Keepsake	Yr.Iss.	6.25	15.50
89-144-016	Balancing Elf 675QX489-5	Keepsake	Yr.Iss.	6.75	22.50
89-144-017	Wiggly Snowman 675QX489-2	Keepsake	Yr.Iss.	6.75	24.50
89-144-018	Cool Swing 625QX487-5	Keepsake	Yr.Iss.	6.25	35.00
89-144-019	Goin' South 425QX410-5	Keepsake	Yr.Iss.	4.25	24.50-30.00
89-144-020	Peppermint Clown 2475QX450-5	Keepsake	Yr.Iss.	24.75	28-35.00

Hallmark Keepsake Ornaments — 1989 Artists' Favorites

Number	Name	Artist	Edition Limit	Issue Price	Quote
89-145-001	Merry-Go-Round Unicorn 1075QX447-2	Keepsake	Yr.Iss.	10.75	19.50
89-145-002	Carousel Zebra 925QX451-5	Keepsake	Yr.Iss.	9.25	19.50
89-145-003	Mail Call 875QX452-2	Keepsake	Yr.Iss.	8.75	19.50
89-145-004	Baby Partridge 675QX452-5	Keepsake	Yr.Iss.	6.75	14.50
89-145-005	Playful Angel 675QX453-5	Keepsake	Yr.Iss.	6.75	15-20.00
89-145-006	Cherry Jubilee 500QX453-2	Keepsake	Yr.Iss.	5.00	15-22.00
89-145-007	Bear-i-Tone 475QX454-2	Keepsake	Yr.Iss.	4.75	14.50

Hallmark Keepsake Ornaments — 1989 Special Edition

Number	Name	Artist	Edition Limit	Issue Price	Quote
89-146-001	The Ornament Express 2200QX580-5	Keepsake	Yr.Iss.	22.00	35-50.00

Hallmark Keepsake Ornaments — 1989 Collectible Series

Number	Name	Artist	Edition Limit	Issue Price	Quote
89-147-001	Christmas Kitty-First Ed.1475QX544-5	Keepsake	Yr.Iss.	14.75	25-28.50
89-147-002	Winter Surprise-First Ed.1075QX427-2	Keepsake	Yr.Iss.	10.75	25.00
89-147-003	Hark! It's Herald-First Ed.675QX455-5	Keepsake	Yr.Iss.	6.75	20.00
89-147-004	Crayola Crayon-First Ed.875QX435-2	Keepsake	Yr.Iss.	8.75	20-35.00
89-147-005	The Gift Bringers-First Ed.500QX279-5	Keepsake	Yr.Iss.	5.00	20-25.00
89-147-006	Mary's Angels-Second Ed.575QX454-5	Keepsake	Yr.Iss.	5.75	15-25.00
89-147-007	Collector's Plate-Third Ed.825QX461-2	Keepsake	Yr.Iss.	8.25	15-35.00
89-147-008	Mr. and Mrs. Claus-Fourth Ed.1325QX457-5	Keepsake	Yr.Iss.	13.25	28-35.00
89-147-009	Reindeer Champs-Fourth Ed.775QX456-2	Keepsake	Yr.Iss.	7.75	15-20.00
89-147-010	Betsey Clark: Home for Christmas-Fourth Edition 500QX230-2	Keepsake	Yr.Iss.	5.00	19.50
89-147-011	Windows of the World-Fifth Ed.1075QX462-5	Keepsake	Yr.Iss.	10.75	15-25.00
89-147-012	Miniature Creche-Fifth Ed.925QX459-2	Keepsake	Yr.Iss.	9.25	19.50
89-147-013	Nostalgic Houses and Shops-Sixth Edition 1425QX458-2	Keepsake	Yr.Iss.	14.25	35-40.00
89-147-014	Wood Childhood Ornaments-Sixth Edition 775QX459-5	Keepsake	Yr.Iss.	7.75	12-20.00
89-147-015	Twelve Days of Christmas-Sixth Ed. 675QX381-2	Keepsake	Yr.Iss.	6.75	17.50
89-147-016	Porcelain Bear-Seventh Ed.875QX461-5	Keepsake	Yr.Iss.	8.75	16.50
89-147-017	Tin Locomotive-Eighth Ed.1475QX460-2	Keepsake	Yr.Iss.	14.75	34.50
89-147-018	Rocking Horse-Ninth Ed.1075QX462-2	Keepsake	Yr.Iss.	10.75	34.50
89-147-019	Frosty Friends-Tenth Ed.925QX457-2	Keepsake	Yr.Iss.	9.25	26.50
89-147-020	Here Comes Santa-Eleventh Ed.1475QX458-5	Keepsake	Yr.Iss.	14.75	33-39.50
89-147-021	Thimble-Twelfth Edition 575QX455-2	Keepsake	Yr.Iss.	5.75	12-18.00

Hallmark Keepsake Ornaments — 1989 Keepsake Magic Collection

Number	Name	Artist	Edition Limit	Issue Price	Quote
89-148-001	Baby's First Christmas 3000QLX727-2	Keepsake	Yr.Iss.	30.00	45-60.00
89-148-002	First Christmas Together1750QLX734-2	Keepsake	Yr.Iss.	17.50	45.00
89-148-003	Forest Frolics-First Edition2450QLX728-2	Keepsake	Yr.Iss.	24.50	50-60.00
89-148-004	Christmas Classics-Fourth Ed.1350QLX724-2	Keepsake	Yr.Iss.	13.50	29.50
89-148-005	Chris Mouse-Fifth Edition 950QLX722-5	Keepsake	Yr.Iss.	9.50	30-35.00
89-148-006	Joyous Carolers 3000QLX729-5	Keepsake	Yr.Iss.	30.00	60.00
89-148-007	Tiny Tinker 1950QLX717-4	Keepsake	Yr.Iss.	19.50	40.00
89-148-008	Rudolph the Red-Nosed Reindeer 1950QLX725-2	Keepsake	Yr.Iss.	19.50	43-50.00
89-148-009	Loving Spoonful 1950QLX726-2	Keepsake	Yr.Iss.	19.50	37.50
89-148-010	Holiday Bell 1750QLX722-2	Keepsake	Yr.Iss.	17.50	35.00
89-148-011	Busy Beaver 1750QLX724-5	Keepsake	Yr.Iss.	17.50	40-50.00
89-148-012	Backstage Bear 1350QLX721-5	Keepsake	Yr.Iss.	13.50	30.00
89-148-013	The Animals Speak 1350QLX723-2	Keepsake	Yr.Iss.	13.50	50.00
89-148-014	Angel Melody 950QLX720-2	Keepsake	Yr.Iss.	9.50	15-17.00
89-148-015	Unicorn Fantasy 950QLX723-5	Keepsake	Yr.Iss.	9.50	19.00
89-148-016	Moonlit Nap 875QLX713-4	Keepsake	Yr.Iss.	8.75	22.50
89-148-017	Kringle's Toy Shop 2450QLX701-7	Keepsake	Yr.Iss.	24.50	40-60.00
89-148-018	Metro Express 2800QLX727-5	Keepsake	Yr.Iss.	28.00	60-75.00
89-148-019	Spirit of St. Nick 2450QLX728-5	Keepsake	Yr.Iss.	24.50	65.00

Hallmark Keepsake Ornaments — 1989 Keepsake Miniature Ornaments

Number	Name	Artist	Edition Limit	Issue Price	Quote
89-149-001	Baby's First Christmas 600QXM573-2	Keepsake	Yr.Iss.	6.00	15.00
89-149-002	Mother 600QXM564-5	Keepsake	Yr.Iss.	6.00	14.50
89-149-003	First Christmas Together 850QXM564-2	Keepsake	Yr.Iss.	8.50	15.00
89-149-004	Lovebirds 600QXM563-5	Keepsake	Yr.Iss.	6.00	14.50
89-149-005	Special Friend 450QXM565-2	Keepsake	Yr.Iss.	4.50	14.00
89-149-006	Sharing a Ride 850QXM576-5	Keepsake	Yr.Iss.	8.50	15.00
89-149-007	Little Star Bringer 600QXM562-2	Keepsake	Yr.Iss.	6.00	25.00
89-149-008	Santa's Roadster 600QXM566-5	Keepsake	Yr.Iss.	6.00	25.00
89-149-009	Load of Cheer 600QXM574-5	Keepsake	Yr.Iss.	6.00	17.50
89-149-010	Slow Motion 600QXM575-2	Keepsake	Yr.Iss.	6.00	16.50
89-149-011	Merry Seal 600QXM575-5	Keepsake	Yr.Iss.	6.00	15.00
89-149-012	Starlit Mouse 450QXM565-5	Keepsake	Yr.Iss.	4.50	22.00
89-149-013	Little Soldier 450QXM567-5	Keepsake	Yr.Iss.	4.50	10.00
89-149-014	Acorn Squirrel 450QXM568-2	Keepsake	Yr.Iss.	4.50	9.00
89-149-015	Happy Bluebird 450QXM566-2	Keepsake	Yr.Iss.	4.50	9.50
89-149-016	Stocking Pal 450QXM567-2	Keepsake	Yr.Iss.	4.50	9.50
89-149-017	Scrimshaw Reindeer 450QXM568-5	Keepsake	Yr.Iss.	4.50	8-10.00
89-149-018	Folk Art Bunny 450QXM569-2	Keepsake	Yr.Iss.	4.50	9.00
89-149-019	Brass Snowflake 450QXM570-2	Keepsake	Yr.Iss.	4.50	8-14.00
89-149-020	Pinecone Basket 450QXM573-4	Keepsake	Yr.Iss.	4.50	8.00
89-149-021	Strollin' Snowman 450QXM574-2	Keepsake	Yr.Iss.	4.50	9.00
89-149-022	Brass Partridge 300QXM572-5	Keepsake	Yr.Iss.	3.00	5-12.00
89-149-023	Cozy Skater 450QXM573-5	Keepsake	Yr.Iss.	4.50	7-9.50
89-149-024	Old-World Santa 300QXM569-5	Keepsake	Yr.Iss.	3.00	6.00
89-149-025	Roly-Poly Ram 300QXM570-5	Keepsake	Yr.Iss.	3.00	10-15.00
89-149-026	Roly-Poly Pig 300QXM571-2	Keepsake	Yr.Iss.	3.00	8-10.00
89-149-027	Puppy Cart 300QXM571-5	Keepsake	Yr.Iss.	3.00	15.00
89-149-028	Kitty Cart 300QXM572-2	Keepsake	Yr.Iss.	3.00	15.00
89-149-029	Holiday Deer 300QXM577-2	Keepsake	Yr.Iss.	3.00	12.00
89-149-030	Bunny Hug 300QXM577-5	Keepsake	Yr.Iss.	3.00	11.00
89-149-031	Rejoice 300QXM578-2	Keepsake	Yr.Iss.	3.00	10.00
89-149-032	Holy Family 850QXM561-1	Keepsake	Yr.Iss.	8.50	14.50
89-149-033	Three Little Kitties 600QXM569-4	Keepsake	Yr.Iss.	6.00	18.50
89-149-034	Country Wreath 450QXM573-1	Keepsake	Yr.Iss.	4.50	12.00
89-149-035	Noel R.R.-First Edition 850QXM576-2	Keepsake	Yr.Iss.	8.50	35.00
89-149-036	The Kringles-First Edition600QXM562-2	Keepsake	Yr.Iss.	6.00	25.00
89-149-037	Old English Village-Second Ed.850QXM561-5	Keepsake	Yr.Iss.	8.50	20-25.00
89-149-038	Penguin Pal-Second Ed.450QXM560-2	Keepsake	Yr.Iss.	4.50	22.50
89-149-039	Rocking Horse-Second Ed. 450QXM560-5	Keepsake	Yr.Iss.	4.50	16-30.00
89-149-040	Kittens in Toyland-Second Ed.450QXM561-2	Keepsake	Yr.Iss.	4.50	20.00
89-149-041	Santa's Magic Ride 850QXM563-2	Keepsake	Yr.Iss.	8.50	19.50

Hallmark Keepsake Ornaments — 1989 Hallmark Keepsake Ornament Collector's Club

Number	Name	Artist	Edition Limit	Issue Price	Quote
89-150-001	Visit from Santa QXC580-2	Keepsake	Yr.Iss.	Unkn.	50.00
89-150-002	Collect a Dream 900QXC428-5	Keepsake	Yr.Iss.	9.00	65.00
89-150-003	Christmas is Peaceful 1850QXC451-2	Keepsake	Yr.Iss.	18.50	45.00
89-150-004	Noelle 1975QXC448-3	Keepsake	Yr.Iss.	19.75	40.00
89-150-005	Holiday Heirloom-Third Ed.2500QXC460-5	Keepsake	Yr.Iss.	25.00	35.00
89-150-006	Sitting Purrty QXC581-2	Keepsake	Yr.Iss.	Unkn.	45.00

Hallmark Keepsake Ornaments — 1990 Commemoratives

Number	Name	Artist	Edition Limit	Issue Price	Quote
90-151-001	Baby's First Christmas 975QX4853	Keepsake	Yr.Iss.	9.75	22.50
90-151-002	Baby's First Christmas 675QX3036	Keepsake	Yr.Iss.	6.75	23.00
90-151-003	Baby's First Christmas-Baby Boy475QX2063	Keepsake	Yr.Iss.	4.75	15.00
90-151-004	Baby's First Christmas-Baby Girl475QX2066	Keepsake	Yr.Iss.	4.75	15.00
90-151-005	Baby's First Christmas-Photo Holder 775QX4843	Keepsake	Yr.Iss.	7.75	15.50
90-151-006	Granddaughter's First Christmas675QX3106	Keepsake	Yr.Iss.	6.75	13.50
90-151-007	Mom-to-Be 575QX4916	Keepsake	Yr.Iss.	5.75	15-25.00
90-151-008	Grandson's First Christmas 675QX3063	Keepsake	Yr.Iss.	6.75	13.50
90-151-009	Dad-to-Be 575QX4913	Keepsake	Yr.Iss.	5.75	20.00
90-151-010	Baby's First Christmas 775QX4856	Keepsake	Yr.Iss.	7.75	25.00
90-151-011	Baby's Second Christmas675QX4683	Keepsake	Yr.Iss.	6.75	20.00
90-151-012	Child's Third Christmas 675QX4866	Keepsake	Yr.Iss.	6.75	14.50
90-151-013	Child's Fourth Christmas 675QX4873	Keepsake	Yr.Iss.	6.75	15.00
90-151-014	Child's Fifth Christmas 675QX4876	Keepsake	Yr.Iss.	6.75	15.00
90-151-015	Sweetheart 1175QX4893	Keepsake	Yr.Iss.	11.75	22.50
90-151-016	Our First Christmas Together975QX4883	Keepsake	Yr.Iss.	9.75	15.00
90-151-017	Our First Christmas Together -Photo Holder Ornament 775QX4886	Keepsake	Yr.Iss.	7.75	15.50
90-151-018	Our First Christmas Together 675QX3146	Keepsake	Yr.Iss.	6.75	15.50
90-151-019	Our First Christmas Together 475QX2136	Keepsake	Yr.Iss.	4.75	15.00
90-151-020	Time for Love 475QX2133	Keepsake	Yr.Iss.	4.75	15.50
90-151-021	Peaceful Kingdom 475QX2106	Keepsake	Yr.Iss.	4.75	12.00
90-151-022	Jesus Loves Me 675QX3156	Keepsake	Yr.Iss.	6.75	13.50

Number	Name	Artist	Edition Limit	Issue Price	Quote
90-151-023	Five Years Together 475QX2103	Keepsake	Yr.Iss.	4.75	15.00
90-151-024	Ten Years Together 475QX2153	Keepsake	Yr.Iss.	4.75	15.00
90-151-025	Twenty-Five Years Together 975QX4896	Keepsake	Yr.Iss.	9.75	19.50
90-151-026	Forty Years Together 975QX4903	Keepsake	Yr.Iss.	9.75	19.50
90-151-027	Fifty Years Together 975QX4906	Keepsake	Yr.Iss.	9.75	19.50
90-151-028	Mother 875QX4536	Keepsake	Yr.Iss.	8.75	15.50
90-151-029	Dad 675QX4533	Keepsake	Yr.Iss.	6.75	13.50
90-151-030	Mom and Dad 875QX4593	Keepsake	Yr.Iss.	8.75	20.00
90-151-031	Grandmother 475QX2236	Keepsake	Yr.Iss.	4.75	15.00
90-151-032	Grandparents 475QX2253	Keepsake	Yr.Iss.	4.75	15.00
90-151-033	Godchild 675QX3167	Keepsake	Yr.Iss.	6.75	13.50
90-151-034	Son 575QX4516	Keepsake	Yr.Iss.	5.75	12.50
90-151-035	Daughter 575QX4496	Keepsake	Yr.Iss.	5.75	12.50
90-151-036	Brother 575QX4493	Keepsake	Yr.Iss.	5.75	15.00
90-151-037	Sister 475QX2273	Keepsake	Yr.Iss.	4.75	17.50
90-151-038	Grandson 475QX2293	Keepsake	Yr.Iss.	4.75	17.50
90-151-039	Granddaughter 475QX2286	Keepsake	Yr.Iss.	4.75	15.00
90-151-040	Friendship Kitten 675QX4142	Keepsake	Yr.Iss.	6.75	19.75
90-151-041	New Home 675QX4343	Keepsake	Yr.Iss.	6.75	20.00
90-151-042	Across The Miles 675QX3173	Keepsake	Yr.Iss.	6.75	13.50-17.50
90-151-043	From Our Home to Yours 475QX2166	Keepsake	Yr.Iss.	4.75	9.50
90-151-044	Teacher 775QX4483	Keepsake	Yr.Iss.	7.75	15.50
90-151-045	Copy of Cheer 775QX4486	Keepsake	Yr.Iss.	7.75	15.50
90-151-046	Child Care Giver 675QX3166	Keepsake	Yr.Iss.	6.75	13.50

Hallmark Keepsake Ornaments — 1990 New Attractions

Number	Name	Artist	Edition Limit	Issue Price	Quote
90-152-001	S. Claus Taxi 1175QX4686	Keepsake	Yr.Iss.	11.75	17-29.50
90-152-002	Coyote Carols 875QX4993	Keepsake	Yr.Iss.	8.75	19.50
90-152-003	King Klaus 775QX4106	Keepsake	Yr.Iss.	7.75	9-18.00
90-152-004	Hot Dogger 775QX4976	Keepsake	Yr.Iss.	7.75	17.50
90-152-005	Poolside Walrus 775QX4986	Keepsake	Yr.Iss.	7.75	15.50
90-152-006	Three Little Piggies 775QX4996	Keepsake	Yr.Iss.	7.75	15.50
90-152-007	Billboard Bunny 775QX5196	Keepsake	Yr.Iss.	7.75	10-15.50
90-152-008	Mooy Christmas 675QX4933	Keepsake	Yr.Iss.	6.75	20.00
90-152-009	Pepperoni Mouse 675QX4973	Keepsake	Yr.Iss.	6.75	20.00
90-152-010	Santa Schnoz 675QX4983	Keepsake	Yr.Iss.	6.75	20.00
90-152-011	Cozy Goose 575QX4966	Keepsake	Yr.Iss.	5.75	12.25
90-152-012	Two Peas in a Pod 475QX4926	Keepsake	Yr.Iss.	4.75	20-30.00
90-152-013	Chiming In 975QX4366	Keepsake	Yr.Iss.	9.75	22.50
90-152-014	Christmas Croc 775QX4373	Keepsake	Yr.Iss.	7.75	15.50
90-152-015	Born to Dance 775QX5043	Keepsake	Yr.Iss.	7.75	12-20.00
90-152-016	Stocking Pals 1075QX5493	Keepsake	Yr.Iss.	10.75	21.50
90-152-017	Home for the Owlidays 675QX5183	Keepsake	Yr.Iss.	6.75	13.50
90-152-018	Baby Unicorn 975QX5486	Keepsake	Yr.Iss.	9.75	19.50
90-152-019	Spoon Rider 975QX5496	Keepsake	Yr.Iss.	9.75	19.50
90-152-020	Lovable Dears 875QX5476	Keepsake	Yr.Iss.	8.75	17.50
90-152-021	Meow Mart 775QX4446	Keepsake	Yr.Iss.	7.75	19.50
90-152-022	Perfect Catch 775QX4693	Keepsake	Yr.Iss.	7.75	15.50
90-152-023	Nutshell Chat 675QX5193	Keepsake	Yr.Iss.	6.75	15.50
90-152-024	Gingerbread Elf 575QX5033	Keepsake	Yr.Iss.	5.75	20.00
90-152-025	Stitches of Joy 775QX5186	Keepsake	Yr.Iss.	7.75	22.00
90-152-026	Little Drummer Boy 775QX5233	Keepsake	Yr.Iss.	7.75	19.50
90-152-027	Goose Cart 775QX5236	Keepsake	Yr.Iss.	7.75	15.50
90-152-028	Holiday Cardinals 775QX5243	Keepsake	Yr.Iss.	7.75	17.50
90-152-029	Christmas Partridge 775QX5246	Keepsake	Yr.Iss.	7.75	15.50
90-152-030	Joy is in the Air 775QX5503	Keepsake	Yr.Iss.	7.75	23.25
90-152-031	Happy Voices 675QX4645	Keepsake	Yr.Iss.	6.75	14.50
90-152-032	Jolly Dolphin 675QX4683	Keepsake	Yr.Iss.	6.75	14-28.00
90-152-033	Long Winter's Nap 675QX4703	Keepsake	Yr.Iss.	6.75	17.50
90-152-034	Hang in There 675QX4713	Keepsake	Yr.Iss.	6.75	15.00
90-152-035	Kitty's Best Pal 675QX4716	Keepsake	Yr.Iss.	6.75	15-19.50
90-152-036	SNOOPY and WOODSTOCK 675QX4723	Keepsake	Yr.Iss.	6.75	11-15.00
90-152-037	Beary Good Deal 675QX4733	Keepsake	Yr.Iss.	6.75	13.50
90-152-038	Country Angel 675QX5046	Keepsake	Yr.Iss.	6.75	19.50
90-152-039	Feliz Navidad 675QX5173	Keepsake	Yr.Iss.	6.75	14.50
90-152-040	Bearback Rider 975QX5483	Keepsake	Yr.Iss.	9.75	19.50
90-152-041	Polar Sport 775QX5156	Keepsake	Yr.Iss.	7.75	15.50
90-152-042	Polar Pair 575QX4626	Keepsake	Yr.Iss.	5.75	15.00
90-152-043	Polar Video 575QX4633	Keepsake	Yr.Iss.	5.75	11.50
90-152-044	Polar V.I.P. 575QX4663	Keepsake	Yr.Iss.	5.75	11.50
90-152-045	Polar TV 775QX5166	Keepsake	Yr.Iss.	7.75	15.00
90-152-046	Polar Jogger 575QX4666	Keepsake	Yr.Iss.	5.75	11.50
90-152-047	Garfield 475QX2303	Keepsake	Yr.Iss.	4.75	20.00
90-152-048	Peanuts 475QX2233	Keepsake	Yr.Iss.	4.75	19.50
90-152-049	Norman Rockwell Art 475QX2296	Keepsake	Yr.Iss.	4.75	15.00

Hallmark Keepsake Ornaments — 1990 Artists' Favorites

Number	Name	Artist	Edition Limit	Issue Price	Quote
90-153-001	Donder's Diner 1375QX4823	Keepsake	Yr.Iss.	13.75	18-27.50
90-153-002	Welcome, Santa 1175QX4773	Keepsake	Yr.Iss.	11.75	23.00
90-153-003	Happy Woodcutter 975QX4763	Keepsake	Yr.Iss.	9.75	19.50
90-153-004	Angel Kitty 875QX4746	Keepsake	Yr.Iss.	8.75	15-20.00
90-153-005	Gentle Dreamers 875QX4756	Keepsake	Yr.Iss.	8.75	19.50
90-153-006	Mouseboat 775QX4753	Keepsake	Yr.Iss.	7.75	15.50

Hallmark Keepsake Ornaments — 1990 Special Edition

Number	Name	Artist	Edition Limit	Issue Price	Quote
90-154-001	Dickens Caroler Bell-Mr. Ashbourne 2175QX5056	Keepsake	Yr.Iss.	21.75	28-45.00

Hallmark Keepsake Ornaments — 1990 Collectible Series

Number	Name	Artist	Edition Limit	Issue Price	Quote
90-155-001	Merry Olde Santa-First Edition 1475QX4736	Keepsake	Yr.Iss.	14.75	40-65.00
90-155-002	Greatest Story-First Edition 1275QX4656	Keepsake	Yr.Iss.	12.75	15-25.50
90-155-003	Heart of Christmas-First Edition 1375QX4726	Keepsake	Yr.Iss.	13.75	33-60.00
90-155-004	Fabulous Decade-First Edition 775QX4466	Keepsake	Yr.Iss.	7.75	10-20.00
90-155-005	Christmas Kitty-Second Edition 1475QX4506	Keepsake	Yr.Iss.	14.75	20-35.00
90-155-006	Winter Surprise-Second Edition 1075QX4443	Keepsake	Yr.Iss.	10.75	23-25.00
90-155-007	CRAYOLA Crayon-Bright Moving Colors-Second Edition 875QX4586	Keepsake	Yr.Iss.	8.75	25-35.00
90-155-008	Hark! It's Herald-Second Edition 675QX4463	Keepsake	Yr.Iss.	6.75	11-20.00
90-155-009	The Gift Bringers-St. Lucia-Second Edition 500QX2803	Keepsake	Yr.Iss.	5.00	8-20.00
90-155-010	Mary's Angels-Rosebud-Third Edition 575QX4423	Keepsake	Yr.Iss.	5.75	15-19.50
90-155-011	Cookies for Santa-Fourth Edition 875QX4436	Keepsake	Yr.Iss.	8.75	12-20.00
90-155-012	Popcorn Party-Fifth Edition 1375QX4393	Keepsake	Yr.Iss.	13.75	30-35.00
90-155-013	Reindeer Champs-Comet-Fifth Edition 775QX4433	Keepsake	Yr.Iss.	7.75	9-18.00
90-155-014	Betsey Clark: Home forChristmas-Fifth Edition 500QX2033	Keepsake	Yr.Iss.	5.00	10-17.50
90-155-015	Holiday Home-Seventh Edition 1475QX4696	Keepsake	Yr.Iss.	14.75	35-38.00
90-155-016	Seven Swans A-Swimming-Seventh Edition 675QX3033	Keepsake	Yr.Iss.	6.75	10-18.00
90-155-017	Rocking Horse-Tenth Edition 1075QX4646	Keepsake	Yr.Iss.	10.75	62.00
90-155-018	Frosty Friends-Eleventh Edition 975QX4396	Keepsake	Yr.Iss.	9.75	15-23.00
90-155-019	Festive Surrey-Twelfth Edition 1475QX4923	Keepsake	Yr.Iss.	14.75	30-34.50
90-155-020	Irish-Sixth Edition 1075QX4636	Keepsake	Yr.Iss.	10.75	15-22.00
90-155-021	Cinnamon Bear-Eighth Edition 875QX4426	Keepsake	Yr.Iss.	8.75	19.50

Hallmark Keepsake Ornaments — 1990 Keepsake Magic Ornaments

Number	Name	Artist	Edition Limit	Issue Price	Quote
90-156-001	Children's Express 2800QLX7243	Keepsake	Yr.Iss.	28.00	50-70.00
90-156-002	Hop 'N Pop Popper 2000QLX7353	Keepsake	Yr.Iss.	20.00	40-45.00
90-156-003	Baby's First Christmas 2800QLX7246	Keepsake	Yr.Iss.	28.00	53-58.00
90-156-004	Christmas Memories 2500QLX7276	Keepsake	Yr.Iss.	25.00	55.00
90-156-005	Forest Frolics 2500QLX7236	Keepsake	Yr.Iss.	25.00	50-60.00
90-156-006	Santa's Ho-Ho-Hoedown 2500QLX7256	Keepsake	Yr.Iss.	25.00	50-65.00
90-156-007	Mrs. Santa's Kitchen 2500QLX7263	Keepsake	Yr.Iss.	25.00	55-60.00
90-156-008	Song and Dance 2000QLX7253	Keepsake	Yr.Iss.	20.00	65.00
90-156-009	Elfin Whittler 2000QLX7265	Keepsake	Yr.Iss.	20.00	25-45.00
90-156-010	Deer Crossing 1800QLX7213	Keepsake	Yr.Iss.	18.00	45.00
90-156-011	Our First Christmas Together 1800QLX7255	Keepsake	Yr.Iss.	18.00	38-45.00
90-156-012	Holiday Flash 1800QLX7333	Keepsake	Yr.Iss.	18.00	36.00
90-156-013	Starship Christmas 1800QLX7336	Keepsake	Yr.Iss.	18.00	25-40.00
90-156-014	Partridges in a Pear 1400QLX7212	Keepsake	Yr.Iss.	14.00	28.00
90-156-015	Letter to Santa 1400QLX7226	Keepsake	Yr.Iss.	14.00	28.00
90-156-016	Starlight Angel 1400QLX7306	Keepsake	Yr.Iss.	14.00	19-28.00
90-156-017	The Littlest Angel 1400QLX7303	Keepsake	Yr.Iss.	14.00	28.00
90-156-018	Blessings of Love 1400QLX7363	Keepsake	Yr.Iss.	14.00	49.50
90-156-019	Chris Mouse Wreath 1000QLX7296	Keepsake	Yr.Iss.	10.00	15-25.00
90-156-020	Beary Short Nap 1000QLX7326	Keepsake	Yr.Iss.	10.00	22.50
90-156-021	Elf of the Year 1000QLX7356	Keepsake	Yr.Iss.	10.00	20.00

Hallmark Keepsake Ornaments — 1990 Keepsake Miniature Ornaments

Number	Name	Artist	Edition Limit	Issue Price	Quote
90-157-001	Thimble Bells 600QXM5543	Keepsake	Yr.Iss.	6.00	20.00
90-157-002	Nature's Angels 450QMX5733	Keepsake	Yr.Iss.	4.50	22.50
90-157-003	Cloisonne Poinsettia 1050QMX5533	Keepsake	Yr.Iss.	10.50	20-24.50
90-157-004	Coal Car 850QXM5756	Keepsake	Yr.Iss.	8.50	19.50
90-157-005	School 850QXM5763	Keepsake	Yr.Iss.	8.50	19.50
90-157-006	The Kringles 600QXM5753	Keepsake	Yr.Iss.	6.00	14.50
90-157-007	Kittens in Toyland 450QXM5736	Keepsake	Yr.Iss.	4.50	15.00
90-157-008	Rocking Horse 450QXM5743	Keepsake	Yr.Iss.	4.50	20.00
90-157-009	Penguin Pal 450QXM5746	Keepsake	Yr.Iss.	4.50	14.50
90-157-010	Santa's Streetcar 850QQXM5766	Keepsake	Yr.Iss.	8.50	17.00
90-157-011	Snow Angel 600QXM5773	Keepsake	Yr.Iss.	6.00	12.00
90-157-012	Baby's First Christmas 850QXM5703	Keepsake	Yr.Iss.	8.50	17.00
90-157-013	Grandchild's First Christmas 600QXM5723	Keepsake	Yr.Iss.	6.00	12.00
90-157-014	Special Friends 600QXM5726	Keepsake	Yr.Iss.	6.00	13.50
90-157-015	Mother 450QXM5716	Keepsake	Yr.Iss.	4.50	12.00
90-157-016	Warm Memories 450QXM5713	Keepsake	Yr.Iss.	4.50	10.00
90-157-017	First Christmas Together 600QXM5536	Keepsake	Yr.Iss.	6.00	13.50
90-157-018	Loving Hearts 300QXM5523	Keepsake	Yr.Iss.	3.00	6.00
90-157-019	Stringing Along 850QXM5606	Keepsake	Yr.Iss.	8.50	17.00
90-157-020	Santa's Journey 850QXM5826	Keepsake	Yr.Iss.	8.50	25.00
90-157-021	Wee Nutcracker 850QXM5843	Keepsake	Yr.Iss.	8.50	20.00
90-157-022	Bear Hug 600QXM5633	Keepsake	Yr.Iss.	6.00	12.00
90-157-023	Acorn Wreath 600QXM5686	Keepsake	Yr.Iss.	6.00	12.00
90-157-024	Puppy Love 600QXM5666	Keepsake	Yr.Iss.	6.00	12.00
90-157-025	Madonna and Child 600QXM5643	Keepsake	Yr.Iss.	6.00	12.00
90-157-026	Basket Buddy 600QXM5696	Keepsake	Yr.Iss.	6.00	12.00
90-157-027	Ruby Reindeer 600QXM5816	Keepsake	Yr.Iss.	6.00	12.00
90-157-028	Perfect Fit 450QXM5516	Keepsake	Yr.Iss.	4.50	12.50
90-157-029	Panda's Surprise 450QXM5616	Keepsake	Yr.Iss.	4.50	13.50
90-157-030	Stamp Collector 450QXM5623	Keepsake	Yr.Iss.	4.50	9.50
90-157-031	Christmas Dove 450QXM5636	Keepsake	Yr.Iss.	4.50	12.00
90-157-032	Type of Joy 450QXM5646	Keepsake	Yr.Iss.	4.50	12.00
90-157-033	Teacher 450QXM5653	Keepsake	Yr.Iss.	4.50	9.50
90-157-034	Air Santa 450QXM5656	Keepsake	Yr.Iss.	4.50	12.50
90-157-035	Sweet Slumber 450QXM5663	Keepsake	Yr.Iss.	4.50	12.00
90-157-036	Busy Carver 450QXM5673	Keepsake	Yr.Iss.	4.50	10.00
90-157-037	Lion and Lamb 450QXM5676	Keepsake	Yr.Iss.	4.50	10.00
90-157-038	Going Sledding 450QXM5683	Keepsake	Yr.Iss.	4.50	9.50
90-157-039	Country Heart 450QXM5693	Keepsake	Yr.Iss.	4.50	9.50
90-157-040	Nativity 450QXM5706	Keepsake	Yr.Iss.	4.50	12.50
90-157-041	Holiday Cardinal 300QXM5526	Keepsake	Yr.Iss.	3.00	12.00
90-157-042	Brass Bouquet 600QMX5776	Keepsake	Yr.Iss.	6.00	6.50
90-157-043	Brass Santa 300QXM5786	Keepsake	Yr.Iss.	3.00	7.00
90-157-044	Brass Horn 300QXM5793	Keepsake	Yr.Iss.	3.00	6.50
90-157-045	Brass Peace 300QXM5796	Keepsake	Yr.Iss.	3.00	7.00
90-157-046	Brass Year 300QXM5833	Keepsake	Yr.Iss.	3.00	7.00

Hallmark Keepsake Ornaments — 1990 Limited Edition

Number	Name	Artist	Edition Limit	Issue Price	Quote
90-158-001	Dove of Peace 2475QXC447-6	Keepsake	25,400	24.75	69.50
90-158-002	Christmas Limited1975 QXC476-6	Keepsake	38,700	19.75	75-85.00
90-158-003	Sugar Plum Fairy 2775QXC447-3	Keepsake	25,400	27.75	55.00

Hallmark Keepsake Ornaments — 1990 Keepsake Collector's Club

Number	Name	Artist	Edition Limit	Issue Price	Quote
90-159-001	Club Hollow QXC445-6	Keepsake	Yr.Iss.	Unkn.	40.00
90-159-002	Crown Prince QXC560-3	Keepsake	Yr.Iss.	Unkn.	40.00
90-159-003	Armful of Joy 800QXC445-3	Keepsake	Yr.Iss.	8.00	45.00

Hallmark Keepsake Ornaments — 1991 Commemoratives

Number	Name	Artist	Edition Limit	Issue Price	Quote
91-160-001	Baby's First Christmas 1775QX5107	Keepsake	Yr.Iss.	17.75	35-39.50
91-160-002	Baby's First Christmas-Baby Boy475QX2217	Keepsake	Yr.Iss.	4.75	17.50
91-160-003	Baby's First Christmas-Baby Girl475QX2227	Keepsake	Yr.Iss.	4.75	17.50
91-160-004	Baby's First Christmas-Photo Holder 775QX4869	Keepsake	Yr.Iss.	7.75	19.50
91-160-005	Mom-to-Be 575QX4877	Keepsake	Yr.Iss.	5.75	20.00
91-160-006	Dad-to-Be 575QX4879	Keepsake	Yr.Iss.	5.75	20.00
91-160-007	Grandson's First Christmas 675QX5117	Keepsake	Yr.Iss.	6.75	15.00
91-160-008	Granddaughter's First Christmas675QX5119	Keepsake	Yr.Iss.	6.75	15.00
91-160-009	A Child's Christmas 975QX4887	Keepsake	Yr.Iss.	9.75	15.50
91-160-010	Baby's First Christmas 775QX4889	Keepsake	Yr.Iss.	7.75	22.50
91-160-011	Baby's Second Christmas 675QX4897	Keepsake	Yr.Iss.	6.75	19.50
91-160-012	Child's Third Christmas 675QX4899	Keepsake	Yr.Iss.	6.75	22.50
91-160-013	Child's Fourth Christmas 675QX4907	Keepsake	Yr.Iss.	6.75	15.50
91-160-014	Child's Fifth Christmas 675QX4909	Keepsake	Yr.Iss.	6.75	15.50
91-160-015	Sweetheart 975QX4957	Keepsake	Yr.Iss.	9.75	17.50
91-160-016	Our First Christmas Together-Photo Holder 875QX4917	Keepsake	Yr.Iss.	8.75	20.00
91-160-017	Our First Christmas Together 875QX4919	Keepsake	Yr.Iss.	8.75	17.50
91-160-018	Our First Christmas Together 675QX3139	Keepsake	Yr.Iss.	6.75	20.00
91-160-019	Our First Christmas Together 475QX2229	Keepsake	Yr.Iss.	4.75	20.00
91-160-020	Under the Mistletoe 875QX4949	Keepsake	Yr.Iss.	8.75	20.00
91-160-021	Jesus Loves Me 775QX3147	Keepsake	Yr.Iss.	7.75	15.50
91-160-022	Five Years Together 775QX4927	Keepsake	Yr.Iss.	7.75	15.50
91-160-023	Ten Years Together 775QX4929	Keepsake	Yr.Iss.	7.75	15.50
91-160-024	Twenty -Five Years Together 875QX4937	Keepsake	Yr.Iss.	8.75	19.50
91-160-025	Forty Years Together 775QX4939	Keepsake	Yr.Iss.	7.75	19.50

Company / Number	Name	Series / Artist	Edition Limit	Issue Price	Quote
91-160-026	Fifty Years Together 875QX4947	Keepsake	Yr.Iss.	8.75	19.50
91-160-027	Mother 975QX5457	Keepsake	Yr.Iss.	9.75	22.50
91-160-028	Dad 775QX5127	Keepsake	Yr.Iss.	7.75	19.50
91-160-029	Mom and Dad 975QX5467	Keepsake	Yr.Iss.	9.75	20.00
91-160-030	Grandmother 475QX2307	Keepsake	Yr.Iss.	4.75	15.50
91-160-031	Grandparents 475QX2309	Keepsake	Yr.Iss.	4.75	15.50
91-160-032	Godchild 675QX5489	Keepsake	Yr.Iss.	6.75	15.50
91-160-033	Son 575QX5469	Keepsake	Yr.Iss.	5.75	15.50
91-160-034	Daughter 575QX5477	Keepsake	Yr.Iss.	5.75	15.50
91-160-035	Brother 675QX5479	Keepsake	Yr.Iss.	6.75	19.50
91-160-036	Sister 675QX5487	Keepsake	Yr.Iss.	6.75	19.50
91-160-037	Grandson 475QX2297	Keepsake	Yr.Iss.	4.75	15.50
91-160-038	Granddaughter 475QX2299	Keepsake	Yr.Iss.	4.75	15.50
91-160-039	Friends Are Fun 975QX5289	Keepsake	Yr.Iss.	9.75	19.50
91-160-040	Extra-Special Friends 475QX2279	Keepsake	Yr.Iss.	4.75	15.50
91-160-041	New Home 675QX5449	Keepsake	Yr.Iss.	6.75	15.50
91-160-042	Across the Miles 675QX3157	Keepsake	Yr.Iss.	6.75	15.50
91-160-043	From Our Home to Yours 475QX2287	Keepsake	Yr.Iss.	4.75	12.50
91-160-044	Terrific Teacher 675QX5309	Keepsake	Yr.Iss.	6.75	13.50
91-160-045	Teacher 475QX2289	Keepsake	Yr.Iss.	4.75	13.50
91-160-046	Gift of Joy 875QX5319	Keepsake	Yr.Iss.	8.75	19.50
91-160-047	The Big Cheese 675QX5327	Keepsake	Yr.Iss.	6.75	17.50
Hallmark Keepsake Ornaments		**1991 New Attractions**			
91-161-001	Winnie-the Pooh 975QX5569	Keepsake	Yr.Iss.	9.75	29.50
91-161-002	Piglet and Eeyore 975QX5577	Keepsake	Yr.Iss.	9.75	35.00
91-161-003	Christopher Robin 975QX5579	Keepsake	Yr.Iss.	9.75	27.50
91-161-004	Rabbit 975QX5607	Keepsake	Yr.Iss.	9.75	25.00
91-161-005	Tigger 975QX5609	Keepsake	Yr.Iss.	9.75	40-50.00
91-161-006	Kanga and Roo 975QX5617	Keepsake	Yr.Iss.	9.75	28-35.00
91-161-007	Look Out Below 875QX4959	Keepsake	Yr.Iss.	8.75	19.50
91-161-008	Yule Logger 875QX4967	Keepsake	Yr.Iss.	8.75	19.50
91-161-009	Glee Club Bears 87566QX4969	Keepsake	Yr.Iss.	8.75	19.50
91-161-010	Plum Delightful 875QX4977	Keepsake	Yr.Iss.	8.75	19.50
91-161-011	Snow Twins 875QX4979	Keepsake	Yr.Iss.	8.75	22.50
91-161-012	Loving Stitches 875QX4987	Keepsake	Yr.Iss.	8.75	25-29.50
91-161-013	Fanfare Bear 875QX5337	Keepsake	Yr.Iss.	8.75	19.50
91-161-014	Mrs. Cratchit 1375QX4999	Keepsake	Yr.Iss.	13.75	22.50
91-161-015	Merry Carolers 2975QX4799	Keepsake	Yr.Iss.	29.75	49.50
91-161-016	Ebenezer Scrooge 1375QX4989	Keepsake	Yr.Iss.	13.75	27.50
91-161-017	Bob Cratchit 1375QX4997	Keepsake	Yr.Iss.	13.75	22.50
91-161-018	Tiny Tim 1075QX5037	Keepsake	Yr.Iss.	10.75	22.50
91-161-019	Evergreen Inn 875QX5389	Keepsake	Yr.Iss.	8.75	15.50
91-161-020	Santa's Studio 875QX5397	Keepsake	Yr.Iss.	8.75	15.50
91-161-021	Holiday Cafe 875QX5399	Keepsake	Yr.Iss.	8.75	15.50
91-161-022	Jolly Wolly Santa 775QX5419	Keepsake	Yr.Iss.	7.75	27.50
91-161-023	Jolly Wolly Snowman 775QX5427	Keepsake	Yr.Iss.	7.75	22.50
91-161-024	Jolly Wolly Soldier 775QX5429`	Keepsake	Yr.Iss.	7.75	19.50
91-161-025	Partridge in a Pear Tree 975QX5297	Keepsake	Yr.Iss.	9.75	19.50
91-161-026	Christmas Welcome 975QX5299	Keepsake	Yr.Iss.	9.75	19.50
91-161-027	Night Before Christmas 975QX5307	Keepsake	Yr.Iss.	9.75	19.50
91-161-028	SNOOPY and WOODSTOCK 675QX5197	Keepsake	Yr.Iss.	6.75	19.50
91-161-029	PEANUTS 500QX2257	Keepsake	Yr.Iss.	5.00	17.50
91-161-030	GARFIELD 775QX5177	Keepsake	Yr.Iss.	7.75	19.50
91-161-031	Norman Rockwell Art 500QX2259	Keepsake	Yr.Iss.	5.00	15.50
91-161-032	Mary Engelbreit 475QX2237	Keepsake	Yr.Iss.	4.75	19.50
91-161-033	Up 'N'Down Journey 975QX5047	Keepsake	Yr.Iss.	9.75	22.50
91-161-034	Old-Fashioned Sled 875QX4317	Keepsake	Yr.Iss.	8.75	19.50
91-161-035	Folk Art Reindeer 875QX5359	Keepsake	Yr.Iss.	8.75	15.50
91-161-036	Sweet Talk 875QX5367	Keepsake	Yr.Iss.	8.75	17.50
91-161-037	Snowy Owl 775QX5269	Keepsake	Yr.Iss.	7.75	19.50
91-161-038	Dinoclaus 775QX5277	Keepsake	Yr.Iss.	7.75	19.50
91-161-039	Basket Bell Players 775QX5377	Keepsake	Yr.Iss.	7.75	22.50
91-161-040	Nutshell Nativity 675QX5176	Keepsake	Yr.Iss.	6.75	19.50
91-161-041	Cuddly Lamb 675QX5199	Keepsake	Yr.Iss.	6.75	19.50
91-161-042	Feliz Navidad 675QX5279	Keepsake	Yr.Iss.	6.75	13.50
91-161-043	Polar Classic 675QX5287	Keepsake	Yr.Iss.	6.75	17.50
91-161-044	All-Star 675QX5329	Keepsake	Yr.Iss.	6.75	17.50
91-161-045	Chilly Chap 675QX5339	Keepsake	Yr.Iss.	6.75	19.50
91-161-046	On a Roll 675QX5347	Keepsake	Yr.Iss.	6.75	19.50
91-161-047	Joyous Memories-Photoholder 675QX5369	Keepsake	Yr.Iss.	6.75	17.50
91-161-048	Ski Lift Bunny 675QX5447	Keepsake	Yr.Iss.	6.75	15.50
91-161-049	Nutty Squirrel 575QX4833	Keepsake	Yr.Iss.	5.75	15.50
91-161-050	Notes of Cheer 575QX5357	Keepsake	Yr.Iss.	5.75	15.50
Hallmark Keepsake Ornaments		**1991 Artists' Favorites**			
91-162-001	Polar Circus Wagon 1375QX4399	Keepsake	Yr.Iss.	13.75	29.50
91-162-002	Noah's Ark 1375QX4867	Keepsake	Yr.Iss.	13.75	35.00
91-162-003	Santa Sailor 975QX4389	Keepsake	Yr.Iss.	9.75	21.50
91-162-004	Hooked on Santa 775QX4109	Keepsake	Yr.Iss.	7.75	19.50
91-162-005	Fiddlin' Around 775QX4387	Keepsake	Yr.Iss.	7.75	17.50
91-162-006	Tramp and Laddie 775QX4397	Keepsake	Yr.Iss.	7.75	25.00
Hallmark Keepsake Ornaments		**1991 Special Edition**			
91-163-001	Dickens Caroler Bell-Mrs. Beaumont -2175QX5039	Keepsake	Yr.Iss.	21.75	35-45.00
Hallmark Keepsake Ornaments		**1991 Collectible Series**			
91-164-001	1957 Corvette-First Edition1275QX4319	Keepsake	Yr.Iss.	12.75	35-45.00
91-164-002	Peace on Earth-Italy First Ed. 1175QX5129	Keepsake	Yr.Iss.	11.75	24.50
91-164-003	Heavenly Angels-First Edition 775QX4367	Keepsake	Yr.Iss.	7.75	19.50
91-164-004	Puppy Love-First Edition 775QX5379	Keepsake	Yr.Iss.	7.75	25-32.50
91-164-005	Merry Olde Santa-Second Ed. 1475QX4359	Keepsake	Yr.Iss.	14.75	35-50.00
91-164-006	Heart of Christmas-Second Ed. 1375QX4357	Keepsake	Yr.Iss.	13.75	25-30.00
91-164-007	Greatest Story-Second Edition 1275QX4129	Keepsake	Yr.Iss.	12.75	25.50
91-164-008	Fabulous Decade-Second Ed. 775QX4119	Keepsake	Yr.Iss.	7.75	19.50
91-164-009	Winter Surprise-Third Ed. 1075QX4277	Keepsake	Yr.Iss.	10.75	21.50
91-164-010	CRAYOLA CRAYON-Bright Vibrant Carols-Third Edition 975QX4219	Keepsake	Yr.Iss.	9.75	24.50
91-164-011	Hark! It's Herald Third Edition 675QX4379	Keepsake	Yr.Iss.	6.75	15.50
91-164-012	The Gift Bringers-Christkind Third Edition 500QX2117	Keepsake	Yr.Iss.	5.00	15.00
91-164-013	Mary's Angels-Iris Fourth Ed. 675QX4279	Keepsake	Yr.Iss.	6.75	17.50
91-164-014	Let It Snow! Fifth Ediiton 875QX4369	Keepsake	Yr.Iss.	8.75	22.50
91-164-015	Checking His List Sixth Edition 1375QX4339	Keepsake	Yr.Iss.	13.75	29.50
91-164-016	Reindeer Champ-Cupid Sixth Ed. 775QX4347	Keepsake	Yr.Iss.	7.75	19.50
91-164-017	Fire Station-Eigth Edition 1475QX4139	Keepsake	Yr.Iss.	14.75	28-35.00
91-164-018	Eight Maids A-Milking-Eigth Ed. 675QX3089	Keepsake	Yr.Iss.	6.75	15.50
91-164-019	Rocking Horse-11th Ed. 1075QX4147	Keepsake	Yr.Iss.	10.75	20-25.50
91-164-020	Frosty Friends-Twelfth Edition 975QX4327	Keepsake	Yr.Iss.	9.75	27.50
91-164-021	Santa's Antique Car-13th Ed. 1475QX4349	Keepsake	Yr.Iss.	14.75	32.50
91-164-022	Christmas Kitty-Third Edition 1475QX4377	Keepsake	Yr.Iss.	14.75	29.50

Company / Number	Name	Series / Artist	Edition Limit	Issue Price	Quote
91-164-023	Betsey Clark: Home for Christmas Sixth Edition 500QX2109	Keepsake	Yr.Iss.	5.00	10.00
Hallmark Keepsake Ornaments		**1991 Keepsake Magic Ornaments**			
91-165-001	PEANUTS 1800QLX7229	Keepsake	Yr.Iss.	18.00	35-43.00
91-165-002	Santa Special 4000QLX7167	Keepsake	Yr.Iss.	40.00	59.50
91-165-003	Salvation Army Band 3000QLX7273	Keepsake	Yr.Iss.	30.00	59.50
91-165-004	Forest Frolics 2500QLX7219	Keepsake	Yr.Iss.	25.00	49.50
91-165-005	Chris Mouse Mail 1000QLX7207	Keepsake	Yr.Iss.	10.00	25-30.00
91-165-006	Arctic Dome 2500QLX7117	Keepsake	Yr.Iss.	25.00	49.50
91-165-007	Baby's First Christmas 3000QLX7247	Keepsake	Yr.Iss.	30.00	55.50
91-165-008	Bringing Home the Tree-2800QLX7249	Keepsake	Yr.Iss.	28.00	55.50
91-165-009	Ski Trip 2800QLX7266	Keepsake	Yr.Iss.	28.00	45-59.50
91-165-010	Kringles's Bumper Cars-2500QLX7119	Keepsake	Yr.Iss.	25.00	49.50
91-165-011	Our First Christmas Together-2500QXL7137	Keepsake	Yr.Iss.	25.00	49.50
91-165-012	Jingle Bears 2500QLX7323	Keepsake	Yr.Iss.	25.00	49.50
91-165-013	Toyland Tower 2000QLX7129	Keepsake	Yr.Iss.	20.00	39.50
91-165-014	Mole Family Home 2000QLX7149	Keepsake	Yr.Iss.	20.00	39.50
91-165-015	Starship Enterprise 2000QLX7199	Keepsake	Yr.Iss.	20.00	100-175.
91-165-016	It's A Wonderful Life 2000QLX7237	Keepsake	Yr.Iss.	20.00	35-42.50
91-165-017	Sparkling Angel 1800QLX7157	Keepsake	Yr.Iss.	18.00	29.50
91-165-018	Santa's Hot Line 1800QLX7159	Keepsake	Yr.Iss.	18.00	35.50
91-165-019	Father Christmas 1400QLX7147	Keepsake	Yr.Iss.	14.00	29.50
91-165-020	Holiday Glow 1400QLX7177	Keepsake	Yr.Iss.	14.00	29.50
91-165-021	Festive Brass Church 1400QLX7179	Keepsake	Yr.Iss.	14.00	24.50
91-165-022	Friendship Tree 1000QLX7169	Keepsake	Yr.Iss.	10.00	24.50
91-165-023	Elfin Engineer 1000QLX7209	Keepsake	Yr.Iss.	10.00	19.50
91-165-024	Angel of Light 3000QLT7239	Keepsake	Yr.Iss.	30.00	59.50
Hallmark Keepsake Ornaments		**1991 Keepsake Miniature Ornaments**			
91-166-001	Woodland Babies 600QXM5667	Keepsake	Yr.Iss.	6.00	19.50
91-166-002	Thimble Bells-Second Edition 600QXM5659	Keepsake	Yr.Iss.	6.00	17.50
91-166-003	Nature's Angels-Second Ed. 450QXM5657	Keepsake	Yr.Iss.	4.50	15.00
91-166-004	Passenger Car-Third Ed. 850QXM5649	Keepsake	Yr.Iss.	8.50	19.50
91-166-005	The Kringles-Third Edition 600QXM5647	Keepsake	Yr.Iss.	6.00	19.50
91-166-006	Inn-Fourth Edition 850QXM5627	Keepsake	Yr.Iss.	8.50	19.50
91-166-007	Rocking Horse-Fourth Ed. 450QXM5637	Keepsake	Yr.Iss.	4.50	19.50
91-166-008	Kittens in Toyland-Fourth Ed. 450QXM5639	Keepsake	Yr.Iss.	4.50	17.50
91-166-009	Penquin Pal-Fourth Ed. 450QXM5629	Keepsake	Yr.Iss.	4.50	17.50
91-166-010	Ring-A-Ding Elf 850QXM5669	Keepsake	Yr.Iss.	8.50	17.50
91-166-011	Lulu & Family 600QXM5677	Keepsake	Yr.Iss.	6.00	19.50
91-166-012	Silvery Santa 975QXM5679	Keepsake	Yr.Iss.	9.75	22.50
91-166-013	Heavenly Minstrel 975QXM5687	Keepsake	Yr.Iss.	9.75	22.50
91-166-014	Tiny Tea Party Set of 6 2900QXM5827	Keepsake	Yr.Iss.	29.00	100-125.
91-166-015	Special Friends 850QXM5797	Keepsake	Yr.Iss.	8.50	19.50
91-166-016	Mom 600QXM5699	Keepsake	Yr.Iss.	6.00	19.50
91-166-017	Baby's First Christmas 600QXM5799	Keepsake	Yr.Iss.	6.00	14.50
91-166-018	Our First Christmas Together 600QXM5819	Keepsake	Yr.Iss.	6.00	19.50
91-166-019	Key to Love 450QXM5689	Keepsake	Yr.Iss.	4.50	19.50
91-166-020	Grandchild's First Christmas 450QXM5697	Keepsake	Yr.Iss.	4.50	17.50
91-166-021	Treeland Trio 850QXM5899	Keepsake	Yr.Iss.	8.50	19.50
91-166-022	Wee Toymaker 850QXM5967	Keepsake	Yr.Iss.	8.50	17.50
91-166-023	Feliz Navidad 600QXM5887	Keepsake	Yr.Iss.	6.00	17.50
91-166-024	Top Hatter 600QXM5889	Keepsake	Yr.Iss.	6.00	19.50
91-166-025	Upbeat Bear 600QXM5907	Keepsake	Yr.Iss.	6.00	19.50
91-166-026	Friendly Fawn 600QXM5947	Keepsake	Yr.Iss.	6.00	19.50
91-166-027	Caring Shepherd 600QXM5949	Keepsake	Yr.Iss.	6.00	19.50
91-166-028	Cardinal Cameo 600QXM5957	Keepsake	Yr.Iss.	6.00	17.50
91-166-029	Courier Turtle 450QXM5857	Keepsake	Yr.Iss.	4.50	17.50
91-166-030	Fly By 450QXM5859	Keepsake	Yr.Iss.	4.50	19.50
91-166-031	Love Is Born 600QXM5959	Keepsake	Yr.Iss.	6.00	19.50
91-166-032	Cool 'n' Sweet 450QXM5867	Keepsake	Yr.Iss.	4.50	22.50
91-166-033	All Aboard 450QXM5869	Keepsake	Yr.Iss.	4.50	19.50
91-166-034	Bright Boxers 450QXM5877	Keepsake	Yr.Iss.	4.50	17.50
91-166-035	Li'l Popper 450QXM5897	Keepsake	Yr.Iss.	4.50	20.00
91-166-036	Kitty in a Mitty 450QXM5879	Keepsake	Yr.Iss.	4.50	14.50
91-166-037	Seaside Otter 450QXM5909	Keepsake	Yr.Iss.	4.50	14.50
91-166-038	Fancy Wreath 450QXM5917	Keepsake	Yr.Iss.	4.50	17.50
91-166-039	N. Pole Buddy 450QXM5927	Keepsake	Yr.Iss.	4.50	22.50
91-166-040	Vision of Santa 450QXM5937	Keepsake	Yr.Iss.	4.50	17.50
91-166-041	Busy Bear 450QXM5939	Keepsake	Yr.Iss.	4.50	12.50
91-166-042	Country Sleigh 450QXM5999	Keepsake	Yr.Iss.	4.50	14.50
91-166-043	Brass Church 300QXM5979	Keepsake	Yr.Iss.	3.00	9.50
91-166-044	Brass Soldier 300QXM5987	Keepsake	Yr.Iss.	3.00	9.50
91-166-045	Noel 300QXM5989	Keepsake	Yr.Iss.	3.00	12.50
91-166-046	Holiday Snowflake 300QXM5997	Keepsake	Yr.Iss.	3.00	12.50
Hallmark Keepsake Ornaments		**1991 Club Limited Editions**			
91-167-001	Secrets for Santa 2375QXC4797	Keepsake	28,700	23.75	50.00
91-167-002	Galloping Into Christmas 1975QXC4779	Keepsake	28,400	19.75	50.00
Hallmark Keepsake Ornaments		**1991 Keepsake Collector's Club**			
91-168-001	Hidden Treasure/Li'l Keeper 1500QXC4769	Keepsake	Yr.Iss.	15.00	35.00
91-168-002	Beary Artistic 1000QXC7259	Keepsake	Yr.Iss.	10.00	35.00
Hallmark Keepsake Ornaments		**1992 Collectible Series**			
92-169-001	Tobin Fraley Carousel-First Ed. 2800QX4891	Keepsake	Yr.Iss.	28.00	28.00
92-169-002	Owliver-First Ed. 775QX4544	Keepsake	Yr.Iss.	7.75	7.75
92-169-003	Betsey's Country Christmas-First Ed. 500QX2104	Keepsake	Yr.Iss.	5.00	5 .00
92-169-004	1966 Mustang-Second Ed. 1275QX4284	Keepsake	Yr.Iss.	12.75	12.75
92-169-005	Peace On Earth-Spain Second Ed. 1175QX5174	Keepsake	Yr.Iss.	11.75	11.75
92-169-006	Heavenly Angels-Second Ed.775QX4454	Keepsake	Yr.Iss.	7.75	7.75
92-169-007	Puppy Love-Second Ed. 775QX4484	Keepsake	Yr.Iss.	7.75	7.75
92-169-008	Merry Olde Santa-Third Ed. 1475QX4414	Keepsake	Yr.Iss.	14.75	14.75
92-169-009	Heart of Christmas-Third Ed. 1375QX4411	Keepsake	Yr.Iss.	13.75	13.75
92-169-010	Fabulous Decade-Third Ed. 775QX4244	Keepsake	Yr.Iss.	7.75	7.75
92-169-011	CRAYOLA CRAYON-Bright Colors Fourth Ed. 975QX4264	Keepsake	Yr.Iss.	9.75	9.75
92-169-012	The Gift Bringers-Kolyada Fourth Ed. 500QX2124	Keepsake	Yr.Iss.	5.00	5.00
92-169-013	Mary's Angels-Lily Fifth Ed. 675QX4274	Keepsake	Yr.Iss.	6.75	6.75
92-169-014	Gift Exchange Seventh Ed. 1475QX4294	Keepsake	Yr.Iss.	14.75	14.75
92-169-015	Reindeer Champs-Donder Seventh Ed. 875QX5284	Keepsake	Yr.Iss.	8.75	8.75
92-169-016	Five-and-Ten-Cent Store Ninth Ed. 1475QX4254	Keepsake	Yr.Iss.	14.75	14.75
92-169-017	Nine Ladies Dancing Ninth Ed. 675QX3031	Keepsake	Yr.Iss.	6.75	6.75
92-169-018	Rocking Horse Twelfth Ed. 1075QX4261	Keepsake	Yr.Iss.	10.75	10.75
92-169-019	Frosty Friends 13th Ed. 975QX4291	Keepsake	Yr.Iss.	9.75	9.75
92-169-020	Kringle Tours 14th Ed. 1475QX4341	Keepsake	Yr.Iss.	14.75	14.75
92-169-021	Greatest Story Third Ed. 1275QX4251	Keepsake	Yr.Iss.	12.75	12.75

Company / Number	Name	Series / Artist	Edition Limit	Issue Price	Quote
92-169-022	Winter Surprise Fourth Ed. 1175QX4271	Keepsake	Yr.Iss.	11.75	11.75
92-169-023	Hark! It's Herald Fourth Ed. 775QX4464	Keepsake	Yr.Iss.	7.75	7.75
92-169-024	Sweet Holiday Harmony Sixth Ed. 875QX4461	Keepsake	Yr.Iss.	8.75	8.75
Hallmark Keepsake Ornaments		**1992 Artists' Favorites**			
92-170-001	Mother Goose 1375QX4984	Keepsake	Yr.Iss.	13.75	13.75
92-170-002	Elfin Marionette1175QX5931	Keepsake	Yr.Iss.	11.75	11.75
92-170-003	Polar Post 875QX4914	Keepsake	Yr.Iss.	8.75	8.75
92-170-004	Turtle Dreams 875QX4991	Keepsake	Yr.Iss.	8.75	8.75
92-170-005	Uncle Art's Ice Cream 875QX5001	Keepsake	Yr.Iss.	8.75	8.75
92-170-006	Stocked With Joy 775QX5934	Keepsake	Yr.Iss.	7.75	7.75
Hallmark Keepsake Ornaments		**1992 Special Edition**			
92-171-001	Dickens Caroler Bell-Lord Chadwick Third Ed. 2175QX4554	Keepsake	Yr.Iss.	21.75	21.75
Hallmark Keepsake Ornaments		**1992 Commemoratives**			
92-172-001	Baby's First Christmas1875QX4581	Keepsake	Yr.Iss.	18.75	18.75
92-172-002	Baby's First Christmas 775QX4641	Keepsake	Yr.Iss.	7.75	7.75
92-172-003	Baby's First Christmas-Baby Girl 475QX2204	Keepsake	Yr.Iss.	4.75	4.75
92-172-004	Baby's First Christmas-Baby Boy 475QX2191	Keepsake	Yr.Iss.	4.75	4.75
92-172-005	For My Grandma 775QX5184	Keepsake	Yr.Iss.	7.75	7.75
92-172-006	A Child's Christmas 975QX4574	Keepsake	Yr.Iss.	9.75	9.75
92-172-007	Grandson's First Christmas 675QX4621	Keepsake	Yr.Iss.	6.75	6.75
92-172-008	Grandaughter's First Christmas 675QX4634	Keepsake	Yr.Iss.	6.75	6.75
92-172-009	Mom-to-Be 675QX4614	Keepsake	Yr.Iss.	6.75	6.75
92-172-010	Dad-to-Be 675QX4611	Keepsake	Yr.Iss.	6.75	6.75
92-172-011	Baby's First Christmas 775QX4644	Keepsake	Yr.Iss.	7.75	7.75
92-172-012	Baby's Second Christmas 675QX4651	Keepsake	Yr.Iss.	6.75	6.75
92-172-013	Child's Third Christmas 675QX4654	Keepsake	Yr.Iss.	6.75	6.75
92-172-014	Child's Fourth Christmas 675QX4661	Keepsake	Yr.Iss.	6.75	6.75
92-172-015	Child's Fifth Christmas 675QX4664	Keepsake	Yr.Iss.	6.75	6.75
92-172-016	For The One I Love 975QX4884	Keepsake	Yr.Iss.	9.75	9.75
92-172-017	Our First Christmas Together 975QX5061	Keepsake	Yr.Iss.	9.75	9.75
92-172-018	Out First Christmas Together 875QX4694	Keepsake	Yr.Iss.	8.75	8.75
92-172-019	Our First Christmas Together 675QX3011	Keepsake	Yr.Iss.	6.75	6.75
92-172-020	Love To Skate 875QX4841	Keepsake	Yr.Iss.	8.75	8.75
92-172-021	Anniversary Year 975QX4851	Keepsake	Yr.Iss.	9.75	9.75
92-172-022	Dad 775QX4674	Keepsake	Yr.Iss.	7.75	7.75
92-172-023	Mom 775QX5164	Keepsake	Yr.Iss.	7.75	7.75
92-172-024	Brother 675QX4684	Keepsake	Yr.Iss.	6.75	6.75
92-172-025	Sister 675QX4681	Keepsake	Yr.Iss.	6.75	6.75
92-172-026	Son 675QX5024	Keepsake	Yr.Iss.	6.75	6.75
92-172-027	Daughter 675QX5031	Keepsake	Yr.Iss.	6.75	6.75
92-172-028	Mom and Dad 975QX4671	Keepsake	Yr.Iss.	9.75	9.75
92-172-029	Grandparents 475QX2004	Keepsake	Yr.Iss.	4.75	4.75
92-172-030	Grandmother 475QX2011	Keepsake	Yr.Iss.	4.75	4.75
92-172-031	Godchild 675QX5941	Keepsake	Yr.Iss.	6.75	6.75
92-172-032	Grandaughter 675QX5604	Keepsake	Yr.Iss.	6.75	6.75
92-172-033	Grandson 675QX5611	Keepsake	Yr.Iss.	6.75	6.75
92-172-034	Friendship Line 975QX5034	Keepsake	Yr.Iss.	9.75	9.75
92-172-035	Friendly Greetings 775QX5041	Keepsake	Yr.Iss.	7.75	7.75
92-172-036	New Home 875QX5191	Keepsake	Yr.Iss.	8.75	8.75
92-172-037	Across the Miles 675QX3044	Keepsake	Yr.Iss.	6.75	6.75
92-172-038	From Our Home To yours 475QX2131	Keepsake	Yr.Iss.	4.75	4.75
92-172-039	Secret Pal 775QX5424	Keepsake	Yr.Iss.	7.75	7.75
92-172-040	Teacher 475QX2264	Keepsake	Yr.Iss.	4.75	4.75
92-172-041	World-Class Teacher 775QX5054	Keepsake	Yr.Iss.	7.75	7.75
92-172-042	V. P. of Important Stuff 675QX5051	Keepsake	Yr.Iss.	6.75	6.75
92-172-043	Holiday Memo 775QX5044	Keepsake	Yr.Iss.	7.75	7.75
92-172-044	Special Dog 775QX5421	Keepsake	Yr.Iss.	7.75	7.75
92-172-045	Special Cat 775QX5414	Keepsake	Yr.Iss.	7.75	7.75
Hallmark Keepsake Ornaments		**1992 New Attractions**			
92-173-001	Eric the Baker 875QX5244	Keepsake	Yr.Iss.	8.75	8.75
92-173-002	Otto the Carpenter 875QX5254	Keepsake	Yr.Iss.	8.75	8.75
92-173-003	Max the Tailor 875QX5251	Keepsake	Yr.Iss.	8.75	8.75
92-173-004	Franz the Artist 875QX5261	Keepsake	Yr.Iss.	8.75	8.75
92-173-005	Freida the Animals' Friend 875QX5264	Keepsake	Yr.Iss.	8.75	8.75
92-173-006	Ludwig the Musician 875QX5281	Keepsake	Yr.Iss.	8.75	8.75
92-173-007	Silver Star 2800QX5324	Keepsake	Yr.Iss.	28.00	28.00
92-173-008	Locomotive 975QX5311	Keepsake	Yr.Iss.	9.75	9.75
92-173-009	Coal Car 975QX5401	Keepsake	Yr.Iss.	9.75	9.75
92-173-010	Stock Car 975QX5314	Keepsake	Yr.Iss.	9.75	9.75
92-173-011	Caboose 975QX5321	Keepsake	Yr.Iss.	9.75	9.75
92-173-012	Gone Wishin' 875QX5171	Keepsake	Yr.Iss.	8.75	8.75
92-173-013	Skiing 'Round 875QX5214	Keepsake	Yr.Iss.	8.75	8.75
92-173-014	North Pole Fire Fighter 975QX5104	Keepsake	Yr.Iss.	9.75	9.75
92-173-015	Rapid Delivery 875QX5094	Keepsake	Yr.Iss.	8.75	8.75
92-173-016	Green Thumb Santa 775QX5101	Keepsake	Yr.Iss.	7.75	7.75
92-173-017	Golf's a Ball 675QX5984	Keepsake	Yr.Iss.	6.75	6.75
92-173-018	A Santa-Full! 975QX5991	Keepsake	Yr.Iss.	9.75	9.75
92-173-019	Tasty Christmas 975QX5994	Keepsake	Yr.Iss.	9.75	9.75
92-173-020	Santa's Roundup 875QX5084	Keepsake	Yr.Iss.	8.75	8.75
92-173-021	Deck the Hogs 875QX5204	Keepsake	Yr.Iss.	8.75	8.75
92-173-022	Patridge IN a Pear Tree 875QX5234	Keepsake	Yr.Iss.	8.75	8.75
92-173-023	Spirit of Christmas Stress 875QX5231	Keepsake	Yr.Iss.	8.75	8.75
92-173-024	Please Pause Here 1475QX5291	Keepsake	Yr.Iss.	14.75	14.75
92-173-025	SNOOPY® and WOODSTOCK 875QX5954	Keepsake	Yr.Iss.	8.75	8.75
92-173-026	Mary Engelbreit Santa Jolly Wolly 775QX5224	Keepsake	Yr.Iss.	7.75	7.75
92-173-027	GARFIELD 775QX5374	Keepsake	Yr.Iss.	7.75	7.75
92-173-028	Norman Rockwell Art 500QX2224	Keepsake	Yr.Iss.	5.00	5.00
92-173-029	PEANUTS® 500QX2244	Keepsake	Yr.Iss.	5.00	5.00
92-173-030	Owl 975QX5614	Keepsake	Yr.Iss.	9.75	9.75
92-173-031	Santa Maria 1275QX5074	Keepsake	Yr.Iss.	12.75	12.75
92-173-032	Fun on a Big Scale 1075QX5134	Keepsake	Yr.Iss.	10.75	10.75
92-173-033	Genius at Work 1075QX5371	Keepsake	Yr.Iss.	10.75	10.75
92-173-034	Hello-Ho-Ho 975QX5141	Keepsake	Yr.Iss.	9.75	9.75
92-173-035	Cheerful Santa 975QX5154	Keepsake	Yr.Iss.	9.75	9.75
92-173-036	Memories to Cherish 1075QX5161	Keepsake	Yr.Iss.	10.75	10.75
92-173-037	Tread Bear 875QX5091	Keepsake	Yr.Iss.	8.75	8.75
92-173-038	Merry "Swiss" Mouse 775QX5114	Keepsake	Yr.Iss.	7.75	7.75
92-173-039	Honest George 775QX5064	Keepsake	Yr.Iss.	7.75	7.75
92-173-040	Bear Bell Champ 775QX5071	Keepsake	Yr.Iss.	7.75	7.75
92-173-041	Egg Nog Nest 775QX5121	Keepsake	Yr.Iss.	7.75	7.75
92-173-042	Jesus Loves Me 775QX3024	Keepsake	Yr.Iss.	7.75	7.75
92-173-043	Loving Shepherd 775QX5151	Keepsake	Yr.Iss.	7.75	7.75
92-173-044	Toboggan Tail 775QX5459	Keepsake	Yr.Iss.	7.75	7.75
92-173-045	Down-Under Holiday 775QX5144	Keepsake	Yr.Iss.	7.75	7.75
92-173-046	Holiday Wishes 775QX5131	Keepsake	Yr.Iss.	7.75	7.75
92-173-047	Feliz Navidad 675QX5181	Keepsake	Yr.Iss.	6.75	6.75

Company / Number	Name	Series / Artist	Edition Limit	Issue Price	Quote
92-173-048	Holiday Teatime 1475QX5431	Keepsake	Yr.Iss.	14.75	14.75
92-173-049	Santa's Hook Shot 1275QX5434	Keepsake	Yr.Iss.	12.75	12.75
92-173-050	Cool Fliers 1075QX5474	Keepsake	Yr.Iss.	10.75	10.75
Hallmark Keepsake Ornaments		**1992 Magic Ornaments**			
92-174-001	PEANUTS-Second Ed. 1800QLX7214	Keepsake	Yr.Iss.	18.00	18.00
92-174-002	Forest Frolics-Fourth Ed. 2800QLX7254	Keepsake	Yr.Iss.	28.00	28.00
92-174-003	Chris Mouse Tales-Eighth Ed. 1200QLX7074	Keepsake	Yr.Iss.	12.00	12.00
92-174-004	Santa Special 4000QLX7167	Keepsake	Yr.Iss.	40.00	40.00
92-174-005	Continental Express 3200QLX7264	Keepsake	Yr.Iss.	32.00	32.00
92-174-006	Look! It's Santa 1400QLX7094	Keepsake	Yr.Iss.	14.00	14.00
92-174-007	The Dancing Nutcracker 3000QLX7261	Keepsake	Yr.Iss.	30.00	30.00
92-174-008	EnchantedClock 3000QLX7274	Keepsake	Yr.Iss.	30.00	30.00
92-174-009	Christmas Parade 3000QLX7271	Keepsake	Yr.Iss.	30.00	30.00
92-174-010	Good Sledding Ahead 2800QLX7244	Keepsake	Yr.Iss.	28.00	28.00
92-174-011	Yuletide Rider 2800QLX7314	Keepsake	Yr.Iss.	28.00	28.00
92-174-012	Santa's Answering Machine 2200QLX7241	Keepsake	Yr.Iss.	22.00	22.00
92-174-013	Baby's First Christmas 2200QLX7281	Keepsake	Yr.Iss.	22.00	22.00
92-174-014	Out First Christmas Together 2000QLX7221	Keepsake	Yr.Iss.	20.00	20.00
92-174-015	Santa Sub 1800QLX7321	Keepsake	Yr.Iss.	18.00	18.00
92-174-016	Lighting the Way 1800QLX7231	Keepsake	Yr.Iss.	18.00	18.00
92-174-017	Under Construction 1800QLX7324	Keepsake	Yr.Iss.	18.00	18.00
92-174-018	Feathered Friends 1400QLX7091	Keepsake	Yr.Iss.	14.00	14.00
92-174-019	Watch Owls 1200QLX7084	Keepsake	Yr.Iss.	12.00	12.00
92-174-020	Nut Sweet Nut 1000QLX7081	Keepsake	Yr.Iss.	10.00	10.00
92-174-021	Angel Of Light 3000QLT7239	Keepsake	Yr.Iss.	30.00	30.00
Hallmark Keepsake Ornaments		**1992 Miniature Ornaments**			
92-175-001	The Night Before Christmas-1375QXM5541	Keepsake	Yr.Iss.	13.75	13.75
92-175-002	The Bearymores-First Ed.-575QXM5544	Keepsake	Yr.Iss.	5.75	5.75
92-175-003	Woodland Babies-Second Ed.-600QXM5444	Keepsake	Yr.Iss.	6.00	6.00
92-175-004	Thimble Bells-Third Ed.-600QXM5461	Keepsake	Yr.Iss.	6.00	6.00
92-175-005	Nature's Angels-Third Ed.-450QXM5451	Keepsake	Yr.Iss.	4.50	4.50
92-175-006	Box Car-Fourth Ed/Noel R.R.-700QXM5441	Keepsake	Yr.Iss.	7.00	7.00
92-175-007	The Kringles-Fourth Ed.-600QXM5381	Keepsake	Yr.Iss.	6.00	6.00
92-175-008	Church-Fifth Ed./Old English V.-700QXM5384	Keepsake	Yr.Iss.	7.00	7.00
92-175-009	Rocking Horse-Fifth Ed.-450QXM5454	Keepsake	Yr.Iss.	4.50	4.5
92-175-010	Kittens in Toyland-Fifth Ed.-450QXM5391	Keepsake	Yr.Iss.	4.50	4.50
92-175-011	Feeding Time-575QXM5481	Keepsake	Yr.Iss.	5.75	5.75
92-175-012	Black-Capped Chickadee-300QXM5484	Keepsake	Yr.Iss.	3.00	3.00
92-175-013	Holiday Holly-975QXM5364	Keepsake	Yr.Iss.	9.75	9.75
92-175-014	Harmony Trio-Set of Three-1175QXM5471	Keepsake	Yr.Iss.	11.75	11.75
92-175-015	Grandchild's First Christmas-575QXM5501	Keepsake	Yr.Iss.	5.75	5.75
92-175-016	Baby's First Christmas-450QXM5494	Keepsake	Yr.Iss.	4.50	4.50
92-175-017	Mom-450QXM5504	Keepsake	Yr.Iss.	4.50	4.50
92-175-018	Grandma-450QXM5514	Keepsake	Yr.Iss.	4.50	4.50
92-175-019	Friends Are Tops-450QXM5521	Keepsake	Yr.Iss.	4.50	4.50
92-175-020	A+ Teacher-375QXM5511	Keepsake	Yr.Iss.	3.75	3.75
92-175-021	Inside Story-725QXM5881	Keepsake	Yr.Iss.	7.25	7.25
92-175-022	Holiday Splash-575QXM5834	Keepsake	Yr.Iss.	5.75	5.75
92-175-023	Christmas Copter-575QXM5844	Keepsake	Yr.Iss.	5.75	5.75
92-175-024	"Coca-Cola" Santa-575QXM5884	Keepsake	Yr.Iss.	5.75	5.75
92-175-025	Wee Three Kings-575QXM5531	Keepsake	Yr.Iss.	5.75	5.75
92-175-026	Angelic Harpist-450QXM5524	Keepsake	Yr.Iss.	4.50	4.50
92-175-027	Polar Polka-450QXM5534	Keepsake	Yr.Iss.	4.50	4.50
92-175-028	Buck-A-Roo-450QXM5814	Keepsake	Yr.Iss.	4.50	4.50
92-175-029	Ski For Two-450QXM5821	Keepsake	Yr.Iss.	4.50	4.50
92-175-030	Hoop It Up-450QXM5831	Keepsake	Yr.Iss.	4.50	4.50
92-175-031	Visions Of Acorns-450QXM5851	Keepsake	Yr.Iss.	4.50	4.50
92-175-032	Friendly Tin Soldier-450QXM5874	Keepsake	Yr.Iss.	4.50	4.50
92-175-033	Bright Stringers-375QXM5841	Keepsake	Yr.Iss.	3.75	3.75
92-175-034	Fast Finish-375QXM5301	Keepsake	Yr.Iss.	3.75	3.75
92-175-035	Cozy Kayak-375QXM5551	Keepsake	Yr.Iss.	3.75	3.75
92-175-036	Snug Kitty-375QXM5554	Keepsake	Yr.Iss.	3.75	3.75
92-175-037	Snowshoe Bunny-375QXM5564	Keepsake	Yr.Iss.	3.75	3.75
92-175-038	Gerbil Inc.-375QXM5924	Keepsake	Yr.Iss.	3.75	3.75
92-175-039	Hickory, Dickory, Dock-375QXM5861	Keepsake	Yr.Iss.	3.75	3.75
92-175-040	Going Places-375QXM5871	Keepsake	Yr.Iss.	3.75	3.75
92-175-041	Minted For Santa-375QXM5854	Keepsake	Yr.Iss.	3.75	3.75
92-175-042	Cool Uncle Sam-300QXM5561	Keepsake	Yr.Iss.	3.00	3.00
92-175-043	Perfect Balance-300QXM5571	Keepsake	Yr.Iss.	3.00	3.00
92-175-044	Puppet Show-300QXM5574	Keepsake	Yr.Iss.	3.00	3.00
92-175-045	Christmas Bonus-300QXM5811	Keepsake	Yr.Iss.	3.00	3.00
92-175-046	Spunky Monkey-300QXM5921	Keepsake	Yr.Iss.	3.00	3.00
92-175-047	Little Town of Bethlehem-300QXM5864	Keepsake	Yr.Iss.	3.00	3.00
92-175-048	Sew Sew Tiny (set of 6)2900QXM5794	Keepsake	Yr.Iss.	29.00	29.00
Hallmark Keepsake Ornaments		**1992 Collectors' Club**			
92-176-001	Santa's Club List	Keepsake	Yr.Iss.	15.00	15.00
Hallmark Keepsake Ornaments		**1992 Limited Edition Ornaments**			
92-177-001	Victorian Skater (w/ base)	Keepsake	14,700	25.00	25.00
Hamilton Gifts		**Maud Humphrey Bogart Ornaments**			
89-01-001	Sarah H1367	M. Humphrey	19,500	35.00	38.00
90-01-002	Victoria H1365	M. Humphrey	19,500	35.00	38.00
90-01-003	Michelle H1370	M. Humphrey	19,500	35.00	38.00
90-01-004	Catherine H1366	M. Humphrey	19,500	35.00	38.00
90-01-005	Gretchen H1369	M. Humphrey	19,500	35.00	38.00
90-01-006	Rebecca H5513	M. Humphrey	19,500	35.00	38.00
91-01-007	Cleaning House-915084	M. Humphrey	Open	24.00	24.00
91-01-008	Gift of Love-915092	M. Humphrey	Open	24.00	24.00
91-01-009	My First Dance-915106	M. Humphrey	Open	24.00	24.00
91-01-010	Special Friends-915114	M. Humphrey	Open	24.00	24.00
91-01-011	Susanna-915122	M. Humphrey	Open	24.00	24.00
91-01-012	Sarah-915165	M. Humphrey	Open	24.00	24.00
92-01-013	Hollies For You-915726	M. Humphrey	Yr.Iss.	24.00	24.00
Hand & Hammer		**Hand & Hammer Ornaments**			
80-01-001	Icicle-009	De Matteo	490	25.00	30.00
81-01-002	Roundel -109	De Matteo	220	25.00	45.00
81-01-003	Gabriel with Liberty Cap-301	De Matteo	275	25.00	50.00
81-01-004	Gabriel -320	De Matteo	Suspd.	25.00	32.00
82-01-005	Fleur de Lys Angel-343	De Matteo	320	28.00	35.00
82-01-006	Madonna & Child-388	De Matteo	175	28.00	50.00
84-01-007	Beardsley Angel-398	De Matteo	Open	28.00	48.00
82-01-008	Carved Heart -425	De Matteo	Suspd.	29.00	48.00
82-01-009	Straw Star -448	De Matteo	590	25.00	40.00
83-01-010	Fire Angel -473	De Matteo	315	25.00	28-36.00
83-01-011	Indian-494	De Matteo	190	29.00	50.00
83-01-012	Pollock Angel-502	De Matteo	Suspd.	35.00	50.00
83-01-013	Calligraphic Deer-511	De Matteo	Suspd.	25.00	29.00
83-01-014	Egyptian Cat-521	De Matteo	Unkn.	13.00	13.00

Company		Series			
Number	**Name**	**Artist**	**Edition Limit**	**Issue Price**	**Quote**
83-01-015	Dove-522	De Matteo	Unkn.	13.00	13.00
83-01-016	Sargent Angel-523	De Matteo	690	29.00	34.00
83-01-017	Cherub-528	De Matteo	295	29.00	50.00
83-01-018	Japanese Snowflake-534	De Matteo	350	29.00	35.00
83-01-019	Sunburst-543	De Matteo	Unkn.	13.00	50.00
83-01-020	Wise Man-549	De Matteo	Suspd.	29.00	36.00
84-01-021	Freer Star-553	De Matteo	Unkn.	13.00	30.00
84-01-022	Pineapple-558	De Matteo	Suspd.	30.00	38.00
84-01-023	Crescent Angel-559	De Matteo	Suspd.	30.00	32.00
84-01-024	Rosette-571	De Matteo	220	32.00	50.00
84-01-025	Nine Hearts-572	De Matteo	275	34.00	50.00
84-01-026	USHS 1984 Angel-574	De Matteo	Suspd.	35.00	50.00
84-01-027	Wreath-575	De Matteo	Unkn.	13.00	30.00
84-01-028	Praying Angel-576	De Matteo	Suspd.	29.00	30.00
84-01-029	Rocking Horse-581	De Matteo	Unkn.	13.00	13.00
84-01-030	Bunny-582	De Matteo	Unkn.	13.00	30.00
84-01-031	Ibex-584	De Matteo	400	29.00	50.00
84-01-032	Bird & Cherub-588	De Matteo	Unkn.	13.00	30.00
84-01-033	Wild Swan-592	De Matteo	Suspd.	35.00	50.00
84-01-034	Moravian Star-595	De Matteo	Open	38.00	50.00
84-01-035	Manger-601	De Matteo	Suspd.	29.00	32.00
84-01-036	Mt. Vernon Weathervane-602	De Matteo	Suspd.	32.00	39.00
85-01-037	Peacock-603	De Matteo	470	34.00	37.00
85-01-038	Model A Ford-604	De Matteo	Unkn.	13.00	30.00
85-01-039	Crane-606	De Matteo	150	39.00	50.00
85-01-040	Angel-607	De Matteo	225	36.00	50.00
85-01-041	Militiaman-608	De Matteo	460	25.00	30.00
85-01-042	Nutcracker-609	De Matteo	510	30.00	50.00
85-01-043	Liberty Bell-611	De Matteo	Suspd.	32.00	40.00
85-01-044	Angel-612	De Matteo	217	32.00	50.00
85-01-045	Abigail-613	De Matteo	500	32.00	50.00
85-01-046	Audubon Swallow-614	De Matteo	Suspd.	48.00	60.00
85-01-047	Audubon Bluebird-615	De Matteo	Suspd.	48.00	60.00
85-01-048	Guardian Angel-616	De Matteo	1,340	35.00	39.00
85-01-049	Shepherd-617	De Matteo	1,770	35.00	39.00
85-01-050	Carousel Pony-618	De Matteo	Unkn.	13.00	13.00
85-01-051	Art Deco Deer-620	De Matteo	Suspd.	34.00	38.00
85-01-052	Halley's Comet-621	De Matteo	432	35.00	50.00
85-01-053	Mermaid-622	De Matteo	Suspd.	35.00	39.00
85-01-054	George Washington-629	De Matteo	Suspd.	35.00	39.00
85-01-055	USHS Madonna-630	De Matteo	Suspd.	35.00	50.00
85-01-056	USHS Bluebird-631	De Matteo	Suspd.	29.00	50.00
85-01-057	USHS Swallow-632	De Matteo	Suspd.	29.00	50.00
85-01-058	Grasshopper-634	De Matteo	Open	32.00	39.00
85-01-059	Hosanna-635	De Matteo	715	32.00	50.00
85-01-060	Teddy-637	De Matteo	Suspd.	37.00	40.00
85-01-061	Herald Angel-641	De Matteo	Suspd.	36.00	40.00
85-01-062	Cherub-642	De Matteo	815	37.00	37.00
85-01-063	Butterfly-646	De Matteo	Suspd.	39.00	39.00
85-01-064	French Quarter Heart-647	De Matteo	Open	37.00	36.00
85-01-065	Samantha-648	De Matteo	Suspd.	35.00	36.00
85-01-066	Eagle-652	De Matteo	375	30.00	50.00
85-01-067	Piazza-653	De Matteo	Suspd.	32.00	50.00
85-01-068	Camel-655	De Matteo	Unkn.	13.00	30.00
85-01-069	Reindeer-656	De Matteo	Unkn.	13.00	30.00
85-01-070	Lafarge Angel-658	De Matteo	Suspd.	32.00	50.00
85-01-071	Family-659	De Matteo	915	32.00	40.00
85-01-072	Unicorn-660	De Matteo	Suspd.	37.00	37.00
85-01-073	Old North Church-661	De Matteo	Open	35.00	39.00
85-01-074	Madonna-666	De Matteo	227	35.00	50.00
85-01-075	Bicycle-669	De Matteo	Unkn.	13.00	30.00
85-01-076	St. Nicholas-670	De Matteo	Unkn.	13.00	30.00
86-01-077	Nativity-679	De Matteo	Suspd.	36.00	38.00
86-01-078	Winged Dove-680	De Matteo	Suspd.	35.00	36.00
86-01-079	Nutcracker-681	De Matteo	1,356	37.00	37.00
86-01-080	Phaeton-683	De Matteo	Unkn.	13.00	13.00
86-01-081	Archangel-684	De Matteo	Suspd.	29.00	30.00
86-01-082	Teddy Bear-685	De Matteo	Suspd.	38.00	40.00
86-01-083	Hallelujah-686	De Matteo	Unkn.	38.00	38.00
86-01-084	Bear Claus-692	De Matteo	Unkn.	13.00	13.00
86-01-085	Prancer-698	De Matteo	Open	38.00	38.00
86-01-086	USHS Angel-703	De Matteo	Suspd.	35.00	50.00
86-01-087	Teddy-707	De Matteo	Unkn.	13.00	30.00
86-01-088	Christmas Tree-708	De Matteo	Unkn.	13.00	13.00
86-01-089	Lafarge Angel-710	De Matteo	Suspd.	31.00	50.00
86-01-090	Salem Lamb-712	De Matteo	Suspd.	32.00	40.00
86-01-091	Snowflake-713	De Matteo	Suspd.	36.00	40.00
86-01-092	Wreath-714	De Matteo	Suspd.	36.00	38.00
86-01-093	Santa Skates-715	De Matteo	Suspd.	36.00	36.00
86-01-094	Nightingale-716	De Matteo	Suspd.	35.00	50.00
86-01-095	Mother Goose-719	De Matteo	Open	34.00	40.00
86-01-096	Kringle Bear-723	De Matteo	Unkn.	13.00	30.00
86-01-097	Victorian Santa-724	De Matteo	250	32.00	35.00
87-01-098	Noel-731	De Matteo	Open	38.00	38.00
87-01-099	Naptime-732	J. Walpole	Suspd.	32.00	32.00
87-01-100	Hunting Horn-738	De Matteo	Open	37.00	37.00
87-01-101	Santa Star-739	J. Walpole	Suspd.	32.00	32.00
87-01-102	Sweetheart Star-740	De Matteo	Suspd.	39.50	39.50
87-01-103	Santa-741	De Matteo	Unkn.	13.00	13.00
87-01-104	Pegasus-745	De Matteo	Unkn.	13.00	13.00
87-01-105	Snow Queen-746	De Matteo	Suspd.	35.00	39.00
87-01-106	Dove-747	De Matteo	Unkn.	13.00	13.00
87-01-107	USHS Gloria Angel-748	De Matteo	Suspd.	39.00	50.00
87-01-108	Angel with Lyre-750	De Matteo	Suspd.	32.00	40.00
87-01-109	Santa and Sleigh-751	De Matteo	Suspd.	32.00	40.00
87-01-110	Reindeer-752	De Matteo	Open	38.00	38.00
87-01-111	Snowman-753	De Matteo	825	38.00	38.00
87-01-112	Cat-754	De Matteo	Open	37.00	37.00
87-01-113	Clipper Ship-756	De Matteo	Suspd.	35.00	35.00
87-01-114	Ride a Cock Horse-757	De Matteo	Suspd.	34.00	39.00
87-01-115	Art Deco Angel-765	De Matteo	Suspd.	38.00	40.00
87-01-116	Old Ironsides-767	De Matteo	Open	35.00	39.00
87-01-117	First Christmas-771	De Matteo	Unkn.	13.00	13.00
87-01-118	Stocking-772	De Matteo	Unkn.	13.00	13.00
88-01-119	Drummer Bear-773	De Matteo	Unkn.	13.00	13.00
88-01-120	Stocking-774	De Matteo	Unkn.	13.00	13.00
87-01-121	Minuteman-776	De Matteo	Suspd.	35.00	40.00
87-01-122	Buffalo-777	De Matteo	Suspd.	36.00	36.00
88-01-123	Star of the East-785	De Matteo	Suspd.	35.00	35.00
88-01-124	Dove-786	De Matteo	112	36.00	50.00
88-01-125	Madonna-787	De Matteo	600	35.00	35.00
88-01-126	Magi-788	De Matteo	Suspd.	39.50	39.50
88-01-127	Jack in the Box-789	De Matteo	Suspd.	39.50	39.50
88-01-128	Skaters-790	De Matteo	Suspd.	39.50	39.50
88-01-129	Angel-797	De Matteo	Unkn.	13.00	13.00
88-01-130	Christmas Tree-798	De Matteo	Unkn.	13.00	13.00
88-01-131	Thumbelina-803	De Matteo	Suspd.	35.00	40.00
88-01-132	Star-806	De Matteo	311	50.00	150.00
88-01-133	Madonna-809	De Matteo	15	39.00	50.00
89-01-134	Carousel Horse-811	De Matteo	2,150	34.00	34.00
88-01-135	Bank-812	De Matteo	400	40.00	40.00
88-01-136	Santa with Scroll-814	De Matteo	250	34.00	37.00
88-01-137	Madonna-815	De Matteo	Suspd.	39.00	50.00
88-01-138	Rabbit-816	De Matteo	Unkn.	13.00	13.00
88-01-139	Buggy-817	De Matteo	Unkn.	13.00	13.00
88-01-140	Angel-818	De Matteo	Suspd.	32.00	40.00
88-01-141	Boston State House-819	De Matteo	Open	34.00	40.00
88-01-142	US Capitol-820	De Matteo	Open	38.00	40.00
88-01-143	Nativity-821	De Matteo	Suspd.	32.00	39.00
88-01-144	Old King Cole-824	De Matteo	Suspd.	34.00	39.00
88-01-145	Stocking-827	De Matteo	Unkn.	13.00	13.00
88-01-146	Conn. State House-833	De Matteo	Open	38.00	38.00
88-01-147	Sleigh-834	De Matteo	Open	34.00	38.00
89-01-148	Stocking Bear-835	De Matteo	Unkn.	13.00	13.00
88-01-149	Night Before Xmas Col.-841	De Matteo	10,000	160.00	160.00
89-01-150	First Christmas-842	De Matteo	Unkn.	13.00	13.00
89-01-151	Locket Bear-844	De Matteo	Unkn.	25.00	25.00
88-01-152	Cable Car-848	De Matteo	Open	38.00	38.00
88-01-153	Star-854	De Matteo	275	32.00	35.00
89-01-154	Santa 1989-856	De Matteo	1,715	35.00	35.00
89-01-155	Goose-857	De Matteo	650	37.00	37.00
89-01-156	Presidential Seal-858	De Matteo	500	39.00	39.00
88-01-157	Eiffel Tower-861	De Matteo	225	38.00	40.00
88-01-158	Coronado-864	De Matteo	Suspd.	38.00	38.00
90-01-159	Carousel Horse -866	De Matteo	1,915	38.00	38.00
90-01-160	Joy-867	De Matteo	1,140	36.00	36.00
90-01-161	Goose & Wreath-868	De Matteo	Open	37.00	37.00
90-01-162	1990 Santa-869	De Matteo	2,250	38.00	38.00
90-01-163	Cardinals-870	De Matteo	Open	39.00	39.00
90-01-164	Angel with Star-871	De Matteo	Open	38.00	38.00
89-01-165	Nutcracker 1989-872	De Matteo	1,790	38.00	38.00
89-01-166	USHS Angel 1989-901	De Matteo	Suspd.	38.00	38.00
89-01-167	Swan Boat-904	De Matteo	Open	38.00	38.00
89-01-168	MFA Noel-905	De Matteo	Suspd.	36.00	42.00
89-01-169	MFA Angel w/Tree-906	De Matteo	Suspd.	36.00	42.00
89-01-170	MFA Durer Snowflake-907	De Matteo	2,000	36.00	42.00
89-01-171	Independence Hall-908	De Matteo	Open	38.00	38.00
90-01-172	Cat on Pillow-915	De Matteo	Unkn.	13.00	13.00
90-01-173	Mouse w/Candy Cane-916	De Matteo	Unkn.	13.00	13.00
89-01-174	L&T Ugly Duckling-917	De Matteo	Suspd.	38.00	38.00
90-01-175	Farmhouse-919	De Matteo	Suspd.	37.00	37.00
90-01-176	Covered Bridge-920	De Matteo	Suspd.	37.00	37.00
90-01-177	Church-921	De Matteo	Suspd.	37.00	37.00
90-01-178	Mill-922	De Matteo	Suspd.	37.00	37.00
90-01-179	Currier & Ives Set -Victorian Village-923	De Matteo	2,000	140.00	140.00
90-01-180	Santa & Reindeer-929	De Matteo	395	39.00	43.00
90-01-181	Christmas Seal-931	De Matteo	Unkn.	25.00	25.00
89-01-182	Bugle Bear-935	De Matteo	Unkn.	12.00	12.00
89-01-183	Jack in the Box Bear-936	De Matteo	Unkn.	12.00	12.00
89-01-184	MFA LaFarge Angel set-937	De Matteo	Suspd.	98.00	98.00
90-01-185	First Christmas Bear-940	De Matteo	Suspd.	35.00	35.00
90-01-186	Santa in the Moon-941	De Matteo	Suspd.	38.00	38.00
90-01-187	Mole & Rat Wind in Will-944	De Matteo	Open	36.00	36.00
90-01-188	Toad Wind in Willows-945	De Matteo	Open	38.00	38.00
90-01-189	Merry Christmas Locket-948	De Matteo	Unkn.	25.00	25.00
90-01-190	Teddy Bear Locket-949	De Matteo	Unkn.	25.00	25.00
89-01-191	Barnesville Buggy 1989-950	De Matteo	Unkn.	13.00	13.00
89-01-192	Victorian Heart-954	De Matteo	Unkn.	13.00	13.00
89-01-193	Stocking Bear-955	De Matteo	Unkn.	12.00	12.00
89-01-194	Stocking w/Toys-956	De Matteo	Unkn.	12.00	12.00
90-01-195	Teddy Bear w/Heart-957	De Matteo	Unkn.	13.00	13.00
90-01-196	Clown w/Dog-958	De Matteo	Unkn.	13.00	13.00
90-01-197	Heart Angel-959	De Matteo	Suspd.	39.00	39.00
90-01-198	Carriage-960	De Matteo	Unkn.	13.00	13.00
90-01-199	Blake Angel-961	De Matteo	Unkn.	36.00	36.00
90-01-200	Colonial Capitol-965	De Matteo	Open	39.00	39.00
90-01-201	Governor's Palace-966	De Matteo	Open	39.00	39.00
90-01-202	Cockatoo-969	De Matteo	Unkn.	13.00	13.00
90-01-203	Father Christmas-970	De Matteo	Suspd.	36.00	36.00
90-01-204	Old Fashioned Santa-971	De Matteo	Suspd.	36.00	36.00
90-01-205	Patriotic Santa-972	De Matteo	Suspd.	36.00	36.00
90-01-206	Santa in Balloon-973	De Matteo	Suspd.	36.00	36.00
90-01-207	Santa on Reindeer-974	De Matteo	Suspd.	36.00	36.00
90-01-208	Santa UpTo Date-975	De Matteo	Suspd.	36.00	36.00
90-01-209	Presidential Homes-990	De Matteo	Open	350.00	350.00
90-01-210	Mrs. Rabbit-991	De Matteo	Open	39.50	39.50
90-01-211	Jeremy Fisher-992	De Matteo	Open	39.50	39.50
90-01-212	Peter Rabbit-993	De Matteo	Open	39.50	39.50
90-01-213	Peter's First Christmas-994	De Matteo	Suspd.	39.50	39.50
90-01-214	Flopsy Bunnies-995	De Matteo	Suspd.	39.50	39.50
90-01-215	First Baptist Angel-997	De Matteo	200	35.00	35.00
91-01-216	I Love Santa-998	De Matteo	Open	36.00	36.00
90-01-217	1990 Peter Rabbit-1018	De Matteo	4,315	39.50	39.50
90-01-218	Peter Rabbit Locket Ornament-1019	De Matteo	Unkn.	30.00	30.00
90-01-219	Jemima Puddleduck-1020	De Matteo	Unkn.	30.00	30.00
90-01-220	Landing Duck-1021	De Matteo	Unkn.	13.00	13.00
90-01-221	White Tail Deer-1022	De Matteo	Unkn.	13.00	13.00
90-01-222	Elk-1023	De Matteo	Unkn.	13.00	13.00
90-01-223	Angel With Violin-1024	De Matteo	Suspd.	39.00	39.00
91-01-224	Carousel Horse-1025	De Matteo	Open	38.00	38.00
91-01-225	Angel With Horn-1026	De Matteo	Open	32.00	32.00
90-01-226	Conestoga Wagon-1027	De Matteo	Open	38.00	38.00
90-01-227	Liberty Bell-1028	De Matteo	Open	38.00	38.00
90-01-228	The Boston Light-1032	De Matteo	Open	39.50	39.50
90-01-229	1990 Snowflake-1033	De Matteo	1,415	36.00	38.00
90-01-230	Pegasus-1037	De Matteo	Suspd.	35.00	35.00
90-01-231	Angels-1039	De Matteo	Suspd.	36.00	36.00
90-01-232	Beardsley Angel-1040	De Matteo	Suspd.	34.00	34.00
90-01-233	Georgia State Capitol-1042	De Matteo	2,000	39.50	39.50
90-01-234	N. Carolina State Capitol-1043	De Matteo	2,000	39.50	39.50
90-01-235	Florida State Capitol-1044	De Matteo	2,000	39.50	39.50
90-01-236	S. Carolina State Capitol-1045	De Matteo	2,000	39.50	39.50
90-01-237	Joy-1047	De Matteo	Suspd.	39.00	39.00
90-01-238	Steadfast Tin Soldier-1050	De Matteo	Suspd.	36.00	36.00
91-01-239	Cow Jumped Over The Moon-1055	De Matteo	Suspd.	38.00	38.00
91-01-240	1991 Santa-1056	De Matteo	3,750	38.00	38.00
90-01-241	USHS Angel 1990-1061	De Matteo	Suspd.	39.00	39.00
90-01-242	San Francisco Row House-1071	De Matteo	Open	39.50	39.50

Company / Number	Series / Name	Artist	Edition Limit	Issue Price	Quote
91-01-243	Mommy & Baby Seal-1075	De Matteo	Suspd.	36.00	36.00
91-01-244	Mommy & Baby Wolves-1076	De Matteo	Suspd.	36.00	36.00
91-01-245	Mommy & Baby Koala Bear-1077	De Matteo	Suspd.	36.00	36.00
91-01-246	Mommy & Baby Kangaroo-1078	De Matteo	Suspd.	36.00	36.00
91-01-247	Mommy & Baby Panda Bear-1079	De Matteo	Suspd.	36.00	36.00
91-01-248	Large Jemima Puddleduck-1083	De Matteo	Open	49.50	49.50
90-01-249	Ferrel's Angel 1990-1084	De Matteo	Unkn.	15.00	15.00
91-01-250	Olivers Rocking Horse-1085	De Matteo	Open	37.00	37.00
91-01-251	Mrs. Rabbit 1991-1086	De Matteo	Suspd.	39.50	39.50
91-01-252	Tailor of Gloucester-1087	De Matteo	Open	39.50	39.50
91-01-253	Pig Robinson-1090	De Matteo	Open	39.50	39.50
91-01-254	Appley Dapply-1091	De Matteo	Open	39.50	39.50
91-01-255	Peter Rabbit With Book-1093	De Matteo	Open	39.50	39.50
90-01-256	Koala San Diego Zoo-1095	De Matteo	Open	36.00	36.00
90-01-257	Locomotive-1100	De Matteo	Suspd.	39.00	39.00
90-01-258	Montpelier-1113	De Matteo	Open	36.00	36.00
90-01-259	Ducklings-1114	De Matteo	Open	38.00	38.00
91-01-260	Large Peter Rabbit-1116	De Matteo	Open	49.50	49.50
91-01-261	Large Tailor of Gloucester-1117	De Matteo	Open	49.50	49.50
91-01-262	Nativity-1118	De Matteo	Open	38.00	38.00
91-01-263	Alice-1119	De Matteo	Open	39.00	39.00
91-01-264	Mad Tea Party-1120	De Matteo	Open	39.00	39.00
91-01-265	White Rabbit-1121	De Matteo	Open	39.00	39.00
91-01-266	Queen of Hearts-1122	De Matteo	Open	39.00	39.00
91-01-267	Waiting For Santa-1123	De Matteo	Open	38.00	38.00
90-01-268	Ember-1124	De Matteo	120	N/A	N/A
91-01-269	USHS Angel 1991-1139	De Matteo	Suspd.	38.00	38.00
91-01-270	Columbus-1140	De Matteo	1,500	39.00	39.00
91-01-271	The Voyages Of Columbus-1141	De Matteo	1,500	39.00	39.00
91-01-272	Precious Planet-1142	De Matteo	2,000	120.00	120.00
91-01-273	MFA Snowflake 1991-1143	De Matteo	Suspd.	36.00	36.00
91-01-274	Fir Tree-1145	De Matteo	Open	39.00	39.00
91-01-275	Nutcracker-1151	De Matteo	Open	49.50	49.50
91-01-276	Paul Revere-1158	De Matteo	Open	39.00	39.00
91-01-277	Alice in Wonderland-1159	De Matteo	Open	140.00	140.00
91-01-278	Nutcracker-1183	De Matteo	Open	38.00	38.00
91-01-279	Nutrcracker Suite-1184	De Matteo	Open	38.00	38.00
91-01-280	Gus-1195	De Matteo	200	N/A	N/A
91-01-281	San Francisco Heart-1196	De Matteo	Open	39.00	39.00
92-01-282	Xmas Tree & Heart-1162	De Matteo	Open	36.00	36.00
92-01-283	Andrea-1163	De Matteo	Open	36.00	36.00
92-01-284	Joy-1164	De Matteo	Open	39.50	39.50
92-01-285	Unicorn-1165	De Matteo	Open	36.00	36.00
92-01-286	Noah's Ark-1166	De Matteo	Open	36.00	36.00
92-01-287	Jemima Puddleduck 1992-1167	De Matteo	Open	39.50	39.50
92-01-288	Mrs. Rabbit-1181	De Matteo	Open	39.50	39.50
92-01-289	Round Teapot-1206	De Matteo	Open	49.50	49.50
92-01-290	Revere Teapot-1207	De Matteo	Open	49.50	49.50
92-01-291	Chocolate Pot-1208	De Matteo	Open	49.50	49.50
92-01-292	Angel W/ Double Horn-1212	De Matteo	2,000	49.50	49.50
92-01-293	Angel-1213	De Matteo	2,000	39.00	39.00
92-01-294	Della Robbia Ornament-1219	De Matteo	Open	39.00	39.00
92-01-295	Fairy Tale Angel-1222	De Matteo	Open	36.00	36.00
92-01-296	Parrot-1233	De Matteo	Open	37.00	37.00
92-01-297	St John Lion-1235	De Matteo	10,000	39.00	39.00
92-01-298	St John Angel-1236	De Matteo	10,000	39.00	39.00
92-01-299	Scrooge-1241	De Matteo	Open	36.00	36.00
92-01-300	Bob & Tiny Tim-1242	De Matteo	Open	36.00	36.00
92-01-301	Marley's Ghost-1243	De Matteo	Open	36.00	36.00
92-01-302	Mrs. Cratchit-1244	De Matteo	Open	36.00	36.00
92-01-303	America At Peace-1245	De Matteo	2,000	85.00	85.00
92-01-304	MFA Snowflake-1246	De Matteo	Open	39.00	39.00
92-01-305	Princess & The Pea-1247	De Matteo	Open	39.00	39.00
92-01-306	Dorothy-1284	De Matteo	Open	36.00	36.00
92-01-307	Tin Man-1285	De Matteo	Open	36.00	36.00
92-01-308	Scarecrow-1286	De Matteo	Open	36.00	36.00
92-01-309	Cowardly Lion-1287	De Matteo	Open	36.00	36.00
92-01-310	Heart of Christmas-1301	De Matteo	Open	N/A	N/A
92-01-311	Jessops Clock-1308	De Matteo	Open	N/A	N/A
Hand & Hammer	**Annual Ornaments**				
87-02-001	Silver Bells-737	De Matteo	2,700	38.00	50.00
88-02-002	Silver Bells-792	De Matteo	3,150	39.50	39.50
89-02-003	Silver Bells-843	De Matteo	3,150	39.50	39.50
90-02-004	Silver Bells-865	De Matteo	3,615	39.00	39.00
90-02-005	Silver Bells Rev.-964	De Matteo	4,490	39.00	39.00
91-02-006	Silver Bells-1080	De Matteo	4,100	39.50	39.50
92-02-007	Silver Bells-1148	De Matteo	4,100	39.50	39.50
John Hine N.A. Ltd.	**David Winter Ornaments**				
92-01-001	Scrooge's Counting House	D. Winter	Closed	15.00	23.00
92-01-002	Hogmanay	D. Winter	Closed	15.00	23.00
92-01-003	A Christmas Carol	D. Winter	Closed	15.00	23.00
92-01-004	Mister Fezziwig's Emporium	D. Winter	Closed	15.00	23.00
92-01-005	Set	D. Winter	Closed	60.00	100.00
92-01-006	Fairytale Castle	D. Winter	Yr.Iss.	15.00	15.00
92-01-007	Fred's Home	D. Winter	Yr.Iss.	15.00	15.00
92-01-008	Suffolk House	D. Winter	Yr.Iss.	15.00	15.00
92-01-009	Tudor Manor	D. Winter	Yr.Iss.	15.00	15.00
Kirk Stieff	**Colonial Williamsburg**				
87-01-001	Rocking Horse, silverplate	D. Bacorn	Open	19.95	30.00
87-01-002	Tin Drum, silverplate	D. Bacorn	Open	19.95	30.00
88-01-003	Lamb, silverplate	D. Bacorn	Open	19.95	22.00
83-01-004	Tree Top Star, silverplate	D. Bacorn	Yr.Iss.	29.50	29.50
89-01-005	Doll ornament, silverplate	D. Bacorn	Yr.Iss.	22.00	22.00
88-01-006	Unicorn, silverplate	D. Bacorn	Yr.Iss.	22.00	22.00
Kirk Stieff	**Twelve Days of Christmas**				
85-02-001	Partridge in a Pear Tree	J. Barata	Yr.Iss.	9.95	10.95
85-02-002	Two Turtle Doves	J. Barata	Yr.Iss.	9.95	10.95
86-02-003	Three French Hens	J. Barata	Yr.Iss.	9.95	10.95
86-02-004	Four Calling Birds	J. Barata	Yr.Iss.	9.95	10.95
87-02-005	Five Golden Rings	J. Barata	Yr.Iss.	9.95	10.95
87-02-006	Six Geese-A-Laying	J. Barata	Yr.Iss.	9.95	10.95
88-02-007	Seven Swans-A-Swimming	J. Barata	Yr.Iss.	9.95	10.95
88-02-008	Eight Maids-A-Milking	J. Barata	Yr.Iss.	9.95	10.95
89-02-009	Nine Ladies Dancing	J. Barata	Yr.Iss.	10.95	10.95
89-02-010	Ten Lords-a-Leaping	J. Barata	Yr.Iss.	10.95	10.95
Kirk Stieff	**The Nutcracker Stained Glass Ornaments**				
86-03-001	Clara's Gift	Kirk Stieff	Closed	17.50	17.50
86-03-002	The Battle	Kirk Stieff	Closed	17.50	17.50
86-03-003	The Nutcracker Prince	Kirk Stieff	Closed	17.50	17.50
86-03-004	The Sugar Plum Fairy	Kirk Stieff	Closed	17.50	17.50
86-03-005	Set of Four	Kirk Stieff	Closed	69.95	69.95
Kirk Stieff	**Kirk Stieff Ornaments**				
84-04-001	Unicorn	D. Bacorn	Closed	17.50	19.95
83-04-002	Charleston Locomotive	D. Bacorn	Closed	17.50	19.95
86-04-003	Icicle, sterling silver	D. Bacorn	Open	35.00	50.00
89-04-004	Smithsonian Carousel Horse	Kirk Stieff	Yr.Iss.	50.00	50.00
89-04-005	Smithsonian Carousel Seahorse	Kirk Stieff	Yr.Iss.	50.00	50.00
90-04-006	Toy Ship	Kirk Stieff	Yr.Iss.	23.00	23.00
Lance Corporation	**Sebastian Christmas Ornaments**				
43-01-001	Madonna of the Chair	P.W. Baston	Closed	2.00	150-200.
81-01-002	Santa Claus	P.W. Baston	Open	28.50	30.00
82-01-003	Madonna of the Chair (Reissue of '43)	P.W. Baston	Closed	15.00	30-45.00
85-01-004	Home for the Holidays	P.W. Baston Jr.	Open	10.00	12.50
86-01-005	Holiday Sleigh Ride	P.W. Baston Jr.	Open	10.00	12.50
87-01-006	Santa	P.W. Baston Jr.	Open	10.00	12.50
88-01-007	Decorating the Tree	P.W. Baston Jr.	Open	12.50	12.50
89-01-008	Final Preparations for Christmas	P.W. Baston Jr.	Open	13.90	13.90
90-01-009	Stuffing the Stockings	P.W. Baston Jr.	Open	14.00	14.00
91-01-010	Merry Christmas	P.W. Baston Jr.	Open	14.50	14.50
92-01-011	Final Check	P.W. Baston Jr.	Open	14.50	14.50
Lenox China	**Annual Ornaments**				
82-01-001	1982 Ornament	Lenox	Yr.Iss.	30.00	50-90.00
83-01-002	1983 Ornament	Lenox	Yr.Iss.	35.00	75.00
84-01-003	1984 Ornament	Lenox	Yr.Iss.	38.00	65.00
85-01-004	1985 Ornament	Lenox	Yr.Iss.	37.50	60.00
86-01-005	1986 Ornament	Lenox	Yr.Iss.	38.50	50.00
87-01-006	1987 Ornament	Lenox	Yr.Iss.	39.00	45.00
88-01-007	1988 Ornament	Lenox	Yr.Iss.	39.00	45.00
89-01-008	1989 Ornament	Lenox	Yr.Iss.	39.00	39.00
90-01-009	1990 Ornament	Lenox	Yr.Iss.	42.00	42.00
91-01-010	1991 Ornament	Lenox	Yr.Iss.	39.00	39.00
92-01-011	1992 Ornament	Lenox	Yr.Iss.	39.00	39.00
Lenox China	**Days of Christmas**				
87-02-001	Partridge	Lenox	Open	22.50	22.50
88-02-002	Two Turtle Doves	Lenox	Open	22.50	22.50
89-02-003	Three French Hens	Lenox	Open	22.50	22.50
90-02-004	Four Calling Birds	Lenox	Open	25.00	25.00
91-02-005	Five Golden Rings	Lenox	Open	25.00	25.00
92-02-006	Six Geese a-Laying	Lenox	Open	25.00	25.00
Lenox China	**Yuletide**				
85-03-001	Teddy Bear	Lenox	Closed	18.00	18.00
85-03-002	Christmas Tree	Lenox	Open	18.00	18.00
89-03-003	Santa with Tree	Lenox	Closed	18.00	18.00
89-03-004	Angel with Horn	Lenox	Open	18.00	18.00
90-03-005	Dove	Lenox	Open	19.50	19.50
91-03-006	Snowman	Lenox	Open	19.50	19.50
92-03-007	Goose	Lenox	Open	20.00	20.00
Lenox China	**Carved**				
87-04-001	Portrait Wreath	Lenox	Closed	21.00	21.00
89-04-002	Georgian Frame	Lenox	Open	25.00	25.00
Lenox China	**Renaissance Angels**				
87-05-001	Angel with Trumpet	Lenox	Closed	21.00	21.00
87-05-002	Angel with Violin	Lenox	Closed	21.00	21.00
87-05-003	Angel with Mandolin	Lenox	Closed	21.00	21.00
Lenox China	**Golden Renaissance Angels**				
91-06-001	Angel with Trumpet	Lenox	Open	25.00	25.00
91-06-002	Angel with Violin	Lenox	Open	25.00	25.00
91-06-003	Angel with Mandolin	Lenox	Open	25.00	25.00
Lenox China	**Nativity**				
89-07-001	Mary &Child	Lenox	Closed	21.00	21.00
89-07-002	Joseph	Lenox	Closed	21.00	21.00
90-07-003	Melchior	Lenox	Closed	22.00	22.00
90-07-004	Gaspar	Lenox	Closed	22.00	22.00
90-07-005	Balthazar	Lenox	Closed	22.00	22.00
Lenox China	**Commemoratives**				
89-08-001	First Christmas Together (Dated)	Lenox	Yr.Iss.	22.50	25.00
89-08-002	Baby's First Christmas (Dated)	Lenox	Yr.Iss.	22.50	25.00
Lenox China	**Holiday Homecoming**				
88-09-001	Hearth	Lenox	Closed	22.50	22.50
89-09-002	Door (Dated)	Lenox	Closed	22.50	22.50
90-09-003	Hutch	Lenox	Open	25.00	25.00
91-09-004	Window (Dated)	Lenox	Yr.Iss.	25.00	25.00
92-09-005	Stove (Dated)	Lenox	Yr.Iss.	25.00	25.00
Lenox China	**Santa's Portraits**				
89-10-001	Santa's Visit	Lenox	Open	27.00	27.00
90-10-002	Santa With Garland	Lenox	Open	29.00	29.00
90-10-003	Santa's Ride	Lenox	Open	29.00	29.00
91-10-004	Santa And Child	Lenox	Open	29.00	29.00
92-10-005	Santa in Chimney	Lenox	Open	29.00	29.00
Lenox China	**Lenox Christmas Village**				
89-11-001	Village Church	Lenox	Open	39.00	39.00
90-11-002	Village Inn	Lenox	Open	39.00	39.00
91-11-003	Village Town Hall (Dated)	Lenox	Yr.Iss.	39.00	39.00
92-11-004	Sweet Shop (Dated)	Lenox	Yr.Iss.	39.00	39.00
Lenox China	**Yuletide Express**				
88-12-001	Locomotive	Lenox	Open	39.00	39.00
89-12-002	Caboose	Lenox	Open	39.00	90.00
90-12-003	Passenger Car	Lenox	Open	39.00	39.00
91-12-004	Dining Car (Dated)	Lenox	Yr.Iss.	39.00	39.00
92-12-005	Tender Car (Dated)	Lenox	Yr.Iss.	39.00	39.00
Lenox China	**Renaissance Angel Treetopper**				
89-13-001	Angel Treetopper	Lenox	Closed	100.00	100.00
Lenox China	**Victorian Homes**				
90-14-001	Sheffield Manor	Lenox	Open	25.00	25.00
91-14-002	Cambridge Manor	Lenox	Open	25.00	25.00

Company		Series			
Number	**Name**	**Artist**	**Edition Limit**	**Issue Price**	**Quote**
Lenox China		**Lenox Christmas Keepsakes**			
90-15-001	Swan	Lenox	Open	42.00	42.00
90-15-002	Rocking Horse	Lenox	Open	42.00	42.00
91-15-003	Sleigh	Lenox	Open	42.00	42.00
92-15-004	Fire Engine	Lenox	Open	42.00	42.00
Lenox China		**Victorian Lace**			
91-16-001	Christmas Tree	Lenox	Open	25.00	25.00
91-16-002	Fan	Lenox	Open	25.00	25.00
Lenox China		**Cathedral Portraits**			
91-17-001	15th Century Madonna & Child	Botticelli	Open	29.00	29.00
91-17-002	16th Century Madonna & Child	Raphael	Open	29.00	29.00
Lenox Collections		**The Christmas Carousel**			
89-01-001	White Horse	Lenox	Open	19.50	19.50
89-01-002	Zebra	Lenox	Open	19.50	19.50
89-01-003	Lion	Lenox	Open	19.50	19.50
89-01-004	Sea Horse	Lenox	Open	19.50	19.50
89-01-005	Pinto	Lenox	Open	19.50	19.50
89-01-006	Goat	Lenox	Open	19.50	19.50
89-01-007	Reindeer	Lenox	Open	19.50	19.50
89-01-008	Polar Bear	Lenox	Open	19.50	19.50
89-01-009	Hare	Lenox	Open	19.50	19.50
89-01-010	Elephant	Lenox	Open	19.50	19.50
89-01-011	Swan	Lenox	Open	19.50	19.50
89-01-012	Unicorn	Lenox	Open	19.50	19.50
89-01-013	Palomino	Lenox	Open	19.50	19.50
89-01-014	Black Horse	Lenox	Open	19.50	19.50
89-01-015	Cat	Lenox	Open	19.50	19.50
89-01-016	Tiger	Lenox	Open	19.50	19.50
90-01-017	Camel	Lenox	Open	19.50	19.50
90-01-018	Rooster	Lenox	Open	19.50	19.50
90-01-019	Giraffe	Lenox	Open	19.50	19.50
90-01-020	Panda	Lenox	Open	19.50	19.50
90-01-021	Frog	Lenox	Open	19.50	19.50
90-01-022	Pig	Lenox	Open	19.50	19.50
90-01-023	St. Bernard	Lenox	Open	19.50	19.50
90-01-024	Medieval Horse	Lenox	Open	19.50	19.50
90-01-025	Set of 24	Lenox	Open	468.00	468.00
Lenox Crystal		**Crystal Ball Ornaments**			
84-01-001	Deep Cut Ball	Lenox	Yr.Iss.	35.00	50.00
85-01-002	Cut Ball	Lenox	Yr.Iss.	35.00	50.00
86-01-003	Cut Ball	Lenox	Yr.Iss.	35.00	45.00
87-01-004	Cut Ball	Lenox	Yr.Iss.	29.00	29.00
88-01-005	Christmas Lights Ball	Lenox	Yr.Iss.	30.00	30.00
89-01-006	Starlight Ornament	Lenox	Open	34.00	34.00
89-01-007	Crystal Lights Ornaments	Lenox	Open	30.00	30.00
91-01-008	Crystal Abbey Ball	Lenox	Open	45.00	45.00
91-01-009	Crystal Starlight Ball-Blue	Lenox	Open	45.00	45.00
91-01-010	Crystal Starlight Ball-Red	Lenox	Open	45.00	45.00
91-01-011	Crystal Starlight Ball-Green	Lenox	Open	45.00	45.00
92-01-012	Crystal Optika	Lenox	Open	37.00	37.00
Lenox Crystal		**Annual Bell Series**			
87-02-001	Partridge Bell	Lenox	Yr.Iss.	45.00	45.00
88-02-002	Angel Bell	Lenox	Open	45.00	45.00
89-02-003	St. Nicholas Bell	Lenox	Open	45.00	45.00
90-02-004	Christmas Tree Bell	Lenox	Open	49.00	49.00
91-02-005	Teddy Bear Bell	Lenox	Yr.Iss.	49.00	49.00
92-02-006	Snowman Bell	Lenox	Yr.Iss.	49.00	49.00
Lenox Crystal		**Crystal Ornaments**			
89-03-001	Candlelight Bell	Lenox	Open	38.00	38.00
89-03-002	Annual Christmas Tree	Lenox	Yr.Iss.	26.00	26.00
89-03-003	Crystal Icicle	Lenox	Open	30.00	30.00
89-03-004	Our First Christmas	Lenox	Yr.Iss.	26.00	26.00
89-03-005	Baby's First Christmas	Lenox	Yr.Iss	26.00	26.00
89-03-006	Nativity	Lenox	Open	26.00	26.00
89-03-007	Snowflake	Lenox	Open	32.00	32.00
89-03-008	Christmas Lights Tree Top Ornament	Lenox	Open	55.00	55.00
90-03-009	Our First Christmas-1990	Lenox	Yr.Iss.	32.00	32.00
90-03-010	Baby's First Christmas-1990	Lenox	Yr.Iss.	30.00	30.00
90-03-011	Candy Cane	Lenox	Open	30.00	30.00
90-03-012	Christmas Tree-1990	Lenox	Yr.Iss.	30.00	30.00
90-03-013	Christmas Goose	Lenox	Open	29.00	29.00
91-03-014	Our First Christmas-1991	Lenox	Yr.Iss.	29.00	29.00
91-03-015	Baby's First Christmas-1991	Lenox	Yr.Iss.	29.00	29.00
91-03-016	Christmas Tree-1991	Lenox	Yr.Iss.	29.00	29.00
91-03-017	Christmas Stocking	Lenox	Open	29.00	29.00
91-03-018	Angel Pendent	Lenox	Open	29.00	29.00
91-03-019	Bird-Clear	Lenox	Open	29.00	29.00
91-03-020	Bird-Blue	Lenox	Open	29.00	29.00
91-03-021	Bird-Red	Lenox	Open	29.00	29.00
91-03-022	Bird-Green	Lenox	Open	29.00	29.00
91-03-023	Herald Angel-Clear	Lenox	Open	29.00	29.00
91-03-024	Herald Angel-Blue	Lenox	Open	29.00	29.00
91-03-025	Herald Angel-Red	Lenox	Open	29.00	29.00
91-03-026	Herald Angel-Green	Lenox	Open	29.00	29.00
91-03-027	Dove	Lenox	Open	32.00	32.00
91-03-028	Snowman	Lenox	Open	32.00	32.00
91-03-029	Abbey Treetopper	Lenox	Open	54.00	54.00
Lilliput Lane Ltd.		**Christmas Ornaments**			
92-26-001	Mistletoe Cottage	Lilliput Lane	Yr.Iss.	27.50	27.50
Lladro		**Miniature Ornaments**			
88-01-001	Miniature Angels-L1604G (Set of 3)	Lladro	Yr.Iss.	75.00	150-200.
89-01-002	Holy Family-L5657G (Set of 3)	Lladro	Yr.Iss.	79.50	100-150.
90-01-003	Three Kings-L5729G (Set of 3)	Lladro	Yr.Iss.	87.50	120.00
91-01-004	Holy Shepherds-L5809G	Lladro	Yr.Iss.	97.50	100.00
Lladro		**Annual Ornaments**			
88-02-001	Christmas Ball-L1603M	Lladro	Yr.Iss.	60.00	75-120.00
89-02-002	Christmas Ball-L5656M	Lladro	Yr.Iss.	65.00	85-100.00
90-02-003	Christmas Ball-L5730M	Lladro	Yr Iss.	70.00	75-90.00
91-02-004	Christmas Ball-L5829M	Lladro	Yr.Iss.	52.00	52.00
92-02-005	Christmas Ball-L5914M	Lladro	Yr.Iss.	52.00	52.00
Lladro		**Tree Topper Ornaments**			
90-03-001	Angel Tree Topper-L5719G-Blue	Lladro	Yr.Iss.	115.00	225.00
91-03-002	Angel Tree Topper-L5831G-Pink	Lladro	Yr.Iss.	115.00	160.00

Company		Series			
Number	**Name**	**Artist**	**Edition Limit**	**Issue Price**	**Quote**
92-03-003	Angel Tree Topper-L5875G-Green	Lladro	Yr.Iss.	120.00	120.00
Lladro		**Ornaments**			
92-04-001	Snowman-L5841G	Lladro	Yr.Iss.	50.00	50.00
92-04-002	Santa-L5842G	Lladro	Yr.Iss.	55.00	55.00
92-04-003	Baby's First-1992-L5922G	Lladro	Yr.Iss.	55.00	55.00
92-04-004	Our First-1992-L5923G	Lladro	Yr.Iss.	50.00	50.00
92-04-005	Elf Ornament-L5938G	Lladro	Yr.Iss.	50.00	50.00
92-04-006	Mrs. Claus-L5939G	Lladro	Yr.Iss.	55.00	55.00
92-04-007	Christmas Morning-L5940G	Lladro	Yr.Iss.	97.50	97.50
Lladro		**Angel Orchestra**			
91-05-001	Heavenly Harpist 15830	Lladro	Yr.Iss.	135.00	135.00
92-05-002	Angelic Cymbalist 5876	Lladro	Yr.Iss.	140.00	140.00
Seymour Mann Inc.		**Christmas Collection**			
85-01-001	Angel Wall Ornament XMAS-523	J. White	Open	12.00	12.00
86-01-002	Cupid Head Ornament XMAS-53	J. White	Open	25.00	25.00
86-01-003	Santa Ornament XMAS-384	J. White	Open	7.50	7.50
89-01-004	Christmas Cat in Teacup XMAS-660	J. White	Open	13.50	13.50
89-01-005	Flat Red Santa Ornament CJ-115R	Jaimy	Open	2.88	2.88
89-01-006	Flat Santa Ornament CJ-115	Jaimy	Open	7.50	7.50
90-01-007	Doll Tree Topper OM-124	J. White	Open	85.00	85.00
90-01-008	Hat w/ Streamers OM-116	J. White	Open	20.00	20.00
90-01-009	Lace Ball OM-120	J. White	Open	10.00	10.00
91-01-010	Elf w/ Reindeer CJ-422	Jaimy	Open	9.00	9.00
Seymour Mann Inc.		**Gingerbread Christmas Collection**			
91-02-001	Gingerbread Angel CJ-411	J. Sauerbrey	Open	7.50	7.50
91-02-002	Gingerbread House CJ-416	J. Sauerbrey	Open	7.50	7.50
91-02-003	Gingerbread Man CJ-415	J. Sauerbrey	Open	7.50	7.50
91-02-004	Gingerbread Mouse/Boot CJ-409	J. Sauerbrey	Open	7.50	7.50
91-02-005	Gingerbread Mrs. Claus CJ-414	J. Sauerbrey	Open	7.50	7.50
91-02-006	Gingerbread Reindeer CJ-410	J. Sauerbrey	Open	7.50	7.50
91-02-007	Gingerbread Santa CJ-408	J. Sauerbrey	Open	7.50	7.50
91-02-008	Gingerbread Sleigh CJ-406	J. Sauerbrey	Open	7.50	7.50
91-02-009	Gingerbread Snowman CJ-412	J. Sauerbrey	Open	7.50	7.50
91-02-010	Gingerbread Tree CJ-407	J. Sauerbrey	Open	7.50	7.50
Seymour Mann Inc.		**Victorian Christmas Collection**			
91-03-001	Couple Against Wind CJ-420	Jaimy	Open	15.00	15.00
June McKenna Collectibles, Inc.		**Flatback Ornaments**			
82-01-001	Santa With Toys	J. McKenna	Closed	14.00	50-80.00
82-01-002	Mama Bear, Blue Cape	J. McKenna	Closed	12.00	75-125.00
82-01-003	Papa Bear, Red Cape	J. McKenna	Closed	12.00	100-275.
82-01-004	Baby Bear, Teeshirt	J. McKenna	Closed	11.00	75-200.00
82-01-005	Candy Cane	J. McKenna	Closed	10.00	250.00
82-01-006	Colonial Man, available in 2 colors	J. McKenna	Closed	12.00	100-125.
82-01-007	Colonial Woman, available in 2 colors	J. McKenna	Closed	12.00	85-100.00
82-01-008	Kate Greenaway Boy	J. McKenna	Closed	12.00	300-500.
82-01-009	Kate Greenaway Girl	J. McKenna	Closed	12.00	350-500.
82-01-010	Angel With Toys	J. McKenna	Closed	14.00	65-75.00
83-01-011	Grandma, available in 4 colors	J. McKenna	Closed	12.00	60-75.00
83-01-012	Grandpa, available in 4 colors	J. McKenna	Closed	12.00	60-85.00
83-01-013	Mother Bear in Dress, available in 2 colors	J. McKenna	Closed	12.00	65-95.00
83-01-014	Father Bear in Suit, available in 2 colors	J. McKenna	Closed	12.00	65-75.00
83-01-015	Baby Bear in Vest, available in 2 colors	J. McKenna	Closed	11.00	55-65.00
83-01-016	Raggedy Ann	J. McKenna	Closed	12.00	175.00
83-01-017	Raggedy Andy	J. McKenna	Closed	12.00	175.00
83-01-018	St. Nick With Lantern	J. McKenna	Closed	14.00	50-75.00
83-01-019	Gloria Angel	J. McKenna	Closed	14.00	350-500.
83-01-020	Baby, available in 2 colors	J. McKenna	Closed	11.00	85.00
84-01-021	Angel with Horn	J. McKenna	Closed	14.00	100-125.
84-01-022	Mr. Claus	J. McKenna	Closed	14.00	85-95.00
84-01-023	Mrs. Claus	J. McKenna	Closed	14.00	85-95.00
84-01-024	Country Boy, available in 2 colors	J. McKenna	Closed	12.00	60-85.00
84-01-025	Country Girl, available in 2 colors	J. McKenna	Closed	12.00	60-85.00
84-01-026	Old World Santa, available in 3 colors	J. McKenna	Closed	14.00	50-95.00
85-01-027	Bride	J. McKenna	Closed	25.00	200.00
85-01-028	Groom	J. McKenna	Closed	25.00	200.00
85-01-029	Baby Pig	J. McKenna	Closed	11.00	95.00
85-01-030	Father Pig	J. McKenna	Closed	12.00	150.00
85-01-031	Mother Pig	J. McKenna	Closed	12.00	150.00
85-01-032	Amish Man	J. McKenna	Closed	13.00	50-275.00
85-01-033	Amish Woman	J. McKenna	Closed	13.00	50-275.00
85-01-034	Primitive Santa	J. McKenna	Closed	17.00	75-150.00
86-01-035	Amish Boy	J. McKenna	Closed	13.00	65-275.00
86-01-036	Amish Girl	J. McKenna	Closed	13.00	65-275.00
86-01-037	Santa with Bells, green	J. McKenna	Closed	14.00	200-400.
86-01-038	Santa with Bells, blue	J. McKenna	Closed	14.00	50-75.00
86-01-039	Santa with Bear	J. McKenna	Closed	14.00	40.00
86-01-040	Santa with Bag	J. McKenna	Closed	16.00	30-40.00
88-01-041	Elizabeth, sill sitter	J. McKenna	Closed	N/A	200-300.
88-01-042	Guardian Angel	J. McKenna	Closed	16.00	40.00
88-01-043	1776 Santa	J. McKenna	Closed	17.00	40.00
88-01-044	Santa With Book (Blue & Red)	J. McKenna	Closed	17.00	40-110.00
88-01-045	Santa With Toys	J. McKenna	Closed	17.00	40.00
88-01-046	Santa With Wreath	J. McKenna	Closed	17.00	40.00
89-01-047	Glorious Angel	J. McKenna	Open	17.00	17.00
89-01-048	Santa With Staff	J. McKenna	Closed	17.00	40.00
89-01-049	Santa WithTree	J. McKenna	Closed	17.00	40.00
89-01-050	Winking Santa	J. McKenna	Closed	17.00	40.00
90-01-051	Ho Ho Ho	J. McKenna	Closed	17.00	40.00
90-01-052	Elf Jeffrey	J. McKenna	Closed	17.00	40.00
90-01-053	Harvest Santa	J. McKenna	Closed	17.00	40.00
91-01-054	Santa With Lights, Black	J. McKenna	Open	20.00	20.00
91-01-055	Santa With Banner	J. McKenna	Closed	20.00	20.00
91-01-056	Elf Joey	J. McKenna	Open	20.00	20.00
91-01-057	Boy Angel	J. McKenna	Closed	20.00	20.00
91-01-058	Girl Angel	J. McKenna	Open	20.00	20.00
92-01-059	Santa With Basket	J. McKenna	Open	25.00	25.00
92-01-060	Santa With Sack	J. McKenna	Open	25.00	25.00
92-01-061	NorthPole News	J. McKenna	Open	25.00	25.00
92-01-062	Elf Scotty	J. McKenna	Open	25.00	25.00
92-01-063	Praying Angel	J. McKenna	Open	25.00	25.00
Midwest Importers		**Wendt und Kuhn Ornaments**			
78-01-001	Angel Clip-on Ornament 07296	Wendt/Kuhn	Open	20.00	20.00
89-01-003	Trumpeting Angel Ornament,2 asst.94029	Wendt/Kuhn	Open	14.00	14.00
91-01-002	Angel in Ring Ornament 12089	Wendt/Kuhn	Open	12.00	12.00

Company / Number	Name	Series / Artist	Edition Limit	Issue Price	Quote
Midwest Importers		**Heritage Santa CollectionOrnaments**			
90-02-001	Scanda Klaus Fabric Mache 05208	Midwest Importers	Retrd.	18.00	18.00
90-02-002	Herr Kristmas Fabric Mache 05216	Midwest Importers	Retrd.	18.00	18.00
90-02-003	MacNicholas Fabric Mache 05224	Midwest Importers	Retrd.	18.00	18.00
90-02-004	Papa Frost Fabric Mache 05232	Midwest Importers	Retrd.	18.00	18.00
91-02-005	Scanda Klaus Dimensional 29414	Midwest Importers	Open	11.50	11.50
91-02-006	Herr Kristmas Dimensional 29422	Midwest Importers	Open	11.50	11.50
91-02-007	MacNicholas Dimensional 29430	Midwest Importers	Open	11.50	11.50
91-02-008	Papa Frost Dimensional 29448	Midwest Importers	Open	11.50	11.50
91-02-009	Father Christmas Dimensional 29456	Midwest Importers	Open	11.50	11.50
91-02-010	Santa Niccolo Dimensional 29464	Midwest Importers	Open	11.50	11.50
92-02-011	Santa Nykolai Dimensional 67745	Midwest Importers	Open	11.50	11.50
92-02-012	Pere Noel Dimensional 67739	Midwest Importers	Open	11.50	11.50
Novelino		**Embroidered Ornaments**			
90-01-001	Snowman EMB101	Novelino	Open	2.00	2.00
90-01-002	Santa EMB102	Novelino	Open	2.00	2.00
90-01-003	Santa EMB103	Novelino	Open	2.00	2.00
90-01-004	Santa EMB104	Novelino	Open	2.00	2.00
90-01-005	Santa EMB105	Novelino	Open	2.00	2.00
90-01-006	Star EMB106	Novelino	Open	2.00	2.00
90-01-007	Teddy Bear EMB107	Novelino	Open	2.00	2.00
90-01-008	Bells EMB108	Novelino	Open	2.00	2.00
90-01-009	Stocking EMB109	Novelino	Open	2.00	2.00
90-01-010	Xmas Tree EMB201	Novelino	Open	3.00	3.00
90-01-011	Angel EMB202	Novelino	Open	3.00	3.00
90-01-012	Angel EMB203	Novelino	Open	3.00	3.00
90-01-013	Wreath EMB204	Novelino	Open	3.00	3.00
90-01-014	Reindeer EMB205	Novelino	Open	3.00	3.00
90-01-015	Angel EMB301	Novelino	Open	4.00	4.00
90-01-016	Angel EMB302	Novelino	Open	4.00	4.00
90-01-017	Angel EMB303	Novelino	Open	4.00	4.00
90-01-018	Santa EMB304	Novelino	Open	4.00	4.00
90-01-019	Santa EMB305	Novelino	Open	4.00	4.00
90-01-020	Santa EMB306	Novelino	Open	4.00	4.00
90-01-021	Nutcracker EMB307	Novelino	Open	4.00	4.00
90-01-022	Nutcracker EMB308	Novelino	Open	4.00	4.00
90-01-023	Nutcracker EMB309	Novelino	Open	4.00	4.00
90-01-024	Nutcracker EMB310	Novelino	Open	4.00	4.00
90-01-025	Nutcracker EMB311	Novelino	Open	4.00	4.00
90-01-026	Nutcracker EMB312	Novelino	Open	4.00	4.00
Novelino		**Old World Santa Ornaments**			
90-02-001	Santa/Bell PLO1001	Novelino	Open	4.00	4.00
90-02-002	Santa/Shoulder Bag PLO1002	Novelino	Open	4.00	4.00
90-02-003	Santa/Xmas List PLO1003	Novelino	Open	4.00	4.00
90-02-004	Santa/Tree PLO1004	Novelino	Open	4.00	4.00
90-02-005	Santa/Drum PLO1005	Novelino	Open	4.00	4.00
90-02-006	Santa/Armed Bag PLO1006	Novelino	Open	4.00	4.00
90-02-007	Santa/Baby PLO1007	Novelino	Open	4.00	4.00
90-02-008	Santa/Wreath PLO1008	Novelino	Open	4.00	4.00
90-02-009	Santa/Toy PLO1009	Novelino	Open	4.00	4.00
90-02-010	Santa/Drum & Horn PLO1010	Novelino	Open	4.00	4.00
Novelino		**Christmas Collectible Ornaments**			
90-03-001	Train PLO1011	Novelino	Open	4.00	4.00
90-03-002	Santa/Sled PLO1012	Novelino	Open	4.00	4.00
90-03-003	Drummer PLO1013	Novelino	Open	4.00	4.00
90-03-004	Unicorn PLO1014	Novelino	Open	4.00	4.00
90-03-005	Church PLO1015	Novelino	Open	4.00	4.00
90-03-006	Teddy Santa PLO1016	Novelino	Open	4.00	4.00
90-03-007	Clown PLO1018	Novelino	Open	4.00	4.00
90-03-008	Xmas Tree PLO1019	Novelino	Open	4.00	4.00
90-03-009	Snowman PLO1020	Novelino	Open	4.00	4.00
Novelino		**Heavenly Angel Ornaments**			
90-04-001	Angel/Harp PLO1021	Novelino	Open	6.00	6.00
90-04-002	Angel/Horn PLO1022	Novelino	Open	6.00	6.00
90-04-003	Angel/Guitar PLO1023	Novelino	Open	6.00	6.00
90-04-004	Angel/Flute PLO1024	Novelino	Open	6.00	6.00
90-04-005	Angel/Ribbon PLO1025	Novelino	Open	6.00	6.00
90-04-006	Angel/Book PLO1026	Novelino	Open	6.00	6.00
Novelino		**Nutcracker Sweet Ornaments**			
90-05-001	Nutcracker, RD/WH PLO1041	Novelino	Open	5.00	5.00
90-05-002	Nutcracker, BL/WH PLO1042	Novelino	Open	5.00	5.00
90-05-003	Nutcracker,DK BL/RD PLO1043	Novelino	Open	5.00	5.00
90-05-004	Nutcracker, DK/LT BL PLO1044	Novelino	Open	5.00	5.00
90-05-005	Nutcracker, RD/DK BL PLO1045	Novelino	Open	5.00	5.00
90-05-006	Nutcracker, RD/YW PLO1045	Novelino	Open	5.00	5.00
Novelino		**Santa Clown Ornaments**			
90-06-001	Caroling Clown PLO1051	Novelino	Open	9.00	9.00
90-06-002	Beard Being Pulled PLO1052	Novelino	Open	9.00	9.00
90-06-003	"Holy" Bag PLO1053	Novelino	Open	9.00	9.00
90-06-004	Driving Santa PLO1054	Novelino	Open	10.00	10.00
90-06-005	Stuck in Chimney PLO1055	Novelino	Open	10.00	10.00
Novelino		**Classic American Santa Ornaments**			
90-07-001	St. Nicholas PLO1624	Novelino	Open	10.00	10.00
90-07-002	Father Christmas PLO1664	Novelino	Open	10.00	10.00
90-07-003	Wilderness Santa PLO1701	Novelino	Open	10.00	10.00
90-07-004	Independence Santa PLO1776	Novelino	Open	10.00	10.00
90-07-005	Reindeer Santa PLO1821	Novelino	Open	10.00	10.00
90-07-006	Clement Moore Santa PLO1829	Novelino	Open	10.00	10.00
90-07-007	Beacon Santa PLO1860	Novelino	Open	10.00	10.00
90-07-008	Bell Ringing Santa PLO1912	Novelino	Open	10.00	10.00
90-07-009	World War II Santa PLO1945	Novelino	Open	10.00	10.00
90-07-010	Modern Santa PLO1990	Novelino	Open	10.00	10.00
Orrefors		**Christmas Ornaments**			
84-01-001	Dove	O. Alberius	Yr.Iss.	30.00	45.00
85-01-002	Angel	O. Alberius	Yr.Iss.	30.00	40.00
86-01-003	Reindeer	O. Alberius	Yr.Iss.	30.00	35.00
87-01-004	Snowman	O. Alberius	Yr.Iss.	30.00	35.00
88-01-005	Sleigh	O. Alberius	Yr.Iss.	30.00	35.00
89-01-006	Christmas Tree "1989"	O. Alberius	Yr.Iss.	35.00	35.00
90-01-007	Holly Leaves And Berries	O. Alberius	Yr.Iss.	35.00	35.00
91-01-008	Stocking	O. Alberius	Yr.Iss.	40.00	40.00
92-01-009	Star	O. Alberius	Yr.Iss.	35.00	35.00
93-01-010	Bell	O. Alberius	Open	35.00	35.00
Reco International		**The Reco Angel Collection Hang-Ups**			
87-01-001	Innocence	J. McClelland	Open	7.50	7.50

Company / Number	Name	Series / Artist	Edition Limit	Issue Price	Quote
87-01-002	Harmony	J. McClelland	Open	7.50	7.50
87-01-003	Love	J. McClelland	Open	7.50	7.50
87-01-004	Gloria	J. McClelland	Open	7.50	7.50
87-01-005	Devotion	J. McClelland	Open	7.50	7.50
87-01-006	Joy	J. McClelland	Open	7.50	7.50
87-01-007	Adoration	J. McClelland	Open	10.00	10.00
87-01-008	Peace	J. McClelland	Open	10.00	10.00
87-01-009	Serenity	J. McClelland	Open	10.00	10.00
87-01-010	Hope	J. McClelland	Open	10.00	10.00
Reco International		**The Reco Ornament Collection**			
88-02-001	Billy	S. Kuck	Yr.Iss.	15.00	15.00
88-02-002	Lisa	S. Kuck	Yr.Iss.	15.00	15.00
89-02-003	Heather	S. Kuck	Yr.Iss.	15.00	15.00
89-02-004	Timothy	S. Kuck	Yr.Iss.	15.00	15.00
90-02-005	Amy	S. Kuck	Yr.Iss.	15.00	15.00
90-02-006	Johnny	S. Kuck	Yr.Iss.	15.00	15.00
90-02-007	Peace On Earth	S. Kuck	17,500	17.50	17.50
Reed & Barton		**Christmas Cross**			
71-01-001	Sterling Silver-1971	Reed & Barton	Yr.Iss.	10.00	300.00
71-01-002	24Kt. Gold over Sterling-V1971	Reed & Barton	Yr.Iss.	17.50	225.00
72-01-003	Sterling Silver-1972	Reed & Barton	Yr.Iss.	10.00	125.00
72-01-004	24Kt. Gold over Sterling-V1972	Reed & Barton	Yr.Iss.	17.50	65-105.
73-01-005	Sterling Silver-1973	Reed & Barton	Yr.Iss.	10.00	60-75.00
73-01-006	24Kt. Gold over Sterling-V1973	Reed & Barton	Yr.Iss.	17.50	55-65.00
74-01-007	Sterling Silver-1974	Reed & Barton	Yr.Iss.	12.95	35-60.00
74-01-008	24Kt. Gold over Sterling-V1974	Reed & Barton	Yr.Iss.	20.00	50-60.00
75-01-009	Sterling Silver-1975	Reed & Barton	Yr.Iss.	12.95	35-55.00
75-01-010	24Kt. Gold over Sterling-V1975	Reed & Barton	Yr.Iss.	20.00	45-50.00
76-01-011	Sterling Silver-1976	Reed & Barton	Yr.Iss.	13.95	55.00
76-01-012	24Kt. Gold over Sterling-V1976	Reed & Barton	Yr.Iss.	19.95	45-50.00
77-01-013	Sterling Silver-1977	Reed & Barton	Yr.Iss.	15.00	35-55.00
77-01-014	24Kt. Gold over Sterling-V1977	Reed & Barton	Yr.Iss.	18.50	45-50.00
78-01-015	Sterling Silver-1978	Reed & Barton	Yr.Iss.	16.00	60.00
78-01-016	24Kt. Gold over Sterling-V1978	Reed & Barton	Yr.Iss.	20.00	45-55.00
79-01-017	Sterling Silver-1979	Reed & Barton	Yr.Iss.	20.00	60.00
79-01-018	24Kt. Gold over Sterling-V1979	Reed & Barton	Yr.Iss.	24.00	32-57.00
80-01-019	Sterling Silver-1980	Reed & Barton	Yr.Iss.	35.00	60.00
80-01-020	24Kt. Gold over Sterling-V1980	Reed & Barton	Yr.Iss.	40.00	45-50.00
81-01-021	Sterling Silver-1981	Reed & Barton	Yr.Iss.	35.00	45.00
81-01-022	24Kt. Gold over Sterling-V1981	Reed & Barton	Yr.Iss.	40.00	45.00
82-01-023	Sterling Silver-1982	Reed & Barton	Yr.Iss.	35.00	53.00
82-01-024	24Kt. Gold over Sterling-V1982	Reed & Barton	Yr.Iss.	40.00	45.00
83-01-025	Sterling Silver-1983	Reed & Barton	Yr.Iss.	35.00	50.00
83-01-026	24Kt. Gold over Sterling-V1983	Reed & Barton	Yr.Iss.	40.00	40-45.00
84-01-027	Sterling Silver-1984	Reed & Barton	Yr.Iss.	35.00	45.00
84-01-028	24Kt. Gold over Sterling-V1984	Reed & Barton	Yr.Iss.	45.00	45.00
85-01-029	Sterling Silver-1985	Reed & Barton	Yr.Iss.	35.00	40.00
85-01-030	24Kt. Gold over Sterling-V1985	Reed & Barton	Yr.Iss.	40.00	40.00
86-01-031	Sterling Silver-1986	Reed & Barton	Yr.Iss.	38.50	38.50
86-01-032	24Kt. Gold over Sterling-V1986	Reed & Barton	Yr.Iss.	40.00	40.00
87-01-033	Sterling Silver-1987	Reed & Barton	Yr.Iss.	35.00	35.00
87-01-034	24Kt. Gold over Sterling-V1987	Reed & Barton	Yr.Iss.	40.00	40.00
88-01-035	Sterling Silver-1988	Reed & Barton	Yr.Iss.	35.00	35.00
88-01-036	24Kt. Gold over Sterling-V1988	Reed & Barton	Yr.Iss.	40.00	40.00
89-01-037	Sterling Silver-1989	Reed & Barton	Yr.Iss.	35.00	35.00
89-01-038	24Kt. Gold over Sterling-V1989	Reed & Barton	Yr.Iss.	40.00	40.00
90-01-039	Sterling Silver-1990	Reed & Barton	Yr.Iss.	40.00	40.00
90-01-040	24Kt. Gold over Sterling-1990	Reed & Barton	Yr.Iss.	45.00	45.00
91-01-041	Sterling Silver-1991	Reed & Barton	Yr.Iss.	40.00	40.00
91-01-042	24Kt Gold over Sterling-1991	Reed & Barton	Yr.Iss.	45.00	45.00
92-01-043	Sterling Silver-1992	Reed & Barton	Yr.Iss.	40.00	40.00
92-01-044	24Kt Gold over Sterling-1992	Reed & Barton	Yr.Iss.	45.00	45.00
Reed & Barton		**Holly Ball**			
76-02-001	1976 Silver plated	Reed & Barton	Yr.Iss.	13.95	50.00
77-02-002	1977 Silver plated	Reed & Barton	Yr.Iss.	15.00	35.00
78-02-003	1978 Silver plated	Reed & Barton	Yr.Iss.	15.00	35.00
79-02-004	1979 Silver plated	Reed & Barton	Yr.Iss.	15.00	35.00
Reed & Barton		**Holly Bell**			
80-03-001	1980 Bell	Reed & Barton	Yr.Iss.	22.50	40.00
80-03-002	Bell, gold plate, V1980	Reed & Barton	Yr.Iss.	25.00	45.00
81-03-003	1981 Bell	Reed & Barton	Yr.Iss.	22.50	35.00
81-03-004	Bell, gold plate, V1981	Reed & Barton	Yr.Iss.	27.50	35.00
82-03-005	1982 Bell	Reed & Barton	Yr.Iss.	22.50	35.00
82-03-006	Bell, gold plate, V1982	Reed & Barton	Yr.Iss.	27.50	35.00
83-03-007	1983 Bell	Reed & Barton	Yr.Iss.	23.50	40.00
83-03-008	Bell, gold plate, V1983	Reed & Barton	Yr.Iss.	30.00	35.00
84-03-009	1984 Bell	Reed & Barton	Yr.Iss.	25.00	30.00
84-03-010	Bell, gold plate, V1984	Reed & Barton	Yr.Iss.	28.50	35.00
85-03-011	1985 Bell	Reed & Barton	Yr.Iss.	25.00	35.00
85-03-012	Bell, gold plate, V1985	Reed & Barton	Yr.Iss.	28.50	28.50
86-03-013	1986 Bell	Reed & Barton	Yr.Iss.	25.00	35.00
86-03-014	Bell, gold plate, V1986	Reed & Barton	Yr.Iss.	28.50	32.50
87-03-015	1987 Bell	Reed & Barton	Yr.Iss.	27.50	30.00
87-03-016	Bell, gold plate, V1987	Reed & Barton	Yr.Iss.	30.00	30.00
88-03-017	1988 Bell	Reed & Barton	Yr.Iss.	27.50	30.00
88-03-018	Bell, gold plate, V1988	Reed & Barton	Yr.Iss.	30.00	30.00
89-03-019	1989 Bell	Reed & Barton	Yr.Iss.	27.50	27.50
89-03-020	Bell, gold plate, V1989	Reed & Barton	Yr.Iss.	30.00	30.00
90-03-021	Bell, gold plate, V1990	Reed & Barton	Yr.Iss.	30.00	30.00
90-03-022	1990 Bell	Reed & Barton	Yr.Iss.	27.50	27.50
91-03-023	Bell, gold plate, V1991	Reed & Barton	Yr.Iss.	30.00	30.00
91-03-024	1991 Bell	Reed & Barton	Yr.Iss.	27.50	27.50
92-03-025	Bell, gold plate, V1992	Reed & Barton	Yr.Iss.	30.00	30.00
92-03-026	Bell, silver plate, 1992	Reed & Barton	Yr.Iss.	27.50	27.50
Reed & Barton		**12 Days of Christmas**			
83-04-001	Partridge in a Pear Tree	Reed & Barton	Yr.Iss.	16.50	20.00
83-04-002	Turtle Doves	Reed & Barton	Yr.Iss.	16.50	20.00
84-04-003	French Hens	Reed & Barton	Yr.Iss.	18.50	20.00
84-04-004	Calling Birds	Reed & Barton	Yr.Iss.	18.50	20.00
85-04-005	Gold Rings	Reed & Barton	Yr.Iss.	20.00	20.00
85-04-006	Geese A'Laying	Reed & Barton	Yr.Iss.	20.00	20.00
86-04-007	Swans A'Swimming	Reed & Barton	Yr.Iss.	20.00	20.00
86-04-008	Maids A'Milking	Reed & Barton	Yr.Iss.	20.00	20.00
87-04-009	Ladies Dancing	Reed & Barton	Yr.Iss.	20.00	20.00
87-04-010	Lords A'Leaping	Reed & Barton	Yr.Iss.	20.00	20.00
88-04-011	Pipers Piping	Reed & Barton	Yr.Iss.	20.00	20.00
88-04-012	Drummers Drumming	Reed & Barton	Yr.Iss.	20.00	20.00

Number	Name	Artist	Edition Limit	Issue Price	Quote
Reed & Barton		**12 Days of Christmas Sterling and Lead Crystal**			
88-05-001	Partridge in a Pear Tree	Reed & Barton	Yr.Iss.	25.00	27.50
89-05-002	Two Turtle Doves	Reed & Barton	Yr.Iss.	25.00	27.50
90-05-003	French Hens	Reed & Barton	Yr.Iss.	27.50	27.50
91-05-004	Colly birds	Reed & Barton	Yr.Iss.	27.50	27.50
92-05-005	Five Golden Rings	Reed & Barton	Yr.Iss.	27.50	27.50
Reed & Barton		**Carousel Horse**			
88-06-001	Silverplate-1988	Reed & Barton	Yr.Iss.	13.50	13.50
88-06-002	Gold-covered-1988	Reed & Barton	Yr.Iss.	15.00	15.00
89-06-003	Silverplate-1989	Reed & Barton	Yr.Iss.	13.50	13.50
89-06-004	Gold-covered-1989	Reed & Barton	Yr.Iss.	15.00	15.00
90-06-005	Silverplate-1990	Reed & Barton	Yr.Iss.	13.50	13.50
90-06-006	Gold-covered-1990	Reed & Barton	Yr.Iss.	15.00	15.00
91-06-007	Silverplate-1991	Reed & Barton	Yr.Iss.	13.50	13.50
91-06-008	Gold-covered-1991	Reed & Barton	Yr.Iss.	15.00	15.00
92-06-009	Silverplate-1992	Reed & Barton	Yr.Iss.	13.50	13.50
92-06-010	Gold-covered-1992	Reed & Barton	Yr.Iss.	15.00	15.00
Norman Rockwell Gallery		**Ornaments**			
91-01-001	Rockwell's Legends of Santa(Set of 4)	Rockwell-Inspired	N/A	49.95	49.95
92-01-002	Rockwell's Classic Santas(Set of 3)	Rockwell-Inspired	N/A	49.95	49.95
Royal Orleans		**Ornaments**			
84-01-001	Jimmy	J. Hagara	2-Yr.	10.00	225.00
84-01-002	Jenny	J. Hagara	2-Yr.	10.00	125.00
84-01-003	Lisa	J. Hagara	2-Yr.	10.00	35-60.00
84-01-004	Anne	J. Hagara	2-Yr.	10.00	60-125.00
Roman, Inc.		**The Discovery of America**			
91-01-001	Kitstopher Kolumbus	I. Spencer	1,992	15.00	15.00
91-01-002	Queen Kitsabella	I. Spencer	1,992	15.00	15.00
Roman, Inc.		**Fontanini Annual Christmas Ornaments**			
91-02-001	1991 Annual (Girl)	E. Simonetti	Yr.Iss.	8.50	8.50
91-02-002	1991 Annual (Boy)	E. Simonetti	Yr.Iss.	8.50	8.50
92-02-003	1992 Annual (Girl)	E. Simonetti	Yr.Iss.	8.50	8.50
92-02-004	1992 Annual (Boy)	E. Simonetti	Yr.Iss.	8.50	8.50
Roman, Inc.		**Catnippers**			
88-03-001	Christmas Mourning	I. Spencer	Open	15.00	15.00
88-03-002	Ring A Ding-Ding	I. Spencer	Open	15.00	15.00
88-03-003	Puss in Berries	I. Spencer	Open	15.00	15.00
89-03-004	Bow Brummel	I. Spencer	Open	15.00	15.00
89-03-005	Happy Holidaze	I. Spencer	Open	15.00	15.00
89-03-006	Sandy Claws	I. Spencer	Open	15.00	15.00
90-03-007	Sock It to Me Santa	I. Spencer	Open	15.00	15.00
90-03-008	Stuck on Christmas	I. Spencer	Open	15.00	15.00
90-03-009	Felix Navidad	I. Spencer	Open	15.00	15.00
91-03-010	Meowy Christmas	I. Spencer	Open	15.00	15.00
91-03-011	Christmas Knight	I. Spencer	Open	15.00	15.00
91-03-012	Faux Paw	I. Spencer	Open	15.00	15.00
91-03-013	Snow Biz	I. Spencer	Open	15.00	15.00
91-03-014	Holly Days Are Happy Days	I. Spencer	Open	15.00	15.00
91-03-015	Pawtridge in a Purr Tree	I. Spencer	Open	15.00	15.00
Sarah's Attic, Inc.		**Santas Of The Month Ornaments**			
88-01-001	Jan. Mini Santa	Sarah's Attic	Closed	14.00	21.00
88-01-002	Feb. Mini Santa	Sarah's Attic	Closed	14.00	21.00
88-01-003	March Mini Santa	Sarah's Attic	Closed	14.00	21.00
88-01-004	April Mini Santa	Sarah's Attic	Closed	14.00	21.00
88-01-005	May Mini Santa	Sarah's Attic	Closed	14.00	21.00
88-01-006	June Mini Santa	Sarah's Attic	Closed	14.00	21.00
88-01-007	July Mini Santa	Sarah's Attic	Closed	14.00	21.00
88-01-008	Aug. Mini Santa	Sarah's Attic	Closed	14.00	21.00
88-01-009	Sept. Mini Santa	Sarah's Attic	Closed	14.00	21.00
88-01-010	Oct. Mini Santa	Sarah's Attic	Closed	14.00	21.00
88-01-011	Nov. Mini Santa	Sarah's Attic	Closed	14.00	21.00
88-01-012	Dec.Mini Santa	Sarah's Attic	Closed	14.00	21.00
Schmid		**Lowell Davis Country Christmas**			
83-01-001	Mailbox	L. Davis	Yr.Iss.	17.50	52-75.00
84-01-002	Cat in Boot	L. Davis	Yr.Iss.	17.50	60-65.00
85-01-003	Pig in Trough	L. Davis	Yr.Iss.	17.50	50-60.00
86-01-004	Church	L. Davis	Yr.Iss.	17.50	35-55.00
87-01-005	Blossom	L. Davis	Yr.Iss.	19.50	25-60.00
88-01-006	Wisteria	L. Davis	Yr.Iss.	19.50	25-50.00
89-01-007	Wren	L. Davis	Yr.Iss.	19.50	30-47.50
90-01-008	Wintering Deer	L. Davis	Yr.Iss.	19.50	30.00
91-01-009	Church at Red Oak II	L. Davis	Yr.Iss.	25.00	25.00
92-01-010	Born On A Starry Night	L. Davis	Yr.Iss.	25.00	25.00
Schmid		**Lowell Davis Glass Ornaments**			
86-02-001	Christmas at Red Oak	L. Davis	Yr.Iss.	5.00	7-10.00
87-02-002	Blossom's Gift	L. Davis	Yr.Iss.	5.50	12.00
88-02-003	Hope Mom Likes It	L. Davis	Yr.Iss.	5.00	10.00
89-02-004	Peter and the Wren	L. Davis	Yr.Iss.	6.50	8.00
90-02-005	Wintering Deer	L. Davis	Yr.Iss.	6.50	6.50
91-02-006	Christmas at Red Oak II	L. Davis	Yr.Iss.	7.50	7.50
92-02-007	Born On A Starry Night Ball	L. Davis	Yr.Iss.	7.50	7.50
Schmid		**Kitty Cucumber Annual**			
89-03-001	Ring Around the Rosie	M. Lillemoe	Yr.Iss.	25.00	25.00
90-03-002	Swan Lake	M. Lillemoe	Yr.Iss.	12.00	12.00
91-03-003	Tea Party	M. Lillemoe	Yr.Iss.	12.00	24.00
92-03-004	Dance 'Round the Maypole	M. Lillemoe	Yr.Iss.	10.00	10.00
Schmid		**Disney Annual**			
85-04-001	Snow Biz	Disney Studios	Yr.Iss.	8.50	20.00
86-04-002	Tree for Two	Disney Studios	Yr.Iss.	8.50	15.00
87-04-003	Merry Mouse Medley	Disney Studios	Yr.Iss.	8.50	10.00
88-04-004	Warm Winter Ride	Disney Studios	Yr.Iss.	11.00	45.00
89-04-005	Merry Mickey Claus	Disney Studios	Yr.Iss.	11.00	11.00
90-04-006	Holly Jolly Christmas	Disney Studios	Yr.Iss.	13.50	30.00
91-04-007	Mickey & Minnie's Rockin' Christmas	Disney Studios	Yr.Iss.	13.50	13.50
Schmid		**Friends of Mine**			
89-05-001	Sun Worshippers	L. Davis	Yr.Iss.	32.50	32.50
90-05-002	Sunday Afternoon Treat	L. Davis	Yr.Iss.	37.50	37.50
91-05-003	Warm Milk	L. Davis	Yr.Iss.	37.50	37.50
92-05-004	Cat and Jenny Wren	L. Davis	Yr.Iss.	35.00	35.00
Sculpture Workshop Designs		**Annual**			
85-01-001	The Return of the Christmas Comet	F. Kreitchet	7,500	39.00	100.00
86-01-002	Liberty/Peace	F. Kreitchet	7,500	49.00	150.00
87-01-003	Christmas at Home	F. Kreitchet	2,500	57.00	90.00
88-01-004	Christmas Doves	F. Kreitchet	2,500	57.00	80.00
89-01-005	Santa's Reindeer	F. Kreitchet	2,500	60.00	75.00
90-01-006	Joyful Angels	F. Kreitchet	2,500	75.00	75.00
91-01-007	Angel & Shepherds	F. Krietchet	2,500	75.00	75.00
Sculpture Workshop Designs		**Annual-Special Commemorative**			
87-02-001	The Bicentennial of the U.S. Constitution	F. Kreitchet	200	95.00	250.00
89-02-002	The Presidential Signatures	F. Kreitchet	200	95.00	125.00
91-02-003	The U.S. Bill of Rights	F. Kreitchet	200	150.00	150.000
Sculpture Workshop Designs		**Santa Series**			
92-03-001	Forever Santa	F. Kreitchet	2,500	68.00	68.00
Swarovski America Ltd.		**Holiday Ornaments**			
86-01-001	Small Angel/Noel	Unknown	Yr.Iss.	18.00	18.00
86-01-002	Small Bell/Merry Christmas	Unknown	Yr.Iss.	18.00	18.00
86-01-003	Small Dove/Peace	Unknown	Yr.Iss.	18.00	18.00
86-01-004	Small Holly/Merry Christmas	Unknown	Yr.Iss.	18.00	18.00
86-01-005	Small Snowflake	Unknown	Yr.Iss.	18.00	18.00
86-01-006	Medium Snowflake	Unknown	Yr.Iss.	22.50	22.50
86-01-007	Medium Bell/Merry Christmas	Unknown	Yr.Iss.	22.50	22.50
86-01-008	Medium Angel/Joyeux Noel	Unknown	Yr.Iss.	22.50	22.50
86-01-009	Large Angel/Noel	Unknown	Yr.Iss.	35.00	35.00
86-01-010	Large Partridge/Merry Christmas	Unknown	Yr.Iss.	35.00	35.00
87-01-011	1987 Holiday Etching-Candle	Unknown	Yr.Iss.	20.00	35.00
88-01-012	1988 Holiday Etching-Wreath	Unknown	Yr.Iss.	25.00	25.00
89-01-013	1989 Holiday Etching-Dove	Unknown	Yr.Iss.	35.00	35.00
90-01-014	1990 Holiday Etching	Unknown	Yr.Iss.	25.00	99.00
91-01-015	1991 Holiday Ornament	Unknown	Yr.Iss.	35.00	35.00
91-01-016	1992 Holiday Ornament	Unknown	Yr.Iss.	37.50	37.50
Towle Silversmiths		**Sterling Twelve Days of Christmas Medallions**			
71-01-001	Partridge in Pear Tree	Towle	15,000	20.00	700.00
72-01-001	Two Turtle Doves	Towle	45,000	20.00	250.00
73-01-003	Three French Hens	Towle	75,000	20.00	150.00
74-01-004	Four Mockingbirds	Towle	60,000	30.00	100.00
75-01-005	Five Golden Rings	Towle	60,000	30.00	65.00
76-01-006	Six Geese-a-Laying	Towle	60,000	30.00	90.00
77-01-007	Seven Swans-a-Swimming	Towle	60,000	35.00	50.00
78-01-008	Eight Maids-a-Milking	Towle	60,000	37.00	50.00
79-01-009	Nine Ladies Dancing	Towle	40,000	Unkn.	50.00
80-01-010	Ten Lords-a-Leaping	Towle	25,000	76.00	50.00
81-01-011	Eleven Pipers Piping	Towle	25,000	50.00	50.00
82-01-012	Twelve Drummers Drumming	Towle	20,000	35.00	40.00
Towle Silversmiths		**Songs of Christmas Medallions**			
78-02-001	Silent Night Medallion	Towle	25,000	35.00	60.00
79-02-002	Deck The Halls	Towle	5,000	Unkn.	50.00
80-02-003	Jingle Bells	Towle	5,000	52.50	60.00
81-02-004	Hark the Hearld Angels Sing	Towle	5,000	52.50	60.00
82-02-005	O Christmas Tree	Towle	2,000	35.00	50.00
83-02-006	Silver Bells	Towle	2,500	40.00	60.00
84-02-007	Let It Snow	Towle	6,500	30.00	50.00
85-02-008	Chestnuts Roasting on Open Fire	Towle	3,000	35.00	50.00
86-02-009	It Came Upon a Midnight Clear	Towle	3,500	35.00	45.00
87-02-010	White Christmas	Towle	3,500	35.00	45.00
Towle Silversmiths		**Sterling Floral Medallions**			
83-03-001	Christmas Rose	Towle	20,000	40.00	50.00
84-03-002	Hawthorne/Glastonbury Thorn	Towle	20,000	40.00	50.00
85-03-003	Poinsettia	Towle	14,000	35.00	50.00
86-03-004	Laurel Bay	Towle	12,000	35.00	40.00
87-03-005	Mistletoe	Towle	10,000	35.00	45.00
88-03-006	Holly	Towle	10,000	40.00	40.00
89-03-007	Ivy	Towle	10,000	35.00	45.00
90-03-008	Christmas Cactus	Towle	10,000	40.00	40.00
91-03-009	Chrysanthemum	Towle	N/A	40.00	40.00
92-03-010	Star of Bethlehem	Towle	N/A	40.00	40.00
Towle Silversmiths		**Sterling Nativity Medallion**			
88-04-001	Angel Gabriel	Towle	7,500	40.00	50-60.00
89-04-002	The Journey	Towle	7,500	40.00	55.00
90-04-003	No Room at the Inn	Towle	7,500	40.00	40.00
91-04-004	Tidings of Joy	Towle	N/A	40.00	40.00
92-04-005	Star of Bethlehem	Towle	N/A	40.00	40.00
Towle Silversmiths		**Twelve Days of Christmas**			
79-05-001	Silverplate Etched	Towle	1,000	3.60	10.00
79-05-002	Silverplate Etched	Towle	1,000	3.60	10.00
79-05-003	Silverplate Etched	Towle	1,000	3.60	10.00
79-05-004	Silverplate Etched	Towle	1,000	3.60	10.00
79-05-005	Silverplate Etched	Towle	1,000	3.60	10.00
79-05-006	Silverplate Etched	Towle	1,000	3.60	10.00
79-05-007	Silverplate Etched	Towle	1,000	3.60	10.00
79-05-008	Silverplate Etched	Towle	1,000	3.60	10.00
79-05-009	Silverplate Etched	Towle	1,000	3.60	10.00
79-05-010	Silverplate Etched	Towle	1,000	3.60	10.00
79-05-011	Silverplate Etched	Towle	1,000	3.60	10.00
79-05-012	Silverplate Etched	Towle	1,000	3.60	10.00
Towle Silversmiths		**Twelve Days of Christmas**			
88-06-001	Goldplate Etched	Towle	2,500	7.00	7.00
88-06-002	Goldplate Etched	Towle	2,500	7.00	7.00
88-06-003	Goldplate Etched	Towle	2,500	7.00	7.00
88-06-004	Goldplate Etched	Towle	2,500	7.00	7.00
88-06-005	Goldplate Etched	Towle	2,500	7.00	7.00
88-06-006	Goldplate Etched	Towle	2,500	7.00	7.00
88-06-007	Goldplate Etched	Towle	2,500	7.00	7.00
88-06-008	Goldplate Etched	Towle	2,500	7.00	7.00
88-06-009	Goldplate Etched	Towle	2,500	7.00	7.00
88-06-010	Goldplate Etched	Towle	2,500	7.00	7.00
88-06-011	Goldplate Etched	Towle	2,500	7.00	7.00
88-06-012	Goldplate Etched	Towle	2,500	7.00	7.00
Towle Silversmiths		**Sterling Christmas Ornaments**			
89-07-001	Faceted Ball	Towle	Open	38.00	38.00
89-07-002	Plain Ball	Towle	Open	38.00	38.00
89-07-003	Fluted Ball	Towle	Open	38.00	38.00
89-07-004	Pomander Ball	Towle	Open	33.00	33.00
Towle Silversmiths		**Remembrance Collection**			
90-08-001	Old Master Snowflake-1990	Towle	N/A	45.00	45.00

CHRISTMAS ORNAMENTS

Company / Number	Name	Series / Artist	Edition Limit	Issue Price	Quote
91-08-002	Old Master Snowflake-1991	Towle	N/A	45.00	45.00
92-08-003	Old Master Snowflake-1992	Towle	N/A	45.00	45.00
Towle Silversmiths		**Twelve Days of Christmas**			
91-09-001	Partridge in Wreath	Towle	N/A	45.00	45.00
92-09-002	Two Turtledoves in Wreath	Towle	N/A	45.00	45.00
Towle Silversmiths		**Christmas Angel**			
91-10-001	1991 Angel	Towle	N/A	45.00	45.00
92-10-002	1992 Angel	Towle	N/A	45.00	45.00
United Design Corporation		**Angels Collection-Tree Ornaments**			
90-01-001	Crystal Angel IBO-401	P.J. Jonas	Open	20.00	20.00
90-01-002	Rose of Sharon IBO-402	P.J. Jonas	Open	20.00	20.00
90-01-003	Star Glory IBO-403	P.J. Jonas	Open	15.00	15.00
90-01-004	Victorian Angel IBO-404	P.J. Jonas	Open	15.00	15.00
90-01-005	Crystal Angel, Ivory IBO-405	P.J. Jonas	Open	20.00	20.00
90-01-006	Rose of Sharon, Ivory IBO-406	P.J. Jonas	Open	20.00	20.00
90-01-007	Star Glory, Ivory IBO-407	P.J. Jonas	Open	15.00	15.00
90-01-008	Victorian Angel, Ivory IBO-408	P.J. Jonas	Open	15.00	15.00
91-01-009	Victorian Cupid, Ivory IBO-409	P.J. Jonas	Open	15.00	15.00
91-01-010	Rosetti Angel, Ivory IBO-410	P.J. Jonas	Open	20.00	20.00
91-01-011	Angel Waif, Ivory IBO-411	P.J. Jonas	Open	15.00	15.00
91-01-012	Peace Descending, Ivory IBO-412	P.J. Jonas	Open	20.00	20.00
91-01-013	Girl Cupid w/Rose, Ivory IBO-413	S. Bradford	Open	15.00	15.00
91-01-014	Fra Angelico Drummer, Blue IBO-414	S. Bradford	Open	20.00	20.00
91-01-015	Fra Angelico Drummer, Ivory IBO-420	S. Bradford	Open	20.00	20.00
91-01-016	Victorian Cupid IBO-415	S. Bradford	Open	15.00	15.00
91-01-017	Rosetti Angel IBO-416	P.J. Jonas	Open	20.00	20.00
91-01-018	Angel Waif IBO-417	P.J. Jonas	Open	15.00	15.00
91-01-019	Peace Descending IBO-418	P.J. Jonas	Open	20.00	20.00
92-01-020	Angel and Tambourine IBO-422	S. Bradford	Open	20.00	20.00
92-01-021	Angel and Tambourine, Ivory IBO-425	S. Bradford	Open	20.00	20.00
92-01-022	Mary and Dove IBO-424	S. Bradford	Open	20.00	20.00
92-01-023	St. Francis and Critters IBO-423	S. Bradford	Open	20.00	20.00
Wallace Silversmiths		**Annual Silverplated Bells**			
71-01-001	1st Edition Sleigh Bell	Wallace	Closed	12.95	1050.00
72-01-002	2nd Edition Sleigh Bell	Wallace	Closed	12.95	400.00
73-01-003	3rd Edition Sleigh Bell	Wallace	Closed	12.95	400.00
74-01-004	4th Edition Sleigh Bell	Wallace	Closed	13.95	300.00
75-01-005	5th Edition Sleigh Bell	Wallace	Closed	13.95	250.00
76-01-006	6th Edition Sleigh Bell	Wallace	Closed	13.95	300.00
77-01-007	7th Edition Sleigh Bell	Wallace	Closed	14.95	150.00
78-01-008	8th Edition Sleigh Bell	Wallace	Closed	14.95	85.00
79-01-009	9th Edition Sleigh Bell	Wallace	Closed	15.95	100.00
80-01-010	10th Edition Sleigh Bell	Wallace	Closed	18.95	50.00
81-01-011	11th Edition Sleigh Bell	Wallace	Closed	18.95	60.00
82-01-012	12th Edition Sleigh Bell	Wallace	Closed	19.95	80.00
83-01-013	13th Edition Sleigh Bell	Wallace	Closed	19.95	80.00
84-01-014	14th Edition Sleigh Bell	Wallace	Closed	21.95	75.00
85-01-015	15th Edition Sleigh Bell	Wallace	Closed	21.95	75.00
86-01-016	16th Edition Sleigh Bell	Wallace	Closed	21.95	35.00
87-01-017	17th Edition Sleigh Bell	Wallace	Closed	21.99	25.00
88-01-018	18th Edition Sleigh Bell	Wallace	Closed	21.99	25.00
89-01-019	19th Edition Sleigh Bell	Wallace	Closed	24.99	25.00
90-01-020	20th Edition Sleigh Bell	Wallace	Yr.Iss.	25.00	25.00
90-01-021	Special Edition Sleigh Bell, gold	Wallace	Yr.Iss.	35.00	35.00
92-01-022	22th Edition Sleigh Bell	Wallace	Yr.Iss.	25.00	25.00
Wallace Silversmiths		**24K Goldplate Sculptures**			
88-02-001	Dove	Wallace	Open	15.99	15.99
88-02-002	Candy Cane	Wallace	Open	15.99	15.99
88-02-003	Christmas Tree	Wallace	Open	15.99	15.99
88-02-004	Angel	Wallace	Open	15.99	15.99
88-02-005	Nativity Scene	Wallace	Open	15.99	15.99
88-02-006	Snowflake	Wallace	Open	15.99	15.99
Wallace Silversmiths		**Christmas Cookie Ornaments**			
88-03-001	Angel	Wallace	Open	8.99	10.00
88-03-002	Dragon	Wallace	Open	8.99	10.00
88-03-003	Goose	Wallace	Open	8.99	10.00
88-03-004	Teddy Bear	Wallace	Open	8.99	10.00
88-03-005	Elephant	Wallace	Open	8.99	10.00
88-03-006	Christmas Village	Wallace	Open	8.99	10.00
88-03-007	The Night Before	Wallace	Open	8.99	10.00
88-03-008	Polar Bear	Wallace	Open	8.99	10.00
88-03-009	Baby Bear	Wallace	Open	8.99	10.00
85-03-010	Clown	Wallace	Closed	6.95	10.00
85-03-011	Unicorn	Wallace	Closed	6.95	10.00
85-03-012	Teddy Bear	Wallace	Open	6.95	10.00
84-03-013	Horn	Wallace	Closed	6.95	10.00
84-03-014	Puppy in Boot	Wallace	Closed	6.95	10.00
83-03-015	Rocking Horse	Wallace	Closed	5.95	10.00
83-03-016	Mrs. Claus	Wallace	Closed	5.95	10.00
83-03-017	Toy Soldier	Wallace	Closed	5.95	10.00
83-03-018	Jack-In-The-Box	Wallace	Closed	5.95	10.00
83-03-019	Gingerbread House	Wallace	Closed	5.95	10.00
80-03-020	Santa	Wallace	Closed	5.95	10.00
86-03-021	Panda	Wallace	Closed	5.95	10.00
86-03-022	Santa Head	Wallace	Closed	6.95	10.00
86-03-023	Penguin	Wallace	Closed	6.95	10.00
86-03-024	Girl Honey Bear	Wallace	Closed	6.95	10.00
86-03-025	Dressed Kitten	Wallace	Closed	6.95	15.00
86-03-026	Tugboat	Wallace	Closed	6.95	10.00
87-03-027	Giraffe	Wallace	Closed	7.95	10.00
87-03-028	Angel with Heart	Wallace	Open	7.95	10.00
87-03-029	Polar Bear	Wallace	Open	7.95	10.00
87-03-030	Ski Cabin	Wallace	Closed	7.95	10.00
85-03-031	Boy Skater	Wallace	Closed	10.95	10.00
85-03-032	Hot-Air Balloon	Wallace	Closed	10.95	10.00
87-03-033	Snowbird	Wallace	Closed	7.95	10.00
81-03-034	Drum	Wallace	Closed	5.95	15.00
80-03-035	Tree	Wallace	Closed	5.95	15.00
80-03-036	Snowman	Wallace	Closed	5.95	15.00
81-03-037	Reindeer	Wallace	Closed	5.95	15.00
81-03-038	Bell	Wallace	Closed	5.95	15.00
82-03-039	Mouse	Wallace	Closed	5.95	15.00
82-03-040	Train	Wallace	Closed	5.95	15.00
83-03-041	Boy Caroler	Wallace	Closed	5.95	15.00
84-03-042	Mother and Child	Wallace	Closed	6.95	15.00
84-03-043	Carol Singer	Wallace	Closed	6.95	15.00
86-03-044	Goose	Wallace	Closed	6.95	15.00
80-03-045	Angel	Wallace	Closed	5.95	20.00
82-03-046	Dove	Wallace	Closed	5.95	20.00
83-03-047	Husky	Wallace	Closed	5.95	20.00
86-03-048	Carrousel Horse	Wallace	Closed	6.95	20.00
86-03-049	Dog on Sled	Wallace	Closed	6.95	20.00
86-03-050	New Design Snowman	Wallace	Closed	6.95	20.00
89-03-051	Snowbird	Wallace	Open	9.99	10.00
89-03-052	Santa	Wallace	Open	9.99	10.00
89-03-053	Rocking Horse	Wallace	Open	9.99	10.00
Wallace Silversmiths		**Antique Pewter Ornaments**			
XX-04-001	Toy Soldier	Wallace	Open	9.99	9.99
XX-04-002	Gingerbread House	Wallace	Open	9.99	9.99
XX-04-003	Teddy Bear	Wallace	Open	9.99	9.99
XX-04-004	Rocking Horse	Wallace	Open	9.99	9.99
XX-04-005	Dove	Wallace	Open	9.99	9.99
XX-04-006	Candy Cane	Wallace	Open	9.99	9.99
89-04-007	Wreath	Wallace	Open	9.99	9.99
89-04-008	Angel with Candles	Wallace	Open	9.99	9.99
89-04-009	Teddy Bear	Wallace	Open	9.99	9.99
89-04-010	Cherub with Horn	Wallace	Open	9.99	9.99
89-04-011	Santa	Wallace	Open	9.99	9.99
Wallace Silversmiths		**Candy Canes**			
81-05-001	Peppermint	Wallace	Closed	8.95	225.00
82-05-002	Wintergreen	Wallace	Closed	9.95	60.00
83-05-003	Cinnamon	Wallace	Closed	10.95	50.00
84-05-004	Clove	Wallace	Closed	10.95	50.00
85-05-005	Dove Motif	Wallace	Closed	11.95	50.00
86-05-006	Bell Motif	Wallace	Closed	11.95	80.00
87-05-007	Teddy Bear Motif	Wallace	Closed	12.95	50.00
88-05-008	Christmas Rose	Wallace	Closed	13.99	40.00
89-05-009	Christmas Candle	Wallace	Closed	14.99	35.00
90-05-010	Reindeer	Wallace	Yr.Iss.	16.00	20.00
Wallace Silversmiths		**Grande Baroque 12 Day Series**			
88-06-001	Partridge	Wallace	Closed	39.99	55.00
89-06-002	Two Turtle Doves	Wallace	Yr.Iss.	39.99	50.00
90-06-003	Three French Hens	Wallace	Yr.Iss.	40.00	40.00
Wallace Silversmiths		**Cathedral Ornaments**			
88-07-001	1988-1st Edition	Wallace	Closed	24.99	35.00
89-07-002	1989-2nd Edition	Wallace	Yr.Iss.	24.99	24.99
90-07-003	1990-3rd Edition	Wallace	Yr.Iss.	25.00	25.00
Wallace Silversmiths		**Sterling Memories**			
89-08-001	Church	Wallace	Open	34.99	34.99
89-08-002	Mother & Child	Wallace	Open	34.99	34.99
89-08-003	Drummer Boy	Wallace	Open	34.99	34.99
89-08-004	Sleigh	Wallace	Open	34.99	34.99
89-08-005	Rocking Horse	Wallace	Open	34.99	34.99
89-08-006	Snowflake	Wallace	Open	34.99	34.99
89-08-007	Dove	Wallace	Open	34.99	34.99
89-08-008	Nativity Angel	Wallace	Open	34.99	34.99
89-08-009	Carolers	Wallace	Open	34.99	34.99
89-08-010	Reindeer	Wallace	Open	34.99	34.99
89-08-011	Bear with Blocks	Wallace	Open	34.99	34.99
89-08-012	Snowman	Wallace	Open	34.99	34.99
Wallace Silversmiths		**Sterling Memories - Hand Enameled with Color**			
89-09-001	Elf with Gift	Wallace	Open	34.99	34.99
89-09-002	Santa	Wallace	Open	34.99	34.99
89-09-003	Train	Wallace	Open	34.99	34.99
89-09-004	Kneeling Angel	Wallace	Open	34.99	34.99
89-09-005	Skater	Wallace	Open	34.99	34.99
89-09-006	Single Candle	Wallace	Open	34.99	34.99
89-09-007	Fireplace	Wallace	Open	34.99	34.99
89-09-008	Candy Cane	Wallace	Open	34.99	34.99
89-09-009	Church	Wallace	Open	34.99	34.99
89-09-010	Toy Soldier	Wallace	Open	34.99	34.99
Wallace Silversmiths		**Antique Pewter Bells**			
89-10-001	Reindeer	Wallace	Open	15.99	15.99
89-10-002	Teddy Bear	Wallace	Open	15.99	15.99
89-10-003	Toy Soldier	Wallace	Open	15.99	15.99
90-10-004	Carousel Horse	Wallace	Open	16.00	16.00
90-10-005	Santa Claus	Wallace	Open	16.00	16.00
Wallace Silversmiths		**Cameo Frame Ornaments**			
89-11-001	Christmas Ball	Wallace	Open	14.99	14.99
89-11-002	Snowman	Wallace	Open	14.99	14.99
89-11-003	Wreath	Wallace	Open	14.99	14.99
89-11-004	Dino	Wallace	Open	14.99	14.99
89-11-005	Angel	Wallace	Open	14.99	14.99
89-11-006	Kitten	Wallace	Open	14.99	14.99
89-11-007	Santa	Wallace	Open	14.99	14.99
89-11-008	Soldier	Wallace	Open	14.99	14.99
89-11-009	Elephant	Wallace	Open	14.99	14.99
Waterford Wedgwood U.S.A.		**Waterford Crystal Christmas Ornaments**			
78-01-001	1978 Ornament	Waterford	Annual	25.00	60.00
79-01-002	1979 Ornament	Waterford	Annual	28.00	50.00
80-01-003	1980 Ornament	Waterford	Annual	28.00	44.50
81-01-004	1981 Ornament	Waterford	Annual	28.00	44.50
82-01-005	1982 Ornament	Waterford	Annual	28.00	44.50
83-01-006	1983 Ornament	Waterford	Annual	28.00	39.00
84-01-007	1984 Ornament	Waterford	Annual	28.00	39.00
85-01-008	1985 Ornament	Waterford	Annual	28.00	39.00
86-01-009	1986 Ornament	Waterford	Annual	28.00	31.00
87-01-010	1987 Ornament	Waterford	Annual	29.00	29.00
88-01-011	1988 Ornament	Waterford	Annual	30.00	30.00
89-01-012	1989 Ornament	Waterford	Annual	32.00	32.00
Waterford Wedgwood U.S.A.		**Wedgwood Christmas Ornaments**			
88-02-001	Jasper Christmas Tree Ornament	Wedgwood	Open	20.00	28.00
89-02-002	Jasper Angel Ornament	Wedgwood	Open	25.00	28.00
90-02-003	Jasper Santa Claus Ornament	Wedgwood	Open	28.00	28.00
91-02-004	Jasper Wreath Ornament	Wedgwood	Open	28.00	28.00
92-02-005	Jasper Stocking Ornament	Wedgwood	Open	25.00	25.00

Company / Number	Name	Series / Artist	Edition Limit	Issue Price	Quote
DOLLS					
Kurt S. Adler/Santa's World		**Christmas In Chelsea Collection**			
92-01-001	Amy W2729	J. Mostrom	Open	21.00	21.00
92-01-001	Allison W2729	J. Mostrom	Open	21.00	21.00
Annalee Mobilitee Dolls		**Santas**			
72-01-001	7" Santa With Mushroom	A. Thorndike	540	Unkn.	275.00
82-01-002	7" Santa Wreath Centerpiece	A. Thorndike	1,150	Unkn.	150.00
74-01-003	7" Black Santa	A. Thorndike	1,157	5.50	225.00
81-01-004	7" Santa With Mistletoe	A. Thorndike	Unkn.	10.50	40.00
79-01-005	7" Santa With Mistletoe	A. Thorndike	Unkn.	7.95	50.00
81-01-006	7" Santa With Pot Belly Stove	A. Thorndike	Unkn.	11.95	75.00
73-01-007	18" Mrs.Santa With Cardholder	A. Thorndike	3,900	14.95	150.00
65-01-008	18" Santa	A. Thorndike	Unkn.	9.00	150.00
73-01-009	18" Mrs. Santa	A. Thorndike	3,700	7.00	150.00
65-01-010	12" Santa	A. Thorndike	Unkn.	5.00	125.00
74-01-011	29" Mrs. Santa With Cardholder	A. Thorndike	Unkn.	28.95	200.00
54-01-112	26" Bean Nose Santa	A. Thorndike	Unkn.	19.95	700.00
78-01-013	7" Santa With Deer And Tree	A. Thorndike	5,813	18.50	400.00
75-01-014	18" Mrs. Santa With Plum Pudding	A. Thorndike	N/A	12.00	300.00
87-01-015	18" Workshop Santa	A. Thorndike	980	N/A	600.00
81-01-016	10" Ballooning Santa	A. Thorndike	1,737	39.95	325.00
74-01-017	7" Santa In Ski Bob	A. Thorndike	704	4.95	450.00
72-01-018	29" Santa With Cardholder Sack	A. Thorndike	686	24.95	150.00
82-01-019	5" Santa With Deer	A. Thorndike	3,072	20.00	235.00
72-01-020	18" Mr. Santa With Sack	A. Thorndike	850	N/A	150.00
88-01-021	30" Victorian Mrs. Santa With Tray	A. Thorndike	N/A	119.95	360.00
56-01-022	12" Santa With Bean Nose	A. Thorndike	N/A	20.00	1000.00
65-01-023	7" Mr. & Mrs. Santa	A. Thorndike	N/A	5.95	325.00
59-01-024	7" Santa With Fur Trim Suit	A. Thorndike	N/A	2.95	225.00
71-01-025	7" Mr. & Mrs. Santa With Basket	A. Thorndike	3,403	5.95	150.00
89-01-026	10" Collector Mrs. Santa, proof	A. Thorndike	1	N/A	300.00
80-01-027	7" Santa With Stocking	A. Thorndike	17,665	9.95	75.00
81-01-028	7" X-Country Ski Santa	A. Thorndike	5,180	10.95	100.00
72-01-029	7" Mr. & Mrs. Tuckered	A. Thorndike	1,187	6.50	375.00
87-01-030	7" Victorian Mr. & Mrs. Santa	A. Thorndike	N/A	23.95	200.00
84-01-031	7" Santa on a Moon	A. Thorndike	N/A	N/A	150.00
82-01-032	5" Mrs. Santa With Gift Box	A. Thorndike	7,566	10.95	75.00
71-01-033	18" Mrs. Santa With Cardholder	A. Thorndike	1,563	8.00	200.00
79-01-034	18" Mr. Santa With Cardholder	A. Thorndike	N/A	N/A	75.00
86-01-035	18" Mrs. Victorian Santa	A. Thorndike	2,000	N/A	200.00
87-01-036	18" Mr. Victorian Santa	A. Thorndike	2,150	57.50	200.00
70-01-037	7" Santa With 10" X-mas Mushroom	A. Thorndike	N/A	7.00	125.00
72-01-038	7" Mrs. Santa With Apron And Cap	A. Thorndike	8,867	5.50	50.00
70-01-039	10" Christmas Mushroom With 7" Santa On Top And 7" Deer Hugging Stem	A. Thorndike	N/A	11.00	600.00
87-01-040	10" Collector Santa Trimming Lighted Tree	A. Thorndike	N/A	130.00	250.00
67-01-041	7" Santa With Toy Bag	A. Thorndike	N/A	3.95	275.00
60-01-042	7" Mr. & Mrs. Tuckered	A. Thorndike	N/A	N/A	500.00
91-01-043	10" Summer Santa, proof	A. Thorndike	1	None	1050.00
73-01-044	7" Santa Mailman	A. Thorndike	3,276	5.00	200.00
73-01-045	7" Mr. & Mrs. Santa in Wicker Loveseat	A. Thorndike	3,973	10.95	250.00
77-01-046	7" Mr. & Mrs. Santa W/ Wicker Loveseat	A. Thorndike	4,935	11.95	175.00
66-01-047	29" Mr. Outdoor Santa	A. Thorndike	N/A	17.00	350.00
68-01-048	18" Mrs. Indoor Santa	A. Thorndike	N/A	7.50	250.00
68-01-049	18" Mr. Indoor Santa	A. Thorndike	N/A	7.50	225.00
86-01-050	7" Victorian Santa W/Sleigh & Deer	A. Thorndike	6,820	44.00	200.00
68-01-051	7" Mr. &Mrs. Santa Tuckered	A. Thorndike	N/A	3.00	200.00
65-01-052	26" Mrs. Santa W/Apron	A. Thorndike	N/A	14.95	1000.00
68-01-053	29" Mr. Santa W/Vest & Sack	A. Thorndike	N/A	16.00	500.00
87-01-054	30" Mrs. Victorian Santa	A. Thorndike	425	150.00	350.00
87-01-055	30" Mr. Victorian Santa	A. Thorndike	450	150.00	350.00
79-01-056	7" C.B. Santa	A. Thorndike	2,206	7.95	75.00
79-01-057	29" Motorized Mr. & Mrs. Santa In Rocking Chair	A. Thorndike	136	400.00	1600.00
92-01-058	10" Santa At Workbench, proof	A. Thorndike	1	N/A	750.00
92-01-059	10" Tennis Santa , proof	A. Thorndike	1	N/A	600.00
92-01-060	10" Santa W/Bank, proof	A. Thorndike	1	N/A	925.00
92-01-061	10" Fishing Mr. & Mrs. Santa, proof	A. Thorndike	1	N/A	1100.00
86-01-062	7" Mr. & Mrs. Victorian Santa	A. Thorndike	N/A	19.95	450.00
70-01-063	18" Mr. & Mrs. All Tuckered Out	A. Thorndike	215	16.00	400.00
78-01-064	29" Animated Santa & Deer	A. Thorndike	10	280.00	1300.00
70-01-065	10" Christmas Mushroom w/7" Santa and Deer	A. Thorndike	424	10.90	375.00
69-01-066	7" Mr. & Mrs. Santa on Ski Bob	A. Thorndike	N/A	7.95	350.00
93-01-067	10" Santa w/Toboggan, Proof	A. Thorndike	1	N/A	375.00
93-01-068	10" Mr. & Mrs. Santa Skating, proof	A. Thorndike	1	N/A	700.00
93-01-069	7" Victorian Santa w/ Sleigh, proof	A. Thorndike	1	N/A	500.00
50-01-070	20" Santa w/ Corkscrew Nose	A. Thorndike	N/A	N/A	3300.00
93-01-071	10" Gardening Santa, proof	A. Thorndike	1	N/A	550.00
93-01-072	10" Santa w/ Fireplace, proof	A. Thorndike	1	N/A	500.00
77-01-073	4" Mrs. Santa	A. Thorndike	147	150.00	500.00
77-01-074	4" Mr .Santa	A. Thorndike	185	150.00	300.00
87-01-075	18" Workshop Santa Animated	A. Thorndike	N/A	119.50	240.00
88-01-076	18" Mr. & Mrs. Fireside Santa	A. Thorndike	2,786	68.95	150.00
Annalee Mobilitee Dolls		**Christmas Animals**			
81-02-001	7" Santa Monkey	A. Thorndike	4,606	10.00	200.00
81-02-002	12" Santa Monkey	A. Thorndike	1,800	24.00	250.00
82-02-003	7" Santa Fox	A. Thorndike	3,726	12.95	250.00
82-02-004	18" Santa Fox	A. Thorndike	1,499	29.95	575.00
80-02-005	10" Santa Frog	A. Thorndike	7,631	9.95	125.00
82-02-006	22" Christmas Giraffe With Elf	A. Thorndike	448	44.00	500.00
85-02-007	18" Christmas Panda	A. Thorndike	2,207	43.95	100.00
84-02-008	5" Duck In Santa Hat	A. Thorndike	2,371	12.95	75.00
73-02-009	7" Christmas Panda	A. Thorndike	1,094	8.95	350.00
85-02-010	10" Panda With Toy Bag	A. Thorndike	1,904	20.00	100.00
81-02-011	18" Cat With 7" Mouse And Mistletoe	A. Thorndike	10,999	46.95	140.00
80-02-012	18" Santa Frog	A. Thorndike	2,126	25.00	145.00
Annalee Mobilitee Dolls		**Reindeer**			
85-03-001	10" Reindeer With Bell	A. Thorndike	6,398	13.95	55.00
78-03-002	18" Reindeer	A. Thorndike	Unkn.	18.00	125.00
78-03-003	36" Reindeer With Saddlebags	A. Thorndike	594	58.00	175.00
81-03-004	18" Reindeer With Saddlebags	A. Thorndike	7,121	27.95	75.00
83-03-005	18" Fawn	A. Thorndike	1,444	32.95	225.00
78-03-006	18" Reindeer	A. Thorndike	5,134	9.00	125.00
70-03-007	10" Reindeer With Hat	A. Thorndike	144	5.00	175.00
83-03-008	18" Fawn	A. Thorndike	N/A	33.00	200.00
84-03-009	18" Fawn With Wreath	A. Thorndike	1,444	32.95	225.00
69-03-010	10" Reindeer With Red Nose	A. Thorndike	N/A	4.95	350.00
65-03-011	10" Reindeer	A. Thorndike	N/A	4.95	550.00
71-03-012	36" Reindeer With Two 18" Gnomes	A. Thorndike	624	38.00	700.00
81-03-013	5" Miniature Reindeer	A. Thorndike	9,080	11.50	120.00
72-03-014	18" Reindeer With 12" Gnome	A. Thorndike	1,617	21.00	400.00
71-03-015	10" Red Nosed Reindeer	A. Thorndike	1,588	4.95	225.00
75-03-016	10" Red Nosed Reindeer	A. Thorndike	4,854	N/A	100.00
68-03-017	36" Red Nosed Reindeer	A. Thorndike	N/A	N/A	300.00
78-03-018	10" Red Nosed Reindeer	A. Thorndike	6,698	N/A	160.00
69-03-019	10" Reindeer w/ Red Nose	A. Thorndike	N/A	4.95	250.00
Annalee Mobilitee Dolls		**Mice**			
82-04-001	12" Nightshirt Mouse	A. Thorndike	2,319	25.95	125.00
69-04-002	12" Nightshirt Mouse	A. Thorndike	Unkn.	Unkn.	225.00
79-04-003	12" Santa Mouse	A. Thorndike	Unkn.	Unkn.	125.00
79-04-004	12" Mrs. Santa Mouse	A. Thorndike	7,210	Unkn.	125.00
79-04-005	7" Santa Mouse	A. Thorndike	12,649	7.95	100.00
84-04-006	7" Nightshirt Mouse	A. Thorndike	Unkn.	11.95	150.00
66-04-007	7" Mouse With Candle	A. Thorndike	Unkn.	Unkn.	225.00
80-04-008	7" Mouse With Chimney	A. Thorndike	4,452	Unkn.	75.00
84-04-009	7" Mouse With Wreath	A. Thorndike	Unkn.	12.95	55.00
64-04-010	7" Christmas Mouse	A. Thorndike	Unkn.	3.95	450.00
78-04-011	29" Caroler Mouse	A. Thorndike	658	50.00	750.00
83-04-012	7" Equestrine Mouse	A. Thorndike	Unkn.	12.95	200.00
81-04-013	7" Woodchopper Mouse	A. Thorndike	2,121	11.00	75.00
82-04-014	7" Woodchopper Mouse	A. Thorndike	1,910	11.95	75.00
80-04-015	7" Pilot Mouse	A. Thorndike	2,011	9.95	100.00
71-04-016	7" Chef Mouse	A. Thorndike	Unkn.	Unkn.	75.00
81-04-017	7" Airplane Pilot Mouse	A. Thorndike	1,910	9.95	325.00
71-04-018	7" Mouse With Inner Tube	A. Thorndike	267	4.00	200.00
75-04-019	7" Fisherman Mouse	A. Thorndike	1,343	5.50	200.00
80-04-020	7" Fishing Mouse	A. Thorndike	Unkn.	7.50	150.00
81-04-021	7" Iceskater Mouse	A. Thorndike	1,429	9.95	150.00
80-04-022	7" Card Playing Girl Mouse	A. Thorndike	1,826	9.50	125.00
81-04-023	7" Card Playing Girl Mouse	A. Thorndike	863	9.95	125.00
84-04-024	7" Bowling Mouse	A. Thorndike	1,472	13.95	75.00
85-04-025	7" Girl Tennis Mouse	A. Thorndike	1,947	14.95	75.00
86-04-026	7" Boating Mouse	A. Thorndike	2,320	16.95	55.00
73-04-027	7' Football Mouse	A. Thorndike	944	4.50	150.00
82-04-028	7" Football Mouse	A. Thorndike	2,164	10.50	200.00
81-04-029	7" Jogger Mouse	A. Thorndike	1,783	9.95	75.00
81-04-030	7" Backpacker Mouse	A. Thorndike	1,008	9.95	100.00
80-04-031	7" Girl Disco Mouse	A. Thorndike	915	9.50	150.00
80-04-032	7" Boy Disco Mouse	A. Thorndike	363	9.50	150.00
80-04-033	7" Volleyball Mouse	A. Thorndike	915	9.50	75.00
84-04-034	7" Hockeyplayer Mouse	A. Thorndike	1,525	5.50	200.00
74-04-035	7" Hunter Mouse With 10" Deer	A. Thorndike	1,282	11.50	175.00
83-04-036	7" Quilting Mouse	A. Thorndike	2,786	11.95	75.00
85-04-037	7" Get-Well Mouse	A. Thorndike	1,425	14.95	75.00
82-04-038	7" Graduate Boy Mouse	A. Thorndike	4,971	12.00	100.00
85-04-039	7" Graduate Girl Mouse	A. Thorndike	2,884	13.95	100.00
78-04-040	7" Gardener Mouse	A. Thorndike	Unkn.	7.00	75.00
80-04-041	7" Greenthumb Mouse	A. Thorndike	1,869	9.50	75.00
77-04-042	7" Groom Mouse	A. Thorndike	1,211	6.95	50.00
87-04-043	7" Groom Mouse	A. Thorndike	1,800	14.50	55.00
82-04-044	7" Groom Mouse	A.Thorndike	3,406	10.95	50.00
87-04-045	7" Bride Mouse	A. Thorndike	1,801	14.50	55.00
82-04-046	7" Bride Mouse	A. Thorndike	3,681	10.95	50.00
85-04-047	7" Bride & Groom Mice	A. Thorndike	2,963	13.95	170.00
80-04-048	7" Bride & Groom Mice	A. Thorndike	2,418	9.50	175.00
64-04-049	7" Bride & Groom Mice	A. Thorndike	Unkn.	2.75	750.00
83-04-050	7" Cheerleader Mouse	A. Thorndike	2,025	11.95	200.00
75-04-051	7" Bicyclist Mouse	A. Thorndike	1,561	5.50	125.00
79-04-052	7" C.B. Mouse	A. Thorndike	1,039	6.95	75.00
78-04-053	7" C.B. Mouse	A. Thorndike	2,396	6.95	75.00
74-04-054	7" Painter Mouse	A. Thorndike	Unkn.	4.00	175.00
81-04-055	7" Baseball Mouse	A. Thorndike	2,380	Unkn.	100.00
74-04-056	7" Cowboy Mouse	A. Thorndike	394	5.50	150.00
83-04-057	7" Cowboy Mouse	A. Thorndike	1,794	12.95	150.00
83-04-058	7" Cowgirl Mouse	A. Thorndike	1,517	12.95	150.00
79-04-059	7" Carpenter Mouse	A. Thorndike	2,024	6.95	175.00
86-04-060	7" Mouse With Wheelborrow	A. Thorndike	2,037	16.95	75.00
73-04-061	7" Waiter Mouse	A. Thorndike	Unkn.	4.00	250.00
79-04-062	7" Fireman Mouse	A. Thorndike	1,773	6.95	200.00
78-04-063	7" Fireman Mouse	A. Thorndike	Unkn.	6.95	200.00
73-04-064	7" Skiing Mouse	A. Thorndike	2,774	4.00	175.00
84-04-065	7" Mrs. Retired Mouse	A. Thorndike	1,356	13.95	95.00
74-04-066	7" Pregnant Mouse	A. Thorndike	820	Unkn.	200.00
84-04-067	7" Devil Mouse	A. Thorndike	3,571	13.95	100.00
75-04-068	7" Beautician Mouse	A. Thorndike	1,349	4.00	300.00
77-04-069	7" Beautician Mouse	A. Thorndike	1,521	5.50	250.00
74-04-070	7" Vacation Mouse	A. Thorndike	Unkn.	Unkn.	175.00
82-04-071	7" Mrs. A.M. Mouse	A. Thorndike	2,184	11.95	80.00
74-04-072	7" Secretary Mouse	A. Thorndike	364	4.00	150.00
79-04-073	7" Skateboard Mouse	A. Thorndike	1,821	6.00	300.00
77-04-074	7" Sweetheart Mouse	A. Thorndike	3,323	5.50	100.00
86-04-075	7" Sweetheart Mouse	A. Thorndike	6,271	12.95	100.00
78-04-076	7" Teacher Mouse	A. Thorndike	2,249	5.50	100.00
84-04-077	7" Teacher Mouse	A. Thorndike	3,150	13.95	75.00
81-04-078	7" Nurse Mouse	A. Thorndike	3,222	11.95	50.00
73-04-079	7" Golfer Mouse	A. Thorndike	Unkn.	5.00	100.00
74-04-080	7" Seamstress Mouse	A. Thorndike	387	4.00	175.00
83-04-081	7" Windsurfer Mouse	A. Thorndike	2,352	13.95	125.00
86-04-082	7" Birthday Girl Mouse	A. Thorndike	3,724	14.95	125.00
78-04-083	7" Policeman Mouse	A. Thorndike	1,189	7.00	150.00
74-04-084	7" Artist Mouse	A. Thorndike	397	5.50	110.00
85-04-085	7" Hiker Mouse	A. Thorndike	1,781	13.95	275.00
77-04-086	7" Bingo Mouse	A. Thorndike	1,221	6.00	150.00
84-04-087	7" Mouse With Strawberry	A. Thorndike	1,776	11.95	75.00
77-04-088	7" Vacationer Mouse	A. Thorndike	1,040	6.00	175.00
84-04-089	12" Devil Mouse	A. Thorndike	1,118	29.95	145.00
83-04-090	12" Bride Mouse	A. Thorndike	854	31.95	200.00
83-04-091	12" Groom Mouse	A. Thorndike	826	31.95	200.00
76-04-092	12" Colonial Boy Mouse	A. Thorndike	838	13.50	400.00
76-04-093	12" Colonial Girl Mouse	A. Thorndike	691	13.50	350.00
70-04-094	7" Architect Mouse	A. Thorndike	2,051	3.95	375.00
79-04-095	7" Chimney Sweep Mouse	A. Thorndike	6,331	7.95	275.00
78-04-096	7" Policeman Mouse	A. Thorndike	1,189	6.95	350.00
80-04-097	7" Backpacker Mouse	A. Thorndike	1,008	9.95	375.00
73-04-098	7" Painter Mouse	A. Thorndike	N/A	4.50	275.00
80-04-099	7" Disco Boy Mouse	A. Thorndike	363	9.50	150.00
80-04-100	7" Disco Girl Mouse	A. Thorndike	N/A	9.50	325.00

Number	Name	Artist	Edition Limit	Issue Price	Quote
67-04-101	7" Santa Mouse	A. Thorndike	N/A	2.00	250.00
73-04-102	12" Nightshirt Mouse	A. Thorndike	122	7.50	350.00
79-04-103	7" Pregnant Mouse	A. Thorndike	1,856	7.95	225.00
79-04-104	7" Gardener Mouse	A. Thorndike	1,939	7.95	375.00
84-04-105	7" Teacher Mouse	A. Thorndike	3,023	13.95	225.00
77-04-106	29" Mrs. Santa Mouse	A. Thorndike	571	49.95	450.00
78-04-107	7" Nightshirt Mouse	A. Thorndike	6,444	7.95	75.00
71-04-108	7" Baseball Mouse	A. Thorndike	553	4.00	150.00
84-04-109	7" Devil Mouse	A. Thorndike	3,571	12.95	100.00
74-04-110	7" Hockey Mouse	A. Thorndike	687	7.95	200.00
82-04-111	7" Witch Mouse On Broom	A. Thorndike	2,798	12.95	75.00
82-04-112	7" Sweetheart Mouse	A. Thorndike	4,110	11.00	75.00
76-04-113	7" Mr. Holly Mouse	A. Thorndike	2,774	5.50	125.00
76-04-114	7" Mrs. Holly Mouse	A. Thorndike	3,078	5.50	125.00
77-04-115	7" Baseball Mouse	A. Thorndike	1,634	6.00	100.00
85-04-116	7" Graduation Mouse	A. Thorndike	1,999	14.00	75.00
78-04-117	7" Doctor Mouse	A. Thorndike	816	6.95	75.00
68-04-118	7" Nightshirt Boy Mouse	A. Thorndike	N/A	3.95	200.00
76-04-119	12" Girl Mouse With Plum Pudding	A. Thorndike	1,482	13.50	400.00
64-04-120	12" George & Sheila, Bride & Groom Mice	A. Thorndike	N/A	12.95	600.00
65-04-121	7" Lawyer Mouse	A. Thorndike	N/A	6.95	425.00
73-04-122	7" Fireman Mouse	A. Thorndike	557	4.50	200.00
72-04-123	7" Pregnant Mouse	A. Thorndike	820	5.50	100.00
89-04-124	7" Sweetheart Mouse	A. Thorndike	N/A	16.95	35.00
86-04-125	7" Tennis Mouse	A. Thorndike	1,947	15.95	80.00
82-04-126	7" Mouse With Strawberry	A. Thorndike	N/A	11.95	75.00
79-04-127	7" Mrs. Santa Mouse With Holly	A. Thorndike	N/A	7.95	50.00
82-04-128	12" Pilgrim Boy Mouse	A. Thorndike	2,151	27.95	175.00
82-04-129	12" Pilgrim Girl Mouse	A. Thorndike	2,017	27.95	175.00
71-04-130	7" Artist Mouse	A. Thorndike	422	3.95	175.00
72-04-131	7" Yachtsman Mouse	A. Thorndike	1,130	3.95	250.00
72-04-132	7" Housewife Mouse	A. Thorndike	1,768	3.95	250.00
79-04-133	7" Boy Golfer Mouse	A. Thorndike	2,743	7.95	100.00
75-04-134	7" Pregnant Mouse	A. Thorndike	879	5.50	150.00
71-04-135	7" Ski Mouse	A. Thorndike	1,326	3.95	175.00
79-04-136	7" Fishing Mouse	A. Thorndike	3,053	7.95	150.00
74-04-137	7" Carpenter Mouse	A. Thorndike	551	5.50	175.00
77-04-138	7" Diet Time Mouse	A. Thorndike	1,478	6.00	200.00
79-04-139	12" Nightshirt Mouse With Candle	A. Thorndike	5,739	16.00	225.00
86-04-140	7" Tennis Mouse	A. Thorndike	1,947	15.95	100.00
82-04-141	7" Girl Tennis Mouse	A. Thorndike	2,443	10.95	135.00
79-04-142	7" Girl Golfer Mouse	A. Thorndike	2,316	7.95	90.00
87-04-143	7" Graduation Boy Mouse	A. Thorndike	N/A	19.95	85.00
78-04-144	7" Girl Golfer Mouse	A. Thorndike	2,215	6.95	100.00
78-04-145	7" Doctor Mouse	A. Thorndike	2,028	6.95	100.00
85-04-146	7" Boy Golfer Mouse	A. Thorndike	2,099	14.95	75.00
72-04-147	7" Girl Golfer Mouse	A. Thorndike	N/A	3.95	100.00
84-04-148	7" Teacher Mouse, Girl	A. Thorndike	5,064	13.95	200.00
89-04-149	7" Tacky Tourist Mouse, proof	A. Thorndike	1	N/A	400.00
89-04-150	7" Business Man Mouse, proof	A. Thorndike	1	N/A	375.00
89-04-151	7" Knitting Mouse, proof	A. Thorndike	1	N/A	550.00
79-04-152	7" C.B. Mouse	A. Thorndike	1,039	7.95	100.00
81-04-153	7" Witch Mouse On Broom With Moon	A. Thorndike	1,585+	24.95	200.00
79-04-154	7" Quilting Mouse	A. Thorndike	213	N/A	150.00
86-04-155	7" Witch Mouse In Pumpkin Balloon	A. Thorndike	868	77.95	275.00
81-04-156	12" Witch Mouse On Broom	A. Thorndike	1,049	34.95	160.00
78-04-157	7" Groom Mouse	A. Thorndike	2,952	9.50	85.00
78-04-158	7" Groom Mouse	A. Thorndike	N/A	14.50	125.00
74-04-159	12" Retired Grandma Mouse	A. Thorndike	1,135	13.50	300.00
74-04-160	12" Retired Grandpa Mouse	A. Thorndike	1,103	13.50	pair
82-04-161	7" Cheerleader Mouse	A. Thorndike	3,441	10.95	150.00
75-04-162	7" Two In Tent Mice	A. Thorndike	914	N/A	85.00
75-04-163	7" Goin' Fishin' Mouse	A. Thorndike	4,507	5.95	125.00
76-04-164	7" Colonial Boy Mouse	A. Thorndike	5,457	N/A	200.00
75-04-165	7" Christmas Mouse In Santa's Mitten	A. Thorndike	3,959	5.95	150.00
76-04-166	7" Birthday Girl Mouse	A. Thorndike	732	5.50	250.00
77-04-167	29" Mr. Niteshirt Mouse	A. Thorndike	309	49.95	650.00
72-04-168	7" Diaper Mouse, It's A Girl	A. Thorndike	2,293	4.50	225.00
72-04-169	7" Diaper Mouse, It's A Boy	A. Thorndike	2,293	4.50	175.00
79-04-170	7" Swimmer Mouse	A. Thorndike	3,640	9.50	225.00
77-04-171	29" Mrs. Santa Mouse With Muff	A. Thorndike	571	49.95	500.00
82-04-172	7" Windsurfer Mouse	A. Thorndike	4,114	13.95	250.00
72-04-173	7" Bar-Be-Que Mouse	A. Thorndike	907	3.95	225.00
86-04-174	7" Indian Girl Mouse With Papoose	A. Thorndike	6,992	24.95	115.00
65-04-175	7" Singing Christmas Mouse	A. Thorndike	N/A	4.95	275.00
86-04-176	7" Ballerina Mouse	A. Thorndike	N/A	N/A	200.00
90-04-177	7" Artist Mouse, Proof	A. Thorndike	1	N/A	750.00
67-04-178	7" Miguel The Mouse	A. Thorndike	N/A	3.95	400.00
90-04-179	7" Maui Mouse, Proof	A. Thorndike	1	N/A	600.00
90-04-180	7" Sailor Mouse, Proof	A. Thorndike	1	N/A	675.00
76-04-181	7" Card Playing Girl Mouse	A. Thorndike	2,878	5.95	175.00
78-04-182	7" Skateboard Mouse	A. Thorndike	3,733	7.95	300.00
87-04-183	7" Baby Mouse	A. Thorndike	2,500	13.95	80.00
70-04-184	7" Plumber Mouse	A. Thorndike	196	3.95	350.00
72-04-185	7" Christmas Mouse	A. Thorndike	2,793	3.95	425.00
84-04-186	7" Angel Mouse	A. Thorndike	2,093	14.95	150.00
75-04-187	7" Retired Grandpa Mouse	A. Thorndike	793	5.50	95.00
87-04-188	7" Bicyclist Boy Mouse	A. Thorndike	1,507	19.95	175.00
78-04-189	7" Policeman Mouse	A. Thorndike	1,189	6.95	200.00
77-04-190	7" Hobo Mouse	A. Thorndike	1,004	5.95	250.00
70-04-191	7" Nightshirt Girl Mouse	A. Thorndike	N/A	3.95	175.00
70-04-192	7" Carpenter Mouse	A. Thorndike	307	3.95	300.00
70-04-193	7" Architect Mouse	A. Thorndike	205	3.95	350.00
75-04-194	7" Ski Mouse	A. Thorndike	5,219	5.50	200.00
76-04-195	7" Colonial Girl Mouse	A. Thorndike	5,457	5.50	225.00
74-04-196	7" Hunter Mouse W/Bird	A. Thorndike	690	5.50	300.00
90-04-197	7" Sailor Mouse	A. Thorndike	6,838	23.95	118.00
75-04-198	7" Bouquet Girl Mouse	A. Thorndike	N/A	3.95	300.00
76-04-199	7" Gardener Mouse	A. Thorndike	1,255	5.50	225.00
67-04-200	7" Conductor Mouse	A. Thorndike	N/A	3.95	300.00
91-04-201	7" Red Cross Nurse Mouse, proof	A. Thorndike	1	N/A	525.00
68-04-202	7" Mr. Holly Mouse	A. Thorndike	N/A	3.95	250.00
91-04-203	7" Desert Storm Mouse	A. Thorndike	1	N/A	800.00
87-04-204	7" Barbeque Mouse	A. Thorndike	1,798	17.95	85.00
89-04-205	7" Knitting Mouse	A. Thorndike	N/A	19.95	75.00
78-04-206	7" Airplane Pilot Mouse	A. Thorndike	2,308	6.95	375.00
74-04-207	7" Doctor Mouse	A. Thorndike	720	5.50	200.00
76-04-208	7" Nurse Mouse	A. Thorndike	5,164	5.95	250.00
67-04-209	7" Mrs. Holly Mouse	A. Thorndike	N/A	3.95	150.00
85-04-210	12" Indian Boy Mouse	A. Thorndike	N/A	34.50	100.00
89-04-211	12" Trick or Treat Mouse	A. Thorndike	N/A	39.95	225.00
93-04-212	7" Baseball Mouse, proof	A. Thorndike	1	N/A	525.00
93-04-213	7" Fireman Mouse, proof	A. Thorndike	1	N/A	425.00
93-04-214	7" Factory in the Woods Mouse, proof	A. Thorndike	1	N/A	550.00
65-04-215	7" Eek, Peek, Squeek Mouse	A. Thorndike	N/A	3.95	500.00
67-04-216	7" Mr. Santa Mouse	A. Thorndike	N/A	3.95	300.00
89-04-217	7" Business Man Mouse	A. Thorndike	5,085	21.95	150.00
82-04-218	7" Cowboy Mouse	A. Thorndike	3,776	28.95	60.00
80-04-219	7" Skating Mouse	A. Thorndike	3,369	10.95	100.00
82-04-220	7" Graduate Girl Mouse	A. Thorndike	3,563	10.95	85.00
75-04-221	7" Housewife Mouse	A. Thorndike	1,632	5.50	250.00
70-04-222	7" Boxing Mouse	A. Thorndike	321	3.95	400.00
70-04-223	7" Professor Mouse	A. Thorndike	248	3.95	225.00
70-04-224	7" Sheriff Mouse	A. Thorndike	11	3.95	500.00
76-04-225	12" Colonial Boy & Girl Mouse	A. Thorndike	N/A	26.90	900.00

Company / Number	Name	Series / Artist	Edition Limit	Issue Price	Quote
Annalee Mobilitee Dolls		**Snowmen**			
84-05-001	4" Snowman	A. Thorndike	Unkn.	169.95	350.00
84-05-002	30" Snowgirl & Boy	A. Thorndike	685	79.95	475.00
78-05-003	18" Snowman	A. Thorndike	3,971	79.95	250.00
83-05-004	7" Snowman	A. Thorndike	15,980	12.95	75.00
71-05-005	29" Snowman With Broom	A. Thorndike	1,075	19.95	200.00
84-05-006	30" Snowman	A. Thorndike	956	79.50	475.00
84-05-007	30" Snowgirl	A. Thorndike	685	79.50	475.00
79-05-008	10" Snowman	A. Thorndike	12,888	7.95	100.00
79-05-009	29" Snowman	A. Thorndike	917	42.95	400.00
78-05-010	10" Snowman	A. Thorndike	9,701	6.95	175.00
71-05-011	7" Snowman	A. Thorndike	1,917	3.95	275.00
Annalee Mobilitee Dolls		**Clowns**			
81-06-001	18" Clown	A. Thorndike	2,742	24.95	200.00
78-06-002	10" Clown	A. Thorndike	4,020	6.50	175.00
80-06-003	18" Clown	A. Thorndike	3,192	24.95	125.00
85-06-004	18" Clown	A. Thorndike	2,275	36.95	200.00
86-06-005	Ballooning Clown	A. Thorndike	2,700	16.95	110.00
85-06-006	18" Clown with Balloon	A. Thorndike	1,485	36.95	150.00
86-06-007	10" Clown	A. Thorndike	3,897	15.50	75.00
80-06-008	10" Clown	A. Thorndike	8,136	12.50	75.00
81-06-009	10" Clown	A. Thorndike	6,479	12.95	100.00
77-06-010	10" Clown	A. Thorndike	4,784	6.00	125.00
71-06-011	10" Clown	A. Thorndike	708	2.00	200.00
87-06-012	10" Clown	A. Thorndike	Unkn.	17.95	55.00
76-06-013	30" Clown	A. Thorndike	466	30.00	650.00
84-06-014	30" Clown	A. Thorndike	387	69.95	400.00
70-06-015	10" Clown	A. Thorndike	2,362	4.00	125.00
76-06-016	18" Clown	A. Thorndike	916	13.50	200.00
77-06-017	18" Clown	A. Thorndike	2,343	13.50	475.00
80-06-018	4' Clown	A. Thorndike	224	150.00	900.00
84-06-019	10" Clown	A. Thorndike	6,383	13.95	95.00
84-06-020	18" Clown	A. Thorndike	N/A	32.95	150.00
70-06-021	18" Clown	A. Thorndike	542	5.00	250.00
80-06-022	18" Clown With Balloon	A. Thorndike	3,192	24.95	100.00
76-06-023	10" Clown	A. Thorndike	2,285	5.50	100.00
81-06-024	10" Clown	A. Thorndike	6,479	9.95	125.00
84-06-025	30" Clown	A. Thorndike	381	165.00	325.00
78-06-026	18" Clown	A. Thorndike	4,000	13.95	225.00
80-06-027	42" Clown w/ Stand	A. Thorndike	224	84.95	600.00
90-06-028	30" Clown w/ Stand	A. Thorndike	530	99.95	150.00
93-06-029	18" Halloween Clown	A. Thorndike	1	N/A	2600.00
90-06-030	10" Yellow Clown	A. Thorndike	3,100	25.95	75.00
90-06-031	10" Clown w/ Base	A. Thorndike	2,750	27.95	75.00
84-06-032	18" Clown	A. Thorndike	1,828	32.95	250.00
Annalee Mobilitee Dolls		**Kids/Babies**			
82-07-001	7" I'm a 10" Baby	A. Thorndike	2,159	12.95	125.00
60-07-002	7" Baby With Bow	A. Thorndike	Unkn.	1.50	125.00
68-07-003	5" Baby In Santa Cap	A. Thorndike	Unkn.	2.00	150.00
63-07-004	5" Baby With Santa Hat	A. Thorndike	Unkn.	2.50	175.00
84-07-005	7" Country Girl With Basket	A. Thorndike	715	16.95	250.00
63-07-006	5" Baby	A. Thorndike	Unkn.	Unkn.	300.00
80-07-007	7" Baby In Bassinette	A. Thorndike	Unkn.	Unkn.	125.00
85-07-008	7" Dressup Girl	A. Thorndike	1,536	18.95	425.00
85-07-009	7" Dressup Boy	A. Thorndike	1,174	18.95	225.00
85-07-010	7" Baseball Kid	A. Thorndike	1,225	Unkn.	75.00
84-07-011	7" Boy With Firecracker	A. Thorndike	1,893	19.95	140.00
85-07-012	7" Kid With Kite	A. Thorndike	1,084	17.95	75.00
84-07-013	7" Jogger Kid	A. Thorndike	Unkn.	17.95	85.00
85-07-014	7" Hockey Player Kid	A. Thorndike	1,578	18.95	125.00
85-07-015	7" Happy Birthday Boy	A. Thorndike	937	19.00	100.00
84-07-016	7" Cupid in Heart	A. Thorndike	2,445	32.95	150.00
84-07-017	7" Cupid Kid	A. Thorndike	6,808	14.95	150.00
83-07-018	7" Fishing Boy	A. Thorndike	Unkn.	12.95	125.00
84-07-019	18" Candy Girl	A. Thorndike	1,333	29.95	125.00
84-07-020	18" Candy Boy	A. Thorndike	1,350	29.95	300.00
82-07-021	18" Girl P.J. Kid	A. Thorndike	5,389	25.50	125.00
84-07-022	18" Girl On Sled	A. Thorndike	2,328	29.95	150.00
84-07-023	18" Boy On Sled	A. Thorndike	2,205	29.95	150.00
87-07-024	3" Baby Witch	A. Thorndike	Unkn.	13.95	55.00
57-07-025	10" Boy Skier	A. Thorndike	N/A	16.00	800.00
57-07-026	10" Girl & Boy in Boat	A. Thorndike	N/A	17.50	900.00
71-07-027	18" Choir Girl	A. Thorndike	424	7.95	400.00
85-07-028	7" Baseball Kid	A. Thorndike	1,221	16.95	425.00
78-07-029	18" Candy Girl	A. Thorndike	1,333	14.95	375.00
68-07-030	5" Baby in Santa Hat	A. Thorndike	N/A	3.00	225.00
85-07-031	7" Birthday Girl	A. Thorndike	1,017	18.95	75.00
75-07-032	10" Lass	A. Thorndike	558	6.00	300.00
84-07-033	7" Baseball Kid	A. Thorndike	2,079	13.00	200.00
75-07-034	18" Lad & Lass On Bike	A. Thorndike	206	24.00	275.00
64-07-035	18" P.J. Boy & Girl	A. Thorndike	N/A	7.00	525.00
65-07-036	7" Dresden China Babies, 2	A. Thorndike	N/A	N/A	525.00
69-07-037	7" X-mas Baby On 3 Hot Boxes	A. Thorndike	N/A	3.00	400.00
87-07-038	7" Indian Boy	A. Thorndike	N/A	19.95	60.00
81-07-039	18" Boy On Sled	A. Thorndike	N/A	12.50	200.00
75-07-040	10" Lad On Bicycle	A. Thorndike	453	6.00	300.00
85-07-041	7" Jogger Kid	A. Thorndike	654	17.95	85.00
86-07-042	7" Cupid In Hot Air Balloon	A. Thorndike	391	54.95	175.00
50-07-043	9" Choir Boy	A. Thorndike	N/A	N/A	400.00
75-07-044	10" Lad & Lass	A. Thorndike	162	12.00	249.00
87-07-045	3" Cupid In Heart Balloon	A. Thorndike	1,715	38.95	175.00
54-07-046	5" Sno Bunny, (Kid)	A. Thorndike	N/A	N/A	300.00
69-07-047	18" Santa Kid	A. Thorndike	N/A	7.45	250.00
87-07-048	7" Girl Graduate	A. Thorndike	2,438	19.95	80.00
87-07-049	7" Boy Graduate	A. Thorndike	2,034	N/A	80.00
69-07-050	25" Country Boy	A. Thorndike	70	7.00	500.00
69-07-051	25" Country Girl	A. Thorndike	69	7.00	pair
86-07-052	7" Skiing Kid	A. Thorndike	8,057	18.45	75.00

Company Number	Name	Series Artist	Edition Limit	Issue Price	Quote
60-07-053	7" Baby With Pink Bow	A. Thorndike	N/A	N/A	450.00
63-07-054	7" Saturday Night Baby	A. Thorndike	N/A	2.95	350.00
60-07-055	7" Baby In Stocking	A. Thorndike	N/A	N/A	275.00
68-07-056	7" Baby I'm Reading	A. Thorndike	N/A	N/A	375.00
68-07-057	7" Baby Vain Jane	A. Thorndike	N/A	2.50	300.00
70-07-058	18" Patchwork Kid	A. Thorndike	496	7.50	250.00
70-07-059	10" Choir Boy	A. Thorndike	3,517	4.50	150.00
76-07-060	10" Girl in Tire Swing	A. Thorndike	357	6.95	225.00
76-07-061	10" Boy In Tire Swing	A. Thorndike	358	6.95	200.00
75-07-062	25" Lass With Basket Of Flowers	A. Thorndike	92	28.95	450.00
71-07-063	18" Santa Fur Kid	A. Thorndike	1,191	7.95	400.00
70-07-064	10" Choir Girl	A. Thorndike	7,245	5.50	225.00
71-07-065	10" Choir Boy	A. Thorndike	904	3.95	175.00
87-07-066	7" Baby W/Blanket & Sweater	A. Thorndike	7,836	21.95	60.00
80-07-067	10" Boy on Raft	A. Thorndike	1,087	28.95	300.00
85-07-068	12" Kid W/Sled	A. Thorndike	4,707	31.50	115.00
65-07-069	10" Fishing Boy	A. Thorndike	N/A	7.95	300.00
54-07-070	8" Boy Skier	A. Thorndike	N/A	N/A	550.00
62-07-071	10" Skeeple (Boy)	A. Thorndike	N/A	9.00	425.00
70-07-072	7" Treasure Baby	A. Thorndike	N/A	3.95	200.00
71-07-073	7" Baby Bunting In Basket	A. Thorndike	195	3.95	350.00
76-07-074	10" Lass w/Planter Basket	A. Thorndike	313	6.95	200.00
67-07-075	10" Surfer Boy	A. Thorndike	N/A	4.95	300.00
57-07-076	10" Easter Holiday Doll	A. Thorndike	N/A	10.00	800.00
65-07-077	10" Fishing Girl	A. Thorndike	N/A	9.95	400.00
67-07-078	7" Garden Club Baby	A. Thorndike	N/A	2.95	350.00
54-07-079	5" Sno-Bunny Child	A. Thorndike	N/A	2.95	350.00
81-07-080	7" Naughty Angel	A. Thorndike	12,359	10.95	75.00
56-07-081	7" Baby Angel With Feather Hair	A. Thorndike	Unkn.	3.95	325.00
84-07-082	7" Baseball Player	A. Thorndike	937	15.95	75.00
84-07-083	7" Cupid Kid	A. Thorndike	6,808	15.50	200.00
93-07-084	7" Fishing Boy, Proof	A. Thorndike	1	N/A	500.00
93-07-085	7" Girl Eating Turkey, Proof	A. Thorndike	1	N/A	525.00
93-07-086	7" Boy Building Snowman, Proof	A. Thorndike	1	N/A	450.00
93-07-087	7" Hot Shot Business Man Kid, Proof	A. Thorndike	1	N/A	600.00
93-07-088	18" P.J. Kid	A. Thorndike	1	N/A	875.00
93-07-089	7" Bedtime Kid, Proof	A. Thorndike	1	N/A	450.00
93-07-090	7" Jump Rope Kid, Proof	A. Thorndike	1	N/A	500.00
93-07-091	7" Basketball Kid, Proof	A. Thorndike	1	N/A	550.00
88-07-092	10" Shepherd Boy w/ Lamb	A. Thorndike	1,300	89.95	175.00
83-07-093	7" Fishing Boy	A. Thorndike	3,927	16.95	175.00
72-07-094	18" P.J. Kid	A. Thorndike	N/A	N/A	125.00
93-07-095	7" Court Jester	A. Thorndike	N/A	3.95	325.00

Annalee Mobilitee Dolls — **Angels**

Company Number	Name	Series Artist	Edition Limit	Issue Price	Quote
85-08-001	12" Naughty Angel	A. Thorndike	1,393	Unkn.	125.00
63-08-002	5" Baby Angel With Halo	A. Thorndike	Unkn.	2.00	300.00
82-08-003	7" Angel With Teardrop	A. Thorndike	3,092	12.95	200.00
84-08-004	7" Naughty Angel	A. Thorndike	4,258	Unkn.	75.00
78-08-005	7" Tree Top Angel With Wreath	A. Thorndike	Unkn.	Unkn.	100.00
68-08-006	5" Baby Angel On Cloud	A. Thorndike	N/A	3.00	300.00
78-08-007	7" Tree Top Angel With Wreath	A. Thorndike	8,613	6.50	100.00
66-08-008	7" Angel, White Wings	A. Thorndike	N/A	N/A	225.00
86-08-009	12" Naughty Angel With Slingshot	A. Thorndike	N/A	36.95	225.00
71-08-010	7" Angel With Paper Wings	A. Thorndike	608	3.00	325.00
64-08-011	7" Angel in A Blanket	A. Thorndike	N/A	2.50	300.00
56-08-012	10" Baby Angel	A. Thorndike	N/A	5.50	550.00
91-08-013	10" Nativity Angel, Proof	A. Thorndike	1	N/A	1200.00
60-08-014	12" Big Angel On Cloud	A. Thorndike	N/A	9.95	350.00
60-08-015	7" Baby Angel	A. Thorndike	N/A	N/A	300.00
60-08-016	7" Baby Angel With Star On Leg	A. Thorndike	N/A	N/A	300.00
76-08-017	7" Mistletoe Angel	A. Thorndike	17,540	6.00	80.00
84-08-018	7" Angel On Star	A. Thorndike	772	32.95	200.00
60-08-019	7" Baby Angel w/Blue Wings	A. Thorndike	N/A	N/A	300.00
63-08-020	7" Baby Angel On Cloud	A. Thorndike	N/A	N/A	300.00
69-08-021	7" Angel w/Blue Wings	A. Thorndike	N/A	2.95	225.00
64-08-022	7" Sat. Nite Angel w/Blanket	A. Thorndike	N/A	2.95	250.00

Annalee Mobilitee Dolls — **Bunnies**

Company Number	Name	Series Artist	Edition Limit	Issue Price	Quote
64-09-001	5" Brown Bunny	A. Thorndike	N/A	N/A	540.00
71-09-002	30" White Bunny With Carrot	A. Thorndike	172	Unkn.	165.00
71-09-003	7" White Bunny With Candlewreath	A. Thorndike	227	4.95.	350.00
86-09-004	30" Boy Bunny With Wheelbarrow	A. Thorndike	252	119.50	200.00
72-09-005	30" Boy Bunny	A. Thorndike	237	25.00	225.00
72-09-006	18" Boy Bunny With Burlap Sack Cardholder	A. Thorndike	326	10.95	450.00
72-09-007	30" Girl Bunny	A. Thorndike	223	25.00	225.00
79-09-008	29" E.P. Mom Bunny	A. Thorndike	662	42.95	200.00
70-09-009	29" Girl Bunny	A. Thorndike	Unkn.	22.00	250.00
70-09-010	18" White Bunny With Butterfly	A. Thorndike	258	10.95	500.00
70-09-011	18" Bunny With Butterfly	A. Thorndike	258	10.95	500.00
73-09-012	7" White Bunny	A. Thorndike	1,600	5.50	125.00
72-09-013	7" Ballerina Bunny	A. Thorndike	4,700	4.00	100.00
79-09-014	7" Ballerina Bunny	A. Thorndike	4,700	7.50	100.00
80-09-015	7" Ballerina Bunny	A. Thorndike	Unkn.	8.95	175.00
82-09-016	7" Ballerina Bunny	A. Thorndike	4,179	9.95	100.00
78-09-017	7" Artist Bunny	A. Thorndike	4,217	7.50	250.00
86-09-018	7" Valentine Bunny	A. Thorndike	Unkn.	14.50	125.00
81-09-019	7" Country Bunnies	A. Thorndike	7,940	Unkn.	185.00
78-09-020	7" Bunnies With Basket	A. Thorndike	2,253	Unkn.	150.00
84-09-021	7" Country Bunnies With Basket	A. Thorndike	2,345	25.95	75.00
87-09-022	18" E.P. Girl Sample Bunny	A. Thorndike	1	Unkn.	300.00
87-09-023	18" E.P. Boy Sample Bunny	A. Thorndike	1	Unkn.	300.00
79-09-024	18" Artist Bunny	A. Thorndike	1,064	15.95	275.00
70-09-025	18" Girl Bunny With Egg	A. Thorndike	1,727	15.95	150.00
82-09-026	4' Boy Bunny	A. Thorndike	186	190.00	450.00
84-09-027	7" E.P. Boy Bunny	A. Thorndike	5,989	12.95	35.00
83-09-028	7" E.P. Girl Bunny	A. Thorndike	Unkn.	12.50	50.00
83-09-029	7" E.P. Boy Bunny	A. Thorndike	Unkn.	12.50	50.00
83-09-030	7" Country Boy Bunny With Butterfly	A. Thorndike	N/A	12.50	100.00
85-09-031	7" Boy Bunny With Carrot	A. Thorndike	3,273	14.95	55.00
86-09-032	7" Boy Bunny With Carrot	A. Thorndike	2,949	15.50	95.00
83-09-033	5" Country Girl Bunny	A. Thorndike	5,163	Unkn.	50.00
83-09-034	5" Floppy-ear Boy Bunny With Basket	A. Thorndike	Unkn.	11.50	55.00
84-09-035	5" Country Bunnies With Basket	A. Thorndike	1,110	Unkn.	150.00
77-09-036	29" Mechanical See Saw Bunny	A. Thorndike	N/A	300.00	900.00
83-09-037	5" Bunny On Music Box	A. Thorndike	N/A	29.95	375.00
70-09-038	7" Bunny On Box	A. Thorndike	N/A	N/A	250.00
73-09-039	7" Bunny On Box	A. Thorndike	795	5.50	125.00
77-09-040	7" Bunny With Butterfly	A. Thorndike	2,721	6.00	125.00
82-09-041	7" Easter Parade Boy Bunny	A. Thorndike	7,108	11.95	50.00
86-09-042	7" Bunny With Egg	A. Thorndike	2,233	16.95	55.00
77-09-043	18" Easter Parade Boy Bunny	A. Thorndike	1,567	13.50	150.00
77-09-044	29" Easter Parade Pop Bunny	A. Thorndike	477	35.00	250.00
72-09-045	29" Easter Parade Mom Bunny	A. Thorndike	508	35.00	250.00
84-09-046	5" Girl Bunny	A. Thorndike	2,594	11.50	65.00
66-09-047	7" Yum Yum Bunny	A. Thorndike	N/A	3.95	525.00
71-09-048	18" Peter Bunny	A. Thorndike	219	10.95	425.00
77-09-049	29" Pop Bunny With Basket	A. Thorndike	N/A	11.50	400.00
65-09-050	7" Dumb Bunny	A. Thorndike	N/A	3.95	400.00
83-09-051	29" Easter Parade Girl Bunny	A. Thorndike	N/A	71.95	200.00
81-09-052	18" Country Boy Bunny With Carrot	A. Thorndike	1,998	23.95	275.00
88-09-053	7" Bunny With Sled	A. Thorndike	3,050	21.95	45.00
88-09-054	7" Set of Three Bunnies On Revolving Music Box Maypole	A. Thorndike	610	69.95	150.00
85-09-055	7" Valentine Bunny	A. Thorndike	5,602	13.95	75.00
84-09-056	7" Two Bunnies With Bushel Basket	A. Thorndike	2,339	25.95	75.00
66-09-057	7" Yum Yum Bunny	A. Thorndike	N/A	3.95	400.00
67-09-058	12" Yum Yum Bunny	A. Thorndike	N/A	9.95	550.00
85-09-059	18" Country Boy Bunny With Watering Can	A. Thorndike	2,355	46.95	N/A
87-09-060	18" Victorian Country Boy Bunny	A. Thorndike	1,394	49.95	350.00
87-09-061	18" Victorian Country Girl Bunny	A. Thorndike	1,492	49.95	pair
72-09-062	7" Bunny, (With Bandana)	A. Thorndike	1,615	3.95	150.00
84-09-063	18" Country Girl Bunny With Basket	A. Thorndike	1,481	31.95	300.00
88-09-064	18" Country Mom Bunny w/Baby	A. Thorndike	1,800	68.95	140.00
70-09-065	7" Bunny w/Butterfly	A. Thorndike	1,264	4.95	150.00
84-09-066	5" Floppy Ear Girl Bunny	A. Thorndike	2,594	11.50	75.00
90-09-067	18" Strawberry Bunny	A. Thorndike	2,365	59.95	200.00
90-09-068	30" Strawberry Bunny	A. Thorndike	582	135.95	300.00
86-09-069	18" C.B. Bunny w/Wheelbarrow	A. Thorndike	1,224	46.95	75.00
86-09-070	18" C.G. Bunny w/Flowers	A. Thorndike	1,205	41.50	75.00
80-09-071	18" C.G. Bunny w/Basket	A. Thorndike	3,964	19.95	150.00
78-09-072	29" E.P. Mom & Pop Bunnies (pair)	A. Thorndike	529	36.95	400.00
77-09-073	7" Bunny w/Egg	A. Thorndike	2,442	5.95	125.00
70-09-074	7" Yellow Bunny	A. Thorndike	N/A	3.95	300.00
77-09-074	7" Yellow Bunny	A. Thorndike	N/A	N/A	275.00
65-09-075	12" Nipsy-Tipsy Hare	A. Thorndike	N/A	7.50	700.00
69-09-076	7" Bunny w/Oversized Carrot	A. Thorndike	N/A	4.95	400.00
84-09-077	7" Valentine Bunny	A. Thorndike	5,603	13.95	125.00
84-09-078	7" Valentine Bunny	A. Thorndike	5,602	13.95	125.00
76-09-079	18" Girl Bunny With Egg	A. Thorndike	789	13.50	375.00
76-09-080	18" Easter Parade Boy Bunny	A. Thorndike	791	13.50	300.00

Annalee Mobilitee Dolls — **Pigs**

Company Number	Name	Series Artist	Edition Limit	Issue Price	Quote
82-10-001	8" Boy BBQ Pig	A. Thorndike	1,044	11.95	55.00
81-10-002	8" Boy BBQ Pig	A. Thorndike	1,159	11.95	100.00
81-10-003	8" Girl BBQ Pig	A. Thorndike	2,596	9.95	250.00
80-10-004	4" Pig	A. Thorndike	1,615	8.50	100.00
81-10-005	4" Pig	A. Thorndike	3,194	7.95	100.00
82-10-006	8" Ballerina Pig	A. Thorndike	1,058	12.95	250.00
81-10-007	3" Pig	A. Thorndike	3,435	7.95	100.00
79-10-008	14" Father Pig	A. Thorndike	1,500	18.95	150.00
79-10-009	14" Mom Pig	A. Thorndike	1,807	18.95	150.00
81-10-010	8" Boy B-B-Q Pig	A. Thorndike	4,072	10.50	200.00
81-10-011	8" Girl B-B-Q Pig	A. Thorndike	3,854	10.50	pair
88-10-012	10" Easter Parade Boy Pig	A. Thorndike	3,005	24.50	180.00
88-10-013	10" Easter Parade Girl Pig	A. Thorndike	3,400	24.50	pair
69-10-014	4" Pig-Bubble Time w/Champagne Glass	A. Thorndike	N/A	4.95	275.00

Annalee Mobilitee Dolls — **Frogs**

Company Number	Name	Series Artist	Edition Limit	Issue Price	Quote
69-11-001	10" Bride & Groom Frogs Courtin'	A. Thorndike	N/A	7.95	550.00
74-11-002	42" Willie Wog Frog	A. Thorndike	223	51.95	700.00
74-11-003	10" Wille Wog Goin' Fishing	A. Thorndike	Unkn.	5.50	200.00
79-11-004	10" Girl Frog	A. Thorndike	5,970	8.50	90.00
79-11-005	18" Girl Frog	A. Thorndike	2,338	18.95	225.00
87-11-006	10" Leap Frogs	A. Thorndike	1,800	31.95	80.00
71-11-007	10" Bride & Groom Frogs On Bike	A. Thorndike	13	17.50	625.00
81-11-008	18" Girl Frog	A. Thorndike	666	24.00	225.00
80-11-009	10" Boy Frog	A. Thorndike	4,185	9.50	125.00
80-11-010	10" Girl Frog	A. Thorndike	421	9.50	125.00
80-11-011	42" Frog	A. Thorndike	202	89.95	500.00
80-11-012	10" Bride Frog	A. Thorndike	1,653	14.95	150.00
80-11-013	10" Groom Frog	A. Thorndike	1,611	14.95	150.00
80-11-014	18" Boy Frog	A. Thorndike	1,285	23.00	150.00
81-11-015	10" Groom Frog	A. Thorndike	2,061	14.95	150.00
81-11-016	10" Bride Frog	A. Thorndike	1,239	14.95	150.00
69-11-017	42" Frog	A. Thorndike	30	29.95	700.00
69-11-018	10" Croaker Frog Band	A. Thorndike	N/A	24.95	3700.00
69-11-019	18" Croaker Crosby Frog With Instrument	A. Thorndike	N/A	10.95	300.00
71-11-020	18" Frog w/Bass Viola	A. Thorndike	224	11.95	1350.00
71-11-021	10" Frog w/Instrument	A. Thorndike	233	3.95	200.00
79-11-022	10" Boy Frog	A. Thorndike	5,642	8.50	90.00
80-11-023	42" Santa Frog	A. Thorndike	206	100.00	700.00
80-11-024	18" Santa Frog	A. Thorndike	2,126	25.00	225.00
92-11-025	10" Frog In Boat, proof	A. Thorndike	1	N/A	900.00

Annalee Mobilitee Dolls — **Assorted Animals**

Company Number	Name	Series Artist	Edition Limit	Issue Price	Quote
81-12-001	18" Escort Fox*	A. Thorndike	Unkn.	28.50	350.00
81-12-002	18" Foxy Lady*	A. Thorndike	Unkn.	28.50	350.00
81-12-003	7" Escort Fox	A. Thorndike	Unkn.	12.50	250.00
81-12-004	7" Foxy Lady	A. Thorndike	Unkn.	12.50	250.00
72-12-005	36" Election Elephant	A. Thorndike	113	Unkn.	550.00
76-12-006	8" Election Elephant	A. Thorndike	1,223	Unkn.	175.00
72-12-007	30" Election Donkey	A. Thorndike	120	23.95	350.00
83-12-008	5" Dragon With Wings & Baby	A. Thorndike	199	22.50	900.00
82-12-009	5" Dragon With Bushboy	A. Thorndike	1,066	17.95	475.00
81-12-010	14" Dragon With Bushboy	A. Thorndike	1,257	28.95	650.00
81-12-011	29" Dragon With Bushboy	A. Thorndike	76	69.95	1050.00
85-12-012	12" Jazz Cat	A. Thorndike	2,622	Unkn.	250.00
87-12-013	10" Bride & Groom Cat	A. Thorndike	727	Unkn.	200.00
76-12-014	36" Election Donkey	A. Thorndike	119	Unkn.	650.00
76-12-015	10" Vote Donkey	A. Thorndike	1,202	5.95	225.00
82-12-016	12" Girl Skunk	A. Thorndike	936	27.95	225.00
82-12-017	12" Boy Skunk	A. Thorndike	935	27.95	225.00
82-12-018	12" Skunk With Snowball	A. Thorndike	1,304	Unkn.	225.00
76-12-019	8" Rooster	A. Thorndike	1,094	5.50	250.00
77-12-020	15" Purple Rooster	A. Thorndike	548	5.48	450.00
70-12-021	7" Blue Monkey	A. Thorndike	293	Unkn.	250.00
81-12-022	7" Monkey With Banana Trapeze	A. Thorndike	3,075	Unkn.	125.00
81-12-023	12" Boy Monkey With Trapeze	A. Thorndike	1,800	23.95	300.00
81-12-024	12" Girl Monkey With Trapeze	A. Thorndike	857	23.95	200.00
73-12-025	12" Girl Nightshirt Monkey	A. Thorndike	Unkn.	7.50	300.00
75-12-026	18" Horse	A. Thorndike	221	17.00	200.00
86-12-027	18" Valentine Cat	A. Thorndike	Unkn.	Unkn.	125.00
72-12-028	12" Cat With Mouse	A. Thorndike	N/A	13.00	450.00
83-12-029	5" Dragon With Wings & Baby	A. Thorndike	199	22.50	300.00
76-12-030	15" Rooster	A. Thorndike	485	13.50	1050.00

Company Number	Name	Series Artist	Edition Limit	Issue Price	Quote
76-12-031	36" Horse	A. Thorndike	27	48.00	500.00
76-12-032	18" Elephant	A. Thorndike	285	16.95	425.00
72-12-033	10" Donkey	A. Thorndike	861	5.95	175.00
77-12-034	8" Rooster	A. Thorndike	1,642	6.00	400.00
68-12-035	12" Ice Pack Cat	A. Thorndike	N/A	6.95	500.00
71-12-036	7" Yellow Kitten	A. Thorndike	103	4.50	575.00
68-12-037	12" Tessie Tar Cat	A. Thorndike	N/A	6.95	450.00
85-12-038	15" Jazz Cat	A. Thorndike	2,622	31.95	250.00
76-12-039	10" Donkey	A. Thorndike	1,202	5.95	150.00
76-12-040	10" Elephant	A. Thorndike	1,223	5.95	225.00
83-12-041	24" Stork With Baby	A. Thorndike	858	36.95	175.00
77-12-042	8" Rooster	A. Thorndike	1,642	5.95	300.00
81-12-043	29" Dragon With Bushboy	A. Thorndike	75	63.95	1050.00
73-12-044	7" Girl Niteshirt Mouse	A. Thorndike	1,740	5.50	105.00
87-12-045	10" Bride Cat	A. Thorndike	727	35.95	250.00
87-12-046	10" Groom Cat	A. Thorndike	762	35.95	pair
85-12-047	18" Valentine Cat With Heart	A. Thorndike	2,129	34.95	225.00
65-12-048	8" Elephant-Republican	A. Thorndike	N/A	4.95	225.00
70-12-049	7" Monkey	A. Thorndike	293	4.95	525.00
87-12-050	24" Christmas Goose With Basket	A. Thorndike	N/A	54.95	150.00
67-12-051	36" Christmas Cat	A. Thorndike	N/A	12.00	350.00
67-12-052	12" Laura May Cat	A. Thorndike	N/A	6.95	850.00
68-12-053	6" Myrtle Turtle	A. Thorndike	N/A	3.95	700.00
86-12-054	10" Christmas Panda w/Toybag	A. Thorndike	4,397	18.95	150.00
76-12-055	18" Vote 76 Donkey	A. Thorndike	285	16.95	300.00
72-12-056	16" Elephant	A. Thorndike	230	12.95	285.00
81-12-057	18" Cat w/Mouse & Mistletoe	A. Thorndike	18,995	46.95	150.00
88-12-058	10" Stork w/3" Baby	A. Thorndike	500	49.95	145.00
86-12-059	10" Kitten w/Yarn & Basket	A. Thorndike	3,917	27.95	125.00
67-12-060	12" Fancy Nancy Cat Christmas	A. Thorndike	N/A	6.95	700.00
82-12-061	7" Santa Fox w/Bag	A. Thorndike	3,622	12.95	400.00
92-12-062	10" Spring Chicken, proof	A. Thorndike	1	N/A	800.00
66-12-063	12" Sneaky Cat	A. Thorndike	Unkn.	6.95	525.00
70-12-064	7" Monkey (Bristol Blue)	A. Thorndike	293	4.95	300.00
70-12-065	22" Monkey (Hot Pink)	A. Thorndike	70	10.95	1650.00
70-12-066	10" Nightshirt Monkey With Candle	A. Thorndike	71	4.95	500.00
73-12-067	12" Nightshirt Monkey	A. Thorndike	835	7.50	225.00
84-12-068	18" Christmas Panda With Toybag	A. Thorndike	4,144	39.95	275.00
72-12-069	8" Elephant	A. Thorndike	966	7.00	200.00
72-12-070	16" Elephant (Republican)	A. Thorndike	230	12.95	600.00
72-12-071	16" Democratic Donkey	A. Thorndike	219	12.95	600.00
73-12-072	7" Bear With Bumblebee	A. Thorndike	694	4.50	250.00
76-12-073	15" Duck	A. Thorndike	1,895	13.50	175.00
81-12-074	18" Cat With 7" Mouse & Mistletoe	A. Thorndike	5,685	31.95	275.00
81-12-075	7" Escort & Lady Fox	A. Thorndike	N/A	N/A	475.00
82-12-076	18" Boy Skunk	A. Thorndike	935	N/A	250.00
85-12-077	12" Jazz Cat With Instrument	A. Thorndike	2,622	31.95	225.00
85-12-078	18" Be My Honey Bear	A. Thorndike	705	39.95	130.00
87-12-079	10" Girl Bear	A. Thorndike	2,200	20.95	225.00
86-12-080	15" Hobo Cat	A. Thorndike	4,130	35.95	250.00
88-12-081	10" Easter Parade Boy Pig	A. Thorndike	N/A	24.50	75.00
88-12-082	10" Easter Parade Girl Pig	A. Thorndike	N/A	24.50	75.00
88-12-083	10" Easter Parade Goose	A. Thorndike	2,450	29.95	60.00
87-12-084	10" Frog In Top Hat & Tails	A. Thorndike	1,325	23.95	95.00
89-12-085	10" Christmas Goose	A. Thorndike	3,007	30.95	55.00
89-12-086	24" Christmas Goose With Basket	A. Thorndike	2,036	57.95	75.00
89-12-087	10" Bear On Sled	A. Thorndike	3,563	28.95	60.00
89-12-088	10" Country Boy Goose	A. Thorndike	N/A	N/A	65.00
89-12-089	10" Country Girl Goose	A. Thorndike	N/A	N/A	65.00
90-12-090	24" Spring Swan	A. Thorndike	671	62.95	150.00
93-12-091	10" Cooking Bear	A. Thorndike	1	N/A	900.00
93-12-092	10" Skating Penguin	A. Thorndike	1	N/A	525.00
93-12-094	10" Doctor Bear	A. Thorndike	1	N/A	600.00
93-12-095	10" Beach Bear	A. Thorndike	1	N/A	850.00
88-12-096	10" Eskimo Bear	A. Thorndike	7,500	31.95	100.00

Annalee Mobilitee Dolls — **Ducks**

Company Number	Name	Series Artist	Edition Limit	Issue Price	Quote
83-13-001	5" Sweetheart Duck	A. Thorndike	1,530	Unkn.	40.00
83-13-002	5" E.P. Boy Duck	A. Thorndike	5,133	Unkn.	50.00
83-13-003	5" E.P. Girl Duck	A. Thorndike	5,577	Unkn.	50.00
84-13-004	5" Pilot Duckling	A. Thorndike	4,396	14.95	150.00
86-13-005	5" Duck with Raincoat	A. Thorndike	5,029	Unkn.	200.00
85-13-006	12" Duck with Raincoat	A. Thorndike	Unkn.	Unkn.	275.00
82-13-007	12" Duck with Kerchief	A. Thorndike	5,861	26.95	125.00
75-13-008	5" Baby Duck	A. Thorndike	1,333	4.00	135.00
76-13-009	8" White Duck	A. Thorndike	3,265	4.95	225.00
87-13-010	12" Duck On Sled	A. Thorndike	300	N/A	500.00

Annalee Mobilitee Dolls — **Elves/Gnomes/Woodsprites/Leprechauns**

Company Number	Name	Series Artist	Edition Limit	Issue Price	Quote
74-14-001	22" Workshop Elf With Apron	A. Thorndike	1,404	10.95	882.00
82-14-002	10" Elf On Butterfly	A. Thorndike	882	Unkn.	275.00
81-14-003	10" Elf On Butterfly	A. Thorndike	1,625	24.95	300.00
60-14-004	5" Elf	A. Thorndike	Unkn.	Unkn.	200.00
54-14-005	10" Elf	A. Thorndike	Unkn.	Unkn.	275.00
70-14-006	10" Elf Skier	A. Thorndike	597	Unkn.	200.00
69-14-007	10" White Elf With Presents	A. Thorndike	Unkn.	Unkn.	180.00
67-14-008	10" Elf with Skis	A. Thorndike	48	3.00	350.00
77-14-009	18" White Elf	A. Thorndike	2,600	Unkn.	150.00
78-14-010	12" Christmas Gnome	A. Thorndike	10,140	Unkn.	125.00
63-14-011	10" Yellow Woodsprite	A. Thorndike	Unkn.	Unkn.	275.00
63-14-012	10" White Woodsprite	A. Thorndike	Unkn.	Unkn.	325.00
63-14-013	10" Elf Skier	A. Thorndike	Unkn.	Unkn.	350.00
83-14-014	10" Workshop Elf	A. Thorndike	Unkn.	Unkn.	75.00
65-14-015	5" Green Gnome	A. Thorndike	Unkn.	Unkn.	125.00
80-14-016	7" Gnome	A. Thorndike	13,238	9.50	150.00
79-14-017	18" Gnome	A. Thorndike	9,048	16.95	350.00
63-14-018	5" Christmas Elf	A. Thorndike	Unkn.	3.00	200.00
81-14-019	10" Jack Frost with Snowflake	A. Thorndike	5,950	31.95	175.00
72-14-020	18" Leprechaun	A. Thorndike	1,372	Unkn.	200.00
81-14-021	12" Elf With Butterfly	A. Thorndike	N/A	27.95	475.00
70-14-022	10" Casualty Elf	A. Thorndike	991	225	300.00
71-14-023	5" Gnome With Candle	A. Thorndike	N/A	3.00	300.00
64-14-024	18" Woodsprite	A. Thorndike	N/A	6.00	325.00
72-14-025	10" Robin Hood Elf	A. Thorndike	N/A	2.50	175.00
82-14-026	10" Jackfrost With Snowflake	A. Thorndike	2,289	13.50	250.00
67-14-027	10" Workshop Elf	A. Thorndike	N/A	N/A	175.00
57-14-028	9" Elf With Musical instrument	A. Thorndike	N/A	3.50	550.00
57-14-029	10" Mr. Holly Elf	A. Thorndike	N/A	N/A	1600.00
64-14-030	10" Imp Skier	A. Thorndike	N/A	4.00	350.00
64-14-031	22" Woodsprite	A. Thorndike	N/A	5.95	325.00
79-14-032	29" Gnome	A. Thorndike	1,762	47.95	400.00
83-14-033	10" Ballooning Elves	A. Thorndike	7,395	59.95	200.00
74-14-034	22" Workshop Elf	A. Thorndike	1,404	10.45	125.00
63-14-035	18" Friar Bottle Cover	A. Thorndike	N/A	3.00	350.00
71-14-036	10" Elf Skier	A. Thorndike	N/A	N/A	100.00
63-14-037	24" Woodsprite	A. Thorndike	N/A	5.45	125.00
67-14-038	10" Elf With Round Box	A. Thorndike	N/A	2.50	350.00
59-14-039	10" Elf With Instrument	A. Thorndike	N/A	3.50	400.00
57-14-040	10" Holly Elf	A. Thorndike	N/A	N/A	500.00
71-14-041	7" Three Gnomes w/Large Candle	A. Thorndike	80	11.95	700.00
63-14-042	10" Christmas Elf w/Tinsel	A. Thorndike	N/A	N/A	250.00
62-14-043	5" Elf w/Feather Hair	A. Thorndike	N/A	9.00	300.00
77-14-044	22" Jack Frost Elf	A. Thorndike	2,600	11.95	400.00
78-14-045	12" Gnome	A. Thorndike	10,140	9.50	175.00
59-14-046	10" Green Woodsprite	A. Thorndike	N/A	6.95	350.00
67-14-047	12" Gnome w/PJ Suit	A. Thorndike	N/A	N/A	425.00
67-14-048	7" Gnome w/PJ Suit	A. Thorndike	N/A	2.50	250.00

Annalee Mobilitee Dolls — **Humans**

Company Number	Name	Series Artist	Edition Limit	Issue Price	Quote
87-15-001	3" Bride & Groom	A. Thorndike	1,250	38.95	135.00
68-15-002	7" Fat Fanny	A. Thorndike	Unkn.	6.00	375.00
84-15-003	10" Aerobic Dancer	A. Thorndike	4,785	Unkn.	75.00
85-15-004	10" Bride	A. Thorndike	318	Unkn.	125.00
85-15-005	10" Groom	A. Thorndike	264	Unkn.	125.00
57-15-006	10" Boy With Straw Hat	A. Thorndike	Unkn.	Unkn.	500.00
59-15-007	10" Boy & Girl On Bike	A. Thorndike	Unkn.	Unkn.	575.00
56-15-008	10" Fishing Girl	A. Thorndike	Unkn.	Unkn.	425.00
57-15-009	10" Boy Building Boat	A. Thorndike	Unkn.	Unkn.	925.00
59-15-010	10" Girl Swimmer	A. Thorndike	Unkn.	Unkn.	550.00
55-15-011	10" Boy Swimmer	A. Thorndike	Unkn.	Unkn.	550.00
63-15-012	10" Girl Waterskier	A. Thorndike	Unkn.	7.50	450.00
59-15-013	10" Boy Golfer	A. Thorndike	Unkn.	Unkn.	475.00
50-15-014	10" Girl Golfer	A. Thorndike	Unkn.	Unkn.	475.00
81-15-015	10" Boy on Raft	A. Thorndike	Unkn.	Unkn.	200.00
57-15-016	10" Valentine Doll	A. Thorndike	Unkn.	Unkn.	925.00
57-15-017	10" Thanksgiving Doll	A. Thorndike	Unkn.	Unkn.	600.00
76-15-018	10" Country Girl In Tire Swing	A. Thorndike	357	Unkn.	200.00
74-15-019	10" Ladd & Lass	A. Thorndike	453	Unkn.	300.00
84-15-020	18" Bob Cratchet	A. Thorndike	1,819	49.95	250.00
84-15-021	18" Martha Cratchet	A. Thorndike	1,751	35.95	350.00
84-15-022	18" Aerobic Dancer	A. Thorndike	622	35.95	175.00
75-15-023	18" Lass	A. Thorndike	224	11.95	95.00
75-15-024	18" Ladd	A. Thorndike	206	11.95	175.00
76-15-025	18" Uncle Sam	A. Thorndike	345	17.00	425.00
57-15-026	10" Girl Skier	A. Thorndike	Unkn.	Unkn.	1000.00
59-15-027	10" Girl Skier	A. Thorndike	Unkn.	Unkn.	825.00
59-15-028	10" Boy Skier	A. Thorndike	Unkn.	Unkn.	800.00
85-15-029	10" Cross Country Skier	A. Thorndike	1,150	Unkn.	75.00
59-15-030	7" Girl Skier	A. Thorndike	Unkn.	Unkn.	675.00
60-15-031	10" Girl Skier	A. Thorndike	Unkn.	Unkn.	400.00
55-15-032	7" Boy Skier	A. Thorndike	Unkn.	Unkn.	1250.00
75-15-033	10" Caroler Boy	A. Thorndike	Unkn.	Unkn.	275.00
76-15-034	18" Choir Boy	A. Thorndike	Unkn.	Unkn.	500.00
76-15-035	10" Drummer Boy	A. Thorndike	Unkn.	6.00	200.00
76-15-036	18" Drummer Boy	A. Thorndike	402	13.50	400.00
87-15-037	5" Monk	A. Thorndike	Unkn.	13.95	50.00
67-15-038	10" Monk	A. Thorndike	Unkn.	Unkn.	200.00
82-15-039	10" Monk	A. Thorndike	6,968	12.95	130.00
83-15-040	16" Monk With Jug	A. Thorndike	Unkn.	27.95	200.00
84-15-041	30" Monk	A. Thorndike	432	78.50	300.00
63-15-042	18" Friar	A. Thorndike	Unkn.	Unkn.	400.00
87-15-043	18" Bottlecover Monk	A. Thorndike	718	29.95	105.00
84-15-044	18" Monk With Jug	A. Thorndike	1,821	34.95	295.00
76-15-045	18" Yankee Doodle Dandy	A. Thorndike	153	Unkn.	425.00
78-15-046	10" Boy Pilgrim	A. Thorndike	3,461	7.00	325.00
78-15-047	10" Boy Pilgrim	A. Thorndike	3,465	7.00	325.00
59-15-048	10" Boy Golfer	A. Thorndike	N/A	10.00	325.00
57-15-049	10" Girl Skier	A. Thorndike	N/A	15.00	1500.00
68-15-050	7" Fat Fanny	A. Thorndike	N/A	5.95	375.00
57-15-051	10" Casualty Ski Group	A. Thorndike	N/A	35.00	3100.00
68-15-052	10" Boy With Beachball	A. Thorndike	N/A	5.95	375.00
59-15-053	10" Boy Square Dancer	A. Thorndike	N/A	10.00	475.00
69-15-054	10" Nun On Skis	A. Thorndike	1,551	4.50	300.00
59-15-055	10" Girl Square Dancer	A. Thorndike	N/A	10.00	475.00
66-15-056	10" Boy Go-Go Dancer	A. Thorndike	N/A	10.00	275.00
57-15-057	10" Casualty Toboggan Group	A. Thorndike	N/A	35.00	900.00
58-15-058	10" Spring Doll	A. Thorndike	N/A	10.00	3500.00
59-15-059	10" Football Player	A. Thorndike	N/A	10.00	600.00
70-15-060	10" Monk With Skis	A. Thorndike	406	4.00	350.00
84-15-061	10" Aerobic Dancer	A. Thorndike	4,875	17.95	150.00
59-15-062	10" Boy & Girl in Fishing Boat	A. Thorndike	N/A	17.00	1000.00
69-15-063	22" Girl Go-Go Dancer	A. Thorndike	N/A	10.00	300.00
71-15-064	10" Nun On Skis	A. Thorndike	617	4.00	300.00
84-15-065	16" Monk With Jug	A. Thorndike	1,767	34.95	200.00
50-15-066	20" Boy & Girl Calypso Dancers	A. Thorndike	N/A	N/A	800.00
59-15-067	10" Dentist	A. Thorndike	N/A	10.00	600.00
59-15-068	10" Texas Oil Man	A. Thorndike	N/A	16.00	1550.00
60-15-069	33" Boy & Girl On Tandem Bike	A. Thorndike	N/A	N/A	3500.00
64-15-070	10" Gendarme	A. Thorndike	N/A	4.00	450.00
65-15-071	10" Back To School, Boy &Girl	A. Thorndike	N/A	19.90	525.00
66-15-072	10" Go-Go Boy &Girl	A. Thorndike	N/A	3.95	500.00
76-15-073	25" Yankee Doodle Dandy On 30" Horse	A. Thorndike	41	77.50	1600.00
89-15-074	10" Two Wisemen, Proof	A. Thorndike	1	N/A	350.00
89-15-075	10" Bob Cratchet &Tiny Tim, Proof	A. Thorndike	1	N/A	450.00
89-15-076	10" Pilgrim Couple, Proof	A. Thorndike	1	N/A	575.00
89-15-077	10" Merlin The Magician, Proof	A. Thorndike	1	N/A	500.00
89-15-078	10" Americana Couple, Proof	A. Thorndike	1	N/A	450.00
89-15-079	10" Wiseman With Camel, Proof	A. Thorndike	1	N/A	600.00
89-15-080	10" Jacob Marley, Proof	A. Thorndike	1	N/A	550.00
84-15-081	10" Downhill Skier	A. Thorndike	3,535	31.95	75.00
84-15-082	8" Monk With Jug	A. Thorndike	3,502	17.95	95.00
65-15-083	10"Monk With Christmas Tree Planting	A. Thorndike	N/A	3.00	275.00
59-15-084	10" Architect	A. Thorndike	N/A	N/A	700.00
57-15-085	10" Fourth Of July Doll	A. Thorndike	N/A	10.00	1600.00
91-15-086	10" Martha Cratchet, Proof	A. Thorndike	1	N/A	650.00
60-15-087	10" Girl Ski Doll	A. Thorndike	N/A	N/A	450.00
64-15-088	10" Monk With Cap	A. Thorndike	N/A	3.00	275.00
57-15-089	10" Skier With Leg In Cast Held By Two Skiers	A. Thorndike	N/A	35.00	1950.00
50-15-090	10" Boy & Girl Skiers	A. Thorndike	N/A	15.00	1250.00
57-15-091	10" Girl Square Dancer	A. Thorndike	N/A	9.95	475.00
57-15-092	10" Boy Square Dancer	A. Thorndike	N/A	9.95	475.00
54-15-093	10" Country Girl	A. Thorndike	N/A	8.95	1000.00
67-15-094	18" Nun	A. Thorndike	296	8.00	525.00
56-15-095	10" Water Skier Girl	A. Thorndike	N/A	9.95	800.00
84-15-096	32" Monk With Holly Garland	A. Thorndike	416	78.50	600.00

Number	Name	Artist	Edition Limit	Issue Price	Quote
57-15-097	10" Valentine Doll	A. Thorndike	N/A	10.00	900.00
87-15-098	10" Huck Fin, #690	A. Thorndike	1,200	102.95	400.00
81-15-099	18" Monk w/Jug	A. Thorndike	494	N/A	290.00
67-15-100	10" Surfer Boy	A. Thorndike	N/A	9.95	400.00
67-15-101	10" Surfer Girl	A. Thorndike	N/A	9.95	400.00
60-15-102	10" Bathing Girl	A. Thorndike	N/A	3.95	300.00
67-15-103	18" Monk w/Plant	A. Thorndike	N/A	7.50	400.00
92-15-104	10" Father Time, proof	A. Thorndike	1	N/A	550.00
89-15-105	10" Merlin	A. Thorndike	3,565	69.95	300.00
71-15-106	10" Choir Girl	A. Thorndike	925	3.95	250.00
77-15-107	8" Drummer Boy	A. Thorndike	6,522	6.00	100.00
76-15-108	10" Uncle Sam	A. Thorndike	1,095	5.95	325.00
63-15-109	22" Bellhop (red)	A. Thorndike	N/A	N/A	700.00
64-15-110	10" Monk (green)	A. Thorndike	N/A	3.00	275.00
50-15-111	10" Frogman (girl diver)	A. Thorndike	N/A	9.95	3800.00
92-15-112	10" Bob Cratchet, proof	A. Thorndike	1	N/A	700.00
92-15-113	10" Scrooge, proof	A. Thorndike	1	N/A	650.00
92-15-114	10" Snow Queen, proof	A. Thorndike	1	N/A	925.00
54-15-115	10" Saks Fifth Ave. Skier	A. Thorndike	50	9.95	1500.00
53-15-116	Girl Water Skier	A. Thorndike	Unkn.	10.00	200.00
Annalee Mobilitee Dolls		**Miscellaneous**			
84-16-001	10" Gingerbread Man	A. Thorndike	4,615	15.95	200.00
83-16-002	18" Gingerbread Man	A. Thorndike	5,027	28.95	250.00
82-16-003	22" Sun	A. Thorndike	838	Unkn.	200.00
83-16-004	22" Sun	A. Thorndike	Unkn.	Unkn.	75.00
76-16-005	42" Scarecrow	A. Thorndike	134	62.00	375.00
83-16-006	18" Scarecrow	A. Thorndike	3,150	32.95	175.00
84-16-007	10" Scarecrow	A. Thorndike	3,008	15.95	125.00
76-16-008	10" Scarecrow	A. Thorndike	2,341	6.00	200.00
83-16-009	18" Scarecrow	A. Thorndike	2,300	28.95	150.00
77-16-010	18" Scarecrow	A. Thorndike	Unkn.	13.50	175.00
85-16-011	10" Scarecrow	A. Thorndike	2,930	15.95	325.00
83-16-012	18" Scarecrow	A. Thorndike	3,896	32.95	200.00
76-16-013	10" Scarecrow	A. Thorndike	2,341	5.95	120.00
77-16-014	10" Scarecrow	A. Thorndike	4,879	5.95	225.00
81-16-015	18" Butterfly w/10" Elf	A. Thorndike	2,517	27.95	400.00
86-16-016	Large Pumpkin w/7" Witch M.	A. Thorndike	668	77.95	250.00
76-16-017	18" Scarecrow	A. Thorndike	916	13.50	250.00
70-16-018	14" Spring Mushroom	A. Thorndike	N/A	N/A	450.00
85-16-019	Christmas Tree Skirt	A. Thorndike	1,332	24.95	110.00
87-16-020	Carrot	A. Thorndike	2,503	9.95	300.00
Annalee Mobilitee Dolls		**Doll Society-Folk Heroes**			
84-17-001	Robin Hood, Proof	A. Thorndike	1	N/A	1200.00
84-17-002	Johnny Appleseed, Proof	A. Thorndike	1	N/A	1000.00
85-17-003	Annie Oakley, Proof	A. Thorndike	1	N/A	1000.00
86-17-004	Mark Twain, Proof	A. Thorndike	1	N/A	1500.00
87-17-005	Ben Franklin, Proof	A. Thorndike	1	N/A	2100.00
88-17-006	Sherlock Holmes, Proof	A. Thorndike	1	N/A	1000.00
89-17-007	Abraham Lincoln, Proof	A. Thorndike	1	N/A	1350.00
90-17-008	Betsy Ross, Proof	A. Thorndike	1	N/A	1500.00
84-17-009	Robin Hood	A. Thorndike	1,500	80.00	N/A
84-17-010	Johnny Appleseed, #627	A. Thorndike	1,500	80.00	900.00
85-17-011	Annie Oakley, #185	A. Thorndike	1,500	95.00	700.00
86-17-012	Mark Twain, #467	A. Thorndike	2,500	119.50	500.00
87-17-013	Ben Franklin, #1776	A. Thorndike	2,500	119.50	525.00
88-17-014	Sherlock Holmes, #391	A. Thorndike	2,500	119.50	500.00
89-17-015	Abraham Lincoln, Current Item	A. Thorndike	2,500	119.50	119.50
90-17-016	Betsy Ross, Current Item	A. Thorndike	2,500	119.50	119.50
91-17-017	10" Christopher Columbus, Proof	A. Thorndike	1	N/A	1600.00
Annalee Mobilitee Dolls		**Doll Society-Logo Kids**			
85-18-001	7" Logo Kid, Proof	A. Thorndike	1	N/A	500.00
86-18-002	7" Logo Kid, Proof	A. Thorndike	1	N/A	575.00
87-18-003	7" Logo Kid, Proof	A. Thorndike	1	N/A	500.00
88-18-004	7" Logo Kid, Proof	A. Thorndike	1	N/A	400.00
89-18-005	7" Logo Kid, Proof	A. Thorndike	1	N/A	550.00
90-18-006	7" Logo Kid, Proof	A. Thorndike	1	N/A	850.00
85-18-007	7" Logo Kid	A. Thorndike	3,562	N/A	250.00
86-18-008	7" Logo Kid	A. Thorndike	6,271	N/A	175.00
87-18-009	7" Logo Kid	A. Thorndike	11,000	N/A	150.00
88-18-010	7" Logo Kid	A. Thorndike	N/A	N/A	100.00
89-18-011	7" Logo Kid	A. Thorndike	N/A	N/A	N/A
90-18-012	7" Logo Kid, Current Item	A. Thorndike	N/A	N/A	N/A
91-18-013	7" Logo Kid, Proof	A. Thorndike	1	N/A	775.00
Annalee Mobilitee Dolls		**Doll Society-Animals**			
85-19-001	10" Penguin With Chick, Proof	A. Thorndike	1	N/A	650.00
86-19-002	10" Unicorn, Proof	A. Thorndike	1	N/A	1050.00
87-19-003	10" Kangaroo, Proof	A. Thorndike	1	N/A	375.00
88-19-004	10" Owl, Proof	A. Thorndike	1	N/A	900.00
89-19-005	10" Polar Bear, Proof	A. Thorndike	1	N/A	1100.00
90-19-006	10" Chicken, Proof	A. Thorndike	1	N/A	1150.00
85-19-007	10" Penguin With Chick, #178	A. Thorndike	3,000	30.00	225.00
86-19-008	10" Unicorn, #268	A. Thorndike	3,000	36.50	350.00
87-19-009	7" Kangaroo	A. Thorndike	3,000	37.50	N/A
88-19-010	5" Owl	A. Thorndike	3,000	37.50	N/A
89-19-011	7" Polar Bear Cub, Current Item	A. Thorndike	3,000	37.50	N/A
90-19-012	7" Chicken, Current Item	A. Thorndike	3,000	37.50	N/A
91-19-013	10" World War II Aviator Frog, Proof	A. Thorndike	1	N/A	775.00
91-19-014	7" Sherrif Mouse, Proof	A. Thorndike	1	N/A	675.00
Annalee Mobilitee Dolls		**Commemoratives**			
66-20-001	10" Central Gas Co. Elf	A. Thorndike	N/A	N/A	350.00
61-20-002	10" Human Red Devil One-Of-A-Kind	A. Thorndike	1	N/A	450.00
81-20-003	7" "I'm Late Bunny"	A. Thorndike	N/A	N/A	575.00
66-20-004	5" New Hampton School Baby (Winter Carnival)	A. Thorndike	300	N/A	200.00
91-20-005	10" Victory Ski Doll, Proof	A. Thorndike	1	N/A	600.00
91-20-006	10" Bamboo Shop Girl	A. Thorndike	1	N/A	650.00
62-20-007	10" Two Realtor Dolls w/Land	A. Thorndike	1	N/A	875.00
ANRI		**Disney Dolls**			
89-01-001	Mickey Mouse, 14"	Disney Studios	Closed	850.00	895.00
89-01-002	Minnie Mouse, 14"	Disney Studios	Closed	850.00	895.00
89-01-003	Pinocchio, 14"	Disney Studios	Closed	850.00	895.00
90-01-004	Donald Duck, 14"	Disney Studios	Closed	895.00	895.00
90-01-005	Daisy Duck, 14"	Disney Studios	Closed	895.00	895.00
ANRI		**Sarah Kay Dolls**			
88-02-001	Jennifer, 14"	S. Kay	Closed	500.00	500.00
88-02-002	Rebecca, 14"	S. Kay	Closed	500.00	500.00
88-02-003	Sarah, 14"	S. Kay	Closed	500.00	500.00
88-02-004	Katherine, 14"	S. Kay	Closed	500.00	500.00
88-02-005	Martha, 14"	S. Kay	Closed	500.00	500.00
88-02-006	Emily, 14"	S. Kay	Closed	500.00	500.00
88-02-007	Rachael, 14"	S. Kay	Closed	500.00	500.00
88-02-008	Victoria, 14"	S. Kay	Closed	500.00	500.00
89-02-009	Bride to Love And To Cherish	S. Kay	750	750.00	775.00
89-02-010	Groom With This Ring Doll	S. Kay	750	550.00	575.00
89-02-011	Charlotte (Blue)	S. Kay	Closed	550.00	575.00
89-02-012	Henry	S. Kay	Closed	550.00	575.00
89-02-013	Elizabeth (Patchwork)	S. Kay	Closed	550.00	575.00
89-02-014	Helen (Brown)	S. Kay	Closed	550.00	575.00
89-02-015	Eleanor (Floral)	S. Kay	Closed	550.00	575.00
89-02-016	Mary (Red)	S. Kay	Closed	550.00	575.00
90-02-017	Polly, 14"	S. Kay	1,000	575.00	680.00
90-02-018	Christina, 14"	S. Kay	1,000	575.00	730.00
90-02-019	Faith, 14"	S. Kay	1,000	575.00	685.00
90-02-020	Sophie, 14"	S. Kay	1,000	575.00	660.00
91-02-021	Jessica, 7"	S. Kay	1,500	300.00	300.00
91-02-022	Michelle, 7"	S. Kay	1,500	300.00	300.00
91-02-023	Peggy, 7"	S. Kay	1,500	300.00	300.00
91-02-024	Annie, 7"	S. Kay	1,500	300.00	300.00
91-02-025	Susan, 7"	S. Kay	1,500	300.00	300.00
91-02-026	Julie, 7"	S. Kay	1,500	300.00	300.00
91-02-027	Janine, 14"	S. Kay	1,500	750.00	750.00
91-02-028	Patricia, 14"	S. Kay	1,500	730.00	730.00
ANRI		**Ferrandiz Dolls**			
89-03-001	Gabriel, 14"	J. Ferrandiz	Closed	550.00	575.00
89-03-002	Maria, 14"	J. Ferrandiz	Closed	550.00	575.00
90-03-003	Margarite, 14"	J. Ferrandiz	1,000	575.00	730.00
90-03-004	Philipe, 14"	J. Ferrandiz	1,000	575.00	680.00
91-03-005	Carmen, 14"	J. Ferrandiz	1,000	730.00	730.00
91-03-006	Fernando, 14"	J. Ferrandiz	1,000	730.00	730.00
91-03-007	Miguel, 7"	J. Ferrandiz	1,500	300.00	300.00
91-03-008	Juanita, 7"	J. Ferrandiz	1,500	300.00	300.00
Artaffects		**Art Doll Collection**			
86-01-001	Morning Star 17-1/2"	G. Perillo	1,000	250.00	250.00
88-01-002	Sunflower 12"	G. Perillo	2,500	175.00	175.00
90-01-003	Little Dove	G. Perillo	5,000	175.00	175.00
90-01-004	Straight Arrow	G. Perillo	5,000	175.00	175.00
92-01-005	Brave and Free	G. Perillo	N/A	111.00	111.00
Ashton-Drake Galleries		**Yolanda's Picture - Perfect Babies**			
85-01-001	Jason	Y. Bello	Closed	48.00	695-1150.
86-01-002	Heather	Y. Bello	Closed	48.00	400-550.
87-01-003	Jennifer	Y. Bello	Closed	58.00	300-550.
87-01-004	Matthew	Y. Bello	Closed	58.00	225-325.
87-01-005	Sarah	Y. Bello	Closed	58.00	125-300.
88-01-006	Amanda	Y. Bello	Closed	63.00	125-225.
89-01-007	Jessica	Y. Bello	Closed	63.00	70-85.00
90-01-008	Michael	Y. Bello	Closed	63.00	100-115.
90-01-009	Lisa	Y. Bello	Closed	63.00	75-115.
91-01-010	Emily	Y. Bello	Closed	63.00	63.00
91-01-011	Danielle	Y. Bello	Closed	69.00	69.00
Ashton-Drake Galleries		**Children of Mother Goose**			
87-02-001	Little Bo Peep	Y. Bello	Closed	58.00	200-350.
87-02-002	Mary Had a Little Lamb	Y. Bello	Closed	58.00	150-250.
88-02-003	Little Jack Horner	Y. Bello	Closed	63.00	125.00
89-02-004	Miss Muffet	Y. Bello	Closed	63.00	78-150.00
Ashton-Drake Galleries		**Yolanda's Lullaby Babies**			
91-03-001	Christy (Rock-a-Bye)	Y. Bello	Closed	69.00	69.00
92-03-002	Joey (Twinkle, Twinkle)	Y. Bello	12/93	69.00	69.00
Ashton-Drake Galleries		**Moments To Remember**			
91-04-001	Justin	Y. Bello	Closed	75.00	75.00
92-04-002	Jill	Y. Bello	12/93	75.00	75.00
Ashton-Drake Galleries		**Yolanda's Precious Playmates**			
92-05-001	David	Y. Bello	Closed	69.95	69.95
Ashton-Drake Galleries		**Parade of American Fashion**			
87-06-001	The Glamour of the Gibson Girl	Stevens/Siegel	Closed	77.00	195-250.
88-06-002	The Southern Belle	Stevens/Siegel	Closed	77.00	175-250.
90-06-003	Victorian Lady	Stevens/Siegel	Closed	82.00	82.00
91-06-004	Romantic Lady	Stevens/Siegel	Closed	85.00	85.00
Ashton-Drake Galleries		**Heroines from the Fairy Tale Forests**			
88-07-001	Little Red Riding Hood	D. Effner	Closed	68.00	150-295.
89-07-002	Goldilocks	D. Effner	Closed	68.00	75-85.00
90-07-003	Snow White	D. Effner	Closed	73.00	85-125.00
91-07-004	Rapunzel	D. Effner	Closed	79.00	79.00
92-07-005	Cinderella	D. Effner	Closed	79.00	79.00
Ashton-Drake Galleries		**International Festival of Toys and Tots**			
89-08-001	Chen, a Little Boy of China	K. Hippensteel	Closed	78.00	175-350.
89-08-002	Natasha	K. Hippensteel	Closed	78.00	100.00
90-08-003	Molly	K. Hippensteel	Closed	83.00	83.00
91-08-004	Hans	K. Hippensteel	Closed	88.00	88.00
Ashton-Drake Galleries		**Born To Be Famous**			
89-09-001	Little Sherlock	K. Hippensteel	Closed	87.00	110-125.
90-09-002	Little Florence Nightingale	K. Hippensteel	Closed	87.00	87.00
91-09-003	Little Davey Crockett	K. Hippensteel	Closed	92.00	92.00
92-09-004	Little Christopher Columbus	K. Hippensteel	12/93	95.00	95.00
Ashton-Drake Galleries		**Baby Book Treasures**			
90-10-001	Elizabeth's Homecoming	K. Hippensteel	Closed	58.00	80.00
91-10-002	Catherine's Christening	K. Hippensteel	Closed	58.00	58.00
91-10-003	Christopher's First Smile	K. Hippensteel	Closed	63.00	63.00
Ashton-Drake Galleries		**Growing Young Minds**			
91-11-001	Alex	K. Hippensteel	12/93	79.00	79.00
Ashton-Drake Galleries		**Happiness Is...**			
91-12-001	Patricia (My First Tooth)	K. Hippensteel	Closed	69.00	69.00
92-12-002	Crystal	K. Hippensteel	12/93	69.95	69.95
Ashton-Drake Galleries		**Cindy's Playhouse Pals**			
89-13-001	Meagan	C. McClure	Closed	87.00	125-150.
89-13-002	Shelly	C. McClure	Closed	87.00	87-110.00
90-13-003	Ryan	C. McClure	Closed	89.00	89.00

Company / Number	Name	Series / Artist	Edition Limit	Issue Price	Quote
91-13-004	Samantha	C. McClure	Closed	89.00	89.00
Ashton-Drake Galleries		**A Children's Circus**			
90-14-001	Tommy The Clown	J. McClelland	Closed	78.00	78-95.00
91-14-002	Katie The Tightrope Walker	J. McClelland	Closed	78.00	78.00
91-14-003	Johnnie The Strongman	J. McClelland	Closed	83.00	83.00
92-14-004	Maggie The Animal Trainer	J. McClelland	Closed	83.00	83.00
Ashton-Drake Galleries		**Maude Fangel's Cover Babies**			
90-15-001	Peek-A-Boo Peter	Fangel-Inspired	Closed	73.00	73.00
90-15-002	Benjamin's Ball	Fangel-Inspired	Closed	73.00	73.00
Ashton-Drake Galleries		**Amish Blessings**			
90-16-001	Rebeccah	J. Good-Kruger	Closed	68.00	68.00
91-16-002	Rachel	J. Good-Kruger	Closed	69.00	69.00
91-16-003	Adam	J. Good-Kruger	Closed	75.00	75.00
92-16-004	Ruth	J. Good-Kruger	12/93	75.00	75.00
92-16-005	Eli	J. Good-Kruger	12/93	79.95	79.95
Ashton-Drake Galleries		**Polly's Tea Party**			
90-17-001	Polly	S. Krey	Closed	78.00	90-125.00
91-17-002	Lizzie	S. Krey	Closed	79.00	79.00
92-17-003	Annie	S. Krey	12/93	83.00	83.00
Ashton-Drake Galleries		**Yesterday's Dreams**			
90-18-001	Andy	M. Oldenburg	Closed	68.00	68.00
91-18-002	Janey	M. Oldenburg	Closed	69.00	69.00
Ashton-Drake Galleries		**My Closest Friend**			
91-19-001	Boo Bear 'N Me	J. Goodyear	Closed	78.00	100-145.
91-19-002	Me and My Blankie	J. Goodyear	12/92	79.00	79.00
Ashton-Drake Galleries		**The Littlest Clowns**			
91-20-001	Sparkles	M. Tretter	Closed	63.00	63.00
91-20-002	Bubbles	M. Tretter	Closed	65.00	65.00
91-20-003	Smooch	M. Tretter	Closed	69.00	69.00
92-20-004	Daisy	M. Tretter	12/93	69.95	69.95
Ashton Drake Galleries		**Romantic Flower Maidens**			
88-21-001	Rose, Who is Love	M. Roderick	Closed	87.00	125-150.
89-21-002	Daisy	M. Roderick	Closed	87.00	87-150.00
90-21-003	Violet	M. Roderick	Closed	92.00	92.00
90-21-004	Lily	M. Roderick	Closed	92.00	92.00
Ashton-Drake Galleries		**Precious Memories of Motherhood**			
90-22-001	Loving Steps	S. Kuck	Closed	125.00	150-195.
90-22-002	Lullaby	S. Kuck	Closed	125.00	125.00
91-22-003	Expectant Moments	S. Kuck	Closed	149.00	149.00
92-22-004	Bedtime	S. Kuck	12/93	149.95	149.95
Ashton-Drake Galleries		**Brides of The Century**			
90-23-001	Flora, The 1900s Bride	E. Williams	Closed	145.00	145.00
91-23-002	Jennifer, The 1980s Bride	E. Williams	Closed	149.00	149.00
92-23-002	Cathleen, The 1990s Bride	E. Williams	12/93	149.95	149.95
Ashton-Drake Galleries		**My Fair Lady**			
91-24-001	Eliza at Ascot	P. Ryan Brooks	Closed	125.00	250-285.
Ashton-Drake Galleries		**The King & I**			
91-25-001	Shall We Dance?	P. Ryan Brooks	Closed	175.00	250.00
Ashton-Drake Galleries		**Stepping Out**			
91-26-001	Millie	Akers/Girardi	Closed	99.00	99.00
Ashton-Drake Galleries		**Year Book Memories**			
91-27-001	Peggy Sue	Akers/Girardi	Closed	87.00	87.00
Ashton-Drake Galleries		**Winterfest**			
91-28-001	Brian	S. Sherwood	Closed	89.00	89.00
92-28-002	Michelle	S. Sherwood	12/93	89.95	89.95
Ashton-Drake Galleries		**Dianna Effner's Mother Goose**			
90-29-001	Mary, Mary, Quite Contrary	D. Effner	Closed	78.00	88.00
91-29-002	The Little Girl With The Curl (Horrid)	D. Effner	Closed	79.00	79.00
91-29-003	The Little Girl With The Curl (Good)	D. Effner	Closed	79.00	79.00
Ashton-Drake Galleries		**New Bonnet Babies**			
91-30-001	Grandma's Little Girl	H. Hunt	12/92	69.00	69.00
Ashton-Drake Galleries		**A Child's Garden of Verses**			
91-31-001	Nathan (The Land of Nod)	J. Singer	Closed	79.00	79.00
Ashton-Drake Galleries		**Down The Garden Path**			
91-32-001	Rosemary	P. Coffer	Closed	79.00	79.00
91-32-002	Angelica	P. Coffer	12/93	85.00	85.00
Ashton-Drake Galleries		**Beautiful Dreamers**			
92-33-001	Katrina	G. Rademann	Closed	89.00	89.00
92-33-002	Nicolette	G. Rademann	12/93	89.95	89.95
Ashton-Drake Galleries		**Great Moments From Hollywood**			
91-34-001	Shall We Dance?	P. Brooks	Closed	175.00	175.00
Ashton-Drake Galleries		**International Spirit Of Christmas**			
89-35-001	American Santa	F. Wick	Closed	125.00	125.00
Ashton-Drake Galleries		**From The Heart**			
92-36-001	Carolin	T. Menzenbach	Closed	79.95	79.95
92-36-002	Erik	T. Menzenbach	12/93	79.95	79.95
Ashton-Drake Galleries		**Little House On The Prarie**			
92-37-001	Laura	J. Ibarolle	12/93	79.95	79.95
Ashton-Drake Galleries		**Rockwell Christmas**			
90-38-001	Scotty Plays Santa	Rockwell-Inspired	Closed	48.00	48.00
91-38-002	Scotty Gets His Tree	Rockwell-Inspired	Closed	59.00	59.00
Ashton-Drake Galleries		**Holy Hunt's Bonnet Babies**			
91-39-001	Missy (Grandma's Little Girl)	H. Hunt	Closed	69.00	69.00
92-39-002	Susie (Somebody Loves Me)	H. Hunt	12/93	69.00	69.00
Ashton-Drake Galleries		**Heavenly Inspirations**			
92-40-001	Every Cloud Has a Silver Lining	C. MC Clure	12/93	59.95	59.95
Ashton-Drake Galleries		**Elvis: Lifetime Of A Legend**			
92-41-001	'68 Comeback	L. Di Leo	12/93	99.95	99.95
Ashton-Drake Galleries		**Caught In The Act**			
92-42-001	Stevie, Catch Me If You Can	M. Tretter	12/93	49.95	49.95
Ashton-Drake Galleries		**Your Heart's Desire**			
91-43-001	Julia	M. Stauber	Closed	99.00	99.00
Ashton-Drake Galleries		**My Closest Friends**			
92-44-001	Boo Bear (Evie)	J. Goodyear	Closed	78.00	78.00
92-44-002	Me/Blankie (Steffie)	J. Goodyear	Closed	79.00	79.00
92-44-003	My Secret Pal (Robbie)	J. Goodyear	12/93	85.00	85.00
The Collectables Inc.		**The Collectibles Inc. Dolls**			
86-01-001	Tatiana	P. Parkins	1,000	270.00	800-1200.
87-01-002	Tasha	P. Parkins	1,000	290.00	1400.00
87-01-003	Storytime By Sarah Jane	P. Parkins	1,000	330.00	500.00
89-01-004	Michelle	P. Parkins	250	270.00	400-450.
89-01-005	Welcome Home	D. Effner	1,000	330.00	465.00
90-01-006	Lizbeth Ann	D. Effner	1,000	420.00	420.00
90-01-007	Bassinet Baby	P. Parkins	2,000	130.00	130.00
90-01-008	Danielle	P. Parkins	1,000	400.00	400.00
90-01-009	In Your Easter Bonnet	P. Parkins	1,000	350.00	350.00
91-01-010	Yvette	P. Parkins	300	580.00	580.00
91-01-011	Lauren	P. Parkins	S/O	490.00	490.00
91-01-012	Bethany	P. Parkins	Closed	450.00	450.00
91-01-013	Natasha	P. Parkins	Closed	510.00	510.00
91-01-014	Adrianna	P. Parkins	Closed	1350.00	1350.00
91-01-015	Kelsie	P. Parkins	500	320.00	320.00
92-01-016	Karlie	P. Parkins	500	380.00	380.00
92-01-017	Marissa	P. Parkins	300	350.00	350.00
92-01-018	Shelley	P. Parkins	300	450.00	450.00
92-01-019	Angel on My Shoulder (Lillianne w/CeCe)	P. Parkins	500	530.00	530.00
92-01-020	Molly	P. Parkins	450	350.00	350.00
92-01-021	Matia	P. Parkins	250	190.00	190.00
92-01-022	Marty	P. Parkins	250	190.00	190.00
92-01-023	Missy	P. Parkins	Open	59.00	59.00
The Collectables Inc.		**Mother's Little Treasures**			
85-02-001	1st Edition	D. Effner	1,000	380.00	700.00
90-02-002	2nd Edition	D. Effner	1,000	440.00	600.00
The Collectables Inc.		**Yesterday's Child**			
82-03-001	Jason And Jessica	D. Effner	1,000	150.00	300.00
82-03-002	Cleo	D. Effner	1,000	180.00	250.00
82-03-003	Columbine	D. Effner	1,000	180.00	250.00
83-03-004	Chad And Charity	D. Effner	1,000	190.00	190.00
83-03-005	Noel	D. Effner	1,000	190.00	240.00
84-03-006	Kevin And Karissa	D. Effner	1,000	190.00	250-300.
84-03-007	Rebecca	D. Effner	1,000	250.00	250-300.
86-03-008	Todd And Tiffany	D. Effner	1,000	220.00	250.00
86-03-009	Ashley	P. Parkins	1,000	220.00	275.00
The Collectables Inc.		**Cherished Memories**			
86-04-001	Amy And Andrew	P. Parkins	1,000	220.00	325.00
88-04-002	Jennifer	P. Parkins	1,000	380.00	500-600.
88-04-003	Brittany	P. Parkins	1,000	240.00	300.00
88-04-004	Heather	P. Parkins	1,000	280.00	300-350.
88-04-005	Leigh Ann And Leland	P. Parkins	1,000	250.00	250-300.
88-04-006	Tea Time	D. Effner	1,000	380.00	450.00
90-04-007	Cassandra	P. Parkins	Closed	500.00	550.00
89-04-008	Generations	P. Parkins	1,000	480.00	500.00
90-04-009	Twinkles	P. Parkins	Closed	170.00	275.00
The Collectables Inc.		**Fairy**			
88-05-001	Tabatha	P. Parkins	1,500	370.00	400-450.
The Collectables Inc.		**Butterfly Babies**			
89-06-001	Belinda	P. Parkins	Closed	270.00	375.00
90-06-002	Willow	P. Parkins	Closed	240.00	240.00
92-06-003	Laticia	P. Parkins	500	320.00	320.00
The Collectables Inc.		**Enchanted Children**			
90-07-001	Kristin	P. Parkins	S/O	550.00	650.00
90-07-002	Tiffy	P. Parkins	S/O	370.00	500.00
90-07-003	Kara	P. Parkins	Closed	550.00	550.00
90-07-004	Katlin	P. Parkins	Closed	550.00	550.00
The Collectables Inc.		**Collector's Club Doll**			
90-08-001	Mandy	P. Parkins	Closed	360.00	360.00
91-08-002	Kallie	P. Parkins	Closed	410.00	410.00
92-08-003	Mommy and Me	P. Parkins	Yr.Iss.	N/A	N/A
The Collectables Inc.		**Tiny Treasures**			
91-09-001	Little Girl	P. Parkins	1,000	140.00	140.00
91-09-002	Toddler Girl	P. Parkins	1,000	130.00	130.00
91-09-003	Toddler Boy	P. Parkins	1,000	130.00	130.00
91-09-004	Victorian Girl	P. Parkins	1,000	150.00	150.00
91-09-005	Victorian Boy	P. Parkins	1,000	150.00	150.00
91-09-006	Holly	P. Parkins	1,000	150.00	150.00
92-09-007	Nicole	P. Parkins	500	180.00	180.00
92-09-008	Nicolaus	P. Parkins	500	160.00	160.00
92-09-009	Tori	P. Parkins	1,000	170.00	170.00
92-09-010	Tommie	P. Parkins	1,000	160.00	160.00
The Collectables Inc.		**Limited Edition Vinyl Dolls**			
92-10-001	Jessica	P. Parkins	2,500	190.00	190.00
92-10-002	Jenny and Jeremy (Puppy Love)	P. Parkins	2,500	180.00	180.00
92-10-003	Brent	P. Parkins	2,500	190.00	190.00
92-10-004	Annie	P. Parkins	2,500	190.00	190.00
92-10-005	Brenda (Blue Dress)	P. Parkins	2,500	180.00	180.00
92-10-006	Brenda (Spring)	P. Parkins	250	240.00	240.00
92-10-007	Brenda (Christmas)	P. Parkins	250	240.00	240.00
Corolle/Catherine Refabert		**Collector Dolls**			
89-01-001	Melisande	C. Refabert	Closed	256.00	256.00
89-01-002	Diane	C. Refabert	Closed	214.00	214.00
89-01-003	Aurelia	C. Refabert	Closed	214.00	214.00
90-01-004	Ondine	C. Refabert	Closed	268.00	268.00
90-01-005	Melusine	C. Refabert	Closed	260.00	260.00
90-01-006	Ophelie	C. Refabert	Closed	450.00	450.00
91-01-007	Melisande As A Baby	C. Refabert	Closed	460.00	460.00
91-01-008	Ludivine	C. Refabert	Closed	1000.00	1000.00

Number	Name	Artist	Edition Limit	Issue Price	Quote
91-01-009	Angeline	C. Refabert	Closed	1000.00	1000.00
91-01-010	Ombeline	C. Refabert	Closed	1000.00	1000.00
92-01-011	Angelique, La Mariee	C. Refabert	1 Yr.	500.00	500.00
92-01-012	Danielle	C. Refabert	100	900.00	900.00
Corolle/Catherine Refabert		**Liberty Of London**			
91-02-001	Laurent	C. Refabert	Closed	200.00	200.00
91-02-002	Lorene	C. Refabert	Closed	220.00	220.00
91-02-003	Lucille	C. Refabert	Closed	220.00	220.00
91-02-004	Laurence	C. Refabert	Closed	260.00	260.00
91-02-005	Lilas	C. Refabert	Closed	220.00	220.00
91-02-006	Lilliane	C. Refabert	Closed	260.00	260.00
91-02-007	Loic	C. Refabert	Closed	330.00	330.00
92-02-008	Baptiste	C. Refabert	1 Yr.	200.00	200.00
92-02-009	Berangere	C. Refabert	1 Yr.	200.00	200.00
Corolle/Catherine Refabert		**White Symphony**			
92-03-001	Christina/Benoit	C. Refabert	1 Yr.	100.00	100.00
92-03-002	Benjamin	C. Refabert	1 Yr.	150.00	150.00
92-03-003	Blandine	C. Refabert	1 Yr.	240.00	240.00
92-03-004	Bettina	C. Refabert	1 Yr.	240.00	240.00
Corolle/Catherine Refabert		**Friends Around Our World**			
92-04-001	Katie-Alsace	C. Refabert	1 Yr.	100.00	100.00
92-04-002	Katioucha-Russia	C. Refabert	1 Yr.	100.00	100.00
92-04-003	Kaatje-Holland	C. Refabert	1 Yr.	100.00	100.00
Corolle/Catherine Refabert		**English Garden**			
92-05-001	Jenny	C. Refabert	1 Yr.	190.00	190.00
92-05-002	Justine	C. Refabert	1 Yr.	300.00	300.00
92-05-003	Juliette	C. Refabert	1 Yr.	300.00	300.00
Corolle/Catherine Refabert		**History Of Costumes**			
92-06-001	Ana, La Ballerine	C. Refabert	1 Yr.	350.00	350.00
92-06-002	Carolina/Hortense	C. Refabert	1 Yr.	350.00	350.00
92-06-003	Lea	C. Refabert	1 Yr.	350.00	350.00
92-06-004	Camille	C. Refabert	1 Yr.	350.00	350.00
Corolle/Catherine Refabert		**They Changed Our World**			
92-07-001	Columbus	C. Refabert	1 Yr.	200.00	200.00
92-07-002	Isabella	C. Refabert	1 Yr.	200.00	200.00
92-07-003	Marie Antoinette	C. Refabert	1 Yr.	350.00	350.00
92-07-004	Le Dauphin	C. Refabert	1 Yr.	200.00	200.00
Corolle/Catherine Refabert		**Porcelain**			
91-08-001	Esperence	C. Refabert	Closed	1800.00	1800.00
92-08-002	Bebe Desire	C. Refabert	1,000	1000.00	1000.00
Corolle/Catherine Refabert		**Dolls From Around The World**			
89-09-001	Jasmine	C. Refabert	Closed	228.00	228.00
89-09-002	Sabrina	C. Refabert	Closed	206.00	206.00
89-09-003	Cannelle	C. Refabert	Closed	228.00	228.00
89-09-004	Mei Mei	C. Refabert	Closed	214.00	214.00
89-09-005	Tania	C. Refabert	Closed	236.00	236.00
90-09-006	Princess Maya	C. Refabert	Closed	260.00	260.00
91-09-007	Yukka	C. Refabert	Closed	300.00	300.00
91-09-008	Niki	C. Refabert	Closed	300.00	300.00
Corolle/Catherine Refabert		**Belleepoque**			
91-10-001	La Danseuse	C. Refabert	Closed	300.00	300.00
91-10-002	Marie Lavande	C. Refabert	Closed	330.00	330.00
91-10-003	Marie Claudine	C. Refabert	Closed	330.00	330.00
91-10-004	Colombe	C. Refabert	Closed	500.00	500.00
91-10-005	Valentine	C. Refabert	Closed	220.00	220.00
91-10-006	Marie Flore	C. Refabert	Closed	330.00	330.00
Department 56		**Heritage Village Doll Collection**			
87-01-001	Christmas Carol Dolls1000-6 4/set(Tiny Tim, Bob Crachet, Mrs. Crachet, Scrooge)	Department 56	250	1500.00	1500.00
87-01-002	Christmas Carol Dolls5907-2 4/set(Tiny Tim, Bob Crachet, Mrs. Crachet, Scrooge)	Department 56	Open	250.00	250.00
88-01-003	Christmas Carol Dolls1001-4 4/set(Tiny Tim, Bob Crachet, Mrs. Crachet, Scrooge)	Department 56	350	800.00	800.00
88-01-004	Mr. & Mrs. Fezziwig 5594-8-Set of 2	Department 56	Open	172.00	172.00
Department 56		**Snowbabies Dolls**			
88-02-001	Allison & Duncan- Set of 2, 7730-5	Department 56	Closed	200.00	200-500.
Dolls by Jerri		**Dolls by Jerri**			
84-01-001	Clara	J. McCloud	1,000	320.00	1500.00
84-01-002	Emily	J. McCloud	1,000	330.00	2400-3500.
85-01-003	Scotty	J. McCloud	1,000	340.00	1200-2000.
85-01-004	Uncle Joe	J. McCloud	1,000	160.00	250-300.
85-01-005	Miss Nanny	J. McCloud	1,000	160.00	250-300.
85-01-006	Bride	J. McCloud	1,000	350.00	350-400.
86-01-007	David-2 Years Old	J. McCloud	1,000	330.00	550.00
86-01-008	Princess and the Unicorn	J. McCloud	1,000	370.00	370.00
86-01-009	Charlotte	J. McCloud	1,000	330.00	450-500.
86-01-010	Cane	J. McCloud	1,000	350.00	1200.00
86-01-011	Clown-David 3 Yrs. Old	J. McCloud	1,000	340.00	450.00
86-01-012	Tammy	J. McCloud	1,000	350.00	900.00
86-01-013	Samantha	J. McCloud	1,000	350.00	500.00
86-01-014	Elizabeth	J. McCloud	1,000	340.00	340.00
86-01-015	Audrey	J. McCloud	300	550.00	550.00
86-01-016	Yvonne	J. McCloud	300	500.00	500.00
86-01-017	Annabelle	J. McCloud	300	600.00	600.00
86-01-018	Ashley	J. McCloud	1,000	350.00	450-500.
86-01-019	Allison	J. McCloud	1,000	350.00	450-500.
86-01-020	Nobody	J. McCloud	1,000	350.00	550.00
86-01-021	Somebody	J. McCloud	1,000	350.00	550.00
86-01-022	Danielle	J. McCloud	1,000	350.00	500.00
86-01-023	Helenjean	J. McCloud	1,000	350.00	500-550.
86-01-024	David-Magician	J. McCloud	1,000	350.00	350-500.
86-01-025	Amber	J. McCloud	1,000	350.00	875.00
86-01-026	Joy	J. McCloud	1,000	350.00	350.00
86-01-027	Mary Beth	J. McCloud	1,000	350.00	350.00
86-01-028	Jacqueline	J. McCloud	300	500.00	500.00
86-01-029	Lucianna	J. McCloud	300	500.00	500.00
86-01-030	Bridgette	J. McCloud	300	500.00	500.00
86-01-031	The Fool	J. McCloud	1,000	350.00	350.00
86-01-032	Alfalfa	J. McCloud	1,000	350.00	350.00
85-01-033	Candy	J. McCloud	1,000	340.00	1000-2000.
82-01-034	Baby David	J. McCloud	538	290.00	2000.00

Number	Name	Artist	Edition Limit	Issue Price	Quote
88-01-035	Holly	J. McCloud	1,000	370.00	750-825.
89-01-036	Laura Lee	J. McCloud	1,000	370.00	575.00
XX-01-037	Boy	J. McCloud	1,000	350.00	425.00
XX-01-038	Uncle Remus	J. McCloud	500	290.00	400-450.
XX-01-039	Gina	J. McCloud	1,000	350.00	475.00
XX-01-040	Laura	J. McCloud	1,000	350.00	425-500.
89-01-041	Goose Girl, Guild	J. McCloud	Closed	300.00	700-875.
XX-01-042	Little Bo Peep	J. McCloud	1,000	340.00	395-450.
XX-01-043	Little Miss Muffet	J. McCloud	1,000	340.00	395-450.
XX-01-044	Megan	J. McCloud	750	420.00	550.00
XX-01-045	Denise	J. McCloud	1,000	380.00	550.00
XX-01-046	Meredith	J. McCloud	750	430.00	600.00
XX-01-047	Goldilocks	J. McCloud	1,000	370.00	450-600.
XX-01-048	Jamie	J. McCloud	800	380.00	450.00
Dynasty Doll		**Annual**			
89-01-001	Amber	Unknown	Yr.Iss.	90.00	90.00
90-01-002	Marcella	Unknown	Yr.Iss.	90.00	90.00
91-01-003	Butterfly Princess	Unknown	Yr.Iss.	110.00	110.00
Dynasty Doll		**Christmas**			
87-02-001	Merrie	Unknown	3,500	60.00	60.00
88-02-002	Noel	Unknown	3,500	80.00	80.00
90-02-003	Faith	Unknown	5,000	110.00	110.00
91-02-004	Joy	Unknown	5,000	125.00	125.00
Dynasty Doll		**Ballerina Series**			
91-03-001	Masha-Nutcracker	Lee Po Nan	7,500	190.00	190.00
Dynasty Doll		**Anna Collection**			
92-04-001	Pocahontas	Unknown	3,500	95.00	95.00
92-01-004	Communion Girl	G. Hoyt	Yr.Iss.	125.00	125.00
Elke's Originals, Ltd.		**Elke Hutchens**			
89-01-001	Annabelle	E. Hutchens	250	575.00	1295.00
90-01-002	Aubra	E. Hutchens	250	575.00	1295.00
90-01-003	Aurora	E. Hutchens	250	595.00	1295.00
91-01-004	Alicia	E. Hutchens	250	595.00	1295.00
91-01-005	Braelyn	E. Hutchens	400	595.00	1150-1500.
91-01-006	Bellinda	E. Hutchens	400	595.00	800-1000.
91-01-007	Brianna	E. Hutchens	400	595.00	1000.00
92-01-008	Bethany	E. Hutchens	400	595.00	1000.00
92-01-009	Cecilia	E. Hutchens	435	635.00	950.00
92-01-010	Cherie	E. Hutchens	435	635.00	N/A
90-01-011	Little Liebchen	E. Hutchens	250	475.00	1000.00
90-01-012	Victoria	E. Hutchens	500	645.00	N/A
90-01-013	Kricket	E. Hutchens	500	575.00	1000.00
Enesco Corporation		**Precious Moments Dolls**			
81-01-001	Mikey, 18"- E-6214B	S. Butcher	Suspd.	150.00	225.00
81-01-002	Debbie, 18"- E-6214G	S. Butcher	Suspd.	150.00	230.00
82-01-003	Cubby, 18"- E-7267B	S. Butcher	5,000	200.00	450.00
82-01-004	Tammy, 18"- E-7267G	S. Butcher	5,000	300.00	700.00
83-01-005	Katie Lynne, 16"- E-0539	S. Butcher	Suspd.	165.00	175-185.
84-01-006	Mother Sew Dear, 18"- E-2850	S. Butcher	Retrd.	350.00	350-375.
84-01-007	Kristy, 12"- E-2851	S. Butcher	Suspd.	150.00	185.00
84-01-008	Timmy, 12"- E-5397	S. Butcher	Open	125.00	150-175.
85-01-009	Aaron, 12"- 12424	S. Butcher	Suspd.	135.00	150.00
85-01-010	Bethany, 12"- 12432	S. Butcher	Suspd.	135.00	150.00
85-01-011	P.D., 7"- 12475	S. Butcher	Suspd.	50.00	75.00
85-01-012	Trish, 7" - 12483	S. Butcher	Suspd.	50.00	75.00
86-01-013	Bong Bong, 13" - 100455	S. Butcher	12,000	150.00	225.00
86-01-014	Candy, 13" - 100463	S. Butcher	12,000	150.00	250.00
86-01-015	Connie, 12" - 102253	S. Butcher	7,500	160.00	225.00
87-01-016	Angie, The Angel of Mercy - 12491	S. Butcher	12,000	160.00	200.00
90-01-017	The Voice of Spring-408786	S. Butcher	2 Yr.	150.00	150.00
90-01-018	Summer's Joy-408794	S. Butcher	2 Yr.	150.00	150.00
90-01-019	Autumn's Praise-408808	S. Butcher	2 Yr.	150.00	150.00
90-01-020	Winter's Song-408816	S. Butcher	2 Yr.	150.00	150.00
91-01-021	You HaveTouched So Many Hearts-427527	S. Butcher	2 Yr.	90.00	90.00
91-01-022	May You Have An Old Fashioned Christmas-417785	S. Butcher	2 Yr.	150.00	150.00
91-01-023	The Eyes Of The Lord Are Upon You (Boy, Action Muscial)-429570	S. Butcher	Open	65.00	65.00
91-01-024	The Eyes Of The Lord Are Upon You (Girl, Action Musical)-429589	S. Butcher	Open	65.00	65.00
Enesco Corporation		**Precious Moments-Jack-In-The-Boxes**			
91-02-001	You Have Touched So Many Hearts-422282	S. Butcher	2 Yr.	175.00	175.00
91-02-002	May You Have An Old Fashioned Christmas-417777	S. Butcher	2 Yr.	200.00	200.00
Enesco Corporation		**Jack-In-The-Boxes-4 Seasons**			
90-03-001	Voice of Spring-408735	S. Butcher	2 Yr.	200.00	200.00
90-03-002	Summer's Joy-408743	S. Butcher	2 Yr.	200.00	200.00
90-03-003	Autumn's Praise-408751	S. Butcher	2 Yr.	200.00	200.00
90-03-004	Winter's Song-408778	S. Butcher	2 Yr.	200.00	200.00
Georgetown Collection, Inc.		**Nursery Babies**			
90-01-001	Baby Bunting	T. DeHetre	Closed	118.20	225.00
90-01-002	Patty Cake	T. DeHetre	Closed	118.20	118.20
91-01-003	Diddle, Diddle	T. DeHetre	Closed	118.20	118.20
91-01-004	Little Girl	T. DeHetre	100-day	118.20	118.20
91-01-005	This Little Piggy	T. DeHetre	100-day	118.20	118.20
Georgetown Collection, Inc.		**Baby Kisses**			
92-02-001	Michelle	T. DeHetre	100-day	118.60	118.60
Georgetown Collection, Inc.		**Let's Play**			
92-03-001	Peek-A-Boo Beckie	T. DeHetre	100-day	118.60	118.60
92-03-002	Eentsy Weentsy Willie	T. DeHetre	100-day	118.60	118.60
Georgetown Collection, Inc.		**Sugar & Spice**			
91-04-001	Little Sweetheart	L. Mason	100-day	118.25	118.25
91-04-002	Red Hot Pepper	L. Mason	100-day	118.25	118.25
92-04-003	Little Sunshine	L. Mason	100-day	141.10	141.10
Georgetown Collection, Inc.		**American Diary Dolls**			
90-05-001	Jennie Cooper	L. Mason	100-day	129.25	129.25
91-05-002	Bridget Quinn	L. Mason	100-day	129.25	129.25
91-05-003	Christina Merovina	L. Mason	100-day	129.25	129.25
91-05-004	Many Stars	L. Mason	100-day	129.25	129.25
92-05-005	Rachel Williams	L. Mason	100-day	129.25	129.25

Company Number	Name	Series Artist	Edition Limit	Issue Price	Quote
Georgetown Collection, Inc.		**Little Loves**			
90-06-001	Laura	B. Deval	Closed	139.20	139.20
89-06-002	Katie	B. Deval	Closed	139.20	139.20
88-06-003	Emma	B. Deval	Closed	139.20	139.20
89-06-004	Megan	B. Deval	Closed	138.00	160.00
Georgetown Collection, Inc.		**Small Wonders**			
90-07-001	Corey	B. Deval	100-day	97.60	97.60
91-07-002	Abbey	B. Deval	100-day	97.60	97.60
92-07-003	Sarah	B. Deval	100-day	97.60	97.60
Georgetown Collection, Inc.		**Faerie Princess**			
89-08-001	Faerie Princess	B. Deval	Closed	248.00	248.00
Georgetown Collection, Inc.		**Miss Ashley**			
89-09-001	Miss Ashley	P. Thompson	Closed	228.00	228.00
Georgetown Collection, Inc.		**Tansie**			
88-10-001	Tansie	P. Coffer	Closed	81.00	81.00
Georgetown Collection, Inc.		**Kindergarten Kids**			
92-11-001	Nikki	V. Walker	100-day	129.60	129.60
Goebel, Inc.		**Victoria Ashlea Originals**			
88-01-001	Campbell Kid-Girl-758700	B. Ball	Closed	13.80	13.80
88-01-002	Campbell Kid-Boy-758701	B. Ball	Closed	13.80	13.80
84-01-003	Claude-901032	B. Ball	Closed	110.00	225.00
84-01-004	Claudette-901033	B. Ball	Closed	110.00	225.00
84-01-005	Henri-901035	B. Ball	Closed	100.00	200.00
84-01-006	Henrietta-901036	B. Ball	Closed	100.00	200.00
84-01-007	Jeannie-901062	B. Ball	Closed	200.00	550.00
84-01-008	Victoria-901068	B. Ball	Closed	200.00	1500.00
84-01-009	Laura-901106	B. Ball	Closed	300.00	575.00
83-01-010	Deborah-901107	B. Ball	Closed	220.00	400.00
84-01-011	Barbara-901108	B. Ball	Closed	57.00	110.00
84-01-012	Diana-901119	B. Ball	Closed	55.00	135.00
84-01-013	Clown-901136	B. Ball	Closed	90.00	120.00
84-01-014	Sabina-901155	B. Ball	Closed	75.00	N/A
85-01-015	Dorothy-901157	B. Ball	Closed	130.00	275.00
85-01-016	Claire-901158	B. Ball	Closed	115.00	160.00
85-01-017	Adele-901172	B. Ball	Closed	145.00	275.00
85-01-018	Roxanne-901174	B. Ball	Closed	155.00	275.00
86-01-019	Gina-901176	B. Ball	Closed	300.00	300.00
86-01-020	Cat/Kitty Cheerful Gr Dr-901179	B. Ball	Closed	60.00	60.00
85-01-021	Garnet-901183	B. Ball	Closed	160.00	295.00
86-01-022	Pepper Rust Dr/Appr-901184	B. Ball	Closed	125.00	200.00
86-01-023	Patty Artic Flower Print-901185	B. Ball	Closed	140.00	140.00
87-01-024	Lillian-901199	B. Ball	Closed	85.00	100.00
87-01-025	Suzanne-901200	B. Ball	Closed	85.00	100.00
87-01-026	Kitty Cuddles-901201	B. Ball	Closed	65.00	65.00
87-01-027	Bonnie Pouty-901207	B. Ball	Closed	100.00	100.00
87-01-028	Amanda Pouty-901209	B. Ball	Closed	150.00	215.00
87-01-029	Tiffany Pouty-901211	B. Ball	Closed	120.00	160.00
87-01-030	Alice-901212	B. Ball	Closed	95.00	135.00
88-01-031	Elizabeth-901214	B. Ball	Closed	90.00	90.00
87-01-032	Bride Allison-901218	B. Ball	1,500	180.00	180.00
87-01-033	Dominique-901219	B. Ball	Closed	170.00	225.00
87-01-034	Sarah-901220	B. Ball	1,500	350.00	350.00
87-01-035	Tasha-901221	B. Ball	Closed	115.00	130.00
87-01-036	Michelle-901222	B. Ball	Closed	90.00	90.00
87-01-037	Nicole-901225	B. Ball	Closed	575.00	575.00
87-01-038	Clementine-901226	B. Ball	Closed	75.00	75.00
87-01-039	Catanova-901227	B. Ball	Closed	75.00	75.00
87-01-040	Caitlin-901228	B. Ball	Closed	260.00	260.00
88-01-041	Christina-901229	B. Ball	Closed	350.00	400.00
88-01-042	Melissa-901230	B. Ball	Closed	110.00	110.00
82-01-043	Marie-901231	B. Ball	Closed	95.00	95.00
82-01-044	Trudy-901232	B. Ball	Closed	100.00	100.00
82-01-045	Holly-901233	B. Ball	Closed	160.00	200.00
88-01-046	Brandon-901234	B. Ball	Closed	90.00	90.00
88-01-047	Ashley-901235	B. Ball	Closed	110.00	110.00
88-01-048	April-901239	B. Ball	1,000	225.00	225.00
88-01-049	Sandy-901240	K. Kennedy	Closed	115.00	115.00
88-01-050	Erin-901241	B. Ball	Closed	170.00	170.00
88-01-051	Catherine-901242	B. Ball	Closed	240.00	240.00
88-01-052	Susan-901243	B. Ball	Closed	100.00	100.00
88-01-053	Paulette-901244	B. Ball	Closed	90.00	90.00
88-01-054	Bernice-901245	B. Ball	Closed	90.00	90.00
88-01-055	Ellen-901246	B. Ball	Closed	100.00	100.00
88-01-056	Cat Maude-901247	B. Ball	2,500	85.00	85.00
88-01-057	Jennifer-901248	B. Ball	Closed	150.00	150.00
90-01-058	Helene-901249	K. Kennedy	Closed	160.00	160.00
89-01-059	Ashlea-901250	B. Ball	1,000	550.00	550.00
90-01-060	Matthew-901251	B. Ball	Closed	100.00	100.00
89-01-061	Marissa-901252	K. Kennedy	Closed	225.00	225.00
89-01-062	Holly-901254	B. Ball	1,000	180.00	180.00
89-01-063	Valerie-901255	B. Ball	Closed	175.00	175.00
90-01-064	Justine-901256	B. Ball	Closed	200.00	200.00
89-01-065	Claudia-901257	K. Kennedy	1,000	225.00	225.00
90-01-066	Rebecca-901258	B. Ball	1,000	250.00	250.00
89-01-067	Megan-901260	B. Ball	Closed	120.00	120.00
90-01-068	Carolyn-901261	K. Kennedy	1,000	200.00	200.00
90-01-069	Amy-901262	B. Ball	1,000	110.00	110.00
89-01-070	Lindsey-901263	B. Ball	Closed	100.00	100.00
90-01-071	Heidi-901266	B. Ball	2,000	150.00	150.00
84-01-072	Tobie-912023	B. Ball	Closed	30.00	30.00
84-01-073	Sheila-912060	B. Ball	Closed	75.00	135.00
84-01-074	Jamie-912061	B. Ball	Closed	65.00	100.00
85-01-075	Michelle-912066	B. Ball	Closed	100.00	225.00
85-01-076	Phyllis-912067	B. Ball	Closed	60.00	60.00
85-01-077	Clown Casey-912078	B. Ball	Closed	40.00	40.00
85-01-078	Clown Jody-912079	B. Ball	Closed	100.00	150.00
85-01-079	Clown Christie-912084	B. Ball	Closed	60.00	90.00
85-01-080	Chauncey-912085	B. Ball	Closed	75.00	110.00
86-01-081	Baby Lauren Pink-912086	B. Ball	Closed	120.00	120.00
85-01-082	Rosalind-912087	B. Ball	Closed	145.00	225.00
86-01-083	Clown Cyd-912093	B. Ball	Closed	70.00	70.00
82-01-084	Charleen-912094	B. Ball	Closed	65.00	65.00
86-01-085	Clown Christabel-912095	B. Ball	Closed	100.00	150.00
86-01-086	Clown Clarabella-912096	B. Ball	Closed	80.00	80.00
86-01-087	Baby Brock Beige Dress-912103	B. Ball	Closed	60.00	60.00
86-01-088	Clown Calypso-912104	B. Ball	Closed	70.00	70.00
86-01-089	Girl Frog Freda-912105	B. Ball	Closed	20.00	20.00

Company Number	Name	Series Artist	Edition Limit	Issue Price	Quote
86-01-090	Googley German Astrid-912109	B. Ball	Closed	60.00	60.00
86-01-091	Clown Clarissa-912123	B. Ball	Closed	75.00	110.00
86-01-092	Baby Courtney-912124	B. Ball	Closed	120.00	120.00
85-01-093	Mary-912126	B. Ball	Closed	60.00	90.00
86-01-094	Clown Lollipop-912127	B. Ball	Closed	125.00	225.00
86-01-095	Clown Cat Cadwalader-912132	B. Ball	Closed	55.00	55.00
86-01-096	Clown Kitten-Cleo-912133	B. Ball	Closed	50.00	50.00
85-01-097	Millie-912135	B. Ball	Closed	70.00	125.00
85-01-098	Lynn-912144	B. Ball	Closed	90.00	135.00
86-01-099	Ashley-912147	B. Ball	Closed	125.00	125.00
87-01-100	Megan-912148	B. Ball	Closed	70.00	70.00
87-01-101	Joy-912155	B. Ball	Closed	50.00	50.00
87-01-102	Kittle Cat-912167	B. Ball	Closed	55.00	55.00
87-01-103	Christine-912168	B. Ball	Closed	75.00	75.00
87-01-104	Noel-912170	B. Ball	Closed	125.00	125.00
87-01-105	Sophia-912173	B. Ball	Closed	40.00	40.00
87-01-106	Julia-912174	B. Ball	Closed	80.00	80.00
87-01-107	Clown Champagne-912180	B. Ball	Closed	95.00	95.00
82-01-108	Clown Jolly-912181	B. Ball	Closed	70.00	70.00
87-01-109	Baby Doll-912184	B. Ball	Closed	75.00	75.00
87-01-110	Baby Lindsay-912190	B. Ball	Closed	80.00	80.00
87-01-111	Caroline-912191	B. Ball	Closed	80.00	80.00
87-01-112	Jacqueline-912192	B. Ball	Closed	80.00	80.00
87-01-113	Jessica-912195	B. Ball	Closed	120.00	135.00
87-01-114	Doreen-912198	B. Ball	Closed	75.00	75.00
88-01-115	Clown Cotton Candy-912199	B. Ball	Closed	67.00	67.00
88-01-116	Baby Daryl-912200	B. Ball	Closed	85.00	85.00
88-01-117	Angelica-912204	B. Ball	Closed	150.00	150.00
88-01-118	Karen-912205	B. Ball	Closed	200.00	250.00
88-01-119	Polly-912206	B. Ball	Closed	100.00	125.00
88-01-120	Brittany-912207	B. Ball	Closed	130.00	145.00
88-01-121	Melissa-912208	B. Ball	Closed	125.00	125.00
88-01-122	Baby Jennifer-912210	B. Ball	Closed	75.00	75.00
88-01-123	Molly-912211	K. Kennedy	Closed	75.00	75.00
88-01-124	Lauren-912212	B. Ball	Closed	110.00	110.00
88-01-125	Anne-912213	B. Ball	Closed	130.00	150.00
89-01-126	Alexa-912214	B. Ball	Closed	195.00	195.00
88-01-127	Diana-912218	B. Ball	1,000	270.00	270.00
88-01-128	Sarah w/Pillow-912219	B. Ball	Closed	105.00	105.00
88-01-129	Betty Doll-912220	B. Ball	1,000	90.00	90.00
88-01-130	Jennifer-912221	B. Ball	Closed	80.00	80.00
88-01-131	Baby Katie-912222	B. Ball	5,000	70.00	70.00
88-01-132	Maritta Spanish-912224	B. Ball	Closed	140.00	140.00
88-01-133	Laura-912225	B. Ball	Closed	135.00	135.00
88-01-134	Crystal-912226	B. Ball	Closed	75.00	75.00
88-01-135	Jesse-912231	B. Ball	1,000	110.00	110.00
88-01-136	Whitney Blk-912232	B. Ball	1,000	62.50	62.50
88-01-137	Goldilocks-912234	K. Kennedy	1,500	65.00	65.00
88-01-138	Snow White-912235	K. Kennedy	Closed	65.00	65.00
88-01-139	Stephanie-912238	B. Ball	Closed	200.00	200.00
88-01-140	Morgan-912239	K. Kennedy	Closed	75.00	75.00
XX-01-141	Charity-912244	B. Ball	Closed	70.00	70.00
88-01-142	Renae-912245	B. Ball	Closed	120.00	120.00
88-01-143	Amanda-912246	B. Ball	Closed	180.00	180.00
88-01-144	Heather-912247	B. Ball	Closed	135.00	135.00
89-01-145	Merry-912249	B. Ball	1,000	200.00	200.00
90-01-146	January Birthstone Doll-912250	K. Kennedy	5,000	25.00	25.00
90-01-147	February Birthstone Doll-912251	K. Kennedy	5,000	25.00	25.00
90-01-148	March Birthstone Doll-912252	K. Kennedy	5,000	25.00	25.00
90-01-149	April Birthstone Doll-912253	K. Kennedy	5,000	25.00	25.00
90-01-150	May Birthstone Doll-912254	K. Kennedy	5,000	25.00	25.00
90-01-151	June Birthstone Doll-912255	K. Kennedy	5,000	25.00	25.00
90-01-152	July Birthstone Doll-912256	K. Kennedy	5,000	25.00	25.00
90-01-153	August Birthstone Doll-912257	K. Kennedy	5,000	25.00	25.00
90-01-154	September Birthstone Doll-912258	K. Kennedy	Closed	25.00	25.00
90-01-155	October Birthstone Doll-912259	K. Kennedy	5,000	25.00	25.00
90-01-156	November Birthstone Doll-912260	K. Kennedy	5,000	25.00	25.00
90-01-157	December Birthstone Doll-912261	K. Kennedy	5,000	25.00	25.00
89-01-158	Tammy-912264	B. Ball	Closed	110.00	110.00
89-01-159	Maria-912265	B. Ball	Closed	90.00	90.00
89-01-160	Nancy-912266	B. Ball	Closed	110.00	110.00
89-01-161	Pinky Clown-912268	K. Kennedy	1,000	70.00	70.00
89-01-162	Margot-912269	B. Ball	Closed	110.00	110.00
89-01-163	Jingles-912271	B. Ball	Closed	60.00	60.00
89-01-164	Vanessa-912272	B. Ball	Closed	110.00	110.00
89-01-165	Alexandria-912273	B. Ball	Closed	275.00	275.00
89-01-166	Lisa-912275	B. Ball	Closed	160.00	160.00
89-01-167	Loni-912276	B. Ball	1,200	125.00	125.00
89-01-168	Diana Bride-912277	B. Ball	Closed	180.00	180.00
90-01-169	Annabelle-912278	B. Ball	2,000	200.00	200.00
89-01-170	Sara-912279	B. Ball	Closed	175.00	175.00
89-01-171	Terry-912281	B. Ball	2,000	125.00	125.00
89-01-172	Sigrid-912282	B. Ball	2,000	145.00	145.00
89-01-173	Missy-912283	B. Ball	1,000	110.00	110.00
89-01-174	Melanie-912284	K. Kennedy	Closed	135.00	135.00
89-01-175	Kristin-912285	K. Kennedy	1,000	90.00	90.00
89-01-176	Suzanne-912286	B. Ball	Closed	120.00	120.00
90-01-177	Ginny-912287	K. Kennedy	1,000	140.00	140.00
89-01-178	Candace-912288	K. Kennedy	Closed	70.00	70.00
89-01-179	Joy-912289	K. Kennedy	Closed	110.00	110.00
90-01-180	Licorice-912290	B. Ball	Closed	75.00	75.00
89-01-181	Jimmy Baby w/ Pillow-912291	K. Kennedy	1,000	165.00	165.00
89-01-182	Hope Baby w/ Pillow-912292	B. Ball	1,000	110.00	110.00
90-01-183	Fluffer-912293	B. Ball	1,000	135.00	135.00
90-01-184	Marshmallow-912294	K. Kennedy	Closed	75.00	75.00
89-01-185	Suzy-912295	B. Ball	Closed	110.00	110.00
90-01-186	Alice-912296	K. Kennedy	Closed	65.00	65.00
90-01-187	Baryshnicat-912298	K. Kennedy	Closed	25.00	25.00
90-01-188	Tasha-912299	K. Kennedy	Closed	25.00	25.00
90-01-189	Priscilla-912300	B. Ball	1,000	185.00	185.00
90-01-190	Mrs. Katz-912301	B. Ball	1,000	140.00	140.00
89-01-200	Pamela-912302	B. Ball	Closed	95.00	95.00
89-01-201	Emily-912303	B. Ball	Closed	150.00	150.00
90-01-202	Brandy-912304	K. Kennedy	Closed	150.00	150.00
90-01-203	Sheri-912305	K. Kennedy	Closed	115.00	115.00
90-01-204	Gigi-912306	K. Kennedy	1,000	150.00	150.00
90-01-205	Joanne-912307	K. Kennedy	Closed	165.00	165.00
89-01-206	Melinda-912309	K. Kennedy	Closed	70.00	70.00
90-01-207	Bettina-912310	B. Ball	1,000	100.00	100.00
90-01-208	Stephanie-912312	B. Ball	2,000	150.00	150.00
90-01-209	Amie-912313	K. Kennedy	Closed	150.00	150.00
90-01-210	Samantha-912314	B. Ball	2,000	185.00	185.00
90-01-211	Tracie-912315	B. Ball	2,500	125.00	125.00

Company Number	Name	Series Artist	Edition Limit	Issue Price	Quote
90-01-212	Paula-912316	B. Ball	Closed	100.00	100.00
90-01-213	Debra-912319	K. Kennedy	2,000	120.00	120.00
90-01-214	Robin-912321	B. Ball	2,000	160.00	160.00
90-01-215	Heather-912322	B. Ball	2,000	150.00	150.00
90-01-216	Jillian-912323	B. Ball	2,000	150.00	150.00
90-01-217	Angela-912324	K. Kennedy	2,000	130.00	130.00
90-01-218	Penny-912325	K. Kennedy	2,000	130.00	130.00
90-01-219	Tiffany-912326	K. Kennedy	Closed	180.00	180.00
90-01-220	Susie-912328	B. Ball	2,000	115.00	115.00
90-01-221	Jacqueline-912329	K. Kennedy	2,000	136.00	136.00
90-01-222	Kelly-912331	B. Ball	Closed	95.00	95.00
90-01-223	Annette-912333	K. Kennedy	1,500	85.00	85.00
90-01-224	Julia-912334	K. Kennedy	1,500	85.00	85.00
90-01-225	Monique-912335	K. Kennedy	1,500	85.00	85.00
90-01-226	Monica-912336	K. Kennedy	1,000	100.00	100.00
90-01-227	Helga-912337	B. Ball	1,000	325.00	325.00
90-01-228	Sheena-912338	B. Ball	Closed	115.00	115.00
90-01-229	Kimberly-912341	B. Ball	1,000	140.00	140.00
84-01-230	Amelia-933006	B. Ball	Closed	100.00	100.00
84-01-231	Stephanie-933012	B. Ball	Closed	115.00	115.00
92-01-232	Wendy-912330	K. Kennedy	1,000	125.00	125.00
92-01-233	Margaret-912354	K. Kennedy	1,000	150.00	150.00
92-01-234	Cassandra-912355	K. Kennedy	1,000	165.00	165.00
92-01-235	Noelle-912360	K. Kennedy	1,000	165.00	165.00
92-01-236	Kelly-912361	B. Ball	1,000	160.00	160.00
92-01-237	Ashley-911004	B. Ball	2,000	99.00	99.00
92-01-238	Lauren-912363	K. Kennedy	1,000	190.00	190.00
92-01-239	Denise-912362	K. Kennedy	1,000	145.00	145.00
92-01-240	Kris-912345	K. Kennedy	1,000	160.00	160.00
92-01-241	Hilary-912353	B. Ball	1,000	130.00	130.00
92-01-242	Toni-912367	K. Kennedy	1,000	120.00	120.00
92-01-243	Angelica-912339	B. Ball	1,000	145.00	145.00
92-01-244	Marjorie-912357	B. Ball	1,000	180.00	180.00
92-01-245	Brittany-912365	K. Kennedy	1,000	140.00	140.00
92-01-246	Allison-912358	B. Ball	1,000	160.00	160.00
92-01-247	Jenny-912374	K. Kennedy	1,000	150.00	150.00
92-01-248	Holly Belle-912380	B. Ball	500	125.00	125.00
92-01-249	Michelle-912381	K. Kennedy	500	175.00	175.00
92-01-250	Tamika-912382	B. Ball	500	185.00	185.00
92-01-251	Sherise-912383	K. Kennedy	500	145.00	145.00
92-01-252	Cindy-912384	B. Ball	1,000	185.00	185.00
92-01-253	Tulip-912385	K. Kennedy	500	145.00	145.00
92-01-254	Carol-912387	K. Kennedy	1,000	140.00	140.00
92-01-255	Alicia-912388	B. Ball	500	135.00	135.00
92-01-256	Iris-912389	K. Kennedy	500	165.00	165.00
92-01-257	Betsy-912390	B. Ball	500	150.00	150.00
92-01-258	Trudie-912391	B. Ball	500	135.00	135.00
92-01-259	Dottie-912393	K. Kennedy	1,000	160.00	160.00
Goebel/Schmid		**M. I. Hummel Collectibles Dolls**			
64-01-001	Gretel 1901	M. I. Hummel	Closed	55.00	125.00
64-01-002	Hansel 1902	M. I. Hummel	Closed	55.00	110.00
64-01-003	Rosa-Blue Baby 1904/B	M. I. Hummel	Closed	45.00	85.00
64-01-004	Rosa-Pink Baby 1904/P	M. I. Hummel	Closed	45.00	75.00
64-01-005	Little Knitter 1905	M. I. Hummel	Closed	55.00	75.00
64-01-006	Merry Wanderer 1906	M. I. Hummel	Closed	55.00	90.00
64-01-007	Chimney Sweep 1908	M. I. Hummel	Closed	55.00	110.00
64-01-008	School Girl 1909	M. I. Hummel	Closed	55.00	75.00
64-01-009	School Boy 1910	M. I. Hummel	Closed	55.00	80.00
64-01-010	Goose Girl 1914	M. I. Hummel	Closed	55.00	80.00
64-01-011	For Father 1917	M. I. Hummel	Closed	55.00	90.00
64-01-012	Merry Wanderer 1925	M. I. Hummel	Closed	55.00	110.00
64-01-013	Lost Stocking 1926	M. I. Hummel	Closed	55.00	75.00
64-01-014	Visiting and Invalid 1927	M. I. Hummel	Closed	55.00	75.00
64-01-015	On Secret Path 1928	M. I. Hummel	Closed	55.00	80.00
Goebel/Schmid		**M. I. Hummel Porcelain Dolls**			
84-02-001	Birthday Serenade/Boy	M. I. Hummel	Closed	225.00	250-300.
84-02-002	Birthday Serenade/Girl	M. I. Hummel	Closed	225.00	250-300.
84-02-003	On Holiday	M. I. Hummel	Closed	225.00	250-300.
84-02-004	Postman	M. I. Hummel	Closed	225.00	250-300.
85-02-005	Carnival	M. I. Hummel	Closed	225.00	250-300.
85-02-006	Easter Greetings	M. I. Hummel	Closed	225.00	250-300.
85-02-007	Lost Sheep	M. I. Hummel	Closed	225.00	250-300.
85-02-008	Signs of Spring	M. I. Hummel	Closed	225.00	250-300.
Gorham		**Gorham Dolls**			
81-01-001	Jillian, 16"	S. Stone Aiken	Closed	200.00	475.00
81-01-002	Alexandria, 18"	S. Stone Aiken	Closed	250.00	575.00
81-01-003	Christopher, 19"	S. Stone Aiken	Closed	250.00	850-950.
81-01-004	Stephanie, 18"	S. Stone Aiken	Closed	250.00	1800-2100.
81-01-005	Cecile, 16"	S. Stone Aiken	Closed	200.00	950.00
81-01-006	Christina, 16"	S. Stone Aiken	Closed	200.00	475.00
81-01-007	Danielle, 14"	S. Stone Aiken	Closed	150.00	350-375.
81-01-008	Melinda, 14"	S. Stone Aiken	Closed	150.00	350-375.
81-01-009	Elena, 14"	S. Stone Aiken	Closed	150.00	750.00
81-01-010	Rosemond, 18"	S. Stone Aiken	Closed	250.00	650-675.
82-01-011	Mlle. Monique, 12"	S. Stone Aiken	Closed	125.00	295.00
82-01-012	Mlle. Jeanette, 12"	S. Stone Aiken	Closed	125.00	195-225.
82-01-013	Mlle. Lucille, 12"	S. Stone Aiken	Closed	125.00	450-475.
82-01-014	Benjamin, 18"	S. Stone Aiken	Closed	200.00	550-600.
82-01-015	Ellice, 18"	S. Stone Aiken	Closed	200.00	550-600.
82-01-016	Corrine, 21"	S. Stone Aiken	Closed	250.00	595.00
82-01-017	Baby in Blue Dress, 12"	S. Stone Aiken	Closed	150.00	350-375.
82-01-018	Baby in Apricot Dress, 16"	S. Stone Aiken	Closed	175.00	375.00
82-01-019	Baby in White Dress, 18"	Gorham	Closed	250.00	395.00
82-01-020	Melanie, 23"	S. Stone Aiken	Closed	300.00	725.00
82-01-021	Jeremy, 23"	S. Stone Aiken	Closed	300.00	750-800.
82-01-022	Mlle. Yvonne, 12"	Unknown	Closed	125.00	450.00
82-01-023	M. Anton, 12"	Unknown	Closed	125.00	195.00
82-01-024	Mlle. Marsella, 12"	Unknown	Closed	125.00	295.00
82-01-025	Kristin, 23"	S. Stone Aiken	Closed	300.00	575-700.
83-01-026	Jennifer, 19" Bridal Doll	S. Stone Aiken	Closed	325.00	825.00
85-01-027	Linda, 19"	S. Stone Aiken	Closed	275.00	475.00
85-01-028	Odette, 19"	S. Stone Aiken	Closed	250.00	450.00
85-01-029	Amelia, 19"	S. Stone Aiken	Closed	275.00	400.00
85-01-030	Nanette, 19"	S. Stone Aiken	Closed	275.00	400.00
85-01-031	Alexander, 19"	S. Stone Aiken	Closed	275.00	400-425.
85-01-032	Gabrielle, 19"	S. Stone Aiken	Closed	225.00	395.00
86-01-033	Julia, 16"	S. Stone Aiken	Closed	225.00	375.00
86-01-034	Lauren, 14"	S. Stone Aiken	Closed	175.00	375.00
86-01-035	Emily, 14"	S. Stone Aiken	Closed	175.00	375.00
86-01-036	Fleur, 19"	S. Stone Aiken	Closed	300.00	395.00
87-01-037	Juliet	S. Stone Aiken	Closed	325.00	395.00
86-01-038	Meredith	S. Stone Aiken	Closed	295.00	400-425.
86-01-039	Alissa	S. Stone Aiken	Closed	245.00	375.00
86-01-040	Jessica	S. Stone Aiken	Closed	195.00	350.00
Gorham		**Limited Edition Dolls**			
82-02-001	Allison, 19"	S. Stone Aiken	1,000	300.00	4800.00
83-02-002	Ashley, 19"	S. Stone Aiken	2,500	350.00	1200.00
84-02-003	Nicole, 19"	S. Stone Aiken	2,500	350.00	1000.00
84-02-004	Holly (Christmas), 19"	S. Stone Aiken	2,500	300.00	875-925.
85-02-005	Lydia,19"	S. Stone Aiken	1,500	550.00	1800.00
85-02-006	Joy (Christmas), 19"	S. Stone Aiken	2,500	350.00	500-725.
86-02-007	Noel (Christmas), 19"	S. Stone Aiken	2,500	400.00	795.00
87-02-008	Jacqueline, 19"	S. Stone Aiken	1,500	500.00	600-850.
87-02-009	Merrie (Christmas), 19"	S. Stone Aiken	2,500	500.00	795.00
88-02-010	Andrew, 19"	S. Stone Aiken	1,000	475.00	625.00
88-02-011	Christa (Christmas), 19"	S. Stone Aiken	2,500	550.00	1500.00
90-02-012	Amey (10th Anniversary Edition)	S. Stone Aiken	Closed	650.00	1100.00
Gorham		**Gorham Holly Hobbie Childhood Memories**			
85-03-001	Mother's Helper	Holly Hobbie	Closed	45.00	125.00
85-03-002	Best Friends	Holly Hobbie	Closed	45.00	125.00
85-03-003	First Day of School	Holly Hobbie	Closed	45.00	125.00
85-03-004	Christmas Wishes	Holly Hobbie	Closed	45.00	125.00
Gorham		**Gorham Holly Hobbie For All Seasons**			
84-04-001	Summer Holly 12"	Holly Hobbie	Closed	42.50	195.00
84-04-002	Fall Holly 12"	Holly Hobbie	Closed	42.50	195.00
84-04-003	Winter Holly 12"	Holly Hobbie	Closed	42.50	195.00
84-04-004	Spring Holly 12"	Holly Hobbie	Closed	42.50	195.00
Gorham		**Holly Hobbie**			
83-05-001	Blue Girl, 14"	Holly Hobbie	Closed	80.00	325.00
83-05-002	Christmas Morning, 14"	Holly Hobbie	Closed	80.00	275.00
83-05-003	Heather, 14"	Holly Hobbie	Closed	80.00	275.00
83-05-004	Little Amy, 14"	Holly Hobbie	Closed	80.00	275.00
83-05-005	Robbie, 14"	Holly Hobbie	Closed	80.00	275.00
83-05-006	Sweet Valentine, 16"	Holly Hobbie	Closed	100.00	350.00
83-05-007	Yesterday's Memories, 18"	Holly Hobbie	Closed	125.00	450.00
83-05-008	Sunday Best, 18"	Holly Hobbie	Closed	115.00	350.00
83-05-009	Blue Girl, 18"	Holly Hobbie	Closed	115.00	395.00
Gorham		**Little Women**			
83-06-001	Beth, 16"	S. Stone Aiken	Closed	225.00	575.00
83-06-002	Amy, 16"	S. Stone Aiken	Closed	225.00	575.00
83-06-003	Meg, 19"	S. Stone Aiken	Closed	275.00	695.00
83-06-004	Jo, 19"	S. Stone Aiken	Closed	275.00	675.00
Gorham		**Kezi Doll For All Seasons**			
85-07-001	Ariel 16"	Kezi	Closed	135.00	500.00
85-07-002	Aubrey 16"	Kezi	Closed	135.00	500.00
85-07-003	Amber 16"	Kezi	Closed	135.00	500.00
85-07-004	Adrienne 16"	Kezi	Closed	135.00	500-525.
Gorham		**Kezi Golden Gifts**			
84-08-001	Faith 18"	Kezi	Closed	95.00	195-225.
84-08-002	Felicity 18"	Kezi	Closed	95.00	195.00
84-08-003	Patience 18"	Kezi	Closed	95.00	195.00
84-08-004	Prudence 18"	Kezi	Closed	85.00	195.00
84-08-005	Hope 16"	Kezi	Closed	85.00	175-225.
84-08-006	Grace 16"	Kezi	Closed	85.00	175.00
84-08-007	Charity 16"	Kezi	Closed	85.00	175-195.
84-08-008	Merrie 16"	Kezi	Closed	85.00	175-195.
Gorham		**Limited Edition Sister Set**			
88-09-001	Kathleen	S. Stone Aiken	1,000	550.00	850.00
88-09-002	Katelin	S. Stone Aiken	Set	Set	Set
Gorham		**Southern Belles**			
85-10-001	Amanda, 19"	S. Stone Aiken	Closed	300.00	850.00
86-10-002	Veronica, 19"	S. Stone Aiken	Closed	325.00	750.00
87-10-003	Rachel, 19"	S. Stone Aiken	Closed	375.00	825.00
88-10-004	Cassie, 19"	S. Stone Aiken	Closed	500.00	700.00
Gorham		**Valentine Ladies**			
87-11-001	Jane	P. Valentine	2,500	145.00	350-400.
87-11-002	Lee Ann	P. Valentine	2,500	145.00	325.00
87-11-003	Elizabeth	P. Valentine	2,500	145.00	450.00
87-11-004	Rebecca	P. Valentine	2,500	145.00	325.00
87-11-005	Patrice	P. Valentine	2,500	145.00	325.00
87-11-006	Anabella	P. Valentine	2,500	145.00	395-425.
87-11-007	Sylvia	P. Valentine	2,500	160.00	395.00
87-11-008	Rosanne	P. Valentine	2,500	145.00	325.00
87-11-009	Marianna	P. Valentine	Closed	160.00	400.00
88-11-010	Maria Theresa	P. Valentine	2,500	225.00	425.00
88-11-011	Priscilla	P. Valentine	2,500	195.00	325.00
88-11-012	Judith Anne	P. Valentine	2,500	195.00	325.00
88-11-013	Felicia	P. Valentine	2,500	225.00	395.00
89-11-014	Julianna	P. Valentine	2,500	225.00	275-325.
89-11-015	Rose	P. Valentine	Closed	225.00	275-325.
Gorham		**Precious as Pearls**			
86-12-001	Colette	S. Stone Aiken	2,500	400.00	1500.00
87-12-002	Charlotte	S. Stone Aiken	2,500	425.00	795-895.
88-12-003	Chloe	S. Stone Aiken	2,500	525.00	925.00
89-12-004	Cassandra	S. Stone Aiken	1,500	525.00	1300.00
Gorham		**Gorham Baby Doll Collection**			
87-13-001	Christening Day	Aiken/Matthews	Closed	245.00	295.00
87-13-002	Leslie	Aiken/Matthews	Closed	245.00	325.00
87-13-003	Matthew	Aiken/Matthews	Closed	245.00	285.00
Gorham		**Beverly Port Designer Collection**			
87-14-001	Silver Bell 17"	B. Port	2,500	175.00	295.00
87-14-002	Kristobear Kringle 17"	B. Port	2,500	200.00	325.00
87-14-003	Tedwina Kimelina Bearkin 10"	B. Port	2,500	95.00	150.00
87-14-004	Christopher Paul Bearkin 10"	B. Port	2,500	95.00	150.00
87-14-005	Molly Melinda Bearkin 10"	B. Port	2,500	95.00	150.00
87-14-006	Tedward Jonathan Bearkin 10"	B. Port	2,500	95.00	150.00
88-14-007	Baery Mab 9-1/2"	B. Port	2,500	110.00	150.00
88-14-008	Miss Emily 18"	B. Port	2,500	350.00	450.00
88-14-009	T.R. 28-1/2"	B. Port	1,000	400.00	600.00
88-14-010	The Amazing Calliope Merriweather 17"	B. Port	2,500	275.00	425.00

Company Number	Name	Series Artist	Edition Limit	Issue Price	Quote
88-14-011	Hollybeary Kringle 15"	B. Port	2,500	350.00	395.00
88-14-012	Theodore B. Bear 14"	B. Port	2,500	175.00	195.00
Gorham		**Bonnets & Bows**			
88-15-001	Belinda	B. Gerardi	2,500	195.00	395.00
88-15-002	Annemarie	B. Gerardi	2,500	195.00	395.00
88-15-003	Allessandra	B. Gerardi	2,500	195.00	395.00
88-15-004	Lisette	B. Gerardi	2,500	285.00	495.00
88-15-005	Bettina	B. Gerardi	2,500	285.00	495.00
88-15-006	Ellie	B. Gerardi	2,500	285.00	495.00
88-15-007	Alicia	B. Gerardi	2,500	385.00	800.00
88-15-008	Bethany	B. Gerardi	2,500	385.00	1350.00
88-15-009	Jesse	B. Gerardi	1,000	525.00	795.00
88-15-010	Francie	B. Gerardi	1,000	625.00	895.00
Gorham		**Small Wonders**			
88-16-001	Patina	B. Gerardi	1,000	265.00	265.00
88-16-002	Madeline	B. Gerardi	Closed	365.00	365.00
88-16-003	Marguerite	B. Gerardi	1,000	425.00	425.00
Gorham		**Joyful Years**			
89-17-001	William	B. Gerardi	1,000	295.00	295.00
89-17-002	Katrina	B. Gerardi	1,000	295.00	295.00
Gorham		**Victorian Cameo Collection**			
90-18-001	Victoria	B. Gerardi	1,500	375.00	375.00
91-18-002	Alexandra	B. Gerardi	1,500	375.00	375.00
Gorham		**Children Of Christmas**			
89-19-001	Clara, 16"	S. Stone Aiken	1,500	325.00	675.00
90-19-002	Natalie, 16"	S. Stone Aiken	1,500	350.00	395-450.
91-19-003	Emily	S. Stone Aiken	1,500	375.00	375.00
92-19-004	Virginia	S. Stone Aiken	1,500	375.00	375.00
Gorham		**Les Belles Bebes Collection**			
91-20-001	Cherie	S. Stone Aiken	1,500	375.00	375-600.
91-20-002	Desiree	S. Stone Aiken	1,500	375.00	375.00
93-20-003	Camille	S. Stone Aiken	1,500	375.00	375.00
Gorham		**Childhood Memories**			
91-21-001	Amanda	D. Valenza	Open	98.00	98.00
91-21-002	Kimberly	D. Valenza	Open	98.00	98.00
91-21-003	Jessica	D. Valenza	Open	98.00	98.00
91-21-004	Jennifer	D. Valenza	Open	98.00	98.00
Gorham		**Gifts of the Garden**			
91-22-001	Priscilla	S. Stone Aiken	2,500	125.00	125.00
91-22-002	Lauren	S. Stone Aiken	2,500	125.00	125.00
91-22-003	Irene	S. Stone Aiken	2,500	125.00	125.00
91-22-004	Valerie	S. Stone Aiken	2,500	125.00	125.00
91-22-005	Deborah	S. Stone Aiken	2,500	125.00	125.00
91-22-006	Alisa	S. Stone Aiken	2,500	125.00	125.00
91-22-007	Maria	S. Stone Aiken	2,500	125.00	125.00
91-22-008	Joelle (Christmas)	S. Stone Aiken	Yr.Iss.	150.00	195.00
91-22-009	Holly (Christmas)	S. Stone Aiken	Yr.Iss.	150.00	150.00
Gorham		**Dolls of the Month**			
91-23-001	Miss January	Gorham	Open	79.00	79.00
91-23-002	Miss February	Gorham	Open	79.00	79.00
91-23-003	Miss March	Gorham	Open	79.00	79.00
91-23-004	Miss April	Gorham	Open	79.00	79.00
91-23-005	Miss May	Gorham	Open	79.00	79.00
91-23-006	Miss June	Gorham	Open	79.00	79.00
91-23-007	Miss July	Gorham	Open	79.00	79.00
91-23-008	Miss August	Gorham	Open	79.00	79.00
91-23-009	Miss September	Gorham	Open	79.00	79.00
91-23-010	Miss October	Gorham	Open	79.00	79.00
91-23-011	Miss November	Gorham	Open	79.00	79.00
91-23-012	Miss December	Gorham	Open	79.00	79.00
Gorham		**Legendary Heroines**			
91-24-001	Jane Eyre	S. Stone Aiken	1,500	245.00	245.00
91-24-002	Guinevere	S. Stone Aiken	1,500	245.00	245.00
91-24-003	Juliet	S. Stone Aiken	1,500	245.00	245.00
91-24-004	Lara	S. Stone Aiken	1,500	245.00	245.00
Gorham		**Gift of Dreams**			
91-25-001	Samantha	Young/Gerardi	1,000	495.00	495.00
91-25-002	Katherine	Young/Gerardi	1,000	495.00	495.00
91-25-003	Melissa	Young/Gerardi	1,000	495.00	495.00
91-25-004	Elizabeth	Young/Gerardi	1,000	495.00	495.00
91-25-005	Christina (Christmas)	Young/Gerardi	500	695.00	695.00
Gorham		**The Friendship Dolls**			
91-26-001	Peggy-The American Traveler	P. Seaman	Open	98.00	98.00
91-26-002	Meagan-The Irish Traveler	L. O'Connor	Open	98.00	98.00
91-26-003	Angela-The Italian Traveler	S. Nappo	Open	98.00	98.00
91-26-004	Kinuko-The Japanese Traveler	S. Ueki	Open	98.00	98.00
Gorham		**Special Moments**			
91-27-001	Baby's First Christmas	E. Worrell	Open	135.00	135.00
92-27-002	Baby's Christening	E. Worrell	Open	135.00	135.00
92-27-003	Baby's First Birthday	E. Worrell	Open	135.00	135.00
92-27-004	Baby's First Steps	E. Worrell	Open	135.00	135.00
Gorham		**Dollie And Me**			
91-28-001	Dollie's First Steps	J. Pilallis	Open	160.00	160.00
Gorham		**The Victoriana Collection**			
92-29-001	Victoria's Jubilee	E. Woodhouse	Yr.Iss.	295.00	295.00
Gorham		**Days Of The Week**			
92-30-001	Monday's Child	R./L. Schrubbe	Open	98.00	98.00
92-30-002	Tuesday's Child	R./L. Schrubbe	Open	98.00	98.00
92-30-003	Wednesday's Child	R./L. Schrubbe	Open	98.00	98.00
92-30-004	Thurday's Child	R./L. Schrubbe	Open	98.00	98.00
92-30-005	Friday's Child	R./L. Schrubbe	Open	98.00	98.00
92-30-006	Saturday's Child	R./L. Schrubbe	Open	98.00	98.00
92-30-007	Sunday's Child	R./L. Schrubbe	Open	98.00	98.00
Gorham		**Times To Treasure**			
90-31-001	Storytime	L. Di Leo	Open	195.00	195.00
91-31-002	Bedtime	L. Di Leo	Open	195.00	195.00
93-31-003	Playtime	L. Di Leo	Open	195.00	195.00
93-31-004	Cradletime	L. Di Leo	Open	195.00	195.00
Gorham		**Victorian Children**			
92-32-001	Sarah's Tea Time	S. Stone Aiken	1,000	495.00	495.00
Gorham		**Bride Dolls**			
93-33-001	Victorian Bride	D. Valenza	9,500	295.00	295.00
Gorham		**Carousel Dolls**			
93-34-001	Ribbons And Roses	C. Shafer	Open	95.00	95.00
Gorham		**Pillow Baby Dolls**			
93-35-001	Baby In Pink	L. Gordon	Open	39.00	39.00
93-35-002	Baby In Blue	L. Gordon	Open	39.00	39.00
93-35-002	Baby In Yellow	L. Gordon	Open	39.00	39.00
Gorham		**Victorian Flower Dolls**			
93-36-001	Rose	J. Pillalis	Open	98.00	98.00
Gorham		**Celebrations Of Childhood**			
92-37-003	Happy Birthday Amy	L. Di Leo	Open	160.00	160.00
Gorham		**Littlest Angel Dolls**			
92-38-001	Merriel	L. Di Leo	Open	49.50	49.50
93-38-002	Noelle	L. Di Leo	Open	49.50	49.50
Gorham		**Puppy Love Dolls**			
92-39-001	Katie And Kyle	R./ L. Schrubbe	Open	225.00	225.00
Gorham		**Daydreamer Dolls**			
92-40-001	Heather's Daydream	S. Stone Aiken	Open	119.00	119.00
Gorham		**Children With Pets**			
93-41-001	Play Ball	R./ L. Schrubbe	Open	98.00	98.00
Gorham		**Kids With Stuffed Toys**			
93-42-001	Tara And Teddy	R./ L. Schrubbe	Open	119.00	119.00
Gorham		**Raggedy Ann And Andy**			
93-43-001	Raggedy Ann & Andy	Unknown	9,500	119.00	119.00
Green Valley World		**Norman Rockwell Character Doll**			
XX-01-001	Mimi	M. Moline	Closed	200.00	200.00
XX-01-002	Anne	M. Moline	Closed	200.00	200.00
XX-01-003	Davey	M. Moline	Closed	200.00	200.00
XX-01-004	Susie	M. Moline	Closed	200.00	200.00
XX-01-005	Willma	M. Moline	20,000	200.00	200.00
XX-01-006	Nell	M. Moline	Closed	200.00	200.00
XX-01-007	Tina	M. Moline	Closed	200.00	200.00
XX-01-008	Junior	M. Moline	Closed	200.00	200.00
XX-01-009	Polly	M. Moline	20,000	200.00	200.00
XX-01-010	Dr. Chrisfield	M. Moline	Closed	200.00	200.00
XX-01-011	Jane	M. Moline	Closed	200.00	200.00
XX-01-012	Beth	M. Moline	20,000	200.00	200.00
XX-01-013	Amy	M. Moline	20,000	200.00	200.00
XX-01-014	John	M. Moline	Closed	200.00	200.00
XX-01-015	Mary	M. Moline	Closed	200.00	200.00
XX-01-016	Sally	M. Moline	20,000	200.00	200.00
XX-01-017	Laura	M. Moline	20,000	200.00	200.00
XX-01-018	Santa	M. Moline	Closed	200.00	200.00
XX-01-019	Molly	M. Moline	Closed	200.00	200.00
XX-01-020	Rockwell	M. Moline	Closed	200.00	200.00
H & G Studios, Inc.		**Brenda Burke Dolls**			
89-01-001	Arabelle	B. Burke	500	695.00	1400.00
89-01-002	Angelica	B. Burke	50	1495.00	3000.00
89-01-003	Adelaine	B. Burke	25	1795.00	3600.00
89-01-004	Amanda	B. Burke	25	1995.00	6000.00
89-01-005	Alicia	B. Burke	125	895.00	1800.00
89-01-006	Alexandra	B. Burke	125	995.00	2000.00
89-01-007	Bethany	B. Burke	45	2995.00	2995.00
89-01-008	Beatrice	B. Burke	85	2395.00	2395.00
89-01-009	Brittany	B. Burke	75	2695.00	2695.00
90-01-010	Belinda	B. Burke	12	3695.00	3695.00
91-01-011	Tender Love	B. Burke	25	3295.00	3295.00
91-01-012	Sleigh Ride	B. Burke	20	3695.00	3695.00
91-01-013	Charlotte	B. Burke	20	2395.00	2395.00
91-01-014	Clarissa	B. Burke	15	3595.00	3595.00
92-01-015	Dorothea	B. Burke	500	395.00	395.00
H & G Studios, Inc.		**Childhood Memories**			
89-02-001	Early Days	B. Burke	95	2595.00	2595.00
91-02-002	Playtime	B. Burke	35	2795.00	2795.00
H & G Studios, Inc.		**The Four Seasons**			
90-03-001	Spring	B. Burke	125	1995.00	1995.00
H & G Studios, Inc.		**Dancing Through The Ages**			
90-04-001	Minuet	B. Burke	95	2495.00	2495.00
H & G Studios, Inc.		**Birthday Party**			
90-05-001	Suzie	B. Burke	500	695.00	695.00
Hamilton Collection		**Songs of the Seasons Hakata Doll Collection**			
85-01-001	Winter Song Maiden	T. Murakami	9,800	75.00	75.00
85-01-002	Spring Song Maiden	T. Murakami	9,800	75.00	75.00
85-01-003	Summer Song Maiden	T. Murakami	9,800	75.00	75.00
85-01-004	Autumn Song Maiden	T. Murakami	9,800	75.00	75.00
Hamilton Collection		**Dolls of America's Colonial Heritage**			
86-02-001	Katrina	A. Elekfy	Open	55.00	55.00
86-02-002	Nicole	A. Elekfy	Open	55.00	55.00
87-02-003	Maria	A. Elekfy	Open	55.00	55.00
87-02-004	Priscilla	A. Elekfy	Open	55.00	55.00
87-02-005	Colleen	A. Elekfy	Open	55.00	55.00
88-02-006	Gretchen	A. Elekfy	Open	55.00	55.00
Hamilton Collection		**Star Trek Doll Collection**			
88-03-001	Mr. Spock	E. Daub	Closed	75.00	150.00
88-03-002	Captain Kirk	E. Daub	Closed	75.00	175.00
89-03-003	Dr. Mc Coy	E. Daub	Closed	75.00	120.00
89-03-004	Scotty	E. Daub	Closed	75.00	120.00

Company / Number	Name	Series / Artist	Edition Limit	Issue Price	Quote
90-03-005	Sulu	E. Daub	Closed	75.00	120.00
90-03-006	Chekov	E. Daub	Closed	75.00	120.00
91-03-007	Uhura	E. Daub	Closed	75.00	120.00
Hamilton Collection		**The Antique Doll Collection**			
89-04-001	Nicole	Unknown	Open	195.00	195.00
90-04-002	Colette	Unknown	Open	195.00	195.00
91-04-003	Lisette	Unknown	Open	195.00	195.00
91-04-004	Katrina	Unknown	Open	195.00	195.00
Hamilton Collection		**The Bessie Pease Gutmann Doll Collection**			
89-05-001	Love is Blind	B.P. Gutmann	Open	135.00	135.00
89-05-002	He Won't Bite	B.P. Gutmann	Open	135.00	135.00
91-05-003	Virginia	B.P. Gutmann	Open	135.00	135.00
91-05-004	First Dancing Lesson	B.P. Gutmann	Open	195.00	195.00
91-05-005	Good Morning	B.P. Gutmann	Open	195.00	195.00
91-05-006	Love At First Sight	B.P. Gutmann	Open	195.00	195.00
Hamilton Collection		**The Maud Humphrey Bogart Doll Collection**			
89-06-001	Playing Bride	M.H. Bogart	Open	135.00	135.00
90-06-002	First Party	M.H. Bogart	Open	135.00	135.00
90-06-003	The First Lesson	M.H. Bogart	Open	135.00	135.00
91-06-004	Seamstress	M.H. Bogart	Open	135.00	135.00
91-06-005	Little Captive	M.H. Bogart	Open	135.00	135.00
Hamilton Collection		**Connie Walser Derrick Baby Doll**			
90-07-001	Jessica	C.W. Derrick	Closed	155.00	200-300.
91-07-002	Sara	C.W. Derrick	Open	155.00	155.00
91-07-003	Andrew	C.W. Derrick	Open	155.00	155.00
91-07-004	Amanda	C.W. Derrick	Open	155.00	155.00
Hamilton Collection		**I Love Lucy**			
90-08-001	Lucy	Unknown	Open	95.00	95.00
91-08-002	Ricky	Unknown	Open	95.00	95.00
Hamilton Collection		**Russian Czanna Dolls**			
91-09-001	Alexandra	Unknown	4,950	295.00	295.00
Hamilton Collection		**Storyboook Dolls**			
91-10-001	Alice in Wonderland	L. Di Leo	Open	75.00	75.00
Hamilton Collection		**International Children**			
91-11-001	Miko	C. Woodie	Closed	49.50	80.00
91-11-002	Anastasia	C. Woodie	Open	49.50	49.50
91-11-003	Angelina	C. Woodie	Open	49.50	49.50
92-11-004	Lian	C. Woodie	Open	49.50	49.50
92-11-005	Monique	C. Woodie	Open	49.50	49.50
92-11-006	Lisa	C. Woodie	Open	49.50	49.50
Hamilton Collection		**Central Park Skaters**			
91-12-001	Central Park Skaters	C. Woodie	Open	245.00	245.00
Hamilton Collection		**Jane Zidjunas Toddler Dolls**			
91-13-001	Jennifer	J. Zidjunas	Open	135.00	135.00
91-13-002	Megan	J. Zidjunas	Open	135.00	135.00
92-13-003	Kimberly	J. Zidjunas	Open	135.00	135.00
92-13-004	Amy	J. Zidjunas	Open	135.00	135.00
Hamilton Collection		**Jane Zidjunas Party Dolls**			
91-14-001	Kelly	J. Zidjunas	Open	135.00	135.00
92-14-002	Katie	J. Zidjunas	Open	135.00	135.00
Hamilton Collection		**The Royal Beauty Dolls**			
91-15-001	Chen Mai	Unknown	Open	195.00	195.00
Hamilton Collection		**Abbie Williams Doll Collection**			
92-16-001	Molly	A. Williams	2,500	155.00	155.00
Hamilton Collection		**Zolan Dolls**			
91-17-001	A Christmas Prayer	D. Zolan	Open	95.00	95.00
Hamilton Collection		**Baby Portrait Dolls**			
91-18-001	Melissa	B. Parker	Open	135.00	135.00
92-18-002	Janna	B. Parker	Open	135.00	135.00
92-18-003	Bethany	B. Parker	Open	135.00	135.00
Hamilton Collection		**Helen Kish Dolls**			
91-19-001	Ashley	H. Kish	Open	135.00	135.00
92-19-002	Elizabeth	H. Kish	Open	135.00	135.00
92-19-003	Hannah	H. Kish	Open	135.00	135.00
Hamilton Collection		**Picnic In The Park**			
91-20-001	Rebecca	J. Esteban	Open	155.00	155.00
92-20-002	Emily	J. Esteban	Open	155.00	155.00
92-20-003	Victoria	J. Esteban	Open	155.00	155.00
Hamilton Collection		**Bride Dolls**			
91-21-001	Portrait of Innocence	Unknown	Open	195.00	195.00
92-21-002	Portrait of Loveliness	Unknown	Open	195.00	195.00
Hamilton Collection		**Maud Humphrey Bogart Dolls**			
92-22-001	Playing Bridesmaid	Unknown	Closed	195.00	195.00
Hamilton Collection		**Year Round Fun**			
92-23-001	Alison	D. Schurig	Open	95.00	95.00
Hamilton Collection		**Laura Cobabe Dolls**			
92-24-001	Amber	L. Cobabe	Open	195.00	195.00
Hamilton Collection		**Belles Of The Countryside**			
92-25-001	Erin	C. Beath Oran	Open	135.00	135.00
Hamilton Collection		**Dolls By Kay McKee**			
92-26-001	Shy Violet	K. McKee	Open	135.00	135.00
Hamilton Collection		**Parker-Levi Toddlers**			
92-27-001	Courtney	B. Parker	Open	135.00	135.00
Hamilton Collection		**Parkins Treasures**			
92-28-001	Tiffany	P. Parkins	Open	55.00	55.00
Hamilton Gifts		**Maud Humphrey Bogart Porcelain Dolls**			
91-01-001	Sarah H5617	M. Humphrey	Open	37.00	37.00
91-01-002	Susanna H5648	M. Humphrey	Open	37.00	37.00
91-01-003	My First Party H5686	M. Humphrey	Open	135.00	135.00
91-01-004	Playing Bride H5618	M. Humphrey	Open	135.00	135.00
Edna Hibel Studios		**Child's Fancy**			
85-01-001	Jenny's Lady Jennifer	E. Hibel	800	395.00	700-1000.
Edna Hibel Studios		**Wax Doll Collection**			
86-02-001	Wax Doll	E. Hibel	12	2500.00	3000-3400.
Annette Himstedt		**Barefoot Children**			
87-01-001	Fatou	A. Himstedt	Closed	329.00	950-1250.
87-01-002	Bastian	A. Himstedt	Closed	329.00	600-850.
87-01-003	Ellen	A. Himstedt	Closed	329.00	650-950.
87-01-004	Paula	A. Himstedt	Closed	329.00	650-950.
87-01-005	Lisa	A. Himstedt	Closed	329.00	650-950.
87-01-006	Kathe	A. Himstedt	Closed	329.00	600-950.
Annette Himstedt		**Heartland Series**			
88-02-001	Timi	A. Himstedt	Closed	329.00	500-550.
88-02-002	Toni	A. Himstedt	Closed	329.00	500-550.
Annette Himstedt		**Blessed Are The Children**			
88-03-001	Friederike	A. Himstedt	Closed	499.00	800-950.
88-03-002	Makimura	A. Himstedt	Closed	499.00	600-950.
88-03-003	Kasimir	A. Himstedt	Closed	499.00	900-1200.
88-03-004	Michiko	A. Himstedt	Closed	499.00	800-850.
88-03-005	Malin	A. Himstedt	Closed	499.00	800-950.
Annette Himstedt		**Reflection of Youth**			
89-04-001	Adrienne (France)	A. Himstedt	Closed	558.00	600.00
89-04-002	Kai (German)	A. Himstedt	Closed	558.00	600-750.
89-04-003	Janka (Hungry)	A. Himstedt	Closed	558.00	600-750.
89-04-004	Ayoka (Africa)	A. Himstedt	Closed	558.00	700-1200.
Annette Himstedt		**Fiene And The Barefoot Babies**			
90-05-001	Annchen-German Baby Girl	A. Himstedt	2 Yr.	498.00	498.00
90-05-002	Taki-Japanese Baby Girl	A. Himstedt	2 Yr.	498.00	498.00
90-05-003	Mo-American Baby Boy	A. Himstedt	2 Yr.	498.00	498.00
90-05-004	Fiene-Belgian Girl	A. Himstedt	2 Yr.	598.00	598.00
Annette Himstedt		**Faces of Friendship**			
91-06-001	Liliane (Netherlands)	A. Himstedt	2 Yr.	598.00	598.00
91-06-002	Shireem (Bali)	A. Himstedt	2 Yr.	598.00	598.00
91-06-003	Neblina (Switzerland)	A. Himstedt	2 Yr.	598.00	598.00
Annette Himstedt		**Summer Dreams**			
91-07-001	Sanga	A. Himstedt	2 Yr.	598.00	598.00
91-07-002	Pemba	A. Himstedt	2 Yr.	598.00	598.00
91-07-003	Jule	A. Himstedt	2 Yr.	598.00	598.00
91-07-004	Enzo	A. Himstedt	2 Yr.	598.00	598.00
Kaiser Porcelain		**Dolls**			
90-01-001	Newborn/Christening Dress-17"	Unknown	1,000	74.00	82.00
90-01-002	Amanda-17"	Unknown	1,000	74.00	82.00
90-01-003	Nicole-17"	Unknown	1,000	74.00	82.00
90-01-004	Susan-17"	Unknown	1,000	74.00	82.00
90-01-005	Ashley-19"	Unknown	1,000	98.00	106.00
90-01-006	Kelly-19"	Unknown	1,000	98.00	106.00
90-01-007	Amy-19"	Unknown	1,000	98.00	106.00
90-01-008	Elizabeth-19"	Unknown	1,000	98.00	106.00
90-01-009	Sarah-22"	Unknown	1,000	116.00	126.00
90-01-010	Jennifer-22"	Unknown	1,000	116.00	126.00
90-01-011	Jessica-22"	Unknown	1,000	116.00	126.00
90-01-012	Heather-22"	Unknown	1,000	116.00	126.00
90-01-013	Kristy-24"	Unknown	1,000	128.00	138.00
90-01-014	Ann-24"	Unknown	1,000	128.00	138.00
90-01-015	Laura-24"	Unknown	1,000	128.00	138.00
90-01-016	Jill-24"	Unknown	1,000	128.00	138.00
Ladie and Friends™		**The Family and Friends of Lizzie High®**			
85-01-001	Lizzie High®-1100	B.K. Wisber	Open	36.00	36.00
85-01-002	Sabina Valentine (First Edition)-1101	B.K. Wisber	Closed	32.00	32.00
88-01-003	Sabina Valentine (Second Edition)-1101	B.K. Wisber	Open	41.00	41.00
85-01-004	Nettie Brown (First Edition)-1102	B.K. Wisber	Closed	32.00	32.00
88-01-005	Nettie Brown (Second Edition)-1102	B.K. Wisber	Open	37.00	37.00
85-01-006	Emma High-1103	B.K. Wisber	Closed	32.00	32.00
85-01-007	Rebecca Bowman (First Edition)-1104	B.K. Wisber	Closed	32.00	32.00
89-01-008	Rebecca Bowman (Second Edition)-1104	B.K. Wisber	Open	58.00	58.00
85-01-009	Mary Valentine-1105	B.K. Wisber	Closed	32.00	32.00
85-01-010	Wendel Bowman (First Edition)-1106	B.K. Wisber	Closed	32.00	32.00
92-01-011	Wendel Bowman (Second Edition)-1106	B.K. Wisber	Open	60.00	60.00
85-01-012	Russell Dunn-1107	B.K. Wisber	Closed	32.00	32.00
85-01-013	Luther Bowman-1108	B.K. Wisber	Closed	32.00	32.00
85-01-014	Elizabeth Sweetland (First Edition)-1109	B.K. Wisber	Closed	32.00	32.00
91-01-015	Elizabeth Sweetland (Second Edition)-1109	B.K. Wisber	Open	56.00	56.00
85-01-016	Christian Bowman-1110	B.K. Wisber	Closed	32.00	32.00
85-01-017	Amanda High (First Edition)-1111	B.K. Wisber	Closed	32.00	32.00
90-01-018	Amanda High (Second Edition)-1111	B.K. Wisber	Open	56.00	56.00
85-01-019	Louella Valentine-1112	B.K. Wisber	Closed	35.00	35.00
85-01-020	Peter Valentine-1113	B.K. Wisber	Closed	36.00	36.00
85-01-021	Nettie Brown (Christmas)-1114	B.K. Wisber	Closed	32.00	32.00
85-01-022	Cora High-1115	B.K. Wisber	Closed	32.00	32.00
85-01-023	Ida Valentine-1116	B.K. Wisber	Closed	32.00	32.00
85-01-024	Martin Bowman-1117	B.K. Wisber	Closed	36.00	36.00
85-01-025	Esther Dunn (First Edition)-1127	B.K. Wisber	Closed	45.00	45.00
91-01-026	Esther Dunn (SecondEdition)-1127	B.K. Wisber	Open	60.00	60.00
91-01-027	Cynthia High-1127A	B.K. Wisber	Open	60.00	60.00
85-01-028	Benjamin Bowman-1129	B.K. Wisber	Closed	32.00	32.00
85-01-029	Flossie High (First Edition)-1128	B.K. Wisber	Closed	45.00	45.00
89-01-030	Flossie High (Second Edition)-1128	B.K. Wisber	Open	55.00	55.00
85-01-031	Hannah Brown-1131	B.K. Wisber	Closed	45.00	45.00
85-01-032	Benjamin Bowman (Santa)-1134	B.K. Wisber	Open	39.00	39.00
85-01-033	Katrina Valentine-1135	B.K. Wisber	Closed	32.00	32.00
86-01-034	Grace Valentine (First Edition)-1146	B.K. Wisber	Closed	33.00	33.00
90-01-035	Grace Valentine (Second Edition)-1146	B.K. Wisber	Open	48.00	48.00
86-01-036	Juliet Valentine (First Edition)-1147	B.K. Wisber	Closed	33.00	33.00
90-01-037	Juliet Valentine (Second Edition)-1147	B.K. Wisber	Open	49.00	49.00
86-01-038	Alice Valentine-1148	B.K. Wisber	Closed	33.00	33.00
85-01-039	Susanna Bowman-1149	B.K. Wisber	Closed	45.00	45.00
86-01-040	Annie Bowman (First Edition)-1150	B.K. Wisber	Closed	33.00	33.00
93-01-041	Annie Bowman (Second Edition)-1150	B.K. Wisber	Open	N/A	N/A
93-01-042	Boy with Bunny Hutch	B.K. Wisber	Open	N/A	N/A

Company Number	Name	Series Artist	Edition Limit	Issue Price	Quote
86-01-043	Martha High-1151	B.K. Wisber	Closed	33.00	33.00
86-01-044	Dora High (First Edition)-1152	B.K. Wisber	Closed	32.00	32.00
92-01-045	Dora High (Second Edition)-1152	B.K. Wisber	Open	48.00	48.00
86-01-046	Delia Valentine-1153	B.K. Wisber	Closed	33.00	33.00
86-01-047	Sarah Valentine-1154	B.K. Wisber	Open	37.00	37.00
86-01-048	Sally Bowman-1155	B.K. Wisber	Closed	35.00	35.00
86-01-049	Tillie Brown-1156	B.K. Wisber	Closed	34.00	34.00
86-01-050	Andrew Brown-1157	B.K. Wisber	Closed	45.00	45.00
86-01-051	Edward Bowman-1158	B.K. Wisber	Closed	45.00	45.00
86-01-052	Thomas Bowman-1159	B.K. Wisber	Closed	32.00	32.00
86-01-053	Maggie High-1160	B.K. Wisber	Closed	32.00	32.00
86-01-054	Karl Valentine-1161	B.K. Wisber	Closed	32.00	32.00
86-01-055	Willie Bowman-1162	B.K. Wisber	Closed	35.00	35.00
86-01-056	Sadie Valentine-1163	B.K. Wisber	Open	47.00	47.00
86-01-057	Sophie Valentine-1164	B.K. Wisber	Closed	47.00	47.00
86-01-058	Katie Bowman-1178	B.K. Wisber	Open	38.00	38.00
86-01-059	Cassie Yocum-1179	B.K. Wisber	Closed	37.00	37.00
86-01-060	Jillian Bowman-1180	B.K. Wisber	Closed	34.00	34.00
86-01-061	Jenny Valentine-1181	B.K. Wisber	Closed	34.00	34.00
86-01-062	Christopher High-1182	B.K. Wisber	Closed	35.00	35.00
86-01-063	Marland Valentine-1183	B.K. Wisber	Closed	33.00	33.00
86-01-064	Marie Valentine (First Edition)-1184	B.K. Wisber	Closed	48.00	48.00
92-01-065	Marie Valentine (Second Edition)-1184	B.K. Wisber	Open	68.00	68.00
86-01-066	Emily Bowman (First Edition)-1185	B.K. Wisber	Closed	34.00	34.00
90-01-067	Emily Bowman (Second Edition)-1185	B.K. Wisber	Open	48.00	48.00
86-01-068	Matthew Yocum-1186	B.K. Wisber	Closed	33.00	33.00
86-01-069	Madaleine Valentine (First Edition)-1187	B.K. Wisber	Closed	34.00	34.00
89-01-070	Madaleine Valentine (Second Edition)-1187	B.K. Wisber	Open	38.00	38.00
86-01-071	Rachel Bowman (First Edition)-1188	B.K. Wisber	Closed	34.00	34.00
89-01-072	Rachel Bowman (Second Edition)-1188	B.K. Wisber	Open	36.00	36.00
86-01-073	Molly Yocum (First Edition)-1189	B.K. Wisber	Closed	34.00	34.00
89-01-074	Molly Yocum(Second Edition)-1189	B.K. Wisber	Open	40.00	40.00
86-01-075	Carrie High (First Edition)-1190	B.K. Wisber	Closed	45.00	45.00
89-01-076	Carrie High (Second Edition)-1190	B.K. Wisber	Open	47.00	47.00
86-01-077	William Valentine-1191	B.K. Wisber	Closed	37.00	37.00
86-01-078	Jeremy Bowman-1192	B.K. Wisber	Closed	37.00	37.00
86-01-079	Marisa Valentine (w/ Brother Petey)-1194	B.K. Wisber	Open	48.00	48.00
86-01-080	Marisa Valentine (alone)-1194A	B.K. Wisber	Open	37.00	37.00
86-01-081	David Yocum-1195	B.K. Wisber	Open	35.00	35.00
86-01-082	Little Ghosts-1197	B.K. Wisber	Open	17.00	17.00
87-01-083	Johanna Valentine-1198	B.K. Wisber	Closed	37.00	37.00
87-01-084	Abigail Bowman-1199	B.K. Wisber	Open	44.00	44.00
87-01-085	Naomi Valentine-1200	B.K. Wisber	Open	43.00	43.00
87-01-086	Amy Bowman-1201	B.K. Wisber	Open	40.00	40.00
87-01-087	Addie High-1202	B.K. Wisber	Open	40.00	40.00
87-01-088	The Wedding (Bride)-1203	B.K. Wisber	Open	39.00	39.00
87-01-089	The Wedding (Groom)-1203A	B.K. Wisber	Open	35.00	35.00
87-01-090	The Flower Girl-1204	B.K. Wisber	Open	22.00	22.00
87-01-091	Olivia High-1205	B.K. Wisber	Open	40.00	40.00
87-01-092	Imogene Bowman-1206	B.K. Wisber	Open	39.00	39.00
87-01-093	Rebecca's Mother-1207	B.K. Wisber	Open	42.00	4200
87-01-094	Penelope High-1208	B.K. Wisber	Closed	41.00	41.00
87-01-095	Margaret Bowman-1213	B.K. Wisber	Open	40.00	40.00
87-01-096	Patsy Bowman-1214	B.K. Wisber	Open	51.00	51.00
87-01-097	Ramona Brown-1215	B.K. Wisber	Closed	40.00	40.00
87-01-098	Gretchen High-1216	B.K. Wisber	Open	43.00	43.00
87-01-099	Cat on Chair-1217	B.K. Wisber	Closed	17.00	17.00
87-01-100	Katie and Barney-1219	B.K. Wisber	Open	40.00	40.00
87-01-101	Melanie Bowman (First Edition)-1220	B.K. Wisber	Closed	36.00	36.00
92-01-102	Melanie Bowman (Second Edition)-1220	B.K. Wisber	Open	46.00	46.00
87-01-103	Charles Bowman (First Edition)-1221	B.K. Wisber	Closed	34.00	34.00
92-01-103	Charles Bowman (Second Edition)-1221	B.K. Wisber	Open	46.00	46.00
87-01-104	Bridget Bowman-1222	B.K. Wisber	Open	45.00	45.00
87-01-105	Laura Valentine-1223	B.K. Wisber	Open	38.00	38.00
87-01-106	Santa Claus (sitting)-1224	B.K. Wisber	Closed	51.00	51.00
87-01-107	Little Witch-1225	B.K. Wisber	Open	21.00	21.00
87-01-108	Priscilla High-1226	B.K. Wisber	Open	60.00	60.00
88-01-109	Megan Valentine-1227	B.K. Wisber	Open	47.00	47.00
87-01-110	Pauline Bowman-1228	B.K. Wisber	Open	47.00	47.00
88-01-111	Allison Bowman-1229	B.K. Wisber	Open	58.00	58.00
88-01-112	Jacob High-1230	B.K. Wisber	Open	45.00	45.00
88-01-113	Janie Valentine-1231	B.K. Wisber	Open	40.00	40.00
88-01-114	Ruth Anne Bowman-1232	B.K. Wisber	Open	45.00	45.00
88-01-115	Daphne Bowman-1235	B.K. Wisber	Open	39.00	39.00
88-01-116	Mary Ellen Valentine-1236	B.K. Wisber	Open	42.00	42.00
88-01-117	Kinch Bowman-1237	B.K. Wisber	Open	48.00	48.00
88-01-118	Samantha Bowman-1238	B.K. Wisber	Open	48.00	48.00
88-01-119	Hattie Bowman-1239	B.K. Wisber	Open	43.00	43.00
88-01-120	Eunice High-1240	B.K. Wisber	Open	57.00	57.00
88-01-121	Bess High-1241	B.K. Wisber	Open	47.00	47.00
88-01-122	Bessie Valentine-1245	B.K. Wisber	Open	43.00	43.00
88-01-123	Phoebe High-1246	B.K. Wisber	Closed	49.00	49.00
89-01-124	Vanessa High-1247	B.K. Wisber	Open	47.00	47.00
89-01-125	Amelia High-1248	B.K. Wisber	Open	47.00	47.00
89-01-126	Victoria Bowman-1249	B.K. Wisber	Open	41.00	41.00
89-01-127	Johann Bowman-1250	B.K. Wisber	Open	41.00	41.00
89-01-128	Emmy Lou Valentine-1251	B.K. Wisber	Open	46.00	46.00
89-01-129	Peggy Bowman-1252	B.K. Wisber	Open	59.00	59.00
89-01-130	Jessica High (with Mother)-1253	B.K. Wisber	Open	59.00	59.00
89-01-131	Jessica High (alone)-1253A	B.K. Wisber	Open	22.00	22.00
89-01-132	Jason High (with Mother)-1254	B.K. Wisber	Open	59.00	59.00
89-01-133	Jason High (alone)-1254A	B.K. Wisber	Open	22.00	22.00
89-01-134	Lucy Bowman-1255	B.K. Wisber	Open	46.00	46.00
89-01-135	Miriam High-1256	B.K. Wisber	Open	47.00	47.00
89-01-136	Santa (with Tub)-1257	B.K. Wisber	Open	60.00	60.00
89-01-137	Mrs. Claus-1258	B.K. Wisber	Open	43.00	43.00
90-01-138	Marlene Valentine-1259	B.K. Wisber	Open	49.00	49.00
90-01-139	Albert Valentine-1260	B.K. Wisber	Open	43.00	43.00
90-01-140	Nancy Bowman-1261	B.K. Wisber	Open	49.00	49.00
91-01-141	Annabelle Bowman-1267	B.K. Wisber	Open	68.00	68.00
91-01-142	Michael Bowman-1268	B.K. Wisber	Open	52.00	52.00
91-01-143	Trudy Valentine-1269	B.K. Wisber	Open	64.00	64.00
91-01-144	The Department Store Santa-1270	B.K. Wisber	Open	76.00	76.00
91-01-145	Santa's Helper-1271	B.K. Wisber	Open	52.00	52.00
91-01-146	Barbara Helen-1274	B.K. Wisber	Open	58.00	58.00
92-01-147	Edwin Bowman-1281	B.K. Wisber	Open	70.00	70.00
92-01-148	Carol Anne Bowman-1282	B.K. Wisber	Open	70.00	70.00
92-01-149	Joseph Valentine-1283	B.K. Wisber	Open	62.00	62.00
92-01-150	Natalie Valentine-1284	B.K. Wisber	Open	62.00	62.00
92-01-151	Kathryn Bowman (Limited Edition)-1285	B.K. Wisber	3,000	140.00	140.00
92-01-152	Wendy Bowman-1293	B.K. Wisber	Open	78.00	78.00
92-01-153	Timothy Bowman-1294	B.K. Wisber	Open	56.00	56.00
92-01-154	Joanie Valentine-1295	B.K. Wisber	Open	48.00	48.00

Company Number	Name	Series Artist	Edition Limit	Issue Price	Quote
Ladie and Friends™		**The Little Ones**			
85-02-001	White Girl (First Edition)-1130	B.K. Wisber	Closed	15.00	15.00
85-02-002	Black Girl (First Edition)-1130	B.K. Wisber	Closed	15.00	15.00
85-02-003	White Boy (First Edition)-1130	B.K. Wisber	Closed	15.00	15.00
85-02-004	Black Boy (First Edition)-1130	B.K. Wisber	Closed	15.00	15.00
89-02-005	White Girl-pastels (Second Edition)-1130D	B.K. Wisber	Open	22.00	22.00
89-02-006	Black Girl-pastels (Second Edition)-1130E	B.K. Wisber	Open	22.00	22.00
89-02-007	White Girl-country color (2nd Edition)-1130F	B.K. Wisber	Open	22.00	22.00
89-02-008	Black Girl-country color(2nd Edition)-1130G	B.K. Wisber	Open	22.00	22.00
89-02-009	White Boy (Second Edition)-1130H	B.K. Wisber	Open	22.00	22.00
89-02-010	Black Boy (Second Edition)-1130I	B.K. Wisber	Open	22.00	22.00
92-02-011	Little One w/Beach Bucket-1275	B.K. Wisber	Open	26.00	26.00
92-02-012	Little One w/Easter Eggs-1276	B.K. Wisber	Open	26.00	26.00
92-02-013	Little One wApples-1277	B.K. Wisber	Open	26.00	26.00
92-02-014	Little One w/Kitten and Yarn-1278	B.K. Wisber	Open	34.00	34.00
92-02-015	Little One w/Birthday Gift-1279	B.K. Wisber	Open	26.00	26.00
92-02-016	Little One w/Kitten and Milk-1280	B.K. Wisber	Open	32.00	32.00
92-02-017	Little One Reading-1286	B.K. Wisber	Open	36.00	36.00
92-02-018	Little One w/Christmas Lights-1287	B.K. Wisber	Open	34.00	34.00
92-02-019	Little One w/Snowman-1288	B.K. Wisber	Open	36.00	36.00
92-02-020	Little One w/Sled-1289	B.K. Wisber	Open	30.00	30.00
92-02-021	Little One Clown-1290	B.K. Wisber	Open	32.00	32.00
92-02-022	Little One w/Valentine-1291	B.K. Wisber	Open	30.00	30.00
Ladie and Friends™		**The Little Ones at Christmas**			
90-03-001	Little One w/Basket of Greens-1263	B.K. Wisber	Open	24.00	24.00
90-03-002	Little One w/Cookie-1264	B.K. Wisber	Open	24.00	24.00
90-03-003	Little One w/Tree Garland-1265	B.K. Wisber	Open	24.00	24.00
90-03-004	Little One w/Gift-1266	B.K. Wisber	Open	24.00	24.00
91-03-005	White Girl w/Santa Photo-1272	B.K. Wisber	Open	26.00	26.00
91-03-006	Black Girl w/Santa Photo-1272A	B.K. Wisber	Open	26.00	26.00
91-03-007	White Boy w/Santa Photo-1273	B.K. Wisber	Open	26.00	26.00
91-03-008	Black Boy w/Santa Photo-1273A	B.K. Wisber	Open	26.00	26.00
Ladie and Friends™		**The Pawtuckets™ of Sweet Briar Lane**			
86-04-001	Aunt Minnie Pawtucket™-1136	B.K. Wisber	Closed	45.00	45.00
86-04-002	Grammy Pawtucket™-1137	B.K. Wisber	Closed	34.00	34.00
86-04-003	Uncle Harley Pawtucket™-1138	B.K. Wisber	Closed	34.00	34.00
86-04-004	Sister Flora Pawtucket™-1139	B.K. Wisber	Closed	34.00	34.00
86-04-005	Brother Noah Pawtucket™-1140	B.K. Wisber	Closed	34.00	34.00
86-04-006	Aunt Lillian Pawtucket™-1141	B.K. Wisber	Closed	34.00	34.00
86-04-007	Mama Pawtucket™-1142	B.K. Wisber	Closed	36.00	36.00
86-04-008	Pappy Pawtucket™-1143	B.K. Wisber	Closed	34.00	34.00
86-04-009	Cousin Clara Pawtucket™-1144	B.K. Wisber	Closed	34.00	34.00
86-04-010	The Little One Bunnies-girl-1145	B.K. Wisber	Closed	15.00	15.00
86-04-011	The Little One Bunnies-boy-1145	B.K. Wisber	Closed	15.00	15.00
87-04-012	Cousin Isabel Pawtucket™-1209	B.K. Wisber	Closed	36.00	36.00
87-04-013	Cousin Alberta Pawtucket™-1210	B.K. Wisber	Closed	36.00	36.00
87-04-014	Sister Clemmie Pawtucket™-1211	B.K. Wisber	Closed	34.00	34.00
87-04-015	Aunt Mabel Pawtucket™-1212	B.K. Wisber	Closed	45.00	45.00
87-04-016	Bunny Bed-1218	B.K. Wisber	Closed	16.00	16.00
88-04-017	Cousin Winnie Pawtucket™-1233	B.K. Wisber	Closed	49.00	49.00
88-04-018	Cousin Jed Pawtucket™-1234	B.K. Wisber	Closed	34.00	34.00
Ladie and Friends™		**The Grummels™ of Log Hollow**			
86-05-001	Cousin Miranda Grummel™-1165	B.K. Wisber	Closed	47.00	47.00
86-05-002	Uncle Hollis Grummel™-1166	B.K. Wisber	Closed	34.00	34.00
86-05-003	Ma Grummel™-1167	B.K. Wisber	Closed	36.00	36.00
86-05-004	Teddy Bear Bed-1168	B.K. Wisber	Closed	15.00	15.00
86-05-005	Aunt Polly Grummel™-1169	B.K. Wisber	Closed	34.00	34.00
86-05-006	Cousin Lottie Grummel™-1170	B.K. Wisber	Closed	36.00	36.00
86-05-007	Aunt Gertie Grummel™-1171	B.K. Wisber	Closed	34.00	34.00
86-05-008	Pa Grummel™-1172	B.K. Wisber	Closed	34.00	34.00
86-05-009	Grandma Grummel™-1173	B.K. Wisber	Closed	45.00	45.00
86-05-010	Aunt Hilda Grummel™-1174	B.K. Wisber	Closed	34.00	34.00
86-05-011	Washline-1175	B.K. Wisber	Closed	15.00	15.00
86-05-012	Grandpa Grummel™-1176	B.K. Wisber	Closed	36.00	36.00
86-05-013	Sister Nora Grummel™-1177	B.K. Wisber	Closed	34.00	34.00
86-05-014	The Little Ones-Grummels™ (boy/girl)-1196	B.K. Wisber	Closed	15.00	15.00
Ladie and Friends™		**The Thanksgiving Play**			
88-06-001	Pilgrim Boy-1242	B.K. Wisber	Open	41.00	41.00
88-06-002	Pilgrim Girl-1243	B.K. Wisber	Open	49.00	49.00
88-06-003	Indian Squaw-1244	B.K. Wisber	Open	37.00	37.00
Ladie and Friends™		**The Christmas Pageant**			
85-07-001	Mary and Baby Jesus-1118	B.K. Wisber	Open	36.00	36.00
85-07-002	Joseph and Donkey-1119	B.K. Wisber	Open	36.00	36.00
85-07-003	"Peace" Angel-1120	B.K. Wisber	Closed	32.00	32.00
85-07-004	"On" Angel-1121	B.K. Wisber	Closed	32.00	32.00
85-07-005	"Earth" Angel-1122	B.K. Wisber	Closed	32.00	32.00
89-07-006	"Peace" Angel (Second Edition)-1120	B.K. Wisber	Open	49.00	49.00
85-07-007	"Noel" Angel (First Edition)-1126	B.K. Wisber	Closed	32.00	32.00
89-07-008	"Noel" Angel (Second Edition)-1126	B.K. Wisber	Open	49.00	49.00
85-07-009	Wiseman #1-1123	B.K. Wisber	Open	36.00	36.00
85-07-010	Wiseman #2-1124	B.K. Wisber	Open	36.00	36.00
85-07-011	Wiseman #3-1125	B.K. Wisber	Open	36.00	36.00
85-07-012	Wooden Creche-1132	B.K. Wisber	Open	30.00	30.00
85-07-013	Christmas Wooly Lamb-1133	B.K. Wisber	Closed	12.00	12.00
86-07-014	Shepherd-1193	B.K. Wisber	Open	36.00	36.00
Ladie and Friends™		**The Christmas Concert**			
90-08-001	Claire Valentine-1262	B.K. Wisber	Open	56.00	56.00
92-08-002	Judith High-1292	B.K. Wisber	Open	70.00	70.00
Lawtons		**Childhood Classics**			
83-01-001	Alice In Wonderland	W. Lawton	Closed	225.00	2000-3000.
84-01-002	Heidi	W. Lawton	Closed	325.00	650-850.00
85-01-003	Hans Brinker	W. Lawton	Closed	325.00	1000-1800.
86-01-004	Anne Of Green Gables	W. Lawton	Closed	325.00	2000-2400.
86-01-005	Pollyanna	W. Lawton	Closed	325.00	1000-1600.
86-01-006	Laura Ingals	W. Lawton	Closed	325.00	500-900.
87-01-007	Mary Lennox	W. Lawton	Closed	325.00	500-950.
87-01-008	Just David	W. Lawton	Closed	325.00	700-1100.
87-01-009	Polly Pepper	W. Lawton	Closed	325.00	450-700.
88-01-010	Rebecca	W. Lawton	Closed	350.00	500-850.
88-01-011	Eva	W. Lawton	Closed	350.00	500-1000.
88-01-012	Topsy	W. Lawton	Closed	350.00	750-1200.
89-01-013	Little Princess	W. Lawton	Closed	395.00	650-950.
89-01-014	Honey Bunch	W. Lawton	Closed	350.00	550-800.
90-01-015	Mary Frances	W. Lawton	Closed	350.00	425.00
90-01-016	Poor Little Match Girl	W. Lawton	Closed	350.00	475.00
91-01-017	The Bobbsey Twins	W. Lawton	Closed	725.00	795.00

Company / Number	Series / Name	Artist	Edition Limit	Issue Price	Quote
91-01-018	Hiawatha	W. Lawton	Closed	395.00	500.00
91-01-019	Little Black Sambo	W. Lawton	Closed	395.00	595.00
Lawtons	**Childhood Classics II**				
92-02-001	Peter And The Wolf	W. Lawton	750	495.00	495.00
92-02-002	Marigold Garden	W. Lawton	750	450.00	450.00
92-02-003	Oliver Twist	W. Lawton	750	450.00	450.00
Lawtons	**Sugar 'n' Spice**				
86-03-001	Kimberly	W. Lawton	Closed	250.00	550-800.
86-03-002	Kersten	W. Lawton	Closed	250.00	550-800.
86-03-003	Jason	W. Lawton	Closed	250.00	800-1700.
86-03-004	Jessica	W. Lawton	Closed	250.00	800-1700.
87-03-005	Marie	W. Lawton	Closed	275.00	450.00
87-03-006	Ginger	W. Lawton	Closed	275.00	395-550.
Lawtons	**Newcomer Collection**				
87-04-001	Ellin Elizabeth	W. Lawton	Closed	335.00	900-1200.
87-04-002	Ellin Elizabeth, Eyes Closed	W. Lawton	Closed	335.00	750-1000.
Lawtons	**Timeless Ballads**				
87-05-001	Highland Mary	W. Lawton	Closed	550.00	600-875.
87-05-002	Annabel Lee	W. Lawton	Closed	550.00	600-695.
87-05-003	Young Charlotte	W. Lawton	Closed	550.00	850-900.
85-05-004	She Walks In Beauty	W. Lawton	Closed	550.00	600.00
Lawtons	**One-Of-A Kind Issues**				
89-06-001	Amelia	W. Lawton	1	N/A	N/A
90-06-002	Goldilocks And Baby Bear	W. Lawton	1	N/A	4250.00
91-06-003	Felicity Minds The Quints	W. Lawton	1	N/A	N/A
Lawtons	**Special Edition**				
88-07-001	Marcella And Raggedy Ann	W. Lawton	Closed	395.00	650.00
Lawtons	**Christmas Dolls**				
88-08-001	Christmas Joy	W. Lawton	Closed	325.00	750-1200.
89-08-002	Noel	W. Lawton	Closed	325.00	325-750.
90-08-003	Christmas Angel	W. Lawton	Closed	325.00	325.00
91-08-004	Yuletide Carole	W. Lawton	Closed	395.00	395.00
Lawtons	**Special Occasion**				
88-09-001	Nanthy	W. Lawton	Closed	325.00	450-525.
88-09-002	First Day Of School	W. Lawton	Closed	325.00	450-550.
90-09-003	First Birthday	W. Lawton	Closed	295.00	350.00
Lawtons	**Seasons**				
88-10-001	Amber Autumn	W. Lawton	Closed	325.00	400-525.
89-10-002	Summer Rose	W. Lawton	Closed	325.00	375-475.
90-10-003	Crystal Winter	W. Lawton	Closed	325.00	325.00
91-10-004	Spring Blossom	W. Lawton	Closed	350.00	350.00
Lawtons	**Wee Bits**				
88-11-001	Wee Bit O'Heaven	W. Lawton	Closed	295.00	450-600.
88-11-002	Wee Bit O'Woe	W. Lawton	Closed	295.00	450-700.
88-11-003	Wee Bit O'Sunshine	W. Lawton	Closed	295.00	450-600.
89-11-004	Wee Bit O'Bliss	W. Lawton	Closed	295.00	350.00
89-11-005	Wee Bit O'Wonder	W. Lawton	Closed	295.00	395.00
Lawtons	**Playthings Past**				
89-12-001	Victoria And Teddy	W .Lawton	Closed	395.00	395.00
89-12-002	Edward And Dobbin	W. Lawton	Closed	395.00	495-600.
89-12-003	Elizabeth And Baby	W. Lawton	Closed	395.00	495-650.
Lawtons	**Cherished Customs**				
90-13-001	The Blessing/Mexico	W. Lawton	Closed	395.00	800-1200.
90-13-002	Midsommar/Sweden	W. Lawton	Closed	395.00	395.00
90-13-003	Girls Day/Japan	W. Lawton	Closed	395.00	450-600.
90-13-004	High Tea/Great Britain	W. Lawton	Closed	395.00	450-550.
91-13-005	Ndeko/Zaire	W. Lawton	Closed	395.00	550-750.
91-13-006	Frolic/Amish	W. Lawton	Closed	395.00	395.00
92-13-007	Pascha/Ukraine	W. Lawton	750	495.00	495.00
92-13-008	Carnival/Brazil	W. Lawton	750	425.00	425.00
92-13-009	Cradleboard/Navajo	W. Lawton	750	425.00	425.00
Lawtons	**Guild Dolls**				
89-14-001	Baa Baa Black Sheep	W. Lawton	Closed	395.00	750-1000.
90-14-002	Lavender Blue	W. Lawton	Closed	395.00	450-600.
91-14-003	To Market, To Market	W. Lawton	Closed	495.00	495.00
92-14-004	Little Boy Blue	W. Lawton	Open	395.00	395.00
Lawtons	**The Children's Hour**				
91-15-001	Grave Alice	W. Lawton	Closed	395.00	395.00
91-15-002	Laughing Allegra	W. Lawton	Closed	395.00	395.00
91-15-003	Edith With Golden Hair	W. Lawton	Closed	395.00	395.00
Lawtons	**Store Exclusives**				
91-16-001	Main Street, USA	W. Lawton	Closed	350.00	350.00
91-16-002	Liberty Square	W. Lawton	Closed	350.00	395.00
91-16-003	Little Colonel	W. Lawton	Closed	395.00	395.00
91-16-004	Garden Song Marta	W. Lawton	Closed	335.00	335.00
91-16-005	Tish	W. Lawton	Closed	395.00	395.00
Lawtons	**Christmas Legends**				
91-17-001	The Legend Of The Poinsettia	W. Lawton	750	395.00	395.00
Lawtons	**Folk Tales And Fairy Stories**				
92-18-001	Little Red Riding Hood	W. Lawton	750	450.00	450.00
92-18-002	The Little Emperor's Nightingale	W. Lawton	750	425.00	425.00
92-18-003	William Tell, The Younger	W. Lawton	750	395.00	395.00
92-18-004	Swan Princess	W. Lawton	750	495.00	495.00
Lenox Collections	**Lenox China Dolls**				
84-01-001	Maryanne, 20"	J. Grammer	Unkn.	425.00	2000.00
84-01-002	Abigail, 20"	J. Grammer	Unkn.	425.00	2000.00
84-01-003	Jessica, 20"	J. Grammer	Unkn.	450.00	1900.00
84-01-004	Rebecca, 16"	J. Grammer	Unkn.	375.00	1700.00
84-01-005	Amanda, 16"	J. Grammer	Unkn.	385.00	1700.00
84-01-006	Maggie, 16"	J. Grammer	Unkn.	375.00	1700.00
84-01-007	Melissa, 16"	J. Grammer	Unkn.	450.00	3100.00
84-01-008	Samantha, 16"	J. Grammer	500	500.00	2800.00
Lenox Collections	**China Dolls -Cloth Bodies**				
85-02-001	Amy, 14"	J. Grammer	Unkn.	250.00	995.00
85-02-002	Elizabeth, 14"	J. Grammer	Unkn.	250.00	995.00
85-02-003	Sarah, 14"	J. Grammer	Unkn.	250.00	995.00
85-02-004	Annabelle, 14"	J. Grammer	Unkn.	250.00	995.00
85-02-005	Miranda, 14"	J. Grammer	Unkn.	250.00	995.00
85-02-006	Jennifer, 14"	J. Grammer	Unkn.	250.00	995.00
Lenox Collections	**Lenox Victorian Dolls**				
89-03-001	The Victorian Bride	Unknown	Open	295.00	295.00
90-03-002	Christmas Doll, Elizabeth	Unknown	Open	195.00	195.00
91-03-003	Victorian Christening Doll	Unknown	Open	295.00	295.00
92-03-004	Lady at Gala	Unknown	Open	295.00	295.00
Lenox Collections	**Children of the World**				
89-04-001	Hannah, The Little Dutch Maiden	Unknown	Open	119.00	119.00
90-04-002	Heather, Little Highlander	Unknown	Open	119.00	119.00
91-04-003	Amma-The African Girl	Unknown	Open	119.00	119.00
91-04-004	Sakura-The Japanese Girl	Unknown	Open	119.00	119.00
92-04-005	Gretchen, German Doll	Unknown	Open	119.00	119.00
Lenox Collections	**Sibling Dolls**				
91-05-001	Skating Lesson	A. Lester	Open	195.00	195.00
Lenox Collections	**Ellis Island Dolls**				
91-06-001	Megan	P. Thompson	12/92	150.00	150.00
91-06-002	Stefan	P. Thompson	12/92	150.00	150.00
92-06-003	Angelina	P. Thompson	12/92	150.00	150.00
92-06-004	Catherine	P. Thompson	12/92	152.00	152.00
92-06-005	Anna	P. Thompson	12/92	152.00	152.00
Lenox Collections	**Musical Baby Dolls**				
91-07-001	Patrick's Lullabye	Unknown	Open	95.00	95.00
Lenox Collections	**Bolshoi Nutcracker Dolls**				
91-08-001	Clara	Unknown	Open	195.00	195.00
Lenox Collections	**Country Decor Dolls**				
91-09-001	Molly	Unknown	Open	150.00	150.00
Lenox Collections	**Children With Toys Dolls**				
91-10-001	Tea For Teddy	Unknown	Open	136.00	136.00
Lenox Collections	**Little Women**				
92-11-001	Amy	Unknown	Open	150.00	150.00
92-11-002	Amy, The Inspiring Artist	Unknown	Open	152.00	152.00
Lenox Collections	**Bonnet Baby Dolls**				
92-12-001	Easter Bonnet	Unknown	Open	95.00	95.00
Lenox Collections	**First Collector Doll**				
92-13-001	Lauren	Unknown	Open	152.00	152.00
Lenox Collections	**Inspirational Doll**				
92-14-001	Blessed Are The Peacemakers	Unknown	Open	119.00	119.00
Lenox Collections	**International Baby Doll**				
92-15-001	Natalia, Russian Baby	Unknown	Open	119.00	119.00
Lenox Collections	**Nutcracker Dolls**				
92-16-001	Sugarplum	Unknown	Open	195.00	195.00
93-16-002	Nutcracker	Unknown	Open	195.00	195.00
Lenox Collections	**Prima Ballerina Collection**				
92-17-001	Odette, Queen of the Swans	Unknown	Open	195.00	195.00
93-17-002	Sleeping Beauty	Unknown	Open	195.00	195.00
Seymour Mann Inc.	**Connossieur Doll Collection**				
84-01-001	Miss Debutante Debi	E. Mann	N/A	75.00	180.00
85-01-002	Christmas Cheer-124	E. Mann	N/A	40.00	100.00
85-01-003	Wendy-C120	E. Mann	Closed	45.00	150.00
86-01-004	Camelot Fairy-C84	E. Mann	N/A	75.00	225.00
87-01-005	Audrina-YK200	E. Mann	Closed	85.00	140.00
87-01-006	Dawn-C185	E. Mann	Closed	75.00	175.00
87-01-007	Linda-C190	E. Mann	Closed	60.00	120.00
87-01-008	Marcy-YK122	E. Mann	Closed	55.00	100.00
87-01-019	Rapunzel-C158	E. Mann	Closed	95.00	165.00
87-01-010	Sabrina-C208	E. Mann	Closed	65.00	95.00
87-01-011	Sailorette-DOM217	E. Mann	Closed	70.00	150.00
88-01-012	Brittany-TK-5	E. Mann	2,500	120.00	120.00
88-01-013	Cissie-DOM263	E. Mann	Closed	65.00	135.00
88-01-014	Crying Courtney-PS75	E. Mann	2,500	115.00	115.00
88-01-015	Cynthia-DOM-211	E. Mann	3,500	85.00	85.00
88-01-016	Doll Oliver-FH392	E. Mann	2,500	100.00	100.00
88-01-017	Giselle on Goose-FH176	E. Mann	N/A	105.00	225.00
88-01-018	Jessica-DOM-267	E. Mann	2,500	90.00	90.00
88-01-019	Joanne Cry Baby-PS50	E. Mann	25,000	100.00	100.00
88-01-020	Jolie-C231	E. Mann	N/A	65.00	150.00
88-01-021	Julie-C245A	E. Mann	Closed	65.00	160.00
88-01-022	Juliette Bride Musical-C246LTM	E. Mann	25,000	150.00	150.00
88-01-023	Kirsten-PS-40G	E. Mann	2,500	70.00	70.00
88-01-024	Lionel-FH206B	E. Mann	Closed	50.00	120.00
88-01-025	Lucinda-DOM-293	E. Mann	2,500	90.00	90.00
88-01-026	Michelle & Marcel-YK176	E. Mann	N/A	70.00	150.00
88-01-027	Sister Agnes 14"-C250	E. Mann	25,000	75.00	75.00
88-01-030	Sister Ignatius Notre Dame-FH184	E. Mann	25,000	75.00	75.00
88-01-031	Sister Teresa-FH187	E. Mann	25,000	80.00	80.00
88-01-032	Tracy-C-3006	E. Mann	Closed	95.00	150.00
88-01-033	Vivian-C201P	E. Mann	3,500	80.00	80.00
89-01-034	Ashley-C-278	E. Mann	3,500	80.00	80.00
89-01-035	Amber-DOM-281A	E. Mann	Closed	85.00	85.00
89-01-036	Betty-PS27G	E. Mann	Closed	65.00	125.00
89-01-037	Brett-PS27B	E. Mann	Closed	65.00	125.00
89-01-038	Brittany-TK-4	E. Mann	Closed	150.00	150.00
89-01-039	Baby John-PS-49B	E. Mann	2,500	85.00	85.00
89-01-040	Daphne Ecru/Mint Green-C3025	E. Mann	25,000	85.00	85.00
89-01-041	Elizabeth-C-246P	E. Mann	3,500	150.00	200.00
89-01-042	Emily-PS-48	E. Mann	2,500	110.00	110.00
89-01-043	Frances-C233	E. Mann	Closed	80.00	125.00
89-01-044	Happy Birthday-C3012	E. Mann	2,500	80.00	125.00
89-01-045	Heidi-260	E. Mann	Closed	50.00	95.00
89-01-046	Jaqueline-DOLL-254M	E. Mann	2,500	85.00	85.00
89-01-047	Kayoko-PS24	E. Mann	Closed	75.00	175.00
89-01-048	Ling-Ling-PS-87G	E. Mann	2,500	90.00	90.00
89-01-049	[illegible]-YK-269	E. Mann	2,500	70.00	100.00

Number	Name	Artist	Edition Limit	Issue Price	Quote
89-01-050	Mai-Ling-PS-79	E. Mann	2,500	100.00	100.00
89-01-051	Margaret-245	E. Mann	Closed	100.00	150.00
89-01-052	Maureen-PS-84	E. Mann	2,500	90.00	90.00
89-01-053	Meimei-PS22	E. Mann	Closed	75.00	225.00
89-01-054	Melissa-LL-794	E. Mann	2,500	95.00	95.00
89-01-055	Miss Kim-PS-25	E. Mann	Closed	75.00	175.00
89-01-056	Patricia/Patrick-215GBB	E. Mann	3,500	105.00	135.00
89-01-057	Pauline Bonaparte-OM68	E. Mann	25,000	120.00	120.00
89-01-058	Rosie-290M	E. Mann	2,500	55.00	85.00
89-01-059	Sister Mary-C-249	E. Mann	3,500	75.00	125.00
89-01-060	Suzie-PS-32	E. Mann	2,500	80.00	80.00
89-01-061	Tatiana Pink Ballerina-OM-60	E. Mann	2,500	120.00	120.00
89-01-062	Terri-PS-104	E. Mann	2,500	85.00	85.00
89-01-063	Wendy-PS-51	E. Mann	2,500	105.00	105.00
90-01-064	Anabelle-C-3080	E. Mann	2,500	85.00	85.00
90-01-065	Angel-DOM-335	E. Mann	2,500	105.00	105.00
90-01-066	Angela-C-3084	E. Mann	2,500	105.00	105.00
90-01-067	Angela-C-3084M	E. Mann	2,500	115.00	115.00
90-01-068	Anita-FH-277G	E. Mann	2,500	65.00	65.00
90-01-069	Ashley-FH-325	E. Mann	2,500	75.00	75.00
90-01-070	Audrey-YK-4089	E. Mann	3,500	125.00	125.00
90-01-071	Baby Betty-YK-4087	E. Mann	3,500	125.00	125.00
90-01-072	Baby Bonnie-SP-341	E. Mann	2,500	55.00	55.00
90-01-073	Baby Brent-EP-15	E. Mann	2,500	85.00	85.00
90-01-074	Baby Ecru-WB-17	E. Mann	2,500	65.00	65.00
90-01-075	Baby Kate-WB-19	E. Mann	2,500	85.00	85.00
90-01-076	Baby Nelly-PS-163	E. Mann	2,500	95.00	95.00
90-01-077	Baby Sue-DOLL-402B	E. Mann	2,500	27.50	27.50
90-01-058	Baby Sunshine-C-3055	E. Mann	3,500	90.00	90.00
90-01-079	Beth-YK-4099A/B	E. Mann	2,500	125.00	125.00
90-01-080	Bettina-TR-4	E. Mann	2,500	125.00	125.00
90-01-081	Beverly-DOLL-335	E. Mann	2,500	110.00	110.00
90-01-082	Caitlin-DOLL-11PH	E. Mann	2,500	60.00	60.00
90-01-083	Carole-YK-4085W	E. Mann	3,500	125.00	125.00
90-01-084	Charlene-YK-4112	E. Mann	3,500	90.00	90.00
90-01-085	Chin Fa-C-3061	E. Mann	2,500	95.00	95.00
90-01-086	Chinook-WB-24	E. Mann	2,500	85.00	85.00
90-01-087	Chrissie-WB-2	E. Mann	2,500	75.00	75.00
90-01-088	Daisy-EP-6	E. Mann	2,500	90.00	90.00
90-01-089	Dianna-TK-31	E. Mann	Closed	175.00	175.00
90-01-090	Diane-FH-275	E. Mann	Closed	90.00	90.00
90-01-091	Domino-C-3050	E. Mann	3,500	145.00	145.00
90-01-092	Dorri-DOLL-16PH	E. Mann	2,500	85.00	85.00
90-01-093	Dorothy-TR-10	E. Mann	2,500	135.00	135.00
90-01-094	Eileen-FH-367	E. Mann	2,500	100.00	100.00
90-01-095	Felicia-TR-9	E. Mann	2,500	115.00	115.00
90-01-096	Francesca-C-3021	E. Mann	2,500	100.00	175.00
90-01-097	Gerri Beige-YK4094	E. Mann	25,000	95.00	95.00
90-01-098	Ginny-YK-4119	E. Mann	3,500	100.00	100.00
90-01-099	Hyacinth-DOLL-15PH	E. Mann	2,500	85.00	85.00
90-01-100	Janette-DOLL-385	E. Mann	2,500	85.00	85.00
90-01-101	Joanne-TR-12	E. Mann	2,500	175.00	175.00
90-01-102	Julie-WB-35	E. Mann	2,500	70.00	70.00
90-01-103	Karen-PS-198	E. Mann	2,500	150.00	150.00
90-01-104	Kate-C-3060	E. Mann	3,500	95.00	95.00
90-01-105	Kathy w/Bear-TE1	E. Mann	25,000	70.00	70.00
90-01-106	Kiku-EP-4	E. Mann	2,500	100.00	100.00
90-01-107	Lauren-SP-300	E. Mann	2,500	85.00	85.00
90-01-108	Lavender Blue-YK-4024	E. Mann	3,500	95.00	135.00
90-01-109	Lien Wha-YK-4092	E. Mann	3,500	100.00	100.00
90-01-110	Ling-Ling-DOLL	E. Mann	25,000	50.00	50.00
90-01-111	Lisa-FH-379	E. Mann	2,500	100.00	100.00
90-01-112	Lisa Beige Accordian Pleat-YK4093	E. Mann	25,000	125.00	125.00
90-01-113	Liza-C-3053	E. Mann	2,500	100.00	100.00
90-01-114	Lola-SP-79	E. Mann	2,500	105.00	105.00
90-01-115	Loretta-FH-321	E. Mann	2,500	90.00	90.00
90-01-116	Madame De Pompadour-C-3088	E. Mann	2,500	250.00	250.00
90-01-117	Maggie-PS-151P	E. Mann	2,500	90.00	90.00
90-01-118	Maggie-WB-51	E. Mann	2,500	105.00	105.00
90-01-119	Maria-YK-4116	E. Mann	3,500	85.00	85.00
90-01-120	Melanie-YK-4115	E. Mann	3,500	80.00	80.00
90-01-121	Melissa-DOLL-390	E. Mann	2,500	75.00	75.00
90-01-122	Merry Widow-C-3040	E. Mann	3,500	145.00	145.00
90-01-123	Merry Widow 20"-C-3040M	E. Mann	2,500	140.00	140.00
90-01-124	Nanook-WB-23	E. Mann	2,500	75.00	75.00
90-01-125	Natasha-PS-102	E. Mann	Closed	100.00	100.00
90-01-126	Odessa-FH-362	E. Mann	2,500	65.00	65.00
90-01-127	Ping-Ling-DOLL-363RV	E. Mann	25,000	50.00	50.00
90-01-128	Princess Fair Skies-FH-268B	E. Mann	2,500	75.00	75.00
90-01-129	Priscilla-WB-50	E. Mann	2,500	105.00	105.00
90-01-130	Sabrina-C3050	E. Mann	2,500	105.00	105.00
90-01-131	Sally-WB-20	E. Mann	2,500	95.00	95.00
90-01-132	Shirley-WB-37	E. Mann	2,500	65.00	65.00
90-01-133	Sister Mary-WB-15	E. Mann	2,500	70.00	70.00
90-01-134	Sophie-OM-1	E. Mann	2,500	65.00	65.00
90-01-135	Stacy-TR-5	E. Mann	2,500	105.00	105.00
90-01-136	Sunny-FH-331	E. Mann	2,500	70.00	70.00
90-01-137	Susan Blue-DOLL-364MC	E. Mann	25,000	75.00	75.00
90-01-138	Tania-DOLL-376P	E. Mann	2,500	65.00	65.00
90-01-139	Tina-DOLL-371	E. Mann	2,500	85.00	85.00
90-01-140	Tina-WB-32	E. Mann	2,500	65.00	65.00
90-01-141	Tommy-C-3064	E. Mann	2,500	75.00	75.00
90-01-142	Wendy-TE-3	E. Mann	2,500	75.00	75.00
90-01-143	Wilma-PS-174	E. Mann	2,500	75.00	75.00
90-01-144	Yen Yen-YK-4091	E. Mann	3,500	95.00	95.00
91-01-145	Abigail-EP-3	E. Mann	2,500	100.00	100.00
91-01-146	Abby 16" Pink Dress-C3145	E. Mann	25,000	100.00	100.00
91-01-147	Alexis 24" Beige Lace-EP32	E. Mann	25,000	220.00	220.00
91-01-148	Amanda Toast-OM-182	E. Mann	25,000	260.00	260.00
91-01-149	Ariel 34" Blue/White-Ep-33	E. Mann	25,000	175.00	175.00
91-01-150	Aurora Gold 22"-OM-181	E. Mann	25,000	260.00	260.00
91-01-151	Baby Beth-DOLL-406P	E. Mann	2,500	27.50	27.50
91-01-152	Baby Bonnie w/Walker Music-DOLL-409	E. Mann	25,000	40.00	40.00
91-01-153	Baby Carrie-DOLL-402P	E. Mann	2,500	27.50	27.50
91-01-154	Baby Ellie Ecru Musical-DOLL-402E	E. Mann	25,000	27.50	27.50
91-01-155	Baby Gloria Black Baby-PS-289	E. Mann	2,500	75.00	75.00
91-01-156	Baby Linda-DOLL-406E	E. Mann	2,500	27.50	27.50
91-01-157	Betsy-AM-6	E. Mann	2,500	105.00	105.00
91-01-158	Bo-Peep w/Lamb-C-3128	E. Mann	2,500	105.00	105.00
91-01-159	Christina-PS-261	E. Mann	2,500	115.00	115.00
91-01-160	Colette-WB-7	E. Mann	2,500	65.00	65.00
91-01-161	Courtney-LL-859	E. Mann	2,500	150.00	150.00
91-01-162	Creole-AM-17	E. Mann	2,500	160.00	160.00
91-01-163	Danielle-AM-5	E. Mann	2,500	125.00	125.00
91-01-164	Daria-C-3122	E. Mann	2,500	130.00	130.00
91-01-165	Denise-LL-852	E. Mann	2,500	105.00	105.00
91-01-166	Dephine-SP-308	E. Mann	2,500	135.00	135.00
91-01-167	Duana-SP-366	E. Mann	2,500	85.00	85.00
91-01-168	Dulcie-YK-4131V	E. Mann	3,500	100.00	100.00
91-01-169	Dwayne-C-3123	E. Mann	2,500	120.00	120.00
91-01-170	Elise -PS-259	E. Mann	2,500	105.00	105.00
91-01-171	Emmaline Beige/Lilac-OM197	E. Mann	2,500	300.00	300.00
91-01-172	Emmy-C-3099	E. Mann	2,500	125.00	125.00
91-01-173	Erin-DOLL-4PH	E. Mann	2,500	60.00	60.00
91-01-174	Evelina-C-3124	E. Mann	2,500	135.00	135.00
91-01-175	Francesca-AM-14	E. Mann	2,500	175.00	175.00
91-01-176	Georgia-YK-4143	E. Mann	3,500	100.00	100.00
91-01-177	Gigi-C-3107	E. Mann	2,500	135.00	135.00
91-01-178	Honey Bunny-WB-9	E. Mann	2,500	70.00	70.00
91-01-179	Indira-AM-4	E. Mann	2,500	125.00	125.00
91-01-180	Jane-PS-243L	E. Mann	2,500	115.00	115.00
91-01-181	Janice Beige-OM-194	E. Mann	2,500	300.00	300.00
91-01-182	Jessica-FH-423	E. Mann	2,500	95.00	95.00
91-01-183	Joy-EP-23V	E. Mann	2,500	130.00	130.00
91-01-184	Julia-C-3102	E. Mann	2,500	135.00	135.00
91-01-185	Karen-EP-24	E. Mann	2,500	115.00	115.00
91-01-186	Kelly-AM-8	E. Mann	2,500	125.00	125.00
91-01-187	Kerry-FH-396	E. Mann	2,500	100.00	100.00
91-01-188	Kristi-FH-402	E. Mann	2,500	100.00	100.00
91-01-189	Laura-WB-110P	E. Mann	2,500	85.00	85.00
91-01-190	Leila-AM-2	E. Mann	2,500	125.00	125.00
91-01-191	Libby-EP-18	E. Mann	2,500	85.00	85.00
91-01-192	Lila-AM-10	E. Mann	2,500	125.00	125.00
91-01-193	Lola-SP-363	E. Mann	2,500	90.00	90.00
91-01-194	Lucy-LL-853	E. Mann	2,500	80.00	80.00
91-01-195	Madeleine-C-3106	E. Mann	2,500	95.00	95.00
91-01-196	Mariel 18" Ivory-C-3119	E. Mann	2,500	125.00	125.00
91-01-197	Melissa-AM-9	E. Mann	2,500	120.00	120.00
91-01-198	Meredith-FH-391-P	E. Mann	2,500	95.00	95.00
91-01-199	Michael w/School Books-FH-439B	E. Mann	2,500	95.00	95.00
91-01-200	Michelle Lilac/Green-EP36	E. Mann	2,500	95.00	95.00
91-01-201	Michelle w/School Books-FH-439G	E. Mann	2,500	95.00	95.00
91-01-202	Miranda-DOLL-9PH	E. Mann	2,500	75.00	75.00
91-01-203	Mon Yun w/Parasol-TR33	E. Mann	2,500	115.00	115.00
91-01-204	Nancy 21" Pink w/Rabbit-EP-31	E. Mann	2,500	165.00	165.00
91-01-205	Nellie-EP-1B	E. Mann	2,500	75.00	75.00
91-01-206	Nicole-AM-12	E. Mann	2,500	135.00	135.00
91-01-207	Pia-PS-246L	E. Mann	2,500	115.00	115.00
91-01-208	Prissy White/Blue-C-3140	E. Mann	2,500	100.00	100.00
91-01-209	Rosalind-C-3090	E. Mann	2,500	150.00	150.00
91-01-210	Sandra-DOLL-6PHE	E. Mann	2,500	65.00	65.00
91-01-211	Sharon 21" Blue-EP-34	E. Mann	2,500	120.00	120.00
91-01-212	Stephanie-AM-11	E. Mann	2,500	105.00	105.00
91-01-213	Stephanie Pink & White-OM-196	E. Mann	2,500	300.00	300.00
91-01-214	Sybil 20" Beige-C-3131	E. Mann	2,500	135.00	135.00
91-01-215	Sybil Pink-DOLL-12PHMC	E. Mann	2,500	75.00	75.00
91-01-216	Tina-AM-16	E. Mann	2,500	130.00	130.00
91-01-217	Vicki-C-3101	E. Mann	2,500	200.00	200.00
91-01-218	Wah-Ching Watching Oriental Toddler-YK-4175	E. Mann	2,500	110.00	110.00
Seymour Mann Inc.		**Signature Doll Series**			
91-02-001	Amber-MS-1	M. Severino	5,000	95.00	95.00
91-02-002	Becky-MS-2	M. Severino	5,000	95.00	95.00
91-02-003	Bianca-PK-101	M. Severino	5,000	120.00	120.00
91-02-004	Bridgette-PK-104	P. Kolesar	5,000	120.00	120.00
91-02-005	Clair-Ann-PK-252	P. Kolesar	5,000	100.00	100.00
91-02-006	Daddy's Little Darling-MS-8	M. Severino	5,000	165.00	165.00
91-02-007	Dozy Elf w/ Featherbed-MAB-100	M.A. Byerly	5,000	110.00	110.00
91-02-008	Duby Elf w/ Featherbed-MAB-103	M.A. Byerly	5,000	110.00	110.00
91-02-009	Dudley Elf w/ Featherbed-MAB-101	M.A. Byerly	5,000	110.00	110.00
91-02-010	Duffy Elf w/ Featherbed-MAB-102	M.A. Byerly	5,000	110.00	110.00
91-02-011	Enoc-PK-100	P. Kolesar	5,000	100.00	100.00
91-02-012	Mikey-MS-3	M. Severino	5,000	95.00	95.00
91-02-013	Mommy's Rays of Sunshine-MS-9	M. Severino	5,000	165.00	165.00
91-02-014	Paulette-PAC-2	P. Aprile	5,000	250.00	250.00
91-02-015	Paulette-PAC-4	P. Aprile	5,000	250.00	250.00
91-02-016	Precious Baby-SB-100	S. Bilotto	5,000	250.00	250.00
91-02-017	Precious Pary Time-SB-102	S. Bilotto	5,000	250.00	250.00
91-02-018	Precious Spring Time-SB-104	S. Bilotto	5,000	250.00	250.00
91-02-019	Shun Lee-PK-102	P. Kolesar	5,000	120.00	120.00
91-02-020	Sparkle-PK-250	P. Kolesar	5,000	100.00	100.00
91-02-021	Stephie-MS-6	M. Severino	5,000	125.00	125.00
91-02-022	Alice-MS-7	M. Severino	5,000	120.00	120.00
91-02-023	Su Lin-MS-5	M. Severino	5,000	105.00	105.00
91-02-024	Susan Marie-PK-103	P. Kolesar	5,000	120.00	120.00
91-02-025	Sweet Pea-PK-251	P. Kolesar	5,000	100.00	100.00
91-02-026	Yawning Kate-MS-4	M. Severino	5,000	105.00	105.00
92-02-027	Abigail-MS-11	M. Severino	5,000	125.00	125.00
92-02-028	Adora-MS-14	M. Severino	5,000	185.00	185.00
92-02-029	Baby Cakes Crumbs-PK-CRUMBS	P. Kolesar	5,000	17.50	17.50
92-02-030	Baby Cakes Crumbs/Black-PK-CRUMBS/B	P. Kolesar	5,000	17.50	17.50
92-02-031	Bride & Flower Girl-PAC-6	P. Aprile	5,000	600.00	600.00
92-02-032	Cassandra-PAC-8	P. Aprile	5,000	450.00	450.00
92-02-033	Cassie Flower Girl-PAC-9	P. Aprile	5,000	175.00	175.00
92-02-034	Celine-PAC-11	P. Aprile	5,000	165.00	165.00
92-02-035	Clarissa-PAC-3	P. Aprile	5,000	165.00	165.00
92-02-036	Creole Black-HP-202	H. Payne	5,000	250.00	250.00
92-02-037	Cynthia-PAC-10	P. Aprile	5,000	165.00	165.00
92-02-038	Darla-HP-204	H. Payne	5,000	250.00	250.00
92-02-039	Dulcie-HP-200	H. Payne	5,000	250.00	250.00
92-02-040	Dustin-HP-201	H. Payne	5,000	250.00	250.00
92-02-041	Eugenie Bride-PAC-1	P. Aprile	5,000	165.00	165.00
92-02-042	Evening Star-PAC-5	P. Aprile	5,000	500.00	500.00
92-02-043	Kate-MS-15	M. Severino	5,000	190.00	190.00
92-02-044	"Little Turtle" Indian-PK-110	P. Kolesar	5,000	150.00	150.00
92-02-045	Megan-MS-12	M. Severino	5,000	125.00	125.00
92-02-046	Raven Eskimo-PK-106	P. Kolesar	5,000	130.00	130.00
92-02-047	Sally-MS-25	M. Severino	5,000	110.00	110.00
92-02-048	Spanky-HP-25	H. Payne	5,000	250.00	250.00
92-02-049	Stacy-MS-24	M. Severino	5,000	110.00	110.00
92-02-050	Victoria w/Blanket-MS-10	M. Severino	5,000	110.00	110.00
Jan McLean Originals		**Flowers of the Heart Collection**			
90-01-001	Pansy	J. McLean	100	2200.00	2800-3200.
90-01-002	Poppy	J. McLean	100	2200.00	2400-2800.

Company / Number	Name	Series / Artist	Edition Limit	Issue Price	Quote
91-01-003	Primrose	J. McLean	100	2500.00	2500.00
91-01-004	Marigold	J. McLean	100	2400.00	2400.00
Jan McLean Originals		**Jan McLean Originals**			
90-02-001	Phoebe I	J. McLean	25	2700.00	2700.00
91-02-00	Lucrezia	J. McLean	15	6000.00	6000.00
Middleton Doll Company		**Porcelain Limited Edition Series**			
88-01-001	Cherish-1st Edition	L. Middleton	750	350.00	500.00
88-01-002	Sincerity -1st Edition-Nettie/Simplicity	L. Middleton	750	330.00	350-475.
89-01-003	My Lee	L. Middleton	629	500.00	500.00
89-01-004	Devan	L. Middleton	525	500.00	500.00
90-01-005	Baby Grace	L. Middleton	500	500.00	500.00
90-01-006	Johanna	L. Middleton	500	500.00	500.00
91-01-007	Molly Rose	L. Middleton	500	500.00	500.00
Middleton Doll Company		**Limited Edition Vinyl**			
81-02-001	Little Angel-Kingdom (Hand Painted)	L. Middleton	800	40.00	300.00
85-02-002	Little Angel-King-2 (Hand Painted)	L. Middleton	400	40.00	200.00
87-02-003	Christmas Angel 1987	L. Middleton	4,174	130.00	200.00
88-02-004	Christmas Angel 1988	L. Middleton	6,385	130.00	160.00
89-02-005	Christmas Angel 1989	L. Middleton	7,500	150.00	160.00
89-02-006	Angel Fancy	L. Middleton	10,000	120.00	130.00
90-02-007	Baby Grace	L. Middleton	5,000	190.00	190.00
90-02-008	Christmas Angel 1990	L. Middleton	5,000	150.00	150.00
90-02-009	Sincerity-Apricots n' Cream	L. Middleton	5,000	250.00	250.00
90-02-010	Sincerity-Apples n' Spice	L. Middleton	5,000	250.00	250.00
90-02-011	Forever Cherish	L. Middleton	5,000	170.00	170.00
90-02-012	First Moments-Twin Boy	L. Middleton	5,000	180.00	180.00
90-02-013	First Moments-Twin Girl	L. Middleton	5,000	180.00	180.00
90-02-014	Angel Locks	L. Middleton	10,000	140.00	150.00
90-02-015	Missy- Buttercup	L. Middleton	5,000	160.00	170.00
90-02-016	Dear One-Sunday Best	L. Middleton	5,000	140.00	140.00
91-02-017	Bubba Batboy	L. Middleton	5,000	190.00	190.00
91-02-018	My Lee Candy Cane	L. Middleton	2,500	170.00	170.00
91-02-019	Devan Delightful	L. Middleton	5,000	170.00	170.00
91-02-020	Gracie Mae	L. Middleton	5,000	250.00	250.00
91-02-021	Christmas Angel 1991	L. Middleton	5,000	180.00	180.00
91-02-022	Johanna	L. Middleton	5,000	190.00	190.00
Middleton Doll Company		**First Moments Series**			
84-03-001	First Moments (Sleeping)	L. Middleton	41,000	69.00	150.00
86-03-002	First Moments Blue Eyes	L. Middleton	15,000	120.00	150.00
86-03-003	First Moments Brown Eyes	L. Middleton	5,490	120.00	150.00
87-03-004	First Moments Boy	L. Middleton	6,075	130.00	160.00
87-03-005	First Moments Christening (Asleep)	L. Middleton	Open	160.00	180.00
87-03-006	First Moments Christening (Awake)	L. Middleton	Open	160.00	180.00
90-03-007	First Moments Sweetness	L. Middleton	Open	180.00	180.00
Middleton Doll Company		**Vinyl Collectors Series**			
86-04-001	Bubba Chubbs	L. Middleton	5,600	100.00	150-200.
88-04-002	Bubba Chubbs Railroader	L. Middleton	Open	140.00	170.00
86-04-003	Little Angel - 3rd Edition	L. Middleton	Open	90.00	110.00
85-04-004	Angel Face	L. Middleton	20,200	90.00	150.00
87-04-005	Missy	L. Middleton	Open	100.00	120.00
87-04-006	Amanda - 1st Edition	L. Middleton	4,200	140.00	160.00
86-04-007	Dear One - 1st Edition	L. Middleton	4,935	90.00	200.00
88-04-008	Cherish	L. Middleton	Open	160.00	160.00
88-04-009	Sincerity - Limited 1st Ed. -Nettie/Simplicity	L. Middleton	4,380	160.00	160.00
89-04-010	My Lee	L. Middleton	Open	170.00	170.00
89-04-011	Devan	L. Middleton	Open	170.00	170.00
89-04-012	Sincerity-Schoolgirl	L. Middleton	Open	180.00	180.00
Middleton Doll Company		**Littlest Ballet Company**			
88-05-001	April (Dressed in Pink)	S. Wakeen	7,500	100.00	110.00
88-05-002	Melanie (Dressed in Blue)	S. Wakeen	7,500	100.00	110.00
88-05-003	Jeanne (Dressed in White)	S. Wakeen	7,500	100.00	110.00
88-05-004	Lisa (Black Leotards)	S. Wakeen	7,500	100.00	110.00
89-05-005	April (In Leotard)	S. Wakeen	7,500	100.00	110.00
89-05-006	Melanie (In Leotard)	S. Wakeen	7,500	100.00	110.00
89-05-007	Jeannie (In Leotard)	S. Wakeen	7,500	100.00	110.00
Middleton Doll Company		**First Collectibles**			
90-06-001	Sweetest Little Dreamer (Asleep)	L. Middleton	Open	40.00	40.00
90-06-002	Day Dreamer (Awake)	L. Middleton	Open	42.00	42.00
91-06-003	Day Dreamer Sunshine	L. Middleton	Open	49.00	49.00
91-06-004	Teenie	L. Middleton	Open	59.00	59.00
Nahrgang Collection		**Porcelain Doll Series**			
89-01-001	Palmer	J. Nahrgang	250	270.00	270.00
90-01-002	Grant (Take Me Out To The Ball Game)	J. Nahrgang	500	390.00	390.00
90-01-003	Maggie	J. Nahrgang	500	295.00	295.00
90-01-004	Kelsey	J. Nahrgang	250	350.00	350.00
90-01-005	Kasey	J. Nahrgang	250	450.00	450.00
90-01-006	Alicia	J. Nahrgang	250	330.00	330.00
90-01-007	Karman (Gypsy)	J. Nahrgang	250	350.00	350.00
90-01-008	Karissa	J. Nahrgang	500	350.00	395.00
91-01-009	McKinsey	J. Nahrgang	250	350.00	350.00
91-01-010	Rae	J. Nahrgang	250	350.00	350.00
91-01-011	Aubry	J. Nahrgang	250	390.00	390.00
91-01-012	Laura	J. Nahrgang	250	450.00	450.00
91-01-013	Sophie	J. Nahrgang	250	450.00	450.00
91-01-014	Carson	J. Nahrgang	250	350.00	350.00
91-01-015	Erin	J. Nahrgang	250	295.00	295.00
91-01-016	Ana Marie	J. Nahrgang	250	390.00	390.00
91-01-017	Holly	J. Nahrgang	175	295.00	295.00
92-01-018	Brooke	J. Nahrgang	250	390.00	390.00
92-01-019	Alexis	J. Nahrgang	250	390.00	390.00
92-01-020	Katie	J. Nahrgang	250	295.00	295.00
92-01-021	Pocahontas	J. Nahrgang	100	395.00	395.00
92-01-022	Molly Pitcher	J. Nahrgang	100	395.00	395.00
92-01-023	Harriet Tubman	J. Nahrgang	100	395.00	395.00
92-01-024	Florence Nightingale	J. Nahrgang	100	395.00	395.00
92-01-025	Dolly Madison	J. Nahrgang	100	395.00	395.00
92-01-026	Annie Sullivan	J. Nahrgang	25	895.00	895.00
92-01-027	Taylor	J. Nahrgang	250	395.00	395.00
Nahrgang Collection		**Vinyl Doll Series**			
90-02-001	Karman (Gypsy)	J. Nahrgang	2,000	190.00	190.00
91-02-002	Aubry	J. Nahrgang	1,000	225.00	225.00
91-02-003	Laura	J. Nahrgang	1,000	250.00	250.00
91-02-004	Ann Marie	J. Nahrgang	500	225.00	225.00
91-02-005	Molly	J. Nahrgang	500	190.00	190.00

Company / Number	Name	Series / Artist	Edition Limit	Issue Price	Quote
91-02-006	Alexis	J. Nahrgang	500	250.00	250.00
91-02-007	Brooke	J. Nahrgang	500	250.00	250.00
91-02-008	Beatrix	J. Nahrgang	500	250.00	250.00
91-02-009	Angela	J. Nahrgang	500	190.00	190.00
91-02-010	Vanessa	J. Nahrgang	250	250.00	250.00
91-02-011	Chelsea	J. Nahrgang	250	190.00	190.00
91-02-012	Polly	J. Nahrgang	250	270.00	270.00
92-02-013	Pocahontas	J. Nahrgang	500	199.00	199.00
92-02-014	Molly Pitcher	J. Nahrgang	500	199.00	199.00
92-02-015	Harriet Tubman	J. Nahrgang	500	199.00	199.00
92-02-016	Florence Nightingale	J. Nahrgang	500	199.00	199.00
92-02-017	Dolly Madison	J. Nahrgang	500	199.00	199.00
Original Appalachian Artworks		**Little People**			
78-01-001	Helen, Blue	X. Roberts	1,000	150.00	3000-7600.
80-01-002	SP, Preemie	X. Roberts	5,000	100.00	400-700.
80-01-003	Celebrity	X. Roberts	5,000	200.00	400-800.
80-01-004	Nicholas	X. Roberts	2,500	200.00	1500-2000.
80-01-005	Noel	X. Roberts	2,500	200.00	700.00
82-01-006	Baby Rudy	X. Roberts	1,000	200.00	800-900.
82-01-007	Christy Nicole	X. Roberts	1,000	200.00	800.00
82-01-008	Amy	X. Roberts	2,500	125.00	700-800.
82-01-009	Bobbie	X. Roberts	2,500	125.00	700-800.
82-01-010	Billie	X. Roberts	2,500	125.00	700-800.
82-01-011	Gilda	X. Roberts	2,500	125.00	1400-1600.
82-01-012	Tyler	X. Roberts	2,500	125.00	1700-2500.
82-01-013	Sybil	X. Roberts	2,500	125.00	700-1000.
82-01-014	Marilyn	X. Roberts	2,500	125.00	700-800.
82-01-015	Otis	X. Roberts	2,500	125.00	800-1000.
82-01-016	Rebecca	X. Roberts	2,500	125.00	700-900.
82-01-017	Dorothy	X. Roberts	2,500	125.00	700-900.
82-01-018	PE, New 'ears Preemie	X. Roberts	5,000	140.00	300-450.
Original Appalachian Artworks		**Cabbage Patch Kids International**			
83-02-001	Oriental	X. Roberts	1,000	150.00	1200-1500.
83-02-002	American Indian	X. Roberts	1,000	150.00	800-1800.
Original Appalachian Artworks		**Cabbage Patch Kids**			
83-03-002	Andre / Madeira	X. Roberts	2,000	250.00	1500-2000.
84-03-003	Daddy's Darlins'-Pun'kin	X. Roberts	2,000	300.00	500-700.
84-03-004	Daddy's Darlins'-Tootsie	X. Roberts	2,000	300.00	500-700.
84-03-005	Daddys Darlins'-Princess	X. Roberts	2,000	300.00	500-700.
84-03-006	Daddy's Darlins'-Kitten	X. Roberts	2,000	300.00	500-700.
88-03-007	Tiger's Eye-Valentine's Day	X. Roberts	5,000	150.00	200-400.
89-03-008	Tiger's Eye-Mother's Day	X. Roberts	5,000	150.00	150-400.
90-03-009	Joy	X. Roberts	500	250.00	400-750.
Original Appalachian Artworks		**Cabbage Patch Kids Circus Parade**			
87-04-001	Big Top Clown-Baby Cakes	X. Roberts	2,000	180.00	425-550.
89-04-002	Happy Hobo-Bashful Billy	X. Roberts	1,000	180.00	225-400.
91-04-003	Mitzi	X. Roberts	1,000	220.00	220.00
Original Appalachian Artworks		**Collectors Club Editions**			
89-05-001	Anna Ruby	X. Roberts	Closed	250.00	400.00
90-05-002	Lee Ann	X. Roberts	Closed	250.00	250.00
91-05-003	Richard Russell	X. Roberts	Closed	250.00	250.00
Original Appalachian Artworks		**Convention Baby**			
89-06-001	Ashley	X. Roberts	Closed	150.00	1000.00
90-06-002	Bradley	X. Roberts	Closed	175.00	600.00
91-06-003	Caroline	X. Roberts	Closed	200.00	200.00
Princeton Gallery		**Little Ladies of Victorian England**			
90-01-001	Victoria Anne	Unknown	Open	59.00	59.00
91-01-002	Abigail	Unknown	Open	59.00	59.00
91-01-003	Valerie	Unknown	Open	58.50	58.50
92-01-004	Caroline	Unknown	Open	58.50	58.50
92-01-005	Heather	Unknown	Open	58.50	58.50
93-01-006	Beverly	Unknown	Open	58.50	58.50
Princeton Gallery		**Best Friend Dolls**			
91-02-001	Sharing Secrets	Unknown	Open	78.00	78.00
Princeton Gallery		**Childhood Songs Dolls**			
91-03-001	It's Raining, It's Pouring	Unknown	Open	78.00	78.00
Princeton Gallery		**Dress Up Dolls**			
91-04-001	Grandma's Attic	Unknown	Open	95.00	95.00
Princeton Gallery		**Fabrique Santa**			
91-05-001	Christmas Dream	Unknown	Open	76.00	76.00
Princeton Gallery		**Santa Doll**			
91-06-001	Checking His List	Unknown	Open	119.00	119.00
Princeton Gallery		**Rock-N-Roll Dolls**			
91-07-001	Cindy at the Hop	M. Sirko	Open	95.00	95.00
92-07-002	Chantilly Lace	M. Sirko	Open	95.00	95.00
93-07-003	Yellow Dot Bikini	Unknown	Open	95.00	95.00
Princeton Gallery		**Terrible Twos Dolls**			
91-08-001	One Man Band	M. Sirko	Open	95.00	95.00
Princeton Gallery		**Imaginary People**			
92-09-001	Melinda, Tooth Fairy	Unknown	Open	95.00	95.00
Reco International		**Precious Memories of Motherhood**			
90-01-001	Loving Steps	S. Kuck	Yr.Iss.	125.00	140-195.
91-01-002	Lullaby	S. Kuck	Yr.Iss.	125.00	125.00
92-01-003	Expectant Moments	S. Kuck	Yr.Iss.	149.00	149.00
93-01-004	Bedtime	S. Kuck	Yr.Iss.	149.00	149.00
Reco International		**Children's Circus Doll Collection**			
91-02-001	Tommy The Clown	J. McClelland	Yr.Iss.	78.00	78.00
91-02-002	Katie The Tightrope Walker	J. McClelland	Yr.Iss.	78.00	78.00
91-02-003	Johnny The Strongman	J. McClelland	Yr.Iss.	83.00	83.00
92-02-004	Maggie The Animal Trainer	J. McClelland	Yr.Iss.	83.00	83.00
Rhodes Studio		**A Norman Rockwell Christmas**			
90-01-001	Scotty Plays Santa	Rockwell-Inspired	Yr.Iss.	48.00	48.00
91-01-002	Scotty Gets His Tree	Rockwell-Inspired	Yr.Iss.	59.00	59.00

Company / Number	Name	Series / Artist	Edition Limit	Issue Price	Quote
Roman, Inc.		**Ellen Williams Doll**			
89-01-001	Noelle	E. Williams	5,000	125.00	125.00
89-01-002	Rebecca 999	E. Williams	7,500	195.00	195.00
Roman, Inc.		**A Christmas Drasm**			
90-02-001	Chelsea	E. Williams	5,000	125.00	125.00
90-02-002	Carole	E. Williams	5,000	125.00	125.00
Roman, Inc.		**Tyrolean Treasures: Wood Body, Moveable Joint**			
90-03-001	Nadia	Unkn.	2,000	650.00	650.00
90-03-002	Susie	Unkn.	2,000	650.00	650.00
90-03-003	Verena	Unkn.	2,000	650.00	650.00
90-03-004	Monica	Unkn.	2,000	650.00	650.00
90-03-005	Melissa	Unkn.	2,000	650.00	650.00
90-03-006	Karin	Unkn.	2,000	650.00	650.00
90-03-007	Tina	Unkn.	2,000	650.00	650.00
90-03-008	Ann	Unkn.	2,000	650.00	650.00
90-03-009	Lisa	Unkn.	2,000	650.00	650.00
90-03-010	David	Unkn.	2,000	650.00	650.00
Roman, Inc.		**Tyrolean Treasures: Soft Body, Human Hair**			
90-04-001	Erika	Unkn.	2,000	575.00	575.00
90-04-002	Ellan	Unkn.	2,000	575.00	575.00
90-04-003	Marisa	Unkn.	2,000	575.00	575.00
90-04-004	Sarah	Unkn.	2,000	575.00	575.00
90-04-005	Andrew	Unkn.	2,000	575.00	575.00
90-04-006	Matthew	Unkn.	2,000	575.00	575.00
Roman, Inc.		**Classic Brides of the Century**			
90-05-001	Flora	E. Williams	Open	145.00	145.00
91-05-002	Jennifer	E. Williams	Open	149.50	149.50
Roman, Inc.		**Abbie Williams Collection**			
91-06-001	Molly	E. Williams	5,000	155.00	155.00
Sally-Lynne Dolls		**French Replicas**			
85-01-001	Victoria, 30"	S. Beatty	100	1050.00	3100.00
85-01-002	Charles, 30"	S. Beatty	100	1050.00	2500.00
85-01-003	Annabelle, 28"	S. Beatty	Closed	950.00	3100.00
85-01-004	Candice	S. Beatty	100	950.00	2500.00
86-01-005	Victoria at Christmas, 30"	S. Beatty	Closed	2500.00	4100.00
Sarah's Attic, Inc.		**Angels in The Attic Collection**			
89-01-001	Joy Angel	Sarah's Attic	Closed	50.00	50.00
89-01-002	Holly Angel	Sarah's Attic	Closed	50.00	50.00
89-01-003	Liberty Angel	Sarah's Attic	Closed	50.00	50.00
89-01-004	Glory Angel	Sarah's Attic	Closed	50.00	50.00
Sarah's Attic Inc.		**Beary Adorables Collection**			
90-02-001	Betty Bear Sunday	Sarah's Attic	Closed	160.00	160.00
90-02-002	Teddy Bear Sunday	Sarah's Attic	Closed	160.00	160.00
90-02-003	Teddy School Bear	Sarah's Attic	Closed	160.00	160.00
90-02-004	Americana Bear	Sarah's Attic	Closed	160.00	160.00
91-02-005	Christmas Betty Bear	Sarah's Attic	Closed	160.00	160.00
91-02-006	Christmas Teddy Bear	Sarah's Attic	Closed	160.00	160.00
91-02-007	Springtime Betty Bear	Sarah's Attic	Closed	160.00	160.00
91-02-008	Springtime Teddy Bear	Sarah's Attic	Closed	160.00	160.00
Sarah's Attic Inc.		**Black Heritage Collection**			
90-03-001	School Days Sassafras	Sarah's Attic	2,000	140.00	150-175.
90-03-002	Sweet Dreams Sassafras	Sarah's Attic	2,000	140.00	150-175.
90-03-003	Playtime Sassafras	Sarah's Attic	2,000	140.00	150-175.
90-03-004	Beachtime Sassafras	Sarah's Attic	2,000	140.00	150-175.
90-03-005	Sunday's Best Sassafras	Sarah's Attic	2,000	150.00	150-175.
90-03-006	Americana Sassafras	Sarah's Attic	2,000	150.00	150-175.
90-03-007	School Days Hickory	Sarah's Attic	2,000	140.00	150-175.
90-03-008	Sweet Dreams Hickory	Sarah's Attic	2,000	140.00	150-175.
90-03-009	Playtime Hickory	Sarah's Attic	2,000	140.00	150-175.
90-03-010	Beachtime Hickory	Sarah's Attic	2,000	140.00	150-175.
90-03-011	Sunday's Best Hickory	Sarah's Attic	2,000	150.00	150-175.
90-03-012	Americana Hickory	Sarah's Attic	2,000	150.00	150-175.
91-03-013	Christmas Sassafras	Sarah's Attic	2,000	150.00	150-175.
91-03-014	Christmas Hickory	Sarah's Attic	2,000	150.00	150-175.
91-03-015	Springtime Sassafras	Sarah's Attic	2,000	150.00	150-175.
91-03-016	Springtime Hickory	Sarah's Attic	2,000	150.00	150-175.
Sarah's Attic, Inc.		**Happy Collection**			
89-04-001	Harmony Clown	Sarah's Attic	Closed	150.00	150.00
89-04-002	X-Mas Clown Noel	Sarah's Attic	Closed	150.00	150.00
89-04-003	Freedom Clown	Sarah's Attic	Closed	150.00	150.00
88-04-004	Smiley Clown	Sarah's Attic	Closed	118.00	118.00
Sarah's Attic, Inc.		**Little Charmers Collection**			
89-05-001	Beverly Jane Black	Sarah's Attic	Closed	160.00	160.00
89-05-002	Becky	Sarah's Attic	Closed	120.00	120.00
89-05-003	Bobby	Sarah's Attic	Closed	120.00	120.00
89-05-004	Sunday's a Best-Bevie Jane	Sarah's Attic	Closed	160.00	160.00
89-05-005	Green Beverly Jane	Sarah's Attic	Closed	160.00	160.00
89-05-006	Red Beverly Jane	Sarah's Attic	Closed	160.00	160.00
90-05-007	Megan Doll	Sarah's Attic	Closed	70.00	100.00
90-05-008	Scott Doll	Sarah's Attic	Closed	70.00	100.00
87-05-009	Molly Small 5 Piece Doll	Sarah's Attic	Closed	36.00	36.00
87-05-010	Sunshine 5 Piece Doll	Sarah's Attic	Closed	79.00	79.00
88-05-011	Michael 5 Piece Doll	Sarah's Attic	Closed	44.00	44.00
91-05-012	Victorian Emily	Sarah's Attic	500	250.00	250.00
91-05-013	Country Emily	Sarah's Attic	500	250.00	250.00
91-05-014	Victorian Hilary	Sarah's Attic	500	200.00	200.00
91-05-015	Country Hilary	Sarah's Attic	500	200.00	200.00
91-05-016	Victorian Edie	Sarah's Attic	500	170.00	170.00
91-05-017	Country Edie	Sarah's Attic	500	170.00	170.00
91-05-018	Playtime Edie	Sarah's Attic	500	170.00	170.00
91-05-019	Victorian Emma	Sarah's Attic	500	160.00	160.00
91-05-020	Country Emma	Sarah's Attic	500	160.00	160.00
91-05-021	Playtime Emma	Sarah's Attic	500	160.00	160.00
Sarah's Attic, Inc.		**Spirit Of Christmas**			
89-06-001	Spirit of America Santa	Sarah's Attic	500	150.00	150.00
88-06-002	Mrs. Claus 5 Piece Doll	Sarah's Attic	Closed	120.00	120.00
88-06-003	Santa 5 Piece Doll	Sarah's Attic	Closed	120.00	120.00
Sarah's Attic, Inc.		**Tattered 'N Torn**			
91-07-001	All Cloth Opie White Doll	Sarah's Attic	Closed	90.00	90.00
91-07-002	All Cloth Polly White Doll	Sarah's Attic	Closed	90.00	90.00
91-07-003	All Cloth Puffin Black Doll	Sarah's Attic	Closed	90.00	90.00
91-07-004	All Cloth Muffin Black Doll	Sarah's Attic	Closed	90.00	90.00
Sarah's Attic, Inc.		**Heavenly Wings**			
91-08-001	All Cloth Enos Angel	Sarah's Attic	Closed	90.00	90.00
91-08-002	All Cloth Adora Angel	Sarah's Attic	Closed	90.00	90.00
Schmid		**June Amos Grammer**			
88-01-001	Rosamund	J. Amos Grammer	750	225.00	225.00
89-01-002	Katie	J. Amos Grammer	1,000	180.00	180.00
89-01-003	Vanessa	J. Amos Grammer	1,000	180.00	210.00
90-01-004	Lauren	J. Amos Grammer	1,000	279.00	280.00
90-01-005	Jester Love	J. Amos Grammer	1,000	195.00	210.00
90-01-006	Leigh Ann	J. Amos Grammer	1,000	195.00	210.00
90-01-007	Megan	J. Amos Grammer	750	380.00	380.00
91-01-008	Lauren	J. Amos Grammer	1,000	280.00	280.00
91-01-009	Mitsuko	J. Amos Grammer	1,000	210.00	210.00
91-01-010	Heather	J. Amos Grammer	1,000	210.00	210.00
Sports Impressions		**Porcelain Dolls**			
90-01-001	Mickey Mantle	Sports Impressions	1,956	150.00	150.00
90-01-002	Don Mattingly	Sports Impressions	1,990	150.00	150.00
Turner Dolls Inc.		**Turner Dolls**			
83-01-001	Kristi	J. Turner	Closed	1000.00	1000.00
83-01-002	Baby Nell	J. Turner	Closed	970.00	970.00
84-01-003	Mindy	J. Turner	Closed	720.00	720.00
84-01-004	Petunia	J. Turner	Closed	720.00	720.00
84-01-005	Winston	J. Turner	Closed	900.00	900.00
84-01-006	Sonny	J. Turner	Closed	640.00	640.00
84-01-007	Leslie	J. Turner	Closed	970.00	970.00
85-01-008	Sun Hee	J. Turner	Closed	720.00	720.00
85-01-009	Yong Mi	J. Turner	Closed	720.00	720.00
85-01-010	Cassandra (open)	J. Turner	Closed	900.00	900.00
85-01-011	Cassandra (closed)	J. Turner	Closed	900.00	900.00
85-01-012	Baby Teri	J. Turner	Closed	390.00	390.00
86-01-013	Chelsea	J. Turner	Closed	1000.00	1000.00
86-01-014	Concha	J. Turner	Closed	390.00	390.00
86-01-015	Carrie	J. Turner	Closed	390.00	390.00
86-01-016	Darci	J. Turner	Closed	390.00	390.00
86-01-017	Tressy	J. Turner	Closed	390.00	390.00
86-01-018	Amelia	J. Turner	Closed	640.00	640.00
86-01-019	Timothy/Tabitha	J. Turner	Closed	390.00	390.00
87-01-020	Freddie	J. Turner	Closed	500.00	500.00
87-01-021	Phoebe	J. Turner	Closed	500.00	500.00
87-01-022	Keisha	J. Turner	Closed	410.00	410.00
87-01-023	Senji	J. Turner	Closed	450.00	450.00
87-01-024	Shizuko	J. Turner	Closed	450.00	450.00
87-01-025	Lollie	J. Turner	Closed	450.00	450.00
88-01-026	Jena	J. Turner	Closed	410.00	410.00
88-01-027	Julie D	J. Turner	Closed	450.00	450.00
88-01-028	Susan Jayne	J. Turner	Closed	450.00	450.00
88-01-029	Seth	J. Turner	Closed	450.00	450.00
88-01-030	Tara Renee Baby	J. Turner	Closed	570.00	570.00
88-01-031	Tara Renee Toddler	J. Turner	Closed	570.00	570.00
88-01-032	Melinda	J. Turner	Closed	820.00	1100.00
89-01-033	Bretta	J. Turner	Closed	450.00	450.00
89-01-034	Cami	J. Turner	Closed	450.00	450.00
89-01-035	Cameron	J. Turner	Closed	450.00	450.00
89-01-036	Gabaree	J. Turner	Closed	1000.00	1000.00
89-01-037	Jilli	J. Turner	Closed	640.00	640.00
89-01-038	Lindsey	J. Turner	Closed	450.00	450.00
89-01-039	Selena	J. Turner	Closed	1050.00	1050.00
89-01-040	Jeannie	V.. Turner	Closed	420.00	420.00
89-01-041	Molly	V. Turner	Closed	420.00	420.00
90-01-042	Chad w/sled	J. Turner	Closed	590.00	590.00
90-01-043	Chad w/airplane	J. Turner	Closed	500.00	500.00
90-01-044	Lynette	J. Turner	Closed	900.00	900.00
90-01-045	Marci	J. Turner	Closed	570.00	570.00
90-01-046	Rudy	J. Turner	Closed	700.00	700.00
90-01-047	Whitney	J. Turner	Closed	770.00	770.00
90-01-048	Rudy	J. Turner	Closed	700.00	700.00
90-01-049	Alli	V. Turner	Closed	570.00	570.00
90-01-050	Christina	V. Turner	Closed	570.00	570.00
90-01-051	Tori	V. Turner	Closed	570.00	570.00
90-01-052	Katrina	V. Turner	Closed	620.00	620.00
90-01-053	Melodie	V. Turner	Closed	470.00	470.00
90-01-054	Jenalee	V. Turner	Closed	620.00	620.00
90-01-055	Cymbre	V. Turner	Closed	620.00	620.00
91-01-056	Christmas Marta	J. Turner	Closed	1100.00	1100.00
91-01-057	Marta	J. Turner	Closed	900.00	900.00
91-01-058	Mei Chun	J. Turner	Closed	900.00	900.00
91-01-059	Heather	V. Turner	Closed	700.00	700.00
91-01-060	Kitty Kay	V. Turner	Closed	450.00	450.00
91-01-061	Suzette (small)	V. Turner	Closed	700.00	700.00
91-01-062	Suzette (large)	V. Turner	Closed	1300.00	1300.00
91-01-063	Christmas Hannah	V. Turner	Closed	1100.00	1100.00
91-01-064	Hannah	V. Turner	Closed	900.00	900.00
92-01-065	Baby Joe Michael	V. Turner	Open	470.00	470.00
92-01-066	Nikkeya	V. Turner	350	800.00	800.00
92-01-067	Terrace	V. Turner	350	750.00	750.00
92-01-068	Sarah Chang	V. Turner	150	600.00	600.00
92-01-069	Sarah Chang (Ballerina)	V. Turner	50	1200.00	1200.00
92-01-070	Bucky the Newsboy	V. Turner	200	650.00	650.00
92-01-071	Christmas Bucky	V. Turner	50	900.00	900.00
92-01-072	Christmas Raven	V. Turner	50	1100.00	1100.00
92-01-073	Spring Raven	V. Turner	250	900.00	900.00
92-01-074	Autumn Raven	V. Turner	150	900.00	900.00
92-01-075	Makenzie	V. Turner	250	600.00	600.00
U.S. Historical Society		**Children of the Past**			
84-01-001	Holly	F. Zeller	950	625.00	625.00
85-01-002	Michael	P. Wright	950	350.00	350.00
Susan Wakeen Doll Co. Inc.		**The Littlest Ballet Company**			
85-01-001	Jeanne	S. Wakeen	375	198.00	800.00
85-01-002	Patty	S. Wakeen	375	198.00	500.00
85-01-003	Cynthia	S. Wakeen	375	198.00	350.00
87-01-004	Elizabeth	S. Wakeen	250	425.00	1000.00

Number	Name	Artist	Edition Limit	Issue Price	Quote
FIGURINES					
Kurt S. Adler/Santa's World	**Camelot Steinbach Nutcracker Series**				
91-01-001	Merlin The Magician ES610	K.S. Adler	Retrd.	185.00	185.00
92-01-002	King Arthur ES621	K.S. Adler	10,000	195.00	195.00
Kurt S. Adler/Santa's World	**Great Americans Steinbach Nutcracker Series**				
92-02-001	Abraham Lincoln ES622	K.S. Adler	12,000	195.00	195.00
92-02-002	George Washington ES623	K.S. Adler	12,000	195.00	195.00
Kurt S. Adler/Santa's World	**Steinbach Smoking Figure Collection**				
92-03-001	Merlin The Magician ES830	K.S. Adler	7,500	150.00	1000.00
92-03-002	The Breadbaker ES806	K.S. Adler	Open	105.00	105.00
92-03-003	The Musical Artist ES804	K.S. Adler	Open	104.00	104.00
92-03-004	Happy Santa ES831	K.S. Adler	Open	105.00	105.00
92-03-005	The Musical Octoberfest ES829	K.S. Adler	Open	157.00	157.00
92-03-006	The Florist ES748	K.S. Adler	Open	105.00	105.00
92-03-007	The Tournament Rider ES783	K.S. Adler	Open	95.00	95.00
92-03-008	The Skier ES776	K.S. Adler	Open	125.00	125.00
92-03-009	The Fairy Tale King ES789	K.S. Adler	Open	130.00	130.00
92-03-010	The Little Drummer Boy ES787	K.S. Adler	Open	130.00	130.00
92-03-011	The Musical Photographer ES822	K.S. Adler	Open	155.00	155.00
92-03-012	The Fisherman ES781	K.S. Adler	Open	125.00	125.00
Kurt S. Adler/Santa's World	**Zuber Nutcracker Collection**				
92-04-001	The Pilgrim EK14	K.S. Adler	5,000	125.00	125.00
92-04-002	The Indian EK15	K.S. Adler	5,000	135.00	135.00
92-04-003	The Bavarian EK16	K.S. Adler	5,000	130.00	130.00
92-04-004	The Fisherman EK17	K.S. Adler	5,000	125.00	125.00
92-04-005	The Gold Prospector EK18	K.S. Adler	5,000	125.00	125.00
92-04-006	The Country Singer EK19	K.S. Adler	5,000	125.00	125.00
92-04-007	Gepetto, The Toymaker EK9	K.S. Adler	5,000	125.00	125.00
92-04-008	The West Point Cadet With Canon EK8	K.S. Adler	5,000	130.00	130.00
92-04-009	The Chimney Sweep EK6	K.S. Adler	5,000	125.00	125.00
92-04-010	The Annapolis Midshipman EK7	K.S. Adler	5,000	125.00	125.00
92-04-011	The Golfer EK5	K.S. Adler	5,000	125.00	125.00
92-04-012	Bronco Billy The Cowboy EK1	K.S. Adler	5,000	125.00	125.00
92-04-013	The Nor' Easter Sea Captain EK3	K.S. Adler	5,000	125.00	125.00
92-04-014	TheTyrolean EK4	K.S. Adler	5,000	125.00	125.00
92-04-015	Paul Bunyan The Lumberjack EK2	K.S. Adler	5,000	125.00	125.00
Kurt S. Adler/Santa's World	**Steinbach Nutcracker Collection**				
92-05-001	Happy Santa ES601	K.S. Adler	Open	190.00	190.00
92-05-002	James Cook The Explorer ES628	K.S. Adler	Open	166.00	166.00
92-05-003	The Aviator ES642	K.S. Adler	Open	176.00	176.00
92-05-004	Tchaikovsky ES619	K.S. Adler	Open	185.00	185.00
92-05-005	The Texas Sherriff ES700	K.S. Adler	Open	176.00	176.00
92-05-006	King Neptune ES629	K.S. Adler	Open	176.00	176.00
92-05-007	The Wizard Of Oz ES624	K.S. Adler	Open	176.00	176.00
92-05-008	The Dentist ES627	K.S. Adler	Open	176.00	176.00
92-05-009	The Mailman ES626	K.S. Adler	Open	176.00	176.00
92-05-010	The Cowboy Sitting at Player Piano ES607	K.S. Adler	Open	180.00	180.00
92-05-011	The Skier ES640	K.S. Adler	Open	176.00	176.00
92-05-012	Father And Son ES688	K.S. Adler	Open	190.00	190.00
92-05-013	The Bavarian ES708	K.S. Adler	Open	165.00	165.00
92-05-014	The Bagpiper ES682	K.S. Adler	Open	176.00	176.00
92-05-015	The Fisherman ES704	K.S. Adler	Open	165.00	165.00
92-05-016	The Viking ES730	K.S. Adler	Open	150.00	150.00
92-05-017	Christopher Columbus ES697	K.S. Adler	Open	176.00	176.00
92-05-018	The Hunter ES706	K.S. Adler	Open	165.00	165.00
92-05-019	The Druggist ES685	K.S. Adler	Open	176.00	176.00
92-05-020	The Chef Cook ES663	K.S. Adler	Open	176.00	176.00
92-05-021	The Irish Leprechaun ES686	K.S. Adler	Open	176.00	176.00
92-05-022	The Lottoman ES612	K.S. Adler	Open	176.00	176.00
92-05-023	The Napoleanic Guard ES615	K.S. Adler	Open	176.00	176.00
92-05-024	The Basket Vendor ES617	K.S. Adler	Open	176.00	176.00
92-05-025	Einstein ES602	K.S. Adler	Open	176.00	176.00
92-05-026	The Shoemaker ES613	K.S. Adler	Open	176.00	176.00
92-05-027	King Wilhelm Of Prussia ES698	K.S. Adler	Open	176.00	176.00
92-05-028	The Linen Weaver ES611	K.S. Adler	Open	176.00	176.00
92-05-029	The Tyrolean Mountain Climber ES606	K.S. Adler	Open	176.00	176.00
92-05-030	Rosenkavalier The Florist ES603	K.S. Adler	Open	176.00	176.00
92-05-031	Sherlock Holmes ES681	K.S. Adler	Open	150.00	150.00
92-05-032	Dr. Watson ES680	K.S. Adler	Open	150.00	150.00
92-05-033	The Fireman ES699	K.S. Adler	Open	176.00	176.00
92-05-034	The Guard Soldier ES711	K.S. Adler	Open	165.00	165.00
92-05-035	The Shepherd ES710	K.S. Adler	Open	176.00	176.00
92-05-036	The Nutcracker Maker ES696	K.S. Adler	Open	176.00	176.00
92-05-037	The Golfer ES692	K.S. Adler	Open	176.00	176.00
92-05-038	The Chimney Sweep ES707	K.S. Adler	Open	165.00	165.00
92-05-039	The Saxophonist ES609	K.S. Adler	Open	145.00	145.00
92-05-040	The Conductor ES605	K.S. Adler	Open	145.00	145.00
92-05-041	Chopin ES701	K.S. Adler	Open	190.00	190.00
92-05-042	Mozart ES679	K.S. Adler	Open	150.00	150.00
92-05-043	Paganini ES604	K.S. Adler	Open	145.00	145.00
Kurt S. Adler/Santa's World	**Disney Christmas Nutcracker Collection**				
92-06-001	Goofy H1216	K.S. Adler	Open	78.00	78.00
92-06-002	Mickey Mouse Sorcerer H1221	K.S. Adler	Open	100.00	100.00
92-06-003	Mickey Mouse Soldier H1194	K.S. Adler	Open	72.00	72.00
Kurt S. Adler/Santa's World	**German Erzgebirge Nutcracker Collection**				
92-07-001	The Santa E95	K.S. Adler	Open	75.00	75.00
92-07-002	The Swedish Officer E163	K.S. Adler	Open	75.00	75.00
92-07-003	The Fireman E45	K.S. Adler	Open	84.00	84.00
92-07-004	The Royal Hunter E176	K.S. Adler	Open	75.00	75.00
92-07-005	The Soldier Guard E99	K.S. Adler	Open	60.00	60.00
92-07-006	British Tambour Major E175	K.S. Adler	Open	75.00	75.00
92-07-007	The Buckingham Guard E160	K.S. Adler	Open	160.00	160.00
92-07-008	The Royal Hussar E177	K.S. Adler	Open	75.00	75.00
92-07-009	The Red And Blue King E42	K.S. Adler	Open	84.00	84.00
92-07-010	The Natural Wood King E117	K.S. Adler	Open	80.00	80.00
92-07-011	The Fur Trapper E96	K.S. Adler	Open	60.00	60.00
92-07-012	The Old Fashioned Santa E153	K.S. Adler	Open	55.00	55.00
92-07-013	The Chimney Sweep E122	K.S. Adler	Open	55.00	55.00
92-07-014	The Chimney Sweep E37	K.S. Adler	Open	84.00	84.00
92-07-015	The Santa E23	K.S. Adler	Open	84.00	84.00
92-07-016	The Red And Green King E40	K.S. Adler	Open	90.00	90.00
92-07-017	The Old Fashioned King E152	K.S. Adler	Open	55.00	55.00
92-07-018	The Prussian Drummer E43	K.S. Adler	Open	75.00	75.00
92-07-019	The British General E174	K.S. Adler	Open	60.00	60.00
92-07-020	The White King E35	K.S. Adler	Open	95.00	95.00
92-07-021	The Blue King E41	K.S. Adler	Open	80.00	80.00
92-07-022	The Hussar E100	K.S. Adler	Open	60.00	60.00
92-07-023	The Seiffen King E94	K.S. Adler	Open	55.00	55.00
92-07-024	The Seiffen King E91	K.S. Adler	Open	70.00	70.00
Kurt S. Adler/Santa's World	**The Wizard Of Oz Nutcracker Collection**				
92-08-001	The Cowardly Lion C206	K.S. Adler	Open	19.00	19.00
92-08-002	The Tin Man C206	K.S. Adler	Open	19.00	19.00
92-08-003	The Scarecrow C206	K.S. Adler	Open	19.00	19.00
92-08-004	The Dorothy & Toto C206	K.S. Adler	Open	19.00	19.00
Kurt S. Adler/Santa's World	**Fabriché Collection**				
91-09-001	Santa Fiddler W1549	K.S. Adler	Open	100.00	100.00
91-09-002	Hello! Little One W1552	K.S. Adler	12,000	90.00	90.00
92-09-003	Bringin in the Yule Log W1589	M. Rothenberg	5,000	200.00	200.00
92-09-004	A Stitch in Time W1591	M. Rothenberg	5,000	135.00	135.00
92-09-005	Santa's Ice Capades W1588	M. Rothenberg	Open	110.00	110.00
92-09-006	Santa Steals A Kiss & A Cookie W1581	M. Rothenberg	Open	150.00	150.00
92-09-007	Apron Full of Love W1582	M. Rothenberg	Open	75.00	75.00
92-09-008	Christmas is in the Air W1590	K.S. Adler	Open	110.00	110.00
92-09-009	Bundles of Joy W1578	K.S. Adler	Open	78.00	78.00
92-09-010	Homeward Bound W1568	K.S. Adler	Open	61.00	61.00
92-09-011	Master Toymaker W1566	K.S. Adler	Open	61.00	61.00
92-09-012	Special Delivery W1558	K.S. Adler	Open	56.00	56.00
92-09-013	Jolly Old Nick W1557	K.S. Adler	Open	56.00	56.00
92-09-014	Old Father Frost W1559	K.S. Adler	Open	56.00	56.00
92-09-015	Merry Kissmas W1548	M. Rothenberg	Open	140.00	140.00
92-09-016	Santa's Cat Nap W1504	M .Rothenberg	Open	98.00	98.00
92-09-017	Sitting Santa Workshop J2903	K.S. Adler	Open	70.00	70.00
92-09-018	Singing Santa With Toy Sack J2943	K.S. Adler	Open	48.00	48.00
92-09-019	Patriotic Santa J2911	K.S. Adler	Open	60.00	60.00
92-09-020	Santa On Wooden Bench J662	K.S. Adler	Open	69.00	69.00
92-09-021	Santa Holding Girl On Lap J655	K.S. Adler	Open	78.00	78.00
92-09-022	Laughing All The Way J1567	K.S. Adler	Open	83.00	83.00
92-09-023	Santa J7936	K.S. Adler	Open	37.00	37.00
92-09-024	Santa With Elf And Santa J7943	K.S. Adler	Open	150.00	150.00
92-09-025	Santa With Elves J7944	K.S. Adler	Open	160.00	160.00
92-09-026	Santa In Burgundy Coat W1506	K.S. Adler	Open	49.00	49.00
92-09-027	Santa In Beige Coat W1523	K.S. Adler	Open	49.00	49.00
92-09-028	Santa In Red Coat W1524	K.S. Adler	Open	49.00	49.00
92-09-039	Workshop Santa Toymaker Master W1566	K.S. Adler	Open	61.00	61.00
92-09-030	St. Nicholas The Bishop W1532	K.S. Adler	Open	78.00	78.00
92-09-031	Checking Santa's Book W1550	K.S. Adler	Open	80.00	80.00
92-09-032	Ringing In Christmas W1551	K.S. Adler	Open	62.00	62.00
92-09-033	Sled Santa W1555	K.S. Adler	Open	67.00	67.00
92-09-034	Hugs and Kisses W1531	K.S. Adler	Open	67.00	67.00
92-09-035	Not A Creature Was Stirring W1534	K.S. Adler	Open	67.00	67.00
Kurt S. Adler/Santa's World	**Thomas Nast Fabriché Reproduction Series**				
92-10-001	Christmas Sing-A-Long W1576	K.S. Adler	12,000	110.00	110.00
92-10-002	Caught in the Act W1577	K.S. Adler	12,000	133.00	133.00
Kurt S. Adler/Santa's World	**Smithsonian Museum Fabriché Collection**				
91-11-001	Santa On A Bicycle W1527	K.S. Adler	Open	150.00	150.00
92-11-002	Holiday Drive W1556	K.S. Adler	Open	155.00	155.00
92-11-003	Peace on Earth Angel Treetop W1583	K.S. Adler	Open	52.00	52.00
92-11-004	Peace on Earth Flying Angel W1585	K.S. Adler	Open	49.00	49.00
Kurt S. Adler/Santa's World	**Fabriché Angel Collection**				
92-12-001	Heavenly Messenger W1584	K.S. Adler	Open	41.00	41.00
Kurt S. Adler/Santa's World	**Christmas In Chelsea**				
92-13-001	Large Black Forest Santa W2717	J. Mostrom	3,000	110.00	110.00
92-13-002	Small Grandfather Frost W2718	J. Mostrom	3,000	106.00	106.00
92-13-003	Large Father Christmas W2719	J. Mostrom	3,000	106.00	106.00
92-13-004	Patriotic Santa W2720	J. Mostrom	3,000	128.00	128.00
92-13-005	Chelsea Garden Santa W2721	J. Mostrom	5,000	33.50	33.50
92-13-006	Small Father Christmas W2712	J. Mostrom	5,000	33.50	33.50
92-13-007	Pere Noel W2723	J. Mostrom	5,000	33.50	33.50
92-13-008	Small Black Forest Santa W2712	J. Mostrom	5,000	40.00	40.00
92-13-009	St. Nickolas W2713	J. Mostrom	5,000	30.00	30.00
92-13-010	Mrs. Claus W2714	J. Mostrom	5,000	37.00	37.00
92-13-011	Workshop Santa W2715	J. Mostrom	5,000	43.00	43.00
92-13-012	Small Grandfather Frost W2716	J. Mostrom	5,000	43.00	43.00
Kurt S. Adler/Santa's World	**Fabric Mache Collection**				
92-14-001	I'm Late, I'm Late J7947	T. Rubel	Open	100.00	100.00
92-14-002	It's Time To Go J7943	T. Rubel	Open	150.00	150.00
92-14-003	He Did It Again J7944	T. Rubel	Open	160.00	160.00
Kurt S. Adler/Santa's World	**Steinbach Musical Smoking Figurine Collection**				
92-15-001	Ski Lift Musical ES27	K.S. Adler	2,000	150.00	150.00
92-15-002	The Black Forest Mill ES71	K.S. Adler	Open	170.00	170.00
92-15-003	The Fisherman In Boat ES767	K.S. Adler	Open	165.00	165.00
92-15-004	The Mushroom Man ES825	K.S. Adler	Open	165.00	165.00
92-15-005	The Grandpa Rocker ES755	K.S. Adler	Open	150.00	150.00
92-15-006	Santa on Sled ES766	K.S. Adler	Open	157.00	157.00
92-15-007	The Grandma Rocker ES756	K.S. Adler	Open	150.00	150.00
Kurt S. Adler/Santa's World	**Oscar & Bertie Waterglobe Collection**				
92-16-001	Santa Bear With Packages J1033	K.S. Adler	Open	41.00	41.00
92-16-002	Bears on Rocking Horse J1034	K.S. Adler	Open	56.00	56.00
Kurt S. Adler/Santa's World	**Saturday Evening Post Waterglobe Collection**				
92-17-001	Christmas Trio Norman Rockwell Reproduction J1035	K.S. Adler	Open	40.00	40.00
92-17-002	Santa's Surprise J.C. Leyendecker Reproduction J1036	K.S. Adler	Open	40.00	40.00
Kurt S. Adler/Santa's World	**Currier & Ives Waterglobe Collection**				
92-18-001	Our First Christmas J1037	K.S. Adler	Open	40.00	40.00
92-18-002	We Wish You A Merry Christmas J1048	K.S. Adler	Open	40.00	40.00
Kurt S. Adler/Santa's World	**Waterglobe Collection**				
92-19-001	Santa With Two Girls J1038	K.S. Adler	Open	40.00	40.00
Kurt S. Adler/Santa's World	**Smithsonian Museum Carousel Series**				
XX-20-001	The Antique Carousel Goat S3027/1	K.S. Adler	Retrd.	14.50	14.50
XX-20-002	The Antique Carousel Bunny S3027/2	K.S. Adler	Retrd.	14.50	14.50
XX-20-003	The Antique Carousel Horse S3027/3	K.S. Adler	Open	14.50	14.50
XX-20-004	The Antique Carousel Giraffe S3027/4	K.S. Adler	Open	14.50	14.50
XX-20-005	The Antique Carousel Lion S3027/5	K.S. Adler	Open	14.50	14.50
XX-20-006	The Antique Carousel Cat S3027/6	K.S. Adler	Open	14.50	14.50

Company / Number	Name	Series / Artist	Edition Limit	Issue Price	Quote
XX-20-007	The Antique Carousel Zebra S3027/7	K.S. Adler	Open	14.50	14.50
XX-20-008	The Antique Carousel Seahorse S3027/8	K.S. Adler	Open	14.50	14.50
XX-20-009	The Antique Carousel Rooster S3027/9	K.S. Adler	Open	14.50	14.50
XX-20-010	The Antique Carousel Horse S3027/10	K.S. Adler	Open	14.50	14.50
Kurt S. Adler/Santa's World		**Visions Of Santa Collection**			
92-21-001	Workshop Santa J825	T. Rubel	7,500	27.00	27.00
92-21-002	Santa Holding Child J826	T. Rubel	7,500	24.50	24.50
92-21-003	Santa With Sack Holding Toy J827	T. Rubel	7,500	24.50	24.50
92-21-004	Santa Spilling Bag Of Toys J1022	T. Rubel	7,500	25.50	25.50
92-21-005	Santa Coming Out Of Fireplace J1023	T. Rubel	7,500	29.00	29.00
92-21-006	Santa With Little Girls On Lap J1024	T. Rubel	7,500	24.50	24.50
All God's Children		**All God's Children**			
85-01-001	Abe -1357	M. Holcolme	Retrd.	24.95	800-1200.
86-01-002	Annie Mae 8 1/2" -1310	M. Holcolme	Retrd.	26.95	100-125.
86-01-003	Annie Mae 6" -1311	M. Holcolme	Retrd.	18.95	70-100.00
87-01-004	Aunt Sarah - blue -1440	M. Holcolme	Retrd.	45.00	100-155.
87-01-005	Aunt Sarah - red-1440	M. Holcolme	Retrd.	45.00	150-300.
89-01-006	Bean (Clear Water)-1521	M. Holcolme	Retrd.	36.00	90-115.00
87-01-007	Becky with Patch - 1402W	M. Holcolme	Retrd.	18.95	115-150.
87-01-008	Ben - 1504	M. Holcolme	Retrd.	21.95	175-350.
88-01-009	Betsy (Clear Water)- 1513	M. Holcolme	Retrd.	36.00	90-125.00
89-01-010	Beverly - 1525	M. Holcolme	Retrd.	50.00	350-500.
87-01-011	Blossom - blue - 1500	M. Holcolme	Retrd.	59.95	125-180.
87-01-012	Blossom - red- 1500	M. Holcolme	Retrd.	59.95	120-180.
85-01-013	Booker T - 1320	M. Holcolme	Retrd.	18.95	800-1250.
88-01-014	Boone - 1510	M. Holcolme	Retrd.	16.00	45-65.00
85-01-015	Callie 4 1/2" - 1361	M. Holcolme	Retrd.	18.95	200-375.
85-01-016	Callie 2 1/4" - 1362	M. Holcolme	Retrd.	12.00	200-280.
88-01-017	Calvin - 777	M. Holcolme	Retrd.	200.00	1000-1050.
87-01-018	Cassie - 1503	M. Holcolme	Retrd.	21.95	60-100.00
91-01-019	Dori (green dress) - 1544	M. Holcolme	Retrd.	30.00	175-350.
85-01-020	Emma - 1322	M. Holcolme	Retrd.	26.95	1350-1700.
87-01-021	Ginnie - 1508	M. Holcolme	Retrd.	22.00	200-350.
86-01-022	Grandma - 1323	M. Holcolme	Retrd.	29.95	3000-3200.
89-01-023	Jessica and Jeremy -1522-1523	M. Holcolme	Retrd.	195.00	1350-1400.
87-01-024	Jessie (no base) -1501W	M. Holcolme	Retrd.	18.95	275-350.
88-01-025	John -1514	M. Holcolme	Retrd.	30.00	75-130.00
86-01-026	Lil' Emmie 4 1/2" -1344	M. Holcolme	Retrd.	15.99	40-80.00
86-01-027	Lil' Emmie 3 1/2"-1345	M. Holcolme	Retrd.	12.99	45-58.00
88-01-028	Lisa -1512	M. Holcolme	Retrd.	30.00	75-125.00
88-01-029	Meg (blue dress, long hair) -1505	M. Holcolme	Retrd.	21.00	300-325.
88-01-030	Meg (blue dress, short hair) -1505	M. Holcolme	Retrd.	21.00	275-325.
88-01-031	Meg (beige dress) -1505	M. Holcolme	Retrd.	21.00	850-1000.
88-01-032	Peanut -1509	M. Holcolme	Retrd.	16.00	45-75.00
87-01-033	Primas Jones -1377	M. Holcolme	Retrd.	39.95	400-550.
87-01-034	Primas Jones (w/base) -1377	M. Holcolme	Retrd.	39.95	600.00
87-01-035	Prissy with Yarn Hair (6 strands) -1343	M. Holcolme	Retrd.	18.95	20-135.00
87-01-036	Prissy with Yarn Hair (9 strands) -1343	M. Holcolme	Retrd.	18.95	200-250.
87-01-037	Prissy with Basket -1346	M. Holcolme	Retrd.	16.00	70-100.00
87-01-038	Pud- 1550	M. Holcolme	Retrd.	10.00	1000-1200.
88-01-039	Sally -1507	M. Holcolme	Retrd.	18.95	60-100.00
86-01-040	Selina Jane (6 strands) -1338	M. Holcolme	Retrd.	21.95	75-125.00
86-01-041	Selina Jane (9 strands) -1338	M. Holcolme	Retrd.	21.95	100-250.
86-01-042	St. Nicholas-W -1315	M. Holcolme	Retrd.	29.95	80-110.00
86-01-043	St. Nicholas-B -1316	M. Holcolme	Retrd.	29.95	80-110.00
88-01-044	Tansi & Tedi (green socks, collar, cuffs)-1516	M. Holcolme	Retrd.	30.00	125-150.
90-01-045	Thaliyah- 778	M. Holcolme	Retrd.	150.00	1100-1200.
86-01-046	Toby 4 1/2"- 1331	M. Holcolme	Retrd.	15.99	50-80.00
86-01-047	Toby 3 1/2"- 1332	M. Holcolme	Retrd.	12.99	50-60.00
85-01-048	Tom- 1353	M. Holcolme	Retrd.	15.95	225-265.
86-01-049	Uncle Bud 8 1/2"- 1303	M. Holcolme	Retrd.	26.95	70-150.00
86-01-050	Uncle Bud 6"- 1304	M. Holcolme	Retrd.	18.95	60-100.00
87-01-051	Willie (no base)- 1406W	M. Holcolme	Retrd.	18.95	275-350.
All God's Children		**Christmas**			
87-02-001	1987 Father Christmas-W -1750	M. Holcolme	Retrd.	145.00	450-500.
87-02-002	1987 Father Christmas-B -1751	M. Holcolme	Retrd.	145.00	450-510.
88-02-003	1988 Father Christmas-W -1757	M. Holcolme	Retrd.	195.00	425-450.
88-02-004	1988 Father Christmas-B -1758	M. Holcolme	Retrd.	195.00	400-450.
88-02-005	Santa Claus-W -1767	M. Holcolme	Retrd.	185.00	400-450.
88-02-006	Santa Claus-B -1768	M. Holcolme	Retrd.	185.00	400-500.
89-02-007	1989 Father Christmas-W -1769	M. Holcolme	Retrd.	195.00	450-550.
89-02-008	1989 Father Christmas-B -1770	M. Holcolme	Retrd.	195.00	450-550.
91-02-009	1990-91 Father Christmas-W -1771	M. Holcolme	Retrd.	195.00	450-500.
91-02-010	1990-91 Father Christmas-B -1772	M. Holcolme	Retrd.	195.00	275-500.
All God's Children		**Sugar And Spice**			
87-03-001	God is Love (Angel) -1401	M. Holcolme	Retrd.	21.95	375-500.
87-03-002	Friend Show Love (Becky) -1402	M. Holcolme	Retrd.	21.95	375-500.
87-03-003	Blessed are the Peacemakers (Eli) -1403	M. Holcolme	Retrd.	21.95	375-500.
87-03-004	Old Friends are Best (Rachel) -1404	M. Holcolme	Retrd.	21.95	375-500.
87-03-005	Jesus Loves Me (Amy) -1405	M. Holcolme	Retrd.	21.95	375-500.
87-03-006	Sharing with Friends (Willie) -1406	M. Holcolme	Retrd.	21.95	375-500.
87-03-007	Friendship Warms the Heart (Jacob) -1407	M. Holcolme	Retrd.	21.95	375-500.
All God's Children		**Collectors' Club**			
89-04-001	Molly -1524	M. Holcolme	Retrd.	38.00	300-400.
90-04-002	Joey -1539	M. Holcolme	Retrd.	32.00	150-200.
91-04-003	Mandy	M. Holcolme	Retrd.	36.00	36.00
American Artists		**Fred Stone Figurines**			
85-01-001	The Black Stallion, porcelain	F. Stone	2,500	125.00	260.00
85-01-002	The Black Stallion, bronze	F. Stone	1,500	150.00	175.00
86-01-003	Arab Mare & Foal	F. Stone	2,500	150.00	225.00
86-01-004	Tranquility	F. Stone	2,500	175.00	275.00
87-01-005	Rearing Black Stallion (Porcelain)	F. Stone	3,500	150.00	175.00
87-01-006	Rearing Black Stallion (Bronze)	F. Stone	1,250	175.00	195.00
ANRI		**Ferrandiz Shepherds of the Year**			
77-01-001	Friendships, 6"	J. Ferrandiz	Annual	110.00	500-675.
77-01-002	Friendships, 3"	J. Ferrandiz	Annual	53.50	330.00
78-01-003	Spreading the Word, 6"	J. Ferrandiz	Annual	270.50	500.00
78-01-004	Spreading the Word, 3"	J. Ferrandiz	Annual	115.00	275.00
79-01-005	Drummer Boy, 6"	J. Ferrandiz	Annual	220.00	425.00
79-01-006	Drummer Boy, 3"	J. Ferrandiz	Annual	80.00	250.00
80-01-007	Freedom Bound, 6"	J. Ferrandiz	Annual	225.00	400.00
80-01-008	Freedom Bound, 3"	J. Ferrandiz	Annual	90.00	225.00
81-01-009	Jolly PipeLr, 6"	J. Ferrandiz	2,250	225.00	275-375.
82-01-010	Companions, 6"	J. Ferrandiz	2,250	220.00	300.00
83-01-011	Good Samaritan, 6"	J. Ferrandiz	2,250	220.00	320.00
84-01-012	Devotion, 6"	J. Ferrandiz	2,250	180.00	250.00

Company / Number	Name	Series / Artist	Edition Limit	Issue Price	Quote
84-01-013	Devotion, 3"	J. Ferrandiz	2,250	82.50	125.00
ANRI		**Ferrandiz Matching Number Woodcarvings**			
88-02-001	Dear Sweetheart, 6"	J. Ferrandiz	100	525.00	900.00
88-02-002	For My Sweetheart, 6"	J. Ferrandiz	Set	Set	Set
88-02-003	Dear Sweetheart, 3"	J. Ferrandiz	100	285.00	495.00
88-02-004	For My Sweetheart, 3"	J. Ferrandiz	Set	Set	Set
88-02-005	Extra, Extra!, 6"	J. Ferrandiz	100	665.00	665.00
88-02-006	Sunny Skies, 6"	J. Ferrandiz	Set	Set	Set
88-02-007	Extra, Extra!, 3"	J. Ferrandiz	100	315.00	315.00
88-02-008	Sunny Skies, 3"	J. Ferrandiz	Set	Set	Set
88-02-009	Picnic for Two, 6"	J. Ferrandiz	500	845.00	845.00
88-02-010	Bon Appetit, 6"	J. Ferrandiz	Set	Set	Set
88-02-011	Picnic for Two, 3"	J. Ferrandiz	500	390.00	390.00
88-02-012	Bon Appetit, 3"	J. Ferrandiz	Set	Set	Set
89-02-013	Baker / Pastry, 6"	J. Ferrandiz	100	680.00	680.00
89-02-014	Baker / Pastry, 3"	J. Ferrandiz	100	340.00	340.00
90-02-015	Alpine Music / Friend, 6"	J. Ferrandiz	100	900.00	900.00
90-02-016	Alpine Music / Friend, 3"	J. Ferrandiz	100	450.00	450.00
91-02-017	Catalonian Boy/Girl, 6"	J. Ferrandiz	100	1000.00	1000.00
91-02-018	Catalonian Boy/Girl, 3"	J. Ferrandiz	100	455.00	455.00
ANRI		**Ferrandiz Boy and Girl**			
76-03-001	Cowboy, 6"	J. Ferrandiz	1,500	75.00	700.00
76-03-002	Harvest Girl, 6"	J. Ferrandiz	1,500	75.00	800.00
77-03-003	Tracker, 6"	J. Ferrandiz	1,500	100.00	375.00
77-03-004	Leading the Way, 6"	J. Ferrandiz	1,500	100.00	375.00
78-03-005	Peace Pipe, 6"	J. Ferrandiz	1,500	140.00	325-450.
78-03-006	Basket of Joy, 6"	J. Ferrandiz	1,500	140.00	350-450.
79-03-007	Happy Strummer, 6"	J. Ferrandiz	2,250	160.00	395.00
79-03-008	First Blossom, 6"	J. Ferrandiz	2,250	135.00	375.00
80-03-009	Friends, 6"	J. Ferrandiz	2,250	200.00	350.00
80-03-010	Melody for Two, 6"	J. Ferrandiz	2,250	200.00	350.00
81-03-011	Merry Melody, 6"	J. Ferrandiz	2,250	210.00	300-350.
81-03-012	Tiny Sounds, 6"	J. Ferrandiz	2,250	210.00	300-350.
82-03-013	Guiding Light, 6"	J. Ferrandiz	2,250	225.00	275.00
82-03-014	To Market, 6"	J. Ferrandiz	2,250	220.00	250.00
83-03-015	Bewildered, 6"	J. Ferrandiz	2,250	196.00	250.00
83-03-016	Admiration, 6"	J. Ferrandiz	2,250	220.00	250.00
84-03-017	Wanderer's Return, 6"	J. Ferrandiz	2,250	196.00	250.00
84-03-018	Wanderer's Return, 3"	J. Ferrandiz	2,250	93.00	125.00
84-03-019	Friendly Faces, 6"	J. Ferrandiz	2,250	210.00	225.00
84-03-020	Friendly Faces, 3"	J. Ferrandiz	2,250	93.00	110.00
85-03-021	Tender Love, 6"	J. Ferrandiz	2,250	225.00	250.00
85-03-022	Tender Love, 3"	J. Ferrandiz	2,250	100.00	125.00
85-03-023	Peaceful Friends, 6"	J. Ferrandiz	2,250	250.00	250.00
85-03-024	Peaceful Friends, 3"	J. Ferrandiz	2,250	120.00	120.00
86-03-025	Season's Bounty, 6"	J. Ferrandiz	2,250	245.00	245.00
86-03-026	Season's Bounty, 3"	J. Ferrandiz	2,250	125.00	125.00
86-03-027	Golden Sheaves, 6"	J. Ferrandiz	2,250	245.00	245.00
86-03-028	Golden Sheaves, 3"	J. Ferrandiz	2,250	125.00	125.00
87-03-029	Dear Sweetheart, 6"	J. Ferrandiz	2,250	250.00	250.00
87-03-030	Dear Sweetheart, 3"	J. Ferrandiz	2,250	130.00	130.00
87-03-031	For My Sweetheart, 6"	J. Ferrandiz	2,250	250.00	250.00
87-03-032	For My Sweetheart, 3"	J. Ferrandiz	2,250	130.00	130.00
88-03-033	Extra, Extra!, 6"	J. Ferrandiz	2,250	320.00	320.00
88-03-034	Extra, Extra!, 3"	J. Ferrandiz	2,250	145.00	145.00
88-03-035	Sunny Skies, 6"	J. Ferrandiz	2,250	320.00	320.00
88-03-036	Sunny Skies, 3"	J. Ferrandiz	2,250	145.00	145.00
89-03-037	Baker Boy, 6"	J. Ferrandiz	1,500	340.00	340.00
89-03-038	Baker Boy, 3"	J. Ferrandiz	1,500	170.00	170.00
89-03-039	Pastry Girl, 6"	J. Ferrandiz	1,500	340.00	340.00
89-03-040	Pastry Girl, 3"	J. Ferrandiz	1,500	170.00	170.00
90-03-041	Alpine Music, 6"	J. Ferrandiz	1,500	450.00	450.00
90-03-042	Alpine Music, 3"	J. Ferrandiz	1,500	225.00	225.00
90-03-043	Alpine Friend, 6"	J. Ferrandiz	1,500	450.00	450.00
90-03-044	Alpine Friend, 3"	J. Ferrandiz	1,500	225.00	225.00
91-03-045	Catalonian Boy, 6"	J. Ferrandiz	1,500	500.00	500.00
91-03-046	Catalonian Boy, 3"	J. Ferrandiz	1,500	227.50	227.50
91-03-047	Catalonian Girl, 6"	J. Ferrandiz	1,500	500.00	500.00
91-03-048	Catalonian Girl,3"	J. Ferrandiz	1,500	227.50	227.50
ANRI		**Ferrandiz Woodcarvings**			
69-04-001	Sugar Heart, 6"	J. Ferrandiz	Closed	25.00	525.00
69-04-002	Sugar Heart, 3"	J. Ferrandiz	Closed	12.50	450.00
69-04-003	Angel Sugar Heart, 6"	J. Ferrandiz	Closed	25.00	2500.00
69-04-004	Heavenly Quintet, 6"	J. Ferrandiz	Closed	25.00	2000.00
69-04-005	Heavenly Gardener, 6"	J. Ferrandiz	Closed	25.00	2000.00
69-04-006	Love's Messenger, 6"	J. Ferrandiz	Closed	25.00	2000.00
74-04-007	Greetings, 6"	J. Ferrandiz	Closed	55.00	475.00
74-04-008	Greetings, 3"	J. Ferrandiz	Closed	30.00	300.00
74-04-009	New Friends, 6"	J. Ferrandiz	Closed	55.00	550.00
74-04-010	New Friends, 3"	J. Ferrandiz	Closed	30.00	275.00
74-04-011	Tender Moments, 6"	J. Ferrandiz	Closed	55.00	575.00
74-04-012	Tender Moments, 3"	J. Ferrandiz	Closed	30.00	375.00
74-04-013	Helping Hands, 6"	J. Ferrandiz	Closed	55.00	700.00
74-04-014	Helping Hands, 3"	J. Ferrandiz	Closed	30.00	350.00
74-04-015	Spring Outing, 6"	J. Ferrandiz	Closed	55.00	900.00
74-04-016	Spring Outing, 3"	J. Ferrandiz	Closed	30.00	625.00
73-04-017	Sweeper, 6"	J. Ferrandiz	Closed	75.00	425.00
73-04-018	Sweeper, 3"	J. Ferrandiz	Closed	35.00	130.00
74-04-019	The Bouquet, 6"	J. Ferrandiz	Closed	75.00	325.00
74-04-020	The Bouquet, 3"	J. Ferrandiz	Closed	35.00	175.00
70-04-021	Artist, 6"	J. Ferrandiz	Closed	25.00	350.00
74-04-022	Artist, 3"	J. Ferrandiz	Closed	30.00	175.00
74-04-023	Little Mother, 6"	J. Ferrandiz	Closed	85.00	285.00
74-04-024	Little Mother, 3"	J. Ferrandiz	Closed	136.00	290.00
74-04-025	Romeo, 6"	J. Ferrandiz	Closed	85.00	375.00
74-04-026	Romeo, 3"	J. Ferrandiz	Closed	50.00	225.00
75-04-027	Inspector, 6"	J. Ferrandiz	Closed	80.00	350.00
75-04-028	Inspector, 3"	J. Ferrandiz	Closed	40.00	225.00
76-04-029	Girl with Rooster, 6"	J. Ferrandiz	Closed	60.00	275.00
76-04-030	Girl with Rooster, 3"	J. Ferrandiz	Closed	32.50	175.00
75-04-031	The Gift, 6"	J. Ferrandiz	Closed	70.00	250.00
75-04-032	The Gift, 3"	J. Ferrandiz	Closed	40.00	150.00
75-04-033	Love Gift, 6"	J. Ferrandiz	Closed	70.00	250.00
75-04-034	Love Gift, 3"	J. Ferrandiz	Closed	40.00	150.00
77-04-035	The Blessing, 6"	J. Ferrandiz	Closed	125.00	250.00
77-04-036	The Blessing, 3"	J. Ferrandiz	Closed	45.00	150.00
69-04-037	Love Letter, 6"	J. Ferrandiz	Closed	25.00	250.00
69-04-038	Love Letter, 3"	J. Ferrandiz	Closed	12.50	150.00
75-04-039	Courting, 6"	J. Ferrandiz	Closed	150.00	450.00
75-04-040	Courting, 3"	J. Ferrandiz	Closed	70.00	235.00

Company		Series			
Number	Name	Artist	Edition Limit	Issue Price	Quote
75-04-041	Wanderlust, 6"	J. Ferrandiz	Closed	70.00	450.00
76-04-042	Wanderlust, 3"	J. Ferrandiz	Closed	32.50	125.00
75-04-043	Catch a Falling Star, 6"	J. Ferrandiz	Closed	75.00	250.00
76-04-044	Catch a Falling Star, 3"	J. Ferrandiz	Closed	35.00	150.00
75-04-045	Mother and Child, 6"	J. Ferrandiz	Closed	90.00	250.00
75-04-046	Mother and Child, 3"	J. Ferrandiz	Closed	45.00	125.00
77-04-047	Journey, 6"	J. Ferrandiz	Closed	120.00	400.00
77-04-048	Journey, 3"	J. Ferrandiz	Closed	67.50	175.00
77-04-049	Night Night, 6"	J. Ferrandiz	Closed	67.50	250-315.
77-04-050	Night Night, 3"	J. Ferrandiz	Closed	45.00	120.00
76-04-051	Sharing, 6"	J. Ferrandiz	Closed	75.00	225-275.
76-04-052	Sharing, 3"	J. Ferrandiz	Closed	32.50	130.00
82-04-053	Clarinet, 6"	J. Ferrandiz	Closed	175.00	200.00
82-04-054	Clarinet, 3"	J. Ferrandiz	Closed	80.00	100.00
82-04-055	Violin, 6"	J. Ferrandiz	Closed	175.00	195.00
82-04-056	Violin, 3"	J. Ferrandiz	Closed	80.00	95.00
82-04-057	Bagpipe, 6"	J. Ferrandiz	Closed	175.00	190.00
82-04-058	Bagpipe, 3"	J. Ferrandiz	Closed	80.00	95.00
82-04-059	Flute, 6"	J. Ferrandiz	Closed	175.00	190.00
82-04-060	Flute, 3"	J. Ferrandiz	Closed	80.00	95.00
82-04-061	Guitar, 6"	J. Ferrandiz	Closed	175.00	190.00
82-04-062	Guitar, 3"	J. Ferrandiz	Closed	80.00	95.00
82-04-063	Harmonica, 6"	J. Ferrandiz	Closed	175.00	190.00
82-04-064	Harmonica, 3"	J. Ferrandiz	Closed	80.00	95.00
82-04-065	Harmonica, 3"	J. Ferrandiz	Closed	80.00	95.00
82-04-066	Lighting the Way, 6"	J. Ferrandiz	Closed	225.00	255.00
82-04-067	Lighting the Way, 3"	J. Ferrandiz	Closed	105.00	120.00
81-04-068	Musical Basket, 6"	J. Ferrandiz	Closed	200.00	225.00
81-04-069	Musical Basket, 3"	J. Ferrandiz	Closed	90.00	115.00
82-04-070	The Good Life, 6"	J. Ferrandiz	Closed	225.00	250.00
82-04-071	The Good Life, 3"	J. Ferrandiz	Closed	100.00	200.00
82-04-072	Star Bright, 6"	J. Ferrandiz	Closed	250.00	260.00
82-04-073	Star Bright, 3"	J. Ferrandiz	Closed	110.00	125.00
82-04-074	Encore, 6"	J. Ferrandiz	Closed	225.00	235.00
82-04-075	Encore, 3"	J. Ferrandiz	Closed	100.00	115.00
82-04-076	Play It Again, 6"	J. Ferrandiz	Closed	250.00	255.00
82-04-077	Play It Again, 3"	J. Ferrandiz	Closed	100.00	120.00
73-04-078	Girl with Dove, 6"	J. Ferrandiz	Closed	50.00	205.00
73-04-079	Girl with Dove, 3"	J. Ferrandiz	Closed	30.00	110.00
79-04-080	Stitch in Time, 6"	J. Ferrandiz	Closed	150.00	235.00
79-04-081	Stitch in Time, 3"	J. Ferrandiz	Closed	75.00	125.00
79-04-082	He's My Brother, 6"	J. Ferrandiz	Closed	155.00	240.00
79-04-083	He's My Brother, 3"	J. Ferrandiz	Closed	70.00	130.00
81-04-084	Stepping Out, 6"	J. Ferrandiz	Closed	220.00	252.00
81-04-085	Stepping Out, 3"	J. Ferrandiz	Closed	95.00	110-140.
79-04-086	High Riding, 6"	J. Ferrandiz	Closed	340.00	475.00
79-04-087	High Riding, 3"	J. Ferrandiz	Closed	145.00	200.00
80-04-088	Umpapa, 4"	J. Ferrandiz	Closed	125.00	140.00
81-04-089	Jolly Piper, 3"	J. Ferrandiz	Closed	100.00	120.00
77-04-090	Tracker, 3"	J. Ferrandiz	Closed	70.00	120.00
81-04-091	Merry Melody, 3"	J. Ferrandiz	Closed	90.00	115.00
82-04-092	Guiding Light, 3"	J. Ferrandiz	Closed	100.00	115.00
82-04-093	Companions, 3"	J. Ferrandiz	Closed	95.00	115.00
77-04-094	Leading the Way, 3"	J. Ferrandiz	Closed	62.50	120.00
82-04-095	To Market, 3"	J. Ferrandiz	Closed	95.00	115.00
78-04-096	Basket of Joy, 3"	J. Ferrandiz	Closed	65.00	120.00
81-04-097	Tiny Sounds, 3"	J. Ferrandiz	Closed	90.00	105.00
78-04-198	Spring Dance, 12"	J. Ferrandiz	Closed	950.00	1750.00
78-04-199	Spring Dance, 24"	J. Ferrandiz	Closed	4750.00	6200.00
76-04-100	Gardener, 3"	J. Ferrandiz	Closed	32.00	195.00
76-04-101	Gardener, 6"	J. Ferrandiz	Closed	65.00	275.00
79-04-102	First Blossom, 3"	J. Ferrandiz	Closed	70.00	110.00
81-04-103	Sweet Arrival Pink, 6"	J. Ferrandiz	Closed	225.00	225.00
81-04-104	Sweet Arrival Pink, 3"	J. Ferrandiz	Closed	105.00	110.00
81-04-105	Sweet Arrival Blue, 6"	J. Ferrandiz	Closed	225.00	255.00
81-04-106	Sweet Arrival Blue, 3"	J. Ferrandiz	Closed	105.00	110.00
82-04-107	The Champion, 6"	J. Ferrandiz	Closed	225.00	225.00
82-04-108	The Champion, 3"	J. Ferrandiz	Closed	98.00	110.00
82-04-109	Sweet Melody, 6"	J. Ferrandiz	Closed	198.00	210.00
82-04-110	Sweet Melody, 3"	J. Ferrandiz	Closed	80.00	90.00
73-04-111	Trumpeter, 6"	J. Ferrandiz	Closed	120.00	240.00
73-04-112	Trumpeter, 3"	J. Ferrandiz	Closed	69.00	115.00
80-04-113	Trumpeter, 10"	J. Ferrandiz	Closed	500.00	500.00
84-04-114	Trumpeter, 20"	J. Ferrandiz	Closed	2350.00	3050.00
79-04-115	Peace Pipe, 3"	J. Ferrandiz	Closed	85.00	120.00
83-04-116	Peace Pipe, 10"	J. Ferrandiz	Closed	460.00	480.00
84-04-117	Peace Pipe, 20"	J. Ferrandiz	Closed	2200.00	3500.00
74-04-118	Happy Wanderer, 6"	J. Ferrandiz	Closed	70.00	200.00
74-04-119	Happy Wanderer, 3"	J. Ferrandiz	Closed	40.00	105.00
73-04-120	Happy Wanderer, 10"	J. Ferrandiz	Closed	120.00	500.00
74-04-121	Flight Into Egypt, 6"	J. Ferrandiz	Closed	70.00	500.00
74-04-122	Flight Into Egypt, 3"	J. Ferrandiz	Closed	35.00	125.00
77-04-123	Poor Boy, 6"	J. Ferrandiz	Closed	125.00	215.00
77-04-124	Poor Boy, 3"	J. Ferrandiz	Closed	50.00	110.00
79-04-125	Happy Strummer, 3"	J. Ferrandiz	Closed	75.00	110.00
78-04-126	Harvest Girl, 3"	J. Ferrandiz	Closed	75.00	110-140.
82-04-127	Hitchhiker, 6"	J. Ferrandiz	Closed	125.00	230.00
82-04-128	Hitchhiker, 3"	J. Ferrandiz	Closed	98.00	110.00
84-04-129	High Hopes, 6"	J. Ferrandiz	Closed	170.00	247.50
84-04-130	High Hopes, 3"	J. Ferrandiz	Closed	81.00	81.00
88-04-131	Abracadabra, 6"	J. Ferrandiz	3,000	315.00	345.00
88-04-132	Abracadabra, 3"	J. Ferrandiz	3,000	145.00	165.00
88-04-133	Peace Maker, 6"	J. Ferrandiz	3,000	360.00	395.00
88-04-134	Peace Maker, 3"	J. Ferrandiz	3,000	180.00	200.00
88-04-135	Picnic for Two, 6"	J. Ferrandiz	500	425.00	465.00
88-04-136	Picnic for Two, 3"	J. Ferrandiz	500	190.00	210.00
88-04-137	Bon Appetit, 6"	J. Ferrandiz	500	395.00	440.00
88-04-138	Bon Appetit, 3"	J. Ferrandiz	500	175.00	195.00
69-04-139	The Good Sheperd, 3"	J. Ferrandiz	Closed	12.50	120.50
69-04-140	The Good Shepherd, 6"	J. Ferrandiz	Closed	25.00	236.50
71-04-141	The Good Shepherd, 10"	J. Ferrandiz	Closed	90.00	90.00
75-04-142	Going Home, 3"	J. Ferrandiz	Closed	40.00	110.00
75-04-143	Going Home, 6"	J. Ferrandiz	Closed	70.00	240.00
75-04-144	Holy Family, 3"	J. Ferrandiz	Closed	75.00	250.00
75-04-145	Holy Family, 6"	J. Ferrandiz	Closed	200.00	670.00
73-04-146	Nature Girl, 3"	J. Ferrandiz	Closed	30.00	30.00
73-04-147	Nature Girl, 6"	J. Ferrandiz	Closed	60.00	272.00
73-04-148	Girl in the Egg, 3"	J. Ferrandiz	Closed	30.00	127.00
73-04-149	Girl in the Egg, 6"	J. Ferrandiz	Closed	60.00	272.00
76-04-150	Flower Girl, 3"	J. Ferrandiz	Closed	40.00	40.00
76-04-151	Flower Girl, 6"	J. Ferrandiz	Closed	90.00	310.00
76-04-152	The Letter, 3"	J. Ferrandiz	Closed	40.00	40.00
76-04-153	The Letter, 6"	J. Ferrandiz	Closed	90.00	600.00
69-04-154	Talking to the Animals, 3"	J. Ferrandiz	Closed	12.50	125.00
69-04-155	Talking to the Animals, 6"	J. Ferrandiz	Closed	45.00	45.00
71-04-156	Talking to the Animals, 10"	J. Ferrandiz	Closed	90.00	90.00
71-04-157	Talking to Animals, 20"	J. Ferrandiz	Closed	Unkn.	3000.00
70-04-158	Duet, 3"	J. Ferrandiz	Open	36.00	165.00
70-04-159	Duet, 6"	J. Ferrandiz	Open	Unkn.	355.00
73-04-160	Spring Arrivals, 3"	J. Ferrandiz	Open	30.00	145.00
73-04-161	Spring Arrivals, 6"	J. Ferrandiz	Open	50.00	340.00
80-04-162	Spring Arrivals, 10"	J. Ferrandiz	Open	435.00	500.00
80-04-163	Spring Arrivals, 20"	J. Ferrandiz	250	2,000	3300.00
75-04-164	Summertime, 3"	J. Ferrandiz	Closed	35.00	35.00
75-04-165	Summertime, 6"	J. Ferrandiz	Closed	70.00	258.00
76-04-166	Cowboy, 3"	J. Ferrandiz	Closed	35.00	140.00
84-04-167	Cowboy, 10"	J. Ferrandiz	Closed	370.00	500.00
83-04-168	Cowboy, 20"	J. Ferrandiz	Closed	2100.00	2100.00
87-04-169	Serenity, 3"	J. Ferrandiz	Closed	125.00	150.50
84-04-170	Bird's Eye View, 3"	J. Ferrandiz	Closed	88.00	129.00
84-04-171	Bird's Eye View, 6"	J. Ferrandiz	Closed	216.00	700.00
86-04-172	God's Little Helper, 2"	J. Ferrandiz	3,500	170.00	255.00
86-04-173	God's Little Helper, 4"	J. Ferrandiz	2,000	425.00	550.00
85-04-174	Butterfly Boy, 3"	J. Ferrandiz	Closed	95.00	140.00
85-04-175	Butterfly Boy, 6"	J. Ferrandiz	Closed	220.00	322.00
84-04-176	Shipmates, 3"	J. Ferrandiz	Closed	81.00	118.50
84-04-177	Shipmates, 6"	J. Ferrandiz	Closed	170.00	247.50
78-04-178	Spreading the Word, 3"	J. Ferrandiz	Closed	115.00	193.50
78-04-179	Spreading the Word, 6"	J. Ferrandiz	Closed	270.00	494.50
82-04-180	Bundle of Joy, 3"	J. Ferrandiz	Closed	100.00	300.00
82-04-181	Bundle of Joy, 6"	J. Ferrandiz	Closed	225.00	322.50
77-04-182	Riding Thru the Rain, 5"	J. Ferrandiz	Open	145.00	399.00
77-04-183	Riding Thru the Rain, 10"	J. Ferrandiz	Open	400.00	1000.00
81-04-184	Sweet Dreams, 3"	J. Ferrandiz	Closed	100.00	140.00
77-04-185	Hurdy Gurdy, 3"	J. Ferrandiz	Closed	53.00	150.00
77-04-186	Hurdy Gurdy, 6"	J. Ferrandiz	Closed	112.00	390.00
77-04-187	Proud Mother, 3"	J. Ferrandiz	Closed	52.50	150.00
77-04-188	Proud Mother, 6"	J. Ferrandiz	Closed	130.00	350.00
80-04-189	Drummer Boy, 3"	J. Ferrandiz	Closed	130.00	200.00
80-04-190	Drummer Boy, 6"	J. Ferrandiz	Closed	300.00	400.00
82-04-191	Circus Serenade, 3"	J. Ferrandiz	Closed	100.00	160.00
82-04-192	Circus Serenade, 6"	J. Ferrandiz	Closed	220.00	220.00
82-04-193	Surprise, 3"	J. Ferrandiz	Closed	100.00	150.00
82-04-194	Surprise, 6"	J. Ferrandiz	Closed	225.00	325.00
75-04-195	Cherub, 2"	J. Ferrandiz	Closed	32.00	90.00
75-04-196	Cherub, 4"	J. Ferrandiz	Closed	32.00	275.00
69-04-197	The Quintet, 3"	J. Ferrandiz	Closed	12.50	140.00
69-04-198	The Quintet, 6"	J. Ferrandiz	Closed	25.00	340.00
71-04-199	The Quintet, 10"	J. Ferrandiz	Closed	100.00	600.00
71-04-200	The Quintet, 20"	J. Ferrandiz	Closed	Unkn.	3000.00
87-04-201	Serenity, 6"	J. Ferrandiz	3,000	245.00	290.50
87-04-202	Nature's Wonder, 3"	J. Ferrandiz	3,000	125.00	150.50
87-04-203	Nature's Wonder, 6"	J. Ferrandiz	3,000	245.00	290.50
87-04-204	Black Forest Boy, 3"	J. Ferrandiz	Closed	125.00	150.50
87-04-205	Black Forest Boy, 6"	J. Ferrandiz	Closed	250.00	301.00
87-04-206	Black Forest Girl, 3"	J. Ferrandiz	Closed	125.00	150.50
87-04-207	Black Forest Girl, 6"	J. Ferrandiz	Closed	250.00	300.00
87-04-208	Heavenly Concert, 2"	J. Ferrandiz	3,500	200.00	200.00
87-04-209	Heavenly Concert, 4"	J. Ferrandiz	2,000	450.00	550.00
86-04-210	Swiss Girl, 3"	J. Ferrandiz	Open	122.00	122.00
86-04-211	Swiss Girl, 6"	J. Ferrandiz	Open	245.00	303.50
86-04-212	Swiss Boy, 3"	J. Ferrandiz	Open	122.00	161.50
86-04-213	Swiss Boy, 6"	J. Ferrandiz	Open	245.00	323.50
86-04-214	A Musical Ride, 4"	J. Ferrandiz	Closed	165.00	236.50
86-04-215	A Musical Ride, 8"	J. Ferrandiz	Closed	395.00	559.00
82-04-216	Sweet Dreams, 6"	J. Ferrandiz	Closed	225.00	330.00
83-04-217	Love Message, 3"	J. Ferrandiz	Closed	105.00	150.50
83-04-218	Love Message, 6"	J. Ferrandiz	Closed	240.00	365.50
83-04-219	Edelweiss, 3"	J. Ferrandiz	Open	95.00	140.00
83-04-220	Edelweiss, 6"	J. Ferrandiz	Open	220.00	325.00
86-04-221	Edelweiss, 10"	J. Ferrandiz	Open	500.00	750.00
86-04-222	Edelweiss, 20"	J. Ferrandiz	250	3300.00	5160.00
83-04-223	Golden Blossom, 3"	J. Ferrandiz	Open	95.00	140.00
83-04-224	Golden Blossom, 6"	J. Ferrandiz	Open	220.00	325.00
86-04-225	Golden Blossom, 10"	J. Ferrandiz	Open	500.00	750.00
86-04-226	Golden Blossom, 20"	J. Ferrandiz	250	3300.00	5160.00
86-04-227	Golden Blossom, 40"	J. Ferrandiz	50	8300.00	12950.00
88-04-228	Winter Memories, 3"	J. Ferrandiz	1,500	180.00	195.00
88-04-229	Winter Memories, 6"	J. Ferrandiz	1,500	398.00	440.00
87-04-230	Among Friends, 3"	J. Ferrandiz	Closed	125.00	150.50
87-04-231	Among Friends, 6"	J. Ferrandiz	Closed	245.00	290.50
89-04-232	Mexican Girl, 3"	J. Ferrandiz	1,500	170.00	175.00
89-04-233	Mexican Girl, 6"	J. Ferrandiz	1,500	340.00	350.00
89-04-234	Mexican Boy, 3"	J. Ferrandiz	1,500	170.00	175.00
89-04-235	Mexican Boy, 6"	J. Ferrandiz	1,500	340.00	350.00
ANRI		**Ferrandiz Message Collection**			
89-05-001	He is the Light, 4 1/2"	J. Ferrandiz	5,000	300.00	300.00
89-05-002	Heaven Sent, 4 1/2"	J. Ferrandiz	5,000	300.00	300.00
89-05-003	God's Precious Gift, 4 1/2"	J. Ferrandiz	5,000	300.00	300.00
89-05-004	Love Knows No Bounds, 4 1/2"	J. Ferrandiz	5,000	300.00	300.00
89-05-005	Love So Powerful, 4 1/2"	J. Ferrandiz	5,000	300.00	300.00
89-05-006	Light From Within, 4 1/2"	J. Ferrandiz	5,000	300.00	300.00
89-05-007	He Guides Us, 4 1/2"	J. Ferrandiz	5,000	300.00	300.00
89-05-008	God's Miracle, 4 1/2"	J. Ferrandiz	5,000	300.00	300.00
89-05-009	He is the Light, 9"	J. Ferrandiz	5,000	600.00	600.00
90-05-010	God's Creation 4 1/2"	J. Ferrandiz	5,000	300.00	300.00
90-05-011	Count Your Blessings, 4 1/2"	J. Ferrandiz	5,000	300.00	300.00
90-05-012	Christmas Carillon, 4 1/2"	J. Ferrandiz	2,500	299.00	299.00
ANRI		**Ferrandiz Mini Nativity Set**			
84-06-001	Mary, 1 1/2"	J. Ferrandiz	Open	300.00	540.00
84-06-002	Joseph, 1 1/2"	J. Ferrandiz	Open	Set	Set
84-06-003	Infant, 1 1/2"	J. Ferrandiz	Open	Set	Set
84-06-004	Leading the Way, 1 1/2"	J. Ferrandiz	Open	Set	Set
84-06-005	Ox Donkey, 1 1/2"	J. Ferrandiz	Open	Set	Set
84-06-006	Sheep Standing, 1 1/2"	J. Ferrandiz	Open	Set	Set
84-06-007	Sheep Kneeling, 1 1/2"	J. Ferrandiz	Open	Set	Set
85-06-008	Reverence, 1 1/2"	J. Ferrandiz	Open	45.00	53.00
85-06-009	Harmony, 1 1/2"	J. Ferrandiz	Open	45.00	53.00
85-06-010	Rest, 1 1/2"	J. Ferrandiz	Open	45.00	53.00
85-06-011	Thanksgiving, 1 1/2"	J. Ferrandiz	Open	45.00	53.00
85-06-012	Small Talk, 1 1/2"	J. Ferrandiz	Open	45.00	53.00
85-06-013	Camel, 1 1/2"	J. Ferrandiz	Open	45.00	53.00
85-06-014	Camel Guide, 1 1/2"	J. Ferrandiz	Open	45.00	53.00
85-06-015	Baby Camel, 1 1/2"	J. Ferrandiz	Open	45.00	53.00

Company Number	Name	Series Artist	Edition Limit	Issue Price	Quote
86-06-016	Mini Melchoir, 1 1/2"	J. Ferrandiz	Open	45.00	53.00
86-06-017	Mini Caspar, 1 1/2"	J. Ferrandiz	Open	45.00	53.00
86-06-018	Mini Balthasar, 1 1/2"	J. Ferrandiz	Open	45.00	53.00
86-06-019	Mini Angel, 1 1/2"	J. Ferrandiz	Open	45.00	53.00
86-06-020	Mini Free Ride, plus Mini Lamb, 1 1/2"	J. Ferrandiz	Open	45.00	53.00
86-06-021	Mini Weary Traveller, 1 1/2"	J. Ferrandiz	Open	45.00	53.00
86-06-022	Mini The Stray, 1 1/2"	J. Ferrandiz	Open	45.00	53.00
86-06-023	Mini The Hiker, 1 1/2"	J. Ferrandiz	Open	45.00	53.00
86-06-024	Mini Star Struck, 1 1/2"	J. Ferrandiz	Open	45.00	53.00
88-06-025	Jolly Gift, 1 1/2"	J. Ferrandiz	Open	53.00	53.00
88-06-026	Sweet Inspiration, 1 1/2"	J. Ferrandiz	Open	53.00	53.00
88-06-028	Sweet Dreams, 1 1/2"	J. Ferrandiz	Open	53.00	53.00
88-06-029	Long Journey, 1 1/2"	J. Ferrandiz	Open	53.00	53.00
88-06-030	Devotion, 1 1/2"	J. Ferrandiz	Open	53.00	53.00
ANRI		**Limited Edition Couples**			
85-07-001	Springtime Stroll, 8"	J. Ferrandiz	750	590.00	950.00
85-07-002	First Kiss, 8"	J. Ferrandiz	750	590.00	900.00
86-07-003	A Tender Touch, 8"	J. Ferrandiz	750	590.00	850.00
86-07-004	My Heart Is Yours, 8"	J. Ferrandiz	750	590.00	850.00
87-07-005	Heart to Heart, 8"	J. Ferrandiz	750	590.00	850.00
88-07-006	A Loving Hand, 8"	J. Ferrandiz	750	795.00	850.00
ANRI		**Sarah Kay Figurines**			
83-08-001	Morning Chores,6"	S. Kay	Closed	210.00	495.00
83-08-002	Morning Chores, 4"	S. Kay	Closed	95.00	300.00
83-08-003	Morning Chores, 1 1/2"	S. Kay	Closed	45.00	110.00
83-08-004	Helping Mother, 6"	S. Kay	Closed	210.00	495.00
83-08-005	Helping Mother, 4"	S. Kay	Closed	95.00	300.00
83-08-006	Helping Mother,1 1/2"	S. Kay	Closed	45.00	110.00
83-08-007	Sweeping, 6"	S. Kay	Closed	195.00	435.00
83-08-008	Sweeping, 4"	S. Kay	Closed	95.00	230.00
83-08-009	Sweeping, 1 1/2"	S. Kay	Closed	45.00	110.00
83-08-010	Playtime, 6"	S. Kay	Closed	195.00	445.00
83-08-011	Playtime, 4"	S. Kay	Closed	95.00	230.00
83-08-012	Playtime, 1 1/2"	S. Kay	Closed	45.00	110.00
83-08-013	Feeding the Chickens, 6"	S. Kay	Closed	195.00	435.00
83-08-014	Feeding the Chickens, 4"	S. Kay	Closed	95.00	230.00
83-08-015	Feeding the Chickens, 1 1/2"	S. Kay	Closed	45.00	110.00
83-08-016	Waiting for Mother, 6"	S. Kay	Closed	195.00	445.00
83-08-017	Waiting for Mother, 4"	S. Kay	Closed	95.00	230.00
83-08-018	Waiting for Mother, 1 1/2"	S. Kay	Closed	45.00	110.00
83-08-019	Waiting for Mother, 11"	S. Kay	Closed	495.00	795.00
83-08-020	Bedtime, 6"	S. Kay	Closed	195.00	435.00
83-08-021	Bedtime, 4"	S. Kay	Closed	95.00	230.00
83-08-022	Bedtime, 1 1/2"	S. Kay	Closed	45.00	110.00
83-08-023	From the Garden, 6"	S. Kay	Closed	195.00	450.00
83-08-024	From the Garden, 4"	S. Kay	Closed	95.00	235.00
83-08-025	From the Garden, 1 1/2"	S. Kay	Closed	45.00	110.00
83-08-026	Wake Up Kiss, 6"	S. Kay	Closed	210.00	550.00
84-08-027	Wake Up Kiss, 4"	S. Kay	Closed	95.00	155.00
84-08-028	Wake Up Kiss, 1 1/2"	S. Kay	Closed	45.00	550.00
84-08-029	Finding R Way, 6"	S. Kay	Closed	210.00	495.00
84-08-030	Finding R Way, 4"	S. Kay	Closed	95.00	245.00
84-08-031	Finding R Way, 1 1/2"	S. Kay	Closed	45.00	135.00
84-08-032	Daydreaming, 6"	S. Kay	Closed	195.00	445.00
84-08-033	Daydreaming, 4"	S. Kay	Closed	95.00	235.00
84-08-034	Daydreaming,1 1/2"	S. Kay	Closed	45.00	125.00
84-08-035	Off to School, 6"	S. Kay	4,000	195.00	325.00
84-08-036	Off to School, 4"	S. Kay	4,000	95.00	185.00
84-08-037	Off to School,1 1/2"	S. Kay	7,500	45.00	125.00
84-08-038	Off to School, 11"	S. Kay	750	Unkn.	770.00
84-08-039	Off to School, 20"	S. Kay	100	Unkn.	4000.00
84-08-040	Flowers for You, 6"	S. Kay	Closed	195.00	430.00
84-08-041	Flowers for You, 4"	S. Kay	Closed	95.00	230.00
84-08-042	Flowers for You, 1 1/2"	S. Kay	Closed	45.00	125.00
84-08-043	Watchful Eye, 6"	S. Kay	Closed	195.00	445.00
84-08-044	Watchful Eye, 4"	S. Kay	Closed	95.00	235.00
84-08-045	Watchful Eye,1 1/2"	S. Kay	Closed	45.00	125.00
84-08-046	Special Delivery, 6"	S. Kay	Closed	195.00	312.00
84-08-047	Special Delivery, 4"	S. Kay	Closed	95.00	172.00
84-08-048	Special Delivery ,1 1/2"	S. Kay	Closed	45.00	125.00
84-08-049	Tag Along, 6"	S. Kay	4,000	195.00	290.00
84-08-050	Tag Along, 4"	S. Kay	4,000	95.00	225.00
84-08-051	Tag Along,1 1/2"	S. Kay	7,500	45.00	130.00
85-08-052	A Special Day, 6"	S. Kay	Closed	195.00	325.00
85-08-053	A Special Day, 4"	S. Kay	Closed	95.00	185.00
85-08-054	Afternoon Tea, 6"	S. Kay	Closed	195.00	325.00
85-08-055	Afternoon Tea, 4"	S. Kay	Closed	95.00	185.00
85-08-056	Afternoon Tea, 11"	S. Kay	Closed	Unkn.	770.00
85-08-057	Afternoon Tea, 20"	S. Kay	Closed	Unkn.	3500.00
85-08-058	Nightie Night, 6"	S. Kay	Closed	195.00	325.00
85-08-059	Nightie Night, 4"	S. Kay	Closed	95.00	185.00
85-08-060	Yuletide Cheer, 6"	S. Kay	Closed	210.00	435.00
85-08-061	Yuletide Cheer, 4"	S. Kay	4,000	95.00	185.00
85-08-062	'Tis the Season, 6"	S. Kay	Closed	210.00	425.00
85-08-063	'Tis the Season, 4"	S. Kay	4,000	95.00	185.00
85-08-064	Giddyap!, 6"	S. Kay	Closed	195.00	325.00
85-08-065	Giddyap!, 4"	S. Kay	Closed	95.00	185.00
86-08-066	Our Puppy, 4"	S. Kay	Closed	95.00	185.00
86-08-067	Our Puppy, 6"	S. Kay	Closed	210.00	355.00
86-08-068	Our Puppy, 1-1/2"	S. Kay	Closed	45.00	90.00
86-08-069	Always By My Side,4"	S. Kay	Closed	95.00	195.00
86-08-070	Always By My Side, 6"	S. Kay	Closed	195.00	375.00
86-08-071	Always By My Side, 1-1/2"	S. Kay	Closed	45.00	95.00
86-08-072	Finishing Touch, 4"	S. Kay	4,000	95.00	172.00
86-08-073	Finishing Touch, 6"	S. Kay	Closed	195.00	312.00
86-08-074	Finishing Touch, 1-1/2"	S. Kay	7,500	45.00	85.00
86-08-075	Good As New, 4"	S. Kay	4,000	95.00	185.00
86-08-076	Good As New, 6"	S. Kay	4,000	195.00	325.00
86-08-077	Good As New, 1-1/2"	S. Kay	7,500	45.00	90.00
86-08-078	Bunny Hug, 4"	S. Kay	4,000	95.00	172.00
86-08-079	Bunny Hug, 6"	S. Kay	2,000	210.00	395.00
86-08-080	Bunny Hug, 1-1/2"	S. Kay	7,500	45.00	85.00
86-08-081	Sweet Treat, 4"	S. Kay	4,000	95.00	172.00
86-08-082	Sweet Treat, 6"	S. Kay	4,000	195.00	312.00
86-08-083	Sweet Treat, 1-1/2"	S. Kay	7,500	45.00	85.00
86-08-084	To Love And To Cherish, 4"	S. Kay	Closed	95.00	172.00
86-08-085	To Love And To Cherish, 6"	S. Kay	Closed	195.00	312.00
86-08-086	To Love And To Cherish, 1-1/2"	S. Kay	Closed	45.00	85.00
86-08-087	To Love and To Cherish, 11"	S. Kay	Closed	Unkn.	667.00
86-08-088	To Love and To Cherish, 20"	S. Kay	Closed	Unkn.	3600.00
86-08-089	With This Ring, 4"	S. Kay	Closed	95.00	172.00
86-08-090	With This Ring, 6"	S. Kay	Closed	195.00	312.00
86-08-091	With This Ring, 1-1/2"	S. Kay	Closed	45.00	85.00
86-08-092	With This Ring, 11"	S. Kay	Closed	Unkn.	667.50
86-08-093	With This Ring, 20"	S. Kay	Closed	Unkn.	3600.00
87-08-094	All Aboard, 6"	S. Kay	Closed	265.00	355.00
87-08-095	All Aboard, 4"	S. Kay	Closed	130.00	185.00
87-08-096	All Aboard, 1-1/2"	S. Kay	Closed	49.50	90.00
87-08-097	Let's Play, 6"	S. Kay	Closed	265.00	355.00
87-08-098	Let's Play, 4"	S. Kay	Closed	130.00	185.00
87-08-099	Let's Play, 1-1/2"	S. Kay	Closed	49.50	90.00
87-08-100	A Loving Spoonful, 6"	S. Kay	4,000	295.00	400.00
87-08-101	A Loving Spoonful, 4"	S. Kay	4,000	150.00	200.00
87-08-102	A Loving Spoonful, 1-1/2"	S. Kay	7,500	49.50	90.00
87-08-103	Little Nanny, 6"	S. Kay	Closed	295.00	400.00
87-08-104	Little Nanny, 4"	S. Kay	Closed	150.00	200.00
87-08-105	Little Nanny, 1-1/2"	S. Kay	Closed	49.50	90.00
87-08-106	All Mine, 6"	S. Kay	Closed	245.00	465.00
87-08-107	All Mine, 4"	S. Kay	Closed	130.00	225.00
87-08-108	All Mine, 1-1/2"	S. Kay	Closed	49.50	95.00
87-08-109	Cuddles, 6"	S. Kay	Closed	245.00	465.00
87-08-110	Cuddles, 4"	S. Kay	Closed	130.00	225.00
87-08-111	Cuddles, 1-1/2"	S. Kay	Closed	49.50	95.00
88-08-112	My Little Brother, 6"	S. Kay	2,000	375.00	450.00
88-08-113	My Little Brother, 4"	S. Kay	2,000	195.00	225.00
88-08-114	My Little Brother, 1-1/2"	S. Kay	3,700	70.00	90.00
88-08-115	Purrfect Day, 6"	S. Kay	2,000	265.00	455.00
88-08-116	Purrfect Day 4"	S. Kay	2,000	184.00	215.00
88-08-117	Purrfect Day, 1-1/2"	S. Kay	3,700	70.00	90.00
88-08-118	Penny for Your Thoughts, 6"	S. Kay	2,000	365.00	455.00
88-08-119	Penny for Your Thoughts 4"	S. Kay	2,000	185.00	215.00
88-08-120	Penny for Your Thoughts, 1-1/2"	S. Kay	3,700	70.00	90.00
88-08-121	New Home, 6"	S. Kay	2,000	365.00	500.00
88-08-122	New Home, 4"	S. Kay	2,000	185.00	240.00
88-08-123	New Home, 1-1/2"	S. Kay	3,700	70.00	90.00
88-08-124	Ginger Snap, 6"	S. Kay	Closed	300.00	355.00
88-08-125	Ginger Snap, 4"	S. Kay	Closed	150.00	185.00
88-08-126	Ginger Snap, 1-1/2"	S. Kay	Closed	70.00	90.00
88-08-127	Hidden Treasures, 6"	S. Kay	Closed	300.00	355.00
88-08-128	Hidden Treasures, 4"	S. Kay	Closed	150.00	185.00
88-08-129	Hidden Treasures, 1-1/2"	S. Kay	Closed	70.00	90.00
89-08-130	First School Day, 6"	S. Kay	2,000	550.00	630.00
89-08-131	First School Day, 4"	S. Kay	2,000	290.00	295.00
89-08-132	First School Day, 1 1/2"	S. Kay	3,500	85.00	95.00
89-08-133	Yearly Check-Up, 6"	S. Kay	2,000	390.00	390.00
89-08-134	Yearly Check-Up, 4"	S. Kay	2,000	190.00	195.00
89-08-135	Yearly Check-Up, 1 1/2"	S. Kay	3,500	85.00	95.00
89-08-136	House Call, 6"	S. Kay	2,000	390.00	390.00
89-08-137	House Call, 4"	S. Kay	2,000	190.00	195.00
89-08-138	House Call, 1 1/2"	S. Kay	3,500	85.00	95.00
89-08-139	Take Me Along, 6"	S. Kay	1,000	440.00	475.00
89-08-140	Take Me Along, 4"	S. Kay	2,000	220.00	240.00
89-08-141	Take Me Along, 1 1/2"	S. Kay	3,500	85.00	95.00
89-08-142	Garden Party, 6"	S. Kay	2,000	440.00	475.00
89-08-143	Garden Party, 4"	S. Kay	2,000	220.00	240.00
89-08-144	Garden Party, 1 1/2"	S. Kay	3,500	85.00	95.00
89-08-145	Fisherboy, 6"	S. Kay	1,000	440.00	475.00
89-08-146	Fisherboy, 4"	S. Kay	2,000	220.00	240.00
89-08-147	Fisherboy, 1 1/2"	S. Kay	3,500	85.00	95.00
89-08-148	Cherish, 6"	S. Kay	2,000	398.00	450.00
89-08-149	Cherish, 4"	S. Kay	2,000	199.00	225.00
89-08-150	Cherish, 1 1/2"	S. Kay	3,500	80.00	95.00
90-08-151	Holiday Cheer, 6"	S. Kay	1,000	450.00	495.00
90-08-152	Holiday Cheer, 4"	S. Kay	2,000	225.00	240.00
90-08-153	Holiday Cheer, 1 1/2"	S. Kay	3,500	90.00	95.00
90-08-154	Tender Loving Care, 6"	S. Kay	2,000	440.00	475.00
90-08-155	Tender Loving Care, 4"	S. Kay	2,000	220.00	240.00
90-08-156	Tender Loving Care, 1 1/2"	S. Kay	3,500	90.00	95.00
90-08-157	Spring Fever, 6"	S. Kay	2,000	450.00	495.00
90-08-158	Spring Fever, 4"	S. Kay	2,000	225.00	240.00
90-08-159	Spring Fever, 1 1/2"	S. Kay	3,500	90.00	95.00
90-08-160	Batter Up, 6"	S. Kay	2,000	440.00	450.00
90-08-161	Batter Up, 4"	S. Kay	2,000	220.00	225.00
90-08-162	Batter Up, 1 1/2"	S. Kay	3,500	90.00	95.00
90-08-163	Seasons Greetings, 6"	S. Kay	1,000	450.00	495.00
90-08-164	Seasons Greetings, 4"	S. Kay	2,000	225.00	240.00
90-08-165	Seasons Greetings, 1 1/2"	S. Kay	3,500	90.00	95.00
90-08-166	Shootin' Hoops, 6"	S. Kay	2,000	440.00	450.00
90-08-167	Shootin' Hoops, 4"	S. Kay	2,000	220.00	225.00
90-08-168	Shootin' Hoops,1 1/2"	S. Kay	3,500	90.00	95.00
91-08-169	Figure Eight, 6"	S. Kay	2,000	550.00	550.00
91-08-170	Figure Eight, 4"	S. Kay	2,000	270.00	270.00
91-08-171	Figure Eight, 1 1/2"	S. Kay	3,750	110.00	110.00
91-08-172	Season's Joy, 6"	S. Kay	1,000	550.00	550.00
91-08-173	Season's Joy, 4"	S. Kay	2,000	270.00	270.00
91-08-174	Season's Joy, 1 1/2"	S. Kay	3,750	110.00	110.00
91-08-175	Winter Surprise, 6"	S. Kay	1,000	550.00	550.00
91-08-176	Winter Surprise, 4"	S. Kay	2,000	270.00	270.00
91-08-177	Winter Surprise, 1 1/2"	S. Kay	3,750	110.00	110.00
91-08-178	Dress Up, 6"	S. Kay	2,000	550.00	550.00
91-08-179	Dress Up, 4"	S. Kay	2,000	270.00	270.00
91-08-180	Dress Up, 1 1/2"	S. Kay	3,750	110.00	110.00
91-08-181	Touch Down, 1 1/2"	S. Kay	3,750	110.00	110.00
91-08-182	Touch Down, 6"	S. Kay	2,000	550.00	550.00
91-08-183	Touch Down, 4"	S. Kay	2,000	270.00	270.00
91-08-184	Touch Down, 1 1/2"	S. Kay	3,750	110.00	110.00
91-08-185	Fore!!, 6"	S. Kay	2,000	550.00	550.00
91-08-186	Fore!!, 4"	S. Kay	2,000	270.00	270.00
91-08-187	Fore!!, 1 1/2"	S. Kay	3,750	110.00	110.00
ANRI		**Sarah Kay Santas**			
88-09-001	Jolly St. Nick, 6"	S. Kay	Closed	398.00	850.00
88-09-002	Jolly St. Nick, 4"	S. Kay	Closed	199.00	300-550.
88-09-003	Jolly Santa, 6"	S. Kay	Closed	480.00	600.00
88-09-004	Jolly Santa, 4"	S. Kay	Closed	235.00	300.00
89-09-005	Jolly Santa, 12"	S. Kay	Closed	1300.00	1300.00
89-09-006	Santa, 6"	S. Kay	750	480.00	480.00
89-09-007	Santa, 4"	S. Kay	750	235.00	235.00
90-09-008	Kris Kringle Santa, 6"	S. Kay	750	550.00	550.00
90-09-009	Kris Kringle Santa, 4"	S. Kay	750	275.00	275.00
91-09-010	A Friend To All, 6"	S. Kay	750	590.00	590.00
91-09-011	A Friend To All, 4"	S. Kay	750	300.00	300.00

Company / Number	Name	Series / Artist	Edition Limit	Issue Price	Quote
ANRI		**Sarah Kay Mini Santas**			
91-10-001	Jolly St. Nick, 1 1/2"	S. Kay	2,500	110.00	110.00
91-10-002	Jolly Santa, 1 1/2"	S. Kay	2,500	110.00	110.00
91-10-003	Sarah Kay Santa, 1 1/2"	S. Kay	2,500	110.00	110.00
91-10-004	Kris Kringle, 1 1/2"	S. Kay	2,500	110.00	110.00
ANRI		**Club ANRI**			
83-11-001	Welcome 4"	J. Ferrandiz	Closed	110.00	395.00
84-11-002	My Friend 4"	J. Ferrandiz	Closed	110.00	400.00
84-11-003	Apple of My Eye 4-1/2"	S. Kay	Closed	135.00	385.00
85-11-004	Harvest Time 4"	J. Ferrandiz	Closed	125.00	175-385.
85-11-005	Dad's Helper 4-1/2"	S. Kay	Closed	135.00	150-375.
86-11-006	Harvest's Helper 4"	J. Ferrandiz	Closed	135.00	175-335.
86-11-007	Romantic Notions 4"	S. Kay	Closed	135.00	175-310.
86-11-008	Celebration March 5"	J. Ferrandiz	Closed	165.00	225-295.
87-11-009	Will You Be Mine 4"	J. Ferrandiz	Closed	135.00	175-310.
86-11-010	Make A Wish 4"	S. Kay	Closed	165.00	215-325.
87-11-011	A Young Man's Fancy 4"	S. Kay	Closed	135.00	165-265.
88-11-012	Forever Yours 4"	J. Ferrandiz	Closed	170.00	250.00
88-11-013	I've Got a Secret 4"	S. Kay	Closed	170.00	205.00
88-11-014	Maestro Mickey 4 1/2"	Disney Studios	Closed	170.00	200-215.
89-11-015	Diva Minnie 41/2"	Disney Studios	5,000	190.00	190.00
89-11-016	I'll Never Tell 4"	S. Kay	Closed	190.00	190.00
89-11-017	Twenty Years of Love 4"	J. Ferrandiz	Closed	190.00	190.00
90-11-018	You Are My Sunshine 4"	J. Ferrandiz	Yr.Iss.	220.00	220.00
90-11-019	A Little Bashful 4"	S. Kay	Yr.Iss.	220.00	220.00
90-11-020	Dapper Donald 4"	Disney Studio	5,000	199.00	199.00
91-11-021	With All My Heart 4"	J. Ferrandiz	N/A	250.00	250.00
91-11-022	Kiss Me 4"	S.Kay	N/A	250.00	250.00
91-11-023	Daisy Duck 4 1/2"	Disney Studio	N/A	250.00	250.00
92-11-024	You Are My All 4"	J. Ferrandiz	N/A	260.00	260.00
92-11-025	My Present For You 4"	S. Kay	N/A	270.00	270.00
ANRI		**Disney Woodcarving**			
87-12-001	Mickey Mouse, 4"	Disney Studio	Closed	150.00	210.00
87-12-002	Minnie Mouse, 4"	Disney Studio	Closed	150.00	210.00
87-12-003	Pinocchio, 4"	Disney Studio	Closed	150.00	195.00
87-12-004	Donald Duck, 4"	Disney Studio	Closed	150.00	195.00
87-12-005	Goofy, 4"	Disney Studio	Closed	150.00	195.00
87-12-006	Mickey & Minnie, 6" (matching numbers)	Disney Studio	Closed	625.00	1650.00
88-12-007	Donald Duck, 6"	Disney Studio	Closed	350.00	700.00
88-12-008	Goofy, 6"	Disney Studio	Closed	380.00	700.00
88-12-009	Mickey Mouse, 4"	Disney Studio	Closed	180.00	199.00
88-12-010	Pluto, 4"	Disney Studio	Closed	180.00	199.00
88-12-011	Pinocchio, 4"	Disney Studio	Closed	180.00	199.00
88-12-012	Donald Duck, 4"	Disney Studio	Closed	180.00	199.00
88-12-013	Goofy, 4"	Disney Studio	Closed	180.00	199.00
88-12-014	Mickey Mouse, 1-3/4"	Disney Studio	Closed	80.00	100.00
88-12-015	Pluto, 1-3/4"	Disney Studio	Closed	80.00	100.00
88-12-016	Pinocchio, 1-3/4"	Disney Studio	Closed	80.00	100.00
88-12-017	Donald Duck, 1-3/4"	Disney Studio	Closed	80.00	100.00
88-12-018	Goofy, 1-3/4"	Disney Studio	Closed	80.00	100.00
89-12-019	Pluto, 4"	Disney Studio	Closed	190.00	205.00
88-12-020	Pluto, 6"	Disney Studio	Closed	350.00	350.00
88-12-021	Goofy, 6"	Disney Studio	Closed	350.00	350.00
89-12-022	Mickey, 4"	Disney Studio	Closed	190.00	205.00
89-12-023	Minnie, 4"	Disney Studio	Closed	190.00	205.00
89-12-024	Donald, 4"	Disney Studio	Closed	190.00	205.00
89-12-025	Daisy, 4"	Disney Studio	Closed	190.00	205.00
89-12-026	Goofy, 4"	Disney Studio	Closed	190.00	205.00
89-12-027	Mini Mickey, 2"	Disney Studio	Closed	85.00	100.00
89-12-028	Mini Minnie, 2"	Disney Studio	Closed	85.00	100.00
89-12-029	Mini Donald, 2"	Disney Studio	Closed	85.00	100.00
89-12-030	Minnie Daisy, 2"	Disney Studio	Closed	85.00	100.00
89-12-031	Mini Goofy, 2"	Disney Studio	Closed	85.00	100.00
89-12-032	Mini Pluto, 2"	Disney Studio	Closed	85.00	100.00
89-12-033	Mickey, 10"	Disney Studio	Closed	700.00	750.00
89-12-034	Minnie, 10"	Disney Studio	Closed	700.00	750.00
89-12-035	Mickey, 20"	Disney Studio	Closed	3500.00	3500.00
89-12-036	Minnie, 20"	Disney Studio	Closed	3500.00	3500.00
89-12-037	Mickey & Minnie, 20" matched set	Disney Studio	Closed	7000.00	7000.00
89-12-038	Mickey & Minnie Set, 6"	Disney Studio	Closed	700.00	700.00
88-12-039	Mickey Sorcerer's Apprentice, 6"	Disney Studio	Closed	350.00	700.00
88-12-040	Mickey Sorcerer's Apprentice, 4"	Disney Studio	Closed	180.00	199.00
88-12-041	Mickey Sorcerer's Apprentice, 2"	Disney Studio	Closed	80.00	100.00
89-12-042	Pinocchio, 6"	Disney Studio	Closed	350.00	350.00
89-12-043	Pinocchio, 4"	Disney Studio	Closed	190.00	199.00
89-12-044	Pinocchio, 2"	Disney Studio	Closed	85.00	100.00
89-12-045	Pinocchio, 10"	Disney Studio	Closed	700.00	700.00
89-12-046	Pinocchio, 20"	Disney Studio	Closed	3500.00	3500.00
90-12-047	Mickey Mouse, 4"	Disney Studio	Closed	199.00	205.00
90-12-045	Mickey Mouse, 2"	Disney Studio	Closed	100.00	100.00
90-12-049	Minnie Mouse, 4"	Disney Studio	Closed	199.00	205.00
90-12-050	Minnie Mouse, 2"	Disney Studio	Closed	100.00	100.00
90-12-051	Chef Goofy, 5"	Disney Studio	Closed	265.00	265.00
90-12-052	Chef Goofy, 2 1/2"	Disney Studio	Closed	125.00	125.00
90-12-053	Donald & Daisy, 6" (Matched Set)	Disney Studio	Closed	700.00	700.00
91-12-054	Mickey Skating, 4"	Disney Studio	Closed	250.00	250.00
91-12-055	Minnie Skating, 4"	Disney Studio	Closed	250.00	250.00
91-12-056	Mickey Skating, 2"	Disney Studio	Closed	120.00	120.00
91-12-057	Minnie Skating, 2"	Disney Studio	Closed	120.00	120.00
91-12-058	Bell Boy Donald, 4"	Disney Studio	Closed	250.00	250.00
91-12-059	Bell Boy Donald, 6"	Disney Studio	Closed	400.00	400.00
ANRI		**Mickey Mouse Thru The Ages**			
90-13-001	Steam Boat Willie, 4"	Disney Studio	Closed	295.00	295.00
91-13-002	The Mad Dog, 4"	Disney Studio	Closed	500.00	500.00
Armani		**Wildlife**			
83-01-001	Eagle 3213	G. Armani	Open	210.00	425.00
83-01-002	Royal Eagle with Babies 3553	G. Armani	Open	215.00	400.00
82-01-003	Snow Bird 5548	G. Armani	Open	100.00	180.00
88-01-004	Peacock 455S	G. Armani	5,000	600.00	650.00
88-01-005	Peacock 458S	G. Armani	5,000	630.00	675.00
88-01-006	Bird Of Paradise 454S	G. Armani	5,000	475.00	550.00
90-01-007	Three Doves 996S	G. Armani	5,000	670.00	700.00
90-01-008	Soaring Eagles 970S	G. Armani	5,000	620.00	650.00
90-01-009	Bird of Paradise 718S	G. Armani	5,000	550.00	550.00
Armani		**My Fair Ladies**			
87-02-001	Lady With Peacock 385C	G. Armani	Retrd.	380.00	650-1800.
87-02-002	Lady with Mirror 386C	G. Armani	Retrd.	300.00	400.00
87-02-003	Lady with Muff 388C	G. Armani	5,000	250.00	450.00
87-02-004	Lady With Fan 387C	G. Armani	5,000	300.00	400.00
87-02-005	Flamenco Dancer 389C	G. Armani	5,000	400.00	500.00
87-02-006	Lady With Book 384C	G. Armani	5,000	300.00	450.00
87-02-007	Lady & Great Dane 429C	G. Armani	5,000	375.00	475.00
87-02-008	Mother & Child 405C	G. Armani	5,000	410.00	550.00
89-02-009	Lady With Parrot 616C	G. Armani	Retrd.	400.00	500.00
Armani		**Wedding**			
82-03-001	Wedding Couple 5132	G. Armani	Open	110.00	190.00
87-03-002	Wedding Couple 407C	G. Armani	Open	525.00	550.00
88-03-003	Bride & Groom Wedding 475P	G. Armani	Open	270.00	285.00
90-03-003	Just Married 827C	G. Armani	5,000	950.00	1000.00
91-03-004	Wedding Couple 813C	G. Armani	7,500	400.00	400.00
91-03-005	Wedding Couple 814C	G. Armani	7,500	600.00	600.00
91-03-006	Wedding Couple 815C	G. Armani	7,500	500.00	500.00
Armani		**Special Times**			
82-04-001	Sledding 111E	G. Armani	Open	115.00	250.00
82-04-002	Girl with Sheep Dog 5117E	G. Armani	Open	100.00	210.00
82-04-003	Girl with Chicks 5122E	G. Armani	Suspd.	95.00	165.00
82-04-004	Shy Kiss 5138E	G. Armani	Open	125.00	280.00
82-04-005	Soccer Boy 5109	G. Armani	Open	75.00	180.00
82-04-006	Card Players (Cheaters) 3280	G. Armani	Open	400.00	1000.00
91-04-007	Couple in Car 862C	G. Armani	5,000	1000.00	1000.00
91-04-008	Lady with Car 861C	G. Armani	3,000	900.00	900.00
Armani		**Premiere Ballerina**			
88-05-001	Ballerina Group in Flight 518C	G. Armani	7,500	810.00	900.00
88-05-002	Ballerina with Drape 504C	G. Armani	10,000	450.00	550.00
88-05-003	Ballerina 508C	G. Armani	10,000	430.00	530.00
88-05-004	Two Ballerinas 515C	G. Armani	7,500	620.00	775.00
88-05-005	Ballerina in Flight 503C	G. Armani	10,000	420.00	500.00
88-05-006	Ballerina 517C	G. Armani	10,000	325.00	530.00
Armani		**Religious**			
87-06-001	Choir Boys 900	G. Armani	5,000	350.00	620.00
88-06-002	Crucifix 1158C	G. Armani	Retrd.	155.00	325-350.
90-06-003	Crucifix Plaque 711C	G. Armani	15,000	265.00	265.00
91-06-004	Crucifix 790C	G. Armani	15,000	180.00	180.00
Armani		**Pearls Of The Orient**			
89-07-001	Madame Butterfly 610C	G. Armani	10,000	450.00	500.00
89-07-002	Turnadot 611C	G. Armani	10,000	475.00	500.00
89-07-003	Chu Chu San 612C	G. Armani	10,000	500.00	550.00
89-07-004	Lotus Blossom 613C	G. Armani	10,000	450.00	475.00
Armani		**Moonlight Masquerade**			
90-08-001	Harlequin Lady 740C	G. Armani	7,500	450.00	450.00
90-08-002	Lady Pierrot 741C	G. Armani	7,500	390.00	390.00
90-08-003	Lady Clown with Cane 742C	G. Armani	7,500	390.00	390.00
90-08-004	Lady Clown with Doll 743C	G. Armani	7,500	410.00	410.00
90-08-005	Queen of Hearts 744C	G. Armani	7,500	450.00	450.00
Armani		**Renaissance**			
92-09-001	Abundance 870C	G. Armani	5,000	600.00	600.00
92-09-002	Vanity 871C	G. Armani	5,000	585.00	585.00
92-09-003	Twilight 872C	G. Armani	5,000	560.00	560.00
92-09-004	Dawn 874C	G. Armani	5,000	500.00	500.00
Armani		**Special Issues**			
91-10-001	Discovery of America 867C	G. Armani	2,500	400.00	400.00
Armani		**G. Armani Society Members Only Figurine**			
90-11-001	Awakening 591C	G. Armani	Closed	137.50	600-1500.
90-11-002	My Fine Feathered Friends (Bonus)122S	G. Armani	Closed	175.00	175.00
91-11-003	Ruffles 745E	G. Armani	Closed	139.00	300-450.
91-11-004	Peace & Harmony (Bonus) 824C	G. Armani	7,500	300.00	300.00
91-11-005	Eve 590T	G. Armani	Closed	250.00	500-650.
92-11-006	Ascent 866C	G. Armani	Yr.Iss.	195.00	195.00
92-11-007	Lady with Basket of Flowers 961C	G. Armani	Yr.Iss.	250.00	250.00
92-11-008	Boy with Dog 409S	G. Armani	Yr.Iss.	200.00	200.00
Armani		**Garden Series**			
91-12-001	Lady with Cornucopie 870C	G. Armani	10,000	600.00	600.00
91-12-002	Lady with Peacock 871C	G. Armani	10,000	585.00	585.00
91-12-003	Lady with Violin 872C	G. Armani	10,000	560.00	560.00
91-12-004	Lady with Harp 874C	G. Armani	10,000	500.00	500.00
Armani		**Can-Can Dancers**			
89-13-001	Two Can-Can Dancers 516C	G. Armani	1,000	820.00	975.00
Armani		**Four Seasons**			
90-14-001	Lady With Bicycle (Spring) 539C	G. Armani	Open	550.00	550.00
90-14-002	Lady With Umbrella (Fall) 541C	G. Armani	Open	475.00	475.00
90-14-003	Lady With Ice Skates (Winter) 542C	G. Armani	Open	400.00	400.00
90-14-004	Lady on Seashore (Summer) 540C	G. Armani	Open	440.00	440.00
Armstrong's		**The Red Skelton Collection**			
81-01-001	Freddie in the Bathtub	R. Skelton	7,500	80.00	80.00
81-01-002	Freddie on the Green	R. Skelton	7,500	80.00	80.00
81-01-003	Freddie the Freeloader	R. Skelton	7,500	70.00	150.00
81-01-004	Sheriff Deadeye	R. Skelton	7,500	75.00	75.00
81-01-005	Clem Kadiddlehopper	R. Skelton	7,500	75.00	75.00
81-01-006	Jr., The Mean Widdle Kid	R. Skelton	7,500	75.00	150.00
81-01-007	San Fernando Red	R. Skelton	7,500	75.00	150.00
Armstrong's		**Armstrong's/Ron Lee**			
84-02-001	Captain Freddie	R. Skelton	7,500	85.00	150.00
84-02-002	Freddie the Torchbearer	R. Skelton	7,500	110.00	190.00
Armstrong's		**Happy Art**			
82-03-001	Woody's Triple Self-Portrait	W. Lantz	5,000	95.00	300.00
Armstrong's		**Ceramic Plaque**			
85-04-001	Flamborough Head	A. D'Estrehan	500	195.00	195.00
85-04-002	Flamborough Head (Artist's Proof)	A. D'Estrehan	50	295.00	295.00
88-04-003	Katrina	L. De Winne	500	195.00	195.00
Armstrong's		**Ceramic Plaque**			
85-05-001	The Stamp Collector	M. Paredes	400	195.00	195.00
85-05-002	The Stamp Collector (Artist's Proof)	M. Paredes	50	295.00	295.00
85-05-003	Mother's Pride	M. Paredes	400	195.00	195.00
85-05-004	Mother's Pride (Artist's Proof)	M. Paredes	50	295.00	295.00

Company / Number	Name / Series	Artist	Edition Limit	Issue Price	Quote
Armstrong's	**Pro Autographed Ceramic Baseball Card Plaque**				
85-06-001	Brett, Garvey, Jackson, Rose, Seaver, auto, 3-1/4X5	Unknown	1,000	149.75	149.75
Armstrong's	**Pro Classic Ceramic Baseball Card Plaques**				
85-07-001	George Brett, 2-1/2" x 3-1/2"	Unknown	Open	9.95	9.95
85-07-002	Steve Garvey, 2-1/2" x 3-1/2"	Unknown	Open	9.95	9.95
85-07-003	Reggie Jackson, 2-1/2" x 3-1/2"	Unknown	Open	9.95	9.95
85-07-004	Pete Rose, 2-1/2" x 3-1/2"	Unknown	Open	9.95	9.95
85-07-005	Tom Seaver, 2-1/2" x 3-1/2"	Unknown	Open	9.95	9.95
Artaffects	**Heavenly Blessings**				
85-01-001	First Step	Unknown	Open	15.00	19.00
85-01-002	Heaven Scent	Unknown	Open	15.00	19.00
85-01-003	Bubbles	Unknown	Open	15.00	19.00
85-01-004	So Soft	Unknown	Open	15.00	19.00
85-01-005	See!	Unknown	Open	15.00	19.00
85-01-006	Listen!	Unknown	Open	15.00	19.00
85-01-007	Happy Birthday	Unknown	Open	15.00	19.00
85-01-008	Day Dreams	Unknown	Open	15.00	19.00
85-01-009	Just Up	Unknown	Open	15.00	19.00
85-01-010	Beddy Bye	Unknown	Open	15.00	19.00
85-01-011	Race You!	Unknown	Open	15.00	19.00
85-01-012	Yum, Yum!	Unknown	Open	15.00	19.00
Artaffects	**Musical Figurines**				
84-02-001	The Wedding	R. Sauber	Open	65.00	70.00
86-02-002	The Anniversary	R. Sauber	Open	65.00	70.00
87-02-003	Home Sweet Home	R. Sauber	Open	65.00	70.00
87-02-004	Newborn	R. Sauber	Open	65.00	70.00
87-02-005	Motherhood	R. Sauber	Open	65.00	70.00
87-02-006	Fatherhood	R. Sauber	Open	65.00	70.00
87-02-007	Sweet Sixteen	R. Sauber	Open	65.00	70.00
Artaffects	**Christian Collection**				
87-03-001	Bring To Me the Children	A. Tobey	Open	65.00	100.00
88-03-002	The Healer	A. Tobey	Open	65.00	65.00
Artaffects	**Reflections of Youth**				
88-04-001	Julia	MaGo	N/A	29.50	70.00
89-04-002	Jessica	MaGo	14-day	29.50	60.00
89-04-003	Sebastian	MaGo	14-day	29.50	40.00
Artaffects	**Single Issue**				
84-05-001	Babysitter Musical Fig.	G. Perillo	2,500	65.00	90.00
Artaffects	**The Professionals**				
80-06-001	The Big Leaguer	G. Perillo	10,000	65.00	150.00
80-06-002	Ballerina's Dilemma	G. Perillo	10,000	65.00	75.00
81-06-003	The Quarterback	G. Perillo	10,000	65.00	75.00
82-06-004	Rodeo Joe	G. Perillo	10,000	65.00	75.00
82-06-005	Major Leaguer	G. Perillo	10,000	65.00	175.00
83-06-006	Hockey Player	G. Perillo	10,000	65.00	125.00
Artaffects	**The Storybook Collection**				
80-07-001	Little Red Ridinghood	G. Perillo	10,000	65.00	95.00
81-07-002	Cinderella	G. Perillo	10,000	65.00	95.00
82-07-003	Hansel and Gretel	G. Perillo	10,000	80.00	110.00
82-07-004	Goldilocks & 3 Bears	G. Perillo	10,000	80.00	110.00
Artaffects	**The Princesses**				
84-08-001	Lily of the Mohawks	G. Perillo	1,500	65.00	155.00
84-08-002	Pocahontas	G. Perillo	1,500	65.00	125.00
84-08-003	Minnehaha	G. Perillo	1,500	65.00	125.00
84-08-004	Sacajawea	G. Perillo	1,500	65.00	125.00
Artaffects	**The Chieftains**				
83-09-001	Sitting Bull	G. Perillo	5,000	65.00	500.00
83-09-002	Joseph	G. Perillo	5,000	65.00	250.00
83-09-003	Red Cloud	G. Perillo	5,000	65.00	275.00
83-09-004	Geronimo	G. Perillo	5,000	65.00	135.00
83-09-005	Crazy Horse	G. Perillo	5,000	65.00	200.00
Artaffects	**Child Life**				
83-10-001	Siesta	G. Perillo	2,500	65.00	75.00
84-10-002	Sweet Dreams	G. Perillo	1,500	65.00	75.00
Artaffects	**Special Issue**				
85-11-001	Lovers	G. Perillo	N/A	70.00	125.00
Artaffects	**Special Issue**				
84-12-001	Papoose	G. Perillo	325	500.00	500-975.
Artaffects	**Special Issue**				
82-13-001	The Peaceable Kingdom	G. Perillo	950	750.00	1500.00
Artaffects	**Perillo Collector Club**				
83-14-001	Apache Brave	G. Perillo	N/A	50.00	150.00
92-14-002	Sunbeam	G. Perillo	Yr.Iss.	35.00	35.00
93-14-003	Little Shadow	G. Perillo	Yr.Iss.	35.00	35.00
Artaffects	**The Little Indians**				
82-15-001	Blue Spruce	G. Perillo	10,000	50.00	75.00
82-15-002	White Rabbit	G. Perillo	10,000	50.00	75.00
82-15-003	Tender Love	G. Perillo	10,000	65.00	75-250.00
Artaffects	**Special Issue**				
84-16-001	Apache Boy Bust	G. Perillo	N/A	40.00	75.00
84-16-002	Navajo Girl Bust	G. Perillo	N/A	40.00	75.00
Artaffects	**The War Pony**				
83-17-001	Sioux War Pony	G. Perillo	495	150.00	250.00
83-17-002	Nez Perce Pony	G. Perillo	495	150.00	250.00
83-17-003	Apache War Pony	G. Perillo	495	150.00	250.00
Artaffects	**The Tribal Ponies**				
84-18-001	Arapaho	G. Perillo	1,500	65.00	200.00
84-18-002	Comanche	G. Perillo	1,500	65.00	200.00
84-18-003	Crow	G. Perillo	1,500	65.00	250.00
Artaffects	**Pride of America's Indians**				
88-19-001	Brave and Free	G. Perillo	N/A	50.00	150.00
89-19-002	Dark Eyed Friends	G. Perillo	10-day	45.00	75.00

Company / Number	Name / Series	Artist	Edition Limit	Issue Price	Quote
89-19-003	Noble Companions	G. Perillo	10-day	45.00	50.00
89-19-004	Kindred Spirits	G. Perillo	10-day	45.00	50.00
89-19-005	Loyal Alliance	G. Perillo	10-day	45.00	75.00
89-19-006	Small & Wise	G. Perillo	10-day	45.00	50.00
89-19-007	Winter Scouts	G. Perillo	10-day	45.00	50.00
89-19-008	Peaceful Comrades	G. Perillo	10-day	45.00	50.00
Artaffects	**Sagebrush Kids**				
85-20-001	Hail to the Chief	G. Perillo	Closed	19.50	52.00
85-20-002	Dressing Up	G. Perillo	Closed	19.50	52.00
85-20-003	Favorite Kachina	G. Perillo	Closed	19.50	52.00
85-20-004	Message of Joy	G. Perillo	Closed	19.50	52.00
85-20-005	Boots	G. Perillo	Closed	19.50	52.00
85-20-006	Stay Awhile	G. Perillo	Closed	19.50	52.00
85-20-007	Room for Two?	G. Perillo	Closed	19.50	52.00
85-20-008	Blue Bird	G. Perillo	Closed	19.50	52.00
85-20-009	Ouch!	G. Perillo	Closed	19.50	52.00
85-20-010	Take One	G. Perillo	Closed	19.50	52.00
86-20-011	The Long Wait	G. Perillo	Closed	19.50	52.00
86-20-012	Westward Ho!	G. Perillo	Closed	19.50	52.00
86-20-013	Finishing Touches	G. Perillo	Closed	19.50	52.00
86-20-014	Deputies	G. Perillo	Closed	19.50	52.00
86-20-015	Country Music	G. Perillo	Closed	19.50	52.00
86-20-016	Practice Makes Perfect	G. Perillo	Closed	19.50	52.00
86-20-017	The Hiding Place	G. Perillo	Closed	19.50	52.00
86-20-018	Prarie Prayers	G. Perillo	Closed	19.50	52.00
87-20-019	Just Picked	G. Perillo	Closed	19.50	52.00
87-20-020	Row, Row	G. Perillo	Closed	19.50	52.00
87-20-021	My Papoose	G. Perillo	Closed	19.50	52.00
87-20-022	Playing House	G. Perillo	Closed	19.50	52.00
87-20-023	Wagon Train	G. Perillo	Closed	19.50	52.00
87-20-024	Small Talk	G. Perillo	Closed	19.50	52.00
89-20-025	Santa's Lullaby	G. Perillo	Closed	45.00	45.00
89-20-026	Harmony	G. Perillo	Closed	37.50	82.00
89-20-027	Melody	G. Perillo	Closed	37.50	50.00
90-20-028	How! Do I Love Thee?	G. Perillo	Closed	37.50	50.00
90-20-029	Easter Offering	G. Perillo	Closed	27.50	50.00
90-20-030	Just Married	G. Perillo	Closed	45.00	45.00
91-20-031	Baby Bronc	G. Perillo	Closed	27.50	80.00
91-20-032	Little Warriors	G. Perillo	Closed	27.50	35.00
91-20-033	Toy Totem	G. Perillo	Closed	27.50	35.00
91-20-034	Just Baked	G. Perillo	Closed	27.50	35.00
91-20-035	Lovin Spoonful	G. Perillo	Closed	27.50	35.00
91-20-036	Teddy Too??	G. Perillo	Closed	27.50	35.00
Artaffects	**Sagebrush Kids Christmas Caravan**				
87-21-001	Leading the Way	G. Perillo	Open	90.00	120.00
87-21-002	Sleepy Sentinels	G. Perillo	Open	45.00	50.00
87-21-003	Singing Praises	G. Perillo	Open	45.00	50.00
87-21-004	Gold, Frankincense & Presents	G. Perillo	Open	35.00	35.00
87-21-005	Complete Set	G. Perillo	Open	185.00	255.00
Artaffects	**Sagebrush Kids Nativity**				
86-22-001	Christ Child	G. Perillo	Open	12.50	13.50
86-22-002	Mary	G. Perillo	Open	17.50	19.50
86-22-003	Joseph	G. Perillo	Open	17.50	19.50
86-22-004	Tee Pee	G. Perillo	Open	17.50	22.50
86-22-005	4-pc. Set	G. Perillo	Open	50.00	65.00
86-22-006	King with Corn	G. Perillo	Open	17.50	22.50
86-22-007	King with Pottery	G. Perillo	Open	17.50	22.50
86-22-008	King with Jewelry	G. Perillo	Open	17.50	22.50
86-22-009	Shepherd with Lamb	G. Perillo	Open	17.50	22.50
86-22-010	Shepherd Kneeling	G. Perillo	Open	17.50	22.50
86-22-011	Cow	G. Perillo	Open	12.00	13.50
86-22-012	Donkey	G. Perillo	Open	12.00	13.50
86-22-013	Lamb	G. Perillo	Open	6.00	8.00
86-22-014	Goat	G. Perillo	Open	8.00	9.50
86-22-015	Backdrop Dove	G. Perillo	Open	17.50	21.50
86-22-016	Backdrop Pottery	G. Perillo	Open	17.50	21.50
89-22-017	Pig	G. Perillo	Open	15.00	15.00
89-22-018	Racoon	G. Perillo	Open	12.50	12.50
89-22-019	Cactus	G. Perillo	Open	24.50	24.50
89-22-020	Buffalo	G. Perillo	Open	17.50	17.50
Artaffects	**Sagebrush Kids Banks**				
90-23-001	Perillo's Piggy Bank	G. Perillo	Open	39.50	39.50
90-23-002	Buckaroo Bank	G. Perillo	Open	39.50	39.50
90-23-003	Wampum Wig-Wam Bank	G. Perillo	Open	39.50	39.50
Artaffects	**Sagebrush Kids Wedding Party**				
90-24-001	Bride	G. Perillo	Open	24.50	24.50
90-24-002	Groom	G. Perillo	Open	24.50	24.50
90-24-003	Flower Girl	G. Perillo	Open	22.50	22.50
90-24-004	Ring Bearer	G. Perillo	Open	22.50	22.50
90-24-005	Donkey	G. Perillo	Open	22.50	22.50
90-24-006	Chief	G. Perillo	Open	24.50	24.50
90-24-007	Wedding Backdrop	G. Perillo	Open	27.50	27.50
90-24-008	Wedding Party Of 7	G. Perillo	Open	165.00	165.00
Artaffects	**Sagebrush Kids-Flight Into Egypt**				
90-25-001	3/Set (Mary With Baby,Joseph, Donkey)	G. Perillo	Open	65.00	65.00
Artaffects	**Perillo Limited Edition Porcelain Figurines**				
91-26-001	One Nation Under God	G. Perillo	5,000	195.00	195.00
91-26-002	Safe And Dry (Umbrella Boy)	G. Perillo	5,000	95.00	95.00
91-26-003	Out Of The Rain (Umbrella Girl)	G. Perillo	5,000	95.00	95.00
91-26-004	Angel of the Plains	G. Perillo	5,000	75.00	75.00
92-26-005	The Sioux Carousel Horse	G. Perillo	5,000	95.00	95.00
92-26-006	The Cheyenne Carousel Horse	G. Perillo	5,000	95.00	95.00
Artaffects	**Musical Figurines**				
89-27-001	A Boys Prayer	G. Perillo	N/A	45.00	65.00
89-27-002	A Girls Prayer	G. Perillo	N/A	45.00	65.00
Artaffects	**Wildlife Figurines**				
91-28-001	Mustang	G. Perillo	Open	85.00	85.00
91-28-002	White-Tailed Deer	G. Perillo	Open	95.00	95.00
91-28-003	Mountain Lion	G. Perillo	Open	75.00	75.00
91-28-004	Bald Eagle	G. Perillo	Open	65.00	65.00
91-28-005	Buffalo	G. Perillo	Open	75.00	75.00
91-28-006	Timber Wolf	G. Perillo	Open	85.00	85.00
91-28-007	Polar Bear	G. Perillo	Open	65.00	65.00
91-28-008	Bighorn Sheep	G. Perillo	Open	75.00	75.00

Company Number	Name	Series Artist	Edition Limit	Issue Price	Quote
Artaffects		**The Great Chieftains**			
91-29-001	Crazy Horse (Club Piece)	G. Perillo	N/A	195.00	195.00
91-29-002	Sitting Bull	G. Perillo	5,000	195.00	195.00
91-29-003	Red Cloud	G. Perillo	5,000	195.00	195.00
91-29-004	Chief Joseph	G. Perillo	5,000	195.00	195.00
91-29-005	Cochise	G. Perillo	5,000	195.00	195.00
91-29-006	Geronimo	G. Perillo	5,000	195.00	195.00
Artaffects		**Simple Wonders**			
91-30-001	Joseph	C. Roeda	N/A	45.00	45.00
91-30-002	Joseph (Black)	C. Roeda	N/A	45.00	45.00
91-30-003	Mary	C. Roeda	N/A	40.00	40.00
91-30-004	Mary (Black)	C. Roeda	N/A	40.00	40.00
91-30-005	Baby Jesus	C. Roeda	N/A	35.00	35.00
91-30-006	Baby Jesus (Black)	C. Roeda	N/A	35.00	35.00
91-30-007	Sheep Dog	C. Roeda	N/A	15.00	15.00
91-30-008	Off To School	C. Roeda	N/A	49.50	49.50
91-30-009	Playing Hookey	C. Roeda	N/A	49.50	49.50
91-30-010	Mommy's Best	C. Roeda	N/A	49.50	49.50
91-30-011	Made With Love	C. Roeda	N/A	49.50	49.50
91-30-012	Bride	C. Roeda	N/A	55.00	55.00
91-30-013	Groom	C. Roeda	N/A	45.00	45.00
91-30-014	The Littlest Angel	C. Roeda	N/A	29.50	29.50
91-30-015	Star Light, Star Bright	C. Roeda	N/A	35.00	35.00
91-30-016	Lighting the Way	C. Roeda	N/A	39.50	39.50
91-30-017	Forever Friends	C. Roeda	N/A	39.50	39.50
91-30-018	Song of Joy	C. Roeda	N/A	39.50	39.50
91-30-019	I Love Ewe	C. Roeda	N/A	37.50	37.50
91-30-020	The Littlest Angel (Black)	C. Roeda	N/A	29.50	29.50
92-30-021	Ten Penny Serenade	C. Roeda	N/A	45.00	45.00
92-30-022	Ten Penny Serenade (Black)	C. Roeda	N/A	45.00	45.00
92-30-023	Rainbow Patrol	C. Roeda	N/A	39.50	39.50
92-30-024	The Three Bears	C. Roeda	N/A	45.00	45.00
92-30-025	Trick or Treat	C. Roeda	N/A	39.50	39.50
92-30-026	A Perfect Fit	C. Roeda	N/A	45.00	45.00
92-30-027	Pocketful of Love	C. Roeda	N/A	35.00	35.00
92-30-028	Pocketful of Love (Black)	C. Roeda	N/A	35.00	35.00
92-30-029	This Too Shall Pass	C. Roeda	N/A	35.00	35.00
92-30-030	Fallen Angel	C. Roeda	N/A	35.00	35.00
92-30-031	Lil' Dumplin	C. Roeda	N/A	25.00	25.00
92-30-032	Lil' Dumplin (Black)	C. Roeda	N/A	25.00	25.00
92-30-033	Little Big Shot	C. Roeda	N/A	35.00	35.00
92-30-034	With Open Arms (Wisechild)	C. Roeda	N/A	39.50	39.50
92-30-035	Following the Star (Wisechild)	C. Roeda	N/A	45.00	45.00
92-30-036	Catch the Spirit (Wisechild)	C. Roeda	N/A	35.00	35.00
Artaffects		**Village of the Sun**			
92-31-001	Rolling Thunder (Medicine Man)	G. Perillo	N/A	39.50	39.50
92-31-002	Cloud Catcher (Boy with Dog)	G. Perillo	N/A	37.50	37.50
92-31-003	Smiling Eyes (Baby with Lamb)	G. Perillo	N/A	27.50	27.50
92-31-004	Many Bears (Farmer)	G. Perillo	N/A	39.50	39.50
92-31-005	Cactus Flower (Weaver)	G. Perillo	N/A	55.00	55.00
92-31-006	Lambs	G. Perillo	N/A	17.50	17.50
92-31-007	Dancing Waters (Tortilla Maker)	G. Perillo	N/A	37.50	37.50
92-31-008	Red Bird (Jewelry Maker)	G. Perillo	N/A	39.50	39.50
92-31-009	Bright Sky (Cook)	G. Perillo	N/A	39.50	39.50
92-31-010	Summer Breeze (Maiden)	G. Perillo	N/A	39.50	39.50
92-31-011	Standing Deer (Brave)	G. Perillo	N/A	39.50	39.50
92-31-012	Large Cactus	G. Perillo	N/A	19.50	19.50
92-31-013	Medium Cactus	G. Perillo	N/A	17.50	17.50
92-31-015	Small Cactus (Yellow Flowers)	G. Perillo	N/A	12.00	12.00
92-31-016	Small Cactus (Pink Flowers)	G. Perillo	N/A	12.00	12.00
92-31-017	Noble Guardian (Horse)	G. Perillo	N/A	55.00	55.00
92-31-018	Hogan	G. Perillo	N/A	85.00	85.00
Artists of the World		**DeGrazia Figurines**			
84-01-001	Flower Girl	T. DeGrazia	Open	65.00	110.00
84-01-002	Flower Boy	T. DeGrazia	Open	65.00	110.00
84-01-003	Sunflower Boy	T. DeGrazia	Closed	65.00	250-300.
84-01-004	My First Horse	T. DeGrazia	Closed	65.00	110.00
84-01-005	White Dove	T. DeGrazia	Open	45.00	80-85.00
84-01-006	Wondering	T. DeGrazia	Closed	85.00	135-175.
84-01-007	Flower Girl Plaque	T. DeGrazia	Closed	45.00	95.00
85-01-008	Little Madonna	T. DeGrazia	Open	80.00	125.00
85-01-009	Mary	T. DeGrazia	Open	55.00	80.00
85-01-010	Joseph	T. DeGrazia	Open	55.00	90.00
85-01-011	Jesus	T. DeGrazia	Open	25.00	55.00
85-01-012	Nativity Set-3 pieces	T. DeGrazia	Open	135.00	195.00
86-01-013	The Blue Boy	T. DeGrazia	Open	70.00	95.00
86-01-014	Festival Lights	T. DeGrazia	Open	75.00	95.00
86-01-015	Merry Little Indian	T. DeGrazia	12,500	175.00	245.00
85-01-016	Pima Drummer Boy	T. DeGrazia	Closed	65.00	110.00
87-01-017	Love Me	T. DeGrazia	Open	95.00	110.00
87-01-018	Wee Three	T. DeGrazia	Closed	180.00	195.00
88-01-019	Christmas Prayer Angel	T. DeGrazia	Closed	70.00	70-80.00
88-01-020	Los Niños	T. DeGrazia	5,000	595.00	645.00
88-01-021	Beautiful Burden	T. DeGrazia	Closed	175.00	185-200.
88-01-022	Merrily, Merrily, Merrily	T. DeGrazia	Closed	95.00	110-150.
88-01-023	Flower Boy Plaque	T. DeGrazia	Closed	80.00	79.50
89-01-024	Two Little Lambs	T. DeGrazia	Open	70.00	79.50
89-01-025	My First Arrow	T. DeGrazia	Open	95.00	110.00
89-01-026	My Beautiful Rocking Horse	T. DeGrazia	Open	225.00	245.00
89-01-027	Los Ninos	T. DeGrazia	48	695.00	695.00
90-01-028	Alone	T. DeGrazia	Open	395.00	475.00
90-01-029	El Burrito	T. DeGrazia	Open	60.00	75.00
90-01-030	Sunflower Girl	T. DeGrazia	Open	95.00	95.00
90-01-031	Crucifixion	T. DeGrazia	Yr.Iss.	295.00	295.00
90-01-032	Navajo Boy	T. DeGrazia	Yr.Iss.	110.00	125.00
90-01-033	Desert Harvest	T. DeGrazia	5,000	135.00	145.00
90-01-034	Biggest Drum	T. DeGrazia	Yr.Iss.	110.00	125.00
90-01-035	Little Prayer	T. DeGrazia	Yr.Iss.	85.00	85.00
91-01-036	Navajo Mother	T. DeGrazia	3,500	295.00	295.00
91-01-037	Wanderer	T. DeGrazia	Yr.Iss.	75.00	75.00
91-01-038	Shepherd Boy	T. DeGrazia	Open	95.00	95.00
92-01-039	Sun Showers	T. DeGrazia	5,000	195.00	195.00
92-01-040	Navajo Madonna	T. DeGrazia	Open	135.00	135.00
92-01-041	Coming Home	T. DeGrazia	3,500	165.00	165.00
93-01-042	Feliz Navidad	T. DeGrazia	Yr.Iss.	195.00	195.00
93-01-043	Saddle Up	T. DeGrazia	5,000	195.00	195.00
93-01-044	El Toro	T. DeGrazia	Open	95.00	95.00
93-01-045	Little Medicine Man	T. DeGrazia	Open	175.00	175.00

Company Number	Name	Series Artist	Edition Limit	Issue Price	Quote
Boehm Studios		**Boehm**			
83-01-001	Great Egret	Boehm	Yr.Iss.	1200.00	2400.00
84-01-002	Whooping Crane	Boehm	Yr.Iss.	1800.00	2000.00
85-01-003	Trumpeter Swan	Boehm	Yr.Iss.	1500.00	1800.00
Boehm Studios		**Bird Sculptures**			
57-02-001	American Eagle, large	Boehm	31	225.00	1100.00
57-02-002	American Eagle, small	Boehm	76	225.00	19200.00
58-02-003	American Redstarts	Boehm	500	350.00	2000.00
80-02-004	Arctic Tern	Boehm	350	1400.00	2850.00
69-02-005	Black-headed Grosbeak	Boehm	675	1250.00	2000.00
56-02-006	Black-tailed Bantams, pair	Boehm	57	350.00	4700.00
58-02-007	Black-throated Blue Warbler	Boehm	500	400.00	1875.00
76-02-008	Black-throated Blue Warbler	Boehm	200	900.00	1100.00
67-02-009	Blue Grosbeak	Boehm	750	1050.00	1500.00
62-02-010	Blue Jays, pair	Boehm	250	2000.00	12750.00
64-02-011	Bobolink	Boehm	500	550.00	1550.00
53-02-012	Bob White Quail, pair	Boehm	750	400.00	2600.00
72-02-013	Brown Pelican	Boehm	100	10500.00	14500.00
73-02-014	Brown Thrasher	Boehm	260	1850.00	1875.00
72-02-015	Cactus Wren	Boehm	225	3000.00	3300.00
57-02-016	California Quail, pair	Boehm	500	400.00	2900.00
78-02-017	Canada Geese, pair	Boehm	100	4200.00	4200.00
77-02-018	Cape May Warbler	Boehm	400	825.00	950.00
55-02-019	Cardinals, pair	Boehm	500	550.00	3750.00
77-02-020	Cardinals	Boehm	200	3500.00	3850.00
57-02-021	Carolina Wrens	Boehm	100	750.00	5500.00
65-02-022	Catbird	Boehm	500	900.00	2135.00
56-02-023	Cedar Waxwings, pair	Boehm	100	600.00	7750.00
57-02-024	Cerulean Warblers	Boehm	100	800.00	4335.00
68-02-025	Common Tern	Boehm	500	1400.00	6200.00
67-02-026	Crested Flycatcher	Boehm	500	1650.00	2925.00
57-02-027	Downy Woodpeckers	Boehm	500	450.00	1775.00
76-02-028	Eagle of Freedom I	Boehm	15	35000.00	53000.00
59-02-029	Eastern Bluebirds, pair	Boehm	100	1800.00	12000.00
75-02-030	Eastern Kingbird	Boehm	100	3500.00	3900.00
73-02-031	Everglades Kites	Boehm	50	5800.00	7200.00
77-02-032	Fledgling Brown Thrashers	Boehm	400	500.00	655.00
67-02-033	Fledgling Canada Warbler	Boehm	750	550.00	2275.00
65-02-034	Fledgling Great Horned Owl	Boehm	750	350.00	1475.00
71-02-035	Flicker	Boehm	250	2400.00	2950.00
56-02-036	Golden-crowned Kinglets	Boehm	500	1400.00	2400.00
54-02-037	Golden Pheasant, decorated	Boehm	7	350.00	19000.00
54-02-038	Golden Pheasant, bisque	Boehm	7	200.00	11250.00
61-02-039	Goldfinches	Boehm	500	400.00	1800.00
66-02-040	Green Jays, pair	Boehm	400	1850.00	4200.00
74-02-041	Hooded Warbler	Boehm	100	2400.00	3150.00
73-02-042	Horned Larks	Boehm	200	3800.00	5000.00
68-02-043	Kestrels, pair	Boehm	460	2300.00	3000.00
64-02-044	Killdeer, pair	Boehm	300	1750.00	4500.00
74-02-045	Lark Sparrow	Boehm	150	,100.00	2200.00
73-02-046	Lazuli Buntings	Boehm	250	1800.00	2300.00
79-02-047	Least Tern	Boehm	350	1275.00	3100.00
62-02-048	Lesser Prairie Chickens, pair	Boehm	300	1200.00	2400.00
52-02-049	Mallards, pair	Boehm	500	650.00	1700.00
57-02-050	Meadowlark	Boehm	750	350.00	3100.00
63-02-051	Mearn's Quail, pair	Boehm	350	950.00	3450.00
68-02-052	Mergansers, pair	Boehm	440	2200.00	2825.00
61-02-053	Mockingbirds, pair	Boehm	500	650.00	3800.00
78-02-054	Mockingbirds	Boehm	Unkn.	2200.00	2800.00
63-02-055	Mountain Bluebirds	Boehm	300	1900.00	5850.00
58-02-056	Mourning Doves	Boehm	500	550.00	1250.00
71-02-057	Mute swans, life-size, pair	Boehm	3	Unkn.	Unkn.
71-02-058	Mute Swans, small size, pair	Boehm	400	4000.00	8200.00
74-02-059	Myrtle Warblers	Boehm	210	1850.00	2075.00
58-02-060	Nonpareil Buntings	Boehm	750	250.00	1075.00
67-02-061	Northern Water Thrush	Boehm	500	800.00	1400.00
70-02-062	Orchard Orioles	Boehm	550	1750.00	2200.00
70-02-063	Oven-bird	Boehm	450	1400.00	1800.00
65-02-064	Parula Warblers	Boehm	400	1500.00	3150.00
75-02-065	Pekin Robins	Boehm	100	7000.00	8550.00
62-02-066	Ptarmigan, pair	Boehm	350	800.00	3575.00
74-02-067	Purple Martins	Boehm	50	6700.00	8450.00
75-02-068	Red-billed Blue Magpie	Boehm	100	4600.00	5950.00
57-02-069	Red-winged Blackbirds, pair	Boehm	100	700.00	5250.00
54-02-070	Ringed-necked Pheasants, pair	Boehm	500	650.00	1825.00
68-02-071	Roadrunner	Boehm	500	2600.00	3700.00
64-02-072	Robin (Daffodils)	Boehm	500	600.00	5700.00
77-02-073	Robin (nest)	Boehm	350	1650.00	1840.00
60-02-074	Ruffed Grouse, pair	Boehm	250	950.00	4950.00
66-02-075	Rufous Hummingbirds	Boehm	500	850.00	1900.00
77-02-076	Scarlet Tanager	Boehm	4	1800.00	4000.00
77-02-077	Scissor-tailed Flycatcher	Boehm	100	3200.00	3200.00
79-02-078	Scops Owl	Boehm	300	975.00	1500.00
80-02-079	Screech Owl	Boehm	350	2100.00	3100.00
70-02-080	Slate-colored Junco	Boehm	NA	1600.00	2000.00
81-02-081	Snow Buntings	Boehm	350	2400.00	2950.00
56-02-082	Song Sparrows, pair	Boehm	50	2000.00	38000.00
61-02-083	Sugarbirds	Boehm	100	2500.00	13250.00
63-02-084	Towhee	Boehm	500	350.00	2600.00
65-02-085	Tufted Titmice	Boehm	500	600.00	2000.00
65-02-086	Varied Buntings	Boehm	300	2200.00	4500.00
74-02-087	Varied Thrush	Boehm	NA	2500.00	3000.00
69-02-088	Verdins	Boehm	575	1150.00	1525.00
69-02-089	Western Bluebirds	Boehm	300	5500.00	6600.00
71-02-090	Western Meadowlark	Boehm	350	1425.00	1675.00
54-02-091	Woodcock	Boehm	500	300.00	1950.00
51-02-092	Wood Thrush	Boehm	2	375.00	Unkn.
66-02-093	Wood Thrushes, pair	Boehm	400	4200.00	8400.00
72-02-094	Yellow-bellied Sapsucker	Boehm	NA	2700.00	3000.00
74-02-095	Yellow-bellied Cuckoo	Boehm	NA	2800.00	3000.00
74-02-096	Yellow-headed Blackbird	Boehm	75	3200.00	3600.00
73-02-097	Young American Eagle, Inaugural	Boehm	100	1500.00	2100.00
69-02-098	Young American Eagle	Boehm	850	700.00	1400.00
75-02-099	Young & Spirited 1976	Boehm	1,121	950.00	1800.00
79-02-100	Avocet	Boehm	175	1200.00	1200.00
72-02-101	Barn Owl	Boehm	350	3600.00	5600.00
73-02-102	Blackbirds, pair	Boehm	75	5400.00	6300.00
72-02-103	Black Grouse	Boehm	175	2800.00	3025.00
73-02-104	Blue Tits	Boehm	300	3000.00	3000.00
74-02-105	Chaffinch	Boehm	125	2000.00	2200.00
74-02-106	Crested Tit	Boehm	400	1150.00	1250.00
75-02-107	European Goldfinch	Boehm	225	1150.00	1350.00

Company Number	Name	Series Artist	Edition Limit	Issue Price	Quote
72-02-108	Goldcrest	Boehm	500	650.00	1200.00
73-02-109	Green Woodpeckers	Boehm	50	4200.00	4800.00
79-02-110	Grey Wagtail	Boehm	150	1050.00	1260.00
76-02-111	Kingfishers	Boehm	200	1900.00	2300.00
73-02-112	Lapwing	Boehm	100	2600.00	2975.00
71-02-113	Little Owl	Boehm	350	700.00	1325.00
73-02-114	Long Tail Tits	Boehm	200	2600.00	2900.00
71-02-115	Nuthatch	Boehm	350	650.00	1100.00
73-02-116	Peregrine Falcon	Boehm	350	4400.00	5450.00
76-02-117	Rivoli's Hummingbird	Boehm	350	950.00	1550.00
74-02-118	Ruby-throated Hummingbird	Boehm	200	1900.00	2650.00
73-02-119	Screech Owl	Boehm	50	850.00	1425.00
74-02-120	Song Thrushes	Boehm	100	2800.00	3350.00
74-02-121	Stonechats	Boehm	150	2200.00	2400.00
74-02-122	Swallows	Boehm	125	3400.00	4100.00
72-02-123	Tree Creepers	Boehm	200	3200.00	4200.00
71-02-124	Winter Robin	Boehm	225	1150.00	1440.00
73-02-125	Yellowhammers	Boehm	350	3300.00	4200.00
Boehm Studios		**Animal Sculptures**			
69-03-001	Adios	Boehm	130	1500.00	1800.00
52-03-002	Hunter	Boehm	250	600.00	1300.00
57-03-003	Polo Player	Boehm	100	850.00	4450.00
78-03-004	Thoroughbred with Jockey	Boehm	25	2600.00	2800.00
77-03-005	African Elephant	Boehm	50	9500.00	14400.00
76-03-006	American Mustangs	Boehm	75	3700.00	5700.00
80-03-007	Asian Lion	Boehm	100	1500.00	1500.00
78-03-008	Black Rhinoceros	Boehm	50	9500.00	11000.00
71-03-009	Bobcats	Boehm	200	1600.00	2000.00
78-03-010	Camel & Calf	Boehm	50	3500.00	3900.00
80-03-011	Cheetah	Boehm	100	2700.00	2900.00
79-03-012	Fallow Deer	Boehm	30	7500.00	7500.00
71-03-013	Foxes	Boehm	200	1800.00	2550.00
75-03-014	Giant Panda	Boehm	100	3800.00	6350.00
78-03-015	Gorilla	Boehm	50	3800.00	4400.00
79-03-016	Hunter Chase	Boehm	20	4000.00	4000.00
73-03-017	Nyala Antelope	Boehm	100	4700.00	6500.00
76-03-018	Otter	Boehm	75	1100.00	1450.00
75-03-019	Puma	Boehm	50	5700.00	6800.00
71-03-020	Raccoons	Boehm	200	1600.00	2250.00
72-03-021	Red Squirrels	Boehm	100	2600.00	2800.00
78-03-022	Snow Leopard	Boehm	75	3500.00	5500.00
79-03-023	Young & Free Fawns	Boehm	160	1875.00	1875.00
Boehm Studios		**Floral Sculptures**			
79-04-001	Cactus Dahlia	Boehm	300	800.00	960.00
72-04-002	Chrysanthemums	Boehm	350	1100.00	1950.00
71-04-003	Daisies	Boehm	350	600.00	975.00
74-04-004	Debutante Camellia	Boehm	500	625.00	800.00
73-04-005	Dogwood	Boehm	250	625.00	975.00
78-04-006	Double Clematis Centerpiece	Boehm	150	1500.00	1950.00
74-04-007	Double Peony	Boehm	275	575.00	1050.00
75-04-008	Emmett Barnes Camellia	Boehm	425	550.00	780.00
74-04-009	Gentians	Boehm	350	425.00	725.00
79-04-010	Grand Floral Centerpiece	Boehm	15	7500.00	8700.00
78-04-011	Helen Boehm Camellia	Boehm	500	600.00	1050.00
78-04-012	Helen Boehm Daylily	Boehm	175	975.00	1160.00
78-04-013	Helen Boehm Iris	Boehm	175	975.00	1175.00
79-04-014	Honeysuckle	Boehm	200	900.00	1080.00
75-04-015	Magnolia Grandiflora	Boehm	750	650.00	1350.00
76-04-016	Orchid Cactus	Boehm	100	650.00	975.00
76-04-017	Queen of the Night Cactus	Boehm	125	650.00	850.00
78-04-018	Rhododendron Centerpiece	Boehm	350	1150.00	1750.00
80-04-019	Rose, Alec's Red	Boehm	500	1050.00	1300.00
78-04-020	Rose, Blue Moon	Boehm	500	650.00	900.00
78-04-021	Rose, Pascali	Boehm	500	950.00	1375.00
76-04-022	Rose, Supreme Peace	Boehm	250	850.00	1575.00
76-04-023	Rose, Supreme Yellow	Boehm	250	850.00	1575.00
78-04-024	Rose, Tropicana	Boehm	500	475.00	1085.00
78-04-025	Spanish Iris	Boehm	500	600.00	600.00
73-04-026	Streptocalyx Poeppigii	Boehm	50	3400.00	4300.00
71-04-027	Swan Centerpiece	Boehm	135	1950.00	2725.00
76-04-028	Swan Lake Camellia	Boehm	750	825.00	1725.00
76-04-029	Sweet Viburnum	Boehm	35	650.00	1425.00
74-04-030	Waterlily	Boehm	350	400.00	660.00
78-04-031	Watsonii Magnolia	Boehm	250	575.00	690.00
Boehm Studios		**Figurines**			
77-05-001	Beverly Sills	Boehm	100	950.00	1500.00
77-05-002	Jerome Hines	Boehm	12	825.00	1000.00
Byers' Choice Ltd.		**Carolers**			
82-01-001	Victorian Adult Caroler (1st Version)	J. Byers	Closed	32.00	300.00
82-01-002	Victorian Child Caroler (1st Version)	J. Byers	Closed	32.00	300.00
83-01-003	Victorian Adult Caroler (2nd Version)	J. Byers	Open	35.00	46.00
83-01-004	Victorian Child Caroler (2nd Version)	J. Byers	Open	33.00	46.00
86-01-005	Traditional Grandparents	J. Byers	Open	35.00	41.00-50.00
86-01-006	Singing Dogs	J. Byers	Open	13.00	13.00
88-01-007	Victorian Grand Parent Carolers	J. Byers	Open	40.00	45.00
88-01-008	Children with Skates	J. Byers	Open	40.00	46.00
88-01-009	Singing Cats	J. Byers	Open	13.50	15.00
91-01-010	Adult Skaters	J. Byers	Open	50.00	50.00
91-01-011	Toddler on Sled	J. Byers	Closed	30.00	30.00
92-01-012	Children Skaters	J. Byers	Open	50.00	50.00
92-01-013	Lil' Dickens-Shovel	J. Byers	Open	17.00	17.00
92-01-014	Lil' Dickens-Snowball (Lg.)	J. Byers	Open	17.00	17.00
92-01-015	Lil' Dickens-Sled	J. Byers	Open	17.00	17.00
Byers' Choice Ltd.		**Special Characters**			
81-02-001	Thanksgiving Man (Clay Hands)	J. Byers	Closed	Unkn.	2000.00
81-02-002	Thanksgiving Lady (Clay Hands)	J. Byers	Closed	Unkn.	2000.00
82-02-003	Icabod	J. Byers	Closed	32.00	1150.00
82-02-004	Choir Children, boy and girl	J. Byers	Closed	32.00	250.00
82-02-005	Valentine Boy	J. Byers	Closed	32.00	450.00
82-02-006	Valentine Girl	J. Byers	Closed	32.00	450.00
82-02-007	Easter Boy	J. Byers	Closed	32.00	450.00
82-02-008	Easter Girl	J. Byers	Closed	32.00	450.00
82-02-009	Leprechauns	J. Byers	Closed	34.00	1200.00
82-02-010	Conductor	J. Byers	Open	32.00	42.00
82-02-011	Drummer Boy	J. Byers	Open	34.00	46.00
83-02-012	Boy on Rocking Horse	J. Byers	300	85.00	1500.00
84-02-013	Chimney Sweep (Adult)	J. Byers	Closed	36.00	1200.00
85-02-014	Pajama Children	J. Byers	Closed	35.00	150.00

Company Number	Name	Series Artist	Edition Limit	Issue Price	Quote
87-02-015	Boy on Sled	J. Byers	Closed	50.00	175.00
87-02-016	Caroler with Lamp	J. Byers	Closed	40.00	150.00
87-02-017	Mother's Day	J. Byers	225	125.00	350.00
88-02-018	Mother's Day (Son)	J. Byers`	Closed	125.00	225-275.
88-02-019	Mother's Day (Daughter)	J. Byers	Closed	125.00	225.00
88-02-020	Angel Tree Top	J. Byers	100	Unkn.	150.00
88-02-021	Mother Holding Baby	J. Byers	Open	40.00	47.00
89-02-022	Newsboy with Bike	J. Byers	Open	78.00	80.00
89-02-023	Girl with Hoop	J. Byers	Closed	44.00	50.00
89-02-024	Mother's Day (with Carriage)	J. Byers	3,000	75.00	200.00
90-02-025	Postman	J. Byers	Open	45.00	47.00
90-02-026	Parson	J. Byers	Open	44.00	46.00
90-02-027	Girl On Rocking Horse	J. Byers	Closed	70.00	72.00
91-02-028	Chimney Sweep (Child)	J. Byers	Open	50.00	50.00
91-02-029	Boy W/Tree	J. Byers	Open	49.00	49.00
92-02-030	Schoolteacher	J. Byers	Open	48.00	48.00
92-02-031	Salvation Army-Woman With Kettle	J. Byers	Open	64.00	64.00
92-02-032	Victorian Mother With Toddler	J. Byers	Open	60.00	60.00
Byers' Choice Ltd.		**Santas**			
78-03-001	Old World Santa	J. Byers	Closed	33.00	2000.00
78-03-002	Velvet Santa	J. Byers	Open	Unkn.	46.00
82-03-003	Santa in a Sleigh (1st Version)	J. Byers	Closed	46.00	800.00
83-03-004	Working Santa	J. Byers	Closed	38.00	46.00
84-03-005	Santa in Sleigh (2nd Version)	J. Byers	Closed	70.00	500.00
84-03-006	Mrs. Claus	J. Byers	Closed	38.00	46.00
86-03-007	Mrs. Claus on Rocker	J. Byers	Closed	73.00	400.00
86-03-008	Victorian Santa	J. Byers	Closed	39.00	175.00
87-03-009	Velvet Mrs. Claus	J. Byers	Open	44.00	44.00
88-03-010	Saint Nicholas	J. Byers	Open	44.00	50.00
88-03-011	Knecht Ruprecht	J. Byers	Closed	38.00	65.00
89-03-012	Russian Santa	J. Byers	Closed	85.00	150.00
90-03-013	Weihnachtsmann	J. Byers	Closed	56.00	56.00
91-03-014	Father Christmas	J. Byers	Open	48.00	48.00
92-03-015	Mrs. Claus (2nd Version)	J. Byers	Open	50.00	50.00
92-03-016	Working Santa (2nd Version)	J. Byers	Open	52.00	52.00
Byers' Choice Ltd.		**Dickens Series**			
83-04-001	Scrooge (1st Edition)	J. Byers	Closed	36.00	1000-2000.
84-04-002	Mrs. Cratchit (1st Edition)	J. Byers	Closed	38.00	1000-1700.
84-04-003	Scrooge (2nd Edition)	J. Byers	Open	38.00	38.00
85-04-004	Mrs. Fezziwig (1st Edition)	J. Byers	Closed	43.00	500-650.
85-04-005	Mr. Fezziwig (1st Edition)	J. Byers	Closed	43.00	500.00
85-04-006	Mrs. Cratchit (2nd Edition)	J. Byers	Open	39.00	39.00
86-04-007	Marley's Ghost (1st Edition)	J. Byers	Closed	40.00	300-500.
86-04-008	Mrs. Fezziwig (2nd Edition)	J. Byers	Closed	43.00	65.00
86-04-009	Mr. Fezziwig (2nd Edition)	J. Byers	Closed	43.00	65.00
87-04-010	Spirit of Christmas Past (1st Edition)	J. Byers	Closed	42.00	150-200.
87-04-011	Marley's Ghost (2nd Edition)	J. Byers	Open	42.00	42.00
88-04-012	Spirit of Christmas Present (1st Edition)	J. Byers	Closed	44.00	65-150.00
88-04-013	Spirit of Christmas Past (2nd Edition)	J. Byers	Closed	46.00	46.00
89-04-014	Spirit of Christmas Future (1st Edition)	J. Byers	Closed	46.00	100.00
89-04-015	Spirit of Christmas Present (2nd Edition)	J. Byers	Closed	48.00	48.00
90-04-016	Bob Cratchit & Tiny Tim (1st Edition)	J. Byers	Closed	84.00	84.00
90-04-017	Spirit of Christmas Future (2nd Edition)	J. Byers	Closed	48.00	48.00
91-04-018	Happy Scrooge (1st Edition)	J. Byers	Closed	50.00	50.00
91-04-019	Bob Cratchit & Tiny Tim (2nd Edition)	J. Byers	Open	86.00	86.00
92-04-020	Happy Scrooge (2nd Edition)	J. Byers	Open	50.00	50.00
Byers' Choice Ltd		**Musicians**			
83-05-001	Violin Player Man (1st Version)	J. Byers	Closed	38.00	800.00
84-05-002	Violin Player Man (2nd Version)	J. Byers	Closed	38.00	1500.00
85-05-003	Horn Player, chubby face	J. Byers	Closed	37.00	900.00
85-05-004	Horn Player	J. Byers	Closed	38.00	450.00
86-05-005	Victorian Girl with Violin	J. Byers	Closed	39.00	175.00
89-05-006	Musician with Clarinet	J. Byers	Closed	44.00	125-150.
90-05-007	Musician With Mandolin	J. Byers	Closed	46.00	50-100.00
91-05-008	Musician with Accordian	J. Byers	Closed	48.00	48.00
91-05-009	Boy W/Mandolin	J. Byers	Closed	48.00	48.00
92-05-010	Musician With French Horn	J. Byers	Open	52.00	52.00
Byers' Choice Ltd		**Nativity**			
87-06-001	Black Angel	J. Byers	Closed	36.00	125.00
87-06-002	Angel-Great Star (Blonde)	J. Byers	Closed	40.00	75.00
87-06-003	Angel-Great Star (Brunette)	J. Byers	Closed	40.00	75.00
87-06-004	Angel-Great Star (Red Head)	J. Byers	Closed	40.00	75.00
88-06-005	Shepherds	J. Byers	Closed	37.00	40.00
89-06-006	King Gasper	J. Byers	Closed	40.00	42.00
89-06-007	King Melchior	J. Byers	Closed	40.00	42.00
89-06-008	King Balthasar	J. Byers	Closed	40.00	42.00
90-06-009	Holy Family	J. Byers	Closed	90.00	90.00
Byers' Choice Ltd		**Display Figures**			
81-07-001	Display Man	J. Byers	Closed	Unkn.	2000.00
81-07-002	Display Lady	J. Byers	Closed	Unkn.	2000.00
82-07-003	Display Drummer Boy-1st	J. Byers	Closed	96.00	600.00
85-07-004	Display Drummer Boy-2nd	J. Byers	Closed	160.00	300.00
82-07-005	Display Santa	J. Byers	Closed	96.00	600.00
83-07-006	Display Carolers	J. Byers	Closed	200.00	500.00
84-07-007	Display Working Santa	J. Byers	Closed	260.00	400.00
85-07-008	Display Old World Santa	J. Byers	Closed	260.00	500.00
85-07-009	Display Children	J. Byers	Closed	140.00	500.00
86-07-010	Display Adults	J. Byers	Closed	170.00	500.00
90-07-011	Display Santa-Red	J. Byers	Closed	250.00	250.00
90-07-012	Display Santa-Bayberry	J. Byers	Closed	250.00	250.00
Byers' Choice Ltd		**Cries Of London**			
91-08-001	Cry of London-Apple Lady	J. Byers	Closed	80.00	200.00
92-08-002	Cry of London-Baker	J. Byers	Open	62.00	62.00
Byers' Choice		**Wayside Country Store Exclusives**			
86-09-001	Colonial Lamplighter s/n	J. Byers	600	46.00	500.00
87-09-002	Colonial Watchman s/n	J. Byers	600	49.00	400.00
88-09-003	Colonial Lady s/n	J. Byers	600	49.00	350.00
Byers' Choice		**Snow Goose Exclusive**			
88-10-001	Man with Goose	J. Byers	600	60.00	350.00
Byers' Choice		**Country Christmas Store Exclusive**			
88-11-001	Toymaker	J. Byers	600	59.00	875.00
Byers' Choice		**Woodstock Inn Exclusives**			
87-12-001	Skier Boy	J. Byers	200	40.00	400.00

Company / Number	Name	Series / Artist	Edition Limit	Issue Price	Quote
87-12-002	Skier Girl	J. Byers	200	40.00	400.00
88-12-003	Woodstock Lady	J. Byers	N/A	41.00	250.00
88-12-004	Woodstock Man	J. Byers	N/A	41.00	250.00
88-12-005	Sugarin Kids (Woodstock)	J. Byers	N/A	41.00	250.00
Byers' Choice		**Stacy's Gifts & Collectibles Exclusives**			
87-13-001	Santa in Rocking Chair with Boy	J. Byers	100	130.00	550.00
87-13-002	Santa in Rocking Chair with Girl	J. Byers	100	130.00	450.00
The Cat's Meow		**Series I**			
83-01-001	Federal House	F. Jones	Retrd.	8.00	35-76.00
83-01-002	Inn	F. Jones	Retrd.	8.00	56-200.00
83-01-003	Garrison House	F. Jones	Retrd.	8.00	56-80.00
83-01-004	Victorian House	F. Jones	Retrd.	8.00	35-75.00
83-01-005	School	F. Jones	Retrd.	8.00	56-75.00
83-01-006	Barbershop	F. Jones	Retrd.	8.00	50-100.00
83-01-007	Sweetshop	F. Jones	Retrd.	8.00	50-100.00
83-01-008	Book Store	F. Jones	Retrd.	8.00	50-100.00
83-01-009	Antique Shop	F. Jones	Retrd.	8.00	50-75.00
83-01-010	Florist Shop	F. Jones	Retrd.	8.00	50-100.00
83-01-011	Toy Shoppe	F. Jones	Retrd.	8.00	50-100.00
83-01-012	Apothecary	F. Jones	Retrd.	8.00	35-100.00
83-01-013	Set	F. Jones	Retrd.	96.00	850-2000.
The Cat's Meow		**Series II**			
84-02-001	Grandinere House	F. Jones	Retrd.	8.00	46-56.00
84-02-002	Brocke House	F. Jones	Retrd.	8.00	46-56.00
84-02-003	Eaton House	F. Jones	Retrd.	8.00	36-56.00
84-02-004	Church	F. Jones	Retrd.	8.00	30-110.00
84-02-005	Town Hall	F. Jones	Retrd.	8.00	45-76.00
84-02-006	Music Shop	F. Jones	Retrd.	8.00	45-100.00
84-02-007	Attorney/Bank	F. Jones	Retrd.	8.00	45-76.00
84-02-008	S&T Clothiers	F. Jones	Retrd.	8.00	45-76.00
84-02-009	Millinery/Quilt	F. Jones	Retrd.	8.00	36-100.00
84-02-010	Tobacconist/Shoemaker	F. Jones	Retrd.	8.00	46-76.00
84-02-011	Set	F. Jones	Retrd.	96.00	475-800.
The Cat's Meow		**Series III**			
85-03-001	Hobart-Harley House	F. Jones	Retrd.	8.00	25-27.00
85-03-002	Kalorama Guest House	F. Jones	Retrd.	8.00	25-27.00
85-03-003	Allen-Coe House	F. Jones	Retrd.	8.00	20-27.00
85-03-004	Opera House	F. Jones	Retrd.	8.00	25-27.00
85-03-005	Connecticut Ave. FireHouse	F. Jones	Retrd.	8.00	25-35.00
85-03-006	Dry Goods Store	F. Jones	Retrd.	8.00	25-27.00
85-03-007	Fine Jewelers	F. Jones	Retrd.	8.00	25-27.00
85-03-008	Edinburgh Times	F. Jones	Retrd.	8.00	25-27.00
85-03-009	Main St. Carriage Shop	F. Jones	Retrd.	8.00	25-27.00
85-03-010	Ristorante	F. Jones	Retrd.	8.00	25-27.00
The Cat's Meow		**Series IV**			
86-04-001	John Belville House	F. Jones	Retrd.	8.00	15-19.00
86-04-002	Westbrook House	F. Jones	Retrd.	8.00	19.00
86-04-003	Bennington-Hull House	F. Jones	Retrd.	8.00	15-19.00
86-04-004	Vandenberg House	F. Jones	Retrd.	8.00	15-19.00
86-04-005	Chepachet Union Church	F. Jones	Retrd.	8.00	15-19.00
86-04-006	Chagrin Falls Popcorn Shop	F. Jones	Retrd.	8.00	15-19.00
86-04-007	O'Malley's Livery Stable	F. Jones	Retrd.	8.00	15-19.00
86-04-008	The Little House Giftables	F. Jones	Retrd.	8.00	15-19.00
86-04-009	Jones Bros. Tea Co.	F. Jones	Retrd.	8.00	15-19.00
86-04-010	Village Clock Shop	F. Jones	Retrd.	8.00	19.00
The Cat's Meow		**Series V**			
87-05-001	Murray Hotel	F. Jones	Retrd.	8.00	8.00
87-05-002	Congruity Tavern	F. Jones	Retrd.	8.00	8.00
87-05-003	M. Washington House	F. Jones	Retrd.	8.00	8.00
87-05-004	Creole House	F. Jones	Retrd.	8.00	8.00
87-05-005	Police Department	F. Jones	Retrd.	8.00	8.00
87-05-006	Markethouse	F. Jones	Retrd.	8.00	8.00
87-05-007	Southport Bank	F. Jones	Retrd.	8.00	8.00
87-05-008	Amish Oak/Dixie Shoe	F. Jones	Retrd.	8.00	8.00
87-05-009	Dentist/Physician	F. Jones	Retrd.	8.00	8.00
87-05-010	Architect/Tailor	F. Jones	Retrd.	8.00	8.00
The Cat's Meow		**Series VI**			
88-06-001	Burton Lancaster House	F. Jones	Open	8.00	9.00
88-06-002	Ohliger House	F. Jones	Open	8.00	9.00
88-06-003	Stiffenbody Funeral Home	F. Jones	Open	8.00	9.00
88-06-004	Pruyn House	F. Jones	Open	8.00	9.00
88-06-005	First Baptist Church	F. Jones	Open	8.00	9.00
88-06-006	City Hospital	F. Jones	Open	8.00	9.00
88-06-007	Lincoln School	F. Jones	Open	8.00	9.00
88-06-008	Fish/Meat Market	F. Jones	Open	8.00	9.00
88-06-009	New Masters Gallery	F. Jones	Open	8.00	9.00
88-06-010	Williams & Sons	F. Jones	Open	8.00	9.00
The Cat's Meow		**Series VII**			
89-07-001	Thorpe House Bed & Breakfast	F. Jones	Open	8.00	9.00
89-07-002	Justice of the Peace	F. Jones	Open	8.00	9.00
89-07-003	Old Franklin Book Shop	F. Jones	Open	8.00	9.00
89-07-004	Octagonal School	F. Jones	Open	8.00	9.00
89-07-005	Winkler Bakery	F. Jones	Open	8.00	9.00
89-07-006	Black Cat Antiques	F. Jones	Open	8.00	9.00
89-07-007	Village Tinsmith	F. Jones	Open	8.00	9.00
89-07-008	Williams Apothecary	F. Jones	Open	8.00	9.00
89-07-009	Handcrafted Toys	F. Jones	Open	8.00	9.00
89-07-010	Hairdressing Parlor	F. Jones	Open	8.00	9.00
The Cat's Meow		**Series VIII**			
90-08-001	Puritan House	F. Jones	Open	8.00	9.00
90-08-002	Haberdashers	F. Jones	Open	8.00	9.00
90-08-003	Walldorff Furniture	F. Jones	Open	8.00	9.00
90-08-004	Victoria's Parlour	F. Jones	Open	8.00	9.00
90-08-005	Globe Corner Bookstore	F. Jones	Open	8.00	9.00
90-08-006	Medina Fire Department	F. Jones	Open	8.00	9.00
90-08-007	Piccadilli Pipe & Tobacco	F. Jones	Open	8.00	9.00
90-08-008	Noah's Ark Veterinary	F. Jones	Open	8.00	9.00
90-08-009	F.J. Realty Company	F. Jones	Open	8.00	9.00
90-08-010	Nell's Stems & Stitches	F. Jones	Open	8.00	9.00
The Cat's Meow		**Series IX**			
91-09-001	Central City Opera House	F. Jones	Open	8.00	9.00
91-09-002	All Saints Chapel	F. Jones	Open	8.00	9.00
91-09-003	City Hall	F. Jones	Open	8.00	9.00
91-09-004	Gov. Snyder Mansion	F. Jones	Open	8.00	9.00
91-09-005	American Red Cross	F. Jones	Open	8.00	9.00
91-09-006	The Treble Clef	F. Jones	Open	8.00	9.00
91-09-007	Osbahr's Upholstery	F. Jones	Open	8.00	9.00
91-09-008	Spanky's Hardware Co.	F. Jones	Open	8.00	9.00
91-09-009	CPA/Law Office	F. Jones	Open	8.00	9.00
91-09-010	Jeweler/Optometrist	F. Jones	Open	8.00	9.00
The Cat's Meow		**Series X**			
92-10-001	Henyan's Athletic Shop	F. Jones	Open	8.50	9.00
92-10-002	Grand Haven	F. Jones	Open	8.50	9.00
92-10-003	Fudge Kitchen	F. Jones	Open	8.50	9.00
92-10-004	United Church of Acworth	F. Jones	Open	8.50	9.00
92-10-005	City News	F. Jones	Open	8.50	9.00
92-10-006	Pure Gas Station	F. Jones	Open	8.50	9.00
92-10-007	Pickles Pub	F. Jones	Open	8.50	9.00
92-10-008	Madeline's Dress Shop	F. Jones	Open	8.50	9.00
92-10-009	Owl And The Pussycat	F. Jones	Open	8.50	9.00
92-10-010	Leppert's 5 &10¢	F. Jones	Open	8.50	9.00
The Cat's Meow		**Roscoe Village**			
86-11-001	Roscoe General Store	F. Jones	Retrd.	8.00	14-16.00
86-11-002	Jackson Twp. Hall	F. Jones	Retrd.	8.00	14-16.00
86-11-003	Old Warehouse Rest.	F. Jones	Retrd.	8.00	14-16.00
86-11-004	Canal Company	F. Jones	Retrd.	8.00	14-16.00
The Cat's Meow		**Fall**			
86-12-001	Mail Pouch Barn	F. Jones	Retrd.	8.00	14-18.00
86-12-002	Vollant Mills	F. Jones	Retrd.	8.00	14-18.00
86-12-003	Grimm's Farmhouse	F. Jones	Retrd.	8.00	14-18.00
86-12-004	Golden Lamb Buttery	F. Jones	Retrd.	8.00	14-18.00
The Cat's Meow		**Nautical**			
87-13-001	Monhegan Boat Landing	F. Jones	Retrd.	8.00	8.00
87-13-002	Lorain Lighthouse	F. Jones	Retrd.	8.00	8.00
87-13-003	Yacht Club	F. Jones	Retrd.	8.00	8.00
87-13-004	H & E Ships Chandlery	F. Jones	Retrd.	8.00	8.00
The Cat's Meow		**Main St.**			
87-14-001	Historical Museum	F. Jones	Retrd.	8.00	8.00
87-14-002	Franklin Library	F. Jones	Retrd.	8.00	8.00
87-14-003	Garden Theatre	F. Jones	Retrd.	8.00	8.00
87-14-004	Telegraph/Post Office	F. Jones	Retrd.	8.00	8.00
The Cat's Meow		**Nantucket**			
87-15-001	Nantucket Atheneum	F. Jones	Retrd.	8.00	8.00
87-15-002	Unitarian Church	F. Jones	Retrd.	8.00	8.00
87-15-003	Maria Mitchell House	F. Jones	Retrd.	8.00	8.00
87-15-004	Jared Coffin House	F. Jones	Retrd.	8.00	8.00
The Cat's Meow		**Hagerstown**			
88-16-001	The Yule Cupboard	F. Jones	Open	8.00	9.00
88-16-002	J Hager House	F. Jones	Open	8.00	9.00
88-16-003	Miller House	F. Jones	Open	8.00	9.00
88-16-004	Woman's Club	F. Jones	Open	8.00	9.00
The Cat's Meow		**Tradesman**			
88-17-001	Hermannhof Winery	F. Jones	Open	8.00	9.00
88-17-002	Jenney Grist Mill	F. Jones	Open	8.00	9.00
88-17-003	Buckeye Candy & Tobacco	F. Jones	Open	8.00	9.00
88-17-004	C.O. Wheel Company	F. Jones	Open	8.00	9.00
The Cat's Meow		**Liberty St.**			
88-18-001	County Courthouse	F. Jones	Open	8.00	9.00
88-18-002	Wilton Railway Depot	F. Jones	Open	8.00	9.00
88-18-003	Graf Printing Co.	F. Jones	Open	8.00	9.00
88-18-004	Z. Jones Basketmaker	F. Jones	Open	8.00	9.00
The Cat's Meow		**Painted Ladies**			
88-19-001	Lady Elizabeth	F. Jones	Open	8.00	9.00
88-19-002	Lady Iris	F. Jones	Open	8.00	9.00
88-19-003	Lady Amanda	F. Jones	Open	8.00	9.00
88-19-004	Andrews Hotel	F. Jones	Open	8.00	9.00
The Cat's Meow		**Wild West**			
89-20-001	F.C. Zimmermann's Gun Shop	F. Jones	Open	8.00	9.00
89-20-002	Drink 'em up Saloon	F. Jones	Open	8.00	9.00
89-20-003	Wells, Fargo & Co.	F. Jones	Open	8.00	9.00
89-20-004	Marshal's Office	F. Jones	Open	8.00	9.00
The Cat's Meow		**Market St.**			
89-21-001	Schumacher Mills	F. Jones	Open	8.00	9.00
89-21-002	Seville Hardware Store	F. Jones	Open	8.00	9.00
89-21-003	West India Goods Store	F. Jones	Open	8.00	9.00
89-21-004	Yankee Candle Company	F. Jones	Open	8.00	9.00
The Cat's Meow		**Lighthouse**			
90-22-001	Split Rock Lighthouse	F. Jones	Open	8.00	9.00
90-22-002	Cape Hatteras Lighthouse	F. Jones	Open	8.00	9.00
90-22-003	Sandy Hook Lighthouse	F. Jones	Open	8.00	9.00
90-22-004	Admiralty Head	F. Jones	Open	8.00	9.00
The Cat's Meow		**Ohio Amish**			
91-23-001	Jonas Troyer Home	F. Jones	Open	8.00	9.00
91-23-002	Ada Mae's Quilt Barn	F. Jones	Open	8.00	9.00
91-23-003	Eli's Harness Shop	F. Jones	Open	8.00	9.00
91-23-004	Brown School	F. Jones	Open	8.00	9.00
The Cat's Meow		**Washington, D.C.**			
91-24-001	U.S. Capitol	F. Jones	Open	8.00	9.00
91-24-002	White House	F. Jones	Open	8.00	9.00
91-24-003	National Archives	F. Jones	Open	8.00	9.00
91-24-004	U.S. Supreme Court	F. Jones	Open	8.00	9.00
The Cat's Meow		**American Barns**			
92-25-001	Ohio Barn	F. Jones	Open	8.50	9.00
92-25-002	Bank Barn	F. Jones	Open	8.50	9.00
92-25-003	Crib Barn	F. Jones	Open	8.50	9.00
92-25-004	Vermont Barn	F. Jones	Open	8.50	9.00
The Cat's Meow		**Accessories**			
83-26-001	Summer Tree	F. Jones	Retrd.	4.00	17-46.00
83-26-002	Fall Tree	F. Jones	Retrd.	4.00	17-46.00

Company Number	Name	Series Artist	Edition Limit	Issue Price	Quote
83-26-003	Pine Tree	F. Jones	Retrd.	4.00	17-46.00
83-26-004	XMas Pine Tree	F. Jones	Retrd.	4.00	25-46.00
83-26-005	XMas Pine Tree w/Red Bows	F. Jones	Retrd.	3.00	100-175.
84-26-006	5" Picket Fence	F. Jones	Retrd.	3.00	5.50
84-26-007	8" Picket Fence	F. Jones	Retrd.	3.25	23-46.00
84-26-008	5" Hedge	F. Jones	Retrd.	3.00	7.00-46.00
84-26-009	8" Hedge	F. Jones	Retrd.	3.25	45.00
84-26-010	Gas Light	F. Jones	Open	3.25	4.10
84-26-011	Dairy Wagon	F. Jones	Retrd.	4.00	5.00-10.00
84-26-012	Horse & Carriage	F. Jones	Retrd.	4.00	5.00-10.00
84-26-013	Horse & Sleigh	F. Jones	Retrd.	4.00	4.00
85-26-014	Band Stand	F. Jones	Retrd.	6.50	6.50
85-26-015	Lilac Bushes	F. Jones	Retrd.	3.00	90-125.00
85-26-016	Telephone Booth	F. Jones	Open	3.00	4.10
85-26-017	FJ Real Estate Sign	F. Jones	Retrd.	3.00	5.00-10.00
85-26-018	U.S. Flag	F. Jones	Open	3.25	4.10
85-26-019	Chickens	F. Jones	Retrd.	3.25	5-8.00
85-26-020	Ducks	F. Jones	Retrd.	3.25	5-9.00
85-26-021	Cows	F. Jones	Retrd.	4.00	5.00-10.00
85-26-022	Main St. Sign	F. Jones	Open	3.25	4.10
85-26-023	Flower Pots	F. Jones	Open	3.00	4.10
86-26-024	Carolers	F. Jones	Retrd.	4.00	8.00-10.00
86-26-025	5" Iron Fence	F. Jones	Retrd.	3.00	46.00
86-26-026	8" Iron Fence	F. Jones	Retrd.	3.25	46-50.00
86-26-027	Wishing Well	F. Jones	Retrd.	3.25	5.00-9.00
86-26-028	Skipjacks	F. Jones	Open	6.50	6.50
86-26-029	Ice Wagon	F. Jones	Retrd.	4.00	8-10.00
86-26-030	Mail Wagon	F. Jones	Open	4.00	4.10
86-26-031	Iron Gate	F. Jones	Retrd.	3.00	55-60.00
86-26-032	Wooden Gate	F. Jones	Retrd.	3.00	3.00
86-26-033	Poplar Tree	F. Jones	Retrd.	4.00	17-46.00
86-26-034	Street Clock	F. Jones	Open	3.25	4.10
86-26-035	Cherry Tree	F. Jones	Retrd.	4.00	20-65.00
87-26-036	FJ Express	F. Jones	Retrd.	4.00	4.00
87-26-037	Liberty St. Sign	F. Jones	Retrd.	3.25	5.00-9.00
87-26-038	Railroad Sign	F. Jones	Retrd.	3.00	3.00
87-26-039	Windmill	F. Jones	Retrd.	3.25	3.25
87-26-040	Cable Car	F. Jones	Retrd.	4.00	6.00-10.00
88-26-041	Butch & T.J.	F. Jones	Retrd.	4.00	4.00
88-26-042	Charlie & Co.	F. Jones	Retrd.	4.00	4.00
88-26-043	Ada Belle	F. Jones	Open	4.00	4.10
88-26-044	Colonial Bread Wagon	F. Jones	Open	4.00	4.10
89-26-045	Pony Express Rider	F. Jones	Open	4.00	4.10
89-26-046	Wells, Fargo Wagon	F. Jones	Retrd.	4.00	8.00-12.00
89-26-047	Market St. Sign	F. Jones	Retrd.	3.25	5.00-9.00
89-26-048	Passenger Train Car	F. Jones	Open	4.00	4.10
89-26-049	Harry's Hotdogs	F. Jones	Open	4.00	4.10
89-26-050	Clothesline	F. Jones	Open	4.00	4.10
89-24-051	Touring Car	F. Jones	Retrd.	4.00	8.00
89-26-052	Pumpkin Wagon	F. Jones	Open	3.25	4.10
89-26-053	Nanny	F. Jones	Retrd.	4.00	4.00
89-26-054	Rudy & Aldine	F. Jones	Open	4.00	4.10
89-26-055	Tad & Toni	F. Jones	Open	4.00	4.10
89-26-056	Snowmen	F. Jones	Open	4.00	4.10
89-26-057	Rose Trellis	F. Jones	Open	3.25	4.10
89-26-058	Quaker Oats Train Car	F. Jones	Open	4.00	4.10
90-26-059	Gerstenslager Buggy	F. Jones	Open	4.00	4.10
90-26-060	1914 Fire Pumper	F. Jones	Open	4.00	4.10
90-26-061	1913 Peerless Touring Car	F. Jones	Open	4.00	4.10
90-26-062	1909 Franklin Limousine	F. Jones	Open	4.00	4.10
90-26-063	Watkins Wagon	F. Jones	Open	4.00	4.10
90-26-064	Veterinary Wagon	F. Jones	Open	4.00	4.10
90-26-065	Amish Buggy	F. Jones	Open	4.00	4.10
90-26-066	Victorian Outhouse	F. Jones	Open	4.00	4.10
90-26-067	Bus Stop	F. Jones	Open	4.00	4.10
90-26-068	Eugene	F. Jones	Open	4.00	4.10
90-26-069	Christmas Tree Lot	F. Jones	Open	4.00	4.10
90-26-070	Santa & Reindeer	F. Jones	Open	4.00	4.10
90-26-071	5" Wrought Iron Fence	F. Jones	Open	3.00	4.10
90-26-072	Little Red Caboose	F. Jones	Open	4.00	4.10
90-26-073	Red Maple Tree	F. Jones	Open	4.00	4.10
90-26-074	Tulip Tree	F. Jones	Open	4.00	4.10
90-26-075	Blue Spruce	F. Jones	Open	4.00	4.10
90-26-076	XMas Spruce	F. Jones	Open	4.00	4.10
91-26-077	School Bus	F. Jones	Open	4.00	4.10
91-26-078	Popcorn Wagon	F. Jones	Open	4.00	4.10
91-26-079	Scarey Harry (Scarecrow)	F. Jones	Open	4.00	4.10
91-26-080	Amish Garden	F. Jones	Open	4.00	4.10
91-26-081	Chessie Hopper Car	F. Jones	Open	4.00	4.10
91-26-082	USMC War Memorial	F. Jones	Open	6.50	6.50
91-26-083	Village Entrance Sigh	F. Jones	Open	6.50	6.50
91-26-084	Concert in the Park	F. Jones	Open	4.00	4.10
91-26-085	Martin House	F. Jones	Open	3.25	4.10
91-26-086	Marble Game	F. Jones	Open	4.00	4.10
91-26-087	Barnyard	F. Jones	Open	4.00	4.10
91-26-088	Ski Party	F. Jones	Open	4.00	4.10
91-26-089	On Vacation	F. Jones	Open	4.00	4.10
91-26-090	Jack The Postman	F. Jones	Open	3.25	4.10
92-26-091	Forsythia Bush	F. Jones	Open	3.98	4.10
92-26-092	Police Car	F. Jones	Open	3.98	4.10
92-26-093	Delivery Truck	F. Jones	Open	3.98	4.10
92-26-094	School Crossing	F. Jones	Open	3.98	4.10
92-26-095	Mr. Softee Truck	F. Jones	Open	3.98	4.10
92-26-096	Gasoline Truck	F. Jones	Open	3.98	4.10
92-26-097	Silo	F. Jones	Open	3.98	4.10
92-26-098	Springhouse	F. Jones	Open	3.25	4.10
92-26-099	Nutcracker Billboard	F. Jones	Open	3.98	4.10
The Cat's Meow		**Williamsburg Christmas**			
83-27-001	Christmas Church	F. Jones	Retrd.	6.00	N/A
83-27-002	Garrison House	F. Jones	Retrd.	6.00	N/A
83-27-003	Federal House	F. Jones	Retrd.	6.00	N/A
83-27-004	Georgian House	F. Jones	Retrd.	6.00	N/A
83-27-005	Set	F. Jones	Retrd	24.00	N/A
The Cat's Meow		**Nantucket Christmas**			
84-28-001	Powell House	F. Jones	Retrd.	6.50	N/A
84-28-002	Shaw House	F. Jones	Retrd.	6.50	N/A
84-28-003	Wintrop House	F. Jones	Retrd.	6.50	N/A
84-28-004	Christmas Shop	F. Jones	Retrd.	6.50	N/A
84-28-005	Set	F. Jones	Retrd.	26.00	400-1350.

Company Number	Name	Series Artist	Edition Limit	Issue Price	Quote
The Cat's Meow		**Ohio Western Reserve Christmas**			
85-29-001	Western Reserve Academy	F. Jones	Retrd.	7.00	35-175.00
85-29-002	Olmstead House	F. Jones	Retrd.	7.00	35-175.00
85-29-003	Bellevue House	F. Jones	Retrd.	7.00	35-175.00
85-29-004	Gates Mills Church	F. Jones	Retrd.	7.00	35-175.00
85-29-005	Set	F. Jones	Retrd.	27.00	400-700.
The Cat's Meow		**Savannah Christmas**			
86-30-001	J.J. Dale Row House	F. Jones	Retrd.	7.25	150.00
86-30-002	Liberty Inn	F. Jones	Retrd.	7.25	150.00
86-30-003	Lafayette Square House	F. Jones	Retrd.	7.25	150.00
86-30-004	Simon Mirault Cottage	F. Jones	Retrd.	7.25	150.00
86-30-005	Set	F. Jones	Retrd.	29.00	600-1050.
The Cat's Meow		**Maine Christmas**			
87-31-001	Damariscotta Church	F. Jones	Retrd.	7.75	125.00
87-31-002	Portland Head Lighthouse	F. Jones	Retrd.	7.75	125.00
87-31-003	Cappy's Chowder House	F. Jones	Retrd.	7.75	125.00
87-31-004	Captain's House	F. Jones	Retrd.	7.75	125.00
87-31-005	Set	F. Jones	Retrd.	31.00	750-1350
The Cat's Meow		**Philadelphia Christmas**			
88-32-001	Graff House	F. Jones	Retrd.	7.75	50-75.00
88-32-002	Hill-Physick-Keith House	F. Jones	Retrd.	7.75	75.00
88-32-003	Elfreth's Alley	F. Jones	Retrd.	7.75	50-75.00
88-32-004	The Head House	F. Jones	Retrd.	7.75	50-75.00
88-32-005	Set	F. Jones	Retrd.	31.00	350-450.
The Cat's Meow		**Christmas In New England**			
89-33-001	The Old South Meeting House	F. Jones	Retrd.	8.00	32-55.00
89-33-002	Hunter House	F. Jones	Retrd.	8.00	32-55.00
89-33-003	Sheldon's Tavern	F. Jones	Retrd.	8.00	32-55.00
89-33-004	The Vermont Country Store	F. Jones	Retrd.	8.00	32-55.00
89-33-005	Set	F. Jones	Retrd.	32.00	200-325.
The Cat's Meow		**Colonial Virginia Christmas**			
90-34-001	Rising Sun Tavern	F. Jones	Retrd.	8.00	10-25.00
90-34-002	St. John's Church	F. Jones	Retrd.	8.00	15-25.00
90-34-003	Dulany House	F. Jones	Retrd.	8.00	35.00
90-34-004	Shirley Plantation	F. Jones	Retrd.	8.00	10-25.00
90-34-005	Set	F. Jones	Retrd.	32.00	100.00
The Cat's Meow		**Rocky Mountain Christmas**			
91-35-001	First Presbyterian Church	F. Jones	Retrd.	8.20	15-45.00
91-35-002	Tabor House	F. Jones	Retrd.	8.20	15-45.00
91-35-003	Western Hotel	F. Jones	Retrd.	8.20	15-45.00
91-35-004	Wheller-Stallard House	F. Jones	Retrd.	8.20	15-45.00
91-35-005	Set	F. Jones	Retrd.	32.80	72.00
The Cat's Meow		**Hometown Christmas**			
92-36-001	Wayne Co. Courthouse	F. Jones	Retrd.	8.50	8.50
92-36-002	Overholt House	F. Jones	Retrd.	8.50	8.50
92-36-003	August Imgard House	F. Jones	Retrd.	8.50	8.50
92-36-004	Howey House	F. Jones	Retrd.	8.50	8.50
92-36-005	Set	F. Jones	Retrd.	34.00	34.00
The Cat's Meow		**Collector Club Gift - Houses**			
89-37-001	Betsy Ross House	F. Jones	Closed	Gift	150.00
90-37-002	Amelia Earhart	F. Jones	Closed	Gift	80.00
91-37-003	Limberlost Cabin	F. Jones	Closed	Gift	N/A
92-37-004	Abigail Adams Birthplace	F. Jones	Closed	Gift	N/A
93-37-005	Pearl S. Buck House	F. Jones	Yr.Iss.	Gift	N/A
The Cat's Meow		**Collector Club Pieces - Famous Authors**			
89-38-001	Harriet Beecher Stowe	F. Jones	Closed	8.75	85.00
89-38-002	Orchard House	F. Jones	Closed	8.75	85.00
89-38-003	Longfellow House	F. Jones	Closed	8.75	85.00
89-38-004	Herman Melville's Arrowhead	F. Jones	Closed	8.75	85.00
89-38-005	Set	F. Jones	Closed	35.00	750.00
The Cat's Meow		**Collector Club Pieces - Great Inventors**			
90-39-001	Thomas Edison	F. Jones	Closed	9.25	30.00
90-39-002	Ford Motor Co.	F. Jones	Closed	9.25	30.00
90-39-003	Seth Thomas Clock Co.	F. Jones	Closed	9.25	30.00
90-39-004	Wright Cycle Co.	F. Jones	Closed	9.25	30.00
90-39-005	Set	F. Jones	Closed	37.00	450.00
The Cat's Meow		**Collector Club Pieces - American Songwriters**			
91-40-001	Benjamin R. Hanby House	F. Jones	Closed	9.25	N/A
91-40-002	Anna Warner House	F. Jones	Closed	9.25	N/A
91-40-003	Stephen Foster Home	F. Jones	Closed	9.25	N/A
91-40-004	Oscar Hammerstein House	F. Jones	Closed	9.25	N/A
The Cat's Meow		**Collector Club Pieces - Signers of the Declaration**			
92-41-001	Josiah Bartlett Home	F. Jones	Closed	9.75	9.75
92-41-002	George Clymer Home	F. Jones	Closed	9.75	9.75
92-41-003	Stephen Hopkins Home	F. Jones	Closed	9.75	9.75
92-41-004	John Witherspoon Home	F. Jones	Closed	9.75	9.75
The Cat's Meow		**Collector Club Pieces - 19th Century Master Builders**			
93-42-001	Henry Hobson Richardson	F. Jones	Yr.Iss.	10.25	10.25
93-42-002	Samuel Sloan	F. Jones	Yr.Iss.	10.25	10.25
93-42-003	Alexander Jackson Davis	F. Jones	Yr.Iss.	10.25	10.25
93-42-004	Andrew Jackson Downing	F. Jones	Yr.Iss.	10.25	10.25
The Cat's Meow		**Miscellaneous**			
85-43-001	Pencil Holder	F. Jones	Closed	3.95	210.00
85-43-002	Recipe Holder	F. Jones	Closed	3.95	210.00
The Constance Collection		**Santa Claus By Constance**			
86-01-001	Jolly St. Nick	C. Guerra	4,000	72.00	72.00
86-01-002	Victorian Santa	C. Guerra	4,000	90.00	90.00
86-01-003	Victorian Santa With Bear	C. Guerra	4,000	80.00	80.00
87-01-004	Animal Santa	C. Guerra	4,000	78.00	78.00
88-01-005	Midnight Visit	C. Guerra	4,000	112.00	112.00
88-01-006	American Traditional Santa	C. Guerra	4,000	90.00	90.00
88-01-007	Santas Delivery	C. Guerra	4,000	90.00	90.00
88-01-008	Saint Nicholas of Myra	C. Guerra	4,000	90.00	90.00
89-01-009	Santa With Lamb	C. Guerra	4,000	112.00	112.00
89-01-010	Santa With Deer	C. Guerra	4,000	112.00	112.00
89-01-011	Cobblestone Santa	C. Guerra	4,000	112.00	112.00
89-01-012	Kitty Christmas	C. Guerra	4,000	112.00	112.00
89-01-013	Thomas Nast Santa	C. Guerra	4,000	112.00	112.00

Number	Name	Artist	Edition Limit	Issue Price	Quote
89-01-014	Siberian Santa	C. Guerra	1,000	190.00	190.00
89-01-015	Santa With Girl	C. Guerra	1,000	90.00	90.00
89-01-016	Santa With Boy	C. Guerra	1,000	90.00	90.00
89-01-017	Santas Sleigh	C. Guerra	1,000	190.00	190.00
90-01-018	Elf Santa	C. Guerra	1,000	298.00	298.00
90-01-019	Candy Cane Santa	C. Guerra	1,000	124.00	124.00
90-01-020	Rockinghorse Santa	C. Guerra	1,000	124.00	124.00
90-01-021	Kitty Claus	C. Guerra	1,000	78.00	78.00
90-01-022	Hunt Santa	C. Guerra	1,000	158.00	158.00
91-01-023	First Frost	C. Guerra	1,000	250.00	250.00
91-01-024	Santa's Day Off	C. Guerra	1,000	90.00	90.00
91-01-025	Santa's Dance	C. Guerra	1,000	95.00	95.00
91-01-026	Little Boy's Santa	C. Guerra	1,000	95.00	95.00
91-01-027	Heavenly Blessing	C. Guerra	1,000	79.00	79.00
91-01-028	Santa's Girl	C. Guerra	1,000	95.00	95.00
91-01-029	First Christmas	C. Guerra	1,000	79.00	79.00
92-01-030	Peace on Earth	C. Guerra	2,500	64.00	64.00
92-01-031	Touch Up Santa	C. Guerra	2,500	64.00	64.00
92-01-032	Hush! Hush! Santa	C. Guerra	2,500	59.90	59.90
92-01-033	Test Run Santa	C. Guerra	2,500	79.00	79.00
92-01-034	Old English Santa	C. Guerra	500	90.00	90.00
92-01-035	Ringing In Christmas	C. Guerra	500	112.00	112.00
92-01-036	Wassail Santa	C. Guerra	500	90.00	90.00
92-01-037	Santa w/Birdhouse	C. Guerra	500	112.00	112.00
92-01-038	Midnight Blue	C. Guerra	500	112.00	112.00
The Constance Collection		**Annual Santa Claus By Constance**			
91-02-001	Teddy Claus	C. Guerra	Yr.Iss.	90.00	90.00
92-02-002	Reach For The Star Santa	C. Guerra	Yr.Iss.	90.00	90.00
The Constance Collection		**The Briar Patch**			
90-03-001	Bernard Bunny	C. Guerra	1,500	30.00	30.00
90-03-002	Betsey Bunny	C. Guerra	1,500	30.00	30.00
90-03-003	Barbara Bunny	C. Guerra	1,500	30.00	30.00
90-03-004	Buster Bunny	C. Guerra	1,500	30.00	30.00
90-03-005	Bonnie Bunny	C. Guerra	1,500	30.00	30.00
90-03-006	Benedict Bunny	C. Guerra	1,500	30.00	30.00
90-03-007	Bernice Bunny	C. Guerra	1,500	30.00	30.00
90-03-008	Bertrum Bunny	C. Guerra	1,500	30.00	30.00
90-03-009	Brotherly Bunny	C. Guerra	1,500	30.00	30.00
90-03-010	Birtha Bunny	C. Guerra	1,500	30.00	30.00
90-03-011	Brownie Bunny	C. Guerra	1,500	30.00	30.00
90-03-012	Bartholemue Bunny	C. Guerra	1,500	30.00	30.00
90-03-013	Braida Bunny	C. Guerra	1,500	30.00	30.00
90-03-014	Blossum Bunny	C. Guerra	1,500	30.00	30.00
92-03-015	Grandfather Bun	C. Guerra	2,500	21.90	21.90
92-03-016	Mother w/ Twins	C. Guerra	2,500	21.90	21.90
92-03-017	Pappa Bunny	C. Guerra	2,500	21.90	21.90
92-03-018	Grandmother Bunny	C. Guerra	2,500	21.90	21.90
92-03-019	Proud Pappa Bunny	C. Guerra	2,500	21.90	21.90
92-03-020	New Mamma Bunny	C. Guerra	2,500	21.90	21.90
92-03-021	Woodland Bunny	C. Guerra	2,500	31.50	31.50
92-03-022	Number One Bun	C. Guerra	2,500	21.90	21.90
92-03-023	Love Bun	C. Guerra	2,500	21.90	21.90
92-03-024	Bunny's Basket	C. Guerra	2,500	21.90	21.90
92-03-025	Pondering Bun	C. Guerra	2,500	21.90	21.90
The Constance Collection		**Kitty Kat Klub**			
90-04-001	Konrad Kitty	C. Guerra	1,500	30.00	30.00
90-04-002	Klara Kitty	C. Guerra	1,500	30.00	30.00
90-04-003	Klarence Kitty	C. Guerra	1,500	30.00	30.00
90-04-004	Kockey Kitty	C. Guerra	1,500	30.00	30.00
90-04-005	Koquette Kitty	C. Guerra	1,500	30.00	30.00
90-04-006	Kassandra Kitty	C. Guerra	1,500	30.00	30.00
90-04-007	Katrina Kitty	C. Guerra	1,500	30.00	30.00
90-04-008	Klaudius Kitty	C. Guerra	1,500	30.00	30.00
The Constance Collection		**The Golden Americans**			
91-05-001	Belinda	C. Guerra	1,500	31.00	31.00
91-05-002	Andres And Sam	C. Guerra	1,500	37.00	37.00
91-05-003	Gilbert	C. Guerra	1,500	31.00	31.00
91-05-004	Effie And Company	C. Guerra	1,500	31.00	31.00
91-05-005	Ruby Rae And Tom-tom	C. Guerra	1,500	37.00	37.00
91-05-006	Lettie The Dollmaker	C. Guerra	1,500	48.00	48.00
91-05-007	Hannah And Kitty	C. Guerra	1,500	42.00	42.00
91-05-008	Emma And Nickie	C. Guerra	1,500	37.00	37.00
91-05-009	Puppy Love	C. Guerra	1,500	37.00	37.00
91-05-010	Missing You	C. Guerra	1,500	37.00	37.00
91-05-011	Penny Pincher	C. Guerra	1,500	48.00	48.00
91-05-012	Glorya	C. Guerra	1,500	75.00	75.00
91-05-013	Grandmas Love	C. Guerra	1,500	65.00	65.00
91-05-014	Puddles	C. Guerra	1,500	37.00	37.00
91-05-015	Sunday Morning	C. Guerra	1,500	75.00	75.00
91-05-016	Frozen Friends	C. Guerra	1,500	42.00	42.00
91-05-017	Felicia & Fluff	C. Guerra	1,500	37.00	37.00
91-05-018	Sweet Dreams	C. Guerra	1,500	37.00	37.00
91-05-019	New Pups	C. Guerra	1,500	31.00	31.00
91-05-020	Learning to Braid	C. Guerra	1,500	42.00	42.00
91-05-021	School Daze	C. Guerra	1,500	31.00	31.00
91-05-022	Endless Love	C. Guerra	1,500	48.00	48.00
91-05-023	Daddy's Darling	C. Guerra	1,500	48.00	48.00
91-05-024	Party Time Pals	C. Guerra	1,500	55.00	55.00
91-05-025	Blessed With Love	C. Guerra	1,500	55.00	55.00
91-05-026	Sweet Assurance	C. Guerra	1,500	48.00	48.00
91-05-027	Preacher Man	C. Guerra	1,500	31.00	31.00
91-05-028	Play Time	C. Guerra	1,500	31.00	31.00
91-05-029	Into The Light	C. Guerra	1,500	31.00	31.00
91-05-030	Praying Pals	C. Guerra	1,500	31.00	31.00
92-05-031	Annelle	C. Guerra	2,500	37.00	37.00
92-05-032	First Position	C. Guerra	2,500	31.00	31.00
92-05-033	Prima Dona	C. Guerra	2,500	31.00	31.00
92-05-034	Balla Rena	C. Guerra	2,500	31.00	31.00
92-05-035	Puppy Loving	C. Guerra	2,500	37.00	37.00
92-05-036	Prepie Winthrop	C. Guerra	2,500	31.00	31.00
92-05-037	Prepie Gregory	C. Guerra	2,500	37.00	31.00
92-05-038	Church Lady Ellie	C. Guerra	2,500	37.00	37.00
92-05-039	Church Lady Ethel	C. Guerra	2,500	37.00	37.00
92-05-040	Church Lady Pearle	C. Guerra	2,500	37.00	37.00
92-05-041	Too Much Homework	C. Guerra	2,500	48.00	48.00
92-05-042	Chris Miss	C. Guerra	2,500	31.00	31.00
92-05-043	Joy Boy	C. Guerra	2,500	31.00	31.00
92-05-044	Bestest Friends	C. Guerra	2,500	31.00	31.00
92-05-045	Mandas Nabbit	C. Guerra	2,500	31.00	31.00

Number	Name	Artist	Edition Limit	Issue Price	Quote
92-05-046	Little Magic	C. Guerra	2,500	31.00	31.00
92-05-047	Quarterback Jack	C. Guerra	2,500	31.00	31.00
92-05-048	P.S. I Love You	C. Guerra	2,500	42.00	42.00
92-05-049	Valentine of Mine	C. Guerra	2,500	31.00	31.00
92-05-050	Dutchie	C. Guerra	2,500	31.00	31.00
92-05-051	Loving Ewe	C. Guerra	2,500	31.00	31.00
92-05-052	Loving Ewe Too!	C. Guerra	2,500	33.00	33.00
92-05-053	Little Chase	C. Guerra	2,500	31.00	31.00
92-05-054	Bunny Love	C. Guerra	2,500	31.00	31.00
92-05-055	School Girl Sal	C. Guerra	2,500	31.00	31.00
92-05-056	School Girl Sue	C. Guerra	2,500	31.00	31.00
92-05-057	Victory	C. Guerra	2,500	31.00	31.00
92-05-058	Free Kick Dick	C. Guerra	2,500	31.00	31.00
92-05-059	There You Are!	C. Guerra	2,500	48.00	48.00
The Constance Collection		**Victoriana Collection**			
91-06-001	Rosie	C. Guerra	1,500	37.00	37.00
91-06-002	Julia	C. Guerra	1,500	37.00	37.00
91-06-003	Victoria	C. Guerra	1,500	37.00	37.00
91-06-004	Penelope	C. Guerra	1,500	37.00	37.00
91-06-005	Fritz	C. Guerra	1,500	37.00	37.00
The Constance Collection		**Friends & Family Collection**			
92-07-001	First Love	C. Guerra	2,500	57.00	57.00
92-07-002	Christopher	C. Guerra	2,500	37.00	37.00
92-07-003	Chelsea's Easter	C. Guerra	2,500	37.00	37.00
92-07-004	Mothers' Day Bouquet	C. Guerra	2,500	42.00	42.00
92-07-005	Rachel's Blue Bird	C. Guerra	2,500	42.00	42.00
92-07-006	Annette & Christian	C. Guerra	2,500	48.00	48.00
92-07-007	Pitz and Sara	C. Guerra	500	48.00	48.00
92-07-008	A Moment w/ Margo	C. Guerra	2,500	55.00	55.00
92-07-009	Pillow Talk	C. Guerra	2,500	42.00	42.00
92-07-010	Little Sis	C. Guerra	2,500	48.00	48.00
92-07-011	Elizabeth and Phillip	C. Guerra	2,500	55.00	55.00
92-07-012	Michelli Belle	C. Guerra	2,500	31.00	31.00
92-07-013	Missy	C. Guerra	2,500	31.00	31.00
92-07-014	Party Pammy	C. Guerra	2,500	31.00	31.00
92-07-015	One on One Father/Son	C. Guerra	2,500	55.00	55.00
92-07-016	Special Sisters	C. Guerra	2,500	51.00	51.00
92-07-017	Grandpops Angel	C. Guerra	2,500	51.00	51.00
92-07-018	Forever Friends	C. Guerra	2,500	51.00	51.00
92-07-019	Togetherness	C. Guerra	2,500	49.00	49.00
92-07-020	Covered with Love	C. Guerra	2,500	59.90	59.90
92-07-021	Timeout to Love	C. Guerra	2,500	37.00	37.00
92-07-022	Buttercups	C. Guerra	2,500	35.00	35.00
92-07-023	Loves Tender Touch	C. Guerra	2,500	33.00	33.00
The Constance Collection		**Seasonal Santas**			
92-08-001	Fresh Powder Fun	C. Guerra	2,500	72.00	72.00
92-08-002	Fishing Day Fun	C. Guerra	2,500	90.00	90.00
92-08-003	Lost Ball Santa	C. Guerra	2,500	90.00	90.00
92-08-004	Bases Loaded	C. Guerra	2,500	90.00	90.00
92-08-005	Spring Serenity	C. Guerra	2,500	112.00	112.00
The Constance Collection		**Heaven Sent**			
92-09-001	Enduring Faith	C. Guerra	2,500	55.00	55.00
92-09-002	Alleluia	C. Guerra	2,500	45.00	45.00
92-09-003	Christening Day	C. Guerra	2,500	55.00	55.00
92-09-004	Love is Patient	C. Guerra	2,500	49.00	49.00
The Constance Collection		**Tender Tots**			
92-10-001	First Day Home (Girl)	C. Guerra	2,500	35.00	35.00
92-10-002	First Day Home (Boy)	C. Guerra	2,500	35.00	35.00
92-10-003	Night-Night	C. Guerra	2,500	31.00	31.00
92-10-004	Baby Buns	C. Guerra	2,500	31.00	31.00
92-10-005	PlayMates	C. Guerra	2,500	33.00	33.00
92-10-006	First Words	C. Guerra	2,500	37.00	37.00
92-10-007	First Crawl	C. Guerra	2,500	37.00	37.00
92-10-008	Baby's Blocks	C. Guerra	2,500	37.00	37.00
92-10-009	Baby's First ABC's	C. Guerra	2,500	37.00	37.00
92-10-010	Toyland	C. Guerra	2,500	37.00	37.00
92-10-011	Sugarplum Darlings	C. Guerra	2,500	37.00	37.00
The Constance Collection		**Ti Ti and Me**			
92-11-001	Angel Christine	C. Guerra	500	45.00	45.00
92-11-002	Angel Amanda	C. Guerra	500	45.00	45.00
92-11-003	Angel Christen	C. Guerra	500	45.00	45.00
Creart		**African Wildlife**			
86-01-001	Running Elephant -73	Perez	2,500	260.00	320.00
87-01-002	African Elephant -10	Perez	S/O	410.00	410.00
87-01-003	African Elephant With Leaf -22	Martinez	2,500	230.00	280.00
87-01-004	Giraffe -43	Perez	2,500	250.00	320.00
87-01-005	Cob Antelope -46	Perez	2,500	310.00	370.00
87-01-006	African Lion -61	Martinez	2,500	260.00	320.00
87-01-007	Zebra -67	Perez	2,500	305.00	380.00
87-01-008	White Rhinoceros -136	Perez	2,500	330.00	410.00
90-01-009	Symbol of Power Lion -40	Quezada	2,500	450.00	470.00
90-01-010	Hippopotamus -55	Quezeda	2,500	420.00	420.00
91-01-011	Breaking Away Gazelles -256	Quezeda	1,500	650.00	650.00
91-01-012	Sound of Warning Elephant -268	Perez	2,500	500.00	500.00
92-01-013	Small African Elephant- 271	Perez	2,500	320.00	320.00
Creart		**American Wildlife**			
85-02-001	Pigeons- 64	Perez	Closed	265.00	265.00
86-02-002	Polar Bear- 58	Martinez	2,500	200.00	240.00
86-02-003	Bald Eagle- 70	Martinez	Susp.	730.00	730.00
86-02-004	American Bison- 121	Perez	Susp.	400.00	400.00
87-02-005	Grizzley Bear- 31	Perez	2,500	210.00	270.00
87-02-006	Royal Eagle- 49	Martinez	Closed	545.00	545.00
87-02-007	Puma- 130	Perez	2,500	370.00	470.00
88-02-008	Mammoth-112	Martinez	2,500	450.00	550.00
88-02-009	Flamingo Upright-169	Perez	2,500	230.00	294.00
88-02-010	Flamingo Head Down-172	Perez	2,500	230.00	294.00
88-02-011	Flamingo Flapping-175	Perez	2,500	230.00	298.00
89-02-012	Jaguar- 79	Gonzalez	500	700.00	750.00
89-02-013	Rooster- R40	Martinez	Closed	290.00	290.00
89-02-014	Penguins- R76	Del Valle	Closed	175.00	175.00
90-02-015	The Challenge, Rams- 82	Gonzalez	1,500	698.00	698.00
90-02-016	Over the Clouds Falcon- 85	Martinez	2,500	520.00	520.00
90-02-017	Gray Wolf- 88	Quezada	2,500	365.00	370.00
90-02-018	Dolphin, Front- 142	Perez	2,500	210.00	236.00
90-02-019	Dolphin, Middle- 145	Perez	2,500	210.00	236.00

Company		Series			
Number	**Name**	**Artist**	**Edition Limit**	**Issue Price**	**Quote**
90-02-020	Dolphin, Back- 148	Perez	2,500	210.00	236.00
90-02-021	White Tail Deer- 151	Martinez	2,500	380.00	460.00
90-02-022	White Tail Doe- 154	Martinez	2,500	330.00	400.00
90-02-023	White Tail Fawn- 157	Martinez	2,500	220.00	280.00
91-02-024	White Hunter Polar Bear- 250	Gonzalez	2,500	380.00	390.00
91-02-025	Royal Eagle With Snake- 259	Martinez	2,500	700.00	700.00
91-02-026	Mischievous Raccoon- 262	Quezada	2,500	370.00	370.00
91-02-027	Playmates Sparrows- 265	Martinez	2,500	500.00	500.00
92-02-028	Soaring Royal Eagle- 52	Martinez	2,500	580.00	580.00
92-02-029	Penguins- 76	Perez	2,500	100.00	100.00
92-02-030	Standing Whitetail Deer- 109	Martinez	2,500	364.00	364.00
Creart		**Wild America Edition**			
92-03-001	Puma Head- 334	Perez	900	320.00	320.00
92-03-002	Twelve Pointer Deer- 337	Perez	900	472.00	472.00
Creart		**Horses And Cattle**			
85-04-001	Running Horse- 7	Martinez	2,500	360.00	420.00
85-04-002	Arabian Horse- 34	Martinez	2,500	230.00	280.00
85-04-003	Bull- 28	Martinez	Susp.	285.00	285.00
87-04-004	Horse In Passage- 127	Martinez	2,500	500.00	550.00
88-04-005	Horse Head- 139	Martinez	2,500	440.00	480.00
89-04-006	Quarter Horse Recoil- 1	Gonzalez	Closed	310.00	310.00
89-04-007	Brahma Bull- 13	Gonzalez	2,500	420.00	470.00
89-04-008	Arabian Horse- 91	Perez	2,500	260.00	260.00
89-04-009	Lippizzan Horse- 94	Perez	2,500	260.00	260.00
89-04-010	Thoroughbred Horse-97	Perez	2,500	260.00	260.00
89-04-011	Apaloosa Horse- 100	Martinez	2,500	260.00	260.00
89-04-012	Quarter Horse II- 103	Perez	2,500	260.00	260.00
92-04-013	Pegasus- 106	Perez	2,500	420.00	420.00
Creart		**From Asia & Europe**			
85-05-001	Indian Elephant Mother- 25	Perez	Susp.	485.00	485.00
85-05-002	Marco Polo Sheep- 37	Martinez	2,500	270.00	300.00
85-05-003	Tiger- R55	Martinez	Closed	200.00	200.00
86-05-004	Deer- 4	Martinez	Closed	560.00	560.00
86-05-005	Indian Elephant Baby- 16	Perez	Susp.	200.00	200.00
87-05-006	Drover of Camels- 124	Martinez	2,500	650.00	700.00
87-05-007	Royal Owl- 133	Perez	Closed	340.00	340.00
88-05-008	Bengal Tiger- 115	Perez	2,500	440.00	480.00
90-05-009	Giant Panda- 244	Martinez	2,500	280.00	290.00
Creart		**Pets**			
87-06-001	Labrador Retriever- 19	Martinez	2,500	300.00	350.00
89-06-002	Cocker Spaniel American- 184	Martinez	Susp.	100.00	100.00
89-06-003	Boxer- 187	Martinez	Susp.	135.00	135.00
89-06-004	Schnauzer Miniature- 190	Perez	Susp.	110.00	110.00
89-06-005	Great Dane, Brown- 193	Martinez	Susp.	140.00	140.00
89-06-006	Great Dane, Harlequi- 196	Martinez	Susp.	140.00	140.00
89-06-007	Pointer, Brown- 199	Perez	Susp.	132.00	132.00
89-06-008	Pointer, Black- 202	Perez	Susp.	132.00	132.00
89-06-009	Poodle- 205	Perez	Susp.	120.00	120.00
89-06-010	Saint Bernard- 208	Perez	Susp.	130.00	130.00
89-06-011	Labrador, Golden- 211	Martinez	Susp.	130.00	130.00
89-06-012	Labrador, Black- 214	Martinez	Susp.	130.00	130.00
91-06-013	German Shepherd Dog- 253	Martinez	2,500	360.00	360.00
C.U.I./Carolina Collection/Dram Tree		**Legends of Santa Claus**			
91-01-001	Checkin' it Twice	Christjohn	2,500	60.00	60.00
91-01-002	Have You Been a Good Little Boy	Christjohn	2,500	60.00	60.00
91-01-003	Have You Been a Good Little Girl	Christjohn	2,500	60.00	60.00
91-01-004	Mrs. Claus	Christjohn	2,500	60.00	60.00
91-01-005	Won't You Guide My Sleigh Tonight	Christjohn	2,500	60.00	60.00
91-01-006	With A Finger Aside His Nose	Christjohn	2,500	60.00	60.00
Cybis		**Animal Kingdom**			
71-01-001	American Bullfrog	Cybis	Closed	250.00	600.00
75-01-002	American White Buffalo	Cybis	250	1250.00	4000.00
71-01-003	Appaloosa Colt	Cybis	Closed	150.00	300.00
80-01-004	Arctic White Fox	Cybis	100	4500.00	4700.00
84-01-005	Australian Greater Sulpher Crested Cockatoo	Cybis	25	9850.00	9850.00
85-01-006	Baxter and Doyle	Cybis	400	450.00	450.00
68-01-007	Bear	Cybis	Closed	85.00	400.00
85-01-008	Beagles, Branigan and Clancy	Cybis	Open	375.00	625.00
81-01-009	Beavers, Egbert and Brewster	Cybis	400	285.00	335.00
68-01-010	Buffalo	Cybis	Closed	115.00	185.00
XX-01-011	Bull	Cybis	100	150.00	4500.00
76-01-012	Bunny, Muffet	Cybis	Closed	85.00	150.00
77-01-013	Bunny Pat-a-Cake	Cybis	Closed	90.00	150.00
85-01-014	Bunny, Snowflake	Cybis	Open	65.00	75.00
84-01-015	Chantilly, Kitten	Cybis	Open	175.00	210.00
76-01-016	Chipmunk w/Bloodroot	Cybis	225	625.00	675.00
69-01-017	Colts, Darby and Joan	Cybis	Closed	295.00	475.00
82-01-018	Dall Sheep	Cybis	50	Unkn.	4250.00
86-01-019	Dapple Grey Foal	Cybis	Open	195.00	250.00
70-01-020	Deer Mouse in Clover	Cybis	Closed	65.00	160.00
78-01-021	Dormouse, Maximillian	Cybis	Closed	250.00	285.00
78-01-022	Dormouse, Maxine	Cybis	Closed	195.00	225.00
68-01-023	Elephant	Cybis	100	600.00	5000.00
85-01-024	Elephant, Willoughby	Cybis	Open	195.00	245.00
61-01-025	Horse	Cybis	100	150.00	2000.00
86-01-026	Huey, the Harmonious Hare	Cybis	Open	175.00	275.00
67-01-027	Kitten, Blue Ribbon	Cybis	Closed	95.00	500.00
75-01-028	Kitten, Tabitha	Cybis	Closed	90.00	150.00
75-01-029	Kitten, Topaz	Cybis	Closed	90.00	150.00
86-01-030	Mick, The Melodious Mutt	Cybis	Open	175.00	275.00
85-01-031	Monday, Rhinoceros	Cybis	Open	85.00	150.00
71-01-032	Nashua	Cybis	100	2000.00	3000.00
78-01-033	Pinky Bunny/Carrot	Cybis	200	200.00	265.00
72-01-034	Pinto Colt	Cybis	Closed	175.00	250.00
76-01-035	Prairie Dog	Cybis	Closed	245.00	345.00
65-01-036	Raccoon, Raffles	Cybis	Closed	110.00	365.00
68-01-038	Snail, Sir Escargot	Cybis	Closed	50.00	300.00
65-01-039	Squirrel, Mr. Fluffy Tail	Cybis	Closed	90.00	350.00
80-01-040	Squirrel, Highrise	Cybis	400	475.00	525.00
68-01-041	Stallion	Cybis	350	475.00	850.00
66-01-042	Thoroughbred	Cybis	350	425.00	1500.00
86-01-043	White Tailed Deer	Cybis	50	9500.00	11500.00
Cybis		**Biblical**			
60-02-001	Exodus	Cybis	50	350.00	2600.00
60-02-002	Flight Into Egypt	Cybis	50	175.00	2500.00
56-02-003	Holy Child of Prague	Cybis	10	1500.00	75000.00
XX-02-004	Holywater Font "Holy Ghost"	Cybis	Closed	15.00	145.00
57-02-005	Madonna, House of Gold	Cybis	8	125.00	4000.00
60-02-006	Madonna Lace & Rose	Cybis	Open	15.00	295.00
63-02-007	Moses, The Great Lawgiver	Cybis	750	250.00	5500.00
84-02-008	Nativity, Mary	Cybis	Open	Unkn.	325.00
84-02-009	Nativity, Joseph	Cybis	Open	Unkn.	325.00
84-02-010	Christ Child with Lamb	Cybis	Open	Unkn.	290.00
84-02-011	Nativity, Angel, Color	Cybis	Open	395.00	575.00
84-02-012	Nativity, Camel, Color	Cybis	Open	625.00	825.00
85-02-013	Nativity, Cow, Color	Cybis	Open	175.00	195.00
85-02-014	Nativity, Cow, White	Cybis	Open	125.00	225.00
85-02-015	Nativity, Donkey, Color	Cybis	Open	195.00	225.00
85-02-016	Nativity, Donkey, White	Cybis	Open	130.00	150.00
85-02-017	Nativity, Lamb, Color	Cybis	Open	150.00	195.00
85-02-018	Nativity, Lamb, White	Cybis	Open	115.00	125.00
84-02-019	Nativity, Shepherd, Color	Cybis	Open	395.00	475.00
76-02-020	Noah	Cybis	500	975.00	2800.00
64-02-021	St. Peter	Cybis	500	Unkn.	1250.00
60-02-022	The Prophet	Cybis	50	250.00	3500.00
Cybis		**Birds & Flowers**			
85-03-001	American Bald Eagle	Cybis	300	2900.00	3595.00
72-03-002	American Crested Iris	Cybis	400	975.00	1150.00
76-03-003	American White Turkey	Cybis	75	1450.00	1600.00
76-03-004	American Wild Turkey	Cybis	75	1950.00	2200.00
77-03-005	Apple Blossoms	Cybis	400	350.00	550.00
72-03-006	Autumn Dogwood w/Chickadees	Cybis	350	1100.00	1200.00
XX-03-007	Birds & Flowers	Cybis	250	500.00	4500.00
61-03-008	Blue-Grey Gnatcatchers, pair	Cybis	200	400.00	2500.00
60-03-009	Blue Headed Virio Building Nest	Cybis	Closed	60.00	1100.00
60-03-010	Blue Headed Virio with Lilac	Cybis	275	1200.00	2200.00
XX-03-011	Butterfly w/Dogwood	Cybis	200	Unkn.	350.00
68-03-012	Calla Lily	Cybis	500	750.00	1750.00
65-03-013	Christmas Rose	Cybis	500	250.00	750.00
77-03-014	Clematis	Cybis	Closed	210.00	315.00
69-03-015	Clematis with House Wren	Cybis	350	1300.00	1400.00
76-03-016	Colonial Basket	Cybis	100	2750.00	5500.00
76-03-017	Constancy Flower Basket	Cybis	Closed	345.00	400.00
64-03-018	Dahlia, Yellow	Cybis	350	450.00	1800.00
76-03-019	Devotion Flower Basket	Cybis	Closed	345.00	400.00
62-03-020	Duckling "Baby Brother"	Cybis	Closed	35.00	140.00
77-03-021	Duckling "Buttercup & Daffodil"	Cybis	Closed	165.00	295.00
70-03-022	Dutch Crocus	Cybis	350	550.00	750.00
76-03-023	Felicity Flower Basket	Cybis	Closed	325.00	345.00
61-03-024	Golden Clarion Lily	Cybis	100	250.00	4500.00
74-03-025	Golden Winged Warbler	Cybis	200	1075.00	1150.00
75-03-026	Great Horned Owl, Color	Cybis	50	3250.00	7500.00
75-03-027	Great Horned Owl, White	Cybis	150	1950.00	4500.00
64-03-028	Great White Heron	Cybis	350	850.00	3750.00
77-03-029	Hermit Thrush	Cybis	150	1450.00	1450.00
59-03-030	Hummingbird	Cybis	Closed	95.00	950.00
63-03-031	Iris	Cybis	250	500.00	4500.00
77-03-032	Krestrel	Cybis	175	1875.00	1925.00
78-03-033	Kinglets on Pyracantha	Cybis	175	900.00	1100.00
71-03-034	Little Blue Heron	Cybis	500	425.00	1500.00
63-03-035	Magnolia	Cybis	Closed	350.00	450.00
76-03-036	Majesty Flower Basket	Cybis	Closed	345.00	400.00
70-03-037	Mushroom with Butterfly	Cybis	Closed	225.00	450.00
68-03-038	Narcissus	Cybis	500	350.00	550.00
78-03-039	Nestling Bluebirds	Cybis	Closed	235.00	250.00
72-03-040	Pansies, China Maid	Cybis	1,000	275.00	350.00
75-03-041	Pansies, Chinolina Lady	Cybis	750	295.00	400.00
60-03-042	Pheasant	Cybis	150	750.00	5000.00
XX-03-043	Sandpipers	Cybis	400	700.00	1500.00
85-03-044	Screech Owl & Siblings	Cybis	100	3250.00	3925.00
XX-03-045	Skylarks	Cybis	350	330.00	1800.00
62-03-046	Sparrow on a Log	Cybis	Closed	35.00	450.00
82-03-047	Spring Bouquet	Cybis	200	750.00	750.00
57-03-048	Turtle Doves	Cybis	500	350.00	5000.00
68-03-049	Wood Duck	Cybis	500	325.00	800.00
80-03-050	Yellow Rose	Cybis	Closed	80.00	450.00
80-03-051	Yellow Condesa Rose	Cybis	Closed	Unkn.	255.00
Cybis		**Children to Cherish**			
64-04-001	Alice in Wonderland	Cybis	Closed	50.00	850.00
78-04-002	Alice (Seated)	Cybis	Closed	350.00	550.00
78-04-003	Allegra	Cybis	Closed	310.00	350.00
63-04-004	Ballerina on Cue	Cybis	Closed	150.00	700.00
68-04-005	Ballerina, Little Princess	Cybis	Closed	125.00	750.00
85-04-006	Ballerina, Recital	Cybis	Open	275.00	275.00
60-04-007	Ballerina Red Shoes	Cybis	Closed	75.00	1200.00
85-04-008	Ballerina, Swanilda	Cybis	Open	450.00	725.00
68-04-009	Baby Bust	Cybis	239	375.00	1000.00
85-04-010	Beth	Cybis	Open	235.00	275.00
77-04-011	Boys Playing Marbles	Cybis	Closed	285.00	425.00
84-04-012	The Choirboy	Cybis	Open	325.00	345.00
85-04-013	Clara	Cybis	Open	395.00	395.00
86-04-014	Clarissa	Cybis	Open	165.00	195.00
78-04-015	Edith	Cybis	Closed	310.00	325.00
76-04-016	Elizabeth Ann	Cybis	Closed	195.00	275.00
85-04-017	Felicia	Cybis	Open	425.00	525.00
86-04-018	"Encore" Figure Skater	Cybis	750	625.00	675.00
85-04-019	Figure Eight	Cybis	750	625.00	750.00
XX-04-020	First Bouquet	Cybis	250	150.00	300.00
66-04-021	First Flight	Cybis	Closed	50.00	475.00
81-04-022	Fleurette	Cybis	1,000	725.00	1075.00
73-04-023	Goldilocks	Cybis	Closed	145.00	525.00
74-04-024	Gretel	Cybis	Closed	260.00	425.00
74-04-025	Hansel	Cybis	Closed	270.00	550.00
62-04-026	Heide, White	Cybis	Closed	165.00	550.00
62-04-027	Heide, Color	Cybis	Closed	165.00	550.00
84-04-028	Jack in the Beanstalk	Cybis	750	575.00	575.00
85-04-029	Jody	Cybis	Open	235.00	275.00
86-04-030	Kitri	Cybis	Open	450.00	550.00
78-04-031	Lisa and Lynette	Cybis	Closed	395.00	475.00
78-04-032	Little Boy Blue	Cybis	Closed	425.00	500.00
84-04-033	Little Champ	Cybis	Open	325.00	375.00
80-04-034	Little Miss Muffet	Cybis	Closed	335.00	365.00
73-04-035	Little Red Riding Hood	Cybis	Closed	110.00	475.00
86-04-036	Lullaby, Pink	Cybis	Open	125.00	160.00
86-04-037	Lullaby, Blue	Cybis	Open	125.00	160.00
86-04-038	Lullaby, Ivory	Cybis	Open	125.00	160.00

Company / Number	Name	Series / Artist	Edition Limit	Issue Price	Quote
85-04-039	Marguerite	Cybis	Open	425.00	525.00
74-04-040	Mary, Mary	Cybis	500	475.00	750.00
76-04-041	Melissa	Cybis	Closed	285.00	425.00
84-04-042	Michael	Cybis	Open	235.00	350.00
67-04-043	Pandora Blue	Cybis	Closed	265.00	325.00
58-04-044	Peter Pan	Cybis	Closed	80.00	1000.00
71-04-045	Polyanna	Cybis	Closed	195.00	550.00
75-04-046	Rapunzel, Apricot	Cybis	1,500	475.00	1200.00
78-04-047	Rapunzel, Lilac	Cybis	1,000	675.00	1000.00
72-04-048	Rapunzel, Pink	Cybis	1,000	425.00	1100.00
64-04-049	Rebecca	Cybis	Closed	110.00	360.00
85-04-050	Recital	Cybis	Open	275.00	275.00
82-04-051	Robin	Cybis	1,000	475.00	850.00
82-04-052	Sleeping Beauty	Cybis	750	695.00	1475.00
63-04-053	Springtime	Cybis	Closed	45.00	775.00
57-04-054	Thumbelina	Cybis	Closed	45.00	525.00
59-04-055	Tinkerbell	Cybis	Closed	95.00	1500.00
85-04-056	Vanessa	Cybis	Open	425.00	525.00
75-04-057	Wendy with Flowers	Cybis	Unkn.	250.00	375.00
75-04-058	Yankee Doodle Dandy	Cybis	Closed	275.00	325.00
Cybis		**Commemoratives**			
81-05-001	Arion, Dolphin Rider	Cybis	1,000	575.00	1150.00
69-05-002	Apollo II Moon Mission	Cybis	111	1500.00	2500.00
72-05-003	Chess Set	Cybis	10	30000.00	60000.00
67-05-004	Columbia	Cybis	200	1000.00	2500.00
86-05-005	1986 Commemorative Egg	Cybis	Open	365.00	365.00
67-05-006	Conductor's Hands	Cybis	250	250.00	1500.00
71-05-007	Cree Indian	Cybis	100	2500.00	5500.00
84-05-008	Cree Indian "Magic Boy"	Cybis	200	4250.00	4995.00
75-05-009	George Washington Bust	Cybis	Closed	275.00	350.00
85-05-010	Holiday Ornament	Cybis	Open	75.00	75.00
81-05-011	Kateri Takakwitha	Cybis	100	2875.00	2975.00
86-05-012	Little Miss Liberty	Cybis	Open	295.00	350.00
77-05-013	Oceania	Cybis	200	1250.00	975-1550.
81-05-014	Phoenix	Cybis	100	950.00	950.00
80-05-015	The Bride	Cybis	100	6500.00	10500.00
84-05-016	1984 Cybis Holiday	Cybis	Open	145.00	145.00
85-05-017	Liberty	Cybis	100	1875.00	4000.00
Cybis		**Fantasia**			
74-06-001	Cybele	Cybis	500	675.00	800.00
81-06-002	Desiree, White Deer	Cybis	400	575.00	595.00
84-06-003	Flight and Fancy	Cybis	1,000	975.00	1175.00
80-06-004	Pegasus	Cybis	500	1450.00	3750.00
80-06-005	Pegaus, Free Spirit	Cybis	1,000	675.00	775.00
81-06-006	Prince Brocade Unicorn	Cybis	500	2200.00	2600.00
78-06-007	"Satin" Horse Head	Cybis	500	1100.00	2800.00
77-06-008	Sea King's Steed "Oceania"	Cybis	200	1250.00	1450.00
78-06-009	"Sharmaine" Sea Nymph	Cybis	250	1450.00	1650.00
82-06-010	Theron	Cybis	350	675.00	850.00
69-06-011	Unicorn	Cybis	500	1250.00	3750.00
77-06-012	Unicorns, Gambol and Frolic	Cybis	1,000	425.00	2300.00
85-06-013	Dore'	Cybis	1,000	575.00	1075.00
Cybis		**Land of Chemeric**			
77-07-001	Marigold	Cybis	Closed	185.00	550.00
81-07-002	Melody	Cybis	1,000	725.00	800.00
79-07-003	Pip, Elfin Player	Cybis	1,000	450.00	665.00
77-07-004	Queen Titania	Cybis	750	725.00	2500.00
77-07-005	Tiffin	Cybis	Closed	175.00	550.00
85-07-006	Oberon	Cybis	750	825.00	825.00
Cybis		**North American Indian**			
74-08-001	Apache, "Chato"	Cybis	350	1950.00	3300.00
69-08-002	Blackfeet "Beaverhead Medicine Man"	Cybis	500	2000.00	2775.00
82-08-003	Choctaw "Tasculusa"	Cybis	200	2475.00	4050.00
77-08-004	Crow Dancer	Cybis	200	3875.00	8500.00
69-08-005	Dakota "Minnehaha Laughing Water"	Cybis	500	1500.00	2500.00
73-08-006	Eskimo Mother	Cybis	200	1875.00	2650.00
79-08-007	Great Spirit "Wankan Tanka"	Cybis	200	3500.00	4150.00
73-08-008	Iriquois "At the Council Fire"	Cybis	500	4250.00	4975.00
69-08-009	Onondaga "Haiwatha"	Cybis	500	1500.00	2450.00
71-08-010	Shoshone "Sacajawea"	Cybis	500	2250.00	2775.00
85-08-011	Yaqui "Deer Dancer"	Cybis	200	2095.00	2850.00
Cybis		**Portraits in Porcelain**			
76-09-001	Abigail Adams	Cybis	600	875.00	1300.00
73-09-002	Ballet-Princess Aurora	Cybis	200	1125.00	1500.00
73-09-003	Ballet-Prince Florimond	Cybis	200	975.00	1100.00
84-09-004	Bathsheba	Cybis	500	1975.00	3250.00
65-09-005	Beatrice	Cybis	700	225.00	1800.00
79-09-006	Berengaria	Cybis	500	1450.00	2000-4700.
86-09-007	Carmen	Cybis	500	1675.00	1975.00
82-09-008	Desdemona	Cybis	500	1850.00	4000.00
71-09-009	Eleanor of Aquitaine	Cybis	750	875.00	4250.00
67-09-010	Folk Singer	Cybis	283	300.00	850.00
78-09-011	Good Queen Anne	Cybis	350	975.00	1500.00
67-09-012	Guinevere	Cybis	800	250.00	2400.00
68-09-013	Hamlet	Cybis	500	350.00	2000.00
81-09-014	Jane Eyre	Cybis	500	975.00	1500.00
65-09-015	Juliet	Cybis	800	175.00	4000.00
85-09-016	King Arthur	Cybis	350	2350.00	3450.00
85-09-017	King David	Cybis	350	1475.00	2175.00
72-09-018	Kwan Yin	Cybis	350	1250.00	2000.00
82-09-019	Lady Godiva	Cybis	200	1875.00	3250.00
75-09-020	Lady Macbeth	Cybis	750	850.00	1350.00
79-09-021	Nefertiti	Cybis	500	2100.00	3000.00
69-09-022	Ophelia	Cybis	800	750.00	3500.00
85-09-023	Pagliacci	Cybis	Open	325.00	325.00
82-09-024	Persephone	Cybis	200	3250.00	5250.00
73-09-025	Portia	Cybis	750	825.00	3750.00
76-09-026	Priscilla	Cybis	500	825.00	1500.00
74-09-027	Queen Esther	Cybis	750	925.00	1800.00
85-09-028	Romeo and Juliet	Cybis	500	2200.00	3400.00
68-09-029	Scarlett	Cybis	500	450.00	3250-3500.
85-09-030	Tristan and Isolde	Cybis	200	2200.00	2200.00
Cybis		**Theatre of Porcelain**			
81-10-001	Columbine	Cybis	250	2250.00	2250.00
78-10-002	Court Jester	Cybis	250	1450.00	1750.00
80-10-003	Harlequin	Cybis	250	1575.00	1875.00
81-10-004	Puck	Cybis	250	2300.00	2450.00
Cybis		**Carousel-Circus**			
75-11-001	"Barnaby" Bear	Cybis	Closed	165.00	325.00
81-11-002	Bear, "Bernhard"	Cybis	325	1125.00	1150.00
75-11-003	Bicentennial Horse Ticonderoga	Cybis	350	925.00	4000.00
75-11-004	"Bosun" Monkey	Cybis	Closed	195.00	425.00
81-11-005	Bull, Plutus	Cybis	325	1125.00	2050.00
85-11-006	Carousel Unicorn	Cybis	325	1275.00	2750.00
79-11-007	Circus Rider "Equestrienne Extraordinaire"	Cybis	150	2275.00	3500.00
77-11-008	"Dandy" Dancing Dog	Cybis	Closed	145.00	295.00
81-11-009	Frollo	Cybis	1,000	750.00	825.00
76-11-010	"Funny Face" Child Head/Holly	Cybis	Closed	325.00	750.00
82-11-011	Giraffe	Cybis	750	Unkn.	1750.00
73-11-012	Carousel Goat	Cybis	325	875.00	1750.00
73-11-013	Carousel Horse	Cybis	325	925.00	7500.00
74-11-014	Lion	Cybis	325	1025.00	1350.00
76-11-015	Performing Pony "Poppy"	Cybis	1,000	325.00	1200.00
84-11-016	Phineas, Circus Elephant	Cybis	Open	325.00	425.00
86-11-017	Pierre, the Performing Poodle	Cybis	Open	225.00	275.00
81-11-018	Pony	Cybis	750	975.00	975.00
76-11-019	"Sebastian" Seal	Cybis	Closed	195.00	200.00
74-11-020	Tiger	Cybis	325	925.00	1500.00
85-11-021	Jumbles and Friend	Cybis	750	675.00	725.00
85-11-022	Valentine	Cybis	Open	335.00	375.00
Cybis		**Children of the World**			
72-12-001	Eskimo Child Head	Cybis	Closed	165.00	400.00
75-12-002	Indian Girl Head	Cybis	Closed	325.00	900.00
75-12-003	Indian Boy Head	Cybis	Closed	425.00	900.00
78-12-004	Jason	Cybis	Closed	285.00	375.00
78-12-005	Jennifer	Cybis	Closed	325.00	375.00
77-12-006	Jeremy	Cybis	Closed	315.00	475.00
79-12-007	Jessica	Cybis	Closed	325.00	475.00
Cybis		**Sport Scenes**			
80-13-001	Jogger, Female	Cybis	Closed	345.00	425.00
80-13-002	Jogger, Male	Cybis	Closed	395.00	475.00
Cybis		**Everyone's Fun Time (Limnettes)**			
72-14-001	Country Fair	Cybis	500	125.00	200.00
72-14-002	Windy Day	Cybis	500	125.00	200.00
72-14-003	The Pond	Cybis	500	125.00	200.00
72-14-004	The Seashore	Cybis	500	125.00	200.00
Cybis		**The Wonderful Seasons (Limnettes)**			
72-15-001	Autumn	Cybis	500	125.00	200.00
72-15-002	Spring	Cybis	500	125.00	200.00
72-15-003	Summer	Cybis	500	125.00	200.00
72-15-004	Winter	Cybis	500	125.00	200.00
Cybis		**When Bells are Ringing (Limnettes)**			
72-16-001	Easter Egg Hunt	Cybis	500	125.00	200.00
72-16-002	Independence Celebration	Cybis	500	125.00	200.00
72-16-003	Merry Christmas	Cybis	500	125.00	200.00
72-16-004	Sabbath Morning	Cybis	500	125.00	200.00
Danbury Mint		**Rockwell Figurines**			
80-01-001	Trick or Treat	N. Rockwell	Closed	55.00	60.00
80-01-002	Gramps at the Reins	N. Rockwell	Closed	55.00	75.00
80-01-003	Grandpa Snowman	N. Rockwell	Closed	55.00	60.00
80-01-004	Caught in the Act	N. Rockwell	Closed	55.00	75.00
80-01-005	Boy on Stilts	N. Rockwell	Closed	55.00	60.00
80-01-006	Young Love	N. Rockwell	Closed	55.00	125.00
Department 56		**Dickens' Village Collection**			
84-01-001	The Original Shops of Dickens' Village 6515-3, Set of 7	Department 56	Closed	175.00	1100-1800.
84-01-002	Crowntree Inn 6515-3	Department 56	Closed	25.00	325-425.
84-01-003	Candle Shop 6515-3	Department 56	Closed	25.00	175-250.
84-01-004	Green Grocer 6515-3	Department 56	Closed	25.00	175-250.
84-01-005	Golden Swan Baker 6515-3	Department 56	Closed	25.00	150-200.
84-01-006	Bean And Son Smithy Shop 6515-3	Department 56	Closed	25.00	175-220.
84-01-007	Abel Beesley Butcher 6515-3	Department 56	Closed	25.00	110-190.
84-01-008	Jones & Co. Brush & Basket Shop 6515-3	Department 56	Closed	25.00	275-400.
84-01-009	Dickens' Village Church (cream) 6516-1	Department 56	Closed	35.00	225-375.
85-01-010	Dickens' Village Church(tan) 6516-1	Department 56	Closed	35.00	125-175.
85-01-011	Dickens' Village Church(green) 6516-1	Department 56	Closed	35.00	225-375.
85-01-012	Dickens' Cottages 6518-8 Set of 3	Department 56	Closed	75.00	900-1100.
85-01-013	Thatched Cottage	Department 56	Closed	25.00	200-350.
85-01-014	Stone Cottage	Department 56	Closed	25.00	350-450.
85-01-015	Tudor Cottage	Department 56	Closed	25.00	350-450.
85-01-016	Dickens' Village Mill 6519-6	Department 56	2,500	35.00	4500-5800.
86-01-017	Christmas Carol Cottages 6500-5, Set of 3 (Fezziwig's Warehouse, Scrooge and Marley Counting House, The Cottage of Bob Cratchit & Tiny Tim)	Department 56	Open	75.00	90.00
86-01-018	Norman Church 6502-1	Department 56	3,500	40.00	3000-4000.
86-01-019	Dickens' Lane Shops 6507-2, Set of 3	Department 56	Closed	80.00	425-650.
86-01-020	Thomas Kersey Coffee House 6507-2	Department 56	Closed	27.00	125-225.
86-01-021	Cottage Toy Shop 6507-2	Department 56	Closed	27.00	175-275.
86-01-022	Tuttle's Pub 6507-2	Department 56	Closed	27.00	200-250.
86-01-023	Blythe Pond Mill House 6508-0	Department 56	Closed	37.00	125-225.
86-01-024	By The Pond Mill House 6508-0	Department 56	Closed	37.00	90-175.00
86-01-025	Chadbury Station and Train 6528-5	Department 56	Closed	65.00	325-425.
87-01-026	Barley Bree 5900-5,Set of 2 (Farmhouse, Barn)	Department 56	Closed	60.00	275-375.
87-01-027	The Old Curiosity Shop 5905-6	Department 56	Open	32.00	37.50
87-01-028	Kenilworth Castle 5916-1	Department 56	Closed	70.00	375-475.
87-01-029	Brick Abbey 6549-8	Department 56	Closed	33.00	329-450.
87-01-030	Chesterton Manor House 6568-4	Department 56	7,500	45.00	1650-2000.
88-01-031	Counting House & Silas Thimbleton Barrister 5902-1	Department 56	Closed	32.00	75-150.00
88-01-032	C. Fletcher Public House 5904-8	Department 56	12,500	35.00	550-850.
88-01-033	Cobblestone Shops 5924-2, Set of 3	Department 56	Closed	95.00	400.00
88-01-034	The Wool Shop 5924-2	Department 56	Closed	32.00	125-200.
88-01-035	Booter and Cobbler 5924-2	Department 56	Closed	32.00	90-150.00
88-01-036	T. Wells Fruit & Spice Shop 5924-2	Department 56	Closed	32.00	80-150.00
88-01-037	Nicholas Nickleby 5925-0, Set of 2	Department 56	Closed	72.00	150-190.
88-01-038	Nicholas Nickleby Cottage 5925-0	Department 56	Closed	36.00	85-140.
88-01-039	Wackford Squeers Boarding School 5925-0	Department 56	Closed	36.00	90-125.00
88-01-040	Nickolas Nickleby Cottage 5925-0-misspelled	Department 56	Closed	36.00	100-135.
88-01-041	Merchant Shops 5926-9, 5/set(Poulterer, Geo. Weeton Watchmaker, The Mermaid Fish Shoppe, White Horse Bakery,Walpole Tailors	Department 56	Open	150.00	175.00

Number	Name	Artist	Edition Limit	Issue Price	Quote
88-01-042	Ivy Glen Church 5927-7	Department 56	Closed	35.00	80-125.00
89-01-043	David Copperfield 5550-6, Set of 3 (Mr. Wickfield Solicitor, Betsy Trotwood's Cottage, Peggotty's Seaside Cottage	Department 56	Open	125.00	125.00
89-01-044	Peggotty's Seaside Cottage(tan)	Department 56	Closed	42.50	125-225.
89-01-045	Victoria Station 5574-3	Department 56	Open	100.00	100.00
89-01-046	Knottinghill Church 5582-4	Department 56	Open	50.00	50.00
89-01-047	Cobles Police Station 5583-2	Department 56	Closed	37.50	80-125.00
89-01-048	Theatre Royal 5584-0	Department 56	Open	45.00	45.00
89-01-049	Ruth Marion Scotch Woolens 5585-9	Department 56	17,500	65.00	350-450.
89-01-050	Green Gate Cottage 5586-7	Department 56	22,500	65.00	275-350.
89-01-051	The Flat of Ebenezer Scrooge 5587-5	Department 56	Open	37.50	37.50
90-01-052	Bishops Oast House 5567-0	Department 56	Open	45.00	45.00
90-01-053	Kings Road 5568-9, Set of 2 (Tutbury Printer, C.H. Watt Physician)	Department 56	Open	72.00	72.00
91-01-054	Fagin's Hide-A-Way 5552-2	Department 56	Open	68.00	68.00
91-01-055	Oliver Twist 5553-0 Set of 2, (Brownlow House, Maylie Cottage)	Department 56	Open	75.00	75.00
91-01-056	Ashbury Inn 5555-7	Department 56	Open	55.00	55.00
91-01-057	Nephew Fred's Flat 5557-3	Department 56	Open	35.00	35.00
92-01-058	Crown & Cricket Inn (Charles Dickens' Signature Series), 5750-9	Department 56	Yr.Iss.	100.00	100.00
92-01-059	Old Michael Church, 5562-0	Department 56	Open	42.00	42.00
Department 56	**New England Village Collection**				
86-02-001	New England Village 6530-7, Set of 7	Department 56	Closed	170.00	750-1000.
86-02-002	Apothecary Shop 6530-7	Department 56	Closed	25.00	70-120.00
86-02-003	General Store 6530-7	Department 56	Closed	25.00	200-325.
86-02-004	Nathaniel Bingham Fabrics 6530-7	Department 56	Closed	25.00	100-150.
86-02-005	Livery Stable & Boot Shop 6530-7	Department 56	Closed	25.00	90-125.00
86-02-006	Steeple Church 6530-7	Department 56	Closed	25.00	80-150.
86-02-007	Brick Town Hall 6530-7	Department 56	Closed	25.00	110-250.
86-02-008	Red Schoolhouse 6530-7	Department 56	Closed	25.00	150-325.
86-02-009	Jacob Adams Farmhouse and Barn 6538-2	Department 56	Closed	65.00	275-400.
86-02-010	Steeple Church 6539-0	Department 56	Closed	30.00	80-150.00
87-02-011	Craggy Cove Lighthouse 5930-7	Department 56	Open	35.00	44.00
87-02-012	Weston Train Station 5931-5	Department 56	Closed	42.00	200-265.
87-02-013	Smythe Woolen Mill 6543-1	Department 56	7,500	42.00	1000-1300.
87-02-014	Timber Knoll Log Cabin 6544-7	Department 56	Closed	28.00	90-150.00
88-02-015	Old North Church 5932-3	Department 56	Open	40.00	42.00
88-02-016	Cherry Lane Shops 5939-0, Set of 3	Department 56	Closed	80.00	190-250.
88-02-017	Ben's Barbershop 5939-0	Department 56	Closed	27.00	65-125.00
88-02-018	Otis Hayes Butcher Shop 5939-0	Department 56	Closed	27.00	65-125.00
88-02-019	Anne Shaw Toys 5939-0	Department 56	Closed	27.00	95-125.
88-02-020	Ada's Bed and Boarding House (lemon yellow) 5940-4	Department 56	Closed	36.00	125-310.
88-02-021	Ada's Bed and Boarding House (pale yellow) 5940-4	Department 56	Closed	36.00	85-130.
89-02-022	Berkshire House (medium blue) 5942-0	Department 56	Closed	40.00	85-125.00
89-02-023	Berkshire House (teal) 5942-0	Department 56	Closed	40.00	70-95.00
89-02-024	Jannes Mullet Amish Farm House 5943-9	Department 56	Open	32.00	32.00
89-02-025	Jannes Mullet Amish Barn 5944-7	Department 56	Open	48.00	48.00
90-02-026	Shingle Creek House 5946-3	Department 56	Open	37.50	37.50
90-02-027	Captain's Cottage 5947-1	Department 56	Open	40.00	40.00
90-02-028	Sleepy Hollow 5954-4, Set of 3 (Sleepy Hollow School, Van Tassel Manor Ichabod Crane's Cottage)	Department 56	Open	96.00	96.00
90-02-029	Sleepy Hollow Church 5955-2	Department 56	Open	36.00	36.00
91-02-030	McGrebe-Cutters & Sleighs 5640-5	Department 56	Open	45.00	45.00
Department 56	**Alpine Village Collection**				
86-03-001	Alpine Village 6540-4, 5/set(Bessor Bierkeller, Gasthof Eisl, Apotheke, E. Staubr Backer, Milch-Kase)	Department 56	Open	150.00	185.00
87-03-002	Josef Engel Farmhouse 5952-8	Department 56	Closed	33.00	250-450.
87-03-003	Alpine Church 6541-2	Department 56	Closed	32.00	85-135.00
88-03-004	Grist Mill 5953-6	Department 56	Open	42.00	44.00
90-03-005	Bahnhof 5615-4	Department 56	Open	42.00	42.00
91-03-006	St. Nikolaus Kirche 5617-0	Department 56	Open	37.50	37.50
Department 56	**Christmas In the City Collection**				
87-04-001	Sutton Place Brownstones 5961-7	Department 56	Closed	80.00	625-850.
87-04-002	The Cathedral 5962-5	Department 56	Closed	60.00	250-350.
87-04-003	Palace Theatre 5963-3	Department 56	Closed	45.00	750-1000.
87-04-004	Christmas In The City 6512-9, Set of 3	Department 56	Closed	112.00	275-400.
87-04-005	Toy Shop and Pet Store 6512-9	Department 56	Closed	37.50	100-130.
87-04-006	Bakery 6512-9	Department 56	Closed	37.50	80-220.00
87-04-007	Tower Restaurant 6512-9	Department 56	Closed	37.50	110-150.
88-04-008	Chocolate Shoppe 5968-4	Department 56	Closed	40.00	80-150.00
88-04-009	City Hall (standard) 5969-2	Department 56	Closed	65.00	125-185.
88-04-010	City Hall (small) 5969-2	Department 56	Closed	65.00	250.00
88-04-011	Hank's Market 5970-6	Department 56	Open	40.00	45.00
88-04-012	Variety Store 5972-2	Department 56	Closed	45.00	100-150.
89-04-013	Ritz Hotel 5973-0	Department 56	Open	55.00	55.00
89-04-014	Dorothy's Dress Shop 5974-9	Department 56	12,500	70.00	325-475.
89-04-015	Dorothy's Dress Shop (proof) 5974-9	Department 56	12,500	70.00	250-300.
89-04-016	5607 Park Avenue Townhouse 5977-3	Department 56	Open	48.00	48.00
89-04-017	5609 Park Avenue Townhouse 5978-1	Department 56	Open	48.00	48.00
90-04-018	Red Brick Fire Station 5536-0	Department 56	Open	55.00	55.00
90-04-019	Wong's In Chinatown 5537-9	Department 56	Open	55.00	55.00
91-04-020	Hollydale's Department Store 5534-4	Department 56	Open	75.00	75.00
91-04-021	"Little Italy" Ristorante 5538-7	Department 56	Open	50.00	50.00
91-04-022	All Saints Corner Church 5542-5	Department 56	Open	96.00	96.00
91-04-023	Arts Academy 5543-3	Department 56	Open	45.00	45.00
90-04-024	The Doctor's Office 5544-1	Department 56	Open	60.00	60.00
92-04-025	Cathedral Church of St. Marks 5549-2	Department 56	17,500	120.00	120.00
Department 56	**Little Town of Bethlehem Collection**				
87-05-001	Little Town of Bethlehem 5975-7, Set of 12	Department 56	Open	150.00	150.00
Department 56	**The Original Snow Village Collection**				
76-06-001	Mountain Lodge 5001-3	Department 56	Closed	20.00	400-650.
76-06-002	Gabled Cottage 5002-1	Department 56	Closed	20.00	400-415.
76-06-003	The Inn 5003-9	Department 56	Closed	20.00	440-625.
76-06-004	Country Church 5004-7	Department 56	Closed	18.00	325-440.
76-06-005	Steepled Church 5005-4	Department 56	Closed	25.00	525-750.
76-06-006	Small Chalet 5006-2	Department 56	Closed	15.00	300-375.
77-06-007	Victorian House 5007-0	Department 56	Closed	30.00	325-600.
77-06-008	Mansion 5008-8	Department 56	Closed	30.00	500-625.
77-06-009	Stone Church 5009-6 (10")	Department 56	Closed	35.00	525-1100.
78-06-010	Homestead 5011-2	Department 56	Closed	30.00	225-250.
78-06-011	General Store 5012-0	Department 56	Closed	25.00	350-600.
78-06-012	Cape Cod 5013-8	Department 56	Closed	20.00	350-400.
78-06-013	Nantucket 5014-6	Department 56	Closed	25.00	200-275.
78-06-014	Skating Rink, Duck Pond (Set) 5015-3	Department 56	Closed	16.00	1150-1850.
78-06-016	Small Double Trees 5016-1	Department 56	Closed	13.50	35-50.00
79-06-017	Thatched Cottage 5050-0 Meadowland Series	Department 56	Closed	30.00	400-1400.
79-06-018	Countryside Church 5051-8 Meadowland Series	Department 56	Closed	25.00	275-1800.
79-06-019	Victorian 5054-2	Department 56	Closed	30.00	350-400.
79-06-020	Knob Hill 5055-9	Department 56	Closed	30.00	300-450.
79-06-021	Brownstone 5056-7	Department 56	Closed	36.00	425-500.
79-06-022	Log Cabin 5057-5	Department 56	Closed	22.00	425-500.
79-06-023	Countryside Church 5058-3	Department 56	Closed	27.50	250-400.
79-06-024	Stone Church 5059-1 (8")	Department 56	Closed	32.00	475-900.
79-06-025	School House 5060-9	Department 56	Closed	30.00	350-400.
79-06-026	Tudor House 5061-7	Department 56	Closed	25.00	325-440.
79-06-027	Mission Church 5062-5	Department 56	Closed	30.00	880-1250.
79-06-028	Mobile Home 5063-3	Department 56	Closed	18.00	1000-2000.
79-06-029	Giant Trees 5065-8	Department 56	Closed	20.00	275-400.
79-06-030	Adobe House 5066-6	Department 56	Closed	18.00	1000-2000.
80-06-031	Cathedral Church 5067-4	Department 56	Closed	36.00	825-2200.
80-06-032	Stone Mill House 5068-2	Department 56	Closed	30.00	525-830.
80-06-033	Colonial Farm House 5070-9	Department 56	Closed	30.00	375-575.
80-06-034	Town Church 5071-7	Department 56	Closed	33.00	325-375.
80-06-035	Train Station with 3 Train Cars 5085-6	Department 56	Closed	100.00	300-400.
81-06-036	Wooden Clapboard 5072-5	Department 56	Closed	32.00	275-300.
81-06-037	English Cottage 5073-3	Department 56	Closed	25.00	275-375.
81-06-038	Barn 5074-1	Department 56	Closed	32.00	420-500.
81-06-039	Corner Store 5076-8	Department 56	Closed	30.00	225-440.
81-06-040	Bakery 5077-6	Department 56	Closed	30.00	275-300.
81-06-041	English Church 5078-4	Department 56	Closed	30.00	300-330.
81-06-042	Large Single Tree 5080-6	Department 56	Closed	17.00	40-55.00
82-06-043	Skating Pond 5017-2	Department 56	Closed	25.00	275-375.
82-06-044	Street Car 5019-9	Department 56	Closed	16.00	300-350.
82-06-045	Centennial House 5020-2	Department 56	Closed	32.00	300-450.
82-06-046	Carriage House 5021-0	Department 56	Closed	28.00	325-450.
82-06-047	Pioneer Church 5022-9	Department 56	Closed	30.00	270-425.
82-06-048	Swiss Chalet 5023-7	Department 56	Closed	28.00	200-500.
82-06-049	Bank 5024-5	Department 56	Closed	32.00	350-650.
82-06-050	Gabled House 5081-4	Department 56	Closed	30.00	350-550.
82-06-051	Flower Shop 5082-2	Department 56	Closed	25.00	375-475.
82-06-052	New Stone Church 5083-0	Department 56	Closed	32.00	200-325.
83-06-053	Town Hall 5000-8	Department 56	Closed	32.00	300-415.
83-06-054	Grocery 5001-6	Department 56	Closed	35.00	275-400.
83-06-055	Victorian Cottage 5002-4	Department 56	Closed	35.00	340-385.
83-06-056	Governor's Mansion 5003-2	Department 56	Closed	32.00	275-300.
83-06-057	Turn of the Century 5004-0	Department 56	Closed	36.00	250-325.
83-06-058	Gingerbread HouseBank(Non-lighted)5025-3	Department 56	Closed	24.00	300-700.
83-06-059	Village Church 5026-1	Department 56	Closed	30.00	275-475.
83-06-060	Gothic Church 5028-8	Department 56	Closed	36.00	200-330.
83-06-061	Parsonage 5029-6	Department 56	Closed	35.00	300-385.
83-06-062	Wooden Church 5031-8	Department 56	Closed	30.00	350-475.
83-06-063	Fire Station 5032-6	Department 56	Closed	32.00	500-750.
83-06-064	English Tudor 5033-4	Department 56	Closed	30.00	200-300.
83-06-065	Chateau 5084-9	Department 56	Closed	35.00	300-425.
84-06-066	Main Street House 5005-9	Department 56	Closed	27.00	200-300.
84-06-067	Stratford House 5007-5	Department 56	Closed	28.00	150-225.
84-06-068	Haversham House 5008-3	Department 56	Closed	37.00	225-450.
84-06-069	Galena House 5009-1	Department 56	Closed	32.00	285-310.
84-06-070	River Road House 5010-5	Department 56	Closed	36.00	120-180.
84-06-071	Delta House 5012-1	Department 56	Closed	32.00	300-375.
84-06-072	Bayport 5015-6	Department 56	Closed	30.00	220-250.
84-06-073	Congregational Church 5034-2	Department 45	Closed	28.00	250-330.
84-06-074	Trinity Church 5035-0	Department 56	Closed	32.00	220-300.
84-06-075	Summit House 5036-9	Department 56	Closed	28.00	275-450.
84-06-076	New School House 5037-7	Department 56	Closed	35.00	225-300.
84-06-077	Parish Church 5039-3	Department 56	Closed	32.00	300-400.
85-06-078	Stucco Bungalow 5045-8	Department 56	Closed	30.00	125-440.
85-06-079	Williamsburg House 5046-6	Department 56	Closed	37.00	85-150.00
85-06-080	Plantation House 5047-4	Department 56	Closed	37.00	90-150.00
85-06-081	Church of the Open Door 5048-2	Department 56	Closed	34.00	100-150.
85-06-082	Spruce Place 5049-0	Department 56	Closed	33.00	225-300.
85-06-083	Duplex 5050-4	Department 56	Closed	35.00	100-150.
85-06-084	Depot and Train with 2 Train Cars 5051-2	Department 56	Closed	65.00	110-175.
85-06-085	Ridgewood 5052-0	Department 56	Closed	35.00	150-200.
86-06-086	Waverly Place 5041-5	Department 56	Closed	35.00	200-325.
86-06-087	Twin Peaks 5042-3	Department 56	Closed	32.00	200-365.
86-06-088	2101 Maple 5043-1	Department 56	Closed	32.00	250-400.
86-06-089	Lincoln Park Duplex 5060-1	Department 56	Closed	33.00	100-150.
86-06-090	Sonoma House 5062-8	Department 56	Closed	33.00	88-125.00
86-06-091	Highland Park House 5063-6	Department 56	Closed	35.00	100-225.
86-06-092	Beacon Hill House 5065-2	Department 56	Closed	31.00	100-220.
86-06-093	Pacific Heights House 5066-0	Department 56	Closed	33.00	90-120.00
86-06-094	Ramsey Hill House 5067-9	Department 56	Closed	36.00	90-150.00
86-06-095	Saint James Church 5068-7	Department 56	Closed	37.00	100-120.
86-06-096	All Saints Church 5070-9	Department 56	Open	38.00	45.00
86-06-097	Carriage House 5071-7	Department 56	Closed	29.00	100-175.
86-06-098	Toy Shop 5073-3	Department 56	Closed	36.00	90-105.00
86-06-099	Apothecary 5076-8	Department 56	Closed	34.00	75-125.00
86-06-100	Bakery 5077-6	Department 56	Closed	35.00	75-90.00
86-06-101	Mickey's Diner 5078-4	Department 56	Closed	22.00	325-475.
87-06-102	St. Anthony Hotel & Post Office 5006-7	Department 56	Closed	40.00	85-150.00
87-06-103	Snow Village Factory 5013-0	Department 56	Closed	45.00	80-150.00
87-06-104	Cathedral Church 5019-9	Department 56	Closed	50.00	80-115.00
87-06-105	Cumberland House 5024-5	Department 56	Open	42.00	44.00
87-06-106	Springfield House 5027-0	Department 56	Closed	40.00	85-125.00
87-06-107	Lighthouse 5030-0	Department 56	Closed	36.00	300-385.
87-06-108	Red Barn 5081-4	Department 56	Open	38.00	42.00
87-06-109	Jefferson School 5082-2	Department 56	Closed	36.00	75-100.00
87-06-110	Farm House 5089-0	Department 56	Open	40.00	44.00
87-06-111	Fire Station No. 2 5091-1	Department 56	Closed	40.00	100-145.
87-06-112	Snow Village Resort Lodge 5092-0	Department 56	Closed	55.00	90-150.00
88-06-113	Village Market 5044-0	Department 56	Closed	39.00	75-100.00
88-06-114	Kenwood House 5054-7	Department 56	Closed	50.00	90-175.00
88-06-115	Maple Ridge Inn 5121-7	Department 56	Closed	55.00	100-150.
88-06-116	Village Station and Train 5122-5	Department 56	Open	65.00	70.00
88-06-117	Cobblestone Antique Shop 5123-3	Department 56	Open	36.00	37.50
88-06-118	Corner Cafe 5124-1	Department 56	Closed	37.00	65-115.00
88-06-119	Single Car Garage 5125-0	Department 56	Closed	22.00	45-65.00
88-06-120	Home Sweet Home/House & Windmill5126-8	Department 56	Closed	60.00	85-120.00
88-06-121	Redeemer Church 5127-6	Department 56	Open	42.00	45.00
88-06-122	Service Station 5128-4	Department 56	Closed	37.50	70-125.00
88-06-123	Stonehurst House 5140-3	Department 56	Open	37.50	37.50
88-06-124	Palos Verdes 5141-1	Department 56	Closed	37.50	65-95.00
89-06-125	Jingle Belle Houseboat 5114-4	Department 56	Closed	42.00	85-95.00

Number	Name	Artist	Edition Limit	Issue Price	Quote
89-06-126	Colonial Church 5119-5	Department 56	Open	60.00	60.00
89-06-127	North Creek Cottage 5120-9	Department 56	Open	45.00	45.00
89-06-128	Paramount Theater 5142-0	Department 56	Open	42.00	42.00
89-06-129	Doctor's House 5143-8	Department 56	Open	56.00	56.00
89-06-130	Courthouse 5144-6	Department 56	Open	65.00	65.00
89-06-131	Village Warming House 5145-4	Department 56	Open	42.00	42.00
89-06-132	J. Young's Granary 5149-7	Department 56	Open	45.00	45.00
89-06-133	Pinewood Log Cabin 5150-0	Department 56	Open	37.50	37.50
90-06-134	56 Flavors Ice Cream Parlor 5151-9	Department 56	Open	42.00	4200
90-06-135	Morningside House 5152-7	Department 56	Open	45.00	45.00
90-06-136	Mainstreet Hardware Store 5153-5	Department 56	Open	42.00	42.00
90-06-137	Village Realty 5154-3	Department 56	Open	42.00	42.00
90-06-138	Spanish Mission Church 5155-1	Department 56	Open	42.00	42.00
90-06-139	Prairie House (American Architecture Series), 5156-0	Department 56	Open	42.00	42.00
90-06-140	Queen Anne Victorian (American Architecture Series), 5157-8	Department 56	Open	48.00	48.00
91-06-141	Oak Grove Tudor 5400-3	Department 56	Open	42.00	42.00
91-06-142	Honeymooner Motel 5401-1	Department 56	Open	42.00	42.00
91-06-143	The Christmas Shop 5097-0	Department 56	Open	37.50	37.50
91-06-144	Village Greenhouse 5402-0	Department 56	Open	35.00	35.00
91-06-145	Southern Colonial (American Architecture Series), 5403-8	Department 56	Open	48.00	48.00
91-06-146	Gothic Farmhouse (American Architecture Series), 5404-6	Department 56	Open	48.00	48.00
91-06-147	Finklea's Finery: Costume Shop 5405-4	Department 56	Open	45.00	45.00
91-06-148	Jack's Corner Barber Shop 5406-2	Department 56	Open	42.00	42.00
91-06-149	Double Bungalow, 5407-0	Department 56	Open	45.00	45.00
92-06-150	Post Office 5422-4	Department 56	Open	35.00	35.00
92-06-151	Grandma's House 5420-8	Department 56	Open	42.00	42.00
92-06-152	St. Luke's Church 5421-6	Department 56	Open	45.00	45.00
Department 56	**North Pole Collection**				
90-07-001	Santa's Workshop 5600-6	Department 56	Open	72.00	72.00
90-07-002	North Pole 5601-4 Set of 2 (Reindeer Barn, Elf Bunkhouse)	Department 56	Open	70.00	70.00
91-07-003	Neenee's Dolls & Toys 5620-0	Department 56	Open	37.50	36.00
91-07-004	North Pole Shops, Set of 2 5621-9 (Orly's Bell & Harness Supply, Rimpy's Bakery)	Department 56	Open	75.00	75.00
91-07-005	Tassy's Mittens & Hassel's Woolies 5622-7	Department 56	Open	50.00	50.00
92-07-006	North Pole Post Office 5623-5	Department 56	Open	45.00	45.00
Department 56	**Event Piece - Heritage Village Collection Accessory**				
92-08-001	Gate House 5530-1	Department 56	Sp.Iss.	22.50	22.50
Department 56	**Retired Heritage Village Collection Accessories**				
84-09-001	Carolers 6526-9, Set Of 3 w/ Lamppost(wh)	Department 56	Closed	10.00	115-200.
84-09-002	Carolers 6526-9, Set Of 3 w/ Lamppost(bl)	Department 56	Closed	10.00	25-60.00
85-09-003	Village Train 6527-7, Set Of 3	Department 56	Closed	12.00	300-470.
86-09-004	Christmas Carol Figures 6501-3, Set of 3	Department 56	Closed	12.50	25-43.00
86-09-005	Lighted Tree With Children & Ladder 6510-2	Department 56	Closed	35.00	225-300.
86-09-006	Sleighride 6511-0	Department 56	Closed	19.50	35-80.00
86-09-007	Covered Wooden Bridge 6531-5	Deaprtment 56	Closed	10.00	25-50.00
86-09-008	New England Winter Set 6532-3, Set of 5	Department 56	Closed	18.00	30-65.00
87-09-009	Farm People And Animals 5901-3, Set Of 5	Department 56	Closed	24.00	50-75.00
87-09-010	Blacksmith 5934-0, Set of 3	Department 56	Closed	20.00	35-75.00
87-09-011	City People 5965-0, Set of 5	Department 56	Closed	27.50	50-75.00
87-09-012	Silo And Hay Shed 5950-1	Department 56	Closed	18.00	80-112.00
87-09-013	Ox Sled 5951-0	Department 56	Closed	20.00	75-130.00
87-09-014	Shopkeepers 5966-8, Set Of 4	Department 56	Closed	15.00	25-45.00
87-09-015	City Workers 5967-6, Set Of 4	Department 56	Closed	15.00	30-45.00
87-09-016	Skating Pond 6545-5	Department 56	Closed	24.00	50-80.00
87-09-017	Stone Bridge 6546-3	Department 56	Closed	12.00	50-75.00
87-09-018	Village Well And Holy Cross 6547-1, Set Of 2	Department 56	Closed	13.00	80-125.00
87-09-019	Maple Sugaring Shed 6589-7, Set Of 3	Department 56	Closed	19.00	115-145.
87-09-020	Dover Coach 6590-0	Department 56	Closed	18.00	45-90.00
87-09-021	Dover Coach w/o Mustache 6590-0	Department 56	Closed	18.00	75-150.
88-09-022	Fezziwig and Friends 5928-5, Set Of 3	Department 56	Closed	12.50	30-40.00
88-09-023	Village Train Trestle 5981-1	Department 56	Closed	17.00	35-70.00
88-09-024	Woodcutter And Son 5986-2, Set Of 2	Department 56	Closed	10.00	25-45.00
88-09-025	Childe Pond and Skaters 5903-0, Set of 4	Department 56	Closed	30.00	55-95.00
88-09-026	Nicholas Nickleby Characters 5929-3,Set of 4	Department 56	Closed	20.00	35-50.00
88-09-027	Village Harvest People 5941-2 Set of4	Department 56	Closed	27.50	30-55.00
88-09-028	City Newsstand 5971-4, Set of 4	Department 56	Closed	25.00	40-60.00
88-09-029	City Bus & Milk Truck 5983-8, Set of 2	Department 56	Closed	15.00	25-35.00
88-09-030	Salvation Army Band 5985-4, Set of 6	Department 56	Closed	24.00	40-60.00
89-09-031	Constables 5579-4, Set Of 3	Department 56	Closed	17.50	35-60.00
89-09-032	Farm Animals 5945-5, Set of 4	Department 56	Closed	15.00	30-50.00
89-09-033	Organ Grinder 5957-9, Set of 3	Department 56	Closed	21.00	35-45.00
89-09-034	River Street Ice House Cart 5959-5	Department 56	Closed	20.00	35-46.00
Department 56	**The Original Snow Village Collection Accessories Retired**				
79-10-001	Aspen Trees 5052-6, Meadowland Series	Department 56	Closed	16.00	32.00
79-10-002	Sheep, 9 White, 3 Black 5053-4 Meadowland Series	Department 56	Closed	12.00	24.00
79-10-003	Carolers 5064-1	Department 56	Closed	12.00	55-140.00
80-10-004	Ceramic Car 5069-0	Department 56	Closed	5.00	30-75.00
81-10-005	Ceramic Sleigh 5079-2	Department 56	Closed	5.00	30-75.00
82-10-006	Snowman With Broom 5018-0	Department 56	Closed	3.00	10-25.00
83-10-007	Monks-A-Caroling (butterscotch) 6459-9	Department 56	Closed	6.00	65-125.00
84-10-008	Scottie With Tree 5038-5	Department 56	Closed	3.00	90-165.00
84-10-009	Monks-A-Caroling (brown) 5040-7	Department 56	Closed	6.00	30.00
85-10-010	Singing Nuns 5053-9	Department 56	Closed	6.00	60-75.00
85-10-011	Snow Kids Sled, Skis 5056-3	Department 56	Closed	11.00	30-55.00
85-10-012	Family Mom/Kids, Goose/Girl 5057-1	Department 56	Closed	11.00	30-44.00
85-10-013	Santa/Mailbox 5059-8	Department 56	Closed	11.00	30-50.00
86-10-014	Girl/Snowman, Boy 5095-4	Department 56	Closed	11.00	30-50.00
86-10-015	Shopping Girls With Packages 5096-2	Department 56	Closed	11.00	25-50.00
86-10-016	Kids Around The Tree 5094-6	Department 56	Closed	15.00	30-66.00
87-10-017	3 Nuns With Songbooks 5102-0	Department 56	Closed	6.00	50-75.00
87-10-018	Praying Monks 5103-9	Department 56	Closed	6.00	35.00
87-10-019	Children In Band 5104-7	Department 56	Closed	15.00	25-40.00
87-10-020	Caroling Family 5105-5, Set Of 3	Department 56	Closed	20.00	25-45.00
87-10-021	Christmas Children 5107-1, Set Of 4	Department 56	Closed	20.00	30-40.00
87-10-022	Snow Kids 5113-6, Set of 4	Department 56	Closed	20.00	30-36.00
88-10-023	Hayride 5117-9	Department 56	Closed	30.00	45-75.00
88-10-024	School Children 5118-7, Set of 3	Department 56	Closed	15.00	25-40.00
88-10-025	Apple Girl/Newspaper Boy 5129-2, Set of 2	Department 56	Closed	11.00	20-39.00
88-10-026	Woodsman and Boy 5130-6, Set of 2	Department 56	Closed	13.00	25-33.00
88-10-027	Woody Station Wagon 5136-5	Department 56	Closed	6.50	15-30.00
88-10-028	Water Tower 5133-0	Department 56	Closed	20.00	30-85.00
88-10-029	School Bus, Snow Plow 5137-3, Set of 2	Department 56	Closed	16.00	25-45.00
88-10-030	Sisal Tree Lot 8183-3	Department 56	Closed	45.00	60-75.00
89-10-031	Special Delivery 5148-9 Set of 2	Department 56	Closed	16.00	36-75.00
89-10-032	Mailbox 5179-9	Department 56	Closed	3.50	15-30.00
89-10-033	Kids Tree House 5168-3	Department 56	Closed	25.00	40-53.00
89-10-034	Skate Faster Mom 5170-5	Department 56	Closed	13.00	25-75.00
89-10-035	Through the Woods 5172-1, Set of 2	Department 56	Closed	18.00	35-45.00
89-10-036	Statue of Mark Twain 5173-0	Department 56	Closed	15.00	20-30.00
89-10-037	Calling All Cars 5174-8, Set of 2	Department 56	Closed	15.00	25-33.00
Department 56	**Snowbabies**				
86-11-001	Give Me A Push 7955-3	Department 56	Closed	12.00	35-60.00
86-11-002	Hold On Tight 7956-1	Department 56	Open	12.00	12.00
86-11-003	Best Friends 7958-8	Department 56	Closed	12.00	75-100.00
86-11-004	Snowbaby Nite-Lite 7959-6	Department 56	Closed	15.00	250-350.
86-11-005	I'm Making Snowballs 7962-6	Department 56	Open	12.00	12.00
86-11-006	Climbing on Snowball 7965-0	Department 56	Closed	15.00	35-80.00
86-11-007	Hanging Pair 7966-9	Department 56	Closed	15.00	50-85.00
86-11-008	Snowbaby Holding Picture Fram7970-7 2/set	Department 56	Closed	15.00	325-400.
87-11-009	Tumbling In the Snow, 5/set 7957-0	Department 56	Open	35.00	35.00
87-11-010	Down The Hill We Go 7960-0	Department 56	Open	20.00	20.00
87-11-011	Don't Fall Off 7968-5	Department 56	Closed	12.50	35-60.00
87-11-012	Climbing On Tree, Set Of 2 7971-5	Department 56	Closed	25.00	350-500.
87-11-013	Winter Surprise 7974-0	Department 56	Open	15.00	15.00
88-11-014	Are All These Mine? 7977-4	Department 56	Open	10.00	10.00
88-11-015	Polar Express 7978-2	Department 56	Open	22.00	22.00
88-11-016	Tiny Trio, Set Of 3 7979-0	Department 56	Closed	20.00	70-115.00
88-11-017	Frosty Frolic 7981-2	Department 56	4,800	35.00	550-850.
89-11-018	Helpful Friends 7982-0	Department 56	Open	30.00	30.00
89-11-019	Frosty Fun 7983-9	Department 56	Closed	27.50	50-75.00
89-11-020	All Fall Down, Set Of 4 7984-7	Department 56	Closed	36.00	60-90.00
89-11-021	Finding Fallen Stars 7985-5	Department 56	6,000	32.50	125-175.
89-11-022	Penguin Parade 7986-3	Department 56	Open	25.00	25.00
89-11-023	Icy Igloo 7987-1	Department 56	Open	37.50	37.50
90-11-024	Twinkle Little Stars 7942-1 Set of 2	Department 56	Open	37.50	37.50
90-11-025	Wishing on a Star 7943-0	Department 56	Open	20.00	20.00
90-11-026	Read Me a Story 7945-6	Department 56	Open	25.00	25.00
90-11-027	We Will Make it Shine 7946-4	Department 56	Open	45.00	45.00
90-11-028	Playing Games Is Fun 7947-2	Department 56	Open	30.00	30.00
90-11-029	A Special Delivery 7948-0	Department 56	Open	13.50	13.50
90-11-030	Who Are You? 7949-9	Department 56	12,500	32.50	100-175.
91-11-031	I Will Put Up The Tree 6800-4	Department 56	Open	24.00	24.00
91-11-032	Why Don't You Talk To Me 6801-2	Department 56	Open	24.00	24.00
91-11-033	I Made This Just For You 6802-0	Department 56	Open	15.00	15.00
91-11-034	Is That For Me 6803-9 Set of 2	Department 56	Open	32.50	32.50
91-11-035	Snowbaby Polar Sign 6804-7	Department 56	Open	20.00	20.00
91-11-036	This Is Where We Live 6805-5	Department 56	Open	60.00	60.00
91-11-037	Can I Help You? 6806-3	Department 56	18,500	48.00	48.00
91-11-038	Waiting For Christmas 6807-1	Department 56	Open	27.50	27.50
91-11-039	Dancing To a Tune 6808-0, Set of 3	Department 56	Open	30.00	30.00
91-11-040	Fishing For Dreams 6809-8	Department 56	Open	28.00	28.00
92-11-041	I Need A Hug 6813-6	Department 56	Open	20.00	20.00
92-11-042	Let's Go Skiing 6815-2	Department 56	Open	15.00	15.00
92-11-043	Wait For Me 6812-8	Department 56	Open	48.00	48.00
92-11-044	Winken, Blinken, and Nod 6814-4	Department 56	Open	60.00	60.00
92-11-045	This Willl Cheer You Up 6816-0	Department 56	Open	30.00	30.00
Department 56	**Village CCP Miniatures**				
87-12-001	Dickens' Village Original, set of 7 6558-7	Department 56	Closed	72.00	125-210.
87-12-002	Crowntree Inn 6558-7	Department 56	Closed	12.00	27.50
87-12-003	Candle Shop 6558-7	Department 56	Closed	12.00	30-40.00
87-12-004	Green Grocer 6558-7	Department 56	Closed	12.00	30-38.00
87-12-005	Golden Swan Baker 6558-7	Department 56	Closed	12.00	25-30.00
87-12-006	Bean and Son Smithy Shop 6558-7	Department 56	Closed	12.00	25.00
87-12-007	Abel Beesley Butcher 6558-7	Department 56	Closed	12.00	25-42.00
87-12-008	Jones & Co. Brush & Basket Shop 6558-7	Department 56	Closed	12.00	40.00
87-12-009	Dickens' Cottages, set of 3 6559-5	Department 56	Closed	30.00	175.00
87-12-010	Thatched Cottage 6559-5	Department 56	Closed	10.00	50-80.00
87-12-011	Stone Cottage 6559-5	Department 56	Closed	10.00	45-82.00
87-12-012	Tudor Cottage 6559-5	Department 56	Closed	10.00	100-150.
87-12-013	Dickens' Village Assorted, set of 3 6560-9	Department 56	Closed	48.00	N/A
87-12-014	Dickens Village Church 6560-9	Department 56	Closed	16.00	32-49.00
87-12-015	Norman Church 6560-9	Department 56	Closed	16.00	55-60.00
87-12-016	Blythe Pond Mill House 6560-9	Department 56	Closed	16.00	36-45.00
87-12-017	Christmas Carol Cottages, set of 3 6561-7	Department 56	Closed	30.00	50-75.00
87-12-018	Fezziwig's Warehouse 6561-7	Department 56	Closed	10.00	25-35.00
87-12-019	Scrooge & Marley Countinghouse 6561-7	Department 56	Closed	10.00	26-28.00
87-12-020	The Cottage of Bob Cratchit & Tiny Tim 6561-7	Department 56	Closed	10.00	26.00
87-12-021	Dickens' Village Assorted, set of 4 6562-5	Department 56	Closed	60.00	N/A
87-12-022	The Old Curiosity Shop 6562-5	Department 56	Closed	15.00	42.00
87-12-023	Brick Abbey 6562-5	Department 56	Closed	15.00	50-75.00
87-12-024	Chesterton Manor House 6562-5	Department 56	Closed	15.00	60-75.00
87-12-025	Barley Bree Farmhouse 6562-5	Department 56	Closed	15.00	32-39.00
88-12-026	Dickens' Kenilworth Castle 6565-0	Department 56	Closed	30.00	70-85.00
87-12-027	Dickens' Lane Shops, set of 3 6591-9	Department 56	Closed	30.00	78-90.00
87-12-028	Thomas Kersey Coffee House 6591-9	Department 56	Closed	10.00	26-39.00
87-12-029	Cottage Toy Shop 6591-9	Department 56	Closed	10.00	26-32.00
87-12-030	Tuttle's Pub 6591-9	Department 56	Closed	10.00	26-40.00
87-12-031	Dickens' Chadbury Station & Train 6592-7	Department 56	Closed	27.50	50-60.00
88-12-032	New England Village Original, set of 7 5935-8	Department 56	Closed	72.00	275-300.
88-12-033	Apothecary Shop 5935-8	Department 56	Closed	10.50	30-40.00
88-12-034	General Store 5935-8	Department 56	Closed	10.50	40-50.00
88-12-035	Nathaniel Bingham Fabrics 5935-8	Department 56	Closed	10.50	40.00
88-12-036	Livery Stable & Boot Shop 5935-8	Department 56	Closed	10.50	40.00
88-12-037	Steeple Church 5935-8	Department 56	Closed	10.50	40-120.00
88-12-038	Brick Town Hall 5935-8	Department 56	Closed	10.50	40.00
88-12-039	Red Schoolhouse 5935-8	Department 56	Closed	10.50	40-65.00
88-12-040	New England Village Assorted, set of 6 5937-4	Department 56	Closed	85.00	N/A
88-12-041	Timber Knoll Log Cabin 5937-4	Department 56	Closed	14.50	30-42.00
88-12-042	Smythe Wollen Mill 5937-4	Department 56	Closed	14.50	65-70.00
88-12-043	Jacob Adams Farmhouse 5937-4	Department 56	Closed	14.50	42-50.00
88-12-044	Jacob Adams Barn 5937-4	Department 56	Closed	14.50	30-60.00
88-12-045	Craggy Cove Lighthouse 5937-4	Department 56	Closed	14.50	100-110.
88-12-046	Maple Sugaring Shed 5937-4	Department 56	Closed	14.50	32-48.00
87-12-047	Little Town of Bethlehem, set of 12 5976-5	Department 56	Closed	85.00	140-230.
86-12-048	Victorian Miniatures, set of 5 6563-3	Department 56	Closed	65.00	N/A
86-12-049	Victorian Miniatures, set of 2 6564-1	Department 56	Closed	45.00	300.00
86-12-050	Estate 6564-1	Department 56	Closed	22.50	N/A
86-12-051	Church 6564-1	Department 56	Closed	22.50	N/A
86-12-052	Williamsburg Snowhouse Series, set of 6 6566-8	Department 56	Closed	60.00	N/A
86-12-053	Williamsburg House, White 6566-8	Department 56	Closed	10.00	40.00

Company / Number	Name	Series / Artist	Edition Limit	Issue Price	Quote
86-12-054	Williamsburg House, Blue 6566-8	Department 56	Closed	10.00	60.00
86-12-055	Williamsburg House, Brown Brick 6566-8	Department 56	Closed	10.00	40.00
86-12-056	Williamsburg House, Brown Clapboard 6566-8	Department 56	Closed	10.00	40.00
86-12-057	Williamsburg House, Red 6566-8	Department 56	Closed	10.00	60.00
86-12-059	Williamsburg House, White 6566-8	Department 56	Closed	10.00	75.00
Walt Disney		**Classics Collection**			
92-01-001	Cinderella 6" 41000	Disney Studios	Open	195.00	195.00
92-01-002	Lucifer 2 3/5" 41001	Disney Studios	Open	69.00	69.00
92-01-003	Bruno 4 2/5" 41002	Disney Studios	Open	69.00	69.00
92-01-004	Cinderella's Sewing Book 41003	Disney Studios	Open	69.00	69.00
92-01-005	Needle Mouse 5 4/5" 41004	Disney Studios	Open	69.00	69.00
92-01-006	Birds With Sash 6 2/5" 41005	Disney Studios	Open	149.00	149.00
92-01-007	Chalk Mouse 3 2/5" 41006	Disney Studios	Open	65.00	65.00
92-01-008	Gus 3 2/5" 41007	Disney Studios	Open	65.00	65.00
92-01-009	Jaq 4 1/5" 41008	Disney Studios	Open	65.00	65.00
92-01-010	Opening Title 41009	Disney Studios	Open	29.00	29.00
92-01-011	Bambi & Flower 6" 41010	Disney Studios	10,000	298.00	298.00
92-01-012	Friend Owl 8 3/5" 41011	Disney Studios	Open	195.00	195.00
92-01-013	Field Mouse 5 3/5" 41012	Disney Studios	7,500	195.00	195.00
92-01-014	Thumper 3" 41013	Disney Studios	Open	55.00	55.00
92-01-015	Thumper's Sisters 3 3/5" 41014	Disney Studios	Open	69.00	69.00
92-01-016	Opening Title 41015	Disney Studios	Open	29.00	29.00
92-01-017	Sorcerer Mickey 5 1/5" 41016	Disney Studios	Open	195.00	195.00
92-01-018	Broom (Two) 5 4/5" 41017	Disney Studios	Open	150.00	150.00
92-01-019	Opening Title 41018	Disney Studios	Open	29.00	29.00
92-01-020	Opening Title 41019	Disney Studios	Open	29.00	29.00
92-01-021	Mickey 6" 41020	Disney Studios	Open	125.00	125.00
92-01-022	Minnie 6" 41021	Disney Studios	Open	125.00	125.00
92-01-023	Pluto 3 3/5" 41022	Disney Studios	Open	65.00	65.00
Duncan Royale		**History of Santa Claus I**			
83-01-001	St. Nicholas	P. Apsit	Retrd.	175.00	650-1800.
83-01-002	Dedt Moroz	P. Apsit	Retrd.	145.00	325-600.
83-01-003	Black Peter	P. Apsit	Retrd.	145.00	200-450.
83-01-004	Victorian	P. Apsit	Retrd.	120.00	225-450.
83-01-005	Medieval	P. Apsit	Retrd.	220.00	1200-3500.
83-01-006	Russian	P. Apsit	Retrd.	145.00	400-825.
83-01-007	Wassail	P. Apsit	Retrd.	90.00	250-600.
83-01-008	Kris Kringle	P. Apsit	Retrd.	165.00	1200-2500.
83-01-009	Soda Pop	P. Apsit	Retrd.	145.00	1000-3500.
83-01-010	Pioneer	P. Apsit	Retrd.	145.00	300-825.
83-01-011	Civil War	P. Apsit	10,000	145.00	250-600.
83-01-012	Nast	P. Apsit	Retrd.	90.00	2500-6900.
Duncan Royale		**Special Release**			
92-02-001	Nast & Sleigh	Duncan Royale	5,000	500.00	500.00
Duncan Royale		**History of Santa Claus II**			
86-03-001	Odin	P. Apsit	10,000	200.00	250.00
86-03-002	Lord of Misrule	P. Apsit	10,000	160.00	200.00
86-03-003	Mongolian/Asian	P. Apsit	10,000	240.00	300.00
86-03-004	The Magi	P. Apsit	10,000	350.00	400.00
86-03-005	St. Lucia	P. Apsit	10,000	180.00	225.00
86-03-006	Befana	P. Apsit	10,000	200.00	250.00
86-03-007	Babouska	P. Apsit	10,000	170.00	200.00
86-03-008	Bavarian	P. Apsit	10,000	250.00	300.00
86-03-009	Alsace Angel	P. Apsit	10,000	250.00	300.00
86-03-010	Frau Holda	P. Apsit	10,000	160.00	180.00
86-03-011	Sir Christmas	P. Apsit	10,000	150.00	175.00
86-03-012	The Pixie	P. Apsit	10,000	140.00	175.00
Duncan Royale		**History of Santa Claus III**			
90-04-001	St. Basil	Duncan Royale	10,000	300.00	300.00
90-04-002	Star Man	Duncan Royale	10,000	300.00	300.00
90-04-003	Julenisse	Duncan Royale	10,000	200.00	200.00
90-04-005	Ukko	Duncan Royale	10,000	250.00	250.00
90-04-006	Druid	Duncan Royale	10,000	250.00	250.00
91-04-007	Saturnalia King	Duncan Royale	10,000	200.00	200.00
91-04-008	Judah Maccabee	Duncan Royale	10,000	300.00	300.00
91-04-009	King Wenceslas	Duncan Royale	10,000	300.00	300.00
91-04-010	Hoteisho	Duncan Royale	10,000	200.00	200.00
91-04-011	Knickerbocker	Duncan Royale	10,000	300.00	300.00
91-04-012	Samichlaus	Duncan Royale	10,000	350.00	350.00
91-04-013	Grandfather Frost & Snow Maiden	Duncan Royale	10,000	400.00	400.00
91-04-014	Signature Piece	Duncan Royale	Open	50.00	50.00
Duncan Royale		**History of Santa Claus**			
87-05-001	St. Nicholas-8" wood	P. Apsit	500	450.00	450.00
87-05-002	Dedt Moroz-8" wood	P. Apsit	500	450.00	450.00
87-05-003	Black Peter-8" wood	P. Apsit	500	450.00	450.00
87-05-004	Victorian-8" wood	P. Apsit	500	450.00	450.00
87-05-005	Medieval-8" wood	P. Apsit	500	450.00	450.00
87-05-006	Russian-8" wood	P. Apsit	500	450.00	450.00
87-05-007	Wassail-8" wood	P. Apsit	500	450.00	450.00
87-05-008	Kris Kringle-8" wood	P. Apsit	500	450.00	450.00
87-05-009	Soda Pop-8" wood	P. Apsit	Retrd.	450.00	450.00
87-05-010	Pioneer-8" wood	P. Apsit	500	450.00	450.00
87-05-011	Civil War-8" wood	P. Apsit	500	450.00	450.00
87-05-012	Nast-8" wood	P. Apsit	Retrd.	450.00	450.00
89-05-013	St. Nicholas-18"	P. Apsit	1,000	1500.00	1500.00
89-05-014	Medieval-18"	P. Apsit	1,000	1500.00	1500.00
89-05-015	Russian-18"	P. Apsit	1,000	1500.00	1500.00
89-05-016	Kris Kringle-18"	P. Apsit	1,000	1500.00	1500.00
89-05-017	Soda Pop-18"	P. Apsit	1,000	1500.00	1500.00
89-05-018	Nast-18"	P. Apsit	1,000	1500.00	1500.00
Duncan Royale		**Miniature Collection**			
88-06-001	St. Nicholas-6" porcelain	P. Apsit	6,000/yr.	70.00	80.00
88-06-002	Dedt Moroz -6" porcelain	P. Apsit	6,000/yr.	70.00	80.00
88-06-003	Black Peter-6" porcelain	P. Apsit	6,000/yr.	70.00	80.00
88-06-004	Victorian-6" porcelain	P. Apsit	6,000/yr.	60.00	80.00
88-06-005	Medieval-6" porcelain	P. Apsit	6,000/yr.	70.00	80.00
88-06-006	Russian-6" porcelain	P. Apsit	6,000/yr.	70.00	80.00
88-06-007	Wassail-6" porcelain	P. Apsit	6,000/yr.	60.00	80.00
88-06-008	Kris Kringle-6" porcelain	P. Apsit	6,000/yr.	60.00	80.00
88-06-009	Soda Pop-6" porcelain	P. Apsit	6,000/yr.	60.00	80.00
88-06-010	Pioneer-6" porcelain	P. Apsit	6,000/yr.	60.00	80.00
88-06-011	Civil War-6" porcelain	P. Apsit	6,000/yr.	60.00	80.00
88-06-012	Nast-6" porcelain	P. Apsit	6,000/yr.	60.00	80.00
88-06-013	Odin-6" porcelain	P. Apsit	6,000/yr.	80.00	90.00
88-06-014	Lord of Misrule-6" porcelain	P. Apsit	6,000/yr.	60.00	80.00
88-06-015	Mongolian/Asian-6" porcelain	P. Apsit	6,000/yr.	80.00	90.00
88-06-016	Magi-6" porcelain	P. Apsit	6,000/yr.	130.00	150.00
88-06-017	St. Lucia-6" porcelain	P. Apsit	6,000/yr.	70.00	80.00
88-06-018	Befana-6" porcelain	P. Apsit	6,000/yr.	70.00	80.00
88-06-019	Babouska-6" porcelain	P. Apsit	6,000/yr.	70.00	80.00
88-06-020	Bavarian-6" porcelain	P. Apsit	6,000/yr.	90.00	100.00
88-06-021	Alsace Angel-6" porcelain	P. Apsit	6,000/yr.	80.00	90.00
88-06-022	Frau Holda-6" porcelain	P. Apsit	6,000/yr.	50.00	80.00
88-06-023	Sir Christmas-6" porcelain	P. Apsit	6,000/yr.	60.00	80.00
88-06-024	Pixie-6" porcelain	P. Apsit	6,000/yr.	50.00	80.00
90-06-025	Bob Hope-6" porcelain	P. Apsit	6,000/yr.	130.00	130.00
Duncan Royale		**History of Classic Entertainers**			
87-07-001	Greco-Roman	P. Apsit	20,000	180.00	200.00
87-07-002	Jester	P. Apsit	20,000	410.00	450.00
87-07-003	Pierrot	P. Apsit	20,000	180.00	200.00
87-07-004	Harlequin	P. Apsit	20,000	250.00	270.00
87-07-005	Grotesque	P. Apsit	20,000	230.00	250.00
87-07-006	Pantalone	P. Apsit	20,000	270.00	270.00
87-07-007	Pulcinella	P. Apsit	20,000	220.00	220.00
87-07-008	Russian	P. Apsit	20,000	190.00	200.00
87-07-009	Auguste	P. Apsit	20,000	220.00	240.00
87-07-010	Slapstick	P. Apsit	20,000	250.00	270.00
87-07-011	Uncle Sam	P. Apsit	20,000	160.00	160.00
87-07-012	American	P. Apsit	20,000	160.00	200.00
90-07-013	Mime-18"	P. Apsit	1,000	1500.00	1500.00
90-07-014	Bob Hope-18"	P. Aspit	1,000	1500.00	1500.00
Duncan Royale		**History of Classic Entertainers II**			
88-08-001	Goliard	P. Apsit	20,000	200.00	200.00
88-08-002	Touchstone	P. Apsit	20,000	200.00	200.00
88-08-003	Feste	P. Apsit	20,000	250.00	250.00
88-08-004	Tartaglia	P. Apsit	20,000	200.00	200.00
88-08-005	Zanni	P. Apsit	20,000	200.00	200.00
88-08-006	Mountebank	P. Apsit	20,000	270.00	270.00
88-08-007	Pedrolino	P. Apsit	20,000	200.00	200.00
88-08-008	Thomassi	P. Apsit	20,000	200.00	200.00
88-08-009	Tramp	P. Apsit	20,000	200.00	200.00
88-08-010	White Face	P. Apsit	20,000	250.00	250.00
88-08-011	Mime	P. Apsit	20,000	200.00	200.00
88-08-012	Bob Hope	P. Apsit	20,000	250.00	250.00
88-08-013	Signature Piece	P. Apsit	Open	50.00	50.00
Duncan Royale		**Greatest Gift...Love**			
88-09-001	Annunciation, marble	P. Apsit	5,000	270.00	270.00
88-09-002	Annunciation, painted porcelain	P. Apsit	5,000	270.00	270.00
88-09-003	Nativity, marble	P. Apsit	5,000	500.00	500.00
88-09-004	Nativity, painted porcelain	P. Apsit	5,000	500.00	500.00
88-09-005	Crucifixion, marble	P. Apsit	5,000	300.00	300.00
88-09-006	Crucifixion, painted porcelain	P. Apsit	5,000	300.00	300.00
Duncan Royale		**Woodland Fairies**			
88-10-001	Cherry	Duncan Royale	10,000	70.00	70.00
88-10-002	Mulberry	Duncan Royale	10,000	70.00	70.00
88-10-003	Apple	Duncan Royale	10,000	70.00	70.00
88-10-004	Poplar	Duncan Royale	10,000	70.00	70.00
88-10-005	Elm	Duncan Royale	10,000	70.00	70.00
88-10-006	Chestnut	Duncan Royale	10,000	70.00	70.00
88-10-007	Calla Lily	Duncan Royale	10,000	70.00	70.00
88-10-008	Pear Blossom	Duncan Royale	10,000	70.00	70.00
88-10-010	Lime Tree	Duncan Royale	10,000	70.00	70.00
88-10-011	Christmas Tree	Duncan Royale	10,000	70.00	70.00
88-10-012	Sycamore	Duncan Royale	10,000	70.00	70.00
88-10-013	Pine Tree	Duncan Royale	10,000	70.00	70.00
88-10-014	Almond Blossom	Duncan Royale	10,000	70.00	70.00
Duncan Royale		**Calendar Secrets (12")**			
90-11-001	January	D. Aphessetche	5,000	260.00	260.00
90-11-002	February	D. Aphessetche	5,000	370.00	370.00
90-11-003	March	D. Aphessetche	5,000	350.00	350.00
90-11-004	April	D. Aphessetche	5,000	370.00	370.00
90-11-005	May	D. Aphessetche	5,000	390.00	390.00
90-11-006	June	D. Aphessetche	5,000	410.00	410.00
90-11-007	July	D. Aphessetche	5,000	280.00	280.00
90-11-008	August	D. Aphessetche	5,000	300.00	300.00
90-11-009	September	D. Aphessetche	5,000	300.00	300.00
90-11-010	October	D. Aphessetche	5,000	350.00	350.00
90-11-011	November	D. Aphessetche	5,000	410.00	410.00
90-11-012	December	D. Aphessetche	5,000	410.00	410.00
Duncan Royale		**Calendar Secrets II (6")**			
93-12-001	January	D. Aphessetche	6,000	N/A	N/A
93-12-002	February	D. Aphessetche	6,000	N/A	N/A
93-12-003	March	D. Aphessetche	6,000	N/A	N/A
93-12-004	April	D. Aphessetche	6,000	N/A	N/A
93-12-005	May	D. Aphessetche	6,000	N/A	N/A
93-12-006	June	D. Aphessetche	6,000	N/A	N/A
93-12-007	July	D. Aphessetche	6,000	N/A	N/A
93-12-008	August	D. Aphessetche	6,000	N/A	N/A
93-12-009	September	D. Aphessetche	6,000	N/A	N/A
93-12-010	October	D. Aphessetche	6,000	N/A	N/A
93-12-011	November	D. Aphessetche	6,000	N/A	N/A
93-12-012	December	D. Aphessetche	6,000	N/A	N/A
Duncan Royale		**Ebony Collection**			
90-13-001	The Fiddler	Duncan Royale	5,000	90.00	90.00
90-13-002	Harmonica Man	Duncan Royale	5,000	80.00	80.00
90-13-003	Banjo Man	Duncan Royale	5,000	80.00	80.00
91-13-004	Spoons	Duncan Royale	5,000	90.00	90.00
91-13-005	Preacher	Duncan Royale	5,000	90.00	90.00
91-13-006	Female Gospel Singer	Duncan Royale	5,000	90.00	90.00
91-13-007	Male Gospel Singer	Duncan Royale	5,000	90.00	90.00
91-13-008	Jug Man	Duncan Royale	5,000	90.00	90.00
91-13-009	Signature Piece	Duncan Royale	Open	50.00	50.00
92-13-010	Jug Tooter	Duncan Royale	5,000	90.00	90.00
92-13-011	A Little Magic	Duncan Royale	5,000	80.00	80.00
92-13-012	Jazz Man Set	Duncan Royale	5,000	500.00	500.00
92-13-013	Sax	Duncan Royale	5,000	90.00	90.00
92-13-014	Trumpet	Duncan Royale	5,000	90.00	90.00
92-13-015	Bass	Duncan Royale	5,000	90.00	90.00
92-13-016	Piano	Duncan Royale	5,000	130.00	130.00
92-13-017	Bongo	Duncan Royale	5,000	90.00	90.00

Number	Name	Artist	Edition Limit	Issue Price	Quote
Duncan Royale		**Early American (12")**			
91-14-001	Doctor	Duncan Royale	10,000	150.00	150.00
91-14-002	Accountant	Duncan Royale	10,000	170.00	170.00
91-14-003	Lawyer	Duncan Royale	10,000	170.00	170.00
91-14-004	Nurse	Duncan Royale	10,000	150.00	150.00
91-14-005	Fireman	Duncan Royale	10,000	150.00	150.00
91-14-006	Policeman	Duncan Royale	10,000	150.00	150.00
91-14-007	Salesman	Duncan Royale	10,000	150.00	150.00
91-14-008	Storekeeper	Duncan Royale	10,000	150.00	150.00
91-14-009	Dentist	Duncan Royale	10,000	150.00	150.00
91-14-010	Pharmacist	Duncan Royale	10,000	150.00	150.00
91-14-011	Teacher	Duncan Royale	10,000	150.00	150.00
91-14-012	Homemaker	Duncan Royale	10,000	150.00	150.00
91-14-013	Banker	Duncan Royale	10,000	150.00	150.00
91-14-014	Secretary	Duncan Royale	10,000	150.00	150.00
91-14-015	Chiropractor	Duncan Royale	10,000	150.00	150.00
91-14-016	Set of 15	Duncan Royale	10,000	2290.00	2290.00
Duncan Royale		**Early American II (6")**			
92-15-001	Doctor	Duncan Royale	6,000	80.00	80.00
92-15-002	Accountant	Duncan Royale	6,000	80.00	80.00
92-15-003	Lawyer	Duncan Royale	6,000	80.00	80.00
92-15-004	Nurse	Duncan Royale	6,000	80.00	80.00
92-15-005	Fireman	Duncan Royale	6,000	80.00	80.00
92-15-006	Policeman	Duncan Royale	6,000	80.00	80.00
92-15-007	Salesman	Duncan Royale	6,000	80.00	80.00
92-15-008	Storekeeper	Duncan Royale	6,000	80.00	80.00
92-15-009	Dentist	Duncan Royale	6,000	80.00	80.00
92-15-010	Pharmacist	Duncan Royale	6,000	80.00	80.00
92-15-011	Teacher	Duncan Royale	6,000	80.00	80.00
92-15-012	Homemaker	Duncan Royale	6,000	80.00	80.00
92-15-013	Banker	Duncan Royale	6,000	80.00	80.00
92-15-014	Secretary	Duncan Royale	6,000	80.00	80.00
92-15-015	Chiropractor	Duncan Royale	6,000	80.00	80.00
92-15-016	Set of 15	Duncan Royale	6,000	1200.00	1200.00
Duncan Royale		**Christmas Images**			
91-16-001	The Carolers	Duncan Royale	10,000	120.00	120.00
91-16-002	The Christmas Pageant	Duncan Royale	10,000	175.00	175.00
92-16-003	Are You Really Santa?	Duncan Royale	10,000	N/A	N/A
92-16-004	The Midnight Watch	Duncan Royale	10,000	N/A	N/A
92-16-005	The Christmas Angel	Duncan Royale	10,000	N/A	N/A
92-16-006	Sneaking A Peek	Duncan Royale	10,000	N/A	N/A
Duncan Royale		**Painted Pewter Miniatures-Santa 1st Series**			
86-17-001	St. Nicholas	Duncan Royale	500	30.00	30.00
86-17-002	Dedt Moroz	Duncan Royale	500	30.00	30.00
86-17-003	Black Peter	Duncan Royale	500	30.00	30.00
86-17-004	Victorian	Duncan Royale	500	30.00	30.00
86-17-005	Medieval	Duncan Royale	500	30.00	30.00
86-17-006	Russian	Duncan Royale	500	30.00	30.00
86-17-007	Wassail	Duncan Royale	500	30.00	30.00
86-17-008	Kris Kringle	Duncan Royale	500	30.00	30.00
86-17-009	Soda Pop	Duncan Royale	500	30.00	30.00
86-17-010	Pioneer	Duncan Royale	500	30.00	30.00
86-17-011	Civil War	Duncan Royale	500	30.00	30.00
86-17-012	Nast	Duncan Royale	500	30.00	30.00
86-17-013	Set of 12	Duncan Royale	500	360.00	360-495.
Duncan Royale		**Painted Pewter Miniatures-Santa 2nd Series**			
88-18-001	Odin	Duncan Royale	500	30.00	30.00
88-18-002	Lord of Misrule	Duncan Royale	500	30.00	30.00
88-18-003	Mongolian	Duncan Royale	500	30.00	30.00
88-18-004	Magi	Duncan Royale	500	30.00	30.00
88-18-005	St. Lucia	Duncan Royale	500	30.00	30.00
88-18-006	Befana	Duncan Royale	500	30.00	30.00
88-18-007	Babouska	Duncan Royale	500	30.00	30.00
88-18-008	Bavarian	Duncan Royale	500	30.00	30.00
88-18-009	Alsace Angel	Duncan Royale	500	30.00	30.00
88-18-010	Frau Holda	Duncan Royale	500	30.00	30.00
88-18-011	Sir Christmas	Duncan Royale	500	30.00	30.00
88-18-012	Pixie	Duncan Royale	500	30.00	30.00
88-18-013	Set of 12	Duncan Royale	500	360.00	360-495.
Duncan Royale		**Collector Club**			
91-19-001	Today's Nast	Duncan Royale	Yr.Iss.	80.00	95.00
Duncan Royale		**1990 & 1991 Special Event Piece**			
XX-20-001	Nast & Music	Duncan Royale	5,000	79.95	79.95
Duncan Royale		**Buckwheat Collection**			
92-21-001	Petee & Friend	Duncan Royale	5,000	90.00	90.00
92-21-002	Painter	Duncan Royale	5,000	90.00	90.00
92-21-003	O'Tay	Duncan Royale	5,000	90.00	90.00
92-21-004	Smile For The Camera	Duncan Royale	5,000	90.00	90.00
Enesco Corporation		**Precious Moments Special Edition**			
81-01-001	Hello, Lord, It's Me Again-PM-811	S. Butcher	Closed	25.00	425-435.
82-01-002	Smile, God Loves You-PM-821	S. Butcher	Closed	25.00	250.00
83-01-003	Put on a Happy Face-PM-822	S. Butcher	Closed	25.00	190-250.
83-01-004	Dawn's Early Light-PM-831	S. Butcher	Closed	27.50	90.00
84-01-005	God's Ray of Mercy-PM-841	S. Butcher	Closed	25.00	85.00
84-01-006	Trust in the Lord to the Finish-PM-842	S. Butcher	Closed	25.00	65.00
85-01-007	The Lord is My Shepherd-PM-851	S. Butcher	Closed	25.00	75-88.00
85-01-008	I Love to Tell the Story-PM-852	S. Butcher	Closed	27.50	65-125.00
86-01-009	Grandma's Prayer-PM-861	S. Butcher	Closed	25.00	85-115.00
86-01-010	I'm Following Jesus-PM-862	S. Butcher	Closed	25.00	85-95.00
87-01-011	Feed My Sheep-PM-871	S. Butcher	Closed	25.00	85-95.00
87-01-012	In His Time-PM-872	S. Butcher	Closed	25.00	50-65.00
88-01-013	God Bless You for Touching My Life-PM-881	S. Butcher	Closed	27.50	45-85.00
88-01-014	You Just Can't Chuck A Good Friendship-PM-882	S. Butcher	Closed	27.50	45-65.00
89-01-015	You Will Always Be My Choice- PM-891	S. Butcher	Closed	27.50	35-45.00
89-01-016	Mow Power To Ya-PM-892	S. Butcher	Closed	27.50	35-80.00
90-01-017	Ten Years And Still Going Strong-PM-901	S. Butcher	Closed	30.00	35-50.00
90-01-018	You Are A Blessing To Me-PM-902	S. Butcher	Closed	27.50	35-45.00
91-01-019	One Step At A Time-PM-911	S. Butcher	Closed	33.00	33-45.00
91-01-020	Lord, Keep Me In TeePee Top Shape-PM-912	S. Butcher	Closed	27.50	27.50-35.00
92-01-021	Only Love Can Make A Home-PM-921	S. Butcher	Yr.Iss.	30.00	30.00
92-01-022	This Land Is Our Land-527386	S. Butcher	Yr.Iss.	350.00	350-375.
Enesco Corporation		**Precious Moments Collectors Club Welcome Gift**			
82-02-001	But Love Goes On Forever-Plaque-E-0202	S. Butcher	Yr.Iss.	Unkn.	70-85.00

Number	Name	Artist	Edition Limit	Issue Price	Quote
83-02-002	Let Us Call the Club to Order-E-0303	S. Butcher	Yr.Iss.	Unkn.	55-60.00
84-02-003	Join in on the Blessings-E-0404	S. Butcher	Yr.Iss.	Unkn.	40-100.00
85-02-004	Seek and Ye Shall Find-E-0005	S. Butcher	Yr.Iss.	Unkn.	40-50.00
86-02-005	Birds of a Feather Collect Together-E-0006	S. Butcher	Yr.Iss.	Unkn.	35-45.00
87-02-006	Sharing Is Universal-E-0007	S. Butcher	Yr.Iss.	Unkn.	40-45.00
88-02-007	A Growing Love-E-0008	S. Butcher	Yr.Iss.	Unkn.	35-50.00
89-02-008	Always Room For One More-C-0009	S. Butcher	Yr.Iss.	Unkn.	35-50.00
90-02-009	My Happiness-C-0010	S. Butcher	Yr.Iss.	Unkn.	40-75.00
91-02-010	Sharing the Good News Together-C-0011	S. Butcher	Yr.Iss.	Unkn.	40-50.00
92-02-011	The Club Is Out Of This World-C-0012	S. Butcher	Yr.Iss.	Unkn.	40.00
Enesco Corporation		**Precious Moments Inscribed Charter Member Renewal Gift**			
81-03-001	But Love Goes on Forever-E-0001	S. Butcher	Yr.Iss.	Unkn.	160-225.
82-03-002	But Love Goes on Forever-Plaque-E-0102	S. Butcher	Yr.Iss.	Unkn.	70-100.00
83-03-003	Let Us Call the Club to Order-E-0103	S. Butcher	Yr.Iss.	25.00	65-75.00
84-03-004	Join in on the Blessings-E-0104	S. Butcher	Yr.Iss.	25.00	65-90.00
85-03-005	Seek and Ye Shall Find-E-0105	S. Butcher	Yr.Iss.	25.00	50-60.00
86-03-006	Birds of a Feather Collect Together-E-0106	S. Butcher	Yr.Iss.	25.00	50-65.00
87-03-007	Sharing Is Universal -E-0107	S. Butcher	Yr.Iss.	25.00	45-60.00
88-03-008	A Growing Love-E-0108	S. Butcher	Yr.Iss.	25.00	45-55.00
89-03-009	Always Room For One More-C-0109	S. Butcher	Yr.Iss.	35.00	45-60.00
90-03-010	My Happiness-C-0110	S. Butcher	Yr.Iss.	Unkn.	35-45.00
91-03-011	Sharing The Good News Together-C-0111	S. Butcher	Yr.Iss.	Unkn.	40.00
92-03-012	The Club Is Out Of This World-C-0012	S. Butcher	Yr.Iss.	Unkn.	40.00
Enesco Corporation		**Precious Moments Figurines**			
83-04-001	Sharing Our Season Together-E-0501	S. Butcher	Suspd.	50.00	110-145.
83-04-002	Jesus is the Light that Shines-E-0502	S. Butcher	Suspd.	23.00	48-60.00
83-04-003	Blessings from My House to Yours-E-0503	S. Butcher	Suspd.	27.00	65-80.00
83-04-004	God Sent His Son-E-0507	S. Butcher	Suspd.	32.50	65-90.00
83-04-005	Prepare Ye the Way of the Lord-E-0508	S. Butcher	Suspd.	75.00	95-125.00
83-04-006	Bringing God's Blessing to You-E-0509	S. Butcher	Suspd.	35.00	70-100.00
83-04-007	Tubby's First Christmas-E-0511	S. Butcher	Open	12.00	16.50-40.00
83-04-018	It's a Perfect Boy-E-0512	S. Butcher	Suspd.	18.50	40-60.00
83-04-019	Onward Christian Soldiers-E-0523	S. Butcher	Open	24.00	35-95.00
83-04-010	He Upholdeth Those Who Fall-E-0526	S. Butcher	Suspd.	35.00	65-115.00
87-04-011	This Is The Day Which The Lord Has Made-12157	S. Butcher	Suspd.	20.00	55-100.00
79-04-012	Jesus Loves Me-E-1372B	S. Butcher	Open	7.00	25-99.00
79-04-013	Jesus Loves Me-E-1372G	S. Butcher	Open	7.00	25-115.00
79-04-014	Make a Joyful Noise-E-1374G	S. Butcher	Open	8.00	28-125.00
79-04-015	Love Lifted Me-E-1375A	S. Butcher	Open	11.00	35-110.00
79-04-016	Prayer Changes Things-E-1375B	S. Butcher	Suspd.	11.00	125-200.
79-04-017	Love One Another-E-1376	S. Butcher	Open	10.00	35-119.00
79-04-018	He Leadeth Me-E-1377A	S. Butcher	Suspd.	9.00	75-125.00
79-04-019	He Careth For You-E-1377B	S. Butcher	Suspd.	9.00	85-120.00
79-04-020	Love is Kind-E-1379A	S. Butcher	Suspd.	8.00	80-130.00
79-04-021	God Understands-E-1379B	S. Butcher	Suspd.	8.00	95-130.00
79-04-022	Jesus is the Answer-E-1381	S. Butcher	Suspd.	11.50	120-160.
79-04-023	We Have Seen His Star-E-2010	S. Butcher	Suspd.	8.00	80-115.00
79-04-024	Jesus is Born-E-2012	S. Butcher	Suspd.	12.00	90-125.00
79-04-025	Unto Us a Child is Born-E-2013	S. Butcher	Suspd.	12.00	85-130.00
82-04-026	May Your Christmas Be Cozy-E-2345	S. Butcher	Suspd.	23.00	60-80.00
82-04-027	May Your Christmas Be Warm-E-2348	S. Butcher	Suspd.	30.00	88-105.00
82-04-028	Tell Me the Story of Jesus-E-2349	S. Butcher	Suspd.	30.00	75-100.00
82-04-029	Dropping in for Christmas-E-2350	S. Butcher	Suspd.	18.00	70-85.00
82-04-030	I'll Play My Drum for Him-E-2356	S. Butcher	Suspd.	30.00	75-110.00
82-04-031	I'll Play My Drum for Him-E-2360	S. Butcher	Open	16.00	25-50.00
82-04-032	Christmas Joy from Head to Toe-E-2361	S. Butcher	Suspd.	25.00	55-80.00
82-04-033	Camel Figurine-E-2363	S. Butcher	Open	20.00	33-50.00
82-04-034	Goat Figurine-E-2364	S. Butcher	Suspd.	10.00	30-43.00
82-04-035	The First Noel-E-2365	S. Butcher	Suspd.	16.00	45-60.00
82-04-036	The First Noel-E-2366	S. Butcher	Suspd.	16.00	45-65.00
82-04-037	Bundles of Joy-E-2374	S. Butcher	Open	27.50	45-90.00
82-04-038	Our First Christmas Together-E-2377	S. Butcher	Suspd.	35.00	65-95.00
82-04-039	3 Mini Nativity Houses & Palm Tree-E-2387	S. Butcher	Open	45.00	75-110.00
82-04-040	Come Let Us Adore Him-E-2395(11pc. set)	S. Butcher	Open	80.00	130-175.
80-04-041	Come Let Us Adore Him-E2800(9 pc. set)	S. Butcher	Open	70.00	125-175.
80-04-042	Jesus is Born-E-2801	S. Butcher	Suspd.	37.00	225-350.
80-04-043	Christmas is a Time to Share-E-2802	S. Butcher	Suspd.	20.00	65-100.00
80-04-044	Crown Him Lord of All-E-2803	S. Butcher	Suspd.	20.00	65-95.00
80-04-045	Peace on Earth-E-2804	S. Butcher	Suspd.	20.00	115-135.
84-04-046	You Have Touched So Many Hearts-E-2821	S. Butcher	Open	25.00	35-50.00
84-04-047	To God Be the Glory-E-2823	S. Butcher	Suspd.	40.00	70-100.00
84-04-048	To a Very Special Mom-E-2824	S. Butcher	Open	27.50	37.50-55.00
84-04-049	To a Very Special Sister-E-2825	S. Butcher	Open	37.50	65.00
84-04-050	May Your Birthday Be a Blessing-E-2826	S. Butcher	Suspd.	37.50	70-99.00
84-04-051	I Get a Kick Out of You-E-2827	S. Butcher	Suspd.	50.00	85-120.00
84-04-052	Precious Memories-E-2828	S. Butcher	Open	45.00	60-75.00
84-04-053	I'm Sending You a White Christmas-E-2829	S. Butcher	Open	37.50	50-70.00
84-04-054	God Bless the Bride-E-2832	S. Butcher	Open	35.00	50-60.00
86-04-055	Sharing Our Joy Together-E-2834	S. Butcher	Suspd.	30.00	40-60.00
84-04-056	Baby Figurines (set of 6)-E-2852	S. Butcher	Open	12.00	99-168.00
80-04-057	Blessed Are the Pure in Heart-E-3104	S. Butcher	Suspd.	9.00	25-65.00
80-04-058	He Watches Over Us All-E-3105	S. Butcher	Suspd.	11.00	70-90.00
80-04-059	Mother Sew Dear-E-3106	S. Butcher	Open	13.00	27.50-80.
80-04-060	The Hand that Rocks the Future-E-3108	S. Butcher	Suspd.	13.00	60-95.00
80-04-061	The Purr-fect Grandma-E-3109	S. Butcher	Open	13.00	27.50-79.
80-04-062	Loving is Sharing-E-3110B	S. Butcher	Open	13.00	30-95.00
80-04-063	Loving is Sharing-E-3110G	S. Butcher	Open	13.00	30-95.00
80-04-064	Thou Art Mine-E-3113	S. Butcher	Open	16.00	35-90.00
80-04-065	The Lord Bless You and Keep You-E-3114	S. Butcher	Open	16.00	37.50-85.00
80-04-066	But Love Goes on Forever-E-3115	S. Butcher	Open	16.50	35-95.00
80-04-067	Thee I Love-E-3116	S. Butcher	Open	16.50	37.50-100.
80-04-068	Walking By Faith-E-3117	S. Butcher	Open	35.00	70-125.00
80-04-069	It's What's Inside that Counts-E-3119	S. Butcher	Suspd.	13.00	90-130.00
80-04-070	To Thee With Love-E-3120	S. Butcher	Suspd.	13.00	65-95.00
81-04-071	The Lord Bless You and Keep You-E-4720	S. Butcher	Suspd.	14.00	32-48.00
81-04-072	The Lord Bless You and Keep You-E-4721	S. Butcher	Open	14.00	30-80.00
81-04-073	Love Cannot Break a True Friendship-E-4722	S. Butcher	Suspd.	22.50	90-130.00
81-04-074	Peace Amid the Storm-E-4723	S. Butcher	Suspd.	22.50	60-80.00
81-04-075	Rejoicing with You-E-4724	S. Butcher	Open	25.00	45-99.00
81-04-076	Peace on Earth-E-4725	S. Butcher	Suspd.	25.00	60-89.00
81-04-077	Bear Ye One Another's Burdens-E-5200	S. Butcher	Suspd.	20.00	70-105.00
81-04-078	Love Lifted Me-E-5201	S. Butcher	Suspd.	25.00	70-110.00
81-04-079	Thank You for Coming to My Ade-E-5202	S. Butcher	Suspd.	22.50	90-120.00
81-04-080	Let Not the Sun Go Down Upon Your Wrath-E-5203	S. Butcher	Suspd.	22.50	100-140.
81-04-081	To A Special Dad-E-5212	S. Butcher	Open	20.00	35-79.00
81-04-082	God is Love-E-5213	S. Butcher	Suspd.	17.00	60-99.00
81-04-083	Prayer Changes Things-E-5214	S. Butcher	Suspd.	35.00	85-150.00
84-04-084	May Your Christmas Be Blessed-E-5376	S. Butcher	Suspd.	37.50	59-75.00
84-04-085	Joy to the World-E-5378	S. Butcher	Suspd.	18.00	37-45.00

Company Number	Name	Series Artist	Edition Limit	Issue Price	Quote
84-04-086	Isn't He Precious?-E-5379	S. Butcher	Open	20.00	30-45.00
84-04-087	A Monarch is Born-E-5380	S. Butcher	Suspd.	33.00	60-75.00
84-04-088	His Name is Jesus-E-5381	S. Butcher	Suspd.	45.00	70-85.00
84-04-089	For God So Loved the World-E-5382	S. Butcher	Suspd.	70.00	110-135.
84-04-090	Wishing You a Merry Christmas-E-5383	S. Butcher	Yr.Iss.	17.00	45-55.00
84-04-091	I'll Play My Drum for Him-E-5384	S. Butcher	Open	10.00	15-30.00
84-04-092	Oh Worship the Lord-E-5385	S. Butcher	Suspd.	10.00	34-45.00
84-04-093	Oh Worship the Lord-E-5386	S. Butcher	Suspd.	10.00	34-45.00
81-04-094	Come Let Us Adore Him-E-5619	S. Butcher	Suspd.	10.00	30-50.00
81-04-095	Donkey Figurine-E-5621	S. Butcher	Open	6.00	13.50-35.00
81-04-096	They Followed the Star-E-5624	S. Butcher	Open	130.00	200-270.
81-04-097	Wee Three Kings-E-5635	S. Butcher	Open	40.00	75-125.00
81-04-098	Rejoice O Earth-E-5636	S. Butcher	Open	15.00	30-65.00
81-04-099	The Heavenly Light-E-5637	S. Butcher	Open	15.00	27.50-60.0
81-04-100	Cow with Bell Figurine-E-5638	S. Butcher	Open	16.00	30-49.00
81-04-101	Isn't He Wonderful-E-5639	S. Butcher	Suspd.	12.00	40-65.00
81-04-102	Isn't He Wonderful-E-5640	S. Butcher	Suspd.	12.00	40-65.00
81-04-103	They Followed the Star-E-5641	S. Butcher	Suspd.	75.00	160-185.
81-04-104	Nativity Wall (2 pc. set)-E-5644	S. Butcher	Open	60.00	120-145.
84-04-105	God Sends the Gift of His Love-E-6613	S. Butcher	Suspd.	22.50	65-90.00
82-04-106	God is Love, Dear Valentine-E-7153	S. Butcher	Suspd.	16.00	40-59.00
82-04-107	God is Love, Dear Valentine-E-7154	S. Butcher	Suspd.	16.00	40-65.00
82-04-108	Thanking Him for You-E-7155	S. Butcher	Suspd.	16.00	60-75.00
82-04-109	Love Beareth All Things-E-7158	S. Butcher	Open	25.00	37.50-64.00
82-04-110	Lord Give Me Patience-E-7159	S. Butcher	Suspd.	25.00	50-65.00
82-04-111	The Perfect Grandpa-E-7160	S. Butcher	Suspd.	25.00	45-65.00
82-04-112	His Sheep Am I-E-7161	S. Butcher	Suspd.	25.00	55-65.00
82-04-113	Love is Sharing-E-7162	S. Butcher	Suspd.	25.00	130-150.
82-04-114	God is Watching Over You-E-7163	S. Butcher	Suspd.	27.50	65-75.00
82-04-115	Bless This House-E-7164	S. Butcher	Suspd.	45.00	110-150.
82-04-116	Let the Whole World Know-E-7165	S. Butcher	Suspd.	45.00	110-150.
83-04-117	Love is Patient-E-9251	S. Butcher	Suspd.	35.00	65-85.00
83-04-118	Forgiving is Forgetting-E-9252	S. Butcher	Suspd.	37.50	64-85.00
83-04-119	The End is in Sight-E-9253	S. Butcher	Suspd.	25.00	53-75.00
83-04-120	Praise the Lord Anyhow-E-9254	S. Butcher	Open	35.00	50-75.00
83-04-121	Bless You Two-E-9255	S. Butcher	Open	21.00	32.50-44.00
83-04-122	We are God's Workmanship-E-9258	S. Butcher	Open	19.00	27.50-53.00
83-04-123	We're In It Together-E-9259	S. Butcher	Suspd.	24.00	49-65.00
83-04-124	God's Promises are Sure-E-9260	S. Butcher	Suspd.	30.00	55-75.00
83-04-125	Seek Ye the Lord-E-9261	S. Butcher	Suspd.	21.00	37-54.00
83-04-126	Seek Ye the Lord-E-9262	S. Butcher	Suspd.	21.00	45-55.00
83-04-127	How Can Two Walk Together Except They Agree-E-9263	S. Butcher	Suspd.	35.00	90-139.00
53-04-128	Press On-E-9265	S. Butcher	Open	40.00	55-87.00
83-04-129	Animal Collection, Teddy Bear-E-9267A	S. Butcher	Suspd.	6.50	24.30
83-04-130	Animal Collection, Dog W/ Slippers-E-9267B	S. Butcher	Suspd.	6.50	24.30
83-04-131	Animal Collection, Bunny W/ Carrot-E-9267C	S. Butcher	Suspd.	6.50	24.30
83-04-132	Animal Collection, Kitty With Bow-E-9267D	S. Butcher	Suspd.	6.50	24.30
83-04-133	Animal Collection, Lamb With Bird-E-9267E	S. Butcher	Suspd.	6..50	24.30
83-04-134	Animal Collection, Pig W/ Patches-E-9267F	S. Butcher	Suspd.	6.50	24.30
83-04-135	Jesus Loves Me-E-9278	S. Butcher	Open	9.00	15-27.00
83-04-136	Jesus Loves Me-E-9279	S. Butcher	Open	9.00	15-32.00
83-04-137	To Some Bunny Special-E-9282A	S. Butcher	Suspd.	8.00	20-37.00
83-04-138	You're Worth Your Weight In Gold-E-9282B	S. Butcher	Suspd.	8.00	21-37.00
83-04-139	Especially For Ewe-E-9282C	S. Butcher	Suspd.	8.00	20-37.00
83-04-140	If God Be for Us, Who Can Be Against Us-E-9285	S. Butcher	Suspd.	27.50	55-65.00
83-04-141	Peace on Earth-E-9287	S. Butcher	Suspd.	37.50	60-80.00
83-04-142	Sending You a Rainbow-E-9288	S. Butcher	Suspd.	22.50	55-70.00
83-04-143	Trust in the Lord-E-9289	S. Butcher	Suspd.	21.00	50-65.00
85-04-144	Love Covers All-12009	S. Butcher	Suspd.	27.50	45-65.00
85-04-145	Part of Me Wants to be Good-12149	S. Butcher	Suspd.	19.00	40-65.00
85-04-146	Get into the Habit of Prayer-12203	S. Butcher	Suspd.	19.00	37-45.00
85-04-147	Miniature Clown-12238A	S. Butcher	Open	13.50	19-29.00
85-04-148	Miniature Clown-12238B	S. Butcher	Open	13.50	19-29.00
85-04-149	Miniature Clown-12238C	S. Butcher	Open	13.50	19-29.00
85-04-150	Miniature Clown-12238D	S. Butcher	Open	13.50	19-29.00
85-04-151	It is Better to Give than to Receive-12297	S. Butcher	Suspd.	19.00	50-80.00
85-04-152	Love Never Fails-12300	S. Butcher	Open	25.00	35-49.00
85-04-153	God Bless Our Home-12319	S. Butcher	Open	40.00	55-65.00
86-04-154	You Can Fly-12335	S. Butcher	Suspd.	25.00	50-65.00
85-04-155	Jesus is Coming Soon-12343	S. Butcher	Suspd.	22.50	45-55.00
85-04-156	Halo, and Merry Christmas-12351	S. Butcher	Suspd.	40.00	90-120.00
85-04-157	May Your Christmas Be Delightful-15482	S. Butcher	Open	25.00	35-50.00
85-04-158	Honk if You Love Jesus-15490	S. Butcher	Open	13.00	19-35.00
85-04-159	Baby's First Christmas-15539	S. Butcher	Yr.Iss.	13.00	42-45.00
85-04-160	Baby's First Christmas-15547	S. Butcher	Yr.Iss.	13.00	45.00
85-04-161	God Sent His Love-15881	S. Butcher	Yr.Iss.	17.00	30-39.00
86-04-162	To My Favorite Paw-100021	S. Butcher	Suspd.	22.50	50-65.00
87-04-163	To My Deer Friend-100048	S. Butcher	Open	33.00	50-92.00
86-04-164	Sending My Love-100056	S. Butcher	Suspd.	22.50	35-60.00
86-04-165	O Worship the Lord-100064	S. Butcher	Open	24.00	35-49.00
86-04-166	To My Forever Friend-100072	S. Butcher	Open	33.00	50-90.00
87-04-167	He's The Healer Of Broken Hearts-100080	S. Butcher	Open	33.00	50-59.00
86-04-168	Lord I'm Coming Home-100110	S. Butcher	Open	22.50	32.50-72.00
86-04-169	The Joy of the Lord is My Strength-100137	S. Butcher	Open	35.00	50-89.00
86-04-170	God Bless the Day We Found You-100145	S. Butcher	Suspd.	37.50	70-85.00
86-04-171	God Bless the Day We Found You-100153	S. Butcher	Suspd.	37.50	62-85.00
86-04-172	Serving the Lord-100161	S. Butcher	Suspd.	19.00	39-55.00
86-04-173	I'm a Possibility-100188	S. Butcher	Open	21.00	32.50-40.00
87-04-174	The Lord Giveth & the Lord Taketh Away-100226	S. Butcher	Open	33.50	40-49.00
86-04-175	Friends Never Drift Apart-100250	S. Butcher	Open	35.00	50-69.00
86-04-176	He Cleansed My Soul-100277	S. Butcher	Open	24.00	35-42.00
86-04-177	Serving the Lord-100293	S. Butcher	Suspd.	19.00	27.50-47.00
86-04-178	Brotherly Love-100544	S. Butcher	Suspd.	37.00	59-75.00
87-04-179	No Tears Past The Gate-101826	S. Butcher	Open	40.00	60-67.00
86-04-180	O Worship the Lord-102229	S. Butcher	Open	24.00	35-42.00
86-04-181	Shepherd of Love-102261	S. Butcher	Open	10.00	15-24.00
86-04-182	Three Mini Animals-102296	S. Butcher	Suspd.	13.50	19-30.00
86-04-183	Wishing You a Cozy Christmas-102342	S. Butcher	Yr.Iss.	17.00	39-45.00
86-04-184	Love Rescued Me-102393	S. Butcher	Open	21.00	32.50-44.00
86-04-185	Angel of Mercy-102482	S. Butcher	Open	19.00	30-39.00
86-04-186	Sharing our Christmas Together-102490	S. Butcher	Suspd.	35.00	50-70.00
87-04-187	We Are All Precious In His Sight-102903	S. Butcher	Yr.Iss.	30.00	80-120.00
86-04-188	God Bless America-102938	S. Butcher	Yr.Iss.	30.00	65-85.00
86-04-189	It's the Birthday of a King-102962	S. Butcher	Suspd.	18.50	35-47.00
87-04-190	I Would Be Sunk Without You-102970	S. Butcher	Open	15.00	19-29.00
87-04-191	My Love Will Never Let You Go-103497	S. Butcher	Open	25.00	35-45.00
86-04-192	I Believe in the Old Rugged Cross-103632	S. Butcher	Open	25.00	35-47.00
86-04-193	Come Let Us Adore Him-104000 (9 pc. set w/cassette)	S. Butcher	Open	95.00	110-115.
87-04-194	With this Ring I...-104019	S. Butcher	Open	40.00	55-65.00
87-04-195	Love Is The Glue That Mends-104027	S. Butcher	Suspd.	33.50	59-75.00
87-04-196	Cheers To The Leader-104035	S. Butcher	Open	22.50	30-39.00
87-04-197	Happy Days Are Here Again-104396	S. Butcher	Suspd.	25.00	43-70.00
87-04-198	A Tub Full of Love-104817	S. Butcher	Open	22.50	30-35.00
87-04-199	Sitting Pretty-104825	S. Butcher	Suspd.	22.50	43-60.00
87-04-200	Have I Got News For You-105635	S. Butcher	Suspd.	22.50	30-50.00
87-04-201	To Tell The Tooth You're Special-105813	S. Butcher	Suspd.	38.50	65-85.00
88-04-202	Hallelujah Country-105821	S. Butcher	Open	35.00	45-54.00
87-04-203	We're Pulling For You-106151	S. Butcher	Suspd.	40.00	60-75.00
87-04-204	God Bless You Graduate-106194	S. Butcher	Open	20.00	30-35.00
87-04-205	Congratulations Princess-106208	S. Butcher	Open	20.00	30-35.00
87-04-206	Lord Help Me Make the Grade-106216	S. Butcher	Suspd.	25.00	35-70.00
88-04-207	Heaven Bless Your Togetherness-106755	S. Butcher	Open	65.00	80-87.00
88-04-208	Precious Memories-106763	S. Butcher	Open	37.50	50-55.00
88-04-209	Puppy Love Is From Above-106798	S. Butcher	Open	45.00	55-63.00
88-04-210	Happy Birthday Poppy-106836	S. Butcher	Open	27.50	33.50-37.00
88-04-211	Sew In Love-106844	S. Butcher	Open	45.00	55-60.00
87-04-212	They Followed The Star-108243	S. Butcher	Open	75.00	100-115.00
87-04-213	The Greatest Gift Is A Friend-109231	S. Butcher	Open	30.00	37.50-49.00
88-04-214	Believe the Impossible-109487	S. Butcher	Suspd.	35.00	50-105.00
87-04-215	Wishing You A Yummy Christmas-109754	S. Butcher	Open	35.00	45-55.00
87-04-216	We Gather Together To Ask The Lord's Blessing-109762	S. Butcher	Open	130.00	150-169.
87-04-217	Oh What Fun It Is To Ride-109819	S. Butcher	Open	85.00	110-120.
88-04-218	Wishing You A Happy Easter-109886	S. Butcher	Open	23.00	27.50-34.00
88-04-219	Wishing You A Basket Full Of Blessings-109924	S. Butcher	Open	23.00	27.50-33.00
88-04-220	Sending You My Love-109967	S. Butcher	Open	35.00	45-57.00
88-04-221	Mommy, I Love You-109975	S. Butcher	Open	22.50	27.50-34.00
87-04-222	Love Is The Best Gift of All-110930	S. Butcher	Yr.Iss.	22.50	45-49.00
88-04-223	Faith Takes The Plunge-111155	S. Butcher	Open	27.50	33.50-12500.
87-04-224	O Come Let Us Adore Him (4 pc. 9" Nativity)-111333	S. Butcher	Suspd.	200.00	245-275.
88-04-225	Mommy, I Love You-112143	S. Butcher	Open	22.50	27.50-32.00
87-04-226	A Tub Full of Love-112313	S. Butcher	Open	22.50	30-33.00
88-04-227	This Too Shall Pass-114014	S. Butcher	Open	23.00	27.50-37.00
88-04-228	Something's Missing When You're Not Around -105643	S. Butcher	Suspd.	32.50	37.50
88-04-229	Meowie Christmas-109800	S. Butcher	Open	30.00	40-65.00
88-04-230	Tis the Season-111163	S. Butcher	Open	27.50	35-45.00
88-04-231	Some Bunny's Sleeping-115274	S. Butcher	Open	15.00	25-40.00
88-04-232	Our First Christmas Together-115290	S. Butcher	Suspd.	50.00	60-80.00
88-04-233	Time to Wish You a Merry Christmas-115339	S. Butcher	Yr.Iss.	24.00	35-48.00
88-04-234	Rejoice O Earth-520268	S. Butcher	Open	13.00	15-22.00
88-04-235	Jesus the Savior Is Born-520357	S. Butcher	Open	25.00	32.50-40.00
89-04-236	My Heart Is Exposed With Love-520624	S. Butcher	Open	45.00	50-60.00
89-04-237	A Friend Is Someone Who Cares-520632	S. Butcher	Open	30.00	32.50-45.00
89-04-238	Eggspecially For You-520667	S. Butcher	Open	45.00	50-60.00
89-04-239	Your Love Is So Uplifting-520675	S. Butcher	Open	60.00	65-79.00
89-04-240	Just A LineTo Wish You A Happy Day-520721	S. Butcher	Open	65.00	70-79.00
89-04-241	Friendship Hits The Spot-520748	S. Butcher	Open	55.00	60-68.00
89-04-242	Jesus Is The Only Way-520756	S. Butcher	Open	40.00	45-50.00
89-04-243	Puppy Love-520764	S. Butcher	Open	12.50	13.50-22.00
89-04-244	Wishing You Roads Of Happiness-520780	S. Butcher	Open	60.00	65-73.00
89-04-245	My Days Are Blue Without You-520802	S. Butcher	Suspd.	65.00	75-125.00
89-04-246	We Need A Good Friend Through The Ruff Times-520810	S. Butcher	Suspd.	35.00	50-70.00
89-04-247	You Are My Number One-520829	S. Butcher	Open	25.00	27.50-30.00
89-04-248	The Lord Is Your Light To Happiness-520837	S. Bucher	Open	50.00	55-62.00
89-04-249	Wishing You A Perfect Choice-520845	S.Butcher	Open	55.00	60-67.00
89-04-250	I Belong To The Lord-520853	S. Butcher	Suspd.	25.00	35-50.00
89-04-251	Tell It To Jesus-521477	S. Butcher	Open	35.00	37.50-49.00
89-04-252	The Greatest of These Is Love-521868	S. Butcher	Suspd.	27.50	40-54.00
89-04-253	Wishing You A Cozy Season-521949	S. Butcher	Open	42.50	45-53.00
79-04-254	May Your Life Be Blessed With Touchdowns-522023	S. Butcher	Open	45.00	50-58.00
89-04-255	Thank You Lord For Everything-522031	S. Butcher	Open	55.00	60-70.00
89-04-256	Don't Let the Holidays Get You Down-522112	S. Butcher	Open	42.50	45-54.00
89-04-257	Wishing You A Very Successful Season-522120	S. Butcher	Open	60.00	65-70.00
89-04-258	Bon Voyage!-522201	S. Butcher	Open	75.00	80-99.00
89-04-259	He Is The Star Of The Morning-522252	S. Butcher	Open	55.00	60-65.00
89-04-260	To Be With You Is Uplifting-522260	S. Butcher	Open	20.00	22.50-30.00
89-04-261	Merry Christmas Deer-522317	S. Butcher	Open	50.00	55-65.00
89-04-262	Isn't He Precious-522988	S. Butcher	Open	15.00	16.50-20.00
89-04-263	Jesus Is The Sweetest Name I Know-523097	S. Butcher	Open	22.50	25-29.00
90-04-264	Lord, Turn My Life Around-520551	S. Butcher	Open	35.00	35-49.00
90-04-265	Heaven Bless You-520934	S. Butcher	Open	35.00	35-150.00
90-04-266	Hope You're Up And OnThe Trail Again-521205	S. Butcher	Open	35.00	35-45.00
90-04-267	Happy Trip-521280	S. Butcher	Open	35.00	35-73.00
90-04-268	Yield Not To Temptation-521310	S. Butcher	Open	27.50	27.50-37.00
90-04-269	Faith Is A Victory-521396	S. Butcher	Open	25.00	25-34.00
90-04-270	I'll Never Stop Loving You-521418	S. Butcher	Open	37.50	37.50-49.00
90-04-271	Lord, Help Me Stick To My Job-521450	S. Butcher	Open	30.00	30-40.00
90-04-272	Sweep All Your Worries Away-521779	S. Butcher	Open	40.00	40-130.00
90-04-273	Good Friends Are Forever-521817	S. Butcher	Open	50.00	50-57.00
90-04-274	Love Is From Above-521841	S. Butcher	Open	45.00	45-59.00
90-04-275	Easter's On Its Way-521892	S. Butcher	Open	60.00	60-75.00
90-04-276	High Hopes-521957	S. Butcher	Open	30.00	30-37.00
90-04-277	There Shall Be Showers Of Blessings-522090	S. Butcher	Open	60.00	60-69.00
90-04-278	Thinking Of You Is What I Really Like To Do-522287	S. Butcher	Open	30.00	30-35.00
90-04-279	The Good Lord Always Delivers- 523453	S. Butcher	Open	27.50	27.50-35.00
90-04-280	This Day Has Been Made In Heaven-523496	S. Butcher	Open	30.00	30-45.00
90-04-281	God Is Love Dear Valentine-523518	S. Butcher	Open	27.50	27.50-32.00
90-04-282	We're Going To Miss You-524913	S. Butcher	Open	50.00	50-55.00
90-04-283	Time Heals-523739	S. Butcher	Open	37.50	37.50-40.00
90-04-284	Once Upon A Holy Night-523836	S. Butcher	Yr.Iss.	25.00	25-29.00
90-04-285	That's What Friends Are For-521183	S. Butcher	Open	45.00	45-49.00
90-04-286	Blessings From Above-523747	S. Butcher	Open	45.00	45-50.00
90-04-287	Happy Birthday Dear Jesus-524875	S. Butcher	Open	13.50	13.50-16.
90-04-288	Some Bunny's Sleeping-522996	S. Butcher	Open	12.00	12-19.00
91-04-289	Hug One Another-521299	S. Butcher	Open	45.00	45-49.00
91-04-290	Thumb-body Loves You-521698	S. Butcher	Open	55.00	55-59.00
91-04-291	Hoppy Easter Friend-521906	S. Butcher	Open	40.00	40-43.00
91-04-292	To A Special Mum-521965	S. Butcher	Open	30.00	30-33.00
91-04-293	In The Spotlight Of His Grace-520543	S. Butcher	Open	35.00	35.00
91-04-294	I Will Cherish The Old Rugged Cross-523534	S. Butcher	Yr.Iss.	27.50	40-45.00
91-04-295	There's A Light At The End Of The Tunnel-521485	S. Butcher	Open	55.00	55.00

Number	Name	Artist	Edition Limit	Issue Price	Quote
91-04-296	A Reflection Of His Love-522279	S. Butcher	Open	50.00	50.00
91-04-297	Joy On Arrival-523178	S. Butcher	Open	50.00	50.00
91-04-298	He Loves Me -524263	S. Butcher	Yr.Iss.	35.00	35-40.00
91-04-299	I Can't Spell Success Without You-523763	S. Butcher	Open	40.00	40-45.00
91-04-300	May Your Birthday Be A Blessing-524301	S. Butcher	Open	30.00	30-35.00
91-04-301	May Only Good Things Come Your Way-524425	S. Butcher	Open	30.00	30-35.00
91-04-302	May Your Christmas Be Merry-524166	S. Butcher	Yr.Iss.	27.50	27.50
91-04-303	To A Very Special Mom & Dad-521434	S. Butcher	Open	35.00	35.00
91-04-304	A Special Delivery-521493	S. Butcher	Open	30.00	30.00
91-04-305	Good Friends Are For Always-524123	S. Butcher	Open	27.50	27.50
91-04-306	Take Heed When You Stand-521272	S. Butcher	Open	55.00	55.00
91-04-307	Angels We Have Heard On High-524921	S. Butcher	Open	60.00	60.00
91-04-308	May Your World Be Trimmed With Joy-522082	S. Butcher	Open	55.00	55.00
91-04-309	Good News Is So Uplifting-523615	S. Butcher	Open	60.00	60.00
91-04-310	It's A Perfect Boy-525286	S. Butcher	Open	16.50	16.50
91-04-311	We Have Come From Afar-526959	S. Butcher	Open	17.50	17.50
92-04-312	You Are The Type I Love-523542	S. Butcher	Open	40.00	40.00
92-04-313	It's No Yolk When I Say I Love You-522104	S. Butcher	Open	60.00	60.00
92-04-314	My Warmest Thoughts Are You-524085	S. Butcher	Open	55.00	55.00
92-04-315	You Deserve An Ovation-520578	S. Butcher	Open	35.00	35.00
92-04-316	Friendship Grows When You Plant A Seed-524271	S. Butcher	Open	40.00	40.00
92-04-317	Going Home-525979	S. Butcher	Open	60.00	60.00
92-04-318	You Are My Happiness-526185	S. Butcher	Yr.Iss.	37.50	37.50
92-04-319	I Would Be Lost Without You-526142	S. Butcher	Open	27.50	27.50
92-04-320	God Bless The U.S.A.-527564	S. Butcher	Yr.Iss.	32.50	32.50
92-04-321	But The Greatest of These Is Love-527688	S. Butcher	Yr.Iss.	27.50	27.50
92-04-322	It's So Uplifting To Have A Friend Like You-524905	S. Butcher	Open	40.00	40.00
92-04-323	Tubby's First Christmas-525278	S. Butcher	Open	10.00	10.00
92-04-324	You Are My Favorite Star-527378	S. Butcher	Open	55.00	55.00
92-04-325	Wishing You A Ho Ho Ho-527629	S. Butcher	Open	40.00	40.00
92-04-326	Wishing You A Comfy Christmas-527750	S. Butcher	Open	30.00	30.00
92-04-327	The Lord Turned My Life Around-520535	S. Butcher	Open	35.00	35.00
92-04-328	Bring The Little Ones To Jesus-527556	S. Butcher	Open	90.00	90.00
92-04-329	What The World Needs Now-524352	S. Butcher	Open	50.00	50.00
92-04-330	This Land Is Our Land-527777	S. Butcher	Yr.Iss.	35.00	35.00

Enesco Corporation — Precious Moments Bridal Party

Number	Name	Artist	Edition Limit	Issue Price	Quote
84-05-001	Bridesmaid-E-2831	S. Butcher	Open	13.50	20-30.00
85-05-002	Ringbearer-E-2833	S. Butcher	Open	11.00	20-30.00
85-05-003	Flower Girl-E-2835	S. Butcher	Open	11.00	15-25.00
84-05-004	Groomsman-E-2836	S. Butcher	Open	13.50	20-30.00
86-05-005	Groom-E-2837	S. Butcher	Open	13.50	20-40.00
85-05-006	Junior Bridesmaid-E-2845	S. Butcher	Open	12.50	19-30.00
87-05-007	Bride-E-2846	S. Butcher	Open	18.00	25-30.00
87-05-008	God Bless Our Family (Parents of the Groom)-100498	S. Butcher	Open	35.00	50-55.00
87-05-009	God Bless Our Family (Parents of the Bride)-100501	S. Butcher	Open	35.00	50-55.00
87-05-010	Wedding Arch-102369	S. Butcher	Suspd.	22.50	35.00

Enesco Corporation — Precious Moments Baby's First

Number	Name	Artist	Edition Limit	Issue Price	Quote
84-06-001	Baby's First Step-E-2840	S. Butcher	Suspd.	35.00	55-89.00
84-06-002	Baby's First Picture-E-2841	S. Butcher	Retrd.	45.00	110-165.00
85-06-003	Baby's First Haircut-12211	S. Butcher	Suspd.	32.50	65-75.00
86-06-004	Baby's First Trip-16012	S. Butcher	Suspd.	32.50	75-85.00
89-06-005	Baby's First Pet-520705	S. Butcher	Open	45.00	50-60.00
90-06-006	Baby's First Meal-524077	S. Butcher	Open	35.00	35.00
90-06-007	Baby's First Word-527238	S. Butcher	Open	24.00	24.00

Enesco Corporation — Precious Moments Anniversary Figurines

Number	Name	Artist	Edition Limit	Issue Price	Quote
84-07-001	God Blessed Our Years Together With So Much Love And Happiness-E-2853	S. Butcher	Open	35.00	50-60.00
84-07-002	God Blessed Our Year Together With So Much Love And Happiness (1st)-E-2854	S. Butcher	Open	35.00	50-60.00
84-07-003	God Blessed Our Years Together With So Much Love And Happiness (5th)-E-2855	S. Butcher	Open	35.00	50-55.00
84-07-004	God Blessed Our Years Together With So Much Love And Happiness (10th)-E-2856	S. Butcher	Open	35.00	50-55.00
84-07-005	God Blessed Our Years Together With So Much Love And Happiness (25th)-E-2857	S. Butcher	Open	35.00	50-65.00
84-07-006	God Blessed Our Years Together With So Much Love And Happiness (40th)-E-2859	S. Butcher	Open	35.00	50-65.00
84-07-007	God Blessed Our Years Together With So Much Love And Happiness (50th)-E-2860	S. Butcher	Open	35.00	50-65.00

Enesco Corporation — Precious Moments The Four Seasons

Number	Name	Artist	Edition Limit	Issue Price	Quote
85-08-001	The Voice of Spring-12068	S. Butcher	Yr.Iss.	30.00	275-325
85-08-002	Summer's Joy-12076	S. Butcher	Yr.Iss.	30.00	90-110.00
86-08-003	Autumn's Praise-12084	S. Butcher	Yr.Iss.	30.00	60-95.00
86-08-004	Winter's Song-12092	S. Butcher	Yr.Iss.	30.00	90-120.00
86-08-005	Set	S. Butcher	Yr.Iss.	120.00	500-585.

Enesco Corporation — Precious Moments Rejoice in the Lord

Number	Name	Artist	Edition Limit	Issue Price	Quote
85-09-001	There's a Song in My Heart-12173	S. Butcher	Suspd.	11.00	25-45.00
85-09-002	Happiness is the Lord-12378	S. Butcher	Suspd.	15.00	35-60.00
85-09-003	Lord Give Me a Song-12386	S. Butcher	Suspd.	15.00	30-50.00
85-09-004	He is My Song-12394	S. Butcher	Suspd.	17.50	30-60.00
87-09-005	Lord Keep My Life In Tune - 12580	S. Butcher	Suspd.	37.50	80-100.00

Enesco Corporation — Precious Moments Clown

Number	Name	Artist	Edition Limit	Issue Price	Quote
XX-10-001	I Get a Bang Out of You-12262	S. Butcher	Open	30.00	45-55.00
86-10-002	Lord Keep Me On the Ball-12270	S. Butcher	Open	30.00	45-55.00
85-10-003	Waddle I Do Without You-12459	S. Butcher	Retrd.	30.00	65-110.00
86-10-004	The Lord Will Carry You Through-12467	S. Butcher	Retrd.	30.00	60-105.00

Enesco Corporation — Precious Moments Club Fifth Anniversary Commemorative Edition

Number	Name	Artist	Edition Limit	Issue Price	Quote
85-11-001	God Bless Our Years Together-12440	S. Butcher	Closed	175.00	275-325.

Enesco Corporation — Precious Moments Family Christmas Scene

Number	Name	Artist	Edition Limit	Issue Price	Quote
85-12-001	May You Have the Sweetest Christmas-15776	S. Butcher	Suspd.	17.00	35-55.00
85-12-002	The Story of God's Love-15784	S. Butcher	Suspd.	22.50	45-85.00
85-12-003	Tell Me a Story-15792	S. Butcher	Suspd.	10.00	20-50.00
85-12-004	God Gave His Best-15806	S. Butcher	Suspd.	13.00	22-50.00
85-12-005	Silent Night-15814	S. Butcher	Suspd.	37.50	69-120.00
86-12-006	Sharing Our Christmas Together-102490	S. Butcher	Suspd.	40.00	55-80.00
89-12-007	Have A Beary Merry Christmas-522856	S. Butcher	Suspd.	15.00	30-45.00
90-12-008	Christmas Fireplace-524883	S. Butcher	Suspd.	37.50	100-125.

Enesco Corporation — Retired Precious Moments Figurines

Number	Name	Artist	Edition Limit	Issue Price	Quote
79-13-001	Smile, God Loves You-E-1373B	S. Butcher	Retrd.	7.00	80-110.00
79-13-002	Praise the Lord Anyhow-E-1374B	S. Butcher	Retrd.	8.00	105-130.
79-13-003	God Loveth a Cheerful Giver-E-1378	S. Butcher	Retrd.	11.00	850-1000.
79-13-004	O, How I Love Jesus-E-1380B	S. Butcher	Retrd.	8.00	90-135.00
79-13-005	His Burden Is Light-E-1380G	S. Butcher	Retrd.	8.00	90-145.00
79-13-006	Come Let Us Adore Him-E-2011	S. Butcher	Retrd.	10.00	325-350.
80-13-007	Wishing You a Season Filled with Joy-E-2805	S. Butcher	Retrd.	20.00	95-145.00
80-13-008	Blessed are the Peacemakers-E-3107	S. Butcher	Retrd.	13.00	85-115.00
80-13-009	Be Not Weary In Well Doing-E-3111	S. Butcher	Retrd.	14.00	75-130.00
80-13-010	God's Speed-E-3112	S. Butcher	Retrd.	14.00	70-120.00
80-13-011	Eggs Over Easy-E-3118	S. Butcher	Retrd.	12.00	75-125.00
82-13-012	O Come All Ye Faithful-E-2353	S. Butcher	Retrd.	27.50	70-100.00
82-13-013	There is Joy in Serving Jesus-E-7157	S. Butcher	Retrd.	17.00	50-80.00
83-13-014	Taste and See that the Lord is Good-E-9274	S. Butcher	Retrd.	22.50	60-80.00
87-13-015	His Eye Is On The Sparrow-E-0530	S. Butcher	Retrd.	28.50	85-110.00
87-13-016	Holy Smokes-E-2351	S. Butcher	Retrd.	27.00	80-115.00
87-13-017	Love is Kind-E-5377	S. Butcher	Retrd.	27.50	80-100.00
87-13-018	Let Love Reign-E-9273	S. Butcher	Retrd.	27.50	65-85.00
79-13-019	Jesus is the Light-E-1373G	S. Butcher	Retrd.	7.00	55-120.00
84-13-020	This is Your Day to Shine-E-2822	S. Butcher	Retrd.	37.50	75-130.00
83-13-021	Surrounded with Joy-E-0506	S. Butcher	Retrd.	21.00	60-75.00
83-13-022	You Can't Run Away from God-E-0525	S. Butcher	Retrd.	28.50	70-135.00
86-13-023	Lord, Keep Me On My Toes-100129	S. Butcher	Retrd.	22.50	60-85.00
86-13-024	Help, Lord, I'm In a Spot-100269	S. Butcher	Retrd.	18.50	50-65.00
83-13-025	Christmastime Is for Sharing-E-0504	S. Butcher	Retrd.	37.00	70-95.00
83-13-026	Nobody's Perfect-E-9268	S. Butcher	Retrd.	21.00	50-75.00
87-13-027	Make Me A Blessing-100102	S. Butcher	Retrd.	35.00	70-135.00
89-13-028	Many Moons In Same Canoe, Blessum You-520772	S. Butcher	Retrd.	50.00	125-200.
82-13-029	Dropping Over for Christmas-E-2375	S. Butcher	Retrd.	30.00	75-110.00
87-13-030	Smile Along The Way-101842	S. Butcher	Retrd.	30.00	135-190.00
87-13-031	Scent From Above-100528	S. Butcher	Retrd.	19.00	50-80.00
87-13-032	The Spirit Is Willing But The Flesh Is Weak-100196	S. Butcher	Retrd.	19.00	45-60.00
89-13-033	I'm So Glad You Fluttered Into My Life-520640	S. Butcher	Retrd.	40.00	200-300.
82-13-034	I Believe in Miracles-E-7156	S. Butcher	Retrd.	17.00	100-150.
87-13-035	I Believe In Miracles-E-7156R	S. Butcher	Retrd.	22.50	45-90.00
87-13-036	Lord, Help Us Keep Our Act Together-101850	S. Butcher	Retrd.	35.00	95-175.00
88-13-037	Happiness Divine-109584	S. Butcher	Retrd.	25.00	50-75.00
89-13-038	Sending You Showers Of Blessings-520683	S. Butcher	Retrd.	32.50	50-100.00
89-13-039	Someday My Love-520799	S. Butcher	Retrd.	40.00	55-75.00

Enesco Corporation — Precious Moments Collection 10th Anniv. Commemorative Edition

Number	Name	Artist	Edition Limit	Issue Price	Quote
88-14-001	The Good Lord has Blessed Us Tenfold-114022	S. Butcher	Yr.Iss.	90.00	125-175.

Enesco Corporation — Precious Moments Birthday Train Figurines

Number	Name	Artist	Edition Limit	Issue Price	Quote
88-15-001	Isn't Eight Just Great-109460	S. Butcher	Open	18.50	22.50-30.00
88-15-002	Wishing You Grr-eatness-109479	S. Butcher	Open	18.50	22.50-30.00
86-15-003	May Your Birthday Be Warm-15938	S. Butcher	Open	10.00	15-40.00
86-15-004	Happy Birthday Little Lamb-15946	S. Butcher	Open	10.00	15-39.00
86-15-005	Heaven Bless Your Special Day-15954	S. Butcher	Open	11.00	16.50-30.00
86-15-006	God Bless You On Your Birthday-15962	S. Butcher	Open	11.00	16.50-40.00
86-15-007	May Your Birthday Be Gigantic -15970	S. Butcher	Open	12.50	18.50-40.00
86-15-008	This Day Is Something To Roar About-15989	S. Butcher	Open	13.50	20-40.00
86-15-009	Keep Looking Up-15997	S. Butcher	Open	13.50	20-43.00
86-15-010	Bless The Days Of Our Youth-16004	S. Butcher	Open	15.00	22.50-45.00
92-15-011	May Your Birthday Be Mammoth-521825	S. Butcher	Open	25.00	25-40.00
92-15-012	Being Nine Is Just Divine-521833	S. Butcher	Open	25.00	25-40.00

Enesco Corporation — Precious Moments Birthday Club Figurines

Number	Name	Artist	Edition Limit	Issue Price	Quote
86-16-001	Fishing For Friends-BC-861	S. Butcher	Yr.Iss.	10.00	110-140.
87-16-002	Hi Sugar-BC-871	S. Butcher	Yr.Iss.	11.00	75-100.00
88-16-003	Somebunny Cares-BC-881	S. Butcher	Yr.Iss.	13.50	50-85.00
89-16-004	Can't Beehive Myself Without You-BC-891	S. Butcher	Yr.Iss.	13.50	35-75.00
90-16-005	Collecting Makes Good Scents-BC-901	S. Butcher	Yr.Iss.	15.00	15-40.00
90-16-006	I'm Nuts Over My Collection-BC-902	S. Butcher	Yr.Iss.	15.00	15-40.00

Enesco Corporation — Precious Moments Birthday Club Welcome Gift

Number	Name	Artist	Edition Limit	Issue Price	Quote
86-17-001	Our Club Can't Be Beat-B-0001	S. Butcher	Yr.Iss.	Unkn.	75-90.00
87-17-002	A Smile's The Cymbal of Joy-B-0002	S. Butcher	Yr.Iss.	Unkn.	50-65.00
88-17-003	The Sweetest Club Around-B-0003	S. Butcher	Yr.Iss.	Unkn.	35-65.00
89-17-004	Have A Beary Special Birthday- B-0004	S. Butcher	Yr.Iss.	Unkn.	30-55.00
90-17-005	Our Club Is A Tough Act To Follow-B-0005	S. Butcher	Yr.Iss.	Unkn.	25-45.00
91-17-006	Jest To Let You Know You're Tops-B-0006	S. Butcher	Yr.Iss.	Unkn.	45.00

Enesco Corporation — Birthday Club Inscribed Charter Member Renewal Gift

Number	Name	Artist	Edition Limit	Issue Price	Quote
87-18-001	A Smile's the Cymbal of Joy-B-0102	S. Butcher	Yr.Iss.	Unkn.	60-70.00
88-18-002	The Sweetest Club Around-B-0103	S. Butcher	Yr.Iss.	Unkn.	35-65.00
89-18-003	Have A Beary Special Birthday- B-0104	S. Butcher	Yr.Iss.	Unkn.	30-55.00
90-18-004	Our Club Is A Tough Act To Follow-B-0105	S. Butcher	Yr.Iss.	Unkn.	25-40.00
91-18-005	Jest To Let You Know You're Tops-B-0106	S. Butcher	Yr.Iss.	Unkn.	25-40.00

Enesco Corporation — Birthday Series

Number	Name	Artist	Edition Limit	Issue Price	Quote
88-19-001	Friends To The End-104418	S. Butcher	Open	15.00	18.50-35.00
87-19-002	Showers Of Blessings-105945	S. Butcher	Open	16.00	20-35.00
88-19-003	Brighten Someone's Day-105953	S. Butcher	Open	12.50	15-30.00
89-19-004	Hello World!-521175	S. Butcher	Open	13.50	15-30.00
90-19-005	To My Favorite Fan-521043	S. Butcher	Open	16.00	16-50.00
90-19-006	Not A Creature Was Stirring-524484	S. Butcher	Open	17.00	17-25.00
91-19-007	Can't Be Without You-524492	S. Butcher	Open	16.00	16-29.00
91-19-008	How Can I Ever Forget You-526924	S. Butcher	Open	15.00	15.00
92-19-009	Let's Be Friends-527270	S. Butcher	Open	15.00	15.00
92-19-010	Happy Birdie-527343	S. Butcher	Open	8.00	8.00

Enesco Corporation — Precious Moments Events Figurines

Number	Name	Artist	Edition Limit	Issue Price	Quote
88-20-001	You Are My Main Event-115231	S. Butcher	Yr.Iss.	30.00	50-95.00
89-20-002	Sharing Begins In The Heart-520861	S. Butcher	Yr.Iss.	25.00	45-80.00
90-20-003	I'm A Precious Moments Fan-523526	S. Butcher	Yr.Iss.	25.00	40-65.00
91-20-004	You Can Always Bring A Friend-527122	S. Butcher	Yr.Iss.	27.50	30-40.00
92-20-005	An Event Worth Wading For-527319	S. Butcher	Yr.Iss.	32.50	32.50

Enesco Corporation — Precious Moments Commemorative Easter Seal Figurines

Number	Name	Artist	Edition Limit	Issue Price	Quote
88-21-001	Jesus Loves Me-9" Fig.-104531	S. Butcher	1,000	N/A	1500-1700.
87-21-002	He Walks With Me-107999	S. Butcher	Yr.Iss.	25.00	35-50.00
88-21-003	Blessed Are They That Overcome-115479	S. Butcher	Yr.Iss.	27.50	35-40.00
89-21-004	Make A Joyful Noise-9" Fig.-520322	S. Butcher	1,500	N/A	1000-1300.
89-21-005	His Love Will Shine On You-522376	S. Butcher	Yr.Iss.	30.00	40-50.00
90-21-006	Always In His Care-524522	S. Butcher	Yr.Iss.	30.00	35-60.00

Number	Name	Artist	Edition Limit	Issue Price	Quote
90-21-007	You Have Touched So Many Hearts-9" fig.-523283	S. Butcher	2,000	N/A	650-1000.
91-21-008	Sharing A Gift Of Love-527114	S. Butcher	Yr.Iss.	30.00	30-50.00
91-21-009	We Are God's Workmanship-9" fig.-523879	S. Butcher	2,000	N/A	650-1000.
92-21-010	A Universal Love-527173	S. Butcher	Yr.Iss.	32.50	32.50
92-21-011	You Are Such A Purr-fect Friend9" fig.-526010	S. Butcher	2,000	N/A	N/A
Enesco Corporation	**Precious Moments Musical Figurines**				
87-22-001	You Have Touched So Many Hearts-112577	S. Butcher	Open	50.00	50-60.00
81-22-002	The Lord Bless You And Keep You-E-7180	S. Butcher	Open	55.00	80-100.00
85-22-003	Heaven Bless You-100285	S. Butcher	Open	45.00	60-75.00
80-22-004	My Guardian Angel-E-5205	S. Butcher	Suspd.	22.50	60-75.00
81-22-005	My Guardian Angel-E-5206	S. Butcher	Suspd.	22.50	55-80.00
80-22-006	The Hand That Rocks The Future-E-5204	S. Butcher	Open	30.00	55-85.00
81-22-007	Mother Sew Dear-E-7182	S. Butcher	Open	35.00	55-75.00
81-22-008	The Purr-fect Grandma-E-7184	S. Butcher	Open	35.00	55-80.00
79-22-009	Unto Us A Child Is Born-E-2808	S. Butcher	Suspd.	35.00	65-115.00
84-22-010	Wishing You A Merry Christmas-E-5394	S. Butcher	Suspd.	55.00	80-95.00
80-22-011	Peace On Earth-E-4726	S. Butcher	Suspd.	45.00	95-120.00
86-22-012	Our 1st Christmas Together-101702	S. Butcher	Retrd.	50.00	70-105.00
83-22-013	Let Heaven And Nature Sing-E-2346	S. Butcher	Suspd.	55.00	115-130.
87-22-014	I'm Sending You A White Christmas-112402	S. Butcher	Open	55.00	70-75.00
84-22-015	We Saw A Star-12408	S. Butcher	Suspd.	50.00	65-80.00
80-22-016	Come Let Us Adore Him-E-2810	S. Butcher	Open	45.00	85-125.00
82-22-017	I'll Play My Drum For Him-E-2355	S. Butcher	Suspd.	45.00	125-140.
80-22-018	Jesus Is Born-E-2809	S. Butcher	Suspd.	35.00	90-120.00
79-22-019	Crown Him Lord Of All-E-2807	S. Butcher	Suspd.	35.00	75-100.00
83-22-020	Wee Three Kings-E-0520	S. Butcher	Suspd.	60.00	90-110.00
80-22-021	Silent Knight-E-5642	S. Butcher	Suspd.	45.00	125-150.
81-22-022	Love Is Sharing-E-7185	S. Butcher	Retrd.	40.00	125-165.
79-22-023	Christmas Is A Time To Share-E-2806	S. Butcher	Retrd.	35.00	140-170.
81-22-024	Rejoice O Earth-E-5645	S. Butcher	Retrd.	35.00	80-110.00
83-22-025	Sharing Our Season Together-E-0519	S. Butcher	Retrd.	70.00	100-150.
91-22-026	Lord Help Keep Me In Balance-520691	S. Butcher	Open	60.00	60.00
92-22-027	This Day Has Been Made In Heaven-523682	S. Butcher	Open	60.00	60.00
92-22-028	Do Not Open Till Christmas-522244	S. Butcher	Open	75.00	75.00
81-22-029	Let the Whole World Know	S. Butcher	Suspd.	60.00	135.00
Enesco Corporation	**Precious Moments Calendar Girl**				
88-23-001	January-109983	S. Butcher	Open	37.50	45-67.00
88-23-002	February-109991	S. Butcher	Open	27.50	33.50-67.00
88-23-003	March-110019	S. Butcher	Open	27.50	33.50-64.00
88-23-004	April-110027	S. Butcher	Open	30.00	35-113.00
88-23-005	May -110035	S. Butcher	Open	25.00	30-150.00
88-23-006	June-110043	S. Butcher	Open	40.00	50-112.00
88-23-007	July-110051	S. Butcher	Open	35.00	45-58.00
88-23-008	August-110078	S. Butcher	Open	40.00	50-57.00
88-23-009	September-110086	S. Butcher	Open	27.50	33.50-49.00
88-23-010	October-110094	S. Butcher	Open	35.00	45-59.00
88-23-011	November-110108	S. Butcher	Open	32.50	37.50-50.00
88-23-012	December-110116	S. Butcher	Open	27.50	33.50-50.00
Enesco Corporation	**Bless Those Who Serve Their Country**				
91-24-001	Bless Those Who Serve Their Country (Navy) 526568	S. Butcher	Suspd.	32.50	32.50
91-24-002	Bless Those Who Serve Their Country (Army) 526576	S. Butcher	Suspd.	32.50	32.50
91-24-003	Bless Those Who Serve Their Country (Air Force) 526584	S. Butcher	Suspd.	32.50	32.50
91-24-004	Bless Those Who Serve Their Country (Girl Soldier) 527289	S. Butcher	Suspd.	32.50	32.50
91-24-005	Bless Those Who Serve Their Country (Soldier) 527297	S. Butcher	Suspd.	32.50	32.50
91-24-006	Bless Those Who Serve Their Country (Marine) 527521	S. Butcher	Suspd.	32.50	32.50
Enesco Corporation	**Sugartown**				
92-25-001	Christmas Tree-528684	S. Butcher	Open	15.00	15.00
92-25-002	Chapel-529621	S. Butcher	Open	85.00	85.00
92-25-003	Nativity-529508	S. Butcher	Open	20.00	20.00
92-25-004	Grandfather-529516	S. Butcher	Open	15.00	15.00
92-25-005	Sam Butcher-529567	S. Butcher	Yr. Iss.	22.50	22.50
92-25-006	Aunt Ruth & Aunt Dorothy-529486	S. Butcher	Open	20.00	20.00
92-25-007	Philip-529494	S. Butcher	Open	17.00	17.00
Enesco Corporation	**Memories of Yesterday Special Edition**				
88-26-001	Mommy, I Teared It-523488	M. Attwell	10,000	25.00	175-325.
89-26-002	As Good As His Mother Ever Made-522392	M. Attwell	9,600	32.50	100-150.
90-26-003	A Lapful of Luck -525014	M. Attwell	5,000	30.00	75-180.00
Enesco Corporation	**Memories of Yesterday -Charter 1988**				
88-27-001	Mommy, I Teared It-114480	M. Attwell	Open	25.00	32-55.00
88-27-002	Now I Lay Me Down To Sleep-114499	M. Attwell	Open	20.00	25-40.00
88-27-003	We's Happy! How's Yourself?-114502	M. Attwell	Open	40.00	45-60.00
88-27-004	Hang On To Your Luck!-114510	M. Attwell	Open	25.00	27.50-50.00
88-27-005	How Do You Spell S-O-R-R-Y?-114529	M. Attwell	Retrd.	25.00	35-70.00
88-27-006	What Will I Grow Up To Be?-114537	M. Attwell	Open	40.00	45-65.00
88-27-007	Can I Keep Her Mommy?-114545	M. Attwell	Open	25.00	27-50.00
88-27-008	Hush!-114553	M. Attwell	Retrd.	45.00	60-100.00
88-27-009	It Hurts When Fido Hurts-114561	M. Attwell	Retrd.	30.00	32.50-45.00
88-27-010	Anyway, Fido Loves Me-114588	M. Attwell	Open	30.00	32.50-45.00
88-27-011	If You Can't Be Good, Be Careful-114596	M. Attwell	Open	50.00	55-80.00
88-27-012	Mommy, I Teared It, 9"-115924	M. Attwell	Closed	85.00	140-200.
88-27-013	Welcome Santa-114960	M. Attwell	Open	45.00	50-75.00
88-27-014	Special Delivery-114979	M. Attwell	Retrd.	30.00	32.50-50.00
88-27-015	How 'bout A Little Kiss?-114987	M. Attwell	Open	25.00	27.50-50.00
88-27-016	Waiting For Santa-114995	M. Attwell	Open	40.00	45-60.00
88-27-017	Dear Santa. . .-115002	M. Attwell	Open	50.00	55-75.00
88-27-018	I Hope Santa Is Home . . .-115010	M. Attwell	Open	30.00	32.50-40.00
88-27-019	It's The Thought That Counts.-115029	M. Attwell	Open	25.00	27.50-45.00
88-27-020	Is It Really Santa?-115347	M. Attwell	Open	50.00	55-65.00
88-27-021	He Knows IF You've Been Bad Or Good-115355	M. Attwell	Open	40.00	45-60.00
88-27-022	Now He Can Be Your Friend, Too!-115363	M. Attwell	Open	45.00	50-65.00
88-27-023	We Wish You A Merry Christmas-115371	M. Attwell	Open	70.00	75-125.00
88-27-024	Good Morning Mr. Snowman-115401	M. Attwell	Retrd.	75.00	80-170.00
Enesco Corporation	**Memories of Yesterday Figurines**				
89-28-001	Blow Wind, Blow-520012	M. Attwell	Open	40.00	40.00
89-28-002	Let's Be Nice Like We Was Before-520047	M. Attwell	Open	50.00	50.00
89-28-003	I'se Spoken For-520071	M. Attwell	Retrd.	30.00	30-45.00
89-28-004	Daddy, I Can Never Fill Your Shoes-520187	M. Attwell	Open	30.00	30.00
89-28-005	This One's For You, Dear-520195	M. Attwell	Open	50.00	50.00
89-28-006	Should I . . . ?-520209	M. Attwell	Open	50.00	50.00
89-28-007	Here Comes The Bride-God Bless Her! -9"-5205272	M. Attwell	Closed	95.00	100-125.
89-28-008	We's Happy! How's Yourself?-520616	M. Attwell	Retrd.	70.00	85-100.00
89-28-009	Here Comes The Bride & Groom God Bless 'Em-520896	M. Attwell	Open	50.00	50.00
89-28-010	The Long and Short of It-522384	M. Attwell	Open	32.50	32.50
89-28-011	As Good As His Mother Ever Made-522392	M. Attwell	Open	32.50	32.50
89-28-012	Must Feed Them Over Christmas-522406	M. Attwell	Open	38.50	38.50
89-28-013	Knitting You A Warm & Cozy Winter-522414	M. Attwell	Open	37.50	37.50
89-28-014	Joy To You At Christmas-522449	M. Attwell	Open	45.00	45.00
89-28-015	For Fido And Me-522457	M. Attwell	Open	70.00	70.00
90-28-016	Hold It! You're Just Swell-520020	M. Attwell	Open	50.00	50.00
90-28-017	Kiss The Place And Make It Well-520039	M. Attwell	Open	50.00	50.00
90-28-018	Where's Muvver?-520101	M. Attwell	Open	30.00	30.00
90-28-019	Here Comes The Bride And Groom God Bless 'Em!-520136	M. Attwell	Open	80.00	80.00
90-28-020	Luck At Last! He Loves Me-520217	M. Attwell	Retrd.	35.00	35.00
90-28-021	I'm Not As Backwards As I Looks-523240	M. Attwell	Open	32.50	32.50
90-28-022	I Pray The Lord My Soul To Keep-523259	M. Attwell	Open	25.00	25.00
90-28-023	He Hasn't Forgotten Me-523267	M. Attwell	Open	30.00	30.00
90-28-024	Time For Bed 9"-523275	M. Attwell	Closed	95.00	95-125.00
90-28-025	Got To Get Home For The Holidays-524751	M. Attwell	Open	100.00	100.00
90-28-026	Hush-A-Bye Baby-524778	M. Attwell	Open	80.00	80.00
90-28-027	Let Me Be Your Guardian Angel-524670	M. Attwell	Open	32.50	32.50
90-28-028	I'se Been Painting-524700	M. Attwell	Open	37.50	37.50
90-28-029	A Lapful Of Luck-524689	M. Attwell	Open	15.00	15.00
90-28-030	The Greatest Treasure The World Can Hold-524808	M. Attwell	Open	50.00	50.00
90-28-031	Hoping To See You Soon-524824	M. Attwell	Open	30.00	30.00
90-28-032	A Dash of Something With Something For the Pot-524727	M. Attwell	Open	55.00	55.00
90-28-033	Not A Creature Was Stirrin'-524697	M. Attwell	Open	45.00	45.00
90-28-034	Collection Sign-513156	M. Attwell	Open	7.00	7.00
91-28-035	He Loves Me -9" -525022	M. Attwell	2 Yr.	100.00	100.00
91-28-036	Give It Your Best Shot-525561	M. Attwell	Open	35.00	35.00
91-28-037	Wishful Thinking-522597	M. Attwell	Open	45.00	45.00
91-28-038	Them Dishes Nearly Done-524611	M. Attwell	Open	50.00	50.00
91-28-039	Just Thinking 'bout You-523461	M. Attwell	Open	70.00	70.00
91-28-040	Who Ever Told Mother To Order Twins?-520063	M. Attwell	Open	33.50	33.50
91-28-041	Tying The Knot-522678	M. Attwell	Open	60.00	60.00
91-28-042	Pull Yourselves Together Girls, Waists Are In-522783	M. Attwell	Open	30.00	30.00
91-28-043	I Must Be Somebody's Darling-524832	M. Attwell	Open	30.00	30.00
91-28-044	We All Loves A Cuddle-524832	M. Attwell	Retrd.	30.00	30.00
91-28-045	Sitting Pretty-522708	M. Attwell	Open	40.00	40.00
91-28-046	Why Don't You Sing Along?-522600	M. Attwell	Open	55.00	55.00
91-28-047	Wherever I Am, I'm Dreaming of You-522686	M. Attwell	Open	40.00	40.00
91-28-048	Opening Presents Is Much Fun!-524735	M. Attwell	Open	37.50	37.50
91-28-049	I'm As Comfy As Can Be-525480	M. Attwell	Open	50.00	50.00
91-28-050	Friendship Has No Boundaries (Special Understamp)-525545	M. Attwell	Yr.Iss.	30.00	30-40.00
91-28-051	Could You Love Me For Myself Alone?-525618	M. Attwell	Open	30.00	30.00
91-28-052	Good Morning, Little Boo-Boo-525766	M. Attwell	Open	40.00	40.00
91-28-053	S'no Use Lookin' Back Now!-527203	M. Attwell	Open	75.00	75.00
92-28-054	I Pray the Lord My Soul To Keep (Musical)-525596	M. Attwell	Open	65.00	65.00
92-28-055	Time For Bed-527076	M. Attwell	Open	30.00	30.00
92-28-056	Now Be A Good Dog Fido-524581	M. Attwell	Open	45.00	45.00
92-28-057	A Kiss From Fido-523119	M. Attwell	Open	35.00	35.00
92-28-058	I'se Such A Good Little Girl Sometimes-522759	M. Attwell	Open	30.00	30.00
92-28-059	Send All Life's Little Worries Skipping-527505	M. Attwell	Open	30.00	30.00
92-28-060	A Whole Bunch of Love For You-522732	M. Attwell	Open	40.00	40.00
92-28-061	Hurry Up For the Last Train to Fairyland-525863	M. Attwell	Open	40.00	40.00
92-28-062	I'se So Happy You Called-526401	M. Attwell	2 Yr.	100.00	100.00
92-28-063	I'm Hopin' You're Missing Me Too-525499	M. Attwell	Open	55.00	55.00
92-28-064	You'll Always Be My Hero-524743	M. Attwell	Open	50.00	50.00
92-28-065	Things Are Rather Upside Down-522775	M. Attwell	Open	30.00	30.00
92-28-066	The Future-God Bless 'Em!-524719	M. Attwell	Open	37.50	37.50
92-28-067	Making Something Special For You-525472	M. Attwell	Open	45.00	45.00
92-28-068	Home's A Grand Place To Get Back To Musical-525553	M. Attwell	Open	100.00	100.00
92-28-069	Five Years Of Memories-525669 (Five Year Anniversary Figurine)	M. Attwell	Yr.Iss.	50.00	50.00
92-28-070	Good Night and God Bless You In Every Way!-525634	M. Attwell	Open	50.00	50.00
92-28-071	Collection Sign-527300	M. Attwell	Open	30.00	30.00
92-28-072	Merry Christmas, Little Boo-Boo-528803	M. Attwell	Open	37.50	37.50
92-28-073	Five Years Of Memories. Celebrating Our Five Years1992-525669A	M. Attwell	500	N/A	N/A
Enesco Corporation	**Memories of Yesterday Once Upon A Fairy Tale™...**				
92-29-001	Mother Goose-526428	M. Attwell	18,000	50.00	50.00
92-29-002	Mary Had A Little Lamb-526479	M. Attwell	18,000	45.00	45.00
92-29-003	Simple Simon-526452	M. Attwell	18,000	35.00	35.00
Enesco Corporation	**Memories of Yesterday-Exclusive Membership Figurine**				
91-30-001	We Belong Together-S0001	M. Attwell	Yr.Iss.	Gift	30.00
92-30-002	Waiting For The Sunshine-S0002	M. Attwell	Yr.Iss.	Gift	N/A
Enesco Corporation	**Memories of Yesterday-Exclusive Charter Membership Figurine**				
92-31-001	Waiting For The Sunshine-S0102	M. Attwell	Yr.Iss.	Gift	N/A
Enesco Corporation	**Memories of Yesterday-Society Figurines**				
91-32-001	Welcome To Your New Home-M4911	M. Attwell	Yr.Iss.	30.00	85.00
91-32-002	I Love My Friends-MY921	M. Attwell	Yr.Iss.	32.50	32.50
Enesco Corporation	**Memories of Yesterday-Exclusive Heritage Dealer Figurine**				
91-33-001	A Friendly Chat and a Cup of Tea-525510	M. Attwell	Yr.Iss.	50.00	50.00
Flambro Imports	**Emmett Kelly, Jr. Figurines**				
81-01-001	Looking Out To See	Undis.	12,000	75.00	1700-3300.
81-01-002	Sweeping Up	Undis.	12,000	75.00	1000-1600.
82-01-003	Wet Paint	Undis.	15,000	80.00	500-950.
82-01-004	The Thinker	Undis.	15,000	60.00	900-1700.
82-01-005	Why Me?	Undis.	15,000	65.00	600-900.

Company Number	Name	Series Artist	Edition Limit	Issue Price	Quote
83-01-006	The Balancing Act	Undis.	10,000	75.00	600-950.
83-01-007	Wishful Thinking	Undis.	10,000	65.00	500-700.
83-01-008	Hole In The Sole	Undis.	10,000	75.00	450-600.
83-01-009	Balloons For Sale	Undis.	10,000	75.00	500-550.
83-01-010	Spirit of Christmas I	Undis.	3,500	125.00	1500-3500.
84-01-011	Eating Cabbage	Undis.	12,000	75.00	375-600.
84-01-012	Big Business	Undis.	9,500	110.00	650-950.
84-01-013	Piano Player	Undis.	9,500	160.00	400-750.
84-01-014	Spirit of Christmas II	Undis.	3,500	270.00	300-800.
85-01-015	Man's Best Friend	Undis.	9,500	98.00	325-600.
85-01-016	No Strings Attached	Undis.	9,500	98.00	150-325.
85-01-017	In The Spotlight	Undis.	12,000	103.00	250-375.
85-01-018	Emmett's Fan	Undis.	12,000	80.00	325-650.
85-01-019	Spirit of Christmas III	Undis.	3,500	220.00	400-700.
86-01-020	The Entertainers	Undis.	12,000	120.00	140-165.
86-01-021	Cotton Candy	Undis.	12,000	98.00	300-400.
86-01-022	Bedtime	Undis.	12,000	98.00	150-325.
86-01-023	Making New Friends	Undis.	9,500	140.00	200-450.
86-01-024	Fair Game	Undis.	2,500	450.00	900-1800.
86-01-025	Spirit of Christmas IV	Undis.	3,500	150.00	400-600.
87-01-026	On The Road Again	Undis.	9,500	109.00	200-350.
87-01-027	My Favorite Things	Undis.	9,500	109.00	400-800.
87-01-028	Saturday Night	Undis.	7,500	153.00	400-750.
87-01-029	Toothache	Undis.	12,000	98.00	121.00
87-01-030	Spirit of Christmas V	Undis.	2,400	170.00	500-600.
88-01-031	Over a Barrel	Undis.	9,500	130.00	200-225.
88-01-032	Wheeler Dealer	Undis.	7,500	160.00	200-250.
88-01-033	Dining Out	Undis.	12,000	120.00	150-250.
88-01-034	Amen	Undis.	12,000	120.00	150-350.
88-01-035	Spirit of Christmas VI	Undis.	2,400	194.00	300-600.
89-01-036	Making Up	Undis.	7,500	200.00	264.00
89-01-037	No Loitering	Undis	7,500	200.00	264.00
89-01-038	Hurdy-Gurdy Man	Undis.	9,500	150.00	175-200.
89-01-039	65th Birthday Commemorative	Undis.	1,989	275.00	1200-2500.
90-01-040	Watch the Birdie	Undis.	9,500	200.00	210.00
90-01-041	Convention-Bound	Undis.	7,500	225.00	230.00
90-01-042	Balloons for Sale II	Undis.	7,500	250.00	250.00
90-01-043	Misfortune?	Undis.	3,500	400.00	400-525.
90-01-044	Spirit Of Christmas VII	Undis.	3,500	275.00	350-700.
91-01-045	Finishing Touch	Undis.	7,500	245.00	245.00
91-01-046	Artist At Work	Undis.	7,500	295.00	295.00
91-01-047	Follow The Leader	Undis.	7,500	200.00	200.00
91-01-048	Spirit Of Christmas VIII	Undis.	3,500	250.00	250-425.
92-01-049	No Use Crying	Undis.	7,500	200.00	200.00
92-01-050	Ready-Set-Go	Undis.	7,500	200.00	200.00
92-01-051	Peanut Butter?	Undis.	7,500	200.00	200.00
Flambro Imports		**Circus World Museum Clowns**			
85-02-001	Paul Jerome (Hobo)	Undis.	9,500	80.00	80-150.00
85-02-002	Paul Jung (Neat)	Undis.	9,500	80.00	110-120.
85-02-003	Felix Adler (Grotesque)	Undis.	9,500	80.00	80-110.00
87-02-004	Paul Jerome with Dog	Undis.	7,500	90.00	90.00
87-02-005	Paul Jung, Sitting	Undis.	7,500	90.00	90.00
87-02-006	Felix Adler with Balloon	Undis.	7,500	90.00	90.00
87-02-007	Abe Goldstein, Keystone Kop	Undis.	7,500	90.00	90.00
Flambro Imports		**Emmett Kelly, Jr, Miniatures**			
86-03-001	Looking Out To See	Undis.	Retrd.	25.00	75-125.00
86-03-002	Sweeping Up	Undis.	Retrd.	25.00	75-100.00
86-03-003	Wet Paint	Undis.	Retrd.	25.00	38.50
86-03-004	Why Me?	Undis.	Retrd.	25.00	45-100.00
86-03-005	The Thinker	Undis.	Retrd.	25.00	50-70.00
86-03-006	Balancing Act	Undis.	Retrd.	25.00	40-65.00
86-03-007	Hole in the Sole	Undis.	Retrd.	25.00	50-125.00
86-03-008	Balloons for Sale	Undis.	Retrd.	25.00	40-55.00
86-03-009	Wishful Thinking	Undis.	Retrd.	25.00	60-75.00
87-03-010	Emmett's Fan	Undis.	Retrd.	30.00	40-50.00
87-03-011	Eating Cabbage	Undis.	Retrd.	30.00	40-65.00
88-03-012	Spirit of Christmas I	Undis.	Retrd.	40.00	55-150.00
88-03-013	Big Business	Undis.	Numbrd.	35.00	38.50
90-03-014	Saturday Night	Undis.	Numbrd.	50.00	50.00
90-03-015	My Favorite Things	Undis.	Numbrd.	45.00	45.00
90-03-016	Spirit Of Christmas III	Undis.	Retrd.	50.00	50.00
89-03-017	Man's Best Friend?	Undis.	Numbrd.	35.00	35.00
89-03-018	Cotton Candy	Undis.	Retrd.	30.00	30-50.00
91-03-019	In The Spotlight	Undis.	Numbrd.	35.00	35.00
91-03-020	No Strings Attached	Undis.	Numbrd.	35.00	35.00
92-03-021	Spirit of Christmas II	Undis.	Numbrd.	50.00	50.00
92-03-022	Making New Friends	Undis.	Numbrd.	40.00	40.00
92-03-023	Piano Player	Undis.	Numbrd.	50.00	50.00
92-03-024	On the Road Again	Undis.	Numbrd.	35.00	35.00
93-03-025	Spirit of Christmas IV	Undis.	Numbrd.	40.00	40.00
Flambro Imports		**Raggedy Ann & Andy**			
88-04-001	70 Years Young	C. Beylon	2,500	95.00	110.00
88-04-002	Giddy Up	C. Beylon	3,500	95.00	110.00
88-04-003	Wet Paint	C. Beylon	3,500	70.00	80.00
88-04-004	Oops!	C. Beylon	3,500	80.00	90.00
Flambro Imports		**Annual Emmett Kelly Jr. Nutcracker**			
90-05-001	1990 Nutcracker	Undis.	Yr.Iss.	50.00	50-75.00
Flambro Imports		**Pleasantville 1893**			
90-06-001	Sweet Shoppe & Bakery	J. Berg Victor	Open	40.00	40.00
90-06-002	Toy Store	J. Berg Victor	Open	30.00	30.00
90-06-003	1st Church Of Pleasantville	J. Berg Victor	Open	35.00	35.00
90-06-004	Department Store	J. Berg Victor	Open	25.00	25.00
90-06-005	Pleasantville Library	J. Berg Victor	Open	32.00	32.00
90-06-006	The Band Stand	J. Berg Victor	Open	12.00	12.00
90-06-007	The Gerber House	J. Berg Victor	Open	30.00	30.00
90-06-008	Reverend Littlefield's House	J. Berg Victor	Open	34.00	34.00
90-06-009	Mason's Hotel and Saloon	J. Berg Victor	Open	35.00	35.00
91-06-010	Methodist Church	J. Berg Victor	Open	40.00	40.00
91-06-011	Fire House	J. Berg Victor	Open	40.00	40.00
91-06-012	Court House	J. Berg Victor	Open	36.00	36.00
91-06-013	School Houe	J. Berg Victor	Open	36.00	36.00
92-06-014	Railroad Station	J. Berg Victor	Open	N/A	N/A
92-06-015	Blacksmith/Livery	J. Berg Victor	Open	N/A	N/A
92-06-016	Bank/Real Estate Office	J. Berg Victor	Open	N/A	N/A
92-06-017	Apothecary/Ice Cream Shop	J. Berg Victor	Open	N/A	N/A
92-06-018	Tubbs, Jr. House	J. Berg Victor	Open	N/A	N/A
92-06-019	Miss Fountains	J. Berg Victor	Open	N/A	N/A
92-06-021	Covered Bridge	J. Berg Victor	Open	N/A	N/A
93-06-022	Balcombs Farm	J. Berg Victor	Open	N/A	N/A
93-06-023	Blacksmith Shop	J. Berg Victor	Open	N/A	N/A
93-06-024	Blacksmith/Livery Stable	J. Berg Victor	Open	N/A	N/A
93-06-025	New Sculpted Bandstand/Gazebo	J. Berg Victor	Open	N/A	N/A
93-06-026	Catholic Church	J. Berg Victor	Open	N/A	N/A
93-06-027	Sacred Heart Catholic Church	J. Berg Victor	Open	N/A	N/A
93-06-028	Sacred Heart Rectory	J. Berg Victor	Open	N/A	N/A
93-06-029	Pleasantville Gazette Building	J. Berg Victor	Open	N/A	N/A
Flambro Imports		**Daddy Loves You**			
91-07-001	Make You....Giggle!	C. Pracht	2,500	100.00	100.00
91-07-002	You're Sooo....Sweet	C. Pracht	2,500	100.00	100.00
91-07-003	C'mon, Daddy!	C. Pracht	2,500	100.00	100.00
91-07-004	Soo....You Like It?	C. Pracht	2,500	100.00	100.00
Flambro Imports		**Emmett Kelly Jr. Metal Sculptures**			
91-08-001	Carousel Rider	Undis.	5,000	125.00	125.00
91-08-002	The Magician	Undis.	5,000	125.00	125.00
91-08-003	Emmett's Pooches	Undis.	5,000	125.00	125.00
91-08-004	Balancing Act, Too	Undis.	5,000	125.00	125.00
Flambro Imports		**Emmett Kelly Jr. A Day At The Fair**			
90-09-001	Step Right Up	Undis.	Numbrd.	65.00	65.00
90-09-002	Three For A Dime	Undis.	Numbrd.	65.00	65.00
90-09-003	Look At You	Undis.	Retrd.	65.00	65.00
90-09-004	75 Please	Undis.	Numbrd.	65.00	65.00
90-09-005	The Stilt Man	Undis.	Retrd.	65.00	65.00
90-09-006	Ride The Wild Mouse	Undis.	Numbrd.	65.00	65.00
90-09-007	You Can Do It, Emmett	Undis.	Retrd.	65.00	65.00
90-09-008	Thanks Emmett	Undis.	Numbrd.	65.00	65.00
90-09-009	You Go First, Emmett	Undis.	Retrd.	65.00	65.00
91-09-010	The Trouble With Hot Dogs	Undis.	N/A	65.00	65.00
91-09-011	Popcorn!	Undis.	N/A	65.00	65.00
91-09-012	Coin Toss	Undis.	N/A	65.00	65.00
92-09-013	Stilt Man	Undis.	N/A	65.00	65.00
Flambro Imports		**Emmett Kelly Jr. Appearance Only Figurine**			
92-10-001	Now Appearing	Undis.	N/A	100.00	100.00
Flambro Imports		**Emmett Kelly Jr. Limited Edition Figurine**			
93-11-001	After the Parade	Undis.	7,500	200.00	200.00
93-11-001	World Traveler	Undis.	7,500	200.00	200.00
93-11-003	Kittens for Sale	Undis.	7,500	190.00	190.00
Flambro Imports		**Gnomes Limited Edition**			
92-12-001	Welcome Home Gnome	Poortvliet	1,500	55.00	55.00
92-12-002	The Garden Gnome	Poortvliet	1,500	100.00	100.00
92-12-003	The Farm Gnome	Poortvliet	1,500	100.00	100.00
Flambro Imports		**Gnome Miniatures**			
92-13-001	Bill & Bella	Poortvliet	Open	27.00	27.00
92-13-002	Harold	Poortvliet	Open	25.00	25.00
92-13-003	Daniel & Dede	Poortvliet	Open	27.00	27.00
92-13-004	Al Jo	Poortvliet	Open	27.00	27.00
92-13-005	Patrick	Poortvliet	Open	23.00	23.00
92-13-006	George	Poortvliet	Open	22.00	22.00
92-13-007	Julius	Poortvliet	Open	23.00	23.00
92-13-008	Tilly	Poortvliet	Open	19.00	19.00
92-13-009	Wilbur	Poortvliet	Open	25.00	25.00
92-13-010	Mary & Michael	Poortvliet	Open	30.00	30.00
92-13-011	Oscar	Poortvliet	Open	20.00	20.00
92-13-012	Benjamin	Poortvliet	Open	23.00	23.00
92-13-013	Catrina & Charles	Poortvliet	Open	30.00	30.00
92-13-014	Henry	Poortvliet	Open	23.00	23.00
Flambro Imports		**Gnomes**			
92-14-001	Snorri	Poortvliet	Open	51.00	51.00
92-14-002	Genevieve	Poortvliet	Open	49.00	49.00
92-14-003	Abram	Poortvliet	Open	55.00	55.00
92-14-004	Ritkig	Poortvliet	Open	27.00	27.00
92-14-005	Pieter & Hattie	Poortvliet	Open	47.00	47.00
92-14-006	Marta with Bunny	Poortvliet	Open	50.00	50.00
92-14-007	David	Poortvliet	Open	46.00	46.00
92-14-008	Theodor	Poortvliet	Open	40.00	40.00
92-14-009	Tobias	Poortvliet	Open	38.00	40.00
92-14-010	Jacob	Poortvliet	Open	37.00	37.00
92-14-011	Gabriel	Poortvliet	Open	20.00	20.00
92-14-012	Quentin	Poortvliet	Open	30.00	30.00
92-14-013	Hannah & Josh	Poortvliet	Open	27.00	27.00
92-14-014	Franz with Christoph & Katya	Poortvliet	Open	45.00	45.00
92-14-015	Claire	Poortvliet	Open	36.00	36.00
92-14-016	Slumber Chief	Poortvliet	Open	40.00	40.00
92-14-017	Ollie	Poortvliet	Open	27.00	27.00
92-14-018	Purdy & Pippin	Poortvliet	Open	39.00	39.00
92-14-019	Columbine	Poortvliet	Open	25.00	25.00
92-14-020	Sigfried	Poortvliet	Open	52.00	52.00
92-14-021	Sophia	Poortvliet	Open	52.00	52.00
92-14-022	Brina & Borg	Poortvliet	Open	45.00	45.00
92-14-023	Ahni with Max & Molly	Poortvliet	Open	55.00	55.00
92-14-024	Stephie & Stoffie	Poortvliet	Open	19.00	19.00
92-14-025	Trudy & Frederick	Poortvliet	Open	50.00	50.00
92-14-026	Richard & Rosemary	Poortvliet	Open	53.00	53.00
92-14-027	Otto	Poortvliet	Open	40.00	40.00
92-14-028	Willie	Poortvliet	Open	37.00	37.00
92-14-029	Gideon	Poortvliet	Open	40.00	40.00
92-14-030	Nicolas (Siberian)	Poortvliet	Open	35.00	35.00
92-14-031	Jonathan (Snowman)	Poortvliet	Open	40.00	40.00
92-14-032	Pepi (Skiing)	Poortvliet	Open	42.00	42.00
92-14-033	Gobby & Lou (Goblin)	Poortvliet	Open	39.00	39.00
Flambro Imports		**Emmett Kelly Jr. Members Only Figurine**			
90-15-001	Merry-Go-Round	Undis.	Closed	125.00	200-550.
91-15-002	10 Years Of Collecting	Undis.	N/A	100.00	100-180.
92-15-003	All Aboard	Undis.	N/A	75.00	75.00
93-15-004	Ringmaster	Undis.	N/A	N/A	N/A
Franklin Mint		**Joys of Childhood**			
76-01-001	Hopscotch	N. Rockwell	3,700	120.00	175.00
76-01-002	The Fishing Hole	N. Rockwell	3,700	120.00	175.00
76-01-003	Dressing Up	N. Rockwell	3,700	120.00	175.00
76-01-004	The Stilt Walker	N. Rockwell	3,700	120.00	175.00
76-01-005	Trick or Treat	N. Rockwell	3,700	120.00	175.00
76-01-006	Time Out	N. Rockwell	3,700	120.00	175.00

Number	Name	Artist	Edition Limit	Issue Price	Quote
76-01-007	The Marble Champ	N. Rockwell	3,700	120.00	175.00
76-01-008	The Nurse	N. Rockwell	3,700	120.00	175.00
76-01-009	Ride 'Em Cowboy	N. Rockwell	3,700	120.00	175.00
76-01-010	Coasting Along	N. Rockwell	3,700	120.00	175.00
Gartlan USA, Inc.		**Plaques**			
85-01-001	Pete Rose-"Desire to Win", signed	T. Sizemore	4,192	75.00	75.00
86-01-002	George Brett-"Royalty in Motion", signed	J. Martin	2,000	85.00	85-250.00
86-01-003	Reggie Jackson-"The Roundtripper", signed	J. Martin	500	150.00	175-300.
86-01-004	Reggie Jackson Artist Proof-"The Roundtripper", signed	J. Martin	44	175.00	250-450.
87-01-005	Roger Staubach, signed	C. Soileau	1,979	85.00	200-250.
Gartlan USA, Inc.		**Baseball/Football/Hockey Card Series**			
85-02-001	Pete Rose Ceramic Baseball Card	T. Sizemore	Open	9.95	18.00
85-02-002	Pete Rose Ceramic Baseball Card, signed	T. Sizemore	4,192	39.00	60-100.00
86-02-003	George Brett Baseball Rounder	J. Martin	Open	9.95	14.00
86-02-004	George Brett Baseball Rounder, signed	J. Martin	2,000	30.00	30.00
86-02-005	George Brett Ceramic Baseball	J. Martin	Open	20.00	20.00
86-02-006	Gerorge Brett Ceramic Baseball, signed	J. Martin	2,000	39.75	39.75
87-02-007	Roger Staubach Ceramic Football Card	C. Soileau	Open	9.95	18.00
87-02-008	Roger Staubach Ceramic Football Card, signed	C. Soileau	1,979	39.00	39.00
90-02-009	Wayne Gretzky Ceramic Hockey Card	M. Taylor	Open	16.00	18.00
91-02-010	Joe Montana CeramicFootball Card	M. Taylor	Open	18.00	18.00
92-02-011	Carlton Fisk Ceramic Baseball Card	M. Taylor	Open	18.00	18.00
92-02-012	Tom Seaver	M. Taylor	Open	18.00	18.00
92-02-013	Gordon Howe	M. Taylor	Open	18.00	18.00
92-02-014	Phil Esposito	M. Taylor	Open	18.00	18.00
Gartlan USA, Inc.		**Magic Johnson Gold Rim Collection**			
88-03-001	Magic Johnson Artist Proof-"Magic in Motion", signed	Roger	250	175.00	1500-2900.
88-03-002	Magic Johnson-"Magic in Motion"	Roger	1,737	125.00	300-600.
88-03-003	Magic Johnson Commemorative	Roger	32	275.00	2800-7200.
Gartlan USA, Inc.		**Mike Schmidt "500th" Home Run Edition**			
87-04-001	Figurine-signed	Roger	1,987	150.00	550-850.
87-04-002	Figurine-signed, Artist Proof	Roger	20	275.00	275-1200.
87-04-003	Plaque-"Only Perfect"-signed	Paluso	500	150.00	175-350.
87-04-004	Plaque-"Only Perfect", Artist Proof	Paluso	20	200.00	200.00
Gartlan USA, Inc.		**Pete Rose Diamond Collection**			
88-05-001	Farewell Ceramic Baseball Card-signed	Forbes	4,256	39.00	50-100.00
88-05-002	Farewell Ceramic Baseball Card	Forbes	Open	9.95	18.00
Gartlan USA, Inc.		**Reggie Jackson "500th" Home Run Edition**			
86-06-001	Ceramic Baseball Card, signed	J. Martin	1,986	39.00	50-75.00
86-06-002	Ceramic Baseball Card	J. Martin	Open	9.95	18.00
Gartlan USA, Inc.		**Kareem Abdul-Jabbar Sky-Hook Collection**			
89-07-001	Kareem Abdul-Jabbar "The Captain"-signed	L. Heyda	1,989	175.00	375-400.
89-07-002	Kareem Abdul-Jabbar, Artist Proof	L. Heyda	100	200.00	325-650.
89-07-003	Kareem Abdul-Jabbar, Commemorative	L. Heyda	33	275.00	300-1000.
Gartlan USA, Inc.		**Signed Figurines**			
85-08-001	Pete Rose-"For the Record", signed	H. Reed	4,192	125.00	950-1100.
89-08-002	Carl Yastrzemski-"Yaz"	L. Heyda	1,989	150.00	250-350.
89-08-003	Carl Yastrzemski-"Yaz" , Artist Proof	L. Heyda	250	150.00	300-400.
89-08-004	Johnny Bench	L. Heyda	1,989	150.00	275-350.
89-08-005	Johnny Bench, Artist Proof	L. Heyda	250	150.00	450.00
89-08-006	Joe DiMaggio	L. Heyda	2,214	275.00	850-1100.
90-08-007	Joe DiMaggio- Pinstripe Yankee Clipper	L. Heyda	325	695.00	1200-1750.
89-08-008	John Wooden-Coaching Classics	L. Heyda	1,975	175.00	175.00
89-08-009	John Wooden-Coaching Classics, Artist Pr.	L. Heyda	250	350.00	350.00
89-08-010	Ted Williams	L. Heyda	2,654	295.00	400-600.
89-08-011	Ted Williams, Artist Proof	L. Heyda	250	650.00	N/A
89-08-012	Wayne Gretzky	L. Heyda	1,851	225.00	500-900.
89-08-013	Wayne Gretzky, Artist Proof	L. Heyda	300	695.00	900-1600.
89-08-014	Yogi Berra	F. Barnum	2,150	225.00	225-250.
89-08-015	Yogi Berra, Artist Proof	F. Barnum	250	350.00	350.00
89-08-016	Steve Carlton	L. Heyda	3,290	175.00	175-350.
89-08-017	Steve Carlton, Artist Proof	L. Heyda	300	350.00	350.00
90-08-018	Whitey Ford	S. Barnum	2,360	225.00	225.00
90-08-019	Whitey Ford, Artist Proof	S. Barnum	250	350.00	350.00
90-08-020	Luis Aparicio	J. Slockbower	1,984	225.00	225.00
90-08-021	Darryl Strawberry	L. Heyda	2,500	225.00	225.00
90-08-022	George Brett	F. Barnum	2,250	225.00	225.00
91-08-023	Ken Griffey, Jr	J. Slockbower	1,989	225.00	225.00
91-08-024	Warren Spahn	J. Slockbower	1,973	225.00	225.00
91-08-025	Rod Carew - Hitting Splendor	J. Slockbower	1,991	225.00	225.00
91-08-026	Brett Hull - The Golden Brett	L. Heyda	1,986	250.00	250.00
92-08-027	Brett Hull, Artist Proof	L. Heyda	300	500.00	500.00
91-08-028	Bobby Hull - The Golden Jet	L. Heyda	1,983	250.00	250.00
92-08-029	Bobby Hull, Artist Proof	L. Heyda	300	500.00	500.00
91-08-030	Hull Matched Figurines	L. Heyda	950	500.00	500.00
91-08-031	Al Barlick	V. Bova	1,989	175.00	175.00
91-08-032	Monte Irvin	V. Bova	1,973	225.00	225.00
91-08-033	Joe Montana	F. Barnum	2,250	325.00	325.00
91-08-034	Joe Montana, Artist Proof	F. Barnum	250	500.00	650-700.
92-08-035	Isiah Thomas	J. Slockbower	1,990	225.00	225.00
92-08-036	Hank Aaron	F. Barnum	1,982	225.00	225.00
92-08-037	Carlton Fisk	J. Slockbower	1,972	225.00	225.00
92-08-038	Carlton Fisk, Artist Proof	J. Slockbower	300	350.00	350.00
92-08-039	Gordie Howe	L. Heyda	2,358	225.00	225.00
92-08-040	Gordie Howe, Artist Proof	L. Heyda	250	500.00	500.00
92-08-041	Phil Esposito	L. Heyda	1, 984	225.00	225.00
92-08-042	Phil Esposito, Artist Proof	L. Heyda	250	500.00	500.00
92-08-043	Hank Aaron Commemorative	F. Barnum	755	295.00	295.00
92-08-044	Hank Aaron, Artist Proof	F. Barnum	300	325.00	325.00
92-08-045	Stan Musial	J. Slockbower	1,969	325.00	325.00
92-08-046	Stan Musial, Artist Proof	J. Slockbower	300	500.00	500.00
92-08-047	Ralph Kiner	J. Slockbower	1,975	225.00	225.00
92-08-048	Tom Seaver	J. Slockbower	1,992	225.00	225.00
Gartlan USA, Inc.		**All-Star Gems Miniature Figurines**			
89-09-001	Carl Yastrzemski	L. Heyda	10,000	75.00	79.00
89-09-002	Johnny Bench	L. Heyda	10,000	75.00	75.00
89-09-003	Ted Williams	L. Heyda	10,000	75.00	79.00
89-09-004	Steve Carlton	L. Heyda	10,000	75.00	79.00
90-09-005	John Wooden	L. Heyda	10,000	75.00	79.00
90-09-006	Wayne Gretzky	L. Heyda	10,000	75.00	79.00
90-09-007	Pete Rose	F. Barnum	10,000	75.00	79.00
90-09-008	Mike Schmidt	Roger	10,000	75.00	79.00
90-09-009	Yogi Berra	F. Barnum	10,000	75.00	79.00
90-09-010	George Brett	F. Barnum	10,000	75.00	79.00
90-09-011	Whitey Ford	F. Barnum	10,000	75.00	79.00
90-09-012	Luis Aparicio	J. Slockbower	10,000	75.00	79.00
90-09-013	Darryl Strawberry	L. Heyda	10,000	75.00	79.00
90-09-014	Kareem Abdul-Jabbar	L. Heyda	10,000	75.00	75.00
91-09-015	Ken Griffey, Jr.	J. Slockbower	10,000	75.00	79.00
91-09-016	Warren Spahn	J. Slockbower	10,000	75.00	79.00
91-09-017	Rod Carew	J. Slockbower	10,000	75.00	79.00
91-09-018	Brett Hull	L. Heyda	10,000	75.00	79.00
91-09-019	Bobby Hull	L. Heyda	10,000	75.00	79.00
91-09-020	Monte Irvin	V. Bova	10,000	75.00	79.00
91-09-021	Joe Montana	F. Barnum	10,000	79.00	79.00
92-09-022	Isiah Thomas	J. Slockbower	10,000	79.00	79.00
92-09-023	Hank Aaron	F. Barnum	10,000	79.00	79.00
92-09-024	Carlton Fisk	J. Slockbower	10,000	79.00	79.00
92-09-025	Phil Esposito	L. Heyda	10,000	79.00	79.00
92-09-026	Stan Musial	J. Slockbower	2, 269	99.00	99.00
92-09-027	Tom Seaver	J. Slockbower	10,000	79.00	79.00
92-09-028	Ralph Kiner	J. Slockbower	10,000	79.00	79.00
92-09-029	Gordie Howe	L. Heyda	10,000	79.00	79.00
Gartlan USA, Inc.		**Members Only Figurine**			
90-10-001	Wayne Gretzky-Home Uniform	L. Heyda	N/A	75.00	200-225.
91-10-002	Joe Montana-Road Uniform	F. Barnum	N/A	75.00	125.00
91-10-003	Kareem Abdul-Jabbar	L. Heyda	N/A	75.00	75.00
92-10-004	Mike Schmidt	J. Slockbower	N/A	79.00	79.00
Gartlan USA, Inc.		**Club Gift**			
89-11-001	Pete Rose, Plate (8 1/2")	B. Forbes	Closed	Gift	100.00
90-11-002	Al Barlick, Plate (8 1/2")	M. Taylor	Closed	Gift	30.00
91-11-003	Joe Montana (8 1/2")	M. Taylor	Closed	Gift	30.00
92-11-004	Ken Griffey Jr., Plate (8 1/2")	M. Taylor	Yr.Iss.	30.00	30.00
Gartlan USA, Inc.		**Master's Museum Collection**			
91-12-001	Kareem Abdul-Jabbar	L. Heyda	500	3000.00	3000-3200.
91-12-002	Wayne Gretzky	L. Heyda	500	set	set
91-12-003	Joe Montana	F. Barnum	500	set	set
91-12-004	Ted Williams	L. Heyda	500	set	set
Gartlan USA, Inc.		**Negro League Series**			
91-13-001	James "Cool Papa" Bell	V. Bova	1,499	195.00	195.00
91-13-002	Ray Dandridge	V. Bova	1,987	195.00	195.00
91-13-003	Buck Leonard	V. Bova	1,972	195.00	195.00
91-13-004	Matched-Number set #1-950	V. Bova	950	500.00	500.00
Goebel Inc.		**Goebel Figurines**			
63-01-001	Little Veterinarian (Mysterious Malady)	N. Rockwell	Closed	15.00	400.00
63-01-002	Boyhood Dreams (Adventurers between Adventures)	N. Rockwell	Closed	12.00	400.00
63-01-003	Mother's Helper (Pride of Parenthood)	N. Rockwell	Closed	15.00	400.00
63-01-004	His First Smoke	N. Rockwell	Closed	9.00	400.00
63-01-005	My New Pal (A Boy Meets His Dog)	N. Rockwell	Closed	12.00	400.00
63-01-006	Home Cure	N. Rockwell	Closed	16.00	400.00
63-01-007	Timely Assistance (Love Aid)	N. Rockwell	Closed	16.00	400.00
63-01-008	She Loves Me (Day Dreamer)	N. Rockwell	Closed	8.00	400.00
63-01-009	Buttercup Test (Beguiling Buttercup)	N. Rockwell	Closed	10.00	400.00
63-01-010	First Love (A Scholarly Pace)	N. Rockwell	Closed	30.00	400.00
63-01-012	Patient Anglers (Fisherman's Paradise)	N. Rockwell	Closed	18.00	400.00
63-01-013	Advertising Plaque	N. Rockwell	Closed	Unkn.	600.00
Goebel Inc.		**Blumenkinder- First Edition**			
66-02-001	Her First Bouquet	Lore	Closed	30.00	Unkn.
66-02-002	A Butterfly's Kiss	Lore	Closed	27.50	Unkn.
66-02-003	St. Valentine's Messenger	Lore	Closed	30.00	Unkn.
66-02-004	Nature's Treasures	Lore	Closed	25.00	Unkn.
66-02-005	Flute Recital	Lore	Closed	25.00	Unkn.
66-02-006	Bearer of Gifts	Lore	Closed	27.50	Unkn.
66-02-007	Apronful of Flowers	Lore	Closed	25.00	Unkn.
66-02-008	The Flower Farmer	Lore	Closed	30.00	Unkn.
66-02-009	Tender Loving Care	Lore	Closed	30.00	Unkn.
66-02-010	Garden Romance	Lore	Closed	50.00	Unkn.
66-02-011	Barefoot Lad	Lore	Closed	27.50	Unkn.
66-02-012	Her Kitten	Lore	Closed	27.50	Unkn.
66-02-013	Display Plaque	Lore	Closed	4.00	Unkn.
Goebel Inc.		**Blumenkinder-Second Edition**			
69-03-001	Summer Magic	Lore	Closed	50.00	Unkn.
69-03-002	Garden Princes	Lore	Closed	50.00	Unkn.
69-03-003	First Journey	Lore	Closed	25.00	Unkn.
69-03-004	First Love	Lore	Closed	25.00	Unkn.
71-03-005	Country Lad	Lore	Closed	35.00	Unkn.
71-03-006	Country Maiden	Lore	Closed	35.00	Unkn.
71-03-007	The Boy Friend	Lore	Closed	65.00	Unkn.
71-03-008	Bird Song	Lore	Closed	65.00	Unkn.
71-03-009	Cello Recital	Lore	Closed	80.00	Unkn.
71-03-010	Courting Country Style	Lore	Closed	80.00	Unkn.
Goebel Inc.		**Blumenkinder-Third Edition**			
72-04-001	Party Guest	Lore	Closed	95.00	Unkn.
72-04-002	First Date	Lore	Closed	95.00	Unkn.
73-04-003	The Patient	Lore	Closed	95.00	Unkn.
73-04-004	The Hitchhiker	Lore	Closed	80.00	Unkn.
73-04-005	The Accompanist	Lore	Closed	95.00	Unkn.
73-04-006	By A Garden Pond	Lore	Closed	75.00	Unkn.
73-04-007	Kittens	Lore	Closed	75.00	Unkn.
73-04-008	Easter Time	Lore	Closed	80.00	Unkn.
Goebel Inc.		**Blumenkinder-Fourth Edition**			
75-05-001	The Lucky One	Lore	Closed	150.00	Unkn.
75-05-002	With Love	Lore	Closed	150.00	Unkn.
75-05-003	Both in Harmony	Lore	Closed	95.00	Unkn.
75-05-004	Happy Minstrel	Lore	Closed	95.00	Unkn.
75-05-005	Springtime	Lore	Closed	95.00	Unkn.
75-05-006	For You-With Love	Lore	Closed	95.00	Unkn.
75-05-007	Companions	Lore	Closed	85.00	Unkn.
75-05-008	Loyal Friend	Lore	Closed	85.00	Unkn.
Goebel Inc.		**Blumenkinder-Fifth Edition**			
79-06-001	Garden Friends	Lore	Closed	175.00	Unkn.
79-06-002	Farmhouse Companions	Lore	Closed	175.00	Unkn.
79-06-003	Harvest Treat	Lore	Closed	149.00	Unkn.

Company		Series			
Number	Name	Artist	Edition Limit	Issue Price	Quote
79-06-004	Sweet Treat	Lore	Closed	149.00	Unkn.
79-06-005	Loving Touch	Lore	Closed	201.00	Unkn.
79-06-006	Birthday Morning	Lore	Closed	201.00	Unkn.
Goebel Inc.		**Blumenkinder-Sixth Edition**			
80-07-001	Flutist	Lore	Closed	175.00	Unkn.
80-07-002	Drummer Boy	Lore	Closed	180.00	Unkn.
80-07-003	Violinist	Lore	Closed	180.00	Unkn.
80-07-004	Spring Song	Lore	Closed	180.00	Unkn.
80-07-005	Dancing Song	Lore	Closed	175.00	Unkn.
80-07-006	Romance	Lore	Closed	175.00	Unkn.
Goebel Inc.		**Blumenkinder-Seventh Edition**			
82-08-001	Happy Sailing	Lore	Closed	150.00	Unkn.
82-08-002	The Spinning Top	Lore	Closed	150.00	Unkn.
82-08-003	Mail Call	Lore	Closed	165.00	Unkn.
82-08-004	Little Mommy	Lore	Closed	165.00	Unkn.
82-08-005	Autumn Delight	Lore	Closed	165.00	Unkn.
82-08-006	Play Bell	Lore	Closed	165.00	Unkn.
Goebel Inc.		**Co-Boy**			
71-09-001	Robby the Vegetarian	G. Skrobek	Closed	16.00	28.00
71-09-002	Mike the Jam Maker	G. Skrobek	Closed	16.00	28.00
71-09-003	Bit the Bachelor	G. Skrobek	Closed	16.00	28-80.00
71-09-004	Tom the Honey Lover	G. Skrobek	Closed	16.00	28.00
71-09-005	Sam the Gourmet	G. Skrobek	Closed	16.00	28.00
71-09-006	Plum the Pastry Chef	G. Skrobek	Closed	16.00	28-60.00
71-09-007	Wim the Court Supplier	G. Skrobek	Closed	16.00	28.00
71-09-008	Fips the Foxy Fisherman	G. Skrobek	Closed	16.00	28.00
71-09-009	Porz the Mushroom Muncher	G. Skrobek	Closed	20.00	28.00
72-09-010	Sepp the Beer Buddy	G. Skrobek	Closed	20.00	28-72.00
72-09-011	Kuni the Big Dipper	G. Skrobek	Closed	20.00	28-50.00
71-09-012	Fritz the Happy Boozer	G. Skrobek	Closed	16.00	42-50.00
72-09-013	Bob the Bookworm	G. Skrobek	Closed	20.00	42-50.00
72-09-014	Brum the Lawyer	G. Skrobek	Closed	20.00	42-72.00
72-09-015	Utz the Banker	G. Skrobek	Closed	20.00	42-50.00
72-09-016	Co-Boy Plaque	G. Skrobek	Closed	20.00	42-50.00
XX-09-017	Jack the Village Pharmacist	G. Skrobek	Closed	Unkn.	42-50.00
XX-09-018	John the Hawkeye Hunter	G. Skrobek	Closed	Unkn.	42-50.00
XX-09-019	Petrl the Village Angler	G. Skrobek	Closed	Unkn.	42-72.00
XX-09-020	Conny the Night Watchman	G. Skrobek	Closed	Unkn.	42-50.00
XX-09-021	Ed the Wine Cellar Steward	G. Skrobek	Closed	Unkn.	42-50.00
XX-09-022	Toni the Skier	G. Skrobek	Closed	Unkn.	42-72.00
XX-09-023	Candy the Baker's Delight	G. Skrobek	Closed	Unkn.	42-50.00
XX-09-024	Mark-Safety First	G. Skrobek	Closed	Unkn.	42-50.00
XX-09-025	Bert the Soccer Star	G. Skrobek	Closed	Unkn.	50.00
XX-09-026	Jim the Bowler	G. Skrobek	Closed	Unkn.	50.00
XX-09-027	Max the Boxing Champ	G. Skrobek	Closed	Unkn.	50.00
78-09-028	Gil the Goalie	G. Skrobek	Closed	34.00	50.00
78-09-029	Pat the Pitcher	G. Skrobek	Closed	34.00	50.00
78-09-030	Tommy Touchdown	G. Skrobek	Closed	34.00	50.00
80-09-031	Ted the Tennis Player	G. Skrobek	Closed	49.00	50.00
80-09-032	Herb the Horseman	G. Skrobek	Closed	49.00	50.00
80-09-033	Monty the Mountain Climber	G. Skrobek	Closed	49.00	50-72.00
80-09-034	Carl the Chef	G. Skrobek	Closed	49.00	72-80.00
80-09-035	Doc the Doctor	G. Skrobek	Closed	49.00	50-72.00
80-09-036	Gerd the Diver	G. Skrobek	Closed	49.00	50.00
81-09-037	George the Gourmand	G. Skrobek	Closed	45.00	50-72.00
81-09-038	Greg the Gourmet	G. Skrobek	Closed	45.00	50.00
81-09-039	Ben the Blacksmith	G. Skrobek	Closed	45.00	50.00
81-09-040	Al the Trumpet Player	G. Skrobek	Closed	45.00	50.00
81-09-041	Peter the Accordionist	G. Skrobek	Closed	45.00	50.00
81-09-042	Niels the Strummer	G. Skrobek	Closed	45.00	50.00
81-09-043	Greta the Happy Housewife	G. Skrobek	Closed	45.00	50.00
81-09-044	Nick the Nightclub Singer	G. Skrobek	Closed	45.00	50.00
81-09-045	Walter the Jogger	G. Skrobek	Closed	45.00	50.00
84-09-046	Rudy the World Traveler	G. Skrobek	Closed	45.00	50-80.00
84-09-047	Sid the Vintner	G. Skrobek	Closed	45.00	50.00
84-09-048	Herman the Butcher	G. Skrobek	Closed	45.00	50.00
84-09-049	Rick the Fireman	G. Skrobek	Closed	45.00	50-80.00
84-09-050	Chuck the Chimney Sweep	G. Skrobek	Closed	45.00	50.00
84-09-051	Chris the Shoemaker	G. Skrobek	Closed	45.00	50.00
84-09-052	Felix the Baker	G. Skrobek	Closed	45.00	50-80.00
84-09-053	Marthe the Nurse	G. Skrobek	Closed	45.00	50.00
84-09-054	Paul the Dentist	G. Skrobek	Closed	45.00	50.00
84-09-055	Homer the Driver	G. Skrobek	Closed	45.00	50-80.00
84-09-056	Brad the Clockmaker	G. Skrobek	Closed	75.00	95.00
87-09-057	Clock-Cony the Watchman	G. Skrobek	Closed	125.00	125.00
87-09-058	Clock-Sepp and the Beer Keg	G. Skrobek	Closed	125.00	125.00
87-09-059	Bank-Pete the Pirate	G. Skrobek	Closed	80.00	80.00
87-09-060	Bank-Utz the Money Bags	G. Skrobek	Closed	80.00	80.00
87-09-061	Chuck on His Pig	G. Skrobek	Closed	75.00	75.00
Goebel Inc.		**Fashions on Parade**			
82-10-001	The Garden Fancier	G. Bochmann	Open	30.00	50.00
82-10-002	The Visitor	G. Bochmann	Open	30.00	50.00
82-10-003	The Cosmopolitan	G. Bochmann	Open	30.00	50.00
82-10-004	At The Tea Dance	G. Bochmann	Open	30.00	50.00
82-10-005	Strolling On The Avenue	G. Bochmann	Open	30.00	50.00
82-10-006	Edwardian Grace	G. Bochmann	Open	30.00	50.00
83-10-007	Gentle Thoughts	G. Bochmann	Open	32.50	50.00
83-10-008	Demure Elegance	G. Bochmann	Open	32.50	50.00
83-10-009	Reflections	G. Bochmann	Open	32.50	50.00
83-10-010	Impatience	G. Bochmann	Closed	32.50	50.00
83-10-011	Waiting For His Love-Groom	G. Bochmann	Open	32.50	50.00
83-10-012	Her Treasured Day-Bride	G. Bochmann	Open	32..50	50.00
83-10-013	Bride and Groom	G. Bochmann	Open	65.00	100.00
84-10-014	On The Fairway	G. Bochmann	Closed	32.50	45.00
84-10-015	Center Court	G. Bochmann	Closed	32.50	45.00
84-10-016	Skimming Gently	G. Bochmann	Closed	32.50	45.00
85-10-017	A Lazy Day	G. Bochmann	Closed	22.50	35.00
85-10-018	A Gentle Moment	G. Bochmann	Closed	22.50	35.00
85-10-019	Afternoon Tea	G. Bochmann	Open	32.50	50.00
85-10-020	River Outing	G. Bochmann	Open	32.50	50.00
85-10-021	To The Hunt	G. Bochmann	Open	32.50	50.00
85-10-022	Gentle Breezes	G. Bochmann	Open	32.50	50.00
86-10-023	Equestrian	G. Bochmann	Open	36.00	50.00
86-10-024	Southern Belle	G. Bochmann	Open	36.00	50.00
86-10-025	Fashions on Parade Plaque	G. Bochmann	Open	10.00	12.50
87-10-026	Say Please	G. Bochmann	Open	55.00	55.00
87-10-027	The Viscountess Diana	G. Bochmann	Open	55.00	55.00
87-10-028	The Shepherdess	G. Bochmann	Open	55.00	55.00
87-10-029	Paris In Fall	G. Bochmann	Open	55.00	55.00

Company		Series			
Number	Name	Artist	Edition Limit	Issue Price	Quote
87-10-030	Promenade in Nice	G. Bochmann	Open	55.00	55.00
87-10-031	Silver Lace and Rhinestones	G. Bochmann	Open	55.00	55.00
88-10-032	The Promise-Groom	G. Bochmann	Open	55.00	55.00
88-10-033	Forever and Always-Bride	G. Bochmann	Open	55.00	55.00
88-10-034	Bride and Groom-2nd Set	G. Bochmann	Open	110.00	110.00
Goebel Inc.		**Betsey Clark Figurines**			
72-11-001	Bless You	G. Bochmann	Closed	18.00	275.00
72-11-002	Friends	G. Bochmann	Closed	21.00	400.00
72-11-003	So Much Beauty	G. Bochmann	Closed	24.50	350.00
72-11-004	Little Miracle	G. Bochmann	Closed	24.50	350.00
Goebel/Schmid		**M.I. Hummel Collectibles Figurines**			
88-02-001	A Budding Maestro 477	M.I. Hummel	Open	Unkn.	90.00
XX-02-002	A Fair Measure 345	M.I. Hummel	Open	Unkn.	230.00
93-02-003	A Free Flight 569	M.I. Hummel	Open	Unkn.	N/A
XX-02-004	A Gentle Glow 439	M.I. Hummel	Open	Unkn.	175.00
91-02-005	A Nap 534	M.I. Hummel	Open	Unkn.	100.00
XX-02-006	Accordion Boy 185	M.I. Hummel	Open	Unkn.	160.00
XX-02-007	Adoration 23/I	M.I. Hummel	Open	Unkn.	300.00
XX-02-008	Adoration 23/III	M.I. Hummel	Open	Unkn.	470.00
XX-02-009	Adventure Bound 347	M.I. Hummel	Open	Unkn.	3300.00
89-02-010	An Apple A Day 403	M.I. Hummel	Open	Unkn.	240.00
XX-02-011	Angel Duet 261	M.I. Hummel	Open	Unkn.	180.00
XX-02-012	Angel Serenade 214/O	M.I. Hummel	Open	Unkn.	70.00
XX-02-013	Angel Serenade with Lamb 83	M.I. Hummel	Open	Unkn.	180.00
XX-02-014	Angel with Accordion 238/B	M.I. Hummel	Open	Unkn.	45.00
XX-02-015	Angel with Lute 238/A	M.I. Hummel	Open	Unkn.	45.00
XX-02-016	Angel With Trumpet 238/C	M.I. Hummel	Open	Unkn.	45.00
XX-02-017	Angelic Song 144	M.I. Hummel	Open	Unkn.	125.00
XX-02-018	Apple Tree Boy 142/3/0	M.I. Hummel	Open	Unkn.	120-200.
XX-02-019	Apple Tree Boy 142/1	M.I. Hummel	Open	Unkn.	225.00
XX-02-020	Apple Tree Boy 142/V	M.I. Hummel	Open	Unkn.	1000.00
XX-02-021	Apple Tree Girl 141/3/0	M.I. Hummel	Open	Unkn.	120-170.
XX-02-022	Apple Tree Girl 141/1	M.I. Hummel	Open	Unkn.	225.00
XX-02-023	Apple Tree Girl 141/V	M.I. Hummel	Open	Unkn.	600-1000.
91-02-024	Art Critic 318	M.I. Hummel	Open	Unkn.	240.00
XX-02-025	Artist 304	M.I. Hummel	Open	Unkn.	200.00
XX-02-026	Auf Wiedersehen 153/0	M.I. Hummel	Open	Unkn.	200.00
XX-02-027	Auf Wiedersehen 153/1	M.I. Hummel	Open	Unkn.	250.00
XX-02-028	Autumn Harvest 355	M.I. Hummel	Open	Unkn.	180.00
XX-02-029	Baker 128	M.I. Hummel	Open	Unkn.	160.00
XX-02-030	Baking Day 330	M.I. Hummel	Open	Unkn.	220.00
XX-02-031	Band Leader 129	M.I. Hummel	Open	Unkn.	170.00
XX-02-032	Band Leader 129/4/0	M.I. Hummel	Open	Unkn.	80.00
XX-02-033	Barnyard Hero 195/2/0	M.I. Hummel	Open	Unkn.	140-400.
XX-02-034	Barnyard Hero 195/1	M.I. Hummel	Open	Unkn.	265.00
XX-02-035	Bashful 377	M.I. Hummel	Open	Unkn.	170.00
90-02-036	Bath Time 412	M.I. Hummel	Open	Unkn.	350.00
XX-02-037	Begging His Share 9	M.I. Hummel	Open	Unkn.	200.00
XX-02-038	Be Patient 197/2/0	M.I. Hummel	Open	Unkn.	160.00
XX-02-039	Be Patient 197/I	M.I. Hummel	Open	Unkn.	230.00
XX-02-040	Big Housecleaning 363	M.I. Hummel	Open	Unkn.	230.00
XX-02-041	Bird Duet 169	M.I. Hummel	Open	Unkn.	120.00
XX-02-042	Bird Watcher 300	M.I. Hummel	Open	Unkn.	190.00
89-02-043	Birthday Cake 338	M.I. Hummel	Open	Unkn.	120.00
XX-02-044	Birthday Serenade 218/2/0	M.I. Hummel	Open	Unkn.	150.00
XX-02-045	Birthday Serenade 218/0	M.I. Hummel	Open	Unkn.	200-250.
XX-02-046	Blessed Event 333	M.I. Hummel	Open	Unkn.	280.00
XX-02-047	Bookworm 8	M.I. Hummel	Open	Unkn.	180.00
XK-02-048	Bookworm 3/I	M.I. Hummel	Open	Unkn.	250.00
XX-02-049	Boots 143/0	M.I. Hummel	Open	Unkn.	160.00
XX-02-050	Boots 143/1	M.I. Hummel	Open	Unkn.	270.00
XX-02-051	Botanist 351	M.I. Hummel	Open	Unkn.	185.00
XX-02-052	Boy with Accordion 390	M.I. Hummel	Open	Unkn.	70.00
XX-02-053	Boy with Horse 239C	M.I. Hummel	Open	Unkn.	45.00
XX-02-054	Boy with Toothache 217	M.I. Hummel	Open	Unkn.	145-185.
XX-02-055	Brother 95	M.I. Hummel	Open	Unkn.	165.00
XX-02-056	Builder 305	M.I. Hummel	Open	Unkn.	200.00
XX-02-057	Busy Student 367	M.I. Hummel	Open	Unkn.	140.00
XX-02-058	Carnival 328	M.I. Hummel	Open	Unkn.	190.00
XX-02-059	Celestial Musician 188/0	M.I. Hummel	Open	Unkn.	180.00
XX-02-060	Celestial Musician 188/I	M.I. Hummel	Open	Unkn.	230.00
93-02-061	Celestial Musician (mini) 188/4/0	M.I. Hummel	Open	Unkn.	N/A
XX-02-062	Chick Girl 57/2/0	M.I. Hummel	Open	Unkn.	125.00
XX-02-063	Chick Girl 57/0	M.I. Hummel	Open	Unkn.	145.00
XX-02-064	Chick Girl 57/I	M.I. Hummel	Open	Unkn.	220.00
XX-02-065	Chicken-Licken 385	M.I. Hummel	Open	Unkn.	240.00
XX-02-066	Chicken-Licken 385/4	M.I. Hummel	Open	Unkn.	85.00
XX-02-067	Chimney Sweep 12/2/0	M.I. Hummel	Open	Unkn.	110.00
XX-02-068	Chimney Sweep 12/I	M.I. Hummel	Open	Unkn.	180.00
89-02-069	Christmas Angel 301	M.I. Hummel	Open	Unkn.	210.00
XX-02-070	Christmas Song 343	M.I. Hummel	Open	Unkn.	180.00
XX-02-071	Cinderella 337	M.I. Hummel	Open	Unkn.	240.00
XX-02-072	Close Harmony 336	M.I. Hummel	Open	Unkn.	240.00
XX-02-073	Confidentially 314	M.I. Hummel	Open	Unkn.	230.00
XX-02-074	Congratulations 17/0	M.I. Hummel	Open	Unkn.	160.00
XX-02-075	Coquettes 179	M.I. Hummel	Open	Unkn.	230.00
XX-02-076	Crossroads (Original) 331	M.I. Hummel	Open	Unkn.	350.00
XX-02-077	Crossroads (Commemorative) 331	M.I. Hummel	10,000	Unkn.	900-2000.
XX-02-078	Culprits 56/A	M.I. Hummel	Open	Unkn.	245.00
89-02-079	Daddy's Girls 371	M.I. Hummel	Open	Unkn.	200.00
XX-02-080	Doctor 127	M.I. Hummel	Open	Unkn.	135.00
XX-02-081	Doll Bath 319	M.I. Hummel	Open	Unkn.	230.00
XX-02-082	Doll Mother 67	M.I. Hummel	Open	Unkn.	190.00
XX-02-083	Duet 130	M.I. Hummel	Open	Unkn.	225.00
XX-02-084	Easter Greetings 378	M.I. Hummel	Open	Unkn.	185.00
XX-02-085	Easter Time 384	M.I. Hummel	Open	Unkn.	225.00
92-02-086	Evening Prayer 495	M.I. Hummel	Open	Unkn.	95.00
XX-02-087	Eventide 99	M.I. Hummel	Open	Unkn.	290.00
XX-02-088	Farewell 65	M.I. Hummel	Open	Unkn.	220.00
XX-02-089	Farm Boy 66	M.I. Hummel	Open	Unkn.	190.00
XX-02-090	Favorite Pet 361	M.I. Hummel	Open	Unkn.	230.00
XX-02-091	Feathered Friends 344	M.I. Hummel	Open	Unkn.	220.00
XX-02-092	Feeding Time 199/0	M.I. Hummel	Open	Unkn.	160.00
XX-02-093	Feeding Time 199/I	M.I. Hummel	Open	Unkn.	220.00
XX-02-094	Festival Harmony, with Mandolin 172/0	M.I. Hummel	Open	Unkn.	260.00
XX-02-095	Festival Harmony, with Flute 173/0	M.I. Hummel	Open	Unkn.	260.00
XX-02-096	Flower Vendor 381	M.I. Hummel	Open	Unkn.	200.00
XX-02-097	Follow the Leader 369	M.I. Hummel	Open	Unkn.	1000.00
XX-02-098	For Father 87	M.I. Hummel	Open	Unkn.	135-550.
XX-02-099	For Mother 257/2/0	M.I. Hummel	Open	Unkn.	105.00
XX-02-100	For Mother 257	M.I. Hummel	Open	Unkn.	170.00

Company Number	Name	Series Artist	Edition Limit	Issue Price	Quote
XX-02-101	Forest Shrine 183	M.I. Hummel	Open	Unkn.	345-460.00
91-02-102	Friend Or Foe 434	M.I. Hummel	Open	Unkn.	195.00
XX-02-103	Friends 136/I	M.I. Hummel	Open	Unkn.	180.00
XX-02-104	Friends 136/V	M.I. Hummel	Open	Unkn.	1000.00
XX-02-105	Gay Adventure 356	M.I. Hummel	Open	Unkn.	160.00
XX-02-106	Girl with Doll 239/B	M.I. Hummel	Open	Unkn.	45.00
XX-02-107	Girl with Nosegay 239/A	M.I. Hummel	Open	Unkn.	45.00
XX-02-108	Girl with Sheet Music 389	M.I. Hummel	Open	Unkn.	70.00
XX-02-109	Girl with Trumpet 391	M.I. Hummel	Open	Unkn.	70.00
XX-02-110	Going Home 383	M.I. Hummel	Open	Unkn.	260.00
XX-02-111	Going to Grandma's 52/0	M.I. Hummel	Open	Unkn.	230.00
XX-02-112	Good Friends 182	M.I. Hummel	Open	Unkn.	160.00
XX-02-113	Good Hunting 307	M.I. Hummel	Open	Unkn.	200-400.
XX-02-114	Good Night 214/C	M.I. Hummel	Open	Unkn.	70.00
XX-02-115	Good Shepherd 42/0	M.I. Hummel	Open	Unkn.	200.00
XX-02-116	Goose Girl 47/3/0	M.I. Hummel	Open	Unkn.	145-600.
XX-02-117	Goose Girl 47/0	M.I. Hummel	Open	Unkn.	185.00
XX-02-118	Goose Girl 47/II	M.I. Hummel	Open	Unkn.	380.00
XX-02-119	Grandma's Girl 561	M.I. Hummel	Open	Unkn.	125.00
XX-02-120	Grandpa's Boy 562	M.I. Hummel	Open	Unkn.	125.00
XX-02-121	Guiding Angel 357	M.I. Hummel	Open	Unkn.	70.00
XX-02-122	Happiness 86	M.I. Hummel	Open	Unkn.	110.00
XX-02-123	Happy Birthday 176/0	M.I. Hummel	Open	Unkn.	180.00
XX-02-124	Happy Birthday 176/I	M.I. Hummel	Open	Unkn.	250.00
XX-02-125	Happy Days 150/2/0	M.I. Hummel	Open	Unkn.	150.00
XX-02-126	Happy Days 150/0	M.I. Hummel	Open	Unkn.	250.00
XX-02-127	Happy Days 150/I	M.I. Hummel	Open	Unkn.	400.00
XX-02-128	Happy Pastime 69	M.I. Hummel	Open	Unkn.	135.00
XX-02-129	Happy Traveler 109/0	M.I. Hummel	Open	Unkn.	120.00
XX-02-130	Hear Ye! Hear Ye! 15/0	M.I. Hummel	Open	Unkn.	170.00
XX-02-131	Hear Ye! Hear Ye! 15/I	M.I. Hummel	Open	Unkn.	200.00
XX-02-132	Hear Ye! Hear Ye! 15/II	M.I. Hummel	Open	Unkn.	400.00
XX-02-133	Hear Ye! Hear Ye! 15/2/0	M.I. Hummel	Open	Unkn.	125.00
XX-02-134	Heavenly Angel 21/0	M.I. Hummel	Open	Unkn.	100.00
XX-02-135	Heavenly Angel 21/0 1/2	M.I. Hummel	Open	Unkn.	170.00
XX-02-136	Heavenly Angel 21/I	M.I. Hummel	Open	Unkn.	200.00
XX-02-137	Heavenly Angel 21/II	M.I. Hummel	Open	Unkn.	390.00
XX-02-138	Heavenly Lullaby 262	M.I. Hummel	Open	Unkn.	155.00
XX-02-139	Heavenly Protection 88/1	M.I. Hummel	Open	Unkn.	370.00
XX-02-140	Heavenly Protection 88/11	M.I. Hummel	Open	Unkn.	590.00
XX-02-141	Hello 124/0	M.I. Hummel	Open	Unkn.	180.00
XX-02-142	Home from Market 198/2/0	M.I. Hummel	Open	Unkn.	450.00
XX-02-143	Home from Market 198/I	M.I. Hummel	Open	Unkn.	300-450.
XX-02-144	Homeward Bound 334	M.I. Hummel	Open	Unkn.	295.00
90-02-145	Horse Trainer 423	M.I. Hummel	Open	Unkn.	185.00
89-02-146	Hosanna 480	M.I. Hummel	Open	Unkn.	80.00
89-02-147	I'll Protect Him 483	M.I. Hummel	Open	Unkn.	70.00
89-02-148	I'm Here 478	M.I. Hummel	Open	Unkn.	85.00
89-02-149	In D Major 430	M.I. Hummel	Open	Unkn.	170.00
XX-02-150	In The Meadow 459	M.I. Hummel	Open	Unkn.	170.00
XX-02-151	In Tune 414	M.I. Hummel	Open	Unkn.	230.00
XX-02-152	Is It Raining? 420	M.I. Hummel	Open	Unkn.	225.00
XX-02-153	Joyful 53	M.I. Hummel	Open	Unkn.	100.00
XX-02-154	Joyous News 27/III	M.I. Hummel	Open	Unkn.	180.00
XX-02-155	Just Resting 112/3/0	M.I. Hummel	Open	Unkn.	125.00
XX-02-156	Just Resting 112/I	M.I. Hummel	Open	Unkn.	225.00
XX-02-157	Kindergartner 467	M.I. Hummel	Open	Unkn.	170.00
XX-02-158	Kiss Me 311	M.I. Hummel	Open	Unkn.	230.00
XX-02-159	Knitting Lesson 256	M.I. Hummel	Open	Unkn.	440.00
XX-02-160	Knit One, Purl One 432	M.I. Hummel	Open	Unkn.	105.00
92-02-161	Land in Sight 530	M.I. Hummel	30,000	Unkn.	1600.00
XX-02-162	Latest News 184/0	M.I. Hummel	Open	Unkn.	240-650.
XX-02-163	Let's Sing 110/0	M.I. Hummel	Open	Unkn.	105.00
XX-02-164	Let's Sing 110/I	M.I. Hummel	Open	Unkn.	140.00
XX-02-165	Letter to Santa Claus 340	M.I. Hummel	Open	Unkn.	285.00
93-02-166	Little Architect 410/I	M.I. Hummel	Open	Unkn.	N/A
XX-02-167	Little Bookkeeper 306	M.I. Hummel	Open	Unkn.	240.00
XX-02-168	Little Cellist 89/I	M.I. Hummel	Open	Unkn.	180.00
XX-02-169	Little Cellist 89/II	M.I. Hummel	Open	Unkn.	380.00
XX-02-170	Little Drummer 240	M.I. Hummel	Open	Unkn.	125.00
XX-02-171	Little Fiddler 2/4/0	M.I. Hummel	Open	Unkn.	80.00
XX-02-172	Little Fiddler 4	M.I. Hummel	Open	Unkn.	170.00
XX-02-173	Little Fiddler 2/0	M.I. Hummel	Open	Unkn.	190.00
XX-02-174	Little Fiddler 2/I	M.I. Hummel	Open	Unkn.	370.00
XX-02-175	Little Gabriel 32	M.I. Hummel	Open	Unkn.	115.00
XX-02-176	Little Gardener 74	M.I. Hummel	Open	Unkn.	100.00
XX-02-177	Little Goat Herder 200/0	M.I. Hummel	Open	Unkn.	160.00
XX-02-178	Little Goat Herder 200/I	M.I. Hummel	Open	Unkn.	200.00
XX-02-179	Little Guardian 145	M.I. Hummel	Open	Unkn.	125.00
XX-02-180	Little Helper 73	M.I. Hummel	Open	Unkn.	100.00
XX-02-181	Little Hiker 16/2/0	M.I. Hummel	Open	Unkn.	100.00
XX-02-182	Little Hiker 16/I	M.I. Hummel	Open	Unkn.	180.00
XX-02-183	Little Nurse 376	M.I. Hummel	Open	Unkn.	210.00
XX-02-184	Little Pharmacist 322	M.I. Hummel	Open	Unkn.	200.00
XX-02-185	Little Scholar 80	M.I. Hummel	Open	Unkn.	180-220.
XX-02-186	Little Shopper 96	M.I. Hummel	Open	Unkn.	120.00
XX-02-187	Little Sweeper 171/4/0	M.I. Hummel	Open	Unkn.	80.00
88-02-188	Little Sweeper 171	M.I. Hummel	Open	Unkn.	110.00
XX-02-189	Little Tailor 308	M.I. Hummel	Open	Unkn.	200.00
XX-02-190	Little Thrifty 118	M.I. Hummel	Open	Unkn.	130.00
XX-02-191	Little Tooter 214/H	M.I. Hummel	Open	Unkn.	90.00
XX-02-192	Little Tooter 214/H	M.I. Hummel	Open	Unkn.	100.00
XX-02-193	Lost Sheep 68/2/0	M.I. Hummel	Open	Unkn.	125.00
XX-02-194	Lost Sheep 68/0	M.I. Hummel	Open	Unkn.	180.00
XX-02-195	Lost Stocking 374	M.I. Hummel	Open	Unkn.	120.00
XX-02-196	Mail is Here 226	M.I. Hummel	Open	Unkn.	470.00
89-02-197	Make A Wish 475	M.I. Hummel	Open	Unkn.	160.00
XX-02-198	March Winds 43	M.I. Hummel	Open	Unkn.	135.00
XX-02-199	Max and Moritz 123	M.I. Hummel	Open	Unkn.	190.00
XX-02-200	Meditation 13/2/0	M.I. Hummel	Open	Unkn.	120.00
XX-02-201	Meditation 13/0	M.I. Hummel	Open	Unkn.	190.00
XX-02-202	Merry Wanderer 11/2/0	M.I. Hummel	Open	Unkn.	115-200.
XX-02-203	Merry Wanderer 11/0	M.I. Hummel	Open	Unkn.	160.00
XX-02-204	Merry Wanderer 7/0	M.I. Hummel	Open	Unkn.	220.00
XX-02-205	Merry Wanderer 7/I	M.I. Hummel	Open	Unkn.	350.00
XX-02-206	Merry Wanderer 7/II	M.I. Hummel	Open	Unkn.	900.00
XX-02-207	Mischief Maker 342	M.I. Hummel	Open	Unkn.	220.00
XX-02-208	Mother's Darling 175	M.I. Hummel	Open	Unkn.	180.00
XX-02-209	Mother's Helper 133	M.I. Hummel	Open	Unkn.	160.00
XX-02-210	Mountaineer 315	M.I. Hummel	Open	Unkn.	180.00
XX-02-211	Not For You 317	M.I. Hummel	Open	Unkn.	200.00
89-02-212	One For You, One For Me 482	M.I. Hummel	Open	Unkn.	85.00
93-02-213	One Plus One 556	M.I. Hummel	Open	Unkn.	N/A

Company Number	Name	Series Artist	Edition Limit	Issue Price	Quote
XX-02-214	On Holiday 350	M.I. Hummel	Open	Unkn.	145.00
XX-02-215	On Secret Path 386	M.I. Hummel	Open	Unkn.	210.00
XX-02-216	Out of Danger 56/B	M.I. Hummel	Open	Unkn.	245.00
93-02-217	Parade Of Lights 616	M.I. Hummel	Open	Unkn.	N/A
XX-02-218	Photographer 178	M.I. Hummel	Open	Unkn.	230.00
XX-02-219	Playmates 58/2/0	M.I. Hummel	Open	Unkn.	125.00
XX-02-220	Playmates 58/0	M.I. Hummel	Open	Unkn.	145.00
XX-02-221	Playmates 58/I	M.I. Hummel	Open	Unkn.	220.00
XX-02-222	Postman 119	M.I. Hummel	Open	Unkn.	115-135.
89-02-223	Postman 119/2/0	M.I. Hummel	Open	Unkn.	170.00
XX-02-224	Prayer Before Battle 20	M.I. Hummel	Open	Unkn.	145.00
XX-02-225	Retreat to Safety 201/2/0	M.I. Hummel	Open	Unkn.	140.00
XX-02-226	Retreat to Safety 201/1	M.I. Hummel	Open	Unkn.	250.00
XX-02-227	Ride into Christmas 396/2/0	M.I. Hummel	Open	Unkn.	200.00
XX-02-228	Ride into Christmas 396/I	M.I. Hummel	Open	Unkn.	360.00
XX-02-229	Ring Around the Rosie 348	M.I. Hummel	Open	Unkn.	2300.00
XX-02-230	Run-A-Way 327	M.I. Hummel	Open	Unkn.	210.00
XX-02-231	St. George 55	M.I. Hummel	Open	Unkn.	280.00
92-02-232	Scamp 553	M.I. Hummel	Open	Unkn.	95.00
XX-02-233	School Boy 82/2/0	M.I. Hummel	Open	Unkn.	120.00
XX-02-234	School Boy 82/0	M.I. Hummel	Open	Unkn.	160.00
XX-02-235	School Boy 82/II	M.I. Hummel	Open	Unkn.	380.00
XX-02-236	School Boys 170/I	M.I. Hummel	Open	Unkn.	1000.00
XX-02-237	School Girl 81/2/0	M.I. Hummel	Open	Unkn.	120.00
XX-02-238	School Girl 81/0	M.I. Hummel	Open	Unkn.	160-175.
XX-02-239	School Girls 177/I	M.I. Hummel	Open	Unkn.	1000.00
XX-02-240	Sensitive Hunter 6/0	M.I. Hummel	Open	Unkn.	160.00
XX-02-241	Sensitive Hunter 6/I	M.I. Hummel	Open	Unkn.	210.00
XX-02-242	Sensitive Hunter 6/2/0	M.I. Hummel	Open	Unkn.	125.00
XX-02-243	Serenade 85/0	M.I. Hummel	Open	Unkn.	110.00
XX-02-244	Serenade 85/4/0	M.I. Hummel	Open	Unkn.	80.00
XX-02-245	Shepherd's Boy 64	M.I. Hummel	Open	Unkn.	185.00
XX-02-246	She Loves Me, She Loves Me Not 174	M.I. Hummel	Open	Unkn.	150.00
XX-02-247	Shining Light 358	M.I. Hummel	Open	Unkn.	70.00
XX-02-248	Sing Along 433	M.I. Hummel	Open	Unkn.	240.00
XX-02-249	Singing Lesson 63	M.I. Hummel	Open	Unkn.	100.00
XX-02-250	Sing With Me 405	M.I. Hummel	Open	Unkn.	260.00
XX-02-251	Sister 98/2/0	M.I. Hummel	Open	Unkn.	120.00
XX-02-252	Sister 98/0	M.I. Hummel	Open	Unkn.	165.00
XX-02-253	Skier 59	M.I. Hummel	Open	Unkn.	185.00
90-02-254	Sleep Tight 424	M.I. Hummel	Open	Unkn.	185.00
XX-02-255	Smart Little Sister 346	M.I. Hummel	Open	Unkn.	210.00
XX-02-256	Soldier Boy 332	M.I. Hummel	Open	Unkn.	180.00
XX-02-257	Soloist 135/4/0	M.I. Hummel	Open	Unkn.	80.00
XX-02-258	Soloist 135	M.I. Hummel	Open	Unkn.	110.00
88-02-259	Song of Praise 454	M.I. Hummel	Open	Unkn.	80.00
88-02-260	Sound the Trumpet 457	M.I. Hummel	Open	Unkn.	80.00
88-02-261	Sounds of the Mandolin 438	M.I. Hummel	Open	Unkn.	100.00
XX-02-262	Spring Dance 353/0	M.I. Hummel	Open	Unkn.	255.00
XX-02-263	Star Gazer 132	M.I. Hummel	Open	Unkn.	180.00
XX-02-264	Stitch in Time 255	M.I. Hummel	Open	Unkn.	230.00
XX-02-265	Stitch in Time 255	M.I. Hummel	Open	Unkn.	80.00
XX-02-266	Stormy Weather 71/I	M.I. Hummel	Open	Unkn.	400.00
XX-02-267	Stormy Weather 71/2/0	M.I. Hummel	Open	Unkn.	250.00
92-02-268	Storybook Time 458	M.I. Hummel	Open	Unkn.	330.00
XX-02-269	Street Singer 131	M.I. Hummel	Open	Unkn.	155.00
XX-02-270	Surprise 94/3/0	M.I. Hummel	Open	Unkn.	130.00
XX-02-271	Surprise 94/I	M.I. Hummel	Open	Unkn.	235.00
XX-02-272	Sweet Greetings 352	M.I. Hummel	Open	Unkn.	185.00
XX-02-273	Sweet Music 186	M.I. Hummel	Open	Unkn.	160.00
XX-02-274	Telling Her Secret 196/0	M.I. Hummel	Open	Unkn.	250.00
88-02-275	The Accompanist 453	M.I. Hummel	Open	Unkn.	80.00
91-02-276	The Guardian 455	M.I. Hummel	Open	Unkn.	145.00
92-02-277	The Professor 320/0	M.I. Hummel	Open	Unkn.	180.00
XX-02-278	Thoughtful 415	M.I. Hummel	Open	Unkn.	190.00
XX-02-279	Timid Little Sister 394	M.I. Hummel	Open	Unkn.	360.00
XX-02-280	To Market 49/3/0	M.I. Hummel	Open	Unkn.	140.00
XX-02-281	To Market 49/0	M.I. Hummel	Open	Unkn.	225.00
XX-02-282	Trumpet Boy 97	M.I. Hummel	Open	Unkn.	110.00
89-02-283	Tuba Player 437	M.I. Hummel	Open	Unkn.	225.00
XX-02-284	Tuneful Angel 359	M.I. Hummel	Open	Unkn.	70.00
XX-02-285	Umbrella Boy 152/0/A	M.I. Hummel	Open	Unkn.	490.00
XX-02-286	Umbrella Boy 152/II/A	M.I. Hummel	Open	Unkn.	1200.00
XX-02-287	Umbrella Girl 152/0/B	M.I. Hummel	Open	Unkn.	490.00
XX-02-288	Umbrella Girl 152/II/B	M.I. Hummel	Open	Unkn.	1200.00
XX-02-289	Village Boy 51/3/0	M.I. Hummel	Open	Unkn.	100.00
XX-02-290	Village Boy 51/2/0	M.I. Hummel	Open	Unkn.	115.00
XX-02-291	Village Boy 51/0	M.I. Hummel	Open	Unkn.	195.00
XX-02-292	Visiting an Invalid 382	M.I. Hummel	Open	Unkn.	185.00
XX-02-293	Volunteers 50/2/0	M.I. Hummel	Open	Unkn.	190.00
XX-02-294	Volunteers 50/0	M.I. Hummel	Open	Unkn.	250.00
XX-02-295	Waiter 154/0	M.I. Hummel	Open	Unkn.	180.00
XX-02-296	Waiter 154/I	M.I. Hummel	Open	Unkn.	240.00
XX-02-297	Wash Day 321	M.I. Hummel	Open	Unkn.	230.00
89-02-298	Wash Day 321/4/0	M.I. Hummel	Open	Unkn.	80.00
XX-02-299	Watchful Angel 194	M.I. Hummel	Open	Unkn.	270.00
XX-02-300	Wayside Devotion 28/II	M.I. Hummel	Open	Unkn.	370.00
XX-02-301	Wayside Devotion 28/III	M.I. Hummel	Open	Unkn.	480.00
XX-02-302	Wayside Harmony 111/3/0	M.I. Hummel	Open	Unkn.	125.00
XX-02-303	Wayside Harmony 111/I	M.I. Hummel	Open	Unkn.	220.00
XX-02-304	Weary Wanderer 204	M.I. Hummel	Open	Unkn.	200.00
XX-02-305	We Congratulate 214/E/11	M.I. Hummel	Open	Unkn.	140.00
XX-02-306	We Congratulate 220	M.I. Hummel	Open	Unkn.	135.00
90-02-307	What's New 418	M.I. Hummel	Open	Unkn.	240.00
XX-02-308	Which Hand? 258	M.I. Hummel	Open	Unkn.	165.00
92-02-309	Whistler's Duet 413	M.I. Hummel	Open	Unkn.	235.00
XX-02-310	Whitsuntide 163	M.I. Hummel	Open	Unkn.	270.00
88-02-311	Winter Song 476	M.I. Hummel	Open	Unkn.	95.00
XX-02-312	With Loving Greetings 309	M.I. Hummel	Open	Unkn.	160.00
XX-02-313	Worship 84/0	M.I. Hummel	Open	Unkn.	135.00
Goebel/Schmid		**M.I. Hummel's Temp. Out of Production**			
XX-03-001	Apple Tree Boy 142/X	M.I. Hummel	Suspd.	Unkn.	17000.00
XX-03-002	Apple Tree Girl 141/X	M.I. Hummel	Suspd.	Unkn.	17000.00
XX-03-003	Blessed Child 78/1/11	M.I. Hummel	Suspd.	Unkn.	35.00
XX-03-004	Blessed Child 78/11/11	M.I. Hummel	Suspd.	Unkn.	40.00
XX-03-005	Blessed Child 78/111/11	M.I. Hummel	Suspd.	Unkn.	50.00
XX-03-006	Bookworm 3/11	M.I. Hummel	Suspd.	Unkn.	900-1200.
XX-03-007	Bookworm 3/111	M.I. Hummel	Suspd.	Unkn.	975-1300.
XX-02-008	Christ Child 18	M.I. Hummel	Suspd.	Unkn.	120-300.
XX-03-009	Festival Harmony, with Mandolin 172/11	M.I. Hummel	Suspd.	Unkn.	325-400.
XX-03-010	Festival Harmony, with Flute 173/11	M.I. Hummel	Suspd.	Unkn.	325-400.
XX-03-011	Flower Madonna, color 10/111/11	M.I. Hummel	Suspd.	Unkn.	375-475.

Number	Name	Artist	Edition Limit	Issue Price	Quote
XX-03-012	Flower Madonna, white 10/111/W	M.I. Hummel	Suspd.	Unkn.	250-310.
XX-03-013	Going to Grandma's 52/1	M.I. Hummel	Suspd.	Unkn.	325-390.
XX-03-014	Good Night 260D	M.I. Hummel	Suspd.	Unkn.	120.00
XX-03-015	Happy Traveler 109/11	M.I. Hummel	Suspd.	Unkn.	350-750.
XX-03-016	Hello 124/1	M.I. Hummel	Suspd.	Unkn.	160-230.
XX-03-017	Holy Child 70	M.I. Hummel	Suspd.	Unkn.	135-160.
XX-03-018	"Hummel" Display Plaque 187	M.I. Hummel	Suspd.	Unkn.	150-200.
XX-03-019	Little Band 392	M.I. Hummel	Suspd.	Unkn.	132-225.
XX-03-020	Little Fiddler 2/11	M.I. Hummel	Suspd.	Unkn.	900-1200.
XX-03-021	Little Fiddler 2/111	M.I. Hummel	Suspd.	Unkn.	975-1300.
XX-03-022	Lullaby 24/111	M.I. Hummel	Suspd.	Unkn.	285-450.
XX-03-023	Madonna Holding Child, color 151	M.I. Hummel	Suspd.	Unkn.	700-825.
XX-03-024	Madonna Holding Child, color 151/II	M.I. Hummel	Suspd.	Unkn.	N/A
XX-03-025	Madonna with Halo, color 45/0/6	M.I. Hummel	Suspd.	Unkn.	65.00
XX-03-026	Madonna with Halo, 45/111/W	M.I. Hummel	Suspd.	Unkn.	110.00
XX-03-027	Madonna with Halo, 45/111/6	M.I. Hummel	Suspd.	Unkn.	155.00
XX-03-028	Madonna Praying, color 46/0/6	M.I. Hummel	Suspd.	Unkn.	65.00
XX-03-029	Madonna Praying, color 46/111/6	M.I. Hummel	Suspd.	Unkn.	155.00
XX-03-030	Madonna Praying, white 46/0/W	M.I. Hummel	Suspd.	Unkn.	45.00
XX-03-031	Madonna Praying, white 46/1/W	M.I. Hummel	Suspd.	Unkn.	75-95.00
XX-03-032	Meditation 13/11	M.I. Hummel	Suspd.	Unkn.	275-360.
XX-03-033	Meditation 13V	M.I. Hummel	Suspd.	Unkn.	975-1250.
XX-03-034	Merry Wanderer 7/III	M.I. Hummel	Suspd.	Unkn.	975-1200.
XX-03-035	Merry Wanderer 7/X	M.I. Hummel	Suspd.	Unkn.	17000.00
XX-03-036	School Boys 170/111	M.I. Hummel	Suspd.	Unkn.	1850-5000.
XX-03-037	School Girls 177/111	M.I. Hummel	Suspd.	Unkn.	1850-5000.
XX-03-038	Sensitive Hunter 6/11	M.I. Hummel	Suspd.	Unkn.	300-400.
XX-03-039	Spring Cheer 72	M.I. Hummel	Suspd.	Unkn.	150-200.
XX-03-040	Spring Dance 353/1	M.I. Hummel	Suspd.	Unkn.	265-500.
XX-03-041	Telling Her Secret 196/1	M.I. Hummel	Suspd.	Unkn.	240-375.
XX-03-042	To Market 49/1	M.I. Hummel	Suspd.	Unkn.	240-420.
XX-03-043	Volunteers 50/1	M.I. Hummel	Suspd.	Unkn.	240-425.
XX-03-044	Village Boy 51/1	M.I. Hummel	Suspd.	Unkn.	110-250.
XX-03-045	Worship 84V	M.I. Hummel	Suspd.	Unkn.	925-1050.

Goebel/Schmid — **M.I. Hummel Collectibles Figurines Retired**

Number	Name	Artist	Edition Limit	Issue Price	Quote
XX-04-001	Jubilee 416	M.I. Hummel	Closed	200.00	200-450.
XX-04-002	Supreme Protection 364	M.I. Hummel	Closed	150.00	150-400.
XX-04-003	Puppy Love 1	M.I. Hummel	Closed	125.00	300-750.
XX-04-004	Strolling Along 5	M.I. Hummel	Closed	115.00	225-625.
XX-04-005	Signs Of Spring 203/2/0	M.I. Hummel	Closed	120.00	150-400.
XX-04-006	Signs Of Spring 203/1	M.I. Hummel	Closed	155.00	200-450.
XX-02-007	Globe Trotter 79	M.I. Hummel	Closed	Unkn.	180.00

Goebel/Schmid — **M.I. Hummel Collectibles-Century Collection**

Number	Name	Artist	Edition Limit	Issue Price	Quote
86-05-001	Chapel Time 442	M.I. Hummel	Yr.Iss.	500.00	1350-2000.
87-05-002	Pleasant Journey 406	M.I. Hummel	Yr.Iss.	500.00	1100-2000.
88-05-003	Call to Worship 441	M.I. Hummel	Yr.Iss.	600.00	650-900.
89-05-004	Harmony in Four Parts 471	M.I. Hummel	Yr.Iss.	850.00	900-1250.
90-05-005	Let's Tell the World 487	M.I. Hummel	Yr.Iss.	875.00	900-1250.
91-05-006	We Wish You The Best 600	M.I. Hummel	Yr.Iss.	1300.00	1300-1500.
92-05-007	On Our Way 472	M.I. Hummel	Yr.Iss.	950.00	950.00
93-05-008	Welcome Spring 635	M.I. Hummel	Yr.Iss.	N/A	N/A

Goebel/Schmid — **M.I. Hummel Collectibles Nativity Components**

Number	Name	Artist	Edition Limit	Issue Price	Quote
XX-06-001	Madonna 214/A/M/11	M.I. Hummel	Open	Unkn.	150.00
XX-06-002	Infant Jesus 214/A/K/11	M.I. Hummel	Open	Unkn.	50.00
XX-06-003	St. Joseph color 214/B/11	M.I. Hummel	Open	Unkn.	110.00
XX-06-004	Goodnight 214/C/11	M.I. Hummel	Open	Unkn.	70.00
XX-06-005	Angel Serenade 214/D/11	M.I. Hummel	Open	Unkn.	70.00
XX-06-006	We Congratulate 214/E/11	M.I. Hummel	Open	Unkn.	140.00
XX-06-007	Shepherd with Sheep 214/F/11 1 piece	M.I. Hummel	Open	Unkn.	155.00
XX-06-008	Shepherd Boy 214/G/11	M.I. Hummel	Open	Unkn.	110.00
XX-06-009	Little Tooter 214/H/11	M.I. Hummel	Open	Unkn.	100.00
XX-06-010	Donkey 214/J/11	M.I. Hummel	Open	Unkn.	60.00
XX-06-011	Ox 214/K/11	M.I. Hummel	Open	Unkn.	60.00
XX-06-012	King (standing) 214/L/11	M.I. Hummel	Open	Unkn.	155.00
XX-06-013	King (kneeling on one knee) 214/M/11	M.I. Hummel	Open	Unkn.	150.00
XX-06-014	King (kneeling on two knees) 214/N/11	M.I. Hummel	Open	Unkn.	140.00
XX-06-015	Lamb 214/0/11	M.I. Hummel	Open	Unkn.	18.00
XX-06-016	Flying Angel/color 366	M.I. Hummel	Open	Unkn.	105.00
XX-06-017	Madonna-260A	M.I. Hummel	Suspd.	Unkn.	470.00
XX-06-018	St. Joseph 260B	M.I. Hummel	Suspd.	Unkn.	470.00
XX-06-019	Infant Jesus 260C	M.I. Hummel	Suspd.	Unkn.	95.00
XX-06-020	Good Night 260D	M.I. Hummel	Suspd.	Unkn.	120.00
XX-06-021	Angel Serenade 260E	M.I. Hummel	Suspd.	Unkn.	115.00
XX-06-022	We Congratulate 260F	M.I. Hummel	Suspd.	Unkn.	330.00
XX-06-023	Shepherd. standing 260G	M.I. Hummel	Suspd.	Unkn.	475.00
XX-06-024	Sheep (standing) with Lamb 260H	M.I. Hummel	Suspd.	Unkn.	80.00
XX-06-025	Shepherd Boy (kneeing) 260J	M.I. Hummel	Suspd.	Unkn.	270.00
XX-06-026	Little Tooter 260K	M.I. Hummel	Suspd.	Unkn.	140.00
XX-06-027	Donkey 260L	M.I. Hummel	Suspd.	Unkn.	115.00
XX-06-028	Ox 260M	M.I. Hummel	Suspd.	Unkn.	130.00
XX-06-029	Moorish King 260N	M.I. Hummel	Suspd.	Unkn.	450.00
XX-06-030	King (standing) 290 O	M.I. Hummel	Suspd.	Unkn.	450.00
XX-06-031	King (kneeling) 260P	M.I. Hummel	Suspd.	Unkn.	430.00
XX-06-032	Sheep (lying) 260R	M.I. Hummel	Suspd.	Unkn.	40.00
XX-06-033	Holy Family,3 pc ,Color 214/A/M/0, B/0,A/K/0	M.I. Hummel	Open	Unkn.	255.00
XX-06-034	Holy Family 3 Pieces 214/A & B/11	M.I. Hummel	Open	Unkn.	350.00
XX-06-035	12-Set Figs. Only,.Color, 214/A-B, F-G, J-0/11 366	M.I. Hummel	Open	Unkn.	1300.00
89-06-036	Holy Family Set 214/AM/0. 214/B/0. 214/AK/0	M.I. Hummel	Open	Unkn.	240.00
XX-06-037	16 -Set Figs. only ,Color, 214/A-H, J-0/11366	M.I. Hummel	Open	Unkn.	1680.00
XX-06-038	(17 Pc Set) Large Color 16 Figs.& Stable 260 A-S	M.I. Hummel	Suspd.	Unkn.	4540.00
XX-06-039	Stable only fit 12 or16 pc HUM214S1	M.I. Hummel	Open	Unkn.	100.00
XX-06-040	Stable only fit 3 pc HUM214 Set 214/S11	M.I. Hummel	Open	Unkn.	45.00
XX-06-041	Stable only to fit 12 or 16 piece HUM260 Set 260/S	M.I. Hummel	Open	Unkn.	400.00
89-06-042	Madonna 214/AM/0	M.I. Hummel	Open	Unkn.	110.00
89-06-043	Infant Jesus 214/AK/0	M.I. Hummel	Open	Unkn.	35.00
89-06-044	St. Joseph 214/B/0	M.I. Hummel	Open	Unkn.	110.00
89-06-045	Donkey 214/J/0	M.I. Hummel	Open	Unkn.	45.00
89-06-046	Lamb 214/0/0	M.I. Hummel	Open	Unkn.	15.00
89-06-047	Ox,214/K/0	M.I. Hummel	Open	Unkn.	45.00
89-06-048	Flying Angel 366/0	M.I. Hummel	Open	Unkn.	85.00
89-06-049	King (kneeling, one knee) 214/M/0	M.I. Hummel	Open	Unkn.	115.00
90-06-050	King (kneeling, both knees) 214/N/0	M.I. Hummel	Open	Unkn.	95.00
XX-06-051	King (kneeling) 214M	M.I. Hummel	Open	Unkn.	120.00
XX-06-052	King (kneeling with box) 214/M	M.I. Hummel	Open	Unkn.	115.00
XX-06-053	King Morrish 214L	M.I. Hummel	Open	Unkn.	130.00
XX-06-054	Shepherd (kneeling) 214/0	M.I. Hummel	Open	Unkn.	100.00
XX-06-055	Shepherd (standing) 214/F	M.I. Hummel	Open	Unkn.	135.00
XX-06-056	Shepherd With Sheep 214/F/11	M.I. Hummel	Open	Unkn.	155.00

Goebel/Schmid — **M.I. Hummel Collectibles-Madonna Figurines**

Number	Name	Artist	Edition Limit	Issue Price	Quote
XX-07-001	Flower Madonna, color 10/I/II	M.I. Hummel	Open	Unkn.	350.00
XX-07-002	Flower Madonna, white 10/I/W	M.I. Hummel	Open	Unkn.	165.00
XX-07-003	Madonna Holding Child, white 151/W	M.I. Hummel	Suspd.	Unkn.	320.00
XX-07-004	Madonna with Halo, color 45/I/6	M.I. Hummel	Suspd.	Unkn.	105.00
XX-07-005	Madonna with Halo, white 45/I/W	M.I. Hummel	Suspd.	Unkn.	70.00
XX-07-006	Madonna without Halo, color 46/I/6	M.I. Hummel	Suspd.	Unkn.	75.00
XX-07-007	Madonna without Halo, white 46/I/W	M.I. Hummel	Suspd.	Unkn.	50.00

Goebel/Schmid — **M.I. Hummel Collectors Club Exclusives**

Number	Name	Artist	Edition Limit	Issue Price	Quote
77-08-001	Valentine Gift 387	M.I. Hummel	Closed	45.00	300-600.
78-08-002	Smiling Through Plaque 690	M.I. Hummel	Closed	50.00	75-150.00
79-08-003	Bust of Sister-M.I.Hummel HU-3	G. Skrobek	Closed	75.00	165-300.
80-08-004	Valentine Joy 399	M.I. Hummel	Closed	95.00	200-300.
81-08-005	Daisies Don't Tell 380	M.I. Hummel	Closed	80.00	200-250.
82-08-005	It's Cold 421	M.I. Hummel	Closed	80.00	200-600.
83-08-007	What Now? 422	M.I. Hummel	Closed	90.00	200-300.
83-08-008	Valentine Gift Mini Pendant	R. Olszewski	Closed	85.00	175-300.
84-08-009	Coffee Break 409	M.I. Hummel	Closed	90.00	225-350.
85-08-010	Smiling Through 408/0	M.I. Hummel	Closed	125.00	200-250.
86-08-011	Birthday Candle 440	M.I. Hummel	Closed	95.00	150-200.
86-08-012	What Now? Mini Pendant	R. Olszewski	Closed	125.00	175-225.
87-08-013	Morning Concert 447	M.I. Hummel	Closed	98.00	175-250.
87-08-014	Little Cocopah Indian Girl	T. DeGrazia	Closed	140.00	175-300.
88-08-015	The Surprise 431	M.I. Hummel	Closed	125.00	150-250.
89-08-016	Mickey and Minnie	H. Fischer	10,000	275.00	350-500.
89-08-017	Hello World 429	M.I. Hummel	Closed	130.00	165-250.
90-08-018	I Wonder 486	M.I. Hummel	Open	140.00	175.00
91-08-019	Gift From A Friend 485	M.I. Hummel	Open	160.00	160.00
91-08-020	Miniature Morning Concert	R. Olszewski	Open	175.00	175.00
92-08-021	My Wish Is Small 463/0	M.I. Hummel	Open	170.00	170.00
92-08-022	Cheeky Fellow 554	M.I. Hummel	Open	120.00	120.00

Goebel/Schmid — **Special Edition M.I. Hummel Anniversary Figurine For 5 & 10 Year Club Members**

Number	Name	Artist	Edition Limit	Issue Price	Quote
90-09-001	Flower Girl 548	M.I. Hummel	Open	105.00	115.00
90-09-002	The Little Pair 449	M.I. Hummel	Open	170.00	185.00
91-09-003	Honey Lover 312	M.I. Hummel	Open	190.00	190.00

Goebel Miniatures — **First Edition M.I. Hummel Miniatures**

Number	Name	Artist	Edition Limit	Issue Price	Quote
89-20-001	Little Fiddler 250-P	M.I. Hummel	10,000	90.00	120-200.
89-20-002	Little Sweeper 253-P	M.I. Hummel	10,000	90.00	125-200.
89-20-003	Merry Wanderer 254-P	M.I. Hummel	10,000	95.00	120-200.
89-20-004	Doll Bath 252-P	M.I. Hummel	10,000	95.00	115-175.
89-20-005	Stormy Weather 251-P	M.I. Hummel	10,000	115.00	175-250.
88-20-006	Bavarian Village 954-D	M.I. Hummel	10,000	100.00	100.00
88-20-007	Bavarian Cottage 953-D	M.I. Hummel	10,000	60.00	64.00
89-20-008	Visiting an Invalid 256-P	M.I. Hummel	10,000	105.00	115-130.
89-20-009	Apple Tree Boy 257-P	M.I. Hummel	10,000	115.00	125-250.
89-20-010	Postman 255-P	M.I. Hummel	10,000	95.00	100-200.
90-20-011	Baker 262-P	M.I. Hummel	10,000	100.00	105-125.
90-20-012	Waiter 263-P	M.I. Hummel	10,000	100.00	125-250.
90-20-013	Cinderella 264-P	M.I. Hummel	10,000	115.00	115.00
91-20-014	Serenade 265-P	M.I. Hummel	10,000	105.00	105.00
91-20-015	Accordion Boy 266-P	M.I. Hummel	10,000	105.00	105.00
91-20-016	We Congratulate 267-P	M.I. Hummel	10,000	130.00	130.00
91-20-017	Busy Student 268-P	M.I. Hummel	10,000	105.00	105.00
91-20-018	Merry Wanderer Dealer Plaque 280-P	M.I. Hummel	10,000	130.00	130.00
90-20-019	Bavarian Marketsquare 960-D	M.I. Hummel	Open	110.00	110.00
90-20-020	Marketsquare Hotel 961-D	M.I. Hummel	Open	70.00	70.00
90-20-021	Marketsquare Flower Stand 962-D	M.I. Hummel	Open	35.00	35.00
90-20-022	Bavarian Marketsquare Bridge 963-D	M.I. Hummel	Open	30.00	30.00
91-20-023	Bavarian Country School 974-D	M.I. Hummel	Open	100.00	100.00
91-20-024	Wayside Shrine 975-D	M.I. Hummel	Open	60.00	60.00
92-20-025	School Boy 281-P	M.I. Hummel	10,000	120.00	120.00
92-20-028	Wayside Harmony 282-P	M.I. Hummel	10,000	140.00	140.00
92-20-026	Goose Girl 283-P	M.I. Hummel	10,000	130.00	130.00

Goebel Miniatures — **Goebel Miniatures: Children's Series**

Number	Name	Artist	Edition Limit	Issue Price	Quote
80-21-001	Blumenkinder-Courting 630-P	R. Olszewski	Closed	55.00	265-400.
81-21-002	Summer Days 631-P	R. Olszewski	Closed	65.00	265.00
82-21-003	Out and About 632-P	R. Olszewski	Closed	85.00	385.00
83-21-004	Backyard Frolic 633-P	R. Olszewski	Closed	65.00	125-250.
85-21-005	Snow Holiday 635-P	R. Olszewski	Closed	75.00	100-125.
86-21-006	Clowning Around 636-P	R. Olszewski	Closed	85.00	175.00
87-21-007	Carrousel Days 637-P	R. Olszewski	Closed	85.00	150-165.
88-21-008	Little Ballerina 638-P	R. Olszewski	Closed	85.00	110-150.
88-21-009	Children's Display (small)	R. Olszewski	Closed	45.00	50.00
84-21-010	Grandpa 634-P	R. Olszewski	Closed	75.00	125-165.
90-21-011	Building Blocks Castle (large) 968-D	R. Olszewski	Closed	75.00	90.00

Goebel Miniatures — **Goebel Miniatures: Wildlife Series**

Number	Name	Artist	Edition Limit	Issue Price	Quote
80-22-001	Chipping Sparrow 620-P	R. Olszewski	Open	55.00	270-525.
81-22-002	Owl-Daylight Encounter 621-P	R. Olszewski	Open	65.00	250-365.
82-22-003	Western Bluebird 622-P	R. Olszewski	Open	65.00	195.00
83-22-004	Red-Winged Blackbird 623-P	R. Olszewski	Closed	65.00	150-225.
84-22-005	Winter Cardinal 624-P	R. Olszewski	Open	65.00	150-225.
85-22-006	American Goldfinch 625-P	R. Olszewski	Open	65.00	120.00
86-22-007	Autumn Blue Jay 626-P	R. Olszewski	Open	65.00	150-205.
87-22-008	Mallard Duck 627-P	R. Olszewski	Open	75.00	195.00
88-22-009	Spring Robin 628-P	R. Olszewski	Open	75.00	165-195.
87-22-010	Country Display (small) 940-D	R. Olszewski	Open	45.00	55.00
90-22-011	Wildlife Display (large) 957-D	R. Olszewski	Open	85.00	95.00
89-22-012	Hooded Oriole 629-P	R. Olszewski	Open	80.00	115-175.
90-22-013	Hummingbird 696-P	R. Olszewski	Open	85.00	125-150.

Goebel Miniatures — **Goebel Miniatures: Women's Series**

Number	Name	Artist	Edition Limit	Issue Price	Quote
80-23-001	Dresden Dancer 610-P	R. Olszewski	Closed	55.00	400-550.
81-23-002	The Hunt With Hounds 611-P	R. Olszewski	Closed	75.00	200-445.
82-23-003	Precious Years 612-P	R. Olszewski	Closed	65.00	315.00
83-23-004	On The Avenue 613-P	R. Olszewski	Closed	65.00	100-150.
84-23-005	Roses 614-P	R. Olszewski	Closed	65.00	105-150.
86-23-006	I Do 615-P	R. Olszewski	Closed	85.00	195.00
89-23-007	Women's Display (small) 950-D	R. Olszewski	Closed	40.00	59.00

Goebel Miniatures — **Goebel Miniatures: Historical Series**

Number	Name	Artist	Edition Limit	Issue Price	Quote
80-24-001	Capodimonte 600-P	R. Olszewski	Closed	90.00	565.00
81-24-002	Masquerade-St. Petersburg 601-P	R. Olszewski	Closed	65.00	150-325.

Company Number	Name	Series Artist	Edition Limit	Issue Price	Quote
83-24-003	The Cherry Pickers 602-P	R. Olszewski	Open	85.00	285.00
84-24-004	Moor With Spanish Horse 603-P	R. Olszewski	Open	85.00	100-200.
85-24-005	Floral Bouquet Pompadour 604-P	R. Olszewski	Open	85.00	130.00
87-24-006	Meissen Parrot 605-P	R. Olszewski	Open	85.00	100-150.
88-24-007	Minton Rooster 606-P	R. Olszewski	7,500	85.00	95-195.00
89-24-008	Farmer w/Doves 607-P	R. Olszewski	Open	85.00	95-150.00
90-24-009	Gentleman Fox Hunt 616-P	R. Olszewski	Open	145.00	145.00
88-24-010	Historical Display 943-D	R. Olszewski	Suspd.	45.00	50.00
90-24-011	English Country Garden 970-D	R. Olszewski	Open	85.00	110.00
92-24-012	Poultry Seller 608-G	R. Olszewski	Open	165.00	165.00
Goebel Miniatures		**Goebel Miniatures: Oriental Series**			
80-25-001	Kuan Yin 640-W	R. Olszewski	Closed	40.00	150-225.
82-25-002	The Geisha 641-P	R. Olszewski	Open	65.00	150-195.
85-25-003	Tang Horse 642-P	R. Olszewski	Open	65.00	100-175.
86-25-004	The Blind Men and the Elephant 643-P	R. Olszewski	Open	70.00	100-175.
87-25-005	Chinese Water Dragon 644-P	R. Olszewski	Open	70.00	175.00
87-25-006	Oriental Display (small) 945-D	R. Olszewski	Suspd.	45.00	59.00
89-25-007	Tiger Hunt 645-P	R. Olszewski	Open	85.00	105.00
90-25-008	Chinese Temple Lion 646-P	R. Olszewski	Open	90.00	90.00
90-25-009	Empress' Garden 967-D	R. Olszewski	Open	95.00	110.00
Goebel Miniatures		**Goebel Miniatures: Americana Series**			
81-26-001	The Plainsman 660-B	R. Olszewski	Closed	45.00	265.00
82-26-002	American Bald Eagle 661-B	R. Olszewski	Closed	45.00	345.00
83-26-003	She Sounds the Deep 662-B	R. Olszewski	Closed	45.00	145.00
84-26-004	Eyes on the Horizon 663-B	R. Olszewski	Closed	45.00	125.00
85-26-005	Central Park Sunday 664-B	R. Olszewski	Closed	45.00	115.00
86-26-006	Carrousel Ride 665-B	R. Olszewski	Closed	45.00	115.00
87-26-007	To The Bandstand 666-B	R. Olszewski	Closed	45.00	110.00
89-26-008	Blacksmith 676-B	R. Olszewski	Closed	55.00	145.00
86-26-009	Americana Display 951-D	R. Olszewski	Suspd.	80.00	95.00
Goebel Miniatures		**Goebel Miniatures: DeGrazia**			
85-27-001	Flower Girl 501-P	R. Olszewski	Suspd.	85.00	85-125.00
85-27-002	Flower Boy 502-P	R. Olszewski	Suspd.	85.00	85-125.00
85-27-003	My First Horse 503-P	R. Olszewski	Suspd.	85.00	85-125.00
85-27-004	Sunflower Boy 551- P	R. Olszewski	Suspd.	93.00	150.00
85-27-005	White Dove 504-P	R. Olszewski	Suspd.	80.00	80-125.00
85-27-006	Wondering 505-P	R. Olszewski	Suspd.	93.00	95-150.00
86-27-007	Little Madonna 552-P	R. Olszewski	Suspd.	93.00	150.00
86-27-008	Pima Drummer Boy 506-P	R. Olszewski	Suspd.	85.00	250-300.
86-27-009	Festival of Lights 507-P	R. Olszewski	Suspd.	85.00	225-250.
87-27-010	Merry Little Indian 508-P	R. Olszewski	Suspd.	95.00	295.00
88-27-011	Adobe Display 948D	R. Olszewski	Suspd.	45.00	59.00
89-27-013	Beautiful Burden 554-P	R. Olszewski	Suspd.	110.00	110.00
90-27-012	Adobe Hacienda (large) Display 958-D	R. Olszewski	Suspd.	85.00	95.00
90-27-015	Chapel Display 971-D	R. Olszewski	Suspd.	95.00	100.00
91-27-014	My Beautiful Rocking Horse 555-P	R. Olszewski	Suspd.	110.00	110.00
Goebel Miniatures		**Goebel Miniatures: The American Frontier Collection**			
87-28-001	The End of the Trail 340-B	Frazier	Open	80.00	80-90.00
87-28-002	The First Ride 330-B	Rogers	Open	85.00	85.00
87-28-003	Eight Count 310-B	Pounder	Open	75.00	75.00
87-28-004	Grizzly's Last Stand 320-B	Jonas	Open	65.00	65.00
87-28-005	Indian Scout and Buffalo 300-B	Bonheur	Open	95.00	95.00
87-28-006	The Bronco Buster 350-B	Remington	Open	80.00	80.00
87-28-006	American Frontier-947-D Display	R. Olszewski	Open	80.00	95.00
Goebel Miniatures		**Goebel Miniatures: Portrait of America**			
88-29-001	The Doctor and the Doll 361-P	N. Rockwell	Open	85.00	95.00
88-29-002	No Swimming 360-P	N. Rockwell	Open	85.00	95.00
88-29-003	Marbles Champion 362-P	N. Rockwell	Open	85.00	95.00
88-29-004	Check-Up 363-P	N. Rockwell	Open	85.00	105.00
88-29-005	Triple Self-Portrait 364-P	N. Rockwell	Open	85.00	175.00
88-29-006	Bottom of the Sixth 365-P	N. Rockwell	Open	85.00	95.00
89-29-007	Bottom Drawer 366-P	N. Rockwell	7,500	85.00	95.00
88-29-008	Rockwell Display-952-D	N. Rockwell	Open	80.00	93.00
Goebel Miniatures		**Disney-Snow White**			
87-31-001	Sneezy 161-P	R. Olszewski	19,500	60.00	85.00
87-31-002	Doc 162-P	R. Olszewski	19,500	60.00	85.00
87-31-003	Sleepy 163-P	R. Olszewski	19,500	60.00	85.00
87-31-004	Happy 164-P	R. Olszewski	19,500	60.00	85.00
87-31-005	Bashful 165-P	R. Olszewski	19,500	60.00	85.00
87-31-006	Grumpy 166-P	R. Olszewski	19,500	60.00	85.00
87-31-007	Dopey 167-P	R. Olszewski	19,500	60.00	85.00
87-31-008	Snow White 168-P	R. Olszewski	19,500	60.00	90.00
90-31-009	Snow White's Prince 170-P	R. Olszewski	19,500	80.00	85.00
87-31-010	Cozy Cottage Display 941-D	R. Olszewski	Closed	35.00	185.00
88-31-011	House In The Woods Display 944-D	R. Olszewski	Open	60.00	105.00
90-31-012	The Wishing Well Display 969-D	R. Olszewski	Open	65.00	70.00
91-31-013	Snow White Queen 182-P	R. Olszewski	Open	Unkn.	Unkn.
91-31-014	Castle Courtyard Display 981-D	R. Olszewski	Open	105.00	105.00
92-31-015	Snow White's Witch 183-P	R. Olszewski	Open	100.00	100.00
92-31-016	Snow White's Queen 182-P	R. Olszewski	Open	100.00	100.00
92-31-017	Path In The Woods 996-D	R. Olszewski	Open	140.00	140.00
Goebel Miniatures		**Disney-Pinocchio**			
90-32-001	Geppetto/Figaro 682-P	R. Olszewski	Open	90.00	95.00
90-32-002	Gideon 683-P	R. Olszewski	Open	75.00	85.00
90-32-003	J. Worthington Foulfellow 684-P	R. Olszewski	Open	95.00	95.00
90-32-004	Jiminy Cricket 685-P	R. Olszewski	Open	75.00	85.00
90-32-005	Pinocchio 686-P	R. Olszewski	Open	75.00	85.00
91-32-006	Little Street Lamp Display 964-D	R. Olszewski	Open	65.00	65.00
90-32-007	Geppetto's Toy Shop Display 965-D	R. Olszewski	Open	95.00	105.00
91-32-008	Stromboli 694-P	R. Olszewski	Open	95.00	95.00
91-32-009	Blue Fairy 693-P	R. Olszewski	Open	95.00	95.00
91-32-010	Stromboli's Street Wagon 979-D	R. Olszewski	Open	105.00	105.00
92-32-011	Monstro The Whale 985-D	R. Olszewski	Open	135.00	135.00
Goebel Miniatures		**Disney-Cinderella**			
91-33-001	Anastasia 172-P	R.Olszewski	Open	85.00	85.00
91-33-002	Jaq 173-P	R.Olszewski	Open	80.00	80.00
91-33-003	Drizella 174-P	R.Olszewski	Open	85.00	85.00
91-33-004	Lucifer 175-P	R.Olszewski	Open	80.00	80.00
91-33-005	Cinderella 176-P	R.Olszewski	Open	85.00	85.00
91-33-006	Gus 177-P	R.Olszewski	Open	80.00	80.00
91-33-007	Stepmother 178-P	R.Olszewski	Open	85.00	85.00
91-33-008	Prince Charming 179-P	R.Olszewski	Open	85.00	85.00
91-33-009	Fairy Godmother 180-P	R.Olszewski	Open	85.00	85.00
91-33-010	Footman 181-P	R.Olszewski	Open	85.00	85.00
91-33-011	Cinderella's Dream Castle 976-D	R.Olszewski	Open	95.00	95.00

Company Number	Name	Series Artist	Edition Limit	Issue Price	Quote
91-33-012	Cinderella's Coach Display 978-D	R.Olszewski	Open	95.00	95.00
Goebel Miniatures		**Mickey Mouse**			
90-34-001	The Sorcerer's Apprentice 171-P	R. Olszewski	Open	80.00	80.00
90-34-002	Fantasia Living Brooms 972-D	R. Olszweski	Open	85.00	85.00
Goebel Miniatures		**Night Before Christmas (1st Edition)**			
90-35-001	Sugar Plum Boy 687-P	R. Olszewski	5,000	70.00	85.00
90-35-002	Yule Tree 688-P	R. Olszewski	5,000	90.00	95.00
90-35-003	Sugar Plum Girl 689-P	R. Olszewski	5,000	70.00	85.00
90-35-004	St. Nicholas 690-P	R. Olszewski	5,000	95.00	105.00
90-35-005	Eight Tiny Reindeer 691-P	R. Olszewski	5,000	110.00	110.00
90-35-006	Mama & Papa 692-P	R. Olszewski	5,000	110.00	120.00
91-35-007	Up To The Housetop 966-D	R. Olszewski	5,000	95.00	95.00
Goebel Miniatures		**Special Release-Alice in Wonderland**			
82-36-001	Alice in the Garden 670-P	R. Olszewski	5,000	60.00	485-785.
83-36-002	Down the Rabbit Hole 671-P	R. Olszewski	5,000	75.00	450-480.
84-36-003	The Cheshire Cat 672-P	R. Olszewski	5,000	75.00	350-415.
Goebel Miniatures		**Special Release-Wizard of Oz**			
84-37-001	Scarecrow 673-P	R. Olszewski	5,000	75.00	425.00
85-37-002	Tinman 674-P	R. Olszewski	5,000	80.00	285.00
86-37-003	The Cowardly Lion 675-P	R. Olszewski	5,000	85.00	240.00
87-37-004	The Wicked Witch 676-P	R. Olszewski	5,000	85.00	110-170.
88-37-005	The Munchkins 677-P	R. Olszewski	5,000	85.00	100-200.
87-37-006	Oz Display 942-D	R. Olszewski	Closed	45.00	210.00
92-37-007	Dorothy/Glinda 695-P	R. Olszewski	5,000	135.00	135.00
92-37-008	Good-Bye to Oz Display 980-D	R. Olszewski	5,000	120.00	120.00
92-37-009	Set	R. Olszewski	5,000	730.00	1275-1400.
Goebel Miniatures		**Three Little Pigs**			
89-38-001	Little Sticks Pig 678-P	R. Olszewski	7,500	75.00	85.00
90-38-002	Little Straw Pig 679-P	R. Olszewski	7,500	75.00	85.00
91-38-003	Little Bricks Pig 680-P	R. Olszewski	7,500	75.00	75.00
91-38-004	The Hungry Wolf 681-P	R. Olszewski	7,500	80.00	80.00
89-38-005	Three Little Pigs House 956-D	R. Olszewski	7,500	50.00	55.00
Goebel Miniatures		**Pendants**			
85-39-001	Flower Girl Pendant 561-P	R. Olszewski	Open	125.00	150.00
87-39-002	Festival of Lights 562-P	R. Olszewski	Open	90.00	195.00
88-39-003	Mickey Mouse 169-P	R. Olszewski	5,000	92.00	185.00
90-39-004	Hummingbird 697-P	R. Olszewski	Open	125.00	135.00
86-39-005	Camper Bialosky 151-P	R. Olszewski	Open	95.00	145.00
91-39-006	Rose Pendant 220-P	R. Olszewski	Open	135.00	135.00
91-39-007	Daffodil Pendant 221-P	R. Olszewski	Open	135.00	135.00
91-39-008	Chrysanthemum Pendant 222-P	R. Olszewski	Open	135.00	135.00
91-39-009	Poinsettia Pendant 223-P	R. Olszewski	Open	135.00	135.00
Goebel Miniatures		**Nativity Collection**			
91-40-001	Mother/Child 440-P	R. Olszewski	10,000	120.00	120.00
91-40-002	Joseph 401-P	R. Olszewski	10,000	95.00	95.00
91-40-003	Joyful Cherubs 403-P	R. Olszewski	10,000	130.00	130.00
91-40-004	The Stable Donkey 402-P	R. Olszewski	10,000	95.00	95.00
91-40-005	Holy Family Display 982-D	R. Olszewski	10,000	85.00	85.00
92-40-006	Balthazar 405-P	R. Olszewski	10,000	135.00	135.00
92-40-007	Melchoir 404-P	R. Olszewski	10,000	135.00	135.00
92-40-008	Caspar 406-P	R. Olszewski	10,000	135.00	135.00
92-40-009	3 Kings Display 987-D	R. Olszewski	10,000	85.00	85.00
Goebel Miniatures		**Special Releases**			
91-41-001	Portrait Of The Artist 658-P	R. Olszewski	Open	195.00	195.00
92-41-002	Summer Days Collector Plaque 659-P	R. Olszewski	Open	130.00	130.00
Goebel Miniatures		**Saturday Evening Post**			
91-42-001	Soldier 368-P	N. Rockwell	Open	Unkn.	Unkn.
91-42-002	Mother 369-P	N. Rockwell	Open	Unkn.	Unkn.
91-42-003	Home Coming Vignette 990-D	N. Rockwell	Open	Unkn.	Unkn.
Goebel Miniatures		**Disney-Peter Pan**			
92-43-001	Peter Pan 184-P	R. Olszewski	Open	90.00	90.00
92-43-002	Wendy 185-P	R. Olszewski	Open	90.00	90.00
92-43-003	John 186-P	R. Olszewski	Open	90.00	90.00
92-43-004	Michael 187-P	R. Olszewski	Open	90.00	90.00
92-43-005	Nana 189-P	R. Olszewski	Open	95.00	95.00
92-43-006	Peter Pan's London 986-D	R. Olszewski	Open	125.00	125.00.
Goebel Miniatures		**Archive Releases**			
92-44-001	Autumn Blue Jay 626-P	R. Olszewski	Open	125.00	125.00
93-44-002	Cherry Pickers 602-P	R. Olszewski	Open	175.00	175.00
93-44-003	Kuan Yin 640-W	R. Olszewski	Open	100.00	100.00
Gorham		**A Boy And His Dog (Four Seasons)**			
72-01-001	A Boy Meets His Dog	N. Rockwell	2,500	200.00	1575.00
72-01-002	Adventurers Between Adventures	N. Rockwell	2,500	Set	Set
72-01-003	The Mysterious Malady	N. Rockwell	2,500	Set	Set
72-01-004	Pride of Parenthood	N. Rockwell	2,500	Set	Set
Gorham		**Young Love (Four Seasons)**			
73-02-001	Downhill Daring	N. Rockwell	2,500	250.00	1100.00
73-02-002	Beguiling Buttercup	N. Rockwell	2,500	Set	Set
73-02-003	Flying High	N. Rockwell	2,500	Set	Set
73-02-004	A Scholarly Pace	N. Rockwell	2,500	Set	Set
Gorham		**Four Ages of Love (Four Seasons)**			
74-03-001	Gaily Sharing Vintage Times	N. Rockwell	2,500	300.00	1250.00
74-03-002	Sweet Song So Young	N. Rockwell	2,500	Set	Set
74-03-003	Flowers In Tender Bloom	N. Rockwell	2,500	Set	Set
74-03-004	Fondly Do We Remember	N. Rockwell	2,500	Set	Set
Gorham		**Grandpa and Me (Four Seasons)**			
75-04-001	Gay Blades	N. Rockwell	2,500	300.00	900.00
75-04-002	Day Dreamers	N. Rockwell	2,500	Set	Set
75-04-003	Goin' Fishing	N. Rockwell	2,500	Set	Set
75-04-004	Pensive Pals	N. Rockwell	2,500	Set	Set
Gorham		**Me and My Pal (Four Seasons)**			
76-05-001	A Licking Good Bath	N. Rockwell	2,500	300.00	900.00
76-05-002	Young Man's Fancy	N. Rockwell	2,500	Set	Set
76-05-003	Fisherman's Paradise	N. Rockwell	2,500	Set	Set
76-05-004	Disastrous Daring	N. Rockwell	2,500	Set	Set

Company / Number	Name	Series / Artist	Edition Limit	Issue Price	Quote
Gorham		**Grand Pals (Four Seasons)**			
77-06-001	Snow Sculpturing	N. Rockwell	2,500	350.00	675.00
77-06-002	Soaring Spirits	N. Rockwell	2,500	Set	Set
77-06-003	Fish Finders	N. Rockwell	2,500	Set	Set
77-06-004	Ghostly Gourds	N. Rockwell	2,500	Set	Set
Gorham		**Going On Sixteen (Four Seasons)**			
78-07-001	Chilling Chore	N. Rockwell	2,500	400.00	675.00
78-07-002	Sweet Serenade	N. Rockwell	2,500	Set	Set
78-07-003	Shear Agony	N. Rockwell	2,500	Set	Set
78-07-004	Pilgrimage	N. Rockwell	2,500	Set	Set
Gorham		**Tender Years (Four Seasons)**			
79-08-001	New Year Look	N. Rockwell	2,500	500.00	550.00
79-08-002	Spring Tonic	N. Rockwell	2,500	Set	Set
79-08-003	Cool Aid	N. Rockwell	2,500	Set	Set
79-08-004	Chilly Reception	N. Rockwell	2,500	Set	Set
Gorham		**A Helping Hand (Four Seasons)**			
80-09-001	Year End Court	N. Rockwell	2,500	650.00	700.00
80-09-002	Closed For Business	N. Rockwell	2,500	Set	Set
80-09-003	Swatter's Right	N. Rockwell	2,500	Set	Set
80-09-004	Coal Seasons Coming	N. Rockwell	2,500	Set	Set
Gorham		**Dad's Boy (Four Seasons)**			
81-10-001	Ski Skills	N. Rockwell	2,500	750.00	800.00
81-10-002	In His Spirit	N. Rockwell	2,500	Set	Set
81-10-003	Trout Dinner	N. Rockwell	2,500	Set	Set
81-10-004	Careful Aim	N. Rockwell	2,500	Set	Set
Gorham		**Rockwell**			
74-11-001	Weighing In	N. Rockwell	Closed	40.00	125.00
74-11-002	Missing Tooth	N. Rockwell	Closed	30.00	70.00
74-11-003	Tiny Tim	N. Rockwell	Closed	30.00	75.00
74-11-004	At The Vets	N. Rockwell	Closed	25.00	65.00
74-11-005	Fishing	N. Rockwell	Closed	50.00	100.00
74-11-006	Batter Up	N. Rockwell	Closed	40.00	90.00
74-11-007	Skating	N. Rockwell	Closed	37.50	85.00
74-11-008	Captain	N. Rockwell	Closed	45.00	95.00
75-11-009	Boy And His Dog	N. Rockwell	Closed	37.50	85.00
75-11-010	No Swimming	N. Rockwell	Closed	35.00	80.00
75-11-011	Old Mill Pond	N. Rockwell	Closed	45.00	95.00
76-11-012	Saying Grace	N. Rockwell	Closed	75.00	120.00
76-11-013	God Rest Ye Merry Gentlemen	N. Rockwell	Closed	50.00	800.00
76-11-014	Tackled (Ad Stand)	N. Rockwell	Closed	35.00	85.00
76-11-015	Independence	N. Rockwell	Closed	40.00	150.00
76-11-016	Marriage License	N. Rockwell	Closed	50.00	175.00
76-11-017	The Occultist	N. Rockwell	Closed	50.00	175.00
81-11-018	Day in the Life Boy II	N. Rockwell	Closed	75.00	85.00
81-11-019	Wet Sport	N. Rockwell	Closed	85.00	85.00
82-11-020	April Fool's (At The Curiosity Shop)	N. Rockwell	Closed	55.00	110.00
82-11-021	Tackled (Rockwell Name Signed)	N. Rockwell	Closed	45.00	70.00
82-11-022	A Day in the Life Boy III	N. Rockwell	Closed	85.00	85.00
82-11-023	A Day in the Life Girl III	N. Rockwell	Closed	85.00	85.00
81-11-024	Christmas Dancers	N. Rockwell	7,500	130.00	130.00
82-11-025	Marriage License	N. Rockwell	5,000	110.00	400.00
82-11-026	Saying Grace	N. Rockwell	5,000	110.00	450.00
82-11-027	Triple Self Portrait	N. Rockwell	5,000	300.00	500.00
80-11-028	Jolly Coachman	N. Rockwell	7,500	75.00	125.00
82-11-029	Merrie Christmas	N. Rockwell	7,500	75.00	75.00
83-11-030	Facts of Life	N. Rockwell	7,500	110.00	110.00
83-11-031	Antique Dealer	N. Rockwell	7,500	130.00	130.00
83-11-032	Christmas Goose	N. Rockwell	7,500	75.00	75.00
84-11-033	Serenade	N. Rockwell	7,500	95.00	95.00
84-11-034	Card Tricks	N. Rockwell	7,500	110.00	110.00
84-11-035	Santa's Friend	N. Rockwell	7,500	75.00	75.00
85-11-036	Puppet Maker	N. Rockwell	7,500	130.00	130.00
85-11-037	The Old Sign Painter	N. Rockwell	7,500	130.00	130.00
86-11-038	Drum For Tommy	N. Rockwell	Annual	90.00	90.00
87-11-039	Santa Planning His Annual Visit	N. Rockwell	7,500	95.00	95.00
88-11-040	Home for the Holidays	N. Rockwell	7,500	100.00	100.00
88-11-041	Gary Cooper in Hollywood	N. Rockwell	15,000	90.00	90.00
88-11-042	Cramming	N. Rockwell	15,000	80.00	80.00
88-11-043	Dolores & Eddie	N. Rockwell	15,000	75.00	75.00
88-11-044	Confrontation	N. Rockwell	15,000	75.00	75.00
88-11-045	The Diary	N. Rockwell	15,000	80.00	80.00
Gorham		**Miniature Christmas Figurines**			
79-12-001	Tiny Tim	N. Rockwell	Yr.Iss.	15.00	15.00
80-12-002	Santa Plans His Trip	N. Rockwell	Yr.Iss.	15.00	15.00
81-12-003	Yuletide Reckoning	N. Rockwell	Yr.Iss.	20.00	20.00
82-12-004	Checking Good Deeds	N. Rockwell	Yr.Iss.	20.00	20.00
83-12-005	Santa's Friend	N. Rockwell	Yr.Iss.	20.00	20.00
84-12-006	Downhill Daring	N. Rockwell	Yr.Iss.	20.00	20.00
85-12-007	Christmas Santa	T. Nast	Yr.Iss.	20.00	20.00
86-12-008	Christmas Santa	T. Nast	Yr.Iss.	25.00	25.00
87-12-009	Annual Thomas Nast Santa	T. Nast	Yr.Iss.	25.00	25.00
Gorham		**Miniatures**			
81-13-001	Young Man's Fancy	N. Rockwell	Closed	55.00	55.00
81-13-002	Beguiling Buttercup	N. Rockwell	Closed	45.00	45.00
81-13-003	Gay Blades	N. Rockwell	Closed	45.00	70.00
81-13-004	Sweet Song So Young	N. Rockwell	Closed	55.00	55.00
81-13-005	Snow Sculpture	N. Rockwell	Closed	45.00	70.00
81-13-006	Sweet Serenade	N. Rockwell	Closed	45.00	45.00
81-13-007	At the Vets	N. Rockwell	Closed	27.50	39.50
81-13-008	Boy Meets His Dog	N. Rockwell	Closed	37.50	37.50
81-13-009	Downhill Daring	N. Rockwell	Closed	45.00	70.00
81-13-010	Flowers in Tender Bloom	N. Rockwell	Closed	60.00	60.00
82-13-011	Triple Self Portrait	N. Rockwell	Closed	60.00	175.00
82-13-012	Marriage License	N. Rockwell	Closed	60.00	70.00
82-13-013	The Runaway	N. Rockwell	Closed	50.00	50.00
82-13-014	Vintage Times	N. Rockwell	Closed	50.00	50.00
82-13-015	The Annual Visit	N. Rockwell	Closed	50.00	75.00
83-13-016	Trout Dinner	N. Rockwell	15,000	60.00	60.00
84-13-017	Ghostly Gourds	N. Rockwell	Closed	60.00	60.00
84-13-018	Years End Court	N. Rockwell	Closed	60.00	60.00
84-13-019	Shear Agony	N. Rockwell	Closed	60.00	60.00
84-13-020	Pride of Parenthood	N. Rockwell	Closed	50.00	50.00
84-13-021	Goin Fishing	N. Rockwell	Closed	60.00	60.00
84-13-022	Careful Aims	N. Rockwell	Closed	55.00	55.00
84-13-023	In His Spirit	N. Rockwell	Closed	60.00	60.00
85-13-024	To Love & Cherish	N. Rockwell	Closed	32.50	32.50
85-13-025	Spring Checkup	N. Rockwell	Closed	60.00	60.00
85-13-026	Engineer	N. Rockwell	Closed	55.00	55.00
85-13-027	Best Friends	N. Rockwell	Closed	27.50	27.50
85-13-028	Muscle Bound	N. Rockwell	Closed	30.00	30.00
85-13-029	New Arrival	N. Rockwell	Closed	32.50	32.50
85-13-030	Little Red Truck	N. Rockwell	Closed	25.00	25.00
86-13-031	The Old Sign Painter	N. Rockwell	Closed	70.00	70.00
86-13-032	The Graduate	N. Rockwell	Closed	30.00	30.00
86-13-033	Football Season	N. Rockwell	Closed	60.00	60.00
86-13-034	Lemonade Stand	N. Rockwell	Closed	60.00	60.00
86-13-035	Welcome Mat	N. Rockwell	Closed	70.00	70.00
86-13-036	Shoulder Ride	N. Rockwell	Closed	50.00	50.00
86-13-037	Morning Walk	N. Rockwell	Closed	60.00	60.00
86-13-038	Little Angel	N. Rockwell	Closed	50.00	60.00
87-13-039	Starstruck	N. Rockwell	15,000	75.00	75.00
87-13-040	The Prom Dress	N. Rockwell	15,000	75.00	75.00
87-13-041	The Milkmaid	N. Rockwell	15,000	80.00	80.00
87-13-042	Cinderella	N. Rockwell	15,000	70.00	70.00
87-13-043	Springtime	N. Rockwell	15,000	65.00	65.00
87-13-044	Babysitter	N. Rockwell	15,000	75.00	75.00
87-13-045	Between The Acts	N. Rockwell	15,000	60.00	60.00
Gorham		**Old Timers (Four Seasons Miniatures)**			
82-14-001	Canine Solo	N. Rockwell	2,500	250.00	250.00
82-14-002	Sweet Surprise	N. Rockwell	2,500	Set	Set
82-14-003	Lazy Days	N. Rockwell	2,500	Set	Set
82-14-004	Fancy Footwork	N. Rockwell	2,500	Set	Set
Gorham		**Life With Father (Four Seasons Miniatures)**			
83-15-001	Big Decision	N. Rockwell	2,500	250.00	250.00
83-15-002	Blasting Out	N. Rockwell	2,500	Set	Set
83-15-003	Cheering The Champs	N. Rockwell	2,500	Set	Set
83-15-004	A Tough One	N. Rockwell	2,500	Set	Set
Gorham		**Old Buddies (Four Seasons)**			
84-16-001	Shared Success	N. Rockwell	2,500	250.00	250.00
84-16-002	Hasty Retreat	N. Rockwell	2,500	Set	Set
84-16-003	Final Speech	N. Rockwell	2,500	Set	Set
84-16-004	Endless Debate	N. Rockwell	2,500	Set	Set
Gorham		**Traveling Salesman (Four Seasons)**			
85-17-001	Horse Trader	N. Rockwell	2,500	275.00	275.00
85-17-002	Expert Salesman	N. Rockwell	2,500	Set	Set
85-17-003	Traveling Salesman	N. Rockwell	2,500	Set	Set
85-17-004	Country Pedlar	N. Rockwell	2,500	Set	Set
Gorham		**Vasari Figurines**			
71-18-001	Mercenary Warrior	Vasari	250	250.00	500.00
71-18-002	Ming Warrior	Vasari	250	200.00	400.00
71-18-003	Swiss Warrior	Vasari	250	250.00	1000.00
73-18-004	Austrian Hussar	Vasari	250	300.00	600.00
73-18-005	D'Artagnan	Vasari	250	250.00	800.00
73-18-006	English Crusader	Vasari	250	250.00	500.00
73-18-007	French Crusader	Vasari	250	250.00	500.00
73-18-008	German Hussar	Vasari	250	250.00	500.00
73-18-009	German Mercenary	Vasari	250	250.00	500.00
73-18-010	Italian Crusader	Vasari	250	250.00	500.00
73-18-011	Pirate	Vasari	250	200.00	400.00
73-18-012	Porthos	Vasari	250	250.00	500.00
73-18-013	Roman Centurion	Vasari	250	200.00	400.00
73-18-014	Spanish Grandee	Vasari	250	200.00	400.00
73-18-015	The Cossack	Vasari	250	250.00	500.00
73-18-016	Venetian Nobleman	Vasari	250	200.00	400.00
73-18-017	Viking	Vasari	250	200.00	400.00
73-18-018	Cellini	Vasari	250	400.00	800.00
73-18-019	Christ	Vasari	250	250.00	500.00
73-18-020	Creche	Vasari	250	500.00	1000.00
73-18-021	Leonardo Da Vinci	Vasari	200	250.00	500.00
73-18-022	Michelangelo	Vasari	200	250.00	500.00
73-18-023	Three Kings, (Set of 3)	Vasari	200	750.00	1500.00
73-18-024	Three Musketeers, (Set of 3)	Vasari	200	750.00	1500.00
Gorham		**Leyendecker Annual Christmas Figurines**			
88-19-001	Christmas Hug	J.C. Leyendecker	7,500	95.00	95.00
Granget		**Granget Wood Carvings**			
XX-01-001	Barn Owl, 20 inches	G. Granget	250	2000.00	7000.00
73-01-002	Black Grouse, large	G. Granget	250	2800.00	8600.00
73-01-003	Golden Eagle, large	G. Granget	250	2000.00	8000.00
73-01-004	Lynx, large	G. Granget	250	1600.00	6000.00
73-01-005	Mallard, large	G. Granget	250	2000.00	6500.00
XX-01-006	Peregrine Falcon, large	G. Granget	250	2250.00	6500.00
73-01-007	Rooster, large	G. Granget	250	2400.00	6000.00
73-01-008	Black Grouse, small	G. Granget	1,000	700.00	1500.00
73-01-009	Fox, small	G. Granget	1,000	650.00	1500.00
73-01-010	Golden Eagle, small	G. Granget	1,000	550.00	1500.00
73-01-011	Lynx, small	G. Granget	1,000	400.00	700.00
73-01-012	Mallard, small	G. Granget	1,000	500.00	700.00
73-01-013	Partridge, small	G. Granget	1,000	550.00	1200.00
XX-01-014	Peregrine Falcon, small	G. Granget	1,000	500.00	600.00
73-01-015	Rooster, small	G. Granget	1,000	600.00	1000.00
73-01-016	Wild Boar, small	G. Granget	1,000	275.00	1200.00
XX-01-017	Wild Sow with Young, large	G. Granget	1,000	2800.00	8000.00
73-01-018	Fox, large	G. Granget	200	2800.00	9000.00
73-01-019	Partridge. large	G. Granget	200	2400.00	8000.00
73-01-020	Wild Boar, large	G. Granget	200	2400.00	8000.00
XX-01-021	Wild Sow with Young, small	G. Granget	200	600.00	1500.00
XX-01-022	Barn Owl, 10 inches	G. Granget	2,500	600.00	700.00
XX-01-023	Barn Owl, 12.5 inches	G. Granget	1,500	700.00	1200.00
XX-01-024	Peregrine Falcon, medium	G. Granget	1,500	700.00	1200.00
XX-01-025	Ring-necked Pheasant, large	G. Granget	Unkn.	2250.00	8000.00
XX-01-026	Ring-necked Pheasant, small	G. Granget	Unkn.	500.00	1000.00
Dave Grossman Creations		**Saturday Evening Post**			
90-01-001	No Swimming NRP-901	Rockwell-Inspired	Retrd.	50.00	50.00
90-01-002	Daydreamer NRP-902	Rockwell-Inspired	Retrd.	55.00	55.00
90-01-003	Prom Dress NRP-903	Rockwell-Inspired	Retrd.	60.00	60.00
90-01-004	Bedside Manner NRP-904	Rockwell-Inspired	Retrd.	65.00	65.00
90-01-005	Runaway NRP-905	Rockwell-Inspired	Retrd.	130.00	130.00
90-01-006	Big Moment NRP-906	Rockwell-Inspired	Retrd.	100.00	100.00
90-01-007	Doctor and Doll NRP-907	Rockwell-Inspired	Retrd.	110.00	110.00
90-01-008	Bottom of the Sixth NRP-908	Rockwell-Inspired	Retrd.	165.00	165.00
91-01-009	Catching The Big One NRP-909	Rockwell-Inspired	Retrd.	75.00	75.00

Company / Number	Name / Series	Artist	Edition Limit	Issue Price	Quote
91-01-010	Gramps NRP-910	Rockwell-Inspired	Retrd.	85.00	85.00
91-01-011	The Pharmacist NRP-911	Rockwell-Inspired	Retrd.	70.00	70.00
92-01-012	Choosin Up NRP-912	Rockwell-Inspired	7,500	110.00	110.00
Dave Grossman Creations	**Saturday Evening Post-Miniatures**				
91-02-001	A Boy Meets His Dog BMR-01	Rockwell-Inspired	Retrd.	35.00	35.00
91-02-002	Downhill Daring BMR-02	Rockwell-Inspired	Retrd.	40.00	40.00
91-02-003	Flowers in Tender Bloom BMR-03	Rockwell-Inspired	Retrd.	32.00	32.00
91-02-004	Fondly Do We Remember BMR-04	Rockwell-Inspired	Retrd.	30.00	30.00
91-02-005	In His Spirit BMR-05	Rockwell-Inspired	Retrd.	30.00	30.00
91-02-006	Pride of Parenthood BMR-06	Rockwell-Inspired	Retrd.	35.00	35.00
91-02-007	Sweet Serenade BMR-07	Rockwell-Inspired	Retrd.	32.00	32.00
91-02-008	Sweet Song So Young BMR-08	Rockwell-Inspired	Retrd.	30.00	30.00
Dave Grossman Creations	**Norman Rockwell America Collection-Large Limited Edition**				
89-03-001	Doctor and Doll NRP-300	Rockwell-Inspired	Retrd.	150.00	150.00
89-03-002	Bottom of the Sixth NRP-307	Rockwell-Inspired	Retrd.	190.00	190.00
89-03-003	Runaway NRP-310	Rockwell-Inspired	Retrd.	190.00	190.00
89-03-004	Weigh-In NRP-311	Rockwell-Inspired	Retrd.	160.00	160.00
Dave Grossman Creations	**Norman Rockwell America Collection**				
89-04-001	Doctor and Doll NRP-600	Rockwell-Inspired	Retrd.	90.00	90.00
89-04-002	Locomotive NRC-603	Rockwell-Inspired	Retrd.	110.00	110.00
89-04-003	First Haircut NRC-604	Rockwell-Inspired	Retrd.	75.00	75.00
89-04-004	First Visit NRC-605	Rockwell-Inspired	Retrd.	110.00	110.00
89-04-005	First Day Home NRC-606	Rockwell-Inspired	Retrd.	80.00	80.00
89-04-006	Bottom of the Sixth NRC-607	Rockwell-Inspired	Retrd.	140.00	140.00
89-04-007	Runaway NRC-610	Rockwell-Inspired	Retrd.	140.00	140.00
89-04-008	Weigh-In NRC-611	Rockwell-Inspired	Retrd.	120.00	120.00
Dave Grossman Creations	**Norman Rockwell America Collection-Miniatures**				
89-05-001	First Haircut MRC-904	Rockwell-Inspired	Retrd.	45.00	45.00
89-05-002	First Day Home MRC-906	Rockwell-Inspired	Retrd.	45.00	45.00
Dave Grossman Creations	**Emmett Kelly-Circus Collection**				
92-06-001	Christmas Tunes	B. Leighton-Jones	15,000	40.00	40.00
92-06-002	Emmett The Caddy	B. Leighton-Jones	15,000	45.00	45.00
92-06-003	Emmett At The Organ	B. Leighton-Jones	15,000	50.00	50.00
92-06-004	Emmett At Work	B. Leighton-Jones	15,000	45.00	45.00
92-06-005	Look At The Birdie	B. Leighton-Jones	15,000	40.00	40.00
Dave Grossman Creations	**Native American Series**				
91-07-001	Lone Wolf	E. Roberts	7,500	55.00	55.00
92-07-002	Tortoise Lady	E. Roberts	7,500	60.00	60.00
Dave Grossman Creations	**Gone With The Wind Series**				
92-08-001	Scarlett in Green Dress	Unknown	2 Yr.	70.00	70.00
Dave Grossman Designs	**Norman Rockwell Collection**				
73-01-001	Redhead NR-01	Rockwell-Inspired	Retrd.	20.00	200.00
73-01-002	Back To School NR-02	Rockwell-Inspired	Retrd.	20.00	35.00
73-01-003	Caroller NR-03	Rockwell-Inspired	Retrd.	22.50	35.00
73-01-004	Daydreamer NR-04	Rockwell-Inspired	Retrd.	22.50	50.00
73-01-005	No Swimming NR-05	Rockwell-Inspired	Retrd.	25.00	50.00
73-01-006	Love Letter NR-06	Rockwell-Inspired	Retrd.	25.00	60.00
73-01-007	Lovers NR-07	Rockwell-Inspired	Retrd.	45.00	66.00
73-01-008	Lazybones NR-08	Rockwell-Inspired	Retrd.	30.00	300.00
73-01-019	Leapfrog NR-09	Rockwell-Inspired	Retrd.	50.00	550.00
73-01-010	Schoolmaster NR-10	Rockwell-Inspired	Retrd.	55.00	225.00
73-01-011	Marble Players NR-11	Rockwell-Inspired	Retrd.	60.00	450.00
73-01-012	Doctor & Doll NR-12	Rockwell-Inspired	Retrd.	65.00	150.00
74-01-013	Friends In Need NR-13	Rockwell-Inspired	Retrd.	45.00	96.00
74-01-014	Springtime '33 NR-14	Rockwell-Inspired	Retrd.	30.00	45.00
74-01-015	Summertime '33 NR-15	Rockwell-Inspired	Retrd.	45.00	45.00
74-01-016	Baseball NR-16	Rockwell-Inspired	Retrd.	45.00	120.00
74-01-017	See America First NR-17	Rockwell-Inspired	Retrd.	50.00	85.00
74-01-018	Take Your Medicine NR-18	Rockwell-Inspired	Retrd.	50.00	95.00
75-01-019	Discovery NR-20	Rockwell-Inspired	Retrd.	55.00	160.00
75-01-020	Big Moment NR-21	Rockwell-Inspired	Retrd.	60.00	120.00
75-01-021	Circus NR-22	Rockwell-Inspired	Retrd.	55.00	100.00
75-01-022	Barbershop Quartet NR-23	Rockwell-Inspired	Retrd.	100.00	1400.00
76-01-023	Drum For Tommy NRC-24	Rockwell-Inspired	Retrd.	40.00	80.00
77-01-024	Springtime '35 NR-19	Rockwell-Inspired	Retrd.	50.00	55.00
77-01-025	Pals NR-25	Rockwell-Inspired	Retrd.	60.00	75.00
78-01-026	Young Doctor NRD-26	Rockwell-Inspired	Retrd.	100.00	100.00
78-01-027	First Day of School NR-27	Rockwell-Inspired	Retrd.	100.00	135.00
78-01-028	Magic Potion NR-28	Rockwell-Inspired	Retrd.	84.00	100.00
78-01-029	At the Doctor NR-29	Rockwell-Inspired	Retrd.	108.00	160.00
79-01-030	Teacher's Pet NRA-30	Rockwell-Inspired	Retrd.	35.00	80.00
79-01-031	Dreams of Long Ago NR-31	Rockwell-Inspired	Retrd.	100.00	160.00
79-01-032	Grandpa's Ballerina NR-32	Rockwell-Inspired	Retrd.	100.00	110.00
79-01-033	Back From Camp NR-33	Rockwell-Inspired	Retrd.	96.00	110.00
80-01-034	The Toss NR-34	Rockwell-Inspired	Retrd.	110.00	110.00
80-01-035	Exasperated Nanny NR-35	Rockwell-Inspired	Retrd.	96.00	96.00
80-01-036	Hankerchief NR-36	Rockwell-Inspired	Retrd.	110.00	110.00
80-01-037	Santa's Good Boys NR-37	Rockwell-Inspired	Retrd.	90.00	90.00
81-01-038	Spirit of Education NR-38	Rockwell-Inspired	Retrd.	96.00	110.00
82-01-039	A Visit With Rockwell NR-40	Rockwell-Inspired	Retrd.	120.00	120.00
82-01-040	Croquet NR-41	Rockwell-Inspired	Retrd.	100.00	110.00
82-01-041	American Mother NRG-42	Rockwell-Inspired	Retrd.	100.00	110.00
83-01-042	Country Critic NR-43	Rockwell-Inspired	Retrd.	75.00	75.00
83-01-043	Graduate NR-44	Rockwell-Inspired	Retrd.	30.00	35.00
83-01-044	Scotty's Surprise NRS-20	Rockwell-Inspired	Retrd.	25.00	25.00
84-01-045	Scotty's Home Plate NR-46	Rockwell-Inspired	Retrd.	30.00	40.00
86-01-046	Red Cross NR-47	Rockwell-Inspired	Retrd.	67.00	75.00
87-01-047	Young Love NR-48	Rockwell-Inspired	Retrd.	70.00	70.00
88-01-048	Wedding March NR-49	Rockwell-Inspired	Retrd.	110.00	110.00
Dave Grossman Designs	**Norman Rockwell Collection Miniatures**				
79-02-001	Redhead NR-201	Rockwell-Inspired	Retrd.	18.00	48.00
79-02-002	Back To School NR-202	Rockwell-Inspired	Retrd.	18.00	25.00
79-02-003	Caroller NR-203	Rockwell-Inspired	Retrd.	20.00	25.00
79-02-004	Daydreamer NR-204	Rockwell-Inspired	Retrd.	20.00	30.00
79-02-005	No Swimming NR-205	Rockwell-Inspired	Retrd.	22.00	30.00
79-02-006	Love Letter NR-206	Rockwell-Inspired	Retrd.	26.00	30.00
79-02-007	Lovers NR-207	Rockwell-Inspired	Retrd.	28.00	30.00
79-02-008	Lazybones NR-208	Rockwell-Inspired	Retrd.	22.00	30.00
79-02-009	Leapfrog NR-209	Rockwell-Inspired	Retrd.	32.00	32.00
79-02-010	Schoolmaster NR-210	Rockwell-Inspired	Retrd.	34.00	40.00
79-02-011	Marble Players NR-211	Rockwell-Inspired	Retrd.	36.00	38.00
79-02-012	Doctor and Doll NR-212	Rockwell-Inspired	Retrd.	40.00	40.00
80-02-013	Friends In Need NR-213	Rockwell-Inspired	Retrd.	30.00	40.00
80-02-014	Springtime '33 NR-214	Rockwell-Inspired	Retrd.	24.00	80.00
80-02-015	Summertime '33 NR-215	Rockwell-Inspired	Retrd.	22.00	25.00
80-02-016	Baseball NR-216	Rockwell-Inspired	Retrd.	40.00	50.00
80-02-017	See America First NR-217	Rockwell-Inspired	Retrd.	28.00	35.00
80-02-018	Take Your Medicine NR-218	Rockwell-Inspired	Retrd.	36.00	40.00
82-02-019	Springtime '35 NR-219	Rockwell-Inspired	Retrd.	24.00	30.00
82-02-020	Discovery NR-220	Rockwell-Inspired	Retrd.	35.00	45.00
82-02-021	Big Moment NR-221	Rockwell-Inspired	Retrd.	36.00	40.00
82-02-022	Circus NR-222	Rockwell-Inspired	Retrd.	35.00	40.00
82-02-023	Barbershop Quartet NR-223	Rockwell-Inspired	Retrd.	40.00	50.00
82-02-024	Drum For Tommy NRC-224	Rockwell-Inspired	Retrd.	25.00	30.00
83-02-025	Santa On the Train NR-245	Rockwell-Inspired	Retrd.	35.00	55.00
84-02-026	Pals NR-225	Rockwell-Inspired	Retrd.	25.00	25.00
84-02-027	Young Doctor NRD-226	Rockwell-Inspired	Retrd.	30.00	50.00
84-02-028	First Day of School NR-227	Rockwell-Inspired	Retrd.	35.00	35.00
84-02-029	Magic Potion NR-228	Rockwell-Inspired	Retrd.	30.00	40.00
84-02-030	At the Doctor's NR-229	Rockwell-Inspired	Retrd.	35.00	35.00
84-02-031	Dreams of Long Ago NR-231	Rockwell-Inspired	Retrd.	30.00	30.00
Dave Grossman Designs	**Norman Rockwell Collection-Large Limited Editions**				
74-03-001	Doctor and Doll NR-100	Rockwell-Inspired	Retrd.	300.00	1600.00
74-03-002	See America First NR-103	Rockwell-Inspired	Retrd.	100.00	300.00
75-03-003	No Swimming NR-101	Rockwell-Inspired	Retrd.	150.00	450.00
75-03-004	Baseball NR-102	Rockwell-Inspired	Retrd.	125.00	450.00
79-03-005	Leapfrog NR-104	Rockwell-Inspired	Retrd.	440.00	600.00
81-03-006	Dreams of Long Ago NR-105	Rockwell-Inspired	Retrd.	500.00	750.00
82-03-007	Circus NR-106	Rockwell-Inspired	Retrd.	500.00	550.00
84-03-008	Marble Players NR-107	Rockwell-Inspired	Retrd.	500.00	500.00
Dave Grossman Designs	**Norman Rockwell Collection-American Rockwell Series**				
81-04-001	Breaking Home Ties NRV-300	Rockwell-Inspired	Retrd.	2000.00	2300.00
82-04-002	Lincoln NRV-301	Rockwell-Inspired	Retrd.	300.00	375.00
82-04-003	Thanksgiving NRV-302	Rockwell-Inspired	Retrd.	2500.00	2650.00
Dave Grossman Designs	**Norman Rockwell Collection-Lladro Series**				
82-05-001	Lladro Love Letter RL-400	Rockwell-Inspired	Retrd.	650.00	650.00
82-05-002	Summer Stock RL-401	Rockwell-Inspired	Retrd.	750.00	750.00
82-05-003	Practice Makes Perfect RL-402	Rockwell-Inspired	Retrd.	725.00	725.00
82-05-004	Young Love RL-403	Rockwell-Inspired	Retrd.	450.00	475.00
82-05-005	Daydreamer RL-404	Rockwell-Inspired	Retrd.	450.00	450.00
82-05-006	Court Jester RL-405	Rockwell-Inspired	Retrd.	600.00	600.00
82-05-007	Springtime RL-406	Rockwell-Inspired	Retrd.	450.00	470.00
Dave Grossman Designs	**Norman Rockwell Collection-Rockwell Club Series**				
81-06-001	Young Artist RCC-01	Rockwell-Inspired	Retrd.	96.00	105.00
82-06-002	Diary RCC-02	Rockwell-Inspired	Retrd.	35.00	50.00
83-06-003	Runaway Pants RCC-03	Rockwell-Inspired	Retrd.	65.00	75.00
84-06-004	Gone Fishing RCC-04	Rockwell-Inspired	Retrd.	30.00	55.00
Dave Grossman Designs	**Norman Rockwell Collection-Tom Sawyer Series**				
75-07-001	Whitewashing the Fence TS-01	Rockwell-Inspired	Retrd.	60.00	200.00
76-07-002	First Smoke TS-02	Rockwell-Inspired	Retrd.	60.00	200.00
77-07-003	Take Your Medicine TS-03	Rockwell-Inspired	Retrd.	63.00	170.00
78-07-004	Lost In Cave TS-04	Rockwell-Inspired	Retrd.	70.00	145.00
Dave Grossman Designs	**Norman Rockwell Collection-Tom Sawyer Miniatures**				
83-08-001	Whitewashing the Fence TSM-01	Rockwell-Inspired	Retrd.	40.00	50.00
83-08-002	First Smoke TSM-02	Rockwell-Inspired	Retrd.	40.00	45.00
83-08-003	Take Your Medicine TSM-04	Rockwell-Inspired	Retrd.	40.00	45.00
83-08-004	Lost In Cave TSM-05	Rockwell-Inspired	Retrd.	40.00	45.00
Dave Grossman Designs	**Norman Rockwell Collection-Huck Finn Series**				
79-09-001	The Secret HF-01	Rockwell-Inspired	Retrd.	110.00	130.00
80-09-002	Listening HF-02	Rockwell-Inspired	Retrd.	110.00	120.00
80-09-003	No Kings HF-03	Rockwell-Inspired	Retrd.	110.00	110.00
80-09-004	Snake Escapes HF-04	Rockwell-Inspired	Retrd.	110.00	120.00
Dave Grossman Designs	**Norman Rockwell Collection-Boy Scout Series**				
81-10-001	Can't Wait BSA-01	Rockwell-Inspired	Retrd.	30.00	50.00
81-10-002	Scout Is Helpful BSA-02	Rockwell-Inspired	Retrd.	38.00	45.00
81-10-003	Physically Strong BSA-03	Rockwell-Inspired	Retrd.	56.00	60.00
81-10-004	Good Friends BSA-04	Rockwell-Inspired	Retrd.	58.00	65.00
81-10-005	Good Turn BSA-05	Rockwell-Inspired	Retrd.	65.00	100.00
81-10-006	Scout Memories BSA-06	Rockwell-Inspired	Retrd.	65.00	70.00
82-10-007	Guiding Hand BSA-07	Rockwell-Inspired	Retrd.	58.00	60.00
83-10-008	Tomorrow's Leader BSA-08	Rockwell-Inspired	Retrd.	45.00	55.00
Dave Grossman Designs	**Norman Rockwell Collection-Country Gentlemen Series**				
82-11-001	Turkey Dinner CG-01	Rockwell-Inspired	Retrd.	85.00	N/A
82-11-002	Bringing Home the Tree CG-02	Rockwell-Inspired	Retrd.	60.00	N/A
82-11-003	Pals CG-03	Rockwell-Inspired	Retrd.	36.00	45.00
82-11-004	The Catch CG-04	Rockwell-Inspired	Retrd.	50.00	60.00
82-11-005	On the Ice CG-05	Rockwell-Inspired	Retrd.	50.00	N/A
82-11-006	Thin Ice CG-06	Rockwell-Inspired	Retrd.	50.00	60.00
Dave Grossman Designs	**Norman Rockwell Collection-Select Collection, Ltd.**				
82-12-001	Boy & Mother With Puppies SC-1001	Rockwell-Inspired	Retrd.	27.50	N/A
82-12-002	Girl With Dolls In Crib SC-1002	Rockwell-Inspired	Retrd.	26.50	N/A
82-12-003	Young Couple SC-1003	Rockwell-Inspired	Retrd.	27.50	N/A
82-12-004	Football Player SC-1004	Rockwell-Inspired	Retrd.	22.00	N/A
82-12-005	Father With Child SC-1005	Rockwell-Inspired	Retrd.	22.00	N/A
82-12-006	Girl Bathing Dog SC-1006	Rockwell-Inspired	Retrd.	26.50	N/A
82-12-007	Helping Hand SC-1007	Rockwell-Inspired	Retrd.	32.00	N/A
82-12-008	Lemonade Stand SC-1008	Rockwell-Inspired	Retrd.	32.00	N/A
82-12-009	Shaving Lesson SC-1009	Rockwell-Inspired	Retrd.	30.00	N/A
82-12-010	Save Me SC-1010	Rockwell-Inspired	Retrd.	35.00	N/A
Dave Grossman Designs	**Norman Rockwell Collection-Pewter Figurines**				
80-13-001	Back to School FP-02	Rockwell-Inspired	Retrd.	25.00	N/A
80-13-002	Caroller FP-03	Rockwell-Inspired	Retrd.	25.00	N/A
80-13-003	No Swimming FP-05	Rockwell-Inspired	Retrd.	25.00	N/A
80-13-004	Lovers FP-07	Rockwell-Inspired	Retrd.	25.00	N/A
80-13-005	Doctor and Doll FP-12	Rockwell-Inspired	Retrd.	25.00	N/A
80-13-006	See America First FP-17	Rockwell-Inspired	Retrd.	25.00	N/A
80-13-007	Take Your Medicine FP-18	Rockwell-Inspired	Retrd.	25.00	N/A
80-13-008	Big Moment FP-21	Rockwell-Inspired	Retrd.	25.00	N/A
80-13-009	Circus FP-22	Rockwell-Inspired	Retrd.	25.00	N/A
80-13-010	Barbershop Quartet FP-23	Rockwell-Inspired	Retrd.	25.00	N/A
80-13-011	Magic Potion FP-28	Rockwell-Inspired	Retrd.	25.00	N/A
80-13-012	Grandpa's Ballerina FP-32	Rockwell-Inspired	Retrd.	25.00	N/A
80-13-013	Figurine Display Rack FDR-01	Rockwell-Inspired	Retrd.	60.00	N/A
Hamilton/Boehm	**Roses of Disctinction**				
83-01-001	Peace Rose	Boehm	9,800	135.00	195.00

Number	Name	Artist	Edition Limit	Issue Price	Quote
83-01-002	White Masterpiece Rose	Boehm	9,800	135.00	180.00
83-01-003	Angel Face Rose	Boehm	9,800	135.00	175.00
83-01-004	Queen Elizabeth Rose	Boehm	9,800	135.00	175.00
83-01-005	Elegance Rose	Boehm	9,800	135.00	175.00
83-01-006	Royal Highness Rose	Boehm	9,800	135.00	175.00
83-01-007	Tropicana Rose	Boehm	9,800	135.00	175.00
83-01-008	Mr. Lincoln Rose	Boehm	9,800	135.00	175.00
Hamilton/Boehm		**Favorite Garden Flowers**			
85-02-001	Morning Glory	Boehm	9,800	195.00	225.00
85-02-002	Hibiscus	Boehm	9,800	195.00	225.00
85-02-003	Tulip	Boehm	9,800	195.00	225.00
85-02-004	Sweet Pea	Boehm	9,800	195.00	225.00
85-02-005	Rose	Boehm	9,800	195.00	225.00
85-02-006	Carnation	Boehm	9,800	195.00	225.00
85-02-007	California Poppy	Boehm	9,800	195.00	225.00
85-02-008	Daffodil	Boehm	9,800	195.00	225.00
Hamilton Collection		**American Wildlife Bronze Collection**			
79-01-001	Cougar	H./N. Deaton	7,500	60.00	125.00
79-01-002	White-Tailed Deer	H./N. Deaton	7,500	60.00	105.00
79-01-003	Bobcat	H./N. Deaton	7,500	60.00	75.00
80-01-004	Beaver	H./N. Deaton	7,500	60.00	65.00
80-01-005	Polar Bear	H./N. Deaton	7,500	60.00	65.00
80-01-006	Sea Otter	H./N. Deaton	7,500	60.00	65.00
Hamilton Collection		**Rockwell Home of The Brave**			
82-02-001	Reminiscing	N. Rockwell	7,500	75.00	75.00
82-02-002	Hero's Welcome	N. Rockwell	7,500	75.00	75.00
82-02-003	Uncle Sam Takes Wings	N. Rockwell	7,500	75.00	75.00
82-02-004	Back to His Old Job	N. Rockwell	7,500	75.00	75.00
82-02-005	Willie Gillis in Church	N. Rockwell	7,500	75.00	75.00
82-02-006	Taking Mother over the Top	N. Rockwell	7,500	75.00	75.00
Hamilton Collection		**Ringling Bros. Circus Animals**			
83-03-001	Miniature Show Horse	P. Cozzolino	9,800	49.50	68.00
83-03-002	Baby Elephant	P. Cozzolino	9,800	49.50	55.00
83-03-003	Acrobatic Seal	P. Cozzolino	9,800	49.50	49.50
83-03-004	Skating Bear	P. Cozzolino	9,800	49.50	49.50
83-03-005	Mr. Chimpanzee	P. Cozzolino	9,800	49.50	49.50
83-03-006	Performing Poodles	P. Cozzolino	9,800	49.50	49.50
84-03-007	Roaring Lion	P. Cozzolino	9,800	49.50	49.60
84-03-008	Parade Camel	P. Cozzolino	9,800	49.50	49.50
Hamilton Collection		**Great Animals of the American Wilderness**			
83-04-001	Mountain Lion	H. Deaton	7,500	75.00	75.00
83-04-002	Grizzly Bear	H. Deaton	7,500	75.00	75.00
83-04-003	Timber Wolf	H. Deaton	7,500	75.00	75.00
83-04-004	Pronghorn Antelope	H. Deaton	7,500	75.00	75.00
83-04-005	Plains Bison	H. Deaton	7,500	75.00	75.00
83-04-006	Elk	H. Deaton	7,500	75.00	75.00
83-04-007	Mustang	H. Deaton	7,500	75.00	75.00
83-04-008	Bighorn Sheep	H. Deaton	7,500	75.00	75.00
Hamilton Collection		**American Garden Flowers**			
87-05-001	Camelia	D. Fryer	9,800	55.00	75.00
87-05-002	Gardenia	D. Fryer	15,000	75.00	75.00
87-05-003	Azalea	D. Fryer	15,000	75.00	75.00
87-05-004	Rose	D. Fryer	15,000	75.00	75.00
88-05-005	Day Lily	D. Fryer	15,000	75.00	75.00
88-05-006	Petunia	D. Fryer	15,000	75.00	75.00
88-05-007	Calla Lilly	D. Fryer	15,000	75.00	75.00
89-05-008	Pansy	D. Fryer	15,000	75.00	75.00
Hamilton Collection		**Celebration of Opera**			
86-06-001	Cio-Cio-San	J. Villena	7,500	95.00	95.00
86-06-002	Carmen	J. Villena	7,500	95.00	95.00
87-06-003	Figaro	J. Villena	7,500	95.00	95.00
88-06-004	Mimi	J. Villena	7,500	95.00	95.00
88-06-005	Aida	J. Villena	7,500	95.00	95.00
88-06-006	Canio	J. Villena	7,500	95.00	95.00
Hamilton Collection		**Exotic Birds of the World**			
84-07-001	The Cockatoo	Francesco	7,500	75.00	115.00
84-07-002	The Budgerigar	Francesco	7,500	75.00	105.00
84-07-003	The Rubenio Parakeet	Francesco	7,500	75.00	95.00
84-07-004	The Quetzal	Francesco	7,500	75.00	95.00
84-07-005	The Red Lorg	Francesco	7,500	75.00	95.00
84-07-006	The Fisher's Whydah	Francesco	7,500	75.00	95.00
84-07-007	The Diamond Dove	Francesco	7,500	75.00	95.00
84-07-008	The Peach-faced Lovebird	Francesco	7,500	75.00	95.00
Hamilton Collection		**Majestic Wildlife of North America**			
85-08-001	White-tailed Deer	H. Deaton	7,500	75.00	75.00
85-08-002	Ocelot	H. Deaton	7,500	75.00	75.00
85-08-003	Alaskan Moose	H. Deaton	7,500	75.00	75.00
85-08-004	Black Bear	H. Deaton	7,500	75.00	75.00
85-08-005	Mountain Goat	H. Deaton	7,500	75.00	75.00
85-08-006	Coyote	H. Deaton	7,500	75.00	75.00
85-08-007	Barren Ground Caribou	H. Deaton	7,500	75.00	75.00
85-08-008	Harbour Seal	H. Deaton	7,500	75.00	75.00
Hamilton Collection		**Magnificent Birds of Paradise**			
85-09-001	Emperor of Germany	Francesco	12,500	75.00	95.00
85-09-002	Greater Bird of Paradise	Francesco	12,500	75.00	95.00
85-09-003	Magnificent Bird of Paradise	Francesco	12,500	75.00	95.00
85-09-004	Raggiana Bird of Paradise	Francesco	12,500	75.00	95.00
85-09-005	Princess Stephanie Bird of Paradise	Francesco	12,500	75.00	95.00
85-09-006	Goldie's Bird of Paradise	Francesco	12,500	75.00	95.00
85-09-007	Blue Bird of Paradise	Francesco	12,500	75.00	95.00
85-09-008	Black Sickle-Billed Bird of Paradise	Francesco	12,500	75.00	95.00
Hamilton Collection		**Legendary Flowers of the Orient**			
85-10-001	Iris	Ito	15,000	55.00	55.00
85-10-002	Lotus	Ito	15,000	55.00	55.00
85-10-003	Chinese Peony	Ito	15,000	55.00	55.00
85-10-004	Gold Band Lily	Ito	15,000	55.00	55.00
85-10-005	Chrysanthemum	Ito	15,000	55.00	55.00
85-10-006	Cherry Blossom	Ito	15,000	55.00	55.00
85-10-007	Japanese Orchid	Ito	15,000	55.00	55.00
85-10-008	Wisteria	Ito	15,000	55.00	55.00

Number	Name	Artist	Edition Limit	Issue Price	Quote
Hamilton Collection		**The Splendor of Ballet**			
87-11-001	Juliet	E. Daub	15,000	95.00	95.00
87-11-002	Odette	E. Daub	15,000	95.00	95.00
87-11-003	Giselle	E. Daub	15,000	95.00	95.00
87-11-004	Kitri	E. Daub	15,000	95.00	95.00
88-11-005	Aurora	E. Daub	15,000	95.00	95.00
89-11-006	Swanilda	E. Daub	15,000	95.00	95.00
89-11-007	Firebird	E. Daub	15,000	95.00	95.00
89-11-008	Clara	E. Daub	15,000	95.00	95.00
Hamilton Collection		**The Noble Swan**			
85-12-001	The Noble Swan	G. Granget	5,000	295.00	295.00
Hamilton Collection		**The Gibson Girls**			
86-13-001	The Actress	Unknown	Open	75.00	75.00
87-13-002	The Career Girl	Unknown	Open	75.00	75.00
87-13-003	The College Girl	Unknown	Open	75.00	75.00
87-13-004	The Bride	Unknown	Open	75.00	75.00
87-13-005	The Sportswoman	Unknown	Open	75.00	75.00
88-13-006	The Debutante	Unknown	Open	75.00	75.00
88-13-007	The Artist	Unknown	Open	75.00	75.00
88-13-008	The Society Girl	Unknown	Open	75.00	75.00
Hamilton Collection		**The Romance of Flowers**			
87-14-001	Springtime Bouquet	Maruri	15,000	95.00	95.00
87-14-002	Summer Bouquet	Maruri	15,000	95.00	95.00
88-14-003	Autumn Bouquet	Maruri	15,000	95.00	95.00
88-14-004	Winter Bouquet	Maruri	15,000	95.00	95.00
Hamilton Collection		**Wild Ducks of North America**			
87-15-001	Common Mallard	C. Burgess	15,000	95.00	95.00
87-15-002	Wood Duck	C. Burgess	15,000	95.00	95.00
87-15-003	Green Winged Teal	C. Burgess	15,000	95.00	95.00
87-15-004	Hooded Merganser	C. Burgess	15,000	95.00	95.00
88-15-005	Northern Pintail	C. Burgess	15,000	95.00	95.00
88-15-006	Ruddy Duck Drake	C. Burgess	15,000	95.00	95.00
88-15-007	Bufflehead	C. Burgess	15,000	95.00	95.00
88-15-008	American Widgeon	C. Burgess	15,000	95.00	95.00
Hamilton Collection		**Snuggle Babies**			
88-16-001	Baby Bunnies	Jacqueline B.	Open	35.00	35.00
88-16-002	Baby Bears	Jacqueline B.	Open	35.00	35.00
88-16-003	Baby Skunks	Jacqueline B.	Open	35.00	35.00
88-16-004	Baby Foxes	Jacqueline B.	Open	35.00	35.00
89-16-005	Baby Chipmunks	Jacqueline B.	Open	35.00	35.00
89-16-006	Baby Raccoons	Jacqueline B.	Open	35.00	35.00
89-16-007	Baby Squirrels	Jacqueline B.	Open	35.00	35.00
89-16-008	Baby Fawns	Jacqueline B.	Open	35.00	35.00
Hamilton Collection		**Tropical Treasures**			
89-17-001	Sail-finned Surgeonfish	M. Wald	Open	37.50	37.50
89-17-002	Flag-tail Surgeonfish	M. Wald	Open	37.50	37.50
89-17-003	Pennant Butterfly Fish	M. Wald	Open	37.50	37.50
89-17-004	Sea Horse	M. Wald	Open	37.50	37.50
90-17-005	Zebra Turkey Fish	M. Wald	Open	37.50	37.50
90-17-006	Spotted Angel Fish	M. Wald	Open	37.50	37.50
90-17-007	Blue Girdled Angel Fish	M. Wald	Open	37.50	37.50
90-17-008	Beaked Coral Butterfly Fish	M. Wald	Open	37.50	37.50
Hamilton Collection		**A Celebration of Roses**			
89-18-001	Tiffany	N/A	Open	55.00	55.00
89-18-002	Color Magic	N/A	Open	55.00	55.00
89-18-003	Honor	N/A	Open	55.00	55.00
89-18-004	Brandy	N/A	Open	55.00	55.00
89-18-005	Miss All-American Beauty	N/A	Open	55.00	55.00
90-18-006	Oregold	N/A	Open	55.00	55.00
91-18-007	Paradise	N/A	Open	55.00	55.00
91-18-008	Ole'	N/A	Open	55.00	55.00
Hamilton Collection		**Heroes of Baseball-Porcelain Baseball Cards**			
90-19-001	Brooks Robinson	N/A	Open	19.50	19.50
90-19-002	Roberto Clemente	N/A	Open	19.50	19.50
90-19-003	Willie Mays	N/A	Open	19.50	19.50
90-19-004	Duke Snider	N/A	Open	19.50	19.50
91-19-005	Whitey Ford	N/A	Open	19.50	19.50
91-19-006	Gil Hodges	N/A	Open	19.50	19.50
91-19-007	Mickey Mantle	N/A	Open	19.50	19.50
91-19-008	Casey Stengel	N/A	Open	19.50	19.50
91-19-009	Jackie Robinson	N/A	Open	19.50	19.50
91-19-010	Ernie Banks	N/A	Open	19.50	19.50
91-19-011	Yogi Berra	N/A	Open	19.50	19.50
91-19-012	Satchel Page	N/A	Open	19.50	19.50
Hamilton Collection		**Little Night Owls**			
90-20-001	Tawny Owl	D.T. Lyttleton	Open	45.00	45.00
90-20-002	Barn Owl	D.T. Lyttleton	Open	45.00	45.00
90-20-003	Snowy Owl	D.T. Lyttleton	Open	45.00	45.00
91-20-004	Barred Owl	D.T. Lyttleton	Open	45.00	45.00
91-20-005	Great Horned Owl	D.T. Lyttleton	Open	45.00	45.00
Hamilton Collection		**Puppy Playtime Sculpture Collection**			
90-21-001	Double Take	J. Lamb	Open	29.50	29.50
91-21-002	Catch of the Day	J. Lamb	Open	29.50	29.50
91-21-003	Cabin Fever	J. Lamb	Open	29.50	29.50
91-21-004	Weekend Gardner	J. Lamb	Open	29.50	29.50
91-21-005	Hanging Out	J. Lamb	Open	29.50	29.50
91-21-006	Getting Acquainted	J. Lamb	Open	29.50	29.50
91-21-007	A New Leash on Life	J. Lamb	Open	29.50	29.50
Hamilton Collection		**Freshwater Challenge**			
91-22-001	The Strike	M. Wald	Open	75.00	75.00
91-22-002	Rainbow Lure	M. Wald	Open	75.00	75.00
91-22-003	Sun Catcher	M. Wald	Open	75.00	75.00
92-22-004	Prized Catch	M. Wald	Open	75.00	75.00
Hamilton Collection		**Puss in Boots**			
92-23-001	Caught Napping	P. Cooper	Open	35.00	35.00
92-23-002	Sweet Dreams	P. Cooper	Open	35.00	35.00
Hamilton Collection		**International Santa**			
92-24-001	Father Christmas	N/A	Open	55.00	55.00
92-24-002	Santa Claus	N/A	Open	55.00	55.00

Hamilton Gifts — Maud Humphrey Bogart Figurines

Number	Name	Artist	Edition Limit	Issue Price	Quote
88-01-001	Tea And Gossip H1301	M. Humphrey	Retrd.	65.00	85-120.00
88-01-002	Cleaning House H1303	M. Humphrey	Retrd.	60.00	60-100.00
88-01-003	Susanna H 1305	M. Humphrey	Retrd.	60.00	150-250.
88-01-004	Little Chickadees H1306	M. Humphrey	Retrd.	65.00	70-100.00
88-01-005	The Magic Kitten H1308	M. Humphrey	Retrd.	66.00	80-115.00
88-01-006	Seamstress H1309	M. Humphrey	Retrd.	66.00	90-125.00
88-01-006	A Pleasure To Meet You H1310	M. Humphrey	Retrd.	65.00	100.00
88-01-008	My First Dance H1311	M. Humphrey	Retrd.	60.00	175-300.
88-01-009	Sarah H1312	M. Humphrey	Retrd.	60.00	250-425.
89-01-010	The Bride H1313	M. Humphrey	19,500	90.00	90.00
89-01-011	Sealed With A Kiss H1316	M. Humphrey	Retrd.	45.00	55-105.00
88-01-012	Special Friends H1317	M. Humphrey	Retrd.	66.00	100-140.
89-01-013	School Days H1318	M. Humphrey	Retrd.	42.50	60-100.00
89-01-014	Gift Of Love H1319	M. Humphrey	Retrd.	65.00	67.00
89-01-015	My 1st Birthday H1320	M. Humphrey	Retrd.	47.00	50.00
90-01-016	A Little Robin H1347	M. Humphrey	19,500	55.00	58.00
90-01-017	Autumn Days H1348	M. Humphrey	24,500	45.00	49.00
90-01-018	Little Playmates H1349	M. Humphrey	19,500	48.00	53.00
89-01-019	No More Tears H1351	M. Humphrey	24,500	44.00	49.00
89-01-020	Winter Fun H1354	M. Humphrey	Retired	46.00	54.00
89-01-021	Kitty's Lunch H1355	M. Humphrey	19,500	60.00	66.00
90-01-022	School Lesson H1356	M. Humphrey	19,500	77.00	79.00
89-01-023	In The Orchard H1373	M. Humphrey	24,500	33.00	36.00
89-01-024	The Little Captive H1374	M. Humphrey	19,500	55.00	58.00
89-01-025	Little Red Riding Hood H1381	M. Humphrey	24,500	42.50	46.00
89-01-026	Little Bo Peep H1382	M. Humphrey	24,500	45.00	49.00
90-01-027	Playtime H1383	M. Humphrey	19,500	60.00	66.00
90-01-028	Kitty's Bath H1384	M. Humphrey	19,500	103.00	109.00
89-01-029	Springtime Gathering H1385	M. Humphrey	7,500	295.00	299.00
89-01-030	A Sunday Outing H1386	M. Humphrey	15,000	135.00	139.50
89-01-031	Spring Beauties H1387	M. Humphrey	15,000	135.00	139.50
89-01-032	The Bride-Porcelain H1388	M. Humphrey	15,000	125.00	128.00
89-01-033	Little Chickadees-Porcelain H1389	M. Humphrey	15,000	125.00	128.00
89-01-034	Special Friends-Porcelain H1390	M. Humphrey	15,000	125.00	128.00
89-01-035	Playing Bridesmaid H5500	M. Humphrey	19,500	125.00	135.00
89-01-036	The Magic Kitten-Porcelain H5543	M. Humphrey	15,000	125.00	125.00
90-01-037	A Special Gift H5550	M. Humphrey	19,500	70.00	99.00
90-01-038	Holiday Surprise H5551	M. Humphrey	24,500	50.00	55.00
90-01-039	Winter Friends H5552	M. Humphrey	19,500	64.00	69.00
90-01-040	Winter Days H5553	M. Humphrey	24,500	50.00	55.00
90-01-041	My Winter Hat H5554	M. Humphrey	24,500	40.00	46.00
91-01-042	The Graduate H5559	M. Humphrey	19,500	75.00	75.00
90-01-043	A Chance Acquaintance H5589	M. Humphrey	19,500	70.00	135.00
91-01-044	Spring Frolic H5590	M. Humphrey	15,000	170.00	170.00
90-01-045	Sarah (Waterball) H5594	M. Humphrey	19,500	75.00	79.00
90-01-046	Susanna (Waterball) H5595	M. Humphrey	19,500	75.00	79.00
91-01-047	Spring Bouquet H5598	M. Humphrey	24,500	44.00	44.00
91-01-048	The Pinwheel H5600	M. Humphrey	24,500	45.00	45.00
91-01-049	Little Boy Blue H5612	M. Humphrey	19,500	55.00	55.00
91-01-050	Little Miss Muffet H5621	M. Humphrey	24,500	75.00	75.00
91-01-051	My First Dance-Porcelain H5650	M. Humphrey	15,000	110.00	110.00
91-01-052	Sarah-Porcelain H5651	M. Humphrey	15,000	110.00	110.00
91-01-053	Susanna-Porcelain H5652	M. Humphrey	15,000	110.00	110.00
91-01-054	Tea And Gossip-Porcelain H5653	M. Humphrey	15,000	132.00	132.00
91-01-055	Cleaning House (Waterball) H5654	M. Humphrey	19,500	75.00	75.00
91-01-056	My First Dance (Waterball) H5655	M. Humphrey	19,500	75.00	75.00
91-01-057	Hush A Bye Baby H5695	M. Humphrey	19,500	62.00	62.00
91-01-058	All Bundled Up -910015	M. Humphrey	19,500	85.00	85.00
91-01-059	Doubles -910023	M. Humphrey	19,500	70.00	70.00
91-01-060	Melissa -910031	M. Humphrey	24,500	55.00	55.00
91-01-061	My Snow Shovel -910058	M. Humphrey	19,500	7000	70.00
91-01-062	Winter Ride -910066	M. Humphrey	19,500	60.00	60.00
91-01-063	Melissa (Waterball) -910074	M. Humphrey	19,500	40.00	40.00
91-01-064	Winter Days (Waterball) -915130	M. Humphrey	19,500	75.00	75.00
91-01-065	Winter Friends (Waterball) -915149	M. Humphrey	19,500	75.00	75.00
91-01-066	My Winter Hat -921017	M. Humphrey	15,000	80.00	80.00
91-01-067	Winter Fun -921025	M. Humphrey	15,000	90.00	90.00
92-01-068	Spring's Child 910244	M. Humphrey	24,500	50.00	50.00
92-01-069	Summer's Child 910252	M. Humphrey	24,500	50.00	50.00
92-01-070	Autumn's Child 910260	M. Humphrey	24,500	50.00	50.00
92-01-071	Winter's Child 910279	M. Humphrey	24,500	50.00	50.00
92-01-072	Jack and Jill 910155	M. Humphrey	19,500	75.00	75.00
92-01-073	The Young Artist 910228	M. Humphrey	19,500	75.00	75.00
92-01-074	Stars and Stripes Forever 910201	M. Humphrey	Open	75.00	75.00
92-01-075	New Friends 910171	M. Humphrey	15,000	125.00	125.00
92-01-076	Under The Mistletoe 910309	M. Humphrey	19,500	75.00	75.00
92-01-077	Hollies For You 910317	M. Humphrey	24,500	55.00	55.00
92-01-078	Hush! Santa's Coming 915378	M. Humphrey	19,500	50.00	50.00
92-01-079	A Melody For You 915432	M. Humphrey	Open	60.00	60.00
92-01-080	The Christmas Carol 915823	M. Humphrey	19,500	75.00	75.00
92-01-081	Susanna (Musical) 921084	M. Humphrey	7,500	125.00	125.00
92-01-082	Sarah (Musical) 921076	M. Humphrey	7,500	125.00	125.00
92-01-083	Hollies For You (Musical) 921092	M. Humphrey	5,000	125.00	125.00

Hamilton Gifts — Maud Humphrey Bogart Gallery Figurines

Number	Name	Artist	Edition Limit	Issue Price	Quote
91-02-001	Mother's Treasures H5619	M. Humphrey	15,000	118.00	118.00
91-02-002	Sharing Secrets-910007	M. Humphrey	15,000	120.00	120.00

Hamilton Gifts — Maud Humphrey Bogart Symbol Of Membership Figurines

Number	Name	Artist	Edition Limit	Issue Price	Quote
91-03-001	A Flower For You H5596	M. Humphrey	Closed	Unkn.	Unkn.
92-03-002	Sunday Best M0002	M. Humphrey	Open	Unkn.	Unkn.

Hamilton Gifts — Maud Humphrey Bogart Collectors' Club Members Only

Number	Name	Artist	Edition Limit	Issue Price	Quote
91-04-001	Friends For Life MH911	M. Humphrey	Closed	60.00	120.00
92-04-002	Nature's Little Helper MH921	M. Humphrey	Open	65.00	65.00

John Hine N.A. Ltd. — David Winter Cottages

Number	Name	Artist	Edition Limit	Issue Price	Quote
80-01-001	The Wine Merchant	D. Winter	Open	28.90	50.00
80-01-002	Little Market	D. Winter	Open	28.90	50.00
80-01-003	Rose Cottage	D. Winter	Open	28.90	50.00
80-01-004	Market Street	D. Winter	Open	48.80	80.00
81-01-005	Single Oast	D. Winter	Open	22.00	50-130.00
81-01-006	Triple Oast	D. Winter	Open	59.90	106.00
81-01-007	Stratford House	D. Winter	Open	74.80	118.00
81-01-008	The Village	D. Winter	Open	362.00	550.00
82-01-009	Drover's Cottage	D. Winter	Open	22.00	30.00
82-01-010	Ivy Cottage	D. Winter	Open	22.00	38.00
82-01-011	Sussex Cottage	D. Winter	Open	22.00	38.00
82-01-012	The Village Shop	D. Winter	Open	22.00	30.00
82-01-013	The Dower House	D. Winter	Open	22.00	30.00
82-01-014	Cotswold Cottage	D. Winter	Open	22.00	30.00
82-01-015	The Old Distillery	D. Winter	Open	312.20	530.00
83-01-016	The Bakehouse	D. Winter	Open	31.40	54.00
83-01-017	The Bothy	D. Winter	Open	31.40	54.00
83-01-018	Fisherman's Wharf	D. Winter	Open	31.40	54.00
83-01-019	The Green Dragon Inn	D. Winter	Open	31.40	54.00
83-01-020	Pilgrim's Rest	D. Winter	Open	48.80	80.00
83-01-021	Hertford Court	D. Winter	Open	87.00	138.00
84-01-022	The Chapel	D. Winter	Open	48.80	78.00
84-01-023	Snow Cottage	D. Winter	Open	74.80	118.00
84-01-024	The Parsonage	D. Winter	Open	390.00	530.00
85-01-025	The Cooper's Cottage	D. Winter	Open	57.90	78.00
85-01-026	Kent Cottage	D. Winter	Open	48.80	94.00
85-01-027	The Schoolhouse	D. Winter	Open	24.10	42.00
85-01-028	Craftsmen's Cottages	D. Winter	Open	24.10	38.00
85-01-029	The Vicarage	D. Winter	Open	24.10	38.00
85-01-030	The Hogs Head Tavern	D. Winter	Open	24.10	42.00
85-01-031	Blackfriars Grange	D. Winter	Open	24.10	38.00
85-01-032	Shirehall	D. Winter	Open	24.10	42.00
85-01-033	The Apothecary Shop	D. Winter	Open	24.10	42.00
85-01-034	Yeoman's Farmhouse	D. Winter	Open	24.10	38.00
85-01-035	Meadowbank Cottages	D. Winter	Open	24.10	38.00
85-01-036	St. George's Church	D. Winter	Open	24.10	42.00
87-01-037	Smuggler's Creek	D. Winter	Open	390.00	490.00
87-01-038	Devoncombe	D. Winter	Open	73.00	106.00
87-01-039	Tamar Cottage	D. Winter	Open	45.30	70.00
87-01-040	There was a Crooked House	D. Winter	Open	96.90	144.00
87-01-041	Devon Creamery	D. Winter	Open	62.90	94.00
88-01-042	Windmill	D. Winter	Open	37.50	50.00
88-01-043	Lock-keepers Cottage	D. Winter	Open	65.00	80.00
88-01-044	Derbyshire Cotton Mill	D. Winter	Open	65.00	80.00
88-01-045	Gunsmiths	D. Winter	Open	78.00	94.00
88-01-046	John Benbow's Farmhouse	D. Winter	Open	78.00	92.00
88-01-047	Coal Miner's Row	D. Winter	Open	90.00	106.00
88-01-048	Lacemaker's Cottage	D. Winter	Open	120.00	144.00
88-01-049	Cornish Harbour	D. Winter	Open	120.00	144.00
88-01-050	Cornish Engine House	D. Winter	Open	120.00	144.00
91-01-051	Inglenook Cottage	D. Winter	Open	60.00	66.00
91-01-052	The Weaver's Lodgings	D. Winter	Open	65.00	72.00
91-01-053	The Printers and The Bookbinders	D. Winter	Open	120.00	132.00
91-01-054	Moonlight Haven	D. Winter	Open	120.00	132.00
91-01-055	Castle in the Air	D. Winter	Open	675.00	675.00
92-01-056	Scrooge's School	D. Winter	Yr.Iss.	160.00	160.00

John Hine N.A. Ltd. — David Winter Retired Cottages

Number	Name	Artist	Edition Limit	Issue Price	Quote
80-02-001	Mill House	D. Winter	Closed	50.00	2000-2800.
80-02-002	Little Mill	D. Winter	Closed	40.00	1700-2300.
80-02-003	Three Ducks Inn	D. Winter	Closed	60.00	2000-2500.
80-02-004	Dove Cottage	D. Winter	Closed	60.00	1700-2300.
80-02-005	The Forge	D. Winter	Closed	60.00	1800-2500.
80-02-006	Little Forge	D. Winter	Closed	40.00	5625.00.
80-02-007	Mill House-remodeled	D. Winter	Closed	Unkn.	Unkn.
80-02-008	Little Mill-remodeled	D. Winter	Closed	Unkn.	Unkn.
80-02-009	The Coaching Inn	D. Winter	Closed	165.00	4500-7000.
80-02-010	Quayside	D. Winter	Closed	60.00	1800-2600.
81-02-011	St. Paul's Cathedral	D. Winter	Closed	40.00	2000-2800.
81-02-012	Castle Keep	D. Winter	Closed	30.00	1800-2400.
81-02-013	Chichester Cross	D. Winter	Closed	50.00	3400-3600.
81-02-014	Double Oast	D. Winter	Closed	60.00	2800.00
81-02-015	The Old Curiosity Shop	D. Winter	Closed	40.00	1200-2000.
81-02-016	Tythe Barn	D. Winter	Closed	39.30	2500-4000.
82-02-017	Sabrina's Cottage	D. Winter	Closed	30.00	2000-3000.
82-02-018	William Shakespeare's Birthplace(large)	D. Winter	Closed	60.00	600-1650.
82-02-019	Cornish Cottage	D. Winter	Closed	30.00	1000-2800.
82-02-020	Blacksmith's Cottage	D. Winter	Closed	22.00	400-500.
82-02-021	Moorland Cottage	D. Winter	Closed	22.00	250-450.
82-02-022	The Haybarn	D. Winter	Closed	22.00	300-600.
82-02-023	Miner's Cottage	D. Winter	Closed	22.00	275-375.
83-02-024	The Alms Houses	D. Winter	Closed	59.90	475-750.
82-02-025	The House on Top	D. Winter	Closed	92.30	300-400.
84-02-026	House of the Master Mason	D. Winter	Closed	74.80	250-500.
83-02-027	Woodcutter's Cottage	D. Winter	Closed	87.00	275-550.
85-02-028	Hermit's Humble Home	D. Winter	Closed	87.00	250-500.
83-02-029	The Cotton Mill	D. Winter	Closed	41.30	700-950.
83-02-030	Cornish Tin Mine	D. Winter	Closed	22.00	60-150.00
87-02-031	Ebenezer Scrooge's Counting House	D. Winter	Closed	96.90	200-550.
88-02-032	Jim'll Fixit	D. Winter	Closed	350.00	2100-3500.
82-02-033	Fairytale Castle	D. Winter	Closed	115.40	220-500.
85-02-034	Suffolk House	D. Winter	Closed	48.80	95-145.00
86-02-035	Crofter's Cottage	D. Winter	Closed	51.00	90-125.00
88-02-036	Hogmanay	D. Winter	Closed	100.00	125-300.
89-02-037	A Christmas Carol	D. Winter	Closed	135.00	120-325.
88-02-038	The Grange	D. Winter	Closed	120.00	1500.00
86-02-039	Falstaff's Manor	D. Winter	Closed	242.00	325-650.
82-02-040	Cotswold Village	D. Winter	Closed	59.90	100-220.
85-02-041	Squires Hall	D. Winter	Closed	92.30	130-230.
90-02-042	Mr. Fezziwig's Emporium	D. Winter	Closed	135.00	150-275.
81-02-043	Tudor Manor House	D. Winter	Closed	48.80	125-250.
82-02-044	Brookside Hamlet	D. Winter	Closed	74.80	100-250.
84-02-045	Spinner's Cottage	D. Winter	Closed	28.90	75-125.00
87-02-046	Orchard Cottage	D. Winter	Closed	91.30	150-225.
88-02-047	Bottle Kilns	D. Winter	Closed	78.00	90-175.00
91-02-048	Fred's Home:"A Merry Christmas, Uncle Ebeneezer," said Scrooge's nephew Fred, "and a Happy New Year."	D. Winter	Closed	145.00	175-185.
92-02-049	Audrey's Tea Room	D. Winter	Closed	90.00	200-300.
84-02-050	Tollkeeper's Cottage	D. Winter	Closed	87.00	120-160.
84-02-051	Castle Gate	D. Winter	Closed	154.90	250-370.

John Hine N.A. Ltd. — David Winter Retired Cottages-Tiny Series

Number	Name	Artist	Edition Limit	Issue Price	Quote
80-03-001	William Shakespeare's Birthplace	D. Winter	Closed	Unkn.	1000-1200.
80-03-002	Ann Hathaway's Cottage	D. Winter	Closed	Unkn.	1200.00
80-03-003	Sulgrave Manor	D. Winter	Closed	Unkn.	1000-1200.
80-03-004	Cotswold Farmhouse	D. Winter	Closed	Unkn.	1000-1200.
80-03-005	Crown Inn	D. Winter	Closed	Unkn.	1000-1200.
80-03-006	St. Nicholas' Church	D. Winter	Closed	Unkn.	1000-1500.

John Hine N.A. Ltd. — Collectors Guild Exclusives

Number	Name	Artist	Edition Limit	Issue Price	Quote
87-04-001	Robin Hood's Hideaway	D. Winter	Closed	54.00	350-600.
87-04-002	The Village Scene	D. Winter	Closed	Unkn.	200-350.
88-04-003	Queen Elizabeth Slept Here	D. Winter	Closed	183.00	350-475.
88-04-004	Black Bess Inn	D. Winter	Closed	60.00	200-300.
88-04-005	The Pavillion	D. Winter	Closed	52.00	200-275.
89-04-007	Homeguard	D. Winter	Closed	105.00	150-250.
89-04-008	Coal Shed	D. Winter	Closed	112.00	200-300.

Number	Name	Artist	Edition Limit	Issue Price	Quote
89-04-009	Street Scene	D. Winter	Closed	Unkn.	150-250.
90-04-010	The Cobblers	D. Winter	Closed	40.00	75-150.00
90-04-011	The Pottery	D. Winter	Closed	40.00	75-150.00
90-04-012	Cartwrights Cottage	D. Winter	Closed	45.00	100-200.
90-04-013	Plucked Duck	D. Winter	Closed	N/A	100-200.
91-04-014	Pershore Mill	D. Winter	Closed	Unkn.	110-125.
91-04-015	Tomfool's Cottage	D. Winter	12/92	100.00	100.00
91-04-016	Will O' The Wisp	D. Winter	12/92	120.00	120.00
92-04-017	Candle Maker's	D. Winter	12/92	65.00	65.00
92-04-018	Bee Keeper's	D. Winter	12/92	65.00	65.00
92-04-019	Irish Water Mill	D. Winter	12/92	N/A	N/A
John Hine N.A. Ltd.		**Scottish Collection**			
89-05-001	Scottish Crofter	D. Winter	Open	42.00	54.00
89-05-002	House on the Loch	D. Winter	Open	65.00	80.00
89-05-003	Gillie's Cottage	D. Winter	Open	65.00	80.00
89-05-004	Gatekeeper's	D. Winter	Open	65.00	80.00
89-05-005	MacBeth's Castle	D. Winter	Open	200.00	244.00
89-05-006	Old Distillery	D. Winter	Open	450.00	530.00
John Hine N.A. Ltd.		**Irish Collection**			
92-06-001	Irish Round Tower	D. Winter	Open	65.00	65.00
92-06-002	Secret Shebeen	D. Winter	Open	70.00	70.00
92-06-003	Fogartys	D. Winter	Open	75.00	75.00
92-06-004	Only A Span Apart	D. Winter	Open	80.00	80.00
92-06-005	Murphys	D. Winter	Open	100.00	100.00
92-06-006	O'Donovan's Castle	D. Winter	Open	145.00	145.00
John Hine N.A. Ltd.		**British Traditions**			
90-07-001	Burns' Reading Room	D. Winter	Open	31.00	34.00
90-07-002	Stonecutters Cottage	D. Winter	Open	48.00	52.00
90-07-003	The Boat House	D. Winter	Open	37.50	42.00
90-07-004	Pudding Cottage	D. Winter	Open	78.00	86.00
90-07-005	Blossom Cottage	D. Winter	Open	59.00	64.00
90-07-006	Knight's Castle	D. Winter	Open	59.00	64.00
90-07-007	St. Anne's Well	D. Winter	Open	48.00	52.00
90-07-008	Grouse Moor Lodge	D. Winter	Open	48.00	52.00
90-07-009	Staffordshire Vicarage	D. Winter	Open	48.00	52.00
90-07-010	Harvest Barn	D. Winter	Open	31.00	34.00
90-07-011	Guy Fawkes	D. Winter	Open	31.00	34.00
90-07-012	Bull & Bush	D. Winter	Open	37.50	42.00
John Hine N.A. Ltd.		**David Winter Cameos**			
92-08-001	Brooklet Bridge	D. Winter	Open	12.50	12.50
92-08-002	Poultry Ark	D. Winter	Open	12.50	12.50
92-08-003	The Potting Shed	D. Winter	Open	12.50	12.50
92-08-004	Lych Gate	D. Winter	Open	12.50	12.50
92-08-005	One Man Jail	D. Winter	Open	12.50	12.50
92-08-006	Market Day	D. Winter	Open	12.50	12.50
92-08-007	Welsh Pig Pen	D. Winter	Open	12.50	12.50
92-08-008	The Privy	D. Winter	Open	12.50	12.50
92-08-009	Greenwood Wagon	D. Winter	Open	12.50	12.50
92-08-010	Saddle Steps	D. Winter	Open	12.50	12.50
92-08-011	Barley Malt Kilns	D. Winter	Open	12.50	12.50
92-08-012	Penny Wishing Well	D. Winter	Open	12.50	12.50
John Hine N.A. Ltd.		**American Collection**			
89-09-001	The Out House	M. Wideman	Open	15.00	16.00
89-09-002	Colonial Wellhouse	M. Wideman	Open	15.00	16.00
89-09-003	Wisteria	M. Wideman	Open	15.00	22.00
89-09-004	The Blockhouse	M. Wideman	Closed	25.00	25.00
89-09-005	Garconniere	M. Wideman	Open	25.00	28.00
89-09-006	The Log Cabin	M. Wideman	Open	45.00	56.00
89-09-007	Cherry Hill School	M. Wideman	Open	45.00	56.00
89-09-008	The Maple Sugar Shack	M. Wideman	Open	50.00	56.00
89-09-009	The Kissing Bridge	M. Wideman	Open	50.00	56.00
89-09-010	The Gingerbread House	M. Wideman	Open	60.00	72.00
89-09-011	The New England Church	M. Wideman	Open	79.00	100.00
89-09-012	The Opera House	M. Wideman	Open	89.00	100.00
89-09-013	The Pacific Lighthouse	M. Wideman	Open	89.00	110.00
89-09-014	King William Tavern	M. Wideman	Closed	99.00	100-200.
89-09-015	The Mission	M. Wideman	Open	99.00	110.00
89-09-016	New England Lighthouse	M. Wideman	Open	99.00	110.00
89-09-017	The River Bell	M. Wideman	Open	99.00	120.00
89-09-018	Plantation House	M. Wideman	Closed	119.00	120-185.
89-09-019	Town Hall	M. Wideman	Open	129.00	144.00
89-09-020	Dog House	M. Wideman	Open	10.00	12.00
89-09-021	Star Cottage	M. Wideman	Open	30.00	34.00
89-09-022	Sod House	M. Wideman	Open	40.00	44.00
89-09-023	Barber Shop	M. Wideman	Open	40.00	44.00
89-09-024	Octagonal House	M. Wideman	Open	40.00	44.00
89-09-025	Cajun Cottage	M. Wideman	Open	50.00	56.00
89-09-026	Prairie Forge	M. Wideman	Open	65.00	72.00
89-09-027	Oxbow Saloon	M. Wideman	Open	90.00	100.00
89-09-028	Sierra Mine	M. Wideman	Open	120.00	132.00
89-09-029	California Winery	M. Wideman	Open	180.00	198.00
89-09-030	Railhead Inn	M. Wideman	Open	250.00	276.00
89-09-031	Haunted House	M. Wideman	Open	100.00	110.00
89-09-032	Tobacconist	M. Wideman	Open	45.00	50.00
89-09-033	Hawaiian Grass Hut	M. Wideman	Open	45.00	50.00
89-09-034	The Old Mill	M. Wideman	Open	100.00	110.00
89-09-035	Band Stand	M. Wideman	Open	90.00	100.00
89-09-036	Seaside Cottage	M. Wideman	Open	225.00	248.00
89-09-037	Tree House	M. Wideman	Open	45.00	50.00
89-09-038	Hacienda	M. Wideman	Open	51.00	56.00
89-09-039	Sweetheart Cottage	M. Wideman	Open	45.00	50.00
89-09-040	Forty-Niner Cabin	M. Wideman	Open	50.00	56.00
91-09-041	Desert Storm Tent	M. Wideman	Closed	75.00	75.00
91-09-042	Paul Revere's House	M. Wideman	Closed	90.00	100.00
91-09-043	Mo At Work	M. Wideman	Closed	35.00	35-70.00
91-09-044	Church in the Dale	M. Wideman	Open	130.00	144.00
91-09-045	Milk House	M. Wideman	Open	20.00	22.00
91-09-046	Moe's Diner	M. Wideman	Open	100.00	110.00
91-09-047	Fire Station	M. Wideman	Open	160.00	176.00
91-09-048	Joe's Service Station	M. Wideman	Open	90.00	100.00
92-09-049	News Stand	M. Wideman	Open	30.00	30.00
92-09-050	Village Mercantile	M. Wideman	Open	60.00	60.00
92-09-051	Grain Elevator	M. Wideman	Open	110.00	110.00
92-09-052	Telephone Booth	M. Wideman	Open	15.00	15.00
92-09-053	Topper's Drive-In	M. Wideman	Open	120.00	120.00
John Hine N.A. Ltd.		**Mushrooms**			
89-10-001	Royal Bank of Mushland	C. Lawrence	2,500	235.00	235.00
89-10-002	The Elders Mushroom	C. Lawrence	2,500	175.00	175.00

Number	Name	Artist	Edition Limit	Issue Price	Quote
89-10-003	The Cobblers	C. Lawrence	2,500	265.00	265.00
89-10-004	The Mush Hospital for Malingerers	C. Lawrence	2,500	250.00	250.00
89-10-005	The Ministry	C. Lawrence	2,500	185.00	185.00
89-10-006	The Gift Shop	C. Lawrence	1,200	350.00	420.00
89-10-007	The Constables	C. Lawrence	2,500	200.00	200.00
89-10-008	The Princess Palace	C. Lawrence	750	600.00	730.00
John Hine N.A. Ltd.		**Bugaboos**			
89-11-001	Arnold	John Hine Studio	Closed	45.00	45.00
89-11-002	Edna	John Hine Studio	Closed	45.00	45.00
89-11-003	Wilbur	John Hine Studio	Closed	45.00	45.00
89-11-004	Beryl	John Hine Studio	Closed	45.00	45.00
89-11-005	Gerald	John Hine Studio	Closed	45.00	45.00
89-11-006	Wesley	John Hine Studio	Closed	45.00	45.00
89-11-007	Oscar	John Hine Studio	Closed	45.00	45.00
89-11-008	Lizzie	John Hine Studio	Closed	45.00	45.00
89-11-009	Enid	John Hine Studio	Closed	45.00	45.00
John Hine N.A. Ltd.		**Great British Pubs**			
89-12-001	Smith's Arms	M. Cooper	Open	28.00	28.00
89-12-002	The Plough	M. Cooper	Open	28.00	28.00
89-12-003	King's Arms	M. Cooper	Closed	28.00	28.00
89-12-004	White Tower	M. Cooper	Open	35.00	35.00
89-12-005	Old Bridge House	M. Cooper	Open	37.50	37.50
89-12-006	White Horse	M. Cooper	Open	39.50	39.50
89-12-007	Jamaica Inn	M. Cooper	Open	39.50	39.50
89-12-008	The George	M. Cooper	Open	57.50	57.50
89-12-009	Montague Arms	M. Cooper	Open	57.50	57.50
89-12-010	Blue Bell	M. Cooper	Open	57.50	57.50
89-12-011	The Lion	M. Cooper	Open	57.50	57.50
89-12-012	Coach & Horses	M. Cooper	Open	79.50	79.50
89-12-013	Ye Olde Spotted Horse	M. Cooper	Open	79.50	79.50
89-12-014	The Crown Inn	M. Cooper	Open	79.50	79.50
89-12-015	The Bell	M. Cooper	Closed	79.50	100-350.
89-12-016	Black Swan	M. Cooper	Closed	79.50	100-350.
89-12-017	Ye Grapes	M. Cooper	Open	87.50	87.50
89-12-018	Old Bull Inn	M. Cooper	Open	87.50	87.50
89-12-019	Dickens Inn	M. Cooper	Open	100.00	100.00
89-12-020	Sherlock Holmes	M. Cooper	Closed	100.00	200.00
89-12-021	George Somerset	M. Cooper	Open	100.00	100.00
89-12-022	The Feathers	M. Cooper	Open	200.00	200.00
89-12-023	Hawkeshead	M. Cooper	Open	Unkn.	900.00
John Hine N.A. Ltd.		**Great British Pubs-Yard of Pubs**			
89-13-001	Grenadier	M. Cooper	Closed	25.00	25.00
89-13-002	Black Friars	M. Cooper	Closed	25.00	25.00
89-13-003	Falkland Arms	M. Cooper	Closed	25.00	25.00
89-13-004	George & Pilgrims	M. Cooper	Closed	25.00	25.00
89-13-005	Dirty Duck	M. Cooper	Closed	25.00	25.00
89-13-006	Wheatsheaf	M. Cooper	Closed	35.00	35.00
89-13-007	Lygon Arms	M. Cooper	Closed	35.00	35.00
89-13-008	Suffolk Bull	M. Cooper	Closed	35.00	35.00
89-13-009	The Swan	M. Cooper	Closed	35.00	35.00
89-13-010	The Falstaff	M. Cooper	Closed	35.00	35.00
89-13-011	The Eagle	M. Cooper	Closed	35.00	35.00
89-13-012	The Green Man	M. Cooper	Closed	Unkn.	Unkn.
John Hine N.A. Ltd.		**Father Christmas**			
88-14-001	Standing	J. King	Closed	70.00	70.00
88-14-002	Feet	J. King	Closed	70.00	70.00
88-14-003	Falling	J. King	Closed	70.00	70.00
John Hine N.A. Ltd.		**The Shoemaker's Dream**			
91-15-001	The Jester Boot	J. Herbert	Open	29.00	29.00
91-15-002	The Crooked Boot	J. Herbert	Open	35.00	35.00
91-15-003	Rosie's Cottage	J. Herbert	Open	40.00	40.00
91-15-004	Baby Booty (pink)	J. Herbert	Open	45.00	45.00
91-15-005	Baby Booty (blue)	J. Herbert	Open	45.00	45.00
91-15-006	Shoemaker's Palace	J. Herbert	Open	50.00	50.00
91-15-007	Tavern Boot	J. Herbert	Open	55.00	55.00
91-15-008	River Shoe Cottage	J. Herbert	Open	55.00	55.00
91-15-009	The Chapel	J. Herbert	Open	55.00	55.00
91-15-010	Castle Boot	J. Herbert	Open	55.00	55.00
91-15-011	The Clocktower Boot	J. Herbert	Open	60.00	60.00
91-15-012	Watermill Boot	J. Herbert	Open	60.00	60.00
91-15-013	Windmill Boot	J. Herbert	Open	65.00	65.00
91-15-014	The Gate Lodge	J. Herbert	Open	65.00	65.00
92-15-015	Wishing Well Shoe	J. Herbert	Open	32.00	32.00
92-15-016	The Golf Shoe	J. Herbert	Open	35.00	35.00
92-15-017	The Sports Shoe	J. Herbert	Open	35.00	35.00
92-15-018	Clown Boot	J. Herbert	Open	45.00	45.00
92-15-019	Upside Down Boot	J. Herbert	Open	45.00	45.00
92-15-020	Christmas Boot	J. Herbert	Open	55.00	55.00
John Hine N.A. Ltd.		**Heartstrings**			
92-16-001	Hush, It's Sleepytime	S. Kuck	15,000	97.50	97.50
92-16-002	Taking Tea	S. Kuck	15,000	92.50	92.50
92-16-003	Day Dreaming	S. Kuck	15,000	92.50	92.50
92-16-004	Watch Me Waltz	S. Kuck	15,000	97.50	97.50
John Hine N.A. Ltd.		**Sandra Kuck Collectors Club**			
92-17-001	Friends For Keeps	S. Kuck	Yr.Iss.	Gift	N/A
92-17-002	Friends For Keeps Lithograph	S. Kuck	Yr.Iss.	Gift	N/A
92-17-003	La Belle	S. Kuck	Yr Iss.	Gift	N/A
Hoyle Products		**Various**			
82-01-001	The Horsetrader	N. Rockwell	1,500	180.00	Unkn.
80-01-002	The Country Pedlar	N. Rockwell	1,500	160.00	Unkn.
81-01-003	The Traveling Salesman	N. Rockwell	1,500	175.00	175.00
Hutschenreuther		**Portrait Figurines**			
77-01-001	Catherine The Great	D. Valenza	500	500.00	1100.00
77-01-002	Helen of Troy	D. Valenza	500	500.00	1050.00
77-01-003	Jennie Churchhill	D. Valenza	500	500.00	925.00
77-01-004	Queen Isabelle	D. Valenza	500	500.00	925.00
77-01-005	Judith	D. Valenza	500	500.00	1575.00
77-01-006	Isolde	D. Valenza	500	500.00	2650.00
77-01-007	Lillian Russell	D. Valenza	500	500.00	1825.00
Hutschenreuther		**American Limited Edition Collection**			
XX-02-001	A Family Affair	Granget	200	Unkn.	3700.00
XX-02-002	Take Cover	Granget	125	Unkn.	14000.00
XX-02-003	The Challenge	Granget	150	Unkn.	14000.00
XX-02-004	Heading South	Granget	150	Unkn.	14000.00

Number	Name	Artist	Edition Limit	Issue Price	Quote
XX-02-005	First Lesson	Granget	175	Unkn.	3550.00
XX-02-006	Safe at Home	Granget	350	Unkn.	9000.00
XX-02-007	Off Season	Granget	125	Unkn.	4125.00
XX-02-008	Disdain-Owl	Granget	175	Unkn.	5200.00
XX-02-009	Friendly Enemies-Woodpecker	Granget	175	Unkn.	5200.00
XX-02-010	Engaged	Granget	250	Unkn.	1750.00
XX-02-011	Spring is Here	Granget	175	Unkn.	4500.00
XX-02-012	Anxious Moment	Granget	175	Unkn.	5225.00
XX-02-013	It's Spring Again	Granget	250	Unkn.	3475.00
XX-02-014	Freedom in Flight	Granget	200	Unkn.	9000.00
XX-02-015	Reluctant Fledgling	Granget	350	Unkn.	3475.00
XX-02-016	Proud Parent	Granget	250	Unkn.	13750.00
XX-02-017	Joe-Stag	Granget	150	Unkn.	12000.00
XX-02-018	Olympic Champion	Granget	500	Unkn.	3650.00
XX-02-019	The Sentinel-Springbok	Granget	150	Unkn.	5200.00
XX-02-020	Sea Frolic-Sea Lion	Granget	500	Unkn.	3500.00
XX-02-021	The Dance-Crowncrested Crane	Granget	25	Unkn.	30000.00
XX-02-022	The Contest	Granget	100	Unkn.	14000.00
XX-02-023	The Fish Hawk	Granget	500	Unkn.	12000.00
XX-02-024	To Ride the Wind	Granget	500	Unkn.	8650.00
XX-02-025	Decorated Sea Lions	Granget	100	Unkn.	6000.00
XX-02-026	Dolphin Group	Granget	500	Unkn.	4000.00
XX-02-027	Silver Heron	Netzsch	500	Unkn.	5000.00
XX-02-028	Sparrowhawk w/Kingbird	Granget	500	Unkn.	8250.00
XX-02-029	Saw Whet Owl	Granget	750	Unkn.	3575.00
XX-02-030	Pygmy Owls	Granget	650	Unkn.	6225.00
XX-02-031	Arabian Stallion	Achtziger	300	Unkn.	8525.00
XX-02-032	Whooping Cranes	Netzsch	300	Unkn.	8000.00
XX-02-033	Wren on Wild Rose	Netzsch	250	Unkn.	1675.00
XX-02-034	Redstart on Quince Branch	Netzsch	250	Unkn.	1300.00
XX-02-035	Linnet on Ear of Rye	Netzsch	250	Unkn.	1175.00
XX-02-036	Quince	Netzsch	375	Unkn.	2850.00
XX-02-037	Water Lily	O'Hara	375	Unkn.	4150.00
XX-02-038	Christmas Rose	O'Hara	375	Unkn.	3050.00
XX-02-039	Blue Dolphins	Granget	100	Unkn.	10000.00
Kaiser		**Birds of America Collection**			
72-01-001	Blue Bird-496, color/base	W. Gawantka	2,500	120.00	480.00
73-01-002	Blue Jay-503, color/base	W. Gawantka	1,500	475.00	1198.00
76-01-003	Baltimore Oriole-536, color/base	G. Tagliariol	1,000	280.00	746.00
73-01-004	Cardinal-504, color/base	W. Gawantka	1,500	60.00	600.00
75-01-005	Sparrow-516, color/base	G. Tagliariol	1,500	300.00	596.00
70-01-006	Scarlet Tanager, color/base	Kaiser	Closed	60.00	90.00
XX-01-007	Sparrow Hawk-749, color/base	Kaiser	3,000	575.00	906.00
82-01-008	Hummingbird Group-660, color/base	G. Tagliariol	3,000	650.00	1232.00
81-01-009	Kingfisher-639, color/base	G. Tagliariol	Closed	45.00	60.00
73-01-010	Robin-502, color/base	W. Gawantka	1,500	340.00	718.00
XX-01-011	Robin II-537, color/base	Kaiser	1,000	260.00	888.00
XX-01-012	Robin & Worm, color/base	Kaiser	Closed	60.00	90.00
XX-01-013	Baby Titmice-501, white/base	W. Gawantka	1,200	200.00	754.00
XX-01-014	Baby Titmice-501, color/base	W. Gawantka	Closed	400.00	500.00
78-01-015	Baby Titmice-601, color/base	G. Tagliariol	2,000	Unkn.	956.00
78-01-016	Baby Titmice-601, white/base	G. Tagliariol	2,000	Unkn.	562.00
68-01-017	Pidgeon Group-475, white/base	U. Netzsch	2,000	60.00	412.00
68-01-018	Pidgeon Group-475, color/base	U. Netzsch	1,500	150.00	812.00
76-01-019	Pheasant-556, color/base	G. Tagliariol	1,500	3200.00	6020.00
84-01-020	Pheasant-715, color/base	G. Tagliariol	1,500	1000.00	1962.00
76-01-021	Pelican-534, color/base	G. Tagliariol	1,200	925.00	1768.00
XX-01-022	Pelican-534, white/base	G. Tagliariol	Closed	Unkn.	625.00
84-01-023	Peregrine Falcon-723, color/base	M. Tandy	1,500	850.00	4946.00
72-01-024	Goshawk-491, white/base	W. Gawantka	1,500	850.00	1992.00
72-01-025	Goshawk-491, color/base	W. Gawantka	1,500	2400.00	4326.00
XX-01-026	Roadrunner-492, color/base	Kaiser	Closed	350.00	900.00
72-01-027	Seagull-498, white/base	W. Gawantka	700	550.00	1586.00
72-01-028	Seagull-498, color/base	W. Gawantka	Closed	850.00	1150.00
73-01-028	Seagull-498, color bisque	W. Gawantka	Closed	Unkn.	1150.00
75-01-029	Woodpeckers-515, color/base	G. Tagliariol	800	900.00	1762.00
76-01-030	Screech Owl-532, white/base	W. Gawantka	Closed	175.00	199.00
76-01-031	Screech Owl-532, color bisque	W. Gawantka	Closed	Unkn.	175.00
XX-01-032	Horned Owl II-524, white/base	G. Tagliariol	1,000	Unkn.	918.00
XX-01-033	Horned Owl II- 524, color/base	G. Tagliariol	1,000	650.00	2170.00
69-01-034	Owl-476, color bisque	W. Gawantka	Closed	Unkn.	550.00
69-01-035	Owl -476, white bisque	W. Gawantka	Closed	Unkn.	180.00
77-01-036	Owl IV-559, color/base	G. Tagliariol	1,000	Unkn.	1270.00
XX-01-037	Snowy Owl -776, white/base	Kaiser	1,500	Unkn.	668.00
XX-01-038	Snowy Owl -776, color/base	Kaiser	1,500	Unkn.	1146.00
68-01-039	Pair of Mallards-456, white/base	U. Netzsch	2,000	75.00	518.00
68-01-040	Pair of Mallards-456, color/base	U. Netzsch	Closed	150.00	500.00
78-01-041	Pair of Mallards II-572, color/base	G. Tagliariol	1,500	Unkn.	1156.00
78-01-042	Pair of Mallards II-572, white/base	G. Tagliariol	1,500	Unkn.	2366.00
75-01-043	Wood Ducks-514, color/base	G. Tagliariol	800	Unkn.	2804.00
85-01-044	Pintails-747, white/base	Kaiser	1,500	Unkn.	364.00
85-01-045	Pintails-747, color/base	Kaiser	1,500	Unkn.	838.00
76-01-046	Canadian Geese-550, white/base	G. Tagliariol	1,500	1500.00	3490.00
81-01-047	Quails-640, color/base	G. Tagliariol	1,500	Unkn.	2366.00
79-01-048	Swan-602, color/base	G. Tagliariol	2,000	Unkn.	1370.00
69-01-049	Bald Eagle I -464, color	U. Netzsch	Closed	Unkn.	650.00
69-01-050	Bald Eagle I -464, white	U. Netzsch	Closed	Unkn.	250.00
73-01-051	Bald Eagle II -497, color bisque	G. Tagliariol	Closed	Unkn.	1300.00
74-01-052	Bald Eagle III -513, color bisque	W. Gawantka	Closed	Unkn.	850.00
74-01-053	Bald Eagle III -513,white bisque	W. Gawantka	Closed	Unkn.	378.00
76-01-054	Bald Eagle IV-552, white/base	W. Gawantka	1,500	210.00	572.00
76-01-055	Bald Eagle IV-552, color/base	W. Gawantka	1,500	450.00	998.00
78-01-056	Bald Eagle V-600, color/base	G. Tagliariol	1,500	Unkn.	3848.00
80-01-057	Bald Eagle VI-634, white/base	W. Gawantka	3,000	Unkn.	672.00
XX-01-058	Bald Eagle VII-637, color/base	G. Tagliariol	200	Unkn.	20694.00
82-01-059	Bald Eagle VIII-656, color/base	G. Tagliariol	Closed	800.00	880.00
82-01-060	Bald Eagle VIII-656, white/base	G. Tagliariol	1,000	400.00	904.00
84-01-061	Bald Eagle IX-714, white/base	W. Gawantka	4,000	190.00	374.00
84-01-062	Bald Eagle IX-714, color/base	W. Gawantka	3,500	500.00	850.00
85-01-063	Bald Eagle X-746, white/base	W. Gawantka	1,500	375.00	672.00
85-01-064	Bald Eagle X-746, color/base	W. Gawantka	1,500	Unkn.	1198.00
85-01-065	Bald Eagle XI-751, white/base	W. Gawantka	1,000	Unkn.	902.00
85-01-066	Bald Eagle XI-751, color/base	W. Gawantka	1,000	880.00	1422.00
81-01-067	Rooster-642, white/base	G. Tagliariol	1,500	380.00	688.00
81-01-068	Rooster-642, color/base	G. Tagliariol	1,500	860.00	1304.00
74-01-069	Falcon-507, color/base	W. Gawantka	1,500	820.00	1928.00
86-01-070	Sparrow Hawk-777, white bisque	M. Tandy	1,000	440.00	716.00
86-01-071	Sparrow Hawk-777, colored bisque	M. Tandy	10,000	950.00	1336.00
XX-01-072	Bald Eagle II-497, Colored	Kaiser	Closed	Unkn.	1300.00
XX-01-073	Paradise Bird-318, white bisque	Kaiser	Closed	Unkn.	135.00
XX-01-074	Fighting Peacocks -337, color glaze	G. Bochman	Closed	Unkn.	340.00
XX-01-075	Wild Ducks-456, color bisque	Kaiser	Closed	Unkn.	500.00
68-01-076	Wild Ducks-456, white bisque	Kaiser	2,000	Unkn.	175.00
72-01-077	Roadrunner-492, color bisque	W. Gawantka	1,000	175.00	199.00
Kaiser		**Horse Sculpture**			
69-02-001	Arabian Stallion-Comet, color/bisque	W. Gawantka	Closed	Unkn.	850.00
76-02-002	Hassan/Arabian-553, white/base	W. Gawantka	Closed	250.00	600.00
76-02-003	Hassan/Arabian-553, color/base	W. Gawantka	1,500	600.00	1204.00
80-02-004	Orion/Arabian-629, color/base	W. Gawantka	2,000	600.00	1038.00
80-02-005	Orion/Arabian-629, white/base	W. Gawantka	2,000	250.00	442.00
78-02-006	Capitano/Lipizzaner- 597, white	W. Gawantka	Closed	275.00	574.00
78-02-007	Capitano/Lipizzaner- 597, color	W. Gawantka	1,500	625.00	1496.00
75-02-008	Mare & Foal II-510, color/base	W. Gawantka	Closed	650.00	775.00
75-02-009	Mare & Foal II-510, white/bisque	W. Gawantka	Closed	Unkn.	775.00
80-02-010	Mare & Foal III-636, white/base	W. Gawantka	1,500	300.00	646.00
80-02-011	Mare & Foal III-636, color/base	W. Gawantka	1,500	950.00	1632.00
71-02-012	Pony Group-488, white/base	W. Gawantka	2,500	50.00	418.00
71-02-013	Pony Group-488, color/base	W. Gawantka	Closed	Unkn.	350.00
71-02-014	Pony Group-488, color bisque	W. Gawantka	Closed	Unkn.	350.00
87-02-015	Trotter-780, white/base	W. Gawantka	1,500	574.00	652.00
87-02-016	Trotter-780, color/base	W. Gawantka	1,500	1217.00	1350.00
87-02-017	Pacer-792, white/base	W. Gawantka	1,500	574.00	652.00
87-02-018	Pacer-792, color/base	W. Gawantka	1,500	1217.00	1350.00
90-02-019	Argos-633101/wht. bisq./base	W. Gawantka	1,000	578.00	672.00
90-02-020	Argos-633103/lt. color/base	W. Gawantka	1,000	1194.00	1388.00
90-02-021	Argos-633143/color/base	W. Gawantka	1,000	1194.00	1388.00
75-02-022	Lipizzaner/Maestoso-517/color bisque	W. Gawantka	Closed	Unkn.	1150.00
75-02-023	Lipizzaner/Maestoso-517white bisque	W. Gawantka	Closed	Unkn.	750.00
Kaiser		**Animals**			
75-03-001	German Shepherd-528, white bisque	W. Gawantka	Closed	185.00	420.00
75-03-002	German Shepherd-528, color bisque	W. Gawantka	Closed	250.00	652.00
76-03-003	Irish Setter-535, color bisque	W. Gawantka	1,000	290.00	652.00
76-03-004	Irish Setter-535, white/base	W. Gawantka	1,500	Unkn.	424.00
79-03-005	Bear & Cub-521, white bisque	W. Gawantka	Closed	125.00	378.00
79-03-006	Bear & Cub-521, color bisque	W. Gawantka	900	400.00	1072.00
85-03-007	Trout-739, color bisque	W. Gawantka	Open	95.00	488.00
85-03-008	Rainbow Trout-739, color bisque	W. Gawantka	Open	250.00	488.00
85-03-009	Brook Trout-739, color bisque	W. Gawantka	Open	250.00	488.00
85-03-010	Pike-737, color bisque	W. Gawantka	Open	350.00	682.00
69-03-011	Porpoise Group (3)-478, white bisque	W. Gawantka	Closed	85.00	375.00
78-03-012	Dolphin Group (4)-596/4, white bisque	W. Gawantka	4,500	75.00	956.00
75-03-013	Dolphin Group (4)-508, white bisque	W. Gawantka	Closed	Unkn.	575.00
75-03-014	Dolphin Group (5)-520/5, white bisque	W. Gawantka	800	850.00	3002.00
78-03-015	Killer Whale-579, color/bisque	W. Gawantka	2,000	420.00	798.00
78-03-016	Killer Whale-579, white/bisque	W. Gawantka	2,000	85.00	404.00
78-03-017	Killer Whales (2)-594, color	W. Gawantka	2,000	925.00	2008.00
78-03-018	Killer Whales (2)-594, white	W. Gawantka	2,000	425.00	1024.00
82-03-019	Two wild Boars-664, color bisque	H. Liederly	1,000	650.00	890.00
80-03-020	Bison-630, color bisque	G. Tagliariol	2,000	620.00	1044.00
80-03-021	Bison-690, white bisque	G. Tagliariol	2,000	350.00	488.00
91-03-022	Lion-701203, color bisque	W. Gawantka	1,500	1300.00	1300.00
91-03-023	Lion-701201, white bisque	W. Gawantka	1,500	650.00	650.00
Kaiser		**Human Figures**			
82-04-001	Father & Son-659, white/base	W. Gawantka	2,500	100.00	384.00
82-04-002	Father & Son-659, color/base	W. Gawantka	2,500	400.00	712.00
83-04-003	Mother & Child/bust-696, white	W. Gawantka	4,000	225.00	428.00
83-04-004	Mother & Child/bust-696, color	W. Gawantka	3,500	500.00	1066.00
XX-04-005	Father & Daughter-752, white	Kaiser	2,500	175.00	362.00
XX-04-006	Father & Daughter-752, color	Kaiser	2,500	390.00	710.00
82-04-007	Swan Lake Ballet-641, white	W. Gawantka	2,500	200.00	974.00
82-04-008	Swan Lake Ballet-641, color	W. Gawantka	2,500	650.00	1276.00
82-04-009	Ice Princess-667, white	W. Gawantka	5,000	200.00	416.00
82-04-010	Ice Princess-667, color	W. Gawantka	5,000	375.00	732.00
XX-04-011	Mother & Child-757, white	Kaiser	4,000	300.00	430.00
XX-04-012	Mother & Child-757, color	Kaiser	3,500	600.00	864.00
XX-04-013	Mother & Child-775, white	Kaiser	4,000	300.00	430.00
XX-04-014	Mother & Child-775, color	Kaiser	3,500	600.00	864.00
60-04-015	Mother & Child-398, white bisque	G. Bochmann	Open	Unkn.	312.00
Lance Corporation		**Chilmark Pewter American West**			
74-01-001	Cheyenne	D. Polland	S/O	200.00	2700-3000.
74-01-002	Counting Coup	D. Polland	S/O	225.00	1600-1900.
74-01-003	Crow Scout	D. Polland	S/O	250.00	1500-1700.
75-01-004	Maverick Calf	D. Polland	S/O	250.00	1500-1700.
76-01-005	Cold Saddles, Mean Horses	D. Polland	S/O	200.00	1100-1600.
75-01-006	The Outlaws	D. Polland	S/O	450.00	900-1180.
76-01-007	Buffalo Hunt	D. Polland	S/O	300.00	1200-2200.
76-01-008	Rescue	D. Polland	S/O	275.00	1300-2700.
76-01-009	Painting the Town	D. Polland	S/O	300.00	1550-1700.
76-01-010	Monday Morning Wash	D. Polland	S/O	200.00	1300-1800.
78-01-011	Dangerous Encounter	B. Rodden	Retrd.	475.00	600-950.
79-01-012	Border Rustlers	D. Polland	S/O	1295.00	1500.00
79-01-013	Mandan Hunter	D. Polland	S/O	65.00	780-900.
79-01-014	Getting Acquainted	D. Polland	S/O	215.00	875-1100.
79-01-015	Cavalry Officer	D. LaRocca	S/O	125.00	225-400.
79-01-016	Cowboy	D. LaRocca	S/O	125.00	600-750.
79-01-017	Mountain Man	D. LaRocca	Retrd.	95.00	500-650.
79-01-018	Indian Warrior	D. LaRocca	Retrd.	95.00	400.00
79-01-019	Running Battle	B. Rodden	Retrd.	400.00	750-900.
81-01-020	Buffalo Robe	D. Polland	2,500	235.00	315-600.
81-01-021	When War Chiefs Meet	D. Polland	S/O	300.00	850-900.
81-01-022	War Party	D. Polland	Retrd.	550.00	975-1150.
81-01-023	Dog Soldier	D. Polland	2,500	235.00	350-700.
81-01-024	Enemy Tracks	D. Polland	S/O	225.00	700-725.
81-01-025	Ambushed	D. Polland	Retrd.	2370.00	2700.00
81-01-026	U.S. Marshal	D. Polland	S/O	95.00	450-600.
81-01-027	Plight of the Huntsman	M. Boyette	S/O	495.00	1100-1300.
82-01-028	Last Arrow	D. Polland	S/O	95.00	370-400.
82-01-029	Sioux War Chief	D. Polland	S/O	95.00	375-480.
82-01-030	Navajo Kachina Dancer	D. Polland	2,500	95.00	110-250.
82-01-031	Arapaho Drummer	D. Polland	2,500	95.00	175-250.
82-01-032	Apache Hostile	D. Polland	2,500	95.00	110.00
82-01-033	Buffalo Prayer	D. Polland	S/O	95.00	245-400.
82-01-034	Jemez Eagle Dancer	D. Polland	S/O	95.00	250-450.
82-01-035	Flathead War Dancer	D. Polland	2,500	95.00	110-400.
82-01-036	Hopi Kachina Dancer	D. Polland	2,500	95.00	110.00
82-01-037	Apache Gan Dancer	D. Polland	2,500	95.00	110.00
82-01-038	Crow Medicine Dancer	D. Polland	2,500	95.00	110.00
82-01-039	Comanche Plaines Drummer	D. Polland	2,500	95.00	110.00
82-01-040	Yakima Salmon Fisherman	D. Polland	S/O	200.00	900-1230.
82-01-041	Mustanger	D. Polland	2,500	425.00	550.00
82-01-042	Blood Brothers	M. Boyett	Retrd.	250.00	610-995.

Number	Name	Artist	Edition Limit	Issue Price	Quote
83-01-043	Line Rider	D. Polland	S/O	195.00	1000-1410.
83-01-044	Bounty Hunter	D. Polland	S/O	250.00	300-600.
83-01-045	The Wild Bunch	D. Polland	S/O	200.00	225-400.
83-01-046	Too Many Aces	D. Polland	2,500	400.00	495.00
83-01-047	Eye to Eye	D. Polland	2,500	350.00	475.00
83-01-048	Now or Never	D. Polland	Retrd.	265.00	800.00
84-01-049	Flat Out for Red River Station	M. Boyett	S/O	3000.00	6200-6850.
85-01-050	Postal Exchange	S. York	Retrd.	300.00	400-600.
85-01-051	Bear Meet	S. York	Retrd.	500.00	600-800.
85-01-052	Horse of A Different Color	S. York	Retrd.	500.00	600-800.
90-01-053	Pequot Wars	D. Polland	S/O	395.00	450-800.
90-01-054	Tecumseh's Rebellion	D. Polland	S/O	350.00	700.00
90-01-055	Red River Wars	D. Polland	S/O	425.00	700-850.
Lance Corporation	**Chilmark Pewter American West Annual Special**				
83-02-001	The Chief	D. Polland	Yr.Iss.	275.00	1650-2050.
84-02-002	Unit Colors	D. Polland	Yr.Iss.	250.00	1250-1350.
85-02-003	Oh Great Spirit	D. Polland	Yr.Iss.	300.00	1000-1300.
86-02-004	Eagle Catcher	M. Boyett	Yr.Iss.	300.00	850-1200.
87-02-005	Surprise Encounter	F. Barnum	Yr.Iss.	250.00	700-750.
88-02-005	I Will Fight No More Forever	D. Polland	Yr.Iss.	350.00	700-830.
89-02-007	Geronimo	D. Polland	Yr.Iss.	375.00	700-785.
90-02-008	Cochise	D. Polland	Yr.Iss.	400.00	600-750.
91-02-009	Crazy Horse	D. Polland	Yr.Iss.	295.00	600.00
92-02-010	Strong Hearts to the Front	D. Polland	Yr.Iss.	425.00	425.00
Lance Corporation	**Chilmark Pewter American West Christmas Special**				
91-03-001	Merry Christmas Neighbor	D. Polland	Annual	395.00	675.00
92-03-002	Merry Christmas My Love	D. Polland	Annual	350.00	350.00
Lance Corporation	**Chilmark Pewter American West Event Specials**				
91-04-001	Uneasy Truce	D. Polland	Annual	125.00	215.00
92-04-002	Irons In The Fire	D. Polland	Annual	125.00	125.00
Lance Corporation	**Chilmark Pewter Civil War Annual Specials**				
89-05-001	Lee To The Rear	F. Barnum	Yr.Iss.	300.00	450-800.
90-05-002	Lee And Jackson	F. Barnum	Yr.Iss.	375.00	450-700.
91-05-003	Stonewall Jackson	F. Barnum	Yr.Iss.	295.00	295-695.
Lance Corporation	**Chilmark Pewter Civil War Event Specials**				
91-06-001	Boots and Saddles	F. Barnum	Annual	95.00	250.00
92-06-002	140th NY Zouave	F. Barnum	Annual	95.00	95.00
Lance Corporation	**Chilmark Pewter Civil War Christmas Specials**				
92-07-001	Merry Christmas Yank	F. Barnum	Annual	350.00	350.00
Lance Corporation	**Chilmark Pewter Wildlife**				
78-08-001	Buffalo	B. Rodden	S/O	170.00	375-400.
79-08-002	Elephant	D. Polland	S/O	315.00	450-550.
79-08-003	Giraffe	D. Polland	S/O	145.00	145.00
79-08-004	Kudu	D. Polland	S/O	160.00	160.00
79-08-005	Rhino	D. Polland	S/O	135.00	135-550.
80-08-006	Ruby-Throated Hummingbird	V. Hayton	S/O	275.00	350.00
80-08-007	Prairie Sovereign	M. Boyett	Retrd.	550.00	800.00
80-08-008	Duel of the Bighorns	M. Boyett	Retrd.	650.00	1200.00
Lance Corporation	**Chilmark Pewter Horses**				
76-09-001	Stallion	B. Rodden	S/O	75.00	260.00
76-09-002	Running Free	B. Rodden	S/O	75.00	300.00
77-09-003	Rise and Shine	B. Rodden	S/O	135.00	200.00
77-09-004	The Challenge	B. Rodden	S/O	175.00	250-300.
78-09-005	Paddock Walk	A. Petito	Retrd.	85.00	215.00
80-09-006	Born Free	B. Rodden	S/O	250.00	500-680.
81-09-007	Clydesdale Wheel Horse	C. Keim	Retrd.	120.00	430.00
82-09-008	Tender Persuasion	J. Mootry	Retrd.	950.00	1250.00
85-09-009	Fighting Stallions	D. Polland	2,500	225.00	300.00
85-09-010	Wild Stallion	D. Polland	Retrd.	145.00	350.00
Lance Corporation	**Chilmark Pewter Rodeo**				
85-10-001	Saddle Bronc Rider	D. Polland	2,500	250.00	300.00
85-10-002	Bareback Rider	D. Polland	2,500	225.00	300.00
85-10-003	Bull Rider	D. Polland	2,500	265.00	335.00
85-10-004	Steer Wrestling	D. Polland	2,500	500.00	600.00
85-10-005	Team Roping	D. Polland	2,500	500.00	625.00
85-10-006	Calf Roper	D. Polland	2,500	300.00	375.00
85-10-007	Barrel Racer	D. Polland	2,500	275.00	325.00
Lance Corporation	**Chilmark Pewter Legacy of Courage**				
81-11-001	Apache Signals	M. Boyett	Retrd.	175.00	575-750.
81-11-002	Iroquois Warfare	M. Boyett	Retrd.	125.00	600.00
81-11-003	Victor Cheyenne	M. Boyett	Retrd.	175.00	500.00
81-11-004	Buffalo Stalker	M. Boyett	Retrd.	175.00	560.00
81-11-005	Comanche	M. Boyett	Retrd.	175.00	530-670.
81-11-006	Unconquered Seminole	M. Boyett	Retrd.	175.00	540.00
81-11-007	Blackfoot Snow Hunter	M. Boyett	Retrd.	175.00	650.00
82-11-008	Shoshone Eagle Catcher	M. Boyett	S/O	225.00	1650-2040.
82-11-009	Plains Talk-Pawnee	M. Boyett	Retrd.	195.00	625.00
82-11-010	Kiowa Scout	M. Boyett	Retrd.	195.00	525.00
82-11-011	Mandan Buffalo Dancer	M. Boyett	Retrd.	195.00	610.00
82-11-012	Listening For Hooves	M. Boyett	Retrd.	150.00	400.00
82-11-013	Arapaho Sentinel	M. Boyett	Retrd.	195.00	500.00
82-11-014	Dance of the Eagles	M. Boyett	Retrd.	150.00	215.00
82-11-015	The Tracker Nez Perce	M. Boyett	Retrd.	150.00	575.00
83-11-016	Moment of Truth	M. Boyett	Retrd.	295.00	550-620.
83-11-017	Winter Hunt	M. Boyett	Retrd.	295.00	370.00
83-11-018	Along the Cherokee Trace	M. Boyett	Retrd.	295.00	720.00
83-11-019	Forest Watcher	M. Boyett	Retrd.	215.00	540.00
83-11-020	Rite of the Whitetail	M. Boyett	Retrd.	295.00	400.00
83-11-021	Circling the Enemy	M. Boyett	Retrd.	295.00	395.00
83-11-022	A Warrior's Tribute	M. Boyett	Retrd.	335.00	635.00
Lance Corporation	**Chilmark Pewter Off Canvas**				
90-12-001	Smoke Signal	A. T. McGrory	S/O	345.00	700-770.
90-12-002	Vigil	A. T. McGrory	S/O	345.00	500-700.
90-12-003	Warrior	A. T. McGrory	S/O	300.00	350-600.
Lance Corporation	**Chilmark Pewter Sculptures**				
79-13-001	Unicorn	R. Sylvan	S/O	115.00	550.00
79-13-002	Carousel	R. Sylvan	S/O	115.00	115.00
79-13-003	Moses	B. Rodden	S/O	140.00	235.00
81-13-004	Freedom Eagle	G. deLodzia	S/O	195.00	750-900.
82-13-005	Wings of Liberty	M. Boyett	S/O	625.00	1565.00
84-13-006	Cheyenne (Remington)	C. Rousell	Retrd.	400.00	600.00
84-13-007	Garden Unicorn	J. Royce	Retrd.	160.00	200.00
85-13-008	Bronco Buster (Large)	C. Rousell	Retrd.	400.00	400.00
86-13-009	Camelot Chess Set	P. Jackson	Retrd.	2250.00	2250.00
88-13-010	Dragon Slayer	D. LaRocca	Retrd.	385.00	500.00
88-13-011	End of the Trail (Mini)	A. McGrory	S/O	225.00	250.00
Lance Corporation	**Chilmark Pewter The Sorcerer's Apprentice Collectors Series**				
90-14-001	The Sorcerer's Apprentice	Disney Studios	2,500	225.00	225.00
90-14-002	The Incantation	Disney Studios	2,500	150.00	150.00
90-14-003	The Dream	Disney Studios	2,500	225.00	225.00
90-14-004	The Whirlpool	Disney Studios	2,500	225.00	225.00
90-14-005	The Repentant Apprentice	Disney Studios	2,500	195.00	195.00
Lance Corporation	**Chilmark Pewter Disney Figurines**				
89-15-001	Hollywood Mickey	Disney Studios	2,500	165.00	170.00
89-15-002	"Gold Edition" Hollywood Mickey	Disney Studios	Retrd.	200.00	200.00
91-15-003	Mickey's Carousel Ride	Disney Studios	2,500	150.00	150.00
92-15-004	Minnie's Carousel Ride	Disney Studios	2,500	150.00	150.00
92-15-005	Cruising (Metal Art™)	Disney Studios	350	275.00	275.00
Lance Corporation	**Chilmark Pewter Generations of Mickey**				
87-16-001	Antique Mickey	Disney Studios	S/O	130.00	350.00
89-16-002	Steam Boat Willie	Disney Studios	2,500	165.00	175.00
89-16-003	Sorcerer's Apprentice	Disney Studios	2,500	150.00	160.00
89-16-004	Mickey's Gala Premiere	Disney Studios	2,500	150.00	150.00
90-16-005	Disneyland Mickey	Disney Studios	2,500	150.00	150.00
90-16-006	The Band Concert	Disney Studios	2,000	185.00	185.00
90-16-007	The Band Concert (Painted)	Disney Studios	500	215.00	215.00
91-16-008	Plane Crazy-1928	Disney Studios	2,500	175.00	175.00
91-16-009	The Mouse-1935	Disney Studios	1,200	185.00	185.00
Lance Corporation	**Chilmark Pewter The Adversaries**				
91-17-001	Robert E. Lee	F. Barnum	S/O	350.00	350.00
92-17-002	Ulysses S. Grant	F. Barnum	S/O	350.00	350.00
Lance Corporation	**Chilmark Pewter Civil War**				
87-18-001	Saving The Colors	F. Barnum	Retrd.	350.00	350.00
88-18-002	Johnny Shiloh	F. Barnum	S/O	100.00	110.00
92-18-003	Kennesaw Mountain	F. Barnum	S/O	650.00	650.00
Lance Corporation	**Chilmark Metal Art™ The Great Chiefs**				
92-19-001	Chief Joseph	J. Slockbower	S/O	975.00	975-1500.
Lance Corporation	**Chilmark Pewter/Metal Art™ The Warriors**				
92-20-001	Spirit of the Wolf (pewter)	D. Polland	S/O	350.00	350-500.
Lance Corporation	**Sebastian Miniature Figurines**				
80-21-001	S.M.C. Society Plaque ('80 Charter)	P.W. Baston	Yr.Iss.	Unkn.	20-30.00
83-21-002	Harry Hood	P.W. Baston, Jr.	S/O	Unkn.	200-250.
85-21-003	It's Hoods (Wagon)	P.W. Baston, Jr.	S/O	Unkn.	150-175.
86-21-004	Statue of Liberty (AT & T)	P.W. Baston, Jr.	S/O	Unkn.	175-200.
87-21-005	White House (Gold, Oval Base)	P.W. Baston, Jr.	S/O	17.00	75-100.00
91-21-006	America Salutes Desert Storm-painted	P.W. Baston, Jr.	S/O	49.50	49.50
91-21-007	America Salutes Desert Storm-bronze	P.W. Baston, Jr.	1,641	26.50	26.50
91-21-008	Happy Hood Holidays	P.W. Baston, Jr.	2,000	32.50	32.50
Lance Corporation	**Sebastian Miniatures Children At Play**				
78-22-001	Sidewalk Days Boy	P.W. Baston	S/O	19.50	35-50.00
78-22-002	Sidewalk Days Girl	P.W. Baston	S/O	19.50	30-50.00
79-22-003	Building Days Boy	P.W. Baston	S/O	19.50	20-40.00
79-22-004	Building Days Girl	P.W. Baston	S/O	19.50	20-40.00
80-22-005	Snow Days Boy	P.W. Baston	S/O	19.50	20-40.00
80-22-006	Snow Days Girl	P.W. Baston	S/O	19.50	20-40.00
81-22-007	Sailing Days Boy	P.W. Baston	S/O	19.50	20-30.00
81-22-008	Sailing Days Girl	P.W. Baston	S/O	19.50	20-30.00
82-22-009	School Days Boy	P.W. Baston	S/O	19.50	20-30.00
82-22-010	School Days Girl	P.W. Baston	S/O	19.50	20-30.00
Lance Corporation	**Sebastian Miniatures America Remembers**				
79-23-001	Family Sing	P.W. Baston	Yr.Iss.	29.50	90-125.00
80-23-002	Family Picnic	P.W. Baston	Yr.Iss.	29.50	45-60.00
81-23-003	Family Reads Aloud	P.W. Baston	Yr.Iss.	34.50	34.50
82-23-004	Family Fishing	P.W. Baston	Yr.Iss.	34.50	34.50
83-23-005	Family Feast	P.W. Baston	Yr.Iss.	37.50	100-150.
Lance Corporation	**Sebastian Miniatures Jimmy Fund**				
83-24-001	Schoolboy	P.W. Baston	Yr.Iss.	24.50	50-75.00
84-24-002	Catcher	P.W. Baston	Yr.Iss.	24.50	50-75.00
85-24-003	Hockey Player	P.W. Baston,Jr.	Yr.Iss.	24.50	25-50.00
86-24-004	Soccer Player	P.W. Baston,Jr.	Yr.Iss.	25.00	25.00
87-24-005	Football Player	P.W. Baston,Jr.	Yr.Iss.	26.50	26.50
88-24-006	Santa	P.W. Baston,Jr.	Closed	32.50	32.50
Lance Corporation	**Sebastian Miniatures Exchange Figurines**				
83-25-001	Newspaper Boy	P.W. Baston	Yr.Iss.	28.50	40-60.00
84-25-002	First Things First	P.W. Baston,Jr.	Yr.Iss.	30.00	30.00
85-25-003	Newstand	P.W. Baston,Jr.	Yr.Iss.	30.00	30.00
86-25-004	News Wagon	P.W. Baston,Jr.	Yr.Iss.	35.00	35.00
87-25-005	It's About Time	P.W. Baston,Jr.	Yr.Iss.	25.00	25.00
Lance Corporation	**Sebastian Miniatures Washington Irving-Member Only**				
80-26-001	Rip Van Winkle	P.W. Baston	Closed	19.50	19.50
81-26-002	Dame Van Winkle	P.W. Baston	Closed	19.50	19.50
81-26-003	Ichabod Crane	P.W. Baston	Closed	19.50	19.50
82-26-004	Katrina Van Tassel	P.W. Baston	Closed	19.50	19.50
82-26-005	Brom Bones(Headless Horseman)	P.W. Baston	Closed	22.50	22.50
83-26-006	Diedrich Knickerbocker	P.W. Baston	Closed	22.50	22.50
Lance Corporation	**Sebastian Miniatures Shakespearean-Member Only**				
84-27-001	Henry VIII	P.W. Baston	Yr.Iss.	19.50	19.50
84-27-002	Anne Boyeln	P.W. Baston	6 month	17.50	17.50
85-27-003	Falstaff	P.W. Baston	Yr.Iss.	19.50	19.50
85-27-004	Mistress Ford	P.W. Baston	6 month	17.50	17.50
86-27-005	Romeo	P.W. Baston	Yr.Iss.	19.50	19.50
86-27-006	Juliet	P.W. Baston	6 month	17.50	17.50
87-27-007	Malvolio	P.W. Baston	Yr.Iss.	21.50	21.50
87-27-008	Countess Olivia	P.W. Baston	6 month	19.50	19.50
88-27-009	Touchstone	P.W. Baston	Yr.Iss.	22.50	22.50
88-27-010	Audrey	P.W. Baston	6 month	22.50	22.50
89-27-011	Mark Anthony	P.W. Baston	Yr.Iss.	27.00	27.00
89-27-012	Cleopatra	P.W. Baston	6 month	27.00	27.00
88-27-013	Shakespeare	P.W. Baston,Jr.	Yr.Iss.	23.50	23.50

Company Number	Name	Series Artist	Edition Limit	Issue Price	Quote
Lance Corporation		**Sebastian Miniatures Member Only**			
89-28-001	The Collectors	P.W. Baston,Jr.	Yr.Iss.	39.50	39.50
92-28-002	Christopher Columbus	P.W. Baston,Jr.	Yr.Iss.	28.50	28.50
Lance Corporation		**Sebastian Miniatures Holiday Memories-Member Only**			
90-29-001	Thanksgiving Helper	P.W. Baston,Jr.	Yr.Iss.	39.50	39.50
90-29-002	Leprechaun	P.W. Baston,Jr.	Yr.Iss.	27.50	27.50
91-29-003	Trick or Treat	P.W. Baston,Jr.	Yr.Iss.	25.50	25.50

Also see Sebastian Studios

Company Number	Name	Series Artist	Edition Limit	Issue Price	Quote
Lance Corporation		**Hudson Pewter Figures**			
69-30-001	George Washington (Cannon)	P.W. Baston	Closed	35.00	75-100.00
69-30-002	John Hancock	P.W. Baston	Closed	15.00	100-125.
69-30-003	Colonial Blacksmith	P.W. Baston	Closed	30.00	100-125.
69-30-004	Betsy Ross	P.W. Baston	Closed	30.00	100-125.
72-30-005	Benjamin Franklin	P.W. Baston	Closed	15.00	75-100.00
72-30-006	Thomas Jefferson	P.W. Baston	Closed	15.00	75-100.00
72-30-007	George Washington	P.W. Baston	Closed	15.00	75-100.00
72-30-008	John Adams	P.W. Baston	Closed	15.00	75-100.00
72-30-009	James Madison	P.W. Baston	Closed	15.00	50-75.00
75-30-010	Declaration Wall Plaque	P.W. Baston	Closed	Unkn.	300-500.
75-30-011	Washington's Letter of Acceptance	P.W. Baston	Closed	Unkn.	300-400.
75-30-012	Lincoln's Gettysburg Address	P.W. Baston	Closed	Unkn.	300-400.
75-30-013	Lee's Ninth General Order	P.W. Baston	Closed	Unkn.	300-400.
75-30-014	The Favored Scholar	P.W. Baston	Closed	Unkn.	600-1000.
75-30-015	Neighboring Pews	P.W. Baston	Closed	Unkn.	600-1000.
75-30-016	Weighing the Baby	P.W. Baston	Closed	Unkn.	600-1000.
75-30-017	Spirit of '76	P.W. Baston	Closed	Unkn.	750-1500.
76-30-018	Great Horned Owl	H. Wilson	Closed	Unkn.	41.50
76-30-019	Bald Eagle	H. Wilson	Closed	100.00	112.50
Lance Corporation		**Hudson Pewter Crystals of Zorn**			
88-31-001	Guarding the Crystal	D. Liberty	950	450.00	460.00
88-31-002	Charging the Stone	D. Liberty	950	375.00	395.00
88-31-003	USS Strikes Back	D. Liberty	500	650.00	675.00
88-31-004	Response of Ornic Force	D. Liberty	950	275.00	285.00
88-31-005	Battle on the Plains of Xenon	D. Liberty	950	250.00	265.00
88-31-006	Restoration	D. Liberty	950	425.00	435.00
90-31-007	Struggle For Supremacy	D. Liberty	950	395.00	400.00
90-31-008	Asmund's Workshop	D. Liberty	950	275.00	275.00
90-31-009	Vesting The Grail	D. Liberty	950	200.00	200.00
Lance Corporation		**Military Commemoratives**			
91-32-001	Desert Liberator (Pewter)	D. LaRocca	Retrd.	295.00	295.00
91-32-002	Desert Liberator (Painted Porcelain)	D. LaRocca	5,000	125.00	125.00
Lance Corporation		**Hudson Pewter The Villagers**			
87-33-001	Mr. Bosworth	Hudson Studios	Retrd.	35.00	35.00
87-33-002	Emily	Hudson Studios	Retrd.	23.00	23.00
87-33-003	Reginald	Hudson Studios	Retrd.	23.00	23.00
87-33-004	Oliver	Hudson Studios	Retrd.	20.00	20.00
87-33-005	Jenny	Hudson Studios	Retrd.	20.00	20.00
87-33-006	Thomas	Hudson Studios	Retrd.	20.00	20.00
88-33-007	Melissa	Hudson Studios	Retrd.	18.00	18.00
88-33-008	Tully's Pond	Hudson Studios	Retrd.	49.00	49.00
88-33-009	Main Street	Hudson Studios	Retrd.	47.00	47.00
88-33-010	Bosworth Manor	Hudson Studios	Retrd.	57.00	57.00
88-33-011	Santa	Hudson Studios	Retrd.	28.00	28.00
89-33-012	Grandpa Todd	Hudson Studios	Retrd.	23.00	23.00
89-33-013	Grandma Todd & Sarah	Hudson Studios	Retrd.	29.00	29.00
89-33-014	Rascal	Hudson Studios	Retrd.	25.00	25.00
89-33-015	Seated Santa	Hudson Studios	Yr.Iss.	25.00	25.00
89-33-016	Creche	Hudson Studios	Retrd.	15.00	15.00
89-33-017	Ben Torpey	Hudson Studios	Retrd.	28.00	28.00
89-33-018	Villagers Plaque	Hudson Studios	Retrd.	27.00	27.00
90-33-019	Santa & Holly	Hudson Studios	Yr.Iss.	32.00	32.00
91-33-020	Santa and Matthew	Hudson Studios	Yr.Iss.	35.00	35.00
92-33-021	Crack the Whip	Hudson Studios	1,500	95.00	95.00
92-33-022	1992 Annual Santa	Hudson Studios	Yr.Iss.	32.00	32.00
Lance Corporation		**Hudson Pewter Noah's Ark**			
82-34-001	Toucan Pair	Hudson Studios	Retrd.	18.00	18.00
83-34-002	Male Rhino	Hudson Studios	Retrd.	13.00	13.00
83-34-003	Female Rhino	Hudson Studios	Retrd.	13.00	13.00
83-34-004	Panda Pair	Hudson Studios	Retrd.	18.00	18.00
84-34-005	Male Tiger	Hudson Studios	Retrd.	13.00	13.00
84-34-006	Female Tiger	Hudson Studios	Retrd.	13.00	13.00
84-34-007	Male Deer	Hudson Studios	Retrd.	13.00	13.00
84-34-008	Female Deer	Hudson Studios	Retrd.	13.00	13.00
84-34-009	Mice Pair	Hudson Studios	Retrd.	14.00	14.00
84-34-010	Raccoon Pair	Hudson Studios	Retrd.	14.00	14.00
87-34-011	Cat Pair	Hudson Studios	Retrd.	18.00	18.00
87-34-012	Female Dog	Hudson Studios	Retrd.	13.00	13.00
87-34-013	Male Dog	Hudson Studios	Retrd.	16.00	16.00
87-34-014	Ram	Hudson Studios	Retrd.	16.00	16.00
87-34-015	Ewe	Hudson Studios	Retrd.	16.00	16.00
88-34-016	Geese Pair	Hudson Studios	Retrd.	18.00	18.00
Ron Lee's World of Clowns		**The Original Ron Lee Collection**			
76-01-001	Pinky Upside Down 111	R. Lee	Closed	25.00	32-84.00
76-01-002	Pinky Lying Down 112	R. Lee	Closed	25.00	32-84.00
76-01-003	Hobo Joe Hitchiking 116	R. Lee	Closed	55.00	65.00
76-01-004	Hobo Joe with Umbrella 117	R. Lee	Closed	58.00	65-160.00
76-01-005	Pinky Sitting 119	R. Lee	Closed	25.00	32-84.00
76-01-006	Hobo Joe with Balloons 120	R. Lee	Closed	63.00	90.00
76-01-007	Hobo Joe with Pal 115	R. Lee	Closed	63.00	85-170.00
76-01-008	Clown and Dog Act 101	R. Lee	Closed	48.00	78-140.00
76-01-009	Clown Tightrope Walker 104	R. Lee	Closed	50.00	82-155.00
76-01-010	Clown and Elephant Act 107	R. Lee	Closed	56.00	85-140.00
76-01-011	Pinky Standing 118	R. Lee	Closed	25.00	45-100.00
76-01-012	Owl With Guitar 500	R. Lee	Closed	15.00	35-78.00
76-01-013	Turtle On Skateboard 501	R. Lee	Closed	15.00	35-78.00
76-01-014	Frog Surfing 502	R. Lee	Closed	15.00	35-78.00
76-01-015	Penguin on Snowskis 503	R. Lee	Closed	15.00	35-78.00
76-01-016	Alligator Bowling 504	R. Lee	Closed	15.00	35-78.00
76-01-017	Hippo on Scooter 505	R. Lee	Closed	15.00	35-78.00
76-01-018	Rabbit Playing Tennis 507	R. Lee	Closed	15.00	35-78.00
76-01-019	Kangaroos Boxing 508	R. Lee	Closed	15.00	35-78.00
76-01-020	Pig Playing Violin 510	R. Lee	Closed	15.00	35-78.00
76-01-021	Bear Fishing 511	R. Lee	Closed	15.00	35-78.00
76-01-022	Dog Fishing 512	R. Lee	Closed	15.00	35-78.00
77-01-023	Koala Bear In Tree 514	R. Lee	Closed	15.00	35-78.00
77-01-024	Koala Bear With Baby 515	R. Lee	Closed	15.00	35-78.00
77-01-025	Koala Bear On Log 516	R. Lee	Closed	15.00	35-78.00
77-01-026	Mr. Penguin 518	R. Lee	Closed	18.00	39-85.00
77-01-027	Owl Graduate 519	R. Lee	Closed	22.00	44-90.00
77-01-028	Mouse and Cheese 520	R. Lee	Closed	18.00	30-80.00
77-01-029	Monkey With Banana 521	R. Lee	Closed	18.00	30-80.00
77-01-030	Pelican and Python 522	R. Lee	Closed	18.00	30-80.00
77-01-031	Bear On Rock 523	R. Lee	Closed	18.00	30-80.00
78-01-032	Polly, the Parrot & Crackers 201	R. Lee	Closed	63.00	100-170.
78-01-033	Driver the Golfer 211	R. Lee	Closed	55.00	72-177.00
78-01-034	Skippy Swinging 239	R. Lee	Closed	52.00	65-85.00
78-01-035	Sailfish 524	R. Lee	Closed	18.00	40-95.00
78-01-036	Dolphins 525	R. Lee	Closed	22.00	40-85.00
78-01-037	Prince Frog 526	R. Lee	Closed	22.00	40-85.00
78-01-038	Seagull 527	R. Lee	Closed	22.00	40-85.00
78-01-039	Hummingbird 528	R. Lee	Closed	22.00	40-85.00
78-01-040	Butterfly and Flower 529	R. Lee	Closed	22.00	40-85.00
78-01-041	Turtle on Rock 530	R. Lee	Closed	22.00	40-85.00
78-01-042	Sea Otter on Back 531	R. Lee	Closed	22.00	40-85.00
78-01-043	Sea Otter on Rock 532	R. Lee	Closed	22.00	40-85.00
78-01-044	Corky, the Drummer Boy 202	R. Lee	Closed	53.00	85-130.00
78-01-045	Tinker Bowing 203	R. Lee	Closed	37.00	55-110.00
78-01-046	Bobbi on Unicyle 204	R. Lee	Closed	45.00	65-98.00
78-01-047	Clara-Bow 205	R. Lee	Closed	52.00	70-120.00
78-01-048	Sparky Skating 206	R. Lee	Closed	55.00	72-260.00
78-01-049	Pierrot Painting 207	R. Lee	Closed	50.00	80-170.00
78-01-050	Cuddles 208	R. Lee	Closed	37.00	55-110.00
78-01-051	Poppy with Puppet 209	R. Lee	Closed	60.00	75-140.00
78-01-052	Clancy, the Cop 210	R. Lee	Closed	55.00	72-130.00
78-01-053	Sad Sack 212	R. Lee	Closed	48.00	62-210.00
78-01-054	Elephant on Stand 213	R. Lee	Closed	26.00	42-80.00
78-01-055	Elephant on Ball 214	R. Lee	Closed	26.00	42-80.00
78-01-056	Elephant Sitting 215	R. Lee	Closed	26.00	42-80.00
78-01-057	Fireman with Hose 216	R. Lee	Closed	62.00	85-140.00
78-01-058	Tobi-Hands Outstretched 217	R. Lee	Closed	70.00	98-260.00
78-01-059	Coco-Hands on Hips 218	R. Lee	Closed	70.00	95-150.00
78-01-060	Jeri In a Barrel 219	R. Lee	Closed	75.00	110-180.
78-01-061	Hey Rube 220	R. Lee	Closed	35.00	53-92.00
78-01-062	Jocko with Lollipop 221	R. Lee	Closed	67.50	93-215.00
78-01-063	Bow Tie 222	R. Lee	Closed	67.50	93-215.00
78-01-064	Oscar On Stilts 223	R. Lee	Closed	55.00	90-120.00
78-01-065	Fancy Pants 224	R. Lee	Closed	55.00	90-120.00
79-01-066	Timmy Tooting 225	R. Lee	Closed	35.00	52-85.00
79-01-067	Tubby Tuba 226	R. Lee	Closed	35.00	55-90.00
79-01-068	Lilli 227	R. Lee	Closed	75.00	105-145.
79-01-069	Doctor Sawbones 228	R. Lee	Closed	75.00	110-150.
79-01-070	Buttons Bicycling 229	R. Lee	Closed	75.00	110-150.
79-01-071	Kelly in Kar 230	R. Lee	Closed	164.00	210-380.
79-01-072	Kelly's Kar 231	R. Lee	Closed	75.00	90-230.00
79-01-073	Carousel Horse 232	R. Lee	Closed	119.00	130-195.
79-01-074	Harry and the Hare 233	R. Lee	Closed	69.00	102-180.
79-01-075	Fearless Fred in Cannon 234	R. Lee	Closed	80.00	105-300.
79-01-076	Darby with Flower 235	R. Lee	Closed	35.00	60-140.00
79-01-077	Darby with Umbrella 236	R. Lee	Closed	35.00	60-140.00
79-01-078	Darby With Violin 237	R. Lee	Closed	35.00	60-140.00
79-01-079	Darby Tipping Hat 238	R. Lee	Closed	35.00	60-140.00
79-01-080	Kelly at the Piano 241	R. Lee	Closed	185.00	280-510.
80-01-081	Cubby Holding Balloon 240	R. Lee	Closed	50.00	65-70.00
80-01-082	Chuckles Juggling 244	R. Lee	Closed	98.00	105-150
80-01-083	Jo-Jo at Make-up Mirror 250	R. Lee	Closed	86.00	125-185
80-01-084	Hobo Joe in Tub 259	R. Lee	Closed	96.00	105-125
80-01-085	Jingles Telling Time 242	R. Lee	Closed	75.00	90-190.00
80-01-086	Donkey What 243	R. Lee	Closed	60.00	92-250.00
80-01-087	P. T. Dinghy 245	R. Lee	Closed	65.00	80-190.00
80-01-088	Roni Riding Horse 246	R. Lee	Closed	115.00	180-290.
80-01-089	Peanuts Playing Concertina 247	R. Lee	Closed	65.00	150-285.
80-01-090	Carousel Horse 248	R. Lee	Closed	88.00	115-285.
80-01-091	Carousel Horse 249	R. Lee	Closed	88.00	115-285.
80-01-092	Monkey 251	R. Lee	Closed	60.00	85-210.00
80-01-093	Dennis Playing Tennis 252	R. Lee	Closed	74.00	95-185.00
80-01-094	Jaque Downhill Racer 253	R. Lee	Closed	74.00	90-210.00
80-01-095	Ruford 254	R. Lee	Closed	43.00	82-190.00
80-01-096	Happy Waving 255	R. Lee	Closed	43.00	82-190.00
80-01-097	Zach 256	R. Lee	Closed	43.00	82-190.00
80-01-098	Emile 257	R. Lee	Closed	43.00	82-190.00
80-01-099	Banjo Willie 258	R. Lee	Closed	68.00	85-195.00
80-01-100	Doctor Jawbones 260	R. Lee	Closed	85.00	110-305.
80-01-101	Alexander's One Man Band 261	R. Lee	Closed	N/A	N/A
80-01-102	The Menagerie 262	R. Lee	Closed	N/A	N/A
80-01-103	Horse Drawn Chariot 263	R. Lee	Closed	N/A	N/A
81-01-104	Louie on Park Bench 268	R. Lee	Closed	56.00	85-160.00
81-01-105	Hobo Joe Praying 298	R. Lee	Closed	57.00	65-85.00
81-01-106	Executive Reading 264	R. Lee	Closed	23.00	45-110.00
81-01-107	Executive with Umbrella 265	R. Lee	Closed	23.00	45-110.00
81-01-108	Executive Resting 266	R. Lee	Closed	23.00	45-110.00
81-01-109	Executive Hitchiking 267	R. Lee	Closed	23.00	45-110.00
81-01-110	Louie Hitching A Ride 269	R. Lee	Closed	47.00	58-135.00
81-01-111	Louie On Railroad Car 270	R. Lee	Closed	77.00	95-180.00
81-01-112	Elephant Reading 271	R. Lee	Closed	N/A	N/A
81-01-113	Pistol Pete 272	R. Lee	Closed	76.00	85-180.00
81-01-114	Barbella 273	R. Lee	Closed	N/A	N/A
81-01-115	Larry and His Hotdogs 274	R. Lee	Closed	76.00	90-200.00
81-01-116	Cashew On One Knee 275	R. Lee	Closed	N/A	N/A
81-01-117	Bojangles 276	R. Lee	Closed	N/A	N/A
81-01-118	Bozo Playing Cymbols 277	R. Lee	Closed	28.00	49-185.00
81-01-119	Bozo Riding Car 278	R. Lee	Closed	28.00	49-185.00
81-01-120	Bozo On Unicycle 279	R. Lee	Closed	28.00	49-185.00
81-01-120	Carousel Horse 280	R. Lee	Closed	88.00	125-240.
81-01-121	Carousel Horse 281	R. Lee	Closed	88.00	125-240.
81-01-122	Ron Lee Trio 282	R. Lee	Closed	144.00	280-435.
81-01-123	Kevin at the Drums 283	R. Lee	Closed	50.00	92-150.00
81-01-124	Al at the Bass 284	R. Lee	Closed	48.00	52-112.00
81-01-125	Ron at the Piano 285	R. Lee	Closed	46.00	55-110.00
81-01-126	Timothy In Big Shoes 286	R. Lee	Closed	37.00	50-95.00
81-01-127	Perry Sitting With Balloon 287	R. Lee	Closed	37.00	50-95.00
81-01-128	Perry Standing With Balloon 288	R. Lee	Closed	37.00	50-95.00
81-01-129	Nicky Sitting on Ball 289	R. Lee	Closed	39.00	48-92.00
81-01-130	Nicky Standing on Ball 290	R. Lee	Closed	39.00	48-92.00
81-01-131	Mickey With Umbrella 291	R. Lee	Closed	50.00	75-140.00
81-01-132	Mickey Tightrope Walker 292	R. Lee	Closed	50.00	75-140.00
81-01-133	Mickey Upside Down 293	R. Lee	Closed	50.00	75-140.00
81-01-134	Rocketman 294	R. Lee	Closed	77.00	92-180.00
81-01-135	My Son Darren 295	R. Lee	Closed	57.00	72-140.00

Company Number	Name	Series Artist	Edition Limit	Issue Price	Quote
81-01-136	Harpo 296	R. Lee	Closed	120.00	190-350.
81-01-137	Pickles and Pooch 297	R. Lee	Closed	90.00	140-240.
81-01-138	Bosom Buddies 299	R. Lee	Closed	135.00	90-280.00
81-01-139	Carney and Seal Act 300	R. Lee	Closed	63.00	75-140.00
82-01-140	Self Portrait 702	R. Lee	Closed	1000.00	1250-2500.
82-01-141	Ron Lee Carousel	R. Lee	Closed	10000.00	12500.00
82-01-142	Georgie Going Anywhere 302	R. Lee	Closed	95.00	125-256.
82-01-143	Carney and Dog Act 301	R. Lee	Closed	63.00	75-149.00
82-01-144	Fireman Watering House 303	R. Lee	Closed	99.00	99-180.00
82-01-145	Quincy Lying Down 304	R. Lee	Closed	80.00	92-210.00
82-01-146	Denny Eating Ice Cream 305	R. Lee	Closed	39.00	50-170.00
82-01-147	Denny Holding Gift Box 306	R. Lee	Closed	39.00	50-170.00
82-01-148	Denny Juggling Ball 307	R. Lee	Closed	39.00	50-170.00
82-01-149	Buster in Barrel 308	R. Lee	Closed	85.00	90-120.00
82-01-150	Sammy Riding Elephant 309	R. Lee	Closed	90.00	102-182.
82-01-151	Benny Pulling Car 310	R. Lee	Closed	190.00	235-360.
82-01-152	Dr. Painless and Patient 311	R. Lee	Closed	195.00	240-385.
82-01-153	Too Loose-L'Artiste 312	R. Lee	Closed	150.00	180-290.
82-01-154	Slim Charging Bull 313	R. Lee	Closed	195.00	265-410.
82-01-155	Norman Painting Dumbo 314	R. Lee	Closed	126.00	150-210.
82-01-156	Barnum Feeding Bacon 315	R. Lee	Closed	120.00	160-270.
82-01-157	Kukla and Friend 316	R. Lee	Closed	100.00	140-210.
82-01-158	Marion With Marrionette 317	R. Lee	Closed	105.00	135-225.
82-01-159	Two Man Valentinos 318	R. Lee	Closed	45.00	60-130.00
82-01-160	Three Man Valentinos 319	R. Lee	Closed	55.00	70-120.00
82-01-161	Captain Cranberry 320	R. Lee	Closed	115.00	145-180.
82-01-162	Charlie in the Rain 321	R. Lee	Closed	80.00	90-160.00
82-01-163	Hobo Joe on Cycle 322	R. Lee	Closed	125.00	170-280.
82-01-164	Tou Tou 323	R. Lee	Closed	70.00	90-190.00
82-01-165	Toy Soldier 324	R. Lee	Closed	95.00	140-270.
82-01-166	Herbie Dancing 325	R. Lee	Closed	26.00	40-110.00
82-01-167	Herbie Hands Outstretched 326	R. Lee	Closed	26.00	40-110.00
82-01-168	Herbie Balancing Hat 327	R. Lee	Closed	26.00	40-110.00
82-01-169	Herbie Lying Down 328	R. Lee	Closed	26.00	40-110.00
82-01-170	Herbie Legs in Air 329	R. Lee	Closed	26.00	40-110.00
82-01-171	Herbie Touching Ground 330	R. Lee	Closed	26.00	40-110.00
82-01-172	Clarence - The Lawyer 331	R. Lee	Closed	100.00	140-230.
82-01-173	Pinball Pal 332	R. Lee	Closed	150.00	195-287.
82-01-174	Clancy, the Cop and Dog 333	R. Lee	Closed	115.00	140-250.
82-01-175	Burrito Bandito 334	R. Lee	Closed	150.00	190-260.
82-01-176	Ali on His Magic Carpet 335	R. Lee	Closed	105.00	150-210.
82-01-177	Chico Playing Guitar 336	R. Lee	Closed	70.00	95-180.00
82-01-178	Murphy On Unicycle 337	R. Lee	Closed	115.00	160-288.
82-01-179	Robin Resting 338	R. Lee	Closed	110.00	125-210.
82-01-180	Nappy Snoozing 346	R. Lee	Closed	110.00	125-210.
82-01-181	Laurel & Hardy 700	R. Lee	Closed	225.00	290-500.
82-01-182	Charlie Chaplain 701	R. Lee	Closed	230.00	285-650.
82-01-183	Self Portrait 702	R. Lee	Closed	355.00	550-816.
82-01-184	Captain Mis-Adventure 703	R. Lee	Closed	250.00	300-550.
82-01-185	Steppin' Out 704	R. Lee	Closed	325.00	390-700.
82-01-186	Limousine Service 705	R. Lee	Closed	330.00	375-750.
82-01-187	Pig Brick Layer 800	R. Lee	Closed	23.00	35-92.00
82-01-188	Rabbit With Egg 801	R. Lee	Closed	23.00	35-92.00
82-01-189	Smokey, the Bear 802	R. Lee	Closed	23.00	35-92.00
82-01-190	Fish With Shoe 803	R. Lee	Closed	23.00	35-92.00
82-01-191	Seal Blowing His Horns 804	R. Lee	Closed	23.00	35-92.00
82-01-192	Dog Playing Guitar 805	R. Lee	Closed	23.00	35-92.00
82-01-193	Fox In An Airplane 806	R. Lee	Closed	23.00	35-92.00
82-01-193	Beaver Playing Accordian 807	R. Lee	Closed	23.00	35-92.00
82-01-194	Rooster With Barbell 808	R. Lee	Closed	23.00	35-92.00
82-01-196	Parrot Rollerskating 809	R. Lee	Closed	23.00	35-92.00
82-01-197	Walrus With Umbrella 810	R. Lee	Closed	23.00	35-92.00
82-01-198	Turtle With Gun 811	R. Lee	Closed	57.00	75-150.00
82-01-199	Reindeer 812	R. Lee	Closed	57.00	75-150.00
82-01-200	Ostrich 813	R. Lee	Closed	57.00	75-150.00
82-01-201	Tiger 814	R. Lee	Closed	57.00	75-150.00
82-01-202	Rooster 815	R. Lee	Closed	57.00	75-150.00
82-01-203	Giraffe 816	R. Lee	Closed	57.00	75-150.00
82-01-204	Lion 817	R. Lee	Closed	57.00	75-150.00
82-01-205	Camel 818	R. Lee	Closed	57.00	75-150.00
82-01-206	Horse 819	R. Lee	Closed	57.00	75-150.00
83-01-207	Clyde Juggling 339	R. Lee	Closed	39.00	45-100.00
83-01-208	Clyde Upside Down 340	R. Lee	Closed	39.00	45-105.00
83-01-209	Hobi in His Hammock 344	R. Lee	Closed	85.00	175-225.
83-01-210	Little Saturday Night 348	R. Lee	Closed	53.00	100-140.
83-01-211	Tatters and Balloons 352	R. Lee	Closed	65.00	85-167.00
83-01-212	I Love You From My Heart 360	R. Lee	Closed	35.00	50-95.00
83-01-213	Singin' In The Rain 362	R. Lee	Closed	105.00	225-275.
83-01-214	Up, Up and Away 364	R. Lee	Closed	50.00	100-125.
83-01-215	Lou Proposing 365	R. Lee	Closed	57.00	75-116.00
83-01-216	Riches to Rags 374	R. Lee	Closed	55.00	85-250.00
83-01-217	Gilbert Tee'd Off 376	R. Lee	Closed	60.00	100-155.
83-01-218	Matinee Jitters 378	R. Lee	Closed	175.00	180-225.
83-01-219	The Bandwagon 707	R. Lee	Closed	900.00	1200-2570.
83-01-220	Little Horse - Head Up 341	R. Lee	Closed	29.00	72.00
83-01-221	Little Horse - Head Down 342	R. Lee	Closed	29.00	72.00
83-01-222	Rufus and His Refuse 343	R. Lee	Closed	65.00	160.00
83-01-223	Flipper Diving 345	R. Lee	Closed	115.00	140-205.
83-01-224	Ride 'em Roni 347	R. Lee	Closed	125.00	145-190.
83-01-225	Tottie Scottie 349	R. Lee	Closed	39.00	45-75.00
83-01-226	Teeter Tottie Scottie 350	R. Lee	Closed	55.00	70-105.00
83-01-227	Casey Cruising 351	R. Lee	Closed	57.00	70-95.00
83-01-228	Bumbles Selling Balloons 353	R. Lee	Closed	80.00	95-170.00
83-01-229	Cecil and Sausage 354	R. Lee	Closed	90.00	120-190.
83-01-230	On The Road Again 355	R. Lee	Closed	220.00	290-500.
83-01-231	Engineer Billie 356	R. Lee	Closed	190.00	275-480.
83-01-232	My Daughter Deborah 357	R. Lee	Closed	63.00	65-125.00
83-01-233	Beethoven's Fourth Paws 358	R. Lee	Closed	59.00	60-110.00
83-01-234	Say It With Flowers 359	R. Lee	Closed	35.00	50-95.00
83-01-235	Chef's Cuisine 361	R. Lee	Closed	57.00	70-93.00
83-01-236	Buster and His Balloons 363	R. Lee	Closed	47.00	55-90.00
83-01-237	Knickers Balancing Feather 366	R. Lee	Closed	47.00	55-116.00
83-01-238	Daring Dudley 367	R. Lee	Closed	65.00	75-172.00
83-01-239	Wilt the Stilt 368	R. Lee	Closed	49.00	55-92.00
83-01-240	Coco and His Compact 369	R. Lee	Closed	55.00	70-145.00
83-01-241	Josephine 370	R. Lee	Closed	55.00	70-145.00
83-01-242	The Jogger 372	R. Lee	Closed	75.00	80-115.00
83-01-243	Door to Door Dabney 373	R. Lee	Closed	100.00	140-210.
83-01-244	Captain Freddy 375	R. Lee	Closed	85.00	200-425.
83-01-245	Cotton Candy 377	R. Lee	Closed	150.00	170-325.
83-01-246	The Last Scoop 379	R. Lee	Closed	175.00	200-350.
83-01-247	Cimba the Elephant 706	R. Lee	Closed	225.00	290-450.
83-01-248	Catch the Brass Ring 708	R. Lee	Closed	510.00	750-1150.
83-01-249	The Last Scoop 900	R. Lee	Closed	325.00	286-400.
83-01-250	The Last Scoop 379	R. Lee	Closed	175.00	200-350.
83-01-251	Matinee Jitters 901	R. Lee	Closed	325.00	350-450.
83-01-252	No Camping or Fishing 902	R. Lee	Closed	325.00	350-400.
83-01-253	Black Carousel Horse 1001	R. Lee	Closed	450.00	525-750.
83-01-254	Chestnut Carousel Horse 1002	R. Lee	Closed	450.00	525-750.
83-01-255	White Carousel Horse 1003	R. Lee	Closed	450.00	525-750.
83-01-256	Gazebo 1004	R. Lee	Closed	750.00	950-1250.
84-01-257	Rudy Holding Balloons 713	R. Lee	Closed	230.00	270-410.
84-01-258	Saturday Night 714	R. Lee	Closed	250.00	500-600.
84-01-259	No Camping or Fishing 380	R. Lee	Closed	175.00	190-275.
84-01-260	Wheeler Sheila 381	R. Lee	Closed	75.00	90-175.00
84-01-261	Mortimer Fishing 382	R. Lee	Closed	N/A	N/A
84-01-262	Give a Dog a Bone 383	R. Lee	Closed	95.00	95-182.00
84-01-263	The Peppermints 384	R. Lee	Closed	150.00	180-240.
84-01-264	T.K. and OH!! 385	R. Lee	Closed	85.00	95-210.00
84-01-265	Just For You 386	R. Lee	Closed	110.00	150-275.
84-01-266	Baggy Pants 387	R. Lee	Closed	98.00	110-250.
84-01-267	Look at the Birdy 388	R. Lee	Closed	138.00	160-255.
84-01-268	Bozo's Seal of Approval 389	R. Lee	Closed	138.00	165-240.
84-01-269	A Bozo Lunch 390	R. Lee	Closed	148.00	160-300.
84-01-270	My Fellow Americans 391	R. Lee	Closed	138.00	150-400.
84-01-271	No Loitering 392	R. Lee	Closed	113.00	115-205.
84-01-272	Tisket and Tasket 393	R. Lee	Closed	93.00	105-190.
84-01-273	White Circus Horse 709	R. Lee	Closed	305.00	350-520.
84-01-274	Chestnut Circus Horse 710A	R. Lee	Closed	305.00	350-520.
84-01-275	Black Circus Horse 711A	R. Lee	Closed	305.00	350-520.
84-01-276	Rudy Holding Balloons 713	R. Lee	Closed	230.00	270-410.
85-01-277	Whiskers Sweeping 744	R. Lee	Closed	240.00	N/A
85-01-278	Whiskers Hitchhiking 745	R. Lee	Closed	240.00	N/A
85-01-279	Whiskers Holding Balloons 746	R. Lee	Closed	265.00	N/A
85-01-280	Whiskers Holding Umbrella 747	R. Lee	Closed	265.00	N/A
85-01-281	Whiskers Bathing 749	R. Lee	Closed	305.00	N/A
85-01-282	Whiskers On The Beach 750	R. Lee	Closed	230.00	N/A
85-01-283	Giraffe Getting a Bath 428	R. Lee	Closed	160.00	235-450.
85-01-284	Clowns of the Caribbean PS101	R. Lee	Closed	1250.00	1750-2200.
86-01-285	Wet Paint 436	R. Lee	Closed	80.00	100-150.
86-01-286	Bathing Buddies 450	R. Lee	Closed	145.00	150-245.
86-01-287	Hari and Hare 454	R. Lee	Closed	57.00	65-85.00
86-01-288	Ride 'Em Peanuts 463	R. Lee	Closed	55.00	68.00
86-01-289	Captain Cranberry 469	R. Lee	Closed	140.00	150-185.
86-01-290	Getting Even 485	R. Lee	Closed	85.00	98-120.00
87-01-291	Heartbroken Harry L101	R. Lee	Closed	63.00	100-150.
87-01-292	Lovable Luke L102	R. Lee	8,500	70.00	70.00
87-01-293	Puppy Love L103	R. Lee	8,500	71.00	71.00
87-01-294	Would You Like To Ride? L104	R. Lee	Closed	246.00	275-325.
87-01-295	Sugarland Express L109	R. Lee	Closed	342.00	200-375.
87-01-296	First & Main L110	R. Lee	Closed	368.00	400-650.
88-01-297	New Ron Lee Carousel	R. Lee	Closed	7000.00	9500.00
88-01-298	The Fifth Wheel L117	R. Lee	Closed	250.00	295.00
88-01-299	Tunnel of Love L123	R. Lee	Closed	490.00	550.00
88-01-300	To The Rescue L127	R. Lee	Closed	130.00	160-550.
88-01-301	When You're Hot, You're Hot! L128	R. Lee	Closed	221.00	250-800.
89-01-302	Be It Ever So Humble L111	R. Lee	Closed	900.00	950-1250.
89-01-303	Wishful Thinking L114	R. Lee	Closed	230.00	250-500.
89-01-304	If I Were A Rich Man L133	R. Lee	Closed	315.00	375-500.
89-01-305	I Pledge Allegiance L134	R. Lee	3,750	131.00	131-150.
89-01-306	In Over My Head L135	R. Lee	Closed	95.00	125.00
89-01-307	O' Solo Mia L139	R. Lee	Closed	85.00	90-150.00
89-01-308	Tee for Two L141	R. Lee	Closed	125.00	150.00
89-01-309	Circus Little L143	R. Lee	Closed	990.00	1250.00
89-01-310	Hughie Mungus L144	R. Lee	Closed	250.00	300-825.
89-01-311	Sh-h-h-h! L146	R. Lee	Closed	210.00	400-1000.
89-01-312	Today's Catch L147	R. Lee	Closed	230.00	245-325.
89-01-313	Catch A Falling Star L148	R. Lee	Closed	57.00	N/A
89-01-314	Snowdrifter L163	R. Lee	Closed	230.00	275-450.
89-01-315	The Policeman L165	R. Lee	Closed	68.00	75-85.00
89-01-316	The Fireman L169	R. Lee	Closed	68.00	85.00
89-01-317	The Lawyer 171	R. Lee	Closed	68.00	75.00
89-01-318	The Golfer L188	R. Lee	Closed	72.00	90.00
89-01-319	The Fisherman L194	R. Lee	7,500	72.00	72.00
89-01-320	The Greatest Little Shoe on Earth L210	R. Lee	Closed	165.00	195-225.
90-01-321	Candy Man L217	R. Lee	2,750	350.00	350.00
90-01-322	The New Self Portrait L218	R. Lee	Closed	800.00	950.00
90-01-323	Me Too! L231	R. Lee	3,500	70.00	70-80.00
90-01-324	Heartbroken Hobo L233	R. Lee	Closed	116.00	160.00
90-01-325	Scooter L234	R. Lee	2,750	240.00	275.00
90-01-326	Tandem Mania L235	R. Lee	2,750	360.00	360.00
90-01-327	The Big Wheel L236	R. Lee	2,750	240.00	240.00
90-01-328	Uni-Cycle L237	R. Lee	2,750	240.00	240.00
90-01-329	Fill'er Up L248	R. Lee	2,250	280.00	280.00
90-01-330	Push and Pull L249	R. Lee	2,250	260.00	260.00
90-01-331	Snowdrifter II L250	R. Lee	1,250	340.00	340-350.
90-01-332	Kiss! Kiss! L251	R. Lee	2,750	37.00	37.00
90-01-333	Na! Na! L252	R. Lee	2,750	33.00	33.00
90-01-334	Henry 8-3/4 L260	R. Lee	2,750	37.00	37.00
90-01-335	Horsin' Around L262	R. Lee	2,750	37.00	37-50.00
91-01-336	Cruising L265	R. Lee	1,500	170.00	170-175.
91-01-337	Business is Business L266	R. Lee	1,500	110.00	110.00
91-01-338	I'm Singin' In The Rain L268	R. Lee	1,500	135.00	135.00
91-01-339	Anywhere? L269	R. Lee	1,500	125.00	125-145.
91-01-340	Gilbert's Dilemma L270	R. Lee	1,750	90.00	90.00
91-01-341	Puppy Love Scootin' L275	R. Lee	1,750	73.00	73-80.00
91-01-342	Puppy Love's Free Ride L276	R. Lee	1,750	73.00	73-80.00
91-01-343	Puppy Love's Treat L277	R. Lee	1,750	73.00	73-80.00
91-01-344	Happy Birthday Puppy Love L278	R. Lee	1,750	73.00	73-80.00
91-01-345	Winter L279	R. Lee	1,500	115.00	115-125.
91-01-346	Spring L280	R. Lee	1,500	95.00	95-100.00
91-01-347	Summer L281	R. Lee	1,500	95.00	95-110.00
91-01-348	Fall L282	R. Lee	1,500	120.00	120-125.
91-01-349	TA DA L294	R. Lee	1,500	220.00	220-225.
91-01-350	Lit'l Snowdrifter L298	R. Lee	1,750	70.00	70-75.00
91-01-351	Our Nation's Pride L312	R. Lee	1,776	150.00	150.00
91-01-352	Give Me Liberty L313	R. Lee	1,776	155.00	155-165.
91-01-353	United We Stand L314	R. Lee	1,776	150.00	150.00
Ron Lee's World of Clowns		**The Ron Lee Disney Collection Exclusives**			
90-02-001	The Bandleader MM100	R. Lee	2,750	75.00	75.00
90-02-002	The Sorcerer MM200	R. Lee	Closed	85.00	120.00
90-02-003	Steamboat Willie MM300	R. Lee	2,750	95.00	95.00
90-02-004	Mickey's Christmas MM400	R. Lee	2,750	95.00	95.00
90-02-005	Pinocchio MM500	R. Lee	2,750	85.00	85.00
90-02-006	Dumbo MM600	R. Lee	2,750	110.00	110.00

Company		Series			
Number	Name	Artist	Edition Limit	Issue Price	Quote
90-02-007	Uncle Scrooge MM700	R. Lee	2,750	110.00	110.00
90-02-008	Snow White & Grumpy MM800	R. Lee	2,750	140.00	140.00
91-02-009	Goofy MM110	R. Lee	2,750	115.00	115.00
91-02-010	Dopey MM120	R. Lee	2,750	80.00	80.00
91-02-011	The Witch MM130	R. Lee	2,750	115.00	115.00
91-02-012	Two Gun Mickey MM140	R. Lee	2,750	115.00	115.00
91-02-013	Mickey's Adventure MM150	R. Lee	2,750	195.00	195.00
91-02-014	Mt. Mickey MM900	R. Lee	2,750	175.00	175.00
91-02-015	Tugboat Mickey MM160	R. Lee	2,750	180.00	180.00
91-02-016	Minnie Mouse MM170	R. Lee	2,750	80.00	80.00
91-02-017	Mickey & Minnie at the Piano MM180	R. Lee	2,750	195.00	195.00
91-02-018	Decorating Donald MM210	R. Lee	2,750	60.00	60.00
91-02-019	Mickey's Delivery MM220	R. Lee	2,750	70.00	70.00
91-02-020	Goofy's Gift MM230	R. Lee	2,750	70.00	70.00
91-02-021	Pluto's Treat MM240	R. Lee	2,750	60.00	60.00
91-02-022	Jimminy's List MM250	R. Lee	2,750	60.00	60.00
91-02-023	Lady and the Tramp MM280	R. Lee	1,500	295.00	295.00
91-02-024	Lion Around MM270	R. Lee	2,750	140.00	140.00
91-02-025	The Tea Cup Ride (Disneyland Exclusive) MM260	R. Lee	1,250	225.00	225.00
Ron Lee's World of Clowns		**The Ron Lee Emmett Kelly, Sr. Collection**			
91-03-001	That-A-Way EK201	R. Lee	1,750	125.00	125.00
91-03-002	Help Yourself EK202	R. Lee	1,750	145.00	145.00
91-03-003	Spike's Uninvited Guest EK203	R. Lee	1,750	165.00	165.00
91-03-004	Love at First Sight EK204	R. Lee	1,750	197.00	197.00
91-03-005	Time for a Change EK205	R. Lee	1,750	190.00	190.00
91-03-006	God Bless America EK206	R. Lee	1,750	130.00	130.00
91-03-007	My Protege EK207	R. Lee	1,750	160.00	160.00
91-03-008	Emmett Kelly, Sr. Sign E208	R. Lee	1,750	110.00	110.00
Ron Lee's World of Clowns		**The Ron Lee Looney Tunes Collection**			
91-04-001	Western Daffy Duck LT105	R. Lee	2,750	87.00	87-90.00
91-04-002	Michigan J. Frog LT110	R. Lee	2,750	115.00	115.00
91-04-003	Porky Pig LT115	R. Lee	2,750	97.00	97-100.00
91-04-004	Tasmanian Devil LT120	R. Lee	2,750	105.00	105.00
91-04-005	Elmer Fudd LT125	R. Lee	2,750	87.00	87-90.00
91-04-006	Yosemite Sam LT130	R. Lee	2,750	110.00	110.00
91-04-007	Sylvester & Tweety LT135	R. Lee	2,750	110.00	110-115.
91-04-008	Daffy Duck LT140	R. Lee	2,750	80.00	80-85.00
91-04-009	Pepe LePew & Penelope LT145	R. Lee	2,750	115.00	115.00
91-04-010	Bugs Bunny LT150	R. Lee	2,750	123.00	123.00
91-04-011	Tweety LT155	R. Lee	2,750	110.00	110-115.
91-04-012	Foghorn Leghorn & Henry Hawk LT160	R. Lee	2,750	115.00	115.00
91-04-013	1940 Bugs Bunny LT165	R. Lee	2,750	85.00	85.00
91-04-014	Marvin the Martian LT170	R. Lee	2,750	75.00	75.00
91-04-015	Wile E. Coyote & Roadrunner LT175	R. Lee	2,750	165.00	165-175.
91-04-016	Mt. Yosemite LT180	R. Lee	850	160.00	160-300.
Ron Lee's World of Clowns		**The Ron Lee Warner Bros. Collection**			
91-05-001	The Maltese Falcon WB100	R. Lee	1,250	175.00	175.00
91-05-002	Robin Hood Bugs WB200	R. Lee	1,000	190.00	190.00
Ron Lee's World of Clowns		**The Flintstones**			
91-06-001	The Flinstones HB100	R. Lee	2,750	410.00	410.00
91-06-002	Yabba-Dabba-Doo HB110	R. Lee	2,750	230.00	230.00
91-06-003	Saturday Blues HB120	R. Lee	2,750	105.00	105.00
91-06-004	Bedrock Serenade HB130	R. Lee	2,750	250.00	250.00
91-06-005	Joyride-A-Saurus HB140	R. Lee	2,750	107.00	107.00
91-06-006	Bogey Buddies HB150	R. Lee	2,750	143.00	143.00
91-06-007	Vac-A-Saurus HB160	R. Lee	2,750	105.00	105.00
91-06-008	Buffalo Brothers HB170	R. Lee	2,750	134.00	134.00
Ron Lee's World of Clowns		**The Jetsons**			
91-07-001	The Jetsons HB500	R. Lee	2,750	500.00	500.00
91-07-002	The Cosmic Couple HB510	R. Lee	2,750	105.00	105.00
91-07-003	Astro: Cosmic Canine HB520	R. Lee	2,750	275.00	275.00
91-07-004	I Rove Roo HB530	R. Lee	2,750	105.00	105.00
91-07-005	Scare-D-Dog HB540	R. Lee	2,750	160.00	160.00
91-07-006	4 O'Clock Tea HB550	R. Lee	2,750	203.00	203.00
Ron Lee's World of Clowns		**The Classics**			
91-08-001	Yogi Bear & Boo Boo HB800	R. Lee	2,750	95.00	95.00
91-08-002	Quick Draw McGraw HB805	R. Lee	2,750	90.00	90.00
91-08-003	Scooby Doo & Shaggy HB810	R. Lee	2,750	114.00	114.00
91-08-004	Huckleberry Hound HB815	R. Lee	2,750	90.00	90.00
Ron Lee's World of Clowns		**The Ron Lee Collector's Club Gifts**			
87-09-001	Hooping It Up CCG1	R. Lee	Closed	Gift	N/A
88-09-002	Pudge CCG2	R. Lee	Closed	Gift	N/A
89-09-003	Pals CCG3	R. Lee	Closed	Gift	N/A
90-09-004	Potsie CCG4	R. Lee	Closed	Gift	N/A
91-09-005	Hi! Ya! CCG5	R. Lee	Closed	Gift	N/A
92-09-005	Bashful Beau CCG6	R. Lee	Yr.Iss.	Gift	N/A
Ron Lee's World of Clowns		**The Ron Lee Collector's Club Renewal Sculptures**			
87-10-001	Doggin' Along CC1	R. Lee	Yr.Iss.	75.00	115.00
88-10-002	Midsummer's Dream CC2	R. Lee	Yr.Iss.	97.00	140.00
89-10-003	Peek-A-Boo Charlie CC3	R. Lee	Yr.Iss.	65.00	100.00
90-10-004	Get The Message CC4	R. Lee	Yr.Iss.	65.00	N/A
91-10-005	I'm So Pretty CC5	R. Lee	Yr Iss.	65.00	N/A
92-10-006	It's For You CC6	R. Lee	Yr.Iss.	65.00	N/A
Ron Lee's World of Clowns		**Rocky & Bullwinkle And Friends Collection**			
92-11-001	Rocky & Bullwinkle RB600	R. Lee	1,750	120.00	120.00
92-11-002	The Swami RB605	R. Lee	1,750	175.00	175.00
92-11-003	Dudley Do-Right RB610	R. Lee	1,750	175.00	175.00
92-11-004	My Hero RB615	R. Lee	1,750	275.00	275.00
92-11-005	KA-BOOM! RB620	R. Lee	1,750	175.00	175.00
Ron Lee's World of Clowns		**The Wizard Of Oz Collection**			
92-12-001	Kansas WZ400	R. Lee	750	550.00	550.00
92-12-002	The Munchkins WZ405	R. Lee	750	620.00	620.00
92-12-003	The Ruby Slippers WZ410	R. Lee	750	620.00	620.00
92-12-004	The Scarecrow WZ415	R. Lee	750	510.00	510.00
92-12-005	The Tin Man WZ420	R. Lee	750	530.00	530.00
92-12-006	The Cowardly Lion WZ425	R. Lee	750	620.00	620.00
Ron Lee's World of Clowns		**The Woody Woodpecker And Friends Collection**			
92-13-001	Birdy for Woody WL005	R. Lee	1,750	117.00	117.00
92-13-002	Peck of My Heart WL010	R. Lee	1,750	370.00	370.00
92-13-003	Woody Woodpecker WL015	R. Lee	1,750	73.00	73.00
92-13-004	1940 Woody Woodpecker WL020	R. Lee	1,750	73.00	73.00
92-13-005	Andy and Miranda Panda WL025	R. Lee	1,750	140.00	140.00
92-13-006	Pals WL030	R. Lee	1,750	179.00	179.00
Ron Lee's World of Clowns		**The Popeye Collection**			
92-14-001	Liberty P001	R. Lee	1,750	184.00	184.00
92-14-002	Men!!! P002	R. Lee	1,750	230.00	230.00
92-14-003	Strong to The Finish P003	R. Lee	1,750	95.00	95.00
92-14-004	That's My Boy P004	R. Lee	1,750	145.00	145.00
92-14-005	Oh Popeye P005	R. Lee	1,750	230.00	230.00
92-14-006	Par Excellence P006	R. Lee	1,750	220.00	220.00
Ron Lee's World of Clowns		**The Ron Lee Looney Tunes II Collection**			
92-15-001	Speedy Gonzales LT185	R. Lee	2,750	73.00	73.00
92-15-002	For Better or Worse LT190	R. Lee	1,500	285.00	285.00
92-15-003	What The ...? LT195	R. Lee	1,500	240.00	240.00
92-15-004	Ditty Up LT200	R. Lee	2,750	110.00	110.00
92-15-005	Leopold & Giovanni LT205	R. Lee	1,500	225.00	225.00
92-15-006	No Pain No Gain LT210	R. Lee	950	270.00	270.00
92-15-007	What's up Doc? LT215	R. Lee	950	950.00	950.00
92-15-008	Beep Beep LT220	R. Lee	1,500	115.00	115.00
92-15-009	Rackin' Frackin' Varmint LT225	R. Lee	950	260.00	260.00
92-15-010	Van Duck LT230	R. Lee	950	335.00	335.00
92-15-011	The Virtuosos LT235	R. Lee	950	350.00	350.00
Legends		**The Legendary West Premier Edition**			
88-01-001	Red Cloud's Coup	C. Pardell	S/O	480.00	4000-5000.
89-01-002	Pursued	C. Pardell	S/O	750.00	2500-4000.
89-01-003	Songs of Glory	C. Pardell	S/O	850.00	2200-3500.
90-01-004	Crow Warrior	C. Pardell	S/O	1225.00	2000-3500.
91-01-005	Triumphant	C. Pardell	S/O	1150.00	1500-2000.
92-01-006	The Final Charge	C. Pardell	S/O	1250.00	1250.00
Legends		**The Legacies Of The West Premier Edition**			
90-02-001	Mystic Vision	C. Pardell	S/O	990.00	2000-3200.
90-02-002	Victorious	C. Pardell	S/O	1275.00	2000-3500.
91-02-003	Defiant Comanche	C. Pardell	S/O	1300.00	1500-2100.
91-02-004	No More, Forever	C. Pardell	S/O	1500.00	1750-2000.
92-02-005	Esteemed Warrior	C. Pardell	S/O	1750.00	1750-1950.
Legends		**The Legendary West Collection**			
87-03-001	White Feather's Vision	C. Pardell	S/O	310.00	500-650.
87-03-002	Pony Express	C. Pardell	Retrd.	320.00	390-450.
87-03-003	Johnson's Last Fight	C. Pardell	S/O	590.00	850-1000.
Legends		**American West Premier Edition**			
91-04-001	Unexpected Rescuer	C. Pardell	S/O	990.00	1500-1900.
91-04-002	First Coup	C. Pardell	S/O	1150.00	1150-1500.
92-04-003	American Horse Takes His Name	C. Pardell	950	1300.00	1300.00
Legends		**The Endangered Wildlife Collection**			
90-05-001	Forest Spirit	K. Cantrell	S/O	290.00	750-1250.
90-05-002	Savannah Prince	K. Cantrell	950	290.00	290.00
91-05-003	Mountain Majesty	K. Cantrell	950	350.00	350.00
91-05-004	Old Tusker	K. Cantrell	950	390.00	390.00
92-05-005	Plains Monarch	K. Cantrell	950	350.00	350.00
92-05-006	Spirit Song	K. Cantrell	950	350.00	350.00
92-05-007	Unchallenged	K. Cantrell	950	350.00	350.00
92-05-008	Songs of Autumn	K. Cantrell	950	390.00	390.00
Legends		**Annual Collectors Edition**			
90-06-001	The Night Before	C. Pardell	S/O	990.00	1500-1900.
91-06-002	Medicine Gift of Manhood	C. Pardell	S/O	990.00	1200-1900.
92-06-003	Spirit of the Wolf	C. Pardell	500	950.00	950-1250.
Legends		**The Great Outdoorsman**			
88-07-001	Both Are Hooked (Bronze)	C. Pardell	Retrd.	320.00	320.00
88-07-002	Both Are Hooked (Pewter)	C. Pardell	Retrd.	320.00	320.00
Legends		**Classic Equestrian Collection**			
88-08-001	Lippizzaner (Bronze)	C. Pardell	Retrd.	200.00	200.00
Legends		**Wild Realm Collection**			
88-09-001	Fly Fisher (Bronze)	C. Pardell	Retrd.	330.00	330.00
88-09-002	Fly Fisher (Pewter)	C. Pardell	Retrd.	330.00	330.00
88-09-003	Alpha Pair (Bronze)	C. Pardell	Retrd.	330.00	330.00
88-09-004	Alpha Pair (Pewter)	C. Pardell	Retrd.	330.00	330.00
88-09-005	Alpha Pair (Mixed Media)	C. Pardell	S/O	390.00	500-900.
Legends		**Oceanic World**			
89-10-001	Freedom's Beauty (Bronze)	D. Medina	Retrd.	330.00	330.00
89-10-002	Freedom's Beauty (Pewter)	D. Medina	Retrd.	130.00	130.00
89-10-003	Together (Bronze)	D. Medina	Retrd.	140.00	140.00
89-10-004	Together (Pewter)	D. Medina	Retrd.	130.00	130.00
Legends		**North American Wildlife**			
88-11-001	Double Trouble (Bronze)	D. Edwards	Retrd.	300.00	300.00
88-11-002	Double Trouble (Pewter)	D. Edwards	Retrd.	320.00	320.00
88-11-003	Grizzly Solitude (Bronze)	D. Edwards	Retrd.	310.00	310.00
88-11-004	Grizzly Solitude (Pewter)	D. Edwards	Retrd.	330.00	330.00
88-11-005	Defenders of Freedom (Bronze)	D. Edwards	Retrd.	340.00	340.00
88-11-006	Defenders of Freedom (Pewter)	D. Edwards	Retrd.	370.00	370.00
88-11-007	The Proud American (Bronze)	D. Edwards	Retrd.	330.00	330.00
88-11-008	The Proud American (Pewter)	D. Edwards	Retrd.	340.00	340.00
88-11-009	Downhill Run (Bronze)	D. Edwards	Retrd.	330.00	330.00
88-11-010	Downhill Run (Pewter)	D. Edwards	Retrd.	340.00	340.00
88-11-011	Sudden Alert (Bronze)	D. Edwards	Retrd.	300.00	300.00
88-11-012	Sudden Alert (Pewter)	D. Edwards	Retrd.	320.00	320.00
88-11-013	Ridge Runners (Bronze)	D. Edwards	Retrd.	300.00	300.00
88-11-014	Ridge Runners (Pewter)	D. Edwards	Retrd.	310.00	310.00
88-11-014	Last Glance (Bronze)	D. Edwards	Retrd.	300.00	300.00
88-11-015	Last Glance (Pewter)	D. Edwards	Retrd.	320.00	320.00
Legends		**American Heritage**			
87-12-001	Grizz Country (Bronze)	D. Edwards	Retrd.	350.00	350.00
87-12-002	Grizz Country (Pewter)	D. Edwards	Retrd.	370.00	370.00
87-12-003	Winter Provisions (Bronze)	D. Edwards	Retrd.	340.00	340.00
87-12-004	Winter Provisions (Pewter)	D. Edwards	Retrd.	370.00	370.00
87-12-005	Wrangler's Dare (Bronze)	D. Edwards	Retrd.	630.00	630.00
87-12-006	Wrangler's Dare (Pewter)	D. Edwards	Retrd.	660.00	660.00
Legends		**Special Commissions**			
87-13-001	Mama's Joy (Bronze)	D. Edwards	Retrd.	200.00	200.00
87-13-002	Mama's Joy (Pewter)	D. Edwards	Retrd.	250.00	250.00

Company Number	Name	Series Artist	Edition Limit	Issue Price	Quote
87-13-003	Wild Freedom (Bronze)	D. Edwards	Retrd.	320.00	320.00
87-13-004	Wild Freedom (Pewter)	D. Edwards	Retrd.	330.00	330.00
Legends		**Indian Arts Collection**			
89-14-001	Chief's Blanket	C. Pardell	S/O	350.00	450-600.
Legends		**Gallery Editions**			
92-15-001	Resolute	C. Pardell	S/O	7950.00	7950.00
Lenox Collections		**American Fashion**			
83-01-001	Springtime Promenade	Unknown	Open	95.00	95.00
84-01-002	Tea at the Ritz	Unknown	Open	95.00	95.00
84-01-003	First Waltz	Unknown	Open	95.00	95.00
85-01-004	Governor's Garden Party	Unknown	Open	95.00	95.00
86-01-005	Grand Tour	Unknown	Open	95.00	95.00
86-01-006	Belle of the Ball	Unknown	Open	95.00	95.00
87-01-007	Centennial Bride	Unknown	Open	95.00	95.00
87-01-008	Gala at the Whitehouse	Unknown	Open	95.00	95.00
92-01-009	Royal Reception	Unknown	Open	95.00	95.00
Lenox Collections		**Wildlife of the Seven Continents**			
84-02-001	North American Bighorn Sheep	Unknown	Open	120.00	120.00
85-02-002	Australian Koala	Unknown	Open	120.00	120.00
85-02-003	Asian Elephant	Unknown	Open	120.00	120.00
86-02-004	South American Puma	Unknown	Open	120.00	120.00
87-02-005	European Red Deer	Unknown	Open	136.00	136.00
87-02-006	Antarctic Seals	Unknown	Open	136.00	136.00
88-02-007	African Lion	Unknown	Open	136.00	136.00
Lenox Collections		**Legendary Princesses**			
85-03-001	Rapunzel	Unknown	Open	119.00	136.00
86-03-002	Sleeping Beauty	Unknown	Open	119.00	136.00
87-03-003	Snow Queen	Unknown	Open	119.00	136.00
88-03-004	Cinderella	Unknown	Open	136.00	136.00
89-03-005	Swan Princess	Unknown	Open	136.00	136.00
89-03-006	Snow White	Unknown	Open	136.00	136.00
90-03-007	Juliet	Unknown	Open	136.00	136.00
90-03-008	Guinevere	Unknown	Open	136.00	136.00
90-03-009	Cleopatra	Unknown	Open	136.00	136.00
91-03-010	Peacock Maiden	Unknown	Open	136.00	136.00
91-03-011	Pocohontas	Unknown	9,500	136.00	136.00
92-03-012	Firebird	Unknown	Open	156.00	156.00
92-03-013	Sheherezade	Unknown	Open	156.00	156.00
93-03-014	Little Mermaid	Unknown	Open	156.00	156.00
Lenox Collections		**Carousel Animals**			
87-04-001	Carousel Horse	Unknown	Open	136.00	152.00
88-04-002	Carousel Unicorn	Unknown	Open	136.00	152.00
89-04-003	Carousel Circus Horse	Unknown	Open	136.00	152.00
89-04-004	Carousel Reindeer	Unknown	Open	136.00	152.00
90-04-005	Carousel Elephant	Unknown	Open	136.00	152.00
90-04-006	Carousel Lion	Unknown	Open	136.00	152.00
90-04-007	Carousel Charger	Unknown	Open	136.00	152.00
91-04-008	Carousel Polar Bear	Unknown	Open	152.00	152.00
91-04-009	Pride of America	Unknown	12/92	152.00	152.00
91-04-010	Western Horse	Unknown	Open	152.00	152.00
92-04-011	Camelot Horse	Unknown	Open	152.00	152.00
92-04-012	Statement Piece	Unknown	Open	395.00	395.00
92-04-013	Victorian Romance Horse	Unknown	Open	156.00	156.00
92-04-014	Tropical Horse	Unknown	Open	156.00	156.00
92-04-015	Christmas Horse	Unknown	Open	156.00	156.00
93-04-016	Nautical Horse	Unknown	Open	156.00	156.00
Lenox Collections		**Nativity**			
86-05-001	Holy Family	Unknown	Open	119.00	136.00
87-05-002	Three Kings	Unknown	Open	119.00	152.00
88-05-003	Shepherds	Unknown	Open	119.00	152.00
88-05-004	Animals of the Nativity	Unknown	Open	119.00	152.00
89-05-005	Angels of Adoration	Unknown	Open	136.00	152.00
90-05-006	Children of Bethlehem	Unknown	Open	136.00	152.00
91-05-007	Townspeople of Bethlehem	Unknown	Open	136.00	152.00
91-05-008	Standing Camel & Driver	Unknown	9,500	152.00	152.00
Lenox Collections		**Garden Birds**			
85-06-001	Chickadee	Unknown	Open	39.00	45.00
86-06-002	Blue Jay	Unknown	Open	39.00	45.00
86-06-003	Eastern Bluebird	Unknown	Open	39.00	45.00
86-06-004	Tufted Titmouse	Unknown	Open	39.00	45.00
87-06-005	Red-Breasted Nuthatch	Unknown	Open	39.00	45.00
87-06-006	Cardinal	Unknown	Open	39.00	45.00
87-06-007	Turtle Dove	Unknown	Open	39.00	45.00
87-06-008	American Goldfinch	Unknown	Open	39.00	45.00
88-06-009	Hummingbird	Unknown	Open	39.00	45.00
88-06-010	Cedar Waxwing	Unknown	Open	39.00	45.00
89-06-011	Robin	Unknown	Open	39.00	45.00
89-06-012	Downy Woodpecker	Unknown	Open	39.00	45.00
89-06-013	Saw Whet Owl	Unknown	Open	45.00	45.00
90-06-014	Baltimore Oriole	Unknown	Open	45.00	45.00
90-06-015	Wren	Unknown	Open	45.00	45.00
90-06-016	Chipping Sparrow	Unknown	Open	45.00	45.00
90-06-017	Wood Duck	Unknown	Open	45.00	45.00
91-06-018	Purple Finch	Unknown	Open	45.00	45.00
91-06-019	Golden Crowned Kinglet	Unknown	Open	45.00	45.00
91-06-020	Dark Eyed Junco	Unknown	Open	45.00	45.00
91-06-021	Broadbilled Hummingbird	Unknown	Open	45.00	45.00
91-06-022	Rose Grosbeak	Unknown	Open	45.00	45.00
92-06-023	Scarlet Tanger	Unknown	Open	45.00	45.00
92-06-024	Magnificent Hummingbird	Unknown	Open	45.00	45.00
92-06-025	Western Meadowlark	Unknown	Open	45.00	45.00
93-06-026	Statement Piece	Unknown	Open	345.00	345.00
93-06-027	Mockingbird	Unknown	Open	45.00	45.00
93-06-028	Barn Swallow	Unknown	Open	45.00	45.00
93-06-029	Indigo Bunting	Unknown	Open	45.00	45.00
93-06-030	Sparrow	Unknown	Open	45.00	45.00
Lenox Collections		**Floral Sculptures**			
86-07-001	Rubrum Lily	Unknown	Open	119.00	136.00
87-07-002	Iris	Unknown	Open	119.00	136.00
88-07-003	Magnolia	Unknown	Open	119.00	136.00
88-07-004	Peace Rose	Unknown	Open	119.00	136.00
Lenox Collections		**Garden Flowers**			
88-08-001	Tea Rose	Unknown	Open	39.00	45.00
88-08-002	Cattleya Orchid	Unknown	Open	39.00	45.00
88-08-003	Parrot Tulip	Unknown	Open	39.00	39.00
89-08-004	Iris	Unknown	Open	45.00	45.00
90-08-005	Day Lily	Unknown	Open	45.00	45.00
90-08-006	Carnation	Unknown	Open	45.00	45.00
90-08-007	Daffodil	Unknown	Open	45.00	45.00
91-08-008	Morning Glory	Unknown	Open	45.00	45.00
91-08-009	Magnolia	Unknown	Open	45.00	45.00
91-08-010	Calla Lily	Unknown	Open	45.00	45.00
91-08-011	Camelia	Unknown	Open	45.00	45.00
91-08-012	Poinsettia	Unknown	Open	39.00	39.00
Lenox Collections		**Mother & Child**			
86-09-001	Cherished Moment	Unknown	Open	119.00	119.00
86-09-002	Sunday in the Park	Unknown	Open	119.00	119.00
87-09-003	Storytime	Unknown	Open	119.00	119.00
88-09-004	The Present	Unknown	Open	119.00	119.00
89-09-005	Christening	Unknown	Open	119.00	119.00
90-09-006	Bedtime Prayers	Unknown	Open	119.00	119.00
91-09-007	Afternoon Stroll	Unknown	7,500	136.00	136.00
91-09-008	Evening Lullaby	Unknown	7,500	136.00	136.00
92-09-009	Morning Playtime	Unknown	Open	136.00	136.00
Lenox Collections		**Owls of America**			
88-10-001	Snowy Owl	Unknown	Open	136.00	136.00
89-10-002	Barn Owl	Unknown	Open	136.00	136.00
90-10-003	Screech Owl	Unknown	Open	136.00	136.00
91-10-004	Great Horned Owl	Unknown	9,500	136.00	136.00
Lenox Collections		**International Horse Sculptures**			
88-11-001	Arabian Knight	Unknown	Open	136.00	136.00
89-11-002	Thoroughbred	Unknown	Open	136.00	136.00
90-11-003	Lippizan	Unknown	Open	136.00	136.00
90-11-004	Appaloosa	Unknown	Open	136.00	136.00
Lenox Collections		**Nature's Beautiful Butterflies**			
89-12-001	Blue Temora	Unknown	Open	39.00	45.00
90-12-002	Yellow Swallowtail	Unknown	Open	39.00	45.00
90-12-003	Monarch	Unknown	Open	39.00	45.00
90-12-004	Purple Emperor	Unknown	Open	45.00	45.00
91-12-005	Malachite	Unknown	Open	45.00	45.00
91-12-006	Adonis	Unknown	Open	45.00	45.00
93-12-007	Black Swallowtail	Unknown	Open	45.00	45.00
93-12-008	Great Orange Wingtip	Unknown	Open	45.00	45.00
Lenox Collections		**Kings of the Sky**			
89-13-001	American Bald Eagle	Unknown	Open	195.00	195.00
91-13-002	Golden Eagle	Unknown	Open	234.00	234.00
91-13-003	Defender of Freedom	Unknown	12/92	234.00	234.00
92-13-004	Take Off	Unknown	Open	234.00	234.00
Lenox Collections		**Endangered Baby Animals**			
90-14-001	Panda	Unknown	Open	39.00	39.00
91-14-002	Elephant	Unknown	Open	57.00	57.00
91-14-003	Baby Florida Panther	Unknown	Open	57.00	57.00
91-14-004	Baby Grey Wolf	Unknown	Open	57.00	57.00
92-14-005	Baby Rhinocerous	Unknown	Open	57.00	57.00
93-14-006	Indian Elephant Calf	Unknown	Open	57.00	57.00
Lenox Collections		**Lenox Baby Book**			
90-15-001	Baby's First Shoes	Unknown	Open	57.00	57.00
91-15-002	Baby's First Steps	Unknown	Open	57.00	57.00
91-15-003	Baby's First Christmas	Unknown	Open	57.00	57.00
92-15-004	Baby's First Portrait	Unknown	Open	57.00	57.00
Lenox Collections		**Lenox Puppy Collection**			
90-16-001	Beagle	Unknown	Open	76.00	76.00
91-16-002	Cocker Spaniel	Unknown	Open	76.00	76.00
92-16-003	Poodle	Unknown	Open	76.00	76.00
Lenox Collections		**International Brides**			
90-17-001	Russian Bride	Unknown	Open	136.00	136.00
92-17-002	Japanese Bride, Kiyoshi	Unknown	Open	136.00	136.00
Lenox Collections		**Life of Christ**			
90-18-001	The Children's Blessing	Unknown	Open	95.00	95.00
90-18-002	Madonna And Child	Unknown	Open	95.00	95.00
90-18-003	The Good Shepherd	Unknown	Open	95.00	95.00
91-18-004	The Savior	Unknown	Open	95.00	95.00
91-18-005	Jesus, The Teacher	Unknown	9,500	95.00	95.00
92-18-006	A Child's Prayer	Unknown	Open	95.00	95.00
92-18-007	Childrens's Devotion (Painted)	Unknown	Open	195.00	195.00
92-18-008	Mary & Christ Child (Painted)	Unknown	Open	195.00	195.00
92-18-009	A Child's Comfort	Unknown	Open	95.00	95.00
93-18-010	Jesus, The Carpenter	Unknown	Open	95.00	95.00
Lenox Collections		**North American Bird Pairs**			
90-19-001	Hummingbirds	Unknown	Open	119.00	119.00
91-19-002	Chickadees	Unknown	Open	119.00	119.00
91-19-003	Blue Jay Pairs	Unknown	Open	119.00	119.00
92-19-004	Cardinal	Unknown	Open	119.00	119.00
Lenox Collections		**Santa Claus Collections**			
90-20-001	Father Christmas	Unknown	Open	136.00	136.00
91-20-002	Americana Santa	Unknown	Open	136.00	136.00
91-20-003	Kris Kringle	Unknown	Open	136.00	136.00
92-20-004	Grandfather Frost	Unknown	Open	136.00	136.00
92-20-005	Pere Noel	Unknown	Open	136.00	136.00
93-20-006	St. Nick	Unknown	Open	136.00	136.00
Lenox Collections		**Woodland Animals**			
90-21-001	Red Squirrel	Unknown	Open	39.00	39.00
90-21-002	Raccoon	Unknown	Open	39.00	39.00
91-21-003	Chipmunk	Unknown	Open	39.00	39.00
92-21-004	Rabbit	Unknown	Open	39.00	39.00
93-21-005	Fawn	Unknown	Open	39.00	39.00
Lenox Collections		**Gentle Majesty**			
90-22-001	Bear Hug Polar Bear	Unknown	Open	76.00	76.00
90-22-002	Penguins	Unknown	Open	76.00	76.00
91-22-003	Keeping Warm (Foxes)	Unknown	Open	76.00	76.00

Company / Number	Name	Series / Artist	Edition Limit	Issue Price	Quote
Lenox Collections		**Street Crier Collection**			
90-23-001	French Flower Maiden	Unknown	Open	136.00	136.00
91-23-002	Belgian Lace Maker	Unknown	Open	136.00	136.00
Lenox Collections		**Country Kids**			
91-24-001	Goose Girl	Unknown	Open	75.00	75.00
Lenox Collections		**Doves & Roses**			
91-25-001	Love's Promise	Unknown	Open	95.00	95.00
91-25-002	Dove's of Peace	Unknown	Open	95.00	95.00
92-25-003	Dove's of Honor	Unknown	Open	119.00	119.00
Lenox Collections		**Exotic Birds**			
91-26-001	Cockatoo	Unknown	Open	45.00	45.00
93-26-002	Parakeet	Unknown	Open	49.50	49.50
Lenox Collections		**Jessie Willcox Smith**			
91-27-001	Rosebuds	J.W.Smith	Open	60.00	60.00
91-27-002	Feeding Kitty	J.W.Smith	Open	60.00	60.00
Lenox Collections		**Baby Bears**			
91-28-001	Polar Bear	Unknown	Open	45.00	45.00
Lenox Collections		**Baby Bird Pairs**			
91-29-001	Robins	Unknown	Open	64.00	64.00
92-29-002	Orioles	Unknown	Open	64.00	64.00
92-29-003	Chickadee	Unknown	Open	64.00	64.00
Lenox Collections		**Lenox Sea Animals**			
91-30-001	Dance of the Dolphins	Unknown	Open	119.00	119.00
93-30-002	Flight of the Dolphins	Unknown	Open	119.00	119.00
Lenox Collections		**North American Wildlife**			
91-31-001	White Tailed Deer	Unknown	Open	195.00	195.00
Lenox Collections		**Porcelain Duck Collection**			
91-32-001	Wood Duck	Unknown	Open	45.00	45.00
91-32-002	Mallard Duck	Unknown	Open	45.00	45.00
92-32-003	Blue Winged Teal Duck	Unknown	Open	45.00	45.00
93-32-004	Pintail Duck	Unknown	Open	45.00	45.00
Lenox Collections		**Biblical Characters**			
92-33-001	Moses, The Lawgiver	Unknown	Open	95.00	95.00
Lenox Collections		**Parent & Child Bird Pairs**			
92-34-001	Blue Jay Pairs	Unknown	Open	119.00	119.00
Lenox Collections		**Renaissance Nativity**			
91-35-001	Holy Family	Unknown	Open	195.00	195.00
91-35-002	Shepherds of Bethlehem	Unknown	Open	195.00	195.00
91-35-003	Three Kings	Unknown	Open	195.00	195.00
91-35-004	Animals of the Nativity	Unknown	Open	195.00	195.00
91-35-005	Angels	Unknown	Open	195.00	195.00
Lenox Collections		**International Songbirds**			
92-36-001	European Goldfinch	Unknown	Open	152.00	152.00
92-36-002	American Goldfinch	Unknown	Open	152.00	152.00
Lenox Collections		**Challenge of the Eagles**			
93-37-001	Double Eagle	Unknown	Open	275.00	275.00
Lenox Collections		**Classical Goddesses**			
92-38-001	Aphrodite, Painted	Unknown	Open	136.00	136.00
92-38-002	Aphrodite	Unknown	Open	95.00	95.00
Lilliput Lane Ltd.		**Lilliput Lane Cottage Collection-English Cottages**			
82-01-001	Old Mine	D. Tate	Retrd.	15.95	2500.00
82-01-002	Drapers	D. Tate	Retrd.	15.95	325.00
82-01-003	Dale House	D. Tate	Retrd.	25.00	500-1000.
82-01-004	Sussex Mill	D. Tate	Retrd.	25.00	450-500.
82-01-005	Lakeside House	D. Tate	Retrd.	40.00	575-950.
82-01-006	Stone Cottage	D. Tate	Retrd.	40.00	175-300.
82-01-007	Acorn Cottage	D. Tate	Retrd.	30.00	80-400.
82-01-008	Bridge House	D. Tate	Retrd.	15.95	50-200.00
82-01-009	April Cottage	D. Tate	Retrd.	Unkn.	75-150.00
82-01-010	Honeysuckle	D. Tate	Retrd.	45.00	100-150.
82-01-011	Oak Lodge	D. Tate	Retrd.	40.00	100-200.
82-01-012	Dale Farm	D. Tate	Retrd.	30.00	400-1100.
82-01-013	The Old Post Office	D. Tate	Retrd.	35.00	600-800.
82-01-014	Coach House	D. Tate	Retrd.	100.00	1100-1875.
82-01-015	Castle Street	D. Tate	Retrd.	130.00	460-650.
82-01-016	Holly Cottage	D. Tate	Retrd.	42.50	90-175.00
82-01-017	Burnside	D. Tate	Retrd.	30.00	400-600.
83-01-018	Coopers	D. Tate	Retrd.	15.00	300-500.
83-01-019	Millers	D. Tate	Retrd.	15.00	125-150.
83-01-020	Miners	D. Tate	Retrd.	15.00	350-500.
83-01-021	Toll House	D. Tate	Retrd.	15.00	100-200.
83-01-022	Woodcutters	D. Tate	Retrd.	15.00	125-250.
83-01-023	Tuck Shop	D. Tate	Retrd.	35.00	500-900.
83-01-024	Warwick Hall	D. Tate	Retrd.	185.00	1200-1800.
83-01-025	Anne Hathaway's	D. Tate	Retrd.	40.00	400-600.
83-01-026	William Shakespeare	D. Tate	Retrd.	55.00	200-300.
83-01-027	Red Lion	D. Tate	Retrd.	125.00	300-400.
83-01-028	Thatcher's Rest	D. Tate	Retrd.	185.00	225-375.
83-01-029	Troutbeck Farm	D. Tate	Retrd.	125.00	250-400.
83-01-030	Dove Cottage	D. Tate	Retrd.	35.00	100-175.
84-01-031	Old School House	D. Tate	Retrd.	Unkn.	1000-1440.
84-01-032	Tintagel	D. Tate	Retrd.	39.50	175-250.
85-01-033	Old Curiosity Shop	D. Tate	Retrd.	62.50	100-250.
85-01-034	St. Mary's Church	D. Tate	Retrd.	40.00	100-300.
85-01-035	Clare Cottage	D. Tate	Open	30.00	65.00
85-01-036	Fisherman's Cottage	D. Tate	Retrd.	30.00	65-100.00
85-01-037	Sawrey Gill	D. Tate	Retrd.	30.00	50.00
85-01-038	Ostlers Keep	D. Tate	Retrd.	55.00	100-200.
85-01-039	Moreton Manor	D. Tate	Retrd.	55.00	110-175.
85-01-040	Kentish Oast	D. Tate	Retrd.	55.00	100-175.
85-01-041	Watermill	D. Tate	Open	40.00	65-105.00
85-01-042	Bronte Parsonage	D. Tate	Retrd.	72.00	150-200.
85-01-043	Farriers	D. Tate	Retrd.	40.00	80-125.00
86-01-044	Dale Head	D. Tate	Retrd.	75.00	125-300.
86-01-045	Bay View	D. Tate	Retrd.	39.50	100-125.
86-01-046	Cobblers Cottage	D. Hall	Open	42.00	60.00
86-01-047	Gulliver	Unknown	Retrd.	65.00	200-275.
86-01-048	Three Feathers	D. Tate	Retrd.	115.00	200-275.
86-01-049	Spring Bank	D. Tate	Retrd.	42.00	95.00
86-01-050	Scroll on the Wall	D. Tate	Retrd.	55.00	120-275.
86-01-051	Tudor Court	Lilliput Lane	Retrd.	260.00	350.00
87-01-052	Beacon Heights	Lilliput Lane	Retrd.	125.00	175-210.
87-01-053	Wealden House	D. Tate	Retrd.	125.00	200-500.
87-01-054	The Gables	Lilliput Lane	Retrd.	145.00	200-210.
87-01-055	Secret Garden	M. Adkinson	Open	145.00	210.00
87-01-056	Rydal View	D. Tate	Retrd.	220.00	275-400.
87-01-057	Stoneybeck	D. Tate	Retrd.	45.00	60.00
87-01-058	Riverview	D. Tate	Open	27.50	34.00
87-01-059	Clover Cottage	D. Tate	Open	27.50	34.00
87-01-060	Inglewood	D. Tate	Open	27.50	34.00
87-01-061	Tanners Cottage	D. Tate	Retrd.	27.50	34.00
87-01-062	Holme Dyke	D. Tate	Retrd.	50.00	150-250.
87-01-063	Saddlers Inn	M. Adkinson	Retrd.	50.00	95-125.00
87-01-064	Four Seasons	M. Adkinson	Retrd.	70.00	110-150.
87-01-065	Magpie Cottage	D. Tate	Retrd.	70.00	150-300.
87-01-066	Izaak Waltons Cottage	D. Tate	Retrd.	75.00	100-200.
87-01-067	Keepers Lodge	D. Tate	Retrd.	75.00	120-175.
87-01-068	Summer Haze	D. Tate	Open	90.00	120.00
87-01-069	Street Scene No. 1	Unknown	Retrd.	40.00	125-200.
87-01-070	Street Scene No. 2	Unknown	Retrd.	45.00	125-200.
87-01-071	Street Scene No. 3	Unknown	Retrd.	45.00	125-200.
87-01-072	Street Scene No. 4	Unknown	Retrd.	45.00	125-200.
87-01-073	Street Scene No. 5	Unknown	Retrd.	40.00	125-200.
87-01-074	Street Scene No. 6	Unknown	Retrd.	40.00	125-200.
87-01-075	Street Scene No. 7	Unknown	Retrd.	40.00	125-200.
87-01-076	Street Scene No. 8	Unknown	Retrd.	40.00	125-200.
87-01-077	Street Scene No. 9	Unknown	Retrd.	45.00	125-200.
87-01-078	Street Scene No. 10	Unknown	Retrd.	45.00	125-200.
88-01-079	Brockbank	D. Tate	Open	58.00	72.50
88-01-080	St. Marks	D. Tate	Retrd.	75.00	150.00
88-01-081	Swift Hollow	D. Tate	Retrd.	75.00	160-250.
88-01-082	Pargetters Retreat	D. Tate	Retrd.	75.00	165-250.
88-01-083	Swan Inn	D. Tate	Retrd.	120.00	150.00
88-01-084	Ship Inn	Lilliput Lane	Retrd.	210.00	250.00
88-01-085	Saxon Cottage	D. Tate	Retrd.	245.00	350-500.
88-01-086	Smallest Inn	D. Tate	Retrd.	42.50	95-150.00
88-01-087	Rising Sun	D. Tate	Retrd.	58.00	72.50
88-01-088	Crown Inn	D. Tate	Retrd.	120.00	140.00
88-01-089	Royal Oak	D. Tate	Retrd.	145.00	175-250.
88-01-090	Bredon House	D. Tate	Retrd.	145.00	175-450.
89-01-091	Chine Cot	D. Tate	Open	36.00	46.50
89-01-092	Fiveways	D. Tate	Open	42.50	50.00
89-01-093	Ash Nook	D. Tate	Open	47.50	55.00
89-01-094	The Briary	D. Tate	Open	47.50	55.00
89-01-095	Victoria Cottage	D. Tate	Open	52.50	60.00
89-01-096	Butterwick	D. Tate	Open	52.50	65.00
89-01-097	Greensted Church	D. Tate	Open	72.50	90.00
89-01-098	Beehive Cottage	D. Tate	Open	72.50	90.00
89-01-099	Tanglewood Lodge	D. Tate	Retrd.	97.00	120.00
89-01-100	Anne Hathaway's Cottage 1989	D. Tate	Open	130.00	150.00
89-01-101	St. Peter's Cove	D. Tate	Closed	1375.00	2000-3600.
89-01-102	Wight Cottage	D. Tate	Open	52.50	60.00
89-01-103	Helmere	D. Tate	Open	65.00	75.00
89-01-104	Titmouse Cottage	D. Tate	Open	92.50	110.00
89-01-105	St. Lawrence Church	D. Tate	Open	110.00	130.00
89-01-106	William Shakespeare 1989	D. Tate	Retrd.	130.00	150.00
90-01-107	Strawberry Cottage	D. Tate	Open	36.00	42.50
90-01-108	Buttercup Cottage	D. Tate	Retrd.	40.00	46.50
90-01-109	Bramble Cottage	D. Tate	Open	55.00	65.00
90-01-110	Mrs. Pinkerton's Post Office	D. Tate	Open	72.50	82.50
90-01-111	Sulgrave Manor	D. Tate	Retrd.	120.00	140.00
90-01-112	Periwinkle Cottage	D. Tate	Open	165.00	200.00
90-01-113	Robin's Gate	D. Tate	Open	33.50	40.00
90-01-114	Cherry Cottage	D. Tate	Open	33.50	40.00
90-01-115	Otter Reach	D. Tate	Open	33.50	40.00
90-01-116	Runswick House	D. Tate	Open	62.50	72.50
90-01-117	The King's Arms	D. Tate	Open	450.00	525.00
90-01-118	Convent in The Woods	D. Tate	Open	175.00	210.00
91-01-119	Armada House	D. Tate	Open	175.00	175.00
91-01-120	Moonlight Cove	D. Tate	Open	82.50	82.50
91-01-121	Pear Tree House	D. Tate	Open	82.50	82.50
91-01-122	Lapworth Lock	D. Tate	Open	82.50	82.50
91-01-123	Micklegate Antiques	D. Tate	Open	90.00	90.00
91-01-124	Bridge House 1991	D. Tate	Open	25.00	25.00
91-01-125	Tillers Green	D. Tate	Open	60.00	60.00
91-01-126	Wellington Lodge	D. Tate	Open	55.00	55.00
91-01-127	Primrose Hill	D. Tate	Open	46.50	46.50
91-01-128	Daisy Cottage	D. Tate	Open	37.50	37.50
91-01-129	Farthing Lodge	D. Tate	Open	37.50	37.50
91-01-130	Dovetails	D. Tate	Open	90.00	90.00
91-01-131	Lace Lane	D. Tate	Open	90.00	90.00
91-01-132	The Flower Sellers	D. Tate	Open	110.00	110.00
91-01-133	Witham Delph	D. Tate	Open	110.00	110.00
91-01-134	Village School	D. Tate	Open	120.00	120.00
91-01-135	Hopcroft Cottage	D. Tate	Open	120.00	120.00
91-01-136	John Barleycorn Cottage	D. Tate	Open	130.00	130.00
91-01-137	Paradise Lodge	D. Tate	Open	130.00	130.00
91-01-138	The Priest's House	D. Tate	Open	180.00	180.00
91-01-139	Old Shop at Bignor	D. Tate	Open	215.00	215.00
91-01-140	Chatsworth View	D. Tate	Open	250.00	250.00
91-01-141	Anne of Cleves	D. Tate	Open	360.00	360.00
91-01-142	Saxham St. Edmunds	D. Tate	4,500	1550.00	1550.00
92-01-143	Bow Cottage	D. Tate	Open	127.50	127.50
92-01-144	Granny Smiths	D. Tate	Open	60.00	60.00
92-01-145	Oakwood Smithy	D. Tate	Open	450.00	450.00
92-01-146	Pixie House	D. Tate	Open	55.00	55.00
92-01-147	Puffin Row	D. Tate	Open	127.50	127.50
92-01-148	Rustic Roof House	D. Tate	Open	110.00	110.00
92-01-149	Wheyside Cottage	Lilliput Lane	Open	46.50	46.50
92-01-150	Wedding Bells	Lilliput Lane	Open	75.00	75.00
92-01-151	Derwent-le-Dale	Lilliput Lane	Open	75.00	75.00
92-01-152	The Nutshell	Lilliput Lane	Open	75.00	75.00
92-01-153	Finchingfields	Lilliput Lane	Open	82.50	82.50
92-01-154	The Chocolate House	Lilliput Lane	Open	130.00	130.00
92-01-155	Grantchester Meadows	Lilliput Lane	Open	275.00	275.00
92-01-156	High Ghyll Farm	Lilliput Lane	Open	360.00	360.00
Lilliput Lane Ltd.		**Collectors Club Specials**			
86-02-001	Packhorse Bridge	D. Tate	Retrd.	Unkn.	400-950.
86-02-002	Crendon Manor	D. Tate	Retrd.	285.00	600-1600.

Company / Number	Name	Series / Artist	Edition Limit	Issue Price	Quote
87-02-003	Little Lost Dog	D. Tate	Retrd.	Unkn.	200-350.
87-02-004	Yew Tree Farm	D. Tate	Retrd.	160.00	250-500.
88-02-005	Wishing Well	D. Tate	Retrd.	Unkn.	100-175.
89-02-006	Wenlock Rise	D. Tate	Retrd.	175.00	225-400.
89-02-007	Dovecot	D. Tate	Retrd.	Unkn.	100-200.
90-02-008	Lavender Cottage	D. Tate	Retrd.	50.00	125-200.
90-02-009	Bridle Way	D. Tate	Retrd.	100.00	200-300.
90-02-010	Cosy Corner	D. Tate	Retrd.	Unkn.	100-150.
91-02-011	Puddlebrook	D. Tate	Retrd.	Unkn.	85-125.00
91-02-012	Gardeners Cottage	D. Tate	Retrd.	120.00	150-200.
91-02-013	Wren Cottage	D. Tate	Retrd.	13.95	150-200.
92-02-014	Pussy Willow	D. Tate	Retrd.	N/A	N/A
92-02-015	Forget-Me-Not	D. Tate	4/93	130.00	130.00
Lilliput Lane Ltd.		**German Collection**			
87-03-001	Meersburger Weinstube	D. Tate	Open	82.50	82.50
87-03-002	Jaghutte	D. Tate	Open	82.50	82.50
87-03-003	Das Gebirgskirchlein	D. Tate	Open	120.00	120.00
87-03-004	Nurnberger Burgerhaus	D. Tate	Open	140.00	140.00
87-03-005	Schwarzwaldhaus	D. Tate	Open	140.00	140.00
87-03-006	Moselhaus	D. Tate	Open	140.00	140.00
87-03-007	Haus Im Rheinland	D. Tate	Open	220.00	220.00
88-03-008	Der Familienschrein	D. Tate	Retrd.	52.50	52.50
88-03-009	Das Rathaus	D. Tate	Open	140.00	140.00
88-03-010	Die Kleine Backerei	D. Tate	Open	68.00	68.00
92-03-011	Alte Schmiede	D. Tate	Open	175.00	175.00
92-03-012	Der Bücherwurm	D. Tate	Open	140.00	140.00
92-03-013	Rosengartenhaus	D. Tate	Open	120.00	120.00
92-03-014	Strandvogthaus	D. Tate	Open	120.00	120.00
Lilliput Lane Ltd.		**Christmas**			
88-04-001	Deer Park Hall	D. Tate	Retrd.	120.00	200-400.
89-04-002	St. Nicholas Church	D. Tate	Retrd.	130.00	200-250.
90-04-003	Yuletide Inn	D. Tate	Retrd.	145.00	200-400.
91-04-004	The Old Vicarage at Christmas	D. Tate	Retrd.	180.00	200-300.
92-04-005	Chestnut Cottage	Lilliput Lane	Open	46.50	46.50
92-04-006	Cranberry Cottage	Lilliput Lane	Open	46.50	46.50
92-04-007	Hollytree House	Lilliput Lane	Open	46.50	46.50
92-04-008	Highland Lodge	Lilliput Lane	Yr.Iss.	180.00	180.00
Lilliput Lane Ltd.		**Blaise Hamlet Collection**			
89-05-001	Diamond Cottage	D. Tate	Open	110.00	127.50
89-05-002	Oak Cottage	D. Tate	Open	110.00	127.50
89-05-003	Circular Cottage	D. Tate	Open	110.00	127.50
90-05-004	Dial Cottage	D. Tate	Open	110.00	127.50
90-05-005	Vine Cottage	D. Tate	Open	110.00	127.50
90-05-006	Sweetbriar Cottage	D. Tate	Open	110.00	127.50
91-05-007	Double Cottage	D. Tate	Open	200.00	200.00
91-05-008	Jasmine Cottage	D. Tate	Open	140.00	140.00
91-05-009	Rose Cottage	D. Tate	Open	140.00	140.00
Lilliput Lane Ltd.		**Irish Cottages**			
87-06-001	Donegal Cottage	D. Tate	Retrd.	29.00	34.00
89-06-002	Kennedy Homestead	D. Tate	Open	33.50	40.00
89-06-003	Magilligans	D. Tate	Open	33.50	40.00
89-06-004	St. Columba's School	D. Tate	Open	47.50	55.00
89-06-005	St. Kevin's Church	D. Tate	Open	55.00	65.00
89-06-006	O'Lacey's Store	D. Tate	Open	68.00	79.00
89-06-007	Hegarty's Home	D. Tate	Retrd.	68.00	79.00
89-06-008	Kilmore Quay	D. Tate	Retrd.	68.00	79.00
89-06-009	Quiet Cottage	D. Tate	Retrd.	72.50	85.00
89-06-010	Thoor Ballylee	D. Tate	Retrd.	105.00	120.00
89-06-011	Pat Cohan's Bar	D. Tate	Open	110.00	130.00
89-06-012	Limerick House	D. Tate	Retrd.	110.00	130.00
89-06-013	St. Patrick's Church	D. Tate	Open	185.00	215.00
89-06-014	Ballykerne Croft	D. Tate	Open	75.00	85.00
Lilliput Lane Ltd.		**Scottish Cottages**			
82-07-001	The Croft (without sheep)	D. Tate	Retrd.	29.00	800-1250.
84-07-002	The Croft (Renovated)	D. Tate	Retrd.	36.00	50-100.00
85-07-003	Preston Mill	D. Tate	Retrd.	45.00	150.00
85-07-004	Burns Cottage	D. Tate	Retrd.	35.00	100-150.
85-07-005	7 St. Andrews Square	A. Yarrington	Retrd.	15.95	100-150.
87-07-006	East Neuk	D. Tate	Retrd.	29.00	60.00
87-07-007	Preston Mill (Renovated)	D. Tate	Retrd.	62.50	72.50
89-07-008	Culloden Cottage	D. Tate	Open	36.00	42.50
89-07-009	Inverlochie Hame	D. Tate	Open	47.50	55.00
89-07-010	Carrick House	D. Tate	Open	47.50	55.00
89-07-011	Stockwell Tenement	D. Tate	Open	62.50	72.50
89-07-012	John Knox House	D. Tate	Retrd.	68.00	79.00
89-07-013	Claypotts Castle	D. Tate	Open	72.50	85.00
89-07-014	Kenmore Cottage	D. Tate	Open	87.00	100.00
89-07-015	Craigievar Castle	D. Tate	Retrd.	185.00	225-300.
89-07-016	Blair Atholl	D. Tate	Retrd.	275.00	400-500.
90-07-017	Fishermans Bothy	D. Tate	Open	36.00	42.50
90-07-018	Hebridean Hame	D. Tate	Retrd.	55.00	65.00
90-07-019	Kirkbrae Cottage	D. Tate	Open	55.00	65.00
90-07-020	Kinlochness	D. Tate	Open	79.00	79.00
90-07-021	Glenlochie Lodge	D. Tate	Open	110.00	110.00
90-07-022	Ellean Donan	D. Tate	Open	145.00	170.00
90-07-023	Cawdor Castle	D. Tate	Retrd.	295.00	550-800.
92-07-024	Culross House	D. Tate	Open	90.00	90.00
92-07-025	Duart Castle	D. Tate	3,000	450.00	450.00
92-07-026	Eriskay Croft	D. Tate	Open	50.00	50.00
92-07-027	Mair Haven	D. Tate	Open	46.50	46.50
Lilliput Lane Ltd.		**Lakeland Bridge Plaques**			
89-08-001	Aira Force	D. Simpson	Retrd.	35.00	35.00
89-08-002	Birks Bridge	D. Simpson	Retrd.	35.00	35.00
89-08-003	Stockley Bridge	D. Simpson	Retrd.	35.00	35.00
89-08-004	Hartsop Packhorse	D. Simpson	Retrd.	35.00	35.00
89-08-005	Bridge House	D. Simpson	Retrd.	35.00	35.00
89-08-006	Ashness Bridge	D. Simpson	Retrd.	35.00	35.00
Lilliput Lane Ltd.		**Countryside Scene Plaques**			
89-09-001	Country Inn	D. Simpson	Retrd.	49.50	49.50
89-09-002	Norfolk Windmill	D. Simpson	Retrd.	49.50	49.50
89-09-003	Watermill	D. Simpson	Retrd.	49.50	49.50
89-09-004	Parish Church	D. Simpson	Retrd.	49.50	49.50
89-09-005	Bottle Kiln	D. Simpson	Retrd.	49.50	49.50
89-09-006	Cornish Tin Mine	D. Simpson	Retrd.	49.50	49.50
89-09-007	Lighthouse	D. Simpson	Retrd.	49.50	49.50
89-09-008	Cumbrian Farmhouse	D. Simpson	Retrd.	49.50	49.50
89-09-009	Post Office	D. Simpson	Retrd.	49.50	49.50
89-09-010	Village School	D. Simpson	Retrd.	49.50	49.50
89-09-011	Old Smithy	D. Simpson	Retrd.	49.50	49.50
89-09-012	Oasthouse	D. Simpson	Retrd.	49.50	49.50
Lilliput Lane Ltd.		**Framed Scottish Plaques**			
90-10-001	Preston Oat Mill	D. Tate	Retrd.	59.50	59.50
90-10-002	Barra Black House	D. Tate	Retrd.	59.50	59.50
90-10-003	Kyle Point	D. Tate	Retrd.	59.50	59.50
90-10-004	Fife Ness	D. Tate	Retrd.	59.50	59.50
Lilliput Lane Ltd.		**Unframed Plaques**			
89-11-001	Small Stoney Wall Lea	D. Tate	Retrd.	47.50	47.50
89-11-002	Small Woodside Farm	D. Tate	Retrd.	47.50	47.50
89-11-003	Medium Cobble Combe Cottage	D. Tate	Retrd.	68.00	68.00
89-11-004	Medium Wishing Well	D. Tate	Retrd.	75.00	75.00
89-11-005	Large Lower Brockhampton	D. Tate	Retrd.	120.00	120.00
89-11-006	Large Somerset Springtime	D. Tate	Retrd.	130.00	130.00
Lilliput Lane Ltd.		**London Plaques**			
89-12-001	Buckingham Palace	D. Simpson	Retrd.	39.50	39.50
89-12-002	Trafalgar Square	D. Simpson	Retrd.	39.50	39.50
89-12-003	Tower Bridge	D. Simpson	Retrd.	39.50	39.50
89-12-004	Tower of London	D. Simpson	Retrd.	39.50	39.50
89-12-005	Big Ben	D. Simpson	Retrd.	39.50	39.50
89-12-006	Piccadilly Circus	D. Simpson	Retrd.	39.50	39.50
Lilliput Lane Ltd.		**Framed Irish Plaques**			
90-13-001	Ballyteag House	D. Tate	Retrd.	59.50	59.50
90-13-002	Shannons Bank	D. Tate	Retrd.	59.50	59.50
90-13-003	Pearses Cottages	D. Tate	Retrd.	59.50	59.50
90-13-004	Crockuna Croft	D. Tate	Retrd.	59.50	59.50
Lilliput Lane Ltd.		**Framed English Plaques**			
90-14-001	Huntingdon House	D. Tate	Retrd.	59.50	59.50
90-14-002	Coombe Cot	D. Tate	Retrd.	59.50	59.50
90-14-003	Ashdown Hall	D. Tate	Retrd.	59.50	59.50
90-14-004	Flint Fields	D. Tate	Retrd.	59.50	59.50
90-14-005	Fell View	D. Tate	Retrd.	59.50	59.50
90-14-006	Cat Slide Cottage	D. Tate	Retrd.	59.50	59.50
90-14-007	Battleview	D. Tate	Retrd.	59.50	59.50
90-14-008	Stowside	D. Tate	Retrd.	59.50	59.50
90-14-009	Jubilee Lodge	D. Tate	Retrd.	59.50	59.50
90-14-010	Trevan Cove	D. Tate	Retrd.	59.50	59.50
Lilliput Lane Ltd.		**Special Event Collection**			
89-15-001	Commemorative Medallion-1989 South Bend	D. Tate	Closed	Unkn.	95-220.00
90-15-002	Rowan Lodge-1990 South Bend	D. Tate	Closed	Unkn.	200-450.
91-15-003	Gamekeepers Cottage-1991 South Bend	D. Tate	Closed	Unkn.	200-425.
92-15-004	Ashberry Cottage-1992 South Bend	D. Tate	Closed	Unkn.	N/A
Lilliput Lane Ltd.		**Specials**			
83-16-001	Cliburn School	D. Tate	Retrd.	22.50	4950-5800.
83-16-002	Bridge House Dealer Sign	D. Tate	Retrd.	Unkn.	900.00
85-16-003	Bermuda Cottage (3 Colors)	D. Tate	Open	29.00	29-49.00
86-16-004	Seven Dwarf's Cottage	D. Tate	Retrd.	Unkn.	275-450.
87-16-005	Clockmaker's Cottage	D. Tate	Retrd.	40.00	200-250.
87-16-006	Guildhall	D. Tate	Retrd.	Unkn.	175-275.
88-16-007	Chantry Chapel	D. Tate	Retrd.	Unkn.	200-325.
89-16-008	Chiltern Mill	D. Tate	Open	87.50	100.00
89-16-009	Mayflower House	D. Tate	Retdr.	87.50	125-300.
89-16-010	Olde York Toll	D. Tate	Retrd.	82.50	95.00
90-16-011	Rowan Lodge	D. Tate	Retrd.	50.00	150-200.
91-16-012	Gamekeeper's Cottage	Lilliput Lane	Retrd.	75.00	75.00
Lilliput Lane Ltd		**American Landmark Series**			
89-17-001	Countryside Barn	R. Day	Retrd.	75.00	115.00
89-17-002	Mail Pouch Barn	R. Day	Open	75.00	100.00
89-17-003	Falls Mill	R. Day	Retrd.	130.00	150.00
90-17-004	Sign Of The Times	R. Day	Open	27.50	33.75
90-17-005	Pioneer Barn	R. Day	Retrd.	30.00	75-100.00
90-17-006	Great Point Light	R. Day	Open	39.50	50.00
90-17-007	Hometown Depot	R. Day	Open	68.00	87.50
90-17-008	Country Church	R. Day	Retrd.	82.50	120.00
90-17-009	Riverside Chapel	R. Day	Open	82.50	120.00
90-17-010	Pepsi Cola Barn	R. Day	Retrd.	87.00	150-250.
90-17-011	Roadside Coolers	R. Day	Open	75.00	100.00
90-17-012	Covered Memories	R. Day	Open	110.00	150.00
91-17-013	Rambling Rose	R. Day	Open	60.00	60.00
91-17-014	School Days	R. Day	Open	60.00	75.00
91-17-015	Fire House 1	R. Day	Open	87.50	100.00
91-17-016	Victoriana	R. Day	Retrd.	295.00	400-700.
92-17-017	Home Seet Home	R. Day	Open	120.00	120.00
92-17-018	Small Town Library	R. Day	Open	130.00	130.00
92-17-019	16.9 Cents Per Gallon	R. Day	Open	150.00	150.00
92-17-020	Gold Miners' Claim	R. Day	Open	110.00	110.00
92-17-021	Winnie's Place	R. Day	2,000	395.00	395.00
Lilliput Lane Ltd.		**American Collection**			
84-18-001	Adobe Church	D. Tate	Retrd.	22.50	450-650.
84-18-002	Adobe Village	D. Tate	Retrd.	60.00	700-1000.
84-18-003	Cape Cod	D. Tate	Retrd.	22.50	400-600.
84-18-004	Covered Bridge	D. Tate	Retrd.	22.50	500-1000.
84-18-005	Country Church	D. Tate	Retrd.	22.50	450-800.
84-18-006	Forge Barn	D. Tate	Retrd.	22.50	550-660.
84-18-007	Grist Mill	D. Tate	Retrd.	22.50	500-785.
84-18-008	Log Cabin	D. Tate	Retrd.	22.50	500-650.
84-18-009	General Store	D. Tate	Retrd.	22.50	650-750.
84-18-010	Light House	D. Tate	Retrd.	22.50	700-1000.
84-18-011	Midwest Barn	D. Tate	Retrd.	22.50	150-425.
84-18-012	Wallace Station	D. Tate	Retrd.	22.50	350-1000.
84-18-013	San Francisco House	D. Tate	Retrd.	22.50	500-1000.
Lilliput Lane Ltd.		**Welsh Collection**			
85-19-001	Hermitage	D. Tate	Retrd.	30.00	150-200.
87-19-002	Hermitage Renovated	D. Tate	Retrd.	42.50	65-85.00
86-19-003	Brecon Bach	D. Tate	Open	42.00	85.00
91-19-004	Tudor Merchant	D. Tate	Open	90.00	90.00
91-19-005	Ugly House	D. Tate	Open	55.00	55.00
91-19-006	Bro Dawel	D. Tate	Open	37.50	37.50
92-19-007	St. Govan's Chapel	Lilliput Lane	Open	75.00	75.00

Company / Number	Name	Series / Artist	Edition Limit	Issue Price	Quote
Lilliput Lane Ltd.		**Dutch Collection**			
91-20-001	Aan de Amstel	D. Tate	Open	79.00	79.00
91-20-002	Begijnhof	D. Tate	Open	55.00	55.00
91-20-003	Bloemenmarkt	D. Tate	Open	79.00	79.00
91-20-004	De Branderij	D. Tate	Open	72.50	72.50
91-20-005	De Diamantair	D. Tate	Open	79.00	79.00
91-20-006	De Pepermolen	D. Tate	Open	55.00	55.00
91-20-007	De Wolhandelaar	D. Tate	Open	72.50	72.50
91-20-008	De Zijdewever	D. Tate	Open	79.00	79.00
91-20-009	Rembrant van Rijn	D. Tate	Open	120.00	120.00
91-20-010	Rozengracht	D. Tate	Open	72.50	72.50
Lilliput Lane Ltd.		**French Collection**			
91-21-001	L' Auberge d'Armorique	D. Tate	Open	220.00	220.00
91-21-002	La Bergerie du Perigord	D. Tate	Open	230.00	230.00
91-21-003	La Cabane du Gardian	D. Tate	Open	55.00	55.00
91-21-004	La Chaumiere du Verger	D. Tate	Open	120.00	120.00
91-21-005	La Maselle de Nadaillac	D. Tate	Open	130.00	130.00
91-21-006	La Porte Schoenenberg	D. Tate	Open	75.00	75.00
91-21-007	Le Manoir de Champfleuri	D. Tate	Open	265.00	265.00
91-21-008	Le Mas du Vigneron	D. Tate	Open	120.00	120.00
91-21-009	Le Petite Montmartre	D. Tate	Open	130.00	130.00
91-21-010	Locmaria	D. Tate	Open	65.00	65.00
Lilliput Lane Ltd.		**Village Shop Collection**			
92-22-001	The Greengrocers	D. Tate	Open	120.00	120.00
92-22-002	Penny Sweets	Lilliput Lane	Open	N/A	N/A
Lladro		**Capricho**			
87-01-001	Orchid Arrangement C1541	Lladro	Closed	500.00	1700-1925.
87-01-002	Iris Basket C1542	Lladro	Closed	800.00	1250.00
87-01-003	Fan C1546	Lladro	Closed	650.00	1600.00
87-01-004	Fan C1546.3	Lladro	Closed	650.00	1600.00
87-01-005	Iris with Vase C1551	Lladro	Closed	110.00	375.00
Lladro		**Lladro**			
71-02-001	Shepherdess with Goats L1001	Lladro	Closed	80.00	460.00
71-02-002	Girl With Lamb L1010G	Lladro	Open	26.00	170.00
71-02-003	Girl With Pig L1011G	Lladro	Open	13.00	82.00
71-02-004	Centaur Girl L1012	Lladro	Closed	45.00	250.00
71-02-005	Centaur Boy L1013	Lladro	Closed	45.00	375.00
71-02-006	Dove L1015 G	Lladro	Open	21.00	100.00
71-02-007	Dove L1016 G	Lladro	Open	36.00	170.00
71-02-008	Idyl L1017G/M	Lladro	Closed	115.00	565.00
71-02-009	King Gaspar L1018 M	Lladro	Open	345.00	1795.00
71-02-010	King Melchior L1019 M	Lladro	Open	345.00	1795.00
71-02-011	King Balthasar L1020 M	Lladro	Open	345.00	1795.00
71-02-012	King Gaspar L1018	Lladro	Open	345.00	1600.00
71-02-013	King Melchior L1019	Lladro	Open	345.00	1600.00
71-02-014	King Baltasar L1020	Lladro	Open	345.00	1600.00
84-02-015	Horse Group L1021	Lladro	Closed	950.00	1950.00
71-02-016	Horse Group/All White L1022M	Lladro	Open	465.00	2000.00
69-02-017	Flute Player L1025	Lladro	Closed	73.00	870.00
85-02-018	Clown with Concertina L1027G	Lladro	Open	95.00	700.00
71-02-019	Don Quixote w/Stand L1030G	Lladro	Open	225.00	1375.00
71-02-020	Sancho Panza L1031	Lladro	Closed	65.00	400.00
69-02-021	Old Folks L1033	Lladro	Closed	140.00	1100.00
71-02-022	Girl with Basket L1034	Lladro	Closed	30.00	225.00
71-02-023	Girl with Geese L1035G	Lladro	Open	37.50	170.00
71-02-024	Girl Geese L1036 G/M	Lladro	Open	Unkn.	155.00
71-02-025	Violinist and Girl L1039	Lladro	Closed	120.00	1000.00
71-02-026	Girl with Duck L1052G	Lladro	Open	30.00	195.00
71-02-027	Beagle Puppy L1071 G/M	Lladro	Open	17.50	135.00
71-02-028	Girl Seated with Flowers L1088	Lladro	Closed	45.00	650.00
71-02-029	Pelusa Clown L1125	Lladro	Closed	70.00	875.00
XX-02-030	Clown with Violin L1126	Lladro	Closed	71.00	1400.00
71-02-031	Puppy Love L1127G	Lladro	Open	50.00	270.00
71-02-032	Elephants (3) L1150G	Lladro	Open	100.00	775.00
71-02-033	Elephants (2) L1151G	Lladro	Open	45.00	375.00
72-02-034	Dog w/Microphone L1155	Lladro	Closed	35.00	475.00
74-02-035	Kissing Doves L1169 G	Lladro	Open	32.00	140.00
71-02-036	Girl With Flowers L1172 G	Lladro	Open	27.00	285.00
73-02-037	Boy with Donkey L1181	Lladro	Closed	50.00	260.00
84-02-038	Boy Meets Girl L1188	Lladro	Closed	310.00	310.00
74-02-039	Eskimo L1195 G	Lladro	Open	30.00	125.00
74-02-040	Bear, White L1207 G	Lladro	Open	16.00	70.00
74-02-041	Bear, White L1208 G	Lladro	Open	16.00	70.00
74-02-042	Bear, White L1209 G	Lladro	Open	16.00	70.00
73-02-043	Girl With Doll L1211 G	Lladro	Open	72.00	420.00
74-02-044	Young Harlequin L1229G	Lladro	Open	70.00	495.00
74-02-045	Friendship L1230G/M	Lladro	Closed	68.00	325.00
74-02-046	Angel with Lute L1231	Lladro	Closed	60.00	375.00
74-02-047	Angel with Clarinet L1232	Lladro	Closed	60.00	375.00
74-02-048	Angel with Flute L1233	Lladro	Closed	60.00	375.00
74-02-049	Caress L1246	Lladro	Closed	50.00	190.00
74-02-050	Honey Lickers L1248	Lladro	Closed	100.00	600.00
74-02-051	The Race L1249	Lladro	Closed	450.00	1800-2250.
74-02-052	Lovers from Verona L 1250	Lladro	Closed	330.00	1250.00
74-02-053	Hamlet and Yorick L1254	Lladro	Closed	325.00	1050.00
74-02-054	Seesaw L1255G	Lladro	Open	110.00	525.00
74-02-055	Flying Duck L1263 G	Lladro	Open	20.00	85.00
74-02-056	Flying Duck L1264 G	Lladro	Open	20.00	85.00
74-02-057	Flying Duck L1265 G	Lladro	Open	20.00	85.00
74-02-058	Girl with Ducks L1267G	Lladro	Open	55.00	250.00
80-02-059	Reminiscing L1270	Lladro	Closed	975.00	1375.00
83-02-060	Thoughts L1272G	Lladro	Closed	87.50	3050.00
76-02-061	Lovers in the Park L1274G	Lladro	Open	450.00	1300.00
75-02-062	Feeding Time L1277G	Lladro	Open	120.00	360.00
75-02-063	Devotion L1278	Lladro	Closed	140.00	450.00
75-02-064	The Wind L1279M	Lladro	Open	250.00	765.00
75-02-065	Playtime L1280	Lladro	Closed	160.00	475.00
75-02-066	Little Gardener L1283G	Lladro	Open	250.00	765.00
75-02-067	"My Flowers" L1284G	Lladro	Open	200.00	525.00
75-02-068	"My Goodness" L1285G	Lladro	Open	190.00	395.00
75-02-069	Flower Harvest L1286G	Lladro	Open	200.00	470.00
75-02-070	Picking Flowers L1287G	Lladro	Open	170.00	420.00
75-02-071	Agressive Duck L1288G	Lladro	Open	170.00	450.00
76-02-072	Victorian Girl on Swing L1297	Lladro	Closed	520.00	2100.00
76-02-073	Valencian Lady with Flowers L1304G	Lladro	Open	200.00	595.00
77-02-074	"On the Farm" L1306	Lladro	Closed	130.00	240.00
77-02-075	Ducklings L1307G	Lladro	Open	47.50	145.00
76-02-076	Girl with Cats L1309G	Lladro	Open	120.00	295.00
76-02-077	Girl with Puppies in Basket L1311G	Lladro	Open	120.00	325.00
76-02-078	Schoolgirl L1313	Lladro	Closed	200.50	650-750.
80-02-079	IBIS L1319G	Lladro	Open	1550.00	2500.00
76-02-080	The Helmsman L1325M	Lladro	Closed	600.00	6400.00
XX-02-081	Card Players, numbered L1327	Lladro	Open	3800.00	6400.00
XX-02-082	Playing Cards L1327 M, numbered	Lladro	Open	N/A	6400.00
84-02-083	Dove Group L1335	Lladro	Closed	950.00	1700.00
80-02-084	Blooming Roses L1339	Lladro	Closed	325.00	425.00
77-02-085	Wrath of Don Quixote L1343	Lladro	Closed	250.00	850.00
80-02-086	Under the Willow L1346	Lladro	Closed	1600.00	2000.00
78-02-087	Nautical Vision L1349	Lladro	Closed	Unkn.	3000.00
80-02-088	In the Gondola L1350G, numbered	Lladro	Open	1850.00	3100.00
79-02-089	Growing Roses L1354	Lladro	Closed	485.00	635.00
78-02-090	Phyllia L1356 G	Lladro	Open	75.00	165.00
78-02-091	Shelley L1357 G	Lladro	Open	75.00	165.00
78-02-092	Beth L1358 G	Lladro	Open	75.00	165.00
78-02-093	Heather L1359 G	Lladro	Open	75.00	165.00
78-02-094	Laura L1360 G	Lladro	Open	75.00	165.00
78-02-095	Julia L1361 G	Lladro	Open	75.00	165.00
79-02-096	Swinging L1366	Lladro	Closed	825.00	1375.00
79-02-097	Spring Birds L1368	Lladro	Closed	1600.00	2500.00
79-02-098	Anniversary Waltz L1372G	Lladro	Open	260.00	530.00
80-02-099	Waiting in the Park L1374G	Lladro	Open	235.00	425.00
79-02-100	Watering Flowers L1376	Lladro	Closed	400.00	1100.00
80-02-101	A Rickshaw Ride L1383G	Lladro	Open	1500.00	2100.00
83-02-102	The Brave Knight L1385	Lladro	Closed	350.00	500.00
82-02-103	St. Joseph L1386G	Lladro	Open	250.00	375.00
82-02-104	Mary L1387G	Lladro	Open	240.00	365.00
82-02-105	Baby Jesus L1388G	Lladro	Open	85.00	135.00
82-02-106	Donkey L1389G	Lladro	Open	95.00	175.00
82-02-107	Cow L1390G	Lladro	Open	95.00	175.00
80-02-108	Holy Mary, numbered L1394G	Lladro	Open	1000.00	1400.00
83-02-109	Full of Mischief L1395G	Lladro	Open	420.00	730.00
83-02-110	Appreciation L1396G	Lladro	Open	420.00	730.00
83-02-111	Second Thoughts L1397G	Lladro	Open	420.00	730.00
83-02-112	Reverie L1398G	Lladro	Open	490.00	860.00
82-02-113	Dutch Woman with Tulips L1399	Lladro	Closed	Unkn.	700.00
83-02-114	Valencian Boy L1400	Lladro	Closed	297.50	400.00
83-02-115	Sleeping Nymph L1401	Lladro	Closed	210.00	525-750.
83-02-116	Daydreaming Nymph L1402	Lladro	Closed	210.00	525-625.
83-02-117	Pondering Nymph L1403	Lladro	Closed	210.00	525-625.
83-02-118	Matrimony L1404G	Lladro	Open	320.00	560.00
83-02-119	Illusion L1413G	Lladro	Open	115.00	235.00
83-02-120	Fantasy L1414G	Lladro	Open	115.00	235.00
83-02-121	Mirage L1415G	Lladro	Open	115.00	235.00
83-02-122	From My Garden L1416G	Lladro	Open	140.00	260.00
83-02-123	Nature's Bounty L1417G	Lladro	Open	160.00	295.00
83-02-124	Flower Harmony L1418G	Lladro	Open	130.00	235.00
83-02-125	A Barrow of Blossoms L1419G	Lladro	Open	390.00	650.00
83-02-126	Born Free L1420G	Lladro	Open	1520.00	2785.00
83-02-127	Mariko L1421G	Lladro	Open	860.00	1500.00
83-02-128	Ms. Valencia L1422G	Lladro	Open	175.00	335.00
83-02-129	King Melchor L1423G	Lladro	Open	225.00	420.00
83-02-130	King Gaspar L1424G	Lladro	Open	265.00	450.00
83-02-131	King Baltasar L1425G	Lladro	Open	315.00	565.00
83-02-132	Male Tennis Player L1426	Lladro	Closed	200.00	275.00
83-02-133	Female Tennis Player L1427	Lladro	Closed	200.00	275.00
83-02-134	Afternoon Tea L1428G/M	Lladro	Open	115.00	245.00
83-02-135	Winter Wonderland L1429G	Lladro	Open	1025.00	1895.00
83-02-136	High Society L1430G	Lladro	Open	305.00	565.00
83-02-137	The Debutante L1431G/M	Lladro	Open	115.00	240.00
84-02-138	Vows L1434	Lladro	Closed	600.00	950.00
84-02-139	Blue Moon L1435	Lladro	Closed	98.00	375.00
84-02-140	Moon Glow L1436	Lladro	Closed	98.00	375.00
84-02-141	Moon Light L1437	Lladro	Closed	98.00	375.00
84-02-142	Full Moon L1438	Lladro	Closed	115.00	500.00
84-02-143	"How Do You Do!" L1439G	Lladro	Open	185.00	295.00
84-02-144	Pleasantries L1440	Lladro	Closed	960.00	1900.00
84-02-145	A Litter of Love L1441G	Lladro	Open	385.00	625.00
84-02-146	Kitty Confrontation L1442G	Lladro	Open	155.00	275.00
84-02-147	Purr-Fect L1444G	Lladro	Open	350.00	595.00
84-02-148	Springtime in Japan L1445G	Lladro	Open	965.00	1750.00
84-02-149	"Here Comes the Bride" L1446G	Lladro	Open	517.50	945.00
84-02-150	Michiko L1447G	Lladro	Open	235.00	440.00
84-02-151	Yuki L1448G	Lladro	Open	285.00	525.00
84-02-152	Mayumi L1449G	Lladro	Open	235.00	440.00
84-02-153	Kiyoko L1450G	Lladro	Open	235.00	440.00
84-02-154	Teruko L1451G	Lladro	Open	235.00	440.00
84-02-155	On the Town L1452G	Lladro	Open	220.00	420.00
84-02-156	Golfing Couple L1453G	Lladro	Open	248.00	480.00
84-02-157	Flowers of the Season L1454G	Lladro	Open	1460.00	2500.00
84-02-158	Reflections of Hamlet L1455	Lladro	Closed	1000.00	1260.00
84-02-159	Cranes L1456G	Lladro	Open	1000.00	1850.00
85-02-160	Carefree Angel with Flute L1463	Lladro	Closed	220.00	575-650.
85-02-161	Carefree Angel with Lyre L1464	Lladro	Closed	220.00	575.00
85-02-162	Girl on Carousel Horse L1469G	Lladro	Open	470.00	825.00
85-02-163	Boy on Carousel Horse L1470G	Lladro	Open	470.00	825.00
85-02-164	Wishing On A Star L1475	Lladro	Closed	130.00	350.00
85-02-165	Star Light Star Bright L1476	Lladro	Closed	130.00	350.00
85-02-166	Star Gazing L1477	Lladro	Closed	130.00	350.00
85-02-167	Hawaiian Dancer L1478G	Lladro	Open	230.00	420.00
85-02-168	In a Tropical Garden L1479G	Lladro	Open	230.00	420.00
85-02-169	Aroma of the Islands L1480G	Lladro	Open	260.00	455.00
85-02-170	Eve L1482	Lladro	Closed	145.00	575.00
86-02-171	Lady of the East L1488G	Lladro	Open	625.00	1050.00
86-02-172	Valencian Children L1489G	Lladro	Open	700.00	1150.00
86-02-173	My Wedding Day L1494G	Lladro	Open	800.00	1395.00
86-02-174	A Lady of Taste L1495G	Lladro	Open	575.00	995.00
86-02-175	Don Quixote & The Windmill L1497G	Lladro	Open	1100.00	1950.00
86-02-176	Tahitian Dancing Girls L1498G	Lladro	Open	750.00	1250.00
86-02-177	Blessed Family L1499G	Lladro	Open	200.00	340.00
86-02-178	Ragamuffin L1500G/M	Lladro	Closed	125.00	200.00
86-02-179	Rag Doll L1501G/M	Lladro	Closed	125.00	200.00
86-02-180	Forgotten L1502G/M	Lladro	Closed	125.00	200.00
86-02-181	Neglected L1503G/M	Lladro	Closed	125.00	200.00
86-02-182	The Reception L1504	Lladro	Closed	625.00	650.00
86-02-183	Nature Boy L1505G/M	Lladro	Closed	100.00	180.00
86-02-184	A New Friend L1506G/M	Lladro	Closed	110.00	180.00
86-02-185	Boy & His Bunny L1507G/M	Lladro	Closed	90.00	160.00
86-02-186	In the Meadow L1508G/M	Lladro	Closed	100.00	180.00
86-02-187	Spring Flowers L1509G/M	Lladro	Closed	100.00	185.00
87-02-188	Cafe De Paris L1511G	Lladro	Open	1900.00	2800.00
87-02-189	Hawaiian Beauty L1512	Lladro	Closed	575.00	725.00
87-02-190	A Flower for My Lady L1513	Lladro	Closed	1150.00	1375.00

Company Number	Name	Series Artist	Edition Limit	Issue Price	Quote
87-02-191	Gaspar 's Page L1514	Lladro	Closed	275.00	450.00
87-02-192	Melchior's Page L1515	Lladro	Closed	290.00	450.00
87-02-193	Balthasar's Page L1516	Lladro	Closed	275.00	475-600.
87-02-194	Circus Train L1517G	Lladro	Open	2900.00	4200.00
87-02-195	Valencian Garden L1518G	Lladro	Closed	1100.00	1650.00
87-02-196	Stroll in the Park L1519G	Lladro	Open	1600.00	2500.00
87-02-197	The Landau Carriage L1521G	Lladro	Open	2500.00	3750.00
87-02-198	I am Don Quixote L1522G	Lladro	Open	2600.00	3850.00
87-02-199	Valencian Bouquet L1524G	Lladro	Closed	250.00	375.00
87-02-200	Valencian Dreams L1525G	Lladro	Closed	240.00	360.00
87-02-201	Valencian Flowers L1526G	Lladro	Closed	375.00	550.00
87-02-202	Tenderness L1527G	Lladro	Open	260.00	395.00
87-02-203	I Love You Truly L1528G	Lladro	Open	375.00	565.00
87-02-204	Momi L1529	Lladro	Closed	275.00	340.00
87-02-205	Leilani L1530	Lladro	Closed	275.00	500.00
87-02-206	Malia L1531	Lladro	Closed	275.00	340.00
87-02-207	Lehua L1532	Lladro	Closed	275.00	575.00
89-02-208	Fluttering Crane L1598G	Lladro	Open	115.00	135.00
89-02-209	Nesting Crane L1599G	Lladro	Open	95.00	110.00
89-02-210	Landing Crane L1600G	Lladro	Open	115.00	135.00
89-02-211	Latest Addition L1606G	Lladro	Open	385.00	475.00
89-02-212	Courting Cranes L1611G	Lladro	Open	565.00	670.00
89-02-213	Preening Crane L1612G	Lladro	Open	385.00	465.00
89-02-214	Bowing Crane L1613G	Lladro	Open	385.00	465.00
89-02-215	Dancing Crane L1614G	Lladro	Open	385.00	465.00
71-02-216	Shepherdess with Lamb L2005	Lladro	Closed	100.00	710.00
75-02-217	Oriental L2056M	Lladro	Closed	35.00	95.00
75-02-218	Oriental L2057M	Lladro	Closed	30.00	95.00
75-02-219	Thailandia L2058M	Lladro	Closed	650.00	1650.00
84-02-220	Monk L2060M	Lladro	Closed	60.00	120.00
77-02-221	Thai Dancers L2069M	Lladro	Closed	300.00	690.00
79-02-222	A New Hairdo L2070	Lladro	Closed	1060.00	1430.00
77-02-223	Graceful Duo L2073M	Lladro	Closed	775.00	1575.00
78-02-224	Nuns L2075M	Lladro	Closed	90.00	220.00
78-02-225	Rain in Spain L2077	Lladro	Closed	190.00	550.00
83-02-226	The Whaler L2121	Lladro	Closed	820.00	1050.00
82-02-227	Lost in Thought L2125	Lladro	Closed	210.00	250.00
82-02-228	American Heritage L2127	Lladro	Closed	525.00	950.00
82-02-229	Venus L2128M	Lladro	Closed	650.00	1150.00
XX-02-230	Mother & Son L2131M, numbered	Lladro	Closed	850.00	1350.00
84-02-231	Nautical Watch L2134	Lladro	Closed	450.00	750.00
84-02-232	Mystical Joseph L2135	Lladro	Closed	427.50	700.00
84-02-233	The King L2136	Lladro	Closed	510.00	710.00
84-02-234	Fairy Ballerina L2137	Lladro	Closed	500.00	625.00
84-02-235	Friar Juniper L2138M	Lladro	Open	160.00	275.00
84-02-236	Aztec Indian L2139	Lladro	Closed	552.50	600.00
84-02-237	Sea Harvest L2142	Lladro	Closed	535.00	700.00
84-02-238	Aztec Dancer L2143	Lladro	Closed	462.50	650.00
84-02-239	Head of Gongolese Woman L2148	Lladro	Closed	55.00	150.00
85-02-240	Young Madonna L2149	Lladro	Closed	400.00	675.00
85-02-241	A Tribute to Peace L2150M	Lladro	Open	470.00	825.00
85-02-242	Hawaiian Flower Vendor L2154M	Lladro	Open	245.00	400.00
90-02-243	Mother's Pride L2189 M	Lladro	Open	300.00	330.00
80-02-244	To The Well L2190 M	Lladro	Open	250.00	285.00
90-02-245	Forest Born L2191 M	Lladro	Closed	230.00	250.00
90-02-246	King Of The Forest L2192 M	Lladro	Closed	290.00	310.00
80-02-247	Heavenly Strings L2194 M	Lladro	Open	170.00	185.00
90-02-248	Heavenly Sounds L2195 M	Lladro	Open	170.00	185.00
90-02-249	Heavenly Solo L2196 M	Lladro	Open	170.00	185.00
90-02-250	Heavenly Song L2197 M	Lladro	Open	175.00	175.00
90-02-251	A King is Born L2198 M	Lladro	Open	750.00	840.00
90-02-252	Devoted Friends L2199 M	Lladro	Open	700.00	785.00
90-02-253	A Big Hug L2200 M	Lladro	Open	250.00	275.00
90-02-254	Our Daily Bread L2201 M	Lladro	Open	150.00	175.00
90-02-255	A Helping Hand L2202 M	Lladro	Open	150.00	175.00
90-02-256	Afternoon Chores L2203 M	Lladro	Open	150.00	175.00
90-02-257	Farmyard Grace L2204 M	Lladro	Open	180.00	200.00
90-02-258	Prayerful Stitch L2205 M	Lladro	Open	160.00	180.00
90-02-259	Sisterly Love L2206 M	Lladro	Open	300.00	330.00
90-02-260	What A Day L2207 M	Lladro	Open	550.00	600.00
90-02-261	Let's Rest L2208 M	Lladro	Open	550.00	600.00
92-02-262	Underfoot L2219M	Lladro	Open	360.00	360.00
92-02-263	Free Spirit L2220M	Lladro	Open	235.00	235.00
92-02-264	Spring Beauty L2221M	Lladro	Open	285.00	285.00
92-02-265	Tender Moment L2222M	Lladro	Open	400.00	400.00
92-02-266	New Lamb L2223M	Lladro	Open	365.00	365.00
92-02-267	Cherish L2224M	Lladro	Open	1750.00	1750.00
92-02-268	Friendly Sparrow L2225M	Lladro	Open	295.00	295.00
92-02-269	Boy's Best Friend L2226M	Lladro	Open	390.00	390.00
92-02-270	Artic Allies L2227M	Lladro	Open	585.00	585.00
92-02-271	Snowy Sunday L2228M	Lladro	Open	550.00	550.00
92-02-272	Seasonal Gifts L2229M	Lladro	Open	450.00	450.00
92-02-273	Mary's Child L2230M	Lladro	Open	525.00	525.00
92-02-274	Afternoon Verse L2231M	Lladro	Open	580.00	580.00
92-02-275	Poor Little Bear L2232M	Lladro	Open	250.00	250.00
92-02-276	Guess What I Have L2233M	Lladro	Open	340.00	340.00
92-02-277	Playful Push L2234M	Lladro	Open	850.00	850.00
78-02-278	Native L3502	Lladro	Open	700.00	2350.00
80-12-279	Letters to Dulcinea, numbered L3509M	Lladro	Open	1275.00	2050.00
79-02-280	Horse Heads L3511	Lladro	Closed	260.00	700.00
80-02-281	A Wintry Day L3513	Lladro	Closed	525.00	750.00
79-02-282	Pensive L3514M	Lladro	Open	500.00	1000.00
79-02-283	Nude with Rose L3517M	Lladro	Open	225.00	725.00
82-02-284	Mother's Love L3521	Lladro	Closed	1000.00	1100.00
82-02-285	Weary L3525M	Lladro	Open	360.00	595.00
82-02-286	Contemplation L3526M	Lladro	Open	265.00	515.00
83-02-287	Stormy Sea L3554M	Lladro	Open	675.00	1250.00
XX-02-288	Innocence/Green L3558M	Lladro	Closed	960.00	1650.00
XX-02-289	Innocence/Red L3558/3	Lladro	Closed	960.00	1200.00
85-02-290	Peace Offering L3559M	Lladro	Open	397.00	655.00
71-02-291	Girl with Lamb L4505G	Lladro	Open	20.00	105.00
71-02-292	Girl with Parasol and Geese L4510G	Lladro	Open	40.00	235.00
72-02-293	Female Equestrian L4516G	Lladro	Open	170.00	685.00
71-02-294	Flamenco Dancers L4519G	Lladro	Open	495.00	1050.00
71-02-295	Angel, Chinese L4536G/M	Lladro	Open	45.00	85.00
71-02-296	Angel, Black L4537G/M	Lladro	Open	13.00	85.00
71-02-297	Angel, Praying L4538G/M	Lladro	Open	13.00	85.00
71-02-298	Angel, Thinking L4539G/M	Lladro	Open	13.00	85.00
71-02-299	Angel with Horn L4540G/M	Lladro	Open	13.00	85.00
71-02-300	Angel Reclining L4541G/M	Lladro	Open	13.00	85.00
71-02-301	Group of Angels L4542G/M	Lladro	Open	31.00	180.00
74-02-302	Sad Harlequin L4558G	Lladro	Open	110.00	485.00
74-02-303	Waiting Backstage L4559G	Lladro	Open	110.00	420.00
71-02-304	Girl with Geese L4568G	Lladro	Open	45.00	210.00
71-02-305	Mother & Child L4575G	Lladro	Open	50.00	250.00
71-02-306	Girl with Sheep L4584G	Lladro	Open	27.00	160.00
71-02-307	Shepherdess with Basket and Rooster L4591G	Lladro	Open	20.00	130.00
73-02-308	Fairy L4595G	Lladro	Open	27.50	130.00
71-02-309	Playfull Horses L4597	Lladro	Closed	240.00	1000.00
71-02-310	Doctor L4602.3G	Lladro	Open	33.00	180.00
71-02-311	Nurse-L4603.3G	Lladro	Open	35.00	185.00
71-02-312	Nuns L4611G/M	Lladro	Open	37.50	145.00
71-02-313	Clown L4618G	Lladro	Open	70.00	395.00
71-02-314	Sea Captain L4621G	Lladro	Open	45.00	255.00
71-02-315	Angel with Child L4635G	Lladro	Open	15.00	95.00
71-02-316	Flamenco Dancers on Horseback L4647	Lladro	Closed	412.00	1000-1250.
87-02-317	Valencian Couple on Horseback L4648	Lladro	Closed	900.00	1200.00
71-02-318	Girl with Calla Lillies L4650G	Lladro	Open	18.00	130.00
71-02-319	Horses L4655G	Lladro	Open	110.00	725.00
71-02-320	Shepherdess L4660G	Lladro	Open	21.00	165.00
71-02-321	Girl with Milkpail L4682	Lladro	Closed	28.00	350.00
71-02-322	Dressmaker L4700G	Lladro	Open	45.00	340.00
71-02-323	Mother & Child L4701G	Lladro	Open	45.00	290.00
XX-02-324	Dentist L4723	Lladro	Closed	36.00	500-750.
71-02-325	Romeo and Juliet L4750G	Lladro	Open	150.00	1200.00
74-02-326	Lady with Dog L4761G	Lladro	Open	60.00	245.00
71-02-327	Obstetrician L4763-3G	Lladro	Open	40.00	225.00
77-02-328	Geisha L4807G	Lladro	Open	190.00	420.00
75-02-329	Wedding L4808G/M	Lladro	Open	50.00	170.00
73-02-330	Going Fishing L4809G	Lladro	Open	33.00	155.00
73-02-331	Young Sailor L4810G	Lladro	Open	33.00	155.00
73-02-332	Getting her Goat L4812	Lladro	Closed	55.00	275.00
73-02-333	Girl with Geese L4815G/M	Lladro	Closed	72.00	295.00
73-02-334	Male Golfer L4824G	Lladro	Open	66.00	285.00
73-02-335	Girl with Rabbit L4826G	Lladro	Open	40.00	175.00
73-02-336	Cinderella L4828G	Lladro	Open	47.00	220.00
73-02-337	Shepherdess L4835G	Lladro	Closed	42.00	225.00
73-02-338	Oriental Flower Arranger L4840G/M	Lladro	Open	90.00	490.00
74-02-339	Girl from Valencia L4841G	Lladro	Open	35.00	195.00
73-02-340	Pharmacist L4844	Lladro	Closed	70.00	1000-2000.
74-02-341	Lady Golfer L4851G	Lladro	Open	70.00	245.00
74-02-342	Don Quixote L4854G	Lladro	Open	40.00	200.00
74-02-343	Ballerina L4855G	Lladro	Open	45.00	315.00
84-02-344	Ballerina, white L4855.3	Lladro	Closed	110.00	250.00
74-02-345	Embroiderer L4865G	Lladro	Open	115.00	615.00
71-02-346	Girl with Swan and Dog L4866G	Lladro	Open	26.00	195.00
71-02-347	Seesaw L4867G	Lladro	Open	55.00	335.00
74-02-348	Lady with Parasol L4879G	Lladro	Open	48.00	285.00
74-02-349	Carnival Couple L4882G	Lladro	Open	60.00	285.00
76-02-350	"My Dog" L4893G	Lladro	Open	85.00	200.00
75-02-351	Lady with Shawl L4914G	Lladro	Open	220.00	650.00
75-02-352	Girl with Pigeons L4915	Lladro	Closed	110.00	215.00
76-02-353	Windblown Girl L4922G	Lladro	Open	150.00	355.00
76-02-354	Sad Clown L4924	Lladro	Closed	200.00	675.00
76-02-355	"Closing Scene" L4935G	Lladro	Open	180.00	495.00
84-02-356	"Closing Scene"/white L4935.3	Lladro	Closed	202.50	265.00
76-02-357	Spring Breeze L4936G	Lladro	Open	145.00	390.00
76-02-358	Baby's Outing L4938G	Lladro	Open	250.00	695.00
77-02-359	Cherub, Puzzled L4959G	Lladro	Open	40.00	98.00
77-02-360	Cherub, Smiling L4960G	Lladro	Open	40.00	98.00
77-02-361	Cherub, Dreaming L4961G	Lladro	Open	40.00	98.00
77-02-362	Cherub, Wondering L4962G	Lladro	Open	40.00	98.00
77-02-363	Girl with Calla Lillies sitting L4972G	Lladro	Open	65.00	165.00
XX-02-364	Choir Lesson L4973	Lladro	Closed	Unkn.	1175.00.
78-02-365	Naughty Dog L4982G	Lladro	Open	130.00	240.00
80-02-366	Gossip L4984	Lladro	Closed	260.00	525-825.00
78-02-367	Oriental Spring L4988G	Lladro	Open	125.00	310.00
78-02-368	Sayonara L4989G	Lladro	Open	125.00	285.00
78-02-369	Chrysanthemum L4990G	Lladro	Open	125.00	295.00
78-02-370	Butterfly L4991G	Lladro	Open	125.00	285.00
78-02-371	Don Quijote & Sancho L4998	Lladro	Closed	875.00	2675.00
80-02-372	Reading L5000G	Lladro	Open	150.00	245.00
80-02-373	Sunny Day L5005	Lladro	Open	192.50	310.00
78-02-374	Daughters L5013	Lladro	Closed	425.00	750.00
79-02-375	Flower Curtsy L5027G	Lladro	Open	230.00	450.00
79-02-376	Wildflower L5030G	Lladro	Open	360.00	670.00
79-02-377	Little Friskies L5032G	Lladro	Open	107.50	210.00
79-02-378	Avoiding the Duck L5033G	Lladro	Open	160.00	330.00
79-02-379	Act II L5035G	Lladro	Open	700.00	1350.00
79-02-380	Jockey with Lass L5036G	Lladro	Open	950.00	1950.00
80-02-381	Sleighride L5037G	Lladro	Open	585.00	995.00
79-02-382	Dancer L5050G	Lladro	Open	85.00	185.00
81-02-383	Clown with Clock L5056	Lladro	Closed	290.00	625.00
81-02-384	Clown with Violin and Top Hat L5057	Lladro	Closed	270.00	725.00
81-02-385	Clown with Concertina L5058	Lladro	Closed	290.00	675.00
81-02-386	Clown with Saxaphone L5059	Lladro	Closed	320.00	575-610.
81-02-387	Girl Clown with Trumpet L5060	Lladro	Closed	290.00	500-575.
81-02-388	Gretel L5064	Lladro	Closed	255.00	375.00
81-02-389	Ingrid L5065	Lladro	Closed	370.00	400.00
81-02-390	Ilsa L5066	Lladro	Closed	275.00	300.00
84-02-391	Nostalgia L5071G	Lladro	Open	185.00	295.00
84-02-392	Courtship L5072	Lladro	Closed	327.00	525.00
81-02-393	My Hungry Brood L5074G	Lladro	Open	295.00	395.00
83-02-394	Roses for My Mom L5088	Lladro	Closed	645.00	810.00
89-02-395	Her Ladyship, numbered L5097G	Lladro	Closed	5900.00	6700.00
82-02-396	August Moon L5122G	Lladro	Open	185.00	295.00
82-02-397	My Precious Bundle L5123G	Lladro	Open	150.00	220.00
82-02-398	Amparo L5125	Lladro	Closed	130.00	200-250.
85-02-399	Nippon Lady L5327	Lladro	Open	325.00	470.00
82-02-400	Lost Love L5128	Lladro	Closed	400.00	750.00
82-02-401	Jester L5129G	Lladro	Open	220.00	385.00
82-02-402	Pensive Clown L5130G	Lladro	Open	250.00	395.00
82-02-403	Cervantes L5132	Lladro	Closed	925.00	1175.00
82-02-404	A New Doll House L5139	Lladro	Closed	185.00	375.00
83-02-405	Balloons for Sale L5141G	Lladro	Open	145.00	240.00
83-02-406	Scooting L5143	Lladro	Closed	575.00	735-850.
82-02-407	Amy L5145	Lladro	Closed	110.00	1500.00
82-02-408	Ellen L5146	Lladro	Closed	110.00	1200.00
82-02-409	Ivy L5147	Lladro	Closed	100.00	700.00
82-02-410	Olivia L5148	Lladro	Closed	100.00	400.00
82-02-411	Ursula L5149	Lladro	Closed	100.00	400.00
83-02-412	Monks at Prayer L5155G	Lladro	Open	130.00	240.00
81-02-413	Cycling To A Picnic L5161	Lladro	Closed	2000.00	3000.00
83-02-414	A Toast by Sancho L5165	Lladro	Closed	100.00	250-325.
83-02-415	Sea Fever L5166G	Lladro	Open	130.00	245.00

FIGURINES

Company Number	Name	Series Artist	Edition Limit	Issue Price	Quote
83-02-416	Jesus L5167G	Lladro	Open	130.00	255.00
83-02-417	Moses L5170G	Lladro	Open	175.00	340.00
83-02-418	Madonna with Flowers L5171G	Lladro	Open	172.50	295.00
83-02-419	Fish A'Plenty L5172G	Lladro	Open	190.00	365.00
83-02-420	Pondering L5173G	Lladro	Open	300.00	490.00
83-02-421	Roaring 20's L5174G	Lladro	Open	172.50	280.00
83-02-402	Flapper L5175G	Lladro	Open	185.00	345.00
81-02-422	Rhapsody in Blue L5176	Lladro	Closed	325.00	1250.00
83-02-423	Stubborn Mule L5178G	Lladro	Open	250.00	400.00
83-02-424	Dante L5177	Lladro	Closed	263.00	475.00
83-02-425	Three Pink Roses w/base L5179	Lladro	Closed	70.00	110.00
83-02-426	Dahlia L5180	Lladro	Closed	65.00	95.00
83-02-427	Japanese Camelia w/base L5181	Lladro	Closed	60.00	90.00
83-02-428	White Peony L5182	Lladro	Closed	85.00	125.00
83-02-429	Two Yellow Roses L5183	Lladro	Closed	57.50	85.00
83-02-430	White Carnation L5184	Lladro	Closed	65.00	100.00
83-02-431	Lactiflora Peony L5185	Lladro	Closed	65.00	100.00
83-02-432	Begonia L5186	Lladro	Closed	67.50	100.00
83-02-433	Rhododendrom L5187	Lladro	Closed	67.50	100.00
83-02-434	Miniature Begonia L5188	Lladro	Closed	80.00	120.00
83-02-435	Chrysanthemum L5189	Lladro	Closed	100.00	150.00
83-02-436	California Poppy L5190	Lladro	Closed	97.50	180.00
83-02-437	Say "Cheese!" L5195	Lladro	Closed	170.00	475.00
83-02-438	"Maestro, Music Please!" L5196	Lladro	Closed	135.00	250.00
83-02-439	Female Physician L5197	Lladro	Open	120.00	230.00
84-02-440	Boy Graduate L5198G	Lladro	Open	160.00	260.00
84-02-441	Girl Graduate L5199G	Lladro	Open	160.00	260.00
83-02-442	Male Soccer Player L5200	Lladro	Closed	155.00	450-725.
83-02-443	Josefa Feeding Duck L5201G	Lladro	Closed	125.00	215.00
83-02-444	Aracely with Ducks L5202G	Lladro	Closed	125.00	220.00
83-02-445	Sharpening the Cutlery L5204	Lladro	Closed	210.00	700.00
83-02-446	Lamplighter L5205G	Lladro	Open	170.00	340.00
83-02-447	Yachtsman L5206G	Lladro	Open	110.00	200.00
83-02-448	A Tall Yarn L5207G	Lladro	Open	260.00	490.00
83-02-449	Professor L5208	Lladro	Closed	205.00	750.00
83-02-450	School Marm L5209	Lladro	Closed	205.00	500-850.
83-02-451	Lawyer L5213G	Lladro	Open	250.00	495.00
83-02-452	Architect L5214	Lladro	Open	140.00	220.00
83-02-453	Fishing with Gramps L5215G	Lladro	Open	410.00	760.00
83-02-454	On the Lake L5216	Lladro	Closed	660.00	825.00
83-02-455	Spring L5217G/M	Lladro	Open	90.00	165.00
83-02-456	Autumn L5218G/M	Lladro	Open	90.00	165.00
83-02-457	Summer L5219G/M	Lladro	Open	90.00	165.00
83-02-458	Winter L5220G/M	Lladro	Open	90.00	165.00
83-02-459	Sweet Scent L5221G/M	Lladro	Open	80.00	130.00
83-02-460	Pretty Pickings L5222G/M	Lladro	Open	80.00	130.00
83-02-461	Spring is Here L5223G/M	Lladro	Open	80.00	130.00
84-02-462	The Quest L5224G	Lladro	Open	125.00	260.00
83-02-463	Storytime L5229	Lladro	Closed	245.00	360.00
84-02-464	Charlie the Tramp L5233	Lladro	Closed	150.00	675-700.
84-02-465	Artistic Endeavor L5234	Lladro	Closed	225.00	450.00
84-02-466	Ballet Trio L5235G	Lladro	Open	785.00	1475.00
84-02-467	Wine Taster L5239G	Lladro	Open	190.00	340.00
84-02-468	Lady from Majorca L5240	Lladro	Closed	120.00	375.00
84-02-469	St. Cristobal L5246	Lladro	Closed	265.00	330.00
84-02-470	Torch Bearer L5251	Lladro	Closed	100.00	300.00
84-02-471	Dancing the Polka L5252G	Lladro	Open	205.00	385.00
84-02-472	Making Paella L5254G	Lladro	Open	215.00	385.00
84-02-473	Folk Dancing L5256	Lladro	Closed	205.00	300.00
85-02-474	Bust of Lady from Elche L5269	Lladro	Closed	432.00	750.00
85-02-475	Racing Motor Cyclist L5270	Lladro	Closed	360.00	700-850.
85-02-476	Gazelle L5271	Lladro	Closed	205.00	400.00
85-02-477	Biking in the Country L5272	Lladro	Closed	295.00	775-825.
85-02-478	Wedding Day L5274G	Lladro	Open	240.00	395.00
85-02-479	Sailor Serenades His Girl L5276	Lladro	Closed	315.00	475.00
85-02-480	Pierrot with Puppy L5277G	Lladro	Open	95.00	155.00
85-02-481	Pierrot with Puppy and Ball L5278G	Lladro	Open	95.00	155.00
85-02-482	Pierrot with Concertina L5279G	Lladro	Open	95.00	155.00
85-02-483	Hiker L5280	Lladro	Closed	195.00	250.00
85-02-484	Nativity Scene "Haute Relief" L5281	Lladro	Closed	210.00	450.00
85-02-485	Over the Threshold L5282G	Lladro	Open	150.00	265.00
85-02-486	Socialite of the Twenties L5283G	Lladro	Open	175.00	330.00
85-02-487	Glorious Spring L5284G	Lladro	Open	355.00	630.00
85-02-488	Summer on the Farm L5285G	Lladro	Open	235.00	420.00
85-02-489	Fall Clean-up L5286G	Lladro	Open	295.00	525.00
85-02-490	Winter Frost L5287G	Lladro	Open	270.00	495.00
85-02-491	Love in Bloom L5292G	Lladro	Open	225.00	395.00
85-02-492	Mother and Child and Lamb L5299	Lladro	Closed	180.00	425.00
85-02-493	Medieval Courtship L5300	Lladro	Closed	735.00	850.00
85-02-494	Waiting to Tee Off L5301G	Lladro	Open	145.00	270.00
85-02-495	Playing with Ducks at the Pond L5303	Lladro	Closed	425.00	700.00
85-02-496	Children at Play L5304	Lladro	Closed	220.00	550.00
85-02-497	A Visit with Granny L5305G	Lladro	Open	275.00	490.00
85-02-498	Young Street Musicians L5306	Lladro	Closed	300.00	750-875.
85-02-499	Wistful Centaur Girl L5319	Lladro	Closed	157.00	225.00
85-02-500	Demure Centaur Girl L5320	Lladro	Closed	157.00	300.00
85-02-501	Parisian Lady L5321G	Lladro	Open	192.50	310.00
85-02-502	Viennese Lady L5322G	Lladro	Open	160.00	285.00
85-02-503	Milanese Lady L5323G	Lladro	Open	180.00	325.00
85-02-504	English Lady L5324G	Lladro	Open	225.00	390.00
85-02-505	Ice Cream L5325G	Lladro	Open	380.00	625.00
85-02-506	The Tailor L5326	Lladro	Closed	335.00	450.00
85-02-507	Nippon Lady L5327G	Lladro	Open	325.00	520.00
85-02-508	Lady Equestrian L5328	Lladro	Closed	160.00	375.00
85-02-509	Gentleman Equestrian L5329	Lladro	Closed	160.00	325.00
85-02-510	Concert Violinist L5330	Lladro	Closed	220.00	400.00
85-02-511	"La Giaconda" L5337	Lladro	Closed	350.00	450.00
86-02-512	A Stitch in Time L5344G	Lladro	Open	425.00	715.00
86-02-513	A New Hat L5345	Lladro	Closed	200.00	445.00
86-02-514	Nature Girl L5346	Lladro	Closed	450.00	900.00
86-02-515	Bedtime L5347G	Lladro	Open	300.00	520.00
86-02-516	On Guard L5350	Lladro	Closed	50.00	100.00
86-02-517	Woe is Me L5351	Lladro	Closed	45.00	70.00
86-02-518	Hindu Children L5352G	Lladro	Open	250.00	390.00
86-02-519	Eskimo Riders L5353G/M	Lladro	Open	150.00	240.00
86-02-520	A Ride in the Country L5354G	Lladro	Open	225.00	395.00
86-02-521	Consideration L5355	Lladro	Closed	100.00	225.00
86-02-522	Wolf Hound L5356	Lladro	Closed	45.00	55.00
86-02-523	Oration L5357G	Lladro	Open	170.00	265.00
86-02-524	Little Sculptor L5358	Lladro	Closed	160.00	300.00
86-02-525	El Greco L5359	Lladro	Closed	300.00	675.00
86-02-526	Sewing Circle L5360	Lladro	Closed	600.00	1000.00
86-02-527	Try This One L5361G	Lladro	Open	225.00	365.00
86-02-528	Still Life L5363G	Lladro	Open	180.00	350.00
86-02-529	Litter of Fun L5364G	Lladro	Open	275.00	445.00
86-02-530	Sunday in the Park L5365G	Lladro	Open	375.00	595.00
86-02-531	Can Can L5370	Lladro	Closed	700.00	1400.00
86-02-532	Family Roots L5371G	Lladro	Open	575.00	895.00
86-02-533	Lolita L5372G	Lladro	Open	120.00	190.00
86-02-534	Carmencita L5373G	Lladro	Open	120.00	190.00
86-02-535	Pepita L5374G	Lladro	Open	120.00	190.00
86-02-536	Teresita L5375G	Lladro	Open	120.00	190.00
86-02-537	This One's Mine L5376G	Lladro	Open	300.00	495.00
86-02-538	A Touch of Class L5377G	Lladro	Open	475.00	785.00
86-02-539	Time for Reflection L5378G	Lladro	Open	425.00	710.00
86-02-540	Children's Games L5379	Lladro	Open	325.00	480.00
86-02-541	Sweet Harvest L5380	Lladro	Closed	450.00	700-750.
86-02-542	Serenade L5381	Lladro	Closed	450.00	625.00
86-02-543	Lovers Serenade L5382	Lladro	Closed	350.00	600.00
86-02-544	Petite Maiden L5383	Lladro	Closed	110.00	150.00
86-02-545	Petite Pair L5384	Lladro	Closed	225.00	375.00
86-02-546	Scarecrow & the Lady L5385G	Lladro	Open	350.00	595.00
86-02-547	St. Vincent L5387	Lladro	Closed	190.00	350.00
86-02-548	Sidewalk Serenade L5388	Lladro	Closed	750.00	1300.00
86-02-549	Deep in Thought L5389	Lladro	Closed	170.00	225.00
86-02-550	Spanish Dancer L5390	Lladro	Closed	170.00	275.00
86-02-551	A Time to Rest L5391	Lladro	Closed	170.00	375.00
86-02-552	Balancing Act L5392	Lladro	Closed	35.00	50.00
86-02-553	Curiosity L5393	Lladro	Closed	25.00	40.00
86-02-554	Poor Puppy L5394	Lladro	Closed	25.00	40.00
86-02-555	Valencian Boy L5395G	Lladro	Closed	200.00	325.00
86-02-556	The Puppet Painter L5396G	Lladro	Open	500.00	825.00
86-02-557	The Poet L5397	Lladro	Closed	425.00	550.00
86-02-558	At the Ball L5398G	Lladro	Closed	375.00	620.00
87-02-559	Time To Rest L5399G	Lladro	Open	175.00	280.00
87-02-560	The Wanderer L5400G	Lladro	Open	150.00	235.00
87-02-561	My Best Friend L5401G	Lladro	Open	150.00	235.00
87-02-562	Desert Tour L5402	Lladro	Closed	950.00	1050.00
87-02-563	The Drummer Boy L5403	Lladro	Closed	225.00	320-550.
87-02-564	Cadet Captain L5404	Lladro	Closed	175.00	325.00
87-02-565	The Flag Bearer L5405	Lladro	Closed	200.00	400.00
87-02-566	The Bugler L5406	Lladro	Closed	175.00	300-400.
87-02-567	At Attention L5407	Lladro	Closed	175.00	325.00
87-02-568	Sunday Stroll L5408	Lladro	Closed	250.00	450.00
87-02-569	Courting Time L5409	Lladro	Closed	425.00	550.00
87-02-570	Pilar L5410	Lladro	Closed	200.00	325.00
87-02-571	Teresa L5411	Lladro	Closed	225.00	330-350.
87-02-572	Isabel L5412	Lladro	Closed	225.00	350.00
87-02-573	Mexican Dancers L5415G	Lladro	Open	800.00	1100.00
87-02-574	In the Garden L5416G	Lladro	Open	200.00	310.00
87-02-575	Artist's Model L5417	Lladro	Closed	425.00	475.00
87-02-576	Short Eared Owl L5418	Lladro	Closed	200.00	225.00
87-02-577	Great Gray Owl L5419	Lladro	Closed	190.00	195-225.
87-02-578	Horned Owl L5420	Lladro	Closed	150.00	180.00
87-02-579	Barn Owl L5421	Lladro	Closed	120.00	145.00
87-02-580	Hawk Owl L5422	Lladro	Closed	120.00	145.00
87-02-581	Intermezzo L5424	Lladro	Closed	325.00	500.00
87-02-582	Studying in the Park L5425G/M	Lladro	Closed	675.00	950.00
87-02-583	One, Two, Three L5426G	Lladro	Open	240.00	350.00
87-02-584	Saint Nicholas L5427G	Lladro	Closed	425.00	635.00
87-02-585	Feeding the Pigeons L5428	Lladro	Closed	490.00	700.00
87-02-586	Happy Birthday L5429G	Lladro	Open	100.00	155.00
87-02-587	Music Time L5430	Lladro	Closed	500.00	610.00
87-02-588	Midwife L5431	Lladro	Closed	175.00	400.00
87-02-589	Monkey L5432	Lladro	Closed	60.00	100-150.
87-02-590	Kangaroo L5433	Lladro	Closed	65.00	150.00
87-02-591	Polar Bear L5434G	Lladro	Open	65.00	95.00
87-02-592	Cougar L5435	Lladro	Closed	65.00	150.00
87-02-593	Lion L5436	Lladro	Closed	50.00	150.00
87-02-594	Rhino L5437	Lladro	Closed	50.00	150.00
87-02-595	Elephant L5438	Lladro	Closed	50.00	100-150.
87-02-596	The Bride L5439G	Lladro	Open	250.00	375.00
87-02-597	Poetry of Love L5442G	Lladro	Open	500.00	785.00
87-02-598	Sleepy Trio L5443G	Lladro	Open	190.00	290.00
87-02-599	Will You Marry Me? L5447G	Lladro	Open	750.00	1200.00
87-02-600	Naptime L5448G/M	Lladro	Open	135.00	220.00
87-02-601	Goodnight L5449	Lladro	Open	225.00	340.00
87-02-602	I Hope She Does L5450G	Lladro	Open	190.00	300.00
89-02-603	Puppy Dog Tails L5539	Lladro	Open	1200.00	1300.00
89-02-604	Melancholy L5542	Lladro	Open	375.00	375.00
89-02-605	"Hello Flowers" L5543	Lladro	Open	385.00	420.00
89-02-606	Pretty Posies L5548	Lladro	Open	425.00	460.00
89-02-607	My New Pet L5549G	Lladro	Open	150.00	340.00
89-02-608	"Let's Make Up" L5555G	Lladro	Open	215.00	260.00
89-02-609	Fine Melody L5585G	Lladro	Open	225.00	280.00
89-02-610	Sad Note L5586G	Lladro	Open	185.00	260.00
89-02-612	Wedding Cake L5587G	Lladro	Open	595.00	725.00
89-02-612	Playful Romp L5594G	Lladro	Open	215.00	260.00
89-02-613	Joy in a Basket L5595G	Lladro	Open	215.00	260.00
89-02-614	A Gift of Love L5596G	Lladro	Open	400.00	495.00
89-02-615	Bride's Maid L5598G	Lladro	Open	150.00	175.00
89-02-616	The Blues L5600G	Lladro	Open	265.00	325.00
89-02-617	Baby Doll L5608G	Lladro	Open	150.00	175.00
89-02-618	Star Struck L5610G	Lladro	Open	335.00	400.00
89-02-619	Sad Clown L5611G	Lladro	Open	335.00	400.00
89-02-620	Reflecting L5612G	Lladro	Open	335.00	400.00
90-02-621	Cat Nap L5640 G	Lladro	Open	125.00	140.00
90-02-622	The King's Guard L5642 G	Lladro	Open	950.00	1050.00
90-02-623	Cathy L5643G	Lladro	Open	200.00	225.00
90-02-624	Susan L5644 G	Lladro	Open	190.00	210.00
90-02-625	Elizabeth L5645 G	Lladro	Open	190.00	210.00
90-02-626	Cindy L5646 G	Lladro	Open	190.00	210.00
90-02-627	Sara L5647 G	Lladro	Open	200.00	220.00
90-02-628	Courtney L5648 G	Lladro	Open	200.00	220.00
90-02-629	Nothing To Do L5649 G	Lladro	Open	190.00	210.00
90-02-630	Anticipation L5650 G	Lladro	Open	300.00	325.00
90-02-631	Musical Muse L5651 G	Lladro	Open	375.00	420.00
90-02-632	Venetian Carnival L5658 G	Lladro	Open	500.00	555.00
90-02-633	Barnyard Scene L5659 G	Llsdro	Open	200.00	225.00
90-02-634	Sunning In Ipanema L5660 G	Lladro	Open	370.00	400.00
90-02-635	Traveling Artist L5661 G	Lladro	Open	250.00	275.00
90-02-636	May Dance L5662 G	Lladro	Open	170.00	185.00
90-02-637	Spring Dance L5663 G	Lladro	Open	170.00	185.00
90-02-638	Giddy Up L5664 G	Lladro	Open	190.00	220.00
90-02-639	Hang On! L5665 G	Lladro	Open	225.00	250.00
90-02-640	Trino At The Beach L5666 G	Lladro	Open	390.00	440.00

Company Number	Name	Series Artist	Edition Limit	Issue Price	Quote
90-02-641	Valencian Harvest L5668 G	Lladro	Open	175.00	195.00
90-02-642	Valencian FLowers L5669 G	Lladro	Open	370.00	400.00
90-02-643	Valencian Beauty L5670 G	Lladro	Open	175.00	195.00
90-02-644	Little Dutch Gardener L5671 G	Lladro	Open	400.00	450.00
90-02-645	Hi There! L5672 G	Lladro	Open	450.00	495.00
90-02-646	A Quiet Moment L5673 G	Lladro	Open	450.00	495.00
90-02-647	A Fawn And A Friend L5674 G	Lladro	Open	450.00	495.00
90-02-648	Tee Time L5675 G	Lladro	Open	280.00	300.00
90-02-649	Wandering Minstrel L5676 G	Lladro	Open	270.00	295.00
90-02-650	Twilight Years L5677 G	Lladro	Open	370.00	400.00
90-02-651	I Feel Pretty L5678 G	Lladro	Open	190.00	220.00
90-02-652	In No Hurry L5679 G	Lladro	Open	550.00	615.00
90-02-653	Traveling In Style L5680 G	Lladro	Open	425.00	480.00
90-02-654	On The Road L5681 G	Lladro	Closed	320.00	345.00
90-02-655	Breezy Afternoon L5682 G/M	Lladro	Open	180.00	195.00
90-02-656	Beautiful Burro L5683 G	Lladro	Open	280.00	310.00
90-02-657	Barnyard Reflections L5684 G	Lladro	Open	460.00	510.00
90-02-658	Promenade L5685 G	Lladro	Open	275.00	310.00
90-02-659	On The Avenue L5686 G	Lladro	Open	275.00	310.00
90-02-660	Afternoon Stroll L5687 G	Lladro	Open	275.00	310.00
90-02-661	Dog's Best Friend L5688 G	Lladro	Open	250.00	280.00
90-02-662	Can I Help? L5689 G	Lladro	Open	250.00	280.00
90-02-663	Marshland Mates L5691 G	Lladro	Open	950.00	1150.00
90-02-664	Street Harmonies L5692 G	Lladro	Open	3200.00	3600.00
90-02-665	Circus Serenade L5694 G	Lladro	Open	300.00	340.00
90-02-666	Concertina L5695 G	Lladro	Open	300.00	340.00
90-02-667	Mandolin Serenade L5696 G	Lladro	Open	300.00	340.00
90-02-668	Over The Clouds L5697 G	Lladro	Open	275.00	300.00
90-02-669	Don't Look Down L5698 G	Lladro	Open	330.00	370.00
90-02-670	Sitting Pretty L5699 G	Lladro	Open	300.00	330.00
90-02-671	Southern Charm L5700 G	Lladro	Open	675.00	995.00
90-02-672	Just A Little Kiss L5701 G	Lladro	Open	320.00	355.00
90-02-673	Back To School L5702 G	Lladro	Open	350.00	385.00
90-02-674	Behave! L5703 G	Lladro	Open	230.00	255.00
90-02-675	Swan Song L5704 G	Lladro	Open	350.00	390.00
90-02-676	The Swan And The Princess L5705 G	Lladro	Open	350.00	390.00
90-02-677	We Can't Play L5706 G	Lladro	Open	200.00	225.00
90-02-678	After School L5707G	Lladro	Open	280.00	300.00
90-02-679	My First Class L5708 G	Lladro	Open	280.00	300.00
90-02-680	Between Classes L5709 G	Lladro	Open	280.00	300.00
90-02-681	Fantasy Friend L5710 G	Lladro	Open	420.00	470.00
90-02-682	A Christmas Wish L5711 G	Lladro	Open	350.00	390.00
90-02-683	Sleepy Kitten L5712 G	Lladro	Open	110.00	125.00
90-02-684	The Snow Man L5713 G	Lladro	Open	300.00	340.00
90-02-685	First Ballet L5714 G	Lladro	Open	370.00	400.00
90-02-686	Mommy, it's Cold!L5715G	Lladro	Open	360.00	395.00
90-02-687	Land of The Giants L5716 G	Lladro	Open	275.00	300.00
90-02-688	Rock A Bye Baby L5717 G	Lladro	Open	300.00	340.00
90-02-689	Sharing Secrets L5720 G	Lladro	Open	290.00	320.00
90-02-690	Once Upon A Time L5721 G	Lladro	Open	550.00	595.00
90-02-691	Follow Me L5722 G	Lladro	Open	140.00	155.00
90-02-692	Heavenly Chimes L5723 G	Lladro	Open	100.00	115.00
90-02-693	Angelic Voice L5724 G	Lladro	Open	125.00	140.00
90-02-694	Making A Wish L5725 G	Lladro	Open	125.00	140.00
90-02-695	Sweep Away The Clouds L5726 G	Lladro	Open	125.00	140.00
90-02-696	Angel Care L5727 G	Lladro	Open	190.00	200.00
90-02-697	Heavenly Dreamer L5728 G	Lladro	Open	100.00	115.00
91-02-698	Carousel Charm L5731G	Lladro	Open	1700.00	1785.00
91-02-699	Carousel Canter L5732G	Lladro	Open	1700.00	1785.00
91-02-700	Horticulturist L5733G	Lladro	Open	450.00	470.00
91-02-701	Pilgrim Couple L5734G	Lladro	Open	490.00	500.00
91-02-702	Big Sister L5735G	Lladro	Open	650.00	675.00
91-02-703	Puppet Show L5736G	Lladro	Open	280.00	295.00
91-02-704	Little Prince L5737G	Lladro	Open	295.00	300.00
91-02-705	Best Foot Forward L5738G	Lladro	Open	280.00	290.00
91-02-706	Lap Full Of Love L5739G	Lladro	Open	275.00	285.00
91-02-707	Alice In Wonderland L5740G	Lladro	Open	440.00	460.00
91-02-708	Dancing Class L5741G	Lladro	Open	340.00	350.00
91-02-709	Bridal Portrait L5742G	Lladro	Open	480.00	495.00
91-02-710	Don't Forget Me L5743G	Lladro	Open	150.00	155.00
91-02-711	Bull & Donkey L5744G	Lladro	Open	250.00	260.00
91-02-712	Baby Jesus L5745G	Lladro	Open	170.00	175.00
91-02-713	St. Joseph L5746G	Lladro	Open	350.00	365.00
91-02-714	Mary L5747G	Lladro	Open	275.00	285.00
91-02-715	Shepherd Girl L5748G	Lladro	Open	150.00	155.00
91-02-716	Shepherd Boy L5749G	Lladro	Open	225.00	235.00
91-02-717	Little Lamb L5750G	Lladro	Open	40.00	40.00
91-02-718	Walk With Father L5751G	Lladro	Open	375.00	390.00
91-02-719	Little Virgin L5752G	Lladro	Open	295.00	310.00
91-02-720	Hold Her Still L5753G	Lladro	Open	650.00	680.00
91-02-721	Singapore Dancers L5754G	Lladro	Open	950.00	995.00
91-02-722	Claudette L5755G	Lladro	Open	265.00	275.00
91-02-723	Ashley L5756G	Lladro	Open	265.00	275.00
91-02-724	Beautiful Tresses L5757G	Lladro	Open	725.00	760.00
91-02-725	Sunday Best L5758G	Lladro	Open	725.00	760.00
91-02-726	Presto! L5759G	Lladro	Open	275.00	285.00
91-02-727	Interrupted Nap L5760G	Lladro	Open	325.00	340.00
91-02-728	Out For A Romp L5761G	Lladro	Open	375.00	390.00
91-02-729	Checking The Time L5762G	Lladro	Open	560.00	585.00
91-02-730	Musical Partners L5763G	Lladro	Open	625.00	650.00
91-02-731	Seeds Of Laughter L5764G	Lladro	Open	525.00	550.00
91-02-732	Hats Off To Fun L5765G	Lladro	Open	475.00	495.00
91-02-733	Charming Duet L5766G	Lladro	Open	575.00	595.00
91-02-734	First Sampler L5767G	Lladro	Open	625.00	650.00
91-02-735	Academy Days L5768G	Lladro	Open	280.00	295.00
91-02-736	Faithful Steed L5769G	Lladro	Open	370.00	385.00
91-02-737	Out For A Spin L5770G	Lladro	Open	390.00	400.00
91-02-738	The Magic Of Laughter L5771G	Lladro	Open	950.00	980.00
91-02-739	Little Dreamers L5772G/M	Lladro	Open	230.00	235.00
91-02-740	Graceful Offering L5773G	Lladro	Open	850.00	885.00
91-02-741	Nature's Gifts L5774G	Lladro	Open	900.00	940.00
91-02-742	Gift Of Beauty L5775G	Lladro	Open	850.00	889.00
91-02-743	Lover's Paradise L5779G	Lladro	Open	2250.00	2350.00
91-02-744	Walking The Fields L5780G	Lladro	Open	725.00	755.00
91-02-745	Not Too Close L5781G	Lladro	Open	365.00	380.00
91-02-746	My Chores L5782G	Lladro	Open	325.00	335.00
91-02-747	Special Delivery L5783G	Lladro	Open	525.00	545.00
91-02-748	A Cradle Of Kittens L5784G	Lladro	Open	360.00	375.00
91-02-749	Ocean Beauty L5785G	Lladro	Open	625.00	650.00
91-02-750	Story Hour L5786G	Lladro	Open	550.00	570.00
91-02-751	Sophisticate L5787G	Lladro	Open	185.00	195.00
91-02-752	Talk Of The Town L5788G	Lladro	Open	185.00	195.00
91-02-754	The Flirt L5789G	Lladro	Open	185.00	195.00

Company Number	Name	Series Artist	Edition Limit	Issue Price	Quote
91-02-755	Carefree L5790G	Lladro	Open	300.00	315.00
91-02-756	Fairy Godmother L5791G	Lladro	Open	375.00	390.00
91-02-757	Reverent Moment L5792G	Lladro	Open	295.00	305.00
91-02-758	Precocious Ballerina L5793G	Lladro	Open	575.00	595.00
91-02-759	Precious Cargo L5794G	Lladro	Open	460.00	480.00
91-02-760	Floral Getaway L5795G	Lladro	Open	625.00	650.00
91-02-761	Holy Night L5796G	Lladro	Open	330.00	345.00
91-02-762	Come Out And Play L5797G	Lladro	Open	275.00	285.00
91-02-763	Milkmaid L5798G	Lladro	Open	450.00	470.00
91-02-764	Shall We Dance? L5799G	Lladro	Open	600.00	625.00
91-02-765	Elegant Promenade L5802G	Lladro	Open	775.00	795.00
91-02-766	Playing Tag L5804G	Lladro	Open	170.00	180.00
91-02-767	Tumbling L5805G/M	Lladro	Open	130.00	135.00
91-02-768	Tickling L5806G/M	Lladro	Open	130.00	135.00
91-02-769	My Puppies L5807G	Lladro	Open	325.00	340.00
91-02-770	Musically Inclined L5810G	Lladro	Open	235.00	240.00
91-02-771	Littlest Clown L5811G	Lladro	Open	225.00	235.00
91-02-772	Tired Friend L5812G	Lladro	Open	225.00	235.00
91-02-773	Having A Ball L5813G	Lladro	Open	225.00	235.00
91-02-774	Curtain Call L5814G/M	Lladro	Open	490.00	495.00
91-02-775	In Full Relave L5815G/M	Lladro	Open	490.00	495.00
91-02-776	Prima Ballerina L5816G/M	Lladro	Open	490.00	495.00
91-02-777	Backstage Preparation L5817G/M	Lladro	Open	490.00	495.00
91-02-778	On Her Toes L5818G/M	Lladro	Open	490.00	495.00
91-02-779	Allegory Of Liberty L5819G	Lladro	Open	1950.00	2000.00
91-02-780	Dance Of Love L5820G	Lladro	Open	575.00	595.00
91-02-781	Minstrel's Love L5821G	Lladro	Open	525.00	550.00
91-02-782	Little Unicorn L5826G/M	Lladro	Open	275.00	285.00
91-02-783	I've Got It L5827G	Lladro	Open	170.00	175.00
91-02-784	Next At Bat L5828G	Lladro	Open	170.00	175.00
91-02-785	Jazz Horn L5832G	Lladro	Open	295.00	295.00
91-02-786	Jazz Sax L5833G	Lladro	Open	295.00	295.00
91-02-787	Jazz Bass L5834G	Lladro	Open	395.00	395.00
91-02-788	I Do L5835G	Lladro	Open	165.00	170.00
91-02-789	Sharing Sweets L5836G	Lladro	Open	220.00	235.00
91-02-790	Sing With Me L5837G	Lladro	Open	240.00	240.00
91-02-791	On The Move L5838G	Lladro	Open	340.00	350.00
92-02-792	A Quiet Afternoon L5843G	Lladro	Open	1050.00	1050.00
92-02-793	Flirtatious Jester L5844G	Lladro	Open	890.00	890.00
92-02-794	Dressing The Baby L5845G	Lladro	Open	295.00	295.00
92-02-795	All Tuckered Out L5846G/M	Lladro	Open	220.00	220.00
92-02-796	The Loving Family L5848G	Lladro	Open	950.00	950.00
92-02-797	Inspiring Muse L5850G	Lladro	Open	1200.00	1200.00
92-02-798	Feathered Fantasy L5851G	Lladro	Open	1200.00	1200.00
92-02-799	Easter Bonnets L5852G	Lladro	Open	265.00	265.00
92-02-800	Floral Admiration L5853G	Lladro	Open	690.00	690.00
92-02-801	Floral Fantasy L5854G	Lladro	Open	690.00	690.00
92-02-802	Afternoon Jaunt L5855G	Lladro	Open	420.00	420.00
92-02-803	Grand Entrance L5857G	Lladro	Open	265.00	265.00
92-02-804	Waiting to Dance L5858G	Lladro	Open	295.00	295.00
92-02-805	At The Ball L5859G	Lladro	Open	295.00	295.00
92-02-806	Fairy Garland L5860G	Lladro	Open	630.00	630.00
92-02-807	Fairy Flowers L5861G	Lladro	Open	630.00	630.00
92-02-808	Fragrant Bouquet L5862G	Lladro	Open	350.00	350.00
92-02-809	Dressing For The Ballet L5865G	Lladro	Open	395.00	395.00
92-02-810	Final Touches L5866G	Lladro	Open	395.00	395.00
92-02-811	Serene Valenciana L5867G	Lladro	Open	365.00	365.00
92-02-812	Loving Valenciana L5868G	Lladro	Open	365.00	365.00
92-02-813	Fallas Queen L5869G	Lladro	Open	420.00	420.00
92-02-814	Modern Mother L5873G	Lladro	Open	325.00	325.00
92-02-815	Off We Go L5874G	Lladro	Open	365.00	365.00
92-02-816	Guest Of Honor L5877G	Lladro	Open	195.00	195.00
92-02-817	Sister's Pride L5878G	Lladro	Open	595.00	595.00
92-02-818	Shot On Goal L5879G	Lladro	Open	1100.00	1100.00
92-02-819	Playful Unicorn L5880G/M	Lladro	Open	295.00	295.00
92-02-820	Mischievous Mouse L5881G	Lladro	Open	285.00	285.00
92-02-821	Restful Mouse L5882G	Lladro	Open	285.00	285.00
92-02-822	Loving Mouse L5883G	Lladro	Open	285.00	285.00
92-02-823	From This Day Forward L5885G	Lladro	Open	265.00	265.00
92-02-824	Hippity Hop L5886G	Lladro	Open	95.00	95.00
92-02-825	Washing Up L5887G	Lladro	Open	95.00	95.00
92-02-826	That Tickles L5888G	Lladro	Open	95.00	95.00
92-02-827	Snack Time L5889G	Lladro	Open	95.00	95.00
92-02-828	The Aviator L5891G	Lladro	Open	375.00	375.00
92-02-829	Circus Magic L5892G	Lladro	Open	470.00	470.00
92-02-830	Friendship In Bloom L5893G	Lladro	Open	650.00	650.00
92-02-831	Bouquet of Blossoms L5895G	Lladro	Open	295.00	295.00
92-02-832	The Loaves & Fishes L5896G	Lladro	Open	695.00	695.00
92-02-833	Trimming The Tree L5897G	Lladro	Open	900.00	900.00
92-02-834	Spring Splendor L5898G	Lladro	Open	440.00	440.00
92-02-835	Just One More L5899G	Lladro	Open	450.00	450.00
92-02-836	Sleep Tight L5900G	Lladro	Open	450.00	450.00
92-02-837	Surprise L5901G	Lladro	Open	325.00	325.00
92-02-838	Easter Bunnies L5902G	Lladro	Open	240.00	240.00
92-02-839	Down The Aisle L5903G	Lladro	Open	295.00	295.00
92-02-840	Sleeping Bunny L5904G	Lladro	Open	75.00	75.00
92-02-841	Attentive Bunny L5905G	Lladro	Open	75.00	75.00
92-02-842	Preening Bunny L5906G	Lladro	Open	75.00	75.00
92-02-843	Sitting Bunny L5907G	Lladro	Open	75.00	75.00
92-02-844	Just A Little More L5908G	Lladro	Open	370.00	370.00
92-02-845	All Dressed Up L5909G	Lladro	Open	440.00	440.00
92-02-846	Making A Wish L5910G	Lladro	Open	790.00	790.00
92-02-847	Swans Take Flight L5912G	Lladro	Open	2850.00	2850.00
92-02-848	Swan Ballet L5920G	Lladro	Open	210.00	210.00
92-02-849	Take Your Medicine L5921G	Lladro	Open	360.00	360.00
92-02-850	Jazz Clarinet L5928G	Lladro	Open	295.00	295.00
92-02-851	Jazz Drums L5929G	Lladro	Open	595.00	595.00
92-02-852	Jazz Duo L5930G	Lladro	Open	795.00	795.00
92-02-853	Garden Song L7618G	Lladro	Open	295.00	295.00
Lladro		**Limited Edition**			
71-03-001	Hamlet LL 1144	Lladro	Closed	250.00	2500.00
71-03-002	Othello and Desdemona LL 1145	Lladro	Closed	275.00	2500-3300.
71-03-003	Antique Auto LL1146	Lladro	Closed	1000.00	16000.00
73-03-004	Sea Birds LL1174	Lladro	Closed	600.00	2750.00
74-03-005	Floral LL1184	Lladro	Closed	400.00	2200.00
74-03-006	Floral LL1185	Lladro	Closed	475.00	1800.00
74-03-007	Floral LL1186	Lladro	Closed	575.00	2200.00
73-03-008	Eagles LL1189	Lladro	Closed	900.00	3200.00
73-03-009	Sea Birds with Nest LL1194	Lladro	Closed	600.00	2750.00
73-03-010	Turkey Group LL1196	Lladro	Closed	650.00	1800.00
73-03-011	Peace LL1202	Lladro	Closed	550.00	7500.00
73-03-012	Eagle Owl LL1223	Lladro	Closed	450.00	1650.00

Number	Name	Artist	Edition Limit	Issue Price	Quote
73-03-013	Hansom Carriage LL1225	Lladro	Closed	1250.00	10-12000
74-03-014	Hunting Scene LL1238	Lladro	Closed	800.00	3000.00
74-03-015	Turtle Doves LL1240	Lladro	Closed	500.00	2300-2500.
74-03-016	The Forest LL1243	Lladro	Closed	1250.00	3300.00
74-03-017	Soccer Players LL1266	Lladro	Closed	2000.00	7500.00
75-03-018	Man From LaMancha LL1269	Lladro	Closed	700.00	5000.00
83-03-019	Queen Elizabeth II LL 1275	Lladro	Closed	3650.00	4600.00
75-03-020	Judge LL1281	Lladro	Closed	325.00	1400.00
74-03-021	The Hunt LL1308	Lladro	Closed	4750.00	6900.00
77-03-022	Ducks at Pond LL1317	Lladro	Closed	4250.00	6900.00
77-03-023	Impossible Dream LL1318	Lladro	Closed	2400.00	5000.00
77-03-024	Comforting Baby LL1329	Lladro	Closed	700.00	2000.00
77-03-025	Mountain Country Lady LL1330	Lladro	Closed	900.00	1850.00
77-03-026	My Baby LL1331	Lladro	Closed	550.00	2000.00
83-03-027	Flight of Gazelles LL1352	Lladro	Closed	2450.00	3100.00
79-03-028	Car in Trouble LL1375	Lladro	Closed	3000.00	8250.00
83-03-029	Fearful Flight LL1377	Lladro	750	7000.00	13500.00
84-03-030	Henry VIII LL 1384	Lladro	1,200	650.00	940.00
82-03-031	Venus and Cupid LL1392	Lladro	Closed	1100.00	2800.00
82-03-032	First Date LL1393	Lladro	1,500	3800.00	5600.00
84-03-033	Columbus LL 1432	Lladro	Closed	575.00	1100-1500.
84-03-034	Venetian Serenade LL 1433	Lladro	Closed	2600.00	3750.00
85-03-035	Festival in Valencia LL1457	Lladro	3,000	1475.00	2250.00
85-03-036	Camelot LL1458	Lladro	3,000	1000.00	1550.00
85-03-037	Napoleon Planning Battle LL 1459	Lladro	1,500	875.00	1350.00
85-03-038	Youthful Beauty LL1461	Lladro	5,000	800.00	1150.00
85-03-039	Flock of Birds LL1462	Lladro	1,500	1125.00	1650.00
85-03-040	Classic Spring LL1465	Lladro	Closed	650.00	1050-1100.
85-03-041	Classic Fall LL1466	Lladro	Closed	650.00	1000.00
85-03-042	Valencian Couple on Horse LL1472	Lladro	3,000	1175.00	1450.00
85-03-043	Coach XVIII Century LL1485	Lladro	500	14000.00	24000.00
86-03-044	The New World LL 1486	Lladro	4,000	700.00	1300.00
XX-03-045	Fantasia LL1487	Lladro	5,000	1500.00	2550.00
86-03-046	Floral Offering LL1490	Lladro	3,000	2500.00	4250.00
86-03-047	Oriental Music LL1491	Lladro	5,000	1350.00	2300.00
86-03-048	Three Sisters LL1492	Lladro	3,000	1850.00	3100.00
XX-03-049	At the Stroke of Twelve LL1493	Lladro	1,500	4250.00	7100.00
86-03-050	Hawaiian Festival LL1496	Lladro	4,000	1850.00	3000.00
87-03-051	A Sunday Drive LL1510	Lladro	1,000	2600.00	4950.00
87-03-052	Listen to Don Quixote LL1520	Lladro	750	1800.00	2750.00
87-03-053	A Happy Encounter LL1523	Lladro	1,500	2900.00	4700.00
89-03-054	"Jesus the Rock" LL1615	Lladro	1,000	1175.00	1450.00
91-03-055	Valencian Cruise LL1731	Lladro	1,000	2700.00	2800.00
91-03-056	Venice Vows LL1732	Lladro	1,500	3750.00	3900.00
91-03-057	Liberty Eagle LL1738	Lladro	1,500	1000.00	1050.00
91-03-058	Heavenly Swing LL1739	Lladro	1,000	1900.00	1975.00
91-03-059	Columbus, Two Routes LL1740	Lladro	1,000	1500.00	1575.00
91-03-060	Columbus Reflecting LL1741	Lladro	1,000	1850.00	1900.00
91-03-061	Onward! LL1742	Lladro	1,000	2500.00	2600.00
91-03-062	The Princess And The Unicorn LL1755	Lladro	1,500	1750.00	1800.00
91-03-063	Outing In Seville LL1756	Lladro	500	23000.00	23750.00
92-03-064	Hawaiian Ceremony LL1757	Lladro	1,000	9800.00	9800.00
92-03-065	Circus Time LL1758	Lladro	2,500	9200.00	9200.00
92-03-066	Tea In The Garden LL1759	Lladro	2,000	9500.00	9500.00
73-03-067	Girl with Guitar LL2016	Lladro	Closed	650.00	1800.00
73-03-068	Madonna with Child LL2018	Lladro	Closed	450.00	1650.00
73-03-069	Oriental Man LL2021	Lladro	Closed	500.00	1650.00
73-03-070	Three Graces LL2028	Lladro	Closed	950.00	3500.00
73-03-071	Eve at Tree LL2029	Lladro	Closed	450.00	3000.00
73-03-072	Oriental Horse LL2030	Lladro	Closed	1100.00	3500-5000.
73-03-073	Lyric Muse LL2031	Lladro	Closed	750.00	2100.00
73-03-074	Madonna and Child LL2043	Lladro	Closed	400.00	1500.00
74-03-075	Peasant Woman LL2049	Lladro	Closed	400.00	1300.00
74-03-076	Passionate Dance LL2051	Lladro	Closed	450.00	2750.00
84-03-077	St. Theresa LL2061	Lladro	Closed	775.00	1600.00
82-03-078	Concerto LL2063	Lladro	Closed	1000.00	1235.00
84-03-079	Flying Partridges LL2064	Lladro	Closed	3500.00	4300.00
90-03-080	Invincible LL2188	Lladro	300	1100.00	1250.00
83-03-081	Dawn LL3000	Lladro	300	325.00	525.00
83-03-082	Monks LL3001	Lladro	300	1675.00	2400.00
83-03-083	Waiting LL3002	Lladro	Closed	1550.00	1900.00
83-03-084	Indolence LL3003	Lladro	Closed	1465.00	1800.00
83-03-085	Venus in the Bath LL3005	Lladro	Closed	1175.00	1450.00
90-03-086	Daydreamlng LL3022	Lladro	500	550.00	730.00
90-03-087	After The Bath LL3023	Lladro	Closed	350.00	750.00
90-03-088	Discoveries LL3024	Lladro	100	1500.00	1650.00
91-03-089	Resting Nude LL3025	Lladro	200	650.00	670.00
91-03-090	Unadorned Beauty LL3026	Lladro	200	1700.00	1750.0
84-03-091	Elk LL3501	Lladro	Closed	950.00	1200.00
79-03-092	Nude with Dove LL3503	Lladro	Closed	500.00	1400.00
81-03-093	The Rescue LL3506	Lladro	Closed	3500.00	4450.00
84-03-094	St. Michael LL3515	Lladro	1,500	2200.00	4100.00
83-03-095	Turtledove Nest LL3519	Lladro	1,200	3600.00	5750.00
83-03-096	Turtle Doves LL3520	Lladro	750	6800.00	10900.00
82-03-097	Philippine Folklore LL3522	Lladro	1,500	1450.00	2300.00
83-03-098	Nest of Eagles LL3523	Lladro	300	6900.00	10900.00
82-03-099	Drum Beats LL3524	Lladro	1,500	1875.00	2900.00
81-03-100	Togetherness LL3527	Lladro	Closed	750.00	975.00
81-03-101	Wrestling LL3528	Lladro	Closed	950.00	1125.00
81-03-102	Companionship LL3529	Lladro	Closed	1000.00	1450.00
81-03-103	Anxiety LL3530	Lladro	125	1075.00	1775.00
81-03-104	Victory LL3531	Lladro	Closed	1500.00	1800.00
81-03-105	Plentitude LL3532	Lladro	Closed	1000.00	1375.00
81-03-106	Observer LL3533	Lladro	115	900.00	1575.00
81-03-107	In the Distance LL3534	Lladro	Closed	525.00	1275.00
81-03-108	Slave LL3535	Lladro	Closed	950.00	1150.00
81-03-109	Relaxation LL3536	Lladro	Closed	525.00	1000.00
81-03-110	Dreaming LL3537	Lladro	Closed	950.00	1300.00
81-03-111	Youth LL3538	Lladro	Closed	525.00	1120.00
81-03-112	Dantiness LL3539	Lladro	Closed	1000.00	1400.00
81-03-113	Pose LL3540	Lladro	Closed	1250.00	1450.00
81-03-114	Tranquility LL3541	Lladro	Closed	1000.00	1400.00
81-03-115	Yoga LL3542	Lladro	Closed	650.00	900.00
81-03-116	Demure LL3543	Lladro	Closed	1250.00	1700.00
81-03-117	Reflections LL3544	Lladro	Closed	650.00	975.00
81-03-118	Adoration LL3545	Lladro	Closed	1050.00	1600.00
81-03-119	African Woman LL3546	Lladro	Closed	1300.00	2000.00
81-03-120	Reclining Nude LL3547	Lladro	Closed	650.00	875.00
81-03-121	Serenity LL3548	Lladro	300	925.00	1450.00
81-03-122	Reposing LL3549	Lladro	Closed	425.00	575.00
81-03-123	Boxer LL3550	Lladro	300	850.00	1365.00
81-03-124	Bather LL3551	Lladro	Closed	975.00	1300.00
84-03-125	Blue God LL3552	Lladro	1,500	900.00	1500.00
84-03-126	Fire Bird LL3553	Lladro	1,500	800.00	1250.00
83-03-127	Desert People w/Base LL3555	Lladro	750	1680.00	2975.00
83-03-128	Road to Mandalay LL3556	Lladro	Closed	1390.00	2500.00
83-03-129	Jesus in Tiberias LL3557	Lladro	1,200	2600.00	4300.00
92-03-130	The Reader LL3560	Lladro	200	2650.00	2650.00
86-03-131	Fox Hunt LL3562	Lladro	Closed	5200.00	6275.00
81-03-132	Successful Hunt LL5098	Lladro	1,000	5200.00	7750.00
85-03-133	Napoleon Bonaparte LL 5338	Lladro	5,000	275.00	470.00
85-03-134	Beethoven LL 5339	Lladro	3,000	800.00	1250.00
85-03-135	Thoroughbred Horse LL5340	Lladro	1,000	625.00	985.00
85-03-136	I Have Found Thee, Dulcinea LL5341	Lladro	Closed	1850.00	2000-3000.
85-03-137	Pack of Hunting Dogs LL5342	Lladro	3,000	925.00	1575.00
85-03-138	Love Boat LL5343	Lladro	3,000	825.00	1300.00
86-03-139	Rey De Copas LL5366	Lladro	2,000	325.00	575.00
86-03-140	Rey De Oros LL5367	Lladro	2,000	325.00	575.00
86-03-141	Rey De Espadas LL5368	Lladro	2,000	325.00	575.00
86-03-142	Rey De Bastos LL5369	Lladro	2,000	325.00	575.00
86-03-143	Pastoral Scene LL5386	Lladro	Open	1100.00	2000.00
87-03-144	Inspiration LL5413	Lladro	500	1200.00	1975.00
87-03-145	Carnival Time LL5423	Lladro	1,000	2400.00	3750.00
89-03-146	"Pious" LL5541	Lladro	Closed	1075.00	1500-2000.
89-03-147	Freedom LL5602	Lladro	Closed	875.00	950.00
90-03-148	A Ride In The Park LL5718	Lladro	1,000	3200.00	3675.00
91-03-149	Youth LL5800	Lladro	500	650.00	680.00
91-03-150	Charm LL5801	Lladro	500	650.00	680.00
91-03-151	New World Medallion LL5808	Lladro	5,000	200.00	200.00
92-03-152	The Voyage of Columbus LL5847	Lladro	1,500	1450.00	1450.00
92-03-153	Sorrowful Mother LL5849	Lladro	1,500	1750.00	1750.00
92-03-154	Justice Eagle LL5863	Lladro	1,500	1700.00	1700.00
92-03-155	Maternal Joy LL5864	Lladro	1,500	1600.00	1600.00
92-03-156	Motoring In Style LL5884	Lladro	1,500	3700.00	3700.00
92-03-157	The Way Of The Cross LL5890	Lladro	2,000	975.00	975.00
92-03-158	Presenting Credentials LL5911	Lladro	1,500	19500.00	19500.00
92-03-159	Young Mozart LL5915	Lladro	1,500	500.00	500.00

Lladro — **Lladro Collectors Society**

Number	Name	Artist	Edition Limit	Issue Price	Quote
85-04-001	Little Pals S7600	Lladro	Closed	95.00	2250-4000.
86-04-002	Little Traveler S7602	Lladro	Closed	95.00	1000-1800.
87-04-003	Spring Bouquets S7603	Lladro	Closed	125.00	700-900.
88-04-004	School Days S7604	Lladro	Closed	125.00	400-750.
88-04-005	Flower Song S7607	Lladro	Closed	175.00	550-850.
89-04-006	My Buddy S7609	Lladro	Closed	145.00	250-650.
90-04-007	Can I Play? S7610	Lladro	Closed	150.00	250-600.
91-04-008	Summer Stroll S7611	Lladro	Closed	195.00	195-300.
91-04-009	Picture Perfect S7612	Lladro	Closed	350.00	425-700.
92-04-010	All Aboard S7619	Lladro	Yr.Iss.	165.00	165.00

Lynell Studios — **Rockwell**

Number	Name	Artist	Edition Limit	Issue Price	Quote
81-01-001	Snow Queen	N. Rockwell	10,000	85.00	85.00
81-01-002	Cradle of Love	N. Rockwell	10,000	85.00	85.00
81-01-003	Scotty	N. Rockwell	7,500	125.00	125.00

Seymour Mann, Inc. — **Wizard Of Oz - 40th Anniversary**

Number	Name	Artist	Edition Limit	Issue Price	Quote
79-01-001	Dorothy, Scarecrow, Lion, Tinman	E. Mann	N/A	7.50	45.00
79-01-002	Dorothy, Scarecrow, Lion, Tinman, Musical	E. Mann	N/A	12.50	75.00

Seymour Mann, Inc. — **Christmas In America**

Number	Name	Artist	Edition Limit	Issue Price	Quote
88-02-001	Doctor's Office Lite Up	Nork	Open	27.50	27.50
89-02-002	Santa in Sleigh	E. Mann	Open	25.00	45.00
90-02-003	Cart With People	E. Mann	Open	25.00	35.00
88-02-004	Set Of 3, Capitol, White House, Mt. Vernon	E. Mann	Retrd.	75.00	150.00

Seymour Mann, Inc. — **Christmas Village**

Number	Name	Artist	Edition Limit	Issue Price	Quote
91-03-001	The Fire Station	L. Sciola	Open	60.00	60.00
91-03-002	Curiosity Shop	L. Sciola	Open	45.00	45.00
91-03-003	Scrooge/Marley's Counting House	L. Sciola	Open	45.00	45.00
91-03-004	The Playhouse	L. Sciola	Open	60.00	60.00
91-03-005	Ye Old Gift Shoppe	L. Sciola	Open	50.00	50.00
91-03-006	Emily's Toys	L. Sciola	Open	45.00	45.00
91-03-007	Counsil House	L. Sciola	Open	60.00	60.00
91-03-008	Public Library	L. Sciola	Open	50.00	50.00
91-03-009	On Thin Ice	L. Sciola	Open	30.00	30.00
91-03-010	Away, Away	L. Sciola	Open	30.00	30.00
91-03-011	Story Teller	L. Sciola	Open	20.00	20.00

Seymour Mann, Inc. — **Christmas Collection**

Number	Name	Artist	Edition Limit	Issue Price	Quote
85-04-001	Trumpeting Angel w/Jesus XMAS-527	J. White	Open	40.00	40.00
85-04-002	Virgin w/Christ Musical XMAS-528	J. White	Open	33.50	33.50
86-04-003	Antique Santa Musical XMAS-364	J. White	Open	20.00	20.00
86-04-004	Jumbo Santa/Toys XMAS-38	J. White	Open	45.00	45.00
89-04-005	Cat in Teacup Musical XMAS-600	J. White	Open	30.00	30.00
89-04-006	Cats in Basket XMAS-664	Mann	Open	7.50	7.50
89-04-007	Santa in Sled w/Reindeer CJ-3	Jaimy	Open	25.00	25.00
89-04-008	Santa Musicals CJ-1/4	Jaimy	Open	27.50	27.50
89-04-009	Santa on Horse CJ-33A	Jaimy	Open	33.50	33.50
89-04-010	Santa w/List CJ-23	Jaimy	Open	27.50	27.50
90-04-011	2 Tone Stone Church Lite Up House MER-360	B J. White	Open	35.00	35.00
90-04-012	Antique Shope Lite Up House MER-376	J. White	Open	27.50	27.50
90-04-013	Bakery Lite Up House MER-373	J. White	Open	27.50	27.50
90-04-014	Brick Church Lite Up House MER-360C	J. White	Open	35.00	35.00
90-04-015	Cathedral Lite Up House MER-362	J. White	Open	37.50	37.50
90-04-016	Church Lite Up House MER-310	J. White	Open	27.50	27.50
90-04-017	Church w/Blue Roof Lite Up House MER-360	J. White	Open	35.00	35.00
90-04-018	Deep Gold Church Lite Up House MER-360D	J. White	Open	35.00	35.00
90-04-019	Double Store Lite Up House MER-311	J. White	Open	27.50	27.50
90-04-020	Fire Station Lite Up House XMS-1550C	Mann	Open	25.00	25.00
90-04-021	Grist Mill Lite Up House MER-372	J. White	Open	27.50	27.50
90-04-022	Inn Lite Up House MER-316	J. White	Open	27.50	27.50
90-04-023	Leatherworks Lite Up House MER-371	J. White	Open	27.50	27.50
90-04-024	Library Lite Up House MER-317	J. White	Open	27.50	27.50
90-04-025	Light House Lite Up House MER-370	J. White	Open	27.50	27.50
90-04-026	Mansion Lite Up House MER-319	J. White	Open	27.50	27.50
90-04-027	Mr/Mrs Santa Musical CJ-281	Jaimy	Open	37.50	37.50
90-04-028	New England Church Lite Up House MER-375	J. White	Open	27.50	27.50
90-04-029	New England General Store Lite Up House MER-377	J. White	Open	27.50	27.50
90-04-030	Railroad Station Lite Up House MER-374	J. White	Open	27.50	27.50
90-04-031	Santa on Chimney Musical CJ-212	Jaimy	Open	33.50	33.50
90-04-032	Santa Packing Bag CJ-210	Jaimy	Open	33.50	33.50
90-04-033	School Lite Up House MER-320	J. White	Open	27.50	27.50

Number	Name	Artist	Edition Limit	Issue Price	Quote
90-04-034	Town Hall Lite Up House MER-315	J. White	Open	27.50	27.50
90-04-035	Roly Poly Santas 3 Asst. CJ-253/4/7	Jaimy	Open	17.50	17.50
90-04-036	Bethlehem Lite Up Set 3 CP-59893	J. White	Open	120.00	120.00
90-04-037	Soup Seller Waterball CJ-209	Jaimy	Open	25.00	25.00
91-04-038	Reindeer Barn Lite Up House CJ-421	Jaimy	Open	55.00	55.00
91-04-039	Restaurant Lite Up House MER-354	J. White	Open	27.50	27.50
91-04-040	Toy Store Lite Up House MER-355	J. White	Open	27.50	27.50
Seymour Mann, Inc.		**Dickens Collection**			
89-05-001	Cratchits Lite Up XMS-7000A	J. White	Open	30.00	30.00
89-05-002	Fezziwigs Lite Up XMS-7000C	J. White	Open	30.00	30.00
89-05-003	Gift Shoppe Lite Up XMS-7000D	J. White	Open	30.00	30.00
89-05-004	Scrooge/Marley Lite Up XMS-7000B	J. White	Open	30.00	30.00
90-05-005	Black Swan Inn Lite Up XMS-7000E	J. White	Open	30.00	30.00
90-05-006	Hen Poultry Lite Up XMS-7000H	J. White	Open	30.00	30.00
90-05-007	Tea and Spice Lite Up XMS-7000F	J. White	Open	30.00	30.00
90-05-008	Waite Fish Store Lite Up XMS-7000G	J. White	Open	30.00	30.00
90-05-009	Cratchit/Tiny Tim Musical MER-105	J. White	Open	33.50	33.50
Seymour Mann, Inc.		**Gingerbread Christmas Collection**			
91-06-001	Gingerbread Church Lite Up House CJ403	J. Sauerbrey	Open	65.00	65.00
91-06-002	Gingerbread House Lite Up CJ404	J. Sauerbrey	Open	65.00	65.00
91-06-003	Gingerbread Mansion Lite Up CJ405	J. Sauerbrey	Open	70.00	70.00
91-06-004	Gingerbread Rocking Horse Music CJ460	J. Sauerbrey	Open	33.50	33.50
91-06-005	Gingerbread Swan Musical CJ462	J. Sauerbrey	Open	33.50	33.50
91-06-006	Gingerbread Sweet Shop Lite Up House CJ401	J. Sauerbrey	Open	60.00	60.00
91-06-007	Gingerbread Teddy Bear Music CJ461	J. Sauerbrey	Open	33.50	33.50
91-06-008	Gingerbread Toy Shop Lite Up House CJ402	J. Sauerbrey	Open	60.00	60.00
91-06-009	Gingerbread Village Lite Up House CJ400	J. Sauerbrey	Open	60.00	60.00
Seymour Mann, Inc.		**Victorian Christmas Collection**			
90-07-001	Two Boys w/Snowman CJ-106	Jaimy	Open	12.00	12.00
90-07-002	Toy/Doll House Lite Up MER-314	J. White	Open	27.50	27.50
90-07-003	Victorian House Lite Up House MER-312	J. White	Open	27.50	27.50
90-07-004	Yarn Shop Lite Up House MER-313	J. White	Open	27.50	27.50
91-07-005	Antique Shop Lite Up House MER-353	J. White	Open	27.50	27.50
91-07-006	Beige Church Lite Up House MER-351	J. White	Open	35.00	35.00
91-07-007	Book Store Lite Up House MER-351	J. White	Open	27.50	27.50
91-07-008	Church Lite Up House MER-350	J. White	Open	37.50	37.50
91-07-009	Country Store Lite Up House MER-356	J. White	Open	27.50	27.50
91-07-010	Inn Lite Up House MER-352	J. White	Open	27.50	27.50
91-07-011	Little Match Girl CJ-419	Jaimy	Open	9.00	9.00
Seymour Mann, Inc.		**Cat Musical Figurines**			
85-08-001	Cats Ball Shape MH-303A/G	Kenji	Open	25.00	25.00
86-08-002	Cats w/Ribbon MH-481A/C	Kenji	Open	30.00	30.00
87-08-003	Cat in Garbage Can MH-490	Kenji	Open	35.00	35.00
87-08-004	Cat on Tipped Garbage Can MH-498	Kenji	Open	35.00	35.00
87-08-005	Cat in Rose Teacup MH-600VG	Kenji	Open	30.00	30.00
87-08-006	Cat in Teapot Brown MH-600VGB	Kenji	Open	30.00	30.00
87-08-007	Brown Cat in Teacup MH-600VGB16	Kenji	Open	30.00	30.00
87-08-008	Cat in Teacup MH-600VGG	Kenji	Open	30.00	30.00
87-08-009	Valentine Cat in Teacup MH-600VLT	Kenji	Open	33.50	33.50
87-08-010	Musical Bear MH-602	Kenji	Open	27.50	27.50
87-08-011	Kittens w/Balls of Yarn MH-612	Kenji	Open	30.00	30.00
87-08-012	Cat in Bag MH-614	Kenji	Open	30.00	30.00
87-08-013	Cat in Bag MH-617	Kenji	Open	30.00	30.00
87-08-014	Brown Cat in Bag MH-617B/6	Kenji	Open	30.00	30.00
87-08-015	Valentine Cat in Bag Musical MH-600	Kenji	Open	33.50	33.50
87-08-016	Teapot Cat MH-631	Kenji	Open	30.00	30.00
88-08-017	Cat in Hat Box MH-634	Kenji	Open	35.00	35.00
88-08-018	Cat in Hat MH-634B	Kenji	Open	35.00	35.00
88-08-019	Brown Cat in Hat MH-634B/6	Kenji	Open	35.00	35.00
89-08-020	Cat w/Coffee Cup Musical MH-706	Kenji	Open	35.00	35.00
89-08-021	Cat in Flower MH-709	Kenji	Open	35.00	35.00
89-08-022	Cat w/Swing Musical MH-710	Kenji	Open	35.00	35.00
89-08-023	Cat in Water Can Musical MH-712	Kenji	Open	35.00	35.00
89-08-024	Cat on Basket MH-713	Kenji	Open	35.00	35.00
89-08-025	Cat in Basinet MH-714	Kenji	Open	35.00	35.00
89-08-026	Cat in Basket MH-713B	Kenji	Open	35.00	35.00
89-08-027	Cat in Shoe MH-718	Kenji	Open	30.00	30.00
90-08-028	Cat in Bootie MH-728	Kenji	Open	35.00	35.00
90-08-029	Grey Cat in Bootie MH-728G/6	Kenji	Open	35.00	35.00
89-08-030	Cat in Gift Box Musical MH-732	Kenji	Open	40.00	40.00
90-08-031	Cat Sailor in Rocking Boat MH-734	Kenji	Open	45.00	45.00
90-08-032	Cat Asleep MH-735	Kenji	Open	37.50	37.50
90-08-033	Cat on Gift Box Music MH-740	Kenji	Open	40.00	40.00
90-08-034	Cat w/Bow on Pink Pillow MH-741P	Kenji	Open	33.50	33.50
90-08-035	Kitten Trio in Carriage MH-742	Kenji	Open	37.50	37.50
90-08-036	Cat Calico in Easy Chair MH-743VG	Kenji	Open	27.50	27.50
90-08-037	Cats Graduation MH-745	Kenji	Open	27.50	27.50
90-08-038	Cat in Dress MH-751VG	Kenji	Open	37.50	37.50
91-08-039	Brown Cat in Bag	Kenji	Open	30.00	30.00
91-08-040	Brown Cat in Hat	Kenji	Open	35.00	35.00
91-08-041	Brown Cat in Teacup	Kenji	Open	30.00	30.00
91-08-042	Cat in Bag	Kenji	Open	30.00	30.00
91-08-043	Cat in Bag	Kenji	Open	30.00	30.00
91-08-044	Cat in Bootie	Kenji	Open	35.00	35.00
91-08-045	Cat in Garbage Can	Kenji	Open	35.00	35.00
91-08-046	Cat in Hat	Kenji	Open	35.00	35.00
91-08-047	Cat in Hat Box	Kenji	Open	35.00	35.00
91-08-048	Cat in Rose Teacup	Kenji	Open	30.00	30.00
91-08-049	Cat in Teacup	Kenji	Open	30.00	30.00
91-08-050	Cat in Teapot Brown	Kenji	Open	30.00	30.00
91-08-051	Cat on Tipped Garbage Can	Kenji	Open	35.00	35.00
91-08-052	Cats Ball Shape	Kenji	Open	25.00	25.00
91-08-053	Cats w/Ribbon	Kenji	Open	30.00	30.00
91-08-054	Grey Cat in Bootie	Kenji	Open	35.00	35.00
91-08-055	Kittens w/Balls of Yarn	Kenji	Open	30.00	30.00
91-08-056	Musical Bear	Kenji	Open	27.50	27.50
91-08-057	Teapot Cat	Kenji	Open	30.00	30.00
91-08-058	Cat in Basket MH-768	Kenji	Open	35.00	35.00
91-08-059	Cat With Bow on Pink Pillow MH-741P	Kenji	Open	33.50	33.50
91-08-060	Family Cat MH-770	Kenji	Open	35.00	35.00
91-08-061	Kitten Picking Tulips MH-756	Kenji	Open	40.00	40.00
91-08-062	Revolving Cat with Butterfly MH-759	Kenji	Open	40.00	40.00
Maruri USA		**Birds of Prey**			
81-01-001	Screech Owl	W. Gaither	300	960.00	960.00
81-01-002	American Bald Eagle I	W. Gaither	Closed	165.00	1150-1750.
82-01-003	American Bald Eagle II	W. Gaither	Closed	245.00	1000-2750.
83-01-004	American Bald Eagle III	W. Gaither	Closed	445.00	600-1750.

Number	Name	Artist	Edition Limit	Issue Price	Quote
84-01-005	American Bald Eagle IV	W. Gaither	Closed	360.00	500-1250.
86-01-006	American Bald Eagle V	W. Gaither	Closed	325.00	500-1250.
Maruri USA		**North American Waterfowl I**			
81-02-001	Blue Winged Teal	W. Gaither	200	980.00	980.00
81-02-002	Wood Duck, decoy	W. Gaither	950	480.00	480.00
81-02-003	Flying Wood Ducks	W. Gaither	Closed	880.00	880.00
81-02-004	Canvasback Ducks	W. Gaither	300	780.00	780.00
81-02-005	Mallard Drake	W. Gaither	Closed	2380.00	2380.00
Maruri USA		**North American Waterfowl II**			
81-03-001	Mallard Ducks Pair	W. Gaither	1,500	225.00	225.00
82-03-002	Goldeneye Ducks Pair	W. Gaither	Closed	225.00	225.00
82-03-003	Bufflehead Ducks Pair	W. Gaither	1,500	225.00	225.00
82-03-004	Widgeon, male	W. Gaither	Closed	225.00	225.00
82-03-005	Widgeon, female	W. Gaither	Closed	225.00	225.00
82-03-006	Pintail Ducks Pair	W. Gaither	1,500	225.00	225.00
83-03-007	Loon	W. Gaither	Closed	245.00	245.00
Maruri USA		**North American Songbirds**			
82-05-001	Cardinal, male	W. Gaither	Closed	95.00	95.00
82-05-002	Chickadee	W. Gaither	Closed	95.00	95.00
82-05-003	Bluebird	W. Gaither	Closed	95.00	95.00
82-05-004	Mockingbird	W. Gaither	Closed	95.00	95.00
82-05-005	Carolina Wren	W. Gaither	Closed	95.00	95.00
83-05-006	Cardinal, female	W. Gaither	Closed	95.00	95.00
83-05-007	Robin	W. Gaither	Closed	95.00	95.00
Maruri USA		**North American Game Birds**			
81-06-001	Canadian Geese, pair	W. Gaither	Closed	2000.00	2000.00
81-06-002	Eastern Wild Turkey	W. Gaither	Closed	300.00	300.00
82-06-003	Ruffed Grouse	W. Gaither	Closed	1745.00	1745.00
83-06-004	Bobtail Quail, male	W. Gaither	Closed	375.00	375.00
83-06-005	Bobtail Quail, female	W. Gaither	Closed	375.00	375.00
83-06-006	Wild Turkey Hen with Chicks	W. Gaither	Closed	300.00	300.00
Maruri USA		**Baby Animals**			
81-07-001	African Lion Cubs	W. Gaither	1,500	195.00	195.00
81-07-002	Wolf Cubs	W. Gaither	Closed	195.00	195.00
81-07-003	Black Bear Cubs	W. Gaither	Closed	195.00	195.00
Maruri USA		**Upland Birds**			
81-08-001	Mourning Doves	W. Gaither	Closed	780.00	780.00
Maruri USA		**Americana**			
81-09-001	Grizzley Bear and Indian	W. Gaither	Closed	650.00	650.00
82-09-002	Sioux Brave and Bison	W. Gaither	Closed	985.00	985.00
Maruri USA		**Stump Animals**			
82-10-001	Red Fox	W. Gaither	Closed	175.00	175.00
83-10-002	Raccoon	W. Gaither	Closed	175.00	175.00
83-10-003	Owl	W. Gaither	Closed	175.00	175.00
84-10-004	Gray Squirrel	W. Gaither	1,200	175.00	175.00
84-10-005	Chipmunk	W. Gaither	Closed	175.00	175.00
84-10-006	Bobcat	W. Gaither	Closed	175.00	175.00
Maruri USA		**Shore Birds**			
84-11-001	Pelican	W. Gaither	Closed	260.00	260.00
84-11-002	Sand Piper	W. Gaither	Closed	285.00	285.00
Maruri USA		**North American Game Animals**			
84-12-001	White Tail Deer	W. Gaither	950	285.00	285.00
Maruri USA		**African Safari Animals**			
83-13-001	African Elephant	W. Gaither	Closed	3500.00	3500.00
83-13-002	Southern White Rhino	W. Gaither	150	3200.00	3200.00
83-13-003	Cape Buffalo	W. Gaither	Closed	2200.00	2200.00
83-13-004	Black Maned Lion	W. Gaither	Closed	1450.00	1450.00
83-13-005	Southern Leopard	W. Gaither	300	1450.00	1450.00
83-13-006	Southern Greater Kudu	W. Gaither	Closed	1800.00	1800.00
83-13-007	Southern Impala	W. Gaither	Closed	1200.00	1200.00
81-13-008	Nyala	W. Gaither	300	1450.00	1450.00
83-13-009	Sable	W. Gaither	Closed	1200.00	1200.00
83-13-010	Grant's Zebras, pair	W. Gaither	500	1200.00	1200.00
Maruri USA		**Special Commissions**			
81-14-001	White Bengal Tiger	W. Gaither	240	340.00	340.00
82-14-002	Cheetah	W. Gaither	Closed	995.00	995.00
83-14-003	Orange Bengal Tiger	W. Gaither	240	340.00	340.00
Maruri USA		**Signature Collection**			
85-15-001	American Bald Eagle	W. Gaither	Closed	60.00	60.00
85-15-002	Canada Goose	W. Gaither	Closed	60.00	60.00
85-15-003	Hawk	W. Gaither	Closed	60.00	60.00
85-15-004	Snow Goose	W. Gaither	Closed	60.00	60.00
85-15-005	Pintail Duck	W. Gaither	Closed	60.00	60.00
85-15-006	Swallow	W. Gaither	Closed	60.00	60.00
Maruri USA		**Legendary Flowers of the Orient**			
85-16-001	Iris	Ito	15,000	45.00	55.00
85-16-002	Lotus	Ito	15,000	45.00	45.00
85-16-003	Chinese Peony	Ito	15,000	45.00	55.00
85-16-004	Lily	Ito	15,000	45.00	55.00
85-16-005	Chrysanthemum	Ito	15,000	45.00	55.00
85-16-006	Cherry Blossom	Ito	15,000	45.00	55.00
85-16-007	Orchid	Ito	15,000	45.00	55.00
85-16-008	Wisteria	Ito	15,000	45.00	55.00
Maruri USA		**American Eagle Gallery**			
85-17-001	E-8501	Maruri Studios	Closed	45.00	50.00
85-17-002	E-8502	Maruri Studios	Open	55.00	65.00
85-17-003	E-8503	Maruri Studios	Open	60.00	65.00
85-17-004	E-8504	Maruri Studios	Open	65.00	75.00
85-17-005	E-8505	Maruri Studios	Closed	65.00	70.00
85-17-006	E-8506	Maruri Studios	Open	75.00	90.00
85-17-007	E-8507	Maruri Studios	Open	75.00	90.00
85-17-008	E-8508	Maruri Studios	Closed	75.00	85.00
85-17-009	E-8509	Maruri Studios	Closed	85.00	85.00
85-17-010	E-8510	Maruri Studios	Open	85.00	95.00
85-17-011	E-8511	Maruri Studios	Closed	85.00	95.00
85-17-012	E-8512	Maruri Studios	Open	295.00	325.00
87-17-013	E-8721	Maruri Studios	Open	40.00	50.00
87-17-014	E-8722	Maruri Studios	Open	45.00	55.00

Company / Number	Name	Series / Artist	Edition Limit	Issue Price	Quote
87-17-015	E-8723	Maruri Studios	Closed	55.00	60.00
87-17-016	E-8724	Maruri Studios	Open	175.00	195.00
89-17-017	E-8931	Maruri Studios	Open	55.00	60.00
89-17-018	E-8932	Maruri Studios	Open	75.00	80.00
89-17-019	E-8933	Maruri Studios	Open	95.00	95.00
89-17-020	E-8934	Maruri Studios	Open	135.00	140.00
89-17-021	E-8935	Maruri Studios	Open	175.00	185.00
89-17-022	E-8936	Maruri Studios	Open	185.00	195.00
91-17-023	E-9141 Eagle Landing	Maruri Studios	Open	60.00	60.00
91-17-024	E-9142 Eagle w/ Totem Pole	Maruri Studios	Open	75.00	75.00
91-17-025	E-9143 Pair in Flight	Maruri Studios	Open	95.00	95.00
91-17-026	E-9144 Eagle w/Salmon	Maruri Studios	Open	110.00	110.00
91-17-027	E-9145 Eagle w/Snow	Maruri Studios	Open	135.00	135.00
91-17-028	E-9146 Eagle w/Babies	Maruri Studios	Open	145.00	145.00
Maruri USA		**Wings of Love Doves**			
87-18-001	D-8701 Single Dove	Maruri Studios	Open	45.00	55.00
87-18-002	D-8702 Double Dove	Maruri Studios	Open	55.00	65.00
87-18-003	D-8703 Single Dove	Maruri Studios	Open	65.00	70.00
87-18-004	D-8704 Double Dove	Maruri Studios	Open	75.00	85.00
87-18-005	D-8705 Single Dove	Maruri Studios	Open	95.00	95.00
87-18-006	D-8706 Double Dove	Maruri Studios	Open	175.00	195.00
90-18-007	D-9021 Double Dove	Maruri Studios	Open	50.00	55.00
90-18-008	D-9022 Double Dove	Maruri Studios	Open	75.00	75.00
90-18-009	D-9023 Double Dove	Maruri Studios	Open	115.00	120.00
90-18-010	D-9024 Double Dove	Maruri Studios	Open	150.00	160.00
Maruri USA		**Majestic Owls of the Night**			
87-19-001	Burrowing Owl	D. Littleton	15,000	55.00	55.00
88-19-002	Barred Owl	D. Littleton	15,000	55.00	55.00
88-19-003	Elf Owl	D. Littleton	15,000	55.00	55.00
Maruri USA		**Studio Collection**			
90-20-001	Majestlc Eagles-MS100	Maruri Studios	Closed	350.00	350.00
91-20-002	Delicate Motion-MS200	Maruri Studios	3,500	325.00	325.00
92-20-003	Imperial Panda-MS300	Maruri Studios	3,500	350.00	350.00
Maruri USA		**Polar Expedition**			
90-21-001	Baby Emperor Penguin-P-9001	Maruri Studios	Open	45.00	50.00
90-21-002	Baby Arctic Fox-P-9002	Maruri Studios	Open	50.00	55.00
90-21-003	Polar Bear Cub Sliding-P-9003	Maruri Studios	Open	50.00	55.00
90-21-004	Polar Bear Cubs Playing-P-9004	Maruri Studios	Open	60.00	65.00
90-21-005	Baby Harp Seals-P-9005	Maruri Studios	Open	65.00	70.00
90-21-006	Mother & Baby Emperor Penguins -P-9006	Maruri Studios	Open	80.00	85.00
90-21-007	Mother & Baby Harp Seals-P-9007	Maruri Studios	Open	90.00	95.00
90-21-008	Mother & Baby Polar Bears-P-9008	Maruri Studios	Open	125.00	130.00
90-21-009	Polar Expedition Sign-PES-001	Maruri Studios	Open	18.00	18.00
92-21-010	Baby Harp Seal-P-9221	Maruri Studios	Open	55.00	55.00
92-21-011	Emperor Penguins-P-9222	Maruri Studios	Open	60.00	60.00
92-21-012	Arctic Fox Cubs Playing-P-9223	Maruri Studios	Open	65.00	65.00
92-21-013	Polar Bear Family-P-9224	Maruri Studios	Open	90.00	90.00
Maruri USA		**Eyes Of The Night**			
90-22-001	Single Screech Owl-0-8801	Maruri Studios	Open	50.00	55.00
90-22-002	Single Snowy Owl-0-8802	Maruri Studios	Open	50.00	55.00
90-22-003	Single Great Horned Owl-0-8803	Maruri Studios	Open	60.00	65.00
90-22-004	Single Tawny Owl-0-8804	Maruri Studios	Open	60.00	65.00
90-22-005	Single Snowy Owl-0-8805	Maruri Studios	Open	80.00	85.00
90-22-006	Single Screech Owl-0-8806	Maruri Studios	Open	90.00	95.00
90-22-007	Double Barn Owl 0-8807	Maruri Studios	Open	125.00	130.00
90-22-008	Single Great Horned Owl-0-8808	Mauurl Studios	Open	145.00	150.00
90-22-009	Double Snowy Owl-0-8809	Maruri Studios	Open	245.00	250.00
Maruri USA		**Songbirds Of Beauty**			
91-23-001	Chickadee With Roses SB-9101	Maruri Studios	Open	85.00	85.00
91-23-002	Goldfinch With Hawthorne SB-9102	Maruri Studios	Open	85.00	85.00
91-23-003	Cardinal With Cherry Blossom SB-9103	Maruri Studios	Open	85.00	85.00
91-23-004	Robin With Lilies SB-9104	Maruri Studios	Open	85.00	85.00
91-23-005	Bluebird With Apple Blossom SB-9105	Maruri Studios	Open	85.00	85.00
91-23-006	Robin & Baby With Azalea SB-9106	Maruri Studios	Open	115.00	115.00
91-23-007	Dbl. Bluebird With Peach Blossom SB-9107	Maruri Studios	Open	145.00	145.00
91-23-008	Dbl. Cardinal With Dogwood SB-9108	Maruri Studios	Open	145.00	145.00
Maruri USA		**Hummingbirds**			
91-24-001	Rufous w/Trumpet Creeper H-8901	Maruri Studios	Open	70.00	75.00
91-24-002	Anna's w/Lily H-8905	Maruri Studios	Open	160.00	160.00
91-24-003	Allew's w/Hibiscus H-8906	Maruri Studios	Open	195.00	195.00
91-24-004	Ruby-Throated w/Azalea H-8911	Maruri Studios	Open	75.00	75.00
91-24-005	White-Eared w/Morning Glory H-8912	Maruri Studios	Open	75.00	75.00
91-24-006	Violet-Crowned w/Gentian H-8913	Maruri Studios	Open	75.00	75.00
91-24-007	Ruby-Throated w/Orchid H-8914	Maruri Studios	Open	150.00	150.00
Maruri USA		**Graceful Reflections**			
91-25-001	Single Mute Swan SW-9151	Maruri Studios	Open	85.00	85.00
91-25-002	Mute Swan w/Baby SW-9152	Maruri Studios	Open	95.00	95.00
91-25-003	Pair-Mute Swan SW-9153	Maruri Studios	Open	145.00	145.00
91-25-004	Pair-Mute Swan SW-9154	Maruri Studios	Open	195.00	195.00
Maruri USA		**Precious Panda**			
92-26-001	Snack Time PP-9201	Maruri Studios	Open	60.00	60.00
92-26-002	Lazy Lunch PP-9202	Maruri Studios	Open	60.00	60.00
92-26-003	Tug Of War PP-9203	Maruri Studios	Open	70.00	70.00
92-26-004	Mother's Cuddle-PP-9204	Maruri Studios	Open	120.00	120.00
June McKenna Collectibles, Inc.		**Limited Edition**			
83-01-001	Father Christmas	J. McKenna	Closed	90.00	2300-6000.
84-01-002	Old Saint Nick	J. McKenna	Closed	100.00	1500-3000.
85-01-003	Woodland	J. McKenna	Closed	140.00	1600-3000.
86-01-004	Victorian	J. McKenna	Closed	150.00	1000-1500.
87-01-005	Christmas Eve	J. McKenna	Closed	170.00	1600.00
87-01-006	Kris Kringle	J. McKenna	Closed	350.00	500-1300.
88-01-007	Bringing Home Christmas	J. McKenna	Closed	170.00	475-1300.
88-01-008	Remembrance of Christmas Past	J. McKenna	4,000	400.00	450.00
89-01-009	Seasons Greetings	J. McKenna	Closed	200.00	225-300.
89-01-010	Santa's Wardrobe	J. McKenna	Closed	750.00	750.00
90-01-011	Wilderness	J. McKenna	Closed	200.00	200.00
90-01-012	Night Before Christmas	J. McKenna	Closed	750.00	750.00
91-01-013	Coming to Town	J. McKenna	4,000	220.00	220.00
91-01-014	Hot Air Balloon	J. McKenna	1,500	800.00	800.00
91-01-015	Bedtime Stories	J. McKenna	2,000	500.00	500.00
92-01-016	Christmas Gathering	J. McKenna	4,000	220.00	220.00

Company / Number	Name	Series / Artist	Edition Limit	Issue Price	Quote
June McKenna Collectibles, Inc.		**Registered Edition**			
86-02-001	Colonial	J. McKenna	Closed	150.00	350-450.
87-02-002	White Christmas	J. McKenna	Closed	170.00	2000-3000.
88-02-003	Jolly Ole St.. Nick	J. McKenna	Closed	170.00	250-350.
89-02-004	Traditional	J. McKenna	Closed	180.00	250-300.
90-02-005	Toy Maker	J. McKenna	Open	200.00	200-250.
91-02-006	Checking His List	J. McKenna	Open	230.00	230.00
92-02-007	Forty Winks	J. McKenna	Open	250.00	250.00
June McKenna Collectibles, Inc.		**Special Limited Edition**			
89-03-001	Santa & His Magic Sleigh	J. McKenna	4,000	280.00	280.00
89-03-002	Last Gentle Nudge	J. McKenna	Closed	280.00	N/A
90-03-003	Up On The Rooftop	J. McKenna	Closed	280.00	N/A
90-03-004	Santa's Reindeer	J. McKenna	1,500	400.00	400.00
90-03-005	Christmas Dreams	J. McKenna	Closed	280.00	280.00
92-03-006	Santa's Arrival	J. McKenna	2,000	300.00	300.00
June McKenna Collectibles, Inc.		**June McKenna Figurines**			
84-04-001	Tree Topper	J. McKenna	Closed	70.00	225.00
85-04-002	Soldier	J. McKenna	Closed	40.00	150-200.
85-04-003	Father Times - 3D	J. McKenna	Closed	40.00	N/A
86-04-004	Male Angel	J. McKenna	Closed	44.00	1000-2000.
86-04-005	Little St. Nick	J. McKenna	Closed	50.00	75-125.00
87-04-006	Patriotic Santa	J. McKenna	Closed	50.00	100-150.
87-04-007	Name Plaque	J. McKenna	Open	50.00	N/A
87-04-008	Country Rag Boy	J. McKenna	Closed	40.00	N/A
87-04-009	Country Rag Girl	J. McKenna	Closed	40.00	N/A
88-04-010	Mrs. Santa	J. McKenna	Closed	50.00	100-125.
88-04-011	Mr. Santa - 3D	J. McKenna	Closed	44.00	N/A
89-04-012	16th Century Santa - 3D	J. McKenna	Closed	60.00	N/A
89-04-013	17th Century Santa - 3D	J. McKenna	Closed	70.00	N/A
89-04-014	Jolly Ole Santa - 3D	J. McKenna	Closed	44.00	N/A
90-04-015	Noel - 3D	J. McKenna	Open	50.00	50.00
92-04-016	Taking A Break	J. McKenna	Open	60.00	60.00
92-04-017	Christmas Santa	J. McKenna	Open	60.00	60.00
92-04-018	Choir of Angels	J. McKenna	Open	60.00	60.00
92-04-019	Let It Snow	J. McKenna	Open	60.00	60.00
June McKenna Collectibles, Inc.		**Carolers**			
85-05-001	Man Caroler	J. McKenna	Closed	36.00	75.00
85-05-002	Woman Caroler	J. McKenna	Closed	36.00	75.00
85-05-003	Girl Caroler	J. McKenna	Closed	36.00	75.00
85-05-004	Boy Caroler	J. McKenna	Closed	36.00	75.00
91-05-005	Carolers, Man With Girl	J. McKenna	Open	50.00	50.00
91-05-006	Carolers, Woman With Boy	J. McKenna	Open	50.00	50.00
92-05-007	Carolers, Grandparents	J. McKenna	Open	70.00	70.00
June McKenna Collectibles, Inc.		**Limited Edition Flatback**			
88-06-001	Toys of Joy	J. McKenna	Closed	30.00	N/A
88-06-002	Mystical Santa	J. McKenna	Closed	30.00	N/A
89-06-003	Blue Christmas	J. McKenna	Closed	32.00	N/A
89-06-004	Victorian	J. McKenna	Closed	32.00	N/A
90-06-006	Old Time Santa	J. McKenna	10,000	34.00	34.00
90-06-007	Medieval Santa	J. McKenna	10,000	34.00	34.00
91-06-008	Farewell Santa	J. McKenna	10,000	34.00	34.00
91-06-009	Bag of Stars	J. McKenna	10,000	34.00	34.00
92-06-010	Good Tidings	J. McKenna	10,000	34.00	34.00
92-06-011	Deck The Halls	J. McKenna	10,000	34.00	34.00
June McKenna Collectibles, Inc.		**7" Limited Edition**			
88-07-001	Joyful Christmas	J. McKenna	Closed	90.00	N/A
88-07-002	Christmas Memories	J. McKenna	Closed	90.00	N/A
89-07-003	Old Fashioned Santa	J. McKenna	Closed	100.00	N/A
89-07-004	Santa's Bag of Surprises	J. McKenna	Closed	100.00	N/A
90-07-005	Christmas Delight	J. McKenna	7,500	100.00	100.00
90-07-006	Ethnic Santa	J. McKenna	7,500	100.00	100.00
91-07-007	Christmas Bishop	J. McKenna	7,500	110.00	110.00
92-07-008	Christmas Wizard	J. McKenna	7,500	110.00	110.00
June McKenna Collectibles, Inc.		**Nativity Set**			
88-08-001	Nativity - 6 Pieces	J. McKenna	Open	130.00	130.00
89-08-002	Three Wise Men	J. McKenna	Open	60.00	60.00
91-08-003	Sheep With Shepherds - 2 Pieces	J. McKenna	Open	60.00	60.00
June McKenna Collectibles, Inc.		**Black Folk Art**			
85-09-001	Mammie With Kids - 3D	J. McKenna	Closed	90.00	N/A
85-09-002	Kids in a Tub - 3D	J. McKenna	Closed	30.00	60.00
85-09-003	Toaster Cover	J. McKenna	Closed	50.00	N/A
85-09-004	Kissing Cousins - sill sitter	J. McKenna	Closed	36.00	60.00
83-09-005	Black Boy With Watermelon	J. McKenna	Closed	12.00	40.00
83-09-006	Black Girl With Watermelon	J. McKenna	Closed	12.00	40.00
84-09-007	Black Man With Pig	J. McKenna	Closed	13.00	40.00
84-09-008	Black Woman With Broom	J. McKenna	Closed	13.00	40.00
84-09-009	Mammie Cloth Doll	J. McKenna	Closed	90.00	N/A
84-09-010	Remus Cloth Doll	J. McKenna	Closed	90.00	N/A
85-09-011	Watermelon Patch Kids	J. McKenna	Closed	24.00	63.00
85-09-012	Mammie With Spoon	J. McKenna	Closed	13.00	N/A
86-09-013	Black Butler	J. McKenna	Closed	13.00	40.00
87-09-014	Aunt Bertha - 3D	J. McKenna	Closed	36.00	72.00
87-09-015	Uncle Jacob- 3D	J. McKenna	Closed	36.00	72.00
87-09-016	Lil' Willie -3D	J. McKenna	Closed	36.00	72.00
87-09-017	Sweet Prissy -3D	J. McKenna	Closed	36.00	72.00
88-09-018	Renty	J. McKenna	Closed	16.00	40.00
88-09-019	Netty	J. McKenna	Closed	16.00	40.00
89-09-020	Jake	J. McKenna	Closed	16.00	40.00
89-09-021	Delia	J. McKenna	Closed	16.00	40.00
90-09-022	Tasha	J. McKenna	Closed	17.00	40.00
90-09-023	Tyree	J. McKenna	Closed	17.00	40.00
90-09-024	Let's Play Ball -3D	J. McKenna	Open	45.00	N/A
90-09-025	Sunday's Best -3D	J. McKenna	Open	45.00	N/A
92-09-026	Fishing John -3D	J. McKenna	1,000	160.00	N/A
92-09-027	Sweet Sister Sue -3D	J. McKenna	1,000	160.00	N/A
June McKenna Collectibles, Inc.		**Victorian Limited Edition**			
90-10-001	Edward - 3D	J. McKenna	Closed	180.00	450.00
90-10-002	Elizabeth - 3D	J. McKenna	Closed	180.00	450.00
90-10-003	Joseph - 3D	J. McKenna	Closed	50.00	50.00
90-10-004	Victoria - 3D	J. McKenna	Closed	50.00	50.00
Midwest Importers		**Christian Ulbricht Nutcracker Collection**			
86-01-001	Pilgrim Nutcracker, 16 1/2" 03939	C. Ulbricht	Open	145.00	145.00
92-01-002	Father Christmas Nutcracker 70946	C. Ulbricht	Closed	190.00	190.00

Number	Name	Artist	Edition Limit	Issue Price	Quote
Midwest Importers	**Nutcracker Fantasy Nutcrackers**				
91-02-001	Herr Drosselmeyer Nutcracker, 16 1/4" 36568	C. Ulbricht	Open	170.00	170.00
91-02-002	Clara Nutcracker, 11 1/2" 36576	C. Ulbricht	Open	125.00	125.00
91-02-003	Prince Nutcracker, 17" 36659	C. Ulbricht	Open	160.00	160.00
91-02-004	Toy Soldier, 14" 36667	C. Ulbricht	Open	160.00	160.00
91-02-005	Mouse King Nutcracker, 13 1/2" 45105	C. Ulbricht	Open	170.00	170.00
Midwest Importers	**Erzgebirge Nutcracker Collection**				
92-03-001	Christopher Columbus Nutcracker 01529	Midwest Importers	Open	80.00	80.00
84-03-002	Pinocchio Nutcracker 01602	Midwest Importers	Open	60.00	60.00
92-03-003	Victorian Santa Nutcracker 01876	Midwest Importers	Open	130.00	130.00
92-03-004	Pilgrim Nutcracker 01884	Midwest Importers	Open	96.00	96.00
92-03-005	Indian Nutcracker 01959	Midwest Importers	Open	96.00	96.00
92-03-006	Ringmaster Nutcracker 01967	Midwest Importers	Open	135.00	135.00
92-03-007	Cowboy Nutcracker 02981	Midwest Importers	Open	97.00	97.00
92-03-008	Farmer Nutcracker 11099	Midwest Importers	Open	65.00	65.50
92-03-009	Santa with Skis Nutcracker 13053	Midwest Importers	Open	100.00	100.00
91-03-010	Clown Nutcracker 35619	Midwest Importers	Open	115.00	118.00
91-03-011	Nutcracker-Maker Nutcracker 36013	Midwest Importers	Open	62.00	64.50
90-03-012	Elf Nutcracker 41541	Midwest Importers	Open	70.00	73.00
90-03-013	Sea Captain Nutcracker 41575	Midwest Importers	Open	86.00	89.50
90-03-014	Witch Nutcracker 41591	Midwest Importers	Open	75.00	78.00
90-03-015	Windsor Club Nutcracker 41608	Midwest Importers	Open	85.00	86.50
90-03-016	Woodland Santa Nutcracker 41913	Midwest Importers	Open	105.00	109.00
90-03-017	Uncle Sam Nutcracker 42060	Midwest Importers	Open	50.00	61.50
90-03-018	Merlin the Magician Nutcracker 42078	Midwest Importers	Open	67.00	70.00
88-03-019	Santa with Tree & Toys Nutcracker 76663	Midwest Importers	Open	76.00	79.00
88-03-020	Nordic Santa Nutcracker 88725	Midwest Importers	Open	84.00	87.50
89-03-021	Golfer Nutcracker 93253	Midwest Importers	Open	85.00	87.50
89-03-022	Country Santa Nutcracker 93261	Midwest Importers	Open	95.00	98.50
89-03-023	Fisherman Nutcracker 93279	Midwest Importers	Open	90.00	94.00
Midwest Importers	**Erzgebirge Easter Nutcrackers**				
91-09-001	Bunny with Egg Nutcracker 01454	Midwest Importers	Open	77.00	80.00
84-09-002	March Hare Nutcracker 03129	Midwest Importers	Open	77.00	80.00
92-09-003	Bunny Painter Nutcracker 64808	Midwest Importers	Open	77.00	77.00
Midwest Importers	**Erzgebirge "Nutcracker Fantasy" Nutcrackers**				
91-10-001	Clara Nutcracker, 8" 12542	Midwest Importers	Open	77.00	80.00
88-10-002	Her Drosselmeyer Nutcracker, 14 1/2" 75061	Midwest Importers	Open	75.00	78.00
88-10-003	The Prince Nutcracker, 12 3/4" 75079	Midwest Importers	Open	75.00	78.00
88-10-004	The Toy Soldier Nutcracker, 11" 75087	Midwest Importers	Open	70.00	72.00
88-10-005	The Mouse King Nutcracker, 10" 75095	Midwest Importers	Open	60.00	61.00
Midwest Importers	**Wendt and Kuhn Collection**				
79-11-001	Angel Playing Violin 04036	Wendt/Kuhn	Open	34.00	35.00
83-11-002	Angel Percussion Musicians, set/6 04432	Wendt/Kuhn	Open	110.00	115.00
84-11-003	Angels Bearing Toys, set/6 04515	Wendt/Kuhn	Open	97.00	101.00
83-11-004	Angel String Musicians, set/6 04557	Wendt/Kuhn	Open	105.00	109.00
83-11-005	Angel String & Woodwind Musicians, set/6 04656	Wendt/Kuhn	Open	108.00	112.50
83-11-006	Angel Conductor on Stand 04698	Wendt/Kuhn	Open	21.00	21.50
83-11-007	Angel Brass Musicians, set/6 04705	Wendt/Kuhn	Open	92.00	96.00
79-11-008	Angel Trio, set/3 04713	Wendt/Kuhn	Open	140.00	146.00
76-11-009	Santa with Angel 04739	Wendt/Kuhn	Open	50.00	52.00
83-11-010	Margarita Birthday Angels, set/3 04804	Wendt/Kuhn	Open	44.00	46.00
80-11-011	Angel Pulling Wagon 05539	Wendt/Kuhn	Open	43.00	45.00
81-11-012	Angel w/ Tree & Basket 11908 (wasMI#0468)	Wendt/Kuhn	Open	24.00	25.00
81-11-013	Santa w/Angel in Sleigh 11924(wasMI#0414)	Wendt/Kuhn	Open	52.00	54.00
81-11-014	Angels at Cradle, set/4 11932 (wasMI#0554)	Wendt/Kuhn	Open	73.00	76.00
83-11-015	Girl w/Wagon 11966 (was MI#2935)	Wendt/Kuhn	Open	27.00	28.00
79-11-016	Girl w/Scissors 11974 (was MI#2941)	Wendt/Kuhn	Open	25.00	25.00
79-11-017	Girl w/Porridge Bowl 11982 (was MI#2942)	Wendt/Kuhn	Open	29.00	30.00
91-11-018	Girl with Doll 12005	Wendt/Kuhn	Open	31.50	32.50
91-11-019	Boy on Rocking Horse, 2 asst. 12021	Wendt/Kuhn	Open	35.00	36.50
79-11-020	Girl w/Cradle, set/2 12039 (was MI#2801)	Wendt/Kuhn	Open	37.50	39.00
91-11-021	White Angel with Violin 12055	Wendt/Kuhn	Open	25.50	26.50
78-11-022	Madonna w/Child 12071 (was MI#0428)	Wendt/Kuhn	Open	120.00	125.00
91-11-023	Birdhouse 12097	Wendt/Kuhn	Open	22.50	23.00
91-11-024	Flower Children, set/6 12138	Wendt/Kuhn	Open	130.00	135.50
91-11-025	Display Base for Wendt und Kuhn Figures, 12 1/2 x2" 12146	Wendt/Kuhn	Open	32.00	33.50
79-11-026	Pied Piper and Children, set/7 28432	Wendt/Kuhn	Open	120.00	125.00
79-11-027	Bavarian Moving Van 28549	Wendt/Kuhn	Open	133.50	138.50
79-11-028	Magarita Angels, set/6 29381	Wendt/Kuhn	Open	94.00	98.00
76-11-029	Angel with Sled 29406	Wendt/Kuhn	Open	36.50	38.00
80-11-030	Little People Napkin Rings, 6 asst. 35049	Wendt/Kuhn	Open	21.00	21.50
90-11-031	Angel Duet in Celestial Stars 41583	Wendt/Kuhn	Open	60.00	62.50
87-11-032	Child on Skis, 2 asst. 60830	Wendt/Kuhn	Open	28.00	29.00
87-11-033	Child on Sled 60856	Wendt/Kuhn	Open	25.50	26.50
92-11-034	Wendt und Kuhn Display Sign w/ Sitting Angel 75350	Wendt/Kuhn	Open	20.00	20.50
88-11-035	Lucia Parade Figures, set/3 76671	Wendt/Kuhn	Open	75.00	78.00
88-11-036	Children Carrying Lanterns Procession, set/6 76697	Wendt/Kuhn	Open	117.00	122.00
89-11-037	Angel at Piano 94037	Wendt/Kuhn	Open	31.00	32.25
Midwest Importers	**Wendt and Kuhn Figurines Candleholders**				
76-12-001	Angel Candleholder Pair 04721	Wendt/Kuhn	Open	70.00	70.00
91-12-002	Angel with Friend Candleholder 11916	Wendt/Kuhn	Open	33.30	33.50
91-12-003	Small Angel Candleholder Pair 11958	Wendt/Kuhn	Open	60.00	60.00
80-12-004	Large Angel Candleholder Pair 12013 (wasMI#0463)	Wendt/Kuhn	Open	270.00	270.00
86-12-005	Pair of Angels Candleholder 12047(was MI#0410)	Wendt/Kuhn	Open	30.00	30.00
91-12-006	White Angel Candleholder 12063	Wendt/Kuhn	Open	28.00	28.00
87-12-007	Santa Candleholder 60822	Wendt/Kuhn	Open	53.00	53.00
Midwest Importers	**Wendt and Kuhn Collection Music Boxes**				
91-13-001	Angels & Santa Around Tree 12112	Wendt/Kuhn	Open	300.00	300.00
78-13-002	Rotating Angels 'Round Cradle 19118	Wendt/Kuhn	Open	270.00	270.00
78-13-003	Angel at Pipe Organ 19291	Wendt/Kuhn	Open	176.00	176.00
76-13-004	Girl Rocking Cradle 92156 (was MI#1941)	Wendt/Kuhn	Open	180.00	180.00
Midwest Importers	**Belenes Puig Nativity Collection**				
85-14-001	Nativity, set/6: Holy Family, Angel, Animals 6 3/4" 02056	J.P. Llobera	Open	250.00	250.00
85-14-002	Shepherd, set/2 04581	J.P. Llobera	Open	110.00	110.00
85-14-003	Wise Men, set/3 04599	J.P. Llobera	Open	185.00	185.00
86-14-004	Sheep, set/3 04755	J.P. Llobera	Open	28.00	28.00
89-14-005	Wise Man with Gold on Camel 20751	J.P. Llobera	Open	155.00	155.00
89-14-006	Wise Man with Myrrh on Camel 20769	J.P. Llobera	Open	155.00	155.00
89-14-007	Wise Man with Frankincense on Camel 20777	J.P. Llobera	Open	155.00	155.00
89-14-008	Donkey 20826	J.P. Llobera	Open	26.00	26.00
89-14-009	Ox 20834	J.P. Llobera	Open	26.00	26.00
89-14-010	Mother Mary 20842	J.P. Llobera	Open	62.00	62.00
89-14-011	Baby Jesus 20850	J.P. Llobera	Open	62.00	62.00
89-14-012	Joseph 20868	J.P. Llobera	Open	62.00	62.00
89-14-013	Angel 20876	J.P. Llobera	Open	50.00	50.00
89-14-014	Wise Man with Frankincense 20884	J.P. Llobera	Open	66.00	66.00
89-14-015	Wise Man with Gold 20892	J.P. Llobera	Open	66.00	66.00
89-14-016	Wise Man with Myrrh 20909	J.P. Llobera	Open	66.00	66.00
89-14-017	Shepherd with Staff 20917	J.P. Llobera	Open	56.00	56.00
89-14-018	Shepherd Carrying Lamb 20925	J.P. Llobera	Open	56.00	56.00
90-14-019	Resting Camel 40254	J.P. Llobera	Open	115.00	115.00
87-14-020	Shepherd & Angel Scene, set/7 60848	J.P. Llobera	Open	305.00	305.00
88-14-021	Standing Camel 87925	J.P. Llobera	Open	115.00	115.00
Midwest Importers	**Leo R. Smith III Collection**				
91-15-001	Stars and Stripes Santa 17435	L.R. Smith	5,000	190.00	198.00
91-15-002	Woodsman Santa 33100	L.R. Smith	5,000	230.00	240.00
91-15-003	Pilgrim Riding Turkey 33126	L.R. Smith	5,000	230.00	240.00
91-15-004	Milkmaker 35411	L.R. Smith	5,000	170.00	177.00
91-15-005	'Tis a Witching Time 35445	L.R. Smith	Closed	140.00	145.00
91-15-006	Toymaker 35403	L.R. Smith	5,000	120.00	125.00
91-15-007	Cossack Santa 10926	L.R. Smith	5,000	95.00	98.50
91-15-008	Pilgrim Man 33134	L.R. Smith	5,000	78.00	81.00
91-15-009	Pilgrim Lady 33150	L.R. Smith	5,000	78.00	81.00
91-15-010	Fisherman Santa 33118	L.R. Smith	5,000	270.00	280.00
92-15-011	Dreams of Night Buffalo 79998	L.R. Smith	5,000	250.00	250.00
92-15-012	Santa of Peace 73289	L.R. Smith	5,000	250.00	250.00
92-15-013	Great Plains Santa 80490	L.R. Smith	5,000	270.00	270.00
92-15-014	Ms. Liberty 78669	L.R. Smith	5,000	190.00	190.00
92-15-015	Woodland Brave 78677	L.R. Smith	5,000	87.00	87.00
Midwest Importers	**Heritage Santa Collection**				
90-16-001	Scanda Klaus 05365	Midwest Importers	Open	26.50	27.50
90-16-002	Herr Kristmas 05373	Midwest Importers	Open	26.50	27.50
90-16-003	MacNicholas 05381	Midwest Importers	Open	26.50	27.50
90-16-004	Papa Frost 05399	Midwest Importers	Open	26.50	27.50
91-16-005	Father Christmas 17980	Midwest Importers	Open	26.50	27.50
91-16-006	Santa Niccolo 17972	Midwest Importers	Open	26.50	27.50
92-16-007	Santa Nykolai 67729	Midwest Importers	Open	26.50	26.50
92-16-008	Pere Noel 67688	Midwest Importers	Open	26.50	26.50
Midwest Importers	**Heritage Santa Roly-Polys**				
90-17-001	Scanda Klaus Roly-Poly 05282	Midwest Importers	Open	24.00	25.00
90-17-002	Herr Kristmas Roly-Poly 05290	Midwest Importers	Open	24.00	25.00
90-17-003	MacNicholas Roly-Poly 05307	Midwest Importers	Open	24.00	25.00
90-17-004	Papa Frost Roly-Poly 05315	Midwest Importers	Open	24.00	25.00
91-17-005	Father Christmas Roly-Poly 17964	Midwest Importers	Open	24.00	25.00
91-17-006	Santa Niccolo Roly-Poly 17956	Midwest Importers	Open	24.00	25.00
92-17-007	Santa Nykolai Roly-Poly 67696	Midwest Importers	Open	24.00	24.00
92-17-008	Pere Noel Roly-Poly 67711	Midwest Importers	Open	24.00	24.00
Midwest Importers	**Heritage Santa Collection Fabric Mache**				
90-18-001	Scanda Klaus Fabric Mache set 05141	Midwest Importers	Open	160.00	160.00
90-18-002	Herr Kristmas Fabric Mache set 05159	Midwest Importers	Open	160.00	160.00
90-18-003	MacNicholas Fabric Mache set 05167	Midwest Importers	Open	160.00	160.00
90-18-004	Papa Frost Fabric Mache set 05175	Midwest Importers	Open	160.00	160.00
91-18-005	Father Christmas Fabric Mache set 18003	Midwest Importers	Open	160.00	160.00
91-18-006	Santa Niccolo Fabric Mache set 17998	Midwest Importers	Open	160.00	160.00
92-18-007	Santa Nykolai Fabric Mache set 67670	Midwest Importers	Open	160.00	160.00
92-18-008	Pere Noel Fabric Mache set 67662	Midwest Importers	Open	160.00	160.00
Midwest Importers	**Heritage Santa Collection Music Boxes**				
90-19-001	Scanda Klaus Music Box 05323	Midwest Importers	Open	53.00	55.00
90-19-002	Herr Kristmas Music Box 05331	Midwest Importers	Open	53.00	55.00
90-19-003	MacNicholas Music Box 05349	Midwest Importers	Open	53.00	55.00
90-19-004	Papa Frost Music Box 05357	Midwest Importers	Open	53.00	55.00
91-19-005	Father Christmas Music Box 18029	Midwest Importers	Open	53.00	55.00
91-19-006	Santa Niccolo Music Box 18011	Midwest Importers	Open	53.00	55.00
92-19-007	Santa Nykolai Music Box 67901	Midwest Importers	Open	53.00	53.00
92-19-008	Pere Noel Music Box 67894	Midwest Importers	Open	53.00	53.00
Midwest Importers	**Heritage Santa Collection Snowglobes**				
90-20-001	Scanda Klaus Snowglobe 05240	Midwest Importers	Open	40.00	41.50
90-20-002	Herr Kristmas Snowglobe 05258	Midwest Importers	Open	40.00	41.50
90-20-003	MacNicholas Snowglobe 05266	Midwest Importers	Open	40.00	41.50
90-20-004	Papa Frost Snowglobe 05274	Midwest Importers	Open	40.00	41.50
91-20-005	Father Christmas Snowglobe 17948	Midwest Importers	Open	40.00	41.50
91-20-006	Santa Niccolo Snowglobe 17930	Midwest Importers	Open	40.00	41.50
92-20-007	Santa Nykolai Snowglobe 67836	Midwest Importers	Open	40.00	40.00
92-20-008	Pere Noel Snowglobe 67787	Midwest Importers	Open	40.00	40.00
Museum Collections, Inc.	**American Family I**				
79-01-001	Baby's First Step	N. Rockwell	22,500	90.00	220.00
80-01-002	Happy Birthday, Dear Mother	N. Rockwell	22,500	90.00	150.00
80-01-003	Sweet Sixteen	N. Rockwell	22,500	90.00	90.00
80-01-004	First Haircut	N. Rockwell	22,500	90.00	195.00
80-01-005	First Prom	N. Rockwell	22,500	90.00	90.00
80-01-006	Wrapping Christmas Presents	N. Rockwell	22,500	90.00	110.00
80-01-007	The Student	N. Rockwell	22,500	110.00	140.00
80-01-008	Birthday Party	N. Rockwell	22,500	110.00	150.00
80-01-009	Little Mother	N. Rockwell	22,500	110.00	110.00
80-01-010	Washing Our Dog	N. Rockwell	22,500	110.00	110.00
81-01-011	Mother's Little Helpers	N. Rockwell	22,500	110.00	110.00
81-01-012	Bride and Groom	N. Rockwell	22,500	110.00	180.00
Museum Collections, Inc.	**Christmas**				
80-02-001	Checking His List	N. Rockwell	Yr.Iss.	65.00	85.00
81-02-002	Ringing in Good Cheer	N. Rockwell	Yr.Iss.	95.00	95.00
82-02-003	Waiting for Santa	N. Rockwell	Yr.Iss.	95.00	95.00
83-02-004	High Hopes	N. Rockwell	Yr.Iss.	95.00	95.00
84-02-005	Space Age Santa	N. Rockwell	Yr.Iss.	65.00	65.00
Museum Collections, Inc.	**Classic**				
80-03-001	Lighthouse Keeper's Daughter	N. Rockwell	Closed	65.00	65.00
80-03-002	The Cobbler	N. Rockwell	Closed	65.00	85.00
80-03-003	The Toymaker	N. Rockwell	Closed	65.00	85.00
80-03-004	Bedtime	N. Rockwell	Closed	65.00	95.00
80-03-005	Memories	N. Rockwell	Closed	65.00	65.00
80-03-006	For A Good Boy	N. Rockwell	Closed	65.00	75.00
81-03-007	A Dollhouse for Sis	N. Rockwell	Closed	65.00	65.00
81-03-008	Music Master	N. Rockwell	Closed	65.00	65.00
81-03-009	The Music Lesson	N. Rockwell	Closed	65.00	65.00

Number	Name	Artist	Edition Limit	Issue Price	Quote
81-03-010	Puppy Love	N. Rockwell	Closed	65.00	65.00
81-03-011	While The Audience Waits	N. Rockwell	Closed	65.00	65.00
81-03-012	Off to School	N. Rockwell	Closed	65.00	65.00
82-03-013	The Country Doctor	N. Rockwell	Closed	65.00	65.00
82-03-014	Spring Fever	N. Rockwell	Closed	65.00	65.00
82-03-015	Words of Wisdom	N. Rockwell	Closed	65.00	65.00
82-03-016	The Kite Maker	N. Rockwell	Closed	65.00	65.00
82-03-017	Dreams in the Antique Shop	N. Rockwell	Closed	65.00	65.00
83-03-018	Winter Fun	N. Rockwell	Closed	65.00	65.00
83-03-019	A Special Treat	N. Rockwell	Closed	65.00	65.00
83-03-020	High Stepping	N. Rockwell	Closed	65.00	65.00
83-03-021	Bored of Education	N. Rockwell	Closed	65.00	65.00
83-03-022	A Final Touch	N. Rockwell	Closed	65.00	65.00
83-03-023	Braving the Storm	N. Rockwell	Closed	65.00	65.00
84-03-024	Goin' Fishin'	N. Rockwell	Closed	65.00	65.00
84-03-025	The Big Race	N. Rockwell	Closed	65.00	65.00
84-03-026	Saturday's Hero	N. Rockwell	Closed	65.00	65.00
84-03-027	All Wrapped Up	N. Rockwell	Closed	65.00	65.00
Museum Collections, Inc.	**Commemorative**				
81-04-001	Norman Rockwell Display	N. Rockwell	5,000	125.00	150.00
82-04-002	Spirit of America	N. Rockwell	5,000	125.00	125.00
83-04-003	Norman Rockwell, America's Artist	N. Rockwell	5,000	125.00	125.00
84-04-004	Outward Bound	N. Rockwell	5,000	125.00	125.00
85-04-005	Another Masterpiece by Norman Rockwell	N. Rockwell	5,000	125.00	150.00
86-04-006	The Painter and the Pups	N. Rockwell	5,000	125.00	150.00
Novelino	**Classic American Santa**				
90-01-001	St. Nicholas CAS1624	Novelino	9,500	45.00	45.00
90-01-002	Father Christmas CAS1664	Novelino	9,500	40.00	40.00
90-01-003	Wilderness Santa CAS1701	Novelino	9,500	40.00	40.00
90-01-004	Independence War Santa CAS1776	Novelino	9,500	55.00	55.00
90-01-005	Reindeer Santa CAS1821	Novelino	9,500	45.00	45.00
90-01-006	Clement Moore Santa CAS1829	Novelino	9,500	50.00	50.00
90-01-007	T.C. Bogey Santa CAS1840	Novelino	9,500	40.00	40.00
90-01-008	Beacon Santa CAS1060	Novelino	9,500	45.00	45.00
90-01-009	Bell Ringing Santa CAS1912	Novelino	9,500	50.00	50.00
90-01-010	North Pole Santa CAS1928	Novelino	9,500	55.00	55.00
90-01-011	World War II Santa CAS1945	Novelino	9,500	40.00	40.00
90-01-012	Modern Santa CAS1990	Novelino	9,500	55.00	55.00
Novelino	**Pewter Old World Santa Figurines (2 1/2" H)**				
90-02-001	Hand Painted Santa/Bell PT1001	Novelino	9,500	6.00	6.00
90-02-002	Hand Painted Santa/Shldr Bag PT1002	Novelino	9,500	6.00	6.00
90-02-003	Hand Painted Santa/Xmas List PT1003	Novelino	9,500	6.00	6.00
90-02-004	Hand Painted Santa/Tree PT1004	Novelino	9,500	6.00	6.00
90-02-005	Hand Painted Santa/Drum PT1005	Novelino	9,500	6.00	6.00
90-02-006	Hand Painted Santa/Armed Bag PT1006	Novelino	9,500	6.00	6.00
90-02-007	Hand Painted Santa/Babyl PT1007	Novelino	9,500	6.00	6.00
90-02-008	Hand Painted Santa/Wreath PT1008	Novelino	9,500	6.00	6.00
90-02-009	Hand Painted Santa/Toy PT1009	Novelino	9,500	6.00	6.00
90-02-010	Hand Painted Santa/Drum/Horn PT1010	Novelino	9,500	6.00	6.00
Novelino	**Pewter Christmas Collectible Figurines (2 1/2" H)**				
90-03-001	Hand Painted Train PT1011	Novelino	9,500	6.00	6.00
90-03-002	Hand Painted Santa/Sled PT1012	Novelino	9,500	6.00	6.00
90-03-003	Hand Painted Drummer PT1013	Novelino	9,500	6.00	6.00
90-03-004	Hand Painted Unicorn PT1014	Novelino	9,500	6.00	6.00
90-03-005	Hand Painted Church PT1015	Novelino	9,500	6.00	6.00
90-03-006	Hand Painted Teddy Santa PT1016	Novelino	9,500	6.00	6.00
90-03-007	Hand Painted Clown PT1018	Novelino	9,500	6.00	6.00
90-03-008	Hand Painted Christmas Tree PT1019	Novelino	9,500	6.00	6.00
90-03-009	Hand Painted Snowman PT1020	Novelino	9,500	6.00	6.00
Novelino	**Pewter Heavenly Angel Figurines (3" H)**				
90-04-001	Hand Painted Angel/Harp PT1021	Novelino	9,500	9.00	9.00
90-04-002	Hand Painted Angel/Horn PT1022	Novelino	9,500	9.00	9.00
90-04-003	Hand Painted Angel/Guitar PT1023	Novelino	9,500	9.00	9.00
90-04-004	Hand Painted Angel/Flute PT1024	Novelino	9,500	9.00	9.00
90-04-005	Hand Painted Angel/Ribbon PT1025	Novelino	9,500	9.00	9.00
90-04-005	Hand Painted Angel/Book PT1026	Novelino	9,500	9.00	9.00
Novelino	**Pewter Nutcracker Sweet Figurines (3" H)**				
90-05-001	Hand Painted RD/WH Nutcracker PT1041	Novelino	9,500	8.00	8.00
90-05-002	Hand Painted BL/WH Nutcracker PT1042	Novelino	9,500	8.00	8.00
90-05-003	Hand Painted DK BL/RD Nutcracker PT1043	Novelino	9,500	8.00	8.00
90-05-004	Hand Painted DK/LT BL Nutcracker PT1044	Novelino	9,500	8.00	8.00
90-05-005	Hand Painted RD/DK BL Nutcracker PT1045	Novelino	9,500	8.00	8.00
90-05-006	Hand Painted RD/YW Nutcracker PT1046	Novelino	9,500	8.00	8.00
Novelino	**Pewter Santa Clown Figurines (2 1/4" H)**				
90-06-001	Hand Painted Caroling Clown PT1051	Novelino	9,500	13.00	13.00
90-06-002	Hand Painted Beard Being Pulled PT1052	Novelino	9,500	13.00	13.00
90-06-003	Hand Painted "Holy" Bag PT1053	Novelino	9,500	13.00	13.00
Novelino	**William Holden Wildlife Foundation Collection**				
91-07-001	Hippopotamus WHWF001	Novelino	9,500	50.00	50.00
91-07-002	Masai Ostrich WHWF002	Novelino	9,500	55.00	55.00
91-07-003	Colobus Monkey WHWF003	Novelino	9,500	55.00	55.00
91-07-004	Grevy's Zebra WHWF004	Novelino	9,500	60.00	60.00
91-07-005	Crested Crane WHWF005	Novelino	9,500	60.00	60.00
91-07-006	Chimpanzee WHWF006	Novelino	9,500	65.00	65.00
91-07-007	Black-Maned Lion WHWF007	Novelino	9,500	75.00	75.00
91-07-008	Grant's Gazelle WHWF008	Novelino	9,500	75.00	75.00
91-07-009	Spotted Leopard WHWF009	Novelino	9,500	75.00	75.00
91-07-010	Black Rhinocerous WHWF010	Novelino	9,500	80.00	80.00
91-07-011	Reticulated Giraffe WHWF011	Novelino	9,500	85.00	85.00
91-07-012	African Elephant WHWF012	Novelino	9,500	90.00	90.00
91-07-013	Set of 12, 1 of each above WHWF100	Novelino	9,500	825.00	825.00
91-07-014	Bongo Antelope WHWF500	Novelino	2,500	250.00	250.00
Novelino	**William Holden Wildlife Foundation Single Animal Figurines**				
92-08-001	Grevy's Zebra WHF104	Novelino	9,500	39.00	39.00
92-08-002	Spotted Leopard WHF109	Novelino	9,500	39.00	39.00
92-08-003	African Elephant WHF112	Novelino	9,500	45.00	45.00
92-08-004	Black-Maned Lion WHF107	Novelino	9,500	39.00	39.00
92-08-005	Rhinoceros WHF110	Novelino	9,500	45.00	45.00
92-08-006	Reticulated Giraffe WHF111	Novelino	9,500	45.00	45.00
Novelino	**William Holden Wildlife Foundation Pewter Figurines**				
92-09-001	Hippopotamus WHWF5001	Novelino	Open	15.00	15.00
92-09-002	Colobus Monkey WHWF5003	Novelino	Open	15.00	15.00
92-09-003	Grevy's Zebra WHWF5004	Novelino	Open	15.00	15.00
92-09-004	Crested Crane WHWF5005	Novelino	Open	15.00	15.00
92-09-005	Chimpanzee WHWF5006	Novelino	Open	15.00	15.00
92-09-006	Black Maned Lion WHWF 5007	Novelino	Open	15.00	15.00
92-09-007	Spotted Leopard WHWF5009	Novelino	Open	15.00	15.00
92-09-008	African Elephant WHWF5012	Novelino	Open	15.00	15.00
92-09-009	Black Rhinoceros WHWF5010	Novelino	Open	15.00	15.00
92-09-010	Reticulated Giraffe WHWF5011	Novelino	Open	15.00	15.00
Novelino	**William Holden Wildlife Foundation Musical Waterglobes**				
92-10-001	Grevy's Zebra PWG5004	Novelino	Open	40.00	40.00
92-10-002	Chimpanzee PWG5006	Novelino	Open	40.00	40.00
92-10-003	Grant's Gazelle PWG5008	Novelino	Open	40.00	40.00
92-10-004	Spotted Leopard PWG5009	Novelino	Open	40.00	40.00
92-10-005	Reticulated Giraffe PWG5011	Novelino	Open	40.00	40.00
92-10-006	African Elephant PWG5012	Novelino	Open	40.00	40.00
Novelino	**National Wildlife Federation**				
92-11-001	Jaguar NWF102	Novelino	9,500	44.00	44.00
92-11-002	Moose With Calf NWF103	Novelino	9,500	70.00	70.00
92-11-003	Red Fox NWF104	Novelino	9,500	39.00	39.00
92-11-004	Eastern Fox Squirrel NWF105	Novelino	9,500	35.00	35.00
92-11-005	Grizzly Bear With Cub NWF106	Novelino	9,500	70.00	70.00
92-11-006	Big Horn Sheep NWF107	Novelino	9,500	50.00	50.00
92-11-007	Wapati Elk With Fawn NWF108	Novelino	9,500	60.00	60.00
92-11-008	Mountain Lion With Cub NWF109	Novelino	9,500	60.00	60.00
92-11-019	Orca (Killer Whale) NWF110	Novelino	9,500	44.00	44.00
92-11-010	Bison NWF111	Novelino	9,500	44.00	44.00
92-11-011	White Tailed Deer With Fawn NWF112	Novelino	9,500	60.00	60.00
92-11-012	Polar Bear With Cub NWF113	Novelino	9,500	75.00	75.00
Novelino	**My Friend And Me**				
92-12-001	Flower Basket MFM101	Novelino	Open	27.00	27.00
92-12-002	Fishing Buddies MFM102	Novelino	Open	27.00	27.00
92-12-003	Bathtime MFM103	Novelino	Open	27.00	27.00
92-12-004	Summer Stroll MFM104	Novelino	Open	22.00	22.00
92-12-005	Grooming Time MFM105	Novelino	Open	27.00	27.00
92-12-006	Playtime MFM106	Novelino	Open	30.00	30.00
92-12-007	Yarn Balls MFM107	Novelino	Open	30.00	30.00
92-12-008	Dolly Meets Kitty MFM108	Novelino	Open	30.00	30.00
92-12-009	Reading To A Friend MFM109	Novelino	Open	25.00	25.00
92-12-010	Buggy Ride MFM110	Novelino	Open	22.00	22.00
92-12-011	Walking To School MFM111	Novelino	Open	22.00	22.00
92-12-012	Castle Building MFM112	Novelino	Open	25.00	25.00
Pemberton & Oakes	**Zolan's Children**				
82-01-001	Erik and the Dandelion	D. Zolan	17,000	48.00	90.00
83-01-002	Sabina in the Grass	D. Zolan	6,800	48.00	130.00
84-01-003	Winter Angel	D. Zolan	8,000	28.00	150.00
85-01-004	Tender Moment	D. Zolan	10,000	29.00	60.00
PenDelfin	**Nursery Rhymes**				
56-01-001	Wee Willie Winkie	J. Heap	Retrd.	Unkn.	N/A
56-01-002	Little Bo Peep	J. Heap	Retrd.	Unkn.	N/A
56-01-003	Miss Muffet	J. Heap	Retrd.	Unkn.	N/A
56-01-004	Mary Mary Quite Contrary	J. Heap	Retrd.	Unkn.	N/A
56-01-005	Tom Tom the Piper's Son	J. Heap	Retrd.	Unkn.	N/A
56-01-006	Little Jack Horner	J. Heap	Retrd.	Unkn.	N/A
53-01-007	Pendle Witch	J. Heap	Retrd.	Unkn.	N/A
53-01-008	Pixie House	J. Heap	Retrd.	Unkn.	N/A
53-01-009	Tipsy Witch	J. Heap	Retrd.	Unkn.	N/A
53-01-010	Cauldron Witch	J. Heap	Retrd.	Unkn.	N/A
54-01-011	Rhinegold Lamp	J. Heap	Retrd.	Unkn.	N/A
55-01-012	Old Adam	J. Heap	Retrd.	Unkn.	N/A
55-01-013	Balloon Woman	J. Heap	Retrd.	Unkn.	N/A
55-01-014	Bell Man	J. Heap	Retrd.	Unkn.	N/A
55-01-015	Elf	J. Heap	Retrd.	Unkn.	N/A
55-01-016	Toper	J. Heap	Retrd.	Unkn.	N/A
55-01-017	Flying Witch	J. Heap	Retrd.	Unkn.	N/A
55-01-018	Phynnodderee (Commissioned-Exclusive)	J. Heap	Retrd.	Unkn.	N/A
55-01-019	Margot	J. Heap	Retrd.	Unkn.	N/A
55-01-020	Old Father	J. Heap	Retrd.	Unkn.	900.00
56-01-021	Desmond Duck	J. Heap	Retrd.	Unkn.	N/A
56-01-022	Bobbin Woman	J. Heap	Retrd.	Unkn.	N/A
56-01-023	Manx Kitten	J. Heap	Retrd.	Unkn.	N/A
56-01-024	Midge (Replaced by Picnic Midge)	J. Heap	Retrd.	Unkn.	N/A
56-01-025	Original Robert	J. Heap	Retrd.	Unkn.	N/A
56-01-026	Timber Stand	J. Heap	Retrd.	Unkn.	N/A
57-01-027	Romeo & Juliet	J. Heap	Retrd.	Unkn.	N/A
57-01-028	Old Mother	J. Heap	Retrd.	Unkn.	N/A
59-01-029	Cha Cha	J. Heap	Retrd.	Unkn.	N/A
58-01-030	Rabbit Book Ends	J. Heap	Retrd.	Unkn.	N/A
60-01-031	Gussie	J. Heap	Retrd.	Unkn.	N/A
60-01-032	Shiner	J. Heap	Retrd.	Unkn.	N/A
60-01-033	Squeezy	J. Heap	Retrd.	Unkn.	N/A
60-01-034	Model Stand	J. Heap	Retrd.	Unkn.	N/A
60-01-035	Lucy Pocket	J. Heap	Retrd.	Unkn.	N/A
61-01-036	Megan	J. Heap	Retrd.	Unkn.	N/A
61-01-037	Lollipop (Mouse)	J. Heap	Retrd.	Unkn.	N/A
61-01-038	Mother Mouse	J. Heap	Retrd.	Unkn.	N/A
61-01-039	Father Mouse	J. Heap	Retrd.	Unkn.	N/A
62-01-040	Cornish Prayer (Corny)	J. Heap	Retrd.	Unkn.	N/A
63-01-041	Cyril Squirrel	J. Heap	Retrd.	Unkn.	N/A
63-01-042	Aunt Agatha	J. Heap	Retrd.	Unkn.	N/A
65-01-043	Mouse House	J. Heap	Retrd.	Unkn.	N/A
65-01-044	Picnic Stand	J. Heap	Retrd.	Unkn.	N/A
65-01-045	Muncher	D. Roberts	Retrd.	Unkn.	N/A
65-01-046	Pixie Bods	J. Heap	Retrd.	Unkn.	N/A
66-01-047	Picnic Basket	J. Heap	Retrd.	Unkn.	N/A
66-01-048	Milk Jug Stand	J. Heap	Retrd.	Unkn.	N/A
66-01-049	Cakestand	J. Heap	Retrd.	Unkn.	200.00
67-01-050	Maud	J. Heap	Retrd.	Unkn.	300.00
67-01-051	Robert	D. Roberts	Retrd.	Unkn.	100.00
67-01-052	The Bath Tub	J. Heap	Retrd.	Unkn.	N/A
67-01-053	Picnic Table	J. Heap	Retrd.	Unkn.	N/A
69-01-054	The Gallery Series: Wakey, Pieface, Poppet, Robert, Dodger	J. Heap	Retrd.	Unkn.	N/A
71-01-055	Totty	J. Heap	Retrd.	Unkn.	N/A
59-01-056	Uncle Soames	J. Heap	Retrd.	Unkn.	300.00
67-01-057	Phumf	J. Heap	Retrd.	Unkn.	N/A
57-01-058	Tammy	D. Roberts	Retrd.	Unkn.	N/A
62-01-059	Pooch	D. Roberts	Retrd.	Unkn.	N/A
66-01-060	Pieface	D. Roberts	Retrd.	Unkn.	N/A
64-01-061	Bongo	D. Roberts	Retrd.	Unkn.	N/A

Company Number	Name	Series Artist	Edition Limit	Issue Price	Quote
80-01-062	Crocker	D. Roberts	Retrd.	Unkn.	N/A
81-01-063	Nipper	D. Roberts	Retrd.	Unkn.	N/A
84-01-064	Blossom	D. Roberts	Retrd.	Unkn.	N/A
PenDelfin		**Bed Series**			
XX-02-001	Dodger	J. Heap	Open	24.00	24.00
XX-02-002	Peeps	J. Heap	Open	21.00	21.00
XX-02-003	Poppet	D. Roberts	Open	23.00	23.00
XX-02-004	Snuggles	J. Heap	Open	20.00	20.00
XX-02-005	Twins	J. Heap	Open	25.00	25.00
XX-02-006	Wakey	J. Heap	Open	24.00	24.00
XX-02-007	Victoria	J. Heap	Open	47.50	47.50
XX-02-008	Parsley	D. Roberts	Open	25.00	25.00
XX-02-009	Chirpy	D. Roberts	Open	60.00	60.00
XX-02-010	Snuggles Awake	J. Heap	Open	60.00	60.00
PenDelfin		**Band Series**			
XX-03-001	Rocky	J. Heap	Open	32.00	32.00
XX-03-002	Rolly	J. Heap	Open	17.50	17.50
XX-03-003	Thumper	J. Heap	Open	25.00	25.00
XX-03-004	Piano	D. Roberts	Open	25.00	25.00
XX-03-005	Casanova	J. Heap	Open	35.00	35.00
XX-03-006	Clanger	J. Heap	Open	35.00	35.00
XX-03-007	Rosa	J. Heap	Open	40.00	40.00
XX-03-008	Solo	D. Roberts	Open	40.00	40.00
XX-03-009	Jingles	D. Roberts	Open	22.50	22.50
XX-03-010	Bandstand	J. Heap	Open	70.00	70.00
PenDelfin		**Picnic Series**			
XX-04-001	Picnic Midge	J. Heap	Open	25.00	25.00
XX-04-002	Barrow Boy	J. Heap	Open	35.00	35.00
XX-04-003	Oliver	D. Roberts	Open	25.00	25.00
XX-04-004	Apple Barrel	D. Roberts	Open	15.00	15.00
XX-04-005	Scrumpy	J. Heap	Open	35.00	35.00
XX-04-006	Picnic Island	J. Heap	Open	85.00	85.00
PenDelfin		**Toy Shop Series**			
XX-05-001	Jacky	D. Roberts	Open	45.00	45.00
XX-05-002	The Toy Shop	D. Roberts	Open	325.00	325.00
PenDelfin		**Fisherman Series**			
XX-06-001	Whopper	D. Roberts	Open	35.00	35.00
XX-06-002	Jim-Lad	D. Roberts	Open	45.00	45.00
XX-06-003	Little Mo	D. Roberts	Open	35.00	35.00
XX-06-004	The Raft	J. Heap	Open	70.00	70.00
XX-06-005	Shrimp Stand	D. Roberts	Open	70.00	70.00
XX-06-006	The Jetty	J. Heap	Open	180.00	180.00
PenDelfin		**Sport Series**			
XX-07-001	Birdie	J. Heap	Open	47.50	47.50
XX-07-002	Tennyson	D. Roberts	Open	35.00	35.00
XX-07-003	Humphrey Go-Kart	J. Heap	Open	70.00	70.00
XX-07-004	Rambler	D. Roberts	Open	65.00	65.00
XX-07-005	Scout	D. Roberts	Open	N/A	N/A
PenDelfin		**School Series**			
XX-08-001	Boswell	J. Heap	Open	37.50	37.50
XX-08-002	Euclid	J. Heap	Open	35.00	35.00
XX-08-003	Digit	D. Roberts	Open	35.00	35.00
XX-08-004	Duffy	J. Heap	Open	50.00	50.00
XX-08-005	Old School House	J. Heap	Open	250.00	250.00
XX-08-006	Angelo	J. Heap	Open	90.00	90.00
XX-08-007	New Boy	D. Roberts	Open	50.00	50.00
XX-08-008	Wordsworth	D. Roberts	Open	60.00	60.00
PenDelfin		**Various**			
XX-09-001	Dandy	D. Roberts	Open	50.00	50.00
XX-09-002	Barney	J. Heap	Open	18.00	18.00
XX-09-003	Honey	D. Roberts	Open	40.00	40.00
XX-09-004	Charlotte	D. Roberts	Open	50.00	50.00
XX-09-005	Butterfingers	D. Roberts	Open	55.00	55.00
XX-09-006	Scoffer	D. Roberts	Open	55.00	55.00
XX-09-007	Mother with baby	J. Heap	Open	150.00	150.00
XX-09-008	Father	J. Heap	Open	150.00	150.00
PenDelfin		**Village Series**			
XX-10-001	Fruit Shop	J. Heap	Open	125.00	125.00
XX-10-002	Castle Tavern	D. Roberts	Open	120.00	120.00
XX-10-003	Caravan	D. Roberts	Open	350.00	350.00
XX-10-004	Large House	J. Heap	Open	275.00	275.00
XX-10-005	Cobble Cottage	D. Roberts	Open	80.00	80.00
XX-10-006	Curiosity Shop	J. Heap	Open	350.00	350.00
XX-10-007	Balcony Scene	D. Roberts	Open	175.00	175.00
XX-10-008	Grand Stand	J. Heap	Open	150.00	150.00
PenDelfin		**PenDelfin Family Circle Collectors' Club**			
92-11-001	Herald	J. Heap	Yr. Iss.	30.00	30.00
Polland Studios		**Collectible Bronzes**			
67-01-001	Bull Session	D. Polland	11	200.00	1200.00
69-01-002	Blowin' Cold	D. Polland	30	375.00	1250.00
69-01-003	The Breed	D. Polland	30	350.00	975.00
68-01-004	Buffalo Hunt	D. Polland	30	450.00	1250.00
69-01-005	Comanchero	D. Polland	30	350.00	750.00
69-01-006	Dancing Indian with Lance	D. Polland	50	250.00	775.00
69-01-007	Dancing Indian with Tomahawk	D. Polland	50	250.00	775.00
69-01-008	Dancing Medicine Man	D. Polland	50	250.00	775.00
69-01-009	Drawn Sabers	D. Polland	50	2000.00	5650.00
69-01-010	Lookouts	D. Polland	30	375.00	1300.00
69-01-011	Top Money	D. Polland	30	275.00	800.00
69-01-012	Trail Hazzard	D. Polland	30	700.00	1750.00
69-01-013	War Cry	D. Polland	30	350.00	975.00
69-01-014	When Enemies Meet	D. Polland	30	700.00	2350.00
70-01-015	Coffee Time	D. Polland	50	1200.00	2900.00
70-01-016	The Lost Dispatch	D. Polland	50	1200.00	2950.00
70-01-017	Wanted	D. Polland	50	500.00	1150.00
70-01-018	Dusted	D. Polland	50	400.00	1175.00
71-01-019	Ambush at Rock Canyon	D. Polland	5	20000.00	45000.00
71-01-020	Oh Sugar!	D. Polland	40	700.00	1525.00
71-01-021	Shakin' Out a Loop	D. Polland	40	500.00	1075.00
72-01-022	Buffalo Robe	D. Polland	50	1000.00	2350.00
73-01-023	Bunch Quitter	D. Polland	60	750.00	1975.00
73-01-024	Challenge	D. Polland	60	750.00	1800.00

Company Number	Name	Series Artist	Edition Limit	Issue Price	Quote
73-01-025	War Party	D. Polland	60	1500.00	5500.00
73-01-026	Tracking	D. Polland	60	500.00	1150.00
75-01-027	Cheyenne	D. Polland	6	1300.00	1800.00
75-01-028	Counting Coup	D. Polland	6	1450.00	1950.00
75-01-029	Crow Scout	D. Polland	6	1300.00	1800.00
75-01-030	Buffalo Hunt	D. Polland	6	2200.00	3500.00
76-01-031	Rescue	D. Polland	6	2400.00	3000.00
76-01-032	Painting the Town	D. Polland	6	3000.00	4200.00
76-01-033	Monday Morning Wash	D. Polland	6	2800.00	2800.00
76-01-034	Mandan Hunter	D. Polland	12	775.00	775.00
80-01-035	Buffalo Prayer	D. Polland	25	375.00	675.00
Polland Studios		**Collector Society**			
87-02-001	I Come In Peace	D. Polland	Closed	35.00	300-495.
87-02-002	Silent Trail	D. Polland	Closed	300.00	1200.00
87-02-003	I Come In Peace, Silent Trail-Matched Numbered Set	D. Polland	Closed	335.00	1500-1895.
88-02-004	The Hunter	D. Polland	Closed	35.00	300-380.
88-02-005	Disputed Trail	D. Polland	Closed	300.00	700-775.
88-02-006	The Hunter, Disputed Trail-Matched Numbered Set	D. Polland	Closed	335.00	1100-1450.
89-02-007	Crazy Horse	D. Polland	Closed	35.00	300-550.
89-02-008	Apache Birdman	D. Polland	Closed	300.00	700-960.
89-02-009	Crazy Horse, Apache Birdman-Matched Numbered Set	D. Polland	Closed	335.00	1300-1700.
90-02-010	Chief Pontiac	D. Polland	Closed	35.00	200-430.
90-02-011	Buffalo Pony	D. Polland	Closed	300.00	600-725.
90-02-012	Chief Pontiac, Buffalo Pony-Matched Numbered Set	D. Polland	Closed	335.00	900-1350.
91-02-013	War Dancer	D. Polland	Closed	35.00	150-300.
91-02-014	The Signal	D. Polland	Closed	350.00	500-650.
91-02-015	War Drummer & The Signal-Matched Numbered Set	D. Polland	Closed	385.00	900-1150.
92-02-016	Cabinet Sign	D. Polland	Yr.Iss.	35.00	35.00
92-02-017	Warrior's Farewell	D. Polland	Yr.Iss.	350.00	350.00
92-02-018	Cabinet Sign & Warrior's Farewell-Matched Numbered Set	D. Polland	Yr.Iss.	385.00	385.00
Polland Studios		**Pewter Collection**			
84-03-001	Federal Stallion	D. Polland	1,500	145.00	185.00
85-03-003	Running Free	D. Polland	1,500	250.00	300.00
86-03-003	Hunting Cougar	D. Polland	1,500	145.00	180.00
91-03-004	Mermaid	D. Polland	2,000	250.00	250.00
91-03-005	Mermaid (Tinted)	D. Polland	2,500	275.00	275.00
91-03-006	Turtle Hounds (Tinted)	D. Polland	2,500	150.00	150.00
91-03-007	Double Play	D. Polland	2,500	150.00	150.00
91-03-008	Double Play (Tinted)	D. Polland	2,500	165.00	165.00
91-03-009	4th And Goal	D. Polland	2,500	150.00	150.00
91-03-010	4th And Goal (Tinted)	D. Polland	2,500	165.00	165.00
91-03-011	Ballerina	D. Polland	1,500	100.00	100.00
91-03-012	Ballerina (Tinted)	D. Polland	1,500	115.00	115.00
91-03-013	Ballerina (Porcelain)	D. Polland	1,500	125.00	125.00
91-03-014	Stalking Cougar (Porcelain)	D. Polland	2,500	85.00	85.00
91-03-015	Indian Pony Grey (Porcelain)	D. Polland	2,500	115.00	115.00
91-03-016	Indian Pony Bay (Porcelain)	D. Polland	2,500	115.00	115.00
91-03-017	Indian Pony Buckskin (Porcelain)	D. Polland	2,500	115.00	115.00
Possible Dreams®		**Clothtique® The Saturday Evening Post Norman Rockwell Collection**			
90-01-001	Dear Santa-3050	N. Rockwell	Closed	160.00	180.00
90-01-002	Santa with Globe-3051	N. Rockwell	Closed	154.00	175.00
90-01-003	Hobo-3052	N. Rockwell	Open	159.00	159.00
90-01-004	Love Letters-3053	N. Rockwell	Open	172.00	172.00
91-01-005	Gone Fishing-3054	N. Rockwell	Open	250.00	250.00
91-01-006	Doctor and Doll-3055	N. Rockwell	Open	196.00	196.00
91-01-007	Springtime-3056	N. Rockwell	Open	130.00	130.00
91-01-008	The Gift-3057	N. Rockwell	Open	160.00	160.00
91-01-009	Gramps at the Reins-3058	N. Rockwell	Open	290.00	290.00
91-01-010	Man with Geese-3059	N. Rockwell	Open	120.00	120.00
91-01-011	Plotting His Course-3060	N. Rockwell	Open	160.00	160.00
92-01-012	Triple Self Portrait-3061	N. Rockwell	Open	230.00	230.00
92-01-013	Marriage License-3062	N. Rockwell	Open	195.00	195.00
92-01-014	Santa's Helpers-3063	N. Rockwell	Open	170.00	170.00
92-01-015	Balancing the Budget-3064	N. Rockwell	Open	120.00	120.00
Possible Dreams®		**Clothtique® The Saturday Evening Post J.C. Leyendecker Collection**			
90-02-001	Santa and Baby-3600	J. Leyendecker	Closed	100.00	110.00
91-02-002	Hugging Santa-3599	J. Leyendecker	Open	129.00	129.00
92-02-003	Santa on Ladder-3598	J. Leyendecker	Open	135.00	135.00
Possible Dreams®		**Clothtique® The American Artist Collection**			
91-03-001	Magic of Christmas-15001	L. Bywaters	Open	132.00	132.00
91-03-002	A Peaceful Eve-15002	L. Bywaters	Open	99.50	99.50
91-03-003	Alpine Christmas-15003	J. Brett	Open	129.00	129.00
91-03-004	Traditions-15004	T. Blackshear	Open	50.00	50.00
91-03-005	A Friendly Visit-15005	T. Browning	Open	99.50	99.50
91-03-006	Santa's Cuisine-15006	T. Browning	Open	137.50	137.50
91-03-007	Father Christmas-15007	J. Vaillancourt	Open	59.50	59.50
92-03-008	An Angel's Kiss-15008	J. Griffith	Open	85.00	85.00
92-03-009	Peace on Earth-15009	M. Alvin	Open	87.50	87.50
92-03-010	Lighting the Way-15012	L. Bywaters	Open	85.00	85.00
92-03-011	Out of the Forrest-15013	J. Vaillancourt	Open	60.00	60.00
92-03-012	Heralding the Way-15014	J. Griffith	Open	72.00	72.00
92-03-013	Music Makers-15010	T. Browning	Open	135.00	135.00
92-03-014	Christmas Company-15011	T. Browning	Open	73.00	73.00
Possible Dreams®		**Clothtique® Limited Edition Santas**			
88-04-001	Patriotic Santa-3000	Unknown	10,000	240.00	240.00
88-04-002	Father Christmas-3001	Unknown	10,000	240.00	240.00
88-04-003	Kris Kringle-3002	Unknown	Closed	240.00	240.00
89-04-004	Traditional Santa 40's-3003	Unknown	10,000	240.00	240.00
Possible Dreams®		**Clothtique® Pepsi® Santa Collection**			
90-05-001	Traditional Pepsi Santa 1940's-3601	Unknown	Open	68.00	70.00
91-05-002	Pepsi Santa 1952-3602	N. Rockwell	Open	75.00	77.50
92-05-003	Santa and Friend-3603	Unknown	Open	84.00	84.00
Possible Dreams®		**Clothtique® Santas Collection**			
87-06-001	Traditional Santa-713028	Unknown	Closed	34.50	34.50
87-06-002	Ukko-713031	Unknown	Closed	38.00	38.00
87-06-003	Colonial Santa-713032	Unknown	Closed	38.00	38.00
87-06-004	Christmas Man-713027	Unknown	Closed	34.50	34.50
87-06-005	Santa with Pack-713026	Unknown	Closed	34.50	34.50
87-06-006	Traditional Deluxe Santa-713030	Unknown	Closed	38.00	38.00

Number	Name	Artist	Edition Limit	Issue Price	Quote
Company		**Series**			
88-06-007	Frontier Santa-713034	Unknown	Closed	40.00	42.00
88-06-008	St. Nicholas-713035	Unknown	Closed	40.00	42.00
88-06-009	Weinachtsmann-713037	Unknown	Closed	40.00	43.00
88-06-010	Carpenter Santa-713033	Unknown	Closed	38.00	44.00
88-06-011	Russian St. Nicholas-713036	Unknown	Closed	40.00	43.00
88-06-012	Traditional Santa-713038	Unknown	Closed	42.00	43.00
89-06-013	Pelze Nichol-713039	Unknown	Open	40.00	47.00
89-06-014	Mrs. Claus w/doll-713041	Unknown	Closed	42.00	43.00
89-06-015	Baby's First Christmas-713042	Unknown	Closed	42.00	46.00
89-06-016	Exhausted Santa-713043	Unknown	Closed	60.00	65.00
89-06-017	Santa with Embroidered Coat-713040	Unknown	Closed	43.00	43.00
90-06-018	Santa At Workbench-713044	Unknown	Open	72.00	75.50
90-06-019	Santa "Please Stop Here"-713045	Unknown	Closed	63.00	66.00
90-06-020	Harlem Santa-713046	Unknown	Open	46.00	52.50
90-06-021	Santa Skiing-713047	Unknown	Closed	62.00	65.00
90-06-022	Blue Robed Santa-713048	Unknown	Closed	46.00	50.00
91-06-023	The True Spirit of Christmas-713075	Unknown	Closed	97.00	97.00
91-06-024	Santa in Bed-713076	Unknown	Open	76.00	79.50
91-06-025	Siberian Santa-713077	Unknown	Open	49.00	51.50
91-06-026	Mrs. Claus in Coat -713078	Unknown	Open	47.00	49.50
91-06-027	Decorating the Tree-713079	Unknown	Closed	60.00	60.00
91-06-028	Father Christmas-713087	Unknown	Open	43.00	45.20
91-06-029	Kris Kringle-713088	Unknown	Open	43.00	45.20
91-06-030	Santa Shelf Sitter-713089	Unknown	Open	55.50	58.00
92-06-031	1940's Traditional Santa-713049	Unknown	Open	44.00	44.00
92-06-032	Santa on Sled-713050	Unknown	Open	75.00	75.00
92-06-033	Nicholas-713052	Unknown	Open	57.50	57.50
92-06-034	Fireman Santa-713053	Unknown	Open	60.00	60.00
92-06-035	African American Santa-713056	Unknown	Open	65.00	65.00
92-06-036	Engineer Santa-713057	Unknown	Open	130.00	130.00
92-06-037	Santa on Reindeer-713058	Unknown	Open	75.00	79.00
92-06-038	Santa in Rocking Chair-713090	M. Monteiro	Open	85.00	85.00
92-06-039	Santa on Sleigh-713091	Unknown	Open	79.00	79.00
92-06-040	Santa on Motorbike-713054	Unknown	Open	115.00	115.00
Possible Dreams®		**The Citizens of Londonshire**			
92-07-001	Beth-713417	Unknown	Open	35.00	35.00
92-07-002	Albert-713426	Unknown	Open	65.00	65.00
89-07-003	Lady Ashley-713405	Unknown	Open	65.00	65.00
89-07-004	Lord Winston of Riverside-713403	Unknown	Open	65.00	65.00
89-07-005	Sir Robert-713401	Unknown	Open	65.00	65.00
89-07-006	Rodney-713404	Unknown	Open	65.00	65.00
90-07-007	Dr. Isaac-713409	Unknown	Open	65.00	65.00
90-07-008	Admiral Waldo-713407	Unknown	Open	65.00	65.00
91-07-009	Sir Red-713415	Unknown	Open	72.00	72.00
91-07-010	Bernie-713414	Unknown	Open	68.00	68.00
92-07-011	Tiffany Sorbet-713416	Unknown	Open	65.00	65.00
90-07-012	Margaret of Foxcroft-713408	Unknown	Open	65.00	65.00
90-07-013	Officer Kevin-713406	Unknown	Open	65.00	65.00
89-07-014	Lord Nicholas-713402	Unknown	Open	72.00	72.00
92-07-015	Countess of Hamlett-713419	Unknown	Open	65.00	65.00
89-07-016	Earl of Hamlett-713400	Unknown	Open	65.00	65.00
92-07-017	Rebecca-713424	Unknown	Open	35.00	35.00
90-07-018	Dianne-713413	Unknown	Open	33.00	33.00
90-07-019	Phillip-713412	Unknown	Open	33.00	33.00
90-07-020	Walter-713410	Unknown	Open	33.00	33.00
90-07-021	Wendy-713411	Unknown	Open	33.00	33.00
92-07-022	Jean Claude-713421	Unknown	Open	35.00	35.00
92-07-023	Nicole-713420	Unknown	Open	35.00	35.00
92-07-024	David-713423	Unknown	Open	37.50	37.50
92-07-025	Debbie-713422	Unknown	Open	37.50	37.50
92-07-026	Christopher-713418	Unknown	Open	35.00	35.00
92-07-027	Richard-713425	Unknown	Open	35.00	35.00
Possible Dreams®		**Collectors Club**			
92-08-001	The Gift Giver	Unknown	Yr. Iss.	40.00	40.00
Precious Art/Panton		**World of Krystonia**			
87-01-001	Small Graffyn/Grunch-1012	Panton	Retrd.	45.00	165-250.
87-01-002	Small N'Borg-1091	Panton	Retrd.	50.00	250-300.
87-01-003	Large Rueggan-1701	Panton	Retrd.	55.00	160-450.
87-01-004	Owhey-1071	Panton	Retrd.	32.00	80-125.00
87-01-005	Medium Stoope-1101	Panton	Retrd.	52.00	200.00
87-01-006	Small Shepf-1152	Panton	Retrd.	40.00	85-100.00
87-01-007	Large Wodema-1301	Panton	Retrd.	50.00	100-300.
88-01-008	Large N'Grall-2201	Panton	Retrd.	108.00	250-400.
87-01-009	Large Krak N'Borg-3001	Panton	Retrd.	240.00	500-800.
87-01-010	Large Moplos-1021	Panton	Retrd.	90.00	250-300.
87-01-011	Large Myzer-1201	Panton	Retrd.	50.00	150-250.
87-01-012	Large Turfen-1601	Panton	Retrd.	50.00	75-150.00
87-01-013	Large Haapf-1901	Panton	Retrd.	38.00	85-125.00
88-01-014	Small Tulan Captain-2502	Panton	Retrd.	44.00	75-125.00
87-01-015	Small Groc-1042B	Panton	Retrd.	24.00	4600.00
87-01-016	Large Graffyn on Grumblypeg Grunch-1011	Panton	Retrd.	52.00	86-120.00
87-01-017	Grumblypeg Grunch-1081	Panton	Retrd.	52.00	84-120.00
88-01-018	Tarnhold - Med.-3202	Panton	Retrd.	120.00	140-185.
89-01-019	Caught At Last!-1107	Panton	Retrd.	150.00	175-240.
89-01-020	Stoope (waterglobe) -9003	Panton	Retrd.	40.00	N/A
89-01-021	Graffyn on Grunch (waterglobe) -9006	Panton	Retrd.	42.00	N/A
Precious Art/Panton		**Krystonia Collector's Club**			
89-02-001	Pultzr w/ Key	Panton	Retrd.	55.00	150.00
89-02-002	Pultzr	Panton	Retrd.	55.00	175-260.
89-02-003	Key	Panton	Retrd.	Gift	100.00
91-02-004	Dragons Play	Panton	Retrd.	65.00	65.00
91-02-005	Kephrens Chest	Panton	Retrd.	Gift	N/A
92-02-006	Vaaston	Panton	Yr. Iss.	65.00	65.00
92-02-007	Lantern	Panton	Yr. Iss.	Gift	N/A
Princeton Gallery		**Unicorn Collection**			
90-01-001	Love's Delight	Unknown	Open	75.00	75.00
90-01-002	Love's Sweetness	Unknown	Open	75.00	75.00
91-01-003	Love's Devotion	Unknown	Open	119.00	119.00
91-01-004	Love's Purity	Unknown	Open	95.00	95.00
91-01-005	Love's Majesty	Unknown	Open	95.00	95.00
91-01-006	Christmas Unicorn	Unknown	Yr.Iss.	85.00	85.00
92-01-007	Love's Fancy	Unknown	Open	95.00	95.00
93-01-008	Love's Courtship	Unknown	Open	95.00	95.00
Princeton Gallery		**Playful Pups**			
90-02-001	Dalmation-Where's The Fire	Unknown	Open	19.50	19.50
90-02-002	Beagle	Unknown	Open	19.50	19.50
91-02-003	St. Bernard	Unknown	Open	19.50	19.50
91-02-004	Labrador Retriever	Unknown	Open	19.50	19.50
91-02-005	Wrinkles (Shar Pei)	Unknown	Open	19.50	19.50
Princeton Gallery		**Garden Capers**			
90-03-001	Any Mail?	Unknown	Open	29.50	29.50
91-03-002	Blue Jays	Unknown	Open	29.50	29.50
91-03-003	Robin	Unknown	Open	29.50	29.50
92-03-004	Goldfinch, Home Sweet Home	Unknown	Open	29.50	29.50
92-03-005	Bluebird, Spring Planting	Unknown	Open	29.50	29.50
Princeton Gallery		**Baby bird Trios**			
91-04-001	Woodland Symphony (Bluebirds)	Unknown	Open	45.00	45.00
91-04-002	Cardinals	Unknown	Open	45.00	45.00
Princeton Gallery		**Pegasus**			
92-05-001	Wings of Magic	Unknown	Open	95.00	95.00
Princeton Gallery		**Enchanted Nursery**			
92-06-001	Caprice	Unknown	Open	57.00	57.00
93-06-002	Pegasus	Unknown	Open	57.00	57.00
Princeton Gallery		**Lady And The Unicorn**			
92-07-001	Love's Innocence	Unknown	Open	119.00	119.00
Reco International		**Granget Crystal Sculpture**			
73-01-001	Long Earred Owl, Asio Otus	G. Granget	350	2250.00	2250.00
XX-01-002	Ruffed Grouse	G. Granget	350	1000.00	1000.00
Reco International		**Porcelains in Miniature by John McClelland**			
XX-02-001	John	J. McClelland	10,000	34.50	34.50
XX-02-002	Alice	J. McClelland	10,000	34.50	34.50
XX-02-003	Chimney Sweep	J. McClelland	10,000	34.50	34.50
XX-02-004	Dressing Up	J. McClelland	10,000	34.50	34.50
XX-02-005	Autumn Dreams	J. McClelland	Open	29.50	29.50
XX-02-006	Tuck-Me-In	J. McClelland	Open	29.50	29.50
XX-02-007	Country Lass	J. McClelland	Open	29.50	29.50
XX-02-008	Sudsie Suzie	J. McClelland	Open	29.50	29.50
XX-02-009	Smooth Smailing	J. McClelland	Open	29.50	29.50
XX-02-010	The Clown	J. McClelland	Open	29.50	29.50
XX-02-011	The Baker	J. McClelland	Open	29.50	29.50
XX-02-012	Quiet Moments	J. McClelland	Open	29.50	29.50
XX-02-013	The Farmer	J. McClelland	Open	29.50	29.50
XX-02-014	The Nurse	J. McClelland	Open	29.50	29.50
XX-02-015	The Policeman	J. McClelland	Open	29.50	29.50
XX-02-016	The Fireman	J. McClelland	Open	29.50	29.50
XX-02-017	Winter Fun	J. McClelland	Open	29.50	29.50
XX-02-018	Cowgirl	J. McClelland	Open	29.50	29.50
XX-02-019	Cowboy	J. McClelland	Open	29.50	29.50
XX-02-020	Doc	J. McClelland	Open	29.50	29.50
XX-02-021	Lawyer	J. McClelland	Open	29.50	29.50
XX-02-022	Farmer's Wife	J. McClelland	Open	29.50	29.50
XX-02-023	First Outing	J. McClelland	Open	29.50	29.50
XX-02-024	Club Pro	J. McClelland	Open	29.50	29.50
XX-02-025	Batter Up	J. McClelland	Open	29.50	29.50
XX-02-026	Love 40	J. McClelland	Open	29.50	29.50
XX-02-027	The Painter	J. McClelland	Open	29.50	29.50
XX-02-028	Special Delivery	J. McClelland	Open	29.50	29.50
XX-02-029	Center Ice	J. McClelland	Open	29.50	29.50
XX-02-030	First Solo	J. McClelland	Open	29.50	29.50
XX-02-031	Highland Fling	J. McClelland	7,500	34.50	34.50
XX-02-032	Cheerleader	J. McClelland	Open	29.50	29.50
Reco International		**The Reco Clown Collection**			
85-03-001	Whoopie	J. McClelland	Open	12.00	13.00
85-03-002	The Professor	J. McClelland	Open	12.00	13.00
85-03-003	Top Hat	J. McClelland	Open	12.00	13.00
85-03-004	Winkie	J. McClelland	Open	12.00	13.00
85-03-005	Scamp	J. McClelland	Open	12.00	13.00
85-03-006	Curly	J. McClelland	Open	12.00	13.00
85-03-007	Bow Jangles	J. McClelland	Open	12.00	13.00
85-03-008	Sparkles	J. McClelland	Open	12.00	13.00
85-03-009	Ruffles	J. McClelland	Open	12.00	13.00
85-03-010	Arabesque	J. McClelland	Open	12.00	13.00
85-03-011	Hobo	J. McClelland	Open	12.00	13.00
85-03-012	Sad Eyes	J. McClelland	Open	12.00	13.00
87-03-013	Love	J. McClelland	Open	12.00	13.00
87-03-014	Mr. Big	J. McClelland	Open	12.00	13.00
87-03-015	Twinkle	J. McClelland	Open	12.00	13.00
87-03-016	Disco Dan	J. McClelland	Open	12.00	13.00
87-03-017	Smiley	J. McClelland	Open	12.00	13.00
87-03-018	The Joker	J. McClelland	Open	12.00	13.00
87-03-019	Jolly Joe	J. McClelland	Open	12.00	13.00
87-03-020	Zany Jack	J. McClelland	Open	12.00	13.00
87-03-021	Domino	J. McClelland	Open	12.00	13.00
87-03-022	Happy George	J. McClelland	Open	12.00	13.00
87-03-023	Tramp	J. McClelland	Open	12.00	13.00
87-03-024	Wistful	J. McClelland	Open	12.00	13.00
Reco International		**The Reco Angel Collection**			
86-04-001	Innocence	J. McClelland	Open	12.00	12.00
86-04-002	Harmony	J. McClelland	Open	12.00	12.00
86-04-003	Love	J. McClelland	Open	12.00	12.00
86-04-004	Gloria	J. McClelland	Open	12.00	12.00
86-04-005	Praise	J. McClelland	Open	20.00	20.00
86-04-006	Devotion	J. McClelland	Open	15.00	15.00
86-04-007	Faith	J. McClelland	Open	24.00	24.00
86-04-008	Joy	J. McClelland	Open	15.00	15.00
86-04-009	Adoration	J. McClelland	Open	24.00	24.00
86-04-010	Peace	J. McClelland	Open	24.00	24.00
86-04-011	Serenity	J. McClelland	Open	24.00	24.00
86-04-012	Hope	J. McClelland	Open	24.00	24.00
88-04-013	Reverence	J. McClelland	Open	12.00	12.00
88-04-014	Minstral	J. McClelland	Open	12.00	12.00
Reco International		**Sophisticated Ladies Figurines**			
87-05-001	Felicia	A. Fazio	9,500	29.50	32.50
87-05-002	Samantha	A. Fazio	9,500	29.50	32.50
87-05-003	Phoebe	A. Fazio	9,500	29.50	32.50
87-05-004	Cleo	A. Fazio	9,500	29.50	32.50
87-05-005	Cerissa	A. Fazio	9,500	29.50	32.50
87-05-006	Natasha	A. Fazio	9,500	29.50	32.50
87-05-007	Bianka	A. Fazio	9,500	29.50	32.50
87-05-008	Chelsea	A. Fazio	9,500	29.50	32.50

Company / Number	Name	Series / Artist	Edition Limit	Issue Price	Quote
Reco International		**Clown Figurines by John McClelland**			
87-06-001	Mr. Tip	J. McClelland	9,500	35.00	35.00
87-06-002	Mr. Cure-All	J. McClelland	9,500	35.00	35.00
87-06-003	Mr. One-Note	J. McClelland	9,500	35.00	35.00
87-06-004	Mr. Lovable	J. McClelland	9,500	35.00	35.00
88-06-005	Mr. Magic	J. McClelland	9,500	35.00	35.00
88-06-006	Mr. Cool	J. McClelland	9,500	35.00	35.00
88-06-007	Mr. Heart-Throb	J. McClelland	9,500	35.00	35.00
Reco International		**The Reco Angel Collection Miniatures**			
87-07-001	Innocence	J. McClelland	Open	7.50	7.50
87-07-002	Harmony	J. McClelland	Open	7.50	7.50
87-07-003	Love	J. McClelland	Open	7.50	7.50
87-07-004	Gloria	J. McClelland	Open	7.50	7.50
87-07-005	Devotion	J. McClelland	Open	7.50	7.50
87-07-006	Joy	J. McClelland	Open	7.50	7.50
87-07-007	Adoration	J. McClelland	Open	10.00	10.00
87-07-008	Peace	J. McClelland	Open	10.00	10.00
87-07-009	Serenity	J. McClelland	Open	10.00	10.00
87-07-010	Hope	J. McClelland	Open	10.00	10.00
87-07-011	Praise	J. McClelland	Open	10.00	10.00
87-07-012	Faith	J. McClelland	Open	10.00	10.00
Reco International		**Faces of Love**			
88-08-001	Cuddles	J. McClelland	Open	29.50	32.50
88-08-002	Sunshine	J. McClelland	Open	29.50	32.50
Reco International		**Reco Creche Collection**			
87-09-001	Holy Family (3 Pieces)	J. McClelland	Open	49.00	49.00
87-09-002	Lamb	J. McClelland	Open	9.50	9.50
87-09-003	Shepherd-Kneeling	J. McClelland	Open	22.50	22.50
87-09-004	Shepherd-Standing	J. McClelland	Open	22.50	22.50
88-09-005	King/Frankincense	J. McClelland	Open	22.50	22.50
88-09-006	King/Myrrh	J. McClelland	Open	22.50	22.50
88-09-007	King/Gold	J. McClelland	Open	22.50	22.50
88-09-008	Donkey	J. McClelland	Open	16.50	16.50
88-09-009	Cow	J. McClelland	Open	15.00	15.00
Reco International		**The Reco Collection Clown Busts**			
88-10-001	Hobo	J. McClelland	5,000	40.00	40.00
88-10-002	Love	J. McClelland	5,000	40.00	40.00
88-10-003	Sparkles	J. McClelland	5,000	40.00	40.00
88-10-004	Bow Jangles	J. McClelland	5,000	40.00	40.00
88-10-005	Domino	J. McClelland	5,000	40.00	40.00
Reco International		**Wedding Gifts**			
91-11-001	Cake Topper Bride & Groom	J. McClelland	Open	35.00	35.00
91-11-002	Bride & Groom- Musical	J. McClelland	Open	90.00	90.00
91-11-003	Bride-Blond-Musical	J. McClelland	Open	80.00	80.00
91-11-004	Bride-Brunette-Musical	J. McClelland	Open	80.00	80.00
91-11-005	Bride & Groom	J. McClelland	Open	85.00	85.00
91-11-006	Bride-Blond	J. McClelland	Open	60.00	60.00
91-11-007	Bride-Brunette	J. McClelland	Open	60.00	60.00
Rhodes Studio		**Rockwell's Main Street**			
90-01-001	Rockwell's Studio	Rockwell-Inspired	150-day	28.00	28.00
90-01-002	The Antique Shop	Rockwell-Inspired	150-day	28.00	28.00
90-01-003	The Town Offices	Rockwell-Inspired	150-day	32.00	32.00
90-01-004	The Country Store	Rockwell-Inspired	150-day	32.00	32.00
91-01-005	The Library	Rockwell-Inspired	150-day	36.00	36.00
91-01-006	The Bank	Rockwell-Inspired	150-day	36.00	36.00
91-01-007	Red Lion Inn	Rockwell-Inspired	150-day	39.00	39.00
Rhodes Studio		**Rockwell's Hometown**			
91-02-001	Rockwell's Residence	Rhodes	Closed	34.95	34.95
91-02-002	Greystone Church	Rhodes	12/92	34.95	34.95
91-02-003	Bell Tower	Rockwell-Inspired	3/93	36.95	36.95
91-02-004	Firehous	Rockwell-Inspired	3/93	36.95	36.95
91-02-005	Church On The Green	Rockwell-Inspired	9/93	39.95	39.95
92-02-006	Town Hall	Rockwell-Inspired	12/93	39.95	39.95
92-02-007	Citizen's Hall	Rockwell-Inspired	3/94	42.95	42.95
92-02-008	The Berkshire Playhouse	Rockwell-Inspired	6/94	42.95	42.95
Rhodes Studio		**Rockwell's Heirloom Santa Collection**			
90-03-001	Santa's Workshop	Rockwell-Inspired	150-day	49.95	49.95
91-03-002	Christmas Dream	Rockwell-Inspired	150-day	49.95	49.95
92-03-003	Making His List	Rockwell-Inspired	12/93	49.95	49.95
Rhodes Studio		**Rockwell's Age of Wonder**			
91-04-001	Splish Splash	Rockwell-Inspired	Closed	34.95	34.95
91-04-002	Hush-A-Bye	Rockwell-Inspired	12/92	34.95	34.95
91-04-003	Stand by Me	Rockwell-Inspired	3/93	36.95	36.95
91-04-004	School Days	Rockwell-Inspired	6/93	36.95	36.95
91-04-005	Summertime	Rockwell-Inspired	9/93	39.95	39.95
92-04-006	The Birthday Party	Rockwell-Inspired	12/93	39.95	39.95
Rhodes Studios		**Rockwell's Beautiful Dreamers**			
91-05-001	Sitting Pretty	Rockwell-Inspired	12/92	37.95	37.95
91-05-002	Dear Diary	Rockwell-Inspired	6/93	37.95	37.95
91-05-003	Secret Sonnets	Rockwell-Inspired	9/93	39.95	39.95
91-05-004	Springtime Serenade	Rockwell-Inspired	12/93	39.95	39.95
92-05-005	Debutante's Dance	Rockwell-Inspired	3/94	42.95	42.95
Rhodes Studio		**Rockwell's Gems of Wisdom**			
91-06-001	Love Cures All	Rockwell-Inspired	12/92	39.95	39.95
91-06-002	Practice Makes Perfect	Rockwell-Inspired	9/93	39.95	39.95
91-06-003	A Stitch In Time	Rockwell-Inspired	12/93	42.95	42.95
Also see Norman Rockwell Gallery					
River Shore		**Loveable-Baby Animals**			
78-01-001	Akiku-Seal	R. Brown	15,000	37.50	150.00
78-01-002	Alfred-Raccoon	R. Brown	15,000	42.50	45.00
79-01-003	Scooter-Chipmunk	R. Brown	15,000	45.00	55.00
79-01-004	Matilda-Koala	R. Brown	15,000	45.00	45.00
River Shore		**Wildlife Baby Animals**			
78-02-001	Fanny-Fawn	R. Brown	15,000	45.00	90.00
79-02-002	Roosevelt-Bear	R. Brown	15,000	50.00	65.00
79-02-003	Roscoe-Red Fox	R. Brown	15,000	50.00	50.00
80-02-004	Priscilla-Skunk	R. Brown	15,000	50.00	50.00
River Shore		**Rockwell Single Issues**			
81-03-001	Looking Out To Sea	N. Rockwell	9,500	85.00	225.00
82-03-002	Grandpa's Guardian	N. Rockwell	9,500	125.00	125.00
River Shore		**Babies of Endangered Species**			
84-04-001	Sidney (Cougar)	R. Brown	15,000	45.00	45.00
84-04-002	Baxter (Bear)	R. Brown	15,000	45.00	45.00
84-04-003	Caroline (Antelope)	R. Brown	15,000	45.00	45.00
84-04-004	Webster (Timberwolf)	R. Brown	15,000	45.00	45.00
84-04-005	Violet (Otter)	R. Brown	15,000	45.00	45.00
84-04-006	Chester (Prairie Dog)	R. Brown	15,000	45.00	45.00
84-04-007	Trevor (Fox)	R. Brown	15,000	45.00	45.00
84-04-008	Daisy (Wood Bison)	R. Brown	15,000	45.00	45.00
River Shore		**Wilderness Babies**			
85-05-001	Penelope (Deer)	R. Brown	15,000	45.00	45.00
85-05-002	Carmen (Burro)	R. Brown	15,000	45.00	45.00
85-05-003	Rocky (Bobcat)	R. Brown	15,000	45.00	45.00
85-05-004	Abercrombie (Polar Bear)	R. Brown	15,000	45.00	45.00
85-05-005	Elrod (Fox)	R. Brown	15,000	45.00	45.00
85-05-006	Reggie (Raccoon)	R. Brown	15,000	45.00	45.00
85-05-007	Arianne (Rabbit)	R. Brown	15,000	45.00	45.00
85-05-008	Annabel (Mountain Goat)	R. Brown	15,000	45.00	45.00
River Shore		**Lovable Teddies Musical Figurine Collection**			
87-06-001	Gilbert	M. Hague	Open	29.50	29.50
87-06-002	William	M. Hague	Open	29.50	29.50
87-06-003	Austin	M. Hague	Open	29.50	29.50
87-06-004	April	M. Hague	Open	29.50	29.50
88-06-005	Henry	M. Hague	Open	29.50	29.50
88-06-006	Harvey	M. Hague	Open	29.50	29.50
88-06-007	Adam	M. Hague	Open	29.50	29.50
88-06-008	Katie	M. Hague	Open	29.50	29.50
Norman Rockwell Gallery		**Rockwell's Family Album**			
91-01-001	Baby's First Steps	Rockwell-Inspired	6/93	39.95	39.95
91-01-002	Little Shaver	Rockwell-Inspired	12/93	39.95	39.95
92-01-003	Happy Birthday Dear Mother	Rockwell-Inspired	3/94	22.95	22.95
Norman Rockwell Gallery		**Young At Heart**			
92-02-001	Batter up	Rockwell-Inspired	N/A	34.95	34.95
Norman Rockwell Gallery		**Rockwell's Sugar And Spice**			
92-03-001	Dressing Up	Rockwell-Inspired	N/A	39.95	39.95
92-03-002	The Valedictorian	Rockwell-Inspired	N/A	39.95	39.95
Norman Rockwell Gallery		**Rockwell's Joys Of Motherhood**			
92-04-001	Mother's Little Angels	Rockwell-Inspired	N/A	34.95	34.95
92-04-002	Sweet Dreams	Rockwell-Inspired	N/A	34.95	34.95
Norman Rockwell Gallery		**Rockwell's Living Treasures**			
91-05-001	Grandpa's Gift Of Love	Rockwell-Inspired	N/A	39.95	39.95
92-05-002	Grandpa's Expert Advise	Rockwell-Inspired	N/A	39.95	39.95
92-05-003	Grandpa's First Mate	Rockwell-Inspired	N/A	39.95	39.95
Norman Rockwell Gallery		**Rockwell's Puppy Love**			
91-06-001	Buttercup	Rockwell-Inspired	6/93	44.95	44.95
91-06-002	Swingin'	Rockwell-Inspired	9/93	44.95	44.95
91-06-003	Schoolin'	Rockwell-Inspired	12/93	44.95	44.95
91-06-004	Sleddin'	Rockwell-Inspired	3/93	44.95	44.95
Norman Rockwell Gallery		**Rockwell's Best Friends**			
91-07-001	Bark If They Bite	Rockwell-Inspired	6/93	39.95	39.95
92-07-002	Two-Part Harmony	Rockwell-Inspired	9/93	39.95	39.95
92-07-003	Day Dreamers	Rockwell-Inspired	12/94	42.95	42.95
92-07-004	Gone Fishin'	Rockwell-Inspired	3/95	42.95	42.95
Norman Rockwell Gallery		**Reflections of Rockwell**			
91-08-001	When I Grow Up	Rockwell-Inspired	12/93	39.95	39.95
92-08-002	A Young Girl's Dream	Rockwell-Inspired	3/94	39.95	39.95
92-08-003	The Finishing Touch	Rockwell-Inspired	6/94	39.95	39.95
Norman Rockwell Gallery		**Rockwell's Winter Wonderland Snowglobes**			
91-09-001	Skater's Waltz	Rockwell-Inspired	12/93	29.95	29.95
92-09-002	All Wrapped Up	Rockwell-Inspired	6/94	29.95	29.95
92-09-003	Young At Heart	Rockwell-Inspired	9/94	32.95	32.95
Norman Rockwell Gallery		**Rockwell's Classic Santa Snowglobes**			
92-10-001	Santa's Workshop	Rockwell-Inspired	N/A	29.95	29.95
Also See Rhodes Studio					
Roman, Inc.		**Fontanini, The Collectible Creche**			
73-01-001	10cm., (15 piece Set)	E. Simonetti	Open	63.60	88.50
73-01-002	12cm., (15 piece Set)	E. Simonetti	Open	76.50	102.00
79-01-003	16cm., (15 piece Set)	E. Simonetti	Open	178.50	285.00
82-01-004	17cm., (15 piece Set)	E. Simonetti	Open	189.00	305.00
73-01-005	19cm., (15 piece Set)	E. Simonetti	Open	175.50	280.00
80-01-006	30cm., (15 piece Set)	E. Simonetti	Open	670.00	758.50
Roman, Inc.		**A Child's World 1st Edition**			
80-02-001	Nighttime Thoughts	F. Hook	15,000	25.00	65.00
80-02-002	Kiss Me Good Night	F. Hook	15,000	29.00	40.00
80-02-003	Sounds of the Sea	F. Hook	15,000	45.00	140.00
80-02-004	Beach Buddies, signed	F. Hook	15,000	29.00	600.00
80-02-005	My Big Brother	F. Hook	15,000	39.00	200.00
80-02-006	Helping Hands	F. Hook	15,000	45.00	75.00
80-02-007	Beach Buddies, unsigned	F. Hook	15,000	29.00	450.00
Roman, Inc.		**A Child's World 2nd Edition**			
81-03-001	Making Friends	F. Hook	15,000	42.00	46.00
81-03-002	Cat Nap	F. Hook	15,000	42.00	100.00
81-03-003	The Sea and Me	F. Hook	15,000	39.00	43.00
81-03-004	Sunday School	F. Hook	15,000	39.00	70.00
81-03-005	I'll Be Good	F. Hook	15,000	36.00	70.00
81-03-006	All Dressed Up	F. Hook	15,000	36.00	70.00
Roman, Inc.		**A Child's World 3rd Edition**			
81-04-001	Pathway to Dreams	F. Hook	15,000	47.00	50.00
81-04-002	Road to Adventure	F. Hook	15,000	47.00	50.00
81-04-003	Sisters	F. Hook	15,000	64.00	69.00
81-04-004	Bear Hug	F. Hook	15,000	42.00	45.00
81-04-005	Spring Breeze	F. Hook	15,000	37.50	40.00

Company / Number	Name	Series / Artist	Edition Limit	Issue Price	Quote
81-04-006	Youth	F. Hook	15,000	37.50	40.00
Roman, Inc.		**A Child's World 4th Edition**			
82-05-001	All Bundled Up	F. Hook	15,000	37.50	40.00
82-05-002	Bedtime	F. Hook	15,000	35.00	38.00
82-05-003	Birdie	F. Hook	15,000	37.50	40.00
82-05-004	My Dolly!	F. Hook	15,000	39.00	40.00
82-05-005	Ring Bearer	F. Hook	15,000	39.00	40.00
82-05-006	Flower Girl	F. Hook	15,000	42.00	45.00
Roman, Inc.		**A Child's World 5th Edition**			
83-06-001	Ring Around the Rosie	F. Hook	15,000	99.00	105.00
83-06-002	Handful of Happiness	F. Hook	15,000	36.00	40.00
83-06-003	He Loves Me...	F. Hook	15,000	49.00	55.00
83-06-004	Finish Line	F. Hook	15,000	39.00	42.00
83-06-005	Brothers	F. Hook	15,000	64.00	70.00
83-06-006	Puppy's Pal	F. Hook	15,000	39.00	42.00
Roman, Inc.		**A Child's World 6th Edition**			
84-07-001	Good Doggie	F. Hook	15,000	47.00	50.00
84-07-002	Sand Castles	F. Hook	15,000	37.50	40.00
84-07-003	Nature's Wonders	F. Hook	15,000	29.00	31.00
84-07-004	Let's Play Catch	F. Hook	15,000	33.00	35.00
84-07-005	Can I Help?	F. Hook	15,000	37.50	40.00
84-07-006	Future Artist	F. Hook	15,000	42.00	45.00
Roman, Inc.		**A Child's World 7th Edition**			
85-08-001	Art Class	F. Hook	15,000	99.00	105.00
85-08-002	Please Hear Me	F. Hook	15,000	29.00	30.00
85-08-003	Don't Tell Anyone	F. Hook	15,000	49.00	50.00
85-08-004	Mother's Helper	F. Hook	15,000	45.00	50.00
85-08-005	Yummm!	F. Hook	15,000	36.00	39.00
85-08-006	Look at Me!	F. Hook	15,000	42.00	45.00
Roman, Inc.		**A Child's World 8th Edition**			
85-09-001	Private Ocean	F. Hook	15,000	29.00	31.00
85-09-002	Just Stopped By	F. Hook	15,000	36.00	40.00
85-09-003	Dress Rehearsal	F. Hook	15,000	33.00	35.00
85-09-004	Chance of Showers	F. Hook	15,000	33.00	35.00
85-09-005	Engine	F. Hook	15,000	36.00	40.00
85-09-006	Puzzling	F. Hook	15,000	36.00	40.00
Roman, Inc.		**A Child's World 9th Edition**			
87-10-001	Li'l Brother	F. Hook	15,000	60.00	65.00
87-10-002	Hopscotch	F. Hook	15,000	67.50	70.00
Roman, Inc.		**Rohn's Clowns**			
84-15-001	White Face	E. Rohn	7,500	95.00	95.00
84-15-002	Auguste	E. Rohn	7,500	95.00	95.00
84-15-003	Hobo	E. Rohn	7,500	95.00	95.00
Roman, Inc.		**The Masterpiece Collection**			
79-16-001	Adoration	F. Lippe	5,000	73.00	73.00
80-16-002	Madonna with Grapes	P. Mignard	5,000	85.00	85.00
81-16-003	The Holy Family	G. delle Notti	5,000	98.00	98.00
82-16-004	Madonna of the Streets	R. Ferruzzi	5,000	65.00	65.00
Roman, Inc.		**Ceramica Excelsis**			
77-17-001	Madonna and Child with Angels	Unknown	5,000	60.00	60.00
77-17-002	What Happened to Your Hand?	Unknown	5,000	60.00	60.00
77-17-003	Madonna with Child	Unknown	5,000	65.00	65.00
77-17-004	St. Francis	Unknown	5,000	60.00	60.00
77-17-005	Christ Knocking at the Door	Unknown	5,000	60.00	60.00
78-17-006	Infant of Prague	Unknown	5,000	37.50	60.00
78-17-007	Christ in the Garden of Gethsemane	Unknown	5,000	40.00	60.00
78-17-008	Flight into Egypt	Unknown	5,000	59.00	90.00
78-17-009	Christ Entering Jerusalem	Unknown	5,000	96.00	96.00
78-17-010	Holy Family at Work	Unknown	5,000	96.00	96.00
78-17-011	Assumption Madonna	Unknown	5,000	56.00	56.00
78-17-012	Guardian Angel with Girl	Unknown	5,000	69.00	69.00
78-17-013	Guardian Angel with Boy	Unknown	5,000	69.00	69.00
79-17-014	Moses	Unknown	5,000	77.00	77.00
79-17-015	Noah	Unknown	5,000	77.00	77.00
79-17-016	Jesus Speaks in Parables	Unknown	5,000	90.00	90.00
80-17-017	Way to Emmaus	Unknown	5,000	155.00	155.00
80-17-018	Daniel in the Lion's Den	Unknown	5,000	80.00	80.00
80-17-019	David	Unknown	5,000	77.00	77.00
81-17-020	Innocence	Unknown	5,000	95.00	95.00
81-17-021	Journey to Bethlehem	Unknown	5,000	89.00	89.00
81-17-022	Way of the Cross	Unknown	5,000	59.00	59.00
81-17-023	Sermon on the Mount	Unknown	5,000	56.00	56.00
83-17-024	Good Shepherd	Unknown	5,000	49.00	49.00
83-17-025	Holy Family	Unknown	5,000	72.00	72.00
83-17-026	St. Francis	Unknown	5,000	59.50	59.50
83-17-027	St. Anne	Unknown	5,000	49.00	49.00
83-17-028	Jesus with Children	Unknown	5,000	74.00	74.00
83-17-029	Kneeling Santa	Unknown	5,000	95.00	95.00
Roman, Inc.		**Hook**			
82-18-001	Sailor Mates	F. Hook	2,000	290.00	315.00
82-18-002	Sun Shy	F. Hook	2,000	290.00	315.00
Roman, Inc.		**Frances Hook's Four Seasons**			
84-19-001	Winter	F. Hook	12,500	95.00	100.00
85-19-002	Spring	F. Hook	12,500	95.00	100.00
85-19-003	Summer	F. Hook	12,500	95.00	100.00
85-19-004	Fall	F. Hook	12,500	95.00	100.00
Roman, Inc.		**Jam Session**			
85-20-001	Trombone Player	E. Rohn	7,500	145.00	145.00
85-20-002	Bass Player	E. Rohn	7,500	145.00	145.00
85-20-003	Banjo Player	E. Rohn	7,500	145.00	145.00
85-20-004	Coronet Player	E. Rohn	7,500	145.00	145.00
85-20-005	Clarinet Player	E. Rohn	7,500	145.00	145.00
85-20-006	Drummer	E. Rohn	7,500	145.00	145.00
Roman, Inc.		**Spencer**			
85-21-001	Moon Goddess	I. Spencer	5,000	195.00	195.00
85-21-002	Flower Princess	I. Spencer	5,000	195.00	195.00
Roman, Inc.		**Hook**			
86-22-001	Carpenter Bust	F. Hook	Yr.Iss.	95.00	95.00
86-22-002	Carpenter Bust-Heirloom Edition	F. Hook	Yr.Iss.	95.00	95.00
87-22-003	Madonna and Child	F. Hook	15,000	39.50	39.50
87-22-004	Little Children, Come to Me	F. Hook	15,000	45.00	45.00
Roman, Inc.		**Catnippers**			
85-23-001	The Paw that Refreshes	I. Spencer	15,000	45.00	45.00
85-23-002	A Christmas Mourning	I. Spencer	15,000	45.00	49.50
85-23-003	A Tail of Two Kitties	I. Spencer	15,000	45.00	45.00
85-23-004	Sandy Claws	I. Spencer	15,000	45.00	45.00
85-23-005	Can't We Be Friends	I. Spencer	15,000	45.00	45.00
85-23-006	A Baffling Yarn	I. Spencer	15,000	45.00	45.00
85-23-007	Flying Tiger-Retired	I. Spencer	15,000	45.00	45.00
85-23-008	Flora and Felina	I. Spencer	15,000	45.00	49.50
Roman, Inc.		**Heartbeats**			
86-24-001	Miracle	I. Spencer	5,000	145.00	145.00
87-24-002	Storytime	I. Spencer	5,000	145.00	145.00
Roman, Inc.		**Classic Brides of the Century**			
89-25-001	1900-Flora	E. Williams	5,000	175.00	175.00
89-25-002	1910-Elizabeth Grace	E. Williams	5,000	175.00	175.00
89-25-003	1920-Mary Claire	E. Williams	5,000	175.00	175.00
89-25-004	1930-Kathleen	E. Williams	5,000	175.00	175.00
89-25-005	1940-Margaret	E. Williams	5,000	175.00	175.00
89-25-006	1950-Barbara Ann	E. Williams	5,000	175.00	175.00
89-25-007	1960-Dianne	E. Williams	5,000	175.00	175.00
89-25-008	1970-Heather	E. Williams	5,000	175.00	175.00
89-25-009	1980-Jennifer	E. Williams	5,000	175.00	175.00
92-25-010	1990-Stephanie Helen	E. Williams	5,000	175.00	175.00
Roman Inc.		**Dolfi Original-5" Wood**			
89-26-001	My First Kitten	L. Martin	5,000	230.00	230.00
89-26-002	Flower Child	L. Martin	5,000	230.00	230.00
89-26-003	Pampered Puppies	L. Martin	5,000	230.00	230.00
89-26-004	Wrapped In Love	L. Martin	5,000	230.00	230.00
89-26-005	Garden Secrets	L. Martin	5,000	230.00	230.00
89-26-006	Puppy Express	L. Martin	5,000	230.00	230.00
89-26-007	Sleepyhead	L. Martln	5,000	230.00	230.00
89-26-008	Mother Hen	L. Martin	5,000	230.00	230.00
89-26-009	Holiday Herald	L. Martln	5,000	230.00	230.00
89-26-010	Birdland Cafe	L. Martin	5,000	230.00	230.00
89-26-011	My First Cake	L. Martin	5,000	230.00	230.00
89-26-012	Mud Puddles	L. Martin	5,000	230.00	230.00
89-26-013	Study Break	L. Martin	5,000	250.00	250.00
89-26-014	Dress Rehearsal	L. Martin	5,000	375.00	375.00
89-26-015	Friends & Flowers	L. Martln	5,000	300.00	300.00
89-26-016	Merry Little Light	L. Martin	5,000	250.00	250.00
89-26-017	Mary & Joey	L. Martin	5,000	375.00	375.00
89-26-018	Little Santa	L. Martin	5,000	250.00	250.00
89-26-019	Sing a Song of Joy	L. Martin	5,000	300.00	300.00
89-26-020	Barefoot In Spring	L. Martin	5,000	300.00	300.00
89-26-021	My Favorite Things	L. Martin	5,000	300.00	300.00
89-26-022	Have I Been That Good	L. Martin	5,000	375.00	375.00
89-26-023	A Shoulder to Lean On	L. Martin	5,000	300.00	300.00
89-26-024	Big Chief Sitting Dog	L. Martin	5,000	250.00	250.00
Roman, Inc.		**Dolfi Original-7" Stoneart**			
89-27-001	My First Kitten	L. Martin	Open	110.00	110.00
89-27-002	Flower Child	L. Martin	Open	110.00	110.00
89-27-003	Pampered Puppies	L. Martin	Open	110.00	110.00
89-27-004	Wrapped In Love	L. Martin	Open	110.00	110.00
89-27-005	Garden Secrets	L. Martin	Open	110.00	110.00
89-27-006	Puppy Express	L. Martin	Open	110.00	110.00
89-27-007	Sleepyhead	L. Martln	Open	110.00	110.00
89-27-008	Mother Hen	L. Martin	Open	110.00	110.00
89-27-009	Holiday Herald	L. Martin	Open	110.00	110.00
89-27-010	Birdland Cafe	L. Martin	Open	110.00	110.00
89-27-011	My First Cake	L. Martin	Open	110.00	110.00
89-27-012	Mud Puddles	L. Martin	Open	110.00	110.00
89-27-013	Study Break	L. Martin	Open	120.00	120.00
89-27-014	Dress Rehearsal	L. Martin	Open	185.00	185.00
89-27-015	Friends & Flowers	L. Martin	Open	150.00	150.00
89-27-016	Merry Little Light	L. Martin	Open	120.00	120.00
89-27-017	Mary & Joey	L. Martin	Open	185.00	185.00
89-27-018	Little Santa	L. Martin	Open	120.00	120.00
89-27-019	Sing a Song of Joy	L. Martin	Open	150.00	150.00
89-27-020	Barefoot In Spring	L. Martin	Open	150.00	150.00
89-27-021	My Favorite Things	L. Martin	Open	150.00	150.00
89-27-022	Have I Been That Good	L. Martin	Open	185.00	185.00
89-27-023	A Shoulder to Lean On	L. Martin	Open	150.00	150.00
89-27-024	Big Chief Sitting Dog	L. Martin	Open	120.00	120.00
Roman, Inc.		**Dolfi Original-10" Stoneart**			
89-28-001	My First Kitten	L. Martin	Open	300.00	300.00
89-28-002	Flower Child	L. Martin	Open	300.00	300.00
89-28-003	Pampered Puppies	L. Martin	Open	300.00	300.00
89-28-004	Wrapped in Love	L. Martin	Open	300.00	300.00
89-28-005	Garden Secrets	L. Martin	Open	300.00	300.00
89-28-006	Puppy Express	L. Martin	Open	300.00	300.00
89-28-007	Sleepyhead	L. Martin	Open	300.00	300.00
89-28-008	Mother Hen	L. Martin	Open	300.00	300.00
89-28-009	Holiday Herald	L. Martin	Open	300.00	300.00
89-28-010	Birdland Cafe	L. Martin	Open	300.00	300.00
89-28-011	My First Cake	L. Martin	Open	300.00	300.00
89-28-012	Mud Puddles	L. Martin	Open	300.00	300.00
89-28-013	Study Break	L. Martin	Open	325.00	325.00
89-28-014	Dress Rehearsal	L. Martin	Open	495.00	495.00
89-28-015	Friends & Flowers	L. Martin	Open	400.00	400.00
89-28-016	Merry Little Light	L. Martin	Open	325.00	325.00
89-28-017	Mary & Joey	L. Martin	Open	495.00	495.00
89-28-018	Little Santa	L. Martin	Open	325.00	325.00
89-28-019	Sing a Song of Joy	L. Martin	Open	400.00	400.00
89-28-020	Barefoot In Spring	L. Martin	Open	400.00	400.00
89-28-021	My Favorite Things	L. Martin	Open	400.00	400.00
89-28-022	Have I Been That Good	L. Martin	Open	495.00	495.00
89-28-023	A Shoulder to Lean On	L. Martin	Open	400.00	400.00
89-28-024	Big Chief Sitting Dog	L. Martin	Open	325.00	325.00
Roman, Inc.		**Dolfi Original-10" Wood**			
89-29-001	My First Kitten	L. Martin	2,000	750.00	750.00
89-29-002	Flower Child	L. Martin	2,000	750.00	750.00
89-29-003	Pampered Puppies	L. Martin	2,000	750.00	750.00
89-29-004	Wrapped in Love	L. Martin	2,000	750.00	750.00
89-29-005	Garden Secrets	L. Martin	2,000	750.00	750.00

Company / Number	Name	Series / Artist	Edition Limit	Issue Price	Quote
89-29-006	Puppy Express	L. Martin	2,000	750.00	750.00
89-29-007	Sleepyhead	L. Martin	2,000	750.00	750.00
89-29-008	Mother Hen	L. Martin	2,000	750.00	750.00
89-29-009	Holiday Herald	L. Martin	2,000	750.00	750.00
89-29-010	Birdland Cafe	L. Martin	2.000	750.00	750.00
89-29-011	My First Cake	L. Martin	2,000	750.00	750.00
89-29-012	Mud Puddles	L. Martin	2,000	750.00	750.00
89-29-013	Study Break	L. Martin	2,000	825.00	825.00
89-29-014	Dress Rehearsal	L. Martin	2,000	1250.00	1250.00
89-29-015	Friends & Flowers	L. Martin	2,000	1000.00	1000.00
89-29-016	Merry Little Light	L. Martin	2,000	825.00	825.00
89-29-017	Mary & Joey	L. Martin	2,000	1250.00	1250.00
89-29-018	Little Santa	L. Martin	2,000	825.00	825.00
89-29-019	Sing a Song of Joy	L. Martin	2,000	1000.00	1000.00
89-29-020	Barefoot In Spring	L. Mariin	2,000	1000.00	1000.00
89-29-021	My Favorite Things	L. Martin	2,000	1000.00	1000.00
89-29-022	Have I Been That Good	L. Martin	2,000	1250.00	1250.00
89-29-023	A Shoulder to Lean On	L. Martin	2,000	1000.00	1000.00
89-29-024	Big Chief Sitting Dog	L. Martin	2,000	825.00	825.00
Roman, Inc.		**The Museum Collection by Angela Tripi**			
90-30-001	The Mentor	A. Tripi	1,000	290.00	290.00
91-30-002	The Fiddler	A. Tripi	1,000	175.00	175.00
91-30-003	Christopher Columbus	A. Tripi	1,000	250.00	250.00
91-30-004	St. Francis of Assisi	A. Tripi	1,000	175.00	175.00
91-30-005	The Caddie	A. Tripi	1,000	135.00	135.00
91-30-006	A Gentleman's Game	A. Tripi	1,000	175.00	175.00
91-30-007	Tee Time at St. Andrew's	A. Tripi	1,000	175.00	175.00
92-30-008	Prince of the Plains	A. Tripi	1,000	175.00	175.00
92-30-009	The Fur Trapper	A. Tripi	1,000	175.00	175.00
92-30-010	Justice for All	A. Tripi	1,000	95.00	95.00
92-30-011	Flying Ace	A. Tripi	1,000	95.00	95.00
92-30-012	Our Family Doctor	A. Tripi	1,000	95.00	95.00
92-30-013	To Serve and Protect	A. Tripi	1,000	95.00	95.00
92-30-014	Ladies' Day	A. Tripi	1,000	175.00	175.00
92-30-015	Ladies' Tee	A. Tripi	1,000	250.00	250.00
92-30-016	The Tap In	A. Tripi	1,000	175.00	175.00
92-30-017	Fore!	A. Tripi	1,000	175.00	175.00
Roman, Inc.		**Fontanini Heirloom Nativity**			
74-31-001	5" Mary (5")	E. Simonetti	Closed	2.50	9.50
74-31-002	Jesus (5")	E. Simonetti	Closed	2.50	9.50
74-31-003	Joseph (5")	E. Simonetti	Closed	2.50	9.50
Roman, Inc.		**Fontanini Presepio Collection**			
92-32-001	Ariel	E. Simonetti	Yr.Iss.	29.50	29.50
Roman, Inc.		**Fontanini Collectors' Club Member Only**			
91-33-001	The Pilgrimage	E. Simonetti	Yr.Iss	24.95	24.95
92-33-002	She Rescued Me	E. Simonetti	Yr.Iss	23.50	23.50
Royal Doulton		**Royal Doulton Figurines**			
XX-01-001	Indian Brave	P. Davies	500	2500.00	5700.00
XX-01-002	The Palio	P. Davies	500	2500.00	6500.00
XX-01-003	Beethoven	R. Garbe	25	N/A	6500.00
Royal Doulton		**Royalty**			
XX-02-001	Queen Elizabeth II	P. Davies	750	200.00	1950-2050.
XX-02-002	Queen Mother	P. Davies	1,500	650.00	1200.00
XX-02-003	Duchess Of York	E. Griffiths	1,500	495.00	650.00
XX-02-004	Duke Of Edinburgh	P. Davies	750	395.00	395.00
XX-02-005	Prince Of Wales HN2883	E. Griffiths	1,500	395.00	450-850.
XX-02-006	Prince Of Wales HN2884	E. Griffiths	1,500	750.00	750.00
XX-02-007	Princess Of Wales HN2887	E. Griffiths	1,500	750.00	1250.00
XX-02-008	Lady Diana Spencer	E. Griffiths	1,500	395.00	650-750.
Royal Doulton		**Lady Musicians**			
XX-03-001	Cello	P. Davies	750	250.00	1000.00
XX-03-002	Chitarrone	P. Davies	750	250.00	600-1200.
XX-03-003	Cymbals	P. Davies	750	325.00	600-950.
XX-03-004	Dulcimer	P. Davies	750	375.00	600-1500.
XX-03-005	Flute	P. Davies	750	250.00	950-1100.
XX-03-006	French Horn	P. Davies	750	400.00	550-950.
XX-03-007	Harp	P. Davies	750	275.00	1300-1800.
XX-03-008	Hurdy Gurdy	P. Davies	750	375.00	600-1300.
XX-03-009	Lute	P. Davies	750	250.00	900.00
XX-03-010	Viola d'Amore	P. Davies	750	400.00	550-1000.
XX-03-011	Violin	P. Davies	750	250.00	900-950.
XX-03-012	Virginals	P. Davies	750	250.00	1200-1500.
Royal Doulton		**Dancers Of The World**			
XX-04-001	Dancers, Balinese	P. Davies	750	950.00	950.00
XX-04-002	Dancers, Breton	P. Davies	750	850.00	850-900.
XX-04-003	Dancers, Chinese	P. Davies	750	750.00	750-900.
XX-04-004	Dancers, Indian Temple	P. Davies	750	400.00	900-1100.
XX-04-005	Dancers, Kurdish	P. Davies	750	550.00	600-900.
XX-04-006	Dancers, Mexican	P. Davies	750	550.00	550-900.
XX-04-007	Dancers, No. American Indian	P. Davies	750	950.00	950.00
XX-04-008	Dancers, Philippine	P. Davies	750	450.00	850-900.
XX-04-009	Dancers, Polish	P. Davies	750	750.00	850-1500.
XX-04-010	Dancers, Scottish	P. Davies	750	450.00	850-1200.
XX-04-011	Dancers, Flamenco	P. Davies	750	400.00	1250-1500.
XX-04-012	Dancers, West Indian	P. Davies	750	850.00	550-900.
Royal Doulton		**Soldiers of The Revolution**			
XX-05-001	Soldiers, New York	E. Griffiths	350	750.00	750.00
XX-05-002	Soldiers, New Hampshire	E. Griffiths	350	750.00	750.00
XX-05-003	Soldiers, New Jersey	E. Griffiths	350	750.00	2000.00
XX-05-004	Soldiers, Connecticut	E. Griffiths	350	750.00	750.00
XX-05-005	Soldiers, Delaware	E. Griffiths	350	750.00	750.00
XX-05-006	Soldiers, Georgia	E. Griffiths	350	750.00	850.00
XX-05-007	Soldiers, Massachusetts	E. Griffiths	350	750.00	750.00
XX-05-008	Soldiers, Pennsylvania	E. Griffiths	350	750.00	750.00
XX-05-009	Soldiers, Rhode Island	E. Griffiths	350	750.00	750.00
XX-05-010	Soldiers, South Carolina	E. Griffiths	350	750.00	850.00
XX-05-011	Soldiers, North Carolina	E. Griffiths	350	750.00	750.00
XX-05-012	Soldiers, Maryland	E. Griffiths	350	750.00	750.00
XX-05-013	Soldiers, Virginia	E. Griffiths	350	1500.00	2500.00
XX-05-014	Soldiers, Washington	Ispanky	750	N/A	2000.00
Royal Doulton		**Femmes Fatales**			
XX-06-001	Cleopatra	P. Davies	750	750.00	1350.00
XX-06-002	Helen of Troy	P. Davies	750	1250.00	1250-1400.

Company / Number	Name	Series / Artist	Edition Limit	Issue Price	Quote
XX-06-003	Queen of Sheba	P. Davies	750	1250.00	1250-1400.
XX-06-004	Tz'u-Hsi	P. Davies	750	1250.00	1250.00
XX-06-005	Eve	P. Davies	750	1250.00	1250.00
XX-06-006	Lucrezia Borgia	P. Davies	750	1250.00	1250.00
Royal Doulton		**Myths & Maidens**			
XX-07-001	Lady & Unicorn	R. Jefferson	S/O	2500.00	2500-3500.
XX-07-002	Leda & Swan	R. Jefferson	300	2950.00	2950-3200.
XX-07-003	Juno & Peacock	R. Jefferson	300	2950.00	2950-3200.
XX-07-004	Europa & Bull	R. Jefferson	300	2950.00	2950-3200.
XX-07-005	Diana The Huntress	R. Jefferson	300	2950.00	2950-3200.
Royal Doulton		**Gentle Arts**			
XX-08-001	Spinning	P. Davies	750	1250.00	1250-1400.
XX-08-002	Tapestry Weaving	P. Parsons	750	1250.00	1250.00
XX-08-003	Writing	P. Parsons	750	1350.00	1350.00
XX-08-004	Painting	P. Parsons	750	1350.00	1350.00
XX-08-005	Adornment	N/A	750	1350.00	1350.00
XX-08-006	Flower Arranging	N/A	750	1350.00	1350.00
Royal Doulton		**Ships Figureheads**			
XX-09-001	Ajax	S. Keenan	950	N/A	550-700.
XX-09-002	Benmore	S. Keenan	950	N/A	550-700.
XX-09-003	Chieftain	S. Keenan	950	N/A	750.00
XX-09-004	Hibernia	S. Keenan	950	N/A	950.00
XX-09-005	Lalla Rookh	S. Keenan	950	N/A	750.00
XX-09-006	Mary, Queen of Scots	S. Keenan	950	N/A	1200.00
XX-09-007	Lord Nelson	S. Keenan	950	N/A	850.00
XX-09-008	Pocahontas	S. Keenan	950	N/A	950.00
Royal Doulton		**Les Saisons**			
XX-10-001	Automne	R. Jefferson	300	850.00	950.00
XX-10-002	Printemps	R. Jefferson	300	850.00	850.00
XX-10-003	L'Hiver	R. Jefferson	300	850.00	850.00
XX-10-004	L'Ete	R. Jefferson	300	850.00	895.00
Royal Doulton		**Queens of Realm**			
XX-11-001	Queen Elizabeth I	P. Parsons	S/O	495.00	495-1200.
XX-11-002	Queen Victoria	P Parsons	S/O	495.00	950-1000
XX-11-003	Queen Anne	N/A	5,000	525.00	550.00
XX-11-004	Mary, Queen of Scots	N/A	S/O	550.00	650-950.
Royal Doulton		**Gainsborough Ladies**			
XX-12-001	Mary, Countess Howe	P. Gee	5,000	650.00	650-700.
91-12-002	Lady Sheffield	P. Gee	5,000	650.00	650-700.
91-12-003	Hon Frances Duncombe	P. Gee	5,000	650.00	650-700.
91-12-004	Countess of Sefton	P. Gee	5,000	650.00	650-700.
Royal Doulton		**Reynolds Collection**			
91-13-001	Lady Worsley HN3318	P. Gee	5,000	550.00	550-600.
92-13-002	Countess Harrington HN3317	P. Gee	5,000	550.00	550-600.
92-13-003	Mrs. Hugh Bonfoy HN3319	P. Gee	5,000	550.00	550-600.
93-13-004	Countess Spencer HN3320	P. Gee	5,000	550.00	550-600.
Royal Doulton		**Age of Innocence**			
91-14-001	Feeding Time	N. Pedley	9,500	245.00	250.00
91-14-002	Making Friends	N. Pedley	9,500	270.00	275.00
91-14-003	Puppy Love	N. Pedley	9,500	270.00	275.00
92-14-004	First Outing	N. Pedley	9,500	275.00	275.00
Royal Doulton		**Character Jugs**			
91-15-001	Henry VIII	W. Harper	1,991	395.00	600-850.
91-15-002	Santa Claus Miniature	N/A	5,000	50.00	50-75.00
91-15-003	Fortune Teller	N/A	Yr.Iss.	130.00	130.00
92-15-004	Winston Churchill	N/A	Yr.Iss.	195.00	195.00
92-15-005	King Charles I	W. Harper	2,500	450.00	450.00
Royal Doulton		**Star Crossed Lovers Character Jugs**			
86-16-001	Napoleon & Josephine	M. Abberley	9,500	195.00	195.00
XX-16-002	Anthony & Cleopatra	M. Abberley	S/O	195.00	195.00
89-16-003	King Arthur & Guinevere	S. Taylor	9,500	195.00	195.00
88-16-004	Samson & Delilah	S. Taylor	9,500	195.00	195.00
Royal Doulton		**Antagonists Character Jugs**			
86-17-001	George III & George Washington	M. Abberley	9,500	195.00	195.00
Royal Doulton		**Prestige Figures**			
91-18-001	Columbine	N/A	N/A	1250.00	1250.00
91-18-002	Fighter Elephant	N/A	N/A	2500.00	2500.00
91-18-003	Fox	N/A	N/A	1550.00	1550.00
91-18-004	Harlequin	N/A	N/A	1250.00	1250.00
91-18-005	Jack Point	N/A	N/A	2900.00	2900.00
91-18-006	King Charles	N/A	N/A	2500.00	2500.00
91-18-007	Leopard on Rock	N/A	N/A	3000.00	3000.00
91-18-008	Lion on Rock	N/A	N/A	3000.00	3000.00
91-18-009	Matador and Bull	N/A	N/A	21500.00	21500.00
91-18-010	The Moor	N/A	N/A	2500.00	2500.00
91-18-011	Princess Badoura	N/A	N/A	28000.00	28000.00
91-18-012	St George and Dragon	N/A	N/A	13600.00	13600.00
91-18-013	Tiger	N/A	N/A	1950.00	1950.00
91-18-014	Tiger on Rock	N/A	N/A	3000.00	3000.00
92-18-015	Christopher Columbus	A. Maslankowski	1,492	1950.00	1950.00
92-18-016	Napoleon at Waterloo	A. Maslankowski	1,500	1900.00	1900.00
Royal Doulton		**Figure of the Year**			
91-19-001	Amy	P. Gee	Closed	195.00	195.00
92-19-002	Mary	P. Gee	Yr.Iss.	225.00	225.00
Royal Doulton		**Royal Doulton Collectors' Club**			
80-20-001	John Doulton Jug (8 O'Clock)	N/A	Yr.Iss.	70.00	125.00
81-20-002	Sleepy Darling Figure	N/A	Yr.Iss.	100.00	195.00
82-20-003	Dog of Fo	N/A	Yr.Iss.	50.00	150.00
82-20-004	Prized Possessions Figure	N/A	Yr.Iss.	125.00	475.00
83-20-005	Loving Cup	N/A	Yr.Iss.	75.00	275.00
83-20-006	Springtime	N/A	Yr.Iss.	125.00	350.00
84-20-007	Sir Henry Doulton Jug	N/A	Yr.Iss.	50.00	125.00
84-20-008	Pride & Joy Figure	N/A	Yr.Iss.	125.00	225.00
85-20-009	Top of the Hill Plate	N/A	Yr.Iss.	34.95	75.00
85-20-010	Wintertime Figure	N/A	Yr.Iss.	125.00	195.00
86-20-011	Albert Sagger Toby Jug	N/A	Yr.Iss.	34.95	70.00
86-20-012	Auctioneer Figure	N/A	Yr.Iss.	150.00	195.00
87-20-013	Collector Bunnykins	N/A	Yr.Iss.	40.00	295.00
87-20-014	Summertime Figurine	N/A	Yr.Iss.	140.00	150.00

Number	Name	Artist	Edition Limit	Issue Price	Quote
88-20-015	Top of the Hill Miniature Figurine	N/A	Yr.Iss.	95.00	125.00
88-20-016	Beefeater Tiny Jug	N/A	Yr.Iss.	25.00	125.00
88-20-017	Old Salt Tea Pot	N/A	Yr.Iss.	135.00	250.00
89-20-018	Geisha Flambe Figure	N/A	Yr.Iss.	195.00	195.00
90-20-019	Flower Sellers Children Plate	N/A	Yr.Iss.	190.00	190.00
90-20-020	Autumntime Figure	N/A	Yr.Iss.	190.00	190.00
90-20-021	Jester Mini Figure	N/A	Yr.Iss.	115.00	115.00
90-20-022	Old King Cole Tiny Jug	N/A	Yr.Iss.	35.00	95.00
91-20-023	Bunny's Bedtime Figure	N/A	Yr.Iss.	195.00	250.00
91-20-024	Charles Dickens Jug	N/A	Yr.Iss.	100.00	100.00
91-20-025	L'Ambiteuse Figure	N/A	Yr.Iss.	295.00	295.00
91-20-026	Christopher Columbus Jug	N/A	Yr.Iss.	95.00	95.00
92-20-027	Discovery Figure	N/A	Yr.Iss.	160.00	160.00
Royal Worcester		**Dorothy Doughty Porcelains**			
35-01-001	American Redstarts and Hemlock	D. Doughty	66	Unkn.	5500.00
41-01-002	Apple Blossoms	D. Doughty	250	400.00	1400-3750.
63-01-003	Audubon Warblers	D. Doughty	500	1350.00	2100-4200.
38-01-004	Baltimore Orioles	D. Doughty	250	350.00	Unkn.
56-01-005	Bewick's Wrens & Yellow Jasmine	D. Doughty	500	600.00	2100-3800.
36-01-006	Bluebirds	D. Doughty	350	500.00	8500-9000.
64-01-007	Blue Tits & Pussy Willow	D. Doughty	500	250.00	3000.00
40-01-008	Bobwhite Quail	D. Doughty	22	275.00	11000.
59-01-009	Cactus Wrens	D. Doughty	500	1250.00	1700-4500.
60-01-010	Canyon Wrens	D. Doughty	500	750.00	2000-4000.
37-01-011	Cardinals	D. Doughty	500	500.00	20000-9250.
68-01-012	Carolina Paroquet, Color	D. Doughty	350	1200.00	1900-2200.
68-01-013	Carolina Paroquet, White	D. Doughty	75	600.00	Unkn.
65-01-014	Cerulean Warblers & Red Maple	D. Doughty	500	1350.00	1400-3000.
38-01-015	Chickadees & Larch	D. Doughty	300	350.00	8500-8900.
65-01-016	Chuffchaff	D. Doughty	500	1500.00	1300-2900.
42-01-017	Crabapple Blossom Sprays And A Butterfly	D. Doughty	250	Unkn.	800.00
40-01-018	Crabapples	D. Doughty	250	400.00	3700-4250.
67-01-019	Downy Woodpecker & Pecan, Color	D. Doughty	400	1500.00	1000-2400.
67-01-020	Downy Woodpecker & Pecan, White	D. Doughty	75	1000.00	1900.00
59-01-021	Elf Owl	D. Doughty	500	875.00	Unkn.
55-01-022	Gnatcatchers	D. Doughty	500	600.00	2700-4900.
72-01-023	Goldcrests, Pair	D. Doughty	500	4200.00	Unkn.
36-01-024	Goldfinches & Thistle	D. Doughty	250	350.00	2000-7000.
68-01-025	Gray Wagtail	D. Doughty	500	600.00	Unkn.
61-01-026	Hooded Warblers	D. Doughty	500	950.00	4300.00
50-01-027	Hummingbirds And Fuchsia	D. Doughty	500	Unkn.	2800.00
42-01-028	Indigo Bunting And Plum Twig	D. Doughty	5,000	Unkn.	Unkn.
42-01-029	Indigo Buntings, Blackberry Sprays	D. Doughty	500	375.00	1700-3500.
65-01-030	Kingfisher Cock & Autumn Beech	D. Doughty	500	1250.00	1900-2300.
52-01-031	Kinglets & Noble Pine	D. Doughty	500	450.00	1300-4800.
66-01-032	Lark Sparrow	D. Doughty	500	750.00	Unkn.
62-01-033	Lazuli Bunting & Chokecherries, Color	D. Doughty	500	1350.00	3000-4500.
62-01-034	Lazuli Bunting & Chokecherries, White	D. Doughty	100	1350.00	2600-3000.
64-01-035	Lesser Whitethroats	D. Doughty	500	350.00	1200-4000.
50-01-036	Magnolia Warbler	D. Doughty	150	1100.00	1900-3600.
77-01-037	Meadow Pipit	D. Doughty	500	1800.00	1800.00
50-01-038	Mexican Feijoa	D. Doughty	250	600.00	2600-4900.
40-01-039	Mockingbirds	D. Doughty	500	450.00	7200-7750.
42-01-040	Mockingbirds and Peach Blossom	D. Doughty	500	Unkn.	Unkn.
64-01-041	Moorhen Chick	D. Doughty	500	1000.00	Unkn.
64-01-042	Mountain Bluebirds	D. Doughty	500	950.00	1700-2300.
55-01-043	Myrtle Warblers	D. Doughty	500	550.00	1300-4000.
71-01-044	Nightingale & Honeysuckle	D. Doughty	500	2500.00	2500-2750.
47-01-045	Orange Blossoms & Butterfly	D. Doughty	250	500.00	4200-4500.
57-01-046	Ovenbirds	D. Doughty	250	650.00	4500.00
57-01-047	Parula Warblers	D. Doughty	500	600.00	1700-3600.
58-01-048	Phoebes On Flame Vine	D. Doughty	500	750.00	2200-5500.
52-01-049	Red-Eyed Vireos	D. Doughty	500	450.00	2000.00
68-01-050	Redstarts & Gorse	D. Doughty	500	1900.00	2300.00
64-01-051	Robin	D. Doughty	500	750.00	Unkn.
56-01-052	Scarlet Tanagers	D. Doughty	500	675.00	3000-4200.
62-01-053	Scissor-Tailed Flycatcher, Color	D. Doughty	250	950.00	Unkn.
62-01-054	Scissor-Tailed Flycatcher, White	D. Doughty	75	950.00	1300-1600.
63-01-055	Vermillion Flycatchers	D. Doughty	500	250.00	1100-3400.
64-01-056	Wrens & Burnet Rose	D. Doughty	500	650.00	1000.00
52-01-057	Yellow-Headed Blackbirds	D. Doughty	350	650.00	2000-2400.
58-01-058	Yellowthroats on Water Hyacinth	D. Doughty	350	750.00	1700-4000.
Royal Worcester		**Ronald Van Ruyckevelt Porcelains**			
XX-02-001	Alice	R. Van Ruyckevelt	500	1875.00	1875.00
70-02-002	American Pintail, Pair	R. Van Ruyckevelt	500	Unkn.	3000.00
69-02-003	Argenteuil A-108	R. Van Ruyckevelt	338	Unkn.	Unkn.
68-02-004	Blue Angel Fish	R. Van Ruyckevelt	500	375.00	900.00
67-02-005	Bluefin Tuna	R. Van Ruyckevelt	500	500.00	Unkn.
65-02-006	Blue Marlin	R. Van Ruyckevelt	500	500.00	1000.00
69-02-007	Bobwhite Quail, Pair	R. Van Ruyckevelt	500	Unkn.	2000.00
67-02-008	Butterfly Fish	R. Van Ruyckevelt	500	375.00	1600.00
69-02-009	Castelneau Pink	R. Van Ruyckevelt	429	Unkn.	825-875.
69-02-010	Castelneau Yellow	R. Van Ruyckevelt	163	Unkn.	825-875.
XX-02-011	Cecilia	R. Van Ruyckevelt	500	1875.00	1875.00
68-02-012	Dolphin	R. Van Ruyckevelt	500	500.00	900.00
71-02-013	Elaine	R. Van Ruyckevelt	750	600.00	600-650.
62-02-014	Flying Fish	R. Van Ruyckevelt	300	400.00	450.00
71-02-015	Green-Winged Teal	R. Van Ruyckevelt	500	1450.00	1450.00
62-02-016	Hibiscus	R. Van Ruyckevelt	500	300.00	350.00
56-02-017	Hogfish & Sergeant Major	R. Van Ruyckevelt	500	375.00	650.00
68-02-018	Honfleur A-105	R. Van Ruyckevelt	290	Unkn.	600.00
68-02-019	Honfleur A-106	R. Van Ruyckevelt	290	Unkn.	600.00
71-02-020	Languedoc	R. Van Ruyckevelt	216	Unkn.	1150.00
68-02-021	Mallards	R. Van Ruyckevelt	500	Unkn.	2000.00
68-02-022	Mennecy A-101	R. Van Ruyckevelt	338	Unkn.	675-725.
68-02-023	Mennecy A-102	R. Van Ruyckevelt	334	Unkn.	675-725.
61-02-024	Passionflower	R. Van Ruyckevelt	500	300.00	400.00
76-02-025	Picnic	R. Van Ruyckevelt	250	2850.00	2850.00
76-02-026	Queen Elizabeth I	R. Van Ruyckevelt	250	3850.00	3850.00
77-02-027	Queen Elizabeth II	R. Van Ruyckevelt	250	Unkn.	Unkn.
76-02-028	Queen Mary I	R. Van Ruyckevelt	250	4850.00	4850.00
68-02-029	Rainbow Parrot Fish	R. Van Ruyckevelt	500	1500.00	1500.00
58-02-030	Red Hind	R. Van Ruyckevelt	500	375.00	900.00
68-02-031	Ring-Necked Pheasants	R. Van Ruyckevelt	500	Unkn.	3200-3400.
64-02-032	Rock Beauty	R. Van Ruyckevelt	500	425.00	850.00
62-02-033	Sailfish	R. Van Ruyckevelt	500	400.00	550.00
69-02-034	Saint Denis A-109	R. Van Ruyckevelt	500	Unkn.	925-950.
61-02-035	Squirrelfish	R. Van Ruyckevelt	500	400.00	9000.00
66-02-036	Swordfish	R. Van Ruyckevelt	500	575.00	650.00
64-02-037	Tarpon	R. Van Ruyckevelt	500	500.00	975.00
72-02-038	White Doves	R. Van Ruyckevelt	25	3600.00	27850.00

Number	Name	Artist	Edition Limit	Issue Price	Quote
Royal Worcester		**Ruth Van Ruyckevelt Porcelains**			
60-03-001	Beatrice	R. Van Ruyckevelt	500	125.00	Unkn.
69-03-002	Bridget	R. Van Ruyckevelt	500	300.00	600-700.
60-03-003	Caroline	R. Van Ruyckevelt	500	125.00	Unkn.
68-03-004	Charlotte and Jane	R. Van Ruyckevelt	500	1000.00	1500-1650.
67-03-005	Elizabeth	R. Van Ruyckevelt	750	300.00	750-800.
69-03-006	Emily	R. Van Ruyckevelt	500	300.00	600.00
78-03-007	Esther	R. Van Ruyckevelt	500	Unkn.	Unkn.
71-03-008	Felicity	R. Van Ruyckevelt	750	600.00	600.00
59-03-009	Lisette	R. Van Ruyckevelt	500	100.00	Unkn.
62-03-010	Louisa	R. Van Ruyckevelt	500	400.00	975.00
68-03-011	Madeline	R. Van Ruyckevelt	500	300.00	750-800.
68-03-012	Marion	R. Van Ruyckevelt	500	275.00	575-625.
64-03-013	Melanie	R. Van Ruyckevelt	500	150.00	Unkn.
59-03-014	Penelope	R. Van Ruyckevelt	500	100.00	Unkn.
64-03-015	Rosalind	R. Van Ruyckevelt	500	150.00	Unkn.
63-03-016	Sister of London Hospital	R. Van Ruyckevelt	500	Unkn.	475-500.
63-03-017	Sister of St. Thomas Hospital	R. Van Ruyckevelt	500	Unkn.	475-500.
70-03-018	Sister of the Red Cross	R. Van Ruyckevelt	750	Unkn.	525-500.
66-03-019	Sister of University College Hospital	R. Van Ruyckevelt	500	Unkn.	475-500.
64-03-020	Tea Party	R. Van Ruyckevelt	250	400.00	7000.00
Royal Worcester		**Bicentennial L.E. Commemoratives**			
73-04-001	Potter	P.W. Baston	500	Unkn.	300-400.
73-04-002	Cabinetmaker	P.W. Baston	500	Unkn.	300-400.
73-04-003	Blacksmith	P.W. Baston	500	Unkn.	500.00
75-04-004	Clockmaker	P.W. Baston	Unkn.	Unkn.	500.00
Sarah's Attic, Inc.		**Angels In The Attic**			
89-01-001	St. Gabbe	Sarah's Attic	Closed	30.00	33.00
89-01-002	St. Anne	Sarah's Attic	Closed	29.00	32.00
89-01-003	Angel Wendall	Sarah's Attic	Closed	10.00	14.00
89-01-004	Angel Winnie	Sarah's Attic	Closed	10.00	14.00
89-01-005	Angel Wendy	Sarah's Attic	Closed	10.00	14.00
89-01-006	Angel Wilbur	Sarah's Attic	Closed	9.50	21.50
89-01-007	Angel Bonnie	Sarah's Attic	Closed	17.00	20.00
89-01-008	Angel Clyde	Sarah's Attic	Closed	17.00	20.00
89-01-009	Angel Floppy	Sarah's Attic	Closed	10.00	20.00
89-01-010	Angel Eddie	Sarah's Attic	Closed	10.00	10.00
89-01-011	Angel Jessica	Sarah's Attic	Closed	14.00	14.00
89-01-012	Angel Jeffrey	Sarah's Attic	Closed	14.00	14.00
89-01-013	Angel Amelia	Sarah's Attic	Closed	10.00	14.00
89-01-014	Angel Alex	Sarah's Attic	Closed	10.00	14.00
89-01-015	Angel Abbee	Sarah's Attic	Closed	9.50	13.00
89-01-016	Angel Ashbee	Sarah's Attic	Closed	9.50	13.00
89-01-017	Angel Rayburn	Sarah's Attic	Closed	12.00	19.00
89-01-018	Angel Reggie	Sarah's Attic	Closed	12.00	15.00
89-01-019	Angel Reba	Sarah's Attic	Closed	12.00	12.00
89-01-020	Angel Ruthie	Sarah's Attic	Closed	12.00	12.00
89-01-021	Angel Daisy	Sarah's Attic	Closed	14.00	14.00
89-01-022	Angel Patsy	Sarah's Attic	Closed	13.00	13.00
89-01-023	Angel Ashlee	Sarah's Attic	Closed	14.00	14.00
89-01-024	Angel Shooter	Sarah's Attic	Closed	12.50	18.00
89-01-025	Angel Grams	Sarah's Attic	Closed	17.00	35.00
89-01-026	Angel Gramps	Sarah's Attic	Closed	17.00	95.00
89-01-027	Angel Dusty	Sarah's Attic	Closed	12.00	95.00
89-01-028	Angel Emmy Lou	Sarah's Attic	Closed	12.00	12.00
89-01-029	Saint Willie Bill	Sarah's Attic	Closed	30.00	40.00
89-01-030	Angel Bevie	Sarah's Attic	Closed	10.00	10.00
89-01-031	St. George	Sarah's Attic	Closed	60.00	65.00
90-01-032	Angel Rabbit in Basket	Sarah's Attic	Closed	25.00	25.00
90-01-033	Angel Bear in Basket	Sarah's Attic	Closed	23.00	23.00
90-01-034	Angel Billi	Sarah's Attic	Closed	18.00	22.00
90-01-035	Angel Cindi	Sarah's Attic	Closed	18.00	22.00
90-01-036	Angel Lena	Sarah's Attic	Closed	36.00	40.00
90-01-037	Angel Trudy	Sarah's Attic	Closed	36.00	36.00
90-01-038	Angel Trapper	Sarah's Attic	Closed	17.00	20.00
90-01-039	Angel Louise	Sarah's Attic	Closed	17.00	20.00
90-01-040	Angel Flossy	Sarah's Attic	Closed	15.00	15.00
90-01-041	Angel Buster	Sarah's Attic	Closed	15.00	15.00
91-01-042	Angel Donald with Dog	Sarah's Attic	Closed	50.00	50.00
91-01-043	Angel Bert Golfing	Sarah's Attic	Closed	60.00	60.00
91-01-044	Contentment	Sarah's Attic	Closed	100.00	100.00
91-01-045	Love	Sarah's Attic	Closed	80.00	80.00
92-01-046	Angelle Guardian Angel 3569	Sarah's Attic	2,000	170.00	170.00
92-01-047	Kiah Guardian Angel 3570	Sarah's Attic	2,000	170.00	170.00
92-01-048	Heavenly Caring 3661	Sarah's Attic	2,500	70.00	70.00
92-01-049	Heavenly Sharing 3662	Sarah's Attic	2,500	70.00	70.00
92-01-050	Heavenly Giving 3663	Sarah's Attic	2,500	70.00	70.00
92-01-051	Heavenly Loving 3664	Sarah's Attic	2,500	70.00	70.00
Sarah's Attic, Inc.		**Americana Collection**			
88-02-001	Amer. Bear	Sarah's Attic	Closed	17.50	17.50
88-02-002	Betsy Ross	Sarah's Attic	Closed	34.00	40.00
88-02-003	Americana Bear	Sarah's Attic	Closed	70.00	70.00
88-02-004	Americana Bunny	Sarah's Attic	Closed	70.00	70.00
88-02-005	Betsy Bear W/Flag	Sarah's Attic	Closed	22.50	27.50
88-02-006	Colonial Bear W/Hat	Sarah's Attic	Closed	22.50	25.00
88-02-007	Turkey	Sarah's Attic	Closed	10.00	12.00
88-02-008	Indian Brave	Sarah's Attic	Closed	10.00	10.00
88-02-009	Indian Girl	Sarah's Attic	Closed	10.00	10.00
88-02-010	Pilgrim Boy	Sarah's Attic	Closed	12.50	12.50
88-02-011	Pilgrim Girl	Sarah's Attic	Closed	12.50	12.50
88-02-012	Americana Clown	Sarah's Attic	Closed	80.00	80.00
90-02-013	Iron Hawk	Sarah's Attic	Closed	70.00	70.00
90-02-014	Bright Sky	Sarah's Attic	Closed	70.00	70.00
90-02-015	Little Dove	Sarah's Attic	Closed	40.00	40.00
90-02-016	Spotted Eagle	Sarah's Attic	Closed	30.00	30.00
Sarah's Attic, Inc.		**Beary Adorables Collection**			
87-03-001	Alex Bear	Sarah's Attic	Closed	11.50	11.50
87-03-002	Amelia Bear	Sarah's Attic	Closed	11.50	11.50
87-03-003	Abbee Bear	Sarah's Attic	Closed	10.00	10.00
87-03-004	Ashbee Bear	Sarah's Attic	Closed	10.00	10.00
87-03-005	Collectible Bear	Sarah's Attic	Closed	16.00	16.00
88-03-006	Ghost Bear	Sarah's Attic	Closed	12.00	12.00
88-03-007	Lefty Bear	Sarah's Attic	Closed	80.00	80.00
89-03-008	Sid Bear	Sarah's Attic	Closed	18.00	25.00
89-03-009	Sophie Bear	Sarah's Attic	Closed	18.00	25.00
89-03-010	Daisy Bear	Sarah's Attic	Closed	48.00	55.00
89-03-011	Griswald Bear	Sarah's Attic	Closed	48.00	55.00
89-03-012	Missy Bear	Sarah's Attic	Closed	26.00	30.00
89-03-013	Mikey Bear	Sarah's Attic	Closed	26.00	26.00

Number	Name	Artist	Edition Limit	Issue Price	Quote
89-03-014	Angel Bear	Sarah's Attic	Closed	24.50	24.50
89-03-015	Sugar Bear	Sarah's Attic	Closed	12.00	12.00
89-03-016	Mini Teddy Bear	Sarah's Attic	Closed	5.00	5.00
89-03-017	Sammy Bear	Sarah's Attic	Closed	12.00	15.00
89-03-018	Spice Bear	Sarah's Attic	Closed	12.00	15.00
90-03-019	Bailey 50's Bear	Sarah's Attic	Closed	25.00	30.00
90-03-020	Beulah 50's Bear	Sarah's Attic	Closed	25.00	30.00
90-03-021	Birkey 50's Bear	Sarah's Attic	Closed	20.00	25.00
90-03-022	Belinda 50's Bear	Sarah's Attic	Closed	20.00	25.00
88-03-023	Bear in Basket	Sarah's Attic	Closed	48.00	48.00
87-03-024	Bear On Trunk	Sarah's Attic	Closed	20.00	20.00
88-03-025	Einstein Bear	Sarah's Attic	Closed	8.50	8.50
88-03-026	Benni Bear	Sarah's Attic	Closed	7.00	7.00
88-03-027	Jester Clown Bear	Sarah's Attic	Closed	12.50	12.50
88-03-028	Honey Picnic Bear	Sarah's Attic	Closed	16.50	20.00
88-03-029	Rufus Picnic Bear	Sarah's Attic	Closed	15.00	20.00
88-03-030	Marti Picnic Bear	Sarah's Attic	Closed	12.50	20.00
88-03-031	Arti Picnic Bear	Sarah's Attic	Closed	7.00	15.00
90-03-032	Miss Love Brown Bear	Sarah's Attic	Closed	42.00	42.00
90-03-033	Dudley Brown Bear	Sarah's Attic	Closed	32.00	32.00
90-03-034	Margie Brown Bear	Sarah's Attic	Closed	32.00	32.00
90-03-035	Joey Brown Bear	Sarah's Attic	Closed	32.00	32.00
90-03-036	Franny Brown Bear	Sarah's Attic	Closed	32.00	32.00
90-03-037	Oliver Black Bear	Sarah's Attic	Closed	32.00	32.00
Sarah's Attic, Inc.		**Black Heritage Collection**			
89-04-001	Quilting Ladies	Sarah's Attic	Closed	80.00	200-295.
89-04-002	Pappy Jake	Sarah's Attic	Closed	33.00	100-135.
90-04-003	Susie Mae	Sarah's Attic	Open	20.00	22.00
90-04-004	Caleb	Sarah's Attic	Open	21.00	23.00
90-04-005	Hattie	Sarah's Attic	4,000	35.00	100-135.
90-04-006	Whoopie & Wooster	Sarah's Attic	Closed	50.00	75-235.00
90-04-007	Carpet Bag	Sarah's Attic	Closed	10.00	25.00
90-04-008	Portia	Sarah's Attic	Closed	26.00	30-45.00
90-04-009	Harpster W/Banjo	Sarah's Attic	Closed	60.00	200-220.
90-04-010	Libby W/Bibs	Sarah's Attic	Closed	36.00	70-110.00
90-04-011	Lucas W/Bibs	Sarah's Attic	Closed	36.00	75-135.00
90-04-012	Praise the Lord I (Preacher I)	Sarah's Attic	Closed	50.00	75-135.00
90-04-013	Pearl-Tap Dancer	Sarah's Attic	Closed	40.00	47.00
90-04-014	Percy-Tap Dancer	Sarah's Attic	5,000	40.00	47.00
90-04-015	Brotherly Love	Sarah's Attic	Closed	80.00	80.00
87-04-016	Gramps	Sarah's Attic	Closed	16.00	16.00
87-04-017	Grams	Sarah's Attic	Closed	16.00	16.00
90-04-018	Nighttime Pearl	Sarah's Attic	10,000	50.00	50.00
90-04-019	Nighttime Percy	Sarah's Attic	10,000	50.00	50.00
90-04-020	Sadie & Osie Mae	Sarah's Attic	8,000	70.00	70.00
90-04-021	Corporal Pervis	Sarah's Attic	8,000	60.00	60.00
90-04-022	Victorian Portia	Sarah's Attic	Closed	35.00	35.00
90-04-023	Victorian Webster	Sarah's Attic	Closed	35.00	35.00
90-04-024	Caleb W/Vegetables	Sarah's Attic	Closed	50.00	50.00
90-04-025	Praise the Lord II	Sarah's Attic	5,000	100.00	100.00
90-04-026	Harpster W/Harmonica	Sarah's Attic	8,000	60.00	60.00
90-04-027	Whoopie & Wooster II	Sarah's Attic	8,000	70.00	70.00
90-04-028	Libby W/Puppy	Sarah's Attic	10,000	50.00	50.00
90-04-029	Lucas W/Dog	Sarah's Attic	10,000	50.00	50.00
90-04-030	Black Baby Tansy	Sarah's Attic	10,000	40.00	40.00
90-04-031	Uncle Reuben	Sarah's Attic	8,000	70.00	70.00
91-04-032	Pappy Jake & Susie Mae	Sarah's Attic	6,000	60.00	60.00
91-04-033	Hattie Quilting	Sarah's Attic	6,000	60.00	60.00
91-04-034	Portia Quilting	Sarah's Attic	6,000	40.00	40.00
91-04-035	Caleb With Football	Sarah's Attic	6,000	40.00	40.00
91-04-036	Black Teacher Miss Lettie	Sarah's Attic	6,000	50.00	50.00
91-04-037	Buffalo Soldier	Sarah's Attic	5,000	80.00	80.00
91-04-038	Clarence - Porter	Sarah's Attic	5,000	80.00	80.00
91-04-039	Cricket - Black Girl Graduate	Sarah's Attic	6,000	46.00	46.00
91-04-040	Chips - Black Boy Graduate	Sarah's Attic	6,000	46.00	46.00
91-04-041	Music Masters	Sarah's Attic	Closed	300.00	300.00
91-04-042	"Gen. of Love" Cookstove	Sarah's Attic	Unkn.	100.00	100.00
91-04-043	Granny Wynne & Olivia	Sarah's Attic	5,000	85.00	85.00
91-04-044	Esther with Butter Churn	Sarah's Attic	5,000	70.00	70.00
91-04-045	Braided Rug	Sarah's Attic	Unkn.	35.00	35.00
91-04-046	Pie	Sarah's Attic	Unkn.	7.00	7.00
91-04-047	Kettles	Sarah's Attic	Unkn.	13.00	13.00
92-04-048	Rhythm & Blues 3620	Sarah's Attic	5,000	80.00	80.00
92-04-049	Music Masters II 3621	Sarah's Attic	1,000	250.00	250.00
92-04-050	Sojourner Truth 3629	Sarah's Attic	3,000	80.00	80.00
92-04-051	Booker T. Washington 3648	Sarah's Attic	3,000	80.00	80.00
92-04-052	Ida B. Wells & Frederick Douglass 3642	Sarah's Attic	3,000	160.00	160.00
92-04-053	Jomo 3652	Sarah's Attic	4,000	27.00	27.00
92-04-054	Kaminda 3679	Sarah's Attic	4,000	50.00	50.00
92-04-055	Shamba 3680	Sarah's Attic	4,000	50.00	50.00
92-04-056	Boys Night Out 3660	Sarah's Attic	2,000	350.00	350.00
Sarah's Attic, Inc.		**Cuddly Critters Collection**			
87-05-001	Sparky	Sarah's Attic	Closed	9.00	10.00
88-05-002	Kitty Cat W/Bonnet	Sarah's Attic	Closed	12.00	12.00
89-05-003	Madam Donna	Sarah's Attic	Closed	35.50	45.00
89-05-004	Messieur Pierre	Sarah's Attic	Closed	35.50	45.00
88-05-005	Cow W/Bell	Sarah's Attic	Closed	35.00	35.00
88-05-006	Papa Mouse	Sarah's Attic	Closed	17.50	22.00
89-05-007	Whiskers Boy Cat	Sarah's Attic	Closed	10.00	10.00
89-05-008	Puddin Girl Cat	Sarah's Attic	Closed	10.00	10.00
89-05-009	Otis Papa Cat	Sarah's Attic	Closed	13.00	13.00
89-05-010	Wiggly Pig	Sarah's Attic	Closed	17.00	25.00
90-05-011	Pa Squirrel Sherman	Sarah's Attic	Closed	19.00	19.00
90-05-012	Ma Squirrel Sasha	Sarah's Attic	Closed	19.00	19.00
90-05-013	Boy Squirrel Sonny	Sarah's Attic	Closed	18.00	18.00
90-05-014	Girl Squirrel Sis	Sarah's Attic	Closed	18.00	18.00
90-05-015	Horace & Sissy Dogs	Sarah's Attic	Closed	50.00	50.00
90-05-016	Rebecca Mom Dog	Sarah's Attic	Closed	40.00	40.00
90-05-017	Penny Girl Dog	Sarah's Attic	Closed	35.00	35.00
90-05-018	Scooter Boy Dog	Sarah's Attic	Closed	30.00	30.00
90-05-019	Jasper Dad Cat	Sarah's Attic	Closed	36.00	36.00
90-05-020	Winnie Mom Cat	Sarah's Attic	Closed	36.00	36.00
90-05-021	Scuffy Boy Cat	Sarah's Attic	Closed	26.00	26.00
90-05-022	Lulu Girl Cat	Sarah's Attic	Closed	26.00	26.00
88-05-023	Lila Mrs. Mouse	Sarah's Attic	Closed	17.50	26.00
88-05-024	Lucky Boy Mouse	Sarah's Attic	Closed	13.00	16.00
88-05-025	Lucky Girl Mouse	Sarah's Attic	Closed	12.00	16.00
88-05-026	Rocking Horse	Sarah's Attic	Closed	56.00	56.00
88-05-027	Lazy-cat On Back	Sarah's Attic	Closed	13.00	13.00
88-05-028	Buster Boy Cat	Sarah's Attic	Closed	14.00	14.00
88-05-029	Flossy Girl Cat	Sarah's Attic	Closed	9.50	15.00
88-05-030	Trapper Papa Cat	Sarah's Attic	Closed	20.00	25.00
88-05-031	Louise Mama Cat	Sarah's Attic	Closed	20.00	25.00
88-05-032	Sleeping Cat	Sarah's Attic	Closed	6.00	6.00
88-05-033	Carousel Horse	Sarah's Attic	Closed	31.00	31.00
88-05-034	Myrtle The Pig	Sarah's Attic	Closed	38.00	45.00
91-05-035	Jiggs - Sleeping Cat	Sarah's Attic	Unkn.	10.00	10.00
Sarah's Attic, Inc.		**Classroom Memories**			
88-06-001	Miss Pritchett	Sarah's Attic	Open	28.00	35.00
91-06-002	Achieving Our Goals	Sarah's Attic	10,000	80.00	80.00
91-06-003	Classroom Memories	Sarah's Attic	6,000	80.00	80.00
Sarah's Attic, Inc.		**Cotton Tale Collection**			
87-07-001	Winnie Mom Rabbit	Sarah's Attic	Closed	17.00	17.00
88-07-002	Girl Rabbit Res. Candle	Sarah's Attic	Closed	14.00	14.00
88-07-003	Boy Rabbit Res. Candle	Sarah's Attic	Closed	14.00	14.00
88-07-004	Lizzy Hare	Sarah's Attic	Closed	10.00	10.00
88-07-005	Izzy Hare	Sarah's Attic	Closed	10.00	10.00
88-07-006	Maddy Hare	Sarah's Attic	Closed	11.00	11.00
88-07-007	Amos Hare	Sarah's Attic	Closed	11.00	11.00
89-07-008	Crumb Rabbit	Sarah's Attic	Closed	29.00	35-40.00
89-07-009	Cookie Rabbit	Sarah's Attic	Closed	29.00	35-40.00
89-07-010	Papa Rabbit	Sarah's Attic	Closed	50.00	60-65.00
89-07-011	Nana Rabbit	Sarah's Attic	Closed	50.00	60-65.00
89-07-012	Thelma Rabbit	Sarah's Attic	Closed	33.00	40.00
89-07-013	Thomas Rabbit	Sarah's Attic	Closed	33.00	40.00
89-07-014	Tessy Rabbit	Sarah's Attic	Closed	15.00	20.00
89-07-015	Toby Rabbit	Sarah's Attic	Closed	17.00	20.00
89-07-016	Sleeping Baby Bunny	Sarah's Attic	Closed	15.50	25.00
90-07-017	Zeb W/Carrots	Sarah's Attic	Closed	18.00	18.00
90-07-018	Zelda W/Carrots	Sarah's Attic	Closed	18.00	18.00
90-07-019	Zeke W/Carrots	Sarah's Attic	Closed	17.00	17.00
90-07-020	Zoe W/Carrots	Sarah's Attic	Closed	17.00	17.00
90-07-021	Olly Rabbit W/Vest	Sarah's Attic	Closed	65.00	75.00
90-07-022	Molly Rabbit W/Vest	Sarah's Attic	Closed	65.00	75.00
90-07-023	Henry Rabbit W/Pipe	Sarah's Attic	Open	30.00	32.00
90-07-024	Hannah Rabbit Ouilting	Sarah's Attic	Open	30.00	32.00
90-07-025	Herbie Rabbit W/Book	Sarah's Attic	Open	20.00	22.00
90-07-026	Hether Rabbit W/Doll	Sarah's Attic	Open	20.00	22.00
90-07-027	X-Mas Toby	Sarah's Attic	12/92	20.00	20.00
90-07-028	Zeb Sailor Dad	Sarah's Attic	Closed	26.00	28.00
90-07-029	Zelda Sailor Mom	Sarah's Attic	Closed	26.00	28.00
90-07-030	Zeke Sailor Boy	Sarah's Attic	Closed	24.00	26.00
90-07-031	Zoe Sailor Girl	Sarah's Attic	Closed	24.00	26.00
88-07-032	Rabbit In Basket	Sarah's Attic	Closed	48.00	55.00
87-07-033	Wendall Pa Rabbit	Sarah's Attic	Closed	17.00	25.00
87-07-034	Wendy Girl Rabbit	Sarah's Attic	Closed	15.00	25.00
87-07-035	Wilbur Boy Rabbit	Sarah's Attic	Closed	13.00	25.00
87-07-036	Bonnle	Sarah's Attic	Closed	38.00	38.00
87-07-037	Clyde	Sarah's Attic	Closed	38.00	38.00
87-07-038	Floppy	Sarah's Attic	Closed	21.00	21.00
88-07-039	Mini Papa Rabbit	Sarah's Attic	Closed	8.50	12.00
88-07-040	Mini Boy Rabbit	Sarah's Attic	Closed	7.50	12.00
88-07-041	Mini Girl Rabbit	Sarah's Attic	Closed	7.50	12.00
88-07-042	Mini Mama Rabbit	Sarah's Attic	Closed	8.50	12.00
88-07-043	Cind Rabbit	Sarah's Attic	Closed	27.00	35.00
88-07-044	Billi Rabbit	Sarah's Attic	Closed	27.00	35.00
90-07-045	Papa Farm Rabbit	Sarah's Attic	6/93	80.00	80.00
90-07-046	Nana Farm Rabbit	Sarah's Attic	6/93	100.00	100.00
90-07-047	Chuckles Farm Rabbit	Sarah's Attic	6/93	53.00	53.00
90-07-048	Cookie Farm Rabbit	Sarah's Attic	6/93	47.00	47.00
90-07-049	Crumb Farm Rabbit	Sarah's Attic	6/93	53.00	53.00
90-07-050	Sleepy Farm Rabbit	Sarah's Attic	6/93	35.00	35.00
90-07-051	Victorian Thomas	Sarah's Attic	6/93	60.00	60.00
90-07-052	Victorian Thelma	Sarah's Attic	6/93	60.00	60.00
90-07-053	Victorian Toby	Sarah's Attic	6/93	40.00	40.00
90-07-054	Victorian Tessy	Sarah's Attic	6/93	20.00	20.00
90-07-055	Victorian Tabitha	Sarah's Attic	6/93	30.00	30.00
90-07-056	Victorian Tucker	Sarah's Attic	6/93	37.00	37.00
Sarah's Attic, Inc.		**Daisy Collection**			
89-08-001	Sally Booba	Sarah's Attic	Open	30.00	40.00
90-08-002	Jack Boy Ball & Glove	Sarah's Attic	Open	30.00	40.00
90-08-003	Sparky	Sarah's Attic	6/93	53.00	55.00
90-08-004	Spike	Sarah's Attic	34,121	44.00	46.00
90-08-005	Bomber	Sarah's Attic	34,121	50.00	52.00
90-08-006	Jewel	Sarah's Attic	34,121	60.00	62.00
90-08-007	Stretch	Sarah's Attic	34,121	50.00	52.00
Sarah's Atttic, Inc.		**Ginger Babies Collection**			
89-09-001	Ginger	Sarah's Attic	Closed	17.00	17.00
89-09-002	Molasses	Sarah's Attic	Closed	17.00	17.00
90-09-003	Ginger Girl Cinnamon	Sarah's Attic	Closed	15.50	20.00
90-09-004	Ginger Boy Nutmeg	Sarah's Attic	Closed	15.50	20.00
92-09-005	Home Sweet Home 3608	Sarah's Attic	12/93	100.00	100.00
92-09-006	Cookie Base 3609	Sarah's Attic	12/93	50.00	50.00
92-09-007	Ginger Bench w/Cat 3610	Sarah's Attic	12/93	10.00	10.00
92-09-008	Gingerbread Fence 3611	Sarah's Attic	12/93	13.00	1300
92-09-009	Vanilla Gingerbread Girl 3612	Sarah's Attic	12/93	18.00	18.00
92-09-010	Almond Gingerbread Boy 3613	Sarah's Attic	12/93	18.00	18.00
92-09-011	Cinnamon & Nutmeg w/Wagon 3614	Sarah's Attic	12/93	36.00	36.00
92-09-012	Ginger Tree 3615	Sarah's Attic	12/93	20.00	20.00
Sarah's Attic, Inc.		**Happy Collection**			
87-10-001	Sitting Happy	Sarah's Attic	Closed	26.00	26.00
87-10-002	Happy W/Balloons	Sarah's Attic	Closed	22.00	22.00
90-10-003	Encore Clown W/Dog	Sarah's Attic	Closed	100.00	100.00
87-10-004	Lge. Happy Clown	Sarah's Attic	Closed	22.00	22.00
88-10-005	Lady Clown	Sarah's Attic	Closed	20.00	20.00
Sarah's Attic, Inc.		**Heavenly Wings Collection**			
89-11-001	Angelica Angel	Sarah's Attic	Closed	21.00	25.00
89-11-002	Regina	Sarah's Attic	Closed	24.00	30.00
89-11-003	Heavenly Guardian	Sarah's Attic	Closed	40.00	40.00
90-11-004	Boy Angel Inst. Adair	Sarah's Attic	Closed	29.00	29.00
90-11-005	Enos W/ Blue Gown	Sarah's Attic	Closed	33.00	75-135.00
90-11-006	Adora W/Pink Gown	Sarah's Attic	Closed	35.00	75-135.00
90-11-007	Adora W/Bunny	Sarah's Attic	10,000	50.00	50.00
90-11-008	Enos W/Frog	Sarah's Attic	10,000	50.00	50.00
Sarah's Attic, Inc.		**Little Charmers Collection**			
89-12-001	Jennifer & Dog	Sarah's Attic	Closed	57.00	57.00
87-12-002	Daisy	Sarah's Attic	Closed	36.00	36.00

Company / Number	Name	Series / Artist	Edition Limit	Issue Price	Quote
88-12-003	Girl W/Teacup	Sarah's Attic	Closed	37.00	37.00
88-12-004	Girl W/Dog	Sarah's Attic	Closed	43.00	43.00
89-12-005	Moose Boy Sitting	Sarah's Attic	Open	18.00	20.00
88-12-006	Jessica	Sarah's Attic	Closed	44.00	44.00
87-12-007	Bevie	Sarah's Attic	Closed	18.00	18.00
87-12-008	Dusty	Sarah's Attic	Closed	19.00	19.00
87-12-009	Twinkle W/Pole	Sarah's Attic	Closed	19.00	19.00
87-12-010	Willie Bill	Sarah's Attic	Closed	20.00	20.00
87-12-011	Shooter	Sarah's Attic	Closed	19.00	19.00
87-12-012	Emmy Lou	Sarah's Attic	Closed	14.00	14.00
87-12-013	Cupcake W/Rope	Sarah's Attic	Closed	19.00	19.00
87-12-014	Cheerleader	Sarah's Attic	Closed	16.00	16.00
87-12-015	Eddie	Sarah's Attic	Closed	18.00	18.00
87-12-016	Ashlee	Sarah's Attic	Closed	60.00	60.00
87-12-017	Corky-Boy Sailor Suit	Sarah's Attic	Closed	14.50	14.50
87-12-018	Clementine-Girl Sailor Suit	Sarah's Attic	Closed	14.50	14.50
87-12-019	Butch-Boy Book Sitting	Sarah's Attic	Closed	16.00	16.00
87-12-020	Blondie-Girl Doll Sitting	Sarah's Attic	Closed	16.00	16.00
87-12-021	Amber-Sm. Girl Standing	Sarah's Attic	Closed	15.00	15.00
87-12-022	Archie-Sm.Boy Standing	Sarah's Attic	Closed	15.00	15.00
87-12-023	Bare Bottom Baby	Sarah's Attic	Closed	9.50	9.50
87-12-024	Baseball Player	Sarah's Attic	Closed	24.00	24.00
87-12-025	Football Player	Sarah's Attic	Closed	24.00	24.00
87-12-026	Woman Golfer	Sarah's Attic	Closed	24.00	24.00
87-12-027	Man Golfer	Sarah's Attic	Closed	24.00	24.00
87-12-028	Beau-Cupie Boy	Sarah's Attic	Closed	20.00	20.00
87-12-029	Buttons-Cupie Girl	Sarah's Attic	Closed	20.00	20.00
87-12-030	Boy W/Clown Doll	Sarah's Attic	Closed	40.00	40.00
88-12-031	Bowler	Sarah's Attic	Closed	24.00	24.00
88-12-032	Basketball Player	Sarah's Attic	Closed	24.00	24.00
90-12-033	White Baby Tansy	Sarah's Attic	10,000	40.00	40.00
Sarah's Attic, Inc.		**Memory Lane Collection**			
89-13-001	Fire Station	Sarah's Attic	Closed	20.00	20.00
89-13-002	Post Office	Sarah's Attic	Closed	25.00	25.00
89-13-003	Mini Depot	Sarah's Attic	Closed	7.00	7.00
89-13-004	Mini Bank	Sarah's Att!c	Closed	6.00	6.00
89-13-005	Briton Church	Sarah's Attic	Closed	25.00	25.00
87-13-006	House W/Dormers	Sarah's Attic	Closed	15.00	15.00
87-13-007	Barn	Sarah's Attic	Closed	16.50	16.50
87-13-008	Mill	Sarah's Attic	Closed	16.50	16.50
87-13-009	Cottage	Sarah's Attic	Closed	13.00	13.00
87-13-010	Barber Shop	Sarah's Attic	Closed	13.00	13.00
87-13-011	Grandma's House	Sarah's Attic	Closed	13.00	13.00
87-13-012	Church	Sarah's Attic	Closed	19.00	19.00
87-13-013	School	Sarah's Attic	Closed	14.00	14.00
87-13-014	General Store	Sarah's Attic	Closed	13.00	13.00
87-13-015	Drug Store	Sarah's Attic	Closed	13.00	13.00
88-13-016	Mini Barber Shop	Sarah's Attic	Closed	6.50	6.50
88-13-017	Mini Drug Store	Sarah's Attic	Closed	6.00	6.00
88-13-018	Mini General Store	Sarah's Attic	Closed	6.00	6.00
88-13-019	Mini Salt Box	Sarah's Attic	Closed	6.00	6.00
88-13-020	Mini Church	Sarah's Attic	Closed	6.50	6.50
88-13-021	Mini School	Sarah's Attic	Closed	6.50	6.50
88-13-022	Mini Barn	Sarah's Attic	Closed	6.00	6.00
88-13-023	Mini Grandma's House	Sarah's Attic	Closed	7.00	7.00
88-13-024	Mini Mill	Sarah's Attic	Closed	6.50	6.50
88-13-025	Bank	Sarah's Attic	Closed	13.00	13.00
88-13-026	Train Depot	Sarah's Attic	Closed	13.50	13.50
Sarah's Attic, Inc.		**Rose Collection**			
89-14-001	Sweet Rose	Sarah's Attic	Closed	50.00	50.00
90-14-002	Victorian Boy Cody	Sarah's Attic	Closed	46.00	46.00
90-14-003	Tyler Vict. Boy	Sarah's Attic	Closed	40.00	40.00
90-14-004	Tiffany Vict. Girl	Sarah's Attic	Closed	40.00	40.00
92-14-005	Misty 3616	Sarah's Attic	4,000	60.00	60.00
Sarah's Attic, Inc.		**Snowflake Collection**			
89-15-001	Flurry	Sarah's Attic	Open	10.00	12.00
89-15-002	Boo Mini Snowman	Sarah's Attic	Open	6.00	6.00
89-15-003	Winter Frolic	Sarah's Attic	Closed	60.00	70.00
90-15-004	Amer. Snow Old Glory	Sarah's Attic	Closed	24.00	26.00
Sarah's Attic, Inc.		**Sarah's Gang Collection**			
89-16-001	Small Country Willie	Sarah's Attic	Closed	13.00	26.00
89-16-002	Small Country Tillie	Sarah's Attic	Closed	13.00	26.00
87-16-003	Sitting Whimpy	Sarah's Attic	Closed	14.00	20.00
87-16-004	Sitting Katie	Sarah's Attic	Closed	14.00	20.00
87-16-005	Willie Candle Holder	Sarah's Attic	Closed	15.00	20.00
87-16-006	Tillie Candle Holder	Sarah's Attic	Closed	15.00	20.00
87-16-007	Original Tillie	Sarah's Attic	Closed	14.00	20.00
87-16-008	Original Willie	Sarah's Attic	Closed	14.00	20.00
87-16-009	Original Whimpy	Sarah's Attic	Closed	14.00	20.00
87-16-010	Original Katie	Sarah's Attic	Closed	14.00	20.00
87-16-011	Originl Twinkie	Sarah's Attic	Closed	14.00	20.00
87-16-012	Original Cupcake	Sarah's Attic	Closed	14.00	20.00
89-16-013	Americana Willie	Sarah's Attic	Open	17.00	21.00
89-16-014	Americana Tillie	Sarah's Attic	Open	17.00	21.00
89-16-015	Americana Katie	Sarah's Attic	Open	19.00	21.00
89-16-016	Americana Whimpy	Sarah's Attic	Open	19.00	21.00
89-16-017	Americana Cupcake	Sarah's Attic	Open	19.00	21.00
89-16-018	Americana Twinkie	Sarah's Attic	Open	19.00	21.00
90-16-019	Americana Rachel	Sarah's Attic	Open	30.00	30.00
89-16-020	Baby Rachel	Sarah's Attic	Open	17.00	20.00
89-16-021	Small Sailor Katie	Sarah's Attic	Closed	14.00	20.00
89-16-022	Small Sailor Whimpy	Sarah's Attic	Closed	14.00	20.00
89-16-023	Small School Cupcake	Sarah's Attic	Closed	11.00	20.00
89-16-024	Small School Twinkie	Sarah's Attic	Closed	11.00	20.00
89-16-025	Beachtime Katie & Whimpy	Serah's Attic	Closed	53.00	60.00
90-16-026	Beachtime Cupcake	Sarah's Attic	Closed	30.00	35.00
90-16-027	Beachtime Twinkie	Sarah's Attic	Closed	30.00	35.00
90-16-028	Beachtime Willie	Sarah's Attic	Closed	30.00	35.00
90-16-029	Beachtime Tillie	Sarah's Attic	Closed	30.00	35.00
90-16-030	Beachtime Baby Rachel	Sarah's Attic	Closed	30.00	35.00
90-16-031	Witch Katie	Sarah's Attic	Open	40.00	40.00
90-16-032	Scarecrow Whimpy	Sarah's Attic	Open	40.00	40.00
90-16-033	Devil Cupcake	Sarah's Attic	Open	36.00	40.00
90-16-034	Devil Twinkie	Sarah's Attic	Open	36.00	40.00
90-16-035	Clown Tillie	Sarah's Attic	Open	40.00	40.00
90-16-036	Clown Willie	Sarah's Attic	Open	40.00	40.00
90-16-037	Pumpkin Rachel	Sarah's Attic	Open	36.00	40.00
88-16-038	Cupcake	Sarah's Attic	Open	18.00	20.00
88-16-039	Twinkie	Sarah's Attic	Open	18.00	20.00
88-16-040	Katie	Sarah's Attic	Open	18.00	20.00
88-16-041	Whimpy	Sarah's Attic	Open	18.00	20.00
88-16-042	Willie	Sarah's Attic	Open	18.00	20.00
88-16-043	Tillie	Sarah's Attic	Open	18.00	20.00
87-16-044	Cupcake On Heart	Sarah's Attic	Closed	12.00	20.00
87-16-045	Katie On Heart	Sarah's Attic	Closed	12.00	20.00
87-16-046	Whimpy On Heart	Sarah's Attic	Closed	12.00	20.00
87-16-047	Twinkie On Heart	Sarah's Attic	Closed	12.00	20.00
87-16-048	Tillie On Heart	Sarah's Attic	Closed	12.00	20.00
87-16-049	Willie On Heart	Sarah's Attic	Closed	12.00	20.00
91-16-050	Whimpy - White Groom	Sarah's Attic	12/94	47.00	47.00
91-16-051	Katie - White Bride	Sarah's Attic	12/94	47.00	47.00
91-16-052	Rachel - White Flower Girl	Sarah's Attic	12/94	40.00	40.00
91-16-053	Tyler - White Ring Bearer	Sarah's Attic	12/94	40.00	40.00
91-16-054	Cracker - Cocker Spanial	Sarah's Attic	12/94	9.00	9.00
91-16-055	Twinkle - White Minister	Sarah's Attic	12/94	50.00	50.00
91-16-056	Tillie - Black Bride	Sarah's Attic	12/94	47.00	47.00
91-16-057	Willie - Black Groom	Sarah's Attic	12/94	47.00	47.00
91-16-058	Peaches - Black Flower Girl	Sarah's Attic	12/94	40.00	40.00
91-16-059	Pug - Black Ring Bearer	Sarah's Attic	12/94	40.00	40.00
91-16-060	Percy - Black Minister	Sarah's Attic	12/94	50.00	50.00
91-16-061	Thanksgiving Katie	Sarah's Attic	10,000	32.00	32.00
91-16-062	Thanksgiving Whimpy	Sarah's Attic	10,000	32.00	32.00
91-16-063	Thanksgiving Tillie	Sarah's Attic	10,000	32.00	32.00
91-16-064	Thanksgiving Willie	Sarah's Attic	10,000	32.00	32.00
91-16-065	Thanksgiving Rachel	Sarah's Attic	10,000	32.00	32.00
91-16-066	Nurse Cupcake	Sarah's Attic	6,000	46.00	46.00
91-16-067	Doctor Twinkie	Sarah's Attic	6,000	50.00	50.00
91-16-068	Teacher Tillie	Sarah's Attic	6,000	50.00	50.00
91-16-069	Executive Whimpy	Sarah's Attic	6,000	46.00	46.00
Sarah's Attic, Inc.		**Santas Of The Month**			
88-17-001	January Santa	Sarah's Attic	Closed	50.00	125-225.
88-17-002	February Santa	Sarah's Attic	Closed	50.00	125-225.
88-17-003	March Santa	Sarah's Attic	Closed	50.00	125-225.
88-17-004	April Santa	Sarah's Attic	Closed	50.00	125-225.
88-17-005	May Santa	Sarah's Attic	Closed	50.00	125-225.
88-17-006	June Santa	Sarah's Attic	Closed	50.00	125-225.
88-17-007	July Santa	Sarah's Attic	Closed	50.00	125-225.
88-17-008	August Santa	Sarah's Attic	Closed	50.00	125-225.
88-17-009	September Santa	Sarah's Attic	Closed	50.00	125-225.
88-17-010	October Santa	Sarah's Attic	Closed	50.00	125-225.
88-17-011	November Santa	Sarah's Attic	Closed	50.00	125-225.
88-17-012	December Santa	Sarah's Attic	Closed	50.00	125-225.
88-17-013	Mini January Santa	Sarah's Attic	Closed	14.00	20.00
88-17-014	Mini February Santa	Sarah's Attic	Closed	14.00	20.00
88-17-015	Mini March Santa	Sarah's Attic	Closed	14.00	20.00
88-17-016	Mini April Santa	Sarah's Attic	Closed	14.00	20.00
88-17-017	Mini May Santa	Serah's Attic	Closed	14.00	20.00
88-17-018	Mini June Santa	Sarah's Attic	Closed	14.00	20.00
88-17-019	Mini July Santa	Sarah's Attic	Closed	14.00	20.00
88-17-020	Mini August Santa	Sarah's Attic	Closed	14.00	20.00
88-17-021	Mini September Santa	Sarah's Attic	Closed	14.00	20.00
88-17-022	Mini October Santa	Sarah's Attic	Closed	14.00	20.00
88-17-023	Mini November Santa	Sarah's Attic	Closed	14.00	20.00
88-17-024	Mini December Santa	Sarah's Attic	Closed	14.00	20.00
90-17-025	Jan. Santa Winter Fun	Sarah's Attic	Closed	80.00	80.00
90-17-026	Feb. Santa Cupids Help	Sarah's Attic	Closed	120.00	120.00
90-17-027	Mar. Santa Irish Delight	Sarah's Attic	Closed	120.00	120.00
90-17-028	Apr. Santa Spring/Joy	Sarah's Attic	Closed	150.00	150.00
90-17-029	May Santa Par For Course	Sarah's Attic	Closed	100.00	100.00
90-17-030	June Santa Graduation	Sarah's Attic	Closed	70.00	70.00
90-17-031	July Santa God Bless	Sarah's Attic	Closed	100.00	100.00
90-17-032	Aug. Santa Summers Trn.	Sarah's Attic	Closed	110.00	110.00
90-17-033	Sep. Santa Touchdown	Sarah's Attic	Closed	90.00	90.00
90-17-034	Oct. Santa Seasons Plenty	Sarah's Attic	Closed	120.00	120.00
90-17-035	Nov. Santa Give Thanks	Sarah's Attic	Closed	100.00	100.00
90-17-036	Dec. Santa Peace	Sarah's Attic	Closed	120.00	120.00
90-17-037	Mrs. January	Sarah's Attic	Closed	80.00	80.00
90-17-038	Mrs. February	Sarah's Attic	Closed	110.00	110.00
90-17-039	Mrs. March	Sarah's Attic	Closed	80.00	80.00
90-17-040	Mrs. April	Sarah's Attic	Closed	110.00	110.00
90-17-041	Mrs. May	Sarah's Attic	Closed	80.00	80.00
90-17-042	Mrs. June	Sarah's Attic	Closed	70.00	70.00
90-17-043	Mrs. July	Sarah's Attic	Closed	100.00	100.00
90-17-044	Mrs. August	Sarah's Attic	Closed	90.00	90.00
90-17-045	Mrs. September	Sarah's Attic	Closed	90.00	90.00
90-17-046	Mrs. October	Sarah's Attic	Closed	90.00	90.00
90-17-047	Mrs. November	Sarah's Attic	Closed	90.00	90.00
90-17-048	Mrs. December	Sarah's Attic	Closed	110.00	110.00
90-17-049	Jan. Fruits of Love	Sarah's Attic	12/94	90.00	90.00
90-17-050	Feb. From The Heart	Sarah's Attic	12/94	90.00	90.00
90-17-051	Mar. Irish Love	Sarah's Attic	12/94	100.00	100.00
90-17-052	Apr. Spring Time	Sarah's Attic	12/94	90.00	90.00
90-17-053	May Caddy Chatter	Sarah's Attic	12/94	100.00	100.00
90-17-054	June Homerun	Sarah's Attic	12/94	90.00	90.00
90-17-055	July Celebrate Amer.	Sarah's Attic	12/94	90.00	90.00
90-17-056	Aug. Fun In The Sun	Sarah's Attic	12/94	90.00	90.00
90-17-057	Sept. Lessons In Love	Sarah's Attic	12/94	90.00	90.00
90-17-058	Oct. Masquerade	Sarah's Attic	12/94	120.00	120.00
90-17-059	Nov. Harvest Of Love	Sarah's Attic	12/94	120.00	120.00
90-17-060	Dec. A Gift Of Peace	Sarah's Attic	12/94	90.00	90.00
90-17-061	Masquerade Tillie	Sarah's Attic	12/94	45.00	45.00
Sarah's Attic, Inc.		**Sarah's Neighborhood Friends**			
90-18-001	Bubba W/Lantern	Sarah's Attic	12/92	35.00	35.00
90-18-002	Pansy W/Sled	Sarah's Attic	12/92	30.00	30.00
90-18-003	Bud W/Book	Sarah's Attic	12/92	35.00	35.00
90-18-004	Weasel W/Cap	Sarah's Attic	12/92	35.00	35.00
90-18-005	Annie W/Violin	Sarah's Attic	12/92	35.00	35.00
90-18-006	Hewett W/Drum	Sarah's Attic	12/92	35.00	35.00
90-18-007	Waldo Dog	Sarah's Attic	12/92	10.00	10.00
90-18-008	Hewett W/Apples	Sarah's Attic	12/92	40.00	40.00
90-18-009	Bud W/Newspaper	Sarah's Attic	12/92	40.00	40.00
90-18-010	Waldo W/Flowers	Sarah's Attic	12/92	14.00	14.00
90-18-011	Annie W/Flower Basket	Sarah's Attic	12/92	56.00	56.00
90-18-012	Pansy W/Buggy	Sarah's Attic	12/92	50.00	50.00
90-18-013	Bubba W/Lemonade	Sarah's Attic	12/92	54.00	54.00
90-18-014	Weasel W/Paper	Sarah's Attic	12/92	40.00	40.00
91-18-015	Dolly - White Baby Jesus	Sarah's Attic	12/94	20.00	20.00
91-18-016	Annie - White Mary	Sarah's Attic	12/94	30.00	30.00
91-18-017	Bud - White Joseph	Sarah's Attic	12/94	34.00	34.00
91-18-019	Kitten in Basket	Sarah's Attic	12/94	15.00	15.00

Company / Number	Name	Series / Artist	Edition Limit	Issue Price	Quote
91-18-020	Bubba - Black King	Sarah's Attic	12/94	40.00	40.00
91-18-021	Weasel - White King W/Kitten	Sarah's Attic	12/94	40.00	40.00
91-18-022	Hewitt - White King W/Drum	Sarah's Attic	12/94	40.00	40.00
91-18-023	Pansy - Black Angel	Sarah's Attic	12/94	30.00	30.00
91-18-024	Waldo - Dog W/Shoe	Sarah's Attic	12/94	15.00	15.00
91-18-025	Babes - Black Baby Jesue	Sarah's Attic	12/94	20.00	20.00
91-18-026	Noah - Black Joseph	Sarah's Attic	12/94	36.00	36.00
91-18-027	Shelby - Black Mary	Sarah's Attic	12/94	30.00	30.00
91-18-028	Crate of Love - White	Sarah's Attic	12/94	40.00	40.00
91-18-029	Crate of Love - Black	Sarah's Attic	12/94	40.00	40.00
91-18-030	Nurse Pansy	Sarah's Attic	6,000	46.00	46.00
91-18-031	Dr. Bubba	Sarah's Attic	6,000	60.00	60.00
91-18-032	Teacher Annie	Sarah's Attic	6,000	55.00	55.00
91-18-033	Executive Noah	Sarah's Attic	6,000	46.00	46.00
92-18-034	Stitches Donkey 3656	Sarah's Attic	12/94	26.00	26.00
92-18-035	Rags Cow 3657	Sarah's Attic	12/94	30.00	30.00
92-18-036	Patches Sheep 3658	Sarah's Attic	12/94	20.00	20.00
92-18-037	Angel Hope 3659	Sarah's Attic	12/94	40.00	40.00
Sarah's Attic, Inc.		**Tattered n' Torn Collection**			
90-19-001	Boy Rag Doll Opie	Sarah's Attic	Closed	50.00	50.00
90-19-002	Girl Rag Doll Polly	Sarah's Attic	Closed	50.00	50.00
90-19-003	Muffin Black Rag Doll	Sarah's Attic	Closed	30.00	30.00
90-19-004	Puffin Black Rag Doll	Sarah's Attic	Closed	30.00	30.00
90-19-005	White Prissy & Peanut	Sarah's Attic	Closed	120.00	120.00
90-19-006	White Muffin & Puffin	Sarah's Attic	Closed	55.00	55.00
90-19-007	Black Prissy & Peanut	Sarah's Attic	Closed	120.00	120.00
90-19-008	Black Muffin & Puffin	Sarah's Attic	Closed	55.00	55.00
Sarah's Attic, Inc.		**Spirit of Christmas Collection**			
87-20-001	Naughty Or Nice Santa At D	Sarah's Attic	Closed	100.00	100.00
87-20-002	Father Snow	Sarah's Attic	Closed	46.00	46.00
87-20-003	Jingle Bells	Sarah's Attic	Closed	28.00	28.00
87-20-004	Long Journey	Sarah's Attic	Closed	28.00	35.00
88-20-005	Joseph-Natural	Sarah's Attic	Closed	11.00	11.00
88-20-006	Mary-Natural	Sarah's Attic	Closed	11.00	11.00
88-20-007	Jesus-Natural	Sarah's Attic	Closed	7.00	7.00
88-20-008	Mini Mary-Natural	Sarah's Attic	Closed	5.00	5.00
88-20-009	Mini Joseph-Natural	Sarah's Attic	Closed	5.00	5.00
88-20-010	Mini Jesus-Natural	Sarah's Attic	Closed	3.50	3.50
88-20-011	Cow/Ox	Sarah's Attic	Closed	16.50	16.50
88-20-012	Sheep	Sarah's Attic	Closed	8.00	8.00
88-20-013	Spirit of Christmas 2320	Sarah's Attic	4,000	80.00	80.00
89-20-014	Slient Night	Sarah's Attic	Closed	33.00	40.00
89-20-015	Woodland Santa	Sarah's Attic	Closed	100.00	125.00
89-20-016	Jolly 2	Sarah's Attic	6,000	15.00	17.00
89-20-017	Yule Tidings 2	Sarah's Attic	Closed	23.00	30.00
89-20-018	St. Nick 2	Sarah's Attic	Closed	43.00	43.00
88-20-019	Blessed Christmas	Sarah's Attic	7,500	100.00	100.00
89-20-020	Father Snow 2	Sarah's Attic	Closed	32.00	36.00
87-20-021	Santa W/Pockets	Sarah's Attic	Closed	34.00	34.00
87-20-022	Santa's Workshop	Sarah's Attic	Closed	54.00	54.00
87-20-023	Colonel Santa	Sarah's Attic	Closed	40.00	40.00
88-20-024	Mini Mary	Sarah's Attic	Closed	8.00	8.00
88-20-025	Mini Joseph	Sarah's Attic	Closed	8.00	8.00
88-20-026	Mini Jesus	Sarah's Attic	Closed	8.00	8.00
88-20-027	Elf Grabbing Hat	Sarah's Attic	Closed	10.00	10.00
88-20-028	Santa W/Elf	Sarah's Attic	Closed	90.00	90.00
88-20-029	Lge. Santa Res. Candle	Sarah's Attic	Closed	14.50	14.50
88-20-030	Lge. Mrs. Claus Res. Candle	Sarah's Attic	Closed	14.50	14.50
88-20-031	Sm. Angel Res. Candle	Sarah's Attic	Closed	9.50	9.50
88-20-032	Sm. Santa Res. Candle	Sarah's Attic	Closed	10.50	10.50
88-20-033	Sm. Mrs. Claus Res. Candle	Sarah's Attic	Closed	10.50	10.50
88-20-034	Mini Santa Res. Candle	Sarah's Attic	Closed	8.00	8.00
89-20-035	Christmas Joy	Sarah's Attic	Closed	32.00	32.00
89-20-036	Jingle Bells 2	Sarah's Attic	Closed	25.50	25.50
89-20-037	Colonel Santa 2	Sarah's Attic	Closed	35.00	35.00
89-20-038	Papa Santa Sitting	Sarah's Attic	Closed	30.00	40.00
69-20-039	Mama Santa Sitting	Sarah's Attic	Closed	30.00	40.00
89-20-040	Papa Santa Stocking	Sarah's Attic	Closed	50.00	60.00
89-20-041	Mama Santa Stocking	Sarah's Attic	Closed	50.00	60.00
89-20-042	Long Journey 2	Sarah's Attic	Closed	35.00	40.00
89-20-043	Stinky Elf Sitting	Sarah's Attic	Closed	16.00	20.00
89-20-044	Winky Elf Letter	Sarah's Attic	Closed	16.00	20.00
89-20-045	Blinkey Elf Ball	Sarah's Attic	Closed	16.00	20.00
89-20-046	Mini Colonel Santa	Sarah's Attic	Closed	14.00	20.00
89-20-047	Mini St. Nick	Sarah's Attic	Closed	14.00	14.00
89-20-048	Mini Jingle Bells	Sarah's Attic	Closed	16.00	16.00
89-20-049	Mini Father Snow	Sarah's Attic	Closed	16.00	16.00
88-20-050	Mini Long Journey	Sarah's Attic	Closed	11.00	11.00
89-20-051	Mini Jolly	Sarah's Attic	Closed	10.00	10.00
89-20-052	Mini Naughty Or Nice	Sarah's Attic	Closed	20.00	20.00
90-20-053	X-Mas Wonder Santa	Sarah's Attic	Closed	50.00	50.00
90-20-054	Santa Claus Express	Sarah's Attic	4,000	150.00	150.00
90-20-055	Christmas Music	Sarah's Attic	Closed	60.00	60.00
90-20-056	Love The Children	Sarah's Attic	5,000	75.00	75.00
90-20-057	Christmas Wishes	Sarah's Attic	5,000	50.00	50.00
90-20-058	Bells of X-Mas	Sarah's Attic	Closed	35.00	35.00
88-20-059	Santa Kneeling	Sarah's Attic	Closed	22.00	22.00
88-20-060	Santa In Chimney	Sarah's Attic	Closed	110.00	110.00
88-20-061	Christmas Clown	Sarah's Attic	Closed	88.00	88.00
87-20-062	Santa Sitting	Sarah's Attic	Closed	20.50	20.50
87-20-063	Mini Santa W/Cane	Sarah's Attic	Closed	11.00	11.00
87-20-064	Large Santa W/Cane	Sarah's Attic	Closed	33.00	33.00
87-20-065	Sm. Santa W/Tree	Sarah's Attic	Closed	17.00	17.00
87-20-066	Mrs. Claus	Sarah's Attic	Closed	28.00	28.00
87-20-067	Kris Kringle	Sarah's Attic	Closed	120.00	120.00
88-20-068	Sitting Elf	Sarah's Attic	Closed	7.00	7.00
88-20-069	Elf W/Gift	Sarah's Attic	Closed	8.50	8.50
88-20-070	Sm.Sitting Santa	Sarah's Attic	Closed	11.00	11.00
88-20-071	Sm. Mrs. Claus	Sarah's Attic	Closed	8.50	8.50
91-20-072	Treasures of Love Santa	Sarah's Attic	3,000	140.00	140.00
91-20-073	Sharing Love Santa	Sarah's Attic	3,000	120.00	120.00
92-20-074	Peace on Earth Santa Doll 3564	Sarah's Attic	Closed	320.00	320.00
92-20-075	Small Blessed Christmas Flat Back 3669	Sarah's Attic	5,000	40.00	40.00
92-20-076	Small Emily & Gideon Flat Back 3670	Sarah's Attic	5,000	40.00	40.00
92-20-077	Small Enos & Adora Flat Back 3671	Sarah's Attic	5,000	35.00	35.00
92-20-078	Small Love the Children Flat Back 3672	Sarah's Attic	5,000	35.00	35.00
92-20-079	Small Toby w/Train Flat Back 3673	Sarah's Attic	5,000	35.00	35.00
92-20-080	Small Christmas Love Flat Back 3674	Sarah's Attic	5,000	30.00	30.00
Sarah's Attic		**United Hearts Collection**			
91-21-001	Tillie With Skates	Sarah's Attic	Closed	32.00	32.00
91-21-002	Willie on Sled	Sarah's Attic	Closed	32.00	32.00
91-21-003	Chilly Snowman	Sarah's Attic	Closed	33.00	33.00
91-21-004	Valentine Prissy with Dog	Sarah's Attic	Closed	36.00	36.00
91-21-005	Valentine Peanut w/Candy	Sarah's Attic	Closed	32.00	32.00
91-21-006	Shelby w/Shamrock	Sarah's Attic	Closed	36.00	36.00
91-21-007	Noah w/Pot of Gold	Sarah's Attic	Closed	36.00	36.00
91-21-008	Hawitt w/Leprechaun	Sarah's Attic	Closed	56.00	56.00
91-21-009	Tabitha Rabbit w/Bunny	Sarah's Attic	Closed	32.00	32.00
91-21-010	Toby & Tessie w/Wheelbarrow	Sarah's Attic	Closed	44.00	44.00
91-21-011	Wooly Lamb	Sarah's Attic	Closed	16.00	16.00
91-21-012	Emily w/Buggy	Sarah's Attic	Closed	53.00	53.00
91-21-013	Gideon with Bear & Rose	Sarah's Attic	Closed	40.00	40.00
91-21-014	Sally Booba Graduation	Sarah's Attic	Closed	45.00	45.00
91-21-015	Jack Boy Graduation	Sarah's Attic	Closed	40.00	40.00
91-21-016	Sparky Dog Graduation	Sarah's Attic	Closed	16.00	16.00
91-21-017	Bibi - Miss Liberty Bear	Sarah's Attic	Closed	30.00	30.00
91-21-018	Liberty Papa Barney & Biff	Sarah's Attic	Closed	64.00	64.00
91-21-019	Beach Pansy with Kitten	Sarah's Attic	Closed	34.00	34.00
91-21-020	Beach Annie & Waldo	Sarah's Attic	Closed	40.00	40.00
91-21-021	Beach Bubba w/Innertube	Sarah's Attic	Closed	34.00	34.00
91-21-022	School Cookie Rabbit w/Kit	Sarah's Attic	Closed	28.00	28.00
91-21-023	School Crumb Rabbit-Dunce	Sarah's Attic	Closed	32.00	32.00
91-21-024	School Chuckles Rabbit	Sarah's Attic	Closed	26.00	26.00
91-21-025	School Desk with Book	Sarah's Attic	Closed	15.00	15.00
91-21-026	Barney the Great Bear	Sarah's Attic	Closed	40.00	40.00
91-21-027	Clown Bibi & Biff Bears	Sarah's Attic	Closed	35.00	35.00
91-21-028	Thanksgiving Cupcake	Sarah's Attic	Closed	36.00	36.00
91-21-029	Thanksgiving Twinkie	Sarah's Attic	Closed	32.00	32.00
91-21-030	Thanksgiving Cornstalk	Sarah's Attic	Closed	30.00	30.00
91-21-031	Christmas Adora	Sarah's Attic	Closed	36.00	36.00
91-21-032	Christmas Enos	Sarah's Attic	Closed	36.00	36.00
91-21-033	Christmas Tree with Hearts	Sarah's Attic	Closed	40.00	40.00
92-21-034	Hether Rabbit w/Doll 3617	Sarah's Attic	12/93	26.00	26.00
92-21-035	Herbie Rabbit sitting 3618	Sarah's Attic	12/93	26.00	26.00
92-21-036	Mr. Carrotman 3619	Sarah's Attic	12/93	30.00	30.00
92-21-037	Fluffy Bear on blanket 3625	Sarah's Attic	12/93	35.00	35.00
92-21-038	Puffy Bear w/Roses 3626	Sarah's Attic	12/93	35.00	35.00
92-21-039	Young Kim w/Kite 3627	Sarah's Attic	12/93	40.00	40.00
92-21-040	Kyu Lee w/Sailboat 3628	Sarah's Attic	12/93	40.00	40.00
92-21-041	Jewel w/Umbrella 3630	Sarah's Attic	12/93	60.00	60.00
92-21-042	Stretch w/Rabbit 3661	Sarah's Attic	12/93	50.00	50.00
92-21-043	Angel Adora w/Doll 3632	Sarah's Attic	12/93	50.00	50.00
92-21-044	Angel Enos w/Bear 3633	Sarah's Attic	12/93	50.00	50.00
92-21-045	May Pole 3634	Sarah's Attic	12/93	35.00	35.00
92-21-046	Toby w/Bat 3635	Sarah's Attic	12/93	34.00	34.00
92-21-047	Tabitha w/Ball 3636	Sarah's Attic	12/93	34.00	34.00
92-21-048	Tessie on Blanket w/Ball 3637	Sarah's Attic	12/93	34.00	34.00
92-21-049	Cookie w/Torch 3638	Sarah's Attic	12/93	34.00	34.00
92-21-050	Crumb w/Flag 3639	Sarah's Attic	12/93	34.00	34.00
92-21-051	Zena w/Shells 3640	Sarah's Attic	12/93	46.00	46.00
92-21-052	Ethan w/Sandcastle 3641	Sarah's Attic	12/93	46.00	46.00
92-21-053	Katie w Planner 3643	Sarah's Attic	12/93	35.00	35.00
92-21-054	Willie w/Pail 3644	Sarah's Attic	12/93	35.00	35.00
92-21-055	Teacher's Desk 3645	Sarah's Attic	12/93	36.00	36.00
92-21-056	Pug w/Pumpkin 3646	Sarah's Attic	12/93	47.00	47.00
92-21-057	Peaches w/Cat 3647	Sarah's Attic	12/93	30.00	30.00
92-21-058	Cupcake w/Pumkins 3649	Sarah's Attic	12/93	35.00	35.00
92-21-059	Twinkie w/Basket 3650	Sarah's Attic	12/93	35.00	35.00
92-21-060	Hay Bales 3651	Sarah's Attic	12/93	23.00	23.00
92-21-061	Mrs. Claus w/Ribbon 3653	Sarah's Attic	12/93	45.00	45.00
92-21-062	Santa w/Train 3654	Sarah's Attic	12/93	45.00	45.00
92-21-063	Tree of Love 3655	Sarah's Attic	12/93	40.00	40.00
Sarah's Attic		**Children of Love**			
91-22-001	Charity Sewing Flags	Sarah's Attic	10,000	46.00	46.00
91-22-002	Benjamin with Drums	Sarah's Attic	10,000	46.00	46.00
91-22-003	Susie Painting Train	Sarah's Attic	10,000	46.00	46.00
91-22-004	Skip Building House	Sarah's Attic	10,000	50.00	50.00
91-22-005	Blossom w/Wash Tub	Sarah's Attic	5,000	50.00	50.00
91-22-006	Madge w/Watering Can	Sarah's Attic	2,500	50.00	50.00
91-22-007	Marty with Shovel	Sarah's Attic	2,500	50.00	50.00
91-22-008	Prayer Time Muffy	Sarah's Attic	5,000	46.00	46.00
91-22-009	Prayer Time Calvin	Sarah's Attic	5,000	46.00	46.00
91-22-010	Guardian Angel Priscilla	Sarah's Attic	5,000	46.00	46.00
91-22-011	Prayer Time Bed	Sarah's Attic	N/A	40.00	40.00
91-22-012	Angel Pup	Sarah's Attic	N/A	14.00	14.00
Sarah's Attic		**Cherished Memories**			
91-23-001	Black Baby Boy (Birth - 1 yr.)	Sarah's Attic	N/A	50.00	50.00
91-23-002	Black Baby Girl (1 - 2 yrs.)	Sarah's Attic	N/A	50.00	50.00
91-23-003	Black Baby Boy (1 - 2 yrs.)	Sarah's Attic	N/A	50.00	50.00
91-23-004	Black Baby Girl (Birth - 1 yr.)	Sarah's Attic	N/A	50.00	50.00
91-23-005	White Baby Boy (Birth - 1 yr.)	Sarah's Attic	N/A	60.00	60.00
91-23-006	White Baby Girl (Birth - 1 yr.)	Sarah's Attic	N/A	60.00	60.00
91-23-007	White Baby Girl (1 - 2 yrs.)	Sarah's Attic	N/A	60.00	60.00
91-23-008	White Baby Boy (1 - 2 yrs.)	Sarah's Attic	N/A	60.00	60.00
92-23-009	White Girl (2-3 yrs.) 3623	Sarah's Attic	N/A	30.00	30.00
92-23-010	White Boy (2-3 yrs.) 3624	Sarah's Attic	N/A	30.00	30.00
92-23-011	Black Girl (2-3 yrs.) 3675	Sarah's Attic	N/A	25.00	25.00
92-23-012	Black Boy (2-3 yrs.) 3676	Sarah's Attic	N/A	25.00	25.00
Sarah's Attic		**Matt & Maggie Series**			
86-24-001	Matt Candle Holder	Sarah's Attic	Closed	12.00	12.00
86-24-002	Maggie Candle Holder	Sarah's Attic	Closed	12.00	12.00
86-24-003	Maggie	Sarah's Attic	Closed	14.00	14.00
86-24-004	Matt	Sarah's Attic	Closed	14.00	14.00
87-24-005	Standing Matt	Sarah's Attic	Closed	11.00	11.00
87-24-006	Standing Maggie	Sarah's Attic	Closed	11.00	11.00
87-24-007	Matt on Heart	Sarah's Attic	Closed	9.00	9.00
87-24-008	Maggie on Heart	Sarah's Attic	Closed	9.00	9.00
87-24-009	Matt & Maggie w/ Bear	Sarah's Attic	Closed	100.00	100.00
88-24-010	Large Matt	Sarah's Attic	Closed	48.00	48.00
88-24-011	Large Maggie	Sarah's Attic	Closed	48.00	48.00
88-24-012	Small Sitting Matt	Sarah's Attic	Closed	11.50	11.50
88-24-013	Small Sitting Maggie	Sarah's Attic	Closed	11.50	11.50
89-24-014	Mini Matt	Sarah's Attic	Closed	6.00	6.00
89-24-015	Mini Maggie	Sarah's Attic	Closed	6.00	6.00
89-24-016	Matt Bench Sitter	Sarah's Attic	Closed	32.00	32.00
89-24-017	Maggie Bench Sitter	Sarah's Attic	Closed	32.00	32.00
Sarah's Attic		**Dreams of Tomorrow**			
92-25-001	Executive Katie 3665	Sarah's Attic	6,000	23.00	23.00
92-25-002	Executive Shelby 3666	Sarah's Attic	6,000	23.00	23.00

Number	Name	Artist	Edition Limit	Issue Price	Quote
92-25-003	Fireman Wilie 3667	Sarah's Attic	6,000	23.00	23.00
92-25-004	Fireman Bud 3668	Sarah's Attic	6,000	25.00	25.00

Sarah's Attic — **Forever Friends Collector's Club**

Number	Name	Artist	Edition Limit	Issue Price	Quote
91-26-001	Ruby	Sarah's Attic	Closed	36.00	36.00
91-26-002	Diamond	Sarah's Attic	Closed	42.00	42.00
91-26-003	Forever Frolicking Friends	Sarah's Attic	Closed	Gift	40.99
92-26-004	Love Starts With Children	Sarah's Attic	Closed	Gift	70.00
92-26-005	Sharing Dreams	Sarah's Attic	Closed	75.00	75.00
92-26-006	Lifetime Friends	Sarah's Attic	Closed	75.00	75.00

Schmid/B.F.A. — **Don Polland Figurines I**

Number	Name	Artist	Edition Limit	Issue Price	Quote
83-01-001	Young Bull	D. Polland	2,750	125.00	250.00
83-01-002	Escape	D. Polland	2,500	175.00	650.00
83-01-003	Fighting Bulls	D. Polland	2,500	200.00	600.00
83-01-004	Hot Pursuit	D. Polland	2,500	225.00	550.00
83-01-005	The Hunter	D. Polland	2,500	225.00	500.00
83-01-006	Downed	D. Polland	2,500	250.00	600.00
83-01-007	Challenge	D. Polland	2,000	275.00	600.00
83-01-008	A Second Chance	D. Polland	2,000	350.00	650.00
83-01-009	Dangerous Moment	D. Polland	2,000	250.00	350.00
83-01-010	The Great Hunt	D. Polland	350	3750.00	3750.00
86-01-011	Running Wolf-War Chief	D. Polland	2,500	170.00	295.00
86-01-012	Eagle Dancer	D. Polland	2,500	170.00	295.00
86-01-013	Plains Warrior	D. Polland	1,250	350.00	550.00
86-01-014	Second Chance	D. Polland	2,000	125.00	650.00
86-01-015	Shooting the Rapids	D. Polland	2,500	195.00	495.00
86-01-016	Down From The High Country	D. Polland	2,250	225.00	295.00
86-01-017	War Trophy	D. Polland	2,250	225.00	500.00

Schmid/B.F.A. — **RFD America**

Number	Name	Artist	Edition Limit	Issue Price	Quote
79-02-001	Country Road 25030	L. Davis	Closed	100.00	650-700.
79-02-002	Ignorance is Bliss 25031	L. Davis	Closed	165.00	950-1150.
79-02-003	Blossom 25032	L. Davis	Closed	180.00	1300-1400.
79-02-004	Fowl Play 25033	L. Davis	Closed	100.00	275-325.
79-02-005	Slim Pickins 25034	L. Davis	Closed	165.00	825-850.
79-02-006	Broken Dreams 25035	L. Davis	Closed	165.00	925-975.
80-02-007	Good, Clean Fun 25020	L. Davis	Closed	40.00	125-160.
80-02-008	Strawberry Patch 25021	L. Davis	Closed	25.00	95.00
80-02-009	Forbidden Fruit 25022	L. Davis	Closed	25.00	175-225.
80-02-010	Milking Time 25023	L. Davis	Closed	20.00	200-240.
80-02-011	Sunday Afternoon 25024	L. Davis	Closed	22.50	225-250.
80-02-012	New Day 25025	L. Davis	Closed	20.00	165.00
80-02-013	Wilbur 25029	L. Davis	Closed	100.00	475-500.
80-02-014	Itching Post 25037	L. Davis	Closed	30.00	115.00
80-02-015	Creek Bank Bandit 25038	L. Davis	Closed	37.50	400.00
81-02-016	Split Decision 25210	L. Davis	Closed	45.00	175-325.
81-02-017	Double Trouble 25211	L. Davis	Closed	35.00	475.00
81-02-018	Under the Weather 25212	L. Davis	Closed	25.00	85.00
81-02-019	Country Boy 25213	L. Davis	Closed	37.50	250-325.
81-02-020	Hightailing It 25214	L. Davis	Closed	50.00	375-500.
81-02-021	Studio Mouse 25215	L. Davis	Closed	60.00	275-325.
81-02-022	Dry as a Bone 25216	L. Davis	Closed	45.00	325.00
81-02-023	Rooted Out 25217	L. Davis	Closed	45.00	115.00
81-02-024	Up To No Good 25218	L. Davis	Closed	200.00	850-950.
81-02-025	Punkin' Seeds 25219	L. Davis	Closed	225.00	1200-1400.
81-02-026	Scallawags 25221	L. Davis	Closed	65.00	125-130.
82-02-027	Baby Bobs 25222	L. Davis	Closed	47.50	200-250.
82-02-028	Stray Dog 25223	L. Davis	Closed	35.00	60-75.00
82-02-029	Two's Company 25224	L. Davis	Closed	43.50	200-250.
82-02-030	Moving Day 25225	L. Davis	Closed	43.50	225-292.
82-02-031	Brand New Day 25226	L. Davis	Closed	23.50	150-175.
82-02-032	Baby Blossom 25227	L. Davis	Closed	40.00	175-300.
82-02-033	When Mama Gets Mad 25228	L. Davis	Closed	37.50	300-375.
82-02-034	A Shoe to Fill 25229	L. Davis	Closed	37.50	150-175.
82-02-035	Idle Hours 25230	L. Davis	Closed	37.50	225-300.
82-02-036	Thinking Big 25231	L. Davis	Closed	35.00	75.00
82-02-037	Country Crook 25280	L. Davis	Closed	37.50	300-350.
82-02-038	Waiting for His Master 25281	L. Davis	Closed	50.00	175-225.
82-02-039	Moon Raider 25325	L. Davis	Closed	190.00	325-400.
82-02-040	Blossom and Calf 25326	L. Davis	Closed	250.00	700-950.
82-02-041	Treed 25327	L. Davis	Closed	155.00	250-300.
83-02-042	Woman's Work 25232	L. Davis	Closed	35.00	90-95.00
83-02-043	Counting the Days 25233	L. Davis	Closed	40.00	60.00
83-02-044	Licking Good 25234	L. Davis	Closed	35.00	200-250.
83-02-045	Mama's Prize Leghorn 25235	L. Davis	Closed	55.00	100-135.
83-02-046	Fair Weather Friend 25236	L. Davis	Closed	25.00	50-60.00
83-02-047	False Alarm 25237	L. Davis	Closed	65.00	100-185.
83-02-048	Makin' Tracks 25238	L. Davis	Closed	70.00	70-125.00
83-02-049	Hi Girls, The Name's Big Jack 25328	L. Davis	Closed	200.00	325.00
83-02-050	City Slicker 25329	L. Davis	Closed	150.00	250-375.
83-02-051	Happy Hunting Ground 25330	L. Davis	Closed	160.00	240.00
83-02-052	Stirring Up Trouble 25331	L. Davis	Closed	160.00	250.00
83-02-053	His Eyes Are Bigger Than His Stomach 25332	L. Davis	Closed	235.00	325-350.
84-02-054	Courtin' 25220	L. Davis	Closed	45.00	100-125.
84-02-055	Anybody Home 25239	L. Davis	Closed	35.00	100-120.
84-02-056	Headed Home 25240	L. Davis	Closed	25.00	50.00
84-02-057	One for the Road 25241	L. Davis	Open	37.50	60-70.00
84-02-058	Huh? 25242	L. Davis	Closed	40.00	95.00
84-02-059	Gonna Pay for His Sins 25243	L. Davis	Open	27.50	75.00
84-02-060	His Master's Dog 25244	L. Davis	Closed	45.00	120-175.
84-02-061	Pasture Pals 25245	L. Davis	Closed	52.00	75.00
84-02-062	Country Kitty 25246	L. Davis	Closed	52.00	100-120.
84-02-063	Catnapping Too? 25247	L. Davis	Closed	70.00	100-125.
84-02-064	Gossips 25248	L. Davis	Closed	110.00	250.00
84-02-066	Prairie Chorus 25333	L. Davis	Closed	135.00	1000-1500.
84-02-067	Mad As A Wet Hen 25334	L. Davis	Closed	185.00	700-800.
85-02-068	Country Crooner 25256	L. Davis	Open	25.00	60.00
85-02-069	Barn Cats 25257	L. Davis	Open	39.50	80.00
85-02-070	Don't Play with Your Food 25258	L. Davis	Open	28.50	50.00
85-02-071	Out-of-Step 25259	L. Davis	Open	45.00	90.00
85-02-072	Renoir 25261	L. Davis	Closed	45.00	80.00
85-02-073	Too Good to Waste on Kids 25262	L. Davis	Open	70.00	130.00
85-02-074	Ozark Belle 25264	L. Davis	Closed	35.00	78.50
85-02-075	Will You Still Respect Me in the Morning 25265	L. Davis	Open	35.00	75.00
85-02-076	Country Cousins 25266	L. Davis	Open	42.50	80.00
85-02-077	Love at First Sight 25267	L. Davis	Open	70.00	105.00
85-02-078	Feelin' His Oats 25275	L. Davis	1,500	150.00	300.00
85-02-079	Furs Gonna Fly 25335	L. Davis	1,500	145.00	175-225.
85-02-080	Hog Heaven 25336	L. Davis	1,500	165.00	260-450.
86-02-081	Comfy? 25273	L. Davis	Open	40.00	80.00
86-02-082	Mama? 25277	L. Davis	Closed	15.00	40.00
86-02-083	Bit Off More Than He Could Chew 25279	L. Davis	Open	15.00	30.00
87-02-084	Mail Order Bride 25263	L. Davis	Closed	150.00	185-325.
87-02-085	Glutton for Punishment 25268	L. Davis	Closed	95.00	135.00
87-02-086	Easy Pickins 25269	L. Davis	Closed	45.00	70.00
87-02-087	Bottoms Up 25270	L. Davis	Open	80.00	117.00
87-02-088	The Orphans 25271	L. Davis	Open	50.00	80.00
87-02-089	When the Cat's Away 25276	L. Davis	Open	40.00	60.00
87-02-090	Two in the Bush 25337	L. Davis	Closed	150.00	245-350.
87-02-091	Chicken Thief 25338	L. Davis	Closed	200.00	325-350.
88-02-092	Sawin' Logs 25260	L. Davis	Open	85.00	105.00
88-02-093	Fleas 25272	L. Davis	Open	20.00	24.00
88-02-094	Making a Bee Line 25274	L. Davis	Closed	75.00	125.00
88-02-095	Missouri Spring 25278	L. Davis	Open	115.00	130.00
88-02-096	Perfect Ten 25282	L. Davis	Closed	95.00	105-177.
88-02-097	Goldie and Her Peeps 25283	L. Davis	Open	25.00	36.50
88-02-098	In a Pickle 25284	L. Davis	Open	40.00	50.00
88-02-099	Wishful Thinking 25285	L. Davis	Open	55.00	70.00
88-02-100	Brothers 25286	L. Davis	Closed	55.00	65.00
88-02-101	Happy Hour 25287	L. Davis	Open	57.50	65-80.00
88-02-102	When Three Foot's a Mile 25315	L. Davis	Closed	230.00	295.00
88-02-103	No Private Time 25316	L. Davis	Closed	200.00	250-325.
88-02-104	Wintering Lamb 25317	L. Davis	Closed	200.00	270.00
89-02-105	New Friend 25288	L. Davis	Open	45.00	60.00
89-02-106	Family Outing 25289	L. Davis	Open	45.00	60.00
89-02-107	Left Overs 25290	L. Davis	Open	90.00	100.00
89-02-108	Coon Capers 25291	L. Davis	Open	67.50	90.00
89-02-109	Mother Hen 25292	L. Davis	Open	37.50	50.00
89-02-110	Meeting of Sheldon 25293	L. Davis	Open	120.00	125.00
89-02-111	Boy's Night Out 25339	L. Davis	1,500	190.00	140-200.
89-02-112	A Tribute to Hooker 25340	L. Davis	Closed	180.00	250-300.
89-02-113	Woodscolt 25342	L. Davis	Closed	300.00	350-500.
90-02-114	Corn Crib Mouse 25295	L. Davis	Open	35.00	45.00
90-02-115	Seein' Red 25296	L. Davis	Open	35.00	47.00
90-02-116	Little Black Lamb (Baba) 25297	L. Davis	Open	30.00	37.50
90-02-117	Hanky Panky 25298	L. Davis	Open	65.00	100.00
90-02-118	Finder's Keepers 25299	L. Davis	Open	39.50	45.00
90-02-119	Foreplay 25300	L. Davis	Open	59.50	79.50
90-02-120	The Last Straw 25301	L. Davis	Open	125.00	147-162.50
90-02-121	Long Days, Cold Nights 25344	L. Davis	2,500	175.00	190.00
90-02-122	Piggin' Out 25345	L. Davis	Closed	190.00	300-400.
90-02-123	Tricks Of The Trade 25346	L. Davis	Closed	300.00	300-375.
91-02-124	First Offense 25304	L. Davis	Open	70.00	70.00
91-02-125	Gun Shy 25305	L. Davis	Open	70.00	70.00
91-02-126	Heading For The Persimmon Grove 25306	L. Davis	Open	80.00	80.00
91-02-127	Kissin' Cousins 25307	L. Davis	Open	80.00	80.00
91-02-128	Washed Ashore 25308	L. Davis	Open	70.00	70.00
91-02-129	Long, Hot Summer 25343	L. Davis	1,950	250.00	250.00
91-02-130	Cock Of The Walk 25347	L. Davis	2,500	300.00	300.00
91-02-131	Sooieee 25360	L. Davis	1,500	350.00	350.00
92-02-132	Ozark's Vittles 25318	L. Davis	Open	60.00	60.00
92-02-133	Don't Play With Fire 25319	L. Davis	Open	120.00	120.00
92-02-134	Safe Haven 25320	L. Davis	Open	95.00	95.00
92-02-135	Free Lunch 25321	L. Davis	Open	85.00	85.00
92-02-136	Headed South 25327	L. Davis	Open	45.00	45.00
92-02-137	My Favorite Chores 25362	L. Davis	1,500	750.00	750.00
92-02-138	OH Sheeeit . . . 25363	L. Davis	Open	120.00	120.00
92-02-139	She Lay Low 25364	L. Davis	Open	120.00	120.00
92-02-140	Snake Doctor 25365	L. Davis	Open	70.00	70.00
92-02-141	The Grass is Always Greener 25367	L. Davis	Open	195.00	195.00
92-02-142	School Yard Dogs 25369	L. Davis	Open	100.00	100.00
92-02-143	The Honeymoon's Over 25370	L. Davis	1,950	300.00	300.00

Schmid/B.F.A. — **Farm Set**

Number	Name	Artist	Edition Limit	Issue Price	Quote
85-03-001	Privy 25348	L. Davis	Closed	12.50	35.00
85-03-002	Windmill 25349	L. Davs	Closed	25.00	45.00
85-03-003	Remus' Cabin 25350	L. Davis	Closed	42.50	45-65.00
85-03-004	Main House 25351	L. Davis	Closed	42.50	100-125.
85-03-005	Barn 25352	L. Davis	Closed	47.50	250-325.
85-03-006	Goat Yard and Studio 25353	L. Davis	Closed	32.50	45-75.00
85-03-007	Corn Crib and Sheep Pen 25354	L. Davis	Closed	25.00	50-80.00
85-03-008	Hog House 25355	L. Davis	Closed	27.50	60-85.00
85-03-009	Hen House 25356	L. Davis	Closed	32.50	60-85.00
85-03-010	Smoke House 25357	L. Davis	Closed	12.50	35-65.00
85-03-011	Chicken House 25358	L. Davis	Closed	19.00	45.00
85-03-012	Garden and Wood Shed 25359	L. Davis	Closed	25.00	25-65.00

Schmid/B.F.A. — **Davis Cat Tales Figurines**

Number	Name	Artist	Edition Limit	Issue Price	Quote
82-04-001	Right Church, Wrong Pew 25204	L. Davis	Closed	70.00	350-400.
82-04-002	Company's Coming 25205	L. Davis	Closed	60.00	250-275.
82-04-003	On the Move 25206	L. Davis	Closed	70.00	650-675.
82-04-004	Flew the Coop 25207	L. Davis	Closed	60.00	275-300.

Schmid/B.F.A. — **Davis Special Edition Figurines**

Number	Name	Artist	Edition Limit	Issue Price	Quote
83-05-001	The Critics 23600	L. Davis	Closed	400.00	1350-1650.
85-05-002	Home from Market 23601	L. Davis	Closed	400.00	1100-1500.
89-05-003	From A Friend To A Friend 23602	L. Davis	1,200	750.00	1000-2000.
90-05-004	What Rat Race? 23603	L. Davis	1,200	800.00	800.00
92-05-005	Last Laff 23604	L. Davis	1,200	900.00	900.00

Schmid/B.F.A. — **Davis Country Christmas Figurines**

Number	Name	Artist	Edition Limit	Issue Price	Quote
83-06-001	Hooker at Mailbox with Presents 23550	L. Davis	Closed	80.00	750.00
84-06-002	Country Christmas 23551	L. Davis	Closed	80.00	450.00
85-06-003	Christmas at Fox Fire Farm 23552	L. Davis	Closed	80.00	200-250.
86-06-004	Christmas at Red Oak 23553	L. Davis	Closed	80.00	N/A
87-06-005	Blossom's Gift 23554	L. Davis	Closed	150.00	325-350.
88-06-006	Cutting the Family Christmas Tree 23555	L. Davis	Closed	80.00	200-250.
89-06-007	Peter and the Wren 23556	L. Davis	Closed	165.00	300-400.
90-06-008	Wintering Deer 23557	L. Davis	Closed	165.00	250-300.
91-06-009	Christmas At Red Oak II 23558	L. Davis	Closed	250.00	250.00
92-06-010	Born on a Starry Night 23559	L. Davis	2,500	225.00	225.00

Schmid/B.F.A. — **Little Critters**

Number	Name	Artist	Edition Limit	Issue Price	Quote
89-07-001	Gittin' a Nibble 25294	L. Davis	Open	50.00	57.00
90-07-002	Outing With Grandpa 25502	L. Davis	2,500	200.00	250.00
90-07-003	Home Squeezins 25504	L. Davis	Open	90.00	90.00
90-07-004	Punkin' Pig 25505	L. Davis	2,500	250.00	350.00
90-07-005	Private Time 25506	L. Davis	Open	18.00	40.00
91-07-006	Great American Chicken Race 25500	L. Davis	2,500	225.00	275.00
91-07-007	Punkin' Wine 25501	L. Davis	Open	100.00	150.00
91-07-008	Milk Mouse 25503	L. Davis	2,500	175.00	228.00
91-07-009	When Coffee Never Tasted So Good 25507	L. Davis	1,250	800.00	800.00
91-07-010	Toad Strangler 25509	L. Davis	Open	57.00	57.00

Number	Name	Artist	Edition Limit	Issue Price	Quote
91-07-011	Hittin' The Sack 25510	L. Davis	Open	70.00	70.00
91-07-012	Itiskit, Itasket 25511	L. Davis	Open	45.00	45.00
91-07-013	Christopher Critter 25514	L. Davis	1,992	150.00	150.00
92-07-014	Double Yolker 25516	L. Davis	Yr.Iss.	70.00	70.00
92-07-015	Miss Private Time 25517	L. Davis	Yr.Iss.	35.00	35.00
92-07-016	A Wolf in Sheep's Clothing 25518	L. Davis	Yr.Iss.	110.00	110.00
92-07-017	Charivari 25707	L. Davis	950	250.00	250.00

Schmid/B.F.A. — **Lowell Davis Farm Club**

Number	Name	Artist	Edition Limit	Issue Price	Quote
85-08-001	The Bride 221001 / 20993	L. Davis	Closed	45.00	400-475.
87-08-002	The Party's Over 221002 / 20994	L. Davis	Closed	50.00	100-190.
88-08-003	Chow Time 221003 / 20995	L. Davis	Closed	55.00	125-150.
89-08-004	Can't Wait 221004 / 20996	L. Davis	Closed	75.00	125.00
90-08-005	Pit Stop 221005 / 20997	L. Davis	Closed	75.00	125.00
91-08-006	Arrival Of Stanley 221006 / 20998	L. Davis	Yr.Iss.	100.00	100.00
91-08-007	Don't Pick The Flowers 221007 / 21007	L. Davis	Yr.Iss.	100.00	100.00
92-08-008	Hog Wild	L. Davis	Yr.Iss.	100.00	100.00
92-08-009	Check's in the Mail	L. Davis	Yr.Iss.	100.00	100.00

Schmid/B.F.A. — **Lowell Davis Farm Club Renewal Figurine**

Number	Name	Artist	Edition Limit	Issue Price	Quote
85-09-001	Thirsty? 892050 / 92050	L. Davis	Yr.Iss.	Gift	N/A
87-09-002	Cackle Berries 892051 / 92051	L. Davis	Yr.Iss.	Gift	N/A
88-09-003	Ice Cream Churn 892052 / 92052	L. Davis	Yr.Iss.	Gift	39.00
90-09-004	Not A Sharing Soul 892053 / 92053	L. Davis	Yr.Iss.	Gift	40.00
91-09-005	New Arrival 892054 / 92054	L. Davis	Yr.Iss.	Gift	20.00
92-09-006	Garden Toad	L. Davis	Yr.Iss.	Gift	N/A

Schmid/B.F.A. — **Country Pride**

Number	Name	Artist	Edition Limit	Issue Price	Quote
81-10-001	Surprise in the Cellar 25200	L. Davis	Closed	100.00	900-1200.
81-10-002	Plum Tuckered Out 25201	L. Davis	Closed	100.00	600-950.
81-10-003	Bustin' with Pride 25202	L. Davis	Closed	100.00	225-250.
81-10-004	Duke's Mixture 25203	L. Davis	Closed	100.00	375-450.

Schmid/B.F.A. — **Uncle Remus**

Number	Name	Artist	Edition Limit	Issue Price	Quote
81-11-001	Brer Fox 25250	L. Davis	Closed	70.00	900-950.
81-11-002	Brer Bear 25251	L. Davis	Closed	80.00	900-1200.
81-11-003	Brer Rabbit 25252	L. Davis	Closed	85.00	1500-2000.
81-11-004	Brer Wolf 25253	L. Davis	Closed	85.00	425-475.
81-11-005	Brer Weasel 25254	L. Davis	Closed	80.00	475-700.
81-11-006	Brer Coyote 25255	L. Davis	Closed	80.00	425-475.

Schmid/B.F.A. — **Promotional Figurine**

Number	Name	Artist	Edition Limit	Issue Price	Quote
91-12-001	Leavin' The Rat Race 225512	L. Davis	N/A	125.00	175-200.
92-12-002	Hen Scratch Prom 225968	L. Davis	N/A	95.00	95.00

Schmid/B.F.A. — **Route 66**

Number	Name	Artist	Edition Limit	Issue Price	Quote
91-13-001	Just Check The Air 25600	L. Davis	350	700.00	900-1400.
91-13-002	Nel's Diner 25601	L. Davis	350	700.00	900-1400.
91-13-003	Little Bit Of Shade 25602	L. Davis	Open	100.00	100.00
91-13-004	Just Check The Air 25603	L. Davis	2,500	550.00	550.00
91-13-005	Nel's Diner 25604	L. Davis	2,500	550.00	550.00
92-13-006	Relief 25605	L. Davis	Open	80.00	80.00
92-13-007	Welcome Mat (w/ wooden base)25606	L. Davis	1,500	400.00	400.00
92-13-008	Fresh Squeezed? 25608	L. Davis	2,500	450.00	450.00
92-13-009	Fresh Squeezed? (w/ wooden base) 25609	L. Davis	350	600.00	600.00
92-13-010	Quiet Day at Maple Grove 25618	L. Davis	Open	130.00	130.00
92-13-011	Going To Grandma's 25619	L. Davis	Open	80.00	80.00
92-13-012	What Are Pals For? 25620	L. Davis	Open	100.00	100.00

Schmid/B.F.A. — **Friends of Mine**

Number	Name	Artist	Edition Limit	Issue Price	Quote
89-14-001	Sun Worshippers 23620	L. Davis	5,000	120.00	134.00
89-14-002	Sun Worshippers Mini Figurine 23621	L. Davis	Open	32.50	32.50
90-14-003	Sunday Afternoon Treat 23625	L. Davis	5,000	120.00	130-170.
90-14-004	Sunday Afternoon Treat Mini Figurine 23626	L. Davis	Open	32.50	37.50
91-14-005	Warm Milk 23629	L. Davis	5,000	120.00	200.00
91-14-006	Warm Milk Mini Figurine 23630	L. Davis	Open	32.50	37.50
92-14-007	Cat and Jenny Wren 23633	L. Davis	5,000	170.00	170.00
92-14-008	Cat and Jenny Wren Mini Figurine 23634	L. Davis	Open	35.00	35.00

Schmid/B.F.A. — **Dealer Counter Signs**

Number	Name	Artist	Edition Limit	Issue Price	Quote
80-15-001	RFD America 888902	L. Davis	Closed	40.00	175-275.
81-15-002	Uncle Remus 888904	L. Davis	Closed	30.00	300.00
85-15-003	Fox Fire Farm 888907	L. Davis	Closed	30.00	150-275.
90-15-004	Mr. Lowell's Farm 25302	L. Davis	Open	50.00	55-70.00
92-15-005	Little Critters 25515	L. Davis	Open	50.00	50.00

Schmid/B.F.A. — **Kitty Cucumber Musical Figurine**

Number	Name	Artist	Edition Limit	Issue Price	Quote
92-16-001	Dance 'Round the Maypole 30215	M. Lillemoe	5,000	55.00	55.00
92-16-002	Butterfly 30221	M. Lillemoe	5,000	50.00	50.00

Sebastian Studios: See also Lance Corporation

Sebastian Studios — **Large Ceramastone Figures**

Number	Name	Artist	Edition Limit	Issue Price	Quote
39-01-001	Paul Revere Plaque	P.W. Baston	Closed	Unkn.	400-500.
40-01-002	Jesus	P.W. Baston	Closed	Unkn.	300-400.
40-01-003	Mary	P.W. Baston	Closed	Unkn.	600-1000.
40-01-004	Caroler	P.W. Baston	Closed	Unkn.	300-400.
40-01-005	Candle Holder	P.W. Baston	Closed	Unkn.	300-400.
40-01-006	Lamb	P.W. Baston	Closed	Unkn.	300-400.
40-01-007	Basket	P.W. Baston	Closed	Unkn.	300-400.
40-01-008	Horn of Plenty	P.W. Baston	Closed	Unkn.	300-400.
40-01-009	Breton Man	P.W. Baston	Closed	Unkn.	600-1000.
40-01-010	Breton Woman	P.W. Baston	Closed	Unkn.	600-1000.
47-01-011	Large Victorian Couple	P.W. Baston	Closed	Unkn.	600-1000.
48-01-012	Woody at Three	P.W. Baston	Closed	Unkn.	600-1000.
56-01-013	Jell-O Cow Milk Pitcher	P.W. Baston	Closed	Unkn.	175-225.
58-01-014	Swift Instrument Girl	P.W. Baston	Closed	Unkn.	500-750.
59-01-015	Wasp Plaque	P.W. Baston	Closed	Unkn.	500-750.
63-01-016	Henry VIII	P.W. Baston	Closed	Unkn.	600-1000.
63-01-017	Anne Boleyn	P.W. Baston	Closed	Unkn.	600-1000.
63-01-018	Tom Sawyer	P.W. Baston	Closed	Unkn.	600-1000.
63-01-019	Mending Time	P.W. Baston	Closed	Unkn.	600-1000.
63-01-020	David Copperfield	P.W. Baston	Closed	Unkn.	600-1000.
63-01-021	Dora	P.W. Baston	Closed	Unkn.	600-1000.
63-01-022	George Washington Toby Jug	P.W. Baston	Closed	Unkn.	600-1000.
63-01-023	Abraham Lincoln Toby Jug	P.W. Baston	Closed	Unkn.	600-1000.
63-01-024	John F. Kennedy Toby Jug	P.W. Baston	Closed	Unkn.	600-1000.
64-01-025	Colonial Boy	P.W. Baston	Closed	Unkn.	600-1000.
64-01-026	Colonial Man	P.W. Baston	Closed	Unkn.	600-1000.
64-01-027	Colonial Woman	P.W. Baston	Closed	Unkn.	600-1000.
64-01-028	Colonial Girl	P.W. Baston	Closed	Unkn.	600-1000.
64-01-029	IBM Mother	P.W. Baston	Closed	Unkn.	600-1000.
64-01-030	IBM Father	P.W. Baston	Closed	Unkn.	600-1000.
64-01-031	IBM Son	P.W. Baston	Closed	Unkn.	600-1000.
64-01-032	IBM Woman	P.W. Baston	Closed	Unkn.	600-1000.
64-01-033	IBM Photographer	P.W. Baston	Closed	Unkn.	600-1000.
65-01-034	N.E. Home For Little Wanderers	P.W. Baston	Closed	Unkn.	600-1000.
65-01-035	Stanley Music Box	P.W. Baston	Closed	Unkn.	300-500.
65-01-036	The Dentist	P.W. Baston	Closed	Unkn.	600-1000.
66-01-037	Guitarist	P.W. Baston	Closed	Unkn.	600-1000.
67-01-038	Infant of Prague	P.W. Baston	Closed	Unkn.	600-1000.
73-01-039	Potter	P.W. Baston	Closed	Unkn.	300-400.
73-01-040	Cabinetmaker	P.W. Baston	Closed	Unkn.	300-400.
73-01-041	Blacksmith	P.W. Baston	Closed	Unkn.	300-400.
73-01-042	Clockmaker	P.W. Baston	Closed	Unkn.	600-1000.
75-01-043	Minuteman	P.W. Baston	Closed	Unkn.	600-1000.
78-01-044	Mt. Rushmore	P.W. Baston	Closed	Unkn.	400-500.
XX-01-045	Santa Fe...All The Way	P.W. Baston	Closed	Unkn.	600-1000.
XX-01-046	St. Francis (Plaque)	P.W. Baston	Closed	Unkn.	600-1000.

Sebastian Studios — **Sebastian Miniatures**

Number	Name	Artist	Edition Limit	Issue Price	Quote
38-02-001	Shaker Man	P.W. Baston	Closed	Unkn.	75-100.00
38-02-002	Shaker Lady	P.W. Baston	Closed	Unkn.	75-100.00
39-02-003	George Washington	P.W. Baston	Closed	Unkn.	35-75.00
39-02-004	Martha Washington	P.W. Baston	Closed	Unkn.	35-75.00
39-02-005	John Alden	P.W. Baston	Closed	Unkn.	35-50.00
39-02-006	Priscilla	P.W. Baston	Closed	Unkn.	35-50.00
39-02-007	Williamsburg Governor	P.W. Baston	Closed	Unkn.	75-100.00
39-02-008	Williamsburg Lady	P.W. Baston	Closed	Unkn.	75-100.00
39-02-009	Benjamin Franklin	P.W. Baston	Closed	Unkn.	75-100.00
39-02-010	Deborah Franklin	P.W. Baston	Closed	Unkn.	75-100.00
39-02-011	Gabriel	P.W. Baston	Closed	Unkn.	100-125.
39-02-012	Evangeline	P.W. Baston	Closed	Unkn.	100-125.
39-02-013	Coronado	P.W. Baston	Closed	Unkn.	75-100.00
39-02-014	Coronado's Senora	P.W. Baston	Closed	Unkn.	75-100.00
39-02-015	Sam Houston	P.W. Baston	Closed	Unkn.	75-100.00
39-02-016	Margaret Houston	P.W. Baston	Closed	Unkn.	75-100.00
39-02-017	Indian Warrior	P.W. Baston	Closed	Unkn.	100-125.
39-02-018	Indian Maiden	P.W. Baston	Closed	Unkn.	100-125.
40-02-019	Jean LaFitte	P.W. Baston	Closed	Unkn.	75-100.00
40-02-020	Catherine LaFitte	P.W. Baston	Closed	Unkn.	75-100.00
40-02-021	Dan'l Boone	P.W. Baston	Closed	Unkn.	75-100.00
40-02-022	Mrs. Dan'l Boone	P.W. Baston	Closed	Unkn.	75-100.00
40-02-023	Peter Stvyvesant	P.W. Baston	Closed	Unkn.	75-100.00
40-02-024	Ann Stvyvesant	P.W. Baston	Closed	Unkn.	75-100.00
40-02-025	John Harvard	P.W. Baston	Closed	Unkn.	125-150.
40-02-026	Mrs. Harvard	P.W. Baston	Closed	Unkn.	125-150.
40-02-027	John Smith	P.W. Baston	Closed	Unkn.	75-150.00
40-02-028	Pocohontas	P.W. Baston	Closed	Unkn.	75-150.00
40-02-029	William Penn	P.W. Baston	Closed	Unkn.	100-150.
40-02-030	Hannah Penn	P.W. Baston	Closed	Unkn.	100-150.
40-02-031	Buffalo Bill	P.W. Baston	Closed	Unkn.	75-100.00
40-02-032	Annie Oakley	P.W. Baston	Closed	Unkn.	75-100.00
40-02-033	James Monroe	P.W. Baston	Closed	Unkn.	150-175.
40-02-034	Elizabeth Monroe	P.W. Baston	Closed	Unkn.	150-175.
41-02-035	Rooster	P.W. Baston	Closed	Unkn.	600-1000.
41-02-036	Ducklings	P.W. Baston	Closed	Unkn.	600-1000.
41-02-037	Peacock	P.W Baston	Closed	Unkn.	600-1000.
41-02-038	Doves	P.W. Baston	Closed	Unkn.	600-1000.
41-02-039	Pheasant	P.W. Baston	Closed	Unkn.	600-1000.
41-02-040	Swan	P.W. Baston	Closed	Unkn.	600-1000.
41-02-041	Secrets	P.W. Baston	Closed	Unkn.	600-1000.
41-02-042	Kitten (Sleeping)	P.W. Baston	Closed	Unkn.	600-1000.
41-02-043	Kitten (Sitting)	P.W. Baston	Closed	Unkn.	600-1000.
42-02-044	Majorette	P.W. Baston	Closed	Unkn.	325.-375.
42-02-045	Cymbals	P.W. Baston	Closed	Unkn.	325-375.
42-02-046	Horn	P.W. Baston	Closed	Unkn.	325-375.
42-02-047	Tuba	P.W. Baston	Closed	Unkn.	325-375.
42-02-048	Drum	P.W. Baston	Closed	Unkn.	325-375.
42-02-049	Accordion	P.W. Baston	Closed	Unkn.	325-375.
46-02-050	Puritan Spinner	P.W. Baston	Closed	Unkn.	600-1000.
46-02-051	Satchel-Eye Dyer	P.W. Baston	Closed	Unkn.	125-150.
47-02-052	Down East	P.W. Baston	Closed	Unkn.	125-150.
47-02-053	First Cookbook Author	P.W. Baston	Closed	Unkn.	125-150.
47-02-054	Fisher Pair PS	P.W. Baston	Closed	Unkn.	600-1000.
47-02-055	Mr. Beacon Hill	P.W. Baston	Closed	Unkn.	75-125.00
47-02-056	Mrs. Beacon Hill	P.W. Baston	Closed	Unkn.	75-125.00
47-02-057	Dahl's Fisherman	P.W. Baston	Closed	Unkn.	150-175.
47-02-058	Dilemma	P.W. Baston	Closed	Unkn.	275-300.
47-02-059	Princess Elizabeth	P.W. Baston	Closed	Unkn.	200-300.
47-02-060	Prince Philip	P.W. Baston	Closed	Unkn.	200-300.
47-02-061	Howard Johnson Pieman	P.W. Baston	Closed	Unkn.	300-450.
47-02-062	Tollhouse Town Crier	P.W. Baston	Closed	Unkn.	125-175.
48-02-063	Slalom	P.W. Baston	Closed	Unkn.	175-200.
48-02-064	Sitzmark	P.W. Baston	Closed	Unkn.	175-200.
48-02-065	Mr. Rittenhouse Square	P.W. Baston	Closed	Unkn.	150-175.
48-02-066	Mrs. Rittenhouse Square	P.W. Baston	Closed	Unkn.	150-175.
48-02-067	Swedish Boy	P.W. Baston	Closed	Unkn.	300-500.
48-02-068	Swedish Girl	P.W. Baston	Closed	Unkn.	300-500.
48-02-069	Democratic Victory	P.W. Baston	Closed	Unkn.	350-500.
48-02-070	Republican Victory	P.W. Baston	Closed	Unkn.	600-1000.
48-02-071	Nathaniel Hawthorne	P.W. Baston	Closed	Unkn.	175-200.
48-02-072	Jordan Marsh Observer	P.W. Baston	Closed	Unkn.	150-175.
48-02-073	Mr. Sheraton	P.W. Baston	Closed	Unkn.	350-400.
48-02-074	A Harvey Girl	P.W. Baston	Closed	Unkn.	250-300.
48-02-075	Mary Lyon	P.W. Baston	Closed	Unkn.	250-300.
49-02-076	Uncle Mistletoe	P.W. Baston	Closed	Unkn.	250-300.
49-02-077	Eustace Tilly	P.W. Baston	Closed	Unkn.	750-1500.
49-02-078	Menotomy Indian	P.W. Baston	Closed	Unkn.	175-250.
49-02-079	Boy Scout Plaque	P.W. Baston	Closed	Unkn.	300-350.
49-02-080	Patrick Henry	P.W. Baston	Closed	Unkn.	100-125.
49-02-081	Sarah Henry	P.W. Baston	Closed	Unkn.	100-125.
49-02-082	Paul Bunyan	P.W. Baston	Closed	Unkn.	250.00
49-02-083	Emmett Kelly	P.W. Baston	Closed	Unkn.	250-300.
49-02-084	Giant Royal Bengal Tiger	P.W. Baston	Closed	Unkn.	1000-1500.
49-02-085	The Thinker	P.W. Baston	Closed	Unkn.	175-250.
49-02-086	The Mark Twain Home in Hannibal, MO	P.W. Baston	Closed	Unkn.	600-1000.
49-02-087	Dutchman's Pipe	P.W. Baston	Closed	Unkn.	175-225.
49-02-088	Gathering Tulips	P.W. Baston	Closed	Unkn.	225-250.
50-02-089	Phoebe, House of 7 Gables	P.W. Baston	Closed	Unkn.	150-175.
50-02-090	Mr. Obocell	P.W. Baston	Closed	Unkn.	75-125.00
50-02-091	National Diaper Service	P.W. Baston	Closed	Unkn.	250-300.
51-02-092	Judge Pyncheon	P.W. Baston	Closed	Unkn.	175-225.
51-02-093	Seb. Dealer Plaque (Marblehead)	P.W. Baston	Closed	Unkn.	300-350.
51-02-094	Great Stone Face	P.W. Baston	Closed	Unkn.	600-1000.
51-02-095	Christopher Columbus	P.W. Baston	Closed	Unkn.	250-300.

Company Number	Series Name	Artist	Edition Limit	Issue Price	Quote
51-02-096	Sir Frances Drake	P.W. Baston	Closed	Unkn.	250-300.
51-02-097	Jesse Buffman (WEEI)	P.W. Baston	Closed	Unkn.	200-350.
51-02-098	Carl Moore (WEEI)	P.W. Baston	Closed	Unkn.	200-300.
51-02-099	Caroline Cabot (WEEI)	P.W. Baston	Closed	Unkn.	200-350.
51-02-100	Mother Parker (WEEI)	P.W. Baston	Closed	Unkn.	200-350.
51-02-101	Charles Ashley (WEEI)	P.W. Baston	Closed	Unkn.	200-350.
51-02-102	E. B. Rideout (WEEI)	P.W. Baston	Closed	Unkn.	200-350.
51-02-103	Priscilla Fortesue (WEEI)	P.W. Baston	Closed	Unkn.	200-350.
51-02-104	Chiquita Banana	P.W. Baston	Closed	Unkn.	350-400.
51-02-105	Mit Seal	P.W. Baston	Closed	Unkn.	350-425.
51-02-106	The Observer & Dame New England.	P.W. Baston	Closed	Unkn.	325-375.
51-02-107	Jordon Marsh Observer Rides the A.W. Horse	P.W. Baston	Closed	Unkn.	300-325.
51-02-108	The Iron Master's House	P.W. Baston	Closed	Unkn.	350-500.
51-02-109	Chief Pontiac	P.W. Baston	Closed	Unkn.	400-700.
52-02-110	The Favored Scholar	P.W. Baston	Closed	Unkn.	200-300.
52-02-111	Neighboring Pews	P.W. Baston	Closed	Unkn.	200-300.
52-02-112	Weighing the Baby	P.W. Baston	Closed	Unkn.	200-300.
52-02-113	The First House, Plimoth Plantation	P.W. Baston	Closed	Unkn.	150-195.
52-02-114	Scottish Girl (Jell-O)	P.W. Baston	Closed	Unkn.	350-375.
52-02-115	Lost in the Kitchen (Jell-O)	P.W. Baston	Closed	Unkn.	350-375.
52-02-116	The Fat Man (Jell-O)	P.W. Baston	Closed	Unkn.	525-600.
52-02-117	Baby (Jell-O)	P.W. Baston	Closed	Unkn.	525-600.
52-02-118	Stork (Jell-O)	P.W. Baston	Closed	Unkn.	425-525.
52-02-119	Tabasco Sauce	P.W. Baston	Closed	Unkn.	400-500.
52-02-120	Aerial Tramway	P.W. Baston	Closed	Unkn.	300-600.
52-02-121	Marblehead High School Plaque	P.W. Baston	Closed	Unkn.	200-300.
52-02-122	St. Joan d'Arc	P.W. Baston	Closed	Unkn.	300-350.
52-02-123	St. Sebastian	P.W. Baston	Closed	Unkn.	300-350.
52-02-124	Our Lady of Good Voyage	P.W. Baston	Closed	Unkn.	200-250.
52-02-125	Old Powder House	P.W. Baston	Closed	Unkn.	250-300.
53-02-126	Holgrave the Daguerrotypist	P.W. Baston	Closed	Unkn.	200-250.
53-02-127	St. Teresa of Lisieux	P.W. Baston	Closed	Unkn.	225-275.
53-02-128	Darned Well He Can	P.W. Baston	Closed	Unkn.	300-350.
53-02-129	R.H. Stearns Chestnut Hill Mall	P.W. Baston	Closed	Unkn.	225-275.
53-02-130	Boy Jesus in the Temple	P.W. Baston	Closed	Unkn.	350-400.
53-02-131	Blessed Julie Billart	P.W. Baston	Closed	Unkn.	400-500.
53-02-132	"Old Put" Enjoys a Licking	P.W. Baston	Closed	Unkn.	300-350.
53-02-133	Lion (Jell-O)	P.W. Baston	Closed	Unkn.	350-375.
53-02-134	The Schoolboy of 1850	P.W. Baston	Closed	Unkn.	350-400.
54-02-135	Whale (Jell-O)	P.W. Baston	Closed	Unkn.	350-375.
54-02-136	Rabbit (Jell-O)	P.W. Baston	Closed	Unkn.	350-375.
54-02-137	Moose (Jell-O)	P.W. Baston	Closed	Unkn.	350-375.
54-02-138	Scuba Diver	P.W. Baston	Closed	Unkn.	400-450.
54-02-139	Stimalose (Woman)	P.W. Baston	Closed	Unkn.	175-200.
54-02-140	Stimalose (Men)	P.W. Baston	Closed	Unkn.	600-1000.
54-02-141	Bluebird Girl	P.W. Baston	Closed	Unkn.	400-450.
54-02-142	Campfire Girl	P.W. Baston	Closed	Unkn.	400-450.
54-02-143	Horizon Girl	P.W. Baston	Closed	Unkn.	400-450.
54-02-144	Kernel-Fresh Ashtray	P.W. Baston	Closed	Unkn.	400-450.
54-02-145	William Penn	P.W. Baston	Closed	Unkn.	175-225.
54-02-146	St. Pius X	P.W. Baston	Closed	Unkn.	400-475.
54-02-147	Resolute Ins. Co. Clipper PS	P.W. Baston	Closed	Unkn.	300-325.
54-02-148	Dachshund (Audiovox)	P.W. Baston	Closed	Unkn.	300-350.
54-02-149	Our Lady of Laleche	P.W. Baston	Closed	Unkn.	300-350.
54-02-150	Swan Boat Brooch-Enpty Seats	P.W. Baston	Closed	Unkn.	600-1000.
54-02-151	Swan Boat Brooch-Full Seats	P.W. Baston	Closed	Unkn.	600-1000.
55-02-152	Davy Crockett	P.W. Baston	Closed	Unkn.	225-275.
55-02-153	Giraffe (Jell-O)	P.W. Baston	Closed	Unkn.	350-375.
55-02-154	Old Woman in the Shoe (Jell-O)	P.W. Baston	Closed	Unkn.	500-600.
55-02-155	Santa (Jell-O)	P.W. Baston	Closed	Unkn.	500-600.
55-02-156	Captain Doliber	P.W. Baston	Closed	Unkn.	300-350.
55-02-157	Second Bank-State St. Trust PS	P.W. Baston	Closed	Unkn.	300-325.
55-02-158	Horse Head PS	P.W. Baston	Closed	Unkn.	350-375.
56-02-159	Robin Hood & Little John	P.W. Baston	Closed	Unkn.	400-500.
56-02-160	Robin Hood & Friar Tuck	P.W. Baston	Closed	Unkn.	400-500.
56-02-161	77th Bengal Lancer (Jell-O)	P.W. Baston	Closed	Unkn.	600-1000.
56-02-162	Three Little Kittens (Jell-O)	P.W. Baston	Closed	Unkn.	375-400.
56-02-163	Texcel Tape Boy	P.W. Baston	Closed	Unkn.	350-425.
56-02-164	Permacel Tower of Tape Ashtray	P.W. Baston	Closed	Unkn.	600-1000.
56-02-165	Arthritic Hands (J & J)	P.W. Baston	Closed	Unkn.	600-1000.
56-02-166	Rarical Blacksmith	P.W. Baston	Closed	Unkn.	300-500.
56-02-167	Praying Hands	P.W. Baston	Closed	Unkn.	250-300.
56-02-168	Eastern Paper Plaque	P.W. Baston	Closed	Unkn.	350-400.
56-02-169	Girl on Diving Board	P.W. Baston	Closed	Unkn.	400-450.
56-02-170	Elsie the Cow Billboard	P.W. Baston	Closed	Unkn.	600-1000.
56-02-171	Mrs. Obocell	P.W. Baston	Closed	Unkn.	400-450.
56-02-172	Alike, But Oh So Different	P.W. Baston	Closed	Unkn.	300-350.
56-02-173	NYU Grad School of Bus. Admin. Bldg.	P.W. Baston	Closed	Unkn.	300-350.
56-02-174	The Green Giant	P.W. Baston	Closed	Unkn.	400-500.
56-02-175	Michigan Millers PS	P.W. Baston	Closed	Unkn.	200-275.
57-02-176	Mayflower PS	P.W. Baston	Closed	Unkn.	300-325.
57-02-177	Jamestown Church	P.W. Baston	Closed	Unkn.	400-450.
57-02-178	Olde James Fort	P.W. Baston	Closed	Unkn.	250-300.
57-02-179	Jamestown Ships	P.W. Baston	Closed	Unkn.	350-475.
57-02-180	IBM 305 Ramac	P.W. Baston	Closed	Unkn.	400-450.
57-02-181	Colonial Fund Doorway PS	P.W. Baston	Closed	Unkn.	600-1000.
57-02-182	Speedy Alka Seltzer	P.W. Baston	Closed	Unkn.	600-1000.
57-02-183	Nabisco Spoonmen	P.W. Baston	Closed	Unkn.	600-1000.
57-02-184	Nabisco Buffalo Bee	P.W. Baston	Closed	Unkn.	600-1000.
57-02-185	Borden's Centennial (Elsie the Cow)	P.W. Baston	Closed	Unkn.	600-1000.
57-02-186	Along the Albany Road PS	P.W. Baston	Closed	Unkn.	600-1000.
58-02-187	Romeo & Juliet	P.W. Baston	Closed	Unkn.	400-500.
58-02-188	Mt. Vernon	P.W. Baston	Closed	Unkn.	400-500.
58-02-189	Hannah Duston PS	P.W. Baston	Closed	Unkn.	250-325.
58-02-190	Salem Savings Bank	P.W. Baston	Closed	Unkn.	250-300.
58-02-191	CBS Miss Columbia PS	P.W. Baston	Closed	Unkn.	600-1000.
58-02-192	Connecticut Bank & Trust	P.W. Baston	Closed	Unkn.	225-275.
58-02-193	Jackie Gleason	P.W. Baston	Closed	Unkn.	600-1000.
58-02-194	Harvard Trust Colonial Man	P.W. Baston	Closed	Unkn.	275-325.
58-02-195	Jordan Marsh Observer	P.W. Baston	Closed	Unkn.	175-275.
58-02-196	Cliquot Club Eskimo PS	P.W. Baston	Closed	Unkn.	1000-2300.
58-02-197	Commodore Stephen Decatur	P.W. Baston	Closed	Unkn.	125-175.
59-02-198	Siesta Coffee PS	P.W. Baston	Closed	Unkn.	600-1000.
59-02-199	Harvard Trust Co. Town Crier	P.W. Baston	Closed	Unkn.	350-400.
59-02-200	Mrs. S.O.S.	P.W. Baston	Closed	Unkn.	300-350.
59-02-201	H.P. Hood Co. Cigar Store Indian	P.W. Baston	Closed	Unkn.	600-1000.
59-02-202	Alexander Smith Weaver	P.W. Baston	Closed	Unkn.	350-425.
59-02-203	Fleischman's Margarine PS	P.W. Baston	Closed	Unkn.	225-325.
59-02-204	Alcoa Wrap PS	P.W. Baston	Closed	Unkn.	350-400.
59-02-205	Fiorello LaGuardia	P.W. Baston	Closed	Unkn.	125-175.
59-02-206	Henry Hudson	P.W. Baston	Closed	Unkn.	125-175.
59-02-207	Giovanni Verrazzano	P.W. Baston	Closed	Unkn.	125-175.
60-02-208	Peter Stvyvesant	P.W. Baston	Closed	Unkn.	125-175.

Company Number	Series Name	Artist	Edition Limit	Issue Price	Quote
60-02-209	Masonic Bible	P.W. Baston	Closed	Unkn.	300-400.
60-02-210	Son of the Desert	P.W. Baston	Closed	Unkn.	200-275.
60-02-211	Metropolitan Life Tower PS	P.W. Baston	Closed	Unkn.	350-400.
60-02-212	Supp-Hose Lady	P.W. Baston	Closed	Unkn.	300-350.
60-02-213	Marine Memorial	P.W. Baston	Closed	Unkn.	300-400.
60-02-214	The Infantryman	P.W. Baston	Closed	Unkn.	600-1000.
61-02-215	Tony Piet	P.W. Baston	Closed	Unkn.	600-1000.
61-02-216	Bunky Knudsen	P.W. Baston	Closed	Unkn.	600-1000.
61-02-217	Merchant's Warren Sea Capt.	P.W. Baston	Closed	Unkn.	200-250.
61-02-218	Pope John 23rd	P.W. Baston	Closed	Unkn.	400-450.
61-02-219	St. Jude Thaddeus	P.W. Baston	Closed	Unkn.	400-500.
62-02-220	Seaman's Bank for Savings	P.W. Baston	Closed	Unkn.	300-350.
62-02-221	Yankee Clipper Sulfide	P.W. Baston	Closed	Unkn.	600-1000.
62-02-222	Big Brother Bob Emery	P.W. Baston	Closed	Unkn.	600-1000.
62-02-223	Blue Belle Highlander	P.W. Baston	Closed	Unkn.	200-250.
63-02-224	John F. Kennedy Toby Jug	P.W. Baston	Closed	Unkn.	600-1000.
63-02-225	Jackie Kennedy Toby Jug	P.W. Baston	Closed	Unkn.	600-1000.
63-02-226	Naumkeag Indian	P.W. Baston	Closed	Unkn.	225-275.
63-02-227	Dia-Mel Fat Man	P.W. Baston	Closed	Unkn.	375-400.
65-02-228	Pope Paul VI	P.W. Baston	Closed	Unkn.	400-500.
65-02-229	Henry Wadsworth Longfellow	P.W. Baston	Closed	Unkn.	275-325.
65-02-230	State Street Bank Globe	P.W. Baston	Closed	Unkn.	250-300.
65-02-231	Panti-Legs Girl PS	P.W. Baston	Closed	Unkn.	250-300.
66-02-232	Paul Revere Plaque (W.T. Grant)	P.W. Baston	Closed	Unkn.	300-350.
66-02-233	Massachusetts SPCA	P.W. Baston	Closed	Unkn.	250-350.
66-02-234	Little George	P.W. Baston	Closed	Unkn.	350-450.
66-02-235	Gardeners (Thermometer)	P.W. Baston	Closed	Unkn.	300-400.
66-02-236	Gardener Man	P.W. Baston	Closed	Unkn.	250-300.
66-02-237	Gardener Women	P.W. Baston	Closed	Unkn.	250-300.
66-02-238	Town Lyne Indian	P.W. Baston	Closed	Unkn.	600-1000.
67-02-239	Doc Berry of Berwick (yellow shirt)	P.W. Baston	Closed	Unkn.	300-350.
67-02-240	Ortho-Novum	P.W. Baston	Closed	Unkn.	600-1000.
68-02-241	Captain John Parker	P.W. Baston	Closed	Unkn.	300-350.
68-02-242	Watermill Candy Plaque	P.W. Baston	Closed	Unkn.	600-1000.
70-02-243	Uncle Sam in Orbit	P.W. Baston	Closed	Unkn.	350-400.
71-02-244	Town Meeting Plaque	P.W. Baston	Closed	Unkn.	350-400.
71-02-245	Boston Gas Tank	P.W. Baston	Closed	Unkn.	300-500.
72-02-246	George & Hatchet	P.W. Baston	Closed	Unkn.	400-450.
72-02-247	Martha & the Cherry Pie	P.W. Baston	Closed	Unkn.	350-400.
XX-02-248	The King	P.W. Baston	Closed	Unkn.	600-1000.
XX-02-249	Bob Hope	P.W. Baston	Closed	Unkn.	600-1000.
XX-02-250	Coronation Crown	P.W. Baston	Closed	Unkn.	600-1000.
XX-02-251	Babe Ruth	P.W. Baston	Closed	Unkn.	600-1000.
XX-02-252	Sylvania Electric-Bulb Display	P.W. Baston	Closed	Unkn.	600-1000.
XX-02-252	Ortho Gynecic	P.W. Baston	Closed	Unkn.	600-1000.
XX-02-254	Eagle Plaque	P.W. Baston	Closed	Unkn.	1000-1500.
Shelia's, Inc.	**Painted Ladies I**				
90-01-001	San Francisco Stick House-yellow	S.Thompson	Retrd.	10.00	20-35.00
90-01-002	San Francisco Stick House-blue	S.Thompson	Retrd.	10.00	20-35.00
90-01-003	San Francisco Italianate-yellow	S.Thompson	Retrd.	10.00	20-35.00
90-01-004	Colorado Queen Anne	S.Thompson	Retrd.	10.00	20-35.00
90-01-005	Atlanta Queen Anne	S.Thompson	Retrd.	10.00	20-35.00
90-01-006	Savannah Gingerbread	S.Thompson	Retrd.	10.00	20-35.00
90-01-007	Cape May Gothic Revival	S.Thompson	Retrd.	10.00	20-35.00
90-01-008	Malden Mass. Victorian Inn	S.Thompson	Retrd.	10.00	20-35.00
90-01-009	Illinois Queen Anne	S.Thompson	Retrd.	10.00	20-35.00
Shelia's, Inc.	**Painted Ladies II**				
90-02-001	The Gingerbread Mansion	S.Thompson	Open	15.00	15.00
90-02-002	Pitkin House	S.Thompson	Open	15.00	15.00
90-02-003	The Young-Larson House	S.Thompson	Open	15.00	15.00
90-02-004	Queen Anne Rowhouse	S.Thompson	Open	15.00	15.00
90-02-005	Pink Gothic	S.Thompson	Open	15.00	15.00
90-02-006	The Victorian Blue Rose	S.Thompson	Open	15.00	15.00
90-02-007	Morningstar Inn	S.Thompson	Open	15.00	15.00
90-02-008	Cape May Victorian Pink House	S.Thompson	Open	15.00	15.00
Shelia's, Inc.	**Dicken's Village '91**				
91-03-001	Scrooge & Marley's Shop	S.Thompson	7/93	15.00	15.00
91-03-002	Butcher Shop	S.Thompson	7/93	15.00	15.00
91-03-003	Toy Shoppe	S.Thompson	7/93	15.00	15.00
91-03-004	Scrooge's Home	S.Thompson	7/93	15.00	15.00
91-03-005	Victorian Apartment Building	S.Thompson	7/93	15.00	15.00
91-03-006	Gazebo & Carolers	S.Thompson	7/93	12.00	12.00
91-03-007	Victorian Skaters	S.Thompson	7/93	12.00	12.00
91-03-008	Evergreen Tree	S.Thompson	7/93	11.00	11.00
Shelia's, Inc.	**Dicken's Village '92**				
92-04-001	Victorian Church	S.Thompson	7/93	15.00	15.00
Shelia's, Inc.	**Charleston**				
88-05-001	Rainbow Row-rust	S.Thompson	7/93	9.00	9.00
88-05-002	Rainbow Row-rust (gold seal)	S.Thompson	Retrd.	9.00	9.00
88-05-003	Rainbow Row-tan	S.Thompson	7/93	9.00	9.00
88-05-004	Rainbow Row-tan (gold seal)	S.Thompson	Retrd.	9.00	9.00
88-05-005	Rainbow Row-cream	S.Thompson	7/93	9.00	9.00
88-05-006	Rainbow Row-cream (gold seal)	S.Thompson	Retrd.	9.00	9.00
88-05-007	Rainbow Row-green	S.Thompson	7/93	9.00	9.00
88-05-008	Rainbow Row-green (gold seal)	S.Thompson	Retrd.	9.00	9.00
88-05-009	Rainbow Row-lavender	S.Thompson	7/93	9.00	9.00
88-05-010	Rainbow Row-lavender (gold seal)	S.Thompson	Retrd.	9.00	9.00
88-05-011	Rainbow Row-pink	S.Thompson	7/93	9.00	9.00
88-05-012	Rainbow Row-pink (gold seal)	S.Thompson	Retrd.	9.00	9.00
88-05-013	Rainbow Row-blue	S.Thompson	7/93	9.00	9.00
88-05-014	Rainbow Row-blue (gold seal)	S.Thompson	Retrd.	9.00	9.00
88-05-015	Rainbow Row-yellow	S.Thompson	7/93	9.00	9.00
88-05-016	Rainbow Row-yellow (gold seal)	S.Thompson	Retrd.	9.00	9.00
88-05-017	Rainbow Row-lt. yellow	S.Thompson	7/93	9.00	9.00
88-05-018	Rainbow Row-lt. yellow (gold seal)	S.Thompson	Retrd.	9.00	9.00
88-05-019	Pink House (gold seal)	S.Thompson	Retrd.	9.00	9.00
88-05-020	90 Church St. (gold seal)	S.Thompson	Retrd.	9.00	9.00
89-05-021	Middleton Plantation	S.Thompson	Retrd.	9.00	22-50.00
89-05-022	Middleton Plantation (gold seal)	S.Thompson	Retrd.	9.00	N/A
89-05-023	Powder Magazine	S.Thompson	Retrd.	9.00	22-50.00
89-05-024	Powder Magazine (gold seal)	S.Thompson	Retrd.	9.00	N/A
89-05-025	St. Michael's Church (gold seal)	S.Thompson	Retrd.	9.00	N/A
89-05-026	Exchange Building (gold seal)	S.Thompson	Retrd.	9.00	N/A
90-05-027	Beth Elohim Temple	S.Thompson	7/93	15.00	15.00
90-05-028	Manigault House	S.Thompson	Open	15.00	15.00
90-05-029	Heyward-Washington House	S.Thompson	Open	15.00	15.00
90-05-030	Magnolia Plantation House	S.Thompson	Open	16.00	16.00
90-05-031	Edmonston-Alston Church	S.Thompson	Open	15.00	15.00

Number	Name	Artist	Edition Limit	Issue Price	Quote
90-05-032	St. Phillip's Church	S.Thompson	Open	15.00	15.00
90-05-033	#2 Meeting Street	S.Thompson	Open	15.00	15.00
90-05-034	City Market	S.Thompson	Open	15.00	15.00
90-05-035	Dock Street Theater	S.Thompson	Open	15.00	15.00
Shelia's, Inc.		**Texas**			
90-06-001	The Alamo	S.Thompson	Retrd.	15.00	15.00
90-06-001	Mission Concepcion	S.Thompson	Retrd.	15.00	15.00
90-06-001	Mission San Francisco	S.Thompson	Retrd.	15.00	15.00
90-06-001	Mission San Jose'	S.Thompson	Retrd.	15.00	15.00
Shelia's, Inc.		**New England**			
90-07-001	Old North Church	S.Thompson	Retrd.	15.00	15.00
90-07-002	Martha's Vineyard Cottage-blue/mauve	S.Thompson	Retrd.	15.00	15.00
90-07-003	Martha's Vineyard Cottage-blue/orange	S.Thompson	Retrd.	15.00	15.00
90-07-004	President Bush Home	S.Thompson	Retrd.	15.00	15.00
90-07-005	Longfellow's Home	S.Thompson	Retrd.	15.00	15.00
90-07-006	Motif #1 Boathouse	S.Thompson	Retrd.	15.00	15.00
90-07-007	Paul Revere's Home	S.Thompson	Retrd.	15.00	15.00
90-07-008	Faneuil Hall	S.Thompson	Retrd.	15.00	15.00
90-07-009	Stage Harbor Lighthouse	S.Thompson	Retrd.	15.00	15.00
90-07-010	Wedding Cake House	S.Thompson	Retrd.	15.00	15.00
Shelia's, Inc.		**Williamsburg**			
90-08-001	Governor's Palace	S.Thompson	Open	15.00	15.00
90-08-002	Printer-Bookbinder	S.Thompson	7/93	12.00	12.00
90-08-003	Milliner	S.Thompson	Open	12.00	12.00
90-08-004	Silversmith	S.Thompson	Open	12.00	12.00
90-08-005	Nicolson Store	S.Thompson	Open	12.00	12.00
90-08-006	Apothecary	S.Thompson	Open	12.00	12.00
90-08-007	KIng's Arm Tavern	S.Thompson	Open	15.00	15.00
90-08-008	Courthouse	S.Thompson	Open	15.00	15.00
90-08-009	Homesite	S.Thompson	Open	15.00	15.00
Shelia's, Inc.		**Philadelphia**			
90-09-001	Carpenter's Hall	S.Thompson	Open	15.00	15.00
90-09-002	Market St. Post Office	S.Thompson	Open	15.00	15.00
90-09-003	Betsy Ross House	S.Thompson	Open	15.00	15.00
90-09-004	Independence Hall	S.Thompson	Open	15.00	15.00
90-09-005	Elphreth's Alley	S.Thompson	Open	15.00	15.00
90-09-006	Old Tavern	S.Thompson	Open	15.00	15.00
90-09-007	Graff House	S.Thompson	Retrd.	15.00	15.00
90-09-008	Old City Hall	S.Thompson	Open	15.00	15.00
Shelia's, Inc.		**Washington D.C.**			
90-10-001	National Archives	S.Thompson	Open	16.00	16.00
90-10-002	Library of Congress	S.Thompson	Open	16.00	16.00
90-10-003	White House	S.Thompson	Open	16.00	16.00
90-10-004	Washington Monument	S.Thompson	Open	16.00	16.00
90-10-005	Cherry Trees	S.Thompson	Open	12.00	12.00
Shelia's, Inc.		**North Carolina**			
90-11-001	Josephus Hall House	S.Thompson	Open	15.00	15.00
90-11-002	Presbyterian Bell Tower	S.Thompson	Open	15.00	15.00
90-11-003	Cape Hateras Lighthouse	S.Thompson	Open	15.00	15.00
90-11-004	The Tryon Palace	S.Thompson	Open	15.00	15.00
Shelia's, Inc.		**South Carolina**			
90-12-001	The Hermitage	S.Thompson	Open	15.00	15.00
90-12-002	The Governor's Mansion	S.Thompson	Open	15.00	15.00
90-12-003	The Lace House	S.Thompson	Open	15.00	15.00
90-12-004	The State House	S.Thompson	Open	15.00	15.00
90-12-005	All Saints' Church	S.Thompson	Open	15.00	15.00
Shelia's, Inc.		**St. Augustine**			
90-13-001	The "Oldest House"	S.Thompson	Open	15.00	15.00
90-13-002	Old City Gates	S.Thompson	Open	15.00	15.00
90-13-003	Anastasia Lighthouse	S.Thompson	Open	15.00	15.00
90-13-004	Anastasia Lighthousekeeper's house	S.Thompson	Open	15.00	15.00
90-13-005	Mission Nombre deDios	S.Thompson	Open	15.00	15.00
Shelia's, Inc.		**Savannah**			
90-14-001	Olde Pink House	S.Thompson	Open	15.00	15.00
90-14-002	Andrew Low Mansion	S.Thompson	Open	15.00	15.00
90-14-003	Davenport House	S.Thompson	Open	15.00	15.00
90-14-004	Juliette Low House	S.Thompson	Open	15.00	15.00
90-14-005	Herb House	S.Thompson	Open	15.00	15.00
90-14-006	Mikve Israel Temple	S.Thompson	Open	15.00	15.00
90-14-007	Tybee Lighthouse	S.Thompson	Open	15.00	15.00
90-14-008	Gingerbread House	S.Thompson	Retrd.	15.00	15.00
92-14-009	Catherdral of St. John	S.Thompson	Open	16.00	16.00
Shelia's, Inc.		**Collectible Accessories**			
90-15-001	Wrought Iron Gate With Magnolias	S.Thompson	Open	11.00	11.00
90-15-002	Gazebo With Victorian Lady	S.Thompson	Open	11.00	11.00
90-15-003	Oak Bower	S.Thompson	Open	11.00	11.00
90-15-004	Fence 5"	S.Thompson	Open	9.00	9.00
90-15-005	Fence 8"	S.Thompson	Open	10.00	10.00
90-15-006	Lake With Swan	S.Thompson	Open	11.00	11.00
90-15-007	Tree With Bush	S.Thompson	Open	10.00	10.00
Silver Deer, Ltd.		**Crystal Collectibles**			
84-01-001	Pinocchio, 120mm -02059	G. Truex	Closed	195.00	195-320.00
87-01-002	Bloomer-02102	G. Truex	5,000	140.00	140.00
90-01-003	Joe Cool Cruisin'- 02018	G. Truex	Closed	165.00	165.00
90-01-004	Snoopy's Suppertime- 01973	G. Truex	5,000	160.00	160.00
90-01-005	King Of Beasts- 02017	S. Dailey	1,500	170.00	170.00
90-01-006	Romance- 02002	S. Dailey	2,500	250.00	250.00
91-01-007	Dreamland Teddy- 02643	S. Dailey	2,500	97.50	97.50
91-01-008	Tea For Two- 02639	S. Dailey	1,500	150.00	150.00
91-01-009	Flying Ace- 02649	S. Dailey	Open	140.00	140.00
92-01-010	Proud Spirit- 02823	S. Dailey	500	550.00	550.00
92-01-011	Make A Wish!- 02818	S. Dailey	1,500	210.00	210.00
92-01-012	Joe Cool 'Vette- 02807	S. Dailey	1,500	165.00	165.00
92-01-013	Schoolhouse Mouse- 02805	S. Dailey	Open	45.00	45.00
92-01-014	Teetering Twosome- 02808	S. Dailey	Open	75.00	75.00
92-01-015	Checkmate- 02812	S. Dailey	Open	130.00	130.00
92-01-016	Literary Ace- 02810	S. Dailey	Open	90.00	90.00
Silver Deer, Ltd.		**Crystal Zoo Collectors' Club**			
91-02-001	Le Printemps	S. Dailey	Closed	Gift	N/A
91-02-002	Victoriana (Redemption)	S. Dailey	12/92	195.00	195.00
92-02-003	Garden Party	S. Dailey	12/92	Gift	N/A
92-02-004	Garden Guest (Redemption)	S. Dailey	8/93	175.00	175.00
Silver Deer, Ltd.		**Ark Collectors' Club**			
91-03-001	Christmas Puppy	T. Rubel	Closed	Gift	N/A
91-03-002	Snowy Egret (Redemption)	T. Rubel	12/92	75.00	75.00
92-03-003	Snowball	T. Rubel	12/92	Gift	N/A
Sports Impressions		**Baseball Superstar Figurines**			
87-01-001	Wade Boggs	S. Impressions	Closed	90-125.	150-225.
88-01-002	Jose Canseco	S. Impressions	Closed	90-125.	175-200.
89-01-003	Will Clark	S. Impressions	Closed	90-125.	175-250.
88-01-004	Andre Dawson	S. Impressions	2,500	90-125.	125-200.
88-01-005	Bob Feller	S. Impressions	2,500	90-125.	125-200.
89-01-006	Kirk Gibson	S. Impressions	Closed	90-125.	125-200.
87-01-007	Keith Hernandez	S. Impressions	2,500	90-125.	125-200.
88-01-008	Reg Jackson (Yankees)	S. Impressions	Closed	90-125.	150-200.
89-01-009	Reg Jackson (Angels)	S. Impressions	Closed	90-125.	175-250.
88-01-010	Al Kaline	S. Impressions	2,500	90-125.	125.00
87-01-011	Mickey Mantle	S. Impressions	Closed	90-125.	225-475.
87-01-012	Don Mattingly	S. Impressions	Closed	90-125.	225-650.
88-01-013	Paul Molitor	S. Impressions	2,500	90-125.	125.00
89-01-014	Duke Snider	S. Impressions	2,500	90-125.	125.00
89-01-015	Alan Trammell	S. Impressions	2,500	90-125.	125.00
89-01-016	Frank Viola	S. Impressions	2,500	90-125.	125.00
87-01-017	Ted Williams	S. Impressions	Closed	90-125.	200-375.
Sports Impressions		**Collectors' Club Members Only**			
90-02-001	The Mick-Mickey Mantle 5000-1	S. Impressions	Yr.Iss.	75.00	95.00
91-02-002	Rickey Henderson-Born to Run 5001-11	S. Impressions	Yr.Iss.	49.95	49.95
91-02-003	Nolan Ryan-300 Wins 5002-01	S. Impressions	Yr.Iss.	195.00	195.00
91-02-004	Willie, Mickey & Duke plate 5003-04	S. Impressions	Yr.Iss.	39.95	39.95
92-02-005	Babe Ruth 5006-11	S. Impressions	Yr.Iss.	40.00	40.00
92-02-006	Walter Payton 5015-01	S. Impressions	Yr.Iss.	50.00	50.00
Sports Impressions		**Collectors' Club Symbol of Membership**			
91-03-001	Mick/7 plate 5001-02	S. Impressions	Yr.Iss.	Gift	N/A
92-03-002	USA Basketball team plate 5008-30	S. Impressions	Yr.Iss.	Gift	N/A
Summerhill Crystal		**Summerhill Crystal**			
92-01-001	Venus	Summerhill	500	96.00	96.00
92-01-002	Sacre Coeur	Summerhill	5,000	190.00	190.00
92-01-003	L'arc du Triomphe	Summerhill	5,000	220.00	220.00
92-01-004	Bicycle	Summerhill	500	64.00	64.00
92-01-005	Princess Coach	Summerhill	1,500	700.00	700.00
92-01-006	Large Dragon	Summerhill	1,500	320.00	320.00
92-01-007	Mickey Mouse, Lg.	Summerhill	Open	295.00	295.00
92-01-008	Mickey Mouse, Med.	Summerhill	Open	165.00	165.00
92-01-009	Minnie Mouse, Lg.	Summerhill	Open	295.00	295.00
92-01-010	Minnie Mouse, Med.	Summerhill	Open	165.00	165.00
92-01-011	Epcot Center, Lg.	Summerhill	Open	245.00	245.00
92-01-012	Epcot Center, Med.	Summerhill	Open	110.00	110.00
92-01-013	Epcot Center, Sm.	Summerhill	Open	75.00	75.00
Summerhill Crystal		**Warner Brothers Collection**			
92-02-001	Tasmanian Devil.	Summerhill	2,750	220.00	220.00
92-02-002	Speedy Gonzales	Summerhill	2,750	164.00	164.00
92-02-003	Tweety Bird	Summerhill	Open	120.00	120.00
Summerhill Crystal		**Collector Society**			
92-03-001	Robbie Rabbit	Summerhill	Yr.Iss.	125.00	125.00
Swarovski America		**Our Woodland Friends**			
79-01-001	Mini Owl	M. Schreck	Open	16.00	29.50
79-01-002	Small Owl	M. Schreck	Open	59.00	75.00
79-01-003	Large Owl	M. Schreck	Open	90.00	110.00
83-01-004	Giant Owl	M. Schreck	Open	1200.00	1900.00
85-01-005	Mini Bear	M. Schreck	Open	16.00	42.50
82-01-006	Small Bear	M. Schreck	Open	44.00	70.00
81-01-007	Large Bear	M. Schreck	Open	75.00	85.00
87-01-008	Fox	A. Stocker	Open	50.00	70.00
88-01-009	Mini Sitting Fox	A. Stocker	Open	35.00	37.50
88-01-010	Mini Running Fox	A. Stocker	Open	35.00	37.50
85-01-011	Squirrel	M. Schreck	Open	35.00	42.50
89-01-012	Mushrooms	A. Stocker	Open	35.00	37.50
Swarovski America		**African Wildlife**			
89-02-001	Small Elephant	A. Stocker	Open	50.00	65.00
88-02-002	Large Elephant	A. Stocker	Open	70.00	95.00
89-02-003	Small Hippopotamus	A. Stocker	Open	70.00	75.00
90-02-004	Small Rhinoceros	A. Stocker	Open	70.00	75.00
Swarovski America		**Kingdom Of Ice And Snow**			
86-03-001	Mini Baby Seal	A. Stocker	Open	30.00	37.50
85-03-002	Large Seal	M. Schreck	Open	44.00	75.00
84-03-003	Mini Penguin	M. Schreck	Open	16.00	29.50
84-03-004	Large Penguin	M. Schreck	Open	44.00	85.00
86-03-005	Large Polar Bear	A. Stocker	Open	140.00	195.00
89-03-006	Walrus	M. Stamey	Open	120.00	135.00
Swarovski America		**In A Summer Meadow**			
87-04-001	Small Hedgehog	M. Schreck	Open	50.00	55.00
85-04-002	Medium Hedgehog	M. Schreck	Open	70.00	75.00
85-04-003	Large Hedgehog	M. Schreck	Open	120.00	135.00
88-04-004	Mini Lying Rabbit	A. Stocker	Open	35.00.	37.50
88-04-005	Mini Sitting Rabbit	A. Stocker	Open	35.00	37.50
88-04-006	Mother Rabbit	A. Stocker	Open	60.00	70.00
76-04-007	Medium Mouse	M. Schreck	Open	48.00	75.00
86-04-008	Mini Butterfly	Team	Open	16.00	37.50
82-04-009	Butterfly	Team	Open	44.00	75.00
86-04-010	Snail	M. Stamey	Open	35.00	42.50
91-04-011	Field Mouse	A. Stocker	Open	47.50	47.50
92-04-012	Sparrow	Schneiderbauer	Open	29.50	29.50
Swarovski America		**Beauties of the Lake**			
89-05-001	Small Swan	M. Schreck	Open	35.00	47.50
77-05-002	Medium Swan	M. Schreck	Open	44.00	70.00
77-05-003	Large Swan	M. Schreck	Open	55.00	85.00
86-05-004	Mini Standing Duck	A. Stocker	Open	22.00	29.50
86-05-005	Mini Swimming Duck	M. Schreck	Open	16.00	29.50
83-05-006	Mini Drake	M. Schreck	Open	20.00	37.50
86-05-007	Mallard	M. Schreck	Open	80.00	125.00
89-05-008	Giant Mallard	M. Stamey	Open	2000.00	4250.00

Company / Number	Name	Series / Artist	Edition Limit	Issue Price	Quote
Swarovski America		**Silver Crystal City**			
90-06-001	Silver Crystal City-Cathedral	G. Stamey	Open	95.00	110.00
90-06-002	Silver Crystal City-Houses I& II(Set of 2)	G. Stamey	Open	75.00	75.00
90-06-003	Silver Crystal City-Houses III & IV(Set of 2)	G. Stamey	Open	75.00	75.00
90-06-004	Silver Crystal City-Poplars (Set of 3)	G. Stamey	Open	40.00	42.50
91-06-005	City Tower	G. Stamey	Open	37.50	37.50
91-06-006	City Gates	G. Stamey	Open	95.00	95.00
Swarovski America		**Nativity Scene**			
91-07-001	Holy Family With Arch	Team	Open	250.00	250.00
92-07-002	Wise Men (Set of 3)	Team	Open	175.00	175.00
92-07-003	Shepherd	Team	Open	65.00	65.00
92-07-004	Angel	Team	Open	65.00	65.00
Swarovski America		**When We Were Young**			
88-08-001	Locomotive	G. Stamey	Open	150.00	150.00
88-08-002	Tender	G. Stamey	Open	55.00	55.00
88-08-003	Wagon	G. Stamey	Open	85.00	85.00
90-08-004	Petrol Wagon	G. Stamey	Open	75.00	85.00
89-08-005	Old Timer Automobile	G. Stamey	Open	130.00	150.00
90-08-006	Airplane	A. Stocker	Open	135.00	150.00
91-08-007	Santa Maria	G. Stamey	Open	375.00	375.00
Swarovski America		**Exquisite Accents**			
80-09-001	Birdbath	M. Schreck	Open	150.00	175.00
87-09-002	Birds' Nest	Team	Open	90.00	110.00
87-09-003	Small Dinner Bell	M. Schreck	Open	60.00	65.00
87-09-004	Medium Dinner Bell	M. Schreck	Open	80.00	85.00
Swarovski America		**Sparkling Fruit**			
86-10-001	Small Pineapple/Gold	M. Schreck	Open	55.00	85.00
81-10-002	Large Pineapple/Gold	M. Schreck	Open	150.00	225.00
81-10-003	Giant Pineapple/Gold	M. Schreck	Open	1750.00	3000.00
85-10-004	Small Grapes	Team	Open	200.00	225.00
85-10-005	Medium Grapes	Team	Open	300.00	350.00
91-10-006	Apple	M. Stamey	Open	175.00	175.00
91-10-007	Pear	M. Stamey	Open	175.00	175.00
Swarovski America		**A Pet's Corner**			
90-11-001	Beagle Puppy	A. Stocker	Open	40.00	42.50
90-11-002	Scotch Terrier	A. Stocker	Open	60.00	75.00
87-11-003	Mini Dachshund	A. Stocker	Open	20.00	47.50
91-11-004	Sitting Cat	M. Stamey	Open	75.00	75.00
91-11-005	Kitten	M. Stamey	Open	47.50	47.50
92-11-006	Poodle	A. Stocker	Open	125.00	125.00
Swarovski America		**South Sea**			
91-12-001	South Sea Shell	M. Stamey	Open	110.00	110.00
88-12-002	Open Shell With Pearl	M. Stamey	Open	120.00	150.00
87-12-003	Mini Blowfish	Team	Open	22.00	29.50
86-12-004	Small Blowfish	Team	Open	35.00	47.50
91-12-005	Butterfly Fish	M. Stamey	Open	150.00	150.00
Swarovski America		**Endangered Species**			
91-13-001	Kiwi	M. Stamey	Open	37.50	37.50
89-13-002	Mini Koala	A. Stocker	Open	35.00	37.50
87-13-003	Koala	A. Stocker	Open	50.00	65.00
77-13-004	Small Turtle	M. Schreck	Open	35.00	42.50
77-13-005	Large Turtle	M. Schreck	Open	48.00	70.00
81-13-006	Giant Turtle	M. Schreck	Open	2500.00	4250.00
92-13-007	Mother Beaver	A. Stocker	Open	110.00	110.00
92-13-008	Sitting Baby Beaver	A. Stocker	Open	47.50	47.50
92-13-009	Lying Baby Beaver	A. Stocker	Open	47.50	47.50
Swarovski America		**Barnyard Friends**			
82-14-001	Mini Pig	M. Schreck	Open	16.00	29.50
84-14-002	Medium Pig	M. Schreck	Open	35.00	47.50
88-14-003	Mini Chicks (Set of 3)	G. Stamey	Open	35.00	37.50
87-14-004	Mini Rooster	G. Stamey	Open	35.00	42.50
87-14-005	Mini Hen	G. Stamey	Open	35.00	37.50
Swarovski America		**The Game of Kings**			
84-15-001	Chess Set	M. Schreck	Open	950.00	1250.00
Swarovski America		**Among Flowers And Foliage**			
92-16-001	Hummingbird	Schneiderbauer	Open	195.00	195.00
92-16-002	Bumblebee	Schneiderbauer	Open	85.00	85.00
Swarovski America		**Our Candleholders**			
85-17-001	Small Water Lily 7600NR124	M. Schreck	Open	100.00	150.00
83-17-002	Medium Water Lily 7600NR123	M. Schreck	Open	150.00	225.00
85-17-003	Large Water Lily 7600NR125	M. Schreck	Open	200.00	325.00
89-17-004	Medium Star 7600NR143001	Team	Open	200.00	225.00
87-17-005	Large Star 7600NR143	Team	Open	250.00	325.00
Swarovski America		**Decorative Items For The Desk (Paperweights)**			
87-18-001	Small Chaton 7433NR50	M. Schreck	Open	50.00	55.00
87-18-002	Large Chaton 7433NR80	M. Schreck	Open	190.00	225.00
90-18-003	Giant Chaton 7433NR180000	M. Schreck	Open	3900.00	4250.00
87-18-004	Small Pyramid CC/VM7450NR40	M. Schreck	Open	100.00	110.00
87-18-005	Large Pyramid CC/VM7450NR50	M. Schreck	Open	90.00	195.00
Swarovski America		**Crystal Melodies**			
92-19-001	Lute	M. Zendron	Open	125.00	125.00
92-19-002	Harp	M. Zendron	Open	175.00	175.00
Swarovski America		**Collectors Society Editions**			
87-20-001	Togetherness-The Lovebirds	Schreck/Stocker	Retrd.	150.00	2500-3500.
88-20-002	Sharing-The Woodpeckers	A. Stocker	Retrd.	165.00	900-1800.
89-20-003	Amour-The Turtledoves	A. Stocker	Retrd.	195.00	600-1200.
90-20-004	Lead Me-The Dolphins	M. Stamey	Retrd.	225.00	650-1250.
91-20-005	Save Me-The Seals	M. Stamey	Retrd.	225.00	350-600.
92-20-006	Care For Me - The Whales	M. Stamey	12/92	265.00	265.00
92-20-007	5th Anniversary Edition-The Birthday Cake	Unknown	1//93	85.00	85.00
Swarovski America		**Retired**			
84-22-001	Dachshund 7641NR75	M. Schreck	Retrd.	48.00	100-125.
82-22-002	Mini Cat 7659NR31	M. Schreck	Retrd.	16.00	40-50.00
77-22-003	Large Cat 7634NR70	M. Schreck	Retrd.	44.00	90-130.00
84-22-004	Large Blowfish 7644NR41	Team	Retrd.	40.00	100.00
88-22-005	Whale 7628NR80	M. Stamey	Retrd.	70.00	110-200.
86-22-006	Small Falcon Head 7645NR45	M. Schreck	Retrd.	60.00	100-125.
84-22-007	Large Falcon Head 7645NR100	M. Schreck	Retrd.	600.00	950-1150.

Number	Name	Artist	Edition Limit	Issue Price	Quote
XX-22-008	Small Mouse 7631NR30	M. Schreck	Retrd.	35.00	60.00
79-22-009	Mini Sparrow7650NR20	M. Schreck	Retrd.	16.00	30-45.00
84-22-010	Frog 7642NR48	M. Schreck	Retrd.	30.00	55-82.00
XX-22-011	Mini Chicken 7651NR20	Team	Retrd.	16.00	45-52.00
XX-22-012	Mini Rabbit 7652NR20	Team	Retrd.	16.00	45-50.00
XX-22-013	Mini Duck 7653NR45	Team	Retrd.	16.00	36-45.00
XX-22-014	Mini Mouse 7655NR23	Team	Retrd.	16.00	45-60.00
XX-22-015	Mini Swan 7658NR27	M. Schreck	Retrd.	16.00	65-100.00
84-22-016	Mini Bear 7670NR32	M. Schreck	Retrd.	16.00	65-100.00
XX-22-017	Mini Butterfly 7671NR30	Team	Retrd.	16.00	50-100.00
XX-22-018	Mini Dachshund 7672NR42	A. Stocker	Retrd.	20.00	50-100.00
XX-22-019	Small Hedgehog 7630NR30	M. Schreck	Retrd.	38.00	60-100.00
XX-22-020	Medium Hedgehog 7630NR40	M. Schreck	Retrd.	44.00	75-125.00
XX-22-021	Large Hedgehog 7630NR50	M. Schreck	Retrd.	65.00	125-175.
XX-22-022	King Size Hedgehog 7630NR60	M. Schreck	Retrd.	98.00	225-300.
XX-22-023	Large Mouse 7631NR50	M. Schreck	Retrd.	69.00	200-250.
XX-22-024	King Size Mouse 7631NR60	M. Schreck	Retrd.	95.00	250-500.
XX-22-025	King Size Turtle 7632NR75	M. Schreck	Retrd.	58.00	150-200.
XX-22-026	Medium Cat 7634NR52	Team	Retrd.	38.00	100-200.
XX-22-027	Dog 7635NR70	Team	Retrd.	44.00	75-100.00
XX-22-028	King Size Bear7637NR92	M. Schreck	Retrd.	95.00	350-650.
XX-22-029	Giant Size Bear 7637NR112	M. Schreck	Retrd.	125.00	500-950.
XX-22-030	Large Pig 7638NR65	M. Schreck	Retrd.	50.00	180-230.
XX-22-031	Elephant 7640NR55	Team	Retrd.	90.00	150-200.
XX-22-032	Large Sparrow 7650NR32	Team	Retrd.	38.00	95.00
XX-22-033	Large Rabbit 7652NR45	Team	Retrd.	38.00	100.00
XX-22-034	Medium Duck 7653NR55	Team	Retrd.	38.00	100.00
XX-22-035	Large Duck 7653NR75	Team	Retrd.	44.00	100.00
87-22-036	Partridge 7625NR50	A. Stocker	Retrd.	85.00	125-200.
88-22-037	Hippopotamus 7626NR65	A. Stocker	Retrd.	70.00	95.00
88-22-038	Rhinoceros 7622NR70	A. Stocker	Retrd.	70.00	95.00
90-22-039	Kingfisher 7621NR000001	M. Stamey	Retrd.	75.00	85.00
89-22-040	Toucan 7621NR000002	M. Stamey	Retrd.	70.00	85.00
89-22-041	Owl 7621NR000003	M. Stamey	Retrd.	70.00	85.00
89-22-042	Parrot 7621NR000004	M. Stamey	Retrd.	70.00	85.00
XX-22-043	Sm. Apple Photo Stand(Gold) 7504NR030G	Team	Retrd.	40.00	200.00
XX-22-044	Sm. Apple Photo Stand 7504NR030R	Team	Retrd.	40.00	110.00
XX-22-045	Lg. Apple Photo Stand(Gold) 7504NR050G	Team	Retrd.	80.00	265-300.
XX-22-046	Lg. Apple Photo Stand 7504NR050R	Team	Retrd.	80.00	150.00
XX-22-047	Kg Sz Apple Photo Stand(Gold) 7504NR060G	Team	Retrd.	120.00	400.00
XX-22-048	Large Grapes 7550NR30015	Team	Retrd.	250.00	400-600.
85-22-049	Butterfly (Gold) 7551NR100	Team	Retrd.	200.00	450-750.
85-22-050	Butterfly (Rhodium) 7551NR200	Team	Retrd.	200.00	500-750.
85-22-051	Hummingbird (Gold) 7552NR100	Team	Retrd.	200.00	650-800.
85-22-052	Hummingbird (Rhodium) 7552NR200	Team	Retrd.	200.00	700-950.
85-22-053	Bee (Gold) 7553NR100	Team	Retrd.	200.00	650-900.
85-22-054	Bee (Rhodium) 7553NR200	Team	Retrd.	200.00	950-1100.
87-22-055	Sm. Pineapple/Rhodium 7507NR060002	M. Schreck	Retrd.	55.00	150-175.
82-22-056	Lg. Pineapple/Rhodium 7507NR105002	M. Schreck	Retrd.	150.00	330-500.
85-22-057	Giant Pineapple/Rhodium 7507NR26002	M. Schreck	Retrd.	1750.00	3000.00
81-22-058	Large Dinner Bell 7467NR071000	M. Schreck	Retrd.	80.00	150-175.
XX-22-059	Rd. Pprwgt-Green 7404NR40	Team	Retrd.	20.00	75-150.00
XX-22-060	Rd. Pprwgt-Sahara 7404NR40	Team	Retrd.	20.00	75-150.00
XX-22-061	Rd. Pprwgt-Berm Blue 7404NR40	Team	Retrd.	20.00	75-150.00
XX-22-062	Rd. Pprwgt-Green 7404NR30	Team	Retrd.	15.00	50-150.00
XX-22-063	Rd. Pprwgt-Sahara 7404NR30	Team	Retrd.	15.00	50-150.00
XX-22-064	Rd. Pprwgt-Berm. Blue 7404NR30	Team	Retrd.	15.00	50-150.00
XX-22-065	Rd. Pprwgt-Green 7404NR50	Team	Retrd.	40.00	75-150.00
XX-22-066	Rd. Pprwgt-Sahara 7404NR50	Team	Retrd.	40.00	75-150.00
XX-22-067	Rd. Pprwgt-Berm. Blue 7404NR50	Team	Retrd.	40.00	75-150.00
XX-22-068	Carousel Pprwgt-Vitrl Med 7451NR60087	Team	Retrd.	80.00	750-1000.
XX-22-069	Carousel Pprwgt-Crystal Cal 7451NR60095	Team	Retrd.	80.00	750-1000.
XX-22-070	Atomic Pprwgt-Vitrl Med 7454NR60087	Team	Retrd.	80.00	1000-1500.
XX-22-071	Atomic Pprwgt-Crystal Cal 7454NR60095	Team	Retrd.	80.00	960-1200.
XX-22-072	Barrel Pprwgt 7453NR60087 Vitrl Med	Team	Retrd.	80.00	300-500.
XX-22-073	Barrel Pprwgt 7453NR60095 Crystal Cal	Team	Retrd.	80.00	280-420.
XX-22-074	Rd. Pprwgt-Crystal Cal 7404NR30095	Team	Retrd.	15.00	50.00
XX-22-075	Rd. Pprwgt-Vitrl Med 7404NR30087	Team	Retrd.	15.00	50.00
XX-22-076	Rd. Pprwgt-Crystal Cal 7404NR40095	Team	Retrd.	20.00	50-75.00
XX-22-077	Rd. Pprwgt-Vitrl Med 7404NR40087	Team	Retrd.	20.00	50-75.00
XX-22-078	Rd. Pprwgt-Crystal Cal 7404NR50095	Team	Retrd.	40.00	60-90.00
XX-22-079	Rd. Pprwgt-Vitrl Med 7404NR50087	Team	Retrd.	40.00	60-90.00
XX-22-080	Rd. Pprwgt-Crystal Cal 7404NR60095	Team	Retrd.	50.00	150-250.
XX-22-081	Rd. Pprwgt-Vitrl Med 7404NR60087	Team	Retrd.	50.00	150-250.
XX-22-082	Geometric Pprwgt 7432NR57002n	Team	Retrd.	75.00	100-125.
XX-22-083	One Ton Pprwgt 7495NR65	Team	Retrd.	75.00	100-125.
XX-22-084	Octron Pprwgt 7456NR41	Team	Retrd.	75.00	110-125.
XX-22-085	Octron Pprwgt 7456NR1087	Team	Retrd.	90.00	125-200.
XX-22-086	Candleholder 7600NR101	Team	Retrd.	23.00	350-600.
XX-22-087	Candleholder 7600NR131(Set of 6)	Team	Retrd.	43.00	960.00
XX-22-088	Candleholder 7600NR106	Team	Retrd.	85.00	500.00
XX-22-089	Candleholder 7600NR107	Team	Retrd.	100.00	300-500.
XX-22-090	Candleholder 7600NR109	Team	Retrd.	37.00	100-300.
XX-22-091	Candleholder 7600NR111	Team	Retrd.	100.00	300-400.
XX-22-092	Candleholder 7600NR112	Team	Retrd.	75.00	300-400.
XX-22-093	Candleholder 7600NR114	Team	Retrd.	37.00	250-300.
XX-22-094	Candleholder 7600NR116	Team	Retrd.	350.00	550-1000.
XX-22-095	Candleholder 7600NR130	Team	Retrd.	275.00	750-1000.
XX-22-096	Candleholder 7600NR102	Team	Retrd.	35.00	125-150.
XX-22-097	Candleholder 7600NR110	Team	Retrd.	40.00	125-150.
XX-22-098	Candleholder 7600NR115	Team	Retrd.	185.00	300-350.
XX-22-099	Baroque Candleholder 7600NR121	Team	Retrd.	150.00	200-350.
XX-22-100	Pineapple Candleholder 7600NR136	Team	Retrd.	150.00	400-500.
XX-22-101	Candleholder 7600NR138	Team	Retrd.	160.00	300-350.
XX-22-102	Candleholder 7600NR139	Team	Retrd.	140.00	300-350.
XX-22-103	Candleholder 7600NR140	Team	Retrd.	120.00	300-350.
XX-22-104	Sm.Candleholder w/ Flowers 7600NR120	Team	Retrd.	60.00	200-250.
XX-22-105	Sm.Candleholder w/ Leaves 7600NR126	Team	Retrd.	100.00	250.00
XX-22-106	Candleholder 7600NR127	Team	Retrd.	65.00	200-250.
XX-22-107	Candleholder 7600NR128	Team	Retrd.	100.00	200-250.
XX-22-108	Candleholder 7600NR129	Team	Retrd.	120.00	250-300.
XX-22-109	Candleholder 7600NR103	Team	Retrd.	40.00	125-165.
XX-22-110	Candleholder 7600NR104	Team	Retrd.	95.00	300-350.
XX-22-111	Candleholder 7600NR122	Team	Retrd.	85.00	275-300.
XX-22-112	Kingsize Global Candleholder 7600NR135	Team	Retrd.	50.00	150-200.
XX-22-113	Small Global Candleholder (4) 7600NR132	Team	Retrd.	60.00	100-125.
XX-22-114	Med. Global Candleholder (2) 7600NR133	Team	Retrd.	40.00	60-90.00
XX-22-115	Large Global Candleholder 7600NR134	Team	Retrd.	40.00	60-90.00
XX-22-116	Large Candleholderw/Flowers 7600NR137	Team	Retrd.	150.00	190-225.
90-22-117	Sm. Neo-ClassicCandleholder7600NR144070	A. Stocker	Retrd.	170.00	175.00
90-22-118	Med. Neo-ClassicCandlehldr7600NR144080	A. Stocker	Retrd.	190.00	195.00
90-22-119	Large Neo-Classic Candlehldr7600NR144090	A. Stocker	Retrd.	220.00	225.00
XX-22-120	Beetle Bottle Opener 7505NR76	Team	Retrd.	80.00	1300-2500.

Number	Name	Artist	Edition Limit	Issue Price	Quote
XX-22-121	Table Magnifyer 7510NR01	Team	Retrd.	80.00	1200-2000.
XX-22-122	Treasure Box (Round/Butterfly) 7464NR50/100	Team	Retrd.	80.00	150.00
XX-22-123	Treasure Box (Heart/Flower)7465NR52	Team	Retrd.	80.00	125-175.
XX-22-124	Treasure Box (Oval/Butterfly)7466NR063100	Team	Retrd.	80.00	125-175.
XX-22-125	Salt and Pepper Shakers 7508NR068034	Team	Retrd.	80.00	200-225.
XX-22-126	Picture Frame/Oval 7505NR75G	Team	Retrd.	90.00	150-175.
XX-22-127	Picture Frame/Square 7506NR60G	Team	Retrd.	100.00	200.00
XX-22-128	Treasure Box (Round/Flower) 7464NR50	Team	Retrd.	80.00	125-200.
XX-22-129	Treasure Box (Heart/Butterfly)7465NR52/100	Team	Retrd.	80.00	125-200.
XX-22-130	Treasure Box (Oval/Flower) 7466NR063000	Team	Retrd.	80.00	125-200.
XX-22-131	Vase 7511NR70	Team	Retrd.	50.00	110-125.
XX-22-132	Schnapps Glasses, Set of 6-7468NR039000	Team	Retrd.	150.00	180-300.
XX-22-133	Ashtray 7461NR100	Team	Retrd.	45.00	195-250.
XX-22-134	Lighter 7462NR062	Team	Retrd.	160.00	195-250.
XX-22-135	Cigarette Holder 7463NR062	Team	Retrd.	85.00	125-150.
XX-22-136	Small Cardholders, Set of 4 -7403NR20095	Team	Retrd.	25.00	75-150.00
XX-22-137	Large Cardholders, Set of 4 -7403NR30095	Team	Retrd.	45.00	125-250.
82-22-138	Cone Vitriol Medium 7452NR60087	M. Schreck	Retrd.	80.00	175.00
82-22-139	Cone Crystal Cal 7452NR60095	M. Schreck	Retrd.	80.00	175.00
81-22-140	Egg 7458NR63069	M. Schreck	Retrd.	60.00	95.00
81-22-141	Chess Set/Wooden Board	Team	Retrd.	950.00	2500-3000.
Swarovski America	**Commemorative Single Issue**				
90-23-001	Elephant*(Introduced by Swarovski America as a commemorative item test during Design Celebration/January '90 in Walt Disney World)	Team	Closed	125.00	1000-1500.
Tay Porcelains	**Tay Porcelains**				
XX-01-001	Turtledoves, group of two, 10 inches	Unknown	500	Unkn.	500.00
70-01-002	Blue Jay, 13 inches	Unknown	500	375.00	675.00
70-01-003	Eagle, 12 inches x 15 inches	Unknown	500	1000.00	1650.00
70-01-004	European Woodcock 10.5 inches	Unknown	500	325.00	550.00
70-01-005	Limpkin, 20 inches	Unknown	500	600.00	1100.00
71-01-006	Falcon, 13 inches	Unknown	500	500.00	925.00
71-01-007	Pheasant, 30 inches	Unknown	500	1500.00	2-2700.
71-01-008	Quail Group, 10 inches	Unknown	500	400.00	725.00
71-01-009	Roadrunner, 10 x 19 inches	Unknown	500	800.00	Unkn.
72-01-010	Gray Partridge, 11.5 inches	Unknown	500	800.00	1400.00
74-01-011	American Woodcock, 10.5 inches	Unknown	500	625.00	700.00
74-01-012	Mallard Duck, 13.5 inches	Unknown	500	900.00	1050.00
74-01-013	Mallard Duck, Flying, 15 inches	Unknown	500	550.00	675.00
74-01-014	Owl, 10.5 inches	Unknown	500	350.00	450.00
74-01-015	Turtledoves on Roof Tile, 9.5 inches	Unknown	500	335.00	375.00
75-01-016	Carolina Ducks, group of two, 13 inches	Unknown	500	1350.00	1500.00
75-01-017	Smergos Ducks, group of two, 10 inches	Unknown	500	1000.00	1100.00
75-01-018	White-Throated Sparrow, 5.5 inches	Unknown	500	360.00	400.00
76-01-019	Bluebirds, group of two, 9.5 inches	Unknown	500	500.00	550.00
76-01-020	Custer on Horse, 13 x 14.5 inches	Unknown	500	1500.00	1500.00
73-01-021	Austrian Officer on Horseback	Unknown	100	1200.00	12-1500.
74-01-022	Gyrafalcon, 18 inches	Unknown	300	1250.00	1500.00
74-01-023	Boreal Chickadee, 7 inches	Unknown	5,000	275.00	360.00
74-01-024	Great Crested Flycatcher, 9 inches	Unknown	1,000	300.00	360.00
75-01-025	Oriole, 9.5 inches	Unknown	1,000	300.00	325.00
76-01-026	Indian on Horse, 13 x 14.5 inches	Unknown	500	1500.00	1500.00
76-01-027	Robin, 8 inches	Unknown	500	400.00	450.00
United Design Corp.	**Legend of Santa Claus**				
86-01-001	Santa At Rest CF-001	L. Miller	Retrd.	70.00	350-500.
86-01-002	Kris Kringle CF-002	L. Miller	Retrd.	60.00	75.00
86-01-003	Santa With Pups CF-003	S. Bradford	Retrd.	65.00	250-350.
86-01-004	Rooftop Santa CF-004	S. Bradford	Retrd.	65.00	79.00
86-01-005	Elf Pair CF-005	L. Miller	Retrd.	60.00	75.00
87-01-006	Mrs. Santa CF-006	S. Bradford	Retrd.	60.00	75.00
87-01-007	On Santa's Knee-CF007	S. Bradford	15,000	65.00	79.00
87-01-008	Dreaming Of Santa CF-008	S. Bradford	Retrd.	65.00	225-375.
87-01-009	Checking His List CF-009	L. Miller	15,000	75.00	85.00
87-01-010	Loading Santa's Sleigh CF-010	L. Miller	15,000	100.00	100.00
87-01-011	Santa On Horseback CF-011	S. Bradford	Retrd.	75.00	150-350.
88-01-012	St. Nicholas CF-015	L. Miller	Retrd.	75.00	85.00
88-01-013	Load 'Em Up CF-016	S. Bradford	Retrd.	79.00	150-350.
88-01-014	Assembly Required CF-017	L. Miller	7,500	79.00	95.00
88-01-015	Father Christmas CF-018	S. Bradford	7,500	75.00	85.00
89-01-016	A Purrr-Fect Christmas CF-019	S. Bradford	7,500	95.00	95.00
89-01-017	Christmas Harmony CF-020	S. Bradford	Retrd.	85.00	85.00
89-01-018	Hitching Up CF-021	L. Miller	7,500	90.00	90.00
90-01-019	Puppy Love CF-024	L. Miller	7,500	100.00	100.00
90-01-020	Forest Friends CF-025	L. Miller	7,500	90.00	90.00
90-01-021	Waiting For Santa CF-026	S. Bradford	7,500	100.00	100.00
90-01-022	Safe Arrival CF-027	Memoli/Jonas	7,500	150.00	150.00
90-01-023	Victorian Santa CF-028	S. Bradford	Retrd.	125.00	125.00
91-01-024	For Santa CF-029	L. Miller	7,500	99.00	99.00
91-01-025	Santa At Work CF-030	L. Miller	7,500	99.00	99.00
91-01-026	Reindeer Walk CF-031	K. Memoli	7,500	150.00	150.00
91-01-027	Blessed Flight CF-032	K. Memoli	7,500	159.00	159.00
91-01-028	Victorian Santa w/ Teddy CF-033	S. Bradford	7,500	150.00	150.00
92-01-029	Arctic Santa CF-035	S. Bradford	7,500	90.00	90.00
92-01-030	Letters to Santa CF-036	L. Miller	7,500	125.00	125.00
92-01-031	Santa and Comet CF-037	L. Miller	7,500	110.00	110.00
92-01-032	The Christmas Tree CF-038	L. Miller	7,500	90.00	90.00
92-01-031	Santa and Mrs. Claus CF-039	K. Memoli	7,500	150.00	150.00
92-01-032	Earth Home Santa CF-040	S. Bradford	7,500	135.00	135.00
92-01-033	Loads of Happiness CF-041	K. Memoli	7,500	100.00	100.00
92-01-034	Santa and Mrs. Claus, Victorian CF-042	K. Memoli	7,500	135.00	135.00
United Design Corp.	**Legend Of The Little People**				
89-02-001	Woodland Cache LL-001	L. Miller	7,500	35.00	45.00
89-02-002	Adventure Bound LL-002	L. Miller	7,500	35.00	45.00
89-02-003	A Friendly Toast LL-003	L. Miller	7,500	35.00	45.00
89-02-004	Treasure Hunt LL-004	L. Miller	7,500	45.00	45.00
89-02-005	Magical Discovery LL-005	L. Miller	7,500	45.00	45.00
89-02-006	Spring Water Scrub LL-006	L. Miller	7,500	35.00	45.00
89-02-007	Caddy's Helper LL-007	L. Miller	7,500	35.00	45.00
90-02-008	Husking Acorns LL-008	L. Miller	7,500	60.00	60.00
90-02-009	Traveling Fast LL-009	L. Miller	7,500	45.00	45.00
90-02-010	Hedgehog In Harness LL-010	L. Miller	7,500	45.00	45.00
90-02-011	Woodland Scout LL-011	L. Miller	7,500	40.00	45.00
90-02-012	Fishin' Hole LL-012	L. Miller	7,500	35.00	45.00
90-02-013	A Proclamation LL-013	L. Miller	7,500	45.00	50.00
90-02-014	Gathering Acorns LL-014	L. Miller	7,500	100.00	100.00
90-02-015	A Look Through The Spyglass LL-015	L. Miller	7,500	40.00	45.00
90-02-016	Writing The Legend LL-016	L. Miller	7,500	65.00	65.00
90-02-017	Ministral Magic LL-017	L. Miller	7,500	45.00	45.00
90-02-018	A Little Jig LL-018	L. Miller	7,500	45.00	45.00
91-02-019	Viking LL-019	L. Miller	7,500	45.00	45.00
91-02-020	The Easter Bunny's Cart LL-020	L. Miller	7,500	45.00	45.00
91-02-021	Got It LL-021	L. Miller	7,500	45.00	45.00
91-02-022	It's About Time LL-022	L. Miller	7,500	55.00	55.00
91-02-023	Fire it Up LL-023	L. Miller	7,500	50.00	50.00
United Design Corp.	**MusicMakers**				
89-03-001	Coming To Town MM-001	L. Miller	Open	69.00	69.00
89-03-002	Merry Little Christmas MM-002	L. Miller	Open	69.00	69.00
89-03-003	Merry Making MM-003	L. Miller	Retrd.	69.00	80-100.00
89-03-004	Santa's Sleigh MM-004	L. Miller	Open	69.00	69.00
89-03-005	Evening Carolers MM-005	D. Kennicutt	Open	69.00	69.00
89-03-006	Winter Fun MM-006	D. Kennicutt	Open	69.00	69.00
89-03-007	Snowshoe Sled Ride MM-007	D. Kennicutt	Open	69.00	69.00
89-03-008	Christmas Tree MM-008	D. Kennicutt	Open	69.00	69.00
89-03-009	Teddy Drummers MM-009	D. Kennicutt	Open	69.00	69.00
89-03-010	Teddies And Frosty MM-010	D. Kennicutt	Open	69.00	69.00
89-03-011	Herald Angel MM-011	S. Bradford	12,000	79.00	79.00
89-03-012	Teddy Bear Band MM-012	S. Bradford	12,000	99.00	99.00
91-03-013	Dashing Through The Snow MM-013	D. Kennicutt	Open	59.00	59.00
91-03-014	Two Faeries MM-014	D. Kennicutt	Open	59.00	59.00
91-03-015	A Christmas Gift MM-015	D. Kennicutt	Open	59.00	59.00
91-03-016	Crystal Angel MM-017	D. Kennicutt	Open	59.00	59.00
91-03-017	Teddy Soldiers MM-018	D. Kennicutt	Open	69.00	69.00
United Design Corp.	**Easter Bunny Family**				
88-04-001	Bunnies, Basket Of SEC-001	D. Kennicutt	Retrd.	13.00	17.50
88-04-002	Bunny Boy W/Duck SEC-002	D. Kennicutt	Retrd.	13.00	17.50
88-04-003	Bunny, Easter SEC-003	D. Kennicutt	Retrd.	15.00	17.50
88-04-004	Bunny Girl W/Hen SEC-004	D. Kennicutt	Retrd.	13.00	17.50
88-04-005	Rabbit, Grandma SEC-005	D. Kennicutt	Retrd.	15.00	20.00
88-04-006	Rabbit, Grandpa SEC-006	D. Kennicutt	Retrd.	15.00	20.00
88-04-007	Rabbit, Momma w/Bonnet SEC-007	D. Kennicutt	Retrd.	15.00	20.00
89-04-008	Auntie Bunny SEC-008	D. Kennicutt	Retrd.	20.00	23.00
89-04-009	Little Sis W/Lolly SEC-009	D. Kennicutt	Retrd.	14.50	17.50
89-04-010	Bunny W/Prize Egg SEC-010	D. Kennicutt	Open	19.50	20.00
89-04-011	Sis & Bubba Sharing SEC-011	D. Kennicutt	Open	22.50	23.00
89-04-012	Easter Egg Hunt SEC-012	D. Kennicutt	Open	16.50	20.00
89-04-013	Rock-A-Bye Bunny SEC-013	D. Kennicutt	Open	20.00	23.00
89-04-014	Ducky W/Bonnet, Pink SEC-014	D. Kennicutt	Retrd.	10.00	12.00
89-04-015	Ducky W/Bonnet,Blue SEC-015	D. Kennicutt	Retrd.	10.00	12.00
90-04-016	Bubba w/Wagon SEC-016	D. Kennicutt	Open	16.50	17.50
90-04-017	Easter Bunny w/Crystal SEC-017	D. Kennicutt	Open	23.00	23.00
90-04-018	Hen w/Chick SEC-018	D. Kennicutt	Retrd.	23.00	23.00
90-04-019	Momma Making Basket SEC-019	D. Kennicutt	Retrd.	23.00	23.00
90-04-020	Mother Goose SEC-020	D. Kennicutt	Retrd.	16.50	20.00
91-04-021	Bubba In Wheelbarrow SEC-021	D. Kennicutt	Open	20.00	20.00
91-04-022	Lop-Ear W/Crystal SEC-022	D. Kennicutt	Open	23.00	23.00
91-04-023	Nest of Bunny Eggs SEC-023	D. Kennicutt	Open	17.50	17.50
91-04-024	Victorian Momma SEC-024	D. Kennicutt	Open	20.00	20.00
91-04-025	Bunny Boy W/Basket SEC-025	D. Kennicutt	Open	20.00	20.00
91-04-026	Victorian Auntie Bunny SEC-026	D. Kennicutt	Open	20.00	20.00
91-04-027	Baby in Buggy, Boy SEC-027	D. Kennicutt	Open	20.00	20.00
91-04-028	Fancy Find SEC-028	D. Kennicutt	Open	20.00	20.00
91-04-029	Baby in Buggy, Girl SEC-029	D. Kennicutt	Open	20.00	20.00
92-04-030	Easter Bunny w/Back Pack SEC-030	D. Kennicutt	Open	20.00	20.00
92-04-031	Grandma w/ Bible SEC-031	D. Kennicutt	Open	20.00	20.00
92-04-032	Grandpa w/Carrots SEC-032	D. Kennicutt	Open	20.00	20.00
92-04-033	Auntie Bunny w/Cake SEC-033	D. Kennicutt	Open	20.00	20.00
92-04-034	Boy Bunny w/Large Egg SEC-034	D. Kennicutt	Open	20.00	20.00
92-04-035	Girl Bunny w/Large Egg SEC-035	D. Kennicutt	Open	20.00	20.00
United Design Corp.	**Backyard Birds**				
88-05-001	Bluebird, Small BB-001	S. Bradford	Open	10.00	10.00
88-05-002	Cardinal, Small BB-002	S. Bradford	Open	10.00	10.00
88-05-003	Chickadee, Small BB-003	S. Bradford	Open	10.00	10.00
88-05-004	Hummingbird Flying, Small BB-004	S. Bradford	Open	10.00	10.00
88-05-005	Hummingbird Female, Small BB-005	S. Bradford	Retrd.	10.00	10.00
88-05-006	Robin Baby, Small BB-006	S. Bradford	Open	10.00	10.00
88-05-007	Sparrow, Small BB-007	S. Bradford	Open	10.00	10.00
88-05-008	Robin Babies BB-008	S. Bradford	Open	15.00	18.00
88-05-009	Bluebird BB-009	S. Bradford	Open	15.00	20.00
88-05-010	Chickadee BB-010	S. Bradford	Open	15.00	17.00
88-05-011	Cardinal, Female BB-011	S. Bradford	Open	15.00	17.00
88-05-012	Humingbird BB-012	S. Bradford	Open	15.00	17.00
88-05-013	Cardinal, Male BB-013	S. Bradford	Open	15.00	17.00
88-05-014	Red-winged Blackbird BB-014	S. Bradford	Retrd.	15.00	16.50
88-05-015	Robin BB-015	S. Bradford	Open	15.00	20.00
88-05-016	Sparrow BB-016	S. Bradford	Open	15.00	17.00
88-05-017	Bluebird Hanging BB-017	S. Bradford	Retrd.	11.00	16.50
88-05-018	Cardinal Hanging BB-018	S. Bradford	Retrd.	11.00	11.00
88-05-019	Chickadee Hanging BB-019	S. Bradford	Retrd.	11.00	11.00
88-05-020	Robin Hanging BB-020	S. Bradford	Retrd.	11.00	11.00
88-05-021	Sparrow Hanging BB-021	S. Bradford	Retrd.	11.00	11.00
88-05-022	Hummingbird Sm., Hanging BB-022	S. Bradford	Retrd.	11.00	11.00
88-05-023	Humingbird, Lg., Hanging BB-023	S. Bradford	Retrd.	15.00	15.00
89-05-024	Baltimore Oriole BB-024	S. Bradford	Open	19.50	22.00
89-05-025	Hoot Owl BB-025	S. Bradford	Open	15.00	20.00
89-05-026	Blue Jay BB-026	S. Bradford	Open	19.50	22.00
89-05-027	Blue Jay, Baby BB-027	S. Bradford	Open	15.00	15.00
89-05-028	Goldfinch BB-028	S. Bradford	Open	16.50	20.00
89-05-029	Saw-Whet Owl BB-029	S. Bradford	Open	15.00	18.00
89-05-030	Woodpecker BB-030	S. Bradford	Open	16.50	20.00
90-05-031	Bluebird (Upright) BB-031	S. Bradford	Open	20.00	20.00
90-05-032	Cedar Waxwing BB-032	S. Bradford	Open	20.00	20.00
90-05-033	Cedar Waxwing Babies BB-033	S. Bradford	Open	22.00	22.00
90-05-034	Indigo Bunting BB-036	S. Bradford	Open	20.00	20.00
90-05-035	Indigo Bunting, Female BB-039	S. Bradford	Open	20.00	20.00
90-05-036	Nuthatch, White-throated BB-037	S. Bradford	Open	20.00	20.00
90-05-037	Painted Bunting BB-040	S. Bradford	Open	20.00	20.00
90-05-038	Painted Bunting, Female BB-041	S. Bradford	Open	20.00	20.00
90-05-039	Purple Finch BB-038	S. Bradford	Open	20.00	20.00
90-05-040	Rose Breasted Grosbeak BB-042	S. Bradford	Open	20.00	20.00
90-05-041	Evening Grosbeak BB-034	S. Bradford	Open	22.00	22.00
United Design Corp.	**PenniBears™**				
89-06-001	Bouquet Girl PB-001	P.J. Jonas	Retrd.	20.00	22.00
89-06-002	Honey Bear PB-002	P.J. Jonas	Retrd.	20.00	22.00
89-06-003	Bouquet Boy PB-003	P.J. Jonas	Retrd.	20.00	22.00
89-06-004	Beautiful Bride PB-004	P.J. Jonas	12/92	20.00	24.00
89-06-005	Butterfly Bear PB-005	P.J. Jonas	Retrd.	20.00	22.00

Company Number	Name	Series Artist	Edition Limit	Issue Price	Quote
89-06-006	Cookie Bandit PB-006	P.J. Jonas	12/92	20.00	22.00
89-06-007	Baby Hugs PB-007	P.J. Jonas	12/92	20.00	22.00
89-06-008	Doctor Bear PB-008	P.J. Jonas	12/92	20.00	22.00
89-06-009	Lazy Days PB-009	P.J. Jonas	12/92	20.00	22.00
89-06-010	Petite Mademoiselle PB-010	P.J. Jonas	12/92	20.00	22.00
90-06-011	Giddiap Teddy PB-011	P.J. Jonas	Retrd.	20.00	24.00
90-06-012	Buttons & Bows PB-012	P.J. Jonas	Retrd.	20.00	22.00
90-06-013	Country Spring PB-013	P.J. Jonas	Retrd.	20.00	22.00
90-06-014	Garden Path PB-014	P.J. Jonas	Retrd.	20.00	22.00
89-06-015	Handsome Groom PB-015	P.J. Jonas	12/92	20.00	22.00
89-06-016	Nap Time PB-016	P.J. Jonas	12/92	20.00	22.00
89-06-017	Nurse Bear PB-017	P.J. Jonas	12/92	20.00	22.00
89-06-018	Birthday Bear PB-018	P.J. Jonas	12/92	20.00	24.00
89-06-019	Attic Fun PB-019	P.J. Jonas	12/92	20.00	22.00
89-06-020	Puppy Bath PB-020	P.J. Jonas	12/92	20.00	22.00
89-06-021	Puppy Love PB-021	P.J. Jonas	12/92	20.00	22.00
89-06-022	Tubby Teddy PB-022	P.J. Jonas	12/92	20.00	22.00
89-06-023	Bathtime Buddies PB-023	P.J. Jonas	12/92	20.00	22.00
89-06-024	Southern Belle PB-024	P.J. Jonas	12/92	20.00	22.00
90-06-025	Boooo Bear PB-025	P.J. Jonas	4/93	20.00	22.00
90-06-026	Sneaky Snowball PB-026	P.J. Jonas	4/93	20.00	22.00
90-06-027	Count Bearacula PB-027	P.J. Jonas	4/93	22.00	24.00
90-06-028	Dress Up Fun PB-028	P.J. Jonas	4/93	22.00	24.00
90-06-029	Scarecrow Teddy PB-029	P.J. Jonas	4/93	24.00	24.00
90-06-030	Country Quilter PB-030	P.J. Jonas	4/93	22.00	26.00
90-06-031	Santa Bear-ing Gifts PB-031	P.J. Jonas	4/93	24.00	26.00
90-06-032	Stocking Surprise PB-032	P.J. Jonas	4/93	22.00	26.00
91-06-033	Bearly Awake PB-033	P.J. Jonas	12/93	22.00	22.00
91-06-034	Lil' Mer-teddy PB-034	P.J. Jonas	12/93	24.00	24.00
91-06-035	Bump-bear-Crop PB-035	P.J. Jonas	12/93	26.00	26.00
91-06-036	Country Lullabye PB-036	P.J. Jonas	12/93	24.00	24.00
91-06-037	Bear Footin' it PB-037	P.J. Jonas	12/93	24.00	24.00
91-06-038	Windy Day PB-038	P.J. Jonas	12/93	24.00	24.00
91-06-039	Summer Sailing PB-039	P.J. Jonas	12/93	26.00	26.00
91-06-040	Goodnight Sweet Princess PB-040	P.J. Jonas	12/93	26.00	26.00
91-06-041	Goodnight Little Prince PB-041	P.J. Jonas	12/93	26.00	26.00
91-06-042	Bunny Buddies PB-042	P.J. Jonas	12/93	22.00	22.00
91-06-043	Baking Goodies PB-043	P.J. Jonas	12/93	26.00	26.00
91-06-044	Sweetheart Bears PB-044	P.J. Jonas	12/93	28.00	28.00
91-06-045	Bountiful Harvest PB-045	P.J. Jonas	4/94	24.00	24.00
91-06-046	Christmas Reinbear PB-046	P.J. Jonas	4/94	28.00	28.00
91-06-047	Pilgrim Provider PB-047	P.J. Jonas	4/94	32.00	32.00
91-06-048	Sweet Lil 'Sis PB-048	P.J. Jonas	4/94	22.00	22.00
91-06-049	Curtain Call PB-049	P.J. Jonas	4/94	24.00	24.00
91-06-050	Boo Hoo Bear PB-050	P.J. Jonas	4/94	22.00	22.00
91-06-051	Happy Hobo PB-051	P.J. Jonas	4/94	26.00	26.00
91-06-052	A Wild Ride PB-052	P.J. Jonas	4/94	26.00	26.00
92-06-053	Spanish Rose PB-053	P.J. Jonas	12/94	24.00	24.00
92-06-054	Tally Ho! PB-054	P.J. Jonas	12/94	22.00	22.00
92-06-055	Smokey's Nephew PB-055	P.J. Jonas	12/94	22.00	22.00
92-06-056	Cinderella PB-056	P.J. Jonas	12/94	22.00	22.00
92-06-057	Puddle Jumper PB-057	P.J. Jonas	12/94	24.00	24.00
92-06-058	After Every Meal PB-058	P.J. Jonas	12/94	22.00	22.00
92-06-059	Pot O' Gold PB-059	P.J. Jonas	12/94	22.00	22.00
92-06-050	"I Made It" Girl PB-060	P.J. Jonas	12/94	22.00	22.00
92-06-061	"I Made It" Boy PB-061	P.J. Jonas	12/94	22.00	22.00
92-06-062	Dust Bunny Roundup PB-062	P.J. Jonas	12/94	22.00	22.00
92-06-063	Sandbox Fun PB-063	P.J. Jonas	12/94	22.00	22.00
92-06-064	First Prom PB-064	P.J. Jonas	12/94	22.00	22.00
92-06-065	Clowning Around PB-065	P.J. Jonas	12/94	22.00	22.00
92-06-066	Batter Up PB-066	P.J. Jonas	12/94	22.00	22.00
92-06-067	Will You Be Mine? PB-067	P.J. Jonas	12/94	22.00	22.00
92-06-068	On Your Toes PB-068	P.J. Jonas	12/94	24.00	24.00
92-06-069	Apple For Teacher PB-069	P.J. Jonas	12/94	24.00	24.00
92-06-070	Downhill Thrills PB-070	P.J. Jonas	12/94	24.00	24.00
92-06-071	Lil' Devil PB-071	P.J. Jonas	12/94	24.00	24.00
92-06-072	Touchdown PB-072	P.J. Jonas	12/94	22.00	22.00
92-06-073	Bear-Capade PB-073	P.J. Jonas	12/94	22.00	22.00
92-06-074	Lil' Sis Makes Up PB-074	P.J. Jonas	12/94	22.00	22.00
92-06-075	Christmas Cookies PB-075	P.J. Jonas	12/94	22.00	22.00
92-06-076	Decorating The Wreath PB-076	P.J. Jonas	12/94	22.00	22.00
United Design Corp.		**PenniBears™ Collector's Club Members Only Editions**			
91-07-001	First Collection PB-C90	P.J. Jonas	Retrd.	26.00	26.00
92-07-002	Collecting Makes Cents PB-C91	P.J. Jonas	Retrd.	26.00	26.00
93-07-003	Today's Pleasures, Tomorrow's Treasures	P.J. Jonas	Yr.Iss.	26.00	26.00
United Design Corp.		**Faerie Tales™**			
90-08-001	Faerie Flight FT 001	K. Memoli	Retrd.	39.00	39.00
90-08-002	Sleeping Faerie FT 002	K. Memoli	Retrd.	39.00	39.00
90-08-003	Water Sprite FT 003	K. Memoli	Retrd.	39.00	39.00
90-08-004	Wind Sprite FT 004	K. Memoli	Retrd.	39.00	39.00
90-08-005	Winter Faerie FT 005	K. Memoli	Retrd.	39.00	39.00
90-08-006	Wood Sprite FT 006	K. Memoli	Retrd.	39.00	39.00
United Design Corp.		**Party Animals™**			
84-09-001	Democratic Donkey ('84)	D. Kennicutt	Retrd.	14.50	16.00
84-09-002	GOP Elephant ('84)	L. Miller	Retrd.	14.50	16.00
86-09-003	Democratic Donkey ('86)	L. Miller	Retrd.	14.50	14.50
86-09-004	GOP Elephant ('86)	L. Miller	Retrd.	14.50	14.50
88-09-005	Democratic Donkey ('88)	L. Miller	Retrd.	14.50	16.00
88-09-006	GOP Elephant ('88)	L. Miller	Retrd.	14.50	16.00
90-09-007	Democratic Donkey ('90)	D. Kennicutt	Open	16.00	16.00
90-09-008	GOP Elephant ('90)	D. Kennicutt	Retrd.	16.00	16.00
92-09-009	Democratic Donkey ('92)	K. Memoli	Open	20.00	20.00
92-09-010	GOP Elephant ('92)	K. Memol	Open	20.00	20.00
United Design Corp.		**Angels Collection**			
91-10-001	Christmas Angel AA-003	S. Bradford	10,000	125.00	125.00
91-10-002	Trumpeter Angel AA-004	S. Bradford	10,000	99.00	99.00
91-10-003	Classical Angel AA-005	S. Bradford	10,000	79.00	79.00
91-10-004	Messenger of Peace AA-006	S. Bradford	10,000	75.00	75.00
91-10-005	Winter Rose Angel AA-007	S. Bradford	10,000	65.00	65.00
91-10-006	Heavenly Shepherdess AA-008	S. Bradford	10,000	99.00	99.00
91-10-007	The Gift AA-009	S. Bradford	Retrd.	135.00	135.00
91-10-008	Victorian Cupid Angel AA-010	P.J. Jonas	Open	15.00	15.00
91-10-009	Rosetti Angel AA-011	P.J. Jonas	Open	20.00	20.00
91-10-010	Angel Waif AA-012	P.J. Jonas	Open	15.00	15.00
91-10-011	Peace Descending Angel AA-013	P.J. Jonas	Open	20.00	20.00
92-10-012	Joy To The World AA-016	D. Newborn	10,000	90.00	90.00
92-10-013	Peaceful Encounter AA-017	D. Newborn	10,000	100.00	100.00
92-10-014	"The Gift" '92 AA-018	S. Bradford	3,500	140.00	140.00
92-10-015	Winter Angel AA-019	D. Newborn	10,000	75.00	75.00
92-10-016	Angel, Lion & Lamb AA-020	K. Memoli	10,000	135.00	135.00
92-10-017	Angel, Lamb & Critters AA-021	S. Bradford	10,000	90.00	90.00
92-10-018	Crystal Angel AA-022	P.J. Jonas	Open	20.00	20.00
92-10-019	Rose Of Sharon AA-023	P.J. Jonas	Open	20.00	20.00
92-10-020	Victorian Angel AA-024	P.J. Jonas	Open	20.00	20.00
92-10-021	Star Glory AA-025	P.J. Jonas	Open	20.00	20.00
United Design Corp.		**Lil' Dolls**			
91-11-001	Georgie Bear LD-001	P.J. Jonas	10,000	35.00	35.00
91-11-002	Jenny Bear LD-002	P.J. Jonas	10,000	35.00	35.00
91-11-003	Amy LD-003	D. Newburn	10,000	35.00	35.00
91-11-004	Sam LD-004	D. Newburn	10,000	35.00	35.00
91-11-005	Becky Bunny LD-005	D. Newburn	10,000	35.00	35.00
91-11-006	Nutcracker LD-006	P.J. Jonas	10,000	35.00	35.00
91-11-007	Marching In Time LD-007	D. Newburn	10,000	35.00	35.00
91-11-008	Betty Button's Surprise LD-008	Newburn/Jonas	10,000	35.00	35.00
91-11-009	Archibald Bear LD-009	P.J. Jonas	10,000	35.00	35.00
91-11-010	Angela Bear LD-010	P.J. Jonas	10,000	35.00	35.00
91-11-011	Sara LD-011	D. Newburn	10,000	35.00	35.00
91-11-012	Tom LD-012	D. Newburn	10,000	35.00	35.00
91-11-013	Addie LD-013	D. Newburn	10,000	35.00	35.00
91-11-014	Krista LD-014	D. Newburn	10,000	35.00	35.00
91-11-015	Tess LD-015	D. Newburn	10,000	35.00	35.00
92-11-016	Purr-Cila LD-016	D. Newburn	10,000	35.00	35.00
92-11-017	Clara & The Nutcracker LD-017	D. Newburn	10,000	35.00	35.00
92-11-018	Buster Button LD-018	D. Newburn	10,000	35.00	35.00
United Design Corp.		**Storytime Rhymes & Tales**			
91-12-001	Mother Goose-001	H. Henriksen	3,500	64.00	64.00
91-12-002	Mistress Mary-002	H. Henriksen	3,500	64.00	64.00
91-12-003	Simple Simon-003	H. Henriksen	3,500	90.00	90.00
91-12-004	Owl & Pussy Cat-004	H. Henriksen	3,500	100.00	100.00
91-12-005	Three Little Pigs-005	H. Henriksen	3,500	100.00	100.00
91-12-006	Little Miss Muffet-006	H. Henriksen	3,500	64.00	64.00
91-12-007	Little Jack Horner-007	H. Henriksen	3,500	50.00	50.00
91-12-008	Humpty Dumpty-008	H. Henriksen	3,500	64.00	64.00
VickiLane		**Sweet Thumpins**			
90-01-001	Venture into Sweet Thumpins	V. Anderson	2,500	60.00	73.00
91-01-002	Tea Time	V. Anderson	2,500	79.00	82.00
91-01-003	Making Memories	V. Anderson	2,500	70.00	73.00
92-01-004	Cookie Peddler	V. Anderson	1,500	90.00	90.00
VickiLane		**Mice Memories**			
90-02-001	Happiness Together	V. Anderson	2,500	65.00	73.00
WACO Products Corp.		**Melody In Motion/Willie**			
85-01-001	Willie The Trumpeter	S. Nakane	Open	130.00	140.00
85-01-002	Willie The Hobo	S. Nakane	Open	130.00	140.00
85-01-003	Willie The Whistler	S. Nakane	Open	130.00	140.00
87-01-004	Lamppost Willie	S. Nakane	Open	110.00	120.00
91-01-005	Willie The Fisherman	S. Nakane	Open	150.00	150.00
WACO Products Corp.		**Melody In Motion/Vendor**			
87-02-001	Organ Grinder	S. Nakane	Open	130.00	140.00
89-02-002	Peanut Vendor	S. Nakane	Open	140.00	150.00
89-02-003	Ice Cream Vendor	S. Nakane	Open	140.00	150.00
WACO Products Corp.		**Melody In Motion/Santa**			
86-03-001	Santa Claus-1986	S. Nakane	Retrd.	100.00	N/A
87-03-002	Santa Claus-1987	S. Nakane	Retrd.	130.00	N/A
88-03-003	Santa Claus-1988	S. Nakane	Retrd.	130.00	N/A
89-03-004	Willie The Santa-1989	S. Nakane	Retrd.	130.00	N/A
90-03-005	Santa Claus-1990	S. Nakane	Retrd.	150.00	N/A
91-03-006	Santa Claus-1991	S. Nakane	Retrd.	150.00	N/A
92-03-007	Santa Claus -1992	S. Nakane	11,000	160.00	160.00
WACO Products Corp.		**Melody In Motion/Madame**			
88-04-001	Madame Violin Player	S. Nakane	Retrd.	130.00	130.00
88-04-002	Madame Mandolin Player	S. Nakane	Open	130.00	130.00
88-04-003	Madame Cello Player	S. Nakane	Retrd.	130.00	130.00
88-04-004	Madame Flute Player	S. Nakane	Retrd.	130.00	130.00
88-04-005	Madame Harp Player	S. Nakane	Open	130.00	150.00
88-04-006	Madame Harpsichord Player	S. Nakane	Retrd.	130.00	130.00
88-04-007	Madame Lyre Player	S. Nakane	Open	130.00	130.00
WACO Products Corp.		**Melody In Motion/Spotlight Clown**			
89-05-001	Spotlight Clown Cornet	S. Nakane	Retrd.	120.00	120.00
89-05-002	Spotlight Clown Banjo	S. Nakane	Retrd.	120.00	120.00
89-05-003	Spotlight Clown Trombone	S. Nakane	Retrd.	120.00	120.00
89-05-004	Spotlight Clown With Bingo The Dog	S. Nakane	Retrd.	130.00	130.00
89-05-005	Spotlight Clown Tuba	S. Nakane	Retrd.	120.00	120.00
89-05-006	Spotlight Clown With Upright Bass	S. Nakane	Retrd.	130.00	130.00
WACO Products Corp.		**Melody In Motion/Various**			
85-06-001	Salty 'N' Pepper	S. Nakane	Retrd.	88.00	88.00
86-06-002	The Cellist	S. Nakane	Open	130.00	140.00
86-06-003	The Guitarist	S. Nakane	Open	130.00	140.00
86-06-004	The Fiddler	S. Nakane	Open	130.00	140.00
87-06-005	Violin Clown	S. Nakane	Retrd.	84.00	84.00
87-06-006	Clarinet Clown	S. Nakane	Retrd.	110.00	110.00
87-06-007	Saxophone Clown	S. Nakane	Retrd.	110.00	110.00
87-06-008	Accordion Clown	S. Nakane	Retrd.	110.00	110.00
87-06-009	Balloon Clown	S. Nakane	Open	110.00	120.00
87-06-010	The Carousel	S. Nakane	Open	240.00	240.00
89-06-011	The Grand Carousel	S. Nakane	Open	3000.00	3000.00
90-06-012	Shoemaker	S. Nakane	Retrd.	110.00	120.00
90-06-013	Blacksmith	S. Nakane	Retrd.	110.00	120.00
90-06-014	Woodchopper	S. Nakane	Retrd.	110.00	120.00
90-06-015	Accordion Boy	S. Nakane	Retrd.	120.00	125.00
90-06-016	Hunter	S. Nakane	Open	110.00	110.00
91-06-017	Robin Hood	C. Johnson	Retrd.	180.00	180.00
91-06-018	Little John	C. Johnson	7,000	180.00	180.00
91-06-019	Victoria Park Carousel	S. Nakane	Open	300.00	300.00
92-06-020	King of Clown Carousel	S. Nakane	Open	740.00	740.00
WACO Products Corp.		**Melody In Motion/Timepiece**			
89-07-001	Clockpost Willie	S. Nakane	Open	150.00	160.00
89-07-002	Lull'aby Willie	S. Nakane	Retrd.	170.00	170.00
90-07-003	Grandfather's Clock	S. Nakane	Open	200.00	210.00
91-07-004	Hunter Timepiece	S. Nakane	Open	250.00	250.00
92-07-005	Wall Street Willie	S. Nakane	Open	180.00	180.00
92-07-006	Golden Mountain Clock	S. Nakane	Open	250.00	250.00

Company Number	Name	Series Artist	Edition Limit	Issue Price	Quote
WACO Products Corp.		**The Herman Collection**			
90-08-001	Tennis/Wife	J. Unger	Open	32.00	32.00
90-08-002	Doctor/High Cost	J. Unger	Open	32.00	32.00
90-08-003	Bowling/Wife	J. Unger	Open	32.00	32.00
90-08-004	Husband/Check	J. Unger	Open	36.00	36.00
90-08-005	Birthday Cake	J. Unger	Open	36.00	36.00
90-08-006	Doctor/Fat Man	J. Unger	Open	36.00	36.00
90-08-007	Fry Pan	J. Unger	Open	40.00	40.00
90-08-008	Stop Smoking	J. Unger	Open	40.00	40.00
90-08-009	Husband/Newspaper	J. Unger	Open	41.00	41.00
90-08-010	Wedding Ring	J. Unger	Open	41.00	41.00
90-08-011	Golf/Camel	J. Unger	Open	44.00	44.00
90-08-012	Lawyer/Cabinet	J. Unger	Open	44.00	44.00
Wee Forest Folk		**Bunnies**			
72-01-001	Double Bunnies B-1	A. Petersen	Closed	9.00	N/A
72-01-002	Housekeeping Bunny B-2	A. Petersen	Closed	11.00	N/A
73-01-003	Sir Rabbit B-3	W. Petersen	Closed	11.50	N/A
73-01-004	The Professor B-4	A. Petersen	Closed	12.00	N/A
73-01-005	Sunday Bunny B-5	A. Petersen	Closed	9.50	N/A
73-01-006	Broom Bunny B-6	A. Petersen	Closed	9.50	N/A
73-01-007	Muff Bunny B-7	A. Petersen	Closed	9.00	N/A
73-01-008	Market Bunny B-8	A. Petersen	Closed	9.00	N/A
77-01-009	Batter Bunny B-9	A. Petersen	Closed	17.00	275-400.
77-01-010	Tennis Bunny BS-10	A. Petersen	Closed	10.50	250-300.
78-01-011	Wedding Bunnies B-11	W. Petersen	Closed	33.50	300-600.
80-01-012	Professor Rabbit B-12	W. Petersen	Closed	16.00	400-450.
92-01-014	Windy Day B-13	D. Petersen	Open	37.00	37.00
85-01-013	Tiny Easter Bunny B-14	D. Petersen	Closed	25.00	75.00
Wee Forest Folk		**Bears**			
77-02-001	Blueberry Bears BR-1	A. Petersen	Closed	31.50	500-700.
77-02-002	Girl Blueberry Bear BR-2	A. Petersen	Closed	15.00	200-400.
77-02-003	Boy Blueberry Bear BR-3	A. Petersen	Closed	17.00	200-400.
78-02-004	Big Lady Bear BR-4	A. Petersen	Closed	16.00	N/A
78-02-005	Traveling Bear BR-5	A. Petersen	Closed	21.50	250-375.
Wee Forest Folk		**Tiny Teddies**			
83-03-001	Tiny Teddy TT-1	D. Petersen	Closed	16.00	100-200.
84-03-002	Little Teddy T-1	D. Petersen	Closed	26.00	100-150.
84-03-003	Sailor Teddy T-2	D. Petersen	Suspd.	26.00	N/A
84-03-004	Boo Bear T-3	D. Petersen	Suspd.	26.00	N/A
84-03-005	Drummer Bear T-4	D. Petersen	Suspd.	28.00	N/A
84-03-006	Santa Bear T-5	D. Petersen	Suspd.	33.00	N/A
85-03-007	Ride 'em Teddy! T-6	D. Petersen	Suspd.	38.00	N/A
85-03-008	Seaside Teddy T-7	D. Petersen	Suspd.	32.00	N/A
86-03-009	Huggy Bear T-8	D. Petersen	Suspd.	26.00	N/A
87-03-010	Wedding Bears T-9	D. Petersen	Suspd.	54.00	N/A
87-03-011	Christmas Teddy T-10	D. Petersen	Suspd.	26.00	N/A
88-03-012	Hansel & Gretel Bears@Witch's House T-11	D. Petersen	Suspd.	175.00	245.00
89-03-013	Momma Bear T-12	D. Petersen	Suspd.	27.00	N/A
Wee Forest Folk		**Fairy Tale Series**			
80-04-001	Red Riding Hood & Wolf FT-1	A. Petersen	Closed	34.00	850-1300.
80-04-002	Red Riding Hood FT-2	A. Petersen	Closed	14.00	250-400.
Wee Forest Folk		**Wind in the Willows**			
82-05-001	Mole WW-1	A. Petersen	Closed	18.00	200-300.
82-05-002	Badger WW-2	A. Petersen	Closed	18.00	200-300.
82-05-003	Toad WW-3	W. Petersen	Closed	18.00	200-300.
82-05-004	Ratty WW-4	A. Petersen	Closed	18.00	200-300.
Wee Forest Folk		**Frogs**			
74-06-001	Prince Charming F-1	W. Petersen	Closed	7.50	N/A
74-06-002	Frog on Rock F-2	A. Petersen	Closed	6.00	N/A
77-06-003	Frog Friends F-3	W. Petersen	Closed	17.50	N/A
77-06-004	Spring Peepers F-4	A. Petersen	Closed	9.00	N/A
77-06-005	Grampa Frog F-5	W. Petersen	Closed	17.50	N/A
78-06-006	Singing Frog F-6	A. Petersen	Closed	12.00	N/A
Wee Forest Folk		**Owls**			
74-07-001	Mr. and Mrs. Owl O-1	A. Petersen	Closed	19.00	300-375.
74-07-002	Mrs. Owl O-2	A. Petersen	Closed	8.50	100-200.
74-07-003	Mr. Owl O-3	A. Petersen	Closed	10.50	100-200.
75-07-004	Colonial Owls O-4	A. Petersen	Closed	11.50	N/A
79-07-005	"Grad" Owl O-5	W. Petersen	Closed	12.50	N/A
80-07-006	Graduate Owl O-6	W. Petersen	Closed	12.00	N/A
Wee Forest Folk		**Raccoons**			
77-08-001	Mother Raccoon RC-1	A. Petersen	Closed	11.50	300-450.
77-08-002	Hiker Raccoon RC-2	A. Petersen	Closed	12.00	325-475.
78-08-003	Bird Watcher Raccoon RC-3	A. Petersen	Closed	22.50	350-425.
78-08-004	Raccoon Skater RCS-1	A. Petersen	Closed	12.00	200-400.
78-08-005	Raccoon Skier RCS-2	A. Petersen	Closed	14.00	300-450.
Wee Forest Folk		**Foxes**			
77-09-001	Fancy Fox FX-1	A. Petersen	Closed	10.00	325-450.
77-09-002	Dandy Fox FX-2	A. Petersen	Closed	12.50	N/A
78-09-003	Barrister Fox FX-3	A. Petersen	Closed	21.00	450.00
Wee Forest Folk		**Piggies**			
78-10-001	Miss Piggy School Marm P-1	A. Petersen	Closed	12.00	225-300.
78-10-002	Piggy Baker P-2	A. Petersen	Closed	14.50	225-400.
78-10-003	Jolly Tar Piggy P-3	A. Petersen	Closed	10.00	175-225.
78-10-004	Picnic Piggies P-4	A. Petersen	Closed	24.00	200-300.
78-10-005	Girl Piglet/Picnic Piggy P-5	A. Petersen	Closed	12.00	100-125.
78-10-006	Boy Piglet/ Picnic Piggy P-6	A. Petersen	Closed	12.00	100-125.
78-10-007	Piggy Jogger PS-1	A. Petersen	Closed	13.50	125-200.
80-10-008	Piggy Ballerina P-7	A. Petersen	Closed	15.50	175-250.
80-10-009	Piggy Policeman P-8	A. Petersen	Closed	17.50	200-325.
80-10-010	Pig O' My Heart P-9	A. Petersen	Closed	13.50	175-250.
80-10-011	Nurse Piggy P-10	A. Petersen	Closed	15.50	200-250.
81-10-012	Holly Hog P-11	A. Petersen	Closed	25.00	300-400.
Wee Forest Folk		**Animals**			
73-11-001	Miss Ducky D-1	A. Petersen	Closed	8.00	N/A
74-11-002	Miss Hippo H-1	A. Petersen	Closed	8.00	N/A
74-11-003	Baby Hippo H-2	A. Petersen	Closed	7.00	N/A
74-11-004	Miss and Baby Hippo H-3	A. Petersen	Closed	15.00	N/A
75-11-005	Seedy Rat R-1	A. Petersen	Closed	11.50	200-350.
75-11-006	"Doc" Rat R-2	W. Petersen	Closed	12.00	200-350.
77-11-007	Nutsy Squirrel SQ-1	W. Petersen	Closed	6.00	N/A
78-11-008	Beaver Wood Cutter BV-1	W. Petersen	Closed	23.00	225-450.
78-11-009	Mole Scout MO-1	A. Petersen	Closed	9.00	225-375.
79-11-010	Turtle Jogger TS-1	A. Petersen	Closed	9.00	N/A
Wee Forest Folk		**Mouse Sports**			
75-12-001	Bobsled Three MS-1	A. Petersen	Closed	12.00	N/A
75-12-002	Skater Mouse MS-2	A. Petersen	Closed	14.00	300-500.
76-12-003	Mouse Skier MS-3	A. Petersen	Closed	12.50	250-400.
76-12-004	Tennis Star MS-4	A. Petersen	Closed	7.50	100-275.
76-12-005	Tennis Star MS-5	A. Petersen	Closed	10.50	100-275.
77-12-006	Skating Star Mouse MS-6	A. Petersen	Closed	9.00	250-400.
77-12-007	Golfer Mouse MS-7	A. Petersen	Closed	15.50	350-700.
80-12-008	Skater Mouse MS-8	A. Petersen	Closed	18.00	200-375.
80-12-009	Skier Mouse MS-9	A. Petersen	Open	13.00	35.00
81-12-010	Golfer Mouse MS-10	A. Petersen	Closed	17.00	200-350.
82-12-011	Two in a Canoe MS-11	W. Petersen	Open	29.00	56.00
84-12-012	Land Ho! MS-12	A. Petersen	Closed	46.00	150-250.
84-12-013	Tennis Anyone? MS-13	A. Petersen	Closed	18.00	100-125.
85-12-014	Fishin' Chip MS-14	W. Petersen	Closed	46.00	125-150.
89-12-015	Joe Di'Mousio MS-15	A. Petersen	Open	39.00	43.00
Wee Forest Folk		**Forest Scene**			
88-13-001	Woodland Serenade FS-1	W. Petersen	Open	125.00	130.00
89-13-002	Hearts and Flowers FS-2	W. Petersen	Open	110.00	112.00
90-13-003	Mousie Comes A-Calling FS-3	W. Petersen	Open	128.00	130.00
91-13-004	Mountain Stream FS-4	W. Petersen	Open	128.00	130.00
92-13-005	Love Letter FS-5	W. Petersen	Open	98.00	98.00
Wee Forest Folk		**Mice**			
72-14-001	Miss Mouse M-1	A. Petersen	Closed	8.00	300-350.
72-14-002	Market Mouse M-1a	A. Petersen	Closed	8.00	57.00
72-14-003	Miss Mousey M-2	A. Petersen	Closed	7.50	N/A
72-14-004	Miss Mousey Straw Hat M-2a	A. Petersen	Closed	8.00	225-325.
72-14-005	Miss Mousey Bow Hat M-2b	A. Petersen	Closed	8.00	N/A
73-14-006	Miss Nursey M-3	A. Petersen	Closed	7.50	200-400.
74-14-007	Good Knight Mouse M-4	W. Petersen	Closed	7.50	N/A
74-14-008	Farmer Mouse M-5	A. Petersen	Closed	7.00	N/A
74-14-009	Wood Sprite M-6a	A. Petersen	Closed	7.50	300-550.
74-14-010	Wood Sprite M-6b	A. Petersen	Closed	7.50	300-550.
74-14-011	Wood Sprite M-6c	A. Petersen	Closed	7.50	300-550.
75-14-012	Two Mice with Candle M-7	A. Petersen	Closed	8.00	300-400.
75-14-013	Two Tiny Mice M-8	A. Petersen	Closed	7.50	300-500.
75-14-014	Bride Mouse M-9	A. Petersen	Closed	7.50	375-500.
76-14-015	Fan Mouse M-10	A. Petersen	Closed	10.50	N/A
76-14-016	Tea Mouse M-11	A. Petersen	Closed	10.50	N/A
76-14-017	May Belle M-12	A. Petersen	Closed	8.00	225-425.
76-14-018	June Belle M-13	A. Petersen	Closed	7.50	225-425.
76-14-019	Nightie Mouse M-14	A. Petersen	Closed	9.50	300-500.
76-14-020	Mrs. Mousey M-15	A. Petersen	Closed	8.00	N/A
76-14-021	Mrs. Mousey with Hat M-15a	A. Petersen	Closed	8.50	N/A
76-14-022	Mouse with Muff M-16	A. Petersen	Closed	9.00	N/A
76-14-023	Shawl Mouse M-17	A. Petersen	Closed	9.00	N/A
76-14-024	Mama Mouse with Baby M-18	A. Petersen	Closed	12.00	325-450.
77-14-025	King "Tut" Mouse TM-1	A. Petersen	Closed	9.50	450-600.
77-14-026	Queen "Tut" Mouse TM-2	A. Petersen	Closed	9.50	450-600.
77-14-027	Baby Sitter M-19	A. Petersen	Closed	9.50	225-325.
78-14-028	Bridge Club Mouse M-20	A. Petersen	Closed	12.00	N/A
78-14-029	Bridge Club Mouse Partner M-21	A. Petersen	Closed	12.00	N/A
78-14-030	Secretary, Miss Spell/Miss Pell M-22	W. Petersen	Closed	9.50	375-400.
78-14-031	Picnic Mice M-23	W. Petersen	Closed	14.50	325-400.
78-14-032	Wedding Mice M-24	W. Petersen	Closed	15.00	375-550.
78-14-033	Cowboy Mouse M-25	A. Petersen	Closed	12.00	300-500.
78-14-034	Chief Nip-a-Way Mouse M-26	A. Petersen	Closed	14.00	300-400.
78-14-035	Pirate Mouse M-27	A. Petersen	Closed	13.00	300-700.
78-14-036	Town Crier Mouse M-28	A. Petersen	Closed	10.50	N/A
79-14-037	Mouse Duet M-29	A. Petersen	Closed	25.00	550-700.
79-14-038	Mouse Pianist M-30	A. Petersen	Closed	17.00	300-500.
79-14-039	Mouse Violinist M-31	A. Petersen	Closed	9.00	200-300.
79-14-040	Chris-Miss M-32	A. Petersen	Closed	9.00	200-350.
79-14-041	Chris-Mouse M-33	A. Petersen	Closed	9.00	250-350.
79-14-042	Mousey Baby, heart book M-34	A. Petersen	Closed	9.50	250-375.
79-14-043	Rock-a-bye Baby Mouse M-35	A. Petersen	Closed	17.00	300-400.
79-14-044	Raggedy and Mouse M-36	A. Petersen	Closed	12.00	250-350.
79-14-045	Gardener Mouse M-37	A. Petersen	Closed	12.00	375-400.
79-14-046	Mouse Ballerina M-38	A. Petersen	Closed	12.50	N/A
79-14-047	Mouse Artiste M-39	A. Petersen	Closed	12.50	300-450.
80-14-048	Miss Bobbin M-40	A. Petersen	Open	22.00	54.00
80-14-049	Fishermouse M-41	A. Petersen	Closed	16.00	450-650.
80-14-050	Commo-Dormouse M-42	W. Petersen	Closed	14.00	500-700.
80-14-051	Santa Mouse M-43	A. Petersen	Closed	12.50	200-250.
80-14-052	Witch Mouse M-44	A. Petersen	Closed	12.00	125-200.
80-14-053	Miss Teach M-45	A. Petersen	Closed	18.00	350-450.
80-14-054	Miss Polly Mouse M-46	A. Petersen	Closed	23.00	300-450.
80-14-055	Pirate Mouse M-47	W. Petersen	Closed	16.00	400-600.
80-14-056	Photographer Mouse M-48	W. Petersen	Closed	23.00	400-600.
80-14-057	Carpenter Mouse M-49	A. Petersen	Closed	15.00	375-450.
80-14-058	Mrs. Tidy and Helper M-50	A. Petersen	Closed	24.00	450-650.
80-14-059	Mrs. Tidy M-51	A. Petersen	Closed	19.50	350-450.
81-14-060	Mother's Helper M-52	A. Petersen	Closed	11.00	200-300.
81-14-061	Flower Girl M-53	A. Petersen	Closed	15.00	275-350.
81-14-062	Nurse Mousey M-54	A. Petersen	Closed	14.00	200-400.
81-14-063	Doc Mouse & Patient M-55	W. Petersen	Closed	14.00	500.00
81-14-064	School Marm Mouse M-56	A. Petersen	Closed	19.50	450-550.
81-14-065	Barrister Mouse M-57	A. Petersen	Closed	16.00	400-495.
81-14-066	Graduate Mouse M-58	A. Petersen	Closed	15.00	75-125.00
81-14-067	Pearl Knit Mouse M-59	A. Petersen	Closed	20.00	200-250.
81-14-068	Mom and Squeaky Clean M-60	A. Petersen	Open	27.00	51.00
81-14-069	Little Devil M-61	A. Petersen	Open	12.50	26.00
81-14-070	Blue Devil M-61	A. Petersen	Closed	12.50	N/A
81-14-071	Little Ghost M-62	A. Petersen	Open	8.50	19.00
81-14-072	The Carolers M-63	A. Petersen	Closed	29.00	300-450.
81-14-073	Lone Caroler M-64	A. Petersen	Closed	15.50	375-500.
81-14-074	Mousey Express M-65	A. Petersen	Open	22.00	48.00
82-14-075	Baby Sitter M-66	A. Petersen	Open	23.50	41.00
82-14-076	Wedding Mice M-67	W. Petersen	Open	29.50	54.00
82-14-077	Office Mousey M-68	A. Petersen	Closed	23.00	300-400.
82-14-078	Beddy-bye Mousey M-69	A. Petersen	Open	29.00	48.00
82-14-079	Me and Raggedy Ann M-70	A. Petersen	Open	18.50	32.00
82-14-080	Arty Mouse M-71	A. Petersen	Closed	19.00	50-100.
82-14-081	Say "Cheese" M-72	W. Petersen	Closed	15.50	250-450.
82-14-082	Miss Teach & Pupil M-73	A. Petersen	Closed	29.50	350-575.
82-14-083	Tea for Two M-74	A. Petersen	Closed	26.00	300-375.
82-14-084	Mousey's Teddy M-75	A. Petersen	Closed	29.00	300-350.
82-14-085	Beach Mousey M-76	A. Petersen	Open	19.00	32.00

Company Number	Name	Series Artist	Edition Limit	Issue Price	Quote
82-14-086	Little Fire Chief M-77	W. Petersen	Closed	29.00	350-475.
82-14-087	Moon Mouse M-78	A. Petersen	Closed	15.50	375-450.
82-14-088	Sweethearts M-79	A. Petersen	Closed	26.00	375-500.
82-14-089	Girl Sweetheart M-80	A. Petersen	Open	13.50	21.00
82-14-090	Boy Sweetheart M-81	A. Petersen	Closed	13.50	300-350.
82-14-091	Easter Bunny Mouse M-82	A. Petersen	Open	18.00	31.00
82-14-092	Happy Birthday! M-83	A. Petersen	Open	17.50	30.00
82-14-093	Snowmouse & Friend M-84	A. Petersen	Closed	23.50	300-450.
82-14-094	Little Sledders M-85	A. Petersen	Closed	33.50	175-275.
82-14-095	Lamplight Carolers M-86	A. Petersen	Closed	46.00	250-350.
82-14-096	Holly Mouse M-87	A. Petersen	Open	13.50	26.00
82-14-097	Littlest Angel M-88	A. Petersen	Closed	15.00	100.00
82-14-098	Poorest Angel M-89	A. Petersen	Closed	15.00	100.00
83-14-099	Merry Chris-Miss M-90	A. Petersen	Closed	17.50	150-250.
83-14-100	Merry Chris-Mouse M-91	A. Petersen	Closed	16.00	150-250.
83-14-101	Christmas Morning M-92	A. Petersen	Closed	35.00	175-350.
83-14-102	First Christmas M-93	A. Petersen	Closed	16.00	200-350.
83-14-103	Cupid Mouse M-94	W. Petersen	Open	22.00	36.00
83-14-104	Mousey Nurse M-95	A. Petersen	Open	15.00	25.00
83-14-105	Get Well Soon! M-96	A. Petersen	Closed	15.00	225-350.
83-14-106	Mouse Call M-97	W. Petersen	Closed	24.00	250-400.
83-14-107	Clown Mouse M-98	A. Petersen	Closed	22.00	250-350.
83-14-108	Birthday Girl M-99	A. Petersen	Open	18.50	29.00
83-14-109	Mousey's Cone M-100	A. Petersen	Open	22.00	33.00
83-14-110	Mousey's Tricycle M-101	A. Petersen	Open	24.00	42.00
83-14-111	Mousey's Dollhouse M-102	A. Petersen	Closed	30.00	275-475.
83-14-112	Rocking Tot M-103	A. Petersen	Closed	19.50	50-100.00
83-14-113	Harvest Mouse M-104	W. Petersen	Closed	23.00	250-350.
83-14-114	Wash Day M-105	A. Petersen	Closed	23.00	300-350.
83-14-115	Pack Mouse M-106	W. Petersen	Closed	19.00	280-375.
83-14-116	Chief Geronimouse M-107a	A. Petersen	Open	21.00	37.00
83-14-117	Running Doe/Little Deer M-107b	A. Petersen	Open	35.00	39.00
83-14-118	Rope 'em Mousey M-108	A. Petersen	Closed	19.00	200-350.
84-14-119	Campfire Mouse M-109	W. Petersen	Closed	26.00	300-395.
84-14-120	Traveling Mouse M-110	A. Petersen	Closed	28.00	225-275.
84-14-121	Spring Gardener M-111	A. Petersen	Open	26.00	38.00
84-14-122	First Day of School M-112	A. Petersen	Closed	27.00	350-550.
84-14-123	Tidy Mouse M-113	A. Petersen	Closed	38.00	300-350.
84-14-124	Pen Pal Mousey M-114	A. Petersen	Closed	26.00	275-375.
84-14-125	Mom & Ginger Baker M-115	W. Petersen	Open	38.00	58.00
84-14-126	Santa's Trainee M-116	W. Petersen	Closed	36.50	375-475.
84-14-127	Chris-Mouse Pageant M-117	A. Petersen	Open	38.00	52.00
84-14-128	Peter's Pumpkin M-118	A. Petersen	Closed	19.00	32-64.00
84-14-129	Prudence Pie Maker M-119	A. Petersen	Closed	18.50	29-60.00
84-14-130	Witchy Boo! M-120	A. Petersen	Open	21.00	33.00
85-14-131	Pageant Wiseman M-121	A. Petersen	Closed	58.00	125-200.
85-14-132	Wise Man with Turban M-121a	A. Petersen	Open	28.00	32.00
85-14-133	Wise Man in Robe M-121b	A. Petersen	Open	26.00	31.00
85-14-134	Wise Man Kneeling M-121c	A. Petersen	Open	29.00	34.00
85-14-135	Pageant Shepherds M-122	A. Petersen	Closed	35.00	100-200.
85-14-136	Shepherd Kneeling M-122a	A. Petersen	Open	20.00	26.00
85-14-137	Shepherd Standing M-122b	A. Petersen	Open	20.00	26.00
85-14-138	Under the Chris-Mouse Tree M-123	A. Petersen	Open	48.00	71.00
85-14-139	Chris-Mouse Tree M-124	A. Petersen	Open	28.00	42.00
85-14-140	Quilting Bee M-125	W. Petersen	Open	30.00	39.00
85-14-141	Attic Treasure M-126	A. Petersen	Open	42.00	54.00
85-14-142	Family Portrait M-127	A. Petersen	Closed	54.00	225-350.
85-14-143	Strolling with Baby M-128	A. Petersen	Open	42.00	54.00
85-14-144	Piggy-Back Mousey M-129	W. Petersen	Closed	28.00	250-395.
85-14-145	Mouse Talk M-130	A. Petersen	Open	44.00	58.00
85-14-146	Come Play! M-131	A. Petersen	Closed	18.00	50-100.00
85-14-147	Sunday Drivers M-132	W. Petersen	Open	58.00	108.00
85-14-148	Field Mouse M-133	W. Petersen	Open	46.00	79.00
86-14-149	First Date M-134	W. Petersen	Open	60.00	64.00
86-14-150	Waltzing Matilda M-135	W. Petersen	Open	48.00	51.00
86-14-151	Sweet Dreams M-136	A. Petersen	Closed	58.00	100-150.
86-14-152	First Haircut M-137	W. Petersen	Closed	58.00	64-125.00
86-14-153	Fun Float M-138	W. Petersen	Open	34.00	36.00
86-14-154	Mouse on Campus M-139	W. Petersen	Closed	25.00	75-95.00
86-14-155	Just Checking M-140	A. Petersen	Open	34.00	38.00
86-14-156	Come & Get It! M-141	A. Petersen	Closed	34.00	85-125.00
86-14-157	Christ-Mouse Stocking M-142	A. Petersen	Open	34.00	38.00
86-14-158	Down the Chimney M-143	A. Petersen	Closed	48.00	200-295.
87-14-159	Pageant Stable M-144	A. Petersen	Open	56.00	65.00
87-14-160	Pageant Angel M-145	A. Petersen	Open	19.00	23.00
87-14-161	Miss Noel M-146	A. Petersen	Open	32.00	37.00
87-14-162	Choir Mouse M-147	W. Petersen	Closed	23.00	50.00
87-14-163	Tooth Fairy M-148	A. Petersen	Open	32.00	36.00
87-14-164	Don't Cry! M-149	A. Petersen	Closed	33.00	50-100.00
87-14-165	Market Mouse M-150	W. Petersen	Open	49.00	57.00
87-14-166	The Red Wagon M-151	W. Petersen	Closed	59.00	100-150.
87-14-167	Scooter Mouse M-152	W. Petersen	Open	38.00	38.00
87-14-168	Trumpeter M-153a	W. Petersen	Closed	29.00	50-90.00
87-14-169	Drummer M-153b	W. Petersen	Closed	29.00	50-90.00
87-14-170	Tuba Player M-153c	W. Petersen	Closed	29.00	50-90.00
87-14-171	Bat Mouse M-154	A. Petersen	Open	25.00	29.00
87-14-172	Littlest Witch and Skeleton M-155	A. Petersen	Open	49.00	56.00
87-14-173	Littlest Witch M-156	A. Petersen	Open	24.00	28.00
87-14-174	Skeleton Mousey M-157	A. Petersen	Open	27.00	31.00
88-14-175	Aloha! M-158	A. Petersen	Open	32.00	36.00
88-14-176	Forty Winks M-159	W. Petersen	Open	36.00	41.00
88-14-177	Mousey's Easter Basket M-160	A. Petersen	Open	32.00	36.00
89-14-178	Commencement Day M-161	W. Petersen	Open	28.00	31.00
89-14-179	Prima Ballerina M-162	A. Petersen	Open	35.00	38.00
89-14-180	Elf Tales M-163	A. Petersen	Open	48.00	49.00
89-14-181	Father Chris-Mouse M-164	A. Petersen	Open	34.00	36.00
89-14-182	Haunted Mouse House M-165	D. Petersen	Open	125.00	165.00
90-14-183	Chris-Mouse Slipper M-166	A. Petersen	Open	35.00	37.00
90-14-184	Colleen O'Green M-167	A. Petersen	Open	40.00	42.00
90-14-185	Stars & Stripes M-168	A. Petersen	Open	34.00	36.00
90-14-186	Hans & Greta M-169	A. Petersen	Closed	64.00	100-125.
90-14-187	Polly's Parasol M-170	A. Petersen	Open	39.00	42.00
90-14-188	Zelda M-171	A. Petersen	Open	37.00	41.00
91-14-189	Red Riding Hood at Grandmother's House M-172	D. Petersen	Open	295.00	295.00
91-14-190	Silent Night M-173	A. Petersen	Open	64.00	68.00
91-14-191	The Nutcracker M-174	A. Petersen	Open	49.00	52.00
91-14-192	Mousie's Egg Factory M-175	A. Petersen	Open	73.00	78.00
91-14-193	Grammy-Phone M-176	A. Petersen	Open	75.00	79.00
91-14-194	Tea For Three M-177	D. Petersen	Open	135.00	145.00
91-14-195	Night Prayer M-178	A. Petersen	Open	52.00	56.00
91-14-196	Sea Sounds M-179	A. Petersen	Open	34.00	36.00
91-14-197	April Showers M-180	A. Petersen	Open	27.00	29.00
91-14-198	Little Squirt M-181	W. Petersen	Open	49.00	51.00
92-14-199	Miss Daisy M-182	A. Petersen	Open	42.00	42.00
92-14-200	Peekaboo! M-183	A. Petersen	Open	52.00	52.00
92-14-201	Mrs. Mousey's Studio M-184	W. Petersen	Open	150.00	150.00
92-14-202	The Old Black Stove M-185	A. Petersen	Open	130.00	130.00
92-14-203	High on the Hog M-186	A. Petersen	Open	52.00	52.00
92-14-204	Adam's Apples M-187	A. Petersen	Open	148.00	148.00
92-14-205	Snow Buddies M-188	D. Petersen	Open	58.00	58.00
Wee Forest Folk		**Christmas Carol Series**			
87-15-001	Scrooge CC-1	A. Petersen	Open	23.00	29.00
87-15-002	Bob Cratchit and Tiny Tim CC-2	A. Petersen	Open	36.00	43.00
87-15-003	Marley's Ghost CC-3	A. Petersen	Open	24.00	30.00
87-15-004	Ghost of Christmas Past CC-4	A. Petersen	Open	24.00	30.00
87-15-005	Ghost of Christmas Present CC-5	A. Petersen	Open	54.00	60.00
87-15-006	Ghost of Christmas Yet to Come CC-6	A. Petersen	Open	24.00	29.00
88-15-007	The Fezziwigs CC-7	A. Petersen	Open	65.00	79.00
Wee Forest Folk		**Cinderella Series**			
88-16-001	Cinderella's Slipper C-1	A. Petersen	Closed	62.00	150-200.
89-16-002	Cinderella's Slipper C-1a	A. Petersen	Open	32.00	36.00
88-16-003	The Ugly Stepsisters C-2	A. Petersen	Open	62.00	68.00
88-16-004	The Mean Stepmother C-3	A. Petersen	Open	32.00	38.00
88-16-005	The Flower Girls C-4	A. Petersen	Open	42.00	51.00
88-16-006	Cinderella's Wedding C-5	A. Petersen	Open	62.00	72.00
88-16-007	Flower Girl C-6	A. Petersen	Open	22.00	27.00
89-16-008	The Fairy Godmother C-7	A. Petersen	Open	69.00	81.00
Wee Forest Folk		**Robin Hood Series**			
90-17-001	Robin Hood RH-1	A. Petersen	Open	37.00	39.00
90-17-002	Maid Marion RH-2	A. Petersen	Open	32.00	34.00
90-17-003	Friar Tuck RH-3	A. Petersen	Open	32.00	34.00
Wee Forest Folk		**Limited Edition**			
81-18-001	Beauty and the Beast BB-1	W. Petersen	Closed	89.00	N/A
84-18-002	Postmouster LTD-1	W. Petersen	Closed	46.00	500-750.
85-18-002	Helping Hand LTD-2	A. Petersen	Closed	62.00	500-650.
87-18-003	Statue in the Park LTD-3	W. Petersen	Closed	93.00	400-750.
88-18-004	Uncle Sammy LTD-4	A. Petersen	Closed	85.00	150-295.
Wee Forest Folk		**Minutemice**			
74-19-001	Mouse on Drum with Fife MM-1	A. Petersen	Closed	9.00	N/A
74-19-002	Mouse on Drum with Fife Wood Base MM-1a	A. Petersen	Closed	9.00	N/A
74-19-003	Mouse on Drum with Black Hat MM-2	A. Petersen	Closed	9.00	N/A
74-19-004	Mouse Carrying Large Drum MM-3	A. Petersen	Closed	8.00	N/A
74-19-005	Concordian On Drum with Glasses MM-4	A. Petersen	Closed	9.00	N/A
74-19-006	Concordian Wood Base w/Tan Coat MM-4a	A. Petersen	Closed	7.50	N/A
74-19-007	Concordian Wood Base w/Hat MM-4b	A. Petersen	Closed	8.00	N/A
74-19-008	Little Fifer on Drum with Fife MM-5	A. Petersen	Closed	8.00	N/A
74-19-009	Little Fifer on Wood Base MM-5a	A. Petersen	Closed	8.00	N/A
74-19-010	Little Fifer on Drum MM-5b	A. Petersen	Closed	8.00	N/A
79-19-011	Minute Mouse and Red Coat MM-9	W. Petersen	N/A	28.00	N/A
79-19-012	Concord Minute Mouse MM-10	W. Petersen	N/A	14.00	N/A
79-19-013	Red Coat Mouse MM-11	W. Petersen	N/A	14.00	N/A
Wee Forest Folk		**Single Issues**			
72-20-001	Party Mouse in Sailor Suit	A. Petersen	Closed	N/A	N/A
72-20-002	Party Mouse with Bow Tie	A. Petersen	Closed	N/A	N/A
72-20-003	Party Mouse in Plain Dress	A. Petersen	Closed	N/A	N/A
72-20-004	Party Mouse in Polka-Dot Dress	A. Petersen	Closed	N/A	N/A
79-20-005	Ezra Ripley	A. Petersen	N/A	40.00	N/A
79-20-006	Sarah Ripley	A. Petersen	N/A	48.00	N/A
80-20-007	Cave Mouse	W. Petersen	Closed	N/A	500-600.
80-20-008	Cave Mouse with Baby	W. Petersen	Closed	26.00	N/A
83-20-009	Wee Forest Folk Display Piece	A. Petersen	N/A	70.00	N/A

GRAPHICS

Company Number	Name	Series Artist	Edition Limit	Issue Price	Quote
American Legacy		**Etem**			
XX-01-001	Indiana Summer	S. Etem	Closed	150.00	150.00
XX-01-002	Little Bandit	S. Etem	Closed	150.00	150.00
XX-01-003	The Fountain	S. Etem	Closed	150.00	150.00
Anna-Perenna Porcelain		**Krumeich Hector's Window**			
XX-01-001	Genuine Stone Litho	T. Krumeich	325	175.00	225.00
XX-01-002	13-Color Litho, framed	T. Krumeich	995	95.00	95.00
Artaffects		**Perillo**			
77-01-001	Madre, S/N	G. Perillo	500	125.00	250-950.
78-01-002	Madonna of the Plains, S/N	G. Perillo	500	125.00	200-600.
78-01-003	Snow Pals, S/N	G. Perillo	500	125.00	150-550.
79-01-004	Sioux Scout and Buffalo Hunt, matched set	G. Perillo	500	150.00	250-850.
80-01-005	Babysitter, S/N	G. Perillo	3,000	60.00	125-350.
80-01-006	Puppies, S/N	G. Perillo	3,000	45.00	200-450.
82-01-007	Tinker, S/N	G. Perillo	3,000	45.00	100-350.
82-01-008	Tender Love, S/N	G. Perillo	950	75.00	125-450.
82-01-009	Lonesome Cowboy, S/N	G. Perillo	950	75.00	100-450.
81-01-010	Peaceable Kingdom, S/N	G. Perillo	950	100.00	375-800.
82-01-011	Chief Pontiac, S/N	G. Perillo	950	75.00	100.00
82-01-012	Hoofbeats, S/N	G. Perillo	950	100.00	150.00
82-01-013	Indian Style, S/N	G. Perillo	950	75.00	100.00
82-01-014	Maria, S/N	G. Perillo	550	150.00	350.00
83-01-015	The Moment Poster, S/N	G. Perillo	Unkn.	20.00	60.00
85-01-016	Chief Crazy Horse, S/N	G. Perillo	950	125.00	450.00
85-01-017	Chief Sitting Bull, S/N	G. Perillo	500	125.00	350.00
85-01-018	Marigold, S/N	G. Perillo	500	125.00	150-450.
85-01-019	Whirlaway, S/N	G. Perillo	950	125.00	150.00
85-01-020	Secretariat, S/N	G. Perillo	950	125.00	150.00
86-01-021	The Rescue, S/N	G. Perillo	325	150.00	200-550.
84-01-022	Out of the Forest, S/N	G. Perillo	Unkn.	Unkn.	450.00
84-01-023	Navajo Love, S/N	G. Perillo	300	125.00	700.00
86-01-024	War Pony, S/N	G. Perillo	325	150.00	250.00
86-01-025	Learning His Ways, S/N	G. Perillo	325	150.00	250.00
86-01-026	Pout, S/N	G. Perillo	325	150.00	200-450.
88-01-027	Magnificent Seven, S/N	G. Perillo	950	125.00	125.00
88-01-028	By the Stream, S/N	G. Perillo	950	100.00	150.00
90-01-029	The Pack, S/N	G. Perillo	950	150.00	250.00
Artaffects		**Sauber**			
82-02-001	Butterfly	R. Sauber	3,000	45.00	100.00
Artaffects		**Mago**			
88-03-001	Serenity	Mago	950	95.00	200.00
88-03-002	Beth	Mago	950	95.00	200.00

Number	Name	Artist	Edition Limit	Issue Price	Quote
Company		**Series**			
88-03-003	Jessica	Mago	550	225.00	325.00
88-03-004	Sebastian	Mago	Pair	Pair	Pair
Artaffects		**Deneen**			
88-04-001	Twentieth Century Limited	J. Deneen	950	75.00	75.00
88-04-002	Santa Fe	J. Deneen	950	75.00	75.00
88-04-003	Empire Builder	J. Deneen	950	75.00	75.00
Artaffects		**Grand Gallery Collection**			
88-05-001	Tender Love	G. Perillo	2,500	75.00	90.00
88-05-002	Brave & Free	G. Perillo	2,500	75.00	150.00
88-05-003	Noble Heritage	G. Perillo	2,500	75.00	90.00
88-05-004	Chief Crazy Horse	G. Perillo	2,500	75.00	90.00
88-05-005	The Cheyenne Nation	G. Perillo	2,500	75.00	90.00
88-05-006	Late Mail	G. Perillo	2,500	75.00	90.00
88-05-007	The Peaceable Kingdom	G. Perillo	2,500	75.00	100.00
88-05-008	Chief Red Cloud	G. Perillo	2,500	75.00	90.00
88-05-009	The Last Frontier	G. Perillo	2,500	75.00	90.00
88-05-010	Native American	G. Perillo	2,500	75.00	90.00
88-05-011	Blackfoot Hunter	G. Perillo	2,500	75.00	90.00
88-05-012	Lily of the Mohawks	G. Perillo	2,500	75.00	90.00
88-05-013	Amy	MaGo	2,500	75.00	90.00
88-05-014	Mischief	MaGo	2,500	75.00	90.00
88-05-015	Tomorrows	MaGo	2,500	75.00	90.00
88-05-016	Lauren	MaGo	2,500	75.00	90.00
88-05-017	Visiting the Doctor	R. Sauber	2,500	75.00	90.00
88-05-018	Home Sweet Home	R. Sauber	2,500	75.00	90.00
88-05-019	God Bless America	R. Sauber	2,500	75.00	90.00
88-05-020	The Wedding	R. Sauber	2,500	75.00	90.00
88-05-021	Motherhood	R. Sauber	2,500	75.00	90.00
88-05-022	Venice	L. Marchetti	2,500	75.00	90.00
88-05-023	Paris	L. Marchetti	2,500	75.00	90.00
Art World of Bourgeault		**Royal Literary Series**			
89-01-001	John Bunyan Cottage	R. Bourgeault	Unkn.	75.00	175.00
89-01-002	Thomas Hardy Cottage	R. Bourgeault	Unkn.	75.00	175.00
89-01-003	John Milton Cottage	R. Bourgeault	Unkn.	75.00	175.00
89-01-004	Anne Hathaway Cottage	R. Bourgeault	Unkn.	75.00	175.00
Art World of Bourgeault		**The English Countryside Handtouched**			
89-02-001	The Country Squire	R. Bourgeault	550	75.00	475.00
Marty Bell		**Limited Edition Lithographs**			
87-01-001	Alderton Village	M. Bell	500	264.00	450-899.
90-01-002	Arbor Cottage	M. Bell	900	130.00	150-250.
91-01-003	Bay Tree Cottage, Rye	M. Bell	1,100	230.00	430-520.
82-01-004	Bibury Cottage	M. Bell	900	290.00	800-1489.
82-01-005	Big Daddy's Shoe	M. Bell	900	64.00	120-300.
88-01-006	Bishop's Roses, The	M. Bell	2,400	220.00	295-499.
89-01-007	Blush of Spring	M. Bell	1,200	96.00	120-160.
88-01-008	Bodiam Twilight	M. Bell	900	128.00	200-900.
87-01-009	Broughton Village	M. Bell	900	128.00	158-499.
90-01-010	Bryants Puddle Thatch	M. Bell	900	130.00	150-295.
86-01-011	Burford Village Store	M. Bell	500	120.00	400-999.
82-01-012	Castle Combe Cottage	M. Bell	500	264.00	395-1200.
91-01-013	Christmas in Rochester	M. Bell	900	148.00	250-350.
87-01-014	Chaplains Garden, The	M. Bell	500	264.00	1000-2200.
87-01-015	Chippenham Farm	M. Bell	500	120.00	300-900.
88-01-016	Clove Cottage	M. Bell	900	128.00	220-800.
88-01-017	Clover Lane Cottage	M. Bell	1,800	272.00	595-1400.
86-01-018	Cotswold Parish Church	M. Bell	1,800	98.00	500-2000.
88-01-019	Cotswold Twilight	M. Bell	900	128.00	200-495.
82-01-020	Crossroads Cottage	M. Bell	900	38.00	200.00
85-01-021	Devon Roses	M. Bell	1,200	78.00	300-799.
91-01-022	Dorset Roses	M. Bell	1,200	96.00	96.00
87-01-023	Dove Cottage Garden	M. Bell	900	272.00	304-495.
87-01-024	Driftstone Manor	M. Bell	500	440.00	2200-3950.
87-01-025	Ducksbridge Cottage	M. Bell	500	430.00	1200-2500.
87-01-026	Eashing Cottage	M. Bell	900	128.00	190-350.
85-01-027	Fiddleford Cottage	M. Bell	500	78.00	500-1950.
89-01-028	Fireside Christmas	M. Bell	500	136.00	195-599.
89-01-029	The Game Keeper's Cottage	M. Bell	900	560.00	750-2000.
88-01-030	Ginger Cottage	M. Bell	1,800	320.00	450-800.
90-01-031	Goater's Cottage	M. Bell	900	368.00	395-560.
90-01-032	Gomshall Flower Shop	M. Bell	900	396.00	950-1800.
87-01-033	Halfway Cottage	M. Bell	900	272.00	272-799.
86-01-034	Housewives Choice	M. Bell	500	98.00	400-999.
88-01-035	Icomb Village Garden	M. Bell	2,400	620.00	699-1799.
88-01-036	Jasmine Thatch	M. Bell	900	272.00	315-610.
89-01-037	Larkspur Cottage	M. Bell	2,400	220.00	295-450.
85-01-038	Little Boxford	M. Bell	500	78.00	300-900.
87-01-039	Little Tulip Thatch	M. Bell	500	120.00	400-700.
90-01-040	Little Well Thatch	M. Bell	900	130.00	150-250.
90-01-041	Longparrish Cottage	M. Bell	900	130.00	250.00
90-01-042	Longstock Lane	M. Bell	900	130.00	150-250.
86-01-043	Lorna Doone Cottage	M. Bell	500	380.00	1800-8400.
90-01-044	Lower Brockhampton Manor	M. Bell	900	730.00	850-1800.
88-01-045	Lullabye Cottage	M. Bell	2,400	220.00	250-350.
87-01-046	May Cottage	M. Bell	900	128.00	200-699.
85-01-047	Meadowlark Cottage	M. Bell	500	78.00	450-699.
87-01-048	The Millpond, Stockbridge	M. Bell	500	120.00	1000-1699.
87-01-049	Morning Glory Cottage	M. Bell	500	120.00	400-599.
88-01-050	Morning's Glow	M. Bell	1,800	280.00	320-650.
88-01-051	Murrle Cottage	M. Bell	1,800	320.00	450-999.
83-01-052	Nestlewood	M. Bell	500	325.00	1700-4950.
89-01-053	Old Beams Cottage	M. Bell	900	368.00	700.00
90-01-054	Old Hertfordshire Thatch	M. Bell	900	396.00	550-1500.
84-01-055	Penshurst Tea Rooms (Archival)	M. Bell	500	335.00	795-2800.
84-01-056	Penshurst Tea Rooms (Canvas)	M. Bell	1,000	335.00	1200-4950.
89-01-057	Pride of Spring	M. Bell	500	96.00	120-225.
90-01-058	Ready For Christmas	M. Bell	500	148.00	195-1049.
88-01-059	Rodway Cottage	M. Bell	2,400	620.00	700-1799.
88-01-060	Shere Village Antiques	M. Bell	900	272.00	304-699.
91-01-061	Springtime at Scotney	M. Bell	900	730.00	400-1200.
90-01-062	Summer's Garden	M. Bell	900	78.00	350-799.
85-01-063	Summers Glow	M. Bell	500	98.00	750-999.
87-01-064	Sunrise Thatch	M. Bell	900	128.00	158-299.
85-01-065	Surrey Garden House	M. Bell	500	98.00	850-1499.
85-01-066	Sweet Pine Cottage	M. Bell	500	78.00	350-1499.
88-01-067	Sweet Twilight	M. Bell	2,400	220.00	250-600.
91-01-068	Tea Time	M. Bell	900	130.00	350-799.
91-01-069	Upper Chute	M. Bell	900	496.00	350-1400.
87-01-070	The Vicar's Gate	M. Bell	500	110.00	250-899.

Number	Name	Artist	Edition Limit	Issue Price	Quote
Company		**Series**			
87-01-071	Wakehurst Place	M. Bell	900	520.00	1400-2700.
87-01-072	Well Cottage, Sandy Lane	M. Bell	500	440.00	650-1600.
84-01-073	West Kington Dell	M. Bell	500	240.00	480-999.
87-01-074	White Lilac Thatch	M. Bell	900	272.00	304-699.
85-01-075	Windsong Cottage	M. Bell	500	78.00	350-799.
85-01-076	Windward Cottage, Rye	M. Bell	1,200	228.00	550-620.
86-01-077	York Garden Shop	M. Bell	500	110.00	250-999.
Marty Bell		**Members Only Collectors Club**			
91-02-001	Little Thatch Twilight	M. Bell	Yr.Iss.	288.00	320-380.
92-02-002	Candle At Eventide	M. Bell	Yr.Iss.	Gift	N/A
92-02-003	Blossom Lane	M. Bell	Yr.Iss.	288.00	288.00
Circle Fine Art		**Rockwell**			
XX-01-001	Spelling Bee	N. Rockwell	200	Unkn.	6500.00
XX-01-002	Circus	N. Rockwell	200	Unkn.	2650.00
XX-01-003	Doctor and Boy	N. Rockwell	200	Unkn.	9400.00
XX-01-004	Rocket Ship	N. Rockwell	200	Unkn.	3650.00
XX-01-005	Welcome	N. Rockwell	200	Unkn.	3500.00
XX-01-006	Blacksmith Shop	N. Rockwell	200	Unkn.	6300.00
XX-01-007	Jerry	N. Rockwell	200	Unkn.	4700.00
XX-01-008	Family Tree	N. Rockwell	200	Unkn.	5900.00
XX-01-009	The House	N. Rockwell	200	Unkn.	3700.00
XX-01-010	The Homecoming	N. Rockwell	200	Unkn.	3700.00
XX-01-011	The Bridge	N. Rockwell	200	Unkn.	3100.00
XX-01-012	Top of the World	N. Rockwell	200	Unkn.	4200.00
XX-01-013	Aviary	N. Rockwell	200	Unkn.	4200.00
XX-01-014	Barbershop Quartet	N. Rockwell	200	Unkn.	4200.00
XX-01-015	Window Washer	N. Rockwell	200	Unkn.	4800.00
XX-01-016	Outward Bound-Signed	N. Rockwell	200	Unkn.	7900.00
XX-01-017	Shuffelton's Barbershop	N. Rockwell	200	Unkn.	7400.00
XX-01-018	Doctor and Doll-Signed	N. Rockwell	200	Unkn.	11900.00
XX-01-019	Saying Grace-Signed	N. Rockwell	200	Unkn.	7400.00
XX-01-020	Golden Rule-Signed	N. Rockwell	200	Unkn.	4400.00
XX-01-021	Girl at Mirror-Signed	N. Rockwell	200	Unkn.	8400.00
XX-01-022	Freedom from Fear-Signed	N. Rockwell	200	Unkn.	6400.00
XX-01-023	Freedom from Want-Signed	N. Rockwell	200	Unkn.	6400.00
XX-01-024	Freedom of Speech-Signed	N. Rockwell	200	Unkn.	6400.00
XX-01-025	Freedom of Religion-Signed	N. Rockwell	200	Unkn.	6400.00
XX-01-026	Spring Flowers	N. Rockwell	200	Unkn.	5200.00
XX-01-027	Runaway	N. Rockwell	200	Unkn.	5700.00
XX-01-028	The Critic	N. Rockwell	200	Unkn.	4650.00
XX-01-029	Discovery	N. Rockwell	200	Unkn.	5900.00
XX-01-030	Raliegh the Dog	N. Rockwell	200	Unkn.	3900.00
XX-01-031	Marriage License	N. Rockwell	200	Unkn.	6900.00
XX-01-032	Church/Collotype	N. Rockwell	200	Unkn.	4000.00
XX-01-033	Smoking/Collotype	N. Rockwell	200	Unkn.	4000.00
XX-01-034	Cat/Collotype	N. Rockwell	200	Unkn.	4000.00
XX-01-035	Out the Window/ Collotype	N. Rockwell	200	Unkn.	4000.00
XX-01-036	Whitewashing the Fence/Collotype	N. Rockwell	200	Unkn.	4000.00
XX-01-037	Grotto/Collotype	N. Rockwell	200	Unkn.	4000.00
XX-01-038	Spanking/ Collotype	N. Rockwell	200	Unkn.	4000.00
XX-01-039	Saturday People	N. Rockwell	200	Unkn.	3300.00
XX-01-040	Moving Day	N. Rockwell	200	Unkn.	3900.00
XX-01-041	County Agricultural Agent	N. Rockwell	200	Unkn.	3900.00
XX-01-042	Gaiety Dance Team	N. Rockwell	200	Unkn.	4300.00
XX-01-043	Music Hath Charms	N. Rockwell	200	Unkn.	4200.00
XX-01-044	High Dive	N. Rockwell	200	Unkn.	3400.00
XX-01-045	The Texan	N. Rockwell	200	Unkn.	3700.00
XX-01-046	Wet Paint	N. Rockwell	200	Unkn.	3800.00
XX-01-047	The Problem We All Live With	N. Rockwell	200	Unkn.	4500.00
XX-01-048	Football Mascot	N. Rockwell	200	Unkn.	3700.00
XX-01-049	Dressing Up/Pencil	N. Rockwell	200	Unkn.	3700.00
XX-01-050	Dressing Up/Ink	N. Rockwell	60	Unkn.	4400.00
XX-01-051	Children at Window	N. Rockwell	200	Unkn.	3600.00
XX-01-052	Puppies	N. Rockwell	200	Unkn.	3700.00
XX-01-053	Settling In	N. Rockwell	200	Unkn.	3600.00
XX-01-054	The Big Top	N. Rockwell	148	Unkn.	2800.00
XX-01-055	The Inventor	N. Rockwell	200	Unkn.	4100.00
XX-01-056	Three Farmers	N. Rockwell	200	Unkn.	3600.00
XX-01-057	Medicine/Color Litho	N. Rockwell	200	Unkn.	4000.00
XX-01-058	Study for the Doctor's Office	N. Rockwell	200	Unkn.	6000.00
XX-01-059	Lincoln	N. Rockwell	200	Unkn.	11400.00
XX-01-060	Ichabod Crane	N. Rockwell	200	Unkn.	6700.00
XX-01-061	At the Barber	N. Rockwell	200	Unkn.	4900.00
XX-01-062	The Expected and Unexpected	N. Rockwell	200	Unkn.	3700.00
XX-01-063	The Big Day	N. Rockwell	200	Unkn.	3400.00
XX-01-064	Safe and Sound	N. Rockwell	200	Unkn.	3800.00
XX-01-065	Summer Stock	N. Rockwell	200	Unkn.	4900.00
XX-01-066	Summer Stock/Japon	N. Rockwell	25	Unkn.	5000.00
XX-01-067	Bookseller	N. Rockwell	200	Unkn.	2700.00
XX-01-068	Bookseller/Japon	N. Rockwell	25	Unkn.	2750.00
XX-01-069	The Teacher	N. Rockwell	200	Unkn.	3400.00
XX-01-070	The Teacher/Japon	N. Rockwell	25	Unkn.	3500.00
XX-01-071	A Day in the Life of a Boy	N. Rockwell	200	Unkn.	6200.00
XX-01-072	Day in the Life of a Boy/Japon	N. Rockwell	25	Unkn.	6500.00
XX-01-073	Trumpeter	N. Rockwell	200	Unkn.	3900.00
XX-01-074	Trumpeter/Japon	N. Rockwell	25	Unkn.	4100.00
XX-01-075	Ticketseller	N. Rockwell	200	Unkn.	4200.00
XX-01-076	Ticketseller/Japon	N. Rockwell	25	Unkn.	4400.00
XX-01-077	Prescription	N. Rockwell	200	Unkn.	4900.00
XX-01-078	Prescription/Japon	N. Rockwell	25	Unkn.	5000.00
XX-01-079	See America First	N. Rockwell	200	Unkn.	5650.00
XX-01-080	See America First/Japon	N. Rockwell	25	Unkn.	6100.00
XX-01-081	The Schoolhouse	N. Rockwell	200	Unkn.	4500.00
XX-01-082	Schoolhouse/Japon	N. Rockwell	25	Unkn.	4650.00
XX-01-083	Lobsterman	N. Rockwell	200	Unkn.	5500.00
XX-01-084	Lobsterman/Japon	N. Rockwell	25	Unkn.	5750.00
XX-01-085	Gossips	N. Rockwell	200	Unkn.	5000.00
XX-01-086	Gossips/Japon	N. Rockwell	25	Unkn.	5100.00
XX-01-087	Runaway	N. Rockwell	200	Unkn.	3800.00
XX-01-088	The Artist at Work	N. Rockwell	130	Unkn.	3500.00
XX-01-089	Tom Sawyer Folio	N. Rockwell	200	Unkn.	26500.00
XX-01-090	Church	N. Rockwell	200	Unkn.	3400.00
XX-01-091	Smoking	N. Rockwell	200	Unkn.	3400.00
XX-01-092	Cat	N. Rockwell	200	Unkn.	3400.00
XX-01-093	Out the Window	N. Rockwell	200	Unkn.	3400.00
XX-01-094	White Washing	N. Rockwell	200	Unkn.	3400.00
XX-01-095	Grotto	N. Rockwell	200	Unkn.	3400.00
XX-01-096	Spanking	N. Rockwell	200	Unkn.	3400.00
XX-01-097	Medicine	N. Rockwell	200	Unkn.	3400.00
XX-01-098	Huck Finn Folio	N. Rockwell	200	Unkn.	35000.00
XX-01-099	Then Miss Watson	N. Rockwell	200	Unkn.	4500.00

Company / Number	Name	Series / Artist	Edition Limit	Issue Price	Quote
XX-01-100	Jim Got Down on His Knees	N. Rockwell	200	Unkn.	4500.00
XX-01-101	Miss Mary Jane	N. Rockwell	200	Unkn.	4500.00
XX-01-102	My Hand Shook	N. Rockwell	200	Unkn.	4500.00
XX-01-103	Your Eyes is Lookin'	N. Rockwell	200	Unkn.	4500.00
XX-01-104	Then For Three Minutes	N. Rockwell	200	Unkn.	4500.00
XX-01-105	There Warn't No Harm	N. Rockwell	200	Unkn.	4500.00
XX-01-106	When I Lit My Candle	N. Rockwell	200	Unkn.	4500.00
XX-01-107	Tom Sawyer Color Suite	N. Rockwell	200	Unkn.	30000.00
XX-01-108	American Family Folio	N. Rockwell	200	Unkn.	17500.00
XX-01-109	Teacher's Pet	N. Rockwell	200	Unkn.	3600.00
XX-01-110	Fido's House	N. Rockwell	200	Unkn.	3600.00
XX-01-111	Two O'Clock Feeding	N. Rockwell	200	Unkn.	3600.00
XX-01-112	Debut	N. Rockwell	200	Unkn.	3600.00
XX-01-113	Save Me	N. Rockwell	200	Unkn.	3600.00
XX-01-114	School Days Folio	N. Rockwell	200	Unkn.	14000.00
XX-01-115	Baseball	N. Rockwell	200	Unkn.	3600.00
XX-01-116	Golf	N. Rockwell	200	Unkn.	3600.00
XX-01-117	Studying	N. Rockwell	200	Unkn.	3600.00
XX-01-118	Cheering	N. Rockwell	200	Unkn.	3600.00
XX-01-119	Poor Richard's Almanac	N. Rockwell	200	Unkn.	24000.00
XX-01-120	Ben Franklin's Philadelphia	N. Rockwell	200	Unkn.	3600.00
XX-01-121	The Drunkard	N. Rockwell	200	Unkn.	3600.00
XX-01-122	Ben's Belles	N. Rockwell	200	Unkn.	3500.00
XX-01-123	The Village Smithy	N. Rockwell	200	Unkn.	3500.00
XX-01-124	Ye Old Print Shoppe	N. Rockwell	200	Unkn.	3500.00
XX-01-125	The Golden Age	N. Rockwell	200	Unkn.	3500.00
XX-01-126	The Royal Crown	N. Rockwell	200	Unkn.	3500.00
XX-01-127	Four Seasons Folio	N. Rockwell	200	Unkn.	13500.00
XX-01-128	Winter	N. Rockwell	200	Unkn.	3500.00
XX-01-129	Spring	N. Rockwell	200	Unkn.	3500.00
XX-01-130	Summer	N. Rockwell	200	Unkn.	3500.00
XX-01-131	Autumn	N. Rockwell	200	Unkn.	3500.00
XX-01-132	Four Seasons Folio/Japon	N. Rockwell	25	Unkn.	14000.00
XX-01-133	Winter/Japon	N. Rockwell	25	Unkn.	3600.00
XX-01-134	Spring/Japon	N. Rockwell	25	Unkn.	3600.00
XX-01-135	Summer/Japon	N. Rockwell	25	Unkn.	3600.00
XX-01-136	Autumn/Japon	N. Rockwell	25	Unkn.	3600.00
Cross Gallery, Inc.		**Limited Edition Prints**			
83-01-001	Isbaaloo Eetshiileehcheek(Sorting Her Beads)	P.A. Cross	S/O	150.00	1750.00
83-01-002	Ayla-Sah-Xuh-Xah (Pretty Colours, Many Designs)	P.A. Cross	S/O	150.00	450.00
84-01-003	Blue Beaded Hair Ties	P.A. Cross	S/O	85.00	330.00
84-01-004	Profile of Caroline	P.A. Cross	S/O	85.00	185.00
84-01-005	Whistling Water Clan Girl: Crow Indian	P.A. Cross	S/O	85.00	85.00
84-01-006	Thick Lodge Clan Boy: Crow Indian	P.A. Cross	475	85.00	85.00
85-01-007	The Water Vision	P.A. Cross	S/O	150.00	325.00
86-01-008	The Winter Shawl	P.A. Cross	S/O	150.00	1600.00
86-01-009	The Red Capote	P.A. Cross	S/O	150.00	850.00
86-01-010	Grand Entry	P.A. Cross	S/O	85.00	85.00
84-01-011	Winter Morning	P.A. Cross	S/O	185.00	1450.00
84-01-012	Dii-tah-shteh Ee-wihza-ahook (A Coat of much Value)	P.A. Cross	S/O	90.00	740.00
87-01-013	Caroline	P.A. Cross	S/O	45.00	145.00
87-01-014	Tina	P.A. Cross	S/O	45.00	110.00
87-01-015	The Red Necklace	P.A. Cross	S/O	90.00	210.00
87-01-016	The Elkskin Robe	P.A. Cross	S/O	190.00	640.00
88-01-017	Ma-a-luppis-she-La-dus (She is above everything, nothing can touch her)	P.A. Cross	S/O	190.00	525.00
88-01-018	Dance Apache	P.A. Cross	S/O	190.00	360.00
89-01-019	The Dreamer	P.A. Cross	S/O	190.00	600.00
89-01-020	Chey-ayjeh: Prey	P.A. Cross	S/O	190.00	600.00
89-01-021	Teesa Waits To Dance	P.A. Cross	S/O	135.00	180.00
89-01-022	B' Achua Dlubh-bia Bii Noskiiyahi The Gift, Part II	P.A. Cross	S/O	225.00	650.00
89-01-023	Biaachee-itah Bah-achbeh	P.A. Cross	S/O	225.00	525.00
90-01-024	Baape Ochia (Night Wind, Turquoise)	P.A. Cross	S/O	185.00	185.00
90-01-025	Ishia-Kahda #1 (Quiet One)	P.A. Cross	S/O	185.00	185.00
90-01-026	Eshte	P.A. Cross	S/O	185.00	185.00
91-01-027	The Blue Shawl	P.A. Cross	S/O	185.00	185.00
91-01-028	Ashphadua Hagay Ashae-Gyoke (My Home & Heart Is Crow)	P.A. Cross	S/O	225.00	225-350.
Cross Gallery, Inc		**Star Quilt Series**			
85-02-001	Winter Warmth	P.A. Cross	S/O	150.00	900-1215.
86-02-002	Reflections	P.A. Cross	S/O	185.00	865.00
88-02-003	The Quilt Makers	P.A. Cross	S/O	190.00	1200.00
Cross Gallery, Inc.		**Wolf Series**			
85-03-001	Dii-tah-shteh Bii-wik; Chedah-bah liidah	P.A. Cross	S/O	185.00	3275.00
87-03-002	The Morning Star Gives Long Otter His Hoop Medicine Power	P.A. Cross	S/O	190.00	1800-2500.
89-03-003	Biagoht Eecuebeh Hehsheesh-Checah: (Red Ridinghood and Her Wolves)	P.A. Cross	S/O	225.00	1500-2500.
90-03-004	Agnjnaug Amaguut;Inupiag (Women With Her Wolves)	P.A. Cross	1,050	325.00	325-750.
Cross Gallery, Inc.		**Half Breed Series**			
89-04-001	Ach-hua Dlubh: (Body Two), Half Breed	P.A. Cross	S/O	190.00	1450.00
89-04-002	Ach-hua Dlubh: (Body Two), Half Breed II	P.A. Cross	S/O	225.00	1100.00
90-04-003	Ach-hua Dlubh: (Body Two), Half Breed III	P.A. Cross	S/O	225.00	850.00
Cross Gallery, Inc.		**Limited Edition Original Graphics**			
87-05-001	Caroline, Stone Lithograph	P.A. Cross	S/O	300.00	600.00
88-05-002	Maidenhood Hopi, Stone Lithograph	P.A. Cross	S/O	950.00	1150.00
89-05-003	The Red Capote, Serigraph	P.A. Cross	275	750.00	1150.00
89-05-004	Rosapina, Etching	P.A. Cross	74	1200.00	1200.00
90-05-005	Nighteyes, I, Serigraph	P.A. Cross	275	225.00	425.00
Cross Gallery, Inc.		**Miniature Line**			
91-06-001	BJ	P.A. Cross	447	80.00	80.00
91-06-002	Watercolour Study #2 For Half Breed	P.A. Cross	447	80.00	80.00
91-06-003	The Floral Shawl	P.A. Cross	447	80.00	80.00
91-06-004	Kendra	P.A. Cross	447	80.00	80.00
Cross Gallery, Inc.		**The Painted Ladies' Suite**			
92-07-001	The Painted Ladies	P.A. Cross	475	225.00	225.00
92-07-002	Avisola	P.A. Cross	475	185.00	185.00
92-07-003	Itza-chu (Apache; The Eagle)	P.A. Cross	475	185.00	185.00
92-07-004	Kel'hoya (Hopi; Little Sparrow Hawk)	P.A. Cross	475	185.00	185.00
92-07-005	Dah-say (Crow; Heart)	P.A. Cross	475	185.00	185.00
92-07-006	Tze-go-juni (Chiricahua Apache)	P.A. Cross	447	80.00	80.00

Company / Number	Name	Series / Artist	Edition Limit	Issue Price	Quote
92-07-007	Sus(h)gah-daydus(h) (Crow; Quick)	P.A. Cross	447	80.00	80.00
92-07-008	Acoria (Crow; Seat of Honor)	P.A. Cross	447	80.00	80.00
Gartlan USA		**Lithograph**			
86-01-001	George Brett-"The Swing"	J. Martin	2,000	150.00	150.00
87-01-002	Roger Staubach	C. Soileau	1,979	125.00	125.00
89-01-003	Kareem Abdul Jabbar-The Record Setter	M. Taylor	1,989	175.00	175-225.
90-01-004	Darryl Strawberry	M. Taylor	500	295.00	295.00
91-01-005	Darryl Strawberry, signed Artist Proof	M. Taylor	50	395.00	395.00
91-01-006	Joe Montana	M. Taylor	500	495.00	495.00
92-01-007	Isiah Thomas	M. Taylor	500	395.00	395.00
Graphics Buying Service		**Stone**			
79-01-001	Mare and Foal	F. Stone	500	90.00	500.00
79-01-002	Affirmed, Steve Cauthen Up	F. Stone	750	100.00	600.00
79-01-003	The Rivals-Affirmed & Alydar	F. Stone	500	90.00	500.00
79-01-004	Patience	F. Stone	1,000	90.00	1200.00
79-01-005	One, Two, Three	F. Stone	500	100.00	1000.00
79-01-006	The Moment After	F. Stone	500	90.00	350.00
80-01-007	Genuine Risk	F. Stone	500	100.00	700.00
80-01-008	The Belmont-Bold Forbes	F. Stone	500	100.00	375.00
80-01-009	The Kentucky Derby	F. Stone	750	100.00	650.00
80-01-010	The Pasture Pest	F. Stone	500	100.00	875.00
80-01-011	Exceller-Bill Shoemaker	F. Stone	500	90.00	800.00
80-01-012	Spectacular Bid	F. Stone	500	65.00	350-400.
80-01-013	Kidnapped Mare-Franfreluche	F. Stone	750	115.00	575.00
81-01-014	The Shoe-8,000 Wins	F. Stone	395	200.00	7000.00
81-01-015	The Arabians	F. Stone	750	115.00	525.00
81-01-016	The Thoroughbreds	F. Stone	750	115.00	425.00
81-01-017	Contentment	F. Stone	750	115.00	525.00
81-01-018	John Henry-Bill Shoemaker Up	F. Stone	595	160.00	1500.00
82-01-019	Off and Running	F. Stone	750	125.00	250-350.
82-01-020	The Water Trough	F. Stone	750	125.00	575.00
82-01-021	The Power Horses	F. Stone	750	125.00	250.00
82-01-022	Man O'War "Final Thunder"	F. Stone	750	175.00	3100.00
83-01-023	The Duel	F. Stone	750	150.00	400.00
83-01-024	The Andalusian	F. Stone	750	150.00	350.00
83-01-025	Tranquility	F. Stone	750	150.00	525.00
83-01-026	Secretariat	F. Stone	950	175.00	750-1200.
83-01-027	Ruffian-For Only a Moment	F. Stone	750	175.00	1100.00
84-01-028	Turning For Home	F. Stone	750	150.00	425.00
84-01-029	Northern Dancer	F. Stone	950	175.00	625.00
85-01-030	John Henry-McCarron Up	F. Stone	750	175.00	500-750.
85-01-031	Eternal Legacy	F. Stone	950	175.00	950.00
85-01-032	Fred Stone Paints the Sport of Kings	F. Stone	750	265.00	750.00
85-01-033	Kelso	F. Stone	950	175.00	750.00
86-01-034	Ruffian & Foolish Pleasure	F. Stone	950	175.00	375.00
86-01-035	Nijinski II	F. Stone	950	175.00	275.00
86-01-036	Forever Friends	F. Stone	950	175.00	725.00
87-01-037	Lady's Secret	F. Stone	950	175.00	425.00
87-01-038	The First Day	F. Stone	950	175.00	225.00
87-01-039	The Rivalry-Alysheba and Bet Twice	F. Stone	950	195.00	550.00
88-01-040	Alysheba	F. Stone	950	195.00	650.00
88-01-041	Cam-Fella	F. Stone	950	175.00	350.00
89-01-042	Shoe Bald Eagle	F. Stone	950	195.00	675.00
89-01-043	Phar Lap	F. Stone	950	195.00	275.00
89-01-044	Battle For The Triple Crown	F. Stone	950	225.00	650.00
90-01-045	Final Tribute- Secretariat	F. Stone	1,150	265.00	1300.00
90-01-046	Old Warriors Shoemaker-John Henry	F. Stone	1,950	265.00	595.00
91-01-047	Black Stallion	F. Stone	1,500	225.00	250.00
91-01-048	Forego	F. Stone	1,150	225.00	250.00
91-01-049	Go For Wand-A Candle in the Wind	F. Stone	1,150	225.00	225.00
92-01-050	Dance Smartly	F. Stone	950	225.00	325.00
Greenwich Workshop		**Doolittle**			
80-01-001	Bugged Bear	B. Doolittle	1,000	85.00	3000-3800.
83-01-002	Christmas Day, Give or Take a Week	B. Doolittle	4,581	80.00	1950-2500.
82-01-003	Eagle's Flight	B. Doolittle	1,500	185.00	3000-5000.
83-01-004	Escape by a Hare	B. Doolittle	1,500	80.00	950-1100.
84-01-005	Forest Has Eyes, The	B. Doolittle	8,544	175.00	3800-5200.
80-01-006	Good Omen, The	B. Doolittle	1,000	85.00	3500-5000.
87-01-007	Guardian Spirits	B. Doolittle	13,238	295.00	1200-1700.
84-01-008	Let My Spirit Soar	B. Doolittle	1,500	195.00	3600-5000.
79-01-009	Pintos	B. Doolittle	1,000	65.00	10-12000.00
83-01-010	Runs With Thunder	B. Doolittle	1,500	150.00	1800-2400.
83-01-011	Rushing War Eagle	B. Doolittle	1,500	150.00	1500-2000.
81-01-012	Spirit of the Grizzly	B. Doolittle	1,500	150.00	3700-4600.
86-01-013	Two Bears of the Blackfeet	B. Doolittle	2,650	225.00	1100-1850.
85-01-014	Two Indian Horses	B. Doolittle	12,253	225.00	3000-4700.
81-01-015	Unknown Presence	B. Doolittle	1,500	150.00	3000-4000.
86-01-016	Where Silence Speaks, Doolittle The Art of Bev Doolittle	B. Doolittle	3,500	650.00	3500-4200.
80-01-017	Whoo !?	B. Doolittle	1,000	75.00	1600-1800.
85-01-018	Wolves of the Crow	B. Doolittle	2,650	225.00	1900-2900.
81-01-019	Woodland Encounter	B. Doolittle	1,500	145.00	9000-11000.
87-01-020	Calling the Buffalo	B. Doolittle	8,500	245.00	1100-1700.
87-01-021	Season of the Eagle	B. Doolittle	36,548	245.00	675-1000.
88-01-022	Doubled Back	B. Doolittle	15,000	245.00	1350-1900.
89-01-023	Sacred Ground	B. Doolittle	69,996	265.00	700-1200.
90-01-024	Hide and Seek Suite	B. Doolittle	25,000	1200.00	1200.00
91-01-025	The Sentinel	B. Doolittle	35,000	275.00	700-1200.
91-01-026	Sacred Circle (PC)	B. Doolittle	40,192	325.00	480-750.
Greenwich Workshop		**McCarthy**			
80-02-001	A Time Of Decision	F. McCarthy	1,150	125.00	250.00
77-02-002	An Old Time Mountain Man	F. McCarthy	1,000	65.00	275.00
84-02-003	After the Dust Storm	F. McCarthy	1,000	145.00	165.00
82-02-004	Alert	F. McCarthy	1,000	135.00	160.00
84-02-005	Along the West Fork	F. McCarthy	1,000	175.00	225-285.
78-02-006	Ambush, The	F. McCarthy	1,000	125.00	300-345.
82-02-007	Apache Scout	F. McCarthy	1,000	165.00	175-190.
88-02-008	Apache Trackers (C)	F. McCarthy	1,000	95.00	135-150.
82-02-009	Attack on the Wagon Train	F. McCarthy	1,400	150.00	220-395.
77-02-010	The Beaver Men	F. McCarthy	1,000	75.00	500-710.
80-02-011	Before the Charge	F. McCarthy	1,000	115.00	200-400.
78-02-012	Before the Norther	F. McCarthy	1,000	90.00	400-525.
90-02-013	Below The Breaking Dawn	F. McCarthy	1,250	225.00	185-225.
89-02-014	Big Medicine	F. McCarthy	1,000	225.00	375-425.
83-02-015	Blackfoot Raiders	F. McCarthy	1,000	90.00	250.00
86-02-016	The Buffalo Runners	F. McCarthy	1,000	195.00	195-250.
83-02-017	Burning the Way Station	F. McCarthy	1,000	175.00	375-500.
89-02-018	Canyon Lands	F. McCarthy	1,250	225.00	235.00
82-02-019	Challenge, The	F. McCarthy	1,000	175.00	425.00

Number	Name	Artist	Edition Limit	Issue Price	Quote
85-02-020	Charging the Challenger	F. McCarthy	1,000	150.00	200-300.
86-02-021	Children of the Raven	F. McCarthy	1,000	185.00	185-600.
87-02-022	Chiricahua Raiders	F. McCarthy	1,000	165.00	165-275.
77-02-023	Comanche Moon	F. McCarthy	1,000	75.00	250.00
86-02-024	Comanche War Trail	F. McCarthy	1,000	165.00	165-225.
89-02-025	The Coming Of The Iron Horse	F. McCarthy	1,500	225.00	225-375.
89-02-026	The Coming Of The Iron Horse (Print/Pewter Train Special Publ. Ed.)	F. McCarthy	100	1500.00	1650-2150.
81-02-027	The Coup	F. McCarthy	1,000	125.00	375-450.
81-02-028	Crossing the Divide/The Old West	F. McCarthy	1,500	850.00	900-1250.
84-02-029	The Decoys	F. McCarthy	450	325.00	500.00
77-02-030	Distant Thunder	F. McCarthy	1,500	75.00	650-900.
89-02-031	Down From The Mountains	F. McCarthy	1,500	245.00	245-290.
86-02-032	The Drive (C)	F. McCarthy	1,000	95.00	95-175.
77-02-033	Dust Stained Posse	F. McCarthy	1,000	75.00	675-915.
85-02-034	The Fireboat	F. McCarthy	1,000	175.00	200.00
87-02-035	Following the Herds	F. McCarthy	1,000	195.00	250-300.
80-02-036	Forbidden Land	F. McCarthy	1,000	125.00	225.00
78-02-037	The Fording	F. McCarthy	1,000	75.00	300-360.
87-02-038	From the Rim	F. McCarthy	1,000	225.00	225-310.
81-02-039	Headed North	F. McCarthy	1,000	150.00	225-275.
90-02-040	Hoka Hey: Sioux War Cry	F. McCarthy	1,250	225.00	225.00
88-02-041	The Hostile Land	F. McCarthy	1,000	225.00	235.00
76-02-042	The Hostiles	F. McCarthy	1,000	75.00	600.00
74-02-043	The Hunt	F. McCarthy	1,000	75.00	620-930.
88-02-044	In Pursuit of the White Buffalo	F. McCarthy	1,500	225.00	420-450.
83-02-045	In The Land Of The Sparrow Hawk People	F. McCarthy	1,000	165.00	180.00
87-02-046	In The Land Of The Winter Hawk	F. McCarthy	1,000	225.00	350-525.
78-02-047	In The Pass	F. McCarthy	1,500	90.00	200.00
85-02-048	The Last Crossing	F. McCarthy	550	350.00	450-500.
88-02-049	The Last Stand: Little Big Horn	F. McCarthy	2,250	225.00	225-250.
74-02-050	Lone Sentinel	F. McCarthy	1,000	55.00	1465-1800.
79-02-051	The Loner	F. McCarthy	1,000	75.00	400-600.
74-02-052	Long Column	F. McCarthy	1,000	75.00	750-1250.
85-02-053	The Long Knives	F. McCarthy	1,000	175.00	250-275.
89-02-054	Los Diablos	F. McCarthy	1,250	225.00	225-275.
83-02-055	Moonlit Trail	F. McCarthy	1,000	90.00	210.00
78-02-056	Night Crossing	F. McCarthy	1,000	75.00	200-250.
74-02-057	The Night They Needed a Good Ribbon Man	F. McCarthy	1,000	65.00	350-475.
79-02-058	On the Warpath	F. McCarthy	1,000	75.00	195-250.
83-02-059	Out Of The Mist They Came	F. McCarthy	1,000	165.00	225-325.
90-02-060	Out Of The Windswept Ramparts	F. McCarthy	1,250	225.00	225.00
76-02-061	Packing In	F. McCarthy	1,000	65.00	375-500.
91-02-062	Pony Express	F. McCarthy	1,000	225.00	225.00
79-02-063	The Prayer	F. McCarthy	1,500	90.00	550-600.
91-02-064	The Pursuit	F. McCarthy	650	550.00	550.00
81-02-065	Race with the Hostiles	F. McCarthy	1,000	135.00	170-225.
86-02-066	Red Bull's War Party	F. McCarthy	1,000	165.00	165-225.
79-02-067	Retreat to Higher Ground	F. McCarthy	2,000	90.00	350-500.
75-02-068	Returning Raiders	F. McCarthy	1,000	75.00	450.00
80-02-069	Roar of the Norther	F. McCarthy	1,000	90.00	250-450.
77-02-070	Robe Signal	F. McCarthy	850	60.00	420-500.
88-02-071	Saber Charge	F. McCarthy	2,250	225.00	250.00
84-02-072	The Savage Taunt	F. McCarthy	1,000	225.00	250-375.
85-02-073	Scouting The Long Knives	F. McCarthy	1,400	195.00	250-300.
78-02-074	Single File	F. McCarthy	1,000	75.00	300-490.
76-02-075	Sioux Warriors	F. McCarthy	650	55.00	375-450.
75-02-076	Smoke Was Their Ally	F. McCarthy	1,000	75.00	425-455.
80-02-077	Snow Moon	F. McCarthy	1,000	115.00	250-300.
86-02-078	Spooked	F. McCarthy	1,400	195.00	200.00
81-02-079	Surrounded	F. McCarthy	1,000	150.00	195-275.
75-02-080	The Survivor	F. McCarthy	1,000	65.00	350.00
85-02-081	The Traders	F. McCarthy	1,000	195.00	275-195.
80-02-082	The Trooper	F. McCarthy	1,000	90.00	295.00
78-02-083	To Battle	F. McCarthy	1,000	75.00	370.00
88-02-084	Turning The Leaders	F. McCarthy	1,500	225.00	240.00
83-02-085	Under Attack	F. McCarthy	5,676	125.00	295-350.
81-02-086	Under Hostile Fire	F. McCarthy	1,000	150.00	210-250.
75-02-087	Waiting for the Escort	F. McCarthy	1,000	75.00	225-250.
76-02-088	The Warrior	F. McCarthy	650	50.00	450-600.
82-02-089	The Warriors	F. McCarthy	1,000	150.00	200.00
84-02-090	Watching the Wagons	F. McCarthy	1,400	175.00	440.00
87-02-091	When Omens Turn Bad	F. McCarthy	1,000	165.00	490-525.
86-02-092	Where Tracks Will Be Lost	F. McCarthy	550	350.00	350-375.
84-02-093	Whirling He Raced to Meet the Challenge	F. McCarthy	1,000	175.00	275-340.
91-02-094	The Wild Ones	F. McCarthy	1,000	225.00	225.00
90-02-095	Winter Trail	F. McCarthy	1,500	235.00	235-300.
Greenwich Workshop		**Wysocki**			
88-03-001	The Americana Bowl	C. Wysocki	3,500	295.00	295.00
83-03-002	Amish Neighbors	C. Wysocki	1,000	150.00	475-600.
89-03-003	Another Year At Sea	C. Wysocki	2,500	175.00	250-410.
83-03-004	Applebutter Makers	C. Wysocki	1,000	135.00	375-675.
87-03-005	Bach's Magnificat in D Minor	C. Wysocki	2,250	150.00	350-400.
91-03-006	Beauty And The Beast	C. Wysocki	2,000	125.00	125.00
90-03-007	Belly Warmers	C. Wysocki	2,500	150.00	150-225.
84-03-008	Bird House (C)	C. Wysocki	1,000	85.00	175-250.
85-03-009	Birds of a Feather	C. Wysocki	1,250	145.00	300-400.
89-03-010	Bostonians And Beans (PC)	C. Wysocki	6,711	225.00	350-400.
79-03-011	Butternut Farms	C. Wysocki	1,000	75.00	1150-1300.
80-03-012	Caleb's Buggy Barn	C. Wysocki	1,000	80.00	275-325.
84-03-013	Cape Cod Cold Fish Party	C. Wysocki	1,000	150.00	175-250.
81-03-014	Carver Coggins	C. Wysocki	1,000	145.00	800-1200.
89-03-015	Christmas Greeting	C. Wysocki	11,000	125.00	125-250.
82-03-016	Christmas Print, 1982	C. Wysocki	2,000	80.00	600-850.
85-03-017	Clammers at Hodge's Horn	C. Wysocki	1,000	150.00	900-1200.
83-03-018	Commemorative Print, 1983	C. Wysocki	2,000	55.00	55-100.00
84-03-019	Cotton Country	C. Wysocki	1,000	150.00	200-250.
83-03-020	Country Race	C. Wysocki	1,000	150.00	190-325.
86-03-021	Daddy's Coming Home	C. Wysocki	1,250	150.00	1100-1500.
87-03-022	Dahalia Dinalhaven Makes a Dory Deal	C. Wysocki	2,250	150.00	230-375.
86-03-023	Dancing Pheasant Farms	C. Wysocki	1,750	165.00	325-450.
85-03-024	Devilstone Harbor/An American Celebration (B & P)	C. Wysocki	3,500	195.00	350-600.
89-03-025	Dreamers	C. Wysocki	3,000	175.00	175-275.
80-03-026	Derby Square	C. Wysocki	1,000	90.00	825-975.
86-03-027	Devilbelly Bay	C. Wysocki	1,000	145.00	275-375.
79-03-028	Farhaven by the Sea	C. Wysocki	1,000	75.00	750-950.
88-03-029	Feathered Critics	C. Wysocki	2,500	150.00	150-195.
79-03-030	Fox Run	C. Wysocki	1,000	75.00	1400-1900.
84-03-031	The Foxy Fox Outfoxes the Fox Hunters	C. Wysocki	1,500	150.00	500-650.
89-03-032	Fun Lovin' Silly Folks	C. Wysocki	3,000	185.00	185-300.
86-03-033	Hickory Haven Canal	C. Wysocki	1,500	165.00	725-850.

Number	Name	Artist	Edition Limit	Issue Price	Quote
88-03-034	Home Is My Sailor	C. Wysocki	2,500	150.00	150-250.
90-03-035	Jingle Bell Teddy and Friends	C. Wysocki	5,000	125.00	125.00
80-03-036	Jolly Hill Farms	C. Wysocki	1,000	75.00	700-900.
86-03-037	Lady Liberty's Independence Day Enterprising Immigrants	C. Wysocki	1,500	140.00	200-300.
89-03-038	The Memory Maker	C. Wysocki	2,500	165.00	165.00
85-03-039	Merrymakers Serenade	C. Wysocki	1,250	135.00	135.00
86-03-040	Mr. Swallobark	C. Wysocki	2,000	145.00	450-575.
82-03-041	The Nantucket	C. Wysocki	1,000	145.00	145-400.
81-03-042	Olde America	C. Wysocki	1,500	125.00	475-750.
81-03-043	Page's Bake Shoppe	C. Wysocki	1,000	115.00	450-575.
81-03-044	Prairie Wind Flowers	C. Wysocki	1,000	125.00	900-1500.
90-03-045	Robin Hood	C. Wysocki	2,000	165.00	165.00.
91-03-046	Rockland Breakwater Light	C. Wysocki	2,500	165.00	165.00.
85-03-047	Salty Witch Bay	C. Wysocki	475	350.00	1500-2000.
91-03-048	Sea Captain's Wife Abiding	C. Wysocki	1,500	150.00	150-400.
79-03-049	Shall We?	C. Wysocki	1,000	75.00	425-475.
82-03-050	Sleepy Town West	C. Wysocki	1,500	150.00	400-575.
84-03-051	Storin' Up	C. Wysocki	450	325.00	750-1125.
82-03-052	Sunset Hills, Texas Wildcatters	C. Wysocki	1,000	125.00	125-170.
84-03-053	Sweetheart Chessmate	C. Wysocki	1,000	95.00	275-375.
83-03-054	Tea by the Sea	C. Wysocki	1,000	145.00	1200-1950.
87-03-055	'Twas the Twilight Before Christmas	C. Wysocki	7,500	95.00	150.00
84-03-056	Warm Christmas Love, A	C. Wysocki	3,951	80.00	300-450.
90-03-057	Wednesday Night Checkers	C. Wysocki	2,500	175.00	175.00
90-03-058	Where The Bouys Are	C. Wysocki	2,750	175.00	175.00
91-03-059	Whistle Stop Christmas	C. Wysocki	5,000	125.00	125-190.
84-03-060	Yankee Wink Hollow	C. Wysocki	1,000	95.00	900-1125.
87-03-061	Yearning For My Captain	C. Wysocki	2,000	150.00	300-400.
87-03-062	You've Been So Long at Sea, Horatio	C. Wysocki	2,500	150.00	150-350.
Greenwich Workshop		**Lyman**			
90-04-001	Among The Wild Brambles	Lyman	1,750	185.00	180-275.
87-04-002	An Elegant Couple	Lyman	1,000	125.00	150-235.
85-04-003	Autumn Gathering	Lyman	850	115.00	250.00
85-04-004	Bear & Blossoms (C)	Lyman	850	75.00	75-220.00
87-04-005	Canadian Autumn	Lyman	1,500	165.00	175.00
89-04-006	Color In The Snow	Lyman	1,500	165.00	165-250.
86-04-007	Colors of Twilight	Lyman	850	N/A	N/A
91-04-008	Dance of Cloud and Cliff	Lyman	1,500	225.00	325-450.
83-04-009	Early Winter In The Mountains	Lyman	850	95.00	150-500.
91-04-010	Embers at Dawn	Lyman	3,500	225.00	650-1150.
83-04-011	End Of The Ridge	Lyman	850	95.00	200-275.
90-04-012	Evening Light	Lyman	2,500	225.00	525-900.
84-04-013	Free Flight (C)	Lyman	850	70.00	70-120.00
87-04-014	High Creek Crossing	Lyman	1,000	165.00	775-1000.
89-04-015	High Light	Lyman	1,250	165.00	200-350.
86-04-016	High Trail At Sunset	Lyman	1,000	125.00	545-695.
88-04-017	The Intruder	Lyman	1,500	150.00	150.00
89-04-018	Last Light of Winter	Lyman	1,500	175.00	500-600.
87-04-019	Moon Shadows	Lyman	1,500	135.00	135-185.
86-04-020	Morning Solitude	Lyman	850	115.00	150-250.
90-04-021	A Mountain Campfire	Lyman	1,500	195.00	1300-2500.
87-04-022	New Territories	Lyman	1,000	135.00	210-235.
84-04-023	Noisy Neighbors	Lyman	650	95.00	600-900.
84-04-024	Noisy Neighbors (R)	Lyman	25	215.00	520-1800.
83-04-025	The Pass	Lyman	850	95.00	400-575.
89-04-026	Quiet Rain	Lyman	1,500	165.00	260-475.
88-04-027	The Raptor's Watch	Lyman	1,500	150.00	275-325.
88-04-028	Return Of The Falcon	Lyman	1,500	150.00	150.00
88-04-029	Return Of The Falcon (P)	Lyman	Open	20.00	20.00
91-04-030	Secret Watch	Lyman	2,250	150.00	150.00
90-04-031	Silent Snows	Lyman	1,750	210.00	225.00
88-04-032	Snow Hunter	Lyman	1,500	135.00	135.00
86-04-033	Snowy Throne (C)	Lyman	850	85.00	85-295.
87-04-034	Twilight Snow (C)	Lyman	950	85.00	85-225.
88-04-035	Uzumati: Great Bear of Yosemite	Lyman	1,750	150.00	150.00
88-04-036	Uzumati: Great Bear of Yosemite (P)	Lyman	Open	20.00	20.00
Guildhall, Inc.		**De Haan**			
79-01-001	Foggy Mornin' Wait	C. De Haan	650	75.00	2525.00
80-01-002	Texas Panhandle	C. De Haan	650	75.00	1525.00
81-01-003	MacTavish	C. De Haan	650	75.00	1425.00
81-01-004	Forgin' The Keechi	C. De Haan	650	85.00	725.00
81-01-005	Surprise Encounter	C. De Haan	750	85.00	475.00
82-01-006	O' That Strawberry Roan	C. De Haan	750	85.00	125.00
83-01-007	Ridin' Ol' Paint	C. De Haan	750	85.00	625.00
83-01-008	Crossin' Horse Creek	C. De Haan	750	100.00	625.00
83-01-009	Keep A Movin' Dan	C. De Haan	750	85.00	125.00
84-01-010	Jake	C. De Haan	650	100.00	600.00
84-01-011	Spooked	C. De Haan	650	95.00	1825.00
85-01-012	Up the Chisholm	C. De Haan	750	85.00	125.00
85-01-013	Keechi Country	C. De Haan	750	100.00	375.00
85-01-014	Oklahoma Paints	C. De Haan	750	100.00	425.00
85-01-015	Horsemen of the West (Suite of 3)	C. De Haan	650	145.00	975.00
86-01-016	The Mustangers	C. De Haan	750	100.00	400.00
86-01-017	The Searchers	C. De Haan	650	100.00	375.00
86-01-018	Moondancers	C. De Haan	750	100.00	165.00
86-01-019	The Loner (with matching buckle)	C. De Haan	750	145.00	425.00
87-01-020	Snow Birds	C. De Haan	750	100.00	350.00
87-01-021	Murphy's Law	C. De Haan	750	100.00	225.00
87-01-022	Crow Ceremonial Dress	C. De Haan	750	100.00	175.00
87-01-023	Supremacy	C. De Haan	750	100.00	175.00
88-01-024	Mornin' Gather	C. DeHaan	750	100.00	350.00
88-01-025	Stage To Deadwood	C. DeHaan	750	100.00	275.00
88-01-026	Water Breakin'	C. DeHaan	750	125.00	600.00
89-01-027	Kentucky Blue	C. DeHaan	750	125.00	575.00
89-01-028	Village Markers	C. DeHaan	750	125.00	525.00
89-01-029	The Quarter Horse	C. DeHaan	800	125.00	325.00
89-01-030	Crows	C. DeHaan	800	135.00	525.00
90-01-031	War Cry	C. DeHaan	925	135.00	275.00
90-01-032	Crow Autumn	C. DeHaan	925	135.00	250.00
90-01-033	Escape	C. DeHaan	925	135.00	200.00
90-01-034	High Plains Drifters	C. DeHaan	925	140.00	200.00
90-01-035	The Pipe Carrier	C. DeHaan	925	140.00	175.00
Guildhall, Inc.		**Baize**			
88-02-001	Best of Friends	W. Baize	575	85.00	85.00
88-02-002	Winter Arrival	W. Baize	575	85.00	85.00
Guildhall, Inc.		**Moline**			
88-03-001	Companions	B. Moline	575	85.00	85.00
88-03-002	Portraying His Heritage	B. Moline	575	85.00	85.00

Company / Number	Name	Series / Artist	Edition Limit	Issue Price	Quote
Hadley Companies		**Redlin**			
77-01-001	Apple River Mallards	T. Redlin	Open	10.00	150.00
77-01-002	Over the Blowdown	T. Redlin	Open	20.00	70.00
77-01-003	Winter Snows	T. Redlin	Open	20.00	100.00
78-01-004	Back from the Fields	T. Redlin	720	40.00	325.00
78-01-005	Backwater Mallards	T. Redlin	720	40.00	550.00
78-01-006	Old Loggers Trail	T. Redlin	720	40.00	550.00
78-01-007	Over the Rushes	T. Redlin	720	40.00	250.00
78-01-008	Quiet Afternoon	T. Redlin	720	40.00	350.00
78-01-009	Startled	T. Redlin	720	30.00	400.00
79-01-010	Ageing Shoreline	T. Redlin	960	40.00	250.00
79-01-011	Colorful Trio	T. Redlin	960	40.00	400.00
79-01-012	Fighting a Headwind	T. Redlin	960	30.00	250.00
79-01-013	Morning Chores	T. Redlin	960	40.00	950.00
79-01-014	The Loner	T. Redlin	960	40.00	200.00
79-01-015	Whitecaps	T. Redlin	960	40.00	250.00
80-01-016	Autumn Run	T. Redlin	960	60.00	450.00
80-01-017	Breaking Away	T. Redlin	960	60.00	300.00
80-01-018	Clearing the Rail	T. Redlin	960	60.00	325.00
80-01-019	Country Road	T. Redlin	960	60.00	375.00
80-01-020	Drifting	T. Redlin	960	60.00	300.00
80-01-021	The Homestead	T. Redlin	960	60.00	375.00
80-01-022	Intruders	T. Redlin	960	60.00	200.00
80-01-023	Night Watch	T. Redlin	2,400	60.00	400.00
80-01-024	Rusty Refuge	T. Redlin	960	60.00	425.00
80-01-025	Secluded Pon	T. Redlin	960	60.00	250.00
80-01-026	Silent Sunset	T. Redlin	960	60.00	850.00
80-01-027	Spring Thaw	T. Redlin	960	60.00	350.00
80-01-028	Squall Line	T. Redlin	960	60.00	300.00
81-01-029	1981 Mn Duck Stamp Print	T. Redlin	7,800	125.00	200.00
81-01-030	All Clear	T. Redlin	960	150.00	350.00
81-01-031	April Snow	T. Redlin	960	100.00	400.00
81-01-032	Broken Covey	T. Redlin	960	100.00	300.00
81-01-033	High Country	T. Redlin	960	100.00	450.00
81-01-034	Hightailing	T. Redlin	960	75.00	200.00
81-01-035	The Landmark	T. Redlin	960	100.00	400.00
81-01-036	Morning Retreat (AP)	T. Redlin	240	400.00	2500.00
81-01-037	Passing Through	T. Redlin	960	100.00	225.00
81-01-038	Rusty Refuge II	T. Redlin	960	100.00	375.00
81-01-039	Sharing the Bounty	T. Redlin	960	100.00	400.00
81-01-040	Soft Shadows	T. Redlin	960	100.00	225.00
81-01-041	Spring Run-Off	T. Redlin	1,700	125.00	275.00
82-01-042	1982 Mn Trout Stamp Print	T. Redlin	960	125.00	600.00
82-01-043	Evening Retreat (AP)	T. Redlin	300	400.00	2500.00
82-01-044	October Evening	T. Redlin	960	100.00	375.00
82-01-045	Reflections	T. Redlin	960	100.00	400.00
82-01-046	Seed Hunters	T. Redlin	960	100.00	300.00
82-01-047	Spring Mapling	T. Redlin	960	100.00	450.00
82-01-048	The Birch Line	T. Redlin	960	100.00	500.00
82-01-049	The Landing	T. Redlin	Open	30.00	50.00
82-01-050	Whitewater	T. Redlin	960	100.00	400.00
82-01-051	Winter Haven	T. Redlin	500	85.00	750.00
83-01-052	1983 ND Duck Stamp Print	T. Redlin	3,438	135.00	135.00
83-01-053	Autumn Shoreline	T. Redlin	Open	50.00	150.00
83-01-054	Backwoods Cabin	T. Redlin	960	150.00	650.00
83-01-055	Evening Glow	T. Redlin	960	150.00	1200.00
83-01-056	Evening Surprise	T. Redlin	960	150.00	650.00
83-01-057	Hidden Point	T. Redlin	960	150.00	350.00
83-01-058	On the Alert	T. Redlin	960	125.00	400.00
83-01-059	Peaceful Evening	T. Redlin	960	100.00	350.00
83-01-060	Prairie Springs	T. Redlin	960	150.00	325.00
83-01-061	Rushing Rapids	T. Redlin	960	125.00	400.00
84-01-062	1984 Quail Conservation	T. Redlin	1,500	135.00	135.00
84-01-063	Bluebill Point (AP)	T. Redlin	240	300.00	350.00
84-01-064	Changing Seasons-Summer	T. Redlin	960	150.00	600.00
84-01-065	Closed for the Season	T. Redlin	960	150.00	300.00
84-01-066	Leaving the Sanctuary	T. Redlin	960	150.00	450.00
84-01-067	Morning Glow	T. Redlin	960	150.00	1000.00
84-01-068	Night Harvest	T. Redlin	960	150.00	500.00
84-01-069	Nightflight (AP)	T. Redlin	360	600.00	2800.00
84-01-070	Prairie Skyline	T. Redlin	960	150.00	550.00
84-01-071	Rural Route	T. Redlin	960	150.00	350.00
84-01-072	Rusty Refuge III	T. Redlin	960	150.00	400.00
84-01-073	Silent Wings Suite (set of 4)	T. Redlin	960	200.00	450.00
84-01-074	Sundown	T. Redlin	960	300.00	550.00
84-01-075	Sunny Afternoon	T. Redlin	960	150.00	350.00
84-01-076	Winter Windbreak	T. Redlin	960	150.00	450.00
85-01-077	1985 MN Duck Stamp	T. Redlin	4,385	135.00	135.00
85-01-078	Afternoon Glow	T. Redlin	960	150.00	1000.00
85-01-079	Breaking Cover	T. Redlin	960	150.00	325.00
85-01-080	Brousing	T. Redlin	960	150.00	325.00
85-01-081	Clear View	T. Redlin	1,500	300.00	450.00
85-01-082	Delayed Departure	T. Redlin	1,500	150.00	450.00
85-01-083	Evening Company	T. Redlin	960	150.00	400.00
85-01-084	Night Light	T. Redlin	1,500	300.00	500.00
85-01-085	Riverside Pond	T. Redlin	960	150.00	525.00
85-01-086	Rusty Refuge IV	T. Redlin	960	150.00	375.00
85-01-087	The Sharing Season	T. Redlin	Open	60.00	125.00
85-01-088	Whistle Stop	T. Redlin	960	150.00	500.00
85-01-089	Back to the Sanctuary	T. Redlin	960	150.00	350.00
86-01-090	Changing Seasons-Autumn	T. Redlin	960	150.00	325.00
86-01-091	Changing Seasons-Winter	T. Redlin	960	200.00	400.00
86-01-092	Coming Home	T. Redlin	2,400	100.00	1200.00
86-01-093	Hazy Afternoon	T. Redlin	2,560	200.00	650.00
86-01-094	Night Mapling	T. Redlin	960	200.00	500.00
86-01-095	Prairie Monuments	T. Redlin	960	200.00	400.00
86-01-096	Sharing Season II	T. Redlin	Open	60.00	100.00
86-01-097	Silent Flight	T. Redlin	960	150.00	150.00
86-01-098	Stormy Weather	T. Redlin	1,500	200.00	400.00
86-01-099	Sunlit Trail	T. Redlin	960	150.00	325.00
86-01-100	Twilight Glow	T. Redlin	960	200.00	700.00
87-01-101	Autumn Afternoon	T. Redlin	4,800	100.00	750.00
87-01-102	Changing Seasons-Spring	T. Redlin	960	200.00	450.00
87-01-103	Deer Crossing	T. Redlin	2,400	200.00	450.00
87-01-104	Evening Chores (print & book)	T. Redlin	2,400	400.00	400.00
87-01-105	Evening Harvest	T. Redlin	960	200.00	425.00
87-01-106	Golden Retreat (AP)	T. Redlin	500	800.00	1400.00
87-01-107	Prepared for the Season	T. Redlin	Open	70.00	80.00
87-01-108	Sharing the Solitude	T. Redlin	2,400	125.00	700.00
87-01-109	That Special Time	T. Redlin	2,400	125.00	600.00
87-01-110	Together for the Season	T. Redlin	Open	70.00	80.00
88-01-111	Boulder Ridge	T. Redlin	4,800	150.00	150.00
88-01-112	Catching the Scent	T. Redlin	2,400	200.00	200.00

Company / Number	Name	Series / Artist	Edition Limit	Issue Price	Quote
88-01-113	Country Neighbors	T. Redlin	4,800	150.00	300.00
88-01-114	Homeward Bound	T. Redlin	Open	70.00	125.00
88-01-115	Lights of Home	T. Redlin	9,500	125.00	750.00
88-01-116	Moonlight Retreat (AP)	T. Redlin	530	1000.00	1000.00
88-01-117	Prairie Morning	T. Redlin	4,800	150.00	195.00
88-01-118	Quiet of the Evening	T. Redlin	4,800	150.00	850.00
88-01-119	The Master's Domain	T. Redlin	2,400	225.00	700.00
88-01-120	Wednesday Afternoon	T. Redlin	6,800	175.00	225.00
88-01-121	House Call	T. Redlin	6,800	175.00	250.00
89-01-122	Office Hours	T. Redlin	6,800	175.00	175.00
89-01-123	Morning Rounds	T. Redlin	6,800	175.00	350.00
89-01-124	Indian Summer	T. Redlin	4,800	200.00	300.00
89-01-125	Aroma of Fall	T. Redlin	6,800	200.00	1250.00
89-01-126	Homeward Bound	T. Redlin	Open	80.00	100.00
89-01-127	Special Memories (AP Only)	T. Redlin	570	1000.00	1000.00
90-01-128	Family Traditions	T. Redlin	Open	80.00	100.00
90-01-129	Pure Contentment	T. Redlin	9,500	150.00	350.00
90-01-130	Master of the Valley	T. Redlin	6,800	200.00	200.00
90-01-131	Evening Solitude	T. Redlin	9,500	200.00	500-650.
90-01-132	Best Friends (AP Only)	T. Redlin	570	1000.00	1000.00
90-01-133	Heading Home	T. Redlin	Open	80.00	100.00
90-01-134	Welcome to Paradise	T. Redlin	14,500	150.00	250.00
90-01-135	Evening With Friends	T. Redlin	19,500	225.00	375-975.
91-01-136	Morning Solitude	T. Redlin	12,107	250.00	475.00
91-01-137	Flying Free	T. Redlin	14,500	200.00	200.00
91-01-138	Hunter's Haven (AP Only)	T. Redlin	N/A	1000.00	1000.00
91-01-139	Comforts of Home	T. Redlin	N/A	175.00	175.00
91-01-140	Pleasures of Winter	T. Redlin	24,500	150.00	150.00
91-01-141	Comforts of Home	T. Redlin	22,900	175.00	350.00
92-01-142	Summertime	T. Redlin	24,900	225.00	225.00
Edna Hibel Studios		**Hibel Stone Lithography**			
74-01-001	Mother and Four Children	E. Hibel	60	150.00	1550.00
75-01-002	Sandy (Kissing Baby)	E. Hibel	140	75.00	1550.00
XX-01-003	Beggar	E. Hibel	70	250.00	4700.00
76-01-004	Elsa & Baby	E. Hibel	300	150.00	4200.00
76-01-005	Kikue (Silk)	E. Hibel	145	195.00	2700.00
76-01-006	Switzerland	E. Hibel	270	350.00	2300.00
76-01-007	Mother & 4 Children (horizontal)	E. Hibel	300	250.00	2000.00
76-01-008	Japanese Doll	E. Hibel	28	160.00	2600.00
76-01-009	Sophia & Children	E. Hibel	296	325.00	4300.00
77-01-010	Mayan Man	E. Hibel	295	350.00	4300.00
77-01-011	Colette & Child	E. Hibel	275	195.00	1750.00
77-01-012	Museum Suite	E. Hibel	375	1900.00	9700.00
78-01-013	Felicia	E. Hibel	148	900.00	3850.00
79-01-014	Akiko & Children	E. Hibel	335	450.00	2800.00
79-01-015	Petra Mit Kinder	E. Hibel	320	345.00	4000.00
79-01-016	International Year of The Child Suite	E. Hibel	420	900.00	4200.00
79-01-017	Nora	E. Hibel	394	175.00	850.00
79-01-018	Joseph	E. Hibel	335	495.00	1325.00
79-01-019	Thai Princess	E. Hibel	395	495.00	1450.00
80-01-020	Tina	E. Hibel	200	750.00	1625.00
80-01-021	Cheryll & Wendy	E. Hibel	100	3900.00	11500.00
80-01-022	The Spirit of Mainau Suite	E. Hibel	385	1200.00	3150.00
80-01-023	Hope	E. Hibel	396	400.00	1100.00
80-01-024	Cho Cho San	E. Hibel	396	500.00	1050.00
81-01-025	The Little Emperor	E. Hibel	275	1000.00	2250.00
81-01-026	Little Empress	E. Hibel	319	1000.00	2100.00
81-01-027	Jacklin & Child	E. Hibel	197	110.00	400.00
82-01-028	Joelle	E. Hibel	348	295.00	1800.00
82-01-029	Kelly	E. Hibel	347	320.00	1700.00
82-01-030	Rena & Rachel	E. Hibel	329	345.00	1025.00
82-01-031	Naro-San	E. Hibel	322	310.00	675.00
82-01-032	Bettina and Children	E. Hibel	300	395.00	1400.00
82-01-033	Lydia	E. Hibel	298	295.00	650.00
82-01-034	Family of the Mountain Lake	E. Hibel	305	395.00	2900.00
83-01-035	Valerie & Children	E. Hibel	400	295.00	625.00
84-01-036	Nava & Children	E. Hibel	385	385.00	750.00
84-01-037	The Caress	E. Hibel	430	325.00	700.00
84-01-038	Dorene & Child	E. Hibel	331	250.00	525.00
84-01-039	Sandy & Children	E. Hibel	419	365.00	750.00
84-01-040	Natasha & Children	E. Hibel	308	195.00	500.00
84-01-041	Gerard	E. Hibel	200	250.00	725.00
84-01-042	Claire	E. Hibel	206	335.00	975.00
84-01-043	Wendy with Hat	E. Hibel	308	395.00	725.00
84-01-044	Jennifer & Children	E. Hibel	318	445.00	775.00
84-01-045	Beverly & Child	E. Hibel	216	160.00	425.00
84-01-046	Celeste	E. Hibel	256	175.00	400.00
84-01-047	Dream Sketchbook	E. Hibel	298	175.00	475.00
84-01-048	Arielle & Amy	E. Hibel	275	295.00	675.00
84-01-049	Des Fleurs Rouges	E. Hibel	298	245.00	750.00
84-01-050	Sarah & Joshua	E. Hibel	343	475.00	850.00
85-01-051	La Tosca	E. Hibel	355	595.00	725.00
86-01-052	Nancy with Megan	E. Hibel	367	450.00	900.00
86-01-053	Duchess	E. Hibel	320	325.00	525.00
86-01-054	Belinda & Nina	E. Hibel	320	295.00	625.00
87-01-055	Monica Matteao & Vanessa	E. Hibel	300	350.00	650.00
87-01-056	Flowers of Kashmir	E. Hibel	297	275.00	525.00
87-01-057	Finnish Mother & Child	E. Hibel	343	185.00	325.00
87-01-058	Once Upon A Time	E. Hibel	287	365.00	550.00
88-01-059	The New Hat	E. Hibel	298	310.00	550.00
88-01-060	Amelia & Children	E. Hibel	268	675.00	825.00
88-01-061	Xin-Xin of the High Mountains	E. Hibel	325	1300.00	2000.00
88-01-062	Linda "T"	E. Hibel	302	185.00	325.00
88-01-063	John "M"	E. Hibel	308	185.00	325.00
88-01-064	Flowers of the Adriatic	E. Hibel	286	300.00	500.00
89-01-065	Helene & Children	E. Hibel	280	365.00	495.00
90-01-066	Tamara	E. Hibel	254	360.00	500.00
Edna Hibel Studios		**Hibel Lithography on Porcelain**			
80-02-001	Cheryll and Wendy	E. Hibel	100	3900.00	11500.00
78-02-002	Lenore and Child	E. Hibel	395	600.00	2100.00
John Hine		**Rambles**			
89-01-001	Two for Joy	A. Wyatt	Closed	59.90	59.90
89-01-002	Riverbank	A. Wyatt	Closed	59.90	59.90
89-01-003	Waters Edge	A. Wyatt	Closed	59.90	59.90
89-01-004	Summer Harvest	A. Wyatt	Closed	59.90	59.90
89-01-005	Garden Gate	A. Wyatt	Closed	59.90	59.90
89-01-006	Hedgerow	A. Wyatt	Closed	59.90	59.90
89-01-007	Frog	A. Wyatt	Closed	33.00	33.00
89-01-008	Wren	A. Wyatt	Closed	33.00	33.00
89-01-009	Kingfisher	A. Wyatt	Closed	33.00	33.00

Company / Number	Name	Series / Artist	Edition Limit	Issue Price	Quote
89-01-010	Blue Tit	A. Wyatt	Closed	33.00	33.00
89-01-011	Lobster Pot	A. Wyatt	Closed	50.00	50.00
89-01-012	Puffin Rock	A. Wyatt	Closed	50.00	50.00
89-01-013	Otter's Holt	A. Wyatt	Closed	50.00	50.00
89-01-014	Bluebell Cottage	A. Wyatt	Closed	50.00	50.00
89-01-015	Shirelarm	A. Wyatt	Closed	42.00	42.00
89-01-016	St. Mary's Church	A. Wyatt	Closed	42.00	42.00
89-01-017	The Swan	A. Wyatt	Closed	42.00	42.00
89-01-018	Castle Street	A. Wyatt	Closed	42.00	42.00
Lightpost Publishing		**Canvas Editions**			
89-01-001	Carmel, Ocean Avenue	T. Kinkade	Closed	595.00	1800-2000.
89-01-002	San Francisco, Union Square	T. Kinkade	Closed	595.00	950-2200.
89-01-003	Entrance to the Manor House	T. Kinkade	Closed	495.00	900-1000.
89-01-004	Evening at Merritt's Cottage	T. Kinkade	Closed	495.00	850-2000.
90-01-005	Hidden Cottage	T. Kinkade	Closed	495.00	1000-1800.
90-01-006	Chandler's Cottage	T. Kinkade	Closed	495.00	1000-1500.
90-01-007	Christmas Cottage 1990	T. Kinkade	Closed	295.00	600.00
90-01-008	Christmas Eve	T. Kinkade	Closed	395.00	500-800.
90-01-009	Morning Light A/P	T. Kinkade	Closed	695.00	900-950.
90-01-010	Rose Arbor	T. Kinkade	Closed	495.00	N/A
90-01-011	Spring At Stonegate	T. Kinkade	550	295.00	295.00
91-01-012	Home For The Holidays	T. Kinkade	Closed	595.00	900-1000.
91-01-013	Afternoon Light, Dogwoods	T. Kinkade	980	435.00	435.00
91-01-014	The Autumn Gate	T. Kinkade	980	495.00	495.00
91-01-015	Boston	T. Kinkade	550	435.00	435.00
91-01-016	Carmel, Tuck Box Tea Room	T. Kinkade	980	545.00	545.00
91-01-017	Cedar Nook Cottage	T. Kinkade	1,960	165.00	165.00
91-01-018	Flags Over The Capitol	T. Kinkade	980	495.00	495.00
91-01-019	Home For The Evening	T. Kinkade	980	165.00	165.00
91-01-020	The Lit Path	T. Kinkade	1,960	165.00	165.00
91-01-021	McKenna's Cottage	T. Kinkade	980	435.00	435.00
90-01-022	Olde Porterfield Tea Room	T. Kinkade	Closed	435.00	695.00
91-01-023	Open Gate, Sussex	T. Kinkade	980	165.00	165.00
91-01-024	Pye Corner Cottage	T. Kinkade	1,960	165.00	165.00
91-01-025	Victorian Evening	T. Kinkade	980	435.00	435.00
91-01-026	Woodman's Thatch	T. Kinkade	1,960	165.00	165.00
92-01-027	Broadwater Bridge	T. Kinkade	980	435.00	435.00
92-01-028	Swanbrooke Cottage	T. Kinkade	980	495.00	495.00
92-01-029	Sweetheart Cottage	T. Kinkade	980	435.00	435.00
92-01-030	Blossom Hill Church	T. Kinkade	980	495.00	495.00
92-01-031	Cottage-By-The-Sea	T. Kinkade	980	495.00	495.00
92-01-032	Home is Where the Heart Is	T. Kinkade	980	495.00	495.00
92-01-033	Miller's Cottage	T. Kinkade	980	435.00	435.00
92-01-034	Sunday at Apple Hill	T. Kinkade	980	435.00	435.00
92-01-035	Victorian Garden	T. Kinkade	980	695.00	695.00
92-01-036	San Francisco, Nob Hill	T. Kinkade	980	545.00	545.00
92-01-037	Julianne's Cottage	T. Kinkade	980	345.00	345.00
92-01-038	Weathervane Hutch	T. Kinkade	1,960	245.00	245.00
92-01-039	Yosemite	T. Kinkade	980	495.00	495.00
92-01-040	Country Memories	T. Kinkade	980	295.00	295.00
92-01-041	The Garden Party	T. Kinkade	980	435.00	435.00
92-01-042	Victorian Christmas	T. Kinkade	980	495.00	495.00
92-01-043	Moonlit Sleigh Ride	T. Kinkade	980	245.00	245.00
92-01-044	Olde Porterfield Gift Shoppe	T. Kinkade	980	435.00	435.00
92-01-045	Fall Colors Victorian	T. Kinkade	980	435.00	435.00
92-01-046	Silent Night	T. Kinkade	980	345.00	345.00
92-01-047	Evening Carolers	T. Kinkade	980	245.00	245.00
92-01-048	Christmas At the Ahwahnee	T. Kinkade	980	435.00	435.00
92-01-049	Paris, City of Lights	T. Kinkade	980	495.00	495.00
Lightpost Publishing		**Archival Paper**			
85-02-001	Birth of a City	T. Kinkade	Closed	150.00	150-250.
89-02-002	Carmel, Ocean Avenue	T. Kinkade	Closed	225.00	650-850.
90-02-003	Chandler's Cottage	T. Kinkade	Closed	125.00	350.00
90-02-004	Christmas Cottage 1990	T. Kinkade	Closed	95.00	150.00
84-02-005	Dawson	T. Kinkade	Closed	150.00	150.00
89-02-006	Entrance to the Manor House	T. Kinkade	Closed	125.00	500-675.
89-02-007	Evening at Merritt's Cottage	T. Kinkade	Closed	125.00	675.00
85-02-008	Evening Service	T. Kinkade	Closed	90.00	90-200.00
90-02-009	Hidden Cottage	T. Kinkade	Closed	125.00	650.00
85-02-010	Moonlight on the Waterfront	T. Kinkade	Closed	150.00	150-200.
86-02-011	New York, 6th Avenue	T. Kinkade	Closed	150.00	450.00
84-02-012	Placerville, 1916	T. Kinkade	Closed	90.00	1500-2200.
88-02-013	Room with a View	T. Kinkade	Closed	150.00	550.00
86-02-014	San Francisco, 1909	T. Kinkade	Closed	150.00	900-1450.
89-02-015	San Francisco, Union Square	T. Kinkade	Closed	225.00	650-850.
90-02-016	Rose Arbor	T. Kinkade	Closed	125.00	300.00
90-02-017	Spring At Stonegate	T. Kinkade	550	95.00	95.00
91-02-018	Afternoon Light, Dogwoods	T. Kinkade	980	185.00	185.00
91-02-019	The Autumn Gate	T. Kinkade	980	225.00	225.00
91-02-020	Boston	T. Kinkade	550	175.00	175.00
91-02-021	Carmel, Tuck Box Tea Room	T. Kinkade	980	275.00	275.00
91-02-022	Christmas Eve	T. Kinkade	980	125.00	125.00
91-02-023	Flags Over The Capitol	T. Kinkade	1,991	195.00	195.00
91-02-024	Home For The Evening	T. Kinkade	980	100.00	100.00
91-02-025	Home For The Holidays	T. Kinkade	980	225.00	225.00
91-02-026	McKenna's Cottage	T. Kinkade	980	150.00	150.00
91-02-027	Olde Porterfield Tea Room	T. Kinkade	980	150.00	150.00
91-02-028	Open Gate, Sussex	T. Kinkade	980	100.00	100.00
91-02-029	Victorian Evening	T. Kinkade	980	150.00	150.00
92-02-030	Blossom Hill Church	T. Kinkade	980	225.00	225.00
92-02-031	Broadwater Bridge	T. Kinkade	980	225.00	225.00
92-02-032	Swanbrooke Cottage	T. Kinkade	980	250.00	225.00
92-02-033	Sweetheart Cottage	T. Kinkade	980	150.00	150.00
92-02-034	Cottage-By-The-Sea	T. Kinkade	980	250.00	250.00
92-02-035	Home is Where the Heart Is	T. Kinkade	980	225.00	225.00
92-02-036	Miller's Cottage	T. Kinkade	980	175.00	175.00
92-02-037	Sunday At Apple Hill	T. Kinkade	980	175.00	175.00
92-02-038	Victorian Garden	T. Kinkade	980	275.00	275.00
92-02-039	San Francisco	T. Kinkade	980	275.00	275.00
92-02-040	Julianne's Cottage	T. Kinkade	980	185.00	185.00
92-02-041	Yosemite	T. Kinkade	980	225.00	225.00
92-02-042	Country Memories	T. Kinkade	980	185.00	185.00
92-02-043	The Garden Party	T. Kinkade	980	175.00	175.00
92-02-044	Victorian Christmas	T. Kinkade	980	225.00	225.00
92-02-045	Olde Porterfield Gift Shoppe	T. Kinkade	980	175.00	175.00
92-02-046	Fall Colors Victorian	T. Kinkade	980	175.00	175.00
92-02-047	Silent Night	T. Kinkade	980	185.00	185.00
92-02-048	Christmas At the Ahwahnee	T. Kinkade	980	175.00	175.00
92-02-049	Paris, City of Lights	T. Kinkade	980	225.00	225.00
Lightpost Publishing		**Archival Paper/Canvas-Combined Edition**			
90-03-001	Blue Cottage(Paper)	T. Kinkade	750	125.00	125.00
90-03-002	Blue Cottage(Canvas)	T. Kinkade	Combined	435.00	435.00
90-03-003	Moonlit Village(Paper)	T. Kinkade	Closed	225.00	300.00
90-03-004	Moonlit Village(Canvas)	T. Kinkade	Closed	495.00	495-895.
90-03-005	New York, 1932(Paper)	T. Kinkade	935	225.00	225.00
90-03-006	New York, 1932(Canvas)	T. Kinkade	Combined	495.00	495.00
90-03-007	Skating in the Park(Paper)	T. Kinkade	750	275.00	275.00
90-03-008	Skating in the Park(Canvas)	T. Kinkade	Combined	545.00	545.00
Lynn's Prints		**The Amish**			
87-01-001	Backfire	D. Graebner	750	40.00	125.00
87-01-002	Little Apple Picker	D. Graebner	750	40.00	65.00
88-01-003	Cart Full of Apples	D. Graebner	750	25.00	75.00
88-01-004	Mothers Special Day '88	D. Graebner	750	20.00	75.00
88-01-005	Roadside Berry Pickin	D. Graebner	750	25.00	100.00
88-01-006	Sharing the Load	D. Graebner	750	25.00	100.00
87-01-007	Sunday Meeting	D. Graebner	750	25.00	85.00
88-01-008	Sweet Smells	D. Graebner	750	15.00	85.00
88-01-009	Talking With Dolly	D. Graebner	750	15.00	60.00
88-01-010	Back Porch Quilt Fixin	D. Graebner	750	25.00	75.00
87-01-011	Horsey's Treat	D. Graebner	750	40.00	125.00
88-01-012	Sharing	D. Graebner	750	15.00	45.00
89-01-013	In Town Christmas	D. Graebner	300	100.00	250.00
90-01-014	Be Good To Each Other (Stone Lithograph)	D. Graebner	50	100.00	250.00
Mill Pond Press		**Bateman**			
86-01-001	A Resting Place-Cape Buffalo	R. Bateman	950	265.00	265.00
82-01-002	Above the River -Trumpeter Swans	R. Bateman	950	200.00	850-925.
84-01-003	Across the Sky-Snow Geese	R. Bateman	950	220.00	650-750.
80-01-004	African Amber-Lioness Pair	R. Bateman	950	175.00	525-900.
79-01-005	Afternoon Glow-Snowy Owl	R. Bateman	950	125.00	550-625.
90-01-006	Air, The Forest and The Watch	R. Bateman	42,558	325.00	325-400.
84-01-007	Along the Ridge-Grizzly Bears	R. Bateman	950	200.00	700-950.
84-01-008	American Goldfinch-Winter Dress	R. Bateman	950	75.00	200-300.
79-01-009	Among the Leaves-Cottontail Rabbit	R. Bateman	950	75.00	1200.00
80-01-010	Antarctic Elements	R. Bateman	950	125.00	150.00
91-01-011	Arctic Cliff-White Wolves	R. Bateman	13,000	325.00	450-800.
82-01-012	Arctic Evening-White Wolf	R. Bateman	950	185.00	950-1200.
80-01-013	Arctic Family-Polar Bears	R. Bateman	950	150.00	1100-2000.
82-01-014	Arctic Portrait-White Gyrfalcon	R. Bateman	950	175.00	250.00
85-01-015	Arctic Tern Pair	R. Bateman	950	175.00	200.00
81-01-016	Artist and His Dog	R. Bateman	950	150.00	550.00
80-01-017	Asleep on the Hemlock-Screech Owl	R. Bateman	950	125.00	1150.00
91-01-018	At the Cliff-Bobcat	R. Bateman	12,500	325.00	325.00
87-01-019	At the Nest-Secretary Birds	R. Bateman	950	290.00	290.00
82-01-020	At the Roadside-Red-Tailed Hawk	R. Bateman	950	185.00	550.00
80-01-021	Autumn Overture-Moose	R. Bateman	950	245.00	1450.00
80-01-022	Awesome Land-American Elk	R. Bateman	950	245.00	1450.00
89-01-023	Backlight-Mute Swan	R. Bateman	950	275.00	600.00
83-01-024	Bald Eagle Portrait	R. Bateman	950	185.00	300.00
82-01-025	Baobab Tree and Impala	R. Bateman	950	245.00	350.00
80-01-026	Barn Owl in the Churchyard	R. Bateman	950	125.00	775.00
89-01-027	Barn Swallow and Horse Collar	R. Bateman	950	225.00	225.00
82-01-028	Barn Swallows in August	R. Bateman	950	245.00	425.00
85-01-029	Beaver Pond Reflections	R. Bateman	950	185.00	225.00
84-01-030	Big Country, Pronghorn Antelope	R. Bateman	950	185.00	200.00
86-01-031	Black Eagle	R. Bateman	950	200.00	200.00
86-01-032	Black-Tailed Deer in the Olympics	R. Bateman	950	245.00	300.00
86-01-033	Blacksmith Plover	R. Bateman	950	185.00	185.00
91-01-034	Bluebird and Blossoms	R. Bateman	4,500	235.00	235.00
91-01-035	Bluebird and Blossoms-Prestige Ed.	R. Bateman	450	625.00	625.00
80-01-036	Bluffing Bull-African Elephant	R. Bateman	950	135.00	1125.00
81-01-037	Bright Day-Atlantic Puffins	R. Bateman	950	175.00	875.00
89-01-038	Broad-Tailed Hummingbird Pair	R. Bateman	950	225.00	225.00
80-01-039	Brown Pelican and Pilings	R. Bateman	950	165.00	950.00
79-01-040	Bull Moose	R. Bateman	950	125.00	1275.00
78-01-041	By the Tracks-Killdeer	R. Bateman	950	75.00	1200.00
83-01-042	Call of the Wild-Bald Eagle	R. Bateman	950	200.00	250.00
81-01-043	Canada Geese-Nesting	R. Bateman	950	295.00	2950.00
85-01-044	Canada Geese Family(stone lithograph)	R. Bateman	260	350.00	1000.00
85-01-045	Canada Geese Over the Escarpment	R. Bateman	950	135.00	175.00
86-01-046	Canada Geese With Young	R. Bateman	950	195.00	325.00
88-01-047	Cardinal and Wild Apples	R. Bateman	950	235.00	235.00
89-01-048	Catching The Light-Barn Owl	R. Bateman	2,000	295.00	295.00
88-01-049	Cattails, Fireweed and Yellowthroat	R. Bateman	950	235.00	275.00
89-01-050	Centennial Farm	R. Bateman	950	295.00	450.00
80-01-051	Chapel Doors	R. Bateman	950	135.00	375.00
86-01-052	Charging Rhino	R. Bateman	950	325.00	500.00
88-01-053	Cherrywood with Juncos	R. Bateman	950	245.00	245-345.
82-01-054	Cheetah Profile	R. Bateman	950	245.00	500.00
78-01-055	Cheetah With Cubs	R. Bateman	950	95.00	450.00
90-01-056	Chinstrap Penguin	R. Bateman	810	150.00	150.00
92-01-057	Clan of the Raven	R. Bateman	950	235.00	235.00
81-01-058	Clear Night-Wolves	R. Bateman	950	245.00	6500-8100.
88-01-059	Colonial Garden	R. Bateman	950	245.00	245.00
87-01-060	Continuing Generations-Spotted Owls	R. Bateman	950	525.00	1150.00
91-01-061	Cottage Lane-Red Fox	R. Bateman	950	285.00	285.00
84-01-062	Cougar Portrait	R. Bateman	950	95.00	200.00
79-01-063	Country Lane-Pheasants	R. Bateman	950	85.00	300.00
81-01-064	Courting Pair-Whistling Swans	R. Bateman	950	245.00	550.00
81-01-065	Courtship Display-Wild Turkey	R. Bateman	950	175.00	175.00
80-01-066	Coyote in Winter Sage	R. Bateman	950	245.00	3600.00
92-01-067	Cries of Courtship-Red Crowned Cranes	R. Bateman	950	350.00	350.00
80-01-068	Curious Glance-Red Fox	R. Bateman	950	135.00	1200.00
86-01-069	Dark Gyrfalcon	R. Bateman	950	225.00	325.00
82-01-070	Dipper By the Waterfall	R. Bateman	950	165.00	200.00
89-01-071	Dispute Over Prey	R. Bateman	950	325.00	325.00
89-01-072	Distant Danger-Raccoon	R. Bateman	1,600	225.00	225.00
84-01-073	Down for a Drink-Morning Dove	R. Bateman	950	135.00	200.00
78-01-074	Downy Woodpecker on Goldenrod Gall	R. Bateman	950	50.00	1425.00
88-01-075	Dozing Lynx	R. Bateman	950	335.00	1750.00
86-01-076	Driftwood Perch-Striped Swallows	R. Bateman	950	195.00	250.00
83-01-077	Early Snowfall-Ruffed Grouse	R. Bateman	950	195.00	225.00
83-01-078	Early Spring-Bluebird	R. Bateman	950	185.00	450.00
81-01-079	Edge of the Ice-Ermine	R. Bateman	950	175.00	475.00
82-01-080	Edge of the Woods-Whitetail Deer, w/Book	R. Bateman	950	745.00	1400.00
91-01-081	Elephant Cow and Calf	R. Bateman	950	300.00	300.00
86-01-082	Elephant Herd and Sandgrouse	R. Bateman	950	235.00	235.00
91-01-083	Encounter in the Bush-African Lions	R. Bateman	950	295.00	325.00
87-01-084	End of Season-Grizzly	R. Bateman	950	325.00	500.00
91-01-085	Endangered Spaces-Grizzly	R. Bateman	4,008	325.00	325.00
85-01-086	Entering the Water-Common Gulls	R. Bateman	950	195.00	200.00

GRAPHICS

Number	Name	Artist	Edition Limit	Issue Price	Quote
Company		Series			
86-01-087	European Robin and Hydrangeas	R. Bateman	950	130.00	225.00
89-01-088	Evening Call-Common Loon	R. Bateman	950	235.00	525.00
80-01-089	Evening Grosbeak	R. Bateman	950	125.00	1175.00
83-01-090	Evening Idyll-Mute Swans	R. Bateman	950	245.00	525.00
81-01-091	Evening Light-White Gyrfalcon	R. Bateman	950	245.00	1100.00
79-01-092	Evening Snowfall-American Elk	R. Bateman	950	150.00	1900.00
87-01-093	Everglades	R. Bateman	950	360.00	360.00
80-01-094	Fallen Willow-Snowy Owl	R. Bateman	950	200.00	950.00
87-01-095	Farm Lane and Blue Jays	R. Bateman	950	225.00	450.00
86-01-096	Fence Post and Burdock	R. Bateman	950	130.00	130.00
91-01-097	Fluid Power-Orca	R. Bateman	290	2500.00	2500.00
80-01-098	Flying High-Golden Eagle	R. Bateman	950	150.00	975.00
82-01-099	Fox at the Granary	R. Bateman	950	165.00	225.00
92-01-100	Friend or Foe	P. Calle	950	125.00	125.00
82-01-101	Frosty Morning-Blue Jay	R. Bateman	950	185.00	1000.00
82-01-102	Gallinule Family	R. Bateman	950	135.00	135.00
81-01-103	Galloping Herd-Giraffes	R. Bateman	950	175.00	1200.00
85-01-104	Gambel's Quail Pair	R. Bateman	950	95.00	350.00
82-01-105	Gentoo Penguins and Whale Bones	R. Bateman	950	205.00	300.00
83-01-106	Ghost of the North-Great Gray Owl	R. Bateman	950	200.00	2675.00
82-01-107	Golden Crowned Kinglet and Rhododendron	R. Bateman	950	150.00	2575.00
79-01-108	Golden Eagle	R. Bateman	950	150.00	250.00
85-01-109	Golden Eagle Portrait	R. Bateman	950	115.00	175.00
89-01-110	Goldfinch In the Meadow	R. Bateman	1,600	150.00	200.00
83-01-111	Goshawk and Ruffed Grouse	R. Bateman	950	185.00	700.00
88-01-112	Grassy Bank-Great Blue Heron	R. Bateman	950	285.00	285.00
81-01-113	Gray Squirrel	R. Bateman	950	180.00	1250.00
79-01-114	Great Blue Heron	R. Bateman	950	125.00	1300.00
87-01-115	Great Blue Heron in Flight	R. Bateman	950	295.00	550.00
88-01-116	Great Crested Grebe	R. Bateman	950	135.00	135.00
87-01-117	Great Egret Preening	R. Bateman	950	315.00	500.00
83-01-118	Great Horned Owl in the White Pine	R. Bateman	950	225.00	575.00
87-01-119	Greater Kudu Bull	R. Bateman	950	145.00	145.00
91-01-120	Gulls on Pilings	R. Bateman	1,950	265.00	265.00
88-01-121	Hardwood Forest-White-Tailed Buck	R. Bateman	950	345.00	2100.00
88-01-122	Harlequin Duck-Bull Kelp-Executive Ed.	R. Bateman	950	550.00	550.00
88-01-123	Harlequin Duck-Bull Kelp-Gold Plated	R. Bateman	950	300.00	300.00
80-01-124	Heron on the Rocks	R. Bateman	950	75.00	300.00
81-01-125	High Camp at Dusk	R. Bateman	950	245.00	300.00
79-01-126	High Country-Stone Sheep	R. Bateman	950	125.00	325.00
87-01-127	High Kingdom-Snow Leopard	R. Bateman	950	325.00	700-850.
90-01-128	Homage to Ahmed	R. Bateman	290	3300.00	3300.00
84-01-129	Hooded Mergansers in Winter	R. Bateman	950	210.00	650-700.
84-01-130	House Finch and Yucca	R. Bateman	950	95.00	175.00
86-01-131	House Sparrow	R. Bateman	950	125.00	150.00
87-01-132	House Sparrows and Bittersweet	R. Bateman	950	220.00	400.00
86-01-133	Hummingbird Pair Diptych	R. Bateman	950	330.00	475.00
87-01-134	Hurricane Lake-Wood Ducks	R. Bateman	950	135.00	200.00
81-01-135	In for the Evening	R. Bateman	950	150.00	1500.00
84-01-136	In the Brier Patch-Cottontail	R. Bateman	950	165.00	350.00
86-01-137	In the Grass-Lioness	R. Bateman	950	245.00	245.00
85-01-138	In the Highlands-Golden Eagle	R. Bateman	950	235.00	425.00
85-01-139	In the Mountains-Osprey	R. Bateman	950	95.00	125.00
92-01-140	Intrusion-Mountain Gorilla	R. Bateman	2,250	325.00	325.00
90-01-141	Ireland House	R. Bateman	950	265.00	318.00
85-01-142	Irish Cottage and Wagtail	R. Bateman	950	175.00	175.00
90-01-143	Keeper of the Land	R. Bateman	290	3300.00	3300.00
79-01-144	King of the Realm	R. Bateman	950	125.00	675.00
87-01-145	King Penguins	R. Bateman	950	130.00	135.00
81-01-146	Kingfisher and Aspen	R. Bateman	950	225.00	600.00
80-01-147	Kingfisher in Winter	R. Bateman	950	175.00	825.00
80-01-148	Kittiwake Greeting	R. Bateman	950	75.00	550.00
81-01-149	Last Look-Bighorn Sheep	R. Bateman	950	195.00	225.00
87-01-150	Late Winter-Black Squirrel	R. Bateman	950	165.00	165.00
81-01-151	Laughing Gull and Horseshoe Crab	R. Bateman	950	125.00	125.00
82-01-152	Leopard Ambush	R. Bateman	950	245.00	600.00
88-01-153	Leopard and Thomson Gazelle Kill	R. Bateman	950	275.00	275.00
85-01-154	Leopard at Seronera	R. Bateman	950	175.00	280.00
80-01-155	Leopard in a Sausage Tree	R. Bateman	950	150.00	1250.00
84-01-156	Lily Pads and Loon	R. Bateman	950	200.00	1875.00
87-01-157	Lion and Wildebeest	R. Bateman	950	265.00	265.00
80-01-158	Lion at Tsavo	R. Bateman	950	150.00	275.00
78-01-159	Lion Cubs	R. Bateman	950	125.00	800.00
87-01-160	Lioness at Serengeti	R. Bateman	950	325.00	325.00
85-01-161	Lions in the Grass	R. Bateman	950	265.00	1250.00
81-01-162	Little Blue Heron	R. Bateman	950	95.00	275.00
82-01-163	Lively Pair-Chickadees	R. Bateman	950	160.00	450.00
83-01-164	Loon Family	R. Bateman	950	200.00	750.00
90-01-165	Lunging Heron	R. Bateman	1,250	225.00	225.00
78-01-166	Majesty on the Wing-Bald Eagle	R. Bateman	950	150.00	4000.00
88-01-167	Mallard Family at Sunset	R. Bateman	950	235.00	235.00
86-01-168	Mallard Family-Misty Marsh	R. Bateman	950	130.00	175.00
86-01-169	Mallard Pair-Early Winter	R. Bateman	41,740	135.00	200.00
86-01-170	Mallard Pair-Early Winter Gold Plated	R. Bateman	7,691	250.00	375.00
85-01-171	Mallard Pair-Early Winter 24K Gold	R. Bateman	950	1650.00	2000.00
89-01-172	Mangrove Morning-Roseate Spoonbills	R. Bateman	2,000	325.00	325.00
91-01-173	Mangrove Shadow-Common Egret	R. Bateman	1,250	285.00	285.00
86-01-174	Marginal Meadow	R. Bateman	950	220.00	350.00
79-01-175	Master of the Herd-African Buffalo	R. Bateman	950	150.00	2250.00
84-01-176	May Maple-Scarlet Tanager	R. Bateman	950	175.00	825.00
82-01-177	Meadow's Edge-Mallard	R. Bateman	950	175.00	900.00
82-01-178	Merganser Family in Hiding	R. Bateman	950	200.00	525.00
89-01-179	Midnight-Black Wolf	R. Bateman	25,352	325.00	1650-2200.
80-01-180	Mischief on the Prowl-Raccoon	R. Bateman	950	85.00	350.00
80-01-181	Misty Coast-Gulls	R. Bateman	950	135.00	600.00
84-01-182	Misty Lake-Osprey	R. Bateman	950	95.00	300.00
81-01-183	Misty Morning-Loons	R. Bateman	950	150.00	3000.00
86-01-184	Moose at Water's Edge	R. Bateman	950	130.00	225.00
90-01-185	Morning Cove-Common Loon	R. Bateman	950	165.00	165.00
85-01-186	Morning Dew-Roe Deer	R. Bateman	950	175.00	175.00
83-01-187	Morning on the Flats-Bison	R. Bateman	950	200.00	300.00
84-01-188	Morning on the River-Trumpeter Swans	R. Bateman	950	185.00	300.00
90-01-189	Mossy Branches-Spotted Owl	R. Bateman	4,500	300.00	525.00
90-01-190	Mowed Meadow	R. Bateman	950	190.00	190.00
86-01-191	Mule Deer in Aspen	R. Bateman	950	175.00	175.00
83-01-192	Mule Deer in Winter	R. Bateman	950	200.00	350.00
88-01-193	Muskoka Lake-Common Loons	R. Bateman	950	265.00	450.00
89-01-194	Near Glenburnie	R. Bateman	950	265.00	265.00
83-01-195	New Season-American Robin	R. Bateman	950	200.00	450.00
86-01-196	Northern Reflections-Loon Family	R. Bateman	8,631	255.00	2100.00
85-01-197	Old Whaling Base and Fur Seals	R. Bateman	950	195.00	550.00
87-01-198	Old Willow and Mallards	R. Bateman	950	325.00	390.00
80-01-199	On the Alert-Chipmunk	R. Bateman	950	60.00	500.00
85-01-200	On the Garden Wall	R. Bateman	950	115.00	300.00
85-01-201	Orca Procession	R. Bateman	950	245.00	2525.00
81-01-202	Osprey Family	R. Bateman	950	245.00	325.00
83-01-203	Osprey in the Rain	R. Bateman	950	110.00	650.00
87-01-204	Otter Study	R. Bateman	950	235.00	375.00
81-01-205	Pair of Skimmers	R. Bateman	950	150.00	150.00
88-01-206	Panda's At Play (stone lithograph)	R. Bateman	160	400.00	2500.00
84-01-207	Peregrine and Ruddy Turnstones	R. Bateman	950	200.00	350.00
85-01-208	Peregrine Falcon and White-Throated Swifts	R. Bateman	950	245.00	550.00
87-01-209	Peregrine Falcon on the Cliff-Stone Litho	R. Bateman	525	350.00	625.00
83-01-210	Pheasant in Cornfield	R. Bateman	950	200.00	375.00
88-01-211	Pheasants at Dusk	R. Bateman	950	325.00	525.00
82-01-212	Pileated Woodpecker on Beech Tree	R. Bateman	950	175.00	525.00
90-01-213	Pintails in Spring	R. Bateman	9,651	135.00	135.00
82-01-214	Pioneer Memories-Magpie Pair	R. Bateman	950	175.00	250.00
87-01-215	Plowed Field-Snowy Owl	R. Bateman	950	145.00	400.00
90-01-216	Polar Bear	R. Bateman	290	3300.00	3300.00
82-01-217	Polar Bear Profile	R. Bateman	950	210.00	2350.00
82-01-218	Polar Bears at Bafin Island	R. Bateman	950	245.00	875.00
90-01-219	Power Play-Rhinoceros	R. Bateman	950	320.00	320.00
80-01-220	Prairie Evening-Short-Eared Owl	R. Bateman	950	150.00	200.00
88-01-221	Preening Pair-Canada Geese	R. Bateman	950	235.00	300.00
87-01-222	Pride of Autumn-Canada Goose	R. Bateman	950	135.00	200.00
86-01-223	Proud Swimmer-Snow Goose	R. Bateman	950	185.00	185.00
89-01-224	Pumpkin Time	R. Bateman	950	195.00	195.00
82-01-225	Queen Anne's Lace and AmericanGoldfinch	R. Bateman	950	150.00	1000.00
84-01-226	Ready for Flight-Peregrine Falcon	R. Bateman	950	185.00	500.00
82-01-227	Ready for the Hunt-Snowy Owl	R. Bateman	950	245.00	550.00
88-01-228	Red Crossbills	R. Bateman	950	125.00	125.00
84-01-229	Red Fox on the Prowl	R. Bateman	950	245.00	1500.00
82-01-230	Red Squirrel	R. Bateman	950	175.00	700.00
86-01-231	Red Wolf	R. Bateman	950	250.00	525.00
81-01-232	Red-Tailed Hawk by the Cliff	R. Bateman	950	245.00	550.00
81-01-233	Red-Winged Blackbird and Rail Fence	R. Bateman	950	195.00	225.00
84-01-234	Reeds	R. Bateman	950	185.00	575.00
86-01-235	Resting Place-Cape Buffalo	R. Bateman	950	265.00	265.00
87-01-236	Rhino at Ngoro Ngoro	R. Bateman	950	325.00	325.00
86-01-237	Robins at the Nest	R. Bateman	950	185.00	225.00
87-01-238	Rocky Point-October	R. Bateman	950	195.00	275.00
80-01-239	Rocky Wilderness-Cougar	R. Bateman	950	175.00	1425.00
90-01-240	Rolling Waves-Lesser Scaup	R. Bateman	3,330	125.00	125.00
81-01-241	Rough-Legged Hawk in the Elm	R. Bateman	950	175.00	175.00
81-01-242	Royal Family-Mute Swans	R. Bateman	950	245.00	1100.00
83-01-243	Ruby Throat and Columbine	R. Bateman	950	150.00	2200.00
87-01-244	Ruddy Turnstones	R. Bateman	950	175.00	175.00
81-01-245	Sarah E. with Gulls	R. Bateman	950	245.00	2625.00
91-01-246	Sea Otter Study	R. Bateman	950	150.00	150.00
81-01-247	Sheer Drop-Mountain Goats	R. Bateman	950	245.00	2800.00
88-01-248	Shelter	R. Bateman	950	325.00	1000.00
92-01-349	Siberian Tiger	R. Bateman	4,500	325.00	325.00
84-01-250	Smallwood	R. Bateman	950	200.00	500.00
90-01-251	Snow Leopard	R. Bateman	290	2500.00	3500.00
85-01-252	Snowy Hemlock-Barred Owl	R. Bateman	950	245.00	400.00
87-01-253	Snowy Owl and Milkweed	R. Bateman	950	235.00	950.00
83-01-254	Snowy Owl on Driftwood	R. Bateman	950	245.00	1450.00
83-01-255	Spirits of the Forest	R. Bateman	950	170.00	1750.00
86-01-256	Split Rails-Snow Buntings	R. Bateman	950	220.00	220.00
80-01-257	Spring Cardinal	R. Bateman	950	125.00	600.00
82-01-258	Spring Marsh-Pintail Pair	R. Bateman	950	200.00	275.00
80-01-259	Spring Thaw-Killdeer	R. Bateman	950	85.00	150.00
82-01-260	Still Morning-Herring Gulls	R. Bateman	950	200.00	250.00
87-01-261	Stone Sheep Ram	R. Bateman	950	175.00	175.00
85-01-262	Stream Bank June	R. Bateman	950	160.00	175.00
84-01-263	Stretching-Canada Goose	R. Bateman	950	225.00	3600-3900.
85-01-264	Strutting-Ring-Necked Pheasant	R. Bateman	950	225.00	325.00
85-01-265	Sudden Blizzard-Red-Tailed Hawk	R. Bateman	950	245.00	600.00
84-01-266	Summer Morning-Loon	R. Bateman	950	185.00	1250.00
90-01-267	Summer Morning Pasture	R. Bateman	950	175.00	175.00
86-01-268	Summertime-Polar Bears	R. Bateman	950	225.00	475.00
79-01-269	Surf and Sanderlings	R. Bateman	950	65.00	450.00
81-01-270	Swift Fox	R. Bateman	950	175.00	350.00
86-01-271	Swift Fox Study	R. Bateman	950	115.00	150.00
87-01-272	Sylvan Stream-Mute Swans	R. Bateman	950	125.00	125.00
84-01-273	Tadpole Time	R. Bateman	950	135.00	475.00
88-01-274	Tawny Owl In Beech	R. Bateman	950	325.00	600.00
92-01-275	Tembo (African Elephant)	R. Bateman	1,550	350.00	350.00
88-01-276	The Challenge-Bull Moose	R. Bateman	10,671	325.00	325.00
91-01-277	The Scolding-Chickadees & Screech Owl	R. Bateman	12,500	235.00	235.00
84-01-278	Tiger at Dawn	R. Bateman	950	225.00	2500.00
83-01-279	Tiger Portrait	R. Bateman	950	130.00	400.00
88-01-280	Tree Swallow over Pond	R. Bateman	950	290.00	290.00
91-01-281	Trumpeter Swan Family	R. Bateman	290	2500.00	2500.00
85-01-282	Trumpeter Swans and Aspen	R. Bateman	950	245.00	550.00
79-01-283	Up in the Pine-Great Horned Owl	R. Bateman	950	150.00	550.00
80-01-284	Vantage Point	R. Bateman	950	245.00	1200.00
81-01-285	Watchful Repose-Black Bear	R. Bateman	950	245.00	700.00
89-01-286	Vulture And Wildebeest	R. Bateman	550	295.00	295.00
85-01-287	Weathered Branch-Bald Eagle	R. Bateman	950	115.00	300.00
91-01-288	Whistling Swan-Lake Erie	R. Bateman	1,950	325.00	325.00
85-01-289	White-Breasted Nuthatch on a Beech Tree	R. Bateman	950	175.00	300.00
80-01-290	White Encounter-Polar Bear	R. Bateman	950	245.00	4200-4800.
80-01-291	White-Footed Mouse in Wintergreen	R. Bateman	950	60.00	650.00
82-01-292	White-Footed Mouse on Aspen	R. Bateman	950	90.00	180.00
92-01-293	White-Tailed Deer Through the Birches	R. Bateman	10,000	335.00	335.00
84-01-294	White-Throated Sparrow and Pussy Willow	R. Bateman	950	150.00	580.00
90-01-295	White on White-Snowshoe Hare	R. Bateman	950	195.00	590.00
82-01-296	White World-Dall Sheep	R. Bateman	950	200.00	450.00
91-01-297	Wide Horizon-Tundra Swans	R. Bateman	2,862	325.00	135-325.
91-01-298	Wide Horizon-Tundra Swans Companion	R. Bateman	2,862	325.00	325.00
86-01-299	Wildbeest	R. Bateman	950	185.00	185.00
82-01-300	Willet on the Shore	R. Bateman	950	125.00	225.00
79-01-301	Wily and Wary-Red Fox	R. Bateman	950	125.00	1500.00
84-01-302	Window into Ontario	R. Bateman	950	265.00	1500.00
83-01-303	Winter Barn	R. Bateman	950	170.00	400.00
79-01-304	Winter Cardinal	R. Bateman	950	75.00	3550.00
85-01-305	Winter Companion	R. Bateman	950	175.00	500.00
80-01-306	Winter Elm-American Kestrel	R. Bateman	950	135.00	600.00
86-01-307	Winter in the Mountains-Raven	R. Bateman	950	200.00	200.00
83-01-308	Winter-Lady Cardinal	R. Bateman	950	200.00	1500.00
81-01-309	Winter Mist-Great Horned Owl	R. Bateman	950	245.00	900.00
79-01-310	Winter-Snowshoe Hare	R. Bateman	950	95.00	1200.00
80-01-311	Winter Song-Chickadees	R. Bateman	950	95.00	900.00
84-01-312	Winter Sunset-Moose	R. Bateman	950	245.00	2700.00

Company / Number	Name	Series / Artist	Edition Limit	Issue Price	Quote
81-01-313	Winter Wren	R. Bateman	950	135.00	250.00
87-01-314	Wise One, The	R. Bateman	950	325.00	800.00
79-01-315	Wolf Pack in Moonlight	R. Bateman	950	95.00	3000.00
83-01-316	Wolves on the Trail	R. Bateman	950	225.00	700.00
85-01-317	Wood Bison Portrait	R. Bateman	950	165.00	200.00
83-01-318	Woodland Drummer-Ruffed Grouse	R. Bateman	950	185.00	250.00
81-01-319	Wrangler's Campsite-Gray Jay	R. Bateman	950	195.00	550.00
79-01-320	Yellow-Rumped Warbler	R. Bateman	950	50.00	575.00
78-01-321	Young Barn Swallow	R. Bateman	950	75.00	700.00
83-01-322	Young Elf Owl-Old Saguaro	R. Bateman	950	95.00	250.00
91-01-323	Young Giraffe	R. Bateman	290	850.00	850.00
89-01-324	Young Kittiwake	R. Bateman	950	195.00	195.00
88-01-325	Young Sandhill-Cranes	R. Bateman	950	325.00	325.00
89-01-326	Young Snowy Owl	R. Bateman	950	195.00	195.00
Mill Pond Press		**Reece**			
48-02-001	Federal Duck Stamp-Buffleheads	M. Reece	200	15.00	1200.00
51-02-002	Federal Duck Stamp-Gadwalls	M. Reece	250	15.00	1200.00
59-02-003	Federal Duck Stamp-Retriever	M. Reece	400	15.00	3750.00
69-02-004	Federal Duck Stamp-White-Winged Scoters	M. Reece	750	50.00	940.00
71-02-005	Federal Duck Stamp-Cinnamon Teal	M. Reece	950	75.00	2850.00
91-02-006	Offshore Lunch-Common Loons	M. Reece	550	195.00	195.00
91-02-007	The Chase-Wolf Pack	M. Reece	550	150.00	150.00
91-02-008	Upland Series IV-Ruffed Goose	M. Reece	950	125.00	125.00
Mill Pond Press		**Calle**			
84-03-001	A Brace for the Spit	P. Calle	950	110.00	275.00
83-03-002	A Winter Surprise	P. Calle	950	195.00	800.00
81-03-003	Almost Home	P. Calle	950	150.00	150.00
91-03-004	Almost There	P. Calle	950	165.00	165.00
89-03-005	And A Good Book For Company	P. Calle	950	135.00	190.00
81-03-006	And Still Miles to Go	P. Calle	950	245.00	300.00
81-03-007	Andrew At The Falls	P. Calle	950	150.00	175.00
89-03-008	The Beaver Men	P. Calle	950	125.00	125.00
80-03-009	Caring for the Herd	P. Calle	950	110.00	110.00
84-03-010	Chance Encounter	P. Calle	950	225.00	300.00
81-03-011	Chief High Pipe (Color)	P. Calle	950	265.00	275.00
80-03-012	Chief High Pipe (Pencil)	P. Calle	950	75.00	165.00
80-03-013	Chief Joseph-Man of Peace	P. Calle	950	135.00	150.00
90-03-014	Children of Walpi	P. Calle	350	160.00	160.00
90-03-015	The Doll Maker	P. Calle	950	95.00	95.00
82-03-016	Emerging from the Woods	P. Calle	950	110.00	110-160.
81-03-017	End of a Long Day	P. Calle	950	150.00	150-190.
84-03-018	Fate of the Late Migrant	P. Calle	950	110.00	300.00
83-03-019	Free Spirits	P. Calle	950	195.00	325.00
83-03-020	Free Trapper Study	P. Calle	550	75.00	125-300.
81-03-021	Fresh Tracks	P. Calle	950	150.00	165.00
81-03-022	Friend of Foe	P. Calle	950	125.00	125.00
81-03-023	Friends	P. Calle	950	150.00	150.00
89-03-024	The Fur Trapper	P. Calle	550	75.00	175.00
82-03-025	Generations in the Valley	P. Calle	950	245.00	245.00
85-03-026	Grandmother, The	P. Calle	950	150.00	150.00
92-03-027	Hunter of Geese	P. Calle	950	125.00	125.00
83-03-028	In Search of Beaver	P. Calle	950	225.00	600.00
91-03-029	In the Beginning . . . Friends	P. Calle	1,250	250.00	250.00
87-03-030	In the Land of the Giants	P. Calle	950	245.00	780.00
90-03-031	Interrupted Journey	P. Calle	1,750	265.00	265.00
90-03-032	Interrupted Journey-Prestige Ed.	P. Calle	290	465.00	465.00
87-03-033	Into the Great Alone	P. Calle	950	245.00	600.00
81-03-034	Just Over the Ridge	P. Calle	950	245.00	325.00
80-03-035	Landmark Tree	P. Calle	950	125.00	225.00
91-03-036	Man of the Fur Trade	P. Calle	550	110.00	110.00
84-03-037	Mountain Man	P. Calle	950	95.00	250-550.
89-03-038	Navajo Madonna	P. Calle	650	95.00	95.00
81-03-039	One With The Land	P. Calle	950	245.00	325.00
81-03-040	Pause at the Lower Falls	P. Calle	950	110.00	125.00
80-03-041	Prayer to the Great Mystery	P. Calle	950	245.00	400.00
82-03-042	Return to Camp	P. Calle	950	245.00	400.00
80-03-043	Sioux Chief	P. Calle	950	85.00	85-140.00
90-03-044	Son of Sitting Bull	P. Calle	950	95.00	95.00
86-03-045	Snow Hunter	P. Calle	950	150.00	250-410.
80-03-046	Something for the Pot	P. Calle	950	175.00	1000.00
85-03-047	Storyteller of the Mountains	P. Calle	950	225.00	575.00
83-03-048	Strays From the Flyway	P. Calle	950	195.00	250-340.
81-03-049	Teton Friends	P. Calle	950	150.00	200.00
91-03-050	The Silenced Honkers	P. Calle	1,250	250.00	250.00
91-03-051	They Call Me Matthew	P. Calle	950	125.00	125.00
92-03-052	Through the Tall Grass	P. Calle	950	175.00	175.00
82-03-053	Two from the Flock	P. Calle	950	245.00	400.00
80-03-054	View from the Heights	P. Calle	950	245.00	350.00
80-03-055	When Snow Came Early	P. Calle	950	85.00	250-340.
84-03-056	When Trails Cross	P. Calle	950	245.00	750.00
91-03-057	When Trails Grow Cold	P. Calle	2,500	265.00	265.00
91-03-058	When Trails Grow Cold-Prestige Ed.	P. Calle	290	465.00	465-600.
81-03-059	Winter Hunter (Color)	P. Calle	950	245.00	725.00
80-03-060	Winter Hunter (Pencil)	P. Calle	950	65.00	450.00
Mill Pond Press		**Peterson**			
76-04-001	Adelie Penguins	R. Peterson	950	35.00	35.00
74-04-002	Bald Eagle	R. Peterson	950	150.00	440.00
73-04-003	Baltimore Oriole S/N	R. Peterson	450	150.00	300.00
76-04-004	Barn Owl	R. Peterson	950	225.00	300.00
74-04-005	Barn Swallow S/N	R. Peterson	750	150.00	250-350.
76-04-006	Blue Jays	R. Peterson	950	150.00	350.00
77-04-007	BlueBird	R. Peterson	950	75.00	225.00
74-04-008	Bobolink S/N	R. Peterson	750	150.00	275.00
75-04-009	Bobwhites	R. Peterson	950	150.00	285.00
73-04-010	Cardinal S/N	R. Peterson	450	150.00	525.00
73-04-011	Flicker	R. Peterson	450	150.00	225.00
76-04-012	Golden Eagle	R. Peterson	950	200.00	210.00
74-04-013	Great Horned Owl	R. Peterson	950	150.00	450.00
79-04-014	Gyrfalcon	R. Peterson	950	225.00	360.00
78-04-015	Mockingbird	R. Peterson	950	125.00	250-300.
77-04-016	Peregrine Falcon	R. Peterson	950	175.00	300.00
78-04-017	Ring-Necked Pheasant	R. Peterson	950	200.00	250-300.
78-04-018	Robin	R. Peterson	950	125.00	410.00
78-04-019	Rose-Breasted Grosbeak	R. Peterson	950	125.00	125.00
75-04-020	Ruffed Grouse	R. Peterson	950	150.00	350.00
77-04-021	Scarlet Tanager	R. Peterson	950	125.00	200.00
75-04-022	Sea Otters	R. Peterson	950	25.00	100.00
76-04-023	Snowy Owl	R. Peterson	950	175.00	475.00
77-04-024	Sooty Terns S/N	R. Peterson	450	50.00	85.00
77-04-025	Willets S/N	R. Peterson	450	50.00	75.00
73-04-026	Wood Thrush	R. Peterson	450	150.00	295.00
Mill Pond Press		**Machetanz**			
79-05-001	Beginnings	F. Machetanz	950	175.00	425.00
88-05-002	Change of Direction	F. Machetanz	950	320.00	320-670.
89-05-003	The Chief Dances	F. Machetanz	950	235.00	235.00
79-05-004	Decision on the Ice Field	F. Machetanz	950	150.00	450.00
84-05-005	End of a Long Day	F. Machetanz	950	200.00	200-370.
85-05-006	End of the Hunt	F. Machetanz	950	245.00	255.00
78-05-007	Face to Face	F. Machetanz	950	150.00	1500.00
92-05-008	First Day in Harness	F. Machetanz	950	225.00	225.00
90-05-009	Glory of the Trail	F. Machetanz	950	225.00	275.00
81-05-010	Golden Years	F. Machetanz	950	245.00	590.00
90-05-011	The Grass is Always Greener	F. Machetanz	950	200.00	200.00
92-05-012	Harpooner's Moment	F. Machetanz	950	225.00	225.00
84-05-013	The Heritage of Alaska	F. Machetanz	950	400.00	800.00
78-05-014	Hunter's Dawn	F. Machetanz	950	125.00	500.00
78-05-015	Into the Home Stretch	F. Machetanz	950	175.00	700.00
91-05-016	Kayak Man	F. Machetanz	950	215.00	215-275.
80-05-017	King of the Mountain	F. Machetanz	950	200.00	200.00
86-05-018	Kyrok-Eskimo Seamstress	F. Machetanz	950	225.00	225.00
85-05-019	Land of the Midnight Sun	F. Machetanz	950	245.00	245-270.
85-05-020	Language of the Snow	F. Machetanz	950	195.00	195-240.
86-05-021	Leaving the Nest	F. Machetanz	950	245.00	245.00
86-05-022	Lone Musher	F. Machetanz	950	245.00	145-275.
84-05-023	Many Miles Together	F. Machetanz	950	245.00	245-285.
81-05-024	Midday Moonlight	F. Machetanz	950	265.00	425.00
84-05-025	Midnight Watch	F. Machetanz	950	250.00	250-300.
82-05-026	Mighty Hunter	F. Machetanz	950	265.00	400.00
82-05-027	Moonlit Stakeout	F. Machetanz	950	265.00	525.00
82-05-028	Moose Tracks	F. Machetanz	950	265.00	300.00
86-05-029	Mt. Blackburn-Sovereign of the Wrangells	F. Machetanz	950	245.00	245.00
83-05-030	Nanook	F. Machetanz	950	295.00	295.00
80-05-031	Nelchina Trail	F. Machetanz	950	245.00	450.00
79-05-032	Pick of the Litter	F. Machetanz	950	165.00	1050.00
90-05-033	Quality Time	F. Machetanz	950	200.00	200-240.
79-05-034	Reaching the Campsite	F. Machetanz	950	200.00	400.00
85-05-035	Reaching the Pass	F. Machetanz	950	265.00	465.00
84-05-036	Smoke Dreams	F. Machetanz	950	250.00	400-450.
80-05-037	Sourdough	F. Machetanz	950	245.00	1125.00
87-05-038	Spring Fever	F. Machetanz	950	225.00	225.00
84-05-039	Story of the Beads	F. Machetanz	950	245.00	245.00
91-05-040	The Search for Gold	F. Machetanz	950	225.00	225.00
82-05-041	The Tender Arctic	F. Machetanz	950	295.00	750.00
83-05-042	They Opened the North Country	F. Machetanz	950	245.00	245.00
91-05-043	Tundra Flower	F. Machetanz	950	235.00	235-350.
81-05-044	What Every Hunter Fears	F. Machetanz	950	245.00	375.00
80-05-045	When Three's a Crowd	F. Machetanz	950	225.00	825.00
81-05-046	Where Men and Dogs Seem Small	F. Machetanz	950	245.00	400.00
81-05-047	Winter Harvest	F. Machetanz	950	265.00	325.00
Mill Pond Press		**Parker**			
86-06-001	Above the Breakers-Osprey	R. Parker	950	150.00	175.00
86-06-002	At End of Day-Wolves	R. Parker	950	235.00	325.00
86-06-003	Autumn Foraging-Moose	R. Parker	950	175.00	425.00
86-06-004	Autumn Leaves-Red Fox	R. Parker	950	95.00	100.00
89-06-005	Autumn Maples-Wolves	R. Parker	950	195.00	195.00
86-06-006	Autumn Meadow-Elk	R. Parker	950	195.00	200.00
90-06-007	Breaking the Silence-Wolves	R. Parker	1,250	195.00	300.00
86-06-008	Cardinal In Blue Spruce	R. Parker	950	125.00	150.00
86-06-009	Cardinal in Brambles	R. Parker	950	125.00	150.00
84-06-010	Chickadees In Autumn	R. Parker	950	75.00	75.00
86-06-011	Creekside-Cougar	R. Parker	950	225.00	350.00
91-06-012	Deep Snow-Whitetail	R. Parker	950	175.00	175.00
89-06-013	Deep Water-Orcas	R. Parker	1,250	195.00	195.00
89-06-014	Early Snowfall-Elk	R. Parker	950	185.00	185.00
87-06-015	Evening Glow-Wolf Pack	R. Parker	950	245.00	275.00
84-06-016	Face of the North	R. Parker	950	95.00	250.00
89-06-017	Flying Redtail	R. Parker	290	295.00	295.00
86-06-018	Following Mama-Mute Swans	R. Parker	950	165.00	475.00
91-06-019	Forest Trek-Gray Wolf	R. Parker	950	185.00	185.00
87-06-020	Freeze Up-Canada Geese	R. Parker	950	85.00	100.00
91-06-021	Gila Woodpecker	R. Parker	950	135.00	135.00
84-06-022	Gray Wolf Portrait	R. Parker	950	115.00	175.00
90-06-023	Icy Morning-Red Fox	R. Parker	950	150.00	150.00
90-06-024	Inside Passage-Orcas	R. Parker	1,500	195.00	195.00
86-06-025	Just Resting-Sea Otter	R. Parker	950	85.00	250.00
90-06-026	Lioness and Cubs	R. Parker	150	295.00	295.00
83-06-027	Mallard Family	R. Parker	950	95.00	95.00
85-06-028	Misty Dawn-Loon	R. Parker	950	120.00	525.00
91-06-029	Moonlit Tracks-Wolves	R. Parker	1,500	200.00	225-400.
90-06-030	Moose in the Brush	R. Parker	950	195.00	195.00
86-06-031	Morning on the Lagoon-Mute Swan	R. Parker	950	95.00	100.00
91-06-032	Mother and Son-Orcas	R. Parker	950	185.00	185.00
86-06-033	Northern Morning-Arctic Fox	R. Parker	950	125.00	175.00
87-06-034	On the Run-Wolf Pack	R. Parker	950	245.00	300.00
82-06-035	Racoon Pair	R. Parker	950	95.00	400.00
87-06-036	Rail Fence-Bluebirds	R. Parker	950	105.00	125.00
85-06-037	Reflections-Mallard	R. Parker	950	85.00	175.00
86-06-038	Rimrock-Cougar	R. Parker	950	200.00	900.00
83-06-039	Riverside Pause-River Otter	R. Parker	950	95.00	150.00
88-06-040	Silent Passage-Orcas	R. Parker	950	175.00	175.00
84-06-041	Silent Steps-Lynx	R. Parker	950	145.00	325.00
82-06-042	Snow on the Pine-Chickadees	R. Parker	950	95.00	100.00
85-06-043	Spring Arrivals-Canada Geese	R. Parker	950	120.00	200.00
82-06-044	Spring Mist-Gray Wolf	R. Parker	950	155.00	375.00
85-06-045	Waiting Out the Storm	R. Parker	950	105.00	400.00
82-06-046	Weathered Wood-Bluebirds	R. Parker	950	75.00	175.00
84-06-047	When Paths Cross	R. Parker	950	185.00	400.00
86-06-048	Whitetail and Wolves	R. Parker	950	180.00	300.00
85-06-049	Wings Over Winter-Bald Eagle	R. Parker	950	135.00	350.00
87-06-050	Winter Creek and Whitetails	R. Parker	950	185.00	185.00
86-06-051	Winter Creek-Coyote	R. Parker	950	130.00	275.00
87-06-052	Winter Encounter-Wolf	R. Parker	950	235.00	350.00
84-06-053	Winter Jay	R. Parker	950	95.00	150.00
90-06-054	Winter Lookout-Cougar	R. Parker	950	175.00	175.00
87-06-055	Winter Sage-Coyote	R. Parker	950	225.00	350.00
87-06-056	Winter Storm-Coyotes	R. Parker	950	245.00	325.00
83-06-057	Yellow Dawn-American Elk	R. Parker	950	130.00	200.00
Mill Pond Press		**Seerey-Lester**			
86-08-001	Above the Treeline-Cougar	J. Seerey-Lester	950	130.00	175.00
87-08-002	Alpenglow-Artic Wolf	J. Seerey-Lester	950	200.00	275.00

Number	Name	Artist	Edition Limit	Issue Price	Quote
84-08-003	Among the Cattails-Canada Geese	J. Seerey-Lester	950	130.00	425.00
84-08-004	Artic Procession-Willow Ptarmigan	J. Seerey-Lester	950	220.00	600.00
90-08-005	Artic Wolf Pups	J. Seerey-Lester	290	500.00	500.00
87-08-006	Autumn Mist-Barred Owl	J. Seerey-Lester	950	160.00	225.00
92-08-007	Banyan Ambush- Black Panther	J. Seerey-Lester	950	235.00	235.00
84-08-008	Basking-Brown Pelicans	J. Seerey-Lester	950	115.00	125.00
90-08-009	Bittersweet Winter-Cardinal	J. Seerey-Lester	1,250	150.00	275.00
92-08-010	Black Magic-Panther	J. Seerey-Lester	750	195.00	195.00
87-08-011	Canyon Creek-Cougar	J. Seerey-Lester	950	195.00	450.00
85-08-012	Children of the Forest-Red Fox Kits	J. Seerey-Lester	950	110.00	150.00
85-08-013	Children of the Tundra-Artic Wolf Pup	J. Seerey-Lester	950	110.00	225.00
84-08-014	Close Encounter-Bobcat	J. Seerey-Lester	950	130.00	190.00
83-08-015	Cool Retreat-Lynx	J. Seerey-Lester	950	85.00	100.00
89-08-016	Cougar Run	J. Seerey-Lester	950	185.00	450.00
90-08-017	Dawn Majesty	J. Seerey-Lester	1,250	185.00	185.00
91-08-018	Denali Family-Grizzly Bear	J. Seerey-Lester	950	195.00	195.00
88-08-019	Edge of the Forest-Timber Wolves	J. Seerey-Lester	950	500.00	700.00
89-08-020	Evening Duet-Snowy Egrets	J. Seerey-Lester	1,250	185.00	185.00
91-08-021	Evening Encounter-Grizzly & Wolf	J. Seerey-Lester	1,250	185.00	185.00
91-08-022	Face to Face	J. Seerey-Lester	1,250	200.00	200.00
85-08-023	Fallen Birch-Chipmunk	J. Seerey-Lester	950	60.00	250.00
85-08-024	First Light-Gray Jays	J. Seerey-Lester	950	130.00	200.00
83-08-025	First Snow-Grizzly Bears	J. Seerey-Lester	950	95.00	250.00
85-08-026	Gathering-Gray Wolves, The	J. Seerey-Lester	950	165.00	350.00
89-08-027	Gorilla	J. Seerey-Lester	290	400.00	600.00
90-08-028	Grizzly Litho	J. Seerey-Lester	290	400.00	400.00
89-08-029	Heavy Going-Grizzly	J. Seerey-Lester	950	175.00	175.00
86-08-030	Hidden Admirer-Moose	J. Seerey-Lester	950	165.00	275.00
89-08-031	High and Mighty-Gorilla	J. Seerey-Lester	950	185.00	225.00
86-08-032	High Country Champion-Grizzly	J. Seerey-Lester	950	175.00	275.00
84-08-033	High Ground-Wolves	J. Seerey-Lester	950	130.00	325.00
84-08-034	Icy Outcrop-White Gyrfalcon	J. Seerey-Lester	950	115.00	200.00
90-08-035	In Their Presence	J. Seerey-Lester	1,250	200.00	200.00
85-08-036	Island Sanctuary-Mallards	J. Seerey-Lester	950	95.00	175.00
83-08-037	Lone Fisherman-Great Blue Heron	J. Seerey-Lester	950	85.00	300.00
84-08-038	Lying Low-Cougar	J. Seerey-Lester	950	85.00	450.00
91-08-039	Monsoon-White Tiger	J. Seerey-Lester	950	195.00	195.00
91-08-040	Moonlight Chase-Cougar	J. Seerey-Lester	1,250	195.00	195-220.
88-08-041	Morning Display-Common Loons	J. Seerey-Lester	950	135.00	300.00
84-08-042	Morning Mist-Snowy Owl	J. Seerey-Lester	950	95.00	95-180.00
90-08-043	Mountain Cradle	J. Seerey-Lester	1,250	200.00	200.00
90-08-044	Night Run-Artic Wolves	J. Seerey-Lester	1,250	200.00	250.00
87-08-045	Out of the Blizzard-Timber Wolves	J. Seerey-Lester	950	215.00	350.00
92-08-046	Out of the Darkness	J. Seerey-Lester	290	200.00	200.00
91-08-047	Out on a Limb-Young Barred Owl	J. Seerey-Lester	950	185.00	185.00
91-08-048	Panda Trilogy	J. Seerey-Lester	950	375.00	375.00
90-08-049	The Plunge-Northern Sea Lions	J. Seerey-Lester	1,250	200.00	200.00
86-08-050	Racing the Storm-Artic Wolves	J. Seerey-Lester	950	200.00	350.00
92-08-051	Regal Majesty	J. Seerey-Lester	290	200.00	200.00
90-08-052	Seasonal Greeting-Cardinal	J. Seerey-Lester	1,250	150.00	150.00
91-08-053	Sisters-Artic Wolves	J. Seerey-Lester	1,250	185.00	185.00
89-08-054	Sneak Peak	J. Seerey-Lester	950	185.00	185.00
89-08-055	Softly, Softly-White Tiger	J. Seerey-Lester	950	220.00	490.00
91-08-056	Something Stirred (Bengal Tiger)	J. Seerey-Lester	950	195.00	195.00
84-08-057	Spirit of the North-White Wolf	J. Seerey-Lester	950	130.00	185.00
90-08-058	Spout	J. Seerey-Lester	290	500.00	500.00
86-08-059	Spring Mist Chickadees	J. Seerey-Lester	950	105.00	150.00
89-08-060	Spring Flurry-Adelie Penguins	J. Seerey-Lester	950	185.00	185.00
90-08-061	Suitors-Wood Ducks	J. Seerey-Lester	3,313	135.00	135.00
90-08-062	Summer Rain-Common Loons	J. Seerey-Lester	4,500	200.00	200.00
90-08-063	Summer Rain-Common Loons(Prestige)	J. Seerey-Lester	450	425.00	425.00
92-08-064	The Chase-Snow Leopard	J. Seerey-Lester	950	200.00	200.00
83-08-065	The Refuge-Raccoon	J. Seerey-Lester	950	85.00	300.00
90-08-066	Their First Season	J. Seerey-Lester	1,250	200.00	200.00
90-08-067	Togetherness	J. Seerey-Lester	1,250	125.00	185.00
85-08-068	Under the Pines-Bobcat	J. Seerey-Lester	950	95.00	275.00
89-08-069	Water Sport-Bobcat	J. Seerey-Lester	950	185.00	185.00
90-08-070	Whitetail Spring	J. Seerey-Lester	1,250	185.00	185.00
83-08-071	Winter Lookout-Cougar	J. Seerey-Lester	950	85.00	500.00
86-08-072	Winter Perch-Cardinal	J. Seerey-Lester	950	85.00	175.00
85-08-073	Winter Rendezvous-Coyotes	J. Seerey-Lester	950	140.00	225.00
Mill Pond Press		**Brenders**			
88-13-001	A Hunter's Dream	C. Brenders	950	165.00	875.00
90-13-002	A Threatened Symbol	C. Brenders	1,950	145.00	300.00
88-13-003	Apple Harvest	C. Brenders	950	115.00	295.00
87-13-004	Autumn Lady	C. Brenders	950	150.00	375.00
89-13-005	A Young Generation	C. Brenders	1,250	165.00	375.00
86-13-006	Black-Capped Chickadees	C. Brenders	950	40.00	400.00
90-13-007	Blond Beauty	C. Brenders	1,950	185.00	185.00
86-13-008	Bluebirds	C. Brenders	950	40.00	200.00
91-13-009	Calm Before the Challenge-Moose	C. Brenders	1,950	225.00	225.00
87-13-010	Close to Mom	C. Brenders	950	150.00	1450.00
86-13-011	Colorful Playground-Cottontails	C. Brenders	950	75.00	475.00
92-13-012	Den Mother-Pencil Sketch	C. Brenders	2,500	135.00	135.00
92-13-013	Den Mother-Wolf Family	C. Brenders	25,000	250.00	250.00
86-13-014	Disturbed Daydreams	C. Brenders	950	95.00	425.00
87-13-015	Double Trouble-Raccoons	C. Brenders	950	120.00	500-750.
88-13-016	Forest Sentinel-Bobcat	C. Brenders	950	135.00	500.00
90-13-017	Full House-Fox Family	C. Brenders	20,106	235.00	235.00
90-13-018	Ghostly Quiet-Spanish Lynx	C. Brenders	1,950	200.00	200.00
86-13-019	Golden Season-Gray Squirrel	C. Brenders	950	85.00	525.00
86-13-020	Harvest Time-Chipmunk	C. Brenders	950	65.00	250.00
88-13-021	Hidden In the Pines-Immature Great Hor	C. Brenders	950	175.00	1500.00
88-13-022	High Adventure-Black Bear Cubs	C. Brenders	950	105.00	375.00
87-13-023	Ivory-Billed Woodpecker	C. Brenders	950	95.00	500.00
88-13-024	Long Distance Hunters	C. Brenders	950	175.00	2250.00
89-13-025	Lord of the Marshes	C. Brenders	1,250	135.00	175.00
86-13-026	Meadowlark	C. Brenders	950	40.00	150.00
89-13-027	Merlins at the Nest	C. Brenders	1,250	165.00	375.00
85-13-028	Mighty Intruder	C. Brenders	950	95.00	275.00
87-13-029	Migration Fever-Barn Swallows	C. Brenders	950	150.00	350.00
90-13-030	Mountain Baby-Bighorn Sheep	C. Brenders	1,950	165.00	165.00
87-13-031	Mysterious Visitor-Barn Owl	C. Brenders	950	150.00	375.00
91-13-032	The Nesting Season-House Sparrow	C. Brenders	1,950	195.00	250.00
89-13-033	Northern Cousins-Black Squirrels	C. Brenders	950	150.00	250.00
84-13-034	On the Alert-Red Fox	C. Brenders	950	95.00	475.00
90-13-035	On the Old Farm Door	C. Brenders	1,500	225.00	450.00
91-13-036	One to One-Gray Wolf	C. Brenders	10,000	245.00	375-500.
92-13-037	Pathfinder-Red Fox	C. Brenders	5,000	245.00	245.00
84-13-038	Playful Pair-Chipmunks	C. Brenders	950	60.00	400.00
92-13-039	Red Fox Study	C. Brenders	1,250	125.00	125.00
86-13-040	Robins	C. Brenders	950	40.00	125.00
92-13-041	Rocky Kingdom-Bighorn Sheep	C. Brenders	1,750	255.00	255.00
91-13-042	Shadows in the Grass-Young Cougars	C. Brenders	1,950	235.00	235.00
90-13-043	Shoreline Quartet-White Ibis	C. Brenders	1,950	265.00	265.00
84-13-044	Silent Hunter-Great Horned Owl	C. Brenders	950	95.00	450.00
84-13-045	Silent Passage	C. Brenders	950	150.00	400.00
90-13-046	Small Talk	C. Brenders	1,500	125.00	250.00
90-13-047	Spring Fawn	C. Brenders	1,500	125.00	300.00
90-13-048	Squirrel's Dish	C. Brenders	1,950	110.00	110.00
89-13-049	Steller's Jay	C. Brenders	1,250	135.00	175.00
91-13-050	Study for One to One	C. Brenders	1,950	120.00	200.00
88-13-051	Talk on the Old Fence	C. Brenders	950	165.00	725.00
86-13-052	The Acrobat's Meal-Red Squirrel	C. Brenders	950	65.00	275.00
89-13-053	The Apple Lover	C. Brenders	1,500	125.00	275.00
91-13-054	The Balance of Nature	C. Brenders	1,950	225.00	225.00
89-13-055	The Companions	C. Brenders	18,036	200.00	525-1250.
89-13-056	The Predator's Walk	C. Brenders	1,250	150.00	375.00
89-13-057	The Survivors-Canada Geese	C. Brenders	1,500	225.00	850-950.
84-13-058	Waterside Encounter	C. Brenders	950	95.00	1000.00
87-13-059	White Elegance-Trumpeter Swans	C. Brenders	950	115.00	390.00
92-13-060	Wolf Scout #1	C. Brenders	2,500	105.00	105.00
92-13-061	Wolf Scout #2	C. Brenders	2,500	105.00	105.00
91-13-062	Wolf Study	C. Brenders	950	125.00	125.00
87-13-063	Yellow-Bellied Marmot	C. Brenders	950	95.00	425.00
Mill Pond Press		**Daly**			
91-14-001	A New Beginning	J. Daly	5,000	125.00	125.00
90-14-002	The Big Moment	J. Daly	1,500	125.00	125.00
91-14-003	Cat's Cradle Prestige Edition	J. Daly	950	450.00	450.00
90-14-004	Confrontation	J. Daly	1,500	85.00	85.00
90-14-005	Contentment	J. Daly	1,500	95.00	275.00
92-14-006	Dominoes	J. Daly	1,500	155.00	155.00
86-14-007	Flying High	J. Daly	950	50.00	350.00
92-14-008	Her Secret Place	J. Daly	1,500	135.00	135.00
91-14-009	Home Team: Zero	J. Daly	1,500	150.00	150.00
91-14-010	Homemade	J. Daly	1,500	125.00	125.00
90-14-011	Honor and Allegiance	J. Daly	1,500	110.00	110.00
90-14-012	The Ice Man	J. Daly	1,500	125.00	125.00
89-14-013	In the Doghouse	J. Daly	1,500	75.00	250.00
90-14-014	It's That Time Again	J. Daly	1,500	120.00	120.00
92-14-015	Left Out	J. Daly	1,500	110.00	110.00
89-14-016	Let's Play Ball	J. Daly	1,500	75.00	150.00
90-14-017	Make Believe	J. Daly	1,500	75.00	125.00
91-14-018	Pillars of a Nation-Charter Edition	J. Daly	20,000	175.00	175.00
92-14-019	Playmates	J. Daly	1,500	155.00	155.00
90-14-020	Radio Daze	J. Daly	1,500	150.00	150.00
83-14-021	Saturday Night	J. Daly	950	85.00	1125.00
90-14-022	The Scholar	J. Daly	1,500	110.00	110.00
82-14-023	Spring Fever	J. Daly	950	85.00	750.00
89-14-024	The Thief	J. Daly	1,500	95.00	175.00
92-14-025	The Flying Horse	J. Daly	950	325.00	325.00
91-14-026	Time-Out	J. Daly	1,500	125.00	125.00
Moss Portfolio		**Moss**			
XX-01-001	Apple Picker	P. Buckley Moss	1,000	30.00	70.00
XX-01-002	Barelimbed Reflections	P. Buckley Moss	1,000	25.00	70.00
XX-01-003	Becky and Tom	P. Buckley Moss	1,000	10.00	55.00
XX-01-004	Canada Geese	P. Buckley Moss	1,000	60.00	140.00
XX-01-005	Family Outing	P. Buckley Moss	1,000	65.00	300.00
XX-01-006	Flag Boy	P. Buckley Moss	1,000	16.00	40.00
XX-01-007	Four Little Girls	P. Buckley Moss	1,000	30.00	80.00
XX-01-008	Frosty Frolic	P. Buckley Moss	1,000	75.00	400.00
XX-01-009	Ginny and Chris with Lambs	P. Buckley Moss	1,000	35.00	100.00
XX-01-010	Golden Winter	P. Buckley Moss	1,000	150.00	430.00
XX-01-011	Gossip	P. Buckley Moss	1,000	45.00	95.00
XX-01-012	Hungry Baby Bird	P. Buckley Moss	1,000	15.00	50.00
XX-01-013	Joy	P. Buckley Moss	1,000	10.00	40.00
XX-01-014	Little Fellow	P. Buckley Moss	1,000	57.00	115.00
XX-01-015	Love	P. Buckley Moss	1,000	10.00	40.00
XX-01-016	Mary's Lamb, large	P. Buckley Moss	1,000	75.00	215.00
XX-01-017	Moonlit Skater I, large	P. Buckley Moss	1,000	75.00	200.00
XX-01-018	Muffet Boy I	P. Buckley Moss	1,000	10.00	40.00
XX-01-019	Muffet Girl I	P. Buckley Moss	1,000	10.00	40.00
XX-01-020	Orchard Helpers	P. Buckley Moss	1,000	75.00	250.00
XX-01-021	Public Gardens and Beacon Street	P. Buckley Moss	1,000	50.00	210.00
XX-01-022	Quilting Dreams	P. Buckley Moss	1,000	40.00	60.00
XX-01-023	Reluctant Ballerina	P. Buckley Moss	1,000	15.00	48.00
XX-01-024	Shenandoah Silhouette	P. Buckley Moss	1,000	25.00	60.00
XX-01-025	Sisters	P. Buckley Moss	1,000	20.00	70.00
XX-01-026	Skating Lesson	P. Buckley Moss	1,000	50.00	400.00
XX-01-027	Snowy Birches	P. Buckley Moss	1,000	60.00	160.00
XX-01-028	Spirit of Equus	P. Buckley Moss	1,000	100.00	150.00
XX-01-029	Tarry Not	P. Buckley Moss	1,000	35.00	100.00
XX-01-030	Wayside Inn	P. Buckley Moss	1,000	65.00	500.00
XX-01-031	Wedding	P. Buckley Moss	1,000	80.00	300.00
XX-01-032	Winter Cameo	P. Buckley Moss	1,000	30.00	95.00
XX-01-033	Workday's O'er	P. Buckley Moss	1,000	110.00	350.00
XX-01-034	Together	P. Buckley Moss	99	450.00	2000.00
XX-01-035	Adam	P. Buckley Moss	1,000	20.00	85.00
XX-01-036	Alleluia!	P. Buckley Moss	1,000	70.00	160.00
XX-01-037	Allison	P. Buckley Moss	1,000	20.00	60.00
XX-01-038	Amy	P. Buckley Moss	1,000	20.00	90.00
XX-01-039	Amy's Flowers	P. Buckley Moss	1,000	50.00	115.00
XX-01-040	Andrew	P. Buckley Moss	1,000	20.00	65.00
XX-01-041	Annie & Teddy	P. Buckley Moss	1,000	20.00	60.00
XX-01-042	Apple Day	P. Buckley Moss	1,000	80.00	165.00
XX-01-043	Apple Girl	P. Buckley Moss	1,000	30.00	75.00
XX-01-044	Apple Harvest	P. Buckley Moss	1,000	75.00	150.00
XX-01-045	Autumn Ride	P. Buckley Moss	1,000	80.00	160.00
XX-01-046	Autumn Triptych	P. Buckley Moss	1,000	150.00	300.00
XX-01-047	Awake O Earth	P. Buckley Moss	1,000	50.00	90.00
XX-01-048	Balloon Girl	P. Buckley Moss	1,000	20.00	45.00
XX-01-049	Balloon Ride	P. Buckley Moss	1,000	100.00	200.00
XX-01-050	Becky	P. Buckley Moss	1,000	20.00	75.00
XX-01-051	Behold	P. Buckley Moss	1,000	35.00	70.00
XX-01-052	Billy	P. Buckley Moss	1,000	25.00	55.00
XX-01-053	Black Cat	P. Buckley Moss	1,000	50.00	100.00
XX-01-054	Black Cat on a Pink Cushion	P. Buckley Moss	1,000	40.00	80.00
XX-01-055	Blessing, The	P. Buckley Moss	1,000	60.00	265.00
XX-01-056	Blue Bouquet	P. Buckley Moss	1,000	16.00	32.00
XX-01-057	Blue Winter	P. Buckley Moss	1,000	100.00	200.00
XX-01-058	Brandon	P. Buckley Moss	1,000	20.00	50.00
XX-01-059	Brian	P. Buckley Moss	1,000	20.00	50.00
XX-01-060	Brothers	P. Buckley Moss	1,000	35.00	80.00

Company Number	Name	Series Artist	Edition Limit	Issue Price	Quote
XX-01-061	Brower Homestead	P. Buckley Moss	1,000	100.00	200.00
XX-01-062	Cameo Geese	P. Buckley Moss	1,000	40.00	115.00
XX-01-063	Canada Geese (etch)	P. Buckley Moss	99	600.00	1200.00
XX-01-064	Capitol Skaters	P. Buckley Moss	1,000	80.00	160.00
XX-01-065	Caroline	P. Buckley Moss	1,000	30.00	60.00
XX-01-066	Carrie	P. Buckley Moss	1,000	30.00	70.00
XX-01-067	Cathy	P. Buckley Moss	1,000	20.00	70.00
XX-01-068	Central Park	P. Buckley Moss	1,000	80.00	200.00
XX-01-069	Cherished	P. Buckley Moss	1,000	35.00	111.00
XX-01-070	Chicken Farmers	P. Buckley Moss	1,000	40.00	80.00
XX-01-071	Children's Museum Carousel	P. Buckley Moss	1,000	80.00	165.00
XX-01-072	Chris	P. Buckley Moss	1,000	25.00	70.00
XX-01-073	Cindy	P. Buckley Moss	1,000	40.00	110.00
XX-01-074	Christmas Carol	P. Buckley Moss	1,000	60.00	520.00
XX-01-075	Colonial Sleigh Ride	P. Buckley Moss	1,000	125.00	250.00
XX-01-076	Country Church	P. Buckley Moss	1,000	80.00	170.00
XX-01-077	Country Road	P. Buckley Moss	1,000	160.00	320.00
XX-01-078	Crazy Quilt	P. Buckley Moss	1,000	50.00	105.00
XX-01-079	Daily Chores	P. Buckley Moss	1,000	16.00	40.00
XX-01-080	Daniel	P. Buckley Moss	1,000	20.00	80.00
XX-01-081	Daniel Harrison House, The	P. Buckley Moss	1,000	100.00	200.00
XX-01-082	Daredevil Skaters	P. Buckley Moss	1,000	100.00	185.00
XX-01-083	Dashing Away	P. Buckley Moss	1,000	100.00	210.00
XX-01-084	Dear Lord (long)	P. Buckley Moss	1,000	30.00	75.00
XX-01-085	Dear Lord (short)	P. Buckley Moss	1,000	35.00	75.00
XX-01-086	Diana	P. Buckley Moss	1,000	25.00	55.00
XX-01-087	Donkey Boy	P. Buckley Moss	1,000	40.00	80.00
XX-01-088	Ebony's Jet	P. Buckley Moss	1,000	150.00	300.00
XX-01-089	Emily	P. Buckley Moss	1,000	30.00	100.00
XX-01-090	Engagement, The	P. Buckley Moss	1,000	40.00	80.00
XX-01-091	Erin	P. Buckley Moss	1,000	25.00	60.00
XX-01-092	Evelyn	P. Buckley Moss	1,000	40.00	80.00
XX-01-093	Evening Guests	P. Buckley Moss	1,000	60.00	125.00
XX-01-094	Evening Hour, The	P. Buckley Moss	1,000	70.00	130.00
XX-01-095	Evening In Long Grove	P. Buckley Moss	1,000	70.00	165.00
XX-01-096	Evening Run	P. Buckley Moss	1,000	55.00	110.00
XX-01-097	Evening Welcome	P. Buckley Moss	1,000	60.00	125.00
XX-01-098	Every Blessing	P. Buckley Moss	1,000	50.00	100.00
XX-01-099	Everything Nice	P. Buckley Moss	1,000	65.00	130.00
XX-01-100	Family, The	P. Buckley Moss	1,000	125.00	300.00
XX-01-101	Family Heirloom	P. Buckley Moss	1,000	80.00	160.00
XX-01-102	Faneuil Hall	P. Buckley Moss	1,000	40.00	80.00
XX-01-103	Finishing Touches	P. Buckley Moss	1,000	60.00	130.00
XX-01-104	First Born	P. Buckley Moss	1,000	50.00	100.00
XX-01-105	First Love	P. Buckley Moss	1,000	60.00	120.00
XX-01-106	First Promise	P. Buckley Moss	1,000	70.00	150.00
XX-01-107	Flag Girl	P. Buckley Moss	1,000	10.00	40.00
XX-01-108	Flower Girl	P. Buckley Moss	1,000	20.00	50.00
XX-01-109	Fresh Bouquet	P. Buckley Moss	1,000	16.00	40.00
XX-01-110	Friendly Steed	P. Buckley Moss	1,000	50.00	110.00
XX-01-111	Friends	P. Buckley Moss	1,000	35.00	80.00
XX-01-112	Frosty Ride	P. Buckley Moss	1,000	70.00	150.00
XX-01-113	Fruit of The Valley	P. Buckley Moss	1,000	80.00	300.00
XX-01-114	Gaggle of Geese o/1	P. Buckley Moss	1,000	125.00	275.00
XX-01-115	Gaggle of Geese (sc)	P. Buckley Moss	99	600.00	2000.00
XX-01-116	Gentle Swing	P. Buckley Moss	1,000	50.00	95.00
XX-01-117	Ginger	P. Buckley Moss	1,000	40.00	80.00
XX-01-118	Ginny	P. Buckley Moss	1,000	16.00	45.00
XX-01-119	Girls in Green	P. Buckley Moss	1,000	40.00	80.00
XX-01-120	Golden Autumn	P. Buckley Moss	1,000	110.00	250.00
XX-01-121	Governor's Palace	P. Buckley Moss	1,000	50.00	210.00
XX-01-122	Grandma's Bed	P. Buckley Moss	1,000	60.00	225.00
XX-01-123	Grandmother	P. Buckley Moss	1,000	60.00	120.00
XX-01-124	Grandpa's House	P. Buckley Moss	1,000	40.00	110.00
XX-01-125	Granny's Favorite	P. Buckley Moss	1,000	40.00	110.00
XX-01-126	Granny's Girl	P. Buckley Moss	1,000	50.00	100.00
XX-01-127	Hail The Day, Solace	P. Buckley Moss	1,000	75.00	200.00
XX-01-128	Hand in Hand	P. Buckley Moss	1,000	40.00	105.00
XX-01-129	Hark	P. Buckley Moss	1,000	40.00	100.00
XX-01-130	Hay Ride	P. Buckley Moss	1,000	50.00	110.00
XX-01-131	Heartland	P. Buckley Moss	1,000	80.00	170.00
XX-01-132	Heather	P. Buckley Moss	1,000	25.00	60.00
XX-01-133	He Lives	P. Buckley Moss	1,000	25.00	60.00
XX-01-134	Helpers	P. Buckley Moss	1,000	35.00	70.00
XX-01-135	Hitching a Ride	P. Buckley Moss	1,000	60.00	120.00
XX-01-136	Homesteaders (etch)	P. Buckley Moss	99	1200.00	2300.00
XX-01-137	Homeward Bound	P. Buckley Moss	1,000	90.00	200.00
XX-01-138	How Calm The Morn	P. Buckley Moss	1,000	75.00	200.00
XX-01-139	Hurrah!	P. Buckley Moss	1,000	20.00	40.00
XX-01-140	Imperial Majesty (sc)	P. Buckley Moss	99	600.00	1200.00
XX-01-141	Jack	P. Buckley Moss	1,000	25.00	70.00
XX-01-142	Jake	P. Buckley Moss	1,000	25.00	50.00
XX-01-143	John	P. Buckley Moss	1,000	16.00	45.00
XX-01-144	Joshua	P. Buckley Moss	1,000	25.00	60.00
XX-01-145	Katie	P. Buckley Moss	1,000	30.00	90.00
XX-01-146	Kentucky	P. Buckley Moss	1,000	70.00	140.00
XX-01-147	Kim	P. Buckley Moss	1,000	20.00	55.00
XX-01-148	Lancaster Morn	P. Buckley Moss	1,000	275.00	565.00
XX-01-149	Landscape with Geese. Gold o/1	P. Buckley Moss	1,000	500.00	1000.00
XX-01-150	Lesson in Patience	P. Buckley Moss	1,000	150.00	300.00
XX-01-151	Lisa & Tiger	P. Buckley Moss	1,000	30.00	70.00
XX-01-152	Little Apples in a Row	P. Buckley Moss	1,000	100.00	200.00
XX-01-153	Little Girl in Blue	P. Buckley Moss	1,000	16.00	40.00
XX-01-154	Little Girl's Prayer	P. Buckley Moss	1,000	35.00	95.00
XX-01-155	Little Sister	P. Buckley Moss	1,000	35.00	70.00
XX-01-156	Long Grove Church	P. Buckley Moss	1,000	100.00	225.00
XX-01-157	Lords of the Realm	P. Buckley Moss	1,000	80.00	210.00
XX-01-158	Lords of the Valley	P. Buckley Moss	1,000	175.00	350.00
XX-01-159	Loudmouths	P. Buckley Moss	1,000	125.00	250.00
XX-01-160	Maggie	P. Buckley Moss	1,000	30.00	60.00
XX-01-161	Maid Marion	P. Buckley Moss	1,000	50.00	100.00
XX-01-162	Mary & Magnolia	P. Buckley Moss	1,000	15.00	42.00
XX-01-163	Mary Ann	P. Buckley Moss	1,000	20.00	55.00
XX-01-164	Mary Jen	P. Buckley Moss	1,000	20.00	50.00
XX-01-165	Mary's Lambs sm.	P. Buckley Moss	1,000	40.00	100.00
XX-01-166	Mary's Wedding	P. Buckley Moss	1,000	65.00	125.00
XX-01-167	Mike	P. Buckley Moss	1,000	25.00	75.00
XX-01-168	Mike & Jessie	P. Buckley Moss	1,000	60.00	120.00
XX-01-169	Milk Lad	P. Buckley Moss	1,000	15.00	45.00
XX-01-170	Milk Maid	P. Buckley Moss	1,000	15.00	45.00
XX-01-171	Minnesota	P. Buckley Moss	1,000	70.00	165.00
XX-01-172	Molly	P. Buckley Moss	1,000	30.00	70.00
XX-01-173	Momma Apple (blue)	P. Buckley Moss	1,000	10.00	50.00
XX-01-174	Momma Apple (gold)	P. Buckley Moss	1,000	16.00	50.00
XX-01-175	Monarch	P. Buckley Moss	1,000	35.00	55.00
XX-01-176	Moonlit Skaters II sm.	P. Buckley Moss	1,000	40.00	80.00
XX-01-177	My Girls	P. Buckley Moss	1,000	60.00	130.00
XX-01-178	My Hands to Thee	P. Buckley Moss	1,000	75.00	200.00
XX-01-179	My Little Brothers	P. Buckley Moss	1,000	50.00	115.00
XX-01-180	My Place	P. Buckley Moss	1,000	30.00	60.00
XX-01-181	My Sisters	P. Buckley Moss	1,000	40.00	90.00
XX-01-182	Nancy	P. Buckley Moss	1,000	40.00	95.00
XX-01-183	Never Alone	P. Buckley Moss	1,000	35.00	75.00
XX-01-184	Newborn, The	P. Buckley Moss	1,000	55.00	160.00
XX-01-185	Night Before Christmas, The	P. Buckley Moss	1,000	65.00	200.00
XX-01-186	Nine Mennonite Girls	P. Buckley Moss	1,000	40.00	90.00
XX-01-187	Notre Dame	P. Buckley Moss	1,000	90.00	180.00
XX-01-188	Nurses, The	P. Buckley Moss	1,000	70.00	150.00
XX-01-189	Nursing Team	P. Buckley Moss	1,000	70.00	140.00
XX-01-190	O Gentle Friend	P. Buckley Moss	1,000	40.00	90.00
XX-01-191	Oh Life	P. Buckley Moss	1,000	40.00	80.00
XX-01-192	Ohio Star	P. Buckley Moss	1,000	60.00	130.00
XX-01-193	Old Mill House	P. Buckley Moss	1,000	125.00	260.00
XX-01-194	On The Canal	P. Buckley Moss	1,000	60.00	125.00
XX-01-195	On The Swing	P. Buckley Moss	1,000	40.00	80.00
XX-01-196	Orchard Girl	P. Buckley Moss	1,000	40.00	85.00
XX-01-197	Our Big Brother	P. Buckley Moss	1,000	35.00	80.00
XX-01-198	Our Girls	P. Buckley Moss	1,000	60.00	135.00
XX-01-199	Our Little Brother	P. Buckley Moss	1,000	50.00	115.00
XX-01-200	Our Little Sister	P. Buckley Moss	1,000	50.00	110.00
XX-01-201	Pals	P. Buckley Moss	1,000	25.00	50.00
XX-01-202	Pat	P. Buckley Moss	1,000	25.00	60.00
XX-01-203	Pavilion at Wolfeboro	P. Buckley Moss	1,000	40.00	80.00
XX-01-204	Peach Harvest o/1	P. Buckley Moss	1,000	150.00	500.00
XX-01-205	Perfect Pet	P. Buckley Moss	1,000	15.00	30.00
XX-01-206	Picket Fence	P. Buckley Moss	1,000	60.00	120.00
XX-01-207	Pie Makers/ The	P. Buckley Moss	1,000	80.00	165.00
XX-01-208	Pink Ballerina	P. Buckley Moss	1,000	25.00	50.00
XX-01-209	Playmates	P. Buckley Moss	1,000	70.00	140.00
XX-01-210	Please!	P. Buckley Moss	1,000	35.00	70.00
XX-01-211	Please God	P. Buckley Moss	1,000	50.00	150.00
XX-01-212	Please Ma'am	P. Buckley Moss	1,000	50.00	100.00
XX-01-213	Poppa Apple (blue)	P. Buckley Moss	1,000	10.00	50.00
XX-01-214	Poppa Apple (gold)	P. Buckley Moss	1,000	15.00	50.00
XX-01-215	Princely Pair	P. Buckley Moss	1,000	60.00	130.00
XX-01-216	Professor, The	P. Buckley Moss	1,000	40.00	80.00
XX-01-217	Promised	P. Buckley Moss	1,000	40.00	80.00
XX-01-218	Quilt, The	P. Buckley Moss	1,000	90.00	200.00
XX-01-219	Quilting Bee	P. Buckley Moss	1,000	55.00	110.00
XX-01-220	Quilting Ladies	P. Buckley Moss	1,000	40.00	100.00
XX-01-221	Rachel & Jacob	P. Buckley Moss	1,000	150.00	400.00
XX-01-222	Red Bike	P. Buckley Moss	1,000	35.00	80.00
XX-01-223	Red Carriage	P. Buckley Moss	1,000	65.00	130.00
XX-01-224	Red House	P. Buckley Moss	1,000	100.00	220.00
XX-01-225	Red Wagon	P. Buckley Moss	1,000	50.00	120.00
XX-01-226	Ring Around a Rosie	P. Buckley Moss	1,000	40.00	115.00
XX-01-227	Robbie	P. Buckley Moss	1,000	20.00	55.00
XX-01-228	Rocking	P. Buckley Moss	1,000	40.00	98.00
XX-01-229	Rothenburg	P. Buckley Moss	1,000	40.00	80.00
XX-01-230	Sam	P. Buckley Moss	1,000	16.00	55.00
XX-01-231	Sarah	P. Buckley Moss	1,000	16.00	80.00
XX-01-232	School Days	P. Buckley Moss	1,000	70.00	160.00
XX-01-233	School Yard, The	P. Buckley Moss	1,000	60.00	120.00
XX-01-234	Screech Owl Twins	P. Buckley Moss	1,000	75.00	150.00
XX-01-235	Season's Over	P. Buckley Moss	1,000	35.00	90.00
XX-01-236	Secret, The	P. Buckley Moss	1,000	50.00	100.00
XX-01-237	Senators, The	P. Buckley Moss	1,000	275.00	500.00
XX-01-238	Sentinels, The	P. Buckley Moss	1,000	65.00	120.00
XX-01-239	Serenity in Black & White	P. Buckley Moss	1,000	120.00	300.00
XX-01-240	Shenandoah Harvest	P. Buckley Moss	1,000	60.00	125.00
XX-01-241	Showalter's Farm	P. Buckley Moss	1,000	100.00	200.00
XX-01-242	Sisters Four	P. Buckley Moss	1,000	60.00	150.00
XX-01-243	Sitting Pretty	P. Buckley Moss	1,000	60.00	120.00
XX-01-244	Skating Away I	P. Buckley Moss	1,000	70.00	200.00
XX-01-245	Skating Duet	P. Buckley Moss	1,000	40.00	80.00
XX-01-246	Skating Joy	P. Buckley Moss	1,000	200.00	400.00
XX-01-247	Skating Waltz	P. Buckley Moss	1,000	60.00	125.00
XX-01-248	Sleigh Ride	P. Buckley Moss	1,000	50.00	110.00
XX-01-249	Snow Goose	P. Buckley Moss	1,000	50.00	170.00
XX-01-250	Solitary Skater	P. Buckley Moss	1,000	35.00	100.00
XX-01-251	Solitary Skater II	P. Buckley Moss	1,000	35.00	100.00
XX-01-252	Solo	P. Buckley Moss	1,000	15.00	75.00
XX-01-253	Spring Bouquet	P. Buckley Moss	1,000	40.00	85.00
XX-01-254	Spring Love	P. Buckley Moss	1,000	25.00	60.00
XX-01-255	Spring Sheperds	P. Buckley Moss	1,000	40.00	80.00
XX-01-256	Spring Wedding	P. Buckley Moss	1,000	70.00	155.00
XX-01-257	Stack of Boys	P. Buckley Moss	1,000	30.00	70.00
XX-01-258	Stack of Girls	P. Buckley Moss	1,000	25.00	75.00
XX-01-259	Stephanie	P. Buckley Moss	1,000	35.00	85.00
XX-01-260	Stone House (etch)	P. Buckley Moss	99	600.00	1250.00
XX-01-261	Street by The Park o/1	P. Buckley Moss	1,000	200.00	600.00
XX-01-262	Street by The Park II	P. Buckley Moss	1,000	125.00	275.00
XX-01-263	Summer Love	P. Buckley Moss	1,000	50.00	100.00
XX-01-264	Summer's Blessing	P. Buckley Moss	1,000	65.00	130.00
XX-01-265	Sunday Morning	P. Buckley Moss	1,000	60.00	200.00
XX-01-266	Sunday Stroll	P. Buckley Moss	1,000	50.00	100.00
XX-01-267	Sunday's Apples	P. Buckley Moss	1,000	50.00	120.00
XX-01-268	Sunday's Prayer	P. Buckley Moss	1,000	50.00	105.00
XX-01-269	Sunday's Ride	P. Buckley Moss	1,000	60.00	123.00
XX-01-270	Swan House	P. Buckley Moss	1,000	80.00	160.00
XX-01-271	Taking Turns	P. Buckley Moss	1,000	50.00	120.00
XX-01-272	Tender Shepherd	P. Buckley Moss	1,000	50.00	100.00
XX-01-273	Tending Her Flock	P. Buckley Moss	1,000	80.00	170.00
XX-01-274	Terrace Hill	P. Buckley Moss	1,000	110.00	210.00
XX-01-275	Three Little Sisters	P. Buckley Moss	1,000	70.00	140.00
XX-01-276	Three Sisters	P. Buckley Moss	1,000	70.00	160.00
XX-01-277	Timothy	P. Buckley Moss	1,000	30.00	70.00
XX-01-278	Tis Grace	P. Buckley Moss	1,000	20.00	50.00
XX-01-279	To Each Other	P. Buckley Moss	1,000	40.00	85.00
XX-01-280	To Grandmother's House We Go	P. Buckley Moss	1,000	80.00	160.00
XX-01-281	Together (sc)	P. Buckley Moss	99	450.00	2000.00
XX-01-282	Together In The Park	P. Buckley Moss	1,000	80.00	165.00
XX-01-283	Together on Sunday (sc)	P. Buckley Moss	99	600.00	2050.00
XX-01-284	Twilight Ride	P. Buckley Moss	1,000	80.00	160.00
XX-01-285	Two Little Hands	P. Buckley Moss	1,000	35.00	80.00
XX-01-286	Two on a Barrel	P. Buckley Moss	1,000	25.00	65.00

Number	Name	Artist	Edition Limit	Issue Price	Quote
XX-01-287	Two on a Swing	P. Buckley Moss	1,000	50.00	110.00
XX-01-288	Victorian Legacy	P. Buckley Moss	1,000	150.00	315.00
XX-01-289	Visit to The Capitol	P. Buckley Moss	1,000	30.00	65.00
XX-01-290	Waiting For Tom	P. Buckley Moss	1,000	40.00	100.00
XX-01-291	Watch, The	P. Buckley Moss	1,000	70.00	145.00
XX-01-292	Wayside Inn (etch)	P. Buckley Moss	99	1800.00	3250.00
XX-01-293	Wedding II	P. Buckley Moss	1,000	90.00	220.00
XX-01-294	Wedding III	P. Buckley Moss	1,000	90.00	180.00
XX-01-295	Wedding Bouquet	P. Buckley Moss	1,000	75.00	150.00
XX-01-296	Wedding Day	P. Buckley Moss	1,000	160.00	320.00
XX-01-297	Wedding Joy	P. Buckley Moss	1,000	200.00	420.00
XX-01-298	Wedding Morn	P. Buckley Moss	1,000	70.00	150.00
XX-01-299	Wedding Ride, The	P. Buckley Moss	1,000	130.00	260.00
XX-01-300	Wedding Ring	P. Buckley Moss	1,000	75.00	165.00
XX-01-301	Welcome, A	P. Buckley Moss	1,000	45.00	110.00
XX-01-302	White Church	P. Buckley Moss	1,000	80.00	167.00
XX-01-303	Winter at The Mill	P. Buckley Moss	1,000	80.00	250.00
XX-01-304	Winter Duet	P. Buckley Moss	1,000	90.00	200.00
XX-01-305	Winter Geese (etch)	P. Buckley Moss	1,000	400.00	1100.00
XX-01-306	Winter Ride	P. Buckley Moss	1,000	60.00	130.00
XX-01-307	Winter Skater	P. Buckley Moss	1,000	40.00	100.00
XX-01-308	Winter Visitor	P. Buckley Moss	1,000	80.00	180.00
XX-01-309	Winter Wedding	P. Buckley Moss	1,000	80.00	170.00
XX-01-310	Winter's Day	P. Buckley Moss	1,000	50.00	110.00
XX-01-311	Winter's Eve	P. Buckley Moss	1,000	100.00	200.00
XX-01-312	Winter's Glimpse	P. Buckley Moss	1,000	40.00	90.00
XX-01-313	Winter's Glory	P. Buckley Moss	1,000	200.00	350.00
XX-01-314	Winter's House o/I	P. Buckley Moss	1,000	350.00	750.00
XX-01-315	Winter's Joy	P. Buckley Moss	99	500.00	1050.00
XX-01-316	Winter's Mates	P. Buckley Moss	1,000	50.00	110.00
XX-01-317	Winter's Travelers	P. Buckley Moss	1,000	60.00	120.00
XX-01-318	Woman Talk	P. Buckley Moss	1,000	35.00	70.00
XX-01-319	Young Maestro	P. Buckley Moss	1,000	60.00	85.00
New Masters Publishing		**Bannister**			
78-01-001	Bandstand	P. Bannister	250	75.00	450.00
80-01-002	Dust of Autumn	P. Bannister	200	200.00	1225.00
80-01-003	Faded Glory	P. Bannister	200	200.00	1225.00
80-01-004	Gift of Happiness	P. Bannister	200	200.00	2000.00
80-01-005	Girl on the Beach	P. Bannister	200	200.00	1200.00
80-01-006	The Silver Bell	P. Bannister	200	200.00	2000.00
81-01-007	April	P. Bannister	S/O	200.00	1100.00
81-01-008	Crystal	P. Bannister	300	260.00	300.00
81-01-009	Easter	P. Bannister	S/O	260.00	950.00
81-01-010	Juliet	P. Bannister	S/O	260.00	5000.00
81-01-011	My Special Place	P. Bannister	S/O	260.00	1850.00
81-01-012	Porcelain Rose	P. Bannister	S/O	260.00	2000.00
81-01-013	Rehearsal	P. Bannister	S/O	260.00	1850.00
81-01-014	Sea Haven	P. Bannister	S/O	260.00	1100.00
81-01-015	Titania	P. Bannister	S/O	260.00	900.00
82-01-016	Amaryllis	P. Bannister	S/O	285.00	1900.00
82-01-017	Cinderella	P. Bannister	500	285.00	285.00
82-01-018	Emily	P. Bannister	S/O	285.00	800.00
82-01-019	Ivy	P. Bannister	S/O	285.00	700.00
82-01-020	Jasmine	P. Bannister	S/O	285.00	650.00
82-01-021	Lily	P. Bannister	500	235.00	235.00
82-01-022	Mail Order Brides	P. Bannister	S/O	325.00	2300.00
82-01-023	Memories	P. Bannister	S/O	235.00	500.00
82-01-024	Nuance	P. Bannister	S/O	235.00	470.00
82-01-025	Parasols	P. Bannister	500	235.00	235.00
82-01-026	The Present	P. Bannister	S/O	260.00	800.00
83-01-027	The Duchess	P. Bannister	S/O	250.00	1800.00
84-01-028	The Fan Window	P. Bannister	S/O	195.00	450.00
84-01-029	Window Seat	P. Bannister	S/O	150.00	600.00
83-01-030	Ophelia	P. Bannister	S/O	150.00	675.00
84-01-031	Scarlet Ribbons	P. Bannister	S/O	150.00	300.00
83-01-032	Mementos	P. Bannister	S/O	150.00	1400.00
84-01-033	April Light	P. Bannister	S/O	150.00	600.00
84-01-034	Make Believe	P. Bannister	S/O	150.00	600.00
88-01-035	Summer Choices	P. Bannister	300	250.00	800.00
88-01-036	Guinevere	P. Bannister	485	265.00	1000.00
88-01-037	Love Seat	P. Bannister	S/O	230.00	500.00
88-01-038	Apples and Oranges	P. Bannister	S/O	265.00	600.00
89-01-039	Daydreams	P. Bannister	S/O	265.00	530.00
86-01-040	Pride & Joy	P. Bannister	S/O	150.00	300.00
86-01-041	Soiree	P. Bannister	950	150.00	225.00
87-01-042	Autumn Fields	P. Bannister	950	150.00	225.00
87-01-043	September Harvest	P. Bannister	S/O	150.00	300.00
87-01-044	Quiet Corner	P. Bannister	S/O	115.00	300.00
87-01-045	First Prize	P. Bannister	950	115.00	175.00
88-01-046	Floribunda	P. Bannister	S/O	265.00	550.00
88-01-047	March Winds	P. Bannister	S/O	265.00	530.00
89-01-048	Peace	P. Bannister	S/O	265.00	1100.00
89-01-049	The Quilt	P. Bannister	S/O	265.00	900.00
89-01-050	Low Tide	P. Bannister	S/O	265.00	550.00
89-01-051	Chapter One	P. Bannister	S/O	265.00	1300.00
90-01-052	Lavender Hill	P. Bannister	S/O	265.00	625.00
90-01-053	Rendezvous	P. Bannister	S/O	265.00	650.00
90-01-054	Sisters	P. Bannister	S/O	265.00	950.00
90-01-055	Seascapes	P. Bannister	S/O	265.00	550.00
90-01-056	Songbird	P. Bannister	S/O	265.00	550.00
90-01-057	Good Friends	P. Bannister	S/O	265.00	750.00
91-01-058	String of Pearls	P. Bannister	S/O	265.00	850.00
91-01-059	Wildflowers	P. Bannister	S/O	295.00	590.00
91-01-060	Crossroads	P. Bannister	S/O	295.00	590.00
91-01-060	Teatime	P. Bannister	S/O	295.00	600.00
91-01-061	Celebration	P. Bannister	S/O	350.00	700.00
91-01-062	Pudding & Pies	P. Bannister	S/O	265.00	265.00
Past Impressions		**Maley**			
84-01-001	Secluded Garden	A. Maley	Closed	150.00	970.00
84-01-002	Glorious Summer	A. Maley	Closed	150.00	725.00
85-01-003	Secret Thoughts	A. Maley	Closed	150.00	500-730.
85-01-004	Passing Elegance	A. Maley	Closed	150.00	350-600.
86-01-005	Winter Romance	A. Maley	Closed	150.00	550-650.
86-01-006	Tell Me	A. Maley	Closed	150.00	500-850.
88-01-007	Opening Night	A. Maley	Closed	250.00	450-1750.
67-01-008	Love Letter	A. Maley	Closed	200.00	450-550.
87-01-009	Love Letter, artist proof	A. Maley	Closed	300.00	450.00
87-01-010	The Promise	A. Maley	450	200.00	315.00
88-01-011	Day Dreams	A. Maley	500	200.00	350-450.
88-01-012	The Boardwalk	A. Maley	500	250.00	340.00
88-01-013	Tranquil Moment	A. Maley	Closed	250.00	315.00
88-01-014	Joys of Childhood	A. Maley	500	250.00	250.00
88-01-015	Victorian Trio	A. Maley	500	250.00	340.00
89-01-016	English Rose	A. Maley	750	250.00	285.00
89-01-017	Winter Impressions	A. Maley	750	250.00	315.00
89-01-018	In Harmony	A. Maley	750	250.00	250.00
90-01-019	Festive Occasion	A. Maley	750	250.00	250.00
90-01-020	Summer Pastime	A. Maley	750	250.00	250.00
90-01-021	Cafe Royale	A. Maley	750	275.00	275.00
90-01-022	Romantic Engagement	A. Maley	750	275.00	275.00
90-01-023	Gracious Era	A. Maley	750	275.00	275.00
90-01-024	Evening Performance	A. Maley	750	150.00	150.00
91-01-025	Between Friends	A. Maley	750	275.00	275.00
91-01-026	Summer Carousel	A. Maley	750	200.00	200.00
91-01-027	Sunday Afternoon	A. Maley	750	275.00	275.00
91-01-028	Winter Carousel	A. Maley	750	200.00	200.00
92-01-029	Evening Performance	A. Maley	750	150.00	150.00
92-01-030	Intimate Moment	A. Maley	750	250.00	250.00
92-01-031	A Walk in the Park	A. Maley	500	260.00	260.00
92-01-032	An Elegant Affair	A. Maley	500	260.00	260.00
Past Impressions, Inc.		**Women of Elegance**			
89-02-001	Victoria	A. Maley	750	125.00	125.00
89-02-002	Catherine	A. Maley	750	125.00	125.00
89-02-003	Beth	A. Maley	750	125.00	125.00
89-02-004	Alexandra	A. Maley	750	125.00	125.00
Pemberton & Oaks		**Zolan's Children**			
82-01-001	Erik and the Dandelion	D. Zolan	880	98.00	460.00
83-01-002	By Myself	D. Zolan	880	98.00	289.00
84-01-003	Sabina in the Grass	D. Zolan	880	98.00	710.00
86-01-004	Tender Moment	D. Zolan	880	98.00	375.00
87-01-005	Touching the Sky	D. Zolan	880	98.00	290.00
88-01-006	Tiny Treasures	D. Zolan	450	150.00	250.00
88-01-007	Winter Angel	D. Zolan	980	98.00	275.00
88-01-008	Small Wonder	D. Zolan	880	98.00	312.00
88-01-009	Waiting to Play	D. Zolan	1,000	35.00	150.00
88-01-010	Day Dreamer	D. Zolan	1,000	35.00	125-150.
90-01-011	Daddy's Home	D. Zolan	880	98.00	299.00
90-01-012	Crystals Creek	D. Zolan	880	98.00	320.00
90-01-013	Colors of Spring	D. Zolan	880	98.00	325.00
90-01-014	Mother's Angels	D. Zolan	880	98.00	310.00
90-01-015	Snowy Adventure	D. Zolan	880	98.00	175-295.
90-01-016	Brotherly Love	D. Zolan	880	98.00	360.00
90-01-017	Almost Home	D. Zolan	880	98.00	309.00
90-01-018	Christmas Prayer	D. Zolan	880	98.00	150-245.
Reco International		**Limited Edition Print**			
84-01-001	Jessica	S. Kuck	500	60.00	400.00
85-01-002	Heather	S. Kuck	500	75.00	150.00
86-01-003	Ashley	S. Kuck	500	85.00	150.00
Reco International		**McClelland**			
XX-02-001	Olivia	J. McClelland	300	175.00	175.00
XX-02-002	Sweet Dreams	J. McClelland	300	145.00	145.00
XX-02-003	Just for You	J. McClelland	300	155.00	155.00
XX-02-004	Reverie	J. McClelland	300	110.00	110.00
XX-02-005	I Love Tammy	J. McClelland	500	75.00	100.00
Reco International		**Fine Art Canvas Reproduction**			
90-03-001	Beach Play	J. McClelland	350	80.00	80.00
91-03-002	Flower Swing	J. McClelland	350	100.00	100.00
91-03-003	Summer Conversation	J. McClelland	350	80.00	80.00
Norman Rockwell Galleries		**Rockwell Graphics**			
91-01-001	Rockwell's Santa's Workshop (Canvas Reproduction)	Rockwell-Inspired	N/A	34.95	34.95
91-01-002	Rockwell's Main Street (Canvas Reproduction)	Rockwell-Inspired	N/A	69.95	69.95
Roman, Inc.		**Hook**			
81-01-001	The Carpenter	F. Hook	Yr.Iss	100.00	1000.00
81-01-002	The Carpenter (remarque)	F. Hook	Yr.Iss	100.00	3000.00
82-01-003	Frolicking	F. Hook	1,200	60.00	350.00
82-01-004	Gathering	F. Hook	1,200	60.00	350.00
82-01-005	Poulets	F. Hook	1,200	60.00	350.00
82-01-006	Bouquet	F. Hook	1,200	70.00	350.00
82-01-007	Surprise	F. Hook	1,200	50.00	350.00
82-01-008	Posing	F. Hook	1,200	70.00	350.00
82-01-009	Little Children, Come to Me	F. Hook	1,950	50.00	500.00
82-01-010	Little Children, Come to Me, remarque	F. Hook	50	100.00	500.00
Roman, Inc.		**Portraits of Love**			
88-02-001	Sharing	F. Hook	2,500	25.00	25.00
88-02-002	Expectation	F. Hook	2,500	25.00	25.00
88-02-003	Remember When...	F. Hook	2,500	25.00	25.00
88-02-004	My Kitty	F. Hook	2,500	25.00	25.00
88-02-005	In Mother's Arms	F. Hook	2,500	25.00	25.00
88-02-006	Sunkissed Afternoon	F. Hook	2,500	25.00	25.00
Roman, Inc.		**Abble Williams**			
88-03-001	Mary, Mother of the Carpenter	A. Williams	Closed	100.00	100.00
Roman, Inc.		**The Discovery of America Miniature Art Print**			
91-04-001	The Discovery of America	I. Spencer	Open	2.00	2.00
Schmid		**Lowell Davis Lithographs**			
81-01-001	Surprise in the Cellar, remarque	L. Davis	101	100.00	400.00
81-01-002	Surprise in the Cellar, regular edition	L. Davis	899	75.00	375.00
81-01-003	Plum Tuckered Out, remarque	L. Davis	101	100.00	350.00
81-01-004	Plum Tuckered Out, regular edition	L. Davis	899	75.00	300.00
81-01-005	Duke's Mixture, remarque	L. Davis	101	150.00	350.00
81-01-006	Duke's Mixture, regular edition	L. Davis	899	75.00	125.00
82-01-007	Bustin' with Pride, remarque	L. Davis	101	150.00	250.00
82-01-008	Bustin' with Pride, regular edition	L. Davis	899	75.00	125.00
82-01-009	Birth of a Blossom, remarque	L. Davis	50	200.00	450.00
82-01-010	Birth of a Blossom, regular edition	L. Davis	400	125.00	300.00
82-01-011	Suppertime, remarque	L. Davis	50	200.00	450.00
82-01-012	Suppertime, regular edition	L. Davis	400	125.00	300.00
82-01-013	Foxfire Farm, remarque	L. Davis	100	200.00	250.00
82-01-014	Foxfire Farm, regular edition	L. Davis	800	125.00	125.00
85-01-015	Self Portrait	L. Davis	450	75.00	192.00
87-01-016	Blossom's Gift	L. Davis	450	75.00	75.00
89-01-017	Sun Worshippers	L. Davis	750	100.00	100.00

Number	Name	Artist	Edition Limit	Issue Price	Quote
90-01-018	Sunday Afternoon Treat	L. Davis	750	100.00	100.00
91-01-019	Warm Milk	L. Davis	750	100.00	179.00
92-01-020	Cat and Jenny Wren	L. Davis	750	100.00	100.00
Schmid		**Berta Hummel Lithographs**			
80-02-001	Moonlight Return	B. Hummel	900	150.00	850.00
80-02-002	1984 American Visit	B. Hummel	5	550.00	1000.00
81-02-003	A Time to Remember	B. Hummel	720	150.00	300.00
81-02-004	1984 American Visit	B. Hummel	5	550.00	1100.00
81-02-005	Remarqued	B. Hummel	180	250.00	1250.00
81-02-006	1984 American Visit	B. Hummel	2	1100.00	1700.00
82-02-007	Poppies	B. Hummel	450	150.00	650.00
82-02-008	1984 American Visit	B. Hummel	3	250.00	850.00
83-02-009	Angelic Messenger, 75th Anniversary	B. Hummel	195	375.00	700.00
83-02-010	Angelic Messenger, Christmas Message	B. Hummel	400	275.00	450.00
83-02-011	1984 American Visit	B. Hummel	10	275.00	600.00
83-02-012	Regular	B. Hummel	100	175.00	350.00
83-02-013	1984 American Visit	B. Hummel	10	175.00	400.00
85-02-014	Birthday Bouquet, Edition 1	B. Hummel	195	450.00	550.00
85-02-015	Birthday Bouquet, Edition 2	B. Hummel	225	375.00	375.00
85-02-016	Birthday Bouquet, Edition 3	B. Hummel	100	195.00	395.00
Schmid		**Ferrandiz Lithographs**			
80-03-001	Most Precious Gift, remarque	J. Ferrandiz	50	225.00	2800.00
80-03-002	Most Precious Gift, regular edition	J. Ferrandiz	425	125.00	1200.00
80-03-003	My Star, remarque	J. Ferrandiz	75	175.00	1800.00
80-03-004	My Star, regular edition	J. Ferrandiz	675	100.00	650.00
81-03-005	Heart of Seven Colors, remarque	J. Ferrandiz	75	175.00	1300.00
81-03-006	Heart of Seven Colors, regular edition	J. Ferrandiz	600	100.00	395.00
82-03-007	Oh Small Child, remarque	J. Ferrandiz	50	225.00	1450.00
82-03-008	Oh Small Child, regular edition	J. Ferrandiz	450	125.00	495.00
82-03-009	Spreading the Word, remarque	J. Ferrandiz	75	225.00	1075.00
82-03-010	Spreading the Word, regular edition	J. Ferrandiz	675	125.00	190-250.
82-03-011	On the Threshold of Life, remarque	J. Ferrandiz	50	275.00	1350.00
82-03-012	On the Threshold of Life, regular edition	J. Ferrandiz	425	150.00	450.00
82-03-013	Riding Through the Rain, remarque	J. Ferrandiz	100	300.00	950.00
82-03-014	Riding Through the Rain, regular edition	J. Ferrandiz	900	165.00	350.00
82-03-015	Mirror of the Soul, regular edition	J. Ferrandiz	225	150.00	425.00
82-03-016	Mirror of the Soul, remarque	J. Ferrandiz	35	250.00	2400.00
82-03-017	He Seems to Sleep, regular edition	J. Ferrandiz	450	150.00	700.00
82-03-018	He Seems to Sleep, remarque	J. Ferrandiz	25	300.00	3200.00
83-03-019	Friendship, remarque	J. Ferrandiz	15	1200.00	2300.00
83-03-020	Friendship, regular edition	J. Ferrandiz	460	165.00	450.00
84-03-021	Star in the Teapot; regular edition	J. Ferrandiz	410	165.00	165.00
84-03-022	Star in the Teapot; remarque	J. Ferrandiz	15	1200.00	2100.00
V.F. Fine Arts		**Kuck**			
86-01-001	Tender Moments, proof	S. Kuck	50	80.00	295.00
86-01-002	Tender Moments, S/N	S. Kuck	500	70.00	250.00
86-01-003	Summer Reflections, proof	S. Kuck	90	70.00	300.00
86-01-004	Summer Reflections, S/N	S. Kuck	900	60.00	250.00
86-01-005	Silhouette, proof	S. Kuck	25	90.00	250.00
86-01-006	Silhouette, S/N	S. Kuck	250	80.00	220.00
87-01-007	Le Papillion, remarque	S. Kuck	7	150.00	250.00
87-01-008	Le Papillion, proof	S. Kuck	35	110.00	175.00
87-01-009	Le Papillion, S/N	S. Kuck	350	90.00	150.00
87-01-010	The Reading Lesson, proof	S. Kuck	90	70.00	190-250.
87-01-011	The Reading Lesson, S/N	S. Kuck	900	60.00	200.00
87-01-012	The Daisy, proof	S. Kuck	90	40.00	100.00
87-01-013	The Daisy, S/N	S. Kuck	900	30.00	75.00
87-01-014	The Loveseat, proof	S. Kuck	90	40.00	50-75.00
87-01-015	The Loveseat, S/N	S. Kuck	900	30.00	50.00
87-01-016	A Quiet Time, proof	S. Kuck	90	50.00	75.00
87-01-017	A Quiet Time, S/N	S. Kuck	900	40.00	50.00
87-01-018	The Flower Girl, proof	S. Kuck	90	50.00	75.00
87-01-019	The Flower Girl, S/N	S. Kuck	900	40.00	50-60.00
87-01-020	Mother's Love, proof	S. Kuck	12	225.00	1800.00
87-01-021	Mother's Love, S/N	S. Kuck	150	195.00	1200.00
88-01-022	My Dearest, S/N	S. Kuck	350	160.00	775.00
88-01-023	My Dearest, proof	S. Kuck	50	200.00	900.00
88-01-024	My Dearest, remarque	S. Kuck	25	325.00	1100.00
88-01-025	The Kitten, S/N	S. Kuck	350	120.00	1200.00
88-01-026	The Kitten, proof	S. Kuck	50	150.00	1300.00
88-01-027	The Kitten, remarque	S. Kuck	25	250.00	950-1450.
88-01-028	Wild Flowers, S/N	S. Kuck	350	160.00	250.00
88-01-029	Wild Flowers, proof	S. Kuck	50	175.00	300.00
88-01-030	Wild Flowers, remarque	S. Kuck	25	250.00	350.00
88-01-031	Little Ballerina, S/N	S. Kuck	150	110.00	300.00
88-01-032	Little Ballerina, proof	S. Kuck	25	150.00	350.00
88-01-033	Little Ballerina, remarque	S. Kuck	25	225.00	450.00
88-01-034	First Recital, S/N	S. Kuck	150	200.00	900.00
88-01-035	First Recital, proof	S. Kuck	25	250.00	1000.00
88-01-036	First Recital, remarque	S. Kuck	25	400.00	1200.00
89-01-037	Sisters, S/N	S. Kuck	900	95.00	190.00
89-01-038	Sisters, proof	S. Kuck	90	150.00	395.00
89-01-039	Sisters, remarque	S. Kuck	50	200.00	375.00
89-01-040	Rose Garden, S/N	S. Kuck	500	95.00	400.00
89-01-041	Rose Garden, proof	S. Kuck	50	150.00	450.00
89-01-042	Rose Garden, remarque	S. Kuck	50	200.00	600.00
89-01-043	Sonatina, S/N	S. Kuck	900	150.00	350.00
89-01-044	Sonatina, proof	S. Kuck	90	225.00	450.00
89-01-045	Sonatina, remarque	S. Kuck	50	300.00	600.00
89-01-046	Puppy, S/N	S. Kuck	500	120.00	600.00
89-01-047	Puppy, proof	S. Kuck	50	180.00	650.00
89-01-048	Puppy, remarque	S. Kuck	50	240.00	750-950.
89-01-049	Innocence, S/N	S. Kuck	900	150.00	200.00
89-01-050	Innocence, proof	S. Kuck	90	225.00	250.00
89-01-051	Innocence, remarque	S. Kuck	50	300.00	350.00
89-01-052	Bundle of Joy, S/N	S. Kuck	1,000	125.00	250.00
89-01-053	Day Dreaming, S/N	S. Kuck	900	150.00	200.00
89-01-054	Day Dreaming, proof	S. Kuck	90	225.00	225.00
89-01-055	Day Dreaming, remarque	S. Kuck	50	300.00	300.00
90-01-056	Lilly Pond, S/N	S. Kuck	750	150.00	150.00
90-01-057	Lilly Pond, proof	S. Kuck	75	200.00	200.00
90-01-058	Lilly Pond, color remarque	S. Kuck	125	500.00	500.00
90-01-059	First Snow, S/N	S. Kuck	500	95.00	225.00
90-01-060	First Snow, proof	S. Kuck	50	150.00	275.00
90-01-061	First Snow, remarque	S. Kuck	25	200.00	325.00
90-01-062	La Belle, S/N	S. Kuck	1,500	80.00	160.00
90-01-063	La Belle, proof	S. Kuck	150	120.00	200.00
90-01-064	La Belle, remarque	S. Kuck	25	160.00	250.00
90-01-065	Le Beau, S/N	S. Kuck	1,500	80.00	160.00
90-01-066	Le Beau, proof	S. Kuck	150	120.00	200.00
90-01-067	Le Beau, remarque	S. Kuck	25	160.00	250.00
90-01-068	Chopsticks, S/N	S. Kuck	1,500	80.00	80.00
90-01-069	Chopsticks, proof	S. Kuck	150	120.00	120.00
90-01-070	Chopsticks, remarque	S. Kuck	25	160.00	160.00
91-01-071	Memories, S/N	S. Kuck	5,000	195.00	195.00
91-01-072	God's Gift, proof	S. Kuck	150	150.00	150.00
91-01-073	God's Gift, S/N	S. Kuck	1,500	95.00	95.00
92-01-074	Joyous Day S/N	S. Kuck	1,200	125.00	125.00
92-01-075	Joyous Day, proof	S. Kuck	120	175.00	175.00
92-01-076	Joyous Day Canvas Transfer	S. Kuck	250	250.00	250.00
World Art Editions		**Masseria**			
80-01-001	Eduardo	F. Masseria	300	275.00	2700.00
80-01-002	Rosanna	F. Masseria	300	275.00	3200.00
80-01-003	Nina	F. Masseria	300	325.00	1950.00
80-01-004	First Kiss	F. Masseria	300	375.00	2200.00
81-01-005	Selene	F. Masseria	300	325.00	2200.00
81-01-006	First Flower	F. Masseria	300	325.00	2200.00
81-01-007	Elisa with Flower	F. Masseria	300	325.00	2200.00
81-01-008	Solange	F. Masseria	300	325.00	2200.00
81-01-009	Susan Sewing	F. Masseria	300	375.00	2500.00
81-01-010	Jessica	F. Masseria	300	375.00	2300.00
81-01-011	Eleanor	F. Masseria	300	375.00	1900.00
81-01-012	Julie	F. Masseria	300	375.00	950.00
82-01-013	Robin	F. Masseria	300	425.00	975.00
82-01-014	Jodie	F. Masseria	300	425.00	950.00
82-01-015	Jill	F. Masseria	300	425.00	750.00
82-01-016	Jamie	F. Masseria	300	425.00	750.00
82-01-017	Yasmin	F. Masseria	300	425.00	720.00
82-01-018	Yvette	F. Masseria	300	425.00	620.00
82-01-019	Judith	F. Masseria	300	425.00	750.00
82-01-020	Amy	F. Masseria	300	425.00	720.00
83-01-021	Tara	F. Masseria	300	450.00	1100.00
83-01-022	Antonio	F. Masseria	300	450.00	1100.00
84-01-023	Memoirs	F. Masseria	300	450.00	700.00
84-01-024	Christopher	F. Masseria	300	450.00	700.00
84-01-025	Bettina	F. Masseria	250	550.00	700.00
84-01-026	Vincente	F. Masseria	360	550.00	1000.00
85-01-027	Christina	F. Masseria	300	500.00	700.00
85-01-028	Jorgito	F. Masseria	300	500.00	700.00
84-01-029	Regina	F. Masseria	950	395.00	495.00
84-01-030	Peter	F. Masseria	950	395.00	495.00
85-01-031	Marquerita	F. Masseria	950	495.00	495.00
85-01-032	To Catch a Butterfly	F. Masseria	950	495.00	495.00

PLATES

Number	Name	Artist	Edition Limit	Issue Price	Quote
American Artists		**The Horses of Fred Stone**			
82-01-001	Patience	F. Stone	9,500	55.00	145.00
82-01-002	Arabian Mare and Foal	F. Stone	9,500	55.00	125.00
82-01-003	Safe and Sound	F. Stone	9,500	55.00	120.00
83-01-004	Contentment	F. Stone	9,500	55.00	150.00
American Artists		**The Stallion Series**			
83-02-001	Black Stallion	F. Stone	12,500	49.50	100.00
83-02-002	Andalusian	F. Stone	12,500	49.50	80.00
American Artists		**Sport of Kings Series**			
84-03-001	Man O'War	F. Stone	9,500	65.00	150.00
84-03-002	Secretariat	F. Stone	9,500	65.00	295.00
85-03-003	John Henry	F. Stone	9,500	65.00	100.00
86-03-004	Seattle Slew	F. Stone	9,500	65.00	65.00
American Artists		**Mare and Foal Series**			
86-04-001	Water Trough	F. Stone	12,500	49.50	125.00
86-04-002	Tranquility	F. Stone	12,500	49.50	65.00
86-04-003	Pasture Pest	F. Stone	12,500	49.50	100.00
87-04-004	The Arabians	F. Stone	12,500	49.50	49.50
American Artists		**Famous Fillies**			
87-05-001	Lady's Secret	F. Stone	9,500	65.00	85.00
88-05-002	Ruffian	F. Stone	9,500	65.00	85.00
88-05-003	Genuine Risk	F. Stone	9,500	65.00	85.00
92-05-004	Go For The Wand	F. Stone	9,500	65.00	85.00
American Artists		**Fred Stone Classic Series**			
86-06-001	The Shoe-8,000 Wins	F. Stone	9,500	75.00	95.00
86-06-002	The Eternal Legacy	F. Stone	9,500	75.00	95.00
88-06-003	Forever Friends	F. Stone	9,500	75.00	85.00
89-06-004	Alysheba	F. Stone	9,500	75.00	85.00
American Artists		**Family Treasures**			
81-07-001	Cora's Recital	R. Zolan	18,500	39.50	39.50
82-07-002	Cora's Tea Party	R. Zolan	18,500	39.50	39.50
83-07-003	Cora's Garden Party	R. Zolan	18,500	39.50	39.50
American Rose Society		**All-American Rose**			
75-01-001	Oregold	Unknown	9,800	39.00	142.00
75-01-002	Arizona	Unknown	9,800	39.00	142.00
75-01-003	Rose Parade	Unknown	9,800	39.00	137.00
76-01-004	Yankee Doodle	Unknown	9,800	39.00	135.50
76-01-005	America	Unknown	9,800	39.00	135.50
76-01-006	Cathedral	Unknown	9,800	39.00	135.50
76-01-007	Seashell	Unknown	9,800	39.00	135.50
77-01-008	Double Delight	Unknown	9,800	39.00	115.00
77-01-009	Prominent	Unknown	9,800	39.00	115.00
77-01-010	First Edition	Unknown	9,800	39.00	115.00
78-01-011	Color Magic	Unknown	9,800	39.00	107.00
78-01-012	Charisma	Unknown	9,800	39.00	58-89.00
79-01-013	Paradise	Unknown	9,800	39.00	39-58.00
79-01-014	Sundowner	Unknown	9,800	39.00	67-75.00
79-01-015	Friendship	Unknown	9,800	39.00	74-79.00
80-01-016	Love	Unknown	9,800	49.00	80.00
80-01-017	Honor	Unknown	9,800	49.00	55-77.00
80-01-018	Cherish	Unknown	9,800	49.00	80.00
81-01-019	Bing Crosby	Unknown	9,800	49.00	49.00
81-01-020	White Lightnin'	Unknown	9,800	49.00	69.00
81-01-021	Marina	Unknown	9,800	49.00	61-69.00
82-01-022	Shreveport	Unknown	9,800	49.00	50-54.00
82-01-023	French Lace	Unknown	9,800	49.00	54.00
82-01-024	Brandy	Unknown	9,800	49.00	69.00
82-01-025	Mon Cheri	Unknown	9,800	49.00	49.00
83-01-026	Sun Flare	Unknown	9,800	49.00	69.00

Number	Name	Artist	Edition Limit	Issue Price	Quote
83-01-027	Sweet Surrender	Unknown	9,800	49.00	55.00
84-01-028	Impatient	Unknown	9,800	49.00	55.00
84-01-029	Olympiad	Unknown	9,800	49.00	55.00
84-01-030	Intrigue	Unknown	9,800	49.00	58.00
85-01-031	Showbiz	Unknown	9,800	49.50	49.50
85-01-032	Peace	Unknown	9,800	49.50	49.50
85-01-033	Queen Elizabeth	Unknown	9,800	49.50	49.50
Anheuser-Busch, Inc.		**Holiday Plate Series**			
89-01-001	Winters Day N2295	B. Kemper	Retrd.	30.00	50-150.00
90-01-002	An American Tradition N2767	S. Sampson	Retrd.	30.00	35.00
91-01-003	The Season's Best N3034	S. Sampson	25,000	30.00	30.00
92-01-004	A Perfect Christmas N3440	S. Sampson	25,000	27.50	27.50
Anheuser-Busch, Inc.		**Man's Best Friend Series**			
90-02-001	Buddies N2615	M. Urdahl	Retrd.	30.00	40-45.00
90-02-002	Six Pack N3005	M. Urdahl	Retrd.	30.00	30-105.00
92-02-003	Something's Brewing N3147	M. Urdahl	25,000	30.00	30.00
Anheuser-Busch, Inc.		**1992 Olympic Team Series**			
91-03-001	1992 Olympic Team Winter Plate N3180	A-Busch, Inc.	25,000	35.00	35.00
92-03-002	1992 Olympic Team Summer Plate N3122	A-Busch, Inc.	25,000	35.00	35.00
Anheuser-Busch, Inc.		**Civil War Series**			
92-04-001	General Grant N3478	D. Langeneckert	25,000	45.00	45.00
93-04-002	General Robert E. Lee N3590	D. Langeneckert	25,000	45.00	45.00
93-04-003	President Abraham Lincoln N3591	D. Langeneckert	25,000	45.00	45.00
Anheuser-Busch, Inc.		**Archives Plate Series**			
92-05-001	1893 Columbian Exposition N3477	D. Langeneckert	25,000	27.50	27.50
Anna-Perenna Porcelain		**Uncle Tad's Cats**			
79-01-001	Oliver's Birthday	T. Krumeich	5,000	75.00	220.00
80-01-002	Peaches & Cream	T. Krumeich	5,000	75.00	80.00
81-01-003	Princess Aurora	T. Krumeich	5,000	80.00	85.00
81-01-004	Walter's Window	T. Krumeich	5,000	80.00	95.00
Anna-Perenna Porcelain		**Annual Christmas Plate**			
84-02-001	Noel, Noel	P. Buckley Moss	5,000	67.50	325.00
85-02-002	Helping Hands	P. Buckley Moss	5,000	67.50	225.00
86-02-003	Night Before Christmas	P. Buckley Moss	5,000	67.50	150.00
87-02-004	Christmas Sleigh	P. Buckley Moss	5,000	75.00	95.00
88-02-005	Christmas Joy	P. Buckley Moss	7,500	75.00	75.00
89-02-006	Christmas Carol	P. Buckley Moss	7,500	80.00	95.00
90-02-007	Christmas Eve	P. Buckley Moss	7,500	80.00	80.00
91-02-008	The Snowman	P. Buckley Moss	7,500	80.00	80.00
92-02-009	Christmas Warmth	P. Buckley Moss	7,500	85.00	85.00
Anna-Perenna Porcelain		**American Silhouettes-Childrens Series**			
81-03-001	Fiddlers Two	P. Buckley Moss	5,000	75.00	95.00
83-03-002	Mary With The Lambs	P. Buckley Moss	5,000	75.00	85.00
84-03-003	Ring-Around-the-Rosie	P. Buckley Moss	5,000	75.00	200.00
84-03-004	Waiting For Tom	P. Buckley Moss	5,000	75.00	175.00
Anna-Perenna Porcelain		**The Celebration Series**			
86-04-001	Wedding Joy	P. Buckley Moss	5,000	100.00	350.00
87-04-002	The Christening	P. Buckley Moss	5,000	100.00	175.00
88-04-003	The Anniversary	P. Buckley Moss	5,000	100.00	120-190.
89-04-004	Family Reunion	P. Buckley Moss	5,000	100.00	150.00
Anna-Perenna Porcelain		**American Silhouettes Family Series**			
81-05-001	Family Outing	P. Buckley Moss	5,000	75.00	95.00
82-05-002	John and Mary	P. Buckley Moss	5,000	75.00	95.00
82-05-003	Homemakers Quilting	P. Buckley Moss	5,000	75.00	85-195.00
84-05-004	Leisure Time	P. Buckley Moss	5,000	75.00	85.00
Anna-Perenna Porcelain		**American Silhouettes Valley Series**			
81-06-001	Frosty Frolic	P. Buckley Moss	5,000	75.00	85-95.00
82-06-002	Hay Ride	P. Buckley Moss	5,000	75.00	85.00
83-06-003	Sunday Ride	P. Buckley Moss	5,000	75.00	85-100.00
84-06-004	Market Day	P. Buckley Moss	5,000	75.00	120.00
ANRI		**Ferrandiz Christmas**			
72-01-001	Christ In The Manger	J. Ferrandiz	2,500	35.00	230.00
73-01-002	Christmas	J. Ferrandiz	Unkn.	40.00	225.00
74-01-003	Holy Night	J. Ferrandiz	Unkn.	50.00	100.00
75-01-004	Flight into Egypt	J. Ferrandiz	Unkn.	60.00	95.00
76-01-005	Tree of Life	J. Ferrandiz	Unkn.	60.00	60.00
76-01-006	Girl with Flowers	J. Ferrandiz	4,000	65.00	185.00
78-01-007	Leading the Way	J. Ferrandiz	4,000	77.50	180.00
79-01-008	The Drummer	J. Ferrandiz	4,000	120.00	175.00
80-01-009	Rejoice	J. Ferrandiz	4,000	150.00	160.00
81-01-010	Spreading the Word	J. Ferrandiz	4,000	150.00	150.00
82-01-011	The Shepherd Family	J. Ferrandiz	4,000	150.00	150.00
83-01-012	Peace Attend Thee	J. Ferrandiz	4,000	150.00	150.00
ANRI		**Ferrandiz Mother's Day Series**			
72-02-001	Mother Sewing	J. Ferrandiz	2,500	35.00	200.00
73-02-002	Alpine Mother & Child	J. Ferrandiz	1,500	40.00	150.00
74-02-003	Mother Holding Child	J. Ferrandiz	1,500	50.00	150.00
75-02-004	Dove Girl	J. Ferrandiz	1,500	60.00	150.00
76-02-005	Mother Knitting	J. Ferrandiz	1,500	60.00	200.00
77-02-006	Alpine Stroll	J. Ferrandiz	3,000	65.00	125.00
78-02-007	The Beginning	J. Ferrandiz	3,000	75.00	150.00
79-02-008	All Hearts	J. Ferrandiz	3,000	120.00	170.00
80-02-009	Spring Arrivals	J. Ferrandiz	3,000	150.00	165.00
81-02-010	Harmony	J. Ferrandiz	3,000	150.00	150.00
82-02-011	With Love	J. Ferrandiz	3,000	150.00	150.00
ANRI		**Ferrandiz Wooden Wedding Plates**			
72-03-001	Boy and Girl Embracing	J. Ferrandiz	Unkn.	40.00	150.00
73-03-002	Wedding Scene	J. Ferrandiz	Unkn.	40.00	150.00
74-03-003	Wedding	J. Ferrandiz	Unkn.	48.00	150.00
75-03-004	Wedding	J. Ferrandiz	Unkn.	60.00	150.00
76-03-005	Wedding	J. Ferrandiz	Unkn.	60.00	90-150.00
ANRI		**Christmas**			
71-04-001	St. Jakob in Groden	J. Malfertheiner	10,000	37.50	65.00
72-04-002	Pipers at Alberobello	J. Malfertheiner	10,000	45.00	75.00
73-04-003	Alpine Horn	J. Malfertheiner	10,000	45.00	390.00
74-04-004	Young Man and Girl	J. Malfertheiner	10,000	50.00	95.00
75-04-005	Christmas in Ireland	J. Malfertheiner	10,000	60.00	60.00
76-04-006	Alpine Christmas	J. Malfertheiner	6,000	65.00	190.00
77-04-007	Legend of Heligenblut	J. Malfertheiner	6,000	65.00	91.00
78-04-008	Klockler Singers	J. Malfertheiner	6,000	80.00	80.00
79-04-009	Moss Gatherers	Unknown	6,000	135.00	177.00
80-04-010	Wintry Churchgoing	Unknown	6,000	165.00	165.00
81-04-011	Santa Claus in Tyrol	Unknown	6,000	165.00	200.00
82-04-012	The Star Singers	Unknown	6,000	165.00	165.00
83-04-013	Unto Us a Child is Born	Unknown	6,000	165.00	310.00
84-04-014	Yuletide in the Valley	Unknown	6,000	165.00	170.00
85-04-015	Good Morning, Good Cheer	J. Malfertheiner	6,000	165.00	165.00
86-04-016	A Groden Christmas	J. Malfertheiner	6,000	165.00	200.00
87-04-017	Down From the Alps	J. Malfertheiner	6,000	195.00	250.00
88-04-018	Christkindl Markt	J. Malfertheiner	6,000	220.00	230.00
88-04-019	Flight Into Egypt	J. Malfertheiner	6,000	275.00	275.00
90-04-020	Holy Night	J. Malfertheiner	6,000	300.00	300.00
ANRI		**ANRI Mother's Day**			
72-05-001	Alpine Mother & Children	Unknown.	5,000	35.00	50.00
73-05-002	Alpine Mother & Children	Unknown	5,000	40.00	50.00
74-05-003	Alpine Mother & Children	Unknown	5,000	50.00	55.00
75-05-004	Alpine Stroll	Unknown	5,000	60.00	65.00
76-05-005	Knitting	Unknown	5,000	60.00	65.00
ANRI		**ANRI Father's Day**			
72-06-001	Alpine Father & Children	Unknown	5,000	35.00	100.00
73-06-002	Alpine Father & Children	Unknown	5,000	40.00	95.00
74-06-003	Cliff Gazing	Unknown	5,000	50.00	100.00
76-06-004	Sailing	Unknown	5,000	60.00	90.00
ANRI		**Disney Four Star Collection**			
89-07-001	Mickey Mini Plate	Disney Studios	5,000	40.00	45.00
90-07-002	Minnie Mini Plate	Disney Studios	5,000	40.00	45.00
91-07-003	Donald Mini Plate	Disney Studios	5,000	50.00	50.00
Arabia Annual		**Kalevala**			
76-01-001	Vainamoinen's Sowing	R. Uosikkinen	Unkn.	30.00	230.00
77-01-002	Aino's Fate	R. Uosikkinen	Unkn.	30.00	30.00
78-01-003	Lemminkainen's Chase	R. Uosikkinen	2,500	39.00	39.00
79-01-004	Kullervo's Revenge	R. Uosikkinen	Annual	39.50	39.50
80-01-005	Vainomoinen's Rescue	R. Uosikkinen	Annual	45.00	52.00
81-01-006	Vainomoinen's Magic	R. Uosikkinen	Annual	49.50	49.50
82-01-007	Joukahainen Shoots the Horse	R. Uosikkinen	Annual	55.50	56.00
83-01-008	Lemminkainen's Escape	R. Uosikkinen	Annual	60.00	76.00
84-01-009	Lemminkainen's Magic Feathers	R. Uosikkinen	Annual	49.50	87.00
85-01-010	Lemminkainen's Grief	R. Uosikkinen	Annual	60.00	76.00
86-01-011	Osmatar Creating Ale	R. Uosikkinen	Annual	60.00	85.00
87-01-012	Valnamoinen Tricks Ilmarinen	R. Uosikkinen	Annual	65.00	90.00
88-01-013	Hears Vainamolnen Weep	R. Uosikkinen	Annual	69.00	115.00
89-01-014	Four Maidens	R. Uosikkinen	Annual	75.00	87.00
90-01-015	Annikka	R. Uosikkinen	Annual	85.00	105.00
91-01-013	Lemminkain's Mother Says Don't/ War	R. Uosikkinen	Annual	85.00	89.00
Armstrong's		**Infinite Love**			
87-01-001	A Pair of Dreams	S. Etem	14-day	24.50	24.50
87-01-002	The Eyes Say "I Love You"	S. Etem	14-day	24.50	24.50
87-01-003	Once Upon a Smile	S. Etem	14-day	24.50	24.50
87-01-004	Kiss a Little Giggle	S. Etem	14-day	24.50	24.50
88-01-005	Love Goes Forth in Little Feet	S. Etem	14-day	24.50	24.50
88-01-006	Bundle of Joy	S. Etem	14-day	24.50	24.50
88-01-007	Grins For Grandma	S. Etem	14-day	24.50	24.50
89-01-008	A Moment to Cherish	S. Etem	14-day	24.50	24.50
Armstrong's		**Statue of Liberty**			
86-02-001	Dedication	A. D'Estrehan	10,000	39.50	49.50
86-02-002	The Immigrants	A. D'Estrehan	10,000	39.50	49.50
86-02-003	Independence	A. D'Estrehan	10,000	39.50	49.50
86-02-004	Re-Dedication	A. D'Estrehan	10,000	39.50	49.50
Armstrong's		**Commemorative Issues**			
83-03-001	70 Years Young (10 1/2")	R. Skelton	15,000	85.00	125.00
84-03-002	Freddie the Torchbearer (8 1/2")	R. Skelton	15,000	62.50	85.00
Armstrong's		**The Signature Collection**			
86-04-001	Anyone for Tennis?	R. Skelton	9,000	62.50	62.50
86-04-002	Anyone for Tennis? (signed)	R. Skelton	1,000	125.00	650.00
87-04-003	Ironing the Waves	R. Skelton	9,000	62.50	75.00
87-04-004	Ironing the Waves (signed)	R. Skelton	1,000	125.00	175.00
88-04-005	The Cliffhanger	R. Skelton	9,000	62.50	62.50
88-04-006	The Cliffhanger (signed)	R. Skelton	1,000	150.00	150.00
Armstrong's		**Happy Art Series**			
81-05-001	Woody's Triple Self-Portriat, Signed	W. Lantz	1,000	100.00	100.00
81-05-002	Woody's Triple Self-Portrait	W. Lantz	9,000	39.50	39.50
83-05-003	Gothic Woody, Signed	W. Lantz	1,000	100.00	100.00
83-05-004	Gothic Woody	W. Lantz	9,000	39.50	39.50
84-05-005	Blue Boy Woody, Signed	W. Lantz	1,000	100.00	100.00
84-05-006	Blue Boy Woody	W. Lantz	9,000	39.50	39.50
Armstrong's		**The Constitution Series**			
87-06-001	U.S. Constitution vs. Guerriere	A. D'Estrehan	10,000	39.50	39.50
87-06-002	U.S. Constitution vs. Tripoli	A. D'Estrehan	10,000	39.50	50.00
87-06-003	U.S. Constitution vs. Java	A. D'Estrehan	10,000	39.50	39.50
87-06-004	The Great Chase	A. D'Estrehan	10,000	39.50	39.50
Armstrong's		**The Mischief Makers**			
86-07-001	Puddles	S. Etem	10,000	39.95	39.95
86-07-002	Buckles	S. Etem	10,000	39.95	39.95
87-07-003	Trix	S. Etem	10,000	39.95	39.95
88-07-004	Naps	S. Etem	10,000	39.95	45.00
Armstrong's		**Faces of the World**			
88-08-001	Erin (Ireland)	L. De Winne	14-day	24.50	24.50
88-08-002	Clara (Belgium)	L. De Winne	14-day	24.50	24.50
88-08-003	Luisa (Spain)	L. De Winne	14-day	24.50	24.50
88-08-004	Tamiko (Japan)	L. De Winne	14-day	24.50	24.50
88-08-005	Colette (France)	L. De Winne	14-day	24.50	24.50
88-08-006	Heather (England)	L. De Winne	14-day	24.50	24.50
88-08-007	Greta (Austria)	L. De Winne	14-day	24.50	24.50
88-08-008	Maria (Italy)	L. De Winne	14-day	24.50	24.50
Armstrong's/Crown Parlan		**Freddie The Freeloader**			
79-01-001	Freddie in the Bathtub	R. Skelton	10,000	60.00	210-240.
80-01-002	Freddie's Shack	R. Skelton	10,000	60.00	125.00
81-01-003	Freddie on the Green	R. Skelton	10,000	60.00	69.00

Number	Name	Artist	Edition Limit	Issue Price	Quote
Company		**Series**			
82-01-004	Love that Freddie	R. Skelton	10,000	60.00	70.00
Armstrong's/Crown Parlan		**Freddie's Adventures**			
82-02-001	Captain Freddie	R. Skelton	15,000	60.00	95.00
82-02-002	Bronco Freddie	R. Skelton	15,000	60.00	75.00
83-02-003	Sir Freddie	R. Skelton	15,000	62.50	79.00
84-02-004	Gertrude and Heathcliffe	R. Skelton	15,000	62.50	70.00
Artaffects		**Portraits of American Brides**			
86-01-001	Caroline	R. Sauber	10-day	29.50	75.00
86-01-002	Jacqueline	R. Sauber	10-day	29.50	30.00
87-01-003	Elizabeth	R. Sauber	10-day	29.50	37.00
87-01-004	Emily	R. Sauber	10-day	29.50	44.00
87-01-005	Meredith	R. Sauber	10-day	29.50	45.00
87-01-006	Laura	R. Sauber	10-day	29.50	45.00
87-01-007	Sarah	R. Sauber	10-day	29.50	46.00
87-01-008	Rebecca	R. Sauber	10-day	29.50	64.00
Artaffects		**Masterpieces of Rockwell**			
80-02-001	After the Prom	N. Rockwell	17,500	42.50	150.00
80-02-002	The Challenger	N. Rockwell	17,500	50.00	75.00
82-02-003	Girl at the Mirror	N. Rockwell	17,500	50.00	100.00
82-02-004	Missing Tooth	N. Rockwell	17,500	50.00	75.00
Artaffects		**Rockwell Americana**			
81-03-001	Shuffleton's Barbershop	N. Rockwell	17,500	75.00	150.00
82-03-002	Breaking Home Ties	N. Rockwell	17,500	75.00	125.00
83-03-003	Walking to Church	N. Rockwell	17,500	75.00	125.00
Artaffects		**Rockwell Trilogy**			
81-04-001	Stockbridge in Winter 1	N. Rockwell	Open	35.00	50.00
82-04-002	Stockbridge in Winter 2	N. Rockwell	Open	35.00	50.00
82-04-003	Stockbridge in Winter 3	N. Rockwell	Open	35.00	50.00
Artaffects		**Simpler Times Series**			
84-05-001	Lazy Daze	N. Rockwell	7,500	35.00	75.00
84-05-002	One for the Road	N. Rockwell	7,500	35.00	75.00
Artaffects		**Special Occasions**			
82-06-001	Bubbles	F. Tipton Hunter	Open	29.95	50.00
82-06-002	Butterflies	F. Tipton Hunter	Open	29.95	50.00
Artaffects		**Masterpieces of Impressionism**			
80-07-001	Woman with Parasol	Monet/Cassat	17,500	35.00	75.00
81-07-002	Young Mother Sewing	Monet/Cassat	17,500	35.00	60.00
82-07-003	Sara in Green Bonnet	Monet/Cassat	17,500	35.00	60.00
83-07-004	Margot in Blue	Monet/Cassat	17,500	35.00	50.00
Artaffects		**Magical Moment**			
81-08-001	Happy Dreams	B. Pease Gutmann	Open	29.95	100.00
81-08-002	Harmony	B. Pease Gutmann	Open	29.95	90.00
82-08-003	His Majesty	B. Pease Gutmann	Open	29.95	60.00
83-08-003	The Lullaby	B. Pease Gutmann	Open	29.95	50.00
82-08-004	Waiting for Daddy	B. Pease Gutmann	Open	29.95	50.00
82-08-005	Thank You God	B. Pease Gutmann	Open	29.95	50.00
Artaffects		**Masterpieces of the West**			
80-09-001	Texas Night Herder	Johnson	17,500	35.00	75.00
80-09-002	Indian Trapper	Remington	17,500	35.00	100.00
82-09-003	Cowboy Style	Leigh	17,500	35.00	75.00
82-09-004	Indian Style	Perillo	17,500	35.00	150.00
Artaffects		**Playful Pets**			
82-10-001	Curiosity	J. H. Dolph	7,500	45.00	75.00
82-10-002	Master's Hat	J. H. Dolph	7,500	45.00	75.00
Artaffects		**The Tribute Series**			
82-11-001	I Want You	J. M. Flagg	Open	29.95	50.00
82-11-002	Gee, I Wish	H. C. Christy	Open	29.95	50.00
83-11-003	Soldier's Farewell	N. Rockwell	Open	29.95	50.00
Artaffects		**The Carnival Series**			
82-12-001	Knock em' Down	T. Newsom	19,500	35.00	50.00
82-12-002	Carousel	T. Newsom	19,500	35.00	50.00
Artaffects		**Nursery Pair**			
83-13-001	In Slumberland	C. Becker	Open	25.00	60.00
83-13-002	The Awakening	C. Becker	Open	25.00	60.00
Artaffects		**Melodies of Childhood**			
83-14-001	Twinkle, Twinkle Little Star	H. Garrido	19,500	35.00	50.00
83-14-002	Row, Row, Row Your Boat	H. Garrido	19,500	35.00	50.00
83-14-003	Mary had a Little Lamb	H. Garrido	19,500	35.00	50.00
Artaffects		**Unicorn Magic**			
83-15-001	Morning Encounter	J. Terreson	7,500	50.00	60.00
83-15-002	Afternoon Offering	J. Terreson	7,500	50.00	60.00
Artaffects		**Baker Street**			
83-16-001	Sherlock Holmes	M. Hooks	9,800	55.00	150.00
83-16-002	Watson	M. Hooks	9,800	55.00	125.00
Artaffects		**Angler's Dream**			
83-17-001	Brook Trout	J. Eggert	9,800	55.00	75.00
83-17-002	Striped Bass	J. Eggert	9,800	55.00	75.00
83-17-003	Largemouth Bass	J. Eggert	9,800	55.00	75.00
83-17-004	Chinook Salmon	J. Eggert	9,800	55.00	75.00
Artaffects		**On the Road Series**			
84-18-001	Pride of Stockbridge	N. Rockwell	Open	35.00	75.00
84-18-002	City Pride	N. Rockwell	Open	35.00	75.00
84-18-003	Country Pride	N. Rockwell	Open	35.00	75.00
Artaffects		**Mother's Love**			
84-19-001	Daddy's Here	B. P. Gutmann	Open	29.95	60.00
Artaffects		**Bessie's Best**			
84-20-001	Oh! Oh! A Bunny	B. P. Gutmann	Open	29.95	65.00
84-20-002	The New Love	B. P. Gutmann	Open	29.95	65.00
84-20-003	My Baby	B. P. Gutmann	Open	29.95	65.00
84-20-004	Looking for Trouble	B. P. Gutmann	Open	29.95	65.00
84-20-005	Taps	B. P. Gutmann	Open	29.95	65.00

Number	Name	Artist	Edition Limit	Issue Price	Quote
Company		**Series**			
Artaffects		**The Great Trains**			
85-21-001	Santa Fe	J. Deneen	7,500	35.00	100.00
85-21-002	Twentieth Century Ltd.	J. Deneen	7,500	35.00	100.00
86-21-003	Empire Builder	J. Deneen	7,500	35.00	100.00
Artaffects		**Becker Babies**			
83-22-001	Snow Puff	C. Becker	Open	29.95	60.00
84-22-002	Smiling Through	C. Becker	Open	29.95	60.00
84-22-003	Pals	C. Becker	Open	29.95	60.00
Artaffects		**Portrait Series**			
86-23-001	Chantilly	J. Eggert	14-day	24.50	40.00
86-23-002	Dynasty	J. Eggert	14-day	24.50	40.00
86-23-003	Velvet	J. Eggert	14-day	24.50	40.00
86-23-004	Jambalaya	J. Eggert	14-day	24.50	40.00
Artaffects		**Sailing Through History**			
86-24-001	Flying Cloud	K. Soldwedel	14-day	29.50	60.00
86-24-002	Santa Maria	K. Soldwedel	14-day	29.50	60.00
86-24-003	Mayflower	K. Soldwedel	14-day	29.50	60.00
Artaffects		**How Do I Love Thee?**			
82-25-001	Alaina	R. Sauber	19,500	39.95	60.00
82-25-002	Taylor	R. Sauber	19,500	39.95	60.00
83-25-003	Rendezvouse	R. Sauber	19,500	39.95	60.00
83-25-004	Embrace	R. Sauber	19,500	39.95	60.00
Artaffects		**Childhood Delights**			
83-26-001	Amanda	R. Sauber	7,500	45.00	75.00
Artaffects		**Songs of Stephen Foster**			
84-27-001	Oh! Susannah	R. Sauber	3,500	60.00	80.00
84-27-002	Jeanie with the Light Brown Hair	R. Sauber	3,500	60.00	80.00
84-27-003	Beautiful Dreamer	R. Sauber	3,500	60.00	80.00
Artaffects		**Times of Our Lives Collection**			
84-28-001	Happy Birthday-(10 1/4")	R. Sauber	Open	37.50	39.50
88-28-002	Happy Birthday-(6 1/2")	R. Sauber	Open	19.50	22.50
85-28-003	Home Sweet Home-(10 1/4")	R. Sauber	Open	37.50	39.50
88-28-004	Home Sweet Home-(6 1/2")	R. Sauber	Open	19.50	22.50
82-28-005	The Wedding-(10 1/4")	R. Sauber	Open	37.50	39.50
88-28-006	The Wedding-(6 1/2")	R. Sauber	Open	19.50	22.50
86-28-007	The Anniversary-(10 1/4")	R. Sauber	Open	37.50	39.50
88-28-008	The Anniversary-(6 1/2")	R. Sauber	Open	19.50	22.50
86-28-009	Sweethearts-(10 1/4")	R. Sauber	Open	37.50	39.50
88-28-010	Sweethearts-(6 1/2")	R. Sauber	Open	19.50	22.50
86-28-011	The Christening-(10 1/4")	R. Sauber	Open	37.50	39.50
88-28-012	The Christening-(6 1/2")	R. Sauber	Open	19.50	22.50
85-28-013	All Adore Him-(10 1/4")	R. Sauber	Open	37.50	39.50
88-28-014	All Adore Him-(6 1/2")	R. Sauber	Open	19.50	22.50
87-28-015	Motherhood-(10 1/4")	R. Sauber	Open	37.50	39.50
88-28-016	Motherhood-(6 1/2")	R. Sauber	Open	19.50	22.50
87-28-017	Fatherhood-(10 1/4")	R. Sauber	Open	37.50	39.50
88-28-018	Fatherhood-(6 1/2")	R. Sauber	Open	19.50	22.50
87-28-019	Sweet Sixteen-(10 1/4")	R. Sauber	Open	37.50	39.50
89-28-020	God Bless America-(10 1/4")	R. Sauber	14-day	39.50	39.50
89-28-021	God Bless America-(6 1/4")	R. Sauber	14-day	21.50	22.50
89-28-022	Visiting the Doctor-(10 1/4")	R. Sauber	14-day	39.50	39.50
90-28-023	Mother's Joy-(6 1/2")	R. Sauber	Open	22.50	22.50
90-28-024	Mother's Joy-(10 1/4")	R. Sauber	Open	39.50	39.50
Artaffects		**Christian Collection**			
87-29-001	Bring to Me the Children	A. Tobey	Unkn.	35.00	35.00
87-29-002	Wedding Feast at Cana	A. Tobey	Unkn.	35.00	35.00
87-29-003	The Healer	A. Tobey	Unkn.	35.00	35.00
Artaffects		**American Maritime Heritage**			
87-30-001	U.S.S. Constitution	K. Soldwedel	14 Day	35.00	35.00
Artaffects		**Reflections of Youth**			
88-32-001	Julia	Mago	14-day	29.50	40-45.00
88-32-002	Jessica	Mago	14-day	29.50	35.00
88-32-003	Sebastian	Mago	14-day	29.50	35.00
88-32-004	Michelle	Mago	14-day	29.50	37.50
88-32-005	Andrew	Mago	14-day	29.50	35.00
88-32-006	Beth	Mago	14-day	29.50	39.00
88-32-007	Amy	Mago	14-day	29.50	39.00
88-32-008	Lauren	Mago	14-day	29.50	39.00
Artaffects		**The Chieftains**			
79-33-001	Chief Sitting Bull	G. Perillo	7,500	65.00	399.00
79-33-002	Chief Joseph	G. Perillo	7,500	65.00	124-199.
80-33-003	Chief Red Cloud	G. Perillo	7,500	65.00	148-175.
80-33-004	Chief Geronimo	G. Perillo	7,500	65.00	100-199.
81-33-005	Chief Crazy Horse	G. Perillo	7,500	65.00	160-199.
Artaffects		**The Plainsmen**			
78-34-001	Buffalo Hunt (Bronze)	G. Perillo	2,500	300.00	500.00
79-34-002	The Proud One (Bronze)	G. Perillo	2,500	300.00	800.00
Artaffects		**The Professionals**			
79-35-001	The Big Leaguer	G. Perillo	15,000	29.95	30-75.00
80-35-002	Ballerina's Dilemma	G. Perillo	15,000	32.50	33-50.00
81-35-003	Quarterback	G. Perillo	15,000	32.50	40.00
81-35-004	Rodeo Joe	G. Perillo	15,000	35.00	40.00
82-35-005	Major Leaguer	G. Perillo	15,000	35.00	100.00
83-35-006	The Hockey Player	G. Perillo	15,000	35.00	40.00
Artaffects		**Pride of America's Indians**			
86-36-001	Brave and Free	G. Perillo	10-day	24.50	50-125.00
86-36-002	Dark-Eyed Friends	G. Perillo	10-day	24.50	40-85.00
86-36-003	Noble Companions	G. Perillo	10-day	24.50	30-65.00
87-36-004	Kindred Spirits	G. Perillo	10-day	24.50	45-75.00
87-36-005	Loyal Alliance	G. Perillo	10-day	24.50	80-100.00
87-36-006	Small and Wise	G. Perillo	10-day	24.50	35-50.00
87-36-007	Winter Scouts	G. Perillo	10-day	24.50	35-58.00
87-36-008	Peaceful Comrades	G. Perillo	10-day	24.50	40-60.00
Artaffects		**Legends of the West**			
82-37-001	Daniel Boone	G. Perillo	10,000	65.00	80.00
83-37-002	Davy Crockett	G. Perillo	10,000	65.00	80.00
83-37-003	Kit Carson	G. Perillo	10,000	65.00	80.00
83-37-004	Buffalo Bill	G. Perillo	10,000	65.00	80.00

Company		Series			
Number	**Name**	**Artist**	**Edition Limit**	**Issue Price**	**Quote**
Artaffects		**Chieftans 2**			
83-38-001	Chief Pontiac	G. Perillo	7,500	70.00	70-150.00
83-38-002	Chief Victorio	G. Perillo	7,500	70.00	85-110.00
84-38-003	Chief Tecumseh	G. Perillo	7,500	70.00	85-110.00
84-38-004	Chief Cochise	G. Perillo	7,500	70.00	85-110.00
84-38-005	Chief Black Kettle	G. Perillo	7,500	70.00	85-110.00
Artaffects		**Child Life**			
83-39-001	Siesta	G. Perillo	10,000	45.00	100.00
84-39-002	Sweet Dreams	G. Perillo	10,000	45.00	100.00
Artaffects		**Indian Nations**			
83-40-001	Blackfoot	G. Perillo	7,500	140.00	500-1000.
83-40-002	Cheyenne	G. Perillo	7,500	Set	Set
83-40-003	Apache	G. Perillo	7,500	Set	Set
83-40-004	Sioux	G. Perillo	7,500	Set	Set
Artaffects		**The Storybook Collection**			
80-41-001	Little Red Ridinghood	G. Perillo	18-day	45.00	52-65.00
81-41-002	Cinderella	G. Perillo	18-day	45.00	60.00
81-41-003	Hansel & Gretel	G. Perillo	18-day	45.00	52-65.00
82-41-004	Goldilocks & 3 Bears	G. Perillo	18-day	45.00	60.00
Artaffects		**Perillo Santa's**			
80-42-001	Santa's Joy	G. Perillo	Unkn.	29.95	75-100.00
81-42-002	Santa's Bundle	G. Perillo	Unkn.	29.95	75.00
Artaffects		**The Princesses**			
82-43-001	Lily of the Mohawks	G. Perillo	7,500	50.00	150.00
82-43-002	Pocahontas	G. Perillo	7,500	50.00	120.00
82-43-003	Minnehaha	G. Perillo	7,500	50.00	120.00
82-43-004	Sacajawea	G. Perillo	7,500	50.00	85-125.00
Artaffects		**Nature's Harmony**			
82-44-001	The Peaceable Kingdom	G. Perillo	12,500	100.00	250.00
82-44-002	Zebra	G. Perillo	12,500	50.00	150.00
82-44-003	Bengal Tiger	G. Perillo	12,500	50.00	100.00
83-44-004	Black Panther	G. Perillo	12,500	50.00	100.00
83-44-005	Elephant	G. Perillo	12,500	50.00	150.00
Artaffects		**Arctic Friends**			
82-45-001	Siberian Love	G. Perillo	7,500	100.00	400-1000.
82-45-002	Snow Pals	G. Perillo	7,500	Set	Set
Artaffects		**Motherhood Series**			
83-47-001	Madre	G. Perillo	10,000	50.00	150.00
84-47-002	Madonna of the Plains	G. Perillo	3,500	50.00	75-100.00
85-47-003	Abuela	G. Perillo	3,500	50.00	75.00
86-47-004	Nap Time	G. Perillo	3,500	50.00	75.00
Artaffects		**The War Ponies**			
83-48-001	Sioux War Pony	G. Perillo	7,500	60.00	95-125.00
83-48-002	Nez Perce War Pony	G. Perillo	7,500	60.00	149-195.
83-48-003	Apache War Pony	G. Perillo	7,500	60.00	95-125.00
Artaffects		**The Tribal Ponies**			
84-49-001	Arapaho Tribal Pony	G. Perillo	3,500	65.00	150.00
84-49-002	Comanche Tribal Pony	G. Perillo	3,500	65.00	150.00
84-49-003	Crow Tribal Pony	G. Perillo	3,500	65.00	200.00
Artaffects		**The Thoroughbreds**			
84-50-001	Whirlaway	G. Perillo	9,500	50.00	250.00
84-50-002	Secretariat	G. Perillo	9,500	50.00	350.00
84-50-003	Man o' War	G. Perillo	9,500	50.00	150.00
84-50-004	Seabiscuit	G. Perillo	9,500	50.00	150.00
Artaffects		**Special Issue**			
81-51-001	Apache Boy	G. Perillo	5,000	95.00	175.00
83-51-001	Papoose	G. Perillo	3,000	100.00	125.00
84-51-001	The Lovers	G. Perillo	Unkn.	50.00	100.00
84-51-001	Navajo Girl	G. Perillo	3,500	95.00	350.00
86-51-001	Navajo Boy	G. Perillo	3,500	95.00	250.00
87-51-001	We The People	H.C. Christy	Open	35.00	35.00
Artaffects		**The Arabians**			
86-52-001	Silver Streak	G. Perillo	3,500	95.00	150.00
Artaffects		**The Colts**			
85-53-001	Appaloosa	G. Perillo	5,000	40.00	100.00
85-53-002	Pinto	G. Perillo	5,000	40.00	110.00
85-53-003	Arabian	G. Perillo	5,000	40.00	100.00
85-53-004	The Thoroughbred	G. Perillo	5,000	40.00	100.00
Artaffects		**Tender Moments**			
85-54-001	Sunset	G. Perillo	2,000	150.00	250.00
85-54-002	Winter Romance	G. Perillo	2,000	Set	Set
Artaffects		**Young Emotions**			
86-55-001	Tears	G. Perillo	5,000	75.00	250.00
86-55-002	Smiles	G. Perillo	5,000	Set	Set
Artaffects		**The Maidens**			
85-56-001	Shimmering Waters	G. Perillo	5,000	60.00	150.00
85-56-002	Snow Blanket	G. Perillo	5,000	60.00	150.00
85-56-003	Song Bird	G. Perillo	5,000	60.00	150.00
Artaffects		**The Young Chieftains**			
85-57-001	Young Sitting Bull	G. Perillo	5,000	50.00	75-150.00
85-57-002	Young Joseph	G. Perillo	5,000	50.00	100.00
86-57-003	Young Red Cloud	G. Perillo	5,000	50.00	100.00
86-57-004	Young Geronimo	G. Perillo	5,000	50.00	100.00
86-57-005	Young Crazy Horse	G. Perillo	5,000	50.00	100.00
Artaffects		**Perillo Christmas**			
87-58-001	Shining Star	G. Perillo	Yr.Iss	29.50	125-300.
88-58-002	Silent Light	G. Perillo	Yr.Iss	35.00	50-200.00
89-58-003	Snow Flake	G. Perillo	Yr.Iss	35.00	95.00
90-58-004	Bundle Up	G. Perillo	Yr.Iss	35.00	75.00
91-58-005	Christmas Journey	G. Perillo	Yr.Iss	39.50	50.00
Artaffects		**America's Indian Heritage**			
87-59-001	Cheyenne Nation	G. Perillo	10-day	24.50	85.00
88-59-002	Arapaho Nation	G. Perillo	10-day	24.50	45.00

Company		Series			
Number	**Name**	**Artist**	**Edition Limit**	**Issue Price**	**Quote**
88-59-003	Kiowa Nation	G. Perillo	10-day	24.50	45.00
88-59-004	Sioux Nation	G. Perillo	10-day	24.50	30-55.00
88-59-005	Chippewa Nation	G. Perillo	10-day	24.50	50.00
88-59-006	Crow Nation	G. Perillo	10-day	24.50	60.00
88-59-007	Nez Perce Nation	G. Perillo	10-day	24.50	75.00
88-59-008	Blackfoot Nation	G. Perillo	10-day	24.50	95.00
Artaffects		**Mother's Love**			
88-60-001	Feelings	G. Perillo	Yr.Iss	35.00	175.00
89-60-002	Moonlight	G. Perillo	Yr.Iss	35.00	100-125.
90-60-003	Pride & Joy	G. Perillo	Yr.Iss	35.00	50-125.00
91-60-004	Little Shadow	G. Perillo	Yr.Iss	39.50	45.00
Artaffects		**Perillo's Wildlife**			
89-61-001	Mustang	G. Perillo	14-day	29.50	45-50.00
89-61-002	White-Tailed Deer	G. Perillo	14-day	29.50	35.00
89-61-003	Mountain Lion	G. Perillo	14-day	29.50	45.00
90-61-004	American Bald Eagle	G. Perillo	14-day	29.50	29.50
90-61-005	Timber Wolf	G. Perillo	14-day	29.50	35-50.00
90-61-006	Polar Bear	G. Perillo	14-day	29.50	39.00
90-61-007	Buffalo	G. Perillo	14-day	29.50	39.00
90-61-008	Bighorn Sheep	G. Perillo	14-day	29.50	39.00
Artaffects		**Portraits By Perillo-Mini Plates**			
89-62-001	Smiling Eyes-(4 1/4")	G. Perillo	9,500	19.50	19.50
89-62-002	Bright Sky-(4 1/4")	G. Perillo	9,500	19.50	19.50
89-62-003	Running Bear-(4 1/4")	G. Perillo	9,500	19.50	19.50
89-62-004	Little Feather-(4 1/4")	G. Perillo	9,500	19.50	19.50
90-62-005	Proud Eagle-(4 1/4")	G. Perillo	9,500	19.50	19.50
90-62-006	Blue Bird-(4 1/4")	G. Perillo	9,500	19.50	19.50
90-62-007	Wildflower-(4 1/4")	G. Perillo	9,500	19.50	19.50
90-62-008	Spring Breeze-(4 1/4")	G. Perillo	9,500	19.50	19.50
Artaffects		**March of Dimes: Our Children, Our Future**			
89-63-001	A Time to Be Born	G. Perillo	150-day	29.00	35-49.00
Artaffects		**Indian Bridal**			
90-64-001	Yellow Bird (6 1/2")	G. Perillo	14-day	25.00	25.00
90-64-002	Autumn Blossom (6 1/2")	G. Perillo	14-day	25.00	25.00
90-64-003	Misty Waters (6 1/2")	G. Perillo	14-day	25.00	25.00
90-64-004	Sunny Skies (6 1/2")	G. Perillo	14-day	25.00	25.00
Artaffects		**Proud Young Spirits**			
90-65-001	Protector of the Plains	G. Perillo	14-day	29.50	65.00
90-65-002	Watchful Eyes	G. Perillo	14-day	29.50	50.00
90-65-003	Freedoms Watch	G. Perillo	14-day	29.50	35-45.00
90-65-004	Woodland Scouts	G. Perillo	14-day	29.50	35-45.00
90-65-005	Fast Friends	G. Perillo	14-day	29.50	35-45.00
90-65-006	Birds of a Feather	G. Perillo	14-day	29.50	35-45.00
90-65-007	Prairie Pals	G. Perillo	14-day	29.50	35-45.00
90-65-008	Loyal Guardian	G. Perillo	14-day	29.50	35-45.00
Artaffects		**Perillo's Four Seasons**			
91-66-001	Summer (6 1/2")	G. Perillo	14-day	25.00	25.00
91-66-002	Autumn (6 1/2")	G. Perillo	14-day	25.00	25.00
91-66-003	Winter (6 1/2")	G. Perillo	14-day	25.00	25.00
91-66-004	Spring (6 1/2")	G. Perillo	14-day	25.00	25.00
Artaffects		**Council of Nations**			
92-67-001	Strength of the Sioux	G. Perillo	14-day	29.50	45.00
92-67-002	Pride of the Cheyenne	G. Perillo	14-day	29.50	29.50
92-67-003	Dignity of the NezPerce	G. Perillo	14-day	29.50	29.50
92-67-004	Courage of the Arapatto	G. Perillo	14-day	29.50	29.50
92-67-005	Power of the Blackfoot	G. Perillo	14-day	29.50	29.50
92-67-006	Nobility of the Algonquin	G. Perillo	14-day	29.50	29.50
92-67-007	Wisdom of the Cherokee	G. Perillo	14-day	29.50	29.50
92-67-008	Boldness of the Seneca	G. Perillo	14-day	29.50	29.50
Artaffects		**War Ponies of the Plains**			
92-68-001	Nightshadow	G. Perillo	75-day	27.00	27.00
92-68-002	Windcatcher	G. Perillo	75-day	27.00	27.00
92-68-003	Prairie Prancer	G. Perillo	75-day	27.00	27.00
92-68-004	Thunderfoot	G. Perillo	75-day	27.00	27.00
92-68-005	Proud Companion	G. Perillo	75-day	27.00	27.00
92-68-006	Sun Dancer	G. Perillo	75-day	27.00	27.00
92-68-007	Free Spirit	G. Perillo	75-day	27.00	27.00
92-68-008	Gentle Warrior	G. Perillo	75-day	27.00	27.00
Artaffects		**Classic American Trains**			
88-69-001	Homeward Bound	J. Deneen	14-day	35.00	53.00
88-69-002	A Race Against Time	J. Deneen	14-day	35.00	35.00
88-69-003	Midday Stop	J. Deneen	14-day	35.00	35.00
88-69-004	The Silver Bullet	J. Deneen	14-day	35.00	54.00
88-69-005	Traveling in Style	J. Deneen	14-day	35.00	50.00
88-69-006	Round the Bend	J. Deneen	14-day	35.00	35.00
88-69-007	Taking the High Road	J. Deneen	14-day	35.00	45.00
88-69-008	Competition	J. Deneen	14-day	35.00	40.00
Artaffects		**Good Sports**			
89-70-001	Purrfect Game (6 1/2")	S. Miller-Maxwell	14-day	22.50	25.00
89-70-002	Alley Cats (6 1/2")	S. Miller-Maxwell	14-day	22.50	25.00
89-70-003	Tee Time (6 1/2")	S. Miller-Maxwell	14-day	22.50	25.00
89-70-004	Two/Love (6 1/2")	S. Miller-Maxwell	14-day	22.50	25.00
89-70-005	What's the Catch (6 1/2")	S. Miller-Maxwell	14-day	22.50	25.00
89-70-006	Quaterback Sneak (6 1/2")	S. Miller-Maxwell	14-day	22.50	25.00
Artaffects		**Timeless Love**			
89-71-001	The Proposal	R. Sauber	14-day	35.00	38.00
89-71-002	Sweet Embrace	R. Sauber	14-day	35.00	35.00
90-71-003	Afternoon Light	R. Sauber	14-day	35.00	35.00
90-71-004	Quiet Moments	R. Sauber	14-day	35.00	35.00
Artaffects		**Winter Mindscape**			
89-72-001	Peaceful Village	R. Sauber	14-day	29.50	65.00
89-72-002	Snowbound	R. Sauber	14-day	29.50	40.00
90-72-003	Papa's Surprise	R. Sauber	14-day	29.50	40.00
90-72-004	Well Traveled Road	R. Sauber	14-day	29.50	40.00
90-72-005	First Freeze	R. Sauber	14-day	29.50	40.00
90-72-006	Country Morning	R. Sauber	14-day	29.50	40.00
90-72-007	Sleigh Ride	R. Sauber	14-day	29.50	40.00
90-72-008	January Thaw	R. Sauber	14-day	29.50	40.00

Company / Number	Name	Series / Artist	Edition Limit	Issue Price	Quote
Artaffects		**Baby's Firsts**			
89-73-001	Visiting the Doctor (6 1/2")	R. Sauber	14-day	21.50	22.50
89-73-002	Baby's First Step (6 1/2")	R. Sauber	14-day	21.50	22.50
89-73-003	First Birthday (6 1/2")	R. Sauber	14-day	21.50	22.50
89-73-004	Christmas Morn (6 1/2")	R. Sauber	14-day	21.50	22.50
89-73-005	Picture Perfect (6 1/2")	R. Sauber	14-day	21.50	22.50
Artaffects		**Romantic Cities of Europe**			
89-74-001	Venice	L. Marchetti	14-day	35.00	65.00
89-74-002	Paris	L. Marchetti	14-day	35.00	50.00
90-74-003	London	L. Marchetti	14-day	35.00	50.00
90-74-004	Moscow	L. Marchetti	14-day	35.00	35.00
Aftaffects		**Classic American Cars**			
89-75-001	Duesenberg	J. Deneen	14-day	35.00	40.00
89-75-002	Cadillac	J. Deneen	14-day	35.00	35.00
89-75-003	Cord	J. Deneen	14-day	35.00	35.00
89-75-004	Ruxton	J. Deneen	14-day	35.00	35.00
90-75-005	Lincoln	J. Deneen	14-day	35.00	35.00
90-75-006	Packard	J. Deneen	14-day	35.00	35.00
90-75-007	Hudson	J. Deneen	14-day	35.00	35.00
90-75-008	Pierce-Arrow	J. Deneen	14-day	35.00	35.00
Artaffects		**MaGo's Motherhood**			
90-76-001	Serenity	MaGo	14-day	50.00	50.00
Artaffects		**Studies of Early Childhood**			
90-77-001	Christopher & Kate	MaGo	150-day	34.90	36-59.00
90-77-002	Peek-A-Boo	MaGo	150-day	34.90	40-49.00
90-77-003	Anybody Home?	MaGo	150-day	34.90	35-49.00
90-77-004	Three-Part Harmony	MaGo	150-day	34.90	50.00
Artaffects		**Heavenly Angels**			
92-78-001	Hush-A-Bye	MaGo	75-day	27.00	27.00
92-78-002	Heavenly Helper	MaGo	75-day	27.00	27.00
92-78-003	Heavenly Light	MaGo	75-day	27.00	27.00
92-78-004	The Angel's Kiss	MaGo	75-day	27.00	27.00
92-78-005	Caught In The Act	MaGo	75-day	27.00	27.00
92-78-006	My Angel	MaGo	75-day	27.00	27.00
92-78-007	Angel Cake	MaGo	75-day	27.00	27.00
92-78-008	Sleepy Sentinel	MaGo	75-day	27.00	27.00
Artaffects		**The Adventures of Peter Pan**			
90-79-001	Flying Over London	T. Newsom	14-day	29.50	40.00
90-79-002	Look At Me	T. Newsom	14-day	29.50	40.00
90-79-003	The Encounter	T. Newsom	14-day	29.50	40.00
90-79-004	Never land	T. Newsom	14-day	29.50	40.00
Artaffects		**Backstage**			
90-80-001	The Runaway	B. Leighton-Jones	14-day	29.50	29.50
90-80-002	The Letter	B. Leighton-Jones	14-day	29.50	29.50
90-80-003	Bubbling Over	B. Leighton-Jones	14-day	29.50	29.50
Artaffects		**The Life of Jesus**			
92-81-001	The Last Supper	L. Marchetti	25-day	27.00	27.00
92-81-002	The Sermon on the Mount	L. Marchetti	25-day	27.00	27.00
92-81-003	The Agony in the Garden	L. Marchetti	25-day	27.00	27.00
92-81-004	The Entry Into Jerusalem	L. Marchetti	25-day	27.00	27.00
92-81-005	The Blessing of the Children	L. Marchetti	25-day	27.00	27.00
92-81-006	The Resurrection	L. Marchetti	25-day	27.00	27.00
92-81-007	The Healing of the Sick	L. Marchetti	25-day	27.00	27.00
92-81-008	The Descent from the Cross	L. Marchetti	25-day	27.00	27.00
Artaffects		**Great American Trains**			
92-82-001	The Alton Limited	J. Deneen	75-day	27.00	27.00
92-82-002	The Capitol Limited	J. Deneen	75-day	27.00	27.00
92-82-003	The Merchants Limited	J. Deneen	75-day	27.00	27.00
92-82-004	The Broadway Limited	J. Deneen	75-day	27.00	27.00
92-82-005	The Southwestern Limited	J. Deneen	75-day	27.00	27.00
92-82-006	The Blackhawk Limited	J. Deneen	75-day	27.00	27.00
92-82-007	The Sunshine Special Limited	J. Deneen	75-day	27.00	27.00
92-82-008	The Panama Special Limited	J. Deneen	75-day	27.00	27.00
Artists of the World		**Holiday**			
76-01-001	Festival of Lights	T. DeGrazia	9,500	45.00	98-195.00
77-01-002	Bell of Hope	T. DeGrazia	9,500	45.00	53.00
78-01-003	Little Madonna	T. DeGrazia	9,500	45.00	58-95.00
79-01-004	The Nativity	T. DeGrazia	9,500	50.00	85-150.00
80-01-005	Little Pima Drummer	T. DeGrazia	9,500	50.00	60.00
81-01-006	A Little Prayer	T. DeGrazia	9,500	55.00	65.00
82-01-007	Blue Boy	T. DeGrazia	10,000	60.00	65-95.00
83-01-008	Heavenly Blessings	T. DeGrazia	10,000	65.00	65.00
84-01-009	Navajo Madonna	T. DeGrazia	10,000	65.00	125.00
85-01-010	Saguaro Dance	T. DeGrazia	10,000	65.00	100.00
Artists of the World		**Holiday**			
76-02-001	Festival of Lights, signed	T. DeGrazia	500	100.00	350.00
77-02-002	Bell of Hope, signed	T. DeGrazia	500	100.00	200.00
78-02-003	Little Madonna, signed	T. DeGrazia	500	100.00	350.00
79-02-004	The Nativity, signed	T. DeGrazia	500	100.00	200.00
80-02-005	Little Pima Drummer, signed	T. DeGrazia	500	100.00	200.00
81-02-006	A Little Prayer, signed	T. DeGrazia	500	100.00	200.00
82-02-007	Blue Boy, signed	T. DeGrazia	96	100.00	200.00
Artists of the World		**Holiday Mini-Plates**			
80-03-001	Festival of Lights	T. DeGrazia	5,000	15.00	250.00
81-03-002	Bell of Hope	T. DeGrazia	5,000	15.00	95.00
82-03-003	Little Madonna	T. DeGrazia	5,000	15.00	95.00
82-03-004	The Nativity	T. DeGrazia	5,000	15.00	95.00
83-03-005	Little Pima Drummer	T. DeGrazia	5,000	15.00	25.00
83-03-006	Little Prayer	T. DeGrazia	5,000	20.00	25.00
84-03-007	Blue Boy	T. DeGrazia	5,000	20.00	25.00
84-03-008	Heavenly Blessings	T. DeGrazia	5,000	20.00	25.00
85-03-009	Navajo Madonna	T. DeGrazia	5,000	20.00	25.00
85-03-010	Saguaro Dance	T. DeGrazia	5,000	20.00	25.00
Artists of the World		**Children**			
76-04-001	Los Ninos	T. DeGrazia	5,000	35.00	900-1000.
77-04-002	White Dove	T. DeGrazia	5,000	40.00	60-100.00
78-04-003	Flower Girl	T. DeGrazia	9,500	45.00	90.00
79-04-004	Flower Boy	T. DeGrazia	9,500	45.00	69.00
80-04-005	Little Cocopah	T. DeGrazia	9,500	50.00	70.00
81-04-006	Beautiful Burden	T. DeGrazia	9,500	50.00	55.00
82-04-007	Merry Little Indian	T. DeGrazia	9,500	55.00	85.00
83-04-008	Wondering	T. DeGrazia	10,000	60.00	60.00
84-04-009	Pink Papoose	T. DeGrazia	10,000	65.00	65.00
85-04-010	Sunflower Boy	T. DeGrazia	10,000	65.00	65-125.00
Artists of the World		**Children**			
78-05-001	Los Ninos, signed	T. DeGrazia	500	100.00	3000.00
78-05-002	White Dove, signed	T. DeGrazia	500	100.00	450.00
78-05-003	Flower Girl, signed	T. DeGrazia	500	100.00	450.00
79-05-004	Flower Boy, signed	T. DeGrazia	500	100.00	450.00
80-05-005	Little Cocopah Girl, signed	T. DeGrazia	500	100.00	320.00
81-05-006	Beautiful Burden, signed	T. DeGrazia	500	100.00	320.00
81-05-007	Merry Little Indian, signed	T. DeGrazia	500	100.00	450.00
Artists of the World		**Children Mini-Plates**			
80-06-001	Los Ninos	T. DeGrazia	5,000	15.00	300.00
81-06-002	White Dove	T. DeGrazia	5,000	15.00	35.00
82-06-003	Flower Girl	T. DeGrazia	5,000	15.00	35.00
82-06-004	Flower Boy	T. DeGrazia	5,000	15.00	35.00
83-06-005	Little Cocopah Indian Girl	T. DeGrazia	5,000	15.00	25.00
83-06-006	Beautiful Burden	T. DeGrazia	5,000	20.00	53.00
84-06-007	Merry Little Indian	T. DeGrazia	5,000	20.00	25.00
84-06-008	Wondering	T. DeGrazia	5,000	20.00	25.00
85-06-009	Pink Papoose	T. DeGrazia	5,000	20.00	25.00
85-06-010	Sunflower Boy	T. DeGrazia	5,000	20.00	25.00
Artists of the World		**Children of Aberdeen**			
79-07-001	Girl with Little Brother	K. Fung Ng	Undis.	50.00	50.00
80-07-002	Sampan Girl	K. Fung Ng	Undis.	50.00	55.00
81-07-003	Girl with Little Sister	K. Fung Ng	Undis.	55.00	60.00
82-07-004	Girl with Seashells	K. Fung Ng	Undis.	60.00	60.00
83-07-005	Girl with Seabirds	K. Fung Ng	Undis.	60.00	60.00
84-07-006	Brother and Sister	K. Fung Ng	Undis.	60.00	60.00
Artists of the World		**Children at Play**			
85-08-001	My First Horse	T. DeGrazia	15,000	65.00	65.00
86-08-002	Girl With Sewing Machine	T. DeGrazia	15,000	65.00	65.00
87-08-003	Love Me	T. DeGrazia	15,000	65.00	65.00
88-08-004	Merrily, Merrily, Merrily	T. DeGrazia	15,000	65.00	65.00
89-08-005	My First Arrow	T. DeGrazia	15,000	65.00	65.00
90-08-006	Away With My Kite	T. DeGrazia	15,000	65.00	65.00
Artists of the World		**Western**			
86-09-001	Morning Ride	T. DeGrazia	5,000	65.00	65.00
87-09-002	Bronco	T. DeGrazia	5,000	65.00	65.00
88-09-003	Apache Scout	T. DeGrazia	5,000	65.00	65.00
89-09-004	Alone	T. DeGrazia	5,000	65.00	65.00
Artists of the World		**Children of the Sun**			
87-10-001	Spring Blossoms	T. DeGrazia	150-day	34.50	34.50
87-10-002	My Little Pink Bird	T. DeGrazia	150-day	34.50	34.50
87-10-003	Bright Flowers of the Desert	T. DeGrazia	150-day	37.90	37.90
88-10-004	Gifts from the Sun	T. DeGrazia	150-day	37.90	37.90
88-10-005	Growing Glory	T. DeGrazia	150-day	37.90	37.90
88-10-006	The Gentle White Dove	T. DeGrazia	150-day	37.90	37.90
88-10-007	Sunflower Maiden	T. DeGrazia	150-day	39.90	39.90
89-10-008	Sun Showers	T. DeGrazia	150-day	39.90	45.00
Artists of the World		**Fiesta of the Children**			
90-11-001	Welcome tothe Fiesta	T. DeGrazia	150-day	34.50	34.50
90-11-002	Castanets in Bloom	T. DeGrazia	150-day	34.50	34.50
91-11-003	Fiesta Flowers	T. DeGrazia	150-day	34.50	34.50
91-11-004	Fiesta Angels	T. DeGrazia	150-day	34.50	34.50
Art World of Bourgeault		**The English Countryside Series**			
80-01-001	The Country Squire	R. Bourgeault	1,500	70.00	395.00
81-01-002	The Willows	R. Bourgeault	1,500	85.00	395.00
82-01-003	Rose Cottage	R. Bourgeault	1,500	90.00	395.00
83-01-004	Thatched Beauty	R. Bourgeault	1,500	95.00	395.00
Art World of Bourgeault		**The English Countryside-Single Issues**			
84-02-001	The Anne Hathaway Cottage	R. Bourgeault	500	150.00	750.00
85-02-002	Lilac Cottage	R. Bourgeault	500	125.00	395.00
87-02-003	Suffolk Pink	R. Bourgeault	50	220.00	625.00
88-02-004	Stuart House	R. Bourgeault	50	325.00	625.00
89-02-005	Lark Rise	R. Bourgeault	50	450.00	625.00
Art World of Bourgeault		**The Royal Literary Series**			
85-03-001	The John Bunyan Cottage	R. Bourgeault	4,500	60.00	95.00
87-03-002	The Thomas Hardy Cottage	R. Bourgeault	4,500	65.00	95.00
88-03-003	The John Milton Cottage	R. Bourgeault	4,500	65.00	95.00
89-03-004	The Anne Hathaway Cottage	R. Bourgeault	4,500	65.00	95.00
Art World of Bourgeault		**Where Is England Series**			
90-04-001	Forget-Me-Not	R. Bourgeault	50	525.00	705.00
91-04-002	The Fleece Inn	R. Bourgeault	50	525.00	705.00
92-04-003	Millbrook House	R. Bourgeault	50	525.00	525.00
93-04-004	Cotswold Beauty	R. Bourgeault	50	525.00	525.00
Art World of Bourgeault		**Where Is Scotland Series**			
91-05-001	Eilean Donan Castle	R. Bourgeault	50	525.00	705.00
Art World of Bourgeault		**The Royal Gainsborough Series**			
90-06-001	The Lisa-Caroline	R. Bourgeault	N/A	75.00	85.00
91-06-002	A Gainsborough Lady	R. Bourgeault	N/A	N/A	N/A
Bareuther		**Christmas**			
67-01-001	Stiftskirche	H. Mueller	10,000	12.00	85.00
68-01-002	Kapplkirche	H. Mueller	10,000	12.00	25.00
69-01-003	Christkindlesmarkt	H. Mueller	10,000	12.00	18.00
70-01-004	Chapel in Oberndorf	H. Mueller	10,000	12.50	22.00
71-01-005	Toys for Sale From Drawing By	L. Richter	10,000	12.75	27.00
72-01-006	Christmas in Munich	H. Mueller	10,000	14.50	25.00
73-01-007	Sleigh Ride	H. Mueller	10,000	15.00	35.00
74-01-008	Black Forest Church	H. Mueller	10,000	19.00	19.00
75-01-009	Snowman	H. Mueller	10,000	21.50	30.00
76-01-010	Chapel in the Hills	H. Mueller	10,000	23.50	26.00
77-01-011	Story Time	H. Mueller	10,000	24.50	40.00
78-01-012	Mittenwald	H. Mueller	10,000	27.50	31.00
79-01-013	Winter Day	H. Mueller	10,000	35.00	35.00
80-01-014	Mittenberg	H. Mueller	10,000	37.50	39.00
81-01-015	Walk in the Forest	H. Mueller	10,000	39.50	39.50
82-01-016	Bad Wimpfen	H. Mueller	10,000	39.50	43.00

Company Number	Name	Series Artist	Edition Limit	Issue Price	Quote
83-01-017	The Night before Christmas	H. Mueller	10,000	39.50	39.50
84-01-018	Zeil on the River Main	H. Mueller	10,000	42.50	45.00
85-01-019	Winter Wonderland	H. Mueller	10,000	42.50	57.00
86-01-020	Christmas in Forchheim	H. Mueller	10,000	42.50	70.00
87-01-021	Decorating the Tree	H. Mueller	10,000	42.50	85.00
88-01-022	St. Coloman Church	H. Mueller	10,000	52.50	65.00
89-01-023	Sleigh Ride	H. Mueller	10,000	52.50	80-90.00
90-01-024	The Old Forge in Rothenburg	H. Mueller	10,000	52.50	52.50
91-01-025	Christmas Joy	H. Mueller	10,000	56.50	56.50
92-01-026	Market Place in Heppenheim	H. Mueller	10,000	59.50	59.50
Belleek		**Christmas**			
70-01-001	Castle Caldwell	Unknown	7,500	25.00	70-85.00
71-01-002	Celtic Cross	Unknown	7,500	25.00	60.00
72-01-003	Flight of the Earls	Unknown	7,500	30.00	35.00
73-01-004	Tribute To Yeats	Unknown	7,500	38.50	40.00
74-01-005	Devenish Island	Unknown	7,500	45.00	190.00
75-01-006	The Celtic Cross	Unknown	7,500	48.00	80.00
76-01-007	Dove of Peace	Unknown	7,500	55.00	55.00
77-01-008	Wren	Unknown	7,500	55.00	55.00
Berlin Design		**Christmas**			
70-01-001	Christmas in Bernkastel	Unknown	4,000	14.50	125.00
71-01-002	Christmas in Rothenburg	Unknown	20,000	14.50	45.00
72-01-003	Christmas in Michelstadt	Unknown	20,000	15.00	55.00
73-01-004	Christmas in Wendlestein	Unknown	20,000	20.00	55.00
74-01-005	Christmas in Bremen	Unknown	20,000	25.00	53.00
75-01-006	Christmas in Dortland	Unknown	20,000	30.00	35.00
76-01-007	Christmas in Augsburg	Unknown	20,000	32.00	75.00
77-01-008	Christmas in Hamburg	Unknown	20,000	32.00	32.00
78-01-009	Christmas in Berlin	Unknown	20,000	36.00	85.00
79-01-010	Christmas in Greetsiel	Unknown	20,000	47.50	60.00
80-01-011	Christmas in Mittenberg	Unknown	20,000	50.00	55.00
81-01-012	Christmas Eve In Hahnenklee	Unknown	20,000	55.00	55.00
82-01-013	Christmas Eve In Wasserberg	Unknown	20,000	55.00	50.00
83-01-014	Christmas in Oberndorf	Unknown	20,000	55.00	65.00
84-01-015	Christmas in Ramsau	Unknown	20,000	55.00	55.00
85-01-016	Christmas in Bad Wimpfen	Unknown	20,000	55.00	59.00
86-01-017	Christmas Eve in Gelnhaus	Unknown	20,000	65.00	65.00
87-01-018	Christmas Eve in Goslar	Unknown	20,000	65.00	65.00
88-01-019	Christmas Eve in Ruhpolding	Unknown	20,000	65.00	90.00
89-01-020	Christmas Eve in Friedechsdadt	Unknown	20,000	80.00	80.00
90-01-021	Christmas Eve in Partenkirchen	Unknown	20,000	80.00	80.00
91-01-022	Christmas Eve in Allendorf	Unknown	20,000	80.00	80.00
Berlin Design		**Historical**			
75-02-001	Washington Crossing the Delaware	Unknown	Annual	30.00	40.00
76-02-002	Tom Thumb	Unknown	Annual	32.00	35.00
77-02-003	Zeppelin	Unknown	Annual	32.00	35.00
78-02-004	Benz Motor Car Munich	Unknown	10,000	36.00	36.00
79-02-005	Johannes Gutenberg	Unknown	10,000	47.50	48.00
Berlin Design	**Holiday Week of the Family Kappelmann**				
84-03-001	Monday	Unknown	Undis.	33.00	33.00
84-03-002	Tuesday	Unknown	Undis.	33.00	37.00
85-03-003	Wednesday	Unknown	Undis.	33.00	37.00
85-03-004	Thursday	Unknown	Undis.	35.00	38.00
85-03-005	Friday	Unknown	Undis.	35.00	40.00
86-03-006	Saturday	Unknown	Undis.	35.00	40.00
86-03-007	Sunday	Unknown	Undis.	35.00	40.00
Bing & Grondahl		**Christmas**			
95-01-001	Behind The Frozen Window	F.A. Hallin	Annual	.50	4500-5900.
96-01-002	New Moon	F.A. Hallin	Annual	.50	1100-2299.
97-01-003	Sparrows	F.A. Hallin	Annual	.75	1125-1499.
98-01-004	Roses and Star	F. Garde	Annual	.75	700-825.
99-01-005	Crows	F. Garde	Annual	.75	910-1759.
00-01-006	Church Bells	F. Garde	Annual	.75	850-1309.
01-01-007	Three Wise Men	S. Sabra	Annual	1.00	399-480.
02-01-008	Gothic Church Interior	D. Jensen	Annual	1.00	250-429.
03-01-009	Expectant Children	M. Hyldahl	Annual	1.00	300-429.
04-01-010	Fredericksberg Hill	C. Olsen	Annual	1.00	110-175.
05-01-011	Christmas Night	D. Jensen	Annual	1.00	175-186.
06-01-012	Sleighing to Church	D. Jensen	Annual	1.00	97-110.00
07-01-013	Little Match Girl	E. Plockross	Annual	1.00	123-135.
08-01-014	St. Petri Church	P. Jorgensen	Annual	1.00	80-105.
09-01-015	Yule Tree	Aarestrup	Annual	1.50	909-110.00
10-01-016	The Old Organist	C. Ersgaard	Annual	1.50	79-100.00
11-01-017	Angels and Shepherds	H. Moltke	Annual	1.50	92-96.00
12-01-018	Going to Church	E. Hansen	Annual	1.50	94-100.00
13-01-019	Bringing Home the Tree	T. Larsen	Annual	1.50	87-94.00
14-01-020	Amalienborg Castle	T. Larsen	Annual	1.50	92-150.00
15-01-021	Dog Outside Window	D. Jensen	Annual	1.50	90-155.00
16-01-022	Sparrows at Christmas	P. Jorgensen	Annual	1.50	73-87.00
17-01-023	Christmas Boat	A. Friis	Annual	1.50	87-93.00
18-01-024	Fishing Boat	A. Friis	Annual	1.50	87.00
19-01-025	Outside Lighted Window	A. Friis	Annual	2.00	75-126.00
20-01-026	Hare in the Snow	A. Friis	Annual	2.00	82-93.00
21-01-027	Pigeons	A. Friis	Annual	2.00	82-87.00
22-01-028	Star of Bethlehem	A. Friis	Annual	2.00	75-126.00
23-01-029	The Ermitage	A. Friis	Annual	2.00	79-93.00
24-01-030	Lighthouse	A. Friis	Annual	2.50	82-87.00
25-01-031	Child's Christmas	A. Friis	Annual	2.50	82-126.00
26-01-032	Churchgoers	A. Friis	Annual	2.50	82-93.00
27-01-033	Skating Couple	A. Friis	Annual	2.50	87-109.00
28-01-034	Eskimos	A. Friis	Annual	2.50	69-126.00
29-01-035	Fox Outside Farm	A. Friis	Annual	2.50	77-125.00
30-01-036	Christmas Train	A. Friis	Annual	2.50	78-97.00
31-01-037	Town Hall Square	H. Flugenring	Annual	2.50	70-87.00
32-01-038	Life Boat	H. Flugenring	Annual	2.50	82-95.00
33-01-039	Korsor-Nyborg Ferry	H. Flugenring	Annual	3.00	75-101.00
34-01-040	Church Bell in Tower	H. Flugenring	Annual	3.00	75.00
35-01-041	Lillebelt Bridge	O. Larson	Annual	3.00	75-109.00
36-01-042	Royal Guard	O. Larson	Annual	3.00	68-82.00
37-01-043	Arrival of Christmas Guests	O. Larson	Annual	3.00	90.00
38-01-044	Lighting the Candles	I. Tjerne	Annual	3.00	93-162.00
39-01-045	Old Lock-Eye, The Sandman	I. Tjerne	Annual	3.00	89-187.00
40-01-046	Christmas Letters	O. Larson	Annual	4.00	83-187.00
41-01-047	Horses Enjoying Meal	O. Larson	Annual	4.00	85-255.00
42-01-048	Danish Farm	O. Larson	Annual	4.00	74-212.00
43-01-049	Ribe Cathedral	O. Larson	Annual	5.00	79-180.00
44-01-050	Sorgenfri Castle	O. Larson	Annual	5.00	95-107.00
45-01-051	The Old Water Mill	O. Larson	Annual	5.00	98-160.00

Company Number	Name	Series Artist	Edition Limit	Issue Price	Quote
46-01-052	Commemoration Cross	M. Hyldahl	Annual	5.00	75-148.00
47-01-053	Dybbol Mill	M. Hyldahl	Annual	5.00	107-238.
48-01-054	Watchman	M. Hyldahl	Annual	5.50	214.00
49-01-055	Landsoldaten	M. Hyldahl	Annual	5.50	82-250.00
50-01-056	Kronborg Castle	M. Hyldahl	Annual	5.50	123-141.00
51-01-057	Jens Bang	M. Hyldahl	Annual	6.00	100.00
52-01-058	Thorsvaldsen Museum	B. Pramvig	Annual	6.00	95-121.00
53-01-059	Snowman	B. Pramvig	Annual	7.50	89-95.00
54-01-060	Royal Boat	K. Bonfils	Annual	7.00	100-106.
55-01-061	Kaulundorg Church	K. Bonfils	Annual	8.00	95-127.00
56-01-062	Christmas in Copenhagen	K. Bonfils	Annual	8.50	150-164.
57-01-063	Christmas Candles	K. Bonfils	Annual	9.00	144-150.
58-01-064	Santa Claus	K. Bonfils	Annual	9.50	105-119.
59-01-065	Christmas Eve	K. Bonfils	Annual	10.00	127-135.
60-01-066	Village Church	K. Bonfils	Annual	10.00	149-169.
61-01-067	Winter Harmony	K. Bonfils	Annual	10.50	30-107.00
62-01-068	Winter Night	K. Bonfils	Annual	11.00	52-100.00
63-01-069	The Christmas Elf	H. Thelander	Annual	11.00	89-105.00
64-01-070	The Fir Tree and Hare	H. Thelander	Annual	11.50	36-47.00
65-01-071	Bringing Home the Tree	H. Thelander	Annual	12.00	45-49.00
66-01-072	Home for Christmas	H. Thelander	Annual	12.00	28-47.00
67-01-073	Sharing the Joy	H. Thelander	Annual	13.00	25-39.00
68-01-074	Christmas in Church	H. Thelander	Annual	14.00	20-39.00
69-01-075	Arrival of Guests	H. Thelander	Annual	14.00	15-30.00
70-01-076	Pheasants in Snow	H. Thelander	Annual	14.50	15-25.00
71-01-077	Christmas at Home	H. Thelander	Annual	15.00	15-25.00
72-01-078	Christmas in Greenland	H. Thelander	Annual	16.50	16.50-25.00
73-01-079	Country Christmas	H. Thelander	Annual	19.50	19.50-25.00
74-01-080	Christmas in the Village	H. Thelander	Annual	22.00	22-25.00
75-01-081	Old Water Mill	H. Thelander	Annual	27.50	27.50
76-01-082	Christmas Welcome	H. Thelander	Annual	27.50	27.50
77-01-083	Copenhagen Christmas	H. Thelander	Annual	29.50	29.50
78-01-084	Christmas Tale	H. Thelander	Annual	32.00	35.00
79-01-085	White Christmas	H. Thelander	Annual	36.50	50.00
80-01-086	Christmas in Woods	H. Thelander	Annual	42.50	42.50
81-01-087	Christmas Peace	H. Thelander	Annual	49.50	49.50
82-01-088	Christmas Tree	H. Thelander	Annual	54.50	54.50
83-01-089	Christmas in Old Town	H. Thelander	Annual	54.50	54.50
84-01-090	The Christmas Letter	E. Jensen	Annual	54.50	54.50
85-01-091	Christmas Eve at the Farmhouse	E. Jensen	Annual	54.50	54.50
86-01-092	Silent Night, Holy Night	E. Jensen	Annual	54.50	54.50
87-01-093	The Snowman's Christmas Eve	E. Jensen	Annual	59.50	55-70.00
88-01-094	In the Kings Garden	E. Jensen	Annual	64.50	65.00
89-01-095	Christmas Anchorage	E. Jensen	Annual	59.50	60-80.00
90-01-096	Changing of the Guards	E. Jensen	Annual	64.50	60-80.00
91-01-097	Copenhagen Stock Exchange	E. Jensen	Annual	69.50	70-85.00
92-01-098	Christmas At the Rectory	J. Steensen	Annual	69.50	69.50
93-01-099	Father Christmas in Copenhagen	J. Steensen	Annual	69.50	69.50
Bing & Grondahl		**Jubilee-5 Year Cycle**			
15-02-001	Frozen Window	F.A. Hallin	Annual	Unkn.	155.00
20-02-002	Church Bells	F. Garde	Annual	Unkn.	65.00
25-02-003	Dog Outside Window	D. Jensen	Annual	Unkn.	130.00
30-02-004	The Old Organist	C. Ersgaard	Annual	Unkn.	169.00
35-02-005	Little Match Girl	E. Plockross	Annual	Unkn.	720.00
40-02-006	Three Wise Men	S. Sabra	Annual	Unkn.	1839.00
45-02-007	Amalienborg Castle	T. Larsen	Annual	Unkn.	199.00
50-02-008	Eskimos	A. Friis	Annual	Unkn.	199.00
55-02-009	Dybbol Mill	M. Hyldahl	Annual	Unkn.	210.00
60-02-010	Kronborg Castle	M. Hyldahl	Annual	25.00	129.00
65-02-011	Chruchgoers	A. Friis	Annual	25.00	69.00
70-02-012	Amalienborg Castle	T. Larsen	Annual	30.00	30.00
75-02-013	Horses Enjoying Meal	O. Larson	Annual	40.00	50.00
80-02-014	Yule Tree	Aarestrup	Annual	60.00	60.00
85-02-015	Lifeboat at Work	H. Flugenring	Annual	65.00	93.00
90-02-016	The Royal Yacht Dannebrog	J. Bonfils	Annual	95.00	95.00
Bing & Grondahl		**Mother's Day**			
69-03-001	Dogs and Puppies	H. Thelander	Annual	9.75	350-360.
70-03-002	Bird and Chicks	H. Thelander	Annual	10.00	14-25.00
71-03-003	Cat and Kitten	H. Thelander	Annual	11.00	15.00
72-03-004	Mare and Foal	H. Thelander	Annual	12.00	15.00
73-03-005	Duck and Ducklings	H. Thelander	Annual	13.00	15.00
74-03-006	Bear and Cubs	H. Thelander	Annual	16.50	16.50
75-03-007	Doe and Fawns	H. Thelander	Annual	19.50	19.50
76-03-008	Swan Family	H. Thelander	Annual	22.50	22.50
77-03-009	Squirrel and Young	H. Thelander	Annual	23.50	25-35.00
78-03-010	Heron	H. Thelander	Annual	24.50	25.00
79-03-011	Fox and Cubs	H. Thelander	Annual	27.50	27.50
80-03-012	Woodpecker and Young	H. Thelander	Annual	29.50	39.00
81-03-013	Hare and Young	H. Thelander	Annual	36.50	36.50
82-03-014	Lioness and Cubs	H. Thelander	Annual	39.50	39.50
83-03-015	Raccoon and Young	H. Thelander	Annual	39.50	39.50
84-03-016	Stork and Nestlings	H. Thelander	Annual	39.50	39.50
85-03-017	Bear and Cubs	H. Thelander	Annual	39.50	40.00
86-03-018	Elephant with Calf	H. Thelander	Annual	39.50	43.00
87-03-019	Sheep with Lambs	H. Thelander	Annual	42.50	69.00
88-03-020	Crested Ployer & Young	H. Thelander	Annual	47.50	55.00
88-03-021	Lapwing Mother with Chicks	H. Thelander	Annual	49.50	55.00
89-03-022	Cow With Calf	H. Thelander	Annual	49.50	50-65.00
90-03-023	Hen with Chicks	L. Jensen	Annual	52.50	65.00
91-03-024	The Nanny Goat and her Two Frisky Kids	L. Jensen	Annual	54.50	70-75.00
92-03-025	Panda With Cubs	L. Jensen	Annual	59.50	59.50
93-03-026	St. Bernard Dog and Puppies	A. Therkelsen	Annual	59.50	59.50
Bing & Grondahl		**Children's Day Plate Series**			
85-04-001	The Magical Tea Party	C. Roller	Annual	24.50	25.00
86-04-002	A Joyful Flight	C. Roller	Annual	26.50	28.00
86-04-003	The Little Gardeners	C. Roller	Annual	29.50	40.00
88-04-004	Wash Day	C. Roller	Annual	34.50	34.50
89-04-005	Bedtime	C. Roller	Annual	37.00	50.00
90-04-006	My Favorite Dress	S. Vestergaard	Annual	37.00	40-48.00
91-04-007	Fun on the Beach	S. Vestergaard	Annual	45.00	45.00
92-04-008	A Summer Day in the Meadow	S. Vestergaard	Annual	45.00	45.00
93-04-009	The Carousel	S. Vestergaard	Annual	45.00	45.00
Bing & Grondahl		**Statue of Liberty**			
85-05-001	Statue of Liberty	Unknown	10,000	60.00	75-100.00
Bing & Grondahl		**Christmas In America**			
86-06-001	Christmas Eve in Williamsburg	J. Woodson	Annual	29.50	69-150.00
87-06-002	Christmas Eve at the White House	J. Woodson	Annual	34.50	45-80.00
88-06-003	Christmas Eve at Rockefeller Center	J. Woodson	Annual	34.50	45-75.00

Number	Name	Artist	Edition Limit	Issue Price	Quote
Company		**Series**			
89-06-004	Christmas In New England	J. Woodson	Annual	37.00	45-65.00
90-06-005	Christmas Eve at the Capitol	J. Woodson	Annual	39.50	40-55.00
91-06-006	Christmas Eve at Independence Hall	J. Woodson	Annual	45.00	45-85.00
92-06-007	Christmas in San Francisco	J. Woodson	Annual	47.50	47.50
93-06-008	Coming Home For Christmas	J. Woodson	Annual	47.50	47.50
Bing & Grondahl		**Santa Claus Collection**			
89-07-001	Santa's Workshop	H. Hansen	Annual	59.50	60-65.00
90-07-002	Santa's Sleigh	H. Hansen	Annual	59.50	60-85.00
91-07-003	Santa's Journey	H. Hansen	Annual	69.50	60-85.00
92-07-004	Santa's Arrival	H. Hansen	Annual	74.50	74.50
93-07-005	Santa's Gifts	H. Hansen	Annual	74.50	74.50
Bing & Grondahl		**Young Adventurer Plate**			
90-08-001	The Little Viking	S. Vestergaard	Annual	52.50	65.00
Bing & Grondahl		**Christmas in America Anniversary Plate**			
91-09-001	Christmas Eve in Williamsburg	J. Woodson	Annual	69.50	69.50
Bing & Grondahl		**Centennial Collection**			
92-10-001	Crows Enjoying Christmas	D. Jensen	Annual	59.50	59.50
Boehm Studios		**Egyptian Commemorative**			
78-01-001	Tutankhamun	Boehm	5,000	125.00	170.00
78-01-002	Tutankhamun, handpainted	Boehm	225	975.00	975.00
Boehm Studios		**Panda**			
82-16-001	Panda, Harmony	Boehm	5,000	65.00	65.00
82-16-002	Panda, Peace	Boehm	5,000	65.00	65.00
Curator Collection: See Artaffects					
Crown Parian		**American Folk Heroes**			
83-01-001	Johnny Appleseed	G. Boyer	Undis.	35.00	35.00
84-01-002	Davy Crockett	G. Boyer	Undis.	35.00	35.00
85-01-003	Betsy Ross	G. Boyer	Undis.	35.00	35.00
85-01-004	Buffalo Bill	G. Boyer	Undis.	35.00	35.00
86-01-005	Casey Jones	G. Boyer	Undis.	40.00	40.00
86-01-006	Sacajawea	G. Boyer	Undis.	40.00	40.00
C.U.I./Carolina Collection/Dram Tree		**Native American Series**			
91-01-001	Hunt for the Buffalo Edition I	P. Kethley	4,950	39.50	39.50
92-01-002	Story Teller	P. Kethley	4,950	40.00	40.00
C.U.I./Carolina Collection/Dram Tree		**Christmas Series**			
91-02-001	Checkin' it Twice Edition I	CUI	4,950	39.50	39.50
C.U.I./Carolina Collection/Dram Tree		**Environmental Series**			
91-03-001	Rainforest Magic Edition I	C. L. Bragg	4,950	39.50	39.50
92-03-002	First Breath	M. Hoffman	4,950	40.00	40.00
C.U.I./Carolina Collection/Dram Tree		**Girl In The Moon**			
91-04-001	Miller Girl in the Moon Edition I	CUI	9,950	39.50	39.50
C.U.I./Carolina Collection/Dram Tree		**DU Great American Sporting Dogs**			
92-05-001	Black Lab Edition I	J. Killen	20,000	40.00	40.00
93-05-002	Golden Retriever Edition II	J. Killen	28-day	40.00	40.00
93-05-003	Springer Spaniel Edition III	J. Killen	28-day	40.00	40.00
93-05-004	Yellow Labrador Edition IV	J. Killen	28-day	40.00	40.00
93-05-005	English Setter Edition V	J. Killen	28-day	40.00	40.00
93-05-006	Brittany Spaniel Edition VI	J. Killen	28-day	40.00	40.00
C.U.I./Carolina Collection/Dram Tree		**Classic Car Series**			
92-06-001	1957 Chevy	G. Geivette	28-day	40.00	40.00
C.U.I./Carolina Collection/Dram Tree		**Corvette Series**			
92-07-001	1953 Corvette	G. Geivette	28-day	40.00	40.00
D'Arceau Limoges		**Lafayette**			
73-01-001	The Secret Contract	A. Restieau	Unkn.	14.82	20.00
73-01-002	North Island Landing	A. Restieau	Unkn.	19.82	22.00
74-01-003	City Tavern Meeting	A. Restieau	Unkn.	19.82	22.00
74-01-004	Battle of Brandywine	A. Restieau	Unkn.	19.82	22.00
75-01-005	Messages to Franklin	A. Restieau	Unkn.	19.82	23.00
75-01-006	Siege at Yorktown	A. Restieau	Unkn.	19.82	20.00
D'Arceau Limoges		**Christmas**			
75-02-001	La Fruite en Egypte	A. Restieau	Unkn.	24.32	30.00
76-02-002	Dans la Creche	A. Restieau	Unkn.	24.32	29.00
77-02-003	Refus d' Hebergement	A. Restieau	Unkn.	24.32	29.00
78-02-004	La Purification	A. Restieau	Yr.Iss.	26.81	29.00
79-02-005	L' Adoration des Rois	A. Restieau	Yr.Iss.	26.81	31.00
80-02-006	Joyeuse Nouvelle	A. Restieau	Yr.Iss.	28.74	32.00
81-02-007	Guides par L' Etoile	A. Restieau	Yr.Iss.	28.74	30.00
82-02-008	L' Annuciation	A. Restieau	Yr.Iss.	30.74	35.00
Delphi		**Elvis Presley: Looking At A Legend**			
88-01-001	Elvis at/Gates of Graceland	B. Emmett	150-day	24.75	125-150.
89-01-002	Jailhouse Rock	B. Emmett	150-day	24.75	75-99.00
89-01-003	The Memphis Flash	B. Emmett	150-day	27.75	45-85.00
89-01-004	Homecoming	B. Emmett	150-day	27.75	45-95.00
90-01-005	Elvis and Gladys	B. Emmett	150-day	27.75	52-95.00
90-01-006	A Studio Session	B. Emmett	150-day	27.75	28-75.00
90-01-007	Elvis in Hollywood	B. Emmett	150-day	29.75	30-45.00
90-01-008	Elvis on His Harley	B. Emmett	150-day	29.75	29.75
90-01-009	Stage Door Autographs	B. Emmett	150-day	29.75	29.75
91-01-010	Christmas at Graceland	B. Emmett	150-day	32.75	32.75
91-01-011	Entering Sun Studio	B. Emmett	150-day	32.75	32.75
91-01-012	Going for the Black Belt	B. Emmett	150-day	32.75	32.75
91-01-013	His Hand in Mine	B. Emmett	150-day	32.75	32.75
91-01-014	Letters From Fans	B. Emmett	150-day	32.75	32.75
91-01-015	Closing the Deal	B. Emmett	150-day	34.75	34.75
92-01-016	Elvis Returns to the Stage	B. Emmett	150-day	34.75	34.75
Delphi		**Elvis Presley: In Performance**			
90-02-001	'68 Comeback Special	B. Emmett	150-day	24.75	24.75
91-02-002	King of Las Vegas	B. Emmett	150-day	24.75	24.75
91-02-003	Aloha From Hawaii	B. Emmett	150-day	27.75	27.75
91-02-004	Back in Tupelo, 1956	B. Emmett	150-day	27.75	27.75
91-02-005	If I Can Dream	B. Emmett	150-day	27.75	27.75
91-02-006	Benefit for the USS Arizona	B. Emmett	150-day	29.75	29.75
91-02-007	Madison Square Garden, 1972	B. Emmett	150-day	29.75	29.75
91-02-008	Tampa, 1955	B. Emmett	150-day	29.75	29.75

Number	Name	Artist	Edition Limit	Issue Price	Quote
Company		**Series**			
91-02-009	Concert in Baton Rouge, 1974	B. Emmett	150-day	29.75	29.75
92-02-010	On Stage in Wichita, 1974	B. Emmett	150-day	31.75	31.75
Delphi		**Portraits of the King**			
91-03-001	Love Me Tender	D. Zwierz	150-day	27.75	27.75
91-03-002	Are You Lonesome Tonight?	D. Zwierz	150-day	27.75	27.75
91-03-003	I'm Yours	D. Zwierz	150-day	30.75	30.75
91-03-004	Treat Me Nice	D. Zwierz	150-day	30.75	30.75
92-03-005	The Wonder of You	D. Zwierz	150-day	30.75	30.75
Delphi		**The Elvis Presley Hit Parade**			
92-04-001	Heartbreak Hotel	N. Giorgio	150-day	29.75	29.75
Delphi		**Dream Machines**			
88-05-001	'56 T-Bird	P. Palma	150-day	24.75	55.00
88-05-002	'57 'Vette	P. Palma	150-day	24.75	39.00
89-05-003	'58 Biarritz	P. Palma	150-day	27.75	27.75
89-05-004	'56 Continental	P. Palma	150-day	27.75	27.75
89-05-005	'57 Bel Air	P. Palma	150-day	27.75	55.00
89-05-006	'57 Chrysler 300C	P. Palma	150-day	27.75	38.00
Delphi		**Indiana Jones**			
89-06-001	Indiana Jones	V. Gadino	150-day	24.75	24.75
89-06-002	Indiana Jones and His Dad	V. Gadino	150-day	24.75	54.00
90-06-003	Indiana Jones/Dr. Schneider	V. Gadino	150-day	27.75	27.75
90-06-004	A Family Discussion	V. Gadino	150-day	27.75	45.00
90-06-005	Young Indiana Jones	V. Gadino	150-day	27.75	55.00
91-06-006	Indiana Jones/The Holy Grail	V. Gadino	150-day	27.75	63-68.00
Delphi		**The Marilyn Monroe Collection**			
89-07-001	Marilyn Monroe/7 Year Itch	C. Notarile	150-day	24.75	62-75.00
90-07-002	Diamonds/Girls Best Friend	C. Notarile	150-day	24.75	60.00
91-07-003	Marilyn Monroe/River of No Return	C. Notarile	150-day	27.75	50-65.00
92-07-004	How to Marry a Millionaire	C. Notarile	150-day	27.75	27.75
92-07-005	There's No Business/Show Business	C. Notarile	150-day	27.75	27.75
92-07-006	Marilyn Monroe in Niagra	C. Notarile	150-day	29.75	29.75
Delphi		**The Beatles Collection**			
91-08-001	The Beatles, Live In Concert	N. Giorgio	150-day	24.75	24.75
91-08-002	Hello America	N. Giorgio	150-day	24.75	24.75
91-08-003	A Hard Day's Night	N. Giorgio	150-day	27.75	27.75
Department 56		**Dickens' Village**			
87-01-001	Dickens' Village Porcelain Plates, 5917-0 Set of 4	Department 56	Closed	140.00	N/A
Department 56		**A Christmas Carol**			
91-02-001	The Cratchit's Christmas Pudding, 5706-1	R. Innocenti	18,000	60.00	75.00
92-02-002	Marley's Ghost Appears To Scrooge, 5721-5	R. Innocenti	18,000	60.00	60.00
Duncan Royale		**History of Santa Claus I**			
85-01-001	Medieval	S. Morton	Retrd.	40.00	75.00
85-01-002	Kris Kringle	S. Morton	Retrd.	40.00	65.00
85-01-003	Pioneer	S. Morton	10,000	40.00	40.00
86-01-004	Russian	S. Morton	Retrd.	40.00	40.00
86-01-005	Soda Pop	S. Morton	Retrd.	40.00	65.00
86-01-006	Civil War	S. Morton	10,000	40.00	40.00
86-01-007	Nast	S. Morton	Retrd.	40.00	75.00
87-01-008	St. Nicholas	S. Morton	Retrd.	40.00	75.00
87-01-009	Dedt Moroz	S. Morton	10,000	40.00	40.00
87-01-010	Black Peter	S. Morton	10,000	40.00	40.00
87-01-011	Victorian	S. Morton	Retrd.	40.00	40.00
87-01-012	Wassail	S. Morton	Retrd.	40.00	40.00
XX-01-013	Collection of 12 Plates	S. Morton	Retrd.	480.00	480.00
Enesco Corporation		**Precious Moments Inspired Thoughts**			
85-01-001	Love One Another-E-5215	S. Butcher	15,000	40.00	65.00
82-01-002	Make a Joyful Noise-E-7174	S. Butcher	15,000	40.00	40.00
83-01-003	I Believe In Miracles-E-9257	S. Butcher	15,000	40.00	40.00
84-01-004	Love is Kind-E-2847	S. Butcher	15,000	40.00	40-45.00
Enesco Corporation		**Precious Moments Mother's Love**			
81-02-001	Mother Sew Dear-E-5217	S. Butcher	15,000	40.00	70.00
82-02-002	The Purr-fect Grandma-E-7173	S. Butcher	15,000	40.00	40.00
83-02-003	The Hand that Rocks the Future-E-9256	S. Butcher	15,000	40.00	40.00
84-02-004	Loving Thy Neighbor-E-2848	S. Butcher	15,000	40.00	40.00
Enesco Corporation		**Precious Moments Christmas Collection**			
81-03-001	Come Let Us Adore Him-E-5646	S. Butcher	15,000	40.00	60.00
82-03-002	Let Heaven and Nature Sing-E-2347	S. Butcher	15,000	40.00	45.00
83-03-003	Wee Three Kings-E-0538	S. Butcher	15,000	40.00	40.00
84-03-004	Unto Us a Child Is Born-E-5395	S. Butcher	15,000	40.00	40-45.00
Enesco Corporation		**Precious Moments Joy of Christmas**			
82-04-001	I'll Play My Drum For Him-E-2357	S. Butcher	Yr.Iss.	40.00	90.00
83-04-002	Christmastime is for Sharing-E-0505	S. Butcher	Yr.Iss.	40.00	90.00
84-04-003	The Wonder of Christmas-E-5396	S. Butcher	Yr.Iss.	40.00	70.00
85-04-004	Tell Me the Story of Jesus-15237	S. Butcher	Yr.Iss.	40.00	105.00
Enesco Corporation		**Precious Moments The Four Seasons**			
85-05-001	The Voice of Spring-12106	S. Butcher	Yr.Iss.	40.00	80-90.00
85-05-002	Summer's Joy-12114	S. Butcher	Yr.Iss.	40.00	75-80.00
86-05-003	Autumn's Praise-12122	S. Butcher	Yr.Iss.	40.00	55.00
86-05-004	Winter's Song-12130	S. Butcher	Yr.Iss.	40.00	60-65.00
Enesco Corporation		**Precious Moments Open Editions**			
82-06-001	Our First Christmas Together-E-2378	S. Butcher	Suspd.	30.00	45-55.00
81-06-002	The Lord Bless You and Keep You-E-5216	S. Butcher	Suspd.	30.00	40-45.00
82-06-003	Rejoicing with You-E-7172	S. Butcher	Suspd.	30.00	40.00
83-06-004	Jesus Loves Me-E-9275	S. Butcher	Suspd.	30.00	45.00
83-06-005	Jesus Loves Me-E-9276	S. Butcher	Suspd.	30.00	45.00
Enesco Corporation		**Precious Moments Christmas Love**			
86-07-001	I'm Sending You a White Christmas-101834	S. Butcher	Yr.Iss.	45.00	75.00
87-07-002	My Peace I Give Unto Thee-102954	S. Butcher	Yr.Iss.	45.00	90.00
88-07-003	Merry Christmas Deer-520284	S. Butcher	Yr.Iss.	50.00	75.00
89-07-004	May Your Christmas Be A Happy Home-523003	S. Butcher	Yr.Iss.	50.00	75.00
Enesco Corporation		**Precious Moments Christmas Blessings**			
90-08-001	Wishing You A Yummy Christmas-523801	S. Butcher	Yr.Iss.	50.00	70.00
91-08-002	Blessings From Me To Thee-523860	S. Butcher	Yr.Iss.	50.00	60.00
92-08-003	But The Greatest of These Is Love-527742	S. Butcher	Yr.Iss.	50.00	50.00

Company / Number	Name	Series / Artist	Edition Limit	Issue Price	Quote
Ernst Enterprises		**Women of the West**			
79-01-001	Expectations	D. Putnam	10,000	39.50	39.50
81-01-002	Silver Dollar Sal	D. Putnam	10,000	39.50	45.00
82-01-003	School Marm	D. Putnam	10,000	39.50	39.50
83-01-004	Dolly	D. Putnam	10,000	39.50	39.50
Ernst Enterprises		**A Beautiful World**			
81-02-001	Tahitian Dreamer	S. Morton	27,500	27.50	30.00
82-02-002	Flirtation	S. Morton	27,500	27.50	27.50
84-02-003	Elke of Oslo	S. Morton	27,500	27.50	27.50
Ernst Enterprises		**Seems Like Yesterday**			
81-03-001	Stop & Smell the Roses	R. Money	10-day	24.50	24.50
82-03-002	Home by Lunch	R. Money	10-day	24.50	24.50
82-03-003	Lisa's Creek	R. Money	10-day	24.50	24.50
83-03-004	It's Got My Name on It	R. Money	10-day	24.50	24.50
83-03-005	My Magic Hat	R. Money	10-day	24.50	24.50
84-03-006	Little Prince	R. Money	10-day	24.50	24.50
Ernst Enterprises		**Turn of The Century**			
81-04-001	Riverboat Honeymoon	R. Money	10-day	35.00	35.00
82-04-002	Children's Carousel	R. Money	10-day	35.00	37.50
84-04-003	Flower Market	R. Money	10-day	35.00	35.00
85-04-004	Balloon Race	R. Money	10-day	35.00	35.00
Ernst Enterprises		**Hollywood Greats**			
81-05-001	John Wayne	S. Morton	27,500	29.95	50-165.00
81-05-002	Gary Cooper	S. Morton	27,500	29.95	32.50
82-05-003	Clark Gable	S. Morton	27,500	29.95	65-85.00
84-05-004	Alan Ladd	S. Morton	27,500	29.95	60.00
Ernst Enterprises		**Commemoratives**			
81-06-001	John Lennon	S. Morton	30-day	39.50	75-90.00
82-06-002	Elvis Presley	S. Morton	30-day	39.50	150.00
82-06-003	Marilyn Monroe	S. Morton	30-day	39.50	75.00
83-06-004	Judy Garland	S. Morton	30-day	39.50	75.00
84-06-005	John Wayne	S. Morton	2,500	39.50	75.00
Ernst Enterprises		**Classy Cars**			
82-07-001	The 26T	S. Kuhnly	20-day	24.50	32.00
82-07-002	The 31A	S. Kuhnly	20-day	24.50	30.00
83-07-003	The Pickup	S. Kuhnly	20-day	24.50	27.50
84-07-004	Panel Van	S. Kuhnly	20-day	24.50	35.00
Ernst Enterprises		**Star Trek**			
84-08-001	Mr. Spock	S. Morton	90-day	29.50	45-150.00
85-08-002	Dr. McCoy	S. Morton	90-day	29.50	40-95.00
85-08-003	Sulu	S. Morton	90-day	29.50	40-75.00
85-08-004	Scotty	S. Morton	90-day	29.50	40-85.00
85-08-005	Uhura	S. Morton	90-day	29.50	40-75.00
85-08-006	Chekov	S. Morton	90-day	29.50	40-75.00
85-08-007	Captain Kirk	S. Morton	90-day	29.50	50-150.00
85-08-008	Beam Us Down Scotty	S. Morton	90-day	29.50	60-125.00
85-08-009	The Enterprise	S. Morton	90-day	39.50	70-150.00
Ernst Enterprises		**Elvira**			
86-09-001	Night Rose	S. Morton	90-day	29.50	29.50
Fairmont		**Spencer Special**			
78-01-001	Hug Me	I. Spencer	10,000	55.00	150.00
78-01-002	Sleep Little Baby	I. Spencer	10,000	65.00	125.00
Fairmont		**Famous Clowns**			
76-02-001	Freddie the Freeloader	R. Skelton	10,000	55.00	400-550.
77-02-002	W. C. Fields	R. Skelton	10,000	55.00	99.00
78-02-003	Happy	R. Skelton	10,000	55.00	70-110.00
79-02-004	The Pledge	R. Skelton	10,000	55.00	70-99.00
Fenton Art Glass		**American Craftsman Carnival**			
70-01-001	Glassmaker	Unknown	600	10.00	140.00
70-01-002	Glassmaker	Unknown	200	10.00	220.00
70-01-003	Glassmaker	Unknown	Annual	10.00	68.00
71-01-004	Printer	Unknown	Annual	10.00	80.00
72-01-005	Blacksmith	Unknown	Annual	10.00	150.00
73-01-006	Shoemaker	Unknown	Annual	12.50	70.00
74-01-007	Cooper	Unknown	Annual	12.50	55.00
75-01-008	Silversmith Revere	Unknown	Annual	12.50	60.00
76-01-009	Gunsmith	Unknown	Annual	15.00	45.00
77-01-010	Potter	Unknown	Annual	15.00	35.00
78-01-011	Wheelwright	Unknown	Annual	15.00	25.00
79-01-012	Cabinetmaker	Unknown	Annual	15.00	23.00
80-01-013	Tanner	Unknown	Annual	16.50	20.00
81-01-014	Housewright	Unknown	Annual	17.50	18.00
Flambro Imports		**Emmett Kelly, Jr. Plates**			
83-01-001	Why Me? Plate I	C. Kelly	10,000	40.00	275-348.
84-01-002	Balloons For Sale Plate II	C. Kelly	10,000	40.00	175-200.
85-01-003	Big Business Plate III	C. Kelly	10,000	40.00	120-228.
86-01-004	And God Bless America IV	C. Kelly	10,000	40.00	100-300.
88-01-005	Tis the Season	D. Rust	10,000	40.00	40-75.00
89-01-006	Looking Back- 65th Birthday	D. Rust	6,500	50.00	75-150.00
91-01-007	Winter	D. Rust	10,000	30.00	30.00
92-01-008	Spring	D. Rust	10,000	30.00	30.00
92-01-009	Summer	D. Rust	10,000	30.00	30.00
92-01-010	Autumn	D. Rust	10,000	30.00	30.00
Flambro Imports		**Raggedy Ann & Andy**			
88-02-001	70 Years Young	C. Beylon	10,000	35.00	35-55.00
Fleetwood Collection		**Christmas**			
80-01-001	The Magi	F. Wenger	5,000	45.00	75.00
81-01-002	The Holy Child	F. Wenger	7,500	49.50	58.00
82-01-003	The Shepherds	F. Wenger	5,000	50.00	50.00
85-01-004	Coming Home for Christmas	F. Jacques	5,000	50.00	50.00
Fleetwood Collection		**Mother's Day**			
80-02-001	Cottontails	D. Balke	5,000	45.00	75.00
81-02-002	Raccoons	D. Balke	5,000	45.00	58.00
82-02-003	Whitetail Deer	D. Balke	5,000	50.00	50.00
83-02-004	Canada Geese	D. Balke	5,000	50.00	50.00
Fleetwood Collection		**Royal Wedding**			
81-03-001	Prince Charles/Lady Diana	J. Mathews	9,500	49.50	75.00

Company / Number	Name	Series / Artist	Edition Limit	Issue Price	Quote
86-03-002	Prince Andrew/Sarah Ferguson	J. Mathews	10,000	50.00	50.00
Fleetwood Collection		**Statue of Liberty**			
86-04-001	Statue of Liberty Plate	J. Mathews	10,000	50.00	50.00
Fountainhead		**The Wings of Freedom**			
85-01-001	Courtship Flight	M. Fernandez	2,500	250.00	2400.00
86-01-002	Wings of Freedom	M. Fernandez	2,500	250.00	1100.00
Fountainhead		**As Free As The Wind**			
89-02-001	As Free As The Wind	M. Fernandez	Unkn.	295.00	300-600.
Fukagawa		**Warabe No Haiku Series**			
77-01-001	Beneath The Plum Branch	Suetomi	Undis.	38.00	45.00
78-01-002	Child of Straw	Suetomi	Undis.	42.00	47.50
79-01-003	Dragon Dance	Suetomi	Undis.	42.00	45.00
80-01-004	Mask Dancing	Suetomi	Undis.	42.00	90.00
Gartlan USA, Inc.		**Pete Rose Platinum Edition**			
85-01-001	Pete Rose "The Best of Baseball"(3 1/4")	T. Sizemore	Open	12.95	19.00
85-01-002	Pete Rose "The Best of Baseball"(10 1/4")	T. Sizemore	4,192	100.00	300-600.
Gartlan USA, Inc.		**The Round Tripper**			
86-02-001	Reggie Jackson (3 1/4" diameter)	J. Martin	Open	12.95	19.00
Gartlan USA, Inc.		**George Brett Gold Crown Collection**			
86-03-001	George Brett "Baseball's All Star"(3 1/4")	J. Martin	Open	12.95	19.00
86-03-002	George Brett "Baseball's All Star"(10 1/4") signed	J. Martin	2,000	100.00	120-225.
Gartlan USA, Inc.		**Roger Staubach Sterling Collection**			
87-04-001	Roger Staubach (3 1/4" diameter)	C. Soileau	Open	12.95	19.00
87-04-002	Roger Staubach (10 1/4" diameter), signed	C. Soileau	1,979	100.00	100-150.
Gartlan USA, Inc.		**Magic Johnson Gold Rim Collection**			
87-05-001	Magic Johnson-"The Magic Show"(10 1/4") signed	R. Winslow	1,987	100.00	225-600.
87-05-002	Magic Johnson-"The Magic Show"(3 1/4")	R. Winslow	Closed	14.50	25-35.00
Gartlan USA, Inc.		**Mike Schmidt "500th" Home Run Edition**			
87-06-001	Mike Schmidt-"Power at the Plate"(10 1/4") signed	C. Paluso	1,987	100.00	155-450.
87-06-002	Mike Schmidt-"Power at the Plate"(3 1/4")	C. Paluso	Open	14.50	19.00
87-06-003	Mike Schmidt, Artist Proof	C. Paluso	56	150.00	150.00
Gartlan USA, Inc.		**Pete Rose Diamond Collection**			
88-07-001	Pete Rose-"The Reigning Legend" (10 1/4"), signed	Forbes	950	195.00	225-250.
88-07-002	Pete Rose-"The Reigning Legend" (10 1/4"), signed, Artist Proof	Forbes	50	300.00	450.00
88-07-003	Pete Rose-"The Reigning Legend"(3 1/4")	Forbes	Open	14.50	19.00
Gartlan USA, Inc		**Kareem Abdul-Jabbar Sky-Hook Collection**			
89-08-001	Kareem Abdul-Jabbar- "Path of Glory" (10 1/4"), signed	M. Taylor	1,989	100.00	150-300.
89-08-002	Collector plate (3 1/4")	M. Taylor	Closed	16.00	18.00
Gartlan USA, Inc.		**Johnny Bench**			
89-09-001	Collector Plate (10 1/4"), signed	M. Taylor	1,989	100.00	150-200.
89-09-002	Collector Plate (3 1/4"),	M. Taylor	Open	16.00	19.00
Gartlan USA, Inc.		**Coaching Classics-John Wooden**			
89-10-001	Collector Plate (10 1/4"), signed	M. Taylor	1,975	100.00	100.00
89-10-002	Collector Plate (8 1/2")	M. Taylor	10,000	45.00	45.00
89-10-003	Collector Plate (3 1/4")	M. Taylor	Open	16.00	19.00
Gartlan USA, Inc.		**Wayne Gretzky**			
89-11-001	Collector Plate (10 1/4") signed by Gretzky and Howe	M. Taylor	1,851	225.00	225-450.
89-11-002	Collector Plate (10 1/4") Artist Proof, signed by Gretzky and Howe	M. Taylor	300	300.00	425-500.
89-11-003	Collector Plate (8 1/2")	M. Taylor	10,000	45.00	45-75.00
89-11-004	Collector Plate (3 1/4")	M. Taylor	Open	16.00	19.00
Gartlan USA, Inc.		**Yogi Berra**			
89-12-001	Collector Plate (10 1/4"), signed	M. Taylor	2,150	125.00	125.00
89-12-002	Collector Plate (10 1/4"), signed, Artist Proof	M. Taylor	250	175.00	175.00
89-12-003	Collector Plate (3 1/4")	M. Taylor	Open	16.00	19.00
89-12-004	Collector Plate (8 1/2")	M. Taylor	10,000	45.00	45.00
Gartlan USA, Inc.		**Whitey Ford**			
90-13-001	Signed Plate (10 1/4")	M. Taylor	2,360	125.00	125.00
90-13-002	Signed Plate (10 1/4"), Artist Proof	M. Taylor	250	175.00	175.00
90-13-003	Plate (8 1/2")	M. Taylor	10,000	45.00	45.00
90-13-004	Plate (3 1/4")	M. Taylor	Open	16.00	19.00
Gartlan USA, Inc.		**Darryl Strawberry**			
90-14-001	Signed Plate (10 1/4")	M. Taylor	2,500	125.00	125.00
90-14-002	Plate (8 1/2")	M. Taylor	10,000	45.00	45.00
90-14-003	Plate (3 1/4")	M. Taylor	Open	16.00	19.00
Gartlan USA, Inc.		**Luis Aparicio**			
90-15-001	Signed Plate (10 1/4")	M. Taylor	1,984	125.00	125.00
90-15-002	Signed Plate (10 1/4"), Artist Proof	M. Taylor	250	150.00	150.00
90-15-003	Plate (8 1/2")	M. Taylor	10,000	45.00	45.00
90-15-004	Plate (3 1/4")	M. Taylor	Open	16.00	19.00
Gartlan USA, Inc.		**Rod Carew**			
91-16-001	Hitting For The Hall(10 1/4"), signed	M. Taylor	950	150.00	150.00
91-16-002	Hitting For The Hall(8 1/2")	M. Taylor	10,000	45.00	45.00
91-16-003	Hitting For The Hall(3 1/4")	M. Taylor	Open	16.00	19.00
Gartlan USA, Inc.		**Brett & Bobby Hull**			
91-17-001	Hockey's Golden Boys(10 1/4"), signed	M. Taylor	950	250.00	250.00
92-17-002	Plate, Artist Proof	M. Taylor	300	225.00	225.00
91-17-003	Hockey's Golden Boys(8 1/2")	M. Taylor	10,000	45.00	45.00
91-17-004	Hockey's Golden Boys(3 1/4")	M. Taylor	Open	16.00	19.00
Gartlan USA, Inc.		**Joe Montana**			
91-18-001	Signed Plate (10 1/4")	M. Taylor	2,250	125.00	125.00
91-18-002	Signed Plate (10 1/4"), Artist Proof	M. Taylor	250	195.00	195.00
91-18-003	Plate (8 1/2")	M. Taylor	10,000	45.00	45.00
91-18-004	Plate (3 1/4")	M. Taylor	Open	16.00	19.00

Company / Number	Name	Series / Artist	Edition Limit	Issue Price	Quote
Gartlan USA, Inc.		**Al Barlick**			
91-19-001	Plate (3 1/4")	M. Taylor	Open	16.00	19.00
Gartlan USA, Inc.		**Carlton Fisk**			
92-20-001	Signed Plate (10 1/4")	M. Taylor	950	150.00	150.00
92-20-002	Signed Plate (10 1/4"), Artist Proof	M. Taylor	300	175.00	225.00
92-20-003	Plate (8 1/2")	M. Taylor	10,000	45.00	45.00
92-20-004	Plate (3 1/4")	M. Taylor	Open	19.00	19.00
Gartlan USA, Inc.		**Ken Griffey Jr.**			
92-21-001	Signed Plate (10 1/4")	M. Taylor	1,989	125.00	125.00
92-21-002	Signed Plate (10 1/2"), Artist Proof	M. Taylor	300	195.00	195.00
92-21-003	Plate (8 1/2")	M. Taylor	10,000	45.00	45.00
92-21-004	Plate (3 1/4")	M. Taylor	Open	19.00	19.00
Gartlan USA, Inc.		**Phil Esposito**			
92-22-001	Signed Plate (10 1/4")	M. Taylor	1,984	125.00	125.00
92-22-002	Signed Plate (10 1/2"), Artist Proof	M. Taylor	300	195.00	195.00
92-22-003	Plate (8 1/2")	M. Taylor	10,000	45.00	45.00
92-22-004	Plate (3 1/4")	M. Taylor	Open	19.00	19.00
Gartlan USA, Inc.		**Carl Yastrzemski**			
92-23-001	Signed Plate (10 1/4")	M. Taylor	1,989	125.00	125.00
92-23-002	Signed Plate (10 1/2"), Artist Proof	M. Taylor	300	195.00	195.00
92-23-003	Plate (8 1/2")	M. Taylor	10,000	45.00	45.00
92-23-004	Plate (3 1/4")	M. Taylor	Open	19.00	19.00
Gartlan USA, Inc.		**Tom Seaver**			
92-24-001	Signed Plate (10 1/4")	M. Taylor	1,992	150.00	150.00
92-24-002	Signed Plate (10 1/4"), Artist Proof	M. Taylor	250	195.00	195.00
92-24-003	Signed Plate (8 1/2")	M. Taylor	10,000	45.00	45.00
92-24-004	Signed Plate (3 1/4)	M. Taylor	Open	19.00	19.00
Gartlan USA, Inc.		**Gordie Howe**			
92-24-001	Signed Plate (10 1/4")	M. Taylor	2,358	125.00	125.00
92-24-002	Signed Plate (10 1/4"), Artist Proof	M. Taylor	250	195.00	195.00
92-24-003	Signed Plate (8 1/2")	M. Taylor	10,000	45.00	45.00
92-24-004	Signed Plate (3 1/4")	M. Taylor	Open	19.00	19.00
W. S. George		**Gone With the Wind: Golden Anniversary**			
88-01-001	Scarlett and Her Suitors	H. Rogers	150-day	24.50	79.50-99.00
88-01-002	The Burning of Atlanta	H. Rogers	150-day	24.50	75-125.00
88-01-003	Scarlett and Ashley After the War	H. Rogers	150-day	27.50	80-110.00
88-01-004	The Proposal	H. Rogers	150-day	27.50	80-125.00
89-01-005	Home to Tara	H. Rogers	150-day	27.50	42-95.00
89-01-006	Strolling in Atlanta	H. Rogers	150-day	27.50	45-95.00
89-01-007	A Question of Honor	H. Rogers	150-day	29.50	50-68.00
89-01-008	Scarlett's Resolve	H. Rogers	150-day	29.50	70-90.00
89-01-009	Frankly My Dear	H. Rogers	150-day	29.50	50-65.00
89-01-010	Melane and Ashley	H. Rogers	150-day	32.50	32.50
90-01-011	A Toast to Bonnie Blue	H. Rogers	150-day	32.50	32.50
90-01-012	Scarlett and Rhett's Honeymoon	H. Rogers	150-day	32.50	32.50
W. S. George		**Scenes of Christmas Past**			
87-02-001	Holiday Skaters	L. Garrison	150-day	27.50	65-75.00
88-02-002	Christmas Eve	L. Garrison	150-day	27.50	45-50.00
89-02-003	The Homecoming	L. Garrison	150-day	30.50	35-60.00
90-02-004	The Toy Store	L. Garrison	150-day	30.50	30-45.00
91-02-005	The Carollers	L. Garrison	150-day	30.50	45-50.00
W. S. George		**On Gossamer Wings**			
88-03-001	Monarch Butterflies	L. Liu	150-day	24.50	38-50.00
88-03-002	Western Tiger Swallowtails	L. Liu	150-day	24.50	30-47.00
88-03-003	Red-Spotted Purple	L. Liu	150-day	27.50	35-45.00
88-03-004	Malachites	L. Liu	150-day	27.50	40.00
88-03-005	White Peacocks	L. Liu	150-day	27.50	36.00
89-03-006	Eastern Tailed Blues	L. Liu	150-day	27.50	48.00
89-03-007	Zebra Swallowtails	L. Liu	150-day	29.50	37.50
89-03-008	Red Admirals	L. Liu	150-day	29.50	35.00
W. S. George		**Flowers of Your Garden**			
88-04-001	Roses	V. Morley	150-day	24.50	42-60.00
88-04-002	Lilacs	V. Morley	150-day	24.50	70-95.00
88-04-003	Daisies	V. Morley	150-day	27.50	50-55.00
88-04-004	Peonies	V. Morley	150-day	27.50	30-60.00
88-04-005	Chrysanthemums	V. Morley	150-day	27.50	45.00
89-04-006	Daffodils	V. Morley	150-day	27.50	55.00
89-04-007	Tulips	V. Morley	150-day	29.50	30-55.00
89-04-008	Irises	V. Morley	150-day	29.50	35-65.00
W. S. George		**Beloved Hymns of Childhood**			
88-05-001	The Lord's My Shepherd	C. Barker	150-day	29.50	57.00
88-05-002	Away In a Manger	C. Barker	150-day	29.50	31.00
89-05-003	Now Thank We All Our God	C. Barker	150-day	32.50	32.50
89-05-004	Love Divine	C. Barker	150-day	32.50	32.50
89-05-005	I Love to Hear the Story	C. Barker	150-day	32.50	32.50
89-05-006	All Glory, Laud and Honour	C. Barker	150-day	32.50	32.50
90-05-007	All People on Earth Do Dwell	C. Barker	150-day	34.50	34.50
90-05-008	Loving Shepherd of Thy Sheep	C. Barker	150-day	34.50	34.50
W. S. George		**Classic Waterfowl: The Ducks Unlimited**			
88-06-001	Mallards at Sunrise	L. Kaatz	150-day	36.50	70.00
88-06-002	Geese in the Autumn Fields	L. Kaatz	150-day	36.50	40-45.00
89-06-003	Green Wings/Morning Marsh	L. Kaatz	150-day	39.50	45-50.00
89-06-004	Canvasbacks, Breaking Away	L. Kaatz	150-day	39.50	39-50.00
89-06-005	Pintails in Indian Summer	L. Kaatz	150-day	39.50	39.50
90-06-006	Wood Ducks Taking Flight	L. Kaatz	150-day	39.50	60.00
90-06-007	Snow Geese Against November Skies	L. Kaatz	150-day	41.50	45.00
90-06-008	Bluebills Comin In	L. Kaatz	150-day	41.50	41.50
W. S. George		**The Elegant Birds**			
88-07-001	The Swan	J. Faulkner	150-day	32.50	35.00
88-07-002	Great Blue Heron	J. Faulkner	150-day	32.50	35.50
89-07-003	Snowy Egret	J. Faulkner	150-day	32.50	40-45.00
89-07-004	The Anhinga	J. Faulkner	150-day	35.50	35-40.00
89-07-005	The Flamingo	J. Faulkner	150-day	35.50	35-40.00
90-07-006	Sandhill and Whooping Crane	J. Faulkner	150-day	35.50	35-40.00
W. S. George		**Last of Their Kind: The Endangered Species**			
88-08-001	The Panda	W. Nelson	150-day	27.50	50-75.00
89-08-002	The Snow Leopard	W. Nelson	150-day	27.50	35-55.00
89-08-003	The Red Wolf	W. Nelson	150-day	30.50	35-40.00
89-08-004	The Asian Elephant	W. Nelson	150-day	30.50	42.00
90-08-005	The Slender-Horned Gazelle	W. Nelson	150-day	30.50	30.50
90-08-006	The Bridled Wallaby	W. Nelson	150-day	30.50	30.50
90-08-007	The Black-Footed Ferret	W. Nelson	150-day	33.50	33.50
90-08-008	The Siberian Tiger	W. Nelson	150-day	33.50	33.50
91-08-009	The Vicuna	W. Nelson	150-day	33.50	33.50
91-08-010	Przewalski's Horse	W. Nelson	150-day	33.50	33.50
W. S. George		**America the Beautiful**			
88-09-001	Yosemite Falls	H. Johnson	150-day	34.50	42.00
89-09-002	The Grand Canyon	H. Johnson	150-day	34.50	38.00
89-09-003	Yellowstone River	H. Johnson	150-day	37.50	39.00
89-09-004	The Great Smokey Mountains	H. Johnson	150-day	37.50	45.00
90-09-005	The Everglades	H. Johnson	150-day	37.50	45.00
90-09-006	Acadia	H. Johnson	150-day	37.50	45.00
90-09-007	The Grand Tetons	H. Johnson	150-day	39.50	65.00
90-09-008	Crater Lake	H. Johnson	150-day	39.50	49.00
W. S. George		**Bonds of Love**			
89-10-001	Precious Embrace	B. Burke	150-day	29.50	45-60.00
90-10-002	Cherished Moment	B. Burke	150-day	29.50	37-55.00
91-10-003	Tender Caress	B. Burke	150-day	32.50	40-65.00
92-10-004	Loving Touch	B. Burke	150-day	32.50	32.50
W. S. George		**The Golden Age of the Clipper Ships**			
89-11-001	The Twilight Under Full Sail	C. Vickery	150-day	29.50	31.00
89-11-002	The Blue Jacket at Sunset	C. Vickery	150-day	29.50	35.00
89-11-003	Young America, Homeward	C. Vickery	150-day	32.50	38.00
90-11-004	Flying Cloud	C. Vickery	150-day	32.50	50.00
90-11-005	Davy Crocket at Daybreak	C. Vickery	150-day	32.50	45.00
90-11-006	Golden Eagle Conquers Wind	C. Vickery	150-day	32.50	40.00
90-11-007	The Lightning in Lifting Fog	C. Vickery	150-day	34.50	34.50
90-11-008	Sea Witch, Mistress/Oceans	C. Vickery	150-day	34.50	34.50
W. S. George		**Romantic Gardens**			
89-12-001	The Woodland Garden	C. Smith	150-day	29.50	29.50
89-12-002	The Plantation Garden	C. Smith	150-day	29.50	29.50
90-12-003	The Cottage Garden	C. Smith	150-day	32.50	55.00
90-12-004	The Colonial Garden	C. Smith	150-day	32.50	32.50
W. S. George		**Country Nostalgia**			
89-13-001	The Spring Buggy	M. Harvey	150-day	29.50	36.00
89-13-002	The Apple Cider Press	M. Harvey	150-day	29.50	36.00
89-13-003	The Vintage Seed Planter	M. Harvey	150-day	29.50	41.00
89-13-004	The Old Hand Pump	M. Harvey	150-day	32.50	37.00
90-12-005	The Wooden Butter Churn	M. Harvey	150-day	32.50	49.00
90-13-006	The Dairy Cans	M. Harvey	150-day	32.50	32.50
90-13-007	The Forgotten Plow	M. Harvey	150-day	34.50	44-48.00
90-13-008	The Antique Spinning Wheel	M. Harvey	150-day	34.50	34.50
W. S. George		**Hollywood's Glamour Girls**			
89-14-001	Jean Harlow-Dinner at Eight	E. Dzenis	150-day	24.50	50.00
90-14-002	Lana Turner-Postman Ring Twice	E. Dzenis	150-day	29.50	40.00
90-14-003	Carol Lombard-The Gay Bride	E. Dzenis	150-day	29.50	40.00
90-14-004	Greta Garbo-In Grand Hotel	E. Dzenis	150-day	29.50	60.00
W. S. George		**Purebred Horses of the Americas**			
89-15-001	The Appalosa	D. Schwartz	150-day	34.50	34.50
89-15-002	The Tenessee Walker	D. Schwartz	150-day	34.50	34.50
90-15-003	The Quarterhorse	D. Schwartz	150-day	37.50	45.00
90-15-004	The Saddlebred	D. Schwartz	150-day	37.50	55.00
90-15-005	The Mustang	D. Schwartz	150-day	37.50	60.00
90-15-006	The Morgan	D. Schwartz	150-day	37.50	76.00
W. S. George		**Nature's Poetry**			
89-16-001	Morning Serenade	L. Liu	150-day	24.50	40-45.00
89-16-002	Song of Promise	L. Liu	150-day	24.50	40.00
90-16-003	Tender Lullaby	L. Liu	150-day	27.50	45-57.00
90-16-004	Nature's Harmony	L. Liu	150-day	27.50	40-42.00
90-16-005	Gentle Refrain	L. Liu	150-day	27.50	27.50
90-16-006	Morning Chorus	L. Liu	150-day	27.50	27.50
90-16-007	Melody at Daybreak	L. Liu	150-day	29.50	29.50
91-16-008	Delicate Accord	L. Liu	150-day	29.50	29.50
91-16-009	Lyrical Beginnings	L. Liu	150-day	29.50	29.50
91-16-010	Song of Spring	L. Liu	150-day	32.50	32.50
91-16-011	Mother's Melody	L. Liu	150-day	32.50	32.50
91-16-012	Cherub Chorale	L. Liu	150-day	32.50	32.50
W. S. George		**Art Deco**			
89-17-001	A Flapper With Greyhounds	M. McDonald	150-day	39.50	50.00
90-17-002	Tango Dancers	M. McDonald	150-day	39.50	50-65.00
90-17-003	Arriving in Style	M. McDonald	150-day	39.50	69-79.00
90-17-004	On the Town	M. McDonald	150-day	39.50	55-59.00
W. S. George		**Our Woodland Friends**			
89-18-001	Fascination	C. Brenders	150-day	29.50	47-50.00
90-18-002	Beneath the Pines	C. Brenders	150-day	29.50	40-45.00
90-18-003	High Adventure	C. Brenders	150-day	32.50	32.50
90-18-004	Shy Explorers	C. Brenders	150-day	32.50	32.50
91-18-005	Golden Season:Gray Squirrel	C. Brenders	150-day	32.50	32.50
91-18-006	Full House Fox Family	C. Brenders	150-day	32.50	32.50
91-18-007	A Jump Into Life: Spring Fawn	C. Brenders	150-day	34.50	34.50
91-18-008	Forest Sentinel:Bobcat	C. Brenders	150-day	34.50	34.50
W. S. George		**The Federal Duck Stamp Plate Collection**			
90-19-001	The Lesser Scaup	N. Anderson	150-day	27.50	50.00
90-19-002	Mallard	N. Anderson	150-day	27.50	27.50
90-19-003	The Ruddy Ducks	N. Anderson	150-day	30.50	30.50
90-19-004	Canvasbacks	N. Anderson	150-day	30.50	30.50
91-19-005	Pintails	N. Anderson	150-day	30.50	30.50
91-19-006	Wigeons	N. Anderson	150-day	30.50	30.50
91-19-007	Cinnamon Teal	N. Anderson	150-day	32.50	32.50
91-19-008	Fulvous Wistling Duck	N. Anderson	150-day	32.50	32.50
91-19-009	The Redheads	N. Anderson	150-day	32.50	32.50
91-19-010	Snow Goose	N. Anderson	150-day	32.50	32.50
W. S. George		**Dr. Zhivago**			
90-20-001	Zhivago and Lara	G. Bush	150-day	39.50	39.50
91-20-002	Love Poems For Lara	G. Bush	150-day	39.50	39.50
91-20-003	Zhivago Says Farewell	G. Bush	150-day	39.50	39.50
91-20-004	Lara's Love	G. Bush	150-day	39.50	39.50
W. S. George		**Blessed Are The Children**			
90-21-001	Let the/Children Come To Me	W. Rane	150-day	29.50	30-33.00

Company Number	Name	Series Artist	Edition Limit	Issue Price	Quote
90-21-002	I Am the Good Shepherd	W. Rane	150-day	29.50	29.50
91-21-003	Whoever Welcomes/Child	W. Rane	150-day	32.50	32.50
91-21-004	Hosanna in the Highest	W. Rane	150-day	32.50	32.50
91-21-005	Jesus Had Compassion on Them	W. Rane	150-day	32.50	32.50
91-21-006	Blessed are the Peacemakers	W. Rane	150-day	34.50	34.50
91-21-007	I am the Vine, You are the Branches	W. Rane	150-day	34.50	34.50
91-21-008	Seek and You Will Find	W. Rane	150-day	34.50	34.50
W. S. George		The Vanishing Gentle Giants			
91-22-001	Jumping For Joy	A. Casay	150-day	32.50	32.50
91-22-002	Song of the Humpback	A. Casay	150-day	32.50	32.50
91-22-003	Monarch of the Deep	A. Casay	150-day	35.50	35.50
91-22-004	Travelers of the Sea	A. Casay	150-day	35.50	35.50
91-22-005	White Whale of the North	A. Casay	150-day	35.50	35.50
91-22-006	Unicorn of the Sea	A. Casay	150-day	35.50	35.50
W. S. George		Spirit of Christmas			
90-23-001	Silent Night	J. Sias	150-day	29.50	36-55.00
91-23-002	Jingle Bells	J. Sias	150-day	29.50	30-39.50
91-23-003	Deck The Halls	J. Sias	150-day	32.50	32.50
91-23-004	I'll Be Home For Christmas	J. Sias	150-day	32.50	32.50
91-23-005	Winter Wonderland	J. Sias	150-day	32.50	32.50
91-23-006	O Christmas Tree	J. Sias	150-day	32.50	32.50
W. S. George		Flowers From Grandma's Garden			
90-24-001	Country Cuttings	G. Kurz	150-day	24.50	24.50
90-24-002	The Morning Bouquet	G. Kurz	150-day	24.50	24.50
91-24-003	Homespun Beauty	G. Kurz	150-day	27.50	27.50
91-24-004	Harvest in the Meadow	G. Kurz	150-day	27.50	27.50
91-24-005	Gardener's Delight	G. Kurz	150-day	27.50	27.50
91-24-006	Nature's Bounty	G. Kurz	150-day	27.50	27.50
91-24-007	A Country Welcome	G. Kurz	150-day	29.50	29.50
91-24-008	The Springtime Arrangement	G. Kurz	150-day	29.50	29.50
W. S. George		The Secret World Of The Panda			
90-25-001	A Mother's Care	J. Bridgett	150-day	27.50	27.50
91-25-002	A Frolic in the Snow	J. Bridgett	150-day	27.50	27.50
91-25-003	Lazy Afternoon	J. Bridgett	150-day	30.50	30.50
91-25-004	A Day of Exploring	J. Bridgett	150-day	30.50	30.50
91-25-005	A Gentle Hug	J. Bridgett	150-day	32.50	32.50
91-25-006	A Bamboo Feast	J. Bridgett	150-day	32.50	32.50
W. S. George		Wonders Of The Sea			
91-26-001	Stand By Me	R.Harm	150-day	34.50	34.50
91-26-002	Heart to Heart	R.Harm	150-day	34.50	34.50
91-26-003	Warm Embrace	R.Harm	150-day	34.50	34.50
91-26-004	A Family Affair	R.Harm	150-day	34.50	34.50
W. S. George		Critic's Choice: Gone With The Wind			
91-27-001	Marry Me, Scarlett	P. Jennis	150-day	27.50	27.50
91-27-002	Waiting for Rhett	P. Jennis	150-day	27.50	27.50
91-27-003	A Declaration of Love	P. Jennis	150-day	30.50	30.50
91-27-004	The Paris Hat	P. Jennis	150-day	30.50	30.50
91-27-005	Scarlett Asks a Favor	P. Jennis	150-day	30.50	30.50
W. S. George		Gone With The Wind: The Passions of Scarlett O'Hara			
92-28-001	Fiery Embrace	P. Jennis	150-day	29.50	29.50
92-28-002	Pride and Passion	P. Jennis	150-day	29.50	29.50
W. S. George		Victorian Cat			
90-28-001	Mischief With The Hatbox	H. Bonner	150-day	24.50	24.50
91-28-002	String Quartet	H. Bonner	150-day	24.50	24.50
91-28-003	Daydreams	H. Bonner	150-day	27.50	27.50
91-28-004	Frisky Felines	H. Bonner	150-day	27.50	27.50
91-28-005	Kittens at Play	H. Bonner	150-day	27.50	27.50
91-28-006	Playing in the Parlor	H. Bonner	150-day	29.50	29.50
91-28-007	Perfectly Poised	H. Bonner	150-day	29.50	29.50
92-28-008	Midday Repose	H. Bonner	150-day	29.50	29.50
W. S. George		Victorian Cat Capers			
92-29-001	Who's the Fairest of Them All?	F. Paton	150-day	24.50	24.50
92-29-002	Puss in Boots	F. Paton	150-day	24.50	24.50
W. S. George		Glorious Songbirds			
91-30-001	Cardinals on a Snowy Branch	R. Cobane	150-day	29.50	29.50
91-30-002	Indigo Buntings and/Blossoms	R. Cobane	150-day	29.50	29.50
91-30-003	Chickadees Among The Lilacs	R. Cobane	150-day	32.50	32.50
91-30-004	Goldfinches in/Thistle	R. Cobane	150-day	32.50	32.50
91-30-005	Cedar Waxwing/Winter Berries	R. Cobane	150-day	32.50	32.50
91-30-006	Bluebirds in a Blueberry Bush	R. Cobane	150-day	34.50	34.50
91-30-007	Baltimore Orioles/Autumn Leaves	R. Cobane	150-day	34.50	34.50
91-30-008	Robins with Dogwood in Bloom	R. Cobane	150-day	34.50	34.50
W. S. George		Nature's Lovables			
90-31-001	The Koala	C. Frace	150-day	27.50	27.50-50.00
91-31-002	New Arrival	C. Frace	150-day	27.50	27.50
91-31-003	Chinese Treasure	C. Frace	150-day	27.50	27.50
91-31-004	Baby Harp Seal	C. Frace	150-day	30.50	30.50
91-31-005	Bobcat: Nature's Dawn	C. Frace	150-day	30.50	30.50
91-31-006	Clouded Leopard	C. Frace	150-day	32.50	32.50
91-31-007	Zebra Foal	C. Frace	150-day	32.50	32.50
91-31-008	Bandit	C. Frace	150-day	32.50	32.50
W. S. George		Soaring Majesty			
91-32-001	Freedom	C. Frace	150-day	29.50	29.50-55.00
91-32-002	The Northern Goshhawk	C. Frace	150-day	29.50	29.50
91-32-003	Peregrine Falcon	C. Frace	150-day	32.50	32.50
91-32-004	Red-Tailed Hawk	C. Frace	150-day	32.50	32.50
91-32-005	The Ospray	C. Frace	150-day	32.50	32.50
91-32-006	The Gyrfalcon	C. Frace	150-day	34.50	34.50
91-32-007	The Golden Eagle	C. Frace	150-day	34.50	34.50
92-32-008	Red-Shouldered Hawk	C. Frace	150-day	34.50	34.50
W. S. George		The World's Most Magnificent Cats			
91-33-001	Fleeting Encounter	C. Frace	150-day	24.50	24.50
91-33-002	Cougar	C. Frace	150-day	24.50	24.50
91-33-003	Royal Bengal	C. Frace	150-day	27.50	27.50
91-33-004	Powerful Presence	C. Frace	150-day	27.50	27.50
91-33-005	Jaguar	C. Frace	150-day	27.50	27.50
91-33-006	The Clouded Leopard	C. Frace	150-day	29.50	29.50
91-33-007	The African Leopard	C. Frace	150-day	29.50	29.50
91-33-008	Mighty Warrior	C. Frace	150-day	29.50	29.50

Company Number	Name	Series Artist	Edition Limit	Issue Price	Quote
W. S. George		A Loving Look: Duck Families			
90-34-001	Family Outing	B. Langton	150-day	34.50	34.50
91-34-002	Sleepy Start	B. Langton	150-day	34.50	34.50
91-34-003	Quiet Moment	B. Langton	150-day	37.50	37.50
91-34-004	Safe and Sound	B. Langton	150-day	37.50	37.50
91-34-005	Spring Arrivals	B. Langton	150-day	37.50	37.50
91-34-006	The Family Tree	B. Langton	150-day	37.50	37.50
W. S. George		Nature's Legacy			
90-35-001	Blue Snow at Half Dome	J. Sias	150-day	24.50	24.50
91-35-002	Misty Morning/Mt. McKinley	J. Sias	150-day	24.50	24.50
91-35-003	Mount Ranier	J. Sias	150-day	27.50	27.50
91-35-004	Havasu Canyon	J. Sias	150-day	27.50	27.50
91-35-005	Autumn Splendor in the Smoky Mts.	J. Sias	150-day	27.50	27.50
91-35-006	Winter Peace in Yellowstone Park	J. Sias	150-day	29.50	29.50
91-35-007	Golden Majesty/Rocky Mountains	J. Sias	150-day	29.50	29.50
91-35-008	Radiant Sunset Over the Everglades	J. Sias	150-day	29.50	29.50
W. S. George		Symphony of Shimmering Beauties			
91-36-001	Iris Quartet	L. Liu	150-day	29.50	29.50
91-36-002	Tulip Ensemble	L. Liu	150-day	29.50	29.50
91-36-003	Poppy Pastorale	L. Liu	150-day	32.50	32.50
91-36-004	Lily Concerto	L. Liu	150-day	32.50	32.50
91-36-005	Peony Prelude	L. Liu	150-day	32.50	32.50
91-36-006	Rose Fantasy	L. Liu	150-day	34.50	34.50
W. S. George		Portraits of Christ			
91-37-001	Father, Forgive Them	J. Salamanca	150-day	29.50	29.50
91-37-002	Thy Wil Be Done	J. Salamanca	150-day	29.50	29.50
91-37-003	This is My Beloved Son	J. Salamanca	150-day	32.50	32.50
91-37-004	Lo, I Am With You	J. Salamanca	150-day	32.50	32.50
91-37-005	Become as Little Children	J. Salamanca	150-day	32.50	32.50
91-37-006	Peace I Leave With You	J. Salamanca	150-day	34.50	34.50
W. S. George		Portraits of Exquisite Birds			
90-38-001	Backyard Treasure/Chickadee	C. Brenders	150-day	29.50	29.50-50.00
90-38-002	The Beautiful Bluebird	C. Brenders	150-day	29.50	29.50-61.00
91-38-003	Summer Gold: The Robin	C. Brenders	150-day	32.50	32.50
91-38-004	The Meadowlark's Song	C. Brenders	150-day	32.50	32.50
91-38-005	Ivory-Billed Woodpecker	C. Brenders	150-day	32.50	32.50
91-38-006	Red-Winged Blackbird	C. Brenders	150-day	32.50	32.50
W. S. George		Alaska: The Last Frontier			
91-39-001	Icy Majesty	H. Lambson	150-day	34.50	34.50
91-39-002	Autumn Grandeur	H. Lambson	150-day	34.50	34.50
92-39-003	Mountain Monarch	H. Lambson	150-day	37.50	37.50
W. S. George		On Wings of Snow			
91-40-001	The Swans	L. Liu	150-day	34.50	34.50
91-40-002	The Doves	L. Liu	150-day	34.50	34.50
91-40-003	The Peacocks	L. Liu	150-day	37.50	37.50
91-40-004	The Egrets	L. Liu	150-day	37.50	37.50
W. S. George		Nature's Playmates			
91-41-001	Partners	C. Frace	150-day	29.50	29.50
91-41-002	Secret Heights	C. Frace	150-day	29.50	29.50
91-41-003	Recess	C. Frace	150-day	32.50	32.50
91-41-004	Double Trouble	C. Frace	150-day	32.50	32.50
91-41-005	Pals	C. Frace	150-day	32.50	32.50
92-41-006	Curious Trio	C. Frace	150-day	34.50	34.50
W. S. George		Field Birds of North America			
91-42-001	Winter Colors: Ring-Necked Pheasant	D. Bush	150-day	39.50	39.50
91-42-002	In Display: Ruffed Goose	D. Bush	150-day	39.50	39.50
91-42-003	Morning Light: Bobwhite Quail	D. Bush	150-day	42.50	42.50
91-42-004	Misty Clearing: Wild Turkey	D. Bush	150-day	42.50	42.50
91-42-005	Autumn Moment: American Woodcock	D. Bush	150-day	42.50	42.50
W. S. George		Country Bouquets			
91-43-001	Morning Sunshine	G. Kurz	150-day	29.50	29.50
91-43-002	Summer Perfume	G. Kurz	150-day	29.50	29.50
91-43-003	Warm Welcome	G. Kurz	150-day	32.50	32.50
91-43-004	Garden's Bounty	G. Kurz	150-day	32.50	32.50
W. S. George		Gentle Beginnings			
91-44-001	Tender Loving Care	W. Nelson	150-day	34.50	34.50
91-44-002	A Touch of Love	W. Nelson	150-day	34.50	34.50
91-44-003	Under Watchful Eyes	W. Nelson	150-day	37.50	37.50
91-44-004	Lap of Love	W. Nelson	150-day	37.50	37.50
W. S. George		Garden of the Lord			
92-45-001	Love One Another	C. Gillies	150-day	29.50	29.50
W. S. George		The Majestic Horse			
92-46-001	Classic Beauty: Thoroughbred	P. Wildermuth	150-day	34.50	34.50
92-46-002	American Gold: The Quarterhorse	P. Wildermuth	150-day	34.50	34.50
W. S. George		Columbus Discovers America: The 500th Anniversary			
92-47-001	Under Full Sail	J. Penalva	150-day	29.50	29.50
92-47-002	Ashore at Dawn	J. Penalva	150-day	29.50	29.50
92-47-003	Columbus Raises the Flag	J. Penalva	150-day	32.50	32.50
W. S. George		Lena Liu's Basket Bouquets			
92-48-001	Roses	L. Liu	150-day	29.50	29.50
W. S. George		Tomorrow's Promise			
92-49-001	Curiosity: Asian Elephants	W. Nelson	150-day	29.50	29.50
W. S. George		Sonnets in Flowers			
92-50-001	Sonnet of Beauty	G. Kurz	150-day	29.50	29.50
W. S. George		On the Wing			
92-51-001	Winged Splendor	T. Humphrey	150-day	29.50	29.50
92-51-001	Rising Mallard	T. Humphrey	150-day	29.50	29.50
W. S. George		The Sound of Music: Silver Anniversary			
91-52-001	The Hills are Alive	V. Gadino	150-day	29.50	29.50
92-52-002	Let's Start at the Very Beginning	V. Gadino	150-day	29.50	29.50
92-52-003	Something Good	V. Gadino	150-day	32.50	32.50
W. S. George		Grand Safari			
92-53-001	Images of Africa	C. Frace	150-day	29.50	29.50

PLATES

Company Number	Name	Series Artist	Edition Limit	Issue Price	Quote
W. S. George		**Treasury of Songbirds**			
92-54-001	Springtime Splendor	R. Stine	150-day	29.50	29.50
92-54-002	Morning's Glory	R. Stine	150-day	29.50	29.50
Ghent Collection		**April Fool Annual**			
78-01-001	April Fool	N. Rockwell	10,000	35.00	60.00
79-01-002	April Fool	N. Rockwell	10,000	35.00	35.00
80-01-003	April Fool	N. Rockwell	10,000	37.50	45.00
Ghent Collection		**American Bicentennial Wildlife**			
76-02-001	American Bald Eagle	H. Moeller	2,500	95.00	95.00
76-02-002	American Whitetail Deer	E. Bierly	2,500	95.00	95.00
76-02-003	American Bison	C. Frace	2,500	95.00	95.00
76-02-004	American Wild Turkey	A. Gilbert	2,500	95.00	95.00
Goebel/Schmid		**M.I. Hummel Collectibles-Annual Plates**			
71-01-001	Heavenly Angel 264	M.I. Hummel	Closed	25.00	500-875.
72-01-002	Hear Ye, Hear Ye 265	M.I. Hummel	Closed	30.00	40-100.00
73-01-003	Glober Trotter 266	M.I. Hummel	Closed	32.50	96-195.00
74-01-004	Goose Girl 267	M.I. Hummel	Closed	40.00	52-125.00
75-01-005	Ride into Christmas 268	M.I. Hummel	Closed	50.00	100-125.
76-01-006	Apple Tree Girl 269	M.I. Hummel	Closed	50.00	100-125.
77-01-007	Apple Tree Boy 270	M.I. Hummel	Closed	52.50	54-150.00
78-01-008	Happy Pastime 271	M.I. Hummel	Closed	65.00	100-150.
79-01-009	Singing Lesson 272	M.I. Hummel	Closed	90.00	100.00
80-01-010	School Girl 273	M.I. Hummel	Closed	100.00	59-100.00
81-01-011	Umbrella Boy 274	M.I. Hummel	Closed	100.00	90-125.00
82-01-012	Umbrella Girl 275	M.I. Hummel	Closed	100.00	100-200.
83-01-013	The Postman 276	M.I. Hummel	Closed	108.00	150-250.
84-01-014	Little Helper 277	M.I. Hummel	Closed	108.00	85-125.00
85-01-015	Check Girl 278	M.I. Hummel	Closed	110.00	110-175.
86-01-016	Playmates 279	M.I. Hummel	Closed	125.00	125-175.
87-01-017	Feeding Time 283	M.I. Hummel	Closed	135.00	135-350.
88-01-018	Little Goat Herder 284	M.I. Hummel	Closed	145.00	145-175.
89-01-019	Farm Boy 285	M.I. Hummel	Closed	160.00	175.00
90-01-020	Shepherd's Boy 286	M.I. Hummel	Closed	170.00	175-196.
91-01-021	Just Resting 287	M.I. Hummel	Closed	196.00	196.00
92-01-022	Wayside Harmony 288	M.I. Hummel	Yr.Iss.	210.00	210.00
93-01-023	Doll Bath 289	M.I. Hummel	Yr.Iss.	Unkn.	Unkn.
Goebel/Schmid		**M.I. Hummel Collectibles Anniversary Plates**			
75-02-001	Stormy Weather 280	M.I. Hummel	Closed	100.00	100-200.
80-02-002	Spring Dance 281	M.I. Hummel	Closed	225.00	225.00
85-02-003	Auf Wiedersehen 282	M.I. Hummel	Closed	225.00	250-280.
Goebel/Schmid		**M.I. Hummel—Little Music Makers**			
84-03-001	Little Fiddler 744	M.I. Hummel	Closed	30.00	70-125.00
85-03-002	Serenade 741	M.I. Hummel	Closed	30.00	70-125.00
86-03-003	Soloist 743	M.I. Hummel	Closed	35.00	70-125.00
87-03-004	Band Leader 742	M.I. Hummel	Closed	40.00	70-125.00
Goebel/Schmid		**M.I. Hummel Club Exclusive—Celebration**			
86-04-001	Valentine Gift (Hum 738)	M.I. Hummel	Closed	90.00	100-150.
87-04-002	Valentine Joy (Hum 737)	M.I. Hummel	Closed	98.00	130-150.
88-04-003	Daisies Don't Tell (Hum 736)	M.I. Hummel	Closed	115.00	130-150.
89-04-004	It's Cold (Hum 735)	M.I. Hummel	Closed	120.00	130-150.
Goebel/Schmid		**M.I. Hummel-The Little Homemakers**			
88-05-001	Little Sweeper (Hum 745)	M.I. Hummel	Closed	45.00	70-90.00
89-05-002	Wash Day (Hum 746)	M.I. Hummel	Closed	50.00	70-90.00
90-05-003	A Stitch in Time (Hum 747)	M.I. Hummel	Closed	50.00	70-90.00
91-05-004	Chicken Licken (Hum 748)	M.I. Hummel	Closed	70.00	70-99.00
Goebel/Schmid		**M.I. Hummel-Friends Forever**			
92-06-001	Meditation 292	M.I. Hummel	Open	Unkn.	Unkn.
93-06-002	For Father 293	M.I. Hummel	Open	Unkn.	Unkn.
Gorham		**Christmas**			
74-01-001	Tiny Tim	N. Rockwell	Annual	12.50	35.00
75-01-002	Good Deeds	N. Rockwell	Annual	17.50	35.00
76-01-003	Christmas Trio	N. Rockwell	Annual	19.50	20.00
77-01-004	Yuletide Reckoning	N. Rockwell	Annual	19.50	30.00
78-01-005	Planning Christmas Visit	N. Rockwell	Annual	24.50	24.50
79-01-006	Santa's Helpers	N. Rockwell	Annual	24.50	24.50
80-01-007	Letter to Santa	N. Rockwell	Annual	27.50	32.00
81-01-008	Santa Plans His Visit	N. Rockwell	Annual	29.50	50.00
82-01-009	Jolly Coachman	N. Rockwell	Annual	29.50	30.00
83-01-010	Christmas Dancers	N. Rockwell	Annual	29.50	35.00
84-01-011	Christmas Medley	N. Rockwell	17,500	29.95	29.95
85-01-012	Home For The Holidays	N. Rockwell	17,500	29.95	30.00
86-01-013	Merry Christmas Grandma	N. Rockwell	17,500	29.95	65.00
87-01-014	The Homecoming	N. Rockwell	17,500	35.00	52.00
88-01-015	Discovery	N. Rockwell	17,500	37.50	37.50
Gorham		**A Boy and His Dog Four Seasons Plates**			
71-02-001	Boy Meets His Dog	N. Rockwell	Annual	50.00	200-400.
71-02-002	Adventures Between Adventures	N. Rockwell	Annual	Set	Set
71-02-003	The Mysterious Malady	N. Rockwell	Annual	Set	Set
71-02-004	Pride of Parenthood	N. Rockwell	Annual	Set	Set
Gorham		**Young Love Four Seasons Plates**			
72-03-001	Downhill Daring	N. Rockwell	Annual	60.00	140.00
72-03-002	Beguiling Buttercup	N. Rockwell	Annual	Set	Set
72-03-003	Flying High	N. Rockwell	Annual	Set	Set
72-03-004	A Scholarly Pace	N. Rockwell	Annual	Set	Set
Gorham		**Four Ages of Love**			
73-04-001	Gaily Sharing Vintage Time	N. Rockwell	Annual	60.00	229.00
73-04-002	Flowers in Tender Bloom	N. Rockwell	Annual	Set	Set
73-04-003	Sweet Song So Young	N. Rockwell	Annual	Set	Set
73-04-004	Fondly We Do Remember	N. Rockwell	Annual	Set	Set
Gorham		**Grandpa and Me Four Seasons Plates**			
74-05-001	Gay Blades	N. Rockwell	Annual	60.00	200.00
74-05-002	Day Dreamers	N. Rockwell	Annual	Set	Set
74-05-003	Goin' Fishing	N. Rockwell	Annual	Set	Set
74-05-004	Pensive Pals	N. Rockwell	Annual	Set	Set
Gorham		**Me and My Pals Four Seasons Plates**			
75-06-001	A Lickin' Good Bath	N. Rockwell	Annual	70.00	150.00
75-06-002	Young Man's Fancy	N. Rockwell	Annual	Set	Set
75-06-003	Fisherman's Paradise	N. Rockwell	Annual	Set	Set
75-06-004	Disastrous Daring	N. Rockwell	Annual	Set	Set
Gorham		**Grand Pals Four Seasons Plates**			
76-07-001	Snow Sculpturing	N. Rockwell	Annual	70.00	160.00
76-07-002	Soaring Spirits	N. Rockwell	Annual	Set	Set
76-07-003	Fish Finders	N. Rockwell	Annual	Set	Set
76-07-004	Ghostly Gourds	N. Rockwell	Annual	Set	Set
Gorham		**Going on Sixteen Four Seasons Plates**			
77-08-001	Chilling Chore	N. Rockwell	Annual	75.00	110.00
77-08-002	Sweet Serenade	N. Rockwell	Annual	Set	Set
77-08-003	Shear Agony	N. Rockwell	Annual	Set	Set
77-08-004	Pilgrimage	N. Rockwell	Annual	Set	Set
Gorham		**Tender Years Four Seasons Plates**			
78-09-001	New Year Look	N. Rockwell	Annual	100.00	100-275.00
78-09-002	Spring Tonic	N. Rockwell	Annual	Set	Set
78-09-003	Cool Aid	N. Rockwell	Annual	Set	Set
78-09-004	Chilly Reception	N. Rockwell	Annual	Set	Set
Gorham		**A Helping Hand Four Seasons Plates**			
79-10-001	Year End Court	N. Rockwell	Annual	100.00	100-140.00
79-10-002	Closed for Bûsiness	N. Rockwell	Annual	Set	Set
79-10-003	Swatter's Rights	N. Rockwell	Annual	Set	Set
79-10-004	Coal Season's Coming	N. Rockwell	Annual	Set	Set
Gorham		**Dad's Boys Four Seasons Plates**			
80-11-001	Ski Skills	N. Rockwell	Annual	135.00	138-155.
80-11-002	In His Spirits	N. Rockwell	Annual	Set	Set
80-11-003	Trout Dinner	N. Rockwell	Annual	Set	Set
80-11-004	Careful Aim	N. Rockwell	Annual	Set	Set
Gorham		**Old Timers Four Seasons Plates**			
81-12-001	Canine Solo	N. Rockwell	Annual	100.00	100.00
81-12-002	Sweet Surprise	N. Rockwell	Annual	Set	Set
81-12-003	Lazy Days	N. Rockwell	Annual	Set	Set
81-12-004	Fancy Footwork	N. Rockwell	Annual	Set	Set
Gorham		**Life with Father Four Seasons Plates**			
82-13-001	Big Decision	N. Rockwell	Annual	100.00	200-300.
82-13-002	Blasting Out	N. Rockwell	Annual	Set	Set
82-13-003	Cheering the Champs	N. Rockwell	Annual	Set	Set
82-13-004	A Tough One	N. Rockwell	Annual	Set	Set
Gorham		**Old Buddies Four Seasons Plates**			
83-14-001	Shared Success	N. Rockwell	Annual	115.00	115.00
83-14-002	Endless Debate	N. Rockwell	Annual	Set	Set
83-14-003	Hasty Retreat	N. Rockwell	Annual	Set	Set
83-14-004	Final Speech	N. Rockwell	Annual	Set	Set
Gorham		**Bas Relief**			
81-15-001	Sweet Song So Young	N. Rockwell	Undis.	100.00	100.00
81-15-002	Beguiling Buttercup	N. Rockwell	Undis.	62.50	70.00
82-15-003	Flowers in Tender Bloom	N. Rockwell	Undis.	100.00	100.00
82-15-004	Flying High	N. Rockwell	Undis.	62.50	65.00
Gorham		**Single Release**			
74-16-001	Weighing In	N. Rockwell	Annual	12.50	80-99.00
Gorham		**Single Release**			
74-17-001	The Golden Rule	N. Rockwell	Annual	12.50	30.00
Gorham		**Single Release**			
75-18-001	Ben Franklin	N. Rockwell	Annual	19.50	35.00
Gorham		**Boy Scout Plates**			
75-19-001	Our Heritage	N. Rockwell	18,500	19.50	40.00
76-19-002	A Scout is Loyal	N. Rockwell	18,500	19.50	55.00
77-19-003	The Scoutmaster	N. Rockwell	18,500	19.50	60.00
77-19-004	A Good Sign	N. Rockwell	18,500	19.50	50.00
78-19-005	Pointing the Way	N. Rockwell	18,500	19.50	50.00
78-19-006	Campfire Story	N. Rockwell	18,500	19.50	25.00
80-19-007	Beyond the Easel	N. Rockwell	18,500	45.00	45.00
Gorham		**Single Release**			
76-20-001	The Marriage License	N. Rockwell	Numbrd	37.50	52.00
Gorham		**Presidential**			
76-21-001	John F. Kennedy	N. Rockwell	9,800	30.00	65.00
76-21-002	Dwight D. Eisenhower	N. Rockwell	9,800	30.00	35.00
Gorham		**Single Release**			
78-22-001	Triple Self Portrait Memorial Plate	N. Rockwell	Annual	37.50	75.00
Gorham		**Four Seasons Landscapes**			
80-23-001	Summer Respite	N. Rockwell	Annual	45.00	67.50
81-23-002	Autumn Reflection	N. Rockwell	Annual	45.00	65.00
82-23-003	Winter Delight	N. Rockwell	Annual	50.00	62.50
83-23-004	Spring Recess	N. Rockwell	Annual	60.00	60.00
Gorham		**Single Release**			
80-24-001	The Annual Visit	N. Rockwell	Annual	32.50	35.00
Gorham		**Single Release**			
81-25-001	Day in Life of Boy	N. Rockwell	Annual	50.00	80.00
81-25-002	Day in Life of Girl	N. Rockwell	Annual	50.00	80.00
Gorham		**Gallery of Masters**			
71-26-001	Man with a Gilt Helmet	Rembrandt	10,000	50.00	50.00
72-26-002	Self Portrait with Saskia	Rembrandt	10,000	50.00	50.00
73-26-003	The Honorable Mrs. Graham	Gainsborough	7,500	50.00	50.00
Gorham		**Barrymore**			
71-27-001	Quiet Waters	Barrymore	15,000	25.00	25.00
72-27-002	San Pedro Harbor	Barrymore	15,000	25.00	25.00
Gorham		**Barrymore**			
72-28-001	Nantucket, Sterling	Barrymore	1,000	100.00	100.00
72-28-002	Little Boatyard, Sterling	Barrymore	1,000	100.00	145.00
Gorham		**Pewter Bicentennial**			
71-29-001	Burning of the Gaspee	R. Pailthorpe	5,000	35.00	35.00
72-29-002	Boston Tea Party	R. Pailthorpe	5,000	35.00	35.00

Number	Name	Artist	Edition Limit	Issue Price	Quote
Gorham		**Vermeil Bicentennial**			
72-30-001	1776 Plate	Gorham	250	750.00	800.00
Gorham		**Silver Bicentennial**			
72-31-001	1776 Plate	Gorham	500	500.00	500.00
72-31-002	Burning of the Gaspee	R. Pailthorpe	750	500.00	500.00
73-31-003	Boston Tea Party	R. Pailthorpe	750	550.00	575.00
Gorham		**China Bicentennial**			
72-32-001	1776 Plate	Gorham	18,500	17.50	35.00
76-32-002	1776 Bicentennial	Gorham	8,000	17.50	35.00
Gorham		**Remington Western**			
73-33-001	A New Year on the Cimarron	F. Remington	Annual	25.00	35.00
73-33-002	Aiding a Comrade	F. Remington	Annual	25.00	30.00
73-33-003	The Flight	F. Remington	Annual	25.00	30.00
73-33-004	The Fight for the Water Hole	F. Remington	Annual	25.00	30.00
75-33-005	Old Ramond	F. Remington	Annual	20.00	35.00
75-33-006	A Breed	F. Remington	Annual	20.00	35.00
76-33-007	Cavalry Officer	F. Remington	5,000	37.50	75.00
76-33-008	A Trapper	F. Remington	5,000	37.50	75.00
Gorham		**Moppet Plates-Christmas**			
73-34-001	M. Plate Christmas	Unknown	Annual	10.00	35.00
74-34-002	M. Plate Christmas	Unknown	Annual	12.00	12.00
75-34-003	M. Plate Christmas	Unknown	Annual	13.00	13.00
76-34-004	M. Plate Christmas	Unknown	Annual	13.00	15.00
77-34-005	M. Plate Christmas	Unknown	Annual	13.00	14.00
78-34-006	M. Plate Christmas	Unknown	Annual	10.00	10.00
79-34-007	M. Plate Christmas	Unknown	Annual	12.00	12.00
80-34-008	M. Plate Christmas	Unknown	Annual	12.00	12.00
81-34-009	M. Plate Christmas	Unknown	Annual	12.00	12.00
82-34-010	M. Plate Christmas	Unknown	Annual	12.00	12.00
83-34-011	M. Plate Christmas	Unknown	Annual	12.00	12.00
Gorham		**Moppet Plates-Mother's Day**			
73-35-001	M. Plate Mother's Day	Unknown	Annual	10.00	30.00
74-35-002	M. Plate Mother's Day	Unknown	Annual	12.00	20.00
75-35-003	M. Plate Mother's Day	Unknown	Annual	13.00	15.00
76-35-004	M. Plate Mother's Day	Unknown	Annual	13.00	15.00
77-35-005	M. Plate Mother's Day	Unknown	Annual	13.00	15.00
78-35-006	M. Plate Mother's Day	Unknown	Annual	10.00	10.00
Gorham		**Moppet Plates-Anniversary**			
76-36-001	M. Plate Anniversary	Unknown	20,000	13.00	13.00
Gorham		**Julian Ritter, Fall In Love**			
77-37-001	Enchantment	J. Ritter	5,000	100.00	100.00
77-37-002	Frolic	J. Ritter	5,000	Set	Set
77-37-003	Gutsy Gal	J. Ritter	5,000	Set	Set
77-37-004	Lonely Chill	J. Ritter	5,000	Set	Set
Gorham		**Julian Ritter**			
77-38-001	Christmas Visit	J. Ritter	9,800	24.50	29.00
Gorham		**Julian Ritter, To Love a Clown**			
78-39-001	Awaited Reunion	J. Ritter	5,000	120.00	120.00
78-39-002	Twosome Time	J. Ritter	5,000	120.00	120.00
78-39-003	Showtime Beckons	J. Ritter	5,000	120.00	120.00
78-39-004	Together in Memories	J. Ritter	5,000	120.00	120.00
Gorham		**Julian Ritter**			
78-40-001	Valentine, Fluttering Heart	J. Ritter	7,500	45.00	45.00
Gorham		**Christmas/Children's Television Workshop**			
81-41-001	Sesame Street Christmas	Unknown	Annual	17.50	17.50
82-41-002	Sesame Street Christmas	Unknown	Annual	17.50	17.50
83-41-003	Sesame Street Christmas	Unknown	Annual	19.50	19.50
Gorham		**Pastoral Symphony**			
82-42-001	When I Was a Child	B. Felder	7,500	42.50	50.00
82-42-002	Gather the Children	B. Felder	7,500	42.50	50.00
84-42-003	Sugar and Spice	B. Felder	7,500	42.50	50.00
XX-42-004	He Loves Me	B. Felder	7,500	42.50	50.00
Gorham		**Encounters, Survival and Celebrations**			
82-43-001	A Fine Welcome	J. Clymer	7,500	50.00	62.50
83-43-002	Winter Trail	J. Clymer	7,500	50.00	62.50
83-43-003	Alouette	J. Clymer	7,500	62.50	62.50
83-43-004	The Trader	J. Clymer	7,500	62.50	62.50
83-43-005	Winter Camp	J. Clymer	7,500	62.50	62.50
83-43-006	The Trapper Takes a Wife	J. Clymer	7,500	62.50	62.50
Gorham		**Charles Russell**			
80-44-001	In Without Knocking	C. Russell	9,800	38.00	75.00
81-44-002	Bronc to Breakfast	C. Russell	9,800	38.00	75-115.00
82-44-003	When Ignorance is Bliss	C. Russell	9,800	45.00	75-115.00
83-44-004	Cowboy Life	C. Russell	9,800	45.00	45.00
Gorham		**Gorham Museum Doll Plates**			
84-45-001	Lydia	Gorham	5,000	29.00	125.00
84-45-002	Belton Bebe	Gorham	5,000	29.00	55.00
84-45-003	Christmas Lady	Gorham	7,500	32.50	32.50
85-45-004	Lucille	Gorham	5,000	29.00	35.00
85-45-005	Jumeau	Gorham	5,000	29.00	29.00
Gorham		**Time Machine Teddies Plates**			
86-46-001	Miss Emily, Bearing Up	B. Port	5,000	32.50	32.50
87-46-002	Big Bear, The Toy Collector	B. Port	5,000	32.50	32.50
88-46-003	Hunny Munny	B. Port	5,000	37.50	37.50
Gorham		**Leyendecker Annual Christmas Plates**			
88-47-001	Christmas Hug	J. C. Leyendecker	10,000	37.50	37.50
Gorham		**Single Release**			
76-48-001	The Black Regiment 1778	F. Quagon	7,500	25.00	58.00
Gorham		**American Artist**			
76-49-001	Apache Mother & Child	R. Donnelly	9,800	25.00	56.00
Dave Grossman Creations		**Emmett Kelly Plates**			
86-01-001	Christmas Carol	B. Leighton-Jones	Yr.Iss.	20.00	20.00
87-01-002	Christmas Wreath	B. Leighton-Jones	Yr.Iss.	20.00	20.00

Number	Name	Artist	Edition Limit	Issue Price	Quote
88-01-003	Christmas Dinner	B. Leighton-Jones	Yr.Iss.	20.00	20.00
89-01-004	Christmas Feast	B. Leighton-Jones	Yr.Iss.	20.00	20.00
90-01-005	Just What I Needed	B. Leighton-Jones	Yr.Iss.	24.00	24.00
91-01-006	Emmett The Snowman	B. Leighton-Jones	Yr.Iss.	25.00	25.00
92-01-007	Christmas Tunes	B. Leighton-Jones	Yr.Iss.	25.00	25.00
Dave Grossman Creations		**Saturday Evening Post Collection**			
91-02-001	Downhill Daring BRP-91	Rockwell-Inspired	Yr.Iss.	25.00	25.00
91-02-002	Missed BRP-101	Rockwell-Inspired	Yr Iss.	25.00	25.00
92-02-003	Choosin Up BRP-102	Rockwell-Inspired	Y. Iss.	25.00	25.00
Dave Grossman Creations		**Native American Series**			
91-03-001	Lone Wolf	E. Roberts	10,000	45.00	45.00
92-03-002	Tortoise Lady	E. Roberts	10,000	45.00	45.00
Dave Grossman Designs		**Norman Rockwell Collection**			
79-01-001	Leapfrog NRP-79	Rockwell-Inspired	Retrd.	50.00	50.00
80-01-002	Lovers NRP-80	Rockwell-Inspired	Retrd.	60.00	60.00
81-01-003	Dreams of Long Ago NRP-81	Rockwell-Inspired	Retrd.	60.00	60.00
82-01-004	Doctor and Doll NRP-82	Rockwell-Inspired	Retrd.	65.00	95.00
83-01-005	Circus NRP-83	Rockwell-Inspired	Retrd.	65.00	65.00
84-01-006	Visit With Rockwell NRP-84	Rockwell-Inspired	Retrd.	65.00	65.00
80-01-007	Christmas Trio RXP-80	Rockwell-Inspired	Retrd.	75.00	75.00
81-01-008	Santa's Good Boys RXP-81	Rockwell-Inspired	Retrd.	75.00	75.00
82-01-009	Faces of Christmas RXP-82	Rockwell-Inspired	Retrd.	75.00	75.00
83-01-010	Christmas Chores RXP-83	Rockwell-Inspired	Retrd.	75.00	75.00
84-01-011	Tiny Tim RXP-84	Rockwell-Inspired	Retrd.	75.00	75.00
80-01-012	Back To School RMP-80	Rockwell-Inspired	Retrd.	24.00	24.00
81-01-013	No Swimming RMP-81	Rockwell-Inspired	Retrd.	25.00	25.00
82-01-014	Love Letter RMP-82	Rockwell-Inspired	Retrd.	27.00	30.00
83-01-015	Doctor and Doll RMP-83	Rockwell-Inspired	Retrd.	27.00	27.00
84-01-016	Big Moment RMP-84	Rockwell-Inspired	Retrd.	27.00	27.00
79-01-017	Butterboy RP-01	Rockwell-Inspired	Retrd.	40.00	40.00
82-01-018	American Mother RGP-42	Rockwell-Inspired	Retrd.	45.00	45.00
83-01-019	Dreamboat RGP-83	Rockwell-Inspired	Retrd.	24.00	30.00
78-01-020	Young Doctor RDP-26	Rockwell-Inspired	Retrd.	50.00	65.00
Dave Grossman Designs		**Norman Rockwell Collection-Tom Sawyer Plates**			
75-02-001	Whitewashing the Fence TSP-01	Rockwell-Inspired	Retrd.	26.00	35.00
76-02-002	First Smoke TSP-02	Rockwell-Inspired	Retrd.	26.00	35.00
77-02-003	Take Your Medicine TSP-03	Rockwell-Inspired	Retrd.	26.00	40.00
78-02-004	Lost in Cave TSP-04	Rockwell-Inspired	Retrd.	26.00	40.00
Dave Grossman Designs		**Norman Rockwell Collection-Huck Finn Plates**			
79-03-001	Secret HFP-01	Rockwell-Inspired	Retrd.	40.00	40.00
80-03-002	ListeningHFP-02	Rockwell-Inspired	Retrd.	40.00	40.00
80-03-003	No Kings HFP-03	Rockwell-Inspired	Retrd.	40.00	40.00
81-03-004	Snake Escapes HFP-04	Rockwell-Inspired	Retrd.	40.00	40.00
Dave Grossman Designs		**Norman Rockwell Collection-Boy Scout Plates**			
81-04-001	Can't Wait BSP-01	Rockwell-Inspired	Retrd.	30.00	45.00
82-04-002	Guiding Hand BSP-02	Rockwell-Inspired	Retrd.	30.00	35.00
83-04-003	Tomorrow's Leader BSP-03	Rockwell-Inspired	Retrd.	30.00	45.00
Grande Copenhagen		**Christmas**			
75-01-001	Alone Together	Unknown	Undis.	24.50	24.50
76-01-002	Christmas Wreath	Unknown	Undis.	24.50	24.50
77-01-003	Fishwives at Gammelstrand	Unknown	Undis.	26.50	26.50
78-01-004	Hans Christian Anderson	Unknown	Undis.	32.50	32.50
79-01-005	Pheasants	Unknown	Undis.	34.50	56.00
80-01-006	Snow Queen in the Tivoli	Unknown	Undis.	39.50	39.50
81-01-007	Little Match Girl in Nyhavn	Unknown	Undis.	42.50	43.00
82-01-008	Shepherdess/Chimney Sweep	Unknown	Undis.	45.00	49.00
83-01-009	Little Mermaid Near Kronborg	Unknown	Undis.	45.00	104.00
84-01-010	Sandman at Amalienborg	Unknown	Undis.	45.00	50.00
Hadley Companies		**Glow Series**			
85-01-001	Evening Glow	T. Redlin	5,000	55.00	350-450.
85-01-002	Morning Glow	T. Redlin	5,000	55.00	125-250.
85-01-003	Twilight Glow	T. Redlin	5,000	55.00	95-125.00
87-01-004	Morning Retreat	T. Redlin	9,500	65.00	65-125.00
87-01-005	Evening Retreat	T. Redlin	9,500	65.00	65-75.00
88-01-006	Golden Retreat	T. Redlin	9,500	65.00	95.00
89-01-007	Moonlight Retreat	T. Redlin	9,500	65.00	65.00
87-01-008	Coming Home	T. Redlin	9,500	85.00	85.00
88-01-009	Lights of Home	T. Redlin	9,500	85.00	85.00
89-01-010	Homeward Bound	T. Redlin	9,500	85.00	85.00
88-01-011	Afternoon Glow	T. Redlin	5,000	55.00	55.00
Hamilton/Boehm		**Award Winning Roses**			
79-01-001	Peace Rose	Boehm	15,000	45.00	45-62.50
79-01-002	White Masterpiece Rose	Boehm	15,000	45.00	45-62.50
79-01-003	Tropicana Rose	Boehm	15,000	45.00	45-62.50
79-01-004	Elegance Rose	Boehm	15,000	45.00	45-62.50
79-01-005	Queen Elizabeth Rose	Boehm	15,000	45.00	45-62.50
79-01-006	Royal Highness Rose	Boehm	15,000	45.00	45-62.50
79-01-007	Angel Face Rose	Boehm	15,000	45.00	45-62.50
79-01-008	Mr. Lincoln Rose	Boehm	15,000	45.00	45-62.50
Hamilton/Boehm		**Owl Collection**			
80-02-001	Boreal Owl	Boehm	15,000	45.00	75.00
80-02-002	Snowy Owl	Boehm	15,000	45.00	62.50
80-02-003	Barn Owl	Boehm	15,000	45.00	62.50
80-02-004	Saw Whet Owl	Boehm	15,000	45.00	62.50
80-02-005	Great Horned Owl	Boehm	15,000	45.00	62.50
80-02-006	Screech Owl	Boehm	15,000	45.00	62.50
80-02-007	Short Eared Owl	Boehm	15,000	45.00	62.50
80-02-008	Barred Owl	Boehm	15,000	45.00	62.50
Hamilton/Boehm		**Hummingbird Collection**			
80-03-001	Calliope	Boehm	15,000	62.50	80.00
80-03-002	Broadbilled	Boehm	15,000	62.50	62.50
80-03-003	Rufous Flame Bearer	Boehm	15,000	62.50	80.00
80-03-004	Broadtail	Boehm	15,000	62.50	62.50
80-03-005	Streamertail	Boehm	15,000	62.50	80.00
80-03-006	Blue Throated	Boehm	15,000	62.50	80.00
80-03-007	Crimson Topaz	Boehm	15,000	62.50	62.50
80-03-008	Brazilian Ruby	Boehm	15,000	62.50	80.00
Hamilton/Boehm		**Water Birds**			
81-04-001	Canada Geese	Boehm	15,000	62.50	75.00
81-04-002	Wood Ducks	Boehm	15,000	62.50	62.50
81-04-003	Hooded Merganser	Boehm	15,000	62.50	87.00

Company Number	Name	Series Artist	Edition Limit	Issue Price	Quote
81-04-004	Ross's Geese	Boehm	15,000	62.50	62.50
81-04-005	Common Mallard	Boehm	15,000	62.50	62.50
81-04-006	Canvas Back	Boehm	15,000	62.50	62.50
81-04-007	Green Winged Teal	Boehm	15,000	62.50	62.50
81-04-008	American Pintail	Boehm	15,000	62.50	62.50
Hamilton/Boehm		**Gamebirds of North America**			
84-05-001	Ring-Necked Pheasant	Boehm	15,000	62.50	62.50
84-05-002	Bob White Quail	Boehm	15,000	62.50	62.50
84-05-003	American Woodcock	Boehm	15,000	62.50	62.50
84-05-004	California Quail	Boehm	15,000	62.50	62.50
84-05-005	Ruffed Grouse	Boehm	15,000	62.50	62.50
84-05-006	Wild Turkey	Boehm	15,000	62.50	62.50
84-05-007	Willow Partridge	Boehm	15,000	62.50	62.50
84-05-008	Prairie Grouse	Boehm	15,000	62.50	62.50
Hamilton Collection		**Precious Portraits**			
87-01-001	Sunbeam	B. P. Gutmann	14-day	24.50	30-39.50
87-01-002	Mischief	B. P. Gutmann	14-day	24.50	30-39.50
87-01-003	Peach Blossom	B. P. Gutmann	14-day	24.50	36-45.00
87-01-004	Goldilocks	B. P. Gutmann	14-day	24.50	30-39.00
87-01-005	Fairy Gold	B. P. Gutmann	14-day	24.50	36-45.00
87-01-006	Bunny	B. P. Gutmann	14-day	24.50	30-42.00
Hamilton Collection		**Bundles of Joy**			
88-02-001	Awakening	B. P. Gutmann	14-day	24.50	75.00
88-02-002	Happy Dreams	B. P. Gutmann	14-day	24.50	60.00
88-02-003	Tasting	B. P. Gutmann	14-day	24.50	36.00
88-02-004	Sweet Innocence	B. P. Gutmann	14-day	24.50	30.00
88-02-005	Tommy	B. P. Gutmann	14-day	24.50	30.00
88-02-006	A Little Bit of Heaven	B. P. Gutmann	14-day	24.50	75.00
88-02-007	Billy	B. P. Gutmann	14-day	24.50	30.00
88-02-008	Sun Kissed	B. P. Gutmann	14-day	24.50	30.00
Hamilton Collection		**The Nutcracker Ballet**			
78-03-001	Clara	S. Fisher	28-day	19.50	36.00
79-03-002	Godfather	S. Fisher	28-day	19.50	19.50
79-03-003	Sugar Plum Fairy	S. Fisher	28-day	19.50	45.00
79-03-004	Snow Queen and King	S. Fisher	28-day	19.50	40.00
80-03-005	Waltz of the Flowers	S. Fisher	28-day	19.50	19.50
80-03-006	Clara and the Prince	S. Fisher	28-day	19.50	45.00
Hamilton Collection		**Precious Moments Plates**			
79-04-001	Friend in the Sky	T. Utz	28-day	21.50	50.00
80-04-002	Sand in her Shoe	T. Utz	28-day	21.50	27.00
80-04-003	Snow Bunny	T. Utz	28-day	21.50	40.00
80-04-004	Seashells	T. Utz	28-day	21.50	37.50
81-04-005	Dawn	T. Utz	28-day	21.50	27.00
82-04-006	My Kitty	T. Utz	28-day	21.50	36.00
Hamilton Collection		**The Greatest Show on Earth**			
81-05-001	Clowns	F. Moody	10-day	30.00	45.00
81-05-002	Elephants	F. Moody	10-day	30.00	30.00
81-05-003	Aerialists	F. Moody	10-day	30.00	30.00
81-05-004	Great Parade	F. Moody	10-day	30.00	30.00
81-05-005	Midway	F. Moody	10-day	30.00	30.00
81-05-006	Equestrians	F. Moody	10-day	30.00	30.00
82-05-007	Lion Tamer	F. Moody	10-day	30.00	30.00
82-05-008	Grande Finale	F. Moody	10-day	30.00	30.00
Hamilton Collection		**Rockwell Home of the Brave**			
81-06-001	Reminiscing	N. Rockwell	18,000	35.00	75.00
81-06-002	Hero's Welcome	N. Rockwell	18,000	35.00	50.00
81-06-003	Back to his Old Job	N. Rockwell	18,000	35.00	40.00
81-06-004	War Hero	N. Rockwell	18,000	35.00	35.00
82-06-005	Willie Gillis in Church	N. Rockwell	18,000	35.00	35.00
82-06-006	War Bond	N. Rockwell	18,000	35.00	35.00
82-06-007	Uncle Sam Takes Wings	N. Rockwell	18,000	35.00	48.00
82-06-008	Taking Mother over the Top	N. Rockwell	18,000	35.00	35.00
Hamilton Collection		**Japanese Floral Calendar**			
81-07-001	New Year's Day	Shuho/Kage	10-day	32.50	32.50
82-07-002	Early Spring	Shuho/Kage	10-day	32.50	32.50
82-07-003	Spring	Shuho/Kage	10-day	32.50	32.50
82-07-004	Girl's Doll Day Festival	Shuho/Kage	10-day	32.50	32.50
82-07-005	Buddha's Birthday	Shuho/Kage	10-day	32.50	32.50
82-07-006	Early Summer	Shuho/Kage	10-day	32.50	32.50
82-07-007	Boy's Doll Day Festival	Shuho/Kage	10-day	32.50	32.50
82-07-008	Summer	Shuho/Kage	10-day	32.50	32.50
82-07-009	Autumn	Shuho/Kage	10-day	32.50	32.50
83-07-010	Festival of the Full Moon	Shuho/Kage	10-day	32.50	32.50
83-07-011	Late Autumn	Shuho/Kage	10-day	32.50	32.50
83-07-012	Winter	Shuho/Kage	10-day	32.50	32.50
Hamilton Collection		**Portraits of Childhood**			
81-08-001	Butterfly Magic	T. Utz	28-day	24.95	24.95
82-08-002	Sweet Dreams	T. Utz	28-day	24.95	24.95
83-08-003	Turtle Talk	T. Utz	28-day	24.95	36.00
84-08-004	Friends Forever	T. Utz	28-day	24.95	24.95
Hamilton Collection		**Carefree Days**			
82-09-001	Autumn Wanderer	T. Utz	10-day	24.50	24.50
82-09-002	Best Friends	T. Utz	10-day	24.50	24.50
82-09-003	Feeding Time	T. Utz	10-day	24.50	24.50
82-09-004	Bathtime Visitor	T. Utz	10-day	24.50	30.00
82-09-005	First Catch	T. Utz	10-day	24.50	30.00
82-09-006	Monkey Business	T. Utz	10-day	24.50	30.00
82-09-007	Touchdown	T. Utz	10-day	24.50	24.50
82-09-008	Nature Hunt	T. Utz	10-day	24.50	24.50
Hamilton Colletion		**Utz Mother's Day**			
83-10-001	A Gift of Love	T. Utz	Time	27.50	37.50
83-10-002	Mother's Helping Hand	T. Utz	Time	27.50	27.50
83-10-003	Mother's Angel	T. Utz	Time	27.50	27.50
Hamilton Collection		**Single Issues**			
83-11-001	Princess Grace	T. Utz	21-day	39.50	39.50-60.
Hamilton Collection		**Summer Days of Childhood**			
83-12-001	Mountain Friends	T. Utz	10-day	29.50	29.50
83-12-002	Garden Magic	T. Utz	10-day	29.50	29.50
83-12-003	Little Beachcomber	T. Utz	10-day	29.50	29.50
83-12-004	Blowing Bubbles	T. Utz	10-day	29.50	29.50

Company Number	Name	Series Artist	Edition Limit	Issue Price	Quote
83-12-005	The Birthday Party	T. Utz	10-day	29.50	29.50
83-12-006	Playing Doctor	T. Utz	10-day	29.50	29.50
83-12-007	A Stolen Kiss	T. Utz	10-day	29.50	29.50
83-12-008	Kitty's Bathtime	T. Utz	10-day	29.50	29.50
83-12-009	Cooling Off	T. Utz	10-day	29.50	29.50
83-12-010	First Customer	T. Utz	10-day	29.50	29.50
83-12-011	A Jumping Contest	T. Utz	10-day	29.50	29.50
83-12-012	Balloon Carnival	T. Utz	10-day	29.50	29.50
Hamilton Collection		**Passage to China**			
83-13-001	Empress of China	R. Massey	15,000	55.00	55.00
83-13-002	Alliance	R. Massey	15,000	55.00	55.00
85-13-003	Grand Turk	R. Massey	15,000	55.00	55.00
85-13-004	Sea Witch	R. Massey	15,000	55.00	55.00
85-13-005	Flying Cloud	R. Massey	15,000	55.00	55.00
85-13-006	Romance of the Seas	R. Massey	15,000	55.00	55.00
85-13-007	Sea Serpent	R. Massey	15,000	55.00	55.00
85-13-008	Challenge	R. Massey	15,000	55.00	55.00
Hamilton Collection		**Springtime of Life**			
85-14-001	Teddy's Bathtime	T. Utz	14-day	29.50	29.50
85-14-002	Just Like Mommy	T. Utz	14-day	29.50	29.50
85-14-003	Among the Daffodils	T. Utz	14-day	29.50	29.50
85-14-004	My Favorite Dolls	T. Utz	14-day	29.50	29.50
85-14-005	Aunt Tillie's Hats	T. Utz	14-day	29.50	29.50
85-14-006	Little Emily	T. Utz	14-day	29.50	29.50
85-14-007	Granny's Boots	T. Utz	14-day	29.50	29.50
85-14-008	My Masterpiece	T. Utz	14-day	29.50	29.50
Hamilton Collection		**A Child's Best Friend**			
85-15-001	In Disgrace	B. P. Gutmann	14-day	24.50	90-180.00
85-15-002	The Reward	B. P. Gutmann	14-day	24.50	50-95.00
85-15-003	Who's Sleepy	B. P. Gutmann	14-day	24.50	90.00
85-15-004	Good Morning	B. P. Gutmann	14-day	24.50	75.00
85-15-005	Sympathy	B. P. Gutmann	14-day	24.50	54.00
85-15-006	On the Up and Up	B. P. Gutmann	14-day	24.50	75.00
85-15-007	Mine	B. P. Gutmann	14-day	24.50	90.00
85-15-008	Going to Town	B. P. Gutmann	14-day	24.50	60.00
Hamilton Collection		**A Country Summer**			
85-16-001	Butterfly Beauty	N. Noel	10-day	29.50	36.00
85-16-002	The Golden Puppy	N. Noel	10-day	29.50	29.50
86-16-003	The Rocking Chair	N. Noel	10-day	29.50	36.00
86-16-004	My Bunny	N. Noel	10-day	29.50	33.00
88-16-005	The Piglet	N. Noel	10-day	29.50	29.50
88-16-006	Teammates	N. Noel	10-day	29.50	29.50
Hamilton Collection		**The Little Rascals**			
85-17-001	Three for the Show	Unknown	10-day	24.50	30.00
85-17-002	My Gal	Unknown	10-day	24.50	24.50
85-17-003	Skeleton Crew	Unknown	10-day	24.50	24.50
85-17-004	Roughin' It	Unknown	10-day	24.50	24.50
85-17-005	Spanky's Pranks	Unknown	10-day	24.50	24.50
85-17-006	Butch's Challenge	Unknown	10-day	24.50	24.50
85-17-007	Darla's Debut	Unknown	10-day	24.50	24.50
85-17-008	Pete's Pal	Unknown	10-day	24.50	24.50
Hamilton Collection		**The Japanese Blossoms of Autumn**			
85-18-001	Bellflower	Koseki/Ebihara	10-day	45.00	45.00
85-18-002	Arrowroot	Koseki/Ebihara	10-day	45.00	45.00
85-18-003	Wild Carnation	Koseki/Ebihara	10-day	45.00	45.00
85-18-004	Maiden Flower	Koseki/Ebihara	10-day	45.00	45.00
85-18-005	Pampas Grass	Koseki/Ebihara	10-day	45.00	45.00
85-18-006	Bush Clover	Koseki/Ebihara	10-day	45.00	45.00
85-18-007	Purple Trousers	Koseki/Ebihara	10-day	45.00	45.00
Hamilton Collection		**The Star Wars Plate Collection**			
87-19-001	Hans Solo	T. Blackshear	14-day	29.50	36-45.00
87-19-002	R2-D2 and Wicket	T. Blackshear	14-day	29.50	45.00
87-19-003	Luke Skywalker and Darth Vader	T. Blackshear	14-day	29.50	60-75.00
87-19-004	Princess Leia	T. Blackshear	14-day	29.50	60-85.00
87-19-005	The Imperial Walkers	T. Blackshear	14-day	29.50	45-69.00
87-19-006	Luke and Yoda	T. Blackshear	14-day	29.50	60.00
88-19-007	Space Battle	T. Blackshear	14-day	29.50	170-200.
88-19-008	Crew in Cockpit	T. Blackshear	14-day	29.50	60-85.00
Hamilton Collection		**America's Greatest Sailing Ships**			
88-20-001	USS Constitution	T. Freeman	14-day	29.50	36.00
88-20-002	Great Republic	T. Freeman	14-day	29.50	36.00
88-20-003	America	T. Freeman	14-day	29.50	45.00
88-20-004	Charles W. Morgan	T. Freeman	14-day	29.50	36.00
88-20-005	Eagle	T. Freeman	14-day	29.50	48.00
88-20-006	Bonhomme Richard	T. Freeman	14-day	29.50	36.00
88-20-007	Gertrude L. Thebaud	T. Freeman	14-day	29.50	45.00
88-20-008	Enterprise	T. Freeman	14-day	29.50	36.00
Hamilton Collection		**Noble Owls of America**			
86-21-001	Morning Mist	J. Seerey-Lester	15,000	55.00	55.00
87-21-002	Prairie Sundown	J. Seerey-Lester	15,000	55.00	55.00
87-21-003	Winter Vigil	J. Seerey-Lester	15,000	55.00	55.00
87-21-004	Autumn Mist	J. Seerey-Lester	15,000	55.00	75.00
87-21-005	Dawn in the Willows	J. Seerey-Lester	15,000	55.00	55.00
87-21-006	Snowy Watch	J. Seerey-Lester	15,000	55.00	90.00
88-21-007	Hiding Place	J. Seerey-Lester	15,000	55.00	55.00
88-21-008	Waiting for Dusk	J. Seerey-Lester	15,000	55.00	55.00
Hamilton Collection		**Treasured Days**			
87-22-001	Ashley	H. Bond	14-day	29.50	60.00
87-22-002	Christopher	H. Bond	14-day	24.50	45.00
87-22-003	Sara	H. Bond	14-day	24.50	30.00
87-22-004	Jeremy	H. Bond	14-day	24.50	45.00
87-22-005	Amanda	H. Bond	14-day	24.50	45.00
88-22-006	Nicholas	H. Bond	14-day	24.50	45.00
88-22-007	Lindsay	H. Bond	14-day	24.50	45.00
88-22-008	Justin	H. Bond	14-day	24.50	45.00
Hamilton Collection		**Butterfly Garden**			
87-23-001	Spicebush Swallowtail	P. Sweany	14-day	29.50	45.00
87-23-002	Common Blue	P. Sweany	14-day	29.50	37.50
87-23-003	Orange Sulphur	P. Sweany	14-day	29.50	30.00
87-23-004	Monarch	P. Sweany	14-day	29.50	37.50
87-23-005	Tiger Swallowtail	P. Sweany	14-day	29.50	30.00
87-23-006	Crimson Patched Longwing	P. Sweany	14-day	29.50	37.50

Company		Series			
Number	**Name**	**Artist**	**Edition Limit**	**Issue Price**	**Quote**
88-23-007	Morning Cloak	P. Sweany	14-day	29.50	29.50
88-23-008	Red Admiral	P. Sweany	14-day	29.50	37.50
Hamilton Collection		**The Golden Classics**			
87-24-001	Sleeping Beauty	C. Lawson	10-day	37.50	37.50
87-24-002	Rumpelstiltskin	C. Lawson	10-day	37.50	37.50
87-24-003	Jack and the Beanstalk	C. Lawson	10-day	37.50	37.50
87-24-004	Snow White and Rose Red	C. Lawson	10-day	37.50	37.50
87-24-005	Hansel and Gretel	C. Lawson	10-day	37.50	37.50
88-24-006	Cinderella	C. Lawson	10-day	37.50	37.50
88-24-007	The Golden Goose	C. Lawson	10-day	37.50	37.50
88-24-008	The Snow Queen	C. Lawson	10-day	37.50	37.50
Hamilton Collection		**Children of the American Frontier**			
86-25-001	In Trouble Again	D. Crook	10-day	24.50	35.00
86-25-002	Tubs and Suds	D. Crook	10-day	24.50	27.00
86-25-003	A Lady Needs a Little Privacy	D. Crook	10-day	24.50	24.50
86-25-004	The Desperadoes	D. Crook	10-day	24.50	27.00
86-25-005	Riders Wanted	D. Crook	10-day	24.50	30.00
87-25-006	A Cowboy's Downfall	D. Crook	10-day	24.50	24.50
87-25-007	Runaway Blues	D. Crook	10-day	24.50	24.50
87-25-008	A Special Patient	D. Crook	10-day	24.50	24.50
Hamilton Collection		**The Official Honeymooners Plate Collection**			
87-26-001	The Honeymooners	D. Kilmer	14-day	24.50	60-99.00
87-26-002	The Hucklebuck	D. Kilmer	14-day	24.50	67.50-99.00
87-26-003	Baby, You're the Greatest	D. Kilmer	14-day	24.50	60-125.00
88-26-004	The Golfer	D. Kilmer	14-day	24.50	90-140.00
88-26-005	The TV Chefs	D. Kilmer	14-day	24.50	90-140.00
88-26-006	Bang! Zoom!	D. Kilmer	14-day	24.50	60-125.00
88-26-007	The Only Way to Travel	D. Kilmer	14-day	24.50	90-125.00
88-26-008	The Honeymoon Express	D. Kilmer	14-day	24.50	150-190.00
Hamilton Collection		**North American Waterbirds**			
88-27-001	Wood Ducks	R. Lawrence	14-day	37.50	55.00
88-27-002	Hooded Mergansers	R. Lawrence	14-day	37.50	54.00
88-27-003	Pintails	R. Lawrence	14-day	37.50	45.00
88-27-004	Canada Geese	R. Lawrence	14-day	37.50	45.00
89-27-005	American Widgeons	R. Lawrence	14-day	37.50	54.00
89-27-006	Canvasbacks	R. Lawrence	14-day	37.50	55.00
89-27-007	Mallard Pair	R. Lawrence	14-day	37.50	60.00
89-27-008	Snow Geese	R. Lawrence	14-day	37.50	45.00
Hamilton Collection		**Nature's Quiet Moments**			
88-28-001	A Curious Pair	R. Parker	14-day	37.50	37.50
88-28-002	Northern Morning	R. Parker	14-day	37.50	37.50
88-28-003	Just Resting	R. Parker	14-day	37.50	37.50
89-28-004	Waiting Out the Storm	R. Parker	14-day	37.50	37.50
89-28-005	Creekside	R. Parker	14-day	37.50	37.50
89-28-006	Autumn Foraging	R. Parker	14-day	37.50	37.50
89-28-007	Old Man of the Mountain	R. Parker	14-day	37.50	37.50
89-28-008	Mountain Blooms	R. Parker	14-day	37.50	37.50
Hamilton Collection		**Wizard of Oz Commemorative**			
88-29-001	We're Off to See the Wizard	T. Blackshear	14-day	24.50	89-250.00
88-29-002	Dorothy Meets the Scarecrow	T. Blackshear	14-day	24.50	90-99.00
89-29-003	The Tin Man Speaks	T. Blackshear	14-day	24.50	35-105.00
89-29-004	A Glimpse of the Munchkins	T. Blackshear	14-day	24.50	90-99.00
89-29-005	The Witch Casts A Spell	T. Blackshear	14-day	24.50	35-125.00
89-29-006	If I Were King Of The Forest	T. Blackshear	14-day	24.50	35-150.00
89-29-007	The Great and Powerful Oz	T. Blackshear	14-day	24.50	90-150.00
89-29-008	There's No Place Like Home	T. Blackshear	14-day	24.50	99-120.00
Hamilton Collection		**Petals and Purrs**			
88-30-001	Blushing Beauties	B. Harrison	14-day	24.50	45.00
88-30-002	Spring Fever	B. Harrison	14-day	24.50	37.50
88-30-003	Morning Glories	B. Harrison	14-day	24.50	36.00
88-30-004	Forget-Me-Not	B. Harrison	14-day	24.50	36.00
89-30-005	Golden Fancy	B. Harrison	14-day	24.50	30.00
89-30-006	Pink Lillies	B. Harrison	14-day	24.50	30.00
89-30-007	Summer Sunshine	B. Harrison	14-day	24.50	24.50
89-30-008	Siamese Summer	B. Harrison	14-day	24.50	24.50
Hamilton Collection		**The Jeweled Hummingbirds Plate Collection**			
89-31-001	Ruby-throated Hummingbirds	J. Landenberger	14-day	37.50	37.50
89-31-002	Great Sapphire Wing Hummingbirds	J. Landenberger	14-day	37.50	37.50
89-31-003	Ruby-Topaz Hummingbirds	J. Landenberger	14-day	37.50	37.50
89-31-004	Andean Emerald Hummingbirds	J. Landenberger	14-day	37.50	37.50
89-31-005	Garnet-throated Hummingbirds	J. Landenberger	14-day	37.50	37.50
89-31-006	Blue-Headed Sapphire Hummingbirds	J. Landenberger	14-day	37.50	37.50
89-31-007	Pearl Coronet Hummingbirds	J. Landenberger	14-day	37.50	37.50
89-31-008	Amethyst-throated Sunangels	J. Landenberger	14-day	37.50	37.50
Hamilton Collection		**Stained Glass Gardens**			
89-32-001	Peacock and Wisteria	Unknown	15,000	55.00	55.00
89-32-002	Garden Sunset	Unknown	15,000	55.00	55.00
89-32-003	The Cockatoo's Garden	Unknown	15,000	55.00	55.00
89-32-004	Waterfall and Iris	Unknown	15,000	55.00	55.00
90-32-005	Roses and Magnolias	Unknown	15,000	55.00	55.00
90-32-006	A Hollyhock Sunrise	Unknown	15,000	55.00	55.00
90-32-007	Peaceful Waters	Unknown	15,000	55.00	55.00
90-32-008	Springtime in the Valley	Unknown	15,000	55.00	55.00
Hamilton Collection		**The I Love Lucy Plate Collection**			
89-33-001	California, Here We Come	J. Kritz	14-day	29.50	29.50-39.50
89-33-002	It's Just Like Candy	J. Kritz	14-day	29.50	39.50-95.00
90-33-003	The Big Squeeze	J. Kritz	14-day	29.50	45-99.00
90-33-004	Eating the Evidence	J. Kritz	14-day	29.50	45-125.00
90-33-005	Two of a Kind	J. Kritz	14-day	29.50	39.50-85.00
91-33-006	Queen of the Gypsies	J. Kritz	14-day	29.50	45-125.00
92-33-007	Night at the Copa	J. Kritz	14-day	29.50	29.50
92-33-008	A Rising Problem	J. Kritz	14-day	29.50	29.50
Hamilton Collection		**Birds of the Temple Gardens**			
89-35-001	Doves of Fidelity	J. Cheng	14-day	29.50	29.50
89-35-002	Cranes of Eternal Life	J. Cheng	14-day	29.50	29.50
89-35-003	Honorable Swallows	J. Cheng	14-day	29.50	29.50
89-35-004	Oriental White Eyes of Beauty	J. Cheng	14-day	29.50	29.50
89-35-005	Pheasants of Good Fortune	J. Cheng	14-day	29.50	29.50
89-35-006	Imperial Goldcrest	J. Cheng	14-day	29.50	29.50
89-35-007	Goldfinches of Virtue	J. Cheng	14-day	29.50	29.50
89-35-008	Magpies: Birds of Good Omen	J. Cheng	14-day	29.50	29.50

Company		Series			
Number	**Name**	**Artist**	**Edition Limit**	**Issue Price**	**Quote**
Hamilton Collection		**Winter Wildlife**			
89-36-001	Close Encounters	J. Seerey-Lester	15,000	55.00	55.00
89-36-002	Among the Cattails	J. Seerey-Lester	15,000	55.00	55.00
89-36-003	The Refuge	J. Seerey-Lester	15,000	55.00	55.00
89-36-004	Out of the Blizzard	J. Seerey-Lester	15,000	55.00	55.00
89-36-005	First Snow	J. Seerey-Lester	15,000	55.00	55.00
89-36-006	Lying In Wait	J. Seerey-Lester	15,000	55.00	55.00
89-36-007	Winter Hiding	J. Seerey-Lester	15,000	55.00	55.00
89-36-008	Early Snow	J. Seerey-Lester	15,000	55.00	55.00
Hamilton Collection		**Big Cats of the World**			
89-37-001	African Shade	D. Manning	14-day	29.50	29.50
89-37-002	View from Above	D. Manning	14-day	29.50	29.50
90-37-003	On The Prowl	D. Manning	14-day	29.50	29.50
90-37-004	Deep In The Jungle	D. Manning	14-day	29.50	29.50
90-37-005	Spirit Of The Mountain	D. Manning	14-day	29.50	29.50
90-37-006	Spotted Sentinel	D. Manning	14-day	29.50	29.50
90-37-007	Above the Treetops	D. Manning	14-day	29.50	29.50
90-37-008	Mountain Dweller	D. Manning	14-day	29.50	29.50
Hamilton Collection		**Mixed Company**			
90-38-001	Two Against One	P. Cooper	14-day	29.50	29.50
90-38-002	A Sticky Situation	P. Cooper	14-day	29.50	29.50
90-38-003	What's Up	P. Cooper	14-day	29.50	29.50
90-38-004	All Wrapped Up	P. Cooper	14-day	29.50	29.50
90-38-005	Picture Perfect	P. Cooper	14-day	29.50	29.50
91-38-006	A Moment to Unwind	P. Cooper	14-day	29.50	29.50
91-38-007	Ole	P. Cooper	14-day	29.50	29.50
91-38-008	Picnic Prowlers	P. Cooper	14-day	29.50	29.50
Hamilton Collection		**Portraits From Oz**			
89-39-001	Dorothy	T. Blackshear	14-day	29.50	120.00
89-39-002	Scarecrow	T. Blackshear	14-day	29.50	50-96.00
89-39-003	Tin Man	T. Blackshear	14-day	29.50	78-96.00
90-39-004	Cowardly Lion	T. Blackshear	14-day	29.50	54-75.00
90-39-005	Glinda	T. Blackshear	14-day	29.50	66-80.00
90-39-006	Wizard	T. Blackshear	14-day	29.50	75.00
90-39-007	Wicked Witch	T. Blackshear	14-day	29.50	90.00
90-39-008	Toto	T. Blackshear	14-day	29.50	145-150.
Hamilton Collection		**Delights of Childhood**			
89-40-001	Crayon Creations	J. Lamb	14-day	29.50	29.50
89-40-002	Little Mother	J. Lamb	14-day	29.50	29.50
90-40-003	Bathing Beauty	J. Lamb	14-day	29.50	29.50
90-40-004	Is That You, Granny?	J. Lamb	14-day	29.50	29.50
90-40-005	Nature's Little Helper	J. Lamb	14-day	29.50	29.50
90-40-006	So Sorry	J. Lamb	14-day	29.50	33.00
90-40-007	Shower Time	J. Lamb	14-day	29.50	33.00
90-40-008	Storytime Friends	J. Lamb	14-day	29.50	29.50
Hamilton Collection		**Classic Sporting Dogs**			
89-41-001	Golden Retrievers	B. Christie	14-day	24.50	54.00
89-41-002	Labrador Retrievers	B. Christie	14-day	24.50	60.00
89-41-003	Beagles	B. Christie	14-day	24.50	36.00
89-41-004	Pointers	B. Christie	14-day	24.50	30.00
89-41-005	Springer Spaniels	B. Christie	14-day	24.50	39.00
90-41-006	German Short-Haired Pointers	B. Christie	14-day	24.50	30-54.00
90-41-007	Irish Setters	B. Christie	14-day	24.50	24.50
90-41-008	Brittany Spaniels	B. Christie	14-day	24.50	48.00
Hamilton Collection		**Majesty of Flight**			
89-42-001	The Eagle Soars	T. Hirata	14-day	37.50	48.00
89-42-002	Realm of the Red-Tail	T. Hirata	14-day	37.50	39.00
89-42-003	Coastal Journey	T. Hirata	14-day	37.50	37.50
89-42-004	Sentry of the North	T. Hirata	14-day	37.50	37.50
89-42-005	Commanding the Marsh	T. Hirata	14-day	37.50	37.50
90-42-006	The Vantage Point	T. Hirata	14-day	29.50	37.50
90-42-007	Silent Watch	T. Hirata	14-day	29.50	45.00
90-42-008	Fierce and Free	T. Hirata	14-day	29.50	45.00
Hamilton Collection		**The Proud Nation**			
89-43-001	Navajo Little One	R. Swanson	14-day	24.50	45.00
89-43-002	In a Big Land	R. Swanson	14-day	24.50	31.00
89-43-003	Out with Mama's Flock	R. Swanson	14-day	24.50	33.00
89-43-004	Newest Little Sheepherder	R. Swanson	14-day	24.50	35.00
89-43-005	Dressed Up for the Powwow	R. Swanson	14-day	24.50	35.00
89-43-006	Just a Few Days Old	R. Swanson	14-day	24.50	30-49.00
89-43-007	Autumn Treat	R. Swanson	14-day	24.50	45.00
89-43-008	Up in the Red Rocks	R. Swanson	14-day	24.50	30.00
Hamilton Collection		**Thornton Utz 10th Anniversary Commemorative Plate Collection**			
89-44-001	Dawn	T. Utz	14-day	29.50	29.50
89-44-002	Just Like Mommy	T. Utz	14-day	29.50	29.50
89-44-003	Playing Doctor	T. Utz	14-day	29.50	29.50
89-44-004	My Kitty	T. Utz	14-day	29.50	29.50
89-44-005	Turtle Talk	T. Utz	14-day	29.50	29.50
89-44-006	Best Friends	T. Utz	14-day	29.50	29.50
89-44-007	Among the Daffodils	T. Utz	14-day	29.50	39.00
89-44-008	Friends in the Sky	T. Utz	14-day	29.50	29.50
89-44-009	Teddy's Bathtime	T. Utz	14-day	29.50	29.50
89-44-010	Little Emily	T. Utz	14-day	29.50	29.50
Hamilton Collection		**Country Kitties**			
89-45-001	Mischief Makers	G. Gerardi	14-day	24.50	45.00
89-45-002	Table Manners	G. Gerardi	14-day	24.50	27.00
89-45-003	Attic Attack	G. Gerardi	14-day	24.50	33.00
89-45-004	Rock and Rollers	G. Gerardi	14-day	24.50	24.50
89-45-005	Just For the Fern of It	G. Gerardi	14-day	24.50	27.00
89-45-006	All Washed Up	G. Gerardi	14-day	24.50	39.00
89-45-007	Stroller Derby	G. Gerardi	14-day	24.50	39.00
89-45-008	Captive Audience	G. Gerardi	14-day	24.50	39.00
Hamilton Collection		**Winged Reflections**			
89-46-001	Following Mama	R. Parker	14-day	37.50	37.50
89-46-002	Above the Breakers	R. Parker	14-day	37.50	37.50
89-46-003	Among the Reeds	R. Parker	14-day	37.50	37.50
89-46-004	Freeze Up	R. Parker	14-day	37.50	37.50
89-46-005	Wings Above the Water	R. Parker	14-day	37.50	37.50
90-46-006	Summer Loon	R. Parker	14-day	29.50	29.50
90-46-007	Early Spring	R. Parker	14-day	29.50	29.50
90-46-008	At The Water's Edge	R. Parker	14-day	29.50	29.50

Company / Number	Name	Series / Artist	Edition Limit	Issue Price	Quote
Hamilton Collection		**Elvis Remembered**			
89-47-001	Loving You	S. Morton	90-day	37.50	75.00
89-47-002	Early Years	S. Morton	90-day	37.50	65-75.00
89-47-003	Tenderly	S. Morton	90-day	37.50	80-95.00
89-47-004	The King	S. Morton	90-day	37.50	70-85.00
89-47-005	Forever Yours	S. Morton	90-day	37.50	37.50-85.00
89-47-006	Rockin in the Moonlight	S. Morton	90-day	37.50	60-65.00
89-47-007	Moody Blues	S. Morton	90-day	37.50	65-95.00
89-47-008	Elvis Presley	S. Morton	90-day	37.50	75.00
Hamilton Collection		**Fifty Years of Oz**			
89-48-001	Fifty Years of Oz	T. Blackshear	14-day	37.50	90-120.00
Hamilton Collection		**Small Wonders of the Wild**			
89-49-001	Hideaway	C. Frace	14-day	29.50	29.50
90-49-002	Young Explorers	C. Frace	14-day	29.50	29.50
90-49-003	Three of a Kind	C. Frace	14-day	29.50	60.00
90-49-004	Quiet Morning	C. Frace	14-day	29.50	29.50
90-49-005	Eyes of Wonder	C. Frace	14-day	29.50	29.50
90-49-006	Ready for Adventure	C. Frace	14-day	29.50	29.50
90-49-007	Uno	C. Frace	14-day	29.50	29.50
90-49-008	Exploring a New World	C. Frace	14-day	29.50	29.50
Hamilton Collection		**Dear to My Heart**			
90-50-001	Cathy	J. Hagara	14-day	29.50	29.50
90-50-002	Addie	J. Hagara	14-day	29.50	29.50
90-50-003	Jimmy	J. Hagara	14-day	29.50	29.50
90-50-004	Dacy	J. Hagara	14-day	29.50	29.50
90-50-005	Paul	J. Hagara	14-day	29.50	29.50
91-50-006	Shelly	J. Hagara	14-day	29.50	29.50
91-50-007	Jenny	J. Hagara	14-day	29.50	29.50
91-50-008	Joy	J. Hagara	14-day	29.50	29.50
Hamilton Collection		**North American Gamebirds**			
90-51-001	Ring-necked Pheasant	J. Killen	14-day	37.50	37.50
90-51-002	Bobwhite Quail	J. Killen	14-day	37.50	45.00
90-51-003	Ruffed Grouse	J. Killen	14-day	37.50	37.50
90-51-004	Gambel Quail	J. Killen	14-day	37.50	42.00
90-51-005	Mourning Dove	J. Killen	14-day	37.50	45.00
90-51-006	Woodcock	J. Killen	14-day	37.50	45.00
91-51-007	Chukar Partridge	J. Killen	14-day	37.50	45.00
91-51-008	Wild Turkey	J. Killen	14-day	37.50	45.00
Hamilton Collection		**The Saturday Evening Post Plate Collection**			
89-52-001	The Wonders of Radio	N. Rockwell	14-day	35.00	35.00
89-52-002	Easter Morning	N. Rockwell	14-day	35.00	60.00
89-52-003	The Facts of Life	N. Rockwell	14-day	35.00	35.00
90-52-004	The Window Washer	N. Rockwell	14-day	35.00	45.00
90-52-005	First Flight	N. Rockwell	14-day	35.00	54.00
90-52-006	Traveling Companion	N. Rockwell	14-day	35.00	35.00
90-52-007	Jury Room	N. Rockwell	14-day	35.00	35.00
90-52-008	Furlough	N. Rockwell	14-day	35.00	35.00
Hamilton Collection		**Favorite American Songbirds**			
89-53-001	Blue Jays of Spring	D. O'Driscoll	14-day	29.50	35.00
89-53-002	Red Cardinals of Winter	D. O'Driscoll	14-day	29.50	29.50
89-53-003	Robins & Apple Blossoms	D. O'Driscoll	14-day	29.50	35.00
89-53-004	Goldfinches of Summer	D. O'Driscoll	14-day	29.50	35.00
90-53-005	Autumn Chickadees	D. O'Driscoll	14-day	29.50	29.50
90-53-006	Bluebirds and Morning Glories	D. O'Driscoll	14-day	29.50	35.00
90-53-007	Tufted Titmouse and Holly	D. O'Driscoll	14-day	29.50	29.50
91-53-008	Carolina Wrens of Spring	D. O'Driscoll	14-day	29.50	29.50
Hamilton Collection		**Coral Paradise**			
89-54-001	The Living Oasis	H. Bond	14-day	29.50	29.50
90-54-002	Riches of the Coral Sea	H. Bond	14-day	29.50	29.50
90-54-003	Tropical Pageantry	H. Bond	14-day	29.50	29.50
90-54-004	Caribbean Spectacle	H. Bond	14-day	29.50	29.50
90-54-005	Undersea Village	H. Bond	14-day	29.50	29.50
90-54-006	Shimmering Reef Dwellers	H. Bond	14-day	29.50	36.00
90-54-007	Mysteries of the Galapagos	H. Bond	14-day	29.50	33.00
90-54-008	Forest Beneath the Sea	H. Bond	14-day	29.50	29.50
Hamilton Collection		**Noble American Indian Women**			
89-55-001	Sacajawea	D. Wright	14-day	29.50	45.00
90-55-002	Pocahontas	D. Wright	14-day	29.50	45.00
90-55-003	Minnehaha	D. Wright	14-day	29.50	33.00
90-55-004	Pine Leaf	D. Wright	14-day	29.50	45.00
90-55-005	Lily of the Mohawk	D. Wright	14-day	29.50	36.00
90-55-006	White Rose	D. Wright	14-day	29.50	36.00
91-55-007	Lozen	D. Wright	14-day	29.50	33.00
91-55-008	Falling Star	D. Wright	14-day	29.50	45.00
Hamilton Collection		**Little Ladies**			
89-56-001	Playing Bridesmaid	M.H. Bogart	14-day	29.50	60-80.00
90-56-002	The Seamstress	M.H. Bogart	14-day	29.50	60-80.00
90-56-003	Little Captive	M.H. Bogart	14-day	29.50	45-60.00
90-56-004	Playing Mama	M.H. Bogart	14-day	29.50	54-72.00
90-56-005	Susanna	M.H. Bogart	14-day	29.50	60-80.00
90-56-006	Kitty's Bath	M.H. Bogart	14-day	29.50	54-72.00
90-56-007	A Day in the Country	M.H. Bogart	14-day	29.50	60-80.00
91-56-008	Sarah	M.H. Bogart	14-day	29.50	60-80.00
Hamilton Collection		**A Country Season of Horses**			
90-57-001	First Day of Spring	J.M. Vass	14-day	29.50	36.00
90-57-002	Summer Splendor	J.M. Vass	14-day	29.50	33.00
90-57-003	A Winter's Walk	J.M. Vass	14-day	29.50	33.00
90-57-004	Autumn Grandeur	J.M. Vass	14-day	29.50	29.50
90-57-005	Cliffside Beauty	J.M. Vass	14-day	29.50	29.50
90-57-006	Frosty Morning	J.M. Vass	14-day	29.50	29.50
90-57-007	Crisp Country Morning	J.M. Vass	14-day	29.50	29.50
90-57-008	River Retreat	J.M. Vass	14-day	29.50	29.50
Hamilton Collection		**Good Sports**			
90-58-001	Wide Retriever	J. Lamb	14-day	29.50	29.50
90-58-002	Double Play	J. Lamb	14-day	29.50	29.50
90-58-003	Hole in One	J. Lamb	14-day	29.50	29.50
90-58-004	The Bass Masters	J. Lamb	14-day	29.50	29.50
90-58-005	Spotted on the Sideline	J. Lamb	14-day	29.50	29.50
90-58-006	Slap Shot	J. Lamb	14-day	29.50	29.50
91-58-007	Net Play	J. Lamb	14-day	29.50	29.50
91-58-008	Bassetball	J. Lamb	14-day	29.50	29.50
Hamilton Collection		**Curious Kittens**			
90-59-001	Rainy Day Friends	B. Harrison	14-day	29.50	29.50-35.00
90-59-002	Keeping in Step	B. Harrison	14-day	29.50	36.00
91-59-003	Delightful Discovery	B. Harrison	14-day	29.50	36.00
91-59-004	Chance Meeting	B. Harrison	14-day	29.50	36.00
91-59-005	All Wound Up	B. Harrison	14-day	29.50	29.50
91-59-006	Making Tracks	B. Harrison	14-day	29.50	29.50
91-59-007	Playing Cat and Mouse	B. Harrison	14-day	29.50	36.00
91-59-008	A Paw's in the Action	B. Harrison	14-day	29.50	29.50
Hamilton Collection		**The American Civil War**			
90-60-001	General Robert E. Lee	D. Prechtel	14-day	37.50	48.00
90-60-002	Generals Grant and Lee At Appomattox	D. Prechtel	14-day	37.50	48.00
90-60-003	General Thomas "Stonewall" Jackson	D. Prechtel	14-day	37.50	37.50
90-60-004	Abraham Lincoln	D. Prechtel	14-day	37.50	45.00
91-60-005	General J.E.B. Stuart	D. Prechtel	14-day	37.50	45.00
91-60-006	General Philip Sheridan	D. Prechtel	14-day	37.50	45.00
91-60-007	A Letter from Home	D. Prechtel	14-day	37.50	45.00
91-60-008	Going Home	D. Prechtel	14-day	37.50	37.50
Hamilton Collection		**Growing Up Together**			
90-61-001	My Very Best Friends	P. Brooks	14-day	29.50	36.00
90-61-002	Tea for Two	P. Brooks	14-day	29.50	29.50
90-61-003	Tender Loving Care	P. Brooks	14-day	29.50	29.50
90-61-004	Picnic Pals	P. Brooks	14-day	29.50	29.50
91-61-005	Newfound Friends	P. Brooks	14-day	29.50	29.50
91-61-006	Kitten Caboodle	P. Brooks	14-day	29.50	29.50
91-61-007	Fishing Buddies	P. Brooks	14-day	29.50	29.50
91-61-008	Bedtime Blessings	P. Brooks	14-day	29.50	29.50
Hamilton Collection		**Classic TV Westerns**			
90-62-001	The Lone Ranger and Tonto	K. Milnazik	14-day	29.50	33-45.00
90-62-002	Bonanza ™	K. Milnazik	14-day	29.50	36-40.00
90-62-003	Roy Rogers and Dale Evans	K. Milnazik	14-day	29.50	45-60.00
91-62-004	Rawhide	K. Milnazik	14-day	29.50	33-45.00
91-62-005	Wild Wild West	K. Milnazik	14-day	29.50	45-60.00
91-62-006	Have Gun, Will Travel	K. Milnazik	14-day	29.50	33-45.00
91-62-007	The Virginian	K. Milnazik	14-day	29.50	29.50
91-62-008	Hopalong Cassidy	K. Milnazik	14-day	29.50	60-80.00
Hamilton Collection		**Timeless Expressions of the Orient**			
90-63-001	Fidelity	M. Tsang	15,000	75.00	95.00
91-63-002	Femininity	M. Tsang	15,000	75.00	75.00
91-63-003	Longevity	M. Tsang	15,000	75.00	75.00
91-63-004	Beauty	M. Tsang	15,000	55.00	55.00
92-63-005	Courage	M. Tsang	15,000	55.00	55.00
Hamilton Collection		**Star Wars 10th Anniversary Commemorative**			
90-64-001	Star Wars 10th Anniversary Commemorative Plates	T. Blackshear	14-day	39.50	60-90.00
Hamilton Collection		**Romantic Castles of Europe**			
90-65-001	Ludwig's Castle	D. Sweet	19,500	55.00	55.00
91-65-002	Palace of the Moors	D. Sweet	19,500	55.00	55.00
91-65-003	Swiss Isle Fortress	D. Sweet	19,500	55.00	55.00
91-65-004	The Legendary Castle of Leeds	D. Sweet	19,500	55.00	55.00
91-65-005	Davinci's Chambord	D. Sweet	19,500	55.00	55.00
91-65-006	Eilean Donan	D. Sweet	19,500	55.00	55.00
92-65-007	Eltz Castle	D. Sweet	19,500	55.00	55.00
92-65-008	Kylemore Abbey	D. Sweet	19,500	55.00	55.00
Hamilton Collection		**The American Rose Garden**			
88-66-001	American Spirit	P.J. Sweany	14-day	29.50	29.50
88-66-002	Peace Rose	P.J. Sweany	14-day	29.50	29.50
89-66-003	White Knight	P.J. Sweany	14-day	29.50	36.00
89-66-004	American Heritage	P.J. Sweany	14-day	29.50	36.00
89-66-005	Eclipse	P.J. Sweany	14-day	29.50	33.00
89-66-006	Blue Moon	P.J. Sweany	14-day	29.50	36.00
89-66-007	Coral Cluster	P.J. Sweany	14-day	29.50	33.00
89-66-008	President Herbert Hoover	P.J. Sweany	14-day	29.50	29.50
Hamilton Collection		**English Country Cottages**			
90-67-001	Periwinkle Tea Room	M. Bell	14-day	29.50	29.50
91-67-002	Gamekeeper's Cottage	M. Bell	14-day	29.50	45.00
91-67-003	Ginger Cottage	M. Bell	14-day	29.50	45.00
91-67-004	Larkspur Cottage	M. Bell	14-day	29.50	29.50
91-67-005	The Chaplain's Garden	M. Bell	14-day	29.50	29.50
91-67-006	Lorna Doone Cottage	M. Bell	14-day	29.50	29.50
91-67-007	Murrle Cottage	M. Bell	14-day	29.50	29.50
91-67-008	Lullabye Cottage	M. Bell	14-day	29.50	29.50
Hamilton Collection		**The Angler's Prize**			
91-68-001	Trophy Bass	M. Susinno	14-day	29.50	36.00
91-68-002	Blue Ribbon Trout	M. Susinno	14-day	29.50	29.50
91-68-003	Sun Dancers	M. Susinno	14-day	29.50	29.50
91-68-004	Freshwater Barracuda	M. Susinno	14-day	29.50	36.00
91-68-005	Bronzeback Fighter	M. Susinno	14-day	29.50	36.00
91-68-006	Autumn Beauty	M. Susinno	14-day	29.50	36.00
92-68-007	Old Mooneyes	M. Susinno	14-day	29.50	29.50
92-68-008	Silver King	M. Susinno	14-day	29.50	29.50
Hamilton Collection		**Woodland Encounters**			
91-69-001	Want to Play?	G. Giordano	14-day	29.50	29.50
91-69-002	Peek-a-boo!	G. Giordano	14-day	29.50	29.50
91-69-003	Lunchtime Visitor	G. Giordano	14-day	29.50	29.50
91-69-004	Anyone for a Swim?	G. Giordano	14-day	29.50	29.50
91-69-005	Nature Scouts	G. Giordano	14-day	29.50	29.50
91-69-006	Meadow Meeting	G. Giordano	14-day	29.50	29.50
91-69-007	Hi Neighbor	G. Giordano	14-day	29.50	29.50
92-69-008	Field Day	G. Giordano	14-day	29.50	29.50
Hamilton Collection		**Childhood Reflections**			
91-70-001	Harmony	B.P. Gutmann	14-day	29.50	29.50
91-70-002	Kitty's Breakfast	B.P. Gutmann	14-day	29.50	29.50
91-70-003	Friendly Enemies	B.P. Gutmann	14-day	29.50	29.50
91-70-004	Smile, Smile, Smile	B.P. Gutmann	14-day	29.50	29.50
91-70-005	Lullaby	B.P. Gutmann	14-day	29.50	29.50
91-70-006	Oh! Oh! A Bunny	B.P. Gutmann	14-day	29.50	29.50
91-70-007	Little Mother	B.P. Gutmann	14-day	29.50	29.50
91-70-008	Thank You, God	B.P. Gutmann	14-day	29.50	29.50
Hamilton Collection		**Great Mammals of the Sea**			
91-71-001	Orca Trio	Wyland	14-day	35.00	35.00

Company / Number	Name	Series / Artist	Edition Limit	Issue Price	Quote
91-71-002	Hawaii Dolphins	Wyland	14-day	35.00	35.00
91-71-003	Orca Journey	Wyland	14-day	35.00	35.00
91-71-004	Dolphin Paradise	Wyland	14-day	35.00	35.00
91-71-005	Children of the Sea	Wyland	14-day	35.00	35.00
91-71-006	Kissing Dolphins	Wyland	14-day	35.00	35.00
91-71-007	Islands	Wyland	14-day	35.00	35.00
91-71-008	Orcas	Wyland	14-day	35.00	35.00
Hamilton Collection		**The West of Frank McCarthy**			
91-72-001	Attacking the Iron Horse	F. McCarthy	14-day	37.50	37.50
91-72-002	Attempt on the Stage	F. McCarthy	14-day	37.50	37.50
91-72-003	The Prayer	F. McCarthy	14-day	37.50	37.50
91-72-004	On the Old North Trail	F. McCarthy	14-day	37.50	37.50
91-72-005	The Hostile Threat	F. McCarthy	14-day	37.50	37.50
91-72-006	Bringing Out the Furs	F. McCarthy	14-day	37.50	37.50
91-72-007	Kiowa Raider	F. McCarthy	14-day	37.50	37.50
91-72-008	Headed North	F. McCarthy	14-day	37.50	37.50
Hamilton Collection		**The Quilted Countryside: A Signature Collection by Mel Steele**			
91-73-001	The Old Country Store	M. Steele	14-day	29.50	36.00
91-73-002	Winter's End	M. Steele	14-day	29.50	29.50
91-73-003	The Quilter's Cabin	M. Steele	14-day	29.50	33.00
91-73-004	Spring Cleaning	M. Steele	14-day	29.50	29.50
91-73-005	Summer Harvest	M. Steele	14-day	29.50	29.50
91-73-006	The Country Merchant	M. Steele	14-day	29.50	29.50
92-73-007	Wash Day	M. Steele	14-day	29.50	29.50
92-73-008	The Antiques Store	M. Steele	14-day	29.50	29.50
Hamilton Collection		**Sporting Generation**			
91-74-001	Like Father, Like Son	J. Lamb	14-day	29.50	29.50
91-74-002	Golden Moments	J. Lamb	14-day	29.50	29.50
91-74-003	The Lookout	J. Lamb	14-day	29.50	29.50
91-74-004	Picking Up The Scent	J. Lamb	14-day	29.50	29.50
Hamilton Collection		**Seasons of the Bald Eagle**			
91-75-001	Autumn in the Mountains	J. Pitcher	14-day	37.50	37.50
91-75-002	Winter in the Valley	J. Pitcher	14-day	37.50	37.50
91-75-003	Spring on the River	J. Pitcher	14-day	37.50	37.50
91-75-004	Summer on the Seacoast	J. Pitcher	14-day	37.50	37.50
Hamilton Collection		**The STAR TREK 25th Anniversary Commemorative Collection**			
91-76-001	SPOCK	T. Blackshear	14-day	35.00	75.00
91-76-002	Kirk	T. Blackshear	14-day	35.00	35.00
92-76-003	McCoy	T. Blackshear	14-day	35.00	35.00
92-76-004	Uhura	T. Blackshear	14-day	35.00	35.00
92-76-005	Scotty	T. Blackshear	14-day	35.00	35.00
Hamilton Collection		**STAR TREK 25th Anniversary Commemorative Plate**			
91-77-001	STAR TREK 25th Anniversary Commemorative Plate	T. Blackshear	14-day	37.50	75.00
Hamilton Collection		**Vanishing Rural America**			
91-78-001	Quiet Reflections	J. Harrison	14-day	29.50	45.00
91-78-002	Autumn's Passage	J. Harrison	14-day	29.50	45.00
91-78-003	Storefront Memories	J. Harrison	14-day	29.50	45.00
91-78-004	Country Path	J. Harrison	14-day	29.50	36.00
91-78-005	When the Circus Came To Town	J. Harrison	14-day	29.50	36.00
91-78-006	Covered in Fall	J. Harrison	14-day	29.50	45.00
91-78-007	America's Heartland	J. Harrison	14-day	29.50	29.50
91-78-008	Rural Delivery	J. Harrison	14-day	29.50	29.50
Hamilton Collection		**North American Ducks**			
91-79-001	Autumn Flight	R. Lawrence	14-day	29.50	29.50
91-79-002	The Resting Place	R. Lawrence	14-day	29.50	29.50
91-79-003	Twin Flight	R. Lawrence	14-day	29.50	29.50
92-79-004	Misty Morning	R. Lawrence	14-day	29.50	29.50
92-79-005	Springtime Thaw	R. Lawrence	14-day	29.50	29.50
92-79-006	Summer Retreat	R. Lawrence	14-day	29.50	29.50
92-79-007	Overcast	R. Lawrence	14-day	29.50	29.50
92-79-008	Perfect Pintails	R. Lawrence	14-day	29.50	29.50
Hamilton Collection		**Proud Indian Families**			
91-80-001	The Storyteller	K. Freeman	14-day	29.50	29.50
91-80-002	The Power of the Basket	K. Freeman	14-day	29.50	29.50
91-80-003	The Naming Ceremony	K. Freeman	14-day	29.50	29.50
92-80-004	Playing With Tradition	K. Freeman	14-day	29.50	29.50
92-80-005	Preparing the Berry Harvest	K. Freeman	14-day	29.50	29.50
92-80-006	Ceremonial Dress	K. Freeman	14-day	29.50	29.50
92-80-007	Sounds of the Forest	K. Freeman	14-day	29.50	29.50
92-80-008	The Marriage Ceremony	K. Freeman	14-day	29.50	29.50
Hamilton Collection		**Little Shopkeepers**			
90-81-001	Sew Tired	G. Gerardi	14-day	29.50	29.50
91-81-002	Break Time	G. Gerardi	14-day	29.50	29.50
91-81-003	Purrfect Fit	G. Gerardi	14-day	29.50	29.50
91-81-004	Toying Around	G. Gerardi	14-day	29.50	36.00
91-81-005	Chain Reaction	G. Gerardi	14-day	29.50	45.00
91-81-006	Inferior Decorators	G. Gerardi	14-day	29.50	36.00
91-81-007	Tulip Tag	G. Gerardi	14-day	29.50	36.00
91-81-008	Candy Capers	G. Gerardi	14-day	29.50	36.00
Hamilton Collection		**Great Fighter Planes Of World War II**			
92-82-001	Old Crow	R. Waddey	14-day	29.50	29.50
92-82-002	Big Hog	R. Waddey	14-day	29.50	29.50
92-82-003	P-47 Thunderbolt	R. Waddey	14-day	29.50	29.50
92-82-004	P-40 Flying Tiger	R. Waddey	14-day	29.50	29.50
92-82-005	F4F Wildcat	R. Waddey	14-day	29.50	29.50
92-82-006	P-38 Lockhead Lightning	R. Waddey	14-day	29.50	29.50
Hamilton Collection		**Our Cherished Seas**			
92-83-001	Whale Song	S. Barlowe	48-day	37.50	37.50
92-83-002	Lions of the Sea	S. Barlowe	48-day	37.50	37.50
92-83-003	Flight of the Dolphins	S. Barlowe	48-day	37.50	37.50
92-83-004	Palace of the Seals	S. Barlowe	48-day	37.50	37.50
Hamilton Collection		**Republic Pictures Film Library Collection**			
92-84-001	Show With Laredo	S. Morton	28-day	37.50	37.50
92-84-002	The Ride Home	S. Morton	28-day	37.50	37.50
92-84-003	Attack at Tarawa	S. Morton	28-day	37.50	37.50
92-84-004	Thoughts of Angelique	S. Morton	28-day	37.50	37.50
92-84-005	War of the Wildcats	S. Morton	28-day	37.50	37.50
Hamilton Collection		**Unbridled Spirit**			
92-85-001	Surf Dancer	C. DeHaan	28-day	29.50	29.50
92-85-002	Winter Renegade	C. DeHaan	28-day	29.50	29.50
92-85-003	Desert Shadows	C. DeHaan	28-day	29.50	29.50
Hamilton Collection		**Victorian Playtime**			
91-86-001	A Busy Day	M. H. Bogart	14-day	29.50	29.50
92-86-002	Little Masterpiece	M. H. Bogart	14-day	29.50	29.50
92-86-003	Playing Bride	M. H. Bogart	14-day	29.50	29.50
92-86-004	Waiting for a Nibble	M. H. Bogart	14-day	29.50	29.50
92-86-005	Tea and Gossip	M. H. Bogart	14-day	29.50	29.50
92-86-006	Cleaning House	M. H. Bogart	14-day	29.50	29.50
92-86-007	A Little Persuasion	M. H. Bogart	14-day	29.50	29.50
92-86-008	Peek-a-Boo	M. H. Bogart	14-day	29.50	29.50
Hamilton Collection		**Winter Rails**			
92-87-001	Winter Crossing	T. Xaras	28-day	29.50	29.50
Hamilton Collection		**Farmyard Friends**			
92-88-001	Mistaken Identity	J. Lamb	28-day	29.50	29.50
92-88-002	Little Cowhands	J. Lamb	28-day	29.50	29.50
92-88-003	Shreading the Evidence	J. Lamb	28-day	29.50	29.50
Hamilton Collection		**Man's Best Friend**			
92-89-001	Special Delivery	L. Picken	28-day	29.50	29.50
92-89-002	Making Waves	L. Picken	28-day	29.50	29.50
92-89-003	Good Catch	L. Picken	28-day	29.50	29.50
Hamilton Collection		**Nature's Nightime Realm**			
92-90-001	Bobcat	G. Murray	28-day	29.50	29.50
92-90-002	Cougar	G. Murray	28-day	29.50	29.50
92-90-003	Jaguar	G. Murray	28-day	29.50	29.50
Hamilton Collection		**Precious Moments Of Christmas**			
91-91-001	Come Let Us Adore Him	S. Butcher	28-day	29.50	29.50
92-91-002	They Followed The Star	S. Butcher	28-day	29.50	29.50
92-91-003	The Flight Into Egypt	S. Butcher	28-day	29.50	29.50
92-91-004	The Carpenter Shop	S. Butcher	28-day	29.50	29.50
92-91-005	Jesus In The Temple	S. Butcher	28-day	29.50	29.50
92-91-006	The Crucifixion	S. Butcher	28-day	29.50	29.50
92-91-007	He Is Not Here	S. Butcher	28-day	29.50	29.50
Hamilton Collection		**The Wonder Of Christmas**			
91-92-001	Santa's Secret	J. McClelland	28-day	29.50	29.50
92-92-002	My Favorite Ornament	J. McClelland	28-day	29.50	29.50
92-92-003	Waiting For Santa	J. McClelland	28-day	29.50	29.50
Hamilton Collection		**Romantic Victorian Keepsake**			
92-93-001	Dearest Kiss	J. Grossman	28-day	35.00	35.00
Hamilton Collection		**The World Of Zolan**			
92-94-001	First Kiss	D. Zolan	28-day	29.50	29.50
92-94-002	Morning Discovery	D. Zolan	28-day	29.50	29.50
Hamilton Collection		**Mystic Warriors**			
92-95-001	Deliverance	C. Ren	28-day	29.50	29.50
92-95-002	Mystic Warrior	C. Ren	28-day	29.50	29.50
92-95-003	Sun Seeker	C. Ren	28-day	29.50	29.50
92-95-004	Top Gun	C. Ren	28-day	29.50	29.50
92-95-005	Man Who Walks Alone	C. Ren	28-day	29.50	29.50
Hamilton Collection		**Andy Griffith**			
92-96-001	Sheriff Andy Taylor	R. Tannenbaum	28-day	29.50	29.50
92-96-002	A Startling Conclusion	R. Tannenbaum	28-day	29.50	29.50
Hamilton Collection		**Madonna And Child**			
92-97-001	Madonna Della Seida	R. Sanzio	28-day	37.50	37.50
92-97-002	Virgin of the Rocks	L. DaVinci	28-day	37.50	37.50
Hamilton Collection		**Council Of Nations**			
91-98-001	Strength of the Sioux	G. Perillo	28-day	29.50	29.50
92-98-002	Pride of the Cheyenne	G. Perillo	28-day	29.50	29.50
92-98-003	Dignity of the Nez Parce	G. Perillo	28-day	29.50	29.50
92-98-004	Courage of the Arapaho	G. Perillo	28-day	29.50	29.50
92-98-005	Power of the Blackfoot	G. Perillo	28-day	29.50	29.50
92-98-006	Nobility of the Algonqui	G. Perillo	28-day	29.50	29.50
92-98-007	Wisdom of the Cherokee	G. Perillo	28-day	29.50	29.50
Hamilton Collection		**Beauty Of Winter**			
92-99-001	Silent Night	N/A	28-day	29.50	29.50
Hamilton Collection		**Bialosky Bears**			
92-100-001	Family Addition	P./A.Bialosky	28-day	29.50	29.50
Hamilton Collection		**Country Garden Cottages**			
92-101-001	Riverbank Cottage	E. Dartner	28-day	29.50	29.50
92-101-002	Sunday Outing	E. Dartner	28-day	29.50	29.50
Hamilton Collection		**Quiet Moments Of Childhood**			
91-102-001	Elizabeth's Afternoon Tea	D. Green	14-day	29.50	29.50
91-102-002	Christina's Secret Garden	D. Green	14-day	29.50	29.50
91-102-003	Eric & Erin's Storytime	D. Green	14-day	29.50	29.50
92-102-004	Jessica's Tea Party	D. Green	14-day	29.50	29.50
92-102-005	Megan & Monique's Bakery	D. Green	14-day	29.50	29.50
92-102-006	Children's Day By The Sea	D. Green	14-day	29.50	29.50
92-102-007	Jordan's Playful Pups	D. Green	14-day	29.50	29.50
92-102-008	Daniel's Morning Playtime	D. Green	14-day	29.50	29.50
Haviland		**Twelve Days of Christmas**			
70-01-001	Partridge	R. Hetreau	30,000	25.00	54.00
71-01-002	Two Turtle Doves	R. Hetreau	30,000	25.00	25.00
72-01-003	Three French Hens	R. Hetreau	30,000	27.50	27.50
73-01-004	Four Calling Birds	R. Hetreau	30,000	28.50	30.00
74-01-005	Five Golden Rings	R. Hetreau	30,000	30.00	30.00
75-01-006	Six Geese a'laying	R. Hetreau	30,000	32.50	32.50
76-01-007	Seven Swans	R. Hetreau	30,000	38.00	38.00
77-01-008	Eight Maids	R. Hetreau	30,000	40.00	40.00
78-01-009	Nine Ladies Dancing	R. Hetreau	30,000	45.00	67.00
79-01-010	Ten Lord's a'leaping	R. Hetreau	30,000	50.00	50.00
80-01-011	Eleven Pipers Piping	R. Hetreau	30,000	55.00	65.00
81-01-012	Twelve Drummers	R. Hetreau	30,000	60.00	60.00

Company / Number	Name	Series / Artist	Edition Limit	Issue Price	Quote
Haviland & Parlon		**Tapestry I**			
71-01-001	Unicorn in Captivity	Unknown	10,000	35.00	63.00
72-01-002	Start of the Hunt	Unknown	10,000	35.00	50.00
73-01-003	Chase of the Unicorn	Unknown	10,000	35.00	76.00
74-01-004	End of the Hunt	Unknown	10,000	37.50	69.00
75-01-005	Unicorn Surrounded	Unknown	10,000	40.00	70.00
76-01-006	Brought to the Castle	Unknown	10,000	42.50	65.00
Haviland & Parlon		**The Lady and the Unicorn**			
77-02-001	To My Only Desire	Unknown	20,000	45.00	45.00
78-02-002	Sight	Unknown	20,000	45.00	45.00
79-02-003	Sound	Unknown	20,000	47.50	47.50
80-02-004	Touch	Unknown	15,000	52.50	100.00
81-02-005	Scent	Unknown	10,000	59.00	59.00
82-02-006	Taste	Unknown	10,000	59.00	59.00
Haviland & Parlon		**Christmas Madonnas**			
72-03-001	By Raphael	Raphael	5,000	35.00	42.00
73-03-002	By Feruzzi	Feruzzi	5,000	40.00	78.00
74-03-003	By Raphael	Raphael	5,000	42.50	42.50
75-03-004	By Murillo	Murillo	7,500	42.50	42.50
76-03-005	By Botticelli	Botticelli	7,500	45.00	45.00
77-03-006	By Bellini	Bellini	7,500	48.00	48.00
78-03-007	By Lippi	Lippi	7,500	48.00	53.00
79-03-008	Madonna of The Eucharist	Botticelli	7,500	49.50	112.00
Edna Hibel Studios		**Arte Ovale**			
80-01-001	Takara, Gold	E. Hibel	300	1000.00	2500.00
80-01-002	Takara, Blanco	E. Hibel	700	450.00	1100.00
80-01-003	Takara, Cobalt Blue	E. Hibel	1,000	595.00	2000.00
84-01-004	Taro-kun, Gold	E. Hibel	300	1000.00	2500.00
84-01-005	Taro-kun, Blanco	E. Hibel	700	450.00	750.00
84-01-006	Taro-kun, Cobalt Blue	E. Hibel	1,000	595.00	975.00
Edna Hibel Studios		**The World I Love**			
81-02-001	Leah's Family	E. Hibel	17,500	85.00	157.00
82-02-002	Kaylin	E. Hibel	17,500	85.00	200.00
83-02-003	Edna's Music	E. Hibel	17,500	85.00	165.00
83-02-004	O, Hana	E. Hibel	17,500	85.00	165.00
Edna Hibel Studios		**March of Dimes: Our Children, Our Future**			
90-03-001	A Time To Embrace	E. Hibel	150-days	29.00	29.00
John Hine N.A. Ltd.		**David Winter Plate Collection**			
91-01-001	A Christmas Carol	John Hine Studio	10,000	30.00	30.00
91-01-002	Cotswold Village Plate	John Hine Studio	10,000	30.00	30.00
92-01-003	Chichester Cross Plate	M. Fisher	10,000	30.00	30.00
92-01-004	Little Mill Plate	M. Fisher	10,000	30.00	30.00
92-01-005	Old Curiosity Shop	John Hine Studio	10,000	30.00	30.00
92-01-006	Scrooge's Counting House	John Hine Studio	10,000	30.00	30.00
Hutschenreuther		**Gunther Granget**			
72-01-001	American Sparrows	G. Granget	5,000	50.00	150.00
72-01-002	European Sparrows	G. Granget	5,000	30.00	65.00
73-01-003	American Kildeer	G. Granget	2,250	75.00	90.00
73-01-004	American Squirrel	G. Granget	2,500	75.00	75.00
73-01-005	European Squirrel	G. Granget	2,500	35.00	50.00
74-01-006	American Partridge	G. Granget	2,500	75.00	90.00
75-01-007	American Rabbits	G. Granget	2,500	90.00	90.00
76-01-008	Freedom in Flight	G. Granget	5,000	100.00	100.00
76-01-009	Wrens	G. Granget	2,500	100.00	110.00
76-01-010	Freedom in Flight, Gold	G. Granget	200	200.00	200.00
77-01-011	Bears	G. Granget	2,500	100.00	100.00
78-01-012	Foxes' Spring Journey	G. Granget	1,000	125.00	200.00
Hutschenreuther		**The Glory of Christmas**			
82-02-001	The Nativity	W./C. Hallett	25,000	80.00	125.00
83-02-002	The Annunciation	W./C. Hallett	25,000	80.00	115.00
84-02-003	The Shepherds	W./C. Hallett	25,000	80.00	100.00
85-02-004	The Wiseman	W./C. Hallett	25,000	80.00	100.00
Imperial Ching-te Chen		**Beauties of the Red Mansion**			
86-01-001	Pao-chai	Z. HuiMin	115-day	27.92	40.00
86-01-002	Yuan-chun	Z. HuiMin	115-day	27.92	40.00
87-01-003	Hsi-feng	Z. HuiMin	115-day	30.92	40.00
87-01-004	Hsi-chun	Z. HuiMin	115-day	30.92	35.00
88-01-005	Miao-yu	Z. HuiMin	115-day	30.92	35.00
88-01-006	Ying-chun	Z. HuiMin	115-day	30.92	40.00
88-01-007	Tai-yu	Z. HuiMin	115-day	32.92	40.00
88-01-008	Li-wan	Z. HuiMin	115-day	32.92	35.00
88-01-009	Ko-Ching	Z. HuiMin	115-day	32.92	45.00
88-01-010	Hsiang-yun	Z. HuiMin	115-day	34.92	34.92
89-01-011	Tan-Chun	Z. HuiMin	115-day	34.92	39.00
89-01-012	Chiao-chieh	Z. HuiMin	115-day	34.92	34.92
Imperial Ching-te Chen		**Scenes from the Summer Palace**			
88-02-001	The Marble Boat	Z. Song Mao	175-day	29.92	35.00
88-02-002	Jade Belt Bridge	Z. Song Mao	175-day	29.92	30.00
89-02-003	Hall that Dispels the Clouds	Z. Song Mao	175-day	32.92	32.92
89-02-004	The Long Promenade	Z. Song Mao	175-day	32.92	32.92
89-02-005	Garden/Harmonious Pleasure	Z. Song Mao	175-day	32.92	32.92
89-02-006	The Great Stage	Z. Song Mao	175-day	32.92	32.92
89-02-007	Seventeen Arch Bridge	Z. Song Mao	175-day	34.92	34.92
89-02-008	Boaters on Kumming Lake	Z. Song Mao	175-day	34.92	34.92
Imperial Ching-te Chen		**Blessings From a Chinese Garden**			
88-03-001	The Gift of Purity	Z. Song Mao	175-day	39.92	35.00
89-03-002	The Gift of Grace	Z. Song Mao	175-day	39.92	43.00
89-03-003	The Gift of Beauty	Z. Song Mao	175-day	42.92	49.00
89-03-004	The Gift of Happiness	Z. Song Mao	175-day	42.92	44.00
90-03-005	The Gift of Truth	Z. Song Mao	175-day	42.92	42.92
90-03-006	The Gift of Joy	Z. Song Mao	175-day	42.92	42.92
Imperial Ching-te Chen		**Legends of West Lake**			
89-04-001	Lady White	J. Xue-Bing	175-day	29.92	44.00
90-04-002	Lady Silkworm	J. Xue-Bing	175-day	29.92	41.00
90-04-003	Laurel Peak	J. Xue-Bing	175-day	29.92	33.00
90-04-004	Rising Sun Terrace	J. Xue-Bing	175-day	32.92	32.92
90-04-005	The Apricot Fairy	J. Xue-Bing	175-day	32.92	32.92
90-04-006	Bright Pearl	J. Xue-Bing	175-day	32.92	32.92
90-04-007	Thread of Sky	J. Xue-Bing	175-day	34.92	34.92
91-04-008	Phoenix Mountain	J. Xue-Bing	175-day	34.92	34.92
91-04-009	Ancestors of Tea	J. Xue-Bing	175-day	34.92	34.92

Company / Number	Name	Series / Artist	Edition Limit	Issue Price	Quote
91-04-010	Three Pools Mirroring/Moon	J. Xue-Bing	175-day	36.92	36.92
91-04-011	Fly-In Peak	J. Xue-Bing	175-day	36.92	36.92
91-04-012	The Case of the Folding Fans	J. Xue-Bing	175-day	36.92	36.92
Imperial Ching-te Chen		**Flower Goddesses of China**			
91-05-001	The Lotus Goddess	Z. HuiMin	175-day	34.92	34.92
91-05-002	The Chrysanthemum Goddess	Z. HuiMin	175-day	34.92	34.92
91-05-003	The Plum Blossom Goddess	Z. HuiMin	175-day	37.92	37.92
91-05-004	The Peony Goddess	Z. HuiMin	175-day	37.92	37.92
91-05-005	The Narcissus Goddess	Z. HuiMin	175-day	37.92	37.92
91-05-006	The Camellia Goddess	Z. HuiMin	175-day	37.92	37.92
Imperial Ching-te Chen		**The Forbidden City**			
90-06-001	Pavilion of 10,000 Springs	S. Fu	150-day	39.92	39.92
90-06-002	Flying Kites/Spring Day	S. Fu	150-day	39.92	39.92
90-06-003	Pavilion/Floating Jade Green	S. Fu	150-day	42.92	42.92
91-06-004	The Lantern Festival	S. Fu	150-day	42.92	42.92
91-06-005	Nine Dragon Screen	S. Fu	150-day	42.92	42.92
91-06-006	The Hall of the Cultivating Mind	S. Fu	150-day	42.92	42.92
91-06-007	Dressing the Empress	S. Fu	150-day	45.92	45.92
91-06-008	Pavilion of Floating Cups	S. Fu	150-day	45.92	45.92
International Silver		**Bicentennial**			
72-01-001	Signing Declaration	M. Deoliveira	7,500	40.00	310.00
73-01-002	Paul Revere	M. Deoliveira	7,500	40.00	160.00
74-01-003	Concord Bridge	M. Deoliveira	7,500	40.00	115.00
75-01-004	Crossing Delaware	M. Deoliveira	7,500	50.00	80.00
76-01-005	Valley Forge	M. Deoliveira	7,500	50.00	65.00
77-01-006	Surrender at Yorktown	M. Deoliveira	7,500	50.00	60.00
Svend Jensen		**Christmas**			
70-01-001	H. C. Anderson House	G. Sausmark	Annual	14.50	40.00
71-01-002	Little Match Girl	M. Stage	Annual	15.00	38.00
72-01-003	Mermaid of Copenhagen	E. Eriksen	Annual	16.50	40.00
73-01-004	The Fir Tree	S. Otto	Annual	22.00	25.00
74-01-005	The Chimney Sweep	S. Otto	Annual	25.00	25.00
75-01-006	The Ugly Duckling	S. Otto	Annual	27.50	27.50
76-01-007	The Snow Queen	M. Stage	Annual	27.50	27.50
77-01-008	Snowman	S. Otto	Annual	29.50	29.50
78-01-009	Last Dream of the Old Oak Tree	S. Otto	Annual	32.00	34.00
79-01-010	The Old Street Lamp	S. Otto	Annual	36.50	36.50
80-01-011	Willie Winkie	S. Otto	Annual	42.50	42.50
81-01-012	Uttermost Parts Of the Sea	S. Otto	Annual	49.50	49.50
82-01-013	Twelve by the Mailcoach	S. Otto	Annual	54.50	54.50
83-01-014	The Story of the Year	S. Otto	Annual	54.50	54.50
84-01-015	The Nightingale	S. Otto	Annual	54.50	54.50
85-01-016	Kronberg Castle	S. Otto	Annual	60.00	60.00
86-01-017	The Bell	S. Otto	Annual	60.00	77.00
87-01-018	Thumbelina	S. Otto	Annual	60.00	60.00
88-01-019	The Bell Deep	S. Otto	Annual	60.00	60.00
89-01-020	The Old House	S. Otto	Annual	60.00	60.00
90-01-021	Grandfather's Picturebook	S. Otto	Annual	64.50	72.00
91-01-022	The Windmill	S. Otto	Annual	64.50	70.00
Svend Jensen		**Mother's Day**			
70-02-001	Bouquet for Mother	Unknown	Unkn.	14.50	75.00
71-02-002	Mother's Love	Unknown	Unkn.	15.00	40.00
72-02-003	Good Night	Unknown	Unkn.	16.50	35.00
73-02-004	Flowers for Mother	Unknown	Unkn.	20.00	35.00
74-02-005	Daisies for Mother	Unknown	Unkn.	25.00	35.00
75-02-006	Surprise for Mother	Unknown	Unkn.	27.50	27.50
76-02-007	The Complete Gardener	Unknown	Unkn.	27.50	27.50
77-02-008	Little Friends	Unknown	Unkn.	29.50	29.50
78-02-009	Dreams	Unknown	Unkn.	32.00	32.00
79-02-010	Promenade	Unknown	Unkn.	36.50	36.50
80-02-011	Nursery Scene	Unknown	Unkn.	42.50	42.50
81-02-012	Daily Duties	Unknown	Unkn.	49.50	49.50
82-02-013	My Best Friend	Unknown	Unkn.	54.50	54.50
83-02-014	An Unexpected Meeting	Unknown	Unkn.	54.50	54.50
84-02-015	Who are you?	M. Stage	Annual	54.50	54.50
86-02-016	Meeting on the Meadow	M. Stage	Annual	60.00	60.00
87-02-017	The Complete Angler	S. Otto	Annual	60.00	60.00
88-02-018	The Little Bakery	S. Otto	Annual	60.00	60.00
89-02-019	Springtime	S. Otto	Annual	60.00	64.00
90-02-020	The Spring Excursion	S. Otto	Annual	64.50	68.00
91-02-021	Walking at the Beach	S. Otto	Annual	64.50	64.50
Kaiser		**Oberammergau Passion Play**			
70-01-001	Oberammergau	T. Schoener	Closed	25.00	30.00
70-01-002	Oberammergau	K. Bauer	Closed	40.00	40.00
91-01-003	Oberammergau, sepia	Unknown	700	38.00	38.00
91-01-004	Oberammergau, cobalt	Unknown	400	64.00	64.00
Kaiser		**Christmas Plates**			
70-02-001	Waiting for Santa Claus	T. Schoener	Closed	12.50	25.00
71-02-002	Silent Night	K. Bauer	Closed	13.50	23.00
72-02-003	Welcome Home	K. Bauer	Closed	16.50	43.00
73-02-004	Holy Night	T. Schoener	Closed	18.00	44.00
74-02-005	Christmas Carolers	K. Bauer	Closed	25.00	30.00
75-02-006	Bringing Home the Tree	J. Northcott	Closed	25.00	30.00
76-02-007	Christ/Saviour Born	C. Maratti	Closed	25.00	35.00
77-02-008	The Three Kings	T. Schoener	Closed	25.00	25.00
78-02-009	Shepherds in The Field	T. Schoener	Closed	30.00	30.00
79-02-010	Christmas Eve	H. Blum	Closed	32.00	45.00
80-02-011	Joys of Winter	H. Blum	Closed	40.00	43.00
81-02-012	Adoration by Three Kings	K. Bauer	Closed	40.00	41.00
82-02-013	Bringing Home the Tree	K. Bauer	Closed	40.00	45.00
Kaiser		**Memories of Christmas**			
83-03-001	The Wonder of Christmas	G. Neubacher	Closed	42.50	42.50
84-03-002	A Christmas Dream	G. Neubacher	Closed	39.50	42.50
85-03-003	Christmas Eve	G. Neubacher	Closed	39.50	39.50
86-03-004	A Vist with Santa	G. Neubacher	Closed	39.50	39.50
Kaiser		**Mother's Day**			
71-04-001	Mare and Foal	T. Schoener	Closed	13.00	25.00
72-04-002	Flowers for Mother	T. Schoener	Closed	16.50	20.00
73-04-003	Cats	T. Schoener	Closed	17.00	40.00
74-04-004	Fox	T. Schoener	Closed	20.00	40.00
75-04-005	German Shepherd	T. Schoener	Closed	25.00	100.00
76-04-006	Swan and Cygnets	T. Schoener	Closed	25.00	27.50
77-04-007	Mother Rabbit and Young	T. Schoener	Closed	25.00	30.00
78-04-008	Hen and Chicks	T. Schoener	Closed	30.00	50.00

Company / Number	Name	Series / Artist	Edition Limit	Issue Price	Quote
79-04-009	A Mother's Devotion	N. Peterner	Closed	32.00	40.00
80-04-010	Raccoon Family	J. Northcott	Closed	40.00	45.00
81-04-011	Safe Near Mother	H. Blum	Closed	40.00	40.00
82-04-012	Pheasant Family	K. Bauer	Closed	40.00	44.00
83-04-013	Tender Care	K. Bauer	Closed	40.00	65.00
Kaiser		**Anniversary**			
72-05-001	Love Birds	T. Schoener	Closed	16.50	30.00
73-05-002	In the Park	T. Schoener	Closed	16.50	24.50
74-05-003	Canoeing	T. Schoener	Closed	20.00	30.00
75-05-004	Tender Moment	K. Bauer	Closed	25.00	27.50
76-05-005	Serenade	T. Schoener	Closed	25.00	25.00
77-05-006	Simple Gift	T. Schoener	Closed	25.00	25.00
78-05-007	Viking Toast	T. Schoener	Closed	30.00	30.00
79-05-008	Romantic Interlude	H. Blum	Closed	32.00	32.00
80-05-009	Love at Play	H. Blum	Closed	40.00	40.00
81-05-010	Rendezvous	H. Blum	Closed	40.00	40.00
82-05-011	Betrothal	K. Bauer	Closed	40.00	40.00
83-05-012	Sunday Afternoon	T. Schoener	Closed	40.00	40.00
Kaiser		**Great Yachts**			
72-06-001	Cetonia	K. Bauer	Closed	50.00	50.00
72-06-002	Westward	K. Bauer	Closed	50.00	50.00
Kaiser		**Garden and Song Birds**			
73-07-001	Cardinals	W. Gawantka	Closed	200.00	250.00
73-07-002	Titmouse	W. Gawantka	Closed	200.00	250.00
Kaiser		**King Tut**			
78-08-001	King Tut	Unknown	Closed	65.00	100.00
Kaiser		**Feathered Friends**			
78-09-001	Blue Jays	G. Loates	Closed	70.00	100.00
79-09-002	Cardinals	G. Loates	Closed	80.00	90.00
80-09-003	Waxwings	G. Loates	Closed	80.00	85.00
81-09-004	Goldfinch	G. Loates	Closed	80.00	85.00
Kaiser		**Happy Days**			
79-10-001	The Aeroplane	G. Neubacher	Closed	75.00	75.00
80-10-002	Julie	G. Neubacher	Closed	75.00	75.00
81-10-003	Winter Fun	G. Neubacher	Closed	75.00	75.00
82-10-004	The Lookout	G. Neubacher	Closed	75.00	75.00
Kaiser		**Egyptian**			
80-11-001	Nefertiti	Unknown	10,000	275.00	458.00
80-11-002	Tutankhamen	Unknown	10,000	275.00	458.00
Kaiser		**Four Seasons**			
81-12-001	Spring	I. Cenkovcan	Unkn.	50.00	64.00
81-12-002	Summer	I. Cenkovcan	Unkn.	50.00	64.00
81-12-003	Autumn	I. Cenkovcan	Unkn.	50.00	64.00
81-12-004	Winter	I. Cenkovcan	Unkn.	50.00	64.00
Kaiser		**Romantic Portraits**			
81-13-001	Lilie	G. Neubacher	Closed	200.00	210.00
82-13-002	Camelia	G. Neubacher	Closed	175.00	180.00
83-13-003	Rose	G. Neubacher	Closed	175.00	185.00
84-13-004	Daisy	G. Neubacher	Closed	175.00	180.00
Kaiser		**On The Farm**			
81-14-001	The Duck	A. Lohmann	Unkn.	50.00	108.00
82-14-002	The Rooster	A. Lohmann	Unkn.	50.00	108.00
83-14-003	The Pond	A. Lohmann	Unkn.	50.00	108.00
83-14-004	The Horses	A. Lohmann	Unkn.	50.00	108.00
XX-14-005	White Horse	A. Lohmann	Unkn.	50.00	108.00
XX-14-006	Ducks on the Pond	A. Lohmann	Unkn.	50.00	108.00
XX-14-007	Girl with Goats	A. Lohmann	Unkn.	50.00	108.00
XX-14-008	Girl Feeding Animals	A. Lohmann	Unkn.	50.00	108.00
Kaiser		**Classic Fairy Tales Collection**			
82-15-001	Frog King	G. Neubacher	Unkn.	39.50	39.50
83-15-002	Puss in Boots	G. Neubacher	Unkn.	39.50	39.50
83-15-003	Little Red Riding Hood	G. Neubacher	Unkn.	39.50	39.50
84-15-004	Hansel and Gretel	G. Neubacher	Unkn.	39.50	39.50
84-15-005	Cinderella	G. Neubacher	Unkn.	39.50	39.50
84-15-006	Sleeping Beauty	G. Neubacher	Unkn.	39.50	39.50
Kaiser		**Dance, Ballerina, Dance**			
82-16-001	First Slippers	R. Clarke	Closed	47.50	47.50
83-16-002	At the Barre	R. Clarke	Closed	47.50	47.50
XX-16-003	The Recital	R. Clarke	Closed	47.50	47.50
XX-16-004	Pirouette	R. Clarke	Closed	47.50	47.50
XX-16-005	Swan Lake	R. Clarke	Closed	47.50	47.50
XX-16-006	Opening Night	R. Clarke	Closed	47.50	47.50
Kaiser		**Children's Prayer**			
82-17-001	Now I Lay Me Down to Sleep	W. Zeuner	Closed	29.50	29.50
82-17-002	Saying Grace	W. Zeuner	Closed	29.50	29.50
Kaiser		**Famous Horses**			
83-18-001	Snow Knight	A. Lohmann	Closed	95.00	95.00
84-18-002	Northern Dancer	A. Lohmann	Closed	95.00	95.00
Kaiser		**Traditional Fairy Tales**			
83-19-001	Cinderella	D. King	Unkn.	39.50	39.50
83-19-002	Jack and the Beanstalk	D. King	Unkn.	39.50	39.50
84-19-003	Three Little Pigs	D. King	Unkn.	39.50	39.50
84-19-004	Tom Thumb	D. King	Unkn.	39.50	39.50
85-19-005	Goldilocks	D. King	Unkn.	39.50	39.50
85-19-006	Dick Wittington	D. King	Unkn.	39.50	39.50
Kaiser		**Racing for Pride and Profit**			
84-20-001	The Aging Victor	R. Horton	9,500	50.00	50.00
85-20-002	Second Goes Hungry	R. Horton	9,500	50.00	50.00
86-20-003	No Time to Boast	R. Horton	9,500	50.00	50.00
87-20-004	First Fish to Market	R. Horton	9,500	50.00	50.00
88-20-005	Gypsy Traders	R. Horton	9,500	60.00	60.00
XX-20-006	Profit or Prison	R. Horton	9,500	N/A	60.00
Kaiser		**Bird Dog Series**			
XX-21-001	Cocker Spaniel	J. Francis	19,500	39.50	49.50
XX-21-002	Beagle	J. Francis	19,500	39.50	49.50
XX-21-003	English Setter	J. Francis	19,500	39.50	49.50
XX-21-004	Black Labrador	J. Francis	19,500	39.50	49.50
XX-21-005	German Short Hair Pointer	J. Francis	19,500	39.50	49.50
XX-21-006	Golden Labrador	J. Francis	19,500	39.50	49.50
XX-21-007	English Pointer	J. Francis	19,500	39.50	49.50
XX-21-008	Irish Setter	J. Francis	19,500	39.50	49.50
Kaiser		**Childhood Memories**			
85-22-001	Wait a Little	A. Schlesinger	Closed	29.00	29.00
Kaiser		**Harmony and Nature**			
85-23-001	Spring Encore	J. Littlejohn	Closed	39.50	39.50
Kaiser		**Woodland Creatures**			
85-24-001	Springtime Frolic	R. Orr	10-day	37.50	37.50
85-24-002	Fishing Trip	R. Orr	10-day	37.50	37.50
85-24-003	Resting in the Glen	R. Orr	10-day	37.50	37.50
85-24-004	Meadowland Vigil	R. Orr	10-day	37.50	37.50
85-24-005	Morning Lesson	R. Orr	10-day	37.50	37.50
85-24-006	First Adventure	R. Orr	10-day	37.50	37.50
85-24-007	The Hiding Place	R. Orr	10-day	37.50	37.50
85-24-008	Startled Sentry	R. Orr	10-day	37.50	37.50
Kaiser		**Water Fowl**			
85-25-001	Mallard Ducks	E. Bierly	19,500	55.00	89.00
85-25-002	Canvas Back Ducks	E. Bierly	19,500	55.00	89.00
85-25-003	Wood Ducks	E. Bierly	19,500	55.00	89.00
85-25-004	Pintail Ducks	E. Bierly	19,500	55.00	89.00
Kaiser		**Wildflowers**			
86-26-001	Trillium	G. Neubacher	Closed	39.50	65.00
87-26-002	Spring Beauty	G. Neubacher	9,500	45.00	64.00
87-26-003	Wild Asters	G. Neubacher	9,500	49.50	59.00
87-26-004	Wild Roses	G. Neubacher	9,500	49.50	59.00
Kaiser		**Famous Lullabies**			
85-27-001	Sleep Baby Sleep	G. Neubacher	Unkn.	39.50	40.00
86-27-002	Rockabye Baby	G. Neubacher	Unkn.	39.50	41.00
86-27-003	A Mockingbird	G. Neubacher	Unkn.	39.50	46.00
86-27-004	Au Clair De Lune	G. Neubacher	Unkn.	39.50	44.00
87-27-005	Welsh Lullabye	G. Neubacher	Unkn.	39.50	57.00
88-27-006	Brahms' Lullabye	G. Neubacher	Unkn.	39.50	45.00
Kaiser		**Bicentennial Plate**			
76-28-001	Signing Declaration	J. Trumball	Closed	75.00	150.00
Kaiser		**The Graduate**			
86-29-001	Boy	J. McKernan	7,500	39.50	39.50
86-29-002	Girl	J. McKernan	7,500	39.50	39.50
Kaiser		**America, The Beautiful**			
88-30-001	Snowy Egret	G. Neubacher	9,500	49.50	49.50
88-30-002	California Quail	G. Neubacher	9,500	49.50	59.00
90-30-003	Scanning The Territory	G. Neubacher	9,500	49.50	59.00
90-30-004	Browsing For Delicacies	G. Neubacher	9,500	49.50	59.00
Kaiser		**Wallplates: Stable Door Collection**			
88-31-001	The Visitor	D. Twinney	Open	29.50	29.50
88-31-002	First Steps	D. Twinney	Open	29.50	29.50
88-31-003	Impudence	D. Twinney	Open	29.50	29.50
88-31-004	Pride	D. Twinney	Open	29.50	29.50
Kaiser		**Wallplates: Noble Horse Collection**			
88-32-001	Gelderlander	L. Turner	Open	49.50	49.50
88-32-002	Trakehner	L. Turner	Open	49.50	49.50
88-32-003	Holstein	L. Turner	Open	49.50	49.50
88-32-004	Thoroughbred	L. Turner	Open	49.50	49.50
88-32-005	Quarter Horse	L. Turner	Open	49.50	49.50
88-32-006	Arabian	L. Turner	Open	49.50	49.50
Kaiser		**Wallplates: Forest Surprises**			
89-33-001	Deerhead Orchid	G. Neubacher	9,500	49.50	59.00
89-33-002	Marsh Marigold	G. Neubacher	9,500	49.50	59.00
90-33-003	Violets	G. Neubacher	9,500	49.50	59.00
90-33-004	Wild Iris	G. Neubacher	9,500	49.50	59.00
Kaiser		**Wallplates: #837 Water Fowl Collection**			
89-34-001	Pair Of Mallards	Trevor Boyer	15,000	49.50	49.50
89-34-002	Pair Of Pintails	Trevor Boyer	15,000	49.50	49.50
89-34-003	Pair Of Canvasbacks	Trevor Boyer	15,000	49.50	49.50
89-34-004	Pair Of Greenwinged Teals	Trevor Boyer	15,000	49.50	49.50
89-34-005	Pair of Redheads	Trevor Boyer	15,000	49.50	49.50
89-34-006	Pair Of Carolina Wood Ducks	Trevor Boyer	15,000	49.50	49.50
Kaiser		**Wallplates: #202561 Operation Desert Storm**			
91-35-001	America's Fight For Freedom	D. Jean	14-day	29.95	29.95
Kaiser		**Arabian Nights**			
89-36-001	Scheherazade	R. Hersey	9,500	75.00	75.00
Kaiser		**Faithful Companions**			
90-37-001	German Shepherd	R.J. May	9,500	49.50	49.50
90-37-002	English Springer Spaniel	R.J. May	9,500	49.50	49.50
90-37-003	Beagle	R.J. May	9,500	49.50	49.50
90-37-004	Rottweiler	R.J. May	9,500	49.50	49.50
90-37-005	Dashchund	R.J. May	9,500	49.50	49.50
90-37-006	Doberman	R.J. May	9,500	49.50	49.50
90-37-007	Golden Retriever	R.J. May	9,500	49.50	49.50
90-37-008	Cocker Spaniel	R.J. May	9,500	49.50	49.50
Kaiser		**American Cats**			
91-38-001	Taking It Easy, Persians	G. Williams	7,500	30.00	30.00
91-38-002	Lazy River Days, Shorthairs	G. Williams	7,500	30.00	30.00
91-38-003	Tree View, Shorthairs	G. Williams	7,500	30.00	30.00
91-38-004	Kits In A Cradle, Siamese	G. Williams	7,500	30.00	30.00
Edwin M. Knowles		**Wizard of Oz**			
77-01-001	Over the Rainbow	J. Auckland	100-day	19.00	46.00
78-01-002	If I Only Had a Brain	J. Auckland	100-day	19.00	25.00
78-01-003	If I Only Had a Heart	J. Auckland	100-day	19.00	30.00
78-01-004	If I Were King of the Forest	J. Auckland	100-day	19.00	35.00
79-01-005	Wicked Witch of the West	J. Auckland	100-day	19.00	30.00
79-01-006	Follow the Yellow Brick Road	J. Auckland	100-day	19.00	25.00
79-01-007	Wonderful Wizard of Oz	J. Auckland	100-day	19.00	25.00

Company / Number	Name	Series / Artist	Edition Limit	Issue Price	Quote
80-01-008	The Grand Finale	J. Auckland	100-day	24.00	35.00
Edwin M. Knowles		**Gone with the Wind**			
78-02-001	Scarlett	R. Kursar	100-day	21.50	200-280.
79-02-002	Ashley	R. Kursar	100-day	21.50	125-195.
80-02-003	Melanie	R. Kursar	100-day	21.50	80.00
81-02-004	Rhett	R. Kursar	100-day	23.50	40-79.00
82-02-005	Mammy Lacing Scarlett	R. Kursar	100-day	23.50	75-90.00
83-02-006	Melanie Gives Birth	R. Kursar	100-day	23.50	90.00
84-02-007	Scarlet's Green Dress	R. Kursar	100-day	25.50	70.00
85-02-008	Rhett and Bonnie	R. Kursar	100-day	25.50	76.00
85-02-009	Scarlett and Rhett: The Finale	R. Kursar	100-day	29.50	75-85.00
Edwin M. Knowles		**Csatari Grandparent**			
80-03-001	Bedtime Story	J. Csatari	100-day	18.00	18.00
81-03-002	The Skating Lesson	J. Csatari	100-day	20.00	23.00
82-03-003	The Cookie Tasting	J. Csatari	100-day	20.00	20.00
83-03-004	The Swinger	J. Csatari	100-day	20.00	20.00
84-03-005	The Skating Queen	J. Csatari	100-day	22.00	25.00
85-03-006	The Patriot's Parade	J. Csatari	100-day	22.00	22.00
86-03-007	The Home Run	J. Csatari	100-day	22.00	29.00
87-03-008	The Sneak Preview	J. Csatari	100-day	22.00	26.00
Edwin M. Knowles		**Americana Holidays**			
78-04-001	Fourth of July	D. Spaulding	Yr.Iss.	26.00	26.00
79-04-002	Thanksgiving	D. Spaulding	Yr.Iss.	26.00	26.00
80-04-003	Easter	D. Spaulding	Yr.Iss.	26.00	26.00
81-04-004	Valentine's Day	D. Spaulding	Yr.Iss.	26.00	26.00
82-04-005	Father's Day	D. Spaulding	Yr.Iss.	26.00	26.00
83-04-006	Christmas	D. Spaulding	Yr.Iss.	26.00	26.00
84-04-007	Mother's Day	D. Spaulding	Yr.Iss.	26.00	27.00
Edwin M. Knowles		**Annie**			
83-05-001	Annie and Sandy	W. Chambers	100-day	19.00	22-50.00
83-05-002	Daddy Warbucks	W. Chambers	100-day	19.00	21-35.00
83-05-003	Annie and Grace	W. Chambers	100-day	19.00	22-35.00
84-05-004	Annie and the Orphans	W. Chambers	100-day	21.00	24-32.00
85-05-005	Tomorrow	W. Chambers	100-day	21.00	22-32.50
86-05-006	Annie and Miss Hannigan	W. Chambers	100-day	21.00	29.50
86-05-007	Annie, Lily and Rooster	W. Chambers	100-day	24.00	24.00
86-05-008	Grand Finale	W. Chambers	100-day	24.00	24.00
Edwin M. Knowles		**The Four Ancient Elements**			
84-06-001	Earth	G. Lambert	75-day	27.50	27.50
84-06-002	Water	G. Lambert	75-day	27.50	27.50
85-06-003	Air	G. Lambert	75-day	29.50	29.50
85-06-004	Fire	G. Lambert	75-day	29.50	40.00
Edwin M. Knowles		**Biblical Mothers**			
83-07-001	Bethsheba and Solomon	E. Licea	Yr.Iss.	39.50	39.50
84-07-002	Judgment of Solomon	E. Licea	Yr.Iss.	39.50	39.50
84-07-003	Pharaoh's Daughter and Moses	E. Licea	Yr.Iss.	39.50	39.50
85-07-004	Mary and Jesus	E. Licea	Yr.Iss.	39.50	41-52.00
85-07-005	Sarah and Isaac	E. Licea	Yr.Iss.	44.50	51.00
86-07-006	Rebekah, Jacob and Esau	E. Licea	Yr.Iss.	44.50	45.00
Edwin M. Knowles		**Hibel Mother's Day**			
84-08-001	Abby and Lisa	E. Hibel	Yr.Iss.	29.50	45-50.00
85-08-002	Erica and Jamie	E. Hibel	Yr.Iss.	29.50	29.50
86-08-003	Emily and Jennifer	E. Hibel	Yr.Iss.	29.50	55.00
87-08-004	Catherine and Heather	E. Hibel	Yr.Iss.	34.50	45.00
88-08-005	Sarah and Tess	E. Hibel	Yr.Iss.	34.90	34.90
89-08-006	Jessica and Kate	E. Hibel	Yr.Iss.	34.90	34.90
90-08-007	Elizabeth, Jordan & Janie	E. Hibel	Yr.Iss.	36.90	42.00
91-08-008	Michele and Anna	E. Hibel	Yr.Iss.	36.90	40.00
Edwin M. Knowles		**Friends I Remember**			
83-09-001	Fish Story	J. Down	97-day	17.50	17.50
84-09-002	Office Hours	J. Down	97-day	17.50	17.50
85-09-003	A Coat of Paint	J. Down	97-day	17.50	17.50
85-09-004	Here Comes the Bride	J. Down	97-day	19.50	19.50
85-09-005	Fringe Benefits	J. Down	97-day	19.50	19.50
86-09-006	High Society	J. Down	97-day	19.50	19.50
86-09-007	Flower Arrangement	J. Down	97-day	21.50	21.50
86-09-008	Taste Test	J. Down	97-day	21.50	21.50
Edwin M. Knowles		**Father's Love**			
84-10-001	Open Wide	B. Bradley	100-day	19.50	20.00
84-10-002	Batter Up	B. Bradley	100-day	19.50	20.00
85-10-003	Little Shaver	B. Bradley	100-day	19.50	20.00
85-10-004	Swing Time	B. Bradley	100-day	22.50	22.50
Edwin M. Knowles		**The King and I**			
84-11-001	A Puzzlement	W. Chambers	150-day	19.50	19.50
85-11-002	Shall We Dance?	W. Chambers	150-day	19.50	37.00
85-11-003	Getting to Know You	W. Chambers	150-day	19.50	20.00
85-11-004	We Kiss in a Shadow	W. Chambers	150-day	19.50	19.50
Edwin M. Knowles		**Ency. Brit. Birds of Your Garden**			
85-12-001	Cardinal	K. Daniel	100-day	19.50	50.00
85-12-002	Blue Jay	K. Daniel	100-day	19.50	35.00
85-12-003	Oriole	K. Daniel	100-day	22.50	30.00
86-12-004	Chickadees	K. Daniel	100-day	22.50	22.50
86-12-005	Bluebird	K. Daniel	100-day	22.50	25.00
86-12-006	Robin	K. Daniel	100-day	22.50	24.00
86-12-007	Hummingbird	K. Daniel	100-day	24.50	28.00
87-12-008	Goldfinch	K. Daniel	100-day	24.50	30.00
87-12-009	Downy Woodpecker	K. Daniel	100-day	24.50	25-29.00
87-12-010	Cedar Waxwing	K. Daniel	100-day	24.90	29.00
Edwin M. Knowles		**Frances Hook Legacy**			
85-13-001	Fascination	F. Hook	100-day	19.50	22.50
85-13-002	Daydreaming	F. Hook	100-day	19.50	22.50
86-13-003	Discovery	F. Hook	100-day	22.50	22.50
86-13-004	Disappointment	F. Hook	100-day	22.50	25.00
86-13-005	Wonderment	F. Hook	100-day	22.50	25.00
87-13-006	Expectation	F. Hook	100-day	22.50	32.00
Edwin M. Knowles		**Hibel Christmas**			
85-14-001	The Angel's Message	E. Hibel	Yr.Iss.	45.00	44.00
86-14-002	The Gifts of the Magi	E. Hibel	Yr.Iss.	45.00	60.00
87-14-003	The Flight Into Egypt	E. Hibel	Yr.Iss.	49.00	50.00
88-14-004	Adoration of the Shepherd	E. Hibel	Yr.Iss.	49.00	50.00

Company / Number	Name	Series / Artist	Edition Limit	Issue Price	Quote
89-14-005	Peaceful Kingdom	E. Hibel	Yr.Iss.	49.00	49-55.00
90-14-006	Nativity	E. Hibel	Yr.Iss.	49.00	70.00
Edwin M. Knowles		**Upland Birds of North America**			
86-15-001	The Pheasant	W. Anderson	150-day	24.50	25.00
86-15-002	The Grouse	W. Anderson	150-day	24.50	25.00
87-15-003	The Quail	W. Anderson	150-day	27.50	28.00
87-15-004	The Wild Turkey	W. Anderson	150-day	27.50	28.00
87-15-005	The Gray Partridge	W. Anderson	150-day	27.50	28.00
87-15-006	The Woodcock	W. Anderson	150-day	27.90	28.00
Edwin M. Knowles		**Oklahoma!**			
85-16-001	Oh, What a Beautiful Mornin'	M. Kunstler	150-day	19.50	19.50
86-16-002	Surrey with the Fringe on Top'	M. Kunstler	150-day	19.50	19.50
86-16-003	I Cain't Say No	M. Kunstler	150-day	19.50	19.50
86-16-004	Oklahoma	M. Kunstler	150-day	19.50	19.50
Edwin M. Knowles		**Sound of Music**			
86-17-001	Sound of Music	T. Crnkovich	150-day	19.50	22.00
86-17-002	Do-Re-Mi	T. Crnkovich	150-day	19.50	25.00
86-17-003	My Favorite Things	T. Crnkovich	150-day	22.50	25.00
86-17-004	Laendler Waltz	T. Crnkovich	150-day	22.50	35.00
87-17-005	Edelweiss	T. Crnkovich	150-day	22.50	35.00
87-17-006	I Have Confidence	T. Crnkovich	150-day	22.50	22.50
87-17-007	Maria	T. Crnkovich	150-day	24.90	31.00
87-17-008	Climb Ev'ry Mountain	T. Crnkovich	150-day	24.90	33.00
Edwin M. Knowles		**American Innocents**			
86-18-001	Abigail in the Rose Garden	Marsten/Mandrajji	100-day	19.50	19.50
86-18-002	Ann by the Terrace	Marsten/Mandrajji	100-day	19.50	19.50
86-18-003	Ellen and John in the Parlor	Marsten/Mandrajji	100-day	19.50	19.50
86-18-004	William on the Rocking Horse	Marsten/Mandrajji	100-day	19.50	48.00
Edwin M. Knowles		**J. W. Smith Childhood Holidays**			
86-19-001	Easter	J. W. Smith	97-day	19.50	21.00
86-19-002	Thanksgiving	J. W. Smith	97-day	19.50	21.00
86-19-003	Christmas	J. W. Smith	97-day	19.50	24.00
86-19-004	Valentine's Day	J. W. Smith	97-day	22.50	25.00
87-19-005	Mother's Day	J. W. Smith	97-day	22.50	25.00
87-19-006	Fourth of July	J. W. Smith	97-day	22.50	30.00
Edwin M. Knowles		**Living with Nature-Jerner's Ducks**			
86-20-001	The Pintail	B. Jerner	150-day	19.50	60.00
86-20-002	The Mallard	B. Jerner	150-day	19.50	50.00
87-20-003	The Wood Duck	B. Jerner	150-day	22.50	40.00
87-20-004	The Green-Winged Teal	B. Jerner	150-day	22.50	55.00
87-20-005	The Northern Shoveler	B. Jerner	150-day	22.90	34.00
87-20-006	The American Widgeon	B. Jerner	150-day	22.90	35.00
87-20-007	The Gadwall	B. Jerner	150-day	24.90	35.00
88-20-008	The Blue-Winged Teal	B. Jerner	150-day	24.90	38.00
Edwin M. Knowles		**Lincoln Man of America**			
86-21-001	The Gettysburg Address	M. Kunstler	150-day	24.50	25.00
87-21-002	The Inauguration	M. Kunstler	150-day	24.50	26.00
87-21-003	The Lincoln-Douglas Debates	M. Kunstler	150-day	27.50	27.50
87-21-004	Beginnings in New Salem	M. Kunstler	150-day	27.90	30.00
88-21-005	The Family Man	M. Kunstler	150-day	27.90	27.90
88-21-006	Emancipation Proclamation	M. Kunstler	150-day	27.90	45.00
Edwin M. Knowles		**Portraits of Motherhood**			
87-22-001	Mother's Here	W. Chambers	150-day	29.50	35.00
88-22-002	First Touch	W. Chambers	150-day	29.50	32.00
Edwin M. Knowles		**A Swan is Born**			
87-23-001	Hopes and Dreams	L. Roberts	150-day	24.50	30.00
87-23-002	At the Barre	L. Roberts	150-day	24.50	34.00
87-23-003	In Position	L. Roberts	150-day	24.50	40-65.00
88-23-004	Just For Size	L. Roberts	150-day	24.50	45.00
Edwin M. Knowles		**South Pacific**			
87-24-001	Some Enchanted Evening	E. Gignilliat	150-day	24.50	24.50
87-24-002	Happy Talk	E. Gignilliat	150-day	24.50	34.00
87-24-003	Dites Moi	E. Gignilliat	150-day	24.90	40-65.00
88-24-004	Honey Bun	E. Gignilliat	150-day	24.90	24.90
Edwin M. Knowles		**Tom Sawyer**			
87-25-001	Whitewashing the Fence	W. Chambers	150-day	27.50	27.50
87-25-002	Tom and Becky	W. Chambers	150-day	27.90	27.90
87-25-003	Tom Sawyer the Pirate	W. Chambers	150-day	27.90	27.90
88-25-004	First Pipes	W. Chambers	150-day	27.90	27.90
Edwin M. Knowles		**Friends of the Forest**			
87-26-001	The Rabbit	K. Daniel	150-day	24.50	42.00
87-26-002	The Raccoon	K. Daniel	150-day	24.50	60.00
87-26-003	The Squirrel	K. Daniel	150-day	27.90	28-30.00
88-26-004	The Chipmunk	K. Daniel	150-day	27.90	28-30.00
88-26-005	The Fox	K. Daniel	150-day	27.90	43.00
88-26-006	The Otter	K. Daniel	150-day	27.90	29.00
Edwin M. Knowles		**Amy Brackenbury's Cat Tales**			
87-27-001	A Chance Meeting: White American Shorthairs	A. Brackenbury	150-day	21.50	40.00
87-27-002	Gone Fishing: Maine Coons	A. Brackenbury	150-day	21.50	99.00
88-27-003	Strawberries and Cream: Cream Persians	A. Brackenbury	150-day	24.90	75.00
88-27-004	Flower Bed: British Shorthairs	A. Brackenbury	150-day	24.90	30.00
88-27-005	Kittens and Mittens: Silver Tabbies	A. Brackenbury	150-day	24.90	30.00
88-27-006	All Wrapped Up: Himalayans	A. Brackenbury	150-day	24.90	55.00
Edwin M. Knowles		**The Story of Christmas by Eve Licea**			
87-28-001	The Annunciation	E. Licea	Yr.Iss.	44.90	46.00
88-28-002	The Nativity	E. Licea	Yr.Iss.	44.90	45.00
89-28-003	Adoration Of The Shepherds	E. Licea	Yr.Iss.	49.90	53.00
90-28-004	Journey Of The Magi	E. Licea	Yr.Iss.	49.90	59.00
91-28-005	Gifts Of The Magi	E. Licea	Yr.Iss.	49.90	65.00
Edwin M. Knowles		**Carousel**			
87-29-001	If I Loved You	D. Brown	150-day	24.90	24.90
88-29-002	Mr. Snow	D. Brown	150-day	24.90	24.90
88-29-003	The Carousel Waltz	D. Brown	150-day	24.90	55.00
88-29-004	You'll Never Walk Alone	D. Brown	150-day	24.90	47.00
Edwin M. Knowles		**Field Puppies**			
87-30-001	Dog Tired-The Springer Spaniel	L. Kaatz	150-day	24.90	65-70.00

Number	Name	Artist	Edition Limit	Issue Price	Quote
87-30-002	Caught in the Act-The Golden Retriever	L. Kaatz	150-day	24.90	60.00
88-30-003	Missing/Point/Irish Setter	L. Kaatz	150-day	27.90	40.00
88-30-004	A Perfect Set-Labrador	L. Kaatz	150-day	27.90	52.00
88-30-005	Fritz's Folly-German Shorthaired Pointer	L. Kaatz	150-day	27.90	42-44.00
88-30-006	Shirt Tales: Cocker Spaniel	L. Kaatz	150-day	27.90	35.00
89-30-007	Fine Feathered Friends-English Setter	L. Kaatz	150-day	29.90	46.00
89-30-008	Performance: Wiemaraner	L. Kaatz	150-day	29.90	34.00
Edwin M. Knowles		**The American Journey**			
87-31-001	Westward Ho	M. Kunstler	150-day	29.90	29.90
88-31-002	Kitchen With a View	M. Kunstler	150-day	29.90	32.00
88-31-003	Crossing the River	M. Kunstler	150-day	29.90	39.00
88-31-004	Christmas at the New Cabin	M. Kunstler	150-day	29.90	45.00
Edwin M. Knowles		**Precious Little Ones**			
88-32-001	Little Red Robins	M. T. Fangel	150-day	29.90	29.90
88-32-002	Little Fledglings	M. T. Fangel	150-day	29.90	29.90
88-32-003	Saturday Night Bath	M. T. Fangel	150-day	29.90	34.00
88-32-004	Peek-A-Boo	M. T. Fangel	150-day	29.90	47.00
Edwin M. Knowles		**Aesop's Fables**			
88-33-001	The Goose That Laid the Golden Egg	M. Hampshire	150-day	27.90	27.90
88-33-002	The Hare and the Tortoise	M. Hampshire	150-day	27.90	30.00
88-33-003	The Fox and the Grapes	M. Hampshire	150-day	30.90	35.00
89-33-004	The Lion And The Mouse	M. Hampshire	150-day	30.90	33.00
89-33-005	The Milk Maid And Her Pail	M. Hampshire	150-day	30.90	57.00
89-33-006	The Jay And The Peacock	M. Hampshire	150-day	30.90	38.00
Edwin M. Knowles		**Not So Long Ago**			
88-34-001	Story Time	J. W. Smith	150-day	24.90	24.90
88-34-002	Wash Day for Dolly	J. W. Smith	150-day	24.90	24.90
88-34-003	Suppertime for Kitty	J. W. Smith	150-day	24.90	48.00
88-34-004	Mother's Little Helper	J. W. Smith	150-day	24.90	35.00
Edwin M. Knowles		**Jerner's Less Travelled Road**			
88-35-001	The Weathered Barn	B. Jerner	150-day	29.90	29.90
88-35-002	The Murmuring Stream	B. Jerner	150-day	29.90	29.90
88-35-003	The Covered Bridge	B. Jerner	150-day	32.90	36.00
89-35-004	Winter's Peace	B. Jerner	150-day	32.90	36.00
89-35-005	The Flowering Meadow	B. Jerner	150-day	32.90	33.00
89-35-006	The Hidden Waterfall	B. Jerner	150-day	32.90	33.00
Edwin M. Knowles		**Once Upon a Time**			
88-36-001	Little Red Riding Hood	K. Pritchett	150-day	24.90	24.90
88-36-002	Rapunzel	K. Pritchett	150-day	24.90	24.90
88-36-003	Three Little Pigs	K. Pritchett	150-day	27.90	36.00
89-36-004	The Princess and the Pea	K. Pritchett	150-day	27.90	27.90
89-36-005	Goldilocks and the Three Bears	K. Pritchett	150-day	27.90	43.00
89-36-006	Beauty and the Beast	K. Pritchett	150-day	27.90	60.00
Edwin M. Knowles		**Majestic Birds of North America**			
88-37-001	The Bald Eagle	D. Smith	150-day	29.90	45.00
88-37-002	Peregrine Falcon	D. Smith	150-day	29.90	29.90
88-37-003	The Great Horned Owl	D. Smith	150-day	32.90	32.90
89-37-004	The Red-Tailed Hawk	D. Smith	150-day	32.90	32.90
89-37-005	The White Gyrfalcon	D. Smith	150-day	32.90	32.90
89-37-006	The American Kestral	D. Smith	150-day	32.90	32.90
90-37-007	The Osprey	D. Smith	150-day	34.90	34.90
90-37-008	The Golden Eagle	D. Smith	150-day	34.90	34.90
Edwin M. Knowles		**Cinderella**			
88-38-001	Bibbidi, Bobbidi, Boo	Disney Studios	150-day	29.90	44-70.00
88-38-002	A Dream Is A Wish Your Heart Makes	Disney Studios	150-day	29.90	40-90.00
89-38-003	Oh Sing Sweet Nightingale	Disney Studios	150-day	32.90	45-60.00
89-38-004	A Dress For Cinderelly	Disney Studios	150-day	32.90	90-110.00
89-38-005	So This Is Love	Disney Studios	150-day	32.90	32.90-68.00
90-38-006	At The Stroke Of Midnight	Disney Studios	150-day	32.90	54-60.00
90-38-007	If The Shoe Fits	Disney Studios	150-day	34.90	65-69.00
90-38-008	Happily Ever After	Disney Studios	150-day	34.90	34.90
Edwin M. Knowles		**Mary Poppins**			
89-40-001	Mary Poppins	M. Hampshire	150-day	29.90	40.00
89-40-002	A Spoonful of Sugar	M. Hampshire	150-day	29.90	29.90
90-40-003	A Jolly Holiday With Mary	M. Hampshire	150-day	32.90	45.00
90-40-004	We Love To Laugh	M. Hampshire	150-day	32.90	60.00
91-40-005	Chim Chim Cher-ee	M. Hampshire	150-day	32.90	40.00
91-40-006	Tuppence a Bag	M. Hampshire	150-day	32.90	66.00
Edwin M. Knowles		**Home Sweet Home**			
89-41-001	The Victorian	R. McGinnis	150-day	39.90	39.90
89-41-002	The Greek Revival	R. McGinnis	150-day	39.90	39.90
89-41-003	The Georgian	R. McGinnis	150-day	39.90	39.90
90-41-004	The Mission	R. McGinnis	150-day	39.90	39.90
Edwin M. Knowles		**My Fair Lady**			
89-42-001	Opening Day at Ascot	W. Chambers	150-day	24.90	26.00
89-42-002	I Could Have Danced All Night	W. Chambers	150-day	24.90	24.90
89-42-003	The Rain in Spain	W. Chambers	150-day	27.90	27.90
89-42-004	Show Me	W. Chambers	150-day	27.90	27.90
90-42-005	Get Me To/Church On Time	W. Chambers	150-day	27.90	27.90
90-42-006	I've Grown Accustomed/Face	W. Chambers	150-day	27.90	27.90
Edwin M. Knowles		**Sundblom Santas**			
89-43-001	Santa By The Fire	H. Sundblom	Closed	27.90	44.00
90-43-002	Christmas Vigil	H. Sundblom	Closed	27.90	27.90-36.00
91-43-003	To All A Good Night	H. Sundblom	Closed	32.90	45.00
Edwin M. Knowles		**Great Cats Of The Americas**			
89-44-001	The Jaguar	L. Cable	150-day	29.90	65-100.00
89-44-002	The Cougar	L. Cable	150-day	29.90	44.00
89-44-003	The Lynx	L. Cable	150-day	32.90	44.00
90-44-004	The Ocelot	L. Cable	150-day	32.90	50.00
90-44-005	The Bobcat	L. Cable	150-day	32.90	44.00
90-44-006	The Jaguarundi	L. Cable	150-day	32.90	52.00
90-44-007	The Margay	L. Cable	150-day	34.90	44.00
91-44-008	The Pampas Cat	L. Cable	150-day	34.90	50.00
Edwin M. Knowles		**Heirlooms And Lace**			
89-45-001	Anna	C. Layton	150-day	34.90	65.00
89-45-022	Victoria	C. Layton	150-day	34.90	65.00
90-45-003	Tess	C. Layton	150-day	37.90	80-90.00
90-45-004	Olivia	C. Layton	150-day	37.90	135-139.
91-45-005	Bridget	C. Layton	150-day	37.90	110-131.

Number	Name	Artist	Edition Limit	Issue Price	Quote
91-45-006	Rebecca	C. Layton	150-day	37.90	95-125.00
Edwin M. Knowles		**Stately Owls**			
89-46-001	The Snowy Owl	J. Beaudoin	150-day	29.90	47.00
89-46-002	The Great Horned Owl	J. Beaudoin	150-day	29.90	40.00
90-46-003	The Barn Owl	J. Beaudoin	150-day	32.90	40.00
90-46-004	The Screech Owl	J. Beaudoin	150-day	32.90	42.00
90-46-005	The Short-Eared Owl	J. Beaudoin	150-day	32.90	32.90
90-46-006	The Barred Owl	J. Beaudoin	150-day	32.90	32.90
90-46-007	The Great Grey Owl	J. Beaudoin	150-day	34.90	34.90
91-46-008	The Saw-Whet Owl	J. Beaudoin	150-day	34.90	34.90
Edwin M. Knowles		**Singin' In The Rain**			
90-47-001	Singin' In The Rain	M. Skolsky	150-day	32.90	35-38.00
90-47-002	Good Morning	M. Skolsky	150-day	32.90	45.00
91-47-003	Broadway Melody	M. Skolsky	150-day	32.90	32.90-50.00
91-47-004	We're Happy Again	M. Skolsky	150-day	32.90	62.00
Edwin M. Knowles		**Pinocchio**			
89-48-001	Gepetto Creates Pinocchio	Disney Studios	150-day	29.90	48-57.00
90-48-002	Pinocchio And The Blue Fairy	Disney Studios	150-day	29.90	50-55.00
90-48-003	It's an Actor's Life For Me	Disney Studios	150-day	32.90	55.00
90-48-004	I've Got No Strings On Me	Disney Studios	150-day	32.90	55.00
91-48-005	Pleasure Island	Disney Studios	150-day	32.90	65.00
91-48-006	A Real Boy	Disney Studios	150-day	32.90	68.00
Edwin M. Knowles		**Nature's Child**			
90-49-001	Sharing	M. Jobe	150-day	29.90	44.00
90-49-002	The Lost Lamb	M. Jobe	150-day	29.90	35.00
90-49-003	Seems Like Yesterday	M. Jobe	150-day	32.90	40.00
90-49-004	Faithful Friends	M. Jobe	150-day	32.90	43.00
90-49-005	Trusted Companion	M. Jobe	150-day	32.90	55.00
91-49-006	Hand in Hand	M. Jobe	150-day	32.90	32.90
Edwin M. Knowles		**Fantasia: (The Sorcerer's Apprentice) Golden Anniversary**			
90-50-001	The Apprentice's Dream	Disney Studios	150-day	29.90	29.90
90-50-002	Mischievous Apprentice	Disney Studios	150-day	29.90	29.90
91-50-003	Dreams of Power	Disney Studios	150-day	32.90	32.90
91-50-004	Mickey's Magical Whirlpool	Disney Studios	150-day	32.90	32.90
91-50-005	Wizardry Gone Wild	Disney Studios	150-day	32.90	32.90
91-50-006	Mickey Makes Magic	Disney Studios	150-day	34.90	34.90
91-50-007	The Penitent Apprentice	Disney Studios	150-day	34.90	34.90
Edwin M. Knowles		**Casablanca**			
90-51-001	Here's Looking At You, Kid	J. Griffin	150-day	34.90	34.90-62.00
90-51-002	We'll Always Have Paris	J. Griffin	150-day	34.90	34.90
91-51-003	We Loved Each Other Once	J. Griffin	150-day	37.90	37.90
91-51-004	Rick's Cafe Americain	J. Griffin	150-day	37.90	37.90
91-51-005	A Franc For Your Thoughts	J. Griffin	150-day	37.90	37.90
91-51-006	Play it Sam	J. Griffin	150-day	37.90	37.90
Edwin M. Knowles		**Field Trips**			
90-52-001	Gone Fishing	L. Kaatz	150-day	24.90	24.90
91-52-002	Ducking Duty	L. Kaatz	150-day	24.90	24.90
91-52-003	Boxed In	L. Kaatz	150-day	27.90	27.90
91-52-004	Pups 'N Boots	L. Kaatz	150-day	27.90	27.90
91-52-005	Puppy Tales	L. Kaatz	150-day	27.90	27.90
91-52-006	Pail Pals	L. Kaatz	150-day	29.90	29.90
91-52-007	Chesapeake Bay Retrievers	L. Kaatz	150-day	29.90	29.90
91-52-008	Hat Trick	L. Kaatz	150-day	29.90	29.90
Edwin M. Knowles		**The Old Mill Stream**			
90-53-001	New London Grist Mill	C. Tennant	150-day	39.90	39.90
91-53-002	Wayside Inn Grist Mill	C. Tennant	150-day	39.90	39.90
91-53-003	Old Red Mill	C. Tennant	150-day	39.90	39.90
91-53-004	Glade Creek Grist Mill	C. Tennant	150-day	39.90	39.90
Edwin M. Knowles		**Birds of the Seasons**			
90-54-001	Cardinals In Winter	S. Timm	150-day	24.90	24.90-60.00
90-54-002	Bluebirds In Spring	S. Timm	150-day	24.90	24.90-68.00
91-54-003	Nuthatches In Fall	S. Timm	150-day	27.90	27.90
91-54-004	Baltimore Orioles In Summer	S. Timm	150-day	27.90	43.00
91-54-005	Blue Jays In Early Fall	S. Timm	150-day	27.90	27.90
91-54-006	Robins In Early Spring	S. Timm	150-day	27.90	27.90
91-54-007	Cedar Waxwings in Fall	S. Timm	150-day	29.90	29.90
91-54-008	Chickadees in Winter	S. Timm	150-day	29.90	29.90
Edwin M. Knowles		**Cozy Country Corners**			
90-55-001	Lazy Morning	H. H. Ingmire	150-day	24.90	40.00
90-55-002	Warm Retreat	H. H. Ingmire	150-day	24.90	24.90-40.00
91-55-003	A Sunny Spot	H. H. Ingmire	150-day	27.90	27.90
91-55-004	Attic Afternoon	H. H. Ingmire	150-day	27.90	27.90
91-55-005	Mirror Mischief	H. H. Ingmire	150-day	27.90	27.90
91-55-006	Hide and Seek	H. H. Ingmire	150-day	29.90	29.90
91-55-007	Apple Antics	H. H. Ingmire	150-day	29.90	29.90
91-55-008	Table Trouble	H. H. Ingmire	150-day	29.90	29.90
Edwin M. Knowles		**Jewels of the Flowers**			
91-56-001	Sapphire Wings	T.C. Chiu	150-day	29.90	29.90
91-56-002	Topaz Beauties	T.C. Chiu	150-day	29.90	29.90
91-56-003	Amethyst Flight	T.C. Chiu	150-day	32.90	32.90
91-56-004	Ruby Elegance	T.C. Chiu	150-day	32.90	32.90
91-56-005	Emerald Pair	T.C. Chiu	150-day	32.90	32.90
91-56-006	Opal Splendor	T.C. Chiu	150-day	34.90	34.90
92-56-007	Pearl Luster	T.C. Chiu	150-day	34.90	34.90
92-56-008	Aquamarine Glimmer	T.C. Chiu	150-day	34.90	34.90
Edwin M. Knowles		**Pussyfooting Around**			
91-57-001	Fish Tales	C. Wilson	150-day	24.90	24.90
91-57-002	Teatime Tabbies	C. Wilson	150-day	24.90	24.90
91-57-003	Yarn Spinners	C. Wilson	150-day	24.90	24.90
91-57-004	Two Maestros	C. Wilson	150-day	24.90	24.90
Edwin M. Knowles		**Baby Owls of North America**			
91-58-001	Peek-A-Whoo:Screech Owls	J. Thornbrugh	150-day	27.90	27.90
91-58-002	Forty Winks: Saw-Whet Owls	J. Thornbrugh	150-day	29.90	29.90
91-58-003	The Tree House: Northern Pygmy Owls	J. Thornbrugh	150-day	30.90	30.90
91-58-004	Three of a Kind: Great Horned Owls	J. Thornbrugh	150-day	30.90	30.90
91-58-005	Out on a Limb: Great Gray Owls	J. Thornbrugh	150-day	30.90	30.90
91-58-006	Beginning to Explore: Boreal Owls	J. Thornbrugh	150-day	32.90	32.90
92-58-007	Three's Company: Long Eared Owls	J. Thornbrugh	150-day	32.90	32.90

Company / Number	Name	Series / Artist	Edition Limit	Issue Price	Quote
Edwin M. Knowles		**Season For Song**			
91-59-001	Winter Concert	M. Jobe	150-day	34.90	34.90
91-59-002	Snowy Symphony	M. Jobe	150-day	34.90	34.90
91-59-003	Frosty Chorus	M. Jobe	150-day	34.90	34.90
91-59-004	Silver Serenade	M. Jobe	150-day	34.90	34.90
Edwin M. Knowles		**Garden Cottages of England**			
91-60-001	Chandler's Cottage	T. Kinkade	150-day	27.90	30.00
91-60-002	Cedar Nook Cottage	T. Kinkade	150-day	27.90	27.90
91-60-003	Candlelit Cottage	T. Kinkade	150-day	30.90	30.90
91-60-004	Open Gate Cottage	T. Kinkade	150-day	30.90	30.90
91-60-005	McKenna's Cottage	T. Kinkade	150-day	30.90	30.90
91-60-006	Woodsman's Thatch Cottage	T. Kinkade	150-day	32.90	32.90
Edwin M. Knowles		**Sleeping Beauty**			
91-61-001	Once Upon A Dream	Disney Studios	150-day	39.90	39.90
91-61-002	Awakened by a Kiss	Disney Studios	150-day	39.90	39.90
91-61-003	Happy Birthday Briar Rose	Disney Studios	150-day	42.90	42.90
Edwin M. Knowles		**Snow White and the Seven Dwarfs**			
91-62-001	The Dance of Snow White/Seven Dwarfs	Disney Studios	150-day	29.90	29.90
91-62-002	With a Smile and a Song	Disney Studios	150-day	29.90	29.90
91-62-003	A Special Treat	Disney Studios	150-day	32.90	32.90
91-62-004	A Kiss for Dopey	Disney Studios	150-day	32.90	32.90
Edwin M. Knowles		**Classic Fairy Tales**			
91-63-001	Goldilocks and the Three Bears	S. Gustafson	150-day	29.90	29.90
91-63-002	Little Red Riding Hood	S. Gustafson	150-day	29.90	29.90
91-63-003	The Three Little Pigs	S. Gustafson	150-day	32.90	32.90
91-63-004	The Frog Prince	S. Gustafson	150-day	32.90	32.90
92-63-005	Jack and the Beanstalk	S. Gustafson	150-day	32.90	32.90
Edwin M. Knowles		**Wizard of Oz: A National Treasure**			
91-64-001	Yellow Brick Road	R. Laslo	150-day	29.90	29.90
92-64-002	I Haven't Got a Brain	R. Laslo	150-day	29.90	29.90
92-64-003	I'm a Little Rusty Yet	R. Laslo	150-day	32.90	32.90
92-64-004	I Even Scare Myself	R. Laslo	150-day	32.90	32.90
Edwin M. Knowles		**First Impressions**			
91-65-001	Taking a Gander	J. Giordano	150-day	29.90	29.90
91-65-002	Two's Company	J. Giordano	150-day	29.90	29.90
91-65-003	Fine Feathered Friends	J. Giordano	150-day	32.90	32.90
91-65-004	What's Up?	J. Giordano	150-day	32.90	32.90
91-65-005	All Ears	J. Giordano	150-day	32.90	32.90
92-65-006	Between Friends	J. Giordano	150-day	32.90	32.90
Edwin M. Knowles		**Santa's Christmas**			
91-66-001	Santa's Love	T. Browing	150-day	29.90	29.90
91-66-002	Santa's Cheer	T. Browing	150-day	29.90	29.90
91-66-003	Santa's Promise	T. Browing	150-day	32.90	32.90
91-66-004	Santa's Gift	T. Browing	150-day	32.90	32.90
92-66-005	Santa's Surprise	T. Browing	150-day	32.90	32.90
Edwin M. Knowles		**Home for the Holidays**			
91-67-001	Sleigh Ride Home	T. Kinkade	150-day	29.90	29.90
91-67-002	Home to Grandma's	T. Kinkade	150-day	29.90	29.90
91-67-003	Home Before Christmas	T. Kinkade	150-day	32.90	32.90
91-67-004	The Warmth of Home	T. Kinkade	150-day	32.90	32.90
Edwin M. Knowles		**Call of the Wilderness**			
91-68-001	First Outing	K. Daniel	150-day	29.90	29.90
91-68-002	Howling Lesson	K. Daniel	150-day	29.90	29.90
91-68-003	Silent Watch	K. Daniel	150-day	32.90	32.90
91-68-004	Winter Travelers	K. Daniel	150-day	32.90	32.90
92-68-005	Ahead of the Pack	K. Daniel	150-day	32.90	32.90
Edwin M. Knowles		**Old-Fashioned Favorites**			
91-69-001	Apple Crisp	M. Weber	150-day	29.90	29.90
91-69-002	Blueberry Muffins	M. Weber	150-day	29.90	29.90
91-69-003	Peach Cobbler	M. Weber	150-day	29.90	29.90
91-69-004	Chocolate Chip Oatmeal Cookies	M. Weber	150-day	29.90	29.90
Edwin M. Knowles		**Songs of the American Spirit**			
91-70-001	The Star Spangled Banner	H. Bond	150-day	29.90	29.90
91-70-002	Battle Hymn of the Republic	H. Bond	150-day	29.90	29.90
91-70-003	America the Beautiful	H. Bond	150-day	29.90	29.94
91-70-004	My Country 'Tis of Thee	H. Bond	150-day	29.90	29.90
Edwin M. Knowles		**Backyard Harmony**			
91-71-001	The Singing Lesson	J. Thornbrugh	150-day	27.90	27.90
91-71-002	Welcoming a New Day	J. Thornbrugh	150-day	27.90	27.90
91-71-003	Announcing Spring	J. Thornbrugh	150-day	30.90	30.90
92-71-004	The Morning Harvest	J. Thornbrugh	150-day	30.90	30.90
Edwin M. Knowles		**Bambi**			
92-72-001	Bashful Bambi	Disney Studios	150-day	34.90	34.90
92-72-002	Bambi's New Friends	Disney Studios	150-day	34.90	34.90
92-72-003	Hello Little Prince	Disney Studios	150-day	37.90	37.90
Edwin M. Knowles		**Purrfect Point of View**			
92-73-001	Unexpected Visitors	J. Giordano	150-day	29.90	29.90
92-73-002	Wistful Morning	J. Giordano	150-day	29.90	29.90
92-73-003	Afternoon Catnap	J. Giordano	150-day	29.90	29.90
Edwin M. Knowles		**China's Natural Treasures**			
92-74-001	Siberian Tiger	T.C. Chia	150-day	29.90	29.90
92-74-002	Snow Leopard	T.C. Chia	150-day	29.90	29.90
92-74-003	Giant Panda	T.C. Chia	150-day	32.90	32.90
Edwin M. Knowles		**Under Mother's Wing**			
92-75-001	Arctic Spring: Snowy Owls	J. Beaudoin	150-day	29.90	29.90
92-75-002	Forest's Edge: Great Gray Owls	J. Beaudoin	150-day	29.90	29.90
Edwin M. Knowles		**Classic Mother Goose**			
92-76-001	Little Miss Muffet	S. Gustafson	150-day	29.90	29.90
92-76-002	Mary had a Little Lamb	S. Gustafson	150-day	29.90	29.90
92-76-003	Mary, Mary, Quite Contrary	S. Gustafson	150-day	29.90	29.90
Edwin M. Knowles		**Keepsake Rhymes**			
92-77-001	Humpty Dumpty	S. Gustafson	150-day	29.90	29.90
Edwin M. Knowles		**Thomas Kinkade's Thomashire**			
92-78-001	Olde Porterfield Tea Room	T. Kinkade	150-day	29.90	29.90
92-78-002	Olde Thomashire Mill	T. Kinkade	150-day	29.90	29.90
92-78-003	Swanbrook Cottage	T. Kinkade	150-day	32.90	32.90
Edwin M. Knowles		**Small Blessings**			
92-79-001	Now I Lay Me Down to Sleep	C. Layton	150-day	29.90	29.90
92-79-002	Bless Us O Lord	C. Layton	150-day	29.90	29.90
Edwin M. Knowles		**Seasons of Splendor**			
92-80-001	Autumn's Grandeur	K. Randle	150-day	29.90	29.90
Konigszelt Bayern		**Hedi Keller Christmas**			
79-01-001	The Adoration	H. Keller	Unkn.	29.50	29.50
80-01-002	Flight into Egypt	H. Keller	Unkn.	29.50	29.50
81-01-003	Return into Galilee	H. Keller	Unkn.	29.50	29.50
82-01-004	Following the Star	H. Keller	Unkn.	29.50	29.50
83-01-005	Rest on the Flight	H. Keller	Unkn.	29.50	29.50
84-01-006	The Nativity	H. Keller	Unkn.	29.50	29.50
85-01-007	Gift of the Magi	H. Keller	Unkn.	34.50	34.50
86-01-008	Annunciation	H. Keller	Unkn.	34.50	34.50
KPM-Royal Berlin		**Christmas**			
69-01-001	Christmas Star	Unknown	5,000	28.00	380.00
70-01-002	Three Kings	Unknown	5,000	28.00	300.00
71-01-003	Christmas Tree	Unknown	5,000	28.00	290.00
72-01-004	Christmas Angel	Unknown	5,000	31.00	300.00
73-01-005	Christ Child on Sled	Unknown	5,000	33.00	280.00
74-01-006	Angel and Horn	Unknown	5,000	35.00	180.00
75-01-007	Shepherds	Unknown	5,000	40.00	165.00
76-01-008	Star of Bethlehem	Unknown	5,000	43.00	140.00
77-01-009	Mary at Crib	Unknown	5,000	46.00	100.00
78-01-010	Three Wise Men	Unknown	5,000	49.00	54.00
79-01-011	The Manger	Unknown	5,000	55.00	55.00
80-01-012	Shepherds in Fields	Unknown	5,000	55.00	55.00
Lalique		**Annual**			
65-01-001	Deux Oiseaux (Two Birds)	M. Lalique	2,000	25.00	1200.00
66-01-002	Rose de Songerie (Dream Rose)	M. Lalique	5,000	25.00	160.00
67-01-003	Ballet de Poisson (Fish Ballet)	M. Lalique	5,000	25.00	120.00
68-01-004	Gazelle Fantaisie (Gazelle Fantasy)	M. Lalique	5,000	25.00	115.00
69-01-005	Papillon (Butterfly)	M. Lalique	5,000	30.00	80.00
70-01-006	Paon (Peacock)	M. Lalique	5,000	30.00	70.00
71-01-007	Hibou (Owl)	M. Lalique	5,000	35.00	70.00
72-01-008	Coquillage (Shell)	M. Lalique	5,000	40.00	65.00
73-01-009	Petit Geai (Jayling)	M. Lalique	5,000	42.50	125.00
74-01-010	Sous d'Argent (Silver Pennies)	M. Lalique	5,000	47.50	115.00
75-01-011	Duo de Poisson (Fish Duet)	M. Lalique	5,000	50.00	135.00
76-01-012	Aigle (Eagle)	M. Lalique	5,000	60.00	100.00
Lance Corporation		**Sebastian Plates**			
78-01-001	Motif No. 1	P.W. Baston	Closed	75.00	50-75.00
79-01-002	Grand Canyon	P.W. Baston	Closed	75.00	50-75.00
80-01-003	Lone Cypress	P.W. Baston	Closed	75.00	150-175.
80-01-004	In The Candy Store	P.W. Baston	Closed	39.50	39.50
81-01-005	The Doctor	P.W. Baston	Closed	39.50	39.50
83-01-006	Little Mother	P.W. Baston	Closed	39.50	39.50
84-01-007	Switching The Freight	P.W. Baston	Closed	42.50	80-100.00
Lance Corporation		**The American Expansion (Hudson Pewter)**			
75-02-001	Spirit of '76 (6" Plate)	P.W. Baston	Closed	Unkn.	100-120.
75-02-002	American Independence	P.W. Baston	Closed	Unkn.	100-125.
75-02-003	American Expansion	P.W. Baston	Closed	Unkn.	50-75.00
75-02-004	The American War Between the States	P.W. Baston	Closed	Unkn.	150-200.
Lance Corporation		**A Child's Christmas (Hudson Pewter)**			
78-03-001	Bedtime Story	A. Petitto	10,000	35.00	60.00
79-03-002	Littlest Angels	A. Petitto	10,000	35.00	60.00
80-03-003	Heaven's Christmas Tree	A. Petitto	10,000	42.50	60.00
81-03-004	Filling The Sky	A. Petitto	10,000	47.50	60.00
Lance Corporation		**Twas The Night Before Christmas (Hudson Pewter)**			
82-04-001	Not A Creature Was Stirring	A. Hollis	10,000	47.50	60.00
83-04-002	Visions Of Sugar Plums	A. Hollis	10,000	47.50	60.00
84-04-003	His Eyes How They Twinkled	A. Hollis	10,000	47.50	60.00
85-04-004	Happy Christmas To All	A. Hollis	10,000	47.50	60.00
86-04-005	Bringing Home The Tree	J. Wanat	10,000	47.50	60.00
Lance Corporation		**Walt Disney (Hudson Pewter)**			
86-05-001	God Bless Us, Every One	D. Everhart	10,000	47.50	60.00
87-05-002	The Caroling Angels	A. Petitto	10,000	47.50	60.00
87-05-003	Jolly Old Saint Nick	D. Everhart	10,000	55.00	60.00
88-05-004	He's Checking It Twice	D. Everhart	10,000	50.00	60.00
Lance Corporaton		**The Songs of Christmas (Hudson Pewter)**			
88-06-001	Silent Night	A. McGrory	2,500	55.00	60.00
89-06-002	Hark! The Herald Angels Sing	A. McGrory	2,500	60.00	60.00
90-06-003	The First Noel	A. McGrory	2,500	60.00	60.00
91-06-004	We Three Kings	A. McGrory	2,500	60.00	60.00
Lenox China		**Boehm Birds**			
70-01-001	Wood Thrush	E. Boehm	Yr.Iss.	35.00	140.00
71-01-002	Goldfinch	E. Boehm	Yr.Iss.	35.00	65.00
72-01-003	Mountain Bluebird	E. Boehm	Yr.Iss.	37.50	39.00
73-01-004	Meadowlark	E. Boehm	Yr.Iss.	50.00	50.00
74-01-005	Rufous Hummingbird	E. Boehm	Yr.Iss.	45.00	45-50.00
75-01-006	American Redstart	E. Boehm	Yr.Iss.	50.00	50.00
76-01-007	Cardinals	E. Boehm	Yr.Iss.	53.00	55.00
77-01-008	Robins	E. Boehm	Yr.Iss.	55.00	55.00
78-01-009	Mockingbirds	E. Boehm	Yr.Iss.	58.00	75.00
79-01-010	Golden-Crowned Kinglets	E. Boehm	Yr.Iss.	65.00	75.00
80-01-011	Black-Throated Blue Warblers	E. Boehm	Yr.Iss.	80.00	85.00
81-01-012	Eastern Phoebes	E. Boehm	Yr.Iss.	92.50	92.50
Lenox China		**Boehm Woodland Wildlife**			
73-02-001	Racoons	E. Boehm	Yr.Iss.	50.00	50.00
74-02-002	Red Foxes	E. Boehm	Yr.Iss.	52.50	52.50
75-02-003	Cottontail Rabbits	E. Boehm	Yr.Iss.	58.50	58.50
76-02-004	Eastern Chipmunks	E. Boehm	Yr.Iss.	62.50	62.50
77-02-005	Beaver	E. Boehm	Yr.Iss.	67.50	67.50
78-02-006	Whitetail Deer	E. Boehm	Yr.Iss.	70.00	70.00
79-02-007	Squirrels	E. Boehm	Yr.Iss.	76.00	76.00
80-02-008	Bobcats	E. Boehm	Yr.Iss.	82.50	82.50
81-02-009	Martens	E. Boehm	Yr.Iss.	100.00	150.00
82-02-010	River Otters	E. Boehm	Yr.Iss.	100.00	180.00

Company / Number	Name	Series / Artist	Edition Limit	Issue Price	Quote
Lenox China		**Colonial Christmas Wreath**			
81-03-001	Colonial Virginia	Unknown	Yr.Iss.	65.00	76.00
82-03-002	Massachusetts	Unknown	Yr.Iss.	70.00	93.00
83-03-003	Maryland	Unknown	Yr.Iss.	70.00	79.00
84-03-004	Rhode Island	Unknown	Yr.Iss.	70.00	82.00
85-03-005	Connecticut	Unknown	Yr.Iss.	70.00	75.00
86-03-006	New Hampshire	Unknown	Yr.Iss.	70.00	75.00
87-03-007	Pennsylvania	Unknown	Yr.Iss.	70.00	75.00
88-03-008	Delaware	Unknown	Yr.Iss.	70.00	70.00
89-03-009	New York	Unknown	Yr.Iss.	75.00	82.00
90-03-010	New Jersey	Unknown	Yr.Iss.	75.00	78.00
91-03-011	South Carolina	Unknown	Yr.Iss.	75.00	75.00
92-03-012	North Carolina	Unknown	Yr.Iss.	75.00	75.00
Lenox Collections		**American Wildlife**			
82-01-001	Red Foxes	N. Adams	9,500	65.00	65.00
82-01-002	Ocelots	N. Adams	9,500	65.00	65.00
82-01-003	Sea Lions	N. Adams	9,500	65.00	65.00
82-01-004	Raccoons	N. Adams	9,500	65.00	65.00
82-01-005	Dall Sheep	N. Adams	9,500	65.00	65.00
82-01-006	Black Bears	N. Adams	9,500	65.00	65.00
82-01-007	Mountain Lions	N. Adams	9,500	65.00	65.00
82-01-008	Polar Bears	N. Adams	9,500	65.00	65.00
82-01-009	Otters	N. Adams	9,500	65.00	65.00
82-01-010	White Tailed Deer	N. Adams	9,500	65.00	65.00
82-01-011	Buffalo	N. Adams	9,500	65.00	65.00
82-01-012	Jack Rabbits	N. Adams	9,500	65.00	65.00
Lenox Collections		**Garden Bird Plate Collection**			
88-02-001	Chickadee	Unknown	Open	48.00	48.00
88-02-002	Bluejay	Unknown	Open	48.00	48.00
89-02-003	Hummingbird	Unknown	Open	48.00	48.00
91-02-004	Dove	Unknown	Open	48.00	48.00
91-02-005	Cardinal	Unknown	Open	48.00	48.00
92-02-006	Goldfinch	Unknown	Open	48.00	48.00
Lenox Collections		**Christmas Trees Around the World**			
91-03-001	Germany	Unknown	Yr.Iss.	75.00	75.00
92-03-002	France	Unknown	Yr.Iss.	75.00	75.00
Lenox Collections		**Annual Holiday**			
91-04-001	Sleigh	Unknown	Yr.Iss.	75.00	75.00
Lenox Collections		**Nature's Collage**			
92-05-001	Cedar Waxwing, Among The Berries	C. McClung	Open	34.50	34.50
92-05-002	Gold Finches, Golden Splendor	C. McClung	Open	34.50	34.50
Lihs Linder		**Christmas**			
72-01-001	Little Drummer Boy	J. Neubauer	6,000	25.00	35.00
73-01-002	Carolers	J. Neubauer	6,000	25.00	25.00
74-01-003	Peace	J. Neubauer	6,000	25.00	25.00
75-01-004	Christmas Cheer	J. Neubauer	6,000	30.00	34.00
76-01-005	Joy of Christmas	J. Neubauer	6,000	30.00	30.00
77-01-006	Holly Jolly Christmas	J. Neubauer	6,000	30.00	30.00
78-01-007	Holy Night	J. Neubauer	6,000	40.00	40.00
Lightpost Publishing		**Thomas Kinkade Signature Collection**			
91-01-001	Chandler's Cottage	T. Kinkade	2,500	49.95	49.95
91-01-002	Cedar Nook	T. Kinkade	2,500	49.95	49.95
91-01-003	Sleigh Ride Home	T. Kinkade	2,500	49.95	49.95
91-01-004	Home To Grandma's	T. Kinkade	2,500	49.95	49.95
Lilliput Lane, Ltd.		**American Landmarks Collection**			
90-01-001	Country Church	R. Day	5,000	35.00	35.00
90-01-002	Riverside Chapel	R. Day	5,000	35.00	35.00
March of Dimes		**Our Children, Our Future**			
89-01-001	A Time for Peace	D. Zolan	150-day	29.00	30-39.00
89-01-002	A Time To Love	S. Kuck	150-day	29.00	45.00
89-01-003	A Time To Paint	J. McClelland	150-day	29.00	35.00
89-01-004	A Time To Be Born	G. Perillo	150-day	29.00	35-49.00
90-01-005	A Time To Embrace	E. Hibel	150-day	29.00	35.00
90-01-006	A Time To Laugh	A. Williams	150-day	29.00	35.00
Maruri USA		**Eagle Plate Series**			
84-01-001	Free Flight	W. Gaither	Closed	150.00	150-198.
Mingolla/Home Plates		**Christmas**			
73-01-001	Copper, Enamel	Mingolla	1,000	95.00	165.00
74-01-002	Copper, Enamel	Mingolla	1,000	110.00	145.00
75-01-003	Copper, Enamel	Mingolla	1,000	125.00	145.00
76-01-004	Copper, Enamel	Mingolla	1,000	125.00	125.00
77-01-005	Winter Wonderland (Copper Enamel)	Mingolla	2,000	200.00	200.00
Mingolla/Home Plates		**Christmas**			
74-02-001	Porcelain	Mingolla	5,000	35.00	65.00
75-02-002	Porcelain	Mingolla	5,000	35.00	45.00
76-02-003	Porcelain	Mingolla	5,000	35.00	30.00
Museum Collections, Inc.		**American Family I**			
79-01-001	Baby's First Step	N. Rockwell	9,900	28.50	48.00
79-01-002	Happy Birthday Dear Mother	N. Rockwell	9,900	28.50	45.00
79-01-003	Sweet Sixteen	N. Rockwell	9,900	28.50	35.00
79-01-004	First Haircut	N. Rockwell	9,900	28.50	35.00
79-01-005	First Prom	N. Rockwell	9,900	28.50	35.00
79-01-006	Wrapping Christmas Presents	N. Rockwell	9,900	28.50	35.00
79-01-007	The Student	N. Rockwell	9,900	28.50	35.00
79-01-008	Birthday Party	N. Rockwell	9,900	28.50	35.00
79-01-009	Little Mother	N. Rockwell	9,900	28.50	35.00
79-01-010	Washing Our Dog	N. Rockwell	9,900	28.50	35.00
79-01-011	Mother's Little Helpers	N. Rockwell	9,900	28.50	35.00
79-01-012	Bride and Groom	N. Rockwell	9,900	28.50	35.00
Museum Collections, Inc.		**Christmas**			
79-02-001	Day After Christmas	N. Rockwell	Yr.Iss	75.00	75.00
80-02-002	Checking His List	N. Rockwell	Yr.Iss	75.00	75.00
81-02-003	Ringing in Good Cheer	N. Rockwell	Yr.Iss	75.00	75.00
82-02-004	Waiting for Santa	N. Rockwell	Yr.Iss	75.00	75.00
83-02-005	High Hopes	N. Rockwell	Yr.Iss	75.00	75.00
84-02-006	Space Age Santa	N. Rockwell	Yr.Iss	55.00	55.00
Museum Collections, Inc.		**American Family II**			
80-03-001	New Arrival	N. Rockwell	22,500	35.00	55.00
80-03-002	Sweet Dreams	N. Rockwell	22,500	35.00	37.50
80-03-003	Little Shaver	N. Rockwell	22,500	35.00	40.00
80-03-004	We Missed You Daddy	N. Rockwell	22,500	35.00	37.50
80-03-005	Home Run Slugger	N. Rockwell	22,500	35.00	37.50
80-03-006	Giving Thanks	N. Rockwell	22,500	35.00	37.50
80-03-007	Space Pioneers	N. Rockwell	22,500	35.00	37.50
80-03-008	Little Salesman	N. Rockwell	22,500	35.00	37.50
80-03-009	Almost Grown up	N. Rockwell	22,500	35.00	37.50
80-03-010	Courageous Hero	N. Rockwell	22,500	35.00	37.50
81-03-011	At the Circus	N. Rockwell	22,500	35.00	37.50
81-03-012	Good Food, Good Friends	N. Rockwell	22,500	35.00	37.50
Pemberton & Oakes		**Zolan's Children**			
78-01-001	Erik and Dandelion	D. Zolan	Undis.	19.00	250.00
79-01-002	Sabina in the Grass	D. Zolan	Undis.	22.00	225.00
80-01-003	By Myself	D. Zolan	Undis.	24.00	40.00
81-01-004	For You	D. Zolan	Undis.	24.00	45.00
Pemberton & Oakes		**Wonder of Childhood**			
82-02-001	Touching the Sky	D. Zolan	Undis.	19.00	35.00
83-02-002	Spring Innocence	D. Zolan	Undis.	19.00	43.00
84-02-003	Winter Angel	D. Zolan	Undis.	22.00	60.00
85-02-004	Small Wonder	D. Zolan	Undis.	22.00	40.00
86-02-005	Grandma's Garden	D. Zolan	Undis.	22.00	56.00
87-02-006	Day Dreamer	D. Zolan	Undis.	22.00	40.00
Pemberton & Oakes		**Children and Pets**			
84-03-001	Tender Moment	D. Zolan	Undis.	19.00	50.00
84-03-002	Golden Moment	D. Zolan	Undis.	19.00	44.00
85-03-003	Making Friends	D. Zolan	Undis.	19.00	35.00
85-03-004	Tender Beginning	D. Zolan	Undis.	19.00	49-65.00
86-03-005	Backyard Discovery	D. Zolan	Undis.	19.00	39.00
86-03-006	Waiting to Play	D. Zolan	Undis.	19.00	50.00
Pemberton & Oakes		**Children at Christmas**			
81-04-001	A Gift for Laurie	D. Zolan	15,000	48.00	90.00
82-04-002	Christmas Prayer	D. Zolan	15,000	48.00	105.00
83-04-003	Erik's Delight	D. Zolan	15,000	48.00	85.00
84-04-004	Christmas Secret	D. Zolan	15,000	48.00	75.00
85-04-005	Christmas Kitten	D. Zolan	15,000	48.00	95.00
86-04-006	Laurie and the Creche	D. Zolan	15,000	48.00	60.00
Pemberton & Oakes		**Special Moments of Childhood**			
88-05-001	Brotherly Love	D. Zolan	19-day	19.00	60.00
88-05-002	Sunny Surprise	D. Zolan	19-day	19.00	35.00
89-05-003	Summer's Child	D. Zolan	19-day	22.00	40.00
90-05-004	Meadow Magic	D. Zolan	19-day	22.00	32.00
90-05-005	Cone For Two	D. Zolan	19-day	24.00	25.00
90-05-006	Rodeo Girl	D. Zolan	19-day	24.60	25.00
Pemberton & Oakes		**Childhood Friendship**			
86-06-001	Beach Break	D. Zolan	17-day	19.00	55.00
87-06-002	Little Engineers	D. Zolan	17-day	19.00	105.00
88-06-003	Tiny Treasures	D. Zolan	17-day	19.00	48.00
88-06-004	Sharing Secrets	D. Zolan	17-day	19.00	60.00
88-06-005	Dozens of Daisies	D. Zolan	17-day	19.00	45.00
90-06-006	Country Walk	D. Zolan	17-day	19.00	45.00
Pemberton & Oakes		**The Best of Zolan in Miniature**			
85-07-001	Sabina	D. Zolan	S/O	12.50	145.00
86-07-002	Erik and Dandelion	D. Zolan	Undis.	12.50	96.00
86-07-003	Tender Moment	D. Zolan	Undis.	12.50	65.00
86-07-004	Touching the Sky	D. Zolan	Undis.	12.50	52.00
87-07-005	A Gift for Laurie	D. Zolan	Undis.	12.50	44-82.00
87-07-006	Small Wonder	D. Zolan	Undis.	12.50	39.00
Pemberton & Oakes		**Anniversary (10th)**			
88-08-001	Ribbons and Roses	D. Zolan	19-day	24.40	45.00
Pemberton & Oakes		**Fathers Day**			
86-09-001	Daddy's Home	D. Zolan	Undis.	19.00	65-90.00
Pemberton & Oakes		**Mothers Day**			
88-10-001	Mother's Angels	D. Zolan	Undis.	19.00	40.00
Pemberton & Oakes		**Adventures of Childhood**			
89-11-001	Almost Home	D. Zolan	44-day	19.60	69.00
89-11-002	Crystal's Creek	D. Zolan	44-day	19.60	36.00
89-11-003	Summer Suds	D. Zolan	44-day	22.00	27.00
90-11-004	Snowy Adventure	D. Zolan	44-day	22.00	39.00
91-11-005	Forests & Fairy Tales	D. Zolan	44-day	24.40	
Pemberton & Oakes		**Thanksgiving**			
81-12-001	I'm Thankful Too	D. Zolan	Undis.	19.00	79.50
Pemberton & Oakes		**Nutcracker II**			
81-13-001	Grand Finale	S. Fisher	Undis.	24.40	36.00
82-13-002	Arabian Dancers	S. Fisher	Undis.	24.40	67.50
83-13-003	Dew Drop Fairy	S. Fisher	Undis.	24.40	36.00
84-13-004	Clara's Delight	S. Fisher	Undis.	24.40	42.00
85-13-005	Bedtime for Nutcracker	S. Fisher	Undis.	24.40	45.00
86-13-006	The Crowning of Clara	S. Fisher	Undis.	24.40	36.00
87-13-007	Dance of the Snowflakes	D. Zolan	Undis.	24.40	75.00
88-13-008	The Royal Welcome	R. Anderson	Undis.	24.40	24.40
89-13-009	The Spanish Dancer	M. Vickers	Undis.	24.40	24.40
Pemberton & Oakes		**March of Dimes: Our Children, Our Future**			
87-14-001	A Time for Peace (1st in Series)	D. Zolan	150-day	29.00	29.00
Pemberton & Oakes		**Childhood Discoveries (Miniature)**			
90-15-001	Colors of Spring	D. Zolan	19-day	14.40	14.40
90-15-002	Autumn Leaves	D. Zolan	19-day	14.40	14.40
91-15-003	Enchanted Forest	D. Zolan	19-day	16.60	16.60
91-15-004	Just Ducky	D. Zolan	19-day	16.60	16.60
91-15-005	Rainy Day Pals	D. Zolan	19-day	16.60	16.60
92-15-006	Double Trouble	D. Zolan	19-day	16.60	16.60
Pemberton & Oakes		**Special Issue (Miniature)**			
90-16-001	First Kiss (Valentine's Day)	D. Zolan	19-day	14.40	55.00
90-16-002	Flowers for Mother (Mother's Day)	D. Zolan	19-day	14.40	49.00
91-16-003	Easter Morning (Easter)	D. Zolan	19-day	16.60	35.00
92-16-004	Twilight Prayer (Mother's Day)	D. Zolan	19-day	16.60	16.60

Number	Name	Artist	Edition Limit	Issue Price	Quote
PenDelfin		**Plate Series**			
XX-01-001	Mother with baby	J. Heap	Retrd.	40.00	200.00
XX-01-002	Father	J. Heap	7,500	40.00	40.00
XX-01-003	Whopper	D. Roberts	7,500	50.00	50.00
XX-01-004	Gingerbread Day	J. Heap	7,500	55.00	55.00
XX-01-005	Caravan	D. Roberts	7,500	60.00	60.00
XX-01-006	Old Schoolhouse	J. Heap	7,500	60.00	60.00
Pickard		**Lockhart Wildlife**			
70-01-001	Woodcock/Ruffed Grouse, pair	J. Lockhart	2,000	150.00	210.00
71-01-002	Teal/Mallard, pair	J. Lockhart	2,000	150.00	160.00
72-01-003	Mockingbird/Cardinal, pair	J. Lockhart	2,000	162.50	140.00
73-01-004	Turkey/Pheasant, pair	J. Lockhart	2,000	162.50	225.00
74-01-005	American Bald Eagle	J. Lockhart	2,000	150.00	675.00
75-01-006	White Tailed Deer	J. Lockhart	2,500	100.00	100.00
76-01-007	American Buffalo	J. Lockhart	2,500	165.00	165.00
77-01-008	Great Horn Owl	J. Lockhart	2,500	100.00	115.00
78-01-009	American Panther	J. Lockhart	2,000	175.00	175.00
79-01-010	Red Foxes	J. Lockhart	2,500	120.00	120.00
80-01-011	Trumpeter Swan	J. Lockhart	2,000	200.00	200.00
Pickard		**Annual Christmas**			
76-02-001	Alba Madonna	Raphael	7,500	60.00	100.00
77-02-002	The Nativity	L. Lotto	7,500	65.00	65.00
78-02-003	Rest on Flight into Egypt	G. David	10,000	65.00	65.00
79-02-004	Adoration of the Magi	Botticelli	10,000	70.00	70.00
80-02-005	Madonna and Child	Sodoma	10,000	80.00	80.00
81-02-006	Madonna and Child with Angels	Memling	10,000	90.00	90.00
Pickard		**Mother's Love**			
80-03-001	Miracle	I. Spencer	7,500	95.00	95.00
81-03-002	Story Time	I. Spencer	7,500	110.00	110.00
82-03-003	First Edition	I. Spencer	7,500	115.00	115.00
83-03-004	Precious Moment	I. Spencer	7,500	120.00	145.00
Pickard		**Children of Mexico**			
81-04-001	Maria	J. Sanchez	5,000	85.00	85.00
81-04-002	Miguel	J. Sanchez	5,000	85.00	85.00
82-04-003	Regina	J. Sanchez	5,000	90.00	90.00
83-04-004	Raphael	J. Sanchez	5,000	90.00	90.00
Pickard		**Symphony of Roses**			
82-05-001	Wild Irish Rose	I. Spencer	10,000	85.00	95.00
83-05-002	Yellow Rose of Texas	I. Spencer	10,000	90.00	110.00
84-05-003	Honeysuckle Rose	I. Spencer	10,000	95.00	135.00
85-05-004	Rose of Washington Square	I. Spencer	10,000	100.00	175.00
Porsgrund		**Christmas**			
68-01-001	Church Scene	G. Bratile	Annual	12.00	125.00
69-01-002	Three Kings	G. Bratile	Annual	12.00	12.00
70-01-003	Road to Bethlehem	G. Bratile	Annual	12.00	12.00
71-01-004	A Child is Born	G. Bratile	Annual	12.00	12.00
72-01-005	Hark the Herald Angels	G. Bratile	Annual	12.00	12.00
73-01-006	Promise of the Savior	G. Bratile	Annual	12.00	12.00
74-01-007	The Shepherds	G. Bratile	Annual	15.00	36.00
75-01-008	Road to Temple	G. Bratile	Annual	19.50	19.50
76-01-009	Jesus and the Elders	G. Bratile	Annual	22.00	43.00
77-01-010	Draught of the Fish	G. Bratile	Annual	24.00	28.00
Princeton Gallery		**Circus Friends Collection**			
89-01-001	Don't Be Shy	R. Sanderson	Unkn.	29.50	29.50
90-01-002	Make Me A Clown	R. Sanderson	Unkn.	29.50	29.50
90-01-003	Looks Like Rain	R. Sanderson	Unkn.	29.50	29.50
90-01-004	Cheer Up Mr. Clown	R. Sanderson	Unkn.	29.50	29.50
Princeton Gallery		**Cubs Of The Big Cats**			
90-02-001	Cougar Cub	Q. Lemond	Unkn.	29.50	29.50
91-02-002	Lion Cub	Q. Lemond	90-day	29.50	29.50
91-02-003	Snow Leopard	Q. Lemond	90-day	29.50	29.50
91-02-004	Cheetah	Q. Lemond	90-day	29.50	29.50
91-02-005	Tiger	Q. Lemond	90-day	29.50	29.50
92-02-006	Lynx Cub	Q. Lemond	90-day	29.50	29.50
92-02-007	White Tiger Cub	Q. Lemond	90-day	29.50	29.50
Princeton Gallery		**Arctic Wolves**			
91-03-001	Song of the Wilderness	J. Van Zyle	90-day	29.50	29.50
92-03-002	In The Eye of the Moon	J. Van Zyle	90-day	29.50	29.50
Princeton Gallery		**Enchanted World of the Unicorn**			
91-04-001	Rainbow Valley	R. Sanderson	90-day	29.50	29.50
92-04-002	Golden Shore	R. Sanderson	90-day	29.50	29.50
Princeton Gallery		**Darling Dalmatians**			
91-05-001	Dalmatian	L. Picken	90-day	29.50	29.50
92-05-002	Firehouse Frolic	L. Picken	90-day	29.50	29.50
Reco International		**Bohemian Annuals**			
74-01-001	1974	Unknown	500	130.00	155.00
75-01-002	1975	Unknown	500	140.00	160.00
76-01-003	1976	Unknown	500	150.00	160.00
Reco International		**Americanna**			
72-02-001	Gaspee Incident	S. Devlin	1,500	200.00	325.00
Reco International		**Dresden Christmas**			
71-03-001	Shepherd Scene	Unknown	3,500	15.00	50.00
72-03-002	Niklas Church	Unknown	6,000	15.00	25.00
73-03-003	Schwanstein Church	Unknown	6,000	18.00	35.00
74-03-004	Village Scene	Unknown	5,000	20.00	30.00
75-03-005	Rothenburg Scene	Unknown	5,000	24.00	30.00
76-03-006	Village Church	Unknown	5,000	26.00	35.00
77-03-007	Old Mill (Issue Closed)	Unknown	5,000	28.00	30.00
Reco International		**Dresden Mother's Day**			
72-04-001	Doe and Fawn	Unknown	8,000	15.00	20.00
73-04-002	Mare and Colt	Unknown	6,000	16.00	25.00
74-04-003	Tiger and Cub	Unknown	5,000	20.00	23.00
75-04-004	Dachshunds	Unknown	5,000	24.00	28.00
76-04-005	Owl and Offspring	Unknown	5,000	26.00	30.00
77-04-006	Chamois (Issue Closed)	Unknown	5,000	28.00	30.00
Reco International		**Furstenberg Christmas**			
71-05-001	Rabbits	Unknown	7,500	15.00	30.00
72-05-002	Snowy Village	Unknown	6,000	15.00	20.00
73-05-003	Christmas Eve	Unknown	4,000	18.00	35.00
74-05-004	Sparrows	Unknown	4,000	20.00	30.00
75-05-005	Deer Family	Unknown	4,000	22.00	30.00
76-05-006	Winter Birds	Unknown	4,000	25.00	25.00
Reco International		**Furstenberg Deluxe Christmas**			
71-06-001	Wise Men	E. Grossberg	1,500	45.00	45.00
72-06-002	Holy Family	E. Grossberg	2,000	45.00	45.00
73-06-003	Christmas Eve	E. Grossberg	2,000	60.00	65.00
Reco International		**Furstenberg Easter**			
71-07-001	Sheep	Unknown	3,500	15.00	150.00
72-07-002	Chicks	Unknown	6,500	15.00	60.00
73-07-003	Bunnies	Unknown	4,000	16.00	80.00
74-07-004	Pussywillow	Unknown	4,000	20.00	32.50
75-07-005	Easter Window	Unknown	4,000	22.00	30.00
76-07-006	Flower Collecting	Unknown	4,000	25.00	25.00
Reco International		**Furstenberg Mother's Day**			
72-08-001	Hummingbirds, Fe	Unknown	6,000	15.00	45.00
73-08-002	Hedgehogs	Unknown	5,000	16.00	40.00
74-08-003	Doe and Fawn	Unknown	4,000	20.00	30.00
75-08-004	Swans	Unknown	4,000	22.00	23.00
76-08-005	Koala Bears	Unknown	4,000	25.00	30.00
Reco International		**Furstenberg Olympic**			
72-09-001	Munich	J. Poluszynski	5,000	20.00	75.00
76-09-002	Montreal	J. Poluszynski	5,000	37.50	37.50
Reco International		**Grafburg Christmas**			
75-10-001	Black-Capped Chickadee	Unknown	5,000	20.00	60.00
76-10-002	Squirrels	Unknown	5,000	22.00	22.00
Reco International		**King's Christmas**			
73-11-001	Adoration	Merli	1,500	100.00	265.00
74-11-002	Madonna	Merli	1,500	150.00	250.00
75-11-003	Heavenly Choir	Merli	1,500	160.00	235.00
76-11-004	Siblings	Merli	1,500	200.00	225.00
Reco International		**King's Flowers**			
73-12-001	Carnation	A. Falchi	1,000	85.00	130.00
74-12-002	Red Rose	A. Falchi	1,000	100.00	145.00
75-12-003	Yellow Dahlia	A. Falchi	1,000	110.00	162.00
76-12-004	Bluebells	A. Falchi	1,000	130.00	165.00
77-12-005	Anemones	A. Falchi	1,000	130.00	175.00
Reco International		**King's Mother's Day**			
73-13-001	Dancing Girl	Merli	1,500	100.00	225.00
74-13-002	Dancing Boy	Merli	1,500	115.00	250.00
75-13-003	Motherly Love	Merli	1,500	140.00	225.00
76-13-004	Maiden	Merli	1,500	180.00	200.00
Reco International		**Four Seasons**			
73-14-001	Spring	J. Poluszynski	2,500	50.00	75.00
73-14-002	Summer	J. Poluszynski	2,500	50.00	75.00
73-14-003	Fall	J. Poluszynski	2,500	50.00	75.00
73-14-004	Winter	J. Poluszynski	2,500	50.00	75.00
Reco International		**Marmot Father's Day**			
70-15-001	Stag	Unknown	3,500	12.00	100.00
71-15-002	Horse	Unknown	3,500	12.50	40.00
Reco International		**Marmot Christmas**			
70-16-001	Polar Bear, Fe	Unknown	5,000	13.00	60.00
71-16-002	Buffalo Bill	Unknown	6,000	16.00	55.00
72-16-003	Boy and Grandfather	Unknown	5,000	20.00	50.00
71-16-004	American Buffalo	Unknown	6,000	14.50	35.00
73-16-005	Snowman	Unknown	3,000	22.00	45.00
74-16-006	Dancing	Unknown	2,000	24.00	30.00
75-16-007	Quail	Unknown	2,000	30.00	40.00
76-16-008	Windmill	Unknown	2,000	40.00	40.00
Reco International		**Marmot Mother's Day**			
72-17-001	Seal	Unknown	6,000	16.00	60.00
73-17-002	Bear with Cub	Unknown	3,000	20.00	140.00
74-17-003	Penguins	Unknown	2,000	24.00	50.00
75-17-004	Raccoons	Unknown	2,000	30.00	45.00
76-17-005	Ducks	Unknown	2,000	40.00	40.00
Reco International		**Moser Christmas**			
70-18-001	Hradcany Castle	Unknown	400	75.00	170.00
71-18-002	Karlstein Castle	Unknown	1,365	75.00	80.00
72-18-003	Old Town Hall	Unknown	1,000	85.00	85.00
73-18-004	Karlovy Vary Castle	Unknown	500	90.00	100.00
Reco International		**Moser Mother's Day**			
71-19-001	Peacocks	Unknown	350	75.00	100.00
72-19-002	Butterflies	Unknown	750	85.00	90.00
73-19-003	Squirrels	Unknown	500	90.00	95.00
Reco International		**Royale**			
69-20-001	Apollo Moon Landing	Unknown	2,000	30.00	80.00
Reco International		**Royale Christmas**			
69-21-001	Christmas Fair	Unknown	6,000	12.00	125.00
70-21-002	Vigil Mass	Unknown	10,000	13.00	110.00
71-21-003	Christmas Night	Unknown	8,000	16.00	50.00
72-21-004	Elks	Unknown	8,000	16.00	45.00
73-21-005	Christmas Down	Unknown	6,000	20.00	37.50
74-21-006	Village Christmas	Unknown	5,000	22.00	60.00
75-21-007	Feeding Time	Unknown	5,000	26.00	35.00
76-21-008	Seaport Christmas	Unknown	5,000	27.50	30.00
77-21-009	Sledding	Unknown	5,000	30.00	30.00
Reco International		**Royal Mother's Day**			
70-22-001	Swan and Young	Unknown	6,000	12.00	80.00
71-22-002	Doe and Fawn	Unknown	9,000	13.00	55.00
72-22-003	Rabbits	Unknown	9,000	16.00	40.00
73-22-004	Owl Family	Unknown	6,000	18.00	40.00
74-22-005	Duck and Young	Unknown	5,000	22.00	40.00
75-22-006	Lynx and Cubs	Unknown	5,000	26.00	40.00
76-22-007	Woodcock and Young	Unknown	5,000	27.50	32.50

Company Number	Name	Series Artist	Edition Limit	Issue Price	Quote
77-22-008	Koala Bear	Unknown	5,000	30.00	30.00
Reco International		**Royale Father's Day**			
70-23-001	Frigate Constitution	Unknown	5,000	13.00	80.00
71-23-002	Man Fishing	Unknown	5,000	13.00	35.00
72-23-003	Mountaineer	Unknown	5,000	16.00	55.00
73-23-004	Camping	Unknown	4,000	18.00	45.00
74-23-005	Eagle	Unknown	2,500	22.00	35.00
75-23-006	Regatta	Unknown	2,500	26.00	35.00
76-23-007	Hunting	Unknown	2,500	27.50	32.50
77-23-008	Fishing	Unknown	2,500	30.00	30.00
Reco International		**Royale Game Plates**			
72-24-001	Setters	J. Poluszynski	500	180.00	200.00
73-24-002	Fox	J. Poluszynski	500	200.00	250.00
74-24-003	Osprey	W. Schiener	250	250.00	250.00
75-24-004	California Quail	W. Schiener	250	265.00	265.00
Reco International		**Royale Germania Christmas Annual**			
70-25-001	Orchid	Unknown	600	200.00	650.00
71-25-002	Cyclamen	Unknown	1,000	200.00	325.000
72-25-003	Silver Thistle	Unknown	1,000	250.00	290.00
73-25-004	Tulips	Unknown	600	275.00	310.00
74-25-005	Sunflowers	Unknown	500	300.00	320.00
75-25-006	Snowdrops	Unknown	350	450.00	500.00
Reco Inernational		**Royale Germania Crystal Mother's Day**			
71-26-001	Roses	Unknown	250	135.00	650.00
72-26-002	Elephant and Youngster	Unknown	750	180.00	250.00
73-26-003	Koala Bear and Cub	Unknown	600	200.00	225.00
74-26-004	Squirrels	Unknown	500	240.00	250.00
75-26-005	Swan and Young	Unknown	350	350.00	360.00
Reco International		**Western**			
74-27-001	Mountain Man	E. Berke	1,000	165.00	165.00
Reco International		**The World of Children**			
77-28-001	Rainy Day Fun	J. McClelland	10,000	50.00	50.00
78-28-002	When I Grow Up	J. McClelland	15,000	50.00	50.00
79-28-003	You're Invited	J. McClelland	15,000	50.00	51.00
80-28-004	Kittens for Sale	J. McClelland	15,000	50.00	50.00
Reco International		**Mother Goose**			
79-29-001	Mary, Mary	J. McClelland	Yr.Iss.	22.50	120.00
80-29-002	Little Boy Blue	J. McClelland	Yr.Iss.	22.50	35.00
81-29-003	Little Miss Muffet	J. McClelland	Yr.Iss.	24.50	24.50
82-29-004	Little Jack Horner	J. McClelland	Yr.Iss.	24.50	24.50
83-29-005	Little Bo Peep	J. McClelland	Yr.Iss.	24.50	24.50
84-29-006	Diddle, Diddle Dumpling	J. McClelland	Yr.Iss.	24.50	24.50
85-29-007	Mary Had a Little Lamb	J. McClelland	Yr.Iss.	27.50	30.00
86-29-008	Jack and Jill	J. McClelland	Yr.Iss.	27.50	27.50
Reco International		**The McClelland Children's Circus Collection**			
82-30-001	Tommy the Clown	J. McClelland	100-day	29.50	30-37.50
82-30-002	Katie, the Tightrope Walker	J. McClelland	100-day	29.50	30.00
83-30-003	Johnny the Strongman	J. McClelland	100-day	29.50	30.00
84-30-004	Maggie the Animal Trainer	J. McClelland	100-day	29.50	30.00
Reco International		**Becky's Day**			
85-31-001	Awakening	J. McClelland	90-day	24.50	24.50
85-31-002	Getting Dressed	J. McClelland	90-day	24.50	24.50
86-31-003	Breakfast	J. McClelland	90-day	27.50	27.50
86-31-004	Learning is Fun	J. McClelland	90-day	27.50	27.50
86-31-005	Muffin Making	J. McClelland	90-day	27.50	27.50
86-31-006	Tub Time	J. McClelland	90-day	27.50	27.50
86-31-007	Evening Prayer	J. McClelland	90-day	27.50	27.50
Reco International		**Treasured Songs of Childhood**			
87-32-001	Twinkle, Twinkle, Little Star	J. McClelland	150-day	29.50	30-36.00
88-32-002	A Tisket, A Tasket	J. McClelland	150-day	29.50	29.50
88-32-003	Baa, Baa, Black Sheep	J. McClelland	150-day	32.90	32.90-35.00
89-32-004	Round The Mulberry Bush	J. McClelland	150-day	32.90	32.90-35.00
89-32-005	Rain, Rain Go Away	J. McClelland	150-day	32.90	32.90-35.00
89-32-006	I'm A Little Teapot	J. McClelland	150-day	32.90	32.90-38.00
89-32-007	Pat-A-Cake	J. McClelland	150-day	34.90	34.90
90-32-008	Hush Little Baby	J. McClelland	150-day	34.90	34.90
Reco International		**The Wonder of Christmas**			
91-33-001	Santa's Secret	J. McClelland	48-day	29.50	29.50
92-33-002	My Favorite Ornament	J. McClelland	48-day	29.50	29.50
92-33-003	Waiting For Santa	J. McClelland	48-day	29.50	29.50
Reco International		**The Premier Collection**			
91-34-001	Love	J. McClelland	7,500	75.00	75.00
Reco International		**Golf Collection**			
92-35-001	Par Excellence	J. McClelland	180-day	35.00	35.00
Reco International		**March of Dimes: Our Children, Our Future**			
89-36-001	A Time to Love (2nd in Series)	S. Kuck	150-day	29.00	45.00
89-36-002	A Time to Plant (3rd in Series)	J. McClelland	150-day	29.00	29.00
Reco International		**Games Children Play**			
79-37-001	Me First	S. Kuck	10,000	45.00	50.00
80-37-002	Forever Bubbles	S. Kuck	10,000	45.00	48.00
81-37-003	Skating Pals	S. Kuck	10,000	45.00	47.50
82-37-004	Join Me	S. Kuck	10,000	45.00	45.00
Reco International		**The Grandparent Collector's Plates**			
81-38-001	Grandma's Cookie Jar	S. Kuck	Yr.Iss.	37.50	37.50
81-38-002	Grandpa and the Dollhouse	S. Kuck	Yr.Iss.	37.50	37.50
Reco International		**Little Professionals**			
82-39-001	All is Well	S. Kuck	10,000	39.50	47.50-95.
83-39-002	Tender Loving Care	S. Kuck	10,000	39.50	46-110.00
84-39-003	Lost and Found	S. Kuck	10,000	39.50	42.50-85.
85-39-004	Reading, Writing and...	S. Kuck	10,000	39.50	47.50-85.
Reco International		**Days Gone By**			
83-40-001	Sunday Best	S. Kuck	14-day	29.50	58.00
83-40-002	Amy's Magic Horse	S. Kuck	14-day	29.50	35.00
84-40-003	Little Anglers	S. Kuck	14-day	29.50	35.00
84-40-004	Afternoon Recital	S. Kuck	14-day	29.50	63.00

Company Number	Name	Series Artist	Edition Limit	Issue Price	Quote
84-40-005	Little Tutor	S. Kuck	14-day	29.50	29.50
85-40-006	Easter at Grandma's	S. Kuck	14-day	29.50	29.50
85-40-007	Morning Song	S. Kuck	14-day	29.50	29.50
85-40-008	The Surrey Ride	S. Kuck	14-day	29.50	29.50
Reco International		**A Childhood Almanac**			
85-41-001	Fireside Dreams-January	S. Kuck	14-day	29.50	31.00
85-41-002	Be Mine-February	S. Kuck	14-day	29.50	36.00
86-41-003	Winds of March-March	S. Kuck	14-day	29.50	35.00
85-41-004	Easter Morning-April	S. Kuck	14-day	29.50	29.50
85-41-005	For Mom-May	S. Kuck	14-day	29.50	33-35.00
85-41-006	Just Dreaming-June	S. Kuck	14-day	29.50	29.50
85-41-007	Star Spangled Sky-July	S. Kuck	14-day	29.50	35.00
85-41-008	Summer Secrets-August	S. Kuck	14-day	29.50	45.00
85-41-009	School Days-September	S. Kuck	14-day	29.50	50.00
86-41-010	Indian Summer-October	S. Kuck	14-day	29.50	35.00
86-41-011	Giving Thanks-November	S. Kuck	14-day	29.50	35.00
85-41-012	Christmas Magic-December	S. Kuck	14-day	35.00	40.00
Reco International		**Mother's Day Collection**			
85-42-001	Once Upon a Time	S. Kuck	Yr.Iss.	29.50	47-125.00
86-42-002	Times Remembered	S. Kuck	Yr.Iss.	29.50	40-75.00
87-42-003	A Cherished Time	S. Kuck	Yr.Iss.	29.50	30-40.00
88-42-004	A Time Together	S. Kuck	Yr.Iss.	29.50	35-50.00
Reco International		**A Children's Christmas Pageant**			
86-43-001	Silent Night	S. Kuck	Yr.Iss.	32.50	55.00
87-43-002	Hark the Herald Angels Sing	S. Kuck	Yr.Iss.	32.50	32.50
88-43-003	While Shepherds Watched...	S. Kuck	Yr.Iss.	32.50	51.00
89-43-004	We Three Kings	S. Kuck	Yr.Iss.	32.50	32.50
Reco International		**Barefoot Children**			
87-44-001	Night-Time Story	S. Kuck	14-day	29.50	35.00
87-44-002	Golden Afternoon	S. Kuck	14-day	29.50	29.50-35.00
88-44-003	Little Sweethearts	S. Kuck	14-day	29.50	35.00
88-44-004	Carousel Magic	S. Kuck	14-day	29.50	49.00
88-44-005	Under the Apple Tree	S. Kuck	14-day	29.50	35.00
88-44-006	The Rehearsal	S. Kuck	14-day	29.50	35.00
88-44-007	Pretty as a Picture	S. Kuck	14-day	29.50	35.00
88-44-008	Grandma's Trunk	S. Kuck	14-day	29.50	35.00
Reco International		**Special Occasions by Reco**			
88-45-001	The Wedding	S. Kuck	Open	35.00	35.00
89-45-002	Wedding Day (6 1/2")	S. Kuck	Open	25.00	25.00
90-45-003	The Special Day	S. Kuck	Open	25.00	25.00
Reco International		**Victorian Mother's Day**			
89-46-001	Mother's Sunshine	S. Kuck	Yr.Iss.	35.00	42-70.00
90-46-002	Reflection Of Love	S. Kuck	Yr.Iss.	35.00	37.00
91-46-003	A Precious Time	S. Kuck	Yr.Iss.	35.00	37.00
92-46-004	Loving Touch	S. Kuck	Yr.Iss.	35.00	35.00
Reco International Corp.		**Plate Of The Month Collection**			
90-47-001	January	S. Kuck	28-day	25.00	25.00
90-47-002	February	S. Kuck	28-day	25.00	25.00
90-47-003	March	S. Kuck	28-day	25.00	25.00
90-47-004	April	S. Kuck	28-day	25.00	25.00
90-47-005	May	S. Kuck	28-day	25.00	25.00
90-47-006	June	S. Kuck	28-day	25.00	25.00
90-47-007	July	S. Kuck	28-day	25.00	25.00
90-47-008	August	S. Kuck	28-day	25.00	25.00
90-47-009	September	S. Kuck	28-day	25.00	25.00
90-47-010	October	S. Kuck	28-day	25.00	25.00
90-47-011	November	S. Kuck	28-day	25.00	25.00
90-47-012	December	S. Kuck	28-day	25.00	25.00
Reco International Corp.		**Premier Collection**			
91-48-001	Puppy	S. Kuck	7,500	95.00	95.00
91-48-002	Kitten	S. Kuck	7,500	95.00	125.00
92-48-003	La Belle	S. Kuck	7,500	95.00	95.00
92-48-004	Le Beau	S. Kuck	7,500	95.00	95.00
Reco International Corp.		**Hearts And Flowers**			
91-49-001	Patience	S. Kuck	120-day	29.50	29.50
91-49-002	Tea Party	S. Kuck	120-day	29.50	29.50
92-49-003	Cat's In The Cradle	S. Kuck	120-day	32.50	32.50
92-49-004	Carousel of Dreams	S. Kuck	120-day	32.50	32.50
92-49-005	Storybook Memories	S. Kuck	120-day	32.50	32.50
Reco International Corp.		**Tidings Of Joy**			
92-50-001	Peace on Earth	S. Kuck	N/A	35.00	35.00
Reco International		**The Sophisticated Ladies Collection**			
85-51-001	Felicia	A. Fazio	21-day	29.50	32.50
85-51-002	Samantha	A. Fazio	21-day	29.50	32.50
85-51-003	Phoebe	A. Fazio	21-day	29.50	32.50
85-51-004	Cleo	A. Fazio	21-day	29.50	32.50
86-51-005	Cerissa	A. Fazio	21-day	29.50	32.50
86-51-006	Natasha	A. Fazio	21-day	29.50	32.50
86-51-007	Bianka	A. Fazio	21-day	29.50	32.50
86-51-008	Chelsea	A. Fazio	21-day	29.50	32.50
Reco International		**Gardens of Beauty**			
88-52-001	English Country Garden	D. Barlowe	14-day	29.50	29.50
88-52-002	Dutch Country Garden	D. Barlowe	14-day	29.50	29.50
88-52-003	New England Garden	D. Barlowe	14-day	29.50	29.50
88-52-004	Japanese Garden	D. Barlowe	14-day	29.50	29.50
89-52-005	Italian Garden	D. Barlowe	14-day	29.50	29.50
89-52-006	Hawaiian Garden	D. Barlowe	14-day	29.50	29.50
89-52-007	German Country Garden	D. Barlowe	14-day	29.50	29.50
89-52-008	Mexican Garden	D. Barlowe	14-day	29.50	29.50
Reco International		**Gardens of America**			
92-53-001	Colonial Splendor	D. Barlowe	48-day	29.50	29.50
Reco International		**Vanishing Animal Kingdoms**			
86-54-001	Rama the Tiger	S. Barlowe	21,500	35.00	35.00
86-54-002	Olepi the Buffalo	S. Barlowe	21,500	35.00	35.00
87-54-003	Coolibah the Koala	S. Barlowe	21,500	35.00	42.00
87-54-004	Ortwin the Deer	S. Barlowe	21,500	35.00	39.00
87-54-005	Yen-Poh the Panda	S. Barlowe	21,500	35.00	40.00
88-54-006	Mamakuu the Elephant	S. Barlowe	21,500	35.00	59.00

Company Number	Name	Series Artist	Edition Limit	Issue Price	Quote
Reco International Corp.		**Town And Country Dogs**			
90-55-001	Fox Hunt	S. Barlowe	36-day	35.00	35.00
91-55-002	The Retrieval	S. Barlowe	36-day	35.00	35.00
91-55-003	Golden Fields (Golden Retriever)	S. Barlowe	36-day	35.00	35.00
Reco International		**Our Cherished Seas**			
91-56-001	Whale Song	S. Barlowe	48-day	37.50	37.50
91-56-002	Lions of the Sea	S. Barlowe	48-day	37.50	37.50
91-56-003	Flight of the Dolphins	S. Barlowe	48-day	37.50	37.50
92-56-004	Palace of the Seals	S. Barlowe	48-day	37.50	37.50
92-56-005	Orca Whales	S. Barlowe	48-day	37.50	37.50
Reco International		**Great Stories from the Bible**			
87-57-001	Moses in the Bulrushes	G. Katz	14-day	29.50	35.00
87-57-002	King Saul & David	G. Katz	14-day	29.50	35.00
87-57-003	Moses and the Ten Commandments	G. Katz	14-day	29.50	38.00
87-57-004	Joseph's Coat of Many Colors	G. Katz	14-day	29.50	35.00
88-57-005	Rebekah at the Well	G. Katz	14-day	29.50	35.00
88-57-006	Daniel Reads the Writing on the Wall	G. Katz	14-day	29.50	35.00
88-57-007	The Story of Ruth	G. Katz	14-day	29.50	35.00
88-57-008	King Solomon	G. Katz	14-day	29.50	35.00
Reco International		**The Nutcracker Ballet**			
89-58-001	Christmas Eve Party	C. Micarelli	14-day	35.00	35.00
90-58-002	Clara And Her Prince	C. Micarelli	14-day	35.00	37.00
90-58-003	The Dream Begins	C. Micarelli	14-day	35.00	35.00
91-58-004	Dance of the Snow Fairies	C. Micarelli	14-day	35.00	35.00
92-58-005	The Land of Sweets	C. Micarelli	14-day	35.00	35.00
92-58-006	The Sugar Plum Fairy	C. Micarelli	14-day	35.00	35.00
Reco International		**Special Occasions-Wedding**			
91-59-001	From This Day Forward (9 1/2")	C. Micarelli	Open	35.00	35.00
91-59-002	From This Day Forward (6 1/2")	C. Micarelli	Open	25.00	25.00
91-59-003	To Have And To Hold (9 1/2")	C. Micarelli	Open	35.00	35.00
91-59-004	To Have And To Hold (6 1/2")	C. Micarelli	Open	25.00	25.00
Reco International		**The Glory Of Christ**			
92-60-001	The Ascension	C. Micarelli	48-day	29.50	29.50
Reco International		**J. Bergsma Mothers Day Series**			
90-61-001	The Beauty Of Life	J. Bergsma	14-day	35.00	35.00
92-61-002	Life's Blessing	J. Bergsma	14-day	35.00	35.00
Reco International		**Guardians Of The Kingdom**			
90-62-001	Rainbow To Ride On	J. Bergsma	17,500	35.00	37.00
90-62-002	Special Friends Are Few	J. Bergsma	17,500	35.00	35.00
90-62-003	Guardians Of The Innocent Children	J. Bergsma	17,500	35.00	38.00
90-62-004	The Miracle Of Love	J. Bergsma	17,500	35.00	37.00
91-62-005	The Magic Of Love	J. Bergsma	17,500	35.00	35.00
91-62-006	Only With The Heart	J. Bergsma	17,500	35.00	35.00
91-62-007	To Fly Without Wings	J. Bergsma	17,500	35.00	35.00
91-62-008	In Faith I Am Free	J. Bergsma	17,500	35.00	35.00
Reco International		**Castles & Dreams**			
92-63-001	The Birth of a Dream	J. Bergsma	48-day	29.50	29.50
92-63-002	Dreams Come True	J. Bergsma	48-day	29.50	29.50
Reco International		**The Christmas Series**			
90-64-001	Down The Glistening Lane	J. Bergsma	14-day	35.00	39.00
91-64-002	A Child Is Born	J. Bergsma	14-day	35.00	35.00
92-64-003	Christmas Day	J. Bergsma	14-day	35.00	35.00
Reco International		**God's Own Country**			
90-65-001	Daybreak	I. Drechsler	14-day	30.00	30.00
90-65-002	Coming Home	I. Drechsler	14-day	30.00	30.00
90-65-003	Peaceful Gathering	I. Drechsler	14-day	30.00	30.00
90-65-004	Quiet Waters	I. Drechsler	14-day	30.00	30.00
Reco International		**The Flower Fairies Year Collection**			
90-66-001	The Red Clover Fairy	C.M. Barker	14-day	29.50	29.50
90-66-002	The Wild Cherry Blossom Fairy	C.M. Barker	14-day	29.50	29.50
90-66-003	The Pine Tree Fairy	C.M. Barker	14-day	29.50	29.50
90-66-004	The Rose Hip Fairy	C.M. Barker	14-day	29.50	29.50
Reco International		**Oscar & Bertie's Edwardian Holiday**			
91-67-001	Snapshot	P.D. Jackson	48-day	29.50	29.50
92-67-002	Early Rise	P.D. Jackson	48-day	29.50	29.50
92-67-003	All Aboard	P.D. Jackson	48-day	29.50	29.50
92-67-004	Learning To Swim	P.D. Jackson	48-day	29.50	29.50
Reco International		**In The Eye of The Storm**			
91-68-001	First Strike	W. Lowe	120-day	29.50	29.50
92-68-002	Night Force	W. Lowe	120-day	29.50	29.50
92-68-003	Tracks Across The Sand	W. Lowe	120-day	29.50	29.50
92-68-004	The Storm Has Landed	W. Lowe	120-day	29.50	29.50
Reco International		**Celebration Of Love**			
92-69-001	Happy Anniversary (9 1/4")	J. Hall	Open	35.00	35.00
92-69-002	10th (9 1/4")	J. Hall	Open	35.00	35.00
92-69-003	25th (9 1/4")	J. Hall	Open	35.00	35.00
92-69-004	50th (9 1/4")	J. Hall	Open	35.00	35.00
92-69-005	Happy Anniversary (6 1/2")	J. Hall	Open	25.00	35.00
92-69-006	10th (6 1/2")	J. Hall	Open	25.00	35.00
92-69-007	25th (6 1/2")	J. Hall	Open	25.00	35.00
92-69-008	50th (6 1/2")	J. Hall	Open	25.00	35.00
Reco International		**The Heart Of The Family**			
92-70-001	Sharing Secrets	J. York	N/A	29.50	29.50
Reece		**Waterfowl**			
73-01-001	Mallards & Wood Ducks (Pair)	Unknown	900	250.00	375.00
74-01-002	Canvasback & Canadian Geese (Pair)	Unknown	900	250.00	375.00
75-01-003	Pintails & Teal (Pair)	Unknown	900	250.00	425.00
Reed and Barton		**Audubon**			
70-01-001	Pine Siskin	Unknown	5,000	60.00	175.00
71-01-002	Red-Shouldered Hawk	Unknown	5,000	60.00	75.00
72-01-003	Stilt Sandpiper	Unknown	5,000	60.00	70.00
73-01-004	Red Cardinal	Unknown	5,000	60.00	65.00
74-01-005	Boreal Chickadee	Unknown	5,000	65.00	65.00
75-01-006	Yellow-Breasted Chat	Unknown	5,000	65.00	65.00
76-01-007	Bay-Breasted Warbler	Unknown	5,000	65.00	65.00
77-01-008	Purple Finch	Unknown	5,000	65.00	65.00

Company Number	Name	Series Artist	Edition Limit	Issue Price	Quote
Reed and Barton		**'Twas the Night Before Christmas**			
89-02-001	'Twas the Night Before Christmas	J. Downing	4,000	75.00	75.00
90-02-002	Visions of Sugarplums	J. Downing	3,500	75.00	75.00
91-02-003	Away to the Window	J. Downing	3,500	75.00	75.00
River Shore		**Famous Americans**			
76-01-001	Brown's Lincoln	Rockwell-Brown	9,500	40.00	40.00
77-01-002	Rockwell's Triple Self-Portrait	Rockwell-Brown	9,500	45.00	45.00
78-01-003	Peace Corps	Rockwell-Brown	9,500	45.00	45.00
79-01-004	Spirit of Lindbergh	Rockwell-Brown	9,500	50.00	50.00
River Shore		**Norman Rockwell Single Issue**			
79-02-001	Spring Flowers	N. Rockwell	17,000	75.00	145.00
80-02-002	Looking Out to Sea	N. Rockwell	17,000	75.00	130.00
82-02-003	Grandpa's Guardian	N. Rockwell	17,000	80.00	80.00
82-02-004	Grandpa's Treasures	N. Rockwell	17,000	80.00	80.00
River Shore		**Baby Animals**			
79-03-001	Akiku	R. Brown	20,000	50.00	80.00
80-03-002	Roosevelt	R. Brown	20,000	50.00	90.00
81-03-003	Clover	R. Brown	20,000	50.00	65.00
82-03-004	Zuela	R. Brown	20,000	50.00	65.00
River Shore		**Rockwell Four Freedoms**			
81-04-001	Freedom of Speech	N. Rockwell	17,000	65.00	80.00
82-04-002	Freedom of Worship	N. Rockwell	17,000	65.00	80.00
82-04-003	Freedom from Fear	N. Rockwell	17,000	65.00	65-200.00
82-04-004	Freedom from Want	N. Rockwell	17,000	65.00	65-400.00
River Shore		**Puppy Playtime**			
87-05-001	Double Take	J. Lamb	14-day	24.50	32-35.00
88-05-002	Catch of the Day	J. Lamb	14-day	24.50	24.50
88-05-003	Cabin Fever	J. Lamb	14-day	24.50	24.50
88-05-004	Weekend Gardener	J. Lamb	14-day	24.50	24.50
88-05-005	Getting Acquainted	J. Lamb	14-day	24.50	24.50
88-05-006	Hanging Out	J. Lamb	14-day	24.50	24.50
88-05-007	A New Leash On Life	J. Lamb	14-day	24.50	29.50
87-05-008	Fun and Games	J. Lamb	14-day	24.50	29.50
River Shore		**Lovable Teddies**			
85-06-001	Bedtime Blues	M. Hague	10-day	21.50	21.50
85-06-002	Bearly Frightful	M. Hague	10-day	21.50	21.50
85-06-003	Caught in the Act	M. Hague	10-day	21.50	21.50
85-06-004	Fireside Friends	M. Hague	10-day	21.50	21.50
85-06-005	Harvest Time	M. Hague	10-day	21.50	21.50
85-06-006	Missed a Button	M. Hague	10-day	21.50	21.50
85-06-007	Tender Loving Bear	M. Hague	10-day	21.50	21.50
85-06-008	Sunday Stroll	M. Hague	10-day	21.50	21.50
River Shore		**Little House on the Prairie**			
85-07-001	Founder's Day Picnic	E. Christopherson	10-day	29.50	50.00
85-07-002	Women's Harvest	E. Christopherson	10-day	29.50	45.00
85-07-003	Medicine Show	E. Christopherson	10-day	29.50	45.00
85-07-004	Caroline's Eggs	E. Christopherson	10-day	29.50	45.00
85-07-005	Mary's Gift	E. Christopherson	10-day	29.50	45.00
85-07-006	A Bell for Walnut Grove	E. Christopherson	10-day	29.50	45.00
85-07-007	Ingall's Family	E. Christopherson	10-day	29.50	45.00
85-07-008	The Sweetheart Tree	E. Christopherson	10-day	29.50	45.00
River Shore		**We the Children**			
87-08-001	The Freedom of Speech	D. Crook	14-day	24.50	24.50
88-08-002	Right to Vote	D. Crook	14-day	24.50	24.50
88-08-003	Unreasonable Search and Seizure	D. Crook	14-day	24.50	24.50
88-08-004	Right to Bear Arms	D. Crook	14-day	24.50	24.50
88-08-005	Trial by Jury	D. Crook	14-day	24.50	24.50
88-08-006	Self Incrimination	D. Crook	14-day	24.50	24.50
88-08-007	Cruel and Unusual Punishment	D. Crook	14-day	24.50	24.50
88-08-008	Quartering of Soldiers	D. Crook	14-day	24.50	24.50
Rockwell Society		**Christmas**			
74-01-001	Scotty Gets His Tree	N. Rockwell	Yr.Iss.	24.50	90.00
75-01-002	Angel with Black Eye	N. Rockwell	Yr.Iss.	24.50	40.00
76-01-003	Golden Christmas	N. Rockwell	Yr.Iss.	24.50	32.00
77-01-004	Toy Shop Window	N. Rockwell	Yr.Iss.	24.50	24.50
78-01-005	Christmas Dream	N. Rockwell	Yr.Iss.	24.50	29.00
79-01-006	Somebody's Up There	N. Rockwell	Yr.Iss.	24.50	24.50
80-01-007	Scotty Plays Santa	N. Rockwell	Yr.Iss.	24.50	24.50
81-01-008	Wrapped Up in Christmas	N. Rockwell	Yr.Iss.	25.50	26.50
82-01-009	Christmas Courtship	N. Rockwell	Yr.Iss.	25.50	25.50
83-01-010	Santa in the Subway	N. Rockwell	Yr.Iss.	25.50	25.50
84-01-011	Santa in the Workshop	N. Rockwell	Yr.Iss.	27.50	27.50
85-01-012	Grandpa Plays Santa	N. Rockwell	Yr.Iss.	27.90	27.90
86-01-013	Dear Santy Claus	N. Rockwell	Yr.Iss.	27.90	27.90
87-01-014	Santa's Golden Gift	N. Rockwell	Yr.Iss.	27.90	27.90
88-01-015	Santa Claus	N. Rockwell	Yr.Iss.	29.90	29.90
89-01-016	Jolly Old St. Nick	N. Rockwell	Yr.Iss.	29.90	29.90
90-01-017	A Christmas Prayer	N. Rockwell	Yr.Iss.	29.90	40.00
91-01-018	Santa's Helpers	N. Rockwell	Yr.Iss.	32.90	47.00
Rockwell Society		**Mother's Day**			
76-02-001	A Mother's Love	N. Rockwell	Yr.Iss.	24.50	55.00
77-02-002	Faith	N. Rockwell	Yr.Iss.	24.50	35.00
78-02-003	Bedtime	N. Rockwell	Yr.Iss.	24.50	37.00
79-02-004	Reflections	N. Rockwell	Yr.Iss.	24.50	24.50
80-02-005	A Mother's Pride	N. Rockwell	Yr.Iss.	24.50	24.50
81-02-006	After the Party	N. Rockwell	Yr.Iss.	24.50	24.50
82-02-007	TheCooking Lesson	N. Rockwell	Yr.Iss.	24.50	26.00
83-02-008	Add Two Cups and Love	N. Rockwell	Yr.Iss.	25.50	25.50
84-02-009	Grandma's Courting Dress	N. Rockwell	Yr.Iss.	25.50	25.50
85-02-010	Mending Time	N. Rockwell	Yr.Iss.	27.50	28.00
86-02-011	Pantry Raid	N. Rockwell	Yr.Iss.	27.90	32.50
87-02-012	Grandma's Surprise	N. Rockwell	Yr.Iss.	29.90	29.90
88-02-013	My Mother	N. Rockwell	Yr.Iss.	29.90	29.90
89-02-014	Sunday Dinner	N. Rockwell	Yr.Iss.	29.90	29.90
90-02-015	Evening Prayers	N. Rockwell	Yr.Iss.	29.90	35.00
91-02-016	Building Our Future	N. Rockwell	Yr.Iss.	32.90	38.00
91-02-017	Gentle Reassurance	N. Rockwell	Yr.Iss.	32.90	32.90
Rockwell Society		**Heritage**			
77-03-001	Toy Maker	N. Rockwell	Yr.Iss.	14.50	100.00
78-03-002	Cobbler	N. Rockwell	Yr.Iss.	19.50	71.00
79-03-003	Lighthouse Keeper's Daughter	N. Rockwell	Yr.Iss.	19.50	28.00
80-03-004	Ship Builder	N. Rockwell	Yr.Iss.	19.50	25.00

Number	Name	Artist	Edition Limit	Issue Price	Quote
81-03-005	Music maker	N. Rockwell	Yr.Iss.	19.50	19.50
82-03-006	Tycoon	N. Rockwell	Yr.Iss.	19.50	19.50
83-03-007	Painter	N. Rockwell	Yr.Iss.	19.50	19.50
84-03-008	Storyteller	N. Rockwell	Yr.Iss.	19.50	19.50
85-03-009	Gourmet	N. Rockwell	Yr.Iss.	19.50	19.50
86-03-010	Professor	N. Rockwell	Yr.Iss.	22.90	22.90
87-03-011	Shadow Artist	N. Rockwell	Yr.Iss.	22.90	35.00
88-03-012	The Veteran	N. Rockwell	Yr.Iss.	22.90	30.00
88-03-013	The Banjo Player	N. Rockwell	Yr.Iss.	22.90	29.00
90-03-014	The Old Scout	N. Rockwell	Yr.Iss.	24.90	36.00
91-03-015	The Young Scholar	N. Rockwell	Yr.Iss.	24.90	40.00
91-03-016	The Family Doctor	N. Rockwell	Yr.Iss.	27.90	27.90
Rockwell Society		**Rockwell's Rediscovered Women**			
84-04-001	Dreaming in the Attic	N. Rockwell	100-day	19.50	20-25.00
84-04-002	Waiting on the Shore	N. Rockwell	100-day	22.50	23.00
84-04-003	Pondering on the Porch	N. Rockwell	100-day	22.50	23-32.00
84-04-004	Making Believe at the Mirror	N. Rockwell	100-day	22.50	22.50-28.00
84-04-005	Waiting at the Dance	N. Rockwell	100-day	22.50	23.00
84-04-006	Gossiping in the Alcove	N. Rockwell	100-day	22.50	23.00
84-04-007	Standing in the Doorway	N. Rockwell	100-day	22.50	23-30.00
84-04-008	Flirting in the Parlor	N. Rockwell	100-day	22.50	24.00
84-04-009	Working in the Kitchen	N. Rockwell	100-day	22.50	24.00
84-04-010	Meeting on the Path	N. Rockwell	100-day	22.50	23.00
84-04-011	Confiding in the Den	N. Rockwell	100-day	22.50	25-27.00
84-04-012	Reminiscing in the Quiet	N. Rockwell	100-day	22.50	22.50
XX-04-013	Complete Collection	N. Rockwell	100-day	267.00	370.00
Rockwell Society		**Rockwell on Tour**			
83-05-001	Walking Through Merrie Englande	N. Rockwell	150-day	16.00	29.00
83-05-002	Promenade a Paris	N. Rockwell	150-day	16.00	29.00
83-05-003	When in Rome	N. Rockwell	150-day	16.00	29.00
84-05-004	Die Walk am Rhein	N. Rockwell	150-day	16.00	29.00
Rockwell Society		**Rockwell's Light Compaign**			
83-06-001	This is the Room that Light Made	N. Rockwell	150-day	19.50	30.00
84-06-002	Grandpa's Treasure Chest	N. Rockwell	150-day	19.50	19.50
84-06-003	Father's Help	N. Rockwell	150-day	19.50	19.50
84-06-004	Evening's Ease	N. Rockwell	150-day	19.50	19.50
84-06-005	Close Harmony	N. Rockwell	150-day	21.50	21.50
84-06-006	The Birthday Wish	N. Rockwell	150-day	21.50	23.00
Rockwell Society		**Rockwell's American Dream**			
85-07-001	A Young Girl's Dream	N. Rockwell	150-day	19.90	20-35.00
85-07-002	A Couple's Commitment	N. Rockwell	150-day	19.90	20.00
85-07-003	A Family's Full Measure	N. Rockwell	150-day	22.90	22.90
86-07-004	A Mother's Welcome	N. Rockwell	150-day	22.90	35.00
86-07-005	A Young Man's Dream	N. Rockwell	150-day	22.90	34.00
86-07-006	The Musician's Magic	N. Rockwell	150-day	22.90	22.90
87-07-007	An Orphan's Hope	N. Rockwell	150-day	24.90	24.90
87-07-008	Love's Reward	N. Rockwell	150-day	24.90	24.90
Rockwell Society		**Colonials-The Rarest Rockwells**			
85-08-001	Unexpected Proposal	N. Rockwell	150-day	27.90	27.90
86-08-002	Words of Comfort	N. Rockwell	150-day	27.90	27.90
86-08-003	Light for the Winter	N. Rockwell	150-day	30.90	30.90
87-08-004	Portrait for a Bridegroom	N. Rockwell	150-day	30.90	30.90
87-08-005	The Journey Home	N. Rockwell	150-day	30.90	30.90
87-08-006	Clinching the Deal	N. Rockwell	150-day	30.90	30.90
88-08-007	Sign of the Times	N. Rockwell	150-day	32.90	32.90
88-08-008	Ye Glutton	N. Rockwell	150-day	32.90	32.90
Rockwell Society		**A Mind of Her Own**			
86-09-001	Sitting Pretty	N. Rockwell	150-day	24.90	25-35.00
87-09-002	Serious Business	N. Rockwell	150-day	24.90	35.00
87-09-003	Breaking the Rules	N. Rockwell	150-day	24.90	28.00
87-09-004	Good Intentions	N. Rockwell	150-day	27.90	27.90
88-09-005	Second Thoughts	N. Rockwell	150-day	27.90	27.90
88-09-006	World's Away	N. Rockwell	150-day	27.90	30.00
88-09-007	Kiss and Tell	N. Rockwell	150-day	29.90	29.90
88-09-008	On My Honor	N. Rockwell	150-day	29.90	35.00
Rockwell Society		**Rockwell's Golden Moments**			
87-10-001	Grandpa's Gift	N. Rockwell	150-day	19.90	27.00
87-10-002	Grandma's Love	N. Rockwell	150-day	19.90	28.00
88-10-003	End of day	N. Rockwell	150-day	22.90	28.00
88-10-004	Best Friends	N. Rockwell	150-day	22.90	22.90
89-10-005	Love Letters	N. Rockwell	150-day	22.90	22.90
89-10-006	Newfound Worlds	N. Rockwell	150-day	22.90	22.90
89-10-007	Keeping Company	N. Rockwell	150-day	24.90	24.90
89-10-008	Evening's Repose	N. Rockwell	150-day	24.90	24.90
Rockwell Society		**Rockwell's The Ones We Love**			
88-11-001	Tender Loving Care	N. Rockwell	150-day	19.90	40.00
89-11-002	A Time to Keep	N. Rockwell	150-day	19.90	19.90
89-11-003	The Inventor And The Judge	N. Rockwell	150-day	22.90	22.90
89-11-004	Ready For The World	N. Rockwell	150-day	22.90	22.90
89-11-005	Growing Strong	N. Rockwell	150-day	22.90	30.00
90-11-006	The Story Hour	N. Rockwell	150-day	22.90	22.90
90-11-007	The Country Doctor	N. Rockwell	150-day	24.90	35-51.00
90-11-008	Our Love of Country	N. Rockwell	150-day	24.90	35.00
90-11-009	The Homecoming	N. Rockwell	150-day	24.90	35.00
91-11-010	A Helping Hand	N. Rockwell	150-day	24.90	24.90
Rockwell Society		**Coming Of Age**			
90-12-001	Back To School	N. Rockwell	150-day	29.90	35.00
90-12-002	Home From Camp	N. Rockwell	150-day	29.90	29.90
90-12-003	Her First Formal	N. Rockwell	150-day	32.90	49.00
90-12-004	The Muscleman	N. Rockwell	150-day	32.90	37.00
90-12-005	A New Look	N. Rockwell	150-day	32.90	44.00
91-12-006	A Balcony Seat	N. Rockwell	150-day	32.90	35.00
91-12-007	Men About Town	N. Rockwell	150-day	34.90	60.00
91-12-008	Paths of Glory	N. Rockwell	150-day	34.90	34.90
91-12-009	Doorway to the Past	N. Rockwell	150-day	34.90	34.90
91-12-010	School's Out!	N. Rockwell	150-day	34.90	34.90
Rockwell Society		**Innocence and Experience**			
91-13-001	The Sea Captain	N. Rockwell	150-day	29.90	29.90
92-13-002	The Radio Operator	N. Rockwell	150-day	29.90	29.90
Rockwell Society		**Rockwell's Treasured Memories**			
91-14-001	Quiet Reflections	N. Rockwell	150-day	29.90	31.00
91-14-002	Romantic Reverie	N. Rockwell	150-day	29.90	29.90
91-14-003	Tender Romance	N. Rockwell	150-day	32.90	32.90
91-14-004	Evening Passage	N. Rockwell	150-day	32.90	32.90
91-14-005	Heavenly Dreams	N. Rockwell	150-day	32.90	32.90
91-14-006	Sentimental Shores	N. Rockwell	150-day	32.90	32.90
Roman, Inc.		**The Masterpiece Collection**			
79-01-001	Adoration	F. Lippe	5,000	65.00	65.00
80-01-002	Madonna with Grapes	P. Mignard	5,000	87.50	87.50
81-01-003	The Holy Family	G. Delle Notti	5,000	95.00	95.00
82-01-004	Madonna of the Streets	R. Ferruzzi	5,000	85.00	85.00
Roman, Inc.		**A Child's World**			
80-02-001	Little Children, Come to Me	F. Hook	15,000	45.00	49.00
Roman, Inc.		**A Child's Play**			
82-03-001	Breezy Day	F. Hook	30-day	29.95	35.00
82-03-002	Kite Flying	F. Hook	30-day	29.95	35.00
84-03-003	Bathtub Sailor	F. Hook	30-day	29.95	35.00
84-03-004	The First Snow	F. Hook	30-day	29.95	35.00
Roman, Inc.		**Frances Hook Collection-Set I**			
82-04-001	I Wish, I Wish	F. Hook	15,000	24.95	25.00
82-04-002	Baby Blossoms	F. Hook	15,000	24.95	30.00
82-04-003	Daisy Dreamer	F. Hook	15,000	24.95	30.00
82-04-004	Trees So Tall	F. Hook	15,000	24.95	30.00
Roman, Inc.		**Frances Hook Collection-Set II**			
83-05-001	Caught It Myself	F. Hook	15,000	24.95	25.00
83-05-002	Winter Wrappings	F. Hook	15,000	24.95	25.00
83-05-003	So Cuddly	F. Hook	15,000	24.95	25.00
83-05-004	Can I Keep Him?	F. Hook	15,000	24.95	25.00
Roman, Inc.		**Pretty Girls of the Ice Capades**			
83-06-001	Ice Princess	G. Petty	30-day	24.50	24.50
Roman, Inc.		**The Ice Capades Clown**			
83-07-001	Presenting Freddie Trenkler	G. Petty	30-day	24.50	24.50
Roman, Inc.		**Roman Memorial**			
84-08-001	The Carpenter	F. Hook	Yr.Iss.	100.00	125.00
Roman, Inc.		**Roman Cats**			
84-09-001	Grizabella	Unknown	30-day	29.50	29.50
84-09-002	Mr. Mistoffelees	Unknown	30-day	29.50	29.50
84-09-003	Rum Rum Tugger	Unknown	30-day	29.50	29.50
Roman, Inc.		**The Magic of Childhood**			
85-10-001	Special Friends	A. Williams	10-day	24.50	35.00
85-10-002	Feeding Time	A. Williams	10-day	24.50	35.00
85-10-003	Best Buddies	A. Williams	10-day	24.50	35.00
85-10-004	Getting Acquainted	A. Williams	10-day	24.50	35.00
86-10-005	Last One In	A. Williams	10-day	24.50	35.00
86-10-006	A Handful Of Love	A. Williams	10-day	24.50	35.00
86-10-007	Look Alikes	A. Williams	10-day	24.50	35.00
86-10-008	No Fair Peeking	A. Williams	10-day	24.50	35.00
Roman, Inc.		**Frances Hook Legacy**			
85-11-001	Fascination	F. Hook	100-day	19.50	29.00
85-11-002	Daydreaming	F. Hook	100-day	19.50	29.00
85-11-003	Discovery	F. Hook	100-day	22.50	29.00
85-11-004	Disappointment	F. Hook	100-day	22.50	29.00
85-11-005	Wonderment	F. Hook	100-day	22.50	29.00
85-11-006	Expectation	F. Hook	100-day	22.50	29.00
Roman, Inc.		**The Lord's Prayer**			
86-12-001	Our Father	A. Williams	10-day	24.50	24.50
86-12-002	Thy Kingdom Come	A. Williams	10-day	24.50	24.50
86-12-003	Give Us This Day	A. Williams	10-day	24.50	24.50
86-12-004	Forgive Our Trespasses	A. Williams	10-day	24.50	24.50
86-12-005	As We Forgive	A. Williams	10-day	24.50	24.50
86-12-006	Lead Us Not	A. Williams	10-day	24.50	24.50
86-12-007	Deliver Us From Evil	A. Williams	10-day	24.50	24.50
86-12-008	Thine Is The Kingdom	A. Williams	10-day	24.50	24.50
Roman, Inc.		**The Sweetest Songs**			
86-13-001	A Baby's Prayer	I. Spencer	30-day	39.50	45.00
86-13-002	This Little Piggie	I. Spencer	30-day	39.50	39.50
88-13-003	Long, Long Ago	I. Spencer	30-day	39.50	39.50
89-13-004	Rockabye	I. Spencer	30-day	39.50	39.50
Roman, Inc.		**Fontanini Annual Christmas Plate**			
86-14-001	A King Is Born	E. Simonetti	Yr.Iss.	60.00	60.00
87-14-002	O Come, Let Us Adore Him	E. Simonetti	Yr.Iss.	60.00	65.00
88-14-003	Adoration of the Magi	E. Simonetti	Yr.Iss.	70.00	75.00
89-14-004	Flight Into Egypt	E. Simonetti	Yr.Iss.	75.00	85.00
Roman, Inc.		**The Love's Prayer**			
88-15-001	Love Is Patient and Kind	A. Williams	14-day	29.50	29.50
88-15-002	Love Is Never Jealous or Boastful	A. Williams	14-day	29.50	29.50
88-15-003	Love Is Never Arrogant or Rude	A. Williams	14-day	29.50	29.50
88-15-004	Love Does Not Insist on Its Own Way	A. Williams	14-day	29.50	29.50
88-15-005	Love Is Never Irritable or Resentful	A. Williams	14-day	29.50	29.50
88-15-006	Love Rejoices In the Right	A. Williams	14-day	29.50	29.50
88-15-007	Love Believes All Things	A. Williams	14-day	29.50	29.50
88-15-008	Love Never Ends	A. Williams	14-day	29.50	29.50
Roman, Inc.		**March of Dimes: Our Children, Our Future**			
90-16-001	A Time To Laugh	A. Williams	150-day	29.00	29.00
Roman, Inc.		**Abbie Williams Collection**			
91-17-001	Legacy of Love	A. Williams	Open	29.50	29.50
91-17-002	Bless This Child	A. Williams	Open	29.50	29.50
Roman, Inc.		**Catnippers**			
86-18-001	Christmas Mourning	I. Spencer	9,500	34.50	34.50
92-18-002	Happy Holidaze	I. Spencer	9,500	34.50	34.50
Roman, Inc.		**God Bless You, Little One**			
91-19-001	Baby's First Birthday (Girl)	A. Williams	Open	29.50	29.50
91-19-002	Baby's First Birthday (Boy)	A. Williams	Open	29.50	29.50
91-19-003	Baby's First Smile	A. Williams	Open	19.50	19.50
91-19-004	Baby's First Word	A. Williams	Open	19.50	19.50
91-19-005	Baby's First Step	A. Williams	Open	19.50	19.50

Number	Name	Artist	Edition Limit	Issue Price	Quote
91-19-006	Baby's First Tooth	A. Williams	Open	19.50	19.50
Roman, Inc.		**Millenium Series**			
92-20-001	Silent Night	Morcaldo/Lucchesi	2,000	49.50	49.50
Rorstrand		**Christmas**			
68-01-001	Bringing Home the Tree	G. Nylund	Annual	12.00	500.00
69-01-002	Fisherman Sailing Home	G. Nylund	Annual	13.50	18-30.00
70-01-003	Nils with His Geese	G. Nylund	Annual	13.50	13.50-15.00
71-01-004	Nils in Lapland	G. Nylund	Annual	15.00	15.00
72-01-005	Dalecarlian Fiddler	G. Nylund	Annual	15.00	20-22.00
73-01-006	Farm in Smaland	G. Nylund	Annual	16.00	60.00
74-01-007	Vadslena	G. Nylund	Annual	19.00	43.00
75-01-008	Nils in Vastmanland	G. Nylund	Annual	20.00	35.00
76-01-009	Nils in Uapland	G. Nylund	Annual	20.00	43-49.00
77-01-010	Nils in Varmland	G. Nylund	Annual	29.50	29.50
78-01-011	Nils in Fjallbacka	G. Nylund	Annual	32.50	49.00
79-01-012	Nils in Vaestergoetland	G. Nylund	Annual	38.50	38.50
80-01-013	Nils in Halland	G. Nylund	Annual	55.00	60.00
81-01-014	Nils in Gotland	G. Nylund	Annual	55.00	45.00
82-01-015	Nils at Skansen	G. Nylund	Annual	47.50	40.00
83-01-016	Nils in Oland	G. Nylund	Annual	42.50	55.00
84-01-017	Angerman land	G. Nylund	Annual	42.50	35.00
85-01-018	Nils in Jamtland	G. Nylund	Annual	42.50	70.00
86-01-019	Nils in Karlskr	G. Nylund	Annual	42.50	50.00
87-01-020	Christmas	G. Nylund	Annual	47.50	150.00
88-01-021	Christmas	G. Nylund	Annual	55.00	60.00
89-01-022	Nils Visits Gothenborg	G. Nylund	Annual	60.00	61.00
Rosenthal		**Christmas**			
10-01-001	Winter Peace	Unknown	Annual	Unkn.	550.00
11-01-002	Three Wise Men	Unknown	Annual	Unkn.	325.00
12-01-003	Stardust	Unknown	Annual	Unkn.	255.00
13-01-004	Christmas Lights	Unknown	Annual	Unkn.	235.00
14-01-005	Christmas Song	Unknown	Annual	Unkn.	350.00
15-01-006	Walking to Church	Unknown	Annual	Unkn.	180.00
16-01-007	Christmas During War	Unknown	Annual	Unkn.	240.00
17-01-008	Angel of Peace	Unknown	Annual	Unkn.	200.00
18-01-009	Peace on Earth	Unknown	Annual	Unkn.	200.00
19-01-010	St. Christopher with Christ Child	Unknown	Annual	Unkn.	225.00
20-01-011	Manger in Bethlehem	Unknown	Annual	Unkn.	325.00
21-01-012	Christmas in Mountains	Unknown	Annual	Unkn.	200.00
22-01-013	Advent Branch	Unknown	Annual	Unkn.	200.00
23-01-014	Children in Winter Woods	Unknown	Annual	Unkn.	200.00
24-01-015	Deer in the Woods	Unknown	Annual	Unkn.	200.00
25-01-016	Three Wise Men	Unknown	Annual	Unkn.	200.00
26-01-017	Christmas in Mountains	Unknown	Annual	Unkn.	195.00
27-01-018	Station on the Way	Unknown	Annual	Unkn.	200.00
28-01-019	Chalet Christmas	Unknown	Annual	Unkn.	185.00
29-01-020	Christmas in Alps	Unknown	Annual	Unkn.	225.00
30-01-021	Group of Deer Under Pines	Unknown	Annual	Unkn.	225.00
31-01-022	Path of the Magi	Unknown	Annual	Unkn.	225.00
32-01-023	Christ Child	Unknown	Annual	Unkn.	185.00
33-01-024	Thru the Night to Light	Unknown	Annual	Unkn.	190.00
34-01-025	Christmas Peace	Unknown	Annual	Unkn.	190.00
35-01-026	Christmas by the Sea	Unknown	Annual	Unkn.	190.00
36-01-027	Nurnberg Angel	Unknown	Annual	Unkn.	195.00
37-01-028	Berchtesgaden	Unknown	Annual	Unkn.	195.00
38-01-029	Christmas in the Alps	Unknown	Annual	Unkn.	195.00
39-01-030	Schneekoppe Mountain	Unknown	Annual	Unkn.	195.00
40-01-031	Marien Chruch in Danzig	Unknown	Annual	Unkn.	250.00
41-01-032	Strassburg Cathedral	Unknown	Annual	Unkn.	250.00
42-01-033	Marianburg Castle	Unknown	Annual	Unkn.	300.00
43-01-034	Winter Idyll	Unknown	Annual	Unkn.	300.00
44-01-035	Wood Scape	Unknown	Annual	Unkn.	300.00
45-01-036	Christmas Peace	Unknown	Annual	Unkn.	400.00
46-01-037	Christmas in an Alpine Valley	Unknown	Annual	Unkn.	240.00
47-01-038	Dillingen Madonna	Unknown	Annual	Unkn.	985.00
48-01-039	Message to the Shepherds	Unknown	Annual	Unkn.	875.00
49-01-040	The Holy Family	Unknown	Annual	Unkn.	185.00
50-01-041	Christmas in the Forest	Unknown	Annual	Unkn.	185.00
51-01-042	Star of Bethlehem	Unknown	Annual	Unkn.	450.00
52-01-043	Christmas in the Alps	Unknown	Annual	Unkn.	195.00
53-01-044	The Holy Light	Unknown	Annual	Unkn.	195.00
54-01-045	Christmas Eve	Unknown	Annual	Unkn.	195.00
55-01-046	Christmas in a Village	Unknown	Annual	Unkn.	195.00
56-01-047	Christmas in the Alps	Unknown	Annual	Unkn.	195.00
57-01-048	Christmas by the Sea	Unknown	Annual	Unkn.	195.00
58-01-049	Christmas Eve	Unknown	Annual	Unkn.	195.00
59-01-050	Midnight Mass	Unknown	Annual	Unkn.	195.00
60-01-051	Christmas in a Small Village	Unknown	Annual	Unkn.	195.00
61-01-052	Solitary Christmas	Unknown	Annual	Unkn.	225.00
62-01-053	Christmas Eve	Unknown	Annual	Unkn.	195.00
63-01-054	Silent Night	Unknown	Annual	Unkn.	195.00
64-01-055	Christmas Market in Nurnberg	Unknown	Annual	Unkn.	225.00
65-01-056	Christmas Munich	Unknown	Annual	Unkn.	185.00
66-01-057	Christmas in Ulm	Unknown	Annual	Unkn.	275.00
67-01-058	Christmas in Reginburg	Unknown	Annual	Unkn.	185.00
68-01-059	Christmas in Bremen	Unknown	Annual	Unkn.	195.00
69-01-060	Christmas in Rothenburg	Unknown	Annual	Unkn.	220.00
70-01-061	Christmas in Cologne	Unknown	Annual	Unkn.	175.00
71-01-062	Christmas in Garmisch	Unknown	Annual	42.00	100.00
72-01-063	Christmas in Franconia	Unknown	Annual	50.00	95.00
73-01-064	Lubeck-Holstein	Unknown	Annual	77.00	105.00
74-01-065	Christmas in Wurzburg	Unknown	Annual	85.00	100.00
Rosenthal		**Wiinblad Christmas**			
71-02-001	Maria & Child	B. Wiinblad	Undis.	100.00	700.00
72-02-002	Caspar	B. Wiinblad	Undis.	100.00	290.00
73-02-003	Melchior	B. Wiinblad	Undis.	125.00	335.00
74-02-004	Balthazar	B. Wiinblad	Undis.	125.00	300.00
75-02-005	The Annunciation	B. Wiinblad	Undis.	195.00	195.00
76-02-006	Angel with Trumpet	B. Wiinblad	Undis.	195.00	195.00
77-02-007	Adoration of Shepherds	B. Wiinblad	Undis.	225.00	225.00
78-02-008	Angel with Harp	B. Wiinblad	Undis.	275.00	295.00
79-02-009	Exodus from Egypt	B. Wiinblad	Undis.	310.00	310.00
80-02-010	Angel with Glockenspiel	B. Wiinblad	Undis.	360.00	360.00
81-02-011	Christ Child Visits Temple	B. Wiinblad	Undis.	375.00	375.00
82-02-012	Christening of Christ	B. Wiinblad	Undis.	375.00	375.00
Rosenthal		**Nobility of Children**			
76-03-001	La Contessa Isabella	E. Hibel	12,750	120.00	120.00
77-03-002	La Marquis Maurice-Pierre	E. Hibel	12,750	120.00	120.00
78-03-003	Baronesse Johanna	E. Hibel	12,750	130.00	140.00
79-03-004	Chief Red Feather	E. Hibel	12,750	140.00	180.00
Rosenthal		**Oriental Gold**			
76-04-001	Yasuko	E. Hibel	2,000	275.00	650.00
77-04-002	Mr. Obata	E. Hibel	2,000	275.00	500.00
78-04-003	Sakura	E. Hibel	2,000	295.00	400.00
79-04-004	Michio	E. Hibel	2,000	325.00	375.00
Royal Bayreuth		**Christmas**			
72-01-001	Carriage in the Village	Unknown	4,000	15.00	80.00
73-01-002	Scow Scene	Unknown	4,000	16.50	20.00
74-01-003	The Old Mill	Unknown	4,000	24.00	24.00
75-01-004	Forest Chalet "Serenity"	Unknown	4,000	27.50	27.50
76-01-005	Christmas in the Country	Unknown	5,000	40.00	40.00
77-01-006	Peace on Earth	Unknown	5,000	40.00	40.00
78-01-007	Peaceful Interlude	Unknown	5,000	45.00	45.00
79-01-008	Homeward Bound	Unknown	5,000	50.00	50.00
Royal Copenhagen		**Christmas**			
08-01-001	Madonna and Child	C. Thomsen	Annual	1.00	2100-4000.
09-01-002	Danish Landscape	S. Ussing	Annual	1.00	180.00
10-01-003	The Magi	C. Thomsen	Annual	1.00	143.00
11-01-004	Danish Landscape	O. Jensen	Annual	1.00	180.00
12-01-005	Christmas Tree	C. Thomsen	Annual	1.00	180.00
13-01-006	Frederik Church Spire	A. Boesen	Annual	1.50	149.00
14-01-007	Holy Spirit Church	A. Boesen	Annual	1.50	189.00
15-01-008	Danish Landscape	A. Krog	Annual	1.50	194.00
16-01-009	Shepherd at Christmas	R. Bocher	Annual	1.50	112.00
17-01-010	Our Savior Church	O. Jensen	Annual	2.00	99.00
18-01-011	Sheep and Shepherds	O. Jensen	Annual	2.00	102.00
19-01-012	In the Park	O. Jensen	Annual	2.00	102.00
20-01-013	Mary and Child Jesus	G. Rode	Annual	2.00	102.00
21-01-014	Aabenraa Marketplace	O. Jensen	Annual	2.00	93.00
22-01-015	Three Singing Angels	E. Selschau	Annual	2.00	85.00
23-01-016	Danish Landscape	O. Jensen	Annual	2.00	85.00
24-01-017	Sailing Ship	B. Olsen	Annual	2.00	124.00
25-01-018	Christianshavn	O. Jensen	Annual	2.00	102.00
26-01-019	Christianshavn Canal	R. Bocher	Annual	2.00	102.00
27-01-020	Ship's Boy at Tiller	B. Olsen	Annual	2.00	138-169.
28-01-021	Vicar's Family	G. Rode	Annual	2.00	99.00
29-01-022	Grundtvig Church	O. Jensen	Annual	2.00	99.00
30-01-023	Fishing Boats	B. Olsen	Annual	2.50	127.00
31-01-024	Mother and Child	G. Rode	Annual	2.50	127.00
32-01-025	Frederiksberg Gardens	O. Jensen	Annual	2.50	119.00
33-01-026	Ferry and the Great Belt	B. Olsen	Annual	2.50	173.00
34-01-027	The Hermitage Castle	O. Jensen	Annual	2.50	173.00
35-01-028	Kronborg Castle	B. Olsen	Annual	2.50	260.00
36-01-029	Roskilde Cathedral	R. Bocher	Annual	2.50	205.00
37-01-030	Main Street Copenhagen	N. Thorsson	Annual	2.50	100-230.
38-01-031	Round Church in Osterlars	H. Nielsen	Annual	3.00	355.00
39-01-032	Greenland Pack-Ice	S. Nielsen	Annual	3.00	459.00
40-01-033	The Good Shepherd	K. Lange	Annual	3.00	473.00
41-01-034	Danish Village Church	T. Kjolner	Annual	3.00	473.00
42-01-035	Bell Tower	N. Thorsson	Annual	4.00	455.00
43-01-036	Flight into Egypt	N. Thorsson	Annual	4.00	620.00
44-01-037	Danish Village Scene	V. Olson	Annual	4.00	330.00
45-01-038	A Peaceful Motif	R. Bocher	Annual	4.00	495.00
46-01-039	Zealand Village Church	N. Thorsson	Annual	4.00	219.00
47-01-040	The Good Shepherd	K. Lange	Annual	4.50	285.00
48-01-041	Nodebo Church	T. Kjolner	Annual	4.50	245.00
49-01-042	Our Lady's Cathedral	H. Hansen	Annual	5.00	280.00
50-01-043	Boeslunde Church	V. Olson	Annual	5.00	220.00
51-01-044	Christmas Angel	R. Bocher	Annual	5.00	430.00
52-01-045	Christmas in the Forest	K. Lange	Annual	5.00	155.00
53-01-046	Frederiksberg Castle	T. Kjolner	Annual	6.00	155.00
54-01-047	Amalienborg Palace	K. Lange	Annual	6.00	155.00
55-01-048	Fano Girl	K. Lange	Annual	7.00	230.00
56-01-049	Rosenborg Castle	K. Lange	Annual	7.00	217.00
57-01-050	The Good Shepherd	H. Hansen	Annual	8.00	121-177.
58-01-051	Sunshine over Greenland	H. Hansen	Annual	9.00	83-125.00
59-01-052	Christmas Night	H. Hansen	Annual	9.00	130-140.
60-01-053	The Stag	H. Hansen	Annual	10.00	138-169.
61-01-054	Training Ship	K. Lange	Annual	10.00	110-189.
62-01-055	The Little Mermaid	Unknown	Annual	11.00	140-250.
63-01-056	Hojsager Mill	K. Lange	Annual	11.00	51-97.00
64-01-057	Fetching the Tree	K. Lange	Annual	11.00	49-69.00
65-01-058	Little Skaters	K. Lange	Annual	12.00	45-74.00
66-01-059	Blackbird	K. Lange	Annual	12.00	27-35.00
67-01-060	The Royal Oak	K. Lange	Annual	13.00	24-38.00
68-01-061	The Last Umiak	K. Lange	Annual	13.00	15-38.00
69-01-062	The Old Farmyard	K. Lange	Annual	14.00	21-38.00
70-01-063	Christmas Rose and Cat	K. Lange	Annual	14.00	29-40.00
71-01-064	Hare In Winter	K. Lange	Annual	15.00	15-25.00
72-01-065	In the Desert	K. Lange	Annual	16.00	27-45.00
73-01-066	Train Homeward Bound	K. Lange	Annual	22.00	23.00
74-01-067	Winter Twilight	K. Lange	Annual	22.00	23.00
75-01-068	Queen's Palace	K. Lange	Annual	27.50	27.50
76-01-069	Danish Watermill	S. Vestergaard	Annual	27.50	28.00
77-01-070	Immervad Bridge	K. Lange	Annual	32.00	32.00
78-01-071	Greenland Scenery	K. Lange	Annual	35.00	35.00
79-01-072	Choosing Christmas Tree	K. Lange	Annual	42.50	48.00
80-01-073	Bringing Home the Tree	K. Lange	Annual	49.50	49.50
81-01-074	Admiring Christmas Tree	K. Lange	Annual	52.50	52.50
82-01-075	Waiting for Christmas	K. Lange	Annual	54.50	60.00
83-01-076	Merry Christmas	K. Lange	Annual	54.50	54.50
84-01-077	Jingle Bells	K. Lange	Annual	54.50	54.50
85-01-078	Snowman	K. Lange	Annual	54.50	54.50-66.00
86-01-079	Christmas Vacation	K. Lange	Annual	54.50	58.00
87-01-080	Winter Birds	S. Vestergaard	Annual	59.50	59.50
88-01-081	Christmas Eve in Copenhagen	S. Vestergaard	Annual	59.50	59.50
89-01-082	The Old Skating Pond	S. Vestergaard	Annual	59.50	69.00
90-01-083	Christmas at Tivoli	S. Vestergaard	Annual	64.50	76.00
91-01-084	The Festival of Santa Lucia	S. Vestergaard	Annual	69.50	69.50
92-01-085	The Queen's Carriage	S. Vestergaard	Annual	69.50	69.50
93-01-086	Christmas Guests	S. Vestergaard	Annual	69.50	69.50
Royal Cornwall		**Creation**			
77-01-001	In the Beginning	Y. Koutsis	10,000	37.50	90.00
77-01-002	In His Image	Y. Koutsis	10,000	45.00	55.00
78-01-003	Adam's Rib	Y. Koutsis	10,000	45.00	52.50
78-01-004	Banished from Eden	Y. Koutsis	10,000	45.00	47.50
78-01-005	Noah and the Ark	Y. Koutsis	10,000	45.00	45.00

Company / Number	Name	Series / Artist	Edition Limit	Issue Price	Quote
80-01-006	Tower of Babel	Y. Koutsis	10,000	45.00	75.00
80-01-007	Sodom and Gomorrah	Y. Koutsis	10,000	45.00	45.00
80-01-008	Jacob's Wedding	Y. Koutsis	10,000	45.00	45.00
80-01-009	Rebekah at the Well	Y. Koutsis	10,000	45.00	75.00
80-01-010	Jacob's Ladder	Y. Koutsis	10,000	45.00	75.00
80-01-011	Joseph's Coat of Many Colors	Y. Koutsis	10,000	45.00	75.00
80-01-012	Joseph Interprets Pharaoh's Dream	Y. Koutsis	10,000	45.00	75.00
Royal Cornwall		**Creation Calhoun Charter Release**			
77-01-001	In The Beginning	Y. Koutsis	19,500	29.50	152.00
77-01-002	In His Image	Y. Koutsis	19,500	29.50	120.00
77-01-003	Adam's Rib	Y. Koutsis	19,500	29.50	100.00
77-01-004	Banished from Eden	Y. Koutsis	19,500	29.50	90.00
77-01-005	Noah and the Ark	Y. Koutsis	19,500	29.50	90.00
78-01-006	Tower of Babel	Y. Koutsis	19,500	29.50	80.00
78-01-007	Sodom and Gomorrah	Y. Koutsis	19,500	29.50	80.00
78-01-008	Jacob's Wedding	Y. Koutsis	19,500	29.50	80.00
78-01-009	Rebekah at the Well	Y. Koutsis	19,500	29.50	80.00
78-01-010	Jacob's Ladder	Y. Koutsis	19,500	29.50	80.00
78-01-011	Joseph's Coat of Many Colors	Y. Koutsis	19,500	29.50	80.00
78-01-012	Joseph Interprets Pharaoh's Dream	Y. Koutsis	19,500	29.50	80.00
Royal Devon		**Rockwell Christmas**			
75-01-001	Downhill Daring	N. Rockwell	Yr.Iss.	24.50	30.00
76-01-002	The Christmas Gift	N. Rockwell	Yr.Iss.	24.50	35.00
77-01-003	The Big Moment	N. Rockwell	Yr.Iss.	27.50	50.00
78-01-004	Puppets for Christmas	N. Rockwell	Yr.Iss.	27.50	27.50
79-01-005	One Present Too Many	N. Rockwell	Yr.Iss.	31.50	31.50
80-01-006	Gramps Meets Gramps	N. Rockwell	Yr.Iss.	33.00	33.00
Royal Devon		**Rockwell Mother's Day**			
75-02-001	Doctor and Doll	N. Rockwell	Yr.Iss.	23.50	50.00
76-02-002	Puppy Love	N. Rockwell	Yr.Iss.	24.50	104.00
77-02-003	The Family	N. Rockwell	Yr.Iss.	24.50	85.00
78-02-004	Mother's Day Off	N. Rockwell	Yr.Iss.	27.00	35.00
79-02-005	Mother's Evening Out	N. Rockwell	Yr.Iss.	30.00	32.00
80-02-006	Mother's Treat	N. Rockwell	Yr.Iss.	32.50	35.00
Royal Doulton		**Family Christmas Plates**			
91-01-001	Dad Plays Santa	N/A	Yr.Iss.	60.00	60.00
Royal Worcester		**Birth Of A Nation**			
72-01-001	Boston Tea Party	P.W. Baston	10,000	45.00	275-325.
73-01-002	Paul Revere	P.W. Baston	10,000	45.00	250-300.
74-01-003	Concord Bridge	P.W. Baston	10,000	50.00	150.00
75-01-004	Signing Declaration	P.W. Baston	10,000	65.00	150.00
76-01-005	Crossing Delaware	P.W. Baston	10,000	65.00	150.00
77-01-006	Washington's Inauguration	P.W. Baston	1,250	65.00	250-300.
Royal Worcester		**Currier and Ives Plates**			
74-02-001	Road in Winter	P.W. Baston	5,570	59.50	100-125.
75-02-002	Old Grist Mill	P.W. Baston	3,200	59.50	100-125.
76-02-003	Winter Pastime	P.W. Baston	1,500	59.50	125-150.
77-02-004	Home to Thanksgiving	P.W. Baston	546	59.50	200-250.
Royal Worcester		**Water Birds of North America**			
85-03-001	Mallards	J. Cooke	15,000	55.00	55.00
85-03-002	Canvas Backs	J. Cooke	15,000	55.00	55.00
85-03-003	Wood Ducks	J. Cooke	15,000	55.00	55.00
85-03-004	Snow Geese	J. Cooke	15,000	55.00	55.00
85-03-005	American Pintails	J. Cooke	15,000	55.00	55.00
85-03-006	Green Winged Teals	J. Cooke	15,000	55.00	55.00
85-03-007	Hooded Mergansers	J. Cooke	15,000	55.00	55.00
85-03-008	Canada Geese	J. Cooke	15,000	55.00	55.00
Royal Worcester		**Kitten Encounters**			
87-04-001	Fishful Thinking	P. Cooper	14-day	29.50	54.00
87-04-002	Puppy Pal	P. Cooper	14-day	29.50	36.00
87-04-003	Just Ducky	P. Cooper	14-day	29.50	36.00
87-04-004	Bunny Chase	P. Cooper	14-day	29.50	30.00
87-04-005	Flutter By	P. Cooper	14-day	29.50	30.00
87-04-006	Bedtime Buddies	P. Cooper	14-day	29.50	30.00
88-04-007	Cat and Mouse	P. Cooper	14-day	29.50	33.00
88-04-008	Stablemates	P. Cooper	14-day	29.50	48.00
Royal Worcester		**Kitten Classics**			
85-05-001	Cat Nap	P. Cooper	14-day	29.50	36.00
85-05-002	Purrfect Treasure	P. Cooper	14-day	29.50	29.50
85-05-003	Wild Flower	P. Cooper	14-day	29.50	29.50
85-05-004	Birdwatcher	P. Cooper	14-day	29.50	29.50
85-05-005	Tiger's Fancy	P. Cooper	14-day	29.50	33.00
85-05-006	Country Kitty	P. Cooper	14-day	29.50	33.00
85-05-007	Little Rascal	P. Cooper	14-day	29.50	29.50
86-05-008	First Prize	P. Cooper	14-day	29.50	29.50
Sarah's Attic		**Classroom Memories**			
91-01-001	Classroom Memories	Sarah's Attic	6,000	80.00	80.00
Schmid		**Christmas**			
71-01-001	Angel	B. Hummel	Annual	15.00	20.00
72-01-002	Angel With Flute	B. Hummel	Annual	15.00	15.00
73-01-003	The Nativity	B. Hummel	Annual	15.00	73.00
74-01-004	The Guardian Angel	B. Hummel	Annual	18.50	18.50
75-01-005	Christmas Child	B. Hummel	Annual	25.00	25.00
76-01-006	Sacred Journey	B. Hummel	Annual	27.50	27.50
77-01-007	Herald Angel	B. Hummel	Annual	27.50	32.00
78-01-008	Heavenly Trio	B. Hummel	Annual	32.50	32.50
79-01-009	Starlight Angel	B. Hummel	Annual	38.00	38.00
80-01-010	Parade Into Toyland	B. Hummel	Annual	45.00	45.00
81-01-011	A Time To Remember	B. Hummel	Annual	45.00	45.00
82-01-012	Angelic Procession	B. Hummel	Annual	45.00	49.00
83-01-013	Angelic Messenger	B. Hummel	Annual	45.00	45.00
84-01-014	A Gift from Heaven	B. Hummel	Annual	45.00	48.00
85-01-015	Heavenly Light	B. Hummel	Annual	45.00	46.50
86-01-016	Tell The Heavens	B. Hummel	Annual	45.00	56.00
87-01-017	Angelic Gifts	B. Hummel	Annual	47.50	47.50
88-01-018	Cheerful Cherubs	B. Hummel	Annual	53.00	66.00
89-01-019	Angelic Musician	B. Hummel	Annual	53.00	53.00
90-01-020	Angel's Light	B. Hummel	Annual	53.00	57.00
91-01-021	Message From Above	B. Hummel	Annual	60.00	60.00
92-01-022	Sweet Blessings	B. Hummel	Annual	65.00	65.00
Schmid		**Peanuts Christmas**			
72-02-001	Snoopy Guides the Sleigh	C. Schulz	Annual	10.00	32.00
73-02-002	Christmas Eve at Doghouse	C. Schulz	Annual	10.00	90.00
74-02-003	Christmas At Fireplace	C. Schulz	Annual	10.00	55.00
75-02-004	Woodstock and Santa Claus	C. Schulz	Annual	12.50	14.00
76-02-005	Woodstock's Christmas	C. Schulz	Annual	13.00	24-25.00
77-02-006	Deck The Doghouse	C. Schulz	Annual	13.00	26.00
78-02-007	Filling the Stocking	C. Schulz	Annual	15.00	50.00
79-02-008	Christmas at Hand	C. Schulz	15,000	17.50	31.00
80-02-009	Waiting for Santa	C. Schulz	15,000	17.50	23.00
81-02-010	A Christmas Wish	C. Schulz	15,000	17.50	17.50
82-02-011	Perfect Performance	C. Schulz	15,000	18.50	55.00
Schmid		**Mother's Day**			
72-03-001	Playing Hooky	B. Hummel	Annual	15.00	15.00
73-03-002	Little Fisherman	B. Hummel	Annual	15.00	33.00
74-03-003	Bumblebee	B. Hummel	Annual	18.50	20.00
75-03-004	Message of Love	B. Hummel	Annual	25.00	29.00
76-03-005	Devotion For Mother	B. Hummel	Annual	27.50	30.00
77-03-006	Moonlight Return	B. Hummel	Annual	27.50	29.00
78-03-007	Afternoon Stroll	B. Hummel	Annual	32.50	32.50
79-03-008	Cherub's Gift	B. Hummel	Annual	38.00	38.00
80-03-009	Mother's Little Helpers	B. Hummel	Annual	45.00	52.00
81-03-010	Playtime	B. Hummel	Annual	45.00	52.00
82-03-011	The Flower Basket	B. Hummel	Annual	45.00	47.50
83-03-012	Spring Bouquet	B. Hummel	Annual	45.00	54.00
84-03-013	A Joy to Share	B. Hummel	Annual	45.00	45.00
85-03-014	A Mother's Journey	B. Hummel	Annual	45.00	45.00
86-03-015	Home From School	B. Hummel	Annual	45.00	55.00
88-03-016	Young Reader	B. Hummel	Annual	52.50	81.00
89-03-017	Pretty as a Picture	B. Hummel	Annual	53.00	75.00
90-03-018	Mother's Little Athlete	B. Hummel	Annual	53.00	53.00
91-03-019	Soft & Gentle	B. Hummel	Annual	55.00	55.00
Schmid		**Disney Christmas**			
73-04-001	Sleigh Ride	Disney Studio	Annual	10.00	300.00
74-04-002	Decorating The Tree	Disney Studio	Annual	10.00	80.00
75-04-003	Caroling	Disney Studio	Annual	12.50	18.00
76-04-004	Building A Snowman	Disney Studio	Annual	13.00	17.00
77-04-005	Down The Chimney	Disney Studio	Annual	13.00	15.00
78-04-006	Night Before Christmas	Disney Studio	Annual	15.00	35.00
79-04-007	Santa's Suprise	Disney Studio	15,000	17.50	29.00
80-04-008	Sleigh Ride	Disney Studio	15,000	17.50	34.00
81-04-009	Happy Holidays	Disney Studio	15,000	17.50	22.00
82-04-010	Winter Games	Disney Studio	15,000	18.50	29.00
Schmid		**Disney Mother's Day**			
74-05-001	Flowers For Mother	Disney Studio	Annual	10.00	45.00
75-05-002	Snow White & Dwarfs	Disney Studio	Annual	12.50	50.00
76-05-003	Minnie Mouse	Disney Studio	Annual	13.00	25.00
77-05-004	Pluto's Pals	Disney Studio	Annual	13.00	18.00
78-05-005	Flowers For Bambi	Disney Studio	Annual	15.00	40.00
79-05-006	Happy Feet	Disney Studio	10,000	17.50	20.00
80-05-007	Minnie's Surprise	Disney Studio	10,000	17.50	30.00
81-05-008	Playmates	Disney Studio	10,000	17.50	35.00
82-05-009	A Dream Come True	Disney Studio	10,000	18.50	40.00
Schmid		**Davis Red Oak Sampler**			
86-07-001	General Store	L. Davis	5,000	45.00	100-135.
87-07-002	Country Wedding	L. Davis	5,000	45.00	90.00
89-07-003	Country School	L. Davis	5,000	45.00	60.00
90-07-004	Blacksmith Shop	L. Davis	5,000	52.50	60.00
Schmid		**Davis Country Pride Plates**			
81-08-001	Surprise in the Cellar	L. Davis	7,500	35.00	175.00
81-08-002	Plum Tuckered Out	L. Davis	7,500	35.00	150.00
81-08-003	Duke's Mixture	L. Davis	7,500	35.00	100-150.
82-08-004	Bustin' with Pride	L. Davis	7,500	35.00	100.00
Schmid		**Davis Cat Tales Plates**			
82-09-001	Right Church, Wrong Pew	L. Davis	12,500	37.50	100.00
82-09-002	Company's Coming	L. Davis	12,500	37.50	100.00
82-09-003	On the Move	L. Davis	12,500	37.50	100.00
82-09-004	Flew the Coop	L. Davis	12,500	37.50	100.00
Schmid		**Davis Special Edition Plates**			
83-10-001	The Critics	L. Davis	12,500	45.00	65-100.00
84-10-002	Good Ole Days Privy Set 2	L. Davis	5,000	60.00	135-175.
86-10-003	Home From Market	L. Davis	7,500	55.00	115-125.
Schmid		**Davis Christmas Plates**			
83-11-001	Country Christmas	L. Davis	7,500	45.00	85-100.00
84-11-002	Country Christmas	L. Davis	7,500	45.00	100.00
85-11-003	Christmas at Foxfire Farm	L. Davis	7,500	45.00	75-120.00
86-11-004	Christmas at Red Oak	L. Davis	7,500	45.00	75-95.00
87-11-005	Blossom's Gift	L. Davis	7,500	47.50	75.00
88-11-006	Country Christmas	L. Davis	7,500	47.50	75.00
89-11-007	Peter and the Wren	L. Davis	7,500	47.50	75.00
90-11-008	Wintering Deer	L. Davis	7,500	47.50	47.50
91-11-009	Christmas at Red Oak II	L. Davis	7,500	55.00	55.00
92-11-010	Born On A Starry Night	L. Davis	7,500	55.00	55.00
Schmid		**Friends of Mine**			
89-12-001	Sun Worshippers	L. Davis	7,500	53.00	53.00
90-12-002	Sunday Afternoon Treat	L. Davis	7,500	53.00	53.00
91-12-003	Warm Milk	L. Davis	7,500	55.00	55.00
92-12-004	Cat and Jenny Wren	L. Davis	7,500	55.00	55.00
Schmid		**Ferrandiz Music Makers Porcelain Plates**			
81-17-001	The Flutist	J. Ferrandiz	10,000	25.00	25.00
81-17-002	The Entertainer	J. Ferrandiz	10,000	25.00	25.00
82-17-003	Magical Medley	J. Ferrandiz	10,000	25.00	27.50
82-17-004	Sweet Serenade	J. Ferrandiz	10,000	25.00	25.00
Schmid		**Ferrandiz Beautiful Bounty Porcelain Plates**			
82-18-001	Summer's Golden Harvest	J. Ferrandiz	10,000	40.00	40.00
82-18-002	Autumn's Blessing	J. Ferrandiz	10,000	40.00	40.00
82-18-003	A Mid-Winter's Dream	J. Ferrandiz	10,000	40.00	42.50
82-18-004	Spring Blossoms	J. Ferrandiz	10,000	40.00	40.00
Schmid		**Ferrandiz Wooden Birthday Plates**			
72-19-001	Boy	J. Ferrandiz	Unkn.	15.00	150.00
72-19-002	Girl	J. Ferrandiz	Unkn.	15.00	160.00

Number	Name	Artist	Edition Limit	Issue Price	Quote
73-19-003	Boy	J. Ferrandiz	Unkn.	20.00	200.00
73-19-004	Girl	J. Ferrandiz	Unkn.	20.00	150.00
74-19-005	Boy	J. Ferrandiz	Unkn.	22.00	160.00
74-19-006	Girl	J. Ferrandiz	Unkn.	22.00	160.00
Schmid	**Juan Ferrandiz Porcelain Christmas Plates**				
72-20-001	Christ in the Manger	J. Ferrandiz	Unkn.	30.00	179.00
73-20-002	Christmas	J. Ferrandiz	Unkn.	30.00	229.00
Schmid	**Paddington Bear/Musician's Dream Plates**				
83-24-001	The Beat Goes On	Unknown	10,000	17.50	22.50
83-24-002	Knowing the Score	Unknown	10,000	17.50	20.00
83-24-003	Perfect Harmony	Unknown	10,000	17.50	17.50
83-24-004	Tickling The Ivory	Unknown	10,000	17.50	17.50
Schmid	**Raggedy Ann Christmas Plates**				
75-25-001	Gifts of Love	Unknown	Unkn.	12.50	45.00
76-25-002	Merry Blades	Unknown	Unkn.	13.00	37.50
77-25-003	Christmas Morning	Unknown	Unkn.	13.00	22.50
78-25-004	Checking the List	Unknown	Unkn.	15.00	20.00
79-25-005	Little Helper	Unknown	Unkn.	17.50	19.50
Schmid	**A Year With Paddington Bear Plates**				
79-26-001	Pyramid of Presents	Unknown	25,000	12.50	27.50
80-26-002	Springtime	Unknown	25,000	12.50	25.00
81-26-003	Sandcastles	Unknown	25,000	12.50	22.50
82-26-004	School Days	Unknown	25,000	12.50	12.50
Schmid	**Peanuts Mother's Day Plates**				
72-28-001	Linus	C. Schulz	Unkn.	10.00	10.00
73-28-002	Mom?	C. Schulz	Unkn.	10.00	10.00
74-28-003	Snoopy/Woodstock/Parade	C. Schulz	Unkn.	10.00	10.00
75-28-004	A Kiss for Lucy	C. Schulz	Unkn.	12.50	10.00
76-28-005	Linus and Snoopy	C. Schulz	Unkn.	13.00	35.00
77-28-006	Dear Mom	C. Schulz	Unkn.	13.00	30.00
78-28-007	Thoughts That Count	C. Schulz	Unkn.	15.00	25.00
79-28-008	A Special Letter	C. Schulz	Unkn.	17.50	22.50
80-28-009	A Tribute to Mom	C. Schulz	Unkn.	17.50	22.50
81-28-010	Mission for Mom	C. Schulz	Unkn.	17.50	20.00
82-28-011	Which Way to Mother	C. Schulz	Unkn.	18.50	18.50
Schmid	**Peanuts Valentine's Day Plates**				
77-30-001	Home Is Where the Heart is	C. Schulz	Unkn.	13.00	32.50
78-30-002	Heavenly Bliss	C. Schulz	Unkn.	13.00	30.00
79-30-003	Love Match	C. Schulz	Unkn.	17.50	27.50
80-30-004	From Snoopy, With Love	C. Schulz	Unkn.	17.50	25.00
81-30-005	Hearts-A-Flutter	C. Schulz	Unkn.	17.50	20.00
82-30-006	Love Patch	C. Schulz	Unkn.	17.50	17.50
Schmid	**Peanuts World's Greatest Athlete**				
82-31-001	Go Deep	C. Schulz	10,000	17.50	25.00
82-31-002	The Puck Stops Here	C. Schulz	10,000	17.50	22.50
82-31-003	The Way You Play The Game	C. Schulz	10,000	17.50	20.00
82-31-004	The Crowd Went Wild	C. Schulz	10,000	17.50	17.50
Schmid	**Peanuts Special Edition Plate**				
76-33-001	Bi-Centennial	C. Schulz	Unkn.	13.00	30.00
Schmid	**Raggedy Ann Valentine's Day Plates**				
78-34-001	As Time Goes By	Unknown	Unkn.	13.00	25.00
79-34-002	Daisies Do Tell	Unknown	Unkn.	17.50	20.00
Schmid	**Raggedy Ann Annual Plates**				
80-35-001	The Sunshine Wagon	Unknown	10,000	17.50	80.00
81-35-002	The Raggedy Shuffle	Unknown	10,000	17.50	27.50
82-35-003	Flying High	Unknown	10,000	18.50	18.50
83-35-004	Winning Streak	Unknown	10,000	22.50	22.50
84-35-005	Rocking Rodeo	Unknown	10,000	22.50	22.50
Schmid	**Raggedy Ann Bicentennial Plate**				
76-36-001	Bicentennial Plate	Unknown	Unkn.	13.00	30.00
Schmid	**Disney Annual**				
83-45-001	Sneak Preview	Disney Studios	20,000	22.50	22.50
84-45-002	Command Performance	Disney Studios	20,000	22.50	22.50
85-45-003	Snow Biz	Disney Studios	20,000	22.50	22.50
86-45-004	Tree For Two	Disney Studios	20,000	22.50	22.50
87-45-005	Merry Mouse Medley	Disney Studios	20,000	25.00	25.00
88-45-006	Warm Winter Ride	Disney Studios	20,000	25.00	25.00
89-45-007	Merry Mickey Claus	Disney Studios	20,000	32.50	60.00
90-45-008	Holly Jolly Christmas	Disney Studios	20,000	32.50	32.50
91-45-009	Mickey and Minnie's Rockin' Christmas	Disney Studios	20,000	37.00	37.00
Schmid	**Walt Disney Special Edition Plates**				
78-46-001	Mickey Mouse At Fifty	Disney Studios	15,000	25.00	65.00
80-46-002	Happy Birthday Pinocchio	Disney Studios	7,500	17.50	25.00
81-46-003	Alice in Wonderland	Disney Studios	7,500	17.50	17.50
82-46-004	Happy Birthday Pluto	Disney Studios	7,500	17.50	17.50
82-46-005	Goofy's Golden Jubilee	Disney Studios	7,500	18.50	18.50
87-46-006	Snow White Golden Anniversary	Disney Studios	5,000	47.50	47.50
88-46-007	Mickey Mouse & Minnie Mouse 60th	Disney Studios	10,000	50.00	95.00
89-46-008	Sleeping Beauty 30th Anniversary	Disney Studios	5,000	80.00	95.00
90-46-009	Fantasia-Sorcerer's Apprentice	Disney Studios	5,000	59.00	59.00
90-46-010	Pinocchio's Friend	Disney Studios	Annual	25.00	25.00
90-46-011	Fantasia Relief Plate	Disney Studios	20,000	25.00	25.00
Schmid	**Kitty Cucumber Annual**				
89-47-001	Ring Around the Rosie	M. Lillemoe	20,000	25.00	45.00
90-47-002	Swan Lake	M. Lillemoe	20,000	25.00	45.00
91-47-003	Tea Party	M. Lillemoe	2,500	25.00	45.00
92-47-004	Dance 'Round the Maypole	M. Lillemoe	2,500	25.00	45.00
Spode	**Christmas**				
70-01-001	Partridge	G. West	Undis.	35.00	35.00
71-01-002	Angel's Singing	G. West	Undis.	35.00	35.00
72-01-003	Three Ships A'Sailing	G. West	Undis.	35.00	35.00
73-01-004	We Three Kings of Orient	G. West	Undis.	35.00	35.00
74-01-005	Deck the Halls	G. West	Undis.	35.00	35.00
75-01-006	Christbaum	G. West	Undis.	45.00	45.00
76-01-007	Good King Wenceslas	G. West	Undis.	45.00	45.00
77-01-008	Holly & Ivy	G. West	Undis.	45.00	45.00
78-01-009	While Shepherds Watched	G. West	Undis.	45.00	45.00
79-01-010	Away in a Manger	G. West	Undis.	50.00	50.00
80-01-011	Bringing in the Boar's Head	P. Wood	Undis.	60.00	60.00
81-01-012	Make We Merry	P. Wood	Undis.	65.00	65.00
Spode	**American Song Birds**				
72-02-001	Set of Twelve	R. Harm	Undis.	350.00	765.00
Sports Impressions	**Gold Edition Plates**				
86-01-001	Mickey Mantle At Night	R. Simon	Closed	125.00	225-250.
88-01-002	Brooks Robinson	R. Simon	Closed	125.00	225.00
87-01-003	Darryl Strawberry #1	R. Simon	Closed	125.00	125-195.
87-01-004	Ted Williams	R. Simon	Closed	125.00	225-250.
Vague Shadows: See Artaffects					
V-Palekh Art Studios	**Russian Legends**				
88-01-001	Ruslan and Ludmilla	G. Lubimov	195-day	29.87	40.00
88-01-002	The Princess/Seven Bogatyrs	A. Kovalev	195-day	29.87	38.00
88-01-003	The Golden Cockerel	V. Vleshko	195-day	32.87	32.87
88-01-004	Lukomorya	V. Vleshko	195-day	32.87	32.87
89-01-005	Fisherman and the Magic Fish	V. Vleshko	195-day	32.87	32.87
89-01-006	Tsar Saltan	V. Vleshko	195-day	32.87	32.87
89-01-007	The Priest and His Servant	V. Vleshko	195-day	34.87	34.87
90-01-008	Stone Flower	V. Vleshko	195-day	34.87	34.87
90-01-009	Sadko	V. Vleshko	195-day	34.87	34.87
90-01-010	The Twelve Months	V. Vleshko	195-day	36.87	36.87
90-01-011	Silver Hoof	V. Vleshko	195-day	36.87	36.87
90-01-012	Morozko	V. Vleshko	195-day	36.87	36.87
Veneto Flair	**Bellini**				
71-01-001	Madonna	V. Tiziano	500	45.00	400.00
Veneto Flair	**Christmas**				
71-02-001	Three Kings	V. Tiziano	1,500	55.00	160.00
72-02-002	Shepherds	V. Tiziano	2,000	55.00	90.00
73-02-003	Christ Child	V. Tiziano	2,000	55.00	55.00
74-02-004	Angel	V. Tiziano	Pair	55.00	55.00
Veneto Flair	**Wildlife**				
71-03-001	Deer	V. Tiziano	500	37.50	450.00
72-03-002	Elephant	V. Tiziano	1,000	37.50	275.00
73-03-003	Puma	V. Tiziano	2,000	37.50	65.00
74-03-004	Tiger	V. Tiziano	2,000	40.00	50.00
Veneto Flair	**Birds**				
72-04-001	Owl	Unknown	2,000	37.50	100.00
72-04-002	Falcon	Unknown	2,000	37.50	37.50
73-04-003	Mallard	Unknown	2,000	45.00	45.00
Veneto Flair	**Easter**				
73-05-001	Rabbits	Unknown	2,000	50.00	90.00
74-05-002	Chicks	Unknown	2,000	50.00	55.00
75-05-003	Lamb	Unknown	2,000	50.00	55.00
76-05-004	Composite	Unknown	2,000	55.00	55.00
Viletta	**Disneyland**				
76-01-001	Signing The Declaration	Unknown	3,000	15.00	100.00
76-01-002	Crossing The Delaware	Unknown	3,000	15.00	100.00
76-01-003	Betsy Ross	Unknown	3,000	15.00	100.00
76-01-004	Spirit of '76	Unknown	3,000	15.00	100.00
79-01-005	Mickey's 50th Anniversary	Unknown	5,000	37.00	50.00
Villeroy & Boch	**Russian Fairytales Snow Maiden**				
80-01-001	The Snow Maiden	B. Zvorykin	27,500	70.00	130.00
81-01-002	Snegurochka at the Court of Tsar Berendei	B. Zvorykin	27,500	70.00	70.00
81-01-003	Snegurochka and Lei, the Shepherd Boy	B. Zvorykin	27,500	70.00	73.00
Villeroy & Boch	**Russian Fairytales The Red Knight**				
81-02-001	The Red Knight	B. Zvorykin	27,500	70.00	90-135.00
81-02-002	Vassilissa and her Stepsisters	B. Zvorykin	27,500	70.00	77.00
81-02-003	Vassilissa is Presented to the Tsar	B. Zvorykin	27,500	70.00	75.00
Villeroy & Boch	**Russian Fairytales The Firebird**				
81-03-001	In Search of the Firebird	B. Zvorykin	27,500	70.00	112.00
81-03-002	Ivan and Tsarevna on the Grey Wolf	B. Zvorykin	27,500	70.00	78.00
81-03-003	The Wedding of Tsarevna Elena the Fair	B. Zvorykin	27,500	70.00	118.00
Villeroy & Boch	**Russian Fairytales Maria Morevna**				
82-04-001	Maria Morevna and Tsarevich Ivan	B. Zvorykin	27,500	70.00	70.00
82-04-002	Koshchey Carries Off Maria Morevna	B. Zvorykin	27,500	70.00	81.00
82-04-003	Tsarevich Ivan and the Beautiful Castle	B. Zvorykin	27,500	70.00	95.00
Villeroy & Boch	**Flower Fairy**				
79-05-001	Lavender	C. Barker	21-day	35.00	125.00
80-05-002	Sweet Pea	C. Barker	21-day	35.00	125.00
80-05-003	Candytuft	C. Barker	21-day	35.00	89.00
81-05-004	Heliotrope	C. Barker	21-day	35.00	75.00
81-05-005	Blackthorn	C. Barker	21-day	35.00	75.00
81-05-006	Appleblossom	C. Barker	21-day	35.00	95.00
Waterford Wedgwood USA	**Wedgwood Christmas**				
69-01-001	Windsor Castle	T. Harper	Annual	25.00	100.00
70-01-002	Trafalgar Square	T. Harper	Annual	30.00	30.00
71-01-003	Picadilly Circus	T. Harper	Annual	30.00	40.00
72-01-004	St. Paul's Cathedral	T. Harper	Annual	35.00	40.00
73-01-005	Tower of London	T. Harper	Annual	40.00	90.00
74-01-006	Houses of Parliament	T. Harper	Annual	40.00	40.00
75-01-007	Tower Bridge	T. Harper	Annual	45.00	45.00
76-01-008	Hampton Court	T. Harper	Annual	50.00	50.00
77-01-009	Westminister Abbey	T. Harper	Annual	55.00	60.00
78-01-010	Horse Guards	T. Harper	Annual	60.00	60.00
79-01-011	Buckingham Palace	Unknown	Annual	65.00	65.00
80-01-012	St. James Palace	Unknown	Annual	70.00	70.00
81-01-013	Marble Arch	Unknown	Annual	75.00	75.00
82-01-014	Lambeth Palace	Unknown	Annual	80.00	90.00
83-01-015	All Souls, Langham Palace	Unknown	Annual	80.00	80.00
84-01-016	Constitution Hill	Unknown	Annual	80.00	80.00
85-01-017	The Tate Gallery	Unknown	Annual	80.00	80.00
86-01-018	The Albert Memorial	Unknown	Annual	80.00	150.00
87-01-019	Guildhall	Unknown	Annual	80.00	85.00
88-01-020	The Observatory/Greenwich	Unknown	Annual	80.00	90.00
89-01-021	Winchester Cathedral	Unknown	Annual	88.00	88.00

Company Number	Name	Series Artist	Edition Limit	Issue Price	Quote
Waterford Wedgwood USA		**Mother's Day**			
71-02-001	Sportive Love	Unknown	Unkn.	20.00	20.00
72-02-002	The Sewing Lesson	Unknown	Unkn.	20.00	20.00
73-02-003	The Baptism of Achilles	Unknown	Unkn.	20.00	25.00
74-02-004	Domestic Employment	Unknown	Unkn.	30.00	33.00
75-02-005	Mother and Child	Unknown	Unkn.	35.00	37.00
76-02-006	The Spinner	Unknown	Unkn.	35.00	35.00
77-02-007	Leisure Time	Unknown	Unkn.	35.00	35.00
78-02-008	Swan and Cygnets	Unknown	Unkn.	40.00	40.00
79-02-009	Deer and Fawn	Unknown	Unkn.	45.00	45.00
80-02-010	Birds	Unknown	Unkn.	47.50	47.50
81-02-012	Mare and Foal	Unknown	Unkn.	50.00	60.00
82-02-013	Cherubs with Swing	Unknown	Unkn.	55.00	60.00
83-02-014	Cupid and Butterfly	Unknown	Unkn.	55.00	55.00
84-02-015	Musical Cupids	Unknown	Unkn.	55.00	59.00
85-02-016	Cupids and Doves	Unknown	Annual	55.00	80.00
86-02-017	Cupids Fishing	Unknown	Annual	55.00	55.00
87-02-018	Spring Flowers	Unknown	Annual	55.00	80.00
88-02-019	Tiger Lily	Unknown	Annual	55.00	59.00
89-02-020	Irises	Unknown	Annual	65.00	65.00
91-02-021	Peonies	Unknown	Annual	65.00	65.00
Waterford Wedgwood USA		**Bicentennial**			
72-03-001	Boston Tea Party	Unknown	Annual	40.00	40.00
73-03-002	Paul Revere's Ride	Unknown	Annual	40.00	115.00
74-03-003	Battle of Concord	Unknown	Annual	40.00	55.00
75-03-004	Across the Delaware	Unknown	Annual	40.00	105.00
75-03-005	Victory at Yorktown	Unknown	Annual	45.00	53.00
76-03-006	Declaration Signed	Unknown	Annual	45.00	45.00

STEINS

Company Number	Name	Series Artist	Edition Limit	Issue Price	Quote
Anheuser-Busch, Inc.		**Specialty Steins**			
75-01-001	Bud Man CS1	A-Busch,Inc.	Retrd.	N/A	275-350.
75-01-002	A&Eagle CS2	A-Busch,Inc.	Retrd.	N/A	200-275.
75-01-003	A&Eagle Lidded CSL2	A-Busch,Inc.	Retrd.	N/A	275-375.
75-01-004	Katakombe CS3	A-Busch,Inc.	Retrd.	N/A	200-275.
75-01-005	Katakombe Lidded CSL3	A-Busch,Inc.	Retrd.	N/A	250-350.
75-01-006	German Olympia CS4	A-Busch,Inc.	Retrd.	N/A	125-200.
75-01-007	Senior Grande Lidded CSL4	A-Busch,Inc.	Retrd.	N/A	450-600.
75-01-008	German Pilique CS5	A-Busch,Inc.	Retrd.	N/A	275-350.
75-01-009	German Pilique Lidded CSL5	A-Busch,Inc.	Retrd.	N/A	450-550.
75-01-010	Senior Grande CS6	A-Busch,Inc.	Retrd.	N/A	450-550.
75-01-011	German Olympia Lidded CSL6	A-Busch,Inc.	Retrd.	N/A	250-300.
75-01-012	Miniature Bavarian CS7	A-Busch,Inc.	Retrd.	N/A	200-300.
76-01-013	Budweiser Centennial Lidded CSL7	A-Busch,Inc.	Retrd.	N/A	475-600.
76-01-014	U.S. Bicentennial Lidded CSL8	A-Busch,Inc.	Retrd.	N/A	475-600.
76-01-015	Natural Light CS9	A-Busch,Inc.	Retrd.	N/A	100-250.
76-01-016	Clydesdales Hofbrau Lidded CSL9	A-Busch,Inc.	Retrd.	N/A	275-350.
76-01-017	Blue Delft (4 assorted) CS11	A-Busch,Inc.	Retrd.	N/A	N/A
76-01-018	Clydesdales CS12	A-Busch,Inc.	Retrd.	N/A	275-500.
76-01-019	Budweiser Centennial CS13	A-Busch,Inc.	Retrd.	N/A	400-500.
76-01-020	U.S. Bicentennial CS14	A-Busch,Inc.	Retrd.	N/A	400-500.
76-01-021	Clydesdales Grants Farm CS15	A-Busch,Inc.	Retrd.	N/A	225-400.
76-01-022	German Cities (6 assorted) CS16	A-Busch,Inc.	Retrd.	N/A	1500-1800.
76-01-023	Americana CS17	A-Busch,Inc.	Retrd.	N/A	350-450.
76-01-024	Budweiser Label CS18	A-Busch,Inc.	Retrd.	N/A	350-450.
80-01-025	Budweiser Ladies (4 assorted) CS20	A-Busch,Inc.	Retrd.	N/A	2000-2500.
77-01-026	Budweiser Girl CS21	A-Busch,Inc.	Retrd.	N/A	N/A
76-01-027	Budweiser Centennial CS22	A-Busch,Inc.	Retrd.	N/A	350-450.
77-01-028	A&Eagle CS24	A-Busch,Inc.	Retrd.	N/A	350.00
76-01-029	A&Eagle Barrel CS26	A-Busch,Inc.	Retrd.	N/A	95-150.
76-01-030	Michelob CS27	A-Busch,Inc.	Retrd.	N/A	100-175.
76-01-031	A&Eagle Lidded CS28	A-Busch,Inc.	Retrd.	N/A	275-375.
76-01-032	Clydesdales Lidded CS29	A-Busch,Inc.	Retrd.	N/A	250-350.
76-01-034	Coracao Decanter Set (7 piece) CS31	A-Busch,Inc.	Retrd.	N/A	400-500.
76-01-035	Geraman Wine Set (7 piece) CS32	A-Busch,Inc.	Retrd.	N/A	400-500.
76-01-036	Clydesdales Decanter CS33	A-Busch,Inc.	Retrd.	N/A	1000-1200.
76-01-037	Holanda Brown Decanter Set (7 piece) CS34	A-Busch,Inc.	Retrd.	N/A	N/A
76-01-038	Holanda Blue Decanter Set (7 piece) CS35	A-Busch,Inc.	Retrd.	N/A	N/A
76-01-039	Canteen Decanter Set (7 piece) CS36	A-Busch,Inc.	Retrd.	N/A	N/A
76-01-040	St. Louis Decanter CS37	A-Busch,Inc.	Retrd.	N/A	N/A
76-01-041	St. Louis Decanter Set (7 piece) CS38	A-Busch,Inc.	Retrd.	N/A	1000-1200.
80-01-042	Wurzburger Hofbrau CS39	A-Busch,Inc.	Retrd.	N/A	350-450.
80-01-043	Budweiser Chicago Skyline CS40	A-Busch,Inc.	Retrd.	N/A	135-225.
78-01-044	Busch Gardens CS41	A-Busch,Inc.	Retrd.	N/A	350-450.
80-01-045	Oktoberfest-- "The Old Country" CS42	A-Busch,Inc.	Retrd.	N/A	350-450.
80-01-046	Natural Light Label CS43	A-Busch,Inc.	Retrd.	N/A	100-200.
80-01-047	Busch Label CS44	A-Busch,Inc.	Retrd.	N/A	125-200.
80-01-048	Michelob Label CS45	A-Busch,Inc.	Retrd.	N/A	75-125.00
80-01-049	Budweiser Label CS46	A-Busch,Inc.	Retrd.	N/A	100-150.
81-01-050	Budweiser Chicagoland CS51	A-Busch,Inc.	Retrd.	N/A	50-75.00
81-01-051	Budweiser Texas CS52	A-Busch,Inc.	Retrd.	N/A	60-65.00
81-01-052	Budweiser California CS56	A-Busch,Inc.	Retrd.	N/A	50-75.00
83-01-053	Budweiser San Francisco CS59	A-Busch,Inc.	Retrd.	N/A	175-200.
84-01-054	Budweiser Olympic Games CS60	A-Busch,Inc.	Retrd.	N/A	20-50.00
83-01-055	Bud Light Baron CS61	A-Busch,Inc.	Retrd.	N/A	25-50.00
87-01-056	Santa Claus CS79	A-Busch,Inc.	Retrd.	N/A	60-85.00
87-01-057	King Cobra CS80	A-Busch,Inc.	Retrd.	N/A	150.00
87-01-058	Winter Olympic Games, Lidded CS81	A-Busch,Inc.	Retrd.	49.95	65-90.00
88-01-059	Budweiser Winter Olympic Games CS85	A-Busch,Inc.	Retrd.	24.95	27.00
88-01-060	Summer Olympic Games, Lidded CS91	A-Busch,Inc.	Retrd.	54.95	45-65.00
88-01-061	Budweiser Summer Olympic Games CS92	A-Busch,Inc.	Retrd.	54.95	54.95
88-01-062	Budweiser/ Field&Stream Set (4 piece) CS95	A-Busch,Inc.	Retrd.	69.95	175-225.
89-01-063	Bud Man CS100	A-Busch,Inc.	Open	29.95	29.95
90-01-064	Baseball Cardinal Stein CS125	A-Busch,Inc.	Retrd.	30.00	30.00
91-01-065	Bevo Fox Stein CS160	A-Busch,Inc.	10,000	N/A	250.00
92-01-066	U.S. Olympic Team CS168	A-Busch,Inc.	Open	16.00	16.00
92-01-067	1992 Rodeo CS184	A-Busch,Inc.	Open	18.00	18.00
92-01-068	1992 Oktoberfest CS185	A-Busch,Inc.	Open	16.00	16.00
92-01-069	Budweiser Racing-Elliot/Johnson N3553	T. Watts	Open	18.00	18.00
Anheuser-Busch, Inc.		**Clydesdales Holiday Series**			
80-02-001	1st Holiday CS19	A-Busch,Inc.	Retrd.	9.95	100-190.
81-02-002	2nd Holiday CS50	A-Busch,Inc.	Retrd.	9.95	200-275.
82-02-003	3rd Holiday CS57 50th Anniversary	A-Busch,Inc.	Retrd.	9.95	80-140.00
83-02-004	4th Holiday CS58	A-Busch,Inc.	Retrd.	9.95	25-40.00
84-02-005	5th Holiday CS62	A-Busch,Inc.	Retrd.	9.95	20-30.00
85-02-006	6th Holiday CS63	A-Busch,Inc.	Retrd.	9.95	20-30.00
86-02-007	7th Holiday CS66	A-Busch,Inc.	Retrd.	9.95	20-30.00
87-02-008	8th Holiday CS70	A-Busch,Inc.	Retrd.	9.95	13-20.00
88-02-009	9th Holiday CS88	A-Busch,Inc.	Retrd.	9.95	13-20.00
89-02-010	10th Holiday CS89	A-Busch,Inc.	Retrd.	12.95	13-20.00

Company Number	Name	Series Artist	Edition Limit	Issue Price	Quote
Anheuser-Busch, Inc.		**Clydesdales Series**			
87-03-001	Eight Horse Hitch CS74	A-Busch,Inc.	Retrd.	9.95	14-22.00
88-03-002	Mare & Foal CS90	A-Busch,Inc.	Retrd.	11.50	13-23.00
89-03-003	Parade Dress CS99	A-Busch,Inc.	Retrd.	11.50	22-28.00
91-03-004	Training Hitch CS131	A-Busch,Inc.	Retrd.	13.00	16.00
92-03-005	Clydesdales on Parade CS161	A-Busch,Inc.	Open	16.00	16.00
Anheuser-Busch, Inc.		**Horseshoe Series**			
86-04-001	Horseshoe CS68	A-Busch,Inc.	Retrd.	14.95	35-50.00
87-04-002	Horsehead CS76	A-Busch,Inc.	Retrd.	16.00	20-45.00
86-04-003	Horseshoe CS77	A-Busch,Inc.	Retrd.	16.00	20-25.00
87-04-004	Horsehead CS78	A-Busch,Inc.	Retrd.	14.95	40-50.00
88-04-005	Harness CS94	A-Busch,Inc.	Retrd.	16.00	45-75.00
Anheuser-Busch, Inc.		**Limited Edition Series**			
85-05-001	Ltd. Ed. I Brewing & Fermenting CS64	A-Busch,Inc.	Retrd.	29.95	175-250.
86-05-002	Ltd. Ed. II Aging & Cooperage CS65	A-Busch,Inc.	Retrd.	29.95	45-75.00
87-05-003	Ltd. Ed. III Transportation CS71	A-Busch,Inc.	Retrd.	29.95	35-50.00
88-05-004	Ltd. Ed. IV Taverns & Public Houses CS75	A-Busch,Inc.	100,000	29.95	30-35.00
89-05-005	Ltd. Ed.V Festival Scene CS98	A-Busch,Inc.	Retrd.	34.95	34.95
Anheuser-Busch, Inc.		**Historical Landmark Series**			
86-06-001	Brew House CS67 (First)	A-Busch,Inc.	Retrd.	19.95	22-28.00
87-06-002	Stables CS73 (Second)	A-Busch,Inc.	Retrd.	19.95	22-28.00
88-06-003	Grant Cabin CS83 (Third)	A-Busch,Inc.	Retrd.	19.95	22-28.00
88-06-004	Old School House CS84 (Fourth)	A-Busch,Inc.	Retrd.	19.95	22-28.00
Anheuser-Busch, Inc.		**Classic Series**			
88-07-001	1st Edition CS93	A-Busch,Inc.	Retrd.	34.95	145-200.
89-07-002	2nd Edition CS104	A-Busch,Inc.	Retrd.	54.95	100-149.
90-07-003	3rd Edition CS113	A-Busch,Inc.	Retrd.	75.00	75-100.00
91-07-004	4th Edition CS130	A-Busch,Inc.	25,000	75.00	75.00
Anheuser-Busch, Inc.		**Endangered Species Series**			
89-08-001	Bald Eagle CS106(First)	A-Busch,Inc.	Retrd.	24.95	100-150.
90-08-002	Asian Tiger CS126 (Second)	A-Busch,Inc.	Retrd.	27.50	27.50
91-08-003	African Elephant CS135 (Third)	A-Busch,Inc.	100,000	29.00	29.00
92-08-004	Giant Panda CS173(Fourth)	B. Kemper.	100,000	29.00	29.00
Anheuser-Busch, Inc.		**Porcelain Heritage Series**			
90-09-001	Berninghaus CS105	Berninghaus	20,000	75.00	75.00
91-09-002	After The Hunt CS155	A-Busch,Inc.	25,000	100.00	100.00
92-09-003	Cherub CS182	D. Langeneckert	25,000	100.00	100.00
Anheuser-Busch, Inc.		**Discover America Series**			
90-10-001	Nina CS107	A-Busch,Inc.	100,000	40.00	40.00
91-10-002	Pinta CS129	A-Busch,Inc.	100,000	40.00	40.00
92-10-003	Santa Maria CS138	A-Busch,Inc.	100,000	40.00	40.00
Anheuser-Busch, Inc.		**Wholesaler Holdiay Series**			
90-11-001	An American Tradition CS112-Signature Edition, 1990	S. Sampson	Retrd.	13.50	16-75.00
91-11-002	The Season's Best CS133, 1991	S. Sampson	Open	14.50	16-50.00
92-11-003	The Perfect Christmas CS167	S. Sampson	Open	14.50	14.50
Anheuser-Busch, Inc.		**Sports History Series**			
90-12-001	Baseball, America's Favorite Pastime CS124	A-Busch,Inc.	Retrd.	20.00	22-25.00
90-12-002	Football, Gridiron Legacy CS128	A-Busch,Inc.	Retrd.	20.00	22.00
91-12-003	Auto Racing, Chasing The Checkered Flag CS132	A-Busch,Inc.	100,000	22.00	22.00
91-12-004	Basketball, Heroes of the Hardwood CS134	A-Busch,Inc.	100,000	22.00	22.00
92-12-005	Golf, Par For The Course CS165	A-Busch,Inc.	100,000	22.00	22.00
Anheuser-Busch, Inc.		**Bud Label Series**			
89-13-001	Budweiser Label CS101	A-Busch,Inc.	Open	N/A	13.00
90-13-002	Antique Label II CS127	A-Busch,Inc.	Open	14.00	14.00
90-13-003	Bottled Beer III CS136	A-Busch,Inc.	Open	15.00	15.00
Anheuser-Busch, Inc.		**St. Patrick's Day Series**			
91-14-001	1991 St. Patrick's Day CS109	A-Busch,Inc.	Retrd.	15.00	20-50.00
92-14-002	1992 St. Patrick's Day CS166	A-Busch,Inc.	100,000	15.00	15.00
Anheuser-Busch, Inc.		**Sports Legend Series**			
91-15-001	Babe Ruth CS142	A-Busch,Inc.	50,000	85.00	85.00
92-15-002	Jim Thorpe CS171	M. Caito	50,000	85.00	85.00
Anheuser-Busch, Inc.		**Logo Series Steins**			
91-16-001	Budweiser CS143	A-Busch,Inc.	Open	16.00	16.00
91-16-002	Bud Light CS144	A-Busch,Inc.	Open	16.00	16.00
91-16-003	Michelob CS145	A-Busch,Inc.	Open	16.00	16.00
91-16-004	Michelob Dry CS146	A-Busch,Inc.	Open	16.00	16.00
91-16-005	Busch CS147	A-Busch,Inc.	Open	16.00	16.00
91-16-006	A&Eagle CS148	A-Busch,Inc.	Open	16.00	16.00
91-16-007	Bud Dry Draft CS156	A-Busch,Inc.	Open	16.00	16.00
Anheuser-Busch, Inc.		**1992 Olympic Team Series**			
91-17-001	1992 Winter Olympic Stein CS162	A-Busch,Inc.	25,000	85.00	85.00
92-17-002	1992 Summer Olympic Stein CS163	A-Busch,Inc.	25,000	85.00	85.00
Anheuser-Busch, Inc.		**Birds of Prey Series**			
91-18-001	American Bald Eagle CS164	P. Ford	25,000	125.00	125.00
92-18-002	Peregrine Falcon CS183	P. Ford	25,000	125.00	125.00
Anheuser-Busch, Inc.		**Archives Series**			
92-19-001	Columbian Exposition CS169	A-Busch,Inc.	150,000	35.00	35.00
93-19-002	Ganymede CS190	D. Langeneckert	150,000	35.00	35.00
Anheuser-Busch, Inc.		**Civil War Series**			
92-20-001	General Grant CS181	D. Langeneckert	25,000	150.00	150.00
93-20-002	General Robert E. Lee CS188	D. Langeneckert	25,000	150.00	150.00
93-20-003	President Abraham Lincoln CS189	D. Langeneckert	25,000	150.00	150.00
Anheuser-Busch, Inc.		**Sea World Series**			
92-21-001	Killer Whale CS186	A-Busch, Inc.	Open	100.00	100.00
92-21-002	Dolphin CS187	A-Busch, Inc.	Open	90.00	90.00
M. Cornell Importers		**Cornell Steins**			
XX-01-001	Senator's Cup 3321	Unknown	5,000	117.00	224.00
87-01-002	Farmer & Plow Stein 3423	Unknown	10,000	87.50	113.00
87-01-003	Farmer & Plow Stein-Unlidded 3424	Unknown	10,000	35.00	49.00
91-01-004	F-16 Stein 3697	Unknown	3,000	199.00	199.00
XX-01-005	Fox Jug 3704	Unknown	5,000	86.00	164.00
XX-01-006	The Herring Stein 3706	Unknown	5,000	127.00	180.00

Company		Series			
Number	**Name**	**Artist**	**Edition Limit**	**Issue Price**	**Quote**
XX-01-007	The Sieburg Wine Stein-1.5 Ltr 3707	Unknown	5,000	69.50	115.00
XX-01-008	The Sieburg Wine Stein-.40 Ltr 3708	Unknown	5,000	49.00	74.00
XX-01-009	The Sieburg Wine Stein-.13 Ltr 3709	Unknown	5,000	36.00	59.00
89-01-010	Peter Duemler General Tilly Tankard 3715	P. Duemler	5,000	379.50	440.00
89-01-011	Weihnachten(Christmas) Stein 3716	Unknown	10,000	150.00	185.00
89-01-012	Weihnachten(Christmas) Stein 3717	Unknown	10,000	110.00	139.00
89-01-013	Ahrens-Fox Fire Engine Stein 3719	Unknown	10,000	119.00	157.50
89-01-014	Ahrens-Fox Fire Engine Stein Unlidded 3720	Unknown	10,000	35.00	44.00
89-01-015	Bald Eagle Stein 3721	J. Lim	10,000	150.00	175.00
89-01-016	Bald Eagle Stein 3722	J. Lim	10,000	110.00	139.50
89-01-017	Bald Eagle Stein-Unlidded 3723	J. Lim	10,000	40.00	48.00
XX-01-018	The Zeppelin Stein-Unlidded 3751	Unknown	5,000	21.00	40.00
86-01-019	Join Us! Gemuetlichkeit Stein-Unlidded 3766	Unknown	10,000	30.00	40.00
87-01-020	Join Us! Gemuetlichkeit Stein 3767	Unknown	10,000	78.00	99.50
87-01-021	Join Us! Gemuetlichkeit Stein 3768	Unknown	10,000	125.00	149.50
87-01-022	May Stroll Stein-Unlidded 3769	Unknown	10,000	30.00	40.00
87-01-023	May Stroll Stein 3770	Unknown	10,000	79.00	99.50
87-01-024	May Stroll Stein 3771	Unknown	10,000	125.00	149.50
87-01-025	Zither Player Stein-Unlidded 3772	Unknown	10,000	35.00	48.00
87-01-026	Zither Player Stein 3773	Unknown	10,000	85.00	106.00
87-01-027	Zither Player Stein 3774	Unknown	10,000	130.00	159.00
87-01-028	Wedding Parade Stein-Unlidded 3775	Unknown	10,000	35.00	48.00
87-01-029	Wedding Parade Stein 3776	Unknown	10,000	85.00	104.00
87-01-030	Wedding Parade Stein 3777	Unknown	10,000	130.00	159.00
90-01-031	Seppl Stein-Unlidded 3778	Unknown	10,000	42.50	47.00
90-01-032	Seppl Stein 3779	Unknown	10,000	95.00	104.00
90-01-033	Seppl Stein 3780	Unknown	10,000	137.50	150.00
90-01-034	Loreley Stein-Unlidded 3781	Unknown	10,000	42.50	47.00
90-01-035	Loreley Stein 3782	Unknown	10,000	95.00	104.00
90-01-036	Loreley Stein 3783	Unknown	10,000	137.50	150.00
90-01-037	Friedolin Stein-Unlidded 3784	Unknown	10,000	47.00	50.00
90-01-038	Friedolin Stein 3785	Unknown	10,000	99.00	109.50
90-01-039	Friedolin Stein 3786	Unknown	10,000	140.00	155.00
90-01-040	Berlin Wall Stein#1 3787	Unknown	5,000	159.00	159.00
87-01-041	Berlin City Stein 3788	Unknown	5,000	130.00	159.00
87-01-042	Berlin City Stein 3789	Unknown	5,000	87.50	113.00
89-01-043	Munich Stein 3790	Unknown	10,000	115.00	190.00
89-01-044	Gambrinus Stein 3792	Unknown	10,000	125.00	130.00
89-01-045	Gambrinus Stein-Unlidded 3793	Unknown	10,000	40.00	50.00
90-01-046	Wiesbaden Stein 3794	Unknown	2,000	125.00	139.50
90-01-047	Wiesbaden Stein 3795	Unknown	2,000	100.00	115.00
90-01-048	Turnvater Jahn Stein-Unlidded 3796 Originally #1911	Unknown	10,000	42.50	47.00
90-01-049	Turnvater Jahn Stein 3797	Unknown	10,000	95.00	104.00
90-01-050	Turnvater John Stein 3798	Unknown	10,000	137.50	150.00
90-01-051	Thewalt "Exquisit" Stein 3799	Unknown	250	2500.00	2500.00
90-01-052	Berlin Wall#2 Stein 3801	Unknown	5,000	159.00	159.00
90-01-053	Clipper Stein, Unlidded 3811	Unknown	10,000	47.00	50.00
90-01-054	Clipper Stein 3814	Unknown	10,000	168.00	185.00
90-01-055	Clipper Stein 3815	Unknown	10,000	168.00	185.00
90-01-056	Golfer Stein, Unlidded 3816	Unknown	10,000	47.00	50.00
90-01-057	Golfer Stein 3819	Unknown	10,000	168.00	185.00
90-01-058	Golfer Stein 3820	Unknown	10,000	168.00	185.00
91-01-059	Buffalo Hunt Stein 3821	J. Lim	9,000	197.00	197.00
87-01-060	Dr. Faust-Peter Duemler Stein 3851	P.Duemler	10,000	80.00	98.00
87-01-061	Dr. Faust-Peter Duemler Stein 3852	P.Duemler	10,000	30.00	40.00
87-01-062	Dr. Faust-Peter Duemler Stein 3854	P.Duemler	10,000	123.00	159.00
87-01-063	The Bicyclists Stein 3855	P.Duemler	10,000	89.00	110.00
87-01-064	The Bicyclists Stein 3856	P.Duemler	10,000	130.00	148.00
87-01-065	The Bicyclists Stein, Unlidded 3857	P.Duemler	10,000	30.00	42.00
87-01-066	The Bicyclists Stein 3858	P.Duemler	10,000	80.00	100.00
87-01-067	Centurio Stein, Unlidded 3860	P.Duemler	10,000	30.00	42.00
87-01-068	Centurio Stein 3861	P.Duemler	10,000	73.50	88.00
87-01-069	Patrizier Stein, Unlidded 3863	P.Duemler	10,000	30.00	42.00
87-01-070	Patrizier Stein 3864	P.Duemler	10,000	75.00	88.00
87-01-071	The Cardplayer Stein 3866	P.Duemler	10,000	150.00	198.00
87-01-072	The Cardplayer Stein 3867	P.Duemler	10,000	190.00	220.00
87-01-073	The Cardplayer Stein, Unlidded 3868	P.Duemler	10,000	35.00	47.00
87-01-074	Bible Stein, Unlidded 3869	P.Duemler	10,000	30.00	42.00
87-01-075	Bible Stein 3870	P.Duemler	10,000	80.00	99.00
87-01-076	Bible Stein 3871	P.Duemler	10,000	110.00	110.00
87-01-077	Cheruskan Stein, Unlidded 3872	P.Duemler	10,000	40.00	55.00
87-01-078	Cheruskan Stein 3873	P.Duemler	10,000	109.00	148.00
87-01-079	Cheruskan Stein 3874	P.Duemler	10,000	180.00	218.00
87-01-080	Minuet Stein, Unlidded 3875	P.Duemler	10,000	30.00	42.00
87-01-081	Minuet Stein 3876	P.Duemler	10,000	79.00	108.00
87-01-082	Minuet Stein 3877	P.Duemler	10,000	100.00	130.00
88-01-083	Royalty Stein 3878	P.Duemler	10,000	79.50	88.00
88-01-084	Royalty Stein 3880	P.Duemler	10,000	110.00	130.00
88-01-085	Royalty Stein 3881	P.Duemler	10,000	199.00	220.00
89-01-086	Crusader Stein 3883	P.Duemler	10,000	145.00	179.50
89-01-087	Crusader Stein 3884	P.Duemler	10,000	145.00	179.50
89-01-088	Royalty Stein 3887	P.Duemler	10,000	65.00	75.00
89-01-089	Royalty Stein, Unlidded 3888	P.Duemler	10,000	35.00	47.00
91-01-090	Ornament Stein 3929	Unknown	5,000	115.00	115.00
87-01-091	Jugendstil Stein 3930	Unknown	10,000	75.00	88.00
91-01-092	Polar Bear Stein 3955(Great Animals of the World #1)	Unknown	2,500	199.00	199.00
91-01-093	Elephant Stein 3956(Great Animals of the World #2)	Unknown	2,500	199.00	199.00
87-01-094	"A Toast" Stein 3963	Unknown	10,000	87.50	113.00
88-01-095	Proletarian Stein 3970	Unknown	5,000	100.00	118.00
89-01-096	Proletarian Stein, Multicolor 3971	Unknown	5,000	300.00	333.00
89-01-097	Proletarian Stein, Unlidded 3972	Unknown	5,000	45.00	60.00
88-01-098	Dragon Slayer Stein 3980	P. Duemler	10,000	165.00	197.50
88-01-099	Dragon Slayer Stein 3981	P. Duemler	10,000	89.00	99.50
88-01-100	Dragon Slayer Beer Chalice 3982	P. Duemler	10,000	79.00	105.00
88-01-101	Dragon Slayer Beer Chalice 3983	P. Duemler	10,000	50.00	56.00
87-01-102	Mallard Stein 4041	E. Breiden	4,000	100.00	130.00
87-01-103	Wild Boar Stein 4044	E. Breiden	4,000	100.00	130.00
87-01-104	Alpine Flower Stein 4047	Unknown	5,000	90.00	100.00
89-01-105	Wedding Dance Jug 4048	Unknown	1,500	239.00	299.00
90-01-106	Silver Thistle Stein 4049	Unknown	10,000	79.00	79.00
87-01-107	Club Hunt Stein 4402	Unknown	8,000	87.00	106.00
XX-01-108	Boar Hunt Stein 4403	Unknown	12,000	70.00	124.00
89-01-109	St. George Stein 4409	Unknown	6,000	150.00	165.00
88-01-110	Tyrolean Stein 4411	Unknown	9,000	100.00	100.00
88-01-111	Tyrolean Stein 4413	Unknown	9,000	80.00	84.00
88-01-112	Maximilian Stein 4415	Unknown	6,000	95.00	95.00
88-01-113	Diana Jug 4417	Unknown	1,500	199.00	199.00
90-01-114	National Audubon Society Grizzly Bear Stein 4451	Unknown	20,000	175.00	193.00
90-01-115	National Audubon Society Peregrine Falcon Stein 4452	Unknown	20,000	175.00	193.00
90-01-116	National Audubon Society Wood Duck Stein 4453	Unknown	20,000	175.00	193.00
90-01-117	National Audubon Society Humpback Whale Stein 4454	Unknown	20,000	175.00	193.00
90-01-118	Grenzau Castle Stein 4590	Unknown	12,000	119.50	131.50
89-01-119	Bicyclist Stein 4723	Unknown	5,000	68.00	86.00
89-01-120	Bicyclist Stein 4724	Unknown	5,000	84.00	102.00
89-01-121	Firefighter Stein 4765	Unknown	5,000	68.00	86.00
89-01-122	Firefighter Stein 4766	Unknown	5,000	84.00	102.00
89-01-123	Singer Stein, Unlidded 4767	Unknown	5,000	38.00	45.00
89-01-124	Singer Stein 4768	Unknown	5,000	68.00	86.00
89-01-125	Singer Stein 4769	Unknown	5,000	84.00	100.00
89-01-126	Dragon Regimental Stein 4992	J. Lim	5,000	199.00	249.00
90-01-127	Baba Yaga Stein 4993	W. Gossel	5,000	238.00	249.00
91-01-128	Wolf Tracks Stein 4995	P.C. Weir	1,000	285.00	285.00
91-01-129	Pair of Eagles II Stein 4996	M. Sieve	1,000	285.00	285.00
87-01-130	Heidelberg Stein 6278	Unknown	4,000	100.00	125.00
87-01-131	Golden Hops and Malt Stein 6279	Unknown	4,000	159.00	219.00
87-01-132	Beerwagon Stein 6280	Unknown	4,000	110.00	133.00
87-01-133	Happy Dwarf Stein 6282	Unknown	4,000	106.00	137.00
88-01-134	Beer Barrel Stein 6285	Unknown	4,000	130.00	137.00
88-01-135	Summer Stein 6286	Unknown	4,000	80.00	89.00
88-01-136	Royal King Ludwig Stein 6287	Unknown	4,000	194.00	197.50
88-01-137	Father & Son Stein 6291	Unknown	4,000	115.00	135.00
88-01-138	Father & Son Stein 6292	Unknown	4,000	60.00	73.00
89-01-139	Red Baron Stein 6295	Unknown	4,000	100.00	130.00
89-01-140	Apostle Stein 6298	Unknown	2,000	239.00	290.00
89-01-141	Village Blacksmith Stein 6308	Unknown	2,000	110.00	135.00
89-01-142	Cooper (Barrel Maker) Stein 6309	Unknown	2,000	110.00	135.00
91-01-143	Aviation Stein 6310	Unknown	4,000	150.00	150.00
91-01-144	Berlin Wall Stein 6311	Unknown	4,000	110.00	110.00
91-01-145	Brandenburg Gate Stein 6314	Unknown	4,000	175.00	175.00
91-01-146	Columbus Globe Stein 6315	Unknown	8,000	139.00	139.00
91-01-147	Western Railroad Stein 6316	Unknown	4,000	150.00	150.00
89-01-148	Railroad Stein 6317	Unknown	2,000	110.00	135.00
91-01-149	Old Timer Stein 6318	Unknown	4,000	128.00	128.00
91-01-150	Mozart Stein 6319	Unknown	5,000	119.00	119.00
90-01-151	Berlin Wall Stein 6320	Unknown	2,000	100.00	110.00
91-01-152	Reunification Stein 6322	Unknown	4,000	110.00	110.00
91-01-153	Reunification Stein 6323	Unknown	4,000	125.00	125.00
90-01-154	Bicyclist Stein 6325	Unknown	4,000	120.00	130.00
90-01-155	Munich Bier-Wagon Stein 6326	Unknown	4,000	150.00	165.00
90-01-156	Firefighter Stein 6327	Unknown	4,000	120.00	135.00
87-01-157	Grizzly Bear Stein 6331	Unknown	5,000	99.50	120.00
87-01-158	Grizzly Bear Stein, Unlidded 6333	Unknown	5,000	30.00	37.50
87-01-159	Moose Stein 6337	Unknown	5,000	99.50	120.00
87-01-160	Moose Stein, Unlidded 6339	Unknown	5,000	30.00	37.50
87-01-161	Elk Stein 6340	Unknown	5,000	99.50	120.00
87-01-162	Elk Stein, Unlidded 6342	Unknown	5,000	30.00	37.50
87-01-163	White Tail Deer Stein 6343	Unknown	5,000	99.50	120.00
87-01-164	White Tail Deer Stein, Unlidded 6345	Unknown	5,000	30.00	37.50
91-01-165	Lion Stein 6430	Unknown	4,000	150.00	150.00
91-01-166	Clockmaker Stein 6448	Unknown	5,000	110.00	110.00
87-01-167	Hot Air Balloon Stein 6460	Unknown	5,000	100.00	130.00
89-01-168	Carousel Stein 6467	Unknown	5,000	159.00	190.00
89-01-169	Carousel Stein, Musical 6468	Unknown	5,000	184.00	220.00
90-01-170	Noah's Ark Stein 6469	Unknown	5,000	129.00	150.00
90-01-171	Stoneware Nutcracker Stein 6473	Unknown	5,000	139.00	150.00
91-01-172	Circus Stein 6475	Unknown	5,000	95.00	95.00
91-01-173	Stoneware Nutcracker Stein #2 6476	Unknown	5,000	150.00	150.00
91-01-174	Stoneware Functional Nutcracker 6477	Unknown	5,000	196.00	196.00
87-01-175	Mettlach Stein 6601 Peter Pan	Sir J.M.Barrie	10,000	219.00	230.00
87-01-176	Mettlach Stein 6602 Pied Piper	R. Browning	10,000	219.00	230.00
87-01-177	Mettlach Stein 6603 Pinoccio	C. Collodi	10,000	219.00	230.00
87-01-178	Mettlach Stein 6604 Hansel & Gretel	R. Faure	Closed	230.00	230.00
88-01-179	Mettlach Stein 6605 Medical Literary	Unknown	10,000	220.00	250.00
89-01-180	Mercedes Benz Mettlach Stein 6607	Unknown	N/A	300.00	300.00
90-01-181	Bugatti Stein Mettlach 6608	Unknown	10,000	300.00	300.00
90-01-182	Mettlach Ford Stein 6609	Unknown	10,000	300.00	300.00
90-01-183	Mettlach Rolls Royce Stein 6610	Unknown	10,000	300.00	300.00
90-01-184	Mettlach Stein 6615 Tales of the Brothers Grimm	Unknown	10,000	199.00	199.00
90-01-185	Mettlach Stein 6617 Tales of the Brothers Grimm	Unknown	10,000	199.00	199.00
90-01-186	Mettlach Stein 6618 Tales of the Brothers Grimm	Unknown	10,000	199.00	199.00
90-01-187	Mettlach William Tell Stein 6632	Unknown	N/A	219.00	219.00
90-01-188	Mettlach Peasant Stein 6633	Unknown	10,000	200.00	200.00
90-01-189	Mettlach Lepanto Stein 6637	Unknown	N/A	150.00	150.00
90-01-190	Mettlach Spanish Armada Stein 6638	Unknown	N/A	150.00	150.00

CUI/Carolina Collection/Dram Tree		Ducks Unlimited			
87-01-001	Wood Duck Edition I	K. Bloom	Retrd.	80.00	125-150.
88-01-002	Mallard Edition II	M. Bradford	25,000	80.00	80.00
89-01-003	Canvasbacks Edition III	L. Barnicle	25,000	80.00	80.00
90-01-004	Pintails Edition IV	R. Plasschaert	20,000	80.00	80.00
91-01-005	Canada Geese Edition V	J. Meger	20,000	80.00	80.00

CUI/Carolina Collection/Dram Tree		Federal Duck Stamp			
90-02-001	Lesser Scaup Edition I	N. Anderson	6,950	80.00	80.00
91-02-002	Black Bellied Whistling Duck Edition II	J. Hautman	6,950	80.00	80.00
92-02-003	King Eiders Edition III	N. Howe	6,950	80.00	80.00

CUI/Carolina Collection/Dram Tree		National Wild Turkey Federation			
90-03-001	The Apprentice Edition I	M.T. Noe	9,950	125.00	125.00
91-03-002	Sultan's Sunrise Edition II	A. Agnew	6,950	100.00	100.00
92-03-003	Double Gobble Edition III	J.S. Eberhardt	6,950	100.00	100.00

CUI/Carolina Collection		North American Hunting Club			
90-04-001	Deer Crossing Edition I	R. McGovern	6,950	85.00	85.00
92-04-002	Yukon Grizzly Edition II	L. Anderson	6,950	90.00	90.00

CUI/Carolina Collection/Dram Tree		Nat'l. Foundation to Protect America's Eagles			
91-05-001	Great American Patriots Edition I	R.J. McDonald	6,950	80.00	80.00

CUI/Carolina Collection/Dram Tree		American Angler Series Limited Edition			
90-06-001	Large Mouth Bass	J.R. Hook	Retrd.	25.00	25.00

CUI/Carolina Collection/Dram Tree		Big Horn Sheep			
90-07-001	Wind Blown Ridge	J. Antolik	3,950	70.00	70.00

Number	Name	Artist	Edition Limit	Issue Price	Quote
Company		**Series**			
CUI/Carolina Collection/Dram Tree		**Pheasants Forever**			
91-08-001	Jumping Ringnecks Edition I	J. Killen	6,950	100.00	100.00
92-08-002	Foggy Morning Magic Edition II	P. Crowe	6,950	100.00	100.00
CUI/Carolina Collection/Dram Tree		**Trout Unlimited**			
91-09-001	Rainbow Edition I	M. Stidham	6,950	90.00	90.00
92-09-002	Downstream & Across Edition II	E. Hardle	6,950	90.00	90.00
CUI/Carolina Collection/Dram Tree		**Quail Unlimited**			
91-10-001	Hedgerow Bobs Edition I	D. Chapple	6,950	90.00	90.00
92-10-002	California Trio Edition II	J. Garcia	6.950	90.00	90.00
CUI/Carolina Collection/Dram Tree		**Whitetails Unlimited**			
91-11-001	Whitetails in Retreat Edition I	J. Paluh	6,950	90.00	90.00
92-11-002	Indian Summer Flight Edition II	B. Miller	6,950	90.00	90.00
CUI/Carolina Collection/Dram Tree		**Jack Russell Terrier**			
91-12-001	Jack Russell Terrier Edition I	B.B. Atwater	6,950	90.00	90.00
CUI/Carolina Collection/Dram Tree		**Statue of Liberty**			
91-13-001	Lady Liberty	CUI	Open	50.00	50.00
86-13-002	Statue of Liberty	CUI	Retrd.	42.50	42.50
CUI/Carolina Collection/Dram Tree		**Civil War**			
91-14-001	Firing on Fort Sumter Edition I	CUI	4,950	125.00	125.00
92-14-002	Stonewall Jackson Edition II	CUI	4,950	125.00	125.00
CUI/Carolina Collection/Dram Tree		**Native American Series**			
91-15-001	Hunt for the Buffalo Edition I	P. Kethley	4,950	100.00	100.00
92-15-002	Story Teller	P. Kethley	4,950	50.00	50.00
CUI/Carolina Collection/Dram Tree		**Christmas Series**			
91-16-001	Checkin' It Twice Edition I	CUI	4,950	125.00	125.00
92-16-002	With A Finger Aside His Nose	CUI	4,950	125.00	125.00
CUI/Carolina Collection/Dram Tree		**Environmental Series**			
91-17-001	Rain Forest Magic Edition I	C.L. Bragg	4,950	90.00	90.00
92-17-002	First Breath Edition II	M. Hoffman	4,950	90.00	90.00
CUI/Carolina Collection/Dram Tree		**Miller Girl in the Moon**			
90-18-001	Miller Girl in the Moon	CUI	Open	50.00	50.00
CUI/Carolina Collection/Dram Tree		**Great American Achievements**			
86-19-001	First Successful Flight Edition I	CUI	Retrd.	10.95	75-95.00
87-19-002	The Model T Edition II	CUI	Retrd.	12.95	30-50.00
88-19-003	First Transcontinental Railway Edition III	CUI	Retrd.	15.95	28-40.00
89-19-004	The First River Steamer Edition IV	CUI	Retrd.	25.00	25.00
90-19-005	Man's First Walk on the Moon Edition V	CUI	Retrd.	25.00	25.00
CUI/Carolina Collection/Dram Tree		**Birth of a Nation**			
91-20-001	Paul Revere's Ride Edition I	CUI	Open	25.00	25.00
91-20-002	Paul Revere's Ride Lidded Edition I	CUI	10,000	70.00	70.00
92-20-003	Signing Of The Declaration Of Independence-Edition II	CUI	Open	25.00	25.00
92-20-004	Signing Of The Declaration Of Independence-Special Pewter Lidden Edition II	CUI	10,000	70.00	70.00
CUI/Carolina Collection/Dram Tree		**Miller Plank Road**			
91-21-001	Miller Plank Road Edition I	CUI	9,850	90.00	90.00
CUI/Carolina Collection/Dram Tree		**Miller Historical Collection**			
90-22-001	Frederic Miller Edition I	CUI	9,850	136.00	136.00
91-22-002	Miller's Delivery Wagon Edition II	CUI	9,950	130.00	130.00
92-22-003	Coopersmith Edition III	CUI	9,950	130.00	130.00
CUI/Carolina Collection/Dram Tree		**Miller Holiday Series**			
91-23-001	Milwaukee Waterfront Edition I	CUI	9,950	50.00	50.00
92-23-002	Christmas on Old World Third St. EditionII	CUI	9,950	50.00	50.00
CUI/Carolina Collection/Dram Tree		**Coors Historical Collection**			
88-24-001	Rocky Mountain Brewry Edition I	CUI	Retrd.	15.95	15.95
89-24-002	Old Time Delivery Wagon Edition II	CUI	Retrd.	16.95	16.95
90-24-003	Waterfall Edition III	CUI	Retrd.	25.00	25.00
CUI/Carolina Collection/Dram Tree		**Rocky Mountain Legends**			
91-25-001	Skier Edition I	CUI	Open	25.00	25.00
91-25-002	Skier Lidded Edition I	CUI	10,000	70.00	70.00
92-25-003	White Water Rafting Edition II	CUI	Open	25.00	25.00
92-25-004	White Water Rafting Special Lidded Edition II	CUI	10,000	70.00	70.00
CUI/Carolina Collection/Dram Tree		**Coors Rodeo Collection**			
91-26-001	Jack Hammer Edition I	M.H. Scott	20,000	90.00	90.00
92-26-002	Born To Buck Edition II	M.H. Scott	20,000	90.00	90.00
CUI/Carolina Collection/Dram Tree		**Winterfest**			
89-27-001	Outdoor Skating Edition I	T. Stortz	9,950	50.00	50.00
90-27-002	Christmas Square Edition II	T. Stortz	9,950	50.00	50.00
91-27-003	Horsedrawn Sleighs Edition III	T. Stortz	9,950	50.00	50.00
92-27-004	Edition IV	T. Stortz	9,950	50.00	50.00
CUI/Carolina Collection/Dram Tree		**Coors Legacy Series**			
91-28-001	Coors Rams Head Edition I	CUI	6,950	130.00	130.00
92-28-002	Bock Beer Edition II	CUI	6,950	120.00	120.00
CUI/Carolina Collection/Dram Tree		**Miller Racing Team**			
91-29-001	Penske/Wallace	CUI	6,950	50.00	50.00
CUI/Carolina Collection/Dram Tree		**Ruffed Grouse Society**			
90-30-001	Northwoods Grouse Edition I	G. Moss	3,950	50.00	50.00
91-30-002	Edition II	Z. Jones	3,950	50.00	50.00
CUI/Carolina Collection/Dram Tree		**Phillip Morris**			
91-31-001	London's Bond St. Edition I	D. Hilburn	9,950	50.00	50.00
CUI/Carolina Collection/Dram Tree		**The Fleet Reserve**			
91-32-001	The Arizona Edition I	T. Freeman	6,950	60.00	60.00
CUI/Carolina Collection/Dram Tree		**Experimental Aircraft Association**			
91-33-001	Into the Teeth of a Tiger Edition I	W.S. Phillips	4,950	80.00	80.00
92-33-002	Tokyo Raiders Ready For Launch Edition II	J. Dietz	4,950	80.00	80.00

Number	Name	Artist	Edition Limit	Issue Price	Quote
Company		**Series**			
CUI/Carolina Collection/Dram Tree		**National Football League**			
91-34-001	First NFL Championship Game Edition I - Pewter Edition	CUI	4,950	80.00	80.00
CUI/Carolina Collection/Dram Tree		**N.F.L. National Football League**			
91-35-001	Historically Speaking Pewter Edition I	CUI	4,950	80.00	80.00
CUI/Carolina Collection/Dram Tree		**N.B.A. National Basketball Association**			
91-36-001	100 Years of Basketball-Pewter Edition I	CUI	4,950	80.00	80.00
CUI/Carolina Collection/Dram Tree		**Stroh Heritage Collection**			
84-37-001	Horsedrawn Wagon - Heritage I	CUI	Retrd.	11.95	15-22.00
85-37-002	Kirn Inn Germany - Heritage II	CUI	Retrd.	12.95	15-22.00
86-37-003	Lion Brewing Company - Heritage III	CUI	Retrd.	13.95	25-35.00
87-37-004	Bohemian Beer - Heritage IV	CUI	Retrd.	14.95	19.00
88-37-005	Delivery Vehicles - Heritage V	CUI	Open	25.00	25.00
89-37-006	Fire Brewed - Heritage V I	CUI	Retrd.	16.95	19.00
CUI/Carolina Collection/Dram Tree		**Stroh Bavaria Collection**			
90-38-001	Dancers Edition I - Bavaria I	CUI	Open	45.00	45.00
90-38-002	Dancers Pewter Figure Edition I - Bavaria I	CUI	10,000	70.00	70.00
91-38-003	Barrel Pusher Edition II - Bavaria II	CUI	Open	45.00	45.00
91-38-004	Barrel Pusher Pewter Edition II - Bavaria II	CUI	10,000	70.00	70.00
92-38-005	The Aging Cellar-Edition III	CUI	Open	45.00	45.00
92-38-006	The Aging Cellar-Pewter Edition III	CUI	10,000	70.00	70.00
CUI/Carolina Collection/Dram Tree		**Beck's**			
90-39-001	Beck's Purity Law Edition I	CUI	3,950	115.00	115.00
CUI/Carolina Collection/Dra Tree		**Northern Solitude**			
90-40-001	Moosehead Northern Solitude	N. Anderson	3,950	72.00	72.00
CUI/Carolina Collection/Dram Tree		**Team of the Decade - NFL**			
90-41-001	NFL 49ers	CUI	9,950	60.00	60.00
CUI/Carolina Collection/Dram Tree		**SuperBowl XXV - NFL**			
91-42-001	NFL	CUI	4,950	60.00	60.00
CUI/Carolina Collection/Dram Tree		**SuperBowl Champions - NFL**			
91-43-001	NY Giants - NFL	CUI	4,950	60.00	60.00
92-43-002	Washington Redskins - NFL	CUI	4,950	60.00	60.00
CUI/Carolina Collection/Dram Tree		**World Series Champions - MLB**			
90-44-001	Cincinnati Reds - MLB	CUI	4,950	60.00	60.00
91-44-002	Minnesota Twins - MLB	CUI	4,950	60.00	60.00
CUI/Carolina Collection/Dram Tree		**Stanley Cup Champions - NHL**			
91-45-001	Pittsburgh Penguins - NHL	CUI	4,950	60.00	60.00
92-45-002	Pittsburgh Penguins - NHL	CUI	4,950	60.00	60.00
CUI/Carolina Collection/Dram Tree		**World Champions - NBA**			
91-46-001	Chicago Bulls - NBA	CUI	4,950	60.00	60.00
92-46-002	Chicago Bulls - NBA	CUI	4,950	60.00	60.00
CUI/Carolina Collection/Dram Tree		**Chicago Bulls 25th Anniversary**			
91-47-001	NBA	CUI	4,950	60.00	60.00
CUI/Carolina Collection/Dram Tree		**Ducks Unlimited Classic Decoy Series**			
92-48-001	1930's Bert Graves Mallard Decoys Edition I	D. Boncela	20,000	100.00	100.00
CUI/Carolina Collection/Dram Tree		**North American Fishing Club**			
92-49-001	Jumpin' Hog	V. Beck	6,950	90.00	90.00
CUI/Carolina Collection/Dram Tree		**Lighthouse Collectors Series**			
92-50-001	Boston Light Edition I	CUI	4,950	100.00	100.00
92-50-001	Cape Hatteras Lighthouse Edition II	CUI	4,950	100.00	100.00
CUI/Carolina Collection/Dram Tree		**American Conference Champion - NFL**			
91-51-001	Buffalo Bills - 91 ACC	CUI	4,950	60.00	60.00
CUI/Carolina Collection/Dram Tree		**National League Champion - MLB**			
91-52-001	Atlanta Braves - 91 NLC	CUI	4,950	60.00	60.00
CUI/Carolina Collection/Dram Tree		**Ducks Unlimited Edition I**			
92-53-001	Spring Reflections	P. Crowe	4,950	100.00	100.00
CUI/Carolina Collection/Dram Tree		**Classic Car Series**			
92-54-001	1957 Chevy	G. Geivette	6,950	100.00	100.00
CUI/Carolina Collection/Dram Tree		**The Corvette Series**			
92-55-001	1953 Corvette	G. Geivette	6,950	100.00	100.00
CUI/Carolina Collection/Dram Tree		**Moosehead**			
92-56-001	Moosehead 125th Anniversary	CUI	9,950	100.00	100.00
CUI/Carolina Collection/Dram Tree		**Quarterback Legends**			
92-57-001	Hall of Fame - John Unitas Edition I	CUI	4,950	175.00	175.00
92-57-002	Hall of Fame - Y.A. Tittle Edition II	CUI	4,950	175.00	175.00
92-57-003	Hall of Fame - Bart Starr	CUI	4,950	175.00	175.00
CUI/Carolina Collection/Dram Tree		**Cooperstown Collection**			
92-58-001	St. Louis Cardinals 100th Anniversary	CUI	Open	70.00	70.00
CUI/Carolina Collection/Dram Tree		**Cooperstown Team Collection**			
92-59-001	Brooklyn Dodgers	CUI	Open	60.00	60.00
92-59-002	Boston Braves	CUI	Open	60.00	60.00
92-59-003	Washington Senators	CUI	Open	60.00	60.00
Hamilton Collection		**Warriors Of The Plains Tankards**			
92-01-001	Thundering Hooves	G. Stewart	Open	125.00	125.00
Norman Rockwell Gallery		**Rockwell**			
92-01-001	Jolly Santa	Rockwell-Inspired	N/A	49.95	49.95
Norman Rockwell Gallery		**Rockwell Mugs**			
92-02-001	Saturday Evening Post(Set of 4)	Rockwell-Inspired	N/A	29.95	29.95
92-02-002	Santa Mugs(Set of 4)	Rockwell-Inspired	N/A	29.95	29.95

Index

Three Great Collectibles Offers!

COMPLIMENTARY COPY

"The C.I.B. Report"

Published three times annually

Contains the latest collectibles news:

- Recent product introductions
- New collector clubs
- Convention News
- 36 Page Color Newsletter
- Artist Open Houses, Demonstrations
- Retirement Announcements
- $2.50 Value

201 SECONDARY MARKET SOURCES!

Directory To Secondary Market Retailers

Buying and Selling Limited Edition Artwork

- **For:** Collectors who want to buy or sell retired collectibles (plates, figurines, dolls, bells, Christmas ornaments, steins and graphics.)
- $13.95 postpaid
- **Featuring:** A comprehensive listing of today's most respected secondary market dealers and exchanges nationwide!

MID-YEAR PRICE INDEX UPDATE

AVAILABLE APRIL 1993!

Collectors' Information Bureau's:

Collectibles Price Guide: 1993

Limited Edition Plates • Figurines • Bells • Graphics • Ornaments • Dolls • Steins

- C.I.B.'s official 155-page Price Guide
- Updated Mid-year values for nearly 30,000 collectibles!
- Secondary Market Buy-Sell Information
- $11.95 postpaid

Three Great Collectibles Offers!

☐ **Yes!**

Please send me a ***complimentary*** copy of the "C.I.B. Report" newsletter, highlighting the latest collectible news when available.

☐ **Yes!**

Please send me a ***Directory to Secondary Market Retailers*** for $13.95 postpaid. *(Michigan residents please add 4% book sales tax.)*

☐ **Yes!**

Please send me a preferred collectors' order form for the ***Collectibles Price Guide*** when available.

Name ______________________________

Address ______________________________

City ______________ State __________ Zip __________

I purchased this book from ______________________________

I am a collector of ☐ Plates ☐ Figurines ☐ Bells ☐ Graphics ☐ Christmas Ornaments ☐ Dolls ☐ Steins ☐ Other __________

Your comments on this book will be appreciated. ______________________________

____

____

☐ My check or money order is enclosed, made payable to **"Collectors' Information Bureau," at** 2420 Burton S.E., Grand Rapids, MI 49546, (616) 942-6898

☐ Charge to my credit card:

☐ MasterCard ☐ VISA

____

Credit Card Number **Exp. Date**

____

Signature

Canadian and overseas orders: Contact the "CIB" office for current price information.

Collectors' Information Bureau
2420 Burton S.E.
Grand Rapids, MI 49546